Lecture Notes in Computer Science 4113

*Commenced Publication in 1973*
Founding and Former Series Editors:
Gerhard Goos, Juris Hartmanis, and Jan van Leeuwen

De-Shuang Huang
Kang Li
George William Irwin (Eds.)

# Intelligent Computing

International Conference on
Intelligent Computing, ICIC 2006
Kunming, China, August 16-19, 2006
Proceedings, Part I

Springer

Volume Editors

De-Shuang Huang
Chinese Academy of Sciences
Institute of Intelligent Machines
Hefei, Anhui, China
E-mail: dshuang@iim.ac.cn

Kang Li
George William Irwin
Queen's University
Belfast, UK
E-mail: {K.Li,G.Irwin}@qub.ac.uk

Library of Congress Control Number: 2006930410

CR Subject Classification (1998): F.1, F.2, I.2, G.2, I.4, I.5, J.3

LNCS Sublibrary: SL 1 – Theoretical Computer Science and General Issues

ISSN 0302-9743
ISBN-10 3-540-37271-7 Springer Berlin Heidelberg New York
ISBN-13 978-3-540-37271-4 Springer Berlin Heidelberg New York



Springer is a part of Springer Science+Business Media

springer.com


Printed in Germany

Typesetting: Camera-ready by author, data conversion by Scientific Publishing Services, Chennai, India
Printed on acid-free paper SPIN: 11816157 06/3142 5 4 3 2 1 0

# Preface

The International Conference on Intelligent Computing (ICIC) was formed to provide an annual forum with dedication to the emerging and challenging topics in artificial intelligence, machine learning, bioinformatics, and computational biology, etc. It aims to bring together researchers and practitioners from both the academia and industry to share ideas, problems and solutions related to the multifaceted aspects of intelligent computing.

The ICIC 2006 to be held in Kunming, Yunnan, China, 16-19 August 2006 is the second International Conference on Intelligent Computing, which is built upon the success of ICIC 2005 held in Hefei, China, 2005.

This year, the conference mainly concentrates on the theories & methodologies as well as the emerging applications of intelligent computing. It intends to unify the contemporary intelligent computing techniques within an integral framework that highlights the trends in advanced computational intelligence and bridges the theoretical research with the applications. In particular, the bio-inspired computing emerges as a key role in pursuing for novel technology in recently years. The resulting techniques vitalize the life science engineering and daily life applications. In light of this trend, the theme for this conference is the Emerging Intelligent Computing Technology and Applications. Papers related to this theme were especially solicited, including theories, methodologies, and applications in science and technology.

The ICIC 2006 received over 3000 submissions from 36 countries and regions. All papers went through rigorous peer review and each paper received at least three review reports. Based on the review reports, the Program Committee finally selected 703 high-quality papers for presentation at ICIC 2006. These papers cover 29 topics and 16 special sessions, and are included into five volumes of proceedings published by the Springer, including one volume of Lecture Notes in Computer Science (LNCS), one volume of Lecture Notes in Artificial Intelligence (LNAI), one volume of Lecture Notes in Bioinformatics (LNBI), and two volumes of Lecture Notes in Control and Information Sciences (LNCIS).

This volume of Lecture Notes in Computer Science (LNCS) includes 161 papers covering cover relevant 7 topics and 3 special session topics.

The organizers of the ICIC 2006, including the Yunan University, the Institute of Intelligent Machines of the Chinese Academy of Science, and Queen's University Belfast, have made enormous effort to ensure the success of ICIC 2006. We hereby would like to thank the members of the ICIC 2006 Advisory Committee for their guidance and advice, the members of the Program Committee and the referees for their collective effort in reviewing and soliciting the papers, and the members of the Publication Committee for their significant editorial work. We would like to thank Professor Alfred Hofmann, the executive editor from Springer, for his frank and helpful advice and guidance throughout and his support in publishing the proceedings in the Lecture Notes series. In particular, we would like to thank all the authors for contributing their papers. Without the high-quality submissions from the authors, the success of the conference would not have been possible. Finally, we are especially grateful to the IEEE Computational Intelligence Society, The International Neural Network Society and the National Science Foundation of China for the their sponsorship.

10 June 2006

De-Shuang Huang
Institute of Intelligent Machines
Chinese Academy of Sciences, China
Kang Li
Queen's University Belfast, UK
George William Irwin
Queen's University Belfast, UK

# ICIC 2006 Organization

**General Chairs:**

De-Shuang Huang, China
Song Wu, China
George W. Irwin, UK

**International Advisory Committee:**

Aike Guo, China
Alfred Hofmann, Germany
DeLiang Wang, USA
Erke Mao, China
Fuchu He, China
George W. Irwin, UK
Guangjun Yang, China
Guanrong Chen, Hong Kong
Guoliang Chen, China
Harold Szu, USA
John L. Casti, USA
Marios M. Polycarpou, USA
Mengchu Zhou, USA
Michael R. Lyu, Hong Kong
MuDer Jeng, Taiwan
Nanning Zheng, China
Okyay Knynak, Turkey
Paul Werbos, USA
Qingshi Zhu, China
Ruwei Dai, China
Sam Shuzhi GE, Singapore
Sheng Zhang, China
Shoujue Wang, China
Songde Ma, China
Stephen Thompson, UK
Tom Heskes, Netherlands
Xiangfan He, China
Xingui He, China
Xueren Wang, China
Yanda Li, China
Yixin Zhong, China
Youshou Wu, China
Yuanyan Tang, Hong Kong
Yunyu Shi, China
Zheng Bao, China

**Program Committee Chairs:**

Kang Li, UK
Prashan Premaratne, Australia

**Steering Committee Chairs:**

Sheng Chen, UK
Xiaoyi Jiang, Germany
Xiao-Ping Zhang, Canada

**Organizing Committee Chairs:**

Yongkun Li, China
Hanchun Yang, China
Guanghua Hu, China

**Special Session Chair:**

Wen Yu, Mexico

**Tutorial Chair:**

Sudharman K. Jayaweera, USA

**Publication Chair:** Xiaoou Li, Mexico

**International Liasion Chair:** C. De Silva, Liyanage, New Zealand

**Publicity Chairs:** Simon X. Yang, Canada
Jun Zhang, China

**Exhibition Chair:** Cheng Peng, China

## Program Committee:

Aili Han, China
Arit Thammano, Thailand
Baogang Hu, China
Bin Luo, China
Bin Zhu, China
Bing Wang, China
Bo Yan, USA
Byoung-Tak Zhang, Korea
Caoan Wang, Canada
Chao Hai Zhang, Japan
Chao-Xue Wang, China
Cheng-Xiang Wang, UK
Cheol-Hong Moon, Korea
Chi-Cheng Cheng, Taiwan
Clement Leung, Australia
Daniel Coca, UK
Daqi Zhu, China
David Stirling, Australia
Dechang Chen, USA
Derong Liu, USA
Dewen Hu, China
Dianhui Wang, Australia
Dimitri Androutsos, Canada
Donald C. Wunsch, USA
Dong Chun Lee, Korea
Du-Wu Cui, China
Fengling Han, Australia
Fuchun Sun, China
Girijesh Prasad, UK
Guang-Bin Huang, Singapore
Guangrong Ji, China
Hairong Qi, USA
Hong Qiao, China
Hong Wang, China
Hongtao Lu, China
Hongyong Zhao, China
Huaguang Zhang, China
Hui Wang, China
Jiangtao Xi, Australia
Jianguo Zhu, Australia
Jianhua Xu, China
Jiankun Hu, Australia
Jian-Xun Peng, UK
Jiatao Song, China
Jie Tian, China
Jie Yang, China
Jin Li, UK
Jin Wu, UK
Jinde Cao, China
Jinwen Ma, China
Jochen Till, Germany
John Q. Gan, UK
Ju Liu, China
K.R. McMenemy, UK
Key-Sun Choi, Korea
Liangmin Li, UK
Luigi Piroddi, Italy
Maolin Tang, Australia
Marko Hočevar, Slovenia
Mehdi Shafiei, Canada
Mei-Ching Chen, Taiwan
Mian Muhammad Awais, Pakistan
Michael Granitzer, Austria
Michael J. Watts, New Zealand
Michiharu Maeda, Japan
Minrui Fei, China
Muhammad Jamil Anwas, Pakistan
Muhammad Khurram Khan, China
Naiqin Feng, China
Nuanwan Soonthornphisaj, Thailand
Paolo Lino, Italy
Peihua Li, China
Ping Guo, China
Qianchuan Zhao, China
Qiangfu Zhao, Japan
Qing Zhao, Canada
Roberto Tagliaferri, Italy
Rong-Chang Chen, Taiwan
RuiXiang Sun, China
Saeed Hashemi, Canada
Sanjay Sharma, UK
Seán McLoone, Ireland
Seong G. Kong, USA
Shaoning Pang, New Zealand
Shaoyuan Li, China
Shuang-Hua Yang, UK
Shunren Xia, China
Stefanie Lindstaedt, Austria
Sylvia Encheva, Norway
Tai-hoon Kim, Korea
Tai-Wen Yue, Taiwan
Takashi Kuremoto, Japan

## Reviewers

Charasskulchai, Siyao Fu, Wenpeng Ding, Fuzhen Huang, Amal Punchihewa, Geoffrey Macintyre, Xue Feng He, Gang Leng, Lijuan Gao, Ray Gao, Andrey Gaynulin, Gabriella Dellino, D.W. Ggenetic, Geoffrey Wang, YuRong Ge, Guohui He, Gwang Hyun Kim, Gianluca Cena, Giancarlo Raiconi, Ashutosh Goyal, Guan Luo, Guido Maione, Guido Maione, Grigorios Dimitriadis, Haijing Wang, Kayhan Gulez, Tiantai Guo, Chun-Hung Hsieh, Xuan Guo, Yuantao Gu, Huanhuan Chen, Hongwei Zhang, Jurgen Hahn, Qing Han, Aili Han, Dianfei Han, Fei Hao, Qing-Hua Ling, Hang-kon Kim, Han-Lin He, Yunjun Han, Li Zhang, Hathai Tanta-ngai, Hang-Bong Kang, Hsin-Chang Yang, Hongtao Du, Hazem Elbakry, Hao Mei, Zhao L, Yang Yun, Michael Hild, Heajo Kang, Hongjie Xing, Hailli Wang, Hoh In, Peng Bai, Hong-Ming Wang, Hongxing Bai, Hongyu Liu, Weiyan Hou, Huaping Liu, H.Q. Wang, Hyungsuck Cho, Hsun-Li Chang, Hua Zhang, Xia Huang, Hui Chen, Huiqing Liu, Heeun Park, Hong-Wei Ji, Haixian Wang, Hoyeal Kwon, H.Y. Shen, Jonghyuk Park, Turgay Ibrikci, Mary Martin, Pei-Chann Chang, Shouyi Yang, Xiaomin Mu, Melanie Ashley, Ismail Altas, Muhammad Usman Ilyas, Indrani Kar, Jinghui Zhong, Ian Mack, Il-Young Moon, J.X. Peng , Jochen Till, Jian Wang, Quan Xue, James Govindhasamy, José Andrés Moreno Pérez, Jorge Tavares, S.K. Jayaweera, Su Jay, Jeanne Chen, Jim Harkin, Yongji Jia, Li Jia, Zhao-Hui Jiang, Gangyi Jiang, Zhenran Jiang, Jianjun Ran, Jiankun Hu, Qing-Shan Jia, Hong Guo, Jin Liu, Jinling Liang, Jin Wu, Jing Jie, Jinkyung Ryeu, Jing Liu, Jiming Chen, Jiann-Ming Wu, James Niblock, Jianguo Zhu, Joel Pitt, Joe Zhu, John Thompson, Mingguang Shi, Joaquin Peralta, Si Bao Chen, Tinglong Pan, Juan Ramón González González, JingRu Zhang, Jianliang Tang, Joaquin Torres, Junaid Akhtar, Ratthachat Chatpatanasiri, Junpeng Yuan, Jun Zhang, Jianyong Sun, Junying Gan, Jyh-Tyng Yau, Junying Zhang, Jiayin Zhou, Karen Rosemary McMenemy, Kai Yu, Akimoto Kamiya, Xin Kang, Ya-Li Ji, Guo-Shiang Lin, Muhammad Khurram, Kevin Curran, Karl Neuhold, Kyongnam Jeon, Kunikazu Kobayashi, Nagahisa Kogawa, Fanwei Kong, Kyu-Sik Park, Lily D. Li, Lara Giordano, Laxmidhar Behera, Luca Cernuzzi, Luis Almeida, Agostino Lecci, Yan Zuo, Lei Li, Alberto Leva, Feng Liang, Bin Li, Jinmei Liao, Liang Tang, Bo Lee, Chuandong Li, Lidija Janezic, Jian Li, Jiang-Hai Li, Jianxun Li, Limei Song, Ping Li, Jie Liu, Fei Liu, Jianfeng Liu, Jianwei Liu, Jihong Liu, Lin Liu, Manxi Liu, Yi Liu, Xiaoou Li, Zhu Li, Kun-hong Liu, Li Min Cui, Lidan Miao, Long Cheng , Huaizhong Zhang, Marco Lovera, Liam Maguire, Liping Liu, Liping Zhang, Feng Lu, Luo Xiaobin, Xin-ping Xie, Wanlong Li, Liwei Yang, Xinrui Liu, Xiao Wei Li, Ying Li, Yongquan Liang, Yang Bai, Margherita Bresco, Mingxing Hu, Ming Li, Runnian Ma, Meta-Montero Manrique, Zheng Gao, Mingyi Mao, Mario Vigliar, Marios Savvides, Masahiro Takatsuka, Matevz Dular, Mathias Lux, Mutlu Avci, Zhifeng Hao, Zhifeng Hao, Ming-Bin Li, Tao Mei, Carlo Meloni, Gennaro Miele, Mike Watts, Ming Yang, Jia Ma, Myong K. Jeong, Michael Watts, Markus Koch, Markus Koch, Mario Koeppen, Mark Kröll, Hui Wang, Haigeng Luo, Malrey Lee, Tiedong Ma, Mingqiang Yang, Yang Ming, Rick Chang, Nihat Adar, Natalie Schellenberg, Naveed Iqbal, Nur Bekiroglu, Jinsong Hu, Nesan Aluha, Nesan K Aluha, Natascha Esau, Yanhong Luo, N.H. Siddique, Rui Nian, Kai Nickel, Nihat Adar, Ben Niu, Yifeng Niu, Nizar Tayem, Nanlin Jin, Hong-Wei Ji, Dongjun Yu, Norton Abrew, Ronghua Yao, Marco Moreno-Armendariz, Osman Kaan Erol, Oh Kyu Kwon, Ahmet Onat, Pawel Herman,

Peter Hung, Ping Sun, Parag Kulkarni, Patrick Connally, Paul Gillard, Yehu Shen, Paul Conilione, Pi-Chung Wang, Panfeng Huang, Peter Hung, Massimo Pica Ciamarra, Ping Fang, Pingkang Li, Peiming Bao, Pedro Melo-Pinto, Maria Prandini, Serguei Primak, Peter Scheir, Shaoning Pang, Qian Chen, Qinghao Rong, QingXiang Wu, Quanbing Zhang, Qifu Fan, Qian Liu, Qinglai Wei, Shiqun Yin, Jianlong Qiu, Qingshan Liu, Quang Ha, SangWoon Lee , Huaijing Qu, Quanxiong Zhou , Qingxian Gong, Qingyuan He, M.K.M. Rahman, Fengyuan Ren, Guang Ren, Qingsheng Ren, Wei Zhang, Rasoul Milasi, Rasoul Milasi, Roberto Amato, Roberto Marmo, P. Chen, Roderick Bloem, Hai-Jun Rong, Ron Von Schyndel, Robin Ferguson, Runhe Huang, Rui Zhang, Robin Ferguson, Simon Johnston, Sina Rezvani, Siang Yew Chong, Cristiano Cucco, Dar-Ying Jan, Sonya Coleman, Samuel Rodman, Sancho Salcedo-Sanz, Sangyiel Baik, Sangmin Lee, Savitri Bevinakoppa, Chengyi Sun, Hua Li, Seamus McLoone, Sean McLoone, Shafayat Abrar, Aamir Shahzad, Shangmin Luan, Xiaowei Shao, Shen Yanxia, Zhen Shen, Seung Ho Hong, Hayaru Shouno, Shujuan Li, Si Eng Ling, Anonymous, Shiliang Guo, Guiyu Feng, Serafin Martinez Jaramillo, Sangwoo Moon, Xuefeng Liu, Yinglei Song, Songul Albayrak, Shwu-Ping Guo, Chunyan Zhang, Sheng Chen, Qiankun Song, Seok-soo Kim, Antonino Staiano, Steven Su, Sitao Wu, Lei Huang, Feng Su, Jie Su, Sukree Sinthupinyo, Sulan Zhai, Jin Sun, Limin Sun, Zengshun Zhao, Tao Sun, Wenhong Sun, Yonghui Sun, Supakpong Jinarat, Srinivas Rao Vadali, Sven Meyer zu Eissen, Xiaohong Su, Xinghua Sun, Zongying Shi, Tony Abou-Assaleh, Youngsu Park, Tai Yang, Yeongtak Jo, Chunming Tang, Jiufei Tang, Taizhe Tan, Tao Xu, Liang Tao, Xiaofeng Tao, Weidong Xu, Yueh-Tsun Chang, Fang Wang, Timo Lindemann, Tina Yu, Ting Hu, Tung-Kuan Liu, Tianming Liu, Tin Lay Nwe, Thomas Neidhart, Tony Chan, Toon Calders, Yi Wang, Thao Tran, Kyungjin Hong, Tariq Qureshi, Tung-Shou Chen, Tsz Kin Tsui, Tiantian Sun, Guoyu Tu, Tulay Yildirim, Dandan Zhang, Xuqing Tang, Yuangang Tang, Uday Chakraborty, Luciana Cariello, Vasily Aristarkhov, Jose-Luis Verdegay, Vijanth Sagayan Asirvadam, Vincent Lee, Markus Vincze, Duo Chen, Viktoria Pammer, Vedran Sabol, Wajeeha Akram, Cao Wang , Xutao Wang, Winlen Wang, Zhuang Znuang, Feng Wang, Haifeng Wang, Le Wang, Wang Linkun, Meng Wang, Rongbo Wang, Xin Wang, Xue Wang, Yan-Feng Wang, Yong Wang, Yongcai Wang, Yongquan Wang, Xu-Qin Li, Wenbin Liu, Wudai Liao, Weidong Zhou, Wei Li, Wei Zhang, Wei Liang, Weiwei Zhang, Wen Xu, Wenbing Yao, Xiaojun Ban, Fengge Wu, Weihua Mao, Shaoming Li, Qing Wu, Jie Wang, Wei Jiang, W Jiang, Wolfgang Kienreich, Linshan Wang, Wasif Naeem, Worasait Suwannik, Wolfgang Slany, Shijun Wang , Wooyoung Soh, Teng Wang, Takashi Kuremoto, Hanguang Wu, Licheng Wu, Xugang Wang, Xiaopei Wu, ZhengDao Zhang, Wei Yen, Yan-Guo Wang, Daoud Ait-Kadi, Xiaolin Hu, Xiaoli Li, Xun Wang, Xingqi Wang, Yong Feng, Xiucui Guan, Xiao-Dong Li, Xingfa Shen, Xuemin Hong, Xiaodi Huang, Xi Yang, Li Xia, Zhiyu Xiang, Xiaodong Li, Xiaoguang Zhao, Xiaoling Wang, Min Xiao, Xiaonan Wu, Xiaosi Zhan, Lei Xie, Guangming Xie, Xiuqing Wang, Xiwen Zhang, XueJun Li, Xiaojun Zong, Xie Linbo, Xiaolin Li, Xin Ma, Xiangqian Wu, Xiangrong Liu, Fei Xing, Xu Shuzheng, Xudong Xie, Bindang Xue, Xuelong Li, Zhanao Xue, Xun Kruger, Xunxian Wang, Xusheng Wei, Yi Xu, Xiaowei Yang, Xiaoying Wang, Xiaoyan Sun, YingLiang Ma, Yong Xu, Jongpil

Yang, Lei Yang, Yang Tian, Zhi Yang, Yao Qian, Chao-bo Yan, Shiren Ye, Yong Fang, Yanfei Wang, Young-Gun Jang, Yuehui Chen, Yuh-Jyh Hu, Yingsong Hu, Zuoyou Yin, Yipan Deng, Yugang Jiang, Jianwei Yang, Yujie Zheng, Ykung Chen, Yan-Kwang Chen, Ye Mei, Yongki Min, Yongqing Yang, Yong Wu, Yongzheng Zhang, Yiping Cheng, Yongpan Liu, Yanqiu Bi, Shengbao Yao, Yongsheng Ding, Haodi Yuan, Liang Yuan, Qingyuan He, Mei Yu, Yunchu Zhang, Yu Shi, Wenwu Yu, Yu Wen, Younghwan Lee, Ming Kong, Yingyue Xu, Xin Yuan, Xing Yang, Yan Zhou, Yizhong Wang, Zanchao Zhang, Ji Zhicheng, Zheng Du, Hai Ying Zhang, An Zhang, Qiang Zhang, Shanwen Zhang, Shanwen Zhang, Zhang Tao, Yue Zhao, R.J. Zhao, Li Zhao, Ming Zhao, Yan Zhao, Bojin Zheng, Haiyong Zheng, Hong Zheng, Zhengyou Wang, Zhongjie Zhu, Shangping Zhong, Xiaobo Zhou, Lijian Zhou, Lei Zhu, Lin Zhu, Weihua Zhu, Wumei Zhu, Zhihong Yao, Yumin Zhang, Ziyuan Huang, Chengqing Li, Z. Liu, Zaiqing Nie, Jiebin Zong, Zunshui Cheng, Zhongsheng Wang, Yin Zhixiang, Zhenyu He, Yisheng Zhong, Tso-Chung Lee, Takashi Kuremoto, Tao Jianhua, Liu Wenjue, Pan Cunhong, Li Shi, Xing Hongjie, Yang Shuanghong, Wang Yong, Zhang Hua, Ma Jianchun, Li Xiaocui, Peng Changping, Qi Rui, Guozheng Li, Hui Liu, Yongsheng Ding, Xiaojun Liu, Qinhua Huang.

# Table of Contents

## Neural Networks

## Evolutionary Computing and Genetic Algorithms

## Kernel Methods

## Combinatorial and Numerical Optimization

## Multiobjective Evolutionary Algorithms

## Neural Optimization and Dynamic Programming



## Case Based Reasoning and Probabilistic Reasoning



## Special Session on Computational Intelligence Approaches and Methods for Security Engineering

## Special Session on Advances in Intelligent Computing with Applications in Multimedia Systems

## Special Session on Emerging Intelligent Methods for Nonlinear System Modelling



## Other Topics

# A Balanced Learning CMAC Neural Networks Model and Its Application to Identification*

Daqi Zhu and Qingbin Sang

Research Centre of Control Science and Engineering,
Southern Yangtze University, Wuxi, JiangSu, China
zdq367@yahoo.com.cn

**Abstract.** In this paper, a concept of balanced learning is presented, and an improved neural networks learning scheme is proposed to speed up the learning process in cerebellar model articulation controllers (CMAC). In the conventional CMAC learning scheme, the corrected amounts of errors are equally distributed into all addressed hypercubes, regardless of the credibility of those hypercubes. The proposed improved learning approach is to use the inversion of the $k^{\text{th}}$ power of learned times of addressed hypercubes as the credibility, the learning speed is different at different $k$. For every situation it can be found a optimal learning parameter $k$ . To demonstrate the online learning capability of the proposed balanced learning CMAC scheme, two nonlinear system identification example are given.

## 1 Introduction

Learning capability is an very important issue for intelligent system like dynamic nonlinear systems. Because these systems are usually complicated, and the knowledge used for fulfilling intelligent behaviors may not exist or are very difficult to obtain. When learning capability is considered, neural networks are always the first candidates to be taken into account, especially for backpropagation (BP) trained multiplayer feedforward neural networks. However, owing to the gradient descent nature of BP neural networks learning algorithm, the learning process of BP algorithm may need to iterate many times so as to converge to an acceptable error level, or even cannot converge at all. Another unsuccessful property of BP algorithm is its distributed knowledge representation capability [1-2]. So the BP algorithm can hardly be used for online learning. This is because online learning needs to work within real-time constraints, and the training can only be performed for current patterns. As a result, it is hard to find any successful online BP examples in real applications.

Another kind of learning approaches, termed as cerebellar model articulation controllers (CMAC) was proposed in the literatures [3-4], in which several advantages including local generalization and rapid learning convergence have been demonstrated [5-6]. It seems to be a good candidate for online learning. However, the learning of the conventional CMAC approach still needs several cycles (or called

* This project is supported by JiangSu Province Nature Science Foundation (BK 2004021).

D.-S. Huang, K. Li, and G.W. Irwin (Eds.): ICIC 2006, LNCS 4113, pp. 1 – 11, 2006.

epochs) to converge [7-8]. Though the conventional CMAC is much faster than BP algorithm, it still is not good enough for online learning system. Consequently, several approaches have been proposed to improve the learning performance of CMAC [9-10] recently. For instance, the fuzzy concept was introduced into the cell structure of CMAC, it indeed increases the accuracy of the representation of the stored knowledge. However, the speed of convergence still cannot satisfy the requirement for real-time applications.

In order to improve the learning speed of CMAC, a new learning approach that has considered the credibility of the learned values was proposed in the literature [11]. In the conventional CMAC learning schemes, the correcting amounts of errors are equally distributed into all addressed hypercubes, regardless the credibility of those hypercubes. Such an updating algorithm violates the concept of credit assignment, i.e., it requires that the updating effects be proportional to the responsibilities of hypercubes.

From the literature [11], it is indeed shown that the credit assignment CMAC (CA-CMAC) is faster and more accurate than conventional CMAC. However, in the literature [11], the credit assignment is proportional to $\frac{1}{f(j)+1}$, $f(j)$ is the learned times of the $j$ th hypercubes. It did not investigate how to effect the learning result by the degree of $f(j)$ further.

In this paper, a new improved CA-CMAC (ICA-CMAC) learning scheme is presented. This algorithm can guarantee that the credit assignment is proportional to $\frac{1}{(f(j)+1)^k}$, Where $k$ is a learning constant, this is a general credit assigned CMAC learning algorithm. When $k$ is “0” and “1”, ICA-CMAC will become the conventional CMAC and CA-CMAC respectively. The experimental results given by the examples showed that the ICA-CMAC has a optimal value of $k$ in improving the neural networks learning speed and accuracy.

This paper is organized as follows. The conventional CMAC and the credit assigned CMAC (CA-CMAC) are introduced in Section 2. In section 3, a new improved CA-CMAC (ICA-CMAC) learning scheme is described. In section 4, the comparison between the conventional CMAC、CA-CMAC and ICA-CMAC is presented. Moreover, to demonstrate the online learning capability of the proposed balanced learning CMAC scheme, two nonlinear system identification examples are given to support our claim. Finally, Section 5 concludes the whole paper.

## 2 Conventional CMAC and Credit Assigned CMAC

### 2.1 Conventional CMAC

The basic idea of CMAC is to store learned data into overlapping regions in a way that the data can easily be recalled but use less storage space. Taking a two-dimensional (2-D) input vector, or called as two-dimensional CMAC (2-D-CMAC), as an example, the input vector is defined by two input variables, $x_1$ and $x_2$. The corresponding structure of a 2-D-CMAC is shown in Fig.1. In this example, 7 locations, called as bits in the literature, are to be distinguished for each variable. For each state variable, three kinds of segmentation, or called as floors, are used. For the first floor, the variable $x_1$ is divided into three blocks, A, B, and C and the variable $x_2$ is divided into three blocks, a, b, and c. Then the areas, Aa, Ab, Ac, Ba, Bb, Bc, Ca, Cb, and Cc are the addresses or the locations that store data, Such areas are often called hypercubes. Similarly, hypercubes, Dd, De, Df, Ed, Ee, Ef, Fd, Fe, and Ff are defined in the second floor, and Gg, Gh, Gi, Hg, Hh,Hi,Ig,Ih,and Ii are defined in the third floor. Be aware that only the blocks on the same floor can be combined to form a hypercubes. Thus, the hypercubes, such as, Ad and Db, do not exist. In this example, there are 27 hypercubes used to distinguish 49 different states in the 2-D-CMAC.

The basic concept of CMAC is illustrated in Fig.2. There are two phases of operations performed in the CMAC algorithm: the output-producing phase and the learning phase. First, the output-producing phase is discussed. In this phase, CMAC uses a set of indices as an addressed in accordance with the current input vector (or the so-called state) to extract the stored data. The addressed data are added together to produce the output. Let the number of floors be m, the number of hypercubes be N, and the number of total states be n. Then, the output value $y_s$ for the state $s$ ($s$=1， ……， n) is the sum of all addressed data, and it can be computed as:

$$y_s = \sum_{j=1}^{N} C_s w_j \tag{1}$$

where $w_j$ is the stored data of the $j$th hypercube and $C_s$ is the index indicating whether the $j$th hypercube is addressed by the state $s$. Since each state addresses exactly m hypercubes, only those addressed $C_s$ are 1, and the others are 0, As shown in Fig1. let the hypercubes Bb, Ee, and Hh be addressed by the state $s(3,3)$, Then only those three $C_s$, are 1 and the others are 0.

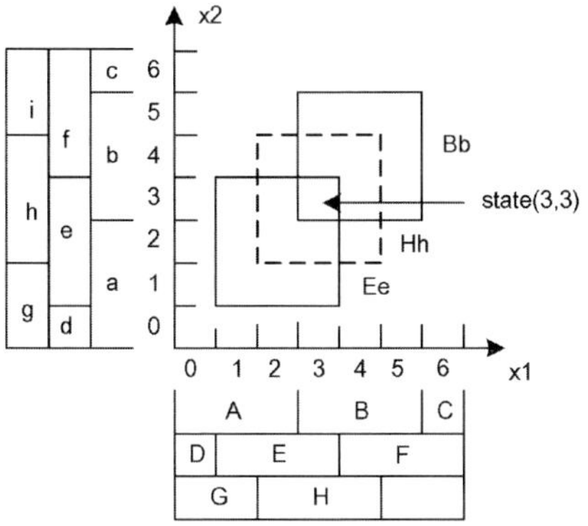


**Fig. 1.** Structure of a 2-D CMAC

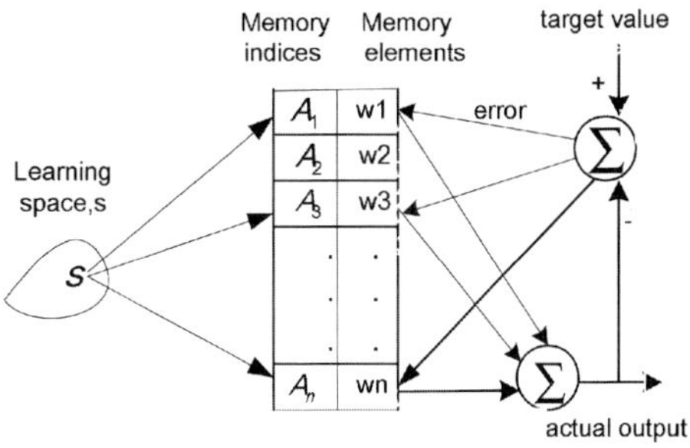


**Fig. 2.** Basic operational concept of CMAC

Whereas the output-producing phase is to generate an output from the CMAC table, the learning phase is to update the data in the CMAC table, according to the error between the desired output and the obtained output. Traditionally, the error is equally distributed to modify the addressed data. Let $s$ be the considered state and $w_j^i$ be the stored values of the $j$ th hypercube after $i$ iterations. The conventional CMAC updating algorithm for $w_j^i$ is

$$w_j^i = w_j^{i-1} + \frac{\alpha}{m} C_s (\overline{y_s} - \sum_{j=1}^{N} C_s w_j^{i-1}) \tag{2}$$

where $\overline{y_s}$ is the desired value for the state $s$ , $\sum_{j=1}^{N} C_s w_j^{i-1}$ is the produced output of the CMAC for the state $s$ , and α is a learning constant. Note that only those addressed hypercubes are updated. It has been proved that if α is not greater than two, then the CMAC learning algorithm will converge[5-6].

In the above learning process, the errors are equally distributed into the hypercubes being addressed. However, after $i-1$ iterations, the original stored data in the CMAC table already contain some knowledge about previous learning. However, not every hypercubes had the same learning history, hence, those hypercubes do not have the same credibility. Disregarding such differences, all addressed hypercubes get equal shares for error correcting in (2). As a result, previous learned information may be corrupted due to large error caused by an unlearned state. When the training process lasts for several cycles, this situation may actually be "smoothed out". This is evident from successful learning in various CMAC applications, However, when the online learning is required, and perhaps only one cycle of training can be performed, there may not have enough time for smoothing out the corrupted data. Thus, the learned results of the updating algorithm may not be acceptable. This can be seen in later simulations.

### 2.2 Credit Assigned CMAC

In the conventional CMAC updating algorithm, unlearned hypercubes may produce the corruption for adjacent hypercubes. Thus the learned results may not be satisfactory in online applications. In order to avoid such corruption effects, the error correction must be distributed according to the creditability of the hypercubes.

Such a concept is often referred to as the credit assignment for learning [12-13]. If possible, the error correction must be distributed according to the creditability of the hypercubes. However, in the CMAC learning process, there is no way of determine which hypercubes is more responsible for the current error, or more accurate than the others. The only information that can be used is how many times the hypercubes have been updated. The assumption used in the literature [11] is that the more times the hypercubes has been trained, the more responsible the stored value is. Hence, the times of updating for hypercubes can be viewed as the creditability of those hypercubes.

With the above assumption, (2) in the literature [11] can be rewritten as

$$w_j^i = w_j^{i-1} + \alpha C_s \{ \frac{(f(j)+1)^{-1}}{\sum_{l=1}^{m} (f(l)+1)^{-1}} \} (\overline{y_s} - \sum_{j=1}^{N} C_s w_j^{i-1}) \tag{3}$$

where $f(j)$ is the learned times of the $j$ th hypercube , and m is the number of addressed hypercubes for a state, i.e. the number of floors. The idea of the updating algorithm is that the effects of error correcting must be proportional to the inversion of learning times for the addressed hypercubes. Note, that the learning times must included the current one to prevent the case divided by zero. In (3) the equal share of error correcting as $1/m$ in (2) is replaced by $(f(j)+1)^{-1} / \sum_{l=1}^{m} (f(l)+1)^{-1}$ . With this modification, the learning effects can be appropriately distributed into the addressed hypercubes according to the creditability of hypercubes. However, this is not the best result, because it did not investigate how to effect the learning result by the degree of $f(j)$ further.

In the paper the credit assignment is proportional to $1/(f(j)+1)^k$ , where $k$ is the balanced learning constant that reflect the weight of the stored value ( or the previous learned information) and unlearned (or new state ) in the neural networks training process.

## 3 Improved Credit Assigned CMCA (ICA-CMAC)

### 3.1 Credit Assigned

According to the analysis above, the concept of the balanced learning is presented here. The updating algorithm for $w_j^i$ can be rewritten as:

$$w_j^i = w_j^{i-1} + \alpha C_s \{ \frac{(f(j)+1)^{-k}}{\sum_{l=1}^{m} (f(j)+1)^{-k}} \} (\overline{y_s} - \sum_{j=1}^{N} C_s w_j^{i-1}) \tag{4}$$

where $k$ is the balanced learning constant, obviously when $k$ is 0 or 1, the ICA-CMAC is the conventional CMAC and the CA-CMAC of the literature [11], respectively. The more $f(j)$ value is, the more updating times of the addressed hypercubes is, the responsible stored value is. When the $k$ value is very much, the stored value is hardly changed for the more $f(j)$ hypercubes. In this situation the addressed hypercubes with unlearned or less $f(j)$ have gotten most correcting amounts of errors.

In addition, when $k$ is very little, the influence of the learned times $f(j)$ to the credit assignment is also very small, the $f(j)$ has no effect on the credit assignment at $k$ =0, In this situation, the error is equally distributed to modify the addressed hypercrubes, all addressed hypercubes have gotten equal credit assignment, regardless of the learned times $f(j)$.

Hence, $k$ is the balanced learning constant that reflects the weight of the stored value (or the previous learned information) and unlearned (or new state) in the neural networks training process. The different $k$ will get the different learning result. Form the following simulations, it can be seen how to influence the learning speed of CMAC by changing balanced learning $k$.

### 3.2 Addressing Function

In the original CMAC described in literatures [3] and [4] , a hashing method is used to reduce the storage space. The hashing method is a way of storing data in a more compact manner, but may lead to the collisions of data, and then may reduce the accuracy of CMAC. In fact, there exists a paper [14] that discusses the applicability of the use of hash coding in CMAC. In our approach, an addressing function is used to simultaneously generate the indices to address the required hypercubes [11]. This approach is to code all possible hypercubes in an array manner, it can saves a lot of time and memory, and will not cause any collisions in data retrieval when compared to simple addressing approaches.

Here, let us take a three dimensional(3-D) CMAC for an example. Suppose that for each dimension, there are $m*(nb-1)+1$ locations to be distinguished, where m is the number of floors in CMAC and nb is the block number for each floor. In this example, each block covers m states and only $N = m*nb^3$ hypercubes are needed to distinguish $(m*(nb-1)+1)^3$ states. Consider a state s, denoted by $(x_1, x_2, x_3)$ representing the locations of the state for those three dimensions, respectively. Let the m addressed hypercubes by the state $s$ be $s(j)$ , for $j = 1,\dots, m$ , The addressing function is to generate $s(j)$ , for $j = 1,\dots, m$ , The addressing function $s(j) = F(x_1, x_2, x_3, j)$, is

① if $j=1$, 则 $i=0$, 其它 $i = m - j + 1$;

② $ax = \text{int}((x_1 + i)/m)$;

③ $ay = \text{int}((x_2 + i)/m)$;

④ $az = \text{int}((x_3 + i)/m)$;

⑤ $s(j) = F(x_1, x_2, x_3, j) = ax + ay + az * nb^2 + (j-1) * nb^3 + 1$.

When a state is defined with this addressing function, the addressed hypercubes can directly be obtained. Thus, no matter what the output-producing phase, or the learning phase is, the required data extraction or data updating can be performed with those hypercubes directly.

## 4 Simulation Results

To illustrate the learning capability of ICA-CMAC, two examples are conducted to compare the learning speed of ICA-CMAC at the different balanced learning constant $k$ .

### 4.1 Two-Dimensional Simulation Results

Let two-dimensional nonlinear function is:

$$y(x_1, x_2) = \sin x_1 \cos x_2 \quad -\pi \le x_1 \le \pi \ \ and \ \ -\pi \le x_1 \le \pi \tag{5}$$

For this example, each variable contains 81 locations. For each variable, 10 floors are used, and each floor contains 9 blocks. The total states are 6561 =81*81, and the number of the used hypercubes is 10*9*9 =810 (only 12.4% of the total states). Here, the learning rate is assumed as α=1.The training data is obtained by equally sampling both variable, and the number of the used training data is 6561.

In the learning process, the learning speed is described by the total absolute error(TAE), the total absolute error can be rewritten as:

$$TAE = \sum_{s=1}^{n} \left| \overline{y_s} - y_s \right| \tag{6}$$

where n is the number of total states, ys is the desired value for the state s, ys is the output value for the state s.

As a result, the learning process for this example is illustrated in Fig.3. All ways of evaluating the errors are considered at the different balanced learning constant $k$ . Note that in this figures, the $k$ value is 0.0, 0.8, 1.2, 2.0 respectively. The detailed and full data is showed in tables 1, here the balanced learning constant $k$ is 0.0, 0.4, 0.8, 1.2, 1.6, 2.0, 2.4 respectively.

In general, online learning schemes are typically used for systems because those schemes can "observe" the changes and then cope with them. In our approach, even though we used the inversion of the $k$ th power of learned times as an index of creditability, such information can be not used to distribute the error amounts. When there are changes (time-varying parameters) in the system, the errors occur to compensate for those changes. Those errors are then distributed into hypercubes according to the used update law.

The error correcting ability of ICA-CMAC is not different from conventional CMAC for this situation. They may be different only in the distributed amount of the errors. Such a distribution in ICA-CMAC is dependent on the learning times of hypercubes, and the learning times of hypercubes areapproximately the same if sufficient learning is conducted. Thus, while facing time-varying systems, there are no differences at different k value in ICA-CMAC for long time. From those figures and tables, It can be seen that after 10 cycles, there is a little difference for different balanced learning consent *k*. In the situation, all CMAC can learn well.

**Table 1.** Total absolute errors in 2-D ICA-CMAC balanced learning

| k | cycle | | | | | | | | | | | | |
|---|---|---|---|---|---|---|---|---|---|---|---|---|---|
| | 1 | 2 | 3 | 4 | 5 | 6 | 7 | 8 | 9 | 10 | 11 | 12 | 13 |
| 0.0 | 108.0 | 121.1 | 55.74 | 79.37 | 48.39 | 50.50 | 47.95 | 39.57 | 44.53 | 39.14 | 39.37 | 38.62 | 38.21 |
| 0.4 | 84.77 | 92.42 | 42.12 | 67.21 | 41.98 | 45.67 | 44.11 | 37.74 | 42.32 | 38.41 | 38.98 | 38.50 | 38.23 |
| 0.8 | 63.30 | 59.17 | 32.72 | 48.80 | 37.77 | 40.33 | 39.81 | 37.57 | 39.70 | 38.60 | 38.65 | 38.59 | 38.49 |
| 1.2 | 61.45 | 44.73 | 31.75 | 41.36 | 36.21 | 39.68 | 39.30 | 38.17 | 39.39 | 38.52 | 38.46 | 38.31 | 38.34 |
| 1.6 | 65.89 | 46.31 | 40.34 | 43.34 | 40.06 | 40.53 | 40.36 | 39.52 | 40.01 | 39.49 | 39.46 | 39.65 | 39.57 |
| 2.0 | 71.56 | 48.14 | 43.56 | 44.68 | 41.73 | 41.40 | 41.17 | 40.20 | 40.48 | 39.87 | 39.74 | 39.95 | 39.85 |
| 2.4 | 102.0 | 58.89 | 52.78 | 50.45 | 46.17 | 44.50 | 43.73 | 42.43 | 42.40 | 41.40 | 41.04 | 41.15 | 40.95 |
| k | cycle | | | | | | | | | | | | |
| | 14 | 15 | 16 | 17 | 18 | 19 | 20 | 21 | 22 | 23 | 24 | 25 | 26 |
| 0.0 | 38.34 | 38.08 | 38.08 | 38.04 | 38.03 | 38.03 | 38.03 | 38.04 | 38.03 | 38.03 | 38.03 | 38.03 | 38.03 |
| 0.4 | 38.30 | 38.14 | 38.15 | 38.13 | 38.14 | 38.14 | 38.15 | 38.15 | 38.16 | 38.17 | 38.16 | 38.17 | 38.17 |
| 0.8 | 38.48 | 38.45 | 38.47 | 38.49 | 38.50 | 38.51 | 38.51 | 38.51 | 38.50 | 38.49 | 38.48 | 38.48 | 38.47 |
| 1.2 | 38.47 | 38.37 | 38.31 | 38.31 | 38.21 | 38.40 | 38.47 | 38.37 | 38.45 | 38.33 | 38.32 | 38.31 | 38.30 |
| 1.6 | 39.64 | 39.71 | 39.76 | 39.77 | 39.75 | 39.73 | 39.68 | 39.64 | 39.59 | 39.54 | 39.48 | 39.43 | 39.38 |
| 2.0 | 39.96 | 40.07 | 40.11 | 40.12 | 40.14 | 40.15 | 40.14 | 40.11 | 40.05 | 39.97 | 39.89 | 38.81 | 39.73 |
| 2.4 | 40.89 | 40.82 | 40.75 | 40.75 | 40.82 | 40.90 | 40.94 | 40.93 | 40.85 | 40.73 | 40.58 | 40.42 | 40.28 |

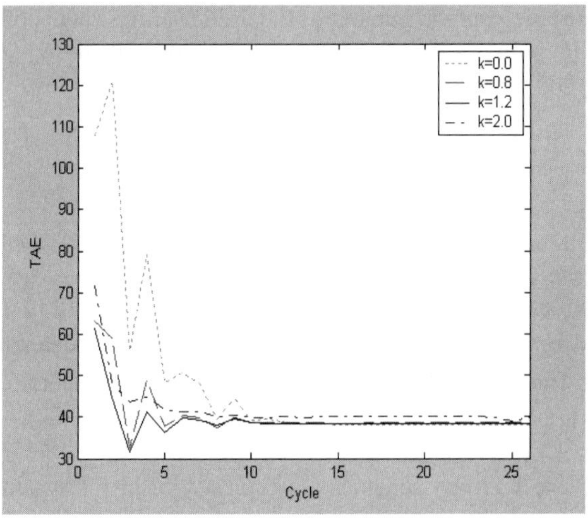


**Fig. 3.** The total absolute error (TAE) of 2-D ICA-CMAC

But in the early learning stage, the learning result is completely different. It can be observed that the errors for $k$ =1.2 is much smaller than others, such as the conventional CMAC ($k$ =0) and CA-CMAC ($k$ =1). So the best balanced learning consent $k$ is 1.2. In other word, at $k$ = 1.2 situation, the stored value (or the previous learned information) and unlearned (or new state) in the neural networks training process achieve the best "balance". From the experimental results given above, it can be found that our proposed balanced learning concept is very right.

### 4.2 Three-Dimensional Simulation Results

Let three-dimensional function is:

$$y(x_1, x_2, x_3) = \sin x_1 \cos x_2 \sin x_3 \quad -\pi \le x_1, x_2, x_3 \le \pi \tag{7}$$

For this example, each variable contains 26 locations. For each variable, 5 floors are used( $m = 5$ ), and each floor contains 6 blocks( $nb = 6$ ). The total states are $(m * (nb - 1) + 1)^3$ =17576= $26 * 26 * 26$ , and the number of the used hypercubes is $m * nb^3 = 5 * 6 * 6 * 6 = 1080$ (only 6.2% of the total states). Here, the learning rate is assumed as $\alpha$ =1. The training data is obtained by equally sampling both variable, and the number of the used training data is 17576.
In the learning process, the total absolute error (TAE) can be rewritten as also:

$$TAE = \sum_{s=1}^{n} \left| \overline{y_s} - y_s \right| \tag{8}$$

**Table 2.** Total absolute errors in 3-D ICA-CMAC balanced learning

| k | cycle | | | | | | | | | | | | |
|---|---|---|---|---|---|---|---|---|---|---|---|---|---|
| | 1 | 2 | 3 | 4 | 5 | 6 | 7 | 8 | 9 | 10 | 11 | 12 | 13 |
| 0.00 | 1298. | 1091. | 967.1 | 952.1 | 846.7 | 862.7 | 840.8 | 835.8 | 849.4 | 832.2 | 841.7 | 832.6 | 836.2 |
| 0.25 | 1199. | 1014. | 958.2 | 934.2 | 814.3 | 867.5 | 827.1 | 833.7 | 830.3 | 822.4 | 828.9 | 819.5 | 826.3 |
| 0.50 | 1107. | 896.7 | 926.7 | 903.8 | 811.7 | 841.3 | 813.8 | 830.1 | 821.7 | 820.6 | 824.2 | 818.5 | 825.0 |
| 0.75 | 1669. | 1177. | 1298. | 1011. | 943.2 | 942.3 | 862.8 | 895.1 | 854.6 | 864.3 | 857.0 | 850.3 | 852.4 |
| 1.00 | 2321. | 1811. | 1613. | 1275. | 1058. | 1081. | 926.6 | 965.5 | 908.9 | 916.4 | 916.1 | 884.6 | 888.1 |
| 1.25 | 2471. | 1953. | 1754. | 1458. | 1249. | 1191. | 959.4 | 986.1 | 956.6 | 951.4 | 964.3 | 932.1 | 932.8 |
| 1.50 | 2927. | 2407. | 2216. | 1954. | 1586. | 1326. | 1236. | 1156 | 1049 | 989.2 | 973.1 | 970.4 | 965.6 |
| k | cycle | | | | | | | | | | | | |
| | 14 | 15 | 16 | 17 | 18 | 19 | 20 | 21 | 22 | 23 | 24 | 25 | 26 |
| 0.00 | 835.4 | 837.1 | 837.5 | 836.9 | 837.3 | 837.6 | 837.5 | 837.4 | 837.5 | 837.2 | 837.0 | 836.8 | 836.7 |
| 0.25 | 824.2 | 825.1 | 825.0 | 824.7 | 825.3 | 825.4 | 826.0 | 826.1 | 826.1 | 826.1 | 826.0 | 826.1 | 826.0 |
| 0.50 | 820.9 | 821.7 | 818.6 | 819.5 | 820.2 | 821.4 | 823.0 | 823.7 | 824.6 | 825.6 | 826.0 | 826.0 | 825.6 |
| 0.75 | 839.7 | 842.6 | 834.1 | 840.4 | 840.7 | 844.1 | 845.5 | 844.7 | 844.5 | 842.1 | 838.7 | 834.7 | 830.5 |
| 1.00 | 869.0 | 886.2 | 879.2 | 889.8 | 889.8 | 890.0 | 887.7 | 880.8 | 876.7 | 869.5 | 862.7 | 857.3 | 851.6 |
| 1.25 | 913.4 | 922.8 | 923.6 | 919.4 | 913.0 | 906.6 | 897.3 | 887.5 | 881.6 | 876.4 | 873.9 | 870.5 | 867.1 |
| 1.50 | 934.0 | 933.1 | 934.8 | 920.4 | 917.9 | 912.1 | 902.0 | 895.8 | 888.4 | 887.1 | 884.1 | 881.6 | 883.2 |

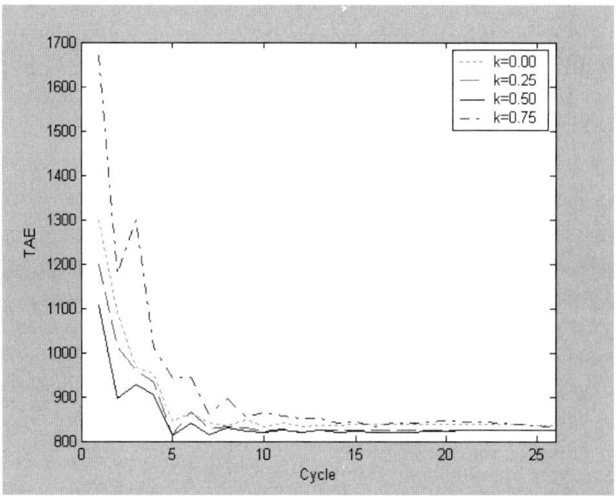


**Fig. 4.** The total absolute error (TAE) of 3-D ICA-CMAC

As a result, the learning process for this example is illustrated in Fig.4. All ways of evaluating the errors are considered at the different balanced learning constant $k$. Note that in Fig.4, the $k$ value is 0.0, 0.25, 0.5, 0.75, respectively.

The total absolute error (TAE) from $k$ =0.0, 0.25, 0.5, 0.75, 1.0, 1.25, 1.5 is all tabulated in tables 2.

From Fig.4 and Table 2, It can be seen that the errors for $k$ =0.5 is much smaller than others, and the learning speed of the conventional CMAC ( $k$ =0) is very slow. So the best balanced learning consent k is 0.5. In other word, at $k$ =0.5 situation in the example, the stored value (or the previous learned information) and unlearned (or new state) in the neural networks training process achieve the best "balance". From the experimental results, it can be found that proposed balanced learning concept is reasonable.

In another, comparing the example 1 with example 2, it can be found that the balanced optimal learning parameter $k$ is different for different object function. But for every situation the balanced optimal learning parameter $k$ always can be found.

## 5 Conclusions

In the paper, a general credit assigned CMAC learning algorithm was proposed based on the concept of balanced learning.

With this idea, the learning speed can indeed become very fast when k is a best value. As a result, the experimental results given by the first example showed that at $k$ =1.2 the improved CMCA is faster and more accurate than the other CMAC in the early learning stage. But $k$ =0.5 is the best balanced learning constant in the second example. In other word, the best balanced learning parameter $k$ is different at different situation.

In addition, an addressing function is used to simultaneously generate the indices to address the required hypercubes without using a huge index matrix or checklist. This method can save a lot of time and memory, and will not cause any collisions in data retrieval when compared to other simple addressing approaches.

## References

1. Hinton G. E., Mcclelland J. L., Rumelhart D.E.: Distributed Representation, Parallel Distributed Proccessing, Rumelhart et al., Eds: MIP Press, vol.l. (1986)
2. Kosko B.: A Dynamical Systems Approach to Machine Intelligence, Neural Networks and Fuzzy Systems, Englewood Cliffs, NJ: Prentice-Hall (1992)
3. Albus J.S.: A New Approach to Manipulator Control: The Cerebellar Model Articulation Controller (cmac), asme J.Dyamic Systems, Measurement, Control.(1975)220-227
4. Albus J.S., Data Storage in Cerebellar Model Articulation Controller (CMAC), ASME J.Dyamic Systems, Measurement, Control.(1975) 228-233
5. Wong Y.F., Sideris A.: Learning Convergence in Cerebellar Model Articulation Controller, IEEE Trans. Neural Networks, vol.3. (1992) 115-121

6. Lin C.S. andChiang C.T., Learning Convergence of CMAC Technique, IEEE Trans.Neural Networks, vol.8, no.6. (1997) 1281-1292
7. Iiguni Y., Hierarchical Image Coding via Cerebellar Model Arithmetic Computers, IEEE Trans. Image Processing, vol.5, no.6. (1996) 1393-1401
8. Hong C.M.,Lin C.H., and Tao T., Grey-CMAC model, Proc. ISTED Int. Conf. High Technology Power Industry. (1997) 39-44
9. Nie J. and Linkens D.A., FCMAC: A Fuzzified Cerebellar Model Articulation Controller with Self-organizing Capacity, Automatica, vol.30, no.4. (1994) 655-664
10. Geng Z.J. and Mccullough C.L, Missile Control using Fuzzy Cerebellar Model Arithmetic Computer Neural Networks, J. Guid., Control, Dyn.,vol.20,no.3. (1997) 557-565
11. Shun-Feng S., Ted T., Hung T.H., Credit Assigned CMAC and Its Application to Online Learning Robust Controllers, IEEE Trans. On Systems, Man, and Cybernetics—part B: Cybernetics, vol.33, no.2.(2003) 202-213
12. Smalz R., Conrad M., Combining Evolution with Credit Apportionment: A new Learning Algorithm for Neural Nets, Neural Networks, vol.7, no.2. (1994) 341-351
13. Plantamura V.L., Soucek B., Visaggio G., Holographic Fuzzy Learning for Credit Scoring, Proc. Int. Joint Conf, Neural Networks, vol.1. (1993) 729-732
14. Wang Z. Q., Schiano J.L, Ginsberg M., Hash-coding in CMAC Neural Networks, IEEE Int'l Conf. Neural Networks. (1996) 1698-1703

# A Cooperative Evolutionary System for Designing Neural Networks

Ben Niu[1,2], Yunlong Zhu[1], Kunyuan Hu[1], Sufen Li[1], and Xiaoxian He[1,2]

[1] Shenyang Institute of Automation, Chinese Academy of Sciences,
Shenyang 110016, China
[2] Graduate School of the Chinese Academy of Sciences,
Beijing 100049, China
{niuben, ylzhu}@sia.cn

**Abstract.** A novel cooperative evolutionary system, i.e., CGPNN, for automatic design artificial neural networks (ANN's) is presented where ANN's structure and parameters are tuned simultaneously. The algorithms used in CGPNN combine genetic algorithm (GA) and particle swarm optimization (PSO) on the basis of a direct encoding scheme. In CGPNN, standard (real-coded) PSO is employed to training ANN's free parameters (weights and bias) and binary-coded GA is used to find optimal ANN's structure. In the simulation part, CGPNN is applied to the predication of tool life. The experimental results show that CGPNN has good accuracy and generalization ability in comparison with other algorithms.

## 1 Introduction

Artificial Neural networks (ANN's), and in particular, the multilayer feed-forward neural networks [1], are widely used in many application areas over the years. It is claimed that a three-layered feed-forward neural network can approximate any nonlinear function with arbitrary accuracy. Nonetheless its drawback is that the design of an efficient architecture and the choice of the synaptic weights require high processing time.

In general, ANN's are designed by means of trial and error and fixed during the learning process and the parameters are trained by gradient-based algorithms such as, error back propagation (BP), conjugate gradient descent, resilient, BFGS quasi-Newton, one-step secant, Levenberg-Marquardt and Bayesian regularization methods [2-7].

The two main disadvantages of such method include:

1) Those algorithms are based on the gradient information of an objective function, easily trapped in local minima, and are limited for applications in complex optimization problems.
2) A fixed structure may not provide the optimal performance within a defined training period. A small network may not provide good performance owing to its limited information processing power. A large network, on the other hand, may lead to overfitting and the implementation cost for a large network is also high.

D.-S. Huang, K. Li, and G.W. Irwin (Eds.): ICIC 2006, LNCS 4113, pp. 12 – 21, 2006.

To obtain ANN's structure automatically, constructive and destructive algorithms can be used [8, 9]. However, Angeline et al. [10] indicated that such structural hill climbing methods are susceptible to becoming trapped at structural local optima and they only investigate restricted topological subset rather than the complete class of network architectures.

The advent of evolutionary computation (EC) has inspired as a new technique for optimal design of neural networks. There have been many applications for both parametric and structural learning [11-13]. These works fall in two broad categories of evolutionary computation: genetic algorithms and evolutionary programming. Although, some attempts have been made in developing evolving networks, few authors have devoted their attention to the cooperative evolutionary system.

This paper aims at giving a cooperative environment to automatic design of ANN's. A cooperative evolutionary system, i.e., CGPNN, is presented by using two evolutionary algorithms: genetic algorithm (GA) and particle swarm optimization (PSO). In CGPNN, standard PSO is used for the weights (including biases) training of ANN's, and binary GA is applied to find the appropriate network architecture. Both algorithms can jointly search the global optimal ANN's structure and parameters. As examples of the application of CGPNN, it is applied to the predication of tool life. The results will be compared with those obtained by traditional feed-forward ANN's with a fixed structure that trained by BP, GA and PSO.

The rest of the paper is organized as follows. Section 2 describes the standard PSO (SPSO), GA and multilayer feed-forward ANN's. Section 3 describes the detailed cooperative evolutionary strategy for multilayer feed-forward ANN's design. Section 4 presents the experimental settings and results for each algorithm. Section 5 concludes the paper.

## 2 Background

This section briefly presents an overview of SPSO, GA and multilayer feed-forward ANN's.

### 2.1 Standard PSO (SPSO)

Particle swarm optimization (PSO) is a novel bio-inspired evolutionary computation technique firstly developed by Kennedy and Eberhart in 1995 [14, 15]. In PSO, the potential solutions, called particles, fly in a *D*-dimension search space with a velocity which is dynamically adjusted according to its own experience and that of its neighbors.

The $i-th$ particle is represented as $x_i=(x_{i1},x_{i2},..x_{iD})$ in the *D*-dimensional space, where $x_{id}\in[l_d,u_d]$, $d\in[1,D]$, $l_d,u_d$ are the lower and upper bounds for the *d*th dimension, respectively. The rate of velocity for particle $i$ is represented as $v_i=(v_{i1},v_{i2},...v_{iD})$, is clamped to a maximum velocity $v_{\max}=(v_{\max,1},...v_{\max,d},v_{\max,D})$, which is specified by the user. In each time step *t*, the particles are manipulated according to the following equations:

$$v_{id} = wv_{id} + R_1c_1(P_{id} - x_{id}) + R_2c_2(p_{gd} - x_{id}) \tag{1}$$

$$x_{id} = x_{id} + v_{id}, \tag{2}$$

where $w$ is inertia weight , $R_1$ and $R_2$ are random values between 0 and 1. $c_1$ and $c_2$ are acceleration constants, which control how far a particle will move in a single iteration. $P_i$ is the best previous position of the $i-th$ particle.

### 2.2 Genetic Algorithm (GA)

Genetic algorithms [16] are inspired by the evolution of populations. In a particular environment, individuals which better fit the environment will be able to survive and hand down chromosomes to their descendants, while less fit individuals will become extinct.

The genetic algorithms create populations of individuals which are often represented by a binary representation. The populations are evolved to find good individuals by performing genetic operations, such as reproduction, crossover, and mutation. A fitness function is defined which measures the fitness of each individual.

As stated above, the task here is to use binary-coded GA for optimal design the neural architectures.

### 2.3 Multilayer Feed-Forward ANN's

In this work, multilayer feed-forward ANN's with each layer consisting of a number of computing neurons have been used. A MFNN represents a nonlinear mapping between input vector and output vector through a system of simple interconnected neurons.

A three-layer feed-forward network composed of one input layer, one hidden layer and one output layer is shown schematically in Fig.1. The number of neurons in hidden layer and output layer are *H* and *O,* respectively.

The neurons in the hidden layer perform computations, and the outputs of these neurons are given by

$$x_j^{(H)} = f_j((\sum_{i=1}^{I} w_{ij}^{(H)} x_i) + b_j^{(H)}), \qquad j = 1, 2, \ldots H \tag{3}$$

The outputs of neurons in the output layer are given by

$$y_j = f_j((\sum_{i=1}^{H} w_{ij} x_i^{(H)}) + b_j), \qquad j = 1, 2, \ldots O \tag{4}$$

$w$ and $b$ are adjustable parameters called weights and biases parameters, which will be tuned. $f(\bullet)$ is the nonlinear activation function

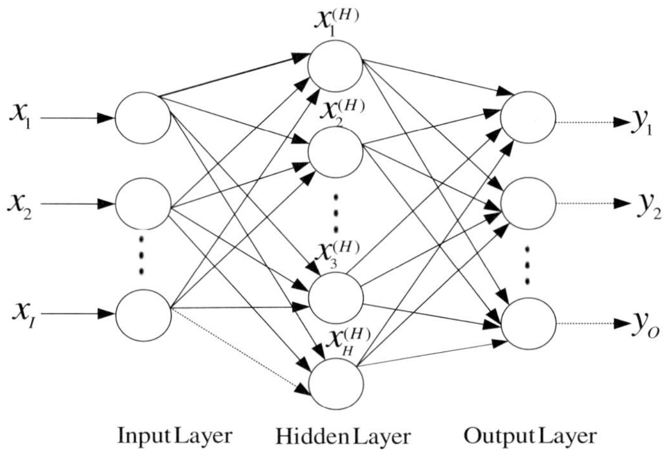


**Fig. 1.** Three-layer BP network architecture

## 3 Designing ANN's Using Cooperative Evolutionary System

The overall learning process of CGPNN can be described as follows:

(1) *Parameter representation*

In our work the direct encoding scheme is applied to encode the architecture of network. Two equal size one-dimensional matrices are used to specify an ANN in CGPNN. One matrix is the weight matrix, *W*, whose entries are real numbers. For the three-layer MFNN mentioned above, the free parameters to be coded include weights and biases, which can be defined as a one-dimensional matrix, i.e.,

$$\left\{ \overbrace{1 \quad 2 \quad \cdots \quad I\times H}^{w^{(IH)}}, \overbrace{1 \quad 2 \quad \cdots \quad H\times O}^{w^{(HO)}}, \overbrace{1 \quad 2 \quad \cdots \quad H}^{b^{(H)}}, \overbrace{1 \quad 2 \quad \cdots \quad O}^{b^{(O)}} \right\}.$$

$w^{(IH)}$ is the weights between input layer and hidden layer. $w^{(HO)}$ is the weights between hidden layer and output layer. $b^{(H)}$ represents the biases of the hidden layer. $b^{(O)}$ represents the biases of the output layer. The size of the matrix can be represented by $D = I \times H + H \times O + H + O$.

The other is connectivity matrix, *C*, corresponding to the weights (bias), whose entries can only be "0" or "1". A bit "0" in an individual indicated the absence of the corresponding weights (bias). Otherwise a bit "1" in an individual indicated the presence of the corresponding weights (bias).

Then the last weight *LW* concerned with the MFNN computation is the multiplication of *W* and *C*, i.e. *LW=W.C'*.

(2) *Initialization*

In CGPNN, PSO and GA both work with the same population, Initially *M* individuals forming the population should be randomly generated and each consists of *D* parameters. These individuals may be regard as chromosomes in terms of GA, or as particles in terms of PSO. In addition, the learning parameters, such as $c_1$ and $c_2$, inertia weight $w$ should be assigned in advance.

(3) *Evaluate the fitness function*
To evaluate the performance of an individual, a predefined fitness function should be formulated. The fitness function takes into account two aspects: mean squared error between network outputs and desired outputs, and the complexity of ANN.

The *SSE* is calculated as the following:

$$SSE = \sum_{p=1}^{\#of\ patterns} \sum_{K=1}^{O} (d_{kp} - y_{kp})^2 \tag{5}$$

where $d_{kp}$ is the *k*-th node of desired output and $y_{kp}$ is the *k*-th network output.

The complexity of the network is simply defines as

$$CNN = \frac{N_{hidden}}{N_{\max hidden}} \tag{6}$$

where $N_{hidden}$ is the number of weights that are involved in networks; $N_{\max hidden}$ is predefined the max number of hidden units.

Then the fitness function of network could be expressed as follows:

$$Fitness = SSE + \lambda \bullet CNN \tag{7}$$

where $\lambda$ is a constant which balances the impact of *SSE* and *CNN.* Designing a network with CGPNN means moving the individuals among the search space to minimize the fitness function.

(4) *Enhancement*
The enhancement mechanism acts as follows: first the weights and bias of the population are updated according to Eqs (1) and (2), then the connectivity bits for the current solution are updated by reproduction, crossover and mutation operation in GA. These two steps can change both structure and parameters to produce new best-performing individuals.

(5) *Termination condition*
The proposed algorithm is performed until the *Fitness* is small enough, or a pre-determined number of epochs is passed. It is expected that, after a certain number of iterations, the near –optimal ANN's architecture can be obtained.

## 4 Experimental Studies

Tool life is usually defined as the period time that tool cutting edges lose their usefulness through wear [17] it is commonly expressed as the actual cutting time to failure but other measures such as the length of work-piece cut, the volume of metal removed and the number of components produced to failure can be also used [18].

From a maintenance point of view, it is very expensive if cutting tool breakage occurs during machining operation due to end of tool life. Therefore, Tool life estimation is very essential for optimizing the cutting performance in turning operations.

In general, mathematical models are available for the prediction of tool life, which require a large number of data for successful implementation. Recent research preferred artificial neural network, which can be trained using a finite set of data. Many works have proved the performance of neural networks to estimate tool life in major machining operations including turning [19] and drilling [20].

**Table 1.** Normalized patterns used for training and testing

| Sample number | Speed ($S$) (m/min) | Feed ($F$)(mm/rev) | Depth of Cut ($D$) (mm) | Flank wear Width ($V_b$) (mm) | Output Tool Life (min) |
|---|---|---|---|---|---|
| 1 | 0.15 | 0.07 | 0.09 | 0.15 | 0.42 |
| 2 | 0.10 | 0.13 | 0.09 | 0.09 | 1.00 |
| 3 | 0.20 | 0.13 | 0.09 | 0.17 | 0.31 |
| 4 | 0.10 | 0.21 | 0.09 | 0.21 | 0.35 |
| 5 | 0.20 | 0.27 | 0.09 | 0.12 | 0.23 |
| 6 | 0.25 | 0.27 | 0.09 | 0.20 | 0.10 |
| 7 | 0.10 | 0.07 | 0.17 | 0.18 | 0.54 |
| 8 | 0.25 | 0.07 | 0.17 | 0.19 | 0.21 |
| 9 | 0.15 | 0.13 | 0.17 | 0.17 | 0.40 |
| 10 | 0.10 | 0.21 | 0.17 | 0.23 | 0.29 |
| 11 | 0.20 | 0.27 | 0.17 | 0.17 | 0.08 |
| 12 | 0.25 | 0.25 | 0.17 | 0.13 | 0.13 |
| 13 | 0.15 | 0.03 | 0.26 | 0.23 | 0.12 |
| 14 | 0.15 | 0.13 | 0.26 | 0.12 | 0.60 |
| 15 | 0.25 | 0.13 | 0.26 | 0.26 | 0.09 |
| 16 | 0.10 | 0.21 | 0.16 | 0.24 | 0.23 |
| 17 | 0.20 | 0.23 | 0.26 | 0.22 | 0.28 |
| 18 | 0.10 | 0.27 | 0.26 | 0.19 | 0.48 |
| 19 | 0.25 | 0.27 | 0.20 | 0.16 | 0.10 |
| 20 | 0.20 | 0.07 | 0.08 | 0.16 | 0.27 |

**Table 2.** Comparison of sum square error (SSE) with different methods

| Method | BPNN | GANN | PSONN | CGPNN |
|---|---|---|---|---|
| SSE (Average) | 0.08975 | 0.0658 | 0.0157 | 0.0087 |
| SSE (Best) | 0.08419 | 0.0625 | 0.0137 | 0.0052 |

In this work, CGPNN is used for designing ANN with speed of work piece ($S$), feed of the tool ($F$), depth of cut the tool ($D$) and flank wear width ($V_b$) as input vectors and cutting tool life as the output vector. As comparison, ANN trained by BP (BPNN), GA (GANN) and PSO (PSONN) are also used for the same task.

The database used for training and testing is taken from [21]. Twenty sets of results are collected as shown in Table 1. The first 15 patterns were used for training and the last 5 patterns were considered for testing. Before the patterns are selected for training and testing, they should be normalized so that they lie between 0 and 1.

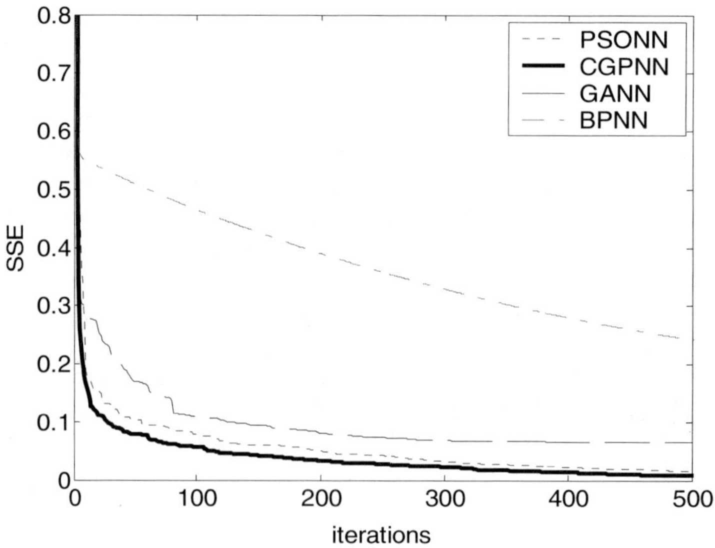


**Fig. 2.** Averaged best-so-far SSE in each generation

**Table 3.** Performance comparisons for ANN'S testing using different methods

| Sample number | Expected output | GANN | BPNN | PSONN | CGPNN |
|---|---|---|---|---|---|
| 16 | 0.23 | 0.2594 | 0.2612 | 0.2518 | 0.2317 |
| 17 | 0.28 | 0.2871 | 0.3204 | 0.2987 | 0.2734 |
| 18 | 0.48 | 0.4248 | 0.4324 | 0.4498 | 0.4621 |
| 19 | 0.10 | 0.0964 | 0.1315 | 0.1151 | 0.1021 |
| 20 | 0.27 | 0.3021 | 0.2928 | 0.2877 | 0.2682 |

In applying CGPNN, GA and PSO are both work with the same population, i.e. the population size of each algorithm $n = 80$, is chosen. The parameters crossover probability $P_c = 0.4$, mutation probability $P_m = 0.1$. inertial weights $w_{max} = 0.9$, $w_{min} = 0.4$, the acceleration constants $c_1 = c_2 = 0.1$. are used.

For fair comparison, all the parameters in PSONN and GANN are set the same as those used in CGPNN. In BP, the learning rate $\eta$ and the momentum $\alpha$ are set as 0.3 and 0.9, respectively. For BPNN, GANN and PSONN the same network configuration with 4-6-1architecture are deigned.

The evolution is processed for 500 generations and is repeated for 20 runs. The averaged best-so-far *SSE* value over 20 runs for each generation is shown in Fig. 2.

The best and averaged *SSE*s for the 20 runs after 500 generations of training are listed in Table 2.

Table 2 illustrates that the average and best *SSE*s of CGPNN are smaller than those of BPNN, GANN and PSONN. Observing from Fig.2, we can see that CGPNN converges with a higher speed compared to BPNN, GANN, PSONN, and obtains a better result. The phenomenon may attribute to the following characteristics:

1) Traditionally, the structure of neural network is based on trial and error, while the CGPNN identify the structure and the parameters of the network simultaneously in a large search space. Therefore, the convergence performance of the neural network could be reasonably enhanced.
2) In training the parameters of the neural networks using GA and PSO, the memory and cooperation features of PSO help it converge faster than GA.
3) Although BP algorithm contributes a lot in the past years, its relatively low convergence speed frequently restricts its application field. As can be seen from the figure, BP converges much slower than other methods.

To test the performance of the designed ANN, the prediction results of the last 5 patterns are listed in Table 3. This comparison is also shown using graphs in Figs. 3 (a)-(d). It should be noted that the BPNN is evolved for 3000 generations repeated for 20 runs. The prediction results of SPSO are more or less the same and slight superior to the BPNN and GANN method, while our proposed method outperforms that of any other approaches. It is shown that CGPNN can predict tool life with high accuracy and the prediction error of the tool life is less than 3.7%.

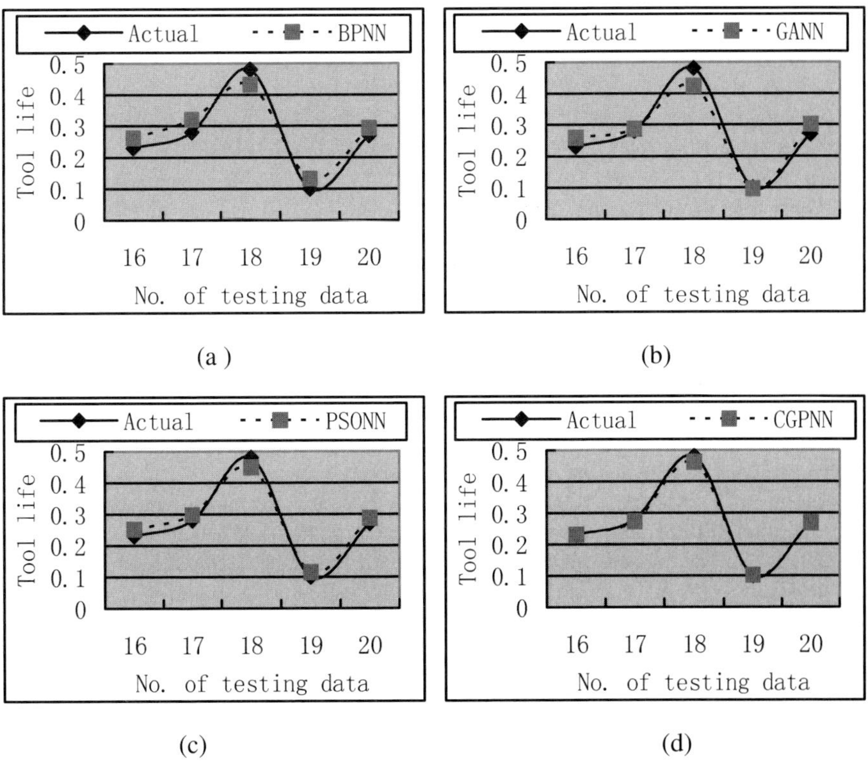


**Fig. 3.** Actual and predicted tool life by different methods: (a) BPNN; (b) GANN; (c) PSONN (d) CGPNN

## 5 Conclusions

In this paper, a cooperative evolutionary system and its learning strategy for predicting tool life were proposed. The hybrid algorithm use GA to evolve the architecture and PSO to learn the free parameters simultaneously. The automatic structure design of neural networks has been a heated problem for a long period. This paper attempt to automatically design a neural network for predicting tool life, and the simulation results demonstrate its superiority compared with some other methods. Further work will be focused on ulteriorly optimize the structure and the parameters of the neural networks, and exploring the effective application in some other fields.

## Acknowledgements

This work is supported by the National Natural Science Foundation of China (Grant No. 70431003) and the National Basic Research Program of China (Grant No. 2002CB312200).

## References

1. Rumelhart, D.E., Hinton, G.E., Williams, R.J.: Learning Internal Representations by ErrorPropagation. The MIT press, Cambridge, Massachusetts (1986)
2. Rumelhar, D.E., Hinton, G.E., Williams, R. J.: Learning Representations by Back-Propagating Errors. Nature. 323 (1986)533-536
3. Vogl, T.P., Mangis, J.K., Rigler, A.K., Zink, W.T., Alkon, D.L.: Accelerating the Convergence of the Back-Propagation Method. Biological Cybernetics. 59(1988)257-263
4. Battit, R: First and Second Order Methods of Learning: Between the Steepest Descent and Newton's Method. Neural Network. 4(1991)141-166
5. Stone, J.V.; Lister, R.: On the Relative Time Complexities of Standard and Conjugate Gradient Back Propagation. In: Proceedings of IEEE World Congress on Computational Intelligence, Orlando Florida USA (1994)84-87
6. Boray, G.K., Srinath, M.D.: Conjugate Gradient Techniques for Adaptive Filtering. IEEE Transactions on Circuits and Systems. 39(1) (1992)1-10.
7. Hagan, M.T., Menhaj, M.B.: Training Feed Forward Networks with the Marquardt Algorithm. IEEE Transactions on Neural Networks. 5 (1994) 989-993
8. Gallant, S.: Neural-Network Learning and Expert Systems. Cambridge, MA: MIT Press (1993)
9. Reed, R.: Pruning algorithms—A Survey. IEEE Transactions on Neural Networks 4(1993)740–747
10. Angeline, P., Saunders, G., Pollack, J.: An Evolutionary Algorithm That Constructs Recurrent Neural Networks. IEEE Trans. Neural Networks. 5 (1994) 54-65
11. Leung, F.H.F., Lam, H.K., Ling, S.H., and Tam, P. K. S.: Tuning of the structure and parameters of neural network using an improved genetic algorithm. IEEE Trans. Neural Networks. 14 (1) (2003)79-88
12. Miller, G. P., Todd, P. M., Hegde, S.U.: Designing neural networks using genetic algorithms. In: Proceedings of the 3rd Int. Conf. Genetic Algorithms Applications, San Mateo, CA. (1989) 379–384.

13. Yao, X., Liu, Y.: A new evolutionary system for evolving artificial neural networks. IEEE Trans. Neural Networks 8 (1997) 694–713
14. Eberchart, R.C., Kennedy, J.: A new optimizer using particle swarm theory. In: proceeding of the 6th international symposium on Micromachine and Human Science, Nagoya, Japan (1995) 39-43
15. Kennedy, J., Eberhart, R.C.: Particle Swarm Optimization. In: proceeding. of IEEE International Conference on Neural Networks, Piscataway, NJ (1995) 1942-1948
16. Holland, J. H.: Adaptation in Natural and Artificial Systems, Ann Arbor, MI: Univ. Michigan Press (1975)
17. Jalali, S.A., Kolarik, W.J.: Tool life and machinability models for drilling steels. International Journal of Machine Tools& Manufacturing 31 (1991) 273–282.
18. Armarego, E.J.A., Brown, R.H.: The Machining of Metals. Prentice-Hall Inc., Englewood Cliffs, NJ (1969)
19. Liu, Q., Altintas. Y.: On-line Monitoring of Flank Wear in Turning with Multi-layered Feed-forward Neural Network. International Journal of Machine Tools& Manufacturing 39 (1999) 1945-1959
20. Lee, B.Y., Liu, H.S., Tarng, Y.S.: Abductive Network for Predicting Tool Life in Drilling. IEEE Transactions on Industry Application. 35 (1999) 190-195
21. Natarajan, U., Saravanan, R., Periasamy, V.M.: Application of particle swarm optimization in artificial neural network for the prediction of tool life, International Journal of Advanced Manufacturing Technology 28 (2006) 1084-1088

# A Neural Network Approach to Medical Image Segmentation and Three-Dimensional Reconstruction

Vitoantonio Bevilacqua, Giuseppe Mastronardi, and Mario Marinelli

Dipartimento di Elettrotecnica ed Elettronica, Polytechnic of Bari,
Via E. Orabona, 4, 70125, Bari, Italy
{bevilacqua, mastrona}@poliba.it

**Abstract.** Medical Image Analysis represents a very important step in clinical diagnosis. It provides image segmentation of the *Region of Interest* (ROI) and the generation of a three-dimensional model, representing the selected object. In this work, was proposed a neural network segmentation based on Self-Organizing Maps (SOM) and a three-dimensional SOM architecture to create a 3D model, starting from 2D data of extracted contours. The utilized dataset consists of a set of CT images of patients presenting a prosthesis' implant, in DICOM format. An application was developed in Visual C++, which provides an user interface to visualize DICOM images and relative segmentation. Moreover it generates a three-dimensional model of the segmented region using Direct3D.

## 1 Introduction

Image Processing, aimed to interpret and classify image content, has attracted research attention since the birth and spread of computers. Technology improvements have brought more applications to image classification such as *Image* and *Scene Analysis*, *Image Understanding*, *Object Recognition* and *Computer Vision*. Recognition, description and automatic classification of structures inside images represent an important issue in a huge set of scientific and engineering subjects.

The medical research has been quite receptive of image processing like X-ray CT and Magnetic Resonance. The output of these techniques, an image of the patient's body (*slice*), allows physicians examining and diagnosing without the need of surgery. In order to perform these complex medical processes, some operations over the images have to be performed.

A standard was introduced by the American College of Radiology (*ACR*) and the National Elecrical Manufactoring Association (*NEMA*) called DICOM (1993) [3] which is now considered the world standard for transferring and managing medical images.

Image Analysis represents an image processing application directed to extract significant informations for describing internal structures. In particular, image segmentation represents a fundamental step in image analysis since it allows extracting the region of interest to recognize and classify. So this is a critical step: precision and quality of the result can heavily affect next processes. Segmentation aim [4] is to decompose an image in distinct parts or ROIs: each ROI is homogeneous to a particular characteristic and it is separate from adjacent regions. The segmentation of an

D.-S. Huang, K. Li, and G.W. Irwin (Eds.): ICIC 2006, LNCS 4113, pp. 22–31, 2006.

image can be carried out by different techniques that are based on the discontinuity and similarity of the grey levels of an image. Some techniques proposed in literature [5, 6] are based on artificial neural networks algorithms. Artificial Neural Networks [7] try to simulate a structure similar to the one that is believed the human brain has got. The area of the brain is organized into several sensory modalities such as speech or hearing. The engineering approach of neural networks develops hardware or software inspired by the brain's structure.

The segmented regions can be processed to generate a three-dimensional model of the selected object. Three-dimensional visualization, in fact, is now a precious tool in biomedical imaging. The medical applicability of 3D image processing is very important, the field of applications are being very large, from the medical statistics to computer assisted tomography [8].

## 2 Self-Organizing Maps (SOM)

Kohonen's Self-Organizing Maps (SOM) [1, 2] are simple analogies of the human brain's way of organizing information in a logical manner. Kohonen's method emulates the unsupervised learning in an elegant, extremely easy manner. It consists of one layer of neurons and uses the method of competitive learning with "*winner takes all*" logic.

Kohonen's Self-Organizing Maps consist of one layer of neurons organized in one, two and multi-dimensional arrays (fig.1).

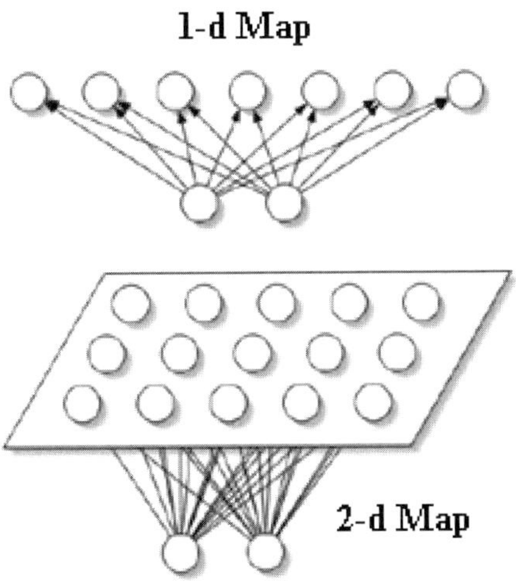


**Fig. 1.** One-dimensional and two-dimensional Kohonen's maps

Each neuron has as many input connections as there are number of attributes to be used in the classification. All the neurons in the map are interconnected and each neuron influences others which are into its neighbourhood. The lateral coupling of the neurons is thought as a function of the distance in two ways: excitatory and inhibitory.

The excitatory is in a short range up to a certain radius, and the inhibitory surrounds the excitatory area up to a bigger radius. A cluster or bubble around one particular node of the network is formed due to the lateral coupling around a given cell. The primary input determines a "winner" node, which will have a certain cluster, and then, following the input, the winner node with its surrounding cluster or neighbourhood will adapt to the input.

The training procedure consists of finding the neuron with weights closest to the input data vector and declaring that neuron as the winning neuron:

$$|w_i - T| \leq |w_k - T| \qquad \forall k = 1 \ldots N$$

where:

$w_i$ is winner neuron
$w_k$ is any neuron
$T$ is the input vector to classify
$N$ is the number of neurons

After finding the winner, the next step is to update the weights' vector of the neurons, as:

$$w_k = w_k(t-1) + \mu \cdot G(i,k)\left(T - w_k(t-1)\right) \quad \forall k = 1 \ldots N$$

where:

$\mu \in [0, 1]$ is the learning rate

$$\begin{cases} t & \text{actual state} \\ t-1 & \text{previous state} \end{cases}$$

The factor $G(i,k)$ is the Gauss function related to the dimension of neuron's neighbourhood. It considers the influence between the winner neuron $i$ and a neuron $k$ in its vicinity. It is defined as:

$$G(i,k) = e^{-\frac{|w_k - w_i|^2}{2\sigma^2}}$$

where σ is the bubble's radius. At the beginning this parameter is set to a certain value which is decreased at each iteration of the training procedure.

So the training algorithm is iterative and this procedure is repeated a certain number of times. The stop criterion of the algorithm is determined by one of the following:

- σ or μ go down under an arranged value;
- the maximum number of epochs is reached;
- weights' values are stable.

At the end of the training algorithm, the network is seen as a "black box" which associates to each sample of the input pattern the index or weights of a neuron in the map. In this way, the net classifies and labels each element in the input pattern.

## 3 Medical Image Segmentation

Image segmentation techniques are based on image properties such as intensity, colour or geometry to identify homogeneous ROIs and their contours. There are two main approaches: the first is based on regions and the second on contours. These are based on two properties: similarity and discontinuity.

We have used two main techniques based on the first approach: *Thresholding* and a *Neural Network segmentation* based on Kohonen's Self-Organizing Maps.

**Thresholding** is the most popular segmentation technique, due to its conceptual and computational simplicity. It uses the property of local similarity of image's pixels to define a certain grey level *T*, called *binarization threshold*, which permits to subdivide an image in significant regions.

Given a couple of grey values ($g_0$, $g_1$), once the threshold value *T* was defined, the segmentation result of an image $I(x,y)$ is a binary one $I_b(x,y)$ which satisfies the following relation:

$$I_b(x, y) = \begin{cases} g_0 & \text{if } I(x, y) < T \\ g_1 & \text{if } I(x, y) \geq T \end{cases}$$

In the case of medical images in DICOM format, we can use a CT Number, expressed in Hounsfield units, as threshold value instead of its associated grey level. This creates a more efficient segmentation, because the Hounsfield scale is larger than the grey one. The limited range of the grey scale, equal to 255, compresses the Hounsfield scale, up to 4000, with consequent loss of voxels' informations. This makes more difficult to distinguish regions among which there is a small difference in Hounsfield values that becomes almost null in the grey scale.

This segmentation process can be made automatic by a neural network approach based on **Kohonen's self-organizing maps**. Their ability of self-organization permits to classify image's pixels basing on some features of the regions to find out. The objective is to label each pixel grouping them in a certain number of clusters.
In particular, the input pattern is represented by the set of slices of the acquired volume, while the output layer represents the regions to be found.

The SOM network is organized as follows (fig. 2):

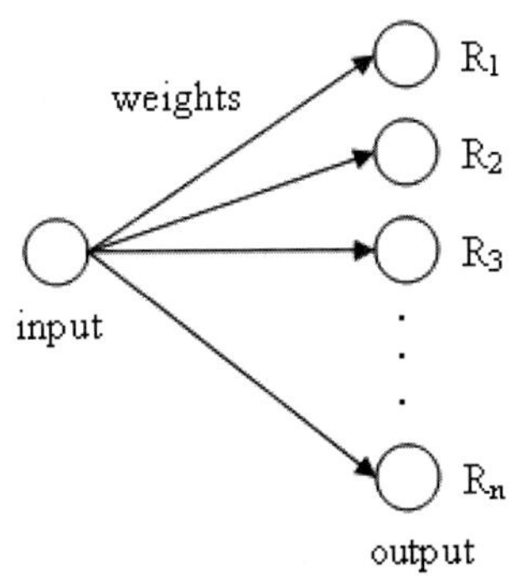


**Fig. 2.** Kohonen's Self-Organizing Map

- one input neuron represented by the voxel's CT Number;
- n output neurons representing the number of ROIs to extract from the original image.

The map is one-dimensional and the neurons are set on a virtual line, so the distance between two consecutive neurons is unitary.

In the initialization step neurons' weights are set to zero, for assuring the same association order to all slices. In the training procedure the weights will adapt to the CT Numbers of the presented slice. This procedure is repeated for each slice of the acquired volume, while the initialization is performed only for the first slice. In this way the weights will adapt to all CT Numbers of the entire volume. At the end of the training procedure, the net is able to assign an index to each voxel representing its own region.

After segmenting all images and extracting the region of interest, the next step is the Edge Detection. This process creates binary images in which activated pixels identify contours of the extracted regions using a particular operator. In the considered case the most significant is the *gradient* operator. It determines the boundary pixels between two different regions. This process is a simple task if we consider the segmented regions for their definition.

Edge detection is the final step before the next three-dimensional reconstruction starting from 2D contours.

## 4 Three-Dimensional Reconstruction

The aim of three-dimensional reconstruction is to generate a 3D model of the object extracted by the segmentation techniques which were described previously. The main problem is to generate a polygonal mesh starting from two-dimensional contours placed on different planes. This consists of establishing an order among contours' points in order to generate a well connected mesh which will represent the external surface of the object. Some techniques were proposed in literature [9] which were based on a geometrical and mathematical approach. We have developed an alternative approach based on artificial neural networks.

This approach consists of a particular SOM architecture that is based on a three-dimensional topology. In this network, neurons represent vertices of the triangular mesh to generate, so weights represent three-dimensional coordinates of the mesh's vertices.

The input pattern contains three-dimensional coordinates of the contours extracted from two contiguous slices, so the SOM input layer is composed of three input neurons representing these three coordinates.

The neurons' weights in the three-dimensional self-organizing map are initialized to create a cylindrical mesh which is the first approximation of the external surface (fig. 3). This is an important step because, in this way, the training procedure and so the algorithm convergence is faster.

The activation bubble, in this case, is seen as a sphere which radius' length is defined by the neighbourhood dimension of a neuron in the map. This sphere must contain only vertices placed on a single slice, because the influence on neurons, placed on a different plane, may cause a wrong mesh's deformation along z-axis. This influence can be reduced by increasing the distance between two contiguous slices.

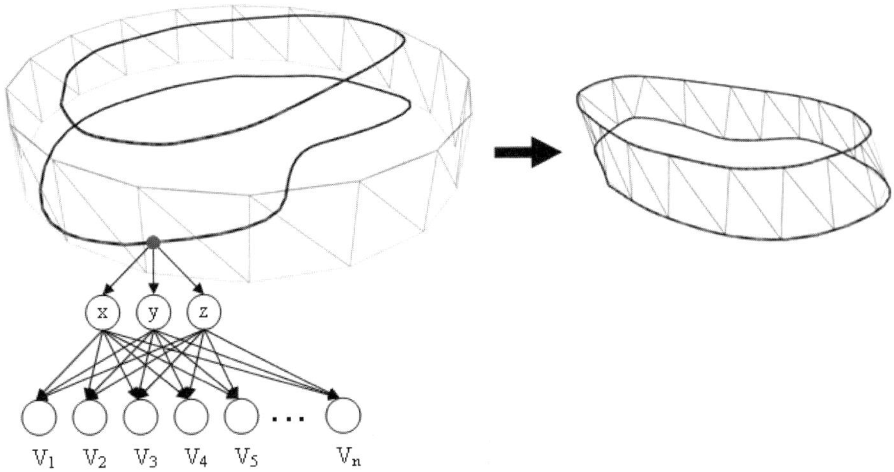


**Fig. 3.** Weights' initialization to create a first cylindrical mesh and resulting mesh at the end of the training procedure

In the training procedure, each contours' point is randomly presented to the network as input which activates the nearest neuron.

So winning neuron's weight vector is updated to bring the corresponding mesh's vertices closer to the point's input data. In order to maintain similarity of topologically closed neurons, weights of all neurons within a selected radius are adjusted. In the case where one neuron is continually the winning neuron, its computed distance is also modified by some amount to allow other neurons winning. At each iteration, the radius of correction is also gradually reduced.

As the training procedure progresses, mesh's vertices will adapt to the contours' points generating an ***adaptive triangular mesh***, approximating the external surface.

The training procedure ends when one of the following stop criteria is satisfied:

- the maximum number of epochs is reached;
- the approximation coefficient is reached.

The *approximation coefficient* is defined as the mean value of distances between each net input and its corresponding neuron (mesh's vertex). A smaller value of this coefficient will bring the adaptive mesh to a better approximation of the external surface. This SOM algorithm is repeated for each set of corresponding contours and for each couple of slices.

## 5 Application and Results

The idea of developing an own application arose from analysis of commercial softwares such as MATLAB and Etdips 2.0.

The application was developed in Visual C++ using Windows APIs to create a graphical and interactive user interface. It is based on a MDI (*Multiple-Document*

*Interface*) application in order to allow the user working with multiple documents within a single application [10].

The application provides functions for reading medical images in DICOM format, making the image thresholding and SOM segmentation, extracting regions' contours and finally generating and visualizing the 3D model of the extracted objects.

The considered dataset contains CT images of a patient presenting a prosthesis' implant. In particular, it consists of a set of 264 DICOM images (512x512 pixels) representing slices which are 0.8mm thick.

Thresholding technique is defined by two values: a minimum and a maximum threshold. In our dataset, the thresholding values for prosthesis identification are set as follows: $T_{min} = 2000$, $T_{max} = 3000$, according to the Hounsfield scale.

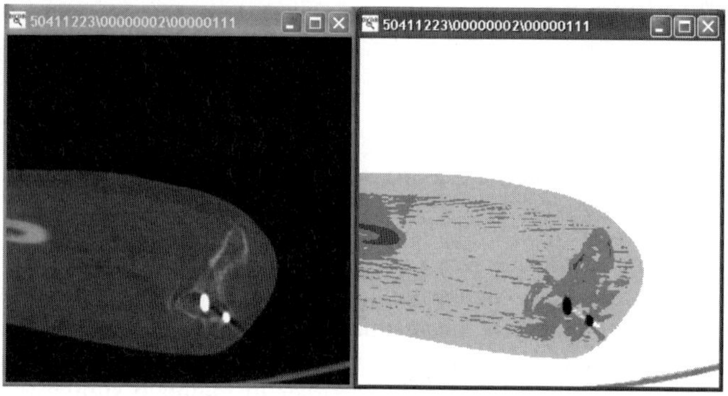


**Fig. 4.** SOM segmentation result after training procedure

The SOM segmentation technique automates this process through the definition of network parameters: number of neurons (regions to identify) and number of epochs (training iterations). After training and labeling each pixel in the dataset, the result is shown in figure 4: the prosthesis is identified with black colour. The streaks in the segmented images are due to the presence of metal streak artifacts in the original images.

After selecting the desired region (prosthesis), edge detection extracts the region's boundary pixels generating the binary image shown in figure 5.

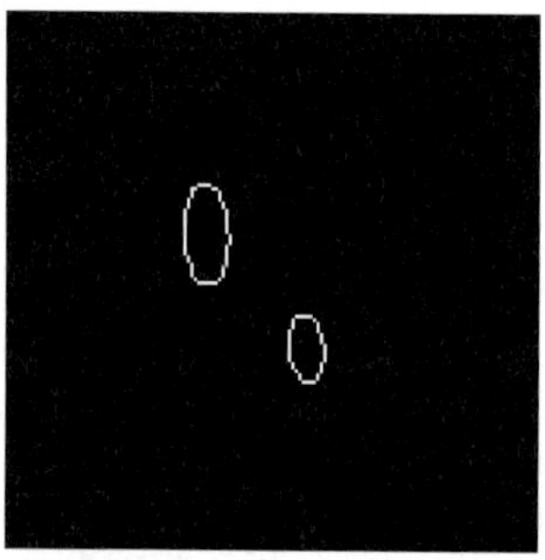

**Fig. 5.** Particular of the binary image after edge detection

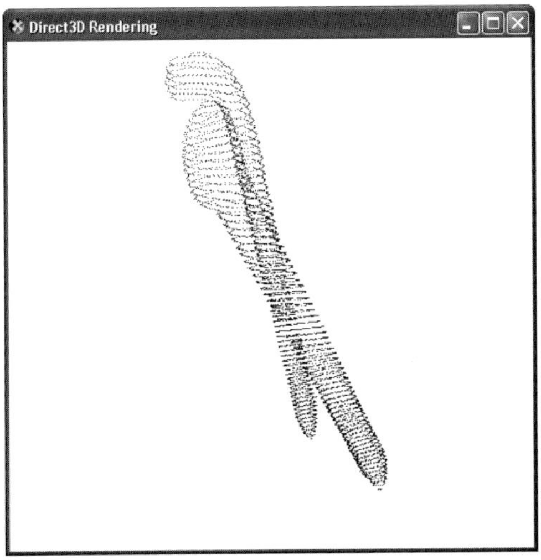


**Fig. 6.** 3D visualization of the extracted contours

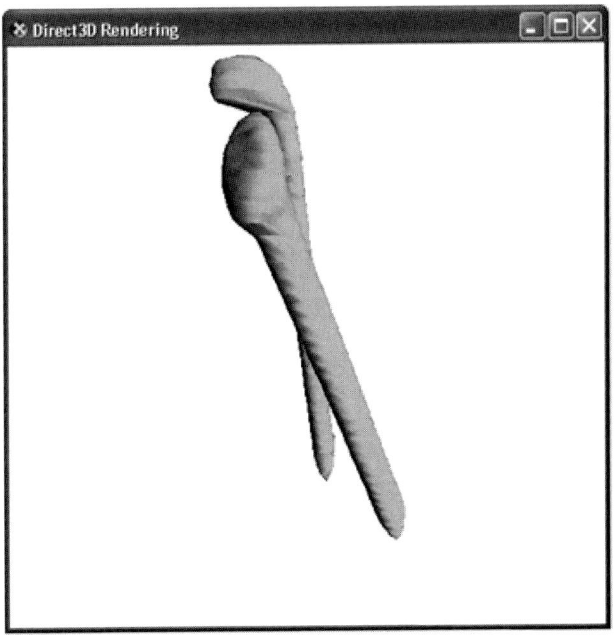


**Fig. 7.** 3D visualization of the resulting triangular mesh

The final step is to generate a three-dimensional model of the prosthesis starting from the set of the extracted contours. We have used Direct3D APIs to render the 3D model, instead of the traditional OpenGL used by most of the commercial clinical applications. A first 3D model consists of rendering the entire set of contours which gives a first idea about the object to be represented (fig. 6).

The second 3D model consists of rendering the adaptive triangular mesh obtained with the proposed neural algorithm. The resulting mesh is shown in figure 7. The mesh consists of 6096 vertices equal to 1/2 of contours' pixels. The application of lights and texture makes the scene more realistic. The visualization is also interactive, so the user can rotate the object in all the directions using mouse pointer.

To evaluate our application's elaboration timings we must consider the dataset's size, the size of the object to be rendered and the resolution of the 3D model. Running our application on a Pentium III (667 MHz) with 256 megabytes of main memory and considering our dataset, data reading and edge detection timings are negligible, while thresholding technique takes few seconds. SOM thresholding method timings depend on epoch's number: it takes about 15 minutes with 200000 epochs for each slice. 3D reconstruction timings mainly depend on the number of neurons (mesh vertices): it takes from few seconds for low mesh resolution (1/5 of contours' pixels) to about 20 minutes for high mesh resolution (1/2 of contours' pixels).

## 6 Conclusions and Future Work

Artificial Neural Networks represents an optimal alternative to some complex algorithms for data analysis and particularly for three-dimensional reconstruction. SOM neural networks, in particular, represents an important tool which can be applied to a lot of different problems thanks to their self-organizing capability. In this work we have proposed two different SOM applications: medical image segmentation and three-dimensional reconstruction. The application of this algorithm to 3D model reconstruction is resulted simpler and more intuitive with respect to some other algorithms which are based on mathematical and geometrical approaches.

With the considered dataset, we have noticed that the presence of metal streak artifacts into original images doesn't permit to make a correct segmentation of all the regions in the acquired volume. So only the prosthesis was correctly identified.

Moreover, Direct3D has represented an optimal alternative to OpenGL for making a fast rendering which has permitted to create an interactive 3D visualization.

Further research will be directed to make the SOM segmentation fully automatic using ART (Adaptive Resonance Theory) networks. It will also provide the implementation of three-dimensional segmentation techniques to identify correctly all the regions inside an acquired volume, characterized by images presenting a great presence of streak artifacts.

## References

1. Kohonen, T.: Self-Organization and Associative Memory, Springer-Verlag, Heidelberg, (1988)
2. Kohonen, T.: Self-Organizing Maps: Optimization and Approaches, ICANN, Espoo, Finland, (1991)
3. Digital Imaging and Communications in Medicine (DICOM), National Electrical Manufacturers Association, ( 2004)

4. Fu, K.S., Mui, J.K.: A Survey of Image Segmentation. Pattern Recognition, vol. 13, n.1,(1981) 3-16
5. Gelenbe, E., Feng, Y., Krishnan, K. R. R.: Neural Network Methods for Volumetric Magnetic Resonance Imaging of the Human Brain. IEEE, (1996) 1488–1496
6. Reddick, W. E., Glass, J. O., Cook, E. N., Elkin, T. D., Deaton, R. J.: Automated Segmentation and Classification of Multispectral Magnetic Resonance Images of Brain Using Artificial Neural Networks. IEEE Trans. Medical Imaging, 16(1997)911–918
7. L. Fausett.: Fundamentals of Neural Networks – Architectures, Algorithms and Applications
8. Stănciulescu, V.: 3D Tomography: Computerized Modeling of 2D scanned images. Results. Advantages. General Inspectorate for Communications and Information Technology Timişoara, Romania
9. Galin, E., Akkouche, S.: Fast Surface Reconstruction from Contours using Implicit Surfaces, Laboratoire d'Informatique Graphique Image et Modèlisation
10. Petzold, C.: Programming Windows, Microsoft Programming Series, (1998)

# A Neural Network with Finite-Time Convergence for a Class of Variational Inequalities*

Xing-Bao Gao and Li-Li Du

College of Mathematics and Information Science
Shaanxi Normal University, Xi'an, Shaanxi 710062, P.R. China
xinbaog@snnu.edu.cn

**Abstract.** In this paper, a new neural network for a class of variational inequalities with linear and nonlinear constraints is proposed by converting it into an extended variational inequality. The proposed neural network with the asymmetric mapping is proved to be stable in the sense of Lyapunov and converge to a solution of the original problem within a finite time under a weaker co-coercivity condition by using a convex energy function. Meanwhile, the finite-time convergence for the proposed network with the gradient mapping is also shown under some mild conditions. Compared with the existing neural networks, the new model is suitable to parallel implementation with lower complexity, and can be applied to solve some nonmonotone problems. The validity and transient behavior of the proposed neural network are demonstrated by numerical examples.

## 1 Introduction

We are concerned with the following variational inequality problem with linear and nonlinear constraints: to find a vector $u^* \in C$ such that

$$\mathbf{VI(F,C)}\ (u-u^*)^T F(u^*) \geq 0, \forall u \in C, \tag{1}$$

where $u \in R^n$, $F$ is a continuous mapping from $R^n$ into $R^n$,

$$C = \{u \in U, |g(u) \geq 0, Au \in V\},$$

$A \in R^{p\times n}$, $U = \{u \in R^n | l_i \leq u_i \leq h_i, i = 1, 2, \cdots, n\}$, $V = \{v \in R^p | a_j \leq v_j \leq b_j, j = 1, 2, \cdots, p\}$ (some $b_j$(or $-a_j$, $-l_i$, $h_i$) could be $+\infty$), $g(u) = (g_1(u), g_2(u), \cdots, g_m(u))^T$, and $g_i(u)$ $(i = 1, 2, \cdots, m)$ is concave on $U$ and continuously differentiable on an open convex set $D$ including $U$.

Problem (1) includes nonlinear complementarity problems($C = R^n_+$), system of nonlinear equations($C = R^n$), and many optimization problems such as linear and quadratic programming, nonlinear programming, extended linear and

* This work was supported in part by NSFC Grant of China No. 10571115.

D.-S. Huang, K. Li, and G.W. Irwin (Eds.): ICIC 2006, LNCS 4113, pp. 32–41, 2006.

quadratic programming[8], minimax problems and so on. Thus it has many important applications(see [1,6,7,8] and the references therein). In many scientific and engineering applications, real-time on-line solutions of problem (1) are desired. However, traditional algorithms[1,6,8,11] are not suitable for a real-time on-line implementation on the computer. Thus it is of great interest in practice to develop some neural network models which could provide a real-time on-line solution.

Recently, neural networks for optimization problems have achieved many significant results[2,3,4,5,9,10]. Friesz *et al.*[2] proposed globally projected dynamic systems, which can be viewed as a neural network model suitable for hardware implementation with the low complexity, but the asymptotical stability of this system for a monotone and asymmetric mapping could not be guaranteed [2,3,5]. Xia and Wang [9] proposed a neural network with a two-layer structure which can be applied to (1) by introducing the Lagrange multipliers to the constraints, yet its structure is quite complex and its asymptotical stability might not be guaranteed when $g(u)$ is nonlinear since the Lispchitz condition is not satisfied even if the mappings $F(u)$ and $g(u)$ are all Lipschitz continuous. To avoid estimating the Lipschitz constant, Gao, Liao and Qi[5] proposed a simple neural network and provided several simple sufficient conditions to ensure its asymptotical stability. In particular, problem (1) can be solved by this model, yet the size of the resulting network must be enlarged since the Lagrange multipliers must be added to the constraints, and thus the model complexity must be increased substantially. More importantly, the stability condition of the model in [5] is so strong that it cannot ascertain the stability for solving Example 2 in Section 4.

Based on the above considerations and to overcome the above shortfalls, in this paper, we will a) propose a new neural network for solving problem (1) by means of the necessary and sufficient conditions of its solution, b) prove the finite-time convergence for the proposed neural network under the weaker monotonicity conditions by defining the proper energy functions. Compared with the existing neural networks for (1), the new model can be applied to solve some nonmonotone problems, and has a much simpler structure. The obtained results for the proposed neural network with the gradient mapping improves the existing ones in [4,5].

Throughout the paper, we assume that problem (1) has a finite solution $u^*$, and satisfies the Slater condition[1], *i.e.*, there exists a $u' \in R^n$ such that

$$u' \in U, \qquad g(u') > 0, \qquad Au' \in V. \tag{2}$$

We let $\|\cdot\|$ denote the Euclidean norm, $\nabla f(u) = [\partial f(u)/\partial u_1,\ \partial f(u)/\partial u_2, \cdots, \partial f(u)/\partial u_n]^T$ denote the gradient vector of the differentiable function $f(u)$ at $u$, $g'(u) = [\nabla g_1(u), \nabla g_2(u), \cdots, \nabla g_m(u)]^T \in R^{m\times n}$ and $c^+ = \max\{0, c\}$. The projection operator $P_\Omega$ on a closed convex set $\Omega \subseteq R^n$ is defined by $P_\Omega(x) = \arg\min_{y\in\Omega} \|x - y\|$. A basic property of the projection mapping on a closed set [4] is

$$[x - P_\Omega(x)]^T [P_\Omega(x) - y] \geq 0, \qquad \forall x \in R^n, y \in \Omega. \tag{3}$$

A neural network is said to be stable in the sense of Lyapunov, and asymptotically stable, if the corresponding dynamical system is so. For the convenience of later discussions, it is necessary to introduce the following definitions.

**Definition 1.** *A neural network is said to have a finite-time convergence to one of its equilibrium point $z^*$ if there exists a time $\tau_0$ such that the output trajectory $z(t)$ of this network reaches $z^*$ for $t \geq \tau_0$ (see [10]).*

**Definition 2.** *A mapping $F$ is said to be a gradient mapping on $\Omega$, if there exists a differentiable function $f : \Omega \to R^1$ such that $\nabla f(u) = F(u)$ for all $u \in \Omega$; otherwise, $F$ is said to be an asymmetric mapping on $\Omega$.*

## 2 The Neural Network Model

In this section, we shall construct a neural network for solving (1), and show the advantages of the new model over the existing ones. First, we state a sufficient and necessary condition for the solution of (1), which provides the theoretical foundation in designing our neural network.

**Theorem 1.** *$u^*$ is a solution of (1) if and only if there exists a $(\lambda^*, \mu^*) \in R^{m+p}$ such that*

$$\begin{cases} u^* \in U, \quad (u-u^*)^T[F(u^*) - (g'(u^*))^T\lambda^* - A^T\mu^*] \geq 0, \quad \forall u \in U, \\ \lambda^* \geq 0, \quad g(u^*) \geq 0, \qquad (\lambda^*)^T g(u^*) = 0, \\ Au^* \in V, \quad (\mu - Au^*)^T\mu^* \geq 0, \quad \forall \mu \in V. \end{cases} \tag{4}$$

*Proof.* Obviously, $u^*$ is a solution of (1) if and only if it is a solution of the following convex problem

$$\min\{u^T F(u^*) | u \in U, y \in V, g(u) \geq 0, Au = y\}. \tag{5}$$

Then the Lagrange function of (5) is

$$L(u, y, \lambda, \mu) = u^T F(u^*) - \lambda^T g(u) - \mu^T(Au - y),$$

which is defined on $U \times V \times R^m_+ \times R^p$. From the Kuhn-Tucker saddle theorem in [1], (4) can be obtained by simple argument.

Obviously, Theorem 1 indicates that problem (1) is equivalent to the extended variational inequality problem EVI$(Q, G, \Omega)$: find a $z^* = ((u^*)^T, (\lambda^*)^T, (\mu^*)^T)^T \in R^{m+n+p}$ such that

$$Q(z^*) \in \Omega, \qquad [z - Q(z^*)]^T G(z^*) \geq 0, \qquad \forall z \in \Omega = U \times R^m_+ \times V,$$

where $z = (u^T, \lambda^T, \mu^T)^T$, $R^m_+ = \{y \in R^m | y \geq 0\}$,

$$Q(z) = \begin{pmatrix} u \\ \lambda \\ Au \end{pmatrix} \quad \text{and} \quad G(z) = \begin{pmatrix} F(u) - (g'(u))^T\lambda - A^T\mu \\ g(u) \\ \mu \end{pmatrix}.$$

Furthermore, using (3), we can easily verify the following result which establishes the relationship between the solution of problem (1) and the solution of a projection system.

**Lemma 1.** *$u^*$ is a solution of (1) if and only if there exists a $(\lambda^*, \mu^*) \in R^{m+p}$ such that*

$$\begin{cases} u^* = P_U\{u^* - \alpha[F(u^*) - (g'(u^*))^T\lambda^* - A^T\mu^*]\}, \\ \lambda^* = [\lambda^* - g(u^*)]^+, \qquad Au^* = P_V(Au^* - \mu^*), \end{cases} \tag{6}$$

*where $\alpha$ is a positive constant, $\lambda^+ = (\lambda_1^+, \lambda_2^+, \cdots, \lambda_m^+)^T$, $P_U(u) = [(P_U(u))_1, (P_U(u))_2, \cdots, (P_U(u))_n]^T$ and $(P_U(u))_i = \min\{h_i, \max\{u_i, l_i\}\}$ for $i = 1, 2, \cdots, n$, and $P_V(\mu)$ is similar as $P_U(u)$.*

Lemma 1 indicates that a solution of problem (1) can be obtained by solving (6). For simplicity, we denote $K = U \times R^{m+p}$, $K^* = \{z \in R^{m+n+p} | z \text{ solves } (6)\}$, and

$$\begin{cases} \tilde{\lambda} = [\lambda - g(u)]^+, \qquad \tilde{\mu} = P_V(Au - \mu), \\ \tilde{u} = P_U\{u - \alpha[F(u) - (g'(u))^T\tilde{\lambda} - A^T(\mu - Au + \tilde{\mu})]\}. \end{cases} \tag{7}$$

Then the above results suggest the following dynamical equation for the proposing neural network model to solve (1):

$$\frac{dz}{dt} = \frac{d}{dt}\begin{pmatrix} u \\ \lambda \\ \mu \end{pmatrix} = -\kappa E(z) = -\kappa \begin{pmatrix} 2(u - \tilde{u}) \\ \lambda - \tilde{\lambda} \\ Au - \tilde{\mu} \end{pmatrix}, \tag{8}$$

where $\kappa > 0$ is a scaling constant.

It is easy to see that the circuit realizing the model (8) consists of $m+n+p$ integrators, $m+n+p$ piecewise-activation functions for $P_U(\cdot)$, $P_V(\cdot)$ and $(\cdot)^+$, $mn+n+m$ processors for $g'(u)$, $F(u)$ and $g(u)$, $mn$ analog multipliers for $(g'(u))^T\tilde{\lambda}$, some amplifiers and summers. Thus the complexity of the proposed network depends only on $F(u)$, $g(u)$, and $g'(u)$ of (1).

To show the advantages of the proposed network (8), we compare it with three existing neural networks. First, let's look at the model in [9]. According to the circuit of the model in [9], the model (8) has no in addition terms $F(u)$, $g(u)$, $F(\bar{u})$, $g(\bar{u})$, $(g'(u))^T\lambda$ and $(g'(\bar{u}))^T\bar{\lambda}$ when $V = \{b\}$, where $\bar{u} = P_U\{u - \alpha[F(u) - (g'(u))^T\lambda - A^T\mu]\}$ and $\bar{\lambda} = [\lambda - \alpha g(u)]^+$. Thus model (8) is much simpler.

Next, we compare the network (8) with the model in [4]. Model (8) can be applied to (1) with the asymmetric mapping, while the model in [4] is only designed to solve convex programming problems, and thus no stability result was given in [4] for the asymmetric mapping. Moreover for (1) with the gradient mapping, even though model (8) with $\alpha = 1$ is model in [4] when $V = \{b\}$, yet the theoretical results for them are different. The model in [4] is asymptotically stable when $F$ is monotone. Model (8) has a finite-time convergence under a weaker monotonicity condition(see Theorem 4 in Section 3), thus it could be applied to solve some nonmonotone problems.

Finally, we compare the network (8) with the model in [5]. First, model in [5] can be applied to (1) by attaching the Lagrange multipliers to the constraints, yet the size of the resulting network must be enlarged to $m + 3n + 2p$ and thus the model complexity must be increased substantially. Second, for (1) with the asymmetric mapping $F$, model (8) has a finite-time convergence under a weaker co-coercivity condition(see Theorem 3 in Section 3), but no such a result holds for the model in [5] at this case. Third, for (1) with a gradient mapping, model in [5] requires the condition that $F$ is monotone at a finite solution $u^*$ of (1) on $R^n$, while the network (8) is only required that $F$ is monotone at a finite solution $u^*$ of (1) on $U$ (See (A3) in Section 3). Thus, the stability and convergence of model in [5] cannot be guaranteed when applied to Example 2 in Section 4 since $F$ in this example is only monotone at a finite solution $u^* \in U$, while model (8) will be shown to have the finite-time convergence for it.

From Theorem 1 and Lemma 1, we know that there must be a finite $z^* \in K^*$ since problem (1) has a finite solution $u^* \in U$. Furthermore, by (4) and (8), we have the following result, which describes the relationship between an equilibrium point of (8) and a solution of problem (1).

**Lemma 2.** *$z \in K^*$ if and only if $z$ is an equilibrium point of network (8).*

## 3 Stability Analysis

In this section, we shall study some theoretical properties for (8). The following assumptions and lemmas are required in our later discussion.

**Assumptions:**

**(A1)** The mappings $F$ and $g'$ are locally Lipschitz continuous on a open convex set $D$ including $U$.

**(A2)** The mapping $F$ is co-coercive at one finite solution $u^* \in U$ of problem (1) with modulus $\nu > 0$, i.e., $(u-u^*)^T[F(u)-F(u^*)] \geq \nu\|F(u)-F(u^*)\|^2$ for all $u \in U$.

**(A3)** The mapping $F$ is monotone at one finite solution $u^* \in U$ of problem (1), i.e., $(u-u^*)^T[F(u)-F(u^*)] \geq 0$ for all $u \in U$.

It should be noted that (A2) implies (A3), but (A2) (or (A3)) does not imply that the mapping $F$ is monotone on $U$(see Example 2 in Section 4 and [11]).

**Lemma 3.** *The followings are true.*

*(i) The function $\|\tilde{\lambda}\|^2$ is continuously differentiable on $D \times R^m$ and convex on $U \times R^m$.*

*(ii) The function $\|Au-\mu-\tilde{\mu}\|^2$ is continuously differentiable and convex on $R^{n+p}$.*

*Proof.* (i) See the proof of Lemma 2 in [4].

(ii) From (3), we have

$$(x-y)^T[P_V(x)-P_V(y)] \leq \|x-y\|^2, \qquad \forall x, y \in R^p. \tag{9}$$

Lct $\psi(w) = \|Au-\mu-\tilde{\mu}\|^2/2$, then $\psi(w) = \|y-P_V(y)\|^2/2$ with $y = Au-\mu$. Thus it is easy to verified that $\psi(w)$ is differentiable on $R^{n+p}$ and

$$\nabla\psi(w) = \begin{pmatrix} A^T(Au-\mu-\tilde{\mu}) \\ \mu+\tilde{\mu}-Au \end{pmatrix}. \tag{10}$$

$\forall w^1 = ((u^1)^T, (\mu^1)^T)^T$, $w^2 = ((u^2)^T, (\mu^2)^T)^T \in R^{n+p}$, let $y^i = Au^i - \mu^i$ for $i = 1, 2$, then

$$\begin{aligned}&(w^1 - w^2)^T[\nabla\psi(w^1) - \nabla\psi(w^2)]\\ &= (y^1 - y^2)^T[y^1 - y^2 - P_V(y^1) + P_V(y^2)] \geq 0,\end{aligned}$$

where the last step follows by setting $x = y^1$ and $y = y^2$ in (9). Therefore $\psi(w)$ is convex [7].

**Lemma 4.** *Let* $\varphi(z) = (\|\tilde{\lambda}\|^2 + \|Au - \mu - \tilde{\mu}\|^2)/2$ *and*

$$\begin{aligned}V_1(z, z^*) = &\alpha[\varphi(z) - \varphi(z^*) - (z - z^*)^T\nabla\varphi(z^*)]\\ &+\frac{1}{2}[\|u - u^*\|^2 + \alpha(\|\lambda - \lambda^*\|^2 + \|\mu - \mu^*\|^2)], \qquad (11)\end{aligned}$$

*where* $z^* = ((u^*)^T, (\lambda^*)^T, (\mu^*)^T)^T \in K^*$ *is finite. Then the followings are true.*

*(i)* $V_1(z, z^*)$ *is convex on* $K$ *and continuously differentiable on* $D \times R^{m+p}$;
*(ii)* $V_1(z, z^*) \geq \min\{1, \alpha\}\|z - z^*\|^2/2$ *for all* $z \in K$;
*(iii) If (A2) holds at* $u^*$, *then* $\nabla V_1(z, z^*)^T E(z) \geq \nu_1\|E(z)\|^2$ *for all* $z \in K$, *where* $\nu_1 = \min\{\alpha, [1 - \alpha/(4\nu)]/2\}$.

*Proof.* From Lemma 3, $\varphi(z)$ is convex on $K$ and continuously differentiable on $D \times R^{m+p}$. Thus (i)-(ii) can be obtained by (11) and [1].

(iii) It is easy to see that

$$\nabla\varphi(z) = \begin{pmatrix} -(g'(u))^T\tilde{\lambda} + A^T(Au - \mu - \tilde{\mu}) \\ \tilde{\lambda} \\ \mu - Au + \tilde{\mu} \end{pmatrix}.$$

Then by (4), (8), (11), and similar to the proof of Lemma 3(iii) in [4], we have

$$\begin{aligned}\nabla V_1(z, z^*)^T E(z) &= 2(u - \tilde{u})^T\{u - u^* + \alpha[(g'(u^*))^T\lambda^* - (g'(u))^T\tilde{\lambda}\\ &\quad +A^T(Au - \mu - \tilde{\mu} - \mu^*)]\} + 2\alpha(\lambda - \tilde{\lambda})^T(\lambda - \lambda^*)\\ &\quad -\alpha(\|\lambda - \tilde{\lambda}\|^2 + \|Au - \tilde{\mu}\|^2) + 2\alpha(\mu - \mu^*)^T(Au - \tilde{\mu})\\ &\geq 2\|u - \tilde{u}\|^2 + \alpha(\|\lambda - \tilde{\lambda}\|^2 + \|Au - \tilde{\mu}\|^2)\\ &\quad +2\alpha(\tilde{u} - u^*)^T[F(u) - F(u^*)], \qquad \forall z \in K. \qquad (12)\end{aligned}$$

By the fact that (A2) holds at $u^*$ of (1), we have

$$\begin{aligned}(\tilde{u} - u^*)^T[F(u) - F(u^*)] &= [(u - u^*) - (u - \tilde{u})]^T[F(u) - F(u^*)]\\ &\geq \nu\|F(u) - F(u^*)\|^2 - \|u - \tilde{u}\|\|F(u) - F(u^*)\|\\ &\geq -\frac{1}{4\nu}\|u - \tilde{u}\|^2, \qquad \forall u \in U.\end{aligned}$$

This (8) and (12) imply (iii) holds.

The results in Lemma 4 pave a way to study the dynamical behavior of (8). From Lemma 4 and similar to the proof in [4,5], we have the following results for (8).

**Theorem 2.** *Assume that (A1)-(A2) hold. If, in addition, $\alpha < 4\nu$, then for any $z^0 \in K$, there exists a unique continuous solution $z(t) \in K$ of (8) with $z(0) = z^0$ for all $t \geq 0$.*

**Theorem 3.** *Assume that (A1)-(A2) hold. If, in addition, $\alpha < 4\nu$, then neural network (8) is stable in the sense of Lyapunov, and for any $z^0 \in K$, the solution $z(t)$ of (8) with $z(0) = z^0$ will converge to $K^*$,* i.e., $\lim_{t\to+\infty} dist\,(z(t), K^*) = 0$, *where $dist(z, K^*) = \inf_{v\in K^*} \|z - v\|$. Furthermore, if problem (1) has a unique solution, or (A2) is verified at any finite solution of (1), then $z(t)$ reaches a point in $K^*$ within a finite time when the designing parameter $\kappa$ is large enough.*

When $F$ is a gradient mapping, *i.e.*, there exists a continuously differentiable function $f : U \to R^1$ such that $\nabla f(u) = F(u)$ for all $u \in U$, with the aid of the function

$$V_2(z, z^*) = V_1(z, z^*) + \alpha[f(u) - f(u^*) - (u - u^*)^T F(u^*)], \tag{13}$$

we can prove that the following finite-time convergence result for (8) by similar argument in [5].

**Theorem 4.** *Suppose that (A1) and (A3) hold. If, in addition, $F$ is a gradient mapping on $U$, then $\forall\alpha > 0$, neural network (8) is stable in the sense of Lyapunov, and for any $z^0 \in K$, the solution $z(t)$ of (8) with $z(0) = z^0$ will converge to $K^*$. Furthermore, if problem (1) has a unique solution, or (A3) is verified at any finite solution of (1), then $z(t)$ reaches a point in $K^*$ within a finite time when the designing parameter $\kappa$ is large enough.*

## 4 Illustrative Examples

In this section, two examples are provided to illustrate both the theoretical results achieved in Section 3 and the simulation performance of neural network (8). The simulation is conducted in **Matlab**, and the ode solver used is **ODE23s**.

*Example 1.* Consider VI$(F, C)$ in (1) with $C = \{u \in R^3 | 2u_1 \geq u_2^3 + u_3^3, u_1 + u_2 + u_3 = 2, 0 \leq u \leq 1\}$ and $F(u) = (4u_1 - 3u_2 - u_3 + 1, -u_1 + 4u_2 - 3u_3 + 1, -3u_1 - u_2 + 4u_3 + 1)^T$. Then this problem satisfies (2), has a unique solution $u^* = (2/3, 2/3, 2/3)^T$, $U = \{u \in R^3 | -1 \leq u \leq 1\}$, $V = \{2\}$, $g(u) = 2u_1 - u_2^3 - u_3^3$, $g'(u) = (2, -3u_2^3, -2u_3^3)$ and $A = (1, 1, 1)$.

It is easy to see that this problem satisfies (A2) with $\nu = 2/13$, and can be solved by neural network (8) on $U \times R^3$. All simulation results show that neural network (8) always converges to $z^* = ((u^*)^T, \lambda^*, \mu^*)^T$ with $\lambda^* = 0$ and $\mu^* = 1$. For example, let $\alpha = 0.6$ and $\kappa = 100$, Fig. 1 depicts that the trajectories of network (8) with 30 random initial points converge to theoretical solutions $z^*$, respectively.

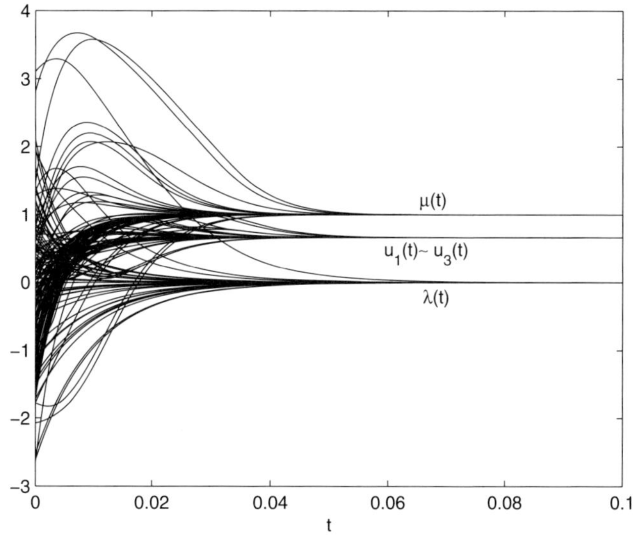


**Fig. 1.** Transient behavior of (8) in Example 1

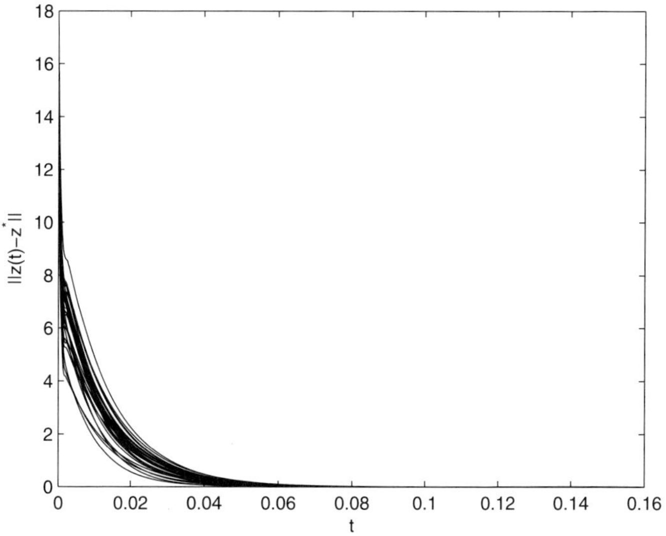


**Fig. 2.** The convergence behavior of the norm $\|z(t) - z^*\|$ based on (8) in Example 2

*Example 2.* Consider the following nonlinear optimization problem:

$$\begin{cases} \min f(u) = (u_1 - 10)^2 + 5(u_2 - 12)^2 + u_3^3 + 3(u_4 - 11)^2 \\ \qquad\qquad\quad +10u_5^5 + 7u_6^2 + u_7^3 - 4u_6u_7 - 10u_6 - 8u_7 \\ \text{s.t. } u \geq 0, \qquad -a \leq Au \leq a, \end{cases}$$

where

$$A = \begin{pmatrix} 2 & 3 & 1 & 4 & 5 & 0 & 0 \\ 7 & 3 & 10 & 1 & -1 & 0 & 0 \\ 23 & 1 & 0 & 0 & 0 & 6 & -8 \\ 4 & 1 & 2 & 0 & 0 & 5 & -11 \end{pmatrix} \quad \text{and} \quad a = \begin{pmatrix} 63 \\ 71 \\ 49 \\ 1 \end{pmatrix}.$$

Then this problem has a unique optimal solutions $u^*= (2.1187, 10.201, 0, 7.0399, 0, 1.2684, 2.1927)^T$ and $\nabla f(u) = [2(u_1-10), 10(u_2-12), 3u_3^3, 6(u_4-11), 50u_5^4, 14u_6-4u_7-10, 3u_7^2-4u_6-8)^T$ .

It is easy to prove that $\nabla f(u)$ is strictly monotone at $u^* \in R_+^7$, but (A3) does not hold at $u^*$ on $R^7$ (in fact, $(u-u^*)^T[\nabla f(u)-\nabla f(u^*)] = -50 < 0$ with $u = u^*$ except for $u_5 = -1$). We use neural network (8) to solve this problem on $R_+^7 \times R^4$, all simulation results show that neural network (8) always converges to $z^* = ((u^*)^T, (\mu^*)^T)^T$, where $\mu^* = (-5.9402, 0, -0.1688, 0)^T$. For example, let $\kappa = 100$, Fig. 2 shows the convergence behavior of the norm $\|z(t) - z^*\|$ based on (8) with 30 random initial points.

## 5 Conclusions

In this paper, we present a new neural network for a class of variational inequalities with linear and nonlinear constraints. We have shown that the proposed neural network with the weaker co-coercive mapping is stable in the sense of Lyapunov and converges to a solution of the original problem within a finite time. Meanwhile, the finite-time convergence for the proposed network with the gradient mapping is also shown under the weaker monotonicity condition. Compared with the existing neural networks, the proposed network does not need to compute any extra terms, has a low complexity and can be used to solve some nonmonotone probems. Theoretical analysis and illustrative examples show that the given conditions can be easily checked in practice.

## References

1. Bazaraa, M.S., Sherali, H.D., Shetty, C.M.: Nonlinear Programming: Theory and Algorithms(2nd ed). Wiley, New York (1993)
2. Friesz, T.L., Bernstein, D.H., Mehta, N.J., Tobin, R. L., Ganjlizadeh, S.: Day-to-day Dynamic Network Disequilibria and Idealized Traveler Information Systems. Operations Research, **42** (1994) 1120–1136
3. Gao, X.B.: Exponential Stability of Globally Projected Dynamic Systems. IEEE Trans. Neural Networks, **14** (2003) 426–431
4. Gao, X.B.:A Novel Neural Network for Nonlinear Convex Programming. IEEE Trans. Neural Networks, **15** (2004) 613–621
5. Gao, X.B., Liao, L.-Z., Qi, L.Q. :A Novel Neural Network for Variational Inequalities With Linear and Nonlinear Constraints. IEEE Trans. Neural Networks, **16** (2005) 1305–1317
6. Harker, P.T., Pang, J.S.: Finite-Dimensional Variational Inequality and Nonlinear Complementarity Problems: a Survey of Theory, Algorithms, and Applications. Mathematical Programming, **48B** (1990) 161–220

7. Ortega, J.M., Rheinboldt, W. C.: Iterative Solution of Nonlinear Equation in Several Variables. Academic, New York (1970)
8. Rockafellar, R.T.:Linear-quadratic Programming and Optimal Control. SIAM J. Control Optim., **25** (1987) 781–814
9. Xia Y.S., Wang J.: A General Methodology for Designing Globally Convergent Optimization Neural Networks. IEEE Trans. Neural Networks, **9** (1998) 1311–1343
10. Xia, Y.S., Feng, G., Wang, J.: A Recurrent Neural Network With Exponential Convergence for Solving Convex Cuadratic Program and Related Linear Piecewise Equations. IEEE Trans. Neural Networks, **17** (2004) 1003–1015
11. Zhu, D.L., Marcotte, P.: Co-coercivity and Its Role in The Convergence of Iterative Schemes for Solving Variational Inequalities. SIAM Journal of Optimizations, **49** (1996) 714–726

# A Novel Multi-class Support Vector Machine Based on Fuzzy Theories

Yong Zhang[1,2], Zhongxian Chi[2], and Yu Sun[2]

[1] Department of Computer, Liaoning Normal University, Dalian 116029, China
ayong_zh@163.com
[2] Department of Computer Science and Engineering, Dalian University of Technology, Dalian 116024, China
czxian@dlut.edu.cn, icf-777@163.com

**Abstract.** Support vector machine (SVM), proposed by Vapnik based on statistical learning theory, is a novel machine learning method. However, there are two problems to be solved in this field: one is the multi-class classification problem, and the other is the sensitivity to the noisy data. In order to overcome these difficulties, a novel method of fuzzy compensation multi-class support vector machine, named as FC-SVM, is proposed in this paper. This method imports a fuzzy compensation function to the penalty in the straightly construction multi-class SVM classification problem proposed by Weston and Watkins. Aim at the dual affects to classification results by each input data, this method has punish item be fuzzy, compensates weight to classification, reconstructs the optimization problem and its restrictions, reconstructs Langrage formula, and presents the theories deduction. This method is applied to the benchmark data sets. The experiment presents our method is feasible.

## 1 Introduction

With the rapid development of nonlinear theories and artificial intelligence, some soft-computing methods, such as rough sets, fuzzy sets, support vector machines, have been strong tools as classifications and forecast in the fields of the money market analysis and evaluating credit.

Support vector machines(SVMs), proposed by Vapnik based on statistical learning theory (SLT) in the nineties of the 20th century, are novel machine learning methods which are based on the VC-dimension theory and the principle of the structural risk minimization. Owe to their higher generalization ability and better classification precision, SVMs can solve the overfitting problem effectively and can be applied to a number of issues [1,2,3]. Now more and more researches focuses on SVMs as well as the pattern recognition and neural network. SVMs play a more and more important role in classification and regression fields. At present, SVMs have already been applied successively to the problems ranging from hand-written character recognition, face detection, speech recognition to medicine diagnosis, spatial data analysis, biology informatics [1].

SVMs have obtained plentiful productions in the fields of utility algorithm research, design and realization, which sum up several research aspects as followings. The first field is how to extend two-class problems to multi-class problems. SVMs for

D.-S. Huang, K. Li, and G.W. Irwin (Eds.): ICIC 2006, LNCS 4113, pp. 42 – 50, 2006.

pattern classification are based on two-class classification problems. Unclassifiable regions exist when SVMs are extended to multi-class problems. Now there are two methods to solve this problem. One method is to construct 2-class classifiers, and then to assemble a multi-class classifier, such as one-against-one, ones-against-all and DAGSVMs [4]. The other method is to construct straight multi-class classifier, such as k-SVM which is proposed by Weston and Watkins [5]. The second field is to improve SVM computing speed convenient for disposing large-scale problems, such as the sequential minimal optimization algorithm [6]. The third field is to use optimization method to improve SVM, and to predigest computing process, such as linear SVM [7], LS-SVM [8]. The fourth field is to put forward novel algorithms according to structural risk minimization and some thoughts, such as v-SVM [9]. The last one is to put forward fuzzy SVM algorithm in order to overcome SVM methods' sensitivity to outlier and noise data. For example, Inoue and Abe presented Fuzzy Support Vector Machines (FSVMs) [11]. They defined the decision functions according to the membership functions in the directions orthogonal to the hyperplane.

Recently, fuzzy set theory has been introduced to support vector machine [16]. Inoue etc. proposed a fuzzy SVM to solve the unclassified regions that exist when extending two-class classification to multi-class case in 2001 [11]. Then, since the optimal hyperplane obtained by SVM depends on only a small part of the data points, it may become sensitive to noises or outliers in the training set. To deal with this problem, another fuzzy SVM was proposed [12]. It employed the fuzzy memberships to evaluate the importance of data points. This method can prevent some points from making narrower margin by setting lower fuzzy membership to the data points that are considered as noises or outliers with higher probability.

This paper presents a novel fuzzy compensation SVM algorithm (FC-SVM) which aims at multi-class classification problem and noise data problem. Compared with other SVM algorithms, FC-SVM is a straight construction method. We first introduce fuzzy compensation function in the punish item of the direct constructing multi-class classifier, which is proposed by Weston and Watkins [6]. So, this method not only makes the punish item in the object function be fuzzy, but also compensates weight to classification. This paper reconstructs the optimization problem and its restrictions, reconstructs Lagrange formula, and presents the theories deduction.

In Section 2, we explain simply two-class support vector machines, and in Section 3 we discuss fuzzy compensation support vector machines for multi-class classification. In Section 4 we compare performance of the fuzzy compensation support vector machine with the other support vector machines for multi-class classification, such as one-against-one, one-against-all.

## 2 Two–Class SVM and Multi-class SVM

For the 2-class classification problem, the support vector approach has been well developed. The main idea is the following: construct a hyperplane to separate the two classes so that the margin is the maximal. This gives the following optimization problem:

$$\begin{aligned} &\min_{\mathrm{w,b},\xi} && \frac{1}{2}\|\mathbf{w}\|^2 + \mathrm{C}\sum_{\mathrm{i=1}}^{\mathrm{n}} \xi_{\mathrm{i}} \\ &\text{s.t.} && \mathrm{y_i}(\mathbf{w}\cdot \mathrm{x} - \mathrm{b}) + \xi_{\mathrm{i}} - 1 \geq 0 \\ & && \xi_{\mathrm{i}} \geq 0 \quad \mathrm{i} = 1,\cdots,n. \end{aligned} \tag{1}$$

The dual solution to this problem is: maximize the quadratic form (1) under the following constraints:

$$\begin{aligned} &\max_{\lambda} && W(\lambda) = \sum_{i=1}^{\mathrm{n}} \lambda_i - \frac{1}{2}\sum_{\mathrm{i=1}}^{\mathrm{n}}\sum_{\mathrm{j=1}}^{\mathrm{n}} \lambda_i \lambda_j y_i y_j \mathbf{x_i}\cdot\mathbf{x_j} \\ &\text{s.t.} && \sum_{i=1}^{\mathrm{n}} \lambda_i y_i = 0 \\ & && C \geq \lambda_i \geq 0 \qquad i = 1,\ldots,\mathrm{n} \end{aligned} \tag{2}$$

Giving the decision function:

$$f(x) = \mathrm{sgn}\left(\sum_{i=1}^{n} \lambda_i \mathrm{y}_i K(x_i \cdot x) - b\right) \tag{3}$$

Currently, for the conventional support vector machines, an multi-class problem is converted into $n$ two-class problems and for the $i$th two-class problem, class $i$ is separated from the remaining classes.

For SVMs are essentially a two-class classifier, some methods have been devised to extend SVMs to multi-class classification such as one-against-one (1-a-1), one-against-all (1-a-a) and directed acyclic graph SVM (SVMDAG) [2]. These methods are based on solving several binary classifications. In other words, SVMs are originally designed for binary classification.

But a more natural way to solve multi-class problems, which is to construct a decision function by considering all classes at once, is proposed by Weston and Watkins [5], which is an extension to the Support Vector method of pattern recognition to solve multi-class problems in one step. It is as the following:

$$\min \phi(w,\xi) = \frac{1}{2}\sum_{m=1}^{k}(w_m \cdot w_m) + C\sum_{i=1}^{l}\sum_{m\neq y_i}\xi_i^m \tag{4}$$

with constraints

$$(w_{y_i} \cdot x_i) + b_{y_i} \geq (w_m \cdot x_i) + b_m + 2 - \xi_i^m, \tag{5a}$$

$$\xi_i^m \geq 0, i = 1,2,\cdots,l, m, y_i \in \{1,2,\cdots,k\}, \quad m \neq y_i \tag{5b}$$

So we have the decision function as follows.

$$f(x) = \mathrm{argmax}[(w_i \cdot x) + b_i], \qquad i = 1,2,\cdots,k \tag{6}$$

This paper presents fuzzy compensation multi-class SVM based on the k-class direct classifiers proposed by Weston and Watkins. We introduce fuzzy compensation function to the punish items so that each data, especially outlier and noise data, can affect more sound influence to classification results. In a word, the fuzzy membership function is introduced to treat data points with different importance.

# 3 Fuzzy Compensation Multi-class SVM

## 3.1 Fuzzy and Fuzzy Compensation

In the theories of SVM, the training process is very sensitive to outlier and noise data. Formula 1 uses parameter $C$ to control the punish degree to error classification samples. If parameter $C$ value is bigger, it denotes to set a bigger punish value to error classification samples, and to decrease error classification data, while a smaller $C$ denotes to ignore some 'negligible' error classification data, and to obtain a bigger classification margin as a result. But parameter $C$ value is invariable in the SVM training process, which means all training data is comparably disposed. So SVM training process is sensitive to some data, such as outlier, noise data, and results in "overfitting".

In this sense, a training datum no longer belongs to the class strictly: a training sample may belong to one class to the 90% degree, and may not belong to this class to the 10% degree. Based on problems above, some scholars propose fuzzy support vector machines.

Presently, most fuzzy SVMs are based on 2-class classification problems, which are not straight to multi-class problems. In addition, we must consider adequately training samples' differences to classification contribution in the training process, and improve the accuracy of classification results. So we present fuzzy compensation SVMs. This method considers not only right classification situation, but also error classification situation to the training sample, so that a training sample may afford two punishes. In this way, our method not only inherits fuzzy SVM merits to overcome "overfitting", but also makes the best of limited samples to enhance classification generalization ability.

FSVMs proposed in [10] solved the overfitting problem by introducing the membership degrees for every data. In order to construct fuzzy compensation function, in this paper we define the member function $t_i$ as

$$t_i = 1 - \frac{\left\| x_i - x^* \right\|}{\max_j \left\| x_j - x^* \right\|} \tag{7}$$

where $x^*$ is the center of class.

The training set becomes a fuzzy set

$$S_f = \{(x_i, y_i, t_i) \mid x_i \in R^d, y_i \in \{1,2,\cdots,k\}, t_i \in [0,1], i = 1,2,\cdots,l\} \tag{8}$$

The membership degrees $t_i$ of fuzzy set $S_f$ are defined through the relative importance of the samples.

### 3.2 Fuzzy Compensation Multi-class SVM

As mentioned above, we select the membership function $t_i$ .The optimal separating hyperplane of fuzzy compensation multi-class SVM is given by the quadratic solution as the following:

$$\min \phi(w,b,\xi,\eta) = \frac{1}{2}\sum_{m=1}^{k}(w_m \cdot w_m) + C\sum_{i=1}^{l}\sum_{m\neq y_i}[t_i^m \xi_i^m + (1-t_i^m)\eta_i^m] \tag{9}$$

with constraints

$$(w_{y_i} \cdot x_i) + b_{y_i} \geq (w_m \cdot x_i) + b_m + 2 - \xi_i^m, \tag{10a}$$

$$(w_{y_i} \cdot x_i) + b_{y_i} \leq (w_m \cdot x_i) + b_m - 2 + \eta_i^m, \tag{10b}$$

$$\begin{gathered} \xi_i^m \geq 0, \eta_i^m \geq 0, i = 1,2,\cdots,l \quad m, y_i \in \{1,2,\cdots,k\}, m \neq y_i \\ 0 \leq t_i^m \leq 1, \quad i = 1,\cdots,l \end{gathered} \tag{11}$$

where $C$ is the constant, $\xi_i^m, \eta_i^m$ are the slack variables, $t_i^m$ is the fuzzy membership function defined as formula (7).

We can find the solution to this optimization problem in dual variables by finding the saddle point of the Lagrangian. Its corresponding Lagrange formula is:

$$\begin{aligned} L(w,b,\xi,\eta) = {} & \frac{1}{2}\sum_{m=1}^{k}(w_m \cdot w_m) + C\sum_{i=1}^{l}\sum_{m=1}^{k}[t_i^m \xi_i^m + (1-t_i^m)\eta_i^m] \\ & - \sum_{i=1}^{l}\sum_{m=1}^{k}\alpha_{1i}^m[(w_{y_i} - w_m)\cdot x_i + b_{y_i} - b_m - 2 + \xi_i^m] - \sum_{i=1}^{k}\beta_{1i}^m \xi_i^m \\ & + \sum_{i=1}^{l}\sum_{m=1}^{k}\alpha_{2i}^m[(w_{y_i} - w_m)\cdot x_i + b_{y_i} - b_m + 2 - \eta_i^m] - \sum_{i=1}^{k}\beta_{2i}^m \eta_i^m \end{aligned} \tag{12}$$

with constraints

$$a_{1i}^m \geq 0, \alpha_{2i}^m \geq 0, \beta_{1i}^m \geq 0, \beta_{2i}^m \geq 0, \tag{13}$$

$$\begin{gathered} \xi_i^m \geq 0, \eta_i^m \geq 0, \quad i = 1,\ldots, l \quad m \in \{1,\ldots, k\} \setminus y_i \\ 0 \leq t_i^m \leq 1, \quad i = 1,\cdots,l \end{gathered} \tag{14}$$

Introducing the notation

$$c_i^n = \begin{cases} 1, & y_i = n \\ 0, & y_i \neq n \end{cases}, \quad A_{1i} = \sum_{m=1}^{k}\alpha_{1i}^m, \quad A_{2i} = \sum_{m=1}^{k}\alpha_{2i}^m \tag{15}$$

and differentiating in $w_n, b_n, \xi_j^n, \eta_j^n$ according to formula (12), we obtain:

$$\begin{aligned}
&\frac{\partial L}{\partial w_n} = w_n + \sum_{i=1}^{l}(\alpha_{1i}^n - \alpha_{2i}^n)x_i - \sum_{i=1}^{l}(A_{1i} - A_{2i})c_i^n x_i \\
&\frac{\partial L}{\partial b_n} = \sum_{i=1}^{l}(\alpha_{1i}^n - \alpha_{2i}^n) + \sum_{i=1}^{l}(A_{2i} - A_{1i})c_i^n \\
&\frac{\partial L}{\partial \xi_i^n} = Ct_i^n - \alpha_{1i}^n - \beta_{1i}^n \\
&\frac{\partial L}{\partial \eta_i^n} = C(1 - t_i^n) - \alpha_{2i}^n - \beta_{2i}^n
\end{aligned} \tag{16}$$

In the saddle point the solution should satisfy the conditions:

$$\begin{aligned}
&\frac{\partial L}{\partial w_n} = 0 \Rightarrow \quad w_n = \sum_{i=1}^{l}(A_{1i} - A_{2i})c_i^n x_i - \sum_{i=1}^{l}(\alpha_{1i}^n - \alpha_{2i}^n)x_i \\
&\frac{\partial L}{\partial b_n} = 0 \Rightarrow \quad \sum_{i=1}^{l}(\alpha_{1i}^n - \alpha_{2i}^n) = \sum_{i=1}^{l}(A_{1i} - A_{2i})c_i^n \\
&\frac{\partial L}{\partial \xi_i^n} = 0 \Rightarrow \quad Ct_i^n = \alpha_{1i}^n + \beta_{1i}^n \\
&\frac{\partial L}{\partial \eta_i^n} = 0 \Rightarrow \quad C(1 - t_i^n) = \alpha_{2i}^n + \beta_{2i}^n
\end{aligned} \tag{17}$$

Substituting (17) back into (12), we obtain:

$$\begin{aligned}
&L(w, b, \xi, \eta) \\
&= \frac{1}{2}\sum_{m=1}^{k}\sum_{i=1}^{l}\sum_{j=1}^{l}[c_i^m(A_{1i} - A_{2i}) - \alpha_{1i}^m + \alpha_{2i}^m] \\
&\qquad [c_j^m(A_{1j} - A_{2j}) - \alpha_{1j}^m + \alpha_{2j}^m](x_i \cdot x_j) \\
&+ \sum_{i=1}^{l}\sum_{m=1}^{k}[(\alpha_{1i}^m + \beta_{1i}^m)\xi_i^m + (\alpha_{2i}^m + \beta_{2i}^m)\eta_i^m] - \sum_{i=1}^{k}\beta_{1i}^m\xi_i^m - \sum_{i=1}^{k}\beta_{2i}^m\eta_i^m \\
&- \sum_{i=1}^{l}\sum_{m=1}^{k}\alpha_{1i}^m[(w_{y_i} - w_m)\cdot x_i + b_{y_i} - b_m - 2 + \xi_i^m] \\
&+ \sum_{i=1}^{l}\sum_{m=1}^{k}\alpha_{2i}^m[(w_{y_i} - w_m)\cdot x_i + b_{y_i} - b_m + 2 - \eta_i^m]
\end{aligned} \tag{18}$$

Using formula (17) and constraints to predigest formula (18), we have:

$$
\begin{aligned}
&L(w,b,\xi,\eta) \\
&= \sum_{i,j,m} [-\frac{1}{2} c_j^{y_i} (A_{1i} - A_{2i})(A_{1j} - A_{2j}) + (\alpha_{1i}^m - \alpha_{2i}^m)(\alpha_{1j}^{y_i} - \alpha_{2j}^{y_i}) \\
&-\frac{1}{2}(\alpha_{1i}^m - \alpha_{2i}^m)(\alpha_{1j}^m - \alpha_{2j}^m)](x_i \cdot x_j) + 2\sum_{i=1}^{l}\sum_{m=1}^{k}(\alpha_{1i}^m + \alpha_{2i}^m)
\end{aligned} \tag{19}
$$

which is a quadratic function in terms of alpha with linear constraints

$$
\sum_{i=1}^{l} \alpha_i^n = \sum_{i=1}^{l} c_i^n A_i, \qquad n = 1, \cdots, k \tag{20}
$$

$$
\begin{aligned}
&0 \le a_{1i}^m \le C t_i^m, 0 \le a_{2i}^m \le C(1 - t_i^m) \\
&a_i^{y_i} = 0, \quad i = 1,\ldots,l \quad m \in \{1,\ldots,k\} \setminus y_i
\end{aligned} \tag{21}
$$

This gives the decision function:

$$
f(x,a) = \arg\max_n [\sum_{i=1}^{l} [c_i^n (A_{1i} - A_{2i}) - (\alpha_{1i}^n - \alpha_{2i}^n)](x_i \cdot x) + b_n] \tag{22}
$$

As usual the inner products $(x_i \cdot x_j)$ in formula (22) can be replaced with the convolution of the inner product $K(x_i, x_j)$.

# 4 Algorithm Experimental Analysis and Comparison

To verify the performance of fuzzy compensation SVM, experiments were performed using some benchmark data in machine learning databases [19].

## 4.1 Benchmark Data Set Experiments

We evaluated our method using a collection of six benchmark data sets from the UCI machine learning repository [19], including iris, wine, glass, soy, vowel and blood-cell data. Their related parameters are listed in Table 1. In the table 1, #pts denotes the number of datum point, #att denotes the number of the attributes, and #class denotes the number of the classifications. Values in the last three columns of Table 1 denote right classification ratio(%).

We randomly select ten times with a third of the data being used as a test data set. The performance of our methods is compared with one-against-one (1-a-1) and one-against-all (1-a-a) classification methods based on support vector machine. To enable comparison, for each algorithm the radial basis kernel $K(x, y)$ is selected, with the same value of the parameter $\xi$ for each algorithm. The results are listed in Table 1.

**Table 1.** Experimental results in the benchmark data sets

| Name | #pts | #att | #class | 1-a-1 | 1-a-a | FC-SVM |
|---|---|---|---|---|---|---|
| iris | 150 | 3 | 4 | 97.24 | 97.24 | 97.32 |
| wine | 178 | 13 | 3 | 97.16 | 97.08 | 97.22 |
| glass | 214 | 9 | 7 | 83.36 | 82.68 | 84.20 |
| soy | 289 | 208 | 17 | 96.84 | 96.84 | 96.84 |
| vowel | 528 | 10 | 11 | 81.26 | 80.80 | 83.72 |
| blood-cell | 3097 | 13 | 12 | 91.48 | 92.02 | 92.36 |

The results show our method is better in right classification ratio than multi-class classification algorithms based on one-against-one (1-a-1) methods and one-against-all (1-a-a) methods.

## 5 Conclusions and Further Working

In this paper, a novel fuzzy compensation multi-class support vector machine is proposed. This method imports a fuzzy compensation membership function to the penalty in the straightly construction multi-class support vector machine classification problem proposed by Weston and Watkins. In our methods, we have punish item be fuzzy, compensate weight to classification, reconstruct the optimization problem and its restrictions, reconstruct Langrage formula, and present the theories deduction.

This method is applied to the benchmark data sets. Results obtained on the benchmark data sets suggest that our methods have better performance compared with the one-against-one method and one-against-all method.

Owe to selecting an array of parameter, it will cost more running time. The proposed method can be used to many classification problems, such as digit recognition, text classification.

Further research involves deceasing algorithm runtime, and testing our method on larger data sets.

## References

1. Burges, J.C.: A Tutorial on Support Vector Machines for Pattern Recognition. Data Mining and Knowledge Discovery. 2 (1998) 121–167
2. Hsu, C.W., Lin, C.J.: A Comparison of Methods for Multi-class Support Vector Machines. IEEE Transactions on Neural Networks. 2 (2002) 415–425
3. Xu, J.H., Zhang, X.G., Li, Y.D.: Advances in Support Vector Machines. Control and Decision. 5 (2004) 481–484
4. Platt J.C., Cristianini N., Shawe-Taylor J.: Large Margin DAG's for Multiclass Classification. Advances in Neural Information Processing Systems. Cambridge, MA: MIT Press. 12 (2000) 547–553

5. Weston J., Watkins C.: Multi-class Support Vector Machines. Department of Computer Science, Royal Holloway University of London Technical Report, SD2TR298204 (1998)
6. Platt J.C.: Fast Training of Support Vector Machines Using Sequential Minimal Optimization. Advances in Kernel Methods --Support Vector Learning. Cambridge: MIT Press. (1999) 185–208
7. Vapnik V.N.: The Nature of Statistical Learning Theory (2nd edition). Springer-Verlag, Berlin Heidelberg New York (1999)
8. Suykens J., Vandewalle J.: Least Squares Support Vector Machines. Neural Processing Letters. 3 (1999) 293–300
9. Scholkopf B., Smola A.J., Williamson R.C., et al: New Support Vector Algorithms. Neural Computation. 5 (2000) 1207–1245
10. Huang, H.P., Liu, Y.H.: Fuzzy Support Vector Machines for Pattern Recognition and Data Mining, International Journal of Fuzzy Systems. 4 (2002) 826–835
11. Takuya Inoue, Shigeo Abe: Fuzzy Support Vector Machines for Pattern Classification. In Proceedings of International Joint Conference on Neural Networks. (2001) 1449–1454
12. Lin, C.F., Wang, S.D.: Fuzzy Support Vector Machines. IEEE Transactions on Neural Networks. 2 (2002) 464–471
13. Sun, Z.H., Sun, Y.X.: Fuzzy Support Vector Machine for Regression Estimation. IEEE International Conference on Systems, Man and Cybernetics. 4 (2003) 3336–3341
14. Hong, D.H., Hwang, C.: Support Vector Fuzzy Regression Machines. Fuzzy Sets and Systems. 2 (2003) 271–281
15. Huang, Z., Chen, H.C., Hsu, C.J., Chen, W.H., Wu, S.S.: Credit Rating Analysis with Support Vector Machines and Neural Networks: a Market Comparative Study. Decision Support Systems. 37 (2004) 543–558
16. Kecman, V.: Learning and Soft Computing, Support Vector Machines, Neural Networks and Fuzzy Logic Models. The MIT Press, Cambridge, MA. (2001)
17. Xie, Z.X., Hu, Q.H., Yu, D.: Fuzzy Output Support Vector Machines for Classification. International Conference on Natural Computation, LNCS Vol. 3612. Springer-Verlag, Berlin Heidelberg New York (2005) 1190–1197
18. Wang, L.P. (Ed.): Support Vector Machines: Theory and Application. Springer, Berlin Heidelberg New York (2005)
19. http:/www.ics.uci.edu/~mlearn/MLRepository.html

# Chaotic Neural Network with Initial Value Reassigned and Its Application

Haipeng Ren[1], Lingjuan Chen[2], Fucai Qian[2], and Chongzhao Han[1]

[1] School of Electronics and Information Engineering, Xi'an Jiaotong University
[2] School of Automation and Information Engineering, Xi'an University of Technology
renhaipeng@xaut.edu.cn

**Abstract.** In this paper, three existing chaotic neural network models are reviewed and the searching ability of these models is analyzed, a novel chaotic neural network with varying initial value is proposed to solve problems of the lower convergence rate and long searching time in the existing method. It is different from the other modified chaotic neural networks in the aspect that it seeks the better initial value that can lead to the global optimized solution in limited steps by means of chaotic iteration instead of enlarging the annealing time or modifying annealing parameters. The new method can get the increasing convergence rate and the decreasing searching time. The controlled numerical experiments with the Travel Salesman Problems (TSP) show that the proposed method has better global searching ability.

## 1 Introduction

In a number of methods proposed to overcome the shortcomings of Hopfield Neural Network (HNN) [1], Chaotic Neural Network (CNN) is claimed to be capable of escaping from local minima [2][3]. CNN can produce a strange attractor, which makes the network states ergodic in its state space. This mechanism increases the possibility of getting the global optimal solution. But it is difficult to determine when and how to eliminate chaos in neural network, so that the optimum solution can be grasped and kept as steady state solution when the states of neural network pass the small neighbor of global optimal point. Chen and Aihara proposed simulated annealing method to eliminate chaos in CNN, which is referred to as Transiently Chaotic Neural Network (TCNN) [4]. Transient chaos is produced by adding a negative self-coupling term to a HNN in TCNN, which can be used for searching and self-organizing. Comparing with HNN, TCNN has a high ability to escape from local minima and to get the global optimal solution [5].

From the theoretical viewpoint, it is sure for a TCNN to get global optimum if the chaos in the network maintains a long enough time because of the ergodic property of chaos. This might mean a low efficiency. In fact, it is almost impossible to maintain chaos with a very long time. TCNN just decays the chaos at a predetermined rate, which means the chaos would disappear within a limited step. Therefore, there still exist local minima solutions for TCNN in solving TSP problem. TCNN can not assure a hundred percent convergence rate.

Some efforts for solving forementioned problem have been made [6]–[8]. A modified chaotic neural network with a chaotic annealing is proposed to improve the

D.-S. Huang, K. Li, and G.W. Irwin (Eds.): ICIC 2006, LNCS 4113, pp. 51 – 62, 2006.

performance of TCNN [6]. The strength of self-feedback term is made chaotic in [6]. This chaotic self-feedback term is faded gradually, which gives a noise-like simulated annealing. Exponential annealing is proposed to replace proportional annealing to extend duration of chaotic state and then to get better convergence rate of TCNN in [7]. The Gauss and Sigmoid (G-S) function is used as activation function for TCNN and exponential annealing is used instead of proportional annealing to improve the performance of TCNN in [8]. All these efforts make the significant improvement to the performance of current TCNN. Motivated by these efforts, we suggest a new method to improve the performance of TCNN.

It has been found in experiments that not only the annealing strategy but also the initial value may affect the optimization performance of TCNN. If "bad" initial values are chosen, then we could not get a global minimum within limited steps by TCNN or its modified forms. To solve this problem, a chaotic neural network method with varying initial values is proposed in this paper. In the proposed method, if the previous initial values can not get the global minima after a setting step of iterations, new initial values are generated by a chaotic mapping until the global minima is reached in the predetermined steps. The proposed method is applied to TSP, comparison is made with the existing methods. Simulation results show this method has a better performance. It not only get a hundred percent convergence rate but also improve the speed of convergence greatly.

This paper is organized as follows: In section 2 three existing chaotic neural network models are reviewed. The mechanism of claimed global search ability is pointed out for each one, the application aspects of three networks are outlined. In section 3 the proposed methods are introduced. In section 4, simulations with TSP are performed, whose results show the better performance of the proposed method. Some conclusion remarks are given in section 5.

## 2 Three Existing Chaotic Neural Network Models and Their Application in TSP

In this section, TCNN and two of its modified models are introduced. The mechanism to produce the global minima solution is analyzed.

### 2.1 TCNN

The TCNN model [4] can be depicted as follows:

$$x_i(t) = \frac{1}{1+\exp(-y_i(t)/u)} \tag{1}$$

$$y_i(t+1) = ky_i(t) - \alpha\left(\sum_{j=1}^{N} w_{ij}x_j(t) + I_i\right) - z_i(t)(x_i(t) - I_0) \tag{2}$$

$$z_i(t+1) = (1-\beta)z_i(t) \tag{3}$$

Where Eq.(1) is the output function of the neuron, Eq. (2) is the neuron dynamics, Eq. (3) is the annealing function, $y_i$ is the internal state of neuron $i$ and $x_i$ is output of neuron $i$, $w_{ij}$ is the connection weight from neuron $j$ to neuron $i$, $I_i$ is the input bias of neuron $i$, $k$ is the damping factor of nerve membrane ($0 \le k \le 1$), $u$ is the steepness parameter of the output function ($u$ >0), $I_0$ is the exterior bias. $z_i(t)$ is the self-feedback connection weight, corresponding the temperature of simulated annealing (it is referred to as annealing function), $\alpha$ ($\alpha > 0$) is positive scaling parameters for input, $\beta$ ($0 \le \beta \le 1$) is damping factor of the annealing function $z_i(t)$, $z_i(0)$ should be selected carefully for the network to be chaotic. From Eq. (3), we have that annealing function $z_i(t)$ approaches to zero as time evolution, and then TCNN becomes a Hopfield-like neural network, which converges to a fixed point. Because $z_i(t+1)$ is proportional to $z_i(t)$ with a ratio ($1-\beta$) less than 1, the speed of $z_i(t)$ tending to zero is determined by $\beta$. Fig.1 shows the anneal function changing versus the iteration steps.

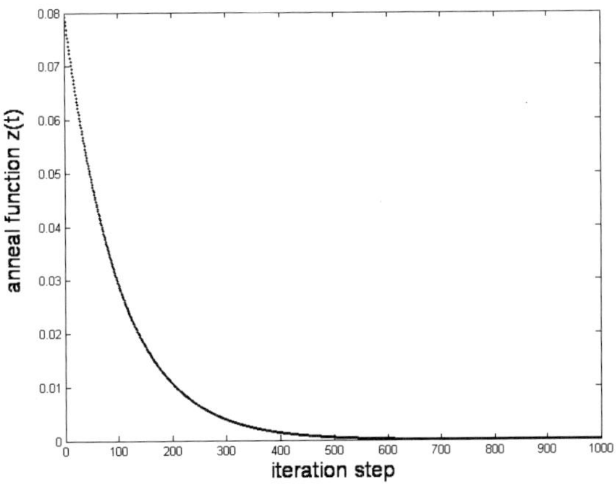


**Fig. 1.** Annealing function $z(t)$ changing curve with $\beta = 0.01$

## 2.2 Noise Chaotic Neural Network

The chaotic neural network with noise-like annealing function in [6] (it is referred to as Noise Chaotic Neural Network (NCNN) for simplicity) is given as:

$$x_i(t) = \frac{1}{1+\exp(-y_i(t)/u)} \tag{4}$$

$$y_i(t+1) = ky_i(t) - \alpha\left(\sum_{j=1}^{N} w_{ij}x_j(t) + I_i\right) - \gamma z_i(t) \tag{5}$$

$$z_i(\mathrm{t}) = \eta_i(t) - h \tag{6}$$

$$\eta_i(t+1) = a(t)\eta_i(t)(1-\eta_i(t)) \tag{7}$$

$$a(t+1) = (1-\beta)a(t) + \beta a_0 \tag{8}$$

$$h = \eta^* = 1 - 1/a_0 \tag{9}$$

Where $1 \le a_0 < 2.9$ ,$0 \le \beta \le 1$, $z_i(t)$ $(0 < z_i(t) < 1)$ is the "noise" to the dynamics of neuron $i$, which corresponds to the self-feedback term of TCNN, $\gamma$ is the positive scaling parameter for the "noise". The noise is generated by Logistic mapping (7). $a(0)=4$, the "noise" is chaotic, according to Eq.(8), $a(t)$ decays gradually, so that $z_i(t)$ is initially chaotic and eventually settle to a fixed point 0; with $z_i$ =0, the network described by Eqs. (4)–(9) reduces to the HNN. The noise term curve $z_i(t)$ and the parameter $a(t)$ changing curve are shown in Fig.2 (a) and (b) respectively.

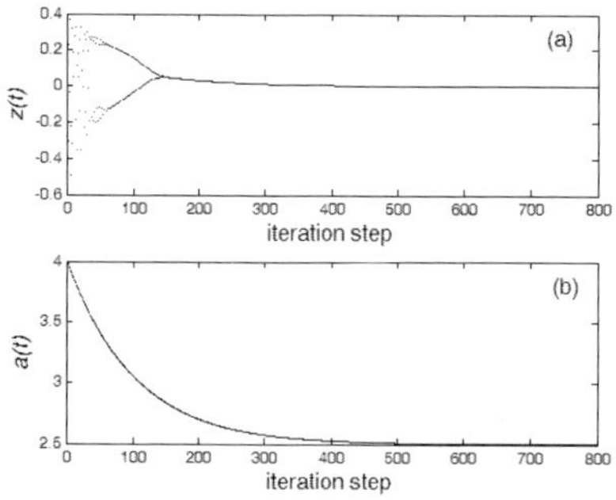


**Fig. 2.** The noise term curve and the parameter changing curve with $\beta = 0.01$

### 2.3 Exponential Annealing TCNN

The new annealing strategy chaotic neural network model [7] (it is referred to as EATCNN for simplicity) can be described as follows:

$$x_i(t) = \frac{1}{1+\exp(-y_i(t)/u)} \tag{10}$$

$$y_i(t+1) = ky_i(t) + \alpha\left(\sum_{j=1}^{N} \omega_{ij} x_i(t) + I_i\right) + z_i(t)(x_i(t) + I_0) \tag{11}$$

$$z_i(t+1) = z_i(t)/(\ln(e + \beta(1-z_i(t)))) \tag{12}$$

By replacing the proportional annealing (3) with exponential annealing (12), EATCNN is obtained. Exponential annealing cause the self-feedback coupling term to decay slower than proportional annealing, which means the chaos is maintain longer than the original TCNN and longer chaotic searching. By this way, the better performance is obtained.

The convergence process of annealing function $z(t)$ is shown in Fig.3. Compared with Fig.1, it is clear that it takes longer time for EATCNN to decay to zero with same parameter $\beta$. This will lead to higher convergence rate and longer searching time.

G-S CNN [8] is similar to EATCNN in annealing strategy, the difference is the activation function which promises to have complex dynamics. In fact, the effectiveness is still open for further research. Therefore we will not discuss it here.

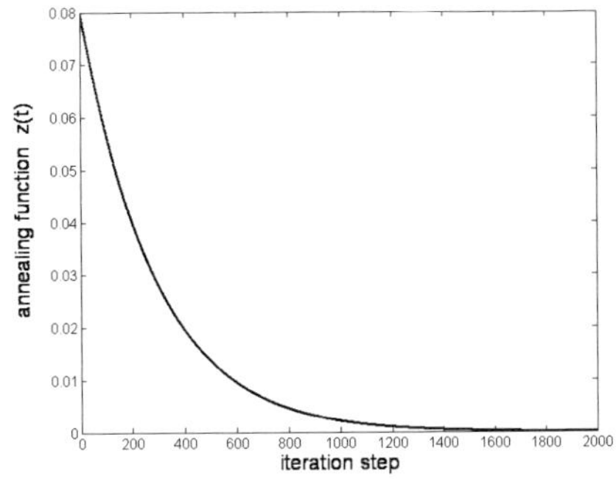


**Fig. 3.** Annealing function $z(t)$ convergence curve with $\beta = 0.01$

### 2.4 Chaotic Neural Network Application in Optimization Problem

When we apply the chaotic neural network in optimization problem, the problem must be mapped into the chaotic neural network. For the traveling salesman problem (TSP), this mapping can be gotten by the energy function. The energy function can be described as follows:

$$E = \frac{A}{2}\left\{\sum_{i=1}^{N}\left(\sum_{k=1}^{N} x_{ik} - 1\right)^2 + \sum_{k=1}^{N}\left(\sum_{i=1}^{N} x_{ik} - 1\right)^2\right\} + \frac{B}{2}\sum_{i=1}^{N}\sum_{\substack{j=1 \\ j\neq i}}^{N}\sum_{k=1}^{N}\left(x_{j(k+1)} + x_{j(k-1)}\right)x_{ik}d_{ij} \tag{13}$$

Where $x_{j0} = x_{jn}$, $x_{j,n+1} = x_{j1}$, $x$ is output, $i$ and $j$ represent city, $k$ represents the order of visiting. A and B are the coupling parameters corresponding to the constraints and the cost function of the tour length, respectively. $d_{ij}$ is the distance between city $i$ and city $j$. For a combinatorial optimizing problem, convergence rate can be defined as the ratio of the times to get global minimum solution to the total number of experiments, which is in fact the possibility of getting global optimum solution if the total number of experiments is quite large.

The optimization process of TCNN consists of two stages: In the first stage the system is in chaotic stage, in which the chaotic searching is performed. At the same time, the annealing function $z_i(t)$ begins to decrease and chaos weakens. When the annealing function tends to zero, the chaos disappeared and the second stage starts. In the second stage, the system becomes a HNN; with the gradient descent dynamics, the network converges to local optimum point. The changing of energy function is show in Fig. 4(a). From Fig. 4(a), we have the TCNN is in chaotic stage within initial several hundreds of steps, and after this stage the TCNN will operate like HNN. The duration of the first stage is determined by annealing function. The larger the annealing function, the stronger the chaos is.

The previous work has shown that the longer duration of chaotic searching the greater possibility of global optimum. From Fig. 4 it can be seen that the duration of chaotic search is determined by the value of the annealing parameter $\beta$ . When the annealing function is small than 0.02, the HNN process starts. This corresponding relation of energy function and annealing function is similar in EATCNN.

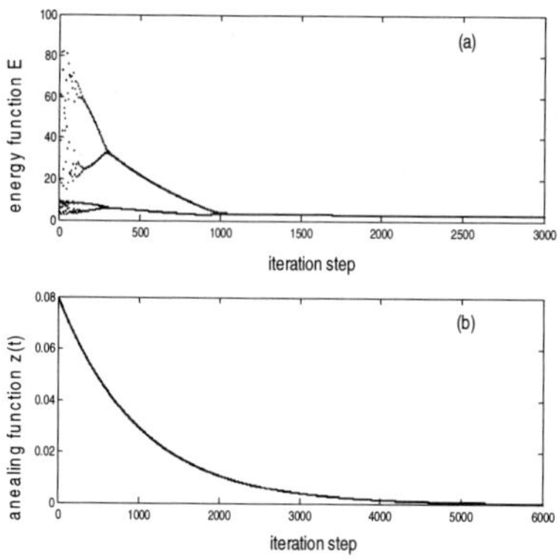


**Fig. 4.** Chaos convergence process with the annealing parameter $\beta$ =0.001: (a) is energy function convergence process; (b) is annealing function convergence curve

Fig. 5 shows four annealing function convergence curves in different annealing parameter $\beta$ . It can be seen that the annealing process decreases slower as $\beta$ becoming smaller, which means chaotic state in the neural network is kept longer, thereby, the possibility of escaping local optimum will increase due to the ergodic property of chaos. Chaotic searching in first stage of TCNN is the key of better convergence rate of TCNN compared with HNN. From Fig.5 we can also derive the conclusion that the longer the chaotic state, the longer time spending on searching procedure, which will cause the low efficiency of TCNN (long searching time).

From Fig.6, it is clear that the chaotic state duration in NCNN is longer than that of TCNN, therefore, NCNN can get better convergence rate than TCNN with same $\beta$.(although $\beta$ of NCNN is different term from that of TCNN, they all determine the time to shift from CNN to HNN ). Because the noise term is irrelevant to the inherent dynamics of the corresponding HNN, the noise term might cause the HNN's dynamics far from its equilibrium (possible local optimum point). Therefore, comparing with TCNN, it takes more time for NCNN to reach its corresponding equilibrium with gradient descend algorithm after chaos is eliminated. This means that longer time might be sped for NCNN and the lower efficiency. The forementioned analysis will prove by the simulation results in Section 4.

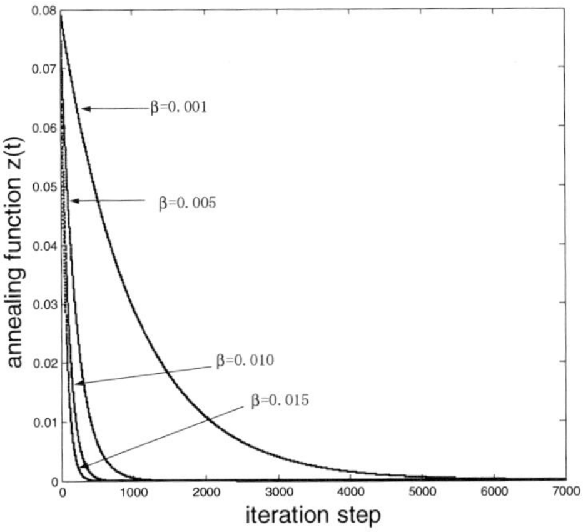


**Fig. 5.** Annealing function curves in different annealing parameter NCNN replaces the self-feedback term in TCNN by a noise generated by Logistic mapping, the energy function curve with $\beta = 0.001$ in NCNN is given in Fig.6

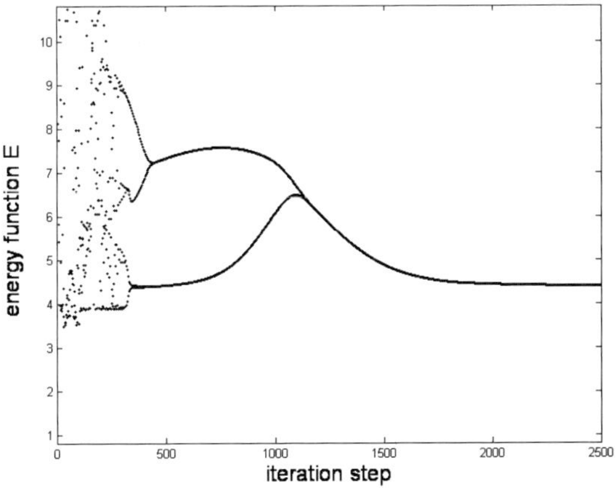


**Fig. 6.** Energy function curve of NCNN with $\beta = 0.001$

The annealing speed parameter $\beta$ of TCNN decreases with an equal proportion mode, which is replaced by exponential mode (expressed by Eq.(12)) in EATCNN. This cause the chaos maintains longer than that of TCNN, which give the EATCNN better convergence rate but longer searching time. These will be illustrated by simulation results in Section 4.

As a word, NCNN and EATCNN rely on modifying the duration of chaotic state to get better performance. Initial values of the networks are neglected on the assumption that the ergodic property of chaos will conquer the bad initial value, which is far from optimum point in sense of trajectory.

But the assumption is not stable if the chaos is not maintained long enough. If the chaos is maintained much longer, the efficiency will be decreased. This can also explain why we cannot get hundred percent of convergence rate of TCNN. From the foregoing analysis, it is clear that there exists conflict between convergence rate and searching efficiency. How to get a tradeoff of these conflict aspects is the key problem in application of TCNN, which also gives the hints to improve the performance of TCNN.

In this paper, to avoid this difficult tradeoff problem, the initial value is reassigned if an iteration limit is reach for one set of initial values. The total spending including changing initial value, chaotic searching and gradient descended searching might decrease compared with existing method. This is the start point and main idea of this paper. The comparison with existing method will prove the effectiveness of the idea.

## 3 Chaotic Neural Network Model of Varying Initial Value

Theoretically, the chaotic neural network can undergo any state in the solution space with an arbitrarily given initial value. So the initial value usually be chosen in [-1.0, 1.0] randomly [4-8]. However, the result is not perfect using the method. If improper initial values are used in chaotic neural network, it takes a very long time iteration to get the global optimal solution despite the ergodicity, and the searching time is very long, so the efficiency is degraded. Once the initial values are selected, these initial values remain unchanged during the iterations in existing method, then after limited time iterations the network could not reach the global optimal solution, and even the suboptimal solution.

In this paper the TCNN with varying initial values is proposed. The proper initial values, which can get global minimum within limited iterations, are searched by the Logistic mapping. At first, one set of initial condition for every neuron in the network is selected randomly. If this set of initial condition can lead to global optimum within predetermined number of iterations, the global optimum is derived without changing the initial conditions. The case is corresponding to the convergent case of the ordinary TCNN, but for some "bad" initial conditions, it can not lead to global optimum solution, within limited iteration. This leads to failure of searching in ordinary TCNN. (Therefore the convergence rate of TCNN is decreased). For the proposed method, if the "bad" initial conditions are selected, it can be detected by the fact that it can not produce global optimum solution within a small number of iterations. Once the initial conditions are conformed to be "bad", a new set of initial condition is generated by one-step iteration of Logistic mapping, the TCNN will start searching with these new initial conditions. The procedure will go on until the global optimum is derived.

The Logistic mapping is given as:

$$v_i(m+1) = 1 - \Phi v_i^2(m) \tag{14}$$

Where $v_i(m)$ is the value of $v_i$ at $m$ th iteration. System (14) is completely chaotic with $\Phi$=2 .The steps to change initial conditions are given as follows:

Step1: $v_i(0), (i=1....N)$ are chosen randomly in [-1, 1], $N$ is the square of city number, $y_i(0) = v_i(0)$, $m = 0$.

Step2: TCNN evolved with the initial conditions $y_i(0)$, if these initial conditions can lead to the global optimum, go to step 4 (In this case, the initial condition changing procedure stops before it starts) ; else go to step 3.

Step3: $v_i(m+1)=1-\Phi v_i^2(m)$, $\Phi=2$ ; $y_i(0)=v_i(m+1)$; $m=m+1$; Go to step 2.

Step 4: The global optimum is output, the searching procedure stops.

The flow chart of proposed TCNN with varying initial value is given in Fig.7. From Fig.7, if the "bad" initial conditions are selected the proposed method can adjust it within predetermined iterations.

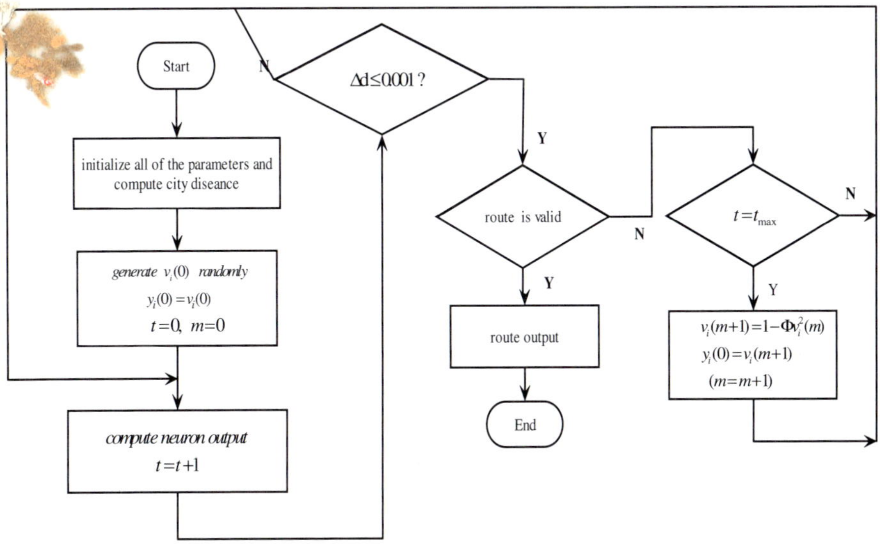


**Fig. 7.** The flow chart of varying initial value method shows the procedure of this method applied to TSP. $\Delta d$ represents the change of distance. $m$ is the step of varying initial value. $t_{max}$ is the predetermined step of detecting "bad" initial values.

This algorithm can help the next iteration to get a better initial value in sense that it can lead to global minima in a limited steps.

Although there is cost for changing initial value, the total cost of changing initial value and corresponding TCNN will decrease, which together with the higher convergence rate will lead to better performance than existing method.

## 4 Comparisons of New Method with Previous CNN

In this section, the Hopfield-Tank original data on TSP with 10-city is used for comparing research of three existing method and the proposed method, the optimal route is 2.6881.

### 4.1 TCNN

TCNN is used for 10-city TSP. The parameters were set as follows: $k = 0.8$, $\alpha = 0.0145$, $u = 1/50$, $I_i = 0$, $I_0 = 0.5$, $z(0) = 0.08$. The results are summarized in Table 1.

**Table 1.** Results of 5000 experiments for each value $\beta$ on 10-city TSP with TCNN

| $\beta$ | NG | RG | NI |
|---|---|---|---|
| 0.015 | 4713 | 94.26% | 161 |
| 0.010 | 4720 | 94.40% | 274 |
| 0.005 | 4729 | 94.58% | 321 |
| 0.001 | 4732 | 94.6% | 573 |

### 4.2 NCNN

NCNN approach is applied to 10-city TSP, the parameters are set as follows: $\alpha = 0.015$, $\gamma = 0.1$, $u = 1/250$, $a(0) = 3.9$, $a_0 = 2.5$, $h = 0.6$, The results are summarized in Table 2.

**Table 2.** Results of 5000 experiments for each value $\beta$ on 10-city TSP with NCNN

| $\beta$ | NG | RG | NI |
|---|---|---|---|
| 0.10 | 5000 | 100% | 168 |
| 0.015 | 5000 | 100% | 500 |
| 0.003 | 5000 | 100% | 1500 |
| 0.001 | 5000 | 100% | 2500 |

### 4.3 EATCNN

EATCNN is applied to 10-city TSP, the parameters are set as same as that of TCNN for each $\beta$ value. The results are summarized in Table 3.

### 4.4 TCNN with Varying Initial Values

The proposed TCNN with varying initial value method is applied to 10-city TSP. The parameters were set as the same as of TCNN, The results are summarized in Table 4.

In table 1–4, NG is the times to get global minimum, RG is the rate of getting global minimum, NI is the average number of iteration to get global minimum. In table 4, T is the average changing times of initial values among 5000 times experiments, and in table 4, NI includes the iteration times for all initial value before the global minimum is derived.

Table 1 shows that with $\beta$ decreasing, NG and RG increase, this conforms foregoing analysis. However, the convergence rate does not reach a hundred percent.

**Table 3.** Results of 5000 experiments for each value $\beta$ on 10-city TSP with EATCNN

| $\beta$ | NG | RG | NI |
|---|---|---|---|
| 0.015 | 4802 | 96.04% | 198 |
| 0.010 | 4851 | 97.02% | 315 |
| 0.005 | 4878 | 97.56% | 523 |
| 0.001 | 4912 | 98.24% | 721 |

**Table 4.** Results of 5000 experiments for each value $\beta$ on 10-city TSP with TCNN with the varying initial value

| $\beta$ | NG | RG | NI | T |
|---|---|---|---|---|
| 0.015 | 5000 | 100% | 53.5 | 0.088 |
| 0.010 | 5000 | 100% | 54 | 0.093 |
| 0.005 | 5000 | 100% | 52.5 | 0.089 |
| 0.001 | 5000 | 100% | 52.4 | 0.079 |

Table 2 shows that NCNN can reach a hundred percent global optimal solution, and with the annealing parameter $\beta$ decreasing, the NI increases dramatically.

Table 3 is the result of EACNN method. It can be seen that NI increase with $\beta$ decreasing. The convergence rate does not reach a hundred percent.

In Table 4 we get a hundred percent global optimal solution by the proposed method with a relative small NI. The average time of initial changing is smaller than one. It shows that the initial value which leads to the global optimal solution within limited time iterations is denseness in the solution space. In fact, this proposed method includes two parts, chaotic searching initial value and chaotic neural network searching global optimal solution, which gives the better performance of proposed method.

## 5 Conclusions

In this paper, we discuss the TCNN optimization method with varying initial value, It is different from another modified chaotic neural networks in the aspect that it does not enlarge the annealing time or modify the annealing parameters, but seeks the better initial value that can lead to the global optimized solution in limited step by means of chaotic iteration, the proposed method is used in 10-city TSP, the better performance is shown in this application.

## References

[1] Hopfield, J., Tank, D. W.: Neural Computation of Decisions in Optimization Problems. Biolog. Cybern, 52 (1985) 141-152

[2] Aihara, K.: Bifurcation Phenomena in Nonlinear Systems and Theory of Dynamical Systems. Chaotic Neural Network in H. Kawakami (ed.), World Scientific, Singapore, (1990) 143-161

[3] Aihara, K., Takabe, T., Toyoda, M.: Chaotic Neural Network. Phys lett. A, 144 (6,7) (1990) 330-340

[4] Chen, L., Aihara, K.: Chaotic Simulated Annealing by a Neural Network Model with Transient Chaos. IEEE Transactions on Neural Networks, 8 (6) (1995) 915-930

[5] Chen, L., Aihara, K.: Global Searching Ability of Chaotic Neural Networks. IEEE Transactions on Circuits and Systems1: Fundamental Theory and Application, 46 (8) (1999) 979-993

[6] He, Y., Wang, L.: Chaotic Neural Networks and Their Application to Optimization Problems. Control Theory and Application, 17 (6) (2000) 847-852

[7] Wang, L., Zheng, D.: A Kind of Chaotic Neural Network Optimization Algorithm Based on Annealing Strategy. Control Theory and Application, 17 (1) (2000) 139-142

[8] Xiu, C., Liu, X.: A Novel Chaotic Neural Network and Its Application. Acta Electronica Sinice, 33 (5) (2005) 868-870

# Chaotic Synchronization of Hindmarsh-Rose Neural Networks Using Special Feedback Function

HongJie Yu[1] and JianHua Peng[2]

[1] Department of Engineering Mechanics, Shanghai Jiao Tong University,
200240 Shanghai, China
yuhongjie@sjtu.edu.cn
[2] Institute for Brain Information Processing and Cognitive Neurodynamics, School of Information Science and Engineering, East China University of Science and Technology,
200237, Shanghai, China

**Abstract.** The chaotic synchronizations of Hindmarsh-Rose (HR) neurons networks linked using the nonlinear coupling feedback functions constructed specially are discussed. The method is an expansion of SC method based on the stability criterion. The stable chaotic synchronization can be achieved without calculation of the maximum Lyapunov exponent when the coupling strength is taken as reference value. The efficiency and robustness of this approach are verified theoretically and numerically. We find that the phenomenon of the phase synchronization occurs in a certain region of coupling strength in the case of networks with three neurons. It is shown that with increasing of the number of the coupled neurons, the coupling strength satisfying stability equation of synchronization decrcases in the case of all-to-all coupling. Besides, the influences of noise to synchronization of two coupling neurons are given.

## 1 Introduction

In recent years the synchronization and the control of chaos and hyperchaos has been widely studied [1-8], and has been experimentally observed in many systems [7,8]. Chaotic synchronizations in neural networks have attracted particular attention [9-14]. It can be expected that the control and synchronization of chaos and hyperchaos will play an important role in the field of biological and artificial neural networks. The observations of synchronous neural activity in the central nervous system have encouraged a great deal of theoretical work on synchronization in coupled neural networks. These observations suggest that the neural activity is a cooperative process of neurons and the synchronization plays a vital role in solving the so-called binding problem of information processing in the brain.

Irregular bursting chaos is seen in the Hindmarsh-Rose (HR) model. The HR model was constructed from voltage clamp data to provide a simple description of the patterned activity seen in molluscan neurons. Wang and Perez [9] investigated the time interval sequences and the spatiotemporal patterns of the firings of coupled neuronal network in 1993. Recently, phase synchronization of two linearly coupled chaotic neurons [10], chaos controlling [12] in the model of HR neurons have been extensively

D.-S. Huang, K. Li, and G.W. Irwin (Eds.): ICIC 2006, LNCS 4113, pp. 63 – 72, 2006.

investigated. A phenomenon of enhancement of neural synchrony by time delay was uncovered in a network of HR neuronal oscillators with time-delayed coupling [14]

We have noticed that synchronization of chaos and hyperchaos are principally studied by using the same linear function of variables from each chaotic oscillator to couple other chaotic oscillators in departed research. Pecora and Carroll gave master stability function for any linear coupling of oscillators [3]. Ali and Fang used nonlinear coupling feedback functions such as triangle functions and their linear superpositions for synchronization of chaotic and hyperchaotic systems [4]. So far, real forms of coupling functions of linked neurons in neural networks are not clear. It maybe is linear coupling functions such as in literature [10]. Furthermore, due to the complexity of information processing in brain, it is greatly possible to possess nonlinear coupling function. In this letter, we report a phenomenon of chaotic synchronization in a HR neural network with nonlinear coupling feedback functions that is specially constructed. A method (SC method) based upon the stability criterion of linear systems for synchronizing chaotic systems was proposed by Yu and Liu in 2003 [6], and is expanded here. In this letter, we focus the attention on the synchronization problem of units of networks linked by special nonlinear coupling function with matrix of all-to-all coupling coefficients. Networks of HR neurons are taken as numerical examples to discuss synchronization behavior of neurons. The phenomenon of stable chaotic synchronization has been found in a certain region around reference value of coupled strength. General master stability equations are given to examine the stability of synchronous state.

## 2 Chaotic Synchronization of Two Coupled Systems

We consider a chaotic continuous system described by

$$\dot{\boldsymbol{X}}(t) = \boldsymbol{F}(\boldsymbol{X}(t)). \tag{1}$$

where $\boldsymbol{X}(t) \in \mathbf{R}^n$ is a $n$-dimensional state vector of the system, and $\boldsymbol{F} : \mathbf{R}^n \to \mathbf{R}^n$ defines a vector field in $n$-dimensional space. We suitably decompose the function $\boldsymbol{F}(\boldsymbol{X}(t))$ as

$$\dot{\boldsymbol{X}}(t) = \boldsymbol{G}(\boldsymbol{X}(t)) - \boldsymbol{D}(\boldsymbol{X}(t)). \tag{2}$$

where function $\boldsymbol{G}(\boldsymbol{X}(t)) = \mathbf{A}\boldsymbol{X}(t)$ is specially disposed as the linear part of $\boldsymbol{F}(\boldsymbol{X}(t))$, and is required that $\mathbf{A}$ is a full rank constant matrix, all eigenvalues of which have negative real parts. Function $-\boldsymbol{D}(\boldsymbol{X}(t)) = \boldsymbol{F}(\boldsymbol{X}(t)) - \boldsymbol{G}(\boldsymbol{X}(t))$ is the nonlinear part of $\boldsymbol{F}(\boldsymbol{X}(t))$, and is called as the nonlinear coupling feedback function. Then the system (1) can be written as

$$\dot{\boldsymbol{X}}(t) = \mathbf{A}\boldsymbol{X}(t) - \boldsymbol{D}(\boldsymbol{X}(t)). \tag{3}$$

We construct a nonlinear coupling between two chaotic systems by the difference of feedback functions $\boldsymbol{D}(\boldsymbol{X}_1(t))$ and $\boldsymbol{D}(\boldsymbol{X}_2(t))$ as follows

$$\dot{\boldsymbol{X}}_1(t) = \mathbf{A}\boldsymbol{X}_1(t) - \boldsymbol{D}(\boldsymbol{X}_1(t)) + \alpha[\boldsymbol{D}(\boldsymbol{X}_1(t)) - \boldsymbol{D}(\boldsymbol{X}_2(t))]. \tag{4}$$

$$\dot{\boldsymbol{X}}_2(t) = \mathbf{A}\boldsymbol{X}_2(t) - \boldsymbol{D}(X_2(t)) + \alpha[\boldsymbol{D}(X_2(t)) - \boldsymbol{D}(X_1(t))]. \tag{5}$$

where $\alpha$ are the coupling strengths. The systems (4) and (5) are driver and response systems each other and they are symmetrically coupled. The synchronization error between system (4) and system (5) is defined as $\boldsymbol{e}(t) = \boldsymbol{X}_1(t) - \boldsymbol{X}_2(t)$. The evolutional equation of the difference $\boldsymbol{e}(t)$ is determined via the linear approximation as follows

$$\dot{\boldsymbol{e}}(t) = [\mathbf{A} + (2\alpha - 1)\frac{\partial \boldsymbol{D}}{\partial \boldsymbol{X}}]\boldsymbol{e}. \tag{6}$$

Obviously the zero point of $\boldsymbol{e}(t)$ corresponds to the equilibrium point. The synchronization between $\boldsymbol{X}_1$ and $\boldsymbol{X}_2$ can be achieved as $\gamma = 2\alpha = 1$. Since all eigenvalues of the matrix $\mathbf{A}$ have negative real parts mentioned as before, according to the stability criterion of linear system $\dot{\boldsymbol{e}} = \mathbf{A}\boldsymbol{e}$, the zero point of synchronization error is asymptotically stable and $\boldsymbol{e}(t)$ tends to zero when $t \to \infty$. Then the state vectors $\boldsymbol{X}_1(t)$ and $\boldsymbol{X}_2(t)$ of systems (4) and (5) are completely synchronized. We notice that the calculation of conditional Lyapunov exponents is not necessary in stability analysis of synchronization when $2\alpha = 1$ is satisfied. When $2\alpha \neq 1$, the synchronization is stable only when all conditional Lyapunov exponents are negative, and it can be examined by solving Eqs.(4),(5) and (6) simultaneously.

## 3 Chaotic Synchronization of HR Neural Network

In order to show the applicability of the proposed approach further, attention is now focused on neural networks. As a network constructed by coupling two neurons nonlinearly, we consider a model of Hindmarsh-Rose neuron described by the following equations of motion

$$\begin{aligned} \dot{x} &= y - ax^3 + bx^2 + I_{ext} - z \\ \dot{y} &= c - dx^2 - y \\ \dot{z} &= r(S(x - \bar{x}) - z) \end{aligned} \tag{7}$$

where $x$ is the membrane potential, $y$ is a recovery variable associated with fast current, $z$ is a slowly changing adaptation current. Here $a = 1.0$, $b = 3.0$, $c = 1.0$,

$d = 5.0$, $S = 4.0$, $r = 0.006$, $\bar{x} = -1.56$, and $I_{ext}$ is the external current input, $I_{ext} = 3.0$. Then the system (7) exhibits a multi-time scaled burst-spike chaotic behavior (see Fig.1).

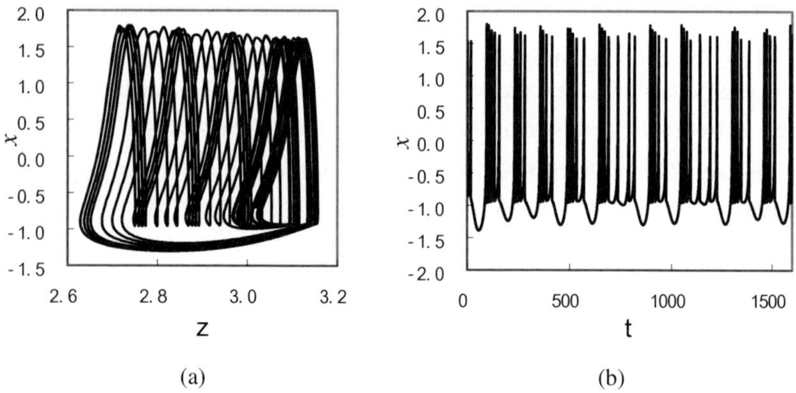


**Fig. 1.** (a) The chaotic attractor of the single HR neuron in $(z, x)$ projection (b) Chaotic spike/burst time series of membrane potential $x$

Considering a network of two HR neurons connected by coupling nonlinear feedback functions as

$$\begin{aligned}\dot{x}_1 &= y_1 - ax_1^3 + bx_1^2 + I_{ext} - z_1 + \alpha(-x_1 + ax_1^3 - bx_1^2 + x_2 - ax_2^3 + bx_2^2)\\ \dot{y}_1 &= c - dx_1^2 - y_1 + \alpha(dx_1^2 - dx_2^2)\\ \dot{z}_1 &= r(S(x_1 - \bar{x}) - z_1)\end{aligned} \tag{8}$$

$$\begin{aligned}\dot{x}_2 &= y_2 - ax_2^3 + bx_2^2 + I_{ext} - z + \alpha(-x_2 + ax_2^3 - bx_2^2 + x_1 - ax_1^3 + bx_1^2)\\ \dot{y}_2 &= c - dx_2^2 - y_2 + \alpha(dx_2^2 - dx_1^2)\\ \dot{z}_2 &= r(S(x_2 - \bar{x}) - z_2)\end{aligned} \tag{9}$$

where the matrices $\mathbf{A}$ and $\boldsymbol{D}(\boldsymbol{x})$ can be considered as

$$\mathbf{A} = \begin{pmatrix} -1 & 1 & -1 \\ 0 & -1 & 0 \\ rS & 0 & -r \end{pmatrix}, \boldsymbol{D}(X) = \begin{pmatrix} -x + ax^3 - bx^2 - I \\ -c + dx^2 \\ rS\bar{x} \end{pmatrix},$$

where the matrix $\mathbf{A}$ has negative real eigenvalues $(-1, -0.975, -0.031)$.

The result of synchronization error $e_1(t) = x_1(t) - x_2(t)$ with different initial condition $x_1(0) = 0.3, y_1(0) = 0.3, z_1(0) = 3.0$, $x_2(0) = 0.35$, $y_2(0) = 0.3$,

$z_2(0) = 3.0$ and coupling strengths $\alpha = 0.5$, are shown in Fig.2 (a). It converges to zero rapidly with evolution of the time. Thus the chaotic synchronization of system (8) and (9) is achieved. The synchronized state is asymptotically stable in the case of $2\alpha = 1$. Fig.2 (b) shows the plot of the maximum Lyapunov exponent with various values of $\gamma = 2\alpha$ for determining the stability of synchronized state. The maximum Lyapunov exponents are negative when $\gamma \in [0.53, 1.22]$, therefore the synchronized state is stable. While $\gamma$ exceeds from the region $[0.53, 1.22]$, the maximum Lyapunov exponents are all positive, and there is no any stable region of synchronized states. We see from Fig.2(b) that there is a region of stability around $\gamma = 1$, where two HR neurons coupled can be synchronized completely. Therefore $\gamma = 1$ can be considered as a reference value of stability coupling strength. It is important to choice of coupling strength $\gamma$.

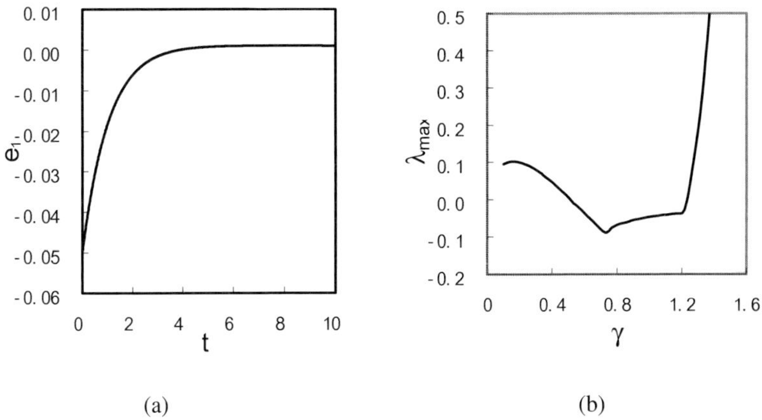


**Fig. 2.** Results of synchronization two chaotic HR neurons when $\alpha = 0.5$ (a) Time history of synchronization error $e_1$ (b) $\lambda_{max}$ vs $\gamma$

In addition, we also consider the influence of noise to synchronization of coupling neurons. Adding term $\varepsilon\xi$ to the right-hand side of the first equation in equations (8), where $\varepsilon$ indicates level of noise, and $\xi$ is a random function, having mean value 0 and mean-squared value 1. Fig.3(a)-(b) shows the time histories of logarithm of synchronization error $e_1$ influenced by noise with two different levels of noise $\varepsilon = 0.001$ and $\varepsilon = 0.01$ respectively. We can see that the synchronization error $e_1$ achieves less than $10^{-3}$ eventually when $\varepsilon = 0.01$ from Fig.3(a), the synchronization

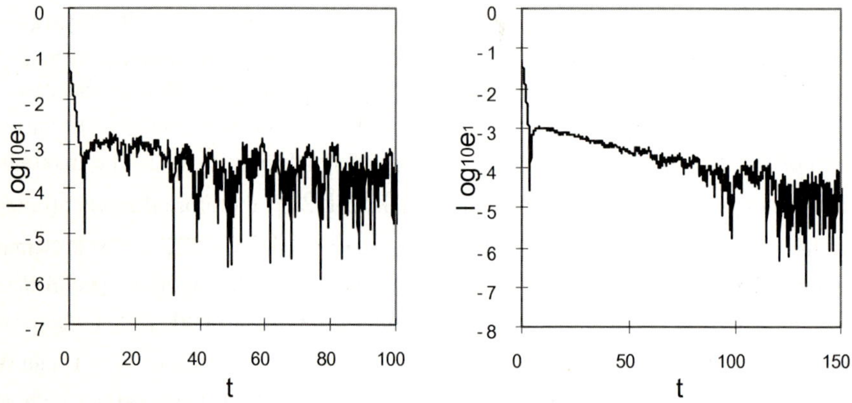


(a) ε = 0.01 (b) ε = 0.001

**Fig. 3.** The time history of the synchronization error $\log_{10} e_1$

error $e_1$ achieves less than $10^{-4}$ when $\varepsilon = 0.001$ from Fig.3(b). The efficiency and robustness of this method are shown even if with the influence of noise.

We now consider a network of coupled nonlinearly by $N$ Hindmarsh-Rose neurons as follows

$$\dot{\boldsymbol{X}}_i(t) = \boldsymbol{A}\boldsymbol{X}_i(t) - \boldsymbol{D}(\boldsymbol{X}_i(t)) + \alpha\sum_{j}^{N} G_{ij}\boldsymbol{D}(\boldsymbol{X}_j(t)), \tag{10}$$

where $\alpha$ is the coupling strength. $\mathbf{G}$ is the matrix of coupling coefficients $\{G_{ij}\}$ and the sum $\sum_{j}^{N} G_{ij} = 0$. The connectivity of HR neurons each other can be modeled by suitable choice of $\mathbf{G}$. $\boldsymbol{D}(\boldsymbol{X})$ is a nonlinear coupling function mentioned before. The connective matrix of $\mathbf{G}$ for all-to-all coupling has all elements equal to 1 for $G_{ij} (i \neq j)$ and $N-1$ for $G_{ii}$.

Let $\boldsymbol{e}_i = \boldsymbol{X}_i - \boldsymbol{X}_{i+1}, i = 1,2\cdots N-1$. The evolutional equations of difference between $i$ th neuron and it's neighbor $i+1$ th neuron can be written via the linear approximation as

$$\dot{\boldsymbol{e}}_i(t) = [\boldsymbol{A} + (N\alpha_{all} - 1)\frac{\partial \boldsymbol{D}}{\partial \boldsymbol{X}}]\boldsymbol{e}_i \text{ , } i = 1,2,\cdots,N-1. \tag{11}$$

Obviously the zero point of synchronization error $\boldsymbol{e}(t)$ is asymptotically stable and $\boldsymbol{e}(t)$ tends to zero when $t \to \infty$ for $\alpha_{all} = 1/N$. Then the neurons

$X_i(t)$ and $X_{i+1}(t)$ of the HR neural network (10) can achieve complete synchronization. We notice that evolutional equations (11) are the same for all the synchronized errors $e_i$ for all-to-all coupling. To examine the stability of synchronized states, it is enough to calculate only $i$ th stability equation in equations (11). Thus it simplifies the calculation process remarkably. The evolutional equations (11) of the errors have a simple form. Giving a coupling strength $\alpha$, we can calculate the maximum conditional Lyapunov exponents to determine the stability of synchronized state. While $\alpha_{all} = 1/N$ for all-to-all coupling, the stability of synchronization holds without calculation of the maximum Lyapunov exponents.

In the case of $N = 3$, by numerical calculation, we obtain a stability region $\alpha_{all} \in [0.177, 0.407]$ around $\alpha_{all} = 1/3$ in which all of the maximum Lyapunov exponents are negative and three HR neurons nonlinearly coupled can be synchronized completely. Therefore $\alpha_{all} = 1/3$ can be regarded as a reference value of stability coupling strength when $N = 3$. We also find that the phenomenon of the phase synchronization occurs in $\alpha_{all} \in [0.11, 0.17]$ in which although the state variables of three neurons can't achieve synchronization completely, but they posses the same phase $\phi(t)$. Using the method proposed in literature [10], the phase of the HR neural model can be defined as $\phi(t) = \arctan[(y - s_{2c})/(x - s_{1c})]$, where the point $(s_{2c}, s_{1c})$ within the rotation center and is selected to be (0,0) in this letter. The phases of three chaotic coupled neurons are illustrated in Fig4 (a), and the time histories of the state variables $x_i, i = 1,2,3$ are shown Fig.4 (b) when $\alpha_{all} = 0.15$. Obviously, they are not identical synchronization, but they are synchronization of phase.

The plot of the maximum Lyapunov exponents with various coupling strength $\alpha_{all}$ is given in Fig.5 for all-to-all coupling when $N = 10$. It is shown that the shape of the curves in Fig.2(b) and Fig.5 are the same, but values of the coupling strength $\alpha_{all}$ in Fig.5 are 1/10 times $\gamma$ in Fig.2(b) for the same Lyapunov exponent. While the region $\alpha_{all} \in [0.053, 0.122]$ of stability of ten coupling neurons is 1/5 times the region $\alpha \in [0.265, 0.61]$ of stability of two coupling neurons in Eq. (8) and Eq. (9). The time history of state component $x(t)$ of ten neurons with $\alpha = 0.1$ is shown in Fig. 6. It is easy to see that the chaotic synchronization of network can be achieved.

Comparing Eq. (11) with Eq. (6), we find that there is a relationship between them, which is $\alpha_{all} = 2\alpha/N$ for the same Lyapunov exponent. Knowing this is very important; we can estimate the region of stability of numerous neurons coupled by coupling matrix from only estimating the region of stability of two neurons. Besides we find that in order to achieve synchronization of a great deal coupling neurons in a network, we only need very low coupling strength. The relationship between coupling strength and number $N$ of coupling neuron is the inverse ratio.

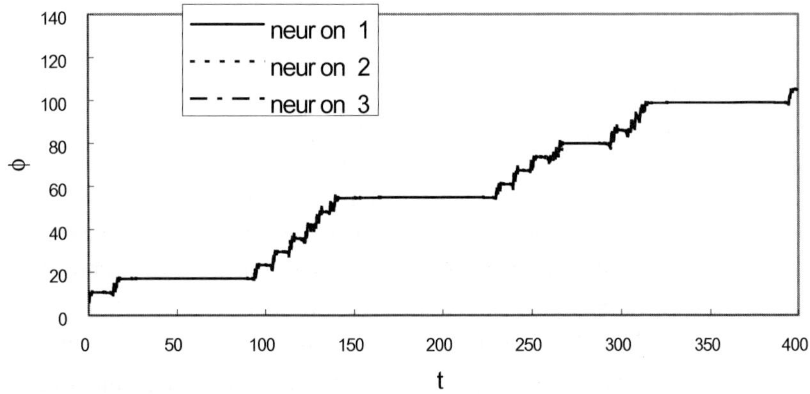


a)

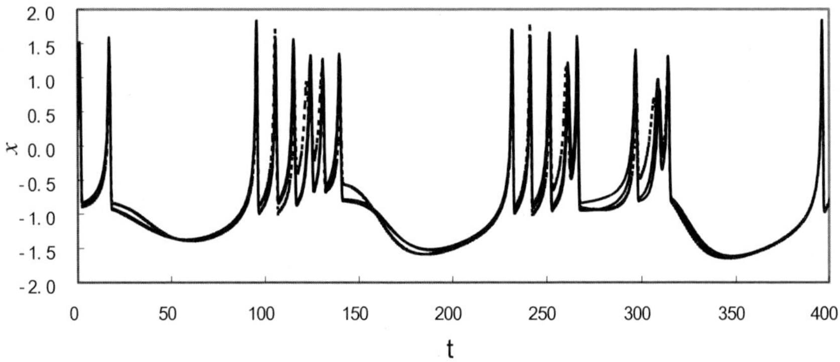


(b)

**Fig. 4.** (a) Time histories of the phase (b) Time histories of the state $x$ with $\alpha = 0.15$ , $N = 3$

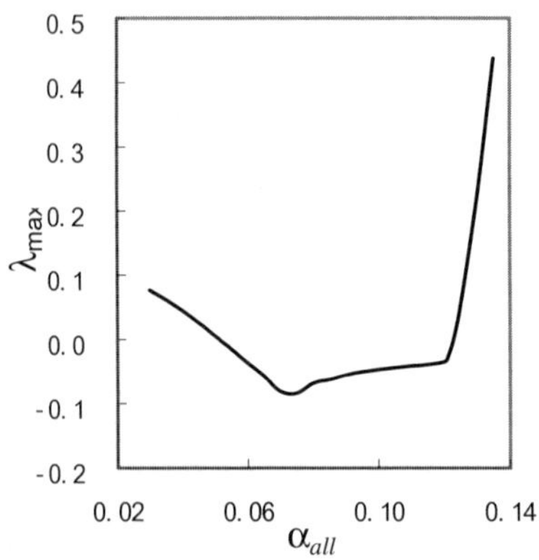


**Fig. 5.** $\lambda_{\max}$ vs $\alpha_{all}$ when $N = 10$

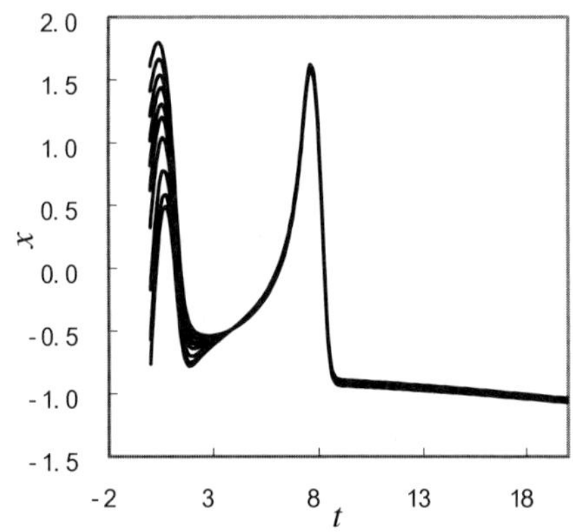


**Fig. 6.** Histories of state $x$ of ten neurons with $\alpha = 0.1$

## 4 Conclusions

In this letter, a new approach of chaotic synchronization through a mutual nonlinear coupling function between the units of HR neural network is proposed. The method expands SC method [6] based on the stability criterion. The evolutional equations of difference for all-to-all coupling HR neurons are given, and it has very simple form. The stable chaotic synchronization can be achieved without the requirement to calculate the maximum Lyapunov exponent when the coupling strength is taken as reference value, and there is a stability region around it. We find that the phenomenon of the phase synchronization occurs in a certain region of coupling strength in the case of networks with three neurons. It is shown that the proposed method is effective for chaotic synchronization of neural network systems and it is robust even if with relative large noise. It is also shown that the stability region of numerous coupling neurons can be expected from estimating stability region of two coupling neurons only. Besides, we also find that with increasing of the number of the coupled neurons, the coupling strength satisfying stability equation of synchronization decreases in the case of all-to-all coupling.

## Acknowledgment

The research is supported by the National Natural Science Foundation of China (Project No.10572086) and Specialized Research Fund for the Doctoral Program of Higher Education of China (Project No. 20050248031).

## References

1. Pecora, L.M., Carroll TL. : Synchronization in Chaotic System. Phys. Rev. Lett. 64 (1990) 821-824
2. Ott, E., Grebogi, C., Yorke, J.A.: Controlling Chaos. Phys. Rev. Lett. 64 (1990) 1196-1199
3. Pecora, L.M., Carroll, T.L.: Master Stability Functions for Synchronized Coupled Systems. Phys. Rev. Lett. 80 (1998) 2109-2112
4. Ali, M.K., Fang, J.Q.: Synchronization of Chaos and Hyperchaos Using Linear and Nonlinear Feedback Functions. Phys. Rev. E. 55 (1997)5285-5290
5. Yu, H.J., Liu, Y.Z., Peng, J.H.: Control Of Chaotic Neural Networks Based On Contraction Mappings. Chaos, Solitons and Fractals. 22(2004) 787-792
6. Yu, H.J., Liu, Y.Z.: Chaotic Synchronization Based on Stability Criterion. Phys. Lett. A. 314 (2003) 292-298
7. Hrshu, J.F., Carroll, T.L., Pecora,L.M.: Sychronous Chaos in Coupled Oscillator Systems. Phys. Rev. E. 50 (1994) 1874-1885
8. Gauthier, D.J., Bienfang, J.C.: Intermittent Loss of Synchronization in Coupled Chaotic Oscillators: Toward a New Criterion for High-Quality Synchronization. Phys. Rev. Lett. 77 (1996) 1751-1754
9. Wang, W., Perez, G., Cerdeira,H.A.: Dynamical Behavior Of The Firings In A Coupled Neuronal System. Phys. Rev. E. 47(1993) 2893-8
10. Shuai, J.W., Durand, D.M.: Phase Synchronization in Two Coupled Chaotic Neurons. Phys.Lett.A 264 (1999)289-297

11. Schäfer, C., Rosenblum, M.G.: Synchronization in the Human Cardiorespiratory System. Phys. Rev. E. 60 (1999) 857-870
12. Sabbagh, H.: Control of chaotic solutions of the Hindmarsh-Rose Equations. Chaos, Solitons and Fractals. 11 (2000) 1213-1218
13. Crook, N., Scheper, T., Pathirana, V.: Self-Organised Dynamic Recognition States for Chaotic Neural Networks. Information Sciences 150(2003) 59-75
14. Dhamala, M., Jirsa, V.K., Ding, M.: Enhancement of Neural Synchrony By Time Delay. Phys.Rev. Lett. 92 (2004) 074104-1-4

# A Comparative Study on Improved Fuzzy Support Vector Machines and Levenberg-Marquardt-Based BP Network

Chao-feng Li[1], Lei Xu[2], and Shi-tong Wang[1]

[1] School of Information Technology, Southern Yangtze University, 214122 Wuxi, China
chaofeng.li@163.com, wxwangst@yahoo.com.cn
[2] Computer Department, Luoyang Normal University, 471022 Luoyang, China
lsf_xl@126.com

**Abstract.** The paper proposes an edge-effect training multi-class fuzzy support vector machine (EFSVM). It treats the training data points with different importance in the training process, and especially emphasizes primary contribution of these points distributed in edge area of data sets for classification, and then assigns them greater fuzzy membership degrees, thus assures that the nearer these points are away from edge area of training sets and the greater their contribution are. At the same time EFSVM is systematically compared to two other fuzzy support vector machines and a Levenberg-Marquardt-based BP algorithm (LMBP). The classification results for both Iris data and remote sensing image show that EFSVM is the best and may effectively enhance pattern classification accuracy.

## 1 Introduction

During recent years, Artificial Neural Networks (ANNs) have become valuable tools to extend the repertoire of statistical methods [1-2] Typical fields are pattern classification and nonlinear interpolation based on learning from examples. But neural network models are based on the so-called Empirical Risk Minimization principle, and the training phase is aimed at achieving the minimum of the error rate on a given training set. A drawback of this approach is the fact that it does not guarantee good generalization ability, and the error probability of the classifier on patterns can be significantly higher than the error rate achieved on the training set.

Recently, Vapnik and his co-workers developed a new kind of classifiers, namely the Support Vector Machines (SVMs) [3-4]. SVMs is a general algorithm based on the guaranteed risk bounds of statistical learning theory, i.e., the so-called Structural Risk Minimization (SRM) principle. SVMs have been gained wide acceptance due to their high generalization ability for a wide range of applications and better performance than other traditional learning machines [5]. In addition, SVMs have been applied to many pattern classification or recognition fields, such as isolated handwritten digit recognition [5], and spatial data analysis [6].

However, as those remarks in [7] and [8], the SVMs are very sensitive to outliers and noise, and easily lead to overfitting phenomenon. So in [9], the author proposes a fuzzy support vector machines (FSVM) which introduces fuzzy membership degree

D.-S. Huang, K. Li, and G.W. Irwin (Eds.): ICIC 2006, LNCS 4113, pp. 73 – 82, 2006.

for training data set to make the influence of training data for classification comes to decrease as it is farther from class center. But that the goal of the SVMs is to find the "optimal" hyper-plane that separates without errors the training set, and at the same time to maximize the distance, named "margin", between the samples points and the hyper-plane. In SVMs, the "optimal" classification hyper-plane is mainly decided by these samples, which are with nearer distance away from it, namely the support vectors. That is to say, the support vectors usually locate in the edge area of training samples set and are generally farther from their class center. If we utilize the method described in [9] to decide fuzzy membership degree value, which will greatly decrease the influence of these points distributing in edge area of data sets, and thus possibly lead to gain a hyper-plane deviating from the optimal classification plane and reduce classification performance of SVMs.

The paper also treats the training data points with different importance during the training process, but the idea is different from [9]. Our study especially emphasizes the central contribution to classification of these samples distributing in edge area of data sets. Greater fuzzy membership degree is assigned to these training samples locating in edge area, which insures that the nearer these samples are away from edge area of training data sets, the greater their effect to classification results is, and we named it as an edge-effect training fuzzy SVMs (EFSVM).

The outline of the paper is as follows: An Introduction of SVM and EFSVM is respectively given in Subsection 2.1 and 2.2. In 2.3 we discuss multi-class fuzzy SVMs. In Section 3, a Levenberg-Marquardt-based BP algorithm (LMBP) is introduced. In Section 4 experiment and comparison is finished for Iris data and remote sensing image classification among SVM, FSVM, EFSVM and LMBP classifier. Conclusions are drawn in Section 5.

## 2 Support Vector Machines for Classification

### 2.1 Overview of Support Vector Machines

In this Section we shortly review some basic work on SVMs for classification problems [4][5]. Given a training set of N data points $\{x_i, y_i\}_{i=1}^{N}$, where $x_i \in R^n$ is the input and $y_i \in \{-1, 1\}$ is the corresponding desired output, and the support vector method aims at constructing a classifier of the following form:

$$f(\mathbf{x}) = Sgn\left[\sum_{SV} y_i \alpha_i K(\mathbf{x}_i, \mathbf{x}_j) + b_0\right] \tag{1}$$

where $a_i$ are positive real constants and $b_0$ is a real constant. For $k(\cdot,\cdot)$ kernel function typically has the following choices: $K(\mathbf{x}, x_i) = [(\mathbf{x} \cdot x_i) + 1]^d$ (polynomial kernel SVM of degree d); $K(\mathbf{x}, x_i) = e^{-\|\mathbf{x}-x_i\|^2 / 2\sigma^2}$ (RBF kernel SVM); $K(\mathbf{x}, x_i) = \tanh(v(x \cdot x_i) + \delta)$ (Sigmoid kernel SVM), where d, $\sigma$, $\delta$ are all constants. The classifier is constructed as follows. One assumes that

$$y_i(w \cdot \varphi(x_i) + b) \geq 1 \quad i = 1, \ldots, l \tag{2}$$

where $\varphi(\cdot)$ is a nonlinear function that maps the input space into a higher dimensional space. However, this function is not explicitly constructed. In order to have the possibility to violate (2), in case a separating hyper-plane in this higher dimensional space does not exist, thus variable $\xi_i$ are introduced such that

$$y_i(\mathbf{w} \cdot \varphi(\mathbf{x}_i) + b) \geq 1 - \xi_i \quad \xi_i \geq 0 \quad i = 1, \ldots, l \tag{3}$$

According to the SRM principle, the risk bound is minimized by formulating the following optimization problem.

$$\min_{w,\xi_i} \Phi(\mathbf{w}, \xi_i) = C(\sum_{i=1}^{l} \xi_i) + \|\mathbf{w}\|^2 \tag{4}$$

Which leads to the solution of the following quadratic programming problem

$$\begin{aligned} &Minimize \quad W(\alpha) = \sum_{i=1}^{n} \alpha_i - \frac{1}{2}\sum_{i,j}^{n} \alpha_i \alpha_j y_i y_j K(\vec{x}_i, \vec{x}) \\ &s.t. \quad \sum_{i=1}^{n} \alpha_i y_i = 0 \\ &\qquad C \geq \alpha_i \geq 0 \qquad\qquad i = 1, \ldots, l \end{aligned} \tag{5}$$

### 2.2 Edge-Effect Training Fuzzy SVMs Classifier

The classical training algorithm of a support vector method usually doesn't treat the training data points with different importance. This paper considers the different contribution of the different training points and introduces a fuzzy factor $s_i$ that stands for the membership degree of this point attaching to a class. It is defined as follows:

$$s_i = e^{-\frac{(x_i - \bar{x})^2}{2\sigma^2}} \tag{6}$$

where $\bar{x}$ is the class center obtained by calculating the average value of its training point, and $\sigma$ is the constant whose value is decided according to practical problems. where $0 < s_i \leq 1$, and when $x_i$ is farer from its clustering center, and $s_i$ is smaller, and the corresponding probability that $x_i$ belongs to this class is also smaller.

Considering the edge points (mainly support vectors) have bigger contributions to classification results in a data set without noise, so we define $u_i = 1/s_i$, thus the nearer the samples is away from edge area in training data set, and the bigger the $u_i$ value is, and the greater their effect to classification result is. Thus adding an attribution $u_i$ to the training data set, namely $(x_i, y_i, u_i)$ . In order to optimize the margin slack vector, we need to introduce slack variables $\xi_i$ to allow the margin constraints to be violated, i.e.

$$\begin{aligned} & y_i(\mathbf{w}\cdot\mathbf{x}_i+b)\geq 1-u_i\xi_i, i=1,\dots,l, \\ & \xi_i\geq 0 \quad i=1,\dots,l. \end{aligned} \tag{7}$$

At last the edge-effect training SVM method can be accomplished by the following quadric programming procedure.

$$\begin{aligned} & Minimize \quad W(\boldsymbol{\alpha})=\frac{1}{2}\sum_{i,j}^{l}\alpha_i\alpha_j y_i y_j K(\mathbf{x}_i\cdot\mathbf{x}_j)-\sum_{i=1}^{l}\alpha_i \\ & s.t. \quad \sum_{i=1}^{l}\alpha_i y_i=0 \\ & Cu_i\geq\alpha_i\geq 0 \qquad i=1,\dots,l \end{aligned} \tag{8}$$

We can solve (8) by using the same SVM algorithm as stated in Subsection 2.1.

### 2.3 Multi-class Fuzzy SVMs

At present fuzzy SVMs has two versions, and one introduces fuzzy factor during the training procedure [9], and the other does fuzzy post-processing for both mixed and missed points after classification [10]. The first version is adopted in this paper.

How to extend two-class problems to multi-class problems for SVMs is one important issue. Several methods have been proposed, such as one-against-one, one-against-all, and directed acyclic graph SVM (DAGSVM)[11] [12]. The computational cost of the one-against-all method is small, so the paper adopts one-against-all method, which firstly decomposes a multi-class problem into a two-class problem and then train again by SVMs. For a N-classification problem, we need to construct N classifiers, and each classifier recognizes one class.

## 3 Levenberg-Marquardt-Based BP Network

Feed-forward networks trained by back-propagation algorithm (Rumelhart, Hinton & Williams, 1991) and its variants are very popular. However the classical gradient descent BP algorithm suffers from its slow convergence, many scholars proposed their improved algorithm, and the Levenberg-Marquardt optimized algorithm is one of the most widely used algorithms.

In the back-propagation algorithm weight update rules are given by

$$w_k = w_{k-1}+\Delta w_k \tag{9}$$

This algorithm performs steepest descent in the connection weight space and an error surface defined by

$$E(w)=\frac{1}{2}\sum_k e(w)^2=\frac{1}{2}\sum_k (t_k-o_k)^2 \tag{10}$$

Suppose

$$e(w)=[e_1(w), e_2(w), \cdots, e_n(w)]^T, \tag{11}$$

Then

$$\nabla E(w)=J^T(w)e(w) \tag{12}$$

$$\nabla^2 E(w)=J^T(w)J(w)+S(w) \tag{13}$$

$$S(w)=\sum_i e_i(w)\nabla^2 e_i(w) \tag{14}$$

where $\nabla^2 E(w)$ stands for Hessian matrix of error function, and $\nabla E(w)$ stands for gradient, and $J(w)$ is Jacobian matrix.

As for Newton's method, its update rule is

$$\Delta w=-[\nabla^2 E(w)]^{-1}\nabla E(w) \tag{15}$$

When being close to a solution $S(w)\cong 0$, and here weight update rule of Gauss-Newton method is:

$$\Delta w=-[J^T(w)J(w)]^{-1}J^T(w)e(w) \tag{16}$$

Levenberg-Marquart algorithm is a blend of Gradient descent and Gauss-Newton iteration (Ananth Ranganathan, 2004), whose update rule is given as

$$\Delta w=-(J^T(w)J(w)+\lambda diag[J^T(w)J(w)])^{-1}J(w)e(w) \tag{17}$$

where $J^T(w)J(w)$ is the Hessian matrix evaluated at $w_i$. This update rule is used as follows. If the error goes down following an update, it implies that our quadratic assumption on e(w) is working and we reduce $\lambda$ (usually by a factor of 10) to reduce the influence of gradient descent. On the other hand, if the error goes up, we would like to follow the gradient more and so $\lambda$ is increased by the same factor. The Levenberg-Marquardt algorithm is thus (Ananth Ranganathan, 2004) -

Step 1: Do an update as directed by the above rule.

Step 2: Evaluate the error at the new parameter vector.

Step 3: If the error has increased as a result of the update, then retract the step (i.e. reset the weights to their previous values) and increase $\lambda$ by a factor of 10 or some such significant factor. Then go to Step 1 and try an update again.

Step 4: If the error has decreased as a result of the update, then accept the step (i.e. keep the weights at their new values) and decrease $\lambda$ by a factor of 10 or so.

Levenberg-Marquardt optimized algorithm converges very quickly and works extremely well in practice. The only flaw is its need for matrix inversion as part of the update, and its cost for computation and memory are much high.

# 4 Experimental Results and Analysis

## 4.1 Iris Data Classification Results

The Iris data set is with 150 random samples of flowers from the iris species Setosa, Versicolor, and Virginica collected by Anderson (1935), and contains 3 classes of 50 instances each. One class is linearly separable from the other 2, and the latter are not linearly separable from each other.

We randomly choose 20 samples for training from each class, the other 30 for testing, and compare above LMBP (our adopted network structure is that number of input layer nodes is 3, number of single hidden nodes is 9 and number of output layer nodes is 3) and three kinds of SVMs algorithm (namely SVM, FSVM, and EFSVM, here SVM adopts RBF-kernel function and SMO algorithm) and obtain classification results shown in table 1(hereinto the results of LMBP classifier is the average value of five times experimental results).

From table 1, we can find that as for Iris-Setosa all the above four kinds of classifier can recognize well and truly, and as for Iris-Versicolor the several classifier is the same and classification accuracy only reach 93.3%, however as for Iris-Virginia they is a little different and only the best EFSVM classifier reach 100%. As a whole EFSVM is superior to FSVM, and FSVM is better than SVM, and SVM is close to LMBP classifier in Iris data set, but the mixed and missed samples via SVM classifier may be reclassified by fuzzy post-processing to enhance classification accuracy [10].

**Table 1.** Comparison for Iris data classification results

| Model | Results / Categories | Classifier1 (Setosa) | Classifier2 (Versicolor) | Classifier3 (Virginia) | Mixed and Missed | Accuracy (%) |
|---|---|---|---|---|---|---|
| SVM | Setosa | 30 | 0 | 0 | 0 | **100** |
| | Versicolor | 0 | 28 | 1 | 1 | 93.3 |
| | Virginia | 0 | 2 | 28 | 2 | 93.3 |
| FSVM | Setosa | 30 | 0 | 0 | 0 | **100** |
| | Versicolor | 0 | 28 | 1 | 2 | 93.3 |
| | Virginia | 0 | 1 | 30 | 1 | 96.7 |
| EFSVM | Setosa | 30 | 0 | 0 | 0 | 100 |
| | Versicolor | 0 | 28 | 2 | 2 | 93.3 |
| | Virginia | 0 | 0 | 30 | 0 | **100** |
| LMBP | Setosa | 30 | | | | **100** |
| | Versicolor | 28 | | | | 93.3 |
| | Virginia | 28 | | | | 93.3 |

### 4.2 Remote Sensing Image Classification Results

An experimental image sampled from satellite TM, which covers Xuzhou city area in China. We make use of band 3, band 4 and band 5 to identify land-use categories. The size of the study area is 220x200 pixels.

According to the terrain map, analyzing the image visually, we divide it into 6 categories, namely road (thereinafter as A class), city area (thereinafter as B class), agriculture land (thereinafter as C class), green-land (thereinafter as D class), woodland (thereinafter as E class), water area (thereinafter as F class), and then choose samples for A class, 3905 for B class, 1949 for C class, 362 for D class, 2706 for E class and 1494 for F class by manual. From these samples data sets we randomly choose 100 as training samples from each class again, and then train and test. As for above three SVMs method we respectively construct six classifiers each, and classifier 1 distinguishes A class from other five categories, and classifier 2 distinguishes B class from other five categories, and the other is analogical.

In order to test performance of our proposed EFSVM method, we respectively use above four kinds of methods to compare. At first we use SVM SMO quick algorithm to obtain classification results shown in table 2 (herein average accuracy calculational equation is $\frac{overall\ samples - mixed\ and\ missed\ samples}{overall\ samples}$), and then use FSVM to obtain classification results shown in table 3, and use EFSVM to gain classification results shown in table 4. All above three results are the optimal value obtained by using suitable parameter (i.e., first training by training samples, and then testing by test samples to adjust sample sets again and again until gaining an appropriate parameters). At last for further comparison we also use LMBP algorithm to obtain classification results shown in table 5 (our adopted LMBP network structure is that number of input layer nodes is 3, number of single hidden nodes is 13 and number of output layer nodes is 6).

**Table 2.** The test results of SVM classifier for remote sensing data

| Results / Categories | Classifier 1 (A) | Classifier 2 (B) | Classifier 3 (C) | Classifier 4 (D) | Classifier 5 (E) | Classifier 6 (F) | Missed and Mixed | Accuracy (%) |
|---|---|---|---|---|---|---|---|---|
| A class (679) | 658 | 14 | 1 | 0 | 0 | 0 | 22 | 96.76 |
| B class (3905) | 321 | 3477 | 0 | 0 | 1 | 19 | 455 | 88.35 |
| C class (1949) | 4 | 0 | 1939 | 7 | 0 | 0 | 17 | 99.13 |
| D class (362) | 2 | 0 | 12 | 313 | 0 | 0 | 49 | 86.46 |
| E class (2706) | 1 | 15 | 26 | 0 | 2601 | 77 | 137 | 94.94 |
| F class (1494) | 0 | 5 | 0 | 0 | 43 | 1400 | 97 | 93.51 |
| Average Accuracy | 93.0% | | | | | | | |

**Table 3.** The test result of FSVM classifier for remote sensing data

| Results / Categories | Classifier 1 (A) | Classifier 2 (B) | Classifier 3 (C) | Classifier 4 (D) | Classifier 5 (E) | Classifier 6 (F) | Missed and Mixed | Accuracy (%) |
|---|---|---|---|---|---|---|---|---|
| A class (679) | 669 | 10 | 1 | 0 | 0 | 0 | 14 | 97.94 |
| B class (3905) | 355 | 3494 | 0 | 0 | 1 | 19 | 445 | 88.60 |
| C class (1949) | 1 | 0 | 1939 | 5 | 0 | 0 | 11 | 99.44 |
| D class (362) | 1 | 1 | 9 | 322 | 0 | 0 | 40 | 88.95 |
| E class (2706) | 0 | 13 | 29 | 0 | 2614 | 76 | 127 | 95.31 |
| F class (1494) | 0 | 4 | 0 | 0 | 41 | 1402 | 97 | 93.51 |
| Average Accuracy | 93.38% | | | | | | | |

**Table 4.** The test result of EFSVM classifier for remote sensing data

| Results / Categories | Classifier 1 (A) | Classifier 2 (B) | Classifier 3 (C) | Classifier 4 (D) | Classifier 5 (E) | Classifier 6 (F) | Missed and Mixed | Accuracy (%) |
|---|---|---|---|---|---|---|---|---|
| A class (679) | 659 | 27 | 1 | 1 | 0 | 0 | 30 | 95.58 |
| B class (3905) | 286 | 3627 | 0 | 0 | 1 | 19 | 317 | 91.88 |
| C class (1949) | 2 | 0 | 1939 | 2 | 9 | 0 | 19 | 99.03 |
| D class (362) | 1 | 1 | 6 | 336 | 0 | 0 | 26 | 92.82 |
| E class (2706) | 1 | 3 | 25 | 0 | 2616 | 76 | 121 | 95.53 |
| F class (1494) | 0 | 6 | 0 | 0 | 36 | 1403 | 93 | 93.78 |
| Average Accuracy | 94.54% | | | | | | | |

From table 2, table 3, table 4 and table 5, we can find that SVM classifier is superior to LMBP classifier and exceed 2.34%; and EFSVM classifier is superior to two other kinds of SVM method and exceeds 1-1.5%. All these data show that edge-effect training SVMs effectively reduces the number of mixed and missed samples after classification, and also exhibits the central contribution to classification of edge samples.

**Table 5.** The test result of LMBP classifier for remote sensing data

| Categories \ Results | A class | B class | C class | D class | E class | F class |
|---|---|---|---|---|---|---|
| A class | 653 | 277 | 0 | 1 | 0 | 1 |
| B class | 22 | 3392 | 186 | 1 | 1 | 3 |
| C class | 0 | 178 | 1708 | 9 | 3 | 4 |
| D class | 0 | 32 | 24 | 285 | 8 | 11 |
| E class | 2 | 10 | 9 | 54 | 2579 | 33 |
| F class | 2 | 16 | 22 | 12 | 115 | 1442 |
| Accuracy | 96.17 | 86.86 | 87.63 | 78.73 | 95.31 | 96.52 |
| Average accuracy | 90.66 | | | | | |

## 5 Conclusions

The paper proposes a kind of edge-effect training multi-class fuzzy SVMs, and at the same time systematically compared it to SVM, FSVM and LMBP algorithm. The classification results for both Iris data and remote sensing image show that SVM classifier is superior to LMBP classifier; and EFSVM classifier is superior to two other kinds of SVMs and may enhance classification accuracy.

## References

1. Atkinson, P. M., Tatnall, A. R. L.: Neural Networks in Remote Sensing. Int. J. Remote Sensing. 18(4)(1997) 699–709
2. Paola,J. D., Schowengerdt R. A.: A Review and Analysis of Back-propagation Neural Networks for Classification of Remotely Sensed Multi-spectral Image. Int. J. GIS. 16(16) (1995) 3033–3058
3. Vapnik, V. N.: Statistical Learning theory. Wiley, New York (1998)
4. Cortes , C., Vapnik, V.: Support Vector Networks. Machine Learning. 20(3)(1995) 273–297
5. Burges, J.C.: A Tutorial on Support Vector Machines for Pattern Recognition. Knowledge Discovery and Data Mining. 2(2) (1998) 121–167
6. Kanevski, M., Pozdnukhov A., Canu S., Maignan M.: Advanced Spatial Data Analysis and Modeling with Support Vector Machines. International Journal of Fuzzy Systems. 4(1)( 2002) 606-615
7. Zhang, X.: Using Class-Center Vectors to Build Support Vector Machines. Proc. IEEE NNSP'99, (1999) 3-11

8. Guyon, I., Matic, N., Vapnik, V. N.: Discovering Information Patterns and Data Cleaning. Cambridge, MA: MIT Press, (1996) 181-203
9. Hung, H.P., Liu, Y.H.: Fuzzy Support Vector Machines for Pattern Recognition and Data Mining. International Journal of Fuzzy Systems, 4(3) (2002) 826-835
10. Li, C. F., Wang, Z. Y.: Remote Sensing Image Classification Method Based on Support Vector Machines and Fuzzy Membership Function. MIPPR 2005: SAR and Multispectral Image Processing, Vol.6043. SPIE, Wuhan (2005) 604324-1–7
11. Hsu, C. W., Lin, C. J.: A Comparison of Methods for Multiclass Support Vector Machines. IEEE Transactions on Neural Networks. 13(2) ( 2002) 415-425,
12. Platt, J. C., Cristianini, N., Shawe-Taylor, J.: Large Margin DAG's for Multiclass Classification. Advances in Neural Information Processing Systems, Cambridge, MA: MIT Press, 12. (2000) 547-553

# Comparative Study on Input-Expansion-Based Improved General Regression Neural Network and Levenberg-Marquardt BP Network

Chao-feng Li, Jun-ben Zhang, and Shi-tong Wang

School of Information Technology, Southern Yangtze University, 214122 Wuxi, China
aofeng.li@163.com, junben@sina.com, wxwangst@yahoo.com.cn

**Abstract.** The paper presents an input-expansion-based improved method for general regression neural network (GRNN) and BP network. Using second-order inner product function or Chebyshev polynomial function to expand input vector of original samples, which makes input vector mapped into a higher-dimension pattern space and thus leads to the samples data more easily separable. The classification results for both Iris data and remote sensing data show that general regression neural network is superior to Levenberg-Marquardt BP network (LMBPN) and moreover input-expansion method may efficiently enhance classification accuracy for neural network models.

## 1 Introduction

During recent years, Artificial Neural Networks (ANNs) have become valuable tools to extend the repertoire of statistical methods. Typical fields are pattern recognition and nonlinear interpolation based on learning from examples [1]. Most popular models are feed-forward networks trained by back-propagation algorithm and its variants [2]. But single gradient descent BP algorithm suffers from its slow convergence problems, many scholars proposed their improve algorithm [3], such as self-adaptation of learning rate, adding a momentum term, Quasi Newton method, conjugate gradient method, and Levenberg-Marquardt (LM) optimized method etc. But they are not universal and still have some limitations.

These limitations can be overcome with the general regression neural network. (GRNN) proposed by Specht D. F. [4]. That does not require an iterative training procedure as in back propagation method. It approximates any arbitrary function between input and output vectors to draw the function estimate directly from the training data. Furthermore, it is consistent; that is, as the training set size becomes large, the estimation error approaches zero, with only mild restrictions on the function [5].

In this paper, the performance of LMBPN (the widely used algorithm in BP models) and of GRNN is systematically compared for pattern classification, in addition we present an input-expand-based improve method for above two neural network model.

The outline of the paper is as follows: An Introduction of LMBPN is given in Section 2. In Section 3 we discuss GRNN and its architecture. An Input-Expansion-based method for neural network models is introduced in Section 4. In Section 5

D.-S. Huang, K. Li, and G.W. Irwin (Eds.): ICIC 2006, LNCS 4113, pp. 83 – 93, 2006.

experimental comparison and analysis is finished for Iris data and remote sensing image classification among several neural network classifier. Conclusions are drawn in Section 6.

## 2 Levenberg-Marquardt-Based BP Network

BP Network is a typical multiplayer feed forward network, and schematic diagram of single hidden layer BP network architecture is presented in Fig.1.

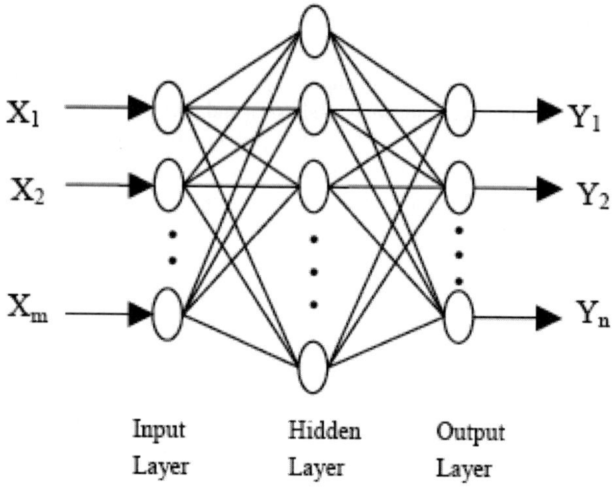


**Fig. 1.** Schematic diagram of a single hidden layer BP network architecture

The standard BP algorithm is based on the gradient descent algorithm, and its weight update rules are given by:

$$w_k = w_{k-1} + \Delta w_k \; . \tag{1}$$

The algorithm performs steepest descent in the connection weight space and an error surface defined by:

$$E(w) = \frac{1}{2}\sum_k e(w)^2 = \frac{1}{2}\sum_k (t_k - o_k)^2 \; . \tag{2}$$

Suppose:

$$e(w) = [e_1(w), e_2(w), \cdots, e_n(w)]^T , \tag{3}$$

Then:

$$\nabla E(w) = J^T(w)e(w) \; . \tag{4}$$

$$\nabla^2 E(w) = J^T(w)J(w) + S(w) \; . \tag{5}$$

$$S(w) = \sum_i e_i(w)\nabla^2 e_i(w) \quad (6)$$

where $\nabla^2 E(w)$ stands for Hessian matrix of error function, and $\nabla E(w)$ stands for gradient, and $J(w)$ is Jacobian matrix.

As for Newton's method, its update rule is

$$\Delta w = -\left[\nabla^2 E(w)\right]^{-1} \nabla E(w) \quad (7)$$

When being close to a solution, and $S(w) \cong 0$, and here weight update rule of Gauss-Newton method is:

$$\Delta w = -\left[J^T(w)J(w)\right]^{-1} J^T(w)e(w) \quad (8)$$

Levenberg-Marquardt algorithm is a blend of Gradient descent and Gauss-Newton iteration (Ananth Ranganathan, 2004), whose update rule is given as

$$\Delta w = -\left(J^T(w)J(w) + \lambda diag\left[J^T(w)J(w)\right]\right)^{-1} J(w)e(w) \quad (9)$$

where $J^T(w)J(w)$ is the Hessian matrix evaluated at $w_i$. This update rule is used as follows. If the error goes down following an update, it implies that our quadratic assumption on e(w) is working and we reduce $\lambda$ (usually by a factor of 10) to reduce the influence of gradient descent. On the other hand, if the error goes up, we would like to follow the gradient more and so $\lambda$ is increased by the same factor. The Levenberg-Marquardt (LM) algorithm is thus (Ananth Ranganathan, 2004) -

(1) Do an update as directed by the rule above.
(2) Evaluate the error at the new parameter vector.
(3) If the error has increased as a result the update, then retract the step (i.e. reset the weights to their previous values) and increase $\lambda$ by a factor of 10 or some such significant factor. Then go to (1) and try an update again.
(4) If the error has decreased as a result of the update, then accept the step (i.e. keep the weights at their new values) and decrease $\lambda$ by a factor of 10 or so.

LM method converges very quickly and works extremely well in practice. The only flaw is its need for matrix inversion as part of the update, and its cost for computation and memory are much high.

## 3 Generalized Regression Neural Network

Generalized Regression Neural Network is a new type of Neural Network proposed by Donald F. Specht in 1991. Compared with the BPNN, GRNN has a lot of advantages [4] [6] that the weights of each layer and the number of hidden layer nodes can be definite only by the training samples; and it needn't iteration during training; when network operating mode changes we only need to modify the corresponding training samples and reconstruct network. That is to say, it has a better generalization [5].

The GRNN is used for estimation of continuous variables, as in standard regression techniques. It is related to the radial basis function network and is based on established statistical principles and converges with an increasing number of samples asymptotically to the optimal regression surface.

Suppose the vector x and scalar y are random variants, and X and Y are observation values, and f (x, y) is defined a joint continuous probability density function. If the f(x, y) is known, then the regression [5] of y on x is given by :

$$E[y|x] = \frac{\int_{-\infty}^{\infty} yf(x,y)dy}{\int_{-\infty}^{\infty} f(x,y)dy} \tag{10}$$

When the density f(x, y) is not known, it must usually be estimated from a sample of observations of x and y. The probability estimator $\hat{f}(x,y)$ is based upon sample values $x_i$ and $y_i$ of the random variables x and y.

$$\hat{f}(x,y) = \frac{1}{(2\pi)^{(m+1)/2}\sigma^{(m+1)}} \cdot \frac{1}{n} \cdot \sum_{i=1}^{n} \exp\left(-\frac{(x-x_i)^T(x-x_i)}{2\sigma^2}\right)\exp\left(-\frac{(y-y_i)^2}{2\sigma^2}\right) \tag{11}$$

where m is the dimension of the vector variable x, and n is the number of sample observations, and $\sigma$ is the spread parameter.

Defining the scalar function $D_i^2$

$$D_i^2 = (x-x_i)^T(x-x_i) \tag{12}$$

And performing the indicated integrations yields the following:

$$\hat{y}(x) = \frac{\sum_{i=1}^{n} y_i \exp(-D_i^2/2\sigma^2)}{\sum_{i=1}^{n} \exp(-D_i^2/2\sigma^2)} \tag{13}$$

Schematic diagram of GRNN architecture is presented in Fig.2. Differing from the LMBPN, the GRNN consists of four layers: input layer, pattern layer, summation layer and output layer. The input layer has m units and receives the input vector. The pattern layer has n units, which calculates and outputs the value of kernel function $\exp\left(-\frac{D_i^2}{2\sigma^2}\right)$. The summation layer has two units, and its output is the value of

$\sum_{i=1}^{n} y_i \exp(-D_i^2/2\sigma^2)$ and $\sum_{i=1}^{n} \exp(-D_i^2/2\sigma^2)$. The output layer has one unit and its output is the value of $\hat{y}(x)$.

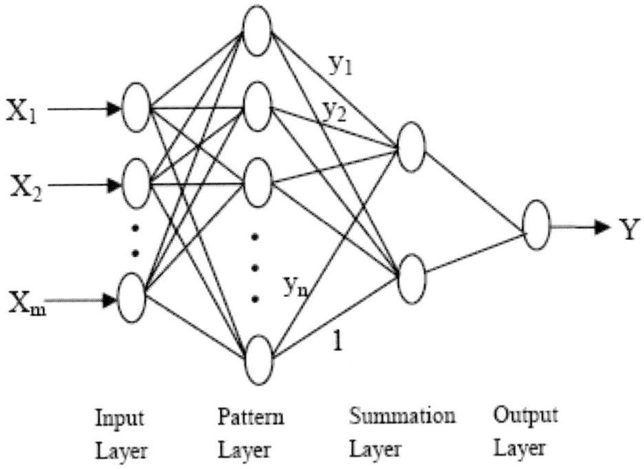


**Fig. 2.** Schematic diagram of GRNN architecture

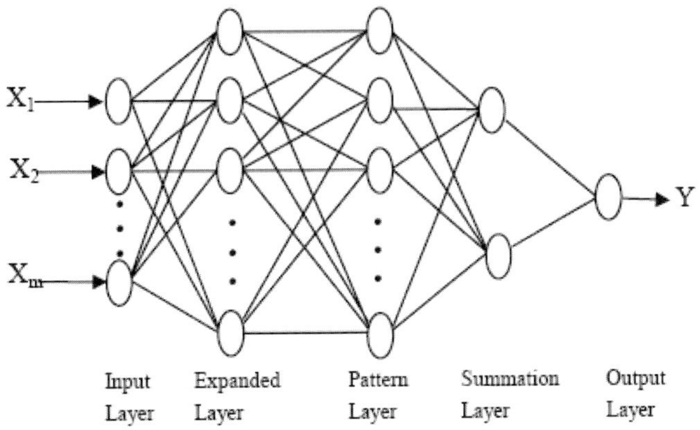


**Fig. 3.** Schematic diagram of Input-Expansion GRNN architecture

## 4 The Expansion Method of Input Vector

In traditional neural network model input vector are only multiplied weight value and then straight sent to the hidden layer for processing. The idea of the paper is different, and we firstly use nonlinear function to expand the input vector, which makes it be mapped into a higher-dimension vector space and leads to the sample sets more easily separable. Supposing (,, ... ,) is original input vector, and is a nonlinear function, and (here ) is the vector after expansion. The used function need satisfy separability of input pattern, and the paper uses second-order inner product function (namely ()) and Chebyshev polynomial function (namely ) to compare and test their effect. Schematic diagram of Input-Expansion GRNN architecture is shown in Fig.3, and schematic diagram of Input-Expansion BP network architecture is shown in Fig.4, both of them are only added an expanded layer after expansion. In the following text the classification results for Iris data and remote sensing data will show the advantage of expanded neural network models in section 5.

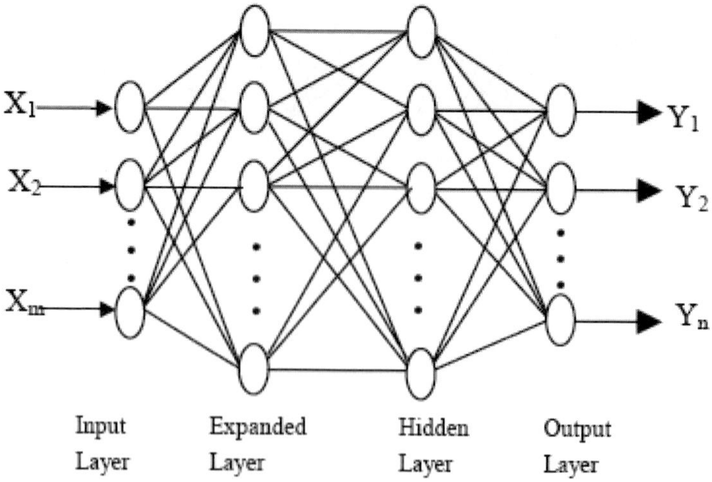


**Fig. 4.** Schematic diagram of Input-Expansion BP network architecture

# 5 Experimental Results and Analysis

## 5.1 Iris Data Classification Results

Iris data set is with 150 random samples of flowers from the Iris species Setosa, Versicolor, and Virginica collected by Anderson (1935), and contains 3 classes of 50 instances each. One class is linearly separable from the other 2, and the latter are not linearly separable from each other.

We randomly choose 20 samples for training from each class, the other 30 for testing, and compare above LMBPN, expanded LMBPN based on second-order inner product function (IELMBPN), expanded LMBPN based on Chebyshev polynomial function (CELMBPN); GRNN, expanded GRNN based on second-order inner product function (IEGRNN) and expanded GRNN based on Chebyshev polynomial function (CEGRNN) (Here our adopted LMBPN network structure is 4-6-3, of which number of input layer nodes 4 is the dimension of input vector, and number of output layer nodes 3 is recognized categories, and number of single hidden layer nodes 6 is received by trial and error. Adopted structure of IELMBPN is 10-6-3 and of

CELMBPN is 9-6-3, of which number of input layer nodes is the dimension of input vector after expansion, and the other is the same as LMBPN. Number of input layer nodes of GRNN or expanded GRNN is the same as corresponding LMBPN or expanded LMBPN). At last we obtain classification results as shown in table 1.

From table 1, we can find that as for Iris-Setosa all the above six kinds of classifier can well and truly recognize, and as for Iris-Versicolor and Iris-Virginia GRNN is superior to LMBPN in classification accuracy, and input-expansion-based method is the best and may efficiently enhance classification effect.

**Table 1.** Comparison for Iris data classification results

| Results<br>Algrithms | Iris-Setosa | Iris-Versicolor | Iris-Virginica |
|---|---|---|---|
| LMBPN | 100% | 93.3% | 93.3% |
| IELMBPN | 100% | 95% | 95% |
| CELMBPN | 100% | 95% | 95% |
| GRNN | 100% | 97.5% | 95% |
| IEGRNN | 100% | **100%** | 95% |
| CEGRNN | 100% | **100%** | 95% |

**Table 2.** The test results of LMBPN for remote sensing image classification

| Results<br>Categories | Road | City | Field | Green | Hill | Water | Accurac (%) | Overall Accuracy | Time (s) |
|---|---|---|---|---|---|---|---|---|---|
| Road | 528 | 49 | 1 | 1 | 0 | 0 | 91.19 | 93.4 | 16.3 |
| City | 136 | 1076 | 17 | 4 | 3 | 45 | 84.00 | | |
| Field | 0 | 3 | 1838 | 0 | 0 | 0 | 99.41 | | |
| Green | 0 | 2 | 6 | 281 | 0 | 0 | 97.23 | | |
| Hill | 47 | 44 | 5 | 0 | 2388 | 123 | 91.60 | | |
| Water | 0 | 2 | 2 | 11 | 17 | 1363 | 97.71 | | |

### 5.2 Remote Sensing Image Classification Results

An experimental remote sensing image sampled from satellite TM, which covers Xuzhou city area in China. We make use of band 3, band 4 and band 5 to identify land-use categories. The size of the study area is 220x200 pixels. According to the terrain map, analyzing the image visually, we divide it into 6 categories, namely road, city area, field, green-land, hill, water, and manually choose samples data set for six categories, and gain 300 samples for training, 8000 for testing.

Whole experimental work is finished in Matlab environment, and our adopted LMBPN structure is 3-8-6, of which number of input layer nodes 3 is the number of bands for remote sensing image, and number of output layer nodes 6 is recognized categories, and number of single hidden layers nodes 8 is received by trial and error. Our adopted structure of IELMBPN is 10-8-6 and of CELMBPN is 9-8-6, of which number of input layer nodes is the dimension of input vector after expansion, and the other received is the same as above LMBPN. During whole training procedure we restrict that error goal is 0.001 and the maximal iteration number is 1000, respectively adopt above LMBPN, IELMBPN, and CELMBPN to train and obtain training convergent curve of three kinds of methods shown in Figure 5, Figure 6, and Figure 7. After finishing training, we use test samples to classify and gain classification results shown in table 2, table 3 and table 4, and whose data is the average value of 5 times experimental results.

**Table 3.** The test results of IELMBPN for remote sensing image classification

| Results Categories | Road | City | Field | Green | Hill | Water | Accuracy (%) | Overall Accuracy | Time (s) |
|---|---|---|---|---|---|---|---|---|---|
| Road | 547 | 29 | 0 | 3 | 0 | 0 | 94.47 | 95.4 | 10.0 |
| City | 114 | 1135 | 22 | 6 | 4 | 0 | 88.60 | | |
| Field | 1 | 5 | 1812 | 31 | 0 | 0 | 98.00 | | |
| Green | 1 | 1 | 0 | 287 | 0 | 0 | 99.31 | | |
| Hill | 0 | 4 | 9 | 29 | 2512 | 53 | 96.36 | | |
| Water | 0 | 2 | 0 | 1 | 51 | 1341 | 96.13 | | |

Comparing table 2 with table 3 and table 4, we can find both IELMBPN and CELMBPN may quicken convergent velocity, and moreover enhance classification accuracy and exceed LMBP about 2%. The performance of IELMBPN is as much as of CELMBPN. All these data show input-expansion-based method is entirely effective.

Number of input layer nodes of GRNN or expanded IEGRNN or CEGRNN is the same as corresponding LMBPN or expanded IELMBPN or CELMBPN. Number of their output layer nodes is 1). We use GRNN, IEGRNN and CEGRNN to obtain classification results as shown in table 5, table 6 and table 7.

**Table 4.** The test results of CELMBPN for remote sensing image classification

| Results Categories | Road | City | Field | Green | Hill | Water | Accuracy (%) | Overall Accuracy | Time (s) |
|---|---|---|---|---|---|---|---|---|---|
| Road | 548 | 31 | 0 | 0 | 0 | 0 | 94.65 | 95.5 | 10.3 |
| City | 98 | 1164 | 4 | 2 | 9 | 4 | 90.87 | | |
| Field | 3 | 1 | 1803 | 35 | 7 | 0 | 97.51 | | |
| Green | 2 | 1 | 5 | 281 | 0 | 0 | 97.23 | | |
| Hill | 3 | 11 | 5 | 4 | 2478 | 106 | 95.05 | | |
| Water | 0 | 2 | 0 | 0 | 26 | 1367 | 97.99 | | |

**Table 5.** The test results of GRNN for remote sensing image classification

| Results Categories | Road | City | Field | Green | Hill | Water | Accuracy (%) | Overall Accuracy | Time (s) |
|---|---|---|---|---|---|---|---|---|---|
| Road | 544 | 32 | 2 | 1 | 0 | 0 | 93.96 | 96.2 | 9.7 |
| City | 93 | 1174 | 9 | 2 | 3 | 0 | 91.65 | | |
| Field | 0 | 1 | 1795 | 53 | 0 | 0 | 97.08 | | |
| Green | 1 | 1 | 0 | 287 | 0 | 0 | 99.31 | | |
| Hill | 1 | 12 | 9 | 7 | 2578 | 0 | 98.89 | | |
| Water | 0 | 5 | 1 | 1 | 70 | 1318 | 94.48 | | |

From table 5, table 6 and table 7, we can find both IELMBPN and CELMBPN only appreciably quicken convergent velocity and improve classification accuracy about 0.4% compared with GRNN. Compared with LMBP, GRNN have biggish advantage and exceed around 3% in classification accuracy.

**Table 6.** The test results of IEGRNN for remote sensing image classification

| Results Categories | Road | City | Field | Green | Hill | Water | Accuracy (%) | Overall Accuracy | Time (s) |
|---|---|---|---|---|---|---|---|---|---|
| Road | 536 | 40 | 2 | 1 | 0 | 0 | 92.57 | 96.6 | 10.9 |
| City | 78 | 1183 | 15 | 1 | 4 | 0 | 92.35 | | |
| Field | 0 | 0 | 1822 | 27 | 0 | 0 | 98.54 | | |
| Green | 1 | 0 | 1 | 287 | 0 | 0 | 99.31 | | |
| Hill | 1 | 14 | 9 | 4 | 2568 | 11 | 98.50 | | |
| Water | 0 | 5 | 2 | 0 | 60 | 1328 | 95.20 | | |

**Table 7.** The test results of CEGRNN for remote sensing image classification

| Results Categories | Road | City | Field | Green | Hill | Water | Accuracy (%) | Overall Accuracy | Time (s) |
|---|---|---|---|---|---|---|---|---|---|
| Road | 535 | 41 | 1 | 2 | 0 | 0 | 92.40 | 96.6 | 10.4 |
| City | 89 | 1172 | 13 | 4 | 3 | 0 | 91.49 | | |
| Field | 0 | 0 | 1828 | 21 | 0 | 0 | 98.86 | | |
| Green | 1 | 0 | 0 | 288 | 0 | 0 | 99.65 | | |
| Hill | 0 | 15 | 8 | 0 | 2567 | 17 | 98.47 | | |
| Water | 0 | 4 | 1 | 0 | 53 | 1337 | 95.84 | | |

## 6 Conclusions

The paper systematically compares the performance of LMBP and GRNN in pattern classification, and experimental results show the definite advantage of GRNN over LMBP. At the same time an input-expansion-based improved method is presented for LMBP and GRNN. Using second-order inner product function or Chebyshev polynomial function to expand input vector of original samples, which may enhance separability of the sample sets. Classification results for Iris data and remote sensing data show input-expansion–based method is entirely effective for neural network models.

## References


1. Tomand, D., Schover, A.: A Modified General Regression Neural Network (MGRNN) with New Efficient Training Algorithms as a Robust 'Black Box'-tool for Data Analysis. Neural networks, 14 (2002) 1023-1034
2. Rumelhart, D.E., Hinton, G.E., Williams, R.J.: Learning Representations by Back-propagating Errors. Nature, 323(1986) 533-536
3. Hagan, M.T., Demuth, H. B.: Neural Network Design. China Machine Press,(2002)
4. Specht, D. F.: A General Regression Neural Network. IEEE Transactions on Neural Networks, 2 (1991) 568-576
5. Cigizoglu H. K., Alp, M.: Generalized Regression Neural Network in Modelling River Sediment Yield, Advances in Engineering Software, 37(2006) 63-68
6. Hyun, B. G., Nam, K.: Faults Diagnoses of Rotaing Machines by Using Neural Nets: GRNN and BPNN. Proceedings of the 1995 IEEE IECON 21st International Conferece on Industrial ECI. Orlando, (1995)

# Deterministic Convergence of an Online Gradient Method with Momentum

Naimin Zhang

School of Mathematics and Information Science, Wenzhou University,
Wenzhou, 325035, P.R. China
nmzhang@wzu.edu.cn

**Abstract.** An online gradient method with momentum for feedforward neural network is considered. The learning rate is set to be a constant and the momentum coefficient an adaptive variable. Both the weak and strong convergence results are proved, as well as the convergence rates for the error function and for the weight.

## 1 Introduction

Online gradient method (see e.g. [2][4]) has been widely used in training neural networks, and the deterministic convergence property of it is also an important topic to discuss (see e.g. [3][6][8][13]). To speed up and stabilize the training iteration procedure, a momentum term [9] [10] is often added to the increment formula for the weights. The convergence of the gradient method with momentum is discussed in [1][12] under the restriction that the error function is quadratic with respect to the weights. In [15] a criterion to choose the coefficient of the momentum term is proposed and a corresponding convergence result is proved, where the learning fashion of training examples is **batch learning**. In this paper, an online gradient method with momentum for a two-layer feedforward neural network with a linearly independent set of training examples is considered. Our contribution in this paper is to prove the convergence of the resulting online gradient method with momentum, whereas we do not assume the error function to be quadratic with respect to the weights.

The rest part of the paper is organized as follows. In Section 2 we introduce the online gradient method with momentum. In Section 3 we establish some preliminary lemmas necessary for the proof of convergence of online gradient method with momentum. In Section 4 we discuss the convergence property of online gradient method with momentum. We set the learning rate $\eta$ a constant and the momentum coefficient $\tau_{m,k}$ an adaptive variable. Both the weak and strong convergence results are proved. In Section 5 we give estimation of convergence rates for both error function and weights. Finally, in section 6 we draw a conclusion which summarizes the paper.

## 2 Online Gradient Method with Momentum

For a given set of training examples $\{\xi^j, O^j\}_{j=1}^J \subseteq R^n \times R$, we describe the neural network approximation problem as follows. Let $g : R \to R$ be a given

D.-S. Huang, K. Li, and G.W. Irwin (Eds.): ICIC 2006, LNCS 4113, pp. 94–105, 2006.

smooth activation function. For a choice of the weight vector $w \in R^n$, the actual output of the neural network is

$$\zeta^j = g(w \cdot \xi^j), \quad j = 1, ..., J \tag{1}$$

where $w \cdot \xi^j$ represents the inner product. Our task is to choose the weight $w$ such that the difference $|O^j - \zeta^j|$ is as small as possible. A simple and popular approach is to minimize the quadratic error function

$$E(w) := \frac{1}{2}\sum_{j=1}^{J}(O^j - \zeta^j)^2 = \frac{1}{2}\sum_{j=1}^{J}(O^j - g(w \cdot \xi^j))^2 \tag{2}$$

that is to look for $w^* \in R^n$ such that

$$E(w^*) = \min_{w \in R^n} E(w) \tag{3}$$

The gradient method is often used to solve the minimization problem (3). Let $E_w(w)$ denote the gradient of the function $E$ at $w$:

$$E_w(w) = -\sum_{j=1}^{J}(O^j - g(w \cdot \xi^j))g'(w \cdot \xi^j)\xi^j \tag{4}$$

We point out that if $g(x) = x$, then the error function $E(w)$ is quadratic with respect to the weights $w$, that is the gradient $E_w(w)$ is a linear function of $w$. Convergence of this case has been studied in e.g. [1][7][11][12] among many others. for nonlinear $g(x)$ such as Sigmoidal type functions, $E(w)$ is no longer quadratic with respect to the weights $w$. In this paper we do not assume the error function to be quadratic with respect to the weights, so it can be adequate for more activation functions.

Denote

$$g_j(t) := \frac{1}{2}(O^j - g(t))^2, \quad j = 1, \cdots, J \tag{5}$$

then

$$E(w) = \sum_{j=1}^{J} g_j(w \cdot \xi^j) \tag{6}$$

and

$$E_w(w) = \sum_{j=1}^{J} g_j^{'}(w \cdot \xi^j)\xi^j \tag{7}$$

Now we consider online gradient method with momentum. Given initial weights $w^{-1}$ and $w^0$, online gradient method with momentum computes weights $w$ iteratively by

$$\begin{aligned} w^{mJ+k} &= w^{mJ+k-1} - \eta g_k^{'}(w^{mJ+k-1} \cdot \xi^k)\xi^k + \tau_{m,k}(w^{mJ+k-1} - w^{mJ+k-2}) \\ & k = 1, ..., J; \; m = 0, 1, ... \end{aligned} \tag{8}$$

where learning rate $\eta$ is a positive constant and momentum coefficient $\tau_{m,k}$ is an adaptive variable chosen by the following equation (13).

Denote

$$\Delta w^{mJ+k-1} = w^{mJ+k-1} - w^{mJ+k-2}, \ k = 1, ..., J; \ m = 0, 1, ... \tag{9}$$

$$p^{(m,k,i)} = g_k'(w^{mJ+i-1} \cdot \xi^k)\xi^k, \ i, k = 1, ..., J; \ m = 0, 1, ... \tag{10}$$

Particularly when $i = 1$ denote

$$p^{(m,k)} \equiv p^{(m,k,1)} = g_k'(w^{mJ} \cdot \xi^k)\xi^k, \ k = 1, ..., J; \ m = 0, 1, ... \tag{11}$$

Then (8) can be rewritten as

$$\Delta w^{mJ+k} = \tau_{m,k} \Delta w^{mJ+k-1} - \eta p^{(m,k,k)}, \ k = 1, ..., J; \ m = 0, 1, ... \tag{12}$$

We choose the momentum coefficients $\tau_{m,k}$ as follows.

$$\tau_{m,k} = \begin{cases} \frac{\tau \|p^{(m,k)}\|}{\|\Delta w^{mJ+k-1}\|} & \text{if } \|\Delta w^{mJ+k-1}\| \neq 0 \\ 0 & \text{else} \end{cases}, \quad k = 1, ..., J; \ m = 0, 1, ... \tag{13}$$

where momentum factor $\tau > 0$ is usually smaller than learning rate $\eta$, in this paper we set $\tau = \eta^2$, and $\| \cdot \|$ is the Euclidian norm.

For the convergence analysis of online gradient method with momentum, Similar to [13], we shall need the following assumptions:

**Assumption 1.** $|g(t)|, |g'(t)|$ and $|g''(t)|$ are uniformly bounded for $t \in R$.

**Assumption 2.** The set of training examples $\{\xi^k\}_{k=1}^J$ is linearly independent.

**Assumption 3.** $E(w)$ is uniformly convex, i.e., there exists a constant $\beta_1 > 0$ such that

$$\beta_1 \|u - v\|^2 \leq (E_w(u) - E_w(v)) \cdot (u - v), \quad \text{for any } u, v \in R^n \tag{14}$$

*Remark 1.* Denote Hessian matrix $H(w) = E_{ww}(w)$, from Assumption 1 and Assumption 3 we know there exist constants $\beta_2 > 0$, $\beta_3 > 0$ such that

$$\beta_2 \|y\|^2 \leq y^T E_{ww}(w) y \leq \beta_3 \|y\|^2 \tag{15}$$

for any $y, w \in R^n$ (see also [15]).

*Remark 2.* Same to [13], one difficulty we met to prove the convergence of online gradient method with momentum is the following equation:

$$\left\| \sum_{j=1}^{J} v^j \right\|^2 \geq C \sum_{j=1}^{J} \|v^j\|^2, \quad \text{for any } v^j \in R^n, \ j = 1, ..., J \tag{16}$$

which is certainly not possible for positive constant $C$ in general. Nevertheless, we observe that (16) is indeed true if $\{v^j\}_{j=1}^J$ is linearly independent. So Assumption 2 is set. The linear independence assumption on the training examples is satisfied in some practical models. For example, it happens in vision problems (see [2]) where the dimension $n$ of the weight vector $w$ is often greater than the size $J$ of the set of training examples.

## 3 Preliminary Lemmas

In this section we construct some lemmas which will be required for the proof of convergence theorems.

Recall equation (6) we get

$$E(w^{mJ}) = \sum_{j=1}^{J} g_j(w^{mJ} \cdot \xi^j) \tag{17}$$

Using Taylor's formula we expand $g_j(w^{(m+1)J} \cdot \xi^j)$ at $w^{mJ} \cdot \xi^j$ as

$$\begin{aligned} g_j(w^{(m+1)J} \cdot \xi^j) &= g_j(w^{mJ} \cdot \xi^j) + g_j^{'}(w^{mJ} \cdot \xi^j)(w^{(m+1)J} - w^{mJ}) \cdot \xi^j \\ &\quad + \tfrac{1}{2} g_j^{''}(t_{m,j})[(w^{(m+1)J} - w^{mJ}) \cdot \xi^j]^2 \\ &= g_j(w^{mJ} \cdot \xi^j) + g_j^{'}(w^{mJ} \cdot \xi^j)(w^{(m+1)J} - w^{mJ}) \cdot \xi^j + \rho_{m,j} \end{aligned} \tag{18}$$

where $t_{m,j}$ lies in between $w^{mJ} \cdot \xi^j$ and $w^{(m+1)J} \cdot \xi^j$, and we denote

$$\rho_{m,j} = \frac{1}{2} g_j^{''}(t_{m,j}) \left[ (w^{(m+1)J} - w^{mJ}) \cdot \xi^j \right]^2 \tag{19}$$

From (17) and (18) we get

$$E(w^{(m+1)J}) - E(w^{mJ}) = \sum_{j=1}^{J} g_j^{'}(w^{mJ} \cdot \xi^j)(w^{(m+1)J} - w^{mJ}) \cdot \xi^j + \sum_{j=1}^{J} \rho_{m,j} \tag{20}$$

Notice

$$w^{(m+1)J} - w^{mJ} = \sum_{k=1}^{J} \Delta w^{mJ+k} = \sum_{k=1}^{J} (\tau_{m,k} \Delta w^{mJ+k-1} - \eta p^{(m,k,k)})$$

and

$$p^{(m,k,k)} = p^{(m,k)} + [g_k^{'}(w^{mJ+k-1} \cdot \xi^k) - g_k^{'}(w^{mJ} \cdot \xi^k)]\xi^k$$

it exists

$$\begin{aligned} & E(w^{(m+1)J}) - E(w^{mJ}) \\ &= \textstyle\sum_{j=1}^{J} g_j^{'}(w^{mJ} \cdot \xi^j) \left[ \sum_{k=1}^{J} \tau_{m,k} \Delta w^{mJ+k-1} - \eta \sum_{k=1}^{J} p^{(m,k)} \right. \\ &\quad \left. -\eta \textstyle\sum_{k=1}^{J} [g_k^{'}(w^{mJ+k-1} \cdot \xi^k) - g_k^{'}(w^{mJ} \cdot \xi^k)]\xi^k \right] \cdot \xi^j + \sum_{j=1}^{J} \rho_{m,j} \\ &= -\eta \left[ \textstyle\sum_{j=1}^{J} g_j^{'}(w^{mJ} \cdot \xi^j)\xi^j \right] \cdot \left[ \sum_{k=1}^{J} p^{(m,k)} \right] + \left[ \sum_{j=1}^{J} g_j^{'}(w^{mJ} \cdot \xi^j)\xi^j \right] \\ &\quad \cdot \left[ \textstyle\sum_{k=1}^{J} \tau_{m,k} \Delta w^{mJ+k-1} \right] - \eta \left[ \sum_{j=1}^{J} g_j^{'}(w^{mJ} \cdot \xi^j)\xi^j \right] \cdot \left[ \sum_{k=1}^{J} [g_k^{'}(w^{mJ+k-1} \cdot \xi^k) \right. \\ &\quad \left. -g_k^{'}(w^{mJ} \cdot \xi^k)]\xi^k \right] + \textstyle\sum_{j=1}^{J} \rho_{m,j} \\ &= -\eta \| \textstyle\sum_{k=1}^{J} p^{(m,k)} \|^2 + \left[ \sum_{j=1}^{J} p^{(m,j)} \right] \cdot \left[ \sum_{k=1}^{J} \tau_{m,k} \Delta w^{mJ+k-1} \right] - \left[ \eta \sum_{j=1}^{J} p^{(m,j)} \right] \\ &\quad \cdot \left[ \textstyle\sum_{k=1}^{J} [g_k^{'}(w^{mJ+k-1} \cdot \xi^k) - g_k^{'}(w^{mJ} \cdot \xi^k)]\xi^k \right] + \sum_{j=1}^{J} \rho_{m,j} \end{aligned}$$

Denote

$$r_{m,k} = [g_k'(w^{mJ+k-1} \cdot \xi^k) - g_k'(w^{mJ} \cdot \xi^k)]\xi^k = p^{(m,k,k)} - p^{(m,k)} \tag{21}$$

So we have

$$\begin{aligned} &E(w^{(m+1)J}) - E(w^{mJ}) \\ &= -\eta \| \textstyle\sum_{k=1}^{J} p^{(m,k)} \|^2 + \left(\sum_{j=1}^{J} p^{(m,j)}\right) \cdot \left(\sum_{k=1}^{J} \tau_{m,k} \Delta w^{mJ+k-1}\right) \\ &\quad - \left(\eta \textstyle\sum_{j=1}^{J} p^{(m,j)}\right) \cdot \left(\sum_{k=1}^{J} r_{m,k}\right) + \sum_{j=1}^{J} \rho_{m,j} \end{aligned} \tag{22}$$

**Lemma 1.** Let $\{\xi^j\}_{j=1}^J$ be linearly independent, then there exists a constant $-1 < \alpha < 1$ such that for all $(\delta_1, ..., \delta_J)^T \in R^J$, it holds the following estimates:

$$\left\| \sum_{j=1}^{J} \delta_j \xi^j \right\|^2 \geq \frac{1 - |\alpha|}{J} \sum_{j=1}^{J} \|\delta_j \xi^j\|^2 \tag{23}$$

*Proof.* See [13] for detail.

**Lemma 2.** If Assumption 1 is satisfied, for $0 < \eta \leq 1$, it exists

$$\|r_{m,j}\| \leq C_1(\tau + \eta) \sum_{k=1}^{j-1} \|p^{(m,k)}\|, \quad j = 2, ..., J \tag{24}$$

where $C_1$ is a positive constant.

*Proof.*

$$\begin{aligned} r_{m,j} &= [g_j'(w^{mJ+j-1} \cdot \xi^j) - g_j'(w^{mJ} \cdot \xi^j)]\xi^j \\ &= g_j''(z_{m,j})[(w^{mJ+j-1} - w^{mJ}) \cdot \xi^j]\xi^j \end{aligned}$$

where $z_{m,j}$ lies in between $w^{mJ+j-1} \cdot \xi^j$ and $w^{mJ} \cdot \xi^j$. It is easy to know that there exists a $\bar{C}_1 > 0$ such that

$$\begin{aligned} \|r_{m,j}\| &\leq \bar{C}_1 \|w^{mJ+j-1} - w^{mJ}\| \\ &= \bar{C}_1 \left\| \textstyle\sum_{k=1}^{j-1} \tau_{m,k} \Delta w^{mJ+k-1} - \eta \sum_{k=1}^{j-1} p^{(m,k)} - \eta \sum_{k=1}^{j-1} r_{m,k} \right\| \\ &\leq \bar{C}_1 \textstyle\sum_{k=1}^{j-1} \left(|\tau_{m,k}| \|\Delta w^{mJ+k-1}\| + \eta \|p^{(m,k)}\| + \eta \|r_{m,k}\|\right) \\ &\leq \bar{C}_1 \textstyle\sum_{k=1}^{j-1} \left((\tau + \eta) \|p^{(m,k)}\| + \eta \|r_{m,k}\|\right) \end{aligned}$$

We prove equation (24) by induction.

For $j = 2$, $r_{m,1} = 0$, set $\bar{C}_2 = \bar{C}_1$, it exists

$$\|r_{m,2}\| \leq \bar{C}_2(\tau + \eta) \sum_{k=1}^{j-1} \|p^{(m,k)}\|$$

For $2 \leq j \leq i - 1$, $3 \leq i \leq J$, suppose

$$\|r_{m,j}\| \leq \bar{C}_j(\tau + \eta) \sum_{k=1}^{j-1} \|p^{(m,k)}\|$$

where $\bar{C}_j > 0$. When $j = i$, set $\hat{C}_{i-1} = max\{\bar{C}_k\}_{k=1}^{i-1}$, it exists

$$\begin{aligned}\|r_{m,i}\| &\leq \bar{C}_1(\tau+\eta)\sum_{k=1}^{i-1}\|p^{(m,k)}\| + \bar{C}_1\eta\sum_{k=1}^{i-1}\|r_{m,k}\| \\ &= \bar{C}_1(\tau+\eta)\sum_{k=1}^{i-1}\|p^{(m,k)}\| + \bar{C}_1\eta\sum_{k=2}^{i-1}\|r_{m,k}\| \\ &\leq \bar{C}_1(\tau+\eta)\sum_{k=1}^{i-1}\|p^{(m,k)}\| + \bar{C}_1\eta\sum_{k=2}^{i-1}\left(\bar{C}_k(\tau+\eta)\sum_{s=1}^{k-1}\|p^{(m,s)}\|\right) \\ &\leq \bar{C}_1(\tau+\eta)\sum_{k=1}^{i-1}\|p^{(m,k)}\| + \bar{C}_1\eta\hat{C}_{i-1}(\tau+\eta)\sum_{k=2}^{i-1}\sum_{s=1}^{k-1}\|p^{(m,s)}\| \\ &\leq \bar{C}_1(\tau+\eta)\sum_{k=1}^{i-1}\|p^{(m,k)}\| + \bar{C}_1\hat{C}_{i-1}(i-2)\eta(\tau+\eta)\sum_{k=1}^{i-1}\|p^{(m,k)}\| \\ &\leq \tilde{C}_i(\tau+\eta)\sum_{k=1}^{i-1}\|p^{(m,k)}\|\end{aligned}$$

where $\tilde{C}_i = \bar{C}_1 + \bar{C}_1\hat{C}_{i-1}(i-2) \geq \bar{C}_1 + \bar{C}_1\hat{C}_{i-1}(i-2)\eta$.

For all the $\bar{C}_k$ and $\tilde{C}_j$ above, set $C_1 = max\{\bar{C}_k, \tilde{C}_j\}$, then

$$\|r_{m,j}\| \leq C_1(\tau+\eta)\sum_{k=1}^{j-1}\|p^{(m,k)}\|, \quad j = 2, ..., J$$

**Lemma 3.** If Assumption 1 is satisfied, then

$$\left|\left(\sum_{j=1}^{J} p^{(m,j)}\right)\cdot\left(\sum_{k=1}^{J}\tau_{m,k}\Delta w^{mJ+k-1}\right)\right| \leq \tau\left(\sum_{k=1}^{J}\|p^{(m,k)}\|\right)^2 \tag{25}$$

$$\left|\eta\left(\sum_{j=1}^{J} p^{(m,j)}\right)\cdot\left(\sum_{k=1}^{J} r_{m,k}\right)\right| \leq JC_1\eta(\tau+\eta)\left(\sum_{k=1}^{J}\|p^{(m,k)}\|\right)^2 \tag{26}$$

$$\left|\sum_{j=1}^{J}\rho_{m,j}\right| \leq C_2(\tau+\eta)^2\left(\sum_{k=1}^{J}\|p^{(m,k)}\|\right)^2 \tag{27}$$

where $C_2$ is a positive constant.

*Proof.* We first prove (25).

$$\begin{aligned}&\left|\left(\sum_{j=1}^{J} p^{(m,j)}\right)\cdot\left(\sum_{k=1}^{J}\tau_{m,k}\Delta w^{mJ+k-1}\right)\right| \\ &\leq \left\|\sum_{j=1}^{J} p^{(m,j)}\right\|\left\|\sum_{k=1}^{J}\tau_{m,k}\Delta w^{mJ+k-1}\right\| \\ &\leq \left(\sum_{j=1}^{J}\|p^{(m,j)}\|\right)\left(\sum_{k=1}^{J}|\tau_{m,k}|\|\Delta w^{mJ+k-1}\|\right) \\ &\leq \left(\sum_{j=1}^{J}\|p^{(m,j)}\|\right)\left(\sum_{k=1}^{J}\tau\|p^{(m,k)}\|\right) \\ &= \tau\left(\sum_{k=1}^{J}\|p^{(m,k)}\|\right)^2\end{aligned}$$

As for (26),

$$\begin{aligned}&\left|\eta\left(\sum_{j=1}^{J} p^{(m,j)}\right)\cdot\left(\sum_{k=1}^{J} r_{m,k}\right)\right| \\ &\leq \eta\left(\sum_{j=1}^{J}\|p^{(m,j)}\|\right)\left(\sum_{k=1}^{J}\|r_{m,k}\|\right) \\ &\leq \eta\left(\sum_{j=1}^{J}\|p^{(m,j)}\|\right)\left(\sum_{k=1}^{J}C_1(\tau+\eta)\sum_{s=1}^{k-1}\|p^{(m,s)}\|\right) \quad \text{(from Lemma 2)} \\ &\leq \eta\left(\sum_{j=1}^{J}\|p^{(m,j)}\|\right)\left(\sum_{k=1}^{J}C_1(\tau+\eta)\sum_{s=1}^{k}\|p^{(m,s)}\|\right) \\ &\leq JC_1\eta(\tau+\eta)\left(\sum_{k=1}^{J}\|p^{(m,k)}\|\right)^2\end{aligned}$$

Now we prove (27), recall the proof of Lemma 2 we have

$$\begin{aligned}
&\left\|w^{(m+1)J} - w^{mJ}\right\| \\
&\leq \textstyle\sum_{k=1}^{J} \left(|\tau_{m,k}|\|\Delta w^{mJ+k-1}\| + \eta\|p^{(m,k)}\| + \|r_{m,k}\|\right) \\
&\leq \textstyle\sum_{k=1}^{J} \left((\tau+\eta)\|p^{(m,k)}\| + \|r_{m,k}\|\right) \\
&= \textstyle\sum_{k=1}^{J} \left((\tau+\eta)\|p^{(m,k)}\|\right) + \sum_{k=2}^{J} \|r_{m,k}\| \quad (\text{Notice } r_{m,1}=0) \\
&\leq \textstyle\sum_{k=1}^{J} \left((\tau+\eta)\|p^{(m,k)}\|\right) + C_1(\tau+\eta)\sum_{k=2}^{J}\sum_{s=1}^{k-1} \|p^{(m,s)}\| \quad (\text{from Lemma 2}) \\
&\leq \textstyle\sum_{k=1}^{J} \left((\tau+\eta)\|p^{(m,k)}\|\right) + JC_1(\tau+\eta)\sum_{k=1}^{J} \|p^{(m,k)}\| \\
&= (1+JC_1)(\tau+\eta)\textstyle\sum_{k=1}^{J} \|p^{(m,k)}\|
\end{aligned}$$

It is easy to know that there exists a $\check{C}_1 > 0$ such that

$$\begin{aligned}
\left|\textstyle\sum_{j=1}^{J} \rho_{m,j}\right| &= \left|\textstyle\sum_{j=1}^{J} \frac{1}{2} g_j''(t_{m,j}) \left[(w^{(m+1)J} - w^{mJ}) \cdot \xi^j\right]^2\right| \\
&\leq \check{C}_1 \textstyle\sum_{j=1}^{J} \|w^{(m+1)J} - w^{mJ}\|^2 \\
&= J\check{C}_1 \|w^{(m+1)J} - w^{mJ}\|^2 \\
&\leq J\check{C}_1 (1+JC_1)^2 (\tau+\eta)^2 \left(\textstyle\sum_{k=1}^{J} \|p^{(m,k)}\|\right)^2 \\
&= C_2 (\tau+\eta)^2 \left(\textstyle\sum_{k=1}^{J} \|p^{(m,k)}\|\right)^2
\end{aligned}$$

where $C_2 = J\check{C}_1(1+JC_1)^2$.

**Lemma 4.** If Assumption 1 and Assumption 2 are satisfied, then

$$E(w^{(m+1)J}) - E(w^{mJ}) \leq -\beta \left(\sum_{k=1}^{J} \|p^{(m,k)}\|\right)^2 \tag{28}$$

where

$$\beta = \frac{\eta}{J^2}(1-|\alpha|) - \tau - JC_1\eta(\tau+\eta) - C_2(\tau+\eta)^2 \tag{29}$$

*Proof.* From Lemma 1 it is easy to know

$$-\eta \left\|\sum_{k=1}^{J} p^{(m,k)}\right\|^2 \leq \frac{-\eta}{J^2}(1-|\alpha|) \left(\sum_{k=1}^{J} \|p^{(m,k)}\|\right)^2$$

and from (22) it exists

$$\begin{aligned}
&E(w^{(m+1)J}) - E(w^{mJ}) \\
&\leq \tfrac{-\eta}{J^2}(1-|\alpha|) \left(\textstyle\sum_{k=1}^{J} \|p^{(m,k)}\|\right)^2 + \left(\textstyle\sum_{j=1}^{J} p^{(m,j)}\right) \cdot \left(\textstyle\sum_{k=1}^{J} \tau_{m,k} \Delta w^{mJ+k-1}\right) \\
&\quad - \left(\eta \textstyle\sum_{j=1}^{J} p^{(m,j)}\right) \cdot \left(\textstyle\sum_{k=1}^{J} r_{m,k}\right) + \textstyle\sum_{j=1}^{J} \rho_{m,j}
\end{aligned}$$

With Lemma 3 we immediately finish the proof.

From Lemma 4 $E(w^{mJ})$ is monotonically decreasing with respect to $m$ when $\beta > 0$. Simply if we set $\tau = \eta^2$, $C_3 = J^2 + 2C_1J^3 + 4J^2C_2$, then it is easy to know $\beta > 0$ when the following inequality exists:

$$\eta < \frac{1-|\alpha|}{C_3} \tag{30}$$

**Lemma 5.** If Assumption 1 and Assumption 2 are satisfied, $\tau = \eta^2$, and (30) exists, then $E(w^{mJ})$ is monotonically decreasing with respect to $m$, furthermore we have the following results:

$$\sum_{m=0}^{\infty}\left(\sum_{k=1}^{J}\|p^{(m,k)}\|\right)^2 < \infty \tag{31}$$

$$\lim_{m\to\infty}\sum_{k=1}^{J}\|p^{(m,k)}\| = 0 \tag{32}$$

$$\lim_{m\to\infty}\|w^{mJ+j} - w^{mJ}\| = 0, \quad j = 1, ..., J \tag{33}$$

*Proof.* We need only prove (33).

$$\begin{aligned}
&\|w^{mJ+j} - w^{mJ}\| \\
&= \left\|\sum_{k=1}^{j}\tau_{m,k}\Delta w^{mJ+k-1} - \eta\sum_{k=1}^{j}p^{(m,k)} - \eta\sum_{k=1}^{j}r_{m,k}\right\| \\
&\leq \sum_{k=1}^{j}(\tau+\eta)\|p^{(m,k)}\| + \eta\sum_{k=1}^{j}\|r_{m,k}\| \\
&= \sum_{k=1}^{j}(\tau+\eta)\|p^{(m,k)}\| + \eta\sum_{k=2}^{j}\|r_{m,k}\| \\
&\leq \sum_{k=1}^{j}(\tau+\eta)\|p^{(m,k)}\| + \eta\sum_{k=2}^{j}\left(C_1(\tau+\eta)\sum_{s=1}^{k-1}\|p^{(m,k)}\|\right) \to 0, \quad m\to\infty
\end{aligned}$$

## 4 Convergence Results

In this section we give the main results for online gradient method with momentum. Firsts we prove the following weak convergence theorem.

**Theorem 1.** If Assumption 1 and Assumption 2 are satisfied, $\tau = \eta^2$, (30) exists, then for the iteration process (12), there exists a $E^* \geq 0$ such that

$$\lim_{i\to\infty} E(w^i) = E^* \tag{34}$$

*Proof.* Since $E(w^{mJ})$ is monotonically decreasing with respect to $m$ and $E(w^{mJ}) \geq 0$, so there exists a $E^* \geq 0$ such that $\lim_{m\to\infty} E(w^{mJ}) = E^*$. Notice

$$\begin{aligned}
E(w^{mJ+j}) - E(w^{mJ}) &= \sum_{k=1}^{J}\left(g_k(w^{mJ+j}\cdot\xi^k) - g_k(w^{mJ}\cdot\xi^k)\right) \\
&= \sum_{k=1}^{J} g_k'(t_{m,j,k})(w^{mJ+j} - w^{mJ})\cdot\xi^k
\end{aligned}$$

where $t_{m,j,k}$ lies between $w^{mJ+j}\cdot\xi^k$ and $w^{mJ}\cdot\xi^k$, so there exists a $C_4 > 0$ such that

$$\left|E(w^{mJ+j}) - E(w^{mJ})\right| \leq C_4\left\|w^{mJ+j} - w^{mJ}\right\|$$

From Lemma 5 it is easy to know that

$$\lim_{m\to\infty}\left|E(w^{mJ+j}) - E(w^{mJ})\right| = 0, \quad j = 1, ..., J$$

For any integer $i$, there exist integers $m_i$ and $j_i$, such that $i = m_iJ + j_i$, $1 \leq j_i < J$.

So

$$\left|E(w^i) - E^*\right| \leq \left|E(w^{m_iJ+j_i}) - E(w^{m_iJ})\right| + \left|E(w^{m_iJ}) - E^*\right| \to 0, \quad i\to\infty$$

If in addition we assume Assumption 3, then we can obtain the following strong convergence result.

**Theorem 2.** If Assumption 1, Assumption 2, and Assumption 3 are satisfied, $\tau = \eta^2$, (30) exists, then for the iteration process (12), there exits a unique $w^* \in R^n$ such that

$$E(w^*) = \inf_{w \in R^n} E(w) \tag{35}$$

$$\lim_{i \to \infty} \|w^i - w^*\| = 0 \tag{36}$$

*Proof.* By Assumption 3 and Remark 1, we know $E$ is a uniformly convex function , and the existence of a unique minimum $w^*$ follows immediately from the property of uniformly convex functions. Now we need only to prove (36).

From Lemma 5 we know

$$E_w(w^{mJ}) = \sum_{k=1}^{J} p^{(m,k)} \to 0, \quad m \to \infty$$

and from (14) it exists

$$\begin{aligned} \beta_1 \|w^{mJ} - w^*\|^2 &\le \left(E_w(w^{mJ}) - E_w(w^*)\right) \cdot (w^{mJ} - w^*) \\ &\le \left\|E_w(w^{mJ}) - E_w(w^*)\right\| \left\|w^{mJ} - w^*\right\| \end{aligned}$$

Notice $E_w(w^*) = 0$, so

$$\|w^{mJ} - w^*\| \le \frac{1}{\beta_1} \left\|E_w(w^{mJ}) - E_w(w^*)\right\| \to 0, \quad m \to \infty$$

From Lemma 5 we also know $\lim_{m \to \infty} \|w^{mJ+j} - w^{mJ}\| = 0, \quad j = 1, ..., J$, and the rest proof is similar to the proof of Theorem 1.

## 5 Estimation of Convergence Rates

In this section we will estimates of the convergence rates for $E(w^{mJ+j})$ and $w^{mJ+j}$. In its proof we shall need $1 - \frac{2\beta\beta_1^2}{\beta_3} > 0$, namely $\beta < \frac{\beta_3}{2\beta_1^2}$, when $\tau = \eta^2$, $\beta = \frac{\eta}{J^2}(1 - |\alpha|) - \tau - JC_1\eta(\tau + \eta) - C_2(\tau + \eta)^2 < \frac{\eta}{J^2}(1 - |\alpha|)$, so we need only $\frac{\eta}{J^2}(1 - |\alpha|) < \frac{\beta_3}{2\beta_1^2}$, that is $\eta < \frac{J^2\beta_3}{2(1-|\alpha|)\beta_1^2}$. Finally we set

$$\eta < min \left\{ \frac{(1 - |\alpha|)}{C_3}, \frac{J^2\beta_3}{2(1 - |\alpha|)\beta_1^2} \right\} \tag{37}$$

**Theorem 3.** If Assumption 1, Assumption 2, and Assumption 3 are satisfied, $\tau = \eta^2$, (37) exists, then for $j = 0, 1, ..., J - 1$ and $m = 0, 1, ...$

$$\left|E(w^{mJ+j}) - E(w^*)\right| \le \left(1 - \frac{2\beta\beta_1^2}{\beta_3}\right)^m \left|E(w^j) - E(w^*)\right| \tag{38}$$

$$\|w^{mJ+j} - w^*\|^2 \le \frac{\beta_3}{\beta_2} \left(1 - \frac{2\beta\beta_1^2}{\beta_3}\right)^m \|w^j - w^*\|^2 \tag{39}$$

*Proof.* Recall the proof of Theorem 2 we have

$$\beta_1\|w^{mJ} - w^*\| \le \|E_w(w^{mJ})\|$$

Using Taylor's formula and noticing $E_w(w^*) = 0$ we have

$$E(w^{mJ}) - E(w^*) = \frac{1}{2}(w^{mJ} - w^*)^T H(\tilde{w})(w^{mJ} - w^*) \tag{40}$$

where $\tilde{w} = w^* + \theta(w^{mJ} - w^*)$, $\theta \in (0,1)$. Using Assumption 1 and Assumption 3 we conclude that

$$\frac{1}{2}\beta_2\|w^{mJ} - w^*\|^2 \le \left|E(w^{mJ}) - E(w^*)\right| \le \frac{1}{2}\beta_3\|w^{mJ} - w^*\|^2 \tag{41}$$

that is

$$\left\|E_w(w^{mJ})\right\|^2 \ge \frac{2\beta_1^2}{\beta_3}\left|E(w^{mJ}) - E(w^*)\right|$$

Notice

$$\left\|E_w(w^{mJ})\right\|^2 = \left\|\sum_{k=1}^{J} p^{(m,k)}\right\|^2 \le \left(\sum_{k=1}^{J} \|p^{(m,k)}\|\right)^2$$

So

$$-\beta\left(\sum_{k=1}^{J} \|p^{(m,k)}\|\right)^2 \le -\beta\left\|E_w(w^{mJ})\right\|^2 \le \frac{-2\beta\beta_1^2}{\beta_3}\left|E(w^{mJ}) - E(w^*)\right|$$

Together with (28) we have

$$\begin{aligned}
\left|E(w^{(m+1)J}) - E(w^*)\right| &= E(w^{(m+1)J}) - E(w^*) \\
&= E(w^{(m+1)J}) - E(w^{mJ}) + E(w^{mJ}) - E(w^*) \\
&\le -\beta\left(\textstyle\sum_{k=1}^{J} \|p^{(m,k)}\|\right)^2 + E(w^{mJ}) - E(w^*) \\
&\le \left(1 - \tfrac{2\beta\beta_1^2}{\beta_3}\right)|E(w^{mJ}) - E(w^*)| \\
&\le \left(1 - \tfrac{2\beta\beta_0^2}{\beta_2}\right)^2 |E(w^{(m-1)J}) - E(w^*)| \\
&\le \cdots \\
&\le \left(1 - \tfrac{2\beta\beta_1^2}{\beta_3}\right)^{m+1} \left|E(w^0) - E(w^*)\right|
\end{aligned}$$

So for $j = 0$ we complete the proof of (38), for $j = 1, ..., J-1$ we need only using $w^j$ instead of $w^0$, and repeat the above process. Now we prove (39) for $j = 0$.

$$\begin{aligned}
\|w^{mJ} - w^*\|^2 &\le \tfrac{2}{\beta_2}\left|E(w^{mJ}) - E(w^*)\right| \\
&\le \tfrac{2}{\beta_2}\left(1 - \tfrac{2\beta\beta_1^2}{\beta_3}\right)^m \left|E(w^0) - E(w^*)\right| \\
&\le \tfrac{2}{\beta_2}\left(1 - \tfrac{2\beta\beta_1^2}{\beta_3}\right)^m \tfrac{1}{2}\beta_3\|w^0 - w^*\|^2 \\
&= \tfrac{\beta_3}{\beta_2}\left(1 - \tfrac{2\beta\beta_1^2}{\beta_3}\right)^m \|w^0 - w^*\|^2
\end{aligned}$$

When $j = 1, ..., J-1$ (39) can be proved similarly.

## 6 Conclusions

In this paper, we consider online gradient method with momentum for two-layer feedforward neural networks. The learning rate $\eta$ is set to be a constant and the momentum coefficient $\tau_k$ an adaptive variable. The corresponding convergence results are established, without assuming the error function to be quadratic as in the existing results.

In particular, a weak convergence result $E(w^i) \to E^*$ as $i \to \infty$ is proved, which indicates that the iteration procedure will converge to a local minimum of the error function $E(w)$. When $E(w)$ is uniformly convex, we can prove the strong convergence $w^i \to w^*$, where $w^*$ is the unique minimum point of the error function $E(w)$ in this case. The convergence rates of the error function and the weight vector are also established.

## Acknowledgment

The author would like to thank the anonymous referees for their valuable comments and suggestions on the revision of this paper.

## References

1. Bhaya, A., Kaszkurewicz, E.: Steepest Descent with Momentum for Quadratic Functions is a Version of the Conjugate Gradient Method. Neural Networks 17(2004)65-71
2. Ellacott, S. W.: The Numerical Approach of Neural Networks. In: Taylor,J.G.(Ed.). Mathematical Approaches to Neural Networks. North-Holland, Amsterdam.(1993)103-138
3. Gaivjoronski, A. A.: Convergence Properties of Backpropagation for Neural Nets via Theory of Stochastic Gradient Methods, Part I. Optimization Methods and Software. 4(1994)117-134
4. Hassoun, M. H.: Foundation of Artificial Neural Networks.Cambrige, MA: MIT Press, 1995
5. Li, Z. X., Wu, W., Tian, Y. L.: Convergence of an Online Gradient Method for Feedforward Neural Networks with Stochastic Inputs. J. Comput. Appl. Math. 163(2004)165-176
6. Luo, Z., Tseng, P.: Analysis of an Approximate Gradient Projection Method with Applications to the Backpropagation Algorithm. Optimization Methods and Software 4(1994)85-101
7. Luo, Z.: On the Convergence of the LMS Algorithm with Adaptive Learning Rate for Linear Feedforward Networks. Neural Comput. 3(1991)226-245
8. Mangagasarian,O. L., Solodov,M. V.: Serial and Parallel Backpropagation Convergence via Nonmonotone Perturbed Minimization. Optimization Methods and Software 4(1994)103-116
9. Rumelhart, D. E., McClelland, J. L. : Parallel Distributed Processing : Explorations in the Microstructure of Cognition. vol. 1. Cambrige, MA: MIT Press. 1986
10. Rumelhart, D. E., Hinton, G. E., Williams, R. J. : Learning Representations by Back-propagating Errors . Nature 323(1986)533-536

11. Sollich, P. , Barber, D. : Online Learning from Finite Training Sets and Robustness Tjo Input Bias. Neural Comput. 10(1998)2201-2217
12. Torii, M., Hagan, M. T. : Stability of Steepest Descent with Momentum for Quadratic Functions . IEEE Transactions on Neural Networks 13(2002)752-756
13. Wu, W., Xu, Y. S.: Deterministic Convergence of an Online Gradient Method for Neural Networks . J. Comput. Appl. Math. 144(2002)335-347
14. Wu, W., Feng, G.R., Li, X. : Training Multilayer Perceptrons via Minimization of Ridge Functions. Advances in Computational Mathematics 17(2002)331-347
15. Zhang, N. M., Wu, W., Zheng, G. F. : Convergence of Gradient Method with Momentum for Two-layer Feedforward Neural Networks . IEEE Transactions on Neural Networks .17(2006)522-525

# Fast Kernel Classifier Construction Using Orthogonal Forward Selection to Minimise Leave-One-Out Misclassification Rate

X. Hong[1], S. Chen[2], and C.J. Harris[2]

[1] Department of Cybernetics
University of Reading, Reading, RG6 6AY, U.K.
x.hong@reading.ac.uk
[2] School of Electronics and Computer Science
University of Southampton
Southampton SO17 1BJ, U.K.
{sqc, cjh}@ecs.soton.ac.uk

**Abstract.** We propose a simple yet computationally efficient construction algorithm for two-class kernel classifiers. In order to optimise classifier's generalisation capability, an orthogonal forward selection procedure is used to select kernels one by one by minimising the leave-one-out (LOO) misclassification rate directly. It is shown that the computation of the LOO misclassification rate is very efficient owing to orthogonalisation. Examples are used to demonstrate that the proposed algorithm is a viable alternative to construct sparse two-class kernel classifiers in terms of performance and computational efficiency.

## 1 Introduction

The two-class classification problems can be configured into a regression framework that solves a separating hyperplane for two classes, with the known class labels used as the desired output examples for model training in supervised learning. Models are usually identified according to some objective criteria. Information based criteria, such as the AIC [1], often include a penalty term to avoid an oversized model which may tend to overfit to the training data set. Parsimonious models are also preferable in engineering applications since a model's computational complexity scales with its model complexity. Moreover a parsimonious model is easier to interpret from the viewpoint of knowledge extraction. Consequently a practical nonlinear modelling principle is to find the smallest model that generalises well. Model construction techniques that have been widely studied include the support vector machine (SVM), relevance vector machine (RVM), and orthogonal forward regression [2,3,4,5]. The orthogonal least square algorithm [6] was developed as a practical linear-in-the-parameters models construction algorithm. A large class of nonlinear representations, e.g. the radial basis function (RBF) network and SVM, can be classified as the linear-in-the-parameters models. An orthogonal forward selection (OFS) procedure can be applied to construct parsimonious two-class classifiers by incrementally maximising the Fisher ratio of class separability measure [7,8]. Alternatively the SVM

D.-S. Huang, K. Li, and G.W. Irwin (Eds.): ICIC 2006, LNCS 4113, pp. 106–114, 2006.

is based on the structural risk minimisation (SRM) principle and approximately minimises an upper bound on the generalisation error [2] via minimising of the norm of weights in the feature space [9]. The SVM is characterised by a kernel function, lending its solution as that of the convex quadratic programming, such that the resultant model is sparse with a subset of the training data set used as support vectors.

In regression, a fundamental concept in the evaluation of model generalisation capability is that of cross validation [10]. The leave-one-out (LOO) cross validation is often used to estimate generalisation error for choosing among different model architectures [10]. LOO errors can be derived using algebraic operation rather than actually splitting the training data set for linear-in-the-parameters models. The calculation of LOO errors however is computational expensive. The generalised cross validation [11] has been introduced as a variant of LOO cross validation to improve computational efficiency. Regressors can incrementally be appended in an efficient OFS procedure while minimising the LOO errors [12,13] to yield a sparse regression model that generalises well.

This paper considers the construction of parsimonious two-class linear-in-the-parameters kernel classifiers using LOO cross validation. The proposed method extends the OFS procedure for regression in [12,13] to the classification problem by using the LOO misclassification rate, the true generalisation capability of a classifier, for model selection. Note that in classification the modelling objective is to minimise the number of misclassified samples rather than the mean square LOO error. An analytic formula for LOO misclassification rate is derived based on the regularised orthogonal least squares (ROLS) parameter estimates [13]. Furthermore it is shown that the orthogonalisation procedure brings the advantage of calculating the LOO misclassification rate via a set of forward recursive updating formula at minimal computational expense. A fast two-class kernel classifier construction algorithm is presented using this OFS procedure by directly minimising the LOO misclassification rate to optimise the model generalisation. Numerical examples are used to demonstrate the effectiveness of the proposed approach, in comparison with other current kernel based classifiers.

## 2 Two-Class Kernel Classifier

Consider the problem of training a two-class classifier $f(\mathbf{x}) : \Re^n \rightarrow \{1, -1\}$ based on a training data set $D_N = \{\mathbf{x}(i), y(i)\}_{i=1}^N$, where $y(i) \in \{1, -1\}$ denotes the class type for each data sample $\mathbf{x}(i) \in \Re^n$. We adopt the linear-in-the-parameters classifier given by

$$\hat{y}(i) = \text{sgn}(f(i)) \quad \text{with} \quad f(i) = \sum_{j=1}^{L} \theta_j p_j(\mathbf{x}(i)) \tag{1}$$

where $\hat{y}(i)$ is the estimated class label for $\mathbf{x}(i)$, $p_j(\bullet)$ denotes the classifier kernels with a known nonlinear basis function, $\theta_j$ are the classifier's coefficients and $L$ is the number of kernels. The Gaussian kernel function

$$p_j(\mathbf{x}) = e^{-\frac{\|\mathbf{x}-\mathbf{c}_j\|^2}{2\sigma^2}} \tag{2}$$

is employed in this study, where $\mathbf{c}_j \in \Re^n$ is the $j^{th}$ kernel centre and $\sigma^2$ the kernel variance. Other kernel functions can obviously be used here.

Define $\xi(i) = y(i) - f(i)$ as the modelling residual sequence. Then the model (1) over the training data set $D_N$ can be written in vector form as

$$\mathbf{y} = \mathbf{P}\boldsymbol{\theta} + \boldsymbol{\Xi} \tag{3}$$

where $\boldsymbol{\Xi} = [\xi(1) \cdots \xi(N)]^T$, $\boldsymbol{\theta} = [\theta_1 \cdots \theta_L]^T$, and $\mathbf{P} = [\mathbf{p}_1 \cdots \mathbf{p}_L] \in \Re^{N \times L}$ is the regression matrix with column vectors $\mathbf{p}_j = [p_j(\mathbf{x}(1)) \cdots p_j(\mathbf{x}(N))]^T$. Denote the row vectors in $\mathbf{P}$ as $\mathbf{p}^T(i) = [p_1(i) \cdots p_L(i)]$, $1 \le i \le N$. Geometrically a parameter vector $\boldsymbol{\theta}$ defines a hyperplane by

$$\sum_{j=1}^{L} \theta_j p_j(\mathbf{x}) = 0 \tag{4}$$

which divides the data into two classes.

Let an orthogonal decomposition of $\mathbf{P}$ be $\mathbf{P} = \mathbf{W}\mathbf{A}$, where $\mathbf{A} = \{a_{ij}\}$ is an $L \times L$ unit upper triangular matrix and $\mathbf{W}$ is an $N \times L$ matrix with orthogonal columns that satisfy

$$\mathbf{W}^T\mathbf{W} = \text{diag}\{\kappa_1, \cdots, \kappa_L\} \tag{5}$$

with

$$\kappa_j = \mathbf{w}_j^T \mathbf{w}_j, \; 1 \le j \le L \tag{6}$$

where $\mathbf{w}_j$ is the $j$th column vector of $\mathbf{W}$. The row vectors of $\mathbf{W}$ are denoted as $\mathbf{w}^T(i) = [w_1(i) \cdots w_L(i)]$, $1 \le i \le N$. The model (3) can alternatively be expressed as

$$\mathbf{y} = (\mathbf{P}\mathbf{A}^{-1})(\mathbf{A}\boldsymbol{\theta}) + \boldsymbol{\Xi} = \mathbf{W}\boldsymbol{\gamma} + \boldsymbol{\Xi} \tag{7}$$

in which $\boldsymbol{\gamma} = [\gamma_1 \cdots \gamma_L]^T$ is an auxiliary weight vector, for which the ROLS parameter estimates are [13]

$$\gamma_j = \frac{\mathbf{w}_j^T \mathbf{y}}{\kappa_j + \lambda_j}, \quad 1 \le j \le L \tag{8}$$

where $\lambda_j$ are small positive regularisation parameters. If all $\lambda_j$ are set to zero, the parameter estimator is the usual least squares estimator. The original model coefficient vector $\boldsymbol{\theta}$ can be calculated from $\mathbf{A}\boldsymbol{\theta} = \boldsymbol{\gamma}$ through back-substitution.

The regularisation parameters $\lambda_j$ can be optimised iteratively using an evidence procedure [14,3,13]. The following updating formula quoted from [13] are used to determine the regularisation parameters.

$$\lambda_j^{new} = \frac{\rho_j^{new}}{N - \rho^{old}} \frac{\boldsymbol{\Xi}^T \boldsymbol{\Xi}}{N - \gamma_j^2}, \quad 1 \le j \le L \tag{9}$$

where

$$\rho_j = \frac{\mathbf{w}_j^T \mathbf{w}_j}{\lambda_j + \mathbf{w}_j^T \mathbf{w}_j} \quad \text{and} \quad \rho = \sum_{j=1}^{L} \rho_j. \tag{10}$$

## 3 Leave-One-Out Misclassification Rate

The misclassification rate for a given two-class classifier based on (1) can be evaluated based on the misclassified data examples as

$$J = \frac{1}{N}\sum_{i=1}^{N} \mathrm{Id}[y(i)f(i)] \tag{11}$$

where Id[•] denotes the misclassification indication function and is defined as

$$\mathrm{Id}[v] = \begin{cases} 1 \text{ if } v < 0, \\ 0 \text{ if } \ v \geq 0. \end{cases} \tag{12}$$

Cross validation criteria are metrics that measures a model's generalisation capability [10]. One commonly used version of cross-validation is the so-called LOO cross-validation. The idea is as follows. For any predictor, each data point in the estimation data set $D_N$ is sequentially set aside in turn, a model is estimated using the remaining $(N-1)$ data, and the prediction error is derived for the data point that was removed from training. By excluding the $i^{th}$ data example in estimation data set, the output of the model for the $i^{th}$ data example using a model estimated by using remaining $(N-1)$ data examples is denoted as $f^{(-i)}(i)$. The associated predicted class label is calculated by

$$\hat{y}^{(-i)}(i) = \mathrm{sgn}(f^{(-i)}(i)). \tag{13}$$

It is highly desirable to derive a classifier with good generalisation capability, i.e. to derive a classifier with a minimal misclassification error rate over a new data set that is not used in model estimation. The LOO cross validation is often used to estimate generalisation error for choosing among different models [10]. The LOO misclassification rate is computed by

$$J^{(-)} = \frac{1}{N}\sum_{i=1}^{N} \mathrm{Id}[y(i)f^{(-i)}(i)] = \frac{1}{N}\sum_{i=1}^{N} \mathrm{Id}[g(i)] \tag{14}$$

where $g(i) = y(i)f^{(-i)}(i)$. If $g(i) < 0$, this means that the $i^{th}$ data sample is misclassified, as the class label produced by the model $f^{(-i)}$ is different from the actual class label $y(i)$.

Instead of directly calculating (13) for the predicted class labels, which requires extensive computational effort, it is shown in the following that the LOO misclassification rate can be evaluated without actually sequentially splitting the estimation data set.

## 4 The Proposed Fast Classifier Construction Algorithm

We propose a fast OFS kernel classifier construction algorithm that directly minimises the LOO misclassification rate (F-OFS-LOO). The LOO modelling residual is given by

$$\xi^{(-i)}(i) = y(i) - f^{(-i)}(i). \tag{15}$$

It has been shown that the LOO model residuals can be derived using an algebraic operation rather than actually splitting the training data set based on the Sherman-Morrison-Woodbury theorem [15]. For models evaluated using the ROLS parameter estimates, it can be shown that the LOO model residuals are given by [13]

$$\xi^{(-i)}(i) = \frac{\xi(i)}{1 - \mathbf{w}(i)^T[\mathbf{W}^T\mathbf{W} + \boldsymbol{\Lambda}]^{-1}\mathbf{w}(i)} = \frac{y(i) - f(i)}{1 - \sum_{j=1}^{L} \frac{w_j^2(i)}{\kappa_j + \lambda_j}} \tag{16}$$

where $\boldsymbol{\Lambda} = \mathrm{diag}\{\lambda_1, \cdots, \lambda_L\}$. Hence

$$y(i) - f^{(-i)}(i) = \frac{y(i) - f(i)}{1 - \sum_{j=1}^{L} \frac{w_j^2(i)}{\kappa_j + \lambda_j}}. \tag{17}$$

Multiplying the both sides of (17) with $y(i)$ and applying $y^2(i) = 1, \forall i$, yields

$$1 - y(i)f^{(-i)}(i) = \frac{1 - f(i)y(i)}{1 - \sum_{j=1}^{L} \frac{w_j^2(i)}{\kappa_j + \lambda_j}}. \tag{18}$$

Thus

$$y(i)f^{(-i)}(i) = \frac{\sum_{j=1}^{L} \gamma_j w_j(i)y(i) - \sum_{j=1}^{L} \frac{w_j^2(i)}{\kappa_j + \lambda_j}}{1 - \sum_{j=1}^{L} \frac{w_j^2(i)}{\kappa_j + \lambda_j}}. \tag{19}$$

In the following it is shown that computational expense associated with classifier regressors determination can be significantly reduced by utilising the OFS process via a recursive formula. In the OFS process, the model size is configured as a growing variable $k$. Consider the model construction by using a subset of $k$ regressors ($k \ll L$), that is, a subset selected from the full model set consisting of the $L$ initial regressors (given by (3)) to approximate the system. By replacing $L$ with a variable model size $k$, and $y(i)f^{(-i)}(i)$ with $g_k(i)$, (19) is represented by

$$g_k(i) = \frac{\sum_{j=1}^{k} \gamma_j w_j(i)y(i) - \sum_{j=1}^{k} \frac{w_j^2(i)}{\kappa_j + \lambda_j}}{1 - \sum_{j=1}^{k} \frac{w_j^2(i)}{\kappa_j + \lambda_j}} = \frac{\alpha_k(i)}{\beta_k(i)} \tag{20}$$

where $\alpha_k(i)$ and $\beta_k(i)$ can be represented using the following recursive formula, respectively

$$\alpha_k(i) = \sum_{j=1}^{k} \gamma_j w_j(i)y(i) - \sum_{j=1}^{k} \frac{w_j^2(i)}{\kappa_j + \lambda_j} = \alpha_{k-1}(i) + \gamma_k w_k(i)y(i) - \frac{w_k^2(i)}{\kappa_k + \lambda_j}, \tag{21}$$

$$\beta_k(i) = 1 - \sum_{j=1}^{k} \frac{w_j^2(i)}{\kappa_j + \lambda_j} = \beta_{k-1}(i) - \frac{w_k^2(i)}{\kappa_k + \lambda_j}. \tag{22}$$

Thus the LOO misclassification rate for a new model with the size increased from $(k-1)$ to $k$ is calculated by

$$J_k^{(-)} = \frac{1}{N} \sum_{i=1}^{N} \mathrm{Id}[g_k(i)]. \tag{23}$$

This is advantageous in that, for a new model whose size is increased from $(k-1)$ to $k$, we only need to adjust both the numerator $\alpha_k(i)$ and the denominator $\beta_k(i)$ based on those of the model size $(k-1)$, with a minimal computational effort. The Gram-Schmidt procedure is used to construct the orthogonal basis $\mathbf{w}_k$ in an OFS manner [12,13]. At the $k$th regression step the regressor that results in the minimum LOO misclassification rate $J_k^{(-)}$ is selected. The detailed algorithm is summarised as follows.

**F-OFS-LOO** based on Gram-Schmidt orthogonalisation:

1. Initialise $\alpha_0(i) = 0$ and $\beta_0(i) = 1$ for $1 \le i \le N$. Set regularisation parameters $\lambda_j$ to a very small positive value $\lambda$.
2. At the $k$th step where $k \ge 1$, for $1 \le l \le L$, $l \ne l_1, \cdots, l \ne l_{k-1}$, compute

$$a_{jk}^{(l)} = \begin{cases} \frac{\mathbf{w}_j^T \mathbf{p}_l}{\mathbf{w}_j^T \mathbf{w}_j}, & 1 \le j < k, \\ 1, & j = k, \end{cases}$$

$$\mathbf{w}_k^{(l)} = \begin{cases} \mathbf{p}_l, & k = 1, \\ \mathbf{p}_l - \sum_{j=1}^{k-1} a_{jk}^{(l)} \mathbf{w}_j, & k \ge 2, \end{cases}$$

$$\kappa_k^{(l)} = (\mathbf{w}_k^{(l)})^T \mathbf{w}_k^{(l)},$$

$$\gamma_k^{(l)} = \frac{(\mathbf{w}_k^{(l)})^T \mathbf{y}}{\kappa_k^{(l)} + \lambda},$$

$$\alpha_k^{(l)}(i) = \alpha_{k-1}(i) + \gamma_k^{(l)} w_k^{(l)}(i) y(i) - \frac{[w_k^{(l)}(i)]^2}{\kappa_k^{(l)} + \lambda},$$

$$\beta_k^{(l)}(i) = \beta_{k-1}(i) - \frac{[w_k^{(l)}(i)]^2}{\kappa_k^{(l)} + \lambda},$$

$$g_k^{(l)}(i) = \frac{\alpha_k^{(l)}(i)}{\beta_k^{(l)}(i)},$$

for $1 \le i \le N$, and

$$J_k^{(-,\, l)} = \frac{1}{N} \sum_{i=1}^{N} \mathrm{Id}[g_k^{(l)}(i)].$$

Find

$$l_k = \arg[\min\{J_k^{(-,\ l)}, 1 \le l \le L, l \ne l_1, \cdots, l \ne l_{k-1}\}]$$

and select $J_k^{(-)} = J_k^{(-,l_k)}$, $a_{jk} = a_{jk}^{(l_k)}$ for $1 \le j \le k$, $\alpha_k(i) = \alpha_k^{(l_k)}(i)$ and $\beta_k(i) = \beta_k^{(l_k)}(i)$ for $1 \le i \le N$, and

$$\mathbf{w}_k = \mathbf{w}_k^{(l_k)} = \begin{cases} \mathbf{p}_{l_k}, & k = 1, \\ \mathbf{p}_{l_k} - \sum_{j=1}^{k-1} a_{jk}\mathbf{w}_j, & k \ge 2. \end{cases}$$

3. The procedure is monitored and terminated at the $k = n_\theta$ step, when $J_k^{(-)} \ge J_{k-1}^{(-)}$. Otherwise, set $k = k + 1$, and go to step 2.

The above procedure derives a model with $n_\theta \ll L$ regressors. Finally with a predetermined number of iterations, the procedure as given in (9) and (10) (with $L$ replaced by $n_\theta$) is applied to optimise the regularisation parameters that are used in the final model.

The computational complexity in the above F-OFS-LOO algorithm is in the order of $O(NL)$. The actual computation cost varies with the final model size, and the smaller the derived model size $n_\theta$, the smaller the computation expense. When $N$ is very large, e.g. over several thousands, a reduced subset of data points can be used as the kernel centres so that $L \ll N$ to control the computational complexity. Note that the proposed procedure for regularisation parameter optimisation is operated based on $n_\theta \ll L$ selected regressors, hence the additional computation cost involved in regularisation parameter optimisation is very small at the level $O(Nn_\theta)$.

## 5 Illustrative Examples

Experiments were performed to compare the proposed F-OFS-LOO algorithm with several existing classification algorithms as published in [16]. Three data sets investigated were Breast Cancer, Diabetes and Heart, which are available from [17]. Each data set contains 100 realizations of training and test data sets, respectively. Kernel classifiers were constructed over 100 training data sets and generalisation performance was evaluated using the average misclassification rate of the corresponding classifiers over the 100 test data sets. The Gaussian kernel function was employed in the experiments. Values of $\sigma^2$ were predetermined to derive individual models for each realization. For each realization of all three data sets, the full training data sets were used as the RBF centres to form the candidate regressor sets. The performance are summarised in Tables 1 to 3, respectively. The results have clearly shown that the proposed approach can construct parsimonious classifiers with competitive classification accuracy for these data sets.

## 6 Conclusions

Based upon the idea of using the orthogonal forward selection procedure to optimise model generalisation, a computationally efficient algorithm has been

**Table 1.** Average misclassification rate in % over 100 realizations of Breast Cancer test data set and classifier size. The results of first 6 methods are quoted from [16,17].

| | Misclassification rate | Model Size |
|---|---|---|
| RBF | $27.6 \pm 4.7$ | 5 |
| Adaboost with RBF | $30.4 \pm 4.7$ | 5 |
| AdaBoost$_{Reg}$ | $26.5 \pm 4.5$ | 5 |
| LP$_{Reg}$-AdaBoost | $26.8 \pm 6.1$ | 5 |
| QP$_{Reg}$-AdaBoost | $25.9 \pm 4.6$ | 5 |
| SVM with RBF kernel | $26.0 \pm 4.7$ | not available |
| Proposed F-OFS-LOO | $25.74 \pm 5$ | $6 \pm 2$ |

**Table 2.** Average misclassification rate in % over 100 realizations of Diabetes test data set and classifier size. The results of first 6 methods are quoted from [16,17].

| | Misclassification rate | Model Size |
|---|---|---|
| RBF | $24.3 \pm 1.9$ | 15 |
| Adaboost with RBF | $26.5 \pm 2.3$ | 15 |
| AdaBoost$_{Reg}$ | $23.8 \pm 1.8$ | 15 |
| LP$_{Reg}$-AdaBoost | $24.1 \pm 1.9$ | 15 |
| QP$_{Reg}$-AdaBoost | $25.4 \pm 2.2$ | 15 |
| SVM with RBF kernel | $23.5 \pm 1.7$ | not available |
| Proposed F-OFS-LOO | $23.0 \pm 1.7$ | $6 \pm 1$ |

**Table 3.** Average misclassification rate in % over 100 realizations of Heart test data set and classifier size. The results of first 6 methods are quoted from [16,17].

| | Misclassification rate | Model Size |
|---|---|---|
| RBF | $17.6 \pm 3.3$ | 4 |
| Adaboost with RBF | $20.3 \pm 3.4$ | 4 |
| AdaBoost$_{Reg}$ | $16.5 \pm 3.5$ | 4 |
| LP$_{Reg}$-AdaBoost | $17.5 \pm 3.5$ | 4 |
| QP$_{Reg}$-AdaBoost | $17.2 \pm 3.4$ | 4 |
| SVM with RBF kernel | $16.0 \pm 3.3$ | not available |
| Proposed F-OFS-LOO | $15.8 \pm 3.7$ | $10 \pm 3$ |

introduced to construct sparse two-class kernel classifiers by directly minimising the leave-one-out misclassification rate. The contribution includes developing a set of forward recursive updating formula of the LOO misclassification rate in the proposed algorithm. Experimental results on three benchmark examples are used to demonstrate the effectiveness of the proposed approach.

## Acknowledgement

S. Chen wishes to thank the support of the United Kingdom Royal Acedemy of Engineering.

## References


1. Akaike,H.: A New Look at the Statistical Model Identification, *IEEE Trans. Automatic Control*, vol.AC-19,(1974)716–723
2. Vapnik,V.: *The Nature of Statictical Learning Theory*, New York: Springer-Verlag, (1995)
3. Tipping,M.E.:Sparse Bayesian Learning and the Relevance Vector Machine, *J. Machine Learning Research*, vol.1,(2001)211–244
4. Scholkopf,B., Smola,A.J.:*Learning with Kernels: Support Vector Machine, Regularization, Optimization and Beyond*, Cambridge, MA: MIT Press, (2002)
5. Hong,X., Harris,C.J .: Nonlinear Model Structure Design and Construction using Orthogonal Least Squares and D-optimality Design, *IEEE Trans. Neural Networks*, vol.13, no.5,(2001)1245–1250
6. Chen,S., Billings, S.A.,W. Luo.: Orthogonal Least Squares Methods and Their Applications to Non-linear System Identification,*Int. J. Control*, vol.50, (1989)1873–1896
7. Mao,K.Z.: RBF Neural Network Center Selection Based on Fisher Ratio Class Separability Measure, *IEEE Trans. Neural Networks*, vol.13, no.5, (2002)1211–1217
8. Chen,S., Wang,X.X., Hong,X., Harris,C.J.: Kernel classifier construction using orthogonal forward selection and boosting with fisher ratio class separability, *IEEE Trans. Neural Networks*, accepted for publication, 2006
9. Vapnik,V.: *Statistical Learning Theory: Adaptive & Learning Systems for Signal Processing, Communication & Control*, J. Wiley, 1998
10. Stone,M.: Cross Validatory Choice and Assessment of Statistical Predictions, *Applied Statistics*, vol.36, pp.117–147, 1974.
11. Golub,G.H., Heath,M., Wahba,G.: Generalized cross-validation as a method for choosing good ridge parameter, *Technometrics*, vol.21, no.2, 1979(215–223)
12. X. Hong, P.M. Sharkey, K. Warwick.:Automatic Nonlinear Predictive Model Construction using Forward Regression and the PRESS Statistic, *IEE Proc. - Control Theory and Applications*, vol.150, no.3,(2003)245–254
13. Chen,S., Hong,X., Harris, C.J., P.M. Sharkey.: Sparse modelling using orthogonal Forward Regression with PRESS Statistic and Regularization, *IEEE Trans. Systems, Man and Cybernetics, Part B: Cybernetics*, vol.34, no.2,(2004)898–911
14. Mackay,D.J.:Bayesian Interpolation, *Neural Computation*, vol.4, no.3, (1992)415–447
15. Myers,R.H.: *Classical and Modern Regression with Applications*, PWS-KENT, Boston, 2nd edition, (1990)
16. G. Rätsch, T. Onoda and K.R. Müller, Soft Margins for AdaBoost, *Machine Learning*, vol.42, no.3, (2001)287–320
17. `http://ida.first.fraunhofer.de/projects/bench/benchmarks.htm`

# Gauss-Morlet-Sigmoid Chaotic Neural Networks

Yao-qun Xu and Ming Sun

Institute of System Engineering, Harbin University of Commerce, 150028, Harbin, China
Xuyq@hrbcu.edu.cn; Snogisun@tom.com

**Abstract.** Chaotic neural networks have been proved to be powerful tools for escaping from local minima. In this paper, we first retrospect Chen's chaotic neural network and then propose a novel Gauss-Morlet-Sigmoid chaotic neural network model. Second, we make an analysis of the largest Lyapunov exponents of the neural units of Chen's and the Gauss-Morlet-Sigmoid model. Third, 10-city traveling salesman problem (TSP) is given to make a comparison between them. Finally we conclude that the novel chaotic neural network model is more effective.

## 1 Introduction

Many combinatorial optimization problems arising from science and technology are often difficult to solve entirely. Hopfield and Tank first applied the continuous-time, continuous-output Hopfield neural network (HNN) to solve TSP [1], thereby initiating a new approach to optimization problems [2, 3]. The Hopfield neural network, one of the well-known models of this type, converges to a stable equilibrium point due to its gradient decent dynamics; however, it causes sever local-minimum problems whenever it is applied to optimization problems.

Chaotic neural networks have been proved to be powerful tools for escaping from local minima. M-SCNN has a more powerful performance than Chen's in solving combinatorial optimization problems, especially in searching global minima of continuous nonlinear function and traveling salesman problems [4]. Now we do research on the activation function in detail.

In this paper, we mainly make research on the effect of Gauss function on the performance of the network. We first review the Chen's chaotic neural network. Second, we propose a novel chaotic neural network model. Third, the time evolution figures of their largest Lyapunov exponents of the neural units are given. At last, we apply them to 10-city traveling salesman problem (TSP) in order to make a comparison. Finally we conclude that the novel chaotic neural network model we proposed is more valid. Because the wavelet function is a kind of basic function, for any function $f(x) \in L_2(R)$ and any wavelet $\Psi$, the known formula can be described as follows:

$$f(x) = \sum_{j,k=-\infty}^{\infty} c_{j,k} \Psi_{j,k}(x) \tag{1}$$

D.-S. Huang, K. Li, and G.W. Irwin (Eds.): ICIC 2006, LNCS 4113, pp. 115 – 125, 2006.

## 2 Chaotic Neural Network Models

In this section, two chaotic neural network models are given. And the first is proposed by Chen, the second proposed by ourselves.

### 2.1 Chaotic Simulated Annealing with Decaying Self-coupling

Chen and Aihara's transiently chaotic neural network [5] is described as follows:

$$x_i(t) = f(y_i(t)) = \frac{1}{1+e^{-y_i(t)/\varepsilon}} \tag{2}$$

$$y_i(t+1) = ky_i(t) + \alpha\left[\sum_j W_{ij}x_j + I_i\right] - z_i(t)(x_i(t) - I_0) \tag{3}$$

$$z_i(t+1) = (1-\beta)z_i(t) \tag{4}$$

where $x_i(t)$ is output of neuron $i$ ; $y_i(t)$ denotes internal state of neuron $i$ ; $W_{ij}$ describes connection weight from neuron $j$ to neuron $i$ , $W_{ij} = W_{ji}$ ; $I_i$ is input bias of neuron $i$ , $a$ a positive scaling parameter for neural inputs, $k$ damping factor of nerve membrane, $0 \le k \le 1$, $z_i(t)$ self-feedback connection weight (refractory strength) $\ge 0$, $\beta$ damping factor of $z_i(t)$ , $0 < \beta < 1$, $I_0$ a positive parameter, $\varepsilon$ steepness parameter of the output function, $\varepsilon > 0$.

### 2.2 Gauss-Morlet-Sigmoid Chaotic Neural Network Model (G-M-SCNN)

Gauss-Sigmoid chaotic neural network is a novel model proposed by ourselves, described as follows:

$$y_i(t+1) = ky_i(t) + \alpha\left[\sum_j W_{ij}x_j + I_i\right] - z_i(t)(x_i(t) - I_0) \tag{5}$$

$$z_i(t+1) = (1-\beta_1)z_i(t) \tag{6}$$

$$x_i(t) = f(y_i(t)) \tag{7}$$

$$f(y_i(t)) = BG((1+r_i(t))y_i(t)) + S(\mu_0(1+\eta_i(t))y_i(t)) + M(\mu_1(1+\eta_i(t))y_i(t)) \tag{8}$$

$$\eta_i(t+1) = \frac{\eta_i(t)}{\ln(e+\lambda(1-\eta_i(t)))} \tag{9}$$

$$r_i(t+1) = \beta_2 r_i(t) \tag{10}$$

$$G(u) = e^{-h(u-a)^2} \tag{11}$$

$$S(u) = \frac{1}{1+e^{-u}} \tag{12}$$

$$M(u) = e^{-u^2/2}cos(5u) \tag{13}$$

where $x_i(t)$, $y_i(t)$, $W_{ij}$, $\alpha$, $k$, $I_i$, $z_i(t)$, $I_0$ are the same with the above. And $\lambda$ is a positive parameter which controls the speed of this annealing process; $r_i(0)$ is an important parameter of activation function which should be varied with kinds of special optimization problems, $0< \beta_1 \leqslant 1$, $0< \beta_2 <1$. $A$, $\mu_0$, $\mu_1$ are positive parameters of Morlet wavelet function and Sigmoid function. $h$, $a$, $b$, $c$ are important parameters of *Gauss* function.

## 3 Research on Lyapunov Exponent of Neural Units

In this section, we mainly make research on the effect of the parameter $\beta_2$ of Gauss function on the largest Lyapunov exponents. We make an analysis of the time evolution figures of the neural units ( $\alpha = 0$ ) of Chen's and G-M-SCNN in the same annealing speed of $\beta = \beta_1$=0.008.

### 3.1 Chen's Chaotic Neural Unit

The parameters are set as follows:

$k$ =0.6, $I_0$=0.1, $\varepsilon$ =1/250 ,z (0)=0.1, y(0)=0.283.

The time evolution figure of the largest Lyapunov exponent is shown as Fig.1:

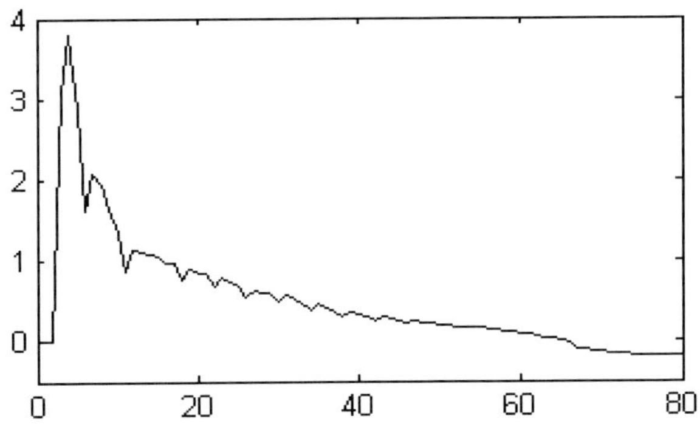


**Fig. 1.** Lyapunov exponent time evolution figure

### 3.2 Gauss-Morlet-Sigmoid Chaotic Neural Unit

We make an analysis of the time evolution figures of the neural unit G-M-SCNN with the change of $\beta_2$.

(1) The parameters are set as follows:

$\beta_2$=0.1, $k$=0.092, $I_0$=0.8, $y(0)$=0.283, $z(0)$=0.8,$\lambda$= 0.008, $\beta_1$=0.008, $\mu_0$=0.8, $\mu_1$=20, $B$=10, $r(0)$=200.5, $\eta(0)$=0.8, $h$=0. 2, $a$=−2. 1, $b$=5. 0, $c$=5. 0.

The time evolution figure of the largest Lyapunov exponent is shown as Fig.2.

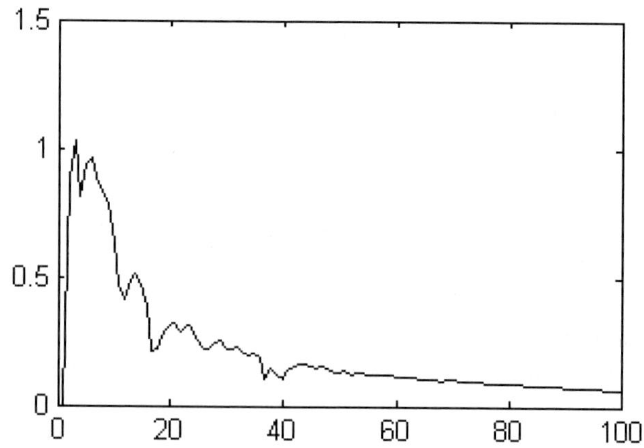


**Fig. 2.** Lyapunov exponent time evolution figure

(2) The parameters are set as follows:

$\beta_2$ =0.5, $k$ =0.092, $I_0$=0.8, $y(0)$ =0.283, $z(0)$ =0.8,λ= 0.008, $\beta_1$=0.008, $\mu_0$=0.8, $\mu_1$=20, $B$ =10, $r(0)$=200.5, $\eta(0)$=0.8, $h$ =0. 2, $a$ =−2. 1, $b$ =5. 0, $c$ =5. 0.

The time evolution figure of the largest Lyapunov exponent is shown as Fig.3.

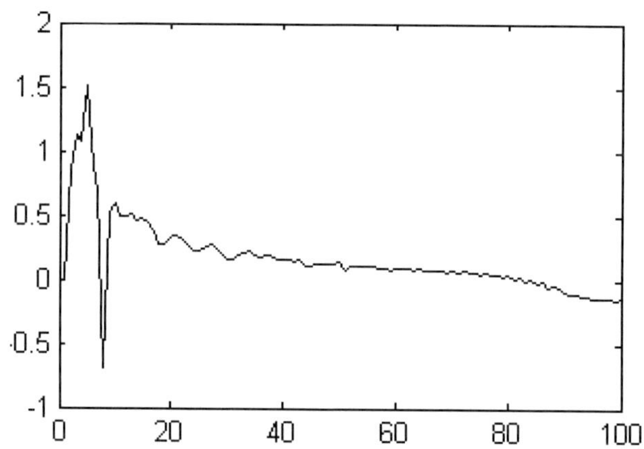


**Fig. 3.** Lyapunov exponent time evolution figure

(3) The parameters are set as follows:

$\beta_2$ =0.9, $k$ =0.092, $I_0$=0.8, $y(0)$ =0.283, $z(0)$ =0.8,λ= 0.008, $\beta_1$=0.008, $\mu_0$=0.8, $\mu_1$=20, $B$ =10, $r(0)$=200.5, $\eta(0)$=0.8, $h$ =0. 2, $a$ =−2. 1, $b$ =5. 0, $c$ =5. 0.

The time evolution figure of the largest Lyapunov exponent is shown as Fig.4.

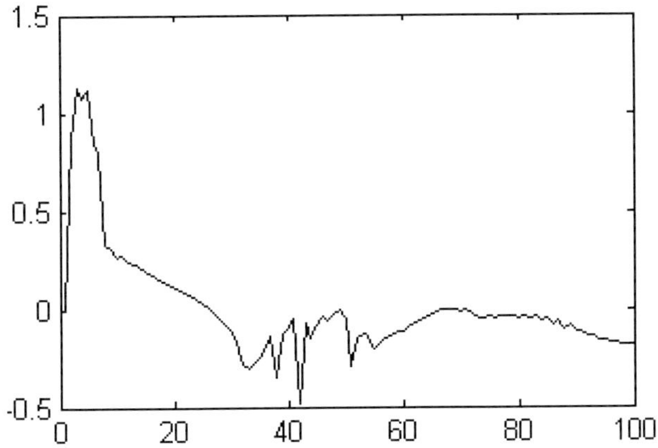


**Fig. 4.** Lyapunov exponent time evolution figure

Seen from the above analysis, we can conclude that the change of $\beta_2$ does have a profound effect on the time evolution of Lyapunov exponent. So, in this paper we will only make analysis of the performance of the network with different $\beta_2$ in solving traveling salesman problem (TSP)

## 4 Application to Traveling Salesman Problem

A solution of TSP with N cities is represented by N×N-permutation matrix, where each entry corresponds to output of a neuron in a network with N×N lattice structure. Assume $v_{xi}$ to be the neuron output which represents city $x$ in visiting order $i$. A computational energy function which is to minimize the total tour length while simultaneously satisfying all constrains takes the follow form [7]:

$$E=\frac{A}{2}(\sum_{x=1}^{N}(\sum_{i=1}^{N}v_{xi}-1)^2+\sum_{i=1}^{N}(\sum_{x=1}^{N}v_{xi}-1)^2)+\frac{D}{2}\sum_{x=1}^{N}\sum_{y=1}^{N}\sum_{i=1}^{N}d_{xy}v_{xi}v_{y,i+1} \tag{14}$$

where $v_{i0}=v_{in}$ and $v_{i,n+1}=v_{i1}$. $A$ and $D$ are the coupling parameters corresponding to the constraint function and the cost function of the tour length, respectively. $d_{xy}$ is the distance between city $x$ and city $y$.

The coordinates of 10-city is as follows:

(0.4, 0.4439),(0.2439, 0.1463),(0.1707, 0.2293),(0.2293, 0.716),(0.5171, 0.9414), (0.8732, 0.6536),(0.6878, 0.5219),(0.8488, 0.3609),(0.6683, 0.2536), (0.6195, 0.2634). The shortest distance of the 10-city is 2.6776.

Here are the results of the test about Chen's and G-M-SCNN.

The coupling parameters corresponding to the constraint function and the cost function of the tour length we adopt are set as follows: $A$ =2.5, $D$ =1.

(1) The parameters of Chen's are set as follows :

$\alpha$=0.2, $k$ =1, $I_0$=0.5, $\varepsilon$ =1/20 ,z (0)=[0.5,0.5].

200 different initial conditions are generated randomly in the region [0, 1] when $\beta$ =0.008, as are shown in table1. (VN= valid number; GN= global number; VP= valid percent; GP=global percent.)

**Table 1.** Simulation result of Chen's chaotic neural network

| Model | VN | GN | VP | GP |
|---|---|---|---|---|
| Chen's | 188 | 188 | 94% | 94% |
| | 185 | 185 | 92.5% | 92.5% |
| | 183 | 183 | 91.5% | 91.5% |
| | 184 | 184 | 92% | 92% |
| | 181 | 180 | 90.5% | 90% |
| | 175 | 175 | 87.5% | 87.5% |
| | 180 | 179 | 90% | 89.5% |
| | 189 | 189 | 94.5% | 94.5% |
| | 187 | 186 | 93.5% | 93% |
| | 178 | 178 | 89% | 89% |
| average | 183 | 182.7 | 91.5% | 91.35% |

In order to gain insight into the effect of $\beta_2$ on the proposed model, the tests are shown as follows:

(2) The parameters of G-M-SCNN are set as follows:

$k$ =1, $I_0$ =0.5, $z(0)$ =0.1,$\lambda$= 0.008, $\beta_1$ =0.008, $\mu_0$ =0.8, $\mu_1$ =20, $B$ =10, $r(0)$ =200.5, $\eta(0)$ =0.8, $h$ =0. 2, $a$ =−2. 1, $b$ =5. 0, $c$ =5. 0.

Let $\beta_2$ =0.1,0.2,0.3,0.4,0.5,0.6,0.7,0.8,0.9, we can get Table2~10.

**Table 2.** Simulation result of G-M-SCNN( $\beta_2$ =0.1)

| Model | VN | GN | VP | GP |
|---|---|---|---|---|
| G-M-SCNN ( $B$ =10, $\beta_2$ =0. 1) | 187 | 178 | 93.5% | 89% |
| | 193 | 188 | 96.5% | 94% |
| | 194 | 187 | 97% | 93.5% |
| | 188 | 183 | 94% | 91.5% |
| | 190 | 176 | 95% | 88% |
| | 193 | 183 | 96.5% | 91.5% |
| | 190 | 184 | 95% | 92% |
| | 192 | 181 | 96% | 90.5% |
| | 188 | 183 | 94% | 91.5% |
| | 189 | 182 | 94.5% | 91% |
| Average | 190.4 | 182.5 | 95.2% | 91.25% |

**Table 3.** Simulation result of G-M-SCNN( $\beta_2$ =0.2)

| Model | VN | GN | VP | GP |
|---|---|---|---|---|
| | 187 | 180 | 93.5% | 90% |
| | 187 | 175 | 93.5% | 87.5% |
| | 191 | 184 | 95.5% | 92% |
| | 187 | 180 | 93.5% | 90% |
| G-M-SCNN ( $B$ =10, $\beta_2$ =0. 2) | 193 | 188 | 96.5% | 94% |
| | 194 | 187 | 97% | 93.5% |
| | 188 | 183 | 94% | 91.5% |
| | 190 | 176 | 95% | 88% |
| | 192 | 182 | 96% | 91% |
| | 190 | 184 | 95% | 92% |
| average | 189.9 | 181.9 | 94.95% | 90.95% |

**Table 4.** Simulation Result of G-M-SCNN( $\beta_2$ =0.3)

| Model | VN | GN | VP | GP |
|---|---|---|---|---|
| | 190 | 183 | 95% | 91.5% |
| | 192 | 181 | 96% | 90.5% |
| | 187 | 182 | 93.5% | 91% |
| | 189 | 183 | 94.5% | 91.5% |
| G-M-SCNN ( $B$ =10, $\beta_2$ =0. 3) | 189 | 175 | 94.5% | 87.5% |
| | 190 | 183 | 95% | 91.5% |
| | 187 | 180 | 93.5% | 90% |
| | 187 | 178 | 93.5% | 89% |
| | 188 | 175 | 94% | 87.5% |
| | 190 | 181 | 95% | 90.5% |
| average | 188.9 | 180.1 | 94.45% | 90.05% |

**Table 5.** Simulation result of G-M-SCNN( $\beta_2$ =0.4)

| Model | VN | GN | VP | GP |
|---|---|---|---|---|
| | 193 | 183 | 96.5% | 91.5% |
| | 188 | 179 | 94% | 89.5% |
| | 182 | 171 | 91% | 85.5% |
| | 191 | 187 | 95.5% | 93.5% |
| G-M-SCNN ( $B$ =10, $\beta_2$ =0. 4) | 191 | 180 | 95.5% | 90% |
| | 194 | 186 | 97% | 93% |
| | 193 | 188 | 96.5% | 94% |
| | 194 | 187 | 97% | 93.5% |
| | 187 | 181 | 93.5% | 90.5% |
| | 188 | 178 | 94% | 89% |
| average | 190.1 | 182 | 95.05% | 91% |

**Table 6.** Simulation result of G-M-SCNN( $\beta_2$ =0.5)

| Model | VN | GN | VP | GP |
|---|---|---|---|---|
| G-M-SCNN ( $B$ =10, $\beta_2$ =0. 5) | 193 | 183 | 96.5% | 91.5% |
| | 191 | 179 | 90.5% | 89.5% |
| | 193 | 183 | 96.5% | 91.5% |
| | 193 | 183 | 96.5% | 91.5% |
| | 193 | 181 | 96.5% | 90.5% |
| | 187 | 182 | 93.5% | 91% |
| | 189 | 183 | 94.5% | 91.5% |
| | 188 | 175 | 94% | 87.5% |
| | 189 | 183 | 94.5% | 91.5% |
| | 188 | 181 | 94% | 90.5% |
| average | 190.4 | 181.5 | 95.2% | 90.75% |

**Table 7.** Simulation result of G-M-SCNN( $\beta_2$ =0.6)

| Model | VN | GN | VP | GP |
|---|---|---|---|---|
| G-M-SCNN ( $B$ =10, $\beta_2$ =0. 6) | 188 | 180 | 94% | 90% |
| | 185 | 171 | 92.5% | 85.5% |
| | 189 | 180 | 94.5% | 90% |
| | 193 | 183 | 96.5% | 91.5% |
| | 181 | 171 | 90.5% | 85.5% |
| | 188 | 177 | 94% | 88.5% |
| | 188 | 182 | 94% | 91% |
| | 190 | 183 | 95% | 91.5% |
| | 193 | 186 | 96.5% | 93% |
| | 187 | 179 | 93.5% | 89.5% |
| average | 188.2 | 178.2 | 94.1% | 89.1% |

**Table 8.** Simulation result of G-M-SCNN( $\beta_2$ =0.7)

| Model | VN | GN | VP | GP |
|---|---|---|---|---|
| G-M-SCNN ( $B$ =10, $\beta_2$ =0. 7) | 190 | 182 | 95% | 91% |
| | 181 | 173 | 90.5% | 86.5% |
| | 193 | 181 | 96.5% | 90.5% |
| | 189 | 180 | 94.5% | 90% |
| | 190 | 185 | 95% | 92.5% |
| | 194 | 187 | 97% | 93.5% |
| | 191 | 189 | 95.5% | 94.5% |
| | 191 | 183 | 95.5% | 91.5% |
| | 189 | 185 | 94.5% | 92.5% |
| | 184 | 170 | 92% | 85% |
| average | 189.2 | 181.5 | 94.6% | 90.75% |

**Table 9.** Simulation result of G-M-SCNN( $\beta_2$ =0.8)

| Model | VN | GN | VP | GP |
|---|---|---|---|---|
| G-M-SCNN ( $B$ =10, $\beta_2$ =0. 8) | 193 | 185 | 96.5% | 92.5% |
| | 192 | 180 | 96% | 90% |
| | 192 | 185 | 96% | 92.5% |
| | 190 | 180 | 95% | 90% |
| | 185 | 175 | 92.5% | 87.5% |
| | 193 | 183 | 96.5% | 91.5% |
| | 191 | 181 | 95.5% | 90.5% |
| | 192 | 178 | 96% | 89% |
| | 193 | 180 | 96.5% | 90% |
| | 183 | 174 | 91.5% | 87% |
| average | 190.4 | 180.1 | 95.2% | 90.05% |

**Table 10.** Simulation result of G-M-SCNN( $\beta_2$ =0.9)

| Model | VN | GN | VP | GP |
|---|---|---|---|---|
| G-M-SCNN ( $B$ =10, $\beta_2$ =0.9) | 188 | 180 | 94% | 90% |
| | 192 | 182 | 96% | 91% |
| | 189 | 180 | 94.5% | 90% |
| | 194 | 183 | 97% | 91.5% |
| | 187 | 175 | 93.5% | 87.5% |
| | 186 | 173 | 93% | 86.5% |
| | 192 | 177 | 96% | 88.5% |
| | 190 | 179 | 95% | 89.5% |
| | 190 | 181 | 95% | 90.5% |
| | 190 | 182 | 95% | 91% |
| average | 189.8 | 179.2 | 94.9% | 89.6% |

An examination of Table2~10 yields the following Table 11.

**Table 11.** Simulation result of G-M-SCNN

| Model | | AVP | AGP |
|---|---|---|---|
| Chen's | | 91.5% | 91.35% |
| G-M-SCNN | $\beta_2$ =0.1 | 95.2% | 91.25% |
| | $\beta_2$ =0.2 | 94.95% | 90.95% |
| | $\beta_2$ =0.3 | 94.45% | 90.05% |
| | $\beta_2$ =0.4 | 95.05% | 91% |
| | $\beta_2$ =0.5 | 95.2% | 90.75% |
| | $\beta_2$ =0.6 | 94.1% | 89.1% |
| | $\beta_2$ =0.7 | 94.6% | 90.75% |
| | $\beta_2$ =0.8 | 95.2% | 90.05% |
| | $\beta_2$ =0.9 | 94.9% | 89.6% |

(AVP=average valid path percent, AGP=average global path percent)

Seen from the Table11, the proposed model can solve the TSP with a higher valid minimum-path percent and a little lower valid-path percent under all the values of $\beta_2$. This means that the proposed model is more valid in only solving TSP than Chen's.

The time evolution figures of the energy function of G-M-SCNN and Chen's in solving TSP are respectively given in Fig.5 and Fig.6.

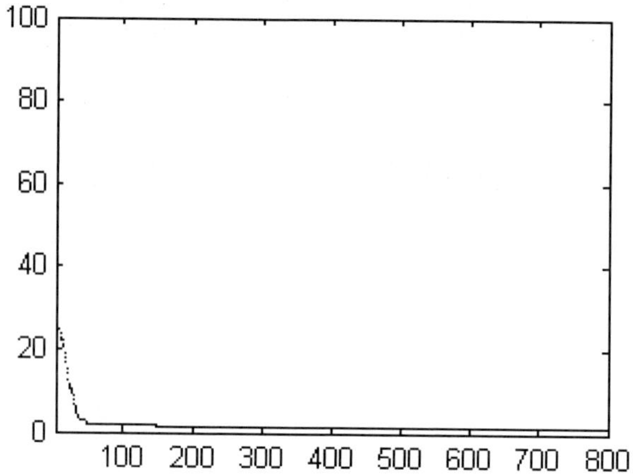


**Fig. 5.** Energy time evolution figure of G-M-SCNN

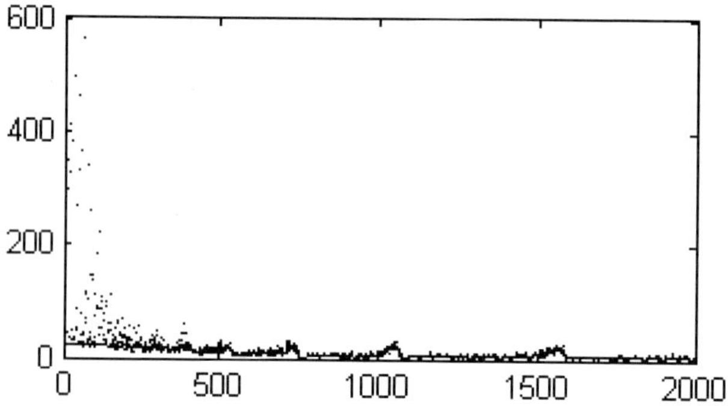


**Fig. 6.** Energy time evolution figure of Chen's

By comparison, it is concluded that M-SCNN is superior to Chen's model. From the Fig.5, Fig.6, one can see that the velocity of convergence of G-M-SCNN is faster than that of Chen's in solving TSP. Because, the state of Fig.5 become stable in 60 iterations while that of Fig.6 become stable in 1500 iterations.

The superiority of G-M-SCNN contributes to several factors: First, because of the higher nonlinear nature of Gauss function, the activation function of G-M-SCNN has a further performance in solving combinatorial optimization problems than Chen's.

Second, it is easier to produce chaotic phenomenon [8] in that the activation function is non-monotonic. Third, the activation function of G-M-SCNN is varied with time. Third, the wavelet function is a kind of basic function.

## 5 Conclusions

We have introduced two models of chaotic neural networks. To verify the effectiveness of it, we have made comparison with Chen's model in optimization problems. By comparison, one can conclude that G-M-SCNN is superior to Chen's in searching global minima of continuous nonlinear function.

Different from Chen's model, the activation function of G-M-SCNN is composed by Gauss, Morlet wavelet and Sigmoid. So, besides it has the quality of sigmoid activation, the activation function of G-M-SCNN has a higher nonlinear nature than Sigmoid, which is easier to produce chaotic phenomenon [7] because of its non-monotonic. Due to these factors, G-M-SCNN is superior to Chen's in solving TSP.

## References


1. Hopfield, J.J., Tank, D.W.: Neural Computation of Decision in Optimization Problems. Biol. Cybern.52 (1985)141-152
2. Hopfield, J.: Neural Networks and Physical Systems with Emergent Collective Computational Abilities. In: Proc. Natl. Acad. Sci., 79 (1982) 2554-2558
3. Hopfield, J.: Neural Networks and Physical Systems with Emergent Collective Computational Abilities. In: Proc. Natl. Acad. Sci., 81 (1984) 3088-3092
4. Xu, Y.Q., Ming, S., Duan, G.R.: Wavelet Chaotic Neural Networks and Their Application to Optimization Problems. Lecture Notes in Computer Science, 3971 Springer Berlin (2006) 379-384
5. Wang, L.P., Tian, F.Y.: Noisy Chaotic Neural Networks for Solving Combinatorial Optimization Problems. International Joint Conference on Neural Networks. Italy: IEEE, (2000)37-40
6. Sun, S.Y., Zhen, J.L.: A Kind of Improved Algorithm and Theory Testify of Solving TSP in Hopfield Neural Network. Journal of electron, 1 (1995)73-78
7. Potapove, A., Kali, M.: Robust Chaos in Neural Networks. Physics Letters A, 277 (2000) 310-322

# Hidden Markov Models for Recognition Using Artificial Neural Networks

V. Bevilacqua, G. Mastronardi, A. Pedone, G. Romanazzi, and D. Daleno

Dipartimento di Elettrotecnica ed Elettronica, Polytechnic of Bari,
via E. Orabona, 4,70125, Bari, Italy
bevilacqua@poliba.it

**Abstract.** In this paper we use a novel neural approach for face recognition with Hidden Markov Models. A method based on the extraction of 2D-DCT feature vectors is described, and the recognition results are compared with a new face recognition approach with Artificial Neural Networks (ANN). ANNs are used to compress a bitmap image in order to represent it with a number of coefficients that is smaller than the total number of pixels. To train HMM has been used the Hidden Markov Model Toolkit v3.3 (HTK), designed by Steve Young from the Cambridge University Engineering Department. However, HTK is able to speakers recognition, for this reason we have realized a special adjustment to use HTK for face identification.

## 1 Introduction

Real world process generally produced observable outputs which can be considered as signals. A problem of fundamental interest is characterizing such real world signals in terms of signal models. In primis, a signal model can provide the basis for a theoretical description of a signal processing system which can be used in order to provide a desiderated output. A second reason why signal models are important is that they are potentially capable of characterising a signal source without having the source available. This property is especially important when the cost of getting signals from the actual source is high. Hidden Markov Models (HMM) are a set of statistical models used to describe the statistical properties of a signal [3][8]. HMM are characterised by two interrelated processes:

1. an unobservable Markov chain with a finite number of states, a state transition probability matrix and an initial state probability distribution. This is the principal aspect of a HMM;
2. a set of probability density functions for each state.

The elements that characterized a HMM are:

- $N=|S|$ is the number of states of the model. If $S$ is the set of states, then $S=\{s_1, s_2, \ldots\ldots, s_N\}$. $s_i \in S$ is one of the states that can be employed by the model. To observe the system are used $T$ observation sequences, where $T$ is the number of observations. The state of the model at time $t$ is given by $q_t \in S$ , $1<t<T$ .

D.-S. Huang, K. Li, and G.W. Irwin (Eds.): ICIC 2006, LNCS 4113, pp. 126–134, 2006.

- $M$=|V| is the number of different observation symbols. If $V$ is the set of all possible observation symbols (also called the *codebook* of the model), then $V = \{v_1, v_2, \ldots\ldots, v_M\}$.
- $A = \{a_{ij}\}$ is the state transition probability matrix, where $a_{ij}$ is the probability that the state $i$ became the state $j$:

$$a_{ij} = p(q_t = s_j \mid q_{t-1} = s_i) \qquad 1 \le i, j \le N \tag{1}$$

- $B = \{b_j(k)\}$ the observation symbol probability matrix, $b_j(k)$ is the probability to have the observation $k$ when the state is $j$:

$$b_j(k) = p(o_t = v_k \mid q_t = s_j) \quad 1 \le j \le N,\ 1 \le k \le M \tag{2}$$

- $\Pi = \{\pi_1, \pi_2, \ldots, \pi_N\}$ is the initial state distribution, where:

$$\pi_i = p(q_1 = s_i) \qquad 1 \le j \le N \tag{3}$$

Using a shorthand notation, a HMM is defined by the following expression:

$$\lambda = (A, B, \Pi) \tag{4}$$

## 2 Hidden Markov Models for Face Recognition

Hidden Markov Models have been successfully used for speech recognition where data are essentially one dimensional because the HMM provide a way of modelling the statistical properties of a one dimensional signal. To apply the HMM also to process images, that are two dimensional data, we consider temporal or space sequences: this question has been considered in [2][6][7], where Samaria suggests to use a space sequence to model an image for HMM. For frontal face images, the significant facial regions are 5: hair, forehead, eyes, nose and mouth [1][5].

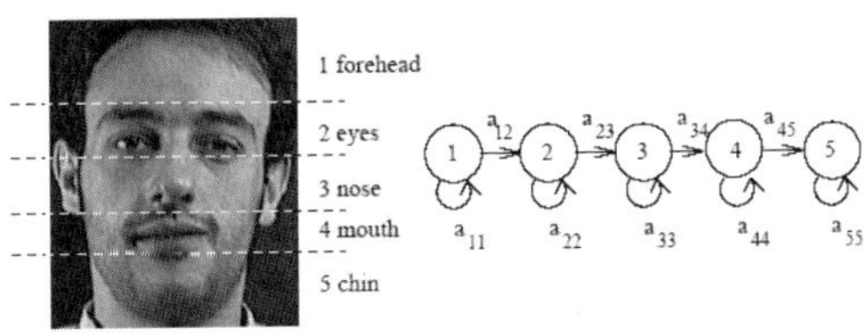


**Fig. 1.** The significant facial regions

Each of these facial regions (facial band) is assigned to a state in a left to right 1D continuous HMM. The Left-to-right HMM used for face recognition is shown in previous figure.To recognize the face $k$ we must trained the following HMM:

$$\lambda^{(k)} = \left(A^{(k)}, B^{(k)}, p^{(k)}\right) \tag{5}$$

To train a HMM we have used 4 different frontal face gray scale image for any person. Each face image of width W and height Y is divided into overlapping blocks of height L and width W. The amount of overlap between consecutive blocks is M. The number of blocks extracted from each face image equals the number of observation vectors T and is given by:

$$T = \frac{(Y - L)}{(L - M)} + 1 \tag{6}$$

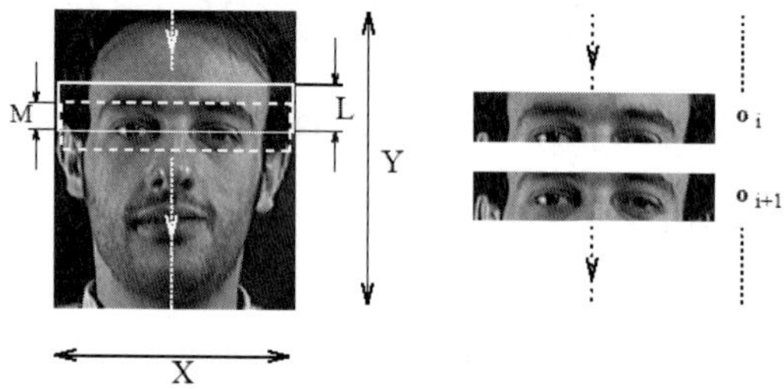


**Fig. 2.** The facial regions overlapped

The choice of parameters M and L can significantly affect the system recognition rate. A high amount of overlap M significantly increases the recognition rate because it allows the features to be captured in a manner that is independent of the vertical position. The choice of parameter L is more delicate. An insufficient amount of information about the observation vector could arise from a small value of the parameter L, while large L increases the probability of cutting across the features. However, the system recognition rate is more sensitive to the variations in M than in L, for this reason is used $M \leq (L-1)$.

We have considered X=92, Y=112, L=10, M=9 [1], then:

- T=103
- X x Y=10304 pixel
- X x L=920 pixel
- X x M=828 pixel

The observation sequence has T element, each of them is characterised by a window X x L=920 pixel. Using the pixel as elements of an observation sequence is the cause of a high complexity computing and a high sensitive to the noise. In this work is presented a new approach based on Artificial Neural Networks (ANNs) with the main goal to extract the principal characters of an image for reducing the complexity of the problem. To train HMM has been used The Hidden Markov Model Toolkit v3.3 (HTK) [4], designed by Steve Young from the Cambridge University Engineering Department. However, HTK is able to speech recognition, for this reason we have realized a special adjustment to use HTK for face identification.

## 3 Recognizing

After the HMM training, it's possible to recognize a frontal face image using the Viterbi's algorithm finding the model $M_i$ that computes the maximum value $P(O \mid M_i)$, where $O$ is the sequence of observation arrays that it's need to recognize. For HTK, the recognition is implemented by the Token Passing Model, an alternative formulation of the Viterbi's algorithm. For recognizing an image is used the tool "HVite":

```
HVite -a -iresult -I transcripts.mlf dict hmmlist foto1
```

*-i* means that the results will be stored into file "result", while "foto1" is the frontal face image to recognize for HTK. "transcrpts.mls","dict","hmmlist" are text files.

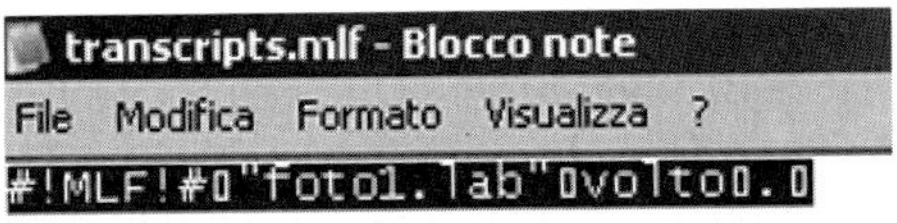
transcripts.mlf - Blocco note
File Modifica Formato Visualizza ?
#!MLF!#□"foto1.lab"□volto□.□

**Fig. 3.** Transcripts.mlf , "foto1" is the name of the image

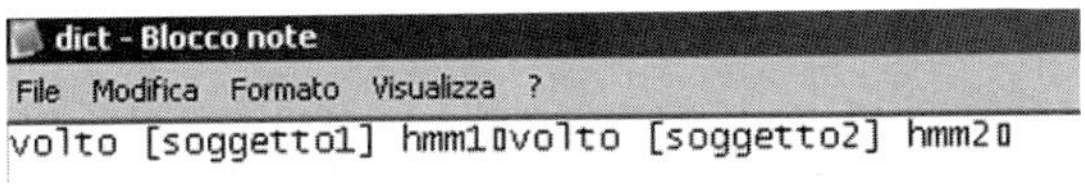
dict - Blocco note
File Modifica Formato Visualizza ?
volto [soggetto1] hmm1□volto [soggetto2] hmm2□

**Fig. 4.** Dict

In Fig. 4 "soggetto1" and "soggetto2" are the names of the frontal face images to recognize, the following *hmm#* is the associated HMM. "hmm2" e "hmm1" are the files stored by the tool "HRest": in the first case has been used the pixels for the observation sequences, while for "hmm1" has been applied the ANN approach introduced by this work.

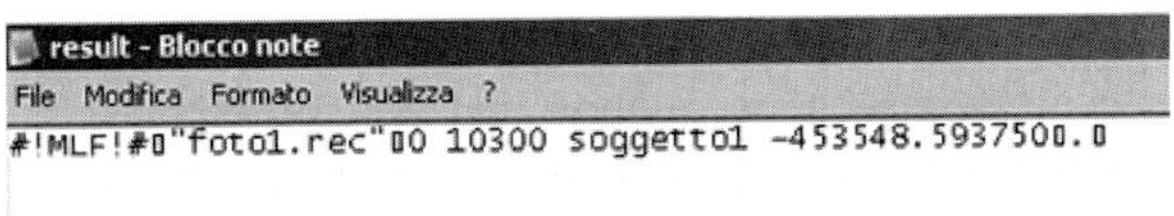
result - Blocco note
File Modifica Formato Visualizza ?
#!MLF!#□"foto1.rec"□0 10300 soggetto1 -453548.593750□.□

**Fig. 5.** Result

The view of the file asserts that the "foto1" has been recognize as "soggetto1" with total logarithmic probability "-453548.593750", for each observation sequence the average probability is the same value divided by T.

## 4 Artificial Neural Networks to Observe an Image for Hidden Markov Models

An Artificial Neural Network (ANN) is an information processing paradigm that is inspired by the way biological nervous systems, such as the brain, process information. The key element of this paradigm is the novel structure of the information processing system. It is composed of a large number of highly interconnected processing elements (neurons) working in unison to solve specific problems. All connections among neurons are characterized by numeric values (*weights*) that are updated during the training. The ANN is trained by a supervised learning process: in the training phase the network processes all the pairs of input-output presented by the user, learning how to associate a particular input to a specific output trying to extend the information acquired also for cases that don't belong to the *training set spectrum*. Any pair of data in the training set is presented to the system a quantity of time determined by the user *a priori*. The learning step is based on the Error *Back Propagation* (EBP) algorithm. The weights of the network are updated sequentially, from the output layer back to the input layer, by propagating an error signal backward along the neural connections (hence the name "back-propagation") according to the gradient-descent learning rule:

$$\Delta w_{ij} = -\eta \cdot \frac{\partial E}{\partial w_{ij}} \qquad 0 < \eta < 1 \tag{7}$$

For this work an ANN is used to compress a bitmap image in order to represent it with a number of coefficients that is smaller than the total number of pixels. Using these coefficients instead of the pixels has been realized a robust facial face recognition system that can operate under a variety conditions, such as varying illuminations and background. The ANN, using the EBP algorithm, extracts the main features from the image to store them in a sequence of 50 bits reducing the complexity computing of the problem. The image is a facial feature of a frontal face image; from this area we consider 103 segments of 920 pixels that represent the observable *states* of the model. Now all of these sections are divided into features of 230 pixels, that are the input of the network. The first layer is formed by 230 neurons, each neuron per pixel, the hidden layer is composed by 50 units and the last layer by 230 neurons. After the training, the network is able to work as a pure linear function, the input of the first layer must be the same of the output of the last layer. The compressed image is described by 50 bits that are the outputs of a hidden layer consisting of a Heaviside function processing elements. For any window of 230 pixels we have an array of 50 elements, so a section of 920 pixels is compressed in a 4 sub windows of 50 binary value array each. The matrix weights, referred to the connections between the inputs and the hidden layer, codifies the image bitmap, while the matrix weights associated to the connections between the hidden layer and the outputs, decodes the sequence of bits.

The ANN has been trained using 10 frontal face image of different persons, after the training phase, the matrix weights is stored and finally the ANN is tested with other images that are similar, but not the same to the training set feature. Finally, we have a face image compressed into an *observation* vector of 103 element of 200 binary (1/0) values that will be computed by the Hidden Markov Models (HMM).

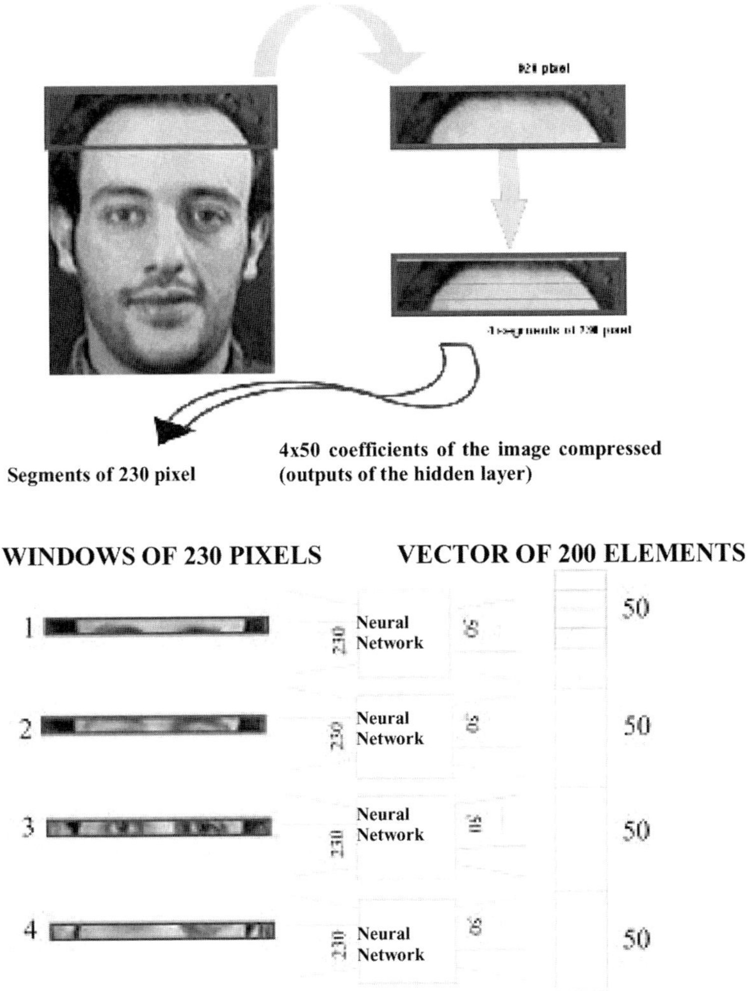


**Fig. 6.** System developed

## 5 Conclusions and Results

Two recognizing systems have been developed: the first uses pixels as observation vectors and the second employs vectors containing the principal components of the images returned by the neural network. The system has been tested using 4 facial face image of 4 different persons:

**Table 1.** Training images

| NOME | Image 1 | Image 2 | Image 3 | Image 4 |
|---|---|---|---|---|
| subject1 |  |  |  |  |
| subject2 |  |  |  |  |
| subject3 |  |  |  |  |
| subject4 |  | 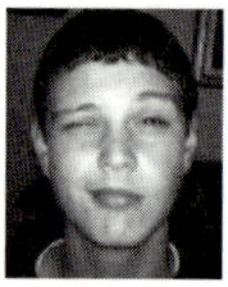 |  |  |

For each face recognized we have computed the total logarithmic probability.

**Table 2.** Results for subject3

| **Subject 3** | **Without ANN** | **Using ANN** |
|---|---|---|
|  | -436165.750000 | -93947.101563 |
|  | -470681.968750 | -99128.085938 |
|  | -478726.531250 | -98591.703125 |
|  | -442659.375000 | -95156.367188 |

**Table 2.** *(continued)*

| | | |
|---|---|---|
|  | -485397.093750 | -104245.335938 |
|  | -497308.093750 | -103274.578125 |
|  | -498396.781250 | -108224.695313 |
|  | -475043.062500 | -99134.726563 |
| 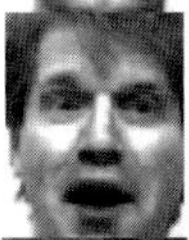 | -491749.812500 | -103642.601563 |
|  | -479394.687500 | -102927.476563 |

**Table 3.** Results for subject 4

| Subject 4 | Without ANN | Using ANN |
|---|---|---|
|  | -435390.937500 | -95473.640625 |
|  | -430359.500000 | -94148.359375 |
|  | -446048.250000 | -98179.273438 |
|  | -441871.812500 | -95641.335938 |
| 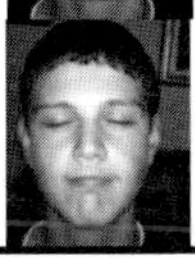 | -516868.187500 | -107430.375000 |

**Table 3.** (*continued*)

| | | |
|---|---|---|
| 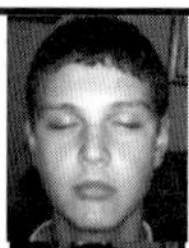 | -443342.437500 | -97138.390625 |
|  | -456531.875000 | -99424.187500 |
|  | -609438.000000 | -127188.664063 |
|  | -635798.500000<br>NOT RECOGNIZED | -122770.937500 |
|  | -658844.000000<br>NOT RECOGNIZED | -131893.875000 |

The logarithmic probability is the possibility that the bitmap will be recognized: it is clear that the system with ANN is more efficient than the system without. In the table 3., there are two images that are not recognized by the system without the neural network.

## References


1. Nefian, A. V., Monson, H.: Hidden Markov Models for Face Recognition. In IEEE International Conference on Acoustics, Speech and Signal Processing (ICASSP98), Seatle (1998) 2721-2724
2. Samaria, F.: Face Identification using Hidden Markov Model. 1st Year Report Cambridge University Engineering Department, London (1992)
3. Rabiner, L., Huang, B.: Fundamentals of Speech Recognition. Englewood Cliffs, Prentice-Hall, New York (1993)
4. Young, S., Evermann, G., Hain, T., Kershaw, D., Moore, G., Odell, J., Ollason, D., Povey, D., Valtchev, V., Woodland, P.: The HTK Book. Cambridge University Engineering Department, Cambridge, UK (2002)
5. Nefian, A. V., Monson, H.: Detection and Recognition Using Hidden Markov Models. International Conference on Image Processing, 1 (1998) 141–145
6. Samaria, F.: Face Recognition Using Hidden Markov Models. PhD Thesis, University of Cambridge, (1994)
7. Samaria, F., Young, S.: Face HMM Based Architecture for Face Identification. Image and Computer Vision, 12 (1994) 537-583
8. Cottrell, G. W., Munro, P., Zipser, D.: Learning Internal Representations from Gray Scale Image: An Example of Extensional Programming. In Ninth Annual Conference of the Cognitive Science Society, (1987) 462-473

# Improved Principal Component Analysis and Neural Network Ensemble Based Economic Forecasting*

Jian Lin[1] and Bangzhu Zhu[1,2]

[1] Institute of System Science and Technology, Wuyi University, Jiangmen 529020 Guangdong, China
Wpzbz@126.com

[2] School of Economics and Management, Beijing University of Aeronautics and Astronautics, Beijing 100083, China
Zhubangzhu@sem.buaa.edu.cn

**Abstract.** The application of neural network ensemble (NNE) to economic forecasting can heighten the generalization ability of learning systems through training multiple neural networks and combining their results. An improved principal component analysis (IPCA) is developed to extract the principal component of the economic data under the prerequisite that the main information of original economic data is not lost, and the input nodes of forecasting model are effectively reduced. Based on Bagging, the NNE constituted by five BP neural networks is employed to forecast GDP of Jiangmen, Guangdong with favorable results obtained, which shows that NNE is generally superior to simplex neural network, and valid and feasible for economic forecasting.

## 1 Introduction

The aim of economic forecasting is to estimate the future values according to the current data. Much attention has been paid to it by scholars home and abroad in recent years. Various approaches have been adopted to solve the problem with success to some degree. Neural network, especially BP neural network, is regarded as a good method widely applied. BP neural network has good learning ability and generalization with its simple structure. However, BP neural network also has some problems such as the difficulty in determining the number of neural cells of the hidden layer, the influences of its initialization and high requirements of the quantity and quality of training samples and so on, which can influence its generalization and make the forecasting results not ideal [1].

In 1990, Hansen and Salamon [2] firstly put forward neural network ensemble (NNE) method. Multiple neural networks learning from their training samples constitute a NNE, and their outputs are combined into NNE's final output, which could remarkably enhance its generalization. NNE has recently been successfully applied to many fields such as function approximation, pattern recognition and probability density estimation and so on. In this paper, NNE is applied for economic forecasting with favorable results obtained, which shows that NNE is generally superior to simplex neural network, and valid and feasible for economic forecasting.

---

* Supported by the National Natural Science Foundation of China under Grant 70471074 and Guangdong Provincial Department of Science and Technology under Grant 2004B36001051.

D.-S. Huang, K. Li, and G.W. Irwin (Eds.): ICIC 2006, LNCS 4113, pp. 135 – 145, 2006.

# 2 Neural Network Ensemble

## 2.1 The Introduction of BP Neural Network

BP neural network (BP NN), a popular multilayer feed-forward network with all the nodes and layers arranged in a feed-forward manner, is always one of the types of models that are able to correctly classify various nonlinearities in the data, and this makes it popular with academics and practitioners.

BP algorithm builds BP neural network on the supervised learning adopting the gradients descend method. The nodes are organized in layers. Via the activation function between the input and hidden layer, hidden and output layer, neural network transmits the input information forwardly to hidden layer's notes, and the hidden layer information to output nodes. The results can get from output layer.

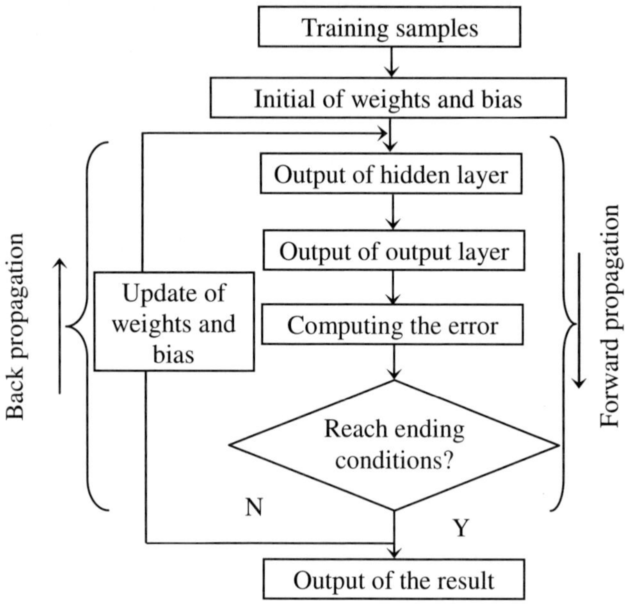


**Fig. 1.** Flow of BP neural network

BP algorithm consists of two parts, that are forward and backward propagation. Scaled data are fed into the network at the input layer. At the beginning of the learning, the interconnection weights are initialized within bound [-1, 1]. In the forward propagation course, the state of neurons in every layer can only affect the next connection layer. There are not couplings between the neurons in the same layer. If the output layer doesn't gain the expected output, then the learning course inverses to back propagation process. As a generalization of the least means squares algorithm, the back propagation algorithm uses a gradient research technique to minimize a cost function equal to the mean square difference of the desired and the actually net output. The weights and thresholds can be modified, and they will reach the proper value by adjusting parameters again and again. When the algorithm reaches the expected errors, the learning course is finished. At the same time, what are output are the final weights and thresholds for sample pattern set in the neural network correspondingly. The flow chart of BP algorithm [3] is given in Fig.1.

## 2.2 Neural Network Ensemble

In this study, multiple BP neural networks are used to build a NNE. Fig.2 is the architecture of NNE. NNE concerns two key problems [4, 5]. One is how to create individual neural networks; the other is how to assemble their outputs as NNE's output.

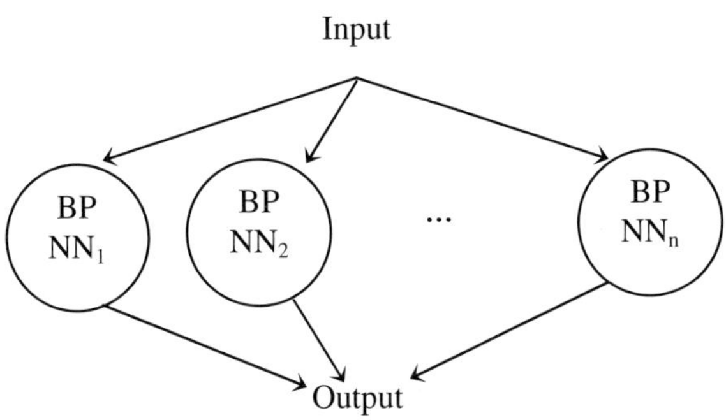


**Fig. 2.** Architecture of NNE

### 2.2.1 Individual Neural Network Creation

Some means have been put forward to create individual neural network, among which Boosting and Bagging are two important techniques [4, 5]. In Boosting, the latter neural network's training set is determined by the former neural network's output, and the samples not correctly learned by the former one should be added to the latter one's training set at a high probability. Therefore, the latter one can learn form the samples better than the former one. However, in Bagging, each NN's training set is determined by bootstrap sampling from the original training set. The main differences between Bagging and Boosting are as follows [4, 5]. In Bagging, neural networks' training sets are determined by bootstrap sampling, which makes neural networks independent of each other so that they can be created in parallel. However, in Boosting, neural networks' training sets aren't independent of but depend on each other, which makes neural networks created in sequence.

It is also proved that in order to build a strong NNE, the individual neural networks should be with high accuracy as well as high diversity. Same or similar individual neural networks are of no help for enhancing the generalization.

### 2.2.2 Output Ensemble Approaches

When NNE is applied to regression, its output can be attained by simple average or weighted average. In general, simple average is applied to bagging; while weighted average is applied to boosting [4, 5].

# 3 Reduce Input Nodes with Improved PCA (IPCA)

## 3.1 The Theory and Method of PCA

Economic forecasting is a very complicated problem with many influential factors. In BP neural network, if every factor is analyzed and evaluated, on one hand the handling process would be complicated because of abundance data, on the other hand the relations between different factors would be separated. In order to reduce the input variables while remain the most information, the original data can be pre-handled with the principal component analysis (PCA) method.

Assume that there are p primary factors that influence the economic forecasting, which are denoted as $x_1$, $x_2$,..., $x_p$. The original data $x_{ij}$ (i=1,2,..., n; j=1,2,..., p) is the value of indicator j in year i.

Firstly the data is standardized [6]:

$$x_{ij}' = \frac{x_{ij} - \bar{x}_j}{\sqrt{\mathrm{var}(x_j)}}, i = 1,2,\cdots,n; j = 1,2,\cdots,p \tag{1}$$

$$\bar{x}_j = \frac{1}{n}\sum_{i=1}^{n} x_{ij} \tag{2}$$

$$\mathrm{var}(x_j) = \frac{1}{n-1}\sum_{i=1}^{n}(x_{ij} - \bar{x}_j)^2 \tag{3}$$

For convenient the standardized data is still denoted as $x_{ij}$. The correlation coefficients matrix R of standardized data can be written as:

$$R = \begin{bmatrix} r_{11} & r_{12} & \cdots & r_{1p} \\ r_{21} & r_{22} & \cdots & r_{2p} \\ \cdots & \cdots & \cdots & \cdots \\ r_{p1} & r_{p2} & \cdots & r_{pp} \end{bmatrix},$$

where $r_{ij}$ is correlation coefficient of standardized data [6]:

$$r_{ij} = \frac{1}{n-1}\sum_{t=1}^{n} x_{ti} x_{tj}, i, j = 1,2,\cdots,p \tag{4}$$

Let $|R-\lambda I|=0$. We can solve the eigenvalue of the correlation coefficient matrix: $\lambda_1 \geq \lambda_2 \geq \ldots \geq \lambda_p$, and the corresponding eigenvectors are: $u_1$, $u_2$, …, $u_p$. We introduce new variables:

$$\begin{cases} F_{i1} = u_1' x_i = u_{11}x_{i1} + u_{12}x_{i2} + \cdots + u_{1p}x_{ip} \\ F_{i2} = u_2' x_i = u_{21}x_{i1} + u_{22}x_{i2} + \cdots + u_{2p}x_{ip} \\ \cdots \\ F_{ip} = u_p' x_i = u_{p1}x_{i1} + u_{p2}x_{i2} + \cdots + u_{pp}x_{ip} \end{cases},$$

where $F_{i1}, F_{i2}, \cdots, F_{ip}$ are respectively the first principal factor, the second principal factor,…, and the pth principal factor.

$$\alpha_k = \lambda_k / \sum_{i=1}^{p} \lambda_i, k = 1,2,\cdots,p \tag{5}$$

$$\beta = \sum_{k=1}^{m} \lambda_k / \sum_{k=1}^{p} \lambda_k \tag{6}$$

where $\alpha_k$ is the percentage of the eigenvalue's variance of $F_{ik}$; β is the accumulated percentage of the eigenvalue's variances of the first m principal factors. The accumulated percentage indicates the ratio of the of the first m principal factors over all the original information, which is set more than a certain value in applications, generally 85%.

### 3.2 The Improved PCA (IPCA)

In general, there are two parts of information in the original data. One is the different information of the variances of the indexes, which is reflected by the mean squared error; the other is the correlative information of the influences of the indexes, which is reflected by the correlation coefficient matrix. The above-mentioned PCA method makes the variances of the indexes be equal to 1, that is, $r_{ij}$ (i=j) is equal to 1, which can eliminate the first part of information and only include the second part of information of the original data. Therefore, it is necessary to improve PCA. In this paper, we adopt mean standardization [7] to improve PCA (IPCA), that means:

$$x'_{ij} = \frac{x_{ij}}{\bar{x}_j}, i = 1,2,\cdots,n; j = 1,2,\cdots,p \tag{7}$$

According the formula (4), $r_{ij}$ (i=j) can be described as:

$$r_{ij} = \frac{\mathrm{var}(x_j)}{\bar{x}_j^2}, i = j \tag{8}$$

The formula (8) can reflect the different information of the variances of the indexes. By using mean standardization, the correlation coefficient matrix can not only eliminate the influences of index dimensions, but also include two parts of information of the original data. Thus, IPCA can not only reduce input nodes, but also remain most original information, which shows that IPCA is an efficient simplification method.

## 4 NNE for Economic Forecasting

In this paper, based on Bagging, NNE is applied to forecast the increasing rates of Gross Domestic Product (GDP) of Jiangmen, Guangdong to illustrate its validity and feasibility, which is realized by MATLAB 7.01.

### 4.1 Economic Forecasting Index System

This paper selects 8 indexes of Jiangmen economic data from 1982 to 2004, which are as follows: $x_1$: GDP of Jiangmen; $x_2$: GDP of China; $x_3$: GDP of Guangdong; $x_4$: Government expenditures; $x_5$: Total exports; $x_6$: Total investment in fixed assets; $x_7$: Total sales of consumer goods; $x_8$: Foreign capital actually utilized.

### 4.2 Data Pretreating

While carrying on the importation of the input variables, this paper uses the increasing rate of the index in order to get rid of the long-term growth trend influence, price fluctuation influence and the difference of index scale. That means:

$$x_i(t)' = \frac{x_i(t)/w_i(t)}{x_i(t-1)/w_i(t-1)} - 1, i = 1,2,\cdots,8; t = 1982,1983,\cdots,2004 \quad (9)$$

where $x_i(t)'$ : the increasing rate of indicator i in t year; $x_i(t)$ : the real value of indicator i in t year; $w_i(t)$ : the price index of indicator in t year; $w_i(t-1)$ : the price index of indicator in t -1 year. The pretreated results are listed in Table 1. In addition, for convenience, let $x_i(t)'$ still be denoted as $x_i(t)$ .

**Table 1.** The pretreated data

| Year | $x_1$ | $x_2$ | $x_3$ | $x_4$ |
|---|---|---|---|---|
| 1983 | 0.099495 | 0.099803 | 0.074073 | 0.104675 |
| 1984 | 0.146769 | 0.131440 | 0.219648 | -0.076540 |
| 1985 | 0.009801 | 0.078192 | 0.086867 | 0.089785 |
| 1986 | 0.153217 | 0.088195 | 0.105362 | 0.811057 |
| 1987 | 0.152476 | 0.157451 | 0.144644 | -0.158030 |
| 1988 | -0.035950 | -0.026440 | 0.043524 | 0.043905 |
| 1989 | -0.062720 | -0.080660 | -0.028710 | -0.078170 |
| 1990 | 0.189334 | 0.150162 | 0.169529 | 0.107578 |
| 1991 | 0.170995 | 0.115266 | 0.203594 | 0.222691 |
| 1992 | 0.243340 | 0.151180 | 0.217246 | 0.085743 |
| 1993 | 0.197495 | 0.112793 | 0.190280 | 0.426691 |
| 1994 | 0.152686 | 0.169033 | 0.102276 | 0.050622 |
| 1995 | 0.128349 | 0.193922 | 0.149918 | 0.004885 |
| 1996 | 0.085521 | 0.126953 | 0.091106 | 0.023269 |
| 1997 | 0.066950 | 0.102500 | 0.122159 | 0.121762 |
| 1998 | 0.071718 | 0.083840 | 0.102344 | 0.046158 |
| 1999 | 0.116112 | 0.077799 | 0.116887 | 0.121276 |
| 2000 | 0.119411 | 0.106170 | 0.158912 | 0.149983 |
| 2001 | 0.107214 | 0.096049 | 0.125635 | 0.147170 |
| 2002 | 0.102894 | 0.095870 | 0.125677 | 0.190504 |
| 2003 | 0.103979 | 0.137328 | 0.149779 | 0.133411 |
| 2004 | 0.107342 | 0.134680 | 0.156675 | 0.115258 |

**Table 1.** *(continued)*

| Year | $x_5$ | $x_6$ | $x_7$ | $x_8$ |
|---|---|---|---|---|
| 1983 | 0.206206 | 0.038243 | -0.961757 | 0.048000 |
| 1984 | 0.102055 | 0.318498 | -0.681502 | -0.124930 |
| 1985 | -0.240760 | 0.333528 | -0.666472 | 0.266601 |
| 1986 | 1.224812 | 0.188219 | -0.811781 | 1.627509 |
| 1987 | -0.024000 | 0.161016 | -0.838984 | 0.462541 |
| 1988 | -0.098700 | 0.046980 | -0.953020 | 0.024446 |
| 1989 | -0.081300 | -0.678790 | -1.678793 | -0.226630 |
| 1990 | 0.696454 | 0.388348 | -0.611652 | 0.072598 |
| 1991 | 0.527487 | 0.345614 | -0.654386 | 0.790504 |
| 1992 | 0.264442 | 0.989359 | -0.010641 | 0.381291 |
| 1993 | 0.296491 | 0.473133 | -0.526867 | 0.703069 |
| 1994 | 0.871993 | -0.023130 | -1.023134 | 0.954271 |
| 1995 | 0.009587 | 0.029388 | -0.970612 | 0.032446 |
| 1996 | -0.040310 | -0.188470 | -1.188471 | -0.037010 |
| 1997 | 0.168984 | -0.109910 | -1.109909 | -0.218230 |
| 1998 | 0.123709 | 0.090174 | -0.909826 | 0.180221 |
| 1999 | -0.147680 | 0.223918 | -0.776082 | 0.214129 |
| 2000 | 0.215448 | 0.146090 | -0.853910 | 0.178396 |
| 2001 | -0.120650 | 0.150910 | -0.849090 | 0.083232 |
| 2002 | 0.178030 | 0.143983 | -0.856017 | -0.090350 |
| 2003 | 0.493333 | 0.174315 | -0.825685 | 0.395680 |
| 2004 | 0.347232 | 0.191299 | -0.808701 | 0.145358 |

**Table 2.** Eigenvalue,eigenvector and accumulated percentage

| Variable | 1 | 2 | 3 | 4 |
|---|---|---|---|---|
| Eigenvalue | 13.8378 | 3.4732 | 1.8657 | 0.9303 |
| Accumulated percentage | 0.6616 | 0.8277 | 0.9169 | 0.9614 |
| Eigenvector | 0.29235 | 0.16799 | 0.27616 | 0.04344 |
| | 0.25417 | 0.16016 | 0.42074 | 0.06263 |
| | 0.25060 | 0.18928 | 0.34873 | -0.10070 |
| | 0.42290 | -0.34568 | -0.25756 | -0.73452 |
| | 0.43409 | -0.36429 | 0.02864 | 0.57409 |
| | 0.43159 | 0.74503 | -0.38362 | 0.00456 |
| | 0.16272 | -0.07996 | 0.59391 | -0.26087 |
| | 0.45508 | -0.31087 | -0.24096 | 0.21650 |

The above-mentioned IPCA method has been applied for dimension reduction, and the results are obtained in Table 2.Three principal factors denoted as $F_1$, $F_2$ and $F_3$ can be extracted from the data of 8 indexes above, which reflect the Jiangmen economic states from 1983 to 2004. The accumulative total variance achieves 91.69%, so to a certain extent, these three factors can be used to describe the main development states

**Table 2.** (*continued*)

| Variable | 5 | 6 | 7 | 8 |
|---|---|---|---|---|
| Eigenvalue | 0.6109 | 0.1231 | 0.0496 | 0.0244 |
| Accumulated percentage | 0.9906 | 0.9965 | 0.9988 | 1 |
| Eigenvector | 0.00831 | -0.35633 | 0.73447 | -0.37640 |
| | -0.05465 | -0.58373 | -0.61686 | -0.06746 |
| | 0.00403 | 0.08415 | 0.20729 | 0.84826 |
| | 0.26087 | -0.16296 | -0.03401 | -0.00588 |
| | 0.56098 | 0.17559 | -0.05404 | 0.00254 |
| | 0.06846 | 0.26787 | -0.13532 | -0.12933 |
| | -0.14820 | 0.62919 | -0.12046 | -0.33763 |
| | -0.76650 | 0.01352 | 0.01311 | 0.05878 |

**Table 3.** The first 3 principal factors

| Year | $F_1$ | $F_2$ | $F_3$ | $x_1$ |
|---|---|---|---|---|
| 1983 | 0.08865 | 0.02589 | -0.5232 | 0.146769 |
| 1984 | 0.11301 | 0.40718 | -0.3018 | 0.009801 |
| 1985 | 0.13479 | 0.30618 | -0.5521 | 0.153217 |
| 1986 | 1.65808 | -0.96760 | -1.0042 | 0.152476 |
| 1987 | 0.18706 | 0.18484 | -0.4727 | -0.035950 |
| 1988 | -0.15430 | 0.12235 | -0.6099 | -0.062720 |
| 1989 | -0.78370 | -0.27330 | -0.7255 | 0.189334 |
| 1990 | 0.58494 | 0.11272 | -0.3629 | 0.170995 |
| 1991 | 0.85589 | -0.11930 | -0.5872 | 0.243340 |
| 1992 | 0.91384 | 0.59966 | -0.2857 | 0.197495 |
| 1993 | 0.88166 | 0.00783 | -0.5969 | 0.152686 |
| 1994 | 0.77097 | -0.4952 | -0.6678 | 0.128349 |
| 1995 | 0.00012 | 0.16523 | -0.4272 | 0.085521 |
| 1996 | -0.21913 | 0.02471 | -0.5230 | 0.066950 |
| 1997 | -0.12627 | 0.02184 | -0.4867 | 0.071718 |
| 1998 | 0.11403 | 0.06773 | -0.5360 | 0.116112 |
| 1999 | 0.13800 | 0.22828 | -0.5283 | 0.119411 |
| 2000 | 0.26396 | 0.05847 | -0.5056 | 0.107214 |
| 2001 | 0.06195 | 0.20470 | -0.5098 | 0.102894 |
| 2002 | 0.12552 | 0.12953 | -0.4733 | 0.103979 |
| 2003 | 0.49435 | -0.08510 | -0.5341 | 0.107342 |
| 2004 | 0.32147 | 0.06492 | -0.4675 | |

of Jiangmen economic in past years. $F_i$ (i=1, 2, 3) can be listed in Table 3, which can be described as the 3 input neural cells of the network.

This paper takes the increasing rate of GDP as the object of economic forecasting and uses the former year's economic data to forecast the latter year's increasing rate of GDP. Therefore, economic forecasting model can be described as:

$$x_1(t) = f(F_1(t-1), F_2(t-1), F_3(t-1)) ,$$

where $f(\cdot)$ is the projection function.

### 4.3 Creating Training and Test Samples

We can define S as the training set made up of the data from1983 to 1999 corresponding to the increasing rates of GDP from 1984-2000 in Table 3, that is to say, the number of the training samples is 17. We can also define the data from 2000 to 2003 corresponding to the increasing rates of GDP from 2001 to 2004 as the test samples and use the data in 2004 to forecast the increasing rate of GDP in 2005.

### 4.4 Creating and Training Individual Neural Networks

Matlab 7.01 neural network toolbox can be used to create and train the individual neural networks of economic forecasting. In this thesis, we use tansig function as the hidden layer's threshold function, purelin as output layer's threshold function and trainlm as BP neural network's training function.

Five neural networks $NN_i$ (i=1, 2,..., 5) are trained Bagging adopted until they all satisfy the request of error. Five training samples, namely $S_i$ (i=1, 2,..., 5), are bootstrap sampling from S at random, and $\|S_i\| \geq 13, i = 1,2,\cdots,5$ . $S_i$ trains $NN_i$. The five neural networks are respective 3-3-1,3-4-1,3-5-1,3-6-1 and 3-7-1 BP NNs with training epochs of 5000, learning rate of 0.001, target error of 0.000001 and initial weights of the random values among [-1,1]. The training effects are listed in Table 4. From the training results, all the individual neural networks have been trained well.

**Table 4.** The training results of $NN_i$ and NNE

| Year | $NN_1$ | $NN_2$ | $NN_3$ | $NN_4$ | $NN_5$ | NNE |
|---|---|---|---|---|---|---|
| 1984 | 0.14023 | 0.14586 | 0.14845 | 0.14533 | 0.14531 | 0.14504 |
| 1985 | 0.00980 | 0.01036 | 0.01062 | 0.00988 | 0.00963 | 0.01006 |
| 1986 | 0.17499 | 0.15294 | 0.15275 | 0.15383 | 0.15443 | 0.15779 |
| 1987 | 0.15448 | 0.15255 | 0.15215 | 0.15308 | 0.15193 | 0.15284 |
| 1988 | 0.01159 | -0.03527 | -0.03595 | -0.03573 | -0.03544 | -0.02616 |
| 1989 | -0.06045 | -0.06260 | -0.06257 | -0.06172 | -0.06301 | -0.06207 |
| 1990 | 0.17322 | 0.18931 | 0.18918 | 0.18956 | 0.18908 | 0.18607 |
| 1991 | 0.17099 | 0.17104 | 0.17091 | 0.17104 | 0.17093 | 0.17098 |
| 1992 | 0.22314 | 0.24541 | 0.24314 | 0.24295 | 0.24358 | 0.24368 |
| 1993 | 0.17531 | 0.19709 | 0.19717 | 0.19770 | 0.19752 | 0.19295 |
| 1994 | 0.15311 | 0.15177 | 0.15301 | 0.15273 | 0.15269 | 0.15266 |
| 1995 | 0.12592 | 0.12738 | 0.12823 | 0.12895 | 0.12826 | 0.12775 |
| 1996 | 0.82580 | 0.08346 | 0.08416 | 0.08586 | 0.08556 | 0.07296 |
| 1997 | 0.07666 | 0.06619 | 0.06623 | 0.06639 | 0.06707 | 0.06851 |
| 1998 | 0.10521 | 0.07366 | 0.07284 | 0.07389 | 0.07149 | 0.08342 |
| 1999 | 0.08588 | 0.11628 | 0.11437 | 0.11816 | 0.11803 | 0.11054 |
| 2000 | 0.10912 | 0.11989 | 0.12066 | 0.11863 | 0.11702 | 0.11912 |

### 4.5 Constituting NNE and Combining Outputs

After having been trained, the five neural networks $NN_i$ (i=1, 2,…, 5) constitutes the NNE, and simple average is adopted to combine NNE's final result. From Table 4, we can find that the training results of NNE are satisfactory. Then, the test samples are introduced into the NNE to checkout its generalization. In addition, we have input the 3 principal factors in 2004 to forecast the increasing rate of GDP in 2005. The test results are given in Table 5.

### 4.6 Results and Discussions

As are shown in the Table 5, all the test results are close to their real values, even though the number of the training samples is only 17. From the results, we can also find that the forecasting ability of NNE is much higher than that of simplex neural network on the whole, and all the errors are less than 7%, with maximal error of 6.33% and minimal error of -0.55%. Therefore, NNE's training and test results are so satisfactory that it can be used for economic forecasting. According to the forecasting result, Jiangmen's increasing rate of GDP in 2005 is much closed to 11%. So in conclusion, using neural network is feasible and effective for economic forecasting.

**Table 5.** The test results with NNE

| Year | | 2001 | 2002 | 2003 | 2004 | 2005 |
|---|---|---|---|---|---|---|
| $x_1$(Real value) | | 0.107214 | 0.102894 | 0.103979 | 0.107342 | |
| $NN_1$ | Predicted value | 0.08588 | 0.08753 | 0.07472 | 0.08594 | 0.09478 |
| | Error (%) | -19.90 | -14.93 | -28.14 | -19.94 | |
| $NN_2$ | Predicted value | 0.12323 | 0.12709 | 0.09892 | 0.09738 | 0.11235 |
| | Error (%) | 14.94 | 23.52 | -4.87 | -0. 93 | |
| $NN_3$ | Predicted value | 0.11037 | 0.11717 | 0.12047 | 0.11323 | 0.12115 |
| | Error (%) | 2.94 | 13.87 | 15.86 | 5.49 | |
| $NN_4$ | Predicted value | 0.11616 | 0.0977 | 0.09865 | 0.12897 | 0.10708 |
| | Error (%) | 8.34 | -5.05 | -5.13 | 20.15 | |
| $NN_5$ | Predicted value | 0.11203 | 0.11757 | 0.12202 | 0.10824 | 0.11194 |
| | Error (%) | 4.49 | 14.26 | 17.35 | 0.84 | |
| NNE | Predicted value | 0.109534 | 0.109412 | 0.102956 | 0.106752 | 0.10946 |
| | Error (%) | 2.16 | 6.33 | -0.98 | -0.55 | |

## 5 Conclusions

All the above is an attempt to applying neural network ensemble to economic forecasting. The model uses the method combing five BP neural networks with improved

PCA, and can achieve more exact forecasting results based on the original data with its excellent learning ability and generalization than simplex neural network on the whole. Neural network ensemble can provide a new and valid way for economic forecasting under a few samples. On the whole, the research into the neural network ensemble in practical economic forecasting is in prospect, particularly under competitive market economic environment at present.

## References

1. Xiao, J.H.: Intelligent Forecasting for the Regional Economic. Mathematics in Economics, Vol.22, No.1 (2005) 57-63
2. Hansen, L.K., Salamon, P.: Neural Network Ensembles. IEEE Trans Pattern Analysis and Machine Intelligence, Vol.12, No.10 (1990) 993-1001
3. Ding, L.Q., Yang, J.Q., Long, C.Y.: A Forecast Method of Generator's Load Based on BP Artificial Neural Networks. Proceedings of 2005 International Conference on Management & Engineering (12th), Harbin (2005) 2319-2322
4. Zhou, Z.H., Chen, S.F.: Neural Network Ensemble. Chinese J.Computers, Vol.25, No.1 (2002) 1-8
5. Shen, X.H., Zhou, Z.H., Wu, J.X., Chen, Z.Q.: Survey of Boosting and Bagging. Computer Engineering and Application, No.12 (2000) 31-32
6. Cui, Y.Q., Li, Z.B.: Application of an Improved Artificial Neural Network in Battlefield Ammunition Consumption Prediction. Proceedings of 2005 International Conference on Management & Engineering (12th) Harbin (2005) 182-186
7. Cheng, Q.Y., Wang, Y.Y., Chen, W.G.: Modified Principal Component Analysis Based on Short-Term Load Forecasting. Power System Technology, Vol.29, No.3 (2005) 64-67

# Improving the Combination Module with a Neural Network

Carlos Hernández-Espinosa, Joaquín Torres-Sospedra, and Mercedes Fernández-Redondo

Departamento de Ingenieria y Ciencia de los Computadores, Universitat Jaume I, Avda. Sos Baynat s/n, C.P. 12071, Castellon, Spain
{ espinosa , jtorres , redondo}@icc.uji.es

**Abstract.** In this paper we propose two versions of *Stacked Generalization* as the combination module of an ensemble of neural networks. The first version only uses the information provided by expert networks. The second one uses the information provided by experts and the input data of the pattern that is being classified. Finally, we have performed a comparison among 6 classical combination methods and the two versions of *Stacked Generalization* in order to get the best method. The results show that the methods based on *Stacked Generalization* are better than classical combination methods.

## 1 Introduction

Probably, the most important property of a neural network is the generalization capability. The ability to correctly respond to inputs which were not used in the training set.

It is clear from the bibliography that the use of an ensemble of neural increases the generalization capability, [1],[2], for the case of Multilayer Feedforward and other classifiers.

The two key factors to design an ensemble are how to train the individual networks and how to combine the different outputs to give a single output.

Among the methods of training the individual networks there are an important number of alternatives. Our research group has performed a comparison among methods of building ensembles detailed in [3] and [4]. These papers show that the *Simple ensemble* method provides a reasonable performance with a lower computational cost.

Moreover, our research group has performed another comparison among combination methods of ensembles in paper [5], which shows that the *Output Average* is the simpler method but it is one of the best combination methods.

In this paper, we present some results on two versions of *Stacked Generalization* and we compare them with six *classic* combination methods. We have built ensembles of 3, 9, 20 and 40 networks with *Simple Ensemble* using six databases from the *UCI repository* to test the performance of the combination methods.

The methods are described in 2. The results we have obtained with these six databases are in subsection 3.2. We have also calculated general measurements of the combination methods to compare them, these results appear in subsetion 3.3.

D.-S. Huang, K. Li, and G.W. Irwin (Eds.): ICIC 2006, LNCS 4113, pp. 146–155, 2006.

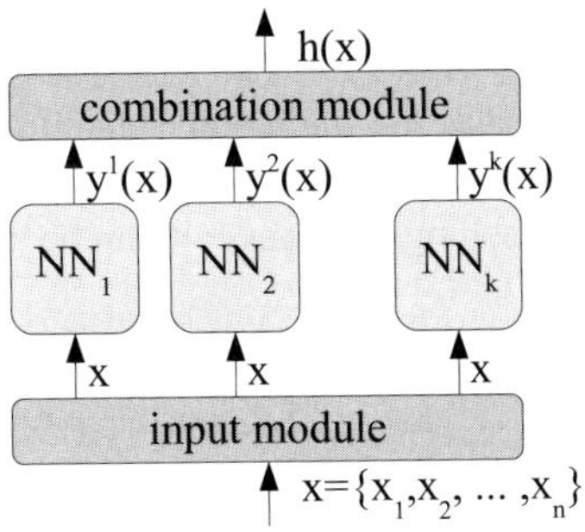


**Fig. 1.** Basic ensemble diagram

## 2 Theory

In this section, first we briefly review the methods of combination that we have used in our experiments for comparison with the methods based on *Stacked Generalization*. Finally, we introduce the two methods we have proposed in subsections 2.7 and 2.8.

### 2.1 Output Average

This approach simply averages the individual classifier outputs across the different classifiers. The output yielding the maximum of the averaged values is chosen as the correct class.

### 2.2 Majority Vote

Each classifier provides a vote to a class, given by its highest output. The correct class is the one most often voted by the classifiers.

### 2.3 Winner Takes All

In this method, the class with overall maximum output across all classifier and outputs is selected as the correct class.

### 2.4 Borda Count

For any class $c$, the Borda count is the sum of the number of classes ranked below $c$ by each classifier. The Borda count for class $class$ is:

$$Borda_{class}(x) = \sum_{net=1}^{k} Borda_{class}^{net}(x). \tag{1}$$

Where $Borda_{class}^{net}(x)$ is the number of classes ranked below the class $class$ by the $net$-th classifier. The final hipothesys is given by the class yielding the highest Borda count.

$$h(x) = \arg \max_{class=1,\dots,q} B_{class}(x). \tag{2}$$

### 2.5 Bayesian Combination

This combination method is based on the belief value, the class with maximum belief value is selected as the correct class. According to [6] this value is the conditional probability that the pattern $x$ belongs to class $i$, it can be approximated by:

$$Belief_{class}(x) = \frac{\prod_{net=1}^{k} p(x \in class|h(y^{net}) = j)}{\sum_{i=1}^{q} \prod_{net=1}^{k} p(x \in i|h(y^{net}) = j)}. \quad (3)$$

$$h(x) = \arg \max_{class=1,\ldots,q} Belief_{class}(x). \quad (4)$$

Where the conditional probability that sample x actually belongs to class $i$, given that classifier $k$ assign it to class $j$ can be estimated from the values of the confusion matrix [7].

$$p(x \in i|class(y^{net}) = j) = \frac{c_{i,j}^{net}}{\sum_{m=1}^{q} c_{m,j}^{net}}. \quad (5)$$

### 2.6 Dinamically Averaged Networks

It is proposed in reference [8]. It is a weighted output average which introduces weights to the outputs of the different networks prior to averaging. The weights values are derived from the network output of the pattern we are classifying. We allow the weights to be proportional to the certainties of the respective network output.

$$\overline{y}_{class}(x) = \sum_{net=1}^{k} w_{class}^{net} \cdot y_{class}^{net}(x). \quad (6)$$

Where the weights are calculated by:

$$w_{class}^{net}(x) = \frac{C_{class}^{net}(x)}{\sum_{i=1}^{k} C_{class}^{k}(x)}. \quad (7)$$

$$C_{class}^{net}(x) = \begin{cases} y_{class}^{net}(x) & \text{if } y_{class}^{net}(x) \geq 0.5 \\ 1 - y_{class}^{net}(x) & \text{otherwise} \\ . \end{cases} \quad (8)$$

The output yielding the maximum of the averaged values is chosen as the correct class.

$$h(x) = \arg \max_{class=1,\ldots,q} \overline{y}_{class}(x). \quad (9)$$

### 2.7 Stacked Generalization

*Stacked Generalization* was introduced by Wolpert [9]. The combination method we propose in this paper is based on the idea of *Stacked Generalization* and it consist on training a neural network to combine the output vectors provided by the networks of the ensemble. The neural network used for combination is called *Combination network*, the networks of the ensemble are also known as *expert networks*. See Figure 2.

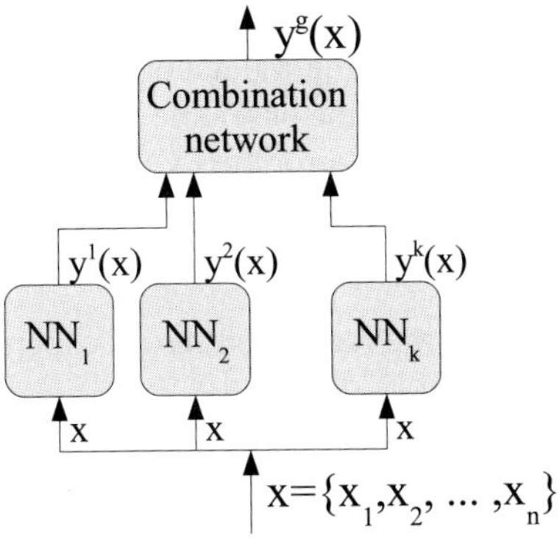


**Fig. 2.** Stacked Generalization diagram

### 2.8 Stacked Generalization Plus

The use of the original pattern input vector is the difference between *Stacked Generalization* and *Stacked Generalization Plus*. The outputs of the expert networks on patterns from the training set and the original pattern input vector are used to train the combination network. In Figure 3 we can see a diagram of the *Staked Generalization Plus*.

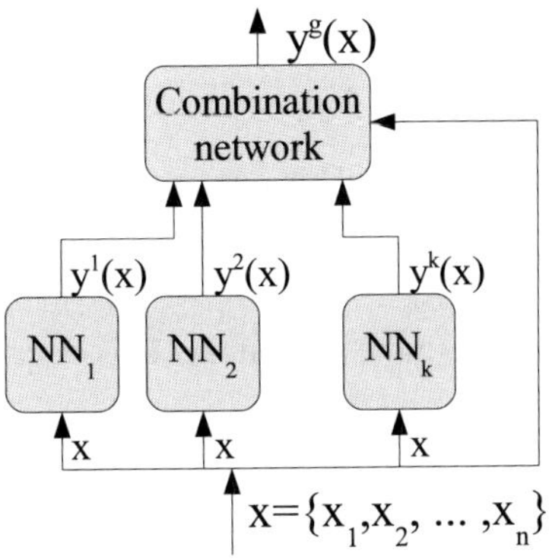


**Fig. 3.** Stacked Generalization Plus diagram

## 3 Experimental Testing

In this section we describe the experimental setup and the datasets we have used in our experiments. Finally, we show and compare the results we have obtained with the combination methods on the different datasets.

To test the performance of the combination methods we have proposed in this paper, we have used ensembles of 3, 9, 20 and 40 MF networks previously trained with *Simple ensemble* on six different classification problems from the *UCI repository of machine learning databases* [10]. In addition, we repeated ten times the whole learning process, using different partitions of data in training, validation and test sets. With this procedure we can obtain a mean performance of the ensemble for each database and an error in the performance calculated by standard error theory.

### 3.1 Datasets

The databases from the *UCI* that we have used in our experiments are the following ones:

**Arrhythmia Database** (aritm)
The aim is to distinguish between the presence and absence of cardiac arrhythmia and to classify it in one of the 16 groups. This dataset contains 443 instances, 277 attributes and 3 classes.

**Glass Identification Database** (glas)
The aim of the dataset is to determinate if the glass analysed was a type of 'float' glass or not for Forensic Science. This dataset contains 2311 instances, 34 attributes and 2 classes.

**Ionosphere Database** (ionos)
Classification of radar returns from the ionosphere. This dataset contains 351 instances, 34 attributes and 2 classes.

**The Monk's Problem 1** (mok1)
Artificial problem with binary inputs. This dataset contains 432 instances, 6 attributes and 2 classes.

**The Monk's Problem 2** (mok2)
Artificial problem with binary inputs. This dataset contains 432 instances, 6 attributes and 2 classes.

**Vowel Database** (vowel)
There is no description about it in the repository. This dataset contains 990 instances, 11 attributes and 11 classes.

Table 1 shows the training parameters (Number of hidden units, Number of iterations, Step and Momentum) of the expert networks and the performance of a single network on each database.

Table 2 shows the training parameters (Number of hidden units, Number of iterations, Step and Momentum) we have used to train the combination networks with *Stacked Generalization* and with *Stacked Generalization Plus*.

### 3.2 Results

In this subsection we present the experimental results. Table 3 shows the results we have obtained with ensembles of 3 networks. Tables 4, 5 and 6 show the results of ensembles of 9, 20 and 40 networks respectively.

**Table 1.** MF training parameters

| Database | Nh | Ite | Step | Mom | Performance |
|---|---|---|---|---|---|
| **aritm** | 9 | 2500 | 0.1 | 0.05 | $75.6 \pm 0.7$ |
| **glas** | 3 | 4000 | 0.1 | 0.05 | $78.5 \pm 0.9$ |
| **ionos** | 8 | 5000 | 0.1 | 0.05 | $87.9 \pm 0.7$ |
| **mok1** | 6 | 3000 | 0.1 | 0.05 | $74.3 \pm 1.1$ |
| **mok2** | 20 | 7000 | 0.1 | 0.05 | $65.9 \pm 0.5$ |
| **vowel** | 15 | 4000 | 0.2 | 0.2 | $83.4 \pm 0.6$ |

**Table 2.** MF training parameters for the Combination Network

| | | **Stacked** | | | | **Stacked Plus** | | | |
|---|---|---|---|---|---|---|---|---|---|
| **DB** | **Nets** | **Mom** | **Step** | **Nh** | **Ite** | **Mom** | **Step** | **Nh** | **Ite** |
| Arrtimia | 3 | 0.01 | 0.05 | 3 | 10000 | 0.01 | 0.05 | 4 | 2500 |
| | 9 | 0.01 | 0.05 | 20 | 500 | 0.01 | 0.05 | 6 | 1500 |
| | 20 | 0.01 | 0.05 | 1 | 100 | 0.01 | 0.05 | 17 | 1500 |
| | 40 | 0.01 | 0.05 | 5 | 100 | 0.01 | 0.05 | 5 | 1500 |
| Glass | 3 | 0.01 | 0.05 | 3 | 10000 | 0.01 | 0.05 | 5 | 10000 |
| | 9 | 0.01 | 0.05 | 3 | 10000 | 0.01 | 0.05 | 4 | 10000 |
| | 20 | 0.01 | 0.05 | 5 | 10000 | 0.01 | 0.05 | 15 | 10000 |
| | 40 | 0.01 | 0.05 | 5 | 10000 | 0.01 | 0.05 | 15 | 10000 |
| Ionos | 3 | 0.01 | 0.05 | 7 | 10000 | 0.01 | 0.05 | 1 | 10000 |
| | 9 | 0.01 | 0.05 | 1 | 10000 | 0.01 | 0.05 | 1 | 10000 |
| | 20 | 0.01 | 0.05 | 5 | 10000 | 0.01 | 0.05 | 4 | 10000 |
| | 40 | 0.01 | 0.05 | 5 | 10000 | 0.01 | 0.05 | 5 | 10000 |
| Monk1 | 3 | 0.01 | 0.05 | 1 | 10000 | 0.01 | 0.05 | 5 | 10000 |
| | 9 | 0.01 | 0.05 | 1 | 10000 | 0.01 | 0.05 | 1 | 10000 |
| | 20 | 0.01 | 0.05 | 1 | 10000 | 0.01 | 0.05 | 5 | 10000 |
| | 40 | 0.01 | 0.05 | 1 | 10000 | 0.01 | 0.05 | 5 | 10000 |
| Monk2 | 3 | 0.01 | 0.05 | 15 | 100 | 0.01 | 0.05 | 4 | 2500 |
| | 9 | 0.01 | 0.05 | 5 | 100 | 0.01 | 0.05 | 5 | 250 |
| | 20 | 0.01 | 0.05 | 5 | 250 | 0.01 | 0.05 | 4 | 10000 |
| | 40 | 0.01 | 0.05 | 25 | 250 | 0.01 | 0.05 | 4 | 10000 |
| Vowel | 3 | 0.01 | 0.05 | 19 | 10000 | 0.01 | 0.05 | 30 | 2500 |
| | 9 | 0.01 | 0.05 | 6 | 7500 | 0.01 | 0.05 | 13 | 5000 |
| | 20 | 0.01 | 0.05 | 20 | 500 | 0.01 | 0.05 | 10 | 2500 |
| | 40 | 0.01 | 0.05 | 10 | 5000 | 0.01 | 0.05 | 7 | 5000 |

### 3.3 Interpretations of Results

Comparing tables 3-6 we can see that both methods based on *Stacked Generalization* are more accurate than the classical methods.

We have calculated the increase of performance of *Stacked Generalization* and *Stacked Generalization Plus* with respect to *Output Average* to see more clearly if *Stacked* combination methods performs better. A positive value of the increase of performance means that the method performance is better on the dataset. There can also be negative values, which means that the performance of the method on the dataset is

**Table 3.** Results for the ensemble of three networks

| | aritm | glas | ionos | mok1 | mok2 | Vowel |
|---|---|---|---|---|---|---|
| **Average** | $73.5 \pm 1.1$ | $94 \pm 0.8$ | $91.1 \pm 1.1$ | $73.8 \pm 1.1$ | $94 \pm 0.7$ | $90.3 \pm 1.1$ |
| **Vote** | $73.1 \pm 1$ | $93.6 \pm 0.9$ | $91.3 \pm 1$ | $73.3 \pm 0.9$ | $93.2 \pm 0.8$ | $90.6 \pm 1.2$ |
| **WTA** | $73.6 \pm 1$ | $94 \pm 0.6$ | $91.1 \pm 1.1$ | $73.3 \pm 1.1$ | $93.8 \pm 0.6$ | $90.9 \pm 1.3$ |
| **Borda** | $73.1 \pm 1$ | $94.4 \pm 0.9$ | $91.3 \pm 1$ | $73.3 \pm 0.9$ | $94.2 \pm 0.7$ | $90.6 \pm 1.2$ |
| **Bayesian** | $73.6 \pm 0.9$ | $94.2 \pm 1$ | $91.4 \pm 1.1$ | $73.6 \pm 0.9$ | $92.2 \pm 0.9$ | $93.1 \pm 1.4$ |
| **DAN** | $73.2 \pm 1.1$ | $92.8 \pm 1.6$ | $90 \pm 1.2$ | $73.6 \pm 1$ | $92.8 \pm 1.1$ | $90 \pm 1.1$ |
| **Stacked** | $75.4 \pm 1.4$ | $95.2 \pm 0.9$ | $92 \pm 0.8$ | $75.1 \pm 1.2$ | $96 \pm 0.7$ | $92.9 \pm 1$ |
| **StackedPlus** | $74.4 \pm 1.4$ | $95.6 \pm 0.9$ | $92 \pm 0.9$ | $73.6 \pm 1.7$ | $95.6 \pm 0.8$ | $92.7 \pm 1$ |

**Table 4.** Results for the ensemble of nine networks

| | aritm | glas | ionos | mok1 | mok2 | Vowel |
|---|---|---|---|---|---|---|
| **Average** | $73.8 \pm 1.1$ | $94 \pm 0.7$ | $90.3 \pm 1.1$ | $98.8 \pm 0.8$ | $90.8 \pm 1.8$ | $88 \pm 0.9$ |
| **Vote** | $73.3 \pm 0.9$ | $93.2 \pm 0.8$ | $90.6 \pm 1.2$ | $98.3 \pm 0.9$ | $90.3 \pm 1.8$ | $88 \pm 0.9$ |
| **WTA** | $73.3 \pm 1.1$ | $93.8 \pm 0.6$ | $90.9 \pm 1.3$ | $99.5 \pm 0.5$ | $90 \pm 1.2$ | $88 \pm 0.9$ |
| **Borda** | $73.3 \pm 0.9$ | $94.2 \pm 0.7$ | $90.6 \pm 1.2$ | $98.3 \pm 0.9$ | $90.3 \pm 1.8$ | $88 \pm 0.9$ |
| **Bayesian** | $73.6 \pm 0.9$ | $92.2 \pm 0.9$ | $93.1 \pm 1.4$ | $99.8 \pm 0.3$ | $89.6 \pm 1.7$ | $88 \pm 0.9$ |
| **DAN** | $73.6 \pm 1$ | $92.8 \pm 1.1$ | $90 \pm 1.1$ | $98.8 \pm 0.9$ | $86.8 \pm 2.8$ | $88 \pm 0.9$ |
| **Stacked** | $75.1 \pm 1.2$ | $96 \pm 0.7$ | $92.9 \pm 1$ | $99.8 \pm 0.3$ | $92.1 \pm 1.2$ | $88 \pm 0.9$ |
| **Stacked Plus** | $73.6 \pm 1.7$ | $95.6 \pm 0.8$ | $92.7 \pm 1$ | $100 \pm 0$ | $91.9 \pm 1.3$ | $92.3 \pm 0.6$ |

**Table 5.** Results for the ensemble of twenty networks

| | aritm | glas | ionos | mok1 | mok2 | Vowel |
|---|---|---|---|---|---|---|
| **Average** | $73.8 \pm 1$ | $94 \pm 0.7$ | $90.4 \pm 1$ | $98.3 \pm 0.9$ | $91.1 \pm 1.1$ | $91.4 \pm 0.8$ |
| **Vote** | $73.3 \pm 1$ | $93.4 \pm 0.9$ | $90 \pm 1.2$ | $98.1 \pm 1$ | $90.4 \pm 1.8$ | $90.6 \pm 0.6$ |
| **WTA** | $73.1 \pm 1.2$ | $94.4 \pm 0.7$ | $91.3 \pm 1.1$ | $100 \pm 0$ | $90 \pm 1.1$ | $89.7 \pm 0.7$ |
| **Borda** | $73.3 \pm 1$ | $94.4 \pm 0.8$ | $90 \pm 1.2$ | $98.1 \pm 1$ | $90.4 \pm 1.8$ | $88 \pm 0.9$ |
| **Bayesian** | $73.8 \pm 1$ | $90.6 \pm 0.9$ | $93.1 \pm 1.4$ | $100 \pm 0$ | $89.9 \pm 1.6$ | $74.9 \pm 1$ |
| **DAN** | $72.8 \pm 1.2$ | $94.2 \pm 1.2$ | $89.6 \pm 1.1$ | $97.6 \pm 1$ | $86.6 \pm 2.1$ | $85.3 \pm 1.1$ |
| **Stacked** | $73.8 \pm 1.3$ | $96.6 \pm 0.8$ | $92.7 \pm 1.1$ | $100 \pm 0$ | $91.5 \pm 1.1$ | $93.3 \pm 0.6$ |
| **Stacked Plus** | $74.7 \pm 1.1$ | $96.6 \pm 0.8$ | $92.9 \pm 1.2$ | $100 \pm 0$ | $91.5 \pm 1.1$ | $93.3 \pm 0.7$ |

**Table 6.** Results for the ensemble of forty networks

| | aritm | glas | ionos | mok1 | mok2 | Vowel |
|---|---|---|---|---|---|---|
| **Average** | $73.8 \pm 1.1$ | $94.2 \pm 0.6$ | $90.3 \pm 1$ | $98.3 \pm 0.9$ | $91.1 \pm 1.2$ | $92.2 \pm 0.7$ |
| **Vote** | $73.5 \pm 1$ | $94 \pm 0.8$ | $90.1 \pm 1.2$ | $98.3 \pm 0.9$ | $91 \pm 1.6$ | $90.5 \pm 0.7$ |
| **WTA** | $73.1 \pm 1.2$ | $93.8 \pm 0.9$ | $91.6 \pm 1.1$ | $99.6 \pm 0.4$ | $90 \pm 1.6$ | $89.5 \pm 0.7$ |
| **Borda** | $73.5 \pm 1$ | $94.4 \pm 0.8$ | $90.1 \pm 1.2$ | $98.3 \pm 0.9$ | $91 \pm 1.6$ | $88.7 \pm 0.8$ |
| **Bayesian** | $74.1 \pm 1.1$ | $90.2 \pm 0.9$ | $93.4 \pm 1.4$ | $100 \pm 0$ | $90.3 \pm 1.5$ | $67.7 \pm 1.3$ |
| **DAN** | $73.2 \pm 1$ | $93.2 \pm 0.9$ | $89 \pm 1.2$ | $98.8 \pm 0.8$ | $86.4 \pm 2.8$ | $84.3 \pm 1.2$ |
| **Stacked** | $73.9 \pm 1.4$ | $95.8 \pm 0.6$ | $92.4 \pm 1$ | $100 \pm 0$ | $92.4 \pm 1.2$ | $94.2 \pm 0.8$ |
| **Stacked Plus** | $74.5 \pm 1.3$ | $96.6 \pm 0.8$ | $92.4 \pm 1.2$ | $100 \pm 0$ | $91.4 \pm 1.2$ | $94.1 \pm 0.7$ |

**Table 7.** *Stacked Generalization* increase of performance respect *Average*

| Database | 3 Nets | 9 Nets | 20 Nets | 40 Nets |
|---|---|---|---|---|
| **aritm** | 1.95 | 1.27 | 0 | 0.11 |
| **glas** | 1.2 | 2 | 2.6 | 1.6 |
| **ionos** | 0.85 | 2.56 | 2.27 | 2.14 |
| **mok1** | 0.12 | 1 | 1.75 | 1.75 |
| **mok2** | 0.75 | 1.38 | 0.37 | 1.25 |
| **vowel** | 1.41 | 1.36 | 1.92 | 2.02 |

**Table 8.** *Stacked Generalization Plus* increase of performance respect *Average*

| Database | 3 Nets | 9 Nets | 20 Nets | 40 Nets |
|---|---|---|---|---|
| **aritm** | 0.92 | −0.24 | 0.91 | 0.68 |
| **glas** | 1.6 | 1.6 | 2.6 | 2.4 |
| **ionos** | 0.85 | 2.41 | 2.42 | 2.14 |
| **mok1** | 1.5 | 1.25 | 1.75 | 1.75 |
| **mok2** | 0.5 | 1.13 | 0.37 | 0.25 |
| **vowel** | 1.81 | 1.36 | 1.92 | 1.92 |

**Table 9.** Mean increase of performance with respect to a single network

| Method | 3 Nets | 9 Nets | 20 Nets | 40 Nets |
|---|---|---|---|---|
| **Average** | 11.2 | 12.15 | 12.23 | 12.38 |
| **Vote** | 10.91 | 11.6 | 11.7 | 11.95 |
| **WTA** | 10.98 | 12.03 | 12.14 | 11.99 |
| **Borda** | 10.88 | 11.42 | 11.44 | 11.72 |
| **Bayesian** | 11.18 | 10.85 | 9.45 | 8.35 |
| **DAN** | 9.85 | 10.34 | 10.07 | 9.88 |
| **Stacked** | 12.25 | 13.75 | 13.72 | 13.86 |
| **Stacked Plus** | 12.4 | 13.41 | 13.9 | 13.9 |

**Table 10.** Mean percentage of error reduction with respect to a single network

| Method | 3 Nets | 9 Nets | 20 Nets | 40 Nets |
|---|---|---|---|---|
| **Average** | 49.17 | 49.66 | 50.16 | 50.94 |
| **Vote** | 46.94 | 47.18 | 47.55 | 48.57 |
| **WTA** | 48.41 | 49.43 | 50.05 | 49.52 |
| **Borda** | 45.68 | 45.87 | 45.73 | 47.05 |
| **Bayesian** | 38.19 | 43.61 | 35.21 | 28.52 |
| **DAN** | 39.35 | 41.05 | 39.65 | 38.09 |
| **Stacked** | 56.78 | 58.3 | 58.56 | 58.98 |
| **Stacked Plus** | 56.91 | 56.8 | 59.4 | 59.4 |

worse. The increase of performance obtained with *Stacked Generalization* and *Stacked Generalization Plus* respect to *Output Average* are in tables 7-8.

Comparing the results showed in tables 7-8 we can sec that the improvement in performance using our method depends on the database and the number of networks used in the ensemble. We can see that, in general the methods based on *Stacked Generalization* are better than *Output Average*.

We have also calculated the percentage of error reduction (PER) of the ensembles with respect to a single network to get a general value for the comparison among all the methods we have studied. We have used equation 10 to calculate the ensemble PER value.

$$PER = 100 \cdot \frac{Error_{singlenetwork} - Error_{ensemble}}{Error_{singlenetwork}}. \qquad (10)$$

The PER value ranges from 0%, where there is no improvement by the use of a particular ensemble method with respect to a single network, to 100%. There can also be negative values, which means that the performance of the ensemble is worse than the performance of the single network. This new measurement is relative and can be used to compare more clearly the different methods.

Furthermore, we have calculated the increase of performance with respect to *Single Network* and the mean PER across all databases for each method to get a global measurement. Table 9 shows the results of the mean increase of performance and Table 10 shows the results of the mean $PER$.

According to these global measurement *Stacked Generalization* methods are the best performing methods. The highest difference between *Stacked Generalizacion* and *Output Average* is in the 40-network ensemble where the mean $PER$ increase is 9.54%. Although, *Stacked Generalization Plus* is slitghly better than *Stacked Generalization* there are some cases where the second method is better.

## 4 Conclusions

In the present paper we have analysed six classic combination methods and we have proposed new combination methods based on *Stacked Generalization*. We have used ensembles of 3, 9, 20 and 40 networks previously trained with *Simple Ensemble* on six databases from the *UCI Repository* to cover a wide spectrum of the number of networks in the classification system.

The results showed that the improvement by the use of *Stacked Generalization* depends on the database. Moreover, we have calculated the mean increase of performance and the mean percentage of error reduction across all databases with respect to a *Single Network* in order to get global measurements to compare the combination methods we have studied.

According to the results of these global measurements *Stacked Generalization* methods perform better than the classical combination methods studied in this paper. In general, *Stacked Generalization* is the best performing combination method for ensembles of 9 networks and *Stacked Generalization Plus* is the best performing combination method for ensembles of 3, 20 and 40 networks.

The use of a *Combination Network* in the module combination of an ensemble increases the generalization capability of the ensemble.

## Acknowledgments

This research was supported by project *P1·1B2004-03* of Universitat Jaume I - Bancaja in Castellón de la Plana, Spain.

## References


1. Tumer, K., Ghosh, J.: Error Correlation and Error Reduction in Ensemble Classifiers. Connection Science **8**(3-4) (1996) 385–403
2. Raviv, Y., Intratorr, N.: Bootstrapping with Noise: An Effective Regularization Technique. Connection Science, Special issue on Combining Estimators **8** (1996) 356–372
3. Hernandez-Espinosa, C., Fernandez-Redondo, M., Torres-Sospedra, J.: Ensembles of Multilayer Feedforward for Classification Problems. In: Neural Information Processing, ICONIP 2004. Volume 3316 of Lecture Notes in Computer Science (2005) 744–749
4. Hernandez-Espinosa, C., Torres-Sospedra, J., Fernandez-Redondo, M.: New Experiments on Ensembles of Multilayer Feedforward for Classification Problems. In: Proceedings of International Conference on Neural Networks, IJCNN 2005, Montreal, Canada (2005) 1120–1124
5. Torres-Sospedra, J., Fernandez-Redondo, M., Hernandez-Espinosa, C.: A Research on Combination Methods for Ensembles of Multilayer Feedforward. In: Proceedings of International Conference on Neural Networks, IJCNN 2005, Montreal, Canada (2005) 1125–1130
6. Xu, L., Krzyzak, A., Suen, C.: Methods of Combining Multiple Classifiers and Their Applications to Handwriting Recognition. IEEE Transactions on Systems, Man, and Cybernetics **22**(3) (1992) 418–435
7. Verikas, A., Lipnickas, A., Malmqvist, K., Bacauskiene, M., Gelzinis, A.: Soft Combination of Neural Classifiers: A Comparative Study. Pattern Recognition Letters **20**(4) (1999) 429–444
8. Jimenez, D., Walsh, N.: Dynamically Weighted Ensemble Neural Networks for Classification. In: IEEE World Congress on Computational Intelligence. Volume 1 (1998) 753–756
9. Wolpert, D.H.: Stacked Generalization. Neural Networks **5**(6) (1994) 1289–1301
10. Newman, D.J., Hettich, S., Blake, C.L., Merz, C.J.: UCI Repository of Machine Learning Databases (1998)

# Improving the Intelligent Prediction Model for Macro-economy*

Jianbo Fan[1], Lidan Shou[2], and Jinxiang Dong[2]

[1] College of Electron & Information Engineering, Ningbo University of Technology, Zhejiang Ningbo 315016
jbfan@163.com

[2] Institute of Artificial Intelligence, Zhejiang University, Zhejiang Hangzhou 310027
{should, djx}@cs.zju.edu.cn

**Abstract.** This paper presents a novel approach to macro-economy forecasting based on the Fuzzy Neural Networks. This method employs the expert opinions, statistical analysis and the Genetic Algorithm, to enhance the model of Fuzzy Neural Network. Our method combines the expert opinions and the results of statistical analysis to determine the input parameters of the prediction model, and adopts the Genetic Algorithm to process the original sample data. We use the fuzzy logic system to establish a set of fuzzy rules and utilize an EBP (Error Back Propagation) algorithm to train the network and adjust the parameters of the membership functions. The experimental results of the system indicates that the method is efficient and robust, producing high-precision results. This method could be extended to other application areas.

## 1 Introduction

Forecast problems have been under intensive study by researchers in the data mining area for more than a decade. In brief, a forecast method uses the known information to predict the future results by making use of prediction operators. There are many techniques developed for accurate forecasting of various problems. For example, Sung-Kwun Oh et al [1] proposed a genetically optimized hybrid fuzzy neural network and the model has been applied to prediction problems such as the three-input nonlinear function, the time series of gas furnace and the $NO_x$ emission process of gas turbine power plant. Wei Li et al [2] adopted fuzzy neural network to control signal lamp of traffic. Weiguo Song et al [3] proposed a method that can set up a haptic model for Liver Cutting. Apart from the wide applications in engineering, FNN has also been used in financial and economic services. For example, Lixin Yu et al [4] proposed an evolutionary fuzzy neural network and the algorithm had been used for financial prediction of bank prime loan rate, federal funds rate and discount rate. In this paper, we shall look at the problem of macro-economy forecasting. Zhibin Xiong et al [5] proposed a fuzzy neural network model to evaluate loan risk. In our research, we will look at the problem of macro-economy forecasting. That is, we shall predict the future economy trend based on the historical data. During the course of our

* The author gratefully acknowledges that this work has been supported by the 2006 K.C. Wong Education Foundation.

D.-S. Huang, K. Li, and G.W. Irwin (Eds.): ICIC 2006, LNCS 4113, pp. 156 – 167, 2006.

research, we observe that a macro-economy forecasting model should address the following difficulties [6]: (1) Predict model will be interfered by external artificial factors and natural factors such as political & economic policies, international affairs, climate affections and natural disasters; (2) Combining the Error Back Propagation algorithm with the fuzzy logic system will be the best choice. (3) If the selection of input variables of the predict model does not suit for the output variable, it will badly affect the predict precision.

In our research, we propose a new method, which combines the opinions from experts and the results of statistics analysis to determine the input variables of the forecast model, and adopts GA (Genetic Algorithm) to optimize the original sample data, afterwards, it uses the fuzzy logic system to establish a set of fuzzy rules and employs the EBP algorithm to train the network which is used thereafter to adjust the parameters of the membership functions. The experimental results of the system show that the prediction algorithm can produce four-year accurate values in the prediction results of a consecutive five years. Furthermore, this method is generic, therefore it can be generalized and applied in many other applications.

## 2 The Differences Between ESGAFNN and Usual Prediction Algorithm

In practice, the selection method of prediction input and output variables are often ad hoc. The selection of prediction input variables versus the predict output variable is critical for the precision of the prediction output. The irrelevance of these variables selection will have a major impact on the prediction precision. In our prediction method, we enhance the NN-based learning method using the economist knowledge, which is regarded as expert opinions. At the same time, the correlation and regression analysis of the 54 variables were done in the production, finance, investment, consumption module. Thus the prediction input and output variables should be chosen based on expertise knowledge. This is important as the expert opinions tend to be less biased compared to any ad hoc solutions given specific economic contexts. For example, the GDP (Gross Domestic Product) stands for the value of the whole final production to be produced and labor services in one nation or region economy in a certainty period (one quarter or one year). GDP is considered one of the most crucial measurements for macro economy [7]. The foreign economists usually consider the GDP to consist of the following items: *consumption*(C), *private investment* (I), *government payout* (P) and *net export value* (E). However, Chinese economists usually consider the GDP to include *fixed assets investment, export* and *inner consumption*. By calculating the correlation coefficient of the 54 variables and combining with the economist's opinions, we choose *Total Retail Sales of Consumer Goods, Total Investment in Fixed Assets, Total Exports Value, Added value of Secondary Industry and Financial Revenue* as predict input variables after the GDP as predict output variable is chosen.

In general, the prediction algorithm often adopts the evolutional computation methods such as NN, FNN, GA or combination of FNN and GA to predict. While our predict algorithm adopts the following approach: (1) To apply the economist's opinions and the results of statistical analysis to determine input variables of predict model; (2) To use genetic algorithm to optimize original sample data; (3) To do normalization processing for optimized data and establish a set of rules using fuzzy logic system; (4) To train the weight of the network and adjust the parameters of the membership function using EBP algorithm; (5) To realize the predict system and calculate predict results. The work flow of the ESGAFNN prediction algorithm is illustrated in fig. 1.

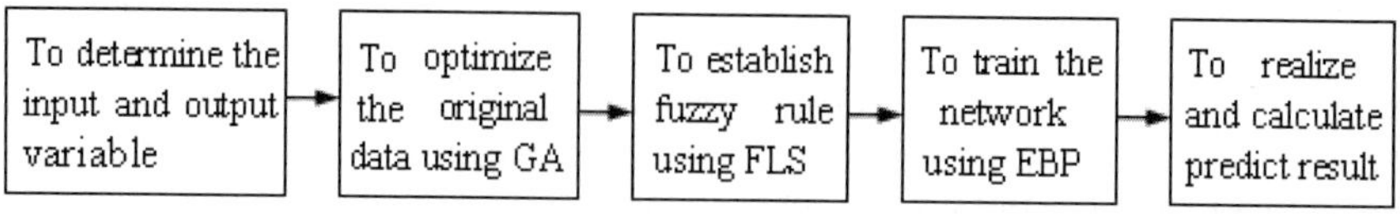


**Fig. 1.** ESGAFNN prediction algorithm workflow

## 3 The Optimization of Original Sample Data Using GA

After all variables of the prediction input and output are determined, we may choose a variable of the prediction output or input as parameter to optimize original sample data. In genetic algorithm, we adopt the binary encoding, random roulette wheel selection, random one point crossover and mutation. The genetic algorithm is described as follows:

Step 1: To give birth to initial population. It needs to be done to encode the parameter. If the mutative bound of the parameter D is $[D_{min}, D_{max}]$ and the width m of binary bits of the $D_{max}$ is worked out, then the binary digit B with m bits may be denoted as:

$$B=(2^m-1)(D-D_{min})/(D_{max}-D_{min}) \in [0, 2^m-1]$$

According to the above formula, we can transform the decimal original sample data into the binary encoding data with *m* bits and give birth to initial populations.

Step 2: To calculate the fitness. With the help of software Origin 7.0, we use quintic polynomial to fit the original sample data. The form to be fit function is such as:

$$y=a0+a1*x+a2*x^2+a3*x^3+a4*x^4+a5*x^5$$

The fitness can be calculated by fit function.

Step 3: To estimate whether the condition satisfies the optimized rule. If the condition satisfies the optimized rule, then go to Step 5. If the condition does not satisfy the optimized rule, then go to Step 4.

Step 4: To do the basic operator of GA. After the random roulette wheel selection and random one point crossover and mutation were done, go to Step 2.

Step 5: To obtain the best individual. According to the formula below we get a set of optimized sample data.

$$D= D_{min}+B*(D_{max}-D_{min})/ (2^m-1)$$

The optimized process for original sample data is shown in fig. 2 below.

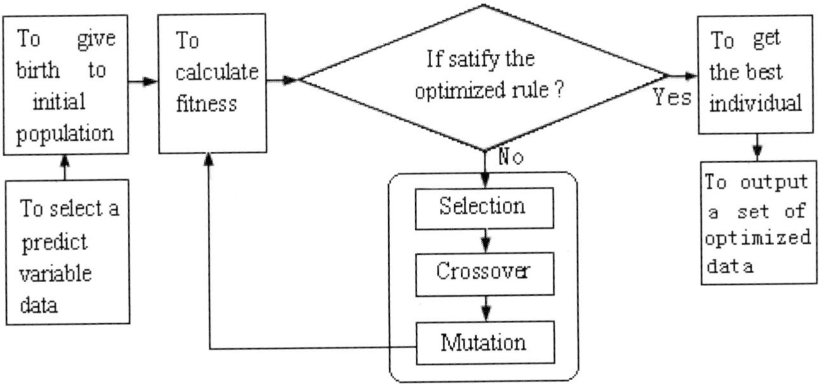


**Fig. 2.** The optimized process for original sample data

In GA, the crossover probability is from 0.4 to 0.8 and mutation probability is from 0.01 to 0.05. The optimized rule adopts a method that the number of the generation exceeds the specified value in advance.

## 4 FNN Forecast Model

### 4.1 Setup of Fuzzy Logic System

Fuzzy Logic System (FLS) is a main body of FNN Forecast System. The first step of system designing and realization is to set up an initial FLS. Fuzzy rules of FLS here is not from experts' experience, but is automatically generated after studying the normalizing data from the optimized sample data.

The data spaces of the system have to be equally divided. For each input variable $x_i$ (i=1,2,…,m),to calculate the min($x_i$) and max($x_i$), we need to divide the input space [min($x_i$),max($x_i$)] into three equal parts. Each equal part corresponds to a fuzzy subset $A_{ij}$(j=1,2,3),here $A_{i1}=\{L,\mu_L(x_i)\}$,$A_{i2}=\{M, \mu_M(x_i)\}$,$A_{i3}=\{H, \mu_H(x_i)\}$. The fuzzy variable $X_i$ may take the value Low (L) or Medium (M) or High (H). The three membership functions corresponding to the fuzzy variable $X_i$ are as follows:

$$\mu_L(x_i)=\frac{1}{1+e^{a(x_i-c1_i)}},\ \mu_M(x_i)=\frac{1}{1+\left(\frac{x_i-c2_i}{d_i}\right)^{2b}},\ \mu_H(x_i)=\frac{1}{1+e^{-a(x_i-c3_i)}}$$

where a=1,b=4,$c1_i$=min($x_i$)+(max($x_i$)-min($x_i$))/3,$c2_i$=min($x_i$)+(max($x_i$)- min($x_i$))/2, $c3_i$=min($x_i$)+(max($x_i$)-min($x_i$))*2/3,$d_i$=($c3_i$-$c1_i$)/2. For output variable y, to calculate the min(y) and max(y), to divide the output space [min(y),max(y)] into five equal parts. Each equal part corresponds to a fuzzy subset $B_j$ (j=1,…,5). The fuzzy variable

Y may take the value Low (L) or Small (S) or Medium (M) or Better (B) or High (H). The membership function value (mfy) corresponding to the fuzzy variable Y is the central value of each equal part. Thus self-adaptable study algorithm of fuzzy rules shows as follows:

Step 1: To the system of multiple input variables and single output variable (MISO), take one sample in order ( $x_1^{(k)}, x_2^{(k)}, \ldots, x_m^{(k)}$, $y^{(k)}$ ) ,k=1,2,...s, s is the number of sample data;

Step 2: To generate one rule out of this sample. For every input variable $x_i^{(k)}$ (i=1,2,...,m),to take the fuzzy subset which is the maximum value of $\mu_L(x_i^{(k)}), \mu_M(x_i^{(k)})$, $\mu_H(x_i^{(k)})$ corresponds to as the fuzzy variable $X_i^{(k)}$ in the rule condition part $x_i^{(k)}$, to take the maximum value as a corresponding membership function value to form a complete rule condition part. For rule conclusion part, to take the fuzzy subset which contains $y^{(k)}$ as the fuzzy variable $Y^{(k)}$ in the rule conclusion part, to take the central value of the fuzzy subset as a corresponding membership function value.

Step 3: To grant each rule with a confidence. To obtain a fuzzy rule k in Step 2, as follows:

$$R(k): \text{if } x_1^{(k)} \text{ is } X_1^{(k)}, x_2^{(k)} \text{ is } X_2^{(k)}, \ldots, x_m^{(k)} \text{ is } X_m^{(k)}, \text{ then } y^{(k)} \text{ is } Y^{(k)}. \tag{1}$$

This rule is taken from the actual sample data, so its confidence is defined as

$$\mu_r = \mu_{X_1^{(k)}}(x_1^{(k)}) \times \mu_{X_2^{(k)}}(x_2^{(k)}) \times \cdots \times \mu_{X_m^{(k)}}(x_m^{(k)}) \tag{2}$$

and the membership function of the fuzzy variable $Y^{(k)}$ is denoted as mfy.

Step 4: Rule set consistency verification. To compare this rule with each rule in the rule set. If one rule is the same as its condition part $X_i^{(k)}$ (i=1,2,...,m), but different to its conclusion part, then retain the rule with a big confidence, delete the other one; otherwise, put this rule into this rule set.

Step 5: Repeat the above steps until exhausting all the sample data and forming a rule set with the number of rules R.

After obtaining the rule set, the fuzzy system with an initial forecast model has had the self-adaptable forecast ability, and its system forecast output is:

$$y^* = \sum_{r=1}^{R} \mu_r \text{mfy}_r \Big/ \sum_{r=1}^{R} \mu_r \tag{3}$$

## 4.2 Structure of FNN Forecast Model

Suppose $y^{(k)}, y^{*(k)}$ is the sample output value (expected value) and forecast output value when the *k*th iteration; $x_i^{(k)}$ is m input variables(i=1,2,...,m);$c1_i^r$, $c2_i^r$, $c3_i^r$ are three center points of membership function corresponding to the fuzzy variable $X_i^{(k)}$ in the *r*th rule; $d_i^r$ is the width of membership function corresponding to $c2_i^r$; $\text{mfy}_r$ is the central value of membership function of the fuzzy variable $Y^{(k)}$ in the conclusion part of the *r*th Rule; $\mu_r$ is confidence of the r*th* rule when $x_i^k$ (i=1,2,...,m) input, then

$$\mu_r = \prod_{i=1}^{m} \mu_{X_i^{(k)}}(x_i^{(k)}) = \prod_{i=1}^{m} \max\{\mu_L(x_i^{(k)}), \mu_M(x_i^{(k)}), \mu_H(x_i^{(k)})\} \tag{4}$$

So the general expression of above FLS is:

$$y^{*(K)} = \frac{\sum_{r=1}^{R} \mathrm{m}fy_{\mathrm{r}}\mu_r}{\sum_{r=1}^{R}\mu_r} = \frac{\sum_{r=1}^{R} \mathrm{m}fy_{\mathrm{r}} \prod_{i=1}^{m} \max\{\mu_L(x_i^{(k)}), \mu_M(x_i^{(k)}), \mu_H(x_i^{(k)})\}}{\sum_{r=1}^{R}\prod_{i=1}^{m} \max\{\mu_L(x_i^{(k)}), \mu_M(x_i^{(k)}), \mu_H(x_i^{(k)})\}} \quad (5)$$

This fuzzy system can be displayed as a forward network in the Fig. 3 below.

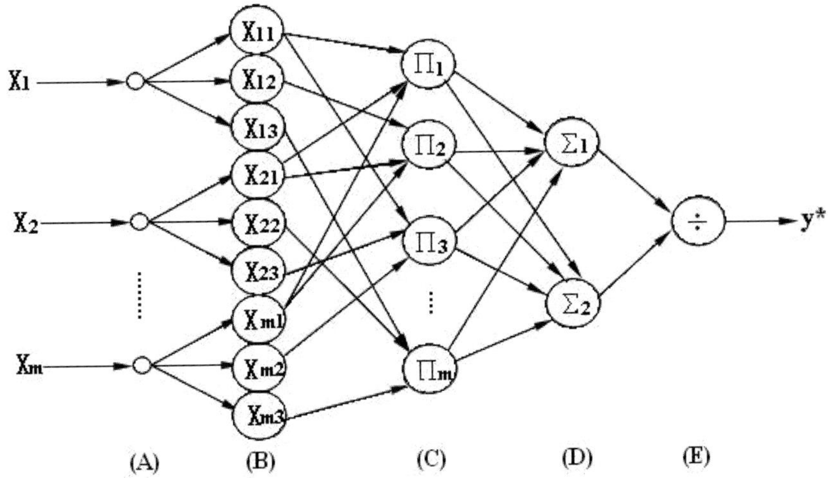


**Fig. 3.** The structure of FNN predict model

Thereinto: (A) is input layer; (E) is output layer ; (B) is fuzzification layer, each neutral cell calculates membership functions corresponding to $x_i^{(k)}(i=1,2,\ldots,m)$,output is $x_{i1}=\mu_L(x_i^{(k)}),x_{i2}=\mu_M(x_i^{(k)}),x_{i3}=\mu_H(x_i^{(k)})$; (C) is fuzzy illations layer, each neutral cell is like a multiplier, confidence $\mu_r$ of each rule is output; (D) is de-fuzzification layer, to work out formula (3) with (E). The membership function value ($\mathrm{mfy}_r$) of the fuzzy variable $Y^{(k)}$ in the conclusion part of each rule equal to weight value connecting (C) with Σ1 neutral cell of (D), other weight value is 1.

After displaying the initial fuzzy forecast model as a forward network, we can use EBP algorithm based on declining grads for study and training. The fuzzy forecast system with optimized parameters will have a stronger self-adaptability and study capability. If back propagation study goes to (C), then it can adjust the central value ($\mathrm{mfy}_r$) of the membership function of the fuzzy variable $Y^{(k)}$ in the rule conclusion part. If going to (B), then all the parameters are adjusted.

## 4.3 The Parameter's Study of Fuzzy Neural Network

For the initial fuzzy forecast model, its adjustable parameters include the central value of membership function in output fuzzy subset and the membership function center and width in input fuzzy subset. If θ stands for any parameter, general formula of study using EBP algorithm is:

$$\theta(k+1) = \theta(k) - \alpha \frac{\partial e(k)}{\partial \theta}\Big|_{\theta=\theta(k)} \tag{6}$$

k is the learning iteration number, α is a parameter to control study speed, the error metric is defined as:

$$e(k) = \frac{1}{2}(y^{(k)} - y^{*(k)})^2 \tag{7}$$

Combining (6) with (7) can get:

$$\theta(k+1) = \theta(k) + \alpha(y^{(k)} - y^{*(k)}) \cdot \frac{\partial y^{*(k)}}{\partial \theta}\Big|_{\theta=\theta(k)} \tag{8}$$

So, if the partial derivative of $y^{*(k)}$ to each parameter is worked out, then（8）can be taken for training. When EBP algorithm goes on to (C), adjusts the central value ($mfy_r$) of the membership function in output fuzzy subset, out of (5), we can get:

$$\frac{\partial y^{*(k)}}{\partial mfy_r} = \mu_r \Big/ \sum_{r=1}^{R} \mu_r \quad , \quad r = 1,2,\cdots,R \tag{9}$$

Iteration formula of study and training can be taken from (8) and (9):

$$mfy_r(k+1) = mfy_r(k) + \alpha(y^{(k)} - y^{*(k)}) \cdot \mu_r \Big/ \sum_{r=1}^{R} \mu_r \tag{10}$$

Thereinto, r=1,2,…,R; k=0,1,2,3,….

When EBP algorithm goes on to (B), adjusts parameters which fuzzy system corresponds to each membership functions of input variables. Suppose the sample of the *k*th study is $(x_1^{(k)}, x_2^{(k)}, \ldots, x_m^{(k)}, y^{(k)})$,use the method to work out partial derivative by functions, put the partial derivative out of (5) into (8), we can get the similar iteration formula which EBP algorithm optimizes and adjusts parameters $c1_i^r$, $c2_i^r$, $c3_i^r$ and $d_i^r$ . Details are omitted.

## 5 The Realization of the Prediction System on Macro-economy

### 5.1 The Sample Data of GDP Predict Model

Based on the above techniques, we implement the intelligent prediction system for Macro-Economy. Table 1 below shows the original sample data chart of GDP(Current Year Price) predict model and table 2 shows the optimized sample data chart of GDP(Current Year Price) predict model (unit:$10^8$ Yuan RMB).

According to the original sample data (Table 1), we use GA to get the optimized sample data (Table 2). With the help of software Origin 7.0, the fitness function uses a *quintic* polynomial to fit the original sample data. The form to be fit function about GDP is as follows:

y=-77.20769+187.9672*x-64.75432*x^2+9.14086*x^3-0.48743*x^4+0.00889*x^5

Here, x is the sequence number of year. For example, x can take the value from 1 to 16. y is the value of GDP. The results log to be fit function about GDP shows in below:

**Table 1.** The original sample data chart of GDP (Current Year Price) Forecast Model [8][9]

| Year | Total Retail Sales of Consumer Goods | Total Investment in Fixed Assets | Total Exports Value | Added value of Secondary Industry | Financial Revenue | GDP (Current year price) |
|---|---|---|---|---|---|---|
| 1985 | 25.33 | 17.67 | 0.04 | 40.40 | 9.12 | 71.05 |
| 1986 | 30.46 | 22.01 | 0.05 | 44.47 | 10.23 | 80.22 |
| 1987 | 35.47 | 29.46 | 0.08 | 53.99 | 11.34 | 95.99 |
| 1988 | 49.05 | 35.81 | 1.15 | 66.43 | 13.34 | 118.62 |
| 1989 | 52.82 | 32.79 | 1.8 | 77.69 | 15.28 | 137.25 |
| 1990 | 54.98 | 39.28 | 2.8 | 79.97 | 15.89 | 144.89 |
| 1991 | 63.38 | 51.42 | 4.75 | 97.93 | 17.79 | 186.93 |
| 1992 | 79.4 | 76.25 | 7.84 | 128.2 | 19.84 | 232.94 |
| 1993 | 118.21 | 129.27 | 11.08 | 186.18 | 28.34 | 328.05 |
| 1994 | 163.41 | 184.6 | 17.5 | 263.25 | 42.02 | 463.51 |
| 1995 | 226.82 | 264.19 | 23.69 | 371.81 | 53.11 | 637.63 |
| 1996 | 259.18 | 313.67 | 26.69 | 450.44 | 65.95 | 795.86 |
| 1997 | 288.58 | 300.57 | 32.55 | 511.25 | 75.04 | 897.43 |
| 1998 | 313.4 | 307.9 | 34.53 | 550.0 | 87.6 | 980.0 |
| 1999 | 345.8 | 318.9 | 34.77 | 598.0 | 104.0 | 1070.0 |
| 2000 | 389.29 | 360.26 | 51.68 | 673.95 | 143.15 | 1191.5 |

**Table 2.** The optimized sample data chart of GDP (Current Year Price) predict model

| *Year* | *Total Retail Sales of Consumer Goods* | *Total Investment in Fixed Assets* | *Total Exports Value* | *Added value of Secondary Industry* | *Financial Revenue* | *GDP (Current year price)* |
|---|---|---|---|---|---|---|
| 1985 | 25.33 | 17.67 | 0.04 | 40.40 | 9.12 | 71.05 |
| 1986 | 30.32 | 21.69 | 0.04 | 44.74 | 10.17 | 80.36 |
| 1987 | 35.30 | 29.74 | 0.04 | 54.02 | 11.22 | 96.23 |
| 1988 | 48.83 | 35.77 | 0.86 | 66.41 | 13.32 | 118.67 |
| 1989 | 53.11 | 33.09 | 1.68 | 77.56 | 15.43 | 137.28 |
| 1990 | 55.24 | 39.12 | 2.50 | 80.04 | 15.95 | 144.94 |
| 1991 | 63.08 | 51.19 | 4.96 | 98.00 | 17.53 | 187.09 |
| 1992 | 79.46 | 76.00 | 8.24 | 128.34 | 19.63 | 233.07 |
| 1993 | 117.92 | 128.96 | 10.70 | 185.94 | 28.57 | 328.31 |
| 1994 | 163.51 | 184.61 | 17.25 | 263.35 | 42.23 | 463.51 |
| 1995 | 226.90 | 264.39 | 23.81 | 371.73 | 53.27 | 637.57 |
| 1996 | 258.95 | 314.00 | 27.09 | 450.38 | 65.89 | 795.76 |
| 1997 | 288.86 | 300.59 | 32.83 | 511.07 | 74.82 | 897.57 |
| 1998 | 313.08 | 307.97 | 34.47 | 550.09 | 87.44 | 980.22 |
| 1999 | 345.84 | 318.69 | 34.47 | 597.78 | 104.26 | 1069.99 |
| 2000 | 389.29 | 360.26 | 51.68 | 673.95 | 143.15 | 1191.50 |

R-Square<COD>=0.99657, SD=28.70266, N=16, P<0.0001

The optimized sample data shown in Table 2 have to be normalized. Suppose x stands for the input variable of predict model and y stands for the output variable of predict model. The yearnum stands for the number of year in the optimized sample data. The formulas of normalization are shown in below:

$$bzx_j = x_{yearnum,j} / x_{yearnum-1,j} \tag{11}$$

$$x_{i,j} = x_{i+1,j} / x_{i,j} - 1 \tag{12}$$

$$x_{yearnum,j} = bzx_j * x_{yearnum-1,j} \tag{13}$$

where, i = 1,2,…,yearnum-1; j=1,2,3,4,5.

$$bzy = y_{yearnum} / y_{yearnum-1} \tag{14}$$

$$y_i = y_{i+2} / y_{i+1} - 1,\ y_{yearnum-1} = y_{yearnum} / y_{yearnum-1} - 1 \tag{15}$$

$$y_{yearnum} = bzy * y_{yearnum-1} \tag{16}$$

where, i = 1,2,…,yearnum-2.

In succession to obtaining the above data, we execute step (3) through (5) in section 2.

## 5.2 Analysis of the Prediction Results

Given the prediction model which selects the GDP as the prediction output variable, we select *total retail sales of consumer goods*, *total investment in fixed assets*, *total exports value*, *added value of secondary industry* and *financial revenue* as predict input variables. We compare the prediction results of ESGAFNN with those of conventional Neural Network (NN). Fig. 4 below shows the prediction curve by comparing with the true value (from 1985 to 2005) and NN prediction value (from 2001 to 2005). Fig. 5 shows the predict curve by comparing the true value (from 1985 to 2005) and prediction values of ESGAFNN (from 2001 to 2005).

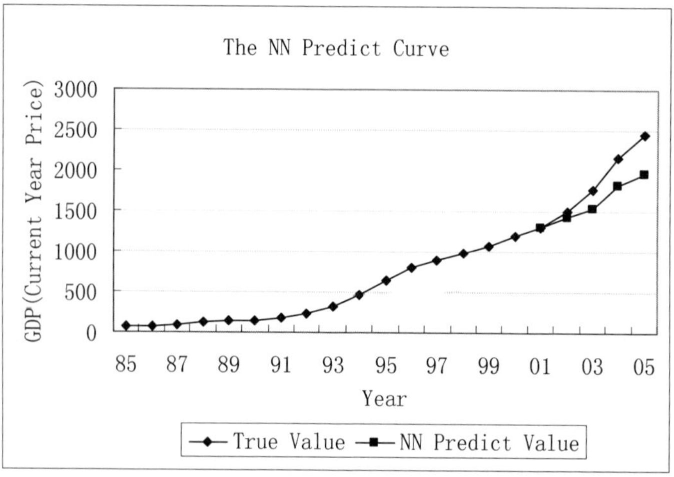


**Fig. 4.** The prediction curve by comparing the true value and NN predict value

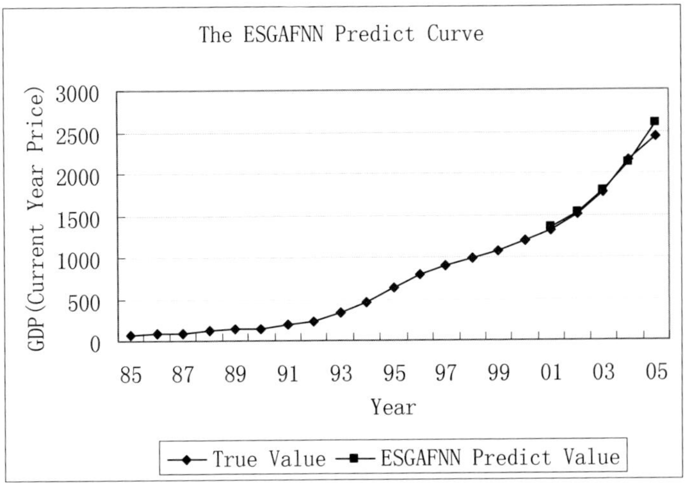


**Fig. 5.** The prediction curve by comparing the true value and ESGAFNN predict value

For the NN prediction system based on four layers EBP network, we analyze that the choice of the node numbers of double hidden layers and the times of network study circulation has had a great influence on the predict precision, and determine that the optimal node numbers of each hidden layer is 7 and the times of network study circulation is 2000. By normalizing the original sample data (Table 1), we firstly calculate the predict value of the 2001 year. Then according to the predict value of year 2001, we obtain the predict value of the 2002 year. We repeat the process until year 2005.

For the ESGAFNN prediction system, by normalizing according to formula (11) to (16) for the optimized sample data (Table 2), we firstly calculate the predict value of the 2001 year. Then according to the predict value of year 2001, we obtain the predict value of the 2002 year. We repeat the process until year 2005.

Table 3 shows the data compared among the true value and the predict value of two methods and the corresponding relative error.

**Table 3.** The data compare among the true value and the predict value of two methods and the corresponding relative error

| Year | True Value | NN Predict Value | NN Predict Relative Error | ESGAFNN Predict Value | ESGAFNN Predict Relative Error |
|---|---|---|---|---|---|
| 2001 | 1310.58 | 1311.38 | 0.0006 | 1342.17 | 0.0241 |
| 2002 | 1500.30 | 1428.08 | 0.0481 | 1533.35 | 0.0220 |
| 2003 | 1769.90 | 1528.11 | 0.1366 | 1782.87 | 0.0073 |
| 2004 | 2158.04 | 1814.23 | 0.1593 | 2120.21 | 0.0175 |
| 2005 | 2446.40 | 1964.51 | 0.1970 | 2597.28 | 0.0617 |

From fig. 4 and fig. 5 and table 3, it is apparent that the ESGAFNN prediction values from 2001 to 2004 are very close to the true values and the mean of each relative error is not greater than 1.78%. The former NN algorithm can only get two years more accurate values in the predict results. While the current ESGAFNN algorithm can get four years very accurate values in the predict result. The result shows that the intelligent prediction system based on ESGAFNN algorithm can play an important role in actual applications. Though this paper only gives out the experimental result of GDP (Current year price) forecastion model of Ningbo in China, other forecast models (such as total retail sales of consumer goods, total investment in fixed assets, total exports value, added value of secondary industry and financial revenue, etc.) and Macro-economic data of Hangzhou in China have all gone through hundreds of experiments. The results are similar to those in this paper. The result of the system implementation indicates that the intelligent forecast algorithm is fast and robust, with high precision in the forecast results. This algorithm can be generalized and applied in other applications.

## 6 Conclusion

In this paper, we presented a novel macro-economy forecasting model based on ESGAFNN. We also presented the implementation of the system and the experimental results. Based on our research, we can make the following conclusions: (1) From the extensive experiments, we found it is important to choose forecast input variables which are close relative to forecast output variables. Whether the variables are chosen reasonably directly affects the forecast precision. (2) The optimization of the original samples data by GA is valuable, since it can adjust some data warped by statistics or interfered by external artificial factors and natural factors. (3) Using fuzzy logic system, FNN can summarize fuzzy rules automatically. Through learning on the optimized sample data, the FNN can not only adjust the central value parameters of fuzzy output subset, but also adjust the parameters of each membership function which specifies the relationship between the fuzzy system and the input variables. Thus the network structure is optimized and its convergence speed and forecasting precision have been greatly improved. (4) The combination and/or amalgamation of each different algorithm in computational intelligence are effective to optimize the result.

For summary, as a challenging work, research on intelligent macro-economy forecasting algorithms requires further investigation concerning the amalgamation of our algorithms. Prediction based on ant colony algorithm is also a promising direction.

## References

1. Oh, S. K., Pedrycz, W.,Park, B.J.: Multilayer Hybrid Fuzzy Neural Networks: Synthesis via Technologies of Advanced Computational Intelligence. Circuits and Systems I: Regular Papers, IEEE Transactions on, Vol. 53 (2006) 688-703
2. Li, W., Li, R. M., He, D.Z., Wang. F. Y.: Intelligent Traffic Signal System Based on Networked Control. Networking, Sensing and Control, 2005. Proceedings. 2005 IEEE 19-22 (2005) 587 - 591

3. Song, W.G., Yuan, K.: Haptic Modeling for Liver Cutting Based on Fuzzy Neural Network, Advanced Intelligent Mechatronics. Proceedings, 2005 IEEE/ASME International Conference on, (2005) 1216 – 1220
4. Yu, L. X., Zhang, Y. Q.: Evolutionary Fuzzy Neural Networks for Hybrid Financial Prediction. Systems, Man and Cybernetics, Part C, IEEE Transactions on, Vol. 35 (2005) 244 - 249
5. Xiong, Z. B., Li, R. J.: Credit Risk Evaluation with Fuzzy Neural Networks on Listed Corporations of China. VLSI Design and Video Technology, 2005. Proceedings of 2005 IEEE International Workshop on May 28-30, (2005) 397 - 402
6. Fan, J.B., Yang, J.G.: The Research of Intelligent Predict Model of Macro-economy. Neural Network and Computational Intelligence. Hangzhou: Zhejiang University Press, (2002) 371 – 377
7. Wessels, W. J.: Economics. Publisher by Barron's Educational Series, (2000)
8. Ningbo Statistic bureau. Ningbo Reform Opening Twenty Years, Vol.1, Vol. 2. Ningbo Press, (1998)
9. Ningbo Statistic Bureau. Ningbo Statistical Communique. URL: http://www.nbnet.com.cn/homepage/njsj/njsj.php, (2006)

# Integrated Structure and Parameter Selection for Eng-genes Neural Models

Patrick Connally, Kang Li, and George W. Irwin

Intelligent Systems and Control Research Group Queen's University Belfast, Belfast BT9 5AH, UK

**Abstract.** A new approach to the construction and optimisation of 'eng-genes' grey-box neural networks is investigated. A forward selection algorithm is used to optimise both the network weights and biases and the parameters of the system-derived activation functions. The algorithm is used for both conventional neural network and eng-genes modelling of a simulated Continuously Stirred Tank Reactor. The resulting eng-genes networks demonstrate superior simulation performance and transparency over a range of network sizes.

## 1 Introduction

### 1.1 Nonlinear Modelling

In modelling a given nonlinear dynamic system, a compromise must often be made between the desired model qualities of accuracy and simplicity.

Physical models of more complex systems may involve large sets of both ordinary and partial differential equations. While numerical methods such as computational fluid dynamics (CFD) are potentially very accurate given adequate system knowledge, these models may not be suited to real-time use due to high computational complexity. On the other hand, data-driven 'black box' models, while far more flexible in terms of complexity, utilise little or no physical insight, and as such their accuracy is dependent almost entirely on the quality of training data available.

Grey-box type models may be constructed in one of two ways. In one category of techniques, the system fundamentals are normally well-understood, and model structure is at least partially known 'a priori'. Physical modelling and system identification form two interacting paths, with the objective of identifying unknown parameters and unmodelled dynamics [1]. The other technique, fundamental grey-box modelling, uses simple system-related nonlinear functions which are known 'a priori' to build a 'pool' of nonlinear model terms. These terms can then be used to construct a model which has both a 'black-box' structure with the corresponding computational advantages, as well as retaining some insight into the physical system [2]. This physical insight is intended to improve both the accuracy and the transparency of the model.

### 1.2 The Eng-genes Concept

One possible interpretation of the second type of grey-box model described is to view the nonlinear functions (and their corresponding parameters) used in

D.-S. Huang, K. Li, and G.W. Irwin (Eds.): ICIC 2006, LNCS 4113, pp. 168–177, 2006.

deriving the model terms as the fundamental 'building blocks' of the system from a mathematical perspective. Perhaps more apt is the analogy to the genes present in the cells of the human brain, which may itself be considered as similar (though very much more complex) in operation to certain types of mathematical model. These 'engineering genes', or 'eng-genes' for short, are extracted from 'a priori' knowledge of the system, and used in the creation of grey-box models [3].

The model structure which most intuitively presents itself as appropriate for this view of a grey-box model is the artificial neural network (ANN). ANNs have been used successfully in many modelling applications in the past, due to their proven ability to model any continuous function to an arbitrary degree of accuracy [4]. This approximation capability is reflected somewhat in Kolmogorov's superposition theorem [5], which states that any multivariate continuous function may be represented as the superposition of a number of univariate ones.

Thus, a natural means of including the fundamental system nonlinearities described in a grey-box model is to use them as the hidden-layer activation functions in a neural network. Because several fundamental nonlinearities may be applicable to a given nonlinear system, it may be necessary to create a heterogeneous neural network, where each hidden node in the same layer has a different activation function. While neural networks have been used as a structural component of grey-box models in the past [6], there is little evidence in the literature relating to the inclusion of fundamental system nonlinearities at any stage in neural network construction or training.

### 1.3 Construction and Optimisation of Eng-genes Models

The first stage in the construction of an eng-genes neural model is to identify the appropriate set of 'eng-genes', or fundamental nonlinear functions, to be used as candidate neural activation functions. In the case where the system's characteristic equations are well known and the objective is to obtain a model with improved computation time, this exercise may be relatively straightforward. However, in the case where the system's behaviour has not been explicitly defined in a mathematical sense, it is likely that less specific 'a priori' knowledge of the system will yield a set of general physical functions which can be used to form a pool of potential activation functions.

Optimisation of the neural structure itself involves two processes. Firstly, the most dominant activation functions must be selected from the pool for inclusion in the final model, and their parameters optimised. While techniques such as the orthogonal least squares (OLS) algorithm [7] exist for selecting the most appropriate nonlinear model terms from a pool, these are typically restricted to the identification of linear-in-the-parameters models such as nonlinear autoregressive models with exogenous inputs (NARX models), rendering them of limited use when some or all of the 'eng-genes' in the pool contain nonlinear parameters. Similarly, the existing methods for neural network construction deal exclusively with conventional architectures, in which the hidden layer activation functions are homogenous and non-parametric.

The second process is common to all neural models, and is that of training, in which the weights and biases in the network are optimised. While many techniques exist for neural network training, such as the one detailed in [8], standard perceptron training algorithms are less than ideal for eng-genes networks, due to their use of nonlinear parameters in the activation functions.

### 1.4 Existing Eng-genes Modelling Methods

A natural and intuitive means for deriving eng-genes models is to use genetic algorithms [3]. These techniques are well suited to the type of mixed-integer optimisation problems encountered in constructing an eng-genes neural network. The genetic algorithm approach also has the advantage of optimising both the structure and the parameters at the same time. However, due to the stochastic nature of the technique, precise convergence on an optimum solution may require a large population size and many evolutionary generations. This large computational burden renders genetic algorithms unsuitable for online use in most cases.

Another technique which has been investigated involves restricting the use of genetic algorithms to the selection of the activation functions and optimisation of their parameters [9]. The network weights and biases are then optimised using standard neural network training methods.

This type of hybrid modelling scheme is useful in that many standard neural network training algorithms have variants which may be used to adjust the weights and biases online. However, as the hybrid scheme optimises the network structure and nonlinear parameters separately from the network weights and biases, the potential advantages of the eng-genes model is mitigated somewhat.

### 1.5 Integrated Selection and Optimisation

It becomes evident that a fast, accurate method of simultaneously selecting activation functions and optimising both linear and nonlinear parameters is desirable. In this paper, a variant on the fast algorithm proposed in [10] is used to construct both eng-genes and standard multilayer perceptron networks.

## 2 Problem Formulation

Consider a MISO nonlinear system, modelled by a single-hidden-layer heterogeneous neural network which may be represented as

$$\hat{y}(t) = \sum\nolimits_{i=1}^{m} w_i \varphi_i(\boldsymbol{\omega}, \mathbf{x}(t)) + b \tag{1}$$

where $\hat{y}(t)$ is the network prediction at time $t$, $w_i$ is the weight applied to the output of node $i$, $\varphi_i$ is the activation function of node $i$, $\boldsymbol{\omega}$ is the set of adjustable parameters (including bias and input weights) to node $i$, $\mathbf{x}(t)$ is the vector of inputs to the network at time $t$, $m$ is the number of hidden nodes in the network, and $b$ is the output layer bias. The network is illustrated in figure 1. Also, let $y(t)$ be the desired network output at time $t$.

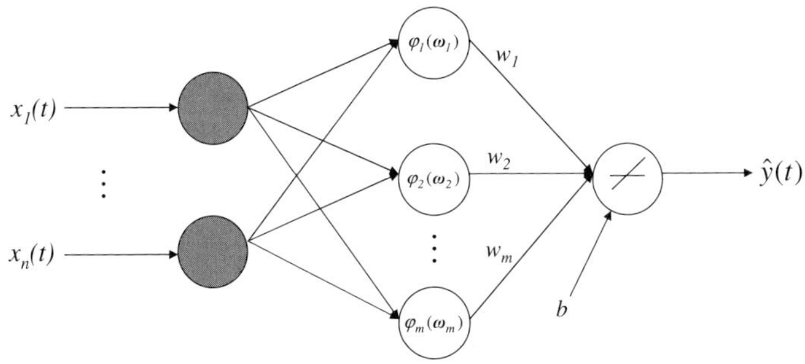


**Fig. 1.** Eng-genes network

If a set of modelling data is given as $\{(\mathbf{x}(t), y(t)), t = 1, \ldots, N\}$, then the desired output vector is $\mathbf{y} = [y(1), \ldots, y(t)]^T$. The objective of constructing the neural model is to produce a model with output vector $\hat{\mathbf{y}} = [\hat{y}(1), \ldots, \hat{y}(t)]^T$ such that the sum-squared error

$$\mathrm{SSE} = (\mathbf{y} - \hat{\mathbf{y}})^T(\mathbf{y} - \hat{\mathbf{y}}) \tag{2}$$

is minimised, by selecting and optimum set of activation functions $\varphi_i, i{=}1, \cdots, m$ from a 'pool' of such functions, with an optimal parameter vector $\boldsymbol{\omega}_i$ for each $\varphi_i$.

## 3 Integrated Selection and Optimisation Algorithm

Let $k$ be the number of nodes in the network. Initially, $k = 0$ and $\mathrm{SSE} = \mathbf{y}^T\mathbf{y}$.
The following three steps are required order to select the $k+1^{th}$ hidden node:

1. For each activation function $\varphi$ in the pool of candidate nodes, search for the optimal parameter vector $\boldsymbol{\omega}$, that is, the value of $\boldsymbol{\omega}$ which maximises the node's contribution $\Delta J_{k+1}(\boldsymbol{\omega})$. Let the initial value for the parameters be $\boldsymbol{\omega} = [\omega_0^{0)}, \omega_1^{0)} \ldots \omega_n^{0)}]$. The search is carried out using the conjugate gradient algorithm, with the direction at each iteration given by

$$\mathbf{h} = -\nabla \Delta J_{k+1}(\boldsymbol{\omega}) \tag{3}$$

where

$$\nabla \Delta J_{k+1}(\boldsymbol{\omega}) = \left[\frac{\delta \Delta J_{k+1}(\boldsymbol{\omega})}{\delta \omega_0}, \frac{\delta \Delta J_{k+1}(\boldsymbol{\omega})}{\delta \omega_1}, \ldots, \frac{\delta \Delta J_{k+1}(\boldsymbol{\omega})}{\delta \omega_n}\right] \tag{4}$$

The individual gradient with respect to a given parameter $\omega_i$ may be obtained by:

$$\frac{\delta \Delta J_{k+1}(\boldsymbol{\omega})}{\delta \omega_i} = \frac{2C(\omega)}{D(\omega)} \left(\mathbf{y} - \frac{C(\omega)}{D(\omega)} \varphi^{(k)}(\boldsymbol{\omega})\right)^T \varphi_{\omega_i}^{(k)}(\boldsymbol{\omega}) \tag{5}$$

where

$$C(\omega) = \sum_{t=1}^{N} [y^{(k)}(t)\varphi^{(k)}(\mathbf{x}(t), \boldsymbol{\omega})] \tag{6}$$

and

$$D(\omega) = \sum_{t=1}^{N} [\varphi^{(k)}(\mathbf{x}(t), \boldsymbol{\omega})]^2 \tag{7}$$

$\mathbf{y}^{(0)} = \mathbf{y}$ and $\boldsymbol{\varphi}^{(k)}$ is given by

$$\boldsymbol{\varphi}^{(k)} = \boldsymbol{\varphi}(\boldsymbol{\omega}) - \sum_{s=1}^{k} \frac{a_{s,k+1}(\boldsymbol{\omega})}{a_{s,s}} \varphi_s^{(s-1)} \tag{8}$$

where

$$a_{s,k+1}(\boldsymbol{\omega}) = (\boldsymbol{\varphi}_s^{(s-1)})^T \boldsymbol{\varphi}^{(s-1)}(\boldsymbol{\omega}), s = 1, \ldots, k \tag{9}$$

$\boldsymbol{\varphi}_{\omega_i}^{(k)}(\boldsymbol{\omega})$ can be obtained by

$$\boldsymbol{\varphi}_{\omega_i}^{(s)}(\boldsymbol{\omega}) = \varphi_{\omega_i}^{(s-1)}(\boldsymbol{\omega}) - \frac{1}{a_{s,s}} \frac{\delta a_{s,k+1}(\boldsymbol{\omega})}{\delta \omega_i} \varphi_{\mathbf{s}}^{\mathbf{i-1}} \tag{10}$$

where $s = 1, \ldots, k$, $i = 0, 1, \ldots, n$ and

$$\frac{\delta a_{s,k+1}(\boldsymbol{\omega})}{\delta \omega_i} = (\boldsymbol{\varphi}_s^{(s-1)})^T \varphi_{\omega_i}^{(s-1)}(\boldsymbol{\omega}) \tag{11}$$

while

$$\boldsymbol{\varphi}_{\omega_i}^{(0)}(\boldsymbol{\omega}) = \varphi_{\omega_i}(\boldsymbol{\omega}) = [\varphi_{(\omega_i)}(\mathbf{x}(1), \boldsymbol{\omega}), \ldots, \varphi_{(\omega_i)}(\mathbf{x}(N), \boldsymbol{\omega})]^T \tag{12}$$

where $\varphi_{\omega_i}^{(j)}(\boldsymbol{\omega}), j = 0, 1, \ldots, k$ denotes the partial differentiation of $\varphi^{(j)}(\boldsymbol{\omega}), j = 0, 1, \ldots, k$ with respect to $\omega_i$.

2. In order to calculate the additional elements of the upper triangular matrix $\mathbf{A}$ and the vector $\mathbf{a}_y$ (for use in the next iteration), first compute the output vector $\boldsymbol{\varphi}_{k+1} = \varphi(\omega_{k+1})$ of the $(k+1)^{th}$ hidden node. Then,

$$\left.\begin{array}{r} a_{s,k+1} = (\boldsymbol{\varphi}_s^{(s-1)})^T \boldsymbol{\varphi}_{k+1}^{(s-1)}, \boldsymbol{\varphi}_{(k+1)}^{(s)} = \boldsymbol{\varphi}_{(k+1)}^{(s-1)} - \dfrac{a_{s,k+1}}{a_{s,s}} \boldsymbol{\varphi}_s^{(s-1)}, s = 1, \ldots, k \\ a_{k+1,k+1} = (\boldsymbol{\varphi}_{k+1)}^{(k)})^T \boldsymbol{\varphi}_{k+1}^{(k)}, a_{k+1,y} = (\mathbf{y}^{(k)})^T \boldsymbol{\varphi}_{k+1}^{(k)} \end{array}\right\} \tag{13}$$

where $\boldsymbol{\varphi}_{k+1}^{(0)} = \boldsymbol{\varphi}_{k+1}$. Update the output vector $\mathbf{y}$ by

$$\mathbf{y}^{(k+1)} = \mathbf{y}^{(k)} - \frac{a_{k+1,y}}{a_{k+1,k+1}} \boldsymbol{\varphi}_{(k+1)}^{(k)} \tag{14}$$

3. Let SSE = SSE $- \Delta J_{k+1}(\boldsymbol{\varphi}_{(k+1)})$. If some condition is satisfied (eg. the desired number of nodes $m$ has been reached, or the reduction in SSE falls below a set threshold), stop network construction. Otherwise, increment $k$ by one and return to step 1 to begin selection of the next hidden node.

# 4 Application Study – Continuously Stirred Tank Reactor

The system studied is a simulated Continuously Stirred Tank Reactor (CSTR) [11].

## 4.1 Physical System

The system is single-input, single-output, where the input variable is the flowrate of a coolant $q_c(t)$, and the output variable is the concentration of the product $C_a(t)$. The reaction is exothermic; if uncooled, the heat generated acts to slow it down. $T(t)$ is the temperature of the solution. Figure 2 shows a simple schematic of the plant, and equations (15) and (16) define the physical relationship between $q_c(t)$, $C_a(t)$ and $T(t)$.

$$\dot{C}_a(t) = \frac{q}{v}(C_{ao} - C_a(t)) - k_o C_a(t)\exp\left(-\frac{E}{RT(t)}\right) \tag{15}$$

$$\begin{aligned}\dot{T}(t) = \frac{q}{v}(T_o - T(t)) + k_1 C_a(t)\exp\left(-\frac{E}{RT(t)}\right) + \cdots \\ k_2 q_c(t)\left(1 - \exp\left(-\frac{k_3}{q_c(t)}\right)\right)(T_{co} - T(t))\end{aligned} \tag{16}$$

where

$$k_1 = -\frac{\Delta H k_0}{\rho C_p}, k_2 = \frac{\rho_c C_{pc}}{\rho C_p v}, k_3 = \frac{h_a}{\rho C_{pc}}$$

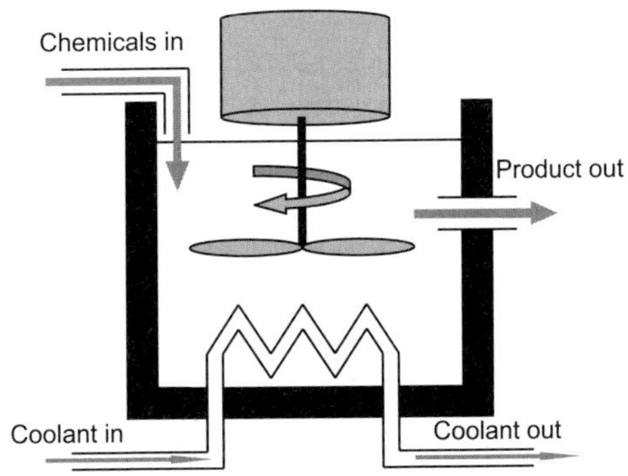


**Fig. 2.** Schematic of a CSTR plant

**Table 1.** Nominal values for CSTR parameters

| Parameter | | Nominal Value |
|---|---|---|
| Process flowrate | $q$ | $100l/\text{min}$ |
| Reactor volume | $v$ | $100l$ |
| Reaction rate constant | $k_0$ | $7.8 \times 10^{10}\text{min}^{-1}$ |
| Activation energy | $E/R$ | $1 \times 10^4\text{K}$ |
| Feed temperature | $T_0$ | 350K |
| Inlet coolant temperature | $T_{co}$ | 350K |
| Heat of reaction | $\Delta H$ | $-2 \times 10^5\text{cal/mol}$ |
| Specific heats | $C_p$, $C_{pc}$ | 1cal/g/K |
| Liquid densities | $\rho$, $\rho_c$ | $1 \times 10^3\text{g}/l$ |
| Heat transfer coefficient | $h_a$ | $7 \times 10^5\text{cal/min/K}$ |
| Inlet feed concentration | $C_{ao}$ | $1.0\text{mol}/l$ |

### 4.2 Modelling Data

For a steady-state output concentration of $C_a(T) = 0.1\text{mol}/l$, and using the nominal parameter values given in table 1, equations (15) and (16) yield equivalent values of $T(t) = 438.54\text{K}$ and $q_c(t) = 103.41l/\text{min}$. The system was simulated with a sampling interval of 0.2 seconds. The input signal for identification consisted of uniformly distributed random step perturbations in the input $q_c(t)$ over the range [-9,9]$l$/min about the operating point with a step duration of 4 seconds, to which was added a small (variance $= 0.1l/\text{min}$) normally distributed noise signal. A normally distributed random noise was also added to the output to simulate measurement error.

### 4.3 Neural Modelling

Two types of network are created using the forward search algorithm. The first is a standard multilayer perceptron, which uses a sigmoid activation function of the form

$$y = \tanh(\omega_0 + \omega_1 u_1 + \omega_2 u_2 + \ldots + \omega_n u_n) \tag{17}$$

where $y$ is the neuron output, $\omega_0$ is the bias, $u_i$ is the $i^{\text{th}}$ input to the neuron, and $\omega_i$ is the corresponding weight value.

The second type of network created is an eng-genes network. From the physical equations (15) and (16), it is evident that the nonlinearity in the plant is due to Arrhenius terms of the form:

$$k = A\exp\left(\frac{-E_a}{RT}\right) \tag{18}$$

where $k$ is the rate coefficient, $A$ is a constant, $E_a$ is the activation energy, $R$ is the universal gas constant, and $T$ is the temperature (in degrees Kelvin).

This ‘a priori’ knowledge leads to the use of an Arrhenius-type activation function for the eng-genes network, of the form:

$$y = \exp\left(\frac{-a}{\omega_0 + \omega_1 u_1 + \omega_2 u_2 + \ldots + \omega_n u_n}\right) \tag{19}$$

where $y$, $\omega_0$, $\omega_i$ and $u_i$ are defined as above, and $a$ is an adjustable parameter. While standard neural network training algorithms optimise only the weights and biases $\boldsymbol{\omega}$, the forward selection algorithm is capable of also selecting an appropriate value for $a$.

In addition to the plant input $q_c(t)$, the regressors $q_c(t-2)$, $q_c(t-4)$, $q_c(t-5)$, $C_a(t-1)$ and $C_a(t-5)$ were chosen as inputs to the CSTR model, as they had been found to be the most significant in previous work [9]. Of the 3000 samples of plant data available, the first 1000 were used in constructing neural models, and the remaining 2000 kept for test purposes.

### 4.4 Results

In order to retain the transparency of the eng-genes models, the networks created are kept small. Ten MLP networks and ten eng-genes networks are created, and the root mean-squared error

$$\text{RMSE} = \sqrt{\sum_{i=1}^{N} \frac{(y_i - \hat{y}_i)^2}{N}} \tag{20}$$

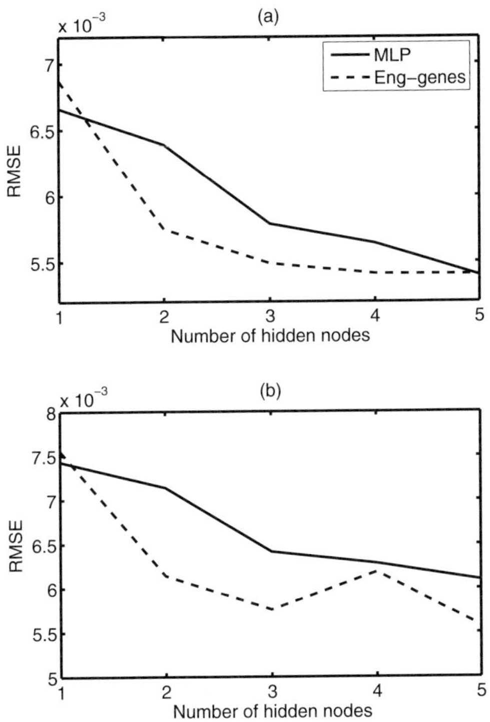


**Fig. 3.** Variation in mean RMS error from 10 candidate networks with number of hidden nodes (a) - Modelling dataset (b) - Validation dataset

is measured under parallel simulation over both the modelling and test datasets, as each subsequent node is added to the network. The mean RMSE values over 10 networks as the networks are created are shown in figure 3.

### 4.5 Computational Complexity

During the network configuration for the CSTR system, the number of floating-point operations (FLOPs) was counted for each of the 10 MLP and 10 eng-genes network models (using the 'flops' function, MATLAB 5.3). The minimum, maximum and mean values are given in Table 2.

**Table 2.** Computational load comparison

| | **FLOPs** $\times 10^6$ | | |
|---|---|---|---|
| **Network Type** | Minimum | Maximum | Mean |
| MLP | 64 | 220 | 124 |
| Eng-genes | 47 | 105 | 63 |

## 5 Conclusions

A method for constructing eng-genes grey-box neural models using an integrated selection and optimisation algorithm is introduced. This method allows for fast, simultaneous selection of hidden-layer nodes and optimisation of nonlinear parameters, as opposed to other methods which are either computationally complex or require combinations of techniques. Results from a simulation study of a continuous stirred-tank process are given, in which both conventional neural models and eng-genes models are produced using the method.

It may be noted that while the conventional MLP models only produce a better performance in the trivial case of a one-hidden-node network, the accuracy of both network types begins to converge as the hidden layer size increases past three nodes. However, as the complexity of the network increases beyond a handful of hidden nodes, the transparency of the model begins to suffer, thus marginalising one of the principal advantages of a grey-box type model. Thus, large 'eng-genes' networks are normally avoided in any case.

From a computational load standpoint, in this case the eng-genes models are consistently quicker to derive than their MLP counterparts, as shown in Table 2. This advantage may, however, be mitigated in a case where multiple potential activation functions are identified and must be evaluated.

## References

1. Bohlin, T.: Case study of grey box identification. Automatica vol.30 (2) (1994) 307–318
2. Li, K., Thompson, S., Peng, J.: Modelling and prediction of nox emission in a coal-fired power generation plant. Control Engineering Practice vol.12 (2004) 707–723

3. Li, K.: Eng-genes: A new genetic modelling approach for nonlinear dynamic systems. In: Proceedings of the 16th IFAC World Congress. (2005)
4. Funahashi, K.I.: On the approximate realization of continuous mappings by neural networks. Neural Networks vol.2 (1989) 183–192
5. Kolmogorov, A.N.: On the representation of continuous functions of many variables by superposition of continuous functions of one variable and addition. Dokl. Akad. Nauk USSR vol.114 (1957) 953–956
6. Psichogios, D.C., Ungar, L.H.: A hybrid neural network - first principles approach to process modeling. AiChE vol.38 (1992) 1499–1511
7. Chen, S., Billings, S.A., Luo, W.: Orthogonal least squares methods and their application to non-linear system identification. International Journal of Control vol.50 (5) (1989) 1873–1896
8. Hagan, M.H., Menhaj, M.B.: Training feedforward networks with the marquardt algorithm. IEEE Transactions on Neural Networks vol.5 (6) (1994) 989–993
9. Connally, P., Li, K., Irwin, G.W.: Two applications of eng-genes bases nonlinear identification. In: Proceedings of the 16th IFAC World Congress. (2005)
10. Li, K., Peng, J.X., Irwin, G.W.: A fast nonlinear model identification method. IEEE Transactions on Automatic Control vol.50 (8) (2005) 1211–16
11. Morningred, J.D., Paden, B.E., Seborg, D.E., Mellichamp, D.A.: An adaptive nonlinear predictive controller. Proc. American Control Conference vol.2 (1990) 1614–1619

# Meta-Learning Evolutionary Artificial Neural Networks Using Cellular Configurations: Experimental Works

Asma Abu Salah and Yahya Al-Salqan

Computer science Department, Al-Quds University, Jerusalem, Palestine
aabusalah@science.alquds.edu, alsalqan@i-jaffa.net

**Abstract.** In this paper, we present the experimental works performed to test and explore the performance of our proposed framework: meta-learning evolutionary artificial neural network by means of cellular automata (MLEANN-CA). This framework based on evolutionary computation with direct and indirect encoding methods (cellular automata) for automatic design of optimal artificial neural networks wherein the neural network architecture, activation function, connection weights, and the learning algorithm with its parameters are adapted according to the problem. We used two toolboxes for simulations: NeuroSolutions and NeuroGenetic Optimizer besides two famous chaotic time series. We compared the performance of the proposed MLEANN-CA with the previous MLEANN framework, which used the direct encoding methods, and with the conventional design of ANNs. We demonstrated how effective is the proposed MLEANN-CA framework to obtain a design of feed-forward neural network that is smaller, faster and with better generalization performance.

## 1 Introduction

Evolutionary algorithms are used to adapt the connection weights, network architecture, and learning algorithms according to the problem environment. Even though evolutionary algorithms are well known as efficient global search algorithms, very often they miss the best local solutions in the complex solution space. In other words, they are inefficiency in fine-tuned local search [1, 2, 9]. This is especially true for GA's. The efficiency of evolutionary algorithms can be improved significantly by using a hybrid learning approach that incorporates the EA's global search ability with local search's ability to fine tune. Thus, the EA is used to locate a good region in the space and then a local search procedure, such as BP or other random search algorithm, is used to find a near-optimal solution in this region [1, 2, 9]. Several hybrid learning approaches had been successfully used for evolving neural network topology and/or weights. One of these hybrid learning approaches is called meta-learning evolutionary artificial neural networks (MLEANN) [1, 2]. It can be considered as an automatic computational framework that used a direct encoding method for the adaptive optimization of ANNs. In the MLEANN, all the randomly generated architecture of the initial population are trained and evolved separately by four different learning algorithms (backpropagation -BP, scaled conjugate gradient -SCG, quasi-Newton algorithm -QNA

D.-S. Huang, K. Li, and G.W. Irwin (Eds.): ICIC 2006, LNCS 4113, pp. 178 – 193, 2006.

and Levenberg-Marquardt -LM) in a parallel environment. Parameters controlling the performance of the learning algorithm (as learning rate and momentum for BP) are adapted according to the problem. The basic Meta-learning algorithm and the chromosome representation of the MLEANN framework can be found in [1, 3].

The MLEANN used the direct encoding methods for the adaptive optimization of artificial neural network architectures. These direct encoding methods base on the codification of the complete network into the chromosome. They are relatively simple and straightforward to implement but requires much larger chromosomes especially for ANNs with complex architectures. This could end in a too huge space search that could make the method impossible in practice. On the other hand, implementation of crossover operator for the chromosome is often difficult due to production of non-functional offsprings [1, 2]. An alternative more interesting for optimizing the ANN architecture is the indirect encoding methods. These methods concentrate on codifying a compact representation of the networks reducing the length of the genotype and avoiding the scalability problem. One of these indirect encoding methods is the cellular automata [6, 8]. This method was used by Gutirrez [6] and according to his experiment he proved that using cellular configurations for designing feed-forward NN architectures is more efficient than using the direct encoding methods. Therefore, we present in this paper an adaptive computational framework: meta-learning evolutionary artificial neural network by means of cellular automata. This framework (MLEANN-CA) combines the local search methods with the evolutionary learning in order to obtain an efficient design of NNs that is smaller, faster and with better generalization performance using direct and indirect encoding methods. The MLEANN-CA framework is explored and simulated using NeuroSolutions and NeuroGenetic Optimizer toolboxes, and two famous chaotic time series [5, 7].

This paper is organized as follows: In section 2, we examined the proposed approach: meta-learning evolutionary artificial neural networks by means of cellular automata (MLEANN-CA). Experiments and Results are provided in section 3. Section 4 provides conclusions and future works for this research. The references are provided at the end of the paper.

## 2 Meta-Learning Evolutionary Artificial Neural Networks by Means of Cellular Automata

Two main stages compose the proposed framework in this research: the cellular configuration stage and the meta-learning stage. The cellular configuration stage includes three main modules for designing small neural network architectures: the genetic algorithm module, the cellular automata module, and the neural network module. The meta-learning stage includes the meta-learning algorithm that is responsible for training and evolving the new generated architectures with the direct codification using different learning algorithms in parallel mode. The system architecture and the modules relationship is shown in figure (1).

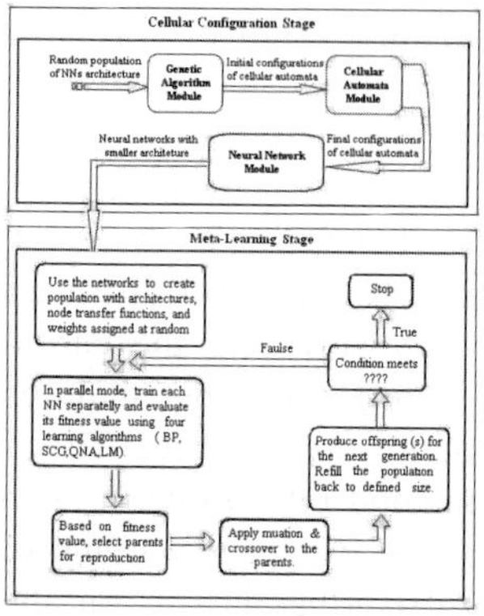


**Fig. 1.** System's architecture and modules relationship

## 2.1 Proposed Approach / MLEANN-CA

The MLEANN-CA approach can be summarized as follows [3]:

1. Randomly, generate an initial population of neural networks with architectures according to the indicated problem.
2. Apply the indirect encoding technique (CA) for optimizing each NN architecture. This is done by the following steps:
   - The GA module takes charge of generating initial configurations of the cellular automata, i.e. seeds positions in a two-dimensional grid.
   - The cellular automata module takes the initial configurations and generates final configurations corresponding to particular NN architectures. This is done using cellular automata rules that allow the convergence of the automata toward a final configuration.
   - The neural network module translates these final cellular configurations into feed-forward NN with smaller architectures.
3. Use the translated NNs to create an initial population with architectures, node transfer functions, and weights assigned at random.
4. In parallel mode, train each translated neural network separately and evaluate the fitness value for each one using the four learning algorithms (BP, SCG, QNA, and LM).
5. Based on the fitness value, select parents for reproduction.
6. Apply mutation to the parents and produce offspring (s) for the next generation Refill the population back to the defined size.
7. Repeat step 4.
8. Stop when the required solution is found or number of iterations reached the required limit.

**Genetic Algorithm Module** [3, 6]**.** This module works with a population of chromosomes that codifies the seeds positions in a two-dimension grid. The size of chromosomes in the GA corresponds with the number of seeds, and it codifies all the possible locations of seeds in the grid. Chromosomes have been codified in base b, where b is the number of rows in the grid and is given through the number of inputs plus the number of outputs of the neural network. Each seed is determined by a co-ordinate (x, y). A unique gene, indicating the row in which the seed is located, represents the first co-ordinate x. The second co-ordinate y will require more than one gene, if, as usual, the maximal number of hidden neurons is bigger than b. In this particular case, two genes have been used to codify the y coordinate, what allows a maximum of b*b hidden neurons. This could be a good estimation of the maximum number of neurons in the hidden layer, but any other consideration could be taken into account without modifying the proposed method. Hence, the chromosome will have 3 genes for each seed to be placed in the grid.

**Cellular Automata Module** [3, 6]**.** For generating neural networks architectures, a two-dimension CA has been used. The size of the two-dimension grid, Dimx*Dimy, is defined as follows: Dimx (rows) is equal to the number of input neurons plus the number of output neurons; Dimy (columns) corresponds with the maximum number of hidden neurons to be considered. Each cell in the grid could be in two different states: active (occupied by a seed) or inactive. Two different kinds of seeds have been introduced: growing seeds and decreasing seeds. The first kind allows making connections and the second one removing connections. Each seed type corresponds with a different type of automata rule, so there are two rules called growing rule and decreasing rule respectively. The rules determine the evolution of the grid configuration and they have been designed allowing the reproduction of growing and decreasing seeds. In the description of the rules, **s** is a specific growing seed, **d** is a decreasing seed, **i** is an inactive state for the cell, and **a** means that the cell could be in any state or contains any type of seed (even a decreasing seed). The growing rules reproduce a particular growing seed when there are at least three identical growing seeds in its neighborhood. There are different configurations, growing seeds located in: rows, columns, or in a corner of the neighborhood. In figure (2) (a) [3, 6], one of those rules is shown. The growing rules allow obtaining feed-forward NN with a large number of connections. The decreasing rules remove connections in the network deactivating a cell in the grid when the cell has a seed and a cell of its neighborhood contains also a decreasing seed. One situation in which the decreasing rules can be applied is shown in figure (2) (b) [3, 6], the others can be obtained symmetrically.

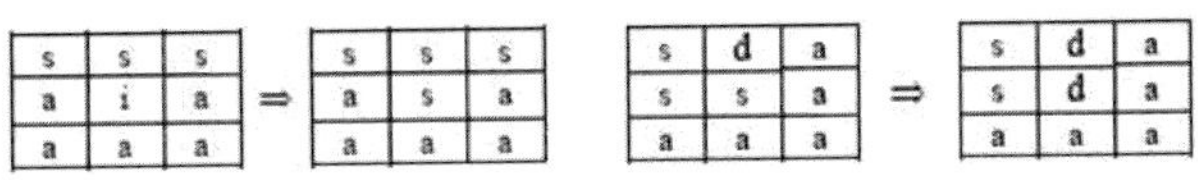

**Fig. 2.** (a): Example of growing rules, (b) Example of decreasing rules

The mechanism of expanding the CA is as follows:

1. The growing seeds are located in the grid.
2. An expansion of the growing seeds takes place. This expansion consists on replicating each seed in turns, over its quadratic neighborhood, in such a way that if a new seed has to be placed in a position previously occupied by another seed, the first one is replaced.
3. The growing rules are applied until no more rules could be fired.
4. The decreasing seeds are placed in the grid. If there are some other seeds in those places, they are replaced.
5. The decreasing rules are applied until the final configuration is reached.
6. The final configuration of the CA is obtained replacing the growing seeds by a **1** and the decreasing seeds or inactive cells by a **0**.

**Neural Network Module** [3, 6]. To relate the final configuration of the CA with an architecture of a NN, the following meaning for a cell in the (x,y) grid is defined: If x < n, with n the number of input neurons, (x,y) represents a connection between the x-th input neuron and the y-th hidden neuron; If x > n, (x,y) represents a connection between the y-th hidden neuron and the (x -n) -th output neuron. In the final configuration, **1** is interpreted as a connection, and **0** as the absence of connection. Thus, the rows and columns in the **matrix** with values 0 are removed. A new and shorter binary matrix (M) is obtained. If Mij=1 then a connection between the i-th input neuron and the j-th hidden neuron is created, or between the j-th hidden neuron and the (i-n)-th output neuron, as is previously described. If Mij=0, there do not exist connection between that neurons. When the final matrix connection is obtained from the final configuration of CA there are cases taken into account, following these steps:

1. If there is a node in hidden layer without any connection to output, this node is eliminated from the net.
2. When a hidden node has no connection from input, but it's connected to output layer, two chances have been considerate: penalizes the net and don't train it, or eliminate that node and is training.
3. If an output node has no connection from hidden layer, the net is penalized and is not trained.

**Table 1.** Parameters used for EANNs

| Parameter | Setting |
|---|---|
| Population size | 40 |
| Maximum no of generations | 40 |
| Number of hidden nodes | 3 to 36 neurons |
| Activation functions | tanh (T), logistic (L), sigmoidal (S). |
| Output neuron | Linear (Li) |
| Training epochs | 500 , 2500 |
| Initialization of weights | + / - 0.3 |
| Ranked based selection | 0.50 |
| Mutation rate | 0.40 |
| Crossover / one point | 0.50 |

**Table 2.** Parameters for the Learning Algorithms

| Learning algorithm | Parameter | Setting |
|---|---|---|
| Backpropagation (BP) | Learning rate | 0.25-0.05 |
| | Momentum rate | 0.25-0.05 |
| Scaled conjugate gradient (SCG) | ---------------- | ------------- |
| Quasi Newton algorithm (QNA) | Step size | 0.1 - 0.6 |
| Levenberg Marquardt (LM) | Learning rate | 0.001 -0.02 |

**Table 3.** Training and test performance for Mackey-glass time series with 4 I/P & 2 O/P

| Mackey-glass time series | | | |
|---|---|---|---|
| Learning algorithm | Hidden neurons | RMSE | |
| | | Training data | Testing data |
| BP | 3 | 0.1188 | 0.1192 |
| | 5 | 0.1165 | 0.1158 |
| | 14 | 0.1088 | 0.1076 |
| | 16 | 0.1006 | 0.1049 |
| | 18 | 0.0938 | 0.0922 |
| | 36 | 0.0490 | 0.0484 |
| SCG | 3 | 0.0106 | 0.0114 |
| | 5 | 0.0095 | 0.0101 |
| | 14 | 0.0062 | 0.0076 |
| | 16 | 0.0085 | 0.0083 |
| | 18 | 0.0084 | 0.0085 |
| | 36 | 0.0058 | 0.0059 |
| QNA | 3 | 0.0091 | 0.0090 |
| | 5 | 0.0073 | 0.0074 |
| | 14 | 0.0050 | 0.0049 |
| | 16 | 0.0040 | 0.0038 |
| | 18 | 0.0052 | 0.0053 |
| | 36 | 0.0042 | 0.0041 |
| LM | 3 | 0.0061 | 0.0072 |
| | 5 | 0.0043 | 0.0052 |
| | 14 | 0.0023 | 0.0023 |
| | 16 | 0.0020 | 0.0020 |
| | 18 | 0.0020 | 0.0020 |
| | 36 | 0.0012 | 0.0012 |

# 3 Experiments and Results

## 3.1 Test Collections and Test Environment

In our experiments, we used two different time series for training the neural networks and evaluating the performance. These two time series are: Mackey-glass [7] and Gas

Furnace [5] time series. The first 50% of such data was used for training and the remaining is for testing. The raw datasets for these two time series could be found in http://neural.cs.nthu.edu.tw/jang/dataset/. The experiments were simulated using two toolboxes: NeuroSolutions (version 5.01), and NeuroGenetic Optimizer (version 2.1). These toolboxes are used for training and optimizing the neural networks. The experiments were carried out on a computer with the following configurations: 1.8 GHz AMD processor, 512 MB RAM, and Windows XP Professional. In our proposed framework (MLEANN-CA), several parameters can influence the experiments. These parameters can be distinguished into two categories: the parameters that are related to the Evolutionary Artificial Neural networks; and the parameters that are related to the learning algorithms. The parameters in tables (1) and (2) were set to be the same for the two data sets, and were finalized after a few trail and error approaches according to Ajith [1].

### 3.2 The Experiments Conducted

For each data set mentioned before, three main experimental simulations are carried out. The first one evaluates the performance of the conventional design of artificial neural networks. The second one explores the performance of the MLEANN framework. The third one test and explore the performance of our proposed approach: MLEANN-CA. These experiments use four different learning algorithms in the training process. By applying these experiments, we (a) should know the best solution, we (b) can carefully control various parameters, and we (c) should know the effect of different learning algorithms namely BP, SCG, QNA and LM on different data sets.

**Artificial Neural Networks: Experiments and Results.** In this subsection, we used two different time series, i.e. Mackey-glass and Gas furnace, for training the artificial neural networks and evaluating their performance. We used a feed-forward neural network with one hidden layer for the two time series. The number of hidden neurons were varied (3, 5, 14, 16, 18, 36) as indicated in table (1). The speed of convergence and generalization error for each of the four learning algorithms was observed. Any required parameter for any learning algorithm is found in table (2). Performances of the four different learning algorithms were evaluated when the architecture is changed. No stopping criterion, and no method of controlling generalization is used other than the maximum number of updates (epochs). All networks were trained for an identical number of stochastic updates: 2500 epochs. We used the same node transfer function for the hidden layer and the output layer: tanh (T) and linear (Li). Table (3) summarizes the empirical results of training and generalization for different architectures with four inputs and two outputs in Mackey-glass time series {x(t −18), x(t −12), x(t −6), x(t), x(t +6), x(t+12)}.

Table (4) summarizes the empirical results of training and generalization for different architectures with three inputs and two outputs in Mackey-glass time series {x(t −12), x(t −6), x(t), x(t +6), x(t+12)}.

**Table 4.** Training and test performance for Mackey-glass time series with 3 I/P & 2 O/P

| **Mackey-glass time series** | | | |
|---|---|---|---|
| **Learning algorithm** | **Hidden neurons** | **RMSE** | |
| | | **Training data** | **Testing data** |
| **BP** | 3 | 0.1426 | 0.1430 |
| | 5 | 0.1398 | 0.1390 |
| | 14 | 0.1306 | 0.1292 |
| | 16 | 0.1207 | 0.1259 |
| | 18 | 0.1126 | 0.1106 |
| | 36 | 0.0588 | 0.0580 |
| **SCG** | 3 | 0.0127 | 0.0137 |
| | 5 | 0.0114 | 0.0121 |
| | 14 | 0.0075 | 0.0091 |
| | 16 | 0.0102 | 0.0099 |
| | 18 | 0.0101 | 0.0102 |
| | 36 | 0.0069 | 0.0071 |
| **QNA** | 3 | 0.0109 | 0.0108 |
| | 5 | 0.0088 | 0.0089 |
| | 14 | 0.0060 | 0.0059 |
| | 16 | 0.0048 | 0.0046 |
| | 18 | 0.0062 | 0.0063 |
| | 36 | 0.0050 | 0.0049 |
| **LM** | 3 | 0.0073 | 0.0086 |
| | 5 | 0.0052 | 0.0062 |
| | 14 | 0.0027 | 0.0027 |
| | 16 | 0.0024 | 0.0024 |
| | 18 | 0.0024 | 0.0024 |
| | 36 | 0.0014 | 0.0014 |

Table (5) summarizes the empirical results of training and generalization for different architectures with four inputs and two outputs in Gas furnace time series {y(t-1), y (t-2), u(t-3),u (t-4), y (t), y(t+1)}.

**Table 5.** Training and test performance for Gas furnace time series with 4 I/P & 2 O/P

| **Gas Furnace time series** | | | |
|---|---|---|---|
| **Learning algorithm** | **Hidden neurons** | **RMSE** | |
| | | **Training data** | **Testing data** |
| **BP** | 3 | 0.0553 | 0.0596 |
| | 5 | 0.0550 | 0.0632 |
| | 14 | 0.0503 | 0.0968 |
| | 16 | 0.0626 | 0.0792 |
| | 18 | 0.0538 | 0.0575 |
| | 36 | 0.0514 | 0.0823 |

**Table 5.** *(continued)*

| | | | |
|---|---|---|---|
| **SCG** | 3 | 0.0148 | 0.0433 |
| | 5 | 0.0138 | 0.0424 |
| | 14 | 0.0120 | 0.0269 |
| | 16 | 0.0118 | 0.0268 |
| | 18 | 0.0124 | 0.0268 |
| | 36 | 0.0112 | 0.0401 |
| **QNA** | 3 | 0.0118 | 0.0442 |
| | 5 | 0.0112 | 0.0431 |
| | 14 | 0.0104 | 0.0446 |
| | 16 | 0.0100 | 0.0378 |
| | 18 | 0.0100 | 0.0306 |
| | 36 | 0.0098 | 0.0427 |
| **LM** | 3 | 0.0097 | 0.0397 |
| | 5 | 0.0092 | 0.0407 |
| | 14 | 0.0089 | 0.0366 |
| | 16 | 0.0098 | 0.0789 |
| | 18 | 0.0088 | 0.0878 |
| | 36 | 0.0077 | 0.1744 |

Table (6) summarizes the empirical results of training and generalization for different architectures with three inputs and two outputs in Gas furnace time series {y(t-1), u(t-3), u(t-4), y(t), y(t+1)}.

*ANN- Results Discussion.* For Mackey-glass series (tables 3 - 4), all the four learning algorithms tend to generalize well (i.e. test set RMSE decreased) as the hidden neurons were increased. The run time also increases for the four learning algorithms as the number of hidden nodes increase. LM showed the fastest convergence regardless of architecture. As an example (in table 3), the LM gave the lowest generalization RMSE of 0.0012 with 36 hidden neurons. However, the run time of LM algorithm is the longest in comparison with the other learning algorithms. On the other hand, for every learning algorithm with the same number of hidden nodes and same number of outputs, the RMSE will increase and the run time will decrease as the number of inputs decrease. This is true for Mackey glass and Gas furnace time series. For Gas furnace series (as shown in tables 5 - 6), the generalization performance were entirely different for the different learning algorithms. Better generalization does not depend on increasing the hidden neurons. For example (in table 5), BP gave the best generalization RMSE of 0.0575 with 18 hidden neurons. RMSE for SCG, QNA and LM were 0.0268 (16 neurons), 0.0306 (18 neurons) and 0.0366 (14 neurons), respectively. However, increasing the number of hidden nodes will cause increasing in execution time for every learning algorithm, and the LM algorithm will have the longest execution time. In spite of execution time, LM performed well for Mackey-glass series. For gas furnace SCG algorithm performed better.

**MLEANN: Experiments and Results.** In this subsection, we explore the performance of the MLEANN approach. We applied this MLEANN approach to the two-time

**Table 6.** Training and test performance for Gas furnace time series with 3 I/P & 2 O/P

| Gas Furnace time series | | | |
|---|---|---|---|
| Learning algorithm | Hidden neurons | RMSE | |
| | | Training data | Testing data |
| BP | 3 | 0.0664 | 0.0715 |
| | 5 | 0.0660 | 0.0759 |
| | 14 | 0.0603 | 0.1162 |
| | 16 | 0.0752 | 0.0950 |
| | 18 | 0.0645 | 0.0689 |
| | 36 | 0.0616 | 0.0987 |
| SCG | 3 | 0.0177 | 0.0520 |
| | 5 | 0.0166 | 0.0509 |
| | 14 | 0.0144 | 0.0323 |
| | 16 | 0.0141 | 0.0322 |
| | 18 | 0.0148 | 0.0322 |
| | 36 | 0.0134 | 0.0481 |
| QNA | 3 | 0.0141 | 0.0530 |
| | 5 | 0.0134 | 0.0518 |
| | 14 | 0.0125 | 0.0535 |
| | 16 | 0.0120 | 0.0453 |
| | 18 | 0.0120 | 0.0367 |
| | 36 | 0.0118 | 0.0513 |
| LM | 3 | 0.0117 | 0.0476 |
| | 5 | 0.0111 | 0.0488 |
| | 14 | 0.0107 | 0.0439 |
| | 16 | 0.0118 | 0.0947 |
| | 18 | 0.0105 | 0.1053 |
| | 36 | 0.0092 | 0.2093 |

series prediction problems discussed before. We used the Neurosolution and Neuro-Genetic optimizer toolboxes in training and optimizing processes. For performance comparison, we used the same set of training and test data that were used for experimentations with conventional design of neural networks. We used the same feed-forward neural network with one hidden layer for the two time series. The number of hidden neurons was varied (from 3 to 36) as indicated in table (1). For performance evaluation, the parameters used in this experiment were set to be the same for the two problems. Fitness value is calculated based on the RMSE achieved on the test set. In this experiment, we have considered the best-evolved neural network as the best individual of the last generation. As the learning process is evolved separately, user has the option to pick the best neural network (e.g. less RMSE, fast convergence, less run time, or small architecture size, etc.) among the four learning algorithms. All the genotypes were represented using binary coding and the initial populations were randomly generated based on the parameters shown in table (1). All networks with different architectures were trained for an identical number of stochastic updates (500 epochs) using the same four learning algorithms. The parameter settings, which were evolved for the different learning algorithms, are found in table (2). The experiments were repeated three times and the worst RMSE values are reported. Tables (7–10) display empirical values of RMSE on test data for the two time series problems using the meta-learning technique with different architectures. They also illustrate the run times of the MLEANN for the two time series with different architectures. For comparison purposes, see the RMSE for the conventional design of ANN that are presented in tables (3–6).

**Table 7.** Performance & run time for MLEANN using Mackey-glass time series (4 I/P – 2 O/P)

| Learning algorithm | EANN | | | ANN | Run time (min) |
|---|---|---|---|---|---|
| | RMSE | | Architecture | Architecture | 4 i/p - 2 o/p |
| | Train | Test | | | |
| BP | 0.0207 | 0.0210 | 3:3T:2Li | 4 : 3T : 2Li | 268.80 |
| | 0.0201 | 0.0204 | 3:5T:2Li | 4 : 5 T: 2 Li | 293.40 |
| | 0.0091 | 0.0096 | 3:11T:2Li | 4 :24T :2 Li | 501.00 |
| | 0.0081 | 0.0085[a] | 3:18T:2Li | 4 :36T :2 Li | 537.60[a] |
| SCG | 0.0074 | 0.0079 | 3:3T:2Li | 4 : 3T : 2Li | 440.41 |
| | 0.0068 | 0.0070 | 3:5T:2Li | 4 : 5 T: 2 Li | 483.64 |
| | 0.0044 | 0.0045 | 3:13T:2Li | 4 :24T :2 Li | 834.32 |
| | 0.0040 | 0.0041[a] | 3:20T:2Li | 4 :36T :2 Li | 906.29[a] |
| QNA | 0.0072 | 0.0071 | 3:3T:2Li | 4 : 3T : 2Li | 465.18 |
| | 0.0061 | 0.0059 | 3:5T:2Li | 4 : 5 T: 2 Li | 511.11 |
| | 0.0034 | 0.0037 | 3:11T:2Li | 4 :24T :2 Li | 885.13 |
| | 0.0030 | 0.0033[a] | 3:18T:2Li | 4 :36T :2 Li | 962.02[a] |
| LM | 0.0027 | 0.0032 | 3:3T:2Li | 4 : 3T : 2Li | 524.75 |
| | 0.0021 | 0.0023 | 3:5T:2Li | 4 : 5 T: 2 Li | 576.08 |
| | 0.0006 | 0.0006 | 3:12T:2Li | 4 :24T :2 Li | 996.92 |
| | 0.0005 | *0.0005[a] | 3:19T:2Li | 4 :36T :2 Li | *1086.35[a] |

**a :** ***Lowest RMSE / Maximum run time in each algorithm***
*** :** ***Lowest RMSE / Maximum run time in all the algorithms***

**Table 8.** Performance & run time for MLEANN using Mackey-glass time series (3 I/P – 2 O/P)

| Learning algorithm | EANN | | | ANN | Run time (min) |
|---|---|---|---|---|---|
| | RMSE | | Architecture | Architecture | 3 i/p - 2 o/p |
| | Train | Test | | | |
| BP | 0.0249 | 0.0252 | 3:3T:2Li | 3: 3T : 2Li | 246.60 |
| | 0.0241 | 0.0245 | 3:4T:2Li | 3: 5T : 2 Li | 269.40 |
| | 0.0110 | 0.0115 | 3:9T:2Li | 3:24T :2 Li | 305.40 |
| | 0.0100 | 0.0102[a] | 3:16T:2Li | 3:36T :2 Li | 400.20[a] |
| SCG | 0.0090 | 0.0094 | 3:3T:2Li | 3: 3T : 2Li | 404.04 |
| | 0.0081 | 0.0083 | 3:5T:2Li | 3: 5T : 2 Li | 444.08 |
| | 0.0052 | 0.0054 | 3:12T:2Li | 3:24T :2 Li | 508.59 |
| | 0.0047 | 0.0049[a] | 3:19T:2Li | 3:36T :2 Li | 674.66[a] |

**Table 8.** *(continued)*

| | | | | | |
|---|---|---|---|---|---|
| **QNA** | 0.0087 | 0.0086 | 3:3T:2Li | 3: 3T : 2Li | 426.76 |
| | 0.0070 | 0.0071 | 3:5T:2Li | 3: 5T : 2 Li | 469.30 |
| | 0.0041 | 0.0044 | 3:10T:2Li | 3:24T :2 Li | 539.56 |
| | 0.0036 | 0.0039[a] | 3:17T:2Li | 3:36T :2 Li | 716.15[a] |
| **LM** | 0.0034 | 0.0038 | 3:3T:2Li | 3:3T:2Li | 481.41 |
| | 0.0026 | 0.0028 | 3:4T:2Li | 3:4T:2Li | 528.96 |
| | 0.0008 | 0.0008 | 3:11T:2Li | 3:11T:2Li | 607.70 |
| | 0.0006 | *0.0006[a] | 3:18T:2Li | 3:18T:2Li | *808.70[a] |

**a : *Lowest RMSE / Maximum run time in each algorithm***
*** : *Lowest RMSE / Maximum run time in all the algorithms***

**Table 9.** Performance & run time for MLEANN using Gas furnace time series (4 I/P – 2 O/P)

| Learning algorithm | EANN | | | ANN | Run time (min) |
|---|---|---|---|---|---|
| | RMSE | | Architecture | Architecture | 4 i/p - 2 o/p |
| | Train | Test | | | |
| **BP** | 0.0145 | 0.0278 | 3:3T:2Li | 4 : 3T : 2Li | 106.80 |
| | 0.0140 | 0.0295 | 3:5T:2Li | 4 : 5T : 2 Li | 111.00 |
| | 0.0121 | 0.0269[a] | 3:10T:2Li | 4 :18T :2 Li | 113.40 |
| | 0.0130 | 0.0385 | 3:20T:2Li | 4 :36T :2 Li | 141.60[a] |
| **SCG** | 0.0146 | 0.0248 | 3:3T:2Li | 4 : 3T : 2Li | 201.25 |
| | 0.0138 | 0.0243 | 3:4T:2Li | 4 : 5T : 2 Li | 213.18 |
| | 0.0090 | *0.0171[a] | 3:12T:2Li | 4 :16T :2 Li | 226.80 |
| | 0.0124 | 0.0217 | 3:23T:2Li | 4 :36T :2 Li | 270.46[a] |
| **QNA** | 0.0127 | 0.0255 | 3:3T:2Li | 4 : 3T : 2Li | 210.69 |
| | 0.0134 | 0.0247 | 3:5T:2Li | 4 : 5T : 2 Li | 225.68 |
| | 0.0094 | 0.0208[a] | 3:11T:2Li | 4 :18T :2 Li | 240.14 |
| | 0.0111 | 0.0228 | 3:22T:2Li | 4 :36T :2 Li | 286.74[a] |
| **LM** | 0.015 | 0.0234 | 3:3T:2Li | 4 : 3T : 2Li | 217.23 |
| | 0.0144 | 0.0239 | 3:4T:2Li | 4 : 5T : 2 Li | 235.23 |
| | 0.0098 | 0.0181[a] | 3:10T:2Li | 4 :14T :2 Li | 254.15 |
| | 0.0108 | 0.0810 | 3:20T:2Li | 4 :36T :2 Li | *296.65[a] |

**a : *Lowest RMSE / Maximum run time in each algorithm***
*** : *Lowest RMSE/ Maximum run time in all the algorithms***

**Table 10.** Performance & run time for MLEANN using Gas furnace time series (3 I/P – 2 O/P)

| Learning algorithm | EANN | | | ANN | Run time (min) |
|---|---|---|---|---|---|
| | RMSE | | Architecture | Architecture | 3 i/p - 2 o/p |
| | Train | Test | | | |
| **BP** | 0.0174 | 0.0334 | 3:3T:2Li | 3: 3T : 2Li | 91.20 |
| | 0.0169 | 0.0355 | 3:4T:2Li | 3: 5T : 2 Li | 100.20 |
| | 0.0144 | 0.0322[a] | 3:8T:2Li | 3:18T :2 Li | 108.60 |
| | 0.0155 | 0.0461 | 3:18T:2Li | 3:36T :2 Li | 132.00[a] |

**Table 10.** *(continued)*

| | | | | | |
|---|---|---|---|---|---|
| **SCG** | 0.0175 | 0.0298 | 3:3T:2Li | 3: 3T : 2Li | 171.85 |
| | 0.0165 | 0.0292 | 3:4T:2Li | 3: 5T : 2 Li | 192.44 |
| | 0.0108 | *0.0205[a] | 3:10T:2Li | 3:16T :2 Li | 217.20 |
| | 0.0148 | 0.0261 | 3:21T:2Li | 3:36T :2 Li | 252.12[a] |
| **QNA** | 0.0153 | 0.0306 | 3:3T:2Li | 3: 3T : 2Li | 179.92 |
| | 0.0161 | 0.0297 | 3:4T:2Li | 3: 5T : 2 Li | 203.72 |
| | 0.0112 | 0.0250[a] | 3:9T:2Li | 3:18T :2 Li | 229.98 |
| | 0.0133 | 0.0273 | 3:20T:2Li | 3:36T :2 Li | 267.30[a] |
| **LM** | 0.0179 | 0.0281 | 3:3T:2Li | 3: 3T : 2Li | 185.50 |
| | 0.0173 | 0.0287 | 3:4T:2Li | 3: 5T : 2 Li | 212.34 |
| | 0.0117 | 0.0217[a] | 3:8T:2Li | 3:14T :2 Li | 243.39 |
| | 0.0129 | 0.0972 | 3:19T:2Li | 3:36T :2 Li | *276.54[a] |

**a : *Lowest RMSE / Maximum run time in each algorithm***
* : *Lowest RMSE / Maximum run time in all the algorithms*

***MLEANN- Results Discussion.*** Tables (7– 10) show the training and testing performance of MLEANN for the two time series problems. The results reveal that EANN design performs more efficiently than conventional ANN design for the two time series. For Mackey-glass series, using 500 epochs of BP learning with architecture of 36 hidden nodes (table7), the RMSE on test set was reduced by 82.4% (BP), 30.6% (SCG), 19.5% (QNA) and 58.3% (LM). At the same time, number of hidden neurons got reduced by approximately 50% (BP), 44.4% (SCG), 50% (QNA) and 47.2% for LM. LM algorithm gave the best RMSE error on test set (0.0005) even though it takes long time (1086.35 minutes) while the BP algorithm takes the shortest time (537.60 minutes) as shown in table (7). For the gas furnace time series, using 500 epochs of BP learning with architectures indicated in table (9), RMSE on test set was reduced by 53.2% (BP with 18 hidden nodes), 36.2% (SCG with 16 hidden nodes), 32% (QNA with 18 hidden nodes) and 50.5% (LM with 14 hidden nodes). Savings in hidden neurons amounted to 44.4% (BP), 25% (SCG), 38.9% (QNA) and 28.6% (LM). SCG training gave the best RMSE value (0.0171) for gas furnace series. To have an empirical comparison, we deliberately terminated the local search after 500 epochs (regardless of early stopping in some cases) for all the training algorithms. In some cases the generalization performance could have been further improved. As depicted in tables (7-10), our experimentations with small architectures also reveal the efficiency of MLEANN technique. The gas furnace time series could be learned just with 3 or 5 hidden neurons using LM algorithm. LM produced best results with few hidden neurons. However, when the hidden neurons were increased, SCG algorithm marginally preformed better than LM. For Mackey-glass series the results were not that encouraging (using 4 hidden neurons) when compared with the conventional design using 36 hidden neurons. The Mackey-glass series requires more hidden neurons to improve the RMSE values.

**MLEANN-CA: Experiment and Results.** In this subsection, we test and explore the performance of the proposed MLEANN-CA approach that used the cellular configurations in optimizing networks architectures. According to Gutteriez experiment [6], he applied the evolutionary cellular configurations for designing feed-forward neural network architecture. He used a network with four inputs, 36 hidden nodes, and two outputs. By using the cellular automata technique, the positions of growing and decreasing seeds in the CA grid are codified into the genotype. The length of chromosome is 30, 3 genes for each growing or decreasing seed. The result is an optimized neural network with three inputs, three hidden nodes, and two outputs. In this experiment, we used the original neural network (4: 36: 2) and the optimized one (3: 3: 2) from Gutteriez experiment. We assumed that the two networks are fully connected as a worst case. We evolved and trained these networks through the Neurosolution and NeuroGenetic optimizer toolboxes using two time series: Mackey-glass and Gas furnace. We used the direct encoding method in training and evolving the networks. We compared the results according to the architecture, RMSE error, and run time. The user has the option to pick the best neural network (e.g. small architecture size, less RMSE, fast convergence, or short run time, etc.) among the four learning algorithms used during the training process. Tables (11– 12) display empirical values of RMSE on test data using the meta-learning technique for the two time series problems with

**Table 11.** Performance of MLEANN for Mackey-glass time series with two architectures

| **Mackey glass time series** | | | | |
|---|---|---|---|---|
| **Learning algorithm** | **ANN** | **MLEANN** | | |
| | **Architecture** | **Architecture** | **RMSE Test** | **Run time (min)** |
| **BP** | 3-3T-2Li | 3:3T:2Li | 0.0252 | 246.60 |
| | 4-36T-2Li | 3:18T:2Li | 0.0085 | 537.60 |
| **SCG** | 3-3T-2Li | 3:3T:2Li | 0.0094 | 404.04 |
| | 4-36T-2Li | 3:20T:2Li | 0.0041 | 906.29 |
| **QNA** | 3-3T-2Li | 3:3T:2Li | 0.0086 | 426.76 |
| | 4-36T-2Li | 3:18T:2Li | 0.0033 | 962.02 |
| **LM** | 3-3T-2Li | 3:3T:2Li | 0.0038 | 481.41 |
| | 4-36T-2Li | 3:19T:2Li | 0.0005 | 1086.35 |

**Table 12.** Performance of MLEANN for Gas furnace time series with two architectures

| **Gas furnace time series** | | | | |
|---|---|---|---|---|
| **Learning algorithm** | **ANN** | **MLEANN** | | |
| | **Architecture** | **Architecture** | **RMSE Test** | **Run time (min)** |
| **BP** | 3-3T-2Li | 3:3T:2Li | 0.0334 | 91.20 |
| | 4-36T-2Li | 3:20T:2Li | 0.0385 | 141.60 |
| **SCG** | 3-3T-2Li | 3:3T:2Li | 0.0298 | 171.85 |
| | 4-36T-2Li | 3:23T:2Li | 0.0217 | 270.46 |
| **QNA** | 3-3T-2Li | 3:3T:2Li | 0.0306 | 179.92 |
| | 4-36T-2Li | 3:22T:2Li | 0.0228 | 286.74 |
| **LM** | 3-3T-2Li | 3:3T:2Li | 0.0281 | 185.50 |
| | 4-36T-2Li | 3:20T:2Li | 0.0810 | 296.65 |

the network architectures: (4:36:2) and (3:3:2). These tables also include the new optimized architectures generated after applying the meta-learning technique. The results are adapted from tables (7-10). The run times using the meta-learning technique for the two time series are also presented in these tables (adapted from tables 7-10). For comparison purposes, see the RMSE values of the conventional design of ANN that are presented in tables (3-6).

***MLEANN-CA**: Results Discussion.* This subsection includes evaluation and summarization of the experimentation results mentioned in section 3.3.3. The cellular automata technique is able to provide more optimal architectures than direct codification methods. According to Gutteriez experiment result [6], the number of hidden neurons got reduced by approximately 91.7% (from 36 to 3 hidden nodes) using the cellular configurations. Using the direct codification in my experiments, for the Mackey glass (table11) the number of hidden neurons (36 hidden nodes) reduced by 50% (BP), 44.4% (SCG), 50% (QNA), and 47.2% (LM). For the Gas furnace (table12), the number of hidden neurons (36 hidden nodes) reduced by 44.4% (BP), 36.1% (SCG), 38.9% (QNA), and 44.4% (LM). Tables (11-12) also show empirical values of RMSE on test data using the meta-learning technique for the two time series problems with the network architectures: (4:36:2) and (3:3:2). For Mackey-glass series (table 11), the results of RMSE on test set were not that encouraging (using 3 hidden neurons) when compared with the architecture design of 36 hidden neurons. The Mackey-glass series requires more hidden neurons to improve the RMSE values. LM algorithm gave the best RMSE error on test set for the architecture of 36 hidden nodes even though it takes the longest time. For the gas furnace time series (table 12), the results of RMSE on test set were much better than in Mackey glass results. For BP and LM algorithms, the RMSE for architecture with 3 hidden nodes was less than in architecture with 36 hidden nodes. This is different in SCG and QNA algorithms, since the RMSE for architecture with 36 hidden nodes was less than in architecture with 3 hidden nodes. The LM algorithm produced the best results of RMSE with 3 hidden neurons while SCG algorithm produced the best results with 36 hidden neurons. For the two time series in tables (11-12), all the learning algorithms take short run time for the architecture with 3 hidden nodes in comparison with 36 hidden nodes. For the Mackey glass, the time for evolving and training was much longer than in Gas furnace for all algorithms with different architectures. In general, these experimentation results reveal the efficiency of our proposed MLEANN–CA approach in designing network architecture that is smaller, faster and with better generalization performance.

## 4 Conclusions and Future Works

In this paper, we had proposed and formulated; MLEANN-CA: an adaptive computational framework based on evolutionary computation and local search procedures for the automatic design of optimal artificial neural networks using direct and indirect encoding methods. In this framework, the evolutionary cellular configurations are used for designing small feed-forward neural network architectures, and then all the generated architectures are trained and evolved separately using the meta-learning algorithm with the direct evolutionary approach, where four different learning algorithms are used in parallel mode. We tested and explored, experimentally, the performance of the MLEANN-CA approach using Neurosolution and NeuroGenetic Optimizer toolboxes, and two famous chaotic time series. We also explored and evaluated the performance of different neural network learning algorithms for the two chaotic time series when the architecture was changed. We compared the performance of the MLEANN-CA approach with the previous MLEANN and with the conventional design of ANNs. Empirical results were promising and illustrated the importance, scalability, and the efficacy of this MLEANN-CA approach in evolving, optimizing, and training neural networks. Similar approach, MLEANN-CA, could be used for optimizing recurrent neural networks, morphological neural networks, and other connectionist networks as a future work. On the other hand, the influence of the rules in the CA evolution and the capability of the rules to generate a complete space of NN architectures could be studied. Besides, some issues about the neural network module and fitness function could be examined in the future works. Also, we can use other different time series, as waste water flow prediction, in training and evolving the neural networks and investigate its effect and performance. Finally, the MLEANN-CA approach could be used in several applications. Example of such applications is: selecting flexible manufacturing systems (FMS), from a group of candidate-FMSs, under disparate level-of-satisfaction of decision maker [4].

## References


1. Abraham, A.: Meta-Learning Evolutionary Artificial Neural Networks, Neurocomputing Journal, Elsevier Science, Netherlands, Vol. 56c, (2004). 1-38
2. Abraham, A.: Optimization of Evolutionary Neural Networks Using Hybrid Learning Algorithms, IEEE International Conference on Neural Networks, Vol. 3, IEEE Press, New York, (2002)2797–2802
3. Abu, S. A., Al-Salqan, Y.: Meta-learning Evolutionary Artificial Neural Networks: By Means of Cellular Automata. In: Proceedings of IEEE International Conference on Computational Intelligence for Modelling, Control and Automation, Vienna-Austria, IEEE press, USA (2006)
4. Bhattacharya, A., Abraham, A., Grosan, C., Vasant, P.: Meta-Learning Evolutionary Artificial Neural Network for Selecting Flexible Manufacturing Systems under Disparate Level-of-Satisfaction of Decision Maker. IEEE International Symposium on Neural Networks, China, Lecture Notes in Computer Science, Springer Verlag, (2006)
5. Box, G. E. P., Jenkins, G. M.: Time Series Analysis, Forecasting and Control, Holden Day, San Francisco (1970)
6. Gutierrez, G., Isasi, P., Molina, J. M., Sanchis, A., Galvan, I. M.: Evolutionary Cellular Configurations for Designing Feedforward Neural Network Architectures, Lecture Notes in Computer Science, Springer, Germany, 2084 (2001) 514–521
7. Mackey, M. C., Glass, L.: Oscillation and Chaos in Physiological Control Systems, Science 197 (1977) 287–289
8. Molina, J. M, Galvan, I, Isasi, P., Sanchis, A.: Grammars and Cellular Automata for Evolving Neural Network Architectures. 2000 IEEE International Conference on Systems, Man, and Cybernetics, 4 (2000) 2497-2502
9. Yao, X.: Evolving Artificial Neural Networks. Proceedings of IEEE, 87 (9) (1999) 423–1447

# Modeling Based on SOFM and the Dynamic $\varepsilon$-SVM for Fermentation Process

Xuejin Gao[1], Pu Wang[1], Chongzheng Sun[1], Jianqiang Yi[2], Yating Zhang[1], and Huiqing Zhang[1]

[1] College of Electronic Information and Control Engineering, Beijing University of Technology, Beijing 100022, China
gaoxuejin@emails.bjut.edu.cn
[2] The Key Laboratory of Complex System and Intelligence Science, Chinese Academy of Sciences, Beijing 100033, China

**Abstract.** To overcome the deficiency of Support Vector Machine (SVM) for regression, dynamic $\varepsilon$-SVM method was proposed. To establish precise mathematical models, a new modeling method was introduced, combining self-organizing feature map (SOFM) with the dynamic $\varepsilon$-SVM. Firstly, SOFM was used as a clustering algorithm to partition the whole input space into several disjointed regions; then, the dynamic $\varepsilon$-SVM modeled for these partitioned regions. This method was illustrated by modeling penicillin fermentation process with plant field data. Results show that the method achieves significant improvement in generalization performance compared with other methods based on SVM.

## 1 Introduction

Microbial fermentation processes are usually time dependent and nonlinear. So it is difficult to establish suitable model for the system by global model. The global modeling method can't always achieve precision required and is complicated to compute [1]. To solve the above problems, samples near input data at a given time instant are used to establish local models. The outputs of the local models are the system outputs with respect to the input vectors [2]. Local Learning Theory (LLT) was proposed based on this idea. It can achieve required system identification precision easily without considering the scope of system input space and its nonlinearity.

A fermentation process can be divided into four phases since inoculation [3], namely log, logarithmic, stationary and death phases, respectively. Each phase has different characteristics. Qian divided the fermentation phases by analyzing the specific growth rate curve [3]. Wang divided the penicillin fermentation phases by analyzing the release of carbon dioxide, pH value and the concentration of sugar [4]. Simon divided the fermentation phases by using artificial neural network (ANN) [5]. These methods could be effective sometimes, but can't guarantee their precision due to the lack of biosensor, the availability of a large number of samples for ANN training, etc. The phase division is the premise of local modeling. So a clustering algorithm was used to partition the whole input samples into several disjointed regions, which realized the phase division. The training data points, which have

D.-S. Huang, K. Li, and G.W. Irwin (Eds.): ICIC 2006, LNCS 4113, pp. 194–203, 2006.

similar characteristics in the input space, will be classified into the same region [6]. The Self-organizing feature map (SOFM) [7] proposed by Kohonen is a kind of ANN models. It simulates the human brain's characteristics of side restrain, self-organizing, etc. It is an unsupervised and non-parametric neural network approach. It can map any input patterns into 1-D or 2-D discrete mapping in the output layer. It can preserve the topological structures and organize automatically the input patterns into clusters or "natural groups". In other words, if two feature vectors are near each other in input space, the corresponding neurons will also be close in output space, and vice versa.

Due to its non-linearity, time dependency and the lack of biosensor along with tight coupling of parameters, classic system theory can hardly describe these processes well [8]. Many authors use ANN to model the fermentation processes [8,9]. But, empirical risk minimization based ANN needs a large number of samples, and leads to over-fitting easily. Moreover structure design of ANN depends on prior knowledge and experience of the designer, and is short of theory instruction. However, SVM [10,11] proposed by Vapnik uses structural risk minimization criterion instead of empirical risk minimization criterion. It overcomes intrinsic limitation of ANN and is powerful for the problem characterized by small sample, non-linearity, high dimension and local minima. SVM can achieve high generalization capability. It has been studied and applied widely to solve pattern recognition, time series forecast, and function approximate problems [6,12,13]. Some papers have proved that SVM is superior to ANN method [14]. SVM provides a new method for modeling fermentation processes.

Each training sample has the same error requirement in the standard SVM for regression [10,11,14]. So it will affect the model 's abilities of fitting and generalization. To overcome the deficiency of SVM, dynamic $\varepsilon$-SVM method was proposed, namely the different training sample uses the different error.

A new modeling method that combined SOFM with the dynamic $\varepsilon$-SVM was presented in this paper. Firstly, SOFM was used as a clustering algorithm to partition the whole input space into several disjointed regions, and then the dynamic $\varepsilon$-SVMs model for all partitioned regions. This method modeled penicillin fermentation process with data collected from real plant in Matlab6.5. Results show that the method achieves significant improvement in the generalization performance compared with other methods.

## 2 SOFM Neural Networks and Self-organizing Learning Algorithm

### 2.1 SOFM Neural Networks

SOFM is an ANN model based on unsupervised and competition learning, can map high-dimension input space into two-dimension space. Every neuron among SOFM neural networks represents a pattern distributing. So SOFM can be used to cluster for complicated high-dimension data [7,15].

The topological structure of SOFM is illustrated in Fig. 1, consists of input layer and output layer. The output layer is also called the competition layer. The nodes of input layer equal to the feature vector dimensions of input samples, so the input layer represents an input sample vector. Every node of output layer is all a vector whose dimensions equal to nodes of input layer. SOFM is totally connective, namely the nodes of input layer and output layer link with each other totally [15].

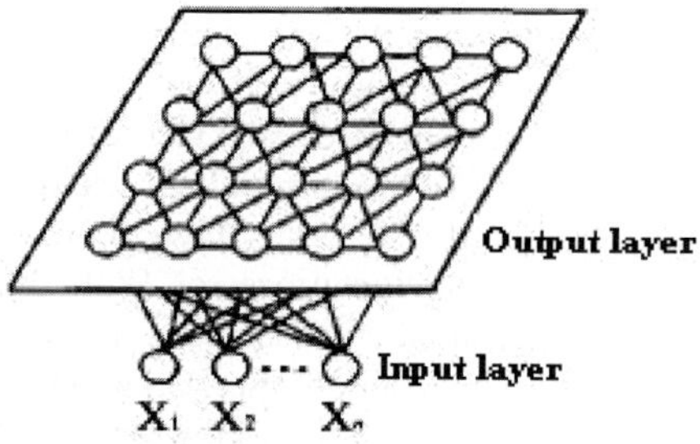


**Fig. 1.** SOFM network structure

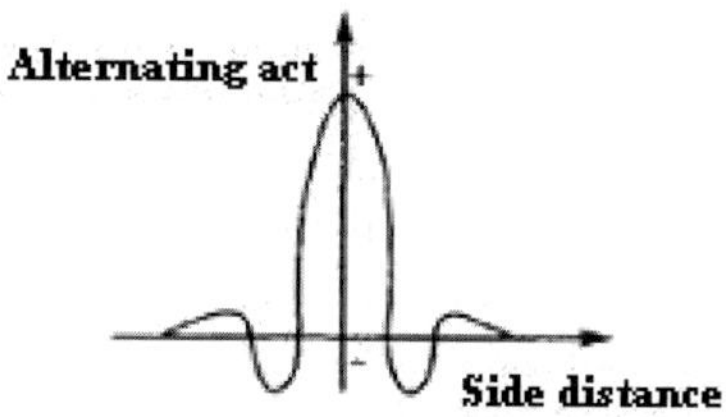


**Fig. 2.** Mexican-hat function

All neurons of competition layer in SOFM networks compete with each other to obtain response opportunities for the input patterns. Finally, only one neuron can win. Taking winning neuron as the center, the winner exhibits the side feedback of excitement to the nearest neighbor neurons. It exhibits the side feedback of restrain to far neighbor neurons. It exhibits the weak inspirit to the farthest neurons. As shown in Fig. 2, the side feedback is usually calculated by using the Mexican-hat function [15].

### 2.2 The Self-organizing Learning Algorithm

The vectors of all input nodes are initialized to small random numbers, and then SOFM networks calculate the Euclidean distance between every input vector and all mapping nodes in the output layer. The mapping node whose Euclidean distance is the smallest is the winning node. The input vector is mapped into the winning node. The weight of the winner is adjusted and the weights in neighborhood are modified too. All input vectors are submitted to SOFM networks to train. Every input vector is usually submitted several times. The input vectors, which are similar, are mapped into the neighborhood in the output layer. Finally, the clustering of input vectors is obtained. At one time, the input samples in high dimensional space are mapped into two-dimensional space via a nonlinear mapping. The topological structure of the networks reflects the distributing of input samples [15]. The steps of the learning algorithm are described as follows:

Step1 Initialize SOFM neural networks: the input vectors are assumed to $X = [x_1(n), x_2(n), \cdots, x_N(n)]^T$, which are called the training samples too. The weight vectors are $W_i = [w_{i1}(n), w_{i2}(n), \cdots, w_{iN}(n)]^T$ , $i = 1,2,\cdots,M$ . The variable $n$ represents the iterative times. To map precisely, the iterative times should be properly large. According to experience, the iterative times should equal to 500 times of $M$ [15]. The value $M$ is the number of neurons in the output layer. The dimension of $X$ may be very great. The weight vectors $W_i$ are assumed to be the random numbers between 0 and 1. The vector $X$ is normalized between 0 and 1.

Step2 Input the training sample vector $x$, let $n=0$.

Step3 Calculate the Euclidean distance between $W_i$ and $X'$, namely

$$d_i = \left\| X'_k - W_i \right\| = [\sum_{j=1}^{N} (x_j'^k - w_{ij})^2]^{\frac{1}{2}} . \tag{1}$$

Step4 Find the minimal distance $d_c$ to determine the winner $c$. The output with respect to $c$ is maximal.

$$d_c = \min[d_i], i = 1,2,\cdots,M . \tag{2}$$

Step5 Update all neuron weight vectors $W_i$ in the neighborhood $N_c(n)$ of the competition layer. The neuron weight vectors out of $N_c(n)$ don't be adjusted.

$$\begin{cases} w_{ij}(n+1) = w_{ij}(n) + a(n)[x_j - w_{ij}(t)], i \in N_c(n) \\ w_{ij}(n+1) = w_{ij}(n), i \notin N_c(n) \end{cases} . \tag{3}$$

Where $a(n)$ denotes the learning factor and decreases along with iterative times. The scope of $a(n)$ is between 0 and 1. The function $N_c(n)$ is the neighborhood of $c$, whose radius decreases along with $n$.

Step6 Let $n = n+1$ and turn to step3.

Step7 When $n = 500M$, stop learning of the current sample and turn to step2.

Step8 Repeat from step2 to step7 until all training samples have been trained.

## 3 The Dynamic $\varepsilon$ -SVM for Regression

The basic idea of SVM is to map training data sets into a high dimensional feature space via a nonlinear mapping and then to solve convex optimization problem in this feature space. The dimensions of feature space may be infinite. SVM is based on structural risk minimization principle to solve the optimal value, so it has stronger generalization ability than other methods. By using the kernel function, SVM transforms inner products computing in a high dimensional feature space into the kernel function computing in original space by the nonlinear mapping, avoids direct computing in high dimensional feature space, reduces computing quantity greatly and avoids dimensional disaster. Moreover, after using the kernel function, SVM needs not know the form of non-linear function [10,11].

In the standard SVM for regression, the selection of $\varepsilon$ insensitive loss function is very important to modeling. The parameter $\varepsilon$ reflects sensitive extent of model to noise that input variables contain and controls the fitting precision of model. If the parameter $\varepsilon$ becomes large the fitting precision will become low, the support vectors will reduce and the model complexity will fall, and vice versa. Each training sample has the same approximation error requirement. Because the output differences of samples at the different time are great, the over-fitting or under-fitting problem easily appears. Of course this will affect the generalization ability. For example, the penicillin titer measured at first is about 5000U/ml, however finally is about 60000U/ml. So each training sample should use different error $\varepsilon$. Aiming at this problem, dynamic $\varepsilon$-SVM was proposed, namely $\varepsilon_i = p \cdot y_i$. The parameter $p$ denotes the relative error ratio. It is chosen according to research objects. The basic principle of the dynamic $\varepsilon$-SVM was described as follows:

Given a training data set of $N$ points $(x_1, y_1)$, $(x_2, y_2)$, …, $(x_n, y_n)$ with input data $x_i \in R^m$ and output data $y_i \in R$, the function $f = w \cdot x + b$ fits $n$ samples. And given all samples are fitted without error under insensitive loss function $\varepsilon_i$, namely:

$$\begin{cases} y_i - w \cdot x_i - b \le \varepsilon_i \\ w \cdot x_i + b - y_i \le \varepsilon_i \end{cases} \quad i = 1, 2, \cdots n \ . \tag{4}$$

Considering the fitting error, the dynamic $\varepsilon$-SVM relaxes constraint conditions by introducing slack variables $\xi_i \ge 0$, $\xi_i^* \ge 0$ and $\xi_i \xi_i^* = 0$. So Eq. (4) becomes:

$$\begin{cases} y_i - w \cdot x_i - b \le \varepsilon_i + \xi_i \\ w \cdot x_i + b - y_i \le \varepsilon_i + \xi_i^* \end{cases} \quad i = 1, 2, \cdots n \ . \tag{5}$$

The non-linear regression method based on the dynamic $\varepsilon$-SVM makes $\frac{1}{2}\|w\|^2 + C \cdot \sum_{i=1}^{n} (\xi_i + \xi_i^*)$ minimize. It constructs Lagrange equation by using Duality theory. Under the conditions of $\sum_{i=1}^{n} (a_i - a_i^*) = 0$ and $0 \le a_i, a_i^* \le C$, $i = 1, 2, \cdots, n$, maximize the objective function:

$$W(a, a^*) = -\varepsilon_i \sum_{i=1}^{n} (a_i^* + a_i) + \sum_{i=1}^{n} y_i (a_i^* - a_i) - \frac{1}{2} \sum_{i,j=1}^{n} (a_i^* - a_i)(a_j^* - a_j)(x_i \cdot x_j) \cdot \tag{6}$$

Where only parts of $a_i$ are not equal to zero, the data points associated to them are called support vectors. For nonlinear problems, the dynamic $\varepsilon$-SVM does not make the nonlinear transform, but uses directly the kernel function $K(x_i, x_j)$ instead of the inner product $(x_i \cdot x_j)$ of Eq. (6).

Obtained a regression model:

$$f(x) = w \cdot x + b = \sum_{i=1}^{n} (a_i^* - a_i) K(x_i, x) + b^* \ . \tag{7}$$

# 4 The Modeling Method Based on SOFM and the Dynamic $\varepsilon$ -SVM for Fermentation Process

As illustrated in Fig. 3, the modeling method based on SOFM and the dynamic $\varepsilon$ -SVM for fermentation process has two stages. In the first stage, SOFM is used as a clustering algorithm to partition the whole input space into several disjointed regions. The number of regions is predetermined according to the research object. Every region has the different characteristic. Then, in the second stage, every region adopts the different dynamic $\varepsilon$ -SVM to model. The validation data is used to select the parameters of the dynamic $\varepsilon$ -SVM. This method is different from the global modeling method based on SVM. The global model is trained in the whole sample space, so the model may not be enough trained in every local area. The steps of this method are outlined as follows:

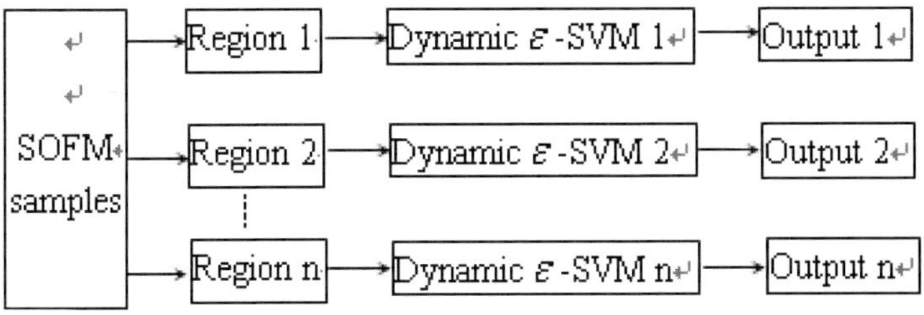


**Fig. 3.** The modeling method based on SOFM and the dynamic $\varepsilon$ -SVM

Step1 Data is divided into three parts. The training data is used to build up the models of the system, the validation data is used to select the parameters of the system that best performs on these data, and the testing data is used to test the model generalization ability.

Step2 Three data sets are normalized between 0 and 1. Establish the corresponding relationship between the data normalized and original data. The data normalized is used to cluster by SOFM neural networks. The original data is used to model, select the model parameters and test the model generalization ability.

Step3 SOFM is used to partition the whole input space into several disjointed regions. The number of regions is predetermined. The samples within every region have the similar characteristics. The differences of samples that locate the different regions are great.

Step4 SOFM that has been trained very well partitions the validation data into several regions. The regions of the validation data are equal to those of the training data.

Step5 According to the clustering results and corresponding relationship, determine the training samples and the validation samples in every region.

Step6 Determine the relative error ratio $p$ and the dynamic $\varepsilon$ -SVM parameters. The original training samples in the different regions are used to train their own dynamic $\varepsilon$ -SVMs. The validation samples in the different regions are used to select their own parameters by experimental method. These parameters make both the fitting and validation error minimal. The model errors are calculated by the mean error ratio $MER = \frac{1}{n}\sum_{i=1}^{n}(\left| y_i - \hat{y}_i \right| / y_i)$, $n$ represents the total number of data patterns, $y_i$ represents actual output value and $\hat{y}_i$ represents predicted value.

Step7 The testing samples test the model generalization ability. The prediction error is calculated by $MER$.

## 5 Modeling for the Penicillin Fermentation Process

### 5.1 The Model Summary

The penicillin is the secondary metabolism of the penicillin producing strain. The penicillin fermentation belongs to the half-continuous fermentation mode. It is a very complicated biochemistry process that possesses the characteristics of non-linearity, time dependency and the lack of biosensor along with tight coupling of parameters. So it is very difficult to establish a precise mathematical model [4]. There are many factors that affect the yield of the penicillin fermentation. These factors include mainly the fermentation temperature, pH value, the substrate concentration, the dissolved oxygen concentration, the biomass concentration, the grown rate of biomass and the hyphal shape. The model for penicillin titer pre-estimate was developed by the modeling method that based on SOFM and the dynamic $\varepsilon$-SVM, namely used the states at fermentation time $t$ to estimate the titer at $t+\Delta t$. The model for state estimate belongs to the dynamic model, covers the entire fermentation process and plays important roles in the online control, optimization control, system pre-estimate, etc. By analyzing the real plant data collected from North China Pharmaceutical Corporation Beta Co., Ltd., we adopted the factors that affect greatly titer as the input variables. These variables are the feeding sugar rate, the feeding ammonia rate, the feeding phenylacetic acid rate, the feeding ammonium sulphate rate, the temperature, pH value, the air flux, the whisking current and the titer at the fermentation time $t$, respectively. At the same time, because the fermentation process is time dependent, the fermentation time is taken as an input variable too. The output variable is the titer at fermentation time $t+\Delta t$. The plant offline measures titer once 4 hour, so the sampling interval $\Delta t$ equals 4 hour.

### 5.2 Modeling

In Matlab6.5, the model for the penicillin fermentation process was established and tested. Six batches data were adopted from the real plant. Every batch data represented an entire fermentation process. This data was divided into three parts: the training data was used to establish the models of the above mentioned system, the validation data was used to select the parameters of the system that best performed on these data, and the testing data was used to test the model generalization ability. The training data comprises 4 batches data, namely 216 data patterns. The validation data comprises 1 batch data, namely 53 data patterns. The testing data comprises 1 batch data, namely 53 data patterns. To reflect the characteristics of the fermentation process, the model adopted the RBF kernel function, namely $K(x, y) = \exp[-\|x-y\|^2 / 2\sigma^2]$. So the parameters of the dynamic $\varepsilon$-SVM include mainly $\varepsilon_i$, $C$ and the kernel parameter $\sigma$. The parameter $\varepsilon_i$ is denoted by the relative error ratio $p$. The penicillin titer is usually measured after log phase and the fermentation process is usually ended before death phase. So the samples were divided into two classes: one class was the logarithmic phase whose characteristic was growth, the other the stationary phase whose characteristic was product synthesis.

The model for the penicillin fermentation process was established and tested. The parameters of SOFM networks were determined. The dimension $N$ of the input vectors $X$ equaled to 10. The neurons of the output layer $M$ equaled to 2. The iterative times $n$ equaled to 1000. According to the effects of the dynamic $\varepsilon$-SVM parameters on models and the fermentation process characteristics, $p$ was assigned to 5%. Results were given in Table 1. Fig. 4 illustrates the learning and actual values in

**Table 1.** The experimental results of this modeling method

| Fermentation phases | $\sigma$ | $C$ | $p$ | Fitting error | Validation error | Prediction error |
|---|---|---|---|---|---|---|
| Logarithmic phase | 4000 | 9000 | 5% | 0.0328 | 0.024645 | 0.028197 |
| Stationary phase | 4000 | 9000 | 5% | 0.02977 | 0.029803 | 0.028879 |
| | | | | The mean error of two phases | | |
| | | | | 0.031285 | 0.027224 | 0.028538 |

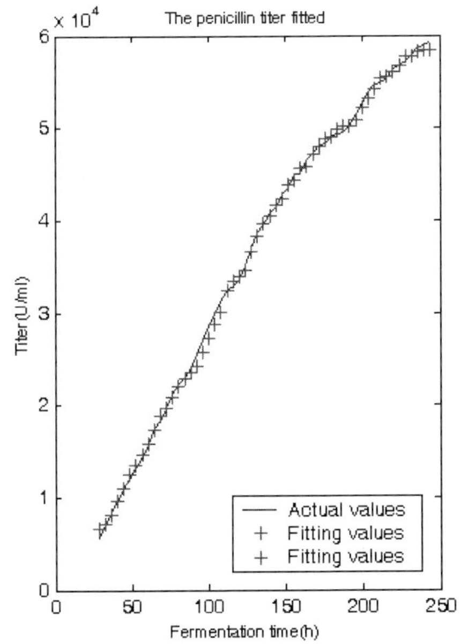


**Fig. 4.** Training results with the 185-th batch

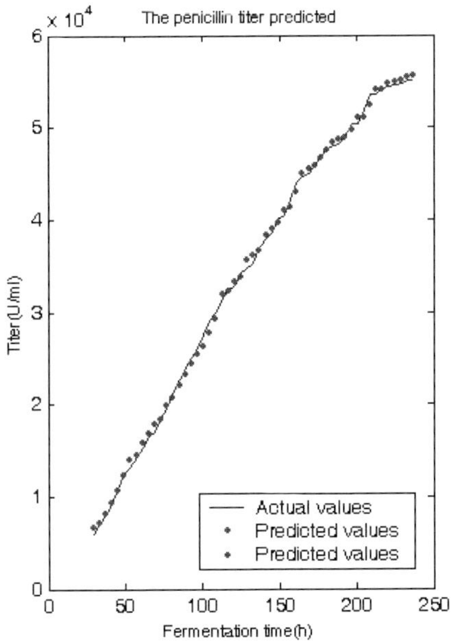


**Fig. 5.** Testing results with the 186-th batch

the 185-th batch data. The green pluses represent the fitted values in logarithmic phase. The red pluses represent the fitted values in stationary phase. Fig. 5 illustrates the predicted and actual values in the 186-th batch data. The green points represent the predicted values in logarithmic phase. The red points represent the predicted values in stationary phase. Obviously, the modeling method that based on SOFM and the dynamic $\varepsilon$-SVM for fermentation process possesses the very strong abilities of fitting and generalization.

## 6 Comparison with Other Modeling Methods

Four penicillin fermentation process models were developed, which adopted the methods based on SOFM and the dynamic $\varepsilon$-SVM (method 1), SOFM and the standard SVM (method 2), the dynamic $\varepsilon$-SVM (method 3) and the standard SVM (method 4), respectively. For comparison, $p$ was assigned to 5%. The parameter $\varepsilon$ was the mean of the product of $y_i$ and $p$. $C$ and $\sigma$ were 9000 and 4000, respectively. The experimental results in Table 2 illustrate that the generalization ability of method 1 is more powerful than that of the other methods.

**Table 2.** The experimental results of four modeling methods

| Methods | Phases | $p/\varepsilon$ | Fitting error | Validation error | Prediction error |
|---|---|---|---|---|---|
| Method 1 | Logarithmic phase | 5% | 0.0328 | 0.024645 | 0.028197 |
| | Stationary phase | 5% | 0.02977 | 0.029803 | 0.028879 |
| | | | The mean error of two phases | | |
| | | | 0.031285 | 0.027224 | 0.028538 |
| Method 2 | Logarithmic phase | 949 | 0.034025 | 0.025415 | 0.026049 |
| | Stationary phase | 2341 | 0.030274 | 0.032253 | 0.031217 |
| | | | The mean error of two phases | | |
| | | | 0.032150 | 0.028834 | 0.028633 |
| Method 3 | Global | 5% | 0.032795 | 0.031991 | 0.031559 |
| Method 4 | Global | 1800 | 0.048218 | 0.048012 | 0.053265 |

## 7 Conclusions

A new method of local modeling for the fermentation process was proposed. To divide the fermentation phases, SOFM neural networks clustered samples according to the intrinsic characteristics of samples. To overcome the deficiencies of the standard SVM, dynamic $\varepsilon$-SVM was proposed. The penicillin fermentation process was modeled based on SOFM and the dynamic $\varepsilon$-SVM with real plant data. Results in Matlab6.5 show that this model possesses the strong capability of fitting and generalization. Compared with other methods based on SVM, this method is more powerful in generalization ability.

## Acknowledgments

This work is supported in part by the Key Laboratory of Complex System and Intelligence Science of Chinese Academy of Sciences, the key (key grant) Project of Chinese Ministry of Education (203002), the Scientific Research Common Program of Beijing Municipal Commission of Education (KM200510005026) and Beijing Hundred-Thousand-Ten Thousand Talent Project (00029).

## References

1. Li Ning, Li Shaoyuan, Xi Yugeng: A Multiple Model Approach to Modeling Based on LPF Algorithm. J of System Engineering and Electronics, 12(3) (2001) 64-70
2. Foss B. A., Johansen T. A., Sorensen A. V.: Nonlinear Predictive Control using Local Models Applied to a Batch Fermentation Process. Control Engineering Practice, 3(3) (1995) 389-396
3. Qian Mingyong: Optimization Control of Fermentation Engineering. Nanjing: Jiangsu Science and Technology Publishing House.(1998)
4. Wang Shuqing, Yuan Yingjin: Automation Technology of Biochemistry Process. Beijing: Chemical Industry Press. (1999)
5. Simon L., Karim M. N., Schreiweis A.: Prediction and Classification of Different Phases in a Fermentation using Neural Networks. Biotechnology Techniques, 12(4) (1998) 301-304
6. Cao Lijuan: Support Vector Machines Experts for Time Series Forecasting. Neurocomputing, 51 (2003) 321-339
7. Kohonen T.: The Self-organizing Map. NY: Springer-Verlag. (1995)
8. Becker T., Enders T., Delgado A.: Dynamic Neural Networks as A Tool for the Online Optimization of Industrial Fermentation. Bioprocess Biosyst Eng, 24(2) (2002) 347-354
9. Zuo K., Wu W. T.: Semi-realtime Optimization and Control of A Fed-batch Fermentation System. Computers and Chemical Eng, 24(2) (2000) 1105-1109
10. Vapnik V. N.: The Nature of Statistical Learning Theory. New York: Springer Verlag, (1995)
11. Vapnik V. N.: An Overview of Statistical Learning Theory. IEEE Trans. on Neural Network, 10(5) (1999) 988-999
12. Guo Guodong, Li Stan Z., Chan Kap Luk: Support Vector Machines for Face Recognition. Image and Vision Computing, 19(9) (2001)631-638
13. Shevade S. K., Keerthi S. S., Bhattacharyya C., et al: Improvements to the SMO Algorithm for SVM Regression. IEEE Trans. on Neural Network, 11(5)(2000)1188-1193
14. Wang Yuhong, Huang Dexian, Gao Dongjie, et al: Nonlinear Predictive Control Based on LS-SVM. Control and Decision, 19(4)(2004) 383-387
15. Zhang Qinggui: Introduction of Artificial Neural Networks. Beijing: China WaterPower Press (2004)

# Neural Network Equalizer

Chulhee Lee, Jinwook Go, Byungjoon Baek, and Hyunsoo Choi

Dept. Electrical and Electronic Engineering, Yonsei University
134 Shinchon-Dong, Seodaumoon-Gu, 120-749 Seoul, South Korea
{chulhee, jinwook, neodion, piyagihs}@yonsei.ac.kr

**Abstract.** In this paper, we view equalization as a multi-class classification problem and use neural networks to detect binary signals in the presence of noise and interference. In particular, we compare the performance of a recently published training algorithm, a multi-gradient, with that of the conventional back-propagation. Then, we apply a feature extraction to obtain more efficient neural networks. Experiments show that neural network equalizers which view equalization as multi-class problems provide significantly improved performance compared to the conventional LMS algorithm while the decision boundary feature extraction method significantly reduces the complexity of the network.

## 1 Introduction

If signal $x(n)$ is transmitted through a linear dispersive channel, the received signal $y(n)$ can be modeled by

$$y(n) = \sum_{k=-L_1}^{L_2} a_k x(n-k) + e(n) \tag{1}$$

where $e(n)$ is Gaussian random noise and $a_k$ is channel impulse response. The input signal $x(n)$ is chosen independently from {-1, 1} with equal probability and equalization is to estimate the original input signal $x(n)$ from the received signal $y(n)$ in the presence of the additive noise and the intersymbol interference which arises due to the finite bandwidth of the channel [1].

Adaptive equalizers have been important in digital communication systems for a reliable data transmission and numerous equalization algorithms have been proposed. Among various equalization methods, the linear transversal equalizer (LTE) with a simple feedforward structure has been widely used and is frequently implemented using the least mean square (LMS) algorithm [2]:

$$W_{n+1} = W_n + c\lambda Y_n \tag{2}$$

However, complex equalization problems in various channel environments may not be effectively solved by linear decision boundaries. In particular, the linear equalizer does not perform well when there is a large amount of intersymbol interference. To compensate shortcomings of the linear equalizer based on the LMS algorithm, many authors have proposed a number of approaches such as the

D.-S. Huang, K. Li, and G.W. Irwin (Eds.): ICIC 2006, LNCS 4113, pp. 204–215, 2006.

maximum likelihood sequence estimation (MLSE) equalizers, decision feedback equalizers (DFE), and neural networks [3-8].

Recently, a new training algorithm for the MLP, a multi-gradient, has been proposed [9]. In the multi-gradient algorithm, each term of the output layer is viewed as a function of weights and the weights are directly adjusted so that the output neurons produce the desired outputs. It has been shown that the multi-gradient algorithm is more efficient for feedforward neural networks when neural networks are used as a classifier for multi-dimensional data. In this paper, we use the multi-gradient algorithm to train neural network equalizers. Comparison with the conventional back-propagation will be provided.

Another problem with neural network equalizers is that the number of operations is significantly larger than that of the linear equalizer, making it difficult to implement the method. We try to solve this problem by applying a feature extraction algorithm to a neural network equalizer. There are not many feature extraction methods for neural networks which can define arbitrary decision boundaries without assuming underlying distributions. Among a few available feature extraction algorithms for neural networks, the decision boundary feature extraction method has been shown to provide consistently good performance [10-11]. In this paper, we use this decision boundary feature extraction method to reduce neural network complexity. Experimental results show that the number of features can be reduced significantly without sacrificing performance.

## 2 Equalization as Multi-class Problems

In equalization, the goal is to estimate $x(n)$ from the received signal $y(n)$. As an easy illustration, it is assumed that $L_1 = L_2 = L = 2$ in (1). If $L = 2$, $\{\, y(n-i) \mid -2 \le i \le 2 \,\}$ will be affected by $x(n)$. In other words, $\{y(n-i) \mid -2 \le i \le 2\}$ contains information on $x(n)$ and can be used to estimate $x(n)$. Furthermore, as can be seen in equation (1), $y(n+2)$ is obtained as follows:

$$\begin{aligned} y(n+2) &= a_2 x(n) + a_1 x(n+1) + a_0 x(n+2) + a_{-1} x(n+3) \\ &\quad + a_{-2} x(n+4) + e(n+2) \end{aligned} \tag{3}$$

Therefore, in order to estimate $x(n)$, $\{y(n-i) \mid -2 \le i \le 2\}$ should be used and $\{x(n-i) \mid -4 \le i \le 4\}$ have effects on $\{y(n-2), y(n-1), y(n), y(n+1), y(n+2)\}$. As a result, it is observed that $\{x(n-i) \mid -4 \le i \le 4\}$ affects the estimation of $x(n)$ at the receiver. Furthermore, $\{y(n-i) \mid -2 \le i \le 2\}$ can be computed in matrix form as follows:

$$Y_{5\dim}(n) = AX_{9\dim}(n) + E_{5\dim}(n) \tag{4}$$

where

$$\begin{aligned} Y_{5\dim}(n) &= [\,y(n-2), y(n-1), y(n), y(n+1), y(n+2)]^T \\ X_{9\dim}(n) &= [x(n-4), x(n-3), x(n-2), x(n-1), x(n), \\ &\qquad x(n+1), x(n+2), x(n+3), x(n+4)]^T \\ N_{5\dim}(n) &= [e(n-2), e(n-1), e(n), e(n+1), e(n+2)]^T \end{aligned}$$

$$A = \begin{bmatrix} a_2 & a_1 & a_0 & a_{-1} & a_{-2} & 0 & 0 & 0 & 0 \\ 0 & a_2 & a_1 & a_0 & a_{-1} & a_{-2} & 0 & 0 & 0 \\ 0 & 0 & a_2 & a_1 & a_0 & a_{-1} & a_{-2} & 0 & 0 \\ 0 & 0 & 0 & a_2 & a_1 & a_0 & a_{-1} & a_{-2} & 0 \\ 0 & 0 & 0 & 0 & a_2 & a_1 & a_0 & a_{-1} & a_{-2} \end{bmatrix}$$

Thus, equalization can be viewed as a classification problem where the equalizer classifies the received vector $Y(n)$ as one of the binary states (1, –1). For instance, if state 1 is transmitted at time *n*, the input vector is expressed as:

$$X_1 : X(n) = [x(n-4), x(n-3), x(n-2), x(n-1), 1, \\ x(n+1), x(n+2), x(n+3), x(n+4)]^T \tag{5}$$

where $X_1$ represents a random vector and the subscript of random vector $X_1$ indicates that state 1 is transmitted (class $\omega_1$). It is noted that $X_1$ is to be understood as a random vector and $X(n)$ represents a sample vector of the input vector at time *n*. On the other hand, if state 1 is transmitted, the received vector can be computed as:

$$Y_1 : Y(n) = AX_1(n) + N(n) \tag{6}$$

We can extend this idea and view equalization as multi-class classification problems. For instance, equalization can be viewed as an 8 class-classification problem when 3 bits are considered. In other words, If state (-1,-1,-1) is transmitted assuming (1), $\{y(n-i) \mid -3 \le i \le 3\}$ contains information on $\{x(n-1), x(n), x(n+1)\}$ and $\{y(n-i) \mid -3 \le i \le 3\}$ is affected by $\{x(n-i) \mid -5 \le i \le 5\}$. In this paradigm, the input vector corresponding to state (-1,-1,-1) is given by

$$X_{-,1,-1,-1} = [x(n-5), x(n-4), x(n-3), x(n-2), -1, -1, -1, x(n+2), \\ x(n+3), x(n+4), x(n+5)]^T \tag{7}$$

For the remaining states, the corresponding input vectors are given by

$$X_{i,j,k} = [x(n-5), x(n-4), x(n-3), x(n-2), i, j, k, \\ x(n+2), x(n+3), x(n+4), x(n+5)]^T \quad \text{where} \quad i = \pm 1,\ j = \pm 1,\ k = \pm 1. \tag{8}$$

On the other hand, if state (*i, j, k*) is transmitted, the received vector can be computed as follows:

$$Y_{i,j,k} = BX_{i,j,k} + N_{7\,\mathrm{dim}} \tag{9}$$

where $i = \pm 1, j = \pm 1, k = \pm 1$, and

$$B = \begin{bmatrix} a_2 & a_1 & a_0 & a_{-1} & a_{-2} & 0 & 0 & 0 & 0 & 0 & 0 \\ 0 & a_2 & a_1 & a_0 & a_{-1} & a_{-2} & 0 & 0 & 0 & 0 & 0 \\ 0 & 0 & a_2 & a_1 & a_0 & a_{-1} & a_{-2} & 0 & 0 & 0 & 0 \\ 0 & 0 & 0 & a_2 & a_1 & a_0 & a_{-1} & a_{-2} & 0 & 0 & 0 \\ 0 & 0 & 0 & 0 & a_2 & a_1 & a_0 & a_{-1} & a_{-2} & 0 & 0 \\ 0 & 0 & 0 & 0 & 0 & a_2 & a_1 & a_0 & a_{-1} & a_{-2} & 0 \\ 0 & 0 & 0 & 0 & 0 & 0 & a_2 & a_1 & a_0 & a_{-1} & a_{-2} \end{bmatrix}$$

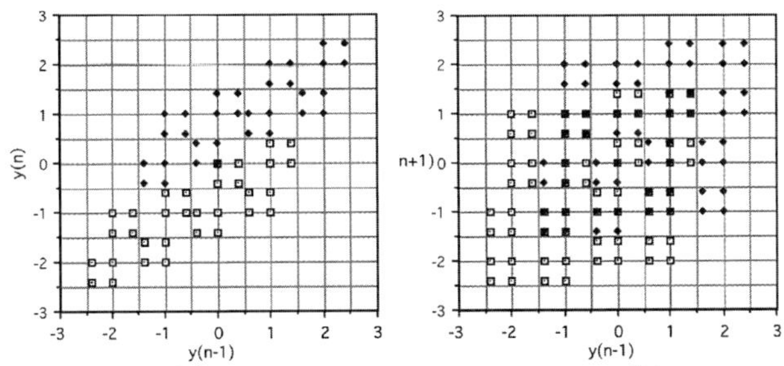

(a) (b)

**Fig. 1.** Distribution of $Y_1$ and $Y_{-1}$ (a) $y(n)-y(n-1)$ plane (b) $y(n+1)-y(n-1)$ plane

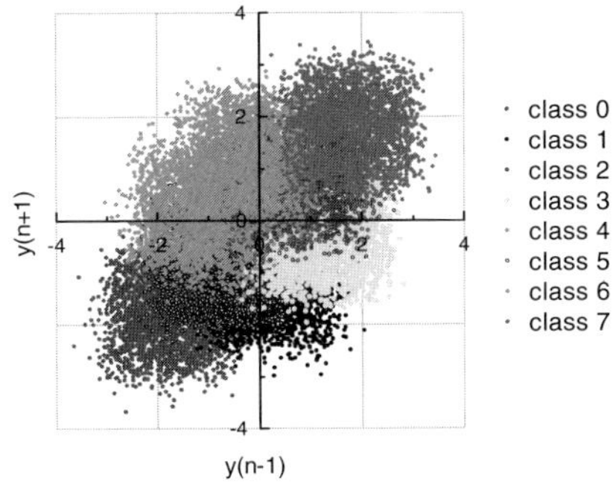


**Fig. 2.** Distribution of the multi-classes in the plane of $y(n+1)$ and $y(n-1)$

Fig. 1a shows the distribution of $Y_1$ and $Y_{-1}$ in the $y(n)-y(n-1)$ space assuming that $a_0=1$, $a_1=a_{-1}=0.5$, $a_2=a_{-2}=0.2$, , $e(n)=0$. Fig. 1b shows the distribution of $Y_1$ and $Y_{-1}$ in the $y(n+1)-y(n-1)$ plane. Fig. 2 shows the distributions of the eight classes in the $y(n+1)-y(n-1)$ plane when 3 bits are considered. As seen in Fig. 2, when equalization is viewed as an 8-class problem, one can obtain better class separability, which will improve overall performance. It is noted that we determine that state -1 is transmitted when the received vector is classified as one the following: state (-1,-1,-1), state (1,-1,-1), state (-1,-1,1) or state (1,-1,1).

## 3 Multi-gradient and Decision Boundary Feature Extraction

Fig. 3 shows an example of 2-layer feedforward neural networks for a 2 pattern-class problem when the decision rule is to choose the class corresponding to the output neuron with the largest output. In Fig. 3, $X=(x_1,x_2,\ldots,x_M)^T$ represents the input vector, $X=(x_1,x_2,\ldots,x_M,x_{M+1})^T$ the input vector which includes the bias term in the input layer. Assuming there are $K$ neurons in the hidden layer, the vector containing all weights is given by

$$W = (w_{1,1}^{hi}, w_{1,2}^{hi}, ..., w_{K,M+1}^{hi}, w_{1,1}^{oh}, w_{1,2}^{oh}, ..., w_{2,K+1}^{oh})^T \\ = (w_1, w_2, w_3, ..., w_L)^T \quad (10)$$

where $L$=(($M$+1)$K$+2($K$+1)), $w_{j,i}^{hi}$ represents the weight between input neuron $i$ and hidden neuron $j$ and $w_{k,j}^{oh}$ is the weight between hidden neuron j and output neuron $k$. Training the neural network is to find $W$ which produces a desirable sequence of output vectors for a given sequence of input vectors. In the previous example, there are (($M$+1)$K$+2($K$+1)) weights to adjust.

In the multi-gradient learning algorithm, the vector containing all weights, $w$ , is viewed as a point in $L$-dimensional space and the learning is treated as finding a solution point in $L$-dimensional space.

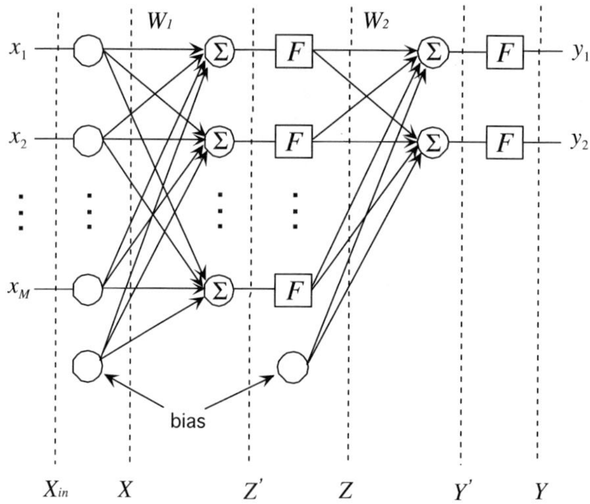


**Fig. 3.** An example of 2-layer feedforward neural networks (2 pattern classes)

In Fig. 3, the output vector $Y$ can be represented as a function of $X$ and $W$ :

$$Y = \begin{bmatrix} y_1 \\ y_2 \end{bmatrix} = \begin{bmatrix} F_1(X,W) \\ F_2(X,W) \end{bmatrix} \quad (11)$$

During learning phase, if $X$ belongs to class $\omega_1$, we move $W$ in such a way that $y_1$ increases and $y_2$ decreases. We can find the direction by computing the gradients of $y_1$ and $y_2$ with respect to $W$ :

$$\nabla y_i = \frac{\partial y_i}{\partial w_1}\overline{w}_1 + \frac{\partial y_i}{\partial w_2}\overline{w}_2 + ... + \frac{\partial y_i}{\partial w_L}\overline{w}_L \quad (12)$$

where $\{\overline{w}_i\}$ is a basis of $L$-dimensional space. Thus, if we update $W$ in the direction of $\alpha\nabla y_1 - \beta\nabla y_2$, where $\alpha, \beta > 0$, $y_1$ will increase and $y_2$ will decrease. If there are $N$ output neurons, then the weight vector $W$ is updated as follows [9]:

$$W^{updated} = W + \gamma(c_1\nabla y_1 + c_2\nabla y_2 + c_3\nabla y_3 + ... + c_N\nabla y_N) \tag{13}$$

where $\gamma$ is the learning rate, otherwise $c_i \geq 0$ if $X$ belongs to class $\omega_i$ and $c_i \leq 0$ .

Assuming the sigmoid function is used as the activation function, it can be shown that differentiating $\{y_1, y_2\}$ with respect to the weights between the hidden layer and the output layer can be obtained as follows:

$$\frac{\partial y_{k'}}{\partial w_{k,j}^{oh}} = \begin{cases} y_{k'}(1-y_{k'})z_j & (k' = k) \\ 0 & (k' \neq k) \end{cases} \tag{14}$$

where $w_{k,j}^{oh}$ is the weight between hidden neuron *j* and output neuron *k* and $z_j$ is the output of hidden neuron *j*. Similarly, differentiating $\{y_1, y_2\}$ with respect to weights between the input layer and hidden layer yields

$$\frac{\partial y_k}{\partial w_{j,i}^{hi}} = y_k(1-y_k)w_{k,j}^{oh} z_j(1-z_j)x_i \tag{15}$$

where $w_{k,j}^{oh}$ is the weight between input neuron *i* and hidden neuron *j*. There are a number of possibilities to set $c_i$ in (13). If we set $c_i$ to be the difference between the target value and the output value, the multi-gradient algorithm is equivalent to the backpropagation algorithm. In [9], assuming that the target value is either 0.1 or 0.9, $c_i$ was set as follows:

$$c_i = \begin{cases} t_i - y_i & \textit{if} \text{ target value } t_i = 0.9 \textit{ and } y_i < 0.9 \\ t_i - y_i & \textit{if} \text{ target value } t_i = 0.1 \textit{ and } y_i > 0.1 \\ 0 & \textit{otherwise} \end{cases} \tag{16}$$

### 3.1 Decision Boundary Feature Extraction [10-11]

For a two-pattern classification problem, the Bayes' decision rule for observation X is given by

$$\text{Decide } \omega_1 \text{ if } h(\mathrm{X}) < t \text{, Otherwise, decide } \omega_2 \tag{17}$$

where $h(\mathrm{X}) = -\ln\left(P(\mathrm{X} \mid \omega_1)/P(\mathrm{X} \mid \omega_2)\right)$ and $t = P(\omega_1)/P(\omega_2)$ . Then feature extraction can be viewed as finding a subspace, W , with the minimum dimension M and the spanning vectors { $\vec{\beta}_k$ } of the subspace such that for any observation X

$$(h(\mathrm{X}) - t)(h(\hat{\mathrm{X}}) - t) > 0 \tag{18}$$

where $\hat{\mathrm{X}}$ is an approximation of X in the subspace W . In the decision boundary feature extraction algorithm, it was shown that discriminantly informative features, which provide useful information for discriminating among classes. Furthermore, discriminantly redundant features, which provide no useful information for discriminating among classes, are related to decision boundaries. In order to extract discriminantly informative features, the decision boundary feature matrix was defined as follows:

$$\Sigma_{DBFM} = \frac{1}{K}\int_{S} \mathrm{N}(\mathrm{X})\mathrm{N}^{\mathrm{T}}(\mathrm{X})p(\mathrm{X})d\mathrm{X} \tag{19}$$

where $p(\mathrm{X})$ is a probability density function, $K = \int_{S} p(\mathrm{X})d\mathrm{X}$ , $S$ is the decision boundary, and the integral is performed over the decision boundary. It is shown the eigenvectors of the decision boundary feature matrix of a pattern recognition problem corresponding to non-zero eigenvalues are the necessary feature vectors to achieve the same classification accuracy as in the original space for the pattern recognition problem. The decision boundary feature extraction algorithm has been successfully applied to the Gaussian maximum likelihood classifier [11], non-parametric classifiers and neural networks [10]. In this paper, we use the decision boundary feature extraction algorithm with analytical computation of normal vectors in order to reduce the complexity of neural network equalizers.

## 4 Experiments and Results

In order to evaluate the performance of the multi-gradient algorithm and the decision boundary feature extraction algorithm for neural network equalizers, experiments are conducted on symmetric and non-symmetric channels. Furthermore, we treat equalization as multi-class classification problems, where the number of classes equals to 8. In other words, 3 bits are considered in order to classify the received signal as one of the binary states (1, –1). As a comparison, the conventional linear equalizer that was implemented using the LMS algorithm is tested. We also provide comparison with the conventional neural network equalizers trained by the backpropagation algorithm.

First, we generated 20,000 samples for the following channel:

$$y(n) = \sum_{k=-L}^{L} a_k x(n-k) + e(n) \tag{20}$$

where $L = 2$ , $a_{-2} = 0.7$ , $a_{-1} = 0.5$ , $a_3 = 1$ , $a_1 = 0.5$ , $a_2 = 0.7$ and noise variance $\sigma_e^2 = 0.4$ . It is noted that the channel is symmetric. The first 8000 samples are used for training and the rest are used for testing. We repeated the experiment 10 times with different initial weights and Fig. 4 shows the average classification accuracies. With backpropagation, the final classification accuracies for the training and test data are 85.2% and 85%, respectively. When the networks are trained by the multi-gradient algorithm, the final classification accuracies for the training and test data are 85.9% and 85.6%, respectively. As can be seen, the multi-gradient algorithm provided better performance than the backpropagation algorithm. The multi-gradient algorithm also converges faster than the backpropagation algorithm.

In the next experiment, we generated 20,000 samples assuming the following non-symmetric channel characteristics:

$L = 2$ , $a_{-2} = 0.3$ , $a_{-1} = 0.7$ , $a_0 = 1$ , $a_1 = 0.8$ , $a_2 = 0.2$, and $\sigma_e^2 = 0.4$ .

As in the previous case, the first 8000 samples were used for training and the rest were used for testing. We repeated the experiment 10 times with different initial weights and Fig. 5 shows the performance comparison. With the multi-gradient algorithm, the final classification accuracies are 89.6% for training data and 89% for test data, while the final classification accuracies of the backprapagation algorithm are 87% for training data and 86.5% for test data. As in the case of the symmetric channel, the multi-gradient algorithm provided better performance than the backpropagation algorithm. The multi-gradient algorithm also converges faster than the backpropagation algorithm.

The following experiments were conducted on the previous symmetric and non-symmetric channels using various noise levels: $\sigma_e{}^2$=0.1, 0.2, 0.3, 0.4, 0.5, 0.6, 0.7, 0.8, 0.9, and 1. Out of the 20,000 samples, the first 8000 samples were used for training and the rest were used for testing. Each experiment was repeated 10 times using different initial weights. Figs. 6-7 show the performance comparison for the symmetric and non-symmetric channels. As can be seen, the multi-gradient algorithm consistently outperforms the backpropagation algorithm. The performance of the linear equalizer trained using the LMS algorithm are also shown. From Figs. 6-7, it can be said that the neural network equalizers which view equalization as multi-class problems provide significantly better performance than the conventional linear equalizer. Furthermore, the multi-gradient algorithm noticeably outperforms the backpropagation algorithm for feedforward neural network equalizers.

Next, we apply the decision boundary feature extraction method to neural network equalizers trained by the multi-gradient algorithm and investigate the performance of the decision boundary feature extraction method. It is noted that the number of input neurons is 7 since equalization is viewed as an 8-class problem. The number of hidden neurons is three times the number of the input neurons. After feature extraction, new features are obtained and the network is trained using the new features. Figs. 8-9 show the results for the symmetric and non-symmetric channels. As can be seen, for the symmetric channel (Fig. 8), one can obtain almost maximum performance with 2-4 features. For the non-symmetric channel (Fig. 9), using the features obtained by applying decision boundary feature extraction, the neural network equalizer can achieve almost maximum classification accuracies with 3-6 features. The decision boundary feature extraction method provides a reduced feature set, which provides almost maximum performance. With the reduced feature set, the complexity of the neural network equalizer can be significantly reduced.

Fig. 10a shows the distributions of the eight classes in the plane spanned by $y(n)$ and $y(n+1)$ for the non-symmetric channel with noise variance $\sigma_e^2 = 0.1$. It is noted that the class samples were preprocessed so that they were in the range of 0 to 2. Fig. 10a shows that the eight classes are mixed and difficult to separate in the $y(n) - y(n+1)$ plane. On the other hand, Fig. 10b shows the distributions of the 8 classes in the plane spanned by the two eigenvectors corresponding to the largest two eigenvalues of the decision boundary feature matrix. Compared to Fig. 10a, the 8 classes are better separated. Fig. 10b demonstrates that the decision boundary feature extraction method can provide better class separability with low dimensionality, which significantly reduces network complexity. The eigenvalues of the decision boundary feature matrix are shown in Table I. It is noted that the largest two eigenvalues account for more than 94% of the total energy.

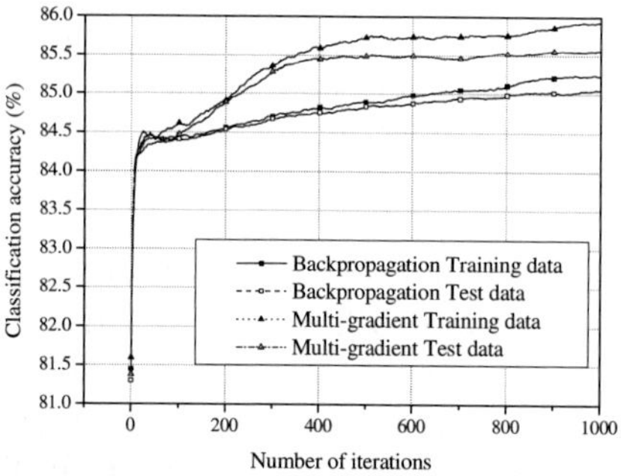


**Fig. 4.** Performance comparison for a symmetric channel

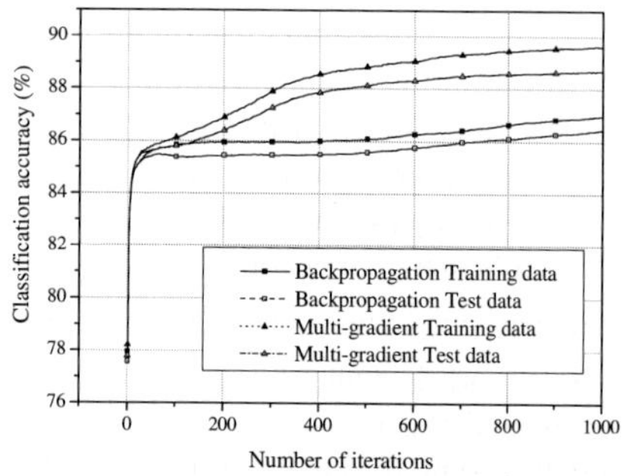


**Fig. 5.** Performance comparison for a non-symmetric channel

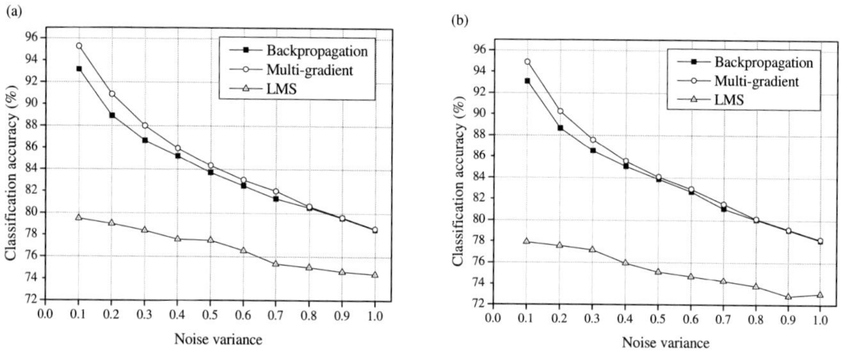


**Fig. 6.** Performance comparison for a symmetric channel: $a_{-2} = 0.7$ , $a_{-1} = 0.5$ , $a_3 = 1$ , $a_1 = 0.5$ , $a_2 = 0.7$ . (a) training data, (b) test data.

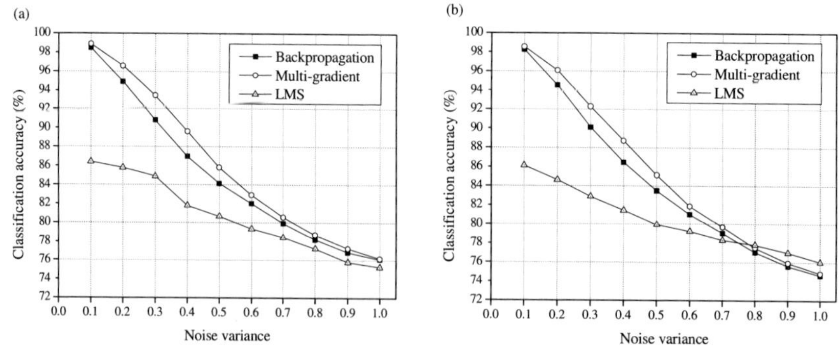


**Fig. 7.** Performance comparison for a non-symmetric channel (a) training (b) test

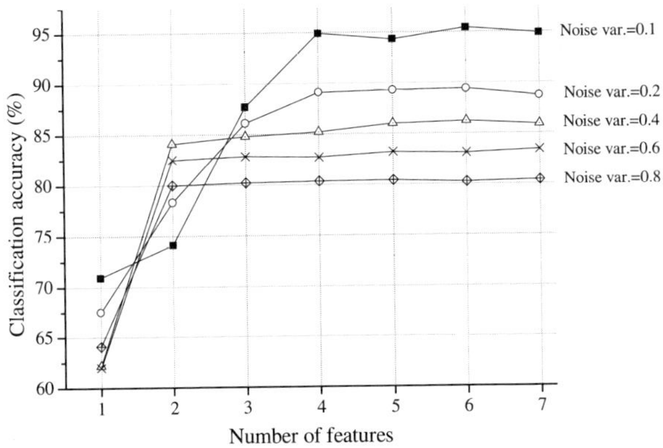


**Fig. 8.** Performance comparison of the decision boundary feature extraction method for various noise variances (symmetric channel)

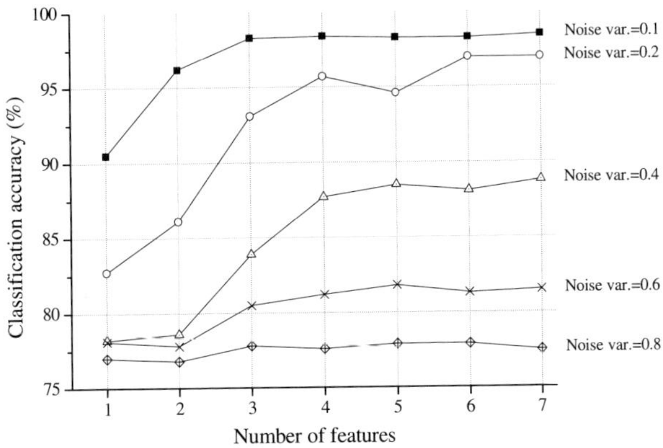


**Fig. 9.** Performance comparison of the decision boundary feature extraction method for various noise variances (non-symmetric channel)

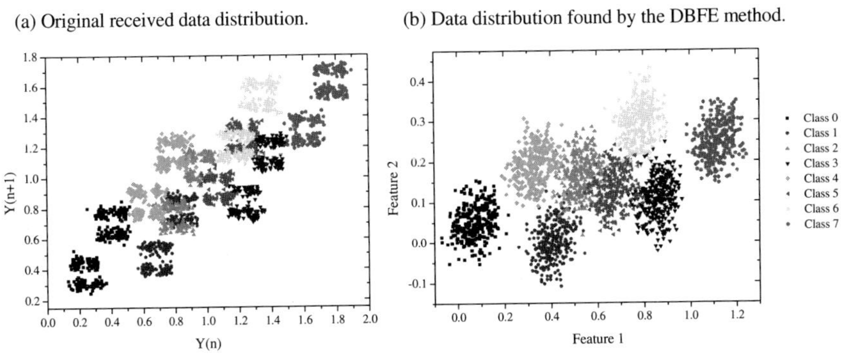


**Fig. 10.** Data distribution found by the decision boundary feature extraction method (non-symmetric channel)

**Table 1.** Eigenvalues of the decision boundary feature matrix

| No. Features | Eigenvalue | Proportion (%) | Accumulation (%) |
|---|---|---|---|
| **1** | 36002 | 65.6 | 65.6 |
| **2** | 16024 | 29.2 | 94.7 |
| **3** | 2474 | 4.5 | 99.2 |
| **4** | 256 | 0.5 | 99.7 |
| **5** | 118 | 0.2 | 99.9 |
| **6** | 30 | 0.1 | 99.9 |
| **7** | 11 | 0 | 100.0 |

## 5 Conclusions

In this paper, we viewed equalization as multi-class problems and used neural networks as a classifier. In particular, we applied the recently published multi-gradient training algorithm to neural networks and applied the decision boundary feature extraction method to simplify the neural networks. We also analyzed the performance of the proposed neural network equalizer and feature extraction at various noise levels. Experiments showed that the proposed algorithm provided noticeable improvements over the conventional LMS algorithm. It is also observed that the multi-gradient algorithm provided improved performance compared to the backpropagation algorithm. On the other hand, the decision boundary feature extraction method provides new features, which can significantly reduce the complexity of neural network equalizers.

## Acknowledgment

This research was supported by the MIC(Ministry of Information and Communication), Korea, under the ITRC(Information Technology Research Center) support program supervised by the IITA(Institute of Information Technology Assessment) (IITA-2005-(C1090-0502-0027)).

## References

1. Qureshi, S.: Adaptive Equalization., IEEE Communications Magazine (1982) 9-16
2. Haykin, S.: Adaptive Filter Theory. 3rd ed. Prentice Hall (1996)
3. Forney, G.D.: Maximum-Likelihood Sequence Estimation of Digital Sequences in the Presence of Intersymbol Interference. IEEE Trans. Information Theory, IT-18 (1972) 363-378
4. George, D.A., Bowen, R.B., Storey, J.R.: An Adaptive Decision Feedback Equalizer. IEEE Trans. Communication Technology, COM-19 (1971) 281-293
5. Johnson, C.R., Schniter, P., Endres, T.J., Behm, J.D., Brown, D.R., Casas, R.A.: Blind Equalization Using the Constant Modulus Criterion: A Review. Proceedings of the IEEE (1998) 1927-1989

6. Mulgrew, B.: Applying Radial Basis Functions. IEEE Signal Processing Magazine, Mar. (1996) 50-65
7. Haykin, S.: Adaptive Digital Communication Receivers. IEEE Communications Magazine, Dec (2000) 106-114
8. Chen, S., Gibson, G. J., Cowan, C.F.N., Grant, P.M.: Adaptive Equalization of Finite Non-linear Channels Using Multilayer Perceptrons. Signal Processing, 20 (1990) 107-119
9. Go, J., Han, G., Kim, H., Lee, C.: Multigradient: A New Neural Network Learning Algorithm for Pattern Classification. IEEE Trans. Geoscience and Remote Sensing, 39, (2001) 986-993
10. Lee, C., Landgrebe, D.A.: Decision Boundary Feature Extraction for Neural Networks. IEEE Trans. Neural Networks, 8 (1997) 75-83
11. Lee, C., Landgrebe, D.A.: Feature Extraction Based on Decision Boundaries. IEEE Trans. Pattern Analysis and Machine Intelligence, 15 (1993) 388-400

# Novel Delay-Dependent Exponential Stability Analysis for a Class of Delayed Neural Networks

Zhiqiang Zuo and Yijing Wang

School of Electrical Engineering & Automation, Tianjin University, Tianjin, 300072, China
{zqzuo, yjwang}@tju.edu.cn

**Abstract.** This paper deals with the problem of exponential stability for a class of delayed neural networks described by nonlinear delay differential equations of neutral type. A less conservative exponential stability condition is derived based on a new Lyapunov-Krasovskii functional in term of linear matrix inequalities. A numerical example is given to illustrate the effectiveness of the proposed methods.

## 1 Introduction

Since Chua and Yang introduced the theory of cellular neural networks [1], the problem of stability of neural networks has attracted the interest of many researchers. There are many applications for neural networks such as pattern recognition, image processing, speed detection of moving objects, optimization problems and so on. In hardware implementation of neural networks, time delays are often encountered in practice. As we know, time delay may be a source of instability or oscillation in neural networks. Therefore, the stability analysis for delayed neural networks has received a great deal of interest for a long time (see e.g., [2]-[9] and the references therein). They can be classified into two categories: delay-independent and delay-dependent. Usually, the delay-dependent stability criterion is less conservative than the delay-independent one in the case when the delay size is small.

As we have know, fast convergence of a system is essential for real-time computation, and the exponentially convergence rate is generally used to determine the speed of neural computations. So it is important to determine the exponential stability and to estimate the exponential convergence rate. Global exponential stability for neural networks without time delay or with delay has been investigated [10]-[17] and the references therein.

Recently, Xu et. al. studied the delay-dependent exponential stability for a class of delayed neural networks which is described by nonlinear delay differential equations of the neutral type. A sufficient exponential stability condition for such systems was proposed in [18]. An inequality was used to derive the result, which brings some conservatism for exponential stability criterion. To overcome the conservatism in [18], we construct a new type of Lyapunov-Krasovskii functional and a less conservative result is obtained by using some free matrices to express the relationship among the terms in system matrix variables. It should be noted

D.-S. Huang, K. Li, and G.W. Irwin (Eds.): ICIC 2006, LNCS 4113, pp. 216–226, 2006.

that our main theorem is given in terms of linear matrix inequalities (LMI) which can be solved efficiently using the interior-point methods [19].

The paper is organized as follows. Section 2 formulates the problem and gives some preliminaries. The main results are proposed in Section 3. A numerical example illustrating our design procedure and its effectiveness is given in Section 4. Finally, in Section 5, concluding remarks end the paper.

**Notations:** The following notations are used throughout this paper. $\Re$ is the set of real numbers. $\Re^n$, $\Re^{m\times n}$ are sets of real vectors with dimension $n$ and real matrices with dimension $m \times n$, respectively. The notation $X \geq Y$ (respectively, $X > Y$), where $X$ and $Y$ are symmetric matrices, means that the matrix $X - Y$ is positive semi-definite (respectively, positive definite). $I$ and $0$ denote the identity matrix and zero matrix with compatible dimensions. In symmetric block matrices, we use an asterisk $\star$ to denote terms that are induced by symmetry.

## 2 Problems Statement and Preliminaries

Consider the following delayed neural network described by a nonlinear delay differential equation of neutral type (see [18])

$$\dot{u}(t) = -A\,u(t) + W_1\,g(u(t)) + W_2\,g(u(t-h)) + D\dot{u}(t-h) + b \tag{1}$$

$$u(t) = \phi(t), \quad -h \leq t \leq 0 \tag{2}$$

or

$$\begin{aligned}\dot{u}_i(t) = -a_i\,u_i(t) &+ \textstyle\sum_{j=1}^{n} w_{ij1}\,g_j(u_j(t)) + \sum_{j=1}^{n} w_{ij2}\,g_j(u_j(t-h)) \\ &+ \textstyle\sum_{j=1}^{n} d_{ij}\dot{u}_j(t-h)) + b_i, \qquad i = 1, 2, \cdots, n\end{aligned} \tag{3}$$

where

$$u(t) = [\,u_1(t)\;\; u_2(t)\;\; \cdots\;\; u_n(t)\,]^T$$

is the neuron state.

$$g(u(t)) = [\,g_1(u_1(t))\;\; g_2(u_2(t))\;\; \cdots\;\; g_n(u_n(t))\,]^T$$

$$g(u(t-h)) = [\,g_1(u_1(t-h))\;\; g_2(u_2(t-h))\;\; \cdots\;\; g_n(u_n(t-h))\,]^T$$

are the activation functions.

$$b = [\,b_1\;\; b_2\;\; \cdots\;\; b_n\,]^T$$

is the constant external input. $A = diag\{a_i\} > 0$ is a positive diagonal matrix. $h > 0$ is the constant time delay. $W_1$ and $W_2$ are interconnection matrices representing the weight coefficients of the neurons. Furthermore, it is assumed that $g_j(\cdot)$, $j = 1, 2, \cdots, n$ satisfies the following assumptions

**Assumption 1**

$$|g_j(\zeta)| \leq m_j \quad j = 1, 2, \cdots, n$$

*for all* $\zeta \in \Re$; $m_j > 0$.

**Assumption 2**

$$0 \le \frac{g_j(\zeta_1) - g_j(\zeta_2)}{\zeta_1 - \zeta_2} \le k_j \quad j = 1, 2, \cdots, n$$

*for all* $\zeta_1, \zeta_2 \in \Re,\ \zeta_1 \neq \zeta_2;\ k_j > 0.$

Here we denote

$$K = diag\{k_1,\ k_2,\ \cdots,\ k_n\} > 0$$

Note that Assumption 1 and Assumption 2 guarantee that there is an equilibrium point for neural network (1).

For the sake of simplicity, we will make the following transformation to neural network (1) using the Brouwer's fix point theorem

$$x(t) = u(t) - u^* \tag{4}$$

where $u^* = [u_1^* \quad u_2^* \quad \cdots \quad u_n^*]^T$ is an equilibrium point of (1). Under this transformation, system (1) can be rewritten as

$$\dot{x}(t) = -A\,x(t) + W_1\,f(x(t)) + W_2\,f(x(t-h)) + D\dot{x}(t-h) \tag{5}$$

where $f_j(x_j(t)) = g_j(x_j(t) + u_j^*) - g_i(u_j^*)$ and $f_j(0) = 0$. It is easy to verify that

$$0 \le \frac{f_j(x_j)}{x_j} \le k_j, \quad \forall x_j \neq 0, \quad j = 1, 2, \cdots, n \tag{6}$$

By (6), we know that for any scalars $r_j \ge 0,\ s_j \ge 0,\ \ j = 1, 2, \cdots, n$

$$2\sum_{j=1}^{n} r_j\, f_j(x_j(t))[\,k_j x_j(t) - f_j(x_j(t))\,] \ge 0 \tag{7}$$

$$2\sum_{j=1}^{n} s_j\, f_j(x_j(t-h(t)))[\,k_j x_j(t-h(t)) - f_j(x_j(t-h(t)))\,] \ge 0 \tag{8}$$

which can be rewritten as

$$2f^T(x(t))RKx(t) - 2f^T(x(t))Rf(x(t)) \ge 0 \tag{9}$$

$$2f^T(x(t-h))SKx(t-h) - 2f^T(x(t-h))Sf(x(t-h)) \ge 0 \tag{10}$$

where

$$R = diag\{r_1,\ r_2,\ \cdots,\ r_n\} \ge 0$$

$$S = diag\{s_1,\ s_2,\ \cdots,\ s_n\} \ge 0$$

It can be seen that the exponential stability of $u^*$ of (1) is equivalent to that of the trivial solution of (5).

**Definition 1.** *System (1) is said to be exponential stable if there exist positive number $k > 0$, $\mu > 1$ such that for every solution $x(t)$ of (1) satisfies*

$$\|x(t)\|^2 \leq \mu e^{-kt} \sup_{-h\leq\theta\leq 0} \{\|x(\theta)\|^2, \|\dot{x}(\theta)\|^2\}$$

In order to obtain our main result in this paper, the following fact is needed.

**Fact 1.** *For any compatible dimensioned matrices $N_j$, $j = 1, 2, \cdots, 6$, it follows that*

$$\begin{aligned}\alpha = 2e^{2kt}\, [\, & x^T(t)N_1 + x^T(t-h)N_2 + f^T(x(t))N_3 + f^T(x(t-h))N_4 \\ & + \dot{x}^T(t)N_5 + \dot{x}^T(t-h)N_6\,] \\ & \times [\,\dot{x}(t) + Ax(t) - W_1 f(x(t)) - W_2 f(x(t-h) - D\dot{x}(t-h)\,] \equiv 0\end{aligned} \tag{11}$$

## 3 Main Results

Now we will present a new delay-dependent exponential stability result for delayed neural network (1).

**Theorem 1.** *The neural network with time delay described by (1) is exponentially stable if there exist matrices $P > 0$, $R = diag\{r_1, r_2, \cdots, r_n\} \geq 0$, $S = diag\{s_1, s_2, \cdots, s_n\} \geq 0$, $N_i (i = 1, \cdots, 6)$, $Q = \begin{bmatrix} Q_{11} & Q_{12} & Q_{13} \\ \star & Q_{22} & Q_{23} \\ \star & \star & Q_{33} \end{bmatrix} > 0$ such that the following condition holds*

$$\Sigma = \begin{bmatrix} \Sigma_{11} & \Sigma_{12} & \Sigma_{13} & \Sigma_{14} & \Sigma_{15} & \Sigma_{16} \\ \star & \Sigma_{22} & \Sigma_{23} & \Sigma_{24} & \Sigma_{25} & \Sigma_{26} \\ \star & \star & \Sigma_{33} & \Sigma_{34} & \Sigma_{35} & \Sigma_{36} \\ \star & \star & \star & \Sigma_{44} & \Sigma_{45} & \Sigma_{46} \\ \star & \star & \star & \star & \Sigma_{55} & \Sigma_{56} \\ \star & \star & \star & \star & \star & \Sigma_{66} \end{bmatrix} < 0 \tag{12}$$

*where*

$$\Sigma_{11} = N_1 A + A^T N_1^T + 2kP + Q_{11}$$

$$\Sigma_{12} = A^T N_2^T$$

$$\Sigma_{13} = A^T N_3^T - N_1 W_1 + Q_{12} + KR$$

$$\Sigma_{14} = A^T N_4^T - N_1 W_2$$

$$\Sigma_{15} = A^T N_5^T + N_1 + P + Q_{13}$$

$$\Sigma_{16} = A^T N_6^T - N_1 D$$

$$\Sigma_{22} = -e^{-2kh} Q_{11}$$

$$\Sigma_{23} = -N_2 W_1$$

$$\Sigma_{24} = -N_2 W_2 - e^{-2kh} Q_{12} + KS$$

$$\Sigma_{25} = N_2$$
$$\Sigma_{26} = -N_2 D - e^{-2kh} Q_{13}$$
$$\Sigma_{33} = -N_3 W_1 - W_1^T N_3^T + Q_{22} - 2R$$
$$\Sigma_{34} = -W_1^T N_4^T - N_3 W_2$$
$$\Sigma_{35} = -W_1^T N_5^T + N_3 + Q_{23}$$
$$\Sigma_{36} = -W_1^T N_6^T - N_3 D$$
$$\Sigma_{44} = -N_4 W_2 - W_2^T N_4^T - e^{-2kh} Q_{22} - 2S$$
$$\Sigma_{45} = -W_2^T N_5^T + N_4$$
$$\Sigma_{46} = -W_2^T N_6^T - N_4 D - e^{-2kh} Q_{23}$$
$$\Sigma_{55} = N_5 + N_5^T + Q_{33}$$
$$\Sigma_{56} = N_6^T - N_5 D$$
$$\Sigma_{66} = -N_6 D - D^T N_6^T - e^{-2kh} Q_{33}$$

*Proof.* Choose the Lyapunov-Krasovskii functional as

$$\begin{aligned} V(x_t) &= e^{2kt} x^T(t) P x(t) + \int_{t-h}^{t} e^{2k\zeta} \begin{bmatrix} x(\zeta) \\ f(x(\zeta)) \\ \dot{x}(\zeta) \end{bmatrix}^T \begin{bmatrix} Q_{11} & Q_{12} & Q_{13} \\ \star & Q_{22} & Q_{23} \\ \star & \star & Q_{33} \end{bmatrix} \begin{bmatrix} x(\zeta) \\ f(x(\zeta)) \\ \dot{x}(\zeta) \end{bmatrix} d\zeta \\ &= e^{2kt} x^T(t) P x(t) + \int_{t-h}^{t} e^{2k\zeta} \varpi^T(\zeta) Q \varpi(\zeta)\, d\zeta \end{aligned} \tag{13}$$

where $\varpi(\zeta) = \begin{bmatrix} x(\zeta) \\ f(x(\zeta)) \\ \dot{x}(\zeta) \end{bmatrix}$ and $Q$ is defined in Theorem 1.

By (9), (10) and (11), the time derivative of $V(x_t)$ along the trajectory of neural network (1) is

$$\begin{aligned} \dot{V}(x_t) &= 2ke^{2kt} x^T(t) P x(t) + 2e^{2kt} x^T(t) P \dot{x}(t) + e^{2kt} \varpi^T(t) Q \varpi(t) \\ &\quad - e^{2kt} e^{-2kh} \varpi^T(t-h) Q \varpi(t-h) \\ &\le 2ke^{2kt} x^T(t) P x(t) + 2e^{2kt} x^T(t) P \dot{x}(t) + e^{2kt} \varpi^T(t) Q \varpi(t) \\ &\quad - e^{2kt} e^{-2kh} \varpi^T(t-h) Q \varpi(t-h) \\ &\quad + \alpha + e^{2kt} \{2f^T(x(t)) RKx(t) - 2f^T(x(t)) Rf(x(t))\} \\ &\quad + e^{2kt} \{2f^T(x(t-h)) SKx(t-h) - 2f^T(x(t-h)) Sf(x(t-h))\} \\ &= e^{2kt} \xi^T(t)\, \Sigma\, \xi(t) \end{aligned} \tag{14}$$

where

$$\xi^T(t) = [\, x^T(t) \;\; x^T(t-h) \;\; f^T(x(t)) \;\; f^T(x(t-h)) \;\; \dot{x}^T(t) \;\; \dot{x}^T(t-h) \,]$$

and $\Sigma$ is defined in (12).

If $\Sigma < 0$, then $\dot{V}(x_t) < 0$ for any $\xi(t) \neq 0$, which guarantees that $V(x_t) \leq V(x(0))$ for $t > 0$. On the other hand, we have

$$\begin{aligned} V(0) &= x^T(0)Px(0) + \int_{-h}^{0} e^{2k\zeta}\varpi^T(\zeta)Q\varpi(\zeta)\,d\zeta \\ &\leq \lambda_{max}(P)\|x(t)\|^2 + \lambda_{max}(Q)(\|x(t)\|^2 + \|f(x(t))\|^2 + \|\dot{x}(t)\|^2)\int_{-h}^{0} e^{2k\zeta}\,d\zeta \\ &\leq \lambda_{max}(P)\|x(t)\|^2 + \lambda_{max}(Q)(\|x(t)\|^2 + k_{max}^2\|x(t)\|^2 + \|\dot{x}(t)\|^2)\tfrac{1-e^{-2kh}}{2k} \\ &= [\,\lambda_{max}(P) + \tfrac{1-e^{-2kh}}{2k}(1+k_{max}^2)\lambda_{max}(Q)\,]\|x(t)\|^2 \\ &\quad + \tfrac{1-e^{-2kh}}{2k}\lambda_{max}(Q)\|\dot{x}(t)\|^2 \\ &\leq [\,\lambda_{max}(P) + \tfrac{1-e^{-2kh}}{2k}(2+k_{max}^2)\lambda_{max}(Q)\,] \sup_{-h\leq\theta\leq 0}\{\|x(\theta)\|^2, \|\dot{x}(\theta)\|^2\} \end{aligned} \tag{15}$$

where

$$k_{max} = max\{k_i\}, \quad i = 1, 2, \cdots, n$$

and

$$V(x_t) \geq e^{2kt}x^T(t)Px(t) \geq \lambda_{min}(P)\|x(t)\|^2 \tag{16}$$

Thus, it follows that

$$\|x(t)\|^2 \leq \frac{\Gamma}{\lambda_{min}(P)}\, e^{-2kt} \sup_{-h\leq\theta\leq 0}\{\|x(\theta)\|^2, \|\dot{x}(\theta)\|^2\}$$

where

$$\Gamma = \lambda_{max}(P) + \frac{1-e^{-2kh}}{2k}(2+k_{max}^2)\lambda_{max}(Q)$$

This completes the proof.

*Remark 1.* Theorem 1 provides a new delay-dependent exponential stability criterion for delayed neural network (1) by using a more general Lyapunov-Krasovskii functional. As we can see, this result is expressed within the framework of linear matrix inequalities which can be easily computed by the interior-point method [19]. Neither model transformation approach nor any bounding technique on the cross term is used. Therefore, we obtain a less conservative stability condition which can be verified in Section 4.

If $D = 0$, then the delayed neural network described by (5) reduces to

$$\dot{x}(t) = -A\,x(t) + W_1\,f(x(t)) + W_2\,f(x(t-h)) \tag{17}$$

Based on the result of Theorem 1, it is easy to obtain the following delay-dependent exponential stability condition for delayed neural network (17).

**Theorem 2.** *The delayed neural network (17) is exponentially stable if there exist matrices* $P > 0$, $R = diag\{r_1, r_2, \cdots, r_n\} \geq 0$, $S = diag\{s_1, s_2, \cdots, s_n\} \geq 0$, $N_i(i = 1, \cdots, 5)$, $Q = \begin{bmatrix} Q_{11} & Q_{12} \\ \star & Q_{22} \end{bmatrix} > 0$ *such that the following condition holds*

$$\Psi = \begin{bmatrix} \Psi_{11} & \Psi_{12} & \Psi_{13} & \Psi_{14} & \Psi_{15} \\ \star & \Psi_{22} & \Psi_{23} & \Psi_{24} & \Psi_{25} \\ \star & \star & \Psi_{33} & \Psi_{34} & \Psi_{35} \\ \star & \star & \star & \Psi_{44} & \Psi_{45} \\ \star & \star & \star & \star & \Psi_{55} \end{bmatrix} < 0 \tag{18}$$

*where*

$$\Psi_{11} = N_1 A + A^T N_1^T + 2kP + Q_{11}$$
$$\Psi_{12} = A^T N_2^T$$
$$\Psi_{13} = A^T N_3^T - N_1 W_1 + Q_{12} + KR$$
$$\Psi_{14} = A^T N_4^T - N_1 W_2$$
$$\Psi_{15} = A^T N_5^T + N_1 + P$$
$$\Psi_{22} = -e^{-2kh} Q_{11}$$
$$\Psi_{23} = -N_2 W_1$$
$$\Psi_{24} = -N_2 W_2 - e^{-2kh} Q_{12} + KS$$
$$\Psi_{25} = N_2$$
$$\Psi_{33} = -N_3 W_1 - W_1^T N_3^T + Q_{22} - 2R$$
$$\Psi_{34} = -W_1^T N_4^T - N_3 W_2$$
$$\Psi_{35} = -W_1^T N_5^T + N_3$$
$$\Psi_{44} = -N_4 W_2 - W_2^T N_4^T - e^{-2kh} Q_{22} - 2S$$
$$\Psi_{45} = -W_2^T N_5^T + N_4$$
$$\Psi_{55} = N_5 + N_5^T$$

*Proof. Choose the Lyapunov-Krasovskii functional as*

$$V(x_t) = e^{2kt} x^T(t) P x(t) + \int_{t-h}^{t} e^{2k\zeta} \begin{bmatrix} x(\zeta) \\ f(x(\zeta)) \end{bmatrix}^T \begin{bmatrix} Q_{11} & Q_{12} \\ \star & Q_{22} \end{bmatrix} \begin{bmatrix} x(\zeta) \\ f(x(\zeta)) \end{bmatrix} d\zeta \tag{19}$$

*The time derivative of $V(x_t)$ along the trajectory of neural network (17) is*

$$\begin{aligned}
\dot{V}(x_t) &= 2ke^{2kt} x^T(t) P x(t) + 2e^{2kt} x^T(t) P \dot{x}(t) \\
&\quad + e^{2kt} \left[ x^T(t) \; f^T(x(t)) \right] \begin{bmatrix} Q_{11} & Q_{12} \\ \star & Q_{22} \end{bmatrix} \begin{bmatrix} x(t) \\ f(x(t)) \end{bmatrix} \\
&\quad - e^{2kt} e^{-2kh} \left[ x^T(t-h) \; f^T(x(t-h)) \right] \begin{bmatrix} Q_{11} & Q_{12} \\ \star & Q_{22} \end{bmatrix} \begin{bmatrix} x(t-h) \\ f(x(t-h)) \end{bmatrix} \\
&\le 2ke^{2kt} x^T(t) P x(t) + 2e^{2kt} x^T(t) P \dot{x}(t) \\
&\quad + e^{2kt} \left[ x^T(t) \; f^T(x(t)) \right] \begin{bmatrix} Q_{11} & Q_{12} \\ \star & Q_{22} \end{bmatrix} \begin{bmatrix} x(t) \\ f(x(t)) \end{bmatrix} \\
&\quad - e^{2kt} e^{-2kh} \left[ x^T(t-h) \; f^T(x(t-h)) \right] \begin{bmatrix} Q_{11} & Q_{12} \\ \star & Q_{22} \end{bmatrix} \begin{bmatrix} x(t-h) \\ f(x(t-h)) \end{bmatrix} \\
&\quad + 2e^{2kt} \left[ x^T(t) N_1 + x^T(t-h) N_2 + f^T(x(t)) N_3 \right. \\
&\qquad \left. + f^T(x(t-h)) N_4 + \dot{x}^T(t) N_5 \right] \\
&\qquad \times \left[ \dot{x}(t) + Ax(t) - W_1 f(x(t)) - W_2 f(x(t-h) \right] \\
&\quad + e^{2kt} \{ 2f^T(x(t)) RKz(t) - 2f^T(x(t)) Rf(x(t)) \} \\
&\quad + e^{2kt} \{ 2f^T(x(t-h)) SKx(t-h) - 2f^T(x(t-h)) Sf(x(t-h)) \} \\
&= e^{2kt} \varphi^T(t) \Psi \varphi(t)
\end{aligned} \tag{20}$$

*where*

$$\varphi^T(t) = [\,x^T(t)\;\; x^T(t-h)\;\; f^T(x(t))\;\; f^T(x(t-h))\;\; \dot{x}^T(t)\,]$$

*and $\Psi$ is defined in (18). The remaining of the proof is similar to that of Theorem 1, thus omitted.*

*Remark 2.* Theorem 1 and Theorem 2 proposed in this paper can be easily extended to the case of time-varying delays.

## 4 Example

In order to demonstrate the effectiveness of the method we have presented, an example is given in this section to compare with the results of the previous methods.

*Example 1.* Consider the delayed neural network (5) described as in [18]

$$A = \begin{bmatrix} 2.7644 & 0 & 0 \\ 0 & 1.0185 & 0 \\ 0 & 0 & 10.2716 \end{bmatrix}, \quad W_1 = \begin{bmatrix} 0.2651 & -3.1608 & -2.0491 \\ 3.1859 & -0.1573 & -2.4687 \\ 2.0368 & -1.3633 & 0.5776 \end{bmatrix}$$

$$W_2 = \begin{bmatrix} -0.7727 & -0.8370 & 3.8019 \\ 0.1004 & 0.6677 & -2.4431 \\ -0.6622 & 1.3109 & -1.8407 \end{bmatrix}, \quad D = \begin{bmatrix} 0.2076 & 0.0631 & 0.3915 \\ -0.0780 & 0.3106 & 0.1009 \\ -0.2763 & 0.1416 & 0.3729 \end{bmatrix}$$

$$K = \begin{bmatrix} 0.1019 & 0 & 0 \\ 0 & 0.3419 & 0 \\ 0 & 0 & 0.0633 \end{bmatrix}$$

Using the Matlab LMI-Toolbox to solve this problem, we can obtain the upper bound of the delay is $h = 6.5$ by Theorem 1 when $k = 0.1$ in this paper. Compared with the result of $h = 1.0344$ in [18], it is obvious that our method gives a less conservative result. For $h = 6.5$, we obtain the following results:

$$P = \begin{bmatrix} 1.9517 & 0.4594 & -0.9535 \\ 0.4594 & 2.2752 & -0.5685 \\ -0.9535 & -0.5685 & 8.1104 \end{bmatrix}$$

$$R = \begin{bmatrix} 78.2566 & 0 & 0 \\ 0 & 16.1190 & 0 \\ 0 & 0 & 77.8660 \end{bmatrix}$$

$$S = 10^3 \times \begin{bmatrix} 46.1195 & 0 & 0 \\ 0 & 5.9277 & 0 \\ 0 & 0 & 217.2068 \end{bmatrix}$$

$$Q_{11} = \begin{bmatrix} 4.1424 & -1.0743 & -0.2263 \\ -1.0743 & 2.8641 & -4.6853 \\ -0.2263 & -4.6853 & 44.0325 \end{bmatrix}$$

$$Q_{12} = \begin{bmatrix} -1.5062 & 4.6804 & 1.1249 \\ -6.3350 & -3.1345 & 4.6472 \\ 4.1797 & 1.4351 & -0.1478 \end{bmatrix}$$

$$Q_{13} = \begin{bmatrix} 0.2285 & -1.2845 & 0.6337 \\ -0.7401 & 1.4757 & -0.4747 \\ 0.2817 & -4.9995 & 2.1561 \end{bmatrix}$$

$$Q_{22} = \begin{bmatrix} 66.4162 & -5.1965 & -7.5045 \\ -5.1965 & 22.7158 & 5.9630 \\ -7.5045 & 5.9630 & 73.2039 \end{bmatrix}$$

$$Q_{23} = \begin{bmatrix} 0.9437 & -6.2783 & -0.1256 \\ 1.2542 & 0.1384 & 0.5883 \\ 0.8236 & 4.3743 & -1.4502 \end{bmatrix}$$

$$Q_{33} = \begin{bmatrix} 0.7416 & -0.4276 & -0.0435 \\ -0.4276 & 3.5544 & -0.9279 \\ -0.0435 & -0.9279 & 1.1551 \end{bmatrix}$$

$$N_1 = 10^3 \times \begin{bmatrix} -0.0074 & -1.0578 & 0.0350 \\ 0.3922 & -0.0052 & -0.0843 \\ -0.1278 & 0.8548 & -0.0040 \end{bmatrix}$$

$$N_2 = \begin{bmatrix} -0.1078 & 0.0240 & -0.0435 \\ -0.2017 & 0.1671 & 0.0198 \\ 1.2666 & -1.1497 & -0.0676 \end{bmatrix}$$

$$N_3 = 10^3 \times \begin{bmatrix} -1.2038 & -0.0671 & 0.2607 \\ 0.0361 & -1.0990 & 0.0270 \\ 0.9584 & -0.8326 & -0.1811 \end{bmatrix}$$

$$N_4 = 10^3 \times \begin{bmatrix} -0.0464 & -0.2411 & 0.0189 \\ -0.2431 & -0.4273 & 0.0660 \\ 0.8876 & 1.6384 & -0.2491 \end{bmatrix}$$

$$N_5 = \begin{bmatrix} -2.7297 & -382.9048 & 12.7118 \\ 385.2540 & -5.1173 & -82.6671 \\ -12.3766 & 83.6259 & -0.9507 \end{bmatrix}$$

$$N_6 = \begin{bmatrix} 27.1456 & 102.1786 & -9.1131 \\ -117.9937 & 13.5255 & 25.0424 \\ -33.3019 & 119.2512 & 3.4301 \end{bmatrix}$$

## 5 Conclusion

In this paper, we have studied the delay-dependent exponential stability for a class of delayed neural networks described by nonlinear delay differential equations of the neutral type. A new type of Lyapunov-Krasovskii functional has been constructed to derive a less conservative stability condition by using some free matrices to express the relationship between the system matrices. Furthermore, a delay-dependent exponential stability criterion has also been obtained for ordinary delayed neural network. Finally, an example has shown that our method gives an improvement over the existing ones.

## Acknowledgment

This work is supported by National Natural Science Foundation of China (No. 60504011) and (No. 60504012).

## References

1. Chua, L.O., Yang, L.: Cellular neural networks: theory and applications. IEEE Trans. Circuits Syst I **35** (1988) 1257–1290
2. Roska, T., Chua, L.O.: Cellular neural networks with nonlinear and delay-type template. Int. J. Circuit Theory Appl. **20** (1992) 469–481
3. Zhang, Q., Ma, R., Xu, J.: Stability of cellular neural networks with delay. Electron Lett. **37** (2001) 575–576
4. Cao, J.: A set of stability criteria for delayed cellular neural networks. IEEE Trans. Circuits Syst. I **48** (2001) 494–498
5. Arik, S.: An improved global stability result for delayed cellular neural networks. IEEE Trans. Circuits Syst. I **49** (2002) 1211-1214
6. Chu, T. G.: Necessary and sufficient condition for absolute stability of normal neural networks. Neural Networks **16** (2003) 1223–1227
7. Chu, T. G.: A decomposition approach to analysis of competitiveCcooperative neural networks with delay. Physics Letters A **312** (2003) 339–347
8. Liao, X.F., Li, C.D.: An LMI approach to asymptotical stability of multi-delayed neural networks. Physica D **200** (2005) 139–155
9. Rong, L.B: LMI approach for global periodicity of neural networks with time-varying delays, IEEE Trans. Circuits Syst. I **52** (2005) 1451–1458
10. Arik, S.: An analysis of exponential stability of delayed neural networks with time-varying delays. Neural Networks **17** (2004) 1027–1031
11. Hunag, X., Cao, J., Huang, D.: LMI-based approach for delay-dependent exponential stability analysis of BAM neural networks. Chaos, Solitons and Fractals **24** (2005) 885–898
12. Li, C. D., Liao, X. F., Zhang, R.: Delay-dependent exponential stability analysis of bi-directional associative memory neural networks with time delay: an LMI approach. Chaos, Solitons and Fractals **24** (2005) 1119–1134
13. Li, Y.K.: Global exponential stability of BAM neural networks with delays and impulses. Chaos Solitons Fractals **24** (2005) 279–285
14. Liao, X. F., Chen, G., Sanchez, E.N.: Delay-dependent exponential stability analysis of delayed neural networks: an LMI approach. Neural Networks **15** (2002) 855–866

15. Chu, T. G.: An exponential convergence estimate for analog neural networks with delay. Physics Letters A **283** (2001) 113–118
16. Xu, S., Lam, J., Ho, D. W. C., Zou, Y., Global robust exponential stability analysis for interval recurrent neural networks. Physics Letters A **325** (2004) 124–133
17. Zhang, Q., Wei, X., Xu, J.: Delay-dependent exponential stability of cellular neural networks with time-varying delays. Chaos, Solitons and Fractals **23** (2005) 1363–1369
18. Xu, S., Lam, J., Ho, D. W. C., Zou, Y., Delay-dependent exponential stability for a class of neural networks with time delays. Journal of Computational and Applied Mathematics **183** (2005) pp. 16-28
19. Boyd, S., El Ghaoui, L., Feron, E., Balakrishnan, V.: Linear Matrix Inequalities in Systems and Control Theory. SIAM, Philadelphia (1994)

# Orthogonal Relief Algorithm for Feature Selection

Jun Yang and Yue-Peng Li

Institute of Acoustics, Chinese Academy of Sciences,
100080 Beijing, China
j_yang@ieee.org

**Abstract.** The Relief is a popular feature selection algorithm. However, it is ineffective in removing redundant features due to its feature evaluation mechanism that all discriminative features are assigned with high relevance scores, regardless of the correlations in between. In the present study, we develop an orthogonal Relief algorithm (O-Relief) to tackle the redundant feature problem. The basic idea of the O-Relief algorithm is to introduce an orthogonal transform to decompose the correlation between features so that the relevance of a feature could be evaluated individually as it is done in the original Relief algorithm. Experiment results on four world problems show that the orthogonal Relief algorithm provides features leading to better classification results than the original Relief algorithm.

## 1 Introduction

Given a machine learning problem, we are provided with a set of training samples, each of which is represented by a high-dimensional vector whose elements are called features. It is these features that provide necessary information for class discrimination. In theory, more features provide larger discriminative power and hence lead to better classifications. But this may not be always true in practice because the performance of a classifier on the test data partly depends on the ratio of the training sample size to the number of features. To obtain a good coverage of the input space, a rule of thumb is to support each feature with a minimum of 10 samples [1]. However, this is often violated in practice. A typical example is the gene microarray data analysis problem, where the number of features, i.e. gene, is often as many as a few thousands, while the number of training samples available is fewer than hundreds. Irrelevant and redundant features must be removed in order to obtain a reasonable ratio of the training sample size to the number of features.

Basically, there are two major types of feature selection [2]. The first type of feature selection evaluates and selects features directly based on classification results. This type of feature selection is called the wrapper method. The wrapper method guarantees good classification results for the training data, but it has a tendency to overfit the training data and generalize unsatisfactorily on the test data. In addition, the wrapper method involves training of a large number of pattern classifiers, which could be computational impractical if complex classifiers such as multi-layer perceptron (MLP) neural networks or nonlinear support vector machines (SVMs) are used. The second type of feature selection is the so called filter method. Instead of using classification results, the filter method employs measures that are independent of classifiers for feature evaluation.

D.-S. Huang, K. Li, and G.W. Irwin (Eds.): ICIC 2006, LNCS 4113, pp. 227 – 234, 2006.

The Relief algorithm is a popular filter feature selection [3]. The basic idea of the Relief algorithm is to consider all features as independent individuals and to estimate the relevance of a feature based on its ability to distinguish samples near to each other. An inherent problem with the Relief algorithm is that it assigns high relevance scores to all discriminative features, even if some of the features are severely correlated. As a consequence, redundant features might not be removed. This problem has been noted, but just a few solutions have been proposed in the literature. In Bins and Draper [4], a multi-step Relief algorithm was proposed, where irrelevant features were first removed using the Relief algorithm and redundant features were then deleted using a redundancy filter. In Ref. [5] by Florez-Lopez, a feature weighted Relief algorithm called WACSA was developed, where feature correlations were taken into account to adjust of the final feature subset. In the present study, we develop an orthogonal Relief algorithm (O-Relief) to address the redundant feature problem. The main idea of the O-Relief algorithm is to introduce an orthogonal transform to decompose the correlation between features so that the relevance of features can be evaluated separately as is done in the original Relief algorithm.

The present study is organized as follows. In Section 2, the basic Relief algorithm is briefly reviewed and the O-Relief is presented. Experiment results are presented in Section 3, and conclusions are given in Section 4.

## 2 The O-Relief Algorithm for Redundant Feature Removal

### 2.1 A Brief Review of Relief Algorithm

The Relief algorithm was first proposed by Kira and Rendell [3]. The idea behind the Relief algorithm is similar to the principle of the K-Nearest Neighbors (K-NN) classification: the closest sample of the same class is expected to be closer than the closest sample of the other classes in dimensions of relevant features. Consider N training samples:

$$\{\mathbf{x}(1), c(1)\}, \{\mathbf{x}(2), c(2)\}, ..., \{\mathbf{x}(N), c(N)\}$$

where $\mathbf{x}(k) = [x_1(k), x_2(k), ..., x_n(k)]$ denote the feature vector of sample $k$, $x_1, x_2, ..., x_n$ are features available, and $c(k)$ is the class label of sample $k$. In the original Relief algorithm, the relevance of a feature, say feature $x_i$, is estimated using the following criterion:

$$C_1 = \frac{1}{N}\sum_{k=1}^{N}[|x_i(k) - x_i^M(k)| - |x_i(k) - x_i^H(k)|] \tag{1}$$

where $x_i^M(k)$ and $x_i^H(k)$ denote values of feature of the nearest-miss and nearest-hit samples of sample $k$. The nearest-hit sample is defined as the nearest neighboring sample of the same class, while the nearest-miss sample is as the nearest neighboring sample of the different class. In the original Relief algorithm, the $N$ samples are re-sampled from the training set, and only one nearest-hit and nearest-miss samples were used in the relevance estimation, but these $N$ samples can also be the entire training set, and if two or more nearest-hit and nearest-miss samples are used, the Relief algorithm could be less sensitive to noise [6].

The Relief algorithm assigns a relevance score to each feature, and high scores are assigned to all discriminative features, regardless of correlations in between. Thus, the discriminative but redundant features might not be removed by the Relief algorithm. Next we develop an algorithm that attempts to alleviate the redundant feature problem through orthogonal decomposition.

## 2.2 The Orthogonal Relief (O-Relief) Algorithm

Consider two features $x_i$ and $x_j$. The projections of training samples on the two dimensions, denoted by $\mathbf{x}_i = [x_i(1), x_i(2), ..., x_i(N)]^T$ and $\mathbf{x}_j = [x_j(1), x_j(2), ..., x_j(N)]^T$ respectively, are illustrated in Figure 1, where ○ and Δ denote samples of two different classes. If the two discriminative features are evaluated separately, high relevance scores, denoted by $w_i$ and $w_j$, will be assigned to both of them. Thus, both features will be selected even if they are highly correlated. If $\mathbf{x}_j$ is projected to a new dimension $z_j$ that is orthogonal to dimension $x_i$, and feature $x_j$ is evaluated based on sample projections on the new dimension, the relevance score is given by:

$$w_j' = w_j \times \sin\alpha = w_j \sqrt{1 - \cos^2\alpha} \tag{2}$$

where $\alpha$ is the angle between vectors $\mathbf{x}_i$ and $\mathbf{x}_j$, and the cosine of the angle is given by:

$$\cos\alpha = \frac{\mathrm{x}_i^T \mathrm{x}_j}{\| \mathrm{x}_i \| \times \| \mathrm{x}_j \|} \tag{3}$$

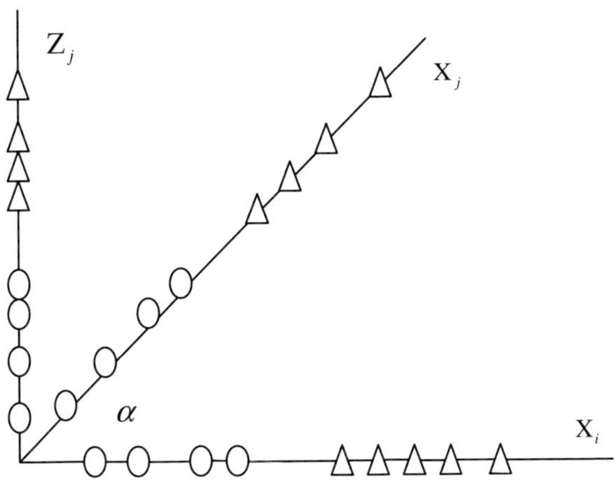


**Fig. 1.** Sample distributions on two correlated dimensions

This means that the cosine of the angle between two vectors is equal to the correlation in between. If feature $x_j$ is severely correlated with $x_i$, the cosine of angle would be close to 1, and the new relevance score $w'_j$ would be close to zero even if the weight $w_j$ is a large value. Thus, feature $x_j$ could be removed if it is evaluated based on the new relevance score. However, if feature $x_j$ is independent of $x_i$, the cosine of angle $\alpha$ would be close to 0, the relevance measure $w'_j$ would not differentiate very much from $w_j$, and hence the orthogonal projection would not affect the relevance estimation of feature $x_j$ much. This actually suggests that redundant features can be removed by the Relief algorithm if orthogonal transform is introduced to decompose the correlations.

Any arbitrary oblique vectors can be transformed into orthogonal vectors using Gram-Schmidt orthogonalization procedure. Gram-Schmidt orthogonal transform was employed in nonlinear system identification [7-8], RBF and PNN neural network neuron selection [9-10] and was recently introduced to feature selection [11]. Define feature matrix **X** as:

$$\mathbf{X} = [\mathbf{x}_1, \mathbf{x}_2, ..., \mathbf{x}_n] = \begin{bmatrix} x_1(1) & x_2(1) & ... & x_n(1) \\ x_1(2) & x_2(2) & ... & x_n(2) \\ \vdots & \vdots & \vdots & \vdots \\ x_1(N) & x_2(N) & ... & x_n(N) \end{bmatrix} \tag{4}$$

Matrix **X** can be factorized as:

$$\mathbf{X} = \mathbf{QR} \tag{5}$$

where **R** is an upper triangular matrix, and **Q** is an orthogonal matrix:

$$\mathbf{Q} = [\mathbf{q}_1, \mathbf{q}_2, ..., \mathbf{q}_n] = \begin{bmatrix} q_1(1) & q_2(1) & ... & q_n(1) \\ q_1(2) & q_2(2) & ... & q_n(2) \\ \vdots & \vdots & \vdots & \vdots \\ q_1(N) & q_2(N) & ... & q_n(N) \end{bmatrix} \tag{6}$$

In the Gram-Schmidt orthogonal decomposition, the orthogonal matrix **Q** is constructed using the following procedure [7]:

$$\mathbf{q}_1 = \mathbf{x}_1 \tag{7}$$

$$\mathbf{q}_i = \mathbf{x}_i - \sum_{j=1}^{i-1} \alpha_{ji} \mathbf{q}_j \tag{8}$$

where

$$\alpha_{ij} = \begin{cases} \dfrac{\mathbf{q}_j^T \mathbf{x}_i}{\mathbf{q}_j^T \mathbf{q}_j} & for\ j=1,2,...i-1 \\ 1 & for\ j=i \end{cases} \tag{9}$$

Column vectors of **Q** actually represent sample projections on dimensions of the orthogonal space, where features are uncorrelated and hence can be evaluated individually in a way similar to the original Relief algorithm. However, the features of the orthogonal space are a set of new variables carrying no clear physical meanings. These physically meaningless orthogonal features need to link back to a subset of the original measurements. As shown in Eqns (7)-(9), the first $m$ features $q_1, q_2, \ldots, q_m$ of the orthogonal space associate with the first $m$ features $x_1, x_2, \ldots, x_m$ only. This means that the features of the orthogonal space can be linked back to the same number of features of the measurement space. But it should be noted that the number of associated features in the measurement space would be larger than the number of features selected in the orthogonal space if irrelevant features are arranged in the first a few columns of **Q**. Arranging relevant features to the first a few columns of matrix **X** can be implemented through a sequential forward selection procedure. The combination of a sequential forward selection procedure, the orthogonal transform and the Relief algorithm form the so called O-Relief algorithm. The pseudo code of the O-Relief algorithm is summarized as follows.

```
(1) Initialize S to an empty set;
(2) Initialize T to the full feature set;
(3) For i =1:n % Each feature is a candidate to be
                 firstly selected;
      Calculate relevance score for each feature using
      the original Relief;
    End
    Add the feature that has the highest relevance
    score, sa x_{k_1} , to set S;
    Take vector x_{k_1} as the first column of Q;
    Remove feature x_{k_1} from set T;
(4) For i=2:m   % Select (m-1) features through (m-1)
                 iterations;
      h=number of features in set T;
      For j=1:h  % Consider each variable in set T as
                 a candidate;
        Orthogonalize variable j to all columns of Q;
        Calculate relevance score of the orthogonal
        column obtained;
      End
      Add the feature that has the highest relevance
      score, say x_{k_2} to S;
      Generate an orthogonal column using x_{k_2} and add it
      to Q;
      Eliminate the feature selected from set T.
    End
```

## 3 Experiment Studies

In the experiment, the O-Relief was tested using 4 real world datasets. These include Wisconsin diagnostic breast cancer (WDBC) data, Ionosphere data and Sonar data from the UCI Machine Learning Databases [12]. The numbers of features in the three datasets are 30, 33 and 60 respectively. The other dataset is gene microarray data [13]. The Gene dataset consists of 38 samples, and each sample is represented by 7129 genes, i.e. features. In the experiment, the genes were first ranked based on Fisher ratio class separability measure, and only 100 significant gene were kept. Thus, the gene dataset used in O-Relief testing has 100 features.

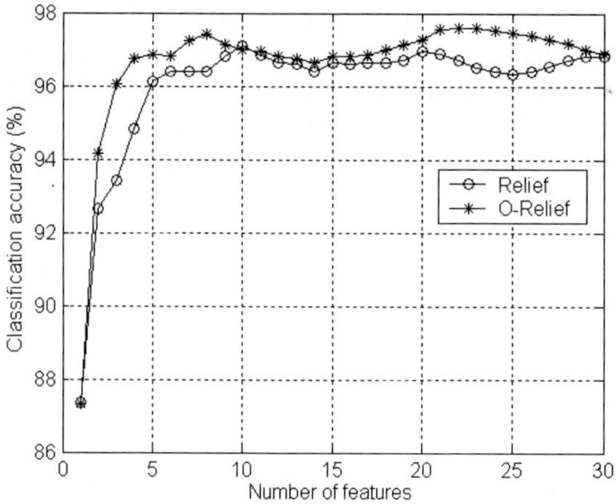


**Fig. 2.** Results of WDBC dataset

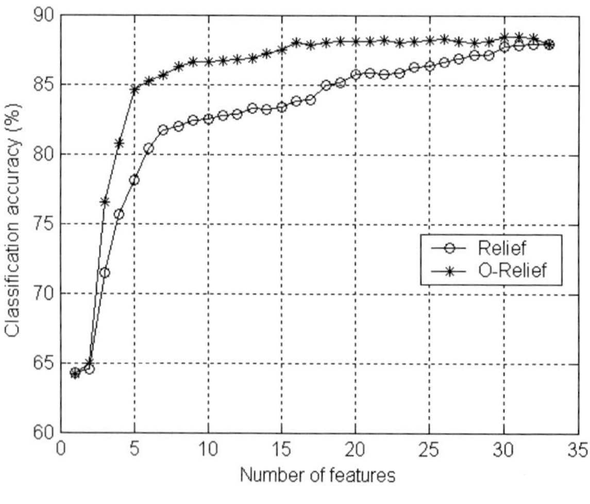


**Fig. 3.** Results of Ionosphere dataset

The Relief and O-Relief algorithms were applied to the 4 datasets described above. Linear support vector machine (SVM) classifiers were then employed to classify the data, and the results are shown in Figures 2-5 respectively. Note that the results illustrated are the average of 30 repeats of 10-fold cross validation. Obviously, improved results were achieved in all the 4 problems.

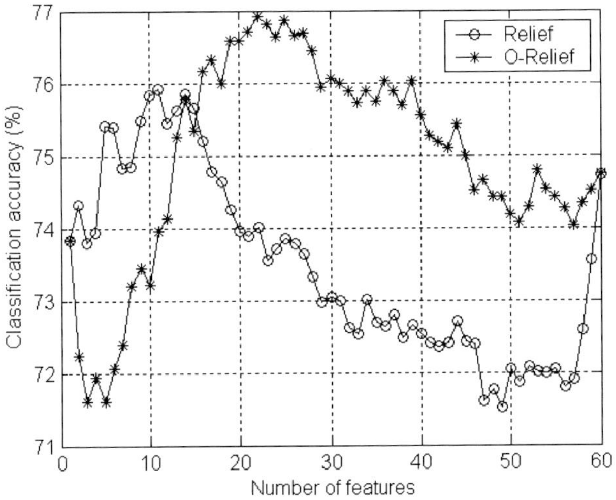


**Fig. 4.** Results of Sonar dataset

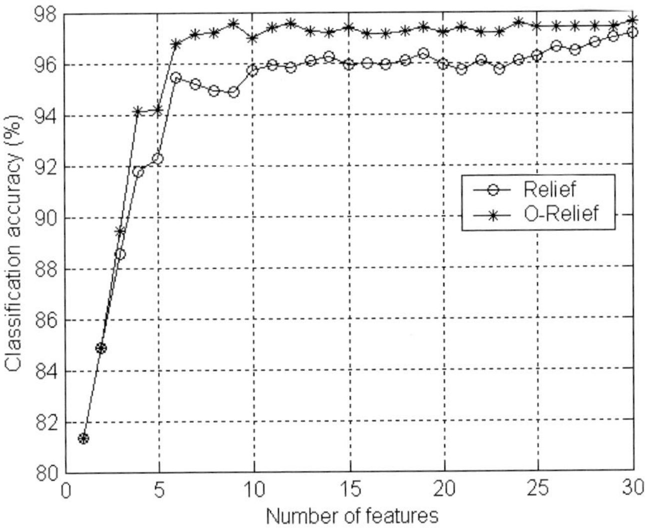


**Fig. 5.** Results of Gene dataset

## 4 Conclusion

In this study, we have developed the orthogonal Relief algorithm to deal with the redundant feature problem inherited in the original Relief algorithm. This has been done by introducing orthogonal transform to decompose correlations between features. In all the 4 datasets used, the orthogonal Relief has achieved improved results compared with the original Relief algorithm.

## Acknowledgements

This research was partially supported by National Natural Science Foundation of China under Grant No. 10474115 and No. 60535030, and Chinese Academy of Science under Grant No. KGCX2-SW-602-7.

## References

1. Jain, A.K., Duin, R.P.W., Mao, J.: Statistical Pattern Recognition: A Review, IEEE Transactions on Pattern Analysis and Machine Intelligence, 22 (2000) 4-37
2. Kohavi, R., John, G.H.: Wrappers for Feature Subset Selection, Artificial Intelligent Journal, 1 (1997) 273-324
3. Kira, K., Rendell, L.A.: The Feature Selection Problem: Traditional Methods and A New Algorithm. Proceedings of AAAI'92, San Jose, USA (1992) 129-134
4. Bins, J., Draper, B.A.: Feature Selection from Huge Feature Sets, Proceedings of ICCV'01, Vancouver, Canada (2001) 159-165
5. Florez-lopez, R.: Reviewing RELIEF and its Extensions: A New Approach for Estimating Attributes Considering High-Correlated Features, Proceedings of IEEE International Conference on Data Mining, Maebashi, Japan (2002) 605-608
6. Kononenko, I.: Estimating Attributes: Analysis and Extensions of RELIEF. Proceedings of European Conference on Machine Learning, Catania, Italy (1994) 171-182
7. Chen, S., Billings, S.A., Luo, W.: Orthogonal Least Square Methods and their Applications to Nonlinear System Identification, International Journal of Control, 50 (1989) 1873-1896
8. Mao, K.Z., Billings S.A.: Algorithms for Minimal Model Structure Detection in Nonlinear Dynamic System Identification, International Journal of Control, 68 (1997)311-330
9. Mao, K.Z., Tan, K.C., Ser W.: Probabilistic Neural Network Structure Determination for Pattern Classification, IEEE Transactions on Neural Networks, 11 (2000) 1009-1016
10. Mao, K.Z.: RBF Neural Network Center Selection Based on Fisher Ratio Class Separability Measure, IEEE Transactions on Neural Networks, 13 (2002) 1211-1217
11. Mao, K.Z.: Orthogonal Forward Selection and Backward Elimination Algorithms for Feature Subset Selection, IEEE Transactions on Systems, Man and Cybernetics, part B, 34 (2004) 629-634
12. Blake, C.L, Merz, C.J.: UCI Repository of Machine Learning Databases, Department of Information and Computer Sciences, University of California, Irvene, CA, USA (1998) [http://www.ics.uci.edu/~mlearn/MLRepository.html]
13. Golub, T.R., et al.: Molecular Classification of Cancer: Class Discovery and Class Prediction by Gene Expression Monitoring, Science, 286 (1999) 531-537

# Concept Features Extraction and Text Clustering Analysis of Neural Networks Based on Cognitive Mechanism

Lin Wang[1], Minghu Jiang[1,2], Shasha Liao[2], Beixing Deng[3], Chengqing Zong[4], and Yinghua Lu[1]

[1] School of Electronic Eng., Beijing Univ. of Post and Telecom, Beijing, 100876, China
[2] Lab of Computational Linguistics, School of Humanities and Social Sciences, Tsinghua University, Beijing, 100084, China
[3] Dept. of Electronic Eng., Tsinghua University, Beijing, 100084, China
[4] State Key Lab of Pattern Recognition, Institute of Automation Chinese Academy of Science, Beijing, 100080, China
jiang.mh@tsinghua.edu.cn

**Abstract.** The feature selection is an important part in automatic classification. In this paper, we use the HowNet to extract the concept attributes, and propose CHI-MCOR method to build a feature set. This method not only selects the highly occurring words, but also selects the word whose occurrence frequency is middle or low occurring words that are important for text classification. The combined method is much better than any one of the weight methods. Then we use the Self-Organizing Map (SOM) to realize automatic text clustering. The experiment result shows that if we can extract the sememes properly, we can not only reduce the feature dimension but also improve the classification precise. SOM can be used in text clustering in large scales and the clustering results are good when the concept feature is selected.

## 1 Introduction

After a decade of emphasis on the study of brain mechanisms at the cellular molecular or genomic level, it is expected that future advances in brain science will promote the study of natural language processing (NLP). With the rapid development of the online information, automatic classification becomes one of the key techniques for handling and organizing the very large scale of text data. In the future, a fundamental breakthrough in text classification could be of benefit to diverse areas such as semantic nets, search engines, and natural language processing.

Text automatic classification based on cognitive science is a cutting-edge research topic both in studying brain cognitive systems and natural language processing. Extraction of brain cognitive principles improves understanding of natural language. Its theoretical models will lead to benefits both the cognitive science and the natural language processing. It will provide feedback to experimental methods concerning the validity of interpretations and suggestions, and enable us to create semantic methods which let the computer to understand language. Our aim is to understand the biological mechanisms of text classification and its role in perception and behavioural

D.-S. Huang, K. Li, and G.W. Irwin (Eds.): ICIC 2006, LNCS 4113, pp. 235 – 246, 2006.

simulation. Although neuroimaging methods by using localization of cognitive operations within the human brain can be applied to studies of neural networks, the conventional syntax techniques are still ineffective in natural language processing due to a lack of semantic understanding of relevance, in addition the concept attributes are much better to reflect the content of the documents, we can get a much better vector space by using the concept attributes and semantic information.

This paper is organized as follows: Section II presents the concept extraction method. Section III presents hierarchical clustering and SOM clustering. Section IV is about experiments and Section V summarizes the conclusions.

## 2 Concept Extractions

The experimental data is 68 words [1] are based on "Dictionary for Modern Chinese Syntax Information" and "Hownet" [2], which are described according to their syntax and semantic attributes, the feature set is consist of 50-dimension syntax features and 132-dimension semantic features. By using SOM neural network to train the 68 Chinese words including nouns, verbs and class-ambiguous words, we compare the fMRI experimental results of Li Ping et al [1] with the map results of neural networks for the three kinds of Chinese words. The neuroimaging localization of LiPing's brain experiments shows that there are obvious the overlapping of brain mapped distributing areas for the three kinds of words. In our SOM experiment [3], when we strengthen the role of syntax features, and weaken the role of semantic features, the overlapping of the mapped distributing areas for the three kinds of words can disappear. Whereas, when we weaken the role of syntax features, and strengthen the role of semantic features, the overlapping of the mapped distributing areas for the three kinds of words is increased. When we adpoted only semantic features to desciribe the three kinds of words, the distributing areas of mapped results are almost entirely overlapped. The experimental result shows that feature description plays an important role in the map area of the three kinds of words. In fact the response of human brain to Chinese lexical information is based mainly on conceptual and semantic attributes, in our accustomed conversation we pay seldom attention to Chinese syntax and grammar features, which is coincident with our experimental results, is also coincident with LiPing's.

We extract the concept attribute from the word as the reflection of the text, which will describe the internal concept information, and get the relationship among the words. The information of the concept extraction comes from HowNet [2] and the synonymy dictionary, use the DEF term of the Chinese word, which descript the word with defined concept attribute, in order to construct the feature reflection of the documents.

### 2.1 Analysis of the Feature Set

When we extract the concept attributes to form the feature set, we convert a lot of words into the concept features, and get rid of the influence of the synonymy and dependence, which makes the classification precise much higher [4]. However, because of the mass of weak concept and the words which are not in the HowNet, some Chinese words are given a comparatively lower weight and become the middle or low occurring feature. In addition there are still some specialty words and proprietary words which are only occur in one category and are not highly occurred in the whole documents and are very important for classification, both of these words need a strategy to get a higher weight and contribute more in text classification, thus we analysis and experiment on the weighting methods in the following parts.

## 2.2 CHI Selection Method

The CHI ($\chi$ statistics) weight method's formula is shown as follows [4]:

$$\chi^2(t,c) = \frac{N*(AD-CB)^2}{(A+C)(B+D)(A+B)(C+D)} \quad (1)$$

$$\mathrm{x}^2_{\max}(t) = \max_{i=1}^{m} \chi^2(t,c_i) \quad (2)$$

Here, N is the total document number of the training set, c is a certain category, t is a certain feature, A is the number of the document which belong to c and t, B is those which do not belong to c but contain t, C is those which belong to c but do not contain t, D is those which do not belong to c and do not contain t.

CHI method is based on such hypothesis: if the feature is highly occurred in a specified category or highly occurred in other categories, it is useful in classification. Because CHI take the occurrence frequency into account, it prefers to select highly occurred words, and ignore the middle and low occurred words which maybe important in classification.

## 2.3 MCOR Selection Method

The MCOR (Multi-Class Odds Ratio) weight method's formula is shown as follows [4]:

$$MCOR(t) = \sum_{i=1}^{m} p(C_i) \left| \log \frac{P(t/C_i)(1-P(t/C_{else})}{(1-P(t/C_i)P(t/C_{else})} \right| . \quad (3)$$

Here, P(Ci) is the occurrence probability of category Ci, P(t / Ci) is the occurrence probability of the feature t when category C is occurred, P(t / Celse) is the occurrence probability of the feature t when category C is not occurred. When P(t / Ci) is higher or P(t / Celse) is lower, the weight of MCOR is higher. Therefore, the MCOR selects the features which are mainly occurred in one category and nearly not occurred in other categories. Because it does not consider the occurrence frequency of the features, it prefers to select the words which are middle or low occurred in the document while highly occurred words are always occurred in more than one categories.

## 2.5 The Comparing Result of Seven Weighing Methods

We select seven common weighing methods of the features and test their performance, and focus mainly on their selection strategy and classification precision. The experimental result is shown in Fig. 1.

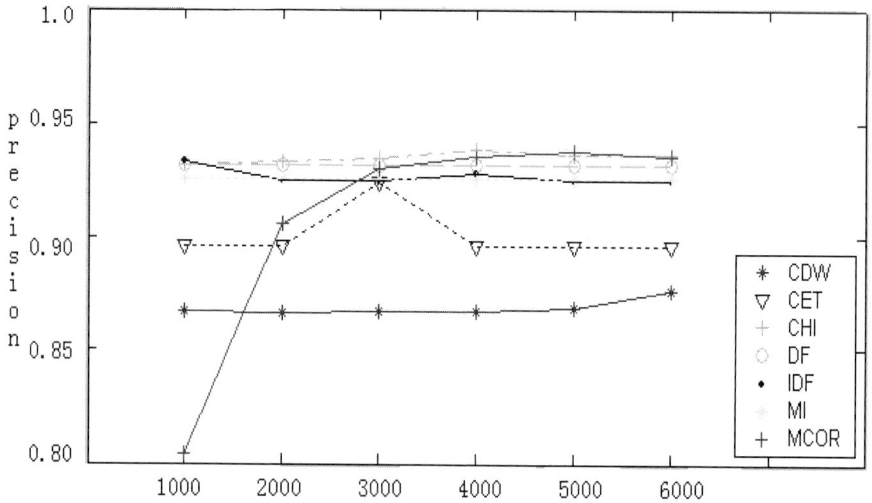


**Fig. 1.** The average of seven different weighing methods. Y axis is the average precision, and x axis is the feature dimension of the training set.

From the analysis of the selected features, we find that:

1. The DF (Document Frequency), TF-IDF (Term Frequency-Inverse Document Frequency), CET (an improved method of Information Gain), CDW (Category-Discriminating Word) and CHI methods prefer the high-occurred words and they are greatly related. In our experiment, CHI is the best method.
2. The MCOR method mainly chooses the middle and low occurred features, so its classification precision is low when the reduction rate is high. But with the increase of the feature dimension, its precision is increased highly and when the feature dimension is above 4000, its precision is higher than CDW, CET, DF, TF-IDF and MI (Mutual Information) methods.
3. The MI method mainly selects the high and middle occurred feature, it can get a good classification precision but with the increase of the feature dimension, the precision is not improved visibly.

### 2.6 Combined Method of CHI-MCOR

Because the MCOR mainly selects the words whose occurrence frequencies are middle or low, its classification precise is low when the reduction of feature dimensions is high. But with the increase of feature dimensions, its precise is improved to an appreciable level. The CHI prefers to select the words whose occurrence frequencies are high, and it is one of the best feature selection methods. As a result, when we combine these two methods, we can make the advantages together and get a high classification precise. Therefore, we give a combined weight method based on the CHI and MCOR:

$$V(t) = \lambda V_{CHI}(t) + (1-\lambda)V_{MCOR}(t), \qquad 0 < \lambda < 1. \tag{4}$$

Where, $V_{CHI}$ is the weight of feature $t$ for the CHI method, $V_{MCOR}$ is the weight of feature $t$ for the MCOR method. When we analysis the weights given by these both methods, we find that the average weight of the features are different. For example, when the reduction of feature dimensions is 50%, the range of the CHI weights is (2.1, 6.81), while that of the MCOR weights is (1.15, 1.76). Because the CHI gives a much higher weight to all the features and its swing is wider, we should give a comparatively lower value to $\lambda$, else the value depends too much on the CHI and the combined weight method is meaningless. Therefore we need a proper value of $\lambda$. According to experience, let us assume that when the average weight of the CHI and MCOR are the same, we can get both advantages of the two and the classification precise will be the highest, therefore the best $\lambda$ cab be evaluated as follows:

$$\frac{\lambda}{1-\lambda} = \frac{Mean(MCOR)}{Mean(CHI)}. \tag{5}$$

From Fig. 2 we can see that the combined weighing method is much better in politics category, it means that there are a lot of important words in politics category which are not highly occurred. Therefore, when the combined CHI-MCOR method is used, its precision is 3.66% higher than the CHI method. In fact, we find that the top ten occurred words in politics category which are not very high in the total statistics.

In order to analysis the best value of $\lambda$, we vary $\lambda$ from 0 to 1.0. From the experiment, we found that when $\lambda$ is 0.3, the classification precise is the highest. This result accords to our hypothesis. Meanwhile, we find that when we use the combined weight method, the precise is always higher than other methods. For example, when $\lambda$ is 0 or 1, it is the precise of the MCOR method or the CHI method. When $\lambda$ is 0.3, the precise is 94.0359%, which is 0.61% higher than the CHI's, 1.074% higher than the MCOR's. When we use the combined CHI-MCOR method, its precise is 3.66% higher than we only use the CHI method. In fact, when we

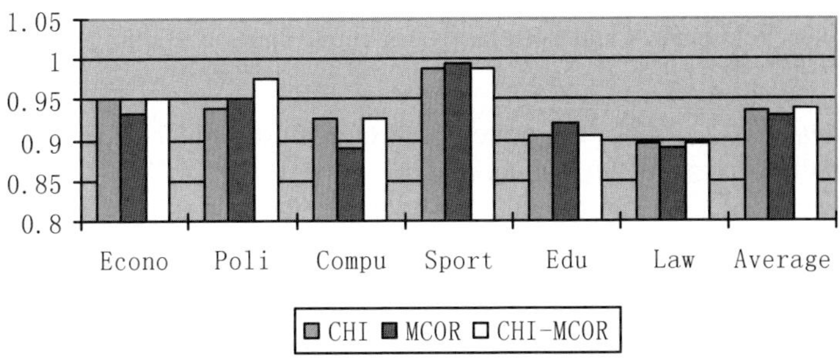


**Fig. 2.** The precision of the six categories in three weighing methods, the CHI, MCOR and CHI-MCOR. Y axis is the classification precision, and x axis is the test categories, the last one is the average precision.

statistic the top ten of the occurred words in politics category, we find that they are not very high in the total statistics. Because there are some words which are not highly occurred but useful and important for text classification, we use the combined CHI-MCOR method to take balance in the high occurring ones and the middle occurring ones. This method not only selects the highly occurring words, but also selects the word whose occurrence frequency is middle or low, and its features only belong to one or two categories. The experimental result shows that the combined method is much better than any one of the weight methods.

## 3 Hierarchical Clustering and SOM Clustering

### 3.1 Hierarchical Clustering

Hierarchical clustering creates a cluster tree to investigate grouping in input data, simultaneously over a variety of scales of distance. The result of hierarchical clustering can be graphically represented by a multi-level hierarchy (dendrogram), where clusters at one level are joined as clusters at the next higher level. The root is the whole input data set, the leaves are the individual elements of input data, and the internal nodes are defined as the union of their children [5]. Each level of the tree represents a partition of the input data into several groups (clusters). We can investigate different scales of grouping in text data, this allows us to decide what scale or level of clustering is most appropriate in our application.

### 3.2 Self-Organizing Map (SOM) Clustering

The SOM is based on research of physiology and brain science which is proposed by Kohonen [6]. By using self-organized learning to the network enables the similar neuron in function to be nearer, the different neuron in function to be more separate. During the learning process, no predefined classes of input data are clustered automatically and enable the weight distribution to be similar to input's probability density distribution. The SOM learns to recognize groups of similar input vectors in such a way that the neurons physically near each other in the output layer respond to the similar input vectors, i.e., the lesser the distance, the greater the degree of similarity and the higher the likelihood of emerging as the winner. The SOM can learn to detect regularities and correlations of input data, its training is based on two principles [6]:

1). *Competitive learning*: the prototype vector most similar to an input vector is updated so that it is even more similar to it.

2). *Cooperative learning*: not only the most similar prototype vector, but also its neighbors on the map are moved towards the input vector.

The SOM not only can adapt the winner node, but also some other neighborhood nodes of the winner are adapted, it can learn topology and represent roughly equal distributive regions of the input space, and similar inputs are mapped to neighboring neurons. The SOM consists of input layer and output layer, which is constructed by competitive learning algorithm based on above two principles. Unlike other cluster methods, the SOM has not distinct cluster boundaries, therefore, it requires some background knowledge to solve it [7]. Here wc adopt the best Davies-Bouldin index to classify cluster boundaries. The choice of the best cluster can be determined by the Davies-Bouldin index [5]. It is a function of the ratio of the sum for within-cluster distance and between-cluster distance. Optimal clustering is determined by [5]:

$$V_{DB} = \frac{1}{N}\sum_{k=1}^{N} \max_{k \neq l} \frac{S_N(D_k) + S(D_l)}{T_N(D_k, D_l)} \tag{6}$$

Where $N$ is the number of clusters, $D$ is a matrix of the data set $X$, $S_N$ *is* the within-cluster distance between the points in a cluster and the centroids for that cluster and $T_N$ *is* the between-cluster distance from the centroid of one cluster to the other. The optimal number of clusters is the one that minimizes $V_{DB}$. If the clusters are well separated, then $V_{DB}$ should decrease monotonically over time as the number of clusters increases until the clustering reaches convergence.

### 3.3 Supervisory Initiative Learning Based on Cognitive Mechanism

A man learns and acquires knowledge by the mode of "learn - practise - relearn - repractise", it suggests us that neural networks are trained by supervisory initiative learning, we introduce the feedback learning to text classification, thus the classification system is extended into a mode of "training - classification - feedback retraining". During the training process, the worth classification results can be selected, it can update the parameters of classification model according to feedback results, and reflect the cerebral cognitive process. We adopt Counterpropagation Networks which is proposed by Robert Hecht-Nielson, it consists of input layer, Kohonen layer and Grossberg output layer. By combining the unsupervisory training and supervisory training to form the network of separate structure, the network structure is closer to brain's one, the semantic concept features of text are preprocessed as input vectors, the unsupervisory training is finished in Kohonen layer, the classification information is extracted by the comparability of input data. The supervisory training is realized in Grossberg layer, the weights are updated by the difference between the expected output and the real output, and realize the category expression. The supervisory training can provide efficient codes and its classifiable boundary approaches a Bayes' boundary.

## 4 Experiments

According to above analysis, we extract the concept attributes by the combined CHI-MCOR method to build a concept feature set of 500 dimensions, is consist of both sememes and words, then we use the SOM network to realize automatic text clustering. The experimental corpus comes from the People Daily from 1996 to 1998. The corpus is unbalanced, and the training set includes 1205 texts (250 economy texts, 175 politics texts, 130 computer texts, 300 sport texts, 150 education texts, 200 law texts). The test set is another 755 texts of above 6 classes.

### 4.1 Hierarchical Clustering Experiment

The concept feature sets is used in clustering experiments. Fig. 3 shows that the clustering results of concept features has obvious cluster groups, form several wave crests and hiberarchy, there are obvious distances among different groups in the 1205 training texts.

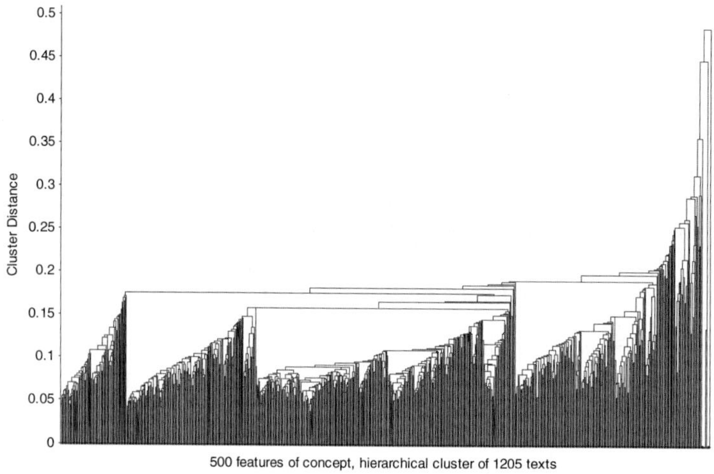


**Fig. 3.** Hierarchical clustering for 500 features of concept and 1205 texts

### 4.2 SOM Clustering Experiment

The SOM's initialization is linear with small random initial weights, and batch training algorithm is used in two phases of rough training and fine-tuning. The size of SOM output layer is 15×11 nodes which depends on dimension number and distribution of input features, the training time is 4+11 seconds which run in a P4 180M computer. Fig. 4 shows the U-matrix (left figure) and D-matrix (right figure) of the SOM clustering by using the 1205 texts of 500 concept features. The 'U-matrix' shows distances between neighboring units and thus visualizes the cluster structure of the map, it has much more hexagons in the visual output planes because each hexagon shows distances between map units. While D-matrix only shows the distance values at the SOM map units. Clusters on the U-matrix are typically uniform areas of low values (white) which mean small distance between neighboring map units, and high values (black) mean large distance between neighboring map units and thus indicate clustering borders. There are more clustering borders of high values (black) in Fig. 4, it shows that there are more small clusters for texts of concept features, several white zones (uniform areas of low values) are encircled by black or gray clustering borders. It shows same as hierarchical clustering that the between-cluster distance of concept features is obvious.

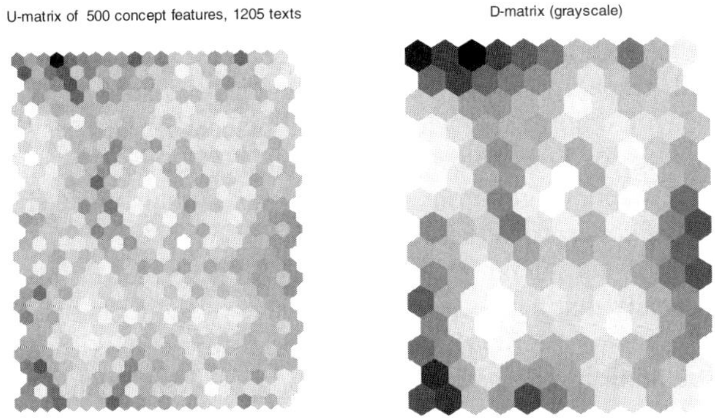


**Fig. 4.** U-matrix (left figure) and D-matrix (right figure) of the SOM, the training data are 1205 texts of 500 concept features, the SOM's initialization is linear, and batch training algorithm is used in two phases of rough training and fine-tuning

Because the SOM has not distinct clustering boundaries, in order to find and show the borders of the SOM clusters, we use the k-means clustering to find an initial partitioning [8], the experimental results show that the values of important variables change very rabidly. We can assign colors to the map units such that similar map units correspond to similar colors. Fig. 5 is the SOM clustering results by using the 1205 texts of 500 concept features, the left figures show the Davies-Boulding (DB) clustering index [5]; and the right figures show the SOM clustering by color code which is minimized with best clustering. According to DB index, we can find that VDB is almost monotonously decreased with increase of clustering groups. The number of the best clusters is 14 (corresponding to their minimum VDB values) for concept features.

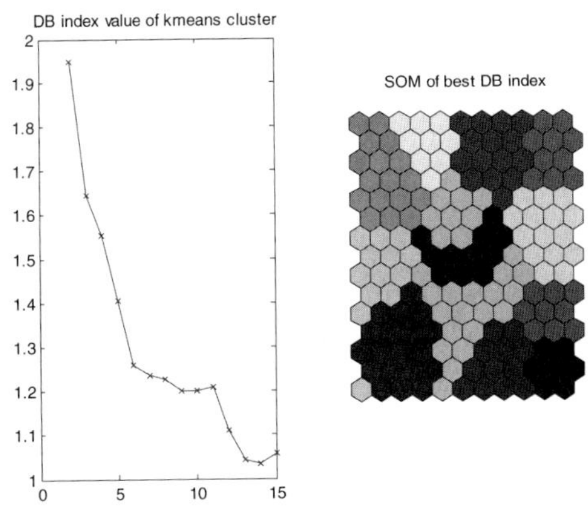


**Fig. 5.** Davies-Boulding clustering index (left figure), and the SOM clustering by color code which is minimized with the best clustering (right figure). Training data are 1205 texts of 500 concept features.

The left figure in Fig. 6 is the number of map samples in each unit; it shows the distribution of the input data on the output map plane. Because the significance of the components with respect to the clustering is harder to visualize, therefore we adopt distance matrix with color codes which is minimized with the best clustering on the right figures of Fig. 6. Small hexagons indicate clustering borders (corresponds to large distance between neighboring map units on U-matrix), it shows more small clusters for texts of concept features.

By comparison of the hierarchical clustering and the SOM clustering, the results show distinctly easily that between-cluster distance of the texts of concept features is obvious. Both results of the SOM clustering and artificial classification have a good corresponding relationship in the rough. A group or several groups in SOM clustering may correspond to some a class of artificial classification. There exist some fuzzy output nodes (hexagon) in Fig. 6, i.e., there are different artificial classes in same output nodes or same color area. The clustering qualities of SOM are evaluated by the precision $P$, recall $R$ and parameter $F1$. The formulas of precision and recall for class $k$ are defined as follows:

$$\mathrm{Pr}\,ecision_k = \frac{AcorrectNum_k}{AtotalNum_k} \tag{7}$$

$$\mathrm{Re}\,call_k = \frac{CorrectNum_k}{TotalNum_k} \tag{8}$$

Where, the $AcorrectNum_k$ is the number of the documents of the class $k$ which are correctly judged by a computer; $AtotalNum_k$ is the number of the documents of the class $k$ which are judged by a computer. The $CorrectNum_k$ is the number of the documents of the class $k$ which are correctly classified; $TotalNum_k$ is the number of the documents of the class $k$ in a standard solution.

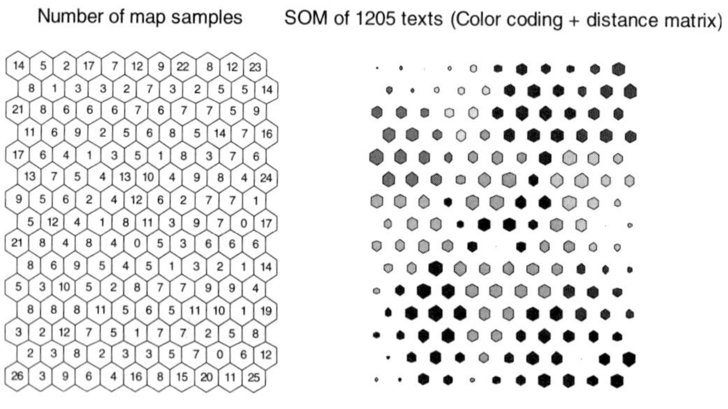


**Fig. 6.** The distribution of the input data on the map (left figure), the digital in each hexagon is the number of map texts; distance matrix with color codes is shown on the right figure, small hexagons on the D-matrix indicate clustering borders (corresponds to large distance between neighboring map units on U-matrix). Training data are 1205 texts of 500 concept features.

Then the average values of precision, recall and $F1$ can be obtained as the clustering results of SOM:

$$P = \frac{\sum_{k=1}^{m} \mathrm{Pr}\,ecision_k}{m} \qquad R = \frac{\sum_{k=1}^{m} \mathrm{Re}\,call_k}{m} \qquad F1 = \frac{2\mathrm{P} \times R}{P + R} \tag{9}$$

Table 1 shows that the clustering performance of concept features. The experimental result shows that the SOM can be used in text clustering in large scales and the clustering results are good when the concept feature is selected. If we can extract the sememes properly, we can not only reduce the feature dimension but also improve the classification precise.

**Table 1.** SOM Clustering Results of Concept Feature sets

| | Economy | Polity | Computer | Sport | Education | Law | Average | $F1$ |
|---|---|---|---|---|---|---|---|---|
| $P$ | 96.5 | 98.0 | 92.8 | 99.1 | 93.1 | 91.6 | 95.18 | 93.16 |
| $R$ | 94.2 | 85.3 | 95.2 | 94.6 | 89.8 | 88.2 | 91.22 | |

## 5 Conclusions

Because there are some words which are not highly occurred but useful in text classification, while the words with high occurrence frequency is usually useful, except the words in the stop word dictionary which are frequently used in the text but useless in classification, our CHI-MCOR method to take balance in the high occurring ones and the middle occurring ones. This method not only selects the highly occurring words, but also selects the words whose occurrence frequencies are middle or low but only occur in one or two categories. It is much better than CHI or MCOR method alone. When we use concept as the feature of text classification, we can efficiently reduce the feature dimension and reflect the original feature space to a more stable one. The experimental result shows that the SOM can be used in text clustering in large scales and the clustering results are good when the concept feature is selected. Between-cluster distance of the texts of concept features is bigger than that of texts of word features.

## References


1. Li, P., Jin, Z., Tan, L. H.: Neural Representations of Nouns and Verbs in Chinese: an fMRI Study. NeuroImage, 21 (2004) 1533-1541
2. http://www.keenage.com
3. Jiang, M., Cai, H., Zhang, B.: Self-organizing Map Analysis Consistent with Neuroimaging for Chinese Noun, Verb and Class-ambiguous Word. Advances in Neural Networks – ISNN2005: Lecture Notes in Computer Science, Springer-Verlag Heidelberg, 3498 (2005) 971-976

4. Liao, S., Jiang, M.: An Improved Method of Feature Selection Based on Concept Attributes in Text Classification. Advances in Natural Computation, Lecture Notes in Computer Science, Springer-Verlag Heidelberg, 3610 (2005) 1140-1149
5. Davies, D., Bouldin, D.: A Cluster Separation Measure. IEEE Transactions on Pattern Analysis and Machine Intelligence - I, 2 (1979) 224-227
6. Kohonen, T.: The Self-organnized Map. Proceedings of the IEEE, 78 (1990) 1464-1480
7. Vesanto, J., Alhoniemi, J.: Clustering of the Self-organizing Map, IEEE Transactions on Neural Networks, 11(3) (2000) 586-600
8. Wang, L., Jiang, M., Lu, Y. et al: Self-organizing Map Clustering Analysis for Molecular Data. ISNN06, Lecture Notes in Computer Science, 3971 (2006) 1250-1255

# The Learning Algorithm for a Novel Fuzzy Neural Network*

Puyin Liu, Qiang Luo, Wenqiang Yang, and Dongyun Yi

Department of Mathematics, National University of Defense Technology, Changsha, Hunan 410073, P.R. China
luoqiang@nudt.edu.cn

**Abstract.** Symmetric polygonal fuzzy numbers are employed to construct a class of novel feedforward fuzzy neural networks (FNN's)—the polygonal FNN's. Their input–output (I/O) relationships are built upon a novel fuzzy arithmetic and extension principle for the polygonal fuzzy numbers. We build the topological architecture of a three layer polygonal FNN, and present its I/O relationship representation. Also the fuzzy BP learning algorithm for the polygonal fuzzy number connection weights and thresholds is developed based on calculus of *max–min* ($\vee - \wedge$) functions. At last some simulation examples are compared to show that our model possess strong I/O ability and generalization capability.

## 1 Introduction

Recently, the theory and application of fuzzy neural networks(FNN) have attracted many scholars' attention[1-16]. However, a regular FNN whose internal operations are based on Zadeh's extension principle and standard fuzzy arithmetic [17] can not be an universal approximator [4, 5] unless some constraint conditions are hold for fuzzy continuous functions [13, 14, 18] which can bring us much inconvenience in application. To broaden the applying areas and to improve input–output capability of regular FNN's, author in [15] presents the polygonal FNN's, which is a novel class of fuzzified neural networks that can be universal approximators of increasing fuzzy functions. This paper aims at an important problem related to the polygonal FNN's-learning algorithm of the fuzzy weights and fuzzy thresholds. So far the learning algorithm uses the BP algorithm to adjust the endpoints of the level sets to determine the fuzzy weights and thresholds [6, 9]. In these BP learning procedures of the level sets of fuzzy weights and thresholds, an essential step is to calculate the derivatives of the *max–min* ($\vee - \wedge$) functions '$x \vee c$' and '$x \wedge c$' with respect to $x$. A basic tool is Gôdel implication [2, 3]. However, the usual derivative rules, such as chain rule for differentiation, do not hold for such derivatives. So the derivative calculi in such BP learning algorithms are only in form, they are lack of strict mathematical sense.

In this paper, we study systematically the BP learning algorithm of polygonal FNN's within a general framework. At first by polygonal fuzzy numbers

* This work was supported by grants from the National Natural Sciences Foundation of China (No.60375023 and No. 60574059) and the National Basic Research Program of China (No. 2005CB321800).

D.-S. Huang, K. Li, and G.W. Irwin (Eds.): ICIC 2006, LNCS 4113, pp. 247–258, 2006.

that generalize the triangular and trapezoidal fuzzy numbers we can express any bounded fuzzy numbers approximately. Then the analytical representation of the I/O relationship of a polygonal FNN is established, and employing derivative computation method for $\vee - \wedge$ functions [19, 20] as mathematical basis, we develop a series of derivative formulas related to the error function of the polygonal FNN. Thus, A fuzzy BP learning algorithm is developed. Our approach is illustrated by a few of numerical examples.

## 2 Symmetric Polygonal Fuzzy Number and Fuzzy Arithmetic

Triangular and trapezoidal fuzzy numbers are widely applied in many real fields [8, 10, 11, 21]. As their generalizations, $n-$symmetric polygonal fuzzy numbers for $n \in \mathbb{N}$ are similar with them.

**Definition 1.** *Let* $\widetilde{A} \in \mathcal{F}_0(\mathbb{R})$. *If there exist* $n \in \mathbb{N}$, *and* $a_0^1, a_1^1, ..., a_n^1, a_n^2, a_{n-1}^2, ..., a_0^2 \in \mathbb{R} : a_0^1 \leq \cdots \leq a_n^1 \leq a_n^2 \leq \cdots \leq a_0^2$, *so that the following conditions hold:*

*(i)* $\text{supp}(\widetilde{A}) = [a_0^1,\, a_0^2]$, $\ker(\widetilde{A}) = [a_n^1,\, a_n^2]$;

*(ii)* $\forall k \in \{1, ..., n\}$, $\widetilde{A}(\cdot)$ *is linear on* $[a_{k-1}^1,\, a_k^1]$ *and* $[a_k^2,\, a_{k-1}^2]$, *respectively;*

*(iii) Let* $k \in \{1, ..., n\}$. *Then we have*

$$a_{k-1}^1 < a_k^1, \Longrightarrow \widetilde{A}(a_{k-1}^1) = \frac{k-1}{n},\ \widetilde{A}(a_k^1 - 0) = \frac{k}{n},$$
$$a_k^2 < a_{k-1}^2, \Longrightarrow \widetilde{A}(a_{k-1}^2) = \frac{k-1}{n},\ \widetilde{A}(a_k^2 + 0) = \frac{k}{n};$$

*where* $\widetilde{A}\,(a_k^1 - 0)$ *is left limit* $\lim\limits_{t \to 0+} \widetilde{A}\,(a_k^1 - t)$, *and* $\widetilde{A}\,(a_k^2 + 0)$ *is right limit* $\lim\limits_{t \to 0+} \widetilde{A}(a_k^2 + t)$. *A is called* $n-$*symmetric polygonal fuzzy number, and we denote* $\widetilde{A}$ *by*

$$\widetilde{A} = \left([a_n^1,\, a_n^2];\, a_0^1, ..., a_{n-1}^1,\, a_{n-1}^2, ..., a_0^2\right).$$

*Define* $\mathcal{F}_{bc}(\mathbb{R})$ *the collection of all fuzzy numbers[21] and the collection of all* $n-$*symmetric polygonal fuzzy numbers is denoted by* $\mathcal{F}_{bc}^{tn}(\mathbb{R})$. *Specifically, let* $n = 1$, *then an* $1-$*symmetric polygonal fuzzy number is triangular or trapezoidal.*

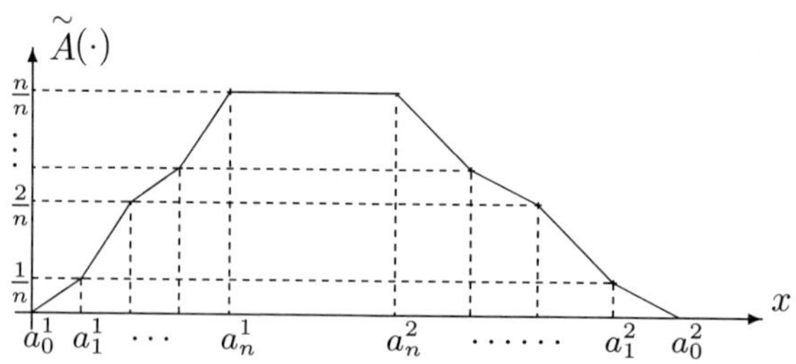


**Fig. 1.** The membership curve of $n$-symmetric polygonal fuzzy number $\widetilde{A}(\cdot)$

If $\widetilde{A}$ is an $n$-symmetric polygonal fuzzy number, the membership curve of $\widetilde{A}$ may be shown by Fig. 1. By $\mathcal{F}_{bc}^{tn}(\mathbb{R}_+)$ we denote the set of all non-negative elements in $\mathcal{F}_{bc}^{tn}(\mathbb{R})$, that is, $\widetilde{A}(x) = 0$ if $x < 0$ for all $\widetilde{A} \in \mathcal{F}_{bc}^{tn}(\mathbb{R}_+)$. In $\mathcal{F}_{bc}^{tn}(\mathbb{R})$ the defines of fuzzy arithmetic operations '+', '−', '·' and the extension operation of the monotone function $\sigma : \mathbb{R} \longrightarrow \mathbb{R}$ can be defined by simply generalizing the fuzzy arithmetic definitions in [21].

## 3 Three-Layer Polygonal Fuzzy Neural Network

In the section, we develop a novel three-layer feedforward FNN-polygonal FNN whose input and output, connection weights are $n-$symmetric polygonal fuzzy numbers. Its internal operations are based on extension operations introduced in section 2. Its input and output neurons are linear, and there is a nonlinear operation which is an activation function $\sigma$ (for example the Sigmoidal function $\sigma(x) = 1/(1+\mathrm{e}^{-x})$, $x \in \mathbb{R}$) in the hidden neurons. Fig. 2 gives the topological structure of the polygonal FNN whose input is fuzzy vector $(\widetilde{X}_1, ..., \widetilde{X}_d)$, where $\widetilde{X}_i \in \mathcal{F}_{bc}^{tn}(\mathbb{R})$ for $i = 1, ..., d$, and the output $\widetilde{Y}$, the fuzzy weights $\widetilde{W}_{ij}$, $\widetilde{V}_j$ and the fuzzy threshold $\widetilde{\Theta}_j$ belong to $\mathcal{F}_{bc}^{tn}(\mathbb{R})$. The I/O relationship of the FNN is represented as follows:

$$\widetilde{Y} \triangleq \Gamma(\widetilde{X}_1, ..., \widetilde{X}_d) = \sum_{j=1}^{m} \widetilde{V}_j \cdot \sigma\Big(\sum_{i=1}^{d} \widetilde{X}_i \cdot \widetilde{W}_{ij} + \widetilde{\Theta}_j\Big). \tag{1}$$

For given I/O pairs $\big((\widetilde{X}_1(1), ..., \widetilde{X}_d(l)), \widetilde{Y}(1)\big), ..., \big((\widetilde{X}_1(L), ..., \widetilde{X}_d(L)), \widetilde{Y}(L)\big)$, our aim is to realize these I/O relationships by learning fuzzy weights $\widetilde{W}_{ij}$, $\widetilde{V}_j$ and fuzzy threshold $\widetilde{\Theta}_j$ $(i = 1, ..., d,\ j = 1, ..., m)$. The polygonal FNN's shown in Fig. 2 can conveniently handle triangular fuzzy information [8], further, by the fact that the space $\bigcup_{n \in \mathbb{N}} \mathcal{F}_{bc}^{tn}(\mathbb{R})$ is dense in $\mathcal{F}_{bc}(\mathbb{R})$ (for details see [15, 22]), we can conclude that the polygonal FNN's can also efficiently deal with general fuzzy data. To this end we at first study the I/O laws of polygonal FNN's.

**Theorem 1.** *Assume that $m \in \mathbb{N}$, and $\widetilde{W}_{ij}, \widetilde{V}_j, \widetilde{\Theta}_j \in \mathcal{F}_{bc}^{tn}(\mathbb{R})$ $(i = 1, ..., d;\ j = 1, ..., m)$. Let $\sigma$ be non-negative and increasing. Then for arbitrary fuzzy vector $(\widetilde{X}_1, ..., \widetilde{X}_d)$, $\widetilde{X}_i \in \mathcal{F}_{bc}^{tn}(\mathbb{R})$, and if let $\mathbf{x}_p^1 = (x_{1(p)}^1, ..., x_{d(p)}^1)$, $\mathbf{x}_p^2 = (x_{1(p)}^2, ..., x_{d(p)}^2)$ $(p = 0, 1, ..., n)$, we have*

$$\begin{aligned}\Gamma(\widetilde{X}_1, ..., \widetilde{X}_d) &= \sum_{j=1}^{m} \widetilde{V}_j \cdot \sigma\Big(\sum_{i=1}^{d} \widetilde{W}_{ij} \cdot \widetilde{X}_i + \widetilde{\Theta}_j\ \Big) \\ &= \big([\gamma_n^1(\mathbf{x}_n^1, \mathbf{x}_n^2),\ \gamma_n^2(\mathbf{x}_n^1, \mathbf{x}_n^2)];\ \gamma_0^1(\mathbf{x}_0^1, \mathbf{x}_0^2), ..., \\ &\quad \gamma_{n-1}^1(\mathbf{x}_{n-1}^1, \mathbf{x}_{n-1}^2), \gamma_{n-1}^2(\mathbf{x}_{n-1}^1, \mathbf{x}_{n-1}^2), ..., \gamma_0^2(\mathbf{x}_0^1, \mathbf{x}_0^2)\big),\end{aligned}$$

*where $\gamma_p^l(\mathbf{x}_p^1, \mathbf{x}_p^2)$ $(l = 1, 2)$ may be represented as follows for $p = 0, 1, ..., n :$*

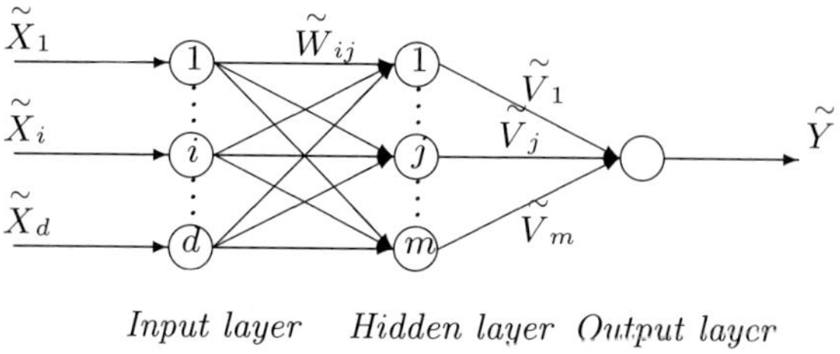


**Fig. 2.** A three-layer feedforward polygonal FNN

$$\begin{cases} \gamma_p^1(\mathbf{x}_p^1, \mathbf{x}_p^2) = \sum_{j=1}^{m} [\{v_{j(p)}^1 \sigma(s_{j(p)}^1\} \wedge \{v_{j(p)}^1 \sigma(s_{j(p)}^2)\}], \\ \gamma_p^2(\mathbf{x}_p^1, \mathbf{x}_p^2) = \sum_{j=1}^{m} [\{v_{j(p)}^2 \sigma(s_{j(p)}^1)\} \vee \{v_{j(p)}^2 \sigma(s_{j(p)}^2)\}], \end{cases}$$

*and*

$$\begin{cases} s_{j(p)}^1 = \theta_{j(p)}^1 + \sum_{i=1}^{d} [\min\{w_{ij(p)}^1 x_{i(p)}^1, \\ \qquad w_{ij(p)}^1 x_{i(p)}^2, \ w_{ij(p)}^2 x_{i(p)}^1, \ w_{ij(p)}^2 x_{i(p)}^2\}], \\ s_{j(p)}^2 = \theta_{j(p)}^2 + \sum_{i=1}^{d} [\max\{w_{ij(p)}^1 x_{i(p)}^1, \\ \qquad w_{ij(p)}^1 x_{i(p)}^2, \ w_{ij(p)}^2 x_{i(p)}^1, \ w_{ij(p)}^2 x_{i(p)}^2\}]. \end{cases}$$

## 4 Learning Algorithm

Two key steps to design learning algorithm for the fuzzy weights and the fuzzy threshold of polygonal FNN's are to derive the error function of fuzzy outputs from output neuron and the corresponding fuzzy targets (desired values) [11,17, 23], and to define the derivatives of the error function in which fuzzy operators '$\vee$' or '$\wedge$' are included. To this end, we at first recall the derivative operations of $\vee - \wedge$ functions introduced in [19,20]. Let

$$\mathrm{lor}(\cdot) : \mathbb{R} \longrightarrow \mathbb{R}, \ \ \mathrm{lor}(x) = \begin{cases} 1, \ x > 0, \\ \frac{1}{2}, \ x = 0, \\ 0, \ x < 0. \end{cases}$$

Before developing self-adaptive learning algorithms, we have to establish the derivative operation laws of $\vee - \wedge$ functions.

**Lemma 1.** *[19] Let the real functions $f, g$ be differentiable on $\mathbb{R}$, and*

$$h_1 = f \vee g, \ \ h_2 = f \wedge g.$$

*Then $h_1$, $h_2$ are almost everywhere differentiable on $\mathbb{R}$, moreover*

$$\frac{\mathrm{d}h_1(x)}{\mathrm{d}x} = \frac{\mathrm{d}(f(x) \vee g(x))}{\mathrm{d}x} = \mathrm{lor}(f(x) - g(x)) \frac{\mathrm{d}f(x)}{\mathrm{d}x} + \mathrm{lor}(g(x) - f(x)) \frac{\mathrm{d}g(x)}{\mathrm{d}x};$$
$$\frac{\mathrm{d}h_2(x)}{\mathrm{d}x} = \frac{\mathrm{d}(f(x) \wedge g(x))}{\mathrm{d}x} = \mathrm{lor}(f(x) - g(x)) \frac{\mathrm{d}g(x)}{\mathrm{d}x} + \mathrm{lor}(g(x) - f(x)) \frac{\mathrm{d}f(x)}{\mathrm{d}x}.$$

*Specifically, if* $a \in \mathbb{R}$, *the following facts hold:*

$$\frac{\mathrm{d}(a \vee f(x))}{\mathrm{d}x} = \mathrm{lor}(f(x) - a)\frac{\mathrm{d}f(x)}{\mathrm{d}x}, \quad \frac{\mathrm{d}(a \wedge f(x))}{\mathrm{d}x} = \mathrm{lor}(a - f(x))\frac{\mathrm{d}f(x)}{\mathrm{d}x}.$$

## 4.1 Error Function and Its Derivatives

Let $\big((\widetilde{X}_1(l), ..., \widetilde{X}_d(1)), \widetilde{Y}(1)\big), ..., \big((\widetilde{X}_1(L), ..., \widetilde{X}_d(L)), \widetilde{Y}(L)\big)$ be the training pairs of fuzzy patterns, that is, when the input of the polygonal FNN is $(\widetilde{X}_1(k), ..., \widetilde{X}_d(k))$ its desired output is $\widetilde{Y}(k)$. And suppose that $\widetilde{O}(k)$ is the real output of the output neuron of the polygonal FNN when input$(\widetilde{X}_1(k), ..., \widetilde{X}_d(k))$ that is, $\widetilde{O}(k) = \Gamma(\widetilde{X}_1(k), ..., \widetilde{X}_d(k))$ $(k = 1, ..., L)$. Our goal is to make $\widetilde{O}(k)$ approximate even equal $\widetilde{Y}(k)$ for each $k = 1, ..., L$ by adjusting the fuzzy weights $\widetilde{W}_{ij}$, $\widetilde{V}_j$ and fuzzy threshold $\widetilde{\Theta}_j$ in Eq. (1). Let

$$\widetilde{O}(k) = \big([o_n^1(k), o_n^2(k)]; o_0^1(k), ..., o_{n-1}^1(k), o_{n-1}^2(k), ..., o_0^2(k)\big);$$
$$\widetilde{Y}(k) = \big([y_n^1(k), y_n^2(k)]; y_0^1(k), ..., y_{n-1}^1(k), y_{n-1}^2(k), ..., y_0^2(k)\big).$$

The second step for designing the learning algorithm is to define a suitable error function:

$$E = \frac{1}{2}\sum_{k=1}^{m} D_E\big(\widetilde{O}(k), \widetilde{Y}(k)\big)^2 \triangleq \frac{1}{2}\sum_{k=1}^{m}\Big(\sum_{i=0}^{n}\{d_E\big([o_i^1(k), o_i^2(k)], [y_i^1(k), y_i^2(k)]\big)\}^2\Big), \tag{2}$$

where $d_E(\cdot,\cdot)$ is the Euclidean metric between intervals [21]. Obviously, $E = 0$ if and only if for each $k = 1, ..., m$, $\widetilde{O}_k = \widetilde{Y}_k$. Since symmetric polygonal fuzzy number weights and thresholds are specified by their finite parameters, we may develop some update rules respectively for such parameters. Finally the polygonal fuzzy numbers can be reconstructed respectively by the updated parameters.

**Theorem 2.** *Let* $E$ *be an error function defined as Eq. (2), and for* $i = 1, ..., d$; $j = 1, ..., m$; $p = 0, 1, ..., n$; $k = 1, ..., L$, *write*

$$\begin{cases} t_p^1(k) = o_p^1(k) - y_p^1(k), \ t_p^2(k) = o_p^2(k) - y_p^2(k); \\ \Gamma_{j(p)}^1(k) = v_{j(p)}^1\sigma'(s_{j(p)}^1(k))\mathrm{lor}(v_{j(p)}^1), \\ \Gamma_{j(p)}^2(k) = v_{j(p)}^1\sigma'(s_{j(p)}^2(k))\mathrm{lor}(-v_{j(p)}^1), \\ \Gamma_{j(p)}^3(k) = v_{j(p)}^2\sigma'(s_{j(p)}^1(k))\mathrm{lor}(-v_{j(p)}^2), \\ \Gamma_{j(p)}^4(k) = v_{j(p)}^2\sigma'(s_{j(p)}^2(k))\mathrm{lor}(v_{j(p)}^2); \\ \underline{\Delta}_{ij(p)}(k) = \big(\{w_{ij(p)}^1 x_{i(p)}^1(k)\} \wedge \{w_{ij(p)}^2 x_{i(p)}^1(k)\}\big) \\ \quad -\big(\{w_{ij(p)}^1 x_{i(p)}^2(k)\} \wedge \{w_{ij(p)}^2 x_{i(p)}^2(k)\}\big); \\ \overline{\Delta}_{ij(p)}(k) = \big(\{w_{ij(p)}^1 x_{i(p)}^1(k)\} \vee \{w_{ij(p)}^2 x_{i(p)}^1(k)\}\big) \\ \quad -\big(\{w_{ij(p)}^1 x_{i(p)}^2(k)\} \vee \{w_{ij(p)}^2 x_{i(p)}^2(k)\}\big). \end{cases} \tag{3}$$

*Then for each* $p = 0,1,...,n;\ i = 1,...,d;\ j = 1,...,m;\ l = 1,2,$ *the following partial derivative formulas hold:*

$$\frac{\partial E}{\partial v^l_{j(p)}} = \sum_{k=1}^{L} t^l_p(k)\Big(\mathrm{lor}(-v^l_{j(p)})\sigma(s^{3-l}_{j(p)}(k)) + \mathrm{lor}(v^l_{j(p)})\sigma(s^l_{j(p)}(k))\Big);$$

$$\begin{aligned}\frac{\partial E}{\partial w^l_{ij(p)}} = \sum_{k=1}^{L}\Big(&\Big(t^1_p(k)\Gamma^1_{j(p)}(k) + t^2_p(k)\Gamma^3_{j(p)}(k)\Big)\\ &\times\Big(\mathrm{lor}(\underline{\Delta}_{ij(p)}(k))\mathrm{lor}((-1)^{l+1}x^2_{i(p)}(k))x^2_{i(p)}(k)\\ &+\mathrm{lor}(-\underline{\Delta}_{ij(p)}(k))\mathrm{lor}((-1)^{l+1}x^1_{i(p)}(k))x^1_{i(p)}(k)\Big)\\ &+\Big(t^1_p(k)\Gamma^2_{j(p)}(k) + t^2_p(k)\Gamma^4_{j(p)}(k)\Big)\\ &\times\Big(\mathrm{lor}(\overline{\Delta}_{ij(p)}(k))\mathrm{lor}((-1)^{l}x^1_{i(p)}(k))x^1_{i(p)}(k)\\ &+\mathrm{lor}(-\overline{\Delta}_{ij(p)}(k))\mathrm{lor}((-1)^{l}x^2_{i(p)}(k))x^2_{i(p)}(k)\Big)\Big);\end{aligned}$$

$$\begin{aligned}\frac{\partial E}{\partial \theta^l_{j(p)}} = \sum_{k=1}^{L}&\Big(t^1_p(k)\mathrm{lor}\big((-1)^{l+1}v^1_{j(p)}\big)v^1_{j(p)}\\ &+t^2_p(k)\mathrm{lor}\big((-1)^{l}v^2_{j(p)}\big)v^2_{j(p)}\Big)\sigma'(s^l_{j(p)}(k)).\end{aligned}$$

## 4.2 Fuzzy BP Learning Algorithm

Using the gradient descent method, we can establish the evolution laws of the fuzzy weights and thresholds of a polygonal FNN. Let $t$ be iterative step, and $\eta > 0$ denote the learning rate, $\alpha > 0$ be the momentum constant. Write for $p = 0,1,...,n;\ i = 1,...,d;\ j = 1,...,m;\ l = 1,2$ that

$$\begin{cases} a^l_{j(p)} = v^l_{j(p)}[t] - \eta\cdot\dfrac{\partial E}{\partial v^l_{j(p)}}\Big|_{v^l_{j(p)}[t]} + \alpha\cdot\triangle v^l_{j(p)}[t-1],\\ b^l_{ij(p)} = w^l_{ij(p)}[t] - \eta\cdot\dfrac{\partial E}{\partial w^l_{ij(p)}}\Big|_{w^l_{ij(p)}[t]} + \alpha\cdot\triangle w^l_{ij(p)}[t-1],\\ c^l_{j(p)} = \theta^l_{j(p)}[t] - \eta\cdot\dfrac{\partial E}{\partial \theta^l_{j(p)}}\Big|_{\theta^l_{j(p)}[t]} + \alpha\cdot\triangle \theta^l_{j(p)}[t-1],\end{cases} \tag{4}$$

where $\triangle v^l_{j(p)}[t] = v^l_{j(p)}[t] - v^l_{j(p)}[t-1]$, $\triangle w^l_{ij(p)}[t] = w^l_{ij(p)}[t] - w^l_{ij(p)}[t-1]$, and $\triangle\theta^l_{j(p)}[t] = \theta^l_{j(p)}[t] - \theta^l_{j(p)}[t-1]$. For each $i = 1,...,d;\ j = 1,...,m$, $\{a^1_{j(0)},...,a^2_{j(0)}\}$, $\{b^1_{ij(0)},...,b^2_{ij(0)}\}$ and $\{c^1_{j(0)},...,c^2_{j(0)}\}$ can be rearranged as the sets $\{a^j_1,...,a^j_{2n+2}\}$, $\{b^{ij}_1,...,b^{ij}_{2n+2}\}$ and $\{c^j_1,...,c^j_{2n+2}\}$ respectively, in such a way that the following inequalities hold:

$$\begin{cases} a_1^j \le a_2^j \le \cdots \le a_{n+1}^j \le \cdots \le a_{2n+2}^j; \\ b_1^{ij} \le b_2^{ij} \le \cdots \le b_{n+1}^{ij} \le \cdots \le b_{2n+2}^{ij}; \\ c_1^j \le c_2^j \le \cdots \le c_{n+1}^j \le \cdots \le c_{2n+2}^j. \end{cases} \tag{5}$$

When the iteration is $t+1$, the fuzzy weights $\widetilde{V}_j[t+1]$, $\widetilde{W}_{ij}[t+1] \in \mathcal{F}_{bc}^{tn}(\mathbb{R})$ and the fuzzy threshold $\widetilde{\Theta}_j[t+1] \in \mathcal{F}_{bc}^{tn}(\mathbb{R})$ $(j = 1, ..., p)$ can be determined with:

$$\begin{cases} v_{j(p)}^1[t+1] = a_{p+1}^j, \ v_{j(p)}^2[t+1] = a_{2n+2-p}^j; \\ w_{ij(p)}^1[t+1] = b_{p+1}^{ij}, \ w_{ij(p)}^2[t+1] = b_{2n+2-p}^{ij}; \\ \theta_{j(p)}^1[t+1] = c_{p+1}^j, \ \theta_{j(p)}^2[t+1] = c_{2n+2-p}^j. \end{cases} \tag{6}$$

The learning algorithm determined by Eqs. (4)-(6) is called the fuzzy BP algorithm. We can realize the algorithm by the following steps:

**The fuzzy BP algorithm**

- *Step 1.* Initialize the fuzzy weights and thresholds. We choose randomly the initial connection weights and thresholds: $\widetilde{V}_j[0]$, $\widetilde{W}_{ij}[0]$, $\widetilde{\Theta}_j[0]$ $(j = 1, ..., p)$. And let $t = 0$.
- *Step 2.* For $j = 1, ..., p$, using to Eqs. (4)–(6), we can compute $\widetilde{V}_j[t]$, $\widetilde{W}_{ij}[t]$, $\widetilde{\Theta}_j[t]$ $(j = 1, ..., p)$.
- *Step 3.* For $j = 1, ..., m$; $p = 0, 1, ..., n$; $i = 1, ..., d$; $l = 1, 2$, complete the following value assignment: $v_{j(p)}^l[t] \longrightarrow v_{j(p)}^l$, $w_{ij(p)}^l[t] \longrightarrow w_{ij(p)}^l$, $\theta_{j(p)}^l[t] \longrightarrow \theta_{j(p)}^l$.
- *Step 4.* For $k = 1, ..., L$; $j = 1, ..., m$; $p = 0, ..., n$; $i = 1, ..., d$; $l = 1, 2$, calculate $t_p^l(k)$,$s_{j(p)}^l(k)$, $\underline{\Delta}_{ij(p)}(k)$ and $\overline{\Delta}_{ij(p)}(k)$ respectively by Eqs. (3) and (7). Consequently we can obtain the following values: $\Gamma_{j(p)}^q(k)$ for $q = 1, ..., 4$.

$$\begin{cases} s_{j'(p)}^1(k) = \sum\limits_{i=1}^{d} \big[\{w_{ij'(p)}^1 x_{i(p)}^1(k)\} \wedge \{w_{ij'(p)}^1 x_{i(p)}^2(k)\} \\ \qquad \wedge \{w_{ij'(p)}^2 x_{i(p)}^1(k)\} \wedge \{w_{ij'(p)}^2 x_{i(p)}^2(k)\}\big] + \theta_{j'(p)}^1, \\ s_{j'(p)}^2(k) = \sum\limits_{i=1}^{d} \big[\{w_{ij'(p)}^1 x_{i(p)}^1(k)\} \vee \{w_{ij'(p)}^1 x_{i(p)}^2(k)\} \\ \qquad \vee \{w_{ij'(p)}^2 x_{i(p)}^1(k)\} \vee \{w_{ij'(p)}^2 x_{i(p)}^2(k)\}\big] + \theta_{j'(p)}^2. \end{cases} \tag{7}$$

- *Step 5.* By Theorem 2, compute $\partial E/\partial v_{j(p)}^l\big|_{v_{j(p)}^l[t]}$, $\partial E/\partial \theta_{j(p)}^l\big|_{\theta_{j(p)}^l[t]}$ and $\partial E/\partial w_{ij(p)}^l\big|_{w_{ij(p)}^l[t]}$, and using Eqs. (4)–(6) we obtain $v_{j(p)}^l[t+1]$, $\theta_{j(p)}^l[t+1]$ and $w_{ij(p)}^l[t+1]$ for $j = 1, ..., m$; $p = 0, 1, ..., n$; $i = 1, ..., d$; $l = 1, 2$.
- *Step 6.* Discriminate analysis: either $t > M$ or $E < \varepsilon$, go to Step 7; otherwise let $t = t + 1$, go to Step 2.
- *Step 7.* Stop and output $\widetilde{V}_j[t]$, $\widetilde{\Theta}_j[t]$, $\widetilde{W}_{ij}[t]$ for $i = 1, ..., d$, $j = 1, ..., m$, and $\widetilde{O}_k$ $(k = 1, ..., L)$.

In Step 6, $M$ is a given upper-bound of iteration steps and $\varepsilon$ is an error bound.

## 5 Simulation Examples

In the section, the proposed fuzzy BP algorithm is demonstrated by computer simulations on a few of numerical examples. In the following simulations, the upper-bound of iterative steps $M$ is assumed to be $2 \times 10^4$, and the error bound $\varepsilon = 0.1$. In the hidden layer of the polygonal FNN there are four five neurons, that is, $m = 5$. Choose $n = 4$. The activation function is chosen as $\sigma : \mathbb{R} \longrightarrow \mathbb{R}_+$, defined as follows: $\forall x \in \mathbb{R}$, $\sigma(x) = 1/(1 + \mathrm{e}^{-x})$, i.e. $\sigma$ is the Sigmoidal function. Obviously it is a increasing, non-negative and differentiable function.

### 5.1 Learning Capability

To examine the learning capability of a polygonal FNN, let us now study a simulation example related to digital image enhancement. Suppose $[0, G]$ to be a grey degree interval, in which includes all grey levels of the digital images related, and here we choose $G = 255$. By some fuzzy sets, such as, 'Bright ($\widetilde{B}_R$)', 'Brighter ($\widetilde{B}_r$)', 'Medium ($\widetilde{M}_e$)', 'Darker ($\widetilde{D}_r$)' and 'Dark ($\widetilde{D}_R$)' we can describe the gray levels of the images [16]. To develop some efficient image filters based on fuzzy inference, the first step is to design a family of suitable fuzzy rules. For example, the following 'IF–THEN' rules are usual cases in designing fuzzy filters [16, 18]:

$$\begin{array}{l} \text{IF } x_1 \text{ is } \widetilde{B}_R \text{ AND } x_2 \text{ is } \widetilde{B}_R \text{ THEN } y \text{ is } \widetilde{B}_R; \\ \text{IF } x_1 \text{ is } \widetilde{B}_R \text{ AND } x_2 \text{ is } \widetilde{D}_R \text{ THEN } y \text{ is } \widetilde{M}_e; \\ \text{IF } x_1 \text{ is } \widetilde{D}_R \text{ AND } x_2 \text{ is } \widetilde{B}_R \text{ THEN } y \text{ is } \widetilde{M}_e; \\ \text{IF } x_1 \text{ is } \widetilde{D}_R \text{ AND } x_2 \text{ is } \widetilde{D}_R \text{ THEN } y \text{ is } \widetilde{D}_R. \end{array} \tag{8}$$

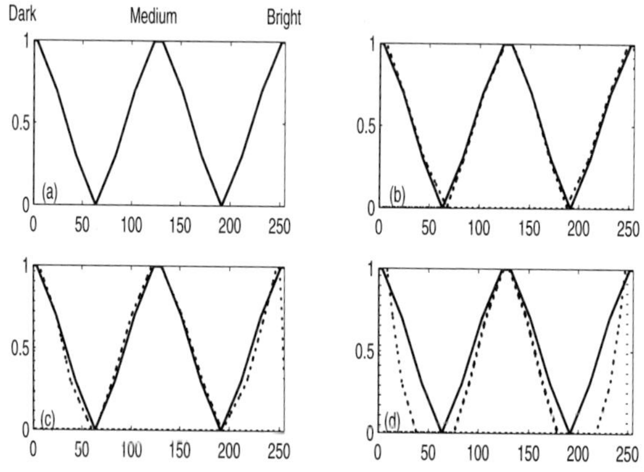


**Fig. 3.** Membership curves of fuzzy numbers 'Dark' 'Medium' 'Bright' : (a) desired curves; (b) desired curves (—) and actual output curves by our model (···); (c) desired curves (—) and actual output curves by Ishibuchi model in [9] (···); (d) desired curves (—) and actual output curves by Ishibuchi model in [10] (···)

The antecedent and consequent fuzzy sets '$\widetilde{D}_R$', '$\widetilde{M}_e$' and '$\widetilde{B}_R$' are fuzzy numbers defined on $[0, G]$, respectively.

Let us now employ the polygonal FNN's to realize the fuzzy IF–THEN inference rules defined by (8), approximately. Also we present the numerical comparison of our model with other fuzzified neural networks developed in [9, 10]. To this end we assume that the input related is a two dimensional variable $(x_1, x_2)$, and the output is an one dimensional variable $y$. The membership curves of fuzzy numbers $\widetilde{B}_R$, $\widetilde{M}_e$, $\widetilde{D}_R$ are shown in (a) of Fig. 3, respectively. Choose

$$\left\{\left((\widetilde{B}_R, \widetilde{B}_R), \widetilde{B}_R\right), \left((\widetilde{B}_R, \widetilde{D}_R), \widetilde{M}_e\right), \left((\widetilde{D}_R, \widetilde{B}_R), \widetilde{M}_e\right), \left((\widetilde{D}_R, \widetilde{D}_R), \widetilde{D}_R\right)\right\}, \tag{9}$$

as the training patterns for designing learning algorithms of the polygonal FNN's as (1) and those in [9,10].

The polygonal FNN as Eq. (1) can be trained by using Algorithm 1, and corresponding to the input patterns in the training set Eq. (9), we can get the actual outputs after 20000 iteration steps, as shown (b) of Fig. 3. Ishibuchi et al use the symmetric triangular fuzzy number weights and thresholds in [10] to build up a regular FNN, whose adjustable parameters are only two kinds of parameters — two endpoints of the $\alpha$−cuts. The BP type learning algorithms are used to train such a FNN model, also it can realize the inference rules in Eq. (8) approximately through the training pattern set Eq. (9). The corresponding actual and desired outputs are shown in (c) of Fig. 3 after 20000 iteration steps. In [9] Ishibuchi et al take the real numbers as the connection weights and thresholds to construct a FNN model. Similarly with the convenient BP algorithm they develop a learning algorithm of the FNN. By iterating 20000 steps, we can get the actual outputs to approximate the rules in Eq. (8), as shown in (d) of Fig. 3. By comparing (b) (c) (d) of Fig. 3, we can easily find that the polygonal FNN as Eq. (1) gives the best results, i.e. the error of the polygonal FNN is significantly lower than those Ishibuchi's FNN models [9,10].

By Fig. 4 we show the curves of the error function defined by Eq. (2), corresponding to above three FNN models, i.e. the polygonal FNN as Eq. (1) and two Ishibuchi's models [9, 10]. Through Fig. 4 we can find that despite larger error at the beginning of iteration, the square error of the polygonal FNN is lowest, and corresponding to Ishibuchi's two FNN models, the square errors are approximately equal. So our result is also the best.

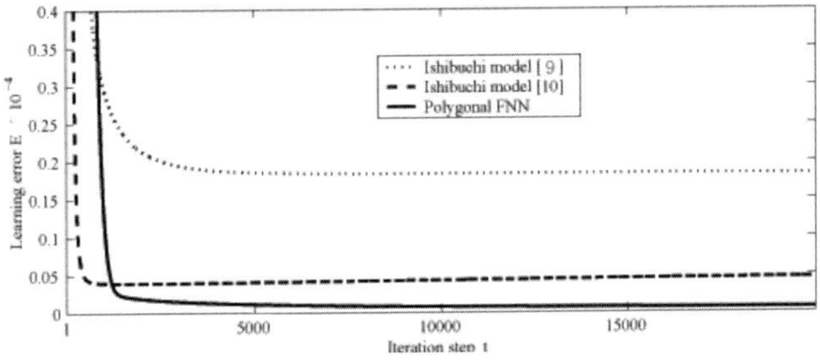


**Fig. 4.** Error curves of different FNN models

| $x_2$ \ $x_1$ | $\tilde{D}_R$ | $\tilde{D}_r$ | $\tilde{M}_e$ | $\tilde{B}_r$ | $\tilde{B}_R$ |
|---|---|---|---|---|---|
| $\tilde{D}_R$ | $\tilde{D}_R$ | | | | $\tilde{M}_e$ |
| $\tilde{D}_r$ | | | | | |
| $\tilde{M}_e$ | | | | | |
| $\tilde{B}_r$ | | | | | |
| $\tilde{B}_R$ | $\tilde{M}_e$ | | | | $\tilde{B}_R$ |

**Fig. 5.** Uncomplete fuzzy rule table

| $x_2$ \ $x_1$ | $\tilde{D}_R$ | $\tilde{D}_r$ | $\tilde{M}_e$ | $\tilde{B}_r$ | $\tilde{B}_R$ |
|---|---|---|---|---|---|
| $\tilde{D}_R$ | $\tilde{D}_R$ | $\tilde{D}_r$ | $\tilde{D}_r$ | $\tilde{D}_r$ | $\tilde{M}_e$ |
| $\tilde{D}_r$ | $\tilde{D}_r$ | $\tilde{D}_r$ | $\tilde{D}_r$ | $\tilde{M}_e$ | $\tilde{B}_r$ |
| $\tilde{M}_e$ | $\tilde{D}_r$ | $\tilde{D}_r$ | $\tilde{M}_e$ | $\tilde{B}_r$ | $\tilde{B}_r$ |
| $\tilde{B}_r$ | $\tilde{D}_r$ | $\tilde{M}_e$ | $\tilde{B}_r$ | $\tilde{B}_r$ | $\tilde{B}_r$ |
| $\tilde{B}_R$ | $\tilde{M}_e$ | $\tilde{B}_r$ | $\tilde{B}_r$ | $\tilde{B}_r$ | $\tilde{B}_R$ |

**Fig. 6.** Fuzzy rule table completed by FNN (1)

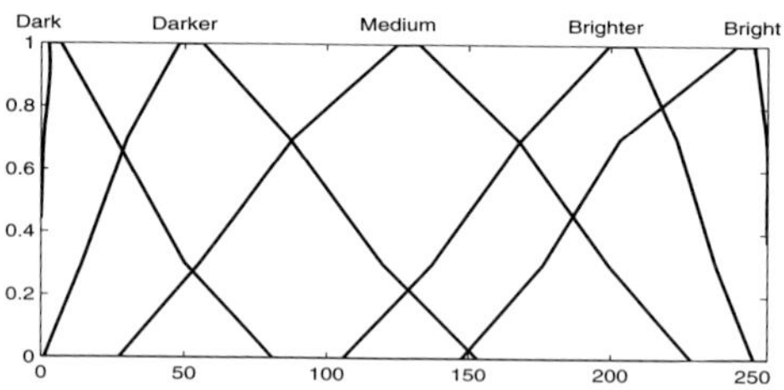


**Fig. 7.** Actual outputs of the polygonal FNN as Eq. (1)

## 5.2 Generalization Capability

Let us proceed to study fuzzy rules to show the generalization capability of polygonal FNN's. The fuzzy rules in (8) are shown as Fig. 5, a fuzzy rule table, in which only four rules out of 25 fuzzy IF—THEN rules are presented and others are missing. Now let us complete the rule table by assigning one of the five fuzzy sets as '$\tilde{B}_R$' '$\tilde{B}_r$' '$\tilde{M}_e$' '$\tilde{D}_r$' and '$\tilde{D}_R$', whose membership curves are shown in (a) of Fig. 3 respectively, to the consequent of each missing rule. For example, when we choose the input $(x_1, x_2)$ to be $\left(\tilde{D}_R, \tilde{D}_r\right)$, $\left(\tilde{D}_R, \tilde{M}_e\right)$, $\left(\tilde{D}_r, \tilde{B}_r\right)$, $\left(\tilde{M}_e, \tilde{B}_R\right)$, and $\left(\tilde{B}_R, \tilde{B}_r\right)$, respectively, the corresponding outputs of the polygonal FNN as Eq. (1) are respectively shown in Fig. 7, from which we can obtain their respective linguistic values: '$\widetilde{D}_R$' '$\widetilde{D}_r$' '$\widetilde{M}_e$' '$\widetilde{B}_r$' and '$\widetilde{B}_R$'. Similarly we can complete the other missing rules, as shown in Fig. 6. Obviously, these consequents conform to inference sense in Eq. (8). So the polygonal FNN's as (1) possesses strong generalization capability, which is advantageous over that of Ishibuchi's model in [10], since the similar rule table is completed based on nine fuzzy rules.

## 6 Conclusions

By modifying the internal operations, this paper defines polygonal FNN's, a class of novel FNN models by which general fuzzy information may be handled. Using the derivatives of the $\vee - \wedge$ functions, we develop an efficient learning algorithm for the fuzzy connection weights and thresholds of the polygonal FNN's. Some simulation examples demonstrate the efficiency of our FNN models. The further problems include developing some improved algorithms, in which the learning rate $\eta$ and the momentum constant $\alpha$ may be adaptively adjusted, with quicker convergence speed and minimal computation complexity, generalizing the polygonal fuzzy numbers to more general cases, and so on.

## References


1. Aliev, R.A., Fazlollahi, B., Vahidov, R. M. : Genetic Algorithm-Based Learning of Fuzzy Neural Networks. Part I: Feed-Forward Fuzzy Neural Networks. Fuzzy Sets and Systems. **118** (2001) 351–358
2. Blanco, A., Delgado, M., Requena I.: Identification of Fuzzy Relational Equations by Fuzzy Neural Networks. Fuzzy Sets and Systems **71** (1995) 215–226
3. Blanco, A., Delgado, M., Requena I.: Improved Fuzzy Neural Networks for Solving Fuzzy Relational Equations. Fuzzy Sets and Systems **72** (1995) 311–322
4. Buckley, J.J., Hayashi, Y.: Can Neural Nets Be Universal Approximators for Fuzzy Functions, Fuzzy Sets and Systems **101** (1999) 323–330
5. Buckley, J.J., Hayashi, Y.: Fuzzy Neural Networks: A Survey. Fuzzy Sets and Systems **66** (1994) 1–13
6. Buckley, J.J., Hayashi, Y.: Direct Fuzzification of Neural Networks. In: Proc. of 1st Asian Fuzzy Sys. Symp. Vol. 1, Singapore (1993) 560–567
7. Dunyak, J., Wunsch D.: Fuzzy Number Neural Networks. Fuzzy Sets and Systems **108** (1999) 49–58
8. Feuring T., Lippe W.M.: The Fuzzy Neural Network Approximation Lemma. Fuzzy Sets and Systems, **102** (1999) 227–236
9. Ishibuchi, H., Fujioka, R., Tanaka, H.: Neural Networks that Learn from Fuzzy If–Then Rules. IEEE Trans. on Fuzzy Systems **1** (1993) 85–97
10. Ishibuchi, H., Kwon K., Tanaka, H.A.: Learning Algorithm of Fuzzy Neural Networks with Triangular Fuzzy Weights. Fuzzy sets and Systems **71** (1995) 277–293
11. Ishibuchi, H., Nii, M.: Numerical Analysis of the Learning of Fuzzified Neural Networks from Fuzzy If–Then Rules. Fuzzy Sets and Systems **120** (2001) 281–307
12. Li, Z., Kecman, V., Ichikawa, A.: Fuzzified Neural Network Based on Fuzzy Number Operations. Fuzzy Sets and Systems **130** (2002) 291–304
13. Liu, P.: Analyses of Regular Fuzzy Neural Networks for Approximation Capability. Fuzzy Sets and Systems **114** (2000) 329–338

14. Liu, P.: On the Approximation Realization of Fuzzy Closure Mapping by Multilayer Regular Fuzzy Neural Networks. Multiple Valued Logic 5(**11**) (2000) 463–480
15. Liu, P.: A Novel Fuzzy Neural Network and Its Approximation Property. Science in China (Series F) 44(**3**) (2001) 184–194
16. Liu, P.: Representation of Digital Image by Fuzzy Neural Networks. Fuzzy Sets and Systems **130** (2002) 109–123
17. Nguyen, H.T.: A Note on the Extension Principle for Fuzzy Set. J. Math. Anal. Appl. **64** (1978) 369–380
18. Liu, P., Li, H.: Fuzzy Neural Network Theory and Application. World Scientific Publishing, Singapore (2004)
19. Zhang, X.H., Tan, S.H., Huang, C.C., et al.: An Efficient Computational Algorithm for Min-Max Operations. Fuzzy Sets and Systems **104** (1999) 297–304
20. Zhang, X.H., Huang, C.C., Tan, S.H., et al.: The Min-Max Function Differentiation and Training of Fuzzy Neural Networks. IEEE Trans. on Neural Networks **7** (1996) 1139–1150
21. Diamond, P., Kloeden, P.: Metric Spaces of Fuzzy Sets. World Scientific Publishing, Singapore (1994)
22. Liu, P., Li, H.: Symmetric Polygonal Fuzzy Numbers. In: The 9th International Conference on Fuzzy Theory and Technology, NC, USA (2003) 26-30
23. Park, S., Han, T.: Iterative Inversion of Fuzzified Neural Networks. IEEE Trans. on Fuzzy Systems **8** (2000) 268–280

# WPSS Communication System Based on CRBF Network Equalizers

Lei Zhou, Jian-Dong Li, and Peng He

Broadband Wireless Communications Laboratory, Information Science Institute,
State Key Laboratory of Integrated Service Networks, Xidian University,
Xi'an 710071, China
{lzhou, jdli, phe}@mail.xidian.edu.cn

**Abstract.** In this paper, novel wavelet packet spread spectrum (WPSS) communication system based on the complex radial basis function (CRBF) network equalizers is studied for multipath fading channels. The complex radial basis function network equalizers technique is adopted to suppress Inter-Symbol Interference (ISI) caused by multipath fading channels and reduce the symbol error rate (SER). The system performance is investigated in multipath fading channels. The theoretical analysis and simulation results show that the proposed CRBF channel equalizer structure which uses least mean square (LMS) algorithm to obtain the optimized equalizer weights offers both fast convergence and low value of the mean square error; the proposed CRBF-WPSS system has a superior SER performance to that of the conventional CRBF-OFDM-SS (spreading spectrum) system, and the proposed CRBF-WPSS system outperforms the WPSS system base on zero-forcing equalizers for multipath fading channels.

## 1 Introduction

Waveform coding [1] is usually employed in a digital communication system to convert the message data into continuous waveforms in order to provide better immunity against noise, fading, or jamming during transmission. To achieve this aim, the various schemes of waveform coding endeavor to make the distance between the waveforms in the coded signal as large as possible, i.e., to make the cross-correlation coefficient between any pair of waveforms as small as possible [2]. To transmit a large number of independent messages over a common channel, the orthogonal waveform coding has been widely used for multiplexing in the form of Frequency Division Multiplexing (FDM) or Time Division Multiplexing (TDM) [3]. However, nonoverlapping spectra of the different channels in FDM results in inefficient use of the bandwidth. Sufficient guard band is needed between adjacent subchannels to isolate them at the receiver using conventional filters.

When much more efficient use of bandwidth is required, one of the popular multiplexing is orthogonal FDM (OFDM), which is now attracting widespread interest from both researcher and product developer. With the wavelet transform developed, several researchers find that a set of basis functions from wavelet and wavelet packet matches the waveform requirement in OFDM. These basis functions are orthogonal with one another and are orthogonal across translations. Using these functions in a multiplexing system guarantees efficient use of the spectrum because of the overlap spectra of these basis functions. Moreover, these functions are essentially generated

D.-S. Huang, K. Li, and G.W. Irwin (Eds.): ICIC 2006, LNCS 4113, pp. 259–267, 2006.

from one function, therefore the problem encountered in OFDM due to inaccurate subcarrier frequency and phase never occur in the multiplexing based on wavelet and wavelet packet. Some researchers have realized the potential of applying wavelet and wavelet packet in spread spectrum and CDMA communications, and various schemes of coding and multiplexing have been proposed [4]–[9]. In this paper, we examine the performance of such a system from a transmission-reception point of view and propose wavelet packet spread spectrum (WPSS) based on neural network equalizers and maximum likelihood algorithm for multipath fading channels.

## 2 System Model

The detailed structure block diagram of WPSS system scheme based on complex radial basis function equalizers can be represented by block diagram of Fig. 1. In this design, the switch $K_1$ and $K_2$ change position P for the training sequence is used in driving the Least Mean Square (LMS) algorithm to update complex radial basis function (CRBF) network equalizer weights. When CRBF network equalizer reaches in its preset target performance, the switch $K_1$ and $K_2$ change position from P to Q. The data symbols are spread individually by Walsh-Hadamard spread spectrum codes after the information bits are mapped into the data symbols by Quadrature Amplitude Modulation (QAM). The spread spectrum chips are then mapped to different subcarriers through an inverse discrete wavelet packet transform. Then the data signal is transmitted in usual way over a channel characterized by multipath fading channels and Additive White Gaussian Noise (AWGN). In this model, before the received symbols are demodulated by the discrete wavelet packet transform, the receiver uses the trained CRBF network equalizer to suppress the Inter-Symbol Interference (ISI) caused by multipath fading channels. The demodulated symbols are de-spread using the corresponding Walsh-Hadamard spread spectrum codes. Finally, the de-spread symbols are determined for M-ARY QAM signals by maximum likelihood (ML) detecting algorithm, and then the determined M-ARY QAM signals are mapped into the information bits.

The detailed transmitter structure of WPSS system is shown in Fig.1.The transmitted signal is generated as follows. A single data symbol is copies into the *M* branches.

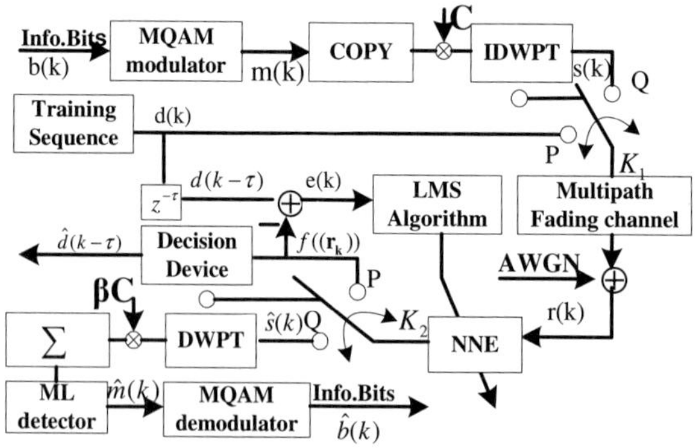


**Fig. 1.** The detailed structure block diagram of WPSS system scheme based on complex radial basis function equalizers

In the $m$th branch, the symbol is multiplied by the $m$th chip of Walsh-Hadamard spread spectrum codes. The spread spectrum chips are then mapped to different sub-carriers through an inverse discrete wavelet packet transform. This mapping is equivalent to the inverse discrete Fourier Transform (IDFT) in the sinusoid waveform-based multicarriers system.

Referring to Fig.1, the transmitted signal is

$$\begin{aligned} s_l(j) &= m(l)\sum_{i=0}^{M-1} c_i\phi_i(j) \qquad j=0,1,\cdots,M-1 \\ &= m(l)W(j) \end{aligned} \tag{1}$$

where $m(l)$ is the $l$th data symbol; $c_i$ is the $i$th chip of Walsh-Hadamard codes; $\phi_i$ is the $i$th wavelet packet waveform; $W$ is the WPSS waveform.The set of wavelet packet waveforms $\phi_0$ to $\phi_{M-1}$ is generated with a full binary wavelet packet tree using a specific pair of QMF $h$(n) and $g$(n).The transmitted signal can be rewritten in matrix form by

$$\begin{aligned} \mathbf{S_l} &= \begin{bmatrix} s_l(0) \\ s_l(1) \\ \vdots \\ s_l(M-1) \end{bmatrix} = \begin{bmatrix} \phi_0(0) & \phi_1(0) & \cdots & \phi_{M-1}(0) \\ \phi_0(1) & \phi_1(1) & \cdots & \phi_{M-1}(1) \\ \vdots & & \ddots & \vdots \\ \phi_0(M-1) & \phi_1(M-1) & \cdots & \phi_{M-1}(M-1) \end{bmatrix} \begin{bmatrix} c_0 \\ c_1 \\ \vdots \\ c_{M-1} \end{bmatrix} m_l \\ &= \mathbf{\Phi C} m_l = \mathbf{W} m_l \end{aligned} \tag{2}$$

where $\mathbf{\Phi}$ is the IDWPT matrix in the modulator. $\mathbf{C}$ is the Walsh-Hadamard spread spectrum codes vector , $\mathbf{W}$ is the WPSS waveform vector.

## 2.1 Adaptive Complex Radial Basis Function (RBF) Network Based Equalizers

The schematic diagram for the LMS-CRBFN equalizers is shown in Fig. 2. To begin with, the switch $K_1$ and $K_2$ change position P for the training sequence is used in driving the Least Mean Square (LMS) algorithm to update complex radial basis function (CRBF) network equalizer weights. The RBF network consists of three different layers as shown in Fig.2. The input layer is constituted by m source nodes. A set of $p$ nonlinear activation functions $\boldsymbol{\beta}_i, i=1,\cdots,p$ , constitutes the hidden second layer. The output of the network is provided by the third layer, which is comprised of output nodes. As shown in Fig.2, using the noisy channel output vector $\mathbf{r_k}$ as the network input and the training symbol $d(k-\tau)$ as the desired output, LMS learning algorithm can readily be applied to train the complex RBF as shown by the dotted lines of Fig.2. During the testing phase, the output $f(\mathbf{r(k)})$ of CRBFN is fed into a nearest neighbor decision device to give an estimate $\hat{d}(k-\tau)$ of the training symbol $d(k-\tau)$ .The channel output observed by the linear $m$th order equalizer can be written in vectorial form as

$$\begin{aligned} \mathbf{r_k} &= [r_k \quad r_{k-1} \quad \cdots \quad r_{k-m+1}]^T \\ &= \begin{bmatrix} h[0] & h[1] & \cdots & h[L] & 0 & \cdots 0 \\ 0 & h[0] & h[1] & \cdots & h[L] & \cdots 0 \\ \vdots & \vdots & \ddots & \ddots & \ddots & \ddots \; \vdots \\ 0 & 0 & \cdots & h[0] & h[1] & \cdots h[L] \end{bmatrix} \begin{bmatrix} d_k \\ d_{k-1} \\ \vdots \\ d_{k-L-m} \end{bmatrix} + \begin{bmatrix} w_k \\ w_{k-1} \\ \vdots \\ w_{k-m+1} \end{bmatrix} \\ &= \mathbf{Hd_k} + \mathbf{w_k} \end{aligned} \tag{3}$$

where **H** is the $m \times (L+m+1)$ channel impulse response matrix. The left part of **H** reflects the interference from the previous symbol while the right part of **H** reflects the multipath effect within the current symbol. $\mathbf{d_k}$ is the training sequence vector defined as $\mathbf{d_k} = [d_k \quad d_{k-1} \quad \cdots \quad d_{k-L-m}]^T$, $\mathbf{w_k}$ is the Gaussian noise sequence vector given by $\mathbf{w_k} = [w_k \quad w_{k-1} \quad \cdots \quad w_{k-m+1}]^T$ .Defining $\boldsymbol{\mu}_\mathbf{i}$ as the m-dimensional complex center vector for the *i*th hidden neuron, the Euclidean distance $\| \bullet \|$ between the two complex-valued vectors is defined as

$$\begin{aligned}\|\mathbf{r_k} - \boldsymbol{\mu}_\mathbf{i}\|^2 &= |r_k - \mu_{1i}|^2 + |r_{k-1} - \mu_{2i}|^2 + \cdots + |r_{k-m+1} - \mu_{mi}|^2 \\ &= (\mathbf{r_k} - \boldsymbol{\mu}_\mathbf{i})^H (\mathbf{r_k} - \boldsymbol{\mu}_\mathbf{i})\end{aligned} \tag{4}$$

where $| \bullet |$ denotes the modulus of a complex number. Therefore, the response $\beta_i$ of hidden neurons to the network input vector $\mathbf{r_k}$ can be expressed as follows:

$$\beta_i(\|\mathbf{r_k} - \boldsymbol{\mu}_\mathbf{i}\|) = \exp\left(-\frac{1}{2\sigma_i^2}(\mathbf{r_k} - \boldsymbol{\mu}_\mathbf{i})^H (\mathbf{r_k} - \boldsymbol{\mu}_\mathbf{i})\right), \quad i = 1, \cdots, p \tag{5}$$

where $\sigma_i$ is the (real valued) width of the Gaussian function and $p$ indicates the total number of hidden neurons in the network. The output layer of the RBF network is essentially a linear combiner. We define the coefficient $\omega_k$ as the weight of the link connecting the *k*th hidden neuron and $\omega_0$ as the bias term. In order to implement complex-valued outputs, we separate the complex valued $\omega_k$ into $\omega_{Rk}$ and $\omega_{Ik}$ for the real and imaginary parts of the network output. Hence, the overall network response is given by

$$\begin{aligned}f(\mathbf{r_k}) &= \left(\omega_{R0} + \sum_{i=1}^{p} \omega_{Ri}\beta_i(\mathbf{r_k})\right) + j\left(\omega_{I0} + \sum_{i=1}^{p} \omega_{Ii}\beta_i(\mathbf{r_k})\right) \\ &= \omega_0 + \sum_{i=1}^{p} \omega_i \exp\left(-\frac{1}{2\sigma_i^2}(\mathbf{r_k} - \boldsymbol{\mu}_\mathbf{i})^H (\mathbf{r_k} - \boldsymbol{\mu}_\mathbf{i})\right)\end{aligned} \tag{6}$$

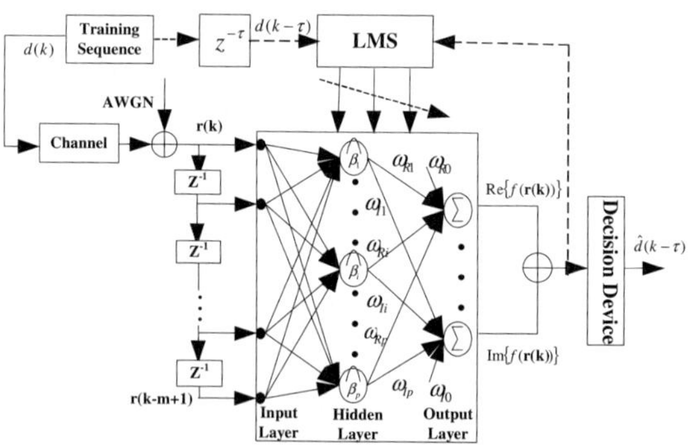


**Fig. 2.** The schematic diagram for the LMS-CRBFN equalizers

When both the network inputs and desired output are real-valued, this complex RBF network degenerates naturally into a real RBF network. An examination of (6) reveals that CRBF network treats the real and imaginary parts of an input as if they were two separate real inputs. Hence it is seen that the complex RBF network is a natural extension of the real RBF network.

## 2.2 Least Mean Square (LMS) Algorithm-Based Supervised Learning

If the assumption of equiprobable symbols is violated, it is advisable to adjust the weights of the RBF networks in order to learn the corresponding scaling factors of the conditional probability density functions in (6) during the training period. The adaptation of the RBF weights can be achieved using the following supervised LMS algorithm:

$$e_k = d_{k-\tau} - f(\mathbf{r_k}) \tag{7}$$

$$\omega_{i,k} = \omega_{i,k-1} + \eta_\omega e_k \beta_i(\|\mathbf{r_k} - \boldsymbol{\mu}_\mathbf{i}\|) \tag{8}$$

where $\eta_\omega$ is the learning rate for the RBF weights. Explicitly, the error $e_k = I_{k-\tau} - f(\mathbf{r_k})$ between the transmitted $I_{k-\tau}$ and the RBF network output is scaled by the RBF learning rate $\eta_\omega$ and this product is then used to weight $\beta_i(\|\mathbf{r_k} - \boldsymbol{\mu}_\mathbf{i}\|)$ in order to update the previous RBF weight $\omega_{i,k-1}$ ,where $\beta_i(\|\mathbf{r_k} - \boldsymbol{\mu}_\mathbf{i}\|)$ is the RBF evaluated at the Euclidean norm $\|\mathbf{r_k} - \boldsymbol{\mu}_\mathbf{i}\|$ characteristic of the distance between the centroid $\boldsymbol{\mu}_\mathbf{i}, i = 1,\cdots,p$ .Based on (5) and (6), (7) and (8) can be rewritten as

$$e_k = I_{k-\tau} - \omega_0 - \sum_{i=1}^{p} \omega_i \exp\left(-\frac{1}{2\sigma_i^2}(\mathbf{r_k} - \boldsymbol{\mu}_\mathbf{i})^H (\mathbf{r_k} - \boldsymbol{\mu}_\mathbf{i})\right) \tag{9}$$

$$\omega_{i,k} = \omega_{i,k-1} + \eta_\omega e_k \exp\left(-\frac{1}{2\sigma_i^2}(\mathbf{r_k} - \boldsymbol{\mu}_\mathbf{i})^\mathbf{H} (\mathbf{r_k} - \boldsymbol{\mu}_\mathbf{i})\right) \tag{10}$$

## 2.3 Receiver Processing

As shown in Fig.1, when CRBF neural network equalizer reaches in its preset target performance, the switch $K_1$ and $K_2$ change position from P to Q. Based on (3), the channel output in vectorial form $\mathbf{r_k}$ can be rewritten by

$$\begin{aligned}\mathbf{r_k} = \begin{bmatrix} r_k \\ r_{k-1} \\ \vdots \\ r_{k-m+1} \end{bmatrix} &= \begin{bmatrix} h[0] & h[1] & \cdots & h[L] & 0 & \cdots 0 \\ 0 & h[0] & h[1] & \cdots & h[L] & \cdots 0 \\ \vdots & \vdots & \ddots & \ddots & \ddots & \ddots \vdots \\ 0 & 0 & \cdots & h[0] & h[1] & \cdots h[L] \end{bmatrix} \begin{bmatrix} s_k \\ s_{k-1} \\ \vdots \\ s_{k-L-m} \end{bmatrix} + \begin{bmatrix} w_k \\ w_{k-1} \\ \vdots \\ w_{k-m+1} \end{bmatrix} \\ &= \mathbf{H}\mathbf{s_k} + \mathbf{w_k}\end{aligned} \tag{11}$$

where $\mathbf{s_k}$ is the transmitted symbol vector. That is

$$\mathbf{s_k} = [s_k \quad s_{k-1} \quad \cdots \quad s_{k-L-m}]^T \tag{12}$$

As shown in Fig.1, based on equation (6) and (11), the output of the CBRF network equalizer is given by

$$\begin{aligned}\hat{s}(k) &= \omega_0 + \sum_{i=1}^{p} \omega_i \exp\left(-\frac{1}{2\sigma_i^2}(\mathbf{r_k}-\boldsymbol{\mu}_\mathbf{i})^H(\mathbf{r_k}-\boldsymbol{\mu}_\mathbf{i})\right) \\ &= \omega_0 + \sum_{i=1}^{p} \omega_i \exp\left(-\frac{1}{2\sigma_i^2}((\mathbf{Hs_k}+\mathbf{w_k})-\boldsymbol{\mu}_\mathbf{i})^\mathbf{H}((\mathbf{Hs_k}+\mathbf{w_k})-\boldsymbol{\mu}_\mathbf{i})\right)\end{aligned} \tag{13}$$

Based on equation (13), the $l$th output vector of the DWPT is written as

$$\mathbf{y_l} = \begin{bmatrix} y_l(0) \\ y_l(1) \\ \vdots \\ y_l(M-1) \end{bmatrix} = \boldsymbol{\Phi}^\mathbf{T}\hat{\mathbf{s}}_\mathbf{l} = \begin{bmatrix} \phi_0(0) & \phi_0(1) & \cdots \phi_0(M-1) \\ \phi_1(0) & \phi_1(1) & \cdots \phi_1(M-1) \\ \vdots & \vdots & \ddots \vdots \\ \phi_{M-1}(0) & \phi_{M-1}(1) & \cdots \phi_{M-1}(M-1) \end{bmatrix} \bullet$$
$$\begin{bmatrix} \omega_0 + \sum_{i=1}^{p} \omega_i \exp\left(-\frac{1}{2\sigma_i^2}((\mathbf{Hs_{l\cdot M}}+\mathbf{w_{l\cdot M}})-\boldsymbol{\mu}_\mathbf{i})^\mathbf{H}((\mathbf{Hs_{l\cdot M}}+\mathbf{w_{l\cdot M}})-\boldsymbol{\mu}_\mathbf{i})\right) \\ \omega_0 + \sum_{i=1}^{p} \omega_i \exp\left(-\frac{1}{2\sigma_i^2}((\mathbf{Hs_{l\cdot M+1}}+\mathbf{w}_{l\cdot \mathbf{M+1}})-\boldsymbol{\mu}_\mathbf{i})^\mathbf{H}((\mathbf{Hs_{l\cdot M+1}}+\mathbf{w_{l\cdot M+1}})-\boldsymbol{\mu}_\mathbf{i})\right) \\ \vdots \\ \omega_0 + \sum_{i=1}^{p} \omega_i \exp\left(-\frac{1}{2\sigma_i^2}((\mathbf{Hs_{l\cdot M+M-1}}+\mathbf{w_{l\cdot M+M-1}})-\boldsymbol{\mu}_\mathbf{i})^\mathbf{H}((\mathbf{Hs_{l\cdot M+M-1}}+\mathbf{w_{l\cdot M+M-1}})-\boldsymbol{\mu}_\mathbf{i})\right) \end{bmatrix} \tag{14}$$

where $\boldsymbol{\Phi}^\mathbf{T}$ is the transposition of $\boldsymbol{\Phi}$ and the DWPT matrix in the demodulator; $\hat{\mathbf{S}}_\mathbf{l}$ is the input vector of DWPT. As shown in Fig.1, the output is obtained by despreading $\mathbf{y_m}$ with the spreading spectrum code $\mathbf{C}$ corresponding to that of the transmitter as

$$\begin{aligned}\hat{m}(k) &= \sum_{i=0}^{M-1} \beta_i c_i y_k(i) \\ &= \sum_{i=0}^{M-1} \beta_i c_i \left\{ \sum_{l=0}^{M-1} \phi_i(l)\omega_0 + \right. \\ & \left. \sum_{j=1}^{M-1} \phi_i(j) \sum_{k=1}^{p} \omega_{ii} \exp\left(-\frac{1}{2\sigma_k^2}((\mathbf{Hs_{k\cdot M+j}}+\mathbf{w_{k\cdot M+j}})-\boldsymbol{\mu}_\mathbf{k})^\mathbf{H}((\mathbf{Hs_{k\cdot M+j}}+\mathbf{w_{k\cdot M+j}})-\boldsymbol{\mu}_\mathbf{k})\right)\right\}\end{aligned} \tag{15}$$

Based on the Euclidean distances between the demodulated signal and all possible transmitted symbols, the most likely transmitted symbol is determined by the ML detector. The simplified decision ruled is based on choosing $x_i$ if and only if

$$dist(\tilde{x}, x_i) \le dist(\tilde{x}, x_j), \quad \forall\, i \ne j \tag{16}$$

where $dist(A, B)$ are the Euclidean distance between signals A and B, and the index j spans all possible transmitted symbols. From equation (16), we can see that the

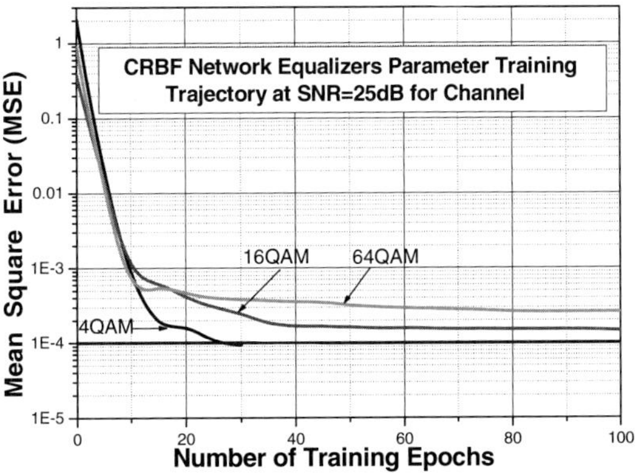


**Fig. 3.** Mean square error of the CRBF network weights for the channel

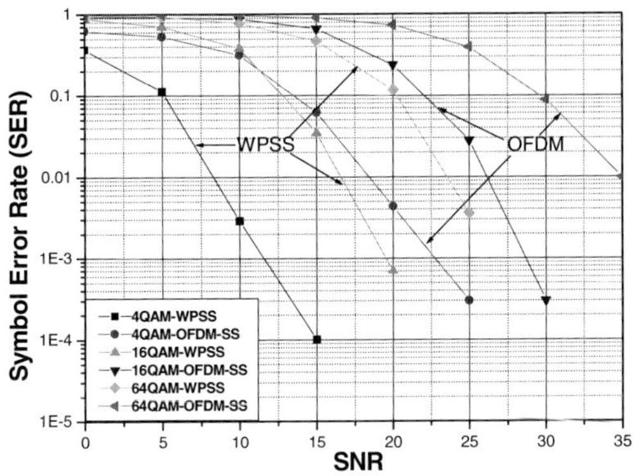


**Fig. 4.** SER performance comparison of WPSS and OFDM-SS

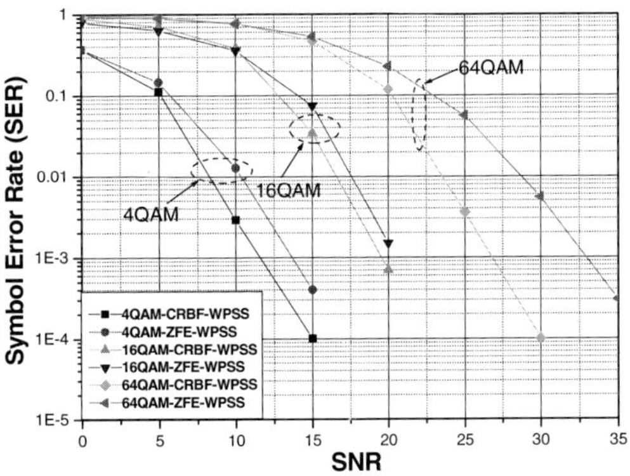


**Fig. 5.** SER performance comparison of CRBF-WPSS and ZFE-WPSS

ML transmitted symbol is the one having the minimum Euclidean distance from the demodulated signal $\tilde{x}$ . According to equation (16), all possible transmitted symbols are denoted by $I(i)$, so that the demodulated signals in (15) are modified as

$$dist[\hat{m}(n), I(i)] \leq dist[\hat{m}(n), I(j)] \ \forall\, i \neq j \tag{17}$$

## 3 Simulation Results

The performances of the wavelet packet spread spectrum system based on CRBF network equalizer and ML detecting algorithm are demonstrated through several simulation examples. We first test the effectiveness and parameter of our CRBF network equalizers for the multipath fading channel. The FIR channel models are taken from [10]. These complex channels cause severe ISI and cross-coupling interference. The DWPT is a three-stage tree and has $M = 2^6 = 64$ input nodes. The wavelet packet function of DWPT is obtained by the known Daubechies wavelet. Walsh – Hadamard codes are used for wavelet domain spreading spectrum. We apply the CRBF network to equalize the channel output. The input layer of the CRBF network is constituted by 17 source nodes. A set of 18 nonlinear activation functions $\beta_i, i = 1, \cdots, 18$ , constitutes the hidden second layer of the CRBF network. The output of the CRBF network is provided by the third layer, which is comprised of 2 output nodes.The rate control parameter of CRBF network is $\eta_w = 10^{-4}$ .The convergence goal of the parameter is $10^4$.In our simulation, we use 4QAM, 16-QAM, and 64QAM signals as the input of channel, for which the minimum distance between consecutive points in the rectangular constellation of the two-dimensional (2-D) signal space representation is two. The additive white Gaussian noise level is taken to be 25dB. 10000 4QAM, 16-QAM, and 64QAM symbols are used to train equalizer and update the equalizer weight, respectively. The mean square error (MSE) of the CRBF network weights versus number of training epochs for 4QAM, 16-QAM, and 64QAM is shown in Figs.3. In Figs.3, the convergence properties of the proposed CRBF network equalizers are also shown. It is evident that the proposed RBF channel equalizer structure offers both fast convergence and low value of the MSE and the lower modulation order is; the faster convergence time is. Performance of OFDM spreading spectrum system which has 64 subcarriers is evaluated in the same channel environment. The Symbol Error Rate (SER) performance comparison of WPSS and OFDM-SS for multipath fading channel is shown in Figs. 4. The simulation results show that the performance of the WPSS is much better than that of the OFDM-SS at all values of Doppler spread. As a comparison, we apply the zero-forcing equalizer method to identify the above channel. The SER performance comparison of CRBF-WPSS and ZFE-WPSS for multipath fading channel is shown in Figs. 5. The simulation result shows that the performance of CRBF-WPSS is much better than that of ZFE-WPSS at all values of Doppler spread.

## 4 Conclusion

In this paper, a novel WPSS communication system based on the CRBF network equalizers and the ML detecting algorithm is presented. The performance of the

WPSS system in multipath fading channel was derived and the CRBF technique is applied to the WPSS system. The CRBF which uses LMS algorithm to obtain the optimized equalizer weight is relatively simple to implement. The simulation results show that in multipath fading channels, the performance of CRBF-WPSS system for M-ary QAM is better than that of CRBF-OFDM-SS for M-ary QAM and the performance of CRBF-WPSS for M-ary QAM is better than that of the ZFE-WPSS for the multipath fading channel. The performances of them are evaluated in the same channel environment. Since mobile channels have fading characterizes, the performance of WPSS in fading channels determines that the WPSS technique applies to mobile communication system.

## Acknowledgments

This work was supported by National Nature Science Foundation of China under contract No.60372048 and Microsoft Research Asia, Teaching Research Award Program for Outstanding Young Teachers in Higher Education Institutions of MOE, P.R.C., sixth subject of Key Project of National Nature Science Foundation of China under contract No. 60496316, National "863" Program of China under contract No. 2005AA123910, and Key Project of Chinese Ministry of Education under contract No. 104171,Research Fund for the Doctoral Program of Higher Education (20050701007).

## References

1. Sklar, B.: Digital Communications. Fundamentals and Applications. 2nd edition, Englewood Cliffs, NJ: Prentice-Hall (2001)
2. Franks, L.E.: Signal Theory. Englewood Cliffs, NJ: Prentice-Hall (1969)
3. Proakis, J.G.: Digital communications, 3rd edition, McGraw-Hill, New York (1995)
4. Wong, K.M., Wu, J.F., Davidson, T.N., Jin, Q., Ching, P.C.: Performance of Wavelet Packet Division Multiplexing In Impulsive and Gaussian Noise. IEEE Trans. Communications. 48 (2000) 1083-1086
5. Wong, K.M., Wu, J.F., Davidson, T.N., Jin, Q.: Wavelet Packet Division Multiplexing And Wavelet Packet Design Under Timing Error Effects. IEEE Trans. Signal Processing. 45 (1997) 2877-2890
6. Jain, V.K., Myers, B.A.: OWSS-A New Signaling System for 100-150 Mb/S Wireless Lans. IEEE Wireless Communications. 10 (2003) 16-24
7. Muayyadi, A., Abu-Rgheff, M.A.: Wavelet-based Multicarrier CDMA System and its Corresponding Multi-user Detection. IEE Proc. Communications. 150 (2003)
8. Yu, X., Zhang, X., Bi, G.: Performance of an MC-CDMA System Based On the Complex Wavelet Packet and Pre-Equalisation Technique. IEE Proc. Communications. 151 (2004)
9. Zhang, H., Fan, H.H., Lindsey, A.R.: Receiver Design for Wavelet-Based Multicarrier CDMA Communications. IEEE Trans. Vehicular Technology. 54 (2005) 615-628
10. Johnson, C.R., Lee, H.J.: On fractionally-spaced equalizer design for microwave radio channels. Proc. Asilomar Conf. on Signals, Systems, and computers. Pacific Grove, CA. (1995) 698-702

# A Big-Neuron Based Expert System

Tao Li[1] and Hongbin Li[2]

[1] Department of Computer Science, Sichuan University, Chengdu 610065, China
litao@scu.edu.cn
[2] Department of Electrical and Computer Engineering, Stevens Institute of Technology, Hoboken, NJ 07030, USA
hli@stevens.edu

**Abstract.** With a new way of knowledge representation and acquirement, inference, and building an expert system based on big-neurons composed of different field expert knowledge presented in this paper, the fundamental theory and architecture of expert system based upon big-neuron theory has thus been built. It is unnecessary to organize a large number of production rules when using big-neurons to build an expert system. The facts and rules of an expert system have already been hidden in big-neurons. And also, it is unnecessary to do a great quantity of tree searching when using this method to do logic reasoning. Machine can do self-organizing and self-learning.

## 1 Introduction

Expert System is one of an active research fields in AI, and has gained many impressive progresses. However, traditional expert systems have gotten big troubles in the fields of knowledge acquirement, self-learning ability, parallel inference, etc [1, 2, 3, 4, 5, 6].

Neural Networks(NN) have the features of massive parallel processing, distributive information store, continuously nonlinear dynamic system, real time processing, self-organizing and self-learning, etc [6, 7]. Hence, we can use these features of NN to solve the problems such as knowledge representation, knowledge acquirement, parallel inference etc. in an expert system [8, 9, 10].

In reference [10] we have presented big-neuron theory, and built the fundamental theory of neuron-oriented programming and system in reference [10, 11]. A new big-neuron can be built based upon the static or dynamic communications (links) among old or new big-neuron objects. The most important contribution of big-neuron theory to the research of neural networks is that it introduces a new way to build neural network systems. Several networks (big-neurons) which are simple and have special functions can produce a larger and more powerful one. In other words, a large complex network can be built out of several simple ones. This paper presents a new way to develop an expert system based upon big-neuron theory.

It is unnecessary to organize a large number of production rules when using big-neurons to build an expert system. The facts and rules of an expert system have already been hidden in big-neurons. Therefore, it is unnecessary to do a great quantity of tree searching when using this method to do logic reasoning. Machine can do self-organizing and self-learning.

D.-S. Huang, K. Li, and G.W. Irwin (Eds.): ICIC 2006, LNCS 4113, pp. 268 – 273, 2006.

## 2 Knowledge Representation Using Big-Neuron

A successful expert system should have the two kinds of knowledge mentioned in [1-5]. Knowledge information processing is the fundaments of an expert system and it has to solve three problems: knowledge representation, acquirement and application.

Although the traditional knowledge representations such as production systems, semantic networks, predicate logic, frame networks etc. have different structures to describe knowledge. However, all of them build their knowledge database by changing the knowledge to the format which can be stored into digital computers. And the inference engine of them is to search the knowledge database depending on a matching algorithm. Thus, these methods have the many disadvantages [8, 9] when the knowledge rules become more and more.

The knowledge representation of traditional expert systems is only one kind of obvious knowledge representation. However, the knowledge representation in big-neuron expert systems is one kind of hidden knowledge representation. Fig.1 shows a big-neuron which has 3 layers and performs the "XOR" operation in logic algebra. If one using production system to describe the "XOR" problem, the network shown in Fig.1 represents the following four rules:

*if* $(x_1 = 0)$ *and* $(x_2 = 0)$ *then* $(y = 0)$ ; *if* $(x_1 = 0)$ *and* $(x_2 = 1)$ *then* $(y = 1)$
*if* $(x_1 = 1)$ *and* $(x_2 = 0)$ *then* $(y = 1)$ ; *if* $(x_1 = 1)$ *and* $(x_2 = 1)$ *then* $(y = 0)$

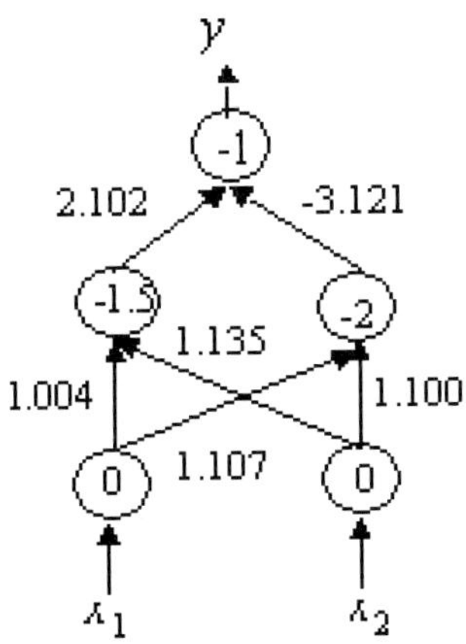


**Fig. 1.** XOR big-neuron

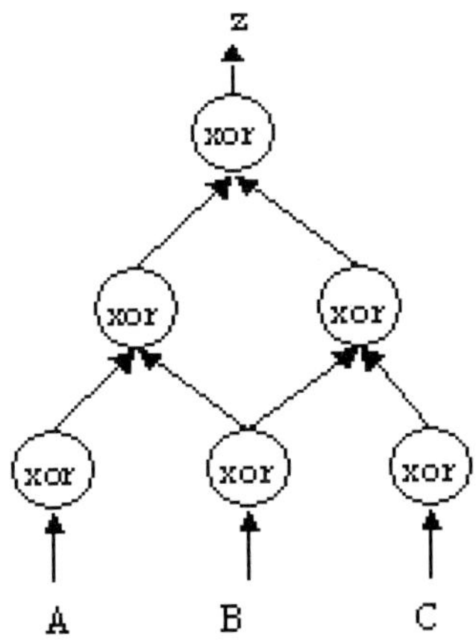


**Fig. 2.** Big-neuron inference

Since the "XOR" operation is complete in logic algebra, thus any logic inference can be implemented by big-neurons which are similar to Fig.1. For example, the big-neuron system shown in Fig.2 performs the following logic reasoning.

$x_1 = A \cdot \overline{B} + \overline{A} \cdot B$ ; $x_2 = B \cdot \overline{C} + \overline{B} \cdot C$ ; $x_3 = A \cdot \overline{C} + \overline{A} \cdot C$ ; $y_1 = x_1 \cdot \overline{x}_2 + \overline{x}_1 \cdot x_2$ ;
$y_2 = x_1 \cdot \overline{x}_2 + \overline{x}_1 \cdot x_2$; $z = y_1 \cdot \overline{y}_2 + \overline{y}_1 \cdot y_2$

## 3 The Architecture of Expert System Based on Big-Neurons

The basic architecture of expert system based on big neurons is shown in Fig.3, where the automatic knowledge acquirement model is used to get the knowledge of experts, the inference system is to solve problems using knowledge database, the interpreting system is used to explain why the decisions have been made, and where the I/O model is a user interface.

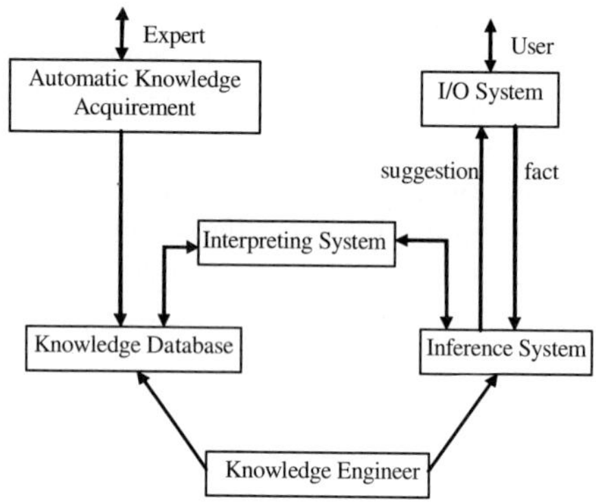


**Fig. 3.** The basic architecture of expert system based on big-neurons

Suppose the inference engine of expert system based upon big-neurons is a computing procedure named $F$ which defined in the following:

- Changing the input logic concepts into input patterns of big-neurons.
- Input the primitive data into the nodes of input layer.
- Forward computing in big-neuron system:
  1) $F(n_i) = y_i$, where $n_i$ is a simple neuron, $y_i$ is the output value of neurons $n_i$ and given by $y_i = f_i(\sum w_{ij} y_j + \theta)$, where $\theta_i$ is the threshold, $w_{ij}$ is link weight and $f_i$ is a nonlinear monotonous function respectively.
  2) $F(N_i) = \bigcup F(n_j), n_j \in N_i, j = 1, \cdots, \#N$, $N_i$ is a big neuron.
- Output pattern interpreting.

The inference engine shown in above has the following features:

- The computing of big-neurons in the same layer of a network and the neurons in the same layer of a big-neuron is completely parallel processing. The message passing between layers can be processed by the method of pipeline parallel processing. Therefore, it is a parallel reasoning procedure.
- There are no "matching conflict" problems.

The inference procedure is only dependent on the parameters of a network that can be adjusted by its learning algorithm. Thus, it is a self-adaptive inference too.

## 4 The Implementation of Expert System Based on Big-Neurons

In a big-neuron expert system, a single knowledge is a big-neuron and the inference is a procedure of the recall of the big-neuron. The knowledge database is a set of big-neurons which is also a big-neuron. Actually, the entire expert system is just only a bigger big-neuron. According to the big-neuron theory, one can build an expert system based upon big-neurons composed of many different field expert knowledge. Since big-neurons have unified internal knowledge representation and input/output structures, thus it is possible to create some links among big-neurons which have different topology. Thus, any big-neuron set can build a large and complex network using link matrix. Therefore, it is possible to build an extensive knowledge expert system composed of different field expert knowledge. Fig.4 shows how to build an extensive knowledge expert system, where $F = \sum_{i=1}^{k} w_i \cdot F_i$ .

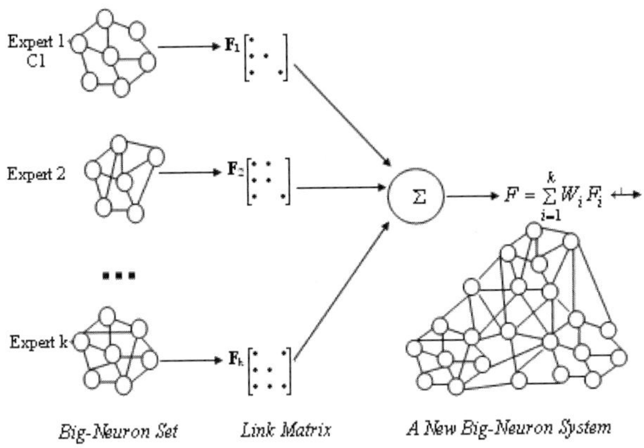


**Fig. 4.** Building an extensive knowledge expert system based on big-neurons

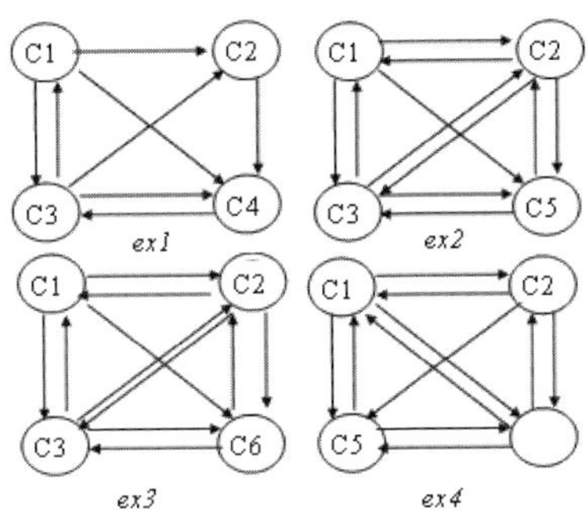


**Fig. 5.** Examples of big-neuron expert system

Consider the simple example shown in Fig.5, where there are only six conceptual nodes and four expert systems named ex1, ex2, ex3 and ex4 respectively. Each expert system uses four conceptual nodes where the corresponding link matrix is shown in following:

$$F_1=\begin{bmatrix}0&1&-1&1&0&0\\0&0&0&-1&0&0\\-1&1&0&-1&0&0\\0&0&1&0&0&0\\0&0&0&0&0&0\\0&0&0&0&0&0\end{bmatrix} F_2=\begin{bmatrix}0&1&-1&0&1&0\\1&0&-1&0&1&0\\-1&-1&0&0&1&0\\0&0&0&0&0&0\\0&1&-1&0&0&0\\0&0&0&0&0&0\end{bmatrix} F_3=\begin{bmatrix}0&1&-1&0&0&0\\-1&0&1&0&0&-1\\-1&-1&0&0&0&1\\0&0&0&0&0&0\\0&0&0&0&0&0\\1&-1&-1&0&0&0\end{bmatrix} F_4=\begin{bmatrix}0&1&0&0&1&-1\\-1&0&0&0&1&1\\0&0&0&0&0&0\\0&0&0&0&0&0\\1&0&0&0&0&-1\\1&-1&0&0&-1&0\end{bmatrix}$$

Fig.6 shows a combinative expert system named EX that includes ex1, ex2, ex3 and ex4 respectively. The link matrix of EX is shown in the Fig. 7:

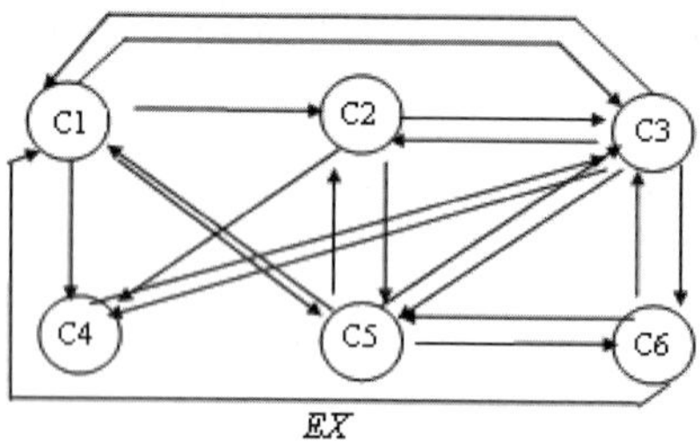


**Fig. 6.** An example of combination expert system

$$F=\begin{bmatrix}0&4&-3&1&2&-1\\-1&0&0&-1&2&0\\-3&-1&0&-1&1&1\\0&0&1&0&0&0\\1&1&-1&0&0&-1\\2&-2&-1&0&-1&0\end{bmatrix}$$

**Fig. 7.** The matrix of EX

In this way, we can design a real "know-all". However, since the disadvantages of traditional knowledge representation, it is impossible for traditional methods to implement the combination of expert systems. The way of expert system based upon the big-neuron theory overcomes the disadvantages of the inference mechanism, knowledge representation and acquirement of traditional expert systems. It develops a new way for modern expert systems. It is convenient to combine many different expert systems and produce a larger, more powerful one. In other words, it is possible to design a real "know-all" expert system.

## 5 Conclusion

With a new way of knowledge representation and acquirement, inference, and building an expert system based on big-neurons composed of different field expert knowledge presented in this paper, the fundamental theory of expert system based upon big-neurons has been built. It is unnecessary to organize a large number of production rules when using big-neurons to build an expert system. The facts and rules have already been hidden in big-neurons. And also, it is unnecessary to do a great quantity of tree searching when using this method to do logic reasoning. Machine can do self-organizing and self-learning.

The theory of big-neuron expert system provides a new way to solve the problems such as knowledge acquirement, parallel inference, ..., etc. which are very difficult to the expert system based on the traditional AI methods.

## Acknowledgments

This work is supported by the National Natural Science Foundation of China under Grant No. 60373110, 60573130 and 60502011, the National Research Foundation for the Doctoral Program of Higher Education of China under Grant No.20030610003, the New Century Excellent Expert Program of Ministry of Education of China under Grant No.NCET-04-0870, and the Innovation Foundation of Sichuan University under Grant No.2004CF10.

## References

1. Mookerjee, V. S., Michael, V. M.: Sequential Decision Models for Expert System Optimization. IEEE Trans. Knowl. Data Eng. 15(5) (2003) 675-687
2. Mookerjee, V. S.: Debiasing Training Data for Inductive Expert System Construction. IEEE Trans. Knowl. Data Eng. 13(3) (2001) 497-512
3. Michael, V. M.: Sequential Decision Models for Expert System Optimization. IEEE Trans. Knowl. Data Eng. 9(5) (1997) 675-687
4. Stephen, I. G.: Connectionist Expert Systems. Commun. ACM 47(2) (2004) 152-169
5. Gurgen, F.: Neural-network-based Decision Making in Diagnostic Applications. IEEE Engineering in Medicine and Biology Magazine, 18(4) (1999) 89 – 93
6. Shi, Z.Z.: Neural Computing. The Publishing House of Ele. Industry, China (1994)
7. Huang, S.H., Endsley, M.R.: Providing Understanding of the Behavior of Feed Forward Neural Networks. IEEE Trans. Syst. Man Cybern., 27 (1997) 465-474
8. Tomsovic, K.: An Expert System Assisting Decision-Making of Reactive Power/Voltage Control. IEEE Trans. on Power Apparatus and Systems, PWRS-1 (1996) 195-201
9. Li, T.: An Intelligent Neuron Network Programming System (NNPS), ACM SIGPLAN Notices, 35(3) (2000) 65-72
10. Reed, R.: Pruning Algorithms—A Survey. IEEE Trans. Neural Networks, 4 (1993) 740–747
11. Li, T.: The Fundamental Theory of Big-Neuron. Proceedings of ICNNSP (1995) 382-386
12. Li, T.: ONPL: A Neuron-Oriented Programming Language. High Tech. Letter, 7, (2001) 56-59

# A Bottom-Up OCR System for Mathematical Formulas Recognition

Wei Wu[1,*], Feng Li[1], Jun Kong[2], Lichang Hou[1], and Bingdui Zhu[1]

[1] Dept. Appl. Math., Dalian University of Technology, Dalian 116024, China
wuweiw@dlut.edu.cn
[2] Northeast Normal University, Changchun 130024, China

**Abstract.** An OCR system is presented to understand mathematical formulas in binary printed document images. The system utilizes a novel component-labeling algorithm for extracting local maximum components from image, and uses these components to locate the mathematical formulas. A character recognition algorithm based on neural networks is then adopted. For segmenting merged characters in the image, a novel segmentation algorithm based on a modified SOM neural network was introduced into the system. With the employment of LL(1) grammar, this system can convert the recognition results into a LaTeX file.

## 1 Introduction

Optical Character Recognition (OCR) has been extensively studied in recent years. The recognition ratio of normal printed text has achieved a high standard. However, there are various kinds of special elements such as tables, pictures, mathematical formulas etc. in document images. In particular, we are interested in the extraction and recognition of mathematical formulas. Anderson [1] has discussed mathematical formula recognition in 1968. Recently, there has been growing interest in formula recognition [2,3].

This paper reports our progress in constructing an OCR system prototype which can understand mathematical formulas. The system analyzes the document image through a bottom-up approach, locates the mathematical formulas, and recognizes the characters in the sub-images with formulas by using an artificial neural network. After character recognition, LL(1) grammar [4] is used to analyze the structure of the formula. Our system eventually convert the output result into LaTeX format. A novel segmentation method is also presented for merged characters by utilizing Self-Organizing Map (SOM) neural network [5].

The remaining of the paper is divided into five sections as follows. Section 2 introduces the definition of local maximum component and the corresponding labeling algorithm. The character recognition method is given in Sect. 3. Section 4 is devoted to the segmentation method for merged characters. Section 5 shows how to analyze the structure of formula and convert the formula image into LaTeX format text. A brief conclusion is given in the last section.

* Corresponding author, supported by the National Natural Science Foundation of China (10471017).

D.-S. Huang, K. Li, and G.W. Irwin (Eds.): ICIC 2006, LNCS 4113, pp. 274–279, 2006.

## 2 Local Maximum Component and Labeling Algorithm

The document image analysis in our system follows a bottom-up approach. The first step is to label the connected components of the image. Let us introduce the definition of local maximum components as follows [6].

**Definition 1.** *Let $A$ and $B$ be two connected components of image $I$, or $A, B \in I$ in symbol, and let their external contours be $C(A)$ and $C(B)$, respectively. When $C(A)$ is completely surrounded by $C(B)$, we write $C(A) \subset C(B)$.*

**Definition 2.** *A connected component $A \in I$ is called a local maximum component of $I$, if $C(A) \not\subset C(B)$ for any other connected component $B \in I$.*

**Definition 3.** *The minimum abscissa, minimum ordinate, maximum abscissa and maximum ordinate of all pixels of a connected component $A \in I$ form a rectangle, called the minimum covering rectangle of $A$ and denoted by $R(A)$.*

For a given image $S$, we associate with it a blank image $T$ of the same size to store the labels assigned to all the components. Scan the source image $S$ line by line. When a black pixel $P$ is encountered, we go clockwise along the external contour $C(A)$ of the connected component $A$ which contains $P$, record the position of $C(A)$ in $T$, and save the location of $R(A)$. Then, scan $R(A)$ line by line, delete all the pixels belong to the interior of $C(A)$ (including $C(A)$) in image $S$. Repeat this process until all black pixels in $S$ are deleted. In the end, the external contours of all the local maximum components in image $S$ have been saved in $T$. See Fig. 1 and Fig. 2 for an illustration.

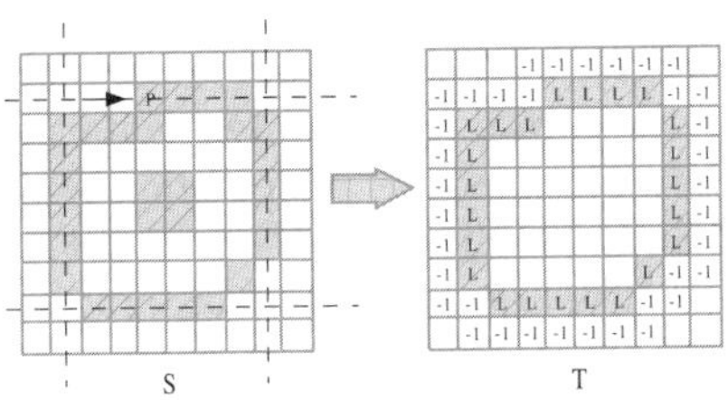

**Fig. 1.** Source image S and target image T

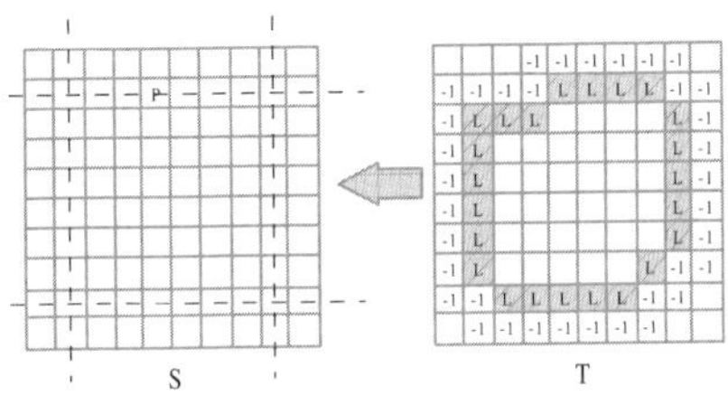

**Fig. 2.** Delete the black pixels in local maximum component

Experiments ([6]) have shown that the new labeling algorithm is more efficient and flexible than the traditional ones [7,8]. After the component labeling, we are to adopt the method of A. Kacem et al. [9,10] to extract the mathematical formula's image from the document image for further processing.

## 3 Symbol Recognition in Mathematical Expression

We use 38-dimensional Zernike moments [11] to extract the feature of characters in the image, and then use a principal component analysis neural network [12]

to compress the dimension of data from 38 to 18. A previous work on junction recognition [13] has indicated that the multi-classifier composed by SOM and BP neural network can achieve a high recognition ratio. Therefore, this multi-classifier is also used in our novel system to recognize the symbols in the mathematical formula image [14]. We utilize SOM neural network to classify 185 mathematical symbols [15] of LaTeX. There are 35 neurons arranged in a ring in our SOM neural network and each neuron is affected only by its two neighboring neurons. The neighborhood function of network is

$$h(d_{jc}, k) = \begin{cases} \eta(k), \|c - j\| \le \Delta(k) \\ 0, \text{otherwise} \end{cases} \tag{1}$$

where $d_{jc}$ is the distance between the winner unit $V_c$ and another unit $V_j$, and $\eta(k)$ and $\Delta(k)$ are functions of the iteration time $k$.

The training of the SOM network is divided into two steps. In the first step, we initialize $\eta(0) = 0.9$, $\Delta(0) = 10$ and the maximum iteration time $K = 10000$, and define $\eta(k) = \eta(0)(1 - k/K)$, $\Delta(k) = \Delta(0)(1 - k/K)$. At the second step we set $\eta(k) \equiv 0.005$, $\Delta(k) \equiv 0$.

The 185 symbols are divided into 35 classes after the training [16]. Then, we train 35 BP neural networks respectively for each class to recognize the symbols which belong to this class, and save the recognition result in LaTeX format. The recognition ratio of each BP neural network exceeds 90% after training [16].

## 4 Merged Characters Segmentation

Our system regards the symbol that fails to be recognized as merged characters and uses an SOM neural network to segment them [17]. Our method utilizes SOM to locate the white regions in the image. We will get several segmentation paths by connecting the centers of larger white pixel regions which often exist between merged characters. The traditional SOM training algorithm will lead the neurons to tend to assemble densely at several large white regions and the distance between neurons becomes very small (see Fig. 3), which may make the segmentation process more sensitive and difficult. We try to overcome this difficulty by modifying the traditional training rule so as to make the neurons repulse, rather than attract, each other (see Fig. 4). So we use the following modified updating rule:

$$\begin{cases} \Delta W_c(k+1) = \eta(k) h(d_c, k) \left(\xi^{(u)} - W_c(k)\right) \\ \Delta W_j(k+1) = m_{jc} \Delta W_c(k+1), j \ne c \end{cases} \tag{2}$$

where $m_{cj}$ represents the repulsion factor between neuron $j$ and neuron $c$ (see Fig. 4). The balance positions of all neurons influence each other via the factor $m_{jc}$. The receptive field $R_j$ is affected by $m_{jc}$, too. All the neurons are arranged in a $3 \times 3$ matrix as shown in Fig. 4.

We select the coordinates of the white pixels $\xi^{(\mu)} = (x_1, x_2)$ as input at each epoch of training and use the off-line training method. Define the step function

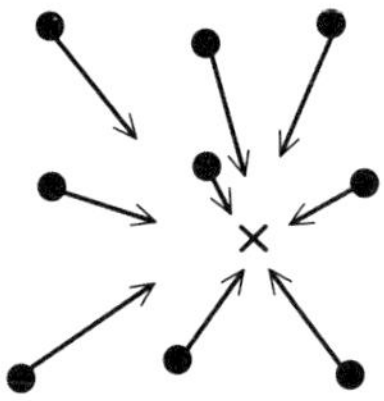

**Fig. 3.** Traditional updating rule for SOM. × :input, •: neurons

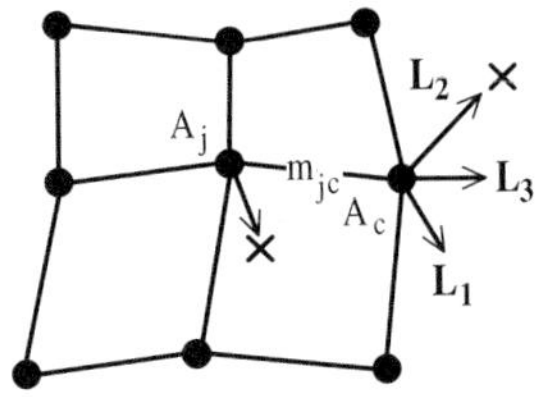


**Fig. 4.** New updating rule for SOM. $L_1$: influence of neuron $j$'s updating on neuron $c$ through $m_{jc}$; $L_2$:influence of the input signal on neuron $c$; $L_3$=$L_1$ + $L_2$.

$\eta(t) = 1/t$, the repulsion factor $m_{ik} = 1/[3\|i-k\|^2]$, and the neighborhood function

$$h(d_{cj},k) = \begin{cases} \exp\left(-\frac{\left(\xi^{(\mu)}-W_j(t)\right)^2}{(\max(n,m))^2}\right), j=c \\ 0, j \neq c \end{cases} \quad (3)$$

The second column nodes (neurons) are chosen as candidate segmentation nodes after network training. These nodes are grouped and connected to form candidate segmentation paths (overall $C_3^1+C_3^2+C_3^3=7$ pathes). For each group of the nodes, draw vertical lines upward/downward from the top/bottom nodes, respectively, to perform a segmentation. Calculate the cost of 7 candidate paths, where a black or white pixel carries a cost of 10 or 1 respectively. Finally, we take a least-cost path as the final segmentation path. We observe that the ratio of successive segmentation improves by properly adjusting the initial position of the second column [18].

From the experiments, we find that the SOM segmentation works particularly good for italic font and is not affected by the stroke's thickness. The SOM segmentation is a bit more time consuming than the most often used shortest-path method [19]. There are 332 merged characters, out of the total 2214 merged characters, that can be segmented by the SOM segmentation, but not by the shortest-path method. Therefore, we suppose that the SOM segmentation can make a good supplement of the shortest-path method.

## 5 Recombination of Mathematical Expressions

A novel formula structure analysis method [20] base on LL(1) grammar [4] is adopted in our system for auto analysis of the formula structure. The syntax of mathematical formula is given by context-free grammar rule [4].

A key step of the structure analysis is the location of the superscripts and subscripts in the formula. We divide all the symbol structures into five classes in terms of the difference of the location of the symbol's superscripts and subscripts (see Table 1). Start from the current symbol, search the successive symbol, and then search the superscripts and subscripts region of it.

**Table 1.** Classification of subscript and superscript domains

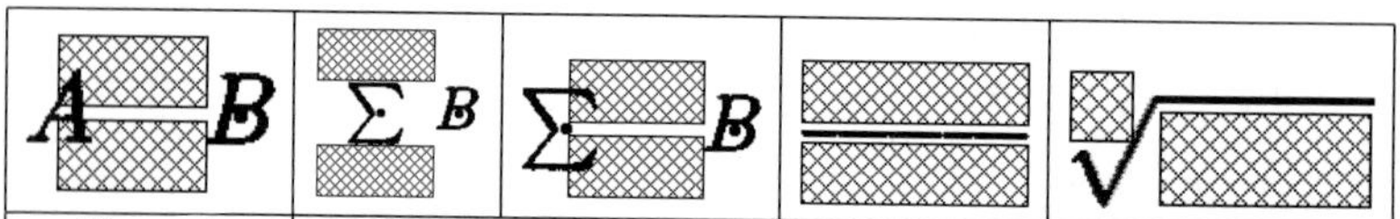

| Normal | Changeable Limit | Fraction Line | Radical Sign |
|---|---|---|---|

**Table 2.** Results of the new OCR system

| Source Image | Result of OCR and Rebuild |
|---|---|
| $\begin{vmatrix} a+b+c & uv \\ a+b & c+d \end{vmatrix} = 7$ | $\begin{vmatrix} a+b+c & uv \\ a+b & c+d \end{vmatrix} = 7$ |
| $E = \frac{A}{2} \sum_{i=1}^{N} \sum_{p=1}^{K} \sum_{q \neq p}^{K} V_{pi} V_{qi}$ | $E = \frac{A}{2} \sum_{i=1}^{N} \sum_{p=i}^{K} \sum_{q \neq p}^{K} V_{pi} V_{qi}$ |
| $x^{(a+b)^{2^{17}}} x_{a_3+7} x_{a_3} + 7$ | $x^{(a+b)^{\# i7}} x_{a_\varepsilon+7} x_{a_s} + 7$ |
| $\int_{-4}^{r^2+1} \frac{x+1}{x+2} dx$ | $\int_{-4}^{r+1} \frac{x+1}{x+2} dx$ |
| $1 + \frac{\sum_{i=2}^{N} \lim_{n \to \infty} y}{\frac{123}{456} * 9999} * 4/5 - 6$ | $1 + \frac{\sum_{i=2}^{N} \lim_{\Psi \leftarrow \infty} y}{\frac{123}{456} * 6999} * 4/5 - 6$ |
| $\lim_{(v,v') \to (0,0)} \frac{H(z+v) - H(z+v') - BH(z)(v-v')}{\lVert v - v' \rVert} = 0$ | $\lim_{(v,v) \leftarrow (0,o)} \frac{H(z+v) - H(z+v), - BH(\#)(v-v)}{\lVert v - v \rVert} = 0$ |

Different from traditional parsers [4], there is an additional symbol stack in our parser. The novel parser searches the next symbol region, superscript region and subscript region of the current symbol and store the most left symbol into the symbol stack. The parser then compares the top element of the symbol stack with the top element of the analysis stack, take the elements out to build the syntax tree if the top elements match, or otherwise write down the index of the parsing table and push the new production into stack. The detailed diagram of the parsing process can be found in [20]. By a single scan of the formula image, our system can convert the recognition result for the printed formula into a LaTeX format file (see Table 2, where "#" indicates a symbol failing to be recognized).

## 6 Conclusion

An OCR system is presented which can successfully recognize the mathematic formula in printed binary document image and output the result into LaTeX format. The grammar and syntax analysis rules used for our novel system to convert the planar distribution of symbols into a symbol tree work effectively. In our future work, we shall try to raise the recognition ratio and to improve the segmentation of merged characters. Since there exist logical relationships between the symbols in formulas, we plan to introduce the semantic analysis into our system.

## References


1. Anderson, R. H.: Syntax-Directed Recognition of Hand-Printed Two-Dimensional Mathematics. In M. Klerer and J. Reinfelds (eds) Interactive Systems for Experimental Applied Matheties. Academic Press. New York (1968) 436–459
2. Lee, H. J., Wang, J. S.: Design of a Mathematical Expression Understanding System. Pattern Recognition Letters **18(3)** (1997) 289–298
3. Eto, Y., Suzuki, M.: Mathematical Formula Recognition Using Virtual Link Network. Proc. ICDAR (2001) 762–767
4. Louden, K. C.: Compiler Construction: Principles and Practice. Brooks Cole.1997
5. Kohonen, T.: The Self-Organizing Map. Proc. IEEE **78(9)** (1990) 1464–1480
6. Li, F., Wu, W.: Local Maximum Component-Labeling Based on Parallel Local Operation Sequence for Layout Analysis. Proc. WCICA (2006) (accepted)
7. Chang, F., Chen, C-J., Lu, C-J.: A Linear-Time Component Labeling Algorithm Using Contour Tracing Technique. Computer Vision Image Understanding **93(2)** (2004) 206–220
8. Drivas, D., Amin, A.: Page Segmentation and Classification Utilising Bottom-Up Approach. Proc. ICDAR (1995) [**11**] 610–614
9. Kacem, A., Belaid, A. and Ben Ahmed, M.: EXTRAFOR: Automatic EXTRAction of Mathematical FORmulas. Proc. ICDAR (1999) [**28**] 527–530
10. Kacem, A., Belaid, A. and Ben Ahmed, M.: Automatic Segmentation of Mathematical Documents. Proc. ACIDCA'00. Monastir - Tunisia (2000) 86–91
11. Mukunkan, R., Ramakrishnan, K. R.: Fast Computation of Legendre and Zernike Moments. Pattern Recognition. **28(9)**(1995) 1433–1442
12. Oja, E., Ogawa, H.: Principal Component Analysis by Homogeneous Neural Network. IEICE. Trans. INF. & SYST., 1992.5, E75-D(3)
13. Guo, L. B, Wu, W.: Recognition of Junctions in Two-Dimensional Images by Neural Networks. Journal of Dalian University of Technology. **43**(2003) 548–550
14. Kong, J., Wu, W., Zhao, W. H.: Neural Networks for Recognition of Mathematical Symbols. Acta Scientiarum Naturalium Universitatis Jilinensis. 2001.3 11–16
15. Deng, J. S., Peng, R. R., Chen, C. S.: LaTeX $2_\varepsilon$ Science and Technology Typesetting Guide. Beijing. Science Press. 2001
16. Hou, L. C.: Design and Implement of Printed Mathematical Formula Recognition System. Master Degree Thesis of Dalian University of Technology. 2004.6
17. Hou, L. C., Wu, W., Zhu, B. D., Li, F.: A Segmentation Method for Merged Characters Using Self-Organizing Map Neural Networks. to appear
18. Zhu, B. D.: Mathematic Expression Recognition. Master Degree Thesis of Dalian University of Technology. 2005.6
19. Wang, J.: Segmentation of Merged Characters by Neural Network and Shortest Path. Pattern Recognition. **27(5)**(1994) 649–658
20. Hou, L. C., Wu, W.: Structure Analysis of Mathematical Expressions Using LL(1) Grammar. To appear in Journal of Dalian University of Technology. **46(3)**(2006)

# A Fast Robust Learning Algorithm for RBF Network Against Outliers

Mei-juan Su and Wei Deng

School of Computer Science & Technology
Soochow University, Suzhou, 215006, China
{210413011, dengw}@suda.edu.cn

**Abstract.** Training data set often contains outliers, which can cause substantial deterioration of the approximation realized by a neural network. In this paper, a fast robust learning algorithm against outliers for RBF network is presented. The algorithm uses the subtractive clustering(SC) method to select hidden node centers of RBF network, and the gradient descent method with the scaled robust loss function(SRLF) as the objective function to adjust hidden node widths and the connection weights of the network. Therefore, the learning of RBF network has robustness on dealing with outliers and fast rate of convergence. The experimental results show the advantages of the learning algorithm over traditional learning algorithms for RBF network.

## 1 Introduction

Radial basis function(RBF) neural networks form a class of artificial neural networks(ANNs), which has certain advantages over other types of ANNs, such as better function approximation capabilities, simpler network structures and faster learning algorithms [1]. Many learning algorithms have been proposed for RBF networks, among them are $k$-means clustering learning algorithm [2], orthogonal least squares(OLS) learning algorithm [3], gradient descent learning algorithm [1], growing and pruning learning algorithm [4].

However, these algorithms generally assume that the training data set does not contain outliers, which can cause substantial deterioration of the approximation realized by a neural network. In 1995, Sánchez presented a robust learning method for RBF network based on scaled robust loss function (SRLF) and conjugate gradient method [5], but it can not select hidden node centers. In 1999, Chien-Cheng et al developed a new kind of robust RBF neural networks which can approximate constant values and have high robustness to outliers [6]. In 2000, Meiqin et al presented a robust learning algorithm incorporating improved genetic algorithm(GA) [7].

In this paper, a new learning algorithm for RBF network is proposed. The algorithm uses the subtractive clustering(SC) method to select hidden node centers of RBF network, and the gradient descent method with SRLF as the objective function to adjust hidden node widths and connection weights of network. Due to approximating underlying mapping rather than interpolating training data set, the algorithm has strong robustness against outliers. At the same time, by

D.-S. Huang, K. Li, and G.W. Irwin (Eds.): ICIC 2006, LNCS 4113, pp. 280–285, 2006.

using the SC method, the rate of the convergence of the algorithm is fast. The experimental results by comparing the performance of the algorithm to that of the traditional algorithms show these advantages of it.

## 2 The SC Method and SRLF

### 2.1 The SC Method

Determination of the hidden node centers is the most crucial step in the development of a successful RBF network model [8]. The SC method[8,12] considers each input data point as a potential hidden node center. A measure of the potential of point $i$ is defined as a function of Euclidean distances to all other points:

$$P_i = \sum_{l=1}^{N} \exp(-a||\boldsymbol{x}_i - \boldsymbol{x}_l||^2) \ . \tag{1}$$

where $\{(\boldsymbol{x}_i, y_i) \mid \boldsymbol{x}_i \in R^n, y_i \in R, i = 1, \ldots, N\}$ is the training data set, $N$ is the number of input data points, $a$ is a design parameter. There are two additional design parameters $\beta$ and $\varepsilon$ in the SC method described as follows:

1. For $i = 1, ..., N$ calculate the potential values $P_i$.
2. Set $L = 1$ and select the data point with highest potential value as the first hidden node center. Let $\boldsymbol{x}_1^*$ be the location of that point and $P_1^*$ its potential value.
3. Revise the potential of each data point $i = 1, ..., N$ by the formula:

$$P_i = P_i - P_1^* \exp(-\beta||\boldsymbol{x}_i - \boldsymbol{x}_1^*||^2) \ . \tag{2}$$

   where $\beta$ is smaller than $a$.
4. If the inequality

$$\max_i P_i \leq \varepsilon P_1^* \ . \tag{3}$$

   is true, stop the algorithm, else set L=L+1 and find the data point corresponding to the highest potential value. Let $\boldsymbol{x}_L^*$ be the location of that point and $P_L^* = \max_i P_i$ its potential value.
5. Select $\boldsymbol{x}_L^*$ as a new hidden node center. Revise the potential of each data point $i = 1, ..., N$ by the formula:

$$P_i = P_i - P_L^* \exp(-\beta||\boldsymbol{x}_i - \boldsymbol{x}_L^*||^2) \ . \tag{4}$$

   and return to 4.

### 2.2 SRLF

The following continuous function for tanh-estimator is used from [9,10,11]:

$$\psi_0(x) = \begin{cases} x & , \ 0 \leq |x| \leq p \ . \\ c_1 \cdot \tanh(c_2(c - |x|))\text{sign(x)} & , \ p < |x| < c \ . \\ 0 & , \ c \leq |x| \ . \end{cases} \tag{5}$$

From (5) and after integration and translation along the $y$-axis, the robust loss function $\rho_0(x)$ is obtained in (6).

$$\rho_0(x) = \begin{cases} \frac{1}{2} \cdot x^2 & , \ 0 \leq |x| \leq p \ . \\ \frac{1}{2} \cdot p^2 + \frac{c_1}{c_2} \cdot \ln\left(\frac{\cosh(c_2 \cdot (c-p))}{\cosh(c_2 \cdot (c-|x|))}\right) & , \ p < |x| < c \ . \\ \frac{p^2}{2} + \frac{c_1}{c_2} \cdot (\cosh(c_2 \cdot (c-p))) & , \ c \leq |x| \ . \end{cases} \tag{6}$$

For a choice of a scale parameter $s$ along $x$-axis, the following *scaled robust loss function*(SRLF) $\rho(x,s)$ and its first derivative $\psi(x,s)$ are obtained:

$$\rho(x,s) = s^2 \cdot \rho_0(x/s) \ . \tag{7}$$

$$\psi(x,s) = s \cdot \psi_0(x/s) \ . \tag{8}$$

The effect of using scaled robust loss function $\rho(x,s)$ instead of quadratic loss function $\frac{1}{2}x^2$ can be explained for three different regions of independent variable $x$. For $|x| \leq sp$, the square of the residuals is taken within the robustization process as when using quadratic loss function. For $sp < |x| < sc$, the influence of the residuals is taken decreasingly with their absolute value. For $sc \leq |x|$, no influence of residuals is taken into consideration, this corresponds to an automatic detection of outliers and at the same time an avoidance of their negative influence on the regression function [5].

## 3 Our Proposed Algorithm

Based on the SC method and SRLF, we proposed a learning algorithm for RBF network, which is described as follows:

1. Select hidden node centers $\{\boldsymbol{c}_j \,|\, \boldsymbol{c}_j \in R^n, j = 1, \cdots, m\}$ using the SC method, where $m$ is the number of hidden nodes .
2. Compute Gaussian widths $\{\sigma_j \mid \sigma_j \in R, j = 1, \cdots, m\}$ using the $K$-nearest neighbor heuristic, $K = \lceil m/4 \rceil$, initialize connection weights $\{w_j \mid w_j \in R, j = 1, \cdots, m\}$ to random values, set the fitting error threshold $\theta$ and maximum number of epochs $P$, let the number of epochs $k = 1$.
3. Calculate the residuals of each input data point $i = 1, \cdots, N$ by the formula:
$$r_i = y_i - \sum_{j=1}^{m} w_j \cdot \varphi(\boldsymbol{x}_i, \boldsymbol{c}_j, \sigma_j) \ . \tag{9}$$
$$\varphi(\boldsymbol{x}_i, \boldsymbol{c}_j, \sigma_j) = \exp(-||\boldsymbol{x}_i - \boldsymbol{c}_j||^2 / 2\sigma_j^2) \ . \tag{10}$$
If the mean sum of squared residuals is smaller than $\theta$, go to 7.
4. Determine the scale parameter $s$. The absolute values of residuals in (9) are sorted in increasing order, resulting $\{|r_i^{'}| | i = 1, \ldots, N\}$. Let $i^* = \lceil N \cdot (1-q) \rceil$, where $q$ is maximal percentage of outliers in the training data set, thus $s$ is obtained in (11).
$$s = |r_{i^*}^{'}| / c \ . \tag{11}$$
where $c$ is defined in (5).

5. Apply gradient descent method to the SRLF. For each input data point $i = 1, \cdots, N$ update $\sigma_j$ and $w_j$ with the adjustments of center width $\Delta\sigma_j$ and connection weight $\Delta w_j$, $j = 1, \cdots, m$ :

$$\Delta\sigma_j = \eta \frac{w_j}{\sigma_j^3} \psi(r_i, s)\varphi(\boldsymbol{x}_i, \boldsymbol{c}_j, \sigma_j)||\boldsymbol{x}_i - \boldsymbol{c}_j||^2 \ . \tag{12}$$

$$\Delta w_j = \eta\psi(r_i, s)\varphi(\boldsymbol{x}_i, \boldsymbol{c}_j, \sigma_j) \ . \tag{13}$$

where $\eta$ is the learning speed.
6. If $k < P$, then set $k = k + 1$ and go to 3.
7. End.

## 4 Experimental Results

In order to test the proposed algorithm, we apply it to approximate function $y = \sin(2\pi x)$. The method presented in [13] is used to obtain the training data and test data. Artificially generated outliers will replace some of the original noise-free training data. The function $f$:$[0, 1] \to [-1, 1]$, $f(x) = \sin(2\pi x)$ and equidistant partitions of interval $[0, 1]$ are used to generate $N = 21$ training data points $(x_i, y_i)$, $y_i = f(x_i)$, where $x_i = i * d$, $i = 0, \ldots, N-1 = 20$, $d = 1/(N-1) = 0.05$, and $M = 20$ test data points $(x_t, y_t)$, $y_t = f(x_t)$, where $x_t = (t+0.5)*d$, $t = 0, \ldots, M-1 = 19$. Table 1 shows how outliers replace some of original values of the training data set. Four original $y$-values are replaced. Table 2 lists the parameter values used in this experiment.

The fitting results of the three algorithms, OLS, gradient descent method, and our proposed algorithm, are compared in Fig.1. Table 3 lists number of hidden nodes, mean sum of squared residuals of training data(MSSRT), mean sum of squared residuals of test data(MSSRS), and running time of each algorithm. We can see that the OLS and gradient descent method are seriously influenced by the outliers and have bad approximation results. In contrast, our proposed algorithm enables the mapping realized by RBF network to fit the function very well, and has a high efficiency.

The SC method to select hidden node centers computes the potential of input data in the form of exponent of the Euclidean distances similar to Gaussian function(10), and requires only one pass, so it obtains better clustering results and greatly reduces the running time of the network. Due to SRLF, if an outlier is presented to the network, no adjustment will be made to the widths and weights, so the negative affect of the outlier is avoided and robustness is achieved.

**Table 1.** Outliers to replace four of $N = 21$ noise-free data

| Outliers | x-value | Original $y$-value | Difference value | New $y$-value |
|---|---|---|---|---|
| 1 | 0.10 | 0.58753 | 0.60 | 1.18753 |
| 2 | 0.45 | 0.31038 | 0.55 | 0.86038 |
| 3 | 0.55 | -0.30735 | -0.50 | -0.80735 |
| 4 | 0.85 | -0.81061 | -0.55 | -1.36061 |

**Table 2.** Parameter values

| $a$ | $\beta$ | $\varepsilon$ | $c$ | $p$ | $c_1$ | $c_2$ | $\theta$ | $K$ | $\eta$ | $q$ |
|---|---|---|---|---|---|---|---|---|---|---|
| 80 | 40 | 0.001 | 6.0 | 1.730683 | 1.731965 | 0.925448 | 0.00001 | 800 | 0.005 | 20% |

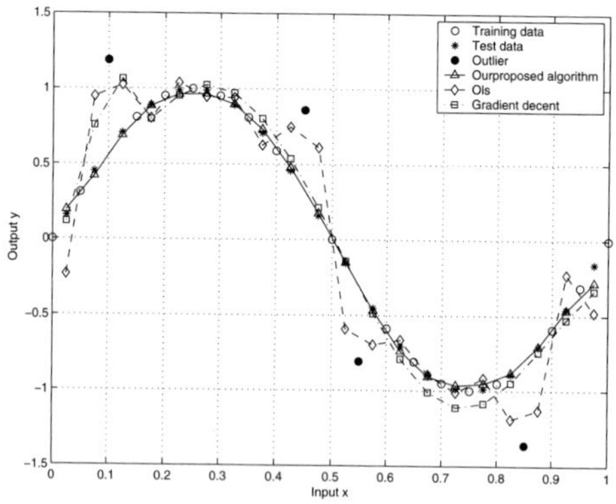


**Fig. 1.** Fitting results of three algorithms

**Table 3.** Running results of three algorithms

| | Our algorithm | OLS | Gradient descent method |
|---|---|---|---|
| No. of hidden nodes | 9 | 20 | 8 |
| MSSRT | 0.0309 | 1.0694e-013 | 0.0139 |
| MSSRS | 5.8140e-004 | 0.1927 | 0.0061 |
| Running time(s) | 1.5620 | 0.2660 | 2.9840 |

## 5 Conclusion

In this work, a new learning algorithm is proposed for RBF network. Since it uses the SC method to select hidden node centers and SRLF as the objective function for gradient descent method, the algorithm has two advantages over the traditional algorithms: strong robustness against outliers, and high speed of convergence. In the future research work, we will apply the algorithm to pattern classification.

## References

1. Haykin, S.: Neural Networks, A Comprehensive Foundation (Second Edition). Tsinghua University Press & Prentice Hall, (2001) 298-305
2. Moody, J., Darken C.: Fast Learning in Networks of Locally-tuned Processing Units. Neural Computation, **1**(2) (1989) 281-294
3. Chen, S., Cowan, C. F. N., Grant, P. M.: Orthogonal Least Squares Learning Algorithm for Radial Basis Function Networks. IEEE Transactions on Neural Networks, **2**(2) (1991) 302-309

4. Guang-Bin, H., Saratchandran, P., Narasimhan, S.: A Generalized Growing and Pruning RBF Neural Network for Function Approximation. IEEE Transactions on Neural Networks, **16** (1) (2005) 57-67
5. Sánchez, V. D. A: Robustization of a learning method for RBF networks. Neurocomputing, **9** (1995) 85-94
6. Chien-Cheng, L., Pau-Choo, C., Jea-Rong, T., Chein-I, C.: Robust Radial Basis Function Neural Networks. IEEE Transactions on Systems, Man, and Cybernetics, **29** (6) (1999) 674-685
7. Meiqin, L., Xiaoxin, L.: A Robust Learning Algorithm for RBF Neural Networks. Journal of Huazhong University of Science and Technology (Nature Science), **28** (2) (2000) 8-10 (In Chinese)
8. Haralambos, S., Alex, A., George, B.: A Fast Training Algorithm for RBF Networks Based on Subtractive Clustering. Neurocomputing, **51** (2003) 501-505
9. Hampel, F. R., Rousseeuw, P. J., & Ronchetti, E.: The Change-of-variance Curve and Optimal Redescending M-estimators. J. American Statistical Assoc., **761** (1981) 643-648
10. Hampel, F. R., Ronchetti, E. M., Rousseeuw, P. J., Stahel, W.A.: Robust Statistics: The Approach Based on Influence Function. Wiley, New York (1986)
11. David, S. C., Ramesh, C. J.: A Robust Back Propagation Learning Algorithm for Function Approximation. IEEE Transactions on Neural Networks, **5** (3) (1994) 467-479
12. Chiu, S. L.: Fuzzy Model Identification Based on Cluster Estimation. J. Intell. Fuzzy Systems, **2** (3) (1994) 267-278
13. Weixiang, Z., Dezhao, C., Shangxu, H.: Detection of Outlier and A Robust BP Algorithm Against Outlier. Computers and Chemical Engineering, **28** (2004) 1403-1408

# A Genetic Algorithm for Constructing Wavelet Neural Networks

Jinhua Xu

Department of Computer Science, East China Normal University
jhxu@cs.ecnu.edu.cn

**Abstract.** In this paper, a new algorithm is proposed for the design of WNNs. The design is performed in an evolutionary way, which allowed us to construct a parsimonious model to satisfy the design requirement. A genetic algorithm (GA) is used to select a wavelet basis, and the fitness of a wavelet is evaluated according to the residue reduction. Output weights are updated using least square techniques. Simulations demonstrate the effectiveness of the proposed algorithm.

## 1 Introduction

Wavelet transforms have emerged as a means of representing a function in a manner which readily reveals properties of the function in localized regions of the joint time-frequency space. The idea of combining wavelets with neural networks has led to the development of wavelet neural networks (WNNs), where wavelets were introduced as activation functions of the hidden neurons in traditional feedforward neural networks [1].

Many issues and problems have to be addressed and resolved when using WNNs. Among them, the determination of a network size and weight parameters is clearly critical. Some research have been done on this problem. In [2], an iterative method which combining genetic algorithms and least squares techniques is proposed for optimizing WNNs. GAs are used for optimal selection of the structure of the WNNs and the parameters of the transfer function of its neurons. Least squares techniques are used to update the weights of the network. In [3], a new class of wavelet networks is proposed, where the model structure for a high dimensional system is chosen to be a superimposition of a number of functions with fewer variables. A forward orthogonal least squares algorithm and the error reduction ratio is applied to select the model terms. In [4], wavelet network is constructed by some selected wavelets from a wavelet basis (or wavelet frame) by exploring the sparseness of training data and using techniques in regression analysis. In [5], an orthogonalized residual based selection (ORBS) algorithm is proposed for WNNs.

The use of evolutionary algorithms (EA) to aid in the artificial neural network (ANN) learning has been a popular approach to address the local optima and design problem of ANN[6]. The typical approach is to combine the strength of backpropagation (BP) in weight learning and EA's capability of searching the architecture space. Some EA methods were proposed to learn both the network structure and connection weights[2],[7],[8].

D.-S. Huang, K. Li, and G.W. Irwin (Eds.): ICIC 2006, LNCS 4113, pp. 286–291, 2006.

Genetic algorithm (GA) is a directed random search technique that is widely applied in optimization problems. This is especially useful for complex optimization problems where the number of parameters is large and the analytical solutions are difficult to obtain. GA can help to find out the optimal solution globally over a domain. In this paper, a genetic algorithm is used to construct wavelet neural networks. A new wavelet to be added to the WNNs will be selected using GA, and output weights are updated using least square techniques. Since the wavelet parameters are integers within a certain range, the search space is greatly reduced compared with the general real-encoded GA in [2].

## 2 Preliminaries

This section briefly review some results on wavelet decompositions and WNNs relevant to the present work.

The wavelet analysis procedure is implemented with dilated and translated versions of a mother wavelet. In theory, the dilation (scale) parameter of a wavelet can be any positive real value and the translation (shift) can be an arbitrary real number. In practice, in order to improve computation efficiency, the values of the shift and scale parameters are often limited to some discrete lattices. This is then referred to as the discrete wavelet transform (DWT). The wavelet decomposition is shown as follows:

$$f(x) = \sum_{j} \sum_{k} c_{j,k} \psi_{j,k}(x), \quad j, k \in \mathbf{Z} \tag{1}$$

where $\psi_{j,k}(x) = 2^{j/2}\psi(2^j x - k)$.

The WNNs stemmed from the DWT have a linear-in-parameter structure[4], [5]. In practical applications, it is unnecessary and impossible to represent a signal using an infinite decomposition of the form (1) in terms of wavelet basis functions. The decomposition (1) are therefore often truncated at an appropriate accuracy. An approximation to a function $f \in L^2(\mathbf{R})$ using the truncated wavelet decomposition with the coarsest resolution $J_{min}$ and the finest resolution $J_{max}$ can be expressed in the following:

$$f(x) = \sum_{j=J_{min}}^{J_{max}} \sum_{k \in K_j} c_{j,k} \psi_{j,k}(x) \tag{2}$$

where $K_j$ are subsets of $\mathbf{Z}$ and often depend on the resolution level $j$ for all compactly supported wavelets and for most rapidly vanishing wavelets. In such a WNN, the positions and dilations of the wavelets are fixed on some discrete lattices and only the weights have to be optimized by training the network using least squares type algorithms.

The wavelet network in (2) may involve a great number of candidate wavelet terms. Experience shows that often many of the terms are redundant and only a small number of significant wavelet terms are necessary to describe a given nonlinear system with a given accuracy. Some basis selection algorithms were proposed to select the significant basis from the candidate wavelet library[4],[5]. However, when the number of the basis in the wavelet library is very large, the heavy computational cost may make the basis selection algorithms not feasible in practice. In this paper, a genetic algorithm is introduced to find the significant wavelets which should be included to the wavelet networks.

## 3 GA-Optimized Wavelet Neural Networks(GA-WNN)

In this section, GA-optimized wavelet neural networks will be described, which start with no wavelet in the WNN and add new wavelets trained using GA.

Suppose the dilation is in the range $[J_{min}, J_{max}]$, where $J_{min}$ and $J_{max}$ are integers which represent the coarsest and finest resolution level respectively. At first stage, no wavelet is added to the network. Use GA to find the dilation and translation parameters of a new wavelet to minimize the residual. If the reduction of the residual error between the desired output and WNN output is greater than a threshold, then add the wavelet to the network, otherwise, retrain a new wavelet using GA. If a wavelet is added to the network successfully, it is orthogonalized to the previously selected wavelet to calculate the optimal weight. Then retrain a new wavelet until a satisfactory solution is found.

Given $N$ pairs of training sample, $\{(x(1), y(1)\}, \cdots, \{x(N), y(N)\}$. Set the desired output $y = [y(1), y(2), \cdots, y(N)]^T$. A WNN with $i-1$ wavelets implements the function given by

$$\hat{y}_{i-1}(x) = \sum_{j=1}^{i-1} w_j \psi_j(x) \tag{3}$$

where $\psi_j(x)$ represents the function implemented by the $j^{th}$ wavelet. Moreover, $r_{i-1}(x) = y(x) - \hat{y}_{i-1}(x)$ is the residual error function for the current network with $i-1$ wavelets. Use GA to train the dilation and translation parameters $\Theta = [d_1, t_1, d_2, t_2, \cdots, d_n, t_n]$, where $n$ is the dimension of the wavelet, which equals to the input dimension of the WNN. The gene number $S$ of the chromosomes is $S = 2n$. In most of the works of WNNs in the literature, for simplicity, it is assumed that the dilations of all dimension for each wavelet are equal, that is, $d_1 = \cdots = d_n = d$. In this case, GA is used to train the dilation and translation parameters $\Theta = [d, t_1, t_2, \cdots, t_n]$. The gene number $S$ of the chromosomes is $S = n + 1$. Set

$$\phi = [\psi(1), \psi(2), \cdots, \psi(N)]^T$$

where $\psi(k) = \prod_{j=1}^{n} \psi(2^{d_j} x_j(k) - t_j)$. Let

$$\hat{y}_i = \hat{y}_{i-1} + w\phi$$
$$r_i = y - \hat{y}_i = r_{i-1} - w\phi$$

with

$$w = (\phi^T \phi)^{-1} \phi^T r_{i-1}. \tag{4}$$

The best $\Theta$ may be selected to minimize the cost function

$$V_i(\Theta) = r_i^T r_i = (r_{i-1} - w\phi)^T (r_{i-1} - w\phi) \\ = r_{i-1}^T r_{i-1} - (\phi^T \phi)^{-1} (\phi^T r_{i-1})^2 \tag{5}$$

Now a genetic algorithm will be proposed to solve the above optimization problem.

1) Encoding Scheme
In this paper, the dilation and translation parameters of a new wavelet, $\Theta$, which are all integers belonging to a certain interval, are encoded into the chromosome. Assume the inputs, $x_j$ are normalized into the unit interval $[0, 1]$ using a priori knowledge and the mother wavelet function is compactly supported on $[s_1, s_2]$, then for a given resolution $d$, the possible values for translation parameter should be between $-(s_2 - 1)$ and $2^d - s_1 - 1$.
2) Evaluation function
Each chromosome in the population will be evaluated by a defined fitness function. The better chromosome will return higher values in this process. From (5), the fitness function to evaluate a chromosome $p_i$ in the population can be chosen as the residue reduction of a new wavelet, which is written as

$$f(p_i) = (\phi^T \phi)^{-1} (\phi^T r_{i-1})^2 \tag{6}$$

3) Selection operation: Spinning the roulette wheel is used.
4) Crossover operator
A conventional one-point crossover operator has been employed. In the offsprings, the parameters for the first $k$ input dimensions are obtained from one parent, the remaining $n - k$ dimensions from another parent.
5)Mutation operator

The offspring undertaken the mutation is coded as

$$os = [\theta_1, \theta_2, \cdots, \theta_S].$$

The following two mutation operators have been applied to the dilation and translation mutations.

(1) Random mutation. An integer generated using uniform random distribution in the corresponding parameter range is assigned to the gene parameter. The dilation range is $[J_{min}, J_{max}]$, the translation range is described in the encoding scheme.
(2) Little perturbation mutation. The gene parameter, $\theta_k$, which can be $d_k$ or $t_k$, will be increased or decreased by 1, which depends on a random number $r$. That is,

$$\theta_k = \begin{cases} \theta_k + 1, & r > 0.5 \\ \theta_k - 1, & r \leq 0.5 \end{cases} \tag{7}$$

If the dilation mutation happens for the input dimension $k$, a random mutation will occur to the translation parameter $t_k$; Otherwise, the little perturbation mutation occurs to $t_k$.

**Table 1.** Comparison of the prediction result of the previous work in [3] on the sunspot data set with the result using the proposed GA algorithm

| Algorithms | Number of nodes (with best $\bar{E}$) | $\bar{E}$ (best) | Number of nodes (Mean) | $\bar{E}$ (Mean) |
|---|---|---|---|---|
| Billings and Wei [3] | 9 | 0.1044 | | |
| GA-WNN1 | 8 | 0.0953 | 7.93 | 0.1419 |
| GA-WNN2 | 10 | 0.0906 | 10.05 | 0.2556 |

## 4 Numerical Examples

Example. The Sunspot Time Series
The sunspot time series considered in this example consists of 300 annually recorded Wolf sunspots of the period from 1700 to 1999. The objective is to construct a WNN model to produce one-step-ahead predictions for the sunspot data set. The data set is separated into two parts: the training set consists of 250 data points corresponding to the period 1700-1949, and the test set consists of 50 data points corresponding to the period 1950-1999.

Following [3], the inputs, $x_i$, of the proposed wavelet network are defined as $x_1 = y(t-1)$, $x_2 = y(t-2)$, and $x_3 = y(t-9)$, where $t$ denotes the year and $y(t)$ is the sunspot number of the year $t$. The tensor product is used for the 3-D wavelets and the 1-D wavelet used is the Mexican hat with support $[-4, 4]$. The coarsest resolution and the finest resolution are -3 and 3 respectively. The population size used for the GA is 10, the maximum generation is 500.

In order to compare the predicted result of the WNN with other work [3], the following index is used to measure the performance of the constructed WNN

$$\bar{E} = \frac{\sum_{k=1}^{N_{test}} |x_k - \hat{x}_k|^2}{\sum_{k=1}^{N_{test}} |x_k - \bar{x}|^2} \tag{8}$$

where $N_{test}$ is the length of the test set, $x_k$ and $\hat{x}_k$ are the measurements over the data set and associated one-step-ahead predictions, respectively, and $\bar{x} = (1/N_{test}) \sum_{k=1}^{N_{test}} x_k$.

Forty independent runs are performed for the WNNs with separate dilations or identical dilations for different input dimensions, respectively, the former is called GA-WNN1, the latter is GA-WNN2. Means of the normalized error $\bar{E}$ and the number of wavelets are shown in Table 1. It can be seen that the GA-WNN1s have a less average number of wavelets and less error than the GA-WNN2s.

## 5 Conclusion

In this paper, a new method has been proposed for the design of WNNs. The design was performed in an evolutionary way, e.g., by adding neurons one at a time, which allowed us to construct a parsimonious model to satisfy the design requirement. GA was used to select a wavelet basis, and the fitness of a wavelet is evaluated according to the residue reduction.

## References


1. Zhang, Q., Benveniste, A. : Wavelet Networks. IEEE Trans. on Neural Networks, VOL.3, (1992) 889-898
2. Alonge, F., Dippolite, F., Raimondi, F.M. : System Identificaton via Optimised Wavelet-Based Neural Networks. IEE Proc.-Control Theory Appl., VOL.150, NO.2, (2003) 147-154
3. Billings, S.A., Wei, H. : A New Class of Wavelet Networks for Nonlinear System Identification. IEEE Trans. on Neural Networks, VOL.16, NO.4, (2005) 862-874
4. Zhang, Q. : Using Wavelet Network in Nonparametric Estimation. IEEE Trans. on Neural Networks, VOL.8, (1997) 227-236
5. Xu, J., Ho, D.W.C. : A Basis Selection Algorithm for Wavelet Neural Networks. Neurocomputing, VOL.48, (2002) 681-689
6. Yao, X. : Evolving Artificial Neural Networks. Proc. IEEE, VOL.87, NO.9, (1999) 1423-1447
7. Leung, F.H.F., Lam, H.K., Ling, S.H., Tam, P.K.S. : Tuning of the Structure and Parameters of a Neural Network Using an Improved Genetic Algorithm. IEEE Trans. on Neural Networks, VOL.14, NO.1, (2003) 79-88
8. Palmes, P.P., Hayasaka, T., Usui, S. : Mutation-Based Genetic Neural Network. IEEE Trans. on Neural Networks, VOL.16, NO.3, (2005) 587-599

# A Neural Network Model for Online Handwritten Mathematical Symbol Recognition

Arit Thammano[1] and Sukhumal Rugkunchon[2]

Computational Intelligence Laboratory
Faculty of Information Technology
King Mongkut's Institute of Technology Ladkrabang,
Bangkok, 10520 Thailand
[1]arit@it.kmitl.ac.th, [2]sukhumalr@gmail.com

**Abstract.** This paper proposes a new handwritten mathematical symbol recognition system that is flexible enough to let the users write the symbols in their own ways. They do not have to learn a completely new way of writing symbols. The proposed approach involves two main stages: online and offline. During the online stage, the input is classified into one of the four groups. During the offline stage, the new neural network, called Hausdorff ARTMAP, which is specifically designed for solving two dimensional binary pattern recognition problems is used to identify the symbols. The proposed model is tested in a writer independent mode using the researcher's own collected database. The result obtained is very encouraging.

## 1 Introduction

As PDAs and Pocket PCs have gained in popularity in recent years, there is an urgent need for powerful handwritten character recognition software. Especially in mobile situations in which a keyboard cannot be used easily, the users are forced to write down the information instead of typing on the keyboard. Typically, the online approaches, which use the temporal information of the writing (the number of strokes, the order of strokes, and the direction of the writing of each stroke [1]), are employed in the recognition process. Although the temporal information of the writing provides useful and distinctive information, it is not stable and has more variation than we could possibly store in the recognition model [2]. On the other hand, the offline recognition systems do not suffer from the above problem because it uses only the image of the handwritten data as the recognition object. However, it is not without its drawback. The offline recognition systems do not work very well with distorted handwriting patterns [3]. Therefore, the trend of the handwritten character recognition is now moving toward a hybrid of online and offline approaches. Many researchers have proposed hybrid models for handwritten recognition such as [2, 3, 4, 5]. These researches show that the online and the offline approaches complemented each other extremely well. The objective of this research is to create a new handwritten mathematical symbol recognition system specifically for the palm-sized computer. The proposed system uses both online and offline data as its input; therefore, there is no limitation on how the users write the symbols.

D.-S. Huang, K. Li, and G.W. Irwin (Eds.): ICIC 2006, LNCS 4113, pp. 292–298, 2006.

Following this introduction, section 2 describes the concept of the proposed model. The architecture of the Hausdorff ARTMAP, which is used as the offline recognition system, and its learning algorithm are presented in section 3. In section 4, the experimental results are demonstrated and discussed.

## 2 The Proposed System

When a user writes a mathematical symbol on the screen of the Pocket PC (Figure 1), each stroke of the symbol will go through a preprocessing step to remove noise that would otherwise complicate the recognition process. Next, the strokes are converted into a bitmap image so that it can be processed by the offline system. If the symbol is composed of more than one stroke, the position of each stroke in reference to the center of the symbol is determined. An example of the method used in finding the positions of the strokes is shown in Figure 2. First of all, the center of each stroke ($X_{Ci}$, $Y_{Ci}$) is calculated as follows:

$$X_{Ci} = (X_{Si\,max} + X_{Si\,min})/2 . \tag{1}$$

$$Y_{Ci} = (Y_{Si\,max} + Y_{Si\,min})/2 . \tag{2}$$

where i is the stroke number. Next, the center of the symbol ($X_C$, $Y_C$) is calculated based on equation 3 and 4.

$$X_C = \frac{\sum_{i=1}^{n} X_{Ci}}{n} . \tag{3}$$

$$Y_C = \frac{\sum_{i=1}^{n} Y_{Ci}}{n} . \tag{4}$$

where n is the number of strokes in the symbol. Finally, the lines are drawn connecting the center of the symbol to the center of the strokes. In this paper, the position of each stroke can only be one of the following: Position 1, 2, 3, 4, and 5. Position 1 represents the connecting line whose angle is between $11\pi/6$ and $\pi/6$; position 2 represents the connecting line whose angle is between $\pi/6$ and $5\pi/6$; position 3 represents the connecting line whose angle is between $5\pi/6$ and $7\pi/6$; position 4 represents the connecting line whose angle is between $7\pi/6$ and $11\pi/6$; and position 5 represents the connecting line whose length is less than 5 pixels. As an example, the stroke positions of the symbol in Figure 2 can be either "2-4" or "4-2," depending on the order of strokes. After the stroke positions of the symbol is identified, its bitmap image will be resized to a 10×10 image. Then the stroke positions of the symbol and its 10×10 image are sent to the offline recognition system. However, if the symbol consists of only one stroke, the process of finding the stroke position of the symbol is not needed. Only its 10×10 bitmap image is sent to the

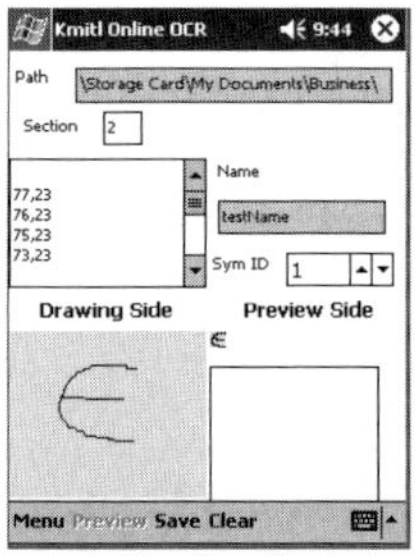


**Fig. 1.** The screen shot of the proposed handwritten recognition software

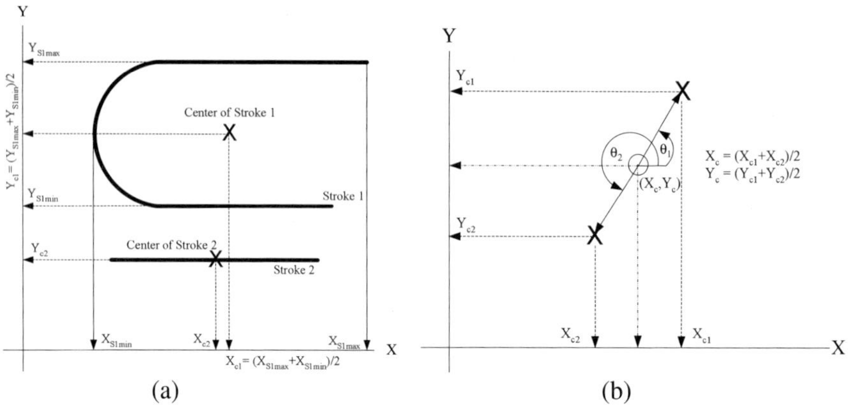


**Fig. 2.** An example of the method used in finding the stroke positions of the symbol

offline recognition system. The offline recognition system used in this research is composed of 4 components (4 Hausdorff ARTMAP neural networks). Each component is for each group of symbols that have the same number of strokes. The architecture of the Hausdorff ARTMAP and its learning algorithm are described in the next section.

## 3 Hausdorff ARTMAP

The architecture of the Hausdorff ARTMAP is a three-layer neural network as shown in Figure 3. The first layer is the input layer, which consists of X×Y nodes. Each node represents a pixel in the input image. In this research, the original images of the mathematical symbols are normalized to the size of 10×10. Hence there are 100 nodes in the input layer. The second layer is the cluster layer. The nodes in this second layer are constructed during the training phase. The third layer is the output layer. Each node in the output layer represents a class that the Hausdorff ARTMAP has to learn to recognize. During the supervised learning, the binary input image $I^m$ is presented to the model, together with its respective target output vector. The input pattern is denoted by

$$I^m_{x,y} = \{1, 0\} \quad : x = 1, 2, ..., 10; \; y = 1, 2, ..., 10 . \tag{5}$$

where m is the $m^{th}$ input pattern.

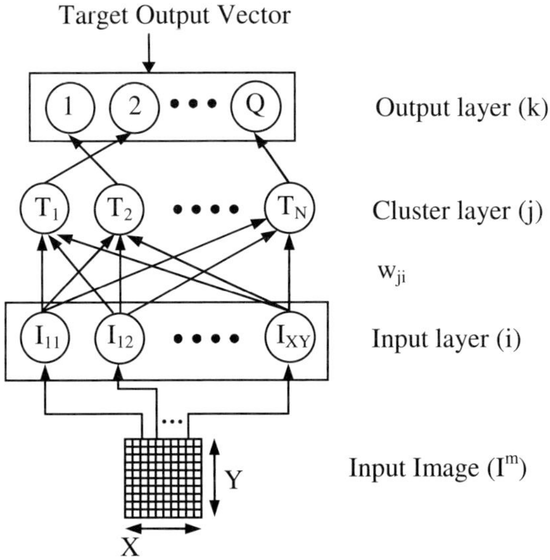


**Fig. 3.** Architecture of the Hausdorff ARTMAP

Each node in the cluster layer is fully connected to the nodes in the input layer via the connections $w_{ji}$. The weight vector $w_j$, which has the same dimension as the input pattern, represents the reference pattern of the $j^{th}$ node in the cluster layer. Once the input pattern is transmitted to the cluster layer, the output of each $j^{th}$ node in the cluster layer is calculated as follows:

$$T_j(I^m) = H(I^m, w_j) . \tag{6}$$

$$H(A,B) = \max\{h(A,B), h(B,A)\} . \tag{7}$$

$$h(A,B) = \max_{a \in A}\{\min_{b \in B}(\|a - b\|)\} . \tag{8}$$

where $H(I^m, w_j)$ is the Hausdorff distance between the input pattern $I^m$ and the reference pattern of the $j^{th}$ node. h(A, B) is the directed Hausdorff distance from set A to set B. $\|a - b\|$ is the Euclidean distance between point a and point b.

Next, the system makes a cluster choice by selecting the winning node J with minimum output value, among all the nodes j in the cluster layer. The cluster choice is indexed by J, where

$$T_J(I^m) = \min\{T_j(I^m)\} \quad : j = 1, 2, ..., N . \tag{9}$$

where N is the number of nodes in the cluster layer. In case of a tie, the node with the smallest index is chosen. Next, the winning node J is examined to check whether it passes the vigilance criterion. A node passes the vigilance criterion if the following condition is met:

$$T_J(I^m) \le \rho . \tag{10}$$

where ρ is the similarity threshold, which has the value between 0 and the length of the diagonal line. The smaller the value of ρ, the more similar the input must be to the reference pattern. If the chosen cluster meets the above criterion, the training process proceeds to the next step. However, if the condition in (10) is not satisfied, a new cluster node J is recruited to code the input pattern based on equation 11 and 12; the connection between a new cluster node and the target output is created. The remaining steps in the training process are skipped and the training is continued with the next input pattern.

$$w_J = I^m . \tag{11}$$

$$SP(J) = SP(I_m) . \tag{12}$$

where $SP(I_m)$ is the positions of the input pattern strokes. SP(J) is the positions of the reference pattern strokes.

Next, the system associates the winning node J in the cluster layer with the target output vector. If the winning node J does not belong to the correct class defined by the target output vector or $SP(I_m) \neq SP(J)$, node J is inhibited and the next best matching node to the input pattern is selected. The system then reevaluates the vigilance criterion (equation 10). However, if the winning node represents the class to which $I^m$ belongs and $SP(I_m) = SP(J)$, the training is continued with the next input pattern.

After all input patterns have been processed, the system proceeds with the cluster reduction algorithm. The cluster reduction algorithm attempts to reduce the number of nodes in the cluster layer by combining the nodes with a few members with the nodes containing a large number of members. The details of the algorithm are as follows:

1. The nodes in the cluster layer are ranked according to their number of members. The cluster node with the largest number of members is indexed as M.
2. Two sets of distances, which are a) the Hausdorff distances between node M and other cluster nodes within the same output class C ($ds_{Mj}$), and b) the Hausdorff distances between node M and other cluster nodes outside the output class C ($dd_{Mj}$), are calculated.

$$ds_{Mj} = H(w_M, w_j) \qquad : j = 1, 2, ..., N; j \in C; j \neq M . \tag{13}$$

$$dd_{Mj} = H(w_M, w_j) \qquad : j = 1, 2, ..., N; j \notin C . \tag{14}$$

3. The system searches for the j* cluster node which satisfies the following 3 conditions: a) it belongs to the same class as node M, b) it has no more than 3 members, and c) $ds_{Mj*} < \min_j\{dd_{Mj}\}$. This node is removed from the cluster layer.

   The similarity threshold of node M, which is initially equal to ρ, is then set to

$$\rho_M^{new} = \begin{cases} ds_{Mj*} & : \text{if } ds_{Mj*} > \rho_M^{old} \\ \rho_M^{old} & : \text{otherwise} \end{cases} \tag{15}$$

   The search continues until no more j* node can be found.

4. Step 2 and 3 are repeated; however, this time M is the cluster node with the next largest number of members. This loop carries on with the next largest nodes in the rank being indexed as M one by one until all cluster nodes with more than 3 members have a chance to act as M.
5. After that, all the input patterns that previously selected the j* nodes are presented to the system again for a new epoch of training. This will allow the remaining clusters to expand their sizes to cover the input space previously covered by the removed clusters.

During testing, the output of each node in the cluster layer is calculated according to equation 6. Then the nodes in the cluster layer are ranked from the lowest to the highest output values. If at least seven out of ten lowest value nodes belong to the same class, that class will be the result of the prediction. However, if not, the class whose j** cluster node belongs to is the result of the prediction.

$$j^{**} = \arg\min_{j=1}^{5}\left[\left(\frac{NS - MS_j + 0.0001}{NS}\right)\left(\frac{T_j(I^m)}{T_{max}(I^m)}\right)\right]. \tag{16}$$

$$T_{max}(I^m) = \max_{j=1}^{5}\left(T_j(I^m)\right). \tag{17}$$

where NS is the number of strokes of the input pattern. $MS_j$ is the number of the j cluster node strokes whose positions match the stroke positions of the input pattern.

## 4 Experimental Results

To test the performance of the proposed model for online handwritten mathematical symbol recognition, five experiments have been conducted on the researcher's own collected database. This database consists of 61 examples which are written by 61 people. Each example contains 89 symbols as shown in Figure 4. For each experiment, thirty examples are randomly chosen from the database to be used as the training data, while the remaining 31 examples are used as the testing data. Results of the experiments are shown in Table 1.

| , | ,, | ,,, | * | ° | ∂ | ⊕ | ⊗ | ∮ | ϕ | ∞ | α | % | Δ | ~ |
|---|---|---|---|---|---|---|---|---|---|---|---|---|---|---|
| ≈ | ≅ | ∫ | ∈ | ∉ | ⊂ | ⊄ | ⊃ | ∪ | ∩ | ⊆ | ⊇ | ∋ | ( | ) |
| { | } | + | - | ± | ∓ | ÷ | < | ≤ | > | ≥ | = | ≠ | ≡ | |
| → | ← | ↔ | ↑ | ↓ | ↕ | ⇕ | ⇐ | ⇒ | ⇑ | ⇓ | ∠ | ∟ | ⊥ | × |
| / | \ | √ | ∀ | ∧ | ∨ | ∣ | ‖ | ∇ | [ | ] | ∃ | # | & | Σ |
| π | θ | *f* | Π | Ω | ◁ | ▷ | ≺ | ≻ | ↵ | ↦ | ⌋ | ⌈ | ⌉ | |

**Fig. 4.** Mathematical symbols used in this research

**Table 1.** The experimental results

| | Exp. 1 | Exp. 2 | Exp. 3 | Exp. 4 | Exp. 5 | Average |
|---|---|---|---|---|---|---|
| % Correct | 87.17 | 87.02 | 86.95 | 87.86 | 88.84 | 87.57 |

## References


1. Koschinski, M., Winkler, H. J., Lang, M.: Segmentation and Recognition of Symbols within Handwritten Mathematical Expressions. Proceedings of the IEEE International Conference on Acoustics, Speech, and Signal Processing, 4 (1995) 2439-2442
2. Tanaka, H., Iwayama, N., Akiyama, K.: Online Handwriting Recognition Technology and Its Applications. Fujitsu Scientific & Technical Journal, 40 (1) (2004) 170-178
3. Tanaka, H., Nakajima, K., Ishigaki, K., Akiyama, K., Nakagawa, M.: Hybrid Pen-Input Character Recognition System Based on Integration of Online-Offline Recognition. Proceedings of the Fifth International Conference on Document Analysis and Recognition, (1999) 209-212
4. Vinciarelli, A., Perrone, M.: Combining Online and Offline Handwriting Recognition. Proceedings of the Seventh International Conference on Document Analysis and Recognition, (2003) 844-848
5. Gauthier, N., Artières, T., Dorizzi, B., Gallinari, P.: Strategies for Combining On-line and Off-line Information in an On-line Handwriting Recognition System. Proceedings of the Sixth International Conference on Document Analysis and Recognition, (2001) 412-416

# A Novel Boundary Extension Approach for Empirical Mode Decomposition

Zhuofu Liu

School of Underwater Acoustic Engineering, Harbin Engineering University, 150001, Harbin, Heilongjiang, P.R. China
liuzoff@yahoo.com.cn

**Abstract.** The Empirical Mode Decomposition (EMD) proposed by Huang et al. in 1998 shows remarkably effective in analyzing nonlinear signals. However, the boundary extension is one of the theoretical problems unsolved in EMD. In this paper, a novel boundary processing technique is proposed to deal with the border effect in EMD. An algorithm based on the sigma-pi neural network is used to extend signals before applying EMD. By virtue of this method, the frequency compression near the end is eliminated and errors caused by end effect are reduced. Verifications of the experimental signals show that the newly proposed boundary extension method is useful in practice.

## 1 Introduction

The empirical mode decomposition (EMD) firstly proposed by Dr. Huang and his colleagues in 1998 is a method of breaking down a signal to a series of zero-mean AM-FM components by iteratively conducting the sifting process. It has shown great utility in time-frequency analysis of dispersive, nonlinear, or non-stationary signals and systems. The EMD process allows time frequency analysis of transient signals for which Fourier based methods have been unsuccessful [1,2].

The decomposed components produced by EMD are called intrinsic mode functions (IMFs) which satisfy two conditions: (1) The number of extrema and thus the number of zero-crossings in the whole data series must be equal or differ at the most by one; and (2) At any instant in time, the mean value of the envelope defined by the local maxima and the envelope of the local minima is zero [3-7].

The EMD is a highly adaptive decomposition. It decomposes any complicated signal into so called intrinsic mode functions (IMF). The IMFs lead to a clean representation of the signal by a few well-behaved signal components. has two steps: (1) construct upper and lower envelopes by connecting all maxima and all minima with cubic splines, respectively; (2) subtract the mean of the upper and lower envelopes from the original signal to get a component. While the sifting process should usually be applied several times because the component created by only one sifting process hardly satisfy all requirements of an IMF. By virtue of EMD, a nonstationary signal is decomposed into several stationary, complete and orthogonal intrinsic mode functions (IMFs). In the procedure of EMD, the cubic spline function is used to construct the upper and lower envelopes of data in order to determine the mean by iterative sifting processes till to satisfy the stop criterion. Once an IMF is created, the same procedure

D.-S. Huang, K. Li, and G.W. Irwin (Eds.): ICIC 2006, LNCS 4113, pp. 299 – 304, 2006.

then is applied on the residual of the signal to obtain the next IMF. The decomposition will stop when no more IMF can be created or the residual is less than a predetermined small value [1-7].

In practice, the EMD has met several unsettled problems, such as boundary extension, curve fitting, stop criteria and so on. In boundary extension, Prof. Huang [1] added two characteristic waves to each end of the data span [4]. However, the characteristic wave approach exists two indefiniteness in the practical application. Firstly, the data only gives information on the extrema inside the data series. Any extension out of the boundary is not reliable. Secondly, by adding different characteristic waves, different results could be produced. Another data extension method, called the Mirror Extension (ME), is proposed by Zhao [4]. The approach eliminates the possible problems in reliability and uniqueness in the data extension. However, a frequency reconstruction process is needed to eliminate common frequency mixture and it is still unsolved efficiently.

To solve the boundary extension problem in EMD, a new boundary process technique based on the sigma-pi neural network [8] is presented in this paper. The paper is organized as follows: the principals of EMD are brought forward in section 2. Section 3 introduces the basic structure of sigma-pi neural network. Some comparisons between existing boundary extension methods and the novel one have been done in section 4. Some conclusions about the newly proposed boundary extension method are stated in Section 5.

## 2 Empirical Mode Decomposition

In this section, the procedure of EMD is introduced briefly, further information can be found in [1-7]:

Let $X(t)$ be the input data series, $u(t)$ and $v(t)$ are the upper and lower envelopes of $X(t)$. The mean envelop $m(t)$ of the series $X(t)$ is calculated:

$$m(t) = [u(t) + v(t)]/2 . \tag{1}$$

A new series $h_1$ with low frequency removed is calculated by subtracting the mean envelop from the series $X(t)$:

$$h_1(t) = X(t) - m(t) . \tag{2}$$

Generally speaking, $h_1$ is still a non-stationary series, so the above procedure must be repeated $k$ times until the mean envelope is approximate to zero, so the first IMF component $C_1(t)$ is obtained:

$$m_{k-1}(t) = [u_{k-1}(t) + v_{k-1}(t)]/2 . \tag{3}$$

$$h_k(t) = h_{k-1}(t) - m_{k-1}(t) . \tag{4}$$

Then, the first IMF component, $c_1(t)$, from the data and its residue, $r_1(t)$, are designated as:

$$c_1(t) = h_k(t)\,. \tag{5}$$

$$r_1(t) = X(t) - c_1(t)\,. \tag{6}$$

Overall, $c_1(t)$ represents the highest frequency component of the original series. Since the residue, $r_1(t)$, still contains information of longer period components, it is treated as the new data series and subjected to new shifting process. The procedure is repeated for all subsequent residues until $r_n(t)$ is less than predetermined small value or a monotonic function. The result is:

$$r_2(t) = r_1(t) - C_2(t), \cdots, r_n(t) = r_{n-1}(t) - C_n(t)\,. \tag{7}$$

Finally, the original series can be presented by a sum of the IMF components and a mean value or trend:

$$X(t) = \sum_{j=1}^{n} C_j(t) + r_n(t)\,. \tag{8}$$

## 3 Structure of Sigma-Pi Neural Network

There are two main types of commonly-used artificial neurons, i.e., distance-based neurons used in radial base function networks (RBFNs), and neurons based on a linear combination of input values as in multilayer perceptrons. In this last case, each neuron computes a scalar product of a variable input vector with a fixed synaptic weight vector, while synaptic weights can only change slowly during learning processes [8,9].

In the literature [8,9], especially in backpropagation context, sigmoidal functions are often defined to be not only bounded but also non-decreasing and differentiable. In our application, smoothness or shape conditions for $\delta$ are not needed and, therefore, we can be more general in our definition of what we mean by a sigmoidal function, as follows:

$$s(\delta) = \begin{cases} 0, & \delta < 0 \\ 1, & \delta \geq 1 \end{cases}\,. \tag{9}$$

For a given sigmoidal function and $f(J) \in R$, $J \in \{0,1\}^n$, the given discrete data set introduced by some underlying function can be defined as:

$$f(x) = 2^{1-n} \sum_{J \in \{0,1\}^n} \delta\left( \prod_{k=1}^{n} \left( x_k - j_k - \frac{1}{2} \right) \right) \Delta_f [J, J+1]\,. \tag{10}$$

As to the implementation of our strategy, a three-layer feed-forward sigma–pi neural network with n simple fan-out input neurons, m hidden sigma–pi neurons, and one usual output neuron performs the following expression [8]:

$$f(x)=\sum_{j=1}^{m}\omega_j\delta\left(\prod_{k=1}^{n}\left(x_k-t_{k,j}\right)\right). \tag{11}$$

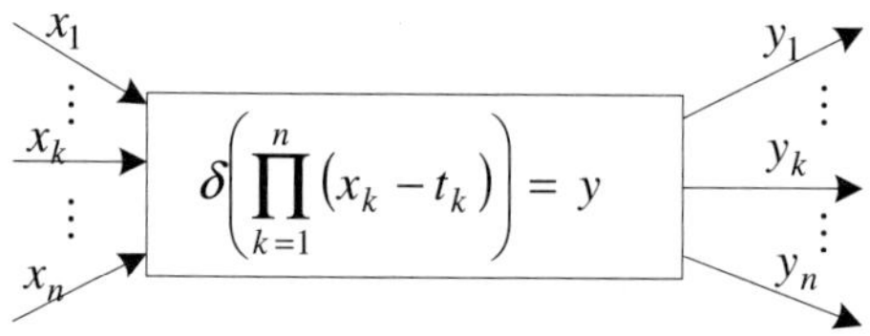


**Fig. 1.** Basic structure of sigma-pi neural network

Fig. 1 gives a sketch look of the sigma-pi neural network. It is clear that the algorithm can be split into two parts: the learning step and the recall step. In the learning phase, the network has to fix the weights depending on the given information and the iterative calculation is:

$$D[J_{n+1}]=D[J_n]+(-1)^{n-i_1-i_2-\cdots-i_n}f(j_1+i_1,\dots j_n+i_n)=\Delta_f[J_n,J_n+1]. \tag{12}$$

Next, comes the recall step of the sigma-pi neural network. Since only negative powers of 2 are involved in this recall scheme, simple left shifts of the binary representation of the values again allow pure integer arithmetics in case that the given evaluation point only consists of integer components. In any fixed step of the n-nested loops we have

$$P=\prod_{k=1}^{n}\left(x_k-j_k-\frac{1}{2}\right). \tag{13}$$

Above is the basic structure of sigma-pi neural network, its application in the boundary extension of EMD will be presented in the next section.

## 4 Application to Boundary Extension

Fig. 2 illustrates the upper and lower envelopes of a series of sample data based on several boundary extension methods, where the sample data are given by:

$$X(t)=\cos(\pi t/10)+\cos((\pi(t-10))/25)+2\cos((\pi t)/55)+2\cos((\pi t)/95). \quad 80\le t\le 160 \tag{14}$$

From Fig. 2, it can be seen that there are only five maxima and four minima in the data set, so several distortions appear in the upper and lower envelopes, especially at both ends of the upper envelops. As the data series is so short that the distortions from the ends of envelopes have influenced the whole series and the results are unbelievable if the distortions cannot be restrained effectively. On the other hand, the occurrence of distortion is normal for the curve fitting by using of cubic spline function, because the cubic spline interpolation needs two neighboring data before and after the given point respectively.

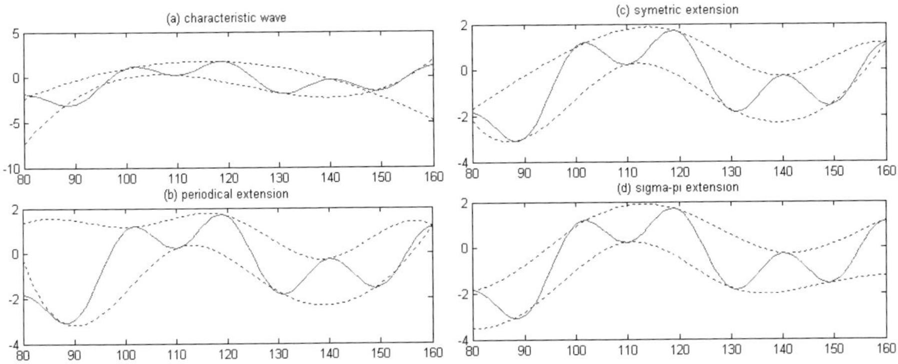


**Fig. 2.** Comparison among the characteristic wave, periodical extension, symmetric extension and sigma-pi neural network for the calculation of upper and lower envelopes in the boundary extension of EMD

Several boundary extension methods have been applied to solve the difficulty. By comparison, it is clear that the method based on sigma-pi neural network performs best. The characteristic wave method causes serve end effect, especially the upper envelope in the right endpoint. Similarly, end effect happens in the left endpoint of the periodical extension. Although the symmetric extension suppresses the border effect, the endpoints are considered as both maxima and minima.

## 5 Conclusions

In the present paper, we proposed the sigma-pi neural network to deal with the border effect in EMD. By applying the neural network to the boundary extension in EMD, a data series can be extended forward and backward, so accurate results are achieved. From the experimental results presented, we see that the proposed method shows obvious advantages by comparing with other boundary extension algorithms.

## Acknowledgements

This work is supported in part through a National Natural Science Foundation of China (Grant No.10504004), Science and Technology Plan Project of Heilongjiang Province (Grant No.GZ04A126) and Harbin Engineering University Science Fund (Grant No. HEUFT0408).

## References

1. Huang, N. E., Shen, Z., Long, S. R. et al.: The Empirical Mode Decomposition and the Hilbert Spectrum for Nonlinear and Nonstationary Time Series Analysis. Proc. R. Soc. Lond. A. 1 (1998) 454–899
2. Anna, Linderhed.: Variable Sampling of the Empirical Mode Decomposition of Two-Dimensional Signals. International Journal of Wavelets, Multiresolution and Information. 4738 (2002) 1-8

3. Zhao, Jinping.: Improvement of the Mirror Extending in Empirical Mode Decomposition Method and the Technology for Eliminating Frequency Mixing. High Technology Letter. 4 (2002) 40–47
4. Kan, Z., Mingxia He.: A Simple Boundary Process Technique for Empirical Mode Decomposition. IEEE Trans. PAMI. 23 (2004) 234-241
5. Jun Shen., Wei Shen., Sun, H.J., J.Y. Yang.: Fuzzy Neural Nets with Non-Symmetric Pi Membership Functions and Applications in Signal Processing and Image Analysis. Signal Processing. 80 (2000) 965–983
6. Marcus Datig., Torsten Schlurmann.: Performance and Limitations of the Hilbert–Huang transformation (HHT) with an Application to Iirregular Water Waves. Ocean Engineering. 31 (2004) 1783–1834
7. Nunes, J.C., Bouaoune, Y., Delechelle, E., Niang, O., Bunel, Ph.: Image Analysis by Bidimensional Empirical Mode Decomposition. Image and Vision Computing 21 (2003) 1019–1026
8. Burkhard Lenze.: Note on Interpolation on the Hypercube by Means of Sigma–pi Neural Networks. Neurocomputing. 61 (2004) 471– 478
9. Pierre Courrieu.: Solving Ttime of Least Square Systems in Sigma-pi Unit Networks. Neural Information Processing. 4 (2004) 39-47

# Adaptive Controller Based on Wavelets Neural Network for a Class of Nonlinear Systems

Zhijun Zhang

Dalian university of technology Dalian China 116024
zzj@dl.cn

**Abstract.** An adaptive control strategy for nonlinear systems is presented. The simple control law is derived based on minimizing a well-chosen performance index. Wavelets neural network model is applied to the scheme that can overcome the problem caused by the local minima when training the neural network. Compared with existing algorithms such as stochastic gradient algorithm, the present algorithm has the advantage of rapid convergence and low computational cost. The proposed approach is finally applied in a chemical reactor control problem. The simulation results proved that the proposed adaptive control method can effectively control unknown nonlinear systems.

## 1 Introduction

Most of practical plants involve nonlinear and un-model feature. The linear-model based controllers are difficult to give a satisfactory control performance when the system involves highly nonlinear dynamics. The fundamental drawbacks of current adaptive control techniques, such as nonlinear control laws which are difficult to derive, geometrically increasing complexity with the number of unknown parameters, have compelled researchers to look for solutions elsewhere. In recent years, a variety of nonlinear system identification techniques have been proposed, the most popular approach is the neural-network-based control [1,2,3]. Among these neural network models, the multilayered feed-forward neural network (MFNN) is one of the most widely used in nonlinear identification and control. Advantages of MFNN are its capability of approximating any continuous function and the computational simplicity of the corresponding back propagation (BP) learning algorithm. But the main drawbacks of BP algorithm and MFNN are that the convergence of BP algorithm is very slow and controller design based on MFNN models is much complex [4]. Many algorithms such as random search techniques and genetic algorithms have been adopted to overcome these problems, however, the algorithm complexity and computation velocity will degrade the performance of real-time control systems [5]. So there is a strong motivation to develop novel network architecture. Recently, wavelet decomposition emerged as a new powerful tool for function approximation in a manner that readily reveals properties of the arbitrary $L_2$ function [6]. Combining adaptive control (MRAC) algorithm is developed based-on wavelet networks. The main idea is to use wavelet functions and scaling functions as the nonlinear functions required in the neurons. Unknown controller functions are constructed on-line using wavelet basis function networks such that the plant output tracks the output of a linear reference

D.-S. Huang, K. Li, and G.W. Irwin (Eds.): ICIC 2006, LNCS 4113, pp. 305 – 310, 2006.

model .The Broyden-Fletcher-Goldfarb-Shanno (BFGS) is incorporated into the RLS algorithm for training neural network off-line and modifying the on-line. It not only increases the computation velocity but also decrease the computation steps. The capabilities and performance of all these new techniques are suitably demonstrated by their application to the modeling and control of a realistic simulation of the typical non-linear continuous stirred tank reactor ( CSTR).

## 2 Wavelet Neural Network Nontroller Structure and Algorithm

### 2.1 Wavelet Neural Network Controller Structure

The wavelet neural network (WNN) controller is constructed with three layers, the first layer is the input layer, the second layer is the hidden layer and the third is the output layer. The network net output can be described by the following equations:

$$\hat{y} = \sum_{j=1}^{L} w_j h\left( \sum_{i=1}^{N} \frac{x_i - b_{ij}}{a_{ij}} \right) \tag{1}$$

Where: $\hat{y} \in R$ is the output vector, $x \in R^n$ is the input vector, $b_{ij}, a_{ij}$ are translation vectors and dilation vectors of the hidden layer respectively, $w_j$ is the connecting weight between the hidden layer and the output layer. $L$ is number of wavelet basis function, $h(\bullet)$ is wavelet basis function.

### 2.2 Wavelet Neural Network Training Algorithm

Many numerical optimization techniques have been successfully used to speed up convergence of back-propagation learning algorithm [7]. In this paper, BFGS+LS algorithm is presented, to (1) wavelet network, the performance index of network may define the following:

$$J = \frac{1}{M} \sum_{t=1}^{M_1} e^2(t)$$
$$e(t) = y(t) - \hat{y}(t) \tag{2}$$

Where: $y\ (t)$ is the set point, $\hat{y}\ (t)$ is the network output value, $e(t)$ is the error between expected value and the network output value. This is done by minimizing the performance index to optimize the controller structure. The required adjusting the parameters of the network are $\theta = \left[ w_j, a_{ij}, b_{ij} \right]^T$, where the non-linear the parameters vector is $\theta_N = [b_{ij}, a_{ij}]^T$ .the linear parameters vector is $\theta_L = \left[ w_j \right]^T$ .The BFGS method is used for updating the non-linear the parameters vector.

Define

$$\theta_{k+1}=\theta_k-\mu_k H_k g_k \tag{3}$$

Where $\mu_k$ is one step of search, $H_k$ is matrix, $g_k$ is gradient of performance index $J$

$$H_{k+1}=H_k-\frac{H_k\Delta g_k\Delta g_k^T H_k}{\Delta g_k^T H_k\Delta g_k}+\frac{\Delta\theta_k\Delta\theta_k^T}{\Delta\theta_k^T\Delta g_k}+\left(\Delta g_k^T H_k\Delta g_k\right)\upsilon_k\upsilon_k^T \tag{4}$$

And

$$\upsilon_k=\frac{\Delta\theta_k}{\Delta\theta_k^T\Delta g_k}-\frac{H_k\Delta g_k}{\Delta g_k^T H_k\Delta g_k} \tag{5}$$

$H_k$ is $N\times N$ positive the symmetrical matrix, $N$ is the number of adjusted parameters. $g_k=\left\{\frac{\partial J}{\partial a}\ \ \frac{\partial J}{\partial b}\right\}$ is $1\times N$ , the derivative of performance index $J$ for translation vectors $b_{ij}$ can be expressed as:

$$\frac{\partial J}{\partial b_{ij}}=-\frac{2}{M}\sum_{i=1}^{M}e\left[x(t)\right]\frac{\partial\hat{y}\left[x(t)\right]}{\partial b_{ij}} \tag{6}$$

$$\frac{\partial J}{\partial a_{ij}}=-\frac{2}{M}\sum_{i=1}^{M}e\left[x(t)\right]\frac{\partial\hat{y}\left[x(t)\right]}{\partial a_{ij}}=-\frac{2}{M}\sum_{i=1}^{M}e\left[x(t)\right]\frac{x_i(t)-b_{ij}}{a^2_{ij}}h'\left(\sum_{i=1}^{n+m}\frac{x_i(t)-b_{ij}}{a_{ij}}\right) \tag{7}$$

$h'(\bullet)$ is derivate of $h(\bullet)$.

Define

$$\phi_t=[h_1,h_2,\cdots,h_L]^T,W_t=[w_1,w_2,\cdots,w_L] \tag{8}$$

Equation (1) can be expressed as

$$\hat{y}=\sum_{j=1}^{L}w_j h\left(\sum_{i=1}^{N}\frac{x_i-b_{ij}}{a_{ij}}\right)=\phi_t^T W_t \tag{9}$$

Let $\lambda_a$ is weighting factor, $0\le\lambda_a\le 1$.Then weights factor of network output layer was calculated as by:

$$K_t=\left(\lambda_a+\phi_t^T P_{t-1}\phi_t\right)^{-1}P_{t-1}\phi_t, P_t=[P_{t-1}-K_t\phi_t^T P_{t-1}]/\lambda_a, W_t=W_{t-1}+K_t[y_t-\phi_t^T W_{t-1}] \tag{10}$$

Where

$$P_i=\left[\phi^T(i)\phi(i)\right]^{-1}, P(0)=\left(10^3\sim 10^6\right)I, \lambda=\left(0.95\sim 0.99\right) \tag{11}$$

## 3 Control Simulation of CSTR Process

In this section, the problem of controller designing is considered. The control system structure is shown in Fig.1. The model reference adaptive control ( MRAC) approach is used to control CSTR. Identifier (WNI) and controller (WNC) consist of proposed wavelet neural network. The first, the WNI and WNC are training off-line by BFGS+RLS algorithm, the neural network is updating on-line, when network satisfies the precision request. Structure of WNC and WNI are 3-12-1. The CSTR is a typical industrial nonlinear systems, the dynamic model is expressed as follows:

$$\dot{C}_a = \frac{q}{v}(C_{ao} - C_a(t)) - k_o C_a(t) e^{-\frac{E}{RT(t)}} \tag{12}$$

$$\dot{T}(t) = \frac{q}{v}(T_o - T(t)) - k_1 C_a(t) e^{-\frac{E}{RT(t)}} + k_2 q_c(t)\left(1 - e^{-k_3/q_c(t)}\right)(T_{co} - T(t)) \tag{13}$$

Where $C_a(t)$ is concentration of product compound, $T(t)$ is the temperature of mixture, $q_c(t)$ is coolant flow rate, $C_{ao}$ is the inlet concentration, $q$ is process flow rate, $v$ is reactor volume $T_0$, and $T_{co}$ is the inlet feed and coolant temperatures respectively, all of which are assumed constant at nominal values. Likewise $k_o$, $E/R, v, k_1$, $k_2$, $k_3$ are thermodynamic and chemical constants. The objective of control is to keep the concentration by manipulating the flow rate $q_c(t)$ ,to ensure product conforms to the requirement.

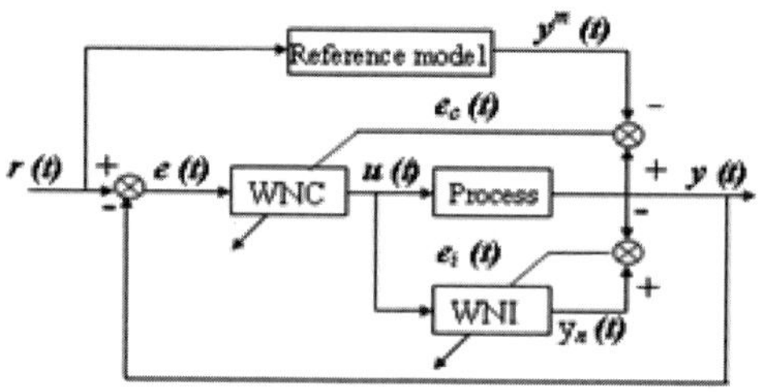


**Fig. 1.** The control system structure

## 4 Results and Discussion

To indicate the effectiveness of the proposed control approach ,comparisons between the CSTR responses using the proposed MARC control the algorithm based on wavelet neural network controller and using the conventional proportional plus integral (PI) controller are performed. The simulation results are shown in Fig. 2 and 3, when reference input setting value 0.08~0.12mol/L change (square-wave signal). Simulation results shows that presented scheme has better characteristics than those obtained using traditional PI controller. System response when value of $k_3$ change to

0.7 $k_3$ is given in Fig.4. The data sampling interval is 0.1 second. Simulation result proves that WNN controller is more robust and adaptive when disturbance or parameter perturbation is imposed on the process.

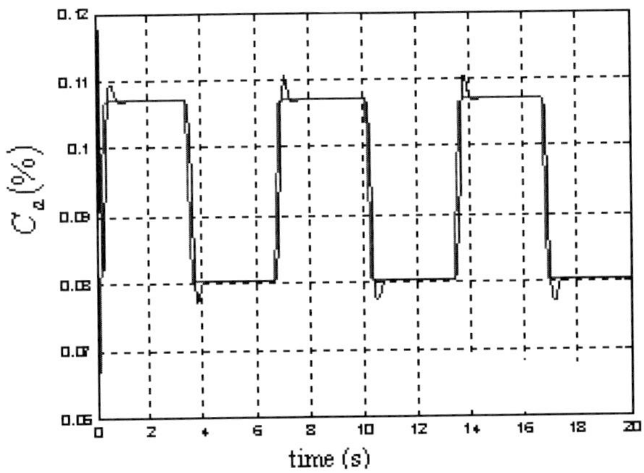


**Fig. 2.** The response trajectory of the CSTR controlled MRAC

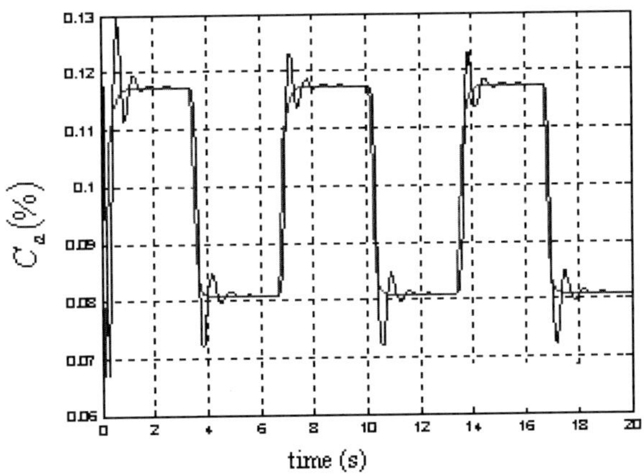


**Fig. 3.** The response trajectory of the CSTR controlled PI

# 5 Conclusions

A new MRAC controller based on wavelet neural network has been developed and applied it to control the non-linear CSTR. The result indicated controller which is trained by BGFS+LS optimizing algorithm big enhancement computation velocity, therefore sped up system convergence, this is helpful to the real-time control implementation. Because the parameters of the wavelet network can rapidly adapt themselves with changes of operating conditions, thus the controller has the good compatibility and robustness. The simulation results show the system performance is improved significantly.

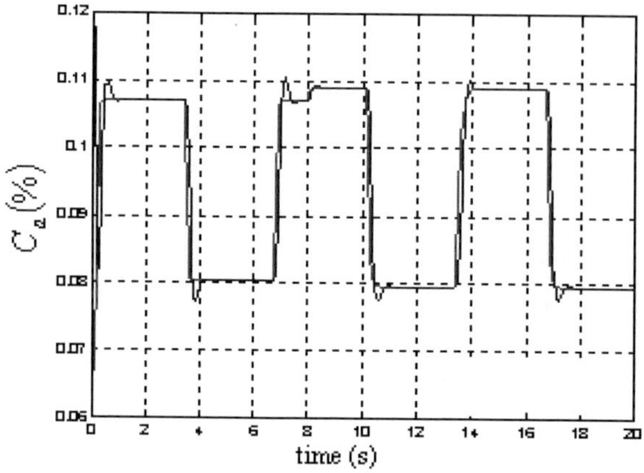


**Fig. 4.** The response trajectory of the CSTR controlled MRAC (the process parametric changed from1 to 0.7)

## References

1. Yasar, B., Ahmet, F. K., Tariq, S.: Intelligent Optimal Control with Dynamic Neural Networks. Neural networks, 16 (2003) 251-259
2. Ahmed, M. S.: Design of a Fixed Neural Controller for Nonlinear Plants, Internat. J. Control, 69 (1998) 65–83
3. Boozarjomehry, R. B., Svrcek, W. L. Y.: Automatic Design of Neural Network Structures. Computer and Chemical Engineering, 25 (2001) 1075-1088
4. Arim, M. N., AI-Duwaish, H.: Use of Multilayer Feedforward Neural Networks in Identification and Control of Wiener Model. IEE Proceedings, Control Theory and Applications, 143 (1996) 255- 258
5. Wang, J.: Adaptive Control for Nonlinear Systems Using Decomposed Neural Networks. Cybernetics and Systems. An International Journal , 29 (1998) 73-83
6. Debnath, L.: Wavelet Transforms and Their Applications. Springer-Verlag Inc., New York (2002)
7. Jose, V., Fernando, M. D., Alexandre, M.: Artificial Neural Networks and Neurofuzzy Systems for Modelling and Controlling Real Systems: a Comparative Study. Engineering Applications of Artificial Intelligence, 17 (2004) 265-273

# An Algorithm for Fuzzy Pattern Recognition Based on Neural Networks

Guohui He and Yinbo Qing

[1] School of information, Wuyi University, Jiangmen, Guangdong, P.R.C. 529020
[2] National Laboratory on Machine Perception, Peking University, Beijing 100871
ghhe@wyu.cn

**Abstract.** According to principles of fuzzy mathematics and neural networks, a new model on neural networks, by which fuzzy patterns can be better recognized, is presented in this paper. This model combines the thoughts of neural networks and maximum membership function. Thus the insufficiency in semantic expressions of neural networks can be compensated for. In the meantime, more objective effect can be obtained than that by fuzzy pattern recognition method in fuzzy mathematics. Experimental results show that the method is valid in practical applications.

## 1 Introduction

There are always some concepts in realistic life, which are very difficult to describe by way of classic mathematics, such as excellent success, general intelligence and good performance etc. All these concepts are fuzzy, and it is difficult to identify their boundary definitely. Is a student excellent or only general? No one can supply an absolutely right answer, because each one has his own criterion. However, fuzzy mathematics provides the solutions to the problems by maximum membership principle and nearest distance principle [1]. These problems can often be solved according to expert's experience. Since the decision of experts is not always right, patterns cannot be recognized correctly by these methods. However, neural networks, which have the advantages of powerful learning and self-adaptive capability, can easily get an reasonable membership function. Therefore, they possess more objective and stronger ability in pattern recognition.

In this paper, a method of fuzzy pattern recognition based on neural networks is presented, which is combined with the thoughts of fuzzy mathematics and the powerful calculation capability of neural networks [2,3]. With unique network structure, the insufficiency in semantic expressions of neural networks can be compensated for. The normalization of samples using membership function can also be finished. Experiments based on test of student physical quality show that the results are promising and near optimal.

## 2 Structures and Algorithm of the Model

Fuzzy patterns are separated into two classes, such as single and composite patterns, for which maximum membership function is commonly used. The principle can be described as follows.

D.-S. Huang, K. Li, and G.W. Irwin (Eds.): ICIC 2006, LNCS 4113, pp. 311 – 316, 2006.

Suppose there are $m$ fuzzy subsets in space $U=\{x_0,x_1,\cdots,x_n\}$, denoted by $A_1, A_2,\cdots, A_m$ respectively, which forms standard fuzzy patterns library. For arbitrary $x_0 \in U$, there exists $i_0 \in \{1,2,\cdots,m\}$, and equation is established

$$A_{i_0} = \bigcup_{k=1}^{m} A_k(x_0), \quad k=1,\cdots,m \tag{1}$$

Where the operator $\bigcup$ expresses solving maximum value. So we can say that $x_0$ belongs to $A_{i_0}$.

Admittedly, patterns can be recognized by this method. But the membership function and operator described above are too subjective to be the best choice. For example, there is an equation

$$A_1(x) = w_1 \times A_1(x_1) + w_2 \times A_2(x_2) + \cdots + w_n \times A_n(x_n) \tag{2}$$

Where weight is completely determined by experts, which results in a bad effect on pattern recognition.

Neural networks not only have the characteristics of non-linear system, but also have powerful learning, generalization and self-adaptive capability, which can be commonly applied in pattern recognition. According to the characteristics of neural networks, a three-layer network model including normalization layer, learning layer and competition layer is considered. Integrated fuzzy pattern recognition and neural networks, the structure and algorithm of the model are presented in this paper, which are discussed in detail.

## 2.1 Model Structures and Algorithm Deduction

Assume the number of fuzzy patterns in the standard fuzzy patterns library is $m$, and each pattern is represented by $n$ fuzzy parameters. The calculation of each parameter can be done by membership function respectively. Therefore, the structure of a $n-m-m$ network model is built, shown in Fig.1, where the first layer is normalization, the second layer is learning, and the third layer is competition [4].

Suppose there exist $k$ training samples, expressed by ( $P_i, D_i$)($i=1,2,\cdots,k$). We can describe them as

$$\begin{gathered}(p_{11}, p_{12},\cdots, p_{1n}; d_{11}, d_{12},\cdots, d_{1m}) \\ \cdots \\ (p_{k1}, p_{k2},\cdots, p_{kn}; d_{k1}, d_{k2},\cdots, d_{km})\end{gathered} \tag{3}$$

From the point of view of network model principles, we know weights of learning layer should meet the following requirements [5]

$$\begin{cases} w_{11}A_1(p_{11}) + w_{12}A_2(p_{12}) + \cdots + w_{1n}A_n(p_{1n}) = d_{11} \\ \cdots \\ w_{m1}A_1(p_{11}) + w_{m2}A_2(p_{12}) + \cdots + w_{mn}A_n(p_{1n}) = d_{1m} \\ w_{11}A_1(p_{k1}) + w_{12}A_2(p_{k2}) + \cdots + w_{1n}A_n(p_{kn}) = d_{k1} \\ \cdots \\ w_{m1}A_1(p_{k1}) + w_{m2}A_2(p_{k2}) + \cdots + w_{mn}A_n(p_{kn}) = d_{km} \end{cases} \tag{4}$$

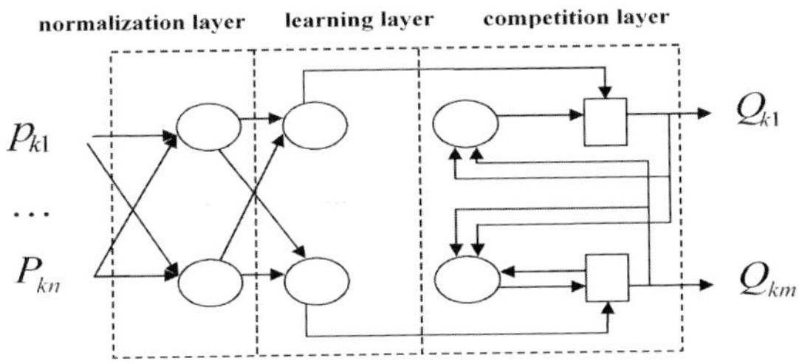


**Fig. 1.** Model structure

To enhance the precision of the network model, the number of training samples should be large enough. Thus suppose $k > n$ . So we need solve equation (**4**) to make sure the structure of this model. In reference [6]

$$R_{ij} = \sum_{h=1}^{n} A_h(p_{ih})w_{jh} - d_{ij}, \quad i = 1,2,\cdots,k; \; j = 1,2,\cdots,m \tag{5}$$

According to least square principles, the sum of square of errors should be minimum. That is

$$F(w_{11}, w_{12}, \cdots, w_{mn}) = \sum_{i=1}^{k}\sum_{j=1}^{m} R_{ij}^2 = \sum_{i=1}^{k}\sum_{j=1}^{m}(\sum_{h=1}^{n} A_h(p_{ih})w_{jh} - d_{ij})^2 \tag{6}$$

Under the conditions of $j = r$ , equation (6) is converted into

$$F(w_{11}, w_{12}, \cdots, w_{mn}) = \sum_{i=1}^{k}(\sum_{h=1}^{n} A_h(p_{ih})w_{rh} - d_{ir})^2 \tag{7}$$

According to the sufficient condition of the existent extreme value of multivariate function, we have

$$\frac{\mathrm{d}F}{\mathrm{d}w_{rs}} = 2\sum_{i=1}^{k}((\sum_{h=1}^{n} A_h(p_{ih})w_{rh} - d_{ir})A_s(p_{is})) = 0 \tag{8}$$

Hence

$$\sum_{i=1}^{k}(\sum_{h=1}^{n} A_h(p_{ih})A_s(p_{is})w_{rh} = \sum_{i=1}^{k} d_{ir}A_s(p_{is}) \tag{9}$$

Let $B_{sh} = \sum_{i=1}^{k} A_h(p_{ih})A_s(p_{is}), E_{sr} = \sum_{i=1}^{k} d_{ir}A_s(p_{is})$, so

$$\sum_{h=1}^{n} B_{sh}w_{rh} = E_{sr}, \quad r = 1,2,\cdots,m; \quad s = 1,2,\cdots,n \tag{10}$$

Obviously, equation (10) is a $m \times n$ norm linear equation group with $m \times n$ unknown coefficients. According to Guass-Seidel method, iterative process can be expressed as

$$\begin{cases} w_{11}^{(k+1)} = -\frac{B_{12}}{B_{11}} w_{12}^{(k)} - \frac{B_{13}}{B_{11}} w_{13}^{(k)} - \cdots - \frac{B_{1n}}{B_{11}} w_{1n}^{(k)} + \frac{E_{11}}{B_{11}} \\ \cdots \\ w_{1n}^{(k+1)} = -\frac{B_{n1}}{B_{nn}} w_{11}^{(k+1)} - \frac{B_{n2}}{B_{nn}} w_{12}^{(k+1)} - \cdots - \frac{B_{1n-1}}{B_{nn}} w_{1n-1}^{(k+1)} + \frac{E_{n1}}{B_{nn}} \\ w_{m1}^{(k+1)} = -\frac{B_{12}}{B_{11}} w_{n2}^{(k)} - \frac{B_{13}}{B_{11}} w_{n3}^{(k)} - \cdots - \frac{B_{1n}}{B_{11}} w_{nn}^{(k)} + \frac{E_{1m}}{B_{11}} \\ \cdots \\ w_{mn}^{(k+1)} = -\frac{B_{n1}}{B_{nn}} w_{n1}^{(k+1)} - \frac{B_{n2}}{B_{nn}} w_{n2}^{(k+1)} - \cdots - \frac{B_{nn-1}}{B_{nn}} w_{nn-1}^{(k+1)} + \frac{E_{nm}}{B_{nn}} \end{cases} \quad (11)$$

Suppose $W^{(l)} = (w_{ij}^{(l)})_{m\times n}$ denotes a weight matrix after updated $l$ times using equation (11). Firstly, each weight was set to a small positive value. The astringency of the algorithm was deduced in reference [6]. If the value on the diagonal of weight matrix $W^{(l)}$ is largest in the same row, iteration process can converge.

## 2.2 Steps of Learning Algorithm

According to what we discussed above, the learning steps of the algorithm are described in detail as follows.

1) The neurons number of each layer is ascertained according to standard fuzzy patterns library and fuzzy parameters. The neurons number of the first layer expresses that of fuzzy parameters; the second expresses that of fuzzy patterns, and the neurons number of the third layer need be equal to that of the second one.
2) The parameters of network model are initialized by way of membership function of fuzzy patterns. The number of iteration is $k$, and the maximum number of iteration is $M$. The precision of iteration is $\varepsilon$.
3) Normal linear equation group (10) of samples is set up according to model structure and algorithm.
4) If $k > M$, step 6) is executed; otherwise $k = k+1$, and weight matrix $W^{(k)}$ is updated according to equation (11).
5) If $\| W^{(k+1)} - W^{(k)} \| < \varepsilon$, step 6) is executed; otherwise step 4) is executed.
6) Weight values are acquired and saved, and all steps are finished.

Since this network model computes weight values of each fuzzy pattern, the insufficiency that experts depend on their experiences can be whole avoided.

# 3 Experimental Results

In reference [1], a research on physical quality of 240 schoolboys is done in Investigation on physical quality of Chinese students. Firstly, 4 main parameters are selected from 18 parameters of physical test. Secondly, physical quality of schoolboys is classified into 5 grades by clustering method. Finally, the class that a student belongs to is recognized by maximum membership principle. However, in this method, the weights of 4 parameters are computed according to expert's experiences and subjective decision. Therefore, the judgment is not correct to physical quality test of students. Training samples are shown in Table 1.

**Table 1.** Training samples

| No. | Stature | Vital capacity | Class |
|---|---|---|---|
| 1 | 160 | 3319 | C |
| 2 | 158 | 3380 | C |
| 3 | 161 | 3250 | C |
| 4 | 157 | 3330 | C |
| 5 | 162 | 3255 | C |
| 6 | 159 | 3384 | C |
| 7 | 163 | 3210 | C |
| 8 | 170 | 3928 | B |
| 9 | 178 | 4000 | B |
| 10 | 168 | 4119 | B |
| 11 | 171 | 3900 | B |
| 12 | 172 | 3891 | B |
| 13 | 167 | 4150 | B |
| 14 | 169 | 4100 | B |
| 15 | 180 | 4336 | A |
| 16 | 179 | 4516 | A |
| 17 | 181 | 4419 | A |
| 18 | 179 | 4777 | A |
| 19 | 180 | 4399 | A |
| 20 | 185 | 4400 | A |

**Table 2.** Checking samples results

| No. | First neuron (A) | Second neuron (B) | Third neuron (C) | Maximum output | Class |
|---|---|---|---|---|---|
| 1 | 0 | 0.022055 | 1.21835 | 1.21835 | C |
| 2 | 0 | 0.019354 | 0.802991 | 0.802991 | C |
| 3 | 0 | 0.023214 | 1.017114 | 1.017114 | C |
| 4 | 0 | 0.017812 | 1.183491 | 1.183491 | C |
| 5 | 0 | 0.024245 | 1.055217 | 1.055217 | C |
| 6 | 0 | 0.020768 | 0.756742 | 0.756742 | C |
| 7 | 0 | 0.025149 | 0.573665 | 0.573665 | C |
| 8 | 0 | 1.067016 | 0.059489 | 1.067016 | B |
| 9 | 0 | 1.278633 | 0.059489 | 1.278633 | B |
| 10 | 0 | 0.940562 | 0.064105 | 0.940562 | B |
| 11 | 0 | 0.899886 | 0.056797 | 0.899886 | B |
| 12 | 0 | 0.835882 | 0.053848 | 0.835882 | B |
| 13 | 0 | 0.711578 | 0.066028 | 0.711578 | B |
| 14 | 0 | 1.052139 | 0.061925 | 1.052139 | B |
| 15 | 1.044027 | 0.02096 | 0.021026 | 1.044027 | A |
| 16 | 1.085326 | 0.022229 | 0.026027 | 1.085326 | A |
| 17 | 1.169935 | 0.019564 | 0.015770 | 1.169935 | A |
| 18 | 0.498652 | 0.022229 | 0.026027 | 0.498652 | A |
| 19 | 1.139585 | 0.02096 | 0.021026 | 1.139585 | A |
| 20 | 0.559541 | 0.012701 | 0 | 0.559541 | A |

**Table 3.** Testing samples results

| No. | Stature | Vital capacity | Class | No. | Stature | Vital capacity | Class | No. | Stature | Vital capacity | Class |
|---|---|---|---|---|---|---|---|---|---|---|---|
| 1 | 160 | 3289 | C | 21 | 164 | 3570 | C | 41 | 169 | 4251 | B |
| 2 | 159 | 3396 | C | 22 | 174 | 3918 | B | 42 | 167 | 4299 | B |
| 3 | 165 | 3150 | C | 23 | 170 | 4102 | B | 43 | 188 | 4239 | A |
| 4 | 167 | 3230 | C | 24 | 167 | 4269 | B | 44 | 176 | 4711 | A |
| 5 | 168 | 3055 | C | 25 | 173 | 3900 | B | 45 | 189 | 4311 | A |
| 6 | 162 | 3384 | C | 26 | 171 | 3999 | B | 46 | 176 | 4878 | A |
| 7 | 164 | 3270 | C | 27 | 173 | 4050 | B | 47 | 190 | 4219 | A |
| 8 | 154 | 3218 | C | 28 | 175 | 4009 | B | 48 | 183 | 4450 | A |
| 9 | 156 | 3280 | C | 29 | 169 | 4028 | B | 49 | 187 | 4336 | A |
| 10 | 163 | 3245 | C | 30 | 175 | 3900 | B | 50 | 181 | 4496 | A |
| 11 | 157 | 3430 | C | 31 | 169 | 4219 | B | 51 | 179 | 4549 | A |
| 12 | 169 | 3155 | C | 32 | 173 | 3890 | B | 52 | 183 | 4677 | A |
| 13 | 165 | 3784 | C | 33 | 170 | 3991 | B | 53 | 182 | 4419 | A |
| 14 | 161 | 3246 | C | 34 | 174 | 4050 | B | 54 | 177 | 4670 | A |
| 15 | 161 | 3279 | C | 35 | 169 | 4290 | B | 55 | 186 | 4339 | A |
| 16 | 157 | 3696 | C | 36 | 168 | 4218 | B | 56 | 178 | 4801 | A |
| 17 | 159 | 3220 | C | 37 | 172 | 4262 | B | 57 | 179 | 4881 | A |
| 18 | 163 | 3280 | C | 38 | 175 | 4119 | B | 58 | 184 | 4654 | A |
| 19 | 165 | 3155 | C | 39 | 171 | 3990 | B | 59 | 191 | 4519 | A |
| 20 | 161 | 3294 | C | 40 | 172 | 4099 | B | 60 | 183 | 4460 | A |

Experiments are done based on the model and algorithm presented in this paper. Let sample space is represented by $U=\{x_1, x_2, \cdots x_i, \cdots, x_{240}\}$, where $x_i$ expresses a sample and $i$ the sequence of a sample. Physical quality of students is classified into 5 grades by clustering method, denoted by $A_1$ (bad), $A_2$ (low middle), $A_3$ (middle), $A_4$ (good), $A_5$ (excellent) respectively. Each class $A_i$ is described by 4 main parameters, such as $A_{i1}$ (stature), $A_{i2}$ (avoirdupois), $A_{i3}$ (circumference), $A_{i4}$ (vital capacity). Thus a fuzzy pattern can be described as $A_i(A_{i1}, A_{i2}, A_{i3}, A_{i4})$. Membership function [1] corresponding to each fuzzy parameter is represented by

$$A_{ij}(x_j)=\begin{cases}0 & when \ |x_j-dx_j|>2s_j \\ 1-(x_j-dx_j)/2s_j & when \ |x_j-dx_j|<2s_j\end{cases} \tag{12}$$

where $dx_j$ is mean value, and $s_j$ is deviation. Samples can be normalized by this equation.

For simplicity, two representative fuzzy parameters such as stature and avoirdupois are chosen from 4 fuzzy parameters. And 3 classes, such as excellent (A), middle (B), bad (C) selected from 5 classes, form standard fuzzy patterns library. Instead of maximum membership principle, a three-layer network model is obtained to test the physical quality of students by 20 training samples shown in Table 1. Then, we apply the method to check training samples, and correct recognition rate reaches 100%, shown in Table 2. When 60 samples are used as testing samples, only 8 testing samples cannot be recognized correctly, and correct recognition rate reaches 86.7%, shown in Table 3.

## 4 Conclusions

From the experiments above, it can be demonstrated that a general fuzzy pattern recognition problem can be completely solved by neural network model. In fact, network structure and model expressed by equation (4) are the same as that by equation (2). The difference between them is mainly in different computing method of weights, thus results in the difference of correct recognition rate. This problem need be further studied in future.

## Acknowledgments

This work is supported by NSF of Guangdong Province, P.R.C. (No.032356) and by the fund of National Laboratory on Machine Perception, Peking University.

## References

1. Xie, J., Liu C.: Fuzzy Mathematic Method and Application. Huazhong University of Science and Technology Rress, Wu Han, China(2000)
2. Pal, S.K., Mitra, S.: Neuro-Fuzzy Pattern Recognition Methods in Soft Computing. John Wiley, New York(1999)
3. Martin, H., T.(ed.): Neural Network Design. PWS Publishing Co. Boston, MA, USA(1997)
4. Stanley, L. E., Hsu-Shih, S., Shih, H. S.: Fuzzy and Multi-level Decision Making. An Interactive Computational Approach. Springer-Verlag, London(2001)
5. Li, P.: A Weighted Fuzzy Reasoning Network and Its Application. Computer Engineering and Design, Vol. 26(1)(2005)188-190
6. Xu, S.: Common Algorithm in Computer. Tsinghua University Press, Beijing, China(1995)

# An Improved Elman Neural Network with Profit Factors and Its Applications

Limin Wang[1,2], Xiaohu Shi[1], Yanchun Liang[1,*], and Xuming Han[1,3]

[1] College of Computer Science and Technology, Jilin University, Key Laboratory of Symbol Computation and Knowledge Engineering of Ministry of Education, Changchun 130012, China
ycliang@jlu.edu.cn

[2] Department of Computer Science and Technology, Changchun Taxation College, Changchun 130117, China

[3] Institute of Information and Spreading Engineering, Changchun University of Technology, Changchun 130012, China

**Abstract.** An improved model is proposed by introducing the direction and time profit factors to Elman neural network (NN) and applied to the fields of the finial investing and atmospheric environment. Simulation results show the effectiveness of the proposed model for stock forecasting and the potential of the forecast and assessment for the atmospheric quality.

## 1 Introduction

Artificial neural network (ANN) has many advantages, such as self-learning, self-organizing, self-adjusting, and some others. It was proved by Hornik that the ANN could approximate any nonlinear functions at any precision if the network structure is selected appropriately [1].

Stock market has important characters with high venture and high profit. Therefore the prediction of the stock index becomes the focus problem of people. Though many methods have been proposed for the prediction of stock indexes, such as moving average method, point drawing method, K drawing method, season change and judge analysis, etc., their prediction results are not very well for the strong nonlinear feature of the stock market. In addition, with the consecutive progress industrialization and the improvement of people's living situation, the air pollution has attracted more and more attention recently. Therefore the studies related to the atmospheric quality, such as the assessment and forecasting of the atmospheric quality, have become noticeable increasingly. Considering the factors, in this paper, in order to obtain more accurate forecasting precision, an improved model based on Elman is proposed by introducing the direction and time profit factors. Then the proposed model is applied to the prediction of the composite index of stock and the field of atmospheric quality forecasting and assessment. Experimental results show that the model is feasible and effective, which could provide novel effective approaches for the finance vesting and useful information for the atmospheric pollution forecasting and assessment.

* Corresponding author.

D.-S. Huang, K. Li, and G.W. Irwin (Eds.): ICIC 2006, LNCS 4113, pp. 317–322, 2006.

## 2 A Brief Introduction of Elman Neural Network

For describing conveniently, Elman neural network (Elman NN) is introduced briefly in this section, the details could be referred to [2]. Elman NN is a dynamic feedback network, it has a particular layer called context layer besides the conventional input, hidden and output layers. The context layer could memory the former value of output layer nodes. It could be regarded as a time-delay operator, so it makes Elman neural network has the capability of the dynamic memory. The structure of Elman NN is shown in Fig.1. The mathematic model of Elman neural network is:

$$x(k) = f(w^{I1} x_C(k) + w^{I2} u(k-1)), \tag{1}$$

$$x_C(k) = \alpha x_C(k-1) + x(k-1), \tag{2}$$

$$y(k) = g(w^{I3} x(k)). \tag{3}$$

Where $w^{I1}$, $w^{I2}$, $w^{I3}$ are , respectively, the weights which link the hidden and context layers, the hidden and input layers, the output and hidden layers, $x_c(k)$ and $x(k)$ are the outputs of context layer and hidden layer, $y(k)$ is the output of output layer, $0 \leq \alpha < 1$ is the feedback gain of the self-connection of context layer, $f(x)$ is usually selected as *sigmoid* function.

Let the given real output of the $k$th sample be denoted by $y_d(k)$, then the objective function is selected as follows:

$$E(k) = \frac{1}{2}(y_d(k) - y(k))^T (y_d(k) - y(k)). \tag{4}$$

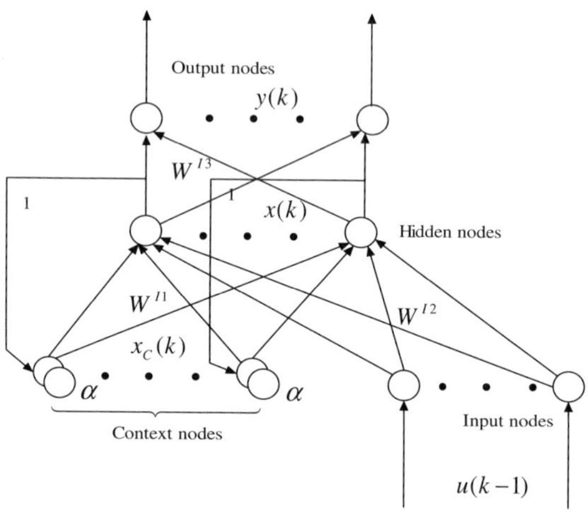


**Fig. 1.** The structure of Elman NN

## 3 Elman Neural Network with Profit Factors

Since the inputs of the neural network are the former sample data, which can be considered as a time series, so the data which are near to the current time should play the more important role than those far from the current time. Therefore a time profit factor $f_{TP}(j)$ [3] is introduced into the objective function of Elman NN to reflect the different effects of different time sample data. In addition, a direction profit factor $f_{DP}(k)$ [4] is introduced to Elman NN which could represent the punishment for the forecasted trend that does not accord with the real value. In this paper, in order to obtain better forecasting results, both direction and time profit factors are introduced into the objective function of Elman NN simultaneously. Therefore the objective function could be defined as follows:

$$E_{DTP}(k) = \sum_{j=1}^{k} f_{DTP}(j)E(j)\,. \tag{5}$$

Where $E(j)$ is defined by Eq. (4), and the profit factor $f_{DTP}(j)$ is defined as the product of the direction profit factor $f_{DP}(j)$ and time profit factor $f_{TP}(j)$, that is

$$f_{DTP}(j)=f_{DP}(j)\times f_{TP}(j). \tag{6}$$

Here $f_{DP}(j)$ and $f_{TP}(j)$ are defined as follows:

$$f_{DP}(j) = \begin{cases} g & if\ (y_d(j) - y_d(j-1))(y(j) - y(j-1)) \le 0 \\ h & otherwise \end{cases}, \tag{7}$$

$$f_{TP}(j) = 1/(1+\exp(a - 2a\cdot j\cdot k^{-1}))\,. \tag{8}$$

Here $g$ is a big value compared with $h$, therefore $f_{DP}(j)$ could represent the punishment, and $a$ is discount rate.

Calculating the partial derivatives of $E_{DTP}(k)$ with respect to weights and let them be zeros, we have the learning algorithm of ENNDTPF as follows:

$$\Delta w_{ij}^{I3}(k) = \sum_{t=1}^{k} \eta_3 f_{DTP}(t)\delta_i^0 x_j(t) \quad (i = 1,2,\cdots,m;\ j = 1,2,\cdots,n)\,, \tag{9}$$

$$\Delta w_{jq}^{I2}(k) = \sum_{t=1}^{k} \eta_2 f_{DTP}(t)\delta_j^h u_q(t-1) \quad (j = 1,2,\cdots,n;\ q = 1,2,\cdots,r)\,, \tag{10}$$

$$\Delta w_{jl}^{I1}(k) = \sum_{t=1}^{k} \eta_1 f_{DTP}(t)\sum_{i=1}^{m}(\delta_i^0 w_{ij}^{I3})\frac{\partial x_j(t)}{\partial w_{jl}^{I1}} \quad (j = 1,2,\cdots,n;\ l = 1,2,\cdots,n)\,, \tag{11}$$

$$\delta_i^0 = (y_{d,i}(k) - y_i(k))\,, \tag{12}$$

$$\delta_j^h = \sum_{i=1}^{m}(\delta_i^0 w_{ij}^{I3}) f_j'(\cdot)\,, \tag{13}$$

$$\frac{\partial x_j(k)}{\partial w_{jl}^{I1}} = f_j'(\cdot)x_l(k-1) + \alpha \frac{\partial x_j(k-1)}{\partial w_{jl}^{I1}} \quad (j=1,2,\cdots,n;\ l=1,2,\cdots,n). \tag{14}$$

Where $\eta_1$, $\eta_2$, $\eta_3$ are the learning steps of the $w^{I1}$, $w^{I2}$, and $w^{I3}$, respectively.

# 4 Applications of the Improved Elman NN Model with Profit Factors

## 4.1 Applications for Stock Market

For convenient calculation, the stock exchange fee is not considered, and we assume that there is only one stock in the market. Therefore we perform the stock exchange according to the following rule: if we predict that the stock price will rise next working day, then we buy the stock as much as money permitted; otherwise we trade off all the stock in hand. The profit could be defined by follows:

$$Profit = ((Remaining\text{-}Seed)/\ Seed) \times 100\%. \tag{15}$$

Where *Profit* is the profit by exchanging stock, *Seed* the value of the initial fund, and *Remaining* the value of the final fund, respectively.

In this paper, the experiment data are selected from the composite indexes in Shanghai Stock Exchange (CISSE) from 4 January 1999 to 29 June 2000. The network structures are selected as 3-10-1, namely with 3 input nodes, 10 hidden and 1 output nodes, respectively. The inputs of the networks are the composite indexes of the stock of three consecutive days, and the output is the forecasting value of the fourth day. Before learning, the input data should be normalized into the unit interval [0, 1]. To evaluate the effectiveness of the prediction models, we use the absolute average error (AAE) and least square error (LSE) functions to represent the forecasting precision.

**Prediction of the Composite Index of Stock**

Firstly, the ENNDTPF is applied to do the prediction of the composite indexes of stock. The parameters selected by trial and error are as follows: $\alpha$=0.1, $\eta_1$=0.1, $\eta_2$=0.1, $\eta_3$=0.1, $a$=3, $g$=1.5, $h$=0.03. The prediction results are shown in Fig.2. It could be found clearly that the forecasting curve obtained from ENNDTPF is closer to the real curve than that obtained by using the Elman NN.

**Comparisons of Stock Profit**

In this section, Elman and ENNDTPF models are applied to forecast the composite indexes of stock. According to their prediction results, the stock exchanges are performed in the following rule: before exchanging, the composite index of the stock of next working day is predicted firstly by using the three consecutive days. If the composite index value predicted is rising, then we buy the stock as much as money permitted; otherwise we trade off all the stock in hand. The initial money funds are set as 1000 RMB. Table 1 shows the results after 50 iterations. In the table, the second column represents the least square error, the third column the absolute average error, the fourth column the final funds, and the fifth column the profits, respectively.

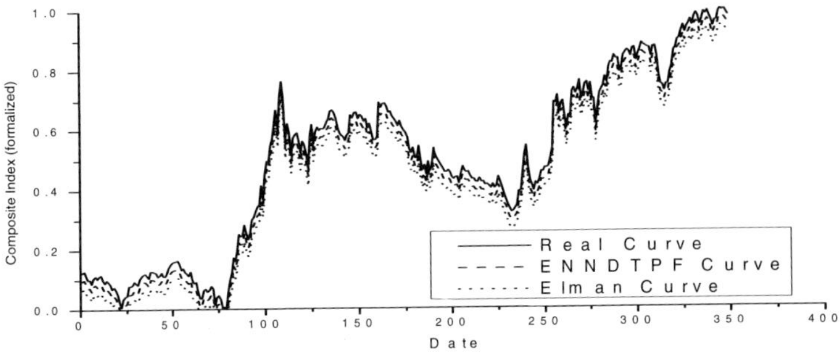


**Fig. 2.** Comparison results of Elman and ENNDTPF models for the stock

It can be seen from Table 1 that the obtained profit of the stock exchange according to the prediction result of ENNDTPF model is higher than Elman NN model evidently, and ENNDTPF model increases 4.3965 times than that of Elman model.

**Table 1.** Errors, remaining and profits using different models (after 50 iterations)

| Model | LSE | AAE | Remaining (RMB) | Profit Rate (%) |
|---|---|---|---|---|
| Elman NN | 0.08831 | 0.20654 | 1084.58 | 8.45830 |
| ENNDTPF | 0.00000 | 0.00054 | 1371.87 | 37.1872 |

## 4.2 Applications to the Forecasting and Assessment Atmospheric Quality

In this section, the improved Elman NN is used to forecast the pollutants ($PM_{10}$, $SO_2$ and $NO_2$) of a city in the Northeast of China. The forecasting density values and assessment results calculated by Reference [5] are listed in Table 2. It could be found from Table 2 that the results obtained by ENNDTPF model are basically accordant with the given real assessment except for one result with a slight difference.

**Table 2.** The assessment results of a city of Northeast of China

| Time | Harm rate $R$ | Assessment | Real results |
|---|---|---|---|
| 2002.4.17 | 0.024068 | good | good |
| 2002.3.18 | 0.017586 | excellent | excellent |
| 2002.4.19 | 0.028258 | good | good |
| 2002.4.20 | 0.067933 | slight | slight |
| 2002.4.21 | 0.029807 | good | good |
| 2002.4.22 | 0.021975 | good | good |
| 2002.4.23 | 0.019396 | excellent | good |
| 2002.4.24 | 0.022019 | good | good |
| 2002.4.25 | 0.020797 | excellent | excellent |
| 2002.4.26 | 0.022513 | good | good |
| 2002.4.27 | 0.023022 | good | good |
| 2002.4.28 | 0.024687 | good | good |
| 2002.4.29 | 0.020423 | excellent | excellent |
| 2002.4.30 | 0.022122 | good | good |

## 5 Conclusions

An improved model is proposed by introducing the direction and time profit factors to Elman neural network. Numerical results show that the proposed model could improve the forecasting precision evidently. Moreover, if the stock exchange is performed according to the prediction results of the composite index of stock, we could obtain more profits. In addition, the ENNDTPF model is also used to forecast and assess atmospheric quality. Experimental results show the improved Elman model is useful in the field of the forecast and assessment for the atmospheric quality.

## Acknowledgment

The first three authors are grateful to the support of the National Natural Science Foundation of China under Grant No. 60433020, the science-technology development project for international collaboration of Jilin Province of China under Grant No. 20050705-2, the doctoral funds of the National Education Ministry of China under Grant No. 20030183060, the Graduate Innovation Lab of Jilin University under Grant No. 503041, the Project of Changchun Taxation College, and "985" Project of Jilin University.

## References

1. Hornik, K., Stinchcombe, M., White, H.: Universal Approximation of An Unknown Mapping and Its Derivatives Using Multilayer Feedforward Networks. Neural Networks, Vol. 3. (1990) 551-560
2. Shi, X. H., Liang, Y. C., Lee, H. P., Lin, W. Z., Xu, X., Lim, S. P.: Improved Elman Networks and Applications for Controlling Ultrasonic Motors. Applied Artificial Intelligence, Vol. 18. (2004) 603-629
3. Refenes, A. N., Brntz, Y., Bunn, D. W., Burgess, A. N., Zapranis, A. D.: Financial Time Series Modeling with Discounted least Squares Back Propagation. Neural Computing, Vol. 14. (1997) 123-138
4. Caldwell, R. B.: Performances Metrics for Neural Network-based Trading System Development. Neuro Ve$t Journal, Vol. 3. (1995) 22-26
5. Wang, L. M., Shi, X. H., Li, M., Chen, G. J., Ge, H. W., Lee, H. P., Liang, Y.C.: Applications of PSO Algorithm and OIF Elman Neural Network to Assessment and Forecasting for Atmospheric Quality, 7th International Conference on Adaptive and Neural Computing Algorithms (2004) 251-254

# Application of Wavelet Network Combined with Nonlinear Dimensionality Reduction on the Neural Dipole Localization

Qing Wu, Lukui Shi, Tao Lin, and Ping He

School of Computer Science and Software, Hebei University of Technology,
Tianjin 300130, China
qingwu@hebut.edu.cn

**Abstract.** A wavelet network (WN) method is presented in this paper, which can be used to estimate the location and moment of an equivalent current dipole source using reduced-dimension data from the original measurement electroencephalography (EEG). In order to handle the large-scale high dimension problems efficiently and provide a real-time EEG dipole source localizer, the ISOMAP algorithm is firstly used to find the low dimensional manifolds from high dimensional EEG signal. Then, a WN is employed to discover the relationship between the observation potentials on the scalp and the internal sources within the brain. In our simulation experiments, satisfactory results are obtained.

## 1 Introduction

The core of the electroencephalography (EEG) inverse problem is the determination of the neuroelectric generators responsible for measured EEG phenomena, which is important in cognitive science and brain pathology research. Generally, the active neurons within small regions of the brain are often modeled as an equivalent current dipole with six parameters $\boldsymbol{y}=[y_1, y_2, y_3, y_4, y_5, y_6]$, where the first three elements denote the dipole location and last three determine the moment. Presently, iterative optimization methods are in widespread use for finding the dipole source. Unfortunately, the computational burden of this kind of methods is inevitably high in order to ensure reasonable solution. To reduce this burden and take the advantage of the high temporal resolution of EEG, we study the use of wavelet network (WN) combined with isometric mapping (ISOMAP) for solving the neural dipole source localization problem in EEG. First, a forward procedure is provided to calculate the measurement variables corresponding with the dipole parameters to generate the sample data. Second, a nonlinear dimensionality reduction mapping - ISOMAP is used to pretreat the data, and find the compact lower dimensional representation of the original data. Third, a wavelet neural network method is applied to get the parameters of the dipole source that corresponds to a certain reduced potential distribution on the scalp.

## 2 Nonlinear Dimensionality Reduction by ISOMAP

Data dimensionality reduction is one of the most important tasks in machine learning. The goal is to compress the data and to gain compact representations of the original

D.-S. Huang, K. Li, and G.W. Irwin (Eds.): ICIC 2006, LNCS 4113, pp. 323 – 328, 2006.

data. Two popular methods for dimensionality reduction are principal component analysis (PCA) and multidimensional scaling (MDS). They are both guaranteed to find the true structure of data lying on or near a linear subspace of the high-dimensional input space. However, linear techniques may be inadequate when the data do not lie approximately on a hyperplane. Thus, it can be beneficial to consider non-linear dimensionality reduction. Recently, several unsupervised learning algorithms, such as ISOMAP [1], LLE [2], and graph Laplacians [3], have been proposed to perform nonlinear dimensionality reduction of low-dimensional nonlinear manifolds embedded in a high dimensional space. The ISOMAP algorithm is the most representative method.

The principle of ISOMAP is that classical multidimensional scaling is applied to the geodesic distances to find a set of low-dimensional points with similar pairwise distances. The crux of the method is to estimate the geodesic distances between points, which represent the shortest paths along the curved surface of the manifold. For a neighboring point, the input space distance provides a good approximation to the geodesic distance. For faraway points, the actual geodesic distances are approximated by a sequence of short hops between neighboring points. For a data set $X$ with $N$ points in the input space, the main idea of the algorithm consists of the following three steps [1]:

Step 1. Determine neighborhoods for each point on the manifold $M$ based on the distances $d_X(i,j)$ between pairs of points $i$ and $j$ in the data set $X$ by a suitable way. For example, one method involves selecting the $k$ nearest neighbors, while another selects all objects within some fixed radius $\varepsilon$. These neighborhood relations are represented as a weighted graph, $G$, over the data set, with edges of weight $d_X(i,j)$ between neighbors.

Step 2. Estimate the geodesic distances $d_M(i,j)$ between all pairs of points by computing approximations as the shortest path distances $d_G(i,j)$ in the graph $G$. Then the final matrix of graph distances $D_G=\{d_G(i,j)\}$ will contain the shortest path distances between all pairs of points in $G$.

Step 3. Apply classical MDS to $D_G$ to construct an embedding of the data in a $d$-dimensional Euclidean space $Y$ that best preserves the manifold's estimated intrinsic geometry.

The ISOMAP algorithm is executed on the Swiss roll data set with 1000 samples. The experimental results are shown in Fig. 1.

In order to use ISOMAP to get the low dimensional representation of multichannel EEG data efficiently, it is expected that when we calculate the distance between two data points, the points with approximate electric potential values become closer and the points with much different electric potential values deviate further. Since the EEG signals under study in this paper are produced by an equivalent dipole, whose electric potential distribution is centered by the potential value produced on the scalp along the dipole moment and decays as approximate concentric circles, the electric potential values can be prearranged according to this regular pattern. By this way, the relatively similar observed data are mapped into near points in the feature space, while the data with quite different shape distribution are mapped into distant points. The ISOMAP can be modified to implement the above aim. First, calculate $k$ nearest neighbors of each sample $x$. The set of the points that have approximate electric potential values as

$x$ is designated as $K$. For each point $x_k$ in the set $K$, reduce the distance between it and $x$ by a certain value, and then execute the rest steps of ISOMAP algorithm. The hidden structure of high dimensional EEG data, which is more easily to cope with in the following procedure, can thus be found.

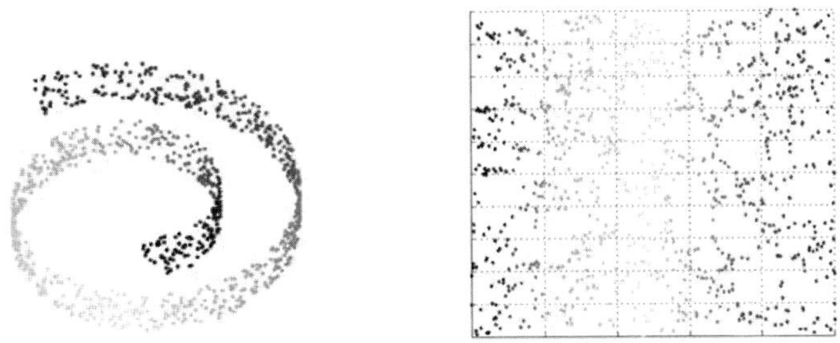

(a) Swiss roll data set (b) 2-dimensional representation

**Fig. 1.** Low-dimensional embeddings from ISOMAP on Swiss roll data set

## 3 Nonlinear Mapping Approximator by Wavelet Network

Radial basis function (RBF) neural network and wavelet transform are both powerful tools in studying nonlinear problems, and there is an inner relationship between the two methods. If mother wavelet is taken as the radial activation function of hidden neurons, the number of wavelet bases determined by training sample sets is corresponding with the number of nodes in the hidden layer, and the dilation and translation of wavelets is corresponding with the radius and centers respectively, the structure of them are very similar. Here, we construct a wavelet network based on a single-scaling wavelet frame [4] and RBF network model to approximate any nonlinear function. A single-scaling radial wavelet frame $F$ of $L^2(R^d)$ can be built by scaling a mother function "Mexican hat" $\psi(\boldsymbol{x}) = (d - \| \boldsymbol{x} \|^2) e^{-\|\boldsymbol{x}\|^2/2}$, $\boldsymbol{x} \in R^d$

$$F = \{\psi_{n,\boldsymbol{m}}(\boldsymbol{x}) = 2^{dn/2}\psi(2^{-n}\boldsymbol{x} - \boldsymbol{m}) : n \in Z, \boldsymbol{m} \in Z^d\}. \tag{1}$$

Consider a sample set $\theta$ of training pairs provided under the mapping $\boldsymbol{f}(\boldsymbol{x})$

$$\theta = \{(\boldsymbol{x}_i, \boldsymbol{y}_i) : \boldsymbol{x}_i \in R^d; \boldsymbol{y}_i \in R^s; \boldsymbol{y}_i = \boldsymbol{f}(\boldsymbol{x}_i); i = 1,2,\cdots,N\}. \tag{2}$$

We would like to obtain a good WN approximation

$$\tilde{\boldsymbol{f}}(\boldsymbol{x}) = \sum\nolimits_{n,\boldsymbol{m}} W_{n,\boldsymbol{m}} \psi_{n,\boldsymbol{m}}(\boldsymbol{x}) \tag{3}$$

of $\boldsymbol{f}$ through self-organization, where $W_{n,\boldsymbol{m}}$ are the weights between the hidden nodes and the output nodes in WN.

Generally speaking, the above kind of WN often suffers from the curse of dimensionality [5]. But fortunately, in the practical neuroelectric source localization, the training samples $\theta$ are often not uniformly distributed in the entire domain of the input space. Rather, they are commonly sparse and distributed in some subspace in the form of clusters. So we start with the analysis of the sparseness of the training samples and focus on reducing the redundancy of $F$ based on localization of wavelets and time-frequency information of the samples' input variable $\boldsymbol{x}$. Then, we use an adaptive orthogonal projective algorithm that can automatically determine the network size and calculate the network weights in the light of the information given by the samples' output variable $\boldsymbol{y}$ [6]. Our main steps of the algorithm are summarized in the following.

Step 1. Determine the range of dilation parameter $n$, and for each dilation $n$, calculate the range of translation parameter $m$ according to input data.

$$\begin{gathered} n_{\min} = \mathrm{int}(-\lg(4\pi / \Delta x\omega)/\lg 2)\,,\ n_{\max} = \mathrm{int}(\lg(x_{\max} - x_{\min})/\lg 2) \\ m_{\min} = \mathrm{int}(x_{\min} / 2^n),\ m_{\max} = \mathrm{int}(x_{\max} / 2^n) \end{gathered} \tag{4}$$

where $\Delta x$ is the spatial interval of the training sample, and $\omega$ is the effective frequency width of $\psi$.

Step 2. Calculate the supports of each wavelet $\varepsilon - \mathrm{supp}(\psi_{n,m})$ for a chosen parameter $\varepsilon$, and eliminate the wavelets whose supports do not contain any input data point $\boldsymbol{x}$. Suppose $F' = \{\psi_1, \psi_2, \cdots, \psi_L\}$ be the resulting set of selected wavelets after the first two steps.

Step 3. According to output vector $\boldsymbol{y}$ to further remove redundant elements in $F'$. Considering the wavelets in $F'$ as regressors, techniques of matching pursuits can be applied. And Gram-Schmidt algorithm is combined to orthonormalize and further selects optimal wavelets. Moreover, WN training is implemented during this executing process. The elements $\psi_j (j = 1,2,\cdots,L)$ in $F'$ and output data rewrite as

$$\begin{gathered} \boldsymbol{\psi}_j = [\psi_j(\boldsymbol{x}_1), \psi_j(\boldsymbol{x}_2), \cdots, \psi_j(\boldsymbol{x}_N)]^{\mathrm{T}} / \| [\psi_j(\boldsymbol{x}_1), \psi_j(\boldsymbol{x}_2), \cdots, \psi_j(\boldsymbol{x}_N)]^{\mathrm{T}} \| \\ \boldsymbol{Y} = [\boldsymbol{y}_1, \boldsymbol{y}_2, \cdots, \boldsymbol{y}_N]^{\mathrm{T}};\ \boldsymbol{y}_i = [y_{i1}, y_{i2}, \cdots, y_{is}];\ \boldsymbol{x}_i, \boldsymbol{y}_i \in \theta;\ i = 1,2,\cdots,N \end{gathered} \tag{5}$$

For the estimation of unknown $\boldsymbol{f}$, the "best" subset of $F' = \{\psi_1, \psi_2, \cdots, \psi_L\}$ is selected by an iterative procedure. Suppose the number of the elements in the subset is finally $h$ and it spans a space "closest" to the matrix $\boldsymbol{Y}$. We first select the wavelet in $F'$ that best fits the observed data. Then, repeatedly select the wavelet in the remainder of $F'$ that best fits the data while combining with the previously selected wavelets. For the sake of computational efficiency, later selected wavelets are orthonormalized to the earlier selected ones. During this procedure, the connection weight $w_{ij}$ between the hidden node $j$ and the output node $i$ is calculated. The resulting WN is

$$\tilde{f}_i(\boldsymbol{x}) = \sum_{j=1}^{h} w_{ij} \psi(2^{-n_j} \boldsymbol{x} - \boldsymbol{m}_j) \quad i = 1,2,\cdots,s\,. \tag{6}$$

According to the above steps, we can design a WN that will provide a good approximation to the unknown map $\boldsymbol{f}$.

## 4 Experimental Results

Since it is a black-box method to use WN to solve the EEG inverse problem based on potential-dipole data, so it has nothing to do with the concrete head model. As to the realistic head model, it is rather complex to obtain samples. The image segmentation of MRI or CT, 3D mesh generation and calculation of BEM or FEM must be completed. To be focused on the inspection of the performance of WN, a four-layer homocentric spherical head model that composed of the brain, cerebrospinal fluid, skull and scalp from inside to outside is firstly employed. Its relative radii and conductivity constants are (0.84, 0.8667, 0.9467, 1) and (0.33, 1.0, 0.0042, 0.33) S/m, respectively. See Fig. 2(a). Since spherical model has analytical solution, numerical calculation error could be avoided.

The EEG forward solution relates the given vector $\boldsymbol{y}_i$ of a certain dipole $i$ to the potential vector $\boldsymbol{x}_i$. We take 138 potentials uniformly distributed on the surface of scalp as the input, and 6 parameters of the corresponding dipole as the output of WN. Random dipole locations whose three components obey the uniform distribution are independently generated. Then, the dipole moments are generated randomly by the zero-mean, unit-variance Gaussian distribution. This procedure yielded 10000 dipoles. We randomly choose 8000 consisting a training set, and the other 2000 consisting a test set. Using the analytic forward algorithm in [7], the data samples can be produced. Subsequently, the 138-dimensional data $\boldsymbol{x}$ is mapped into a 6-dimensional embedding with ISOMAP. Finally, WN is trained based on the dimensionality reduction learning set, and tested with the test set. To evaluate the performance of the WN, we define the average relative mean-square error by

$$\text{Error} = \sum_{i=1}^{N} \sum_{j=1}^{s} (y_j(i) - \tilde{y}_j(i))^2 \Big/ \sum_{i=1}^{N} \sum_{j=1}^{s} y_j^{\,2}(i) \qquad (7)$$

where $y$ and $\tilde{y}$ are the theoretical and network computed parameters. The training and test error is 1.24% and 3.65%, respectively.

In order to decrease the loss in accuracy if a WN is trained on a spherical but applied on a realistic head model in real word problem, we generate the data samples of realistic head model (as shown in Fig. 2(b)) by boundary element method (BEM) [8].

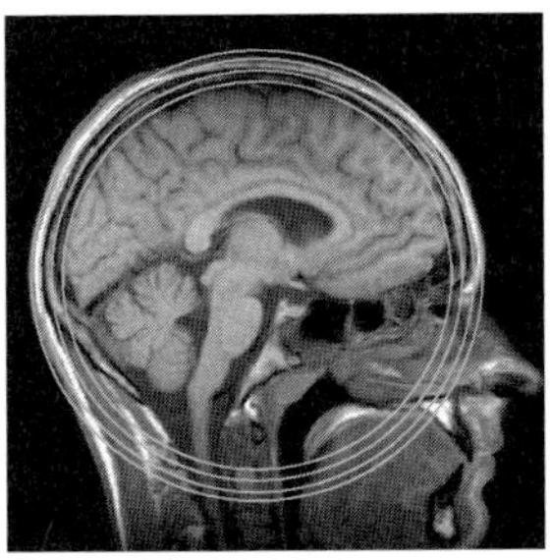

(a) Four-layer concentric sphere model

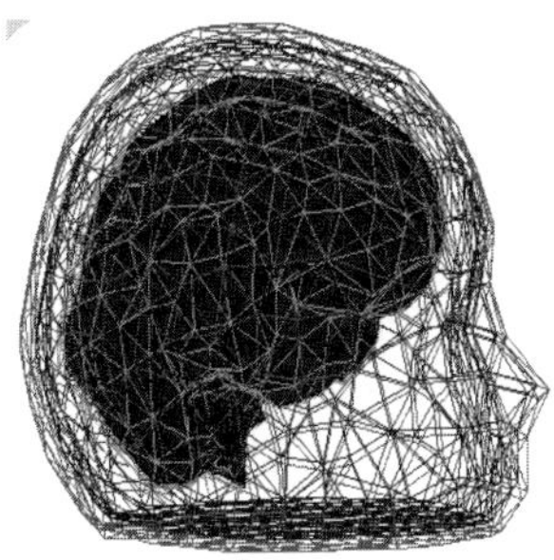

(b) Triangular mesh of realistic model

**Fig. 2.** Head model

Then, we solve the EEG inverse problem by applying the same method as the one used for spherical model. The average relative error for 10000 training samples and 3000 testing samples is 3.96% and 8.74%, respectively.

## 5 Conclusions

Experiments prove that the proposed approach is effective to be used in the EEG dipole source localization. Since the error of realistic head model is higher than that of spherical head model, it could lead us to get the conclusion that the inverse problem is more complex, and thus more difficult to learn, in a realistic geometry. But further analyses show that for spherical model, the error is also higher in the BEM case than in the analytic case. So the higher error is due rather to the use of numerical solution BEM in the forward problem than to the realistic geometry of the head model.

## Acknowledgement

This work was supported by natural science foundation of Hebei province of China under grant number E2005000024, and by the Ph.D. foundation of Hebei education department under grant number B2004107.

## References

1. Tenenbaum, J.B., de Silva, V., Langford, J.C.: A Global Geometric Framework for Nonlinear Dimensionality Reduction. Science, Vol. 290, (2000) 2319-2323
2. Roweis, S.T., Saul, L.K.: Nonlinear Dimensionality Reduction by Locally Linear Embedding. Science, Vol. 290, (2000) 2323-2326
3. Belkin, M., Niyogi, P.: Laplacian Eigenmaps for Dimensionality Reduction and Data Representation. Neural Computation, Vol. 15, (2003) 1373–1396
4. Kugarajah, T., Zhang, Q.: Multidimensional Wavelet Frames. IEEE Transactions on Neural Networks, Vol. 6, (1995) 1552-1556
5. Zhang, Q.: Using Wavelet Network in Non-Parametric Estimation. IEEE Transactions on Neural Networks, Vol. 8, (1997) 227-236
6. Wu, Q., Shen, X.Q., Yan, W.L.: A Multi-dimensional Wavelet Network Construction Algorithm. Chinese Journal of Computers, Vol. 26, (2003) 1206-1210
7. Sun, M.G.: An Efficient Algorithm for Computing Multishell Spherical Volume Conductor Models in EEG Dipole Source Localization. IEEE Trans. Biom. Eng., Vol. 44, (1997) 1243-1252
8. Wu, Q., Wang, L., Li, Y., He, S.J., Yan, W.L.: A Computer Simulation System of the Electric Activity in Brains. The Silver Anniversary International Conference of the IEEE EMBC, Mexico, (2003) 990-993

# Artificial Neural Network Methodology for Soil Liquefaction Evaluation Using CPT Values

Ben-yu Liu, Liao-yuan Ye, Mei-ling Xiao, and Sheng Miao

Institute of Public Safety and Disaster Prevention, Yunnan University,
650091 Kunming, China
{liubenyu, lyye, mlxiao, msheng}@ynu.edu.cn
http://www.srees.ynu.edu.cn/structure/index.html

**Abstract.** With the 413 soil liquefaction records with cone penetration testing values collected after strong earthquakes, the Bayesian Regularization Back Propagation Neural Networks (BRBPNN) method was presented to evaluate the soil liquefaction potential in this paper. Cone resistance ( $q_c$ ), equivalent dynamic shear stress ( $\tau / \sigma_0'$ ), mean grain size ( $D_{50}$ ), total stress ( $\sigma_0$ ), the effective stress ( $\sigma_0'$ ), earthquake magnitude ( $M$ ) and the normalized acceleration horizontal at ground surface ( $a / g$ ) are used as input parameters for networks. Four networks are constructed for different source of input data. The model M7 seems more efficient for the given data, since it only contain 109 records. The model M5 contains 413 samples, and the correct ratio for training data and testing data are 88.5% and 90% respectively. By compared with the square of the weight of the input layer for each network, the importance order of the input parameters should be $q_c$ , $M$ , $\sigma_0'$ , $\sigma_0$ , $a / g$ , $\tau / \sigma_0'$ and $D_{50}$ .

## 1 Introduction

The devastating damage of liquefaction induced ground failures in the Alaska 1964 and Niigata 1964 earthquakes serve as a clear reminder of such events. The liquefaction potential evaluation of a given site under certain seismic forces is a big problem facing engineers. The soil liquefaction prediction methods can be divided into two categories. One is the method developed based on the liquefaction mechanism simulation, such as nonlinear effective stress method, equivalent linear method and elastic-plastic method, etc. The other procedure is constructed based on the liquefaction records collected strong earthquakes, the parameters like the Standard Penetration Test (SPT), the Cone Penetration Test (CPT) and the shear wave velocity of the site are used to predict the liquefaction potential of site [1, 2]. About 40 formulae were constructed to predict the soil liquefaction potential, although most of them were not efficient to use [1]. In the laboratory tests, reliability of the results depends on simulation of idealized filed conditions. Unfortunately, in situ stress states generally cannot be reestablished in the laboratory, and specimens of granular soils retrieved with typical drilling and sampling techniques are too disturbed to yield meaningful results. To avoid the difficulties associated with sampling and laboratory testing, field tests have become the state-of-practice for routine liquefaction investigations. Several field tests

D.-S. Huang, K. Li, and G.W. Irwin (Eds.): ICIC 2006, LNCS 4113, pp. 329 – 336, 2006.

have gained common usage for evaluation of liquefaction resistance, including the standard penetration test (SPT), the cone penetration test (CPT), shear-wave velocity measurements (*Vs*), and the Becker penetration test (BPT).Since the neural network is a nonlinear method which can fit the nonlinear data with great efficiency, the artificial neural networks are employed to predict the soil liquefaction potential in recent years [3-11].

# 2 Neural Network Prediction for Soil Liquefaction Potential

The main characteristics of neural networks are their ability to learn nonlinear functional relationships from examples and to discover patterns or regularities in data through self-organization. The neural network learning process primarily involves the iterative modification of the connection weights until the error between the predicted and expected output values is minimized. It is through the presentation of examples, or training cases, and application of the learning rule that the neural network obtains the relationship embedded in the data.

## 2.1 Back Propagation Neural Networks Design

It is nature that the neural network designed for this problem should be accordance with the sample data. Thus, the input vector of the network contains 7 components. While for the output vector, it includes only one component.

## 2.2 Theory on the Bayesian Regularization Back Propagation Neural Networks

We divided the datasets into two parts: training and testing. In using multiply layer propagation network, the problem of over-fitting on noise data is of major concern in network design strategy. The initial results of using a standard BP algorithm showed poor generalization performance and slow speed of training. To overcome these shortcomings, we incorporated Bayesian learning to this work. In the Bayesian framework, a weight decay term is introduced to the cost function (or performance index) given by

$$F(w) = \alpha E_W + \beta E_D . \tag{1}$$

where $E_W$ is the sum square of the networks weights, $E_D$ is the sum square of the error between network outputs and targets, $\alpha$ and $\beta$ are hyper-parameters for the target function. The relative value of $\alpha$ and $\beta$ determined the emphasis on the network training on minimization of the output errors or the volume of the network. As shown in Equation (1), the main problem with implementing regularization is to set/learn the correct values for the parameters in the cost function. Ref. [12, 13] has presented extensive works on the application of Bayesian rule to neural network training and to optimizing regularization.

In the Bayesian framework, the weights of the network are considered the random variables. The weights in the network are adjusted to the most probable weight parameter, $w_{MP}$, given the data $D\{(x^m, t^m)\}$, network configuration ($M_i$), and hyper-parameters, i.e., $\alpha$ and $\beta$ .

Set the $\alpha$ and $\beta$ as stochastic variables, the Bayesian rule is used for evaluating the posterior probability of $\alpha$ and $\beta$. This is given by

$$P(\alpha,\beta \mid D,M_i)=(P(D \mid \alpha,\beta,M_i)P(\alpha,\beta \mid M_i))/P(D \mid M_i). \tag{2}$$

where $P(\alpha,\beta \mid M_i)$ represents the prior probability of the hyper-parameters and are generally chosen to be uniformly distributed. Since $P(D \mid M_i)$ is independent of $\alpha$ and $\beta$, maximum posterior values for hyper-parameters can be found by maximizing the likelihood term $P(D \mid \alpha,\beta,M_i)$.

Using Bayesian rule, the posterior probability of the weight parameters is:

$$P(w \mid D,\alpha,\beta,M_i)=\frac{(P(D \mid w,\beta,M_i)P(w \mid a,M_i))}{P(D \mid \alpha,\beta,M_i)}. \tag{3}$$

Assume the error and the weight is distributed in Gaussian form,

$$P(D \mid w,\beta,M_i)=\exp(-\beta E_D)/Z_D(\beta). \tag{4}$$

$$P(w \mid \alpha,M_i)=\exp(-\alpha E_W)/Z_W(\alpha). \tag{5}$$

If the $P(D \mid \alpha,\beta,M_i)$ in Equation (3) is regularized factor, $P(w \mid D,\alpha,\beta,M_i)$ must equal to $\exp(-F(w))/Z_F(\alpha,\beta)$. Take them into Equation (2),

$$P(D \mid \alpha,\beta,M_i)=Z_F(\alpha,\beta)/(Z_W(\alpha)Z_D(\beta)). \tag{6}$$

where

$$Z_W(\alpha)=(2\pi/\alpha)^{N/2}. \tag{7}$$

$$Z_D(\beta)=(2\pi/\beta)^{N/2}. \tag{8}$$

$$Z_F(\alpha,\beta)\approx \exp(-F(w_{MP}))(2\pi)^{N/2}|A|^{-1/2}. \tag{9}$$

where $A=\beta\nabla^2 E_D+\alpha\nabla^2 E_W$ is the Hessian matrix of the target function F. Further, the log the Equation (6), then differentiating it with respect to $\alpha$ and $\beta$, and setting it to zero, the optimal values of $\alpha$ and $\beta$ can be obtained by

$$\alpha_{MP}=\gamma/(2E_W(w_{MP})). \tag{10}$$

$$\beta_{MP}=(n-\gamma)/(2E_D(w_{MP})). \tag{11}$$

$$\gamma=N-\alpha_{MP}\text{trace}^{-1}(A_{MP}). \tag{12}$$

where $n$ is the number of sample, $N$ is the number of parameter in the network, $\gamma$ is the number of effective parameters which may reduce the error function for the network in training process.

### 2.3 Training and Testing for BRBPNN Model

For the soil liquefaction evaluation problem, the influence parameters may be divided into three categories. The parameters can be earthquake intensity, the epicenter distance, peak ground acceleration for describing the earthquake ground motion characteristics, and the depth of underground water, the depth of standard penetration test point (soil layer), the thickness of the covered non-liquefied soil layer, effectively overlaying pressure describing the embedding environment of soil layers, and standard penetration blow-count, mean diameter, non-uniformity coefficient, modified standard penetration blow-counts for denoting the sandy soil feature [2]. As in the case of CPT data, cone resistance ($q_c$), equivalent dynamic shear stress ($\tau/\sigma_0'$), mean grain size ($D_{50}$); total stress ($\sigma_0$); the effective stress ($\sigma_0'$); earthquake magnitude ($M$) and the normalized acceleration horizontal at ground surface ($a/g$) was used, and 109 samples were collected [15]. While in [4], only $q_c$, $\sigma_0$, $\sigma_0'$, $M$ and $a/g$ are used, the $D_{50}$ is missed; and 134 samples were recorded. In [5], only $q_c$, $\sigma_0$, $\sigma_0'$, $M$ and $a/g$ are used, the $D_{50}$ and $\tau/\sigma_0'$ is missed; and 170 samples were recorded. Part of data is listed in Table 1.

As for data listed in [4], the equivalent dynamic shear stress $\tau/\sigma_0'$ can be calculated by an expression suggested by Tokimatsu and Yoshini [16]. As per the proposed relation, the value of equivalent dynamic shear stress at a depth $z$ will be

$$\frac{\tau}{\sigma_0'} = 0.1\frac{a}{g}(M-1)\frac{\sigma_0}{\sigma_0'}(1-0.015z). \tag{13}$$

**Table 1.** Parts of training and testing records samples

| $M$ | $\sigma_0$ (kPa) | $\sigma_0'$ (kPa) | $q_c$ (MPa) | $a/g$ | $\tau/\sigma_0'$ | $D_{50}$ (mm) | Remark |
|---|---|---|---|---|---|---|---|
| 7.5 | 53 | 36 | 3.2 | 0.16 | 0.15 | 0.33 | liquefaction |
| 7.5 | 99 | 58 | 7.2 | 0.16 | 0.17 | 0.33 | liquefaction |
| 7.5 | 152 | 83 | 5.6 | 0.16 | 0.17 | 0.33 | liquefaction |
| 7.5 | 86 | 46 | 8 | 0.16 | 0.19 | 0.3 | no |
| 7.5 | 95 | 50 | 14.55 | 0.16 | 0.18 | 0.3 | no |
| 7.7 | 58 | 48 | 10 | 0.23 | 0.18 | 0.32 | no |
| 7.7 | 73 | 54 | 16 | 0.23 | 0.2 | 0.32 | no |
| 7.7 | 54 | 46 | 1.79 | 0.23 | 0.17 | 0.32 | liquefaction |
| 7.7 | 64 | 52 | 4.1 | 0.23 | 0.19 | 0.32 | liquefaction |
| 7.8 | 114 | 69 | 9.4 | 0.4 | 0.41 | 0.25 | liquefaction |
| 7.8 | 148 | 85 | 5.7 | 0.4 | 0.42 | 0.25 | liquefaction |
| 7.7 | 96 | 65 | 15.38 | 0.23 | 0.21 | 0.32 | no |
| 7.5 | 87 | 52 | 1.6 | 0.16 | 0.16 | 0.33 | liquefaction |

Four BRBPNN models are constructed for the problem. The M7 include all the parameters metioned above and only 109 records are used. The M6a include all the parameters metioned above but $D_{50}$ and 243 records are used. The M6b include all the parameters metioned above but $\tau/\sigma_0'$ and 279 records are used. The M5 include all the parameters metioned above except $\tau/\sigma_0'$ and $D_{50}$, and all the 413 records are used. Different types of networks are listed in Table 2 with its sumary of the square of the weight of the input layer, along with the correct ratio for training data and testing data. Figure 1- 4 showed the training and testing errors for the giving data for different neural network models. The errors out of 0.5 can be taken as wrong prediction.

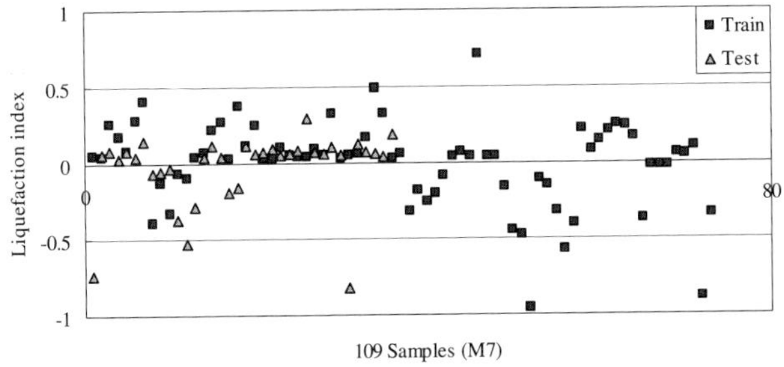


**Fig. 1.** The errors of original data with network simulating data (109 samples) [15]

**Table 2.** The summaration of the square of weight for the input layer and the correct ratio for trainging data and testing data

| Model | $M$ | $\sigma_0$ (kPa) | $\sigma_0'$ (kPa) | $q_c$ (MPa) | $a/g$ | $\tau/\sigma_0'$ | $D_{50}$ (mm) | Correct Ratio Train | Correct Ratio Test |
|---|---|---|---|---|---|---|---|---|---|
| M7 | 1.12 | 0.15 | 0.44 | 2.25 | 0.01 | 0.02 | 0.09 | 93.2% | 91.6% |
| M6a | 6.40 | 0.54 | 0.81 | 8.19 | 0.19 | 0.97 | | 96.7% | 87.1% |
| M6b | 0.33 | 2.44 | 2.42 | 3.32 | 0.11 | | 0.12 | 94.4% | 71.6% |
| M5 | 0.40 | 0.013 | 0.014 | 0.29 | 0.0007 | | | 88.5% | 90% |

From the square of the weight in the first layer, the importance order of these factors is $q_c$, $M$, $\sigma_0'$, $\sigma_0$, $a/g$, $\tau/\sigma_0'$ and $D_{50}$.

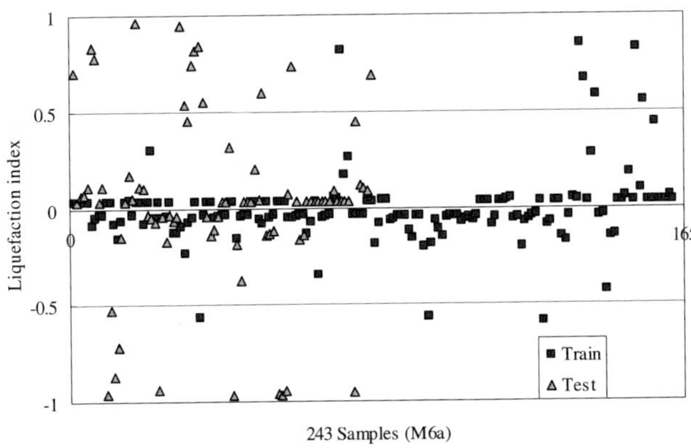


**Fig. 2.** The errors of original data with network simulating data (243 samples) [5, 15]

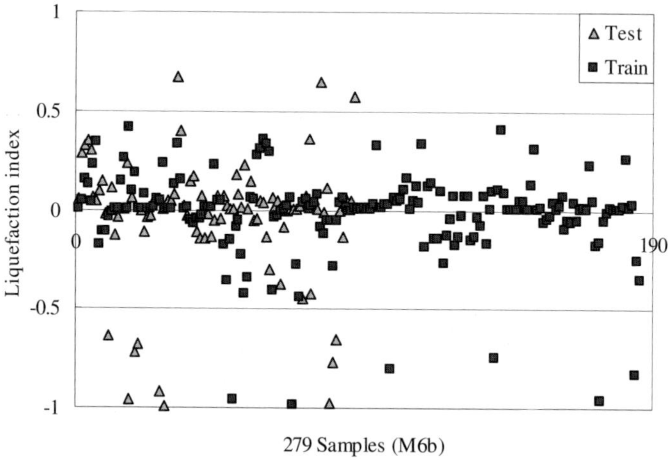


**Fig. 3.** The errors of original data with network simulating data (279 samples) [4, 15]

The model can predict the soil liquefaction with good satisfaction since it cover small samples in M7 (only 109 samples, correct ratio is 91.6% for testing data). When the records increase as for model M5 (413 samples included), the ratio dropped to 89%. Maybe this ratio is the average value for all records for this neural network method.

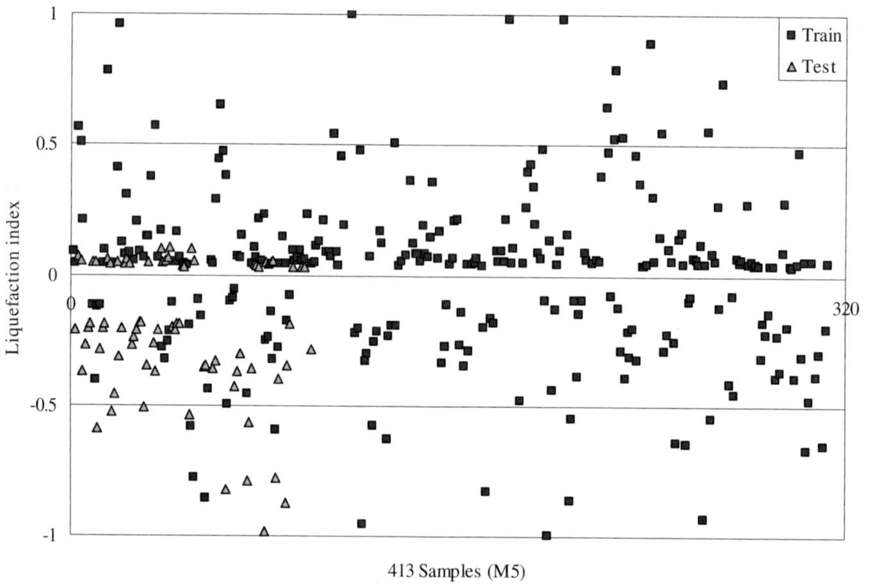


**Fig. 4.** The errors of original data with network simulating data (413 samples) [4, 5, 15]

## 3 Conclusions and Suggestions

413 soil liquefaction records with cone penetration testing values are collected in this paper. After presenting a Bayesian Regularization Back Propagation Neural Networks (BRBPNN) method to evaluate the soil liquefaction potential, the M7, M6a, M6b and M5 model are used according to the sample data. The M7 used 109 samples; the M6a used 243 samples; the M6b used 279 samples and the M5 used 413 samples. The M7 model seems more efficient for the given data since it contains the least records than other models. The M5 contains the all the records discussed in this paper, and the correct ratio for the training and testing are 88.5% and 89% respectively. After checking the square of the weight of the input layer for each network, the importance order of the input parameters should be $q_c$ , $M$ , $\sigma_0'$ , $\sigma_0$ , $a/g$ , $\tau/\sigma_0'$ and $D_{50}$ .

The training and testing of network seems less efficient when the records increase, which demonstrated again the complex nature of the soil liquefaction problem. Of course, the neural network is quite good than the traditional regression equations, which was proved in many literature. Further research of this problem should include more parameters to describe the nature of this phenomenon, and the regression should focus on data collected in certain region.

## Acknowledgements

This research is financial supported by the National Science Foundation of China under the grant number 40564002, the National Science Foundation of Yunnan Province under the grant number 2004E007R and the Science and Engineering Foundation of Yunnan University under the grant number 2004Z005B.

## References

1. Shi, Z. J., Zhang, R. X., Gu, B. H.: Study on Synthetic Methods for Criteria And Appraisal of Sand Liquefaction. Earthquake Engineering and Engineering Vibration (in Chinese), 17 (1) (1997) 82-88
2. Li, F.M., Chen, G.X.: Saturated Sand Liquefaction Potential Estimation Method Based on BP Neural Network. Journal of Natural Disasters (in Chinese), 14 (2) (2005) 108–114
3. Goh, A. T. C.: Seismic Liquefaction Potential Assessed by Neural Networks. Journal of Geotechnical Engineering, ASCE, 120 (9) (1995) 1467-1480
4. Kua, C. S., Leeb, D. H., Wuc, J. H.: Evaluation of Soil Liquefaction in the Chi-Chi, Taiwan earthquake using CPT. Soil Dynamics and Earthquake Engineering, 24(1) (2004) 659–673
5. Anthony, T. C.: Probabilistic Neural Network for Evaluating Seismic Liquefaction Potential. Canadian Geotechnical Journal, 39 (2002) 219-–232
6. Goh, A. T. C.: Neural-Network Modeling of CPT Seismic Liquefaction Data. Journal of Geotechnical Engineering, ASCE, 122 (1) (1996) 7073
7. Juang, C. H., Chen, C. J., Tien, Y.M.: Appraising Cone Penetration Test Based Liquefaction Resistance Evaluation Methods: Artificial Neural Network Approach. Canadian Geotechnical Journal, 36 (1999) 443-454

8. Seed, H. B., Idriss, I. M., Arango, I.: Evaluation of Liquefaction Potential Using Field Performance Data. Journal of Geotechnical Engineering, ASCE, 109 (3) (1983) 458-482
9. Stark, T.D., Olson, S.M.: Liquefaction Resistance using CPT and Field Case Histories. Journal of Geotechnical Engineering, ASCE, 121 (12) (1995) 856-869
10. Ke H., Chen Y. M.: An Improved Method for Evaluating Liquefaction Potential by the Velocity of Shear Waves. Acta Seismologica Sinica, 22 (6) (2000) 637-644
11. Wang M.W., Jin J. L., Li, L.: Application of PP Method Based on Raga to Assessment of Sand Liquefaction Potential. Chinese Journal of Rock Mechanics and Engineering, 23 (4) (2004) 631-634
12. MacKay, D. J. C.: Bayesian Interpolation. Neural Computation, 4 (3) (1992) 415-447
13. MacKay, D. J. C.: A practical Bayesian Framework for Back Propagation Networks. Neural Computation, 4 (3) (1992) 448–472
14. Foresee, F. D., Hagan, M. T.: Gauss-Newton Approximation to Bayesian Regularization. Proceedings of the 1997 International Joint Conference on Neural Networks, (1997) 1930-1935
15. Mahesh, P.: Support Vector Machines-based Modeling of sSeismic Liquefaction Potential. Int. J. Numer. Anal. Meth. Geomech. (www.interscience.wiley.com) (2006) DOI: 10.1002/nag.509
16. Tokimatsu, K, Yoshimi, Y.: Experimental Correlation of Soil Liquefaction Based on SPT N-Value and Fine Content. Soil and Foundations, 23 (4) (1983) 56-74

# Compression of Medical Images by Using Artificial Neural Networks

Zümray Dokur

Department of Electronics and Communication Engineering,
Istanbul Technical University, 34469 Maslak, Istanbul, Turkey
zumray@ehb.itu.edu.tr

**Abstract.** This paper presents a novel lossy compression scheme for medical images by using an incremental self–organized map (ISOM). Three neural networks for lossy compression scheme are comparatively examined: Kohonen map, multi-layer perceptron (MLP) and ISOM. In the compression process of the proposed method, the image is first decomposed into blocks of 8×8 pixels. Two-dimensional discrete cosine transform (2D-DCT) coefficients are computed for each block. The dimension of DCT coefficients vectors (codewords) is reduced by low-pass filtering. Huffman coding is applied to the indexes of codewords obtained by the ISOM. In the decompression process, inverse operations of each stage of the compression are performed in the opposite way. It is observed that the proposed method gives much better compression rates.

## 1 Introduction

Medical images like magnetic resonance (MR) and computer tomography (CT) acquired from various modalities comprise huge amounts of data, rendering them impracticable for storage and transmission. Archiving this large amount of image data in the computer memory is very difficult without any compression. An important issue in lossy compression of medical images is the risk of destroying diagnostically relevant information. Current lossy compression standards, such as JPEG [1] and MPEG, are designed for conventional still-image and video display.

Transform-based techniques have been proposed for the efficient reduction of the high redundancy usually encountered in real life images [2]. Unsupervised neural networks can perform nonlinear principal component analysis as a transform-based method in image compression [3]. They outperform linear principal component analysis, and are relatively easy to implement.

Another common method to compress images is to code them through vector quantization (VQ) techniques. Self-organized Kohonen maps have been used to achieve the VQ process of image compression [4]. They represent an efficient compression scheme based on the fact that consecutive blocks in an image are often similar, and thus coded by similar codewords with a VQ algorithm. Early studies of lossy compressed medical images performed compression using variations on the standard discrete cosine transform coding algorithm combined with scalar quantization and lossless coding. More recent studies of efficient lossy image compression combined with scalar or vector quantization [5]. These algorithms provide several potential

D.-S. Huang, K. Li, and G.W. Irwin (Eds.): ICIC 2006, LNCS 4113, pp. 337 – 344, 2006.

advantages over traditional Fourier-type decompositions, including better concentration of energy, better decorrelation for a wider class of signals. The wavelet-based approach, however, has a filter whose length varies as a function of resolution.

This paper presents a novel compression scheme which is a fusion of DCT [6] of the original image and vector quantization by the ISOM.

## 2 Method

In the study, the medical image is splitted into square blocks of 8×8 pixels. 2D-DCT coefficients are computed for each block. By using the DCT, energy of the image in the square block is compressed into the low frequency band. 2D-DCT coefficients of an 8×8 image block are shown in Fig. 1. Coefficients in dark-colored regions represent the details of the image in the block. In the compression algorithm, some of these coefficients are ignored while the others are stored into the memory. In the proposed method, four coefficients ($C_{11}$, $C_{12}$, $C_{21}$ and $C_{22}$) which are shown inside a bold-bordered square are used to form the codewords. The reconstructed image quality depends on the amount of ignored coefficients. The more coefficients we use in the compression, the better image we can obtain in the reconstruction process.

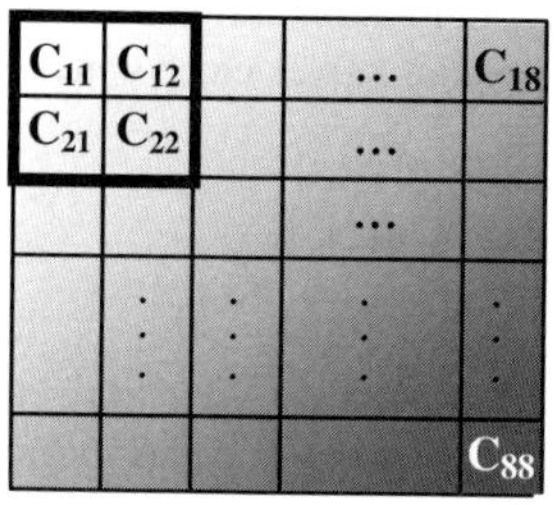


**Fig. 1.** 2D-DCT coefficients of an image block of 8×8 pixels

The lossy compression scheme is described in Fig. 2(a). After splitting the image into square blocks, 2D-DCT coefficients are computed. Then, a low-pass filter is used to eliminate high frequencies not visible to human eyes. By removing a part of the high frequencies, a reduction in the peak-signal-to-noise-ratio is achieved, even though the image visual quality remains more or less unchanged. In other words, before the compression, image quality will be degraded by the filtering. The output of the low pass filter is applied to a neural network for the vector quantization process. At this stage, a single index for each image block is generated by the proposed neural network. At the last stage, Huffman Coding is applied to the indexes of codewords.

The decompression scheme is illustrated in Fig. 2(b). At first, the indexes of the codewords are obtained by the inverse Huffman coding. Then, the corresponding codewords for these indexes are generated from the look-up table. The square image blocks are reconstructed by applying inverse 2D-DCT to the codewords. At the last stage, the original image is reconstructed from these blocks.

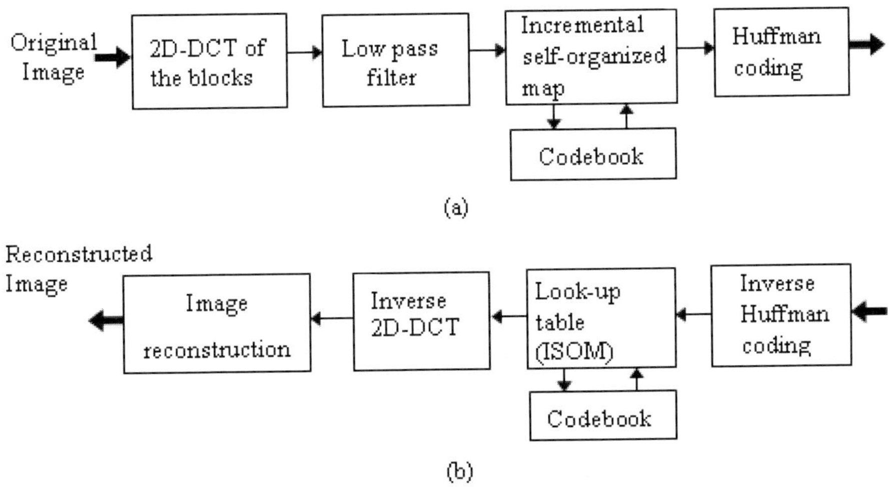


**Fig. 2.** (a) Compression scheme, (b) decompression scheme

## 3 Artificial Neural Networks

Neural networks are frequently used in biomedical signal processing. One of the application areas of neural networks is data compression [7, 8].

In this study, three neural networks are comparatively examined for the compression of medical images: Kohonen map [9], MLP, and ISOM. Kohonen map and ISOM are used in the method explained by Fig. 2. But, the method in which MLP is used is different from the proposed one. Pixel intensities in region of interest are directly presented to MLP without any transformation. MLP is designed with three layers. The first and the second layers are used in the compression scheme while the third layer is used in the decompression. Fig. 3 shows the structure of the network. Pixel intensities in 5×5 image blocks are directly fed into the MLP (no preprocessing is performed on pixel intensities).

### 3.1 Incremental Self-Organized Map

ISOM is a two-layer network as shown in Fig. 4. In the figure, $k$ represents the dimension of the DCT coefficients vectors reduced by the low-pass filter. The DCT coefficients vectors with reduced dimension are called as *codewords*. Codewords are presented to the input of the ISOM. The nodes in the first layer are automatically determined during the training. After the training is completed, the nodes represent codewords distributed homogeneously in the feature space. The winner-takes-all guarantees that there will be only one node activated. Index layer represents the index values of the codewords.

### 3.2 Training of the ISOM

ISOM is a neural network that does not update weights. It may also be called as an adaptive vector quantizer. ISOM has incremental structure for unsupervised learning. The nodes in the first layer represent the codewords formed by 2D-DCT transform.

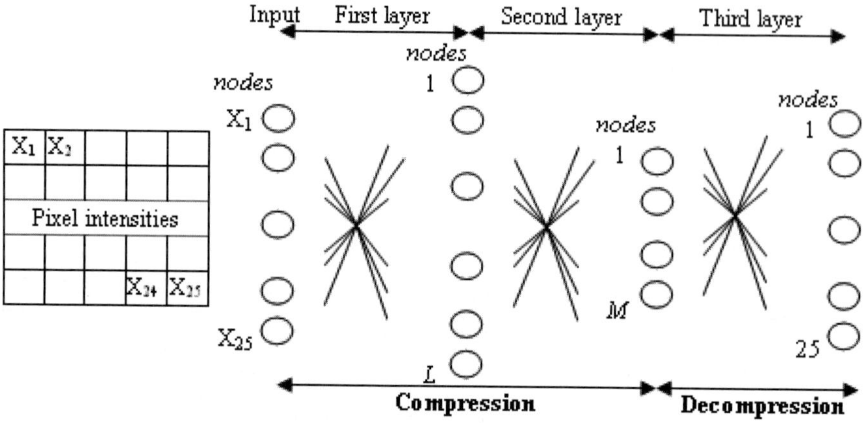


**Fig. 3.** Structure of the MLP used in compression and decompression schemes

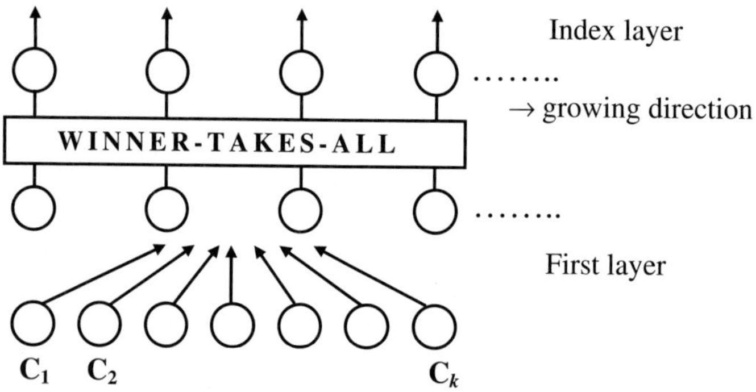


**Fig. 4.** Structure of ISOM

At the beginning, the codeword of the first image block is automatically selected as the first node of the ISOM. Then, the second block is extracted from the image. After the DCT coefficients of this block are computed, a low-pass filter is used to eliminate some amount of high frequency content. Thus, the dimension of the vectors is reduced to increase the compression rate. The distance between the codeword and the first node in the first layer of the ISOM is computed. If the distance exceeds a predetermined threshold value, the codeword is assigned as a new node of the ISOM and a new index is assigned for this codeword. Otherwise, the third image block is extracted and search is continued until all blocks in the image are exhausted.

The training process of the ISOM can be summarized as follows:

*Step 1:* Extract a square block from the image in an order.

*Step 2:* Compute the DCT coefficients of the image in the block to form a codeword. Use the low pass filter to reduce the dimension of the DCT coefficients vectors. Present the reduced dimensional vector (the codeword) to the ISOM.

*Step 3:* Compute the distances between the codeword and the node(s) in the first layer of the ISOM, and find the minimum distance.

*Step 4:* If the minimum distance exceeds the threshold, include the codeword into the ISOM as a new node, increment the index counter by one, and assign the value in the counter as the 'index' of the codeword. Send this index to Huffman coding process. Otherwise, send the index of the node which is the nearest to the codeword, to Huffman coding process.

*Step 5:* Go to *step 1* until all blocks in the image are exhausted.

## 4 Computer Simulations

In this study, MLP, Kohonen map, ISOM and JPEG standard are comparatively examined for medical image compression. MR, CT and ultrasound images are compressed by these four methods. The original medical images are shown in Fig. 5. The size of MR and CT head images is 256×256, and the size of the ultrasound image is 400×288. All simulations are performed by using MATLAB toolbox.

There are three control parameters in the compression processes realized by the Kohonen map and ISOM: (i) Size of the square blocks, (ii) dimension of the DCT coefficients vectors (codewords) determined by the low-pass filtering process, and (iii) the number of nodes in the neural network.

The size of the square blocks affects the compression rate. If the size is high, compression rate increases, however, block effects and edge distortions are observed in the reconstructed image. In the study, the size of the square block for each network is different from each other. Low-pass filter sets high-order 2D-DCT coefficients to zero value. By ignoring zero-valued coefficients, the dimension of the codeword is decreased, and the ignored coefficients are not presented to the neural networks. However, high-order DCT coefficients represent the details in the image. Thus, the amount of ignored coefficients will affect the quality of the reconstructed image.

Table 1 shows mean square error (MSE), compression rate (CR) and number of nodes for the compression methods by artificial neural networks and JPEG. CR for MLP is determined as follows:

$$\text{CR} = \text{number of nodes in input layer / number of nodes in the second layer} \quad (1)$$

In the Kohonen map and ISOM, the size of the compressed image (SOCI) and the CR are calculated as follows:

$$\begin{aligned}&\text{SOCI} = \text{Size of look-up table} + \text{Size of indexes compressed by Huffman coding}\\&\text{CR} = \text{Image size / SOCI}\end{aligned} \quad (2)$$

where, look-up table contains codewords which are assigned as the nodes of the networks. CR value depends on some parameters: (i) (the size of the square block) / (the size of the codeword), (ii) (the size of look-up table) × 8 (bayts), and (iii) performance of the Huffman coding.

The best results obtained in 50 independent runs for each image are given in the table. The best and the average MSE values of ISOM and Kohonen map are similar for 50 independent runs. However, the average MSE value of MLP is higher than the best (lowest) MSE value for 50 independent runs. This is because of the fact that MLP is easily caught by local optimum solutions.

Because the size of the square block for MLP is determined as 5×5 after several trials, training sets of MLP for MR, CT and ultrasound images consist of 2621, 2621 and 4608 square blocks, respectively. The size of the square block for Kohonen map is selected as 8×8 after several trials. Thus, the training sets of the Kohonen map for MR, CT and ultrasound images consist of 1024, 1024 and 1800 square blocks, respectively. Dimension of the codewords is selected as 4×4.

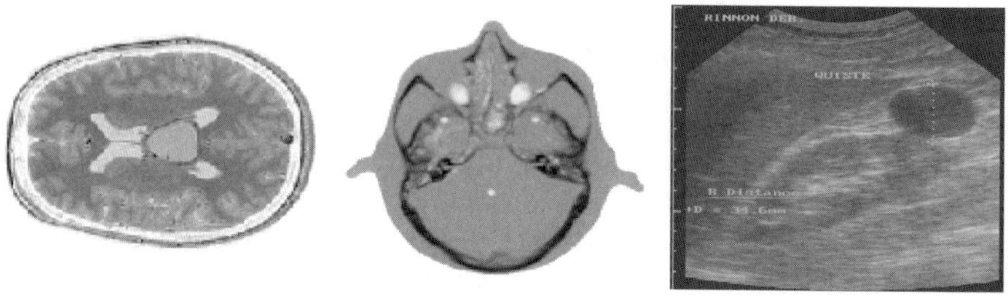

(a) (b) (c)

**Fig. 5.** (a) MR head image, (b) CT head image, (c) Ultrasound image of kidney cyst

**Table 1.** Performance results obtained by artificial neural networks and JPEG

| Method | Images | MSE | Number of nodes | CR |
|---|---|---|---|---|
| | MR | 82.481 | 25–15–10–25 | 2.5 |
| by MLP | CT | 43.561 | 25–20–10–25 | 2.5 |
| | US | 98.274 | 25–10–10–25 | 2.5 |
| | MR | 51.371 | 263 | 35.386 |
| by ISOM | CT | 19.843 | 160 | 63.015 |
| | US | 133.019 | 304 | 38.193 |
| | MR | 52.068 | | 26.131 |
| by JPEG | CT | 19.958 | | 29.735 |
| | US | 138.221 | | 37.586 |
| by | MR | 158.873 | 22 × 22 | 7.670 |
| Kohonen | CT | 64.532 | 22 × 22 | 7.672 |
| map | US | 71.665 | 25 × 25 | 9.020 |

MSE: Mean square error; CR: Compression rate

Fig. 6 shows the three reconstructed images obtained by the ISOM. As the size of the square blocks for ISOM is selected as 8×8 after several trials, training sets of ISOM for MR, CT and ultrasound images consist of 1024, 1024 and 1800 square blocks, respectively. Dimension of the codewords is selected as 2×2. The threshold value is selected as 3000 for each medical image.

Fig. 7 shows the reconstructed images obtained by the JPEG standard.

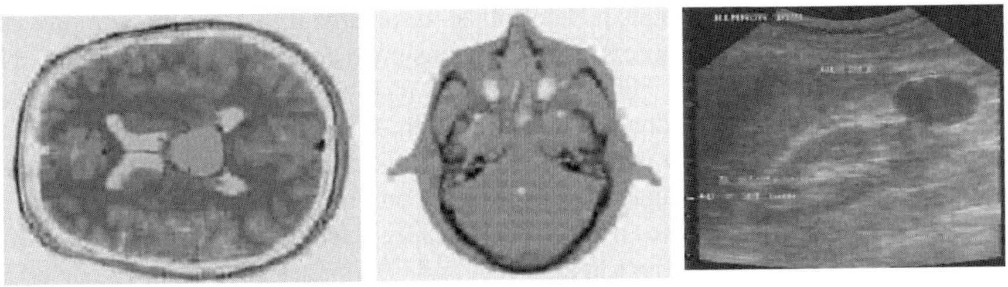

(a) (b) (c)

**Fig. 6.** Reconstructed images by the ISOM

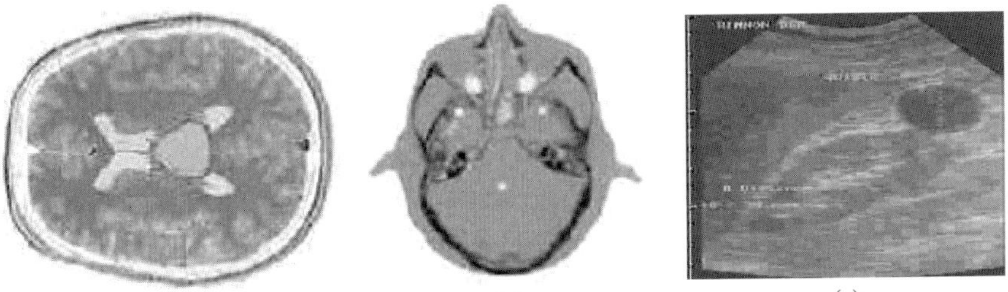

(a) (b) (c)

**Fig. 7.** Reconstructed images by the JPEG

## 5 Conclusions

In Table 1, the parameters of the methods are adjusted so that the MSE values of JPEG standard and ISOM are the same. CRs of the two methods are comparatively examined for approximately the same MSE values.

The CR obtained by using MLP is 2.5. The different structures of the MLP which gave the results in Table 1 are determined after several trials. Each training process for a different trial took approximately half an hour. It is observed that if the CR is increased, the quality of the reconstructed image highly decreases. The CR is controlled by two parameters: (i) Block size, (ii) the number of nodes in the second layer. If the size of the square blocks is increased, block effect and edge distortion are observed in the reconstructed image. The number of nodes in the second layer is determined after 50 different trials. A satisfactory solution could not be found for less than 10 nodes ($M$=10 in Fig. 3) in the second layer. The number of nodes affects the compression rate and the quality of reconstructed image. If the number of nodes is high, compression rate will decrease and the reconstructed image quality will increase.

In the Kohonen map, the number of nodes has to be determined before the compression process. If the number of nodes becomes extremely high, the CR will decrease, but the quality of the reconstructed image will increase. Before the compression process is started, training of the Kohonen map is realized. For this reason, the compression process consumes extra time to learn the map.

In ISOM, the number of nodes is determined automatically during the compression by using a threshold. Thus, no extra time is consumed for the training process. The threshold value is selected as 3000 for the three medical images. The quality of the reconstructed image is determined by the threshold. A low threshold value leads to an excessive number of nodes in the first layer, and a good representation of the image. On the contrary, a high value may lead to a poor representation of the image.

In the study, noise is removed from the images by selecting low-order DCT coefficients. Thus, noise does not affect ISOM. MR and CT images are generally noise-free images. However, ultrasound images have textural content which can be characterized by white noise. Hence, as presented in Table 1, the highest MSE value is obtained for the ultrasound image by the ISOM network.

It is observed that the proposed method gives higher CRs with low MSE. The quality of the reconstructed images by the ISOM is higher than the quality of the images reconstructed by the other methods.

## References

1. Wallace, G.K.: JPEG Still Picture Compression Standard. Comm. ACM, 34(4), (1991) 32-34.
2. Strintzis, M.: Optimal Pyramidal and Subband Decomposition for Hierarchical Coding of Noisy and Quantized Images. IEEE Tran. on Image Pro. 7 (2), (1998), 155–166.
3. Tzovaras, D., Strintzis, M.: Use of Nonlinear Principal Component Analysis and Vector Quantization for Image Coding. IEEE Tran. on Image Pro. 7 (8), (1998), 1218–1223.
4. Amerijckx, C., Verleysen, M., Thissen, P., Legat, J.D.: Image Compression by Self-Organized Kohonen Map. IEEE Trans. on Neural Networks, 9(3), (1998) 503-507.
5. Pal, S., Ghosh, A., Kundu, M.: Soft Computing for Image Processing. Springer, (2000).
6. Ahmed, N., Natarajan, T., Rao, K.R.: Discrete Cosine Transform. IEEE Trans. Comput., C-23 (1974) 90-93.
7. Mougeot, M., Azencott, R., Angeniol, B.: A Study of Image Compression with Backpropagation. NATO ASI Series, Neurocomputing, F-68 (1990) 333-336.
8. Blanchet, P.: Data Compression Using Multilayer Perceptron. NATO ASI Series, Neurocomputing, F 68 (1990) 237-240.
9. Kohonen, T.: An Introduction to Neural Computing. Neural Networks, 1 (1988) 3-16.

# Constraint K-Segment Principal Curves

Junping Zhang[1,3] and Dewang Chen[1,2]

[1] Shanghai Key Lab of Intelligent Information Processing, Fudan University, China
Department of Computer Science and Engineering
Fudan University, Shanghai 200433, China
jpzhang@fudan.edu.cn
[2] School of Electronics and Information Engineering,
Beijing Jiaotong University, China
cdw@telecom.njtu.edu.cn
[3] The Key Laboratory of Complex Systems and Intelligence Science,
Chinese Academy of Sciences, Beijing, China

**Abstract.** To represent the intrinsic regularity of data, one way is to compute the "middle" curves or principal curves (PCs) across the data. However, there are difficulties for current PCs algorithms to discover some known positions that are out of the sampled range of data (Henceforth, out-of-the-samples). Based on principal curves with length constraint proposed by kégl (KPCs), we propose constraint K-segment principal curves (CKPCs) with two refinements. First, out-of-the-samples are introduced as endpoints to improve the performance of the KPCs algorithm. Second, a constraint term is proposed for removing some unexpected vertices and enhancing the stability of the KPCs algorithm. Experiments in three set of practical traffic stream data show that both the stability and the shape of the proposed CKPCs algorithm are better than those of the KPCs algorithm.

## 1 Introduction

Principal Curves (PCs), presented by Hastie and Stuetzle in 1988 [1], denote a smooth one-dimensional curve or high dimensional surface passing through the 'middle' of the data. Under the consideration of highly computational complexity and two biases (model bias and estimation bias), many refinements are proposed [2]. In 1999, Kégl proposed a new principal curves with length constraint (henceforth KPCs) and also proved an approximated convergence rate based on the expected squared distance with statistical learning theory [3]. While the KPCs algorithm makes a remarkable improvement both in theorem and algorithm [3], several problems still remain. First, the first principal component is assumed to be an initial segment in the KPCs algorithm. For complex data, the assumption may result in that the KPCs algorithm fails to converge to a real principal curve. Second, some vertices may go outside the domain of data because the optimization of each vertex is only local minimum. Third, many heuristical parameters need to be adjusted based on human experiences.

D.-S. Huang, K. Li, and G.W. Irwin (Eds.): ICIC 2006, LNCS 4113, pp. 345–350, 2006.

In this paper, two refinements of the KPCs algorithm are proposed to address the first two problems in Section 2. First, we study the influence of the out-of-the-samples to the modeling of principal curves and combine the out-of-the-samples to the KPCs algorithms. Second, a new constraint term is proposed to remove abnormal vertices which may result in the instability of the KPCs algorithm. In Section 3, experiments in three set of practical traffic data show the promising of the proposed CKPCs algorithm. Finally, conclusions are drawn in Section 4.

## 2 The Constraint K-Segment Principal Curves Algorithm

The principal curves satisfy the self-consistent property which means that each point on the curve is the conditional mean of the points projecting there [1]. The basic formula is:

$$f(\lambda) = E(X|\lambda_f(X) = \lambda) \quad \forall \lambda \in \mathbb{R}^1. \tag{1}$$

Where $\lambda$ denotes the projection index, $f(\lambda)$ denotes the corresponding projection coordinates of data $X$, and $E(\cdot)$ denotes expectation value.

When modeling principal curves, most PCs algorithms assume that data belong to a bounded subset of $\mathbb{R}^d$, say $A$. If we define $\mathbb{R}^d$ is a complete set, then $\bar{A} = \mathbb{R}^d - A$ is a null set from which data cannot be sampled. By definition [1], all the principal curves should lie on the range of subset $A$. However, null set has a potential influence to the model of principal curves. If data in the null set is employed, it is obvious that:

$$PCs_A(A) \neq PCs_{A\cup\bar{A}}(A). \tag{2}$$

where the subscripts ($A$ and $A \cup \bar{A}$) denote the subsets used for modeling the PCs, and the letter in the bracket denotes the PCs modelled in the subset $A$.

In the proposed CKPCs algorithm, the out-of-the-samples in the set $\bar{A}$ are assumed to be the start point and/or end point of the principal curves. The assumption bring several advantages into the CKPCs algorithm. First, the refinement can assure that the KPC algorithm obtain a global shape even if data are locally sampled. Second, the curve with the vertices will be different from that one without the vertices. Finally, the influence of some heuristical parameters in the KPCs algorithm may be weakened. It is noticeable that the two vertices will be invariable and independent on the optimization step of the CKPCs algorithm.

Due to the fact that the optimization of vertices is local, furthermore, some vertices may be shifted over the domain of the data even if the optimization steps are iteratively repeated many times in the KPCs algorithm. When vertices are outside the domain, few samples are projected onto the vertices and onto its neighboring segments. It will result in that principal curve cannot go across the "middle" of data and the stability of the KPCs algorithm will suffer. To address the problem, a constraint term is added for verifying and removing the abnormal vertices after the optimizing step. The criterion of removing vertices is formulated as follows:

$$R(v_i) = \begin{cases} 1, \text{ if } (l_{s_{i-1}} \text{ or } l_{s_i}) > r \text{ and } \frac{N_{v_i}}{n} < 0.01 \\ 0, \text{ otherwise} \end{cases} \tag{3}$$

where

$$l_{s_{i-1}} = \|v_i - v_{i-1}\| \quad 2 \le i \le K+1. \tag{4}$$
$$l_{s_i} = \|v_{i+1} - v_i\| \quad 1 \le i \le K. \tag{5}$$

and

$$N_{v_i} = \begin{cases} n_{s_{i-1}} + n_{v_i} + n_{s_i}, & \text{if } 2 \le i \le K \\ n_{s_i} + n_{v_i}, & \text{if } i = 1 \\ n_{v_i} + n_{s_{i-1}}, & \text{if } i = K+1 \end{cases} \tag{6}$$

Where $l_{s_i}$ denotes the length of the $i$th line segment, and $N_{v_{i+1}}$ sums up the number of samples projected into vertex $v_i$ and its neighboring segments ($s_{i-1}$ and/or $s_i$). If $R(v_i) = 1$, then the vertex $v_i$ should be removed according to equation (3). Otherwise, it will be preserved. Here the squared Euclidean distance from a vertex to the domain of data is regarded as a criterion of vertex removal. Once the vertex $v_i$ has been removed, a series of procedures, such as the reassignment of samples which projected into the vertex $v_i$ and its neighboring segments, the re-computation of the average squared distance and so on, will be carried out.

For better understanding the two refinements, a pseudo-code of the CKPCs algorithm is listed as follows:

- (Step 1: Initialization): Different from the KPCs algorithm which assumes that the first principal component be an initial segment, two "out-of-the-samples" are regarded as initial vertices of the CKPCs based on the properties of specific dataset. Let the number of segment be $K = 1$.
- (Step 2: Projection): All of the data are projected into vertices and segments of the $K$-segment principal curve, and corresponding projection index $\lambda_f(x)$ and projection position $f_K^{(m)}(x_{\lambda_f})$ of each sample $x$ in the $m$-th iteration are computed based on Euclidean distance.
- (Step 3: Vertex Optimization): After the projection coordinates of data are assigned, vertices of the CKPCs are optimized through minimizing a penalized distance function. The function $G_n(f_K^{(m)})$ includes $\Delta_n(f_K^{(m)})$(the average squared distance of points in data $X$ from the curve $f_K^{(m)}$), and $P(f_K^{(m)})$ (the curvature penalty imposed at vertex $v_i$, $i = 1, \cdots, K+1$). Actually, the golden section search in one dimension is applied for optimizing the vertices of the KPCs algorithm as well as the proposed CKPCs algorithm.
- (Step 4: Termination of the inner loop): If

$$|1 - \frac{G_n(f_k^{(m)})}{G_n(f_k^{(m-1)})}| \le \delta. \tag{7}$$

is satisfied (where $\delta$ is equal to $1e-3$ without loss of generality), the inner loop of the algorithm terminates, go to step 5. Otherwise, $m = m+1$, return to step 2.

- (Step 5: Length Constraint): If inner loop with $K$ segments is terminated, a heuristical formulation in equation (8) is applied to verify whether the CKPCs algorithm should be stopped [3].

$$c(n, \Delta_n(f_K)) = \beta n^{1/3} \frac{r}{\sqrt{\Delta_n(f_K)}}. \tag{8}$$

where $\beta$ is an experimental parameter which can be set to be a constant value 0.3, and $r$ is the radius of data. If $K$ exceeds the result of equation (8), then the CKPCs algorithm stops. Otherwise, go to step 6.
- (Step 6: Adding vertices): If length constraint of outer loop of the CKPCs algorithm is not exceeded, the number of vertices of principal curves can be added by one each time by partitioning a segment which has the longest length into two line segments.
- (Step 7: Removing Vertices) Detect whether the vertices of the CKPCs need to be removed or not based on equation (3). Let $K = K + 1$, go to step 2 until variable $K$ exceeds the value of equation (8).

## 3 Experiments

In the section, experiments on three set of traffic stream data are performed for traffic flow modeling, a special example of regression analysis, of which a critical problem is to model the relative relationship among the basic parameters of traffic stream [4]. In the field of intelligent transportation system, the density-speed model is the basic model and the fundamental diagram of traffic flow theory. The occupancy (or density)-flow model, is very important to ramp metering. And the flow-speed model is often used to judge the level of service (LOS) of freeways. Furthermore, the traffic model must go through some key points with apparent physical meanings, which include the following situations:

1. Vehicles stop within the detection zone, which means flow= 0 vehicles per hours (Veh/h), speed= 0 kilometer per hours (Km/h), occupancy= 100%. The condition rarely happens in detection.
2. When there are so few vehicles, the drivers can choose the speed freely. In the ultimate, it means occupancy=0, flow= 0 and speed=maxSpeed (Note: maxSpeed is the possible maximal speed, which can not be detected in the reality and is always predefined by experts. We often set it as the detected maximal speed adding a small constant, for example, 120Km/h).

The above-mentioned two points can be regarded as the out-of-the-samples. So, to achieve good interpretation and understandability, an improved PCs algorithm which passes the out-of-the-samples is needed in traffic stream modeling.

To test the effectiveness of the CKPCS algorithm for modeling traffic stream, three set of traffic data were collected in third ring road in Beijing, where a total of 72 RTMS (remote traffic microwave sensor) were set up. The data collection time was from April 1rd, 2005 to April 5th, 2005 [4]. By introducing the out-of-the-samples just discussed as constraint terms, the experimental results of the

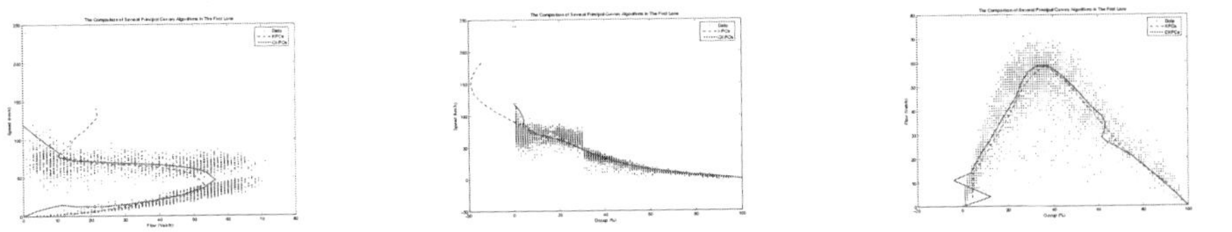

(a) Flow Vs Speed-1 (b) Occupancy Vs Speed-1 (c) Occupancy Vs Flow-1

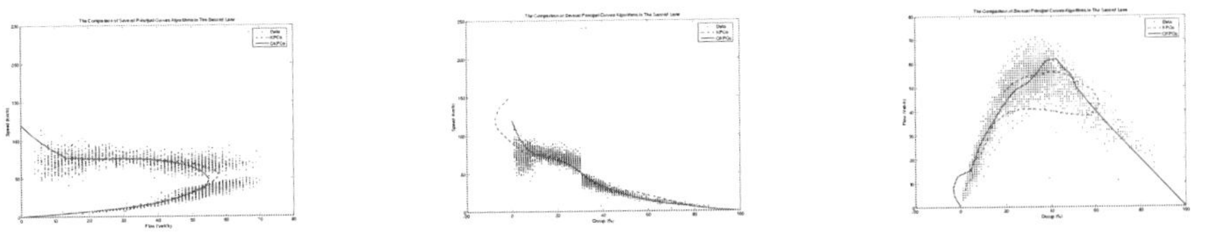

(d) Flow Vs Speed-2 (e) Occupancy Vs Speed-2 (f) Occupancy Vs Flow-2

**Fig. 1.** The illustration of Modeling traffic stream data 1 and 2 with the CKPCs and KPCs algorithms

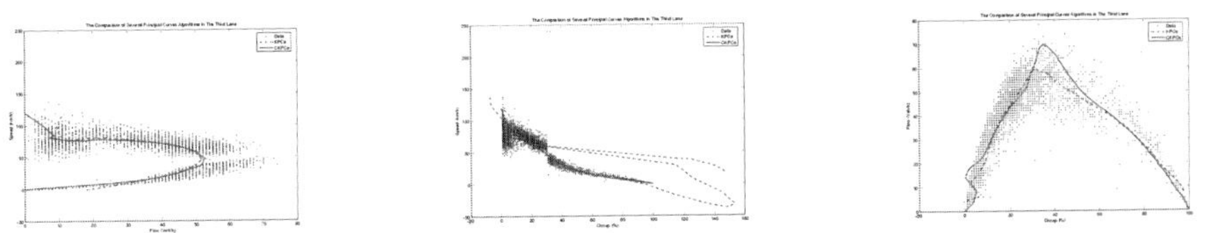

(a) Flow Vs Speed-3 (b) Occupancy Vs Speed-3 (c) Occupancy Vs Flow-3

**Fig. 2.** Modeling traffic stream data 3 with the CKPCs and KPCs algorithms

three lanes based on the KPCs algorithm and the CKPCs algorithm are shown in Fig. 1 to Fig. 2, where 1, 2, and 3 denote the 1th lane, the 2th lane, and the 3th lane, respectively.

Compared with the KPCs (dash-line), it is clear that the proposed CKPCs algorithm (real line) has several advantages for modelling traffic stream data as follows:

- The shapes of constraint K-segment principal curve is more stable and suitable to represent the regularity of traffic stream than those of K-segment principal curve. For example, in Fig. 1(b), it is obvious that occupancy cannot be negative value. However, the curve of the KPCs algorithm has gone outside the positive real number which is insensible to traffic stream model.
- The proposed CKPCs algorithm can automatically removed some vertices. For example, in Fig. 2(b), the KPCs algorithm gives us a very abnormal curve duc to the failure of the optimization step, while the curves obtained by the corresponding CKPCs algorithm is more easier to be explained.

– The KPCs algorithm is more sensitive to abnormal data. For example, in Fig. 1(e), there are some abnormal samples (Occupancy= 40%, Speed= 250 Km/h) because of incorrect sampling from sensors. The KPCs algorithm tries to reflect the properties of abnormal samples because it cannot distinguish the normal and abnormal data, whereas the CKPCs algorithm is not influenced by the abnormal samples because of the introduction of two constraint terms.

## 4 Conclusion

In this paper, we propose the CKPCs algorithm for automatical removing unexpected vertices in which vertex optimization of the KPCs algorithm fails, and introduce some out-of-the-samples for improving the performance of the KPCs algorithm. Experiments on three set of practical traffic stream data show that compared with the KPCs algorithm, the proposed CKPCs algorithm has better interpretation and stability in the modeling of traffic stream data.

## Acknowledgement

This research is sponsored by NSFC under contract No. 60505002, IIPL-04-014 and Beijing Science Foundation under contract No. 8052016.

## References

1. Hastie, T., Stuetzle, W.: Principal curves. J. A. Stat. A. 84 (1988) 502–516
2. Zhang, J., Wang, J.: An overview of principal curves. Chinese J. Computer. 26 (2003) 1–18
3. Kégl, B., Krzyzak, A., et. al.: Learning and design of principal curves. IEEE Trans. on PAMI. 22 (2000) 281–297
4. Chen, D., Zhang, J., Tang S., Wang, J.: Freeway Traffic Stream Modeling Based on Principal Curves and Its Analysis. IEEE Trans. on ITS. 5 (2004) 246–258
5. Chen, D., Gong, X., Zheng, CH.:A wireless traffic information collection system in Beijing urban freeways. IEEE on ITS. Conf. Singapore, (2002) 387–391

# Control of Chaotic Systems with Uncertainties by Orthogonal Function Neural Network

Hongwei Wang[1] and Shuanghe Yu[2]

[1] Department of Automation, Dalian University of Technology
Dalian, 116024, China
wanghw@dlut.edu.cn
[2] Automation Research Center, Dalian Maritime University
Dalian, 116024, China

**Abstract.** The adaptive control method based on orthogonal function neural network is proposed for a class of chaotic nonlinear systems. The adaptive controller is constructed by using a single hidden layer Chebyshev orthogonal function neural network which has advantages such as simple calculation and fast convergence. The adaptive learning law of orthogonal neural network is derived to guarantee that the adaptive weight errors and the tracking error are bounded from Lyapunov stability theory. The uncertain nonlinear system with the external disturbances can track the desired reference trajectory with bounded errors by means of the adaptive feedback controller. Based on the orthogonal function neural network, the control of chaotic systems with uncertainties is studied. The results show that the approach proposed in this paper can overcome effectively the external disturbances.

## 1 Introduction

Different methods were used in the control of chaotic systems such as radical basis function neural network, recurrent neural network and wavelet neural network in the literatures [1-4], which have possessed the abilities to approximate nonlinear systems. However, the specified solution based on the training of these networks is satisfied to the given signal while the specified solution is unsatisfied to the new input signal. In recent years, the control methods for chaotic system have been discussed in many learning methods. Linear feedback control is applied to achieve synchronization of two different chaotic systems by using Lyapunov stability theory [5]. A novel approach to controlling chaos in discrete-time nonlinear autonomous systems is proposed in the paper [6]. A desired unstable periodic orbit is stabilized by small control based on the predicting trajectory of the system. Also, in this research area, there are many attempts to create the control methods and the synchronization of chaotic systems by using fuzzy methods [7].

In the paper, Chebyshev orthogonal polynomial functions are selected as the basic functions of the orthogonal function neural network. The orthogonal function neural network is trained to learn the uncertain information of the systems. When the orthogonal function neural network can be satisfied to estimate the uncertain information of the systems, the orthogonal function neural network is switched to control the chaotic systems. The remainder of this paper is organized as follows. In section 2, the

D.-S. Huang, K. Li, and G.W. Irwin (Eds.): ICIC 2006, LNCS 4113, pp. 351 – 356, 2006.

control problem is proposed. The controller of Chebyshev orthogonal neural network is designed in Section 3. To illustrate the control performance of the proposed method, the numerical example is studied in Section 4. Conclusions are made in Section 5.

## 2 The Description of the Problem

The nonlinear system is shown as the following form.

$$\dot{x} = F(x) + u \,. \tag{1}$$

where the input vector satisfies $x \in R^n$ and $F(x)$ satisfies $F(x)=(f_1(x), f_2(x), ...., f_n(x))^T$, in which $f_i(x)(i=1,2,...,n)$ is a nonlinear function sequence; $u$ is the input vector, satisfying $u \in R^n$.

In the actual system, the nonlinear system is disturbed by the external disturbances, and then Equation (1) can be written as the following equation.

$$\dot{x} = F(x) + \Delta F(x) + u \,. \tag{2}$$

where $\Delta F(x)$ represents the external disturbances.

The reference system is defined as Equation (3)

$$\dot{x}_r = g(x_r) \,. \tag{3}$$

where $x_r$ is a state vector, satisfying $x_r \in R^n$; $g(\cdot)$ is a vector with many slippery nonlinear functions, which has the same as the structure of $F(\cdot)$ or the different from the structure of $F(\cdot)$.

Let $e = x - x_r$, we have the following equation.

$$\lim_{t \to \infty} e(t) = 0 \,. \tag{4}$$

The system (2) can track the reference trajectory of the system (3) under the condition (4).

Matrix A is selected as a matrix with negative real part of the eigenvalues. The error equation is shown as the following equation.

$$\dot{e} = \dot{x} - \dot{x}_r = A(x - x_r) + Ax_r - Ax + F(x) + \Delta F(x) + u - g(x_r) \,. \tag{5}$$

Equation (5) is also described as the following form.

$$\dot{e} = Ae + Ax_r - Ax + F(x) + \Delta F(x) + u - g(x_r) \,. \tag{6}$$

Let $G(x)$ as the following equation.

$$G(x) = Ax_r - Ax + F(x) + \Delta F(x) - g(x_r) \,. \tag{7}$$

Equation (6) is also shown as the following equation.

$$\dot{e} = Ae + G(x) + u \,. \tag{8}$$

The estimated value $\hat{G}(x)$ is used to substitute the function $\hat{G}(x)$ when the function $G(x)$ is unknown.

## 3 The Controller of Orthogonal Function Neural Network

In the paper, Chebyshev orthogonal polynomial functions are selected as the basic functions of orthogonal function neural network.

The global output of the orthogonal function neural network is defined as the following form.

$$y = \sum_{i=1}^{N} \Phi_i W_i \cdot \tag{9}$$

where $\Phi_i = P_{1i}(x_1) \times P_{2i}(x_2) \times \cdots \times P_{ni}(x_n) = \prod_{j=1}^{n} P_{ji}(x_j)$, $P_{ji}(x_j)$ is a Chebyshev polynomial function, satisfying the following forms.

$$P_{j1}(x_j) = 1, P_{j2}(x_j) = x_j, P_{ji}(x_j) = 2x_j P_{j(i-1)}(x_j) - P_{j(i-2)}(x_j), \ j = 1,2,\ldots,N, i \geq 3. \tag{10}$$

Based on (8), $G(x)$ is shown as the following equation.

$$G(x) = W^{*T} \Phi(x) + \eta(x). \tag{11}$$

where $\eta(x)$ is a vector with the smaller norm. Equation (11) is substituted into (8).

$$\dot{e} = Ae + W^{*T} \Phi(x) + \eta(x) + u(t) \tag{12}$$

*Theorem.* Exist a positive definite and symmetric matrix $P$, which satisfies $\dot{W} = \Phi(x) e^T P$, and is the solution of the following Ricattic equation.

$$A^T P + PA + P^T \left(\frac{1}{\rho^2} - \frac{2}{\gamma}\right) P + Q = 0 \cdot \tag{13}$$

where $Q$ is a positive definite and symmetric matrix. The controller is designed as the following form.

$$u = u_1 + u_2 . \tag{14}$$

where $u_1$ satisfies $u_1 = -W^T \Phi(x)$ and $u_2$ satisfies $u_2 = -\frac{1}{\gamma} Pe$.

The state of the equation (8) convergences zero, namely $x \to x_r$, the system (2) can track the reference trajectory of the system (3).

*Proof.* Let $\tilde{W} = W^* - W$, where $W^*$ is an optimization weighted matrix, and $W$ is a weighted matrix, $\tilde{W}$ is an estimated error matrix. The Lyapunov function is shown as the following form.

$$V=\frac{1}{2}e^{T}Pe+\frac{1}{2}tr\left(\widetilde{W}^{T}\widetilde{W}\right). \tag{15}$$

Differentiating (15) with respect to the time is shown as the following steps.

$$\begin{aligned}\dot{V}&=\frac{1}{2}(\dot{e}^{T}Pe+e^{T}P\dot{e})+\frac{1}{2}tr(\dot{\widetilde{W}}^{T}\widetilde{W})=\frac{1}{2}e^{T}\left(A^{T}P+PA-\frac{2}{\gamma}P^{T}P\right)e+\eta^{T}(x)Pe\\&+\Phi^{T}(x)\widetilde{W}Pe+tr(\dot{\widetilde{W}}^{T}\widetilde{W})\end{aligned}. \tag{16}$$

Because of $\Phi^{T}(x)\widetilde{W}Pe=tr(Pe\Phi^{T}(x)\widetilde{W})$, $\dot{\widetilde{W}}=-\dot{W}$, Equation (13) is substituted into Equation (16) as the following form.

$$\dot{V}=-\frac{1}{2}e^{T}Qe-\frac{1}{2}\left(\frac{1}{\rho^{2}}e^{T}PPe-2\eta^{T}(x)Pe\right). \tag{17}$$

Equation (17) is arranged as the following form.

$$\dot{V}=-\frac{1}{2}e^{T}Qe-\frac{1}{2}\left(\frac{1}{\rho}Pe-\rho\eta(x)\right)^{T}\left(\frac{1}{\rho}Pe-\rho\eta(x)\right)+\frac{1}{2}\rho^{2}\eta^{T}(x)\eta(x)\ . \tag{18}$$

Based on the above the equation, we can acquire the following result.

$$\dot{V}\le-\frac{1}{2}e^{T}Qe+\frac{1}{2}\rho^{2}\eta^{T}(x)\eta(x)\le-\frac{1}{2}\lambda_{\min}(Q)\|e\|^{2}+\frac{1}{2}\rho^{2}\eta^{T}(x)\eta(x)\ . \tag{19}$$

where $\lambda_{\min}(Q)$ is the minimum eigenvalue of the matrix $Q$. The error $e$ satisfies the following condition.

Equation (19) represents $\dot{V}\le 0$, and demonstrates the error is bounded. A definite integral is used to $\dot{V}$ from the time 0 to time $T$.

$$V(T)-V(0)\le-\frac{1}{2}\lambda_{\min}(Q)\int_{0}^{T}\|e\|^{2}dt+\rho^{2}\frac{1}{2}\int_{0}^{T}\eta^{T}(x)\eta(x)dt\ . \tag{20}$$

Because of $V(T)\ge 0$, the result is derived from the following form.

$$\int_{0}^{T}\|e\|^{2}dt\le\frac{2V(0)}{\lambda_{\min}(Q)}+\frac{\rho^{2}}{\lambda_{\min}(Q)}\int_{0}^{T}\eta^{T}(x)\eta(x)dt<\infty\ . \tag{21}$$

According to Equation (21), $e\in L_{2}$. Because of Equation (13), $\dot{e}$ is bounded, namely $\dot{e}\in L_{\infty}$, and we have $\lim_{t\to\infty}e=0$.

## 4 Simulation

In the actual system, the Lorenz chaos system is disturbed by the external disturbances, and then the system is represented as the following equation.

$$\begin{cases} \dot{x} = (a + \delta a)(y - x) \\ \dot{y} = (d + \delta d)x - xz - (c + \delta c)y \\ \dot{z} = xy - (b + \delta b)z \end{cases} \cdot \tag{22}$$

There is a chaotic attractive factor with $a = 10$, $b = 2.67$, $c = 1$, $d = 28$. $\delta a$, $\delta b$, $\delta c$, $\delta d$ are the parameter disturbances, $\delta a = 0.2$, $\delta b = 0.1\sin t$, $\delta c = 0.2\cos t$, $\delta d = 0.1\sin t \times \cos t$. The other parameters are shown as $A = diag(-1,-1,-1)$, $Q = diag(2,2,2)$, $\gamma = 0.05$, $\rho = 0.03$. The number of the orthogonal functions sequence is 8. The controller is switched into the system at $t = 600s$. Chebyshev orthogonal neural network are adjusted to accomplish the synchronization between the Lorenz chaotic system and the Lorenz chaotic system with the external disturbances.

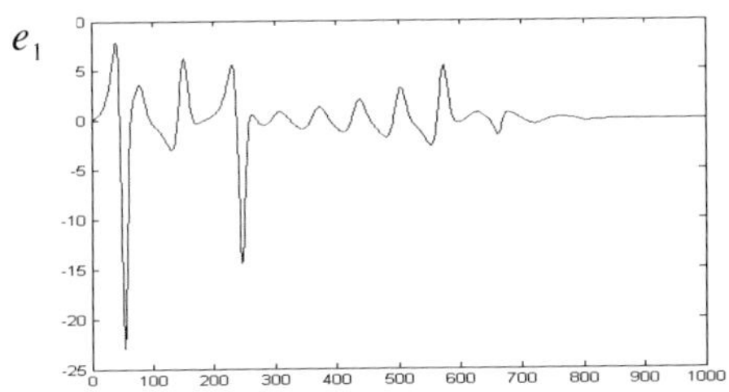


**Fig. 1.** The responding diagram of $e_1$

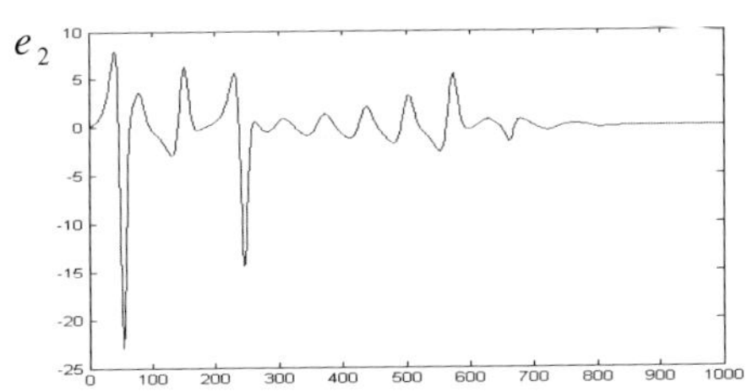


**Fig. 2.** The responding diagram of $e_2$

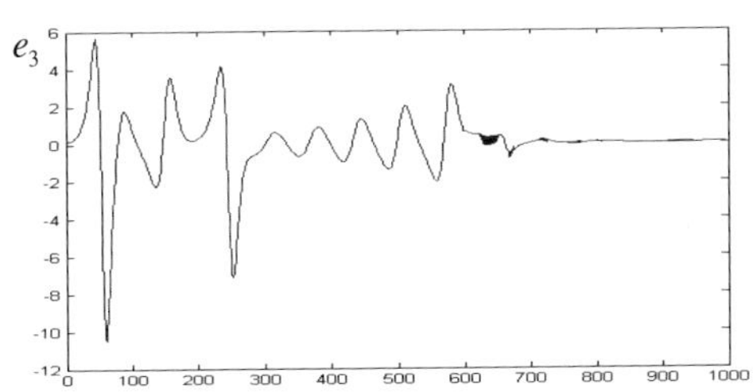


**Fig. 3.** The responding diagram of $e_3$

The error response diagrams are shown as Figure 1 to Figure 3. Based on these response diagrams, the synchronization of the two systems is carried out by the proposed method.

## 5 Conclusion

Chebyshev orthogonal function neural network is trained to learn the uncertain information of the system. When Chebyshev orthogonal function neural network can be satisfied to estimate the uncertain information of the system, the orthogonal function neural network is switched to control the chaotic system. The parameters of orthogonal neural network are adjusted to accomplish the control of chaotic system on the basis of Lyapunov stability theorem. With the demonstration of the simulating result, the proposed method can guarantee the synchronization of the chaotic systems with the external disturbances.

## References

1. Liu, F., Ren, Y., Shan, Qiu, X. M., Z.L.: A Linear Feedback Synchronization Theorem for AClass of Chaotic Systems. Chaos, Solution and Fractals 13(4) (2002) 723-730
2. Shahverdiev, E. M., Sivaprakasam, S., Shore, K. A.: Lag Synchronization in Time-Delayed Systems. Physics Letter A 292(6) (2002) 320-324
3. Li, Z., Han, C. S.: Adaptive Control for A Class of Chaotic Systems with Uncertain Parameters. Chinese Physics Transaction 5(3) (2002) 847-850
4. Sarasola, C., Torrealdea, F. J.: Cost of Synchronizing Different Chaos Systems. Mathematics and Computers in Simulation 58(4) (2002) 309-327
5. Jiang, G. P., Zheng, W. X.: An LMI Criterion for Chaos Synchronization via the Linear-State-Feedback Approach. IEEE International Symposium Computer Aided Control System Design, Taipei, Taiwan, (2004) 368-371
6. G, Grassi., S, Masolo.: Nonlinear Observer Design to Synchronize Hyperchaotic Systems via a Scalar Signal. IEEE Transaction of Circuits Systems 44(3) (1997) 1011-1014
7. Xie, K. M., Chen, Z. H., Xie, G.: Fuzzy Modeling Based on Rough Sets and Fuzzy Sets. The international Symposium on Test and Measurement, Shenzhen, (2003) 977-980

# Exponential Stability of Interval Neural Networks with Variable Delays

Jiye Zhang, Dianbo Ren, and Weihua Zhang

National Traction Power Laboratory, Southwest Jiaotong University,
Chengdu 610031, People's Republic of China
jyzhang@home.swjtu.edu.cn

**Abstract.** In this paper, the conditions ensuring existence, uniqueness, and global exponential stability of the equilibrium point of interval neural networks with variable delays are studied. Applying idea of vector Liapunov function, the sufficient conditions for global exponential stability of interval neural networks are obtained.

## 1 Introduction

In application of neural networks such as associative memories, optimization solution and signal processing, the stability of networks is prerequisite [1]. In hardware implementation of neural networks, time delays often occur due to finite switching speeds of the amplifiers and communication time. Therefore, the study of stability of neural networks with delay is practically required. The conditions ensuring the asymptotic stability of neural networks are given in [2-8]. However, in neural networks, some parameters such as the neurons fire rate, the synaptic interconnection weight and signal transmission delay, etc., are usually acquired and processed by means of statistical estimation. The estimating errors therefore exist. On the other hand, parameter fluctuation in neural networks implementation in large-scale integration chips is also unavoidable. In order to consider the effect of parameters fluctuation, the stability of interval neural networks is studied in [9].

In this paper, we study the global exponential stability of neural networks with variable delays described by the delayed differential equations as follows

$$\frac{\mathrm{d}u_i(t)}{\mathrm{d}t} = -d_i u_i(t) + \sum_{j=1}^{n}[a_{ij} f_j(u_j(t)) + b_{ij} g_j(u_j(t-\tau_{ij}(t)))] + J_i,\ i=1,2,\cdots,n, \tag{1}$$

where $u_i$ is the state of neuron $i$, $i=1,2,\cdots,n$, and $n$ is the number of neurons; $A=(a_{ij})_{n\times n}$, $B=(b_{ij})_{n\times n}$ are connection matrices, $J=(J_1,J_2,\cdots,J_n)^{\mathrm{T}}$ is the constant input. $f(u)=(f_1(u_1),f_2(u_2),\cdots,f_n(u_n))^{\mathrm{T}}$ and $g(u)=(g_1(u_1),g_2(u_2),\cdots,g_n(u_n))^{\mathrm{T}}$ are the activation functions of the neurons, $D=\mathrm{diag}(d_1,d_2,\cdots,d_n)>0$. The variable delays $\tau_{ij}(t)$ ($i,j=1,2,\cdots,n$) are bounded functions, i.e. $0\le\tau_{ij}(t)\le\tau$, $\tau\ge 0$ is a constant. The initial conditions of Eq. (1) is of the form $u_i(s)=\phi_i(s)$, $-\tau\le s\le 0$, where $\phi_i$ is bounded and continuous on $[-\tau,0]$, $i$=1,2,…, $n$.

D.-S. Huang, K. Li, and G.W. Irwin (Eds.): ICIC 2006, LNCS 4113, pp. 357–363, 2006.

Assume the activation functions of the neurons satisfying:

**Assumption 1.** For each $j \in \{1,2,\cdots,n\}$ , $f_j : \mathrm{R} \to \mathrm{R}$ and $g_j : \mathrm{R} \to \mathrm{R}$ , and there exist the real numbers $L_j > 0$, $M_j > 0$ , such that

$$\frac{f_j(z_1)-f_j(z_2)}{z_1-z_2} \geq 0,\ L_j = \sup_{|z_1-z_2|\neq 0} \frac{f_j(z_1)-f_j(z_2)}{z_1-z_2},\ \text{and}\ M_j = \sup_{|z_1-z_2|\neq 0} \left|\frac{g_j(z_1)-g_j(z_2)}{z_1-z_2}\right|.$$

Let $L = \mathrm{diag}(L_1, L_2, \cdots, L_n) > 0$, $M = \mathrm{diag}(M_1, M_2, \cdots, M_n) > 0$ .
Define set of matrices as follows:

$$D_I = \{D = \mathrm{diag}(d_i)_{n\times n} : \underline{D} \leq D \leq \overline{D}, \text{i.e.}, \underline{d}_i \leq d_i \leq \overline{d}_i, i = 1,...,n\},$$
$$A_I = \{A = (a_{ij})_{n\times n} : \underline{A} \leq A \leq \overline{A}, \text{i.e.}, \underline{a}_{ij} \leq a_{ij} \leq \overline{a}_{ij}, i, j = 1,...,n\},$$
$$B_I = \{B = (b_{ij})_{n\times n} : \underline{B} \leq B \leq \overline{B}, \text{i.e.}, \underline{b}_{ij} \leq b_{ij} \leq \overline{b}_{ij}, i, j = 1,...,n\}.$$

**Definition 1.** The interval neural networks system (1) is globally exponentially stable if for each $D \in D_I$ , $A \in A_I$ , $B \in B_I$ , and *J*, systems (1) have an equilibrium point $u^*$ , and there exist constants $\lambda > 0$ and $\eta > 0$ such that

$$\| u(t) - u^* \| \leq \eta \| \phi - u^* \| \mathrm{e}^{-\lambda t}$$

for all $t \geq 0$ , where $\| \phi - u^* \| = \max_{1\leq i\leq n} \sup_{s\in[-\tau,0]} | \phi_i(s) - u_i^* |$ .

Our objective in this paper is to study the existence, uniqueness and global exponential stability of the equilibrium point of interval neural networks with variable delays. From idea of vector Liapunov function, differential inequalities involving variable delays are constructed. From qualitative property of the differential inequalities, the sufficient conditions for global exponential stability of interval neural networks with variable delays are obtained.

For convenience, we introduce some notations: for matrix $A = (a_{ij})_{n\times n}$ , $|A|$ denotes absolute-value matrix given by $|A| = (|a_{ij}|)_{n\times n}$ ; for $x \in \mathrm{R}^n$ , $|x| = (|x_1|,...,|x_n|)^{\mathrm{T}}$ , $\| x \|$ denotes a vector norm defined by $\| x \| = \max_{1\leq i\leq n} \{|x_i|\}$ .

## 2 Existence and Uniqueness of the Equilibrium Point

In the section we will study the existence and uniqueness of the equilibrium point of neural networks (1).

**Lemma 1** [10]. Let $A = (a_{ij})$ be an $n \times n$ matrix with non-positive off-diagonal elements. Then the following statements are equivalent:

(i) $A$ is an M-matrix ;
(ii) The real parts of all eigenvalues of $A$ are positive;
(iii) There exists a vector $\eta > 0$ such that $A\eta > 0$;

(iv) There exists a vector $\xi > 0$ such that $\xi^{T} A > 0$;

(v) There exists a positive definite $n \times n$ diagonal matrix $D$ such that matrix $AD + DA^{T}$ is positive definite.

Define a nonlinear map associated with (1) as follows:

$$H(u) = -Du + Af(u) + Bg(u) + J \ . \quad (2)$$

It is known that the solutions of $H(u) = 0$ are equilibriums of (1). If map $H(u)$ is a homeomorphism on $R^n$, then there exists a unique point $u^*$ such that $H(u^*) = 0$, i.e., systems (1) have a unique equilibrium $u^*$.

**Lemma 2** [2,5]**.** If $H(u) \in C^0$ satisfies (i) $H(u)$ is injective on $R^n$; (ii) $\| H(u) \| \to \infty$ as $\| u \| \to \infty$; then $H(u)$ is a homeomorphism of $R^n$.

From Lemma 2, we can obtain the condition of existence and uniqueness of the equilibrium point of interval neural networks (1).

**Theorem 1.** If Assumption 1 is satisfied, and $\alpha = D^* - (A^* L + B^* M)$ is an M-matrix, then, for each $D \in D_I$, $A \in A_I$, $B \in B_I$, and for every input $J$, system (1) has a unique equilibrium $u^*$, where $D^* = \mathrm{diag}(\underline{d}_1, \ldots, \underline{d}_n)$, $A^* = (a_{ij}^*)_{n \times n}$, with $a_{ii}^* = \max\{0, \overline{a}_{ii}\}$, $a_{ij}^* = \max\{|\underline{a}_{ij}|, |\overline{a}_{ij}|\}\ (i \neq j)$; $B^* = (b_{ij}^*)_{n \times n}$ with $b_{ij}^* = \max\{|\underline{b}_{ij}|, |\overline{b}_{ij}|\}$.

**Proof.** For any $D \in D_I$, $A \in A_I$, $B \in B_I$, let $\beta = D - (A^{+} L + |B| M)$, where $A^{+} = (a_{ij}^{+})_{n \times n}$, $a_{ij}^{+} = \max\{0, a_{ij}\}$. Due to $\alpha$ being an M-matrix, from Lemma 1 we know that, there exist $\xi_i > 0\ (i = 1,2,\ldots,n)$ such that

$$-d_i \xi_i + \sum_{j=1}^{n} \xi_j (L_j a_{ji}^{+} + |b_{ji}| M_j) < 0 \quad (i = 1,2,\ldots,n) \ . \quad (3)$$

From Lemma 1(iv), matrix $\beta$ is an M-matrix. In order to prove that for each input $J$, system (1) has a unique equilibrium point $u^*$, it is only need to prove that $H(u)$ is a homeomorphism on $R^n$. In the following, we shall prove that map $H(u)$ is a homeomorphism in two steps.

**Step 1.** We shall prove that condition (i) in Lemma 2 is satisfied. Suppose, for purposes of contradiction, that there exist $x, y \in R^n$ with $x \neq y$ such that $H(x) = H(y)$. From (2), we get

$$-D(x - y) + A(f(x) - f(y)) + B(g(x) - g(y)) = 0 \ . \quad (4)$$

From Assumption 1, there exist matrices $K = \mathrm{diag}(K_1, \ldots, K_n)\ (-L \le K \le L)$, and $Q = \mathrm{diag}(Q_1, \ldots, Q_n)\ (-M \le Q \le M)$, such that $f(x) - f(y) = K(x - y)$ and $g(x) - g(y) = Q(x - y)$. So (4) can be written as:

$$[-D+(AK+BQ)](x-y)=0\,. \tag{5}$$

In the following, we shall prove that $\det[-D+(AK+BQ)]\neq 0$. Consider the system

$$\dot{z}=[-D+(AK+BQ)]z\,. \tag{6}$$

Since $0\leq K\leq L$ and $-M\leq Q\leq M$, from (3) we have

$$-d_i\xi_i+\sum_{j=1}^{n}\xi_j(a_{ji}^{+}K_j+|b_{ji}Q_j|)<0\quad (i=1,2,...,n)\,. \tag{7}$$

Consider a Liapunov function $V(z)=\sum_{i=1}^{n}\xi_i|z_i|$. Calculating the upper right derivative $D^{+}V$ of $V$ along the solutions of (6), we get

$$D^{+}V(z)=\sum_{i=1}^{n}\xi_i\{\operatorname{sgn} z_i[-d_iz_i+\sum_{j=1}^{n}(a_{ij}K_j+b_{ij}Q_j)z_j]\}$$
$$\leq\sum_{i=1}^{n}[-d_i\xi_i+\sum_{j=1}^{n}\xi_j(a_{ji}^{+}K_j+|b_{ji}Q_j|)]|z_i|\,.$$

From (7), we know that $D^{+}V(z)<0$ $(\|z\|\neq 0)$. By the Liapunov stability Theorem [10], the zero solution of systems (6) is globally asymptotically stable. Thus matrix $-D+(AK+BQ)$ is a stable matrix and $\det[-D+(AK+BQ)]\neq 0$. From (5), we get $x=y$, which is a contradiction. So map $H$ is injective.

**Step 2.** We shall prove that condition (ii) in Lemma 2 is satisfied. Let

$$\overline{H}(u)=-Du+A(f(u)-f(0))+B(g(u)-g(0))\,.$$

To show that $H$ is homeomorphism, it suffices to show that $\overline{H}(u)$ is homeomorphism. According to Assumption 1, we get $u[f_i(u)-f_i(0)]\leq L_iu^2$, $|g_i(u)-g_i(0)|\leq M_i|u|$ (*i*=1,2,…,*n*). Since $\beta=D-(A^{+}L+|B|M)$ is an M-matrix, from Lemma 1(v), there exists a positive definite diagonal matrix $P=\operatorname{diag}(p_1,\cdots,p_n)>0$ such that

$$[P(-D+A^{+}L+|B|M)]^{S}\leq-\varepsilon E_n<0 \tag{8}$$

for sufficiently small $\varepsilon>0$, where $E_n$ is the unit matrix. Calculate

$$[Pu]^{\mathrm{T}}\overline{H}(u)\leq-|u|^{\mathrm{T}}PD|u|+|u|^{\mathrm{T}}PA^{+}|f(u)-f(0)|+|u|^{\mathrm{T}}P|B||g(u)-g(0)|$$
$$\leq|u|^{\mathrm{T}}[P(-D+A^{+}L+|B|M)]^{S}|u|\,.$$

Furthermore, from (8), we have $[Pu]^{\mathrm{T}}\overline{H}(u)\leq-\varepsilon\|u\|^2$. By using Schwartz inequality, we get $\varepsilon\|u\|^2\leq\|P\|\|u\|\|\overline{H}(u)\|$, namely, $\varepsilon\|u\|/\|P\|\leq\|\overline{H}(u)\|$. So $\|\overline{H}(u)\|\to+\infty$, i.e., $\|H(u)\|\to+\infty$ as $\|u\|\to+\infty$. From Lemma 2, we know that for every input $J$, map $H$ is homeomorphism on $\mathrm{R}^n$. So system (1) has a unique equilibrium point $u^*$. The proof is completed.

## 3 Global Exponential Stability of the Equilibrium Point

**Theorem 2.** If Assumption 1 is satisfied and $\alpha = D^* - (A^* L + B^* M)$ is an M-matrix, then, for each $D \in D_I$, $A \in A_I$, $B \in B_I$, and for every input $J$, systems (1) have a unique equilibrium point, which is globally exponentially stable, where $D^* = \mathrm{diag}(\underline{d}_1, \ldots, \underline{d}_n)$, $A^* = (a_{ij}^*)_{n\times n}$, $a_{ii}^* = \max\{0, \overline{a}_{ii}\}$, $a_{ij}^* = \max\{|\underline{a}_{ij}|, |\overline{a}_{ij}|\}\ (i \neq j)$, $B^* = (b_{ij}^*)_{n\times n}$, $b_{ij}^* = \max\{|\underline{b}_{ij}|, |\overline{b}_{ij}|\}$.

**Proof.** Since $\alpha$ is an M-matrix, from Theorem 1, system (1) has a unique equilibrium point $u^*$. Let $x(t) = u(t) - u^*$, Eq. (1) can be written as

$$\frac{dx_i(t)}{dt} = -d_i x_i(t) + \sum_{j=1}^{n} a_{ij} \bar{f}_j(x_j(t)) + \sum_{j=1}^{n} b_{ij} \overline{g}_j(x_j(t - \tau_{ij}(t))),\ i = 1, 2, \cdots, n, \tag{9}$$

where $\bar{f}_j(x_j) = f_j(x_j + u_j^*) - f_j(u_j^*)$, $\overline{g}_j(x_j) = g_j(x_j + u_j^*) - g_j(u_j^*)$ $(j = 1, \cdots, n)$. The initial condition of Eq. (9) is $\psi(s) = \phi(s) - u^*$, $-\tau \le s \le 0$. Due to $\alpha$ being an M-matrix, from the proof of Theorem 1, we know that $\beta = D - (A^+ L + |B| M)$ is an M-matrix, where $A^+ = (a_{ij}^+)_{n\times n}$, $a_{ij}^+ = \max\{0, a_{ij}\}$. From Lemma 1(iii), there exist $\xi_i > 0$ $(i = 1, 2, \ldots, n)$ and $\lambda > 0$ such that

$$-\xi_i(d_i - \lambda) + \sum_{j=1}^{n} \xi_j (a_{ij}^+ L_j + e^{\lambda\tau} |b_{ij}| M_j) < 0 \quad (i = 1, 2, \ldots, n). \tag{10}$$

Here, $\tau \ge 0$ is a fixed number according to assumption of neural networks (1). Let $y_i(t) = e^{\lambda t} x_i(t)$. Calculating the upper right derivative $D^+ |y_i(t)|$ of $|y_i(t)|$ along the solutions of Eq. (9), we get

$$\begin{aligned} D^+ |y_i(t)| &= e^{\lambda t} \operatorname{sgn} x_i \{-d_i x_i(t) + \sum_{j=1}^{n} [a_{ij} \bar{f}_j(x_j(t)) + b_{ij} \overline{g}_j(x_j(t - \tau_{ij}(t)))]\} + \lambda e^{\lambda t} |x_i(t)| \\ &\le e^{\lambda t} \{(-d_i + \lambda)|x_i(t)| + \sum_{j=1}^{n} [a_{ij}^+ |\bar{f}_j(x_j(t))| + |b_{ij}| |\overline{g}_j(x_j(t - \tau_{ij}(t)))|]\} \\ &\le (-d_i + \lambda)|y_i(t)| + \sum_{j=1}^{n} [a_{ij}^+ L_j |y_j(t)| + e^{\lambda\tau} |b_{ij}| M_j \sup_{t-\tau \le s \le t} |y_j(s)|] . \end{aligned} \tag{11}$$

Define the curve $\gamma = \{z(l) : z_i = \xi_i l, l > 0, i = 1, 2, \ldots, n\}$ and the set $\Omega(z) = \{u : 0 \le u \le z, z \in \gamma\}$.

Let $\xi_{\min} = \min_{1\le i\le n}\{\xi_i\}$, $\xi_{\max} = \max_{1\le i\le n}\{\xi_i\}$. Taking $l_0 = (1+\delta)\|\psi\| / \xi_{\min}$, where $\delta > 0$ is a constant, then $\{|y| : |y| = e^{\lambda\tau} |\psi(s)|, -\tau \le s \le 0\} \subset \Omega(z_0(l_0))$, i.e.,

$$|y_i(s)| = e^{\lambda s} |\psi_i(s)| < \xi_i l_0,\ -\tau \le s \le 0,\ i = 1, 2, \ldots, n.$$

We claim that $|y_i(t)|<\xi_i l_0$ for $t\in[0,+\infty)$ and $\forall i$. If it is not true, then there exist some index $i$ and $t_1$ $(t_1>0)$ such that $|y_i(t_1)|=\xi_i l_0$, $D^+|y_i(t_1)|\ge 0$, and $|y_j(t)|\le\xi_j l_0$ for $-\tau\le t\le t_1$, $j$ =1, 2, … , $n$. However, from (11) and (10), we get

$$D^+|y_i(t_1)|\le[(-d_i+\lambda)\xi_i+\sum_{j=1}^{n}(a_{ij}^+L_j+e^{\lambda\tau}|b_{ij}|M_j)\xi_j]l_0<0\,.$$

This is a contradiction. So $|y_i(t)|<\xi_i l_0$ for $t\in[0,+\infty)$, $i=1,2,...,n$. Furthermore,

$$|x_i(t)|<\xi_i l_0\,e^{-\lambda t}\le(1+\delta)\|\psi\|\,\xi_{\max}/\xi_{\min}\,e^{-\lambda t}=\eta\|\psi\|\,e^{-\lambda t}\,,\ i=1,2,...,n\,,$$

for $t\ge 0$, where $\eta=(1+\delta)\xi_{\max}/\xi_{\min}$. From Definition 1, the zero solution of system (9) is globally exponentially stable, i.e., the interval neural networks system (1) is globally exponentially stable. The proof is completed.

In [9], researchers studied the stability of interval neural networks with constant delays. It easy to test that if the conditions in [9] are satisfied, then $\alpha=D^*-(A^*L+B^*M)$ is an M-matrix. On the other hand, the conditions in [9] are more difficult to test than that of Theorem 2 in this work in application.

## 4 Conclusion

In the paper, an analysis of existence, uniqueness, and global exponential stability of the equilibrium point of the interval neural networks with variable delays have been presented. Applying idea of vector Liapunov function method and M-matrix theory, we obtain sufficient conditions for global exponential stability.

## Acknowledgment

This work is supported by Youth Science Foundation of Sichuan (No. 05ZQ026-015), National Program for New Century Excellent Talents in University (No. NCET-04-0889), and Natural Science Foundation of China (No.50375127).

## References

1. Chua, L. O., Yang, L.: Cellular Neural Networks: Theory. IEEE Trans. Circ. Syst. 35 (1988) 1257-1272
2. Forti, M., Tesi, A.: New Conditions for Global Stability of Neural Networks with Application to Linear and Quadratic Programming Problems. IEEE Trans. Circ. Syst.-I 42 (1995) 354-366
3. Van Den Driessche, P., Zou, X.: Global Attractivity in Delayed Hopfield Neural Networks Models. SIAM J. Appl. Math. 58(1998) 1878-1890
4. Arik, S., Tavanoglu, V.: On the Global Asymptotic Stability of Delayed Cellular Neural Networks. IEEE Trans. Circ. Syst.-I 47(2000) 571-574
5. Zhang, J., Jin, X.: Global Stability Analysis in Delayed Hopfield Neural Networks Models. Neural Networks 13(2000) 745-753

6. Zhang, J.: Absolutely Exponential Stability in Delayed Cellular Neural Networks. Int. J. Circ. Theor. Appl. 30 (2002) 395-409
7. Zhang, J.: Globally Exponential Stability of Neural Networks with Variable Delays. IEEE Trans. Circ. Syst.-I 50(2003) 288-291
8. Chen, T.: Global Exponential Stability of Delayed Hopfield Neural Networks. Neural Networks 14(2001) 977-980
9. Liao, X., Wong, K. W., Wu, Z., Chen, G.: Novel Robust Stability Criteria for Interval Delayed Hopfield Neural Networks. IEEE Trans. Circ. Syst.-I 48(2001) 1355-1359
10. Siljak, D. D.: Large-Scale Dynamic Systems-Stability and Structure. Elsevier, New York (1978)

# Exponential Synchronization for a Class of Chaotic Neural Network with Time-Delay

Zhongsheng Wang[1], Jinghuan Chen[1], Wudai Liao[1], and Xiaoxin Liao[2]

[1] School of Electric and Information Engineering,
ZhongYuan University of Technology,
Zhengzhou, Henan, 450007, P.R. China
zswang@zzti.edu.cn
[2] Department of Control Science and Engineering,
Huazhong University of Science and Technology,
Wuhan, Hubei, 430074, P.R. China

**Abstract.** The chaos synchronization between two time-delayed chaotic neural network has been discussed. Based the Lyapuov approaches, we have obtained some new synchronization conditions,the new results improve the earlier works.Numerical simulation is given to demonstrate the validness of the proposed results.

## 1 Introduction

In recent years,neural networks with or without time-delays has attracted the attention of the scientists, due to their promising potential for the tasks of classification, associate memory and parallel computation,communication,etc., and various results were reported,see, e.g.[1-9] and references therein. Complex dynamics behaviors such as chaos exist in time-delayed neural networks.The dimension of Chaotic neural network is infinite, therefore it is more secure to communicate through communication system designed by the time-delayed chaotic system. In this paper,we investigate the chaos synchronization between two time-delayed chaotic neural network with two neurons. Based the Lyapuov approaches, we have obtained some new synchronization conditions,the new results improve the earlier works.Numerical simulation is given to demonstrate the validness of the proposed results.

## 2 System Description and Lemma

We consider the following neural network with time-delay[10]

$$\begin{cases} \dot{y_1} = -y_1 + a_1 f(y_2) - a_1 b_1 f(y_2(t-\tau)) \\ \dot{y_2} = -y_2 + a_2 f(y_1) - a_2 b_2 f(y_1(t-\tau)) \end{cases} \tag{1}$$

Where the neural activation function is f(.), $\tau$ is constant time-delay, $a_1, b_1, a_2, b_2$ are positive constant numbers,and the activation function f(.) satisfies the Lipschitz condition,i.e, there exists a L$<\infty$ such that

$$|f(x_1) - f(x_2)| < L|x_1 - x_2|$$

D.-S. Huang, K. Li, and G.W. Irwin (Eds.): ICIC 2006, LNCS 4113, pp. 364–369, 2006.

for arbitrary $x_1, x_2$. if the parameters in systems(1) satisfy

$$max(|a_1(1-b_1)L|, |a_2(1-b_2)L|) < 1$$

then system(1) possess an equilibrium point $(y_1^*, y_1^*)$ which is unique. Furthermore,if the function f(.) is differentiable and $f'(0) \neq 0, q = \sqrt{1/a_1a_2f'^2(0)} = 1, b_1 = b_2 = 3\pi/2\tau$, hence, there exists Hopf bifurcation phenomena in system(1),the numerical simulation shows that there exists chaos in the neural network.

When we take the system(1) as the following form

$$\dot{x} = -Cx(t) + Af(x(t)) + Bg(x(t-\tau) \tag{2}$$

Where $x(t) = (x_1, x_2, \ldots, x_n)^T$ is state variable, $C = diag(c_1, c_2, \ldots, c_n)$, $f(x(t)) = (f_1(x_1), f_2(x_2), \cdots, f_n(x_n))^T$ ,$g(x(t-\tau)) = (g_1(x_1(t-\tau)), g_2(x_2(t-\tau)), \cdots, g_n(x_n(t-\tau)))^T$, $f(x(t)), g(x(t-\tau))$ satisfy Lipschtiz conditions,that is, for any $j \in 1, 2\cdots, n$,and any $r_1, r_2, r_3, r_4 \in R$,there exist $l_j, k_j$,

$$|f_j(r_1) - f_j(r_2)| \leq l_j|r_1 - r_2|, |g_j(r_3) - g_j(r_4)| \leq k_j|r_3 - r_4|$$

Let $|A| = [|a_{ij}|], \overline{A} = [a_{ij}l_j], \overline{B} = [b_{ij}k_j]$

**Lemma 1**[6]**:** If $C - |\overline{A}| - |\overline{B}|$ is non-singular M-matrix, then system(2) is globally exponentially stable.

Before we give the lemma 2,we consider the following differentiable inequality

$$D^+x_i \leq \sum_{j=1}^n c_{ij}x_j + \sum_{j=1}^n d_{ij}x_j(t-\tau) \tag{3}$$

where $i, j \in 1, 2\cdots, n, x_i, d_{ij} \in C(R, R_+), c_{ij} \in C(R, R_+)(i \neq j), c_{ii} \in C(R, R), R_+ = [0, +\infty)$

**Lemma 2**[7]**:** If there exists a $\eta < 0$ such that for any $i\in 1, 2, \ldots, n$,

$$(c_{ii} - \eta) + \sum_{j=1, j\neq i}^n c_{ij} + \sum_{j=1}^n d_{ij}exp(-\eta\tau) < 0$$

then, any solution $x_i(t)$ of inequality (3) satisfies

$$x_i(t) \leq \overline{x}(t_0)exp(\eta(t-t_0))$$

## 3 Exponential Synchronization for the Chaotic Neural Network with Time-Delay

We select the systems(1)as the drive system, the response system can be obtained by copying system, with state variable form as $\widehat{y}(t)$,we obtained the following coupled system

$$\begin{cases} \dot{\hat{y}}_1 = -\hat{y}_1 + a_1f(\hat{y}_2)) - a_1b_1f(\hat{y}_2(t-\tau)) + k_1(y_1 - \hat{y}_1) \\ \dot{\hat{y}}_2 = -\hat{y}_2 + a_2f(\hat{y}_1) - a_2b_2f(\hat{y}_1(t-\tau)) + k_2(y_2 - \hat{y}_2) \end{cases} \tag{4}$$

Let $e_1 = y_1 - \hat{y}_1, e_2 = y_2 - \hat{y}_2$, then

$$\begin{cases} \dot{e_1} = -(1+k_1)e_1 + a_1(f(y_2) - f(\hat{y}_2)) - a_1 b_1(f(y_2(t-\tau)) - f(\hat{y}_2(t-\tau))) \\ \dot{e_2} = -(1+k_2)e_2 + a_2(f(y_1) - f(\hat{y}_1)) - a_2 b_2(f(y_1(t-\tau)) - f(\hat{y}_1(t-\tau))) \end{cases} \quad (5)$$

In general, we assume $(0,0)$ be the equilibrium point of system and $f^{'}(0) \neq 0$.

**Theorem 1(local exponential stability):** If $(1+k_1)(1+k_2) \geq a_1 a_2 f^{'2}(0)$ $(1+b_1)(1+b_2)$,then the synchronized system is locally exponentially stable.

**Proof:** The linearized equation of (5) is

$$\begin{cases} \dot{e_1} = -(1+k_1)e_1 + a_1 f^{'}(0)e_2 - a_1 b_1 f^{'}(0)e_2(t-\tau) \\ \dot{e_2} = -(1+k_2)e_2 + a_2 f^{'}(0)e_1 - a_2 b_2 f^{'}(0)e_1(t-\tau) \end{cases} \quad (6)$$

Let

$$C = \begin{bmatrix} 1 & 0 \\ 0 & 1+k \end{bmatrix}, \overline{A} = \begin{bmatrix} 0 & a_1 f^{'}(0) \\ a_2 f^{'}(0) & 0 \end{bmatrix}, \overline{B} = \begin{bmatrix} 0 & -a_1 b_1 f^{'}(0) \\ -a_2 b_2 f^{'}(0) & 0 \end{bmatrix}$$

then

$$C = -|\overline{A}| - |\overline{B}| = \begin{bmatrix} 1+k_1 & -a_1(1+b_1)f^{'}(0) \\ -a_2(1+b_2)f^{'}(0) & 1+k_2 \end{bmatrix},$$

from the condition of **Theorem 1**,the above matrix is non-singular M-matrix, then from Lemma 1, the **Theorem 1** is proof.

**Corollary 1**[10]**:** If $b_1 = b_2 = b, k_1 = k_2 > \sqrt{a_1 a_2 f'^2(0)}(1+b) - 1$, then the synchronized system is locally stable.

**Corollary 2:** If $k_1 = 0, k_2 > a_1 a_2 f^{'2}(0)(1+b_1)(1+b_2) - 1$ *or* $k_2 = 0, k_1 > a_1 a_2 f^{'2}(0)(1+b_1)(1+b_2) - 1$,then the synchronized system is locally stable.

**Remark 1: Corollary 2** indicates that we can control the response system with only one feedback.

Now we investigate the global stability condition,we take the Lyapunov function

$$V(e_1, e_2) = (|e_1|/\alpha_1, |e_2|/\alpha_2) = (V_1, V_2)$$

where $\alpha_1, \alpha_2$ is constant numbers, then

$$D^+ V_1 = sgn(e_1).\dot{e}_1/\alpha_1 \leq -(1+k_1)|e_1|/\alpha_1 + \frac{a_1}{\alpha_1} M|e_2| + \frac{a_1}{\alpha_1} M b_1 |e_2(t-\tau)|$$

$$D^+ V_2 = sgn(e_2).\dot{e}_2/\alpha_2 \leq -(1+k_2)|e_2|/\alpha_2 + \frac{a_2}{\alpha_2} M|e_1| + \frac{a_2}{\alpha_2} M b_2 |e_1(t-\tau)|$$

that is

$$\begin{cases} D^+ V_1 \leq -(1+k_1)V_1 + \frac{\alpha_2}{\alpha_1} a_1 M|V_2| + \frac{\alpha_2}{\alpha_1} a_1 M b_1 |V_2(t-\tau)| \\ D^+ V_2 \leq -(1+k_2)V_2 + \frac{\alpha_1}{\alpha_2} a_2 M|V_1| + \frac{\alpha_1}{\alpha_2} a_2 M b_2 |V_1(t-\tau)| \end{cases} \quad (7)$$

Let

$$\theta_1 = \frac{\alpha_2}{\alpha_1}, \theta_2 = \frac{\alpha_1}{\alpha_2}$$

Take a constant number $\eta < 0$.

If

$$\begin{cases} k_1 > \theta_1 a_1 M + \theta_1 a_1 M b_1 | exp(-\eta\tau) - 1 - \eta \\ k_2 > \theta_2 a_2 M + \theta_2 a_2 M b_2 | exp(-\eta\tau) - 1 - \eta \end{cases} \quad (8)$$

Then from Lemma 2, we have

$$\begin{cases} |e_1| \leq |e_1(t_0|exp(\eta(t - t_0)) \\ |e_2| \leq |e_2(t_0|exp(\eta(t - t_0)) \end{cases} \quad (9)$$

**Theorem 2 (globally exponential stability):** If f(.) satisfies the global Lipschitz condition,i.e,there exists a positive M such that $|f(x_1 - x_2| < M|x_1 - x_2|$ for any $x_1, x_2$, then the coupled system(1)and (4) is globally exponentially synchronized when $k_1 > \theta_1 a_1 M + \theta_1 a_1 M b_1 | exp(-\eta\tau) - 1 - \eta,\ k_2 > \theta_2 a_2 M + \theta_2 a_2 M b_2 | exp(-\eta\tau) - 1 - \eta$.

**Corollary 3:** If take $\theta_1 > 0, |\eta|(\eta < 0)$ very small,then the system (1)and (4) can globally exponentially synchronized with $k_1 = 0, k_2 > \theta_2 a_2 M + \theta_2 a_2 M b_2 | exp(-\eta\tau) - 1 - \eta$.

**Corollary 4:** If take $\theta_2 > 0, |\eta|(\eta < 0)$ very small,then the system (1)and (4) can synchronized with $k_1 > \theta_1 a_1 M + \theta_1 a_1 M b_1 | exp(-\eta\tau) - 1 - \eta, k_2 = 0$.

**Remark 2: Corollary 3** and **Corollary 3** indicate that the system (1) and (4)can be globally exponentially synchronized by only one feedback.

## 4 Numerical Example

In this section,we set the parameters to $f(.) = sin(p.), p = 2.81, a_1 = 1, a_2 = 1.71, b1_1 = 1.9, b_2 = 0.61, \tau = 1$. Fig.1 show that system (1) is chaotic. When $k_1 = k_2 = 0$, Fig.2 is the waveform graphs of the synchronous error $e_1$ and $e_2$. Fig.3 is the waveform graphs of $e_1,\ and\ e_2$ when $k_1 = 5, k_2 = 0$. Fig.4 is the

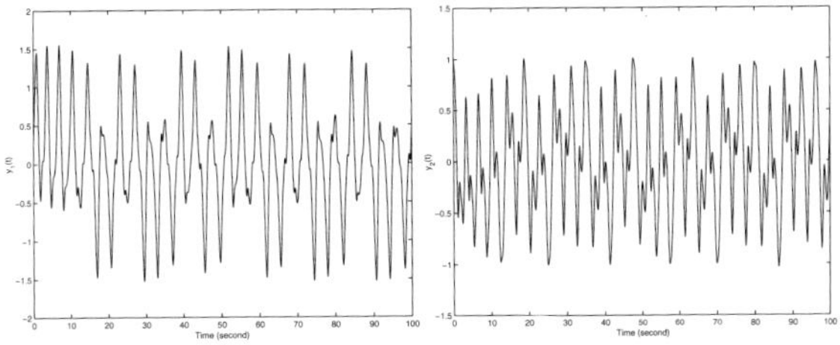


**Fig. 1.** The graphs of state $y_1(t) and y_2(t)$

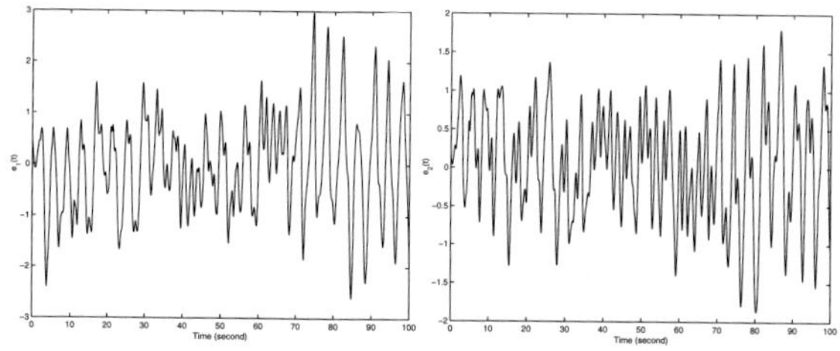

**Fig. 2.** Waveform graphs of $e_1, e_2$ when $k_1 = k_2 = 0$

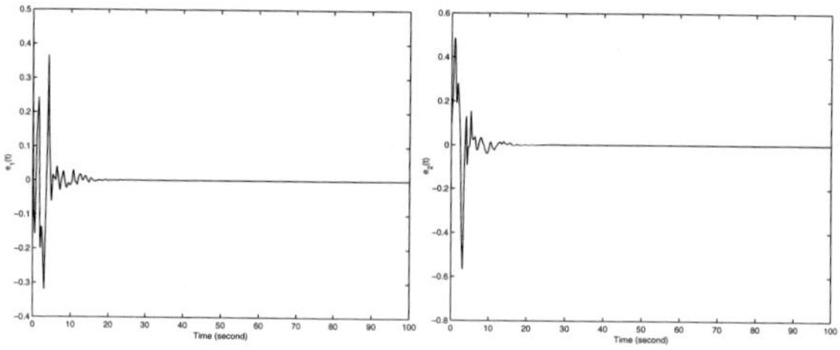

**Fig. 3.** Waveform graphs of $e_1, e_2$ when $k_1 = 5, k_2 = 0$

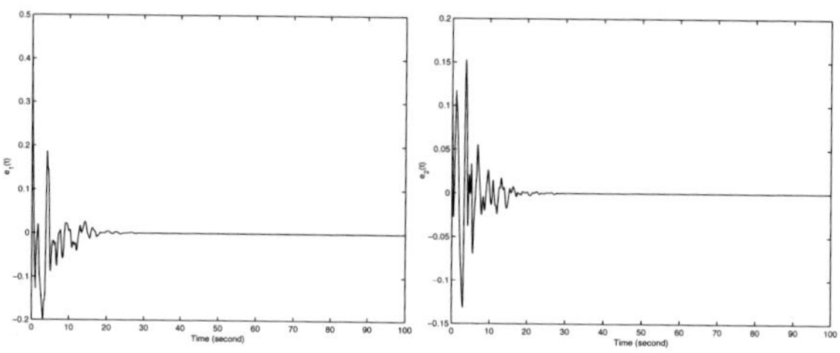

**Fig. 4.** Waveform graphs of $e_1, e_2$ when $k_1 = 0, k_2 = 5$

waveform graphs of $e_1$ *and* $e_2$ when $k_1 = 5, k_2 = 0$. The validness of the results is shown by the numerical simulation.

## Acknowledgement

This work is supported by National Natural Science Foundation (60274007) of China and Foundation of Young Bone Teacher of Henan Province.

## References

1. Liang, X. B., Wu, L. D.: Globally Exponential Stability of Hopfield Neural Networks and Its Applications, Sci. China (series A), vol. 25 (1995) 523-532
2. Forti, M., Tesi, A.: New Conditions for Global Stability of Neural Networks with Application to Linear and Quadratic Programming Problems, IEEE Trans. on Circ. and Sys. I: Fundanmetntal Theory and Application, vol. 42 (1995) 354-366

3. Liao, X. X., Xiao, D. M.: Globally Exponential Stability of Hopfield Neural Networks with Time-Varying Delays, ACTA Electronica Sinica, vol. 28 (2000) 1-4
4. Marco, M. D., Forti, M., Tesi A.: Existence and Characterization of Limit Cycles in Nearly Symmetric Neural Networks, IEEE Trans. on Circ. and Sys. I: Fundanmetntal Theory and Application, vol. 49 (2002) 979-992
5. Forti, M.: Some Extensions of A New Method to Analyze Complete Stability of Neural Networks, IEEE Trans. on Neural Networks, vol. 13 (2002) 1230-1238
6. Zeng, Z. G., Wang J., Liao X. X.: Global Exponential Stability of A General Class of Recurrent Neural Networks with Time-Varying Delays, IEEE Trans. on Circ. and Sys. I: Fundanmetntal Theory and Application, vol. 50 (2003) 1353-1358
7. Zeng, Z.G.,Wang J., Liao, X. X.: Global A Symptotic Stability and Global Exponetial Stability of Networks with Unbounded Time-Varying Delays, IEEE Trans. Circuits Syst. II:express briefs, vol. 52 (2005) 168-173
8. Cao, J. D., Huang, D. S., Qu, Y. Z.: Global Robust Stability of Delayed Recurrent Neural Networks, Chaos, Solitons and Fractals, vol. 23 (2005)221-229
9. Fantacci, R., Forti, M., Marini, M., etc.,: A Neural Network for Vonstrained Optimaization with Application to CDMA Communication Systems, IEEE Trans. on Circ. and Sys. II:Analog and digital signal processing, vol. 50 (2003) 484-487
10. Zhou, S. B., Liao, X. F., Yu, J. B., etc.: Chaos and Its Synchronization in Two-neuron Systems with Discret Delays, Chaos, Solitons and Fractals, vol. 21 (2004) 133-142

# Fault Tolerant Recognition Method of Handwritten Chinese Characters Based on Double Weights Elliptical Neuron

Jian-ping Wang [1], Wei-tao Li[2], and Jin-ling Wang[2]

[1] Hefei University of Technology, School of Electrical Engineering and Automation, Professor
[2] Hefei University of Technology, School of Electrical Engineering and Automation, Graduate Student. 545 P.O. mailbox HFUT south campus, Hefei, Anhui Province, China
xuevic@126.com

**Abstract.** Applied Biomimetic Pattern Recognition to replace "differentiation" of characteristic sample by machine "cognition", a novel method of handwritten Chinese characters recognition is presented. A double weights elliptical neuron is used to cover four basic kinds of handwritten Chinese characters stroke segment. The topological property among the stroke segment neurons is analyzed. Nine style of Chinese characters stroke with fault tolerance are combined. Imitated typing methods of human Chinese characters font code, the style and number of stroke neurons which have redundant fault tolerant shapes are counted. A kind of characteristic knowledge data-base table of handwritten Chinese characters and the sample data-base of standard printed Chinese characters and fault tolerant matching rules are built. Simple and more complex handwritten Chinese characters in SCUT-IRAC database are tested. The method is proved to be close to human fault tolerance and veracity.

## 1 Introduction

Owing to different write style of different person, the recognition of off-line handwritten Chinese characters is hardly reached the recognition degree of human veracity, agility and fault tolerance. Methods of characteristic extraction of off-line handwritten Chinese characters recognition and recognition realized by the nearest neighbor classifier and neural network classifier are widely reported. Used these methods, handwritten Chinese characters are recognized by finite machine "differentiation", not by human "cognition".

The recognizant psychology of Chinese characters indicates [2] human cognizant mechanism for Chinese characters is composed of whole Chinese characters property, layered structure and strokes. According to the shapes, number, relative position and the relative changeless topological structure brought about compounding, connection and crossover of some basic cognized Chinese character strokes, every kind of handwritten Chinese character is compared, judged and recognized agilely and fault tolerantly.

The statistic result of 6763 Chinese characters of the first and second Chinese characters national standard database (*GB2312-80*) indicates the basic Chinese

D.-S. Huang, K. Li, and G.W. Irwin (Eds.): ICIC 2006, LNCS 4113, pp. 370 – 376, 2006.

characters strokes are divided into five strokes: horizontal stroke, vertical stroke, right-diagonal stroke, left-diagonal stroke and break stroke [3]. In this paper, handwritten Chinese characters image is turned into figure which is composed of five different position basic strokes. Imitated typing methods of Chinese characters font code generalized by human in reference [3] and adopted Biomimetic Pattern Recognition, machine is endowed by the ability of "cognized" simple strokes and strokes combination in Chinese characters figure. Imitated the psychological process of human recognizing Chinese characters, obtained basic stroke segment style, stroke shapes and stroke number of redundant combining and representing, the agility and fault tolerance of handwritten Chinese character "cognized" by machine are improved.

## 2 Stroke Segment Extraction

The basic structure of Chinese characters is stroke. A part of stroke is called stroke segment. Stroke is composed of stroke segments. The acquisition of stroke includes stroke segments extraction and combination. Supposed, $f(x,y)$ is a $N \times M$ handwritten Chinese characters bitmap with 256 gray levels and its binarization image $F(x, y)$ is:

$$F(x,y)=\begin{cases}1, (\mathrm{x,y}) \text{ is black pixel}\\ 0, (\mathrm{x,y}) \text{ is white pixel}\end{cases} \quad (\mathrm{x}=1,2,\ldots,\mathrm{N}\,;\mathrm{y}=1,2,\ldots,\mathrm{M}) \tag{1}$$

First the image of handwritten Chinese characters is thinned, then turned into connective thinning aggregation of m dimension, at last normalized into a 40×40 binarization image.

The direction codes $d_i$ ($i$=0,1,2,3) are defined as representing the four basic strokes ($0^\circ$, $45^\circ$, $90^\circ$, $135^\circ$) respectively. The direction run of a stroke is defined as the greatest extended length of a stroke pixel along one direction. First the direction run of every stroke pixel is obtained, then the direction codes $d$ are found out which are the corresponding code of the superiority direction of four directions [4], scilicet:

$$L_{(x,y)}(d)=\max\{L_{(x,y)}(d_i)\} \tag{2}$$

Calculated the direction run of every pixel, the corresponding son images of four basic stroke segments are obtained.

## 3 Biomimetic Pattern Recognition of Handwritten Chinese Characters [1]

The shape of long ellipse is close to the stroke. So set the double weights elliptical neuron to represent every stroke segment, Chinese characters strokes are covered by a set of associated double weights elliptical neurons. Parameters of activation function of double weights elliptical neurons of handwritten Chinese characters stroke segments are set as follows:

Activation function $f(\phi)$ is chosen as:

$$f(\phi)=\begin{cases}1, \phi<0 \\ 0, \phi\geq 0\end{cases} \tag{3}$$

First, activation threshold $\theta$ is chosen as the length of stroke segment; xj is the handwritten Chinese character stroke segment pixel (j=1,2,..., n); wj is the direction weight of xj and wj is the length of half long and short axes of the ellipse. Then the length of half long axis is defined as the length of half stroke segment plus 2, and the length of half short axis is 2; the core weight w'j is the center point of the neuron, and is chosen as the center point of the stroke segment; parameter S and P are defined as 0 and 2 at last.

Every stroke segment is covered by a double weights elliptical neuron mentioned above respectively, so the research of stroke segments is turned into the research of neural network constructed by double weights elliptical neurons.

# 4 Stroke Extraction of Handwritten Chinese Characters

## 4.1 Stroke Segments Combination and Fault Tolerant Shapes of Chinese Characters Strokes

In the process of human handwritten Chinese characters recognition, different stroke segments are combined into another kind of stroke, and different shape distortion strokes are regarded as the same stroke. So some stroke segments belonging to one stroke need to be combined. Fault tolerant shapes of every kind of stroke are generalized and established for shapes distortion of Chinese characters.

Counted and analyzed font style in the SCUT-IRAC database, style of Chinese characters strokes are generalized in Tab.1, in which stroke style and fault tolerant stroke shapes which equal to itself are contained. If the length of a stroke segment on its direction is bigger than 1/3 size of the normalized image, it is defined as a long stroke segment, otherwise is a short stroke segment.

In Tab.1: 1,2,3,4,5,6,7and8 indicate short horizontal, short vertical, short right-diagonal, short left-diagonal, long horizontal, long vertical, long right-diagonal and long left-diagonal stroke segment, respectively

## 4.2 Combination of Chinese Characters Strokes by Neural Network

Chinese characters stroke is combined by extracted stroke segments. Every stroke is decided by associated relation of the double weights elliptical neuron of every stroke segment. So strokes extraction is turned into the topological structure analysis of the double weights elliptical neuron of every stroke segment and position of neurons. First, covered horizontal, vertical, right-diagonal, and left-diagonal stroke segments

**Table 1.** Stroke segments combination and fault tolerant shapes of stroke style

| Stroke style | Stroke shape | Stroke segments combination and fault tolerant shapes of stroke style |
|---|---|---|
| ①.horizontal | ㇐ | 5、1、3+5、3、4 |
| ②.vertical | ㇑ | 6、2、3、4、6+3 |
| ③.right-diagonal | ㇓ | 6+3、6 |
| | ㇀ | 3+5、5 |
| | ㇒ | 3、1 |
| ④.left-diagonal | ㇔ | 4、1、2 |
| | ㇏ | 4、8+1、8、8+3、1、2 |
| ⑤.horizontal break | ㇕ | 5+3、5+2 |
| | ㇆ | 5+6+4、5+6+1、5+6、1+6+4、1+6+1、1+6 |
| | ㇇ | 1+7、1+2+7、3+7、3+2+7 |
| | ㇕ | 5+6、5+2、1+6、1+2 |
| ⑥.vertical break | ㇚ | 6+4、6+1、6 |
| | ㇙ | 6+3、6+1、6 |
| | ㇗ | 6+5、6+1、2+5、2+1 |
| | ㇟ | 6+5+2、6+5+4、6+1+2、6+1+4、2+5+2、2+5+4、2+1+2、2+1+4 |
| ⑦.right-diagonal break | ㇛ | 3+8、3+1、3+4、2+3+1、2+3+4 |
| ⑧.diagonal hook | ㇃ | 4+5+2、6+5+4、4+5+4、6+5+2 |
| | ㇂ | 8+2、8、8+3 |
| ⑨.bended hook | ㇁ | 4+7+4、4+7、2+7+4、2+7+2、2+3、2+3+4、2+3+2 |

by double weights elliptical neurons, four son images are overlain, then in the overlain image it is judged whether two stroke segments need to be combined into a stroke. Combination rules are defined as follows:

**Definition 1.** The foreside of a double weights elliptical neuron $y$ is defined as the elliptical portion from the beginning point of the elliptical long axis to 1/4 length of the elliptical long axis; the middle part is the elliptical portion from 1/4 length of the elliptical long axis to 3/4 length of the elliptical long axis. If the foreside of neuron $y_1$ and the foreside of neuron $y_2$ intersect and neuron style accord with one of stroke segments combination listed in Tab. 1, strokes covered by the neuron $y_1$ and $y_2$ need to be combined. After combination new stroke segment is represented by the neuron $Y_u= y_1 \cup y_2$ $(u=1,2,\ldots, n)$.

According to definition 2, stroke segments are recombined in the image. Until there are no two stroke segments met the condition (1) of definition 2 in the image, strokes combination finish. Finally the combined strokes are represented by $Y_v^w$ (stroke style $v=1,2,\ldots,9$ , stroke number $w=1,2,\ldots, k$).

### 4.3 Acquirement of Characteristic Knowledge of Handwritten Chinese Characters

Combination result used to recognize Chinese characters is obtained by the combination steps mentioned above. Therefore, the characteristic knowledge data-base of handwritten Chinese characters is established.

**Definition 2.** Supposed, the number of stroke segment neurons $y_p$ ($p$=1,2,…, $n$) is $n$ before handwritten Chinese characters strokes combination. According to the result of strokes combination:

(1) Uncombined stroke segment neurons are ascribed to the fault tolerant stroke style listed in Tab. 1, and the number of every stroke segment style is counted after assorted.

(2) Stroke neurons after combination are ascribed to the fault tolerant style listed in Tab. 1, and the number of every stroke style is counted after assorted.

(3) The characteristic knowledge data-base table of handwritten Chinese characters is established.

**Table 2.** Characteristic knowledge database table of handwritten

| Uncombined stroke segments ID | Stroke style | Stroke segment number | Combined strokes ID | Stroke segment style | Stroke number |
|---|---|---|---|---|---|
| 0 | 1 | XX | 1 | 1 | XX |
| 0 | 2 | XX | 1 | 2 | XX |
| 0 | 3 | XX | 1 | 3 | XX |
| 0 | 4 | XX | 1 | 4 | XX |
| 0 | 5 | 00 | 1 | 5 | XX |
| 0 | 6 | 00 | 1 | 6 | XX |
| 0 | 7 | 00 | 1 | 7 | XX |
| 0 | 8 | 00 | 1 | 8 | XX |
| 0 | 9 | 00 | 1 | 9 | XX |

In Tab.2: xx----represent statistic result

## 5 Recognition of Handwritten Chinese Characters

According to stroke segments combination and strokes of fault tolerant representation defined by definition 1 and Tab.1, the sample data-base of GB-2312 standard printed Chinese characters and the characteristic knowledge data-base table of recognized handwritten Chinese characters established by definition 2 are matched.

**Definition 3.** Owing to the difference between shape distortion strokes combination of handwritten and printed, fault tolerant matching rules are defined:

Rule 1: Rule of absolute uniformity. If the characteristic knowledge data-base table of recognized handwritten Chinese characters absolutely accords with the printed, matching succeeds.

Rule 2: Fault tolerant rule of right-diagonal and left-diagonal. Supposed, the characteristic knowledge data-base table of recognized handwritten Chinese characters doesn't absolutely accord with the printed. If the difference of both of the number of stroke segment and stroke style 3(*right-diagonal*) or 4(*left-diagonal*) is less than and equal to±1, and the others absolutely accord with, matching succeeds.

Rule 3: Fault tolerant rule of stroke combination shapes. Supposed, the characteristic knowledge data-base table of recognized handwritten Chinese characters doesn't absolutely accord with the printed. If both of the number of stroke segment and stroke style add equally, and the others absolutely accord with, matching succeeds.

Rule 4: Fault tolerant rule of stroke segments and stroke combination number. Supposed, the characteristic knowledge data-base table of recognized handwritten Chinese characters doesn't absolutely accord with the printed. If both of the number of stroke segment and stroke style 1 and 2 add equally, and the difference of both of the number of stroke style 5 to 9 adds less than and equal to±2, matching succeeds.

## 6 Experiments

100 handwritten Chinese characters in SCUT-IRAC database are tested. Experiment result is listed as follows:

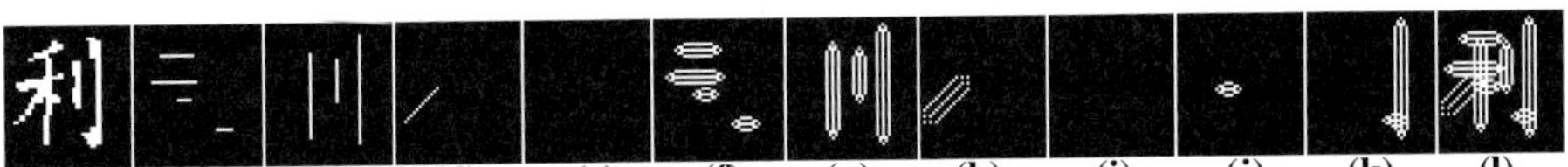

(a) (b) (c) (d) (e) (f) (g) (h) (i) (j) (k) (l)

**Fig. 1A.** (a)Original printed character image. (b)-(e)Horizontal, vertical, right-diagonal and left-diagonal stroke segments image. (f)-(i)Covered horizontal, vertical, right-diagonal and left-diagonal stroke segments by double weights elliptical neurons image. (j)Fault tolerant horizontal stroke shape of left-diagonal stroke style image. (k)Stroke combination image based on definition 1. (l)Overlain neurons image of covered all strokes.

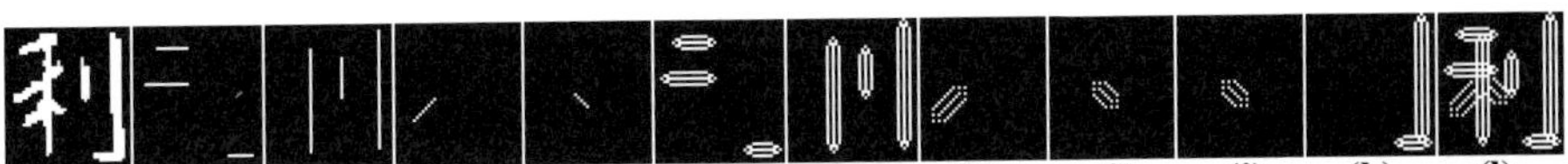

(a) (b) (c) (d) (e) (f) (g) (h) (i) (j) (k) (l)

**Fig. 1B.** (a)Original handwritten character image. (b)-(i)Similar to above. (j)Fault tolerant left-diagonal stroke shape of horizontal stroke style image. (k)-(l)Similar to above.

According to definition 2, the characteristic knowledge data-base of printed and handwritten Chinese character "利" are obtained in Tab.3:

**Table 3.** Characteristic knowledge data-base table of printed and handwritten "利"

| Uncombined stroke segments ID | Stroke style | Stroke segment number | Combined strokes ID | Stroke segment style | Stroke number |
|---|---|---|---|---|---|
| 0 | 1 | 03/02 | 1 | 1 | 00/00 |
| 0 | 2 | 02/02 | 1 | 2 | 00/00 |
| 0 | 3 | 01/01 | 1 | 3 | 00/00 |
| 0 | 4 | 00/01 | 1 | 4 | 00/00 |
| 0 | 5 | 00/00 | 1 | 5 | 00/00 |
| 0 | 6 | 00/00 | 1 | 6 | 01/01 |
| 0 | 7 | 00/00 | 1 | 7 | 00/00 |
| 0 | 8 | 00/00 | 1 | 8 | 00/00 |
| 0 | 9 | 00/00 | 1 | 9 | 00/00 |

In Tab. 3: xx/yy----represent statistic result of printed and handwritten

Based on matching rule 3, the recognized handwritten Chinese character and the printed Chinese character "利" match success, and recognition is finished.

## 7 Conclusion

In order to let machine be close to fault tolerance and veracity of human Chinese characters recognition, Biomimetic Pattern Recognition is used and "cognition" of handwritten Chinese characters is illustrated by the proposed method.

(1) The construction method of double weights elliptical neurons covering horizontal, vertical, right-diagonal and left-diagonal stroke segments is given. The topological structure of the double weights elliptical neuron of every stroke segment and position of neurons are analyzed.

(2) The redundant and fault tolerant characteristic knowledge data-base table of handwritten Chinese characters is established. Imitated human ability of studying, memorizing, comparing and judging, and the agile matching recognition is tested.

It is satisfied for simple and more complex handwritten Chinese characters recognition by the proposed method.

## References

1. Wang, S.J., Qu, Y.F., Li, W.J., Qin, H.: Face Recognition: Biomimetic Pattern Recognition vs. Traditional Pattern Recognition. Acta Electronica Sinic, 32(7) (2004) 1057-1061
2. Zhu, X.P., Gu, H.B.: Current Status of Chinese Characters and Words Recognition. Psychological Science, 15(1) (1992) 40-45
3. Yang, S., Zhang, L.W., Chen, H.M.: Computer Chinese Character Input Code Dictionary. USTC Press, (1995) 581-606, 665-673
4. Zhao, Y.M., Jiang, X.Z., Shi, P.F.: Algorithm for off-line Handwritten Chinese Character Segmentation Based on Extracting and Knowledge-based Merging of Stroke Bounding Boxes. Infrared and Laser Engineering, 31(1) (2002) 23-27

# Global Exponential Stability of Reaction-Diffusion Neural Networks with Both Variable Time Delays and Unbounded Delay

Weifan Zheng, Jiye Zhang, and Weihua Zhang

National Traction Power Laboratory, Southwest Jiaotong University,
Chengdu 610031, People's Republic of China
{wfzheng, jyzhang}@home.swjtu.edu.cn

**Abstract.** In the paper, the reaction-diffusion neural network models with both variable time delays and unbounded delay are investigated. These models contain weaker activation functions than partially or globally Lipschitz continuous functions. Without assuming the boundedness, monotonicity and differentiability of the active functions, algebraic criteria ensuring existence, uniqueness and global exponential stability of the equilibrium point are obtained.

## 1 Introduction

In recent years, there have been increasingly interests in the potential applications of the dynamics of artificial neural networks in many fields [1-2]. Such applications rely on qualitative properties of system. In hardware implementation, time delays are unavoidable due to finite switching speeds of the amplifiers and communication time etc. Time delays may lead to oscillation and furthermore, instability of networks. In most situations, the time delays are variable, and in fact unbounded. Therefore, the stability of neural networks with variable and invariable delays is practically important, and has been extensively studied in the literatures [3-5].

However, diffusion effect can't be avoided in the neural network models when electrons are asymmetric electromagnetic field. The asymptotical stability of neural networks with reaction-diffusion was discussed in [6-10]. But many of systems in these literatures require increasingly monotonic neuron activation functions and non-negative diffusion functions.

In this paper, we study neural networks with reaction-diffusion terms, which contain both variable time delays and unbounded delay. We relax some limits on activation functions and diffusion functions of reaction-diffusion neural network models similar to that discussed in [6-10], By constructing the proper Lyapunov function, we analyze the conditions ensuring the existence, uniqueness and global exponential stability of the equilibrium of the models.

## 2 Notations and Preliminaries

In this paper, we analyze the stability of reaction-diffusion neural networks described by the following differential equations:

D.-S. Huang, K. Li, and G.W. Irwin (Eds.): ICIC 2006, LNCS 4113, pp. 377 – 384, 2006.

$$\frac{\partial u_i(t)}{\partial t} = \sum_{k=1}^{m} \frac{\partial}{\partial x_k}[D_{ik}(t,x,u_i)\frac{\partial u_i}{\partial x_k}] - e_i u_i(t) + \sum_{j=1}^{n} a_{ij} f_j(u_j(t))$$

$$+\sum_{j=1}^{n} b_{ij} g_j(u_j(t-\tau_{ij}(t))) + \sum_{j=1}^{n} c_{ij} \int_{-\infty}^{t} k_{ij}(t-s) h_j(u_j(s))ds + J_i \quad i=[1,...,n], \tag{1}$$

$$\frac{\partial u_i}{\partial \tilde{n}} = \mathrm{col}(\frac{\partial u_i}{\partial x_1},...,\frac{\partial u_i}{\partial x_m}) = 0, i=1,2,...,n, \quad t\in I, \quad x\in \partial\Omega, \tag{2}$$

Where $u_i$ is the state of neuron $i$, $(i=1,2,\cdots,n)$; $D_i(t,x,u_i)$ is smooth reaction-diffusion function, $A=(a_{ij})_{n\times n}$, $B=(b_{ij})_{n\times n}$, $C=(c_{ij})_{n\times n}$ are connection matrices, $J=(J_1,J_2,\cdots,J_n)^T$ is the constant input vector. $f(u)=(f_1(u_1),f_2(u_2),...,f_n(u_n))^{\mathrm{T}}$, $g(u)=(g_1(u_1),g_2(u_2),\cdots, g_n(u_n))^{\mathrm{T}}$, and $h(u)=(h_1(u_1),h_2(u_2),...,h_n(u_n))^{\mathrm{T}}$ are the activation functions of the neurons, $E=\mathrm{diag}(e_1,e_2,\cdots,e_n)>0$. The variable delays $\tau_{ij}(t)$ $(i,j=1,2,\cdots,n)$ are bounded functions, i.e. $0\le\tau_{ij}(t)\le\tau$, and $k_{ij}:[0,\infty)\to[0,\infty)$ $(i,j=1,2,\cdots,n)$ are piecewise continuous. Let $k=(k_{ij})_{n\times n}$.

The conventional conditions for kernel conditions of Eq. (1) satisfy the following assumptions:

**Assumption A:** $\int_0^\infty k_{ij}(s)ds=1$, $\int_0^\infty sk_{ij}(s)ds<+\infty$, $(i,j=1,2,\cdots,n)$;

**Assumption B:** $\int_0^\infty k_{ij}(s)ds=1$, $\int_0^\infty e^{\beta s}k_{ij}(s)ds=K_{ij}<+\infty$, $(i,j=1,2,\cdots,n)$.

In order to study the exponential stability of neural networks (1) conveniently, we inquire kernel functions satisfies the following assumption:

**Assumption C:** $\int_0^\infty e^{\beta s}k_{ij}(s)ds=N_{ij}(\beta)$, $(i,j=1,2,\cdots,n)$, where $N_{ij}(\beta)$ are continuous functions in $[0,\delta)$, $\delta>0$, and $N_{ij}(0)=1$.

It is easy to prove that the Assumption C includes Assumption A and B.

The initial conditions of equation (1) are of the form $u_i(s)=\phi_i(s)$, $-\tau\le s\le 0$, where $\phi_i$ is bounded and continuous on $[-\tau,0]$. Equation (2) is the boundary condition of equation (1), in which $x\in\Omega\subset R^m$, $\Omega$ is a compact set with smooth boundary and $\mathrm{mes}\,\Omega>0$, $\partial\Omega$ is the boundary of $\Omega$, $t\in I=[0,+\infty]$.

For convenience, we introduce some notations. The notation $u=(u_1,u_2,...,u_n)^{\mathrm{T}}\in \mathrm{R}^n$ represents a column vector (the symbol $(\ )^{\mathrm{T}}$ denotes transpose). For matrix $A=(a_{ij})_{n\times n}$, $|A|$ denotes absolute-value matrix given by $|A|=(|a_{ij}|)_{n\times n}$; $[A]^S$ is defined as $(A^T+A)/2$. For $x\in\mathrm{R}^n$, $|x|=(|x_1|,...,|x_n|)^{\mathrm{T}}$, $\|x\|$ denotes a vector norm defined by $\|x\|=\max_{1\le i\le n}\{|x_i|\}$. And

$$D(t,x,u) = \mathrm{col}(\sum_{k=1}^{m}\frac{\partial}{\partial x_k}(D_{1j}(t,x,u_1)\frac{\partial u_1}{\partial x_k}),\ldots,\sum_{k=1}^{m}\frac{\partial}{\partial x_k}(D_{nj}(t,x,u_n)\frac{\partial u_n}{\partial x_k})),$$

So model (1) can be written the following form:

$$\dot{u}(t) = D(t,x,u(t)) - Eu(t) + Af(u(t)) + Bg(u(t-\tau_{ij}(t)) + C\int_{-\infty}^{t} k(t-s)h(u(s))ds + J. \quad (3)$$

System (3) and (1) has the same properties of stability.

If there is a constant $u_0 = u_0^* = const$ (const denotes invariable constant) which is the solution of the following equation:

$$-Eu(t) + Af(u(t)) + Bg(u(t-\tau_{ij}(t)) + C\int_{-\infty}^{t} k(t-s)h(u(s))ds + J = 0, \quad (4)$$

then $\partial u_0^* / \partial x = 0$. From equation (3), we get $D_{ik}(t,x,u_i(t))$ =0, and

$$D(t,x,u(t)) - Eu(t) + Af(u(t)) + Bg(u(t-\tau_{ij}(t)) + C\int_{-\infty}^{t} k(t-s)h(u(s))ds + J = 0.$$

It implies that (4) and (3) has the same equilibrium point, and so, system (4) has the same equilibrium point as that of system (1).

Now we consider that the activation functions of the neurons satisfy the following assumption D.

**Assumption D:** For each $j \in \{1,2,\cdots,n\}$, $f_j : \mathrm{R} \to \mathrm{R}$, $g_j : \mathrm{R} \to \mathrm{R}$ and $h_j : \mathrm{R} \to \mathrm{R}$, there exist real numbers $p_j > 0$, $q_j > 0$ and $r_j > 0$ such that $p_j = \sup_{y \neq z} |\frac{f_j(y) - f_j(z)}{y - z}|$, $q_j = \sup_{y \neq z} |\frac{g_j(y) - g_j(z)}{y - z}|$, $r_j = \sup_{y \neq z} |\frac{h_j(y) - h_j(z)}{y - z}|$ for every $y \neq z$. Let $P = \mathrm{diag}(p_1,\ldots,p_n)$, $Q = \mathrm{diag}(q_1,\ldots,q_n)$ and $R = \mathrm{diag}(r_1,\ldots,r_n)$.

The activation functions such as sigmoid type and piecewise linear type are the special case of the functions satisfying Assumption D.

## 3 Existence and Uniqueness of the Equilibrium Point

In this section, we shall study the necessary and sufficient condition which ensures the existence and uniqueness of the equilibrium point of system (1).

**Definition 1** [11]: A real matrix $A = (a_{ij})_{n \times n}$ is said to be an M-matrix if $a_{ij} \le 0$ $i, j = 1,2,\ldots,n$, $i \neq j$, and all successive principal minors of $A$ are positive.

**Definition 2:** The equilibrium $u^*$ of (1) is said to be globally exponentially stable, if there exist constant $\lambda > 0$ and $\beta > 0$ such that $\| u(t) - u^* \| \le \beta \| \phi - u^* \| \mathrm{e}^{-\lambda t}$ for all $t \ge 0$, where $\| \phi - u^* \| = \max_{1 \le i \le n} \sup_{s \in [-\tau, 0]} | \phi_i(s) - u_i^* |$.

We firstly study the solutions of the nonlinear map associated with (1) as follows:

$$H(u) = -Eu + Af(u) + Bg(u) + Ch(u) + J \,. \tag{5}$$

It is well known that the solutions of $H(u) = 0$ are equilibriums in (1). If $H(u)$ is a homeomorphism, then there exists a unique point $u^*$ such that $H(u^*) = 0$, i.e., system (1) has a unique equilibrium $u^*$. In the following, we shall show the condition that ensures $H(u)$ a homeomorphism.

**Lemma 1:** If $H(u) \in C^0$ satisfies (i) $H(u)$ is injective on $R^n$, (ii) $\| H(u) \| \to \infty$ as $\| u \| \to \infty$, then $H(u)$ is a homeomorphism of $\mathrm{R}^n$.

**Theorem 1:** If Assumption D is satisfied, and $\alpha = E - (|A|P + |B|Q + |C|R)$ is an M-matrix, then, for every input $J$, system (1) has a unique equilibrium.

**Proof:** In order to prove that for every input $J$, system (1) has a unique equilibrium point $u^*$, it is only to prove that $H(u)$ is a homeomorphism on $\mathrm{R}^n$. In following, we shall prove it in two steps.

*Step* 1, we will prove that condition (i) in Lemma 1 is satisfied. Suppose, for purposes of contradiction, that there exist $x, y \in \mathrm{R}^n$ with $x \neq y$ such that $H(x) = H(y)$. Form (5), we get

$$-E(x-y) + A(f(x) - f(y)) + B(g(x) - g(y)) + C(h(x) - h(y)) = 0 \,. \tag{6}$$

From Assumption D, there exist matrices $K = \mathrm{diag}(K_1, ..., K_n)$ ( $-P \le K \le P$ ), $L = \mathrm{diag}(L_1, ..., L_n)$ $(-Q \le L \le Q)$, and $S = \mathrm{diag}(S_1, ..., S_n)$ ( $-R \le S \le R$ ) such that $f(x) - f(y) = K(x-y)$, $g(x) - g(y) = L(x-y)$, and $h(x) - h(y) = S(x-y)$. So (6) can be written as:

$$[-E + (AK + BL + CS)](x-y) = 0 \,. \tag{7}$$

We shall prove that $\det[-E + (AK + BL + CS)] \neq 0$. Considering the system

$$\dot{z} = [-E + (AK + BL + CS)]z \,. \tag{8}$$

Due to $\alpha$ being an M-matrix [11], there exist $\xi_i > 0$ $(i = 1,2,...,n)$ such that $-e_i\xi_i + \sum_{j=1}^{n} \xi_j (|a_{ji}| p_j + |b_{ji}| q_j + |c_{ji}| r_j) < 0$ $(i = 1,2,...,n)$. So

$$-e_i\xi_i + \sum_{j=1}^{n} \xi_j (|a_{ji} K_j| + |b_{ji} L_j| + |c_{ji} S_j|) < 0 \quad (i = 1,2,...,n) \,. \tag{9}$$

Consider a Lyapunov function $V(z) = \sum_{i=1}^{n} \xi_i |z_i|$. Calculating the upper right derivative $D^+V$ of $V$ along the solutions of (8), we get

$$D^+V(z) \le \sum_{i=1}^{n} [-e_i\xi_i + \sum_{j=1}^{n} \xi_j (|a_{ji} K_j| + |b_{ji} L_j| + |c_{ji} S_j|)] |z_i| < 0 \,, \quad (\| z \| \neq 0) \,.$$

So the zero solution of systems (8) is globally asymptotically stable. Thus matrix $-E+(AK+BL+CS)$ is a stable matrix and $\det[-E+(AK+BL+CS)]\neq 0$ . From (7), $x=y$ , which is a contradiction. So map $H(u)$ is injective.

*Step* 2. We now prove that condition (ii) in Lemma 1 is satisfied. Let

$$\overline{H}(u)=-Eu+A(f(u)-f(0))+B(g(u)-g(0))+C(h(u)-h(0)).$$

To show that $H(u)$ is homeomorphism, it suffices to show that $\overline{H}(u)$ is homeomorphism. According to Assumption D, we get

$$|f_i(u)-f_i(0)|\leq p_i|u|,\ |g_i(u)-g_i(0)|\leq q_i|u|,\ |h_i(u)-h_i(0)|\leq r_i|u| \quad (i=1,2,\ldots,n).$$

Since $\alpha=E-(|A|P+|B|Q+|C|R)$ is an M-matrix [11], there exists a positive definite diagonal matrix $D=\mathrm{diag}(d_1,\cdots,d_n)$ such that

$$[D(-E+|A|P+|B|Q+|C|R)]^S\leq-\varepsilon E_n<0, \tag{10}$$

for sufficiently small $\varepsilon>0$, where $E_n$ is the identity matrix. Calculating

$$\begin{aligned}[Du]^{\mathrm{T}}\overline{H}(u)&\leq-|u|^{\mathrm{T}}DE|u|+|u|^{\mathrm{T}}D|A|P|u|+|u|^{\mathrm{T}}D|B|Q|u|+|u|^{\mathrm{T}}D|C|R|u|\\&=|u|^{\mathrm{T}}[D(-E+|A|P+|B|Q+|C|R)]^S|u|\leq-\varepsilon\|u\|^2.\end{aligned} \tag{11}$$

From (11) and using Schwartz inequality, we get $\varepsilon\|u\|^2\leq\|D\|\|u\|\|\overline{H}(u)\|$, namely,

$$\frac{\varepsilon\|u\|}{\|D\|}\leq\left\|\overline{H}(u)\right\|. \tag{12}$$

So, $\|\overline{H}(u)\|\to+\infty$ , i.e., $\|H(u)\|\to+\infty$ as $\|u\|\to+\infty$. From Lemma 1, we know that for every input $J$ , map $H(u)$ is homeomorphism on $R^n$ . So systems (1) have a unique equilibrium point $u^*$ . The proof is completed.

## 4 Global Exponential Stability of Equilibrium Point

In this section, we shall apply the ideal of vector Lyapunov method [6] to analyze global exponential stability of model (1).

**Theorem 2:** If Assumption D be satisfied and $\alpha=E-(|A|P+|B|Q+|C|R)$ is an M-matrix, then for each input $J$ , systems (1) have a unique equilibrium point, which is globally exponentially stable.

**Proof:** Since $\alpha$ is an M-matrix, from Theorem 1, system (1) has a unique equilibrium point $u^*$ . Let $z(t)=u(t)-u^*$ , model (1) can be written as

$$\frac{\partial z_i(t)}{\partial t}=\sum_{k=1}^{m}\frac{\partial}{\partial x_k}[D_{ik}(t,x,(z(t)+u^*))\frac{\partial z_i}{\partial x_k}]-e_i z_i(t)+\sum_{j=1}^{n}a_{ij}f_j(z_j(t))$$
$$+\sum_{j=1}^{n}b_{ij}g_j(z_j(t-\tau_{ij}(t)))+\sum_{j=1}^{n}c_{ij}\int_{-\infty}k_{ij}(t-s)h_j(z_j(s))ds\quad(i=1,2,\ldots,n),\tag{13}$$

Where, $f_j(z_j(t))=f_j(z_j(t)+u_j^*)-f_j(u_j^*)$ , $h_j(z_j(t))=h_j(z_j(t)+u_j^*)-h_j(u_j^*)$ , $j=1,\cdots,n$, and $g_j(z(t-\tau_{ij}(t)))=g_j(z_j(t-\tau_{ij}(t)+u_j^*)-g_j(u_j^*)$. The initial condition of Eq. (13) is $\psi(s)=\phi(s)-u^*, -\tau\le s\le 0$, and Eq. (13) has a unique equilibrium at $z=0$. From Assumption D, we get

$$|f_j(z_j(t))|\le p_j|z_j(t)|,\quad |g_j(z(t-\tau_{ij}(t)))|\le p_j|z_j(t-\tau_{ij}(t))|,\quad |h_j(z_j(t))|\le r_j|z_j(t)|.$$

Due to $\alpha$ being an M-matrix, there exist $\xi_i>0\quad(i=1,2,\ldots,n)$ and a constant $\lambda>0$ satisfy

$$-\xi_i(e_i-\lambda)+\sum_{j=1}^{n}\xi_j(|a_{ij}|p_j+\mathrm{e}^{\lambda\tau}|b_{ij}|q_j+|c_{ij}|N_{ij}(\lambda)r_j)<0.\tag{14}$$

Here, $\tau$ is a fixed number according to assumption of neural networks (1). Let $V_i(t)=\mathrm{e}^{\lambda t}z_i(t)$, and Lyapunov functional $\overline{V_i(t)}=\int_\Omega|V_i(t)|dx\quad(i=1,2,\ldots,n)$, calculating the upper right derivative $D^+\overline{V_i(t)}$ of $\overline{V_i(t)}$ along the solutions of equation (13), we get

$$D^+\overline{V_i(t)}=\int_\Omega D^+|V_i(t)|dx=\int_\Omega(\mathrm{e}^{\lambda t}\operatorname{sgn} z_i\dot{z}_i+\lambda\mathrm{e}^{\lambda t}|z_i|)dx\tag{15}$$

From (13) and (15), according to Assumption D, boundary condition (2) and $\operatorname{mes}\Omega>0$, we get

$$D^+\overline{V_i(t)}\le\mathrm{e}^{\lambda t}\operatorname{sgn} z_i(t)\sum_{k=1}^{m}[D_{ik}(t,x,(z_i(t)+u^*))\frac{\partial u_i}{\partial x_k}]|_{\partial\Omega}$$
$$+\int_\Omega\mathrm{e}^{\lambda t}[(-e_i+\lambda)|z_i(t)|+\sum_{j=1}^{n}(|a_{ij}||f_j(z_j(t))|)+\sum_{j=1}^{n}(|b_{ij}||g_j(z_j(t-\tau_{ij}(t)))|)]dx$$
$$+\int_\Omega[\mathrm{e}^{\lambda t}\sum_{j=1}^{n}|c_{ij}|\int_{-\infty}k_{ij}(t-s)|h_j(s)|ds]dx$$
$$\le\int_\Omega\mathrm{e}^{\lambda t}[-(e_i-\lambda)|z_i|+\sum_{j=1}^{n}(|a_{ij}|p_j|z_j|+\mathrm{e}^{\lambda\tau_{ij}(t)}|b_{ij}|q_j|\mathrm{e}^{\lambda(-\tau_{ij}(t))}z_j(t-\tau_{ij}(t))|]dx$$
$$+\int_\Omega[\sum_{j=1}^{n}|c_{ij}|r_j\int_{-\infty}k_{ij}(t-s)\mathrm{e}^{\lambda(t-s)}\mathrm{e}^{\lambda s}|z_j(s)|ds]dx$$
$$\le\int_\Omega\{-(e_i-\lambda)|V_i(t)|+\sum_{j=1}^{n}[|a_{ij}|p_j|V_j(t)|+\mathrm{e}^{\lambda\tau_{ij}(t)}|b_{ij}|q_j|V_j(t-\tau_{ij}(t))|]\}dx$$
$$+\int_\Omega[\sum_{j=1}^{n}|c_{ij}|r_j\int_{-\infty}k_{ij}(t-s)\mathrm{e}^{\lambda(t-s)}|V_j(s)|ds]dx.\tag{16}$$

Defining the curve $\gamma = \{ y(l) : y_i = \xi_i l, l > 0, i = 1,2,...,n \}$ , and the set $\Omega(y) = \{ u : 0 \le u \le y, y \in \gamma \}$ .

Let $\xi_{\min} = \min_{1 \le i \le n} \{\xi_i\}$ , $\xi_{\max} = \max_{1 \le i \le n} \{\xi_i\}$ . Taking $l_0 = (1+\delta) \| \psi \| / \xi_{\min}$ , where $\delta > 0$ is a constant number, then $\{ |V| : |V| = e^{\lambda s} |\psi(s)|, -\tau \le s \le 0 \} \subset \Omega(z_0(l_0))$ , namely, $|V_i(s)| = e^{\lambda s} |\psi_i(s)| < \xi_i l_0$ , $-\tau \le s \le 0$ , $i$=1,2,…, $n$. We claim that $|V_i(t)| < \xi_i l_0$ , for $t \in [0,+\infty)$ , $i$=1, 2, …, $n$ . If it is not true, then there exist some index $i$ and $t_1$ ( $t_1 > 0$ ) such that $|V_i(t_1)| = \xi_i l_0$ , $D^+ |V_i(t_1)| \ge 0$ , and $|V_j(t)| \le \xi_j l_0$ , for $-\tau < t \le t_1$ , $j$ =1, 2, … , $n$. So we get $D^+ \overline{V_i(t_1)} = \int_\Omega D^+ |V_i(t_1)| dx \ge 0$ . However, from (14) and (16), we get $D^+ \overline{V_i(t_1)} \le [-\xi_i(e_i - \lambda) + \sum_{j=1}^{n} \xi_j (|a_{ij}| p_j + e^{\lambda\tau} |b_{ij}| q_j + |c_{ij}| N_{ij}(\lambda) r_j)] l_0 < 0$ .

There is a contradiction. So $|V_i(t)| < \xi_i l_0$ , for $t \in [0,+\infty)$ , therefore,

$$|z_i(t)| < \xi_i l_0 e^{-\lambda t} \le (1+\delta) \| \psi \| \xi_{\max} / \xi_{\min} \, e^{-\lambda t} = \beta \| \psi \| \, e^{-\lambda t},$$

where $\beta = (1+\delta) \xi_{\max} / \xi_{\min}$ . From Definition 2, the zero solution of systems (13) is globally exponentially stable, i.e., the equilibrium point of systems (1) is globally exponentially stable. The proof is completed.

It is obvious that the result in Theorem 2 includes that in [5~10]. References [6] only discussed asymptotic stability of neural networks, and in [7, 8], only constant time delayed neural networks were discussed.

## 5 Remarks and Conclusions

The similar system is discussed in [6~10], but all of them require nonnegative diffusion function or increasingly monotonic activation functions of neural network models. However, the activation functions of model (1) only need to satisfy Assumption D. It is obvious that Assumption D is weaker than the commonly used partial or global Lipschitz continuous conditions, and piecewise sigmoid functions etc. Our results can be applied to neural networks with reaction-diffusion functions, negative or nonnegative. So these relaxations on parameters of neural networks make the design and verify of these systems more easy in practice.

## Acknowledgments

This work is supported by the National Program for New Century Excellent Talents in University (No.NCET-04-0889), Youth Science Foundation of Sichuan (No. 05ZQ026-015), and Natural Science Foundation of China (No.10272091).

## References


1. Chua, L.O., Yang, L.: Cellular Neural Networks: Theory, IEEE Transactions on Circuits and Systems. 35 (1988)1257–1272
2. Forti, M., Tesi, A.: New Conditions for Global Stability of Neural Networks with Application to Linear and Quadratic Programming Problems, IEEE Trans. Circuits System-I. 42 (1995) 354–366
3. Zheng, W., Zhang, J.: Global Exponential Stability of a Class of Neural Networks with Variable Delays, Computers and Mathematics with Applications, 49 (2005)895–902
4. Zhang, J.: Globally Exponential Stability of Neural Networks with Variable Delays, IEEE Transactions on Circuits and Systems-I, 2 (2003)288–291
5. Zhang, J., Suda, Y., Iwasa, T.: Absolutely Exponential Stability of a Class of Neural Networks with Unbounded Delay. Neural Networks, 17 (2004)391–397
6. Liao, X., Fu, Y.: Stability of Hopfield Neural Networks with Reaction-Diffusion Terms, Acta Electronica Sinica, 1 (2000)78–80
7. Wang, L., Xu, D.: Global Stability of Reaction-Diffusion Hopfield Neural Networks with Variable Time Delay, Science in China (serial E), 6 (2003) 488–495
8. Liang, J., Cao, J.,: Global Exponential Stability of Reaction-Diffusion Recurrent Neural Networks with Time-Varying Delays, Physics letters A, 314 (2003) 434–442
9. Song, Q., Cao, J.: Global Exponential Stability and Existence of Periodic Solutions in BAM Networks with Delays and Reaction-Diffusion Terms, Chaos Solitons and Fractals, 23 (2005) 421–430
10. Song, Q., Zhao, Z., Li, Y.: Global Exponential Stability of BAM Neural Networks with Distributed Delays and Reaction-Diffusion Terms. Physics Letters A, 335 (2005) 213–225
11. Siljak, D.D.: Large-Scale Dynamic Systems — Stability and Structure. New York: Elsevier North-Holland, Inc. (1978)

# Global Exponential Stability of T-S Fuzzy Neural Networks with Time-Varying Delays

Chaojin Fu[1,2] and Zhongsheng Wang[3]

[1] Department of Mathematics, Hubei Normal University,
Huangshi, Hubei, 435002, China
[2] Hubei province Key Laboratory of Bioanalytical Technique,
Hubei Normal University
chaojinfu@126.com
[3] Department of Electric Engineering, ZhongYuan Institute of Technology,
Zhengzhou, Henan, 450007, China
zswang@zzti.edu.cn

**Abstract.** This paper investigates the global exponential stability of Takagi-Sugeno Fuzzy cellular neural networks with time-varying delays. Using the reduction to absurdity, a less conservative delay-independent stability criterion is derived to guarantee the exponential stability of Takagi-Sugeno Fuzzy cellular neural networks with time-varying delays. Since our model is more general than some existing works, the results presented in this paper are the improvement and extension of the existed ones.

## 1 Introduction

Cellular neural networks (CNNs) ([1]) have attracted much attention due to their great perspective of applications. CNNs and delayed cellular neural networks (DCNNs) are arrays of dynamical cells that are suitable for the formulation and solution of many complex computational problems. CNNs and DCNNs have been applied to signal processing, image processing, and pattern recognition ([2]). For example, CNNs with opposite-sign templates have been successfully applied in connected component detection (CCD) in feature extraction [3,4].

Fuzzy logic theory has been efficiently developed to many applications and shown to be an efficient approach to model a complex nonlinear system and deal with its stability. Takagi-Sugeno (T-S) first introduced fuzzy models in [5] and then the T-S fuzzy model is successfully and effectively used in complex nonlinear systems [6]. The main feature of T-S fuzzy model is that a nonlinear system can be approximated by a set of T-S linear models. The overall fuzzy model of the system is achieved by fuzzy blending of the set of T-S linear models. Recently, Huang et al. [7] have extended the T-S fuzzy model to describe the delayed Hopfield neural networks subjected to environmental noise and proposed a sufficient condition to determining the global exponential stability. Fuzzy neural network (FNN) control systems have been extensively studied [8] and successfully used in manufacturing process control, such as tool wear monitoring [9],

D.-S. Huang, K. Li, and G.W. Irwin (Eds.): ICIC 2006, LNCS 4113, pp. 385–390, 2006.

multi-sensor integration for intelligent control of machining, etc. In general, the design of FNN includes (i) the structure, (ii) the learning algorithm and (iii) the stability analysis.

It is well known that the stability of neural networks [10]-[15] is critical for signal processing, especially in image processing and solving nonlinear algebraic and transcendental equations, applied to solve some classes of optimization problems. FNN has inherent connections to mathematical morphology, which is a cornerstone in image processing and pattern recognition. To guarantee that the performance of FNN is what we wanted, it is important to study its equilibrium points and the stability of those equilibrium points. Some papers [9],[16], [17], [18] have studied the stability of FNN. In [16], the stability can be analyzed by the Nyquist stability criterion. In [17], the stability of the T-S model was studied by using a fuzzy block diagram. In [18], an energetic stability algorithm (ESA) was proposed to investigate the local stability of a free dynamic system. In [19], a fuzzy cellular neural network model with flat fuzzy feedback Min templates and flat fuzzy feedback Max templates was proposed and studied. In [20], we introduce a kind of fuzzy neural network which integrates fuzzy logic into the structure of traditional neural network structures, FNN has fuzzy logic between its template and input and/or output besides the "sum of product" operation.

In this paper, a sufficient condition is derived to guarantee the global exponential stability of T-S fuzzy cellular neural networks (TSFCNNs) with time-varying delays.

## 2 Preliminaries

Consider the DCNN described by the following normalized equations:

$$\frac{dx_i(t)}{dt} = -x_i(t) + \sum_{j=1}^{n}(a_{ij}f(x_j(t)) + b_{ij}f(x_j(t-\tau_{ij}(t)))) + u_i, \qquad (1)$$

where $i = 1, \cdots, n$, $x = (x_1, \cdots, x_n)^T \in \Re^n$ is the state vector, $A = (a_{ij})$ and $B = (b_{ij})$ are connection weight matrices, $u = (u_1, \cdots, u_n)^T \in \Re^n$ is the external input vector, $\tau_{ij}(t)$ is the time-varying delay that satisfies $0 \le \tau_{ij}(t) \le \tau_{ij} \le \tau$ ($\tau_{ij}$ and $\tau$ are constant) for all $t \ge t_0$, $f(v) = (|v+1| - |v-1|)/2$. (1) can be rewritten as the following:

$$\frac{dx(t)}{dt} = -x(t) + Af(x(t)) + Bf(x(t-\tau(t))) + u, \qquad (2)$$

where $f(x(t)) = (f(x_1(t)), f(x_2(t)), \cdots, f(x_n(t)))^T$, $f(x(t-\tau(t))) = (f(x_1(t-\tau_1(t))), f(x_2(t-\tau_2(t))), \cdots, f(x_n(t-\tau_n(t))))^T$, $u = (u_1, u_2, \cdots, u_n)^T$.

Let $C([t_0-\tau, t_0], \mathcal{D})$ be the space of continuous functions mapping $[t_0-\tau, t_0]$ into $\mathcal{D} \subset \Re^n$ with norm defined by $||\phi||_{t_0} = \max_{1\le i\le n}\{\sup_{u\in[t_0-\tau,t_0]} |\phi_i(u)|\}$, where $\phi(s) = (\phi_1(s), \phi_2(s), \cdots, \phi_n(s))^T$. Denote $||x|| = \max_{1\le i\le n}\{|x_i|\}$ as the vector norm of the vector $x = (x_1, \cdots, x_n)^T$. The initial condition of DCNN (1) is assumed to be

$$\phi(\vartheta) = (\phi_1(\vartheta), \phi_2(\vartheta), \cdots, \phi_n(\vartheta))^T,$$

where $\phi(\vartheta) \in C([t_0 - \tau, t_0], \Re^n)$. Denote $x(t; t_0, \phi)$ as the state of DCNN (1) with initial condition $\phi(\vartheta)$, it means that $x(t; t_0, \phi)$ is continuous and satisfies (1) and $x(s; t_0, \phi) = \phi(s)$, for $s \in [t_0 - \tau, t_0]$.

The continuous fuzzy system was proposed to represent a nonlinear system. The system dynamics can be captured by a set of fuzzy rules which characterize local relation in the state space. Every local dynamics described by fuzzy IF-THEN rule is with the property of linear input-output relation. Based on the concept of T-S fuzzy model, a model of TSFCNNs with time-varying delays is described as follows:

Model Rule $K$:

If $\theta_1(t)$ is $M_{k1}$ and, $\cdots, \theta_r(t)$ is $M_{kr}$, then

$$\frac{dx(t)}{dt} = -x(t) + A_k f(x(t)) + B_k f(x(t - \tau(t))) + U_k, \tag{3}$$

$$x(t) = \psi_k(t) \in C([t_0 - \tau, t_0], \Re^n), \tag{4}$$

where $A_k, B_k \in \Re^{n \times n}$ are known constant matrices, $\theta_1(t), \theta_2(t), \cdots, \theta_r(t)$ are known premise variables, $M_{kl}$, $k \in \{1, 2, \cdots, m\}$, $l \in \{1, 2, \cdots, r\}$ is the fuzzy set and $m$ is the number of model rules. By inferring the fuzzy models, the final output of TSFCNN is obtained by

$$\begin{aligned}\frac{dx(t)}{dt} &= \frac{\sum_{k=1}^{m} w_k(\theta(t)) \{-x(t) + A_k f(x(t)) + B_k f(x(t - \tau(t))) + U_k\}}{\sum_{k=1}^{m} w_k(\theta(t))} \\ &= \sum_{k=1}^{m} \eta_k(\theta(t)) \{-x(t) + A_k \phi(x(t)) + B_k \phi(x(t - \tau(t))) + U_k\}, \ t \geq 0, \end{aligned}\tag{5}$$

$$x(t) = \sum_{k=1}^{m} \eta_k(\theta(t)) \cdot \psi_k(t), \ t \in [t_0 - \tau, t_0]. \tag{6}$$

The weight and averaged weight of each fuzzy rule are denoted by $w_k(\theta(t)) = \prod_{l=1}^{m} M_{kl}(\theta_l(t))$ and $\eta_k(\theta(t)) = w_k(\theta(t)) / \sum_{k=1}^{m} w_k(\theta(t))$, respectively. The term $M_{kl}(\theta_l(t))$ is the grade of membership of $\theta_l(t)$ in $M_{kl}$. In this paper, we assume that $w_k(\theta(t)) \geq 0$, $k \in \{1, 2, \cdots, m\}$, and $\sum_{k=1}^{m} w_k(\theta(t)) > 0$. Therefore, we have $\eta_k(\theta(t)) \geq 0$, $k \in \{1, 2, \cdots, m\}$ and $\sum_{k=1}^{m} \eta_k(\theta(t)) = 1$, for all $t \geq 0$.

## 3 Main Result

*Theorem.* If $E - \sum_{k=1}^{m} |A_k| - \sum_{k=1}^{m} |B_k|$ is a nonsingular $M$ matrix, then TS-FCNN (5) is globally exponentially stable, where $E$ is an $n \times n$ unit matrix.

*Proof.* It is well known that the equilibrium points of TSFCNN (5) exist by the Schauder fixed-point theorem. Let $x^* = (x_1^*, x_2^*, \cdots, x_n^*)^T$ be an equilibrium point of TSFCNN (5). Denote $z_i(t) = x_i(t) - x_i^*, i = 1, 2, \cdots, n$, then TSFCNN (5) can be rewritten as

$$\begin{aligned}\frac{dz(t)}{dt} &= \sum_{k=1}^{m} w_k(\theta(t)) \{-z(t) + A_k g(z(t)) + B_k g(z(t-\tau(t)))\} \Big/ \sum_{k=1}^{m} w_k(\theta(t)) \\ &= \sum_{k=1}^{m} \eta_k(\theta(t)) \{-z(t) + A_k g(z(t)) + B_k g(z(t-\tau(t)))\}, \ t \geq 0, \end{aligned} \tag{7}$$

$$z(t) = \sum_{k=1}^{m} \eta_k(\theta(t))\varphi_k(t), \ t \in [t_0 - \tau, t_0], \tag{8}$$

where $\varphi_k(t) \in C([t_0 - \tau, t_0], \Re^n)$ is the initial continuous vector function and

$$g(z(t)) = (g_1(z_1(t)), g_2(z_2(t)), \cdots, g_n(z_n(t)))^T,$$

$$g(z(t-\tau(t))) = (g_1(z_1(t-\tau_1(t))), g_2(z_2(t-\tau_2(t))), \cdots, g_n(z_n(t-\tau_n(t))))^T,$$

$$g_i(z_i(t)) = f_i(z_i + x_i^*) - f_i(x_i^*), \ g_i(z_i(t-\tau_i(t))) = f_i(z_i(t-\tau_i(t)) + x_i^*) - f_i(x_i^*).$$

Clearly, the origin, $z = 0$ is an equilibrium point of the system (7). If the origin of the system (7) is globally exponentially stable, then the equilibrium point $x^*$ is also globally exponentially stable.

Since $E - \sum_{k=1}^{m} |A_k| - \sum_{k=1}^{m} |B_k|$ is a nonsingular $M$ matrix, there exist positive numbers $\gamma_1, \cdots, \gamma_n$ such that

$$\gamma_i - \sum_{k=1}^{m}\sum_{j=1}^{n}(|a_{ij}^{(k)}| + |b_{ij}^{(k)})|\gamma_j > 0. \tag{9}$$

Hence, there exists a constant $\nu > 0$ such that

$$\gamma_i - \nu - \sum_{k=1}^{m}\sum_{j=1}^{n}(|a_{ij}^{(k)}| + |b_{ij}^{(k)}|) \exp\{\nu\tau\}\gamma_j > 0. \tag{10}$$

Let $y_i(t) = (x_i(t) - x_i^*)/\gamma_i$, then from (7), for $t \geq 0$,

$$\begin{aligned}\frac{dy_i(t)}{dt} &= \frac{\sum_{k=1}^{m} w_k(\theta(t)) \left\{-\gamma_i y_i(t) + \sum_{j=1}^{n}(a_{ij}^{(k)} g_j(\gamma_j y_j(t)) + b_{ij}^{(k)} g_j(\gamma_j y_j(t-\tau_j(t))))\right\}}{\gamma_i \sum_{k=1}^{m} w_k(\theta(t))} \\ &= \sum_{k=1}^{m} \eta_k(\theta(t)) \left\{-y_i(t) + \frac{\sum_{j=1}^{n}(a_{ij}^{(k)} g_j(\gamma_j y_j(t)) + b_{ij}^{(k)} g_j(\gamma_j y_j(t-\tau_j(t))))}{\gamma_i}\right\} \end{aligned} \tag{11}$$

From (8),

$$y_i(t) = \frac{1}{\gamma_i} \sum_{k=1}^{m} \eta_k(\theta(t))\varphi_k(t), \ t \in [t_0 - \tau, t_0] \tag{12}$$

is the initial continuous function of (11). Hence,

$$||y(t)|| \leq \max_{1\leq i\leq n}\{\max_{t_0-\tau\leq s\leq t_0}\{y_i(s)\}\}\exp\{-\nu(t-t_0)\}. \quad (13)$$

Otherwise, there exist $t_2 > t_1 > t_0$, $q \in \{1, 2, \cdots, n\}$ and sufficiently small $\varepsilon > 0$ such that $\forall s \in [t_0 - \tau, t_1]$, (13) holds, and for $r \in (t_1, t_2]$,

$$|y_p(r)| \leq \max_{1\leq i\leq n}\{\max_{t_0-\tau\leq s\leq t_0}\{y_i(s)\}\}\exp\{-\nu(r-t_0)\} + \varepsilon, \quad (14)$$

$$D^+|y_p(t_2)| + \nu\max_{1\leq i\leq n}\{\max_{t_0-\tau\leq s\leq t_0}\{y_i(s)\}\}\exp\{-\nu(t_2-t_0)\} > 0. \quad (15)$$

But from (10), (11) and (14), (15) does not hold. Hence, from this conclusion of absurdity, it shows that main Theorem holds.

## 4 Concluding Remarks

In this paper, using the reduction to absurdity, for a general class of Takagi-Sugeno Fuzzy cellular neural networks with time-varying delays, we have obtained a sufficient condition to guarantee that the delayed neural network is globally exponentially stable. Since our model is more general than some existing works, the results presented in this paper obviously improve and extend the existing ones.

## Acknowledgement

This work was supported by the Natural Science Foundation of China under Grant 60405002 and the Young Foundation of Hubei Provincial Education Department of China under Grant 2003B001.

## References

1. Chua, L.O., Yang, L.: Cellular Neural Networks: Theory. IEEE Trans. Circuits Syst., 35 (1988) 1257-1272
2. Chua, L.O., Yang, L.: Cellular Neural Networks: Applications. IEEE Trans. Circuits Syst., 35 (1988) 1273-1290
3. Roska, T., Wu, C.W., Balsi, M., Chua, L.O.: Stability and Dynamics of Delay-type General and Cellular Neural Networks. IEEE Trans. Circuits Syst. I, 39 (1992) 487-490
4. Roska, T., Wu, C.W., Chua, L.O.: Stability of Cellular Neural Networks with Dominant Nonlinear and Delay-type Templates. IEEE Trans. Circuits Syst. I, 40 (1993) 270-272
5. Takagi, T., Sugeno, M.: Fuzzy Identification of Systems and Its Applications to Modeling and Control. IEEE Trans. Syst., Man, Cybern. SMC, 15 (1985) 116-132
6. Yamamoto, H., Furuhashi, T.: A New Sufficient Condition for Stable Fuzzy Control System and Its Design Method. IEEE Trans. Fuzzy Syst., 9 (2001) 554-569

7. Huang, H., Ho, D.W.C.,Lam, J.: Stochastic Stability Analysis of Fuzzy Hopfield Neural Networks with Time-varying Delays. IEEE Trans. Circuit Syst., 52 (2005) 251-255
8. Bernard, J.F.: Use of Rule-based System for Process Control. IEEE Contr. System Mag., 8 (1988) 3-13
9. Polycarpou, M.M., Ioannou, P.A.: Learning and Convergence Analysis of Neural-type Structured Networks. IEEE Trans. on Neural Networks, 3 (1992) 39-50
10. Forti, M., Tesi, A.: New Conditions for Global Stability of Neural Networks with Application to Linear and Quadratic Programming Problems. IEEE Trans. Circ. Syst. I, 42 (1995) 354-366
11. Liao, X.X., Wang, J.: Algebraic Criteria for Global Exponential Stability of Cellular Neural Networks with Multiple Time Delays. IEEE Trans. Circuits and Systems I., 50 (2003) 268-275
12. Zeng, Z.G., Wang, J.: Complete Stability of Cellular Neural Networks with Time-varying Delays. IEEE Trans. on Circuits and Systems-I: Regular Papers, 53 (2006) 944-955
13. Zeng, Z.G., Wang, J.: Multiperiodicity and Exponential Attractivity Evoked by Periodic External Inputs in Delayed Cellular Neural Networks. Neural Computation, 18 (2006) 848-870
14. Zeng, Z.G., Huang, D.S., Wang, Z.F.: Global Stability of a General Class of Discrete-time Recurrent Neural Networks. Neural Processing Letters, 22 (2005) 33-47
15. Zeng, Z.G., Wang, J., Liao, X.X.: Global Asymptotic Stability and Global Exponential Stability of Neural Networks with Unbounded Time-varying Delays. IEEE Trans. on Circuits and Systems II, Express Briefs, 52 (2005) 168-173
16. Kumar, S.R., Majumder, D.D.: Application of FCSs to Industrial Processes. Automatica, 13 (1997) 235-242
17. Tanaka, K., Sugeno, M.: Stability Analysis and Design of Fuzzy Control Systems. Fuzzy Sets and Systems, 45 (1992) 135-156
18. Kiszka, J.B., Gupta, M.M., Nikiforuk, P.N.: Energetistic Stability of Fuzzy Dynamic Systems. IEEE Trans. Systems, Man Cybern., 15 (1985) 783-791
19. Yang, T., Yang, L.B.: The Global Stability of Fuzzy Cellular Neural Network. IEEE Trans. Circuits Syst. Part I, 43 (1996) 880-883
20. Fu, C.J., Liao, W.D.: Global Exponential Stability of Fuzzy Neural Networks. Proceedings of the 2004 International Conference on Information Acquisition, (2004) 32-35

# Gradient Descent and Radial Basis Functions

Mercedes Fernández-Redondo, Joaquín Torres-Sospedra, and Carlos Hernández-Espinosa

Departamento de Ingenieria y Ciencia de los Computadores, Universitat Jaume I, Avda. Sos Baynat s/n, C.P. 12071, Castellon, Spain
{redondo, jtorres, espinosa}@icc.uji.es

**Abstract.** In this paper, we present experiments comparing different training algorithms for Radial Basis Functions (RBF) neural networks. In particular we compare the classical training which consists of an unsupervised training of centers followed by a supervised training of the weights at the output, with the full supervised training by gradient descent proposed recently in same papers. We conclude that a fully supervised training performs generally better. We also compare *Batch training* with *Online training* and we conclude that *Online training* suppose a reduction in the number of iterations.

## 1 Introduction

A RBF has two layer of neurons. The first one, in its usual form, is composed of neurons with Gaussian transfer functions (GF) and the second has neurons with linear transfer functions. The output of a RBF can be calculated with the following equation:

$$\hat{y}_{i,k} = \mathbf{w}_i^T \cdot \mathbf{h}_k = \sum_{j=1}^{c} w_{ij} \cdot \exp\left(-\frac{\|\mathbf{x}_k - \mathbf{v}_j\|^2}{\sigma^2}\right). \quad (1)$$

Where $\boldsymbol{v}_j$ are the center of the Gaussian transfer functions, $\sigma$ control the width of the Gaussian transfer functions and $\boldsymbol{w}_i$ are the weights among the Gaussian units (GU) and the output units.

As (1) shows, there are three elements to design in the neural network: the centers and the widths of the Gaussian units and the linear weights among the Gaussian units and output units.

There are two procedures to design the network. One is to train the networks in two steps. First we find the centers and widths by using some unsupervised clustering algorithm and after that we train the weights among hidden and output units by a supervised algorithm. This process is usually fast [1],[2],[3],[4].

The second procedure is to train the centers and weights in a full supervised fashion, similar to the algorithm Backpropagation (BP) for Multilayer Feedforward. This procedure has the same drawbacks of Backpropagation, long training time and high computational cost. However, it has received quite attention recently [5],[6].

In [5],[6] it is used a sensitivity analysis to show that the traditional Gaussian unit (called "*exponential generator function*") of the RBF network has low sensitivity for gradient descent training for a wide range of values of the widths. As an alternative two

D.-S. Huang, K. Li, and G.W. Irwin (Eds.): ICIC 2006, LNCS 4113, pp. 391–396, 2006.

different transfer functions are proposed. They are called in the papers "*lineal generator function*" and "*cosine generator function*".

In contrast, in this paper we present more complete experiments with nine databases from the *UCI Repository*, and include in the experiments four traditional unsupervised training algorithms and a fully gradient descent training with the three transfer functions analysed in papers [5],[6].

Furthermore, we also presents experiments with *Batch* and *Online learning*, in the original references the training was performed in *Batch* mode and we show that Online Traning is the best alternative under the point of view of training speed.

## 2 Theory

### 2.1 Training by Gradient Descent

**"Exponential (EXP) Generator" Function.** This RBF has the usual Gaussian transfer function described in (1). The equation for adapting the weights by gradient descent is in (2).

$$\Delta \mathbf{w}_p = \eta \cdot \sum_{k=1}^{M} \varepsilon_{p,k}^{0} \cdot \mathbf{h}_k. \tag{2}$$

Where $\eta$ is the learning rate, $M$ the number of training patterns and $\varepsilon_{p,k}^{0}$ is the output error, the difference between target and output.

The equation for adapting the centers by gradient descent is the following:

$$\Delta v_q = \eta \cdot \sum_{k=1}^{M} \varepsilon_{p,k}^{h} \cdot (\mathbf{x}_k - \mathbf{v}_q). \tag{3}$$

Where $\eta$ is the learning rate and $\varepsilon_{p,k}^{h}$ is the hidden error given by equation (4).

$$\varepsilon_{p,k}^{h} = \frac{2}{\sigma^2} \cdot \exp\left( - \frac{\left\| \mathbf{x}_k - \mathbf{v}_q \right\|^2}{\sigma^2} \right) \cdot \sum_{i=1}^{n_o} \varepsilon_{i,k}^{0} \cdot w_{iq}. \tag{4}$$

In the above equations $n_o$ is the number of outputs and these equation are for *Batch training*, i.e., we adapt the variables of the network after the presentation of all the patterns of the training set. The equations for *Online training* are basically the same, we only have to omit the sum for k=1, to M in the expressions.

**"Linear (LIN) Generator" Function.** In this case the transfer function of the hidden units is the following:

$$h_{j,k} = \left( \frac{1}{\left\| \mathbf{x}_k - \mathbf{v}_j \right\|^2 + \gamma^2} \right)^{\frac{1}{m-1}}. \tag{5}$$

Where we have used $m = 3$ in our experiments and $\gamma$ is a parameter that should be determined by trial and error and cross-validation.

The above equation (3) is the same, but in this case the hidden erros is (6).

$$\eta_{p,k}^{h} = \frac{2}{m-1} \cdot \left( \|\mathbf{x}_k - \mathbf{v}_q\|^2 + \gamma^2 \right)^{\frac{m}{1-m}} \cdot \sum_{i=1}^{n_o} \varepsilon_{i,k}^{0} \cdot w_{iq}. \tag{6}$$

**"Cosine (COS) Generator" Function.** In this case the transfer function is the following:

$$h_{j,k} = \frac{a_j}{\left( \|\mathbf{x}_k - \mathbf{v}_j\|^2 + a_j^2 \right)^{1/2}}. \tag{7}$$

Equations (3) is the same, but in this case the hidden error is different as in equation (8).

$$\varepsilon_{p,k}^{h} = \left( \frac{h_{j,k}^{3}}{a_j^2} \right) \cdot \sum_{i=1}^{no} \varepsilon_{i,k}^{0} \cdot w_{iq}. \tag{8}$$

The parameter $a_j$ is also adapted during training, the equation is (9).

$$\Delta a_j = \left( \frac{\eta}{a_j} \right) \cdot \sum_{i=1}^{no} h_{j,k} \cdot (1 - h_{j,k}^2) \cdot \varepsilon_{p,k}^{h}. \tag{9}$$

### 2.2 Training by Unsupervised Clustering

**Algorithm 1.** This training algorithm is the simplest one. It was proposed in [1]. It uses adaptive k-means clustering to find the centers of the gaussian units. The process is iterative, we successively present an input pattern and after each presentation we find the closest center and adapt this center toward the input pattern.

**Algorithm 2.** This algorithm is proposed in reference [2]. However, we have slightly modified the algorithm. In the original reference it is used a truncation for the Gaussian functions and non-RBF functions in the hidden layer. We have applied the algorithm without truncation in the Gaussian functions and with only RBF units in the hidden layer. The algorithm is complex and a full description can be found in reference [2].

**Algorithm 3.** It is proposed in reference [3]. They use a one pass algorithm called *APC-III*, clustering the patterns class by class instead of the entire patterns at the same time. The *APC-III* algorithms uses a constant radius to create the clusters. In the reference this radius is calculated as the mean minimum distance between training patterns multiplied by a constant $\alpha$ .

**Algorithm 4.** This algorithm is proposed in reference [4]. However, we have slightly modified the algorithm, in the original reference it is used a truncation for the Gaussian units and a hard limiting function for the output layer. We have applied the algorithm without these modifications of the normal RBF network. The algorithm is complex and a full description can be found in refrence [4].

## 3 Experimental Results

We have applied the training algorithms to nine different classification problems from the UCI repository of machine learning databases.

They are Balance Scale, Cylinders Bands, Liver Disorders, Credit Approval, Glass Identification, Heart Disease, The Monk's Problems and Voting Congresional Records. The complete data and a full description can be found in the repository http://www.ics.uci.edu/∼ mlearn/MLRepository.html) [7].

### 3.1 Results

The first step was to determine the appropriate parameters of the algorithms by trial and error and cross-validation. We have used an extensive trial procedure.

After that, with the final parameters we trained ten networks with different partition of data in training, cross-validation and test set, also with different random initialization of parameters. With this procedure we can obtain a mean performance in the database (the mean of the ten networks) and an error by standard error theory.

These results are in Tables 1, 2 and 3. We have included for each database and training algorithm the mean percentage of correct classification with its error (column Perc.) and the number of gaussian transfer units under the column $Nunit$.

**Table 1.** Performance of Gradient Descent with Exponential Generator Functions

| | Training Algorithm | | | |
|---|---|---|---|---|
| | Exp Batch | | Exp Online | |
| **Database** | **Percentage** | $N_{unit}$ | **Percentage** | $N_{unit}$ |
| **bala** | 90.2±0.5 | 45 | 90.2±0.5 | 60 |
| **band** | 74.1±1.1 | 110 | 74.0±1.1 | 40 |
| **bupa** | 69.8±1.1 | 35 | 70.1±1.1 | 40 |
| **cred** | 86.1±0.7 | 40 | 86.0±0.8 | 30 |
| **glas** | 92.9±0.7 | 125 | 93.0±0.6 | 110 |
| **hear** | 82.0±1.0 | 155 | 82.0±1.0 | 20 |
| **mok1** | 94.7±1.0 | 60 | 98.5±0.5 | 30 |
| **mok2** | 92.1±0.7 | 80 | 91.3±0.7 | 45 |
| **vote** | 95.6±0.4 | 35 | 95.4±0.5 | 5 |

**Table 2.** Performance of Gradient Descent with Linear and Cosine Generator Functions

| | Training Algorithm | | | | | | | |
|---|---|---|---|---|---|---|---|---|
| | Linear Batch | | Linear Online | | Cosine Batch | | Cosine Online | |
| **Database** | **Percentage** | $N_{unit}$ | **Percentage** | $N_{unit}$ | **Percentage** | $N_{unit}$ | **Percentage** | $N_{unit}$ |
| **bala** | 90.1±0.5 | 45 | 90.6±0.5 | 50 | 89.9±0.5 | 25 | 90.0±0.7 | 40 |
| **band** | 74.5±1.1 | 30 | 73.4±1.0 | 35 | 75.0±1.1 | 120 | 74.9±1.1 | 125 |
| **bupa** | 71.2±0.9 | 10 | 69.7±1.3 | 15 | 69.9±1.1 | 15 | 70.2±1.1 | 40 |
| **cred** | 86.2±0.7 | 10 | 85.8±0.8 | 10 | 86.1±0.8 | 10 | 86.1±0.8 | 25 |
| **glas** | 91.4±0.8 | 35 | 92.4±0.7 | 30 | 93.5±0.8 | 105 | 92.6±0.9 | 15 |
| **hear** | 82.1±1.1 | 15 | 81.8±1.1 | 10 | 82.1±1.0 | 25 | 81.9±1.1 | 15 |
| **mok1** | 93.2±0.7 | 15 | 94.5±0.7 | 15 | 89.8±0.8 | 100 | 90.2±1.0 | 145 |
| **mok2** | 82.8±1.2 | 25 | 89.6±1.2 | 50 | 87.9±0.8 | 125 | 86.6±1.1 | 45 |
| **vote** | 95.6±0.4 | 25 | 95.6±0.4 | 10 | 95.6±0.4 | 20 | 95.4±0.4 | 10 |

**Table 3.** Performance of Unsupervised Algorithms 1 and 2

| | Training Algorithm | | | | | |
|---|---|---|---|---|---|---|
| | UC Alg. 1 | | UC Alg. 2 | | UC Alg. 3 | UC Alg. 4 |
| **Database** | **Percentage** | $N_{unit}$ | **Percentage** | $N_{unit}$ | **Percentage** | **Percentage** |
| **bala** | 88.5±0.8 | 30 | 87.6±0.9 | 88.5±1.6 | 88.0±0.9 | 87.4±0.9 |
| **band** | 74.0±1.5 | 60 | 67±2 | 18.7±1.0 | 67±4 | 65.8±1.4 |
| **bupa** | 59.1±1.7 | 10 | 57.6±1.9 | 10.3±1.5 | 60±4 | 47±3 |
| **cred** | 87.3±0.7 | 20 | 87.5±0.6 | 95±14 | 87.9±0.6 | 86.4±0.9 |
| **glas** | 89.6±1.9 | 100 | 79±2 | 30±2 | 82.8±1.5 | 81.2±1.8 |
| **hear** | 80.8±1.5 | 100 | 80.2±1.5 | 26±4 | 72±4 | 78±3 |
| **mok1** | 76.9±1.3 | 90 | 72±2 | 93±8 | 68±3 | 64±2 |
| **mok2** | 71.0±1.5 | 90 | 66.4±1.7 | 26±4 | 66.5±0.8 | 71.6±1.5 |
| **vote** | 95.1±0.6 | 40 | 93.6±0.9 | 53±5 | 94.1±0.8 | 76±5 |

## 3.2 Interpretation of Results

Comparing the results of the same algorithm trained by gradient descent in the case of *Batch training* and *Online training*, we can see that the differences in performance are not significant. The fundamental difference between both training procedures is in the number of iterations and the value of the learning step.

Comparing *EXP*, *LIN* and *COS* generator functions, we can see that the general performance is quite similar except in the case mok1 where the performance of *EXP* is clearly better. In other aspect, *EXP* and *LIN* functions need a higher number of trials for the process of trial and error to design the network, because cosine generator functions adapt all parameters. But in contrast, the number of iterations needed to converge by *COS* functions is usually larger, so globally speaking the computational cost can be considered similar.

Comparing unsupervised training algorithms among them, it seems clear that the classical algorithm 1, $k$-means clustering shows the better performance.

Finally, comparing unsupervised training with gradient descent we can see that the best alternative (under the performance point of view) is supervised training by gradient descent, it achieves a better performance in 6 of 9 databases.

**Table 4.** Performance of Multilayer Feedforward with Backpropagation

| Database | N. Hidden | Percentage |
|---|---|---|
| **bala** | 20 | 87.6±0.6 |
| **Bands** | 23 | 72.4±1.0 |
| **bupa** | 11 | 58.3±0.6 |
| **cred** | 15 | 85.6±0.5 |
| **glas** | 3 | 78.5±0.9 |
| **hear** | 2 | 82.0±0.9 |
| **mok1** | 6 | 74.3±1.1 |
| **mok2** | 20 | 65.9±0.5 |
| **vote** | 1 | 95.0±0.4 |

In order to perform a further comparison, we have included the results of Multilayer Feedforward with Backpropagaion in Table 4. We can see that the results of RBF are better. This is the case in all databases except cred, hear and vote where the performance of both networks is similar.

## 4 Conclusions

In this paper we have presented a comparison of unsupervised and fully supervised training algorithms for RBF networks. The algorithms are compared using nine databases. Our results show that the fully supervised training by gradient descent may be the best alternative under the point of view of performance. The results of RBF are also compared with Multilayer Feedforward with Backpropagation and the performance of a RBF network seems to be better.

Furthermore under the point of view of training speed the alternative of *Online Training* is better than *Batch Training*.

## Acknowledgments

This research was supported by project *P1 ·1B2004-03* of Universitat Jaume I - Bancaja in Castellón de la Plana, Spain.

## References

1. Moody,J., Darken,C.J.:Fast Learning in Networks of Locally-Tuned Procesing Units. *Neural Computation*, vol(1989)1281-294
2. Roy,A. , Govil et alt,S. :A Neural-Network Learning Theory and Polynomial Time RBF Algorithm. *IEEE Trans. on Neural Networks*, vol.8, no. 6(1997)1301-1313
3. Hwang,Y.,Bang, S.:An Efficient Method to Construct a Radial Basis Function Neural Network Classifier. *Neural Network*, Vol.10 no. 8(1997)1495-1503
4. Roy,A. , Govil et alt,S. :An Algorithm to Generate Radial Basis Function (RBF)-Like Nets for Classification Problems., *Neural Networks*, vol.8, no. 2(1995)179-201
5. Krayiannis,N.:Reformulated Radial Basis Neural Networks Trained by Gradient Descent. *IEEE Trans. on Neural Networks*. vol.10, no. 3(1999)657-671
6. Krayiannis,N.,Randolph-Gips,M.: On the Construction and Training of Reformulated Radial Basis Functions. *IEEE Trans. Neural Networks*. vol.14, no. 4(2003)835-846
7. Newman, D.J. , Hettich,S. , Blake,C.L. Merz,C.J.:UCI Repository of machine learning databases, http://www.ics.uci.edu/∼mlearn/MLRepository.html, University of California, Irvine, Dept. of Information and Computer Sciences(1998)

# Improving Adaptive Boosting with $k$-Cross-Fold Validation

Joaquín Torres-Sospedra, Carlos Hernández-Espinosa,
and Mercedes Fernández-Redondo

Departamento de Ingenieria y Ciencia de los Computadores, Universitat Jaume I, Avda. Sos Baynat s/n, C.P. 12071, Castellon, Spain
{jtorres, espinosa, redondo}@icc.uji.es

**Abstract.** As seen in the bibliography, *Adaptive Boosting* (*Adaboost*) is one of the most known methods to increase the performance of an ensemble of neural networks. We introduce a new method based on *Adaboost* where we have applied *Cross-Validation* to increase the diversity of the ensemble. We have used *Cross-Validation* over the whole learning set to generate an specific training set and validation set for each network of the committee. We have tested *Adaboost* and *Crossboost* with seven databases from the *UCI repository*. We have used the mean percentage of error reduction and the mean increase of performance to compare both methods, the results show that *Crossboost* performs better.

## 1 Introduction

Perhaps, the most important property of a neural network is the generalization capability. The ability to correctly respond to inputs which were not used in the training set.

One technique to increase this capability with respect to a single neural network consist on training an ensemble of neural networks, i.e., to train a set of neural networks with different weight initialization or properties and combine the outputs of the different networks in a suitable manner to give a single output.

It is clear from the bibliography that this procedure increases the generalization capability. The error of a neural network can be decomposed into a bias and a variance [1,2]. The use of an ensemble usually keeps the bias constant and reduce the variance if the errors of the different networks are uncorrelated or negatively correlated. Therefore, it increases the generalization performance. The two key factors to design an ensemble are how to train the individual networks to get uncorrelated errors and how to combine the different outputs of the networks to give a single output.

In previouses works, [3] and [4], developed by our research group we presented a comparison among methods to build an ensemble. In these works we concluded that $k$-Cross-Fold Validation (CVC) presented in [5] has a good performance.

Among the methods described in the bibliography we have focused on *Adaptive Boosting* (*Adaboost*). *Adaboost* is a well know method to create an ensemble of neural networks [6] and it has been widely studied by some authors [7,8,9].

*Adaboost* could be improved if we increase the diversity of the ensemble. We can generate an specific validation set $V_{net}$ and training set $T_{net}$ for each network [5] if we apply *Cross Validation* over the learning set in order to get $k$ disjoint subsets.

D.-S. Huang, K. Li, and G.W. Irwin (Eds.): ICIC 2006, LNCS 4113, pp. 397–402, 2006.

To test the performance of the method we have proposed *Cross Validated Boosting* (*Crossboost*), we have built ensembles of 3, 9, 20 and 40 multilayer feedforward networks with seven databases from the *UCI repository*.

The results we have obtained on these seven databases are in subsection 3.1. We have also calculated the global measurements *Mean Increase on performance* and *Mean Percentage of Error Reduction* of *Adaboost* and *Crossboost* to compare both methods, these results appear in subsetion 3.2.

## 2 Theory

### 2.1 Adaptive Boosting

*Adaboost* is a method that constructs a sequence of networks, each network is trained as an individual network, but the training set used to train the network is based on the previous network performance on the original training set.

The successive networks are trained with a training data set $T^{'}$ selected at random from the original training data set $T$, the probability of selecting a pattern from $T$ is given by the sampling distribution associated to the network $d_{net}$. The sampling distribution associated to a network is calculated when the previous network learning process has finished.

Although the *Output Average* and *voting* are the two most used combining methods [10], *Adaboost* use the an specific combination method called (*boosting combiner*) which is described in equation 1 .

$$h_{boosting}(x) = \underset{c=1,\ldots,classes}{\arg\max} \sum_{net:h^{net}(x)\neq d(x)}^{k} \log\left(\frac{1-\epsilon_{net}}{\epsilon_{net}}\right) \tag{1}$$

### 2.2 Cross Validated Boosting

In the method we have proposed, *Crossboost*, we assume that each network has its own version of the training set $T_{net}$ and validation set $V_{net}$. The training process is similar to the training process of *Adaboost*.

In this case, the learning set $L$ has been divided into $k$ disjoint subsets of the same size $L = \{L_1, ..., L_k\}$ with *k-cross-fold validation* in order to create the specific training sets and validation sets. The $i$th-network validation set, $V_i$, is generated by equation 2 and the $i$th-network training set, $T_i$, is generated by equation 3.

$$V_{net} = L_{net} \tag{2}$$

$$T_{net} = \bigcup_{\substack{j=1 \\ j\neq net}}^{k} L_j \tag{3}$$

The algorithm 1 shows the training process of an ensemble of neural networks with *Crossboost*.

**Algorithm 1.** CrossBoost $\{L\ k\}$

Initialize Sampling Distribution $Dist$:

$Dist^{1}_{pattern} = 1/m\ \forall pattern \in L$

Divide Learning set $L$ into $k$ subsets

**for** $net = 1$ to $k$ **do**

Create $T_{net}$ and $V_{net}$

**end for**

**for** $net = 1$ to $k$ **do**

Create $T^{'}$ sampling from $T_{net}$ using $dist^{net}$

MF Network Training $T^{'}_{net}$ , $V^{'}_{net}$

Calculate missclassified vector:

$$miss^{net}_{pattern} = \begin{cases} 1 \text{ if } h^{net}(x_{pattern}) = d(x_{pattern}) \\ 0 \text{ otherwise} \end{cases}$$

Calculate error:

$\epsilon_{net} = \sum^{m}_{pattern=1} Dist^{net}_{pattern} \cdot miss^{net}_{pattern}$

Update sampling distribution:

$$Dist^{net+1}_{pattern} = Dist^{net}_{pattern} \cdot \begin{cases} \frac{1}{2(1-\epsilon_{net})} & \text{if } miss^{net}_{pattern} \\ \frac{1}{(2\epsilon_{net})} & \text{otherwise} \end{cases}$$

**end for**

In our experiments we have used the *Average combiner* (4) and the *boosting combiner* (1) to get the ensemble output/hypothesis of the ensembles generated by *Crossboost*.

$$h_{average}(x) = \underset{class=1\ldots classes}{\arg\max} \left\{ \sum_{net=1}^{k} \frac{1}{k} \cdot y^{net}_{class}(x) \right\} \quad (4)$$

## 3 Experimental Testing

The experimental setup, the datasets we have used in our experiments and the results we have obtained are described in the present section. Finally, the results of *Boosting* methods *Adaboost* and *Crossboost* have been analysed.

For this reason we have trained ensembles of 3, 9, 20 and 40 MF networks with *Adaboost* and *Crossboost* algorithms on seven different classification problems from the *UCI repository of machine learning databases* [11] to test the performance of both methods. The databases we have used are: Balance Scale Database (bala), Australian Credit Approval (credit), Heart Disease Database (hear), Image segmentation Database (img), Ionosphere Database (ionos), MONK Problems 2 (mok2), Wisconsin Breast Cancer Database (wdbc). In addition, we repeated ten times the whole learning process, using different partitions of data in training, validation and test sets. With this procedure we can obtain a mean performance of the ensemble for each database and an error in the performance calculated by standard error theory.

### 3.1 Results

The main results we have obtained with the *Boosting* methods are presented in this subsection. Table 1 shows the results we have obtained with ensembles of 3, 9, 20 and

**Table 1.** Adaboost results

| Database | 3 Nets | 9 Nets | 20 Nets | 40 Nets |
|---|---|---|---|---|
| **bala** | 94.5±0.8 | 95.3±0.5 | 96.1±0.4 | 95.7±0.5 |
| **cred** | 84.9±1.4 | 84.2±0.9 | 84.5±0.8 | 85.1±0.9 |
| **hear** | 80.5±1.8 | 81.2±1.4 | 82±1.9 | 82.2±1.8 |
| **img** | 96.8±0.2 | 97.3±0.3 | 97.29±0.19 | 97.3±0.2 |
| **ionos** | 88.3±1.3 | 89.4±0.8 | 91.4±0.8 | 91.6±0.7 |
| **mok2** | 76.5±2.4 | 78.8±2.5 | 81.1±2.4 | 82.9±2.1 |
| **wdbc** | 95.7±0.6 | 95.7±0.7 | 96.3±0.5 | 96.7±0.9 |

**Table 2.** Crossboost results

| | Average Combiner | | | | Boosting Combiner | | | |
|---|---|---|---|---|---|---|---|---|
| **DB** | **3 Nets** | **9 Nets** | **20 Nets** | **40 Nets** | **3 Nets** | **9 Nets** | **20 Nets** | **40 Nets** |
| **bala** | 96.3±0.5 | 96.3±0.6 | 96.2±0.6 | 95.4±0.6 | 95.1±0.5 | 95.4±0.5 | 96.2±0.6 | 95.8±0.7 |
| **cred** | 84.8±1 | 85±0.8 | 86.5±0.6 | 86.2±0.8 | 85.2±0.9 | 86.4±0.7 | 85.3±0.7 | 84.9±0.7 |
| **hear** | 81.7±1.3 | 80.5±1.8 | 82.4±1.1 | 78.1±1.2 | 80.7±1.3 | 81.2±1.5 | 82.7±1.6 | 81.2±1.5 |
| **img** | 96.6±0.3 | 97.3±0.2 | 97.4±0.2 | 97.4±0.3 | 96.1±0.3 | 97.5±0.2 | 97.5±0.2 | 97.7±0.1 |
| **ionos** | 89.7±0.9 | 91.3±1 | 91.6±1.3 | 91.4±1.8 | 89.1±0.7 | 91.7±0.6 | 90.7±1 | 92.6±0.6 |
| **mok2** | 77.9±2.3 | 85.8±1.3 | 84.1±2 | 77.3±1.6 | 74.8±2 | 86.1±1.4 | 87.3±0.9 | 87.5±1.2 |
| **wdbc** | 96.6±0.2 | 96.5±0.7 | 96±0.5 | 96.1±0.5 | 96.6±0.4 | 96.7±0.5 | 96.4±0.6 | 95.9±0.5 |

40 networks trained with *Adaboost*. Table 2 shows the results we have obtained with ensembles of 3, 9, 20 and 40 networks trained with *Crossboost* combining the outputs with the *Output Average* and the *Boosting Combiner*.

### 3.2 Interpretations of Results

In order to see if the method we have proposed is better, we have calculated the increase of performance of the new method respect the original *Adaboost*. A positive value of the increase of performance means that our method performs better that the original *Adaboost* on the dataset. There can also be negative valies, which means that our method performs worse than original *Adaboost*. The increase on performance obtained with *Crossboost* using *Average Combiner* and *Boosting Combiner* is in table 3.

Comparing the results showed in table 3 we can see that the improvement in performance using our method depends on the database and the number of networks used in the ensemble. For instance, the highest increase of performance of *Crossboost* with respect to *Adaboost* is 9.25 in Database mok2. In contrast we can see that the increase of performance in database bala is not as good as in data base mok2.

But, the increase of performance we have show is an *absolute* measure so we cannot see how important is the increase of performance with respect to the error. To have information about the error reduction, we have also calculated the percentage of error reduction (PER) (5) of the ensembles with respect to a *Single Network*.

$$PER = 100 \cdot \frac{Error_{singlenetwork} - Error_{ensemble}}{Error_{singlenetwork}} \tag{5}$$

**Table 3.** Crossbost increase on performance respect Adaboost

| | Average Combiner | | | | Boosting Combiner | | | |
|---|---|---|---|---|---|---|---|---|
| **DB** | **3 Nets** | **9 Nets** | **20 Nets** | **40 Nets** | **3 Nets** | **9 Nets** | **20 Nets** | **40 Nets** |
| **bala** | 1.83 | 1.03 | 0.08 | -0.25 | 0.64 | 0.15 | 0.16 | 0.15 |
| **cred** | -0.16 | 0.76 | 2.08 | 1.07 | 0.31 | 2.14 | 0.85 | -0.16 |
| **hear** | 1.17 | -0.68 | 0.34 | -4.06 | 0.17 | 0 | 0.67 | -1.02 |
| **img** | -0.18 | 0.03 | 0.14 | 0.1 | -0.69 | 0.18 | 0.16 | 0.4 |
| **ionos** | 1.41 | 1.89 | 0.16 | -0.17 | 0.84 | 2.3 | -0.7 | 0.96 |
| **mok2** | 1.38 | 7 | 3 | -5.63 | -1.76 | 7.38 | 6.12 | 4.62 |
| **wdbc** | 0.93 | 0.74 | -0.3 | 0.39 | 0.84 | 1.03 | 0.06 | 0.2 |

**Table 4.** Global Measures

| | Mean $PER$ | | | | Mean Increase of Performance | | | |
|---|---|---|---|---|---|---|---|---|
| **DB** | **3 Nets** | **9 Nets** | **20 Nets** | **40 Nets** | **3 Nets** | **9 Nets** | **20 Nets** | **40 Nets** |
| **Adaboost)** | 3.57 | 8.52 | 16.95 | 14.95 | 2.07 | 2.73 | 3.71 | 3.96 |
| **CrossBoost (ave)** | 13.19 | 19.34 | 19.76 | 12.48 | 4.27 | 4.5 | 2.74 | -1.46 |
| **CrossBoost (boost)** | 7.01 | 23.01 | 21.25 | 19.95 | 2.12 | 4.62 | 4.76 | 4.7 |

The $PER$ value ranges from $0\%$, where there is no improvement by the use of a particular ensemble method with respect to a single network, to $100\%$. There can also be negative values, which means that the performance of the ensemble is worse than the performance of the single network. This new measurement is relative and can be used to compare more clearly the different methods.

Furthermore, we have calculated the increase of performance with respect to *Adaboost* and the mean PER across all databases for each method to get a global measurement. Table 4 shows these results.

According to this global measurement *Crossboost* performs better than original *Adaboost*. The highest difference between original *Adaboost* and Crossboost is in the 9-network ensemble where the mean $PER$ increase is $14.49\%$. We also see that the ensembles composed by a high number of networks tend to be less accurate than smaller ones. This is becuase the partitioning process of learning set we have apply produces a very small validation set when the number of networks is high.

## 4 Conclusions

In this paper we have presented *Crossboost*, an algortithm based on *Adaboost* and *cross validation*. We have trained ensembles of 3, 9, 20 and 40 networks with *Adaboost* and *Crossboost* to cover a wide spectrum of the number of networks in the ensemble. Altough the results showed that in general the improvement by the use of *Crossboost* depends on the database, in four databases there is a high increase in the performance. Finally, we have obtained the mean percentage of error reduction across all databases. According to the results of this measurement *Conserboost* performs better than *Adaboost*. The most appropriate method to combine the outputs in *Crossboost* is the *Average combiner* for the ensembles of 3 networks and the *Boosting combiner* for the ensembles of 9, 20 and 40 networks. We can conclude that the *Adaboost* variation we have presented in this paper increases the diversity of the classifiers so the performance of the final ensemble is, in general, better.

## Acknowledgments

This research was supported by project *P1·1B2004-03* of Universitat Jaume I - Bancaja in Castellón de la Plana, Spain.

## References

1. Tumer, K., Ghosh, J.: Error Correlation and Error Reduction in Ensemble Classifiers. Connection Science vol.8(3-4) (1996) 385–403
2. Raviv, Y., Intratorr, N.: Bootstrapping with Noise: An Effective Regularization Technique. Connection Science, Special issue on Combining Estimators vol.8 (1996) 356–372
3. Hernandez, E. C., Fernandez, R. M., Torres, S. J.: Ensembles of Multilayer Feedforward for Classification Problems. In: Neural Information Processing, ICONIP 2004. Vol. 3316 of LNCS. (2005) 744–749
4. Hernandez, E. C., Torres, S. J., Fernandez, R. M.: New Experiments on Ensembles of Multilayer Feedforward for Classification Problems. In: Proceedings of International Conference on Neural Networks, IJCNN 2005, Montreal, Canada. (2005) 1120–1124
5. Verikas, A., Lipnickas, A., Malmqvist, K., Bacauskiene, M., Gelzinis, A.: Soft Combination of Neural Classifiers: A Comparative Study. Pattern Recognition Letters vol.20(4) (1999) 429–444
6. Freund, Y., Schapire, R.E.: Experiments with A New Boosting Algorithm. In: International Conference on Machine Learning. (1996) 148–156
7. Kuncheva, L., Whitaker, C.J.: Using Diversity with Three Variants of Boosting: Aggressive. In: Proceedings International Workshop on Multiple Classifier Systems , Calgiari, Italy, June 2002. Springer. Volume 2364 of LNCS., Springer (2002)
8. Oza, N.C.: Boosting with Averaged Weight Vectors. In Windeatt, T., Roli, F., eds.: Multiple Classifier Systems. Vol. 2709 of LNCS., Springer (2003) 15–24
9. Breiman, L.: Arcing Classifiers. The Annals of Statistics vol.26(3) (1998) 801–849
10. Drucker, H., Cortes, C., Jackel, L.D., LeCun, Y., Vapnik, V.: Boosting and Other Ensemble Methods. Neural Computation vol.6(6) (1994) 1289–1301
11. Newman, D.J., Hettich, S., Blake, C.L., Merz, C.J.: UCI Repository of Machine Learning Databases (1998)

# Neural Network Metalearning for Credit Scoring

Kin Keung Lai[1,2], Lean Yu[2,3], Shouyang Wang[1,3], and Ligang Zhou[2]

[1] College of Business Administration, Hunan University, Changsha 410082, China
[2] Department of Management Sciences, City University of Hong Kong,
Tat Chee Avenue, Kowloon, Hong Kong
{mskklai, msyulean, mszhoulg}@cityu.edu.hk
[3] Institute of Systems Science, Academy of Mathematics and Systems Science,
Chinese Academy of Sciences, Beijing 100080, China
{yulean, sywang}@cityu.edu.hk

**Abstract.** In the field of credit risk analysis, the problem that we often encountered is to increase the model accuracy as possible using the limited data. In this study, we discuss the use of supervised neural networks as a metalearning technique to design a credit scoring system to solve this problem. First of all, a bagging sampling technique is used to generate different training sets to overcome data shortage problem. Based on the different training sets, the different neural network models with different initial conditions or training algorithms is then trained to formulate different credit scoring models, i.e., base models. Finally, a neural-network-based metamodel can be produced by learning from all base models so as to improve the reliability, i.e., predict defaults accurately. For illustration, a credit card application approval experiment is performed.

## 1 Introduction

In the financial risk management field, the credit risk analysis is beyond doubt an important branch and credit scoring is one of the key techniques in the credit risk analysis. Especially for any credit-granting institution, such as commercial banks and certain retailers, the ability to discriminate good customers from bad ones is crucial. The need for reliable models that predict defaults accurately is imperative, in order to enable the interested parties to take either preventive or corrective action [1].

As Thomas [2] argued, credit scoring is a technique that helps organizations decide whether or not to grant credit to consumers who apply to them. The generic approach of credit scoring is to apply a classification technique on similar data of previous customers – both faithful and delinquent customers – in order to find a relation between the characteristics and potential failure. One important ingredient needed to accomplish this goal is to seek an accurate classifier in order to categorize new applicants or existing customers as good or bad. Therefore, many different models, including traditional methods, such as linear discriminant analysis [3] and logit analysis [4], and emerging artificial intelligence (AI) techniques, such as artificial neural networks (ANN) [5] and support vector machine (SVM) [1], were widely applied to credit scoring tasks and some interesting results have been obtained. A good recent survey on credit scoring and behavioral scoring is [2].

D.-S. Huang, K. Li, and G.W. Irwin (Eds.): ICIC 2006, LNCS 4113, pp. 403–408, 2006.

However, in the above approaches, it is difficult to say that the performance of one method is consistently better than that of another method in all circumstances, especially for data shortage leading to insufficient estimation. Furthermore, in realistic situation, due to competitive press and privacy, we can only collect few available data about credit risk, making the statistical approaches and intelligent inductive learning algorithm difficult to obtain a consistently good result for credit scoring. In order to improve the performance and overcome data shortage, it is therefore imperative to introduce a new approach to cope with these challenges. In this study, a neural-network based metalearning technique [6] is introduced to solve these problems.

The main motivation of this study is to take full advantage of the flexible mapping capability of neural network and inherent parallelism of metalearning to design a powerful credit scoring system. The rest of this study is organized as follows. In Section 2, a neural-network-based metalearning process is provided in detail. To verify the effectiveness of the proposed metalearning technique, a credit card application approval experiment is performed in Section 3. Finally, Section 4 concludes the paper.

## 2 The Neural-Network-Based Metalearning Process

Metalearning [6], which is defined as learning from learned knowledge, is an emerging technique recently developed to construct a metamodel that deals with the problem of computing a metamodel from data. The basic idea is to use intelligent learning algorithms to extract knowledge from several data sets and then use the knowledge from these individual learning algorithms to create a unified body of knowledge that well represents the entire knowledge about data. Therefore metalearning seeks to compute a metamodel that integrates in some principled fashion the separately learned models to boost overall predictive accuracy.

Broadly speaking, learning is concerned with finding a model $f = f_a[i]$ from a single training set $\{TR_i\}$, while metalearning is concerned with finding a global model or a metamodel $f = f_a$ from several training sets $\{TR_1, TR_2, \ldots, TR_n\}$, each of which has an

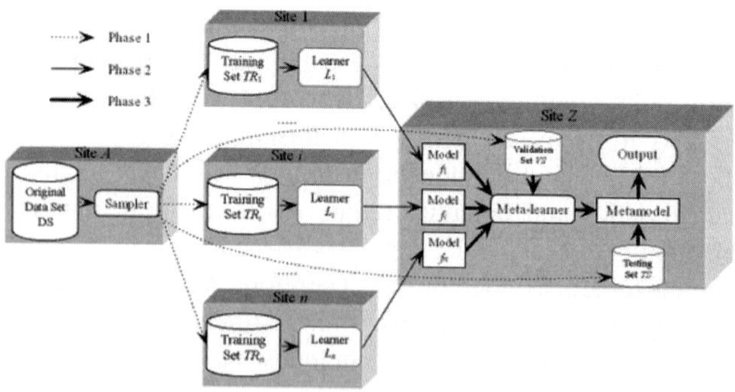


**Fig. 1.** The generic metamodeling process

associated model (i.e., base model) $f = f_a[i]$ ($i$ =1, 2, …, $n$). The $n$ base models derived from the $n$ training sets may be of the same or different types. Similarly, the metamodel may be of a different type than some or all of the component models. Also, the metamodel may use data from a meta-training set (*MT*), which are distinct from the data in the single training set $TR_i$. Generally, the maim process of metalearning is first to generate a number of independent models by applying different learning algorithms to a collection of data sets in parallel. The models computed by learning algorithms are then collected and combined to obtain a metamodel. Fig. 1 shows a generic metalearning process, in which a global model or metamodel is obtained on *Site Z*, starting from the original data set *DS* stored on *Site A*.

As can be seen from Fig. 1, the generic metalearning process consists of three phases, which can be described as follows.

*Phase 1:* on *Site A*, training sets $TR_1$, $TR_2$, …, $TR_n$, validation set *VS* and testing set *TS* are extracted from *DS* with certain sampling algorithm. Then $TR_1$, $TR_2$, …, $TR_n$, *VS* and *TS* are moved from *Site A* to *Site* 1, *Site* 2, …, *Site n* and to *Site Z*.

*Phase 2:* on each *Site i* ($i$ = 1, 2, …, $n$) the different models $f_i$ is trained from $TR_i$ by the different learners $L_i$. Then each $f_i$ is moved from *Site i* to *Site Z*. It is worth noting that the training process of $n$ different models can be implemented in parallel.

*Phase 3:* on *Site Z*, the $f_1$, $f_2$, …, $f_n$ models are combined and validated on *VS* and tested on *TS* by the meta-learner *ML* to produce a metamodel.

### A. Data set partitioning

Due to limitation of the number of data samples available in credit scoring analysis, some approaches, such as bagging [7] have been used for creating samples due to the feature of its random sampling with replacement. Bagging [7] is a widely used data sampling method in the machine learning. Given that the size of the original data set *DS* is *P*, the size of new training data is *N*, and the number of new training data items is *m*, the bagging sampling algorithm can be shown in Fig. 2.

```
Input: original data set DS
Output: The generated new training subsets {TR1, TR2, ..., TRm}
For t = 1 to m
  For i = 1 to N
    RandRow = P * rand ()
    If RandRow <= P
      Pt(i, AllColumns) = DS(RandRow, AllColumns)
    End If
  Next i
Next t
Output the final training subsets {TR1, TR2, ..., TRm}
```

**Fig. 2.** The bagging algorithm

### B. Individual model creation

According to the principle of bias-variance trade-off [9], a metamodel consisting of diverse models (i.e., base models) with much disagreement is more likely to have a good performance. Therefore, how to create the diverse model is the key path to the creation of an effective metamodel. For neural network model, there are several methods for generating diverse models: (1) Initializing different starting weights for each neural network models; (2) Using different training subsets for training each neural network models; (3) Varying the architecture of neural network; and (4) Using different training algorithms. In this study, the single neural network models with different training subsets are therefore used as base learner $L_1$, $L_2$, …, $L_n$, as illustrated in Fig. 1. Through training, base models $f_1$, $f_2$, …, $f_n$ can be formulated in a parallel way.

***C. Neural-network-based metamodel generation***

As Fig. 1 illustrated, the initial data set is first divided into subsets, and then these subsets are input to the different individual neural models which could be executed concurrently. These individual models are called "base models'. In this phase, the main task is to generate a metamodel to assimilate knowledge from different base models. Intuitively, the majority voting can produce a metamodel. But majority voting ignores the fact that some models that lie in a minority sometimes do produce the correct results. In metalearning, it ignores the existence of diversity that can reduce error variance. In this study, another single neural network model different from base neural network model is used to perform this task to generate a metamodel.

Concretely speaking, the base models can be generated based upon different training subsets in previous phase. Using the validation set *VS* and testing set *TS*, the performance of the base models can be assessed. Afterwards, the whole validation set *VS* is applied to these base models and corresponding results produced by these base models are used as input of another individual neural network model. By validation, a metamodel can be generated using the results generated by the base model as input, combined with their expected values. In this sense, neural network learning algorithm is used as a meta-learner (*ML*) shown in Fig. 1 for metamodel generation.

## 3 Experimental Analysis

The research data is about Japanese credit card application approval obtained from UCI Machine Learning Repository (http://www.ics.uci.edu/~mlearn/). For confidentiality all attribute names and values have been changed to meaningless symbols. After deleting the data with missing attribute values, we obtain 653 data, with 357 cases were granted credit and 296 cases were refused. To delete the burden of resolving multi-category, we use the 13 attributes A1-A5, A8-A15. Because we generally should substitute *k*-class attribute with *k*-1 binary attribute, which will greatly increase the dimensions of input space, we don't use two attributes: A6 and A7.

In this empirical analysis, we randomly draw 400 data from the 653 data as the initial training set, 100 data as the validation set and the else as the testing set. In order to increase model accuracy for credit scoring, ten different training subsets are generated by bagging algorithm. Using these different training subsets, different neural network base models with different initial weights are presented. For neural network base models, a three-layer back-propagation neural network with 10 TANSIG neurons in the hidden layer and one PURELIN neuron in the output layer is used. The network training function is the TRAINLM. For the neural-network-based metamodel, a similar three-layer back-propagation neural network with 10 inputs neurons, 8 TANSIG neural in the second layer and one PURELIN neuron in the final layer is adopted for metamodel generation. Besides, the learning rate and momentum rate is set to 0.1 and 0.15. The accepted average squared error is 0.05 and the training epochs are 1600. The above parameters are obtained by trial and error.

For comparison, several typical credit scoring models, linear discriminant analysis (LDA), logit analysis, individual ANN and SVM, are selected as benchmark models. In addition, majority voting based metamodel is also adopted for further comparison. In the ANN model, a three-layer back-propagation neural network with 13 input nodes, 15 hidden nodes and 1 output nodes is used. The hidden nodes use sigmoid transfer function and the output node uses the linear transfer function. In the SVM, the kernel function is Gaussian function with regularization parameter $C$ = 50 and $\sigma^2$=5. Similarly, the above parameters are obtained by trial and error. The classification accuracy (i.e., Type I accuracy and Type II accuracy [1]) in testing set is used as performance evaluation criterion. To overcome the bias of individual models, such a test is repeated ten times and the final Type I and Type II accuracy is the average of the results of the ten individual tests. The computational results are shown in Table 1.

**Table 1.** The prediction performance comparison results

| Model | Type I (%) | Type II (%) |
|---|---|---|
| Linear discriminant analysis | 79.79 | 81.05 |
| Logit regression analysis | 84.17 | 83.11 |
| Single artificial neural network | 81.34 | 83.78 |
| Single support vector machine | 80.58 | 82.36 |
| Majority-voting-based metamodel | 83.41 | 85.16 |
| Neural-Network-based metamodel | 89.56 | 91.19 |

As can be seen from Table 1, we can find the following conclusions. (1) For type I accuracy and Type II accuracy, the neural network based metamodel and the majority voting based metamodel outperforms the single credit scoring model, implying the strong capability of metamodel in credit scoring. (2) In the two metamodels, the performance of the neural-network-based metamodel is much better than that of the majority-voting-based metamodel. The main reason is that neural network has a flexible nonlinear learning capability that can capture subtle relationships between diverse base models. Inversely, the majority voting often ignores the existence of diversity of different base models, as earlier mentioned. (3) In the four individual models, the logit analysis surprisedly outperforms the linear discriminant analysis, the best artificial neural network and the best support vector machine from the view of Type I. For Type II, the artificial neural network is the best of the four individual models. For this example, Type II classification is more important than Type I classification. If a bad customer is classified as a good customer, it may lead to direct economic loss. In this sense, artificial neural network model is very promising approach to credit scoring. (4) Generally, the proposed neural-network-based metamodel perform the best in terms of both Type I accuracy and Type II accuracy, implying that the proposed neural network metalearning technique is a feasible solution to credit scoring.

## 4 Conclusions

In this study, a neural-network-based metalearning technique is proposed to solve the credit scoring with limit data. Through the practical data experiment, we have obtained good classification results and meantime demonstrated that the neural-network-based metamodel outperforms all the benchmark models listed in this study. These advantages imply that the proposed neural-network-based metalearning technique can be used a promising solution to credit scoring. Of course, this neural network metalearning method is also extended to other application areas.

## Acknowledgements

This work is partially supported by National Natural Science Foundation of China (NSFC); Chinese Academy of Sciences (CAS) and Strategic Research Grant of City University of Hong Kong (SRG No. 7001677).

## References

1. Lai, K.K., Yu, L., Zhou, L.G., Wang, S.Y.: Credit Risk Evaluation with Least Square Support Vector Machine. Lecture Notes in Computer Science. (2006)
2. Thomas, L.C.: A Survey of Credit and Behavioral Scoring: Forecasting Financial Risk of Lending to Consumers. International Journal of Forecasting .16 (2002) 149-172
3. Fisher, R.A.: The Use of Multiple Measurements in Taxonomic Problems. Annals of Eugenics. 7 (1936) 179-188
4. Wiginton, J.C.: A Note on the Comparison of Logit and Discriminant Models of Consumer Credit Behaviour. Journal of Financial Quantitative Analysis. 15 (1980) 757-770
5. Malhotra, R., Malhotra, D.K.: Evaluating Consumer Loans Using Neural Networks. Omega 31 (2003) 83-96
6. Chan, P., Stolfo, S.: Meta-Learning for Multistrategy and Parallel Learning. Proceedings of the Second International Workshop on Multistrategy Learning (1993) 150–165
7. Breiman, L.: Bagging Predictors. Machine Learning. 26 (1996) 123-140
8. Lai, K.K., Yu, L., Wang, S.Y., Huang, W.: A Bias-Variance-Complexity Trade-off Framework for Complex System Modeling. Lecture Notes in Computer Science. 3980 (2006) 518-527

# New Results for Global Exponential Stability of Delayed Cohen-Grossberg Neural Networks

Anhua Wan[1], Hong Qiao[1], Bo Zhang[2], and Weihua Mao[3,4]

[1] Institute of Automation, Chinese Academy of Sciences,
100080 Beijing, China
{anhua.wan, hong.qiao}@ia.ac.cn

[2] Institute of Applied Mathematics, Chinese Academy of Sciences,
100080 Beijing, China
b.zhang@amt.ac.cn

[3] College of Automation Science and Engineering,
South China University of Technology, 510641 Guangzhou, China

[4] College of Science, South China Agricultural University,
510642 Guangzhou, China
vhmao@163.com

**Abstract.** The exponential stability is discussed for Cohen-Grossberg neural networks with discrete delays. Without assuming the boundedness, differentiability and monotonicity of the activation functions, the nonlinear measure approach is employed to analyze the existence and uniqueness of an equilibrium, and a novel Lyapunov functional is constructed to investigate the exponential stability of the networks. New general sufficient conditions, which are independent of the delays, are derived for the global exponential stability of the delayed neural networks.

## 1 Introduction

Cohen-Grossberg neural networks model was initially suggested in the pioneering work of Cohen and Grossberg [2]. The model includes a large number of models from neurobiology, population biology and evolutionary theory([4]), among which is the popular Hopfield-type neural networks model([10]). Meanwhile, the model has extensive applications in many areas such as classification, associative memory and optimization problems([4]). Therefore, Cohen-Grossberg neural networks have attracted more and more extensive interest(see, for example, [1,5,13,14,15,17] and references therein).

Due to the finite switching speed of neurons and amplifiers, time delays inevitably exist in biological and artificial neural networks([1,6,8,11]). In this paper, we address Cohen-Grossberg neural networks with discrete delays described by the following difference-differential equations

$$\frac{\mathrm{d}}{\mathrm{d}t}u_i(t) = -a_i(u_i(t))\Big[b_i(u_i(t)) - \sum_{j=1}^{n} w_{ij} f_j(u_j(t-\tau_{ij})) + I_i\Big],\ i = 1, 2, \ldots, n, \quad (1)$$

D.-S. Huang, K. Li, and G.W. Irwin (Eds.): ICIC 2006, LNCS 4113, pp. 409–415, 2006.

where $n \geq 2$ is the number of neurons in the networks, $u_i(t)$ denotes the neuron state vector, $a_i$ denotes an amplification function, $b_i$ denotes a self-signal function, $W = (w_{ij})$ denotes the $n \times n$ connection weight matrix, $f_j$ denotes the activation function, $\tau_{ij} \geq 0$ denotes the delay caused during the switching and transmission processes, and $I_i$ represents the constant external input.

The initial conditions associated with system (1) are of the following form

$$u_i(s) = \phi_i(s) \in C\left([t_0 - \tau, t_0], R\right), \; s \in [t_0 - \tau, t_0], \; i = 1, 2, \ldots, n, \tag{2}$$

where $\tau = \max\limits_{1 \leq i,j \leq n} \{\tau_{ij}\}$ and $C([t_0 - \tau, t_0], R)$ denotes the set of all continuous real-valued functions on $[t_0 - \tau, t_0]$.

As is well known, the stability of neural networks is of crucial importance for the designing and successful applications of networks, and the exponential stability gives a fast convergence rate to the equilibrium([9]). This paper aims to present new sufficient conditions for the exponential stability of delayed neural networks (1), which are milder and more general than those existing ones. In this paper, we only make the following assumptions:

($A_1$) For $i = 1, 2, \ldots, n$, $a_i(\cdot)$ is continuous, and there exist two positive constants $\grave{\alpha}_i$ and $\acute{\alpha}_i$ such that $\grave{\alpha}_i \leq a_i(r) \leq \acute{\alpha}_i$, $\forall r \in R$.

($A_2$) For $i = 1, 2, \ldots, n$, $b_i(\cdot)$ is continuous, and there exists a constant $\lambda_i > 0$ such that for any $r_1, r_2 \in R$, $(r_1 - r_2)\big[b_i(r_1) - b_i(r_2)\big] \geq \lambda_i (r_1 - r_2)^2$.

($A_3$) For $i = 1, 2, \ldots, n$, $f_i(\cdot)$ is Lipschitz continuous. For convenience, we denote $m_i = \sup\limits_{r_1, r_2 \in R, r_1 \neq r_2} \frac{|f_i(r_1) - f_i(r_2)|}{|r_1 - r_2|}$ the minimal Lipschitz constant of $f_i$.

Generally speaking, nonmonotonic activation functions might be better candidates for neuron activation in designing and implementing an artificial neural networks, and the boundedness assumption on activation functions makes the results inapplicable to some important engineering problems([3,7]). Note that we make neither boundedness assumption nor monotonicity or differentiability assumption on $f_i$. In addition, we do not impose any restriction on the matrix $W$, abandoning the usual symmetry assumption. As a consequence, a fairly broader connection topology for the networks is allowed.

## 2 Preliminaries

Let $R^n$ be the $n$-dimensional real vector space with vector norm $\|\cdot\|$. Here, we will always use the $l^2$-norm, that is, for each vector $x = (x_1, x_2, \ldots, x_n)^T \in R^n$, $\|x\|_2 = \left(\sum_{i=1}^n x_i^2\right)^{1/2}$. Let $\langle \cdot, \cdot \rangle$ denote the inner product of any two vectors, and for any two operators $F$ and $G$, $FG(x) = F(G(x))$, $\forall x \in D(G)$.

Let $\Omega$ be an open subset of $R^n$, $F$ is an operator from $\Omega$ to $R^n$ and $x(t) \in \Omega$. Consider the following system

$$\frac{\mathrm{d}x(t)}{\mathrm{d}t} = F(x(t)), \quad t \geq t_0, \tag{3}$$

**Definition 1.** ([12]) *Suppose that $\Omega$ is an open subset of $R^n$, and $F$ is an operator from $\Omega$ to $R^n$. The constant*

$$m_\Omega(F) = \sup_{x,y\in\Omega, x\neq y} \frac{\langle F(x)-F(y), x-y\rangle}{\|x-y\|_2^2} \tag{4}$$

*is called the nonlinear measure of $F$ on $\Omega$.*

The following lemma indicates that the nonlinear measure (4) can exactly characterize the existence and uniqueness of equilibrium of nonlinear systems.

**Lemma 1.** ([12]) *If $m_\Omega(F) < 0$, then $F$ is a one-to-one mapping on $\Omega$. Moreover, if $\Omega = R^n$, then $F$ is a homeomorphism of $R^n$.*

## 3 Global Exponential Stability of Neural Networks (1)

**Theorem 1.** *Suppose that $(A_1), (A_2), (A_3)$ hold. If there exist six sets of real numbers $e_i > 0$, $l_i > 0$, $r_i > 0$, $\eta_i > 0$, $k_i$ and $d_i$ such that*

$$\sum_{j=1}^{n}\left\{\frac{e_j r_j}{e_i\eta_i}|w_{ji}|^{\frac{k_j}{d_i}} + \frac{l_j\eta_j}{l_i r_i}|w_{ij}|^{2-\frac{k_i}{d_j}}\right\} < \frac{2\lambda_i}{m_i}, \quad i=1,2,\ldots,n, \tag{5}$$

*then for each set of external input $I_i$, (1) has a unique equilibrium point $u^*$.*

*Proof.* Define an operator $G: R^n \to R^n$ by $G(x) = \big(G_1(x), G_2(x), \ldots, G_n(x)\big)^T$, $\forall x \in R^n$, where $G_i(x) = -\big[b_i(x_i) - \sum_{j=1}^{n} w_{ij} f_j(x_j) + J_i\big]$, $i = 1, 2, \ldots, n$. Consider the following system

$$\frac{\mathrm{d}x(t)}{\mathrm{d}t} = G(x(t)), \quad t \geq t_0. \tag{6}$$

It is clear that (1) and (6) have the same equilibrium. Let $Q = \mathrm{diag}(e_1, e_2, \ldots, e_n)$ and $P = \mathrm{diag}(\frac{e_1 l_1}{m_1}, \frac{e_2 l_2}{m_2}, \ldots, \frac{e_n l_n}{m_n})$. Consider the following system

$$\frac{\mathrm{d}y(t)}{\mathrm{d}t} = P^{-1}QGQ^{-1}P\big(y(t)\big), \quad t \geq t_0. \tag{7}$$

Note that $y^*$ is the unique equilibrium point of system (7) if and only if $y^*$ is the unique solution of $P^{-1}QGQ^{-1}P(y) = 0$, which is equivalent to $QGQ^{-1}P(y) = 0$.

We have

$$\begin{aligned}
&\langle QGQ^{-1}Py - QGQ^{-1}Pz, y-z\rangle \\
&= \sum_{i=1}^{n}\Big\{-e_i\{b_i(\tfrac{l_i}{m_i}y_i) - b_i(\tfrac{l_i}{m_i}z_i) - \sum_{j=1}^{n} w_{ij}\,[f_j(\tfrac{l_j}{m_j}y_j) - f_j(\tfrac{l_j}{m_j}z_j)]\}(y_i - z_i)\Big\} \\
&\leq \sum_{i=1}^{n}\Big\{-\tfrac{\lambda_i}{m_i}e_i l_i (y_i - z_i)^2 + \sum_{j=1}^{n}\big(e_i l_j |w_{ij}||y_j - z_j||y_i - z_i|\big)\Big\} \\
&\leq -\sum_{i=1}^{n}\tfrac{\lambda_i}{m_i}e_i l_i (y_i - z_i)^2 + \sum_{i=1}^{n}\sum_{j=1}^{n}\Big\{\tfrac{e_i l_j}{2}\Big[\tfrac{r_i}{\eta_j}|w_{ij}|^{\frac{k_i}{d_j}}(y_j - z_j)^2 + \tfrac{\eta_j}{r_i}|w_{ij}|^{2-\frac{k_i}{d_j}}(y_i - z_i)^2\Big]\Big\} \\
&= -\sum_{i=1}^{n}\tfrac{1}{2}e_i l_i\Big\{\tfrac{2\lambda_i}{m_i} - \sum_{j=1}^{n}\tfrac{e_j r_j}{e_i\eta_i}|w_{ji}|^{\frac{k_j}{d_i}} - \sum_{j=1}^{n}\tfrac{l_j\eta_j}{l_i r_i}|w_{ij}|^{2-\frac{k_i}{d_j}}\Big\}(y_i - z_i)^2.
\end{aligned}$$

In view of (5), we derive

$$m_{R^n}(QGQ^{-1}P) \leq -\min_{1\leq i\leq n}\left\{\frac{e_i l_i}{2}\left[\frac{2\lambda_i}{m_i} - \sum_{j=1}^{n}\left(\frac{e_j r_j}{e_i \eta_i}|w_{ji}|^{\frac{k_j}{d_i}} + \frac{l_j \eta_j}{l_i r_i}|w_{ij}|^{2-\frac{k_i}{d_j}}\right)\right]\right\} < 0.$$

By virtue of Lemma 1, we deduce that $QGQ^{-1}P$ is a homeomorphism, thus we conclude that $QGQ^{-1}P(y) = 0$ has a unique solution $y^*$, and therefore (7) has a unique equilibrium point $y^*$. Note that $y(t) = P^{-1}Qx(t)$ is the unique solution of (7) whenever $x(t)$ is a solution of (6), and thus (6) has a unique equilibrium point $x^* = Q^{-1}Py^*$, therefore, system (1) has a unique equilibrium point $u^*$.

*Remark 1.* Theorem 1 presents new general sufficient conditions for the existence and uniqueness of an equilibrium of (1). Wang et al [13] also proved the existence of an equilibrium of (1), but each $f_i$ was additionally assumed to be bounded.

**Theorem 2.** *Suppose that* $(A_1), (A_2), (A_3)$ *hold and there exist five sets of real numbers* $d_i > 0$, $e_i > 0$, $r_i > 0$, $k_i$ *and* $l_i$ *such that*

$$\sum_{j=1}^{n}\left(\frac{m_j e_j}{m_i r_i}|w_{ij}|^{2-\frac{k_i}{l_j}} + \frac{d_j r_j}{d_i e_i}|w_{ji}|^{\frac{k_j}{l_i}}\right) < \frac{2\lambda_i}{m_i}, \quad i = 1, 2, \ldots, n. \tag{8}$$

*Then for each set of external input* $I_i$, *system (1) has a unique equilibrium* $u^*$ *which is globally exponentially stable, and there exists a constant* $\sigma > 0$ *such that the exponential decay estimate of any solution satisfies*

$$\|u(t) - u^*\|_2 \leq \sqrt{c}e^{-\sigma(t-t_0)} \sup_{s\in[t_0-\tau, t_0]} \|\phi(s) - u^*\|_2, \quad t \geq t_0, \tag{9}$$

*where* $c = \max_{1\leq i\leq n}\left\{\frac{d_i}{\dot{\alpha}_i}\left(1 + \frac{\dot{\alpha}_i}{2\sigma}\sum_{j=1}^{n}\frac{r_i}{e_j}m_j|w_{ij}|^{2-\frac{k_i}{l_j}}\left(1 - e^{-2\sigma\tau_{ij}}\right)\right)\right\} \Big/ \min_{1\leq i\leq n}\left(\frac{d_i}{\acute{\alpha}_i}\right)$.

*Proof.* Condition (8) implies (5) holds, and thus it follows from Theorem 1 that (1) has a unique equilibrium $u^*$. Substitution of $x(t) = u(t) - u^*$ into (1) yields

$$\begin{aligned}\frac{dx_i(t)}{dt} &= -a_i(x_i(t) + u_i^*)\Big\{b_i(x_i(t) + u_i^*) - b_i(u_i^*) \\ &\quad - \textstyle\sum_{j=1}^{n} w_{ij}\left(f_j(x_j(t) + u_j^*) - f_j(u_j^*)\right)\Big\}, \quad i = 1, 2, \ldots, n.\end{aligned} \tag{10}$$

Let $p_i(x_i(t)) = a_i(x_i(t) + u_i^*)$, $q_i(x_i(t)) = b_i(x_i(t) + u_i^*) - b_i(u_i^*)$ and $s_j(x_j(t)) = f_j(x_j(t) + u_j^*) - f_j(u_j^*)$. Then system (10) reduces to

$$\frac{dx_i(t)}{dt} = -p_i(x_i(t))\Big\{q_i(x_i(t)) - \sum_{j=1}^{n} w_{ij}s_j(x_j(t - \tau_{ij}))\Big\}, \quad i = 1, 2, \ldots, n. \tag{11}$$

It is clear that 0 is an equilibrium of system (11).

It follows from (8) that for any fixed $\tau_{ij} \geq 0$, we can find a $\sigma > 0$ such that

$$\frac{2\lambda_i}{m_i} - \frac{2\sigma}{m_i\dot{\alpha}_i} - \sum_{j=1}^{n}\left(\frac{m_j e_j}{m_i r_i}|w_{ij}|^{2-\frac{k_i}{l_j}}e^{2\sigma\tau_{ij}} + \frac{d_j r_j}{d_i e_i}|w_{ji}|^{\frac{k_j}{l_i}}\right) > 0. \tag{12}$$

We construct the following Lyapunov functional

$$V(x(t)) = \sum_{i=1}^{n} d_i \Big\{ 2e^{2\sigma t} \int_0^{x_i(t)} \frac{s}{p_i(s)} \mathrm{d}s + \sum_{j=1}^{n} \frac{r_i m_j}{e_j} |w_{ij}|^{\frac{k_i}{l_j}} \int_{t-\tau_{ij}}^{t} e^{2\sigma s} x_j^2(s) \mathrm{d}s \Big\}. \tag{13}$$

We deduce

$$\begin{aligned}
&\frac{\mathrm{d}V(x(t))}{\mathrm{d}t} \\
&= -\sum_{i=1}^{n} 2d_i e^{2\sigma t} x_i(t) \Big\{ q_i(x_i(t)) - \sum_{j=1}^{n} w_{ij} s_j\left(x_j(t-\tau_{ij})\right) \Big\} + \sum_{i=1}^{n} 4d_i \sigma e^{2\sigma t} \int_0^{x_i(t)} \tfrac{s}{p_i(s)} \mathrm{d}s \\
&\quad + \sum_{i=1}^{n}\sum_{j=1}^{n} \tfrac{d_i r_i m_j}{e_j} |w_{ij}|^{\frac{k_i}{l_j}} e^{2\sigma t} x_j^2(t) - \sum_{i=1}^{n}\sum_{j=1}^{n} \tfrac{d_i r_i m_j}{e_j} |w_{ij}|^{\frac{k_i}{l_j}} e^{2\sigma(t-\tau_{ij})} x_j^2(t-\tau_{ij}) \\
&\le e^{2\sigma t} \Big\{ -2\sum_{i=1}^{n} d_i \lambda_i x_i^2(t) + 2\sum_{i=1}^{n}\sum_{j=1}^{n} d_i m_j |w_{ij}| |x_i(t)| |x_j(t-\tau_{ij})| + \sum_{i=1}^{n} \tfrac{2d_i\sigma}{\grave{\alpha}_i} x_i^2(t) \\
&\quad + \sum_{i=1}^{n}\sum_{j=1}^{n} \tfrac{d_i r_i m_j}{e_j} |w_{ij}|^{\frac{k_i}{l_j}} x_j^2(t) - \sum_{i=1}^{n}\sum_{j=1}^{n} \tfrac{d_i r_i m_j}{e_j} |w_{ij}|^{\frac{k_i}{l_j}} e^{-2\sigma\tau_{ij}} x_j^2(t-\tau_{ij}) \Big\} \\
&\le e^{2\sigma t} \Big\{ -2\sum_{i=1}^{n} d_i \lambda_i x_i^2(t) + \sum_{i=1}^{n}\sum_{j=1}^{n} d_i m_j \big[ \tfrac{e_j}{r_i} e^{2\sigma\tau_{ij}} |w_{ij}|^{2-\frac{k_i}{l_j}} x_i^2(t) \\
&\quad + \tfrac{r_i}{e_j} e^{-2\sigma\tau_{ij}} |w_{ij}|^{\frac{k_i}{l_j}} x_j^2(t-\tau_{ij}) \big] + \sum_{i=1}^{n} \tfrac{2d_i\sigma}{\grave{\alpha}_i} x_i^2(t) \\
&\quad + \sum_{i=1}^{n}\sum_{j=1}^{n} \tfrac{d_i r_i m_j}{e_j} |w_{ij}|^{\frac{k_i}{l_j}} x_j^2(t) - \sum_{i=1}^{n}\sum_{j=1}^{n} \tfrac{d_i r_i m_j}{e_j} |w_{ij}|^{\frac{k_i}{l_j}} e^{-2\sigma\tau_{ij}} x_j^2(t-\tau_{ij}) \Big\} \\
&= -e^{2\sigma t} \sum_{i=1}^{n} d_i m_i \Big\{ \tfrac{2\lambda_i}{m_i} - \tfrac{2\sigma}{m_i \grave{\alpha}_i} - \sum_{j=1}^{n} \big( \tfrac{m_j e_j}{m_i r_i} |w_{ij}|^{2-\frac{k_i}{l_j}} e^{2\sigma\tau_{ij}} + \tfrac{d_j r_j}{d_i e_i} |w_{ji}|^{\frac{k_j}{l_i}} \big) \Big\} x_i^2(t) \\
&\le -\min_{1\le i\le n} d_i m_i \Big\{ \tfrac{2\lambda_i}{m_i} - \tfrac{2\sigma}{m_i \grave{\alpha}_i} - \sum_{j=1}^{n} \big( \tfrac{m_j e_j}{m_i r_i} |w_{ij}|^{2-\frac{k_i}{l_j}} e^{2\sigma\tau_{ij}} + \tfrac{d_j r_j}{d_i e_i} |w_{ji}|^{\frac{k_j}{l_i}} \big) \Big\} e^{2\sigma t} \|x(t)\|_2^2 < 0.
\end{aligned}$$

Thus, $V(x(t)) \le V(x(t_0))$ for any $t \ge t_0$, and

$$\begin{aligned}
&V(x(t_0)) \\
&= \sum_{i=1}^{n} d_i \Big\{ 2e^{2\sigma t} \int_0^{x_i(t_0)} \frac{s}{p_i(s)} \mathrm{d}s + \sum_{j=1}^{n} \tfrac{r_i m_j}{e_j} |w_{ij}|^{\frac{k_i}{l_j}} \int_{t_0-\tau_{ij}}^{t_0} e^{2\sigma s} x_j^2(s) \mathrm{d}s \Big\} \\
&\le \sum_{i=1}^{n} d_i \Big\{ \tfrac{1}{\grave{\alpha}_i} e^{2\sigma t_0} x_i^2(t_0) + \sum_{j=1}^{n} \tfrac{r_i m_j}{e_j} |w_{ij}|^{\frac{k_i}{l_j}} \sup_{s\in[t_0-\tau,t_0]} x_j^2(s) \int_{t_0-\tau_{ij}}^{t_0} e^{2\sigma s} \mathrm{d}s \Big\} \\
&\le \max_{1\le i\le n} \Big\{ \tfrac{d_i}{\grave{\alpha}_i} \Big( e^{2\sigma t_0} + \grave{\alpha}_i \sum_{j=1}^{n} \tfrac{r_i m_j}{e_j} |w_{ij}|^{\frac{k_i}{l_j}} \tfrac{1}{2\sigma} \big( e^{2\sigma t_0} - e^{2\sigma(t_0-\tau_{ij})} \big) \Big) \Big\} \sup_{s\in[t_0-\tau,t_0]} \sum_{i=1}^{n} x_i^2(s) \\
&= \max_{1\le i\le n} \Big\{ \tfrac{d_i}{\grave{\alpha}_i} \Big( 1 + \tfrac{\grave{\alpha}_i}{2\sigma} \sum_{j=1}^{n} \tfrac{r_i m_j}{e_j} |w_{ij}|^{\frac{k_i}{l_j}} \big( 1 - e^{-2\sigma\tau_{ij}} \big) \Big) \Big\} e^{2\sigma t_0} \sup_{s\in[t_0-\tau,t_0]} \sum_{i=1}^{n} x_i^2(s).
\end{aligned}$$

By (13), we have $\min_{1\le i\le n} \left(\frac{d_i}{\acute{\alpha}_i}\right) e^{2\sigma t} \sum_{i=1}^{n} x_i^2(t) \le V(x(t))$. Therefore, we obtain $\sum_{i=1}^{n} x_i^2(t) \le ce^{-2\sigma(t-t_0)} \sup_{s\in[t_0-\tau,t_0]} \sum_{i=1}^{n} x_i^2(s)$. In view of $x(t) = u(t) - u^*$, we derive that (9) holds. This completes the proof.

*Remark 2.* Theorem 2 provides new sufficient conditions for the exponential stability of the delayed neural networks (1). The adjustable parameters $d_i, e_i, r_i, k_i, l_i$

in (8) endows the criteria with much flexibility and extensive applicability. As long as (8) suffices for some $d_i, e_i, r_i > 0, k_i$ and $l_i$, (1) is globally exponentially stable. This not only makes it possible that many existing criteria can be deduced from our results through specific choice of $d_i, e_i, r_i, k_i, l_i$([3,5,13,16]), but also can yield some new criteria for the exponential stability of (1).

## 4 Conclusions

This paper is concerned with the exponential stability of Cohen-Grossberg neural networks model with discrete delays. Only assuming the activation functions to be globally Lipschitz continuous, we derive new general sufficient conditions for the global exponential stability of the discrete-delayed neural networks (1), which are less restrictive than many existing results.

## References

1. Chen, T.P., Rong, L.B.: Delay-Independent Stability Analysis of Cohen-Grossberg Neural Networks. Physics Letters A **317** (2003) 436–449
2. Cohen, M.A., Grossberg, S.: Absolute Stability and Global Pattern Formation and Partial Memory Storage by Competitive Neural Networks. IEEE Transactions on Systems, Man and Cybernetics **SMC-13** (1983) 815–826
3. van den Driessche, P., Zou, X.: Global Attractivity in Delayed Hopfield Neural Network Models. SIAM J. Appl. Math. **58** (1998) 1878–1890
4. Grossberg, S.: Nonlinear Neural Networks: Principles, Mechanisms, and Architectures. Neural Networks **1** (1988) 17–61
5. Liao, X.F., Li, C.G., Wong, K.W.: Criteria for Exponential Stability of Cohen-Grossberg Neural Networks. Neural Networks **17** (2004) 1401–1414
6. Marcus, C., Westervelt, R.: Stability of Analog Neural Networks with Delay. Physics Review A **39** (1989) 347–359
7. Morita, M.: Associative Memory with Non-monotone Dynamics. Neural Networks **6**(1) (1993) 115–126
8. Peng, J.G., Qiao, H., Xu, Z.B.: A New Approach to Stability of Neural Networks with Time-Varying Delays. Neural Networks **15** (2002) 95–103
9. Qiao, H., Peng, J.G., Xu, Z.B.: Nonlinear Measures: A New Approach to Exponential Stability Analysis for Hopfield-Type Neural Networks. IEEE Transactions on Neural Networks **12**(2) (2001) 360–370
10. Tank, D.W., Hopfield, J. J.: Simple "Neural" Optimization Networks: An A/D Converter, Signal Decision Circuit, and a Linear Programming Circuit. IEEE Transactions on Circuits and Systems **33**(5) (1986) 533–541
11. Wan, A.H., Peng, J.G., Wang, M.S.: Exponential Stability of a Class of Generalized Neural Networks with Time-Varying Delays. Neurocomputing **69**(7-9) (2006) 959–963
12. Wan, A.H., Wang, M.S., Peng, J.G., Qiao, H., Exponential Stability of Cohen-Grossberg Neural Networks with a General Class of Activation Functions. Physics Letters A **350**(1-2) (2006) 96–102

13. Wang, L., Zou, X.F.: Exponential Stability of Cohen-Grossberg Neural Networks. Neural Networks **15** (2002) 415–422
14. Wang, L., Zou, X.F.: Harmless Delays in Cohen-Grossberg Neural Network. Physica D **170**(2) (2002) 162–173
15. Ye, H., Michel, A.N., Wang, K.: Qualitative Analysis of Cohen-Grossberg Neural Networks with Multiple Delays. Physics Review E **51** (1995) 2611–2618
16. Zhang, J.Y., Jin, X.S.: Global Stability Analysis in Delayed Hopfield Neural Network Models. Neural Networks **13** (2000) 745–753
17. Zhou, L., Zhou, M.R.: Stability Analysis of a Class of Generalized Neural Networks with Delays. Physics Letters A **337** (2005) 203–215

# Nonlinear System Identification Based on Delta-Learning Rules

Xin Tan[1] and Yong Wang[2]

[1] School of Communication,
Chongqing University of Posts and Telecommunications,
400065 Chongqing, China
xintan@vip.163.com

[2] Department of Computer, Chongqing Education College,
400067 Chongqing, China
whoiswangyong@sohu.com

**Abstract.** The neural network can be used to identify unknown systems. A novel method based on delta-learning rules to identify the nonlinear system is proposed. First, a single-input-single-output (SISO) discrete-time nonlinear system is introduced, and Gaussian basis functions are used to represent the nonlinear functions of this system. Then the adjustable parameters of Gaussian basis functions are optimized by using delta-learning rules. In the end, simulation results are illustrated to demonstrate the effectiveness of the proposed method.

## 1 Introduction

The system identification is the theory of how mathematical models for dynamical systems are constructed from observed data [1]. In general, a certain linear or nonlinear model structure contains unknown parameters, and the parameters should be computed so that the errors between estimated (or predicted) and actual outputs of the system should be minimized in order to capture the dynamics of the system as close as possible. The resulting model can be used as a tool for analysis, simulation, prediction, monitoring, diagnosis, and control system design [2].

Typically, system identification is much harder for nonlinear models than for linear models because of the choice of model structure. For nonlinear models there are many more alternatives than for linear models, i.e., a nonlinear function can be nonlinear in so many different ways.

Neural network (NN) models, such as Cabor network, etc, have been successfully applied to the identification of the nonlinear systems [3], [4]. However, NN models share some fundamental drawbacks. One drawback is the fact that, in general, they rely on some type of approximation for computing the partial derivative. The other disadvantage is the inability to obtain analytical results concerning the convergence and stability of these schemes [5].

In this paper, we use Hopfield Neural Networks (HNN) to identify nonlinear systems. First, we introduce a nonlinear discrete-time system and Gaussian basis functions (GBFs) [6], [7], [8] is used to replace the nonlinear function of the equivalent nonlinear system. And then, a method using delta-learning rules to find the

D.-S. Huang, K. Li, and G.W. Irwin (Eds.): ICIC 2006, LNCS 4113, pp. 416 – 421, 2006.

optimal set of GBFs coefficients is proposed in section 3. Simulation results are illustrated in section 4. Finally, some conclusions are pointed out in section 5.

## 2 A Nonlinear System and Gaussian Basis Functions

### 2.1 A Nonlinear Discrete-Time System

A single-input-single-output (SISO) discrete-time nonlinear system is suggested. Use of this system is motivated by the fact that corresponding models have been used in the adaptive systems literature [3], [4], [5] for the identification of linear systems and can be considered as generalizations to nonlinear systems. A nonlinear function of the nonlinear system is assumed to be differentiable functions of their arguments. It is further assumed that the nonlinear function can be approximated to the desired degree of accuracy on compact sets. The system can be written as:

$$y(k) = F[y(k-1), y(k-2), \cdots y(k-m)] + G[u(k-1), u(k-2), \cdots u(k-n)] \quad (1)$$

$y(*)$ is the output vector, $u(*)$ is the input vector, where $F(*)$ and $G(*)$ are two nonlinear functions relating the input to the output, $k$ is the current discrete time, and $m$ and $n$ are the orders of the dynamical systems.

### 2.2 Gaussian Basis Functions

In (1), nonlinear functions $F(*)$, $G(*)$ can be represented by projecting them onto a chosen set of GBFs:

$$\varphi_i^X(x) = e^{-\pi\mu[x(k-i)-p]^2} \quad for\ X = f, g \quad (2)$$

Where $\mu$ is a parameter that determines the width of the GBFs. Let the width $\mu = 0.1$, and the GBFs curve is flat, If $\mu$ becomes to 100 then curve is steep-down, $p \in R$ is the center of GBFs, $k$ is the current discrete time, and $i$ denotes the delay time. Thus, the nonlinear functions $F(*)$, $G(*)$ of the nonlinear systems are given by

$$F(\cdot) = \sum_{i=1}^{m} a_i^f \varphi_i^f(\cdot), \qquad G(\cdot) = \sum_{i=1}^{m} a_i^g \varphi_i^g(\cdot) \quad (3)$$

Where $m$ denotes the number of hidden nodes, $a_i^f$ , $a_i^g$ are the unknown parameters to be identified. And in our research, the number of GBFs is 6.

## 3 The Optimization Method Using Delta-Learning Rules

The delta-learning rule is one of the most important historical developments in neural networks. In this paper, the verification method for the discrete-time nonlinear system is different from the traditional method and GBFs are used to replace the nonlinear functions of the equivalent nonlinear system. Delta-learning rules are used to identify the optimization parameters of GBFs. These weights of the HNN are adjusted using the gradient descent approximation method. For obtaining a good performance in identification of nonlinear systems, the delta-learning rule performs some methods for adjusting weights of Hopfield neural networks and parameters of Gaussian basis functions, and ensuring stability of the trained networks. First, the mean-square-error function (MSE), which measures the system performance, is defined. Second, for the derivative of MSE with respect to the GBFs coefficient $a_i$, we apply the gradient-descent to obtain the GBFs coefficients. Thirdly, the above process produces weight matrix, the bias input vector and coefficient matrix. These matrixes are used to train parameters in the neural network. So, given a training set of data pattern, the delta-learning rule provides a procedure for changing the weights, thresholds and GBFs coefficients in a Hopfield neural network. These weight change are performed for a single training pattern, called a learning step. After a learning step is finished, the next training pattern is submitted and the learning step is repeated. The learning steps proceed until all the patterns in the training set have been exhausted. The complete learning cycle is terminated and known as one epoch. The cumulative cycle error is computed for the complete learning cycle and then compared with the maximum error allowed. If the total error is not satisfied, a new learning cycle is needed.

The nonlinear functions $F(*)$, $G(*)$ can be represented by projecting them onto a chosen set of GBFs in (3). So, the nonlinear discrete-time system is represented by

$$y(k)=\sum_i a_i^y \varphi_i^y\left(y(k-i)\right)+\sum_j a_j^u \varphi_j^u\left(u(k-j)\right) \quad (4)$$

Where $F(*)$ and $G(*)$ are nonlinear functions, $\left[a_i^y, a_j^u\right]$ is a set of adjustable coefficients, where $i=1,\ldots,m$, $j=1,\ldots,n$ and the GBFs, $\varphi_i^y$ and $\varphi_j^u$, are given in (2). We assume that the desired output is $y_d(k)$ and the network output is $y_l(k)$, where $l$ denotes the current learning iteration. The error function of the $l$ th iteration is shown as

$$e_l(k)=y_d(k)-y_l(k)=y_d(k)-\left[\sum_i a_i^y(l)\varphi_i^y\left(y(k-i)\right)+\sum_j a_j^u(l)\varphi_j^u\left(u(k-j)\right)\right] \quad (5)$$

For system identification, the mean-square-error (MSE) is given by

$$MSE=1/n\sum_{k=1}^{n}\left[e_l(k)\right]^2 \quad (6)$$

Theoretically, the minimum mean-square-error (MSE) function (6) along with the optimal coefficients $\left[a_i^y, a_j^u\right]$ and the optimal basis function can be obtained by use of the following delta-learning rule. The derivative of MSE with respect to $a_i$ and $a_j$ can be given by

$$\begin{cases} \Delta a_i^y(l)=\delta MSE/\delta a_i^y(l)=\sum_v a_v^y(l)w_{yvyi}+\sum_j a_j^u(l)w_{ujyi}+I_{yi} \\ \Delta a_j^u(l)=\delta MSE/\delta a_j^u(l)=\sum_i a_i^y(l)w_{yiuj}+\sum_q a_q^u(l)w_{uquj}+I_{uj} \end{cases} \quad (7)$$

The coefficient matrix becomes

$$\begin{bmatrix} a_i^y(l+1) \\ a_j^u(l+1) \end{bmatrix} = \begin{bmatrix} a_i^y(l) \\ a_j^u(l) \end{bmatrix} - \eta \begin{bmatrix} \Delta a_i^y(l) \\ \Delta a_j^u(l) \end{bmatrix} = \begin{bmatrix} a_i^y(l) \\ a_j^u(l) \end{bmatrix} - \eta \left\{ \sum_{ivjq} \begin{bmatrix} w_{yvyi} & w_{ujyi} \\ w_{yiuj} & w_{uquj} \end{bmatrix} \begin{bmatrix} a_i^y(l) \\ a_j^u(l) \end{bmatrix} + \begin{bmatrix} I_{yi} \\ I_{uj} \end{bmatrix} \right\} \quad (8)$$

Then (8) can be written by

$$A(l+1) = A(l) - \eta\left(\sum WA(l) + I(l)\right) = A(l) - \eta \Delta A(l) \quad (9)$$

Where $\eta$ is the learning rate, $W$ and $I$ of (9) are given by

$$\begin{aligned} w_{yvyi} &= 2/N \sum_{k=1}^{N} \varphi_v^y\left(y(k-v)\right)\varphi_i^y\left(y(k-i)\right),\ w_{ujyi} = 2/N \sum_{k=1}^{N} \varphi_j^u\left(y(k-j)\right)\varphi_i^y\left(y(k-i)\right) \\ w_{yiuj} &= 2/N \sum_{k=1}^{N} \varphi_i^y\left(y(k-i)\right)\varphi_j^u\left(u(k-j)\right),\ w_{uquj} = 2/N \sum_{k=1}^{N} \varphi_q^u\left(u(k-q)\right)\varphi_j^u\left(u(k-j)\right) \\ I_{yi} &= -2/N \sum_{k=1}^{N} y_d(k)\varphi_i^y\left(y(k-i)\right), \quad I_{uj} = -2/N \sum_{k=1}^{N} y_d(k)\varphi_j^u\left(u(k-j)\right) \end{aligned} \quad (10)$$

Where $W$ is the weight matrix, $I$ is the bias input vector, and $A$ is coefficient matrix.

## 4 Simulation Results

For the simulation, we use the model in (1) to show the effectiveness of the proposed identification method, and compare the proposed method with the traditional method. The HNN is a GBFs network with 6 GBFs $\varphi_i^y(\cdot)$ and 6 GBFs $\varphi_i^u(\cdot)$. The learning rates

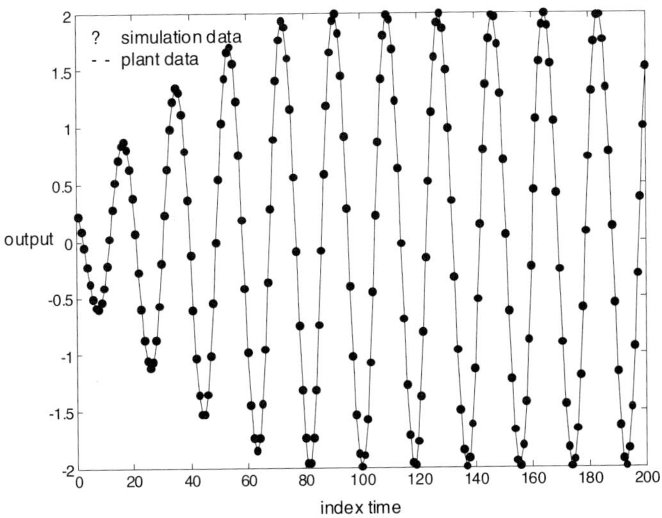


**Fig. 1.** Simulation results of identification output and plant output

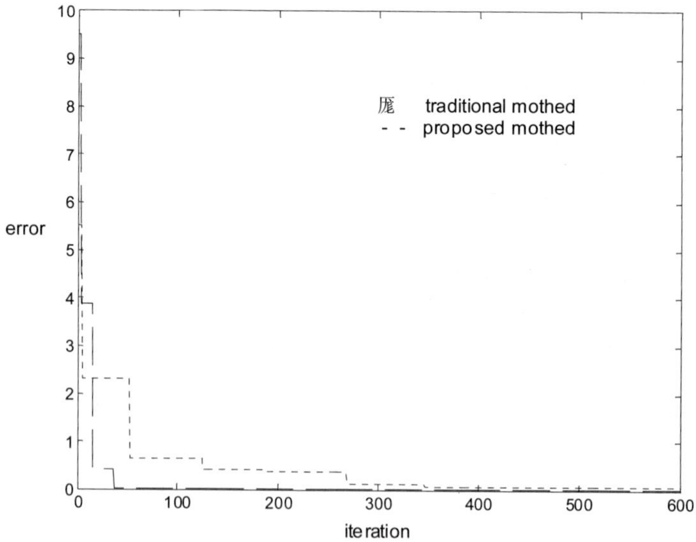


**Fig. 2.** Comparison of the proposed method and the traditional method. Two error curves obviously show that the proposed method converges faster than the traditional method.

are set to be $\eta = 0.01$. The initial values of coefficients $a_i^y(0), a_j^u(0)$ are 0.1. The condition of computation termination is the error $|y_l(k) - y_{l+1}(k)| < 0.00001$, or the error does not change for 5 iterations of learning. Fig.1 shows the outputs of the plant and the identification model.

For comparison purpose, we define the error as $error(k) = y_d(k) - y(k)$, where $y_d(k)$ is the desired plant output, and $y(k)$ is the approximated output. Two error curves using the proposed method and the traditional Hopfield neural network method respectively are shown in Fig.2.

## 5 Conclusions

In this paper, applications of Gaussian-Hopfield neural networks in the identification of nonlinear systems are studied. We introduce a nonlinear discrete-time system and Gaussian basis functions (GBFs) are used to represent its nonlinear functions, then, we apply delta-learning rules for Gaussian-Hopfield neural networks to optimize the set of GBFs coefficients. The simulation results show that the proposed method can be successfully used to identify nonlinear systems with good accuracy of approximation.

## References

1. Ljung, L.: System Identification: Theory for The User, 2nd ed. Prentice-Hall, Englewood Cliffs (1999)
2. Barreto, G.A., Araujo, A.F.R.: Identification and Control of Dynamical Systems Using the Self-Organizing Map. IEEE Trans. on Neural Networks, Vol.15 (2004) 1244–1259

3. Chu, S.R., Shoureshi, R., Tenorio, M.: Neural Networks for System Identification. Proc. 1989Amer. Contr. Conf (1989) 31–35
4. Zhang, C.Q., Fadali, M.S.: Nonlinear System Identification Using a Gabor/Hopfield Network. IEEE Trans. on Systems, Man, and Cybernetics, Vol.26 (1996) 124–134
5. Kosmatopoulos, E.B., Ioannou, P.A., Christodoulou, M.A.: Identification of Nonlinear Systems Using New Dynamic Neural Network Structures. Proc. IEEE Intl. Conf. on Decision and Control, Arizona (1992) 20–25
6. Elramsisi, A.M., Zohdy, M.A., Loh, N.K.: A Joint Frequency-Position Domain Structure Identification of Nonlinear Discrete-time Systems by Neural Networks. IEEE Trans. on Automatic Control, Vol.36(1991) 629–632
7. Jenison, R.L., Fissell, K.: A Comparison of the Von Mises and Gaussian Basis Functions for Approximating Spherical Acoustic Scatter. IEEE Trans. on Neural Networks, Vol.6 (1995) 1284–1287
8. Li, L.X., Fei, M.R., Yang, T.C.: Gaussian-Basis-Function Neural Network Control System with Network-Induced Delays. Proc. IEEE Intl. Conf. on Machine Learning and Cybernetics, Vol. 3 (2002) 1533–1536

# Optical Sensing, Logic and Computations in Brillouin-Active Fiber Based Neural Network in Smart Structures

Yong-Kab Kim[1], Do Geun Huh[1], Kwan-Woong Kim[1], and ChangKug Kim[2]

[1] School of Electrical Electronics & Information Engineering, WonKwang University, 344-2. Sinyong-Dong, Iksan, Chon-Buk 570-749, Korea
ykim@wonkwang.ac.kr
[2] Bioinformatics Div, National Institute of Agricultural Biotechnology, R.D.A. 225 Seodundong, Suwon, 441-707, Korea
ncatcello@hanmail.net

**Abstract.** Nonlinear fiber optics, in the form of stimulated Brillouin scattering (sBs), has now emerged as the essential means for the construction of active optical devices used for all-optic in-line switching, channel selection, amplification, oscillation in optical communications, optical logic elements in optical computation and sensing, and a host of other applications. The controlling of sBs in optical system based smart structures leads to neural networks with multistable periodic states; create optical logic 1 or 0. It can be used for optical logic and computations and optical sensing. It is theoretically possible also to apply the multi-stability regimes as an optical memory device for encoding and decoding series and complex data transmission in optical communications systems.

## 1 Introduction

It is well known that optical fibers have potentials for various [1] uses in the communications field. Research in the past and in recent years has focused on using optical fibers as sensors based neural networks application and hardware implementation; each fiber capable of reacting to measure and changes in its immediate environment. Current research has focused on combining fiber optic sensors and actuation materials to create a system that is capable of sensing, and controlling shape or orientation with respect to its environment, as a first step in creating a smart structure. Specifically, our research focuses on configuring and developing a stimulated Brillouin scattering (sBs) sensing system that behaves as a neural network, in order to acquire the ability to learn by experience, predict future reactions to environmental changes, and execute as prescribed.

A "possible" smart structure system would implement a massively parallel computational architecture with its attendant reduction in processing time while managing the complexity of the system, i.e. the sensing/actuation grid. Our sBs network would learn the correct "algorithms" by example during training and have the ability to generalize to untrained inputs after training is completed. The inputs to the network are the fiber optic sensor signal outputs, and the network outputs are the control signals for actuation controls. The true advantage of this "proposed" system for application to smart structures lies both in its capability to analyze complex sensor signal patterns

D.-S. Huang, K. Li, and G.W. Irwin (Eds.): ICIC 2006, LNCS 4113, pp. 422 – 427, 2006.

and its speed in generating the appropriate control signal for the actuators. The key lies in the implementation of a neuron operation based neural networks using sBs in optical fibers.

## 2 SBS Based Neuron

Nonlinear effects in optical fibers, specifically stimulated Brillouin scattering (sBs), has emerged as a versatile tool for the design of active optical devices for all-optic in-line switching, channel selection, amplification and oscillation, as well as in optical sensing, and optical communications[2, 3, 4]. The backward nature of sBs scattered light, with a frequency shift equal to that of the laser induced acoustic wave in the fiber (known as the Stokes or Brillouin shift), has long been viewed as an ultimate intrinsic loss mechanism in long haul fibers [5, 6]. The very backscattering nature of this nonlinear process and the existence of a threshold provide potential optical device functions, such as optical switching, arithmetic and neural functions.

An artificial neuron, used in neural network research, can be thought of as a device with multiple inputs and single or multiple outputs. The inputs to a neuron are weighted signals. The neuron adds the weighted signals, compares the result with a preset value, and activates if the sum exceeds threshold. In the nonlinear optical phenomenon, the system's combined weighted signals also produce an output if the weighted sum is greater than the threshold. A typical neuron is illustrated in Fig. 1.

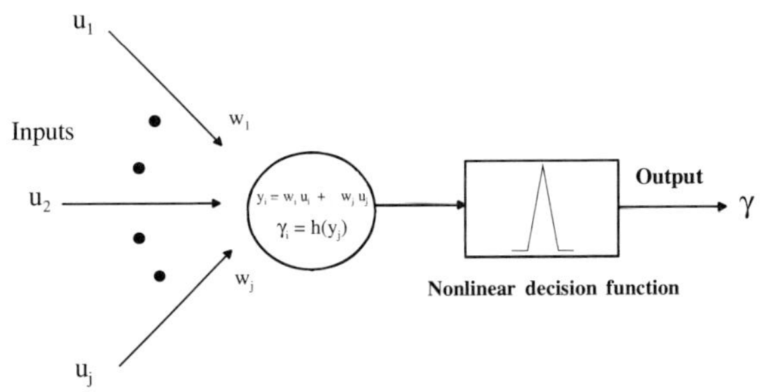


**Fig. 1.** A simplified multi-layered feedward neural network; the processing node between interconnects, where weighted sums are fed to a threshold decision-processing element

The system through sBs mixing combines weighted signals to produce an output if the weighted sum exceeds the threshold. The threshold decision has made by an individual neuron in conjunction with weighted inputs from other neurons. A theoretical sBs based neural network, utilizing sBs threshold sensing with an embedded sensor were explained [7, 8].

## 3 SBS Threshold Logic

Since the Stokes shift is small, the wavelengths in each wave $_p$, $_n$, and $_s$ are almost equal [9]. With these assumptions, the nonlinear coupled equation can be written as

$$\frac{dI_p}{dz} = -\alpha I_p - g_B I_p I_s . \tag{1}$$

$$-\frac{dI_s}{dz} = -\alpha I_s + g_B I_s I_p - g_B I_n Is\ . \quad (2)$$

$$\frac{dI_n}{dz} = -\alpha I_n + g_B I_n Is\ . \quad (3)$$

where $I$ represents wave intensity of the pump "$p$", the backward Stokes wave "$s$" and the acoustic wave "$n$", and and $g_B$ are respectively the fiber attenuation coefficient and Brillouin gain coefficient for all the waves. In the basic optical neuron-type setup based neural networks applications and hardware implementations, the input-output conditions of the waves are given as follows [9]

$$I_p(L) = I_p(0)\, e^{-\alpha L}\ . \quad (4)$$

$$I_n(L) = I_n(0)\, e^{-\alpha L}\ . \quad (5)$$

$$I_s(0) = I_s(L)\, e^{-\alpha L\, g_B L_{eff} \Delta I}\ . \quad (6)$$

where $\Delta I = I_p(0) - I_n(0)$ and $I_p(0)$ is the pump transmission. If the net gain of the sensor signal is close to 0 $dB$, then $I_s(L) \approx I_s(0)$ so that $P_s(0) \approx P_s(L) << \alpha A_{eff}/g_b \leq p_p(0)$, where we have used $I = p/A_{eff.}$ in which $A_{eff} = r^2$ is the effective cross sectional area of the fiber, and $p$ is the power. The ratio $\beta = P_s(L)/P_s(0)$ is on the order of 0.01 or less. Using pump power level for 0 $dB$ gain, we can estimate the pump power value,

$$p_s(L) = 0.001\, p_n(0)\ . \quad (7)$$

if $p_s$ = 1 mw, the pump power $p_n(0)$ required will be 1$W$. The intensity level of each wave is set below the sBs threshold ($I_{th} = 21/g_b L_{eff}$) in order to avoid the generation of backward Stokes from spontaneous scattering. The stokes gain $v_s$ versus total pump power difference $p_p(0) - p_n(0)$ is shown in Figure 2. The gain can be converted to loss and vice versa, simply by changing the pump power levels. The output state of a neuron based neural networks applications and hardware implementations can be changed by changing one or both input pump intensities. The threshold of the neuron can be controlled by changing the power launched in the stokes signal as shown in the Fig.2.

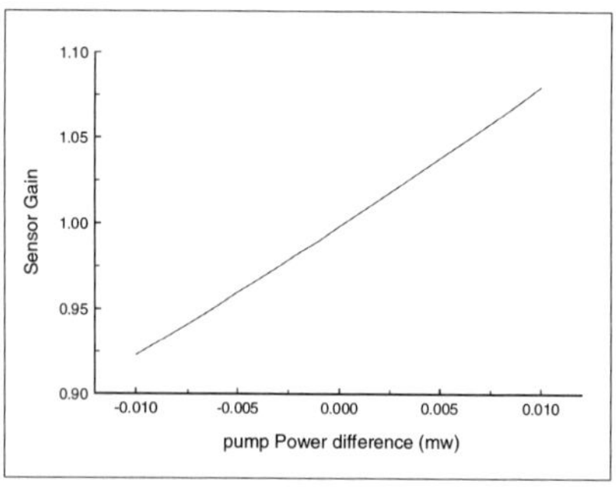


**Fig. 2.** Backward stokes signal *vs.* pump power difference $p_p(0) - p_n(0)$ based neural networks applications and hardware implementations

## 4 SBS Logic Implementation

A practical sBs logic implementation of theoretical neuron based neural networks and hardware implementations calls for all the waves to be generated by the same laser. We are very familiar with this method and a scheme is devised in Figure 3 [10].

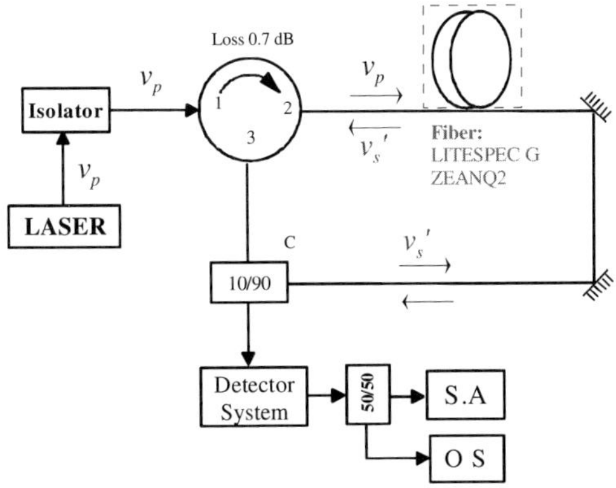


**Fig. 3.** Practical hardware implementation sBs based threshold logic. Optical fibers are used for neuron operation as the medium for providing sBs gain to the stokes wave.

A laser was used as the pump to the system through a coupler. An isolator is installed to prevent any reflected signal back into the laser cavity that may disrupt the performance of the laser. The pump wave travels through the long fiber to an embedded sensing fiber. If the pump signal launched into the fibers exceeds some critical threshold level, then sBs occurs. In this process, the input pump traveling through the fibers may be converted into a Stokes wave, shifted in frequency, and traveling backward towards the laser source. A stabilized *cw* probe laser operating at 1310 *nm* was used as a pump source for low scattering losses in the fiber, yielding a ≈12 *GHz* Brillouin scattering shift. We use a fiber length of 4.28 k*m* *LITESPEC-G-ZEANQ*. Detection is also achieved with a 25*GHz IR* Photodetector Set (New Focus and an amplifier with 20*ps* impulse response) connected to a *HP* Oscilloscope. The temporal repetition rate of which corresponds to a pulse round-trip time in the fiber-ring taken to be less than 10 *nsec*. The Brillouin pulse train amplitudes remain unstable, particularly just below pump threshold. When the observation is made using a long time scale (*μsec /division*), the Brillouin output exhibits randomly distributed trains of periodic pulses. These experimental feature based neural networks in hardware implementation is shown in real time in Figure 4.

To exploit the aspect of the sBs threshold equation for the fiber ring $G_B P_o^{cr} L_{eff}/A_{eff} = 21$ in case, where L value is not a practical consideration, we can actually form that have thresholds $P_o^{cr}$ as low as μw's. This clearly points to the possibility of using a single laser source to energize multiple fibers to perform multiple optical logic and computations. Since sBs thresholds have been rendered so low that multiple Stokes waves can exist in the same systems, serving both as signals and pumps, and exchanging energies among them.

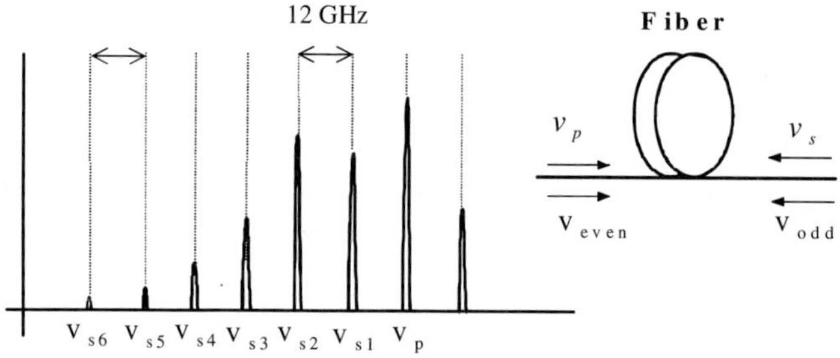


**Fig. 4.** The optical fiber generates multiple Stokes waves for optical logic and computation

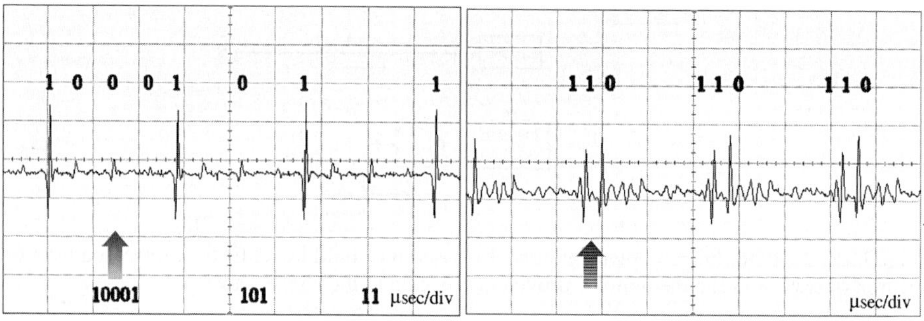


**Fig. 5.** Transiently controlled sBs based on hardware implementation at threshold (a) and high above threshold (b). The examples of sequence of suppression are assigned by '0' and '1' symbols.

The examples of sequence of suppression are assigned by 'low level' and 'high level' states. Multi-stable periodic states, as shown in Figure 5 (a) and (b), can lead to logic '0' or '1' and can in principle create large memory capacity as input bit streams in TDM network systems. Its implementation still requires much engineering improvements, such as arriving at a spatial resolution that is comparable to the references or speckle, and suppression of its tendency to chaos.

## 5 Conclusions

We studied that the controlling of sBs in optical system based smart structures leads to neural networks with multistable periodic states; create optical logic 1 or 0. It can be used for optical logic and computations and optical sensing based neural networks. It is theoretically possible also to apply the multi-stability regimes as an optical memory device for encoding and decoding.

## Acknowledgement

This paper was supported by WonKwang University in 2005.

## References

1. Grossman, B., Alavie, T., Ham, F., Franke, F., Thursby, M.: Fiber-Optic Sensor and Smart Structures Research at Florida Institute of Technology. SPIE. 1170 (1989) 213-218
2. Koyamada, Y., Sato, S., Nakamura, S., Sotobayashi, H., Chujo. W.: Simulating and Designing Brillouin Gain Spectrum in Single-Mode Fibers. J. of Lightwave Tech. 22(2) (2004) 631-639
3. Bernini, R., Minardo, A., Zeni. L.: Stimulated Brillouin Scattering Frequency-Domain Analysis in A Single-Mode Optical Fiber for Distributed Sensing. Optics Letters. 29(17) (2004) 1977-1979
4. Tanemura, T., Takyshima, Y., Kikuchi. K.: Narrowband Optical Filter, with A Variable Transmission Spectrum, Using Stimulated Brillouin Scattering in Optical Fiber. Opt. Lett. 27(17) (2002) 1552-1554
5. Cotter, D.: Stimulated Brillouin Scattering in Monomode Optical Fiber. J. Opt. Com. 4 (1983) 10-19
6. Agrawal, G, P.: Nonlinear Fiber Optics, 3rd, Academic press, London (2001)
7. Yong K. Kim, S. Lim, H. Kim, S. Oh, Chung Y.: Implementation of Brillouin-Active Fiber Based Neural Network in Smart Structures. LNCS 3498 (2005) 987-991
8. Yong K. Kim, J. Kim, S. Lim, D. Kim.: Neuron Operation Using Controlled Chaotic Instabilities in Brillouin-Active Fiber Based Neural Network. LNCS 3612 (2005) 1045-1051
9. Tariq, S., Habib, M, K.: Neural Operation Using Stimulated Brillouin Scattering in Optical Fiber. Opt. Eng. **37** (1998) 1823-1826

# Passivity Analysis for Neuro Identifier with Different Time-Scales

Alejandro Cruz Sandoval[1], Wen Yu[1], and Xiaoou Li[2]

[1] Departamento de Control Automático, CINVESTAV-IPN A.P. 14-740, Av.IPN 2508, México D.F., 07360, México
yuw@ctrl.cinvestav.mx
[2] Sección de Computación, Departamento de Ingeniería Eléctrica CINVESTAV-IPN A.P. 14-740, Av.IPN 2508, México D.F., 07360, México

**Abstract.** Many physical systems contains fast and slow phenomenons. In this paper we propose a dynamic neural networks with different time-scales to model the nonlinear system. Passivity-based approach is used to derive stability conditions for neural identifer. Several stability properties, such as passivity, asymptotic stability, input-to-state stability and bounded input bounded output stability, are guaranteed in certain senses. Numerical examples are also given to demonstrate the effectiveness of the theoretical results.

## 1 Introduction

A wide class of physical systems contains both slow and fast dynamic phenomena occurring in separate time-scales. Resent results show that neural network techniques seem to be very effective to model a wide class of complex nonlinear systems with different time-scales when we have no complete model information, or even when we consider the plant as a "black box". Many applications show that neuro identification has emerged as a effective tool for unknown nonlinear systems. This model-free approach uses the nice features of neural networks, but the lack of model makes it hard to obtain theoretical results on stability and performance of neuro identifiers. It is very important for engineers to assure the stability of neuro identififiers in theory before they apply them to real systems.

Dynamic neural networks with different time-scales can model the dynamics of the short-term memory (neural activity levels) and the long-term memory (dynamics of unsupervised synaptic modifications) [8]. Their capability of storing patterns as stable equilibrium points requires stability criteria which includes the mutual interference between neuron and learning dynamics. The dynamics of neural networks with different time-scales are extremely complex, exhibiting convergence point attractors and periodic attractors [1]. Networks where both short-term and long-term memory are dynamic variables cannot be placed in the form of the Cohen-Grossberg equations [2]. Two kinds of stability for neuro identifiers have been studied: 1) the stability of neural networks may be found in [3] and [11], 2) the stability of learning algorithms was discussed by [10]. We will emphasize this paper on deriving novel stable learning algorithms of the neuro identifier with different time-scales.

D.-S. Huang, K. Li, and G.W. Irwin (Eds.): ICIC 2006, LNCS 4113, pp. 428–433, 2006.

Some of neural networks applications, such as patterns storage and solving optimization problem, require that the equilibrium points of the designed network be stable [5]. So, it is important to study the stability of neural networks. The complete convergence of different time-scales neural networks is proved in [9]. The global exponential stability of the delayed competitive neural networks with different time scales is discussed in [6]. By singularly perturbed technique, [6] investigates the stability problems for both continuous-time and discrete-time fuzzy systems with different time-scales. Global exponential stability of different time-scales neural networks is solved in [8]. A large class of competitive systems have been identified as being "generally" convergent to point attractors even though no Lyapunov functions have found for their flows. The stability of learning algorithms can de derived by analyzing the identification or tracking errors of neural networks. [4] studied the stability conditions of the updating laws when multilayer perceptrons are used to identify and control a nonlinear system. In [11] the dynamic backpropagation was modified with NLq stability constraints. Since neural networks cannot match the unknown nonlinear systems exactly, some robust modifications [3] should be applied on normal gradient or backpropagation algorithm [4] [10]. Passivity approach may deal with the poorly defined nonlinear systems, usually by means of sector bounds, and offers elegant solutions for the proof of absolute stability. It can lead to general conclusion on the stability using only input-output characteristics. The passivity properties of static multilayer neural networks were examined in [?]. By means of analyzing the interconnected of error models, they derived the relationship between passivity and closed-loop stable. Passivity technique can be also applied on dynamic neural networks. Passivity properties of dynamic neural networks may be found in [11]. We concluded that the commonly-used learning algorithms with robust modifications such as dead-zone [4] and $\sigma-$modification [3] are not necessary.

In this paper, we will extend our prior results of normal neuro identifier [11] to multiple time-scales case. Passivity theory is applied to analyze the stability of the neuro identifier with different time-scales. To the best of our knowledge, stabilty analysis for neural identification with different time-scales has not yet been established in the literatures. We show that a backpropagation-like learning law can make the identification error stability, asymptotic stability and input-to-state stability. Simulations of vehicle idle speed identification give the fectiveness of the algorithm proposed in this paper.

## 2 Stability Analysis of Neuro Identifier with Different Time-Scales

The main concern of this section is to understand some concepts of passivity and ISS. Consider a class of nonlinear systems with two time-scales

$$\begin{aligned} \dot{x}_t &= f(x_t, z_t, u_t, v) \\ \epsilon \dot{z}_t &= g(x_t, z_t, u_t, v) \end{aligned} \tag{1}$$

where $x_t, z_t \in \Re^n$ is the state, $u_t \in \Re^m$ is the input vector, $f, g : \Re^n \times \Re^m \to \Re^n$ is locally Lipshitz, $h : \Re^n \times \Re^m \to \Re^m$ is continuous. $x_t$ is slow state and $z_t$ is fast state. $\epsilon > 0$ is known. We construct the following dynamic neural network with two time-scales to identify the nonlinear system (1)

$$\begin{aligned} \dot{\widehat{x}} &= A\widehat{x} + W_1\sigma_1(V_1 [\widehat{x}, \widehat{z}]^T) + W_3\phi_1(V_3 [\widehat{x}, \widehat{z}]^T)u \\ \epsilon\dot{\widehat{z}} &= B\widehat{z} + W_2\sigma_2(V_2 [\widehat{x}, \widehat{z}]^T) + W_4\phi_2(V_4 [\widehat{x}, \widehat{z}]^T)u \end{aligned} \tag{2}$$

where $\widehat{x} \in R^n$ and $\widehat{z} \in R^n$ are slow and fast states, , $W_i \in R^{n\times 2n}$ $(i = 1\cdots 4)$ are the weights in output layers, $V_i \in R^{2n\times 2n}$ $(i = 1\cdots 4)$ are the weights in hidden layers, $\sigma_k = [\sigma_k(\widehat{x}_1)\cdots\sigma_k(\widehat{x}_n), \sigma_k(\widehat{z}_1)\cdots\sigma_k(\widehat{z}_n)]^T \in R^{2n}$ $(k = 1, 2)$, $\phi(\cdot) \in R^{2n\times 2n}$ is diagonal matrix,$\phi_k(\widehat{x}, \widehat{z}) = diag[\phi_k(\widehat{x}_1)\cdots\phi_k(\widehat{x}_n), \phi_k(\widehat{z}_1)\cdots\phi_k(\widehat{z}_n)]$ $(k = 1, 2)$, $u(k) = [u_1, u_2\cdots u_m, 0, \cdots 0]^T \in R^{2n}$. $A \in R^{n\times n}, B \in R^{n\times n}$ are stable matrices (Hurwitz). $\epsilon$ is a small positive constant. When $\epsilon = 0$, the dynamic neural networks (2) have been discussed by many authors, for example [4] and [10]. One may see that Hopfield model is a special case of this kind of neural networks with $A = diag\{a_i\}$, $a_i := -1/R_iC_i$, $R_i > 0$ and $C_i > 0$. $R_i$ and $C_i$ are the resistance and capacitance at the $i$th node of the network respectively. The sub-structure $W_1\sigma_1(V_1 [\widehat{x}, \widehat{z}]^T) + W_3\phi_1(V_3 [\widehat{x}, \widehat{z}]^T)u$ is a multilayer perceptron structure. In order or simplify the theory analysis, we let the hidden layers $V_i = I$. Generally, the nonlinear system (1) can be written as

$$\begin{aligned} \dot{x}_t &= Ax_t + W_1^*\sigma_1(x, z) + W_3^*\phi_1(x, z)u - \widetilde{f}_1 \\ \epsilon\dot{z} &= Bz + W_2^*\sigma_2(x, \widehat{z}) + W_4^*\phi_2(x, z)u - \widetilde{f}_2 \end{aligned} \tag{3}$$

where $W_j^*$ $(j = 1\cdots 4)$ is bounded unknown matrix

$$W_j^*\Lambda_j^{-1}W_j^{*T} \leq \overline{W}_j \tag{4}$$

$\overline{W}_j$ is prior known matrix. Vector function $\widetilde{f}_i$ $(i = 1, 2)$ can be regarded as modelling error and disturbances. Let us define identification error as $\Delta_1 = \widehat{x}_t - x_t$, $\Delta_2 = \widehat{z}_t - z_t$, where $\widehat{X}_t = \left[\widehat{x}_t^T, \widehat{z}_t^T\right]^T$. Because $\sigma_i(\cdot)$ and $\phi_i(\cdot)$ $(i = 1, 2)$, are chosen as sigmoid functions, clearly they satisfy the following *Lipshitz* property

$$\widetilde{\sigma}_i^T\Lambda_i\widetilde{\sigma}_i \leq \Delta_i^T D_{\sigma i}\Delta_i, \quad \left(\widetilde{\phi}_i\gamma(u_t)\right)^T \Lambda_i \left(\widetilde{\phi}_i\gamma(u_t)\right) \leq \overline{u}\Delta_i^T D_{\phi i}\Delta_i, \tag{5}$$

where $\widetilde{\sigma}_i = \sigma_i(\widehat{X}_t) - \sigma_i(X_t)$, $\widetilde{\phi}_i = \phi_i(\widehat{X}_t) - \phi_i(X_t)$, $\Lambda_i$, $D_{\sigma i}$ and $D_{\phi i}$ are known positive constants, $i = 1, 2$. The multilayer dynamics is obtained from (2) and (3)

$$\begin{aligned} \dot{\Delta}_1 &= A\Delta_1 + \widetilde{W}_1\sigma_1(\widehat{X}) + \widetilde{W}_3\phi_1(\widehat{X}_t)\gamma(u_t) + W_1^*\widetilde{\sigma}_1 + W_3^*\widetilde{\phi}_1\gamma(u_t) + \widetilde{f}_1 \\ \epsilon\dot{\Delta}_2 &= B\Delta_2 + \widetilde{W}_2\sigma_2(\widehat{X}) + \widetilde{W}_4\phi_2(\widehat{X}_t)\gamma(u_t) + W_2^*\widetilde{\sigma}_2 + W_4^*\widetilde{\phi}_2\gamma(u_t) + \widetilde{f}_2 \end{aligned} \tag{6}$$

where $\widetilde{W}_j = W_j - W_j^*$ $(j = 1\cdots 4)$. If we define

$$\begin{aligned} R_1 &= \overline{W}_1 + \overline{W}_2, \quad Q_1 = D_{\sigma 1} + \overline{u}D_{\phi 1} + Q_{01} \\ R_2 &= \overline{W}_3 + \overline{W}_4, \quad Q_2 = D_{\sigma 2} + \overline{u}D_{\phi 2} + Q_{02} \end{aligned} \tag{7}$$

and the matrices $A$, $B$, $Q_{01}$ and $Q_{02}$ are selected to fulfill the following conditions:

(1) the pairs $(A, R_1^{1/2})$ and $(B, R_2^{1/2})$ are controllable, the pairs $(Q_1^{1/2}, A)$ and $(Q_2^{1/2}, B)$ are observable,
(2) local frequency conditions [3] satisfies, then the following assumption can be established:

**A1:** There exist a stable matrix $A$ and a strictly positive definite matrix $Q_0$ such that the matrix Riccati equation

$$\begin{array}{c} P_1 A + A^T P_1 + P_1 R_1 P_1 = -Q_1 \\ P_2 B + B^T P_2 + P_2 R_2 P_2 = -Q_2 \end{array} \tag{8}$$

has a positive solution $P_i = P_i^T > 0$, $(i = 1, 2)$.

This conditions is easily fulfilled if we select $A$ as stable diagonal matrix. Next Theorem states the learning procedure of neuro identifier.

**Theorem 1.** *Subject to assumption A1 being satisfied, if the weights* $W_j$ $(j = 1 \cdots 4)$ *is updated as*

$$\begin{array}{c} \dot{W}_1 = -K_1 P_1 \Delta_1 \sigma_1^T(\widehat{X}_t), \dot{W}_2 = -K_2 P_1 \phi_1(\widehat{X}_t)\gamma(u_t)\Delta_1^T \\ \dot{W}_3 = -K_3 P_2 \Delta_2 \sigma_2^T(\widehat{X}_t), \dot{W}_4 = -K_4 P_2 \phi_2(\widehat{X}_t)\gamma(u_t)\Delta_2^T \end{array} \tag{9}$$

*where* $P_1$ *and* $P_2$ *are the solution of Riccati equation (8), then the identification error dynamics (6) is strictly passive from the modeling error* $\widetilde{f}_i$ *to the identification error* $2P\Delta_i$, $i = 1, 2$

*Proof.* Select a Lyapunov function (storage function) as

$$\begin{array}{c} S_t(x, z) = \Delta_1^T P_1 \Delta_1 + \Delta_2^T P_2 \Delta_1 \\ + tr\left\{\widetilde{W}_1^T K_1^{-1} \widetilde{W}_1\right\} + tr\left\{\widetilde{W}_2^T K_2^{-1} \widetilde{W}_2\right\} + tr\left\{\widetilde{W}_3^T K_3^{-1} \widetilde{W}_3\right\} + tr\left\{\widetilde{W}_4^T K_4^{-1} \widetilde{W}_4\right\} \end{array} \tag{10}$$

where $P_i \in \Re^{n \times n}$ is positive definite matrix, $tr\{\cdot\}$ stands for the "trace" and is defined as the sum of all the diagonal elements of a matrix. Since $\Delta_i^T P_i W_j^* \widetilde{\sigma}_i$ is scalar, using (5) and matrix inequality $X^T Y + (X^T Y)^T \leq X^T \Lambda^{-1} X + Y^T \Lambda Y$, where $X, Y, \Lambda \in \Re^{n \times k}$ are any matrices, $\Lambda$ is any positive definite matrix, we obtain

$$\begin{array}{l} 2\Delta_1^T P_1 W_1^* \widetilde{\sigma}_1 \leq \Delta_1^T P_1 W_1^* \Lambda_1^{-1} W_1^{*T} P_1 \Delta_1 + \widetilde{\sigma}_1^T \Lambda_1 \widetilde{\sigma}_1 \leq \Delta_1^T \left(P_1 \overline{W}_1 P_1 + D_{\sigma 1}\right) \Delta_1 \\ 2\Delta_1^T P_1 W_2^* \widetilde{\phi}_1 \gamma(u_t) \leq \Delta_1^T \left(P_1 \overline{W}_2 P_1 + \overline{u} D_{\phi 1}\right) \Delta_1 \end{array} \tag{11}$$

Since $\dot{\widetilde{W}}_j = \dot{W}_j$, if we use the updating law as in (9) and **A1**, we have

$$\dot{S}_t \leq -\Delta_1^T Q_{01} \Delta_1 - \Delta_2^T Q_{02} \Delta_2 + 2\Delta_1^T P_1 \widetilde{f}_1 + 2\Delta_2^T P_2 \widetilde{f}_2 \tag{12}$$

From Definition 1, if we define the input as $\widetilde{f}_i$ and the output as $2P\Delta_i$, then the system is strictly passive with $V_t = \Delta_1^T Q_{01} \Delta_1 + \Delta_2^T Q_{02} \Delta_2 \geq 0$.

*Remark 1.* Since the updating rate is $K_j P_i$ $(j = 1 \cdots 4,\ i = 1, 2)$, and $K_j$ can be selected as any positive matrix, the learning process of the dynamic neural network (9) is free of the solution of Riccati equation (8).

**Corollary 1.** *If only parameters uncertainty present* $(\widetilde{f}_i = 0,\ i = 1, 2)$, *then the updating law as (9) can make the identification error asymptotic stable,* $\lim_{t\to\infty} \Delta_i = 0,\ W_j \in L_\infty,\ \lim_{t\to\infty} \dot{W}_j = 0,\ j = 1 \cdots 4, i = 1, 2$

*Proof.* Since the identification error dynamics (6) is passive and $\widetilde{f}_i = 0$, from the *Property 1* the storage function $S$ satisfies

$$\dot{S} \leq 2\Delta_1^T P_1 \widetilde{f}_1 + 2\Delta_2^T P_2 \widetilde{f}_2 = 0$$

The positive definite $S$ implies $\Delta_i$ and $W_j$are bounded. From the error equation (6) $\dot{\Delta}_i \in L_\infty$

$$\dot{S} \leq -\Delta_1^T Q_{01} \Delta_1 - \Delta_2^T Q_{02} \Delta_2 \leq 0$$

Integrate (12) both sides

$$\int_0^\infty \|\Delta_1\|_{Q_{01}} + \|\Delta_2\|_{Q_{02}} \leq S_0 - S_\infty < \infty$$

So $\Delta_i \in L_2 \cap L_\infty$, using Barlalat's Lemma [3] we have $\lim_{t\to\infty} \Delta_i = 0$. Since $u_t$, $\sigma_i$, $\phi_i$ and $P_i$ are bounded, $\lim_{t\to\infty} \dot{W}_j = 0$ and $\lim_{t\to\infty} \dot{W}_j = 0$.

*Remark 2.* For model matching case, Lyapunov-like analysis can reach the same result (see Corollary 1 and Corollary 2 in [10]). But in present of modeling error, we will give an absolutely different result: the gradient descent algorithm (9) is also robust respected to the bounded unmodeled dynamic and disturbance.

**Theorem 2.** *If assumption A1 is satisfied and there exists a positive definite matrix* $\Lambda_f$ *such that*

$$\begin{array}{c} \lambda_{\max}\left(P_1 \Lambda_{f1} P_1\right) \leq \lambda_{\min}\left(Q_{01}\right) \\ \lambda_{\max}\left(P_2 \Lambda_{f2} P_2\right) \leq \lambda_{\min}\left(Q_{02}\right) \end{array} \tag{13}$$

*then the updating law (9) may make the dynamics of neuro identifier (6) input-to-state stability (ISS).*

**Corollary 2.** *If the modelling error* $\widetilde{f}_i$ *is bounded, then the updating law (9) can make the identification procedure stable* $\Delta_i \in L_\infty$, $W_j \in L_\infty$

*Proof.* We know input-to-state stability means that the behavior of the dynamic neural networks should remain bounded when its input is bounded.

## 3 Conclusion

In this paper, the passivity approach is used to prove that a gradient descent algorithm for weight adjustment of neuro identifier with different time-scales is stable and robust to any bounded uncertainties. A simple gradient learning algorithm can make the neural identifier passive, stability, asymptotic stability, input-to-state stability and bounded input bounded output stability in certain senses.

## References


1. Amari, S., Competitive and Cooperative Aspects in Dynamics of Neural Excitation and Self-organization. Competition Cooperation Neural Networks Vol.20 (1982) 1–28
2. Grossberg, S., Adaptive Pattern Classification and Universal Recording. Biol. Cybern. Vol.23 (1976) 121–134
3. Ioannou, P.A., Sun, J., Robust Adaptive Control, Prentice-Hall (1996)
4. Jagannathan, S., Lewis, F.L., Identification of Nonlinear Dynamical Systems Using Multilayered Neural Networks. Automatica Vol.32 (12) (1996) 1707-1712
5. Jin, L., Gupta, M., Stable Dynamic Dackpropagation Learning in Recurrent Neural Networks. IEEE Trans. Neural Networks Vol.10 (1999) 1321–1334
6. Liu, H., Sun, F., Sun, Z., Stability Analysis and Synthesis of Fuzzy Singularly Perturbed Systems. IEEE Transactions on Fuzzy Systems Vol.13(2) (2005) 273-284
7. Lu, H., He, Z., Global Exponential Stability of Delayed Competitive Neural Networks with Different Time Scales. Neural Networks Vol.18(3) (2005) 243-250
8. Meyer-Baese, A., Pilyugin, S.S., Chen,Y., Global Exponential Stability of Competitive Neural Networks With Different Time Scales. IEEE Trans. on Neural Networks Vol.14(3) (2003) 716-719
9. Ye, M., Zhang, Y., Complete Convergence of Competitive Neural Networks with Different Time Scales. Neural Processing Letters. Vol.21 (1) (2005) 53-60
10. Yu, W., Poznyak, A.S., Indirect Adaptive Control via Parallel Dynamic Neural Networks IEE Proceedings - Control Theory and Applications Vol.146(1) (1999) 25-30
11. Yu , W., Li,X., Some Stability Properties of Dynamic Neural Networks. IEEE Trans. Circuits and Systems, Part I, Vol.48(1) (2001) 256-259

# Power Quality Identification Based on S-transform and RBF Neural Network

Ganyun Lv and Xiaodong Wang

Department of Information Science and Engineering, Zhejiang Normal University, Jinhua,321004 Zhejiang, China
ganyun_lv@yahoo.com

**Abstract.** This paper presents a new power quality (PQ) disturbances identification method based on S-transform time-frequency analysis and RBF network. The proposed technique consists of time-frequency analysis, feature extraction, and pattern classification. Though there are several time-frequency analysis methods existing in the literature, this paper uses S-transform to obtain the time-frequency characteristics of PQ events because of its superior performance under noise. Using the time-frequency characteristics, a set of features is extracted for identification of power quality disturbances. Finally, a RBF network is developed for classification of the power quality disturbances. The proposed method is simple and reached 97.5% identification correct ratio under high signal to noise ratio for those most important disturbances in power system.

## 1 Introduction

The deregulation polices in electric power systems results in the absolute necessity to quantify power quality (PQ). This fact highlights the need for an effective recognition technique capable of detecting and classifying the PQ disturbances. The identification of PQ disturbances is often based on neural network[1],[2], fast match[3], nearest neighbor rule[4], expert system[5] and fuzzy method[6], associated with other PQ detecting methods, such as Fourier transform[6], wavelet[7] and dq transform[1]. These methods may identify some similar PQ disturbances wrong when under strong noise. The BP network has very simple structure and good generalization ability, and could deal PQ data with noise and random varied parameters. Though there are several time-frequency analysis methods existing in the literature, this paper uses S-transform to obtain the time-frequency characteristics of PQ events because of its superior performance under noise. A neural network recognition method based on S-transform time-frequency analysis is proposed for identification of power quality (PQ) disturbances.

## 2 S-transform

### 2.1 S-transform

The S-transform[7] is an extension of continuous wavelet transform (CWT) and short-time Fourier transform (STFT). For its good time-frequency characteristic, it is very suitable for PQ disturbances analysis.

D.-S. Huang, K. Li, and G.W. Irwin (Eds.): ICIC 2006, LNCS 4113, pp. 434 – 439, 2006.

The S-transformation of signal $x(t)$ is defined as followed:

$$S(\tau,f)=\int_{-\infty}^{\infty}x(t)w(\tau-t,f)\exp(-2\pi ift)dt\ . \tag{1}$$

$$w(\tau-t,f)=\frac{|f|}{\sqrt{2\pi}}\exp\left[\frac{-f^2(\tau-t)^2}{2}\right]. \tag{2}$$

Where $w(\tau-t,f)$ is the gauss window function, $\tau$ is a parameter of time position axis. The width and height of gauss window in S-transform varied with change of frequency, while the STFT has fixed width and height of gauss window.

S-transformation could realize fast computing through FFT. The discrete S-transformation is:

$$S[m,n]=\sum_{k=0}^{N-1}X[n+k]\cdot e^{-2\pi^2k^2/n^2}\cdot e^{j2\pi km/N}\ ,n\neq 0\ . \tag{3}$$

$$S[m,n]=\frac{1}{N}\sum_{k=0}^{N-1}x[k]\ \ (n=0). \tag{4}$$

$$\text{Where}\ \ X[n]=\frac{1}{N}\sum_{k=0}^{N-1}x[k]\cdot e^{-j2\pi kn/N}\ . \tag{5}$$

## 2.2 PQ Disturbances Analysis with S-transform

Many analysis results of PQ disturbances could be obtained from S[m,n], including time-frequency distributing curve, amplitude-frequency curve at time, amplitude-time curve at basic frequency and other frequency. Some of detecting results for four important PQ disturbances in power electrical system including sine wave, harmonics, fluctuation and sags, were given in Fig.1 and Fig.2. The signal to noise ratio is 20dB.

From Fig.1 and Fig.2, one could find that with the S-transform one could get both time and frequency characteristics of these PQ disturbances easily and effectively under strong white noise. The identification in the proposed method was just based on those characteristics.

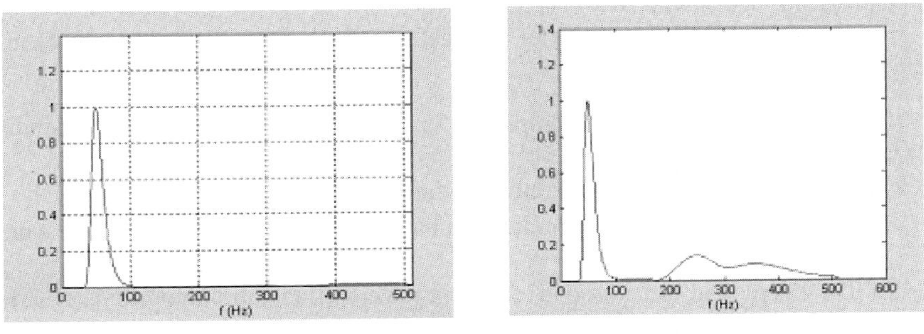


**Fig. 1.** Amplitude-frequency curve of sine wave (left) and harmonics (right)

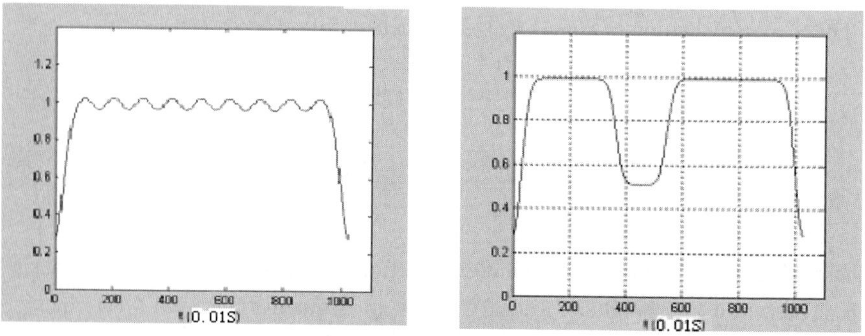


**Fig. 2.** Amplitude-time curve of fluctuation (left) and sags (right) at basic frequency

# 3 PQ Disturbances Identification

The procedure of PQ disturbances identification with neural network includes three steps: extracting features from S-transform analysis results, training networks and identifying disturbances with trained networks. The procedure of the method is shown as Fig. 3.

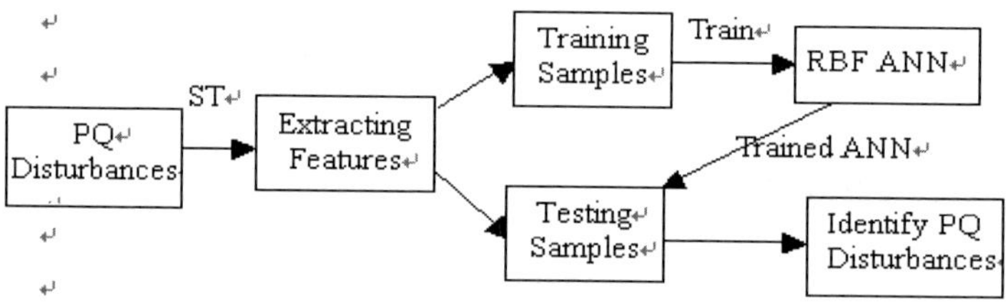


**Fig. 3.** PQ disturbances identification based on RBF ANN and ST

## 3.1 Extracting Features

The identified PQ disturbances included sine wave, harmonics, fluctuations and sags. The training and testing samples of these PQ disturbances were generated by a simulation program according to IEEE 1159.

Through a data dealing process of S-transform result S[m, n], following features were extracted:

1) The three peaks value of amplitude in frequency field and its corresponding frequency.
2) The maximum keeping time in basic frequency field that is larger than 1.1
3) The four peaks value of amplitude in basic frequency field and its corresponding time.
4) The fluctuation times in base frequency which fluctuation amplitude is larger that 0.01.

Thus 16 features were obtained. They reflected the characteristics of harmonics and sine wave, and fluctuation and sags.

### 3.2 Training Networks

In this paper, RBF networks were used in identification of the proposed PQ disturbances. The network included one hidden layer only. The number of input and output components is 16 and 4 respectively. The hidden layer adopts Gaussian function. The output layer adopts linear transfer function. The network was trained with fast back propagation algorithm. The first to the fourth component of output represent the characteristic extent of sine wave, harmonics, fluctuations and sags respectively. During training, each component, except the corresponding one, was set to 0, while he corresponding one was set to 1. For example, the output of a sine wave was set as [1 0 0 0], and the output of a sag sampling was set as [0 0 0 1].

### 3.3 Testing with Trained Networks

The test samples were inputted to trained ANN. The output was composed of four components. From the first to the fourth component represent the characteristic extent of sine wave, harmonics, fluctuations, and sags respectively. The maximum value was regarded as the disturbance type. For example, if a was the maximum component in output vector [a b c d], then the testing sample would identified to be a sine wave signal. If b was the maximum component in output vector, then the testing sample would be identified to be harmonic signal. All testing samples were identified by this way.

## 4 Simulation Result

In this paper, the training and testing samples of PQ disturbances were generated according to the PQ disturbances model in IEEE 1159. The sampling rate was 10k/s. To be mentioned, many parameters of PQ disturbances including amplitude, starting time, ending time, fluctuation frequency, varied randomly. The signal to noise ratio was 20db. Thus the simulation signal could be more like in practical system, and thus ensure reliability of the propose method results.

According to IEEE 1159, 40 training samples were produced by Matlab toolbox, including 10 sine wave, harmonics, voltage fluctuations, and sags respectively. With these small training sample set, the RBF ANN was trained. During the training process, each component, except the corresponding one, was set to 0, while the corresponding one was set to 1. The output of a sinusoidal is $[1\ 0\ \ 0\ \ 0]^T$, the output of harmonic is $[0\ 1\ \ 0\ \ 0]^T$, the output of voltage fluctuation is $[0\ 0\ \ 1\ \ 0]^T$, and the output of sags is $[0\ \ 0\ \ 0\ \ 1]^T$. In this function, Gaussian function was adopted as basis function. Training continued until the sum of squared errors (SSE) is less than 0.01. Then another 40 samples were produced to test the trained ANN. The first 10 samples were sine wave, the second 10 samples were harmonics, the third 10 samples were fluctuations, and the last 10 samples were sags. The test results are shown in Table 1.

It was shown from Table 1 that the network could identify all 40 disturbances correctly. From output components of test sample 1 to10, one could be found that the first component is about 1,while the other three components is almost 0. So test sample 1 to10 were sine wave signals obviously. Other 30 test samples had similar output. From output components of test sample 11 to20, one could find they are harmonics. From output components of test sample 21 to30, one could find they are fluctuations. From output components of test sample 31 to 40, one could find they are sags. The correct ratio of identification reached 100%. The high correct ratio of identification is mainly due to the distinctness of features extracted by data dealing process with S-transform result.

**Table 1.** PQ disturbances identification results

| Test sample | | 1 | 2 | 3 | 4 | 5 | 6 | 7 | 8 | 9 | 10 |
|---|---|---|---|---|---|---|---|---|---|---|---|
| Output Components | 1 | 1.003 | 0.988 | 1.002 | 1.002 | 0.999 | 1.002 | 1.001 | 0.992 | 0.999 | 0.999 |
| | 2 | 0.008 | -0.022 | 0.007 | 0.006 | -0.001 | 0.007 | 0.001 | -0.015 | -0.002 | -0.002 |
| | 3 | 0.001 | 0.001 | 0.002 | 0.001 | 0.002 | 0.001 | 0 | -0.001 | 0.000 | 0.000 |
| | 4 | -0.008 | 0.024 | -0.006 | -0.005 | 0.000 | -0.006 | -0.002 | 0.018 | 0.001 | 0.001 |
| Test sample | | 11 | 12 | 13 | 14 | 15 | 16 | 17 | 18 | 19 | 20 |
| Output Components | 1 | 0.016 | -0.013 | 0.000 | 0.003 | -0.002 | -0.001 | 0.001 | 0.02 | -0.05 | -0.05 |
| | 2 | 0.990 | 0.994 | 1.004 | 1.001 | 1.003 | 1.001 | 0.992 | 1.003 | 1.005 | 1.005 |
| | 3 | -0.006 | 0.001 | 0.001 | -0.006 | 0.001 | 0.001 | 0.001 | -0.010 | 0.005 | 0.005 |
| | 4 | 0 | -0.003 | 0.003 | 0.001 | -0.002 | 0.001 | -0.001 | 0.001 | 0.002 | 0.002 |
| Test sample | | 21 | 22 | 23 | 24 | 25 | 26 | 27 | 28 | 29 | 30 |
| Output Components | 1 | 0 | 0.001 | -0.003 | -0.003 | 0.009 | -0.012 | 0.001 | 0.001 | 0 | 0 |
| | 2 | 0 | 0 | 0 | 0.001 | -0.008 | 0.012 | -0.001 | 0 | 0.001 | 0.001 |
| | 3 | 1.000 | 1.001 | 0.997 | 0.990 | 1.008 | 1.001 | 1.000 | 1.000 | 1.000 | 1.000 |
| | 4 | -0.008 | -0.002 | 0.003 | 0.006 | 0.003 | -0.005 | -0.001 | -0.001 | -0.001 | -0.001 |
| Test sample | | 31 | 32 | 33 | 34 | 35 | 36 | 37 | 38 | 39 | 40 |
| Output components | 1 | -0.029 | -0.013 | 0.003 | 0.011 | -0.005 | 0.014 | -0.014 | 0.001 | 0.013 | 0.013 |
| | 2 | -0.008 | 0.011 | -0.005 | 0 | 0.001 | 0.006 | -0.003 | -0.003 | 0.005 | 0.005 |
| | 3 | 0.027 | -0.006 | -0.001 | -0.004 | 0.003 | -0.019 | 0.001 | 0.019 | -0.011 | -0.011 |
| | 4 | 1.010 | 1.007 | 1.002 | 0.993 | 1.004 | 0.993 | 1.015 | 1.010 | 1.007 | 1.007 |

In order to test more about the proposed method, another new 360 PQ disturbance samples were used to test the trained networks. The parameters of PQ disturbances varied randomly too and the signal to noise ratio was still 20db. The results showed that there were only 9 samples identified wrong. All these samples were sags, and mistaken to be classified as fluctuation samples in the case. The correct ratio of identification had reached 97.5%, while that of most current PQ identification methods is less than 95%. It was much higher than many PQ identification methods.

## 5 Conclusions

This paper presents a PQ disturbances identification method based RBF Networks and S-transform. Some most important PQ disturbances in power electrical system are identified with the proposed method. S-transform could get a good and rich time-frequency characteristics of PQ disturbances, which ensure effect of identification performance. The RBF network has very simple structure and good generalization ability, and could deal PQ data with noise and random varied parameters. The correct ratio of identification could reach 97.5%, which is much better than many other methods. But because the computation of both S-transform analysis and RBF ANN was very large, the training time is relatively long. The method is suitable to be used in off line application.

## References

1. Xu, Y. H., Xiao, X. N., Yang, Y. H.: Power Quality Disturbance Identification Using Dq Conversion-Based Neural Classifiers. Automation of Electric Power System, vol.14, (2001) 24-28
2. Shah, Baki, S.R., Abdullah, M.Z., Abidin, A.F.: Combination Wavelets And Artificial Intelligent For Classification And Detection Transient Overvoltage. Research and Development, SCORED (2002) 177-180
3. Abdel-Galil, T. K., EL- Saadany, E. F., Youssef, A.M.: On-line Disturbance Recognition Utilizing Vector Quantization Based Fast Match. Power Engineering Society Summer Meeting, 2002 IEEE, vol .2, (2002) 1027-1032
4. Gaouda, A. M., Kanoun, S. H., Salama, M. M. A.: On-Line Disturbance Classification Using Nearest Neighbor Rule. J. Electr. Power System Research., vol.57, (2001) 1-8
5. Emmanouil Styvaktakis, Math H. J. Bollen, Irene Y. H. Gu: Expert System For Classification And Analysis of Power System Events. IEEE Trans. Power Delivery, vol.17, (2002) 423-428
6. Dash, P. K., MishraK, S., Salama, M. M. A., Liew, A. C.: Classification Of Power System Disturbances Using A Fuzzy Expert System And A Fourier Linear Combiner. IEEE Trans. Power Delivery, vol. 15, (2000) 472-477
7. Stockwell, R.G., Mansinha, L., Lowe, R.P.: Localization Of The Complex Spectrum: The S transform. IEEE Trans. Signal Process, vol.44,(1996) 998-1001

# Probability Model of Covering Algorithm (PMCA)

Shu Zhao[1], Yan-ping Zhang[1,2], Ling Zhang[1,2], Ping Zhang[3], and Ying-chun Zhang[1]

[1] Key Laboratory of Intelligent Computing & Signal Processing of Ministry of Education, Anhui University, Hefei, , 230039, China
[2] Institute of Artificial intelligence, Anhui University, Hefei, 230039, China
[3] Automation Department, Guangdong Polytechnic Normal University, 510635, China
zhaoshuzs@163.com

**Abstract.** The probability model is introduced into classification learning in this paper. Kernel covering algorithm (KCA) and maximum likelihood principle of the statistic model combine to form a novel algorithm-the probability model of covering algorithm (PMCA) which not only introduces optimization processing for every covering domain, but offers a new way to solve the parameter problem of kernel function. Covering algorithm (CA) is firstly used to get covering domains and approximate interfaces, and then maximum likelihood principle of finite mixture model is used to fit each distributing. Experiments indicate that optimization is surely achieved, classification rate is improved and the neural cells are cut down greatly through with proper threshold value.

## 1 Introduction

Since 1998, CA had been proposed by Professor Zhang Bo and Professor Zhang Ling, it provided a quite satisfactory solution for the design of neural networks[1],[2][3]. Later many improved methods were presented constantly by researchers. They have been widely applied in various fields[4],[5],[6],[7]. But a common problem among them is that the parameters need adjusting and different samples often choose different parameters. The choice of parameters affects the results obviously. The probability model and CA combine to optimize CA from the view of "the maximum likelihood principle" of the probability theory in this paper, which can automatically get different parameters for different samples.

## 2 Probability Model of Covering Algorithm (PMCA)

### 2.1 Probability Model of Covering Algorithm (PMCA)

Training:

S1. Getting k covering sub-sets with CA in literatures [1],[2],[3] $\{C_1^i, C_2^i, \ldots, C_{n_k}^i\}$, i=1,2,…,k (suppose there are k classes samples).

Take the *i*th class samples as examples to illustrate PMCA as follows. Introduce Gauss kernel function to each covering domain;

D.-S. Huang, K. Li, and G.W. Irwin (Eds.): ICIC 2006, LNCS 4113, pp. 440 – 444, 2006.

S2. Let $\alpha_j^{(0)} = d_j$, $d_j$ denotes the amount samples covered by $c_j^i$ occupies the total number of the $i$th class samples, namely the covering domain's density;

Let $\sigma_j^{(0)} = r_j$, $r_j$ is the radius of $c_j^i$; Let $\mu_j^{(0)} = a_j$, $a_j$ is the center of $c_j^i$;

S3. The *(t+1)*th time iteration as follows (n denotes the sample numbers of the $i$th class, $n_i$ denotes the covering domain numbers of the $i$th class):

$$\beta_{ij}^{(t)} = \beta_j(x_i, \theta^{(t)}) = \frac{\alpha_j^{(t)} \frac{1}{\sigma_j^{(t)}} e^{-\frac{(x_i - \mu_j^{(t)})^2}{2\sigma_j^{(t)2}}}}{\sum_{k=1}^{n_i} \alpha_k^{(t)} \frac{1}{\sigma_k^{(t)}} e^{-\frac{(x_i - \mu_k^{(t)})^2}{2\sigma_k^{(t)2}}}} . \tag{1}$$

$$\alpha_j^{(t+1)} = \frac{1}{n} \sum_{i=1}^{n} \beta_{ij}^{(t)}, \ j = 1, 2, \dots, n_i . \tag{2}$$

$$\mu_j^{(t+1)} = \frac{\sum_{i=1}^{n} \beta_{ij}^{(t)} x_i}{\sum_{i=1}^{n} \beta_{ij}^{(t)}}, \ j = 1, 2, \dots, n_i . \tag{3}$$

$$\sigma_j^{(t+1)} = \frac{\sum_{i=1}^{n} \beta_{ij}^{(t)} (x_i - \mu_j^{(t+1)})^2}{\sum_{i=1}^{n} \beta_{ij}^{(t)}}, \ j = 1, 2, \dots, n_i . \tag{4}$$

S4. Take $\mu_j^i$ as the center; get new covering domains by CA.From S3 to S4, iterate for each class samples in turn. Testing:

The decision-function of the $i$th class samples is

$$\sum_{j=1}^{n_i} \alpha_j \mathrm{e}^{-\frac{(\mathrm{x} - \mathrm{u}_j^i)^2}{\sigma_j^2}} . \tag{5}$$

$\alpha_j$ is the density of $c_j^i$, $\mu_j^i$ is the center and $r_j$ is the radius.

### 2.2 The Analysis of PMCA

Comparing with SVM[8],[9],[10],[11] that could attain the global optimization, CA has an advantage that it can handle the classification problem of k-classes simultaneously. However, SVM process two-classes samples one time essentially, it must turn the problem of k-classes into (k-1) classification problems of two-classes.

Furthermore, SVM is a quadratic programming process, its computation at least is O(n3.5), n is the number of samples; the computation of PMCA is just O(n*ni), here n is the number of samples and ni is the number of covering domains, usually ni is one order of magnitude less than n.

Considering the covering domain density $\alpha_j$, the decision function expressed in formula (5) may be thought as the decision function of KCA whose kernel function is Gauss function. But a problem of the kernel function method is how reasonably assign the parameter to the kernel function, namely $\alpha_j$ in the formula. From the view of probability, the formula (5) may be regarded as a finite mixture density probabilistic model. To different samples, PMCA achieves a set of covers firstly, then iterate continuously according to "the maximum likelihood principle" and automatically obtain optimization parameter. It is a reasonable solution for the parameter problem of kernel function. In other words, when the kernel function is thought as the probability distributing function, KCA presents a new angle of view -- probability model.

## 3 Experiments

### 3.1 Data Sources

1) www.ics.uci.edu/~mlearn/mlsumm.html supplies waveform database.
2) www.ics.uci.edu/~mlearn/mlsumm.html supplies waveform+noise database.

### 3.2 Results

**Table 1.** The results of CA, PMCA and SVM for UCI database

| Data | Algorithm | parameter | Correct rate |
|---|---|---|---|
| Wave form | CA | 79 (number of covering) | 78.68% |
| | PMCA | 43 (number of covering) | 83.48% |
| | SVM | 0.0001 | 63.12% |
| | | 0.0005 | 76.6% |
| | | 0.001 | 80.46% |
| | | 0.1 | 84.7% |
| | | 0.5 | 37.74% |
| Wave form + noise | CA | 79 (number of covering) | 75.26% |
| | PMCA | 41 (number of covering) | 80.16% |
| | SVM | 0.0001 | 61.64% |
| | | 0.0005 | 77.22% |
| | | 0.001 | 80.92% |
| | | 0.1 | 46.18% |
| | | 0.5 | 36.84% |

### 3.3 The Explanation and Analysis of Experimental Results

Table 1 shows PMCA is better than the original CA whether there are noises or not. Furthermore, threshold value about covering density is set in PMCA. It deletes the covering domains whose density is very small, and so the neural cell is cut down greatly. Using PMCA not only could enhance the classification rate, but could automatically produce the reasonable parameter by the maximum likelihood principle. However, the parameter has an important role on the results of SVM.

## 4 Conclusions and Directions of Research in the Future

The probability model is introduced into the classification learning to form PMCA in this paper. It combines KCA and maximum likelihood principle of the statistic model to get the parameter of kernel function automatically. The novel algorithm uses CA to get covering sets and interfaces of each class samples approximately, and then uses maximum likelihood fitting of the finite mixture model to get distributing of each class, which can reduce the calculation remarkably. PMCA not only quotes the optimization process for every covering domain, but also offers a new way to solve the parameter problem of kernel function.

There are still many directions of research about PMCA in the future. This paper just discusses the density function with one dimensional gauss density. The density function with multi-dimensional gauss density is to be discussed by further research. Using CA to get each covering set, then the number of component of finite mixture model is confirmed by this new algorithm. The component amount is invariable in latter solution, but it may be not most appropriate, so we need further research to adjust it. Disposing the unknown samplcs will raise classification rate and correct rate, and how to choose the right disposing method is also a developing direction.

## Acknowledgement

The project partially supported by the national natural science fund with grants (60475017), by the 973 project (national main basis research funds) (2004CB318108), by doctor funds of ministry of education(20040357002), by Anhui Province natural science fund and by the science innovation group of Anhui University.

## References

1. Zhang Ling, Zhang Bo.: A Geometrical Representation of M-P Neural Model and Its Application[J].Journal of Software.,Vol.9,No.5 (1998) 334-338
2. Zhang Ling.: An Principle for Design of Multi-layer Neural Networks[J].Journal of Anhui University National Science Edition, Vol.22,No.3 (1998) 31-41
3. Zhang Ling, Zhang Bo, Yin Hai-feng.: An Alternative Covering Design Algorithm of Multi-layer Neural Networks[J]. Journal of Software, Vol.10, No.7 (1999) 737-742
4. Wu Tao, Zhang Yan-ping, Zhang Ling.: An Ameliorating to Alternative Covering Design Algorithm of Multi-layer Neural Networks[J].Microcomputer Development, Vol.13,No.3 (2003) 50-52

5. Zhang Yan-Ping, Zhang Ling, Duan Zhen.: A Constructive Kernel Covering Algorithm and Applying[J].Journal of Image and Graphics, Vol.9,No.11 (2004) 1304-1308
6. Xu Feng, Li Yang, Wu Tao, Zhang Ling.: A Kernel-based Classification Algorithm of Binary-Covering Approach in Constructive Neural Networks[J].Computer Engineering and Application, 9 (2004) 21-23
7. Zhang Min, Cheng Jiaxing.: The Modulation Classification of Signals Based on Granular Computing and Covering Algorithm[J]. Computer Engineering and Application,24 (2003) 56-59
8. Vikas Sindhwani, Subrata Rskshit, Member, IEEE, Dipti Deodhare, Deniz Erdogmus, Member, IEEE, Jose C.Principe, Fellow, IEEE, and Partha Niyogi.: Feature Selection in MLPs and SVMs Based on Maximum Output Informationp[J]. IEEE Transactions on neural networks, vol.15, no.4, july (2004) 937-948
9. Wei Chu, Chong Jin Ong, Sathiya, S., Keerthi.: An Improved Conjugate Gradient Scheme to the Solution of Least Squares SVM[J]. IEEE Transactions on neural networks, vol.16, no.2, march (2005) 498-501
10. Bernard Haasdonk.: Feature Space Interpretation of SVMs with Indefinite Kernelsp[J]. IEEE Transactions on pattern analysis and machine intelligence, vol.27, no.4, (2005) 482-492
11. King-Shy Goh, Edward Y. Chang, Senior Memer, IEEE, Beitao Li.: Using One-Class and Two-Class SVMs for Multiclass Image Annotation[J].IEEE Transactions on knowledge and data engineering, vol.17, no 10, october (2005) 1333-1346

# Robust Control for a Class of Uncertain Neural Networks with Time-Delays on States and Inputs

Qiuxiang Deng and Zhigang Zeng

School of Automation, Wuhan University of Technology,
Wuhan, Hubei, 430070, China
qx_deng@sohu.com, zhigangzeng@mail.whut.edu.cn

**Abstract.** A class of uncertain neural networks with time-delays on states and inputs is studied. The theoretical analysis herein guarantees that the neural networks are robust stable. In addition, a state feedback control law is presented according to matrix inequalities. An example shows the feasibility of these results.

## 1 Introduction

Robust stabilization problem of time-delay systems has been received much attention in recent years. Amounts of efficient methods in analysis and synthesis of robust control were reported not only in theory but also in practice. Yu and Wang focused on analysis and synthesis of robust control for linear systems only with delayed state in [1]. Wang, Su and Chu studied the robust stabilization of uncertain systems only with delayed input in [2]. However, few studies considered the systems with both delay-states and delay-inputs. And most of the literature studied the time-delay systems with linear uncertain condition [1, 2]. Considering practical systems which were existed much non-linear property, Nie and Zhao studied a class of time-delay systems with non-linear uncertainties in [3]. But the delay-inputs have not been studied.

In addition, since Hopfield's seminal work on stability of the Hopfield neural network (HNN) using energy function [4], numerous studies on the quantitative analysis of various neural networks have been reported. In qualitative analysis of recurrent neural networks, the stability properties primarily concerned are uniqueness and stability of equilibria. In recent years, the stability analysis of recurrent neural networks with time delays received much attention [5]-[7].

In this paper, the problem is focused on a class of uncertain neural networks with both delay-states and delay-inputs. It can be seen as the extension of [1], [2] and [3]. Three theorems are given about robust stability, and a non-memory linear state control law is derived from using matrix inequalities and Lyapunov function. The example shows the feasibility of these results.

D.-S. Huang, K. Li, and G.W. Irwin (Eds.): ICIC 2006, LNCS 4113, pp. 445–450, 2006.

## 2 System Description

Consider a uncertain neural networks with both delay-states and delay-inputs as follows,

$$\begin{cases} \dot{x}(t) = A_0x(t) + \Delta f_0(x(t),t) + A_1x(t-d) + \Delta f_1(x(t-d),t) \\ \quad + B_0u(t) + \Delta g_0(u(t),t) + B_1u(t-d) + \Delta g_1(u(t-d),t) + Cw(t), \\ z(t) = Dx(t), \\ x(t) = \varphi(t), \end{cases} \tag{1}$$

where $x(t)$ is the state vector, $u(t)$ is the control input, $d$ is the constant of time-delay $A_0, A_1, B_0$ and $B_1$ are constant matrices with propriety dimension, $w(t)$ is the disturbance input vector which belongs to $L_2[0,\infty]$. Non-linear uncertain functions $\Delta f_0$, $\Delta f_1$, $\Delta g_0$, $\Delta g_1$ satisfy the conditions as follows,

$$\begin{aligned} &\Delta f_0(x(t),t) = E_0\alpha(x(t),t); \\ &\Delta g_0(u(t),t) = F_0\beta(u(t),t); \\ &\Delta f_1(x(t-d),t) = E_1\alpha(x(t-d),t); \\ &\Delta g_1(u(t),t) = F_1\beta(u(t-d),t), \end{aligned} \tag{2}$$

where $E_0, E_1, F_0$ and $F_1$ are the known constant matrices, and $\alpha(\cdot,\cdot), \beta(\cdot,\cdot)$ are the unknown non-linear continuous differentiable vector functions which satisfy the following inequality, $\|\alpha(x(t),t)\| \le \|w_f x(t)\|$, $\|\beta(u(t),t)\| \le \|w_h u(t)\|$, where $w_f$ and $w_h$ are known weight matrices and $||\cdot||$ is Euclidean normal. For (1), a non-memory linear state control law $u = Kx(t)$ is designed to make the system stable, where $K$ is a constant gain matrix with appropriate dimensions. Thus (1) can be turned into the following form:

$$\begin{aligned} \dot{x}(t) = \; & (A_0 + B_0K)x(t) + (A_1 + B_1K)x(t-d) + E_0\alpha(x(t),t) + E_1\alpha(x(t-d),t) \\ & + F_0\beta(Kx(t),t) + F_1\beta(Kx(t-d),t) + Cw(t). \end{aligned} \tag{3}$$

## 3 Robust Stability Analysis

**Lemma.** If $x$ and $y$ are vectors with appropriate dimensions, then $2x^Ty \le \varepsilon x^TQx + \varepsilon^{-1}y^TQ^{-1}y$, where $\varepsilon$ is a positive constant and $Q$ is a positive definite matrix with appropriate dimensions.

**Theorem 1.** Assumed $w(t) = 0$. If there exit a positive symmetric matrix $P$ and a positive constant $\lambda_f$ such that

$$\psi = P(A_0 + B_0K) + (A_0 + B_0K)^TP + PGG^TP + M^TM < 0, \tag{4}$$

where

$$G = \lambda_f^{1/2}[I, E_0, E_1, F_0, F_1], \quad M = (\lambda_f^{-1})^{1/2}[A_1 + B_1K, \sqrt{2}w_f, \sqrt{2}w_hK]^T \tag{5}$$

then (3) is stable.

**Proof.** Choose Lyapunov function

$$V(x(t)) = x^T(t)Px(t) + \lambda_f^{-1} \int_{t-d}^{t} x^T(s)Qx(s)ds,$$

where

$$Q = (A_1 + B_1K)^T(A_1 + B_1K) + w_f^T w_f + (w_hK)^T(w_hK) > 0.$$

The derivative of $V(x)$ along to the closed loop neural network (3) can be gained as follows

$$\begin{aligned}\dot{V}(x(t)) = & \; x^T(t)(P(A_0 + B_0K) + (A_0 + B_0K)^T P)x(t) \\ & +2x^T(t)P(A_1 + B_1K)x(t-d) \\ & +2x^T(t)P(E_0\alpha(x(t),t) + E_1\alpha(x(t-d),t) + F_0\beta(Kx(t),t) \\ & +F_1\beta(Kx(t-d),t)) + \lambda_f^{-1}(x^T(t)Qx(t) - x^T(t-d)Qx(t-d)). \quad (6)\end{aligned}$$

According to Lemma,

$$\begin{aligned}2x^T(t)P(A_1 + B_1K)x(t-d) \le & \; \lambda_f x^T(t)PPx(t) \\ & +\lambda_f^{-1}x^T(t-d)(A_1 + B_1K)^T(A_1 + B_1K)x(t-d), \\ 2x^T(t)PE_0\alpha(x(t),t) \le & \; \lambda_f x^T(t)PE_0E_0^T Px(t) + \lambda_f^{-1}x^T(t)w_f^T w_f x(t), \\ 2x^T(t)PE_1\alpha(x(t-d),t) \le & \; \lambda_f x^T(t)PE_1E_1^T Px(t) \\ & +\lambda_f^{-1}x^T(t-d)w_f^T w_f x(t-d), \\ 2x^T(t)PF_1\beta(Kx(t-d),t) \le & \; \lambda_f x^T(t)PF_1F_1^T Px(t) \\ & +\lambda_f^{-1}x^T(t-d)(w_hK)^T w_hKx(t-d), \\ 2x^T(t)PF_0\beta(Kx(t),t) \le & \; \lambda_f x^T(t)PF_0F_0^T Px(t) \\ & +\lambda_f^{-1}x^T(t)(w_hK)^T w_hKx(t).\end{aligned}$$

From (6),

$$\begin{aligned}\dot{V}(x(t)) \le & \; x^T(t)(P(A_0 + B_0K) + (A_0 + B_0K)^T P + \lambda_f P(I + E_0E_0^T \\ & +E_1E_1^T F_0F_0^T + F_1F_1^T)P + \lambda_f^{-1}((A_1 + B_1K)^T(A_1 + B_1K) \\ & +2w_f w_f^T + 2(w_hK)^T w_hK)))x(t). \qquad (7)\end{aligned}$$

From (4) and (5), $\dot{V}(x(t)) \le x^T(t)\psi x(t)$. From (4), (3) is stable. The proof is completed.

**Theorem 2.** Given a constant $\rho > 0$, if there exists a non-memory state feedback control law such that

$$\bar{\psi} = \psi + D^T D + \rho^{-2}PC^T CP < 0, \qquad (8)$$

then the neural network (1) has the robust $H_\infty$ performance; i.e, the neural network (1) is robust stable via state feedback.

**Proof.** Let $J = \int_0^\infty (z^T(t)z(t) - \rho^{-2}w^T(t)w(t))dt$. In addition, assume the initial states are zero, for all $w \in L_2[0,\infty]$ which is not zero. The following equation can be obtained:

$$J = \int_0^\infty (z^T(t)z(t) - \rho^{-2}w^T(t)w(t) + \dot{V})dt - x^T(\infty)Px(\infty) - V_\infty,$$

where

$$V_\infty = \lim_{t\to+\infty} \lambda_f^{-1} \int_{t-d}^{t} x^T(s)((A_1 + B_1K)^T(A_1 + B_1K) + w_f w_f^T + (w_h K)^T w_h K)x(s)ds.$$

Similar to the proof of Theorem 1, we can get

$$J \le \int_0^\infty (z^T(t)z(t) - \rho^{-2}w(t)w(t) + \psi + 2x^T PCw(t))dt. \tag{9}$$

By Lemma, we can obtain the inequality

$$2x^T PCw(t) \le \rho^2 x^T PC^T CPx + \rho^{-2}w^T(t)w(t) \tag{10}$$

From the inequality (10) and expression (8), we can get $J \le \int_0^\infty x^T(\psi + D^T D + \rho^{-2}PCC^T P)xdt$.

If the inequality (8) is satisfied, then $J \le 0$. According to the corresponding results in [1], the neural network (1) is robust $H_\infty$ via state feedback.

## 4 Design of Robust Controller

**Theorem 3.** For a given constant $\varepsilon > 0$, if there exists a positive symmetric matrix $P$ such that Ricctai equation

$$\begin{aligned}&P(A_0 + \lambda_f^{-1}B_0NB_1^TA_1) + (A_0 + \lambda_f^{-1}B_0NB_1^TA_1)^TP + PGG^T\\&+\rho^{-2}CC^T + B_0NB_0^TP+\\&\lambda_f^{-1}(A_1A_1^T + 2w_fw_f^T) + D^TD + \lambda_f^{-2}A_1^TB_1NB_1^TA_1 + \varepsilon I = 0,\end{aligned} \tag{11}$$

where $N = -\left(\lambda_f^{-1}B_1^TB_1 + 2\lambda_f^{-1}w_h^Tw_h\right)^{-1}$, then $K = N(B_0^TP + \lambda_f^{-1}B_1^TA_1)$ is a state feedback control law of the neural network (1).

**Proof.** According to (7),

$$\begin{aligned}\bar{\psi} = \ & PA_0 + A_0^TP + PGG^TP + \lambda_f^{-1}(A_1A_1^T + 2w_fw_f^T) + D^TD\\&+\rho^{-2}PCC^TP + (B_0^TP + \lambda_f^{-1}B_1^TA_1)TK + K^T(B_0^TP\\&+\lambda_f^{-1}B_1^TA_1) - K^TN^{-1}K\end{aligned} \tag{12}$$

can be received. From $K = N(B_0^TP + \lambda_f^{-1}B_1^TA_1)$ and (13), $\bar{\psi} = -\varepsilon I < 0$ can be gained.

**Remark 1.** If $w(t) = 0$, then (11) can be turned into the following form:

$$\begin{aligned}&P(A_0 + \lambda_f^{-1}B_0NB_1^TA_1) + (A_0 + \lambda_f^{-1}B_0NB_1^TA_1)^TP + PGG^T\\&+B_0NB_0^T + \lambda_f^{-1}(A_1A_1^T + 2w_fw_f^T) + \lambda_f^{-2}A_1^TB_1NB_1^TA_1 + \varepsilon I = 0.\end{aligned} \tag{13}$$

**Remark 2.** If the uncertain function $\Delta f_0$, $\Delta f_1$, $\Delta g_0$, $\Delta g_1$ are linear, that is to say $\Delta f = ETw_f x = E\alpha(\cdot), \Delta g = FTw_f u = F\beta(\cdot)$, where $T^T T \le I$ and $\alpha(\cdot,\cdot), \beta(\cdot,\cdot)$ satisfy condition (2), then Theorems 1, 2 and 3 obviously hold. If $A_1 = 0$, $E_0 = 0$, and $w(t) = 0$, then the obtained results in this paper are the same as that in [1] whose systems are linear uncertainty with delay-states. And if $B_1 = 0$, $F_1 = 0$, then the obtained results in this paper are the same as that in [2] whose systems are linear uncertainty with delay-inputs.

## 5 Simulation Example

Consider the neural network (1), where

$$A_0 = \begin{bmatrix} 2 & 0 \\ 1 & 2 \end{bmatrix}, \quad B_0 = \begin{bmatrix} 3 & 2 \\ 0 & 2 \end{bmatrix}, \quad A_1 = B_1 = \begin{bmatrix} 1 & 0 \\ 0 & 1 \end{bmatrix}, w_f = w_h = I,$$

$$E_0 = E_1 = F_1 = F_0 = \begin{bmatrix} 0.1 \\ 0.1 \end{bmatrix}, \quad \alpha(x(t), t) = \sin(x(t)), \beta(u(t), t) = \cos(u(t)).$$

Simulation results with different initial values are depicted in Figure 1. The trajectories are unstable if the state feedback control is not added.

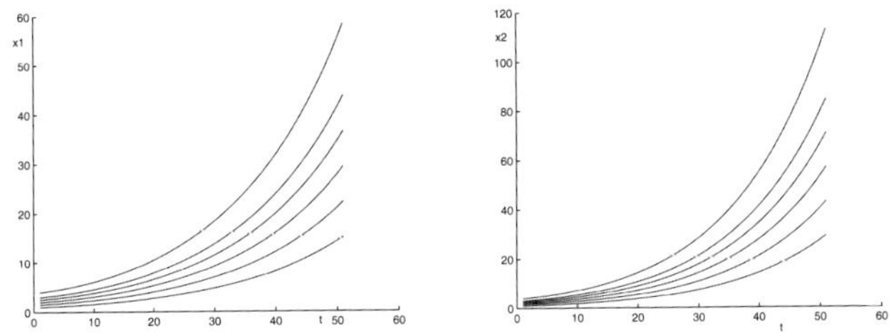


(a) $x_1(t)$ (b) $x_2(t)$

**Fig. 1.** Transient behaviors of $x_1(t)$ and $x_2(t)$ under no control

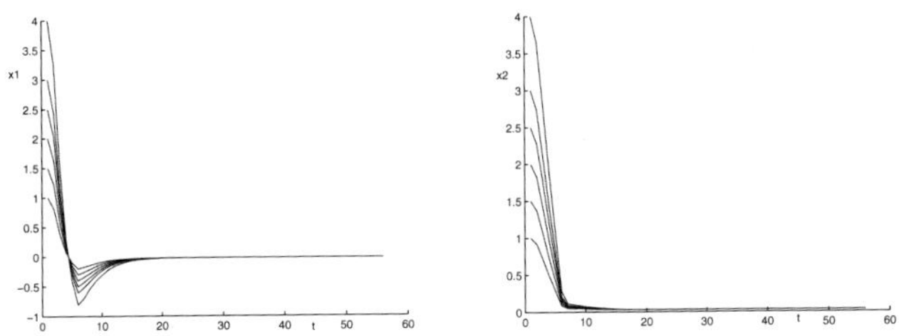


(a) $x_1(t)$ (b) $x_2(t)$

**Fig. 2.** Transient behaviors of $x_1(t)$ and $x_2(t)$ under the state feedback control law

Suppose $\lambda_f = 2$, $\varepsilon = 0.05, w(t) = 0$. According to Theorem 3, from (13), by using Matlab, $P = \begin{bmatrix} 0.2875 & 0.2273 \\ 0.2273 & 1.8350 \end{bmatrix}$ Hence, $K = \begin{bmatrix} -1.2418 & -0.4546 \\ -0.2273 & -1.8350 \end{bmatrix}$.

When the state feedback control is added, simulation results with the same initial value as Figure 1 are depicted in Figure 2, which trajectories are stable.

## 6 Conclusion

This paper focuses on a class of non-linear uncertain neural network with state-delays and input-delays. Some sufficient conditions are presented. The simulation example shows the feasibility of the obtained results.

## Acknowledgement

This work was supported by the Natural Science Foundation of China under Grant 60405002.

## References

1. Yu, L., Wang, W.L.: Design of Output Feedback Stabling Controllers for Uncertain Time-delay Systems. Acta Automatica Sinica, **24** (1998) 225-228
2. Wang, J.C., Su, H. and Chu, J.: Robust $H_\infty$ Output Feedback Controller Design for Linear Time-varying Uncertain Systems with Delayed State. Control Theory and Applications, **16** (1999) 334-337
3. Nie, H., Zhao, J.: Hybrid State Feedback $H_\infty$ Robust Control for A Class of Time-delay Systems with Non-linear Uncertainties. Control Theory and Applications, **22** (2005) 567-570
4. Hopfield, J. J.: Neurons with Graded Response Have Collective Computational Properties Like Those of Two-state Neurons. Proc. Natl. Academy Sci., **81** (1984) 3088-3092
5. Roska, T., Wu, C.W., Balsi, M., and Chua, L.O.: Stability and Dynamics of Delay-type General and Cellular Neural Networks. IEEE Trans. Circuits Syst. I, **39** (1992) 487-490
6. Forti, M., Tesi, A.: New Conditions for Global Stability of Neural Networks with Application to Linear and Quadratic Programming Problems. IEEE Trans. Circ. Syst. I, **42** (1995) 354-366
7. Zeng, Z.G., Wang, J., Liao, X.X.: Stability Analysis of Delayed Cellular Neural Networks Described Using Cloning Templates. IEEE Trans. Circuits and Syst. I, **51** (2004) 2313-2324

# Robust Stability in Interval Delayed Neural Networks of Neutral Type

Jianlong Qiu[1,2] and Qingjun Ren[2]

[1] Department of Mathematics, Southeast University, Nanjing 210096, China
[2] Department of Mathematics, Linyi Normal University, Linyi 276005, China
qjl9916@seu.edu.cn, qjr288@126.com

**Abstract.** In this paper, the problem of global robust stability (GRAS) is investigated for a class of interval neural networks described by nonlinear delayed differential equations of the neutral type. A sufficient criterion is derived by an approach combining the Lyapunov-Krasovskii functional with the linear matrix inequality (LMI). Finally, the effectiveness of the present results is demonstrated by a numerical example.

## 1 Introduction

It is well known, the problem of global stability of delayed neural networks has recently attracted much attention due to its applicability in solving some image processing, signal processing, optimization and pattern recognition problems. Many important results have been reported in the prior literature, see [1-3, 6] and the references therein. Recently in [5], the authors investigated the exponential stability for a class of delayed neural networks described by nonlinear differential equations of the neutral type. However, this stability may be destroyed by some unavoidable uncertainty caused by the existence of modelling errors, external disturbance and parameter fluctuation during the implementation on very-large-scale-integration chips. Therefore, the investigation on robustness of the networks against such errors and fluctuation is very important and significant. There has been some work devoted to the investigation of robust stability for CNNs and DCNNs [7-10].

Motivated by the above discussions, we consider a class of delayed neutral-type neural networks described by a nonlinear differential equation of neutral type:

$$\dot{u}_i(t) = -a_i u_i(t) + \sum_{j=1}^{n} b_{ij} \widetilde{f}_j(u_j(t)) + \sum_{j=1}^{n} c_{ij} \widetilde{g}_j(u_j(t-\tau)) + \sum_{j=1}^{n} d_{ij} \dot{u}_j(t-\tau) + I_i, \quad (1)$$

$$u_i(t) = \phi_i(t), \quad -\tau \le t \le 0, \quad (2)$$

where $i = 1, 2, \cdots, n$ and $n$ denotes the number of neurons in a neural network; $u_i(t)$ denotes the state of the $i$th neuron at time $t$; $\widetilde{f}_j, \widetilde{g}_j$ are activation functions of the $j$th neuron; the scalar $a_i > 0$ is the rate with which the $i$th unit will reset its potential to the resting state in isolation when disconnected from the network and external inputs at time $t$; $b_{ij}, c_{ij}, d_{ij}, i, j = 1, 2, \cdots, n$ are known constants denoting the strength of the $i$th neurons on the $j$th neurons; $\tau$ is non-negative constant, which corresponds to finite speed of axonal signal transmission delay;

D.-S. Huang, K. Li, and G.W. Irwin (Eds.): ICIC 2006, LNCS 4113, pp. 451–456, 2006.

$I_i$ denotes the $i$th component of an external input source. $\phi_i(s,x)$ are bounded and first order continuous differentiable on $[-\tau, 0]$.

The remainder of this paper is organized as follows: In Section 2 some preliminaries are given. The main results are stated in Section 3. In Section 4, an example is provided to show the validity and properties of the stability conditions. In the end, we make concluding remarks.

**Notation.** Throughout this paper, $\mathbb{R}^n$ denotes the $n$-dimensional Euclidean space. $E$ denotes identity matrix. The notation $A > B$ (respectively, $A \geq B$) means that the matrix $A-B$ is symmetric positive definite (respectively, positive semi-definite ), where $A$ and $B$ are matrices of the same dimensions. $A^T$ and $A^{-1}$ denote the transpose and inverse of the matrix $A$. For an arbitrarily real matrix $B$ and two real symmetric matrices $A$ and $C$, $\begin{pmatrix} A & * \\ B & C \end{pmatrix}$ denotes a real symmetric matrix, where $*$ represents the elements above the main diagonal of a symmetric matrix.

## 2 Preliminaries

We make the following assumption:

$(H)$ The neurons activation functions $\widetilde{f}_j$, $\widetilde{g}_j$ are continuous, and there exist constants $l_j > 0, k_j > 0$ such that

$$\|\widetilde{f}_j(\xi_1) - \widetilde{f}_j(\xi_2)\| \leq l_j|\xi_1 - \xi_2|; \quad \|\widetilde{g}_j(\xi_1) - \widetilde{g}_j(\xi_2)\| \leq k_j|\xi_1 - \xi_2|.$$

for any $\xi_1, \xi_2 \in \mathbb{R}, \xi_1 \neq \xi_2, j = 1, 2, \cdots, n$.

In the practical implementation of neural networks, the values of the constant and weight coefficients depend on the resistance and capacitance values which are subject to uncertainties. This may lead to some deviations in the values of $a_i$, $b_{ij}$, $c_{ij}$ and $d_{ij}$. In practice these deviations are bounded, the quantities $a_i$, $b_{ij}$, $c_{ij}$ and $d_{ij}$ may be intervalized as follows:

$$\begin{cases} A_I := \{A = diag(a_i) : \underline{A} \leq A \leq \overline{A}, \text{ i.e., } \underline{a}_i \leq a_i \leq \overline{a}_i, \} \\ B_I := \{B = (b_{ij})_{n\times n} : \underline{B} \leq B \leq \overline{B}, \text{ i.e., } \underline{b}_{ij} \leq b_{ij} \leq \overline{b}_{ij}, \} \\ C_I := \{C = (c_{ij})_{n\times n} : \underline{C} \leq C \leq \overline{C}, \text{ i.e., } \underline{c}_{ij} \leq c_{ij} \leq \overline{c}_{ij}, \} \\ D_I := \{V = (d_{ij})_{n\times n} : \underline{D} \leq D \leq \overline{D}, \text{ i.e., } \underline{d}_{ij} \leq d_{ij} \leq \overline{d}_{ij}, \} \end{cases} \tag{3}$$

Let $U^* = (u_1^*, u_2^*, \cdots, u_n^*)^T$ be an equilibrium point of model (1) for a given $I_i$. To simplify proofs, we will shift the equilibrium point $U^*$ of system (1) to the origin by using the transformation $y_i(t) = u_i(t) - u_i^*, i = 1, 2, \cdots, n$.

It is easy to see that system (1) can be transformed into

$$\dot{y}_i(t) = -a_i y_i(t) + \sum_{j=1}^{n} b_{ij} f_j(y_j(t)) + \sum_{j=1}^{n} c_{ij} g_j(y_j(t-\tau)) + \sum_{j=1}^{n} d_{ij}\dot{y}_j(t-\tau), \tag{4}$$

where $f_j(y_j(t)) = \widetilde{f}_j(y_j(t) + u_j^*) - \widetilde{f}_j(u_j^*)$, $g_j(y_j(t-\tau)) = \widetilde{g}_j(y_j(t-\tau) + u_j^*) - \widetilde{g}_j(u_j^*), j = 1, 2, \cdots, n$. Then it is easy to see that $f_j(0) = 0$, $g_j(0) = 0$, and $f_j(\cdot)$, $g_j(\cdot)$ satisfy assumption $(H)$.

Denote $Y(t) = (y_1(t), y_2(t), \cdots, y_n(t))^T$, $F(Y(t)) = (f_1(y_1(t)), f_2(y_2(t)), \cdots, f_n(y_n(t)))^T$, $G(Y(t-\tau)) = (g_1(y_1(t-\tau)), g_2(y_2(t-\tau)), \cdots, g_n(y_n(t-\tau)))^T$. Then system (4) becomes in the following vector-matrix form

$$\dot{Y}(t) = -AY(t) + BF(Y(t)) + CG(Y(t-\tau)) + D\dot{Y}(t-\tau). \tag{5}$$

**Definition 1.** The neural network model given by (1) is called as interval neural network, if the parameter ranges defined by (3).

**Definition 2.** The neural network model given by (1) with the parameter ranges defined by (3) is globally robust asymptotically stable if the unique equilibrium point $U^* = (u_1^*, u_2^*, \cdots, u_n^*)^T$ of the model is globally asymptotically stable for all $A \in A_I$, $B \in B_I$, $C \in C_I$ and $D \in D_I$.

**Lemma 1** [5]. Suppose $W$, $U$ are any matrices, $\epsilon$ is a positive number and matrix $H = H^T > 0$, then the following inequality holds

$$W^TU + U^TW \le \epsilon W^THW + \epsilon^{-1}U^TH^{-1}U.$$

Moreover, for notational convenience, we define, for $i, j = 1, 2, \cdots, n$,

$$b_{ij}^* = \max\{|\underline{b}_{ij}|, |\bar{b}_{ij}|\}, \quad c_{ij}^* = \max\{|\underline{c}_{ij}|, |\bar{c}_{ij}|\}, \quad d_{ij}^* = \max\{|\underline{d}_{ij}|, |\bar{d}_{ij}|\},$$

and,

$$\begin{cases} u_i = \sum\limits_{j=1}^{n}(b_{ij}^* \sum\limits_{l=1}^{n} b_{lj}^*), v_i = \sum\limits_{j=1}^{n}(c_{ij}^* \sum\limits_{l=1}^{n} c_{lj}^*), w_i = \sum\limits_{j=1}^{n}(d_{ij}^* \sum\limits_{l=1}^{n} d_{lj}^*), \\ U = diag(u_i), \quad V = diag(v_i), \quad W = diag(w_i). \end{cases} \tag{6}$$

**Lemma 2** [11]. For any constant matrix $B \in B_I$, $C \in C_I$ and $D \in D_I$

$$BB^T \le U, \quad CC^T \le V, \quad DD^T \le W$$

where the diagonal matrices $U$, $V$ and $W$ are defined in Eq. (6).

## 3 Main Results

**Theorem.** Under the assumption $(H)$, the equilibrium point $U^*$ of system (1) is globally robust asymptotically stable if there exist positive definite matrix $P$, positive definite diagonal matrix $Q$ and positive constants $\beta$, $\varepsilon_1$, $\varepsilon_2$, $\varepsilon_3$ such that

$$\Psi = \begin{pmatrix} \Sigma & * & * & * & * & * \\ PU^{\frac{1}{2}} & \varepsilon_1 E & * & * & * & * \\ PV^{\frac{1}{2}} & 0 & \varepsilon_2 E & * & * & * \\ PW^{\frac{1}{2}} & 0 & 0 & \varepsilon_3 E & * & * \\ 0 & 0 & 0 & 0 & \Gamma_1 & * \\ 0 & 0 & 0 & 0 & 0 & \Gamma_2 \end{pmatrix} > 0, \tag{7}$$

where $\Sigma = P\underline{A}+\underline{A}P-KQK-\varepsilon_1 L^2-4\beta(\overline{A}^2+LUL), \Gamma_1 = Q-\varepsilon_2 E-4\beta V,\ \Gamma_2 = \beta E-\varepsilon_3 E-4\beta W, L = diag(l_1, l_2, \cdots, l_n),\ \ K = diag(k_1, k_2, \cdots, k_n)$ and $l_i > 0, k_i > 0, i = 1, 2, \cdots, n$ are given in assumption (H). **Proof:** Define a Lyapunov-Krasovskii functional as

$$V(t) = Y^T(t)PY(t) + \int_{t-\tau}^{t} G^T(Y(\xi))QG(Y(\xi))d\xi + \beta\int_{t-\tau}^{t} \dot{Y}(\xi)^T\dot{Y}(\xi)d\xi. \quad (8)$$

Computing the derivative of $V(t)$ along the trajectory of system (5), we have

$$\begin{aligned}\dot{V}(t) = &Y^T(t)[-PA-AP]Y(t) + 2Y^T(t)PBF(Y(t))\\ &+2Y^T(t)PCG(Y(t-\tau)) + 2Y^T(t)PD\dot{Y}(t-\tau)\\ &+G^T(Y(t))QG(Y(t)) - G^T(Y(t-\tau))QG(Y(t-\tau))\\ &+\beta\dot{Y}^T(t)\dot{Y}(t) - \beta\dot{Y}^T(t-\tau)\dot{Y}(t-\tau). \end{aligned} \quad (9)$$

By Lemma 1, Lemma 2 and assumption $(H)$, we have

$$G^T(Y(t))QG(Y(t)) \le Y^T(t)KQKY(t), \quad (10)$$

$$\begin{aligned}2Y^T(t)PBF(Y(t)) &\le \varepsilon_1^{-1}Y^T(t)PBB^TPY(t) + \varepsilon_1 F^T(Y(t))F(Y(t))\\ &\le Y^T(t)[\varepsilon_1^{-1}PUP + \varepsilon_1 L^2]Y(t),\end{aligned} \quad (11)$$

$$\begin{aligned}2Y^T(t)PCG(Y(t-\tau)) &\le \varepsilon_2^{-1}Y^T(t)PCC^TPY(t) + \varepsilon_2 G^T(Y(t-\tau))G(Y(t-\tau))\\ &\le \varepsilon_2^{-1}Y^T(t)PVPY(t) + \varepsilon_2 G^T(Y(t-\tau))G(Y(t-\tau))\end{aligned} \quad (12)$$

$$\begin{aligned}2Y^T(t)PD\dot{Y}(t-\tau) &\le \varepsilon_3^{-1}Y^T(t)PDD^TPY(t) + \varepsilon_3\dot{Y}^T(t-\tau)\dot{Y}(t-\tau)\\ &\le \varepsilon_3^{-1}Y^T(t)PWPY(t) + \varepsilon_3\dot{Y}^T(t-\tau)\dot{Y}(t-\tau),\end{aligned} \quad (13)$$

$$\begin{aligned}\dot{Y}^T(t)\dot{Y}(t) \le\ &4Y^T(t)A^2Y(t) + 4F^T(Y(t))B^TBF(Y(t))\\ &+4G^T(Y(t-\tau))C^TCG(Y(t-\tau)) + 4\dot{Y}^T(t-\tau)D^TD\dot{Y}(t-\tau)\\ \le\ &4Y^T(t)[\overline{A}^2 + LUL]Y(t) + 4G^T(Y(t-\tau))VG(Y(t-\tau))\\ &+4\dot{Y}^T(t-\tau)W\dot{Y}(t-\tau).\end{aligned} \quad (14)$$

Substituting (10)-(14) into (9), we further have

$$\begin{aligned}\dot{V}(t) \le\ &Y^T(t)[-P\underline{A} - \underline{A}P + KQK + \varepsilon_1^{-1}PU^{\frac{1}{2}}U^{\frac{1}{2}T}P + \varepsilon_1 L^2 + \varepsilon_2^{-1}PV^{\frac{1}{2}}V^{\frac{1}{2}T}P\\ &+\varepsilon_3^{-1}PW^{\frac{1}{2}}W^{\frac{1}{2}T}P + 4\beta(\overline{A}^2 + LUL)]Y(t) + \dot{Y}^T(t-\tau)[-\beta E + \varepsilon_3 E + 4\beta W]\\ &\dot{Y}(t-\tau) + G^T(Y(t-\tau))[-Q + \varepsilon_2 E + 4\beta V]G(Y(t-\tau))\\ =\ &\Lambda^T(t)\begin{pmatrix}\widetilde{\Sigma} & 0 & 0 & 0\\ 0 & \widetilde{\Gamma}_1 & 0 & 0\\ 0 & 0 & \widetilde{\Gamma}_2 & 0\\ 0 & 0 & 0 & -\tau\eta\end{pmatrix}\Lambda(t),\end{aligned} \quad (15)$$

where $\widetilde{\Sigma} = -P\underline{A} - \underline{A}P + KQK + \varepsilon_1^{-1}PU^{\frac{1}{2}}U^{\frac{1}{2}T}P + \varepsilon_1 L^2 + \varepsilon_2^{-1}PV^{\frac{1}{2}}V^{\frac{1}{2}T}P + \varepsilon_3^{-1}PW^{\frac{1}{2}}W^{\frac{1}{2}T}P + 4\beta(\overline{A}^2 + LUL), \widetilde{\Gamma}_1 = -Q + \varepsilon_2 E + 4\beta V,\ \ \widetilde{\Gamma}_2 = -\beta E + \varepsilon_3 E + 4\beta W, \Lambda = \left(Y^T(t),\ G^T(Y(t-\tau)), \dot{Y}(t-\tau))^T\right)^T.$

By the Schur complement[4] and the condition (7), $\dot{V}(t) < 0$. So, we can easily see the equilibrium of system (1) is globally asymptotically stable. This completes the proof. □

**Corollary.** Under the assumption $(H)$, the equilibrium point $U^*$ of system (1) is globally robust asymptotically stable if there exist positive definite matrix $P$, positive definite diagonal matrix $Q$ and positive constants $\beta$, $\varepsilon_1$, $\varepsilon_2$, $\varepsilon_3$ such that

$$\widehat{\Psi} = \begin{pmatrix} \widehat{\Sigma} & * & * & * & * & * \\ P & \varepsilon_1 E & * & * & * & * \\ P & 0 & \varepsilon_2 E & * & * & * \\ P & 0 & 0 & \varepsilon_3 E & * & * \\ 0 & 0 & 0 & 0 & \widehat{\Gamma_1} & * \\ 0 & 0 & 0 & 0 & 0 & \widehat{\Gamma_2} \end{pmatrix} > 0, \tag{16}$$

where $\widehat{\Sigma} = P\underline{A} + \underline{A}P - KQK - \varepsilon_1 LUL - 4\beta(\overline{A}^2 + LUL)$, $\widehat{\Gamma_1} = Q - \varepsilon_2 V - 4\beta V$, $\widehat{\Gamma_2} = \beta E - \varepsilon_3 W - 4\beta W$.

**Proof.** The proof is similar to Theorem 1, and omitted here. □

## 4 Simulation Example

**Example.** Let $\widetilde{f}_j = \widetilde{g}_j$, $j = 1, 2$, with the Lipschtiz constant $l_1 = l_2 = 1$. Consider the following delayed neural network of in (1) with parameters as

$$\underline{A} = \begin{pmatrix} 2 & 0 \\ 0 & 2 \end{pmatrix}, \overline{A} = \begin{pmatrix} 3 & 0 \\ 0 & 3 \end{pmatrix}, \underline{B} = \begin{pmatrix} 0.1 & 0.1 \\ 0 & 0.1 \end{pmatrix}, \overline{B} = \begin{pmatrix} 0.5 & 0.1 \\ 0.01 & 0.3 \end{pmatrix},$$
$$\underline{C} = \begin{pmatrix} 0.1 & 0.1 \\ 0 & 0.1 \end{pmatrix}, \overline{C} = \begin{pmatrix} 0.1 & 0.16 \\ 0.05 & 0.1 \end{pmatrix}, \underline{D} = \begin{pmatrix} 0.05 & 0 \\ 0 & 0.05 \end{pmatrix}, \overline{D} = \begin{pmatrix} 0.1 & 0 \\ 0 & 0.1 \end{pmatrix}.$$

Using the Matlab LMI Control Toolbox to solve the LMI in (7), we can obtain the solution as follows

$$\varepsilon_1 = 11.5641,\ \varepsilon_2 = 4.7236,\ \varepsilon_3 = 0.4305,\ \beta = 0.7385,$$
$$P = \begin{pmatrix} 24.7720 & 0 \\ 0 & 25.4904 \end{pmatrix},\ Q = \begin{pmatrix} 16.0100 & 0 \\ 0 & 16.4050 \end{pmatrix}.$$

From Theorem, we derive that the DNN of neutral type is globally robust stable.

## 5 Conclusion

In this paper, the global robust stability for a class of interval neural networks of neutral type has been considered. Based on Lyapunov method and the LMI approach, a series of sufficient conditions have been established to ensure global robust stability of this model. The obtained results improve and extend several earlier works. Simulation result demonstrates the effectiveness of the proposed results.

## References

1. Cao, J., Wang, J.: Global Exponential Stability and Periodicity of Recurrent Neural Networks with Time Delays, IEEE Trans. Circuits Syst. I 52(5) (2005) 925-931
2. Cao, J., Wang, J.: Global Asymptotic Stability of a General Class of Recurrent Neural Networks with Time-varying Delays, IEEE Trans. Circuits Syst. I 50(1) (2003) 34-44
3. Cao, J., Daniel W. C. Ho.: A General Framework for Global Asymptotic Stability Analysis of Delayed Neural Networks Based on LMI Approach. Chaos, Solitons and Fractals 24(5) (2005) 1317-1329
4. Boyd, S., Ghaoui, L.E.I., Feron, E., Balakrishnan, V.: Linear Matrix Inequalities in System and Control Theory, SIAM, Philadelphia (1994)
5. Xu, S., Lam, J., Ho, D.W.C., Zou, Y.: Delay-dependent Exponential Stability for a Class of Neural Networks with Time Delays. J. Comput. Appl. Math. 183 (2005) 16-28
6. Jiang, H., Teng, Z.: Global Exponential Stability of Cellular Neural Networks with Time-varying Coefficients and Delays. Neural Networks 17 (2004) 1415-1425
7. Liao, X.F., Wang, J.: Global and Robust Stability of Interval Hopfield Neural Networks with Time-varying Delays. Int. J. Neural Syst. 13 (2) (2003)
8. Cao, J., Chen, T.: Globally Exponentially Robust Stability and Periodicity of Delayed Neural Networks. Chaos, Solitons and Fractals 22(4) (2004) 957-963
9. Cao, J., Huang, D., Qu, Y.: Global Robust Stability of Delayed Recurrent Neural Networks. Chaos, Solitons and Fractals 23 (2005) 221-229
10. Cao, J., Li, H., Lei H.: Novel Results Concerning Global Robust Stability of Delayed Neural Networks. Nonlinear Analysis, Series B 7(3) (2006) 458-469
11. Li, D.: Matrix Theory and Its Applications. Chongqing University Press, Chongqing, China (1988)
12. Cao, J., Li, X.: Stability in Delayed Cohen-Grossberg Neural Networks: LMI Optimization Approach, Physica D: Nonlinear Phenomena, 212(1-2) (2005) 54-65
13. Cao, J., Li, P., Wang, W.: Global Synchronization in Arrays of Delayed Neural Networks with Constant and Delayed Coupling. Physics Letters A, 353(4) (2006) 318-325

# Segmenting Images of Occluded Humans Using a Probabilistic Neural Network

Yongtae Do

School of Electronic Engineering, Daegu University
Gyeongsan-City, Gyeongbuk, 712-714, South Korea
ytdo@daegu.ac.kr

**Abstract.** When processing an image of multiple occluded humans, segmenting them is a prerequisite for higher-level tasks such as tracking and activity analysis. Although a human observer can easily segment target humans partly occluded among themselves in an image, automatic segmentation in computer vision is difficult. In this paper, the use of a probabilistic neural network is proposed to learn various outline shape patterns of a foreground image blob of occluded humans, and then to segment the blob into its constituents. The segmentation is here regarded as a two-class pattern recognition problem; segmentable positions constitute a class and other positions constitute the other. The technique proposed is useful particularly for low-resolution images where existing image analysis techniques are difficult to be applied.

## 1 Introduction

Recently, a great deal of effort has been expended on video surveillance and monitoring (VSAM) in computer vision society. The goal of VSAM is developing technology to automatically detect and track targets of interest within cluttered scenes, and monitor their activities over long periods of time [1]. Vehicles and humans are two most important targets in VSAM. While significant amount of research work has been carried out for the former, research on the latter became active only lately. One obvious reason is that there have been more commercial demands for automatic vehicle monitoring and traffic control. Another reason is that processing images of humans is more difficult technically. Humans have higher degrees of freedom and their shapes vary flexibly. There are also varieties of colors and texture patterns in human images. They have less limitation in their movement and their motion is less predictable.

A complete VSAM system can be built through threc important steps; detection, tracking, and activity analysis. Collins *et al.* [2] claimed that activity analysis is the most important area of future research in VSAM. However, activity analysis is heavily dependent on the tracking process. A Kalman filter is a popular tool for tracking people in image sequences [3]. As the speed of a human is slow, the total motion of a person is generally small between video image frames. However, the shape of a person may vary significantly. Poor detection of humans in images makes the tracking more difficult. In fact, foreground detection is significantly incomplete occasionally [4].

D.-S. Huang, K. Li, and G.W. Irwin (Eds.): ICIC 2006, LNCS 4113, pp. 457 – 462, 2006.

Even if humans are detected well as foreground in an image, occlusions among themselves make later processing difficult. The simplest method tackling the occlusion problem is avoiding it by placing a camera looking vertically downwards [5]. However, this misses most information of people monitored such as height, color and silhouette. In [6], an occlusion is detected when multiple people are predicted to be located within the same region in the new video image frame based on their velocities. No attempt was made to segment a blob of multiple humans occluded by themselves into constituents but waiting de-occlusion. Another approach is analyzing the outline of a blob of multiple humans, for example using an active contour (snakes) [7]. However, when the image is in low-resolution, it cannot be effective as small error in foreground extraction causes significant change in the contour. Practically, an outdoor surveillance camera is often installed at a far distance from a scene for wide field-of-view.

In this paper, a foreground image blob of multiple humans is segmented into individual constituents using a probabilistic neural network (PNN) [8], which is a neural network implementation of the Bayesian classifier. We regard detecting the vertical segmentation position separating two persons (occluding and occluded) in a foreground blob as a two-class pattern recognition problem; positions need to be segmented constitute a class and others constitute the other class. The use of a PNN is motivated by two factors. First, it is hard to characterize occlusion by some feature variables. Different clothes and postures of people will cause different variable values. Secondly, if images are in low-resolution, it is difficult to build a reliable statistical model. Although a human observer can separate humans in occlusion without difficulty, the method human intelligence implicitly uses is hard to be formulized. In this situation, while most existing techniques cannot provide an effective solution, a PNN is expected to determine the position where a blob of people needs to be segmented by learning based on the shape information of upper body parts of human targets.

## 2 The Overall System

The goal of research work described in this paper is finding the best segmentation position for a foreground image blob of multiple people. We employ a PNN for the goal. Fig. 1 describes the overall system from input image processing to PNN-based segmentation. As shown in the figure, two important steps are required to extract data from images of a VSAM camera for the PNN: extracting humans as foreground and obtaining the shape information.

A background subtraction technique is widely used to extract foreground pixels as it provides more complete feature data than other approaches like temporal differencing [9] or optical flow [10]. In this paper, an adaptive background adaptation method proposed by Lipton *et al.* [4] is used. Morphological operation and size filtering are done on the foreground image extracted to fill holes and to remove noises respectively for obtaining a more complete image.

When processing low-resolution images, it is difficult to build a stable statistical model of a target because the number of pixels belong to the target is small. The foreground detected is frequently not complete also including holes and gaps (*e.g.*, see the binary foreground image extracted in Fig. 1). In this paper, the shape pattern of upper body parts of target humans is checked. We use a line connecting the top pixel of each column in an image blob (we call it 'draping line') as a shape descriptor. Draping is much simpler than existing outline detection techniques such as boundary following or snakes. Although it misses information below the line, it is not a problem here because we will not utilize it. The upper body parts such as head and torso are relatively stable than lower parts like legs and feet in extracted foreground images when a human moves. Draping is thus robust against error in foreground extraction. Incomplete foreground extraction inside a blob does not change the line shape at all. The PNN employed checks local slopes along a draping line to detect segmentation positions for an image blob of occluded humans.

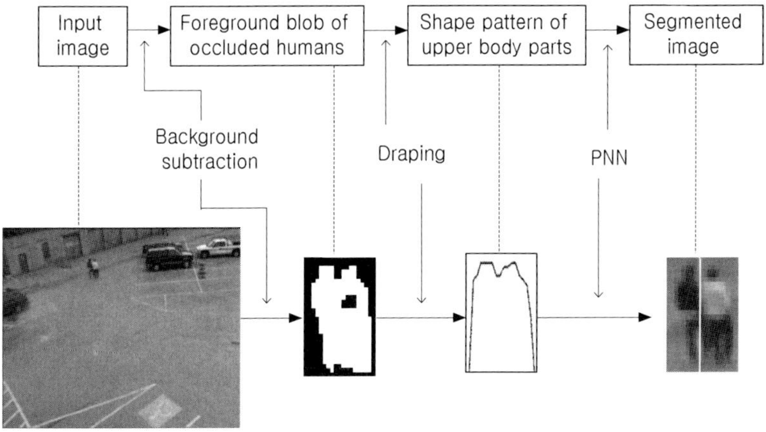


**Fig. 1.** The overall system of PNN-based image segmentation of occluded humans

## 3 PNN for Segmenting an Image Blob of Occluded Humans

The PNN introduced by Specht [8] is based on the well-known Bayesian classifier commonly used in many classical pattern recognition problems. When using a Bayesian classifier, a key step is estimating the probability density functions (pdf) from the training patterns. However, in some cases like the problem being dealt in this paper, estimating the pdf is difficult. In the PNN, a nonparametric estimation technique known as Parzen windows [12] is used to construct the pdf for each class required by Bayes' theorem. This allows determination of the chance a given vector pattern lies within a given class.

One novelty of this paper is that we regard the segmentation problem as a classification problem. Segmentable positions constituent a class (say class S), and other positions constituent the other class (say class N). As there are only limited numbers of segmentation positions in training images (*e.g.*, ideally one if there are two humans in an image), the size of class S is much smaller than that of class N (*i.e.*, much more training data for class N). For image blobs to be used for training the PNN, the best segmentation positions are set manually and used as true output values. The position at which a foreground image blob can be best segmented is actually difficult to precisely specify but it can be within some narrow range. So, two left and two right positions of a user specified segmentation position are also included in class S. In this way, the size of class S becomes larger.

A PNN consists of four layers: input layer, pattern layer, summation layer, and output layer. The input neurons distribute all of the input variables to all the neurons in the pattern layer. We use five consequent signs of slope along a draping line as the network input. This means that the PNN estimates a good segmentation position from the local shape pattern of upper body parts of humans in occlusion. Each pattern layer neuron $k$ performs a dot product of the input pattern vector $\boldsymbol{x}$ with the weight vector $\boldsymbol{w}_k$. Then, a nonlinear operation $\exp[(\boldsymbol{x} \cdot \boldsymbol{w}_k - 1)/\sigma^2]$, where $\sigma$ is an adjustable smoothing parameter, is carried out before outputting to the summation neuron. Training a PNN can be regarded as finding the best smoothing parameter for a set of input vectors which maximizes the classification accuracy [13]. Although $\sigma$ must be found experimentally, a large number of trials are generally not necessary because the curve of the mean squared error versus $\sigma$ exhibits a wide range of values near the minimum [14]. Two neurons in the summation layer are connected to pattern layer neurons which correspond to each of the two classes from which the training patterns were selected. The output represents the goodness of segmentation. In typical pattern recognition problem using PNN, the output is binary. But, in this paper, we get real output values, and the position of the maximum output value is selected.

The main drawback of a PNN is the rapid increase in computing costs by the increase of two factors; the size of the input vector and the size of training data [13]. The PNN employed in this paper has only 5 input nodes and the first factor is not a problem while the second factor may increase computing time. Nevertheless, considering today's context of high-speed computing power, this should no longer be a significant problem.

## 4 Results

To test the PNN designed with various occlusion cases, three people were sampled from real camera images and occlusions between two of them were synthesized randomly. Fig. 2 shows three images of sampled people (person 1, person 2, and person 3) and examples of synthesized occlusions among them. Training data for the PNN were obtained from 30 occlusion cases synthesized using person 1 and person 2, in addition to other 30 cases using person1 and person 3. On the other hand, 30 occlusion cases synthesized using person 2 and person 3 are used for testing the network trained. Additionally 20 real images are collected and used for testing. For each training image, the draping line was found and five slope codes were used as the components of an input vector. In our experiment, the network showed the best result when its smoothing parameter $\sigma$ was set to 0.9. The successful segmentation rates for training images and testing images were 83% and 76% respectively.

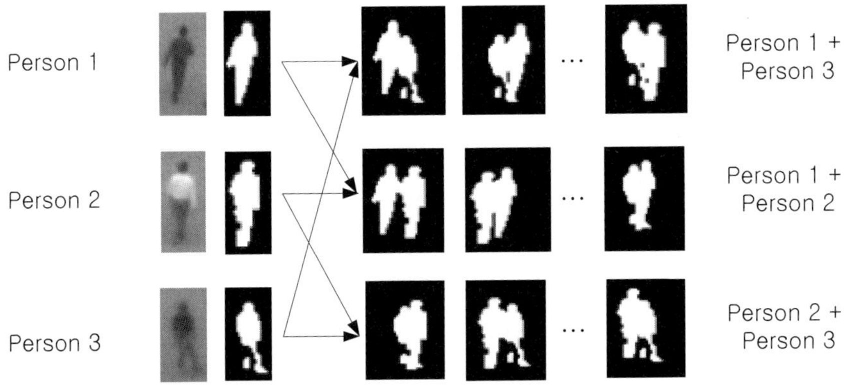


**Fig. 2.** Synthesized occlusions for training and testing the PNN designed

## 5 Conclusion

A PNN is a neural network implementation of the well known Bayesian classifier. This paper describes a PNN employed to segment a foreground image blob of occluded humans for VSAM applications. The network design and steps to extract data for training the network have been presented. It is demonstrated that a PNN is useful to tackle the occlusion problem in low-resolution images, where existing statistical models or contour-based techniques are difficult to be used. Upper body parts of humans are relatively stable during motion, and we checked the shape of upper body parts overlapped by occlusion. We defined 'draping' for the purpose, and the pattern of partial draping line was used for the network learning. Unlike multilayer perceptrons, which are popularly used but need ad hoc design procedures and long training time, the implementation of a PNN is straightforward and simple. In our experiment using images of two occluded humans, a PNN showed around 80% success rates in segmenting each of the images into two properly. The smoothing parameter of the network was set to 0.9 and the size of input vector was 5 in the experiment.

## Acknowledgement

This work was supported by the Korea Research Foundation Grant (KRF-2003-013-D00101).

## References

1. Collins, R.T., Lipton, A.J., Fujiyoshi, H., Kanade, T.: Algorithms for Cooperative Multisensor Surveillance. Proc. IEEE 89 (2001) 1456-1477
2. Collins, R.T., Lipton, A.J., Kanade, T.: Introduction to the Special Section on Video Surveillance. IEEE Trans. Pattern Analysis and Machine Intelligence 22 (2000) 745-746

3. Zhao, T., Nevatia, R., Fengjun, L.: Segmentation and Tracking of Multiple Humans in Complex Situations. In: Proc. Computer Vision and Pattern Recognition, Vol. II (2001) 194-201
4. Lipton, A.J., Fujiyoshi, H., Patil, R.S.: Moving Target Classification and Tracking from Real-Time Video. In: Proc. IEEE Workshop on Application of Computer Vision (1998) 8-14
5. Grimson, W.E.L., Stauffer, C., Romano, R., Lee, L.: Using Adaptive Tracking to Classify and Monitor Activities in a Site. In: Proc. IEEE Computer Vision and Pattern Recognition (1998) 22-29
6. Sindhu, A.J., Morris, T.: A Region Based Approach to Tracking People before, during, and after Occlusions. In: Proc. IASTED Int. Conf. Visualization, Imaging, and Image Processing (2004)
7. Heikkila, J., Silven, O.: A Real-Time System for Monitoring Cyclists and Pedestrians. In: Proc. IEEE Workshop on Visual Surveillance (1999) 74-81
8. Specht, D.F.: Probabilistic Neural Networks for Classification, Mapping, or Associate Memory. In: Proc. IEEE Int. Conf. Neural Networks, Vol. 1 (1988) 525-532
9. Anderson, C., Burt, P., Wal, G. van der: Change Detection and Tracking Using Pyramid Transformation Techniques. In: Proc. SPIE, Vol. 579 (1985) 72-78
10. Barron, J., Fleet, D., Beauchemin, S.: Performance of Optical Flow Techniques. Int. Journal of Computer Vision 12 (1994) 42-77
11. Becanovic, V., Hosseiny, R. Indiveri, G.: Object Tracking Using Multiple Neuromorphic Vision Sensors. In: Proc. RoboCup (2004) 426-433
12. Parzen, E.: On Estimation of a Probability Density Function and Mode. Annals of Mathematical Statistics 33 (1962) 1065-1076
13. Goh, A.T.C.: Probabilistic Neural Network for Evaluating Seismic Liquefaction Potential. Canadian Geotechnical Journal 39 (2002) 219-232
14. Specht, D.F.: Probabilistic Neural Networks. Neural Networks 3 (1990) 109-118

# Simulation Line Design Using BP Neural Network

Hai-yan Zhang, Xin Li, and Shu-feng Tian

Department of Electrical Engineering, Ocean University of China,
Qingdao 266071, China
{hyzhang, eleceng}@mail.ouc.edu.cn

**Abstract.** The simulation line is usually used to imitate the frequency characteristic of a real long transmission line. This paper proposes a novel design scheme of simulation line using back propagation neural network (BP NN). A BP NN is trained to correspond with the line's transfer function and then implemented by field programmable gate array (FPGA) for application in real time. The activation function of NN is approximated with a high-speed symmetric table addition method (STAM), which reduces the amount of memory required. For an underwater coaxial cable that is 10000m long, a simulation line is hardware realized and has been successfully used in the study of digital image transmission.

## 1 Introduction

The simulation line is a designed network to imitate the frequency characteristic of a real long transmission line [1]. It is usually used instead of the real long line when the transmission experiments can't be done on the spot. The simulation line is actually a low-pass filter, but its transfer function is not easy to obtain by inversion means. So it is difficult using general analogy or digital filter to realize the simulation line. This paper presents a new method for simulation line realization using back propagation neural network. The simulation line is realized by FPGA for the real time application. In the hardware implementation of the activation function, STAM algorithm was used to reduce the amount of memory and make the operation simpler [2].

## 2 Simulation Line Design Using BP NN

The simulation line that corresponds to an underwater coaxial cable is hardware implemented using Altera's Stratix-II FPGA and TI's 10 bits high speed DAC. Fig.1 shows the block diagram of the simulation line design.

BP NN has been successfully applied to solve some difficult and diverse problems. It has a powerful ability of nonlinear mapping and pattern recognition [3], [4]. In this paper, a BP NN is trained to correspond with the line's transfer function.

The coaxial cable is 10000m long and 55Ω line characteristic impedance. Signals of information source and sink are sampled on the spot. The information source is a base band signal with HDB3 encoding and transmits through the coaxial cable. The transmission loss of the line leads to the distortion of information sink.

From the analysis of the distorted signal, the output wave not only depends on its corresponding input code cell, but also correlates with the multi code cells around. The

D.-S. Huang, K. Li, and G.W. Irwin (Eds.): ICIC 2006, LNCS 4113, pp. 463 – 469, 2006.

serial 8 code cells play the role of input vector. Each node of the input layer represents a code cell, which is expressed by 2 binary bits in the FPGA implementation. (Let 0.0 denotes 0 of HDB3 encoding, 1.0 denotes +1, 0.1 denotes -1). The information sink signal due to the 5th input code cell serves the role of designed response. Since the sink signal has been distorted, it is necessary to use a high speed DAC to get the analogy value. Considering the precision and speed of DAC, the output layer consists of 10 neurons. Each of them is expressed by 10 binary bits in the FPGA implementation. Selecting the 3-states latch's OE pin in turn, the D/A conversion of each output neuron is completed.

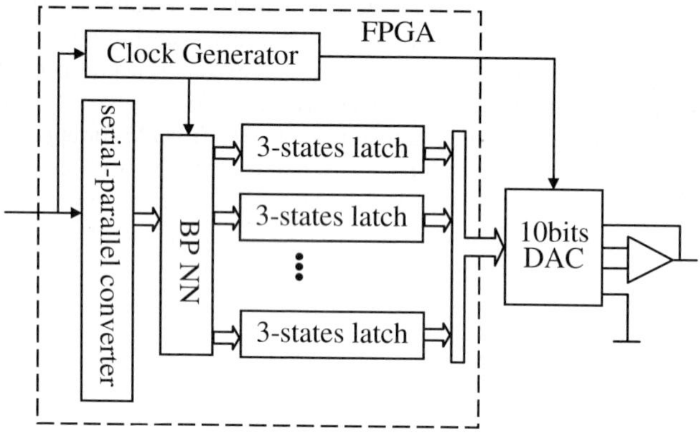


**Fig. 1.** The block diagram of the simulation line design

Considering FPGA implementation resource in addition, the number of hidden neurons is held at 12. So the final network is constructed with 8 input nodes, 12 neurons in the hidden layer and 10 neurons in the output layer.

In the example of this paper, the bit rate of base band signal with $HDB_3$ encoding is 1Mbps and the information sink signal varies acutely. So the tan-s function is selected as the activation function of BP NN. The Tan-s function is defined by

$$f(x) = \tan sig(x) = \frac{e^x - e^{-x}}{e^x + e^{-x}} \tag{1}$$

A training set and a test set are constructed for the BP NN learning in batch mode. The information source and sink signals of the coaxial cable are sampled and 4000 pairs of example are acquired. The front 3000 examples constitute the training set and the test set consists of the rear 1000 examples. After the training and testing phases are found to be successful, the NN can then be put in practical application.

## 3 FPGA Implementation for BP NN

Once the BP NN design is performed, only the forward computation is needed to implement by FPGA. The output signal of neuron $j$ in hidden layer (or output layer) is

$$O_j = f(\sum W_{ij} \cdot x_i - \theta_j) \tag{2}$$

where $O_j$ is the output signal of neuron $j$, $W_{ij}$ is synaptic weight connecting neuron $i$ to neuron $j$, $x_i$ is the input signal of neuron $j$, $\theta_j$ is the bias.

When the network off-line training is over, $W_{ij}$ and $\theta_j$ are fixed and then stored in the RAM of FPGA. The operations for multiplication, addition and subtraction in formula(2) are easily implemented in hardware. How to realize the Tan-s function by FPGA is the key technique.

There are mainly two techniques for hardware implementation of nonlinear function: table-lookup method and polynomial approximation method. Due to the large amount of multiplication operation, it is more complex for real-time hardware implementation of polynomial approximation. For table lookup method, less memory size and simpler operation are required on the premise of satisfying the expression precision.

### 3.1 STAM Algorithm

This paper uses an algorithm named symmetric table addition method for Tan-s function approximation. This method has a close-form solution for the table entries and can be applied to any differentiable function. STAM uses parallel table lookups and multi-operand addition to compute elementary functions. It requires less memory than standard table lookup method[2],[5] and is suitable for high-speed hardware implementation. Symmetry and leading zeroes in the table coefficients are used to further reduce the memory size.

To approximate the function $f(x)$, the $n$ bits input operand $x$ is separated into $m$+1 parts: $x_0$, $x_1$, $\cdots$, $x_m$ with length of $n_0$, $n_1$,$\cdots$, $n_m$ respectively, where $x = x_0+x_1+\cdots+x_m$, $n = n_0+n_1+\cdots+n_m$.

The $i$th table $a_{i-1}(x_0, x_i)$ takes as inputs $x_0$ and $x_i$. The sum of the outputs from the $m$ tables produces an approximation to $f(x)$. This approximation takes the form

$$f(x) \approx \sum_{i=1}^{m} a_{i-1}(x_0, x_i) \tag{3}$$

Accordingly, STAM requires $m$ parallel table lookups followed by a multi-operand adder. The block diagram in Fig.2 is easily implemented in hardware.

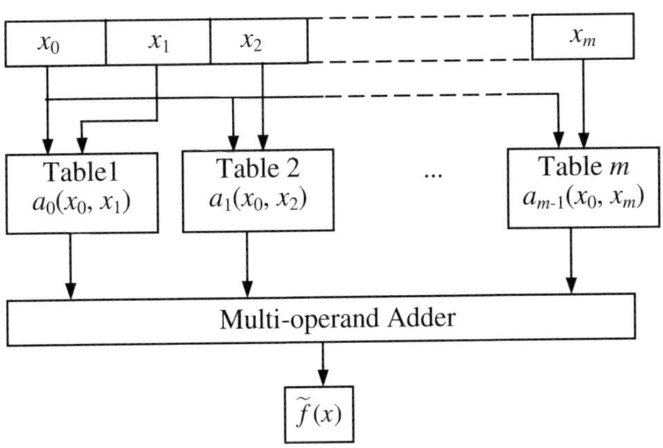


**Fig. 2.** Symmetric table addition method block

### 3.2 Selecting the Coefficients

The approximation for the STAM is based on the Taylor series expansion centered about the point $x = x_{0:1}+\delta_{2:m}$. Using the first two terms of the Taylor series expansion results in the following approximation,

$$f(x) \approx f(x_{0:1}+\delta_{2:m}) + f'(x_{0:1}+\delta_{2:m}) \cdot \sum_{i=2}^{m}(x_i - \delta_i) \tag{4}$$

Where $x_{0:m} = \sum_{i=0}^{m} x_i$ , $\delta_{2:m} = \sum_{i=2}^{m} \delta_i$ .

In order to make the STAM practical, $x_i$ is replaced by $\delta_i$ , which is exactly halfway between the minimum and maximum values for $x_i$.

$$f(x) \approx f(x_{0:1}+\delta_{2:m}) + f'(x_0+\delta_{1:m}) \cdot \sum_{i=2}^{m}(x_i - \delta_i) \tag{5}$$

The first term in Taylor series expansion is selected as the first coefficient $a_0(x_0, x_1)$ and the second term is then distributed into $m$-1 coefficients $a_{i-1}(x_0, x_i)$ ($i$=2,3,···, $m$). Thus the values for the coefficients are

$$a_0(x_0,x_1)=f(x_{0:1}+\delta_{2:m}) \tag{6}$$

$$a_{i-1}(x_0,x_i)=f'(x_0+\delta_{1:m})(x_i-\delta_i) \quad i=2,3,\cdots,m \tag{7}$$

Taking advantage of symmetry and leading zeroes in the table entries, the STAM requires less memory than similar techniques. The input of table $a_0(x_0, x_1)$ has $n_0+n_1$ bits. For another $m$-1 tables, $a_{i-1}(x_0, 2\delta_i-x_i)$ is the one's complement of $a_{i-1}(x_0, x_i)$ . The method for selecting the coefficients causes table $a_1(x_0, x_2)$ through $a_{m-1}(x_0, x_m)$ to be symmetric and allows their inputs have $n_0+n_i$-1 bits.

One benefit of this method is that the magnitude of the $m$-1 coefficients is substantially less than the first coefficient $a_0(x_0, x_1)$. The magnitude is bounded by $|a_{i-1}(x_0, x_i)|<|f'(\xi)|\bullet 2^{-n_{0:i-1}}$, where $\xi$ is the point at which $f'(x)$ takes its maximum value. This results in some leading zeroes (or leading ones). They are not stored in memory and obtained by sign-extending the most significant bit of $a_{i-1}(x_0, x_i)$ before performing the addition.

By controlling the errors of the STAM, the computed result differs from the true result by less than one unit in the last place (ulp) [6].

### 3.3 Approximation of the Tan-s Function and the Express Precision

The two terms Taylor series expansion of the Tan-s function centered about the point $x^*=x_{0:1}+\delta_{2:m}$.

$$\tan sig(x) \approx \tan sig(x^*) + \tan sig'(x^*)(x-x^*) = \frac{e^{x^*}-e^{-x^*}}{e^{x^*}+e^{-x^*}} + \frac{4(x-x^*)}{(e^{x^*}+e^{-x^*})^2} \tag{8}$$

The Tan-s function is symmetric with respect to the origin. The active part is supposed to be located between $-x_a$ and $x_a$. Assuming the final result has $p$ fraction bits, the least expression precision is $2^{-p}$, one ulp=$2^{-p}$. When $x \geq x_a$, tan$sig(x)$ is close to $1-2^{-p}$. So $x_a$ is determined by

$$x_a = \lceil \ln(2^{p+1} - 1)/2 \rceil \tag{9}$$

When $x \geq x_b$, tan*sig*´($x$) is close to 0. Similar to tan*sig* ($x$), $x_b$ is determined by

$$x_b = \lceil \cosh^{-1}(2^{p/2}) \rceil \tag{10}$$

Thus tan*sig*($x$) and tan*sig*´($x$) can be approximated on different intervals [0, $x_a$] and [0, $x_b$]. The final result is accurate within one ulp for any input $x$.

Considering the errors in rounding the coefficient and the final summation result, the bits of actual stored coefficients are $2+log_2(m\text{-}1)$ more than that of the final results[5].

Supposing the input $x$ and the final result have $p$=10 fraction bits, $x_a$=4, $x_b$=4. So the input $x$ has $k$=2 integer bits, its length is $n=k+p=12$. If $x$ is partitioned with $n_0$=4, $n_1$=2, $n_2=n_3$=3, $2+log_2(m\text{-}1)$=3, three tables $a_0(x_0, x_1)$, $a_1(x_0, x_2)$ and $a_2(x_0, x_3)$ are constructed. Each of their inputs has 6 bits(table $a_0$: $n_0+n_1$=6, table $a_1$: $n_0+n_2$-1=6, table $a_2$ : $n_0+n_3$-1=6), and the stored coefficient is 13 fraction bits($p$ +2+$log_2(m\text{-}1)$=13).

Actually, it is not necessary to store the coefficients in 13 fraction bits. For the three tables above, the least significant bit is one. Since it is known in advance, it is not stored. So is the integer bit because of $0 \leq$ tan*sig*($x$) < 1 and 0 < tan*sig*´($x$) $\leq 1$. The table $a_1(x_0, x_2)$ and $a_2(x_0, x_3)$ have 4 and 7 leading zeros respectively, which are not stored. So the length of coefficients stored in the three tables are 12, 8 and 5 bits respectively, the memory size required is 1600bits. If applying standard table lookup on interval [0, 4], the memory size is 40960 bits. For the same express precision of 10 fraction bits, STAM requires 25 times less memory than the standard table lookups.

# 4 Experimental Result

## 4.1 Modelsim Simulation for STAM Algorithm

Using Modelsim software to simulate the VHDL description of the three tables and the adder, the computed results of tan*sig*($x$) differ from the true result by less than one ulp=$2^{-10}$ ($\approx$0.0009765625). Table 1 gives part of the simulation results for tan*sig*($x$).

**Table 1.** Simulation results of tan*sig*($x$) function

| Input $x$ | Simulation Result | True Result | Absolute Error |
|---|---|---|---|
| 0.1269531250 | 0.1261475975 | 0.1262754549 | 0.0001278574 |
| 0.5244140625 | 0.4815655179 | 0.4810996071 | 0.0004659109 |
| 1.0654296875 | 0.7884550059 | 0.7877331282 | 0.0007218778 |
| 1.5205078125 | 0.9090798315 | 0.9087861134 | 0.0002935698 |
| 3.7148437500 | 0.9988123281 | 0.9988139579 | 0.0000016298 |

## 4.2 FPGA Simulation for the Simulation Line

Using Altera's Stratix-II FPGA, the VHDL descriptions are simulated for serial-parallel converter of $HDB_3$ encoding, clock generator and BP NN. Selecting 200 input vectors in the test set, the experiment results show that output signal of BP NN tallies with the actual information sink signal well. Fig.3(a) displays one length of the information source signal which $HDB_3$ encoding is "01001001010110001010111 1110100", Fig.3(b) shows the actual information sink signal corresponding to the source signal in Fig.3(a). The output signal of BP NN (see Fig.3(c)) resembles the actual signal despite the details.

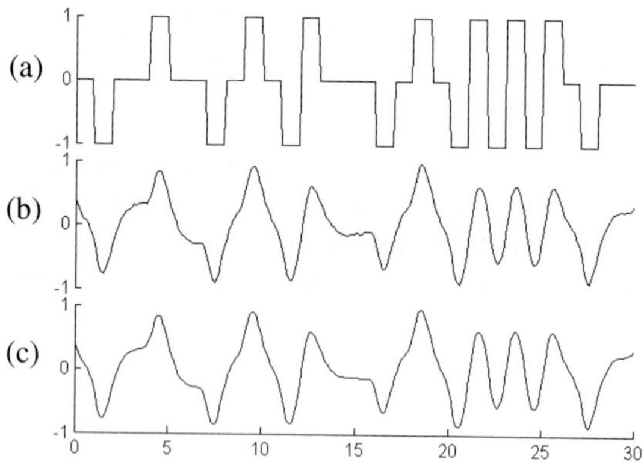


**Fig. 3.** The sampled information source signal(a), sink signal(b) and the simulation output (c)

## 5 Conclusions

This paper applies BP NN to approximate the transfer function of the transmission line. Using STAM algorithm in FPGA implementation, the memory requirements are reduced dramatically. Based on the proposed approach, an underwater coaxial cable is simulated. The implemented simulation line has been successfully used in the study of digital image transmission in the "863" subject.

This technique can be generalized to simulate the transmission path with unknown transfer function.

## Acknowledgments

This work is supported by the Hi-Tech R&D program (863) of China (2001AA612030).

## References

1. China national Standards: General Terminology for telecommunications equipment GB1417-1978, Technical Standards Press of China. (1979)
2. Stine, J.E., Schulte, M.J.: The Symmetric Table Addition Method for Accurate Function Approximation. Journal of VLSI Signal Processing, 21 (1999) 167-177
3. Haykin, S.: Neural Networks. China Machine Press, (2004)

4. Nielsen R.H.: Theory of the Back-Propagation Neural Network. IEEE IJCNN. 1(1989) 593-606
5. Schulte, M.J., Stine, J.E.: Accurate Function Approximations by Symmetric Table Lookup Addition. Proceedings of the 11th International Conference on Application-Specific Systems, Architectures and Processors, (1999) 144-153
6. Sarma, D.D., Matula, D.W.: Measuring the Accuracy of ROM Reciprocal Tables. Proceedings of the 11th Symposium on Computer Arithmetic, (1993) 95-102

# Springback and Geometry Prediction – Neural Networks Applied to the Air Bending Process

M. Luisa Garcia-Romeu and Joaquim Ciurana

Dept. of Mechanical Engineering and Industrial Construction, University of Girona,
Campus Montilivi P-II,
Girona 17071
{mluisa.gromeu, quim.ciurana}@udg.es

**Abstract.** This paper describes the application of neural network techniques to sheet metal bending process, particularly for the prediction of springback phenomenon and bending part final geometry (final radius and bending angle). Springback is an important unwanted change in shape causing accuracy problems. Traditional and new simulation techniques (FEM) of springback minimizing are laborious trial-and-error procedures that involve long cycle times and cost increases. To reduce the trial-an-error procedure, an artificial neural network (ANN) model is developed as an approximator. A back propagation neural network model has been developed using experimental data from several tension and bending tests performed on aluminium and stainless steel. The convergence of the mean square error in training came out very well and the performance of the trained network has been tested with unseen kept back data from experiments and found to be in good agreement.

## 1 Introduction

The capability of predicting the sheet metal part final geometry as well as springback amount is an important feature in the sheet metal bending processes. The sheet metal air bending process has not been recognized as a complex manufacturing process for many years, although in recent works has recovered the research interest. On the one hand, springback is an important unwanted change in shape causing accuracy and assembly problems, that occurs in a bending part when the load is released and the part is taken out of the press. On the other hand, the classical models in air bending assumes a simple bend geometry (two straight legs joint by a circular bent) which it is far from real geometry of a bent part by an air bending process.

Traditional approaches to control these aspects in a sheet metal industry are based on trial-and-error procedures, relying on the experience of the product and process designers or even on the manufacturing craftsmen. They ponder the correctness of the setup and judge whether changes should be made. This traditional proceeding way turns practical production into a slow, laborious and costly approach.

In dealing with the springback problem and bending modeling, three approaches have been commonly used: analytical, experimental and approximate

D.-S. Huang, K. Li, and G.W. Irwin (Eds.): ICIC 2006, LNCS 4113, pp. 470–475, 2006.

methods. Due to the complexities of plasticity, the exact analysis of the metal forming processes is not feasible in most cases, and there was an important growth of approximate methods over the years. Among these techniques, the finite element method (FEM) takes precedence being currently the most popular. In spite of this, the simulations are again a laborious trial-and-error procedure, which is a nontrivial task. This situation points out another drawback for the use of FEM in real industry because it appears the needing of the 12FEM specialist.

It might be meaningful to use an approximation and start from it either to use the traditional approach or FEM simulation. On the one hand, neural networks allow and provide the tool that fit the practical needs of the end-user: it does not demand neither a high user-preparation, a wide experience about the bending process nor an important time investment. On the other hand, neural networks are being applied on manufacturing problems because they allow a good first, quick and reliable approximation to solve the two previous problems related to air bending process, reducing the number of trials and consequently the cycle time and rejection rates. Finally, the non-linear character of the relationships among the influence parameters involve in air bending process and springback phenomenon turn them into an ideal candidate problem for being controlled or/and predicting by a neural network.

The aim of this project underlying this paper is to provide a prediction of a springback value and final geometry (bend radius and angle) that may be used by the process/product designer without the need of being a simulation specialist.

### 1.1 Literature Survey

Although the developed mathematical models behind neural networks exist from the 60s, it has not been until the 90s when neural networks have begun to be developed in manufacturing applications [1]. During the last years several research groups have studied the use of neural networks to control sheet metal forming processes. More specifically,it is also possible to find studies where neural networks are applied to V bending processes. The outstanding and more recent works in this field are detailed next. Forcellese et al.[2] developed a punch displacement control system based on ANN for a V- and U-bending process. In the following Inamdar et al.[3] works, it has been developed a control tool for the prediction of the springback by means of ANN trained by extracted data from experiments and analytical and simulation model predictions.

In this work, a back propagation neural network model has been developed using experimental data from several tension and bending tests performed on aluminium and stainless steel. The model will predict three outputs (springback value($\Delta\beta$), the final geometry expressed by final bend radius($R_f$) at punch-sheet contact and the punch displacement($Z$)) through seven inputs predictors (final bending angle($\beta_f$), sheet thickness($t$), die width($w_d$) and radius($r_d$), yielding stress($S_Y$), Young's modulus($E$) and strain hardening exponent($n$)). The two first outputs neurons fit directly with the title and aim of this work, springback amount and final bending radius as representative variable of the bend part geometry. The third output, the punch displacement was also considered because it is the main process performer parameter, and consequently related to springback and final geometry.

## 2 Experimental Set-Up

Prior knowledge and understanding of the process and the process variables under investigation is necessary for achieving a realistic model. Springback is also sensitive to a range of material parameters such as elastic and plastic anisotropy and the presence of a Bauschinger effect; process parameters such as punch displacement, die width and radius, punch radius, bending force and moment; and geometrical parameters such as bending angle (attempted and final), thickness and part curvature or final part radius.

**Fig. 1.** Test set up with a MTS testing machine

To verify the above relationships and to obtain real parameters from an air bending process it was developed an experimental procedure. It consisted of two stages. In the first one, the material identification for each thickness and material (1, 1.5, 2 and 3 mm. for stainless steel and 1 and 1.35 mm. for aluminium) is carried out by means of tensile test on a laboratory MTS tensile testing machine. In the second stage, bending tests for several specimens were also performed on a laboratory but in this second case, a bending sub-frame has been built and set up on the MTS machine since it allows a very accurate force-displacement registration. As well as bending sub-frame, a loaded bending angle ($\beta_c$) measurement fixture was developed, because its determination is essential for the computation of the springback amount ($\Delta\beta$). By means of a clamp, a linear displacement transducer was added to a bending sub-frame side, as it is presented in Figure 1. The final bending angle ($\beta_f$) measurement of every bending part was done using two techniques, showing a very good agreement. In the first one, a bevel protractor of 5 minutes approximation is used. Whereas in the second one, a digital image processing of the bending parts is carried out. This technique has also supplied the final bend radius at punch-sheet contact as well as a curvature function along the bend[4].

# 3 Back Propagation Neural Network

Neural networks are mathematical models composed by several neurons arranged in different layers, linked through variable weights. These weights are calculated by an iterative method during the training process when the network is fed with a large amount of training data, input and output pairs that represent the pattern attempting to be modeled. On account of this, neural networks are non-linear analysis tools. The relationships among the influence variables in air bending and springback have a non-lineal character with multiple interactions [2,3]. Commonly, a two layer neural network is sufficient to accurately model any type of continuous function if it is provided by a sufficient number of hidden nodes. This universality property [5] is applied for function approximation, which fits with the target of the variables that want to be predicted. Therefore for this work, a multilayer perceptron model with two layers using a back propagation (BP) algorithm, widely used for general engineering applications, is chosen.

## 3.1 Network Design and Important Neural Networks Parameters

Network accuracy and efficiency is dependent upon various parameters as learning rate, momentum factor, hidden nodes, activation functions; and characteristics as normalization, generalization. There is no well-established procedure for finding them and most researchers employ a trial and error procedure to determine some of them. This approach has been adopted in the present work. In the literature there exists a well-known rule of thumb [3,5] for determining the selection of initial training set according to fixed accuracy level:

$$\mathrm{N} > \frac{|W|}{1-a}, \tag{1}$$

where $N$ is the number of patterns (desired), $|W|$ the number of weights to be adjust, and $a$ the accuracy level. This relationship shows the sacrifice that has to carry out in developing the model between a proper generalization and the accuracy that is wanted to be obtained.

## 3.2 Training

The case under study will be broach under a supervised learning strategy, which means that for all the input patterns, the objective outputs are known (from experimentation) and a batch pattern training style is chosen. The classical gradient descent and g.d.with momentum algorithms have been used as well as faster algorithms such as Levenberg-Marquardt.

The training set construction represents a key point of the network generalization property [5], especially for avoiding the overfitting problem. For avoiding it, the early stopping technique is used considering 3 data sets: training, validation and testing. The training set, for training and weights adjustments. The validation set to refine the network by the early stopping technique. And finally the testing data set,an unseeing set during the training that is used to determine the network performance by an error computation. In the present work,

**Table 1.** Available training patterns

| Material | Patterns | Train. set | Valid. set | Test set | Arch. net. |
|---|---|---|---|---|---|
| Aluminum | 50 | 25 | 13 | 12 | 4-1-3 |
| Stainless steel | 82 | 41 | 21 | 20 | 4-1-3 |
| Alum. & Stainless | 132 | 66 | 33 | 133 | 7-1-3 |

fixing the accuracy level at 90% and knowing the number of available training patterns from the experimentation above-mentioned and Eq. (1), it is possible to determine the minimum number of hidden neurons ($h$), Table 1.

One of the options to investigate the network answer in more detail is to carry out a regression analysis between the networks answer with the corresponding objective value. That regression (post-training error analysis) returns three parameters, the first two are the slope and the y-intercept of the best linear regression that relates objective patterns to network outputs. The third parameter is the correlation value between outputs ($A$) and objectives ($T$).

The training of several networks has been carried out designing an algorithm that uses functions and routines from the MATLAB® Neural Network Toolbox. Firstly, in order to maintain the network simple and feasible it has been decided to train two different networks associate to each of the tested materials (material parameters were not taken into account). Secondly, a third network has been trained irrespective of material distinction, that means adding $S_Y$, $E$ and $n$.

## 4 Training Results and Discussion

The initially trained $x$-1-3 networks had not the expected behavior, a bad performance of final bending radius and punch displacement variables led to a redefinition of the network architecture. So finally, there were trained different neural networks, each according to each defined output with an 7-1-1 architecture. The performance improvement can be observed comparing the obtained correlation values. The 7-1-1 network gets a 0.978 correlation value, Figure 2, whereas the obtained from 7-1-3 network for final bending radius was 0.537. For each network, it was stored for being part of the prediction model: the weights, biases, and pre- and postprocessing network values. An algorithm with the above trained networks was built, so it is in position of feeding new unseen parameters and carry out the validation of prediction model output. The predictions quality is good, since it presents good agreement with the real values for each output: springback angle, punch displacement and final bending radius. Finally, by means of the previous structures a total prediction model for the air bending process was built.

## 5 Conclusions

The implementation of the 3 networks in an only model by means of a suitable user interface allows to introduce the required input information and access to

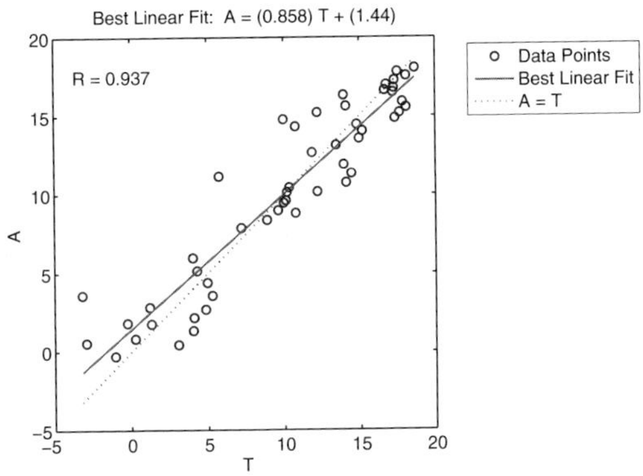


**Fig. 2.** Final bending radius post-training analysis result. 7-1-1 architecture.

the prediction result in an easy and quick way. Hence, a simple performance and a proper displaying eliminates the needing of specific training user. It has to be reminded that the output of the prediction model presented it is a first approximation that is able to be used either during bending sheet metal part design or bending process design. An important advantage from the proposed prediction model is the implementation easiness that the neural networks (core of the model) have for be implemented by a software. Therefore this tool could turn into a computer aided engineering system for a sheet metal final part design and bending process.

## References


1. Vasile, D., Vasile, D., Thamodharan, M., Wolf, A.: The use of neural network in metal industry. IEEE Conference Record . Volume 2. (2000) 1104–1108
2. Forcellese, A., Gabrielli, F., Ruffini, R.: Effect of the training set size on springback control by neural network in an air bending process. J. Mater. Process Tech. **80-81** (1998) 493–500
3. Inamdar, M.V., Date, P.P., Desai, U.B.: Studies on the prediction of springback in air vee bending of metallic sheets using an artificial neural network. J. Mater. Process Tech. **108**(1) (2000) 45–54
4. Garcia-Romeu, M.L.: Contribucion al estudio del doblado al aire de chapa. Modelo prediccion angulo de recuperacion y radio de doblado final. Th. Diss., Girona (2005)
5. Mehrotra, K., Mohan, C.K., Ranka, S.: Elements of artificial neural networks. MIT Press, Cambridge, Mass. (1997)

# Stability Conditions for Discrete Hopfield Neural Networks with Delay

Run-Nian Ma[1,2] and Guo-Qiang Bai[3]

[1] School of Science, Xi'an Jiaotong University, Xi'an, 710049, China
[2] University Key Lab of Information Sciences and Engineering, Dalian University, 116622, China
m314@163.com
[3] Institute of Microelectronics, Tsinghua University, Beijing, 100084, China
baigq@mail.tsinghua.edu.cn

**Abstract.** The stability of discrete Hopfield neural networks with delay is mainly studied by the use of the state transition equation and the energy function, and some results on the stability are given. The sufficient conditions for the networks with delay converging towards a limit cycle with length 4 are presented. Also, one condition ensuring the network with delay having neither a stable state nor a limit cycle with length 2 is given. The obtained results here partially extend some existing results on stability of discrete Hopfield neural network with delay and without delay.

## 1 Introduction

The researches on stability of discrete Hopfield neural networks (DHNN) have attracted considerable interest in Refs.[1-4]. Discrete Hopfield neural network with delay (DHNND) is an extension of DHNN. In Refs.[5-8], the stability of DHNND is mainly investigated. In this paper, we improve the previous stability conditions of DHNND and obtain some new stability conditions for DHNND converging towards a limit cycle with length 4 and other conditions ensuring DHNND having neither a stable state nor a limit cycle with length 2. This paper is organized as follows. Section 2 introduces most of the notations and definitions. Section 3 mainly investigates the stability of DHNND and gives some results. Some conclusions are mainly drawn in section 4.

## 2 Notations and Preliminaries

Discrete Hopfield neural networks with delay having $n$ neurons can be determined by two $n \times n$ real matrices $W^0 = (w_{ij}^0)_{n\times n}$, $W^1 = (w_{ij}^1)_{n\times n}$, and an $n$-dimensional column vector $\theta = (\theta_1, \cdots, \theta_n)^{\mathrm{T}}$, denoted by $N=(W^0 \oplus W^1, \theta)$. There are two possible values for the state of each neuron $i$: 1 or –1. Denote the state of neuron $i$ at time $t \in \{0,1,2,\cdots\}$ as $x_i(t)$, the vector $X(t) = (x_1(t), \cdots, x_n(t))^{\mathrm{T}}$ is the state of the whole neurons at time $t$. In this paper, we assume the vector $\theta = 0$.

D.-S. Huang, K. Li, and G.W. Irwin (Eds.): ICIC 2006, LNCS 4113, pp. 476–481, 2006.

The updating mode of DHNND is determined by the following equations

$$x_i(t+1) = \text{sgn}(\sum_{j=1}^{n} w_{ij}^0 x_j(t) + \sum_{j=1}^{n} w_{ij}^1 x_j(t-1)),\ i \in \mathrm{I} = \{1,2,\cdots,n\}, \tag{1}$$

where $t \in \{0,1,2,\cdots\}$, and the sign function is defined as follows

$$\text{sgn}(u) = \begin{cases} 1, & \text{if } u \geq 0 \\ -1, & \text{if } u < 0 \end{cases}. \tag{2}$$

We rewrite equation (1) in the compact form

$$X(t+1) = \text{sgn}(W^0 X(t) + W^1 X(t-1)). \tag{3}$$

If the state $X^*$ satisfies the following condition

$$X^* = \text{sgn}(W^0 X^* + W^1 X^*), \tag{4}$$

the state $X^*$ is called a stable state (or an equilibrium point).

Let $\mathrm{N}=(W^0 \oplus W^1, \theta)$ start from any initial states $X(0),X(1)$. For $t\geq 2$, if there exists time $t_1 \in \{0,1,2,\cdots\}$ such that the updating sequence $X(0),X(1), X(2),X(3),\cdots$ satisfies that $X(t+T)=X(t)$ for all $t\geq t_1$, where $T$ is the minimum value which satisfies the above condition, then we call that the initial states $X(0),X(1)$ converges towards a limit cycle with length $T$.

A matrix $A=(a_{ij})_{i,j\in \mathrm{I}}$ is called to be negative row diagonally dominant, if the matrix $A$ satisfies the following conditions for each neuron $i \in \mathrm{I} = \{1,2,\cdots,n\}$

$$-a_{ii} \geq \sum_{j\in \mathrm{I}(j\neq i)} |a_{ij}|, \tag{5}$$

If there exists at least one neuron $i$ such that inequality (5) is strict inequality, then we call the matrix A to be a negative row weakly strictly diagonally dominant matrix. If inequality (5) is strict inequality for all neurons $i \in \mathrm{I} = \{1,2,\cdots,n\}$, then we call the matrix A to be a negative row strictly diagonally dominant matrix.

The stability of antisymmetric DHNN and DHNND is respectively studied in Refs. [3] and [5]. In this paper, we assume that the matrix $W^0$ is not antisymmetric. The stability of DHNND is mainly studied and some new conditions ensuring the stability of DHNND are presented. The main contribution of this paper is expressed by the following results.

## 3 Stability of DHNND

**Theorem 1.** Suppose there exists a matrix $D=\text{diag}(d_1,d_2,\cdots,d_n)$ ($d_i>0$, $i=1,2,\cdots,n$) such that matrix $DW^0$ is antisymmetric, and matrix $W^1$ is negative row strictly diagonally dominant, then $\mathrm{N}=(W^0 \oplus W^1, 0)$ converges towards a limit cycle with length 4, i.e., for any initial states $X(0)$, $X(1)$, DHNND (1) converges towards a limit cycle with length 4.

**Proof.** We define energy function (Lyapunov function) of DHNND (1) as follows.

$$E(t) = E(X(t), X(t-1)) = -X^{\mathrm{T}}(t)DW^{0}X(t-1) \tag{6}$$

Then

$$\begin{aligned}
\Delta E(t) &= E(t+1) - E(t) = E(X(t+1), X(t)) - E(X(t), X(t-1)) \\
&= -X^{\mathrm{T}}(t+1)DW^{0}X(t) + X^{\mathrm{T}}(t)DW^{0}X(t-1) \\
&= -(X^{\mathrm{T}}(t+1) + X^{\mathrm{T}}(t-1))DW^{0}X(t) \\
&= -(X^{\mathrm{T}}(t+1) + X^{\mathrm{T}}(t-1))(DW^{0}X(t) + DW^{1}X(t-1)) + \\
&\quad (X^{\mathrm{T}}(t+1) + X^{\mathrm{T}}(t-1))DW^{1}X(t-1) \\
&= -p(t) - q(t)
\end{aligned} \tag{7}$$

where

$$p(t) = (X^{\mathrm{T}}(t+1) + X^{\mathrm{T}}(t-1))(DW^{0}X(t) + DW^{1}X(t-1))$$

$$q(t) = -(X^{\mathrm{T}}(t+1) + X^{\mathrm{T}}(t-1))DW^{1}X(t-1)\,.$$

Firstly, we prove that, if $x_i(t+1)+x_i(t-1)\neq 0$, then

$$x_i(t+1) + x_i(t-1) = 2x_i(t+1) = 2x_i(t-1)\,.$$

Secondly, for each $i\in \mathrm{I}$, we have

$$x_i(t+1)\Big(\sum_{j\in \mathrm{I}} w_{ij}^{0}x_j(t) + \sum_{j\in \mathrm{I}} w_{ij}^{1}x_j(t-1)\Big) \geq 0\,. \tag{8}$$

We further prove that $p(t)\geq 0$ and $q(t)\geq 0$ in (7). To this end, let

$$\mathrm{I}^{*}(t) = \{i\in \mathrm{I} \,|\, x_i(t+1) + x_i(t-1) \neq 0\}. \tag{9}$$

By the equation (8) and the condition $W^1$ being strict negative row-diagonally dominant, we can easily prove that

$$\begin{aligned}
p(t) &= \sum_{i\in \mathrm{I}} (x_i(t+1) + x_i(t-1)) \sum_{j\in \mathrm{I}} (d_i w_{ij}^{0} x_j(t) + d_i w_{ij}^{1} x_j(t-1)) \\
&= 2\sum_{i\in \mathrm{I}^{*}(t)} x_i(t+1)\Big(\sum_{j\in \mathrm{I}} d_i w_{ij}^{0} x_j(t) + \sum_{j\in \mathrm{I}} d_i w_{ij}^{1} x_j(t-1)\Big) \geq 0
\end{aligned} \tag{10}$$

$$q(t) = -\sum_{i\in \mathrm{I}} (x_i(t+1) + x_i(t-1)) \sum_{j\in \mathrm{I}} d_i w_{ij}^{1} x_j(t-1)$$

$$
\begin{aligned}
&= -2\sum_{i\in I^*(t)} x_i(t-1)\sum_{j\in I} d_i w_{ij}^1 x_j(t-1)\\
&= -2\sum_{i\in I^*(t)} d_i(w_{ii}^1 + \sum_{j\in I(j\neq i)} x_i(t-1)w_{ij}^1 x_j(t-1)) \qquad (11)\\
&\geq -2\sum_{i\in I^*(t)} d_i(w_{ii}^1 + \sum_{j\in I(j\neq i)} \left|w_{ij}^1\right|) > 0\cdot
\end{aligned}
$$

Hence, based on (10) and (11), then implies $\Delta E(t)\leq 0$. Furthermore, $\Delta E(t)=0$ if and only if $I^*(t)=\varnothing$, i.e. $X(t+1)+X(t-1)=0$. Therefore, $\Delta E(t)=0$ if and only if $I^*(t)=\varnothing$.

Consequently, for any initial states $X(0)$, $X(1)$, the DHNND (1) converges towards a state which satisfies $\Delta E(t)=0$, i.e., the DHNND (1) converges towards a state $X(t+1)+X(t-1)=0$, i.e. for all states $X(0)$, $X(1)$, there exists time $t_1$ such that when $t\geq t_1$, the states of DHNND (1) satisfy $X(t)=-X(t+2)=X(t+4)$.

If the states $X(t_1)=X(t_1+1)$, then the DHNND (1) converges towards a limit cycle $(X(t_1),X(t_1),-X(t_1),-X(t_1))$ with length 4. If the states $X(t_1)\neq X(t_1+1)$, then the DHNND (1) converges towards a limit cycle $(X(t_1),X(t_1+1),-X(t_1),-X(t_1+1))$ with length 4. Consequently, theorem 1 holds.

**Example 1.** Consider $N=(W^0\oplus W^1,0)$, the expressions of matrices $W^0$ and $W^1$ are respectively in the following

$$
W^0 = \begin{pmatrix} 0 & 4 \\ -2 & 0 \end{pmatrix},\ W^1 = \begin{pmatrix} -4 & 0 \\ 0 & -2 \end{pmatrix}. \qquad (12)
$$

Obviously, matrix $W^0$ is not antiasymmetric, and the DHNND (1) is not strict since $w_{11}^0\times 1 + w_{12}^0\times 1 + w_{11}^1\times 1 + w_{12}^1\times 1 = 0$ or $w_{21}^0\times 1 + w_{22}^0\times 1 + w_{21}^1\times 1 + w_{22}^1\times(-1) = 0$. So, the DHNND (1) converging towards a limit cycle with length 4 is not guaranteed by using the previous results. However, there exists a positive diagonal matrix $D$=diag(1, 2) such that matrix $DW^0$ is antiasymmetric, and matrix $W^1$ is strict negative row-diagonally dominant, i.e., the conditions of theorem 1 are satisfied. Consequently, the DHNND (1) converges towards a limit cycle with length 4 by the theorem 1. In fact, we can test the conclusion being true. For example, the network with delay converges towards a limit cycle $(X(2),X(3),X(4),X(5))$ with length 4 for the initial states $X(0)=X(1)=(1,1)^T$, where $X(2)=(-1,1)^T$, $X(3)=(-1,-1)^T$, $X(4)=(1,-1)^T$, $X(5)=(1,1)^T$. For the initial states $X(0)=X(1)=(-1,-1)^T$, the network converges towards a limit cycle $(X(4),X(5),X(6),X(7))$ with length 4, where $X(4)=(-1,1)^T$, $X(5)=(-1,-1)^T$, $X(6)=(1,-1)^T$, $X(7)=(1,1)^T$. This limit cycle is same as the above limit cycle. For the initial states $X(0)=X(1)=(-1,1)^T$, the network with delay converges towards a limit cycle $(X(2),X(3),X(4),X(5))$ with length 4, where $X(2)=(-1,1)^T$, $X(3)=(1,1)^T$, $X(4)=(1,-1)^T$, $X(5)=(-1,-1)^T$. Also, for the other 14 initial states, the network converges towards a limit cycle with length 4. Theses cases are omitted here.

**Example 2.** Consider $N=(W^0\oplus W^1,0)$, the expressions of matrices $W^0$ and $W^1$ are respectively in the following

$$W^0 = \begin{pmatrix} 0 & 2 & -2 \\ -1 & 0 & 1 \\ 1 & -1 & 0 \end{pmatrix}, W^1 = \begin{pmatrix} 0 & 0 & 0 \\ 0 & 0 & 0 \\ 0 & 0 & 0 \end{pmatrix}. \tag{13}$$

Obviously, there is a positive diagonal matrix $D$=diag(0.5,1,1) such that matrix $DW^0$ is antiasymmetric. However, the conditions of theorem 1 are not satisfied because of matrix $W^1$ being negative row diagonally dominant not being negative row strictly diagonally dominant. So it is not guaranteed that the DHNND (1) converges towards a limit cycle with length 4. In fact, we can test that the DHNND (1) has a stable state $(1,1,1)^T$ and a limit cycle $((-1,1,1)^T, (1,1,-1)^T, (1,-1,1)^T)$ with length 3.

From example 2, we know that the conditions of theorem 1 are needed, otherwise, the result of theorem 1 is not guaranteed. But, we have the other result as follows.

**Theorem 2.** Suppose there exists a matrix $D=\text{diag}(d_1,d_2,\cdots,d_n)$ $(d_i>0, i=1,2,\cdots,n)$ such that matrix $DW^0$ is antisymmetric, and matrix $W^1$ is negative row weakly strictly diagonally dominant, then N=$(W^0 \oplus W^1, 0)$ has neither a stable state nor a limit cycle with length 2.

**Proof.** Reduction to absurdity, if there exists a stable state $X$, then satisfies (4), and, by (4), we have

$$X^T(W^0X+W^1X)\geq 0 \tag{14}$$

So,

$$0\leq X^T(DW^0X+DW^1X)=X^TDW^1X<0 \tag{15}$$

Note that matrix $DW^0$ is antisymmetric, then $X^T(DW^0X+DW^1X)=X^TDW^1X$. Matrix $W^1$ is negative row weakly strictly diagonally dominant, so is matrix $DW^1$. This implies $X^TDW^1X<0$. The conflict in (15) then means that N=$(W^0 \oplus W^1, 0)$ has no one stable state.

In the following, without loss generality, we assume that the network has a limit cycle $(X^1,X^2)$ with length 2. Then, by the definition of sign function, we have

$$(X^1)^T(W^0X^2+W^1X^1)\geq 0,\ (X^2)^T(W^0X^1+W^1X^2)\geq 0. \tag{16}$$

Let $r=(X^1)^T(DW^0X^2+DW^1X^1)$, $s=(X^2)^T(DW^0X^1+DW^1X^2)$. Based on (16), we know that $r\geq 0$, $s\geq 0$. This means $r+s\geq 0$. On the other hand, we have

$$\begin{aligned} r+s&=(X^1)^T(DW^0X^2+DW^1X^1)+(X^2)^T(DW^0X^1+DW^1X^2) \\ &=(X^1)^TDW^0X^2+(X^1)^TDW^1X^1+(X^2)^TDW^0X^1+(X^2)^TDW^1X^2 \\ &=(X^1)^TDW^1X^1+(X^2)^TDW^1X^2. \end{aligned} \tag{17}$$

Since matrix $DW^0$ is antisymmetric, then $(X^1)^TDW^0X^2=-(X^2)^TDW^0X^1$. This means that (17) holds. Matrix $W^1$ is negative row weakly strictly diagonally dominant, so is matrix $DW^1$, and

$$(X^1)^TDW^1X^1<0,\ (X^2)^TDW^1X^2<0. \tag{18}$$

Based on (17) and (18), we have $r+s<0$. This conflict then means that N=$(W^0 \oplus W^1, 0)$ has no one limit cycle with length 2.

## 4 Conclusion

This paper mainly studies the stability of DHNND. The conditions for DHNND converging towards a limit cycle with length 4 and having neither a stable state nor a limit cycle with length 2 are respectively given. From the examples we know that these conditions are only sufficient conditions but not necessary conditions. These results partially generalize the existing results. If matrix $W^1$=0, then DHNND is the same as DHNN. So, the results also partially generalize some results on stability of DHNN.

## Acknowledgments

The work described in this paper is supported by the National Natural Science Foundation of China (No.60273004, 60576027) and partially supported by open Foundation of University Key Lab of Information Sciences and Engineering, Dalian University.

## References

1. Xu, Z., Kwong, C.P.: Global Convergence and Asymptotic Stability of Asymmetrical Hopfield Neural Networks. J. Mathematical Analysis and Applications, 191 (1995) 405-426
2. Lee, D.: New Stability Conditions for Hopfield Neural Networks in Partial Simultaneous Update Mode. IEEE Trans. Neural Networks, 10 (1999) 975-978
3. Goles, E.: Antisymmetrical Neural Networks. Discrete Applied Mathematics, 13 (1986) 97-100
4. Ma, R., Zhang, Q., Xu, J.: Convergence of Discrete-time Cellular Neural Networks. Chinese J. Electronics, 11 (2002) 352-356
5. Ma, R., Liu, N., Xu, J.: Stability Conditions for Discrete Hopfield Neural Networks with Delay. Acta Electronica Sinica, 32 (2004) 1674-1677
6. Qiu, S., Tang, E.-C.C. Yeung, D.S.: Stability of Discrete Hopfield Neural Networks with Time-delay. Proceedings of IEEE International Conference on System, Man Cybernetics, (2000) 2546-2552
7. Ma, R., Xi, Y., Lei, S.: Dynamic Behavior of Discrete Hopfield Neural Networks with Time-Delay. Chinese J. Electronics, 14 (2005) 187-191
8. Ma, R., Lei, S., Zhang, S.: Dynamic Behavior Analysis of Discrete Neural Networks with Delay. In: Wang J., Liao X. and Zhang Y.(eds.): Advance in Neural Networks-ISNN 2005. Lecture Notes in Computer Science 3496 Springer-Verlag Berlin Heidelberg (2005) 259-264

# Subnet Weight Modification Algorithm for Ensemble

Jiang Meng[1], Kun An[2], and Zhijie Wang[3]

[1] College of Mechanical Engineering and Automatization, North University of China, Taiyuan 030051, Shanxi, China
rivermeng@gmail.com

[2] College of Information and Communication Engineering, North University of China, Taiyuan 030051, Shanxi, China
ankun06@gmail.com

[3] School of Mechanical and Automation Engineering, Shanghai Institute of Technology, Shanghai 200235, China
wzjsdstu@163.com

**Abstract.** In view of comparability between neural network ensemble and Adaline, a modification algorithm for ensemble weights is presented based on the gradient descent method. This algorithm can improve the generalization performance by modifying subnet weights after the ensemble subnets are trained individually. Simulation results indicate that the new algorithm is of subnet selection function similar to GASEN but on a different idea, and of better performance than single network, simple-averaged ensemble and GASEN.

## 1 Introduction

Neural network ensemble (ensemble) has been a hotspot in machine learning and artificial intelligence since Hanson et al. [1] proposed it in 1990. Thereafter, Sollich and Kroph [2] gave a well definition that an ensemble is a collection of a finite number of neural networks (called the subnets) or other types of predictors that are trained for the same task. There are two ideas for modification of subnet weights, i.e., the simple averaging and weighted averaging. Bagging [3] is an earlier algorithm of simple averaging, while boosting algorithms, proposed by Schapire [4] and improved by Freund [5][6], are a general designation for a series of algorithms of weighed averaging. Later, Zhou [7] presented a genetic algorithm-based selective ensemble (GASEN), which uses the genetic algorithm to optimize ensemble subnets and improve the generalization performance. GASEN establishes an optimization model based on the simple-averaged ensemble, but the selected weights applied by GASEN shows a non-averaged distribution, as indicates GASEN is a weighted-averaged algorithm too. The non-average weighting ensemble is more reasonable than the simple-averaged one, which is also proved by Perrone and Cooper [8] in 1993. Afterwards, Zhou [9] illuminated a new idea of "*m*any *c*ould be *be*tter *t*han *a*ll" (McBETA), which pointed out the ensemble could improve the generalization by selecting many subnets from all of them in theory. Based on the McBETA idea, there are many methods put forward, such as PLA [10], CLUSENN [11] and PSO-based approach [12].

D.-S. Huang, K. Li, and G.W. Irwin (Eds.): ICIC 2006, LNCS 4113, pp. 482 – 487, 2006.

From the discussion above, the weighted averaging is a potential way to better generalization performance of the ensemble. However, modifying subnet weights is time-consuming using heuristic optimal methods, e.g., genetic algorithm and particle swarm optimization (PSO). Moreover, the ensemble optimized by the methods based on the McBETA idea is still simple averaging, which cannot improve the performance to the extent of maximum. Since the weighted averaging can improve the ensemble performance both theoretically and practically, why not provide a new algorithm for ensemble weights modification on a throughout idea of weighted averaging? The review of Adaline neural network may help the topic.

## 2 Review of Adaline

In 1957, Rosenblatt provided a Perceptron model to simulate the perceptive and learning ability of human; a few years later, Widrow and Hoff presented an *ada*ptive *line*ar (Adaline) neuron model. Both models are of similar topology with input nodes and output layer, but of the different active function in the output neurons, where Perceptron adopts the hard limit function and Adaline uses the linear function for classification and regression tasks, respectively.

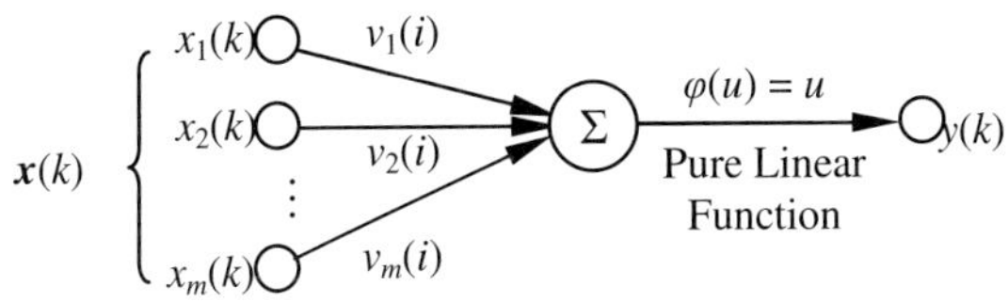


**Fig. 1.** Structure of Adaline

There are a set of training data $T = \{ \boldsymbol{x}(k), d(k) \}$ $(k = 1, 2, \ldots, P)$ with one-dimension output value, where the input vector is $\boldsymbol{x}(k) = [x_1(k), x_2(k), \ldots, x_m(k)]^{\mathrm{T}}$. Given Adaline model (Fig. 1), the neuron weight is $\boldsymbol{v}(k) = [v_1(k), v_2(k), \ldots, v_m(k)]^{\mathrm{T}}$; the active function is pure linear function; and the output relates with the error of $e(k) = d(k) - y(k)$,

$$y(k) = \sum_{j=1}^{m} v_j(k) x_j(k) = \boldsymbol{v}^{\mathrm{T}}(k)\boldsymbol{x}(k) . \tag{1}$$

Considering the $k$-th instant error $e(k)$ in the cost function of Adaline, $\xi(\boldsymbol{v}) = \frac{1}{2} e^2(k)$, the derivative of $\xi(\boldsymbol{v})$ is $\frac{\partial \xi(\boldsymbol{v})}{\partial \boldsymbol{v}} = e(k)\frac{\partial e(k)}{\partial \boldsymbol{v}}$ and we can get $\frac{\partial \xi(\boldsymbol{v})}{\partial \boldsymbol{v}} = -\nabla \xi(\boldsymbol{v})$, and the learning equation for Adaline based on the gradient descent method,

$$\boldsymbol{v}(k+1) = \boldsymbol{v}(k) - \eta \nabla \xi(\boldsymbol{v}) = \boldsymbol{v}(k) + \eta e(k)\boldsymbol{x}(k) . \tag{2}$$

where $\eta$ is the learning rate of Adaline.

## 3 New Algorithm for Subnet Weights Modification

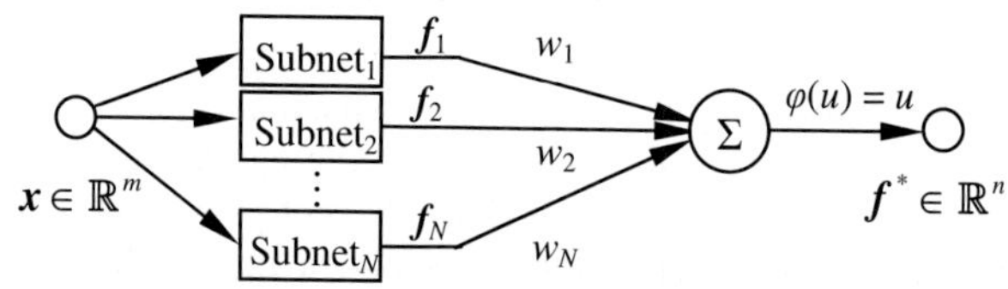


**Fig. 2.** Structure of neural network ensemble

### 3.1 Comparability Between Ensemble and Adaline

Suppose there is an ensemble comprising $N$ subnets (Fig.2) to approximate a function $\boldsymbol{f} : \mathbb{R}^m \to \mathbb{R}^n$, and the subnets are combined in the weighted method. Therefore, the ensemble output $\boldsymbol{f}^*$ is

$$\boldsymbol{f}^* = \sum_{i=1}^{N} w_i \boldsymbol{f}_i \cdot \tag{3}$$

where $\boldsymbol{f}_i$ is the output of the $i$-th subnet; $w_i$ is the weight corresponding to $\boldsymbol{f}_i$, satisfying the following two equations,

$$\sum_{i=1}^{N} w_i = 1 \text{ and } 0 \le w_i \le 1 . \tag{4}$$

**Table 1.** Comparability between the ensemble and Adaline

| Comparability | Ensemble | Adaline |
|---|---|---|
| Input Structure | Subnet outputs and corresponding weights | Input neurons and corresponding weights |
| Output Methods | Weighted average | Linear active function |
| Training Algorithm | Bagging/boosting and then GASEN (if needed) | Least mean square |

There are similarities between Eq.(1) and (3) in their expressions. Both expressions have an operator of weighted sum. But they are different in structures: the former is a simplest neural network with a single layer while the latter is the ensembling model of complex subnets with $w_i$ satisfying Eq.(4). Table 1 lists the comparability of both models. In the input structure item, the subnets are regarded as Adaline neurons and ensemble weights are in the same place as the neuron weights. But they are different in their training algorithms. After the subnets are trained individually (bagging) or sequentially (boosting), the ensemble can optimize the corresponding weights with GASEN if needed. However, Adaline uses gradient descent idea (LMS) to update neuron weights rapidly. Since their weights are equivalent to each other, it would be better to use gradient idea rather than GASEN to optimize ensemble weights and improve the generalization performance.

### 3.2 Subnet Weights Modification Algorithm

Suppose there is an ensemble for the regression task $T = \{\boldsymbol{x}(k), d(k)\}$ ( $k = 1, 2, \ldots, P$ ), which has the output of $f^*(k)$ with the $k$-th training data,

$$f^*(k) = \sum_{i=1}^{N} w_i f_i(k) = \boldsymbol{w}^{\mathrm{T}} \boldsymbol{f}(k) , \tag{5}$$

where $f^*(k)$ is the ensemble output to approximate the regression data $(\boldsymbol{x}(k), d(k))$; $\boldsymbol{f}(k)$ is a vector made up of all the subnets output based on the input of $\boldsymbol{x}(k)$; $\boldsymbol{w}$ is the corresponding weight vector of ensemble subnets.

Defining the ensemble error $e(k) = d(k) - f^*(k)$ and cost function $\xi(\boldsymbol{w}) = \frac{1}{2}\sum_{k=1}^{P} e^2(k)$, and taking derivative of $\xi(\boldsymbol{w})$ with respect to $\boldsymbol{w}$, we can get the weight increment expression similar to Adaline,

$$\Delta \boldsymbol{w} = -\eta \nabla \xi(\boldsymbol{w}) = \eta \sum_{k=1}^{P} e(k) \boldsymbol{f}(k) = \eta\, \boldsymbol{d}(\boldsymbol{w}) , \tag{6}$$

where $\eta$ is a learning rate for subWMA with a very small value, normally $\eta \leq 0.1$.

As an item of subnet weight, $w_i$ should meet the following constraint case,

$$\sum_{i=1}^{N} w_i = 1 , \tag{7}$$

or

$$\sum_{i=1}^{N} \Delta w_i = 0 , \tag{8}$$

but the case above cannot be satisfied by Eq.(6) directly. On this condition, adding an item $\lambda$ to Eq.(6) for modification,

$$\Delta \boldsymbol{w} = \eta \boldsymbol{d}(\boldsymbol{w}) + \lambda , \tag{9}$$

or

$$\Delta w_i = \eta d(w_i) + \lambda , \tag{10}$$

we can get $\sum_{i=1}^{N} \Delta w_i = \eta \sum_{i=1}^{N} d(w_i) + N\lambda = 0$ and solve λ from Eq.(10),

$$\lambda = -\eta \sum_{i=1}^{N} d(w_i) / N = -\eta \bar{d}(w) . \tag{11}$$

Simultaneous Eq.(9) and (11), we can achieve the modification equation for subWMA,

$$\Delta \boldsymbol{w} = \eta\, \boldsymbol{d}(\boldsymbol{w}) - \eta\, \bar{d}(w) = \eta \left[ \sum_{k=1}^{P} e(k) \boldsymbol{f}(k) - \sum_{i=1}^{N} \sum_{k-1}^{P} e(k) f_i(k) / N \right] . \tag{12}$$

Therefore, the procedure of subWMA can be summarized as Table 2.

**Table 2.** Procedure of subWMA

**Input:** validating set *S*, trained ensemble *Nets*, ensemble individuals *N*, iterative times *Epochs*, learning rate *lr*

**Procedure:**

```
init ensemble weight vector w = 1 / N
for t = 1 to Epochs   {
   y = Nets individual output vector from S
   e = individual output error between y and expected S
   d = gradient descent direction by e and y
  dm = sum(d) / N,     (mean of d)
   w = lr * (d – dm),  (updating increment of w)
   w = w +  w           }
```

**Output:** ensemble weights ***w***

## 4 Simulation and Discussion

We use Friedman#1 [13] problem to verify the availability of subWMA and compare the performance with simple averaging and GASEN. The data set $\{x_i ; d\}$ ($i$=1, 2, … , 5) is produced by the equation of $d = 10\sin(\pi x_1 x_2) + 20(x_3 - 0.5)^2 + 10x_4 + 5x_5 + \varepsilon$, where $x_i$ satisfies the uniform distribution U[0, 1] and the noise item $\varepsilon$ satisfies the normal distribution N[0, 1].

For convenient discussion, an ensemble comprising 20 subnets is given for this problem, where each network is with one hidden layer including 6 neurons and has been trained individually with the training set. Given related parameters of subWMA, including $lr$ = 0.005 and $Epochs$ = 50, the following results can be obtained.

Fig. 3 shows the curves of validating error and test error, where the final validation error is 0.2336 and the test error is 0.2745. Table 3 provides the test errors of different

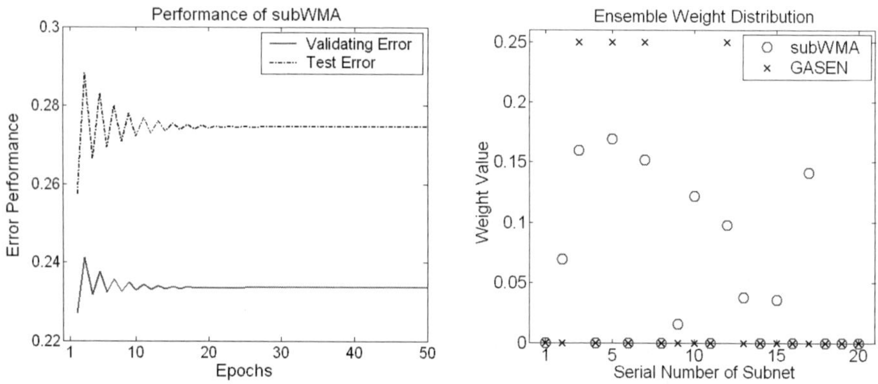


**Fig. 3.** Error curves of subWMA and ensemble weights distributions

algorithms, where the test error of subWMA is the minimum, similar to that of GASEN and the best subnet, the minimal error among all the trained subnets. To avoid the negative cases in subWMA weights, we need to add a *neglect operation* to the main procedure that when some weight is less than a given value, it can be taken as zero. In fact, the neglect operation is of a subnets selection function similar to GASEN, but they are really based on the different ideas, the former is a gradient-based algorithm, the latter is an optimization problem for subnets combination with genetic algorithm.

**Table 3.** Test errors of different algorithms

| Algorithms | SubWMA | GASEN | Best subnet | Simple averaging |
|---|---|---|---|---|
| Test error | 0.2745 | 0.3204 | 0.2795 | 1.1401 |

## 5 Conclusions

By comparing subWMA with other ensembling methods, we can draw a helpful conclusion. On one hand, subWMA is of subnet selection function similar to GASEN but on a different idea of gradient descent; on the other hand, subWMA can achieve better generalization performance than simple averaging method and GASEN.

## References


1. Hanson, L.K., Salamon, P.: Neural Network Ensemble. IEEE Trans. on Pattern Analysis and Machine Intelligence, Vol. PAMA-12 (1990) 993-1002
2. Sollich, P., Kroph, A.: Leaning with Ensembles: How Over-Fitting can be Useful. In: Advances in Neural Information Processing Systems 8, Cambridge, MA (1996) 190-196
3. Breiman, L.: Bagging Predictors. Machine Leaning. Vol. 24 (1996) 123-140
4. Schapire,R.E.: The Strength of Weak Learn Ability. Machine Leaning, Vol. 5 (1990) 197-227
5. Freund, Y.: Boosting a Weak Algorithm by Majority. Information Computation, Vol. 121 (1995) 256–285
6. Freund, Y., Schapire, R.E.: A Decision-theoretic Generalization of On-line Learning and an Application to Boosting. J. Computer and System Science, Vol. 55 (1997) 119-139.
7. Zhou Z.H., Wu J.X., Jiang Y.: Genetic Algorithm Based Selective Neural Network Ensemble. In: Proc. 17th International Joint Conf. on Artificial Intelligence, Seattle, WA, Vol. 2 (2001) 797-802
8. Perrone, M. P., Cooper, J.N.: When Networks Disagree: Ensemble Method for Neural Network. Artificial Neural Networks for Speech and Vision, Chapman and Hall, New York (1993) 126-142
9. Zhou, Z. H., Wu, J. X., Tang, W.: Ensembling Neural Networks: Many Could Be Better Than All. Artificial Intelligence, Vol. 137 (2002) 239-263
10. Wang, Z.Q., Chen, S.F., Chen, Z.Q.: A Parallel Learning Approach for Neural Network Ensemble, Chinese Journal of Computers, Vol.28, No. 3 (2005) 402-408
11. Li, K., Huang, H.K.: A Selective Approach to Neural Network Ensemble Based on Clustering Technology. J. Computer Research and Development, Vol. 42 (2005) 594-598
12. Fu, Q., Hu, S.X., Zhao, S.Y.: PSO-based Approach For Neural Network Ensembles. J. Zhejiang University (Engineering Science), Vol. 38 (2004) 1596-1600
13. Friedman, J.: Multivariate Adaptive Regression Splines. Annals of Statistics, Vol. 19 (1991) 1-141

# The Mixture of Neural Networks Adapted to Multilayer Feedforward Architecture

Joaquín Torres-Sospedra, Carlos Hernández-Espinosa, and Mercedes Fernández-Redondo

Departamento de Ingenieria y Ciencia de los Computadores, Universitat Jaume I, Avda. Sos Baynat s/n, C.P. 12071, Castellon, Spain
{jtorres, espinosa, redondo}@icc.uji.es

**Abstract.** The *Mixture of Neural Networks* (*MixNN*) is a Multi-Net System based on the *Modular Approach*. The *MixNN* employs a neural network to weight the outputs of the expert networks. This method decompose the original problem into subproblems, and the final decision is taken with the information provided by the expert networks and the gating network. The neural networks used in *MixNN* are quite simple so we present a mixture of networks based on the *Multilayer Feedforward* architecure, called *Mixture of Multilayer Feedforward* (*MixMF*). Finally, we have performed a comparison among *Simple Ensemble*, *MixNN* and *MixMF*. The methods have been tested with six databases from the *UCI repository* and the results show that *MixMF* is the best performing method.

## 1 Introduction

The most important property of an artificial neural network is the ability to correctly respond to inputs which were not used in the learning set. One technique commonly used to increase this ability consist on training some Multilayer Feedforward networks with different weights initialization. Then the mean of the outputs are applied to get the output of the ensemble. This method, known as *Simple Ensemble* or *Basic Ensemble Machine*, increases the generalization capability [1,2,3]. The diagram of a *Simple Ensemble* is shown in Figure 1.

Although most of the methods to create a Multi-Net System are based on the *ensemble approach* [4,5], we also focus on a *Mixture of Neural Networks* (*MixNN*) because is one of the most known *modular* methods and we think it could be improved.

*Mixture of Neural Networks* is a method to build a Modular Network which consist on training different neural networks with a gating network. The method divides the problem into subproblems, each subproblem tends to be solved by one network. The gating network is used to combine the outputs of the neural networks to get the final output.

The original *Mixture of Neural Networks* (*MixNN*) [6] is based on a quite simple neural network architecture. We think that *MixNN* could perform better if the method was based on *Multilayer Feedforward* networks. In this paper we present a *Mixture of Multilayer Feedforward Networks* (*MixMF*) which is a modular approach based on Multilayer Feedforward networks trained with Backpropagation.

In section 2 we describe the basic concepts of the MixMF neural network model. We have built multiple classification systems of 3, 9, 20 and 40 networks on six databases

D.-S. Huang, K. Li, and G.W. Irwin (Eds.): ICIC 2006, LNCS 4113, pp. 488–493, 2006.

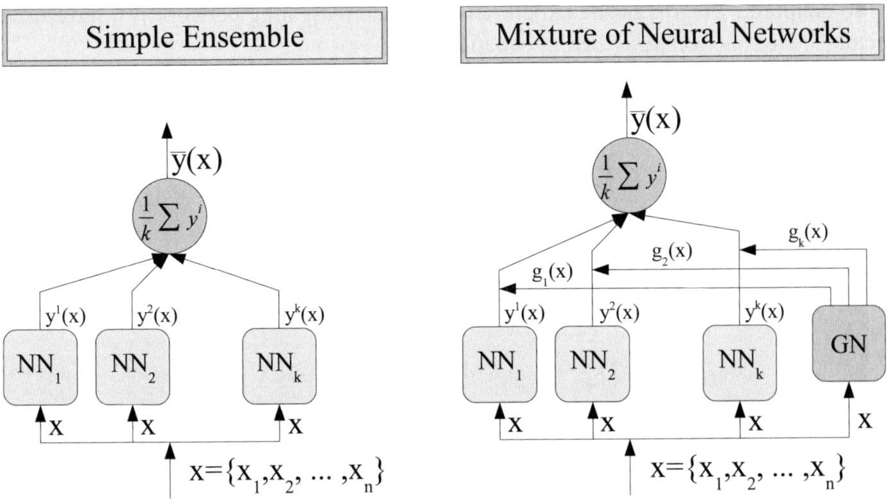


**Fig. 1.** Simple Ensemble and Mixture of Neural Networks diagrams

from the *UCI repository* to test the performance of *Simple Ensemble*, *MixNN* and *MixMF*. The results we have obtained on these six databases are in subsection 3.1. We have also calculated the mean percentage of error reduction, $PER$, of the different networks models to compare the methods, these results appear in subsetion 3.2.

## 2 Theory

In this section, we describe the *Mixture of Neural Networks* and the *Mixture of Multilayer Feedforward*

### 2.1 Mixture of Neural Networks

The *Mixture of Neural Networks* (*MixNN*) is a method to build a Multi-Net System based on the *Modular approach*. It consist on training *k* expert networks and a gating network. The input *x* is applied to the expert networks and the gating network. The modular network output is:

$$\overline{y}_{class} = \sum_{net=1}^{k} y_{class}^{net} \cdot g_{net} \tag{1}$$

Where the output of the expert networks is described in equation 2 and the output of the gating networks is described in equation 3

$$y_{class}^{net} = x^T \cdot w_{class}^{net} \tag{2}$$

$$g_{net} = \frac{\exp\left(x^T \cdot a_{net}\right)}{\sum_{j=1}^{k} \exp\left(x^T \cdot a_j\right)} \tag{3}$$

To adapt the weights of the expert networks and the gating network, we have used the objective function described in equation 4.

$$L = \log \left( \sum_{net=1}^{k} g_{net} \cdot \exp \left( -\frac{1}{2} \cdot \left\| d - y^{net} \right\|^2 \right) \right) \quad (4)$$

The equations used to adapt the weights of the expert networks $w$ and the gating network $a$ are:

$$w_{class}^{net} (ite + 1) = w_{class}^{net} (ite) + \eta \cdot h_{net} \cdot \left( d - y^{net} \right) \cdot x \quad (5)$$

$$a_{net} (ite + 1) = a_{net} (ite) + \eta \cdot h_{net} \cdot (h_{net} - g_{net}) \cdot x \quad (6)$$

where:

$$h_{net} = \frac{g_{net} \cdot \left( -\frac{1}{2} \left| d - y^{net} \right|^2 \right)}{\sum_{j=1}^{k} \left( g_j \cdot \left( -\frac{1}{2} \left| d - y^j \right|^2 \right) \right)} \quad (7)$$

## 2.2 Mixture of Multilayer Feedforward Networks

*Mixture of Multilayer Feedforward Networks* (MixNF) is a method to build a modular network. *MixMF* is an approach of *MixNN* where the expert networks are *Multilayer Feedforward* networks with one hidden layer and threshold nodes. *Multilayer Feedforward* networks are more accurate than the expert networks used in *MixNN* but the training process is slower. In [7] it can be found that MLP network with one hidden layer and threshold nodes can solve any function with a specified precision.

In order to adapt the weights of the expert networks and the gating network we have used the objective function described in equation 4. The equations used to adapt the input layer weights of the expert networks $wi$, the hidden layer weights of the expert networks $wh$ and the gating network $a$ the following ones:

$$wh_{j,k}^{net} (ite + 1) = wh_{j,k}^{net} (ite) + \eta \cdot h_{net} \cdot \delta_k \cdot ho_j \quad (8)$$

$$wi_{i,j}^{net} (ite + 1) = wi_{i,j}^{net} (ite) + \eta \cdot h_{net} \cdot \delta_j^{'} \cdot x_i \quad (9)$$

$$a_{net} (n + 1) = a_{net} (n) + \eta \cdot h_{net} \cdot (h_{net} - g_{net}) \cdot x \quad (10)$$

where:

$$h_{net} = \frac{g_{net} \cdot \left( -\frac{1}{2} \left| d - y^{net} \right|^2 \right)}{\sum_{j=1}^{k} \left( g_j \cdot \left( -\frac{1}{2} \left| d - y^j \right|^2 \right) \right)} \quad (11)$$

$$\delta_k = (d_k - y_k) \cdot (1 - y_k) \cdot (y_k) \quad (12)$$

$$\delta_j^{'} = ho_j \cdot (1 - ho_j) \cdot \sum_{h=1}^{m} \delta_h \cdot wh_{j,h} \quad (13)$$

## 3 Experimental Testing

In this section, we describe the experimental setup, the datasets we have used in our experiments and we show the results we have obtained. Finally we compare the results we have obtained with *Simple Ensemble*, *MixNN* and *MixMF* on the different datasets.

For this reason we have trained multiple classification systems of 3, 9, 20 and 40 MF networks with *Simple Ensemble*, *MixNN* and *MixMF* on eight different classification problems from the *UCI repository of machine learning databases* [8] to test the performance of methods. The databases we have used are: Cylinder Bands Database (band), Australian Credit Approval (cred), Solar Flare Database (flare), Glass Identification Database (glas), The monk's problem 1 (mok1), Congressional Voting Records Database (vote), Wisconsin Breast Cancer Database (wdbc). In addition, we repeated ten times the whole learning process, using different partitions of data in training, validation and test sets. With this procedure we can obtain a mean performance of the ensemble for each database and an error in the performance calculated by standard error theory.

### 3.1 Results

In this subsection we present the experimental results we have obtained with the ensembles of MF networks trained with *Simple Ensemble* and the modular networks.

Table 1 shows the results we have obtained with ensembles of 3, 9, 20 and 40 networks trained with *Simple Ensemble*. Table 2 shows the results we have obtained with a modular network of 3, 9, 20 and 40 networks trained with *Mixture of Neural Networks* and *Mixture of Multilayer Feedforward Networks*.

**Table 1.** Simple Ensemble results

| Database | 3 Nets | 9 Nets | 20 Nets | 40 Nets |
|---|---|---|---|---|
| **band** | 73.5±1.2 | 72.9±1.5 | 73.8±1.3 | 73.8±1.3 |
| **cred** | 86.5±0.7 | 86.4±0.7 | 86.6±0.7 | 86.5±0.7 |
| **flare** | 81.8±0.5 | 81.6±0.4 | 81.5±0.5 | 81.6±0.5 |
| **glas** | 94±0.8 | 94±0.7 | 94±0.7 | 94.2±0.6 |
| **mok1** | 98.3±0.9 | 98.8±0.8 | 98.3±0.9 | 98.3±0.9 |
| **survi** | 74.3±1.3 | 74.2±1.3 | 74.3±1.3 | 74.3±1.3 |
| **vote** | 95.6±0.5 | 95.6±0.5 | 95.6±0.5 | 95.6±0.5 |
| **wdbc** | 96.9±0.5 | 96.9±0.5 | 96.9±0.5 | 96.9±0.5 |

### 3.2 Interpretations of Results

Comparing the results showed in tables 1 and 2 we can see that the improvement in performance using our method depends on the database and the number of networks used in the ensemble. We can also see that, in general, *Mixture of Multilayer Feedforward Networks* is better than *Mixture of Neural Networks*.

We have also calculated the percentage of error reduction (PER) of the ensembles with respect to a single network to get a general value for the comparison among the methods we have studied. We have used equation 14 to calculate the ensemble PER value.

**Table 2.** Mixture Methods $PER$

| | MixNN | | | | MixMF | | | |
|---|---|---|---|---|---|---|---|---|
| **DB** | **3 Nets** | **9 Nets** | **20 Nets** | **40 Nets** | **3 Nets** | **9 Nets** | **20 Nets** | **40 Nets** |
| **band** | 72.7±2.2 | 74.4±1.3 | 74±1.9 | 75.5±1.3 | 75.5±1.9 | 74.2±2 | 74.7±1.7 | 73.8±1.6 |
| **cred** | 86.8±0.5 | 86.9±0.5 | 86.5±0.6 | 86±0.5 | 85.9±0.5 | 86.7±0.7 | 86.5±0.7 | 86.8±0.5 |
| **flare** | 81.5±0.5 | 81.7±0.5 | 81.7±0.6 | 81.8±0.6 | 82.1±0.6 | 81.9±0.6 | 81.6±0.6 | 81.7±0.6 |
| **glas** | 89.4±1 | 91.2±1.1 | 90.2±1.3 | 91±1.1 | 94.6±1 | 94.6±1.2 | 94.2±1.3 | 95±1.2 |
| **mok1** | 87.8±2.2 | 93.6±2.6 | 93.6±2.1 | 93.9±2.5 | 99.3±0.8 | 99.3±0.8 | 98.8±0.9 | 100±0 |
| **survi** | 72.3±1.2 | 72.6±0.9 | 73.8±0.9 | 73.6±1.2 | 74.6±1.3 | 74.9±1.2 | 74.6±1.1 | 75.1±1.2 |
| **vote** | 95±1.2 | 96.1±0.6 | 96.1±0.6 | 96.5±0.7 | 96.1±0.6 | 96.1±0.6 | 96.1±0.6 | 95.8±0.6 |
| **wdbc** | 94.7±0.5 | 94.9±0.4 | 95.1±0.6 | 94.6±0.5 | 96.9±0.5 | 96.9±0.5 | 96.9±0.5 | 96.9±0.5 |

$$PER = 100 \cdot \frac{Error_{singlenetwork} - Error_{ensemble}}{Error_{singlenetwork}} \tag{14}$$

The $PER$ value ranges from $0\%$, where there is no improvement by the use of a particular ensemble method with respect to a single network, to $100\%$. There can also be negative values, which means that the performance of the ensemble is worse than the performance of the single network. This new measurement is relative and can be used to compare more clearly the different methods.

Moreover we have calculated the mean increase of performance and the mean percentage of error reduction across all databases with respect to the single network. Table 3 shows these general measurements.

**Table 3.** Global Measures

| | Mean $PER$ | | | | Mean Increase of Performance | | | |
|---|---|---|---|---|---|---|---|---|
| **DB** | **3 Nets** | **9 Nets** | **20 Nets** | **40 Nets** | **3 Nets** | **9 Nets** | **20 Nets** | **40 Nets** |
| **Simple Ens.)** | 20.96 | 20.63 | 20.98 | 21.1 | 5.17 | 5.1 | 5.19 | 5.21 |
| **MixNN** | -0.12 | 8.58 | 8.92 | 8.51 | 3.67 | 3.99 | 3.93 | 4.17 |
| **MixMF** | 23.77 | 23.93 | 23.11 | 23.43 | 5.62 | 5.63 | 5.48 | 5.69 |

According to this global measurement *MixMF* is the best performing method. The highest difference between *MixMF* and *Simple Ensemble* is in the 9-network ensemble where the mean $PER$ increase is 3.3%. The highest difference between original *MixMF* and *MixNN* is in the 3-network ensemble where the mean $PER$ increase is 23.90%.

## 4 Conclusions

In this paper we have presented *Mixture of Multilayer Feedforward Networks*, a modular method based on *Mixture of Neural Networks* and *Multilayer Feedforward*. We have trained Multiple Classification Systems of 3, 9, 20 and 40 networks with *Simple Ensemble*, *MixNN* and *MMixMF* to cover a wide spectrum of the number of networks in the classification system. The results showed that in general the improvement by the use of *MixMF* depends on the database.

Finally, we have obtained the mean percentage of error reduction across all databases. According to the results of this measurement *MixMF* performs better than *MixNN*. In general, *MixMF* is the best performing method.

We can conclude that the *Mixture of Neural Networks* variation we have presented in this paper uses a better expert networks so the performance of the final classification system is, in general, better.

## Acknowledgments

This research was supported by project *P1·1B2004-03* of Universitat Jaume I - Bancaja in Castellón de la Plana, Spain.

## References

1. Tumer, K., Ghosh, J.: Error Correlation and Error Reduction in Ensemble Classifiers. Connection Science vol.8(3-4) (1996) 385–403
2. Raviv, Y., Intratorr, N.: Bootstrapping with Noise: An Effective Regularization Technique. Connection Science, Special issue on Combining Estimators vol.8 (1996) 356–372
3. Freund, Y., Schapire, R.E.: Experiments with A New Boosting Algorithm. In: International Conference on Machine Learning. (1996) 148–156
4. Hernandez-Espinosa, C., Fernandez-Redondo, M., Torres-Sospedra, J.: Ensembles of Multilayer Feedforward for Classification Problems. In: Neural Information Processing, ICONIP 2004. Volume 3316 of Lecture Notes in Computer Science. (2005) 744–749
5. Hernandez-Espinosa, C., Torres-Sospedra, J., Fernandez-Redondo, M.: New Experiments on Ensembles of Multilayer Feedforward for Classification Problems. In: Proceedings of International Conference on Neural Networks, IJCNN 2005, Montreal, Canada. (2005) 1120–1124
6. Sharkey, A.J., ed.: Combining Artificial Neural Nets: Ensemble and Modular Multi-Net Systems. (1999)
7. Kuncheva, L.I.: Combining Pattern Classifiers: Methods and Algorithms. Wiley-Interscience (2004)
8. Newman, D.J., Hettich, S., Blake, C.L., Merz, C.J.: UCI Repository of Machine Learning Databases (1998)

# The Neural Network for Solving Convex Nonlinear Programming Problem

Yongqing Yang[1,2], Xianyun Xu[1], and Daqi Zhu[3]

[1] School of Science, Southern Yangtze University, Wuxi 214122, China
[2] Department of Mathematics, Southeast University, Nanjing 210096, China
yongqingyang@seu.edu.cn
[3] Industrial Automation Department, Southern Yangtze University, Wuxi 214122, China

**Abstract.** In this paper, a neural network model for solving convex nonlinear programming problems is investigated based on the Fischer-Burmeister function and steepest descent method. The proposed neural network is proved to be stable in the sense of Lyapunov and can converge to an optimal solution of the original optimization problem. An example shows the effectiveness of the proposed neural network model.

## 1 Introduction

Since Hopfield and Tank first proposed a neural network for solving linear programming problems, to construct a neural network for solving linear and nonlinear programming problems has been an active topic [1]-[11]. Neural network is composed of many massively connected neurons and its main advantage is massively paralleled distributed computation. Unlike other parallel algorithms, neural networks can be implemented on analogue circuits. Therefore, the neural network approach is thought of as a good choice of real time solvers for nonlinear programming. At present, there are several neural networks for solving nonlinear programming problems. Kennedy and Chua [6] proposed a neural network which employs both gradient method and penalty function method for solving nonlinear programming problems. Its energy function can be view as an inexact penalty function and thus an approximation optimal solution can only be obtained. Chen *et al.* [7] proposed a neural network for solving convex nonlinear programming problems based on primal-dual method. Its distinguishing features are that the primal and dual problems can be solved simultaneously. But the number of state variables becomes more, which enlarges the scale of network. Based on projection method and Kuhn-Tacker optimality conditions of convex programming, Xia and Wang [8] proposed a projection neural network. To guarantee the stability of the proposed network, stronger conditions, i.e. the objective function is convex and all constraint functions are strictly convex or the objective function is strictly convex and all constraint functions are convex, are needed.

Motivated by the discussions above, in this paper, we proposed a novel neural network for solving convex nonlinear programming problems based on the

D.-S. Huang, K. Li, and G.W. Irwin (Eds.): ICIC 2006, LNCS 4113, pp. 494–499, 2006.

Kuhn-Tacker optimality conditions and the Fischer-Burmeister function. This neural network is simple in structure and proved to be globally stable and can converge to the optimal solution of original optimization problem.

The paper is organized as follows: In Section 2, we will construct a neural network model based on Kuhn-Tacker optimality conditions and the Fischer-Burmeister function and investigate the stability of the equilibrium point. In Section 3, an illustrative example will be given to show the effectiveness of the proposed model. Conclusions are given in Section 4.

## 2 The Neural Network Model and Stability Analysis

Let us consider the following convex nonlinear programming problem

$$\begin{aligned} &\min f(x) \\ &\text{subject to } \ g_j(x) \leq 0, \ j=1,2,...,m. \end{aligned} \tag{1}$$

where $f(x),\ g_j(x),\ j=1,2,...,m,\ x \in R^n$ are twice continuous differentiable convex functions.

It is well known that if a point $x^* \in R^n$ is the optimal solution of (1), if and only if there exists $y^* = (y_1^*,...,y_m^*)^T \in R^m$, such that $(x^*, y^*)$ satisfies the following Kuhn-Tacker system

$$\begin{cases} \nabla f(x) + \nabla g(x) y = 0, \\ y^T g(x) = 0,\ y \geq 0,\ g(x) \leq 0. \end{cases} \tag{2}$$

Now, we construct a neural network model for solving (1).

The Fischer-Burmeister function $\phi:\ R^2 \to R$ is given by

$$\phi(a,b) = \sqrt{a^2+b^2} - a - b. \tag{3}$$

*Proposition 1:*[11] (i) $\phi(a,b)=0$ if and only if $a \geq 0,\ b \geq 0$ and $ab=0$;
(ii) the square of $\phi(a,b)$ is continuously differentiable;
(iii) $\phi$ is twice continuously differentiable everywhere except at the origin.

Let $\alpha = (\alpha_1 \alpha_2,...,\alpha_n),\ \alpha_i > 0,\ i=1,2,...,n$ be constant vector. By Proposition 1, $\nabla f(x) + \nabla g(x) y = 0$ if and only if $\phi(\alpha, \nabla f(x) + \nabla g(x) y) = 0$. Thus, (2) can been reformulated as the following equations

$$\begin{cases} \phi(\alpha, \nabla f(x) + \nabla g(x) y) = 0, \\ \phi(y, -g(x)) = 0. \end{cases} \tag{4}$$

*Proposition 2:* Finding a solution of (1) can be equivalently reformulated as find a solution of the following equation:

$$\phi(x,y) = \begin{bmatrix} \phi(\alpha, \nabla f(x) + \nabla g(x) y) \\ \phi(y, -g(x)) \end{bmatrix} = 0. \tag{5}$$

For simplicity, denote $z = (x, y)$, $\beta = (\alpha, y)$ and

$$F(x, y) = \begin{bmatrix} \nabla f(x) + \nabla g(x) y \\ -g(x) \end{bmatrix}. \tag{6}$$

Thus, solving nonlinear programming problem (1) is equivalent to find a solution for the following equation

$$\phi(z) = \phi(\beta, F(z)) = 0. \tag{7}$$

*Proposition 3:* The Jacobian matrix of $F$ is positive semidefinite matrix.

Define

$$E(z) = \frac{1}{2} \parallel \phi(z) \parallel^2 = \frac{1}{2} \parallel \phi(\alpha, \nabla f(x) + \nabla g(x) y) \parallel^2 + \frac{1}{2} \parallel \phi(y, -g(x)) \parallel^2. \tag{8}$$

We note that $E(z) \geq 0$ for all $z \in R^{n+m}$ and $z$ is the a solution of (5) if and only if $E(z) = 0$. Hence solving nonlinear programming problem (1) is equivalent to finding the global minimizer of the following unconstrained minimization problem:

$$\begin{aligned} &\min E(z) \\ &\text{subject to} \quad z \in R^{n+m}. \end{aligned} \tag{9}$$

Let $z$ depend on time variables. The objective function $E(z)$ in (9) is continuously differentiable for all $z \in R^{n+m}$. Using the steepest descent method, the neural network model can be described by the following nonlinear dynamical system:

$$\begin{aligned} \frac{dz(t)}{dt} &= -\lambda \nabla E(z(t)), \quad \lambda > 0, \\ z(0) &= z_0 \in R^{n+m}. \end{aligned} \tag{10}$$

where $\lambda$ is to scale the convergence rate of system (10).

*Theorem 1:* Suppose that the set of optimal solutions is $\Omega^* = \{z \in R^{n+m} | z = (x, y), x$ is the optimal solution of (1) and $y$ is Lagrangian multiplier vector corresponding to $x\}$, and that the set of equilibrium points of (10) is $\Omega^e = \{z \in R^{n+m} | \nabla E(z) = 0\}$, then $\Omega^* = \Omega^e$.

Proof: From the analysis above, it is easily to see that $x^*$ is an optimal solution of (1) if and only if there exist $y^*$ such that $z^* = (x^*, y^*)$ satisfies

$$\phi(z) = \phi(x, y) = \begin{bmatrix} \phi(\alpha, \nabla f(x) + \nabla g(x) y) \\ \phi(y, -g(x)) \end{bmatrix} = 0. \tag{11}$$

Since $f(x)$, $g_j(x)$, $j = 1, 2, ..., m$, $x \in R^n$ are twice continuous differentiable convex functions, one has

$$\nabla E(z) = \frac{\partial \phi}{\partial z} \phi(z). \tag{12}$$

that is, $\nabla E(z^*) = 0$, i.e. $(x^*, y^*)$ is an equilibrium point of (10). Therefore, $\Omega^* \subseteq \Omega^e$.

Conversely, if $z^e = (x^e, y^e) \in \Omega^e$ is an equilibrium point of (10), $\nabla E(z^e) = 0$. From proposition 3, $\nabla F$ is positive semidefinite matrix. It is well known that $\nabla F$ is positive semidefinite matrix is a sufficient condition for a stationary point to be solution to (1), i.e. $z^e = (x^e, y^e)$ satisfies the following equations.

$$\begin{cases} \nabla f(x^e) + \nabla g(x^e) y^e = 0, \\ (y^e)^T g(x^e) = 0, \; y^e \geq 0, \; g(x^e) \leq 0. \end{cases} \tag{13}$$

thus, $z^e = (x^e, y^e)$ is an optimal solution of (1), i.e. $\Omega^e \subseteq \Omega^*$.
By the discussed above, it is known That $\Omega^e = \Omega^*$. The proof is complete.
Let $L(z_0)$ denote the level set associated with initial point $y_0$ and be given by

$$L(z_0) = \{z \in R^{n+m} : E(z) \leq E(z_0)\}. \tag{14}$$

*Theorem 2:* Suppose that $x^*$ is an optimal solution of (1), then the equilibrium point $z^* = (x^*, y^*)$ of neural network (10) is globally stable.

Proof: First, it is clear that $E(z)$ is nonnegative function over $R^{n+m}$. Since $x^*$ is an optimal solution of (1), there exists $y^*$ such that $z^* = (x^*, y^*)$ satisfies $\phi(z^*) = 0$, i.e. $E(z^*) = 0$. Let $V(z) = E(z) - E(z^*) = E(z) \geq 0$, then

$$\frac{dV(z)}{dt} = [\nabla E(z(t))]^T \frac{dz(t)}{dt} = -\lambda \parallel \nabla E(z(t)) \parallel^2 \leq 0. \tag{15}$$

So, $z^*$ is globally stable in the sense of Lyapunov. The proof is complete.

*Theorem 3:* Suppose that nonlinear programming problem (10) has optimal solutions, and the level set $L(z_0)$ is bound. Let $z = z(t, z_0)$ be a trajectory of (1), then there exists $\bar{z} \in R^{n+m}$ and a sequence $\{t_n\}$ such that

(I) $\lim_{n \to +\infty} z(t_n, z_0) = \bar{z}$.
(II) $z(t, z_0)$ converges to the set of equilibrium points of (10).

Proof: (I) Let $\gamma^+(z_0) = \{z(t, z_0) | t \geq t_0\}$. Calculating the derivative of $E(z)$ along the trajectory $z(t, z_0)$, one has

$$\frac{dE(z)}{dt} = \nabla E(z)^T \frac{dz}{dt} = -\lambda \parallel \nabla E(z(t)) \parallel^2 \leq 0. \tag{16}$$

that is, $E(z)$ is monotone nonincreasing. thus $\gamma^+(z_0) = \{z(t, z_0) | t \geq t_0\} \subseteq L(z_0)$. By the assumption that the level set $L(z_0)$ is bound, it is easily to know that $\gamma^+(z_0)$ is a bounded positive semi-trajectory. Take strictly monotone increasing sequence $\{\bar{t}_n\}$, $0 \leq \bar{t}_1 \leq \bar{t}_2 \leq ... \leq \bar{t}_n \leq ...$, $\bar{t}_n \to +\infty$, then $\{z(\bar{t}_n, z_0)\}$ is a bounded sequence composed of increasing many points. Thus there exists a subsequence $\{t_n\} \subseteq \{\bar{t}_n\}$ such that

$$\lim_{n \to +\infty} z(t_n, z_0) = \bar{z}. \tag{17}$$

(II) By (17), $\bar{z}$ is $\omega-$limits point of trajectory $\gamma^+(z_0)$. Using LaSalle invariance principle, there must be $z(t, z_0) \to \bar{z} \in M \subseteq \Omega^e$, $\nabla E(\bar{z}) = 0$, where $M$ is invariant set of equilibrium points. From (10), it follows that

$$\frac{dz}{dt} = 0 \Leftrightarrow \nabla E(z) = 0. \tag{18}$$

i.e. $\bar{z}$ is an equilibrium point of (10). Therefore, from any initial state $z_0$, the trajectory $z(t, z_0)$ of (10) tent to $\bar{z}$. The proof is complete.

## 3 Simulation Examples

In this section, two simulation examples are given to demonstrate the feasibility and efficiency of the proposed neural networks for solving the convex nonlinear programming problems.

*Example 1:* Consider the following nonlinear programming

$$\begin{aligned} &\min \; f(X) = (x_1 - x_2)^2 + (x_2 - x_3)^2 + (x_3 - x_4)^4 \\ &\text{subject to} \begin{cases} x_1^2 + x_2^2 + x_3^2 + x_4^2 \leq 9 \\ (x_1 - 4)^2 + (x_2 + 4)^2 + (x_3 - 1)^2 + (x_4 + 1)^4 \leq 16. \end{cases} \end{aligned} \tag{19}$$

The nonlinear programming problem has an optimal solution $x^* = [1.6926, -0.9030, -0.0148, -0.5171]^T$ and the optimal value of the objective function is $f(x^*) = 7.5894$. With step size $\Delta t = 0.01$, simulation result shows the trajectory of neural network converges to its optimal solution.

## 4 Conclusions

We have investigated a convex nonlinear programming problem with nonlinear inequality constraints. Based on Kuhn-Tacker optimality conditions of convex programming and the Fischer-Burmeister function, a neural network model for solving this optimization problem has been constructed. This neural network was proved to be globally stable in the sense of Lyapunov and the solution trajectory can converge to an optimal solution of original optimization problem. An illustrative example was given to show the effectiveness of the proposed neural network.[1]

## References

1. Zhang, Y. , Wang, J.: A Dual Neural Network for Convex Quadratic Programming Subject to Linear Equality and Inequality Constraints, Physics Letters A, **298**(2002) 271-278
2. Tao, Q., Cao, J., Xue, M., Qiao, H.: A High Performance Neural Network for Solving Nonlinear Programming Problems with Hybrid Constraints, Physics Letters A, **288**(2001) 88-94

[1] This work was supported by the Natural Science Foundation of Jiangsu Province, China under Grants BK 2004021.

3. Liu, Q., Cao, J., Xia, Y.: A Delayed Neural Network for Solving Linear Projection Equations and Its Analysis, IEEE Transactions on Neural Networks, **16**(2005) 834-843
4. Liu, Q., Wang, J., Cao, J.: A Delayed Lagrangian Network for Solving Quadratic Programming Problems with Equality Constraints, Lecture Note in Computer Science, **3971** (2006) 369-378
5. Xia, Y., Feng, G.: A Modified Neural Network for Quadratic Programming with Real-Time Applications, Neural Information Processing-Letter and Reviews, **3**(2004) 69-75
6. M. P. Kennedy, Chua, L. O.: Neural Networks for Nonlinear Programming, IEEE Trans. Circuits Syst., **35** (1988) 554-562
7. Chen K. Z., Leung Y., Leung K. S., Gao X. B.: A Neural Network for Solving Nonlinear Programming Problem, Neural Computing and Applications, **11** (2002)103-111
8. Xia, Y.,Wang, J.: A Recurrent Neural Networks for Nonlinear Convex Optimization Subject to Nonlinear Inequality Constraints, IEEE Trans. Circuits Syst.-I, **51** (2004) 1385-1394
9. Gao, X. B.: A Novel Neural Network for Nonlinear Convex Programming, IEEE Trans. Neural Networks, **15** (2004) 613-621
10. Cao, J., Li, X.: Stability in Delayed Cohen-Grossberg Neural Networks: LMI Optimization Approach, Physica D: Nonlinear Phenomena, **212**(2005), 54-65
11. S. Effati, A. R. Nazemi: Neural Network Models and Its Application for Solving Linear and Quadratic Programming Problems, Applied mathematics and Computation, **172** (2006) 305-331

# A Hybrid Fuzzy-Genetic Algorithm

Agustin Leon-Barranco[1], Carlos A. Reyes-Garcia[1], and Ramon Zatarain-Cabada[2]

[1] Instituto Nacional de Astrofísica, Óptica y Electrónica (INAOE)
Luis Enrique Erro No. 1, Sta. Ma. Tonanzintla, Puebla, 72840, México
{agustinleonb, kargaxxi}@inaoep.mx
[2] Instituto Tecnológico de Culiacán
Juan de Dios Bátiz s/n, Culiacán, Sinaloa, 80220, México
rzc777@hotmail.com

**Abstract.** In this paper we present a hybrid fuzzy-genetic algorithm for the feature and instance subset selection problem. This algorithm combines a hybrid meta-heuristic algorithm and a fuzzy self-adaptive genetic algorithm with a rotary circular crossover which is based on a half uniform crossover. The best individual in the initial population is used as initial solution of the hybrid meta-heuristic algorithm with the purpose of improving its fitness; this method is a combination of simulated annealing, taboo search and hill-climbers and allows us to speed up the convergence of the initial population. When running, the genetic algorithm adjusts its own control parameters, and the adaptability of control parameters is directed by means of two fuzzy inference systems. Besides the description of the novel evolutionary algorithm, we present the results obtained during the experiments on several known databases and on an infant cry corpus.

## 1 Introduction

Data selection is one important issue in Artificial Intelligence; this is mostly needed when working with very large datasets intending to classify or recognize objects. Searching for feature and instance subsets smaller than the original sets can help to improve performance in prediction tasks using the smallest possible computational resources like time and memory. For optimization of this task, Genetic Algorithms is a recommended option. There is a new algorithm, here introduced, which combines a hybrid meta-heuristic algorithm and a fuzzy self-adaptive genetic algorithm with a modified crossover operator. The combination of these two search techniques forms a hybrid fuzzy-genetic algorithm.

## 2 Methodology

The feature and instance subset selection problem is addressed in this work by means of a hybrid learning methodology that integrates a genetic algorithm (GA) together with a distance weighted k-nearest neighbors classifier (k-NN) 8. The approach described here is an extended version of the *wrapper methodology* for the feature subset selection problem 5. The encoding of the training data subsets is by means of binary strings of length $N + M$ (i.e., $N$ instances and $M$ features of a training set that

D.-S. Huang, K. Li, and G.W. Irwin (Eds.): ICIC 2006, LNCS 4113, pp. 500–510, 2006.

form a search space of $2^{N+M}$ feature and instance subsets) that contain one bit for every feature and instance, and the value of the bit determines whether a feature or instance will be used in the classification process. One bit "1" in the i-*th* position indicates that one feature or instance should be part of the subset and one bit "0" indicates that it should be eliminated. In Figure 1 there is one chromosome, representing a *training subset* composed of 6 ($n$) instances with 3 ($m$) features each. These data are selected from an original *training set* of 11 ($N$) instances with 5 ($M$) features each.

| N – INSTANCES | | | | | | | | | | | M - FEATURES | | | | |
|---|---|---|---|---|---|---|---|---|---|---|---|---|---|---|---|
| 0 | 1 | 1 | 1 | 0 | 0 | 1 | 1 | 0 | 1 | 0 | 1 | 1 | 0 | 0 | 1 |

**Fig. 1.** One chromosome (training set) which has $N$ instances with $M$ features each

Our methodology is the following: For each database 10 experiments were performed in order to find the average performance. At each experiment the instances of the original dataset were randomly shuffled, from them, 60% for training and 20% for evaluating were selected; both directed to the wrapper model. The remaining 20% was left to test the accuracy of the best feature and instance subset found. The training and evaluation sets are used by the wrapper model to maximize the performance of feature and instance subsets according to the fitness evaluation function. From the training set a feature and instance subset is selected to form the k-NN classifier and its classification accuracy is measured by evaluating the evaluation set. The fitness evaluation function used to assess each data subset is composed by both its size and classification accuracy. Once the wrapper model returns the best feature and instance subset found, the accuracy of such a subset is measured by forming the k-NN classifier with this subset and by classifying the test sets. The fitness function $\boldsymbol{F_F}$ is formed by the accuracy of the classifier over the *evaluation set* used in the wrapper model, and the proportion of the *training subset* with regard to the original *training set*. The classifier is induced using a *training subset* taken from the original *training set*. The fitness function was taken from 6 and it is as follows:

$$F_F\,(DataSubset) = P(DataSubset) - \phi \frac{n+m}{N+M}$$

Where *P(DataSubset)* is the percent of the *evaluation set* which was correctly classified using the new *training subset* (*DataSubset*), "$\phi$" is a constant to control the importance given to data reduction over accuracy, "$n$" and "$m$" are the number of instances and features of *DataSubset*, respectively, and finally $N$ and $M$ are the total number of instances and features in the original *training set*, respectively. The value of "$\phi$" in this work is 1.

## 3 The Hybrid Fuzzy-Genetic Algorithm

The hybrid fuzzy-genetic algorithm for feature and instance subset selection combines a Hybrid Meta-Heuristic (HMH) algorithm and a Fuzzy Self-Adaptive Genetic Algorithm whose crossover operator is a Rotary Circular Crossover (RCC) based on

Half Uniform Crossover (HUX). The best individual in the initial population is used as the initial solution of the HMH with the purpose of improving its fitness. This method –also proposed in this work- is a combination of simulated annealing, taboo search and hill-climbers algorithms which allows us to speed up the convergence of the initial population. The genetic algorithm adjusts its own control parameters while running the algorithm by means of two fuzzy inference systems.

### 3.1 The Hybrid Meta-Heuristic Algorithm

The Hybrid Meta-Heuristic (HMH) algorithm is a search technique which combines Simulated Annealing, Taboo Search and two Hill-Climbers (*Record & Sweepers* and *Permutation & Mutation*). The description of every step is given next:

***Record and Sweepers.*** *Record* is the representation of the *Current Solution* (CS) or *Current Chromosome* (CC) by means of two arrays of the same length, one indicates with bits '1' the data present in the CS and the other also indicates with bits '1' the data not present in the CS (these arrays indicate what feature or instance can be removed or added to the CS, respectively), see Figure 2-a. *Sweepers* are two pointers that are on charge of sweeping bit by bit (moving from right to left) searching for bits '1' on their respective array. *Record and Sweepers* are used to create new solutions from CS. For instance, in Figure 2-a Sweeper 1, from bit 8, will pass to bit 7 and will create a new solution that removes from CS that feature or instance (indicated with the bit 1) present in CS. Sweeper 2, from bit 12, will pass to bit 10 and will create a new solution that adds to CS that feature or instance (indicated with the bit 1) not present in CS. We can notice that this is a reduced version of a hill-climbing technique which sweeps bit by bit performing successive changes of one bit to the CS.

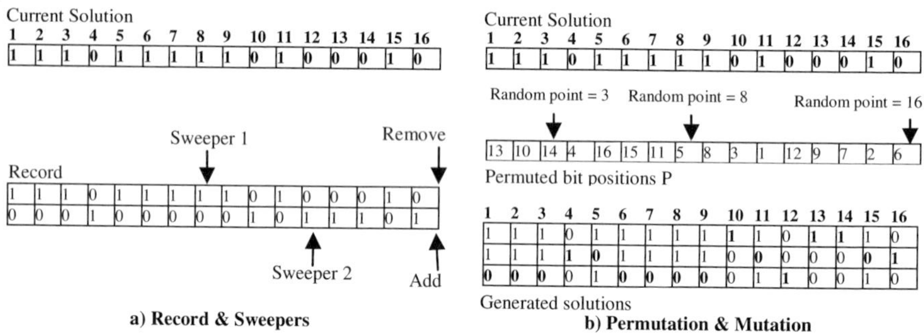


**Fig. 2.** Hill-Climbers

***Permutation and Mutation.*** When *Record and Sweepers* is being used, a *Neighborhood* (a set of solutions around the CS) with a maximum of two and a minimum of one solution can be generated from CS, but else, the *Permutation and Mutation* method is used to generate new solutions. In this case, the *Neighborhood* of a fixed size (20 for the experiments in this work) is formed in the following way: (1) First, a permuted array P is generated with the bit positions of the CS, see Figure 2-b. (2) A point between the last chosen point and the length of P is randomly selected. (3)

A new solution is created by both generating a copy of CS and mutating the bits indicated for the bit positions of the selected segment of P between the last and the new chosen point, i.e., from the next point after the last chosen point up to the new chosen point. (4) The created solution is added to the *Neighborhood.* When the permuted array has been recently generated, the last chosen point is the initial point of P, i.e., the first point of P. A new permuted array P is generated when the last chosen point is the last point of P.

***Taboos.*** The Taboo Search (TS) uses memory structures to record especially recent moves called Taboos that cannot be reached from the current solution during the time these are considered as Taboo. As every feature and instance subset (or chromosome) is hard to evaluate, in this method a Taboo List (TL) of a fixed size $k$ is used to remember the last $k$ evaluations, so, the lifetime of every Taboo solution will be $k$. When the *Neighborhood* has been formed for any of the two methods (*Record & Sweepers* or *Permutation & Mutation*) previously described, the Taboo solutions are deleted from the *Neighborhood.* Finally, the TL is updated by adding the solutions still in the *Neighborhood,* certainly, if this is no empty. When the TL is full, the oldest solutions will be replaced, i.e., they will not be Taboos anymore.

***Simulated Annealing Criterion.*** Once the fitness of every solution in the *Neighborhood* was evaluated, the Best Neighbor (BN) is selected and the difference of fitness between CS and BN (Δ = Fitness(CS) – Fitness(BN)) is calculated. Then BN is accepted as the new CS when one of the following conditions is satisfied:

$$(\Delta \le 0) \text{ or } \left((\Delta > 0) \ \textit{and} \ \left(\exp^{(-\Delta/Tk)} < \textit{Random}\ [0,1)\right)\right)$$

***Update.*** When BN has been accepted by the Simulated Annealing (SA) criterion, CS and *Record* must be updated. The BN will be the new CS and *Record* is updated according to the used method. If *Record & Sweepers* is being used, simply the bit position in the chromosome (CS) is located, which corresponds with the feature or instances removed or added, and finally that bit position in the two arrays of *Record* are mutated. When the *Permutation & Mutation* method is being used we must initialize *Record & Sweepers* again. Once the CS has been updated with BN, the Best Solution (BS) found during the program is also updated if the fitness of CS is strictly better than the fitness of the current BS. If this happens, we continue the program by using *Record & Sweepers*. However, if *Record & Sweepers* is being used, and the number of generated solutions, since the last BS update, is equal to the chromosome's length, then we will work with *Permutation & Mutation* from now on until BS is updated again because maybe a local solution has been reached. Once BS is updated, *Record & Sweepers* is used again.

There are several cooling schedules in the literature. These employ different temperature updating schemes. The rule used in our experiments updates the temperature by the following formula: $T_{k+1} = \propto \cdot T_k$, where $T_k$ is the current temperature and $\propto$ is a temperature factor which is a constant smaller than but close to 1, the recommended values of $\propto \in [0.5, 0.99]$, in this work $\propto = 0.90$. In our experiments the initial temperature $T_i$ was 50, and the final temperature $T_f$ was 0.1 (a value close to 0). $C_{Times}$ is used to calculate the approximate number of times we must update the temperature to be close to the final temperature $T_f$. The number of evaluations of the fitness function to be performed by the HMH algorithm is divided by $C_{Times}$. The result is the number of evaluations of the fitness function to be performed before updating the temperature $T_k$. The number of evaluations of the fitness function to be performed for the HMH algorithm is ¼ of the total for the hybrid fuzzy-genetic algorithm.

$$C_{Times} = \frac{\log T_i}{\log(2-\alpha)} + \frac{\log T_f}{\log(0.9)}$$

## 3.2 The Fuzzy Self-Adaptive Genetic Algorithm

The hybrid fuzzy-genetic algorithm is executed in two stages. In the first stage the HMH algorithm is applied to the best individual of the initial population of the fuzzy genetic algorithm (second stage). The structure of the Fuzzy Self-Adaptive Genetic Algorithm (FSAGA) is based on the self-adaptive genetic algorithm ARGEN+AREPO 7 whose population size, mutation, reproduction and competition rate are adapted during the execution of the algorithm. The description of every step of FSAGA is as follows:

***Population, Meeting and Selection.*** One of the main features of this algorithm is the adaptability of the parameters, including the population. Population size is limited by the maximum allowed size *Mp* and its dynamics is determined by the "*meeting*" probability *Pm* defined as: *Pm = Cp*/*Mp* (population density), where *Cp* is the size of the current population. When two individuals meet they can interact in two ways: by reproducing or by fighting for natural resources. The initial size of the population is a random number (*Cp*) limited by a maximum number of individuals (*Mp*) –given by the user-. *All individuals are unique, ranked in the population by their fitness.* The method used to select two individuals is ***sequential-ranking*** (the first individual selected is the i-*th* individual of the population, for *i*=0,…,*Cp*, and the second individual is selected by ranking 11), which can give us equilibrium between exploration and exploitation.

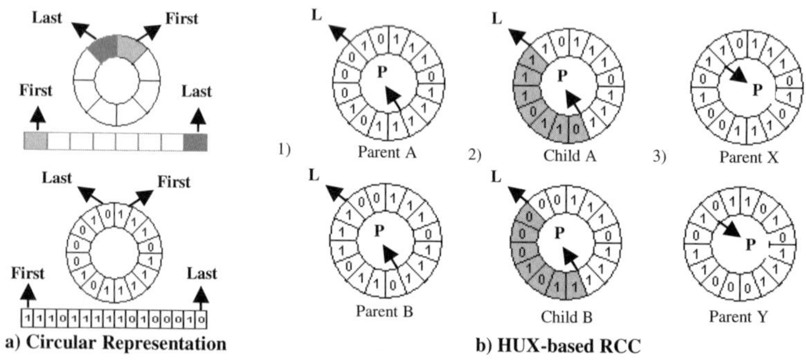


**Fig. 3.** Circular crossover operator

***RCC based on HUX.*** Reproduction is performed according to the adaptive rate *Pr*, and when it occurs, then the HUX-based RCC is applied; the resulting offspring from recombination will not replace the parents, it is only ranked in the population when the offspring is different from all members in the population. In that way, the population size could be increased by two new elements. When the population size reaches its maximum value (*Mp*), the two least fit individuals are removed from the population. When two individuals meet and they do not mate, they fight for survival, the stronger kills the weaker and this one is removed from the population. When two individuals are selected and the reproduction is carried out, we apply the *Rotary Circular Crossover* (RCC), based on the *Half Uniform Crossover* (HUX) 2 operator, by using the circular representation of one chromosome, see Figure 3-a. *P* can be any point in the chromosome and *L (length)* is a random positive number lower than or equal to the chromosome's length which indicates the size of the crossover segments, see Figure 3-b. These two segments on their respective chromosomes are interchanged. Finally, the rotary concept of the circular crossover is reached by keeping memory of the next bit after the segment of the last crossover because it will be the starting point *P* of the next crossover of the new selected individuals.

In RCC based on HUX, the bits that differ between parents are located. If the number of bits that differ in the selected segments is equal to or larger than the half of bits that differ between both parents, the two segments are interchanged. But, whenever the differences between segments is lower than the half of the differences between parents, some bits of the parents that differ from each other and that do not belong to the segments are randomly selected to complete the half of bits in which both parents differ. The reason to apply some ideas of the HUX operator in our crossover operator is based on a previous evaluation and study of six crossover operators under the same circumstances (HUX is included), where a better performance was shown with this crossover operator.

***Reproduction and Competition.*** We said before that this algorithm is based on the self-adaptive GA ARGEN+AREPO whose control parameters are controlled by three rules: meeting probability $Pm = Cp/Mp$, reproduction rate $Pr = 1\text{-}Pm$, and competition rate $Pc = 1\text{-}Pr$ and they are directly formed from the size of the current population *Cp* and the maximum population size *Mp* allowed. To avoid sudden changes in the population a Fuzzy Inference System (FIS) is used to control the Reproduction (R) rate because it does these tasks in an easier and natural way. This FIS-R has as an input the population $Density = Cp/Mp \in [0, 1]$ (the meeting probability *Pm*) and the output is a reproduction rate $Pr \in [0, 1]$, the competition rate $Pc = 1\text{-}Pr$. The input and output of FIS-R on charge of the reproduction rate is presented in Figure 4-a.

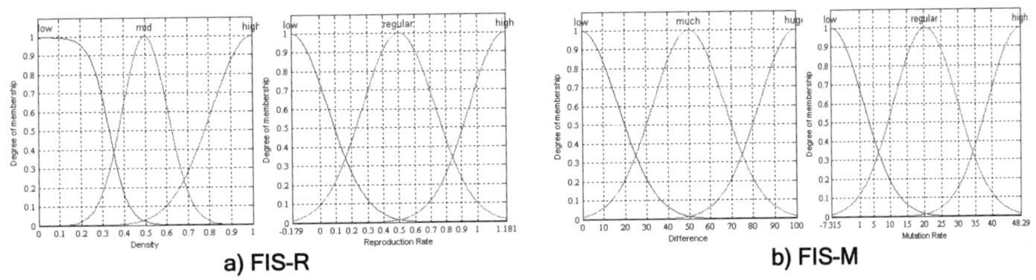


**Fig. 4.** Input and Output variables

The design of FIS-R is simple, the plot indicates that the input is formed by three membership functions: the first is the difference between two sigmoidals (low), the second is a Gaussian (mid) and the third is also a Gaussian (high). The shape of the first membership function has two meanings: when the population density is lower than approximately 0.10, the FIS-R slows down the competition rate up to stopping it, obviously, and this is done by increasing the reproduction rate. When the population density starts growing, the reproduction rate falls smoothly. The output variable *Reproduction Rate* is formed by three Gaussian membership functions (low, regular and high). In the design of FIS-R the defuzzification method used was the *Center of Area,* also called *Centroid.* The rules of FIS-R are the following

- If (Density = low) then (Reproduction Rate = high)
- If (Density = mid) then (Reproduction Rate = regular)
- If (Density = high) then (Reproduction Rate = low)

***The functioning.*** Once two individuals have been selected and also *Pm*, *Pr* and *Pc* have been calculated, we continue with the first part of the algorithm. If a random number *r* in [0, 1] is lower than *Pm* then the individuals proceed to either reproduction or competition. A new random number *r* is generated, and then, if it is lower than *Pr* then we apply the RCC based on HUX without a mutation operator, else, we remove the weaker individual from the population only when a new generated random number *r* is lower than *Pc*. Before applying the RCC based on HUX, the bits that differ between parents are found. If the number of bits that differ between both parents is higher than 1, the crossover operator can be applied, and then, we keep the next bit after the segment of the last crossover because it will be the starting point *P* for the next crossover of the new selected individuals. If the crossover cannot be applied, the starting point *P* for the next crossover of the new selected individuals will be the same.

***Mutation.*** When two individuals meet then they can interact in two ways: by reproducing or fighting, otherwise (If the random number *r* in [0, 1] is not lower than *Pm*) the two current individuals can generate two new individuals by means of mutation. The suitable selection of the Mutation (M) rate, for every individual in the population, is done by means of another fuzzy inference system (FIS-M) according to their fitness. The input and output variables of FIS-M are presented in Figure 4-b. The mutation operator is not always applied, it is carried out just when the two selected individuals do not meet, i.e., when a random number *r* in [0, 1] is not lower than *Pm*.

The input variable *Difference* $\in$ [0, 100] is given by the difference of fitness between the best individual in the population and one of the selected individuals. When the mutation operator is carried out, a mutation rate is computed for each individual because we believe that all the solutions cannot be treated in the same way, we give a higher rate to solutions whose fitness is poorer than the fitness of the best solution into the population. The plot indicates that this input is formed by three Gaussian membership functions (low, much and huge). The output variable *Mutation Rate* is formed also by three Gaussian membership functions (low, regular and high), and its values are in the range [1, 40]. The rules of FIS-M are the following:

- If (Difference = low) then (Mutation Rate = low)
- If (Difference = much) then (Mutation Rate = regular)
- If (Difference = huge) then (Mutation Rate = high)

These rules mean that whenever the difference of fitness between the best individual of the population and a selected individual is given, the Mutation Rate will go from the lowest mutation rate up to the highest. In FIS-M, the defuzzification method *Center of Area* (COA) was used too.

## 4 Preliminary Results

Table 1 presents the performance results of the genetic algorithm. Although the initial population size *Cp* must be a random number lower than the maximum population size *Mp*, the presented results are from experiments with a maximum population size *Mp* = 100 and 1000 and the *Cp* with the totality of the data, i.e., 100 and 1000 respectively. The stop criterion was to reach 8,000 evaluations of the fitness function. All datasets used in the experiments were taken from the Machine Learning Database Repository at the University of California, Irvine.

**Table 1.** Results of generating solutions with the Hybrid Fuzzy-Genetic Algorithm

| | 100 Individuals | | | 1000 Individuals | | |
|---|---|---|---|---|---|---|
| **Database** | **E.A. (%)** | **T.A. (%)** | **Storage (%)** | **E.A. (%)** | **T.A. (%)** | **Storage (%)** |
| B. C. W. | 99.50 | 94.71 | 3.69 | 99.21 | 94.86 | 1.25 |
| Glass | 88.09 | 57.44 | 9.65 | 86.43 | 56.28 | 8.46 |
| Ionosphere | 98.29 | 82.25 | 3.93 | 97.43 | 79.86 | 1.92 |
| Iris | 100 | 93.33 | 3.61 | 100 | 92.67 | 6.64 |
| Liver D. | 90.29 | 57.83 | 12.00 | 88.41 | 58.26 | 9.78 |
| Monks1 | 100 | 100 | 7.10 | 100 | 100 | 7.74 |
| Monks2 | 88.75 | 66.99 | 46.89 | 84.58 | 63.29 | 34.30 |
| Monks3 | 100 | 100 | 6.72 | 100 | 100 | 10.49 |
| **Average** | **95.61** | **82.32** | **11.70** | **94.51** | **80.65** | **10.07** |

The *Evaluation Accuracy* (E.A) column shows the average accuracy of 10 data subsets found over their respective *evaluation sets*, where every subset is the one returned by the wrapper model at each experiment. The *Test Accuracy* (T.A) column shows the average accuracy of 10 data subsets returned by the wrapper model, but these are evaluated over their respective *test sets*. Finally the *Storage* column shows the percentage of the original training set which is necessary when storing to classify new instances. These results are also an average of 10 experiments. The *Average* row in bold, shows the average over the respective columns (over all datasets). The first row (ORIGINAL –training sets-) in Table 2 shows the results of the same evaluations with the whole data sets. It can be easily noticed that there is a clear advantage when selecting a feature and an instance subset over the original training set, in both, classification accuracy and data reduction. Finally, six genetic algorithms were selected to compare their performance in the feature and instance subset selection problem with regard to the Hybrid Fuzzy-Genetic Algorithm. Five are static algorithms based on a population-level adaptation and one is a self-adaptive algorithm based on the population level. The genetic algorithms selected are the following: SGA 3 (*Simple Genetic Algorithm*), sometimes known as Canonical Genetic Algorithm, the

TGA (*Traditional Genetic Algorithm*) which differs from the previous one by the application of elitism, CHC 2 (*Cross-generational elitist selection, Heterogeneous recombination* -by incest prevention- and *Cataclysmic mutation*), GENITOR 11 (*GENetic ImplemenTOR*), CFRSC 4 (*Common Features/Random Sample Climbing*), and AREPO 1 (*ARtificial Evolution of POpulations*).

**Table 2.** Results of generating solutions with all the GAs and of evaluating the ORIGINAL training sets

| Algorithm | E.A. (%) | T.A. (%) | Storage (%) |
|---|---|---|---|
| **ORIGINAL** | **82.62** | **80.59** | **100** |
| SGA | 88.30 | 82.86 | 29.50 |
| TGA | 94.97 | 82.86 | 19.61 |
| CHC | 93.35 | 83.06 | 25.59 |
| CF/RSC | 95.04 | 82.63 | 16.21 |
| GENITOR | 93.39 | 83.42 | 26.21 |
| AREPO | 92.35 | 82.59 | 27.20 |

In all the populations used by these GAs the original training set (the chromosome with 1's only) has been added to consider the original solution. The results are shown in Table 2. The number of evaluations of the fitness function was 8,000 for all algorithms. As the population size was of 50 individuals (SGA, TGA, CHC), the generation number was equal to 160. The control parameters were crossover probability = 0.8 (80%) and mutation probability = 0.01 (1%) for SGA and TGA. 35% was the cataclysmic mutation rate in CHC. The population size of CF/RSC was of 10 individuals and it generates 10 new solutions of each individual by mutating 10 bits of the chromosome. The population size in GENITOR and AREPO was of 1000 individuals.

Table 1 shows that the combination of the Hybrid Fuzzy-GA and the k-NN classifier in the experiments gives up to 95.61% of classification accuracy upon the evaluation sets, which is better than any of the other six GA tested. The data reduction rate obtained with our algorithm was also the highest. Nonetheless, GENITOR found subsets whose classification accuracy upon the test sets were the best.

## 5 The Automatic Infant Cry Recognition

Additionally, the problem of Automatic Infant Cry Recognition (AICR) 9 was chosen to test the performance of the Hybrid Fuzzy-Genetic Algorithm in a real life problem. Automatic Infant Cry Recognition intents to detect pathologies on recently born babies by means of their crying. The goal is to take the wave from the infant's cry as the input pattern, and at the end to obtain the kind of cry or pathology detected. The AICR process is very similar to Automatic Speech Recognition (ASR), which is divided in two main stages, the first one corresponds to signal processing, or acoustic feature extraction, and the second one to pattern classification.

***The Signal Processing Stage.*** The infant cries were collected by recordings done directly by medical doctors. These recordings were first digitalized and stored, and then each signal wave was divided in segments of 1 second, each segment represents a sample. Next, acoustic features were obtained by means of the Mel Frequency

Cepstral Coefficients (MFCC) technique with the help of the program Praat v4.0.8. Every one second a sample is windowed in 50-milliseconds frames, extracting 16 coefficients from each frame. This procedure generates pattern vectors with 304 coefficients by each one second sample. The actual corpus used for the experiments presented here has 1376 vectors or instances of 304 features each. 157 samples belong to normal infant cry, 340 to asphyxia, and 879 to hypo-acoustics (deafness).

***The Pattern Classification Stage.*** It can be observed that the amount of data is very large, so it will be useful to select variables or features just as to select instances with the intention of reducing computational resources and, to improve the accuracy of the classification process. We have 1376 instances or vectors representing infant cry, and each infant cry vector is represented by a vector of 304 features. All the 1376 instances are structured in $r$ classes (three for infant cry: normal, hypo-acoustic and asphyxia). What we want to do is to find a smaller feature and instance subset that can better represent the infant cry dataset avoiding the need of using all data, without degrading the classification accuracy of the system.

The results of evaluating the Hybrid Fuzzy-Genetic Algorithm are presented in Table 3. The baby's crying dataset has 1376 instance with 304 features each. Ten training, evaluation and test sets were formed, i.e., for each experiment 825, 275 and 275 instances for training, evaluation and test respectively were randomly selected from the baby's crying dataset. The presented results are from experiments with a maximum population size Mp = 100. The stop criterion was to reach 8,000 fitness function evaluations.

**Table 3.** Results of generating solutions with the Hybrid Fuzzy-Genetic Algorithm for the infant cry dataset

| Method | E.A. (%) | T.A. (%) | Storage (%) |
|---|---|---|---|
| Hybrid Fuzzy-GA | 100 | 97.35 | 0.08 |

**Table 4.** Results of FRNN and PCA for the infant cry dataset

| # MF | PCA 70% | | PCA 80% | | PCA 90% | | PCA 95% | |
|---|---|---|---|---|---|---|---|---|
| | E.A. (%) | T.A. (%) | E.A. (%) | T.A. (%) | E.A. (%) | T.A. (%) | E.A. (%) | T.A. (%) |
| 3 MF | 87.74 | 86.68 | 85.02 | 84.85 | 65.05 | 62.90 | 65.05 | 62.90 |
| 5 MF | 88.58 | 87.93 | 86.76 | 86.81 | 86.91 | 86.96 | 65.05 | 62.90 |
| Average | **88.16** | **87.30** | **85.89** | **85.83** | **75.98** | **74.93** | **65.05** | **62.90** |

Additionally, the results of an average of 10 experiments with other method that combines vector reduction with PCA and the Fuzzy Relational Neural Network (FRNN) 10 are presented in Table 4. The FRNN receives as input a training set and returns as output a fuzzy relational matrix. Before presenting the training data to the FRNN, PCA is applied to the dataset and the experiments are performed by using 2, 7, 26 and 65 features respectively from the transformed matrix. The training, evaluation and test sets used in the experiments were the same than those used to obtain the results presented in Table 3. Experiments with 3 and 5 linguistic properties are reported, the input membership values were obtained with the Trapezoidal membership function, with $f_d = 6$ and $f_e = 1.5$. Three epochs were completed to train the Neural Network. The classification was performed with the max-min composition.

This process was carried out once each input feature of the training samples was transformed in membership values to each of the assigned linguistic properties, i.e., once a vector containing $m$ features was transformed in a $3m$, or $5m$-dimensional vector, and the fuzzy relational matrix was returned by the FRNN. If we consider that the 825 instances with the 304 features are the 100% of data, then 0.66%, 8.55%, 16.45% and 49.34% was the storage size used for 2, 7, 26 and 65 principal components, respectively.

## 6 Conclusions and Future Work

The Hybrid Fuzzy-Genetic Algorithm gives us a highest classification accuracy of 95.61% upon all the evaluation sets, showing a performance improvement over the other six GAs tested. Moreover, our algorithm delivers the highest data reduction rate. With the infant cry corpus the results show a classification accuracy of up to 97.35%, by using only the 0.08% of the information available in the training set. At present, we are working with more and different membership functions in order to evaluate the performance of our algorithm with more rules for new fuzzy inference systems.

## References


1. Annunziato, Maur, Pizzuti, Stefano.: Adaptive Parameterization of Evolutionary Algorithms Driven by Reproduction and Competition, ESIT, Aachen, Germany,(2000)
2. Eshelman, Larry J.: The CHC Adaptive Search Algorithm: How to Have Safe Search When Engaging in Nontraditional Genetic Recombination, in G. Rawlins, editor, Foundations of Genetic Algorithms. Morgan Kaufmann, (1991)265-283
3. Goldberg, David E.: Genetic Algorithms in Search, Optimizations, and Machine Learning. Addison-Wesley ,(1989)
4. Guerra, Cesar., Chen, Stephen., Whitley, Darrell., Smith, Stephen Fast and Accurate Feature Selection Using Hybrid Genetic Strategies, CEC99: Proceedings of the Congress on Evolutionary Computation,(1999)
5. John, Geoge H., Kohavi, Ron., Pfleger, Karl.: Irrelevant Feature and the Subset Selection Problem, Machine Learning: Proceedings of the Eleventh International Conference,(1994)
6. Kuncheva, Ludmila I., Jain, Lakhmi C.:Nearest Neighbor Classifier: Simultaneous Editing and Feature Selection", Pattern Recognition Letters, 20, (1999) 1149-1156
7. Leon, Agustin , Reyes, Carlos A.: ARGEN + AREPO: Improving the Search Process with Artificial Genetic Engineering, International Work-Conference on Artificial Neural Networks (IWANN), Vilanova i la Geltrú, Barcelona, España ,(2005)
8. Mitchell, Tom M. Machine Learning, McGraw Hill, (1997)
9. Orozco, J. Reyes, Carlos A.: Mel-Frequency Cepstrum Coefficients Extraction from Infant Cry for classification of Normal and Pathological Cry with Feed-Forward Neural Networks, Proceedings of ESANN, Bruges, Belgium ,(2003)
10. Reyes, Carlos A.: On the Design of a Fuzzy Relational Neural Network for Automatic Speech Recognition, Doctoral Dissertation, The Florida State University, Tallahassee, Fl (1994)
11. Whitley, Darrell.: The GENITOR Algorithm and Selective Pressure: Why Rank-Based Allocation of Reproductive Trials is Best, Technical Report CS-89-105,(1989)

# A Hybrid Quantum-Inspired Genetic Algorithm for Multi-objective Scheduling

Bin-Bin Li and Ling Wang

Department of Automation, Tsinghua University, Beijing 100084, China
binbinlee@mails.tsinghua.edu.cn, wangling@tsinghua.edu.cn

**Abstract.** This paper proposes a hybrid quantum-inspired genetic algorithm (HQGA) for multi-objective flow shop scheduling problem. On one hand, a quantum-inspired GA (QGA) based on Q-bit representation is applied for exploration in discrete 0-1 hyperspace by using updating operator of quantum gate and genetic operators of Q-bit. Random key representation is used to convert the Q-bit representation to job permutation. On the other hand, permutation-based GA (PGA) is applied for both performing exploration in permutation-based scheduling space and stressing exploitation for good schedule solutions. To evaluate solutions in multi-objective sense, randomly weighted linear sum function is used in QGA, while non-dominated sorting techniques including classification of Pareto fronts and fitness assignment are applied in PGA regarding to both proximity and diversity of solutions in multi-objective sense. Simulation results and comparisons demonstrate the effectiveness and robustness of the proposed HQGA.

## 1 Introduction

Flow shop scheduling problem (FSSP) is a class of widely studied scheduling problem with strong engineering backgrounds, and has earned a reputation for being a typical strongly NP-complete combinatorial optimization problem [1]. So far, FSSP has gained much attention and wide research in both Computer Science and Operation Research fields.

Permutation FSSP (PFSSP) is a simplification of FSSP, which can be described as follows: Each of $J$ jobs is to be sequentially processed on machine $1,\ldots,M$ . The processing time $p_{i,j}$ of job $i$ on machine $j$ is given. At any time, each machine can process at most one job and each job can be processed on at most one machine. The sequence in which the jobs are to be processed is the same for each machine. The goal is to find a schedule or a set of schedules to minimize one or more objective functions. Until the late 1980s, however, it was a common practice that only one objective function was taken into account. In practice, quality may be a multi-dimensional notion. So, it is very important to develop effective and efficient approaches for multi-objective scheduling problems.

A multi-objective optimization problem can be formulated as follows:

$$\begin{aligned} Min \quad & \mathbf{f}(\mathbf{x}) = (f_1(\mathbf{x}), f_2(\mathbf{x}), \cdots, f_n(\mathbf{x})) \\ s.t. \quad & \mathbf{x} \in \mathbf{X} \end{aligned} \quad (1)$$

D.-S. Huang, K. Li, and G.W. Irwin (Eds.): ICIC 2006, LNCS 4113, pp. 511 – 522, 2006.

where $f_1, f_2, \cdots, f_n$ are objective functions and $\mathbf{x}$ is a feasible solution in the solution space $\mathbf{X}$. A feasible solution $\mathbf{x}_1$ is said to dominate another feasible solution $\mathbf{x}_2$ (denoting this relationship $\mathbf{x}_1 \succ \mathbf{x}_2$ ) if $\forall i \in \{1,2,...,n\}$, $f_i(\mathbf{x}_1) \le f_i(\mathbf{x}_2)$ and $\exists k \in \{1,2,...,n\}$, $f_k(\mathbf{x}_1) < f_k(\mathbf{x}_2)$. A solution $\mathbf{x}^*$ is Pareto optimal (or non-dominated) if there is no such $\mathbf{x} \in \mathbf{X}$ that satisfies $\mathbf{x} \succ \mathbf{x}^*$.

In practical problems, sometimes the considering objectives are conflicting. An improvement in one objective may induce a detriment to another objective, thus an approach should find a set of non-dominates solutions with good proximity and diversity performances to approximate the real Pareto front. In other words, the optimization algorithm should have excellent searching ability to obtain solutions close to the real Pareto front and uniformly distributed along the real Pareto front.

So far, many approaches have been proposed for FSSP, where exact techniques are applicable only to small-scale problems in practice and the qualities of constructive heuristics are often not satisfactory [2]. During the past decade, meta-heuristics have gained wide research, such as simulated annealing [3], genetic algorithm (GA) [4], evolutionary programming [5], tabu search [6], hybrid heuristics [7] and so on. Recently, Han and Kim [8] [9] proposed some quantum-inspired genetic algorithms (QGAs), which were very applicable and effective for solving knapsack problem. Since the solution representation of scheduling problem is completely different from that of knapsack problem, the original QGAs cannot be directly applied to scheduling problem. In this paper, we will propose a hybrid quantum-inspired GA for multi-objective PFSSP. On one hand, it synthesizes the advantages of quantum-inspired genetic search and permutation-based search for well exploration and exploitation. On the other hand, regarding to both proximity and diversity, it applies the non-dominated sorting techniques to handle optimization process under multiple objective functions. Simulation results and comparisons demonstrate the effectiveness and robustness of our proposed algorithm.

## 2 Quantum Genetic Algorithm

### 2.1 Representation

In QGA for a minimization problem, a Q-bit chromosome representation is adopted based on the concept and principle of quantum computing. The characteristic of this representation is that any linear superposition can be represented. The smallest unit of information stored in two-state quantum computer is called a Q-bit, which may be in the “1” state, or in the “0” state, or in any superposition of the two. The state of a Q-bit can be represented as follows:

$$|\Psi\rangle = \alpha|0\rangle + \beta|1\rangle \ . \tag{2}$$

where $\alpha$ and $\beta$ are complex numbers that specify the probability amplitudes of the corresponding states. $|\alpha|^2$ and $|\beta|^2$ denote the probability that the Q-bit will be found in the “1” state and “0” state respectively. Normalization of the state to the unity guarantees $|\alpha|^2 + |\beta|^2 = 1$.

A Q-bit individual as a string of $m$ Q-bit is defined as follows:

$$\left[\begin{array}{c|c|c|c} \alpha_1 & \alpha_2 & \cdots & \alpha_m \\ \beta_1 & \beta_2 & \cdots & \beta_m \end{array}\right]. \quad (3)$$

where $|\alpha_i|^2 + |\beta_i|^2 = 1, \quad i = 1, 2, \ldots, m$.

For example, for a three-Q-bit with three pairs of amplitudes $\left[\begin{array}{c|c|c} 1/\sqrt{2} & 1/\sqrt{2} & 1/2 \\ 1/\sqrt{2} & -1/\sqrt{2} & \sqrt{3}/2 \end{array}\right]$, the states can be represented as $\frac{1}{4}|000\rangle + \frac{\sqrt{3}}{4}|001\rangle - \frac{1}{4}|010\rangle - \frac{\sqrt{3}}{4}|011\rangle + \frac{1}{4}|100\rangle + \frac{\sqrt{3}}{4}|101\rangle - \frac{1}{4}|110\rangle - \frac{\sqrt{3}}{4}|111\rangle$. This means that the probability to represent the states $|000\rangle$, $|001\rangle$, $|010\rangle$, $|011\rangle$, $|100\rangle$, $|101\rangle$, $|110\rangle$ and $|111\rangle$ are $1/16$, $3/16$, $1/16$, $3/16$, $1/16$, $3/16$, $1/16$, $3/16$, respectively. By consequence, the above three-Q-bit system contains the information of eight states. Evolutionary computing with Q-bit represent has a better characteristic of population diversity than other representation, since it can represent linear superposition of state's probabilities.

## 2.2 Solution Evaluation in Multi-objective Sense

In QGA, since the searching solution is a Q-bit string, it is firstly converted to a binary string according to [8] [9]. In particular, for the $i$-th bit ($i = 1, 2, \cdots, m$) of Q-bit string, a random number $\eta$ is generated at interval [0,1], if $|\alpha_i|^2 > \eta$ let the corresponding bit $r_i$ of the binary string be 1, otherwise let $r_i$ be 0. For scheduling problem, such a binary string will be converted to a random key representation [10]. For example, considering a 3-job, 3-machine problem (we use three bits in Q-bit string to represent a job), suppose the resulted binary string is [0 1 1|1 0 1|1 0 1], then its random key representation is [3 5 5]. Obviously, such a random key representation can be easily converted to a job permutation. In particular, if two random key values are different, let smaller random key denote the job with smaller number; otherwise, let the one first appears denotes the job with smaller number. Based on such a rule, the job permutation for above random key representation will be [1 2 3]. Once the job permutation is constructed, the scheduling objectives can be calculated.

After calculating scheduling objectives, a vector of weights is randomly generated to evaluate solutions in multi-objective sense according to the weighted linear sum function. That is, the summed value is used to reflect the fitness value of a solution for multi-objective problem. The smaller the value is, the better the solution is. The one with the smallest summed value is regarded as the best solution (denoted $b$), which will be employed to guide the quantum-gate rotation in current generation. Since the vector of weights is randomly generated, it is helpful to obtain solutions distributed diversely along the Pareto front.

## 2.3 Operations

In this paper, operators used in QGA are designed as follows.

*Selection.* A simple rank-based random selection is designed. All individuals of the population are ordered from the best to the worst after evaluation in multi-objective sense. Then, from the best to the worst every individual randomly chooses a partner from the remaining individuals in the population.

*Crossover.* A two-point crossover operation is used in QGA. First, two different positions are randomly determined (say position $i$ and $j$ ). Then, the sub-string before $i$ , the sub-string between $i$ and $j$ , and the sub-string after $j$ of two parents can be exchanged. In QGA, the above three ways are randomly used in hybrid sense.

*Mutation.* One position is randomly determined (e.g. position $i$ ) for each Q-bit string in the population, and then $\alpha_i$ and $\beta_i$ are exchanged.

*Rotation Operation.* The operation is inspired by quantum computing to adjust the probability amplitudes of each Q-bit. A rotation gate $U(\theta)$ is employed to update $(\alpha_i, \beta_i)$ of the $i$ -th Q-bit as follows:

$$\begin{bmatrix} \alpha_i' \\ \beta_i' \end{bmatrix} = U(\theta_i) \begin{bmatrix} \alpha_i \\ \beta_i \end{bmatrix} = \begin{bmatrix} \cos(\theta_i) & -\sin(\theta_i) \\ \sin(\theta_i) & \cos(\theta_i) \end{bmatrix} \begin{bmatrix} \alpha_i \\ \beta_i \end{bmatrix} . \tag{4}$$

where the rotation angle $\theta_i = s(\alpha_i, \beta_i) \cdot \Delta\theta_i$ . $s(\alpha_i, \beta_i)$ is the sign of $\theta_i$ determining the rotation direction and $\Delta\theta_i$ is the magnitude of rotation angle.

**Table 1.** Lookup table of rotation angle

| $r_i$ | $b_i$ | $r$ better than $b$ | $\Delta\theta_i$ | $s(\alpha_i, \beta_i)$ | | | |
|---|---|---|---|---|---|---|---|
| | | | | $\alpha_i\beta_i > 0$ | $\alpha_i\beta_i < 0$ | $\alpha_i = 0$ | $\beta_i = 0$ |
| 0 | 0 | false | 0 | 0 | 0 | 0 | 0 |
| 0 | 0 | true | 0 | 0 | 0 | 0 | 0 |
| 0 | 1 | false | 0 | 0 | 0 | 0 | 0 |
| 0 | 1 | true | $0.05\pi$ | −1 | +1 | ±1 | 0 |
| 1 | 0 | false | $0.01\pi$ | −1 | +1 | ±1 | 0 |
| 1 | 0 | true | $0.025\pi$ | +1 | −1 | 0 | ±1 |
| 1 | 1 | false | $0.005\pi$ | +1 | −1 | 0 | ±1 |
| 1 | 1 | true | $0.025\pi$ | +1 | −1 | 0 | ±1 |

The lookup table of $\Delta\theta_i$ is shown in Table 1, where $b_i$ and $r_i$ are the $i$ -th bits of the current best solution $b$ (selected in the solution evaluation step) and a binary solution $r$ respectively. Because $b$ is the best solution in QGA, the use of quantum-gate rotation is to emphasize the searching towards $b$ . Since the weights used to evaluate and determine $b$ are randomly generated, the searching directions can be enriched.

*Population Updating.* In QGA, the population obtained after rotation operation is used as the population for the next generation.

### 2.4 Procedure of QGA

The procedure of QGA can be summarized as follows.

*Step 1:* let $t = 0$ and randomly generate an initial population $P_Q(t) = \{p_1^t, \cdots, p_N^t\}$, where $p_j^t = \begin{bmatrix} \alpha_1^t & \alpha_2^t & \cdots & \alpha_m^t \\ \beta_1^t & \beta_2^t & \cdots & \beta_m^t \end{bmatrix}$ denotes the $j$-th individual in the $t$-th generation.

*Step 2:* evaluate population $P_Q(t)$ and record the best solution $b$.

*Step 3:* if stopping condition is satisfied, then output the results; otherwise, go on following steps.

*Step 4:* perform selection, crossover and mutation for $P_Q(t)$ to generate $P_Q'(t)$.

*Step 5:* evaluate $P_Q'(t)$ and update the best solution $b$.

*Step 6:* perform rotation operation for $P_Q'(t)$ to generate $P_Q(t+1)$

*Step 7:* let $t = t+1$ and go back to step 2.

## 3 Hybrid QGA for Multi-objective Flow Shop Scheduling

### 3.1 Permutation-Based GA

As we know, quantum search has high parallel property, based on which QGA is of very strong exploration ability. However, it should be noted that QGA performs search in discrete 0-1 hyperspace while the schedule solutions belong to job permutation space. So, QGA lacks direct search on schedule solution space. Since Q-bit representations must be converted to job permutations for evaluation, we apply permutation-based GA (PGA) as a complementary search for QGA to enhance exploitation ability and improve the algorithm's performance.

#### 3.1.1 Representation

Job permutation is directly used in PGA to perform permutation-based genetic search.

#### 3.1.2 Solution Evaluation in Multi-objective Sense

Since in PGA searching solution is job permutation, it can be directly used to calculate the scheduling objectives. Then, the non-dominated sorting techniques [11] [12] are used to evaluate solutions in multi-objective sense so that the diversity of population and the proximity to the real Pareto front can be stressed. There are two successive procedures, i.e., classification of Pareto fronts and fitness assignment. Firstly, all solutions are divided into $K$ sets $F_1, F_2, \cdots, F_K$, according to the dominance relationship between solutions. $F_1$ corresponds to the set of all non-dominated solutions in the population, and $F_i$, $i = 2, \ldots, K$, contains the non-dominated solutions when the solutions in $F_1, \cdots, F_{i-1}$ are removed from the population. Secondly, every solution's normalized crowding distance is calculated based on its two neighbor solutions in the set it belongs to. Then, this normalized crowding distance is assigned to the solution as its fitness value. We refer to [11] and [12] for detailed introductions about the two procedures.

It is noticed that two basic rules are used to guide the evaluation process. One is that, to solutions in different sets, fitness values of solutions in $F_i$ are greater than those in $F_j$ if $i < j$. This rule stresses the proximity, and the solutions closer to the real Pareto front are assigned larger fitness values. The other is that, to solutions in the same set, those located in less crowded regions of objective space are assigned larger fitness values. This rule stresses the diversity, and those solutions located in more sparse areas of objective space are assigned larger fitness values.

### 3.1.3 Operations

In this paper, operators used in PGA are designed as follows.

*Selection.* The same as QGA, a simple rank-based random selection is used in PGA.

*Crossover.* In PGA, PMX (partial mapping crossover) [10] is applied to perform crossover for two job permutations. In particular, firstly two crossover points are chosen and the sub-sections of the parents between the two points are exchanged, then the chromosomes are filled up by partial map.

*Mutation.* In PGA, two different mutation operators SWAP and INSERT [7] are randomly used in hybrid sense, where SWAP randomly selects two distinct elements and swaps them, and INSERT randomly selects one element and inserts it to another different random position.

*Population Updating.* The operation is very important because it provides an interface for QGA and PGA performing interactions. In PGA, the individuals for next generation are selected from current populations of both QGA and PGA. In particular, all solutions in current two populations obtained by QGA and PGA respectively are combined and evaluated using non-dominates sorting techniques mentioned in 3.1.2, then the best half will be selected as the next generation for genetic operations in PGA. Obviously, the good solution obtained by QGA will have a chance to perform permutation-based search for well exploitation. Moreover, after PGA's genetic operations, the offspring population is combined with the parent population. All the solutions are evaluated again using non-dominates sorting techniques, and the best half will be selected to form a new population.

### 3.1.4 Procedure of PGA

The procedure of PGA can be summarized as follows.

*Step 1:* let $t = 0$, initialize population $P_P(t)$, let $P_{Pt}(t) = P_P(t)$ and go to step 4.

*Step 2:* if the stopping criterion is satisfied, then output the all solutions in elite set $E(t)$; otherwise go on following step.

*Step 3:* denote $P_P(t)$ as the population obtained by QGA. Then, combine $P_P(t)$ with $P_P''(t)$, assign fitness values to all the individuals in the obtained population and select the best half as population $P_{Pt}(t)$.

*Step 4:* apply selection, crossover and mutation for $P_{Pt}(t)$ to generate $P_P^{'}(t)$.

*Step 5:* combine $P_P^{'}(t)$ with $P_{Pt}(t)$, assign fitness values to all individuals in the obtained population and select the best half as population $P_P^{''}(t+1)$.

*Step 6:* select all the non-dominated solutions in $P_P^{''}(t+1)$ to store in $E(t)$, and delete all the dominated solutions in $E(t)$.

*Step 7:* let $t=t+1$, go to step 2.

### 3.2 Hybrid QGA for Multi-objective Flow Shop Scheduling

In this paper, we fuse the above designed QGA and PGA in an integrated framework to propose a hybrid quantum-inspired genetic algorithm for multi-objective PFSSP, which is illustrated in Fig. 1.

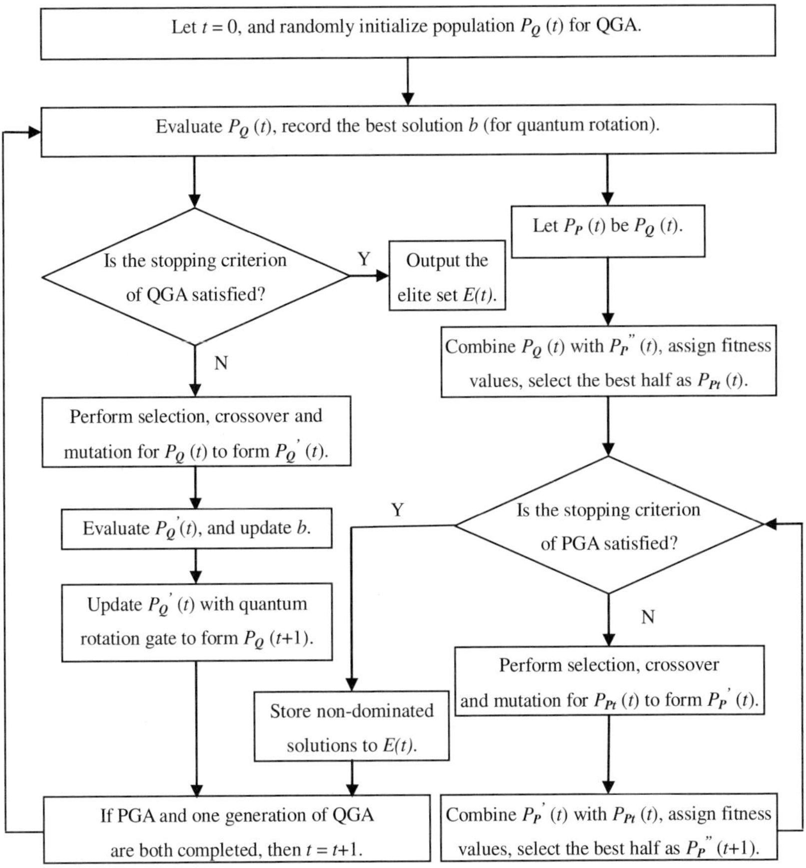


**Fig. 1.** The framework of HQGA for multi-objective PFSSP

In HQGA, quantum-inspired search and genetic-inspired search are hybridized. On one hand, QGA performs exploration in 0-1 hyperspace by using both genetic operations and quantum rotation operation; on the other hand, PGA performs exploration in permutation-based solution space. Moreover, the good solution obtained by QGA has a chance to perform PGA for well exploitation. To evaluate solution in multi-objective sense, the random weighted linear sum functions are used in QGA, while non-dominated sorting techniques are used in PGA.

According to the "No Free Lunch" theorem [13], there is no method that can solve all problems optimally. So, by taking the advantages of different approaches in a hybrid way, the searching behavior can be enriched, the searching ability can be enhanced and the optimization performances can be improved. Due to the hybridization of two different kinds of searching algorithms and the different evaluation approaches in multi-objective sense, the HQGA will have powerful ability to obtain solutions with good proximity and diversity for multi-objective PFSSP.

# 4 Simulations and Comparisons

## 4.1 Testing Problems and Performance Index

To test the performance of the proposed hybrid QGA, computational simulation is carried out on some randomly generated multi-objective PFSSP. There exists a classical way to generate the experiment data [14]. In particular, the processing time of each job in every machine is uniformly distributed in interval [1, 99]. The due date of each job is uniformly distributed in interval $[Q(1-u-v/2), Q(1-u+v/2)]$, where $u$ and $v$ respectively represent the tardiness factor of jobs and dispersion range of due dates, and $Q$ is an estimated lower bound of makespan [14]:

$$Q = \max\{\max_{1\le j\le M}\{\sum_{i=1}^{J} p_{ij} + \min_i \sum_{l=1}^{j-1} p_{il} + \min_i \sum_{l=j+1}^{M} p_{il}\}, \max_i \sum_{j=1}^{M} p_{ij}\} . \tag{5}$$

In this paper, four scenarios about due date are considered according to [14], where each scenario is determined by a different combination of the values of $u$ and $v$. It is said that when $u$ increases the due dates are more restrictive, while when $v$ increases the due dates are more diversified.

**Scenario 1:** low tardiness factor ($u = 0.2$) and small due date range ($v = 0.6$);
**Scenario 2:** low tardiness factor ($u = 0.2$) and wide due date range ($v = 1.2$);
**Scenario 3:** high tardiness factor ($u = 0.4$) and small due date range ($v = 0.6$);
**Scenario 4:** high tardiness factor ($u = 0.4$) and wide due date range ($v = 1.2$).

Since our algorithm is to obtain a set of non-dominated solutions, here we introduce Average Quality (AQ) [15] to measure the quality of the solution set and reflect the algorithm's searching ability:

$$AQ = \sum_{\lambda\in\Lambda} s_a(\mathbf{f}, \mathbf{z}^0, \lambda, \rho) / |\Lambda| . \tag{6}$$

where $s_a(\mathbf{f},\mathbf{z}^0,\boldsymbol{\lambda},\rho)=\min_i\{\max_j\{\lambda_j(f_j(\mathbf{x}_i)-z_j^0)\}+\rho\sum_{j=1}^{n}\lambda_j(f_j(\mathbf{x}_i)-z_j^0)\}$ and $\Lambda=\{\boldsymbol{\lambda}=(\lambda_1,\cdots,\lambda_n)\,|\,\lambda_j\in\{0,1/r,2/r,\cdots,1\},\sum_{j=1}^{n}\lambda_j=1\}$, $\mathbf{z}^0$ is a reference point in the objective space which is set to $(0,0)$ in this paper, and $\rho$ is a sufficiently small number which is set to 0.01 in this paper. Besides, $r$ is a parameter varying according to the number of objectives, which is often set as 50 for two-objective optimization problems. AQ is expressed as the average value of the scalarizing functions over a representative sample of weight vectors. It considers both proximity and diversity of solution set and allows consistent evaluation of the quality of Pareto optimal solutions. A smaller AQ value corresponds to a better solution set.

### 4.2 Simulation Results and Comparisons

The size of investigated problem is 20-job and 10-machine. For each of the four scenarios of the problem, five instances are generated. The considered two objectives are makespan and maximum tardiness.

The parameters in HQGA are set as follows. In QGA, population size is 100, the maximum generation is $J\times M$ (200), crossover probability is 1, mutation probability is 0.05, the length of Q-bit string is $5\times J$ (i.e., every 5 Q-bits correspond to a job). In PGA, population size is 100 (the same as QGA), crossover and mutation probabilities are both 1, and the maximum generation of PGA in every generation of HQGA is 1. To show the effectiveness of hybridization, a pure PGA by removing all the elements of QGA in HQGA and a pure QGA by removing all the elements of PGA in HQGA, are used for comparison, where all parameters and operators are the same as those in HQGA. In order to fairly compare the algorithms, the maximum generations of pure PGA and pure QGA are set to 400, which equals the sum generations of PGA and QGA in HQGA.

In Fig. 2, typical running results by the three algorithms are illustrated; and in Fig. 3, the results by HQGA and pure PGA are shown more clearly. It can be seen that pure QGA without PGA's exploitation on job permutation space can not find non-dominated solutions with good objective values, and pure PGA lacking of QGA's parallel exploration in 0-1 hyperspace also can not obtain very satisfactory Pareto optimal solutions. Obviously, HQGA can obtain more Pareto optimal solutions with better proximity than pure PGA and pure QGA, and most solutions obtained by HQGA can dominate the solutions obtained by pure PGA and pure QGA. Since the solution quality of pure QGA is even worse than that of pure PGA, we only compare the performances of HQGA and pure PGA below.

The AQ values of the solution set obtained by HQGA and pure PGA are shown in Table 2. It can be seen that the AQ values of HQGA are smaller than that of pure PGA in every case. It shows the effectiveness of HQGA, which can obtain solution sets with good proximity and diversity for multi-objective PFSSP. Moreover, it can be found that AQ values of HQGA are similar for different scenarios, which means HQGA can obtain solution sets with good proximity and diversity in sense of multi-objective optimization for PFSSP with different degrees of difficulty. That is, HQGA is of good robustness for different multi-objective PFSSP. Comparing the efficiency, from Table 3 it can be seen that the running times of HQGA are only slightly larger than that of pure PGA, demonstrating that HQGA is also quite efficient.

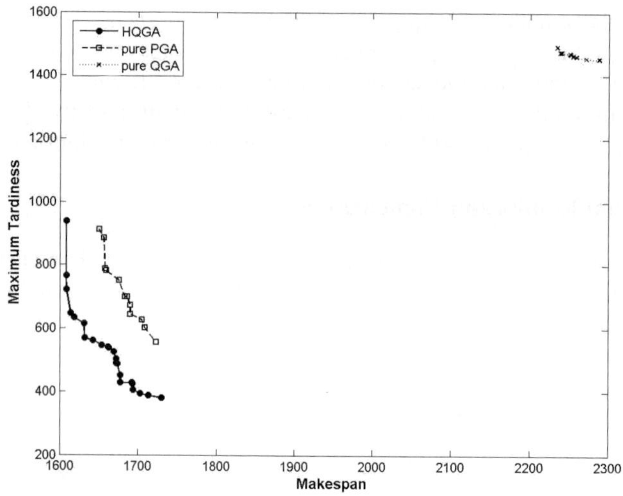


**Fig. 2.** Pareto fronts obtained by HQGA, pure PGA and pure QGA

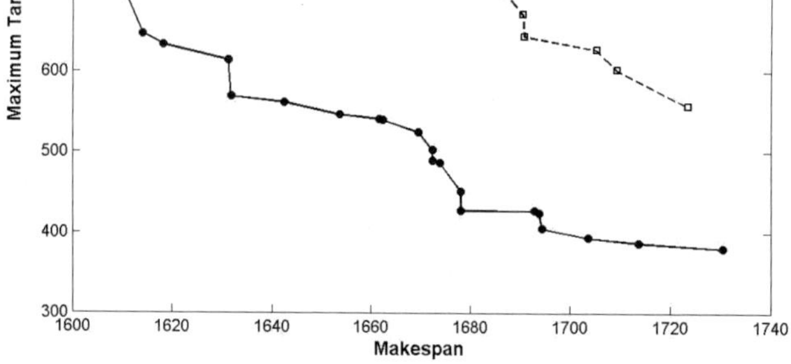


**Fig. 3.** Pareto fronts obtained by HQGA and pure PGA

**Table 2.** AQ values of HQGA and pure PGA

| Scenario | Method | Instance1 | Instance2 | Instance3 | Instance4 | Instance5 | Average |
|---|---|---|---|---|---|---|---|
| 1 | HQGA | 741.92 | 812.41 | 780.85 | 818.65 | 798.87 | 790.54 |
| | PGA | 795.85 | 840.43 | 810.32 | 853.32 | 841.80 | 828.34 |
| 2 | HQGA | 807.57 | 837.70 | 875.58 | 863.23 | 859.90 | 848.80 |
| | PGA | 854.99 | 852.30 | 916.48 | 869.93 | 890.85 | 876.91 |
| 3 | HQGA | 844.70 | 814.87 | 773.82 | 858.09 | 824.26 | 823.15 |
| | PGA | 881.37 | 867.46 | 816.94 | 902.64 | 859.58 | 865.60 |
| 4 | HQGA | 928.57 | 853.67 | 991.69 | 937.61 | 912.72 | 924.85 |
| | PGA | 980.27 | 895.27 | 1023.79 | 980.17 | 967.34 | 969.37 |

**Table 3.** Running times of HQGA and pure PGA

| Scenario | Method | Instance1 | Instance2 | Instance3 | Instance4 | Instance5 | Average |
|---|---|---|---|---|---|---|---|
| 1 | HQGA | 27.30 | 27.48 | 27.95 | 27.75 | 27.64 | 27.62 |
| | PGA | 22.39 | 23.31 | 22.63 | 23.13 | 22.52 | 22.79 |
| 2 | HQGA | 28.08 | 27.72 | 27.91 | 28.25 | 27.91 | 27.97 |
| | PGA | 22.94 | 22.67 | 22.67 | 23.38 | 22.17 | 22.77 |
| 3 | HQGA | 27.47 | 27.77 | 27.42 | 27.95 | 27.77 | 27.67 |
| | PGA | 22.59 | 22.52 | 22.61 | 22.74 | 23.03 | 22.70 |
| 4 | HQGA | 27.41 | 28.31 | 27.64 | 27.27 | 27.44 | 27.61 |
| | PGA | 22.48 | 22.61 | 22.61 | 22.86 | 22.56 | 22.63 |

## 5 Conclusions

This paper presented a hybrid quantum-inspired genetic algorithm for multi-objective PFSSP. The HQGA can be viewed as a fusion of QGA's Q-bit based search and PGA's permutation based search. The Q-bit based search adopts the representation of Q-bit to take use of parallel quantum search in 0-1 hyperspace, which enhances HQGA's exploration ability, and the permutation based search in PGA stresses search in job permutation space, which improves HQGA's exploitation ability. In addition, by adopting multi-objective evaluation methods, HQGA can obtain solutions with good proximity and diversity in sense of multi-objective optimization. Simulation results and comparisons demonstrate its effectiveness and robustness. The future work is to develop more effective hybrid QGA for other kinds of multi-objective combinatorial problems, especially the multi-objective job shop scheduling problems.

## Acknowledgements

This research is partially supported by National Science Foundation of China (Grant No. 60204008, 60374060 and 60574072) as well as the 973 Program (Grant No. 2002CB312200).

## References

1. Garey, M.R., Johonson, D.S.: Computers and Intractability: a Guide to the Theory of NP-Completeness. Freeman, San Francisco, (1979)
2. Nawaz, M., Enscore, E.Jr., Ham, I.: A Heuristic Algorithm for the M-machine, N-job Flowshop Sequencing Problem. Omega, 11 (1983) 91-95
3. Ogbu, F.A., Smith, D.K.: Simulated Annealing for the Permutation Flowshop Problem. Omega, 19 (1990) 64-67
4. Wang, L., Zhang, L., Zheng, D.Z.: A Class of Order-Based Genetic Algorithm for Flow Shop Scheduling. Int. J. Advanced Manufacture Technology, 22 (2003) 828-835
5. Wang, L., Zheng, D.Z.: A Modified Evolutionary Programming for Flow Shop Scheduling. Int. J. Advanced Manufacturing Technology, 22 (2003) 522-527
6. Nowicki, E., Smutnicki, C.: A Fast Tabu Search Algorithm For the Permutation Flow-Shop Problem. European J. Operational Research, 91 (1996) 160-175
7. Wang, L., Zheng, D.Z.: An Effective Hybrid Heuristic for Flow Shop Scheduling. Int. J. Advanced Manufacture Technology, 21 (2003) 38-44
8. Han, K.H., Kim, J.H.: Quantum-Inspired Evolutionary Algorithm for a Class of Combinatorial Optimization. IEEE Trans. Evol. Comput., 6 (2002) 580-593
9. Han, K.H., Kim, J.H.: A Quantum-Inspired Evolutionary Algorithms with a New Termination Criterion, He gate, and Two-Phase Scheme. IEEE Trans. Evol. Comput., 8 (2004) 156-169
10. Bean, J.C.: Genetic Algorithms and Random Keys for Sequencing and Optimization. ORSA Journal on Computing, 6 (1994) 154-160
11. Deb, K., Pratap, A., Agarwal, S., Meyarivan, T.: A Fast and Elitist Multiobjective Genetic Algorithm: NSGA-II. IEEE Trans. Evol. Comput., 6 (2002) 182-197
12. Arroyo, J.E.C., Armentano, V.A.: Genetic Local Search for Multi-Objective Flowshop Scheduling Problems. European J. Operational Research, 167 (2005) 717-738
13. Wolpert, D.H., Macready, W.G.: No Free Lunch Theorems for Optimization. IEEE Trans. Evol. Comput., 1 (1997) 67-82
14. Taillard, E.: Benchmarks for Basic Scheduling Problems. European J. Operational Research, 64 (1993) 278-285
15. Jaszkiewicz, A.: Do Multiple-Objective Metaheuristcs Deliver on their Promises? A Computational Experiment on the Set-Covering Problem. IEEE Trans. Evol. Comput., 7 (2003) 133-143

# An Improved Genetic Algorithm for Cell Placement

Guofang Nan[1], Minqiang Li[1], Wenlan Shi[2], and Jisong Kou[1]

[1] Institute of System Engineering, Tianjin University, 300072, Tianjin, P.R. China
[2] Department of Information Engineering and Automatization, Hebei Institute of Vocation and Technology, Shijiazhuang 050091, China
guofangnan@gmail.com

**Abstract.** Genetic algorithm, an effective methodology for solving combinatorial optimization problems, is a very computationally expensive algorithm and, as such, numerous researchers have undertaken efforts to improve it. In this paper, we presented the partial mapped crossover and cell move or cells exchange mutation operators in the genetic algorithm when applied to cell placement problem. Traditional initially placement method may cause overlaps between two or more cells, so a heuristic initial placement approach and method of timely updating the coordinates of cells involved were used in order to eliminate overlaps between cells, meanwhile, considering the characters of different circuits to be placed, the punishment item in objective function was simplified. This algorithm was applied to test a set of benchmark circuits, and experiments reveal its advantages in placement results and time performance when compared with the traditional simulated annealing algorithm.

## 1 Introduction

There exit many different types of placement problems in our real life, and these problems are all key technologies, which are worth being discussed. Surface mount component placement machines [1] are being widely used in electronic manufacturing industry for automated placement of components on printed wire boards, the core of surface mount component placement machines is placement algorithm. The placement of sensor nodes [2] is critical to develop the technology for improved fault tolerance. Placement of resources in the star network [3] is also an important issue in a large system with many processing elements. Placement of Web server replicas [4] occurs with the increasing deployment of content distribution networks. It is certain that there also have many other placement problems, but the most widely discussed and studied placement problem, I think, is cell placement in VLSI layout, it is an important phase in VLSI design. The VLSI cell placement problem [5] involves placing a set of cells on a VLSI layout, given a netlist, which provides the connectivity between each cell and a library containing layout information for each type of cell. This layout information includes the width and height of the cell, the location of each pin, the presence of equivalent pins, and the possible presence of feed through paths within the cell. The primary goal of cell placement is to determine the best location of each cell so as to minimize the total area of the layout and the wirelength of the nets connecting the cells together. With standard cell design, the layout is organized into equal height rows, and the desired placement should have equal length rows.

D.-S. Huang, K. Li, and G.W. Irwin (Eds.): ICIC 2006, LNCS 4113, pp. 523 – 532, 2006.

The placement problem has been proved to be NP hard, and therefore, it can't be solved exactly in polynomial time. The traditional placement algorithm includes min-cut graph algorithm [6-7], force-directed algorithm [8], tabu search algorithm [9], genetic algorithm [10-11], and simulated annealing [12-13]. Especially, the simulated annealing algorithm was widely and successfully used in most of placement tools, but there are also some problems in traditional simulated annealing, for example, initial temperature shouldn't be a fixed value for all size circuits, and the placement results always differ in the final evaluated wirelength after different computing.

Genetic Algorithms (GAs) have been widely studied, experimented and applied in many fields in engineering worlds. Not only does the GAs provide an alternative method to solving problem, it outperforms other traditional methods in most of the problems. Therefore, a standard cell placement algorithm based on improved genetic algorithm is presented in this paper.

## 2 The Cell Placement Problem

### 2.1 Problem Formulation

The cell placement problem can be defined as follows. Given an electrical circuit consisting of modules with predefined input and output terminals, and interconnection in a predefined way, we need to construct a layout indicating the positions of the cells, so that the estimated wirelength and the layout area are minimized. For a standard placement, minimizing the wirelength is approximately equivalent to minimizing the chip area.

Given a design with $m$ cells need to be placed denoted by $C=\{c_1,c_2,...,c_m\}$, $E=\{e_1,e_2,...,e_n\}$ represents the set of $n$ nets. To each cell $c_i(1\le i\le m)$, the coordination $(x_i,y_i)$ is used to denote the lower left point of the cell. The design area is a rectangle one denoted by points (0,0) and $(X,Y)$. All the circuit modules are placed in $k$ rows, denoted by $R=\{r_1,r_2,...,r_k\}$. In this paper, the main purpose is to get the positions of all modules such that total wirelength $TWL$ of all nets is minimized [14].

$$TWL=\sum_{i=1}^{n} l_i \tag{1}$$

Where $l_i$ represents estimated wirelength of net $i$, $n$ represents net number.

### 2.2 Initial Placement

Traditional initially placement method may cause overlaps between two or more cells, which may bring some difficulties in finding the best placement. In this paper, overlaps are eliminated by a heuristic initial placement method, which is finished in two steps. First, the averaged cell number in each row is calculated according to total cell number and row number, then, these cells are randomly allocated to each row [15]. It should be noted that cells are in the same row should be placed in sequence, so there are no overlaps between cells. Second, the remaining cells are allocated one by one to the rows whose total length is the shortest.

### 2.3 Object Function

The object function in traditional simulated annealing placement algorithm is the sum of three components: the wirelength cost, the cell overlap penalty, and the row length control penalty. In standard cell placement, all cells are of the same height and different width, and each move or position exchange may cause cell overlap penalty, which makes the optimization process more difficult. Moreover, it also results in the row length control penalty, which is a function of the difference between the actual row length and the desired row length. A lot of cxperiments show that too many penalties lead to difficulties in finding the best placement solution, especially for circuits with too many cells, so a heuristic initial placement method and approach of timely updating coordinates of cells involved are employed in this paper to avoid many penalties.

When a cell is moved or when two cells are swapped, it is possible that there is an overlap between cells. So, in order to eliminate overlap, we must update involved cells' coordinate timely. See Fig. 1, cells $(k,j)$ are selected for swap. It is easy to eliminate overlap through updating the involved cells' coordinates, which can also simplify the objective function.

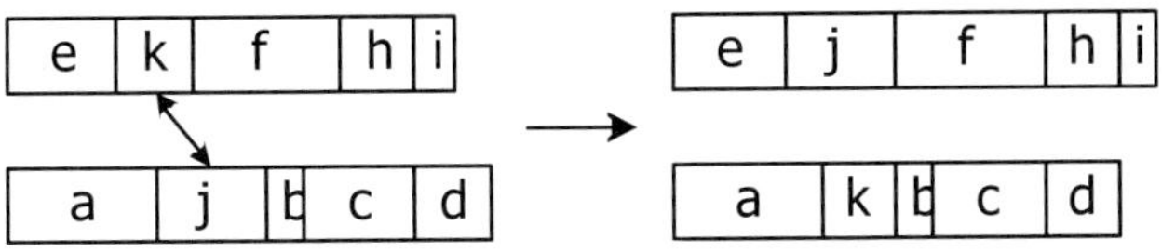


**Fig. 1.** Eliminate Overlap

$$Cost = \gamma_1 + \gamma_2 \tag{2}$$

$$\gamma_1 = \sum_{i=1}^{n} (\alpha_i^H \times X_i + \alpha_i^V \times Y_i) \tag{3}$$

$$\gamma_2 = \omega \sum_{i=1}^{R} |L_A(i) - L_R(i)| \tag{4}$$

where $Cost$ is objective function, $\gamma_1$ is the item of estimated wirelength, $\alpha_i$ is the weight, $X_i, Y_i$ is the horizontal and the vertical length of net $i$ . $\gamma_2$ is the penalty for the length of row exceeding (or falling short of) the expected length, $\omega$ is the weight of unevenness, $R$ is the total row number, and $L_A(i), L_R(i)$ are the desired row length and the real length of row

## 3 Improved Genetic Algorithm

An improved genetic algorithm is presented to deal with the problems discussed in section 2, in which the partial mapped crossover, cell move or cells exchange mutation and other important genetic operations of the genetic algorithm will be discussed in detail when it is applied to cell placement problem.

### 3.1 A Simple Genetic Algorithm

Genetic algorithms are a class of optimization algorithms that seek improve performance by sampling areas of the parameter space that have a high probability for leading to good solutions [16].

As an optimization technique, genetic algorithms simultaneously examine and manipulate a set of possible solutions [17]. Each candidate solution is represented by a string of symbols called chromosome, a chromosome of length $n$ is defined to be $(s_1, s_2, ..., s_n)$. A genetic algorithm starts with an initial population, which consists of a set of solutions. This population then evolves into different populations for a large number of iterations. At last, the algorithm returns the best individual as the final solution to the problem. For each iteration or generation, the evolution process proceeds as follows [18]. Two members (parents) of the population are selected based on some probability distribution. These two parents are then combined through a crossover operator to produce an offspring. With a low probability the offspring is modified by a mutation operator to introduce an unexplored search space to the population, the diversity of the population is then enhanced. We now have a new population, and the evolution process is repeated until a certain condition is met, for example, after a fixed number of generation [19].

### 3.2 Encoding

There is an important character in circuit placement. Every cell can be given a serial number, which represents the cell throughout the placement process. There are $m$ cells in the circuit, and their serial is $1,2,...,m$, so integer encoding based genetic algorithm can be designed to solve these problems, $s = (s_1, s_2, ..., s_m)$ denotes an individual, $s_i (1 \le i \le m, 1 \le s_i \le m)$ is randomly generated and the bits differ in value with each other.

### 3.3 Fitness Evaluation

In formulation (2) (3) (4), $Cost$ is objective function, $\gamma_1$ is the item of estimated wirelength, $\alpha_i$ is the weight, $X_i, Y_i$ is the horizontal and the vertical length of net $i$. $\gamma_2$ is the penalty for the length of row exceeding (or falling short of) the expected length, $\omega$ is the weight of unevenness, $R$ is the total row number, and $L_A(i), L_R(i)$ are the expected length and the real length of row.

So fitness function can be difined as follows:

$$f = \mu / Cost \tag{5}$$

It can ensure that the individual with the maximal fitness has more survival opportunities, here, $\mu$ is a constant, $\mu = 10^5$.

It is also noted that we should timely update coordinates of cells involved in the crossover and mutation operations before computing the fitness of an individual.

### 3.4 Selection

In order to ensure proper selection pressure, roulette wheel selection strategy is used in this paper. Roulette wheel selection is a proportionate selection scheme in which the slots of a roulette wheel are sized according to the fitness of each individual in the population. The probability of selecting an individual is therefore proportional to its fitness. At the same time we adopt elite selection strategy, which is the best individual is retained to the next generation without any modification.

### 3.5 Crossover

There are three styles of crossover operators conventionally used in applications as order crossover, partially mapped crossover and cycle crossover. Here, the partial mapped crossover (PMX) is adopted for the improved genetic algorithm. It is implemented as follows. When a random cut point is chosen, the segments following the cut point in both parents are considered as partial mappings of the modules to be exchanged. We take corresponding modules from the segments of both parents, and locate both these modules in the first parent and exchange them. This process is repeated for all modules in the segment. Thus a module in the segment of the first parent and a module in the same location in the second parent will define which modules in the first parent have to be exchanged to generate the offspring. An example is shown in Figure 2.

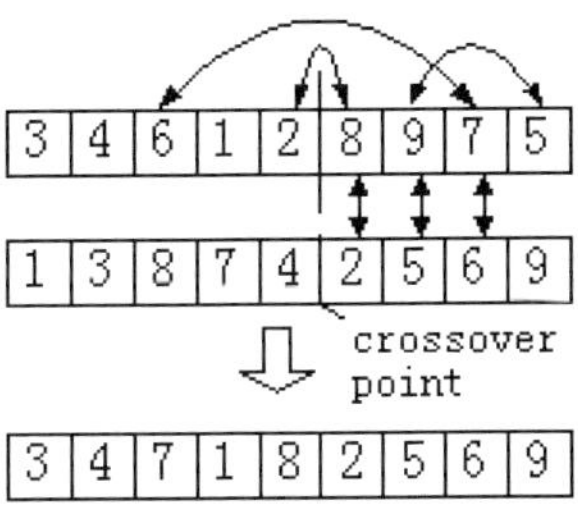


**Fig. 2.** PMX Crossover

### 3.6 Mutation

According to the characters of cell placement problem in VLSI layout, we adopt cell move mutation and position exchange between two any cells mutation methods in this paper.

Cell move means that a single cell (bit) is randomly selected and moved to a new location according to the mutation rate, it can be moved to the same row or to a different row, which we call them same row move and different row move. The same row move can't result in the change of the total row length, while the different row move may cause the change of the total row length.

The position exchange mutation (see Fig.3) is often used for the integer encoding in a GA. When two bits (cells) are randomly selected from an individual to be operated, an exchange between their corresponding nodes will be made.

After the cell move mutation or position exchange mutation, the coordinates of the cells involved should be updated according to the description in Fig.1 in order to compute the fitness correctly.

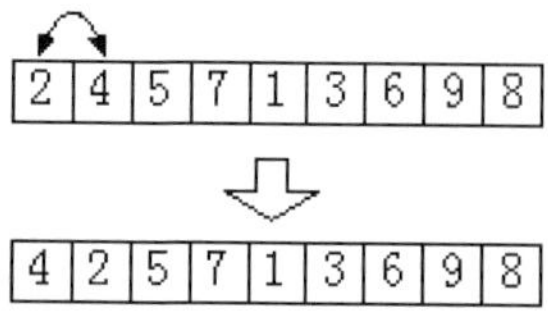


**Fig. 3.** Position Exchange Mutation

The two mutation strategies can be implemented as follows: selecting a cell and a position randomly, if the position is vacant, then move the cell to this position, if the position is occupied by another cell, then change the position of the two cells.

# 4 Experimental Results

## 4.1 Experimental Setup and Benchmarks

In formula (3), $\alpha_i^H = 1, \alpha_i^V = 1$. In formula (4), the value of $\omega$ should satisfy a certain condition, the ratio of the unused length to total length should be less than 1% in each row. Fig. 4 shows the optimization process of $\omega$ when the distance between adjacent rows are zero ($Rowspace = 0$) and a standard cell height (*SCH*: $Rowsapce = SCH$ ).

In Fig 4, X-coordinate represents $\omega$ and Y-coordinate represents $\rho$, where $\rho$ is the ratio of unused length to total length. Therefore, when $Rowspace = 0$, $\omega = 6$, and when $Rowsapce = SCH$, $\omega = 5$. The proposed algorithm are implemented using C++ language on a PC (1 CPU, Intel P4 2.0GHz, 512M RAM, 60G Hard Disk) under the windows XP operating system. In the algorithm, the population size is 50 and crossover probability is 0.6, mutation rate is 0.025, each computing is run 5000 generations. All the experimental data we list in the following table by the improved GA and simulated annealing approach are the average value achieved by 20 runs.

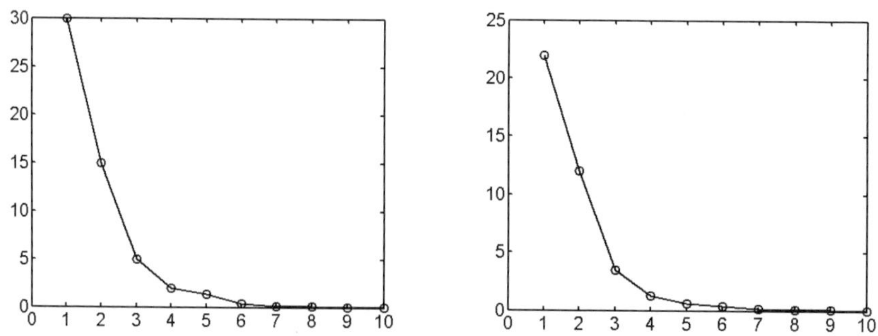

(a) $Rowspace = 0$ (b) $Rowsapce = SCH$

**Fig. 4.** Relationship between $\omega$ and $\rho$

Table 1 shows the statistics of the benchmark circuits used for the experiments, and many researchers have used these benchmark circuits to evaluate their placement algorithms.

**Table 1.** Specification of the Benchmark Circuits

| Benchmarks | Cells | Nets | I/Opads | Pins |
|---|---|---|---|---|
| fract | 149 | 163 | 24 | 510 |
| struct | 1952 | 1920 | 64 | 6207 |
| primary1 | 833 | 904 | 81 | 5526 |
| primary2 | 3014 | 3029 | 108 | 18407 |
| biomed | 6514 | 7052 | 97 | 28257 |

## 4.2 Comparison with Placement Methods

Some parameters mentioned above are used in improved genetic algorithm (IGA) to test some benchmark circuits, and the results including estimated wire-length, chip size, row number, $\rho$ and computation time are listed in Table 2 and Table 3. Meanwhile, we listed some results achieved by simulated annealing (SA), which is used to make a comparison with the IGA. In Table 2, all the data is achieved with $Rowspace = 0$, and in Table 3, all the data is achieved with $Rowsapce = SCH$.

We can see clearly from Table 2 and Table 3 that IGA runs faster and achieve shorter estimated wirelength in most cases that the SA. When $Rowspace = 0$, the IGA runs 9.68% faster and achieves 3.29% shorter estimated wirelength than the SA on average. When $Rowsapce = SCH$, the IGA runs 7.03% faster and achieves 6.15% shorter estimated wirelength than the SA on average.

**Table 2.** Comparison with Two Algorithms when $Rowspace = 0$

| | SA | | | | | IGA | | | | |
|---|---|---|---|---|---|---|---|---|---|---|
| Circuits | Wire-length ($\mu$m) | Row length ($\mu$m) | Rows | $\rho$ (%) | Time (m) | Wire-length ($\mu$m) | Row length ($\mu$m) | Rows | $\rho$ (%) | Time (m) |
| Fract | 46901 | 976 | 8 | 0.41 | 1.48 | 45701 | 976 | 8 | 0.41 | 1.45 |
| Struct | 530214 | 3477 | 29 | 0.55 | 18.3 | 506614 | 3480 | 29 | 0.56 | 16.1 |
| Primary1 | 818366 | 3605 | 23 | 0.97 | 19.4 | 760913 | 3602 | 23 | 0.96 | 16.6 |
| Primary2 | 2799157 | 6153 | 39 | 0.94 | 31.6 | 2751643 | 6148 | 39 | 0.93 | 28.3 |
| Biomed | 2398537 | 7539 | 62 | 0.86 | 32.8 | 2311235 | 7540 | 62 | 0.86 | 31.1 |

**Table 3.** Comparison with two algorithms when *Rowsapce* = *SCH*

| Circuits | SA | | | | | IGA | | | | |
|---|---|---|---|---|---|---|---|---|---|---|
| | Wire-length ($\mu$m) | Row length ($\mu$m) | Rows | $\rho$ (%) | Time (m) | Wire-length ($\mu$m) | Row length ($\mu$m) | Row number | $\rho$ (%) | Time (m) |
| fract | 68654 | 1296 | 6 | 0.97 | 1.64 | 68609 | 1297 | 6 | 0.98 | 1.51 |
| struct | 858971 | 4769 | 21 | 0.84 | 20.1 | 653265 | 4770 | 21 | 0.84 | 19.3 |
| primary1 | 1018625 | 5130 | 17 | 0.85 | 21.8 | 980132 | 5130 | 17 | 0.85 | 20.6 |
| primary2 | 3628335 | 10498 | 22 | 0.91 | 34.2 | 3470321 | 10499 | 22 | 0.91 | 31.4 |
| biomed | 3428721 | 10514 | 44 | 0.93 | 33.6 | 3277672 | 10509 | 44 | 0.93 | 30.7 |

From the above discussion, IGA shows its advantage both in time performance and achieving estimated wirelength. Figure 5 is the final placement of circuit 'fract', which also demonstrates the IGA is feasible and effective for the cell placement in VLSI layout.

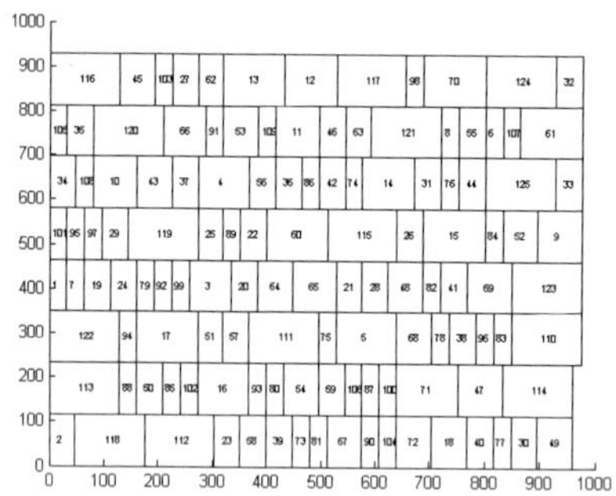

(a) $Rowspace = 0$

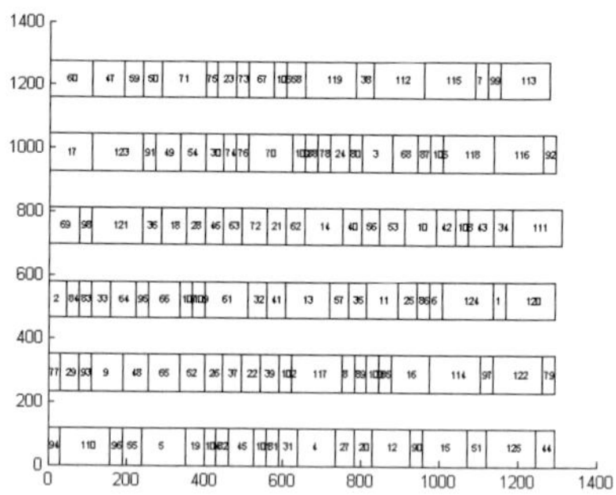

(b) $Rowsapce = SCH$

**Fig. 5.** Final Placement of Circuit 'fract' by IGA

## 5 Conclusions

The cell placement in VLSI layout is a common subject in most placement problems and it is an important phase in VLSI physical design. Many researchers try to solve it by genetic algorithms in order to validate whether the final placement results outperform the traditional simulated annealing placement methods. According to the characters of cell placement, we presented a feasible cell placement algorithm based on improved genetic algorithm, in this paper a heuristic initial placement approach and method of timely updating coordinates of the cells involved were used in order to eliminate overlaps between cells. Meanwhile, the punishment item in objective function was simplified. The partial mapped crossover and cell move or cells' position exchange mutation operators are also designed for the genetic operation. This algorithm is applied to test a set of benchmark circuits after we optimize some important parameters, and experiments show its advantages in placement results and time performance when compared with the traditional simulated annealing.

## Acknowledgements

This research was supported by the National Science Foundation of China (No.70571057) and Postdoctoral Science fund of China (No. 2005038151).

## References

1. Kumar, R., Luo , Z.: Optimizing The Operation Sequence of A Chip Placement Machine Using TSP Model. IEEE Transactions on Electronics Packaging Manufacturing, 26 (1) (2003) 14-21
2. Ishizuka, M., Aida, M.: Achieving Power-law Placement in Wireless Sensor Networks. Autonomous Decentralized Systems, 2005. In Pro. ISADS 2005, (2005) 661-666
3. Alrabady, A. L., Mahud, S. M., Chaudhary, V.: Placement of Resources in the Star Network, Algorithms and Architectures for Parallel Processing, (1996). ICAPP '96. 1996 IEEE Second International Conference on, (1996) 61–67
4. Qiu, L,., Padmanabhan, V. N., Voelker, G. M.: On the Placement of Web Server Replicas. In Pro. Twentieth Annual Joint Conference of the IEEE Computer and Communications Societies (INFOCOM 2001), (2001) 1587-1596
5. John, A. C., Sungho, K.: An Evaluation of Parallel Simulated Annealing Strategies with Application to Standard Cell Placement. IEEE Transactions on Computer-aided Design of Integrated Circuits and Systems, 16 (3) (1997) 398-410
6. Terai, M., Takahashi, K., Sato, K.: A New Min-cut Placement Algorithm for Timing Assurance Layout Design Meeting Net Length Constrain. Design Automation Conference, (1990) 96-102
7. Saurabh, A., Igor, M., Villarrubia, P. G.: Improving Min-cut Placement for VLSI Using Analytical Techniques, IBM ACAS Conference, (2003) 55-62
8. Quinn, J. R., Breuer, M. A.: A Forced Directed Component Placement Procedure for Printed Circuit Boards. IEEE Trans. CAS, 26 (6) (1979) 377-388
9. Suit, S. M., Youssef, H., Barada, H. R., Al-Yamani A.: A Parallel Tabu Search Algorithm for VLSI standard-cell placement. Proceedings of The 2000 IEEE International Symposium on Circuits and Systems (ISCAS 2000), Geneva, 2 (2000) 581-584
10. Manikas, T. W., Mickle, M. H.: A genetic Algorithm for Mixed Macro and Standard Cell Placement. Circuits and Systems, 2 (2002) 4-7
11. Shahookar, K., Mazumder, P.: GASP-a Genetic Algorithm for Standard Cell Placement, Design Automation Conference, 1990 EDAC. Proceedings of the European, (1990) 660-664
12. Grover, L. K.: A New Simulated Annealing Algorithm for Standard Cell Placement. Proc International Conference on CAD, (1986) 378-380
13. Esbensen, H., Mazumder, P.: SAGA: A Unification of The Genetic Algorithm with Simulated Annealing and Its Application to Macro-cell placement. Proceedings of the Seventh International Conference on VLSI Design, (1994) 211-214

14. Yao, B., Hou, W., Hong, X., Cai, Y.: FAME: A Fast Detailed Placement Algorithm for Standard Cell Layout Based on Mixed Min-cut and Enumeration. Chinese Journal of Semiconductors, (2000) 21 (8) 744-753
15. Nan, G., Li, M., Lin, D., Kou, J.: Adaptive Simulated Annealing for Standard Cell Placement. ICNC2005, LNCS 3612, (2005) 943-947
16. Areibi, S.: The Effect of Clustering and Local Search on Genetic Algorithms. Recent Advances In Soft Computing, Leicester, UK (1999) 172-177
17. Kim, C. K., Moon, B R.: Dynamic Embedding for Genetic VLSI Circuit Partitioning,. Engineering Applications of Artificial Intelligence, (1998) 67-76
18. Moon, B. R., Lee, Y. S., Kim, C. K.: GEORG : VLSI Circuit Partitioner with a New Genetic Algorithm Framework. Journal of Intelligent Manufacturing, 9 (1998) 401-412
19. Nan, G., Li, M., Kou, J.: Two Novel Encoding Strategies Based Genetic Algorithms for Circuit Partitioning, Proceedings of 2004 International Conference on Machine Learning and Cybernetics, (2004) 2182-2188

# Conflict Detection in Role-Based Access Control Using Multiple-Attractor Cellular Automata*

Jun-Cheol Jeon and Kee-Young Yoo**

Department of Computer Engineering,
Kyungpook National University,
Daegu, 702-701 Korea
jcjeon33@infosec.knu.ac.kr,
yook@knu.ac.kr

**Abstract.** Cellular automata (CA) have been accepted as a good evolutionary computational model for the simulation of complex physical systems. Meanwhile delegation of role is necessary for scalability of general computing environments. However, this practical principle can lead to conflicts at compile time and run time. Thus, we propose a policy for Separation of Duty (SoD) in Role-based Access Control (RBAC), and demonstrate how conflicts between specified SoD constraints and delegation activities can be detected based on evolutionary computation using Multiple-Attractor CA (MACA).

## 1 Introduction

Techniques adapted from the field of artificial intelligence, especially evolutionary computation, are steadily becoming more and more apparent in the area of computer security, both in network/host security and in the very demanding area of cryptology [1, 2]. In recent years, many algorithms that take advantage of approaches based on evolutionary computation have been proposed; for example, in the design and analysis of a number of new cryptographic primitives, ranging from pseudo-random number generators to block ciphers, in the cryptanalysis of state-of-the-art cryptosystems, and in the detection of network attacking patterns [1-3]. As a result of these recent successes, there is growing interest from the computer security community in evolutionary computation techniques but there still are a number of open problems in the field that should be addressed.

Cellular automata (CA), as introduced by John Von Neumann [4], have been accepted as a good computational model for the simulation of complex physical systems, and have been used in evolutionary computations for over a decade. They can readily simulate complex growth patterns and have been used in various applications, such as parallel processing computations and number theory [5]. Various studies have presented the characteristics of CA based on a group and non-group CA [6, 7]. While in the state-evolution graph of a group CA all states belong to some disjoint set of cycles, non-group CA are characterized by the presence of some non-reachable states in the state-evolution graph.

* This work was supported by the Brain Korea 21 Project in 2006.

** Corresponding author.

D.-S. Huang, K. Li, and G.W. Irwin (Eds.): ICIC 2006, LNCS 4113, pp. 533 – 541, 2006.

Access control is arguably the most fundamental and most pervasive security mechanism in use today. Access control is included in virtually all systems and imposes great architectural and administrative challenges at all levels of enterprise computing. From a business perspective, access control can promote the optimal sharing and exchange of resources, but it also can frustrate users, impose large administrative costs, and cause the unauthorized disclosure or corruption of valuable information [8].

One of the key issues in most access control systems is authorization administration policy, the function of granting and revoking authorizations. Centralized and decentralized administrations are two possible approaches to policy management [9]. In decentralized administration, multiple authorities grant and revoke authorizations, and the ability to manage administrative role is delegated to multiple subjects. It is flexible and apt to the particular requirements of individual subjects. Nevertheless, authorizations become more difficult to control since multiple subjects can grant and revoke authorizations, and the problem of cascading and cyclic authorization may arise.

Two significant areas of extensions to the RBAC96 model have been proposed; one concentrates on the specification of constraints [10, 11], the other describes a framework for role-based delegation [12, 13]. However, these two extensions create a new range of problems within a role-based access control model. The main concern is that specified SoD can conflict with a model allowing for the delegation of authority through role transfer.

Thus, the current study proposes two kinds of exclusion clarified by role, i.e. exclusion specified by role sets and role pair, and divides the exclusion into two types, positive and negative. How to detect conflict in role delegations is demonstrated based on linear non-group CA such as MACA. We propose three algorithms for initialization and activation and show how evolutionary computation is used for the proposed schemes.

The rest of this paper is organized as follows: Section 2 illustrates the characterization of multiple-attractor CA. Section 3 describes the proposed policy and conflict detection algorithms based on evolutionary computation in role-based access control. Section 4 presents an analysis and discussion of our scheme along with the characteristics of our mechanism. Finally, Section 5 gives our concluding remarks.

## 2 Characterization of Linear Non-group Cellular Automata

A CA is a collection of simple cells arranged in a regular fashion. CAs can be characterized based on four properties: cellular geometry, neighborhood specifications, number of states per cell, and the rule to compute to a successor state. The next state of a CA depends on the current state and rules [14]. Only 2-state and 3-neighborhood CAs are considered in this paper. Table 1 shows an example of evolution according to an given initial state and rules. Each mapping is called a 'rule' of the CA.

The next state evolution for the *i*th cell can be represented as a function of the present states of the *i*th, (*i*+1)th, and (*i*-1)th cells for a 3-neighberhood CA: $Q_i(t+1) = f(Q_{i-1}(t), Q_i(t), Q_{i+1}(t))$, where '*f*' represents the combinational logic function as a CA rule implemented by a combinational logic circuit (CL), and $Q(t+1)$ denotes the next state for cell $Q(t)$.

Table 1 illustrates an one-dimensional null hybrid CA of 10 cells with rules 102 and 60 starting at a given binary string (0001110110). CA can also be classified as linear or non-linear. If the neighborhood is only dependent on an XOR operation, the CA is linear, whereas if it is dependent on another operation, the CA is non-linear. If the neighborhood is only dependent on an EXOR or EXNOR operation, then the CA can also be referred to as an additive CA.

**Table 1.** An one-dimensional null hybrid linear CA of 10 cells with rules 102 and 60 starting at a given initial state

| $t$ | 102 | 60 | 60 | 60 | 102 | 102 | 60 | 60 | 60 | 102 |
|---|---|---|---|---|---|---|---|---|---|---|
| 0 | 0 | 0 | 0 | 1 | 1 | 1 | 0 | 1 | 1 | 0 |
| 1 | 0 | 0 | 0 | 1 | 0 | 1 | 1 | 1 | 0 | 0 |
| 2 | 0 | 0 | 0 | 1 | 1 | 0 | 0 | 0 | 1 | 0 |
| 3 | 0 | 0 | 0 | 1 | 1 | 0 | 0 | 0 | 1 | 0 |

Rule 60: $Q_i(t+1) = Q_{i-1}(t) \oplus Q_i(t)$
Rule 102: $Q_i(t+1) = Q_i(t) \oplus Q_{i+1}(t)$

Furthermore, if the same rule applies to all the cells in a CA, the CA is called a uniform or regular CA, whereas if different rules apply to different cells, it is called a hybrid CA. In addition, in the structure of CAs, the boundary conditions must be taken into consideration since there exist no left neighbor of the leftmost cell and right neighbor of the rightmost cell among the cells composing the CA. According to the conditions, they are divided into three types: Null Boundary CA (NBCA), Periodic Boundary CA (PBCA), and Intermediate Boundary CA (IBCA) [14].

## 2.1 Definitions

In this section, we define some notations for use in the later sections.

- Non-group CA: Some of the states are not reachable from any state.
- (Non) Reachable state: In a state evolution diagram of a non-group CA, a state having at least one in-degree is called a reachable state, while a state with no-in-degree is called a non-reachable state.
- Attractor: The cycles in the state-evolution diagram of a non-group CA.
- $\alpha$-tree: The tree rooted at a cyclic state $\alpha$ is denoted as $\alpha$-tree. The set of states in $\alpha$-tree is also referred to as $\alpha$-basin. The terms basin and tree are used interchangeably.
- Depth: The depth of a CA is defined as the minimum number of clock cycles required to reach the nearest cyclic state from any non-reachable state in the state-evolution diagram of the CA.

## 2.2 Characteristics of Multiple Attractor CA

Using the logic function defined in the earlier section, it is also represented by the characteristic matrix $T$ so that the state at the next instant can be represented by

$Q_i(t+1) = T \cdot Q_i(t)$. The state-evolution diagram of a four-cell linear CA is shown in Fig.1. It has attractors 0, 1, 8, and 9, and its characteristic matrix $T$ is given by

$$T = \begin{bmatrix} 1 & 1 & 0 & 0 \\ 0 & 1 & 1 & 0 \\ 0 & 1 & 1 & 0 \\ 0 & 0 & 1 & 1 \end{bmatrix}$$

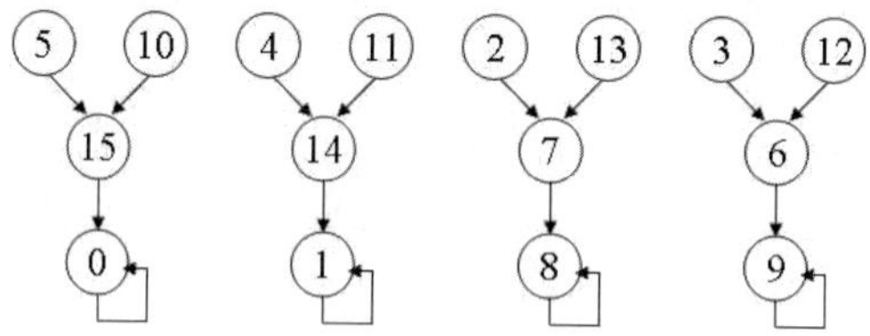


**Fig. 1.** State-Evolution Diagram of a Four-Cell Linear Null Boundary CA with Rule <102, 102, 60, 60>

**Theorem 1** [15]. For any two integer $n$ and $m$ ($0 \le m \le n$) there exists an $n$-cell MACA with $2^m$ attractors.

The algorithm for finding an $n$-cell MACA with $2^m$ attractors is illustrated in [15]. Table 2 notes the number of MACA of different sizes with different numbers of attractors. Table 2 shows there are many MACAs with different numbers of attractors, so we can use any MACAs according to the number of attractors.

**Table 2.** Number of MACA with different number of attractors

| No. of cells | Number of attractors | | | | | | |
|---|---|---|---|---|---|---|---|
| | 2 | 4 | 8 | 16 | 32 | 64 | 128 |
| 4 | 102 | 57 | 12 | | | | |
| 5 | 378 | 301 | 97 | 15 | | | |
| 6 | 1350 | 1421 | 632 | 146 | 18 | | |
| 7 | 4698 | 6217 | 3593 | 1122 | 204 | 21 | |
| 8 | 16038 | 25745 | 18556 | 7407 | 1798 | 271 | 24 |

## 3 Conflict-Detection Based on MACA

SoD is dividing right for critical operations so that no user acting alone can compromise the security of the data processing system. Existing systems typically rely on mutual exclusion of roles to enforce SoD polices and the policy is usually interpreted using mutual exclusion rules between roles [8]. However, there still remain difficult problems related to how strictly the policy is interpreted and how this SoD policy should be implemented in distributed computing environment.

To remedy the problems, we classify the policy of SoD rule and present a detailed explanation of the policy of SoD rules in section 3.1. We also demonstrate an efficient conflict detection algorithm based on multi-attractor CA in section 3.2.

### 3.1 Policy of SoD Rules

We classify two kinds of mutual exclusion clarified by role, i.e. a role set based exclusion and role pair based exclusion. Each kind is divided into two types, positive and negative.

**Definition 1.** (Role-set based mutual exclusion: SE) Positive type (PSE) is clarified based on mutually exclusive role-set while negative type (NSE) is clarified based on mutually non-exclusive role sets.

It is possible to elucidate a set of roles that are mutually exclusive or not. This feature is particularly desirable if the application features elaborate SoD requirements.

**Definition 2.** (Role-pair based mutual exclusion: PE) Positive type (PPE) is clarified based on mutually exclusive role-pair while negative type (NPE) is clarified based on mutually non-exclusive role-pair.

This is a more complex feature since the number of pairs is $n(n\text{-}1)/2$ for $n$ roles

Example 1). There are four roles, $r_1$ through $r_4$, and we assume that a mutual exclusion relationship exists, as shown in Table 3. An '×' in cell $i$, $j$ indicates that $r_i$ is mutually exclusive to $r_j$. Each types has the following result, PSE: $r_1(r_2, r_3)$, $r_2(r_1, r_3)$, $r_3(r_1, r_2, r_4)$, $r_4(r_1, r_3)$, NSE: $r_1(r_4)$, $r_2(r_4)$, $r_3(\phi)$, $r_4(r_2)$, PPE: $(r_1, r_2)$, $(r_1, r_3)$, $(r_2, r_3)$, $(r_3, r_4)$ and NPE: $(r_1, r_4)$, $(r_2, r_4)$.

**Table 3.** Example of a mutual exclusion relationship among $r_1$ through $r_4$

| | $r_1$ | $r_2$ | $r_3$ | $r_4$ |
|---|---|---|---|---|
| $r_1$ | - | × | × | - |
| $r_2$ | × | - | × | - |
| $r_3$ | × | × | - | × |
| $r_4$ | × | - | × | - |

In PSE and NSE, the roles in parentheses represent exclusive sets or non-exclusive sets, respectively, e.g. a user with $r_2$ cannot have $r_3$ at the same time, but $r_4$. In PPE and NPE, all roles are tied by pair, and each pair shows that two roles are mutually exclusive or not. As shown in the above example, PSE and NSE always have the same number of sets as the number of roles. However, if the number of mutually exclusive roles is more than half of them, NSE can reduce the initialization time but both cases have a similar searching time for finding exclusion. It is better to use NPE when the number of mutually exclusive roles is more than $n(n\text{-}1)/4$, as shown in Table 3. This can minimize both the initialization time and searching time.

### 3.2 Conflict Detection in Role Delegation

Let us consider two occasions, initialization and activation, for the whole procedure. Initialization is the point of time when mutually exclusive roles are set to the system, and activation is the point of time when role delegations occur among users. We demonstrate how to detect conflicts corresponding to PSE, NSE, PPE, and NPE based on CA mechanism. As shown in Fig. 2(b) the graph consists of a set of distinct components; each component is an inverted tree containing an equal number of states. The CA states and attractors can be viewed as the addresses connecting user nodes and roles, respectively.

We assume that there are four roles for distribution such as the above example in section 3.1. We could assign one role to each of the four users, but is it essential to have four, or could fewer users suffice? Using graph theory, there is an easy way to determine this number. The chromatic number, $\chi(G)$, of a graph is the minimum number of colors that are required to color vertices so that no two adjacent vertices are the same color [1]. We can model the mutual exclusion relationship with a graph, shown in Fig. 2 (a). The graph is constructed directly from Table 3, so that two roles are connected in the graph whenever they are designated as mutually exclusive.

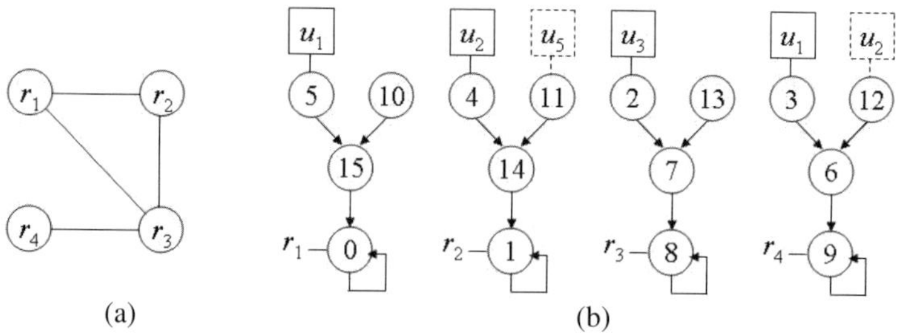


**Fig. 2.** (a) Mutual exclusion relationship and (b) State-Evolution Diagram with assigned users and roles according to Example 1 (a solid and dotted quadrangle denote user nodes after initialization and delegation respectively, and a solid and dotted lines between a user node and a state denote assignments after initialization and delegation respectively, and a solid arrow indicates an evolution direction)

Only three colors are needed to ensure that no edge in Fig. 2 (a) is connected to one vertex of the same color; therefore, SoD requirements can be maintained by assigning roles $r_1$ through $r_4$ to three different users, corresponding to the three colors. In our scheme, a tree and state correspond to a role and the address containing user identification, respectively.

For the sake of clarity, we explain our procedures using Example 1. In initialization procedure, $r_1$ through $r_3$ should be assigned to the different users while $r_4$ can be assigned to $u_1$ or $u_2$, since they have only the roles, $r_1$ or $r_2$ that are not mutually exclusive with $r_4$. However, $r_3$ cannot be assigned to $u_2$ since the two roles, $r_2$ and $r_3$, are mutually exclusive.

[**Algorithm 1.** Assign roles and users to MACA]

Input : $u_i\,(1 \le i \le n)$, $r_j\,(1 \le j \le k$, where $n \le k)$
Output : *Assigned role-tree*

1. Select a $n$-cell MACA with $2^m$ attractors where $2^m$ is more than the number of roles ($2^m \ge j$).
2. Assign roles and users to MACA according to the proposed policy in section 3.1.

**Table 4.** Mutual exclusion relationships among states in MACA according to Example. 1

| Types | 0 | 1 | 8 | 9 |
|---|---|---|---|---|
| PSE | 1, 8 | 0, 8 | 0, 1, 9 | 1, 8 |
| NSE | 9 | 9 | - | 1 |
| PPE | (0, 1), (0, 8), (1, 8), (8, 9) | | | |
| NPE | (0, 9), (1, 9) | | | |

After the initialization procedure, Table 3 can be obtained by mutual exclusion relationships among states in MACA. Current roles and users are assigned to role-tree without any conflicts. If the CA is loaded with a particular address and allowed to run for a number of cycles equal to the depth of such trees, it will evolve through a number of states before reaching the root of the corresponding tree. Thereafter, the evolved state always reaches the attractor autonomously. Let $d$ be the depth of three rooted at any attractors; then the following equation holds.

$$Q_i(t+d) = T^d \cdot Q_i(t) = \alpha \qquad (1)$$

where $\alpha$ is an attractor.

Hence, by autonomous evolution from the CA state of user node, we can obtain the role corresponding to a user. In the activation procedure, there are two possible approaches for delegation. One is that a user wants to delegate a role to a non-specific user; the other is that a user wants to delegate a role to a particular user.

In the former case, our scheme firstly finds a role that is a non-exclusive relationship with the role that a user wants to delegate, and checks if the user assigned the role is assigned a role which is mutually exclusive with the previous role. If not, the user is assigned to the role-tree; otherwise, it is regarded as conflict and a new user is generated and assigned to the role-tree.

[**Algorithm 2.** Delegate a role_to a user]

Input : $u_a$, $r_a$ /* $u_a$ wants to delegate $r_a$ */
Output : $r_a$-tree assigning $u_b$ or $r_a$-tree assigning $u_c$
/* find $u_b$ and assign $r_a$-tree or create $u_c$ and assign $r_a$-tree */

1. Find roles (attractors) that are in a non-mutual exclusion relationship with $r_a$ according to NSE or NPE.
2. Check that the users who are assigned the roles found in step 1 have been assigned to a role which is mutually exclusive with $r_a$ according to PSE or PPE.
3. Assign the user to the $r_a$-tree; otherwise, conflict occurs, and a new user, $u_c$, can be created and assigned to the $r_a$-tree.

For example, we assume that $u_2$ wants to delegate $r_2$ to another user shown in Fig. 2. We can find that $r_4(9)$ is in a non-mutual exclusion relationship with $r_2(1)$ according to Table 4, but $u_1$ assigned $r_4$ has already been assigned to $r_1$ which is in a mutual exclusion relationship with $r_2$. Hence, a new user, $u_5$, should be created and assigned to $r_2$.

In the latter case, we can simply obtain the result by checking whether two roles are mutually exclusive or not.

[**Algorithm 3**. Delegate a role_to a particular user]

Input : $u_a$, $r_a$, $u_b$ /* $u_a$ wants to delegate $r_a$ to $u_b$ */
Output : $r_a$-tree assigning $u_b$ or conflict alerting

1. Check that two roles, $r_a$-tree and $r_b$-tree, where $u_b$ is assigned to, are mutually exclusive.
2. Assign $u_b$ to $r_a$-tree, otherwise, conflict occurs.

For example, we assume that $u_2$ wants to delegate $r_2$ to $u_3$ in Fig. 2. We can find that $r_2(1)$ is in a mutual exclusion relationship with $r_3(8)$ according to Table 4 so that conflict occurs. However, if $u_1$ wants to delegate $r_4$ to $u_2$ then we can get the result with $r_4$-tree assigning $u_2$.

Through the whole proposed algorithm, we could simply find conflict by checking relationships between attractors based on evolution of user nodes. A user node should evolve for a number of cycles equal to the depth of trees then the evolved state always reaches the attractor. After the whole procedures, the previous user node can be deleted from the graph according to the administration policy.

## 4 Analysis and Discussion

In this section, we analyze and discuss our policy and conflict detection technique based on MACA. For elaborate granting rights, we have realized SoD requirements by exclusion of role. In this case, assignment of roles in a SoD environment can become complex. To accomplish this task safely and automatically, a system must first ensure that no single user has all roles needed to accomplish a critical task and then ensure that roles are assigned to individuals in such a way that no individual will have all of these roles through some combination of roles. Users also must be assigned to roles in such a way that no user can violate SoD rules through a combination of roles.

In mutual exclusion of roles, this is more complex and takes more time for initialization. However, there is no problem with assignment of roles to roles and roles to users since mutually exclusive roles cannot be assigned to not only a role but also a user by the proposed policy. We propose two types of policy for SoD requirements according to the number of mutually exclusive relationships. It is a practical alternative plan if the system does not provide enough capability. We find each role by evolution from each user node so that conflicts among users and roles can be simply found by proposed scheme. Thus, initialization and activation can be achieved without any conflicts.

In our proposed algorithm classification, the initialization algorithm should be performed at the first stage, and the activation algorithm can be divided into two types. One is that a user wants to delegate his or her role to whoever he is, and the other is that a user needs to delegate his role to a particular user. Both cases occur frequently in a distributed computing environment so that operating two procedures separately offers much better system performance and capacity.

In RBAC systems, it is hard to manage delegation of roles and permissions. To make a simple and robust administration environment, we propose a strategy in delegation model within CA mechanism. An MACA has the same number of states in each tree so that roles cannot be assigned to more than the number of states. This characteristic can block many roles and permissions being centralized in a particular user. The well-designed distribution of roles can minimize frequent granting operations and user dissatisfaction.

## 5 Conclusion

Administration in RBAC is more difficult to control since multiple subjects can grant authorizations, and the problem of cascading and cyclic authorization may arise. Thus, we have proposed an efficient delegation mechanism based on the policies of SoD requirement and delegation scheme using MACA based on evolutionary computation. The proposed policy for SoD requirement and delegation scheme can block malicious users and minimize delegation time without any conflicts. Thus, we expect that our mechanism can be effectively used for granting strategy in complex automatic system within RBAC.

## References


1. Daemen, J., Govaerts, R., Vandewalle, J.: A Framework for The Design of One-way Hash Functions including Cryptanalysis of Damgaard's One Way Function based on Cellular Automaton. Advances in Cryptology: Proceedings of Asiacrypt'91, Lecture Notes in Computer Science, 739 (1993) 82-96
2. Kanter, I., Kinzel, W., Kanter,E.: Secure Exchange of Information by Synchronization of Neural Networks. Europhyses Letters, 57 (2002) 141-147
3. Hei, S., Zhang, S.: An Evolutionary Approach to the Design of Controllable Cellular Automata Structure for Random Number Generation. IEEE Transactions on Evolutionary Computation, 7 (2003) 23-36
4. Neumann, J. V. (ed.): The Theory of Self-reproducing Automata, University of Illinois Press, Urbana and London (1966)
5. Jeon, J.C., Yoo, K.Y.: Design of Montgomery Multiplication Architecture based on Programmable Cellular Automata. Computational intelligence, 20 (2004) 495-502
6. Seredynski, M., Pienkosz, K., Bouvry, P.: Reversible Cellular Automata Based Encryption. Lecture Notes in Computer Science, Vol. 3222. Springer-Verlag, Berlin Heidelberg New York (2004) 411-418
7. Das, S., Sikdar, B. K., Chaudhuri,P. P.: Charaterization of Reachable/Nonreachable Cellular Automata States. Lecture Notes in Computer Science, Vol. 3305. Springer-Verlag, Berlin Heidelberg New York (2004) 813-822
8. Ruan, C., Varadharajan, V.: A Formal Graph Based Framework for Supporting Authorization Delegations and Conflict Resolutions. Int. J. Inf. Security 10 (2003) 211-222
9. Chen,F., Sandhu,R.: Constraints for RBAC.1st ACM Workshop on Role-Based Access Control, Gaithersburg, MD (1995) 39-46
10. Ahn, G. (ed.): RCL 2000, ph.d dissertation, George Mason University (2000)
11. Lafe, O.: Cellular Automata Transforms: Theory and Applications in Multimedia Compression, Encryption, and Modeling, Kluwer Academic Publishers (2000).

# Evolutionary Algorithm-Based Background Generation for Robust Object Detection

Taekyung Kim[1], Seongwon Lee[2,*], and Joonki Paik[1]

[1] Image Processing and Intelligent Systems Laboratory, Department of Image Engineering, Graduate School of Advanced Imaging Science, Multimedia, and Film, Chung-Ang University, Seoul, Korea
kimktk@wm.cau.ac.kr
http://ipis.cau.ac.kr

[2] Department of Computer Engineering, College of Electronics and Information, Kwangwoon University, Seoul, Korea
swlee@kw.ac.kr

**Abstract.** One of the most fundamental image analysis models is background generation that helps to extract information and features in still images and sequential images. Since conventional approaches generate the background from intensity values of the image affected by illumination, the resulting background is often unsatisfactory. In case of background generation with sequential images, noises and the changes of illumination causes errors in the generated background. In this paper we propose an efficient background generation algorithm based on generic algorithm. The proposed algorithm calculates the suitability of changing regions of sequential images, and then causes evolution to the next generation to obtain a clear background. In the proposed evolutionary algorithm, the chromosome includes edges and intensity values of the images so that the algorithm can effectively exclude incorrect information caused by the change of illumination and generates an image of pure background.

## 1 Introduction

Background generation is one of fundamental, simple approaches for detection and analysis of objects in an image or video. The background generation model provides easy segmentation, and as a result makes it easy to detect and analysis feature information of an object. The outcomes of background generation are a background image and object regions. In the spatial point of view, the generated background should be close to the image of subjective human vision. On the other hand, background is temporally extracted from a video during a certain period of time, and plays a fundamental role in extracting and tracking an object from video. Especially, video-based separation of objects and background is a fundamental technique for surveillance, medical imaging, military tactic weapons, and traffic monitoring, to name a few.

There are many obstacles to get a correct background using intensity-based processing [1]. One typical problem arises with the change of illumination, which can be caused by changes in light source, shadow, and internal reflection. Another problem arises from changes in camera's angle. There are many algorithms to overcome these problems.

* Corresponding author.

D.-S. Huang, K. Li, and G.W. Irwin (Eds.): ICIC 2006, LNCS 4113, pp. 542 – 552, 2006.

One simple approach to background generation accumulates input frames and averaging pixel intensity values at the same position [2]. This approach results in ghost artifacts at the boundary of objects and background, and the situation becomes worse with illumination change during the frame accumulation. In order to solve this problem, an edge-based approach first separates background and objects by generating background only in the static region. This approach, however, requires too many frames to get an acceptable result [3], and is still fragile with illumination change. A more sophisticated method using a median filter has been proposed [4], where background model is generated by the median of pixel intensity values. This method is robust against both noise and illumination change in video because of the nature of median filter. However, this method cannot handle object motion, so it exhibits undesirable ghost artifacts near moving objects.

The proposed approach utilizes generic algorithm (GA) as a background generation model, where the concepts of survival-of-the-fittest and genetic evolution are used to search better, robust background candidates. More specifically, a general GA reproduces the next generation by selecting, mating, and mutating dominance genes [9]. As a result of evolution of the current generation, only dominance genes survive in the suitable environment. The proposed method first detects edges as initial criterions of separating objects and background. The gene structure will be generated from the detected edges, and the evolving parts represent the dynamic regions of the image. The evolving parts are selectively mated and mutated to generate background. By using evolutionary algorithm, the proposed algorithm can significantly reduce the ghost and illumination change problems in the background generation.

This paper is organized as follows. In section 2 a brief survey of existing background generation approaches are presented. The proposed GA-based background generation model is described in section 3. Section 4 summarizes comparison among various methods, and section 5 concludes the paper.

## 2 Background Generation Method and Experiment System

An object can be easily extracted by subtracting the input image from a generated background. This subtraction approach can easily detect change in video and is good for analyzing feature information of an object [4]. More specifically, averaging multiple frames from a video can efficiently remove minor motion and changes, and easily generate a background model [7]. This approach, however, requires too many frames to accumulate, and the extracted background becomes worse as the amount of illumination change increases.

The frame difference method is another simple object extraction method by subtracting two adjacent frames [4]. This can efficiently detects regions that change frame by frame, and be used in many simple background elimination applications.

Abrupt change in illumination affects the generated background, and is finally the major factor to deteriorate the quality of background. Difference between two adjacent frames can be described as

$$Frame(x, y, t) = \left| I(x, y, t) - I(x, y, t-1) \right|. \quad (1)$$

Where $I(x, y, t)$ and $I(x, y, t-1)$ respectively represent the current and previous frames. The desirable property of background is to have constant distribution. Based on this context, change in video should not affect the constant distribution. For this reason W4 algorithm separates objects and background using temporal median filter, and as a result it can provide constant distribution against illumination change [6]. This algorithm can also handle fast motion or abrupt change in the image because of the use of median filter. Figure 1 shows a background generation procedure using median filter.

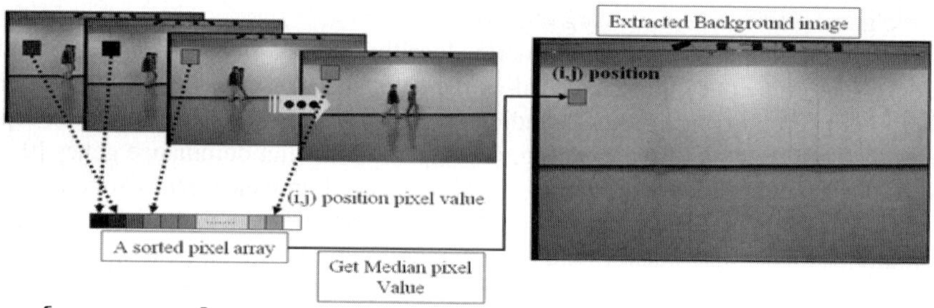


$$F = \{f_1, \ldots\ldots, f_{n-1}\}$$

$$Background(x, y, t-1) = median(F_{x,y,t-1})$$

**Fig. 1.** Background generation using Median Filter

Common drawbacks of existing background generation methods are ghost artifacts due to frame averaging and noisy artifacts near object's boundary. Even the median filter-based method cannot avoid noisy boundary effect. Various methods are classified and compared in Table 1, and their performance is evaluated in Figure2.

**Table 1.** Classification of Background Generation System According to Environment and Methods Technique

| | Area | Sensor | Environment | Object | Methods |
|---|---|---|---|---|---|
| **System** | **Indoor (I) Out-door(O)** | **Color (C) Grayscale (G)** | **Illumination (I) Non-Illumination (NI)** | **People(P) Cars(C) Road(R)** | **Average(A) Edge(E) Frame(F) Median filter(MF) Genetic Algorithm(GA)** |
| Haritaoglu[4] | **O** | **G** | **NI** | P | E |
| Ysauyuki [5] | **O** | **G** | **I** | P | F |
| Shao Yi [6] | **O** | **G** | **I** | R | MF |
| Propased | I,O | G | I, NI | P, C | GA |

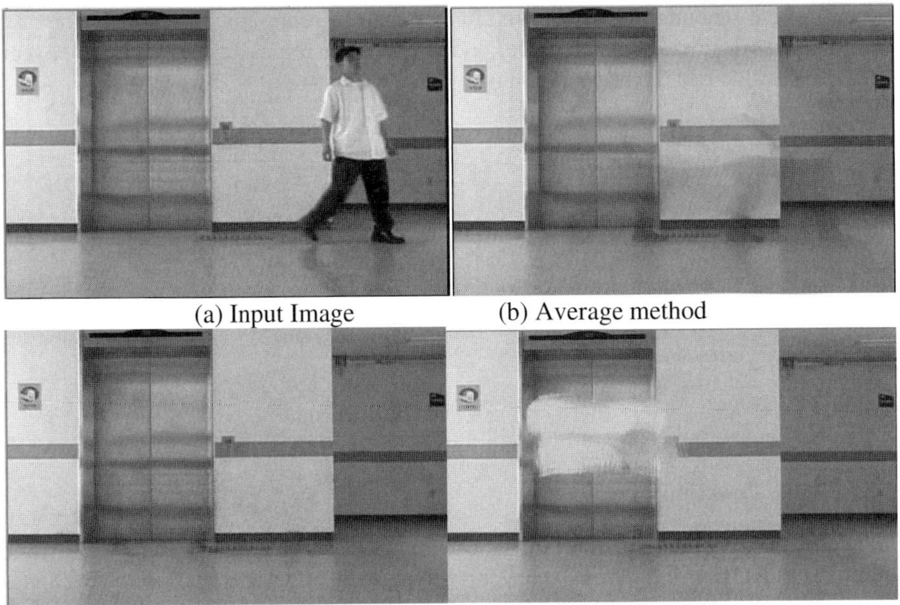

(a) Input Image (b) Average method

(c) Edge Method (d) Median Filter Method

**Fig. 2.** Created Background Generation Model using Number of 50 frames

# 3 Genetic Algorithm for Background Generation

GA can be considered as a natural selection and generation-based search algorithm, which simultaneously evolves multiple populations to obtain the optimal solution. The proposed GA-based background generation algorithm selects parents as a selecting operator, generates population by mutating offsprings obtained by crossover, and finally selects the one best fitting [8]. The gene structure of this algorithm is shown in Figure 3.

## 3.1 Gene Structure

The design of gene structure utilizes variations of input images. The image is generally represented by pixels whose brightness values are distributed between $2^0$ and $2^7$. The big difference of intensity values between objects and background forms edges. Since the edge structure is one of main key features of the input image, we can utilize the edge difference of observed background and object. In the proposed algorithm the chromosome is a bit stream composed of ones and zeros.

Gene structure does not have to be long to include necessary information. To represent the features of input images, the proposed algorithm uses a 7-bit chromosome per single frame of input images. Figure 3 shows the chromosome structure of the proposed algorithm. The chromosome structure represents the edge of the frame with 2 bits. The first bit is set to one if the image has lots of edges, and zero otherwise. The next bit represents the comparison of input edges on the same location between frames. The distribution of the image intensity can be represented by 3 bits. The next bit represents frame edge difference, and the last bit represents difference between input pixel value and the corresponding average.

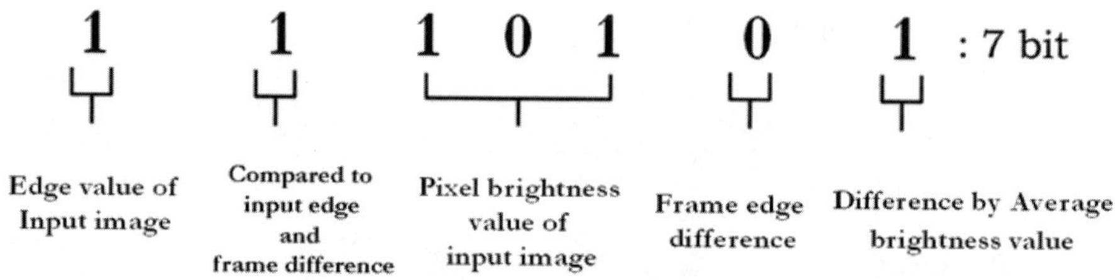


**Fig. 3.** 7-bit chromosome structure

### 3.2 Fitness Function

We calculate the number of pixel to obtain fitness measure. For example, when number of changing edge pixel is less then 10% of the total we measure only changing part because there is no frame difference. This means that the smalls the amount of frame difference, the less background and objects change. Over this range, we just use average in the region of illumination change as shown in the following formulation.

$$Fitness = \frac{number\_edge\_pixel}{\mathrm{Im}\,age(width \times height)} \times 100. \tag{2}$$

where, number_edge_pixel represents the number of pixels in edge difference between two frames, and image (width×height) the total size of the image.

### 3.3 Proposed Background Generation Model (BGM)

Genetic algorithm is based on a survival-of-the-fittest and genetics. It does not require any specific condition for the searching step, and the searching target is the pool because this algorithm evaluates multiple factors simultaneously, the probability to reach the global optimum becomes higher. Such operator in GA includes design of the fitness function, reproduction, crossover, and mutation. Because probabilities for correct reach depend on the above mention operators, we need a training process to find the optimum condition for operations.

Figure 4 shows the proposed GA-based background generation algorithm. In the proposed algorithm, we use the chromosome structure based on edge difference. We evaluate the fitness given in Equation 2. Based on the generated background, reproduction, crossover, and mutation are performed to produce the new pool. The entire process evolves by correcting errors until the convergence criterion is satisfied.

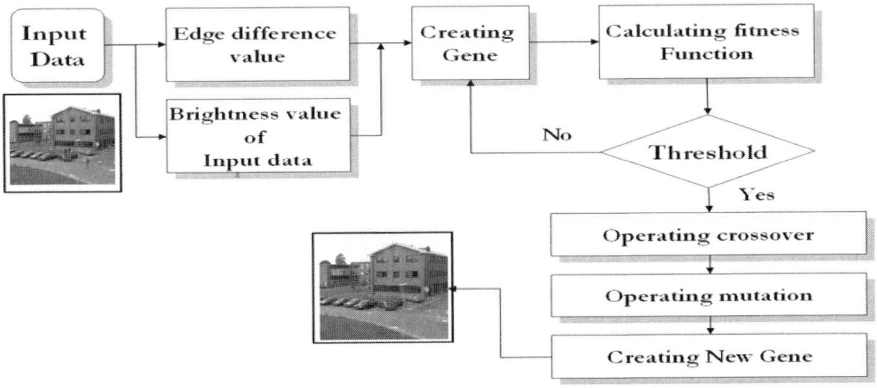


**Fig. 4.** Proposed GA-based background generation algorithm

## 4 Experimental Results

In this paper we used standard test image sets provided by PETS2001 and PETS2002, at well as in-house test image. We tested existing methods using mean, median, and edge to evaluate and compare the performance of the proposed method. The size of the input image is 320×240. From the test images shown in Figure 5 we observed that (a) has big illumination change due to moving cloud, (b) has the reflection problem, and (c) is almost ideal without illumination change.

(a) In-house Image outdoor image

(b) Indoor image provided by PETS2002

(c) Outdoor image by PETS2001

**Fig. 5.** Test images

For the first fifty frame of each video, we tested four different methods and evaluate peak-to-peak signal-to-noise ratio (PSNR) as follows.

$$PSNR = 10\log_{10} \frac{255^2}{\frac{1}{XY}\sum_{x,y}(I_{x,y} - I'_{x,y})^2}. \tag{3}$$

where $I$ represents the original image, $I'$ the modified image, and $X$ and $Y$ respectively represent the horizontal and vertical sizes of the image.

Figure 6 shows the unstable case with big change in intensity. This unstable case occurs when change in edge difference increases. The proposed algorithm minimizes the change by using mean value.

(a) Indoor image provided by PETS2002 (b) The result of unstable chromosome

**Fig. 6.** Original image and its unstable counterpart

Figure 7 shows the background generation results of four different methods using the first fifty frame of PETS2002 image. Three existing methods result in noise background, and are inappropriate to generate clear background.

(a) Average method (b) Edge Method

(c) Median Filter method (d) Proposed Method

**Fig. 7.** Results of four different background generation methods with PETS2002 image

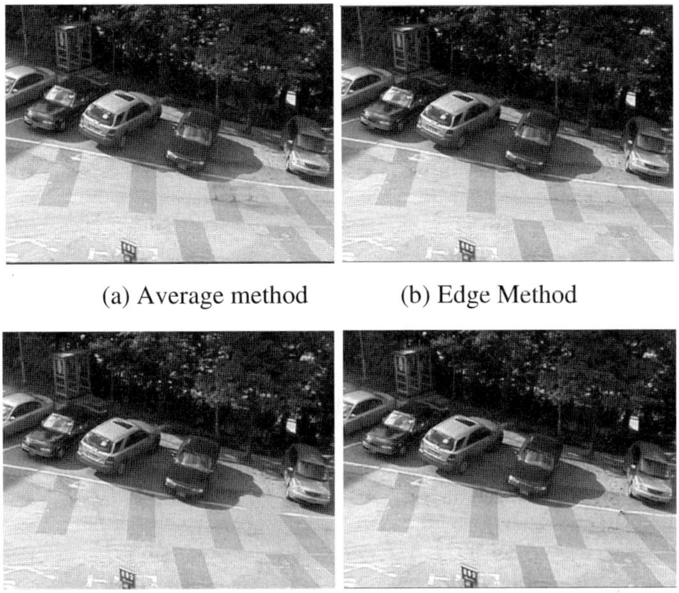

(a) Average method (b) Edge Method

(c) Median Filter method (d) Proposed Method

**Fig. 8.** Results of four different background generation methods with the in-house outdoor image

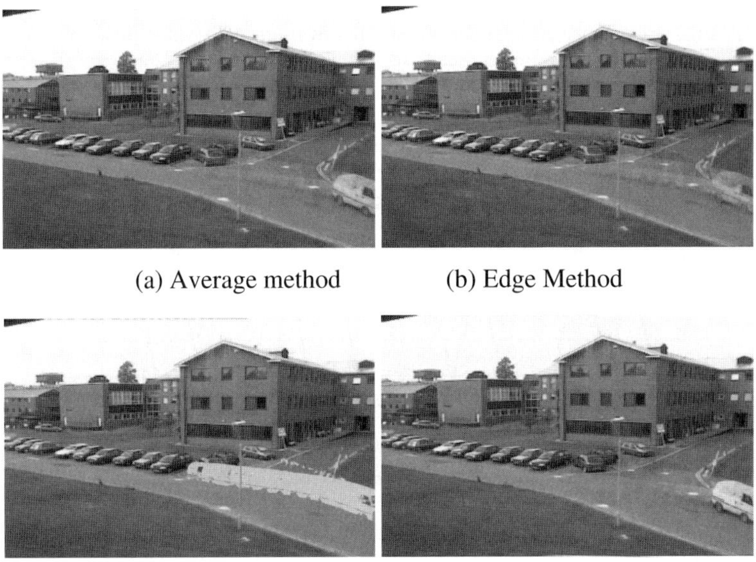

(a) Average method (b) Edge Method

(c) Median Filter method (d) Proposed Method

**Fig. 9.** Results of four different background generation methods with PETS2001 image

Figure 10 shows the distribution of the solution according to the number of generations. Figure 11 shows the fitness of a frame unit. At the $50^{th}$ frame, there is no change in background and objects, and the numbers of generations are correspondingly reduced. On the other hand, if illumination changes in 50, 70, or 110 generations, crossover and mutation take place.

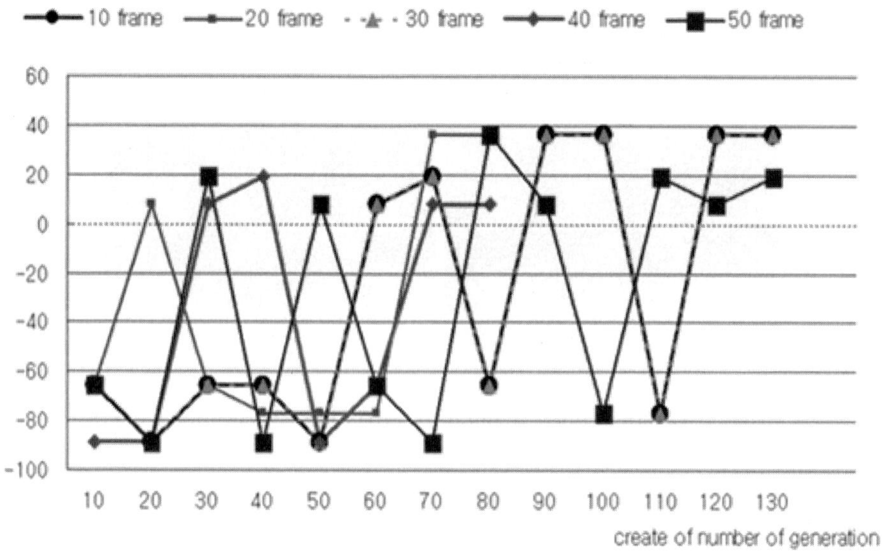


**Fig. 10.** Performance comparison for number of frame Max value [test image (b)]

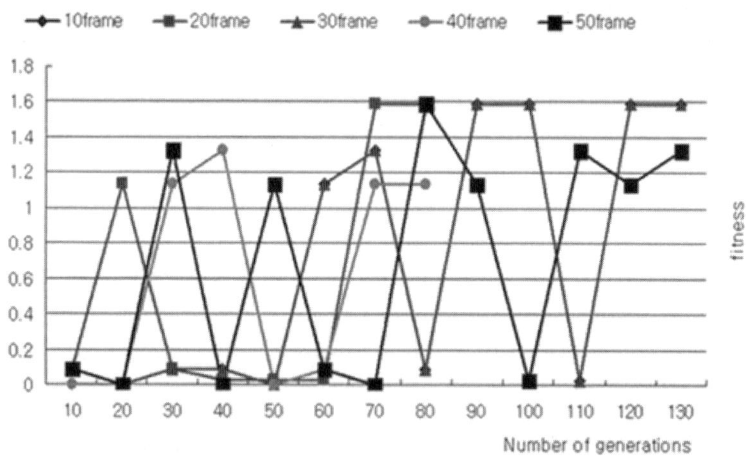


**Fig. 11.** Performance comparison for number of frame for fitness value [test image (b)]

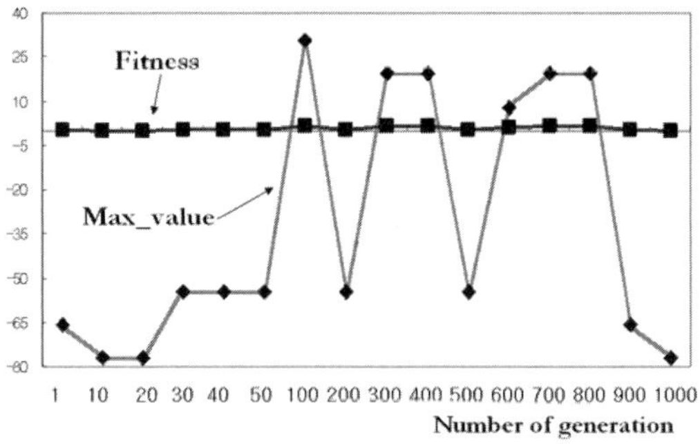


**Fig. 12.** Performance comparison for number of generation for Max_value and fitness [test image (C)]

Figure 13 shows the results of object extraction using the proposed background generation. The proposed method can efficiently generate a difference image of good quality compared to the existing methods.

(a) (b)

**Fig. 13.** Results of object extraction by the proposed method

Results of object extraction using 35 frames by (a) In-house and outdoor image, (b) Outdoor image by PETS2002

Table 2 shows calculated PSNR of created background image the results of existed method and proposed method using $50^{th}$ frame of images in Figure 5. In case of test image (c), the result of the averaging gave better PSNR than the proposed method because the illumination of the test image rarely changes. It should be noticed that the average method provides poor results if the images contain illumination changes or noises.

**Table 2.** The result of proposed method and existed method by PSNR

| Method | Test Image (a) by In-House outdoor | Test Image (b) by PETS2002 | Test Image (c) by PETS2001 |
|---|---|---|---|
| Average method | 12.41 | 19.67 | 24.15 |
| Edge difference | 12.27 | 17.12 | 22.80 |
| Median filter | 12.37 | 20.76 | 22.39 |
| **proposed** | **12.49** | **25.32** | **23.63** |

## 5 Conclusions

The change of illumination in the video sequence is one of the important factors that can cause errors in the background generation. Even with many frames in the calculation, the existing methods still have noises in the generated background due to the accumulated pixel errors. The accumulated errors also affect the separation of the object and background.

In this paper, we proposed a background generation algorithm that can resolve ghost effects and illumination change problems by using generic algorithm. The experimental results show that the proposed algorithm can efficiently generate a good quality of background with small number of frames compared to the existing algorithm. The computational load of the proposed algorithm, thus, is also small. We present the PSNRs of the existing methods and the proposed method to compare the correctness of the generated background. The possible future research includes an object extraction technique and moving object tracking based on the proposed background generation model.

## Acknowledgments

This research was supported by Korean Ministry of Science and Technology under the National Research Laboratory Project, and by Korean Ministry of Education under the BK21 Project, and by Korean Ministry of Information and Communication under HNRC-ITRC program at Chung-Ang University supervised by IITA.

## References

1. Koo, J.H., et al. .: Development of FPGA-based Adaptive Image Enhancement Filter System using Genetic Algorithm. Proc. Congress on Evolutionary Computation, Vol. 2. (2002) 1480-1485
2. Naohiro, A., Akihiro, F.: Detecting Obstructions and Tracking Moving Objects by Image Processing Technique. Electronics and Communications in Japan, Vol. 2. (1999)
3. Wixson, L.: Illumination Assessment for Vision-based Real-time Traffic Monitoring. Proc. Int'l Conf. Pattern Recognition (1996) 56-62
4. Haritaoglu.: W4: Real-Time Surveillance of People and Their Activities. IEEE Trans., Vol. 22. (2000)
5. Yasuyuki M., Ko N., Katsushi I., Msao S.: Illumination Normalization with Time-Dependent Intrinsic Images for Video Surveillance. IEEE Trans. Pattern Analysis and Machine Intelligence, Vol. 26. (2004)
6. Chien, S.Y., Ma, S.Y., Chen, L.G.: Efficient Moving Object Segmentation Algorithm Using Background Registration Technique. IEEE Trans. CIRCUITS and SYSTEMS for Video technology, Vol. 12. (2002)
7. Long, W., Yang, Y.H.: Stationary Background Generation: An alternative to the Difference of two Images. Pattern Recognition, Vol. 23. (1990) 1351-1359
8. Noever, D., Baskaran, S.: Steady-state vs. Generational Genetic Algorithms: A Comparison of Time Complexity and Convergence Properties. Santa Fe Institute Working Papers (1992) 1-33
9. Goldberg, Genetic Algorithms in Search, Optimization, and Machine Learning, Addison-Wesley (1989)

# Fuzzy Anomaly Detection System for IPv6 (FADS6): An Immune-Inspired Algorithm with Hash Function

Yao Li, Zhitang Li, and Li Wang

Network and Computer Center, Huazhong University of Science and Technology, Wuhan, Hubei, P.R. China, 430074
{yaolce, leeying, wtwl}@hust.edu.cn

**Abstract.** This paper presents a novel architecture for an immunological network anomaly detection system in IPv6 environment, Fuzzy Anomaly Detect System for IPv6 (FADS6). In order to perform the anomaly detection based on IPv6, it is necessary to develop more efficient anomaly detection rules generation technology, genetic algorithm is a good choice. A self-adaptive anomaly detection model was developed using fuzzy detection anomaly algorithm with negative selection of biology and proposed a fuzzy anomaly detection rules generation technology for IPv6 using genetic algorithm. In the proposed model, optimized the initial population with hash algorithm, encoded the population with random real values, and detected the anomaly with fuzzy detection rules. This model is flexible, extendible, and adaptable, can meet the needs, preferences of network administrators and supplied for IPv6 environment. Evaluated the model with CERNET2 backbone traffic, it showed that the model has two advantages: algorithm performance and detection effect, and can be applied to protect the next generation Internet.

## 1 Introduction

IPv6 contains numerous features that make it more secure, however, the basic mechanisms for data transporting stay mostly unchanged, IPv6 is not absolute security because there is few security problem derived solely from the IP layer in the network model and IPv6 brings new security issues that did not exist with single IPv4. IPv6 also includes many enhancements, some of which can be exploited by attackers. Attacks, or intrusions, against the IPv6 network will become commonplace events. Recently, researches on building security systems to protect IPv6 network have become increasingly important with the spread of the next generation internet. Many manufacturers and researchers, such as snort[1] and SSL[2], are developing their anomaly detection systems on IPv6. While few of these anomaly detection systems is perfect ,they are just available to decode the IPv6 packets or help counter the threat of the attacks ,and attackers are continually trying to evade detection. Therefore, the time for ignoring IPv6 IDS is past. It is the time to understand it, recognize it and deploy its obvious advantages.

Forrest et al.[3] incorporated the mechanism that detects the "self" or "non-self" in an immune system into a network security system. We purpose a fuzzy anomaly

D.-S. Huang, K. Li, and G.W. Irwin (Eds.): ICIC 2006, LNCS 4113, pp. 553 – 562, 2006.

detection algorithm with negative selection inspired by the artificial immune system. Instead of attempting to describe all that is intrusion in the network try, we describe what is normal use as “self” and define “non-self” as intrusion, it makes the algorithm very suitable for the IPv6 environment, because there are so many new applications in IPv6, and we can’t characterize everyone of them. That’s to say, instead of defining the “black-list” which includes all of the anomaly behaviors, we define the “white-list” which includes all of the normal behaviors. The genetic algorithm (GA) is used to get the best characterizations of the normal behaviors.

There are two main problems in developing an anomaly detection system based on GA for IPv6:

(1) Tremendous IPv6 ad-dresses space. IPv6 has 128-bits address length, which means that the source-destination pair may reach 256-bits. It will be a big problem for the genetic algorithm. So we should improve the efficiency of the genetic algorithm in order to transact all bits in the packets quickly.
(2) Large numbers of un-known attacks. Due to new header format and protocols in IPv6, there are a large number of new attack types. It is impossible for us to characterize all the attacks and define crisp rules for each attack. New type of detection algorithm must be used to detect the anomaly network behaviors.

To overcome these issues, we use hash function to accelerate the genetic algorithm. Then the fuzzy rules are used to detect the unknown attacks in IPv6 environment.

## 2 Genetic Algorithm with Hash Function

Genetic algorithm is inspired by Darwin’s theory of evolution, it is an evolutionary optimization approach which is an alternative to traditional optimization methods. Genetic algorithm is most appropriate for complex non-linear models where location of the global optimum is a difficult task. Genetic algorithms are based on a biological metaphor: They view learning as a competition among a population of evolving candidate problem solutions. A 'fitness' function evaluates each solution to decide whether it will contribute to the next generation of solutions. Then, through operations analogous to gene transfer in sexual reproduction, the algorithm creates a new population of candidate solutions.

The algorithm is started with a set of possible solutions, named as population. Each possible solution within the population is also called chromosome. Each chromosome is assigned with a fitness value based on the fitness function. Solutions from one population are taken and used to construct a new population. This is motivated by a hope that the new population will be fitter than the old one. Solutions, which are selected to construct new solutions, are selected according to their fitness - the fitter they are, the more chances they can have for reproduction. The offspring replaces the old population and a generation is completed. This process is repeated until certain criteria are met. The processing of the genetic algorithm is shown in Figure 1.

A genetic algorithm was used to evolve valid rules that cover the non-self space. This is clearly a multi-objective, multi-model optimization problem.

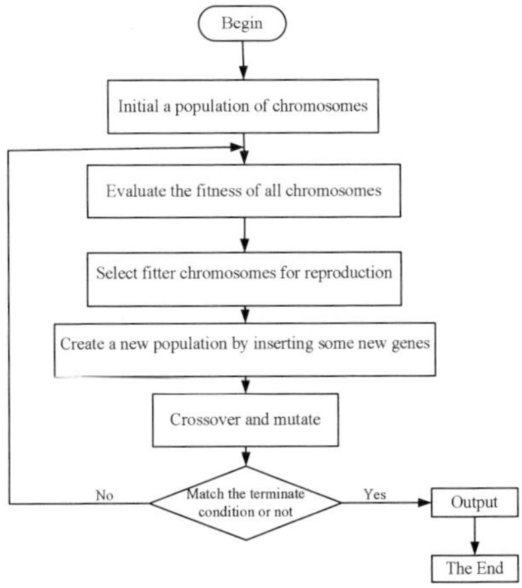


**Fig. 1.** The processing of the genetic algorithm

## 2.1 Chromosomes Encoding

The first step in genetic algorithm is to "translate" the real problem into "biological terms". GA uses a string to represent the population of solution, namely the chromosome. Format of chromosome is called encoding. The genotype is represented as an encoding mode of program. The chromosome is made up of genes. Every gene is a variable of a problem.

The encoding of chromosome is very important for the GA evolution procedure, because the structure of chromosomes encoding influences the solution speed and the space size of solution, and then decide to the GA the efficiency of solution and result. The packet content used as input to the initialization population function must uniquely represent an IP packet. At the same time, it is desirable to limit the size of the population input for performance. Duffield and Grossglauser encountered similar requirements while sampling a subset of forwarded packets in an attempt to measure traffic flows[5]. They masked variant packet content and selecting an appropriate length prefix of the packet to use as input. We use a similar approach to the initialization population. Our choice of invariant fields and prefix length is slightly different, however. Because the application environment of our algorithm is IPv6, the IPv6 header format is slightly simpler but longer compared with IPv4 header. The 40-byte header of IPv6 is shown in Figure 2, fields in green are masked out, including the Version, Priority, Flow label, Payload length, and Hop limit fields.

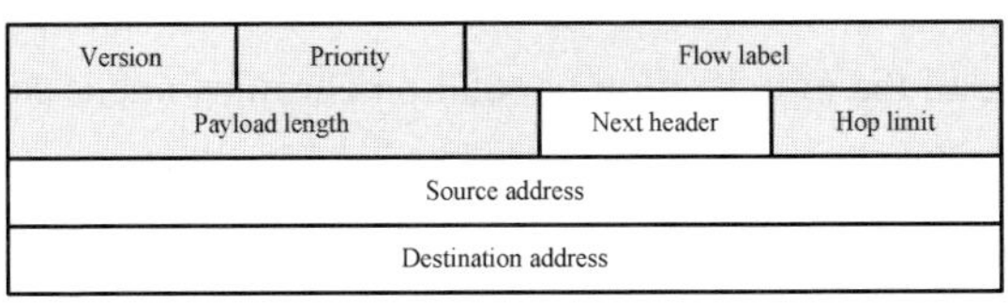


**Fig. 2.** The fields of an IPv6 packet

The globally unique unicast IPv6 addresses are the only type of addresses that can be routed on the Internet. The prefix of the globally unique unicast IPv6 address is '001', that's to say 128-3=125 bits can represent a globally unique unicast IPv6 address adequately. An IPv6 node address and its subnet prefix length can be combined in the following format:

$$Address_{IPv6} = Node-address/Prefix-length \tag{1}$$

On the other hand, we usually detect the anomaly behaviors from the outside network. The destination addresses must be the addresses inside our network, whose prefixes are invariable. The prefix-length for the inside network can be no less than 48, that's to say 128-48=80 bits can represent the destination address adequately. The algorithm of the processing of initialization population encoding is shown as algorithm 1.

**Algorithm 1.** Initialization population encoding.
Input: The source and destination IPv6 address
Output: The initialization population
Begin
1) Initialize the source IPv6 address $S$, the destination IPv6 address $D$, the inside network address space $I$ and the global unicast IPv6 address space $U$.
2) $S = slip(S), D = slip(D)$.
3) IF $D \notin I$ THEN
   $D = \varnothing$, $S = \varnothing$;
   ELSE IF $S \notin U$ THEN
   $D = \varnothing$, $S = \varnothing$;
   ELSE
   $EN = S \cup D$;
4) Return $EN$.

According to the mention above, we can see that the length of the chromosome encoding can be calculated by the equation which is listed as formula (2).

$$l_c = l_n + l_s + l_d. \tag{2}$$

Where $l_c$ represents the length of the chromosome encoding, $l_n$ represents the length of the next header field, $l_s$ and $l_d$ represent the length of the source address and the destination address. In the condition of our research, the $l_n$=8, $l_s$ =125, $l_d$ =80. That's to say, the length of the chromosome encoding $l_c$ =213.

The space of the initialization population chromosome can be represented as formula (3).

$$C = \{c_1, c_2, \cdots, c_i\},\ i = 213 \tag{3}$$

The architecture of the initialization population chromosome is shown as figure 3.

**Definition 1.** The efficiency of the initialization population encoding $f_e$, $f_e = l_c / l$, here $l$ represents the length of the IPv6 address without encoding.

The lower value of $f_e$ means the better efficiency of the encoding. In this case, $f_e$=66.8%.

| C1 | C2 | … | Ci | … | C213 |
|---|---|---|---|---|---|

**Fig. 3.** The architecture of the initialization population chromosome

## 2.2 Initialization Population with Hash Function

When initializing population, it is essential to have a fast IPv6 address lookup process, especially when the frequent user collection is large. To make the initialization population smaller in size, we propose a new scheme for population initialization by using an appropriate hash function to build a single hash table.

Hash Functions take a block of data as input, and produce a hash or message digest as output. Therefore, we can take a block encoding network data as input and produce a hash digest as output. By doing this, we can make the initialization population less in size and improve the performance of the genetic algorithm.

Hashing is the process of running data through a hash function. A hash function is a mapping between a set of input values and a set of integers, known as hash values. A good hash function has the following properties:

(1) The hash value is fully determined by the data being hashed.
(2) The hash function uses all the input data.
(3) The hash function "uniformly" distributes the data across the entire set of possible hash values.
(4) The hash function generates very different hash values for similar strings.

We slipped the destination address into three fields: globe-prefix, local-prefix and interface-ID. The format of the destination address is shown as figure 4.

| 48-bits | 32-bits | 48-bits |
|---|---|---|
| Global prefix | Local prefix | Interface-ID |

**Fig. 4.** Format of IPv6 destination address

Size decrease is one of the key issues in initialization population. In this paper, we initialize the population using compress algorithm based on non-collision hash algorithm and XOR hash algorithm. Hash algorithm allows us to map an element $x$ in a large set into an element $h$ in a small set through the hash function $h = f(x)$ so that we can quickly find the information once we have determined the small set to search for. The XOR hash algorithm introduces XOR operation to obtain a hash key value. The computation of an XOR hash key value structuring the non-collision hash function, which is constructed mainly based on source and destination address field so that the hash function usually can avoid space explosion problem.

XOR fold with the destination IP address, the next header and the interface ID. This hash function can be expressed as formula (4):

$$h(\bullet) = [(d_{ip} << 8) + d_{nh}] \oplus d_{ID} \tag{4}$$

Where $d_{lp}$ represents the local-prefix of the destination address, $d_{nh}$ represents the next header and $d_{ID}$ represents the interface ID of the destination address.

**Algorithm 2.** Initialize population with hash function
Input: Initialization population
Output: chromosome

1) $D = d_{ip}$;
2) For ( i=1 to 8) Do
   $D = D <<, i++$;
3) $D = D \cup d_{nh}$;
4) $D = D \oplus d_{ID}$;
5) $C = S \cup D$;

Return $C$.

By doing this, we can compress the destination address from 128-bit to 48-bits, which is very effective for the population initialization (see figure 5).

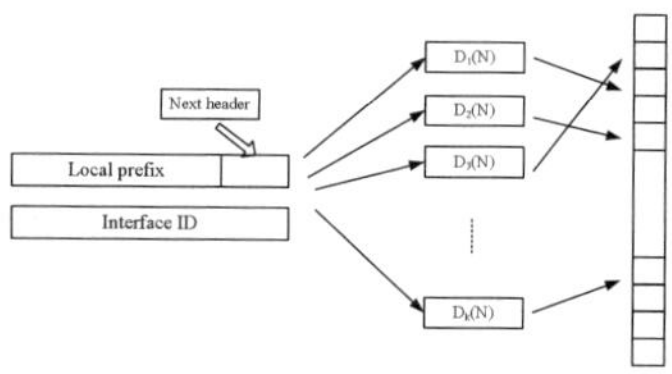


**Fig. 5.** Compression of the IPv6 destination address

## 2.3 Evaluate Fitness

Generally, the genetic algorithm uses fitness value to estimate the purpose function which is represented by a chromosome. In our research, the fitness function of anomaly detection is calculated by the distance between chromosomes (also called individuals).A good measure of distance between individuals is important for genetic algorithm, since it allows the algorithm to replace individuals with closer individuals. We use the Hamming distance because there is a strong relation between each bit in the chromosome with a single fuzzy set of some particular attribute in the search space[6]. The method we used to measure the distance is described as formula 5:

$$dist(c, p) = \frac{1}{2N} \sum_{i=1}^{N} [|\mu_c(x_i) - \mu_p(x_i)| + |\gamma_c(x_i) - \gamma_p(x_i)|] \tag{5}$$

Where c, p represents the IPv6 traffic space elements.We can then calculate the match distance via formula (6) based on the linguistic distance got from formula (5):

$$d_{match}(c, p) = 1 - dist(c, p) \tag{6}$$

Note that the distance measure is not symmetric. The purpose is to give more importance to the area of the parent that is not covered. The justification is as follows: if the child covers a high proportion of the parent, that means that the child is a good generation of it, but if the child covers only a small portion, then it is not so.

It will make computation easy. In general, the lower the fitness value is the lower, the better.

## 3 Fuzzy Rules Detection Algorithm

We extend the algorithm to evolve fuzzy rules instead of crisp rules in order to improve the accuracy of the detection. That is, given a set of self samples, the algorithm will generate fuzzy detection rules in the non-self space that can determine if a new sample is normal or abnormal. The use of fuzzy rules improves the accuracy of the method and produces a measure of deviation from the normal that does not need to partition the non-self space[6].We divide the users' network flow into five type compared with the normal network flow:

(1) Normal $p_0$: All of the network data match with the self-set;

(2) Medium-match $p_1$: A lot of the network data match with the self-set;

(3) Low-match $p_2$: A lot of the network data not match with the self-set, this is the critical status between self and non-self;

(4) Anomaly $p_3$: All of the network data not match with the self-set;

(5) Reset $p_4$: Re-built the self-set.

According to status defined above, a Petri-Net can be set up. A Petri-Net has the same architecture with a continuous time Markov Chain, so a status translation graph of the Petri-Net and the corresponding Markov Chain can be gotten as shown in figure 6 and table 1.

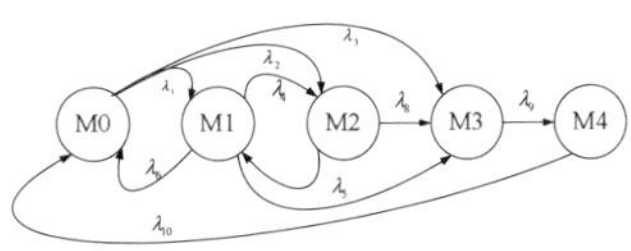


**Fig. 6.** Translation graph of the Petri-Net

**Definition 3.** Translation probability $\lambda = \{\lambda_1, \lambda_2, \cdots, \lambda_{10}\}$, $\lambda_i \in [0,1], 1 \le i \le 10$.

The bigger value of $\lambda_i$ means the higher probability of translation between statuses.

**Table 1.** Markov Chain of the Petri-Net

| | $p_0$ | $p_1$ | $p_2$ | $p_3$ | $p_4$ |
|---|---|---|---|---|---|
| $M_0$ | 1 | 0 | 0 | 0 | 0 |
| $M_1$ | 0 | 1 | 0 | 0 | 0 |
| $M_2$ | 0 | 0 | 1 | 0 | 0 |
| $M_3$ | 0 | 0 | 0 | 1 | 0 |
| $M_4$ | 0 | 0 | 0 | 0 | 1 |

**Definition 4.** The status translation matrix of the Markov Chain $Q=[q_{ij}]$, the status vector $P=(p_0, p_1, p_2, p_3, p_4)$.

$$Q=\begin{bmatrix} -\lambda_1-\lambda_2-\lambda_3 & \lambda_1 & \lambda_2 & \lambda_3 & 0 \\ \lambda_6 & -\lambda_4-\lambda_5-\lambda_6 & \lambda_4 & \lambda_5 & 0 \\ 0 & \lambda_8 & -\lambda_7-\lambda_8 & \lambda_7 & 0 \\ 0 & 0 & 0 & -\lambda_9 & \lambda_9 \\ \lambda_{10} & 0 & 0 & 0 & \lambda_{10} \end{bmatrix}$$

The user's network data flow status can be calculated as the following formula:

$$P\bullet Q=0 \sum p_i =1,0\le i\le 4 \tag{7}$$

So the probability of anomaly can be determined as formula (8):

$$\mu_{non-self}(x)=\frac{\lambda_1\times\lambda_7}{\frac{(1+\lambda_1)(\lambda_1+\lambda_7\times\lambda_8)}{\lambda_1\times\lambda_4+\lambda_2}+\lambda_1(1+2\lambda_7)-\lambda_8(1+\lambda_1)} \tag{8}$$

Where $\mu_{non\_self}(x)$ represents the degree of membership of $x$ to the non-self set; thus, a value close to zero means that $x$ is normal and a value close to 1 indicates that $x$ is abnormal.

## 4 Experiment

Our goal of the design is to implement an anomaly detection system for IPv6 environment. To verify the functionality of the purposed model, we develop several intrusion tools for IPv6. These tools utilized vulnerabilities of IPv6 NDP.

The Neighbor Cache contains information maintained by the Neighbor Unreachability Detection algorithm. A key piece of information is a neighbor's reachability state, which is one of five possible values. For the windows XP system, when received a router advertisement message, it will add a new list in its neighbor cache. When the cache is big enough, the system will be downed. In this way, we develop several IPv6 intrusion tools. Our IPv6 intrusion tools are shown in table 2:

**Table 2.** IPv6 intrusion tools

| Name | Platform | Vulnerability |
|---|---|---|
| Prefix-DOS | Win-XP | Prefix-list |
| RA-DoS-XP | Win-XP | Source link-layer address |
| NS-DoS-XP | Win-XP | Source link-layer address |
| NS-DoS-Linux | Linux | Source link-layer address |
| Vicious-ICMP6-Message | Win-XP, Linux | ICMP6 option |

**Table 3.** The data in experiment

| Data set | Train | Test | |
|---|---|---|---|
| | | Norm | Anomaly |
| IPv6 data set | 9714100 | 5881388 | 13018 |

We use the data of the second week as the test data, which include both normal data and anomaly data. The descriptions of the intrusions are shown in table 4.

**Table 4.** Intrusion description of the test data

| Day | Attack name | Number of data | Number of attack | Type |
|---|---|---|---|---|
| Mon | serverU for IPv6 | 1247366 | 24 | Root acquire |
| Tue | Ra_dos_xp | 1374855 | 2969 | DoS |
| Wed | Ns_dos_Linux | 795287 | 777 | DoS |
| Thu | Prefix-Dos | 1325282 | 1555 | DoS |
| Fri | ICMP big packets | 1151616 | 5238 | Malice code |

**Table 5.** Test result

| Model | Anomaly | false alarms | False alarm rate | Detection rate |
|---|---|---|---|---|
| FADS6 | 13018 | 398 | 2.97% | 97.87% |
| Snort | 13018 | 3943 | 23.2% | 72.2% |

In order to evaluate the efficiency and the performance of the model, we put anomaly system FADS6 on the IPv6 backbone network of CERNET2. CERNET2 is the biggest IPv6 backbone network of China. We use the first week in May 2005 data flow of CERNET2 HuaZhong region network as the training data, and the second week data as the test data which include some intrusion data developed by ourselves.

The self-set is built by the data collected from the detection hosts, we collected 9714,100 packets from the detection host. Encoding the packet according to the method above, eliminating the overlap data, we can use the 1471900 residual data as the self-set. The data used in the experiment is shown in table 3.

We compare the detection rate and false alarm rate of the FADS6 with the open source intrusion system – snort. The test result shown in table 5 and figure 7.

From the consequence, we can see that the algorithm can detect most of the intrusion, which means the performance of the algorithm is very good.

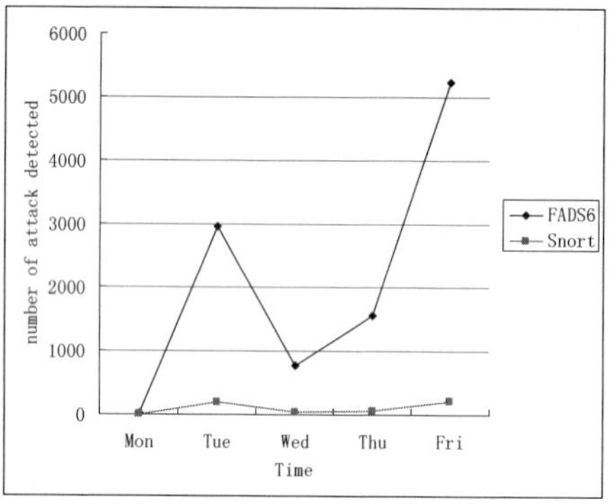


**Fig. 7.** Number of attack detected

## 5 Conclusion

We have developed the prototype of the dynamic immune anomaly detection system for IPv6: built the dynamic detection engine with evolutionary search, evolved the detection rule using the improved GA with hash function. The experiment proved that the proposed method is flexible, extendible, and adaptable, can be supplied for IPv6 environment.

## References

1. Marty, R.: Snort -The Open Source NIDS. http://www.snort.org/ (2004)
2. Michael H. Warfield: Security Implications of IPv6: Internet Security Systems, (2003)
3. Forrest, S.: Using Genetic Algorithms to Explore Pattern Recognition in The Immune System: Evolutionary Computation, 1(3) (1993) 191-211
4. Luger, G. F.: Artificial Intelligence, Structures and Strategies for Complex Problem Solving (Fourth Edition). Harlow, England, Addison-Wesley, 471-474
5. Duffield, N. G., Grossglauser, M.: Trajectory Sampling for Direct Traffic Observation: In Proc. ACM SIGCOMM '00, (2000) 271-282
6. González, F.: A Study of Artificial Immune Systems Applied to Anomaly Detection. Ph.D. Dissertation, The University of Memphis, Egypt(2003)

# Mechanism Design and Analysis of Genetic Operations in Solving Traveling Salesman Problems

Hongwei Ge[1], Yanchun Liang[1,2], Maurizio Marchese[2], and Lu Wang[1]

[1] College of Computer Science, Jilin University, Key Laboratory of Symbol Computation and Knowledge Engineering of the Ministry of Education, Changchun 130012, China
[2] Department of Information and Communication Technology, University of Trento, Via Sommarive 14, 38050, Povo (TN) Italy
ycliang@jlu.edu.cn

**Abstract.** In this paper, some novel improved genetic operations are presented, several combinations of genetic operations are examined and the functions of these operations at different evolutionary stages are analyzed by numerical experiments. The essentiality of the ordering of the gene section, the significance of the evolutionary inversion operation and the importance of the selection model are discussed. Some results provide useful information for the implementation of the genetic operations for solving the traveling salesman problem.

## 1 Introduction

The Traveling Salesperson Problem (TSP) is a well-known non-polynomial time or NP-hard combinatorial optimization problem that has many potential applications and has been studied thoroughly. Early efforts in combinatorial optimization in the field of evolutionary computation focused on the TSP, which is a generalization and simplified form of various complicated problems that have appeared in many fields. Hence, a successful solution for the TSP has not only theoretical significance in computational theory but also important practical value. The first attempt to use simulated evolutionary optimization to address the TSP began in the 1980s. Since then the study on solving the TSP by simulating natural evolutionary processes has been very active, especially, in the recent decade. Among those studies most are based on the genetic algorithm [1-3] and a few on the evolutionary programming [4, 5] and the evolution strategy [6]. In this paper we present some improved genetic operations, examine some combinations of genetic operations, and analyze the functions of these operations.

## 2 Genetic Algorithms for Solving the TSP

The TSP is conceptually simple: a traveling salesperson must visit every city of a specific set of cites exactly once and then return to the starting point. Mathematically, the TSP is one of a search of a permutation $\pi = \{c_1, c_2, \cdots, c_n\}$ of the integer subset $X = \{1,2,\cdots,n\}$, where an element of $X$ represents a serial number of one of $n$ cities, such that

$$T_d = \sum_{i=1}^{n-1} d(c_i, c_{i+1}) + d(c_1, c_n) \tag{1}$$

D.-S. Huang, K. Li, and G.W. Irwin (Eds.): ICIC 2006, LNCS 4113, pp. 563–573, 2006.

reaches a minimum, where $d(c_i, c_{i+1})$ represents the distance from city $c_i$ to city $c_{i+1}$. Note that the size of the search space for the symmetric TSP is $(n-1)!/2$, where $d(c_i, c_{i+1}) = d(c_{i+1}, c_i)$, a number that grows faster than any finite power of $n$.

### 2.1 Coding Pattern and Fitness Function

It is natural to adopt coding methods according to the order of the cities to be visited when using a GA to solve TSPs. When using the city-order coding method, the legal constraint that a city number cannot appear more than once, is implied on initialization of a population of feasible solutions. In this section the linear scaling technique for calculating the fitness function is used.

$$f = \alpha M \sqrt{n} / T_d \tag{2}$$

Where $\alpha$ is a predetermined constant, $n$ the number of cities, $M$ the side-length the smallest square covering all cities and $T_d$ the length of the tour calculated using (1).

### 2.2 Crossover Operations

The crossover is widely acknowledged as critical to the successful operation of a GA and is responsible for exploring the solution space and exploiting or retaining favourable characteristics to yield feasible solutions of higher fitness values. In the simulation experiments seven crossover operators were used in different combinations of genetic operations to compute solutions of the TSP:

1) Partially matched crossover (PMX)[7].
2) Order Crossover (OX)[8].
3) Order Crossover-like1 (OX-1)[9].
4) Order Crossover-like2 (OX-2).

This last operator is an improved version of the OX operator proposed in this paper. Here the gene-segment is replaced with several random positions, as follows.

The two parent strings $A$ and $B$ are:

$$A = 1\ \underline{2}\ 3\ \underline{4}\ 5\ 6\ 7\ 8\ 9 \text{ and } B = 9\ \underline{8}\ 7\ \underline{6}\ 5\ 4\ 3\ 2\ 1.$$

It is assumed that the second and the fourth positions are randomly selected. The corresponding cities concerning these positions are those numbered 2, 4, 8, 6, whose positions are retained in the offspring, and the other cities in the corresponding positions of the two parent strings are swapped. Hence on implementing crossover operator approach one obtains the offspring

$$A' = 9\ 2\ 7\ 4\ 5\ 6\ 3\ 8\ 1 \text{ and } B' = 1\ 8\ 3\ 6\ 5\ 4\ 7\ 2\ 9.$$

5) Mapping approach of single-point crossover.

This is an improved approach to the PMX. Only one crossover point is used instead of two, and is described as follows: two parent strings are denoted $A$ and $B$, and a crossover point is selected randomly as

$$A = 9\ 1\ 4\ 5\ 6 \mid 7\ 8\ 3\ 2 \text{ and } B = 6\ 8\ 1\ 2\ 3 \mid 9\ 5\ 4\ 7.$$

A simple single-point crossover operation, applied to the above two strings yields

$$A' = 9\ 1\ 4\ 5\ 6 \mid 9\ 5\ 4\ 7 \text{ and } B' = 6\ 8\ 1\ 2\ 3 \mid 7\ 8\ 3\ 2.$$

Examine the repeat for the number in front of the crossover point and implement the crossover according to the mapping relation of the position in the rearward of the crossover point. For string $A'$, we have that $9 \to 7$, $5 \to 8$, $4 \to 3$ and $7 \to 2$. From the first and last replacements we have the final result $9 \to 2$. Hence, one obtains

$$A'' = 2\ 1\ 3\ 8\ 6\ 9\ 5\ 4\ 7 \text{ and } B'' = 6\ 5\ 1\ 9\ 4\ 7\ 8\ 3\ 2.$$

6) Order crossover approach of a single point [10].
7) Position information [10].

## 2.3 Mutation Operations

Mutation refers to the process of increasing diversity in the population by introducing random variations in the individuals of the population. Four kinds of mutation operations are employed in different genetic operation combinations, of which two improved crossover operations are proposed in this paper. The four mutation operations are as follows:

1) Reciprocal exchange mutation. Select two points in the string and swap their values.
2) Insertion mutation. Select a number in the string randomly and insert the number into the point between two randomly selected insertion points.
3) Translocation mutation. It is an improved approach proposed in this paper. A decision is made to mutate each number in the string using a Bernoulli approach. The numbers without passing Bernoulli probabilities are kept in their original positions and the others are translocated in turn. For example, for string $A = 1\ 2\ \underline{3}\ 4\ 5\ \underline{6}\ \underline{7}\ 8\ 9$, if the numbers 3, 6 and 7 pass Bernoulli probabilities, then they are translocated in turn and the numbers in the other positions are unchanged: the mutated gene is: $A' = 1\ 2\ 7\ 4\ 5\ 3\ 6\ 8\ 9$.
4) Object-oriented mutation. It is also a novel approach proposed in this paper. A heuristic mutation operator based on a greedy algorithm is proposed, where a local minimization is performed at each step. If the distance of some two adjoining numbers is larger than that of any other adjoining numbers in the string, then the adjoining for the two numbers is irrational. The steps of the algorithm are as follows:

Step 1. Find two adjoining numbers with the largest distance between them and randomly select one: set indicator $i = 0$.
Step 2. Exchange the selected number with another different number selected randomly from the string. If the fitness of the given string does not increase, the operation is implemented again: $i{+}{+}$.
Step 3. If the fitness increases then stop, else if $i < 2$, go to Step 4, else go to Step 5.
Step 4. Select the other number from the two adjoining numbers to repeat Step 2.
Step 5. Implement reciprocal exchange mutation.

## 2.4 Evolutionary Inversion Operator

The evolutionary inversion operator involves selecting two points randomly from the string, and reversing the sub-string between these points. Numerical simulations show that whether or not to implement an evolutionary inversion operator between two numbers in a given string should be determined from a pre-computed judgment. Let the string $A$ be

$$A = c_1, c_2, \cdots, c_i, c_{i+1}, \cdots, c_j, c_{j+1}, \cdots, c_n \tag{3}$$

If $$d(c_i, c_j) + d(c_{i+1}, c_{j+1}) < d(c_i, c_{i+1}) + d(c_j, c_{j+1}) \tag{4}$$

then the inversion section of $A$ is the set of values $\{c_{i+1,} \cdots, c_j\}$. The evolutionary inversion operator is then implemented to yield

$$A = (c_1, c_2, \cdots, c_i \mid c_j, c_{j-1}, \cdots c_{i+1} \mid c_{j+1}, \cdots, c_n) \tag{5}$$

For the implementation of the above mentioned evolutionary inversion judgment, we should first determine the length of inversion judgment according to the requirement and the different genetic operation combinations, then select a sub-string with length $l$ randomly in the parental string and implement the judgment for each number in the sub-string with all others using inequality Eq.(4). The evolutionary inversion adopted here is a continuous inversion operation with increasing fitness, and is implemented continuously until there is no such an operation.

## 3 Experimental Analysis of Genetic Operations

In order to examine and analyze the effect of different operations in computing the TSP, experiments were implemented using certain genetic operations and their combinations. To describe briefly, the names of some operations are abbreviated as follows: mapping approach of single-point crossover (MSPX), order crossover approach of a single point (OSPX), position information (PIX), reciprocal exchange mutation (REM), insertion mutation (IM), translocation mutation (TM), and object-oriented mutation (OOM). Besides, PMX-1 represents the PMX operation without the same numbers required in gene-sequence, and PMX-2 represents the PMX operation no restrictions on numbers in the gene-sequence. $A + B$ represents that operators $A$ and $B$ are used randomly in the evolutional process, and $A \| B$ represents that operator $A$ is used in the early iterations and operator $B$ is used in the later iterations. The algorithms using combinations of genetic operations are shown in Table 1. In all the algorithms, the fitness proportional model and the condition of worst death are adopted.

**Table 1.** Algorithms using different combinations of genetic operations

| GA0 | GA1 | GA2 | GA3 | GA4 | GA5 | GA6 | GA7 | GA8 | GA9 | GA10 | GA11 | GA12 |
|---|---|---|---|---|---|---|---|---|---|---|---|---|
| OX-1 | OX-1 | OX-1 | OX-1 | OX-1 | OX | OX-2 | PMX-1 | PMX-2 | PMX‖OX | MSPX | OSPX | PIX |
| REM | IM | REM+IM | TM | OOM | REM | REM | IM | IM | IM | REM | REM | REM |

### 3.1 Analysis of Crossover and Mutation on Optimization Results

The above algorithms are used in computational experiments and the results are in Table 2. The related parameters employed in the algorithms are as follows: the population size is 100 individuals, the crossover and mutation probabilities are 0.95 and 0.003 respectively, the inversion length $l$ is 1/3 the length of the original string, the permitted renewable times of population is taken as 3000 (units) and the length of a tour is the relative length defined as

$$T = 10^4 / f \tag{6}$$

Where $f$ is the fitness function given by (2), the constant $\alpha$ in (2) is 76.5. For more comprehensive study, we have constructed new instances using randomly-generated two-dimensional point sets. Numerical experiments are performed on a PC with Pentium IV 1.4 GHz processor and 256MB memory.

The data listed in Table 2 are the average values obtained from ten measurements. Each algorithm uses different search techniques for different numbers of cities: 200, 400, 600 and 800. In general, GA4 and GA11 have relatively superior qualities of solution and execution times to the others. From the summation of the relative lengths and elapsed times it can be seen that GA11 and GA12 are the best and worst algorithms respectively. Figs. 1-4 show the best tours for the different sizes and algorithms.

**Table 2.** Comparisons of simulation times and relative lengths using different genetic operator combinations

| Scale | 200 | | 400 | | 600 | | 800 | | Summation | |
|---|---|---|---|---|---|---|---|---|---|---|
| Alg | $T$ | Time | $T$ | Time | $T$ | Time | $T$ | Time | $T$ | Time |
| GA0 | 99.80 | 21.12 | 99.82 | 25.57 | 104.41 | 37.58 | 111.03 | 59.09 | 415.06 | 143.36 |
| GA1 | 99.80 | 23.37 | 99.68 | 25.14 | 104.41 | 37.49 | 110.87 | 59.23 | 414.76 | 145.23 |
| GA2 | 99.80 | 22.14 | 99.64 | 25.56 | 104.37 | 37.44 | 110.65 | 59.01 | 414.46 | 144.15 |
| GA3 | 99.92 | 26.59 | 101.22 | 25.54 | 105.89 | 37.55 | 110.79 | 59.23 | 417.82 | 148.91 |
| GA4 | 98.90 | 23.42 | 99.68 | 26.47 | 103.07 | 38.21 | 110.69 | 59.52 | 412.34 | 147.62 |
| GA5 | 99.80 | 21.01 | 99.92 | 25.52 | 104.35 | 37.59 | 111.06 | 58.57 | 415.13 | 142.69 |
| GA6 | 100.33 | 23.44 | 100.47 | 26.03 | 105.78 | 37.23 | 111.56 | 58.49 | 418.14 | 145.19 |
| GA7 | 101.78 | 19.57 | 102.38 | 30.10 | 104.42 | 38.42 | 113.53 | 73.37 | 422.11 | 161.46 |
| GA8 | 99.76 | 26.51 | 102.81 | 25.07 | 105.54 | 30.29 | 113.47 | 69.36 | 421.58 | 151.23 |
| GA9 | 99.57 | 26.39 | 99.97 | 29.35 | 103.09 | 36.27 | 111.01 | 71.38 | 413.64 | 163.39 |
| GA10 | 100.63 | 49.50 | 106.19 | 25.26 | 105.27 | 31.35 | 112.65 | 73.59 | 424.74 | 179.70 |
| GA11 | 100.01 | 22.47 | 99.57 | 25.16 | 102.36 | 28.10 | 110.30 | 50.50 | 412.24 | 126.23 |
| GA12 | 106.12 | 87.57 | 107.01 | 52.38 | 109.62 | 161.37 | 123.33 | 201.14 | 446.08 | 502.46 |

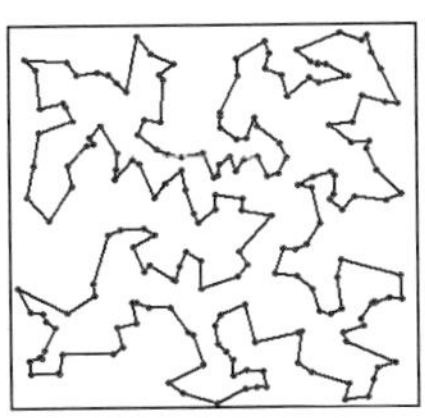

**Fig. 1.** The best tour for 200 cities

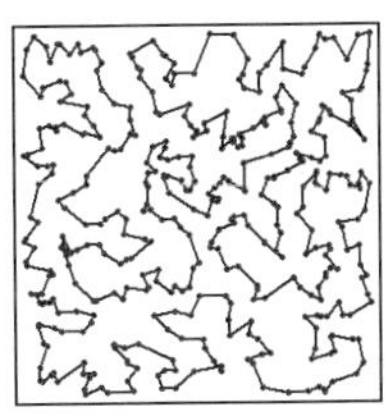

**Fig. 2.** The best tour for 400 cities

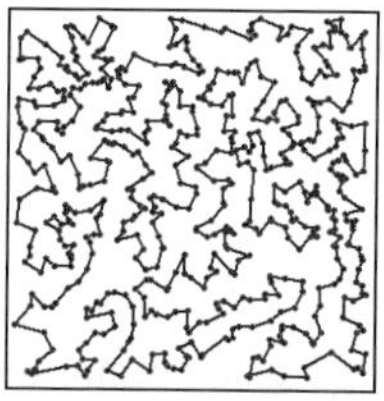

**Fig. 3.** The best tour for 600 cities

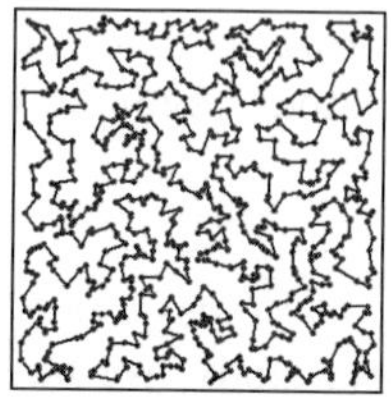

**Fig. 4.** The best tour for 800 cities

From the results in Table 2, the following conclusions may be made:

1) It can be seen that there are few differences between the best results obtained using GA0, GA1 and GA2. This suggests that the mutation operator plays a relative minor role in the search process. In fact, the essentially identical results are due to the small mutation probability, which makes the mutation occur only a few times during the search process. However, it is noticeable that the results of GA2 are better than those of GA0 and GA1, and indicates that using reciprocal exchange mutation and insertion mutation randomly promotes a diversity of the search over the space of possible solutions.
2) The best solutions of GA3 are worse than those of GA0, GA1 and GA2. This is due to the limited use of mutation in the search process. For each position in the string we judge whether it should be mutated by the probability of 0.003 on this condition that the string has passed Bernoulli probabilities. Hence the chance of mutation is greatly reduced, and diversification is minimal resulting in only a small part of the search space being explored.
3) The fitness values of GA4 are better than those of the first four algorithms because of the effect of object-oriented mutation operator presented in this section, but the time of GA4 is greater than those of GA0, GA1 and GA2.
4) The results of GA5 and those of GA0 are almost the same. The order crossover in GA5 retains the position of the gene-sequence while the crossover in GA0 relocates the sequence to the front of the string. Here there is a difference in position of the parent tail forwarded to the offspring. But since there is only one place in the gene sequence, or sequence of cities where the ordering of the cities is rearranged, it does not alter the tour length. Hence the relative lengths are similar.
5) The crossover of GA6 uses several random cities instead of a random point selected to specify the location of the tail segment, as used in GA0 and GA5. However this random selection of cities does not preserve tour order and hence, tours of greater length may result.
6) Both GA0 and GA7 are based on two-point crossover; however, in general, the best solutions in GA0 are superior to those in GA7. If one neglects the differences caused by the mutation, one finds that the algorithms differ in the method of constraint satisfaction. In order to satisfy the constraints, the crossover in GA0 adopts a way of removing the repeated cities outside the transferred gene-sequence, whereas the crossover in GA7 uses a mapping approach to change the city position outside the region of the transferred gene-sequence. For a superior TSP tour, if one retains the city order and remove some cities then the tour may still be of smaller length. However, if cities are removed and replaced with others, tours of greater length may result. Hence, the

crossover method in GA0 is more suitable for solving the TSP than that of GA7, and the fitness values reflecting the tour lengths from GA0 support this conclusion.
7) The crossover methods selected in GA7, GA8, and GA10 use the method of mapping change to satisfy the constraints. These kinds of methods have an adverse effect on maintaining gene structure when crossing over to produce offspring and the results from these algorithms are not better. The difference between GA7 and GA8 is solely that GA7 specifies that there should not be the same city numbers in the tail gene-sequences of two parental strings. If the gene-sequences are too long, then repeated city numbers tends to occur; here the tail sequences in GA7 are typically shorter than that in GA8. A good crossover operator should have the following properties: In order to promote the generation of high fitness individuals at early stages of evolution, the diversity of searching solution space should be greater and the length of the gene section to be ordered should be smaller. In order to retain the structural properties of high fitness individuals at later stages of evolution, the search diversity should be relatively constrained and the length of the gene section to be ordered should be relatively greater. GA7 and GA8 have their respective advantages at the different stage of evolution.
8) GA9 uses the PMX approach in initial evolution and the OX approach at a later stage. The results of GA9 are superior to those of GA 8 and GA5. The ordering ability of PMX is weaker than that of OX but the destructiveness is stronger. GA 9 uses PMX to simulate the process of initial evolution in the early iterations by extending the distribution of offspring in the search space. When fitter genes are obtained, GA 8 using OX has greater potential of retaining their structure and passing this on to future generations. The results of GA 9 support the observations concerning favourable properties of the crossover operator in 7) again.
9) The unique difference between GA0 and GA11 is that two-point crossover and one-point crossover are used respectively. GA11 employs a special two-point crossover operation, where the second point of crossover is not selected randomly but is fixed in the final position. Therefore, the methodology is identical in GA0 and GA11. Their difference is in the average length of the tail gene-sequence. The expectation of the length of the tail sequence in GA0 is one-third of the length of the whole string, while that in GA11 is one half. Relatively speaking, GA11 has greater structural preserving qualities. On one hand the superior gene section is apt to survive, on the other hand the inferior gene section is difficult to evolve.
10) The search ability and efficiency of GA12 are worse than those of the other algorithms. This is because the tail gene-sequence is not retained from one generation to the next in GA12 and much inherited information is lost. It can be seen that in general a suitable selection of the length of the tail gene-sequence, i.e. the ordering of a gene section, is essential.

### 3.2 Effect of Selection Model on Optimization Results

In order to examine the effect of the selection operator using a GA for optimization of the TSP, the fitness proportional model was exchanged for the tournament selection model. The new algorithm is denoted GA0*. The measured process and parameter selection are the same as those used in GA0. The data listed in Table 3 are the average values obtained from ten measurements. The execution time is not listed in these tables as it is similar for both GA0 and GA0*, as both algorithms perform an equal number of iterations.

**Table 3.** Comparisons of effect of selection model on optimization results (600 cities)

| Iterations (n) | 400 | 800 | 1600 | 2500 |
|---|---|---|---|---|
| Algorithm | *T* | *T* | *T* | *T* |
| GA0 | 123.54 | 112.73 | 107.96 | 104.41 |
| GA0* | 120.82 | 110.06 | 108.57 | 106.03 |

From Table 3 it can be seen that the convergence speed of GA0* is faster than GA0's, while the final fitness value of GA0* is worse than that of GA0.

For the case that the initial population is randomly generated, the probability that the best individual exists in the initial population is

$$p_o^0 = 1-(1-m/w)^N \tag{7}$$

Where $w$ is the size of the solution space, $m$ the number of the best individual in the solution space, and $N$ a given population scale. The number of new individuals generated at the t$^{th}$ iteration, when we consider the actions of the crossover and mutation operators, is

$$n = N(p_c + p_m)p_r p_t \tag{8}$$

Where $p_c$ is the crossover probability, $p_m$ the mutation probability, $p_r$ the probability that the individuals generated at the t$^{th}$ iteration are not duplications of each other, $p_t$ the probability that the individuals generated at the t$^{th}$ iteration are not duplicated with individuals generated in all previous generations. The probability that the best individual can be generated at the t$^{th}$ iteration is

$$p_o^t = [1-(1-m/w)^{N(p_c+p_m)p_r p_t}]\cdot\lambda_t \tag{9}$$

Where $\lambda_t$ is the ratio that the best individual is easier to be generated at the t$^{th}$ iteration than in the $(t-1)^{th}$ iteration because of the effect of the selection models. The term $N(p_c + p_m)p_r p_t$ is not only related to the given parameters, but also to the intricate mechanism of crossover and mutation operators. This term is the same for both GA0* and GA0. That is, the selection model determines whether the best individual can be generated as early as possible. The tournament model has larger value of $\lambda_t$ than the proportional model, but it does not ensure the convergence property of the algorithm. However, the selection model of GA0 does ensure convergence. So although GA0* has a relatively fast speed of convergence, it can easily get into local optimization solutions and accordingly it can not find a very good solution.

### 3.3 Effect of Evolutionary Inversion Operation on Best Results

The evolutionary inversion operation is used to improve a given string such that it reaches its local extreme value. To examine the local search function of the GA using the evolutionary inversion operation, the length of the gene sequence to be inverted in GA0 is increased from 1/3 of the string length to the entire string length; the new algorithm is named GA0'. In this way any two city numbers in a string are eligible to be inverted. For GA0' the measured process and parameter selection are the same as those adopted in GA0. The relative length T corresponding to the best tour length for GA0', for $n$=800, is 108.42; this is better than 111.03 using GA0. However, the execution time of GA0' is 127.72, which is about twice times that obtained using GA0 of 59.09 (s). It can be seen that the evolutionary inversion operation is more optimal but more time consuming. Its local search ability enhances diversification, but for the same number of population renewal steps, if the inversion length is extended, greater optimality may be acquired. To increase the speed of computation the number of population renewal steps is reduced from 3000 using GA0, to 1400 using GA0'. The computation was rerun and the results obtained are shown in Table 4.

**Table 4.** Comparison of effect of evolutionary inversion operation on best results

| Scale | 200 | | 400 | | 600 | | 800 | |
|---|---|---|---|---|---|---|---|---|
| Algorithm | $T$ | Time(s) | $T$ | Time(s) | $T$ | Time(s) | $T$ | Time(s) |
| GA0 | 99.80 | 21.12 | 99.82 | 25.57 | 104.41 | 37.58 | 111.03 | 59.09 |
| GA0' | 99.76 | 19.53 | 99.68 | 23.19 | 104.35 | 33.09 | 110.79 | 56.30 |
| GA12 | 106.12 | 87.57 | 107.01 | 52.38 | 109.62 | 161.37 | 123.33 | 201.14 |
| GA12' | 104.85 | 61.42 | 106.64 | 43.52 | 107.38 | 98.77 | 118.06 | 135.18 |

From the results of Table 4, it can be seen that in general the tour lengths and the execution time of GA0' are shorter than those of GA0. The same experiments were also performed for the most worst of the 13 algorithms, that is, GA12. The corresponding modified algorithm denoted GA12' was compared to GA12 and the results obtained are listed in Table 4. It can be seen from the tour lengths and the execution times, that the modified algorithm GA12' is better than the original GA12. It shows that the evolutionary inversion is effective on speeding up the convergence of the search process. The effect of the evolutionary inversion on the entire running time can be reduced to a great extent by decreasing the renewal steps of population. Since the evolutionary inversion operation needs long running time, a suitable string length for the inversion operation may be selected depending on the total number of cities so as to refine the search quality and algorithmic efficiency.

In the experiments it is found that the fluctuation among the best solutions of tours measured each time is large, whereas the fluctuation among the running time is small. These phenomena show that the evolutionary inversion operation plays a part in search process, but some feasible solutions may stick at local optima. In order to change this trend we increase the mutation probability from 0.003 to 0.3, let the renewal steps of population be still 1400, and repeat the above experiment for $n = 600$. We denote the algorithm as GA12". The best relative tours and variance obtained using GA12' and GA12" are shown in Table 5.

**Table 5.** Comparison of effect of evolutionary inversion operation on best results

| | 1 | 2 | 3 | 4 | 5 | 6 | 7 | 8 | 9 | 10 | $\sigma^2$ |
|---|---|---|---|---|---|---|---|---|---|---|---|
| GA12' | 108.08 | 107.17 | 107.15 | 108.29 | 108.20 | 107.09 | 107.81 | 107.69 | 108.31 | 106.71 | 0.38 |
| GA12" | 107.63 | 107.45 | 107.37 | 107.82 | 106.90 | 107.15 | 107.55 | 107.43 | 107.19 | 107.66 | 0.08 |

In Table 5 the mean and variance

$$\bar{x} = \frac{1}{n}\sum_{i=1}^{n} x_i \text{ , } \sigma^2 = \frac{1}{n}\sum_{i=1}^{n}(x_i - \bar{x})^2 \tag{10}$$

are calculated to compare the methods and are used to arrive at conclusions about their relative performance: here $x_i$ is the observed measurement and $n$ the size of the data set.

In the 10 respective measurements using GA12' and GA12", the variance of GA12" is about 21% that of GA12'. The obvious improvement of GA12" over GA12' shows the effect of increasing the mutation probability.

## 4 Conclusions

Some simulation experiments are performed using the improved genetic operations and some combinations of genetic operations in order to analyze the functions of these operations. Genetic operations have a direct effect to optimization result. The same operation is not always favorable to individual evolution at different stages. It has a favorable effect on the genetic evolution to use different operators in different evolutional stages or to use different operators randomly in the same evolutional stage. Different matching range, i.e. different average length of gene section to be ordered, has also a direct impact on the best results of the TSP. A suitable selection on the length of the matching range is essential in genetic algorithms for solving the TSP. The relationship between selection of matching range and different genetic operators is a further question. The evolutionary inversion operation is significant in genetic algorithms for solving the TSP. A suitable selection of the length of the inversion judgment enables the search quality and efficiency to be improved simultaneously.

## Acknowledgment

The authors are grateful to the support of the National Natural Science Foundation of China (60433020), the science-technology development project for international collaboration of Jilin Province of China (20050705-2), the doctoral funds of the National Education Ministry of China (20030183060), and "985" Project of Jilin University. The second and the third authors would like to thank the support of the EuMI project of European Commission.

## References

1. Choi, I.C., Kim, S.I., Kim, H.S.: A Genetic Algorithm with a Mixed Region Search for the Asymmetric Traveling Salesman Problem. Computers & Operations Research, 30 (5) (2003) 773-786
2. Yoon, H.S., Moon, B.R.: An Empirical Study on the Synergy of Multiple Crossover Operators. IEEE Transactions on Evolutionary Computation, 6 (2) (2002) 212-223
3. Tang, L.X., Liu, J.Y., Rong, A.Y., Yang, Z.H.: Modelling and a Genetic Algorithm Solution for the Slab Stack Shuffling Problem When Implementing Steel Rolling Schedules. International Journal of Production Research, 40 (7) (2002) 1583-1595

4. Fogel, D.B.: Applying Evolutionary Programming to Selected Traveling Salesman Problems. Cybernetics and Systems, 24 (1) (1993)27-36
5. Chellapilla, K., Fogel, D.B.: Exploring Self-adaptive Methods to Improve the Efficiency of Generating Approximate Solutions to Traveling Salesman Problems using Evolutionary Programming. Lecture Notes in Computer Science, 1213 (1997) 361
6. Nurnberg, H.T., Beyer, H.G.: Dynamics of Evolution Strategies in the Optimization of Traveling Salesman Problems. Lecture Notes in Computer Science, 1213 (1997) 349
7. Goldberg, D.E., Lingle, R.: Alleles, Loci and Traveling Salesman Problem. In: Proc. of the Int. Conf. on Genetic Algorithms and Their Applications, Carnegie-Mellon University, (1985) 154-159
8. Davis, L.: Job Shop Scheduling with Genetic Algorithms. In: Proc. of the Int. Conf. on Genetic Algorithms and Their Applications, Carnegie-Mellon University, (1985) 136-140
9. Chen, G. L., Wang, X.F., Wang, D.S.: Genetic Algorithms and Applications. Press of Post and Telecommunications, Beijing, (1996) 137-147
10. Liang, Y.C., Ge, H.W., Zhou, C.G., Lee, H.P., Lin, W.Z., Lim, S.P., Lee, K.H.: Solving Traveling Salesman Problems by Genetic Algorithms. Progress in Natural Science, 13 (2) (2003) 135-141

# MURMOEA: A Pareto Optimality Based Multiobjective Evolutionary Algorithm for Multi-UAV Reconnaissance Problem

Jing Tian[1], Lincheng Shen[1], and Yanxing Zheng[2]

[1] Mechatronics and Automation School, National University of Defense Technology, Changsha, P.R. China
jingtian@nudt.edu.cn
[2] Beijing Institute of System Engineering, Beijing, P.R. China
yxzheng@nudt.edu.cn

**Abstract.** The objective of multiple Unmanned Aerial Vehicles(UAVs) reconnaissance is to employ different kinds of UAVs conducting reconnaissance on a set of targets within predefined time windows at minimum cost, without violating the real-world constraints. This paper presents a mathematical formulation for the problem, which is a multi-objective optimization problem. A Pareto optimality based multi-objective evolutionary algorithm, MURMOEA, is put forward to solve the problem. In MURMOEA, an integer string is used to represent the chromosome. Pareto dominance based tournament selection with elitism strategy is introduced, which ensures that MURMOEA converges toward the Pareto set and prevents bias to any object. A novel sequence crossover operator is designed to ensure the feasibilities of the children, and a problem specific forward insert mutation operator is designed to ensure the validity of the mutated individuals. Finally the simulation results show the efficiency of our algorithm.

## 1 Introduction

Unmanned Aerial vehicles (UAVs) provide effective alternatives to manned vehicles for dull, dirty, dangerous, or costly missions. Using a fleet of UAVs equipped with special sensors to conduct air reconnaissance is one of the excellent applications of UAVs, and remains key activities in military operations.

Some literatures have been proposed for the multiple UAVs reconnaissance problem. Ryan[1] formulated the problem as a multiple travelling salesman problem(TSP) with time window constraints and solved by tabu search algorithm. Hutchison[2] proposed a method which divided the operations area into identical sectors and allocated the targets in one sectors to a given UAV. Then TSP defined to find the shortest path connecting each target for an UAV is solved using simulated annealing algorithm. Ousingsawat[3] divided the problem to two issues, minimum-time trajectory problem and task assignment problem. A* search is used to find the shortest path between two points, then the task assignment problem is expressed as a mixed integer linear program solved using the MATLAB optimization toolbox.

D.-S. Huang, K. Li, and G.W. Irwin (Eds.): ICIC 2006, LNCS 4113, pp. 574–585, 2006.

In fact, multi-UAV reconnaissance is a multi-objective optimization problem(MOP). On the one hand, the total travel distance and total consumed time of UAVs should be minimized. On the other hand, the number of UAVs employed in conducting reconnaissance should also be minimized. This paper presents a mathematical model for multi-objective Multi-UAV reconnaissance problem(MOMURP). Then a novel Pareto optimality based multiobjective evolutionary algorithm MURMOEA is proposed to solve MOMURP.

The rest of the paper is organized as follows. Section 2 presents the mathematical model of MOMURP. The proposed MURMOEA is described in detail in section 3. Section 4 shows the simulation results and section 5 concludes the paper.

## 2 Multi-UAV Reconnaissance Problem Formulation

A typical Multi-UAV Reconnaissance Problem can be described as that, $N_V$ kinds of UAVs with different capabilities are asked to conduct reconnaissance on $N_T$ targets with different sites. Mission plans should be quickly made for UAVs that meet the reconnaissance demands of all the targets and can deal with the real-world constraints such as imagery requirements(reconnaissance resolution), time windows, and capabilities of the UAVs(i.e. imagery resolution, maximum permitted travel time etc.).

The reconnaissance targets set is denoted by $T_0 = \{1, 2, ..., N_T\}$, where $N_T$ is the number of targets. $R_i$ is the reconnaissance resolution demand of target $i$. Each target $i$ has a time window $[e_i, l_i]$, where $e_i$ is the earliest time allowed for reconnaissance on it and $l_i$ is the latest time allowed for reconnaissance on it. $T_i$ is the time to begin reconnaissance on target $i$. An UAV may arrive before $e_i$, which incurs the waiting time $w_i$ until reconnaissance is possible. However, no UAV may arrive past $l_i$. The set $T = \{0, 1, 2, ..., N_T\}$ denotes the extended targets set, where 0 indicates the base that UAVs depart from and return to. $V = \{V^1, V^2, ..., V^{N_V}\}$ denotes UAVs set with different capabilities, where $V^k$ denotes the $k$-th kind of UAVs set and $v_q^k$ is the $q$-th UAV in $V^k$. The maximum travel time permitted for UAVs in $V^k$ is $TL_k$, and the reconnaissance resolution is $r_k$. $c_k$ is the cost to employ one UAV in $V^k$. $s_i^k$ denotes the reconnaissance duration for UAV in $V^k$ on target $i$. The routes set between target pairs is denoted by $A = \{(i, j)|i, j \in T \wedge i \neq j\}$. The routes between target pairs can be calculated by classical routing algorithms such as A*. In the rest of the paper, we assume that the routes between target pairs are known. Each route $(i, j) \in A$ is associated with a distance $d_{ij}$ denoting the length of $(i, j)$ and a travel time $t_{ij}^k$ denoting the travel time for UAV in $V^k$ between target $i$ and $j$.

The decision variable of MOMURP is

$$x_{pij}^k = \begin{cases} 1 & \text{if route } (i, j) \text{ is used by UAV } v_p^k \\ 0 & \text{otherwise} \end{cases} \tag{1}$$

The MOMURP model can be mathematically formulated as follows:

$$(\textbf{MOMURP}) \ \min \boldsymbol{f} = (f_1, f_2) \tag{2}$$

$$f_1 = \sum_{V^k \in V} |V^k| c_k \tag{3}$$

$$f_2 = \sum_{V^k \in V} \sum_{v_p^k \in V^k} \sum_{(i,j) \in A} f_{ij}^k x_{pij}^k \tag{4}$$

Where $f_{ij}^k = \alpha d_{ij} + \beta(T_i + s_i^k + t_{ij}^k + w_j)$.
Subject to:

$$\sum_{j \in T_0} x_{p0j}^k = 1, \sum_{j \in T_0} x_{pj0}^k = 1, \forall v_p^k \in V^k, V^k \in V \tag{5}$$

$$\sum_{V^k \in V} \sum_{v_p^k \in V^k} \sum_{i \in T} x_{pij}^k = 1 \quad \forall j \in T_0 \tag{6}$$

$$\sum_{V^k \in V} \sum_{v_p^k \in V^k} \sum_{j \in T} x_{pij}^k = 1 \quad \forall i \in T_0 \tag{7}$$

$$e_i \leq T_i \leq l_i \quad \forall i \in T_0 \tag{8}$$

$$if \;\; x_{pij}^k = 1, \; then \;\; T_i + s_i^k + t_{ij}^k + w_j = T_j \tag{9}$$

$$w_j = max(0, e_j - (T_i + s_i^k + t_{ij}^k)) \tag{10}$$

$$\sum_{(i,j) \in A} x_{pij}^k (t_{ij}^k + s_j^k + w_j) \leq TL_k \;\; \forall v_p^k \in V^k, V^k \in V \tag{11}$$

$$if \;\; x_{pij}^k = 1, \; then \;\; r_k \leq R_j \tag{12}$$

MOMURP has two objectives to minimize. Objective function(3) states that the cost to employ UAVs should be minimized. Objective function(4) means to minimize the total UAVs travel distances and the consumed time for finishing the reconnaissance mission. $f_1$ is called UAV employ cost and $f_2$ is called cooperative reconnaissance cost in the rest of the paper. Eq.(5) specifies that each UAV should begin at the base and return to the base at the end of the mission. Eq.(6) and (7) ensure that each target can be reconnoitred by one and only one UAV. The time feasibility constraints are defined in equations (8)-(11). Inequality (8) imposes the time window constraints. Waiting time is the amount of time that an UAV has to wait if it arrives at a target location before the earliest time for that target. Inequality (11) states that the total travel time of an UAV could not exceed the maximum permitted travel time of it. Inequality (12) restricts that the UAV conducting reconnaissance on a target should satisfy the reconnaissance resolution demand of the target.

## 3 Multiobjective Evolutionary Algorithm for MOMURP: MURMOEA

Multi-objective Evolutionary Algorithm(MOEA) has been increasingly investigated to solve MOP and has been proven to be a general, robust and powerful search mechanism[4][5][6]. This section provides a MOEA based algorithm to solve MOMURP, which is named as MURMOEA.

### 3.1 The Flowchart of MURMOEA

Fig.1 illustrates the flowchart of MURMOEA, which provides an overall view of the algorithm. Each component such as chromosome representation, initial population creation, evolutionary operators and elitism strategy will be described in detail in the following sections.

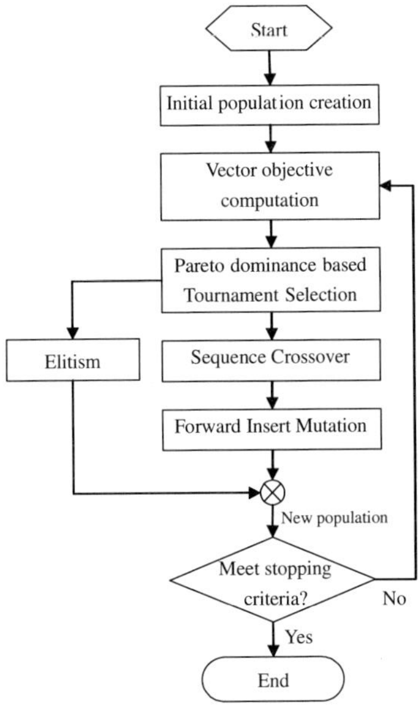


**Fig. 1.** The flowchart of proposed MURMOEA

The initial population is composed of feasible solutions and random solutions. The vector objective of each individual is computed according to Eq.(2)-(4). Then Pareto dominance based tournament selection process is carried out to generate the parent individuals. Elitism process prevents losing of good individuals generated in the evolution process. Evolutionary operators including a sequence crossover and a forward insert mutation will be applied to the selected individuals to generate a new feasible population. Then the new population repeats the evolutionary process until the stopping criteria is met.

### 3.2 Chromosome Representation

To facilitate chromosome representation in MURMOEA, we make the following assumptions (the assumptions will not simplify the problem and are made just for convenience):

(1) The UAVs set is sorted according to the reconnaissance resolutions, i.e. for $V = \{V^1, V^2, ..., V^{N_V}\}$, $r_1 < r_2 < ... < r_{N_v}$ holds.

(2) All targets in $T_0$ are clustered according to their reconnaissance resolution demands. For target $t \in T_0$, if $r_j < R_t < r_{j+1}$, then $t \in C_j$, which means that UAVs in $V^1, V^2, ..., V^j$ can satisfy the reconnaissance resolution demands of target $t$, while UAVs in $V^{j+1}, ..., V^{N_V}$ can not.

In our approach, a chromosome is given by an integer string as shown in Fig.2. A chromosome consists of $N_V$ sequences and is represented as $S$=$\{s_1, s_2, ..., s_{Nv}\}$, where sequence $s_i$ is the reconnaissance targets sequence for UAVs in $V^i$. Each sequence $s_i$ comprises several subsequences and is represented as $s_i = \{s^i_1, ..., s^i_n\}$, where subsequence $s^i_p$ is the reconnaissance targets sequence of UAV $v^i_p$ in $V^i$.

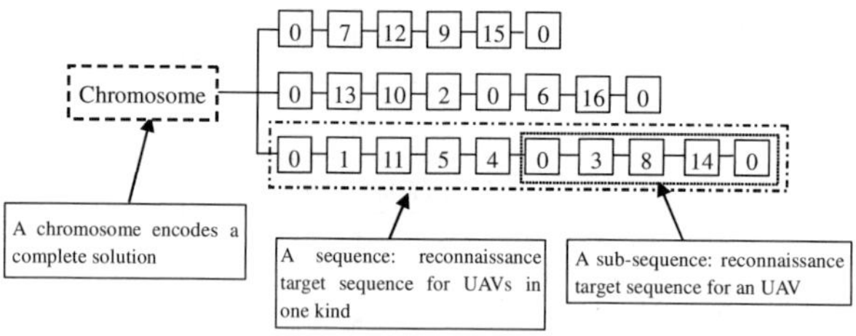


**Fig. 2.** Data structure of chromosome representation

According to the above assumptions, all targets in $C_j$ could appear in one of the sequences in $\{s_i|i \leq j\}$ and could not be in any of the sequences in $\{s_i|i > j\}$. Thus the solution that the chromosome encodes can satisfy the constraint(12). Therefore, the chromosome is an ordered structure, in which different sequences can not exchange positions and the targets in the same subsequence can not exchange positions either.

### 3.3 Creation of Initial Population

In MURMOEA, we generate a mix population comprising feasible solutions and random solutions. The reason for constructing this mix population is that, a population of entirely feasible members gives up the opportunity of exploring the whole regions; and a completely random population may be largely infeasible hence taking a long time to convergence.

**Construction of Feasible Solutions.** We present an algorithm to construct initial feasible solutions for MOMURP. The algorithm is begin with the target categories $C_1, ..., C_{N_V}$ and an empty solution. Fig.3 illustrates the details of the algorithm. Due to the randomness in step(5), repeat running of the algorithm will generate different feasible solutions.

In Fig.3, the step that insert a target $t$ to a sequence $s_k = \{s^k_1, ..., s^k_n\}$ is illustrated in detail by Fig.4, where $n$ is the number of UAVs employed in $V^k$. First all the subsequences $s^k_i$ are sorted according to the mission saturation(MS) $\rho^k_i$ defined as:

$$\rho^k_i = RT_i/TL_k \tag{13}$$

(1) Set all sequences $s_i$=NULL, $i = 1, ..., N_V$
(2) $i = 1$
(3) If $i > N_V$ then go to step (7)
(4) If $C_i$=NULL, then go to step (6)
(5) For a target $t \in C_i$
    Randomly choose a sequence $s_k \in \{s_k | k \leq i\}$
    Insert target $t$ to sequence $s_k$
    Delete target $t$ from $C_i$
    Go to step (4)
(6) $i = i + 1$. Go to step(3)
(7) Stop. Output solution $S = \{s_1, s_2, ..., s_{Nv}\}$

**Fig. 3.** The algorithm of creating feasible solution

Where $RT_i$ is the time spent for UAV $v_i^k$ travelling along subsequence $s_i^k$, and $TL_k$ is the maximum permitted travel time for UAV $v_i^k$. $\rho_i^k > 1$ means that the subsequence $s_i^k$ violates the constraint (11).

Then $t$ is inserted to the subsequence $s_r^k$ with the smallest MS. The cost that inserting $t$ between two adjacent targets $p$ and $q$ in subsequence $s_r^k$ is computed as

$$Cost = \alpha D + \beta W + \gamma O + \eta T \tag{14}$$

Where

$D = \sum_{(i,j) \in s_r^k} d_{ij}$ is the total distance travelled by UAV $v_r^k$.
$W = \sum_{(i,j) \in s_r^k} (T_i + s_i^k + t_{ij}^k + w_j)$ is the total consumed time of UAV $v_r^k$.
$O = \sum_{(i,j) \in s_r^k} \max\{0, (T_i + s_i^k + t_{ij}^k - l_j)\}$ is the penalty for tardiness.
$T = \max\{0, W - TL_k\}$ is the penalty for exceeding the maximum travel time.

According to the insertion cost defined in Eq.(14), target $t$ is inserted to the least cost position between $p^*$ and $q^*$.

**Initial Feasible Ratio.** The initial population is composed of feasible solutions and the random solutions. The ratio of the feasible solutions to the all initial solutions is governed by a parameter *Initial Feasible Ratio(IFR)*

$$IFR = N_F/N \tag{15}$$

Where $N_F$ is number of feasible solutions and $N$ is the population size. *IFR* is a control parameter of MURMOEA and will influence its convergence speed.

### 3.4 Pareto Dominance Based Tournament Selection with Elitism

MOMURP is a typical multiple objective optimization problem and the optimal solutions to MOP are non-dominated solutions known as Pareto-optimal solutions. For the given MOMURP problem, two objective vectors $\boldsymbol{u} = (u_1, u_2)$ and

(1) If $s_k$=NULL, $s_k = (0, t, 0)$. Go to step(10)
(2) Compute MS of all the subsequences as in Eq.(13)
(3) Sort ascending the subsequences according to MS
(4) $r = 1$
(5) If $r > n$ then go to step (9)
(6) For all routes $(p, q)$ in $s_r^k$
 Compute the cost of inserting $t$ between $p$ and $q$ as in Eq.(14)
(7) Select $p^*$ and $q^*$ that has the least insertion cost
 Check the feasibilities defined in Eq.(8)-(11)
 If all the constraints are satisfied
  insert $t$ between $p^*$ and $q^*$
  Go to step (10)
(8) $r = r + 1$. Go to step(5)
(9) Add a new subsequence $s_{n+1}^k = (0, t, 0)$ to $s_k$
(10)Stop. Output $s_k$

**Fig. 4.** The steps of inserting a target to a sequence

$\boldsymbol{v} = (v_1, v_2)$, $\boldsymbol{u}$ is said to dominate $\boldsymbol{v}$ if and only if $\forall i \in \{1, 2\} : u_i \leq v_i \wedge \exists j \in \{1, 2\} : u_i < v_i$, which is denoted as $\boldsymbol{u} \prec \boldsymbol{v}$. A solution $\boldsymbol{x}$ is said to dominate solution $\boldsymbol{y}$ iff $\boldsymbol{f}(\boldsymbol{x}) \prec \boldsymbol{f}(\boldsymbol{y})$. $\boldsymbol{x}_0$ is Pareto optimal if there is no other solution in the search space that dominates $\boldsymbol{x}_0$. The set of all Pareto optimal solutions is called as *Pareto Optimal set.*

To find the approximate Pareto set of the problem and avoid bias to any objective, we introduce a Pareto dominance based tournament selection strategy with elite retaining to generate a new population. Two individuals are randomly selected from the population. Firstly, the feasibilities of the two individuals are checked according to the constraints defined in Eq. (8)-(11). If the two individuals are all infeasible solutions, one is randomly chosen to be the parent. If only one of the two individuals is a feasible solution, the feasible one is chosen to be the parent. If the two individuals are all feasible solutions, the vector objectives of the individuals are computed according to Eq.(2)-(4). Based on the vector objectives, the non-dominated individual is to be the parent. If none of the two individuals dominate the other, one is randomly chosen to be the parent.

Elitism is introduced to avoid losing good solutions during the optimization process due to random effects. we adopt archiving strategies in MURMOEA as most MOEAs did[6]. A secondary population, archive, is maintained during the evolutionary process, to which non-dominated solutions in the population are copied at each generation. An individual in the current population can be copied to archive if and only if that it is non-dominated in the current population and is not dominated by any of the individuals in the archive.

### 3.5 Evolutionary Operators

**Sequence Crossover.** For the special chromosome representation described above, we present a novel sequence crossover operator(SX) in MURMOEA.

Given two parents, $P1 = \{s1_1, ..., s1_{Nv}\}$ and $P2 = \{s2_1, ..., s2_{Nv}\}$, a random integer $pc$ between 1 and $N_V$ is generated. The sequence $s1_{pc}$ and $s2_{pc}$ are exchanged, which results in $C1 = \{s1_1, ..., s2_{pc}, ..., s1_{Nv}\}$ and $C2 = \{s2_1, ..., s1_{pc}, ..., s2_{Nv}\}$. Then the repeated targets are deleted from them. Since each chromosome should contain all the target numbers, the next step is to locate the best possible locations for the missing targets. For a missing target $t$ belonging to $C_{pt}$ to be inserted into a chromosome $C = \{s_1, ..., s_{Nv}\}$, a sequence $s_k$ is selected randomly from $\{s_i | i \leq pt \wedge i \neq pc\}$. Then $t$ is inserted to $s_k$ as Fig.4 describes. SX operator ensures the feasibilities of the children.

Fig.5 illustrates the creation of two offsprings, $C1$ and $C2$, from two parents, $P1$ and $P2$, using an arbitrary problem instance of 3 kind of UAVs conducting reconnaissance on 16 targets. First, a random integer $pc = 2$ is generated. The sequences $s1_2 = (0\ 13\ 10\ 2\ 0\ 6\ 16\ 0)$ and $s2_2 = (0\ 13\ 5\ 0\ 6\ 7\ 0)$ are exchanged, which results in $P1'$ and $P2'$. Then the repeated targets (5,7 in $P1'$ and 2,10,16 in $P2'$) are deleted from them, thus we get $P1''$ and $P2''$. Finally the missing targets (2,10,16 for $P1''$ and 5,7 for $P2''$ ) are inserted followed the steps described in Fig.4, and offsprings $C1$ and $C2$ are generated.

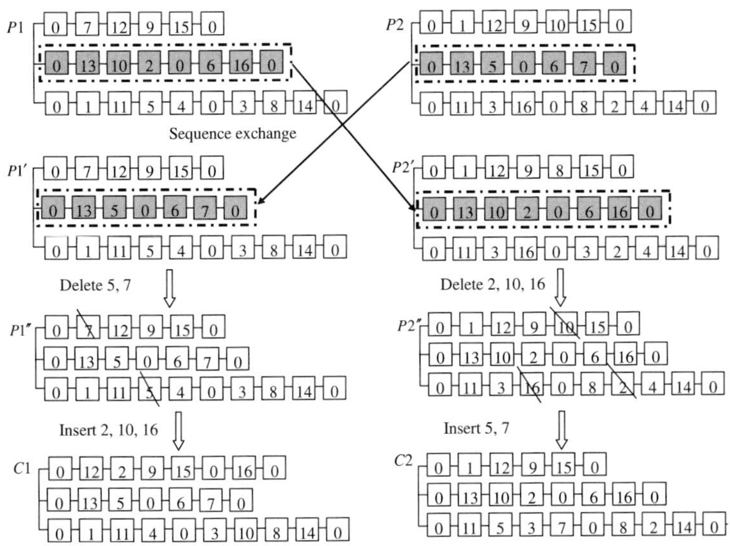


**Fig. 5.** Example of Sequence Crossover operator

**Forward Insert Mutation.** Mutation aids MURMOEA to break away from fixation at any given point in the search space. While using mutation it may be better to introduce the smaller destruction on the good schemas, especially in the MURMOEA, where the reconnaissance resolution constraints and time windows can easily be violated. We put forward a problem specific forward insert mutation(FIM) operator in MURMOEA. A randomly selected target $t$ belonging to sequence $s_i$ is inserted to a sequence $s_k$ selected randomly from $\{s_1, ..., s_{i-1}\}$

following the steps described in Fig.4. Then $t$ is deleted from sequence $s_i$. FIM operator ensures that the mutated chromosome will still satisfy the reconnaissance resolution constraints and time feasibilities.

## 4 Simulation Results

we carry out simulation experiments to verify the MOMURP model and MURMOEA presented. In our experiments, 3 different kind of UAVs with different capabilities are employed in conducting reconnaissance on 100 targets. The reconnaissance resolutions of the 3 kinds UAVs are $r_1 = 1m$, $r_2 = 10m$, $r_3 = 20m$, and the costs of employ one UAV are $c_1 = 200$, $c_2 = 100$, $c_3 = 50$ respectively. The locations and time windows of 100 targets are the same with those of the customers in the Solomon's Vehicle Routing Problems with Time Window instances[7]. The reconnaissance resolution demands of the targets and reconnaissance time are generated randomly.

The parameters of MURMOEA are set as

- population size = 100
- generation span = 1000
- *IFR* = 0.50
- crossover rate = 0.80
- mutation rate = 0.30

### 4.1 Cooperative Reconnaissance Cost and UAV Employ Cost over Generation

The convergence trend is a useful indication to validate the performance of any optimization algorithm. MOMURP has two objectives, the cooperative reconnaissance cost(CR cost) and UAV employ cost(UAVE cost). Both objectives are chosen as measures to show the convergence trend of MURMOEA. We show how minimization of both objective occurs throughout the generations. Fig.6(a) shows the reducing of CR cost over generations and Fig.6(b) shows the reducing of UAVE cost throughout every generation. The decline of the two objectives are faster at the earlier generations as compared to later. Although it is difficult to prove that we have found the optimal solution, it is reasonable to believe that MURMOEA is able to optimize the two objectives of MOMURP concurrently and effectively.

### 4.2 Good Convergence Trace Compared with Single Objective Optimization

In order to verify the multi-objective optimization effort of MURMOEA, we compare it with single objective based methods. Three types of simulations with similar settings but different optimization criteria are performed. The first type of simulation only considers the optimization of CR cost(CRC), the second type of simulation only considers the optimization of UAVE cost (UAVEC) and the

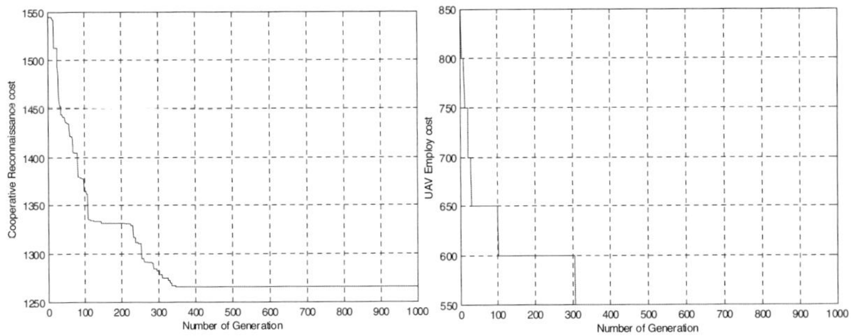


(a) Cooperative Reconnaissance Cost (b) UAV Employ Cost

**Fig. 6.** Cooperative Reconnaissance Cost and UAV Employ cost over generation

**Table 1.** Best objectives in three types of simulations

| Simulations | CR-Cost | UAVE-Cost |
|---|---|---|
| MO | 1310.7 | 550 |
| CRC | 1317.6 | 650 |
| UAVEC | 1398.2 | 550 |

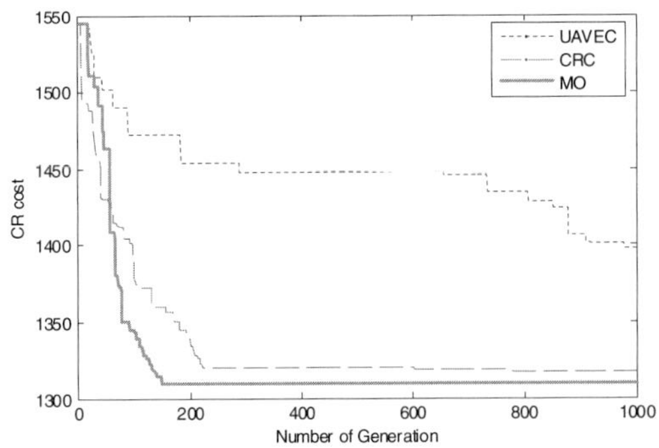


**Fig. 7.** Convergence trace for MO, CRC and UAVEC

third type of simulation concerns the two objectives (MO), i.e. the CR cost and UAVE cost, concurrently.

Table1 shows the smallest CR cost and UAVE cost found by the three types of simulations. Please note that the best CR cost and UAVE cost come from different individuals. Fig.7 shows the convergence trace of the smallest CR cost at each generation along the evolution. From the results in the figure and the table, we can see that UAVEC finds the UAVE cost as small as that MO finds, but it performs poorly in the case of CR cost since it only considers the optimization of UAVE cost. The CR cost convergence trace of CRC appears to be comparable to MO, but CRC performs poorly in the case of UAVE cost since it only considers the optimization of CR cost. On the whole, MO outperforms the other two in the optimization of the two objectives concurrently. This superiority mainly derives from the Pareto dominance based selection during the evolutionary process.

### 4.3 The Impact of IFR on MURMOEA

Finally, an experiment is carried out to observe the influence of initial feasible ratio *IFR* on the convergence speed of MURMOEA. The simulations are computed with different *IFR*=0.1,0.3,0.5,0.7,1.0. The results are presented in Fig.8. We can see that, *IFR* has a great influences on the convergence speed, and simulation with *IFR*=0.5 shows the best performance among all the simulations. The simulations with smaller *IFR* shows slower convergence speed and the simulations with bigger *IFR* constrain MURMOEA to explore more search space.

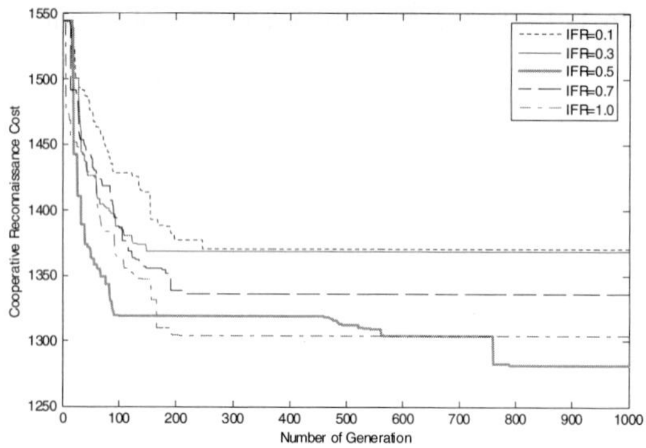


**Fig. 8.** Convergence trace with different *IFR*

## 5 Conclusions

A novel Pareto dominance based evolutionary algorithm MURMOEA is presented for multi-UAV reconnaissance problem. In MURMOEA, the initial population of MURMOEA is composed of feasible solutions and random solutions, thus the algorithm will not fall into the local optimal and will not convergence slowly either. Pareto dominance based tournament selection with elitism is introduced to generate new population, which ensures that MURMOEA converges toward the Pareto set and prevents bias to any objective. Novel problem specific evolutionary operators are designed to ensure the feasibilities of the children. Simulation results show that MURMOEA has good convergence trace in both of the two objectives and outperforms the algorithms with single objective optimization criteria.

## References

1. Ryan,Joel L., Bailey,T.G., Moore,J.T., Carlton, W.B.: Reactive Tabu Search in Unmanned Aerial Reconnaissance Simulations. Proceedings of the 1998 Winter Simulation Conference, Grand Hyatt, Washington D.C. (1998) 873-879

2. Hutchison,M.G.: A Method for Estimating Range Requirements of Tactical Reconnaissance UAVs. AIAA's 1st Technical Conference and Workshop on Unmanned Aerospace Vehicles,Portsmouth, Virginia (2002) 120-124
3. Ousingsawat,J., Campbell,M.E.: Establishing Trajectories for Multi-Vehicle Reconnaissance. AIAA Guidance, Navigation, and Control Conference and Exhibit, Providence, Rhode Island (2004) 1-12
4. Carlos,A. Coello Coello.: A Comprehensive Survey of Evolutionary-Based Multiobjective Optimization Techniques. Knowledge and Information Systems. Vol.1, No.3 (1999) 269-308
5. Van Veldhuizen,D.A. , Lamont,G.B.: Multiobjective Evolutionary Algorithms: Analyzing the State-of-the-Art. Evolutionary Computation, Vol.8, No.2 (2000) 125-147
6. Zitzler,E., Laumanns,M., Bleuler,S.: A Tutorial on Evolutionary Multiobjective Optimization, Metaheuristics for Multiobjective Optimisation. Lecture Notes in Economics and Mathematical Systems. Vol.535 (2004) 3-37
7. Solomon, Marius.M.,: Algorithms for Vehicle Routing and Scheduling Problems with Time Window Constraints. Operations Reasearch. Vol.35, No.2 (1987) 254-265

# Research on Autonomous Planning for AUV in Unstructured Environment

Hongjian Wang, Dehui Zhao, Xinqian Bian, and Xiaocheng Shi

Automation College
Harbin Engineering University
Harbin, 150001, P.R. China
wanghongjian@hrbeu.edu.cn

**Abstract.** Autonomous planning is an important ability for autonomous underwater vehicle (AUV), which is a crucial factor for ensuring and guiding AUV to long-term navigate and accomplish its mission in large range and unstructured oceanic area. In general, the technology of autonomous planning could be sorted into global path planning and local path planning. In this paper, the former is solved by adopting adaptive genetic algorithm (AGA), which aimed at searching an optimized path according to some optimization criteria in a known and certain environment. This algorithm also can be adapted and applied to dynamic plan a collision-free path based on sonar and real-time navigate AUV in unknown and uncertain environment. By analyzing the motion security of AUV, two kinds of regions which are defined as forbidden zone and potential collision zone, and some safety motion criterions are also proposed for AUV. All of above researches are simulated in a semi-physical simulation platform, and the results show that the autonomous planning algorithms are valid, efficient and reliable. The adaptive abilities and autonomy of AUV can make it possible to long-term navigate in ocean and succeed in its mission.

## 1 Introduction

Autonomous underwater vehicle (AUV) has been widely applied to the area of oceanography, geomorphology and physiognomy, marine engineering and some other civil area. Autonomous planning is one of kernel technique for AUV and is widely recognized by more and more researchers.

In general, the technology of autonomous planning embodies two issues, one is global planning which autonomous plan an optimal global path for AUV according to some optimization criteria in a known and certain environment, the other is local planning which dynamic plan an obstacle-free path for AUV based on the real-time feedback of forward looking sonar (FLS) in unknown and uncertain environment. The safe, efficient and economical path makes it possible for AUV to accomplish its mission in succeeded.

We address the general autonomous planning problem for AUV using the following methods, adaptive genetic algorithm (AGA) is proposed for global planning and it is adapted to navigate AUV for local path planning based on FLS. At the same time, by analyzing the motion security of AUV, two kinds of regions which are defined as forbidden zone and potential collision zone, and some safety motion criterions are also proposed for AUV.

D.-S. Huang, K. Li, and G.W. Irwin (Eds.): ICIC 2006, LNCS 4113, pp. 586 – 599, 2006.

In the paper, the known and certain global planning workspace is about 300 sea miles × 300 sea miles, and it can be put some known or unknown obstacles artificially into the planning model in order to meet the need of research. According to the feature of FLS, we are currently building a vision simulating model for FLS to verify the algorithms of obstacle avoidance in laboratory. In future, we will integrate these algorithms into real AUV to test the validity of our approaches during sea trials.

## 2 Planning Spatial Model

### 2.1 Global Planning Spatial Model

Global planning spatial model include two kinds of models, one is just called 2D grid-based workspace model in which each grid includes the whole environment info (such as longitude, latitude, current, altitude), the other is called 3D planning spatial model in which each grid comprises three attributes.

**Definition 1.** The structure of 2D grid-based workspace model $G_{AMAP2}$ is a five elements suit.

$$G_{AMAP2} =< L_{ongitude},\quad L_{atitude},\quad A_{ltitude},\quad C_{urrentv},\quad C_{urrenta} >$$

Where, $L_{ongitude}$ , $L_{atitude}$ , $A_{ltitude}$ , $C_{urrentv}$ and $C_{urrenta}$ are all coming from known chart data. And the top left of grid matrix is the origin coordination, the horizontal rightward is the increase direction of X-axis, and the vertical downward is the increase direction of Y-axis.

Then we can set up a 2D workspace map and stored in computer as a form of 2D structure array.

$$struct \quad G_{AMAP2} \quad M_{ap2}[M][N]$$

Where, $M = 1320, N = 1200$.

**Definition 2.** The structure of 3D planning spatial model is a three elements suit.

$$G_{AMAP3} = < B_{aseAttr},\quad A_{ddAttr},\quad A_{reaDeri} >$$

Where, $\mathrm{B}_{\mathrm{aseAttr}}$ is the basis attribute of grid and comes from the initial known chart data; it uses 1 to represent the surface section, and uses 0 to represent the underwater section.

$\mathrm{A}_{\mathrm{ddAttr}}$ is the additional attribute of grid and used to describe the non-original obstacle in addition. It uses 1 to denote additional obstacle, and 0 to denote no obstacle.

$\mathrm{A}_{\mathrm{reaDeri}}$ is the boundary attribute of a grid, the num 1 denotes that is in viable area, the num 0 denotes that is in unviable area, and in range [2, 9] denotes that is in half viable area. In practice procedure this attribute value is used as domain knowledge of grid to introduce into the path-planning algorithm.

Then we can set up a 3D planning map and stored in computer as form of 3D structure array.

$$struct \quad G_{AMAP3} \quad M_{ap3}[M][N][D]$$

Where, $D = 100$.

Because each grid denotes a very small region in ocean chart, its depth may be a few meters or thousands of meters underwater. A coefficient $D_{epthCoefficient}$ is defined to solve the planning problem among random depth range.

$$D_{epthCoefficient} = \begin{cases} 1.0, & if \ \Delta d_{epth} \le 100 \\ \dfrac{\Delta d_{epth}}{D}, & else \end{cases} \tag{1}$$

Where, $\Delta d_{epth}$ is an absolute difference between the initial depth and the goal depth.

The above two kinds of models and its coordinates are showed as Fig.1.

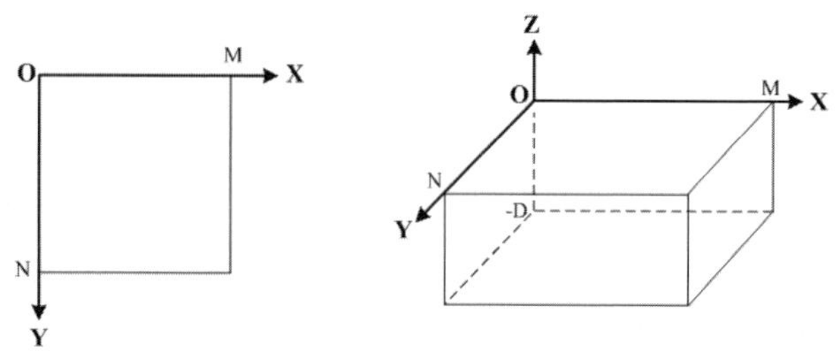


(a) 2D grid-based workspace model (b) 3D planning spatial model

**Fig. 1.** Coordination Systems for global path planning

Based on the above definitions and workspace model described, we can research the autonomous planning approaches to obtain a global optimal path or an obstacle-free path.

## 2.2 Local Planning Spatial Model

Local planning spatial model is a small spatial model shown as fig.2. It is set up when there is some obstacle info returned by FLS in unknown environment and can be updated in real time. Supposed that current coordinate of AUV is $(x_0, y_0, z_0)$ in earth-fixed system. Then we can consider that $(x_0, y_0)$ is a center of $X' - Y'$ plane and sea level is $Z' = 0$. Based on the discrete grid model, the local planning map can be defined alike global planning. The scale of a grid is about 5 meters × 5 meters × 5meters, and the maximum range of data structure is $M' = 100, N' = 100, D' = 20$.

In order to simulate the ability of obstacle avoiding for AUV in lab, a vision simulating model is built and depicted in fig.3. It can provide FLS data without mounting physical FLS on AUV.

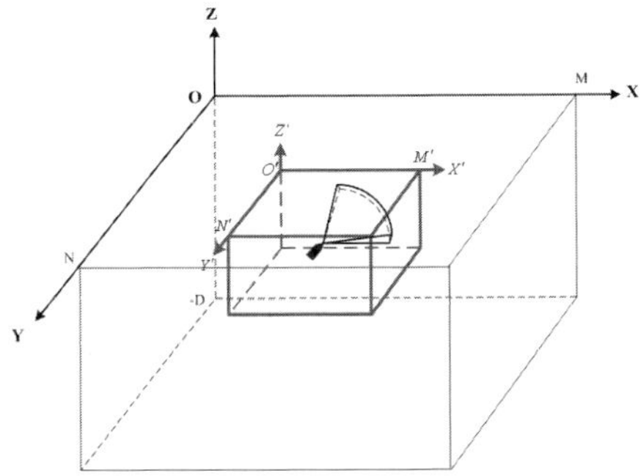


**Fig. 2.** AUV local planning model

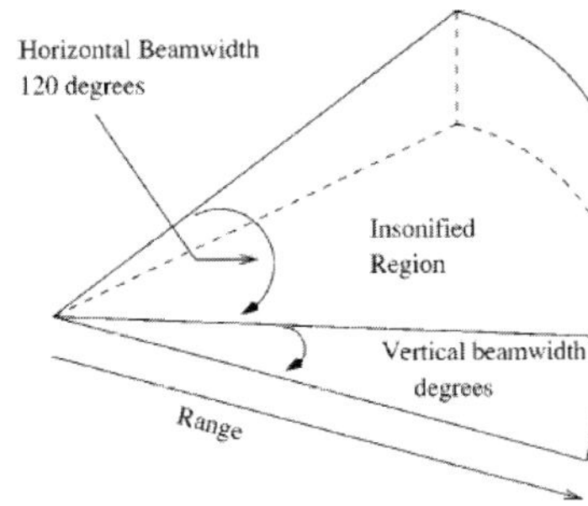


**Fig. 3.** Vision simulation model of the FLS

The shape of sonar vision zone is taper-sector, and the relationship between vision zone and obstacles is described as the following.

Suppose $(x_C, y_C, z_C)$ is mass center of the AUV, $(x_S, y_S, z_S)$ is the position coordinate of FLS, $l_{cs}$ is distance between mass center and sonar position. Both $(x_C, y_C, z_C)$ and $(x_S, y_S, z_S)$ are described in the AUV body-fixed system, $(x_C, y_C, z_C) = (0,0,0)$ and $(x_S, y_S, z_S) = (l_{cs}, 0,0)$. The FLS simulating vision zone can be presented as the following[1].

$$\begin{cases} \dfrac{|y_{bs}|}{\sqrt{x_{bs}^2 + y_{bs}^2}} \le \sin \dfrac{\alpha_v}{2} \\ \sqrt{x_{bs}^2 + y_{bs}^2 + z_{bs}^2} \le R_v \\ \dfrac{|z_{bs}|}{\sqrt{x_{bs}^2 + y_{bs}^2}} \le \sin \dfrac{\beta_v}{2} \end{cases} \tag{2}$$

Where, $\alpha_v$ is horizontal beamwidth, $\beta_v$ is vertical beamwidth, and $R_v$ is operating range.

$(x_{bs}, y_{bs}, z_{bs})$ can be written as the following.

$$\begin{cases} x_{bs} = x'_{obs} - x_s \\ y_{bs} = y'_{obs} - y_s \\ z_{bs} = z'_{obs} - z_s \end{cases} \tag{3}$$

Where, $(x'_{obs}, y'_{obs}, z'_{obs})$ is the obstacle coordinate in the AUV body-fixed system $Ox'_s y'_s z'_z$.

$(x, y, z)$ is the AUV mass point coordinated in the Earth-fixed system, and $(x_{obs}, y_{obs}, z_{obs})$ is the obstacle coordinate in the Earth-fixed system.

So we can propose two kinds of transfer equation between Earth-fixed system and body-fixed system.

$$(x^{'}, y^{'}, z^{'}) = (\xi, \eta, \zeta)S \tag{4}$$

Where, $(x', y', z')$ is the AUV position in the body-fixed system.

$$S = \begin{bmatrix} \cos\phi\cos\theta & \sin\phi\sin\theta\sin\varphi - \sin\phi\cos\varphi & \cos\phi\sin\theta\cos\varphi + \sin\phi\sin\varphi \\ \sin\phi\cos\theta & \sin\phi\sin\theta\sin\varphi + \cos\phi\cos\varphi & \sin\phi\sin\theta\cos\varphi - \cos\phi\cos\varphi \\ -\sin\theta & \cos\theta\sin\varphi & \cos\theta\cos\varphi \end{bmatrix} \tag{5}$$

$$\begin{bmatrix} x'_{obs} \\ y'_{obs} \\ z'_{obs} \end{bmatrix} = \begin{bmatrix} \cos\phi\cos\theta & \sin\phi\cos\theta & -\sin\theta \\ -\sin\phi\cos\varphi + \cos\phi\sin\theta\sin\varphi & \cos\phi\cos\varphi + \sin\phi\sin\varphi\sin\theta & \cos\theta\sin\varphi \\ \sin\phi\sin\varphi + \cos\phi\cos\varphi\sin\theta & -\cos\phi\sin\varphi + \sin\theta\sin\phi\cos\varphi & \cos\theta\cos\varphi \end{bmatrix} \begin{bmatrix} x_{obs} - x \\ y_{obs} - y \\ z_{obs} - z \end{bmatrix} \tag{6}$$

$$\begin{bmatrix} x_{obs} \\ y_{obs} \\ z_{obs} \end{bmatrix} = S \begin{bmatrix} x^{'}_{obs} \\ y^{'}_{obs} \\ z^{'}_{obs} \end{bmatrix} + \begin{bmatrix} x \\ y \\ z \end{bmatrix} \tag{7}$$

## 3 Global Path Planning Based on Adaptive Genetic Algorithm

As we all know that any unfeasible paths do cross over the forbidden zone, which are not only insecurity, but also waste so many times to search a feasible and obstacle-free path during the period of evolution. So in this paper, it takes domain knowledge into account sufficiently on aspect of chromosome encoding, initial population generating, and superior genetic operator designing. Furthermore, it adopts the idea of adaptive genetic algorithm (in short, AGA) and improved by designing adaptive evolution probabilities.

### 3.1 Viable-Length Encoding Method

An individual denotes a path for AUV in the workspace. Gene is the least unit of an individual and uses decimal $(x_i, y_i, z_i)$ to denote a node of the path in grid-based workspace model. For the operating path of AUV is viable, this paper adopts viable-length individual to shorten calculation time of AGA. At beginning, the code length of individual is defined as the maximum length of individual, and it defines the variety of IndividualSize equaling to 100.

### 3.2 Initial Population Generating Based on Domain Knowledge

Initial population is the first step for AGA evolution, and it is making by a count of individuals. When the range of planning workspace is too large and the num of grid in workspace is too big, it makes random individuals in initial population crossing over some blank range and generates more unnecessary searching coursing, and moreover it makes the searching efficiency of AGA too low. On the other hand, it hopes that initial population should distribute at every area in planning workspace to ensure the global optimization of AGA.

Based on the above considering factors, the paper quotes the idea of intervisibility test[7]. This paper only considers the intervisibility problem on condition of point to point, and put the intervisibility of two adjacent points into the generating procedure of initial population as domain knowledge.

### 3.3 Fitness Function

Fitness function is an evaluation criterion for individual. And object function is a tolerance for restriction condition. These two functions will directly affect the convergency speed and calculation efficiency for AGA.

Object function for $individual_i$ is defined as the following.

$$g_i = \alpha \cdot Dis_i^p + \beta \cdot SC_i^q \tag{8}$$

$$Dis_i = \sum_{j=0}^{n-2} \left\| p_j p_{j+1} \right\| \tag{9}$$

$$SC_i = n = population[i].chromamount \tag{10}$$

Where, $Dis_i$ is the 3D Euclid distance from a cell to its adjacent cell.

$SC$ is the length of chromosome, and it is equal the amount of genes which make up of each variable-length chromosome.

$\alpha, \beta$ respectively denote the weight coefficients of $Dis_i$ and $SC_i$, $\alpha, \beta \in (0,1)$ and $\alpha + \beta = 1$.

$p, q$ respectively denote the adjustment coefficients of $Dis_i$ and $SC_i$. Because $Dis_i$ is a 3D Euclid distance which is at least $1320 \times 1200$ range in X-Y plane without considering the depth-degree, $SC_i$ is 300 at most. So it needs to adjust the proportion of $Dis_i$ and $SC_i$ by using $p, q$, and $p \in (0,1), q \in (1,100)$.

Correspondingly the fitness function is defined as follows.

$$f_i = \frac{1}{g_i} \times a \tag{11}$$

Where, $a$ is an amplifier multiple, $a \in [100,10000]$.

### 3.4 Domain Knowledge-Based Adaptive Genetic Operator

#### 3.4.1 Selection Operator

According to the fitness value of an individual, it calculates the probability of an individual in the population and then adopts the Elitist selection strategy to select its offspring.

Selection operation is used to value the individual fitness in an environment. It is a base mode to realize the broadcast of fine gene in the population and decrease the effect of low individual. The paper [6] indicated that selection operator has a function of strict monotony decrease for the population multiformity.

Hence the elitist selection strategy is adopted in the improved planner. It is a sufficient condition to assure the population convergence to an optimal value.

### 3.4.2 Insertion Operator

In this paper, after considering the domain knowledge and the result of intervisibility test in enough, and on the base of some judgment criterions it will inserts some new node into a path (that is so called true inserting) or uses a new optimal node to replace the old path node (that is so called pseudo inserting). The example is shown in fig.4.

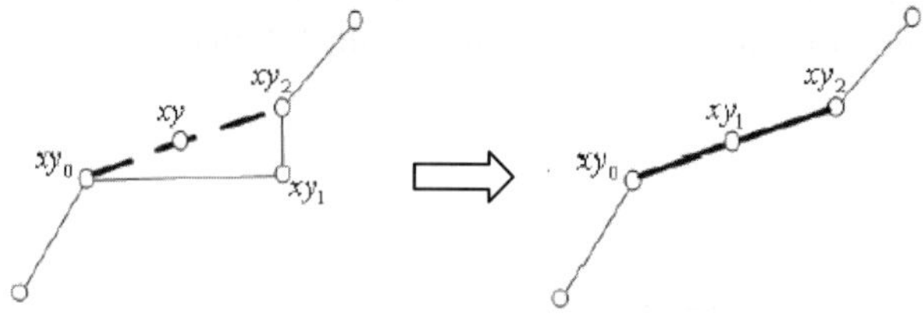


**Fig. 4.** An example of operating case for insertion operator

### 3.4.3 Adaptive Probability Algorithm of Crossover

Crossover operator is particular character to generate new individuals including more complex gene structure, which imitate the gene reform process of propagate in nature.

In this paper, it makes any two paths to crossover at the same loca except for the start gene and the goal gene, but these two gene should be seen each other. So that it can't introduce an unfeasibility node into the path. And its probability should decreases gradually during the evolve process and finally keeps a stable value after a certain generations, all of these change should be related with the evolution generations. So on base of the idea of intervisibility test the crossover strategy can modified, that is, if two random genes in different individual can be seen each other, then one-point crossover can be done at the corresponding genes.

For example, $individual_i$ is composed by a series of genes shown as the following.

$$S \rightarrow P_{i1} \rightarrow P_{i2} \rightarrow ... \rightarrow P_i \rightarrow P_{ik} \rightarrow ... \rightarrow P_{in} \rightarrow G$$

The other $individual_j$ is composed by a series of genes shown as the following.

$$S \rightarrow P_{j1} \rightarrow P_{j2} \rightarrow ... \rightarrow P_j \rightarrow P_{js} \rightarrow ... \rightarrow P_{jm} \rightarrow G$$

By doing intervisibility test, the genes $P_i$ and $p_j$ can be seen each other, and it is accorded with the condition of crossover operation. Two new individuals can be generated as follows.

$$individual_i': S \to P_{i1} \to P_{i2} \to \ldots \to P_j \to P_{js} \to \ldots \to P_{jm} \to G$$

$$individual_j': S \to P_{j1} \to P_{j2} \to \ldots \to P_i \to P_{ik} \to \ldots \to P_{in} \to G$$

An adaptive crossover probability algorithm is proposed, which is related with the evolution generations and be independent of individual fitness.

$$P_{ctemp} = P_{cMax} \times 2^{(-n/N_{Gen})}$$
$$P_c(n) = \begin{cases} P_{ctemp} & if\,(P_{ctemp} > P_{cMin}) \\ P_{cMin} & else \end{cases} \tag{12}$$

Where, $p_{ctemp}$ is a temporary probability of crossover operator, $P_{cMax}$ is a preset maximum probability, $P_{cMin}$ is a preset minimum probability, $n$ is current generation of evolution ( $0 \le n \le N_{Gen}$ ), $N_{Gen}$ is the maximum evolution generation of GA, $P_c(n)$ is the current crossover probability of the population after evolving $n$ generations.

### 3.4.4 Adaptive Probability Algorithm of Mutation

In general, the mutation probability is fixed and very low in standard GA. It can assure the stability of population and avoid generating too many differences between the ancestor and the offspring.

Similarly the designing idea of crossover operator is in accordance with the principle of equal probability; it tests the intervisibility for any two non-adjacent genes PA and PB, and then connects the gene PA to the gene PB and replaces the older gene series of PA $\to \cdots \to$ PB if the result of intervisibility is true, otherwise it do nothing. Of course, the probability of mutation is must low. All above mentioned realizes the planning idea that makes the path being zigzag to the least.

By analyzing the action of mutation operator, it can keep the multiformity of population and efficiently restrain the prematurity phenomena. Its action is subordinate and assistant.

So under the above consideration, an adaptive mutation probability algorithm is proposed, which is related with the fitness at the same evolving generation and be diminishing during the whole evolution process.

$$P_{mtemp} = P_{mMax} \times 2^{(-n/N_{Gen})}$$
$$P_m(n) = \begin{cases} P_{mtemp} & if\,(P_{mtemp} > P_{mMin}) \\ P_{mMin} & else \end{cases} \tag{13}$$

Where, $p_{mtemp}$ is a temporary probability of mutation operator, $P_{mMax}$ is a preset maximum probability, $P_{mMin}$ is a preset minimum probability, $n$ is current generation of evolution ( $0 \le n \le N_{Gen}$ ), $N_{Gen}$ is the maximum evolution generation of GA, $P_m(n)$ is the current mutation probability of the population after evolving $n$ generations.

#### 3.4.5 Deletion Operator

Deletion operator is used to delete all nodes between the same nodes in a path.

For example, there is a $individual_i$ composed by a series of genes.

$$S \to P_1 \to ... \to P \to P_{k1} ... \to P_{km} \to P \to P_j ... \to P_n \to G$$

Obviously there is a circuit at gene $P$. After operated by deletion operator, this individual can be predigested and shown as the following.

$$S \to P_1 \to ... \to P \to P_j ... \to P_n \to G$$

## 4 Local Path Planning Based on Genetic Algorithm

### 4.1 Security Analysis for AUV Maneuvering

The security radius $R_{safe}$ is defined as the minimum distance between obstacle and AUV, which assure AUV has enough time to decision making and dynamic planning based on sonar data.

By analysis the safety for AUV maneuver, forbidden zone and potential collision zone are defined, and accordingly two controlling strategies for obstacle avoiding are proposed.

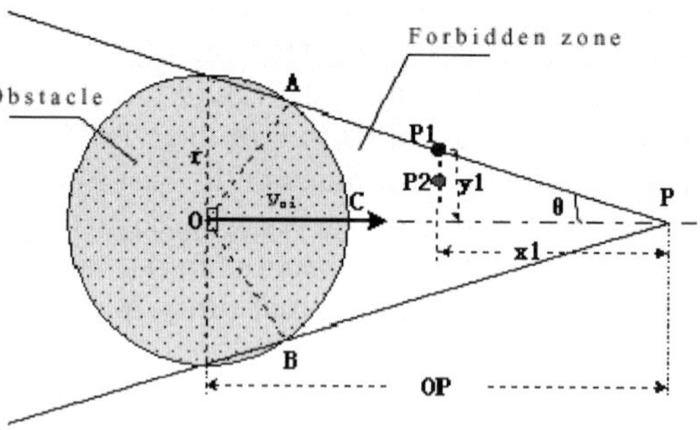


**Fig. 5.** Graph of forbidden zone

It is shown as fig.5. Assume that there is an obstacle $O$ captured by FLS and its coordinate can be gained by transfer from body-fixed system to earth-fixed system. It is also estimated that its radius is $R_{oi}$ and it moves at a constant velocity $\vec{v}_{oi}$. Then we make a circle whose center is $O$ and its radius is $r$.

$$r = l + R_{oi} + R_{safe} \tag{14}$$

Where, $l = \frac{1}{2}L$, and $L$ is the total length of AUV.

It is known that the velocity of AUV is $\vec{v}$ ($\|\vec{v}\| < \|\vec{v}_{oi}\|$) in random directions.

**Definition 3.** Forbidden zone is just constructed by the segments $PA, PB$ and the arc $ACB$. It can be proved that there is an inevitable collision in case of AUV in the zone.

Assume that the AUV is located at $\vec{p}(t)$ when it is $t$-clock, and it is located at $\vec{p}(t+\Delta t)$ when it is $t+\Delta t$ -clock.

$$\vec{p}(t+\Delta t) = \vec{p}(t) + \vec{d}(t) \tag{15}$$

Correspondingly, the obstacle $O_i$ is located at $\vec{p}_{oi}(t)$ when it is $t$ -clock and $\vec{p}_{oi}(t+\Delta t)$ at $t+\Delta t$ -clock.

$\vec{d}_{oi}(t)$ denotes the movement distance of obstacle $O_i$ among $[t, t+\Delta t]$ time-zone.

$$\vec{p}_{oi}(t+\Delta t) = \vec{p}_{oi}(t) + \vec{d}_{oi}(t) \tag{16}$$

$$\|\vec{p}(t) - \vec{p}_{oi}(t)\| \geq R_{safe}, i = 1,2,\cdots,N \tag{17}$$

$$\|\vec{p}(t+\tau) - \vec{p}_{oi}(t+\tau)\| \geq R_{safe}, i = 1,2,\cdots,N, \Delta t \geq \tau \geq 0 \tag{18}$$

$\vec{s}_{voi}(t)$ is the relevant displacement between AUV and obstacle $O_i$ and is equated as the following.

$$\vec{s}_{voi}(t) = \vec{p}(t) - \vec{p}_{oi}(t) \tag{19}$$

$$\vec{v}_{voi}(t) = \frac{d\vec{s}_{voi}(t)}{dt} \tag{20}$$

It is obviously that if and only if $\vec{s}_{voi}(t) = 0$ or $\|\vec{s}_{voi}(t)\| \leq R_{safe}$ then AUV is collided with obstacle.

A constant $R_{border}$ is also introduced to describe the possibility of potential collision for AUV.

$$\|\vec{s}_{voi}(t)\| \leq R_{border}, \text{ when } \vec{v}_{voi}(t) < 0 \tag{21}$$

It is shown that if AUV moves at a direction which makes $\|\vec{s}_{voi}(t)\|$ decreasing, then there is a possibility to collision with obstacle, and ulteriorly it do collision with obstacle once $\|\vec{s}_{voi}(t)\| < R_{safe}$.

## 4.2 Collision Avoidance Strategy for AUV

### 4.2.1 Strategy of Velocity Adjustment

By speed up or slow down the velocity of AUV, it can make AUV maneuver along its initial global planning path without changing its heading. This strategy has a dynamic priority during different kinds of mission.

#### 4.2.2 Strategy of Heading Adjustment

The essential idea of heading adjustment strategy carries the connotation of dynamic path planning. It is suitable not only for static obstacle ($\vec{v}_{oi} = 0$) but also for dynamic obstacle ($\vec{v}_{oi} \neq 0$). When AUV is auto piloting, this strategy has higher priority than the strategy of velocity adjustment. But on the other cases, it is on contrary.

### 4.3 Obstacle Avoiding Based on GA

By comparing with fig.1 and fig.2, it is obviously that the local spatial model is similar to the global planning model. So we can adapt the AGA global planning approach and dynamic plan a local path based on the real-time feedback of FLS to avoid an obstacle.

It also adopt decimal grid-coordinate coding scheme which has variable length chromosome. The generating method of initial population, the evolve strategy and some superiority genetic operators (such as selection, insertion, crossover, mutation and deletion) are all inherited and applied.

We should design a new evolution fitness function to optimize the local planning problem. It is considered the following factor as restriction criteria.

- Economy of Path

$$D(S) = \sum_{i=0}^{SUM-1} \left\| p_{i+1} - p_i \right\| \tag{22}$$

Where, $SUM$ is the gene amount of a chromosome. $D(S)$ is the Euclid distance from the initial point to the goal.

- Security of Path

$$\begin{aligned} Safe(S) &= \max_{i=0}^{SUM-1} safe_i \\ safe_i &= \begin{cases} Dis_{i,AuvObs} - R_{safe} & Dis_{i,AuvObs} \geq R_{safe} \\ MaxValue & \end{cases} \\ Dis_{i,AuvObs} &= \sum_{j=1}^{OM} \min\left(d\left(\overrightarrow{p_i p_{i+1}}, RWxyz_j\right)\right) \end{aligned} \tag{23}$$

Where, $Safe(S)$ is used to evaluate the adjacence degree between AUV and obstacles. $d\left(\overrightarrow{p_i p_{i+1}}, RWxyz_j\right)$ is a vertical distance from the $obstacle_j$ to the path segment $p_i p_{i+1}$, and the $obstacle_j$ is locate at $RWxyz_j$ in the Earth-fixed system. $OM$ is the amount of all obstacles.

- Object Function and Fitness Function

Finally, the object function and fitness function for the *individual S* can be defined as follows.

$$ObjectValue(S) = w_1 \cdot D(S) + w_2 \cdot Safe(S) \tag{24}$$

Where, $w_1, w_2 \in (0,1), and\ w_1 + w_2 = 1$

$$Fitness(S) = \alpha \cdot \frac{1}{ObjectValue(S)} \tag{25}$$

# 5 Experimental Results

## 5.1 Experiments of Global Path Planning

Experimental demand is to search an optimal and obstacle-free path from starting point to goal based on the known large range chart data.

The terminating condition of AGA is when generation reaches the maximum (that is generation>500) or an optimal fitness has keep for a certain evolution generation (in the paper it is ruled as 50), then the genetic evolution can be ended.

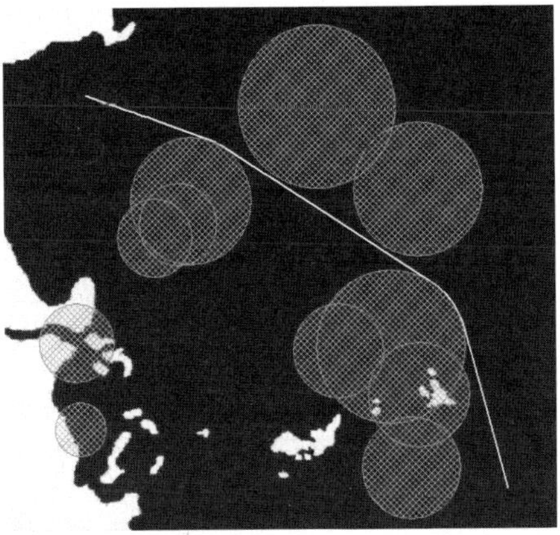

**Fig. 6.** 2-D path in known environment with artificial rotundity obstacles

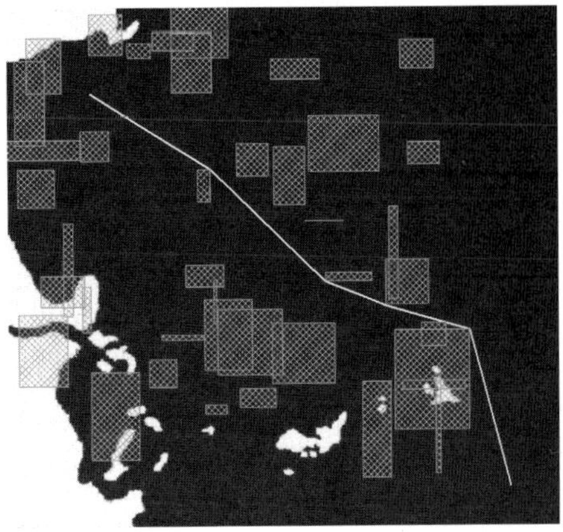

**Fig. 7.** 2-D path in known environment with artificial rectangle obstacles

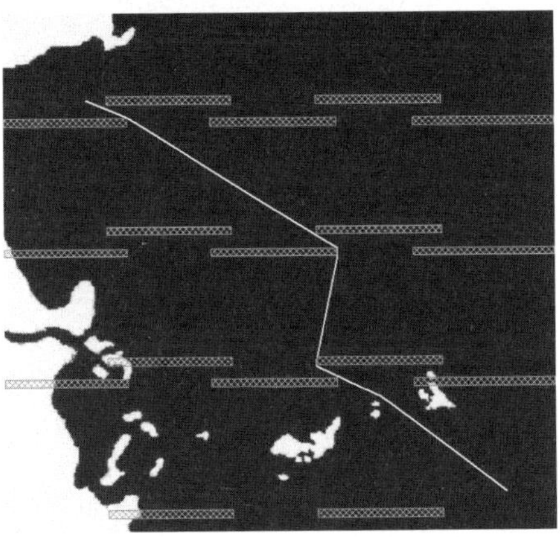

**Fig. 8.** 2-D path in known environment with seventeen artificial pectinate obstacles

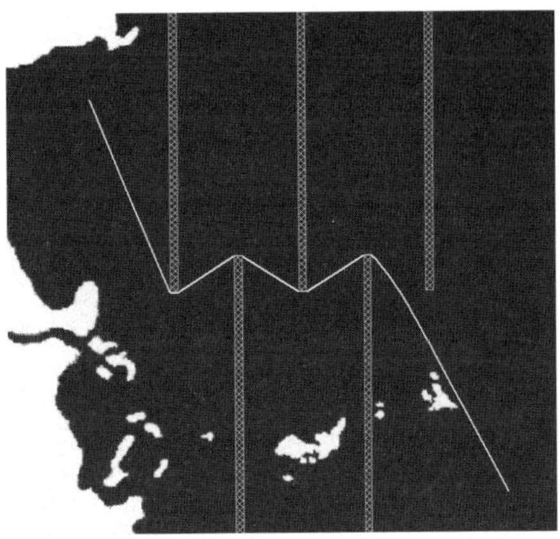

**Fig. 9.** 2-D path in known environment with five artificial pectinate obstacles

Fig.6, 7, 8 and fig.9 show the 2-D planning paths based on AGA in three typical known environments. Fig.10 is the 3-D planning path based on AGA. All of results show that the AGA –based global path planner can search a safe and optimal path for AUV, and it doesn't introduce any unfeasibility node into the planning path. All these mentioned can satisfy the recommend of AUV mission.

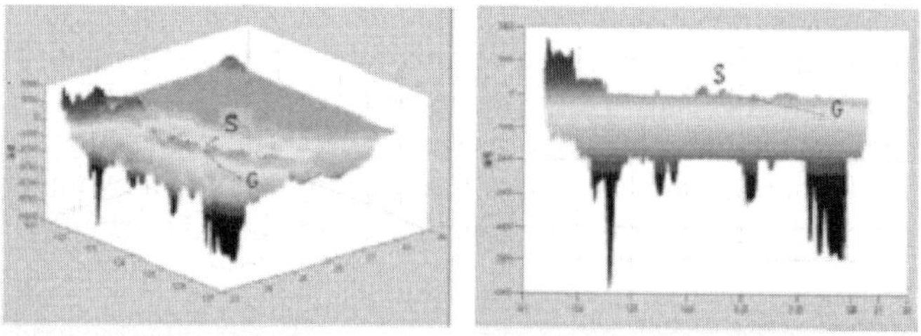


**Fig. 10.** 3D planning path in known environment

## 5.2 Experiments of Local Path Planning

Fig.11 and fig.12 show the simulating vision of FLS and 2-D obstacle-avoiding path respectively. Once the simulator detects the unknown obstacle, then it supplies the feedback sonar data to local path planner, and the local path planner dynamic generates a optimized collision-free path and guides the vehicle to its goal.

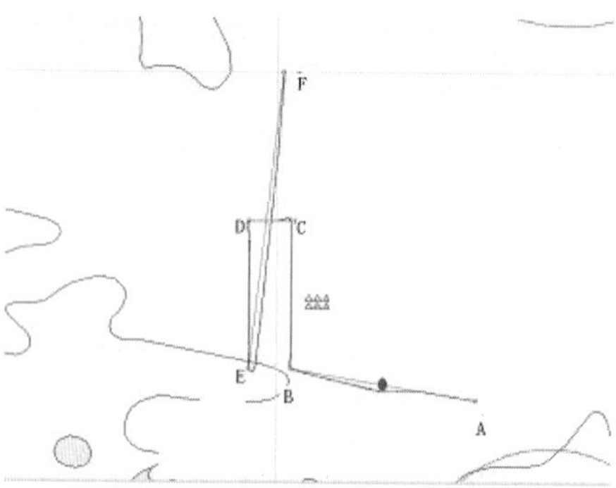


**Fig. 11.** Trajectory of AUV navigated by local planner

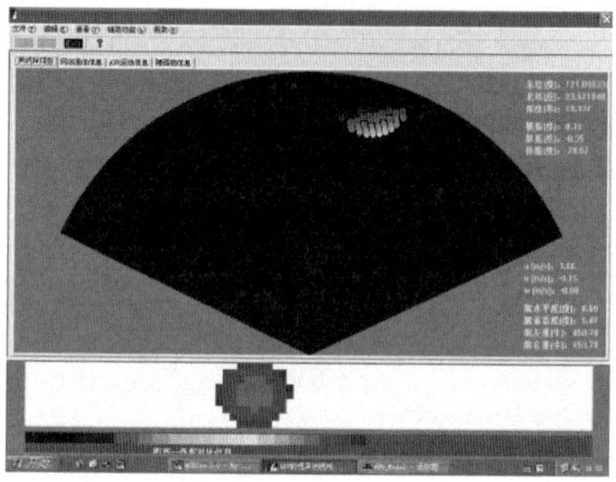

**Fig. 12.** Graph of FLS simulating vision

# 6 Conclusions

This paper mainly aims at the problem of autonomous planning for AUV in partly known environment, which is sorted into global path planning and local path planning. It designs and introduces two kinds of world model based on grid-model for these two planning problems. And it detailed describes an AGA-based global path planner to optimize a global path in a known environment. This planner utilizes domain knowledge adequately to generate initial population and design superiority genetic operators, and further more, some improved adaptive genetic strategies are adopted in the AGA-based planner, which is provided with the excellent character of good stability and high-speed global convergence, more efficiently and effectively adaptive ability. So that it has some advantages, for example, it describes the path more simply and clearly and ensures the planning path through over any blank range to the least. By analyzing the motion security of AUV, two kinds of regions which are defined as forbidden zone and potential collision zone, and some safety motion criterions are also proposed for AUV. The AGA-based global path planner also can be adapted and applied to solve the problem of local path planning. All of above researches are simulated in a semi-physical simulation platform, and the results show that the autonomous planning algorithms are valid, efficient and reliable. The adaptive abilities and autonomy of AUV can make it possible to long-term navigate in ocean and succeed in its mission.

## Acknowledgement

This research work is sponsored by the fund of Heilongjiang Postdoctoral.

## References

1. Nan, Ying., Ying, Low, Eicher..: Real-time 3D Path Planning for Sensor-based Underwater Robotics Vehicles in Unknown Environment, Oceans(1999)2051-2058
2. Petillot, Y., Tena Ruiz, I., Lane, D. M.: Underwater Vehicle Obstacle Avoidance and Path Planning Using a Multi-Beam Forward Looking Sonar. IEEE Journal of OceanicVol.26,No.2, (2001) 240-251
3. Cushieri, J., Negahdaripour, S.: Use of Forward Scan Sonar Images for Positioning and Navigation by an AUV. Oceans,Vol.2, (1998) 752–756
4. Ming, Zhou., Shudong, Sun., Yanwu, Peng: A Simple but Efficient Method for Path Planning of Mobile Robot Using Genetic Algorithm, Journal of Northwestern Polytechnical University (1998):580-583
5. Hongjian, Wang., Xinqian, Bian., etc.: A GA Path Planner Based on Domain Knowledge for AUV, Oceans'04 MTS/IEEE Techno-Ocean'04(2004)1570-1573
6. Mingqiang, Li., Jisong, Kou., etc.: Basic Theory and Application of Genetic Algorithm, Science Publishing Company(2002) 57-68
7. Xiaohui, Liang., Wei, Wu., Qinping, Zhao., etc.: Research on a Global Path Planning Method Based on Genetic Algorithm and Large Scale Real Terrain Data, Journal of Computer Research and Development(2002):301-306

# Research on Reactive Power Optimization Based on Immunity Genetic Algorithm

Keyan Liu[1], Wanxing Sheng[2], and Yunhua Li[1]

[1] Beijing University of Aeronautics and Astronautics, Beijing, China
100083 Beijing, China
liukeyan@asee.buaa.edu.cn, yunhua.l@263.net
[2] China Electric Power Research Institute, Beijing, China
100085 Beijing, China
wxsheng@263.net

**Abstract.** This paper proposed a new kind of immune genetic algorithm (IGA) according to the current algorithms solving the reactive power optimization. The hybrid algorithm is applied in reactive power optimization of power system. Adaptive crossover and adaptive mutation are used according to the fitness of individual. The substitution of individuals is implemented and the multiform of the population is kept to avoid falling into local optimum. The decimal integer encoding and reserving the elitist are used to improve the accuracy and computation speed. The flow chart of improved algorithm is presented and the parameter of the immune genetic algorithm is provided. The procedures of IGA algorithm are designed. A standard test system of IEEE 30-bus has been used to test. The results show that the improved algorithm in the paper is more feasible and effective than current known algorithms.

## 1 Introduction

Genetic algorithm (GA) is a part of evolutionary algorithm which is a branch of artificial intelligence. The method is based on Darwin's survival of the fittest hypothesis. It uses the technology of group searches to make selection, crossover and mutation on current population, which will create new generation, and gradually causes the population to evolve to contain or approaches the optimal solution. It has been applied in the multiple application domains[1] because it has the features of easy to realize, obvious effect and loose initial requirement and so on. Furthermore, being different to the traditional search techniques, which use characteristics of the problem to determine the sampling point, GA can be used to solve multi-modal, discontinuous and none-differentiable functions.

The standard genetic algorithm (SGA) method is a powerful optimization technique analogous to the natural genetic process in biology. In particular, it works very well on mixed (continuous and discrete), combinatorial problems. But it will spend much computation time in iterations to find the global optimum solution theoretically. SGA can converge to the solution with probability one, provided that there are enough time, iterations and computations. Fortunately, the continuing

D.-S. Huang, K. Li, and G.W. Irwin (Eds.): ICIC 2006, LNCS 4113, pp. 600–611, 2006.

price/performance improvements of computational systems have made GA attractive for some types of optimization.

During the past decade there has been a growing concern in power systems about reactive power operation and optimization [2] [3] [4]. Reactive power optimization is a complicated optimization problem that may have several local solutions. The control variables are mixed with continuous and discrete variables. Traditional optimization algorithms, such as linear programming, nonlinear programming, and interior point programming, have the deficiency in solving the reactive power optimization problem while GA can solve the problem with its flexible encoding characteristic.

Immune algorithm has been used to optimize reactive power in some papers[5] [6]. In this paper, a method based on IGA is used for the reactive power optimization problem and its performance is compared to that of SGA, AGA, and EP. Section 2 presents the math models of reactive power optimization problem. Section 3 the IGA algorithm is introduced and explained. To test the validity of proposed algorithm, an IEEE 30-bus test system in reactive power optimization of power system is computed in section 4. The results show the IGA algorithm is an efficient method and will have a good application in reactive power optimization.

## 2 Problem Formulation

The objective of the reactive power optimization is to minimize the active power loss in the transmission network which can be described as follows:

$$f_Q = \min P_L = \sum_{i}^{N_B} V_i \sum_{j \in h} V_j (G_{ij} \cos\delta_{ij} + B_{ij} \sin\delta_{ij}) \qquad i \in N_B,\ j \in N_i . \tag{1}$$

$$P_{Gi} - P_{Di} = V_i \sum_{j=1}^{N} V_j (G_{ij} \cos\theta_{ij} + B_{ij} \sin\theta_{ij}) \tag{2}$$

$$Q_{Gi} - Q_{Di} = V_i \sum_{j=1}^{N} V_j (G_{ij} \sin\theta_{ij} - B_{ij} \cos\theta_{ij}) \tag{3}$$

$$V_{i\min} \le V_i \le V_{i\max} \tag{4}$$

$$Q_{Gi,\min} \le Q_{Gi} \le Q_{Gi,\max} \tag{5}$$

$$C_{i\min} \le C_i \le C_{i\max} \quad i \in S_C \tag{6}$$

$$T_{ik\min} \le T_{ik} \le T_{ik\max} \qquad (i,k) \in S_T \tag{7}$$

The minimization of the function (1) is subject to a number of constraints. The constraints of equations, which are power balance restrictions of nodes, are defined as (2)-(3). The inequation restrictions of control variable and state variable are defined as

(4)-(7). $P_i$, $Q_i$, $V_i$ are the active power, reactive power and voltage in node i; $Y_{ij}$, $\delta_{ij}$ are the conductance and phase angle between node i and j.

In the most of the nonlinear optimization problems, the constraints are considered by generalizing the objective function using penalty terms. In the reactive power optimization, the generator bus voltages, $V_g$, the tap position of transformer, $T_{ik}$, the amount of reactive power source installations $C_i$, are control variables which are self constrained. Voltages of $PQ$ -buses, $V_i$, and injected reactive power of $PV$ -buses, $Q_{Gi}$, are the state variables. By adding the state variables constraints to the objective function (equation (1)) as penalty terms, the above problem can be written in the following form:

$$F = \min\left\{P_L + \lambda_1 \sum_{i=1}^{n} \left(\frac{V_i - V_{i\lim}}{V_{i\max} - V_{i\min}}\right)^2 + \lambda_2 \sum_{i=1}^{n} \left(\frac{Q_i^g - Q_{i\lim}^g}{Q_{i\max}^g - Q_{i\min}^g}\right)^2\right\} \tag{8}$$

where $P_L$ : function of power loss

$\lambda_1$ : penalty coefficient of exceeding voltage

$\lambda_2$ : penalty coefficient of exceeding reactive power limit

$V_i$ : voltage of node $i$

$Q_i$ : reactive power of generator $i$

$G_{ij}$ : imaginary part of network admittance matrix

$B_{ij}$ : real part of network admittance matrix

The definitions of $Q_{i\lim}^g$ and $V_i^{\lim}$ are defined as follows:

$$Q_{i\lim}^g = \begin{cases} Q_{i,\max}^g & (Q_i^g > Q_{i,\max}^g) \\ Q_i^g & (Q_{i,\min}^g \le Q_i^g \le Q_{i,\max}^g) \\ Q_{i,\min}^g & (Q_i^g \le Q_{i,\min}^g) \end{cases} \tag{9}$$

$$U_{i\lim} = \begin{cases} U_{i,\max} & (U_i > U_{i,\max}) \\ U_i & (U_{i,\min} \le U_i \le U_{i,\max}) \\ U_{i,\min} & (U_i < U_{i,\min}) \end{cases} \tag{10}$$

Voltage of generators, ratio of transformers and parallel-connect compensators are adjusted in order to meet the reactive power demand, improve the voltage quality, and decrease the line loss in the power system.

## 3 Immune Genetic Algorithm

The immune algorithm (IA) mimics the basic immune system defending against bacteria, viruses and other disease-related organisms. It is equipped with dramatic and complex mechanisms that recombine the genes to defend invading antigens by reducing the number of antibodies and keeping out the antigens[7]. Using this mechanism, the IA provides good performance as an optimization algorithm. The IA operates simultaneously on a population of points, instead of just on one point, in the search space. The IA is a new optimization algorithm that imitates the immune system to resolve the multi-model function optimization problem. It also holds the capability to obtain accurate results within a short period of time as the GA does. Although the IA is similar to the GA, the IA differs from the GA in the memory education and production system for various antibodies.

The coding structure for the IA is similar to that of the genetic algorithm. The data structure of the genes, the antibody coding, is shown in Fig. 1, where there are $N$ antibodies. Each of antibodies comprise $M$ genes. $N$ represents the number of antibodies in a generation. For those cells marked with k1, k2, . . ., kt, . . ., ks in the antibodies, they are alleles that come from the $i$-th gene of each antibody.

Assuming that the antibody pool comprises $N$ antibodies, each of which having $M$ genes, and with the information entropy approach, we can get

$$X_i^{n,g} = (x_i^{1,g}, x_i^{2,g}, \ldots, x_i^{n,g}) \tag{11}$$

where $X_i^{n,g}$ stands for an allele in the antibody pool, $n$ signifies the antibody number, $g$ denotes the generation number, $i$ represents antibody $n$ 's gene number( $i = 1, 2, \ldots, M$ ).

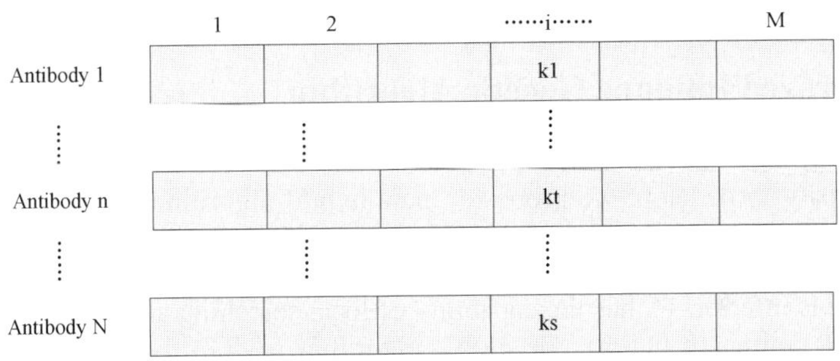


**Fig. 1.** The antibody encoding

Each antibody represents a solution to reactive power optimization, where $M$ , the total number of genes stands for the total number of control variables. The information-entropy mean[8] is defined as (12):

$$H(N) = \frac{1}{M} \sum_{j=1}^{M} H_j(N) \tag{12}$$

$$H_j(N) = -\sum_{j=1}^{N} P_j^{(k)} \log P_j^{(k)} \tag{13}$$

where $H_j(N)$ represents $i$ -th information entropy in antibody $n$ . $P_j^{(k)}$ is the probability of the kt allele coming from the $i$ -th gene. In our sample study case, $P_j^{(k)}$ is set between [0.1, 0.9]. The diversity of the genes is calculated using (13).

where $H_j(N)$ normally lies between 0.1 and 0.05 in our study case. From (12), the entropy can embody the diversity of the antibody population. The affinity expression is considered in this study. The expression observes the diversity between two antibodies and is written as (14):

$$A_{i,j} = \frac{1}{1+H(2)} \tag{14}$$

where $H(2)$ is the affinity between two antibodies. From (14), we observe that the smaller the information entropy difference of antibodies, i.e. $H(2)$ , is, the greater the affinity between two antibodies, $A_{i,j}$ , will be.

The second expression which calculates the affinity between the antigen and antibody is expressed in the following equation:

$$A_i = f(i) / \sum_{i=1}^{N} f(i) \tag{15}$$

where $f(i)$ , a fitness function of antibody fitness, $N$ is the total number of population.

## 4 Improved Immune Genetic Algorithm

Considering GA has the ability of global search and IA is good at partial searching and is easily to develop, we propose a new hybrid algorithm to search the optimal value on the genetic algorithm. The basic idea of IGA is a hybrid optimal algorithm between GA and IA. GA has the merit of searching global solution while the local searching is inferior. IA has the capability of local searching and avoiding be trapped into local optimal solution. The global algorithm of IGA is shown in Fig.2. The proposed procedure is as follows:

Step 1: Input original data and create initial value.
Step 2: Encode, i.e., translated the problem variables into GA chromosome (gene).
Step 3: Create individuals randomly and evaluate the fitness of current population.
Step 4: Extract vaccine and compute the fitness of antibody.
Step 5: Construct the immune operator that is realized by vaccination and immune selection.
Step 6: Crossover and mutation of GA.
Step 7: Decode, i.e., translate the GA chromosome to physical variables.
Step 8: Update population and compute fitness.
Step 9: Judge Convergence. If the current values cannot satisfy the convergence condition, the procedure enters into step3; if the convergence condition can be satisfied, the optimal solution is reached.

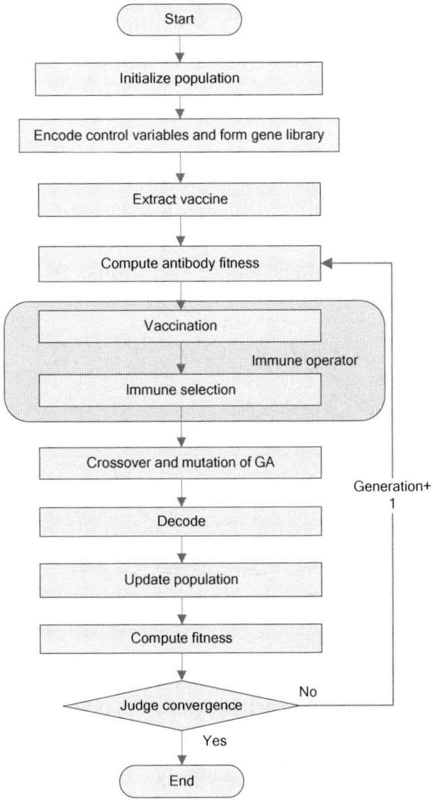


**Fig. 2.** Flow chart of improved IGA

## 4.1 Fitness Function

The selection principle of function fitness is to eliminate the individuals of small fitness at the beginning period, and to preserve the excellent characteristics of individuals to the utmost at the later period of optimization. At the same time, it needs to improve precision and avoid falling into local extreme value. The objective of reactive power optimization is to achieve the minimal values of power loss; however the algorithm of GA is to get the maximal fitness of individuals. So, we can extrude the fitness according to the ideology of SA (Simulated Annealing). The function of fitness can be defined as follows:

$$\mathrm{f}\,(\mathrm{x}) = \exp\left(\frac{1}{K * F(x)}\right) \tag{16}$$

$$\mathrm{K} = \begin{cases} \mathrm{T}_0 & k < \dfrac{N_{\max}}{2} \\ \mathrm{T}_0 * 0.99^k & k > \dfrac{N_{\max}}{2} \end{cases} \tag{17}$$

where $F(x)$ is the function value, f (x) is the fitness of individual, $T_0$ is the initial temperature of SA, $N_{\max}$ is the maximal iteration number, $k$ is the current iteration.

### 4.2 Encoding and Decoding

Although voltage of generators is continuous variable which can be evaluated randomly in the range, the adjustable voltages of generator are a set of discrete values in control center. Ratio of transformers and compensation capacity of parallel-connect compensators can get discrete values within the limits. All control variables can be described as follows:

$$X_c = [x_1 ... x_n] = [T_1 ... T_{n1} | C_1 ... C_{n2} | V_1^g ... V_{n3}^g] \tag{18}$$

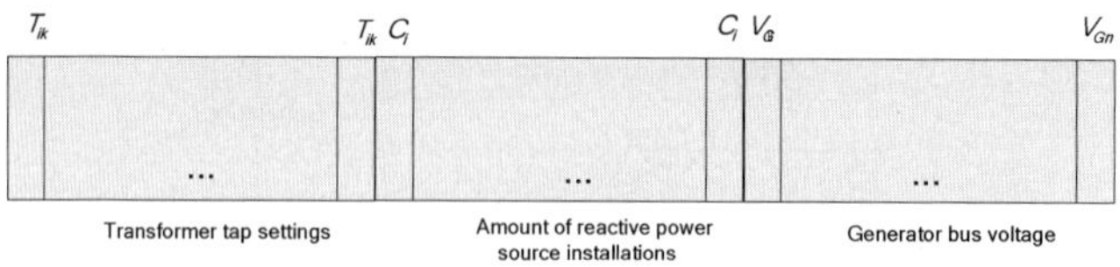


**Fig. 3.** Control variable of reactive power optimization

As (11) shows, the reactive power optimization is a mixed integer non-linear programming problem. The control variables are encoded as decimal integer coding. The chromosome is formed as shown in Fig. 3. There are three chromosome regions (one for each set of control variables), namely, 1) $T_{ik}$ ; 2) $C_i$ ; 3) $V_i^g$ . Encoding is performed using different gene-lengths for each set of control variables, depending on the desired accuracy.

$$X = [x_1 ... x_n] = [N_1^T ... N_{n1}^T | N_1^C ... N_{n2}^C | N_1^{V_g} ... N_{n3}^{V_g}] \tag{19}$$

where $N_i^T$ is the integer number of tap position of transformer, $N_i^C$ is the number of reactive power source installations and $N_i^{V_g}$ is the number of generator bus voltage; $n1$ is the number of OLTC transformer, $n2$ is the number of , $n3$ is the number of generator.

The initial value of $N_i^T$ , $N_i^C$ , $N_i^{V_g}$ can be generated as follows:

$$X_i = \text{int}(rand \times (X_{i\max} - X_{i\min} + 1)) + X_{i\min} \tag{20}$$

$$\begin{aligned} T_{ik} &= T_{ik0} + T_{ik}^{step} \times N_i^T & (i,k) \in S_T \\ C_i &= C_{i0} + C_i^{step} \times N_i^C & i \in S_C \\ V_i^g &= V_0^g + V_i^{step} \times N_i^{V_g} & \end{aligned} \tag{21}$$

where $rand$ is the random number, between 0 and 1, int() is the function of converting decimal to integer. The decoding of a chromosome to the problem physical variable is performed as (21) where $T_{ik}$ , $C_i$ , $V_i^g$ are the ratio of transformer, reactance value and voltage value of generator respectively. $T_{ik0}$, $C_{i0}$, $V_0^g$ correspond to their initial values and $T_{ik}^{step}$ , $C_i^{step}$ , $V_i^{step}$ correspond to their adjustable step value respectively.

### 4.3 Definition of Antigens and Antibodies

Antigens are equivalent to the fitness values defined by (16) and constraints of problem. Antibodies stand for feasible solution as defined in Fig.1. For example, $X_i^{a,u}$ denotes an $a$ antibody at the $u$ -th evolution generation in reactive power optimization, $i$ denotes the $i$ -th code which may be integer number of tap position of transformer, or the number of reactive power source installations, or the number of generator bus voltage.

An allele $X_i^{n,g}$ , corresponds to the $i$ -th composition of integer number ( $N_i^T$ , $N_i^C$ and $N_i^{V_g}$ ) for the $i$ -th solution at the $g$-th evolution generation in an actual reactive power optimization.

### 4.4 Determine the Crossover and Mutation Rates

In simple genetic algorithm (SGA), $P_c$ and $P_m$ are fixed values which is low efficiency for sophisticated multi-variable problem. This paper adopts adaptive crossover and mutation operation. $P_c$ and $P_m$ can be changed by the fitness of function of individuals. When the optimal solution is to fall into local optimization value, $P_c$ and $P_m$ need to improve. When the solution is to disperse, $P_c$ and $P_m$ need to reduce. The values of $P_c$ and $P_m$ should be varied depending on the average value of $f$ .

$$P_c = \begin{cases} k_1 - \dfrac{(k_1 - k_2)(f - f_{avg})}{f_{\max} - f_{avg}} & f \geq f_{avg} \\ k_1 & f < f_{avg} \end{cases} \tag{22}$$

$$P_m = \begin{cases} k_3 - \dfrac{(k_3 - k_4)(f' - f_{avg})}{f_{\max} - f_{avg}} & f' \geq f_{avg} \\ k_3 & f' < f_{avg} \end{cases} \tag{23}$$

where $k_1, k_2, k_3$ and $k_4$ have to less than 1.0 to constraint $P_c$ and $P_m$ to the range 0.0-1.0. $f_{\max}$ is the maximum fitness value, and $f_{avg}$ is the average fitness value of the population. $f$ is the larger of fitness values of the individuals selected for crossover and $f'$ is the fitness of the $i$ -th chromosome to which the mutation with probability $P_m$ is applied. $P_c$ varies from k1 to k2, and $P_m$ changes from k3 to k4. In this paper, k1=0.9, k2=0.5, k3=0.1, k4=0.01.

### 4.5 The Immune Operator

(1) Vaccine inoculation
Evaluate and select the parent-generation antibodies for one having the best fitness value. The best fitness value of previous generation can be computed and achieved by comparing with (16).

(2) Immune selection
Concentration of antibody can be used the following equation:

$$C(j) = \frac{\sum_{j=1}^{N} K(j)}{N} \tag{24}$$

where $K(j) = \begin{cases} 1 & \frac{A_{i,j}}{N} > \lambda \\ 0 & \frac{A_{i,j}}{N} < \lambda \end{cases}$, $\lambda$ is the selected boundary value.

The greater each two solutions' affinity becomes, the denser the solution in the dispatch pool will be, i.e. more similar solutions will exist.

The probability of antibody j selection can be written:

$$p_j = \alpha p_{i,1} + (1-\alpha) p_{i,2} \tag{25}$$

$$p_{i,1} = \frac{A(i)}{\sum_{i=1}^{N} A(i)},\ p_{i,2} = \frac{C(i)}{\sum_{i=1}^{N} C(i)} \tag{26}$$

where $\alpha$ is corrective factor, in our test study $\alpha = 0.5$.

### 4.6 Termination Criterion

The termination criterion for this IGA algorithm is as follows: if the maximal iteration number is reached and the optimal antibody is feasible.

## 5 Test Example

In this section, the proposed immune genetic algorithm is evaluated using the IEEE 30-bus. The test examples have been run on a 3.0-GHz Pentium-4 PC. In order to test the effect of IGA, a simulated annealing genetic algorithm (SAGA) is tested with IGA on the same test computer mentioned above.

**Table 1.** Data of test systems

| Test system | IEEE-30 | Variable constraint | | Step |
|---|---|---|---|---|
| Branch | 41 | Voltage of generator | 0.9~1.1 | 0.01 |
| Generator | 6 | Ratio of transformer | 0.9~1.1 | 0.04 |
| Load | 21 | Reactive compensation | 0~0.5 | 0.05 |

**Table 2.** Control parameters of IGA and SAGA

| | IGA | SAGA |
|---|---|---|
| N | 50 | 50 |
| Max iteration | 100 | 100 |
| Crossover | [0.5,0.9] | 0.6 |
| Mutation | [0.01,0.1] | 0.05 |
| $\lambda_1$ | 10 | 10 |
| $\lambda_2$ | 5 | 5 |

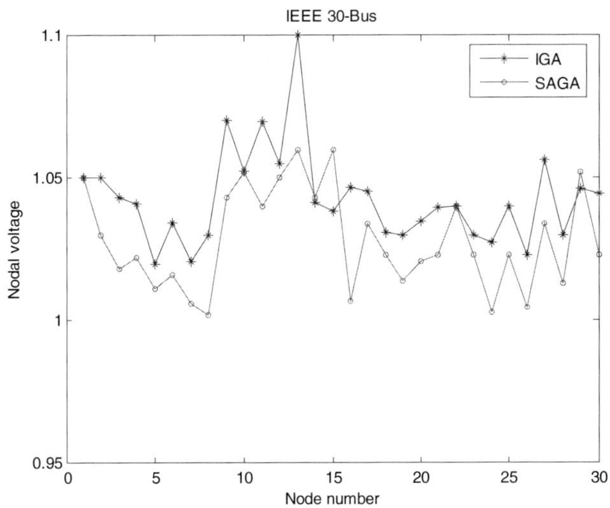


**Fig. 4.** Voltage comparison between SAGA and IGA for IEEE 30-bus

The IEEE 30-bus consists of 41-branch system[9]. It has a total of 11 control variables as follows: five unit active power outputs, six generator-bus voltage magnitudes, four adjustable transformer, and two bus-shunt admittances. The data of test system is illustrated in Table 1. The control parameters of IGA and SGA are listed in Table 2.

**Table 3.** Comparison result of IEEE 30-bus test system

| | Active Power of Generator (MW) [a] | $P_L$ | Percent of decrease | CPU time [b] | Iteration times |
|---|---|---|---|---|---|
| Before optimization | 2.90200 | 0.05988 | ----- | ----- | ----- |
| SGA | 2.88720 | 0.04980 | 17.15% | 76.32s | 80 |
| AGA[c] | 2.88326 | 0.04926 | 17.74% | 54.28s | ----- |
| EP[2] | 2.88362 | 0.04963 | 17.12% | ----- | ----- |
| SAGA | 2.88540 | 0.04894 | 18.27% | 20.14s | 69 |
| IGA | 2.87233 | 0.04787 | 20.01% | 15.21s | 56 |

[a] The base data of power is 100MVA. [b]All the CPU time and iteration times are under the same computer environment. The SGA and IGA were run 20 times with different random seeds to get an average value. [c]Referee the paper of [10] . ---denotes that it is unknown.

The comparison nodal voltage in reactive power optimization between SGA and IGA is shown in Fig.3. The quality of nodal voltage of IGA is better than SGA. Table 3 demonstrates the improvement achieved with IGA algorithm comparing with SGA, AGA[10], and EP[2]. The active line loss is decreased 20.01% and CPU time is reduced to 100 seconds. The global iteration number is decreased.

## 6 Conclusion

An improved immune genetic algorithm method is proposed to solve the reactive power optimization in this paper. This method differs from its counterparts in two main aspects, namely (1) changing the crossover and mutation ratios from a fixed value to a variable value related to fitness function, (2) adding the immune operator and selecting antibody according to computed concentration. The features of improved algorithm are as follows: (1) the IGA can avoid premature and falling into a local optimal solution trap, (2) the IGA can find the most feasible solution for reactive power optimization and has the superiority on multi-variable and discrete optimization problem. Our future work is to further improve performance and add fuzzy logic in the algorithm.

## References

1. Davis, L.: The Handbook of Genetic Algorithms. New York: Van Nostrand Reingold, (1991)
2. Lai, L. L., Ma, J. T.: Application of Evolutionary Programming to Reactive Power Planning-comparison with Nonliear Programming Approach. IEEE Transactions on Power Systems, 12 (1) (1997) 198-204
3. Iba, K.: Reactive Power Optimization by Genetic Algorithm. IEEE Transactions on Power Systems, 9 (2) (1994) 685-692

4. Lee, K. Y., Xiaomin, Bai, X. M., Park, Y. M.: Optimization Method for Reactive Power Planning by Using a Modified Simple Genetic Algorithm. IEEE Transactions on Power Systems, 10 (4) (1995) 1843-1850
5. Wei, H., Eric, H., Khayam, G.: Using Immune Genetic Algorithm to Optimize the Reactive Power. Australasian Universities Power Engineering Conference (AUPEC 2004), Brisbane Australia (2004)
6. Zhong, H. M., Ren, Z., Zhang, Y. G., Liu, B. F.: Immune Algorithm and Its Application in Power System Reactive Power Optimization. Power System Technology, (2004) 16-19 (in Chinese)
7. Dipankar, D.: Special Issue on Artificial Immune System. IEEE Transactions on Evolutionary Computation, 6 (3) (2002) 225-226
8. Liao, G. C.: Short-term Thermal Generation Scheduling Using Improved Immune Algorithm. Electric Power Systems Research, 76 (5) (2006) 360-373
9. Anastasios, G, B., Pandel, N. B., Christoforos, E., Z., Vasilios, P.: Optimal Power Flow by Enhanced Genetic Algorithm. IEEE Transactions on Power Systems. 17 (2) (2002) 229-236
10. Wu, Q. H., Cao, Y. J., Wen, J. Y.: Optimal Reactive Power Dispatch Using an Adaptive Genetic Algorithm. Int. J. Electr Power & Energy Syst., 20 (8) (1998) 563-569

# Stereo-Matching Techniques Optimisation Using Evolutionary Algorithms

Vitoantonio Bevilacqua, Giuseppe Mastronardi, Filippo Menolascina, and Davide Nitti

Dipartimento di Elettrotecnica ed Elettronica, Polytechnic of Bari,
Via E. Orabona, 4, 70125, Bari, Italy
bevilacqua@poliba.it

**Abstract.** In this paper we present a novel approach to 3D stereo-matching which uses an evolutionary algorithm in order to optimise 3D reconstruction. Common techniques in the field of 3D models generation are employed together with a Genetic Algorithm (GA) which is able to improve the results of the matching process. A general overview of the most relevant approaches is given in order to contextualise our method and to analyse its strength-points and potentialities. Details of the implemented GA are discussed with a particular focus on the constraints used in order to obtain better results. Experimental results of the trials carried out are given in a final stage together with concluding remarks and some cues for further research.

## 1 Introduction

The reconstruction of 3D models of real existing object is one of the most challenging task characterizing the field of computer vision. Many techniques exist which can reconstruct a 3D scene from two or more images. The most relevant techniques used in this field are: laser scanner, US or IR sensors, passive stereo-matching techniques, active stereo-matching techniques. The former first two approaches use expensive equipments and, as a matter of fact, this aspect limits the range of contexts these techniques can be used in. The stereo-matching approach uses only two or more photos and consists in the search of couples of points which represent the same 3D point in the real space. The difference between passive and active stereo-matching techniques basically resides in the fact that in the active flavor a structured illumination is used in order to make the matching easier. Stereo-matching algorithms can be classified into feature-based and intensity-based: feature-based methods first looks for edges, corners etc. in the source image, then carry out a matching on these features. Usually feature-based approaches provide robust but sparse information. Moreover complex computation is needed in order to obtain a complete disparity map. Intensity-based methods select a window centered at the each pixel in a image and search the more similar window in the second image. The selection of window size is a critical problem for intensity-based methods. The advantage of similar methods is that dense disparity maps can be estimated.

D.-S. Huang, K. Li, and G.W. Irwin (Eds.): ICIC 2006, LNCS 4113, pp. 612 – 621, 2006.

Traditional stereo matching techniques showed low levels of robustness mainly because each couple of matched points were searched independently from the other couples of matched points. It would be better to find a global and optimal solution (for example entire disparity map) using iterative algorithms. A similar solution should be: meet constraints of the 3D stereo matching, minimize a cost function (it includes distances of corresponding points and other terms). GA is a good solution to this problem, it find a solution that minimize a fitness function, in this work it's used GENOCOP 2 [3] because it allow to fix constraints such as "order constraint" explained in the next paragraphs. So in this work is proposed a passive intensity-based stereo-matching algorithm using a constraint handling GA to search matched points. Approach used search correspondences on corresponding epipolar lines (not on the whole image), then, selected N points on the epipolar line of the first image, N points on the corresponding epipolar line in the second image are researched, the research is carried out for each couple of epipolar lines. Two stereo-matching algorithms are proposed: for generic scenes using images from parallel cameras (or rectified images), for 3D face reconstruction using images from parallel or non parallel cameras (camera calibration is required to compute epipolar lines). In the last case 3D reconstruction process is implemented using these steps: Stereo-matching, calculation of 3D coordinates from matched points using triangulation, generation and visualization of a 3D mesh. Details of implementation proposed are discussed in "3D Stereo-Matching: Approaches and Constraints". In "Experimental Results: parallel cameras, generic scenes case" section, results of general scenes case are reported. After is proposed "The 3D Face Reconstruction Test Case" and relative results. In "Concluding Remarks and Future Works" paragraph, final considerations about this research and clues of further works are reported.

## 2 3D Stereo-Matching: Approaches and Constraints

To search matched points in the images are used these main steps:

Algorithm computes epipolar lines, selects N equidistant points in the epipolar line of the first image and searches the N matched points in the epipolar line of the second image. This step is repeated at different heights. In parallel cameras case, algorithm doesn't compute epipolar lines because they are lines at the same height. The search of N matched points in the second line is performed using GA Algorithm that minimize a fitness function. The main goal is minimize the distance between each couple of points selected in the current epipolar lines, so fitness function must have this distance and eventually others terms. The GA was then set up in order to handle n variables $v_i$ (the number of points the algorithm tries to find correspondences of). Each individual has an n-long chromosome; the GA evolves sets of solutions and, at the end of a predefined number of generations, returns the best individual, that is the individual that minimizes the fitness function described below. For each variable a range was defined in order to exclude erroneous results from the codification in the chromosome: $v_i$ (abscissa of point $P_i$' of line in the right image) must be less then abscissa of the selected point $P_i$ in the left image for geometric reasons, and to implement order constraint: $v_1 \leq v_2 \leq v_3 \ldots \leq v_n$.

All the codified solutions have to meet stereo-matching constraints defined below. Several trials have been carried out in order to obtain an optimal fitness function.

The most important aspects for this algorithm are: define a metric of distance between 2 points, define fitness function to minimize, implement constraints to improve stereo-matching results.

In this work are used Intensity based techniques and several metrics of distances between two windows have been proposed: SSD (Sum of the Squared Error), SSD using gaussian window, SSD on DCT coefficients.

SSD distance is computed considering the two windows of pixels centered on the points and summing the squared differences of pixels intensity in the windows.
In RGB images is summed SSD distance of each color level (red, green, blue). SSD distance using gaussian window respect SSD weigh squared differences of pixels intensity by gaussian function centered on the center of the window to give more importance to pixels near the center.

SSD on DCT coefficients metric computes DCT coefficients of the two windows considered and uses SSD formula on these coefficients.

Usually are compute only low frequencies coefficients to remove noise effects and it's possible to weigh continue DCT coefficient to solve different illuminations problems. Another important aspect of 3D Stereo-Matching techniques lays in the constraints. Most relevant constraints in this context are:

**Epipolar:** which is based on the assumption that the two optical centers of the cameras, the two projections of the point P under observation and the same point P lays on the same plane [11]; this constraint is performed searching matched points in lines at the same height (in parallel cameras) or epipolar lines (in general case);
**Uniqueness:** point in the first image has only one correspondence in the other photograph;
**Smoothness:** accounts for a "smooth" trend of the disparity map;
**Order:** considering N points selected on the first image, the relative points in the second photograph must have the same order, thanks to the possibility offered by Genocop 2 [3] to handle constraints, a simple inequality constraint has been imposed on the variables, so that $v_1<v_2<\ldots<v_n$. (This constraint can, sometimes, lead to mismatching due to particular configurations of the cameras, however the benefits derived from this approach exceed the disadvantages);

## 2.1 Fitness Function

The choose of fitness function is very important to obtain good results in stereo-matching. The main components included in the fitness function are: distance between couples of correspondences, smoothness, occlusion handling, saturation of the components, uniqueness.

**Distance Between Couples of Correspondences**
This contribute in the fitness is the most important and represents the sum of distances between selected points in first image and correspondent points in the second image.

The metric of distance used are SSD, SSD using gaussian window and SSD on DCT coefficients.

**Smoothness**

This contribute isn't essential but can perform better results. This term allows to obtain a smooth disparity map (in parallel cameras case), so it penalizes solutions with discontinuous disparity map probably wrong. This term produces good results in scenes with similar color zones.

Smoothness is defined as:

$$SN_i = d_i - d_{i+1} = (x_i - x_i') - (x_{i+1} - x'_{i+1}) \tag{1}$$

$d_i$ is the disparity of point 'i', $x_i$ is the abscissa of point 'i' in left image, $x_i'$ is the abscissa of point 'i' in right image, STEP is the distance between point 'i' and 'i+1' so:

$$x_{i+1} = x_i + STEP \tag{2}$$

$$SN_i = (x_i - x_i') - (x_i + STEP - x'_{i+1}) = x'_{i+1} - x'_i - STEP \tag{3}$$

The global contribute is:

$$SN = \sum_{i=0}^{n-1} SN_i \tag{4}$$

SN term is multiplied by a coefficient to weigh contribute importance in the fitness function. High coefficients can cause wrong results specially in scenes with object near and far respect the cameras, it is important to find a good compromise.

**Occlusion Handling**

Occluded point is a point visible in a image but not visible in the second image because hidden. Occluded points can cause some problems in the stereo-matching, in fact for each visible point in a image but not visible in the second image ones occurs a matching error because for each point selected is find however a correspondent point, but a not visible point hasn't a correspondent point.

So it is necessary a mechanism to handle occlusions specially in scenes with large occluded parts. In this paper are proposed several techniques to handle occlusions: distances Threshold between two correspondent points, occluded points shifting, uniqueness constraint, saturation of the components.

**Distances Threshold Between Two Correspondent Points**

This technique is used to remove wrong correspondent points after GA optimization. Usually wrong correspondent points have high distance, so to remove this points it is possible define a distance threshold: a couple of matched points is considered correct if distance between points is less then a threshold.

**Occluded Points Shifting**

Selected N points in the first image, GA searches N correspondent points, for each occluded point GA finds a wrong correspondent point; if images have large occluded parts order constraint presence can cause bad results.

To solve this problem it is possible remove from searching high probable occluded points, there are two possible implementation of this solution: scan selected points in the first image ($x_i$) to remove points with: $D_{min12}(x_i)$ > Threshold, $D_{min12}(x_i)$ is the minimum distance between point $x_i$ and all points in epipolar line of second image. Another solution (used in this work) is to use a contribute in fitness function to shift on the left occluded points in second image, so if $D_{min12}(x_i)$ > Threshold this term is added to fitness: $(x'_i-x'_{i-1})$ x beta, $x_i$' is the abscissa of point 'i' in epipolar line of second image and beta is a weight coefficient, and it isn't added distance between $x_i$ and $x_i$' (because point $x_i$ is considered not visible in the second image, therefore to consider distance term leads only matching problems).

In this way variables of GA individuals $v_i=x_i$' of occluded points are shifted near previous $v_{i-1}$ so order constraint doesn't lead problems.

**Uniqueness Constraint**
A point in the first image has only one correspondence in the other photograph, therefore after GA optimization equal variables are removed.

**Saturation of the Components**
Fitness terms (such as smoothness term) can assume big values predominating over the others leading to a bad solution, to avoid this problem it's possible saturate terms.

## 3 Experimental Results: Parallel Cameras, Generic Scenes Case

For test are used benchmark couple of images: tsukuba, sawtooth. The results consist of 2 disparity maps (for both images) on red background to highlight removed matched points because considered wrong (for example occluded points).
Tsukuba and sawtooth disparity maps are:

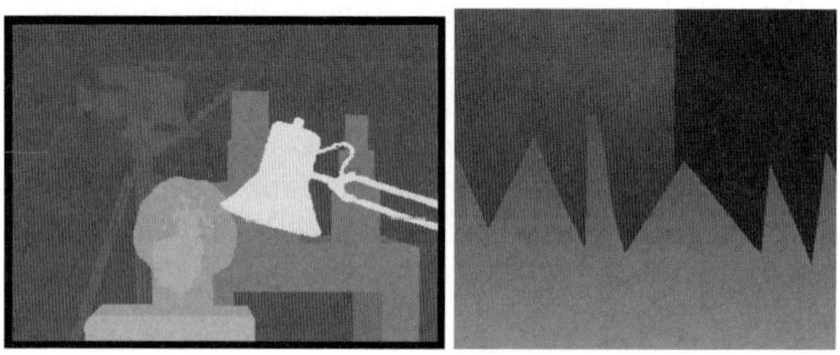

**Fig. 1.** Tsukuba and sawtooth disparity map

**Test 1**
General features are: 5 pixel step between selected points in epipolar line of first image, pixel window size equal to (4 x STEP+1) x (4 x STEP+1), SSD distance with gaussian window using standard deviation equal to 0.8 x STEP, removal of matched points with distance greater then 11*(4 x STEP+1) x (4 x STEP+1), removal of equal variables. GA parameters are: population of 80 individuals, 25000 generations, best solution of previous search to initialize GA. Fitness terms are SSD distances and smoothness with coefficient weight equal to 15.

**Results**

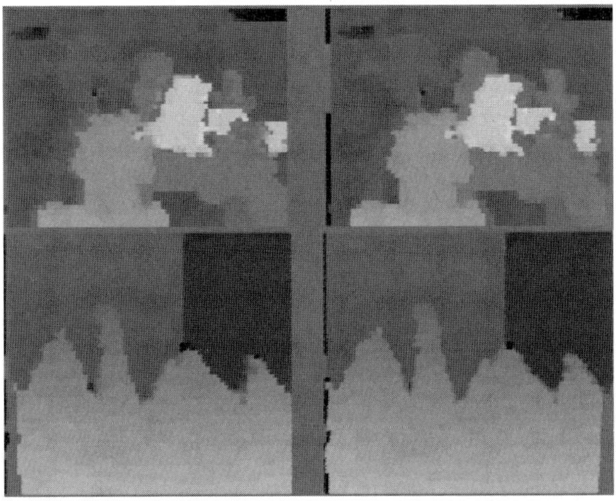

**Fig. 2.** Test 1 results: Tsukuba and sawtooth disparity map

**Comments**

Results are good, only some error is present in limited zones.

**Test 2**

General features are: 4 pixel step between selected points in epipolar line of first image, pixel window size equal to (4 x STEP+1) x (4 x STEP+1), SSD distance with gaussian window using standard deviation equal to 0.8 x STEP, removing matched points with distance greater then 11*(4 x STEP+1) x (4 x STEP+1), removal of equal variables, removal of points with distance greater then a threshold. GA parameters are population of 90 individuals, 35000 generations, best previous solution to initialize the population of the GA. Fitness terms are: SSD distances, smoothness with coefficient weight: 11.

**Results**

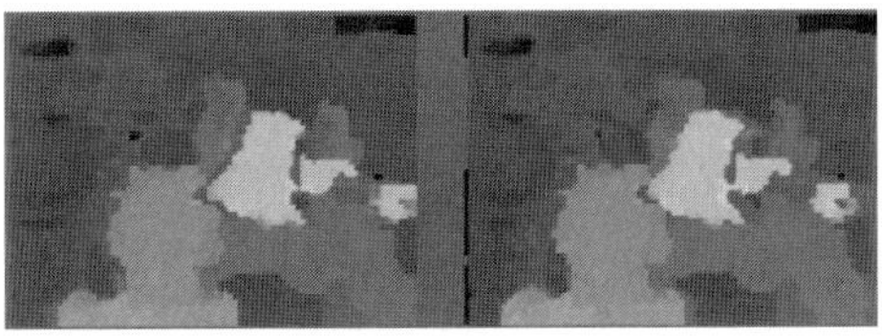

**Fig. 3.** Test 2 results: Tsukuba disparity map

**Comments**

In this test is used a small step (4 pixel instead 5 pixel), results are good but this choose increases computation time.

## 4 The 3D Face Reconstruction Test Case

The developed application has been tested on a common study case for this context: the 3D face reconstruction problem. The 3D face reconstruction experiment has been carried out following these steps: stereo matching of the two photographs using non parallel cameras (without rectification) and computing epipolar lines, save the couples of correspondences, including points' color, coordinates computation through triangulation, surface generation using triangles defined by the obtained 3D points.

### 4.1 Experimental Results

In tests are used images from non parallel cameras (not rectified), so it is needed a previous cameras calibration to compute epipolar lines for stereo-matching. In results are shown matched points using same colors.

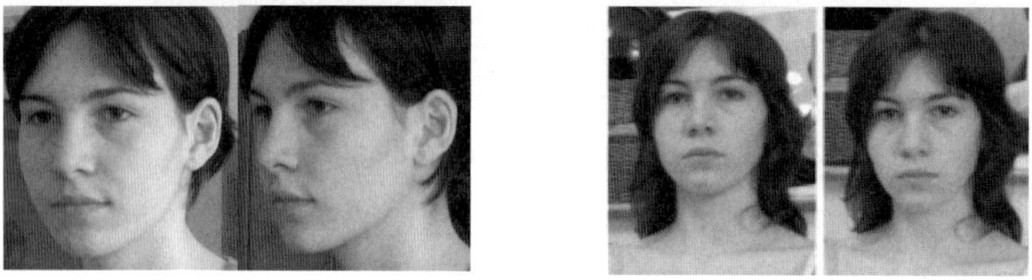

**Fig. 4.** Couples of images used for 3D reconstruction

**Test 3**

General features are: 6 pixel step between selected points in epipolar line of first image, pixel window size: (2 x STEP+1) x (2 x STEP+1). GA parameters are: population of 80 individuals, 25000 generations, best previous solution to initialize the population of the GA. Fitness terms are: SSD distance on DCT coefficients: are computed (2 x STEP+1) / 3 x (2 x STEP+1) / 3 low frequencies coefficients using gaussian window with standard deviation equal to 1.6 x STEP, weight of continue DCT coefficient in the distance formula equal to 1%, smoothness term.

**Results**

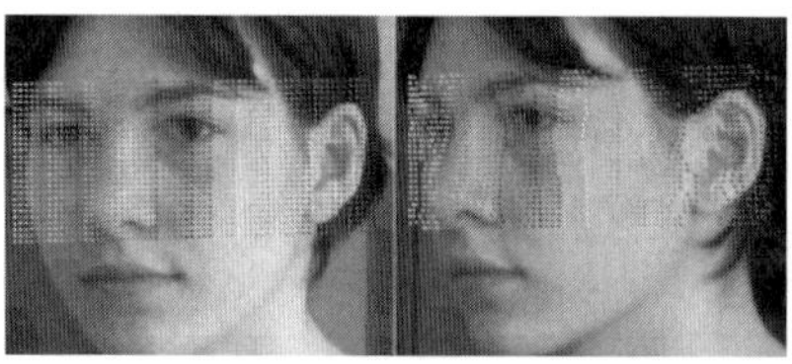

**Fig. 5.** Test 3 results: stereo-matching of first couple of images

**Test 4**

General features are: 6 pixel step between selected points in epipolar line of first image, pixel window size: (4 x STEP+1) x (4 x STEP+1). GA parameters are: population of 80 individuals, 25000 generations, best previous solution to initialize the population of the

GA. Fitness terms are: SSD distance on RGB, with saturation equal to: (4 x STEP+1) x (4 x STEP+1) x 3.4 using gaussian window with standard deviation 1.6 x STEP, smoothness with weight 16 and saturation 80 x STEP, occluded points shifting for point with minimum distance greater then 2 x (4 x STEP+1) x (4 x STEP+1).

**Results**

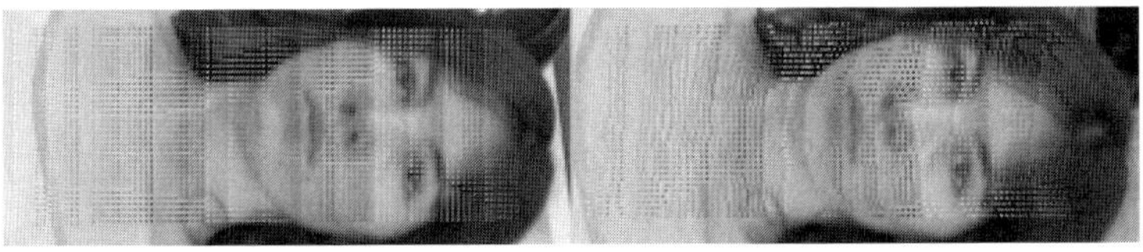

**Fig. 6.** Test 4 results: stereo-matching of second couple of images

**Comments**

Results are visibly very good, using triangulation it is possible compute 3D coordinates of matched points and show them using a 3D engine.

The generation of a surface from a cloud of points is not a trivial task and is an open field of research in the area of computer vision. The implemented algorithm uses the relative positions of points in order to build the surface in an easier way. The mesh is built as in figure 1:

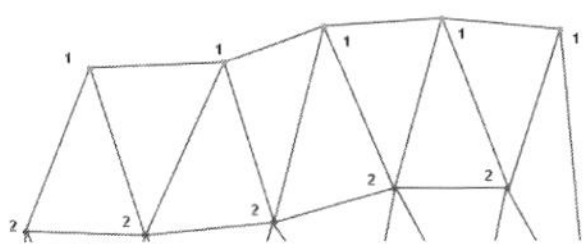

**Fig. 7.** 3D Mesh

The points marked with "1" correspond to the first couple of epipolar lines; the ones marked with "2" to the second epipolar line and so on and so forth. Three dimensional points obtained from the correspondences of two couples of two epipolar adjacent lines are considered (e.g. points marked "1" and "2"); triangles are then built choosing alternatively the points from the first and the second epipolar line, the second and the third and so on and so forth. The mesh structure is then obtained and to each point the pre-saved color is given to draw a visually interpretable surface. A texture taken from the image analysed could also be employed in order to obtain a more accurate final representation of the 3D model. The algorithm for mesh generation and visualisation uses DirectX 3D engine graphic engine.

In the first trial (figure 2) global good results have been reached. The few mismatches derive from the relative positions of the cameras.

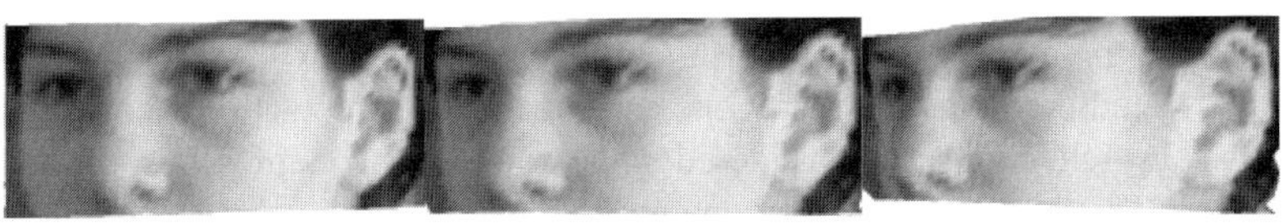

**Fig. 8.** 3D reconstruction of test 3

Results obtained in the second trial are excellent (figure 3). The advantage on the first trial mainly lays in the different relative orientation of the two photograph used for the stereo matching. It is evident that photographs taken from the top to the bottom lead to a more accurate face reconstruction.

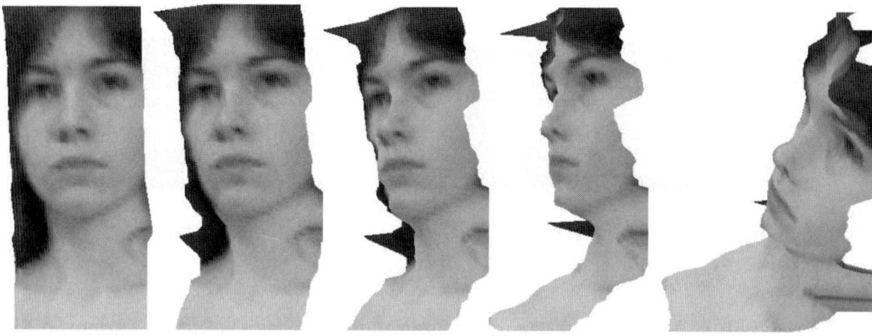

**Fig. 9.** 3D reconstruction of test 4

## 5 Concluding Remarks and Further Works

The results obtained have put in evidence good global performances of the proposed algorithm. An *a posteriori* analysis of the results leads to the conclusion that the main aspect of the implementation described are: employment of the "Smoothness" component in the fitness functions, smoothness saturation, employment of the best previous solution to initialise the population of the GA, use of the DCT in order to solve the issues derived from different lighting, reducing, eliminating or normalizing the continuous component, left shifting of the supposed occluded correspondences.

Moreover the use of the order constraint demonstrated to be quite useful in order to accelerate the convergence rate of the GA. In the case of generic scenes stereo-matching results are good in all tests. In the case of non parallel cameras the results for 3D face reconstruction were quite good; in some cases the model returned proved to be highly accurate even if built on only two images. The position of the cameras showed to be a quite important factor; cameras placed too near lead to a good matching level but even to an higher difficulty in the extraction of an accurate model because errors of one pixel in the correspondence show a greater weight. Instead, if the cameras are placed in more distant places and in different relative orientations, the returned results show lower accuracy but the 3D model extracted is characterised by a higher quality. It is evident that a compromise needs to be looked for. As a matter of fact, better results have been reached when photographs where taken orientating the focal axes of the cameras in order to look at the face from the top to the bottom.

The employment of GA has shown high potentialities in order to solve stereo matching related problems with only one drawback: the computational cost of similar approaches which could be considered unbearable for certain kinds of real-time applications. This last aspect is even one of the most interesting for what concerns the future perspectives of this work. Software level optimisations, on the other hand, are being studied in order to keep limited the computational costs of this approach. A further cue of research can consist in the evaluation of different metrics of distance and, eventually, the application of pre-processing elaboration of the images in order to obtain better results. A more interesting extension to the proposed solution could be represented by the research of the entire disparity map leaving the "line-by-line" approach previously described. This could lead to interesting results even given the fact that vertical constraints would be then required and that, in this situation, it is not possible to use any knowledge about the epipolarity of the lines.

## References


1. Gong, M., Yang, Y.H.: Multi-resolution Stereo Matching Using Genetic Algorithm. IEEE Workshop on Stereo and Multi-Baseline Vision (2001)
2. Sun, C.M.: Fast Stereo Matching Using Rectangular Subregioning and 3D Maximum-Surface Techniques. International Journal of Computer Vision. Vol. 47 (2002) 99-117
3. Michalewicz, Z., Janikow, C. Z.: GENOCOP: a Genetic Algorithm for Numerical Optimization Problems with Linear Constraints. Volume 39, Issue 12es Electronic Supplement to the December issue Article No. 175 (1996)
4. Luo, L. J., Clewer, D. R., Canagarajah, C. N., Bull, D. R.: Genetic Stereo Matching Using Complex Conjugate Wavelet Pyramids
5. Uchida, N., Shibahara, T., Aoki, T., Nakajima, H., Kobayashi, K.: 3D Face Recognition Using Passive Stereo Vision (2005)
6. Klarquist, W.N., Bovik, A.C., Fovea: A Foveated Vergent Active Stereo Vision System For Dynamic Three-Dimensional Scene Recovery, T-RA(14) (1998) 755-770
7. Kanade, T., Okutomi, M.: A Stereo Matching Algorithm with an Adaptive Window: Theory and Experiments. IEEE Transactions on Pattern Analysis and Machine Intelligence, 16(9) (1994) 920-932
8. Egnal, G., Wildes, R. P.: Detecting Binocular Half-Occlusions: Empirical Comparisons of Four Approaches
9. Mordohai, P., Mediani, G.: Dense Multiple View Stereo with General Camera Placement using Tensor Voting
10. Han, K.-P., Song, K.-W., Chung, E.-Y., Cho, S.-J., Ha, Y.-H.: Stereo Matching Using Genetic Algorithm with Adaptive Chromosomes. Pattern Recognition, Vol. 34, No. 9 (2001) 1729-1740

# Weighted Fuzzy C-Means Clustering Based on Double Coding Genetic Algorithm

Duo Chen, Du-Wu Cui, and Chao-Xue Wang

School of Computer Science and Engineering,
Xi'an University of Technology, Xi'an, 710048, China
vkxtfj@163.net, cuidw@xaut.edu.cn

**Abstract.** We propose a double coding scheme in genetic algorithm (GA) and apply it to the fuzzy features-weighting clustering problems. Each individual consists of two segments of codes for cluster centers and feature weights. The two segments are evolved simultaneously in the clustering process. A modified clustering objective function is defined. A weighted fuzzy c-means operator and a feature weights learning operator are designed to guide computing cluster centers and feature weights in an individual respectively. On the basis of the above work, a novel weighed fuzzy c-means clustering algorithm based on double coding GA is advanced.

## 1 Introduction

Clustering analysis is an important research project in knowledge discovery and data mining (KDDM). Clustering algorithms partition data objects into a certain number of clusters such that objects in the same cluster are more similar to each other than objects in different clusters. One of the important problems is to design appropriate dissimilarity measures in cluster analysis. Generally speaking, the traditional clustering algorithms, such as the widely used fuzzy c-means (FCM) algorithm [1], choose Euclidean distance as the dissimilarity measure, which relates to all features, and further supposes that each feature has equal importance. In practical applications, we have the scientific data survey, database analysis, customer relations management, medicine diagnosis, weather forecast, water analysis, etc. The importance of each feature is not often the same, sometimes quite different, and certain features can even be neglected. The method of feature weight assignment can be used to better solve this problem. That is, the larger the feature weight is, the higher the degree of importance of this feature is. The zero value of the feature weight indicates that this feature does not play any role and can be reduced. In fact, feature weights belong to domain knowledge and may be beforehand determined by domain experts. However, in some situation, the domain knowledge is insufficient to determine the feature weights completely. Sometimes the relevant domain knowledge is too deficient to provide effective information for determining feature weights. Consequently, feature weights computing and optimizing have been quite important research topics in cluster analysis. X. Z. Wang el al. [2] proposed the weighted FCM algorithm which was based on the weighted Euclidean distance. The weight assignment was given by

D.-S. Huang, K. Li, and G.W. Irwin (Eds.): ICIC 2006, LNCS 4113, pp. 622–633, 2006.

learning according to the gradient descent technique. E. Y. Chan et al. [3] presented an optimization algorithm for clustering using weighted dissimilarity measures. A new procedure to generate a weight for each feature from each cluster was developed in the algorithm. The W-k-means algorithm [4], proposed by J. Z. Huang et al., can automatically weight features based on the importance of the features in clustering. W-k-means added a new step to the basic k-means [5] algorithm to update feature weights based on the current partition of data. The above-mentioned algorithms belong to the partitional methods in cluster analysis, with a high operation efficiency, but there exists the drawback that clustering results are often dependent on the selection of the initial points and cannot ensure convergence to a global optimum. With global searching ability, GAs are the randomized search and optimization algorithms based on the mechanism of natural selection and genetics. Combining GAs with partitional clustering algorithms is a kind of effective method to avoid converging to a locally optimal solution. GKA clustering algorithm [6] developed by K. Krishna and M. N. Murty combined GA with k-means algorithm to find the global optimum. In GKA, a simple coding scheme was employed; a problem-specific gradient descent operator (KMO) and a distance based mutation (DBM1) were designed. U. Maulik and S. Bandyopadhyay advanced a genetic algorithm-based clustering technique called GA-clustering [7], in which individuals were represented as string of real numbers, encoded the centers of a fixed number of clusters. Y. Y. Dong et al. [8] put forward an improved hybrid cluster algorithm, named GFGA, which achieved the combination of genetic algorithm's global search ability and FCM's local search ability.

The main objective of this paper is to develop a double encoding GA and apply it to the fuzzy features-weighting clustering problems. Appling the double coding scheme of "cluster centers + feature weights", an individual is a sequence of real numbers representing the values of both the cluster centers and the feature weights. The genetic operations are simultaneously applied to the two segments of an individual in each iteration of the algorithm. The modified clustering objective function is defined. The weighted FCM operator is given to update current fuzzy partition and cluster centers. To direct computing the feature weights, we design the feature weights learning operator. On the basis of the above work, a novel weighed FCM clustering algorithm based on double coding GA called DGAFCM is advanced.

The rest of this paper are organized as follows: Section 2 gives the problem statement. Section 3 presents the DGAFCM algorithm. Experimental results on both artificial and real data set are given in Section 4. We conclude the paper and have an outlook for further research in the last section.

## 2 Problem Statement

Let $X=\{X_1,X_2,...,X_n\}$ be a set of $n$ objects and each object $X_i=(x_{i,1},x_{i,2},...x_{i,s})$ in $X$ characterized by $A=\{A_1,A_2,...,A_s\}$, a set of $s$ features, where $x_{i,j}$ is the value of the $jth$ feature of object $X_i$, $\forall$ $1\le i\le n$ and $1\le j\le s$. A fuzzy partition of $X$ can be stated as a constrained nonlinear optimization problem, which minimize Equation (1), under the constraint of Equation (2), with unknown variables $U$ and $V$ as follows:

$$J(U,V)=\sum_{l=1}^{c}\sum_{i=1}^{n}\sum_{j=1}^{s}u_{l,i}^{m}d_{j}(x_{i,j},v_{l,j}) \tag{1}$$

subject to

$$\begin{cases}\sum_{l=1}^{c}u_{l,i}=1 & 1\le i\le n\\ 0\le u_{l,i}\le 1 & 1\le i\le n,\ \ 1\le l\le c\\ 0<\sum_{i=1}^{n}u_{l,i}<n & 1\le l\le c\end{cases} \tag{2}$$

where:

- $c\in(1,n)$ is a known number of clusters and $m>1$ is a parameter;
- $U=[u_{l,i}]$ is a $c\times n$ fuzzy partition matrix;
- $V=\{V_1,V_2,\ldots V_c\}$ is a set of $c$ vectors. Each $V_l=(v_{l,1},v_{l,2},\ldots v_{l,s}),l=1,2,\ldots c$, expresses the center of the $lth$ cluster.
- $d_j(x_{i,j},v_{l,j})$ is a distance or dissimilarity measure between object $i$ and the center of cluster $l$ on the $jth$ feature.

$$d_{j}(x_{i,j},v_{l,j})=(x_{i,j}-v_{l,j})^{2} \tag{3}$$

In FCM algorithm, the above problem is solved by iteratively solving the following two minimization problems:

1. Problem $P_1$: Fix $V=\hat{V}$ and solve the reduced problem $J(U,\hat{V})$;
2. Problem $P_2$: Fix $U=\hat{U}$ and solve the reduced problem $J(\hat{U},V)$;

Problem $P_1$ is solved by

$$u_{l,i}=\left[\sum_{k=1}^{c}\left(\frac{d_{i,l}}{d_{i,k}}\right)^{\frac{1}{m-1}}\right]^{-1} \quad for\ \ 1\le l\le c,\ \ 1\le i\le n \tag{4}$$

where

$$d_{i,l}=\sum_{j=1}^{s}d_{j}(x_{i,j},v_{l,j}) \tag{5}$$

and problem $P_2$ is solved by

$$v_{l,j}=\frac{\sum_{i=1}^{n}(u_{l,i})^{m}x_{i,j}}{\sum_{i=1}^{n}(u_{l,i})^{m}} \quad for\ \ 1\le l\le c,\ \ 1\le j\le s \tag{6}$$

# 3 Clustering Algorithm Based on Double Coding GA

## 3.1 Double Coding Scheme

We give the definition of clustering individual in this section.

**Definition 1.** Let $X=\{X_1,X_2,...,X_n\}$ be a set of $n$ objects to be clustered, and $A=\{A_1,A_2,...,A_s\}$ be a set of $s$ features. $DOM(A_j)\in\Re$ denotes the domain of the feature $A_j$, $j=1,2,...s$. The clustering individual is defined as a finite sequence of real numbers as follows:

$$H=V_1V_2...V_c\omega_1\omega_2...\omega_s \tag{7}$$

where

$$V_l=v_{l,1}v_{l,2}...v_{l,s} \quad l=1,2,...c \tag{8}$$

subject to

$$v_{l,j}\in DOM(A_j), j=1,2,...,s, \quad l=1,2,...,c \tag{9}$$

and

$$\sum_{j=1}^{s}\omega_j=1, \quad 0\le\omega_j\le 1 \tag{10}$$

In Definition 1, $V_1V_2...V_c$ are the centers of $c$ clusters and consist of $c\times s$ words, and $\omega_1\omega_2...\omega_s$ with $s$ words are the weight values of $s$ features. Therefore, the total length of clustering individual is $L=c\times s+s$. Obviously, in the clustering individual the direct encoding method is adopted, so the regularity property is consequentially satisfied. Simplifying the process of coding-decoding, this method is fit for high accuracy computing and searching for a large sample space.

For convenient description, the symbols $H_V=V_1V_2...V_c$ and $H_W=\omega_1\omega_2...\omega_s$ are used to denote the cluster centers and the feature weights in $H$ respectively in the following text.

Let $L$ be the length of an individual, $N$ a known positive integer. Then

$$\Gamma_L=\{H=V_1V_2...V_c\omega_1\omega_2...\omega_s \mid V_i\in H_V, i=1,2,..c, \quad \omega_j\in H_W, j=1,2,...s\} \tag{11}$$

is called the individual space, and the product

$$\Gamma_L^N=\underbrace{\Gamma_L\times\Gamma_L\times...\times\Gamma_L}_{N} \tag{12}$$

is called $N$-population space.

## 3.2 Fitness Function

The definitions of the modified clustering objective function and the fitness function of an individual are discussed in this section.

**Definition 2.** Let $H = H_V H_W$ be an individual. We defined the modified clustering objective function as follows:

$$J_M(H,U) = J_M(H_V, H_W, U) = \sum_{l=1}^{c}\sum_{i=1}^{n}\sum_{j=1}^{s} u_{l,i}^{m}\omega_j^{\beta} d(x_{i,j}, v_{l,j}) \tag{13}$$

where, $\beta > 1$ is an exponent of the feature weight.

**Definition 3.** Let $H = H_V H_W$ be an individual. The fitness function of $H$ is defined as follows:

$$F_U(H) = \frac{1}{J_M(H,U)} \tag{14}$$

Knowing that the fuzzy partition matrix $U$ is not included in an individual, we need first compute it. Using Equation (4), we modify the fuzzy partition matrix computing formula as follows:

$$u_{l,i} = \left[\sum_{k=1}^{c}\left(\frac{d'_{i,l}}{d'_{i,k}}\right)^{\frac{1}{m-1}}\right]^{-1} \quad for\ \ 1 \le l \le c,\ \ 1 \le i \le n \tag{15}$$

where, $d'_{i,j}$ is computed by:

$$d'_{i,l} = \sum_{j=1}^{s} \omega_j d_j(x_{i,j}, v_{l,j}) \tag{16}$$

### 3.3 Selection

The roulette selection strategy is adopted, in which the probability that an individual is selected is proportional to its fitness value in the population.

### 3.4 Crossover

Let $H_1 = H_{V,1}H_{W,1}$ and $H_2 = H_{V,2}H_{W,2}$ be the individuals under consideration, in which, $H_{V,i} = V_1^{(i)}V_2^{(i)}...V_c^{(i)}$ and $H_{W,i} = \omega_1^{(i)}\omega_2^{(i)}...\omega_s^{(i)}$ $i = 1,2$. We deal with the crossover operations to the two segments of the individuals respectively as follows.

For $H_{v,i}$ $i = 1,2$, the arithmetic crossover operator based on gene matching with minimum distance [8] is employed. Let $H_2' = H_{V,2}' H_{W,2}'$ is an empty individual. We compare the distances between the first element $V_1^{(1)} \in H_{V,1}$ and all elements in $H_{V,2}$ one by one, and choose the $V_j^{(2)} \in H_{V,2}$ $(1 \le j \le c)$ such that the distance between $V_j^{(2)}$ and $V_1^{(1)}$ is the minimum and put $V_j^{(2)}$ into $H_{V,2}'$. By the same method, we compare the distances between the other elements in $H_{V,1}$ and the remnant elements in $H_{V,2}$ one by one and put the elements selected into $H_{V,2}'$ in sequence. Therefore we can obtain the $H'_{V,2}$ that is matched with $H_{V,1}$. Performing the common single-point arithmetic crossover operation to $H_{V,1}$ and $H'_{V,2}$ with a fixed crossover probability of $P_c$, the cluster center codes of child individual of $H_1$ and $H'_2$ can be formed.

For $H_{W,i} = \omega_1^{(i)}\omega_2^{(i)}...\omega_s^{(i)}$ $i = 1,2$, the common single-point arithmetic crossover method with the same crossover probability is also adopted. Considering the constraint of $\sum_{j=1}^{s}\omega_j = 1$, a normalization process is required after crossover operations. Let $H_W = \omega_1\omega_2...\omega_s$ be the original weights and $H'_W = \omega'_1\omega'_2...\omega'_s$ the weights after normalization, then they satisfy:

$$\omega'_j = \frac{\omega_j}{\sum_{t=1}^{s}\omega_t} \qquad j = 1,2,...,s \tag{17}$$

### 3.5 Mutation

The common uniform mutation method is adopted. The two segments in an individual undergo mutation with the same fixed mutation probability of $P_m$ . Let $H = H_V H_W = V_1V_2...V_c\omega_1\omega_2...\omega_s$ be an individual. In $H_V$ , for any $v_{l,j} \in V_l$ , we have $v_{l,j} \in DOM(A_j)$, $l = 1,2,...c$ and $j = 1,2,...s$ . Therefore, we can select a value randomly in the range of $DOM(A_j)$ and replace $v_{l,j}$ with it according the mutation probability. For $H_W = \omega_1\omega_2...\omega_s$, the selected $\omega_j \in H_W$ can be replaced with a random value in the range $[0,1]$ according to the mutation probability. After the mutation, we normalize the feature weights by applying Equation (17).

### 3.6 Weighted FCM Operator

Although the FCM is type of iterative and hill climbing algorithm and cannot guarantee convergence to a global optimum, its locally searching capability is strong. As a stochastic optimization approach, GA is good at avoiding convergence to a locally optimal solution but its velocity of convergence is often slow. Combining the both will improves the performances of clustering algorithms. Using a one-step FCM algorithm with the fixed feature weights, we design the weighted FCM operator, called WFCMO, as follows:

Let $H = H_V H_W = V_1V_2...V_c\omega_1\omega_2...\omega_s \in \Gamma_L$ be an individual and $U$ be the fuzzy partition matrix.

1. Fix $H = \hat{H}$ update $U$ by Equation (15)
2. Fix $U = \hat{U}$ update the $H_V = V_1V_2...V_c$ by Equation (6)

In WFCMO, the feature weights are not updated, namely $H_W = \omega_1\omega_2...\omega_m$ being fixed. Under this situation the fuzzy features-weighting fuzzy clustering problem reduces to the optimization problem without considering the feature weights. Therefore, we can utilize the method that is analogous to FCM algorithm for the operator.

### 3.7 Feature Weights Learning Operator

In dealing with the fuzzy features-weighting clustering problems the calculation and optimization of the weights for all features is one of the key problems. Aimed at the problem, the feature weighs learning operator called FWLO is designed in this section.

**Theorem 1.** Let $H = H_V H_W \in \Gamma_L$ be an individual under consideration, $U = \hat{U}$ and $H_V = \hat{H}_v$ be fixed. The minimizer $\hat{H}_W$ of the optimization problem $\min_{H_W} J_M(\hat{H}_V, H_W, \hat{U})$ subject to (10) is given by

$$\hat{\omega}_j = \begin{cases} 0 & \text{if } \delta_j = 0 \\ \left[ \sum_{t=1}^{k} \left( \frac{\delta_j}{\delta_t} \right)^{\frac{1}{\beta-1}} \right]^{-1} & \text{if } \delta_j \neq 0 \end{cases} \tag{18}$$

where

$$\delta_j = \sum_{l=1}^{c} \sum_{i=1}^{n} \hat{u}_{l,i}^m d(x_{i,j}, v_{l,j}) \tag{19}$$

and $k (\leq s)$ is the number of features where $\delta_j \neq 0$

Proof

1. If $\delta_j = 0$, according to Equation (19), these features have a unique value. No matter what values the $\hat{\omega}_j$ is these features have no contribution to $J_M$. So we set $\hat{\omega}_j = 0$ to all features where $\delta_j = 0$.
2. For the $k$ features where $\delta_j \neq 0$, we can adopt the method of Lagrange multiplier. We rewrite Equation (13) as:

$$J_M(\hat{H}_V, H_W, \hat{U}) = \sum_{j=1}^{k} \omega_j^\beta \sum_{l=1}^{c} \sum_{i=1}^{n} \hat{u}_{l,i}^m d(x_{i,j}, v_{l,j}) = \sum_{j=1}^{k} \omega_j^\beta \delta_j \tag{20}$$

Let $\lambda$ be the multiplier and $\Phi(H_W, \lambda)$ be the Lagrangian equation defined by

$$\Phi(H_W, \lambda) = \sum_{j=1}^{k} \omega_j^\beta \delta_j + \lambda \left( \sum_{j=1}^{k} \omega_j - 1 \right) \tag{21}$$

If $(\hat{H}_W, \hat{\lambda})$ is to minimize $\Phi(H_W, \lambda)$, its partial derivative in both sets of variables must be zero, thus

$$\frac{\partial \Phi(\hat{H}_W, \hat{\lambda})}{\partial \hat{\omega}_j} = \beta \hat{\omega}_j^{\beta-1} \delta_j + \hat{\lambda} = 0 \quad \text{for } 1 \leq j \leq k \tag{22}$$

and

$$\frac{\partial \Phi(\hat{H}_W, \hat{\lambda})}{\partial \hat{\lambda}} = \sum_{j=1}^{k} \hat{\omega}_j - 1 = 0 \tag{23}$$

From (22), we have

$$\hat{\omega}_j = \left( \frac{-\hat{\lambda}}{\beta \delta_j} \right)^{\frac{1}{\beta-1}} \quad for \ \ 1 \le j \le k \tag{24}$$

Substituting (24) into (23), we have

$$\left(-\hat{\lambda}\right)^{\frac{1}{\beta-1}} = \left[ \sum_{t=1}^{k} \left( \frac{1}{\beta \delta_t} \right)^{\frac{1}{\beta-1}} \right]^{-1} \tag{25}$$

Substituting (25) into (24), we can obtain

$$\hat{\omega}_j = \left[ \sum_{t=1}^{k} \left( \frac{\delta_j}{\delta_t} \right)^{\frac{1}{\beta-1}} \right]^{-1} \tag{26}$$

According to the theorem, we propose the FWLO as follows:

Let $H = H_V H_W = V_1 V_2 ... V_k \omega_1 \omega_2 ... \omega_s \in \Gamma_L$ be an individual and $U$ be the fuzzy partition matrix. Fix $U = \hat{U}$ and $H_V = \hat{H}_V$ , calculate $H_W$ by Equation (18).

### 3.8 The Proposed Clustering Algorithm

In this section, the weighted fuzzy c-means clustering based on double encoding genetic algorithm, i.e. DGAFCM, is proposed.

**Algorithm DGAFCM**

**Step1** (initialization)**:** Set the size of population *N*, crossover probability $P_c$, mutation probability $P_m$, maximal generation *Maxgen* and *t:=0*. The initial population $G(0) \in \Gamma_L^N$ is formed, in which the cluster centers are randomly selected and the feature weights are generated with uniform distribution. Let $\hat{H}(0)$ be the best individual in $G(0)$.

**Step2** (evolution)**:** For the current population *G(t)* perform the selection, crossover, mutation, WFCMO and FWLO operations respectively to generate the next population *G(t+1)*.

**Step3** (elitist strategy)**:** Let $\tilde{H}(t+1)$ be the best individual in *G(t+1)*, we have $\hat{H}(t+1) = \max\{\hat{H}(t), \tilde{H}(t+1)\}$. Therefore, $\hat{H}(t+1)$ is the best individual so far.

**Step4:** If the algorithm has reached the *Maxgen* generations, outputs the clustering results from the best individual, and then the algorithm stops; else set *t:=t+1* and goes to Step 2.

## 4 Experimental Results

### 4.1 Experiments on Artificial Data Set

The artificial database contains 200 instances that are divided into two clusters, and each cluster has 100 instances. The feature set is $A=\{A_1,A_2,...,A_5\}$, in which the first three features are normally distributed, and the last two features are uniformly distributed. The centers and the standard deviations of the two clusters for all features are shown in Table 1. From Table 1 we can see that the two clusters are well separated in $A_1$ and $A_2$ and overlapped slightly each other in $A_3$, whereas in $A_4$ and $A_5$ with large standard deviations the two clusters cannot nearly be distinguished.

**Table 1.** Centers and standard deviations of clusters in different features

| Cluster | Cluster centers | Standard deviations |
|---|---|---|
| 1 | (0.3155, 0.3157, 0.3656, 0.5410, 0.5240) | (0.0662, 0.1062, 0.1830, 0.2870, 0.3028) |
| 2 | (0.7114, 0.6828, 0.6103, 0.4824, 0.4943) | (0.0787, 0.1035, 0.1798, 0.3007, 0.2687) |

**Table 2.** The clustering results on the artificial data set by FCM, GFGA and DGAFCM

| Algorithm | FCM | GFGA | DGAFCM | | | |
|---|---|---|---|---|---|---|
| | | | $\beta$=2 | $\beta$=3 | $\beta$=4 | $\beta$=5 |
| Number of errors | 11 | 11 | 0 | 0 | 0 | 0 |
| Percentage of errors | 5.5% | 5.5% | 0% | 0% | 0% | 0% |

**Table 3.** The feature weights of the artificial data set by DGAFCM

| $\beta$ | Weight1 | Weight2 | Weight3 | Weight4 | Weight5 | $\beta$ | Weight1 | Weight2 | Weight3 | Weight4 | Weight5 |
|---|---|---|---|---|---|---|---|---|---|---|---|
| 2 | 0.5675 | 0.2687 | 0.0915 | 0.0352 | 0.0372 | 4 | 0.3106 | 0.2502 | 0.1786 | 0.1292 | 0.1313 |
| 3 | 0.3765 | 0.2669 | 0.1586 | 0.0978 | 0.1003 | 5 | 0.2794 | 0.2392 | 0.1867 | 0.1465 | 0.1482 |

We use three algorithms, i.e. FCM [2], GFGA [8], and the DGAFCM proposed in this paper, to run experiments respectively. The parameters that we used are $m$=2.0, $N$=50, $maxgen$=100, $P_c$=0.8 and $P_m$=0.2. All these algorithms are run 100 times and the average number and percentage of misclassifications are reported in Table 2. The results indicate that entirely accurate clusters can be obtained by DGAFCM every time while approximatively correct clusters can only be got in the other two algorithms. The feature weighs obtained by DGAFCM under the case of $\beta$=2,3,4 and 5 respectively are reported in Table 3. The feature $A_1$,$A_2$, and $A_3$ have larger weights and $A_4$, $A_5$ have smaller weights. The results are reasonable.

### 4.2 Experiments on Real Data Set

In this section, we ran run experiments on the iris data set and the wine data set. Both of them can be obtained from the UCI Machine Learning Repository[1].

The iris data set is one of the most popular data sets to examine the performance of novel methods in pattern recognition and machine learning [9]. There are 3 clusters in the data set, each has 50 instances with 4 features, that is sepal length, sepal width, petal length, and petal width, the weights of which are named weight1, weight2, weight3, and weight4 respectively for their short forms.

[1] http://www.ics.uci.edu/~mlearn/MLRepository.html

**Table 4.** The clustering results on the iris data set by DGAFCM

| $\beta$ | 2 | 3 | 4 | 5 |
|---|---|---|---|---|
| Number of errors | 6 | 6 | 6 | 6 |
| Percentage of errors | 4% | 4% | 4% | 4% |

**Table 5.** The feature weights of the iris data set by DGAFCM

| $\beta$ | Weight1 | Weight2 | Weight3 | Weight4 | β | Weight1 | Weight2 | Weight3 | Weight4 |
|---|---|---|---|---|---|---|---|---|---|
| 2 | 0.0874 | 0.1932 | 0.1023 | 0.6170 | 4 | 0.1975 | 0.2514 | 0.2050 | 0.3461 |
| 3 | 0.1681 | 0.2445 | 0.1796 | 0.4078 | 5 | 0.2117 | 0.2528 | 0.2170 | 0.3186 |

**Table 6.** The clustering results on the iris data set by some cluster algorithms

| Algorithm | GFGA [8] | FCM [10] | FPCM [11] | PFCM [11] | Feature weighted FCM [12] |
|---|---|---|---|---|---|
| Number of errors | 16 | 16 | 13,14 | 13,14 | 7 |
| Percentage of errors | 10.6% | 10.6% | 8.7%,9.3% | 8.7%,9.3% | 4.67% |

In experiments on the iris data set we assign $\beta$ values ranging from 2 to 5 and DGAFWC was run 100 times respectively for each value of $\beta$. We use the other parameters as follows: $m$=2.0, $N$=50, $maxgen$=100, $P_c$=0.8 and $P_m$=0.2. The average number and percentage of misclassifications and the features weights for each $\beta$ value are reported in Table 4 and Table 5 respectively. The clustering results of GFGA, FCM, FPCM, PFCM and the feature weighted FCM algorithm reported by Ref. [8], [10], [11] and [12] respectively are shown in Table 6. The experimental results indicate that thc DGAFCM algorithm and the feature weighted FCM algorithm, with feature weights solution strategies, evidently improve the clustering performance on iris data set compared with GFGA, FCM, FPCM, and PFCM algorithms, in which the feature weights are left out of account. Among these clustering algorithms, DGAFWC has the smallest number of misclassifications. From Table 5 we can observe that weight4 is the largest, and then weight2, weight3, weight1 in turns. Also, the difference between feature weighs gets smaller with the increasing of the values of $\beta$.

The wine data set contains 178 instances and each instance has 13 numerical features. The data set is classified into 3 clusters according to the types of wines. We use three algorithms, i.e. FCM [2], GFGA [8], and the DGAFCM proposed in this paper, to run experiments on the data set respectively. For DGAFCM, we assign $\beta$ values ranging from 5 to 8. The other parameters remain unchanged. All these algorithms are run 100 times. The average number and percentage of misclassifications are reported in Table 7. The results indicate that DGAFWC has the smallest number of misclassifications among these clustering algorithms. The feature weighs obtained by DGAFCM under the case of $\beta$=5,6,7 and 8 respectively are reported in Table 8. We can observe that weight8 is the largest, and then weight11, weight3, weight6, weight9, weight12, weight7, weight1, weight2, weight10, weight4, weight5, weight13 in turns.

**Table 7.** The clustering results on the wine data sets by FCM, GFGA and DGAFCM

| Algorithm | FCM | GFGA | DGAFCM | | | |
|---|---|---|---|---|---|---|
| | | | $\beta$=5 | $\beta$=6 | $\beta$=7 | $\beta$=8 |
| Number of errors | 56 | 56 | 25 | 23 | 21 | 21 |
| Percentage of errors | 31.5% | 31.5% | 14.0% | 12.9% | 11.8% | 11.8% |

**Table 8.** The feature weights of the wine data set by DGAFCM

| Feature weights | $\beta$=5 | $\beta$=6 | $\beta$=7 | $\beta$=8 |
|---|---|---|---|---|
| Weight1 | 0.0688 | 0.0732 | 0.0757 | 0.0772 |
| Weight2 | 0.0598 | 0.0653 | 0.0686 | 0.0709 |
| Weight3 | 0.1165 | 0.1111 | 0.1069 | 0.1035 |
| Weight4 | 0.0340 | 0.0415 | 0.0471 | 0.0513 |
| Weight5 | 0.0160 | 0.0228 | 0.0285 | 0.0334 |
| Weight6 | 0.0880 | 0.0890 | 0.0889 | 0.0884 |
| Weight7 | 0.0742 | 0.0777 | 0.0794 | 0.0803 |
| Weight8 | 0.1856 | 0.1603 | 0.1446 | 0.1339 |
| Weight9 | 0.0859 | 0.0872 | 0.0874 | 0.0871 |
| Weight10 | 0.0412 | 0.0486 | 0.0537 | 0.0575 |
| Weight11 | 0.1407 | 0.1293 | 0.1212 | 0.1153 |
| Weight12 | 0.0858 | 0.0872 | 0.0873 | 0.0870 |
| Weight13 | 0.0036 | 0.0069 | 0.0105 | 0.0142 |

## 5 Conclusions

For fuzzy features-weighting clustering problems, we deal with a double encoding scheme in GA. Each individual consists of two segments of codes for cluster centers and feature weights in the scheme. Both of them are evolved in the clustering process at the same time. The modified clustering objective function is defined, from which the fitness value of an individual can be computed. To update the fuzzy partition matrix and the cluster centers in the situation of feature weights being fixed, a one-step weighted fuzzy c-means algorithm operator, i.e. WFCMO, is designed. The operator works on the strategy of FCM algorithm. In dealing with the fuzzy features-weighting clustering problems, the calculation and optimization of the weights for all features is one of the key problems. Targeting the problem we have proven the theorem about the constrained optimization problem of features-weighting in the situation of the fuzzy partition matrix and the cluster centers being fixed, and developed the feature weight leaning operator, that is FWLO. Based on the above work, the double coding GA-based weighted FCM clustering algorithm, DGAFCM, is advanced. DGAFCM is suitable for numeric data. We utilize the roulette selection strategy, the arithmetic crossover and the uniform mutation method to realize the usual genetic operations, and elitist strategy is adopted to guarantee the convergence of the algorithm. Experimental results indicate that the DGAFCM clustering algorithm is stable and adaptive. The future research work will include the further improvement of algorithm efficiency as well as research on clustering algorithms for mixed numeric and categorical data.

## References


1. Bezdek J.C.: Pattern Recognition With Fuzzy Objective Function Algorithms. New York: Plenum, (1981)
2. Wang X. Z., Wang Y. D, Wang L. J.: Improving Fuzzy c-Means Clustering Based on Feature-Weight Learning. Pattern Recognition Letters, Vol.25. (2004)1123-1132
3. Chan E. Y., Ching, W. K., Ng M. K., Huang J. Z.: An Optimization Algorithm for Clustering Using Weighted Dissimilarity Measures. Pattern Recognition, Vol.37. (2004) 943–952
4. Huang J. Z., Ng M. K., Rong H. Q., Li Z.: Automated Variable Weighting in k-Means Type Clustering. IEEE Trans. Pattern Anal. Mach. Intell., Vol. 27, No 5, (2005) 657-668
5. MacQueen J.: Some Methods for Classification and Analysis of Multivariate Observations. In: Proc. Fifth Berkeley Symp. Math. Statistics and Probability, (1967) 281-297
6. Krishna K., Murty M. N.: Genetic K-Means Algorithm. IEEE Trans. Syst., Man, Cybern. B, Cybern., Vol. 29, No. 3, (1999) 433-439
7. Maulik U., Bandyopadhyay S.: Genetic Algorithm-based Clustering Technique. Pattern Recognition, Vol. 33, (2000)1455-1465
8. Dong Y. Y., Zhang Y. J, Chang C. L.: An Improved Hybrid Cluster Algorithm. Fuzzy Systems and Mathematics, Vol. 19, No 2. (2005)128-133 (in Chinese)
9. Xu R., Wunsch II D.: Survey of Clustering Algorithms. IEEE Trans. Neural Networks, Vol. 16, No. 3, (2005) 645-678
10. Hathaway R., Bezdek J: Fuzzy c-Means Clustering of Incomplete Data. IEEE Trans. Syst., Man, Cybern., Vol. 31, No. 5, (2001)735-744
11. Pal N. R., Pal K., Keller J. M., Bezdek J. C.: A Possibilistic Fuzzy c-Means Clustering Algorithm. IEEE Trans. on Fuzzy Systems, Vol.13. No.4. (2005)517-530
12. Li J., Gao X. B., Ji H. B.: A Feature Weighted FCM Clustering Algorithm Based on Evolutionary Strategy. In: Proceedings of the 4th World Congress on Intelligent Control and Automation, Shanghai, China, (2002)1549-1553

# A Genetic Algorithm with Age and Sexual Features

Yani Zhu, Zhongxiu Yang, and Jiatao Song

College of Electronic and Information Engineering,
Ningbo University of Technology,
Ningbo, Zhejiang, 315016, P.R. China
zyn@nbut.cn

**Abstract.** Genetic Algorithm (GA) has been successfully applied to many optimization problems. One problem with Standard GA is its premature convergence for complex multi-modal functions. To overcome it, in this paper a novel genetic algorithm with age and sexual features is proposed. Age and sexual features are provided to individuals to simulate the sexual reproduction popular in nature. During applying age and sexual operators, different evolutionary parameters are given to genetic individuals. As a result, the proposed Genetic Algorithm can combat premature convergence and maintain the diversity of population, and thereby converge on global solutions.

## 1 Introduction

Genetic Algorithm (GA) is a kind of self-adaptive global optimization stochastic searching algorithm based on the principle of nature selection and genetic evolution. It begins with the research of nature and artificial self-adaptive system [1]. The main characteristics of this algorithm are colony search policy and information exchange. It has been abroad applied in combination optimization, machine learning, self-adaptive control, programming design, artificial life and image processing. It is one of the most important technologies in intelligent computing [2].

However, Standard GA faces a problem of premature convergence when used for complex multi-modal functions optimization, for it only simply simulates biology inheritance and evolution procedure without considering sexual reproduction and diploid chromosomes popular in nature [3]. To address this problem, in this paper an improved Genetic Algorithm with age and sexual features is presented.

## 2 Genetic Algorithm with Age and Sexual Features

### 2.1 Algorithm Structure

The genetic individuals in this algorithm are provided with male and female genders. Because the mutation rate of male individuals is higher than female ones, male individuals have more strongly global exploring ability and female ones have more strongly local searching ability. The male and female individuals are all provided with age parameters. They must be matched within some age range. So this algorithm can combat premature convergence and can converge on global optimization solutions rapidly.

D.-S. Huang, K. Li, and G.W. Irwin (Eds.): ICIC 2006, LNCS 4113, pp. 634 – 640, 2006.

The flowchart of the proposed algorithm is depicted in Figure 1:

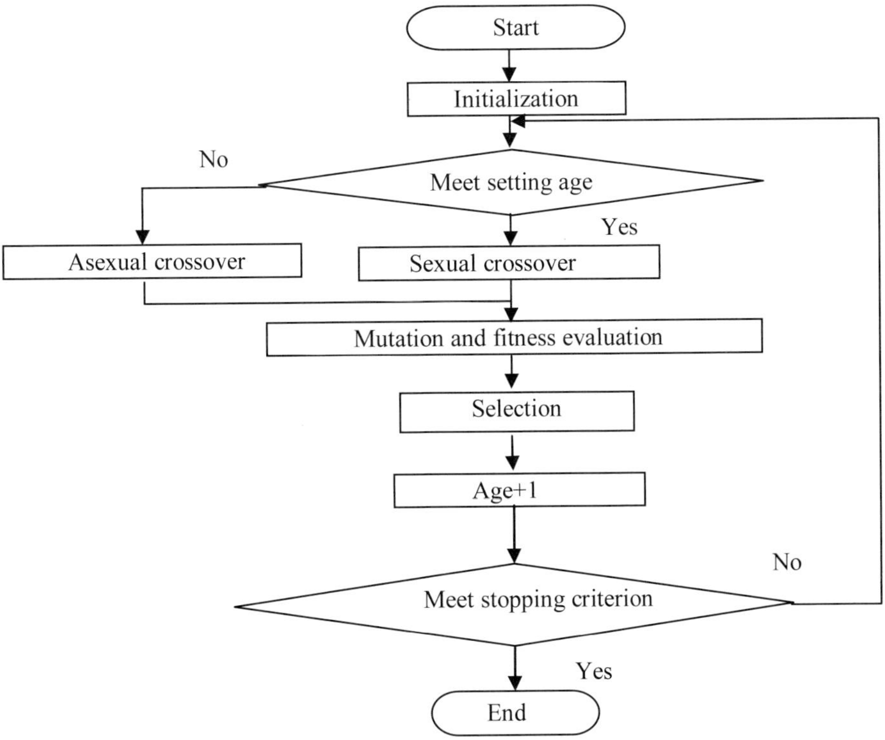


**Fig. 1.** The flowchart of the proposed GA

## 2.2 Encoding

In biology, the diploid structure is composed of a pair of sexual chromosomes that memorize gene information of each individual. On each gene bit, when either of a pair of chromosomes is dominant, the gene behaves dominant; only when both of them are recessive, the gene behaves recessive [4]. Figure 2(a) shows an example of diploid dominant law of binary encoding, where "And" operator is adopted in dominant law. Figure 2(b) shows an example of diploid dominant law of real encoding. The dominant law is:

$$\begin{cases} \alpha\times 312+(1-\alpha)\times 418=410 \\ \alpha\times 218+(1-\alpha)\times 316=312 \end{cases} \cdot \quad \alpha\in(0,1) \tag{1}$$

Diploid structures can memorize useful gene information and can protect them from being damaged by selection operator. In genetic individuals of binary encoding, the last bit of male individuals is "0", and that of female ones is "1"; in genetic individuals of real encoding, the last bit of male individuals is "010", and that of female ones is "110".

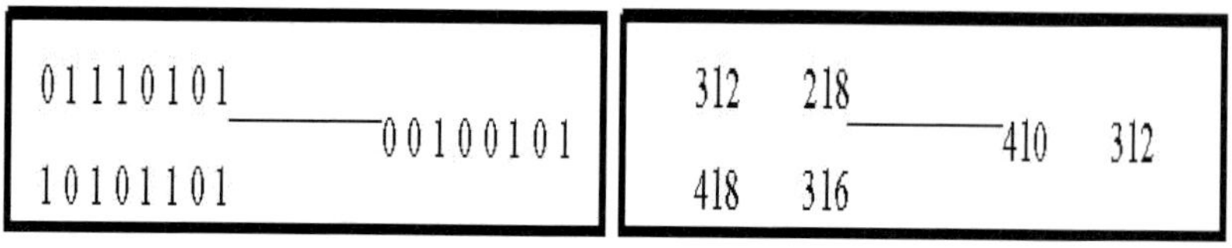


(a) Binary encoding (b) Real encoding

**Fig. 2.** Dominant laws

### 2.3 Matching

In nature, fine male individuals always look for the same fine female individuals to match with in some age range. It is proved that this matching mode is steady. Therefore, we simulate it to design sexual reproduction matching mode. The male individuals on the sequence of fitness values are matched with the female ones on the sequence of fitness values. It is useful for searching global solutions rapidly, while Standard Genetic Algorithm cannot converge on global solutions quickly because of completely random matching mode. Male individuals have strongly global exploring ability and female ones have strongly local searching ability in this mating mode. This matching mode is described as follows:

(1) Estimate individuals' age;
(2) If age<setting age, then male individuals can't be matched with female ones.
(3) If age>=setting age, then male individuals can be matched with female ones in the order of fitness values.

### 2.4 Crossover

One-point crossover is applied in binary encoding. It is important that one-point crossover can protect adjacent gene bit from being damaged by crossover operator. Therefore this crossover mode can't reduce individuals' fitness values [5].

Crossover operation in real code is described as follows：

Parents individuals vectors are：

$$\begin{cases} x_1 = \left(x_1^{(1)}, x_2^{(1)}, \dots, x_m^{(1)}\right) \\ x_2 = \left(x_1^{(2)}, x_2^{(2)}, \dots, x_m^{(2)}\right) \end{cases} \tag{2}$$

Random number $a_i \in (0,1)$, $i = 1, 2, \cdots, m$, offspring individual vectors are:

$$\begin{cases} x_\alpha = \left(y_1^{(1)}, y_2^{(1)}, \dots, y_m^{(1)}\right) \\ x_\beta = \left(y_1^{(2)}, y_2^{(2)}, \dots, y_m^{(2)}\right) \end{cases} \tag{3}$$

Where：

$$\begin{cases} y_i^{(1)} = a_i x_i^{(1)} + (1-a_i) x_i^{(2)} \\ y_i^{(2)} = a_i x_i^{(2)} + (1-a_i) x_i^{(1)} \end{cases}, \qquad i = 1, 2, \dots, m \tag{4}$$

Because this crossover operating can gain many kinds of possible results, it is useful to exchange individuals' gene information and escape from local entrapment. Offspring individual vectors are obtained through modifying parent individual vectors. By means of this purposeful exchanging, offspring individuals are superior to parent ones. The searching method will speed up genetic convergence.

### 2.5 Mutation

In Standard Genetic Algorithm, fixed mutation rate $p_m$ is adopted. If $p_m$ is too low, mutation operator is useless to diversify genetic population and generate a great deal of new individuals. But if $p_m$ is too high, some excellent genetic individuals will be destroyed and the algorithm will not converge on global solutions [6]. In this paper, a new dynamic mutation rate controlled by genetic individuals' age is presented. This is described as follows:

$$p_m = p_o \bullet \beta^j, \qquad j = 1, 2, 3 \cdots, N \cdot \tag{5}$$

Where $p_m$ and $p_o$ are constant parameters, $\beta > 1$, $j$ is genetic individual's age. From formula (5), it can be concluded that mutation rate increases by individuals' age. When individuals are young, mutation rate is low; while individuals are old, mutation rate is high. As a result, many fine genetic individuals are reserved on genetic early stages; while those old ones with low fitness values are displaced on genetic later stages. This mutation operating can not only diversify the gene pool but also escape from possible local entrapment. In addition, mutation rate of male individuals is higher than that of female ones. So the algorithm can obtain good tradeoff between global exploring ability of male individuals and local searching ability of female ones.

### 2.6 Selection

Because the best individuals in parent population are expected to remain to the next generation, best keeping strategy is adopted. This selection strategy allows parent generation to coexist with offspring generation by competing. Best genetic individuals are kept by selecting in the order of fitness values [7].

(1) Find the best and worst individuals from offspring population;
(2) If the fitness of the best individuals from offspring population;
(3) The worst individual in parent population is displayed by the best one in offspring population;
(4) The individuals of parent population at dead age are deleted from the population.

## 3 Experimental Results and Discussion

### 3.1 Test Functions

Five famous testing functions are selected:

$$f_1 = \sum_{i=1}^{3} x_i^2 \qquad -5.12 \le x_i \le 5.12 \tag{6}$$

The global minimal point is $(0,0)$, its minimum is 0.

$$f_2 = 100 \bullet (x_1^2 - x_2)^2 + (1 - x_1)^2, -2.048 \le x_i \le 2.048 \tag{7}$$

The global minimum is 0.

$$f_3 = \sum_{i=1}^{5} \mathrm{int}(x_i), \qquad -5.12 \le x_i \le 5.12 \tag{8}$$

When $x_i \in [-5.12, -5.0]$, the global minimum is –30.

$$f_6 = 0.5 - \frac{\sin^2 \sqrt{x_1^2 + x_2^2} - 0.5}{[1.0 + 0.001(x_1^2 + x_2^2)]^2} \qquad -100 \le x_i \le 100 \tag{9}$$

The global minimal point is $(0,0)$, its maximum is 1.

$$f_8 = \sum_{i=1}^{M} \frac{x_i^2}{4000} - \prod_{i=1}^{M} \cos \frac{x_i}{\sqrt{i}} + 1, \qquad -600 \le x_i \le 600 \tag{10}$$

Only when $x_i = 0$时， the global minimum is 0.

## 3.2 Experimental Results

Table 1 shows the setting of parameters of functions (6)~(10). Because the selected functions are typical ones, the global optimization values are available. Based on these global optimization values, threshold values are set to every function as convergence criterion. The proposed algorithm is considered to converge on global optimization

**Table 1.** Setting of parameters

| Function | Max & min value | Threshold value | Crossover rate | Max age |
|---|---|---|---|---|
| $f_1$ | 0.0 | 0.001 | 0.8 | 100 |
| $f_2$ | 0.0 | 0.001 | 0.8 | 100 |
| $f_3$ | -30 | -30 | 0.8 | 100 |
| $f_6$ | 1.0 | 0.999 | 0.8 | 100 |
| $f_8$(10dim) | 0.0 | 0.001 | 0.8 | 100 |
| $f_8$(10dim) | 0.0 | 0.0001 | 0.8 | 100 |
| $f_8$(100dim) | 0.0 | 0.001 | 0.8 | 100 |
| $f_8$(100dim) | 0.0 | 0.0001 | 0.8 | 100 |

values if the fitness values equal the threshold values. 100 optimization experiments are carried out on $f_1 \sim f_8$. Table 2 shows the performance comparison of the proposed GA with multi-species GA. The data of the multi-species GA in this table is from Ref. [8]. In these two tables, for every function the convergence age equals the average age over 100 experiments, and the convergence time equals the average time over 100 experiments. The computer in the experiments has Pentium IV processor ,a main frequency of 3.0GHz and main memory of 512M.

**Table 2.** Performance comparison with multi-species GA

| Function | multi-species GA | | | this proposed GA | | |
|---|---|---|---|---|---|---|
| | Convergence Rate(%) | Convergence age | time | Convergence Rate(%) | Convergence age | time |
| $f_1$ | 100 | 5.95 | 0.18 | 100 | 3.2 | 0.03 |
| $f_2$ | 100 | 7.68 | 0.19 | 100 | 6.0 | 0.05 |
| $f_3$ | 100 | 6.47 | 0.28 | 100 | 4.5 | 0.17 |
| $f_6$ | 100 | 10.2 | 0.24 | 100 | 7.8 | 0.14 |
| $f_8$(10dim) | 100 | 1400.7 | 67.1 | 100 | 17.5 | 0.46 |
| $f_8$(10dim) | 100 | 2077.9 | 99.3 | 100 | 15.1 | 3.28 |
| $f_8$(100dim) | 100 | 5771.6 | 1889.3 | 100 | 29.7 | 0.77 |
| $f_8$(100dim) | 100 | 15172.6 | 4912.2 | 100 | 22.1 | 4.83 |

From Table 2, the following results can be concluded:

(1) The proposed GA can converge on global solutions by 100 percent for all the selected functions.

(2) For $f_8$, the proposed GA can converge on global solution quickly, while the multi-species Genetic Algorithm is difficult to do so.

(3) For all the selected functions, the convergence time of our proposed GA is less than that of multi-species Genetic Algorithm.

## 4 Conclusion

Genetic algorithm (GA) is a kind of global search and optimization algorithm based on the principles of natural selection and genetic evolution. In view of its briefness and great efficiency, GA has been widely used in many fields. However, many existing genetic algorithms can't converge on global solutions easily. In this paper, an improved GA with age and sexual features is presented. Age and sexual features make the proposed GA possess strongly global exploring and local searching abilities. Therefore, our GA can maintain the diversity of genetic genes in the evolution colony and combat the premature convergence effectively. Experimental results on typical complex multi-modal functions show that our algorithm can achieve good performance.

## Acknowledgements

The work described in this paper was partially supported by two research grants from Zhejiang Provincial Natural Science Foundation of China (Y105239, 602118 ), and a grant from the Scientific Research Foundation for the Returned Overseas Chinese Scholars of Zhejiang Province (72).

## References

1. Holland J H.: Adaptation in Natural and Artificial Systems. The University of Michigan Press, 1975, MIT Press, (1992)
2. Goldberg, D.E.: Genetic Algorithms in Search, Optimization and Machine Learning. Addison-Wesley, (1989)
3. Michalewicz, Z.: Genetic Algorithms + Data Structures = Evolution Programs. Springer, (1992)
4. Hans Ellegren.: Evolution of The Avian Sex Chromosomes And Their Role in Sex Determination. Elesvier Science, Vol. 15, (2000) 188-192
5. Kalyanmoy. Deb, Hans-Georg Beyer.: Self-Adaptive Genetic Algorithms with Simulated Binary Crossover. Evolutionary Computation, vol. 9, no. 2 (2001) 198-221
6. Nicol N Schraudolph ,Richard KBelew,: Dynamic Parameter Encoding for Genetic Algorithms [J ]. Machine Learning July 20, (1992) 1- 8
7. Joanna L is, Eiben. A. E.: A Sexual Genetic Algorithm for Multi-objective Optimization. IEEE Transactions on Evolutionary Computation, Vol.2, (1997) 59-64
8. Zhang Li-fen, Li Ming, Zhou Lin-xia.: Multi-species Genetic Algorithms Based on Multi-encoding. Journal of Image and Graphics,Vol.7, No.9 (2002)980-984

# A New Algorithm of Evolutionary Computation: Bio-Simulated Optimization

Yong Wang[1], Ruijun Zhang[1], Qiumei Pu[2], and Qianxing Xiong[2]

[1] School of Management, Wuhan University of Science and Technology, 430081 Wuhan, China
wangyong_1616@yeah.net

[2] School of Computer Science and Technology, Wuhan University of Technology, 430063 Wuhan, China
qianxx@pubilc.wh.hb.cn

**Abstract.** Genetic algorithm (GA), evolutionary programming (EP) and evolutionary strategy (ES) are called the three kinds of evolutionary computation methods. They have been widely used in many engineering fields. However, selecting individuals directly and random search lead to produce premature problem, and requirement for high precision decreases the search efficiency, these become the obstructs of application in engineering practice. This paper proposes a new algorithm of evolutionary computation, it is called bio-simulated optimization algorithm (BSO). BSO reproduces new generation through asexual propagation and sexual propagation. Here, the evolutionary operators effectively solve the problem of premature convergence. Furthermore, performance of global search and convergence are proved theoretically. Finally, Compared BSO with GA and EP in searching the optimal solution of a continuous multi-peaks function, three kinds of computation procedures are run in Matlab, the result shows that performance of BSO is superior to GA and EP.

## 1 Introduction

To search the optimal solution of optimization problem very precisely is often not an easy thing. So researchers pay close attention to the nearly-best solution. Methods to solve the optimal solution or the nearly-best solution are mainly enumeration and algorithm of random search. Evolutionary computation is a kind of algorithm of random search with power ability of global search; it is widely used in solving many optimization problems, such as GA can be used to solve the function optimization and TSP problems [1].

Methods of evolutionary computation include GA, EP and ES. In 1975, J. H. Holland gets the enlightenment of survival of the fittest, an evolution theory of Darwin, in studying how to create a machine with learning ability, the concept of genetic algorithm is put forward for the first time [2]. As a kind of practical, effective and robust technology in 90s, GA is developed rapidly, and applied extensively in machine learning, pattern recognition, optimization of control system and society science, etc., some frontline issues such as artificial life, genetic programming, and evolutionary computation are researched. In 60s, as a method of random optimization, EP [3], [4] is proposed by L. J. Fogel and other specialists in researching on artificial

D.-S. Huang, K. Li, and G.W. Irwin (Eds.): ICIC 2006, LNCS 4113, pp. 641 – 648, 2006.

intelligence. They use the sequence of symbol on limited set of character indicate the simulated environment. Finite state machine (FSM) represents intelligence system, the output of FMS is a group of activities, the object is to establish an algorithm of optimization make the activities optimal in giving environment. ES [5] originates the idea of natural mutation and natural selection of biologic evolution; it is brought forth by I. Rechenberg and H. P. Schwefel. It emphasizes the change of behavior in individual level. In the model of ES, every components of experiment solution are regarded as the features of behavior instead of gene. Application of EP and ES is still in the primary stage.

Evolutionary computation provides us an effective way to solve optimization problem. Researchers study it deeply in its theory and practical application. However, some problems appear in its application. Firstly, the search ability of GA is not proportional between global search and partial search, this is caused by mismatched position of operator of crossover and mutation and the operation feature of operator of crossover [6]. Secondly, the strategy of evolutionary operation influences largely on the solution and efficiency of algorithm. Finally, three kinds of algorithms are both premature. The author thinks operation of direct selection lead to the problems. According to the natural principle of biologic evolution, this paper put forward a new method of evolutionary computation: algorithm of bio-simulated optimization.

## 2 Algorithm of Bio-Simulated Optimization

### 2.1 Flow of BSO

Living things in nature reproduce new generations through the ways of asexual propagation (AP) or sexual propagation (SP). The fine genes carried to their next generations make them with good adaptability. BSO is established on the principle of biologic evolution, simulates behavior of biologic evolution to search the solution in evolutionary space. Now, let's see a problem of optimization, it can be described as follows.

$$\max\{f(x): x \in R^n\}$$

If $q$ is the current scale of population, $t$ is the evolutionary generation. The flow of BSO is shown as follows.

Step 1: Select individuals randomly in $R^n$, the original population can be expressed as $X^n(t)=\{x_1^n(t), x_2^n(t), \cdots, x_q^n(t)\}$ , $x_p^n(t)=\{x_p^1(t), x_p^2(t), \cdots, x_p^n(t)\}$ , $t$=0, $p \in [1, q]$. $q$ is the quantity of individual.

Step 2: Calculate the fitness of individual, $f_1, f_2, \ldots, f_q$.

Step 3: Consider the condition of end evolution, if the condition is true, end the computation, if not, execute Step 4, $t$=$t$+1.

The condition of end evolution is the evolutionary generation reaches the giving times or acceptable solution appears.

Step 4: Evolutionary operation,

Step 4.1: Select the individuals with better fitness according to probability $P_a$, reproduce the new group $X_a$ of individual through AP.

Step 4.2: Select the individual with the best fitness propagate sexually with the other individuals of this generation, reproduce the new group $X_s$ of individual.

Step 5: Reproduce the new generation, $X^n(t+1)=X_a \cup X_s$, go to Step 2.

Follows is the main distinctions among BSO, GA, EP and ES.

Firstly, BSO has not the operation of selection directly, so it conforms to the principle of biologic evolution. Secondly, the way to reproduce new generation is different from the traditional evolutionary algorithms, AP only changes the arranged order of gene, SP recombines gene between the gene schemas with the longest genetic distance. Lastly, sub-individual inherits the fine gene of parents. Compared BSO with the optimization algorithm of reference [6], its operation of SP ensures the diversity of individuals, enlarges the search space.

## 2.2 Evolutionary Operation of BSO

### 2.2.1 Asexual Propagation

The evolution of BSO has two ways of asexual propagation and sexual propagation. The basic operations of AP are fission and selection. AP does not change the genetic gene, only rearranges the order of gene.

**Definition 1.** Suppose that $D$ is set of all sub-sets in evolutionary space $R^n$, $F : R^n \to D$, for $\forall x \in D$ , $F(x) = \{x, -x, \bar{x}, -\bar{x}\} \in D$ , then, $F$ is the operator of fission on $R^n \to D$ [6].

$-x$, $\bar{x}$ and $-\bar{x}$ respectively stand for reversal, complementary and reversal-complementary of $x$.

**Definition 2.** If $U$ is the ordered set of natural number $N$, $C : N \to U$, for $\forall u \in U$ , $C(u)=u+(-1)^u$, then, $C$ is the operator of complementary on $N \to U$.

**Definition 3.** If $D^*$ is set of fission of $x_i$, $S_1(x') = \min\{f(x_i), f(-x_i), f(\bar{x}_i), f(-\bar{x}_i)\}$ , $x' \in D^*$ , then, $S_1$ is the operator of selection on $D^*$.

$X_a$ is reproduced by AP,

$$X_a = \bigcup_{i=1}^{j} S_1(x_i) \,, \quad j = Int(q * P_a)$$

$Int()$ is the function of integration.

### 2.2.2 Sexual Propagation

SP reproduces the new individuals through selection of gene schema and gene recombination. At first, choose the individual with the best fitness of this population. Then, select a fine gene schema according to some strategies. Lastly, replace the gene schema of other individual with the fine gene schema, the genetic distance between the gene schema replaced and the fine gene schema is longest, this process is called gene recombination. SP conforms to the principle which a different variety of gene indicates a different characteristic of individual. It changes the genetic gene of individual; the new generation inherits the fine gene of their parents.

**Definition 4.** Gene schema is the segment of DNA which consists of one or several genes and indicates some characteristic of individual.

$$z^k(i)=(g_1, g_2, \ldots, g_k),\ i\in[1, m]$$

Where $z^k(i)$ is a gene schema consists of $k$ genes, $k$ is the order of schema, $m$ stands for the size of schema space. The order of sub-schema in the same schema space can be different.

**Definition 5.** If $Z$ is fission set of gene schema of the optimal individual $x_i$ ,$Z=\{z^k(1), z^k(2),\ldots, z^k(m)\}$, $m=\|Z\|$, $S_2(z')=strat(Z)$ , $z'\in Z$ , then, $S_2$ is the operator of selection on Z.

Where *strat* () is the selection function of strategy, for example, the strategy can be random or in sequence.

**Definition 6.** If $z^k(i)$ and $z^k(j)$ are any two schemas in schema space, then, $d_H(z^k(i), z^k(j))$ stands for their genetic distance.

$$d_H(z^k(i),z^k(j))=\sum_{l=1}^{k} d_H(z_l(i),z_l(j))$$

If $z_l(i)= z_l(j)$, then, $d_H(z_l(i), z_l(j))=0$, if not, it is 1.

**Definition 7.** Gene recombination means the gene schema of individual $x_i$ is replaced by the gene schema of the best individual. See the following detailed step.

Firstly, Select a schema $z^k(i)$ using the operator $S_2$ of selection.

Secondly, Calculate the genetic distance between every gene schema of individual $x_i$ and $z^k(i)$, $d_H(z^k(i), z^k(j))$, $j=1, 2,\ldots, m$.

Lastly, If the gene schema $z^k(n)$ of individual $x_i$ is replaced with $z^k(i)$, then,

$$d_H(z^k(i), z^k(n))\geq\max\{d_H(z^k(i), z^k(j)), j=1, 2,\ldots, m\}$$

If there are some gene schemas with the longest genetic distance, then, the first gene schema of these is replaced.

According to the definition 7, recombine all the individuals except for individuals of AP, $X_s$ is reproduced by SP.

### 2.3 Convergence of BSO

BSO is a kind of algorithm of random search, so its global convergence is not only important in theory, but also important in practice. The schema theorem of J. H. Holland [7] analyses the convergence of evolutionary computation qualitatively. D. B. Fogel and reference [8] give the mathematics proof strictly on it. Reference [6] proves its algorithm converge to the optimal global point as probability 1. Convergence of evolutionary computation is usually proved by schema theorem, Markov chain or probability theory. Here we analyze BSO on its ability of global search and nearly-best solution.

### 2.3.1 Global Search in Evolutionary Space

**Theorem 1.** If $X^n(t)$ stands for the population of generation $t$ reproduced by BSO, $X^n(t+1)$ is the population of generation $t+1$, for $\forall\varepsilon > 0$, following inequality is right,

$$\|X^n(t) \setminus X^n(t+1)\| \leq \varepsilon \tag{1}$$

**Proof.** Suppose that the length of individual is $L$, $k$ is the order of schema, $k<L$.

$P_a$ is probability of individuals selected to AP, the quantity of AP individuals is $Int(q*P_a)$, in generation $t$, when the individuals begin to self-reproduction, probability of individuals selected simultaneously as next generation is $P(X_a)$.

$$P(X_a)=(1/4)^{Int(q*Pa)}$$

In SP, $P_s$ is probability of individuals selected to SP, when the genetic distance between the fine gene schema of the best individual and all the gene schemas of individual $x_i(x_i \in X^n(t))$ is 0, $x_i$ will be chosen as an individual of generation $t+1$, the probability is $k/L$ that $x_i$ is chosen. Probability of individuals selected simultaneously as next generation is $P(X_s)$.

$$P(X_s)=(k/L)^{Int(q*Ps)}$$

The probability of population of generation $t$ selected simultaneously in $t+1$ generation is $P(X^n(t))$.

$$P(X^n(t))=P(X_a)\cdot P(X_s)=(1/4)^{Int(q*Pa)}\cdot(k/L)^{Int(q*Ps)} \approx (k/4L)^q\cdot(1/4)^{Pa}\cdot(k/L)^{Ps}$$

$$\|X^n(t) \setminus X^n(t+1)\|=\|X^n(t)\| \cdot P(X^n(t))= q \cdot (k/L)^q \cdot (1/4)^{Pa} \cdot (k/L)^{Ps}$$

Let $q \cdot (k/L)^q \cdot (1/4)^{Pa} \cdot (k/L)^{Ps}=\varepsilon$, for any $q' \geq q$, then,

$$\varepsilon' = q' \cdot (k/4L)^{q'} \cdot (1/4)^{Pa} \cdot (k/L)^{Ps} < \varepsilon$$

Therefore, with the scale of population increasing, there is a great diversity between generation $t$ and generation $t+1$. So we can conclude the formula (1). Because of a great diversity of every generation, a conclusion can be drawn that BSO will extend the whole solution space through enough evolution.

### 2.3.2 Search the Nearly-Best Solution

**Definition 8.** Suppose that $D^t$ is the sequence of population produced by BSO, $D^t \subset R^n$, $D^- = R^n \setminus D^t$. $x^+$ is the optimal solution on $D^t$, and $x^-$ is the optimal solution on $D^-$, $f(x^+) = \max_{x \in D^t} f(x)$, $f(x^-) = \max_{x \in D^-} f(x)$, then, distance between $x^+$ and $x^-$ is called evolutionary distance, use $d(x^+, x^-)$ denote it,

$$d(x^+, x^-) = \sqrt{\sum_{i=1}^{L} (x_i^+ - x_i^-)^2}$$

If $x_i^+ = x_i^-$, $x_i^+ - x_i^- = 0$, otherwise, $x_i^+ - x_i^- = 1$.

Obviously, the evolutionary distance in the same sub-space is 0.

**Theorem 2.** Suppose that $x^*$ is the optimal solution on evolutionary space, $f^* = f(x)|_{x=x^*}$, $x^*(t)$ is the optimal solution of generation *t*, for any ε>0, then,

$$\lim_{t\to\infty} |f(x^*(t)) - f^*| < \varepsilon \tag{2}$$

**Proof.** $D^t$ is the sequence of population produced by BSO, $D^-$ stands for the space which BSO do not search yet. If $x^* \in D^t$, then, according to step of algorithm and definition 8, we know that $d(x^*(t), x^*) = 0$, for any ε>0, the formula (2) is right.

If $x^* \in D^-$, when $t \to \infty$, it is known from theorem 1, the probability $P(x^*)$ that $x^*$ is selected is 1.

$$P(x^*) = \lim_{t\to\infty} \| D_t \| / \| R^n \| = 1$$

Then,

$$\lim_{t\to\infty} d(x^*(t), x^*) = \sqrt{\sum_{i=1}^{L} (x_i^*(t) - x_i^*)^2} = 0, \quad \lim_{t\to\infty} x^*(t) = x^*$$

Following limitation can be deduced.

$$\lim_{t\to\infty} |f(x^*(t)) - f^*| = 0$$

For any ε>0, we can conclude the formula (2).

Theorem 2 indicates the fact that the more evolution, the more near solution. Consider the time and efficiency in practice, we usually search the nearly-best solution.

## 3 Performance Analysis of BSO

The efficiency and precision of solution are a contradiction which is hard to proper attention to both. Time of evolution is more longer, solution is more near the optimal solution, at the same time, and the efficiency of algorithm is more lower. Time of evolution is shorter, efficiency is higher, but the precision of solution is hard to be acceptable. Living things get the fine individuals through very long evolutionary process; therefore, we can not make excessive demands to efficiency in solving practical problem. Fortunately, high performance computer help us solving the efficiency of computation. How is the performance of BSO compared with other evolutionary computation? Here, we compare them by solving the maximum value of a continuous multi-peaks function. Following is the function $f(x)$.

$$f(x)=10^3*(\sin(x+25)*e^{-(x+25)/5})+3$$

Let's search in domain $x$, $x \in [0, 25]$. In fact, $x$ is about 1.50614, the maximum value of $f(x)$ is 7.88865162.

Produce the original population $X(0)$ randomly, $q$=20. Using binary code encode individuals, length of code is 18 bits. The selection probability of GA is 0.5, crossover probability is 0.4 and mutation probability is 0.1. The mutation operator of EP is Gaussian transformation. The schema order $m$ of BSO is 2, The probabilities of AP and SP are both 0.5. Design the procedures of GA, EP and BSO and run in Matlab. We consider following two cases.

### 3.1 Solutions with the Same Evolutionary Generation

When evolutionary generation is the same, we observe the error between the solution searched by three algorithms and the optimal solution. Generation $t$=50 and 300, the computation results of algorithms show as Table 1.

See Table 1, for GA and EP, a premature problem has arisen, with the generation increasing, the computation results are no obvious variation, and the stability of GA is not good. For BSO, when the evolution reaches to 50 generations, the solution is superior to the solutions of GA and EP, to 300 generations, its solution is close to the optimal solution. Because of the random of algorithms, the results maybe have a subtle distinction in every computation.

**Table 1.** Solutions with the same evolutionary generation

| $t$ | Solution | GA | EP | BSO |
|---|---|---|---|---|
| 50 | $x$ | 1.6385 | 1.2684 | 1.3824 |
| | $f(x)$ | 7.8450 | 7.7411 | 7.8491 |
| 300 | $x$ | 0.8192 | 1.2684 | 1.4783 |
| | $f(x)$ | 7.8450 | 7.7411 | 7.8867 |

### 3.2 Evolutionary Generation with the Same Precision of Solution

When the value of function is within the giving precision, we observe how many generations the computation of algorithms reach to the precision need. Here, $\varepsilon$=0.0001, the computation results of algorithms show as Table 2.

**Table 2.** Evolutionary generations with the same precision of solution

| Algorithm | GA | EP | BSO |
|---|---|---|---|
| $f(x)$ | 7.8491 | 7.7417 | 7.8885 |
| Evolutionary Generation | >5000 | >5000 | 491 |

See Table 2, GA and EP have not reached the precision yet after 5000 generations, BSO has reached the precision when it proceeds to 491 generations.

## 4 Conclusion

It is known from analysis of function optimization above, the precision and efficiency of BSO are superior to GA and EP in solving problem of optimization, it is no premature problem, and can converge to a giving precision. BSO can be used to solve extreme of function, the shortest route, multi-object programming and so on. Its performance should be compared with other algorithms, such as genetic programming, simulated annealing algorithm and the immune algorithm, etc. We will compare it with evolutionary computation on solving extreme of multi-variable function and TSP problem, besides this, encoding scheme, strategy selected on gene schema, probability of AP and SP, and gene recombination of BSO are worth to be further researched.

## References

1. Zhang, J.Q., Cao, Y.F., Wang, C.Q.: A Genetic Algorithm Based on Common Path for TSP. Computer Engineering and Applications. 40 (2004) 58-61
2. Holland, J.H.: Building Blocks, Cohort Genetic Algorithms, and Hyperplane-Defines Functions. Evolutionary Computation. 8 (2000) 373-391
3. Fogel, L.J., Angeline, P.J., Back, T.: Evolutionary Programming V. proceedings of the 5th annual conference on evolutionary programming, San Diego CA, MIT Press, Cambridge(1996)488-496. Neurocomputing. 17 (1997) 133-134
4. Zhang, J.H., Xu, X.H.: Development on Simulated Evolutionary Computing. System Engineering and Electrionic Technology. 8 (1998) 44-47
5. Rechenberg, I.: Case Studies in Evolutionary Experimentation and Computation. Computer Methods in Applied Mechanics and Engineering. 186 (2000) 125-140
6. Yu, W., Li, R.H.: A New Evolutionary Approach Based on Reproduction of Asexual Cells. Computer Engineering & Science. 23 (2003) 7-10
7. Tang, F., Teng, H.F., Sun, Z.G.: Schema Theorem of the Decimal-Coded Genetic Algorithm. Mini-Micro System. 21 (2000) 364-367
8. Li, H., Tang, H.W., Guo, C.H.: The Convergence Analysis of A Class of Evolution Strategies. OR Transaction. 3 (1999) 79-83

# Application of a Novel Evolutionary Neural Network for Macro-cell Placement Optimization in VLSI Physical Design

Wei Zhou[1,2], Gaofeng Wang[1], and Xi Chen[1,2]

[1] Institute of Micro-Electronics & Information Tech., Wuhan University
Wuhan, Hubei, 430072, China
[2] School of Electronic Information, Wuhan University
Wuhan, Hubei, 430079, China
weizhou@mail.whu.edu.cn

**Abstract.** As operation frequencies and integration densities of modern very large-scale integration (VLSI) circuits increase while device sizes shrink, the quest for high-speed VLSI applications has highlighted the negligible effects of interconnects. It is important to minimize the interconnect wire lengths during VLSI physical design stage. This paper focuses on the minimization process of the total wire length after placement, that is, macro-cell orientation. A novel evolutionary neural network approach based on the concept of evolutionary programming (EPENN) is proposed to address this combinatorial optimization problem. Numerical experiments and simulation results have shown that the presented approach can obtain high quality solutions with low computational complexity.

## 1 Introduction

High-performance integrated circuit (IC) systems provide infrastructure to a multiple of applications. The race towards large-scale integration comes up against the problem of interconnects, which has become one of the blocking points to the improvement of circuit performances. This behavior is expected to continue due to the continuous scaling of very large-scale integration (VLSI) technology. The quest for high-speed VLSI applications has highlighted the previously negligible signal integrity (SI) effects of interconnects, such as ringing, propagation delay, distortion, reflections, substrate coupling, and crosstalk [1, 2, 3]. With these undesirable effects, future VLSI design may become interconnect-centric design [4], where deep sub-micron or nanometer interconnects dominance impacts all aspects of the top-down design flow including logic synthesis, physical design, and back-end verification.

On one hand, efficient predictions of the behavior and improvements of the performance of high-speed interconnects during back-end verification stage after physical design are becoming a problem of ever-increasing importance. In recent years, many modeling and simulation approaches [1, 2, 3] have been developed, which have been proven to accurately predict and improve these effects in high-speed designs as consideration of SI, so as to guarantee the successful design and fabrication of ICs.

D.-S. Huang, K. Li, and G.W. Irwin (Eds.): ICIC 2006, LNCS 4113, pp. 649 – 654, 2006.

On the other hand, it is necessary to try to minimize the interconnect wire lengths during VLSI physical design stage, which will generate better routing results and less high-frequency effects. This combinatorial and numerical optimization problem is known as standard macro-cell placement, along with circuit partitioning, floor-planning, and clock routing, has been proved NP-hard in VLSI physical design [5]. Many heuristic algorithms in coping with these multi-object optimization problems have been reported, typically in [6, 7, 8].

This work focuses on the further optimization after placement, that is, macro-cell orientation. Thus all statements and results in the work are basing on the facts that macro-cells have been processed by some efficient placement algorithms [7, 8], and that pin positions on each macro-cell have been fixed on cell boundary. Since all macro-cells are located in the same orientation, while different orientations may cause different wire length, then the total wire length can be further minimized by flipping macro-cells with respect to their vertical and/or horizontal axes of symmetry.

Artificial neural networks (ANNs) and evolutionary algorithms (EAs) have been applied to numerous optimization problems. Much research has done in combining the self-adaptability of EAs and learning capability of ANNs [9, 10]. EAs can be divided into three major categories: Genetic Algorithm (GA), Evolutionary Strategies (ES) and Evolutionary Programming (EP). Each approach emphasizes a different aspect of natural evolution. An evolutionary neural network approach based on EP (EPENN) is proposed in this work to address the macro-cell orientation problem.

## 2 Problem Statements and Related Work

Macro-cell placement is an important step in VLSI physical design. However, most placement design algorithms determine only the position of the macro-cells, and the problem of determining the orientation of the macro-cells is left unsolved. In fact, macro-cells orientation is a necessary post-processing step in order to minimize the total wire-length.

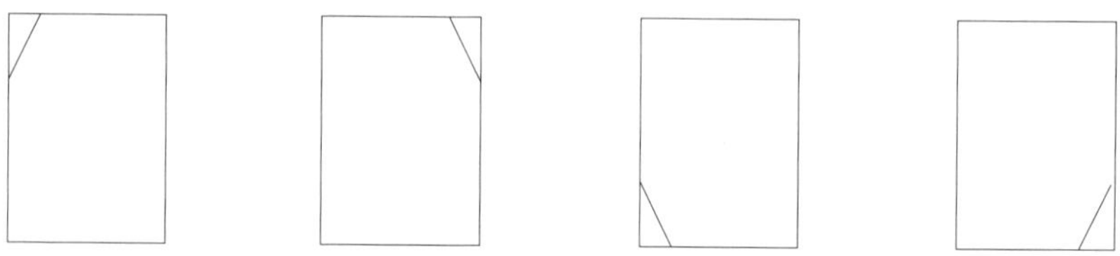

(a) original position (b) vertical flip (c) horizontal flip (d) both

**Fig. 1.** Four possible orientations of a macro-cell

Fig.1 shows the four possible orientations of each macro-cell, in which (a) represents the original position, (b) and (c) represent macro-cells after flips with respect to vertical axes and horizontal axes respectively, while (d) denotes macro-cell after both vertical and horizontal flips.

Thus the aim of macro-cell orientation problem is to further minimize the total wire length by flipping each macro-cell with respect to its vertical and/or horizontal axes of symmetry. All macro-cells are located as the same orientation as Fig. 1(a) after a certain placement algorithm. However, it is not difficult to understand that different orientations may generate totally different total wire lengths. For two pins that belong to the same net, it makes a significant difference whether they are located on the near sides or on the opposite sides of the macro-cells. The wire-length measure used is the Euclidean distance between two pins of a single net. Assuming that a and b are two end pin numbers of the same wire, then the total wire length $L$ can be represented as:

$$L = \sum_{(a,b)\in S} \sqrt{(x_a - x_b)^2 + (y_a - y_b)^2} \; . \tag{1}$$

where $S$ is a set of pairs of pins which belong to the same net. $(x_a, y_a)$ and $(x_b, y_b)$ be the coordinates of pin a and pin b, respectively. Thus minimizing the $L$ is the goal of orientation problem.

Much research has gone into the area of macro-cell orientation in last two decades. Yamada and Liu first introduced this problem in 1988 [11], the proposed approach was proven to be more effective than traditional simulated annealing and hill climbing. Libeskind-Hadas and Liu then applied Hopfield neural network to this problem in 1989 [12], which set the foundation of applying ANNs to this special combinatorial optimization problem. However, the original Hopfield network generates poor quality and invalid solutions and thus a lot of different approaches have been proposed. These techniques have been demonstrated significant improvement in performance over the generic Hopfield network. In 1992, the generalized maximum Hopfield network (GMNN) has been successfully introduced by Lee and Takefuji to solve this problem [13]. However Gloria and Jose stated in [15] that the maximum Hopfield networks do not guarantee the descent of a large class of energy function although these models have been applied to several special cases. Following the basic neuron configuration of GMNN, Nobuo Funabiki *et al.* [14] proposed an evolutionary neural network (ENN) approach in 1998, which was based on GA. A novel evolutionary initialization scheme on neuron states was also proposed. Through simulations on 20 examples with up to 500 macro-cells, they showed that ENN can find better solutions in much shorter time than the existing algorithms.

## 3 EP-Based Evolutionary Neural Network

### 3.1 GA and EP

Both GAs and EPs have been used to search for the neural network structure and weights. Although GAs are successful in finding neural network structure in some cases, Angeline *et al.* [16] suggested that GAs are not well-suited for evolving networks. The reason is that GAs typically rely on two distinct representational spaces. An interpretation function is required to map individuals from recombination space to evaluation space. The selection of the interpretation function may make the network structure fixed, while the crossover operator may destroy the produced good network structure, the mutation operation may produce large jump thus make the searching process unstable.

On the contrary, EPs operate directly with representation type, using mutation as the unique genetic recombination operator, which not only omit the complicated operations of coding and decoding in GAs also avoid the problem produced by crossover operation. It seems that EPs are more suitable for the evolution of network.

### 3.2 Algorithm Description of EPENN

Following the basic network structures of GMNN and ENN, EPENN also consists of $N\times 4$ neurons for the $N$-cell problem. The input vector and the output vector can be represented as,

$$U=(U_{11},U_{12},U_{13},U_{14},\cdots,U_{N1},U_{N2},U_{N3},U_{N4})$$
$$V=(V_{11},V_{12},V_{13},V_{14},\cdots,V_{N1},V_{N2},V_{N3},V_{N4}) \quad (2)$$

For each group $G$ containing 4 neurons, the output is binary, and one and only one neuron may output 1 in a solution state. A more generalized maximum Hopfield neuron model proposed in [15] is adopted here,

$$v_i(k+1)=\begin{cases}1 & if\ u_i(k)-K_{oi}=\max_{j\in G}\{u_j(k)-K_{oj}\}\\ 0 & otherwise\end{cases} \quad (3)$$

where $K_{oj}=-(1/2)(\omega_{oo}+\omega_{jj}-\omega_{oj}-\omega_{jo})$, $o$ is the neuron in $G$ with the output 1 at time $k$, then the energy decrease is maximized at every time $k$.

As to the goal function of minimizing the total wire length $L$, we adopt the energy function $E$ to represent,

$$E=\frac{1}{2}\sum_{i=1}^{N}\sum_{p=1}^{4}\sum_{j=1}^{N}\sum_{q=1}^{4}\omega_{ip\,jq}V_{ip}V_{jq} \quad (4)$$

where $\omega_{ip\,jq}$ represents the sum of wire-lengths between cell $i$ (with orientation $p$) and cell $j$ (with orientation $q$), it can be obtained by Euclidean distance formula.

The whole algorithm flow can be described as follows:

1) Calculate weights $\omega_{ip\,jq}$ for each neuron and initialize parameters.
2) An even number of solutions is given as the initial population.
3) Calculate the performance index (energy function $E$ in (4)) for each individual, and rank the individuals according to their performance indexes.
4) Select the individuals whose performance indices are in the top 50% as offspring of the next generation. Transfer them to the next generation without any change and all other individuals are discarded.
5) In the meanwhile, the selected individuals are designated as the parents of the next generation, copy and then mutate them to produce new offspring.
6) Update the input $U_i$ by $U_i=U_i+\Delta U_i$ for each macro-cell.

7) Update the output $V_i$ by (3).
8) Calculate the change of energy function $E$, and extract the minimum energy function and the best solution.
9) Check the termination condition: if not satisfied, go to 1).

## 4 Numerical Experiments

In this section, the algorithm described above have been implemented and examined on 10 examples, which are generated randomly with various net densities. The configuration of the experimental platform is: Intel 2.0GHz CPU, 512M memory. The configurations and simulation results of these examples are listed in Table 1.

**Table 1.** Simulation results of EPENN on 10 examples

| Example No. | $N$ | Number of Nets | Initial TWLs | EPENN | Reduction Rates |
|---|---|---|---|---|---|
| 1 | 20 | 50 | 2755 | 2322.4 | 15.7% |
| 2 | 50 | 225 | 14776 | 12705.5 | 13.9% |
| 3 | 100 | 300 | 26752 | 24122.5 | 9.82% |
| 4 | 120 | 420 | 42147 | 39152.6 | 7.10% |
| 5 | 150 | 500 | 56752 | 52446.5 | 7.58% |
| 6 | 200 | 600 | 70225 | 64456.4 | 8.21% |
| 7 | 250 | 750 | 114563 | 106253.8 | 7.25% |
| 8 | 300 | 950 | 137586 | 128965.1 | 6.27% |
| 9 | 500 | 1750 | 224537 | 201468.2 | 10.3% |
| 10 | 700 | 2300 | 312467 | 284538.8 | 8.94% |

Note that reduction rates in the table represent the reduced simulated results with respect to the initial TWLs. The results show that EPENN can reduced the TWLs in the range of 7.1% to 15.7%, depending on the placement of the cells and pins. If we change the initial parameters setting, maybe a better or worse result would generate. The run-time of these simulations ranges from 1.5 seconds to 400 seconds.

## 5 Conclusion

Macro-cell placement is an important step in VLSI physical design. In order to obtain the minimized interconnect wire-length and to reduce the high-frequency effects, an evolutionary neural network based on evolutionary programming was proposed to address macro-cell orientation problem. Numerical experiments showed that the proposed approach could obtain a high quality solution in very short time. Further research should focus on the theoretical and practical improvements on the heuristic algorithm with higher efficiencies.

## Acknowledgments

This paper is supported by the National Nature Science Foundation of China (No. 90307017).

## References


1. R.Achar, M.S.Nakhla.: Simulation of High-Speed Interconnects. Proceedings of the IEEE, Vol.89, No.5 (2001) 693-728
2. M.Nakhla, A.Ushida.: Special Issue on Simulation, Modeling, and Electrical Design of High-Speed Interconnects. IEEE Trans, Circuits Syst., Vol.47 (2000) 44-45
3. Gao, D. S., Yang, A. T., Kang, S. M..: Modeling and Simulation of Interconnection Delays and Crosstalk in High-Speed IC. IEEE Trans, Circuit Syst., Vol.37 (1990) 1-9
4. Jason Cong: An Interconnect-Centric Design Flow for Nanometer Technologies. Proc. of Int'l Symp. on VLSI Technology, System, and Applications, (1999) 54-57
5. Melvin A.Breuer, Majid Sarrafzadeh, Fabio Somenzi: Fundamental CAD Algorithms. IEEE Trans, CAD of Integrated Circuits and Syst., Vol.19, No.12 (2000) 1449-1475
6. Nan, G. F., Li, M. Q.: Application of Evolutionary Algorithm to Three Key Problems in VLSI Layout. Proceedings of the 4th ICMLC, Guangzhou (2005)
7. Pinaki Mazumder.: Genetic Algorithms for VLSI Design, Layout & Test Automation. Prentice-Hall (1999)
8. Yao, B., Hou, W. T., Hong, X. L., Cai, Y. C.: FAME: A Fast Detailed Placement Algorithm for Standard Cell Layout Based on Mixed Min-cut and Enumeration. Chinese Journal of Semiconductors, 21 (2005) 744~753
9. Gao, W.: Study on New Evolutionary Neural Network. Proc. of 3rd ICMLC, Xi'an (2003)
10. Fang, J., Xi, Y. G.: Neural Network Design Based on Evolutionary Programming. Artificial Intelligence in Engineering. Elsevier (1997) 155-161
11. M.Yamada, Liu, C. L.: An Analytical Method for Optimal Module Orientation. Proc. Int. Symp. Circuits and Systems (1988) 1679-1682
12. R. Libeskind-Hadas, Liu, C. L.: Solutions to the Module Orientation and Rotation Problems by Neural Computation Networks. Proc. 26th ACM/IEEE Design Automation Conf. (1989) 400–405
13. Lee, K. C., Y. Takefuji: A Generalized Maximum Neural Network for the Module Orientation Problem. Int. J. Electron., Vol. 72, No. 3 (1992) 331–355
14. Nobuo Funabiki, Junji Kitamichi, Seishi Nishikawa: An Evolutionary Neural Network Approach for Module Orientation Problems. IEEE Trans, Systems, Man, and Cybernetics□Part B: Cybernetics, Vol.28, No.6 (1998) 849-856
15. Gloria G., Jose M.: Design and Analysis of Maximum Hopfield Networks. IEEE Trans, Neural Networks, Vol.12, No.2 (2001) 329-339
16. Angeline, Peter J., Saunders, Gregory M., Pollack J.: An Evolutionary Algorithm that Constructs Neural Networks. IEEE Trans, Neural Networks, No.5 (1994) 54-65

# An Integration Method of Artificial Neural Network and Genetic Algorithm for Structure Design of a Scooter

Jinn-Jong Sheu[1] and Chi-Yuan Chen[2]

[1] National Kaohsiung University of Applied Sciences, No. 415 Chien Kung Road, Kaohsiung 807, Taiwan
jjsheu@cc.kuas.edu.tw
[2] Kaohsiung Rapid Transit Corporation, No.1 Tung-An Road Kaohsiung 806, Taiwan
chtyyuan@yahoo.com.tw

**Abstract.** In this paper, an integration method of the artificial neural network (ANN) system and the genetic algorithms (GA) was proposed. Computer aided engineering (CAE) simulations and experiments were carried out to analyze the deformation of a four-wheel scooter under different loading conditions. A prototype of scooter structure was built to verify the simulation and design results. The simulation results of stress, strain and displacement data were adopted for the training and testing of the developed ANN system. The trained ANN system was integrated with the optimization system based on the genetic algorithm to determine the most suitable combination of the structure design. The material types, topological configurations and section geometries of structural beams were taken into consideration of design. The predicted deformation results of the ANN system were in good agreement with the CAE and experiment data.

## 1 Introduction

The ANN system researchers were trying to mimic the working system of a real neuron. McCulloch and Pitts [1] proposed the "MP model" and defined the synapse with the properties of weighting and transferring method. Hebb proposed the "Hebbian learning rule" discussing the method of changing weight of a synapse. If the connected neurons are activated, the weight of the synapse connecting these two neurons will be increased. Rosenblatt [2] combined the MP model and Hebbian learning rule to create the perceptron model of an artificial neural network. The functions of a neuron in ANN system were able to be described in a completely mathematical form.

Rumelhart et al. [3] proposed the "generalized delta rule" to adjust the weights of a multilayer perceptron by using the gradient steepest descent method. A back-propagation (BP) procedure was adopted to minimize the error of the prediction. Holland [4] proposed a genetic algorithm based on the theme of "the survival of the fittest". The design parameters of an engineering problem were coded into chromosomes and the better design was obtained via the genetic evolution. Yang et al. [5] proposed a genetic programming method to optimize the structure of truss. The allowance stress and buckling condition were considered in the fitness function. The existing methods of scooter's structure design in the workshop are based on the trial-and-error process. This paper proposed a systematic method to analyze and design the structure of a scooter.

D.-S. Huang, K. Li, and G.W. Irwin (Eds.): ICIC 2006, LNCS 4113, pp. 655–662, 2006.

## 2 Mathematical Model

In this paper, an artificial neural network system was integrated with the genetic algorithm to predict deformation and obtain the optimal design of a scooter's structure.

### 2.1 The Artificial Neural Network System

A supervised feed forward learning and back propagation network was adopted. The structure of an artificial neural network system with two hidden layers was shown in Fig. 1. The concepts of MP model and generalized delta rule were adopted.

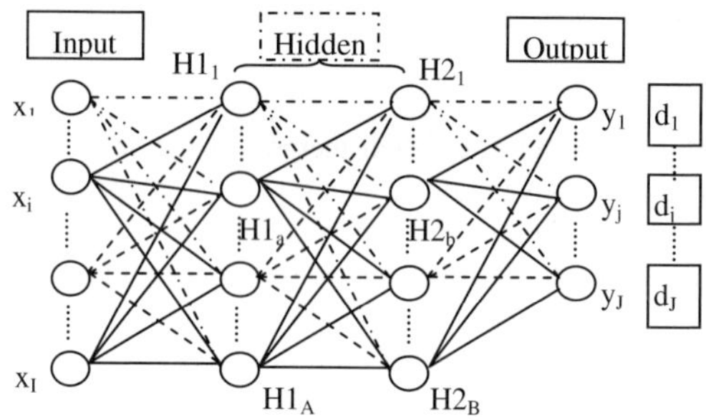


**Fig. 1.** Schematic diagram of the proposed ANN model shows two hidden layers

In Fig. 1, the input and output neuron numbers were not limited. The hidden layer numbers can be chosen arbitrarily. The neurons were created in the input layer($x$), hidden layers ($H$) and output layer ($y$), respectively. The desired outputs ($d$) were compared with the prediction and the errors were minimized to obtain the converged training data. A sigmoid activation function was calculated and controlled the excitement or restraint of a neuron. A back propagation process was performed to minimize the error function. A modified steepest descent method was developed to modify the weight of neurons and minimize the error. The increment of weight of the $j^{th}$ neuron at the $m^{th}$ iteration was given by

$$\Delta w_{ji}^{m} = w_{ji}(t+1) - w_{ji}(t) = -\eta \frac{\partial E}{\partial w_{ji}} + \alpha \Delta w_{ji}^{m-1} \ . \tag{1}$$

where $t$ represents the last step, $i$ is the index of the previous neuron connected to $j$, $\eta$ and $\alpha$ are the learning rate and momentum terms, respectively.

### 2.2 The Genetic Algorithm of the Optimization

A genetic algorithm was adopted to find an optimal design of a scooter's structure. The general form of an optimization problem is described by

$$\text{maximize} \ \ f(x) \ . \tag{2a}$$

$$\text{subject to } l_i \le x_i \le u_i \ . \tag{2b}$$

where the design variable $x_i$ was bounded by the lower and upper limits $l_i$ and $u_i$, respectively. An encoding process was adopted to convert the design variables of optimization into the chromosomes of GA. The bit numbers of a binary chromosome, $n_i$, required for resolution $R$ of the $i^{th}$ design variable was given by

$$n_i = \left[ \frac{\log(((u_i - l_i)/R) + 1)}{\log 2} \right] + 0.5 \ . \tag{3}$$

The reproduction, crossover and mutation process was repeated from generation to generation. A fitness function of chromosome $C$ was defined by

$$fit(C) = 3.\text{-}Delat - Sigma - Epsilon \ . \tag{4}$$

where *Delta*, *Sigma* and *Epsilon* are the normalized maximum displacement, von Mises stress and strain, respectively. It is required to find the displacement, stress and strain in the fitness function.

During reproduction, the chromosomes with higher fitness have higher priority to be kept and reproduced. The roulette wheel method was adopted to select the chromosome of crossover. A single point crossover method was adopted to obtain the mating result. A mutation process was adopted to produce new generation more divergently. The optimized chromosomes were decoded to obtain the real design variables. The value of a design variable, $x_i$, is decoded by using

$$x_i = D_i \times \left( \frac{u_i - l_i}{2^{n_i} - 1} \right) + l_i \ . \tag{5}$$

where $D_i$ is the decimal value of the $i^{th}$ chromosome related to the variable $x_i$.

### 2.3 The Integration of Genetic Algorithm and ANN Model

The fitness value of GA was calculated using the predicted displacement, stress and strain of the integrated ANN module. The new designs were created by GA module and evaluated by the ANN prediction. This integration makes it possible to find the optimal design automatically.

## 3 Implementation and Verification of the Proposed Model

### 3.1 The Implementation of the ANN Model

The proposed ANN model was implemented by using the C++ language. The training and testing data were prepared by using the CAE simulations. The design parameters adopted in the scooter design were shown in Table 1. The desired outputs were the maximum displacement (mm), von Mises stress (Mpa) and equivalent strain ($10^{-3}$) of the structure. The mesh model and loading boundary conditions of a scooter were shown in Fig. 2. The experimental measurement locations were indicated by circles. The section types of tube in the longitudinal direction were same. The lateral direction adopted the same criterion. The loads, $Fz$ and $Fy$ , were applied in the vertical and horizontal directions. The vertical load was 1960 N and kept constant in all simulations. Two levels of horizontal load were considered. The dotted arrow lines in Fig. 2 indicated the wheel centers of scooter. The types of structure designs were shown in Fig. 3. There are 3 designs for each of the main structure layout in the longitudinal and lateral directions, driver's foot supporting area and reinforcement of the driver's seat supporting. There were 75 simulations carried out by using the different combinations of Table 1. The results were divided into two sets, 64 and 11 cases for training and testing, respectively. All of the design variables were normalized to the range of 0 to 1 in the ANN model. The parameters of ANN model and the weights of the neurons after training and testing were saved and integrated to the GA programs.

**Table 1.** The considered design variables of the scooter structure design

| Design variables | Levels | Note |
|---|---|---|
| Factor A :<br>Main layout of the scooter's structure | 1. S-S<br>2. R-R<br>3. S-R | Square or round tubes adopted in the longitudinal and lateral directions, respectively |
| Factor B :<br>Young's module of the structure material | 1. 200 (GPa)<br>2. 193 (GPa)<br>3. 68.9 (GPa) | Material properties of the structural steel, stainless steel and aluminum alloy, respectively |
| Factor C :<br>Section types of the foot supporting area | 1. 1.63(E-8 $m^4$)<br>2. 0.27(E-8 $m^4$)<br>3. 0.55(E-8 $m^4$) | moment of inertia, I, of round tube, plate and square tube, respectively |
| Factor D :<br>Reinforcement design under seat of driver | 1. 0 (E-8 $m^4$)<br>2. 1.01(E-8 $m^4$)<br>3. 1.63(E-8 $m^4$) | Moment of inertia, I, of none, square tube and round tube, respectively |
| Factor E :<br>Side force *Fy* | 1. 245 (N)<br>2. 981 (N) | Consideration of the unbalance of the scooter driver |
| Factor F :<br>Slope of road with respect to x-direction | 1. 0 (degrees)<br>2. 15 (degrees) | Simulate the inclined angle of a road ( climbing up condition) |

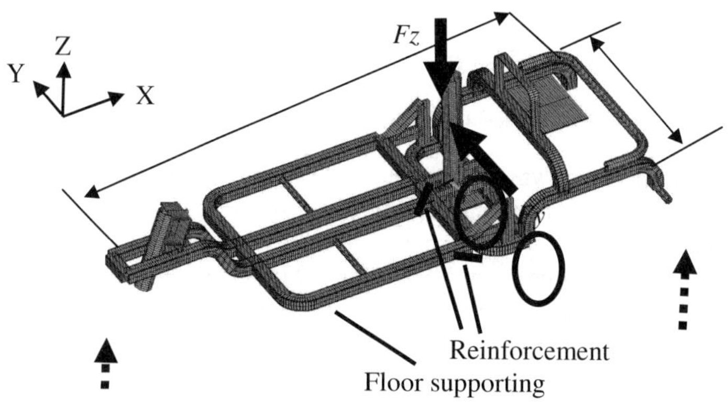


**Fig. 2.** The structure and force boundary conditions applied in CAE mesh of the scooter

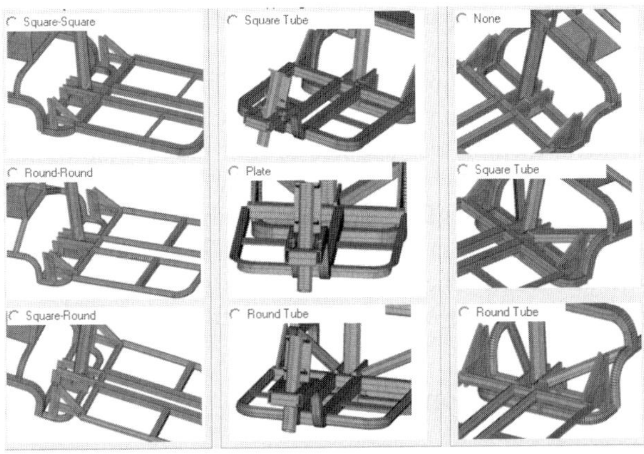


**Fig. 3.** The different structure types of the main layout, foot area supporting and reinforcement

## 3.2 The Implementation of GA and Integration with ANN Model

The proposed GA model was implemented by using the C++ language. The ANN module works in preparation mode for training and testing purpose. It is also capable of working in prediction mode for prediction of deformation. The GA program used the encoding and decoding schemes to pass and retrieve the variables and results of the ANN model. The automatically generated chromosomes of GA were decoded into the normalized design variables required by the ANN module. The ANN module returned the predicted deformation data and a fitness value was calculated in the GA module. The GA module repeated the process of generating populations, calling ANN and evaluating the chromosomes, making evolution until the optimization process converged or the maximum generation limit reached.

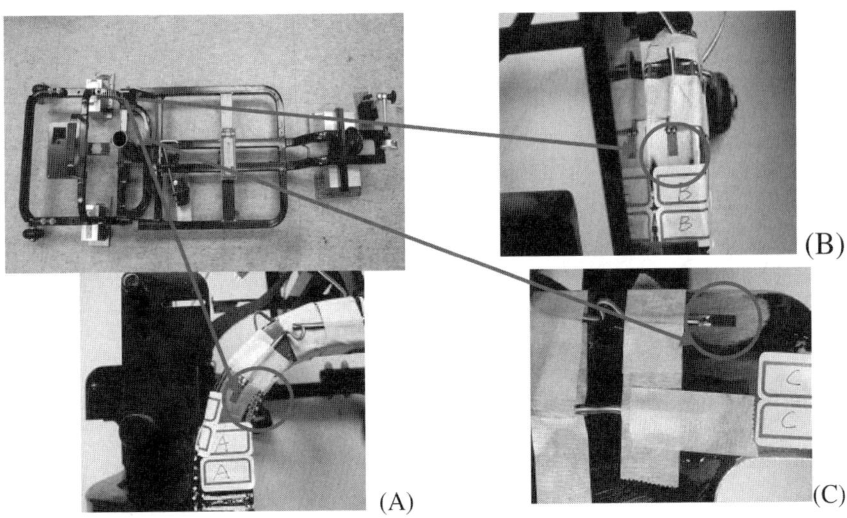


**Fig. 4.** The prototype of scooter and the measurement locations A, B and C of the strain gauges

### 3.3 Verification of the ANN Prediction and GA Optimization

A prototype of optimized scooter structure was built to measure the strains of the structure under loading. The prototype and the attached strain gauges were shown in Fig. 4. The Taguchi method was adopted to find the optimal design of structure for the purpose of comparison. A L9($3^4$) orthogonal array was adopted to setup the combinations of design variables. The parameters of horizontal force and slope of road were treated as noise factors in Taguchi method. The criterion of Taguchi optimum design is lower-the-better. The normalized maximum effective strain, von Mises stress and displacement were weighted and summed to present the design quality.

## 4 Results and Discussion

### 4.1 The Verification of CAE Simulation

The built prototype of a scooter and the setup of strain measurement were shown in Fig. 4. The locations of the attached strain gauges were shown by detailed figures (A), (B) and (C). Three most critical points were measured to study the major deformation of structure. The applied load was 120 Kg at the top center of the vertical tube where the driver's seat will be mounted. The measured strains at A, B and C were -64, -64 and -24 E-6 mm/mm, respectively. The CAE results of the corresponding points were -60.18, -61.33 and -22.56 E-6 mm/mm, respectively. The errors of A, B and C points were about 5%. The experimental data were in good agreement with the CAE results.

### 4.2 The Training and Testing of Artificial Neural Network Model

The training and testing results of the von Mises stress prediction were shown in Fig. 5. The trend and values of the ANN prediction were in good agreement with the training and the testing data. The displacement and effective strain were also shown the same trend.

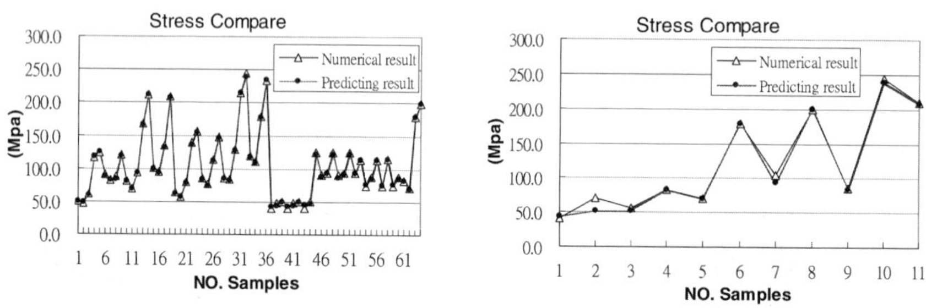


**Fig. 5.** The training (left) and the testing (right) results of the developed ANN model

### 4.3 The Response Chart of Taguchi Method and ANOVA Analysis

Fig. 6 showed the response of the design variables A, B, C and D in Table 1. The S/N (signal-noise) ratio was calculated from the quality index of displacement, strain and

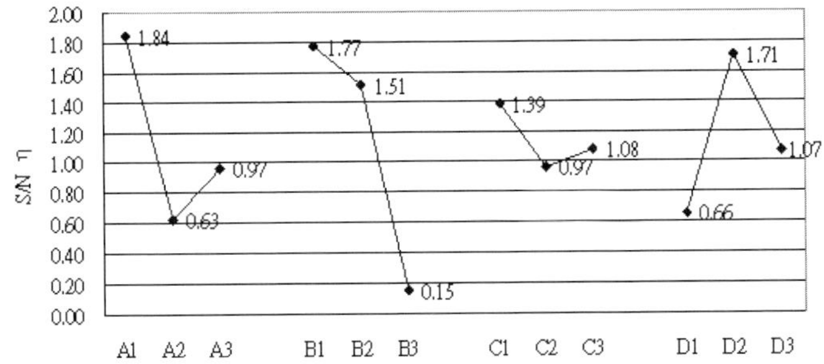


**Fig. 6.** The response chart of the Taguchi method and the optimum prediction

stress. The optimum prediction was the combination of A1, B1, C1 and D2. The significance of factors A, B, C, and D in the ANOVA analysis of displacement consideration was 9.6%, 70%, 5.3% and 15.1%, respectively. The response chart also showed the effect of all factors except C was obvious.

### 4.4 The Integration of GA Program and the Artificial Neural Network Model

The optimal design and the chromosomes of the proposed GA system were shown in Table 2. The optimal design and prediction errors of Taguchi and GA methods were given in Table 3. The results of the proposed system were similar to Taguchi method but the errors of quality prediction were smaller.

**Table 2.** The chromosomes of the optimum design and the decoded design variables

| Factors in Table 1 | Chromosome | Value of design variables |
|---|---|---|
| Factor A | 0 0 0 0 0 0 0 0 0 0 0 0 0 0 | 1 (Square-Square) |
| Factor B | 1 1 1 1 1 1 1 0 0 0 0 0 1 0 | 199.02 (structural steel) |
| Factor C | 1 1 1 1 1 1 1 1 1 0 0 1 1 1 | 1.626(round tube) |
| Factor D | 1 1 1 1 1 1 1 1 1 0 1 1 1 0 | 1.626(round tube) |
| Factor E | 0 0 0 0 0 0 0 0 0 0 0 1 1 0 | 245.53(25 kg unbalance) |
| Factor F | 0 0 0 0 0 1 0 0 0 0 0 0 1 1 | 0.2398( near 0 degree) |

**Table 3.** The optimum design and errors of the proposed GA system and the Taguchi method

| Factors | A | B | C | D | E | F | Disp. | Stress | Strain |
|---|---|---|---|---|---|---|---|---|---|
| GA | 1 | 199.02 | 1.626 | 1.626 | 245.54 | 0.239 | 4.7% | 1.2% | 2.1% |
| Taguchi | 1 | 200.00 | 1.630 | 1.630 | 245.00 | 0.000 | 11.5% | 8.0% | 4.2% |

## 5 Conclusions

An integration system of genetic algorithm and ANN model was proposed and developed successfully. The CAE results were in good agreement with the experimental measurements. The strain prediction of the ANN model was in good agreement with the experimental results. The errors of quality prediction of the proposed system were smaller than Taguchi method. It demonstrated the proposed integration method of GA and ANN was able to find the optimal design and predict the deformation precisely.

## References


1. McCulloch, W.S., Pitts, W.H.: A Logical Calculus of the Ideas Imminent in Nervous Activity. Bulletin of Mathematical Biophysics, 5 (1943) 115–133
2. Rosenblatt, F.: The Perceptron: A Probabilistic Model for Information Storage and Organization in the Brain. Psych. Rev, 65 (1958) 386–408
3. Rumelhart, D.E., Hinton, G.E. Williams, R.J.: Learning Internal Representations by Error Propagation. In: Rumelhart, D.E., McClelland, J.L.: Parallel Distributed Processing: Explorations in the Microstructure of Cognition. MIT Press, Cambridge, (1986) 318-362
4. Holland, J.H.: Adaptation in Natural and Artificial System. University of Michigan Press, Ann Arbor, MI (1975)
5. Yang, Y., Soh, C. K.: Automated Optimum Design of Structures Using Genetic Programming. Computers and Structures, 80 (2002) 1537-1546

# Digital Filter Design Using Evolvable Hardware Chip for Image Enhancement

A. Sumathi[1] and R.S.D. Wahida Banu[2]

[1] Adhiaman college of Engg., Hosur
[2] Government college of Engineering, Salem
ravi_mls@yahoo.com

**Abstract.** Images acquired through modern cameras may be contaminated by a variety of noise sources (e.g. photon or on chip electronic noise) and also by distortions such as shading or improper illumination. Therefore a preprocessing unit has to be incorporated before recognition to improve image quality. General-purpose image filters lacks the flexibility and adaptability for un-modeled noise types. The EHW architecture evolves filters without any apriori information. The approach chosen here is based on functional level evolution The proposed filter considers spatial domain approach and uses the overlapping window to remove the noise in the image.

## 1 Introduction

Many of today's image and signal processing tasks are performed on real-time data. On systems that perform real-time processing of data, performance is often limited by the processing capability of the system. Systems based on software are flexible, but often suffer from insufficient processing capability. Alternately, dedicated hardware can provide the highest processing performance, but is less flexible for changes. Reconfigurable hardware [1] devices offer both the flexibility of computer software, and the ability to construct custom high performance computing circuits. Thus, in many cases they make a good compromise between software and hardware solutions. The structure of a reconfigurable hardware device can be changed any number of times by downloading into the device a software bit string called configuration bits. Field Programmable Gate Arrays (FPGA) and Programmable Logic Devices (PLD) are typical examples of reconfigurable hardware devices.

Evolvable Hardware (EHW) is a new concept in the development of online adaptive machines. In contrast to conventional hardware where the structure is irreversibly fixed in the design process, EHW is designed to adapt to changes in task requirements or changes in the environment through its ability to reconfigure its own hardware structure online and autonomously [2].

In this paper, an EHW chip is configured using evolutionary algorithms to remove the noise and improve the quality of the images. The GA chromosome (architecture bits) is downloaded onto the reconfigurable device during genetic learning [3].

In the field of digital image processing, a broad and disparate range of applications using evolutionary computation can be found in the literature. The functional level EHW architecture is described in [1]. The hardware implementation of the Genetic Algorithm model is explained in [4]. The evolution of spatial masks to detect edges

D.-S. Huang, K. Li, and G.W. Irwin (Eds.): ICIC 2006, LNCS 4113, pp. 663 – 671, 2006.

within gray scale images is described in [8]. [9] has achieved evolutionary design of image filters with virtual reconfigurable circuits in extrinsic EHW environment. This paper presents complete evolvable hardware architecture, dedicated for implementing high performance digital image filters on FPGA, so that the time for the evolution is greatly reduced

## 2 Evolvable Hardware

Evolvable Hardware is the combination of Genetic Algorithms and the software reconfigurable devices. The structure of the reconfigurable device can be determined by downloading binary bit strings called the architecture bits [8]. The architecture bits are treated as chromosomes in the population by the GA, and can be downloaded to the reconfigurable device resulting in changes to the hardware structure. The changed functionality of the device can then be evaluated and the fitness of the chromosome is calculated. The performance of the device is improved as the population is evolved by GA according to fitness. Figures 1 and 2 show the function level and gate level evolution model. The basic concept of evolvable hardware is shown in Figure 3.

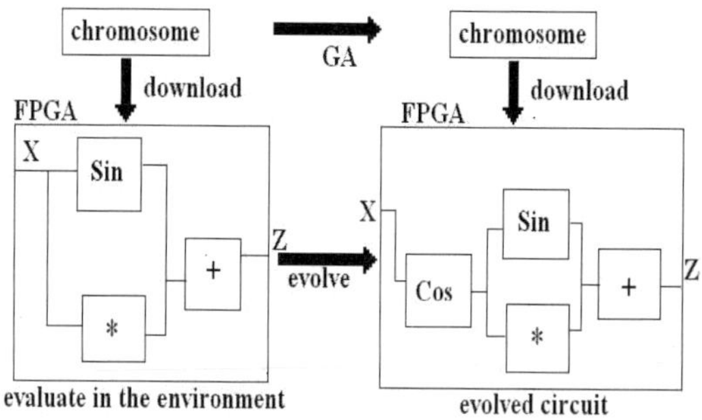


**Fig. 1.** Functional level evolution

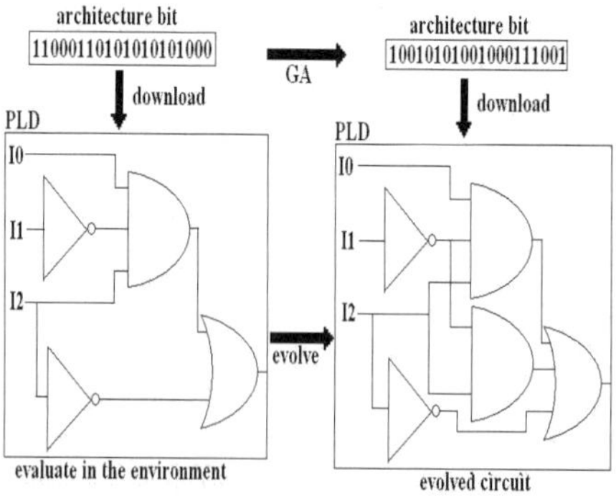


**Fig. 2.** Gate level evolution

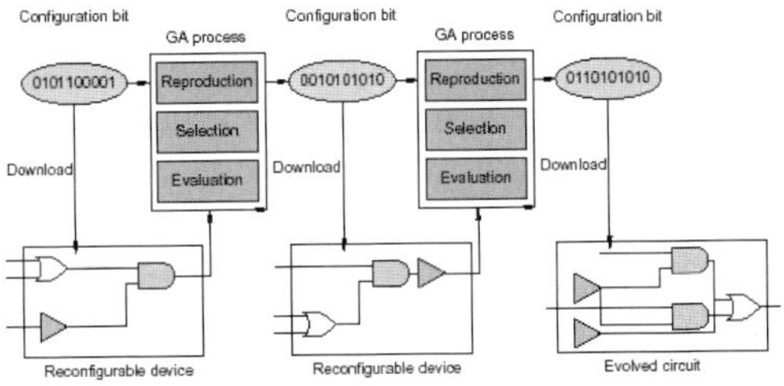


**Fig. 3.** Basic concept of EHW

In gate-level evolution, the hardware evolution is based on primitive gates such as AND-gates and OR-gates. In function level evolution, hardware synthesis involves higher-level hardware functions than the primitive gates of gate-level evolution.

## 3 Genetic Algorithm

Genetic Algorithm [7] determines how the hardware structure should be reconfigured whenever a new hardware structure is needed for an improved performance. GA was proposed to model adaptation of natural and artificial systems through evolution, and is one of the most well known powerful search procedures.

The sequence of operations performed by the GA is shown in Figure 4. In the initial state, chromosomes in the population are generated at random, and processed by many operations, such as evaluation, selection, crossover and mutation. The evaluation assigns the fitness values to the chromosomes, which indicates how well the chromosomes perform as solutions of the given problem.

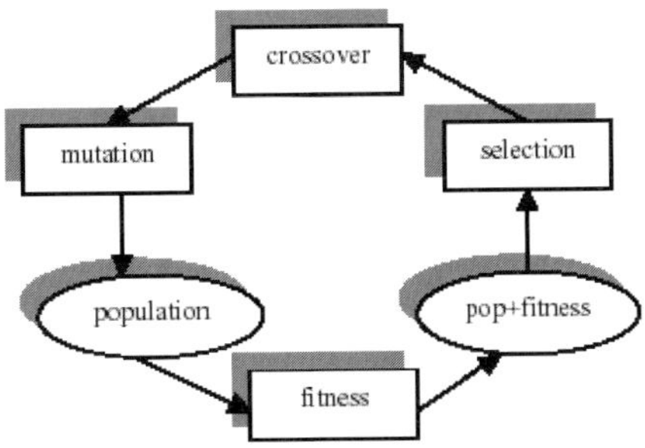


**Fig. 4.** Flow of Genetic algorithm

The major advantages of GA are its robustness and superior search performance particularly in problems without aprior knowledge.

## 4 Hardware Implementation of EHW

A great effort is invested to designing evolvable systems at the level of FPGAs. These solutions can be divided into two groups:

1) FPGA is used for evaluation of circuits produced by evolutionary algorithm, which is executed in software.
2) The whole evolvable system is implemented in the FPGAs. This type of implementation integrates a hardware realization of evolutionary algorithm and a reconfigurable device.

The typical feature of these approaches is that the chromosomes are transformed to configuration bit stream and the configuration bit stream is uploaded into the FPGA.

Virtual Reconfigurable Circuits (VRC) was introduced for digital evolvable hardware as a new kind of rapidly reconfigurable platform utilizing conventional FPGAs [10]. The approach utilizing VRC offers many benefits, such as

1) It is relatively inexpensive, because the whole evolvable system is realized using an ordinary FPGA.
2) The architecture of the reconfigurable device can be designed exactly according the needs of a given problem.
3) Since, the whole evolvable system is available at the level of Hardware Description Language (HDL) code it can easily be modified and synthesized for various target platforms (FPGA families).

## 5 Virtual Reconfigurable Circuit (VRC)

Figure 5 shows the VRC. It is in fact a new reconfigurable circuit consisting of 8 programmable elements realized on top of an ordinary FPGA. Slices have to implement a new array of programmable elements, new routing circuits and new configuration memory. Furthermore, style of reconfiguration and granularity of new virtual reconfigurable circuit can exactly reflect the needs of a given application.

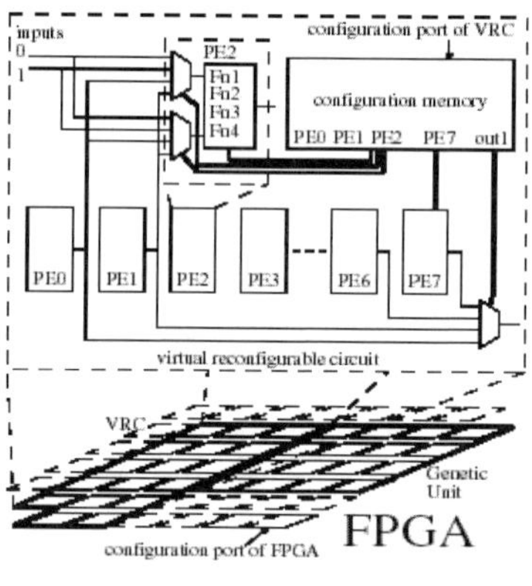


**Fig. 5.** Example of VRC used in EHW

The elements in VRC are referred as Processing Elements (PEs). Configuration bits determine PEs function and the places where its inputs are connected to. The routing circuits are implemented using multiplexers. The configuration memory is composed of flip-flops.

## 6 Digital Image Filter Design

The digital image filter contains virtual reconfigurable circuit together with genetic unit. The corrupted image is given as input to the virtual reconfigurable circuit and the filtered image is obtained. The filtered image is compared with the original image and the fitness is evaluated. This is shown in figure 6.

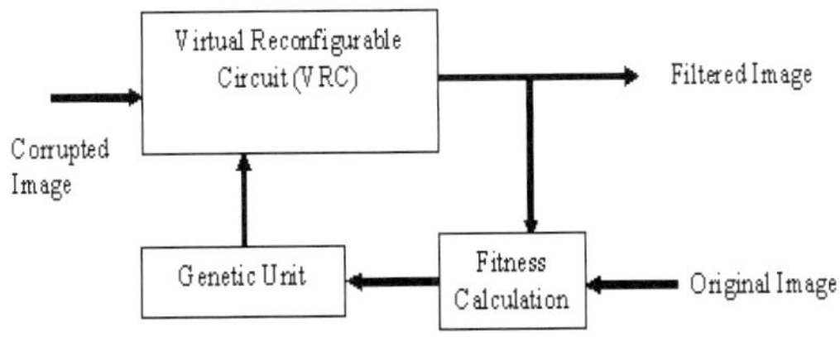


**Fig. 6.** Block diagram of digital image filter using VRC

The VRC processes nine 8-bit inputs I0 – I8 and produces a single 8-bit output. Every pixel value of the filtered image will be calculated using a corresponding pixel and its eight neighbors.

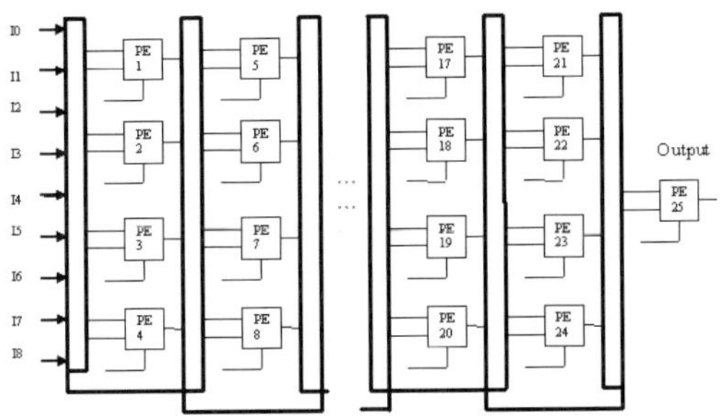


**Fig. 7.** Architecture of VRC with 25 PE's

**Table 1.**

| Function Code | Function | Function Code | Function |
|---|---|---|---|
| 0000 | X >> 1 | 1000 | X & 0x0F |
| 0001 | X | 1001 | X & 0xF0 |
| 0010 | ~ X | 1010 | X \| 0x0F |
| 0011 | X & Y | 1011 | X \| 0x F0 |
| 0100 | X \| Y | 1100 | Min(X,Y) |
| 0101 | X ^ Y | 1101 | Max(X,Y) |
| 0110 | (X+Y)>>2 | 1110 | Y<<1 |
| 0111 | (X+Y) >>1 | 1111 | X+Y |

Each PE has two 8-bit inputs and gives a single 8-bit output. The outputs of PE's are equipped with registers. Every PE executes a certain function from Table 1, depending on the function code configuration, sel3 which is applied to its two inputs.

The architecture of VRC with the 25 PE's is shown in Figure 7. The configuration bit stream consists of ten bits for each PE. First six bits determine the places where PEs inputs will be connected to. One of 16 functions is selected from Table-1 using the last four bits. The output of the PE is given by $\text{Output} = F\{\text{mux(sel1)}, \text{mux(sel2)}, \text{sel3}\}$.

Further functions can be included but this is dependant on the resource requirements, as there is a trade-off between the functionality and the complexity of the hardware structure.

## 7 Details of EHW Chip

The proposed hardware implementation of the complete evolvable system is composed of basic modules; input buffer, virtual reconfigurable circuit, pseudo random number generator, population memory, selection unit, mutation unit, fitness evaluator and output buffer as shown in Figure 8. Both the Genetic unit and the Virtual reconfiguration unit reside in the chip and hence the configuration is complete. The configuration word contains details about the interconnection between the processing elements (PE) of the VRC and the functional operations performed within each PE.

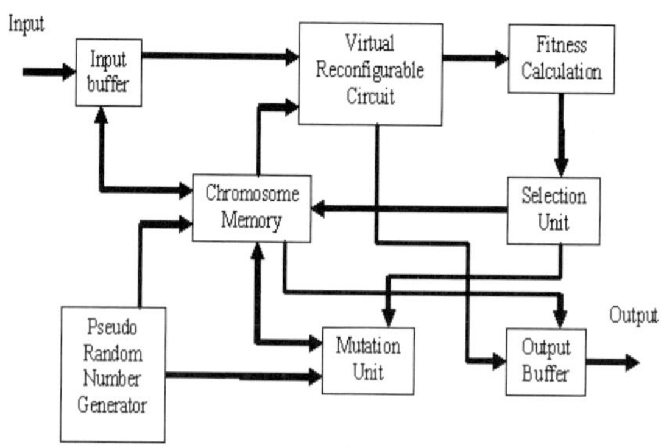


**Fig. 8.** Block diagram of the complete EHW system

## 8 Chromosome Format

The logical configuration of the circuit is defined by a set of 250 bits, 10 bits for each one of the 25 PEs in the reconfigurable architecture as shown

111 000 0000 010 001 1100 110 010 0011 111 011 0010 110 111 0100 ............ 101 000 1000 110 010 1010

The first six bits of each ten bits represent the source of inputs to the PE (sel1& sel2) as labeled in Figure 7. The other four bits of each ten bit (sel3) indexes the function from Table 1 to be applied by the PE.

## 9 Fitness Function

Various approaches exist to measure image visual quality. The Peak Signal-to-Noise Ratio (PSNR) and the Mean difference per pixel (MDPP) are the commonly used approaches. The MDPP fitness function is computationally easier for hardware implementation as compared to PSNR. In this work MDPP fitness function is taken for the fitness calculation.

The fitness function using the PSNR is given by

$$PSNR = 10\log_{10}\frac{255^2}{MSE} \text{ dB}$$

The fitness function using MDPP is given by

$$MDPP = \frac{1}{NxN}\sum_{i,j=1}^{N} | orig(i,j) - filt(i,j) |$$

where |orig(i,j) – filt(i,j)| is the absolute difference between the original and filtered images.

## 10 Discussion of Results

The original and distorted bitmap images are stored in input buffer initially. At the same time using random number generator 16 initial chromosomes are generated.

Simulations were performed using Gaussian noise distorted bitmaps. Bitmap of IEEE test image Lena is used as the target image at different distortion levels for the generality of the EHW architecture. All results were compared with the filtered results from the Gaussian filter. The bitmap images contaminated by Gaussian noise with mean 0 and variance 0.01, 0.02, 0.05, 0.08 and 0.1 were used for the initial evolution. Figure 9 is the original Lena bitmap of 128x128. Figure 10 is the Lena bitmap distorted by Gaussian noise with mean 0 and variance 0.03. Figure 11 is the result from Gaussian filter. Figure 12 is the resulting image of the EHW filter. The MDPP is 135602 for Gaussian filtered image and 127985 for EHW filtered image.

## 11 Chip Implementation Results

The evolved filter is the result of the evolution of an array of 4x6 PEs with one PE at the output. The level back parameter is set as 2. Number of generations is 3000. The hardware evolution took 2 minutes on Xilinx Virtex FPGA xcv800 running at 49 MHz. This compares favorably with software simulations run previously which it took approximately 6 hours (Pentium III/800 MHz system) to achieve the best chromosome. Hardware evolution took 12 minutes in Xilinx VirtexE FPGA xcv2000e. This compares favorably with software simulations run previously which took approximately 6 hours to give the best chromosome. The synthesis report obtained is given in Table-2 below.

**Table 2.** Synthesis Report (Population Size = 16, Chromosome Length = 250)

| Target information: Vendor: Xilinx<br>Device: v800fg680 Speed: -6<br>Optimization Goal: Speed | | |
|---|---|---|
| Number of Slices | 3204 out of 9408 | 34% |
| Number of Slice Flip Flops | 1087 out of 18816 | 5% |
| Number of 4 input LUTs | 6200 out of 18816 | 32% |
| Number of bonded IOBs | 79 out of 516 | 15% |
| Number of BRAMs | 8 out of 28 | 28% |
| Number of GCLKs | 1 out of 4 | 25% |
| Minimum period | 20.160ns | |
| Maximum Frequency | 49.603MHz | |
| Minimum input arrival time before clock | 27.706ns | |
| Maximum output required time after clock | 6.887ns | |

## 12 Conclusion

The work has presented a novel approach to digital image filter design based on the technique of evolvable hardware. FPGA model for the function level evolvable hardware is analyzed and associated with the evolutionary algorithms employed. The evolution time has been greatly reduced by implementing the evolutionary algorithm in hardware. The EHW architecture evolves filters without a priori information and out-performs conventional filter in terms of computational effort, filtered output signal and implementation cost.

**Fig. 9.**

**Fig. 10.**

**Fig. 11.**

**Fig. 12.**

Figure 9 represents Original Lena Image of size 128x128, Figure 10 Image Distorted by Gaussian Noise of Mean 0 and Variance 0.003, Figure 11 Image Filtered by Gaussian Filter, Figure 12 Image Filtered by EHW filter.

## References


1. Vandenberg et al. :Digital image processing techniques, fractal dimensionality and scale-space applied to surface roughness, Wear, (1992),159, 17-30
2. Kiran et al "Evaluation of surface roughness by vision system", International J. Mach. Tools Manufact. Vol. 38, Nos 5-6, (1998), 685-690
3. Suresh et al,:A Genetic algoritm approach for optimization of Surface roughness prediction model, The International Jnl. Of Machine Tools & Manufacture, Vol. 42, (2002), 675-680
4. Samhouri et al,:Surface Roughness in Grinding: Off-line Identification with an Adaptive Neuro Fuzzy Inference system, Paper submitted to NAMRAC 33-2005 conference, May 24-27, Columbia (2005)
5. Higuchi, T., Murakawa, M., Iwata, M., Kajitani, I., Liu W., Salami, M.: Evolvable Hardware at Function Level, Proc. of the *IEEE International Conference on Evolutionary Computation*, Apr (1997), 187-192
6. Layzell, P.:Reducing Hardware Evolution's Dependency on FPGAs, Proc. of the *Seventh International Conference on Microelectronics for Neural, Fuzzy and Bio-Inspired Systems (MicroNeuro '99)*, IEEE 1999, 171-178
7. David E. Goldberg, *Genetic Algorithms in Search, Optimization and Machine Learning*, Pearson Education, 1989
8. Hollingworth, G., Smith, S., Tyrrell, A.:Design of Highly Parallel Edge Detection Nodes using Evolutionary Techniques, Proc. of the *7th Euromicro Workshop on Parallel and Distributed Processing,* IEEE 1999
9. Sekanina, L.:Virtual Reconfigurable Circuits for Real-World Applications of Evolvable Hardware, *Evolvable Systems: From Biology to Hardware: Fifth International Conference, ICES 2003*, pp. 186-198
10. Sekanina, L.:Image Filter Design with Evolvable Hardware, Applications of Evolutionary Computing-Proc. of the 4th Workshop on Evolutionary Computation in Image Analysis and Signal Processing (EvoIASP'02), Springer-Verlag, Berlin, (2002), 255-266

# Efficient Sigmoid Function for Neural Networks Based FPGA Design

Xi Chen[1,2], Gaofeng Wang[1,2], Wei Zhou[1,2], Sheng Chang[2], and Shilei Sun[2]

[1] School of Electronic Information, Wuhan University, Wuhan, Hubei 430079, China
[2] Institute of C.J. Huang Information Technology,
Wuhan University, Wuhan, Hubei 430072, China
robertchenxi@yahoo.com.cn

**Abstract.** Efficient design of sigmoid function for neural networks based FPGA is presented. Employing the hybrid CORDIC algorithm, the sigmoid function is described with VHDL in register transfer level. In order to enhance the efficiency and accuracy of implementation on Altera's FPGA, the technology of pipeline and look-up table have been utilized. Through comparing the results obtained by the post-simulation of EDA tools with the results directly accounted by Matlab, it can be concluded that the designed model works accurately and efficiently.

## 1 Introduction

Artificial neural networks are widely utilized in many fields, such as prediction, pattern recognition, function approximation, numerical analysis, and VLSI (Very large scale integration) design.

Multiple feedforward networks [1], an important class of neural networks, consist of a set of sensory units that constitute the input layer, one or more hidden layers, and an output layer. The input signal propagates through the networks in a forward direction, on a layer-by-layer basis. Each neuron from a previous layer feeds every neuron on the next layer with amplification denoted by the synaptic weight of that connection. Neurons accumulate the sum of each of its inputs scaled by the synaptic weight to generate the net value (this weight sum is called the net function). The output value of the neuron is determined by the activation function of this neuron.

Common examples of activation function $f$ include hard-limiter, saturated linear, hyperbolic tangent function and sigmoid function. The sigmoid function [2], which is given by (1), provides a smooth transition between input and output thereby improving neural response when compared to non-smooth activation (e.g. hard-limiter or saturated linear activation function).

$$y_{ik} = f(s_{ik}) = \frac{1}{1+e^{-s_{ik}}} \tag{1}$$

There are also some researches on how to realize sigmoid function in digital circuit. In [3], the method employing Taylor series expansion is presented, but this approach requires a large of multipliers that take up large silicon areas. In [4], the method of piecewise linear approximation is utilized, but the accuracy of the designed sigmoid function has been weaken.

D.-S. Huang, K. Li, and G.W. Irwin (Eds.): ICIC 2006, LNCS 4113, pp. 672 – 677, 2006.

In this paper, the implementation of sigmoid function for the digital neuron with hybrid CORDIC (Co-ordinate Rotation Digital Computer) is presented. Combining with the technology of LUT (Look Up Table) and pipeline, sigmoid function is designed by VHDL (VHSIC Hardware Description Language) and realized on FPGA (field programmable gate array). The results of post-simulation show that it is accurate and efficient, when compared with the actual results calculated by Matlab.

## 2 Co-ordinate Rotation Digital Computer

The Co-ordinate Rotation Digital Computer algorithm is an efficient algorithm for the computation of elementary functions such as hyperbolic function, multiplication and division etc. It is attractive for hardware implement because it is an iterative method based on bit-level shift-and-add operation. The basic CORDIC iteration equations at the *k*th step are described as follows.

$$\begin{bmatrix} X_{k+1} \\ Y_{k+1} \end{bmatrix} = N_k \begin{bmatrix} 1 & m\delta_k 2^{-k} \\ m\delta_k 2^{-k} & 1 \end{bmatrix} \begin{bmatrix} X_k \\ Y_k \end{bmatrix} \tag{2}$$

$$Z_{k+1} = Z_k + \delta_k \theta_k \tag{3}$$

As described in Table 1, parameter m with the different value of 1,0,-1 identifies the coordinate system type (circular, linear, and hyperbolic coordinate); for rotation ( $Z_K \to 0$ ) or vectoring ( $Y_K \to 0$ ), the rotation direction $\delta_k$ is $-sign(Z_k)$ or $-sign(X_k \cdot Y_k)$ , respectively; for each rotation step, there is a scale $N_k$ which corrects the amplification produced by the rotation in the x and y coordinates, after all iterations, the total scale factor is $N = \prod_{k=1}^{K} N_k$ .

**Table 1.** Operation mode of the CORDIC algorithm

| $m$ | $Z_K \to 0$ (Rotation) | $Y_K \to 0$ (Vectoring) | $\theta_k$ |
|---|---|---|---|
| 1 (Circular) | $X_K = N(X_0 \cos Z_0 - Y_0 \sin Z_0)$ <br> $Y_K = N(Y_0 \cos Z_0 + X_0 \sin Z_0)$ | $X_K = N\sqrt{X_0^2 + Y_0^2}$ <br> $Z_K = Z_0 + \arctan(Y_0 / X_0)$ | $\arctan 2^{-k}$ |
| 0 (Linear) | $X_K = X_0$ <br> $Y_K = Y_0 + X_0 Z_0$ | $X_K = X_0$ <br> $Z_K = Z_0 + Y_0 / X_0$ | $2^{-k}$ |
| -1 (Hyperbolic) | $X_K = N(X_0 \cosh Z_0 + Y_0 \sinh Z_0)$ <br> $Y_K = N(Y_0 \cosh Z_0 + X_0 \sinh Z_0)$ | $X_K = N\sqrt{X_0^2 - Y_0^2}$ <br> $Z_K = Z_0 + \arctan h(Y_0 / X_0)$ | $\arctan h 2^{-k}$ |

The essence of CORDIC algorithm is a representation of an arbitrary angle by using a set of constant angles { $\theta_k$ } instead of a normal radix.For hyperbolic CORDIC iterations, it is more difficult to ensure convergence. This is because unlike $\tan^{-1}(2^{-(k+1)}) \geq 0.5 \tan^{-1}(2^{-k})$ or $2^{-(k+1)}) \geq 0.5 \cdot 2^{-k}$ , the corresponding relationship for tanh, namely, $\tanh^{-1}(2^{-(k+1)}) \geq 0.5\tanh^{-1}(2^{-k})$, does not hold in general. A relatively simple solution is to repeat steps for $k = 4,13,\ldots j,3j+1,\ldots$ to ensure convergence. So for the hyperbolic coordinates, the radix set is:

$$\{\theta_0,\theta_1,\ldots,\theta_{K-1}\} = \{\operatorname{arctanh}2^0, \operatorname{arctanh}2^{-1},\ldots,\operatorname{arctanh}2^{-4},\operatorname{arctanh}2^{-4},\ldots,\operatorname{arctanh}2^{-K+1}\} \tag{4}$$

Which satisfies the CORDIC algorithm theorem [5]:

$$\theta_0 - \sum_{k=1}^{K-1}\theta_k \leq \theta_{K-1} \tag{5}$$

With the different initial values of $X_0, Y_0, Z_0$, various elementary functions can be computed by CORDIC, including the exponential function and division function, as list below:

$$\text{When } m = -1, X_0 = 1/N, Y_0 = 0, Z_0 = \theta$$

$$\Rightarrow X_K = \cosh(Z_0), Y_K = \sinh(Z_0) \Rightarrow e^{-Z_0} = X_K - Y_K \tag{6}$$

$$\text{When } m = 0, X_0 = X, Y_0 = 1, Z_0 = 0$$

$$\Rightarrow Z_K = 1/X \tag{7}$$

In the implementation of elementary functions based on the CORDIC algorithm, the main problem is the iterative nature of CORDIC, which results in slow computation. To overcome this disadvantage, the hybrid CORIDC (HCORDIC) algorithm [6], which combines a traditional LUT with the algorithmic iterative procedures of the CORDIC algorithm, is employed. The iterative CORDIC algorithm is rigorous for infinite bit resolution, permitting in principle arbitrary precision, while the LUT size increases rapidly with resolution and is thus limited to a small-resolution input data regime. If the LUT and the CORDIC portions are properly balanced, the hybrid approach, therefore, offers the advantages of both the fast access and the power efficiency of a reasonably sized LUT and the arbitrary precision obtainable from the systematic iteration algorithm CORDIC.

## 3 Implement Sigmoid Based Hybrid CORDIC with VHDL

### 3.1 System Architecture for Sigmoid Function Model

The Top-Down method is used to design the sigmoid function. As depicted in fig.1, the RTL model of sigmoid function operating on float-point value is divided into two sub-units, exponential function unit and division function unit.

Two formats are used in the model: the first format is used to represent the input rotation signal z. As the result of the output value of sigmoid approaches to 1 or 0 when z>7.5 or z<-7.5, 16-bit signed float point format is used to represent the input

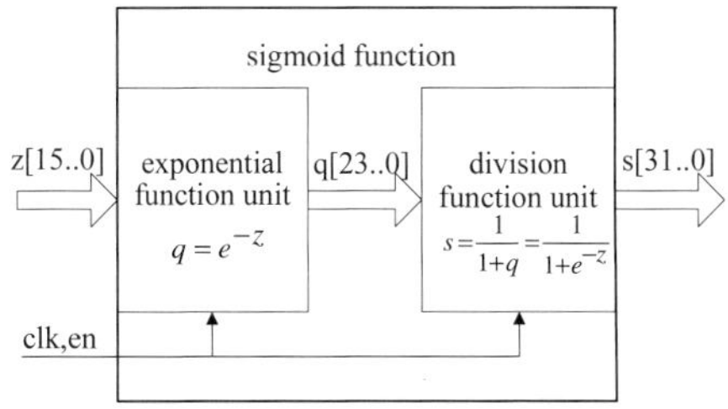


**Fig. 1.** System design for sigmoid function

signal z, 1 bit is used for the sign, 3 bits for encoding the integer portion of the number, and the remaining 12 bits for the fractional representation, with which the ranges of $-7.5<z<7.5$ can be represented; the output value of sigmoid function is in a 32-bit signed float point format. 1 bit is used for the sign, 1 bit is for the integer portion, and the remaining 30 bits for the fractional portion. The reason for employing different formats for input and output is that the output value for sigmoid function is between the ranges from value 0 to 1.

### 3.2 Exponential Function Unit

Considering the range of input signal $Z$, the word length of output signal $q$ of the exponential function unit is defined as 24-bit, in which 1 bit is used for the sign, 11 bits for the integer portion, and the remaining 12 bits for the fractional portion.

According to the hybrid hyperbolic CORDICA, the ROM of $2 \cdot 24 \cdot 2^4$ bits that stores the values of sinh and cosh functions is employed, where the 1 sign bit and 3 integer bits of $Z$ are used as the address. From LUT, the first 7 rotations value of the conventional CORDIC can be directly read and the delay of 7 stages of shift and addition can be saved. Then there are 13 stages for hyperbolic iteration needed which are determined by the remaining 12 bits for the fraction portion of input signal $Z$. Then the value of exponential function can be obtained by correcting the scale and adding $X_{12} - Y_{12}$.

### 3.3 Division Function Unit

A high-speed method based on a hybrid CORDIC for computing the reciprocal function is proposed here. This method uses a look-up table to obtain an initial approximation to the reciprocal. After the initial approximation, several CORDIC rotations are executed to produce an accurate reciprocal.

The reciprocal LUT is constructed by assuming that the value of input signal $q$+1 is normalized such that $1 \le q+1 < 2$ and represented by 32-bit in float point. The high 10 bits of fraction are used to index the LUT, which provides 12 bits output. Excluding the elementary division sub-model, this division function unit consists of another two sub-models: The one is used to count the value of $q$+1; the other is used to normalize the value of $q$+1 to $1 \le q+1 < 2$ and unnormalize corresponding, by which any input data out of the range $1 \le q+1 < 2$ can be shifted into the range, after the reciprocal of the normalized input is obtained, the actual result can be achieved by shifted in the opposite way. As described in Section 2, in the position of linear vectoring, $Z$ will approach to the reciprocal of x closely through iterations. Since the initial value of $Z$ is 0, $Z$ can achieve the result of the reciprocal with $k$-bit width fraction after $k$ iterations. The approximation $l$ from the LUT equals to the value of $Z$ after $k$ iterations, thus with the corresponding initial value, Eqs. (2) Becomes:

$$Y_{k+1} = Y_0 - l \cdot X \tag{8}$$

As a result, the corresponding value of $Y$ after $k$ iterations can be obtained from the approximation of LUT.

The most complicated operation involved is the calculation of $Y_{k+1}$, which involves a multiplication between $l$ and $X$ and a subtraction of this quantity from the initial value $Y_0$. In this unit, 16x16 bits special multiplier unit is used to calculate $l \cdot X$. Then $Y_{k+1}$ and $l$ are used as the initial value for the following iterations, where the number of iterations is 4. The remaining linear vectoring iterations have been done in the same way as the hyperbolic rotation, which has been already described in section 3.2.

## 4 Simulation and Result

The RTL model of sigmoid function described by VHDL is post-simulated in QuartusII 5.0, and the Altera's FPGA EP2S60FC484 is used as the configured device. The input to the model is a list of 16-bit float-point numbers as the variable of the sigmoid function, and the expected output is a list of numbers in the format of 32-bit float-point as the value of the sigmoid function.

**Table 2.** Comparison between the result from QuartusII and Matlab

| Input value (Hex/Dec) | Result from QuartusII (Hex/Dec) | Result from Matlab (Dec) | \|Error\| (%) |
|---|---|---|---|
| 96CB/-6.5754 | 0016D780/0.001394 | 0.001392 | 0.14 |
| BDAD/-4.1453 | 00FF9400/0.01560 | 0.01559 | 0.06 |
| D100/-2.9375 | 03385000/0.05031 | 0.05033 | 0.04 |
| E400/-1.7500 | 097BC000/0.1482 | 0.1481 | 0.07 |
| FA00/-0.3750 | 1A158000/0.4076 | 0.4073 | 0.07 |
| 0600/0.3750 | 25ED0000/0.5926 | 0.5927 | 0.02 |
| 1800/1.5000 | 345F0000/0.8183 | 0.8176 | 0.04 |
| 3468/3.2754 | 3DDA0000/0.9637 | 0.9636 | 0.01 |
| 5253/5.1453 | 3FA10000/0.9942 | 0.9942 | 0 |
| 7635/7.3879 | 40000000/1.0000 | 0.9994 | 0.06 |

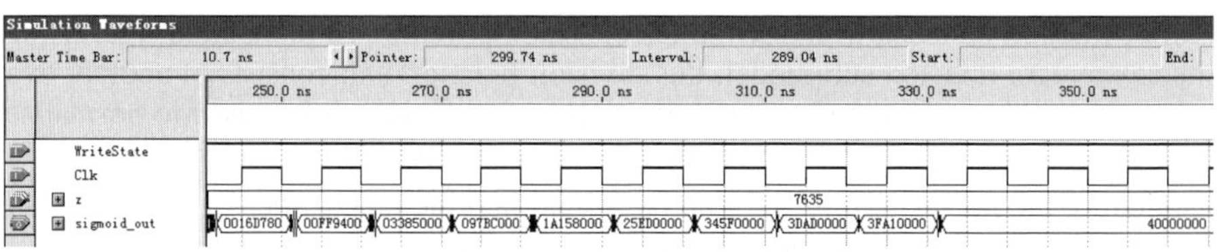


**Fig. 2.** Post-simulation results of the sigmoid function

In order to observe the simulation wave clearly and evaluate the accuracy of the results generated by the post-simulation based Hybrid CORDIC dirctly, a group of 10 values of the input signal $Z$ are random generated with the range $-7.5 < Z < 7.5$ at the falling edge of the clock signal *clk* with the frequency of 100MHz. As depicted in fig.2, after 240ns, one can not only obtain the corresponding simulation result, but also observe that the pipelines of this sigmoid function operate well. Table 2 is proposed to show the comparison between the results obtained from QuartusII and the results directly calculated by Matlab, including the absolute values of error. Obviously, the former results approach to the later one extremely.

## 5 Conclusion

In this work, a scheme to design sigmoid function with VHDL on FPGA has been investigated. Employing the hybrid CORDIC algorithm, RTL model of sigmoid function is divided into exponential function sub-unit and division function sub-unit, which can both be implemented by LUT and iterations. Furthermore, the technology of pipeline has been utilized to make this model work more efficiently in VLSI of neural networks. Through compared the post-simulation results with the Matlab results, it is concluded that the designed model can calculate sigmoid function accurately and efficiently.

## Acknowledgements

This work is supported by the National Nature Science Foundation of China (60444004, 90307017).

## References

1. Hornik, K., Stinchcombe, M., White, H.: Multilayer Feedforward Networks. Neural Networks, 2 (1989) 359-366
2. Martin, T. H., Howard, B., Demuth, M. B.: Neural Networks Design. China Machine Press, (2002)
3. OUALI, J., SAUCIER, G.: Fast Generation of Neuron-ASICs. Proc. Int. Neural Networks Conf, (1990) 563-567
4. Murtagh, P., Tsoi, A. C.: Implementation Issues of Sigmoid Function and Its Derivative for VLSI Digital Neural Networks. IEE Proceedings on Computers and Digital Techniques, (1992) 207-213
5. Walther, J.: A Unified Algorithm for Elementary Functions. Spring Joint Computer Conf. Proc., (1971) 379-385
6. Wang, S., Piuri, V., Wartzlander, E. E. Jr.: Hybrid Cordic Algorithms. IEEE Transactions on Computers, 11(1997) 1202-1206
7. Xia, F.: Efficient Arithmetic Functional Modules for FPGA-based VLSI Design. Master Dissertation, Nan Yang Technological University, Singapore (2005)

# Evolutionary Image Enhancement for Impulsive Noise Reduction

Ung-Keun Cho, Jin-Hyuk Hong, and Sung-Bae Cho

Dept. of Computer Science, Yonsei University
Biometrics Engineering Research Center
134 Sinchon-dong, Seodaemun-ku
Seoul 120-749, Korea
{bearoot, hjinh}@sclab.yonsei.ac.kr, sbcho@cs.yonsei.ac.kr

**Abstract.** Image enhancement with various image filters might be better than that with a single filter, but it is very difficult to find a set of appropriate filters. In this paper, we propose a novel method that uses the genetic algorithm to find a filter set for reducing impulsive noises in images. The proposed method has been verified with benchmark images in image enhancement. Moreover, it does not require any expert knowledge to find the type and order of filters for a given domain, so it can be easily applied to other applications of image processing.

## 1 Introduction

In general non-linear signal processing aims to detect objects on images, but it is often hard to correctly extract features when the quality of images is low. Filtering that reduces image noises and smoothing that removes some forms of misfocus and motion blur are representative image filtering techniques. Histogram-based, mask-based and morphology-based image filters are popular for the enhancement [1].

Impulsive noises are known as salt-and-pepper noises, where the noisy pixels take only the maximum (salt) or the minimum (pepper) values in the dynamic range. Conventional median filters are the most popular non-linear filter to remove impulse noises, but many filters require a complex formulation for better performance [2]. To reduce noises, the usage of various filters together might be effective rather than that of only a single filter, but it requires the expert knowledge to compose a filter set.

Since it is actually impossible to examine all possible combinations of filters, it requires a heuristic algorithm. The genetic algorithm is a representative evolutionary algorithm, which is based on the mechanisms of natural selection and the survival of fittest. It has been successfully applied to many problems such as searching and optimization [3]. In this paper, we adopt the genetic algorithm to find out a set of proper filters for noise reduction in images.

## 2 Related Works

For impulsive noise reduction, the median filter is the most popular non-linear filter because of its good de-noising power and computational efficiency [2]. The

D.-S. Huang, K. Li, and G.W. Irwin (Eds.): ICIC 2006, LNCS 4113, pp. 678 – 683, 2006.

topological median filter [4] is recently introduced as a median filter, and it uses the fuzzy concepts for the extraction of edges in noisy images.

Since impulsive noises are special in which a pixel has only maximum and minimum, the decision-based strategies [5] were proposed. They first identified possible noisy pixels and then replaced them by using the filter, leaving all other pixels unchanged. Especially, they work well for the impulsive noises of high level, but it is limited in detecting noises.

Harvey *et al.* used the genetic algorithm to determine the sequence and structuring element of morphological filters [6], which requires many genes to represent the filter. For image enhancement like impulsive noise reduction, several studies have proposed new filters showing good performance. For combining not only simple filters but also these various filters of good performance, the appropriate method having scalability is required.

## 3 Noise Reduction Based on the Genetic Algorithm

In order to improve the quality of images, noises should be eliminated by using an appropriate image filter. When there are $m$ filters available, the number of possible ordered subsets of $n$ filters is given by $m^n$. Trying all cases to find out the best one is practically impossible when there are lots of filters available. In this paper, the genetic algorithm is used to search a filter set, in which the proper type and order of filters are determined.

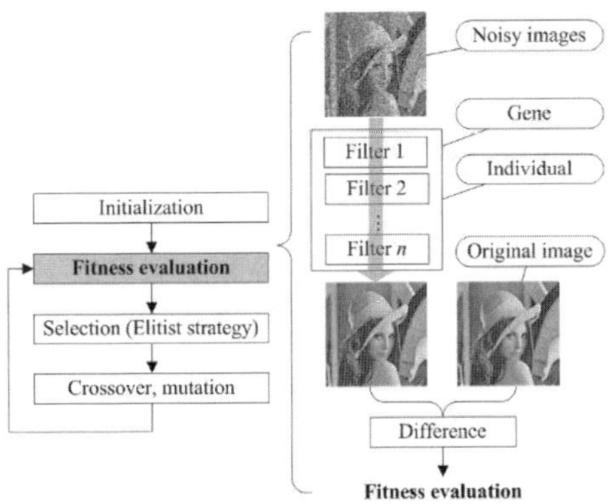


**Fig. 1.** The process of evaluating the fitness (fitness function)

Fig. 1 shows the procedure of the proposed method which also presents the process of evaluating the fitness. In each generation, the fitness of candidate solutions as individuals is evaluated by the fitness function, and individuals with higher fitness are stochastically selected and applied with genetic operators such as crossover and mutation to reproduce the population of the next generation. Elitist-strategy that keeps the best individual of previous generation is used in the process of selection. Genes which compose an individual are represented as numbers representing the

**Table 1.** The description of image filters used in this paper

| Group | Filter | Number |
|---|---|---|
| Histogram | Brightness (3 values), Contrast (3 values), Stretch, Equalize, Logarithm | 1~9 |
| Mask | Blur (6 masks), Sharper (4 masks), Median (10 masks) | 10~29 |
| Morphology | Erosion, Dilation, Opening, Closing (10 masks) | 30~69 |
| | None | 0 |

corresponding filter. Training images including artificial noises are passed through filters of genes, and the fitness is calculated by the difference between the result image and the original image. Table 1 shows the type of 70 image filters used in this paper.

In order to measure the performance of a combination filter in noise reduction, the difference between the filtered image and the original image calculated by using the mean absolute error (MAE) and the peak signal-to-noise ratio (PSNR) [5]. The fitness function of the genetic algorithm is estimated by the equation (1) using the mean absolute error, where an individual that shows good enhancement performance obtains a higher score. Let $MAE_{\max}$ be the maximum MAE for an image, and $MAE_{\max}$ would be 255 for 8-bit grayscale images.

$$f(x) = 1 - \frac{MAE(x)}{MAE_{\max}} \tag{1}$$

## 4 Experiments

In the experiments, LENA and FRUIT are used as the benchmark images. Each image is 256×256 and 512×512 for 8-bit grayscale images. The noisy images will be corrupted by salt (value 255) and pepper (value 0) noises with predefined probability. The noise levels varied from 10% to 70% with increments of 20%. The training images are 4 images as LENA with each noise level, and the test images are 8 images as LENA and FRUIT with each noise level. Table 2 shows the MAE and PSNR of training and test images compared to the original images.

**Table 2.** The analysis of training and test set

| Set | Training | | | | Test | | | | | | | |
|---|---|---|---|---|---|---|---|---|---|---|---|---|
| Image | LENA | | | | LENA | | | | FRUIT | | | |
| Noise level (%) | 10 | 30 | 50 | 70 | 10 | 30 | 50 | 70 | 10 | 30 | 50 | 70 |
| MAE | 12.7 | 38.1 | 63.6 | 89.2 | 12.7 | 38.1 | 63.7 | 89.3 | 12.7 | 38.3 | 63.7 | 89.3 |
| PSNR | 15.5 | 10.8 | 8.57 | 7.10 | 15.5 | 10.8 | 8.5 | 7.09 | 15.4 | 10.6 | 8.44 | 6.96 |

Four filters are obtained for each training image, where there are 4 training images by the noise level. In addition, one filter is evolved for reducing all noises using the fitness as average mean absolute error of 4 images after filtering. Initial values of parameters in the experiments is as follows: 1000 generations, 30 populations, 5 gene

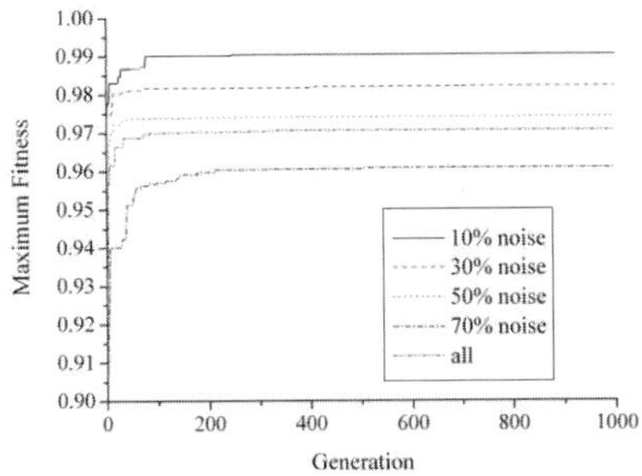


**Fig. 2.** The maximum fitness in each generation

**Table 3.** Type of other filters

| Filter | Filter type | | | | |
|---|---|---|---|---|---|
| Filter I | Median Diamond 3×3 | | | | |
| Filter II | Median Diamond 5×5 | | | | |
| Filter III | Median Rectangle 5×5 | | | | |
| Case I | Median 1×3 | Median Diamond 3×3 | NULL | NULL | NULL |
| Case II | Median Diamond 3×3 | Median 1×3 | Closing 1×3 | Opening 1×3 | Median 3×1 |
| Case III | Median Diamond 5×5 | Median Diamond 5×5 | Median X 3×3 | Median 1×3 | Opening 1×3 |
| Case IV | Median Rectangle 3×3 | Median X 5×5 | Median Rectangle 3×3 | Opening Rectangle 5×5 | Closing Rectangle 5×5 |
| Case V | Median Diamond 5×5 | Median X 5×5 | Median X 5×5 | Median 1×3 | Median Diamond 5×5 |

length, 1 selection rate, 0.7 crossover rate, and 0.05 mutation rate. Fig. 2 shows the change of the maximum fitness in each generation, in which filters with the best performance are found before the 300th generation.

Table 3 shows the image filter of good performance and the filters evolved. The mean absolute error over all image filters was investigated on the training images, and 3 good filters which named filter I~III were obtained for comparing with the filters evolved. The filters which named case I~IV were the results of the evolution for each noisy image, and the filters which named case V were the result of the evolution for all images. Most of them included median filters, since the median filter was suitable for impulsive noise reduction. However, other filters such as opening and closing were also included for better performance.

Fig. 3 shows the comparative performance of the proposed method against other filters. The mean absolute error (MAE) is indicated by logarithm of 2 on y-axis. Total on x-axis indicates the sum MAE and the average PSNR of all images. Case I~IV in each environment performs the best against other filters in the criteria on the MAE and the PSNR. Fig. 4 shows examples of various filters by LENA with 30% noise and FRUIT with 70% noise. Case II and IV are better at reducing noisy pixels than a single filter.

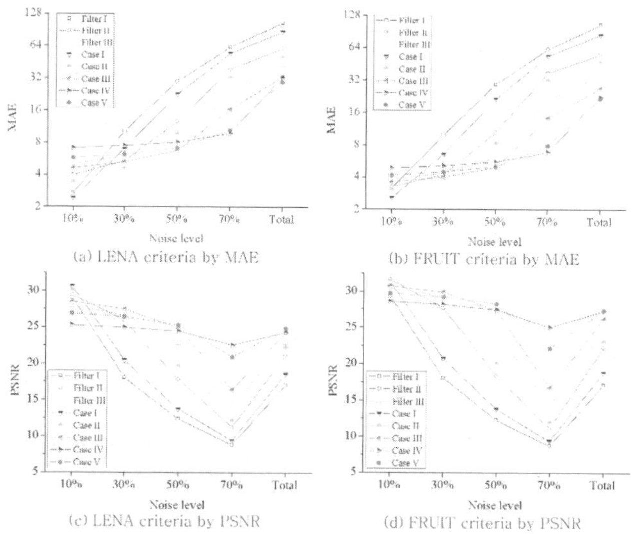


**Fig. 3.** The performance comparison with other filters

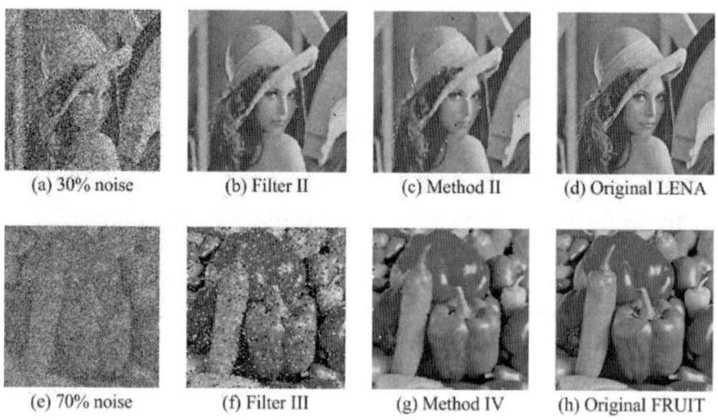


**Fig. 4.** Examples of various filters: (a)~(d) LENA, (e)~(h) FRUIT

Most filters performed well enough in only one environment, not in every environment. For example, case I and filter I worked well at 10% noise level, but not at 70% noise level. Case IV is also better than the other filters for 70% noise level, but it is worse than the other filters for 10% noise level. Case V does not show the best performance in any environment, but there is a little difference of performance compared to the best filter. Since there are many impulsive noise detectors and the noise level is also estimated by detector [5], case I~IV are applied in proper environment. If it is hard to estimate the noise level, case V can be preferred.

## 5 Conclusion

Even though the median filter is popular for impulsive noise reduction, there are many studies investigated to improve the image enhancement performance but they need some complex formula or the expert knowledge. In this paper, the combination of well-known and simple filters is determined by the genetic algorithm for impulsive noise reduction. In the experiments, for real images such as LENA and FRUIT, the filter obtained showed better performance than the other filters on the mean absolute error and the peak signal-to-noise ratio.

For the future work, we would like to apply the proposed method to the other image databases. By changing the fitness function of the genetic algorithm, the method for the better performance of object detection will be also studied. Since the proposed method does not need any expert knowledge, we can also apply the method to various applications for image processing.

## Acknowledgement

This work was supported by the Korea Science and Engineering Foundation (KOSEF) through the Biometrics Engineering Research Center (BERC) at Yonsei University.

## References

1. Gonzalez, R., Woods, R.: Digital Image Processing. Addison Wesley, Reading, MA (1992)
2. Windyga, P.S.: Fast Impulsive Noise Removal. IEEE Transactions on Image Processing, Vol. 10. No. 1 (2001) 173-179
3. Goldberg, D.: Genetic Algorithm in Search, Optimization and Machine Learning, Addison Wesley (1989)
4. Senel, H.G., Peters, R.A., Dawant, B.: Topological Median Filters. IEEE Transactions on Image Processing, Vol. 11, No. 2 (2002) 89-104
5. Chan, R.H., Ho, C.-W., Nikolova, M.: Salt-and-pepper Noise Removal by Median-type Noise Detectors and Detail-preserving Regularization. IEEE Transactions on Image Processing, Vol. 14. No. 10 (2005) 1479-1485
6. Harvey, N.R., Marshall, S.: The Use of Genetic Algorithms in Morphological Filter Design. Signal Processing: Image Communication, Vol. 8 (1996) 55-71

# Expected Value Model and Algorithm for Network Bottleneck Capacity Expansion Under Fuzzy Environment

Yun Wu[1] and Zhou Jian[2]

[1] College of Management, Wuhan University of Technology,
Postfach 430077, Wuhan, Hubei, China
Wuyun1974@hotmail.com
[2] Department of Computer Sciences, University of Angers, France
Zhoujian@hotmail.com

**Abstract.** This paper considers the capacities of the elements in a set E efficiently so that the total cost for the increment of capacity can be decrease to maximum extent while the final expansion capacity of a given family F of subsets of E is with a given limit bound. The paper supposes the cost w is a fuzzy variable. Network bottleneck capacity expansion problem with fuzzy cost is originally formulated as Expected value model according to some criteria. For solving the fuzzy model efficiently, network bottleneck capacity algorithm, fuzzy simulation, neural network(NN) and genetic algorithm(GA) are integrated to produce a hybrid intelligent algorithm.

## 1 Introduction

As we know, during the past years, many experts did relevant researches in the fields of network expansion. Ravindra K.Ahuja and James B.Orlin [1] studied a lot about network flows and network flow model, and they figured out an algorithm for the maximum flows problem with constrained conditions. O.Berman [2] worked over weight problem of decreasing a given tree edge to cut down weight of minimal tree, and proved a strongly polynomial algorithm for this problem. S.O.Krumke [3] presented two improved network flow models, and put forward heuristic algorithm to resolve some network improvement problems. Zhang,J and Yang,C[4] also showed us a strongly polynomial algorithm for a particular network expansion problem. Based on Zhang,J's research, Yang C, etc.[5]took budgets and bottleneck capacity restrictions into consideration, and gave a strongly polynomial algorithm for this kind of network expansion problems. Internally, Wang H.G, et al.[6-7] solved capacity expansion problems of undirected network and directed network by extending Yang C's network bottleneck model. In recent years,some authors have investigated mathematical programming in the presence of fuzziness[8,9,10,11], H.Ishii and Nishida [12] introduced a new problem about fuzzy stochastic bottleneck capacity expansion, afterwards,H.katagiri, H.Hishii [13] discussed a chance-constrained model of bottleneck spanning tree in terms of fuzzy stochastic edge weights. Based on the above algorithms, Hideki Katagiri and Masatoshi Sakawa[14] explored necessary probability

D.-S. Huang, K. Li, and G.W. Irwin (Eds.): ICIC 2006, LNCS 4113, pp. 684 – 689, 2006.

and evaluation problems in fuzzy stochastic bottleneck spanning tree problem. Internally, Liu Baoding, et al.[15] employed genetic algorithm to solve orientation problem in network optimization problem efficiently.

In this paper, based on the above research fruits, few researchers have introduced the expected value model to network bottleneck capacity expansion problem. For solving fuzzy model more efficiently, a strongly polynomial algorithm of network, neural network(NN) and genetic algorithm(GA) are integrated to produce a hybrid intelligent algorithm. Finally, a numerical example is presented.

## 2 Network Bottleneck Capacity Expansion Model with Fuzzy Unit Expansion Cost

Let $G(V,E,C)$ be an undirected network structure, which is composed of vertices set $V=\{v_{1,}\ \ v_{2,}\ \ v_{3,}\ \ \cdots,\ \ v_n\}$ and edge set $E=\{e_{1,}\ \ e_{2,}\ \ e_{3,}\ \ \cdots,\ \ e_m\}\in V*V$. Every edge has an original edge capacity $c_i$. Let original network capacity vector be $C=\{c_{1,}\ \ c_{2,}\ \ c_{3,}\ \ \cdots,\ \ c_m\}$, let unit expansion cost on every edge be $w_i$, and let expansion cost vector $W$ be a fuzzy vector.

Define the capacity of a spanning tree $T$ of network $G(V,E,C)$ be $cap(T,C)$, which is the bottleneck capacity for every edge in $T$, i.e.

$$cap(T,C)=MIN\{c_i\mid \mathrm{e_i}\in T, T\in G(V,E,C)\} \tag{1}$$

We use $T^*(C)$ to show the maximum capacity tree of network $G(V,E,C)$, i.e.

$$cap(T^*,C)=\underset{T}{MAX}\{cap(T,C)\} \tag{2}$$

The beforehand problem of this paper is how to expand original capacity vector $C$ to minimize the total expansion cost while the capacity $cap(T^*,C)$ of maximum expansion tree of expanded network $G(V,E,C)$ meets definite condition and scopes.

$$H(r)=\{\underline{C}\mid \underline{C}\geq C, cap(T^*,\underline{C})\geq r\} \tag{3}$$

### 2.1 Problem 1

Given $r_0$, how to expand $C$ to $\underline{C}$ to minimize expansion cost $(\underline{C}-C)^T W$, and $cap(T^*,\underline{C})\geq r_0$, problem 1 equals the following problem:

$$\begin{aligned}&\min(\underline{C}-C)^T W\\&s.t.\\&\underline{C}\in H(r0)\end{aligned} \tag{4}$$

According to the above analysis, we introduce the expected value model of network bottleneck capacity expansion with fuzzy unit expansion cost, the core idea of this Expected value model is to minimize expected value of total cost and optimize the valuc of objective function in fuzzy conditions, and get reasonable optimized value in reality.

When unit expansion cost vector $W = \{w_{1,} \quad w_{2,} \quad w_{3,} \quad \cdots, \quad w_m\}$ is fuzzy variable, the total expansion cost $COST(\underline{C} \mid W, C) = \min(\underline{C} - C)^T W$ is also a fuzzy variable. The problem we consider here is to let the total cost for the increment of capacity be decrease to maximum extent while the final expansion capacity is under a given limit bound In this section, we offer a new idea to set up a general expected value model of network bottleneck capacity expansion with fuzzy unit expansion cost as follows:

$$\min E \mid COST(\underline{C} \mid W, C) \mid$$
$$or$$
$$\min \int_0^{\infty} Cr\{COST(\underline{C} \mid W, C) \geq r\}dr - \int_{-\infty}^{0} Cr\{COST(\underline{C} \mid W, C) \leq r\}dr \tag{5}$$
$$s.t. \begin{cases} \underline{C} \geq C \\ cap(T, \underline{C}) \geq r0 \end{cases}$$

From the beforehand problem analysis, we could shift to the essential problem in problem 2.

### 2.2 Problem 2

Thus, the ultimate problem of this paper is: considering fuzzy unit expansion cost, how to expand original capacity vector C to minimize the expected value of $COST(\underline{C} \mid W, C)$ while the capacity $cap(T^*, C)$ of maximum expansion tree of expanded network $G(V, E, C)$ satisfies definite condition and scopes. A child problem of bottleneck capacity is included in expected value model of problem 2, $COST(\underline{C} \mid W, C) = \min(\underline{C} - C)^T W$ i.e. problem 1, once choose a value in the fuzzy possibility space $(\Theta, P(\Theta), Pos)$, fuzzy variable $W$ will become a determined value $\underline{W}$. In Yang Chao [4-5], strongly polynomial algorithm has been brought forward for this determined problem. In the next section, we will discuss the general algorithm for this problem.

## 3 Hybrid Intelligent Algorithm for Fuzzy Network Bottleneck Capacity Expansion

### 3.1 Calculate Uncertainty Function

From the above thought, we could work out the algorithm for this expected value mode. First of all, we have a fuzzy simulation algorithm to get the value of uncertainty function.[15]

$$U(\underline{C}) \to E \mid COST(\underline{C} \mid W, C) \mid$$
$$= \int_0^{\infty} Cr\{COST(\underline{C} \mid W, C) \geq r\}dr - \int_{-\infty}^{0} Cr\{COST(\underline{C} \mid W, C) \leq r\}dr \tag{6}$$

Steps:

Step1: set e=0

Step2: generate $\theta_k$ from $\Theta$ evenly, let $Pos\{\theta_k\} \ge \varepsilon$ and $v_k = Pos\{\theta_k\}, k = 1, 2...M$, $\varepsilon$ is very small number.

Step3: set $a = COST(\underline{C} \mid W(\theta_1), C) \wedge ... \wedge COST(\underline{C} \mid W(\theta_M), C)$
$b = COST(\underline{C} \mid W(\theta_1), C) \vee ... \vee COST(\underline{C} \mid W(\theta_M), C)$

Step4: generate r from [a,b] evenly

Step5: if $r \ge 0$, then $e \leftarrow e + Cr\{COST(\underline{C} \mid W, C) \ge r\}$ , in here ,
$Cr\{COST(\underline{C} \mid W, C) \ge r\}$ $\approx$
$\frac{1}{2}(\max_{1\le k\le M}\{v_k \mid COST(\underline{C} \mid W(\theta_k), C) \ge r\} + \min_{1\le k\le M}\{1 - v_k \mid COST(\underline{C} \mid W(\theta_k), C) < r\})$
Employ definitive network bottleneck capacity expansion algorithm, which is designed by Yang Chao [4-5], to calculate problem 1. The algorithm is also a child problem of fuzzy expected value model.

Step6: if $r < 0$, then $e \leftarrow e - Cr\{COST(\underline{C} \mid W, C) \le r\}$
$Cr\{COST(\underline{C} \mid W, C) \le r\}$ $\approx$
$\frac{1}{2}(\max_{1\le k\le M}\{v_k \mid COST(\underline{C} \mid W(\theta_k), C) \le r\} + \min_{1\le k\le M}\{1 - v_k \mid COST(\underline{C} \mid W(\theta_k), C) > r\})$
Employ definitive network bottleneck capacity expansion algorithm, which is designed by Yang Chao [4-5], to calculate problem 1. the algorithm is also a child problem of fuzzy expected value model.

Step7: repeat step 4 to step 6 for M times.

Step8: $E\mid(COST(\underline{C} \mid W, C))\mid = a \vee 0 + b \wedge 0 + e.(b-a)/M$

### 3.2 Approximate Uncertain Function by Neural Network

NNs are inspired by the current understanding of biological NNs. The most popular and useful NN architecture is multilayer feed forward NN, which is widely used for pattern classification and functional approximation, in this paper, NNs are used to approximate uncertain functions. When we solve models (5) by GA, the process of fuzzy simulations to compute U(C), will be repeated for thousands of times , which means large computations, so NNs are trained to approximate these uncertain function, which reduce the computations and speed up the solution process greatly. After making a set of input-output data for uncertain function U(C) by fuzzy simulations, we train an NN to approximate the uncertain function by the back propagation algorithm according to the training data.

$$Err(\omega) = \frac{1}{2}\sum_{i=1}^{N} \| F(w_i, \omega) - u_i \|^2 \tag{7}$$

here $F(W, \omega)$ is the output function of neural network.

### 3.3 Hybrid Intelligent Algorithm

In order to solve the problem of network bottleneck capacity expansion, we combine network bottleneck capacity algorithm, fuzzy simulation, neural network and genetic algorithm to produce a hybrid intelligent algorithm, which will reduce calculation work and manage large-scale problems.

Steps:

(1) Generate training input-out data for uncertain function by fuzzy simulations

(2) Train neural networks to approximate the uncertain function according to the generated training data.

(3) Initialize chromosomes $V_k = (\underline{C}^k) = (\underline{c_1^k}, \underline{c_2^k}, \underline{c_3^k}, ..., \underline{c_m^k})$, $k = 1, 2, 3, \cdots, pop\_size$, check the feasible region $\underline{C} \in H(r_0)$ where the trained neural network will be used

(4) Calculate every chromosome's target value $U^k(\underline{C}^k)$ $k = 1, 2, 3, \cdots, pop\_size$ by the trained neural network. This algorithm includes Yang Chao [4-7]'s strongly polynomial algorithm for determined network bottleneck capacity expansion and employs to solve the problem 1;

(5) Calculate every chromosome's fitness extent, the evaluation function is: $Eval(V_k) = \alpha(1-\alpha)^{k-1}$ $k = 1, 2, 3, \cdots, pop\_size$ $\alpha \in (0.1)$, $\alpha$ is a parameter in genetic algorithm.Rearrange chromosomes $v_1, v_2, v_3, \cdots, v_n$ $pop\_size$, in accordance with the different evaluation values, from good to poor in sequence;

(6) Confirm next generation by circumvolving roulette wheel $pop\_size$ time,

(7) Define $Pc$ as the probability of crossover operation, and update chromosomes $v_k$, $k = 1, 2, 3, \cdots, pop\_size$ by crossover operation.

(8) Renew chromosomes through mutation operation.;

(9) Repeat step 2 to step 6 in terms of the given circulation times;

(10) The best chromosome $V^* = (\underline{c^*_1}, \underline{c^*_2}, \underline{c^*_3}, ... \underline{c^*_m}) = C^*$ is the optimum solution for network bottleneck capacity expansion model with fuzzy unit expansion cost.

## 4 Conclusions

The paper first introduces expected value model to fuzzy network bottleneck capacity expansion problem. For solving the fuzzy model efficiently, network bottleneck capacity algorithm, fuzzy simulation, neural network and genetic algorithm are integrated to produce a hybrid intelligent algorithm.

## References

1. Ahuja, R.K, Magnanti, T.L., Orlin, J.B.: Network Flows Englewood Cliffs. NJ: Prentice-Hall (1993)
2. Averbakh, I., Berman, O., Punnen, A.P.: Constrained Matroidal Bottleneck Problem. Discret Appl. Math. 63 (1995) 201-214
3. Krumke, S.O., Marthe, M.V., Ravi, R., Ravi, S.S.: Approximation Algorithms for Certain Network Improvement. J. Comb. Optim. 2 (1998) 257-288

4. Zhang, J., Yang, C., Lin, Y.: A Class of Bottleneck Expansion Problems. Comput. Oper. Res. 124 (2000) 77-88
5. Yang, C., Liu, J.: A Capacity Expansion Problem with Budget Constraint and Bottleneck Limitation. Acta Math. Sci. 22 (2002) 207-212
6. Wang, H.G., Ma, Z.H.: Capacity Expansion Problems of Undirected Network. J. Shandong Univ. 35 (2000) 418–424
7. Wang, H.G, Ma, Z.H.: Capacity Expansion Problems of Directed Network. J. Coll. Appl. Math.16 (2001) 471-480
8. Sakawa, M.: Fuzzy Sets and Interactive Optimization. Plenum Press (1993)
9. Inuiguchi, M., Ramik, J.: Possibilistic Linear Programming: A Brief Review of Fuzzy Mathematical Programming and a Comparison with Stochastic Programming in Portfolio Selection Problem. Fuzzy Sets Syst. 111 (2000) 3-28
10. Katagiri, H., Ishii, H.: Linear Programming Problem with Fuzzy Random Constraint. Math. Japonica 52 (2000) 123-129
11. Luhandjula, M.K., Gupta, M.M.: On Fuzzy Stochastic Optimization. Fuzzy Sets Syst. 81 (1996) 47-55
12. Ryan S.M.: Capacity Expansion for Random Exponential Demand Growth. Working Paper No. 00-109. Industrial and Manufacturing Systems Engineering, Iowa State University, Ames, IA (2000) 119-121
13. Katagiri, H., Ishii, H.: Chance Constrained Bottleneck Spanning Tree Problem with Fuzzy Random Edge Costs. J. Oper. Res. Soc. Jpn. 43 (2000) 128-137
14. Katagiri, H., Masatoshi, S.: Fuzzy Random Bottleneck Spanning Tree Problem Using Possibility and Necessity Measures. Eur. J. Oper. Res. 152 (2004) 88-95
15. Liu, B.: Uncertain Programming. Wiley, New York (1999)

# Face Recognition: An Optimized Localization Approach and Selected PZMI Feature Vector Using SVM Classifier

Hamidreza Rashidy Kanan, Karim Faez, and Mehdi Ezoji

Image Processing and Pattern Recognition Lab., Electrical Engineering Department, AmirKabir University of Technology (Tehran Polytechnic), Hafez Avenue, Tehran, Iran, 15914
{rashidykanan, kfaez, m_ezoji}@aut.ac.ir

**Abstract.** In this paper a system is developed for face recognition processes. After preprocessing of face images, for omitting the redundant information such as background and hair, the oval shape of face is approximated by an ellipse using shape information. Then the parameters (orientation and center coordinates) of this ellipse are optimized using Genetic Algorithm (GA). High order Pseudo Zernike Moment Invariant (PZMI) which has useful properties is utilized to produce feature vectors. We use GAs in combination with nearest neighbor classifier to select the optimal feature set for classification. Also, Support Vector Machines (SVMs) which has very good generalization ability has been used as a classifier with ERBF kernel function. Proposed approach has been applied on ORL and Yale databases and has shown a high classification rate with small number of feature elements.

## 1 Introduction

Automatic face recognition has become one of the most active research areas of pattern recognition since the early 1990s because of its wide range of applications such as identity authentication, surveillance and intelligent human computer interaction [1].

Face region segmentation or face localization is a fundamental step in the process of face recognition. The accuracy of the localized face center coordinates and orientation has a heavy influence on the recognition performance [2].

Genetic algorithms (GA's) are optimization techniques based on the mechanics of natural selection [3]. Because of their advantages, recently, GA's have been widely used as a tool in pattern recognition applications such as optimization and feature selection.

PZMI is a moment that has been frequently utilized for a number of image processing tasks [2, 4]. The nature of rotation invariance makes the PZMI descriptors very valuable.

SVM is a new type of classifier, which provides a novel approach to the problem of pattern recognition. SVMs are based on a new statistical learning technique developed by Vapnik and his co-workers at AT&T Bell Labs [5].

In this paper, we have proposed a new method for face localization that is utilizes shape information and genetic algorithms approach. After preprocessing, connected components are determined by applying a region growing algorithm (coarse segmentation). Then the best-fit ellipse for the face area is computed. We have used genetic

D.-S. Huang, K. Li, and G.W. Irwin (Eds.): ICIC 2006, LNCS 4113, pp. 690 – 696, 2006.

algorithms to find the best location (including the best orientation and the best position) of face in image. In the feature extraction step, we first extract PZMI of order 1 to 20 and their repetitions for face images and then GAs is employed to select the optimal feature subset for recognition or more precisely the optimal PZMI. Also a SVM classifier which has good generalization ability is employed in this system.

The organization of this paper is as follows: Section 2 presents preprocessing and face localization. Feature extraction is described in section 3 and finally, section 4 and 5 attain the experimental results and conclusion.

## 2 Preprocessing and Face Localization

One of the key problems in building automated systems that perform face recognition task is face localization. Many algorithms have been proposed for face localization and detection [6]. After preprocessing (histogram equalization) of the facial images, we extract connected components by applying a region growing algorithm. Then the ellipse that is a good approximation of connected components is selected by the shape information method [7]. We have used genetic algorithm to find the best location (including the best orientation and the best position) of face in image.

Architecture of this method is shown in Fig. 1.

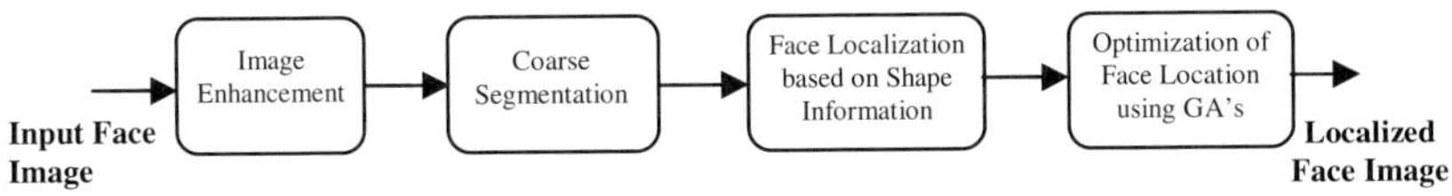


**Fig.1.** Basic flowchart of the localization algorithm

At the first, we extract the face region from the input image using a region growing method that is described in [8].

The oval shape of face can be approximated by an ellipse. Therefore looking for faces in an image means to detect objects with nearly elliptical shape [7].

In the region-based method, the connected components are determined by applying a region growing algorithm, then for each connected component, the best-fit ellipse having the best minimum size, is computed using the properties of the geometric moments [7].

During our experiments it was observed that the ellipse that is obtained in previous part usually covers an area which is not the face region. Because the hair and background was also included in the connected components. In the other words, this ellipse is not the best-fit ellipse. So, we must optimize its orientation and center coordinates.

We calculate the major and minor axes of best-fit ellipse by a shape information method [7] and its exact orientation and center coordinates which uses genetic algorithm is described in following.

In the optimization section, the population was initialized with random points. In order to select the individuals for the next generation, GA's roulette wheel selection method was used.

Further genetic parameters of localization step are summarized in Table 1:

**Table 1.** Genetic Algorithm Parameters (localization step)

| Population size | 30 | Probability of crossover | 0.8 |
|---|---|---|---|
| Chromosome length | 23 | Probability of mutation | 0.003 |

We use two different coding methods (gray and binary) for genotype coding and the symmetric of localized image with respect to major axis of obtained ellipse for fitness function. Using this optimization method, the position of ellipse is found precisely while the Tilt and Translation Errors are lower before optimization. For more details, please see [9].

# 3 PZMI Feature Extraction

The advantages of considering orthogonal moments are that they are shift, rotation and scale invariant and very robust in the presence of noise.

The PZMI of order **n** and repetition **m** can be computed using the scale invariant central moments $CM_{p,q}$ and the radial geometric moments $RM_{p,q}$ as follow [4]:

$$
\begin{aligned}
PZM_{nm} = {} & \frac{n+1}{\pi} \sum_{(n-m-s)even,s=0}^{n-|m|} D_{n,|m|,s} \sum_{a=0}^{k} \sum_{b=0}^{m} \binom{k}{a}\binom{m}{b} (-j)^b \, CM_{2k+m-2a-b,2a+b} \\
& + \frac{n+1}{\pi} \sum_{(n-m-s)odd\,,s=0}^{n-|m|} D_{n,|m|,s} \sum_{a=0}^{d} \sum_{b=0}^{m} \binom{d}{a}\binom{m}{b} (-j)^b \, RM_{2d+m-2a-b,2a+b}
\end{aligned}
\tag{1}
$$

Where $k=(n-s-m)/2$, $d=(n-s-m-1)/2$ and also $D_{n,|m|,s}$, $CM_{p,q}$ and $RM_{p,q}$ are as follow:

$$
D_{n,|m|,s} = (-1)^S \frac{(2n+1-s)!}{s!(n-|m|-s)!(n-|m|-s+1)!} \tag{2}
$$

$$
CM_{p,q} = \frac{\mu_{p,q}}{M_{00}^{(p+q+2)/2}}, \quad RM_{p,q} = \frac{\sum_x \sum_y f(x,y)(\hat{x}^2+\hat{y}^2)^{1/2} \hat{x}^p \hat{y}^q}{M_{00}^{(p+q+2)/2}} \tag{3}
$$

Where $\hat{x} = x - x_0$, $\hat{y} = y - y_0$ and $x_0$, $y_0$, $M_{pq}$ and $\mu_{pq}$ are gravity coordinates, geometric moments and central geometric moments respectively.

## 3.1 GA-Based Feature Selection

After the PZMI features have been extracted over a range of orders, a Genetic Algorithms (GAs) is used to select the features. A block diagram of proposed feature extraction and selection scheme is shown in Fig. 2.

For our problem, we set the length of chromosomes to L (L=20). Each gene $g_i (i = 1,2,...,L)$ corresponds to a specific order of PZMI. If $g_i = 1$, this represents we select this order as one of optimal orders. Otherwise, $g_i = 0$ means discard it. Because most of orders may be selected, the probability of every bit being equal to 1 is set to 0.8 when the initial population of chromosomes is creating. Its purpose is to speed up the convergence.

Given a chromosome **q** the fitness function F(q) is defined as:

$$F(q) = \frac{1}{\sum_{x \in \Omega} \delta(x,q)} \quad (4)$$

Here $\Omega$ is the training image set for GAs and $\delta(x,q)$ is defined as:

$$\delta(x,q) = \begin{cases} 1, & \textit{if } x \textit{ is classified correctly} \\ 0, & \textit{if } x \textit{ is misclassified} \end{cases} \quad (5)$$

For simplicity, we have used the nearest neighbor classifier and the aim is to find a binary vector with the smallest number of **1**'s such that the classifier performance is maximized. In order to select the individuals for the next generation, GA's roulette wheel selection method was used.

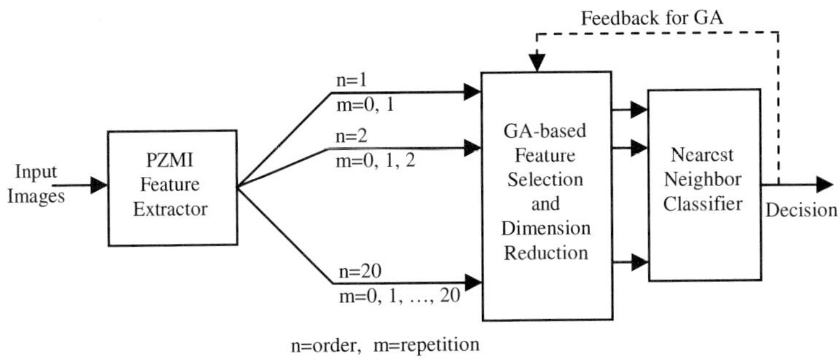


**Fig. 2.** Block Diagram of proposed feature extraction and selection scheme

Further Genetic Algorithms parameters of feature selection step are summarized in Table 2.

**Table 2.** Genetic Algorithm Parameters (feature selection step)

| Population size | 50 | Probability of crossover | 0.7 |
|---|---|---|---|
| Chromosome length | 20 | Probability of mutation | 0.003 |

## 4 Experimental Results

To check the utility of our proposed algorithm, experimental studies are carried out on the ORL and Yale database images. The ORL database contains 400 facial images from 40 individuals in different states and the Yale database contains 165 facial images from 15 individuals in different states.

After preprocessing by means of histogram equalization and face localization that is described in part 2, we have face images in which the redundant information such as background and hair are omitted and also the tilt and translation errors of localized images are reduced. Fig. 3 shows the localized faces before and after using the genetic algorithm optimization.

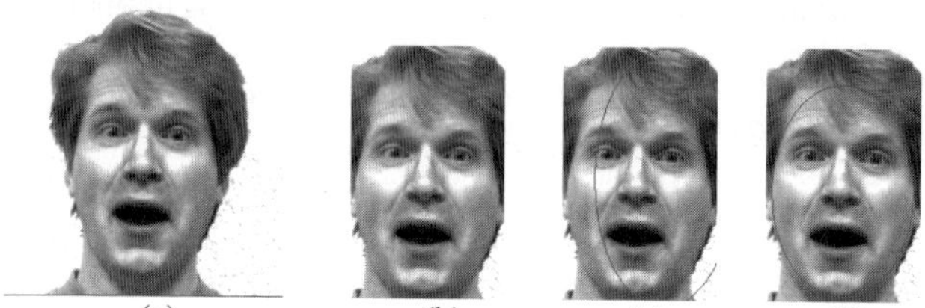

(a) (b) (c) (d)

**Fig. 3.** Localized Face (from Yale database): (a): Original image, (b): After Region growing algorithm, (c): Before optimization ellipse, (c): After optimization ellipse

It is necessary to mention that the ORL database images are not head-shoulder images. So, the coarse segmentation on the ORL database images is not applied.

In the feature extraction step, we extract the PZMI of orders **1** to **20** and their repetitions for face images. I.e. for any **n**, we extract one feature vector of order **n** and all repetitions **m** (**m≤n**). For example if we choose n=5, we have one feature vector which has 6 elements. Then in the selection stage, for any chromosome, we create one feature vector which includes all of the extracted features of GA-based selected orders respectively and for scale invariancy of created feature vector, we normalized it.

In the selection part, the created PZMI over the order range of 1 to 20 were considered and they are applied to GAs. Simulation results of this part show that the high orders PZMI are better for creation of feature vector and the number of optimized feature vector elements is 55.

Further information is summarized in Table 3.

**Table 3.** Experimental results of GAs for feature selection

| Selected Orders (n) | 2, 4, 8, 10, 12, 13 |
|---|---|
| Number of Optimized Feature Vector Elements | *55* |

Also, Fig. 4 shows the selected orders (Best Individuals), Fitness of each individuals and average distance between individuals.

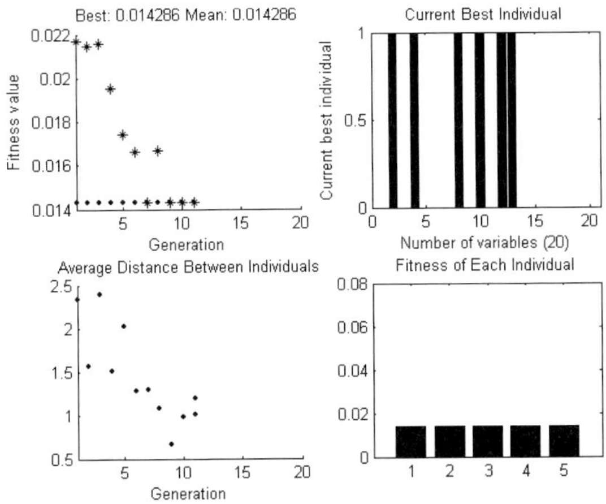


**Fig. 4.** Simulation results of GAs for feature selection

In the classification step, we use SVM with Exponential RBF (ERBF) kernel functions with the best parameters which are obtained by simulation. We use 5 random images in each class for training and the rest for the test. Finally the classifier error rate is computed using the test images. The classifier error rate is computed as the number of misclassifications in the test phase over the total number of test images.

Simulation results on the ORL and Yale databases show that the error rate in face recognition system which uses face localization step is lower than the same system without the face localization step. These results are summarized in Table 4, 5.

**Table 4.** Experimental results for the best orders of PZMI (ORL database)

| Face Recognition System | Errors | | Classification Error Rate |
|---|---|---|---|
| | Tilt Error | Translation Error | |
| Without Face Localization | ** | ** | 4.7% |
| Shape Information Based Method | 17.5 | 26.7 | 4.1% |
| Proposed Method | 4.2 | 5.4 | 1.2% |

**: Not defined

**Table 5.** Experimental results for the best orders of PZMI (Yale database)

| Face Recognition System | Errors | | Classification Error Rate |
|---|---|---|---|
| | Tilt Error | Translation Error | |
| Without Face Localization | ** | ** | 3.6% |
| Shape Information Based Method | 18.7 | 35.1 | 2.2% |
| Proposed Method | 5.1 | 3.6 | 1% |

**: Not defined

## 5 Conclusion

We have proposed a new face recognition approach based on PZMI and GAs. After preprocessing, we find the exact location of oval shape of face (best fit ellipse) in database images with genetic algorithm. Then the high orders PZMI are used as a feature vectors which are fed to classifier stage. Support Vector Machines (SVMs) classifier which has very good generalization ability has been used as a classifier with ERBF kernel function. Experimental results on the ORL and Yale databases indicate that the error rate in the proposed face recognition system which uses face localization step is lower than the same system without face localization step. Also, high order PZMI have more suitable information for classification stage.

## Acknowledgment

This research was supported by the Iran Telecommunication Research Center (ITRC).

## References

1. Chellappa, R., Wilson, C.L., Sirohry, S.: Human and Machine Recognition of faces: A Survey. Proceedings of the IEEE. 83 (1995) 705-740
2. Kanan, H.R., Faez, K.: ZMI and Wavelet Transform Features and SVM Classifier in the Optimized Face Recognition system. Proceeding of the 5th IEEE International Symposium on Signal Processing and Information Technology. (2005) 295-300
3. Srinivas, M., Patnik, L.M.: Genetic Algorithms: A Survey. IEEE, (1994)
4. Teh, C.H., Chin, R.T.: On Image Analysis by the Methods of Moments. IEEE Trans. On Patt. Anal. and Mach. Intell.. 10 (1988) 496-513
5. Osuna, E., Freund, R., Girosi, F.: Support Vector Machine: Training and Applications. Technical Report Massachusetts Institute of Technology. (1997)
6. Daugman, J.: Face Detection: a Survey. Comput. Vis. Imag. Underst. 83 (2001) 236-274
7. Sobotta, K., Pitas, I.: Face Localization and Facial Feature Extraction Based on Shape and Color Information. IEEE Int. Conf. on Image Processing. 3 (1996) 483-486
8. Lin, C.H., Wu, J.L.: Automatic Facial Feature Extraction by Genetic Algorithms. IEEE Transaction of Image Processing. 8 (1999) 834-845
9. Kanan, H.R., Faez, K., Mozaffari, S., Ezoji, M.: Face Localization Using Shape Information and Genetic Algorithm. Proceeding of the First Int. Conference on Modeling, Simulation and Applied Optimization, (2005)

# Genetic Algorithm Based Restructuring of Web Applications Using Web Page Relationships and Metrics*

Byungjeong Lee[1,**], Eunjoo Lee[2], and Chisu Wu[3]

[1] School of Computer Science, University of Seoul, Korea
bjlee@venus.uos.ac.kr
[2] Department of Computer Engineering, Kyungpook National University, Korea
ejlee@knu.ac.kr
[3] School of Computer Science and Engineering, Seoul National University, Korea
wuchisu@selab.snu.ac.kr

**Abstract.** The structure of Web applications tends to deteriorate with time as they undergo maintenance. Web applications with structural flaws increase maintenance costs, decrease component reuses, and reduce software life cycle. In this paper, we describe a genetic algorithm based restructuring approach of Web applications using Web page relationships and metrics. Our approach consists of two parts. First, metrics are derived from Web application. Next, Web application is clustered using the metrics. Then the Web application is refined by software engineers.

## 1 Introduction

Changes of Web applications are unavoidable and tend to cause the application's structure to degrade. This degradation can be reversed only by successively reengineering the structure of Web applications. Web applications have been maintained by restructuring or clustering Web sites/Web pages [1,2,3,4]. However, the previous studies have limits such as the low quality of the restructuring or restructuring in each Web page. In legacy systems a genetic algorithm based clustering has been proposed to improve the structure of declined code by extracting relationships from program code [5]. The method must provide an appropriate model to apply to Web application [1].

In this paper, we describe a genetic algorithm(GA) [6] based restructuring approach of Web applications using Web page relationships and metrics. Our approach consists of two parts. First, metrics are derived from Web application. Next, Web application is clustered using the metrics. Then the Web application is refined by software engineers.

The rest of this paper is organized as follows. Section 2 describes relationships and metrics in Web application. Section 3 provides a genetic algorithm based clustering. Section 4 presents a case study and Section 5 describes our conclusions.

* This work was supported by the second stage of the Brain Korea 21 project.

** Corresponding author.

D.-S. Huang, K. Li, and G.W. Irwin (Eds.): ICIC 2006, LNCS 4113, pp. 697–702, 2006.

## 2 Relationships and Metrics in Web Application

### 2.1 Relationships Between Web Pages

Web application consists of Web pages, which are classified into static and dynamic ones. A static page includes a form, style sheet, script library, etc. A relationship between pages is *link*, *submit*, *redirect*, *include*, *build*, or *load*. Each type of the relationships may be assigned a different weight. For example, a *build* relationship is considered stronger than *link* and *submit* since a static page is dependent on a dynamic page. A *submit* relationship is considered stronger than a *link* since the *submit* relationship is associated with the request and data-flow between pages [2]. The connectivity between pages is measured on the basis of the number of parameters and the number and the type of edges between them: the more the interconnections between items, the stronger their connectivity. A weight between page $u$ and $v$ is defined as follows.

$$W(u,v)=\begin{cases} nlinks(u,v)*nparams(u,v)*w_{ln}, & \text{if there is a } \textit{link} \text{ relationship.} \\ nparams(u,v)*w_{su}, & \text{if a } \textit{submit} \text{ relationship.} \\ nparams(u,v)*w_{re}, & \text{if a } \textit{redirect} \text{ relationship.} \\ nparams(u,v)*w_{ld}, & \text{if a } \textit{load} \text{ relationship.} \\ w_{bu}, & \text{if a } \textit{build} \text{ relationship.} \\ w_{in}, & \text{if an } \textit{include} \text{ relationship.} \end{cases} \tag{1}$$

where

- $w_{ln}, w_{su}, w_{re}, w_{in}, w_{bu}$ and $w_{ld}$ represent the weight of *link*, *submit*, *redirect*, *include*, *build*, and *load* relationships, respectively.($w_{ln}$, $w_{ld}$, $w_{in} \leq w_{re} \leq w_{su} \leq w_{bu}$)
- $nlinks(u,v)$ is the number of hyperlinks from page $u$ to $v$.
- $nparams(u,v)$ is the number of parameters transferred from page $u$ to $v$.

### 2.2 Measures of Web Application

Similarity measure indicates the extent of relatedness between Web pages and is mainly used for clustering [7]. Page similarity measures are classified into content-based, link-based, and usage-based similarity. In this work, because we aim to group interacting related pages we define link-based page similarity(PS), based on the cosine equation, which is derived from page relationship weights.

$$PS(u,v) = \frac{\sum_{w \in WP} W(u,w) * W(v,w)}{\sqrt{\sum_{w \in WP} W(u,w)^2 * \sum_{w \in WP} W(v,w)^2}} . \tag{2}$$

where

- $WP$ is a set of Web pages.

We define cohesion($COH$) and coupling($COP$) metrics using page similarity based on connection strength considering the type and the number of the relationships and the number of parameters transferred between Web pages.

$$COH(C) = \frac{\sum_{u,v \in C} PS(u,v)}{(|C| * |C|)} . \tag{3}$$

$$COP(C_i, C_j) = \sum_{u \in C_i} \sum_{v \in C_j} PS(u,v) . \tag{4}$$

where

- $|C|$ is the number of pages in cluster $C$.

Clustering objective ($CO$) is defined to measure appropriateness of clustering using cohesion and coupling of Web application derived from cluster metrics.

$$COH(WA) = \frac{\sum_{C_i \in WA} COH(C_i)}{NC} . \tag{5}$$

$$COP(WA) = \sum_{C_i, C_j \in WA} COP(C_i, C_j) . \tag{6}$$

$$CO(WA) = \frac{NC * (NC - 1) * w_{coh} * COH(WA)}{2 * w_{cop} * COP(WA)} . \tag{7}$$

where

- $w_{coh}$ and $w_{cop}$ are relative weights of cohesion and coupling, respectively.
- $WA$ represents a Web application with a set of clusters.
- $NC$ is the number of clusters in $WA$.

## 3 Genetic Algorithm Based Clustering

The GA [6] is a non-deterministic search algorithm based on the mechanics of natural selection and natural genetics. We apply a genetic algorithm based clustering approach which uses agglomerative clustering with backtracking (Fig. 1), where each solution is represented by a chromosome. Thus we must define a relevant encoding of chromosomes to solve a problem. In our work, a chromosome consists of genes corresponding to Web pages in a cluster. Hence each chromosome is an $N$-integer string, in which the value of the $i$-th gene is the identifier of the cluster of which the $i$-th Web page of the selected cluster is a member (Fig. 2). Then we must define a fitness function to evaluate a solution during applying GA-operators, as follows.

$$FIT(WA) = \frac{1}{CO(WA)} . \tag{8}$$

The cohesion and coupling of the initial clustering of Web application are computed before applying GA. The cluster with the lowest $COH$ is selected and an initial population of fixed size using the cluster is created. The initial

```
find relationships in Web application;
compute COH(WA) and COP(WA) from the relationships;
do {
  select the cluster with the lowest COH(C);
  create an initial population of fixed size p;
  do {
    select parent1 and parent2 from the population;
    offspring = crossover(parent1, parent2);
    mutation(offspring);
    local improvement(offspring);
    compute the fitness of offspring;
    replace(population, offspring);
  } while (population is not converged);
} while (there exists a cluster to be improved);
return the best clustering;
```

**Fig. 1.** Applying genetic algorithm

| Web page | 1 | 2 | 3 | 4 | 5 | 6 | 7 | 8 | 9 | 10 |
|---|---|---|---|---|---|---|---|---|---|---|
| Cluster | 3 | 1 | 1 | 2 | 4 | 3 | 2 | 2 | 2 | 3 |

**Fig. 2.** Chromosome representation

population consists of chromosomes and evaluate these chromosomes with the fitness function. We then select two chromosomes in decreasing order of fitness, crossover, mutate, and replace a low-quality chromosome with a new one of high quality. As generations pass, the population comes to consist of high-quality chromosomes. However, because the GA takes a long time to find an optimal solution and is not efficient at fine-tuning around local optima, local improvement techniques should be used to alleviate these shortcomings when applying the GA [8]. These processes continue until stopping conditions are satisfied (Fig. 1).

After applying GA, the clustering is refined by software engineer. The following guidelines can be used for refining the clustering. First, if a cluster contains only one page, the cluster is merged with another cluster. Next, if complexity of a cluster is very high, that is, a very big cluster containing too many pages, the cluster is divided. Finally, the refinement might not decrease the fitness, but should improve the cohesion or coupling metric.

## 4 A Case Study

Figure 3 shows contents of a small online community site in UML package diagram. A package stands for a cluster to which Web pages belong. The number in page name is a page identifier and a letter H in index.asp name of Home package

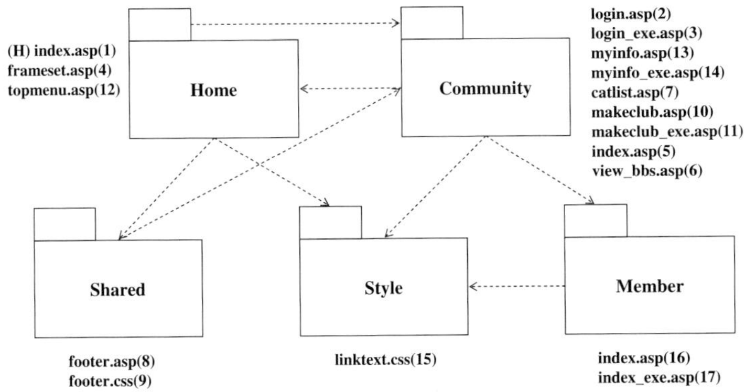


**Fig. 3.** An example structure of a community site

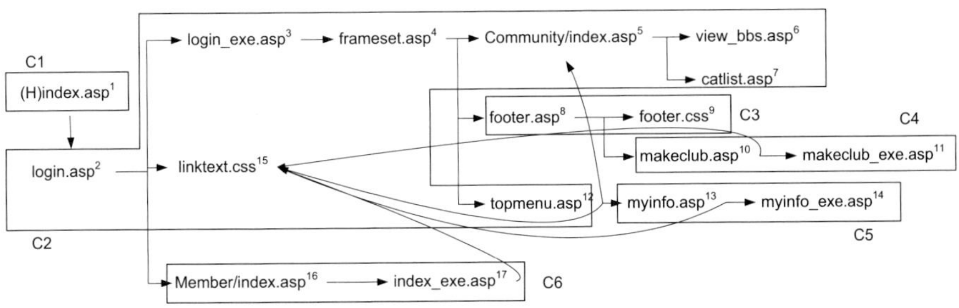


**Fig. 4.** Clustered Web application

indicates the entry page of this site. Each group should be named to represent the semantic after clustering.

For GA-operators the size of the population is 50 and the uniform crossover rate is 0.5. The lower the convergence rate is, the more the mutation occurs. The inner do-while loop in Fig. 1 stops when 80 percent of the population has been occupied by chromosomes with the same quality. Figure 4 shows the navigation starting from the entry page. Two index.asp pages are displayed with path since there are three pages with the same name in different packages. Other pages are unique. Figure 4 shows the structure of a clustered Web application when $w_{ln}$, $w_{su}$, $w_{re}$, $w_{in}$, $w_{ld}$, $w_{coh}$ and $w_{cop}$ are 1, 2, 2, 1, 1, 0.6 and 0.4, respectively. Each polygon represents a cluster. The Web application has been grouped into six clusters which are one more than those in Fig. 3. Figure 5 (a) shows the fitness function when our GA has been applied to the example in Fig. 3. The fitness function value has decreased and converged. The clustered Web application in Fig. 4 can be refined. For example, cluster C1 containing the entry page(index.asp) and cluster C2 might be merged because C1 contains only one file. Figure 5 (b) shows $COH$ and $COP$ metrics of the initial, clustered and refined Web application. We can see that both metrics in the clustered and refined Web application have been improved. Software engineer must decide which clustering is better.

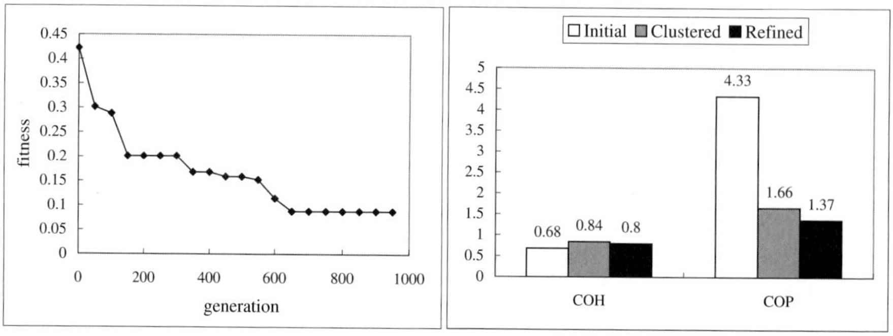


(a) Fitness function (b) Metrics

**Fig. 5.** Fitness and Metrics

## 5 Conclusions

Because this approach finds a clustering with good cohesion and coupling, the approach is expected to help software engineers understand and maintain Web applications. The structure of Web applications has something to do with other quality attributes such as complexity or scalability as well as cohesion and coupling. Our future work will focus on how to achieve multi-objectives including other quality attributes as clustering factors. Thus we plan to study on applying GA for multi-objectives and develop more effective guidelines that can be used for refining the clustered Web application.

## References

1. Lucca, G. A., Fasolino, A. R., Pace, F., Tramontana P., Carlini, U. D.: Comprehending Web Applications by a Clustering Based Approach. In Proc. of International Workshop on Program Comprehension (2002) 261–270
2. Lucca, G. A., Fasolino, A. R., Tramontana, P.: Reverse Engineering Web Applications: the WARE Approach. Journal of Software Maintenance and Evolution: Research and Practice, Vol. 16(1-2). (2004) 71–101
3. Ricca, F., Tonella, P., Baxter, I. D.: Web Applications Transformations Based on Rewrite Rules. Information and Software technology, Vol. 44(13). (2002) 811–825
4. Lucca, G. A., Penta, M., Fasolino, A. R., Tramontana, P.: Supporting Web Application Evolution by Dynamic Analysis. In Proc. of International Workshop on Principles of Software Evoolution (2005) 175–184
5. Mancoridis, S., Mitchell, B., Rorres, C., Chen, Y., Gansner, E.: Using Automatic Clustering to Produce High-Level System Organizations of Source Code. In Proc. of the 6th International Workshop on Program Comprehension (1998)
6. Goldberg, D. E.: Genetic Algorithms in Search, Optimization & Machine Learning. Addison Wesley (1989)
7. Dhyani, D., Keong, W., Bhowmick, S.: A Survey of Web Metrics. ACM Computing Surveys, Vol. 34(4). (2002) 469–503
8. Bui, T. N., Moon, B. R.: Genetic Algorithm and Graph Partitioning. IEEE Transactions on Computers, Vol. 45(7). (1996) 841–855

# Genetic Algorithm-Based Clustering and Its New Mutation Operator

Arit Thammano and Uraiwan Kakulphimp

Computational Intelligence Laboratory
Faculty of Information Technology
King Mongkut's Institute of Technology Ladkrabang,
Bangkok, 10520 Thailand
arit@it.kmitl.ac.th, ukakulphimp@hotmail.com

**Abstract.** This paper proposes an extension to the original GA-clustering algorithm by introducing a new way to mutate the chromosome. The new mutation operator takes the previous values of the chromosome into account when mutating the chromosome. The superiority of the proposed approach over the original GA-clustering algorithm and K-means algorithm is demonstrated by using 6 benchmark data sets.

## 1 Introduction

Clustering is the process of grouping the data into clusters so that objects within a cluster have high similarity in comparison to one another, but are very dissimilar to objects in other clusters [1]. Among all existing clustering algorithms, K-means algorithm is the most widely known; it is rather simple and remarkably effective. However, the K-means algorithm may get stuck at suboptimal solutions, depending on the choice of the initial cluster centers. Maulik and Bandyopadhyay [2] therefore have developed the GA-clustering algorithm, which integrates the capability of the genetic algorithm in avoiding local optima with the K-means algorithm. Their results show that the GA-clustering algorithm provides a performance that is significantly superior to that of the K-means algorithm.

The objective of this paper is to propose a new way to mutate the chromosome. The performance of the original GA-clustering algorithm is further improved when used in conjunction with this new mutation operator.

Following this introduction, section 2 and 3 briefly describe the K-means algorithm and the original GA-clustering algorithm respectively. The proposed mutation operator is presented in section 4. In section 5, the experimental results are demonstrated and discussed.

## 2 K-Means Algorithm

K-means is the most famous clustering algorithm. It groups a set of n objects into K clusters using Euclidean distance as the similarity measure. The steps of the K-means algorithm are described as follows:

D.-S. Huang, K. Li, and G.W. Irwin (Eds.): ICIC 2006, LNCS 4113, pp. 703 – 708, 2006.

A. Arbitrarily select K initial cluster centers ($z_1, z_2, \ldots, z_K$) from the input data.
B. Assign each data pattern $x_i$ to the cluster $C_j$ to which it is the most similar.
C. When all input data has been assigned, update the cluster centers as follows:

$$z_j^* = \frac{1}{n_j} \sum_{x_i \in C_j} x_i \, . \tag{1}$$

where $n_j$ is the number of data belonging to cluster $C_j$.
D. If the stopping criterion is satisfied, terminate the loop. If not, go to step B.

## 3 GA-Clustering Algorithm

A description of the GA-clustering algorithm proposed by Maulik and Bandyopadhyay is given below.

A. Define the size (P) of the population. For each chromosome, randomly select K initial cluster centers ($z_1, z_2, \ldots, z_K$) from the data set and encode them into a chromosome. Therefore, each chromosome is structured as follows:

$$\text{Chromosome} = [z_{11}, \ldots, z_{1Q}, z_{21}, \ldots, z_{2Q}, \ldots, z_{K1}, \ldots, z_{KQ}] \, . \tag{2}$$

where Q is the dimension of each cluster center.
B. Evaluate the fitness of each chromosome in the population. The fitness computation process consists of two phases as follows:
B.1. Assign each data point $x_i$ to the cluster $C_j$ to which it is the most similar. The similarity is defined as

$$d(x_i, z_j) = \sqrt{\sum_{q=1}^{Q} (x_{iq} - z_{jq})^2} \, . \tag{3}$$

where $j = 1, 2, \ldots, K$.
$z_j$ is the center of the cluster $C_j$.
Next, calculate the new cluster centers using

$$z_j^* = \frac{1}{n_j} \sum_{x_i \in C_j} x_i \, . \tag{4}$$

Then replace the previous cluster centers $z_j$ encoded in the chromosome by the new centers $z_j^*$.
B.2. Compute the fitness of chromosomes in the current population using:

$$f = 1/M. \tag{5}$$

$$M = \sum_{j=1}^{K} \sum_{x_i \in C_j} \left\| x_i - z_j \right\| . \tag{6}$$

C. Create a new population by repeating the following steps until there is an appropriate number of chromosomes in the new population:
   C.1. Select two parent chromosomes from a current population using the roulette wheel technique.
   C.2. With a crossover probability, cross over the parent chromosomes to form the new offspring.
   C.3. Perform the mutation on the new offspring as follows:
   - Randomly select mutation positions.
   - With a mutation probability, mutate the value of the selected positions by using the following equation:

$$v^{t+1} = \begin{cases} v^t \pm 2*\delta*v^t & : \text{if } v^t \neq 0 \\ v^t \pm 2*\delta & : \text{if } v^t = 0 \end{cases}. \tag{7}$$

   where $v^t$ is the current value of the selected gene.
   $\delta$ is a small random number in the range of 0 to 1.
   C.4. Place the new offspring into a new population.
D. If a predetermined number of iteration is reached or the end condition is satisfied, stop the loop and return the best chromosome in the current population. If not, go to step B.

## 4 The Proposed Mutation Operator

This paper proposes an extension to the original GA-clustering algorithm (proposed by Maulik and Bandyopadhyay) by introducing a new way to mutate the chromosome. Instead of deciding randomly to add or subtract a small random number to/from the original value of the selected position, the historical information of each chromosome is taken into consideration when mutating the chromosome. In this research, the histories of the chromosome are divided into 2 groups: "good" and "bad." The good consists of all previous stages of the chromosome that have higher fitness value than the current stage, while the bad is composed of all previous stages of the chromosome that have lower fitness value than the current stage. The formula for the proposed mutation operator is as follows:

$$z^{t+1} = z^t + \beta_1 \sum_{i \in g} w_i (z_i - z^t) + \beta_2 \sum_{k \in b} w_k (z_k - z^t). \tag{8}$$

$$w_i = \frac{f_i}{\sum_{j \in g} f_j}. \tag{9}$$

$$w_k = \frac{f_k}{\sum_{j \in b} f_j}. \tag{10}$$

where $z^t$ is the current value of the selected cluster center.

$\beta_1$ and $\beta_2$ are the weight coefficients for "good" and "bad" groups respectively.

$z_i$ and $z_k$ are the past values of the selected cluster center.

## 5 Experimental Results

In this paper, the performance of the proposed approach is compared to the original GA-clustering algorithm and the k-means algorithm. In order to compare the three algorithms, the experiments are conducted using 6 benchmark data sets: "Pima Indians diabetes," "heart disease," "sonar, mines vs. rocks," "satellite image," "vowel recognition," and "letter image recognition." For each data set, one hundred experiments are performed for each algorithm. The performance is measured in terms of the clustering metric as defined in equation 6 and the average time to converge. The experiments are conducted on a 2.8 GHz Pentium IV PC with 1 gigabyte of main memory. Brief descriptions of the data sets are given below:

1. The first data set is the Pima Indians diabetes database. It is publicly available from the UCI machine learning database repository [3]. The problem is to predict whether a patient would test positive (1) or negative (0) for diabetes according to World Health Organization criteria. All patients represented in the data set are females at least 21 years old of Pima Indian heritage living near Phoenix, Arizona, USA. This database contains 768 examples. Each example is described by 8 numerical attributes and belongs to one of two classes (0 or 1). There are 500 examples of class 0 and 268 examples of class 1. Therefore, the value of K is chosen to be 2 for this database.
2. The second data set is the heart disease problem. It is retrieved from Statlog Project Datasets [4]. The problem concerns the prediction of the absence (1) or presence (2) of heart disease given the results of various medical tests carried out on a patient. This data set contains 13 attributes and 270 records. There are 150 records of class 1 and 120 records of class 2. The value of K used for this data set is 2.
3. The third data set is the Sonar, Mines vs. Rocks [3]. The task is to discriminate between sonar signals bounced off a metal cylinder and those bounced off a roughly cylindrical rock. This data set contains 111 patterns obtained by bouncing sonar signals off a metal cylinder at various angles and under various conditions and 97 patterns obtained from rocks under similar conditions. Sixty numerical attributes in the range 0.0 to 1.0 are used to predict the output class (mine or rock). Therefore, the value of K is chosen to be 2 for this data set.
4. The fourth data set is the satellite image data. This data is retrieved from Statlog Project Datasets [4]. This problem concerns the classification of 6 satellite images. Thirty-six numerical attributes are used to predict the output class. There are 6 classes (red soil = 1, cotton crop = 2, grey soil = 3, damp grey soil = 4, soil with vegetation stubble = 5, and very damp grey soil = 7). The value of K is therefore chosen to be 6 for this data set.
5. The fifth is the vowel recognition problem. The vowel data used in this problem was originally collected by Deterding [5], who recorded examples of eleven steady state vowels (hid, hId, hEd, hAd, hYd, had, hOd, hod, hUd, hud, and hed) of British English spoken by fifteen speakers. Each vowel was uttered six times

by each of the fifteen speakers. Therefore, the whole data set contains 990 examples. The data set consists of 10 inputs, which are obtained by low pass filtering the speech signals at 4.7 kHz; digitizing to 12 bits with a 10 kHz sampling rate; extracting the twelfth order linear predictive coefficient (LPC) from six 512 sample Hamming windowed segments; and then using the reflection coefficients to calculate 10 log-area ratio (LAR) parameters. The value of K used for this data set is 11.

6. The sixth data set is the letter image recognition data. The data is taken from the UCI machine learning database repository [3]. Its task is to identify each of the character images as one of the 26 capital letters in the English alphabet. This data set has 20000 instances. Each instance is described by 16 numerical attributes. Therefore, the value of K is chosen to be 26 for this data set.

Tables 1 to 6 summarize the results obtained from the three clustering algorithms for the above data sets. The average time to converge of the K-means algorithm is the lowest among the three algorithms. The proposed algorithm comes second, leaving the original GA-clustering algorithm far behind. However, when considering the clustering metric, the proposed algorithm comes out to be the best among the compared algorithms. For the Pima Indians diabetes database, the heart disease problem, and the satellite image data, the proposed algorithm comes first in the competition, while the K-means and the GA-clustering algorithms tie for second place. For the sonar, mines vs. rocks data, the K-means and the proposed algorithms tie for first place. The vowel recognition problem is the only data for which the proposed algorithm does not win the competition; it comes second. For the letter image recognition data, the proposed algorithm attains the best value of 106944.2, in comparison to 107060.3 of the K-means algorithm and 107103.2 of the GA-clustering algorithm.

**Table 1.** Results for the Pima Indians diabetes database when K = 2

| | Clustering Metric | Time (second) |
|---|---|---|
| K-means Algorithm | 52072.24 | 0.0514 |
| GA-clustering Algorithm | 52072.24 | 1.3231 |
| Proposed Algorithm | 49388.21 | 0.4447 |

**Table 2.** Results for the heart disease problem when K = 2

| | Clustering Metric | Time (second) |
|---|---|---|
| K-means Algorithm | 10695.80 | 0.0334 |
| GA-clustering Algorithm | 10695.80 | 0.6539 |
| Proposed Algorithm | 10686.33 | 0.2238 |

**Table 3.** Results for the sonar, mines vs. rocks data when K = 2

| | Clustering Metric | Time (second) |
|---|---|---|
| K-means Algorithm | 234.7671 | 0.0394 |
| GA-clustering Algorithm | 235.1560 | 4.7724 |
| Proposed Algorithm | 234.7671 | 0.3067 |

**Table 4.** Results for the satellite image data when K = 6

| | Clustering Metric | Time (second) |
|---|---|---|
| K-means Algorithm | 291939.7 | 1.8440 |
| GA-clustering Algorithm | 291939.7 | 164.5408 |
| Proposed Algorithm | 291684.2 | 11.3747 |

**Table 5.** Results for the vowel recognition problem when K = 11

| | Clustering Metric | Time (second) |
|---|---|---|
| K-means Algorithm | 1342.710 | 0.2050 |
| GA-clustering Algorithm | 1343.231 | 274.3829 |
| Proposed Algorithm | 1343.065 | 1.5059 |

**Table 6.** Results for the letter image recognition data when K = 26

| | Clustering Metric | Time (second) |
|---|---|---|
| K-means Algorithm | 107060.3 | 33.2843 |
| GA-clustering Algorithm | 107103.2 | 2504.2886 |
| Proposed Algorithm | 106944.2 | 172.5785 |

## References

1. Han, J., Kamber, M.: Data Mining: Concepts and Techniques. Morgan Kaufmann Publishers, San Francisco (2001)
2. Maulik, U., Bandyopadhyay, S.: Genetic Algorithm-based Clustering Technique. Pattern Recognition, Vol. 33 (2000) 1455-1465
3. Blake, C.L., Merz, C.J.: UCI Repository of Machine Learning Databases: http://www.ics.uci.edu/~mlearn/MLRepository.html. University of California, Department of Information and Computer Science. (1998)
4. Statlog Project Datasets: http://www.liacc.up.pt/ML/statlog/datasets/heart/. (2003)
5. Deterding, D.H.: Speaker Normalization for Automatic Speech Recognition. Ph.D. Dissertation. (1989)

# Genetic Algorithm-Based Watermarking in Discrete Wavelet Transform Domain

Dongeun Lee[1], Taekyung Kim[1], Seongwon Lee[2,*], and Joonki Paik[1]

[1] Image Processing and Intelligent Systems Laboratory, Department of Image Engineering, Graduate School of Advanced Imaging Science, Multimedia, and Film, Chung-Ang University, Seoul, Korea
[2] Department of Computer Engineering, College of Electronics and Information, Kwangwoon University, Seoul, Korea
ehddms98@wm.cau.ac.kr

**Abstract.** This paper presents a watermarking algorithm in the discrete wavelet transform domain using evolutionary algorithm. The proposed algorithm consists of wavelet-domain watermark insertion and genetic algorithm-based watermark extraction. More specifically watermark is inserted to the low-frequency region of wavelet transform domain, and watermark extraction is efficiently performed by using the evolutionary algorithm. The proposed watermarking algorithm is robust against various attacks such as JPEG image compression and geometric transformations.

## 1 Introduction

Digital watermarking is a digital content copyright protection technique against unauthorized uses such as illegal copy, distribution, and forgery. Digital watermarking inserts and extracts copyright information called watermark into the digital contents to prove the ownership of the copyright holder.

Watermark insertion can be done in either spatial domain or frequency domain. The spatial-domain watermark insertion manipulates image pixels, especially on least significant bits that have less perceptual effect on the image. Although the spatial-domain watermark insertion is simple and easy to implement, it is weak at various attacks and noise. On the other hand, the frequency-domain watermark insertion, which is robust at attacks, is made on the frequency coefficients of the image. The existing frequency transformation methods for watermark insertion include *discrete Fourier transform (DFT)* [1, 2], *discrete cosine transform (DCT), and discrete wavelet transform (DWT)* [3, 4].

Despite of recent progresses, existing watermarking algorithms are not sufficiently robust against JPEG compression and geometrical distortions such as translation, rotation, scaling, cropping, change of aspect ratio, and shearing. These geometrical distortions cause the loss of geometric synchronization that is necessary in watermark detection and decoding [5]. Two different types of solutions to resist geometrical

* Corresponding author: swlee@kw.ac.kr

D.-S. Huang, K. Li, and G.W. Irwin (Eds.): ICIC 2006, LNCS 4113, pp. 709–716, 2006.

attacks are: non-blind and blind methods [6]. In the non-blind approach, with the original image, the problem can be well resolved by effective search between the geometrically attacked images and the original ones [7, 8]. The blind solution that extracts watermark without the original image has wider applications but is obviously more challenging.

This paper proposes a more robust blind watermark extraction method using evolutionary algorithm against geometric attacks. The proposed algorithm inserts watermark in the wavelet domain, and the genetic algorithm (GA) searches and automatically extracts watermark. Since the searching process generates lots of local matching, the correct alignment can be determined at the end of exhausted computation. The proposed algorithm can reduce the computational burden by using evolutionary searching method.

This paper is organized as follows. In section 2 we describe the watermark insertion method in the wavelet domain, and in section 3 a watermark extraction method is presented using GA. Experimental results with various types of attacks are given in section 4, and section 5 concludes the paper.

## 2 Watermark Embedding Algorithm

The proposed frequency-domain watermark insertion algorithm is performed in the DWT domain. Since the low frequency band remains robust to attacks, the watermark insertion in the proposed algorithm is carried out in the LL3 band for a 3-level DWT. It should be noted that watermark insertion should be carefully designed since the coefficients of LL3 band have strongest signal energy. Strong watermark could be visible at the LL3 band. Watermark is specially designed user information that is represented by images, text characters, sound data, and so on. In this paper, we used a watermark image because of the convenience of visual analysis and evaluation. Fig. 1 shows the block diagram of watermark insertion of the proposed algorithm. The resolution of the original image is 512×512. A 2-bit watermark image of size 64×64 is used in gray scale space.

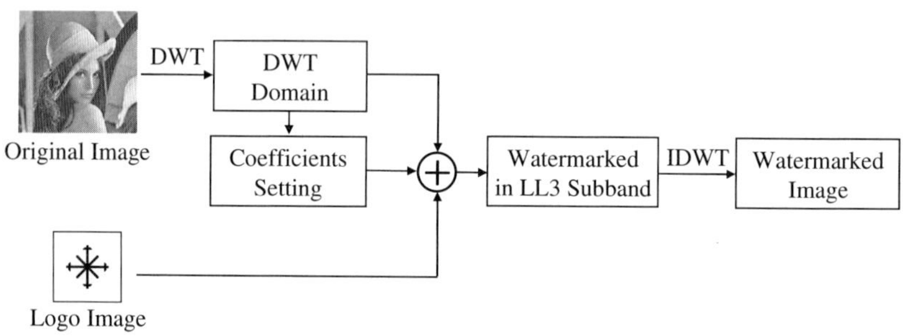


**Fig. 1.** The block diagram of the watermark embedding procedure

The algorithm for embedding the binary watermark is; to apply a 3-level DWT with Daubechies D4 wavelet filters to an input original image *f*(x,y) of size 512×512×8bits, and then to check the magnitude of LL3 coefficients and find the location of bits where the binary logo image will be inserted. Finally, the proposed method inserts bit patterns of watermark using a pre-specified threshold.

# 3 Proposed GA-Based Watermark Detection Algorithm

Watermark detection algorithm consists of two stages; the formation of populations using GA and watermark extraction in the LL3 band in the DWT domain. The watermark is then extracted in the LL3 band. GA realizes efficient watermark extraction by selecting superior genes and mating them to generate mutation. Fig. 2 shows the block diagram of the proposed watermark detection algorithm. The following subsection describes the watermark extraction process in the DWT domain.

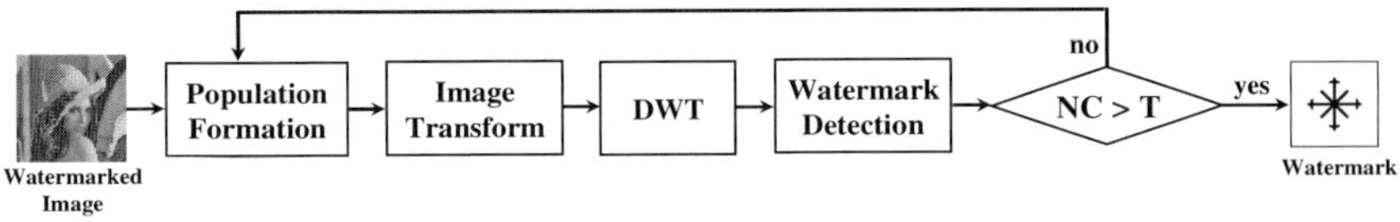


**Fig. 2.** The block diagram of watermark detection procedure

GA is a computational model to solve a real-world problem by simulating a natural evolution process in a computer. Application areas of GA includes nonlinear, non-differentially problems with multiple extremes. GA is particularly suitable for adaptive searches and optimization. The proposed evolutionary algorithm adopts GA to extract the watermark out of the image deformed by geometry attacks such as rotation and translation. Initially, 20 genes (parents) are generated and applied to the attacked image to reverse attacks. Then, the embedded watermark is extracted and the fitness of the extracted watermark is measured. The genes with best fitness are selected and used for the next generation. We generate 20 genes by crossover and mutation with a predetermined rate. The process is repeated until the best gene is found. In the proposed algorithm the chromosome consists of a 16-bit string of 0 and 1. In the chromosome structure, two 4 bits are used for translations in both horizontal and vertical directions respectively and 8 bits are used for rotation attack.

**Table 1.** Parameters of genetic algorithm

| Parameters | Values |
|---|---|
| Population size | 20 |
| Chromosome length | 16 |
| Maximum number of generation | 20 |
| Selection rate | 0.8 |
| Crossover rate | 0.8 |
| Mutation rate | 0.2 |

Table 1 represents the parameters used in the experiments. The parameters are referred to Ali's paper [9] and fixed by experiments. The probability of crossover is empirically set to 0.8%, and that of mutation to 0.5%.

In order to evaluate the feasibility of extracted watermark, normalized correlation (NC) is used. The number of mismatched data between the inserted and the extracted watermarks is used to represent the similarity of watermarks. NC for valid watermarks, which represents the characteristics of the extracted watermark, is defined as

$$NC = \frac{\sum_{x,y} w_{x,y} w'_{x,y}}{\sum_{x,y} w^2_{x,y}}, \tag{1}$$

where $w$ represents the inserted watermark, $w'$ the extracted watermark. Experimental results are rounded to the fourth decimal place. The NC for random noise is about 0.5 and possibility of distinguishing extracted logo is higher than 0.7~0.8 NC.

Fig. 3 (a) shows the variation of the NC of the extracted watermark when the watermarked image is horizontal translation. As shown in the figure, watermark can be extracted every $2^3$ pixels because 3-level DWT was used. Fig. 3 (b) shows the variation of the NC of extracted watermark with rotation. In case of rotation, mutation is generated every 90 degree. Each population is decided to have high feasibility if it has high NC. As the selected genes of high NC are transferred to the next generation, the populations in the new generation also have high NC. Finally, high NC watermark can be extracted.

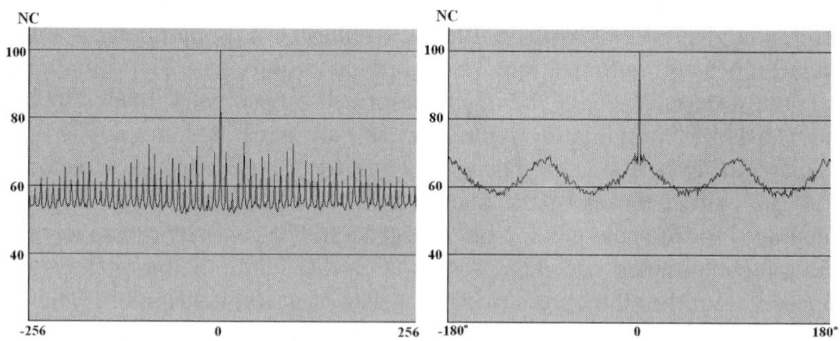


(a) Horizontal translation (b) Rotation

**Fig. 3.** Variation of NC with (a) translation and (b) rotation

The proposed watermark extraction algorithm uses GA to make the watermark extraction process robust against various types of attacks. GA generates populations, and transforms the image for watermark search. The extraction procedure is:

**Step 1:** GA generates populations and their feasibilities are evaluated. Highly feasible genes are selected and mated to generate mutation.

**Step 2**: Watermark-inserted populations are transformed and applied the 3-level DWT to the restored image.

**Step 3:** In order to evaluate the feasibility of extracted watermark, normalized correlation (NC) is measured. If NC is larger than a predetermined value, the extracted watermark is decided to be feasible, and the algorithm terminates. Otherwise go back to step 1.

## 4 Experimental Results

The performance of the proposed algorithm is tested with various types of images. A test image is an 8-bit grayscale Lena image of size 512×512. The watermark is a 64×64 binary image. The original Lena and the watermark image are respectively shown in Fig. 4 (a) and (b). Daubechies D4 filter coefficients are used for 3-level wavelet decomposition. Performance evaluation of the proposed algorithm on test images with various characteristics was studied. Peak signal-to-noise ratio (PSNR) is used to analyze the quality of the watermarked image, which is defined as

$$PSNR = 10\log_{10}\frac{255^2}{\frac{1}{XY}\sum_{x,y}(I_{x,y} - I'_{x,y})^2}, \tag{2}$$

where $I$ represents the original image, $I'$ the modified image, and $X$ and $Y$ represent the horizontal and vertical image sizes respectively.

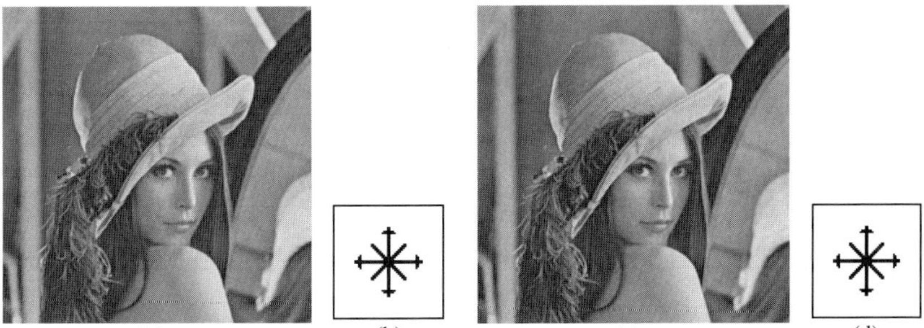

(a) (b) (c) (d)

**Fig. 4.** (a) The original image, (b) the watermark, (c) the watermarked image, and (d) the extracted watermark image

The watermarked Lena image with PSNR 42.11db is shown in Fig. 4(c). There is no perceptual degradation in the watermarked image. The extracted watermark from the watermarked image is shown in Fig. 4(d).

### 4.1 Non-geometric Attacks

We classify the attack patterns into non-geometric attacks and geometric attacks. Watermarked images are first tested for non-geometric attacks such as Gaussian filtering, median filtering and compression. The proposed algorithm can easily cope with wavelet-based JPEG2000 and DCT-based JPEG as shown in Table 2 and 3. Table 2 shows the performance of the proposed algorithm against compression attacks from 0.5 to 0.1 of JPEG2000 compression rates. The extracted watermarks are seriously damaged below the rate 0.1. JPEG compression is also evaluated over various compression rates. Table 3 presents the PSNRs and NCs according to JPEG quality factors. The PSNR values shown value between watermarked image and attacked image. In other words, PSNRs express the extent of degradation by attacks.

We also include non-geometric attacks such as Gaussian, sharpening, and median filter. The PSNR of the attacked images are shown in Table 4. The attack patterns used in the experiment are from the Korean Watermarking Certification [10].

**Table 2.** PSNRs and NCs of watermark embedded images at JPEG2000 compression

| JPEG2000 Rate | Lena | | Lake | | Boat | |
|---|---|---|---|---|---|---|
| | PSNR | NC | PSNR | NC | PSNR | NC |
| 0.50 | 49.87 | 1 | 48.13 | 0.999 | 48.57 | 0.999 |
| 0.45 | 48.54 | 0.998 | 48.13 | 0.974 | 48.13 | 0.999 |
| 0.40 | 48.13 | 0.997 | 45.12 | 0.972 | 48.13 | 0.973 |
| 0.35 | 48.13 | 0.968 | 43.36 | 0.961 | 45.12 | 0.978 |
| 0.30 | 45.12 | 0.969 | 41.14 | 0.973 | 42.11 | 0.894 |
| 0.25 | 43.36 | 0.968 | 39.68 | 0.858 | 40.35 | 0.892 |
| 0.20 | 41.14 | 0.903 | 37.34 | 0.773 | 38.59 | 0.857 |
| 0.15 | 39.68 | 0.854 | 35.58 | 0.692 | 36.99 | 0.731 |
| 0.10 | 37.72 | 0.773 | 33.36 | 0.601 | 34.91 | 0.667 |

**Table 3.** PSNRs and NCs of watermark embedded images at JPEG compression

| JPEG Quality | Lena | | Lake | | Boat | |
|---|---|---|---|---|---|---|
| | PSNR | NC | PSNR | NC | PSNR | NC |
| 10 | 43.36 | 1 | 42.11 | 1 | 42.11 | 1 |
| 8 | 39.68 | 0.998 | 36.67 | 0.999 | 37.72 | 0.992 |
| 6 | 39.10 | 0.988 | 35.58 | 0.989 | 36.99 | 0.991 |
| 4 | 36.67 | 0.915 | 33.51 | 0.917 | 34.71 | 0.917 |
| 2 | 34.15 | 0.832 | 30.97 | 0.830 | 31.80 | 0.823 |
| 0 | 32.11 | 0.622 | 29.27 | 0.614 | 30.00 | 0.622 |

**Table 4.** PSNRs and NCs of watermark embedded images at another attack method

| Attack | Lena | | Lake | | Boat | |
|---|---|---|---|---|---|---|
| | PSNR | NC | PSNR | NC | PSNR | NC |
| Gaussian | 26.52 | 0.808 | 26.99 | 0.854 | 25.80 | 0.892 |
| sharpnening | 18.67 | 0.735 | 15.13 | 0.639 | 16.23 | 0.671 |
| Median(3×3) | 26.23 | 0.873 | 26.28 | 0.811 | 25.19 | 0.854 |
| Median(5×5) | 22.40 | 0.738 | 21.81 | 0.710 | 21.27 | 0.696 |

### 4.2 Geometric Attacks

The geometric attacks are further divided into translation, cropping, rotation, flip, and scale. Fig. 5(a) shows a graph for finding the best fitness using proposed algorithm in the watermarked image with an attack of 15 degree rotation, and (b) shows the extracted watermark with NC value of 7.842. As the generations pass, GA finds the optimal fitness by generating better populations. The geometric parameters are evaluated to determine the geometric attack patterns, and the performance of the watermark extraction is listed in Table 5.

The proposed watermarking algorithm can endure translation attacks if the translation is more than 20%, horizontal or vertical flip attacks, and all degree rotation attacks. The watermark can be identified with cropping attacks up to 50%.

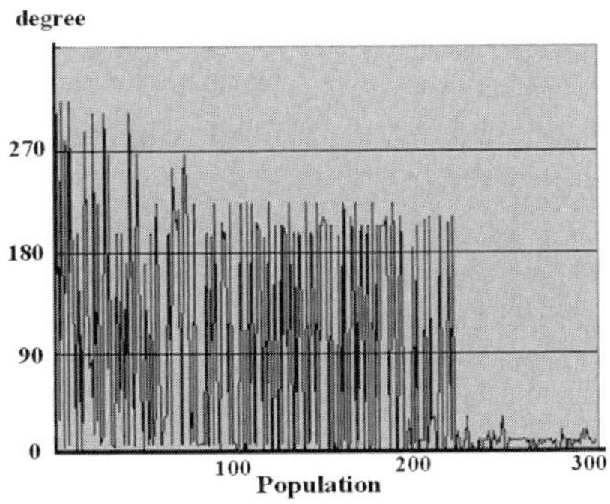


(a)

(b)

**Fig. 5.** (a) A graph of finding the best fitness with an attack of 15 degree rotation, (b) and the extracted watermark

**Table 5.** Experimental results for the geometric attacks

| Geometric attacks | Lena (NC) | Lake (NC) | Boat (NC) | Goldhill (NC) | Drop (NC) | Peppers (NC) |
|---|---|---|---|---|---|---|
| Translation (0.5 pixel) | 0.978 | 0.993 | 0.963 | 0.981 | 0.987 | 0.994 |
| Translation (10 pixel) | 0.977 | 0.981 | 0.976 | 0.979 | 0.986 | 0.980 |
| Translation (30 pixel) | 0.941 | 0.954 | 0.937 | 0.942 | 0.961 | 0.953 |
| Rotation(30°) | 0.711 | 0.719 | 0.704 | 0.730 | 0.778 | 0.718 |
| Rotation(45°) | 0.699 | 0.689 | 0.693 | 0.697 | 0.762 | 0.691 |
| Rotation(90°) | 0.988 | 0.965 | 0.968 | 0.979 | 0.986 | 0.963 |
| Rotation(180°) | 0.970 | 0.975 | 0.984 | 0.973 | 0.984 | 0.986 |
| Cropping(10%) | 0.903 | 0.891 | 0.908 | 0.846 | 0.829 | 0.834 |
| Cropping(20%) | 0.839 | 0.827 | 0.837 | 0.768 | 0.752 | 0.760 |
| Cropping(30%) | 0.791 | 0.656 | 0.802 | 0.669 | 0.654 | 0.659 |
| Cropping(40%) | 0.746 | 0.567 | 0.751 | 0.578 | 0.573 | 0.572 |
| Cropping(50%) | 0.727 | 0.512 | 0.723 | 0.524 | 0.518 | 0.517 |

## 5 Conclusions

In this paper we present a novel watermark extraction algorithm based on DWT and GA. In order to insert the watermark strongly, the proposed algorithm transforms the image into wavelet domain and inserts the watermark into the lowest frequency band. The proposed GA-based watermarking algorithm can effectively extract the watermark with various attacks such as translation and rotation. We also evaluated the performance of the proposed watermarking technique against the attack of image compression such as JPEG and JPEG2000. Further research on other types of geometrical attacks including scaling is in progress in order to ensure more robust watermark extraction.

## Acknowledgments

This research was supported by Korean Ministry of Information and Communication under the HNRC-ITRC program supervised by the IITA.

## References

1. Kang, X., Huang, J., Shi, Y., Lin, Y.: A DWT-DFT Composite Watermarking Scheme Robust to Both Affine Transform and JPEG Compression. IEEE Trans., Vol. 13. Circuits, Systems for Video Technology (2003) 776-786
2. Pereira, S., Pun. T.: "Robust Template Matching for Affine Resistant Image Watermarking. IEEE Trans., Vol. 9. Image Processing (2000) 1123-1129
3. Reddy, A. A., Chatterji, B. N.: A New Wavelet-Based Logo-Watermarking Scheme. Pattern Recognition Letters, Vol. 26. Elsevier (2005) 1019-1027
4. Dawei, Z. L., Guanrong, C., Wenbo L.: A Chaos-Based Robust Wavelet-Domain Watermarking Algorithm. Chaos, Solitons & Fractals, Vol. 22 (2004) 47-54
5. Deguillaume, F., Voloshynovskiy, S., Pun, T.: A Method for the Estimation and Recovering from General Affine Transform in Digital Watermarking Applications. Security and Watermarking of Multimedia Contents IV, Vol. 4675. SPIE (2002) 313-322
6. Dugelay, J. L., Petitcolas, F. A. P.: Possible Counter-Attackers Against Random Geometric Distortions. Security and Watermarking of Multimedia Contents II, Vol. 3971. SPIE (2002) 338-345
7. Braudaway, G. W., Minter, F.: Automatic Recovery of Invisible Image Watermarks from Geometrically Distorted Images. Security and watermarking of multimedia contents I, Vol. 3971. SPIE (2000) 74-81
8. Kang, X., Huang, J., Shi, Y.: An Image Watermarking Algorithm Robust to Geometric Distortion. Lecture Notes in Computer Science, Vol. 2613. Springer-Verlag, Digital Watermarking (2002) 212-223
9. Ali, F. F., Nakao, Z., Chen, Y. W.: An Evolutionary Approach for Graph Coloring. in IEEE, Vol. 5. SMC Conf. (1999) 524-532
10. Oh, W., Kim, H.: The Watermarking Evaluation and Certification Technique of Image. Telecommunications Technology Association, Vol. 90 (2003) 95-103

# Genetic Algorithms for Improving Material Utilization in Manufacturing

Mira Yi[1], Jihyun Hong[2], and Taeho Cho[2]

[1] Division of Marine Electronics & Communication Eng.,
Mokpo National Maritime University, Mokpo, 530-729, S. Korea
yimira@mmu.ac.kr
[2] School of Information & Communication Eng.,
Sungkyunkwan University, Suwon, 440-746, S. Korea
{Jhhong, taecho}@ece.skku.ac.kr

**Abstract.** In modern production industries, computer aided systems have been improving the efficiency and convenience of the various stages of work. However, as the complexity of computerized production systems increases, various techniques are still necessary. The problem we addressed occurs in computer systems that automatically make manufacturing process plans in the metal grating manufacturing industry. In the system, the merging of tasks as a work unit is important to reduce the material loss. However, there is no guarantee that merging always reduces the material loss. So, operators must compare the material loss rates of diverse merging cases to find a near-optimal solution that provides a low material loss rate. In this paper, we apply genetic algorithms to search the near-optimal solution of a planning problem focused on the reduction of material loss. In order to reflect the domain dependent characteristics, we apply genetic algorithms in two levels related each other.

## 1 Introduction

In modern production industries, computer aided systems are common. CAD systems are used for the design stage and CAM systems for the manufacturing stage. Moreover, CIM (Computer Integrated Manufacturing) has been suggested to enhance the efficiency of the manufacturing process by analyzing the overall production process – from design to manufacturing [1,2,3]. This kind of approach increases the complexity of the production system, and needs some techniques to be realized. One of them is to use AI theories and algorithms [4,5] including genetic algorithms.

The genetic algorithm is a randomized search and optimization technique guided by the principle of natural genetic systems [6,7], which is based on the evolution mechanism. A chromosome possessing excellent existence viabilities can generate many offspring compared to other chromosomes. An important characteristic of the genetic algorithm is in that the more superior chromosomes are passed on by selection, crossover and mutation by chance.

Various NP problems have used genetic algorithms to search for a solution [8,9,10]. Most real life problems cannot be solved in a polynomial amount of time

D.-S. Huang, K. Li, and G.W. Irwin (Eds.): ICIC 2006, LNCS 4113, pp. 717 – 724, 2006.

using any deterministic algorithm. Sometimes, near optimal solutions that can be generated quickly are more desirable than optimal solutions, which require a huge amount of time, when the problem can be modeled as an optimization problem.

In this paper, we deal with a problem that occurs in computer systems that automatically make manufacturing process plans in the metal grating manufacturing industry. The grating production system that we face has been using computerized systems, called GPSS (Grating Processing Scheduling System), to improve efficiency of the production process [11]. The most core part in GPSS is the *cutting-planning* module, which automatically arranges grating items in a grating panel to be cut. The cutting-planning module was developed for the purpose of reducing material loss. A task is the unit for the cutting-planning command, and tasks can be merged to reduce the material loss significantly. However, there is no guarantee that the result of cutting-planning by merging of tasks always reduces the material loss. So, operators should compare the material loss rates of diverse merging cases to find a near-optimal merging solution that provides a low material loss rate. To find the optimal task-merging solution is a combination of NP-hard problems.

In this paper, we apply genetic algorithms to search the near-optimal solution of task-merging problem focused on the reduction of material loss. The paper is organized as follows: Chapter 2 briefly reviews genetic algorithms; Chapter 3 describes the metal grating manufacturing system and defines the problem in the target system; Chapter 4 shows the application of genetic algorithms to the problem; finally, Chapter 5 gives the conclusions.

## 2 Genetic Algorithms

A typical process of the genetic algorithm development includes the following steps [12]: specify the problem, and represent (encode) the problem as a chromosome, define a fitness function to evaluate the chromosome's performance, construct the genetic operators, initialize a population and run genetic algorithms.

The first step is to encode the target problem as a chromosome. A chromosome should be able to represent a solution of the problem, and generally a bit string is used for a chromosome because it is easy to deal with.

The second step is to define a fitness evaluation method. The fitness/objective function is chosen, depending on the problem to be solved, in such a way that the strings (possible solutions) representing good points in the search space have high fitness values. This is the only information (also known as the payoff information) that genetic algorithms use while searching for possible solutions.

The third step is to construct the genetic operators. There are three operators for selection, crossover and mutation. First, the *selection* process copies individual strings (called parent chromosomes) into a tentative new population (known as a mating pool) for genetic operations. The second operator is for *crossover*. The main purpose of crossover is to exchange information between randomly selected parent chromosomes by recombining parts of their genetic material. It combines parts of two parent chromosomes to produce offspring for the next generation. The last operation, *mutation*, is the process by which a random alteration in the genetic structure of a chromosome takes place. Its main aim is to introduce genetic diversity into the population.

## 3 Problem in Grating Process Scheduling System

Our domain is a grating metal manufacturing system. A *grating* is a grid shaped product used to cover water drains, or used as a flooring material for various types of production plants and ships. Figure 1 shows the use (a) and construction (b) of a grating. The grid of a grating is composed of *Bearing-Bars (BB)* and *Cross-Bars (CB)*.

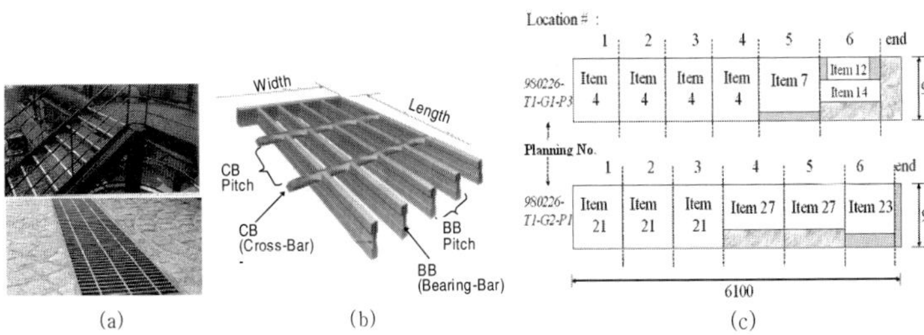


**Fig. 1.** Grating Use (a), Construction (b), and Cutting-planning (c)

The grating production system that we address has been using computerized systems GPSS (Grating Processing Scheduling System) to improve efficiency of the production process. GPSS was developed based on problems provided by the design workers of a factory located near the city of Seoul, South Korea. The core component in GPSS is the *cutting-planning* module, which automatically arranges grating items in a grating panel to be cut. The cutting-planning module was developed for the purpose of reducing the material loss. In Figure 1, (c) shows two panels visualized with the result of cutting planning. In the panels, colored parts are the regions of material loss, and the goal of cutting-planning is to reduce these regions.

For the problem definition, we need to better understand a few terms. A *task* is a set of one or more orders for identical grating uses. A *group* is a set of one or more grating *items*, which have the same grating matrial specification – types of materials (i.e., BB and CB), BB-Pitch and CB-Pitch. A task consists of several groups, and grating items in the same group are manufactured in the same way – e.g., on the same type of machine. In other words, the unit of requirement and delivery is a task, and the unit of process in a production line is a group. Therefore, a task is the unit of the cutting-planning command but the unit of cutting-planning execution is a group.

Tasks (or groups) can be merged to reduce material losses. A task can be merged (henceforth called *'task-merging'*) into a larger task with the constraint that target tasks must have the same type of use ('plant', 'civil', 'frame', etc.), and groups in a merged task can be merged (henceforth called *'group-merging'*) into a larger group if they have the same material specification. Figure 2 shows an example of task-merging, group-merging, and the result of cutting-planning based on merging.

However, there is no guarantee that task-merging and group-merging always reduce the material loss. So, operators should compare the results of cutting-planning according to the various merging cases, repeatedly. It is necessary to search a near-optimal solution of task-merging without cumbersome manual comparison.

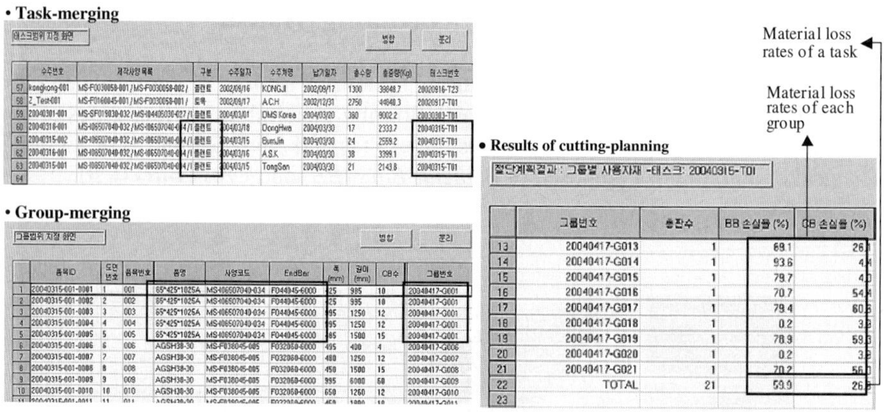


**Fig. 2.** Task-merging, Group-merging and Cutting-planning in GPSS

# 4 Cutting-Planning Using Two-Level Genetic Algorithm

Our approach for the task-merging problem is to use genetic algorithms in two levels. The first level of genetic algorithm is used for task-merging, and the second level is for group-merging to evaluate the fitness of a chromosome for task-merging. Figure 3 shows the relationship between the two levels using the genetic algorithm.

## 4.1 Characteristics of Genetic Algorithms in Two-Level

The first level of Genetic Algorithm is for task-merging. A gene represents the choice of whether or not a task should be merged. A chromosome represents a solution that chooses the tasks to be merged. The number of genes in a chromosome equals to the total number of tasks not planned for machine cutting. We represent each gene as a bit, and each chromosome as a string of bits. The fitness value is the inverse of expected material loss rate based on the task-merging solution. The expected material loss rate is evaluated as follows:

- Material loss rate = ($\sum$ material loss of each task not to be merged + $\sum$ material loss of each group-merging solution for tasks to be merged ) / ($\sum$ material demand of each task not to be merged + $\sum$ material demand of each group-merging solution for tasks to be merged )

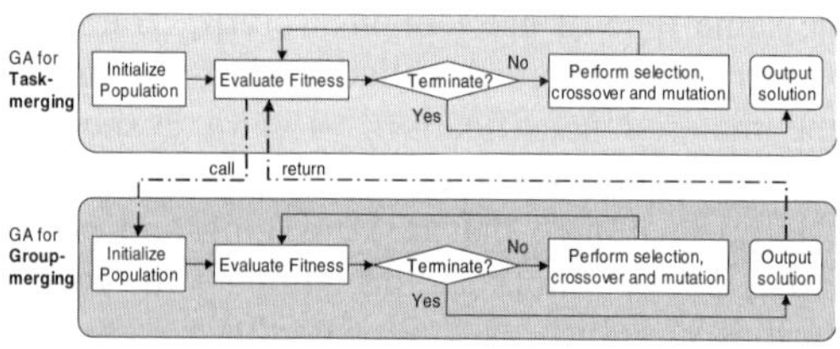


**Fig. 3.** Two-level Genetic Algorithms Flow for Cutting-planning

The second level of Genetic Algorithm is for group-merging. A gene represents the choice of whether or not a group is to be merged, and a chromosome represents a solution that chooses the groups (included in the same merged task) to be merged. The number of genes in a chromosome equals the total number of groups in a merged task. We represent each gene as a bit, and each chromosome as a string of bits. The fitness value is the inverse of the expected material loss rate based on the group-merging solution. The expected material loss rate is evaluated like this:

– Material loss rate = (∑ Material loss of each group not to be merged + Material loss of the groups to be merged) / (∑ Material demand of each group not to be merged + Material demand of the groups to be merged)

There are three generic operators (selection, crossover and mutation) to evolve a population. We used *stochastic universal selection* [13] method to generate a better population from the old population, the single-point-crossover method to exchange information between chromosomes, and the bit-negation mutation method to generate the next new population. We used the probabilities of 0.9 and 0.01 – generally accepted values – for performing crossover and mutation, respectively.

## 4.2 Procedure of Two-Level Genetic Algorithms

This section describes the procedure of the two-level genetic algorithm for a sample task. As shown in Table 1, the sample task is composed of abstract data from the GPSS. There are seven tasks that could be merged.

The first generation of a population for task-merging is initialized at random, such as (1110111, 1111000, 0001111, 0000000). Table 2 describes the populations for group-merging related to the first generation in Level 1, and 1/fitness (not fitness because this domain is more focused on material loss).

For the evolution of the first generation, the first step is to evaluate the fitness of chromosomes. For example, to evaluate the fitness of chromosome 1 (1110111) fromgeneration G1 in Level 1, we need a solution of the group-merging related to the chromosome 1. The target tasks {T1,T2,T3,T4,T5,T6} to be merged have two types of uses: {T1,T2,T5} for 'Plant' and {T3,T6,T7} for 'Civil'. Therefore, two group-merging solutions are needed, and two sets of the groups related to the solutions are

**Table 1.** Sample Tasks Including Groups

| Task ID | Use | Group ID | Material Specification: Grat. Spec. ID | Material Specification: End Bar Type | Items |
|---|---|---|---|---|---|
| T1 | Plant | T1G1 | 1. MS-F0190045-002 | F0190045-6100 | T1-1, T1-2, ... |
| | | T1G2 | 3. MS-F0320030-001 | L040050-6100 | T1-1, T1-2, ... |
| T2 | Plant | T2G1 | 1. MS-F0190045-002 | F0190045-6100 | T2-1, T2-2, ... |
| | | T2G2 | 2. MS-F0380045-005 | F0380045-6100 | T2-1, T2-2, ... |
| | | T2G3 | 3. MS-F0320030-001 | L040050-6100 | T2-1, T2-2, ... |
| T3 | Civil | T4G1 | 4. MS-I06507040-034 | F044045-6000 | T3-1, T3-2, ... |
| | | T4G2 | 5. MS-I05005030-001 | F050050-6100 | T3-1, T3-2, ... |
| T4 | Plant | T4G1 | 3. MS-F0320030-001 | L040050-6100 | T4-1, T4-2, ... |
| | | T4G2 | 1. MS-F0190045-002 | F0190045-6100 | T4-1, T4-2, ... |
| | | T4G3 | 2. MS-F0380045-005 | F0380045-6100 | T4-1, T4-2, ... |
| T5 | Plant | T5G1 | 3. MS-F0320030-001 | L040050-6100 | T5-1, T5-2, ... |
| T6 | Civil | T6G1 | 5. MS-I05005030-001 | F050050-6100 | T6-1, T6-2, ... |
| T7 | Civil | T7G1 | 4. MS-I06507040-034 | F044045-6000 | T7-1, T7-2, ... |
| | | T7G2 | 5. MS-I05005030-001 | F050050-6100 | T7-1, T7-2, ... |

**Table 2.** Populations in Levels 1& 2, and Fitness of Chromosomes

| Level 1 | | | | | Level 2 | | | | | |
|---|---|---|---|---|---|---|---|---|---|---|
| Gen | No | Chromosome {T1,T2,T3,T4,T5,T6,T7} | 1/Fitness BB | 1/Fitness CB | Set | Gen. | No | Chromosome | 1/Fitness BB | 1/Fitness CB |
| G1 | 1 | 1 1 1 0 1 1 1 | 39 | 20 | **S1:{T1G1, T1G2, T2G1, T2G1, T2G3, T5G1}** | | | | | |
| | | | | | | G1 | 1 | 1 1 1 1 1 1 | | |
| | | | | | | | 2 | 1 1 1 0 0 0 | | |
| | | | | | | | 3 | 0 0 0 1 1 1 | | |
| | | | | | | | 4 | 0 0 0 0 0 0 | | |
| | | | | | | G2 | 1 | 1 1 1 1 1 1 | | |
| | | Fitness by the loss rate of **'S1'** group-merging, **'S2'** group-merging, and **T4**. | | | | | 2 | 1 1 1 1 1 1 | | |
| | | | | | | | 3 | 1 1 1 1 1 1 | | |
| | | | | | | | 4 | 1 1 1 1 1 1 | | |
| | | | | | | : | : | : | : | : |
| | | | | | | $Gm_1$ | : | : | 35 | 21 |
| | | | | | **S2:{T3G1, T3G2, T6G1, T7G1, T7G2}** | | | | | |
| | | | | | | G1 | 1 | 1 1 0 1 1 | | |
| | | | | | | | 2 | 1 1 1 0 0 | | |
| | | | | | | | 3 | 0 0 1 1 1 | | |
| | | | | | | | 4 | 0 0 0 0 0 | | |
| | | | | | | : | : | : | : | : |
| | | | | | | $Gm_2$ | : | : | 45 | 18 |
| | 2 | 1 1 1 1 0 0 0 | 30 | 18 | **S1:{T1G1, T1G2, T2G1, T2G1, T2G3, T4G1, T4G1, T4G3}** | | | | | |
| | | Fitness by the loss rate of **'S1'** group-merging, **T3**,.**T5**, **T6** and **T7**. | | | | G1 | 1 | 1 1 1 1 1 1 1 1 1 | | |
| | | | | | | | 2 | 1 1 1 1 0 0 0 0 | | |
| | | | | | | | : | : | : | : |
| | | | | | | : | : | : | : | : |
| | | | | | | $Gm_1$ | : | : | 26 | 15 |
| | 3 | 0 0 0 1 1 1 1 | 54 | 25 | **S1: { T4G1, T4G2, T4G3, T5G1 }** | | | | | |
| | | Fitness by the loss rate of **'S1'** group-merging, **'S2'** group-merging, **T1**, **T2**, **T3** and **T5**. | | | | : | : | : | 41 | 30 |
| | | | | | **S2: { T6G1, T7G1, T7G2 }** | | | | | |
| | | | | | | : | : | : | 46 | 20 |
| | 4 | 0 0 0 0 0 0 0 | 62 | 33 | **No group set to be merged** | | | | | |
| G2 | 1 | 1 1 1 0 1 0 0 | | | **S1:{T1G1, T1G2, T2G1, T2G1, T2G3, T5G1}** | | | | | |
| | 2 | 1 1 1 0 0 1 1 | | | **S1:{T1G1, T1G2, T2G1, T2G1, T2G3}** | | | | | |
| | 3 | 0 0 0 1 0 0 0 | | | **No group set to be merged** | | | | | |
| | 4 | 1 1 1 1 0 1 1 | | | **S1:{T1G1, T1G2, T2G1, T2G1, T2G3, T4G1, T4G1, T4G3}** | | | | | |
| : | : | : | : | : | | | | : | : | : |

* BB and CB represent bearing-bar loss rate and cross-bar loss rate, respectively.

{T1G1,T1G2,T2G1,T2G2, T2G3,T5G1} and {T3G1,T3G2,T6G1,T7G1,T7G2}. Each set of groups is another problem that is dealt with in Level 2. The fitness of the chromosomes in Level 2 is evaluated by using information based on the material specification and the size of items belonging to the groups.

After fitness evaluation, the evolution of generations can be run. Figure 4 describes the procedure of the reproduction that creates the new population (G2) from G1. The main operations are selection of two parent chromosomes based on the fitness values (chromosome 3 is selected twice, while chromosome 4 is not done), crossover of which points are 5 and 4, and mutation at position 4 of the 2nd chromosome and position 5 of the 4th chromosome. The procedure as shown in Figure 4 continues until the average fitness of the chromosomes converges to a near-optimal value.

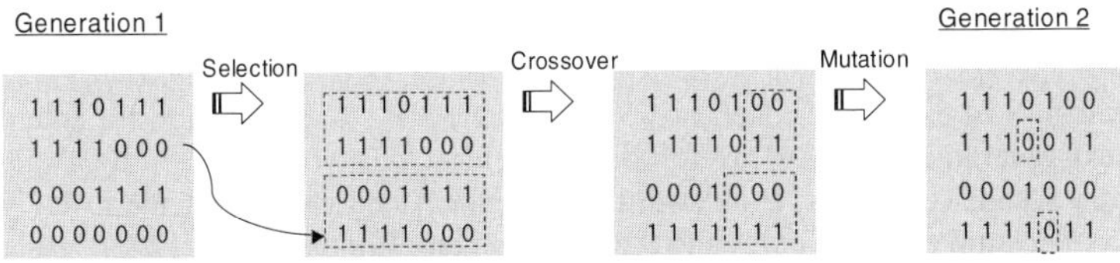


**Fig. 4.** Evolution of Generations

### 4.3 Result of Application of Genetic Algorithms

We applied the above two-level genetic algorithms to real data, and the result was acceptable. We compared two methods of searching for the near-optimal solutions of task-merging: to search for the solution manually and using the two-level genetic algorithm. Figures 5 compare the material loss rate and the number of task-merging occurrences by the two methods. In the manual search method, we executed the task-merging 200 times. In the genetic algorithm search method, the populations were evolved by generating 30 chromosomes 20 times.

As shown in the right, a near-optimal solution is obtained for which the material loss rate converges a low value, while in the left it is not easy to determine which solution is near-optimal. In addition, operators can be freed from the burden of repeatedly comparing the material loss rates according to the diverse merging cases.

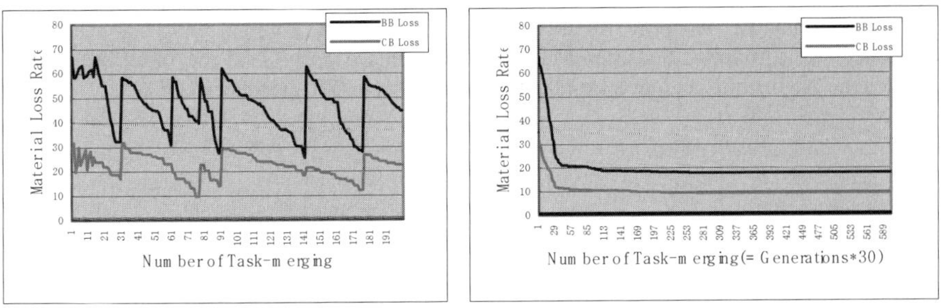


**Fig. 5.** Searching for Merging Solution Manually (left) and Using Genetic Algorithm (right)

## 5 Conclusion

In this paper, we presented how genetic algorithms could be applied to improve material utilization with a real industry example. In order to reflect the domain dependent characteristics, we needed a two-level genetic algorithm with the relationship that the fitness of one level is evaluated based on the near-optimal solution of the other level. We had very good results for the application compared to the traditional method, even though the parameters of the genetic algorithms were tuned roughly. However, more tuning is needed for optimal solutions.

Future work includes the application of genetic algorithms for scheduling systems in grating manufacturing, and the generalization of multi-level genetic algorithms based on the two-level approach of this paper.

## References


1. Szykman, S., Fenves, S.J., Keirouz, W., Shooter, S.B.: A Foundation for Interoperability in Next-generation Product Development Systems. CAD, vol.33, No.7 (2001) 545-559
2. Kalyan-Seshu, U.S., Bras, B.: Towards Computer Aided Design for the Life Cycle. IEEE Int. Symposium on Electronics and the Environment, Illinois, USA (1998) 310-315
3. Swain, J.J., Farrington, P.A.: Designing Simulation Experiments for Evaluating Manufacturing Systems. Proc. of the Winter Simulation Conference (1994) 69-76
4. Monostori, L., Kadar, B., Viharos, Zs. J., Mezgar, I., Stefan, P.: Combined Use of Simulation and AI/Machine Learning Techniques in Designing Manufacturing Process and Systems. CIRP (2000) 199-204
5. 5. Zhang, Y.F., Nee, A.Y.C.: Using Genetic algorithms in Process Planning for Job Shop Machine. IEEE Trans. Evolutionary Computation, Vol.1 (1997) 278-289
6. Bandyopadhyay, S., Maulik, U.: An Improved Evolutionary Algorithm as Function Optimizer. IETE Journal of Research, Jan-Apr (2000) 47-56
7. Goldberg, David E.: Genetic Algorithms. Addison Wesley (1999)
8. Bryant, K.: Genetic Algorithms and the Traveling Salesman Problem. Department of Mathematics, Harvery Mudd College (2000)
9. Hohn, C., Reeves, C.: Graph Partitioning Using Genetic Algorithms. in Proc. of the 2nd Int. Conf. on Massively Parallel Computing Systems, Ischia, Italy (1996) 27-43
10. Jawahar, N., Aravindan, P., Ponnambalam, S. G.: A Genetic Algorithm for Scheduling Flexible Manufacturing Systems. Int. Journal of Advanced Manufacturing Technology, UK, Vol.14, No.7 (1998) 765-771
11. Koh, J., Cho, T.: A Simulation of Production Planning Strategies for the Improvement of a Manufacturing Process. Journal of Korea Society for Simulation, Vol.8, No.2 (1999) 23-35
12. Negnevistsky, M.: Artificial Intelligence. Addison Wesley (2005)
13. Baker, J. E.: Adaptive Selection Methods for Genetic Algorithms. Proc. of an Int. Conf. on Genetic Algorithms and their Application, New Jersey, USA (1985) 101-111

# Improved Differential Evolution with Dynamic Population Size

Fuzhuo Huang, Ling Wang, and Bo Liu

Department of Automation, Tsinghua University, Beijing 100084, China
hfz02@mails.tsinghua.edu.cn, wangling@tsinghua.edu.cn

**Abstract.** As a novel evolutionary computing technique, recently Differential Evolution (DE) has attracted much attention and wide applications due to its simple concept and easy implementation. However, all the control parameters of the classic DE (crossover rate, scaling factor, and population size) keep fixed during the searching process. To improve the performance of DE, an improved DE (IDE) with dynamic population size is proposed in this paper. Simulation results and comparisons based on some well-known benchmarks and an IIR design problem show the good efficiency of the proposed IDE.

## 1 Introduction of DE

Consider the following minimization problem:

$$\min \quad f(X), X = [x_1, ..., x_n], \text{ s.t. } X \in D. \tag{1}$$

where $f$ and $X$ denote the objective function and the decision vector constrained by the domain $D$ respectively.

Recently, evolutionary algorithms (EAs) have been considered as effective methods to solve complex optimization problems. The basic steps of an EA are: select several samples in $D$ to form a population; replace the old sample in the population with the new one according to the objective function of each sample. These two steps should be well designed to enhance the exploration and exploitation abilities to achieve good optimization performances. As a novel EA, Differential Evolution (DE) has attracted much attention and wide applications due to its simple concept and easy implementation. Firstly, DE randomly chooses *NP* samples to form a population, where *NP* denotes population size.

Then, DE creates a competitor for each sample by mutation operation, and combines the old sample and the competitor to a new sample by crossover operation. Finally, DE selects the better sample between the old one and the new one as a solution of the new population. If the best solution found so far keeps fixed for a certain number of generations (see the remark in the Appendix), DE stops and it outputs the best solution.

The *mutation* is implemented as follows:

$$u = a + F(b - c). \tag{2}$$

D.-S. Huang, K. Li, and G.W. Irwin (Eds.): ICIC 2006, LNCS 4113, pp. 725 – 730, 2006.

Where $a$, $b$ and $c$ are three different samples from the old population, $F$ is scaling factor between [0, 1], and $(b-c)$ denotes the differential item.

The *crossover* is implemented as follows:

$$v_{ij} = \begin{cases} x_{ij} & if\,(rand(j) \le CR) \quad or \quad j = rnbr(i) \\ u_{ij} & if\,(rand(j) > CR) \quad and \quad j \ne rnbr(i) \end{cases} \qquad j = 1,2,...,n\,. \tag{3}$$

where $CR$ denotes crossover rate within [0,1], $x_{ij}$ denotes the old sample, $u_{ij}$ denotes the new sample, $rnbr(i)$ denotes a random integer within $[1,n]$ that makes sure that at least one components of $x$ and $v$ are same.

In the classic DE, all the control parameters (crossover rate, scaling factor, and population size) are constant parameters. To improve the performance of DE, we will propose an improved DE (IDE) with dynamic population size in this paper.

## 2 Effect of Population Size on DE

Usually, population size is a crucial parameter of EA. Experimental results [1] showed that with larger $NP$, DE is easier to find the best solution, but larger computational costs are needed. There are two main criterions to judge the performance of DE, i.e., final best solution to show the effectiveness and *nfe* (number of function evaluations) to show the efficiency. Based on seven benchmarks listed in Appendix, ten independent simulations are carried out for each benchmark. The results are listed in Table 1.

From Table 1, firstly it can be seen that *nfe* increases as $NP$ increases. Secondly, the global minimum may not be attained if $NP$ is too small.

So, it is concluded that larger $NP$ causes more calculation but makes DE have higher probability to find the global minimum.

Next, we will design an improved DE with dynamic population size.

**Table 1.** Average result of 10 times experiments

| *NP* | | 5 | 15 | 25 | 35 |
|---|---|---|---|---|---|
| *Fun1* | best value | 0.00 | 0.00 | 0.00 | 0.00 |
| | *nfe* | 940 | 2427 | 4295 | 5677 |
| *Fun2* | best value | 0.10 | 0.00 | 0.00 | 0.00 |
| | *nfe* | 1587 | 2222 | 4185 | 5684 |
| *Fun3* | best value | 2.40 | 0.00 | 0.00 | 0.00 |
| | *nfe* | 1381 | 2892 | 4895 | 6272 |
| *Fun4* | best value | 17.7 | 13.6 | 13.4 | 13.3 |
| | *nfe* | 1662 | 6042 | 8850 | 11189 |
| *Fun5* | best value | 5.88 | 0.998 | 0.998 | 0.998 |
| | *nfe* | 887 | 3114 | 4940 | 5740 |
| *Fun6* | best value | 1.53 | 0.00 | 0.00 | 0.00 |
| | *nfe* | 1870 | 3000 | 4575 | 6559 |
| *Fun7* | best value | 1.83 | 0.004 | 0.000 | 0.000 |
| | *nfe* | 4407 | 10671 | 15840 | 23233 |

## 3 Improved DE

To change $NP$ dynamically, we should firstly make clear the searching behavior of DE. We introduce the following variable $\sigma$ as the variance of samples of population.

$$\sigma = \frac{1}{NP} \sum_{i=1}^{NP} \sum_{j=1}^{n} (x_{ij} - \bar{x}_j)^2 . \tag{4}$$

where $\bar{x}_j$ denotes the average solution of the population. Obviously, if $\sigma$ is zero, all the samples of the population are same.

During our test on the classic DE, it was found that: sometimes the samples converge to the best sample that does not change, but the variance becomes small very quickly; sometimes a new best solution is found, and the variance becomes small but relatively slowly. Thus, in the former situation, we should stress the exploitation to converge to the best solution, so the population can be smaller; in the later situation, we should stress the exploration to find the best solution, so the population should be larger. Therefore, an operation is added in DE after the *selection* operation to adjust $NP$. In particular, the variance of population is calculated first according to Equation (4). To avoid the noise of population, the average variance of last 10 generations is used. If the ratio of average variances between two consecutive generations is greater than 0.98, and the best solution keeps fixed at least 5 generations, then let DE work in Mode 1. That is, decrease the population size by removing the worst sample. If the best changes, then let DE work in Mode 2. That is, increase the population size by adding a new random sample into the population. Besides, during the dynamic searching process, $NP$ is limited within $[NP_{\max}/2, NP_{\max}]$ ( $NP_{\max}$ is predefined number).

To test the performance of the IDE, computational simulations are carried out based on the seven benchmarks. The parameter settings for DE and IDE are shown in Table 2, where $NP$ of DE is fixed and in IDE the $NP_{\max} = NP$ . The two algorithms can both find the best solution, but IDE can find the best solution with less *nfe* as shown in Table 2. In addition, Fig. 1(a)-(e) show the dynamic searching processes of DE and IDE (the average of 10 times running for each method-function pair), from which the superior efficiency of IDE over that of DE is also demonstrated.

**Table 2.** Results and parameter settings of DE and IDE

| *Fun* | DE (*nfe*) | IDE (*nfe*) | *NP* | *CR* | *F* |
|---|---|---|---|---|---|
| 1 | 1023.5 | 935.0 | 5 | 0.1 | 0.9 |
| 2 | 1730.0 | 1382.5 | 10 | 0.9 | 0.9 |
| 3 | 2069.0 | 1919.0 | 10 | 0.0 | 0.9 |
| 4 | 3661.0 | 2691.1 | 10 | 0.0 | 0.9 |
| 5 | 3740.0 | 2670.4 | 20 | 0.2 | 0.5 |
| 6 | 1955.0 | 1533.5 | 10 | 0.0 | 0.5 |
| 7 | 16165.0 | 15707.1 | 25 | 0.2 | 0.5 |

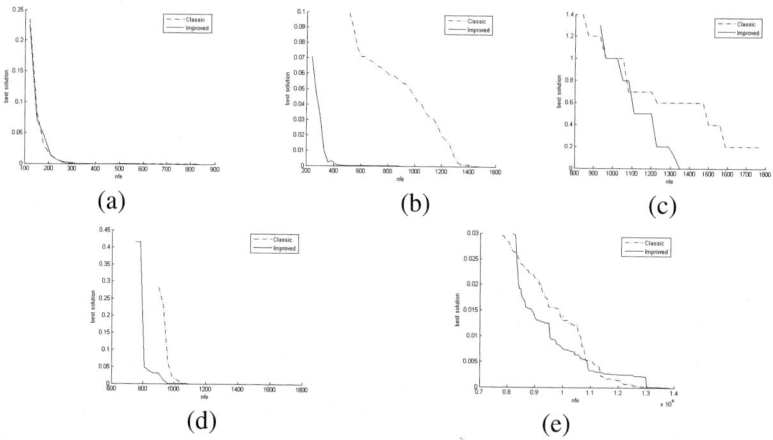


**Fig. 1.** (a) Average curves on Fun 1. (b) Average curves on Fun 2. (c) Average curves on Fun 3. (d) Average curves on Fun 5. (e) Average curves on Fun 7.

# 5 Simulation on IIR Filter Design

Consider the following second-order system and first-order IIR filter:

$$H_p[z^{-1}] = \frac{0.05 - 0.4z^{-1}}{1.0 - 1.1314z^{-1} + 0.25z^{-2}}, \quad H_f[z^{-1}] = \frac{a_0}{1.0 - b_1 z^{-1}}. \tag{5}$$

The system input is a white sequence with unit variance. The output length used in calculating the MSE is 2000. The global minimum is at $a_0 = 0.31$, $b_1 = 0.89$, there is a local minimum $(0.7, -0.4)$. With proper parameters, both DE and IDE can find the best solution. The *nfe* of DE is 6372, while that of IDE is 5843.4. In Fig. 2, the convergence curves of the two methods are illustrated, which demonstrates the good efficiency of the IDE.

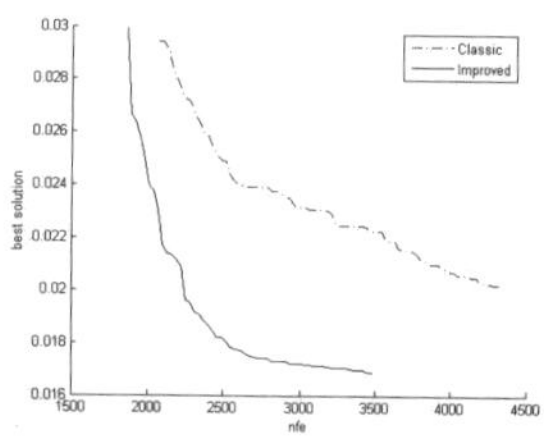


**Fig. 2.** Average curves of DE and IDE

# 6 Conclusions

To enhance the performance of DE, in this paper an improved DE with dynamic population size was proposed. Simulation results demonstrated the good efficiency of the IDE. The future work is to study adaptive mechanism for other parameters.

## Acknowledgements

This research is partially supported by NSF of China (Grant No. 60374060 and 60574072) as well as the 973 Program (Grant No. 2002CB312200).

## References

1. Storn, R., Price, K.: Differential Evolution-A Simple and Efficient Heuristic for Global Optimization over Continuous Spaces. Journal of Global Optimization 11 (1997) 341-359
2. Mayer, D.G., Kinghorn, B.P., Archer, A.A.: Differential Evolution - An Easy and Efficient Evolutionary Algorithm for Model Optimization. Agricultural Systems 83 (2005) 315-328
3. Price, K.V.: Differential Evolution: A Fast and Simple Numerical Optimizer. Proc. of North American Fuzzy Information Processing Society (1996)
4. Kalinlia, A., Karabogab, N.: Artificial Immune Algorithm for IIR Filter Design, Engineering Applications of Artificial Intelligence 18 (2005) 919-929

## Appendix: Seven Benchmarks

*Fun 1*: First De Jong function (sphere)

$$f_1(x)=\sum_{j=1}^{3} x_j^{\,2}, x_j \in [-5.12,5.12], DTG: 1.0\times 10^{-6}. \tag{6}$$

*Fun2*: Second De Jong function (Rosenbrock's sanddle)

$$f_2(x)=100\times(x_2-x_1^{\,2})^2+(1-x_1)^2, x_j\in[-2.084, 2.084], DTG: 1.0\times 10^{-6}. \tag{7}$$

*Fun3*: Modified third De Jong function (step)

$$f_3(x)=\sum_{j=1}^{5}\lfloor x_j \rfloor^2, x_j\in[-5.12,5.12], DTG: 1.0\times 10^{-6}. \tag{8}$$

*Fun4*: Modified fourth De Jong function (quartic)

$$f_4(x)=\sum_{j=1}^{30}(j\times x_j^{\,4}+\eta),\ \eta = random[0,1], x_j\in[-1.28,1.28], DTG: 1.0\times 10^{-6}. \tag{9}$$

*Fun5*: Fifth De Jong fuction (Shekel's Foxholes)

$$f_5(x)=\frac{1}{0.002+\sum_{i=0}^{24}\frac{1}{i+\sum_{j=1}^{2}(x_j-a_{ij})^6}}\quad a_{ij}=\begin{bmatrix}-32,-16,0,16,32,-32...\\ -32,-32,-32,-32,-32,-16...\end{bmatrix}, \tag{10}$$

$x_j \in [-65.536, 65.536], DTG: 1.0\times 10^{-6}$.

*Fun6*:Corana's Parabola Inger (1993), Cornana te al.(1987)

$$f_6(x) = \sum_{j=1}^{4} \begin{cases} 0.15(z_j - 0.05\,\mathrm{sgn}(z_j))^2 \bullet d_j & if \left|x_j - z_j\right| < 0.5 \\ d_j \bullet x_j^{\ 2} & otherwise \end{cases} \quad d_j = \{1,1000,10,100\},$$

$$z_j = \left\lfloor \left|\frac{x_j}{0.2}\right| + 0.49999 \right\rfloor \bullet \mathrm{sgn}(x_j) \bullet 0.2, x_j \in [-100,100], DTG : 1.0\times10^{-6}. \tag{11}$$

*Fun7*: Generalized Griewank Function

$$f_7(x) = \sum_{j=1}^{10} \frac{xj2}{4000} - \prod_{j=1}^{10} \cos(\frac{x_j}{\sqrt{j}}) + 1, x_j \in [-400,400], DTG : 1.0\times10^{-6}. \tag{12}$$

Remark: DTG (difference of two generations) is used to end the algorithm. That is, if the difference of the best solutions of successive two generations is smaller than DTG for successive 50 generations, DE will stop.

# Redundant Space Manipulator Optimization Design Based on Genetic Algorithm of Immunity

Huan Li[1], Jianmin Jiao[2], and Hongfu Zuo[2]

[1] Software College, Dahongying Education Group, Ningbo 315175, China
[2] Civil Aviation College, Nanjing University of Aeronautics and Astronautics, Yudao Street, Nanjing 210016, China
jjmlh@163.com

**Abstract.** To solve the problem of designing a one fault tolerant, one degree of redundancy, space manipulator; a new multi-mode function optimization algorithm is presented. Kinematics redundancy is an important method to improve the reliability of a space manipulator. A kinematics redundant manipulator design bears multi-parameters, non-linearity and multi-mode. This problem can't be solved by a conventional optimization method. By simulating antibody search mechanism, combined with immune system theory, the antibody diversity is maintained, and full-scale searching is carried out- realizing the multi-parameters non-linear multi-mode manipulator design. The design example shows that the presented algorithm is effective.

## 1 Introduction

In harmful circumstances such as radioactive locations, contaminated circumstances, mines, deep sea, or astrospace, the manipulator is very helpful. When the manipulator is used in foul circumstances, it easily malfunctions. We must improve the reliability of manipulators. We must find a way to make the manipulator fulfill its tasks when it goes into trouble. So, the fault tolerant technique is considered in the manipulator designing moment [1-3]. A fault tolerant space manipulator optimal design and analysis method is put forward in this paper, and this method is effective in engineering. All these are carried out on the basis of thorough analysis of a space manipulator. Working with high reliability, with many joints and freedoms, is the demand and characteristic of a space manipulator. The central content of this thesis is how to design a highly reliable redundant manipulator based on the special task.

Every degree of freedom in a serial manipulator is expressed by three character parameters, so an $n$ degree manipulator possesses $3n$ parameters. The designing process is to determine the $3n$ parameters. We can find that manipulator designing possesses multi-parameter characteristics. Based on relations between the freedoms, the serial manipulator kinematics equations can be established, which contains the $3n$ parameters to be determined. Because the equations have inexhaustible roots, so the definite parameters of the manipulator can't be selected exclusively. So the manipulator designing process is an optimization problem. On the other hand, within the sets of parameters, there exist many local optimal ones, so the manipulator designing process

D.-S. Huang, K. Li, and G.W. Irwin (Eds.): ICIC 2006, LNCS 4113, pp. 731 – 736, 2006.

possesses a multi-mode characteristic. At last, there are many trigonometric functions in the equations, so the manipulator designing process possesses nonlinear characteristics.

The object of multi-mode function optimization is to acquire a whole scale optimal solution on the basis of a local optimal solution. The conventional step based optimization method goes to local convergence easily, while the whole scale optimal solution can't be searched out [4]. The genetic algorithm can search out local optimal solutions, but the antibody population converges easily to a single mode. The immune system, as a kind of distributed self-learning system, deals with different antibody evolutional, and effectively identifies antigens, so that the different antibodies survive simultaneously. It possesses an optimization and diversification retaining function [5-8].

Adhering to this idea, the immune concept and theory are applied to the genetic optimization algorithm. The kinematics equations are thoroughly analyzed, and the adaptability function used in the optimization operation is established, a new novel immunity genetic arithmetic is presented. From the practical optimization outcome, we can make sure that the algorithm is feasible, the optimal fault tolerant manipulator is acquired, meeting the design conditions.

## 2 Mathematical Modal of Redundant Manipulator Optimal Design

The operating object of a manipulator is a certain spatial volume in space. The working space can be expressed by some representational characteristic points from the point of engineering. If the manipulator end-effecter can reach these points, then we can say that the manipulator end-effecter can reach any points in the working space. In the design of the manipulator, these characteristic points can be used to test the satisfaction of the design.

The spatial transform between any two adjacent arm reference frames $\{i\}$ and $\{i-1\}$ of a serial manipulator is expressed as:

$$ {}^{i-1}_{i}T = \begin{bmatrix} c\theta_i & -s\theta_i & 0 & a_{i-1} \\ s\theta_i c\alpha_{i-1} & c\theta_i c\alpha_{i-1} & -s\alpha_{i-1} & -d_i s\alpha_{i-1} \\ s\theta_i s\alpha_{i-1} & c\theta_i s\alpha_{i-1} & c\alpha_{i-1} & d_i c\alpha_{i-1} \\ 0 & 0 & 0 & 1 \end{bmatrix} . \tag{1} $$

Parameters $a_{i-1}, \alpha_{i-1}, d_{i-1}, \theta_i$ are the length of arms, torsion angle, translational distance and joint angle. The manipulator kinematics equation is

$$ {}^{0}_{1}T\,{}^{1}_{2}T\,{}^{2}_{3}T \ldots {}^{n-1}_{n}T = {}^{0}_{n}T \ . \tag{2} $$

The manipulator designing process is to find out the $3n$ parameters $v_{dh}$ by (2). For redundancy manipulator, (2) has many roots, we can't make certain $v_{dh}$ uniquely. For a certain object point, if the manipulator can reach it, then the imaginary numbers of joint angles are zero. If the manipulator can't reach the point, then there are complex number joint values. And the farther the manipulator parameters are to perfect, the bigger the absolute values of imaginary numbers are. The penalty function must relate with the degree of the present manipulator parameters to the perfect. The penalty function can be set up as follows:

$$F_1 = \sum_{all\ object\ points} min\begin{pmatrix} the\ \ sum\ \ of\ \ absolute\ \ values \\ of\ \ every\ \ joint\ \ imaginery\ \ value \end{pmatrix} . \tag{3}$$

When penalty function $F_1$changes to zero, it denotes that the manipulator can reach all the object points. At this time, we can only say the manipulator can reach all the points, but the manipulator may not be fault tolerant. For a certain point, every joint works in a certain angle range. So for all points, every joint has a common angle range turning in, and this range may be zero, or non-zero. Accumulate all the common ranges, the bigger the sum is, the bigger the possibility of a manipulator fault tolerant. This sum can be used as penalty function $F_2$ for further optimization.

$$F_2 = \sum_{all\ \ joints} (the\ \ common\ \ range\ \ to\ \ all\ \ object\ \ points\ \ for\ \ a\ \ joint) . \tag{4}$$

Set up final penalty function $F(\theta_1, \theta_2, \theta_3)$, so that the value $F$ relates with the degree of the manipulator parameters to the perfect fault tolerant manipulator parameters.

$$F(\theta_1, \theta_2, \theta_3) = \begin{cases} F_1, & for\ \ F_1 \neq 0 \\ F_2, & for\ \ F_1 = 0\ \ and F_3 = 0 \\ F_3, & for\ \ F_3 = 1 \end{cases} . \tag{5}$$

The process of redundant manipulator design is to change the manipulator parameters continually according to the definite optimization arithmetic, evaluate the corresponding penalties $F_1$ 、 $F_2$ 、 $F_3$, so that $F_1$ turns to zero, then keep $F_1$ being zero, make $F_2$ increase continually, until $F_3$ equals 1. At this time, the manipulator parameters possess the characteristic of one degree of fault tolerant for a special task.

The aforementioned penalty theory is so complex that it can't be discussed in detail, but it has been proven to be correct.

## 3 Implementation of Immunity Genetic Algorithm

Fitness function can express the degree of a set of parameters to optimal. The fitness function can be defined based on penalty function $F(F_1, F_2, F_3)$:

$$fitness = \frac{1}{1+F_1} + F_2 . \tag{6}$$

### 3.1 Basic Definition

*Antigen:* The best optimal mode of the object function, such as a set of redundancy manipulator parameters, expressed as '*ag*'.

*Antibody:* The possible mode of the best optimal mode, expressed as '$ab_i$', it is coded with real number, $ab_i = [ab_i^1, ab_i^2, \ldots ab_i^m, \ldots ab_i^L]$. $ab_i^m$ is real number, it is one element of the set of parameters. $L$ is the length of code, equaling the number of independent variables, it is the number of parameters.

$f_i$: The affinity of $ab_i$ to $ag$, $f_i>0$;  $f_{i,j}$ is the affinity of $ab_i$ to $ab_j$, $f_{i,j}>0$.

*Immunity network:* $AIN = \{ab_i\}, i = [1,2,...,N_1]$ , the carrier of self organized manipulator optimization results, $N_1$ is the number of network antibodies - its value changes with the optimization course.

*AIN*:* memory network.

*New antibody colony:* $NEW = \{ab_i\}, i = [1,2,...,N_2]$ , it is produced randomly to reinforce the imperfect antibodies in immunity network, $N_2$ is the number of new antibodies.

### 3.2 Clone Operation

Set up father antibody $ab_i = [ab_i^1, ab_i^2, ...ab_i^m, ...ab_i^L]$, after clone $ab_i$, a child antibody is produced,

$$ab_i^* = \lfloor ab_i^{1*}, ab_i^{2*}, ..., ab_i^{m*}, ..., ab_i^{L*} \rfloor . \tag{7}$$

'*rand*' is a uniformly distributed random number within [-1.0—1.0], δ is used to confine the degree of aberrance, it is a monotony descending function of $f_i$, the bigger $f_i$ is, the smaller δ. α,β are constants.

$$ab_i^{m*} = ab_i^m + \delta \times rand, \qquad \delta = \alpha e^{-f_i/\beta} . \tag{8}$$

### 3.3 Data Network Regulation

The purpose of network regulation is to delete identical antibodies through restriction between antibodies. Its essence is judgment and deletion of identical antibodies. The detailed arithmetic is: Calculate every affinity between any two antibodies $ab_i(ab_i \in AIN)$ , Set up judgment matrix $A = \{a_{i,j}\}$. When i≠j and $f_{i,j} < k$ , set $a_{i,j} = 1$, otherwise set $a_{i,j} = 0$. $k$ is constant. Examine if all the elements in A are zeros.

1) yes: Then the network has no redundant antibody, set AIN*=AIN, end up regulation.

2) no: i) Calculate line vector $b = A \times [1,1,...,1]^T$ , set the serial number of maximum element in b as $i$, and then set $ab_i$ and all $ab_j$ which $a_{i,j}=1$ as identical antibodies. ii) Delete all the antibodies except the antibody with the biggest affinity to antigen, a new AIN* is produced, the correlative row and line is also deleted in A. iii) Repeat step i) until all elements in A are zeros. Set AIN=AIN*, regulation is finished.

## 4 The Immunity Genetic Based Design of Fault Tolerant Redundant Manipulator

The one degree redundancy one degree fault tolerant spatial position serial manipulator is selected as optimization design object. That is to design a four degrees of freedom serial manipulator. The manipulator end effecter can reach these points on the curve path:(7.4,-1,0),(7.7,-0.6,1.8), (9,1,9),(8,-0.2,3.6), (8.3,0.2,5.4), (8.6,0.6,7.2), If any one joint falls in malfunction, the left three joints can also fulfill the task, making the manipulator reach these task points. The parameters to be optimally determined are the length of every arm, torsional angle, and translational distance. The working range of every joint angle is (-3.14,3.14); The length of arms are *ei2*, its variable range is (0.1,6.0); The translational distance of the arms is zero. The parameters to be optimized are torsional angle and length of arm, *alfa1, alfa2, alfa3, alfa4, ei2*. The optimization outcome is as table 1.

**Table 1.** Optization outcome

| generation | Manipulator parameters |
|---|---|
| 1 | $\alpha_1$=3.068, $\alpha_2$=1.203, $\alpha_3$=-1.622, $\alpha_4$=1.946, $a_2$=5.614 |
| 2 | $\alpha_1$=2.108, $\alpha_2$=-2.136, $\alpha_3$=-2.124, $\alpha_4$=0.047, $a_2$=4.936 |
| 4 | $\alpha_1$=0.414, $\alpha_2$=-1.537, $\alpha_3$=-1.642, $\alpha_4$=-3.040, $a_2$=5.988 |
| 5 | $\alpha_1$=0.414, $\alpha_2$=-1.537, $\alpha_3$=-1.642, $\alpha_4$=-3.040, $a_2$=5.988 |
| 6 | $\alpha_1$=0.414, $\alpha_2$=-1.537, $\alpha_3$=-1.642, $\alpha_4$=-3.040, $a_2$=5.988 |
| 7 | $\alpha_1$=0.414, $\alpha_2$=-1.537, $\alpha_3$=-1.642, $\alpha_4$=-3.040, $a_2$=5.988 |
| 13 | $\alpha_1$=1.853, $\alpha_2$=1.258, $\alpha_3$=2.868, $\alpha_4$=2.229, $a_2$=5.919 |
| 16 | $\alpha_1$=1.853, $\alpha_2$=1.258, $\alpha_3$=2.868, $\alpha_4$=2.229, $a_2$=5.919 |

In the manipulator optimization, the optimized variables are continuous real numbers. If we also adopt binary code, then the effect of these two variations is completely contrary. The second variation will produce a new antibody far away to the original antibody. This is not the original idea of variation. So in this paper, the parameters are decimal coded. The variation will produce a new antibody near to the original antibody. And the degree of variation relates to the fitness of the antibody. The lager the fitness is, the smaller the variation will be. This means it is doing careful optimization. The smaller the fitness is, the larger the variation will be, so as to jump out valley quickly. This immunity system is a kind of distributed auto-study system. From the evolution outcome, we can see that the satisfied manipulator parameters are produced in the second generation, and it becomes more and more optimized in the following generations.

## 5 Conclusion

The biggest characteristic of an immunity algorithm from a genetic algorithm is its' fitness and concentration based antibody promotion and control strategy. The lower fitness antibody can survive normally, at the same time the higher fitness antibody can boost. The cross operation happens not just between better antibodies, so that the new antibodies are produced with diversity. Therefore, the searching space becomes all-sided. This is better for multi-mode function optimization. The perfect parameters are produced in the 64th generation with the penalty optimization method and in the 10th generation with the genetic method. So we can say that the genetic immunity algorithm is best, as it possesses quick optimization speed.

## References

1. Paredis, C.J.J., Khosla, P.K.: Kinematic Design of Serial Link Manipulators from Task Specifications. International Journal of Robotics Research. 12 (1993) 274-287
2. Michael, S., Karol, M.: Optimal Kinematic Design of Spatial Parallel Manipulators: Application to Linear Delta Robot. Transactions of the ASME. 125 (2003)
3. Karol, M.: Design and Applications of Parallel Robots. Robotics Research.. 6 (2003) 161-173
4. Cai, Z.X., Gong, T.: Advance in Research on Immune Algorithms. Control and Decision.19 (2004) 841-846
5. Xu, X.S., Zhu, J.: Immune Algorithm for Multi-modal Function Optimization. Journal of Zhejiang University (Engineering Science). 5 (2004) 530-533
6. Reda, Y., Wenjia, W.: A New Artificial Immune System Algorithm for Clustering. LNCS 3177 (IDEAL 2004) 58–64
7. Chen, T.-C., You, P.-S.: Immune Algorithms based Approach for Redundant Reliability Problems with Multiple Component Choices. Computers in Industry. 56 (2005) 195-205
8. Hao, F., Merlet, J.-P.: Multi-criteria Optimal Design of Parallel Manipulators based on Interval Analysis. Mechanism and Machine Theory. 40 (2005) 157-171

# Two Artificial Intelligence Heuristics in Solving Multiple Allocation Hub Maximal Covering Problem

Ke-rui Weng, Chao Yang, and Yun-feng Ma

School of Management, Huazhong University of Science and Technology
Wuhan 430074, P.R. China
wengkerui100@yahoo.com

**Abstract.** We consider the multiple allocation hub maximal covering problem (MAHMCP): considering a serviced O–D flow was required to reach the destination optionally passing through one or two hubs in a limited time, cost or distance, what is the optimal way to locate $p$ hubs to maximize the serviced flows. By designing a new model for the MAHMCP, we provide two artificial intelligence heuristics based on tabu search and genetic algorithm respectively. Then, we present computational experiments on hub airports location of Chinese aerial freight flows between 82 cities in 2002 and AP data set. By the computational experiments, we find that both GA and TS work well for MAHMCP. We also conclude that genetic algorithm readily finds a better computational result for the MAHMCP, while the tabu search may have a better computational efficiency.

## 1 Introduction

The hub location problem focuses on how to facilitate switching or consolidation nodes, called hubs, to optimize the hub-and-spoke system. In such a system, traffic flow of an origin-destination (O–D) pair is not transported directly between the two nodes, but routed via particular one or two hubs. Due to the consolidated flows between hubs, the hub-and-spoke system achieves economies of scale in hub-to-hub transport costs, which attracted many researches to exploit the advantages of hubs. The existing literatures on hub location have almost exclusively concentrated on hub median problem [1,2] which is to optimize to locate $p$ hubs to minimize the total transport costs of the hub-and-spoke systems. However, the hub median problem neglects an obvious drawback of hub-and-spoke system, which we called bypass costs. Since a flow of an O–D pair must bypass one or two hubs, the travel path of the flow would not necessarily be the shortest path, which leads to added bypass costs for the travel. Therefore, we would prefer that the travel path should be within an acceptable range, which involves the hub maximal covering problem. Considering a serviced O–D flow was required to reach the destination passing through one or two hubs in a limited time, cost or distance, the hub maximal covering problem is to find the optimal way to locate

D.-S. Huang, K. Li, and G.W. Irwin (Eds.): ICIC 2006, LNCS 4113, pp. 737–744, 2006.

$p$ hubs to maximize the serviced flows. The hub maximal covering problem has a wide range application within the design of supply chain, tourism routing, air transportation network, postal delivery network, etc. In supply chain management, the decision-maker would involve the problem of locating logistic hubs to distribute materials or products in a limited delivery time. In tourism routing management, the managers have to locate major travel industry sites as well as subsidiary sites to meet special travel demand within a limited travel time such as *three days tourism* or *five days tourism*. In airline network design, the leaders have to scheme out a hub-and-spoke airline network covering maximal airlines in a limited bypass distance. In postal delivery network, the conductor need locate postal switching sites to reduce the delivery costs within a promised delivery time. The hub maximal covering problem can be categorized into single allocation hub maximal covering problem (SAHMCP) and multiple allocation hub maximal covering problem (MAHMCP) by the way how the points allocated to hubs. The SAHMCP means that each point can send and receive flows via only a single hub, while the MAHMCP suggests more than one hub. The hub covering problem still has not received much attention in literature. It was first formulated by Campbell [3] with an integer programming model by $o(n^4)$ variables and constraints. Then, Kara and Tansel [4,5] designed an improved model with $o(n^2)$ variables and constraints for SAHMCP. Besides these, the MAHMCP still remains essentially unstudied.

At the same time, there have been no direct literatures on algorithms for MAHMCP. However, several researches have successively tried to solve set covering problem or hub median problem with genetic algorithm (GA) as well as tabu search (TS) in existing literatures. Therefore, we are trying to make use of GA and TS to solve MAHMCP on the basis of their experiences. GA is an intelligent randomized search optimization heuristic, which is based on the biological process of natural selection and can be applied to a variety of combinatorial optimization problems. The principles of GA have been applied to solve covering problem or hub location problem in paper [6,7,8]. TS is also an intelligent iterative procedure by moving from a solution to its best neighbor, remarking and avoiding previous local optimization. It has been experimentally applied in the algorithm of hub location in article [9,10,11].

In this article, section 2 presents an improved model for the MAHMCP by $O(n^2)$ variables and constraints. Section 3 and Section 4 provide two artificial intelligence heuristic algorithms based on GA and TS. In section 5, we offer computational experiments on hub airports location of Chinese aerial freight flows between 82 cities in 2002 and hub posts location of Australian Post (AP) data set.

## 2 MAHMCP Model

Given a connected network $G(N, A)$ where $N = \{1, \cdots, n\}$ is the set of nodes, $J = \{(i, j)|h_{ij} > 0,\ i, j \in N\}$ is the set of given $O - D$ pairs where $h_{ij}$ is the flow from node $i$ to node $j$. Let $C_{ij} = C_{ji}$ be the transportation cost from node

$i$ to node $j$ by the shortest path. For every $O-D$ pair of $(i,j)$, let $\beta_{ij}$ denote the limited transportation cost from node $i$ to node $j$. Then we let $C_{ij}^{km} = C_{km} + aC_{km} + C_{mj}$ be the shortest travel cost from node $i$ to node $j$ passing by nodes $k$ and $m$ where $a$, $0 < a < 1$, is the discount factor on inter-hub flows because of scale economies. Now, we can let $a_{ij}^{km}$ be a binary variable, which represents whether the $O-D$ pair $(i,j)$ can be covered by the candidate nodes $k$ and $m$. It is defined as follows:

$$a_{ij}^{km} = \begin{cases} 1 & \text{if } C_{ij}^{km} \le \beta_{ij} \\ 0 & \text{if not} \end{cases} \quad (1)$$

And we let $Z_{ij} = \{0,1\}$ be 1 if flow of the $O-D$ pair $(i,j)$ can be covered by located hubs and 0 otherwise. And let $X_k = \{0,1\}$ be 1 if node $k$ is selected as a hub and 0 otherwise. Then, we let $W_{km} = \{0,1\}$ be 1 if both nodes $k$ and $m$ are selected as hubs and 0 otherwise. Now, we can formulate the MAHMCP as P1:

$$\text{maximize} \quad \sum_i \sum_j h_{ij} Z_{ij} \quad (i,j) \in J \quad (2)$$

$$\text{subject to} \quad Z_{ij} \le \sum_k \sum_m a_{ij}^{km} W_{km} \quad \forall (i,j) \in J \quad (3)$$

$$X_K + X_m \ge 2W_{km} \quad \forall k, m \quad (4)$$

$$\sum_j X_j = p \quad (5)$$

$$X_j = 0,1; \; W_{km} = 0,1; Z_{ij} = 0,1$$

In P1, the objection function (2) accounts for the maximization of the total flows serviced (covered) by located hubs. Constraint (3) requires that the flow of $O-D$ pair $(i,j)$ be serviced if only there were at least one or two hubs ($W_{km}$) which could cover the flow. Constraint (4) ensures that $W_{km}$ could be 1 if only both nodes $i$ and $j$ were selected as hubs. Constraint (5) specifies that exactly $p$ hubs would be chosen. As we can see from P1, it has $2n^2 + n$ variables and $2n^2+1$ constraints at most, while the model of MAHMCP of Campbell's ([1]) has $n^4+n$ variables and $n^4+n^2+1$ constraints. Therefore, P1 has greatly improved on the model of Campbell's. The improvement of model would do great help to solve small-scale MAHMCP more efficiently with exact solution by optimization software such as CPLEX or LINGO. For the large-scale MAHMCP, however, we still may fall back on heuristic approach. If every $O-D$ pair happened to a single node, which occurred when $J = \{(i,i)|h_{ii} > 0, i \in N\}$ , then P1 became a general maximal covering problem (MCP). It means that MCP is a special case of MAHMCP. As a result, MAHMCP is NP-hard since MCP has been proved NP-hard. Therefore, we turn to artificial intelligence heuristics.

## 3 Genetic Algorithm for MAHMCP

### 3.1 Algorithm Elements of Genetic Algorithm

*Representation & Fitness Function.* The schema representation for the MAHMCP uses an $n$-bit string as the chromosome structures where $n$ is the number of potential hubs. A value of 1 for the $i$th bit indicates that the $i$th node was chosen as a hub. The fitness of an individual is directly related to its objective function, which is

$$f(P) = \sum_i \sum_j h_{ij} \min[1, \sum_{P(k)\in P} \sum_{P(m)\in P} a_{ij}^{km} P(k)P(m)]$$

where $P$, $P(k)$ and $P(m)$ represent the chromosome, $k$th, and $m$th gene related to the individual respectively.

*Parent Selection Procedure.* We choose the Binary Tournament Selection Method as the technique for parent selection which has been proved to be implemented very efficiently by Beasley and Chu in set covering problem.

*Crossover Operator.* In location problem, the traditional crossover operators such as one-point or two-point crossover readily produce an offspring identical to their parents. To reduce the probability of identification, we choose the crossover operator fitness-based fusion schema proposed by Beasley and Chu. According to the operator, for the parents $P_1$ , $P_2$ and the offspring $C$, the $C(k)$ would be identical to the $k$th gene of the parents if $P_1(k) = P_2(k)$ , or else $C(k)$ would be $P_1(k)$ or $P_2(k)$ with a probability of $\frac{f(P_1)}{f(P_1)+f(P_2)}$ and $\frac{f(P_2)}{f(P_1)+f(P_2)}$ respectively.

*Mutation Operator.* Mutation operator would help to escape from local optimization by providing genetic diversity and a broader space for MAHMCP. We adopt mutation operator when the offspring is identical to any one of its parents by fixed mutation rate. In our technique, the mutation may happen to the offspring or an individual of its parents in different cases. Though the mutation rate is relatively fixed in one operation, it is actually dynamic since the probability of identification would be increased with the convergence of the population.

*Feasible Operator.* The solution generated by crossover operation or mutation operation may violate constraint (5). We implement feasible operation by greedy add algorithm or greedy drop algorithm, which means that we add the node that can cover the maximal new flow and drop the node that lost the minimal flow respectively at each iteration until $p$ nodes have been selected.

*Replacement Population Operation.* We use the incremental replacement method which makes the best solutions always keep in the population and the newly generated solution immediately available for selection and reproduction. In our GA, we let the number of elite children equal 2.

*Population Size & Initial Population.* In our GA, we let population be $1.2n$ and create the initial population by randomly generation.

### 3.2 Genetic Algorithm Procedure

1. Set $t = 0$. Generate initial population $P(t)$ randomly.
2. Evaluate the fitness of each individual in $P(t)$.
3. If $t \geq 1000$ or the best string didn't change in 50 steps, go end.

4. Select parents $P_1$ and $P_2$ from $P(t)$ by binary tournament selection.
5. Apply crossover operator to $P_1$ and $P_2$ to form an offspring $C_1$. If $C_1 \neq P_1$ and $C_1 \neq P_2$, go step7.
6. Apply mutation operator to the parent with the less fitness to form an offspring $C_1$.
7. Apply feasible operator to $C_1$ to form an offspring $C_2$. If $C_2$ is identical to any string of $P(t)$, apply mutation operator and feasible operator to $C_2$ to form an offspring $C_3$; if not, set $C_3 = C_2$.
8. Keep 2 elite strings of $P(t)$ and let $C_3$ replace an individual selected by roulette wheel selection from the remains of the parents to create the new $P(t)$. Go step 2.
9. End. The final solution is the best elite of $P(t)$.

# 4 Tabu Search Algorithm for MAHMCP

## 4.1 Algorithm Elements of Tabu Search

*Initial solution.* We generate the initial solution by greedy adding algorithm.

*Neighborhood structure.* We determine the neighborhood structure by single exchange. For any solution $T$, defining $N - T$ to be the remainder candidate nodes, we generate the neighborhood as the set of solutions which can be reached by exchanging one node from $N - T$ to $T$. It can be concluded that the set of neighborhood has $p(n - p)$ solutions.

*Tabu list.* We determine the node dropping from the current solution, when moving to its selected neighbor, to be recorded in the tabu list for the purpose of forbidding the reversal of replacement in a number (tabu length) of future iterations. For example, when the solution $(1, 2)$ was replaced by its neighbor $(1, 3)$, node 2 would be added to tabu list, which means that node 2 would not be selected again in a number of upcoming iterations unless an aspiration criteria was awaken.

Besides, we set the *tabu length* by a random integer between $[\sqrt{n/2}, \sqrt{n}]$. Then, we use the *aspiration criteria* when an added node can produce the best known feasible solution. At last, we determine the number of total iterations by 100.

## 4.2 Tabu Search Procedure

Let $N$ be set of $n$ nodes of a given connected network; $T$ the current solution; $N - T$ the remainder candidate nodes; $N(T) = \{T^1, T^2, \cdots, T^{p(n-p)}\}$ the neighborhood of $T$; $V^i$ the node dropped from $T$ relation to $T^i$, $W^i$ the node added from $N - T$ to $T^i$; *tabu_tag*$(i)$ the tabu tag of nodes $i$. For the solution $T$, the objection value will be:

$$Z(T) = \sum_i \sum_j h_{ij} \min(1, \sum_{k \in T} \sum_{m \in T} a_{ij}^{km})$$

The following gives a procedural description of Tabu search for MAHMCP.
*Procedure of tabu search*

1. Generate initial solution $T$ by greedy add algorithm. Initialize tabu list to be empty by set $tabu\_tag(i) = 0 \quad (\forall i \in N)$. Let $T^0 = T$ for the purpose of determining the best known solution. Let the iteration index $t = 0$.
2. Generate the neighborhood $N(T)$.
3. Find the maximal $Z(T^l)$ from $N(T)$. If $tabu\_tag(W^l) = 0$ or $Z(T^l) > Z(T^0)$, set $T = T^l$ and set $tabu\_tag(V^l)$ to a random integer between $[\sqrt{n/2}, \sqrt{n}]$, go to step4; if not, set $N(T) = N(T) - T^l$ and repeat step 3.
4. Set $t = t+1$. If $Z(T) > Z(T^0)$, set $T^0 = T$ to renew the best known solution.
5. If $t < 100$ and $T^0$ did change in 10 steps, set $tabu\_tag(i) = tabu\_tag(i) - 1$ for any node $i$ with $tabu\_tag(i) > 0$ to renew tabu tag, and return to step2.
6. End. The final solution is $T^0$.

## 5 Computational Experiments

To evaluate the computational results of the two heuristics for MAHMCP, this section now presents a large instance on hub airports location of Chinese aerial freight flows between 82 cities in 2002 and several small size cases of AP data set. In the Chinese case, the flow data $h_{ij}$ comes from aerial freight flows between 82 cities in *Annual of Chinese Transportation 2003* (in Chinese) with a total flows of 1.3 million tons (mt). We measure the travel cost by fixed course range which comes from *civil aviation from statistics 2003* (in Chinese). Based on the fixed course range between 82 cities, we calculate the shortest travel cost $C_{ij}$ by Floyd algorithm. When designing the Chinese hub-and-spoke airline network, we require that the flows passing through hubs should not exceed 15% of their shortest path travel cost. That is, we define $a_{ij}^{km}$ by:

$$a_{ij}^{km} = \begin{cases} 1 & \text{if } c_{ik} + ac_{km} + c_{jm} \leq 1.15c_{ij} \\ 0 & \text{if not} \end{cases}$$

We consider the cases of $p$ by 2, 3, 4 and $a$ by 0.8, 0.6, 0.4 respectively. Now, we code the two procedures in matlab 6.5 since we have obtained all coefficients of P1. The parameter values of the GA and TS were all defined as section 3.1 and 4.1 determined about the algorithm elements. At last, we get the outcome listed by Table 1 after the procedures were run in experimental computer which is equipped with 512M of RAM and a Pentium microprocessor running at 1.3GHz. In Table 1, the time means the CPU time (seconds) expended in the algorithm procedures. And the unit of objection value is million tons. As we can see from Table 1, both GA and TS may have superiority and inferiority. According to the experiment, GA readily finds a better computational result for the large scale of MAHMCP, while the TS may have a better computational efficiency. The GA expands more times due to many times of feasible operations. As a result, the TS is more suitable for the instant MAHMCP, while GA is more appropriate for long-term MAHMCP. However, for the cases of $n = 82$ , it may work more than 2 hundred hours to get the optimal solutions by LINGO. Therefore, we still don't know whether the solutions in Table.1 are optimal.

**Table 1.** The computational result of Chinese hub airports location

| p | a | GA | | | TS | | |
|---|---|---|---|---|---|---|---|
| | | Hub location | Objection value | time (s) | Hub location | Objection value | time (s) |
| 2 | 0.8 | Beijing,HangZhou | 0.849 | 220 | Beijing,HangZhou | 0.849 | 108 |
| | 0.6 | Beijing,HangZhou | 0.866 | 278 | Beijing,HangZhou | 0.866 | 106 |
| | 0.4 | Nanjing,Guilin | 0.940 | 209 | Nanjing,Guilin | 0.940 | 351 |
| 3 | 0.8 | Beijing,Nanjing, Shenzhen | 1.042 | 798 | Beijing,Hangzhou, Guangzhou | 1.034 | 468 |
| | 0.6 | Beijing,Nanjing, Shenzhen | 1.061 | 809 | Beijing,Hangzhou, Guangzhou | 1.052 | 465 |
| | 0.4 | Beijing,Nanjing, Guiyang | 1.073 | 755 | Beijing,Hangzhou, Guilin | 1.060 | 462 |
| 4 | 0.8 | Beijing,Shanghai, Guangzhou,Shenzhen | 1.131 | 1788 | Beijing,Shanghai, Guangzhou,Shenzhen | 1.131 | 999 |
| | 0.6 | Beijing,Guiyang, Guangzhou,Hangzhou | 1.144 | 1913 | Beijing,Guangzhou, Hangzhou,Chongqing | 1.141 | 1796 |
| | 0.4 | Beijing,Guangzhou, Hangzhou,Guiyang | 1.156 | 1856 | Beijing,Shanghai, Guangzhou,Chongqing | 1.146 | 993 |

**Table 2.** The computational experiment on AP data set

| n | p | GA | | TS | | Exact solution by B&B | |
|---|---|---|---|---|---|---|---|
| | | Objection value | Time (s) | Objection value | Time (s) | Location | Objection value |
| 15 | 3 | 11.31 | 8 | 11.31 | 0.1 | 1 7 8 | 11.31 |
| | 4 | 11.93 | 10 | 11.93 | 0.8 | 1 7 8 10 | 11.93 |
| | 5 | 12.14 | 14 | 12.14 | 2 | 1 6 7 8 10 | 12.14 |
| 20 | 3 | 30.97 | 55 | 30.97 | 8 | 7 19 20 | 30.97 |
| | 4 | 33.28 | 60 | 33.28 | 15 | 5 7 19 20 | 33.28 |
| | 5 | 35.11 | 72 | 35.11 | 20 | 5 7 16 19 20 | 35.11 |
| 25 | 3 | 37.06 | 109 | 37.06 | 17 | 7 19 24 | 37.06 |
| | 4 | 40.79 | 98 | 40.79 | 25 | 7 16 19 20 | 40.79 |
| | 5 | 43.17 | 130 | 43.17 | 33 | 5 7 16 19 20 | 43.17 |

To test the quality of the solutions, we take another computational experiment on AP data set which is a well known experiment platform for hub location problem and is available at http://people.brunel.ac.uk/ mastjjb. We take the first 15, 20 and 25 data from AP data set. The experiment checks the cases of $p$ by 3, 4, 5 and $a$ by 0.6. And we require that the flows passing through hubs should not exceed 20% of their direct path travel costs. We first use LINGO to solve MAMHCP by branch and bound algorithm to get the exact solution. The test shows that LINGO takes average 30s to solve 15 nodes, 16m to solve 20 nodes and 2h to 25 nodes. The computational result was shown in Table 2. From column 1 to column 8, Table 2 shows the objection value and computational CPU time of GA and TS, and the exact solution obtained by B&B algorithm. According to

Table 2, we can see that both TS and GA work well in relatively small size of MAHMCP since they always converge to the optimal solution in the experimental cases. Again, we see that GA takes more time than TS in the procedures.

## 6 Conclusion

The MAHMCP has a wide range application in supply chain, tourism routing, air transportation network, postal delivery network, etc. The paper first proposes a new model for the MAHMCP. Then, provides two heuristic algorithms based on tabu search and genetic algorithm respectively. At last, we present a large scale instance on hub airports location of Chinese aerial freight flows between 82 cities in 2002 and several small cases on AP data set to test the performance of the two heuristics. According to the experiment, both GA and TS work well. We also find that GA readily finds a better computational result for the MAHMCP, while the TS may have a better computational efficiency. Future researches relation to this article will be computational experiment on different large scale cases, hybrid heuristics for MAHMCP, solving MAHMCP by simulated annealing, neural network approach and so on.

## References


1. Campbell, J.F.: Hub Location and The P-Hub Median Problem. Operations Research. **44** (1996) 923–935
2. O'Kelly, M., Skorin-Kapov, D., Skorin-Kapov, J.: Lower Bounds for The Hub Location Problem. Management Science. **41** (1995) 713–721
3. Campbell, J.F.: Integer Programming Formulations of Discrete Hub Location Problem. European Journal of Operational Research. **72** (1994) 387–405
4. Kara, B.Y., Tansel, B.C.: The Latest Arrival Hub Location Problem. European Journal of Operational Research. **47** (2000) 1408–1420
5. Kara, B.Y., Tansel, B.C.: The Single-Assignment Hub Covering Problem: Models and linearzations. Journal of the Operational Research Society. **54** (2003) 59–64
6. Jaramillo, J.H., Bhadury, J., Batta, R.: On The Use of Genetic Algorithms to Solve Location Problems. Computers & Operations Research. **29** (2002) 761–779
7. Beasley, J.E., Chu, P.C.: A Genetic Algorithm for The Set Covering Problem. European Journal of Operational Research. **94** (1996) 392–204
8. Topcuoglu, H., Corut, F., Ermis, M. et al.: Solving The Uncapacitated Hub Location Problem Using Genetic Algorithms. Computers and Operations Research. **32** (2005) 967–984
9. Skorin-Kapov, D., Skorin-Kapov, J.: On Tabu Search for The Location of Interacting Hub Facilities. European Journal of Operational Research. **73** (1994) 502–509
10. Marianov, V., Serra, D., Revelle, C.: Location of Hubs in A Competitive Environment. European Journal of Operational Research. **114** (1999) 363–371
11. Klincewicz, J.G.: Avoiding Local Optima in The P-Hub Location Problem Using Tabu Search and GRASP. Annals of Operations Research. **40** (1993) 283–302

# Kernel Principal Component Analysis for Large Scale Data Set*

Haixian Wang[1], Zilan Hu[2], and Yu'e Zhao[3]

[1] Research Center for Learning Science, Southeast University, Nanjing, Jiangsu 210096, P.R. China
hxwang@seu.edu.cn

[2] School of Mathematics and Physics, Anhui University of Technology, Maanshan, Anhui 243002, P.R. China
hu_107@hotmail.com

[3] Department of Mathematics, Qingdao University, Qingdao, Shandong 266071, P.R. China
blueskyyu2004@yahoo.com.cn

**Abstract.** Kernel principal component analysis (KPCA) has provided an extremely powerful approach to extracting nonlinear features via kernel trick, and it has been suggested for a number of applications. Whereas the nonlinearity can be allowed by the utilization of Mercer kernels, the standard KPCA could only process limited number of training samples. For large scale data set, it may suffer from computational problem of diagonalizing large matrices, and occupy large storage space. In this paper, by choosing a subset of the entire training samples using Gram-Schmidt orthonormalization and incomplete Cholesky decomposition, we formulate KPCA as another eigenvalue problem of matrix whose size is much smaller than that of the kernel matrix. The theoretical analysis and experimental results on both artificial and real data have shown the advantages of the proposed method for performing KPCA in terms of computational efficiency and storage space, especially when the number of data points is large.

## 1 Introduction

Kernel principal component analysis (KPCA) is to perform linear PCA in a high- (and possibly infinite-) dimensional kernel-defined feature space making use of the dual representation of PCA in terms of dot products between the nonlinearly mapped data points. KPCA was firstly proposed by Schölkopf et al. [1], and has shown to be an extremely powerful tool for the de-noising of handwritten digits [2], feature extraction and de-noising in nonlinear regression [3], face recognition [4]-[6], and complex image modelling [7].

* This work was funded by National Natural Science Foundation of China (Grant No. 60375010, 60503023, and 10571001), and partly by Jiangsu Natural Science Foundation (Grant No. BK2005407) and Program for New Century Excellent Talents in University (Grant No. NCET-05-0467).

D.-S. Huang, K. Li, and G.W. Irwin (Eds.): ICIC 2006, LNCS 4113, pp. 745–756, 2006.

The standard form of KPCA [1], however, can only process limited number of training samples, since it involves in diagonalizing the kernel matrix, whose dimensionality is equal to the number of data points. For large scale data set, KPCA would be very time consuming (with complexity $O(N^3)$, where $N$ is the number of data points) and occupy large memory (to store $N \times N$ kernel matrix $\mathbf{K}$), which prohibit it from being used in many applications. Besides, there is still the attendant problem of numerical accuracy when diagonalizing large matrix directly [8]. To alleviate the computational demand, Rosipal and Girolami proposed an expectation maximization (EM) approach for performing KPCA by considering KPCA from a probabilistic perspective, and the complexity of their method is $O(kN^2)$ per iteration, where $k$ is the number of extracted components [8]. One flaw of this method is that it still needs to store the kernel matrix. Kim et al. provided a new iterative method, the kernel Hebbian algorithm (KHA), to estimate the kernel principal components with only linear order memory complexity [7]. However, this comes at the price that the time complexity depends on the dimensionality of the input data and the number of updates. Zheng et al. presented another training algorithm for KPCA [9]. The basic idea behind their method is to "divide and rule"; that is, they first divided the entire data set into some smaller data sets and then obtained an approximate representation of the sample covariance matrix of each smaller data set via eigenvalue decomposition and kernel trick, and finally combined these approximate covariance matrices to compute kernel principal components again by kernel trick. Their method could reduce computational intensity and memory efficiently; but this depends on the data at hand, the required accuracy of extracted components, and the number of smaller data sets (which is not easy to be determined appropriately).

In the context of function approximation, Baudat and Anouar have suggested choosing a subset of samples as a basis for the entire samples [10]. Their scheme is based on a geometrical consideration, and is rather complex. Moreover, the subset found by their method could not guarantee to be a basis. There are also some greedy algorithms to obtain an approximate kernel matrix $\tilde{\mathbf{K}}$ [11]-[13]. Franc and Hlaváč proposed another greedy algorithm for selecting a set of basis from the training set [14]. Their method, however, is of complexity $O(Nn^3)$, where $n$ is the number of selected samples, and involves inverse matrix operation. Motivated by their idea, we propose a new approach to obtaining a basis for the training points by using Gram-Schmidt orthonormalization and incomplete Cholesky decomposition. Compared with the greedy algorithms aforementioned, the proposed method is more concise; its complexity is $O(Nn^2)$ rather than $O(Nn^3)$. Another contribution of this paper is that we formulate KPCA as another eigenvalue problem using the basis, while still extracting nonlinear principal components from all $N$ samples. By the proposed method for performing KPCA, the size of the matrix that needs to be diagonalized is much smaller than that of the kernel matrix. The theoretical analysis and experimental results on both artificial and real data have shown the advantages of the proposed method in terms of computational efficiency and storage space, especially when the number of data points is large.

The remainder of this paper is organized as follows. Section 2 briefly reviews the standard KPCA, and the novel KPCA algorithm is formulated in Section 3. In Section 4, we present the experimental results, followed by the conclusions that are drawn in Section 5.

## 2 Kernel Principal Component Analysis

Given a set of $N$ observations $\mathbf{x}_i \in R^l, i = 1, \ldots, N$, the thought of KPCA is to first map these input data into some new feature space $\mathcal{F}$ typically via a nonlinear function $\phi : R^l \rightarrow \mathcal{F}$ and then carry out a standard linear PCA in $\mathcal{F}$ using the mapped samples $\phi(\mathbf{x}_i)$. In implementation, the mapping $\phi$ does not need to be computed explicitly, while it and thus the space $\mathcal{F}$ are determined implicitly by the choice of a *kernel function* $k$ which calculates the dot product between two mapped samples $\phi(\mathbf{x}_i)$ and $\phi(\mathbf{x}_j)$ in $\mathcal{F}$ by

$$k(\mathbf{x}_i, \mathbf{x}_j) = (\phi(\mathbf{x}_i) \cdot \phi(\mathbf{x}_j)) \ . \tag{1}$$

Via Mercer's theorem of functional analysis, if $k$ is a positive definite kernel, then there exists a mapping $\phi$ into the dot product space $\mathcal{F}$ such that (1) holds. Examples of Mercer kernels include $d$th-order polynomial, $k(\mathbf{x}_i, \mathbf{x}_j) = (\mathbf{x}_i \cdot \mathbf{x}_j)^d$, Gaussian kernel with width $\sigma > 0$, $k(\mathbf{x}_i, \mathbf{x}_j) = \exp(-\|\mathbf{x}_i - \mathbf{x}_j\|^2/2\sigma^2)$, and sigmoid kernel $k(\mathbf{x}_i, \mathbf{x}_j) = \tanh(a(\mathbf{x}_i \cdot \mathbf{x}_j) + b)$, each of them implying a different mapping and feature space $\mathcal{F}$.

Assuming that the mapped samples are centered, i.e. $\sum_{i=1}^{N} \phi(\mathbf{x}_i) = 0$ (for a method to center the vectors $\phi(\mathbf{x}_i)$ in $\mathcal{F}$, to see [1]), the goal of KPCA is to diagonalize the covariance matrix of mapped samples $\phi(\mathbf{x}_i)$, given by

$$\mathbf{C}^{\phi} = \frac{1}{N} \sum_{i=1}^{N} \phi(\mathbf{x}_i) \phi(\mathbf{x}_i)^{\mathsf{T}} \ , \tag{2}$$

where $\mathsf{T}$ denotes transpose operator. To do this, we find the eigenvalues $\lambda > 0$ and eigenvectors $\mathbf{v} \in \mathcal{F} \setminus \{0\}$ satisfying

$$\lambda \mathbf{v} = \mathbf{C}^{\phi} \mathbf{v} \ . \tag{3}$$

Since all solutions $\mathbf{v}$ with $\lambda \neq 0$ lie within the span of $\{\phi(\mathbf{x}_1), \ldots, \phi(\mathbf{x}_N)\}$, there exists coefficients $\alpha_i$ $(i = 1, \ldots, N)$ such that

$$\mathbf{v} = \sum_{i=1}^{N} \alpha_i \phi(\mathbf{x}_i) \ . \tag{4}$$

Then we may instead consider the following equivalent problem

$$\lambda(\phi(\mathbf{x}_j) \cdot \mathbf{v}) = (\phi(\mathbf{x}_j) \cdot \mathbf{C}^{\phi} \mathbf{v}) \ \textit{for all} \ j = 1, \ldots, N \ . \tag{5}$$

Substituting (2) and (4) into (5), and defining an $N \times N$ kernel matrix $\mathbf{K}$ with elements $\mathbf{K}_{ij} = k(\mathbf{x}_i, \mathbf{x}_j) = (\phi(\mathbf{x}_i) \cdot \phi(\mathbf{x}_j))$ lead to the eigenvalue problem

$$N \lambda \mathbf{K} \alpha = \mathbf{K}^2 \alpha \Rightarrow N \lambda \alpha = \mathbf{K} \alpha \ , \tag{6}$$

where $\alpha$ denotes the column vector with entries $\alpha_1, \ldots, \alpha_N$.

For the purpose of nonlinear principal components extraction, we need to work out the projections onto the eigenvectors $\mathbf{v}$. Let $\mathbf{t}$ be a test point whose image is $\phi(\mathbf{t})$ in $\mathcal{F}$; then the nonlinear principal components corresponding $\phi$ is

$$(\mathbf{v} \cdot \phi(\mathbf{t})) = \sum_{i=1}^{N} \alpha_i (\phi(\mathbf{x}_i) \cdot \phi(\mathbf{t})) = \sum_{i=1}^{N} \alpha_i k(\mathbf{x}_i, \mathbf{t}) \; . \tag{7}$$

Again, there is no need to compute $\phi$ explicitly since everything could be expressed in terms of dot products which are replaced by kernel functions.

## 3 Novel Algorithm for Kernel Principal Component Analysis

In practice, we may indeed observe that the samples in $\mathcal{F}$, $\phi(\mathbf{x}_1), \ldots, \phi(\mathbf{x}_N)$, lie in a subspace of the feature space with lower dimensionality than $N$. In fact, the dimensionality of the subspace spanned by $\{\phi(\mathbf{x}_i)\}$ is just equal to the rank of the matrix $\mathbf{K}$, $rank(\mathbf{K})$, which is often less than $N$. Especially when the training data set is large, $rank(\mathbf{K}) \ll N$ [10]. In other words, the training samples in $\mathcal{F}$ are not linearly independent.

Thinking back in (4), we employ all the training samples $\phi(\mathbf{x}_i)$ $(i = 1, \ldots, N)$ to represent $\mathbf{v}$, and therefore make the size of resulting kernel matrix $\mathbf{K}$ be up to the number of training samples. Now without loss of generality, we assume that $\phi(\mathbf{x}_1), \ldots, \phi(\mathbf{x}_n)$ is a basis of the subspace spanned by entire training samples, where $n$ is the rank of $\mathbf{K}$. Then $\mathbf{v}$ could be rewritten as

$$\mathbf{v} = \sum_{i=1}^{n} \beta_i \phi(\mathbf{x}_i) \; , \tag{8}$$

where $\beta_i$ $(i = 1, \ldots, n)$ are coefficients. Also, for $i = n+1, \ldots, N$, there exist coefficients $p_{ij}$ such that $\phi(\mathbf{x}_i)$ could be expressed as $\phi(\mathbf{x}_i) = \sum_{j=1}^{n} p_{ij}\phi(\mathbf{x}_j)$. As a result, the covariance matrix

$$\begin{aligned} \mathbf{C}^{\phi} &= \frac{1}{N} \sum_{i=1}^{N} \phi(\mathbf{x}_i)\phi(\mathbf{x}_i)^{\mathsf{T}} \\ &= \frac{1}{N} \left( \sum_{i=1}^{n} \phi(\mathbf{x}_i)\phi(\mathbf{x}_i)^{\mathsf{T}} + \sum_{i=n+1}^{N} \sum_{j=1}^{n} \sum_{k=1}^{n} p_{ij} p_{ik} \phi(\mathbf{x}_j)\phi(\mathbf{x}_k)^{\mathsf{T}} \right) \\ &= \frac{1}{N} \sum_{j=1}^{n} \sum_{k=1}^{n} q_{jk} \phi(\mathbf{x}_j)\phi(\mathbf{x}_k)^{\mathsf{T}} \; , \end{aligned} \tag{9}$$

where for $j$, $k = 1, \ldots, n$,

$$q_{jk} = \begin{cases} \sum_{i=n+1}^{N} p_{ij} p_{ik} + 1 & , \quad j = k \\ \sum_{i=n+1}^{N} p_{ij} p_{ik} & , \quad j \neq k . \end{cases} \tag{10}$$

Therefore, equation (3) is equivalent to the set of equations

$$\lambda(\phi(\mathbf{x}_m) \cdot \mathbf{v}) = (\phi(\mathbf{x}_m) \cdot \mathbf{C}^{\phi}\mathbf{v}) \ for \ m = 1, \ldots, n \,. \tag{11}$$

A proof of this proposition is given in appendix. Combining (8), (9) and (11), we get

$$\lambda \sum_{i=1}^{n} \beta_i(\phi(\mathbf{x}_m) \cdot \phi(\mathbf{x}_i)) = \frac{1}{N} \sum_{j=1}^{n} \sum_{k=1}^{n} q_{jk} \left( \phi(\mathbf{x}_m) \cdot \phi(\mathbf{x}_j) \sum_{i=1}^{n} \beta_i(\phi(\mathbf{x}_k) \cdot \phi(\mathbf{x}_i)) \right) \quad for \ m = 1, \ldots, n. \tag{12}$$

Taking an $n \times n$ submatrix $\mathbf{K}^0$ of the kernel matrix $\mathbf{K}$ as

$$\mathbf{K}^0 = (\mathbf{K}_{ij})_{i=1,\ldots,n;\, j=1,\ldots,n} \,, \tag{13}$$

equations (12) read

$$N\lambda \mathbf{K}^0 \beta = \mathbf{K}^0 \mathbf{Q} \mathbf{K}^0 \beta \Rightarrow N\lambda\beta = \mathbf{Q}\mathbf{K}^0\beta \,, \tag{14}$$

where $\mathbf{Q} = (q_{jk})_{j=1,\ldots,n;\, k=1,\ldots,n}$, and $\beta$ is the column vector with elements $\beta_1, \ldots, \beta_n$.

We now turn to consider how to choose $n$ samples as a basis for the entire samples, and how to compute the matrix $\mathbf{Q}$ constructed from the coefficients for samples that are not chosen. We commence by investigating an approach to deriving an orthonormal basis in feature space known as the kernel Gram-Schmidt procedure [15]. If we, for the time being, assume that the training samples $\phi(\mathbf{x}_1), \ldots, \phi(\mathbf{x}_N)$ are linearly independent vectors the method produces the basis by orthogonalizing each vector to all of the earlier vectors. Thus, the first basis vector is specified as $\mathbf{u}_1 = \phi(\mathbf{x}_1)/\|\phi(\mathbf{x}_1)\|$. The $i$th basis vector is given by $\mathbf{u}_i = d_i^{-1}(I - \mathbf{U}_{i-1}\mathbf{U}_{i-1}^{\mathsf{T}})\phi(\mathbf{x}_i)$, where $I$ denotes the identity matrix, $\mathbf{U}_{i-1}$ is the matrix whose $i-1$ columns are the first $i-1$ vectors $\mathbf{u}_1, \ldots, \mathbf{u}_{i-1}$, and $d_i$ is the residual norm $d_i = \|(I - \mathbf{U}_{i-1}\mathbf{U}_{i-1}^{\mathsf{T}})\phi(\mathbf{x}_i)\|$. Clearly, $(\mathbf{u}_i \cdot \mathbf{u}_j) = 0$ for $j = 1, \ldots, i-1$. On the other hand, we could express the training samples using $\mathbf{u}_1, \ldots, \mathbf{u}_N$ as the basis; that is

$$(\phi(\mathbf{x}_1), \ldots, \phi(\mathbf{x}_N)) = \mathbf{U}\mathbf{R}, \tag{15}$$

where $\mathbf{U} = \mathbf{U}_N$ is the matrix containing all the $\mathbf{u}_1, \ldots, \mathbf{u}_N$ as columns, and $\mathbf{R}$ is an upper triangular matrix whose $i$th column $\mathbf{r}_i = \left(\phi(\mathbf{x}_i)^{\mathsf{T}}\mathbf{U}_{i-1}, d_i, 0_{N-i}^{\mathsf{T}}\right)^{\mathsf{T}}$. Here, $0_{N-i}$ is a column vector with all $N-i$ entries being zeros. The computation of $\mathbf{R}$ could be implemented by the Cholesky decomposition row by row in an iterative manner [16]. Taking into account that the entire samples are not linearly independent, we may come to meet a sample, say $\phi(\mathbf{x}_j)$, that lies in the subspace spanned by the earlier samples. And, it could be seen that the corresponding residual norm $d_j$ will be equal to zero when $\phi(\mathbf{x}_j)$ is processed during the Cholesky implementation. So the magnitude of $d_j$ shows how independent the next sample is of the samples processed so far. If we wish to the most independent samples, it is therefore to change the order of the samples that are processed in the Cholesky decomposition by always choosing the samples with largest $d_j$ while those with $d_j$ less than $\theta$ are ignored altogether, where $\theta$ is a positive threshold. This approach is called incomplete Cholesky decomposition [16], since it do not process all the samples.

If let an index array $Ind$ store the indices of the vectors in the order that they are chosen, then $\phi(\mathbf{x}_{Ind(1)}), \ldots, \phi(\mathbf{x}_{Ind(n)})$ are the chosen samples and are also the basis for the entire samples, where $n\,(= rank(\mathbf{K}))$ is number of the chosen samples. Supposing $\mathbf{u}_1, \ldots, \mathbf{u}_n$ are the corresponding orthonormal vectors, then we can factor (15) into

$$(\phi(\mathbf{x}_{Ind(1)}), \ldots, \phi(\mathbf{x}_{Ind(n)})) = (\mathbf{u}_1, \ldots, \mathbf{u}_n)\mathbf{R}_1 \tag{16}$$

and

$$(\phi(\mathbf{x}_i), i \notin Ind) = (\mathbf{u}_1, \ldots, \mathbf{u}_n)\mathbf{R}_2 \, , \tag{17}$$

where $(\phi(\mathbf{x}_i), i \notin Ind)$ denotes the matrix whose columns are the vectors that are not chosen, $\mathbf{R}_1$ is an $n \times n$ upper triangular matrix with positive diagonal entries, and $\mathbf{R}_2$ is an $n \times (N-n)$ matrix. Both $\mathbf{R}_1$ and $\mathbf{R}_2$ could be obtain by virtue of factoring $\mathbf{R}$ that is computed in the incomplete Cholesky decomposition; that is, the $i$th column of $\mathbf{R}_1$ is the $Ind(i)$ column of $\mathbf{R}$, and $\mathbf{R}_2$ is those columns of $\mathbf{R}$ that are not selected by $\mathbf{R}_1$. By (16) and (17), we have

$$(\phi(\mathbf{x}_i), i \notin Ind) = (\phi(\mathbf{x}_{Ind(1)}), \ldots, \phi(\mathbf{x}_{Ind(n)}))\mathbf{R}_1^{-1}\mathbf{R}_2 \, . \tag{18}$$

If let $\mathbf{P} = \mathbf{R}_1^{-1}\mathbf{R}_2$, then the entries of the $i$th column of $n \times (N-n)$ matrix $\mathbf{P}$ is just the coefficients matrix. Therefore, when $j \neq k$,

$$\begin{aligned} q_{jk} &= \sum_{i=n+1}^{N} p_{ij} p_{ik} \\ &= (\mathbf{P}\mathbf{P}^{\mathsf{T}})_{jk} = \left(\mathbf{R}_1^{-1}\mathbf{R}_2\mathbf{R}_2^{\mathsf{T}}(\mathbf{R}_1^{-1})^{\mathsf{T}}\right)_{jk} \\ &= \left(\mathbf{R}_1^{-1}\mathbf{R}_2\mathbf{R}_2^{\mathsf{T}}(\mathbf{R}_1^{-1})^{\mathsf{T}} + I\right)_{jk} \, . \end{aligned} \tag{19}$$

Likewise, for the case $j = k$,

$$\begin{aligned} q_{jj} &= \sum_{i=n+1}^{N} p_{ij}^2 + 1 \\ &= \left(\mathbf{R}_1^{-1}\mathbf{R}_2\mathbf{R}_2^{\mathsf{T}}(\mathbf{R}_1^{-1})^{\mathsf{T}} + I\right)_{jj} \, . \end{aligned} \tag{20}$$

Consequently,

$$\mathbf{Q} = \mathbf{R}_1^{-1}\mathbf{R}_2\mathbf{R}_2^{\mathsf{T}}(\mathbf{R}_1^{-1})^{\mathsf{T}} + I \, . \tag{21}$$

Also, the matrix $\mathbf{K}^0$ in (13) should be rewritten as

$$\mathbf{K}^0 = (\mathbf{K}_{Ind(i), Ind(j)})_{i=1,\ldots,n;\, j=1,\ldots,n} \, . \tag{22}$$

Now let $\lambda_1 \geq \ldots \geq \lambda_n$ denote the eigenvalues of $\mathbf{QK}^0$, namely the solutions $N\lambda$ of equation (14), and $\beta^1, \ldots, \beta^n$ the corresponding eigenvectors. Note that the size of the matrix $\mathbf{QK}^0$ that needed to be diagonalized is $n \times n$. We normalize $\beta^1, \ldots, \beta^n$ by requiring that the corresponding $\mathbf{v}^m$ $(m = 1, \ldots, n)$ have unitary norm. It will suffice to divide $\beta^m$ by $\sqrt{\beta^{m\top}\mathbf{K}^0\beta^m}$ for $m = 1, \ldots, n$. Then the projection of the test point $\mathbf{t}$ onto the eigenvectors $\mathbf{v}^m$ in $\mathcal{F}$ could be calculated as

$$(\mathbf{v}^m \cdot \phi(\mathbf{t})) = \sum_{i=1}^{n} \beta_i^m k(\mathbf{x}_{Ind(i)}, \mathbf{t}), \; m = 1, \ldots, n \; . \tag{23}$$

The procedures of the proposed algorithm for performing KPCA could be summarized as follows:

1. perform incomplete Cholesky decomposition for the data points,
2. compute $\mathbf{Q}$ and $\mathbf{K}^0$ according to (21) and (22), respectively,
3. compute the eigenvalues and corresponding eigenvectors of $\mathbf{QK}^0$, and
4. compute projections of a test point onto the eigenvectors according to (23).

**Complexity analysis.** The proposed method for performing KPCA turns to solve the eigenvalue problem of the matrix $\mathbf{QK}^0$, which has complexity of the order $O(n^3)$. And, the complexity of performing incomplete Cholesky decomposition is of the order $O(n^2N)$. Thus, the entire time complexity of the proposed method is $O(n^2N)$. On the other hand, the storage requirement is $O(nN)$. Both the time and storage complexity compare favorably with those of the methods mentioned in section 1 in the case $n \ll N$. So this, in turn, will depend to a large degree on the problem at hand and the kernel chosen.

# 4 Experiments

## 4.1 Toy Examples

To test the feasibility and efficiency of the proposed method for performing KPCA, we firstly compare it with the standard KPCA on two artificial two-dimensional data sets. In the first toy example, we use the simulated data previously considered by Schölkopf et al. [1], Rosipal and Girolami [8], and Zheng et al. [9]. The data are generated from three two-dimensional Gaussian clusters with means $(-0.5, -0.2; 0.0, 0.6; 0.5, 0.0)$ and common standard deviation 0.1. We generate 500 data points for each cluster and use kernel $k(\mathbf{x}_i, \mathbf{x}_j) = \exp(-\|\mathbf{x}_i - \mathbf{x}_j\|^2/0.1)$ to compute the kernel matrix. We use the standard KPCA and the proposed method to extract the leading principal components of the data set, respectively. In using the proposed method, we choose only 98 linearly independent samples from the entire 1500 samples. Fig. 1 illustrates the first four nonlinear principal components extracted by the standard KPCA [1] and the proposed method, respectively. The principal component values denoted by the gray level and lines of identical principal component values are delineated in Fig. 1. From Fig. 1, we see that the proposed method achieves the same results in coincidence with that of the standard KPCA (ignoring the sign difference). At the same time, the proposed method reduces the time and storage complexity greatly. Table 1 shows the time and space needed in training the two methods.

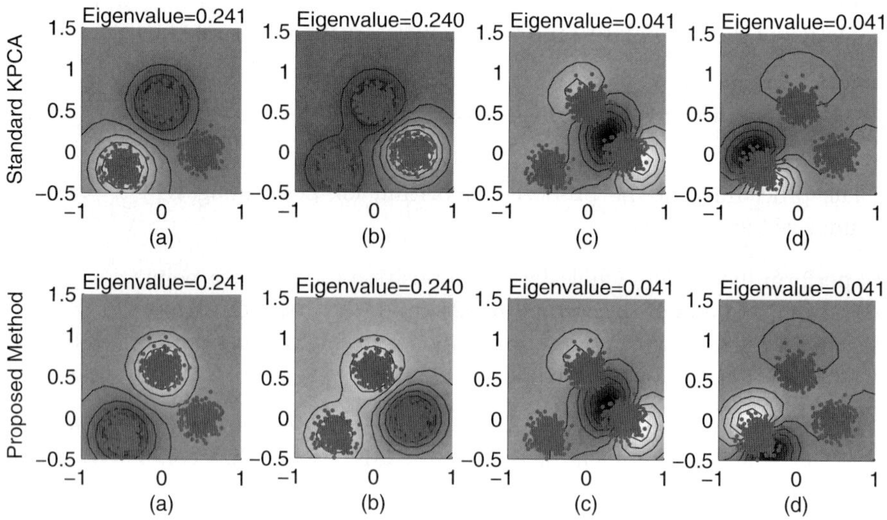


**Fig. 1.** From left to right, the first four nonlinear principal components extracted by standard KPCA (top) and by the proposed method (bottom) using the Gaussian kernel $k(\mathbf{x}_i, \mathbf{x}_j) = \exp(-\|\mathbf{x}_i - \mathbf{x}_j\|^2/0.1)$. The shading shows the principal component values and the constant values are connected by the contour lines.

**Table 1.** Comparison of training time and storage space on the first toy example with 1500 data points (on IntelliStation with 3.06GHz CPU and 3.62GB RAM)

| Methods for performing KPCA | Size of matrix needed to be diagonalized | Training time (seconds) | Storage space (M bytes) |
|---|---|---|---|
| Standard KPCA | $1500 \times 1500$ | 138 | 49 |
| Proposed method | $98 \times 98$ | 5 | 2.5 |

In the second toy example, we generate four parabolic shapes that are vertically and horizontally mirrored by the function $y = x^2 + \delta$, where $x$-values have uniform distribution in $[-1, 1]$ and $\delta$ is normal noise with mean 0.6 and standard deviation 0.1. Each parabolic shape contains 500 data points. The polynomial kernel of degree 2 is adopted. In Fig. 2, we demonstrate the results found by the standard KPCA and the proposed method respectively. Since the dimensionality of the feature space is 3, only 3 linearly independent samples are chosen in using the proposed method. Therefore, the proposed method needs much less time and storage space than the standard KPCA (266 seconds vs. 1 second and 89M bytes vs. 0.5M bytes, to see table 2), while obtaining the same feature values.

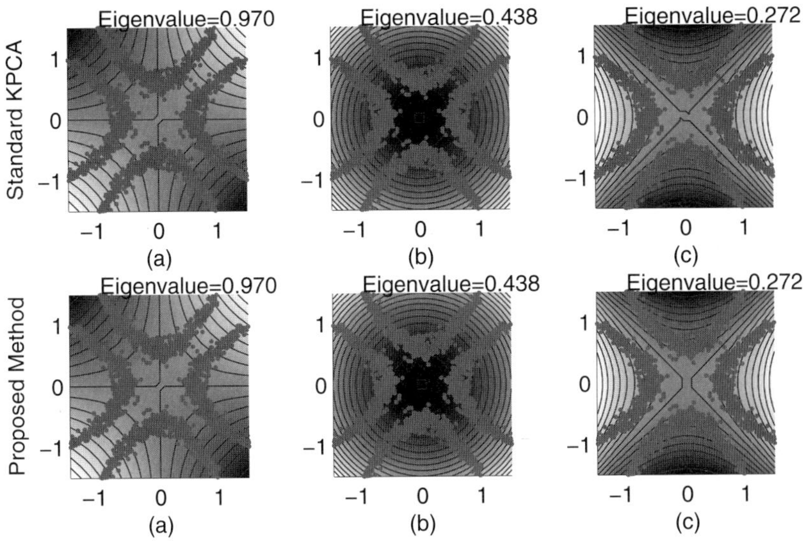


**Fig. 2.** Contour lines of constant values of the first three principal components extracted by standard PCA (top) and the proposed method (bottom) with degree-2 polynomial kernel using 2000 data points

**Table 2.** Comparison of training time and storage space on the second toy example with 2000 data points

| Methods for performing KPCA | Size of matrix needed to be diagonalized | Training time (seconds) | Storage space (M bytes) |
|---|---|---|---|
| Standard KPCA | $2000 \times 2000$ | 266 | 89 |
| Proposed method | $3 \times 3$ | 1 | 0.5 |

### 4.2 Handwritten Digit Recognition

In this experiment, we further compare the performance of the proposed method with that of standard KPCA and Franc and Hlaváč's technique by considering character recognition. We exploit the US Postal Service (USPS) database of handwritten digits collected from mail envelopes in Buffalo, which was also studied by Schölkopf et al. [1] and Zheng et al. [9]. This database contains 7291 samples for training and 2007 ones for testing with dimensionality 256. We use the first 4000 training points to train the standard KPCA, Franc and Hlaváč's method, and the proposed method, respectively, and then use all the 2007 testing points to compare the error rate of recognition. The polynomial kernels of degree 2 through 6 are employed and the *nearest neighbor classifier* is applied to classification. For computational reason, we divide the values of the data vectors by 10. In using Franc and Hlaváč's method, we adopt the same way with this paper to formulate KPCA using the subset selected by their greedy procedure. We set the parameter $\varepsilon = 1$ in their method. In using the proposed method, we also set the threshold $\theta$ to be 1. The experimental results obtained by the three

**Table 3.** Test error rates on the USPS handwritten digit database using three methods, with 4000 training points and 2007 testing points

| Number of | Standard KPCA | | | | | Franc & Hlaváč's method | | | | | Proposed KPCA | | | | |
|---|---|---|---|---|---|---|---|---|---|---|---|---|---|---|---|
| components | d=2 | 3 | 4 | 5 | 6 | 2 | 3 | 4 | 5 | 6 | 2 | 3 | 4 | 5 | 6 |
| 32 | 6.5 | 6.6 | 7.6 | 8.1 | 8.3 | 6.5 | 7.0 | 7.6 | 8.2 | 8.3 | 6.5 | 7.0 | 7.6 | 8.2 | 8.3 |
| 64 | 5.8 | 7.0 | 7.0 | 7.5 | 7.6 | 5.8 | 6.8 | 7.1 | 7.6 | 7.7 | 5.9 | 6.8 | 7.1 | 7.6 | 7.6 |
| 128 | 5.6 | 6.6 | 6.9 | 7.2 | 7.3 | 5.7 | 6.7 | 7.2 | 7.4 | 7.2 | 5.7 | 6.7 | 7.3 | 7.4 | 7.2 |
| 256 | 5.8 | 6.3 | 7.1 | 7.3 | 7.1 | N.A. | 7.2 | 7.2 | 7.4 | 7.1 | N.A. | 7.1 | 7.2 | 7.4 | 7.1 |
| 512 | 5.8 | 6.3 | 7.2 | 8.1 | 8.6 | N.A. | N.A. | 7.9 | 8.3 | 8.6 | N.A. | N.A. | 7.9 | 8.3 | 8.6 |
| 1024 | 5.7 | 6.1 | 7.6 | 9.5 | 10.1 | N.A. | N.A. | N.A. | 9.5 | 10.3 | N.A. | N.A. | N.A. | 9.5 | 10.3 |
| 2048 | 5.6 | 6.0 | 7.2 | 10.1 | 13.2 | N.A. | N.A. | N.A. | N.A. | 13.1 | N.A. | N.A. | N.A. | N.A. | 13.1 |

**Table 4.** Comparison of training time and storage space on the USPS handwritten digit database with 4000 training points

| Methods for performing KPCA | Size of matrix needed to be diagonalized | Training time (seconds) | Storage space (M bytes) |
|---|---|---|---|
| Standard KPCA | 4000 × 4000 | 5508 | 246 |
| Franc and Hlaváč's method (d=2) | 137 × 137 | 201 | 35 |
| Franc and Hlaváč's method (d=3) | 285 × 285 | 549 | 44 |
| Franc and Hlaváč's method (d=4) | 837 × 837 | 1371 | 71 |
| Franc and Hlaváč's method (d=5) | 1631 × 1631 | 2756 | 123 |
| Franc and Hlaváč's method (d=6) | 2392 × 2392 | 6245 | 227 |
| Proposed method (d=2) | 134 × 134 | 12 | 33 |
| Proposed method (d=3) | 274 × 274 | 27 | 39 |
| Proposed method (d=4) | 808 × 808 | 134 | 62 |
| Proposed method (d=5) | 1608 × 1608 | 517 | 115 |
| Proposed method (d=6) | 2364 × 2364 | 1366 | 182 |

approaches are shown in Table 3. Also, we make the comparison of the training time and storage space consumed by the three approaches, as shown in Table 4. From Table 3, we see that the proposed method could achieve similar recognition results as the standard KPCA method. However, from Table 4, we see that the proposed method reduces the time and storage complexity significantly compared with the standard KPCA. When compared with Franc and Hlaváč's method, the proposed method consumes less training time and storage space, and achieves similar recognition accuracy meanwhile.

## 5 Conclusions

Considering that the training samples may lie in a subspace, or close to a subspace, of the feature space with lower dimensionality than the size of samples, we develop a novel algorithm for performing KPCA by choosing some representative samples as a basis for the data. Compared with the standard KPCA method, the proposed method for performing KPCA could reduce the time and storage requirement significantly, especially when the number of training points is large. The methodology of this paper could applied to other kernel-based algorithm provided the algorithm could be expressed by a subset of the entire data points.

## References


1. Schölkopf, B., Smola, A. J., Müller, K.R.: Nonlinear Component Analysis as A Kernel Eigenvalue Prolem. Neural Computation, 10 (1998) 1299-1319
2. Mika, S., Schölkopf, B., Smola, A. J., Müller, K.R., Scholz, M., Rätsch, G.: Kernel PCA and De-noising in Feature Spaces. In: Kearns, M. S., Solla, S. A., Cohn, D. A. (eds.): Advances in Neural Information Processing Systems, Cambridge 11 (1999) 536-542
3. Rosipal, R., Girolami, M., Trejo, L. J., Cichocki, A.: Kernel PCA for Feature Extraction and De-noising in Nonlinear Regression. Neural Comput. Application, 10 (2001) 231-243
4. Kim, K. I., Jung, K., Kim, H. J.: Face Recognition Using Kernel Principal Component Analysis. IEEE Signal Proc. Letter, 19 (2002) 40-42
5. Yang, M. H.: Kernel Eigenfaces vs. Kernel Fisherfaces: Face Recognition Using Kernel Methods. In: Proceedings of the Fifth IEEE International Conference on Automatic Face and Gesture Recognition, Washington (2002) 215-220
6. Kong, H., Wang, L., Teoh, E. K., Li, X., Wang, J. G., Venkateswarlu, R.: Generalized 2D Principal Component Analysis for Face Image Representation and Recognition. Neural Networks, 18 (2005) 585-594
7. Kim, K. I., Franz, M. O., Schölkopf, B.: Iterative Kernel Principal Component Analysis for Image Modelling. IEEE Trans. Patt. Anal. Mach. Intell., 27 (2005) 1351-1366
8. Rosipal, R., Girolami, M.: An Expectation-Maximization Approach to Nonlinear Component Analysis. Neural Computation, 13 (2001) 505-510
9. Zheng, W., Zou, C., Zhao, L.: An Improved Algorithm for Kernel Principal Component Analysis. Neural Proc. Letter, 22 (2005) 49-56
10. Baudat, G., Anouar, F.: Kernel-Based Methods and Function Approximation. In: Proc. Int. Conf. Neural Networks. Washington (2001) 1244-1249
11. Smola, A. J., Schölkopf, B.: Sparse Greedy Matrix Approximation for Machine Learning. In: Langley, P. (eds.): Proceedings of the Seventeenth International Conference on Machine Learning, Morgan Kaufmann, San Francisco (2000) 911-918
12. Tipping, M.: Sparse kernel Principal Component Analysis. In: Leen, T. K., Diettrich, T. G., Tresp, V. (eds.): Advances in Neural Information Processing Systems, Cambridge, 13 (2001) 633-639
13. Ouimet, M., Bengio, Y.: Greedy Spectral Embedding. In: Proceedings of the Tenth International Workshop on Artificial Intelligence and Statistics, Barbade (2005) 253-260
14. Franc, V., Hlaváč, V.: Greedy Algorithm for a Training Set Reduction in the Kernel Methods. In: Petkov, N., Westenberg, M. A. (eds.): Proceedings of the Tenth International Conference on Computer Analysis of Images and Patterns. Lecture Notes in Computer Science, Springer-Verlag, Berlin Heidelberg, 2756 (2003) 426-433
15. Cristianini, N., Lodhi, H., Shawe-Taylor, J.: Latent Semantic Kernels. J. Intell. Inf. Syst., 18 (2002) 127-152
16. Bach, F. R., Jordan, M. I.: Kernel Independent Component Analysis. J. Mach. Learn. Res., 3 (2002) 1-48

## Appendix: The Equivalence of (3) and (11)

Clearly, (11) holds when (3) is true. On the other hand, if (11) is true, we have that, for $m = 1, \ldots, n$,

$$
\begin{aligned}
&\lambda(\phi(\mathbf{x}_m) \cdot \mathbf{v}) = (\phi(\mathbf{x}_m) \cdot C^{\phi}\mathbf{v}) \\
\iff &\lambda\left(\phi(\mathbf{x}_m) \cdot \sum_{i=1}^{n} \beta_i \phi(\mathbf{x}_i)\right) = \\
&\qquad \left(\phi(\mathbf{x}_m) \cdot \frac{1}{N} \sum_{j=1}^{n} \left(\sum_{k=1}^{n}\sum_{i=1}^{n} q_{jk}\beta_i \phi(\mathbf{x}_k)^{\mathsf{T}}\phi(\mathbf{x}_i)\right)\phi(\mathbf{x}_j)\right) \\
\iff &\left(\phi(\mathbf{x}_m) \cdot \sum_{j=1}^{n}\left(\lambda\beta_j - \frac{1}{N}\sum_{k=1}^{n}\sum_{i=1}^{n} q_{jk}\beta_i \phi(\mathbf{x}_k)^{\mathsf{T}}\phi(\mathbf{x}_i)\right)\phi(\mathbf{x}_j)\right) = 0\,.
\end{aligned}
$$

It follows that

$$
\left\| \sum_{j=1}^{n}\left(\lambda\beta_j - \frac{1}{N}\sum_{k=1}^{n}\sum_{i=1}^{n} q_{jk}\beta_i \phi(\mathbf{x}_k)^{\mathsf{T}}\phi(\mathbf{x}_i)\right)\phi(\mathbf{x}_j)\right\| = 0,
$$

which implies (3).

# Kernel-Based Reinforcement Learning

Guanghua Hu[1], Yuqin Qiu[1], and Liming Xiang[2]

[1] School of Mathematics and Statistics, Yunnan University
Kunming, Yunnan, 650091, P.R. China
{ghhu, yqqiu}@ynu.edu.cn
[2] Department of Management Sciences, City University of Hong Kong
83 Tat Chee Avenue, Kowloon, Hong Kong
msxiangl@cityu.edu.hk

**Abstract.** We consider the problem of approximating the cost-to-go functions in reinforcement learning. By mapping the state implicitly into a feature space, we perform a simple algorithm in the feature space, which corresponds to a complex algorithm in the original state space. Two kernel-based reinforcement learning algorithms, the $\varepsilon$ -insensitive kernel based reinforcement learning ( $\varepsilon$ -KRL) and the least squares kernel based reinforcement learning (LS-KRL) are proposed. An example shows that the proposed methods can deal effectively with the reinforcement learning problem without having to explore many states.

## 1 Introduction

The reinforcement learning paradigm can be used to find the optimal behavior for autonomous agents which interact with unmodelled environments. The advantage of using reinforcement learning for robot control is that the desired behaviour need not be completely specified by a human designer. Only the reward function, which is defined in terms of desired outcomes, needs to be specified beforehand.

In the context of reinforcement learning, the most important object is the *cost-to-go* function, which evaluates the expected future cost to be incurred, as a function of the current state. It is used to assess the consequences of any given action at any particular state. Dynamic programming provides a variety of methods for computing cost-to-go functions. Recently, reinforcement learning researchers have developed a number of approaches, including temporal-difference (TD) learning [1] and Q-learning [2]. Due to the curse of dimensionality, however, the practical applications of these methods are somewhat limited. It is essentially impossible to compute the value of the cost-to-go function at every possible state since the state space is huge in practice. Therefore, some methods of approximating cost-to-go functions are proposed such as artificial neural networks [3], temporal-difference learning with function approximation [4] and cost-to-go function with compact representations [5]. These learning methods have the same inadequacy: the convergency requires that the agent explores every state action pair infinite times.

Kernel based learning, which has become a popular technique [6], allows the construction of very powerful nonlinear variants of existing linear scalar product-based algorithms by mapping the date $x$ implicitly into some kernel feature space $\mathcal{F}$ through

D.-S. Huang, K. Li, and G.W. Irwin (Eds.): ICIC 2006, LNCS 4113, pp. 757 – 766, 2006.

some mapping $\varphi:\Re^n \to \mathcal{F}$. Performing a simple linear algorithm in $\mathcal{F}$ then corresponds to a nonlinear algorithm in the input space. The use of kernels enables this technique to be applied without paying the computational penalty implicit in the number of dimensions, since it is possible to evaluate the inner product between the images of two inputs in a feature space without explicitly computing their coordinates.

In this paper, two kernel-based reinforcement learning methods, the $\varepsilon$ -insensitive kernel based reinforcement learning ( $\varepsilon$ -KRL) and the least squares kernel based reinforcement learning (LS-KRL) are proposed and a navigation in a 30×30 maze problem is given. It is shown that the main advantage of these methods is that the agent dose not have to explore as many state-action pairs comparing with the Q-learning.

## 2 Markov Decision Problems and Reinforcement Learning

### 2.1 Markov Decision Problems

Let the tetrad $(S, A, P, r)$ demote the underline irreducible non-periodic Markov decision problem (MDP) model of the environment. Where $S$ is the finite set of states, $A$ the finite set of actions, $P$ the transition law where $p_{ij}(a)$ represents the transition probability from state $i$ to state $j$ when action $a$ is used, and $r(i, j)$ is the scalar reinforcement signal, or the immediate reward the agent received from that transition. Furthermore, the agent does not have all actions available in every state. The nonempty set $A(i) \subseteq A$ denotes the set of admissible actions in state $i$ .

The behavior of the agent is specified by a policy, which is a mapping from situation to action. A stationary closed-loop policy $\mu:\ S \to A$ assigns an action, which is independent on the current time and all previous states and actions, to each state. $\gamma \in (0,1)$ is a discount factor. The cost-to-go function for policy $\mu$ , start from state $i$ is defined by

$$V^{\mu}(i) = E_{\mu}\left[\sum\nolimits_{t=0}^{\infty} \gamma^t r(i_t, i_{t+1}) \mid i_0 = i\right]. \tag{1}$$

*Theorem 1.* [7] Let the stationary policy $\mu$ correspond to a Markov chain with a single recurrent class, then there is a unique vector $V^{\mu}$ such that for all $i \in S$ ,

$$V^{\mu}(i) = \sum_{j \in S} p_{ij}(\mu(i))(r(i, j) + \gamma V^{\mu}(j)) \ . \tag{2}$$

If the cost-to-go function for policy $\mu$ is obtained, an improved policy $\mu^*$ the agent will obtained by taking the so-called greedy policy at every states which defined by

$$\mu^*(i) = \arg\max_{a \in A(i)} \left( r(i,a) + \gamma \sum_{j \in S} P_{ij}(a) V^{\mu}(j) \right) . \tag{3}$$

### 2.2 Reinforcement Learning

Reinforcement learning is process by which an agent improves its behavior in an unknown environment via experience. This means that the $P$ the transition law and the reward function are not known to the agent. In Q-learning, the state-action value $Q(i,a)$ is the long term discounted sum of payoff in state $x$ when action $a$ is performed and the optimal policy is followed thereafter. At the $t$th stage, the agent adjusts its $Q$ -value according to:

$$Q_{t+1}(i,a)=\begin{cases}(1-\alpha_t)Q_t(i,a)+\alpha_t\left[r_t+\gamma V_t(i_{t+1})\right] & \text{if } i=i_t \text{ and } a=a_t\\ Q_t(i,a) & \text{otherwise,}\end{cases} \quad . \tag{4}$$

where $V_t(i)=\max_a Q_t(i,a)$ . When $Q_t$ has converged to the true state-action value, then the greedy policy that selects action according to the following criterion is optimal: $a^*(i)=\arg\max_{a\in A(i)} Q(i,a)$ . Temporal difference learning, a function approximator, approximates $V^*$ using a sequence of function $V_t$ . The traditional implementation of TD($\lambda$) based on eligibility traces is to perform the following update operation to the estimate function at each stage $t$ given that the involved functions are represented as a look-up table.

$$V_{t+1}(i)=V_t(i)+\alpha_t d_t e_i(t) \ . \tag{5}$$

where $d_t=r_t+\gamma V_t(i_{t+1})-V_t(i_t)$, the temporal difference, $e_i(t)$, the eligibility trace function.

## 3 The Support Vector Method of Function Estimation

In this section we review basic ideas of the support vector method (SVM) of function estimation. For further details, one can refer to [8] for the SVM and [9] for the LS-SVM.

Consider regression problem in the following set of function

$$f(x)=w^T\varphi(x) \ . \tag{6}$$

with given training data set $D=\{(x_i,y_i)\}_{i=1}^l$ where $x_i\in\Re^n$ are the input data and $y_i\in\Re$ are the output data. The nonlinear mapping $\varphi:\Re^n\to\mathcal{F}$ maps the input data into a so-called high dimensional feature space $\mathcal{F}$ (which can be infinite dimensional) and $w\in\mathcal{F}$ is the parameter vector. The support vector machines for regression minimizes the structural risk function (7) instead of the empirical risk function

$$\min \quad \frac{\|w\|^2}{2}+C\sum_{i=1}^{l}\left|y_i-w^Tx_i\right|_\varepsilon \ . \tag{7}$$

where $|\square|_\varepsilon$ is the $\varepsilon$ -insensitive loss function defined in (8)

$$|x|_\varepsilon = \begin{cases} 0 & \text{if } |x| < \varepsilon, \\ |x| - \varepsilon & \text{otherwise.} \end{cases} \quad (8)$$

The first term $\|w\|^2$ is called the regularized term. Minimizing $\|w\|^2$ will make a function as flat as possible, thus playing the role of controlling the function capacity. $C$ is a given positive constant which is referred as the regularized constant. This optimization problem is equivalent to (9) by introducing slack variables $\xi_i, \xi_i^*, i = 1,2,...,l$.

$$\begin{aligned} \min \quad & J(w,\xi) = \frac{\|w\|^2}{2} + C\sum_{i=1}^{l}(\xi_i + \xi_i^*) \\ \text{s. t.} \quad & y_i - w^T x_i \le \varepsilon + \xi_i^* \\ & w^T x_i - y_i \le \varepsilon + \xi_i, \quad i = 1,...,l \\ & \xi = (\xi_1,...,\xi_l,\xi_1^*,...,\xi_l^*)^T \ge 0 \end{aligned} \quad (9)$$

Since the feature space is high or even infinite, we consider the dual problem of (9)

$$\begin{aligned} \min \quad & \frac{1}{2}\sum_{i=1}^{l}\sum_{j=1}^{l}(\alpha_i^* - \alpha_i)(\alpha_j^* - \alpha_j)K(x_i,x_j) + \varepsilon\sum_{i=1}^{l}(\alpha_i^* + \alpha_i) - \sum_{i=1}^{l} y_i(\alpha_i^* - \alpha_i) \\ \text{s. t.} \quad & 0 \le \alpha \le Ce, \end{aligned} \quad (10)$$

where the kernel function $K(x,y) = \varphi^T(x)\varphi(y)$ and $\alpha = (\alpha_1,...\alpha_1^*,...,\alpha_l^*)^T$, $e = (1,...,1)^T$. The desired vector has the following expansion:

$$w = \sum_{i=1}^{l}(\alpha_i^* - \alpha_i)\varphi(x_i) . \quad (11)$$

and the regression function is

$$f(x) = \sum_{i=1}^{l}(\alpha_i^* - \alpha_i)\varphi^T(x_i)\varphi(x) = \sum_{i=1}^{l}(\alpha_i^* - \alpha_i)K(x_i,x) . \quad (12)$$

The LS-SVM (13) is obtained simply by using squares loss function instead of $\varepsilon$-insensitive loss function

$$\begin{aligned} \min \quad & R(w) = \frac{1}{2}\|w\|^2 + C\sum_{i=1}^{l}\xi_i^2 \\ \text{s.t.} \quad & \xi_i = y_i - w^T\varphi(x_i) \qquad i = 1,2,...,l, \end{aligned} \quad (13)$$

Similarly, it is easy to obtain that

$$w = \sum_{i=1}^{l}\alpha_i\varphi(x_i) . \quad (14)$$

where the Lagrange multipliers $\alpha$ are the solutions of following equations

$$(C^{-1}I + K)\alpha = y \ . \tag{15}$$

With

$$\alpha = (\alpha_1, \cdots, \alpha_l)^T, y = (y_1, \cdots, y_l)^T \ . \tag{16}$$

and

$$K_{ij} = K(x_i, x_j) = \varphi^T(x_i)\varphi(x_j), \ \ i, j = 1, 2, \cdots, l \ . \tag{17}$$

There fore, the solution of the regression problem is

$$f(x) = \sum_{i=1}^{l} \alpha_i \varphi^T(x_i)\varphi(x) = \sum_{i=1}^{l} \alpha_i K(x_i, x) \ . \tag{18}$$

# 4 Kernel-Based Reinforcement Learning

## 4.1 $\varepsilon$-Kernel Based Reinforcement Learning

Now, suppose the current policy is given and the cost-to-go function of current policy $V(i)$ is approximated as

$$V(i) = w^T\varphi(i), \ \ i \in S \ . \tag{19}$$

where the nonlinear mapping $\varphi: \Re^n \to \mathcal{F}$ maps the state space into the feature space $\mathcal{F}$, we relate the training data $D = \{(x_i, y_i)\}_{i=1}^{l}$ in Eq. (6) to the state and payoff sequences in Eq. (2), i.e. $D = \{i_t, r_t, i_{t+1}\}_{t=0}^{l-1}$. Consider the optimal equation (2) we know that the temporal-differences $d_t$ are close to zero. Therefore, the $\varepsilon$-kernel based reinforcement learning ($\varepsilon$-KRL) proposed is the following optimal problem:

$$\begin{aligned} \min \quad & J(w,\xi) = \frac{1}{2}w^T w + \sum_{t=0}^{l-1} C_t(\xi_t + \xi_t^*) \\ \text{s. t.} \quad & r_t - w^T(\varphi(i_t) - \gamma\varphi(i_{t+1})) \le \varepsilon + \xi_t^* \\ & w^T(\varphi(i_t) - \gamma\varphi(i_{t+1})) - r_t \le \varepsilon + \xi_t, \quad t = 0, \cdots, l-1 \\ & \xi \ge 0. \end{aligned} \ . \tag{20}$$

Where $C_t, t = 0, \cdots, l-1$ give the trade-off between training data set $D = \{i_t, r_t, i_{t+1}\}_{t=0}^{l-1}$. To solve problem (20) we find the saddle point of the Lagrangian

$$\begin{aligned} L(w,\xi,\alpha,\eta) = & \frac{1}{2}w^T w + \sum_{t=0}^{l-1} C_t(\xi_t + \xi_t^*) - \sum_{t=0}^{l-1} \alpha_t \left(\varepsilon + \xi_t^* - r_t + w^T(\varphi(i_t) - \gamma\varphi(i_{t+1}))\right) \\ & - \sum_{t=0}^{l-1} \alpha_t^* \left(\varepsilon + \xi_t^* + r_t - w^T(\varphi(i_t) - \gamma\varphi(i_{t+1}))\right) - \sum_{t=0}^{l-1} (\eta_t\xi_t + \eta_t^*\xi_t^*) \\ & \alpha, \ \ \eta \ge 0. \end{aligned} \ . \tag{21}$$

The parameters that minimize the Lagrangian must satisfy

$$\begin{aligned} &\frac{\partial L}{\partial w}=0 \;\Rightarrow\; w=\sum_{t=0}^{l-1}(\alpha_t^*-\alpha_t)\left(\varphi(i_t)-\gamma\varphi(i_{t+1})\right), \\ &\frac{\partial L}{\partial \xi}=0 \;\Rightarrow\; C-\alpha-\eta=0, \end{aligned} \quad . \tag{22}$$

where $C=\left(C_0,\cdots,C_{l-1},C_0,\cdots C_{l-1}\right)^T$ , $\alpha=\left(\alpha_0,\cdots,\alpha_{l-1},\alpha_0^*,\cdots\alpha_{l-1}^*\right)^T$ and $\eta=\left(\eta_0,\cdots,\eta_{l-1},\eta_0^*,\cdots\eta_{l-1}^*\right)^T$. Substituting (22) into the Lagrangian, we obtain the dual problem of (20)

$$\begin{aligned} \min \;& \frac{1}{2}\sum_{t=0}^{l-1}\sum_{k=0}^{l-1}(\alpha_t^*-\alpha_t)(\alpha_k^*-\alpha_k)\Omega_{tk}+\varepsilon\sum_{t=0}^{l-1}(\alpha_t^*+\alpha_t)-\sum_{t=0}^{l-1}r_t(\alpha_t^*-\alpha_t) \\ \text{s.t. } \;& 0\le\alpha\le C, \end{aligned} \quad . \tag{23}$$

Where

$$\begin{aligned} \Omega_{tk} &=\left(\varphi(i_t)-\gamma\varphi(i_{t+1})\right)^T\left(\varphi(i_k)-\gamma\varphi(i_{k+1})\right) \\ &=K(i_t,i_k)-\gamma\left(K(i_t,i_{k+1})+K(i_k,i_{t+1})\right)+\gamma^2K(i_{t+1},i_{k+1}). \end{aligned} \quad . \tag{24}$$

and the kernel function

$$K(i_t,i_k)=\varphi^T(i_t)\varphi(i_k)\ . \tag{25}$$

After solving problem (23), the cost-to-go function is approximated by

$$\begin{aligned} V(i)&=w^T\varphi(i) \\ &=\sum_{t=0}^{l-1}\left(\alpha_t^*-\alpha_t\right)\left(K(i_t,i)-\gamma K(i_{t+1},i)\right). \end{aligned} \quad . \tag{26}$$

From this approximating value function an approving policy is obtained by greedy strategy

$$\mu^*(i)=\arg\max_{a\in A(i)}\left(r(i,a)+\gamma\sum_{j\in S}P_{ij}(a)V^{\mu}(j)\right)\ . \tag{27}$$

There are variant methods for choice of the kernel. The most popular is the polynomial kernel

$$K(x,y)=\left(<x,y>+c\right)^d\ . \tag{28}$$

and the Gaussian kernel

$$K(x,y)=\exp\left(-\frac{\|x-y\|^2}{\sigma^2}\right)\ . \tag{29}$$

where $<x,y>$ represents the inner production of two vectors $x$ and $y$.

### 4.2 Least Squares Kernel Based Reinforcement Learning

As the LS-SVM, the least squares kernel based reinforcement learning (LS-KRL) proposed in this paper solving the following problem:

$$\begin{aligned} \min \quad & J(w,d) = \frac{1}{2} w^T w + \frac{1}{l} \sum_{t=0}^{l-1} C_t d_t^2 \\ \text{s.t.} \quad & d_t = r_t + \gamma V(i_{t+1}) - V(i_t), \qquad t = 0,1,..,l-1. \end{aligned} \quad (30)$$

which makes the temporal differences $d_t = r_t + \gamma w^T \varphi(i_{t+1}) - w^T \varphi(i_t)$ close to zero as well as low structural complexity . One defines the Lagrangian function

$$L(w,d,\alpha) = J(w,d) - \sum_{t=0}^{l-1} \alpha_t \left( d_t - r_t + w^T (\varphi(i_t) - \gamma\varphi(i_{t+1})) \right) . \quad (31)$$

where $\alpha_t$ are Lagrange multipliers which can be either positive or negative due to the equality constraints. The conditions for optimality

$$\begin{aligned} & \frac{\partial L}{\partial w} = 0 \ \Rightarrow \ w = \sum_{t=0}^{l-1} \alpha_t (\varphi(i_t) - \gamma\varphi(i_{t+1})) \\ & \frac{\partial L}{\partial d_t} = 0 \ \Rightarrow \ \alpha_t = C_t d_t \qquad\qquad t = 0,1,\cdots,l-1 \end{aligned} \quad (32)$$

can be written as the solution to the following set of linear equations after elimination of $w$ and $d$

$$(C^{-1} + \Omega)\alpha = r \ . \quad (33)$$

with

$$C = \text{diag}(C_0,\cdots,C_{l-1}),\ \alpha = (\alpha_0,...,\alpha_{l-1})^T ,\ \text{and}\ \ r = (r_0,...,r_{l-1})^T \ . \quad (34)$$

and the definition of $\Omega$ is the same as in $\varepsilon$-KRL.

The cost-to-go function is approximated by

$$\begin{aligned} V(i) &= w^T \varphi(i) \\ &= \sum_{t=0}^{l-1} \alpha_t \left( K(i_t,i) - \gamma K(i_{t+1},i) \right). \end{aligned} \quad (35)$$

## 5 Experiment and Results

Here we illustrate the $\varepsilon$-KRL and the LS-KRL method on a maze problem. An agent is placed in a 30×30 square maze (Fig.1). The agent can take, in each state, one of four possible actions: *Up*, *Down*, *Left*, or *Right*. Each of these actions has the effect of moving the agent to an adjacent state except that any action, which would ostensibly move the agent outside the maze, has the actual effect of keeping the agent at its current location. At the beginning of each trial, the agent is placed in a random state and the object of the agent is to navigate itself through the maze to the goal states where two goal states are $(6,6)$ and $(25,25)$ marked with '★'.

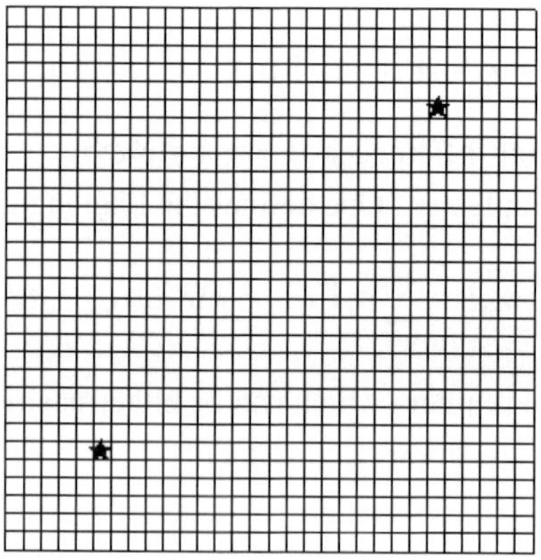

**Fig. 1.** The $30\times30$ maze problem. Two goal states $(6,6)$ and $(25,25)$ are represented as '★.

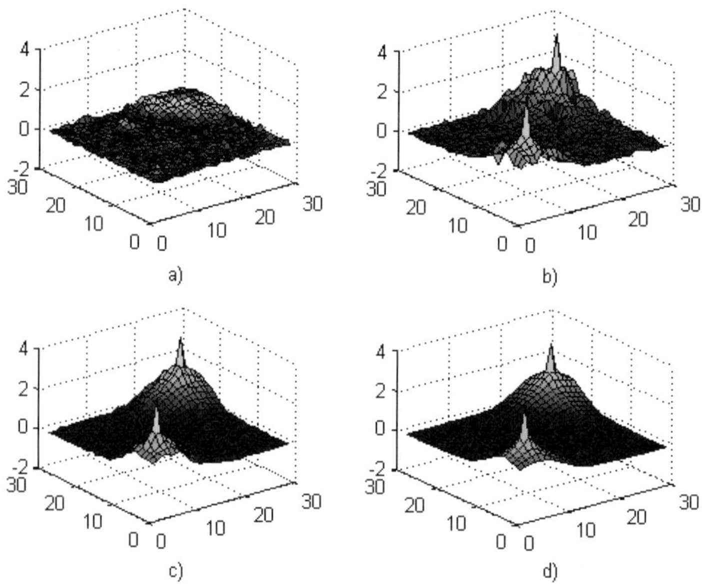


**Fig. 2.** The approximating cost-to-go functions with the $\varepsilon-\mathrm{KRL}$. a) $n=485$, b) $n$ = 631, c) $n=796$ and d) $n=$ 900, where $n$ is the number of states which the agent has explored.

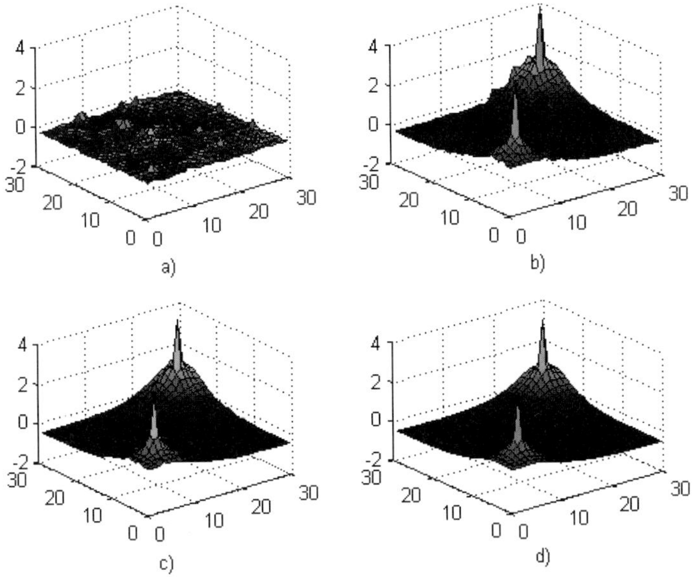


**Fig. 3.** The approximating cost-to-go functions with the LS-KRL. The states the agent has explored are the same as the $\varepsilon-$KRL .

The given policy is the *Uniform* policy, that is, at each state, the agent chooses each action with the same probability. It receives an immediate reinforcement $r=10$ only when it reaches one of the two goal states, otherwise, the reinforcement $r=-0.1$ which means that the cost agent should pay. The approximating cost-to-go function obtained from the $\varepsilon$-KRL and the LS-KRL methods are shown in Fig. 2 and Fig. 3, respectively. Four different approximating functions are given for difference training data sets both in Fig. 2 and Fig. 3. In our experiment, four cases are considered: *a*) *T*=5000, *b*) *T*=10000, *c*) *T*=20000 and *d*) *T*=100000 where *T* is the total number of state transitions. Correspondently, not counting the same state-action pairs, there are 485 difference states the agent has explored in case *a*), 631 states in case *b*) and 796 states in case *c*). In case *d*), the agent has explored all of the states. In the experiment, Gaussian kernel function (29) is used with $\sigma=0.3$, $C_t=50$ and $\varepsilon=0.5$ in the $\varepsilon$-KRL. The greedy policy comes from these is an optimal policy for the case *c*) and case *d*). Here we can see the advantage of the kernel-based reinforcement learning comparing to the classical reinforcement learning methods. The agent does not need too many interactions with the environment. It can approximate satisfyingly the cost-to-go function even when one third of states have not been explored.

## 6 Conclusion

The kernel based learning methods are very powerful learning techniques and have been applied to many fields such as pattern recognition, regression estimation, density estimation, principle component analysis and blind source separation etc. The support vector machines (SVM) is a popular learning method based on these methods. In this paper, the kernel-based methods have been used in a reinforcement learning problem. The $\varepsilon$ -kernel-based reinforcement learning and the least squares kernel-based reinforcement learning methods are proposed. It provides with many advantages of the kernel-based learning methods. However, the methods have suffered some disadvantages the kernel based learning methods have, for example, solving large-scale QP problem in the $\varepsilon$ -KRL and the losing sparsity of the representation in the LS-KRL. Recently, some methods to deal with such issues are proposed in literature [9], [10], [11] and [12]. They will be applied to the $\varepsilon$ -KRL and the LS-KRL context in our future work.

## Acknowledgements

This work is supported by the National Natural Science Foundation of China (10271103). We also acknowledge the referees for their helpful advices.

## References

1. Sutton, R.S.: Learning to Predict by the Methods of Temporal Differences. Machine Learning, Vol. 3 (1988) 9-44
2. Watkins, C.J.C.H.: Q-Learning. Machine Learning, Vol. 8 (1992) 279-292
3. Santharam, G., Sastry, P.S.: A Reinforcement Learning Neural Network for Adaptive Control Markov Chains. IEEE Transactions on System, Man and Cybernetics-Part A, Vol.27 (1997) 588-600
4. Tsitsiklis, J.N., Roy, B.V.: An Analysis of Temporal-Difference Learning with Function Approximation. IEEE Transactions on Automatic Control, Vol. 42 (1997) 674-690
5. Tsitsiklis, J.N., Roy, B.V.: Feature-Based Methods for Large Scale Dynamic Programming. Machine Learning, Vol. 22 (1996) 59-94
6. Shawe-Taylor, J., Cristianini, N.: Kernel Methods for Pattern Analysis. Cambridge University Press, Camgbridge (2004)
7. Bertsekas, D.P.: Dynamic Programming: Deterministic and Stochastic Methods. Prentice-Hall, Englewood Cliffs, NJ, 1987
8. Vapnik, V.N.: Statistical Learning Theory. John Wiley & Sons, New York (1998)
9. Cawley, G.C., Talbot, N.L.C.: Improved Sparse Least-Squares Support Vector Machines. Neurocomputing, Vol. 48 (2002) 1025-1031
10. Flake, G.W. , Lawrence, S.: Efficient SVM Regression Training with SMO. Machine Learning, Vol. 46 (2002) 271-290
11. Suykens, J.A.K., Brabanter, J.D., Lukas, L. , Vandewalle, J.: Weighted Least Squares Support Machines: Robustness and Sparse Approximation. Neurocomputing, Vol. 48(2002) 85-105
12. Platt J.: Fast Training of Support Vector Machines Using Sequential Minimal Optimization. In B Scholkopf, C J Burges, A J Smola, editors, Advances in Kernel Methods – Support Vector Learning. Cambridge, MA: MIT Press., (1999) 185-208

# A Fast Feature Extraction Method for Kernel 2DPCA

Ning Sun[1, 2], Hai-xian Wang[1], Zhen-hai Ji[1, 2], Cai-rong Zou[2], and Li Zhao[1, 2]

[1] Research Center of Learning Science, Southeast University, Nanjing 210096, China
[2] Department of Radio Engineering, Southeast University, Nanjing 210096, China
sunning@seu.edu.cn

**Abstract.** Recently, a new approach called two-dimensional principal component analysis (2DPCA) has been proposed for face representation and recognition. The essence of 2DPCA is that it computes the eigenvectors of the so called image covariance matrix without matrix-to-vector conversion. Kernel principal component analysis (KPCA) is a non-linear generation of the popular principal component analysis via the kernel trick. Similarly, the kernelization of 2DPCA can be benefit to develop the nonlinear structures in the input data. However, the standard K2DPCA always suffers from the computational problem for using the image matrix directly. In this paper, we propose an efficient algorithm to speed up the training procedure of K2DPCA. The results of experiment on face recognition show that the proposed algorithm can achieve much more computational efficiency and remarkably save the memory-consuming compared to the standard K2DPCA. required format.

## 1 Introduction

Feature extraction is the key problem to the pattern recognition task. The aim of feature extraction is to project the high dimensional sample data onto the optimal projection matrix and yield the low dimensional feature data as representative as possible. PCA[1],[2] is one of the most famous technique of feature extraction, which maps the sample vectors considered as a point in high dimensional space into low dimensional subspace. Two dimensional PCA (2DPCA) method, firstly introduced by Yang et al[3], is based on the two dimensional matrix without matrix-to-vector conversion, by which eigenvectors are extracted from the image covariance matrix directly constructed by original image matrices. 2DPCA has three important advantages over PCA. Firstly, the 2D spatial information of the sample is well preserved by directly using original 2D image matrices rather than 1D vector. Secondly, the 2DPCA method is working on the row direction of image, the dimension of which is much smaller than that of covariance in PCA. The last one is that 2DPCA can effectively avoid the Small Sample Size (SSS) problem, which will achieve good recognition accuracy when even only one sample is contained in each class. However, PCA and 2DPCA are all linear techniques of feature extraction, and the pattern recognition problems are mostly nonlinear classification tasks under real situation. So, it is necessary to generalize the 2DPCA method for modeling the nonlinear structure.

KPCA[4] is the nonlinear generalization of the conventional PCA via the kernel trick, which is a powerful method for classification and regression application[4],[5]. The input data are mapped onto a higher or even infinite dimensional Hilbert space F

D.-S. Huang, K. Li, and G.W. Irwin (Eds.): ICIC 2006, LNCS 4113, pp. 767 – 774, 2006.

firstly, and the standard PCA is performed in the feature space F. Likewise, the kernelization of 2DPCA can be benefit to develop the nonlinear structures in the input data. Because the 2DPCA is working on the row of the sample image, the nonlinear generation of 2DPCA need map each row of samples onto feature space via kernel trick. As a result, the dimension of kernel matrix of training sample is very high, and the procedure of diagonalizing the kernel matrix is quite time-consuming. To overcome the suffering of computation cost, we present an efficient algorithm for kernel two-dimensional PCA (K2DPCA). Motivated by the Zheng's method[6], the proposed method divided the kernel matrix into several sub matrices, and then performed dimension reduction on each sub matrix to obtain the approximate new kernel matrix with smaller size. Finally, we diagonalized the new kernel matrix to extract the eigenvectors.

The remainder of this paper is organized as follows: In section 2, we introduce the standard K2DPCA. The efficient method for K2DPCA is developed in section 3. In section 4, experimental results are presented to demonstrate the performance of the proposed method. Finally, the conclusions are presented in section 5.

## 2 Kernel 2DPCA

Given a set of samples $x_i, i = 1 \cdots N$, let $x_i = (x_i^1, \cdots x_i^s)^T$ to be $s \times t$ matrix, where $x_i^j, j = 1, \cdots, s$ is the $j$ row of $i$th samples. Suppose that $\phi$ is an implicit nonlinear map which maps the $x_i^j$ into feature space F:

$$\phi: \ R^t \to F, \ \ x_i^j \to \phi(x_i^j) \ , \ \ (i = 1, \cdots N; j = 1, \cdots, s) \tag{1}$$

The implicit feature vector $\phi$ does not need to compute explicitly, which can just be obtained by computing the dot product of two vectors in F. The dot product can be calculated through a kernel function:

$$k(x_i, x_j) = (\phi(x_i) \cdot \phi(x_j)) \tag{2}$$

And the $\phi$-mapping sample is defined as following:

$$\phi(x_i) = (\phi(x_i^1), \cdots, \phi(x_i^s))^T, \ \ (i = 1, \cdots, N) \tag{3}$$

where we assume that the mapping samples are centered in F.

The aim of kernel 2DPCA is to perform the 2DPCA in the feature space F, and the image covariance matrix is

$$S^\phi = \frac{1}{N} \sum_{i=1}^{N} \phi(x_i)^T \phi(x_i) = \frac{1}{N} \sum_{j=1}^{s} \sum_{i=1}^{N} \phi(x_i^j) \phi(x_i^j)^T \tag{4}$$

so the feature vectors $\beta$ corresponding to the feature values $b \neq 0$ are obtained as:

$$S^\phi \beta = b\beta \tag{5}$$

We solve the Equ.(5) and extract the nonlinear principal component based on the Schölkopf's method[4]. All solution $\beta$ with $b \neq 0$ lie in the span of $\phi(x_1^1), \cdots, \phi(x_N^1), \phi(x_2^1), \cdots, \phi(x_N^s)$ , and the coefficients are denoted as $\delta_i^j \, (i = 1, \cdots, N; j = 1, \cdots, s)$, so the $\beta$ can be rewritten as following forms

$$\beta = \sum_{j=1}^{s} \sum_{i=1}^{N} \delta_i^j \phi(x_i^j) \tag{6}$$

then the Equ.(5) is equal to

$$(S^{\phi} \beta \cdot \phi(x_i^j)) = b(\beta \cdot \phi(x_i^j)) \tag{7}$$

Combined the Equ.(6) and the Equ.(7), we can get

$$K\delta = Nb\delta \tag{8}$$

where $\delta = (\delta_1^1, \cdots, \delta_N^1, \delta_1^2, \cdots, \delta_N^s)$, so the kernel matrix is

$$K = (\phi(x_1^1), \cdots, \phi(x_N^1), \phi(x_1^2), \cdots, \phi(x_N^s))^T (\phi(x_1^1), \cdots, \phi(x_N^1), \phi(x_1^2), \cdots, \phi(x_N^s)) \tag{9}$$

Let $b_1 \geq \cdots \geq b_{sN}$ to be the eigenvalues of *K*, and the corresponding eigenvectors are $\delta^{(1)}, \cdots, \delta^{(sN)}$. From the Equ.(6), the eigenvector $\beta^m$ corresponding to $b_m$ is normalized as:

$$(\beta^m, \beta^m) = b_m (\delta^{(m)}, \delta^{(m)}) = 1 \tag{10}$$

The projection of a test sample $t = (t^1, \cdots, t^s)^T$ onto the eigenvectors $\beta^m$ can be calculated by

$$w_m^{\phi} = \phi(t)\beta^m = \begin{pmatrix} \phi(t^1)^T \\ \vdots \\ \phi(t^s)^T \end{pmatrix} \sum_{j=1}^{s} \sum_{i=1}^{N} \delta_i^{j(m)} \phi(x_i^j) = \begin{pmatrix} \sum_{j=1}^{s} \sum_{i=1}^{N} \delta_i^{j(m)} k(t^1, x_i^j) \\ \vdots \\ \sum_{j=1}^{s} \sum_{i=1}^{N} \delta_i^{j(m)} k(t^s, x_i^j) \end{pmatrix} \tag{11}$$

where $\delta_i^{j(m)} \, (i = 1, \cdots, N; j = 1, \cdots, s)$ is the element of vector $\delta^{(m)}$.

The above algorithm is called standard K2DPCA for two reasons. Firstly, it explicitly develops the model of K2DPCA with analytic solution. Secondly, as concern as the computation complexity, the model is primary. For the size of kernel matrix *K* is the $sN \times sN$ , the complexity of diagonalizing the kernel matrix *K* is $O((sN)^3)$. Because *sN* is always large in the real pattern recognition tasks, the standard K2DPCA suffers from computational problem. In the next section, we propose an efficient algorithm for K2DPCA to reduce the computation complexity.

## 3 Efficient Algorithm for K2DPCA

We divide the kernel matrix K into $s \times s$ block matrix $K(j,l)_{j,l=1,\cdots,s}$, where $K(j,l)$ is $N \times N$ sub matrix:

$$K(j,l) = (\phi(x_1^l),\cdots,\phi(x_N^l))^T (\phi(x_1^l),\cdots,\phi(x_N^l)) \tag{12}$$

Let $S^\phi(j) = (1/N)\sum_{i=1}^N \phi(x_i^j)\phi(x_i^j)^T$ $,(i=1,\cdots,s)$. From Equ.(4 ) we obtain

$$S^\phi = \frac{1}{N}\sum_{j=1}^{s}\sum_{i=1}^{N}\phi(x_i^j)\phi(x_i^j)^T = \sum_{j=1}^{s} S^\phi(j) \tag{13}$$

Suppose that $b_1(j) \geq \cdots \geq b_{n_j}(j)$ are the eigenvalues of $S^\phi(j)$, and the corresponding eigenvectors are $\beta^1(j),\cdots,\beta^{n_j}(j)$, then we get

$$S^\phi(j) = \sum_{m=1}^{n_j} b_m(j)\beta^m(j)\beta^m(j)^T = \sum_{m=1}^{n_j}\breve{\beta}^m(j)\breve{\beta}^m(j)^T \tag{14}$$

$$\breve{\beta}^m(j) = \sqrt{b_m(j)}\beta^m(j) = \sum_{i=1}^N \delta_i^{(m)}(j)\phi(x_i^j) \tag{15}$$

where $\delta^{(m)}(j) = (\delta_1^{(m)}(j),\cdots,\delta_N^{(m)}(j))^T$ is the eigenvector of eigenequation

$$K(j,j)\delta^m(j) = Nb_m(j)\delta^{(m)}(j) \tag{16}$$

its corresponding eigenvalue is $Nb_m(j)$, which satisfied

$$N(\delta^{(m)}(j)\cdot\delta^{(m)}(j)) = 1 \tag{17}$$

To each $S^\phi(j)$, we choose $h_j$ leading eigenvalue such that

$$\sum_{j=1}^s \sum_{m=h_j+1}^{n_j} b_m(j) << \sum_{j=1}^s \sum_{m=1}^{n_j} b_m(j) \tag{18}$$

From Equ.(13) and Equ.(14), we obtain

$$S^\phi = \sum_{j=1}^{s} S^\phi(j) \approx \sum_{j=1}^{s}\sum_{m=1}^{h_j}\breve{\beta}^m(j)\breve{\beta}^m(j)^T = \breve{S}^\phi \tag{19}$$

Thereby, we can turn to solve the eigenvalues problem of matrix $\breve{S}^\phi$ instead of diagonalizing $S^\phi$ since $\breve{S}^\phi$ is approximate to $S^\phi$. Assume that $\breve{\lambda}$ and $\breve{v}$ is the eigenvalue and eigenvectors respectively, then the eigenequation is

$$\breve{S}^\phi\breve{v} = \breve{\lambda}\breve{v} \tag{20}$$

So, $\breve{v}$ can be denoted by

$$\breve{v} = \sum_{j=1}^{s} \sum_{m=1}^{h_j} \eta_m^j \breve{\beta}^m(j) \triangleq \sum_{j=1}^{s} (\phi(x_1^j), \cdots, \phi(x_N^j)) \Delta(j) \eta^j \tag{21}$$

where the weights are $\eta^j = (\eta_1^j, \cdots, \eta_{h_j}^j)^T, (m = 1, \cdots, h_j; j = 1, \cdots, s)$ and the coefficients matrix is $\Delta(j) = (\delta^{(1)}(j), \cdots, \delta^{(h_j)}(j))$. After that the Equ.(20) is equal to

$$\breve{K}\eta = \breve{\lambda}\eta \tag{22}$$

in which $\eta = (\eta_1^1, \cdots, \eta_{h_1}^1, \eta_1^2, \cdots, \eta_{h_s}^s)^T$, $\breve{K} = (\breve{K}(j,l))_{j,l=1,\cdots,s}$ is $s \times s$ block matrix, and the size of each sub matrix is $h_j \times h_l$

$$\breve{K}(j,l) = \Delta(j)^T K(j,l) \Delta(l) \tag{23}$$

Let $\breve{\lambda}_1, \cdots, \breve{\lambda}_Q$ are the $Q$ leading eigenvalues of the $\breve{K}$, the corresponding eigenvectors are $\breve{v}^1, \cdots, \breve{v}^Q$. And the normalization of $\eta^{(r)}$ with nonzero $\breve{\lambda}_r$ are $\breve{\lambda}_r(\eta^{(r)} \cdot \eta^{(r)}) = 1$. Then the projection of a test sample $t = (t^1, \cdots, t^s)^T$ onto the eigenvectors $\breve{v}^r$ can be obtained by

$$w_r^\phi = \phi(t)\breve{v}^r \triangleq \sum_{j=1}^{s} K(j)\Delta(j)\eta^{j(r)}, \quad (r = 1, \cdots, Q) \tag{24}$$

Hence, the nonlinear principal component matrix of $t$ corresponding to $\phi$ is $A^\phi = (w_1^\phi, \cdots, w_Q^\phi)$.

The efficient K2DPCA turns to solve the eigenvalue problem of the new kernel matrix $\breve{K}$ and the diagonal sub matrix $K(j,j)$ $(j = 1, \cdots, s)$. Thus the complexity of the proposed method is $\max(O((\sum_{j=1}^{s} h_j)^3), O(sN^3))$. In addition, the proposed approach just needs to store new kernel matrix $\breve{K}$ with lower dimension rather than the standard kernel matrix $K$.

The procedure of efficient algorithm for K2DPCA is summarized in the following steps:

1. Divide the kernel matrix $K$ into $s \times s$ block matrix $K(j,l)_{j,l=1,\cdots,s}$, where $K(j,l)$ is $N \times N$ sub matrix.
2. Obtain the principal components of the sub matrix $K(j,j)_{j=1,\cdots,s}$.
3. Select the leading principal components of $K(j,l)$ to compute the matrix $\breve{K}(j,l)$, and then construct the $\breve{S}^\phi$
4. Diagonalize $\breve{S}^\phi$ to get eigenvalues $\breve{\lambda}$ and eigenvectors $\breve{v}$ base on Equ.(20).
5. Compute projections of test points onto the eigenvectors $\breve{v}$ using Equ.(24).

## 4 Experiments and Discussion

In this section, we design experiments about face recognition to test the performance of the efficient K2DPCA method on ORL face database. All of our experiments are carried out on a PC with P4 3.0G CPU, 1GMB memory and the matlab 7.0 software platform.

The ORL database contains total 400 images with 112×92 dimension from 40 individuals, each providing 10 different images. To reduce the computation complexity, each face image is downsampled to 28×23 in our experiments.

**Table 1.** Recognition accuracy for degree on face recognition using the standard K2DPCA

| Components percent | Recognition accuracy for degree | | | | | |
|---|---|---|---|---|---|---|
| | 1(2DPCA) | 2 | 3 | 4 | 5 | 6 |
| 95 | 90.41 | 93.33 | 93.33 | 93.33 | 92.91 | 92.08 |
| 90 | 90.83 | 93.33 | 93.75 | 92.91 | 92.50 | 92.08 |
| 85 | 90.83 | 92.91 | 93.75 | 92.92 | 92.50 | 91.67 |
| 80 | 88.75 | 91.67 | 92.50 | 92.50 | 89.17 | 88.75 |
| 75 | 88.33 | 89.17 | 90.83 | 91.25 | 88.33 | 87.50 |
| 70 | 87.50 | 87.92 | 88.33 | 88.75 | 86.67 | 86.67 |

We select 4 images per class (individual) for training and the rest images for testing. Thus, the total number of training samples and testing samples is 160 and 240 respectively. From section 2, the size of kernel matrix $K$ of the standard K2DPCA is $sN \times sN = 4480 \times 4480$ in our experiment, we firstly divide $K$ into $s \times s = 28 \times 28$ block matrix $K(j,l)$, where $K(j,l)$ is $N \times N = 160 \times 160$ sub matrix. To each sub matrix $K(j,j)$, we select the 98% leading components to compute the $\Delta(j)$ and construct the $\breve{S}^{\phi}$. The polynomial kernel $k(x,y) = (x^T y)^d$ is used in the experiment, where $d$ is the degree of the polynomial kernel. Table 1 and Table 2 show the experimental results of the standard K2DPCA and the efficient one. The first column of the two tables means that we select the leading components of $\breve{S}^{\phi}$ just beyond the values. From the two tables, we can find that the efficient K2DPCA method achieves the same best results (=93.75%) as the standard K2DPCA method. And the corresponding results of the two K2DPCA approach are highly alike. As a result, the efficient K2DPCA is the approximate version of the standard K2DPCA, and the difference between the two approaches is very small as concern as the recognition accuracy.

Furthermore, the comparison of the training time and space needed with different samples in our experiments is shown in the table 3. The all highest accuracy listed in the table 3 is achieved when the polynomial kernel degree $d = 2$. In addition, we only show the three pairwise results because the higher number of training samples may cause the out of memory problem. From table 3, we find that the efficient approach can significantly reduce the training time and space compared to the standard K2DPCA.

**Table 2.** Recognition accuracy for degree on face recognition using the efficient K2DPCA

| Components percent | Recognition accuracy for degree | | | | | |
|---|---|---|---|---|---|---|
| | 1(2DPCA) | 2 | 3 | 4 | 5 | 6 |
| 95 | 90.41 | 93.33 | 93.75 | 92.91 | 92.91 | 91.67 |
| 90 | 90.83 | 93.33 | 93.75 | 93.33 | 92.50 | 92.08 |
| 85 | 90.83 | 92.50 | 92.91 | 93.33 | 92.50 | 91.67 |
| 80 | 88.75 | 91.67 | 92.91 | 92.50 | 89.17 | 88.75 |
| 75 | 88.33 | 90.00 | 90.83 | 91.25 | 88.33 | 87.50 |
| 70 | 87.50 | 88.33 | 88.75 | 89.17 | 87.92 | 87.06 |

**Table 3.** Comparison of the training time and space needed with different samples

| *Method* | *Training samples* | *Training time (s)* | *Space (M)* | *Accuracy (%)* |
|---|---|---|---|---|
| Standard K2DPCA | 160 | 6113 | 379 | 93.75 |
| | 120 | 2970 | 259 | 89.17 |
| | 80 | 911 | 217 | 80.94 |
| Efficient K2DPCA | 160 | 648 | 54 | 93.75 |
| | 120 | 241 | 41 | 88.75 |
| | 80 | 107 | 29 | 80.94 |

## 5 Conclusion

In this paper, we generalize the 2DPCA method via kernel trick and propose an efficient algorithm for kernel 2DPCA (K2DPCA) for solving the large computation complexity of the standard K2DPCA method. The detailed theoretical analysis is given in the section 2 and section 3, and the results of face recognition experiments on ORL database are shown that the efficient K2DPCA can effectively speed up the training procedure and remarkably save the memory-consuming compared to the standard K2DPCA.

## Acknowledgment

This work was partly supported by the national natural science foundations of China under grant 60503023, and partly supported by the natural science foundations of Jiangsu province under the grant BK2005407, partly supported by the key laboratory of image processing and image communication of Jiangsu province under the grant ZK205013, and partly supported by Program for New Century Excellent Talents in University (NCET).

## References

1. Kirby ,Y., Sirovich ,L.:Application of the Karhunen-loeve Procedure for the Characterization of Human Faces. IEEE Trans. PAMI. 12, (1990)103-108
2. Turk, M., Pentland, A. : Eigenfaces for Recognition .J Cognitive Neuroscience,(1991) 71-86
3. Yang, J., Zhang, D ., Frangi, A. F., Yang, J. Y.: Two-dimensional PCA: A New Approach to Appearance based Face Representation and Recognition, IEEE Trans. PAMI. 26 (1), (2004) 131-137
4. Schölkopf ,B., Smola,A., Muller,K.R.: Nonlinear Component Analysis as a Kernel Eigenvalue Problem.Neural Computation 10,(1998)1299-1319
5. Rosipal,R.,Rirolami,M.,Trejo,L.,Cichoki,A.: An Expectation-maximization Approach to Nolinear Component Analysis.Neural Computation 13,(2001)505-510
6. Zheng, W. M., Zou, C. R., Zhao, L.: An Improved Algorithm for Kernel Principal Component Analysis. Neural Processing Letters 22,(2005)49-56

# Least Squares Support Vector Machine Based Partially Linear Model Identification*

You-Feng Li, Li-Juan Li, Hong-Ye Su, and Jian Chu

National Key Laboratory of Industrial Control Technology,
Institute of Advanced Process Control, Yuquan campus, Zhejiang University,
Hangzhou, 310027, P.R. China
yfli@iipc.zju.edu.cn

**Abstract.** A nonlinear identification method was proposed for a class of partially linear models (PLM) which consist of a linear component summed with a nonlinear component in nonlinear ARX form. The method extends the standard least squares support vector machine (LSSVM) by replacing the equality constraint in the standard LSSVM with a PLM model. To guarantee the uniqueness of the linear coefficients, we imposed an additional explicit constraint on the feature map instead of an implicit constraint on the regressor vectors. Therefore the resulting PLM is a generalized version of the original one. Two examples show the effectiveness of the presented method.

## 1 Introduction

With higher product quality specifications and increasing productivity demands, tighter environmental regulations and demanding economical considerations in the process industry, linear models are often inadequate to describe the process dynamics and nonlinear models have to be used. Hence modeling and identification of nonlinear systems attracted wide interest in the control community. Under the nonlinear black box modeling setting numerous methods exist such as neural networks, support vector machines (SVM), wavelets, basis expansions, splines, polynomials and so on [6]. With the introduction of a dynamic nonlinear model within the control algorithm, however, the complexity of the control problem increases significantly. By taking advantage of structured nonlinear models, this problem can be addressed to a degree.

In many situations, partially linear models (PLM) composing of a linear part summed with a nonlinear part, are seen to provide a good tradeoff between the complexity of general nonlinear systems and interpretability of linear dynamic systems. Because of the flexible structure and kind of transparency with respect to completely nonlinear regression, this model has received a considerable amount of research in the past two decades. Since Engle et al. [1] applied this

* This work was supported by the National Natural Science Foundation of China (60421002) and Priority supported financially by "the New Century 151 Talent Project" of Zhejiang Province.

D.-S. Huang, K. Li, and G.W. Irwin (Eds.): ICIC 2006, LNCS 4113, pp. 775–781, 2006.

model to analyze the relationship between electricity sales and average daily temperature, the model has been applied in econometrics, statistics, biometrics, and environmental science. In a general sense, PLM is one type of the block-oriented models [5] and hence can be formulated in nonlinear autoregressive with exogenous inputs (NARX) form [2] or in nonlinear state space form [11], [4].

Identification of PLM mainly lies in the way the nonlinearity is represented and in the type of optimization problem that is finally obtained. Existing approaches include the expansion of the nonlinearity as a sum of basis functions and the use of polynomial functions or piecewise linear functions or a finite number of cubic spline functions or neural networks. In [2], least squares support vector machine (LSSVM)was extended to identify a class of nonlinear systems in NARX form where some of the regressors are linear. That method can improve the generalization performance with respect to full black-box models. But the resulting PLM is restrictive in that it requires the regressor for linear part differ from the one for nonlinear part. Clearly this requirement is not kind of practical. For those systems which don't satisfy the requirement, the method in [2] is biased because the model structure is not appropriate. The main aim of this paper is to propose one PLM identification method free from that restriction without loss of generalization performance.

The rest of this paper is organized as follows. Section 2 gives an introduction to partially linear model. The derivation of the proposed method is presented in Section 3. Section 4 applies the method to one example. Finally, some concluding remarks are made in Section 5.

## 2 Partially Linear Model in NARX Form

For a general nonlinear dynamic system, one of the popular parametric model forms is the NARX model. It has the form

$$y(t) = f(z(t)) + e(t) \tag{1}$$

where $z(t) = [y(t-1), \dots, y(t-p), u(t), u(t-1), \dots, u(t-q)]^T$ is the regressor vector, $e(t)$ is a noise term, $f(\cdot)$ is a nonlinear mapping function, $y(t)$ and $u(t)$ are the output and the input of the system respectively. Single input single output system is only concerned in this paper.

When some of the regressors are linear, we get a partially linear model in NARX form

$$y(t) = c^T z^l(t) + f(z^n(t)) + e(t) \tag{2}$$

where $c$ is the linear coefficient vector, $z^l(t) \in \mathbb{R}^{n_a}$and $z^n(t) \in \mathbb{R}^{n_b}$ are the regressors for linear part and for nonlinear part respectively. The regressors are the subset of $\{y(t-1), \dots, y(t-p), u(t), u(t-1), \dots, u(t-q)\}$. Note that the definition of PLM here doesn't require $z^l(t)$ and $z^n(t)$ be independent as [2] does.

## 3 LSSVM for Partially Linear Model

In recent years, least squares support vector machines [3,7,8], a reformulation to the standard support vector machine (SVM)have been used for function estimation. LSSVM involves equality instead of inequality constraints and works with a least squares cost function. This reformulation greatly simplifies the problem in such a way that the solution is characterized by a linear system, more precisely a KKT (Karush-Kuhn-Tucker) system. In LSSVM, the following model is assumed:

$$f(x) = \omega^T \varphi(x) + b \tag{3}$$

where $\varphi(\cdot)$ is a function which maps the input space into a so-called higher dimensional (possibly infinite dimensional) feature space. The term $b$ denotes a bias. Substituting (3) for the nonlinear mapping in (2), we get the following model

$$y(t) = c^T z^l(t) + \omega^T \varphi(z^n(t)) + b + e(t) \tag{4}$$

To guarantee unique representation of the linear coefficients, some additional constraints need to impose. [2] imposed an implicit constraint on the regressors, i.e., $\mathcal{Z}^l \cap \mathcal{Z}^n = \emptyset$ , where $\mathcal{Z} = \{z_i : z_i \text{ is the } i\text{th component of vector } z(t)\}$. Consequently the problem mentioned above appears, that is, the resulting PLM is kind of restrictive. To avoid this problem we impose an explicit constraint on the feature mapping instead

$$\sum_{i=1}^{N} \omega^T \varphi(z^n(t)) = 0 \tag{5}$$

As with the standard LSSVM, the identification of PLM in (4) boils down to the following constrained optimization problem (primal problem)

$$\begin{aligned}
&\min_{\omega,b,e} J = \frac{1}{2}\omega^T \omega + \gamma \frac{1}{2} \sum_{k=1}^{N} e_k^2 \\
&\text{s.t. } y(t) = c^T z^l(t) + \omega^T \varphi(z^n(t)) + b + e(t),\ t = 1, \ldots, N \\
&\qquad \sum_{i=1}^{N} \omega^T \varphi(z^n(t)) = 0
\end{aligned} \tag{6}$$

where $\gamma$ is a regularization parameter.

**Lemma 1.** *Given the problem* (6) *and a positive-definite kernel function* $K$ *, the solution to* (6) *is given by the dual problem*

$$\begin{bmatrix} 0 & 0 & 0 & \mathbf{1}^T \\ 0 & 0 & 0 & X^T \\ 0 & 0 & s & p^T \\ \mathbf{1} & X & p & \Omega + \gamma^{-1} I \end{bmatrix} \begin{bmatrix} b \\ c \\ \beta \\ \alpha \end{bmatrix} = \begin{bmatrix} 0 \\ 0 \\ 0 \\ y \end{bmatrix} \tag{7}$$

*where* $\mathbf{1}$ *is a column vector filled with ones,* $I$ *is the identity matrix,* $\alpha = [\alpha_1, \alpha_2, \ldots, \alpha_N]^T$ *and* $\beta$ *are Lagrange multipliers,* $y = [y(1), y(2), \ldots, y(N)]^T$, $X = [z^l(1)^T; z^l(2); \ldots; z^l(N)^T] \in \mathcal{R}^{N \times n_a}$, $\Omega$ *is the kernel matrix with* $\Omega_{kl} = \varphi(z^n(k))^T \varphi(z^n(l)) = K(z^n(k), z^n(l))$, $p = \sum_{i=1}^N \Omega_{ki}$, $s = \sum_{i=1}^N p_i$.

*Proof.* This directly follows from the Lagrangian of problem (6):

$$
\begin{aligned}
L = J - \beta \sum_{i=1}^{N} \omega^T \varphi(z^n(i)) - \sum_{i=1}^{N} \alpha_i (c^T z^l(t) + \omega^T \varphi(z^n(t)) \\
+ b + e(t) - y(t))
\end{aligned}
$$

by taking the conditions for optimality: $\partial L/\partial e(t) = 0$, $\partial L/\partial \omega = 0$, $\partial L/\partial c = 0$, $\partial L/\partial b = 0$, $\partial L/\partial \alpha_i = 0$, $\partial L/\partial \beta = 0$.

*Remark 1.* $K$ is any nonlinear kernel function satisfying Mercer condition, such as RBF kernel $K(x(i), x(k)) = \exp(-\|x(i) - x(k)\|_2^2/(\sigma)^2)$ ($\sigma$ is the width parameter), polynomial kernel $K(x(i), x(k)) = x(i)^T x(k) + r)^d$ (polynomial of degree $d$, with $r$ a tuning parameter).

*Remark 2.* The nonlinear mapping can be approximated from the kernel matrix by means of the Nyström method [9]. The $i$th component of $\varphi(x)$ is obtained as $\varphi_i(x) \approx (\lambda_i)^{-1/2} \sum_{j=1}^{M} K(x_j, x) u_{ji}$ where $u_{ji}$ is the $j$th element of the $i$th eigenvector of $\Omega$, $\lambda_i$ is the $i$th eigenvalue, $M(\ll N)$ is the number of a fixed subset of data points . In this case a smaller matrix $\Omega_M$ of dimensions $M \times M$ is computed from the subset of $M$ data points to build the approximation.

*Remark 3.* The resulting LSSVM model in terms of the dual variables becomes

$$
\begin{aligned}
y(t) = c^T z^l(t) + \sum_{i=1}^{N} \alpha_i K(z^n(t), z^n(i)) \\
+ \beta \sum_{i=1}^{N} K(z^n(t), z^n(i)) + b + e(t)
\end{aligned}
\tag{8}
$$

*Remark 4.* To obtain a good performance, some parameters in LSSVM have to be chosen carefully. These parameters include the regularization parameter $\gamma$ and the parameter(s) in the kernel function (like $\sigma$ in RBF kernel and $r, d$ in polynomial kernel). These parameters are usually referred as to hyperparameters. Tuning these hyperparameters such that the estimated generalization error is minimized is the so-called *model selection* problem. The standard method to deal with this problem is to use a simple grid search on the log-scale of the parameters in combination with cross-validation on each candidate vector of parameters. If, however, the number of parameters becomes higher, this leads to an explosion of necessary LSSVM trainings.

# 4 Example

We illustrate the method discussed above using simulations of two nonlinear systems. In the first example, linear regressors and nonlinear regressors are not independent. we compare our method with the method in [2]. We will show the effectiveness of our method to a Hammerstein system in the second example. Both examples are carried out with RBF kernel .

## 4.1 Example 1

Consider the following system [2]:

$$\begin{aligned} y(t) = {} & (0.5y(t-1))^3 - 0.5y(t-2)u(t) + 0.3u(t) \\ & - 0.2u(t-1) + e(t) \end{aligned} \tag{9}$$

The input used for simulation was generated from Gaussian white noise with zero mean and unit variance. The noise term $e(t)$ is created from $\mathcal{N}(0, 0.001)$ . We generated 1002 samples of the input and output sequences. Let $z(t) = [y(t-1), y(t-2), u(t), u(t-1)]$, 1000 pairs of the regressor vector and output are available for identification. The first 350 points are discarded to avoid any transient effect; the training set is done with the next 400 points; the last 250 points are used as test set.

For this system, two methods are compared here. One is the method proposed in this paper (referred to as M1) and the other in [2] (referred as to M2). For simplicity we assume the orders of the system for two methods are known. In fact the orders of the system could be estimated by means of minimizing the generalization error. So for M1 we consider $z^l(t) = [u(t), u(t-1)]$, $z^n(t) = [y(t-1), y(t-2), u(t)]$; for M2 $z^l(t) = [u(t-1)]$, $z^n(t) = [y(t-1), y(t-2), u(t)]$ is considered.

As for the measure of performance of both methods, mean square error (MSE) and the variance-accounted-for (VAF) are used; the VAF is defined as [10]

$$\text{VAF} = \max\Big\{1 - \frac{\text{var}(y_k - \widehat{y_k})}{\text{var}(y_k)}, 0\Big\} \times 100\%$$

where $\widehat{y_k}$ denotes the estimated output signal, $y_k$ is the real output signal, and $\text{var}(\cdot)$ denotes the variance of a quasi-stationary signal.

The hyperparameters are selected by grid search as $\sigma = e^2$, $\gamma = e^{12}$ in M1 and $\sigma = e^{-2}$, $\gamma = e^6$ in M2. Table 1 shows a comparison between both methods in terms of MSE on the training set ($\text{MSE}_t$), VAF on the training set ($\text{VAF}_t$), MSE on the test set ($\text{MSE}_v$), VAF on the test set ($\text{VAF}_v$). Such comparisons are presented in the table showing MSE and VAF averaged over 10 realizations of random training data. From Table 1, the generalization performance of M1 is better than that of M2.

## 4.2 Example 2

The following Hammerstein system is considered

$$A(z)y(t) = B(z)g(u(t)) + e(t) \tag{10}$$

**Table 1.** Performance Comparison Between Two Methods For Example 1

| | $\text{MSE}_t$ | $\text{VAF}_t$ | $\text{MSE}_t$ | $\text{VAF}_v$ |
|---|---|---|---|---|
| M1 | 0.0011 | 99.35 | 0.0018 | 99.01 |
| M2 | 0.0010 | 99.39 | 0.0042 | 97.78 |

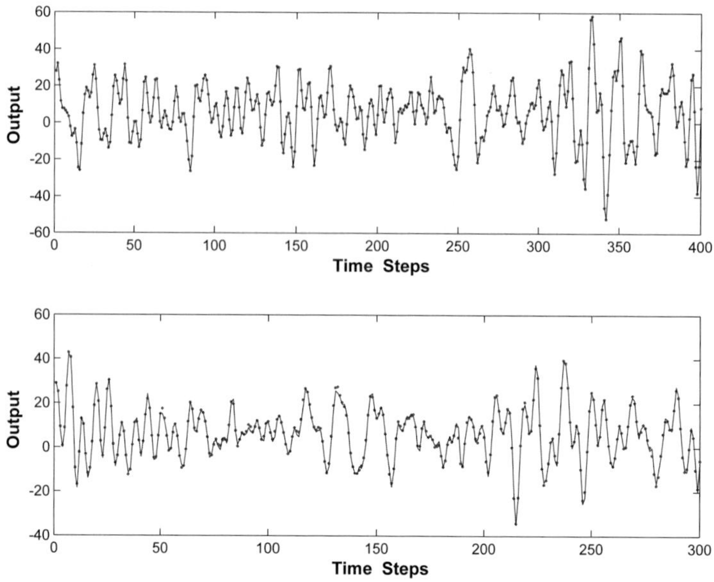


**Fig. 1.** Output signals of Example 2 on the training set (top) and on the test set (bottom). The symbol '·' represents real output and the dash line denotes estimated output.

with $A$ and $B$ polynomials in the forward shift operator $z$ where $B(z) = z^6 + 0.8z^5 + 0.3z^4 + 0.4z^3$, $A(z) = (z - 0.98e^{\pm i})(z - 0.98e^{\pm 1.6i})(z - 0.97e^{\pm 0.4i})$. The static nonlinearity is formulated as $g(u) = sin(u)u$.

A dataset was generated from this system where $u(t) \sim \mathcal{N}(0, 2)$ is a white Gaussian noise sequence for $t = 0, \ldots, N-1$ with $N = 1000$ and $\{e(t)\}_{i=1}^{N}$ is a sequence of Gaussian white noise with a level of 10% of the nonlinearity $f(u)$. Let $z(t) = [y(t-1), \ldots, y(t-6), u(t), \ldots, u(t-3)]$, 994 pairs of the regressor vector and output are available for identification. Like example 1, the dataset was divided sequentially into three subsets with 294, 400, 300 points respectively. The second subset is training set for estimating the model parameters and the third subset is test set for validation.

The hyperparameters in the LSSVM algorithm were selected as $\sigma = e^{-1}$, $\gamma = e^5$ by grid search. MSE and VAF on the test set is 1.3906 and 99.02 respectively. The output signals were displayed in Fig. 1.

## 5 Conclusion

In this paper, we proposed a partially linear model identification method based on least squares support vector machine. By replacing the equality constraints in the standard LSSVM by a PLM, model parameters are estimated from solving a linear system similar to the one in the standard LSSVM. Unlike imposing an implicit constraint on the regressors in the method [2], we impose an explicit constraint on the feature map to guarantee the uniqueness of the linear coefficients. Hence the resulting PLM can be applied to more systems than the model in [2]. The simulation results show the effectiveness of the method.

## References


1. Engle, R.F., Granger, C.W.J., Rice, J., Weiss, A.: Semiparametric Estimates of The Relation Between Weather and Electricity Sales. J. Amer. Statist. Assoc., **81** (1986) 310-320
2. Espinoza, M., Suykens, J.A.K., De Moor, B.: Kernel Based Partially Linear Models and Nonlinear Identification. IEEE Transactions on Automatic Control. **50** (2005) 1602-1606
3. Goethals, I., Pelckmans, K., Suykens, J.A.K., De Moor, B.: Subspce Identification of Hammerstein Systems Using Least Squares Support Vector Machines. IEEE Transactions on Automatic Control. **50** (2005) 1509-1519
4. Qin, S.J., Badgwell, T.A.: Survey of Industrial Model Predictive Control Technology. Control Engineering Practice. **11**(2003) 733-764
5. Schoukens, J., Nemeth, J.G., Crama, P., Rolain, Y., Pintelon, R.: Fast Approximate Identification of Nonlinear Systems. Automatica. **39** (2003) 1267-1274
6. Sjöberg, J., Zhang, Q., Ljung, L., Benveniste, A., Deylon, B., Glorennec, P., Hjalmarsson, H., Juditsky, A.: Nonlinear Black-box Modeling in System Identification: A Unified Overview. Automatica. **31** (1995) 1691-1724
7. Suykens, J.A.K., De Brabanter, J., Lukas, L., Vandewalle, J.: Weighted Least Squares Support Vector Machines: Robustness and Sparse Approximation. Neurocomputing. **48** (2002) 85-105
8. Suykens, J.A.K., Vandewalle, J., De Moor, B.: Optimal Control By Least Squares Support Vector Machines. Neural Networks. **14** (2001) 23-35
9. Van Gestel, T., Suykens, J.A.K., De Moor, B., Vandewalle, J.: Bayesian Inference for LS-SVMs on Large Data Sets Using the Nyström Method. Proceedings of the 2002 International Joint Conference on Neural Networks.**3** (2002) 2779-2784
10. Verdult, V., Verhaegen, M.: Kernel Methods for Subspace Identification of Multivariable LPV and Bilinear Systems. Automatica. **41** (2005) 1557-1565
11. Zhao, H., Guiver, J., Sentoni, G.: An Identifcation Approach to Nonlinear State Space Model for Industrial Multivariable Model Predictive Control. Proceedings of the American Control Conference. (1998) 796-800

# S-transform Based LS-SVM Recognition Method for Identification of PQ Disturbances

Ganyun Lv, Xiushan Cai, Xaidong Wang, and Haoran Zhang

Department of Information Science and Engineering, Zhejiang Normal University Jinhua, Zhejiang 321004, China
ganyun_lv@yahoo.com

**Abstract.** This paper presents a new method based on S-transform time-frequency analysis and multi-lay SVMs classifier for identification of power quality (PQ) disturbances. The proposed technique consists of time-frequency analysis, feature extraction and pattern classification. Though there are several time-frequency analysis methods existing in the literature, this paper uses S-transform to obtain the time-frequency characteristics of PQ disturbances because of its superior performance under noise. With the time-frequency characteristics of ST result, a set of features is extracted for identification of PQ disturbances. Then PQ disturbances training samples were contrsucted with the features, and a multi-lay LS-SVMs classifier was trained by the training sample. Finally, the trained multi-lay LS-SVMs classifier was developed for classification of the PQ disturbances. The proposed method has an excellent performance on training speed and correct ratio. The correct ratio of identification could reach 98.3% and the training time of the N-1 classifier was only about 0.2s.

## 1 Introduction

The deregulation polices in electric power systems results in the absolute necessity to quantify power quality (PQ). This fact highlights the need for an effective recognition technique capable of detecting and classifying the PQ disturbances. The identification of PQ disturbances is often based on neural network[1, 2] and fuzzy method[3], associated with other PQ detecting methods, such as Fourier transform[3, 4], wavelet[2] and dq transform[1]. ANN had attracted great attention because of it inherent pattern recognition capabilities and their ability to handle noisy data. However, ANNs suffer from the danger of over fitting and need of a large training time. The key benefit of FL was that its knowledge representation was explicit in utilizing simple "IF-THEN" relations. At the same time, the use of FL was limited because PQ disturbances, especially transients and flickers, could not be simply described by artificial explicit knowledge. Many other methods, such as fast match, expert system and nearest neighbor rule have also been tried for the identification of PQ disturbances in recent studies[5, 6, 7, 8].

Support vector machines (SVMs) was powerful for the problem with small sampling, nonlinear and high dimension[9], and has been widely used in many applications[10-12]. Though there are several time-frequency analysis methods existing in the literature, this paper uses S-transform to obtain the time-frequency characteristics of PQ events because of its superior performance under noise. A new method based on S-transform

D.-S. Huang, K. Li, and G.W. Irwin (Eds.): ICIC 2006, LNCS 4113, pp. 782–789, 2006.

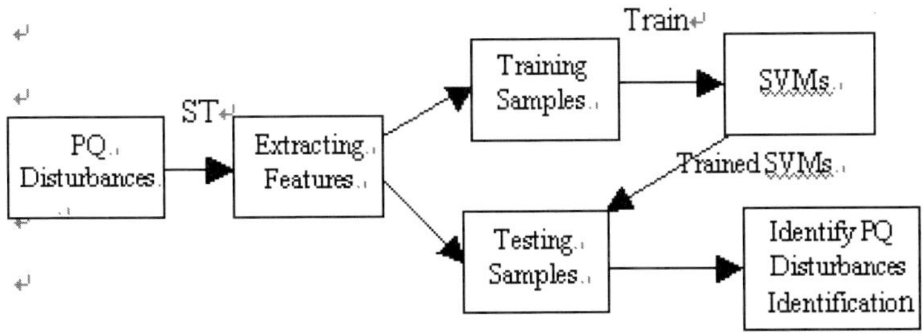


**Fig. 1.** S-transform based SVMs recognition method for identification of PQ disturbances

time-frequency analysis and SVMs is proposed for identification of PQ disturbances. Fig.1 depicted a simplified block diagram for the proposed recognition system.

## 2 S-transform and PQ Time-Frequency Analysis

The S-transform[7] was an extension of continuous wavelet transform (CWT) and short-time Fourier transform(STFT). For its good time-frequency characteristic, it was suitable for PQ disturbances analysis.

The S-transformation of signal $h(t)$ was defined as followed,

$$S(\tau, f) = \int_{-\infty}^{\infty} h(t) w(\tau - t, f) \exp(-2\pi i f t) dt \ . \tag{1}$$

$$w(\tau - t, f) = \frac{|f|}{\sqrt{2\pi}} \exp\left[\frac{-f^2(\tau - t)^2}{2}\right] . \tag{2}$$

Where $w(\tau - t, f)$ is the gauss window function, $\tau$ is a parameter of time position axis. The width and height of gauss window in ST varied with change of frequency, while thus STFT has fixed width and height of gauss window.

S-transformation could realized fast computing through FFT. The discrete S-transformation is:

$$S[m,n] = \sum_{k=0}^{N-1} X[n+k] \cdot e^{-2\pi^2 k^2 / n^2} \cdot e^{j2\pi km/N} \quad (n \neq 0) \ . \tag{3}$$

$$S[m,n] = \frac{1}{N} \sum_{k=0}^{N-1} x[k] \quad (n = 0) \ . \tag{4}$$

$$\text{Where} \quad X[n] = \frac{1}{N} \sum_{k=0}^{N-1} x[k] \cdot e^{-j2\pi kn/N} \ . \tag{5}$$

Many analysis results of PQ disturbances could be obtained with $S[m,n]$, including time-frequency distributing curve, amplitude-frequency curve at given time, amplitude-time curve at given frequency. Detecting results of sine wave, harmonics, flicker and sags were given in following. The signal to noise ratio is 20db.

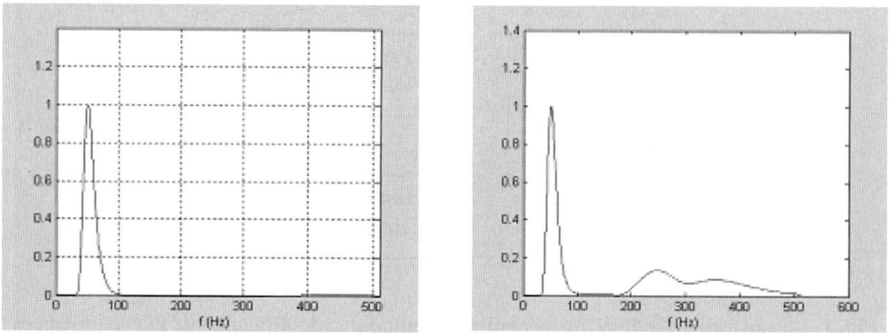


**Fig. 2.** Amplitude-frequency curve of sine wave(the former) and harmonics (the latter)

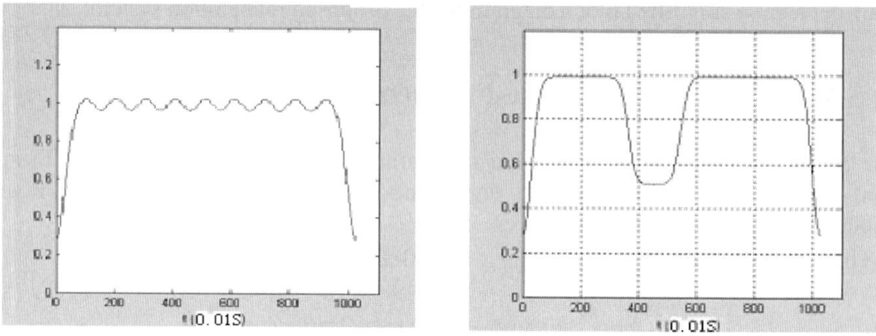


**Fig. 3.** Amplitude-time curve of flicker (the former) and sags (the latter) at basic frequency

From above figures, one could found that the S-transform could get both time and frequency characteristics of these PQ disturbances effectively, even under strong white noise. The identification of the proposed method was just based on those characteristics.

## 3 LS-SVM

The basic idea of the SVM regression is to map the input data into a feature space via a non-linear map. In the feature space, a linear decision function is constructed. The SRM principle is employed in constructing optimum decision function. Then SVM nonlinearly maps the inner product of the feature space to the original space via kernels. The SVM nonlinear regression algorithms are reviewed in this section. Given a set of training data

$$D = \{(x_1, y_1), \cdots, (x_i, y_i) \cdots, (x_l, y_l)\} \in R^n \times R \tag{6}$$

The non-linear function $\psi(\cdot)$ was employed to map original input space $R^n$ to higher dimensional feature space $R^k$: $\phi(x) = (\varphi(x1), \cdots, \varphi(x_l))$, where $k$ ($k >> n$) represents the dimension of feature space. Then an optimum decision function $f(x_i) = w\varphi(x_i) + b$ is constructed in this higher dimensional feature space, where

$w = (w1, \cdots w_k)$ is a vector of weights in this feature space. Nonlinear function estimation in the original space becomes linear function estimation in feature space. Thus, according to principle of structural risk minimization (SRM), when the quadratic ε-insensitive loss function is selected in the LS SVM regression the optimal problem can be formulated as minimization of the following objective function J :

$$\min J(w,\xi) = \frac{1}{2}\left\|w^2\right\| + \frac{1}{2}c\sum_{i=1}^{l}\xi_i^2 \ . \tag{7}$$

subject to the equality constraints

$$y_i = w\varphi(x_i) + b + \xi_i, \quad i = 1,2,...l \ . \tag{8}$$

We define the Lagrangian as

$$L(w,b,\xi,a,\gamma) = \frac{1}{2}ww + \frac{1}{2}c\sum_{i=1}^{l}\xi_i^2 - \sum_{i=1}^{l}a_i(w\varphi(x_i) + b + \xi) \ . \tag{9}$$

where $a_i(i \,.\,.\, 1, \,.\,, l)$ are Lagrange multipliers.

By the optimality conditions

$$\frac{\partial L}{\partial w} = 0, \ \frac{\partial L}{\partial b} = 0, \ \frac{\partial L}{\partial \xi} = 0, \ \frac{\partial L}{\partial a} = 0 . \tag{10}$$

We have

$$\begin{aligned} &\sum_{i-1}^{l} a_{ii} = 0, \qquad w = \sum a_i\varphi(x_i), \qquad a_i = c\xi_i \ . \\ &w\varphi(x_i) + b + \xi_i = y_i \end{aligned} \tag{11}$$

By (7) and (11), the optimization problem can be rewritten as following,

$$\begin{bmatrix} 0 & 1 & \cdots & 1 \\ 1 & K(x1,x1)+\frac{1}{c} & \vdots & K(x1,x_l) \\ \vdots & \vdots & \ddots & \vdots \\ 1 & K(x1,x_l) & \cdots & K(x1,x_l)+\frac{1}{c} \end{bmatrix} \begin{bmatrix} b \\ a1 \\ \vdots \\ a_l \end{bmatrix} = \begin{bmatrix} 0 \\ y1 \\ \vdots \\ y_l \end{bmatrix} . \tag{12}$$

Where $K(x_i, x_j)$ is a symmetric positive definite function in original input space, called kernel function:

$$K(x_i, x_j) = (\varphi(x_i), \varphi(x_j)) \ . \tag{13}$$

Finally, the nonlinear function takes the form:

$$f(x) = \sum_{i=1}^{l} a_i K(x, x_i) + b \ . \tag{14}$$

This nonlinear function is the so-called SVM.

# 4 PQ Disturbances Identification

The procedure of identification of PQ disturbances with N-1 SVMs classifier includes three steps: extracting features from the detecting system output of PQ disturbance signals, training SVMs classifier and identifying PQ disturbances with the trained classifier. The procedure was shown as Fig.4:

## 4.1 Extracting Features

The identified PQ disturbances included sine wave, harmonics, fluctuations and sags. The training and testing samples of these PQ disturbances were generated by a simulation program according to IEEE 1159.

Through a data dealing process of ST result S[m,n], following features were extracted:

1) The three peaks value of amplitude in frequency field and its corresponding frequency.
2) The maxim keeping time when amplitude in basic frequency field is larger than 1.1.
3) The four peaks value of amplitude in basic frequency field and its corresponding time.
4) The fluctuation times in base frequency which fluctuation amplitude is larger that 0.01.

Thus 16 features were obtained. They reflected the characteristics of harmonics and sine wave, flicker and sags.

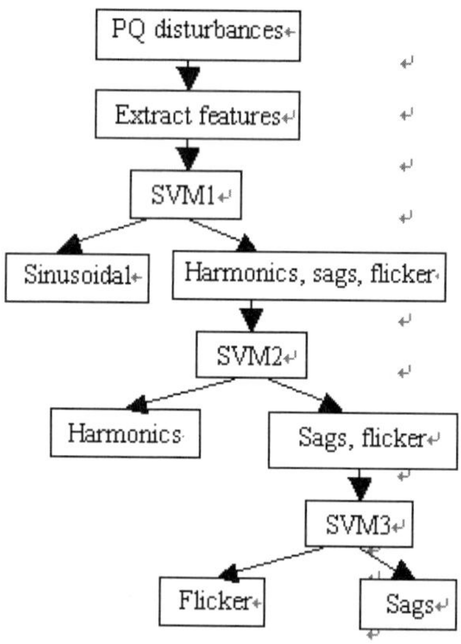


**Fig. 4.** N kinds of PQ Disturbances Identification with N-1 SVMs Classifier

### 4.2 Training Networks of SVMs Classifier

Based on the features of different types of PQ disturbances, N-1 SVMs classifier was adopted to identify sinusoidal and those three types of PQ disturbances, harmonics, flicker and sags. With training samples dropped from above extracting process, the N-1 SVMs classifier was trained. SVM1 was trained with all samples, and separated sinusoidal signal with the three disturbances, harmonics, flicker and sags. If input a sinusoidal signal, SVM1 output was set to +1; otherwise, SVM1 output was set to -1. The second SVM (SVM2) was trained with the three type disturbances samples, and separates harmonics with other two type disturbances. If input a harmonic signal, SVM2 output was set to +1; otherwise, SVM2 output -1. At last, the last SVM (SVM3) was trained with samples of flicker and sags, and separates them. If the input signal was a flicker signal, SVM3 output was set to +1; otherwise, SVM3 output was set to -1. Thus, N-1 SVMs were trained step by step.

### 4.3 Testing with Trained SVMs Classifier

Testing samples were input to N-1 SVMs classifier. With outputs of the classifier, three-layer decision was made. With the outputs of SVM1, one could identify out sinusoidal signal with other three types of PQ disturbances, harmonics, flicker and sags. Then the testing samples of the PQ disturbances are input to SVM2. With the outputs of SVM2, one could identify out harmonics with other two disturbances. Then the testing samples of flicker and sags are input to SVM3. With the outputs of SVM3, one could identify out flicker with sags. Thus, the three types disturbances and sinusoidal were identified with the trained N-1 SVMs classifier, after N-1 times of identification.

## 5 Simulation

In this paper, the training and testing samples of PQ disturbances are generated according to the PQ disturbances model in IEEE 1159. The sampling rate was 10k/s. To be mentioned, many parameters of PQ disturbances including amplitude, starting time, ending time, fluctuation frequency, varied randomly. The signal to noise ratio was 20db. Thus the simulation signal could be more like in practical power system, and thus ensure reliability of the propose method results. The simulations were carried out by a personal computer with PII 733 and 128M memory.

The N-1 SVMs classifier adopted Gaussian radial basis function as its kernel function. 40 samples were generated, including 10 sinusoidal, 10 harmonics, 10 flicker and 10 sags. With S-transform and a feature extracting program, and the training set was composed. Then, the N-1 SVMs classifier was trained with the training set. Then another 40 samples were generated for testing the trained classifier. The first 10 samples were sine wave, the second 10 samples harmonics, the third 10 samples flickers, and the last 10 samples sags. The testing results were shown as following.

Testing samples of SVM1=[10 sinusoidal; 10 harmonics; 10 flicker; 10 sags;]
Output of SVM1 was shown as follow:
[1 1 1 1 1 1 1 1 1 1 -1 -1 -1 -1 -1 -1 -1 -1 -1 -1
-1 -1 -1 -1 -1 -1 -1 -1 -1 -1 -1 -1 -1 -1 -1 -1 -1 -1 -1 –1]

With the above output, one could identify out the 10 sinusoidal and other 30 samples of other three type disturbances. The latter were input to SVM2.

Testing samples of SVM2=[10 harmonics; 10 flicker; 10 sags;]
Output of SVM2 was shown as follow:
[1 1 1 1 1 1 1 1 1 1 -1 -1 -1 -1 -1 -1 -1 -1 -1 -1 -1 -1 -1 -1 -1 -1 -1 -1 -1 -1]

With the above output, one could identify out the 10 harmonics and other 20 samples of other two type PQ disturbances. The 20 samples were input to SVM3.

Testing samples of SVM3=[10 flicker; 10 sags;]
Output of SVM3 was shown as follow:
[1 1 1 1 1 1 1 1 1 1 -1 -1 -1 -1 -1 -1 -1 -1 -1 -1 ]

With the above output, one could identify out the 10 flicker samples with other 10 sags samples.

Through this up-to-down procedure, the identification was carried out from rough to extract, and completed the identification of the whole testing set at last. Among the 40 testing samples, none mistake was made, that was to say, the correct ratio was 100%, despite parameters of disturbance sample of testing and training changing randomly in a wide range. Moreover, the training time of the N-1 classifier was only about 0.2s.

A comparison with BP neural network was made in order to evaluate the proposed method well. The BP network and SVMs was tested with other 240 samples. The target error (TE) of BP networks was set as 0.05, 0.02 and 0.01 respectively. The network was trained with fast back propagation algorithm. The BP network and SVMs were compared with same training and testing sets. The comparison of identification results with two methods was shown as Table 1:

**Table 1.** Comparison of identification result with BP network and n-1 SVMs classifier

| *Method* | *TE* | *Training time* | *Correct ratio* |
|---|---|---|---|
| SVMs | 0.01 | 0.2s | 98.3% |
| BP1 | 0.05 | 3min | 91.7% |
| BP2 | 0.02 | 5min | 93.3% |
| BP3 | 0.01 | 11min | 94.2% |

The results in Table 1 showed that, both BP network and SVMs has a very good identification effect in correct ratio .It is mainly contribute to the good time-frequency characteristics extracted by the S-transform. Compared with BP network, identification of PQ disturbances with N-1 SVMs classifier was more robust, and had a much higher correct ratio. Furthermore, N-1 SVMs classifier needs much less of training time than BP network.

## 6 Conclusions

This paper presents a PQ disturbances identification method based S-transform and SVMs. Some most important PQ disturbances are identified with the proposed method. S-transform could get a good and rich time-frequency characteristics of PQ disturbances, which ensure effect of identification performance. The SVMs classifier has very simple structure and was a strongly regularized method, and could deal PQ dada with noise and random varied parameters. The proposed method has an excellent performance on training speed and correct ratio. The correct ratio of identification could reach 98.3% and the training time of the N-1 classifier was only about 0.2s, which is much better than many other methods.

## References


1. Xu, Y. H., Xiao, X. N., Yang, Y. H., Chen, X. Y.: Power Quality Disturbance Identification Using Dq Conversion-based Neural Classifiers. Automation of Electric Power System, vol.21, (2001) 24-28
2. Sen, O. Y., Wang, J. H., Geng, Y. S., Song, Z. X.: Power Quality Classification Based on Wavelet Transform and Neural Network. Advanced Technology of Electrical Engineering and Energy,Vol.22,(2003) 32-36
3. Dash, P. K., Mishra, S., Salama, M. M. A., Liew, A. C.: Classification of Power System Disturbances Using a Fuzzy Expert System and a Fourier Linear Combiner. IEEE Trans. Power Delivery, vol. 15, (2000) 472-477.
4. Heydt, G. T., Fjeld , P. S., Liu, C. C., Pierce, Tu, D., L., Hensley, G.: Applications of the Windowed FFT to Electric Power Quality Assessment. IEEE Trans. Power Delivery, vol.14, (1999) 1411-1416.
5. Abdel-Galil, T. K., EL-Saadany, E. F., Youssef, A.M., Salama, M. M. A.: On-line Disturbance Recognition Utilizing Vector Quantization Based Fast Match. Power Engineering Society Summer Meeting, 2002 IEEE, Vol 2, (2002) 1027-1032
6. Emmanouil Styvaktakis, Math H. J. Bollen, Irene Y. H. Gu: Expert System for Classification and Analysis of Power System Events. IEEE Trans. Power Delivery, vol.17,(2002) 423- 428
7. Gaouda, A.M., Kanoun, S.H., Salama, M. M. A.: On-line Disturbance Classification Using Nearest Neighbor Rule. J. Electr. Power Syst.Res, vol. 57, (2001) 1-8
8. Lu, J. W., Plataniotis, K.N., Venetsanopoulos A.N: Face Recognition Using Feature Optimization and ν-support Vector Learning. Neural Networks for Signal Processing XI, Proceedings of the 2001 IEEE Signal Processing Society Workshop (2001) 373 - 382
9. Cortes, C, Vapnik, V.: Support-vector Networks. Machine Learning,vol.20, (1995) 273-295
10. Jack, L.B., Nandi, A.K.: Fault Detection Using Support Vector Machines and Artificial Neural Networks,Augmented by Genetic Algorithms. Mechanical Systems and Signal Processing ,vol.16, (2002) 373 -390
11. Francis E.H.Tay , Cao, L. J..: Application of Support Vector Machines in Financial Time Series Forecasting.Omega, Vol.29, (2001) 309-317
12. Chan, W.C., Cheung, K.C., Harris, C.J.: On the Modelling of Nonlinear Dynamic Systems Using Support Vector Neural Networks. Engineering Applications of Artificial Intelligence 14, (2001) 105 -113

# A Global Optimization Method Based on Simulated Annealing and Evolutionary Strategy

DarYun Chiang and JauSung Moh

Department of Aeronautics and Astronautics, National Cheng Kung University
Tainan, Taiwan 701, Republic of China
dchiang@mail.ncku.edu.tw

**Abstract.** A global optimization method is proposed to improve the conventional method of simulated annealing. By introducing the probability distribution function for the objective function and the concept of stable energy for detecting thermal equilibrium during annealing, the selection of initial temperature and equilibrium criterion becomes easy and effective. Furthermore, the efficiency and robustness of the proposed method is retained by employing the technique of region reduction and an adaptive neighborhood structure. In the case where multiple (global) optima may exist, a technique based on the method of simulated evolution is developed to circumvent the difficulty of convergence of population. Numerical studies of some standard test functions and an optimum structural design problem show that the proposed method is effective in solving global optimization problems.

## 1 Introduction

There is a large class of structural optimization problems with non-convexities in the design space, and a mix of continuous and discrete variables. Under such circumstances, standard mathematical programming techniques are usually inefficient, as they are computationally expensive and are almost assured of locating the relative optimum close to the starting design. To overcome these difficulties, the "stochastic" search in structural optimization is considered. Many methods have become possible with the powerful computing facilities available in recent years. Among the stochastic search algorithms, pure random search [1] is the simplest and most robust strategy for optimal design. Some modified versions have been suggested, such as single start, multi-start, and random directions [2, 3]. Methods in this class generally are quite simple to implement but the appropriate stopping rules are very difficult to derive.

Recently, two classes of powerful search methods, which have their philosophical basis in processes found in nature, are widely used in structural optimization. The first class of methods including genetic algorithms [4] and simulated evolution [5] is based on the spirit of Darwinian theory of evolution. The second class of methods is generally referred to as simulated annealing techniques [6], as they are qualitatively derived from a simulation of the behavior of particles in thermal equilibrium at a given temperature. Because of the global capabilities, some research on the utilization of these search methods in design optimization has been studied. [7-11]

In this paper, we propose a method based on simulated annealing which, however, searches from a population as in the method of simulated evolution, instead of from a

D.-S. Huang, K. Li, and G.W. Irwin (Eds.): ICIC 2006, LNCS 4113, pp. 790 – 801, 2006.

single point. The algorithm is referred to as the Region-Reduction Simulated Annealing (RRSA) method because it locates the optimum by successively eliminating the regions with low probability of containing optimum.

## 2 Method of Simulated Annealing

The ideas of simulated annealing (SA) are derived from the principles of statistical thermodynamics. Consider the atoms of a molten metal at some elevated equilibrium temperature $T$. The state of this system $\phi$ is characterized by specific spatial locations of the atoms. The probability $p_T(\phi)$ of the event that at the given equilibrium temperature $T$, the system is in a state $\phi$ is given by the Boltzmann distribution [12, 13],

$$p_T(\phi) = \frac{e^{-E(\phi)/kT}}{\sum_{\Phi} e^{-E(\phi)/kT}}, \tag{1}$$

where $k$ is the Boltzmann constant, $E(\phi)$ is the energy of the state $\phi$, and $\Phi$ represents all possible states that the system can assume at that temperature. At a given temperature, random variations of the system state are considered. If a state results in a lower energy level, it is immediately accepted. If, however, a higher energy state results from the variation, it is only accepted with a probability $p$ given by

$$p = \frac{p_T(\phi_2)}{p_T(\phi_1)} = e^{-[E(\phi_2)-E(\phi_1)]/kT}, \tag{2}$$

where $p_T(\phi_1)$ and $p_T(\phi_2)$ are probabilities of states $\phi_1$ and $\phi_2$, respectively, as obtained from the Boltzmann distribution. Eq.(2) implies that even at low temperature, there is still a chance, though very small, for a system to jump into a state with higher energy. If an annealing schedule is established in which the temperature gets lowered gradually and thermal equilibrium is reached at each temperature, a pure crystalline state corresponding to the lowest energy level is attainable.

SA is an approach simulating the process of annealing for optimization. It takes the objective function value of an optimization problem as the energy level corresponding to a given state, and the candidates (vectors of design variables) in the search space are treated as the possible states at an equilibrium temperature, which is a control parameter in the process. The general scheme of SA is stated as follows:

1. Generate randomly a design candidate $\boldsymbol{x}$.
2. Choose $T>0$ to be the "initial temperature".
3. If a stopping criterion is satisfied then stop; otherwise repeat the following steps:
   a. *if "equilibrium is reached" then exit this loop* ;
   b. *let* $x'$ *be a randomly selected neighbor of* $\boldsymbol{x}$
   c. *generate a uniform random number* $U$ *in* [0, 1]
   d. *if* $exp\{-[f(\boldsymbol{x}')-f(\boldsymbol{x})]/T\}>U$, then $\boldsymbol{x}=\boldsymbol{x}'$
4. Let $T$ be a new (lower) temperature value, and go to 3.

Several decisions have to be made in order to let the conceptual algorithm described above become implementable, including the following:

1. choice of an initial temperature and the corresponding temperature decrement strategy,
2. choice of a criterion for detecting equilibrium at a temperature level,
3. choice of adequate stopping criteria to terminate the search process.

## 3 Concept and Procedures of RRSA

Consider an unconstrained function optimization problem in which the objective function to be minimized is given by

$$f(\boldsymbol{x}) = f(x_1, x_2, \ldots, x_n), \tag{3}$$

To improve the performance of SA, we proposed that the method searches from a population of points instead of from a single design point. The convergence criterion can therefore be set up more easily with a population of design points as discussed later. In order to have a faster rate of convergence and to obtain an appropriate stopping criterion, we introduce the concept of "eliminating" the regions of search that have low probability of containing global optima. To identify whether a region is to be eliminated or not, the probability distribution function for the objective function values (energy levels) is needed, as described below. If it is a problem with multiple global optima, a strategy based on simulated evolution is developed within RRSA to solve such a problem. The concepts and procedures are described in detail as follow.

Firstly, we define the probability distribution function (pdf) for the objective function values as

$$P(f_{\rm r}) = \text{Prob.}(\, f(\boldsymbol{x})\ \text{À}\leqq f_{\rm r}\,), \tag{4}$$

where $f_{\rm r}$ is a reference value and $\boldsymbol{x}$ is arbitrarily selected within the region of interest. Without loss of clarity, $P(f_{\rm r})$ is more conveniently denoted as $P(f)$. Although the true $P(f)$ is usually unknown for an engineering optimization problem, we can use a statistical method through sampling and grouping to get the distribution function of the grouped samples. Using the method of curve fitting we can then obtain an approximate probability distributed function $P(\overline{f})$ for further analysis.

In conventional SA algorithms, the function value $f$, instead of energy $E$, is usually used to calculate the probability of acceptance as defined by Eq.(2). Since the range of function values is different in each problem, it is usually difficult to determine an appropriate value of initial temperature and the decrement of temperature for a particular problem. Observing that the value of $P(\overline{f})$ always lies in [0, 1] gives us an idea that we may treat $P(\overline{f})$ as the state energy $E$. In this way, the probability distribution function $P(\overline{f})$ serves two purposes: firstly, the probability distribution function itself can be used to calculate reliability and to serve as a criterion for reducing the search space; secondly, the energy level of a state $\boldsymbol{x}$ can be used to calculate the probability of acceptance.

The search procedure starts from a population of points, so we need to choose $N_{\rm p}$ initial candidates. Normalize the search space into [0, 1] in each and every dimension. Performing SA once for each of all candidates in the population is called a generation. If the criterion of "system equilibrium" is satisfied after several generations, we then decrease the temperature level $kT$. As all the candidates concentrate into a small region and the convergent condition is satisfied after several temperature levels, we say that it is convergent in this cycle. Then a new cycle starts in the reduced and re-normalized search space. The procedures will be performed repeatedly until the stopping criteria are satisfied. In the following, we discuss the important issues involved in the procedures of RRSA.

### 3.1 Equilibrium Criterion

It is important but difficult to find a criterion for detecting system equilibrium in the process of SA. In this paper, we introduce the concept of "stable energy" to derive the equilibrium criterion for decreasing temperature level.

If the energy level $E$ is continuously distributed in [0, 1], then Eq.(1) becomes

$$p_T(E) = \frac{e^{-E/kT}}{kT(1-e^{-1/kT})}. \tag{5}$$

The probability distribution function of $E$ will be

$$P(E) = \text{Prob}(0 < X \le E)$$

$$= \int_0^E \frac{e^{-\xi/kT}}{kT(1-e^{-1/kT})} \mathrm{d}\xi = \frac{1-e^{-E/kT}}{1-e^{-1/kT}}, \tag{6}$$

For a current state $\boldsymbol{x}$ with corresponding energy $E$, the expectation of energy levels, which is denoted as $E'$, can be calculated as follow:

$$E' = \int_0^E \xi p(\xi) d\xi + \int_E^1 p(\xi)[\xi e^{-(\xi-E)/kT}] d\xi + \int_E^1 E[1-e^{-(\xi-E)/kT}] d\xi, \tag{7}$$

where

$$p(\xi) = \frac{e^{-\xi/kT}}{kT(1-e^{-1/kT})}. \tag{8}$$

The first term in Eq.(6) signifies the case that the energy level of the new state is lower than that of the current state and $\boldsymbol{x}$ is replaced by the new state. The second term indicates the case that the new state has higher energy but is still accepted. The third term signifies the case of rejecting the new state. Eq.(6) can be evaluated explicitly to obtain the energy expectation $E'$ for given $kT$ and $E$. The diagram of $E'$ versus $E$ at different values of $kT$ is shown in Figure 1. It is clear that the curves above the line of $E' = E$ correspond to the states for which the energy expectation of the new state will be higher than the energy level of current state. Obviously, if a state is in that condition, the potential of further decreasing energy may become poor. If we obtain the energy expectation $E'$ from a state energy $E$ at a certain $kT$, and repeatedly treating $E'$ as a new $E$ to calculate the next $E'$, then we can obtain the diagram of $E'$ versus the number of calculations $N$, as sketched in Figure 2. It can be seen that even if we select the highest energy level $E$ = 1 or the lowest energy $E$ = 0 as the initial value, the energy expectation $E'$ will approach the same constant value for a given $kT$. This value is the energy level that the system achieves equilibrium for a given $kT$. We may thus define a "stable energy" $E_S$ which satisfies $E' = E$ and can be solved from Eq.(6) numerically for a given $kT$. Once the average of the population energy is less than, or equal to, $E_S$, we claim that the system equilibrium is achieved at the current temperature. We may then reduce $kT$ to a smaller value in order to further decrease the energy level effectively.

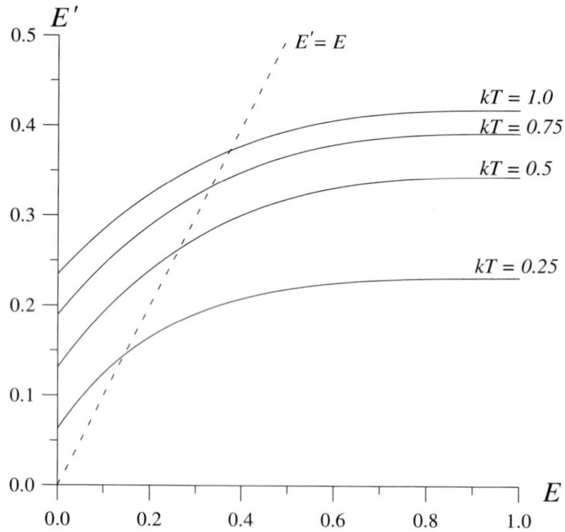


**Fig. 1.** Energy expectation at different temperature

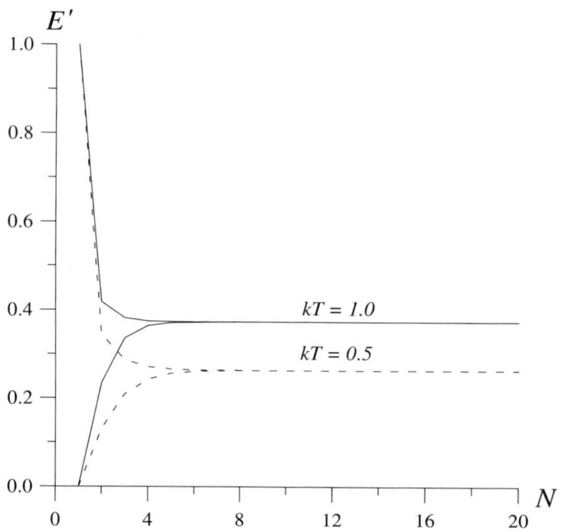


**Fig. 2.** Stable energy at different temperature

### 3.2 Convergence Conditions

As the SA process evolves, the population of candidates should move toward the global optimum and their energy should become lower. Therefore, we may use these two properties to derive the convergent conditions. In order not to get confused, we use $\boldsymbol{y}$ to express the position vector relative to the reduced and normalized search space, and $\boldsymbol{x}$ is used to express the position vector relative to the original search space. If all the candidates are enclosed in a small region in the normalized search space, we defined the reduced region as a hypercube whose side lengths are given by

$$\Delta y_k = y_{kmax} - y_{kmin} \ , \ k = 1, 2, \ldots, \mathrm{n}, \tag{9}$$

where $y_{k\,max}$ and $y_{k\,min}$ are the largest and smallest values of coordinate among the candidates in the $k$th dimension respectively. The condition for terminating a cycle can then be defined as follows:

$$\Delta y_k \le L_c, \forall k \text{ and } E_{max} \le E_c \ , \tag{10}$$

where $E_{max}$ is the highest energy level of these candidates; $L_c$ and $E_c$ are two control parameters to be prescribed for a particular problem.

If the convergent condition (11) is satisfied, then all the candidates would have concentrated into a small region with side length less than $L_c$ in each dimension, and the probability of finding a better candidate is less than $E_c$ (since $E = \mathrm{P}(f)$).

### 3.3 Stopping Criteria

A new cycle starts in a unit hypercube which is obtained by normalizing each dimension of the search space. Searching in the reduccd region can, in general, locate the optimum faster. Besides, we may set up the stopping criterion by using a modified objective function in each new cycle. The procedure is described as follows.

Let $\boldsymbol{x}_i^*$ be the best candidate found in the $i$th cycle, and the corresponding function value $f(\boldsymbol{x}_i^*)$ be denoted as $f_i^*$, then we may replace the objective function $f(\boldsymbol{x})$ by $F_{i+1}(\boldsymbol{x})$ for the $(i+1)$th cycle, where

$$F_{i+1}(\boldsymbol{x}) = f(\boldsymbol{x}) - f_i^* \ . \tag{11}$$

It can be observed that the value of the modified objective function is always negative when a better state is found, and it approaches zero as the cycle evolves. If a cycle is terminated with a positive value of the modified objective function, which usually implies that the candidates converged to a local optimum, we may restart this cycle. If the value of the modified objective function is very close to zero, which means that it is hard to find a better state, we may then terminate the search process. In general, the criterion for terminating the search process can be defined by the following two conditions: (1) all candidates converge into a small region, and (2) the value of the modified objective function approaches zero. When both of the two conditions are satisfied, the region of convergence relative to the original search space becomes very small and it would be difficult to find a better candidate, and so the searching process can be terminated.

### 3.4 Multiple Optima

For the current cycle, it is possible that $kT$ has decreased to a very small value $T_{cv}$ but the candidates still fail to converge. This may be due to the situation that there are several global optima or there are some local optima whose function values are close to the global optimum. In order to solve this problem, we introduce the method of simulated evolution [5] into RRSA. The evolution process consists of four major steps: reproduction, mutation, competition, and selection. To avoid trapping into a local optimum and to improve the convergence rate, Chiang and Huang [14] proposed a rule for competition and employed an adjustable deviation for mutation. In RRSA, we use the simulated evolution in case that a cycle fails to converge as $kT$ is smaller than $T_{cv}$. It should be mentioned that we just use the method of evolution to identify the regions where optima are possibly enclosed, but not to find the exact location of optima. After several generations of evolution, we may obtain regions where some design points concentrate around. Using RRSA algorithm in these regions respectively, we may then find global optima or some local optima whose function values are close to those of global optima.

## 4 Numerical Experiments for Functional Optimization

We will test the effectiveness of RRSA algorithm using some standard problems available in the literature [15]. The following control parameters are used in RRSA for the following problems:

1. The number of samples selected for estimating probability distribution $N = 100$.
2. The number of candidates in a population $N_p = 3$.
3. Temperature decreasing ratio $T_r = 0.6$.
4. Region convergence conditions: (1) $L_c = 0.15$. (2) $E_c = 0.005$.
5. Limit of temperature $T_{cv} = 1\times10^{-6}$
6. Proportional constant of step length $k_r = 5$.
7. Stopping criterions: $\boldsymbol{\varepsilon_x} = 1\times10^{-4}$, $\boldsymbol{\varepsilon_f} = 1\times10^{-6}$

Two test problems are given below along with their domains of interest and optimal function values $f^*$. Each test problem has been solved with ten different seeds for the random number generator. The numerical test results are reported in Table 1 and Table 2 by specifying the following quantities:

NFV = number of function value evaluations;
$N_{opt}$ = number of times that the optimum has been found out of ten times.
$\boldsymbol{x}^*$ = the optimal candidate;
$f^*$ = the optimum function value.
$\boldsymbol{x}^+$ = the highest value of $\boldsymbol{x}^*$ in the ten times
$\boldsymbol{x}^-$ = the lowest value of $\boldsymbol{x}^*$ in the ten times

**Problem 1.** Shubert Function:

$$f(x_1,x_2) = \{\sum_{k=1}^{5} k\cos[(k+1)x_1 + k]\}\{\sum_{k=1}^{5} k\cos[(k+1)x_2 + k]\},$$

$$-10 \le x_i \le 10,\ i = 1,2, \quad f^* \approx -186.73091$$

In the region considered, this function has 760 minima, eighteen of which are also global. Table 1 presents the result of optimization using RRSA. It is seen that all the 18 global optima have been found in the 10 tests and each test individually found 2 to 7 optima. This demonstrates the ability of RRSA to find multiple optima in one search procedure. It is remarkable that because we chose a small population size ($N_p$=3), it is not too difficult for all the candidates to concentrate into a region containing only one or a few of the 18 global optima.

**Table 1.** Result of test problem 1

| | Average of $\boldsymbol{x}^*$ | $N_{opt}$ | | Average of $\boldsymbol{x}^*$ | $N_{opt}$ |
|---|---|---|---|---|---|
| 1. | (-7.708290, 5.482869) | 2 | 2. | (-7.708358, -0.800326) | 2 |
| 3. | (-7.708291, -7.083536) | 3 | 4. | (-7.083523, 4.858068) | 4 |
| 5. | (-7.083505, -1.425145) | 6 | 6. | (-7.083537, -7.708329) | 2 |
| 7. | (-1.425123, 5.482860) | 4 | 8. | (-1.425123, -0.800334) | 3 |
| 9. | (-1.425150, -7.083506) | 2 | 10. | (-0.800314, 4.858037) | 3 |
| 11. | (-0.800268, -1.425149) | 2 | 12. | (-0.800322, -7.708313) | 7 |
| 13. | (4.858054, 5.482848) | 5 | 14. | (4.858051, -0.800311) | 6 |
| 15. | (4.858009, -7.083537) | 2 | 16. | (5.482882, 4.858079) | 4 |
| 17. | (5.482855, -1.425132) | 2 | 18. | (5.482881, -7.708296) | 6 |
| Total NFV | 942451 | Ave. $f^*$ | 186.731 | Ave. reliability | 96.22% |

**Problem 2**

$$f(x)=\frac{\pi}{n}\{10sin^2(\pi y_1)+\sum_{k=1}^{n-1}(y_k-1)^2[1+10sin^2(\pi y_{k+1})]+(y_n-1)^2\},$$

$$y_i=1+\frac{1}{4}(x_i-1),\ -10\le x_i\le 10,\ i=1,2,\cdots,n, \qquad f^*=0$$

This function has roughly $5^n$ local minima and a unique global minimum located at $x_i^*=1, i=1,2,\cdots,n.$ Choose $n$ = 10, and the result of optimization search using RRSA is listed in Table 2.

**Table 2.** Result of test problem 2

| | Average of $\boldsymbol{x}^*$ | $\boldsymbol{x}^-$ | $\boldsymbol{x}^+$ |
|---|---|---|---|
| $x_1$ | 1.000002 | 0.999818 | 1.000137 |
| $x_2$ | 1.000036 | 0.999231 | 1.000921 |
| $x_3$ | 1.000045 | 0.999207 | 1.000786 |
| $x_4$ | 1.000084 | 0.999325 | 1.000988 |
| $x_5$ | 0.999938 | 0.998856 | 1.000816 |
| $x_6$ | 0.999952 | 0.999108 | 1.000993 |
| $x_7$ | 1.000001 | 0.999098 | 1.000545 |
| $x_8$ | 0.999973 | 0.999169 | 1.000748 |
| $x_9$ | 0.999968 | 0.999154 | 1.000931 |
| $x_{10}$ | 1.000017 | 0.999479 | 1.000752 |
| Average of $f^*$ | | Average of reliability | Average of NFV |
| 3.301326E-09 | | 94.67% | 27381 |

## 5 Application to Structural Optimization

Generally a structural design is required to conform to a number of inequality or equality constraints related to stress, deflection, dimensional relationships and other variables. To use RRSA in a structural optimization problem, we may conveniently handle it by using the penalty function approach. To illustrate the procedure of solution by RRSA method, consider the design problem of the ten-bar truss shown in Figure 3. This example has been used by many investigators to demonstrate various methods of solution [16]. The truss is subjected to a single-loading condition and the objective function represents the total volume (or weight) of the truss members:

$$f(x) = \sum_{i=1}^{10} l_i x_i \ , \tag{12}$$

where $l_i$ is the length of each member as given in the figure, and the design variable $x_i$ is the cross-sectional area of each member. The member-size constraints are $0.1 \le x_i$, for $i = 1, 2, ..., 10$. The following 2 cases of stress constraints will be solved:

Case A: $-25 \le \sigma_i \le 25$, for $i = 1, 2, ..., 10$.

Case B: $-25 \le \sigma_i \le 25$, for $i = 1, 2, ..., 8, 10$.

$-50 \le \sigma_9 \le 50$

By employing the exterior penalty function method, the constrained optimization problem can be converted into an unconstrained problem so that RRSA applies directly. Each of the constrained case problems has been solved with ten different seeds for the random number generator. The test results are summarized in Table 3 and 4. The initial value of parameter $r$ for each cycle is chosen as 200 and it changes while the "equilibrium" is reached, i.e. at the time that the temperature parameter $kT$ is to be

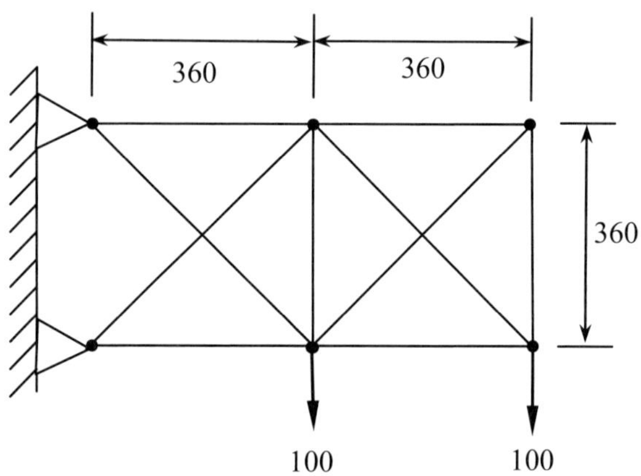


**Fig. 3.** The 10-bar truss

**Table 3.** Result of the ten-bar truss problem

| No. | Hajela | | | Case A | | | Case B | | |
|---|---|---|---|---|---|---|---|---|---|
| | Best $f = 1635$ | | | Exact $f = 15931.8$ | | | Exact $f = 14976.0$ | | |
| | $f^*$ | Error (%) | NFV | $f^*$ | Error (%) | NFV | $f^*$ | Error (%) | NFV |
| 1 | 1678 | 2.63 | 23721 | 15934.6 | 0.02 | 50772 | 15145.4 | 1.13 | 61990 |
| 2 | 1677 | 2.57 | 34971 | 15956.8 | 0.16 | 67010 | 15058.0 | 0.55 | 66369 |
| 3 | 1639 | 0.24 | 14803 | 15972.7 | 0.26 | 63872 | 15256.5 | 1.87 | 49813 |
| 4 | 1635 | 0 | 17906 | 15948.4 | 0.10 | 49849 | 14979.8 | 0.03 | 60707 |
| 5 | 1688 | 3.24 | 16862 | 15933.5 | 0.01 | 62165 | 14983.7 | 0.05 | 63812 |
| 6 | 1666 | 1.90 | 26401 | 15935.6 | 0.02 | 47680 | 15148.1 | 1.15 | 63264 |
| 7 | 1692 | 3.49 | 23399 | 15944.6 | 0.08 | 50080 | 15151.5 | 1.17 | 66496 |
| 8 | 1725 | 5.50 | 14803 | 16015.1 | 0.52 | 67343 | 15158.0 | 1.22 | 59884 |
| 9 | - | - | - | 15940.1 | 0.05 | 55129 | 15308.6 | 2.22 | 62286 |
| 10 | - | - | - | 15949.5 | 0.11 | 46885 | 15113.5 | 0.92 | 66246 |
| Ave. | 1675 | 2.44 | 23992 | 15953.1 | 0.13 | 56079 | 15130.3 | 1.03 | 62087 |

**Table 4.** Detailed result of one typical test for the ten-bar truss problem

| $x$ | Case A | | | Case B | | |
|---|---|---|---|---|---|---|
| | Exact solution | No.10 in Table 3 | Error (%) | Exact solution | No.2 in Table 3 | Error (%) |
| $x_1$ | 7.94 | 7.9243 | -0.20 | 7.90 | 7.7645 | -1.72 |
| $x_2$ | 0.10 | 0.1033 | +3.30 | 0.10 | 0.2355 | +135.50 |
| $x_3$ | 8.06 | 8.0757 | +0.20 | 8.10 | 8.2357 | +1.68 |
| $x_4$ | 3.94 | 3.9243 | -0.40 | 3.90 | 3.7645 | -3.47 |
| $x_5$ | 0.10 | 0.1054 | +5.40 | 0.10 | 0.1017 | +1.70 |
| $x_6$ | 0.10 | 0.1512 | +51.20 | 0.10 | 0.2355 | +135.50 |
| $x_7$ | 5.74 | 5.7639 | +0.42 | 5.80 | 5.9899 | +3.27 |
| $x_8$ | 5.57 | 5.5498 | -0.36 | 5.51 | 5.3238 | -3.38 |
| $x_9$ | 5.57 | 5.5498 | -0.36 | 3.68 | 3.5492 | -3.55 |
| $x_{10}$ | 0.10 | 0.1211 | +21.10 | 0.14 | 0.3330 | +137.86 |

reduced, according to the formula: $r = f_i^* \cdot (\mathrm{N_{RT}} + 1)$, where $\mathrm{N_{RT}}$ is the number of times that $kT$ has been reduced in the $i$th cycle, and $f_i^*$ is the lowest function value found in the $i$th cycle.

In Table 3, the result presented by Hajela [17] is also listed for comparison. The problem is the same as Case A, but the weight was used as the objective function and the problem was solved by the genetic algorithm (GA). It can be seen that the number of function evaluations in RRSA is generally more than that in GA, but the present results are more accurate. If we examine the result of each design point, it can be found that most of the optima found are local minima. Even though their function values are very close to the exact solution, some of the design variables are quite different from those of the global optimum. In Table 4, the detailed result of a typical one of the ten tests for each case is presented. It is noted that some variables near the size constraints are so small (e.g. $x_2$) that they hardly affect the objective function value. Thus, the search is virtually dominated by the variables that have larger values.

## 6 Conclusions

By including the advantages of simulated evolution and genetic algorithms and introducing the idea of stable energy and region reduction, we proposed a global optimization method based on simulated annealing, which is called RRSA. In addition to faster convergence than conventional SA, other advantages of RRSA include the capability of searching multiple optima, and the ease of determining the initial temperature, equilibrium criterion and the stopping rule. All these characteristics make the RRSA algorithm a strong competitor to the existing algorithms. Further studies are merited of the characteristics of the RRSA approach and its application to more complicated engineering optimization problems.

## Acknowledgments

The authors gratefully acknowledge the support provided by the National Science Council of the Republic of China under Grant NSC 93-2212-E-006-043.

## References

1. Brooks, K.H.: A Discussion of Random Methods of Seeking Optima, Operations Research. 6 (1958) 244-251
2. Solis, F.J., Wets, R.J.B.: Minimization by Random Search Techniques, Mathematics of Operations Research, 6 (1981) 19-30
3. Fabio, S.: Stochastic Techniques for Global Optimization: A survey of Recent Advances, Journal of Global Optimization, 1(1991) 207-228
4. Goldberg, D.E.: Genetic Algorithms in Search, Optimization and Machine Learning, Addison-Wesley Reading, MA, (1989)
5. Fogel, L.J., Owens, A.J., Walsh, M.J.: Artificial Intelligence Through Simulated Evolution, Wiley Publishing, New York, (1966)
6. Aarts, E., Korst, J.: Simulated Annealing and Boltzmann Machines, J. Wiley & Sons, (1989)
7. Jenkins, W.M.: Towards Structural Optimization Via the Genetic Algorithm, Computer & Structures, 40 (1991) 1321-1327
8. Riche, R.L., Haftka, R.T.: Optimization of Laminate Stacking Sequence for Buckling Load Maximization by Genetic Algorithm, AIAA Journal, 31 (1993) 951-956
9. Junjiro, O., Yoji, H.: Actuator Placement Optimization by Genetic and Improved Simulated Annealing Algorithms, AIAA Journal, 31 (1992) 1167-1169
10. Atiqullah, M.M., Rao, S.S.: Parallel Processing in Optimal Structural Design Using Simulated Annealing, AIAA Journal, 33 (1995) 2386-2392
11. Srichander, R.: Efficient Schedules for Simulated Annealing, Engineering Optimization, 24 (1995) 161-176

12. Jaynes, E.T.: Information Theory and Statistical Mechanics, Physical Reviews, 106 (1957) 620-630
13. Kirkpatrick, S., Gelatt, C.D., Vecchi, M.P.: Optimization by Simulated Annealing, Science, 220 (1983) 671-680
14. Chiang, D.Y., Huang, S.T.: Modal Parameter Identification Using Simulated Evolution, AIAA Journal, 35 (1997) 1204-1208
15. Lucidi, S., Piccioni, M.: Random Tunneling by Means of Acceptance-Rejection Sampling for Global Optimization, Journal of Optimization Theory & Applications, 62(1989) 255-277
16. Kirsch, U.: Optimum Structural Design, McGraw-Hill, (1981) Chap. 6
17. Hajela, P., Yoo, J.: Constraint Handling in Genetic Search Using Expression Strategies, AIAA Journal, 34 (1996) 2414-2420

# A Hybrid Heuristic for PWB Capacity Expansion Problem*

Zhongsheng Hua and Feihua Huang

School of Management, University of Science & Technology of China,
Hefei, Anhui 230026, People's Republic of China
zshua@ustc.edu.cn, huangfh@mail.ustc.edu.cn

**Abstract.** In the multi-product, flexible manufacturing environment, the line capacity expansion problem for printed wiring board (PWB) assembly systems is a complex combinatorial optimization problem. A model synthesized BOM (Bill of Material) of product families and machine operation flexibility at the aggregate level is described. Since the resulting model is a large-scale two-stage stochastic integer programming problem, it may not be easy to be solved by any standard code. An approximate solution procedure is thus developed, which first reduces the dimensionality of search space by heuristic algorithms, and then deals with the reduced search space by solving a series of knapsack problems. Finally, we demonstrate the financial benefit of the model and the feasibility of our approach by numerical experiments.

## 1 Introduction

The decade of the 1990s has witnessed an increasingly competitive market place characterized by short product life cycles, demand uncertainty, product proliferation, increased customization, and quick response. The most common production process for electronic systems is assembling components on a printed wiring board (PWB). This essential equipment is designed to place components (parts) reliably and accurately, to meet quality requirements and demands of different products or product families. A machine line consists of different machine types that can produce many types of product families. The range of products that can be built on the line, i.e., the diversity of the allowable process recipes, is a key measure of the flexibility of a machine line. Because of the high cost of a machine line with *total flexibility* (i.e., a machine line that can build all products), most manufacturing firms build *partially flexible* machine lines (i.e., a machine line that can build only a subset of all products).

This paper assumes a firm with certain PWB assembly machine lines with installed capacity to produce specific product families which consist of some part types. The planning horizon is divided into several time periods with equal length.

* Supported by Program for New Century Excellent Talents in University of China (Grant No.: NCET-04-0570), NSFC (Grant No.: 70571073) and the Specialized Research Fund for the Doctoral Programme of Higher Education (Grant No.: 20050358002).

D.-S. Huang, K. Li, and G.W. Irwin (Eds.): ICIC 2006, LNCS 4113, pp. 802 – 811, 2006.

The capacity expansion problem is to determine whether capacity should be added at the beginning of each time period at each machine line because of demand fluctuation. Random demand can be met by expanded machines to some assembly lines and/or subcontracting.

Capacity expansion for flexible manufacturing systems (FMS) has been intensively investigated since 1990's. Rajagopalan and Soteriou [1] considered a model of capacity acquisition, disposal, and replacement for a single product on multiple machines over multiple periods, with discrete equipment sizes. He presented an integer programming model and used a linear relaxation together with heuristic interchange in a branch-and-bound procedure to obtain optimal solutions. Fine [2] and Van Mieghem [3] presented optimal line capacity investment (expansion) strategies respectively. Since they addressed choices between dedicated and flexible machine lines, their models and solution methods are not directly applicable to PWB assembly systems. Benjaafar and Gupta [4] used a set of models to compare the effect of product variety and process flexibility on performance under varying operating conditions and control policies. It is in spirit similar to our model, but their models do not associate flexibility with the structure of product. Chen, Li and Tirupati [5] then extended their forementioned result to random demand scenario and the environment characterized by life cycle uncertainty. Catay, Erenguc and Vakharaj [6] discussed strategic level investment decisions on procuring new equipment and aggregate level capacity planning given that the wafer demands are lumpy and time varying. They developed a multi-period mixed-integer programming model to minimize the machine tool operating costs, new tool acquisition costs, and inventory holding costs and proposed a Lagrangian-based relaxation heuristic to find efficient tool procurement plans. Considering a set of possible, discrete demand scenarios with associated probabilities, Hood, Bermon and Barahona [7] presented a model which determined the tools to purchase, under a budget constraint, to minimize weighted average unmet demand, and used stochastic integer programming to find a tool set robust to changes in demand. The resulting robust tool set was proved to deal well with all the scenarios at no or minimal additional cost compared to that for a single demand profile.

In the environment characterized by multi-product, multi-period, deterministic and dynamic market demand, Hua and Banerjee [8] made a pioneer attempt to develop a model of capacity expansion for PWB assembly system, which brings together the feature of structure of product families and machine flexibility. Hua and Liang [10] then extended the model described in Hua and Banerjee [8] to the environment characterized by random market demand. Since capacity is discrete and partially flexible, solving the developed model becomes a challenging task because of excessive or large number of integer decision variables and constraints. An approximate solution procedure is thus developed, which first reduces the dimensionality of search space by heuristic algorithms, and then deals with the reduced search space by solving a series of knapsack problems.

The reminder of the paper is organized as follows. In the next section, a cursory statement of capacity expansion problem and a scenario-based model for PWB assembly systems is presented. An approximate solution process and relative heuristic algorithms to the model are developed in section 3. Numerical experiments in section 4 illustrate financial benefit of the model and the feasibility of the solution approach and algorithms. Section 5 concludes the paper.

## 2 Capacity Extension Problem for PWB Assembly Lines

The PWB assembly system consists of inserting or mounting electrical components, such as resistors, transistors and capacitors, into prespecified positions on a PWB. Each machine can insert certain part types on a PWB, some machines form a machine line which can produce some product families. A machine line makes insertions on PWBs with the only restriction that all the insertions for a product family are done on the same machine line. The placement operations for a given product family are distributed across the available machines in the line. Line capacity layout of PWB assembly system needs to be modified at the beginning of each aggregate period to meet the basic capacity requirement and improve the flexibility of a machine line because of demand fluctuation. Fig. 1 is an illustration of a production system for printed wiring board (PWB) lines. The production system consists of two machine lines, each line consists of some placement machines (boxes in the figure), and each machine is capable of assembling two different types of parts from the list of five categories: small chips (SC), large chips (LC), odd-shaped (OS) parts such as connectors and pins, high-precision (HP) placements such as fine-pitch integrated circuits, and direct chip attach (DCA) parts that require an additional flux dispensing operation. A customized product can be represented by a list of numbers of part types in one unit of the product.

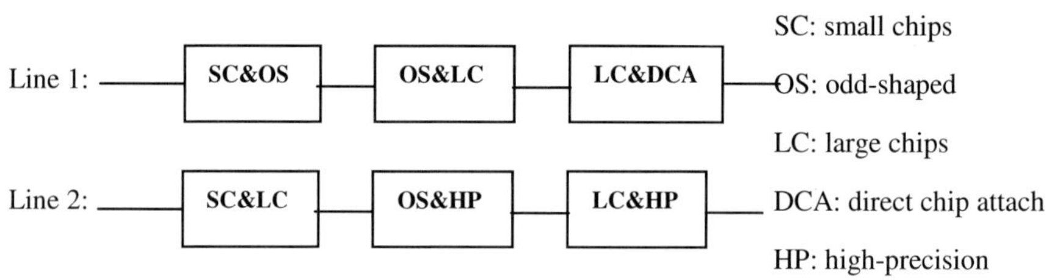


**Fig. 1.** Illustration of a PWB assembly line

We used a scenario approach in which market demand scenarios (or state of nature) were specified for each time period. It is assumed that a finite time horizon (budget period) is divided into a finite number of time periods of equal length. Capacity expansion, if necessary, occurs at the beginning of a time period, and changeover time is assumed negligible. Under the environment that demands in different periods are independent and satisfied by producing and/or subcontracting in each period, the PWB capacity expansion and technology selection model (abbreviated as *GM*) developed by Hua and Banerjee [8] is described as follows. Notations in the model are defined in Table 1.

**Table 1.** Notations

| Indices |
|---|
| $t$ time periods, $t$=1,2,…,$T$ |
| $s$ demand scenarios, $s$=1,2,…,$S$ |
| $l$ machine lines, $l$=1,2,…,$L$ |
| $m$ machine types, $m$=1,2,…,$M$ |
| $j$ product families, $j$=1,2,…,$J$ |
| $i$ part types, $i$=1,2,…,$I$ |
| **Decision Variables** |
| $X(t,s,l,m,j,i)$ production-planning decision variables. Number of part type $i$ for product family $j$ produced on machine $m$ in line $l$ under scenario $s$ in period $t$ |
| $X_{SC}(t,s,j)$ production-planning decision variables. Amount of subcontracting product family $j$ under scenario $s$ in period $t$ |
| $Y(t,l,m)$ capacity-expansion decision variables. Number of machines of type $m$ added to line $l$ in period $t$ |
| **Cost Parameters** |
| $C(s,l,m)$ average unit production cost for given $m$, $s$ , $t$, $l$ |
| $C_{sc}(j)$ unit cost of subcontracting product family $j$ |
| $C_p(m)$ costs of purchasing of a machine of type $m$ |
| **Capacity and Demand Parameters** |
| $N(0,l,m)$ the initial capacity layout. |
| $F(m,i)$ capability of machine type $m$ inserting part type $i$, $F(m,i)=1$ if it can insert part type $i$; 0, otherwise. |
| $Q(m)$ number of insertions machine type $m$ can make in one period |
| $B$ capital limitation on new equipment investment |
| $d(t,s,j)$ demand of product family $j$ under scenario $s$ in period $t$ |
| $S(j,i)$ number of part type $i$ in each of product family $j$ |
| $p(t,s)$ probability that scenario $s$ occurs in period $t$ |

(*GM*)

$$Min\ \ Z = \sum_{t,l,m} C_p(m)Y(t,l,m) + \sum_{t,s,j,i} p(t,s)C_{sc}(j)X_{sc}(t,s,j) + \sum_{t,s,l,m,j,i} p(t,s)C(s,l,m)X(t,s,l,m,j,i) \tag{1}$$

$$\text{s.t.} \sum_{j,i} X(t,s,l,m,j,i) \le \{N(0,l,m) + \sum_{k=1}^{t} Y(k,l,m)\}Q(m) \tag{2}$$

$$t=1,\dots,T,\ \ s=1,\dots,S,\ \ l=1,\dots,L,\ \ m=1,\dots,M$$

$$\sum_j X(t,s,l,m,j,i) \le \{N(0,l,m) + \sum_{k=1}^{t} Y(k,l,m)\} Q(m) F(m,i) \tag{3}$$

$$t=1,\ldots,T,\ s=1,\ldots,S,\ l=1,\ldots,L,\ m=1,\ldots,M,\ i=1,\ldots,I$$

$$\sum_m X(t,s,l,m,j,k) S(j,i') = \sum_m X(t,s,l,m,j,i') S(j,k) \tag{4}$$

$$t=1,\ldots,T;\ s=1,\ldots,S;\ l=1,\ldots,L;\ j=1,\ldots,J;$$

$$S(j,i')S(j,k) \ne 0,\ i'=1,\ldots I\ (i' \ne k),\ \textit{where } k \textit{ is the first } i$$

$$\textit{which } S(j,i) \ne 0 \textit{ when } i \textit{ from } 1 \textit{ to } I \textit{ for every } j$$

$$\sum_{l,m,i} X(t,s,l,m,j,i) + S(j,i) X_{sc}(t,s,j) = S(j,i) d(t,s,j) \tag{5}$$

$$t=1,\ldots,T,\ s=1,\ldots,S,\ j=1,\ldots,J$$

$$\sum_{t,l,m} C_p(t,m) Y(t,l,m) \le B \tag{6}$$

$$X(t,s,l,m,j,i) \ge 0,\ X_{sc}(t,s,j) \ge 0,\ Y(t,l,m) \ge 0 \text{ and integer valued} \tag{7}$$

In the objective function (1), the first term is the cost of purchasing machines; the latter two terms are the sum of expected production cost and expected subcontracting cost. Formulae (2) and (3) are capacity constraints which respectively ensure that a production assignment does not exceed a machine's total capacity and its capacity of inserting part type $i$. Formula (4) is a machine line constraint that requires all insertions for a product family be completed on one machine line. Formula (5) is demand constraint that requires all demand be met by production or subcontracting. Constraint (6) is the capital investment budget limitation, and formula (7) is nonnegative and integer constraint.

Model *GM* is a two-stage stochastic mixed-integer programming problem with recourse, which involves two kinds of decisions. Making choice on the number and types of machines to be added to lines to meet capacity demand is the first stage decision. Determining the number and type of parts assigned to each machine in a line for a given product family to meet market demand is the second stage decision. Note that in the above process, a good capacity adjusting is complicated by the fact that the total capacity decision affects future production planning. The production planning is further complicated by the fact that the demand is characterized by random variables whose values are revealed after the capacity expansion decision.

## 3 Heuristics and Solution Approach

As elaborated in the previous section, a realistic capacity expansion problem for PWB assembly system has thousands of integer capacity-expansion decision variables. The basic idea to solve model (*GM*) is firstly to determine a rough set of machines to be added for each machine line in each period (termed rough addition set) by eliminating part of incompatible capacity expansion decision variables, and then to deal with the reduced search space by solving a series of knapsack problems.

As it was elaborated in [8], when demand is deterministic, a rough addition set for a machine line can be determined by adding a virtual machine to the line, as shown in Fig. 2.

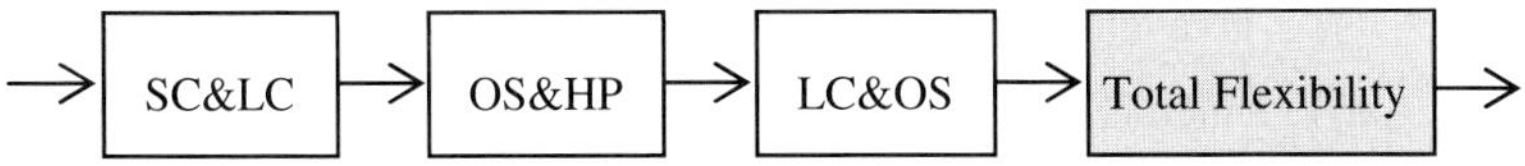


**Fig. 2.** Illustration of an SMT machine line with special machine

In Fig. 2, the virtual machine (shown as shaded box) is totally flexible. It can insert all part types with the unit cost $C_s(t)$ and with infinite capacity. By solving a recursive programming problem [8], we can obtain the volumes of all part types produced by the virtual machine.

When market demand is random and can be forecasted as demand scenarios, each demand scenario can be treated as a deterministic market demand, and its rough addition set can be obtained by applying the above approach. Denote volumes of part types produced by the virtual machine under demand scenario $s$ ( $s=1,...,S$ ) as $X^*(t,l,M+1,j,i)$. Then the rough addition set $\{A'(t,s,l,m)\}$ corresponding to market demand scenario $s$ can be determined by solving the next knapsack problems (*KPs*) for given $s$:

(*KPs*)

$$Min\ \ Z=\sum_{t,l,m} C_p(m)A'(t,s,l,m) \tag{8}$$

$$\text{s.t.} \sum_{m} A'(t,s,l,m)Q(m)F(m,i) \ge \sum_{j} X^*(t,l,M+1,j,i)\ ,t=1,...,T\ \ l=1,...,L, \tag{9}$$

$$\text{int}\ A'(t,s,l,m)\ge 0\ ,\ t=1,...,T\ \ l=1,...,L\ ,m=1,...,M\ . \tag{10}$$

The objective function (8) is to minimize the cost of purchasing machines, and constraints (9) ensure that machines in the rough addition set can produce the volumes of part types assigned to the virtual machine. Formula (10) is nonnegative and integer constraint.

The knapsack problem described in (8)-(10) is still very hard to be solved. For example, the firm described in [10] has 12 assembly lines (*L*=12) and 20 available machine types (*M*=20). When there are two demand scenarios (*S*=2), then even for a single period capacity planning problem (*T*=1), there are 240 integer variables in model (*KPs*), which is hard to be solved by directly applying any programming code. For the capacity planning problem over multiple periods, integer variables will increase linearly with the increase in number of planning periods.

By observing model (*GM*), we know that constraint (5) implies the relative independence of variable in the same period and in the same machine line. This structural property of model (*GM*) hints us that we can apply the variable-grouping based genetic algorithm (VGGA-S) proposed by Hua et al. [9] to effectively solve model (*KPs*). That is, we first put the 240 integer variables in model (*KPs*) into 12 groups, and then apply VGGA-S to the knapsack problem described in (8)-(10).

During the application of VGGA-S, the fitness of a potential solution $A'(t,s,l,m)$, $f(A'(t,s,l,m))$, is evaluated by directly calculating from the objective function $Z(A'(t,s,l,m))$, which is described in formula (11).

$$f(A'(t,s,l,m)) = \begin{cases} 1\big/ Z(A'(t,s,l,m)) \\ 1\big/ (Z(A'(t,s,l,m)) + (0.5g)^2\, penalty) \end{cases} \tag{11}$$

In formula (11), $g$ is the number of GA generations, which will give a larger penalty to an infeasible solutions generated in a later GA generation [9]. Penalty is paid by those infeasible individuals, which is defined as follows:

$$penalty = \sum_{t,l} \max(0, \sum_{j} X^*(t,l,M+1,j,i) - \sum_{m} A'(t,s,l,m) Q(m) F(m,i)). \tag{12}$$

By applying VGGA-S to model (*KPs*), we can obtain $\{A'(t,s,l,m)\}$, $t=1,...,T$, $s$ ($s=1,...,S$), $l=1,...,L$, $m=1,...,M$. We then determine the heuristic solution to model (GM), $\{A(t,l,m)\}$, as follows:

$$A(t,l,m) = \max_{s} A'(t,s,l,m). \tag{13}$$

Formula (13) is actually to determine the heuristic solution to model (*GM*) by getting the maximum value of $\{A'(t,s,l,m)\}$ ($s=1,...,S$) over all market demand scenarios. Formula (13) provides a simple and straightforward method to solve model (*GM*), which is effective if probabilities of all demand scenarios are about the same. When the differences among probabilities of demand scenarios are large, this method may lead to large errors. For this situation, we can interpolate $S$-1 artificial demand scenarios into the demand scenarios. Denote the artificial demand scenario $s'$ between market demand scenarios $s$ and $s$+1 as $d(t,s',j)$, then it can be set as

$$d(t,s',j) = \frac{d(t,s,j) + d(t,s+1,j)}{2}, \quad s' = 1,...,S-1, \ s = 1,...,S. \tag{14}$$

This linear interpolation can also be applied to evaluate the probability of demand scenario $s'$, $p(t,s')$, i.e.,

$$p(t,s') = \frac{p(t,s) + p(t,s+1)}{2}, \quad s' = 1,...,S-1. \tag{15}$$

When $S$-1 artificial demand scenarios are added, the probabilities of all 2$S$-1 demand scenarios, $p'(t,s)$, should be rescaled as follow:

$$p'(t,s) = \frac{p(t,s)}{\sum_{s=1}^{2S-1} p(t,s)}, \quad s = 1, \ldots, 2S-1. \tag{16}$$

After we construct some artificial demand scenarios by linear interpolation, we can then appropriately merge them to let the resulted demand scenarios have the same probabilities.

Denote the average number of linear programming problems solved in a recursive programming problem in each time period and each demand scenarios as $\overline{F}$ , then the computation complexity of the recursive programming problem is $O(T \times S \times L \times \overline{F})$. During applying the VGGA-S, the computation complexity of solving knapsack problem (8)-(10) is $O(T \times S \times L \times M \times GE)$, where $GE$ is the maximal number of generations set for the standard genetic algorithm. Therefore the computation complexity of our method mainly depends on that of solving the knapsack problem (8)-(10), i.e., $O(T \times S \times L \times M \times GE)$, which is an approximate linear function of the number of the integer variables in model (*KPs*).

## 4 Computational Results

In this section, experiment verification of the proposed algorithm is carried out. We apply the proposed approach to model *GM*, and then we compare the results with its optimal solutions on computation quality. We also record the computation time of the proposed algorithm to test its computation complexity. Parameters about the machine lines and structure of product families are all taken from [10]. We report CPU computation times in seconds and perform all calculations in double-precision arithmetic. All computational experiments were conducted on a Dell PowerEdge 1500SC (1266 MHz, dual processor) with Microsoft Visual C++ 6.0. The computation results for all problems in different scale are reported in Table 2 and Table 3.

In Table 2, we report the expected total costs of capacity expansion obtained by the proposed algorithm and by the LP_Solver, a kind of Math Programming software package to solve liner programming problems. In Table 3, when problem scale is small, such as 8 and 30 integer variables, the gaps between the optimal objective values *OPT* to original problem and the objective value $Z(X)$ resulting from the proposed approach, as a percentage of *OPT*, computed as $(Z(X) - OPT)/|OPT| \times 100$. When problem scale is large which can not be solved directly, we replace *OPT* by optimal objective values *LB* to continuous relaxation of *GM*, and report the results of $(Z(X) - LB)/|LB| \times 100$. Which is needed to point out is that, because *LB* is the low bound of the original problem, the actual gaps between the objective value $Z(X)$ and the optimal objective values of the original problem is smaller than $(Z(X) - LB)/|LB| \times 100$.

**Table 2.** Expected total costs for different scale of problems

| Number of integer variables | Expected total costs ($) | |
|---|---|---|
| | Our Approach | *OPT* or *LB* |
| 8 | 1,235,228 | 1,213,647 |
| 30 | 1,935,627 | 1,787,596 |
| 75 | 2,598,463 | 2,195,861 |
| 100 | 3,257,685 | 2,586,895 |

**Table 3.** Computation time and errors of expected total costs for different scale of problems

| Number of integer variables | Errors of expected total costs (%) | Computation time (s) |
|---|---|---|
| 8 | 1.78 | 216 |
| 30 | 8.28 | 698 |
| 75 | 18.33 | 1603 |
| 100 | 25.93 | 2742 |

As shown in Table 2 and Table 3, the proposed approach in this paper can give a good solution to the small scale capacity expansion problems (8 integer variables in our experiment), and can also obtain an approximate solution even when the problem scale is comparatively large (100 integer variables in our experiment). We do not report the computation time of LP_Solver, because it can be omitted compared with the computation time of the proposed algorithm. It means that the computation complexity of the proposed approach is higher than OPT and/or LB which are obtained by using LP_Solver. However, our approach is to deal with large-scale two-stage stochastic integer programming problems, which can not be solved by LP_Solver. Although the computation complexity is higher, the proposed approach is quite valuable.

## 5 Conclusions

We propose a solution method for line capacity expansion problem of PWB assembly systems at the aggregate level. Since capacity is discrete and partially flexible, the model solving becomes a challenging task because of excessive or large number of integer decision variables and constraints. An approximate solution procedure is described, which first reduces the dimensionality of search space by heuristic algorithms, and then deals with the reduced search space by solving a series of knapsack problems. The simulation results show the rationality and the feasibility of the proposed approach.

## References

1. Rajagopalan, S., Soteriou, A. C.: Capacity Acquisition and Disposal with Discrete Facility Sizes. Management Sci, 40 (1994) 903-917
2. Fine, C. H., Freund, R. M.: Optimal Investment in Product-Flexible Manufacturing Capacity. Management Sci, 36 (1990) 449-466

3. Van Mieghem, J. A.: Investment Strategies for Flexible Resources. Management Sci, 44 (1998) 1071-1078
4. Benjaafar, S., Gupta, D.: Scope Versus Focus - Issues of Flexibility, Capacity, and Number of Production Facilities. IIE Trans, 30 (1998) 413-425
5. Chen, Z., Li, S., Tirupati, D.: A Scenario Based Stochastic Programming Approach for Technology and Capacity Planning. Comput. Oper. Res, 29 (2002) 781-806
6. Catay, B., Erenguc, S. S., Vakharaj, A. J.: Tool Capacity Planning in Semiconductor Manufacturing. Comput. Oper. Res, 30 (2003) 1349-1366
7. Hood, S. J., Bermon, S., Barahona, F.: Capacity Planning under Demand Uncertainty for Semiconductor Manufacturing. IEEE Transaction on Semiconductor Manufacturing, 16 (2003) 273-280
8. Hua, Z. S., Banerjee, P.: Aggregate Line Capacity Design for PWB Assembly Systems. Int. J. Prod. Res, 38 (2000) 2417-2441
9. Hua, Z. S., Huang, F. H.: An Effective Genetic Algorithm Approach to Large Scale Mixed Integer Programming Problems. Appl. Math. Comput, 174 (2006) 897-909
10. Hua, Z. S., Liang, L.: Heuristics to Scenario-Based Capacity Expansion Problem of PWB Assembly Systems. Springer-Verlag Berlin Heidelberg, LNAI, 3327 (2004) 135-144

# A New Efficient Parallel Revised Relaxation Algorithm*

Jianjun Zhang[1,2], Qinghua Li[1], Yexin Song[2], and Yong Qu[2]

[1] Department of Computer Science and Technology, Huazhong University of Science and Technology, Wuhan, Hubei 430070, China
Wahh0912@163.com

[2] College of Science, Naval University of Engineering, Wuhan, Hubei 430033, China
Yxsong@21cn.com, qqqyyy0821@21cn.com

**Abstract.** The relaxation algorithm for linear programming is revised in this paper. Based on cluster structure, a parallel revised algorithm is presented. Its performance is analyzed. The experimental results on DAWNING 3000 are also given. Theoretical analysis and experimental results show that the revised relaxation algorithm improves the performance of the relaxation algorithm, and it has good parallelism and is very robust. Therefore, it can expect to be applied to the solution of the large-scale linear programming problems rising from practical application.

## 1 Introduction

Linear programming (LP) is the central problem in the research on discrete algorithms. It plays a very important role in combinatorial optimization problems such as the design of networks, the network router, the task scheduling and the allocation of capital [1]. With the development of the application of linear programming, the scale of LPs increases rapidly. For large-scale linear programs, their computation times still remain intolerable, even the fastest algorithms are applied. Recently, the research on efficient parallel algorithms for solving linear programs with a large number of columns has attracted considerable interest [2]-[4]. The parallel algorithms for linear programs are mainly the parallelism of the simplex algorithm, the interior point method and various variants. Because of the inherent serialization of above algorithms, the parallelism of them is unsatisfactory in terms of the scalability, the parallel efficiency and the practical effect [3].

Recently, Hu and Johnson [5] have developed a primal-dual simplex algorithm that is designed to solve LPs with a very large number of columns. The primal-dual simplex iterates between solving primal sub-problems over a restricted number of columns and dual steps. Later, Klabjan et al. [4] presented a parallel algorithm that parallels the dual steps of Hu-Johnson's algorithm and thus obtains significant speedups. In real world there are only some instances of linear programming problems where the number of constraints is far less than the number of variables. In most cases, the number of constraints can be equal to or surpass the number of variables. This necessitates

* This work is supported by National Natural Science Foundation of China Grant #6027307, Grant #70471031 and Scientific Research Foundation of Naval University of Engineering Grant #HGDJJ05005.

D.-S. Huang, K. Li, and G.W. Irwin (Eds.): ICIC 2006, LNCS 4113, pp. 812 – 821, 2006.

the design and implementation of a version of parallel algorithms that can handle this type of problems efficiently.

The relaxation method is an efficient method for unsymmetric linear programming problems with many constraints [6]. It performs sufficiently in practice, particularly on various types of large scale programming problems such as network programs. To overcome the main deficiency in the choice of relaxation constraints in relaxation algorithms [6], in this paper a necessary condition of LP is presented and proved. It is used to choose the relaxation problems and the simplex pivot variables to improve the performance of the relaxation algorithm. The relaxation algorithm for LP is revised in this paper. Based on cluster structure, a parallel revised algorithm is presented. Its performance is analyzed. The experimental results on DAWNING 3000 are also given. Theoretical analysis and experimental results show that the revised relaxation algorithm improves the performance of the relaxation algorithm, and it has good parallelism and is very robust, which is superior to other related algorithms [2], [3].

The rest of the paper is organized as follows. In Section 2, the traditional relaxation algorithm is stated and the improvement over it is given. The step-by-step description of the proposed parallel revised relaxation algorithm is presented in Section 3, followed by the proof of its correctness and its performance analysis. In Section 4, experimental results are given that demonstrate the power of the proposed algorithm, including the performance results and the comparisons with the traditional relaxation algorithm. Finally, Section 5 contains the conclusions and possible alterations of the proposed algorithm.

## 2 The Revised Relaxation Algorithm

We consider the following primal LP problem

$$\begin{aligned} LP \quad & \min \quad z = cx, \\ & s.t. \quad Ax \geq b,\, x \geq 0, \end{aligned} \tag{1}$$

where $A$ is a $m \times n$ matrix, $c$ and $x$ are $n$-vectors, and $b$ is a $m$-vector. Let $M = \{1,2,\ldots,m\}$ and $M_1 \subset M$. The relaxed problem associated with (1) is

$$\begin{aligned} LP_1 \quad & \min \quad z = cx, \\ & s.t. \quad a_i x \geq b_i,\, i \in M_1,\, x \geq 0. \end{aligned} \tag{2}$$

The main steps of the relaxation algorithm [6] can be described as follows.

*Step 1*: Let $z_0 = -\infty$, and choose an initial $M_1$ such that the objective function value of the relaxed problem $LP_1$ is lower bounded.

*Step 2*: Solve the relaxed problem $LP_1$. If $LP_1$ is infeasible, then LP is infeasible, stop. Otherwise, let $x_1$ be the optimal solution to $LP_1$ and $z_1$ be the corresponding optimal value for $LP_1$.

*Step 3*: If $x_1$ satisfies the condition $Ax \geq b$, then $x_1$ is also the optimal solution to LP, stop. Otherwise set $\Phi \neq F \subseteq \{i \mid a_i x_1 < b_i, i \in M - M_1\}$ and

$$W = \{i \mid a_i x_1 > b_i, i \in M_1\}.$$

*Step 4*: If $z_1 = z_0$ then set $M_1 = M_1 \cup F$ . Go to Step 2.

*Step 5*: If $z_1 > z_0$ then set $z_0 = z_1, M_1 = (M_1 - W) \cup F$ . Go to Step 2.

*Step 1* of the algorithm involves the problem of choosing the initial $M_1$, i.e., the problem of how to choose the constraints to form the initial relaxed problem $LP_1$. Obviously, the efficiency of the relaxation algorithm largely depends on the choice of the initial $M_1$. As to how to choose the constraints to form the relaxed problem, there is no related research result at present.

Now let us begin with the basic theorem in optimization, i.e., Kuhn-Tucker optimal conditions [6], to develop a necessary condition for LP. Using its conclusion we can not only avoid the blindness in the choice of the initial constrained conditions and the added constrained conditions in *Step3* and *Step 4*, but also reduce the number of the iterations in solving each relaxed problem. Because the linear programming problem is just a convex programming problem, the conditions of Kuhn-Tucker theorem [6] are satisfied by it. The constraint $x \geq 0$ can be regarded as $n$ constraints, i.e., $e_i x \geq 0$ , $i = 1,2,...,n$ with $e_i$ being the $i$th unit vector in $R^n$ , and thus the LP problem can be rewritten as

$$\begin{aligned} LP \quad & \min \quad z = cx, \\ & s.t. \quad a_1 x \geq b_1,...,a_m x \geq b_m, e_1 x \geq 0,...,e_n x \geq 0. \end{aligned} \tag{3}$$

By Kuhn-Tucker optimal conditions, we have

$$c = u_1 a_1 + u_2 a_2 + \ldots + u_m a_m + v_1 e_1 + v_2 e_2 + \ldots + v_n e_n ,$$

where $u_i \geq 0, v_j \geq 0$ , $i = 1,\ldots,m, j = 1,\ldots,n$ . Noting that

$$c = (c_1, c_2, \ldots, c_n), a_i = (a_{i1}, a_{i2}, \ldots, a_{in}) , \ i = 1,\ldots,m ,$$

we have

$$\begin{cases} c_1 = u_1 a_{11} + \ldots + u_m a_{m1} + v_1 \\ c_2 = u_1 a_{12} + \ldots + u_m a_{m2} + v_2 \\ \qquad \ldots \\ c_n = u_1 a_{1n} + \ldots + u_m a_{mn} + v_n \end{cases} . \tag{4}$$

Because $u = (u_1, \ldots, u_m) \geq 0$ and $v = (v_1, \ldots, v_n) \geq 0$ , a necessary condition of (4) is that if $c_i \neq 0$ then at least one of the numbers $a_{1i}, a_{2i}, \ldots, a_{mi}, v_i$ must have the same symbol as that of $c_i$ . Let

$$T_i = \{ j \mid c_i \neq 0, a_{ji} c_i > 0 \} \cup \{ i + m \mid c_i \neq 0, v_i c_i > 0 \}$$

or

$$T_i = \{1,2,\ldots,m,m+1,\ldots,m+n \mid c_i = 0\} , \ i = 1,2,\ldots,n .$$

Let $T = T_k$ such that $|T_k| = \min\{|T_i|, i = 1,\ldots,n\}$ . Compare $c = (c_1,\ldots,c_n)$ with $v = (v_1,\ldots,v_n)$ to choose from $c$ the components such that their symbols just differ from that of the corresponding components of $v$ and denote them by $c_{t1}, c_{t2}, \ldots, c_{tk}$. Set $c^t = (c_{t1}, \ldots, c_{tk})$ and $a_i^t = (a_{it1}, \ldots, a_{itk})$, $i = 1, 2, \ldots, m$, and let $v^t = (v_{t1}, \ldots, v_{tk})$. Then the Kuhn-Tucker optimal conditions can be written as

$$c^t = u_1 a_1^t + u_2 a_2^t + \ldots + u_m a_m^t + v^t,$$

hence we have

$$\begin{aligned} \| c^t \|^2 = & u_1 a_1^t \times c^t + u_2 a_2^t \times c^t + \ldots + \\ & u_m a_m^t \times c^t + v^t \times c^t. \end{aligned} \tag{5}$$

Because $\| c^t \|^2 > 0$ and $v^t c^t < 0$, at least one of the $a_i^t c^t$'s should be positive where $i = 1, 2, \ldots, m$. Letting $D = \{i \mid a_i^t c^t > 0, i = 1, 2, \ldots, m\}$, we reach the following theorem:
*Theorem 1.* For the LP problem, if $T = \Phi$ or $D = \Phi$, then it is infeasible. If $T \neq \Phi$, $D \neq \Phi$, and the LP problem has optimal solutions, then in all the critical hyper planes of the optimal solutions there must exists one which has one subscript included in $T$ or $D$.

Using the conclusion of above theorem, the relaxation algorithm performs very surprisingly well in solving LP problems. The causes are:

1. If $T$ or $D$ is empty, then it is sure that the LP problem is infeasible, and it is not necessary to find the initial relaxed problem which makes the objective function lower bounded.
2. If $T$ and $D$ are not empty, then let the constraints for the initial relaxed problem include the hyper planes whose subscript is included in $T$ or $D$ so as to find rapidly a relaxed problem which satisfies the requests, and thus shorten the execution time for solving the LP problem by the relaxation algorithm.
3. Let $T_M = T - \{m+1, \ldots, m+n\}$ and $T_N = T - T_M$. Using $T_N$, the number of the pivot transformations for solving each relaxed problem would decrease and thus further quicken the speed for solving the LP problem.

Using the conclusions of theorem 1 and complementing the relaxation algorithm, our revised relaxation algorithm can be described as follows:

*Step 0*: Find the sets of the subscripts of the hyper planes, i.e., the sets $T$, $D$, $T_M$ and $T_N$. If $T$ or $D$ is empty, then the LP problem is infeasible. Stop.

*Step 1*: Let $z_0 = -\infty$, choose an initial $M_1$ such that it includes the constraints that include the subscript of $T_M$ or $D$ so that the objective value for the relaxed problem $LP_1$ is lower bounded.

*Step 2*, *Step 3* and *Step 4* are the same to the steps mentioned above.

*Step 5*: If $z_1 > z_0$ then set $z_0 = z_1, M_1 = (M_1 - W) \cup F$ and ensure $M_1$ always includes the elements in $T_M$ or $D$. Go to Step 2.

## 3 The Parallel Revised Relaxation Algorithm

Suppose we have $p$ processors and each constraint of LP is assigned with equal probability to a processor. A detailed description of our parallel revised relaxation algorithm follows.

### 3.1 The Description and Correctness of the Algorithm

Algorithm: The parallel revised relaxation algorithm.

Input: A LP problem that includes $n$ variables and $m$ inequality constraints is given;

1. for all $P_i$ where $1 \le i \le p$ in parallel do
2. Compute $T_i, T_{i+p}, \ldots, T_{i+[n/p]p}$;
3. Compute $T(i)$ that satisfies $|T(i)| = \min\{|T_i|, |T_{i+p}|, \ldots, |T_{i+[n/p]p}|\}$;
4. If $T(i) = \Phi$, then LP has not the optimal solution. Stop;
5. end for
6. Compute $T$ that satisfies $|T| = \min\{|T(1)|, |T(2)|, \ldots |T(p)|\}$;
7. Compute the sets of subscripts, i.e., $D$, $T_N$ and $T_M$;
8. If $D = \Phi$, then LP has not the optimal solution. Stop;
9. for all $P_i$ where $1 \le i \le p$ in parallel do
10. Set $z_0 = -\infty$ and find an initial $M_i$ such that $M_i \cap (T_M \cup D) \ne \Phi, M_i \cap M_j = \Phi$ and the objective function value for $LP_i$ is lower bounded;
11. Solve the relaxation problem $LP_i$, if $LP_i$ is infeasible, then LP is infeasible, stop; Otherwise, let $x^i$ be the optimal solution to $LP_i$ and $z_1^i$ be the optimal value for $LP_i$;
12. end for
13. Set $z_1 = \max\{z_1^i, i = 1, \ldots, p\}$ and denote the corresponding optimal solution by $x$, constraints set by $M^1$;
14. Test if $x$ satisfies $Ax \ge b$. If so, then $x$ is just the optimal solution to the LP problem. Stop. Otherwise set
$$\Phi \ne F \subseteq \{i \mid a_i x_1 < b_i, i \in M - M^1\}, W = \{i \mid a_i x_1 > b_i, i \in M^1\};$$
15. for all $P_i$ where $1 \le i \le p$ in parallel do
16. If $z_1 = z_0$, then $M_i \leftarrow M^1 \cup F$
else $z_0 \leftarrow z_1$; $M_i \leftarrow (M^1 - W) \cup F$;
17. Solve the relaxed problem $LP_i$;
18. end for
19. go to step 13.;

Sentence 13 of the algorithm is based on the convergence property of the parallel algorithm as follows:

*Theorem 2.* If all $p$ relaxed problems of the LP problem have the optimal solutions. Denote the optimal solution and the corresponding optimal value by $x^i$ and $z_1^i$ respectively, $i = 1,2,\ldots,p$. Let $z_1 = \max\{z_1^i \mid i = 1,\ldots,p\}$ and $x_1$ be the optimal solution to the relaxed problem corresponding to $z_1$. Then if the LP problem has the optimal solution $x$ and the corresponding optimal value $z$, then $z \geq z_1$ and $z_1$ converges to $z$ after finite number of iterations.

*Proof:* Consider the general form of the LP problem (1). The relaxed problem $LP_i$ is composed of the objective function $z = cx$ and a part of all the inequality constraints $a_i x \geq b_i$ for $i = 1,2,\ldots,m$. Let $G$ and $G_i$ denote the feasible region of the problem LP and $LP_i$, respectively. Since the constraints for problem $LP_i$ is the subset of that of problem LP, clearly we have $G \subseteq G_i$. Hence

$$\{z \mid z = cx, x \in G\} \subseteq \{z \mid z = cx, x \in G_i\}.$$

Noticing

$$z = \min\{z \mid z = cx, x \in G\},\ z_1^i = \min\{z \mid z = cx, x \in G_i\},$$

it easily follows that $z \geq z_1^i$. Noting the arbitrariness of problem $LP_i$ and the finitude of i, it follows that

$$z \geq z_1 = \max\{z_1^i \mid i = 1,\ldots,p\}.$$

In the parallel revised relaxation algorithm, except sentence 13 other sentences do not change the basic steps of the relaxation algorithm. Hence by the correctness of the relaxation algorithm [7], in the last phase of the proposed algorithm $z_1$ converges to $z$.

### 3.2 The Co-operative Structure of the Algorithm

According to the characteristics of the parallel algorithm and the practical computational environment of DAWNING 3000 in The National High Performance Computation Center (NHPCC, in Wuhan, Hubei, China), the program is based on Cluster paralleled processor model and the Master-Slave Message Passing Interface [7] is used as the support environment. In the implementation process of the algorithm, the master process is used to control the slave process to solve each relaxed problem $LP_i$ and execute the basic serial part of the program, and the slave process is used to in parallel solve each relaxed problem generated by the master process. In order to sufficiently make use of the computational ability of the computers and shorten the execution times for solving large-scale LP problems by above algorithm, we harmoniously deal with the master process and the slave process as follows:

(1) In order to eliminate the influence on the performance of the algorithm because of the communication delay between the master process and the slave process, we use the method of overlapping to deal with the computation and communication. While solving the relaxed problem generated from the execution of the algorithm, the message passage that the slave process adds new constraint to form new relaxed problem

and the computation that the master process determine if the current local optimal solution satisfies all the constraints $Ax \geq b$ of LP may process simultaneously. On the other hand, after the slave process has processed its own corresponding relaxed problem, in order to eliminate the possible congestion and conflict generated while various slave processes are passing messages to the master process, different strategies [3] can be used in different processes to solve its corresponding relaxed problem. Because various solving strategies are sensible to problem instances [3], above method can ensure that each slave process can complete its own relaxed problem at various point of time in order to reduce the communication delays.

(2) The practical LP Problems usually contain the relaxed problems that include anomalous numerical values that shall result in the abnormity in the processing time of the corresponding process and then affect the processing of the total problem. In order to improve the stabilization of the algorithm, three types of communication points between the master process and the slave processes named B1, B2 and B3 are set. Of the three communication points B1 and B3 are installed to ensure the normal communication between the slave processes and the master process. On the other hand B2 is a passive communication point, if the slave process has not yet obtained the solution to the corresponding relaxed problem when the upper bound of time assigned in advance is reached, then numeral problems arise in the process. Then the processing of the relaxed problem is terminated and problem-related messages are sent to the master process from the slave process.

### 3.3 The Performance Analysis of the Algorithm

Suppose the computation time for the processor to execute one basic operation to be $\tau_1$ and the communication delay when one processor sends or accepts a unit of data to or from another processor to be $\tau_2$. Firstly we discuss the computation costs of the revised serial relaxation algorithm. It is easy to derive that in the preparation phase the overall average computation costs of the revised serial relaxation algorithm is $2nm + 3n/2 + m/2 - 1$. For LP problems of given size, the relaxation algorithm generally need to solve $g(m)$ (which is usually the linear function of $m$) relaxation problems to achieve the optimal solution. Note that the average time complexity of the dual simplex algorithm is $\Theta(m^2(n+m))$ [6], so the overall computation time of the serial revised relaxation algorithm $T_s$ is

$$T_s = (lm^2(n+m) + 2nm + 3n/2 + m/2 - 1)\tau_1,$$

where $l$ is a constant.

Without loss of generality, suppose that $n$ is exactly divisible by $p$, i.e. $n = kp$, where $k$ is an integer. In the preparation phase the algorithm runs $k(m+1) + mk/2 + mp/2 + mn/(2p) + m/2$ times multiplications or additions, and the most communication costs is $np$. Hence in the preparation phase the execution time of the parallel algorithm is

$$(k(m+1) + mk/2 + mp/2 + mn/(2p) + m/2)\tau_1 + np\tau_2.$$

In the solving phase, the serial part of the algorithm compares the optimal values for the $p$ relaxation problems to determine whether the greatest optimal value is just the optimal solution to the LP problem. The corresponding processing times and communication costs is $(p+mn)\tau_1$ and $p+m$ respectively. Noticing the required time for parallel solving each relaxation problem, in this phase the processing times is

$$\frac{g(m)}{p}((\frac{lm^2(m+n)}{g(m)}+p+mn)\tau_1+(p+m)\tau_2),$$

therefore the overall execution time of the parallel algorithm is

$$\begin{aligned} T_p &= \frac{g(m)}{p}((\frac{lm^2(n+m)}{g(m)}+p+mn)\tau_1+(p+m)\tau_2) \\ &+(k(m+1)+\frac{m(k+p+1)}{2}+\frac{mn}{2p})\tau_1+np\tau_2 \end{aligned} \quad . \tag{6}$$

Hence, when $n$ and $m$ are relatively large the speedup of the algorithm is

$$\begin{aligned} \frac{T_S}{T_p} &\approx \frac{lm^2(n+m)\tau_1}{\frac{lm^2(n+m)\tau_1}{p}+\frac{g(m)}{p}(p+mn)\tau_1+(\frac{m+p}{p}+\frac{np}{g(m)})\tau_2} \\ &\approx p\frac{m}{m+g(m)}. \end{aligned} \tag{7}$$

According to the experiences in computation [6], the range of $g(m)$ is from $m/5$ to $m$, so the range of the speedup of the parallel algorithm is from $p/2$ to $5p/6$ which is an ideal linear speedup. The efficiency of the parallel algorithm is between 50% and 80%, which indicates that the algorithm has better parallelism.

## 4 Experimental Results and Analysis

All computational experiments were performed on DAWNING 3000 in The National High Performance Computation Center in Wuhan. DAWNING 3000 is a cluster based distributed memory multiprocessor system, which offers facilities for parallel computing. The parallel implementation uses the message-passing interface MPI [7] to process the communications between processors. The MPI message passing standard is widely used in the parallel computing community. It offers facilities for creating parallel programs to run across cluster machines and for exchanging information between processes using message passing procedures like broadcast, send, receive and others. The program is written by FORTRAN90. The four test instances are from OR-library [7]. Of them except instance four which is degenerate, the number of variables of problem scale in other three problems is not larger than the number of constraints. Instance four is dedicated to testing if the algorithm can preserve higher efficiency in the case when the problem is degenerate and $m$ is far less than $n$. Using the relaxation algorithm, revised relaxation algorithm and parallel revised relaxation algorithm respectively, the four instances were performed on DAWNING 3000. The experiment results are listed in Table 1 where column time-1, column time-2 and column time-3 denote the execution times of the above three algorithms respectively.

**Table 1.** The experiment results for the parallel revised relaxation algorithm

| Name of Instances | Number of rows | Number of columns | Time-1 (s) | Time-2 (s) | Number of processors | Time-3 (s) | Speed up | Efficiency (%) |
|---|---|---|---|---|---|---|---|---|
| Pr1 | 983 | 704 | 13170 | 9535 | 2 | 6495 | 1.47 | 73.5 |
| | | | | | 4 | 3860 | 2.47 | 61.8 |
| | | | | | 8 | 2137 | 4.46 | 55.1 |
| | | | | | 16 | 1236 | 7.71 | 48.2 |
| Pr2 | 1652 | 617 | 5673 | 19031 | 2 | 14640 | 1.35 | 67.5 |
| | | | | | 4 | 9438 | 2.01 | 50.2 |
| | | | | | 8 | 5857 | 3.25 | 40.7 |
| | | | | | 16 | 2851 | 6.68 | 41.8 |
| Pr3 | 2027 | 893 | 29164 | 19840 | 2 | 14732 | 1.35 | 67.5 |
| | | | | | 4 | 8645 | 2.30 | 57.5 |
| | | | | | 8 | 4972 | 3.98 | 49.7 |
| | | | | | 16 | 2793 | 7.10 | 44.3 |
| Pr4 | 262 | 2640 | 48273 | 42117 | 2 | 25462 | 1.65 | 84.5 |
| | | | | | 4 | 17540 | 2.40 | 60.0 |
| | | | | | 8 | 9562 | 4.41 | 42.6 |
| | | | | | 16 | 6204 | 6.79 | 42.4 |

The experiment results show that the relaxation algorithm, especially the revised relaxation algorithm is very effective for solving LPs where $m > n$. When $n >> m$, as showed in instance four, the computational effect of the relaxation algorithm is somewhat worse. However, the performance of the parallel revised relaxation algorithm is relatively consistent with the theoretical results and its parallel efficiency exceeds 40%, which is not higher than other parallel algorithms [2], [3] for solving the same type of problems, but the proposed algorithm has better parallelism and higher stability.

## 5 Conclusions

The relaxation algorithm for linear programming is revised in this paper. According to the characteristic that revised relaxation algorithm is easy to be paralleled, based on cluster structure a parallel revised algorithm is presented. Its performance is analyzed. The experimental results on DAWNING 3000 are also given. Theoretical analysis and experimental results show that the revised relaxation algorithm improves the performance of the relaxation algorithm considerably, and it has good parallelism and is very robust. Therefore, it can expect to be applied to the solution to the large-scale linear programming problems rising from practical application. We made an initial attempt in this direction but more experimentation needs to be done.

On the other hand, from the experiment results we can see that, although the parallel efficiency is greater than 40%, there are some differences between the experimental results and the best theoretically analyzed results. There are several open questions regarding the efficient implementation of the proposed algorithm. The following aspects could lead to substantial improvement over the proposed algorithm, according to the storage requirements each processor may keep a copy of the LP problem so that the communication costs among the processors could be reduced; how to enable the computation to overlap the communication, and how to optimize the codes of the algorithm according to the practical environment, etc. All the above aspects are the goals for further research.

## References


1. Papadimitrious, C. H., Steiglitz, K.: Combinatorial Optimization. Algorithms and Complexity. Printice-Hall Inc (1992)
2. Lyu, J., Luh, H., Lee, M.: Performance Analysis Of A Parallel Dantzig-Wolfe Decomposition Algorithm for Linear Programming. Computers and Mathematics with Applications, 44 (2002) 1431-1437
3. Maros, I., MitraG.: Investigating the Sparse Simplex Algorithm On a Distributed Memory Multiprocessor. Parallel Computing, 26 (2000) 151-170
4. Klabjan, D., Johnson, E., Nemhauser, G.: A Parallel Primal-dual Simplex Algorithm. Operation Research Letters, 27 (2000) 47-55
5. Johnson, H. E.: Computational Results with a Primal-dual Sub problem Simplex Method. Operation Research Letter, 25 (1999) 149-158
6. Nemhauser, G. L., Wolsey, L. A.: Integer and Combinatorial Optimization. Wiley New York, (1988)
7. Gay, D. M.: Electronic Mail Distribution of Linear Programming Test Problems. Mathematical Programming Society COAL Newsletter, 13 (1985) 10-12

# An Improved Simulated Annealing Algorithm for the Maximum Independent Set Problem

Xinshun Xu, Jun Ma, and Hua Wang

School of Computer Science and Technology, Shandong University
Jinan, Shandong, 250061, China
xuxinshun@sdu.edu.cn

**Abstract.** The maximum independent set problem is a classic graph optimization problem. It is well known that it is an NP-Complete problem. In this paper, an improved simulated annealing algorithm is presented for the maximum independent set problem. In this algorithm, an acceptance function is defined for every vertex. This can help the algorithm find a near optimal solution to a problem. Simulations are performed on benchmark graphs and random graphs. The simulation results show that the proposed algorithm provides a high probability of finding optimal solutions.

## 1 Introduction

Given an undirected graph $G(V, E)$ with a vertex set $V=\{1,2,\ldots,n\}$ and an edge set $E$, an independent set $I$ of $G$ is a subset of nodes such that no two nodes in $I$ are adjacent in $G$. An independent set is maximal if it is not a subset of any larger independent set, and maximum if there are no larger independent sets in the graph. The cardinality of a maximum independent set in $G$ is called the stability number (or the independence number) of $G$. The following is a formal definition of the maximum independent set problem by making use of Stinson's terminology for combinatorial optimization problems [1]:

**Problem instance:** A graph $G=(V, E)$, where $V=\{1, 2, \ldots, n\}$ is the set of vertices and $E \subseteq V \times V$ the set of edges. An edge between vertices $i$ and $j$ is denoted by pair $(i, j) \in E$, and the binary variables $d_{ij}$ $(i, j=1, 2, \ldots, n)$ form the adjacency matrix of $G$. Its value is defined as follows:

$$d_{ij} = \begin{cases} 1 & if\,(i, j) \in E \\ 0 & otherwise \end{cases} \tag{1}$$

**Feasible solution:** A subset $S$ of $V$ such that $\forall i, j \in S$, $(i, j) \notin E$, that is to say, $d_{ij}$ is equal to zero.

**Objective function:** The size $|S|$ of the independent set $S$.

**Optimal solution:** An independent set $S$ that maximizes $|S|$.

As an example, Fig. 1 shows a simple graph with 5 vertices and 6 edges. The black vertex set $\{2, 3, 5\}$ indicates an independent set (it is also a maximum independent set in this graph).

D.-S. Huang, K. Li, and G.W. Irwin (Eds.): ICIC 2006, LNCS 4113, pp. 822–831, 2006.

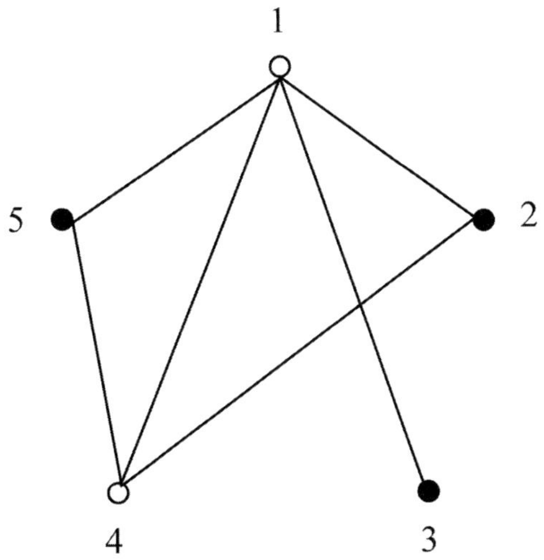


**Fig. 1.** A simple graph showing the maximum independent problem

Along with the maximum independent set problem, the similar problem is the maximum clique problem. A clique $C$ of $G$ is a subset of $V$ such that the subgraph induced by $C$ on $G$ is a complete graph. The maximum clique problem is to find a clique of maximum cardinality. It is easy to see that $I$ is an independent set of $G$ if and only if $I$ is a clique of the complement graph of $G$. It is well known that both the maximum independent set problem and the maximum clique problem are NP-hard problems [2, 3]. Johnson [4] proved that if there is a polynomial time algorithm that can find an independent set whose size is within a constant factor of optimal, then there is a polynomial approximation scheme for the maximum independent set problem, that is, an algorithm that finds an independent set whose size is within $(1 - \varepsilon)$ of optima and whose running time is polynomial for any fixed $\varepsilon > 0$. So far, nobody has devised such a polynomial approximation scheme, and it is somewhat unlikely that it exits. However, because both problems have many important practical applications, especially in information retrieval, signal transmission analysis, classification theory, economics, scheduling, experimental design and computer vision (See [5, 6, 7, 8] for details), both problems are never abandoned. Karp and Wigderson showed that the problem of finding a maximal independent set is in NC which means that there are constants $c$ and $k$ such that it can be solved in time O((log $n)c$) using $O(n^k)$ parallel processors [9]. Since their work, a number of parallel algorithms have been proposed to solve this problem [10, 11, 12]. However a common drawback of all NC-algorithms for the maximal independent set problem is that occasionally they can find a too small set [13]. Any graph with a large independent set and a vertex adjacent to all other vertices is a potential example of such a situation.

In light of those negative results on this problem, much effort has been directed towards devising efficient heuristics, for which no formal guarantee of performance may be provided, but are anyway of interest in practical application. Takefuji et al.

proposed a Hopfield-type neural network for finding a near-maximum independent set of a circle graph [14], and Thomas et al. gave an evolutionary heuristic for this problem[15]. Recently, a heuristic for the maximum independent set problem based on optimization of a quadratic over a sphere was presented in [16]. These algorithms lack a general theory of how the algorithms work, their evaluation is essentially based on massive experiments. In addition, many methods have been presented for some constrained graphs, e.g. the low degree graphs and Hypergraphs [17, 18].

In this paper, we propose an improved simulated annealing algorithm for this problem, we call it ISA. A new acceptance function is introduced to help the ISA find a near optimal solution to a given problem. The experimental results indicate that ISA has higher convergence rate to optimal solutions to benchmark graphs.

## 2 Problem Formulation

For a given undirected graph $G=(V, E)$, $I$ is an independent set and $E$ is edge set. We let $|V|=n$, $|E|=m$. Binary variables $d_{ij}$ ( $i=1,2,\ldots,n$, $j=1,2,\ldots,n$) are defined as those in section 1 and they form the adjacency matrix of graph $G$. For example, for the graph of Fig. 1, we have the following adjacency matrix.

$$D = \begin{pmatrix} 0 & 1 & 1 & 1 & 1 \\ 1 & 0 & 0 & 1 & 0 \\ 1 & 0 & 0 & 0 & 0 \\ 1 & 1 & 0 & 0 & 1 \\ 1 & 0 & 0 & 1 & 0 \end{pmatrix}$$

The state of neuron $i$ is determined by:

$$v_i = \begin{cases} 1 & \text{if the \#i vertex is in the independent set} \\ 0 & \text{otherwise} \end{cases} \tag{2}$$

So the number of vertices of a given graph determines the number of neurons. For example, if there are $n$ vertices in a graph, then $n$ neurons are required. Thus the number of vertices in the independent set can be expressed by:

$$E_1 = \sum_{i=1}^{n} v_i. \tag{3}$$

If a set $I$ is not an independent set, then at least two nodes ($v_i$ and $v_j$) in $I$ are adjacent. That is, both $v_i$ and $v_j$ are equal to one, and $d_{ij}$ is equal to one. Then the constrained condition can be written as:

$$E_2 = \sum_{i=1}^{n} \sum_{\substack{j=1 \\ j\neq i}}^{n} (d_{ij}(v_i \wedge v_j)). \tag{4}$$

where $\wedge$ is the logical AND.

The objective is to maximize $E_1$ with $E_2$ equal to zero. Thus, the objective function for the maximum independent set problem can be described as follows:

$$\begin{aligned} E &= AE_1 + BE_2 \\ &= A\sum_{i=1}^{n} v_i + B\sum_{i=1}^{n}\sum_{\substack{j=1 \\ j\neq i}}^{n} d_{ij} v_i \wedge v_j \\ &= A\sum_{i=1}^{n} v_i + B\sum_{i=1}^{n}\sum_{\substack{j=1 \\ j\neq i}}^{n} d_{ij} v_i v_j . \end{aligned} \tag{5}$$

For simulated annealing algorithm, usually a minimum value has to be calculated for the objective function. Recall that we are working on the maximum independent set problem. If a set I is a maximum independent set, E should take the minimum value. So coefficient A should be smaller than 0. However, once I is not an independent set, then $E_2$ is more than zero. If B takes a value more than 0, E become larger. So we have $A < 0$ and $B > 0$. This can be shown as follows:

Suppose that $I_1$ and $I_2$ are independent sets, then for both $I_1$ and $I_2$, we have

$$\sum_{i=1}^{n}\sum_{\substack{j=1 \\ j\neq i}}^{n} d_{ij} v_i v_j = 0. \tag{6}$$

That is to say, the second part in Eq. (5) is equal to zero. So we have

$$E_{I1} = A\sum_{i=1}^{n} v_i . \tag{7}$$

$$E_{I2} = A\sum_{i=1}^{n} v_i . \tag{8}$$

If $|I_1|>|I_2|$, namely, $I_1$ is a better solution, for $A<0$, then we have

$$E_{I1} < E_{I2} . \tag{9}$$

So if I is a maximum independent set, the objective function will take the minimum value.

## 3 An Improved Simulated Annealing Algorithm

The SA algorithm can be considered as a version of an "iterative improvement algorithm" which considers only specific transitions and terminates in the first local minima found [19]. Unlike this algorithm, simulated annealing allows various types of transitions in which some of them may be opposite towards achieving the goal. For instance, cost-increasing transitions are also accepted along with cost-decreasing transitions whereas an iterative improvement algorithm would allow only cost-decreasing ones to pass. However, it is proven that eventually simulated annealing produces a more optimal solution than the original iterative improvement algorithm [19]. But in most circumstances, the solution SA obtains is just a local optimal one.

SA starts with an initial solution, *s*. A neighbor to this solution *s'*, is then generated as the next solution by SA and the change in cost, $\Delta F(s,s')$ is evaluated. If a reduction in cost is found, the current solution is replaced by the generated neighbor, otherwise we decide with a certain probability whether s remains or s' becomes the current solution. The probability of accepting a transition that causes an increase, $\Delta F$ , in the cost is usually called the acceptance function as follows:

$$p = e^{-\frac{\Delta F}{T}}. \tag{10}$$

where T is the control parameter that corresponds to temperature in the analogy with the physical annealing process.

In SA, the algorithm is started with a relatively high value of T, to have a better chance to avoid being prematurely trapped in a local minimum. The control parameter is lowered in steps until it approaches to zero. After termination, the final configuration is taken as the solution of the problem at hand.

In the ISA, s is the sequence of $v_i$ ($i$=1, 2, …, $n$), and s' is a neighbor of s if one $v_i$ is changed, here $v_i$ is selected randomly. In addition, there is a well-known fact on the independent set problem that the vertices having smaller degrees will be selected into the independent set with higher probability because such a vertex covers fewer edges. Based on this, some algorithms have been presented, such as the minimum degree greedy algorithm [20] and Yuan's method [21]. From this point, we modify the acceptance function as follows:

$$p = \begin{cases} e^{-\frac{\Delta F(1+Deg(v_i))}{T}} & v_i = 1 \\ e^{-\frac{\Delta F(1-Deg(v_i))}{T}} & v_i = 0 \end{cases} \tag{11}$$

$$Deg(v_i) = \frac{Degree(i)}{EdgeNum}. \tag{12}$$

Where *Degree(i)* is the degree of vertex *i*, it's value is equal to the number of edges linking to the *i*th vertex, and *EdgeNum* is a constant, equal to the total number of edges in a given graph.

Once $\Delta F > 0$ then we use Eq. (11) to determine whether a solution is replaced by its neighbor. By using Eq. (11), we have:

- If $v_i$=1 in s', this means $v_i$'s original value is 0. Once we accept s', the *i*th vertex is then selected into the independent set. From Eq. (11), *p* takes a larger value if the degree of the *i*th vertex is smaller. This means s' will be accepted as a new solution with higher probability. That is to say, a vertex with smaller degree will be selected into the independent set with higher probability. In contrast, if vertex *i* has a larger degree, it will then be selected into the independent set with lower probability. For example, there are two vertices- the *i*th and the *j*th, with degree(*i*) > degree(*j*), and at the same T, their reversions (from 0 to 1) make the object function change equally, that is, $\Delta F(v_i) = \Delta F(v_j)$. Taking into account Eq. (11), we have:

$$p(v_i) = e^{-\frac{\Delta F(v_i)(1+Deg(v_i))}{T}}. \tag{13}$$

$$p(v_j) = e^{-\frac{\Delta F(v_j)(1+Deg(v_j))}{T}} . \tag{14}$$

From Eq. (12) and the condition degree($i$) > degree($j$), we then have:

$$Deg(v_i) > Deg(v_j). \tag{15}$$

This means:

$$\frac{\Delta F(v_i)(1+Deg(v_i))}{T} > \frac{\Delta F(v_j)(1+Deg(v_j))}{T}. \tag{16}$$

Then, we have the following relation between p($v_i$) and p($v_j$):

$$p(v_i) < p(v_j). \tag{17}$$

That is to say, the s' resulting from the reversion of $v_j$ will be accepted as a new state with higher probability. On the contrary, p($v_i$) is equal to p($v_j$) with the acceptance function in the standard SA.

- If $v_i$ =0, this means $v_i$'s original value is 1. Once we accept s', the $i$th vertex is then removed from the independent set. From Eq. (11), $p$ takes a smaller value if the degree of the $i$th vertex is smaller. This means s' will be accepted as a new solution with lower probability if vertex has a smaller degree. That is to say, a vertex with a smaller degree will be removed from the independent set with lower probability. In contrast, if vertex $i$ has a large degree, then it will be removed from the independent set with higher probability.

## 4 Simulation Results

In order to assess the effectiveness of the proposed algorithm, extensive simulations were carried out on two type graphs: some benchmark graphs and $p$-random graphs. The parameters used in the proposed algorithm are selected empirically as those in Table 1.

The benchmark graphs are the complement graphs of some the DIMACS clique instances which can be downloaded from the following URL http://dimacs.rutgers.edu/challenges/. The performance of the algorithm on the benchmarks is summarized in Table 2. Columns "Name", "$n$", and "$I(G)$" represent the name of the graph , the number of its vertices, and its maximum independent set size. For comparisons, the results of the original SA are also presented in column "SA". For each graph, two algorithms were run 100 times from different initial solution state. The optimal solution size and the success rate of finding an optimal solution are presented for each algorithm.

From Table 2, the following observations can be made:

1. For the first three problems, the improved simulated annealing algorithm can solve the maximum independent set problem with 100% convergent rate to the best solution. For other four problems, it's convergent rate is near 100%.

2. The original simulated annealing can solve this problem with good solution quality when problem scale is small. However, once the problem scale becomes large, its solution quality is not satisfactory.
3. The improved simulated annealing algorithm can obtain the best solution with high convergent rate when problem scale becomes large.

So we can conclude that the proposed simulated annealing algorithm is effective for the maximum independent set problem.

**Table 1.** Parameters used in the proposed algorithm

| Parameters | Initial value | Meaning |
|---|---|---|
| A | 1.0 | The first coefficient in the object function |
| B | 1.0 | The second coefficient in the object function |
| $T_0$ | 60 | Initial temperature |
| α | 0.96 | A constant to decrease temperature |
| L | 100 | # of steps to run without much change |
| ST | 15 | Maximum steps algorithm runs without much change |

**Table 2.** Simulation results on DIMACS benchmark graphs

| Name | *n* | I(G) | SA | | ISA | |
|---|---|---|---|---|---|---|
| | | | Best | Rate | Best | Rate |
| Johnsom8-2-4 | 28 | 4 | 4 | 100% | 4 | 100% |
| MANN_a9 | 45 | 16 | 16 | 100% | 16 | 100% |
| Hamming6-2 | 64 | 32 | 32 | 100% | 32 | 100% |
| Johnson16-2-4 | 120 | 8 | 8 | 96% | 8 | 98% |
| c-fat200-2 | 200 | 24 | 24 | 93% | 24 | 100% |
| P_hat300-3 | 300 | 36 | 36 | 89% | 36 | 97% |
| c-fat500-1 | 500 | 14 | 14 | 83% | 14 | 95% |

The second type of graphs we used to test on was the complement graph of *p*-random graphs. A *p*-random graph of size *n* is a graph (*V*, *E*) where *V*={1, 2, …, n} and *E* is obtained by selecting $\{i, j\}$ as an edge with probability $p(0 < p < 1)$. For the *p*-random graph, there is an easy way to estimate the maximum clique size. The expected number of cliques of size *k* in a *p*-random graph of size n is $\binom{n}{k} p^{\frac{k(k-1)}{2}}$. For fixed *p* and sufficiently large *n*, let *C*(*n*, *p*) be the real number *k* such that $\binom{n}{k} p^{\frac{k(k-1)}{2}} = 1$, then *C*(*n*, *p*) estimates the maximum clique size quite well [22, 23]. In Table 3, we give 12 *p*-random graphs and the expected size of the maximum clique for *n*=100, 200, 300, 500 and *p*=0.5, 0.8, 0.9. The first column contains the nodes of the graphs; the second is the number of edges, the third is the value of parameter *p* and the expected size of the maximum clique is given in column "*C(G)*". For the *p*-random graph, Jagota's [24] and Funabiki's [25] algorithms are used for comparison. Each algorithm is run 100 times with different initial values. For each algorithm, the size of the best solution and the average CPU time are presented. Recall that we are working with the complement graphs of the $p$-random graphs to get the independent set, and the other two algorithms are working with the $p$-random graphs to get the clique.

From table 3, we have the following observations:

1. The size of solutions that the proposed algorithm is very closed to the expected size of the maximum clique.
2. For 9 problems, the proposed algorithm obtains better solutions than Funabiki's algorithm. For other problems, it obtains solutions as good as Funabiki's algorithm. Comparing with Jagota's algorithm, the proposed algorithm obtains better solutions to six problems, and other solutions are the same as Jaogta's.
3. The proposed algorithm obtains better solutions to six problems than both Jagota's algorithm and Funabiki's algorithm.
4. The proposed algorithm uses a little more CPU time than Jagota's algorithm and Funabiki's algorithm.

The results of numerical experiments suggest that the proposed method is superior to Jagota's and Funabiki's algorithms in light of the solution size.

**Table 3.** Simulation results on $p$-random graphs

| Nodes | Edges | $p$ | C(G) | ISA | | Funabiki | | Jagota | |
|---|---|---|---|---|---|---|---|---|---|
| | | | | Size | Time(s) | Size | Time(s) | Size | Time(s) |
| 100 | 2475 | 0.5 | 9.9 | 9 | 1.29 | 9 | 0.31 | 9 | 0.81 |
| 100 | 3960 | 0.8 | 21.66 | 19 | 1.31 | 19 | 0.56 | 19 | 0.62 |
| 100 | 4455 | 0.9 | 34.82 | 32 | 1.74 | 30 | 0.59 | 31 | 0.74 |
| 200 | 9950 | 0.5 | 11.60 | 11 | 10.91 | 11 | 8.78 | 11 | 6.11 |
| 200 | 15920 | 0.8 | 26.63 | 23 | 11.23 | 21 | 10.46 | 21 | 10.13 |
| 200 | 17910 | 0.9 | 44.90 | 41 | 11.82 | 36 | 12.17 | 39 | 9.51 |
| 300 | 22425 | 0.5 | 12.60 | 11 | 50.12 | 10 | 40.96 | 11 | 26.87 |
| 300 | 35880 | 0.8 | 29.57 | 27 | 51.57 | 25 | 47.24 | 27 | 28.64 |
| 300 | 40365 | 0.9 | 50.93 | 47 | 53.84 | 45 | 58.15 | 46 | 26.91 |
| 500 | 62375 | 0.5 | 13.87 | 12 | 150. 92 | 11 | 96.76 | 11 | 123.92 |
| 500 | 99800 | 0.8 | 33.32 | 31 | 153.44 | 29 | 120.47 | 31 | 127.74 |
| 500 | 112275 | 0.9 | 58.64 | 57 | 167.31 | 52 | 113.14 | 56 | 126.27 |

## 5 Conclusions

We have proposed an improved simulated annealing algorithm for the maximum independent set problem. A new acceptance function is used in the proposed algorithm. With this acceptance function, the proposed algorithm can find an optimal solution to a given graph with higher probability. The experimental results indicate that the algorithm has higher convergence rate, to optimal solutions on benchmark graphs, than the original SA. The results also show that the proposed algorithm is superior to Jagota's and Funabiki's algorithms in light of the solution size on $p$-random graphs.

## Acknowledgements

The authors thank the anonymous reviewers for their helpful suggestions and comments.

## References

1. Stinson, D.R.: An Introduction to the Design and Analysis of Algorithms. 2nd edn. The Charles Babbage Research Center, Winnipeg, Manitoba, Canada (1987)
2. Karp, R. M.: Reducibility among Combinatorial Problems. In: Miller, R.E., Thatcher, J.W. (eds): Complexity of Computer Computation. Plenum Press, New York (1972) 85–103
3. Garey, M.R., Johnson, D.S.: Computers and Intractability: A Guide to the Theory of NP-completeness. Freeman, San Francisco (1979)
4. Johnson, D.: Approximate Algorithms for Combinatorial Problems. Journal of Computer and System Sciences, 9 (1974) 256–278
5. Abello, J., Pardalos, P.M., Resende, M.G.C.: On the Maximum Clique Problems in very Large Graphs. In: Abello, J., Vitter, J.S. (eds): External Memory Algorithms and Visualization. DIMACS series on discrete mathematics and theoretical Computer Science, American Mathematical Society, 50 (1999) 119–130
6. Avondo-Bodeno, G.: Economic Applications of the Theory of Graphs. Gordon and Breach Science, New York (1962)
7. Berge, C.: The Theory of Graphs and Its Applications. John Wiley and Sons, New York (1962)
8. Bomze, I.M., Budinich, M. Pardalos, P.M., Pelillot, M.: The maximum clique problem. In: Du, D.Z., Pardalos, P.M. (eds): Handbook of Combinatorial Optimization, Kluwer Academic Publisher, Dordrecht. (1999) 1–74
9. Karp, R.M., Wigderson, A.: A Fast Parallel Algorithm for the Maximal Independent Set Problem. Journal of the ACM, 32:4 (1985) 762–773
10. Alon, N., Babai, L., Itai, A.: A Fast and Simple Randomized Parallel Algorithm for the Maximal Independent Set Problem. Journal of Algorithms, 7 (1986) 567–583
11. Goldberg, M., Spencer, T.: A New Parallel Algorithm for the Maximal Independent Set Problem. SIAM Journal on Computing, 18 (1989) 419–427
12. Goldberg, M., Spencer, T.: Constructing a Maximal Independent Set in Parallel. SIAM Journal on Discrete Mathematics, 2 (1989) 322–328
13. Goldberg, M., Spencer, T.: An Efficient Parallel Algorithm that Finds Independent Sets of Guaranteed Size. SIAM Journal on Discrete Mathematics, 6 (1993) 443–459
14. Takefuji, Y., Chen, L., Lee, K., Huffman, J.: Parallel Algorithm for Finding a Near Maximum Independent Set of the Circle Graph. IEEE Transaction on Neural Networks, 1 (1990) 263–267
15. Bäck, T., Khuri, S.: An Evolutionary Heuristic for the Maximum Independent Set Problem. In: Michalewicz, Z., Schaffer, J.D., Schwefel, H.P., Fogel, D.B., Kitano, H. (eds): Proceeding of the First IEEE Conference on Evolutionary Computation. IEEE Press, New York (1994) 531–535
16. Busygin, S., Butenko, S., Pardalos, P.: A Heuristic for the Maximum Independent Set Problem Based on Optimization of a Quadratic over a Sphere. Journal of Combinatorial Optimization, 6 (2002) 287–297
17. Berman, P., and Fujito, T.: On Approximation Properties of the Independent Set Problem for Low Degree Graphs. Theory of Computing Systems, 32 (1999) 115-132

18. Dahlhaus, E., Karpinski, M., Kelsen, P.: An Efficient Parallel Algorithm for Computing a Maximal Independent Set in a Hypergraph of Dimension 3. Information Processing Letters, 42 (1992) 309–313
19. Pham, D.T., Karaboga, D.: Intelligent Optimisation Techniques: Genetic Algorithm, Tabu Search, Simulated Annealing, and Neural Networks. Springer-Verlag, London, Heidelber, New York (2000)
20. Halldórsson, M.M., Radhakrishnan, J.: Greed is good: Approximating Independent Sets in Sparse and Bounded-degree Graphs. Algorithmica, 18 (1997) 145–163
21. Shi-Yi Yuan, Sy-Yen Kuo: A New Technique for Optimization Problems in Graph Theory. IEEE Transactions on Computers, 47 (1998) 190–196
22. Matual, D.W.: On the Complete Subgraph of a Random Graph", In: Bose, R., Dowling, T. (eds): Proceeding of the Second Chapel Hill Conference on Combinatory Mathematics and its Applications. Chapel Hill, North Carolina, (1970) 356–369
23. Bertoni, A., Campadelli, P., Grossi, G.: A Neural Algorithm for the Maximum Clique Problem: Analysis, Experiments, and Circuit Implementation. Algorithmica, 33 (2002) 71–88
24. Jagota: Approximating Maximum Clique with a Hopfield Network. IEEE Transactions on Neural Networks, 6 (1995) 724–735
25. Funabiki, N., Nishikawa, S.: Comparisons of Energy-descent Optimization Algorithms for Maximum Clique Problems. IEICE Transactions on Fundamentals E79-A, 4 (1996) 452–460

# Exponential Convergence Flow Control Model for Congestion Control

Weirong Liu[1], Jianqiang Yi[1], Dongbin Zhao[1], and John T. Wen[2]

[1] Laboratory of Complex Systems & Intelligence Science,
Institute of Automation, Chinese Academy of Sciences, Beijing, China
{Weirong.liu, jianqiang.yi, dongbin.zhao}@mail.ia.ac.cn
[2] Department of Electrical, Computer, and Systems,
Rensselaer Polytechnic Institute, NY, USA
wen@cat.rpi.edu

**Abstract.** Recently, many new flow control mechanisms derived from classic Kelly model are proposed to solve network congestion problem. They perform well in stability, fairness or robustness. However, most of their convergence rates are linear since in classic Kelly model, link price is only positive. In addition, some need to introduce extra packet header to get price information. This paper presents a novel flow control model based on Kelly model in which the link price can be negative to improve the convergence rate. Further, The proposed model uses two bits of ECN field to feed back price instead of introducing new packet header data. Thus it can implement flow control scheme achieving exponential convergence in traditional TCP/IP datagram format. NS2 simulation results show that our model can keep fairness and asymptotic stability with more rapid convergence rate.

## 1 Introduction

It is well known that the traditional TCP frame is inefficient in high-speed networks and wireless networks. Over the recent years, many new congestion control mechanisms were developed based on all kinds of theories, such as optimization theory [1], [2], [13], game theory [3], [4], and control theory [5], [6], [7], [8]. In these mechanisms, Kelly flow control model [13], based on optimization theory, can achieve a global optimal solution by decentralized method. The model provides a mathematic analysis method to design distributed congestion control scheme in general networks. And because the model gives a direction to construct asymptotic stable optimal solution, many new schemes [9], [10], [11], [12] have been evolved.

In Kelly model, the network flow control problem can be transferred into the optimal problem,

$$SYSTEM(U,R,C):$$
$$\max \sum_{i=1}^{N} U_i(x_i) \quad \text{subject to} \quad Rx \le C \quad \text{over} \quad x \ge 0. \tag{1}$$

where $x_i$ is the host $i$ send rate, $U_i(x_i)$ is a strictly concave function, which determines rate allocation between hosts. $C$ is link capacity vector and $N$ is the number of users. $R$ is the router matrix.

D.-S. Huang, K. Li, and G.W. Irwin (Eds.): ICIC 2006, LNCS 4113, pp. 832–841, 2006.

Without knowing the information of the router matrix and without corporation among hosts or among links, [13] proposes "primal" and "dual" algorithms to solve the optimal problem. Many recent researches [9],[11],[12] use the primal algorithm to realize the end-to-end congestion control. The primal control model is:

$$\begin{aligned} \dot{x}_i &= f(x_i, q_i) \\ q &= R^T p \\ p_l &= h(y_l) \\ y &= Rx \end{aligned} \tag{2}$$

$y$ is the link aggregate rate, $p$ is the link price and $q$ is the aggregate price. $f(x_i,q_i)$ is the simple first-order control law:

$$\dot{x} = k(w_i - x_i q_i). \tag{3}$$

$h(y)$ is a non-negative, continuous increasing function. One usual form is:

$$p_l = \delta_l [y_l - c_l]^+. \tag{4}$$

we can choose $1/c_l$ or $1/y_l$ as $\delta_l$, and $[z]^+=\max\{z,0\}$.

Some recent researches take the delay time as price, but they have fairness problem such as in [11] and in [15]. And these mechanisms have comparatively long queue delay. REM [16] mechanism uses ECN mark to feedback the price information. It can converge to fairness equilibrium and achieve the asymptotic stability. Moreover, it has very low queue delay. However, in REM, its price is just positive and its convergence rate is linear. In [9], Y. Zhang et al propose to use negative price to achieve exponential convergence rate. However, they add new packet header into the traditional TCP header.

To avoid introducing new packet header while keeping rapid convergence rate, in this paper, we propose a new flow control model, which uses ECN bits in IP header to feed back price information, including negative price. The control model can exponentially converge to fairness equilibrium point without adding any new packet header to convey price information.

Our paper is organized as follows: in Section 2, we introduce the effect of negative price and give our method to realize the negative price; in Section 3, we give the implementation of our flow control model; In Section 4, the simulation results of our flow control mechanism is displayed, which validates that our model achieves the control objective. Finally, we conclude our method.

## 2 Negative Price

### 2.1 Effect of Negative Price

To take insight into the effect of negative price to the network, we consider the discrete form of the primal algorithm in Kelly model with delay [12]:

$$x_i(n) = x_i(n-1) + k_i(w_i - x_i(n-D)\sum_{j \in r_i} p_j(n-D))$$
$$p_l(n) = [(y_l(n) - c_l) / y_l(n)]^+ \tag{5}$$

where $r_i$ is the links sets used by user $i$, and $D$ denotes the feedback delay. $D$=1 means immediate feedback and $D$>2 means delayed feedback. From (5) we can note that when $x(n)<c$, that is, the user should increase its rate, the feed back price is zero, so the increment is $k_i w_i$ for every control step. This is a linear increment. In high-speed network, [13] and [14] have indicated that linear increment is unsatisfactory. If we allow the link can feed back negative price, for every control step, from (5) we can see that the increment is

$$k_i w_i + | x_i(n-D)\sum_{j \in r_i} p_j(n-D) | \tag{6}$$

which is exponential increment. Thus, the negative price will change the primal algorithm from linear convergence to exponential convergence. The local asymptotic stability of Kelly model using negative price has been proved in [9].

To show the effect of negative price, we consider the single-source and single-link case with infinite queue size, that is, no packet losses. In this case, the primal algorithm can be transferred into:

$$x_i(n) = x_i(n-1) + k_i w_i - k_i \max(0, x_i(n-D) - C) \tag{7}$$

Now we assume a special parameter set: $k$=0.5, $w$=10mb/s, $C$=1,000mb/s, $D$=1. Solving the difference equation (7), we show the result in fig. 1.(a). From fig. 1.(a), we can see that it takes 200 steps to converge to its equilibrium point. It is obvious that the convergence rate is linear. Now we use the price update law:

$$p_l(n) = (y_l(n) - c_l) / y_l(n) \tag{8}$$

and the primal algorithm can be transferred into:

$$x_i(n) = x_i(n-1) + k_i w_i - k_i(x_i(n-D) - C). \tag{9}$$

Solving the difference equation (9), we show the result in fig. 1.(b). From fig. 1.(b), we can see that it takes only 10 steps to converge to its equilibrium point. It is obvious that the convergence rate is exponential. Thus, introducing negative price can improve the classic Kelly model performance.

However, with Kelly original framework, the negative price will result in oscillation, even unstableness under large delay [9]. To keep the asymptotic stability, [9] modify the Kelly model by:

$$x_i(n) = x_i(n-D) + k_i(w_i - x_i(n-D)\sum_{j \in r_i} p_j(n-D)) \tag{10}$$

Let$\alpha$=$kw$,$\beta$=$k$, and $q_i$= $\sum_{j \in r_i} p_j(n-D)$ . We can get:

$$x_i(n) = x_i(n-D) + \alpha - \beta q_i(n-D) x_i(n-D) \tag{11}$$

[9] has prove that the local asymptotic stability condition of (11) is 0<$\beta$<2.

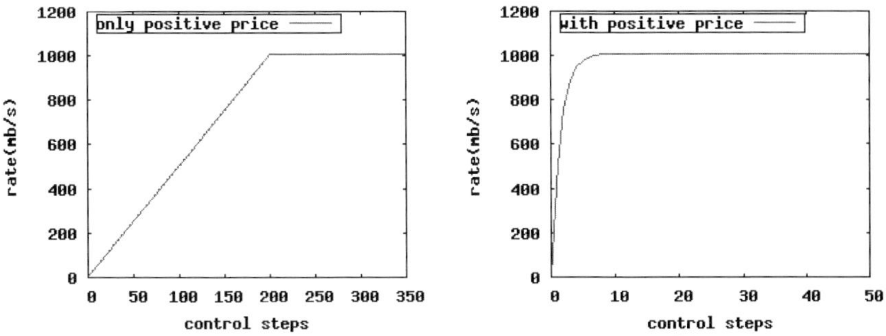


(a) (b)

**Fig. 1.** Convergence rate without and with negative price

## 2.2 Realization of Negative Price

However, to get negative price, [9] uses new packet header added into the traditional TCP/IP header. It adds a new 20 bytes packet header called MKC header to give users the feed back information (IP header has only 20 bytes). It is a going arguable topic whether we need to introduce more cost to deal with congestion [15]. However, as to the negative price, we can avoid introducing extra header data. In REM, the price can be transferred to ECN marks without using extra header. The user can use a series of ECN marks to estimate the link price. Nevertheless, REM mechanism can only provide positive price because it must transfer the price into the mark possibility, which is a limitation to use REM. In this paper, since there are two bits in ECN field of IP header, we propose to use one bit to feed back positive price and another bit to feed back negative price. By using the mark approach, we can let the user get enough price information under the format of IP/TCP datagram, even we use new flow control mechanism.

In REM, if the link price is $p_l$ ($p_l$>0), an ECN bit would be marked at each link with probability:

$$1-\phi^{-p_l} \tag{12}$$

where $\Phi$ is a global constant, which means choosing a range of prices. The selection of $\Phi$ is relative to the parameters setting of the utility function. When $\Phi$=500, the curve of (12) is shown as fig. 2.(a).

After passing all the links in one route, the overall mark probability of the ECN bit in one packet is:

$$P_i = 1-\phi^{-\sum_{j\in r_i} p_j} = 1-\phi^{-q_i} \tag{13}$$

The receiver will copy the ECN bits into ACK and send back to the user, so the user can estimate the sum of prices from marking statistics. The proportion of ECN bit marks provides an estimation of the overall marking probability. To get the mark proportion, the user should keep a register to record the recent $M$ ACKs ECN bits, from which an estimation can be derived.

In our flow control model, we use 2 bits to record the price. When $y_l > c_l$, that is, the link price is positive, our method is similar to REM. Though REM uses the dynamic price update law, as follow discussion, it does not affect using REM mechanism in our algorithm. Now we notice the case $y_l < c_l$, the link price is negative. To keep the absolute value of price $p_l$ between 0 and 1, we modify the price update law by:

$$p_l(n) = (y_l(n) - c_l) / c_l \tag{14}$$

For the bottleneck links, the negative price should be feed back to users to inform the users of increasing rate. However, for the non-bottleneck links, the negative price should be ignored so that the user can increase sending rate based on bottleneck link negative price only. Therefore, for negative price, when the absolute value of link price is big, the probability to mark is small. To realize this, the probability to mark another bit in ECN field should be:

$$1 - \phi^{-(1-|p_l|)} \tag{15}$$

When $\Phi$=500, the curve of (15) is shown as fig. 2.(b).

When the user detects the last $M$ ECN bits, it will calculate two aggregate prices, positive price $q1_i$ and negative price $q2_i$, based on the two series of ECN bits. If $q2_i > 0$, then the final price $q_i = q2_i$, and if the $q2_i = 0$, then the final price $q_i = q1_i$

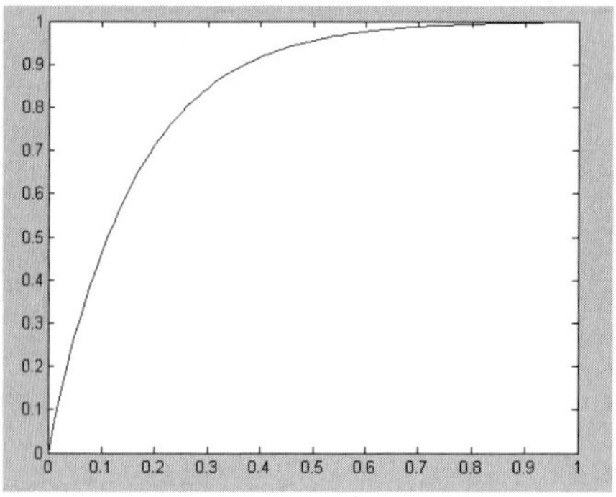


**Fig. 2.(a)** The approximate curve of mark probability versus positive price

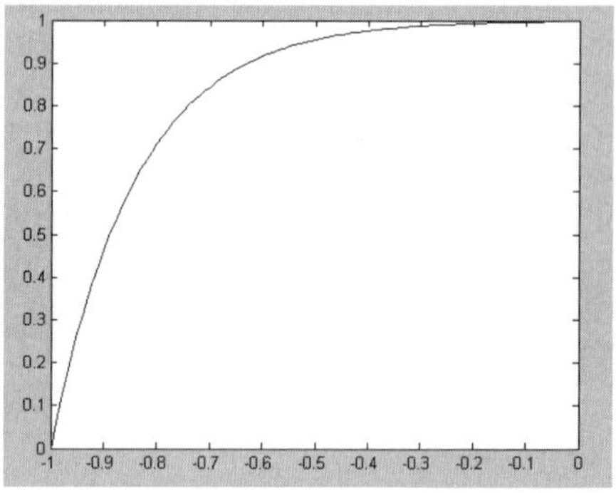


**Fig. 2.(b)** The approximate curve of mark probability versus negative price

## 3 Implementation of Flow Control Model

Now we consider how to realize the flow control model under traditional TCP/IP datagram. In this paper, like many other flow control model such as XCP [21] and EMKC [9], the router or the hosts needs to take average rate rather than instantaneous rate as control variable.

The sending rate update law is:

$$x_i(n) = \overline{x_i}(n) + \alpha - \beta q_i(n-D)\overline{x_i}(n) \tag{16}$$

(16) comes from (11), where $x_i(n)$ is the sending rate, and $\overline{x_i}(n)$ is the recent average rate calculated in sample interval $\tau_u$:

$$\overline{x_i}(n) = (\sum_{k \in u} s_i(k)) / \tau_u \tag{17}$$

$s_i(k)$ is the size of packet $k$, and $u$ is the acknowledgement packet set in interval $\tau_u$.

The link price $p_l(n)$ is calculated by:

$$p_l(n) = \begin{cases} (\overline{y_l}(n) - c_l) / \overline{y_l}(n) & \overline{y_l}(n) \geq c_l \\ (\overline{y_l}(n) - c_l) / c_l & \overline{y_l}(n) < c_l \end{cases} \tag{18}$$

where $\overline{y_l}(n)$ is the input rate of link $l$, which is calculated by:

$$\overline{y_l}(n) = (\sum_{k \in z} s_l(k)) / \tau_v \tag{19}$$

$\tau_v$ is the link sample rate, $s_l(k)$ is the size of packet $k$, and $v$ is the input packet set in interval $\tau_v$. Here we use $c_{0l}$ to replace the real capacity $c_l$. $c_{0l}$ is called virtual capacity and is slight below $c_l$. By using $c_{0l}$, we try to empty the queue in router and utilize the bottleneck link rather fully. In our implementation, like in [11], we let $c_{0l}$ =0.95$c_l$.

The sample interval $\tau_u$ used in hosts should be equal to the sample interval $\tau_v$ used in link. Otherwise, there are some inconsistencies in the feedback loop. In our realization, we set its value to 100ms.

When the host sends data, to smooth the burst data, it does not use the received ACK to inspire new packet, instead, it keep a sending timer to determine the send time. If the current rate is $x_i(n)$, and the interval time is $\tau_u$, then in the next interval, the sending data should be $x_i(n)\tau_u$. And if the packet size is $s$, the number of user sending packets should be:

$$m(n) = x_i(n)\tau_u / s \tag{20}$$

so in next interval, the time space for every packet sending time should be $\tau_u/m(n)=s/x_i(n)$. Thus, after calculating average rate $x_i(n)$, we should update sending timer value to $s/x_i(n)$. When the sending timer times out, the user will send a new packet. The data sending method is similar to the "burstiness control" in FAST TCP [15] and is mentioned as early in [23].

## 4 Simulation

Now we evaluate the performance of the new control model in *NS2* simulation platform. Firstly, we consider the single-link and single-source case, in which the user uses FTP flow to send data. We will give the comparison of the effect with negative price and without negative price. The simulation parameters are set by: the link capacity $c$=4MB/s, the link delay time $T$=10ms, the packet size $s$=1000 bytes, the increment coefficient $\alpha$=40kb/s, the decrement coefficient $\beta$=0.9, the mark base $\Phi$ =500, the virtual capacity $c_l$=0.95$c$, the interval time $\tau$=100ms and the FTP flow start at time 0.

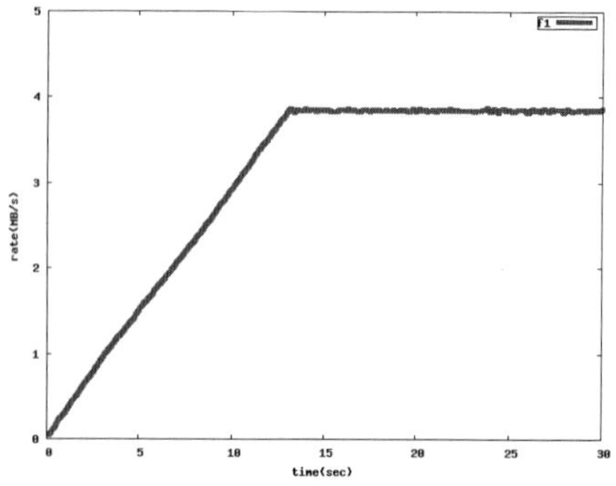


**Fig. 3.** Rate increase without negative price in single-source and single-link case

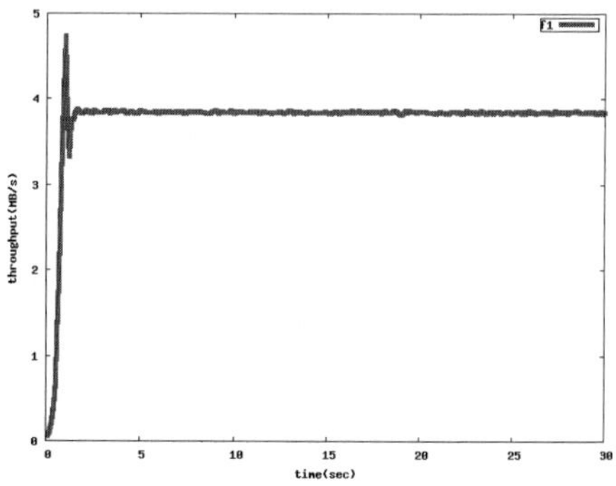


**Fig. 4.** Rate increase with negative price in single-source and single-link case

The result is showed in fig. 3 and fig. 4. From fig. 3, we can see that if the host just uses the positive price, the convergence rate is linear. It will take more than 10 seconds to reach the link capacity. While in fig. 4, the rate is close to link capacity less than 2 seconds. Thus in high-speed network, using negative price can improve the performance greatly. To compare the new mechanism with TCP protocol, we use TCP protocol in the same simulation scene and the result is shown in fig. 5. We can see that TCP does not utilize the capacity adequately and the rate oscillates slightly.

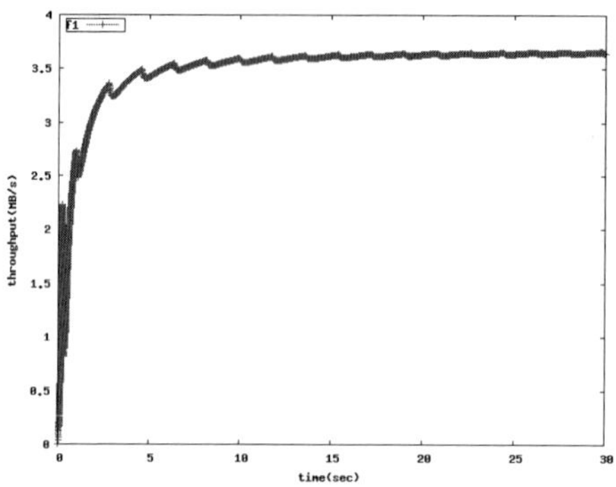


**Fig. 5.** Throughput of TCP in single-link and single-source case

Now we focus on the fairness of our new flow control protocol under heterogeneous delay time. We let two FTP flows go through one single bottleneck. The bottleneck link capacity is 4MB/s. One of the FTP delay time is 40 ms and another is 60 ms. The FTP flow with short delay time starts at time 0 and the FTP flow with long delay time starts at time 10. Other simulation parameters are set the same as the above simulation test. The result is showed as fig. 6. From fig. 6, we can see that the two FTP flow can converge to the same rate even the FTP flow with long delay time starts later. The time to converge to fair equilibrium point is approximately 10 seconds.

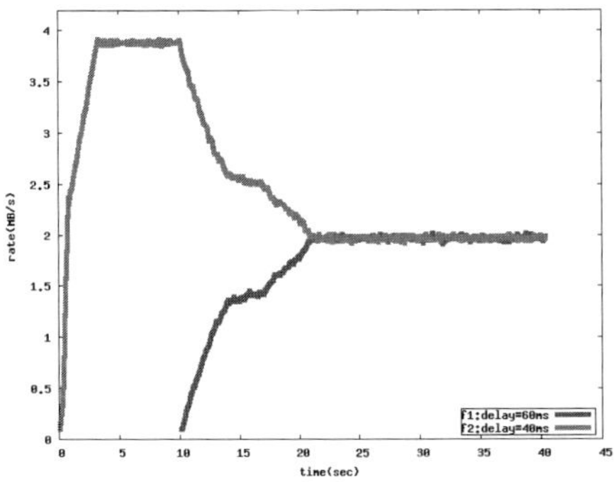


**Fig. 6.** 2 FTP flows using flow control mechanism passing one bottleneck link.

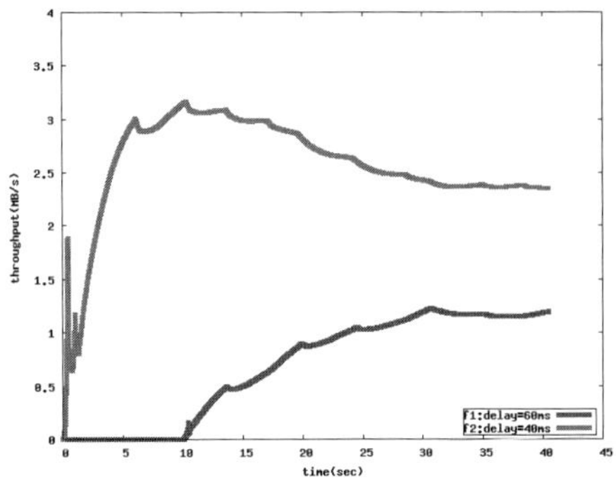


**Fig. 7.** 2 TCP flows with different delay time passing one bottleneck link.

To address it more clearly, we run TCP protocol in this simulation scene. The result is showed as fig. 7. From fig. 7, we can see that TCP can not realize the fairness. The FTP flow with long delay time is pressed and can not share the link capacity equally.

Now we consider more complex simulation scene. In which, 5 flows dynamically enter into and leave the network. These flows start at time 0, 10, 60, 90, 120 respectively, where the flow that starts at 0 ends at time 100, the flow that starts at time 30 ends at time 80. Their delay times are 40, 52, 64, 76 and 88 respectively. The result is shown as fig. 8.

From the simulation, we can see it is feasible to realize the negative price by using our model, which is profitable because the proposed model uses only 2 bits and can be implemented under TCP/IP datagram framework. While the negative price can help users converge to fair, efficient equilibrium point with exponential rate.

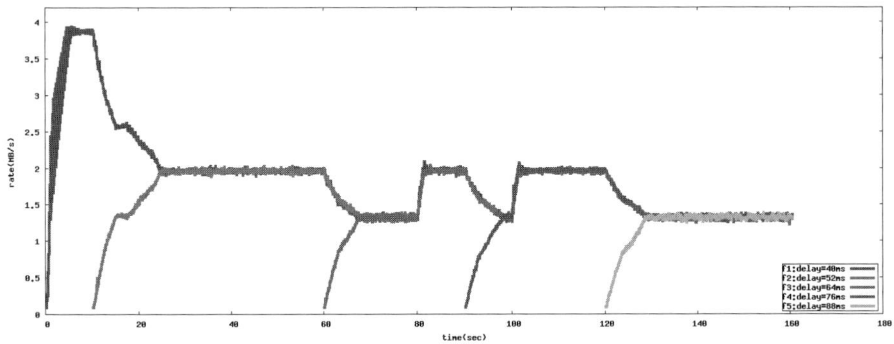


**Fig. 8.** 5 FTP flows passing one bottleneck link in dynamic scene

## 5 Conclusion

In this paper, we discuss the effect of introducing the negative price in Kelly model, and try to implement it in traditional TCP/IP datagram. By theoretical discussion and simulation results, we indicate that introducing negative price can improve convergence rate of flow control model, which is very important in high-speed network. To introduce negative price and keep the TCP/IP header unchanged, we use 2 bits of ECN field in IP header to convey link price, including positive price and negative price. The simulation displays that 2 bits of ECN field can carry the sufficient price information, and our model is fair, robust and stable irrelative to delay.

## Acknowledgments

This work was supported by NSFC Projects (No. 60334020, 60440420130) and the Outstanding Overseas Chinese Scholars Fund of Chinese Academy of Sciences (No. 2005-1-11), China.

## References

1. Low, S. H.: A Duality Model of TCP and Queue Management Algorithms. IEEE/ACM Transactions on Networking.Vol. 11(4) (2003) 525-536
2. Low, S. H., Lapsley, D. E.: Optimization Flow Control I: Basic Algorithm and Convergence. IEEE/ACM Transactions on Networking.Vol. 7(6) (1999) 861-874
3. Kar, K., Sarkar, S., Tassiulas, L.: A Simple Rate Control Algorithm for Maximizing Total User Utility. IEEE INFOCOM., April 2001.
4. Kunniyur, S., Srikant, R.: End-to-End Congestion Control Schemes: Utility Functions, Random Losses and ECN Marks. IEEE/ACM Transactions on Networking.Vol. 11(5) (2003) 689-702.
5. Johari, R., Tan, D. K. H.: End-to-End Congestion Control for the Internet: Delays and Stability. IEEE/ACM Transactions on Networking., Vol. 9(6) (2001) 818-832
6. Kar, K., Sarkar, S., Tassiulas L.: A Simple Rate Control Algorithm for Maximizing Total User Utility. IEEE INFOCOM. (2001).
7. Massoulie, L.: Stability of Distributed Congestion Control with Heterogeneous Feedback Delays. IEEE/ACM Transactions on Networking., Vol. 47(6) 895-902
8. Paganini, Y.F., Doyle, J., Low, S.H.: A Control Theoretical Look at Internet Congestion Control. The Mohammed Dahleh Symposium. (2002)
9. Zhang, Y., Kang, S.K., Loguinov, R.: Delayed Stability and Performance of Distributed Congestion Control. ACM SIGCOMM. (2004)
10. Low, S.H., Paganini, F., Doyle, J.C.: Internet Congestion Control. IEEE Control Systems Magazine. Vol. 22 (2002) 28-43
11. Paganini, F., Wang, Z., Doyle, J. C., Low, S. H.: Congestion control for high performance, stability, and fairness in general networks. IEEE/ACM Transactions on Networking. Vol. 13(1) (2005) 43-56
12. Wen, T., Arcak, M.: A unifying passivity framework for network flow control. IEEE INFOCOM. (2004.)
13. Kelly, F.P., Maulloo, A.K.,Tan, D.K.H.: Rate Control for Communication Networks: Shadow Prices, Proportional Fairness and Stability. Journal of the Operational Research Society. Vol 49(3) (1998) 237-252
14. Kelly, F.P.: Charging and Rate Control for Elastic Traffic. European Transactions on Telecommunications, Vol. 8(1) (1997) 33-37

15. Jin, C., Wei, D.X., Low, S.H.: FAST TCP: motivation, architecture, algorithms, performance. IEEE INFOCOM. (2004)
16. Athuraliya, S., Li, V.H., Low,S.H.,Yin, Q.: REM: Active queue management. IEEE Network, vol. 15 (2001) 48–53
17. Hollot, C., Misra, C., Towsley, D., Gong, W.-B.: Control theoretic analysis of RED. IEEE INFOCOM, (2001) 1510–1519
18. Floyd, S.: High-speed TCP for Large Congestion Windows. RFC 3649 (2003)
19. Kelly, T.: Scalable TCP: Improving Performance in High-speed Wide Area Networks. First International Workshop on Protocols for Fast Long-Distance Networks, (2003)
20. Atkinson, R., Floyd, S.: IAB Concerns and Recommendations Regarding Internet Research and Evolution. RFC3869 (2004)
21. Katabi, D., Handley, M., Rohrs, C.: Congestion Control for High Bandwidth Delay Product Networks. ACM SIGCOMM (2002)
22. Kunniyur, S., Srikant, R.: Analysis and Design of an Adaptive Virtual Queue (AVQ) Algorithm for Active Queue Management ACM SIGCOMM (2001)
23. Jacobson, V.: Congestion avoidance and control. ACM SIGCOMM (1998) 314–329

# Feature Extraction and Evolution Based Pattern Recognition

Mi Young Nam and Phill Kyu Rhee

Dept. of Computer Science & Engineering, Inha University
253, Yong-Hyun Dong, Incheon, South Korea
rera@im.inha.ac.kr, pkrhee@inha.ac.kr

**Abstract.** This paper proposes a novel method of classifier selection for efficient object recognition based on evolutionary computation and data context knowledge called Evolvable Classifier Selection. The proposed method tries to distinguish the data characteristics of input image (data contexts) and selects a classifier system accordingly using the genetic algorithm. It stores its experiences in terms of the data context category and the artificial chromosome so that the context knowledge can be accumulated and used later. The proposed method operates in two modes: the evolution mode and the action mode. It can improve its performance incrementally using GA in the evolution mode. Once sufficient context knowledge is accumulated, the method can operate in real-time. The proposed method has been evaluated in the area of face recognition. Data context-awareness, modeling and identification of input data as data context categories, is carried out using SOM.

## 1 Introduction

The difficulties of object recognition for robust computer vision are caused by the variations in internal object characteristics, viewpoint, viewing distance, illumination, etc. Recognizing objects under such variations is one of the ultimate goals in the research area of computer vision. Much research has been devoted on this problem. However, most object recognition methods today can only operate successfully only for restricted images captured under strongly controlled environments [1, 2, 3]. In this paper, we discuss about an evolvable classifier selection method based on context-awareness that can behave in a robust manner under such variations. We focus on the variation of illumination in input images, what we call data context, that affect the performance of object recognition. However, the proposed method can be readily applied or extended to other kinds of variations. It employs the concept of context-awareness and the genetic algorithm (GA), and determines (selects) a most effective structure of classifier system considering the variation of illumination in input images. Classifier selection is one approach of classifier combination. Classifier combination is expected to produce a superior performance to that of a single classifier system in terms of accuracy and reliability [5, 6]. Classifier combination is divided into classifier selection and classifier fusion [7]. The classifier fusion approaches can be found in the literature of classifier fusion [5, 6, 7], classifier ensemble [7], expert mixture [8], etc. Several researchers have studied theoretically the area of fusion [7, 8]. In classifier selection approaches, input data are partitioned into several regions,

D.-S. Huang, K. Li, and G.W. Irwin (Eds.): ICIC 2006, LNCS 4113, pp. 842 – 852, 2006.

and the best classifier is assigned to each partitioned region [7, 9]. Two types of classifier selection are the static classifier and the dynamic classifier selections. In the static classifier system, the regions are specified first, and the best classifier is selected for the region. Another approach is that classifier systems are given, and region is selected for each classifier system. In dynamic classifier selection, the choice of classifier system is made during run-time [9, 10].

In this paper, we present a novel classifier selection method, called ECS (Evolvable Classifier Selection) aiming at highly efficient object recognition by taking advantage of the evolutionary computing and the context-awareness. Similar research can be found by [7]. We will deal with image objects the spatial boundaries of which can be well estimated in prior, called spatially well-defined object class [11] without loss of generality. Face images are in the class of well-defined image objects, the spatial boundaries of which can be well estimated in prior. Recently, face recognition becomes a popular task in object recognition area [12, 13, 14].

**Fig. 1.** Face images each face database: For images in the fafb category a different facial expression was requested

The paper is organized as follows. In the section 2, we present the proposed model for context-aware evolutionary computation and the overview of the proposed object recognition scheme. In the section 3, we discuss about the illumination context modeling and illumination identification using Self Organization Map. The adaptive and robust face recognition process will be given in the section 4. Finally, we give the experimental results and the concluding remarks in the section 5 and 6, respectively.

## 2 The Model of Evolvable Classifier Selection

A classifier system usually has multiple stages each of which consists of several competitive action primitives. The action primitives are basic functional elements that can be heterogeneous, homogeneous, or hybrid operational entities. The same functional elements with different behavior due to different parameters, threshold, etc. are treated as different action primitives. For example, the action primitives of object recognition can be divided into three stages: preprocessing, feature representation, and class decision.

### 2.1 The Architecture of ECS

In the proposed scheme, two types of inputs are used: context data and action data inputs as discussed before. We use a single input image as both context and action data in this paper. The proposed ECS (Evolvable Classifier Selection) consists of the context identification module (CIM), the action control module (ACM), the action module (AM), the evolution control module (ECM), and the context knowledge base (CKB) (see Fig. 2).

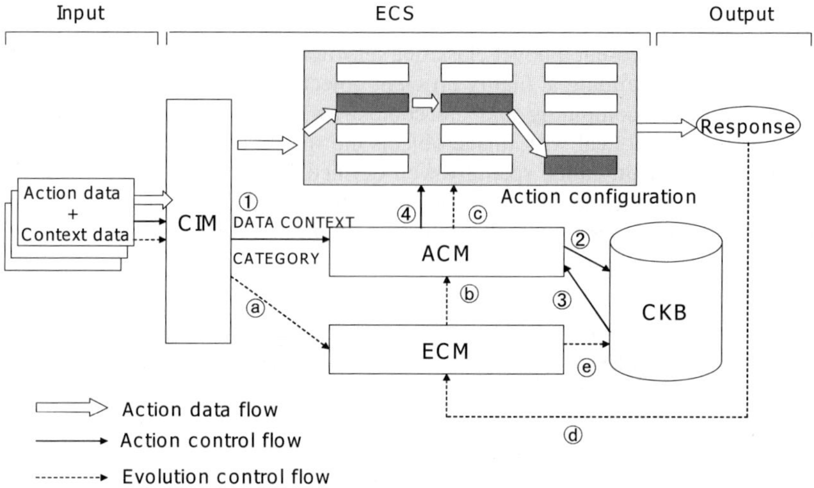


**Fig. 2.** Block diagram of the proposed architecture for object recognition

The system tries to distinguish the data characteristics of input image (data contexts) and selects a classifier system accordingly using the genetic algorithm (GA). It stores its experiences in terms of the data context category and the artificial chromosome, called action configuration chromosome, so that the context knowledge can be accumulated and used later. Each chromosome represents the encoding of the structure of an optimal AM for corresponding data context category. Data context is identified by the CIM. The ACM searches for a best combining structure of action primitives (i.e. classifier system) for an identified data context. The action configuration chromosomes of optimal actions are stored in the CKB with the corresponding data context category.

## 2.2 The Action Mode

In the action mode, data context is identified by the CIM. The ACM searches the action configuration chromosome for the identified data context in the CKB (see ②, ③ in Fig. 2). The AM is reconfigured by the ACM (④), if necessary. Then, the reconfigured AM performs its task using the action data (⑤), and produces the response of the ECS (⑥). Whenever the ACM identifies that the data context is changed, the system reconfigures the AM. If the ECS measures the performance being fell down below a predefined criterion, the ECS activates the evolution mode, or it may evolve the system periodically.

### 2.3 The Evolution Mode

In the evolution mode, the training data are clustered into data context categories by the CIM (see ⓐ a in Fig. 2). The training data of each data context category are used to accumulate the knowledge of the action configuration chromosome of the AM (ⓑ,ⓒ,ⓓ). The evolution process is controlled by the ECM, and the details will be discussed in the next session. The determined action configuration chromosome with its corresponding data context category is stored in the CKB (ⓔ).

## 3 Data Context-Awareness and Context Knowledge Accumulation

Context data is defined as any observable and relevant attributes that affects system behavior, and its interaction with other entities and/or surrounding environment at an instance of time [15]. In this session, we will discuss data context modeling, identification, and knowledge accumulation for efficient object recognition.

### 3.1 Data Context-Awareness

Data context-awareness is carried out by modeling and identification of context data. The context data set should be modeled in association with the input action data (context modeling). An input context data need be identified (context identification), and used to select (reconfigure) a most effective classifier system for an associated action data. We use the same input image as the context data as well as the action data here. The ECS controls the classifier system selection (reconfiguration) based on the identified data context category. Context modeling can be performed by an unsupervised learning algorithm such as SOM, Fuzzy Art, K-means etc. [16, 17].

### 3.2 Context Knowledge Accumulation Using GA

Context knowledge describes a trigger of system action (combined classifier system output) in association with an identified context stored in the context knowledge base over a period of time [8]. Initially, the proposed system learns and accumulates the knowledge of context-action configuration chromosome associations, and stores them in the CKB. The knowledge of context-action association denotes that of a most effective classifier system for an identified context. The AM configuration is encoded by the action configuration chromosome, and the fitness of the GA in the ECM is decided. (The chromosome encoding describes all possible combination of classifier systems using the given classifier system components.)

Various approaches using GA for feature selection problem can be found in [18]. GA based optimization of classifier components can also be found in adaptive preprocessing based recognition [16], and neural network classifier systems [7]. In this paper, all possible classifier system combinations are encoded as artificial chromosomes. However, GA can hardly be used under dynamically changing environment alone since they usually consume too much time to evaluate the population of chromosomes in the genospace until finding an optimal solution. The knowledge of an individual context category and its associated chromosomes of effective classifier systems are stored in the context knowledge base. In addition, once the context knowledge is constructed, the system can react to changing environments at run-time.

The detail of context knowledge accumulation process is given in the followings.

Step1. The context data associated application environments are clustered (learned) as data context categories by the CIM.

Step2. The most effective subset of classifier systems of the AM for each identified data context is decided by the GA using the associated training action data set as follows.

2.1 Generate a random population of the chromosome.

2.2 Evaluate the fitness of each chromosome vector of the population.

2.3 Select only a portion of the population as the population of next generation.

2.4 Repeat 2.2 and 2.3 until a most effective classifier is reached, or a generation exceeds a desired criterion value.

Step3. The classifier system chromosomes with their associated contexts (the knowledge of context-action relations) are stored in the CKB.

## 4 Face Recognition Using ECS Method

The proposed ECS method has been tested in the area of object recognition. We deal with face image objects the spatial boundaries of which can be well estimated in prior. We employ the ECS strategy where the face recognition system structure is allowed to evolve in accordance with changing quality of input image data, i.e. data context. The data sets Inha, FERRET, and Yale were used in our experiments.

### 4.1 The Design of ECS Based Face Recognition

The AM of ECS based face recognition consists of three stages: the preprocessing, feature representation, and class decision. We adopt Gabor vectors with different weight values of individual fiducial points as the action primitives of feature representation. The details of generation of Gabor vector will be discussed later. For the simplicity, we adopt non-parametric classification method k-nn's with different threshold values as the action primitives of the class decision stage. The architecture of face recognition using the ECS is shown in Fig. 3.

In ECS based face recognition, the input images are used as the action data as well as the context data. We assume that the training set of input face image is provided. In the action mode, and the data context category of input face image is identified by the CIM. If the data context category is the same as the previous one, the ACM activates the AM. Finally, the AM produce the recognition result using the action data (input face image).

### 4.2 Context Modeling

We used face image of 128 x 128 spatial resolution and 256 gray levels as input context data y here (seethe session 3.1). Three methods of derived context feature were investigated here as shown in Fig. 4. In the vertical scanning method, the input context data, i.e. 128 x 128 face image is reduced into 6 x 6 images, and the reduced image is scanned in the vertical direction first (from top to bottom) and from left to right. Several types of unsupervised learning methods have been investigated, and SOM is selected to be the most promising algorithm for constructing the data context model for face recognition. SOM can be used to create an intuitive model of the important concepts contained in information [15, 16]. After a sufficient number of input vectors have been presented, network connection weights specify clusters, the point density function of which tends to approximate the probability density function of the input vectors. In addition, the connection weights will be organized such that topologically close nodes are sensitive to inputs that are similar.

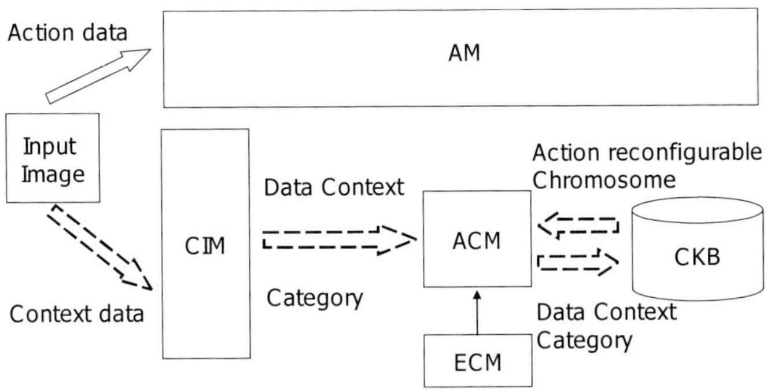


(a) The flows of action and context data in the action mode

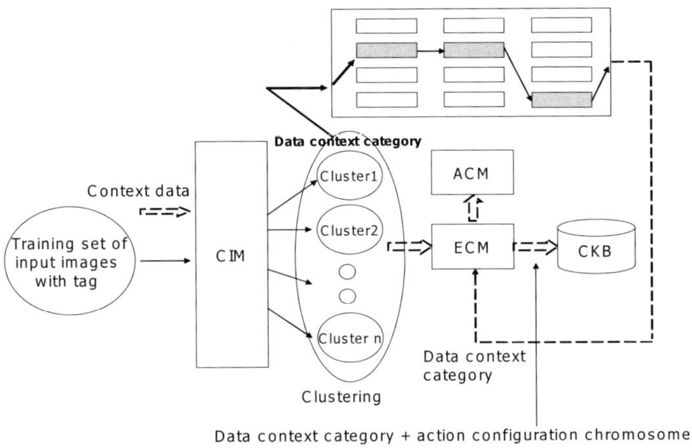


(b) The flow of action and context data in the evolution mode

**Fig. 3.** Two modes of ECS based face recognition: (a) the flow diagram of the action mode, and (b) the flow diagram of the evolution mode

*Gabor Wavelet Based Feature Representation*

The proposed face recognition of the AM employs Gabor feature vector, which is generated using the Gabor wavelet transform. The kernels of the Gabor wavelets show biological relevance to 2-D receptive field profiles of mammalian cortical cells

[28]. The feature vector thus includes all the Gabor transform at the fiducial point $\vec{x}$, $V=(\overrightarrow{F(x_1)}\overrightarrow{F(x_2)}\cdots\overrightarrow{F(x_n)})$.

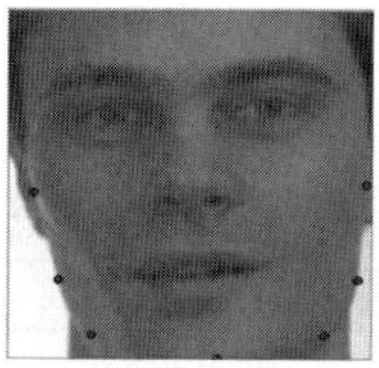

**Fig. 4.** The characteristic vector of the Gabor feature space. The characteristic vectors are generated from 32 fiducial points.

### 4.3 The Chromosome Encoding and Fitness Function of the ECM

The ECM is implemented by employing the genetic algorithm. The design of the chromosome and the fitness function of the GA are discussed in the followings. The GA explores the huge search space of action reconfiguration chromosomes to find an optimal classifier system structures for an identified data context. The optimality of the chromosome, i.e. fitness, is defined by classification accuracy and generalization capability. Fig. 5 shows a possible encoding of the chromosome description.

| $GFR_1$ | $GFR_2$ | $GFR_2$ | … | $GFR_n$ |
|---|---|---|---|---|

**Fig. 5.** Chromosome description of the proposed scheme

$GFR_1$, $GFR_2$, . . ., and $GFR_n$ denote weight values for fidiucial points, and they are represented by 4 bits. As the GA searches the genospace, the GA makes its choices via genetic operators as a function of probability distribution driven by fitness function. The genetic operators used here are selection, crossover, and mutation.

The GA needs a salient fitness function to evaluate current population and chooses offspring for the next generation. Evolution or adaption will be guided by a fitness function defined in terms of the system accuracy and the class scattering criterionThe evolutionary module derives the classifier being balanced between successful recognition and generalization capability. The fitness function adopted here is defined as follows:

$$\eta(V)=\lambda_1\eta_s(V)+\lambda_2\eta_g(V). \tag{1}$$

where $\eta_s(V)$ is the term for the system correctness, i.e., successful recognition rate and $\eta_g(V)$ is the term for class generalization. $\lambda_1$ and $\lambda_2$ are positive parameters that indicate the weight of each term, respectively.

Let $w_1, w_{2,} \cdots, w_k$ be the classes and $N_1, N_2, \cdots, N_k$ be the number of images in each class, respectively. Let $M_1, M_2, \cdots, M_k$ be the means of corresponding classes, and $M_{avg}$ be the total mean in the Gabor feature space. Then, *Mi* can be calculated,

$$M_i = \frac{1}{N} \sum_{j=1}^{N_i} S_j^{(i)} i = 1,2,....,L \cdot \tag{2}$$

where $S_j^{(i)} i = 1,2,....,L$ denotes the sample data in class $w_i$ and

$$M_{avg} = \frac{1}{n} \sum_{i=1}^{k} N_i M_i \cdot \tag{3}$$

where $n = \sum_{i=1}^{k} N_i \cdot$

Then, $\eta_g(V)$ can be calculated as follows:

$$\eta_g(V) = \sqrt{\sum_{k=1}^{k} (M_i - M_{avg})^t (M_i - M_{avg})} \cdot \tag{4}$$

## 5 Experimental Results

The feasibility of the proposed ECS method has been tested in the area of face recognition using Inha, Yale [19], FERET [20] data sets. We used 1000 images from 100 persons in Inha data set, 60 images from 15 persons in Yale Face data set [19], and 2418 images from 1195 persons in FERET data set. The above data sets are merged for the context modeling. The data context of the merged data is analyzed by the SOM as discussed in the session 4.2. We have 10 images for each person in Inha data set. The first experiment was performed using FERRET data set. First, we clustered the images into context models (we investigates six, nine, and twelve cluster models here) by SOM. Second, we evolve classifier systems for individual context models. The evolution of a best classifier system for each context model is carried out by the genetic algorithm using images in the corresponding cluster. The selected (evolved) classifier system is described by an artificial chromosome produced by the genetic algorithm. We will have six, nine, and twelve corresponding selected classifiers in six, nine, and twelve context models, respectively.

We have experimented three types of context feature vectorization as discussed in the session 4.2 in order to investigate the effect of the vectorization methods. Table 1 shows the performance of successful face recognition resulting of six cluster modeling for non-evolutionary face recognition, the system based face recognition with vertical scanning, the system with horizontal scanning, the system with hybrid scanning. Here, the non-evolutionary face recognition indicates a Gabor based face recognition system without using the evolutionary computing method. For the simplicity of experiment, we only evolved the feature representation stage described by Gabor based fiducial points. Tables 1, 2, and 3 show the experimental results of six, nine and twelve category context models, respectively. As you can see in those tables, the vectorization methods used in the context modeling may affect the performance. As the number of context models is increased, we can achieve a higher successful recognition rate. The best recognition can be found as 96.24% in the proposed face recognition with the hybrid scanning when the twelve context model is adopted.

**Table 1.** The comparison of successful recognition rates between the non-evolutionary method and the proposed method based face recognition method with the vertical, horizontal, and hybrid scans when the six context model is adopted

| Data context category | Non-evolutionary method | The proposed face recognition with the hybrid scanning | The proposed face recognition with the vertical scanning | The proposed face recognition with the horizontal scanning |
|---|---|---|---|---|
| Cluster -0 | 91.10% | 94.66% | 95.26% | 91.20% |
| Cluster -1 | 94.27% | 97.45% | 93.43% | 97.30% |
| Cluster-2 | 92.37% | 96.18% | 97.31% | 96.18% |
| Cluster-3 | 92.57% | 96.26% | 93.56% | 93.32% |
| Cluster-4 | 94.27% | 97.45% | 97.62% | 91.32% |
| Cluster-5 | 88.94% | 92.63% | 94.77% | 95.77% |
| Average | 91.93% | 95.51% | 95.51% | 94.18% |

**Table 2.** The comparison of successful recognition rates between the non-evolutionary method and the proposed ECS based face recognition method with the vertical, horizontal, and hybrid scanning when the nine context model is adopted

| Data context category | Non-evolutionary method | The proposed face recognition with the hybrid scanning | The proposed d face recognition with the vertical scanning | The proposed face recognition with the horizontal scanning |
|---|---|---|---|---|
| Cluster -0 | 86.29 | 82.85 | 93.27 | 92.00 |
| Cluster -1 | 93.75 | 96.88 | 97.96 | 96.50 |
| Cluster-2 | 92.00 | 97.33 | 92.00 | 91.02 |
| Cluster-3 | 95.04 | 96.45 | 97.48 | 96.48 |
| Cluster-4 | 83.39 | 92.85 | 97.83 | 97.00 |
| Cluster-5 | 89.90 | 94.95 | 94.25 | 93.5 |
| Clsuter6 | 92.92 | 97.35 | 98.58 | 97.25 |
| Cluster7 | 97.45 | 100.00 | 97.00 | 95.00 |
| Cluster8 | 94.44 | 99.15 | 94.16 | 93.05 |
| Average | 91.93 | 96.06 | 95.78 | 94.65 |

**Table 3.** The comparison of successful recognition rates between the non-evolutionary method and the proposed ECS based face recognition method with the vertical, horizontal, and hybrid scanning when the twelve context model is adopted

| Data context category | Non-evolutionary method | The proposed face recognition with the hybrid scanning | The proposed face recognition with the vertical scanning | The proposed face recognition with the horizontal scanning |
|---|---|---|---|---|
| Cluster -0 | 87.14% | 95.71% | 95.74% | 95.39% |
| Cluster -1 | 96.00% | 97.33% | 92.68% | 95.83% |
| Cluster-2 | 97.14% | 98.10% | 95.92% | 100.00% |
| Cluster-3 | 91.30% | 94.20% | 95.92% | 92.63% |
| Cluster-4 | 89.80% | 100.00% | 98.36% | 88.71% |
| Cluster-5 | 87.65% | 92.59% | 96.72% | 95.81% |
| Clsuter6 | 93.33% | 97.78% | 95.16% | 100.00% |
| Cluster7 | 86.17% | 89.36% | 98.51% | 98.73% |
| Cluster8 | 94.95% | 98.99% | 93.55% | 98.20% |
| Cluster9 | 93.33% | 97.14% | 95.11% | 87.50% |
| Cluster10 | 94.62% | 96.77% | 95.19% | 97.84% |
| Cluster11 | 92.31% | 97.80% | 97.83% | 97.50% |
| Average | 91.93% | 96.24 | 96.05% | 95.97% |

## 6 Conclusion

In this paper, ECS (Evolvable Classifier Selection), a novel method of classifier combination using data context-awareness is proposed and applied to object recognition problem. The proposed method tries to distinguish its input data context and evolves the classifier combination structure accordingly by Genetic algorithm (GA). It stores its experiences in terms of the data context category and the evolved artificial chromosome so that the evolutionary knowledge can be used later. The main difference of the proposed classifier selection method from other methods is that it can select classifiers in accordance with the identified context. In addition, once the context knowledge is constructed, the system can react to changing environments at run-time.

## References

1. Potzsch, M., Kruger, N., Von der Malsburg, C.: Improving Object recognition by Transforming Gabor Filter reponses. Network: Computation in Neural Systems, Vol.7, No.2 (1996) 36~55
2. Liu, C., Wechsler, H.: Evolutionary Pursuit and Its Application to Face recognition. IEEE Trans. on PAMI, Vol. 22, No. 6 ( 2000) 66~78

3. Georghiades, A. S., Belhumeur, P. N., Kriegman, D. J.: From Few to Many: Illumination Cone Models for Face Recognition under Variable Lighting and Pose. IEEE Trans. on PAMI, Vol. 23 No. 6 (2001)45~89
4. Phillips, P.: The FERET Database and Evoluation Procedure for Face Recognition Algorithms. Image and Vision Computing, Vol.16, No.5 (1999) 23~56
5. Kuncheva, L.I., Jain, L.C.: Designing Classifier Fusion Systems by Genetic Algorithms. IEEE Transactions on Evolutionary Computation, Vol.4, No.4 (2000) 12~23
6. Kim, Sang-Woon., Oommen, B.J.: On using Prototype Reduction Schemes and Classifier Fusion Strategies to Optimize Kernel-based Nonlinear Subspace Methods. Pattern Analysis and Machine Intelligence, IEEE Trans. Vol. 27 (2005) 56~78
7. Ludmila, I., Kuncheva.: Switching Between Selection and Fusion in Combining Classifiers: An Experiment. IEEE Transactions on Systems, Man, and Cybernetics - part B: cybernetics, Vol.32, No.2 (2002) 56~82
8. Liu, C., Wechsler, H.: Gabor Feature Classifier for Face Recognition. Computer Vision 8th IEEE International Conference (2001) 56~95
9. Kuncheva, L. , Andreeva, K., DREAM: S Shell-like Software System for Medical Data Analysis and Decision Support. Computer Methods and Programs in Biomedicine, Vol.40, No.2 (1993) 23~71
10. Liang, Y., Kato, H., Taya, M. , Mori, T.: Infinitesimal Approach to the Crystallography of Martensitic Transformation: Application to Ni-Ti , Scripta Materia, Vol. 43 (2000) 99~102
11. In Ja Jeon, Ki Sang Kwon, Phill Kyu Rhee.: Optimal Gabor Encoding Scheme for Face Recognition Using Genetic Algorithm, KES 2004 (2004) 56~78
12. Wang, X., Tang, X.: Random Sampling LDA for Face Recognition. in Proceedings of CVPR, Vol.2 (2004) 79~89
13. Wang, X., Tang, X.: A Unified Framework for Subspace Face Recognition. IEEE Trans. on PAMI, Vol. 26, No. 9 ( 2004) 89~95
14. Kim, H., Kim, D., Bang, S. Y.: Face Recognition Using LDA Mixture Model. in Proceedings of ICPR (2002)
15. Yau, S. , Karim, F., Wang, Y., Wang, B., Gupta, S.: Reconfigurable Context-Sensitive Middleware for Pervasive Computing. IEEE Pervasive Computing, 1(3) (2002)
16. Nam, M.Y., Rhee, P.K.: A Novel Image Preprocessing by Evolvable Neural Network. LNAI3214, Vol.3 (2004)98~121
17. Nam, M.Y., Rhee, P.K.: An Efficient Face Recognition for Variant Illumination Condition, ISPACS2005, Vol.1 (2004)93~102
18. Shafer, S., Brumitt, B., Meyers, B.: The EasyLiving Intelligent Environment System, CHI Workshop on Research Directions in Situated Computing (2000)
19. http://cvc.yale.edu/projects/yalefaces/yalefaces.html
20. Phillips, P.: The FERET Database and Evaluation Procedure for Face Recognition Algorithms. Image and Vision Computing, Vol.16, No.5 (1999) 103~121
21. http://www.nist.gov/

# Partner Selection for Renewable Resources in Construction Supply Chain

Zhenyuan Liu and Hongwei Wang

Institute of Systems Engineering,
Huazhong University of Science and Technology,
Wuhan, Hubei, 430074, China
zyliu.hustise@263.net

**Abstract.** Partner selection is an important problem in supply chain management. The renewable resources suppliers are the most immediate partners for contractor in construction supply chain and their capacity will form constraints to project scheduling. The mathematical model for selecting these suppliers in construction projects is proposed and the principle to reduce the solution space is discussed. Following that, a schema with a hybrid genetic algorithm(GA) to solve the problems is designed wherein chromosome is composed of two parts: one represents partner selection, the other is an activities chain with precedence relationship, and different genetic operators are set on them respectively. Finally, an example is given to show the effectiveness of the algorithm.

## 1 Introduction

When we design the construction supply chain whose kernel is the main contractor or the owner in construction project, there is a critical problem facing the kernel: how to select the appropriate partners. Among these partners, the direct ones are special subcontractors and the prefabricated parts suppliers who provide the renewable resources such as the manpower with special skill and mixer to produce ready mix in construction projects and whose capacity will form constraints for project scheduling. In reality, there are often many supplier candidates to bid for supplying these renewable resources so that project scheduling is correlated with the selection schema of renewable resource suppliers.

Partner Selection is an important problem in supply chain management and virtual enterprize on which much work has been focused. In manufacturing industry, people have paid more attention to suppliers selection, and many rules have been put forward to solve this type of problem. The methods include mathematical programming, activity based costing approach and weighted point plan[1,2]. There are many similar methods in partner selection of virtual enterprize. Wang etc. has proposed a method based on activity network analysis in which activities in project are respectively executed by different partners. And the method to solve the problem is a soft computing approach which combines genetic algorithm with fuzzy decision making[3,4,5]. In addition, much work has been also done on partner selection in construction project, but people usually discussed

D.-S. Huang, K. Li, and G.W. Irwin (Eds.): ICIC 2006, LNCS 4113, pp. 853–862, 2006.

the problem qualitatively[6,7], their work are about concepts or based on surveys. Research on construction supply chain occurred just recently. To our knowledge, there is still no quantitative method to solve this type of problem presented in the literatures.

This paper will discuss renewable-resource suppliers selection in construction supply chain based on project scheduling. The next section describes the problem and defines the mathematical model of the problem as an integer programming. The basic principle to reduce the solution space is also discussed. The third section is to design the genetic algorithm which uses a hybrid encoding schema. Section 4 consists of a numerical example to illustrate the effectiveness of the algorithm.

## 2 Problem Description and Mathematical Model

In construction project, the needed renewable resources are usually not produced or provided by the main contractor. With variety of the requirement, supply of these renewable resources is more dependent on the special resource suppliers. For example, ready mix for placement of bridges in cities is supplied by some commercial ready mix suppliers whose capacity for ready mix is a type of renewable resource in fact. To complete a construction project effectively, people need to select appropriate supplier for each renewable resource to satisfy the requirement, and to reduce the activities' cost in project.

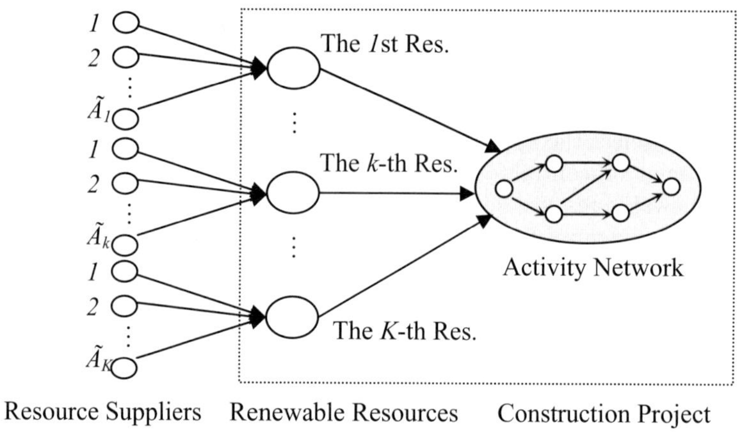


**Fig. 1.** The sketch map of the problem

As Fig.1 shows,we consider a single project which consists of $j = 1, 2, \cdots, J$ activities with a non-preemptive duration of $d_j$ periods, respectively. Due to technological requirement, precedence relationship among the activities enforce that an activity $j = 2, \cdots, J$ may not be started before all its immediate predecessors $i \in P_j$ ($P_j$ is the set of immediate predecessors of activity $j$) have been finished. In the description of activity-on-node method, the structure of the project is a network where the nodes represent the activities and the arcs the precedence relations. The network is acyclic and numerically labelled, where an activity has always a higher label than all its predecessors. Without loss of generalization, we can assume that 1 is the only start activity and activity $J$ is the only finish activity. $K$-types of renewable resources supplied by the partners will be needed during the project. It is assumed that the project needs $q_{jk}$ units of resource $k$ for activity $j$ during every period of its duration. And the cost of activity $j$ is $v_j$. Let $FT_j$ be the finish time of activity $j$.

For resource $k = 1, \cdots, K$, there are $\widetilde{A}_k$ suppliers to respond to the invitation for the tender, and they all promise to supply their resource without delay. The capacity and unit price of candidate $\alpha$ for resource k are $Q_{k\alpha}, C_{k\alpha}$.

In the problem, $h$ is the cost per period of holding completed activities stated as a percent of activity's cost and due date of the project is $H$. Giving $H$, we can get the earliest finish time $EF_j$ and the latest finish time $LF_j$ of activity $j$ by using CPM. The time parameters in the problem are all integer valued. $V_t$ is the holding cost for completed activities of the project through period $t$.

In the mathematical model, we use the following decision variables: $X_{jt} = 1$ for $j = 1, \cdots, J; t = EF_j, \cdots, LF_j$ if activity $j$ is completed in period $t$, 0 otherwise. $Y_{k\alpha} = 1$ if candidate $\alpha$ is selected as the supplier of resource k, 0 otherwise. With the above notations, the problem may be stated as follows:

$$\min \quad TV = h \sum_{t=1}^{FT_J} V_t + \sum_{j=1}^{J} v_j \tag{1}$$

$$\text{s.t.} \quad \sum_{t=EF_i}^{LF_i} tX_{it} \le \sum_{t=EF_j}^{LF_j} [(t - d_j)X_{jt}], \forall i \in P_j, j = 1, \cdots, J \tag{2}$$

$$\sum_{t=EF_j}^{LF_j} X_{jt} = 1, j = 1, \cdots, J \tag{3}$$

$$F_J = \sum_{t=EF_J}^{LF_J} tX_{Jt} \le H \tag{4}$$

$$\sum_{\alpha=1}^{\widetilde{A}_k} Y_{k\alpha} = 1, k = 1, \cdots, K \tag{5}$$

$$\sum_{j=1}^{J} (q_{jk} \sum_{t'=t}^{t+d_j-1} X_{jt'}) \le \sum_{\alpha=1}^{\widetilde{A}_k} Y_{k\alpha} Q_{k\alpha}, k = 1, \cdots, K, t = 1, \cdots, FT_J \tag{6}$$

$$v_j = v_j^{'} + \sum_{k=1}^{K} \sum_{\alpha=1}^{\widetilde{A}_k} Y_{k\alpha} C_{k\alpha} q_{jk} d_j, j = 1, \cdots, J \tag{7}$$

$$V_t = V_{t-1} + \sum_{j=1}^{J} v_j X_{jt}, t = 1, \cdots, FT_J \tag{8}$$

$$X_{jt} \in \{0,1\}, \forall j, t; Y_{k\alpha} \in \{0,1\}, \forall k, \alpha \tag{9}$$

As formula (1), the objective is to minimize $TV$, the activities' total cost of the project which includes two items. The first item is the sum of holding cost of the completed activities from the start time of the project to its finish time. The second is the amount of the activities' fixed cost. Constraints (2) ensure the precedence relations can be satisfied. (3) indicates the activity must be executed within the interval $(EF_j, LF_j)$ and (4) means that the project can not be finished after the due date. Constraints (5) are set to ensure that only one candidate is selected to serve for project for every resource. (6) is the resource-constraint which guarantees that the per-period availabilities of the renewable resources are not violated. (7) gives the composition of the activities' cost which consists of two parts, the first part, $v_j'$, is the part that is not related with the selection of the partners and is constant in fact, the later is the cost for resources needed to complete the activity that is related with the selection of suppliers because different selection will form different price. Finally, (8) illustrates how to get the holding cost for the completed activities through period $t$ where $V_0 = 0$.

From the model, we can see that there are $\prod_{k=1}^{K} \widetilde{A}_k$ combinations for partner selection that is very large in general. Therefore, the reduction of solution space is very important.

**Theorem.** If there are two candidates $\alpha_1, \alpha_2$ for resource $k$ with resource capacity and unit price $Q_{k\alpha_1}, C_{k\alpha_1}, Q_{k\alpha_2}, C_{k\alpha_2}, Q_{k\alpha_1} \leq Q_{k\alpha_2}$ and $C_{k\alpha_1} > C_{k\alpha_2}$, or $Q_{k\alpha_1} < Q_{k\alpha_2}$ and $C_{k\alpha_1} \geq C_{k\alpha_2}$, we can get that $\alpha_2$ is prior to $\alpha_1$.

**Proof.** Assume candidate $\alpha_1$ is selected as the suppliers of resource k. Without loss of generalization, it's assumed that the best objective will be reached when the suppliers for the other resources are $\alpha^{(1)}, \alpha^{(2)}, \cdots, \alpha^{(k-1)}, \alpha^{(k+1)}, \cdots, \alpha^{(K)}$ respectively, and the scheduling variables related with the activities are $X_{1t_1} = 1, \cdots, X_{Jt_J} = 1$.

According to the model, we can transform the objective to the following:

$$\min \quad TV = \sum_{j=1}^{J} (h(\sum_{t=EF_J}^{LF_J} tX_{Jt} - \sum_{t=EF_j}^{LF_j} tX_{jt}) + 1) \tag{10}$$

In addition, it's assumed the cost of the activity $j$ is $v_j^{(1)}$ when candidate $\alpha_1$ is selected ad the supplier of resource k. Then, the objective is:

$$TV_1 = \sum_{j=1}^{J} v_j^{(1)} (h(t_J - t_j) + 1) \tag{11}$$

If we change the selected candidate of resource $k$ to $\alpha_2$ with the cost of activity $j$ $v_j^{(2)}$ (Here, $v_j^{(2)} \leq v_j^{(1)}, j = 1, \cdots, J$).

In the assumption, we have $Q_{k\alpha_1} \leq Q_{k\alpha_2}$. When we select candidate $\alpha_2$ as the supplier of resource $k$, the set $\alpha^{(1)}, \alpha^{(2)}, \cdots, \alpha^{(k-1)}, \alpha^{(k+1)}, \cdots, \alpha^{(K)}$ as the suppliers of the other resources and set the scheduling variables as $X_{1t_1} = 1, \cdots, X_{Jt_J} = 1$, all the constraints will be also satisfied. In this condition, the objective will be:

$$TV_2 = \sum_{j=1}^{J} v_j^{(2)}(h(t_J - t_j) + 1) \tag{12}$$

It's obvious that $TV_2 \leq TV_1$.

If the best objective is $TV_2^*$ when candidate $\alpha_2$ is selected as the supplier of resource $k$, then we have $TV_2^* \leq TV_2 \leq TV_1$. It means that $\alpha_2$ is prior to $\alpha_1$.

Therefore, we can exclude candidate $\alpha_1$ from the set of candidates for resource $k$ in construction supply chain.

## 3 The Solving Framework Based on GA

We can get from the model that if a set of suppliers has been selected to provide renewable resources for the project, the problem will be transferred to be a resource-constrained project scheduling problem(RCPSP) with the objective of minimizing activities' cost. Therefore, if we consider all the combinations based on the current candidate set, and compute the objective under each combination, we can get the minimal objective and find the best combination of supplier candidates for the project. In other word, to select the appropriate candidates combination, we can turn to solve RCPSP with the objective of minimizing activities' cost. In our previous research[8], we have proposed an improved genetic algorithm to solve RCPSP with the objective of minimizing activities' cost wherein we used an activities chain with precedence relationship as chromosome and the decoding procedure is a serial scheduling schema. In addition, we designed the related crossover and mutation operators. The proposed GA was demonstrated to be effective based on the results of a computational study on the updated PSPLIB[9]. Following this, we will extent the above GA to solve the model (1) $\sim$ (9). The framework of the algorithm is shown in Fig. 2.

### 3.1 Encoding and Decoding

In the problem, there are two types of variables: one is related with the selection of suppliers, the other is related with the activities. Here, we use a hybrid chain as chromosome which consists of two parts: the first is entity chain and the second is activities chain with precedence relationship. The entity chain represents the selection of the candidates, and it's divided into $K$ segments and every segment has $\widetilde{A}_k$ bits. If value of bit $l$ in segment $k$ is 1, candidate $l$ is selected as the supplier of resource $k$. The activities chain with precedence relationship represents the order of activities in project scheduling based on which a serial scheduling schema is executed to gain a schedule[8].

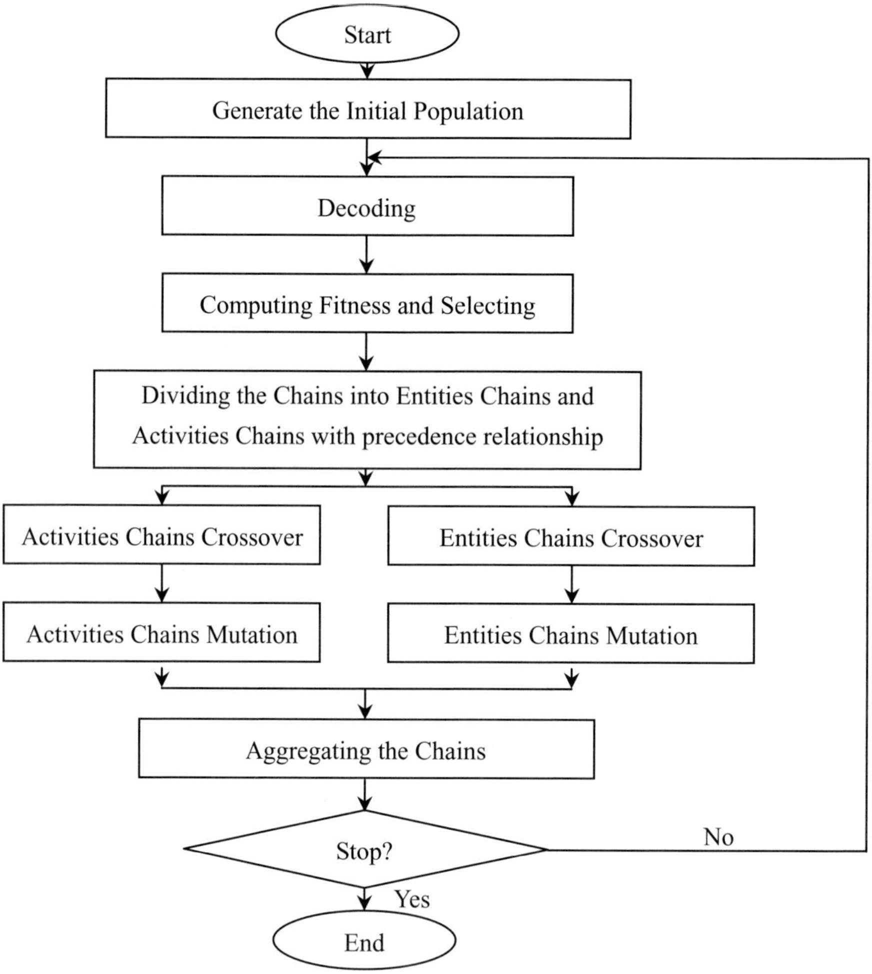


**Fig. 2.** The framework of the algorithm

For example, Fig.3 is an activity network represented by activity-on-node. The activities require 4-type of renewable resources and there are 3 candidates for every renewable resource. The following is a hybrid chains: 001|100|010|010||1 2 3 5 4 7 6 9 8 10 11. Before the mark ||, 001|100|010|010 represents the selection for 4-type of resources is 3,1,2,2 and after ||, 1 2 3 5 4 7 6 9 8 10 11 is an activities chain with precedence relationship.

The decoding procedure is as the following:

Step 1: Decoding the entity chain to get the selected candidates for resources;
Step 2: Form the new RCPSP with the objective of minimizing activities' cost with the parameters of the selected candidates;
Step 3: Based on the above problem, decoding the activities chain using the serial scheduling schema proposed in [8].

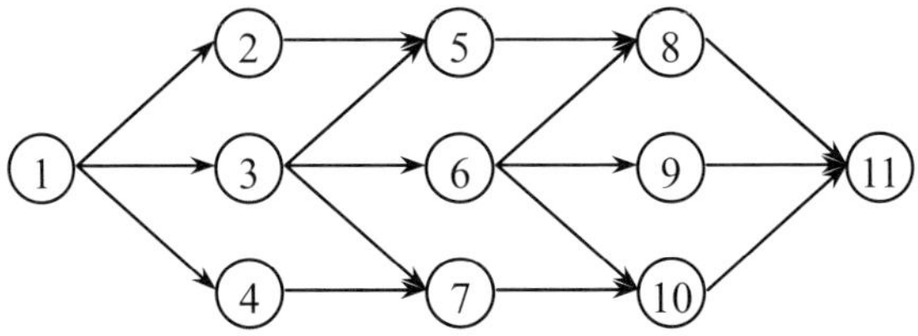

**Fig. 3.** An Example Activity Network

### 3.2 Fitness Function and Selection Scheme

The objective is to minimize the activities' cost so that a fitness measure is proposed according to the general principle of genetic algorithm: $f(s) = TV_m - TV(s)$ where $TV_m$ is a very large constant, and $TV(s)$ is the value of objective after chromosome $s$ has been decoded. Selection scheme is represented by stochastic tournament model with elitist preservation.

### 3.3 Genetic Operators

In the framework, the hybrid chains will be divided into entities chains and activities chains with precedence relationship. Then, the two series of chains will be evolved with different genetic operators. The entity chains consist of some segments which stand for selection schema for renewable resources, so a one-point crossover is set to exchange the content after some segment $k$ between the father chromosomes. For example, giving two father chains:

$$P_1\text{: } 00100|10000|01000|00010\text{ ; } P_2\text{: } 00001|00100|00010|01000$$

Choosing $k = 2$ to exchange the segments after segment 2, we can get the son chains:

$$S_1\text{: } 00100|10000|00010|01000\text{ ; } S_2\text{: } 00001|00100|01000|00010$$

Similarly, the mutation operator for the entity chains is set to change the schema of a segment. Consider as an example:

$$P\text{: } 00001|00100|00010|01000$$

Set $k = 3$ and change the selected status of candidate 2 to be 1, then the son chain is:

$$S\text{: } 00001|00100|01000|01000$$

The genetic operators over the activities chains with precedence relationship are designed to maintain the precedence relationship when evolving. To know the details, we can refer to the literature[8]. After executing the genetic operators, the two series of chains will be aggregated to form a new series of hybrid chains.

## 4 A Numerical Example

An example activity network is shown in Fig. 3 and there are 11 activities in the project in which 4 types of renewable resources are required. The duration, requirement for the resources and the non-resource cost of the activities are shown in Table 1.

Assume that there are 3 candidate suppliers for each renewable resource whose capacity and unit price for each resource is shown in Table 2. Giving $h = 0.01$ and $H = 30$.

The algorithm is coded by Matlab 6.5 and run on a Legend 460 P4-2GHz-256M with Windows XP. In the configuration of parameters of the algorithm, the preservation scale is 2, the population size is 12, the crossover probability is $P_c = 0.7$, the mutation probability is $P_m = 0.1$ and the tournament scale is 2. In addition, the computing procedure will stop when the average variance among the continuous 20-generation is less than 0.01 according to the general principle of genetic algorithm[10].

As Fig.4 shows, the procedure will stop at the 186th generation. The results show that convergence is fine. The best objective we get is $TV = 371.66$ and the selection schema of candidates for resources is 2,1,1,2.

**Table 1.** The Parameters of the Activities

| Activity | Duration | k=1 | k=2 | k=3 | k=4 | $v'$ |
|---|---|---|---|---|---|---|
| 1 | 4 | 4 | 3 | 1 | 5 | 4.1 |
| 2 | 3 | 6 | 2 | 3 | 2 | 2.7 |
| 3 | 2 | 5 | 6 | 1 | 3 | 1.8 |
| 4 | 4 | 3 | 3 | 4.5 | 4 | 1.8 |
| 5 | 3 | 2 | 4 | 3 | 3 | 2.4 |
| 6 | 3 | 4 | 2 | 2 | 2 | 2.2 |
| 7 | 3 | 4 | 1 | 1 | 2 | 0.8 |
| 8 | 2 | 6 | 5 | 2 | 2.5 | 1.8 |
| 9 | 2 | 2 | 3 | 2 | 1.5 | 1.0 |
| 10 | 2 | 2 | 5 | 1 | 2 | 1.8 |
| 11 | 4 | 4 | 7 | 1 | 3 | 3.6 |

**Table 2.** The resource parameters of candidate suppliers

| Candidate Suppliers | | k=1 | k=2 | k=3 | k=4 |
|---|---|---|---|---|---|
| 1 | Unit Price $C_{k\alpha}$ | 1.5 | 0.9 | 0.5 | 0.4 |
| | Capacity $Q_{k\alpha}$ | 10 | 9 | 6 | 8 |
| 2 | Unit Price $C_{k\alpha}$ | 1.2 | 1.0 | 0.8 | 0.35 |
| | Capacity $Q_{k\alpha}$ | 9 | 10 | 12 | 7 |
| 3 | Unit Price $C_{k\alpha}$ | 1.8 | 1.3 | 0.7 | 0.45 |
| | Capacity $Q_{k\alpha}$ | 13 | 12 | 8 | 9 |

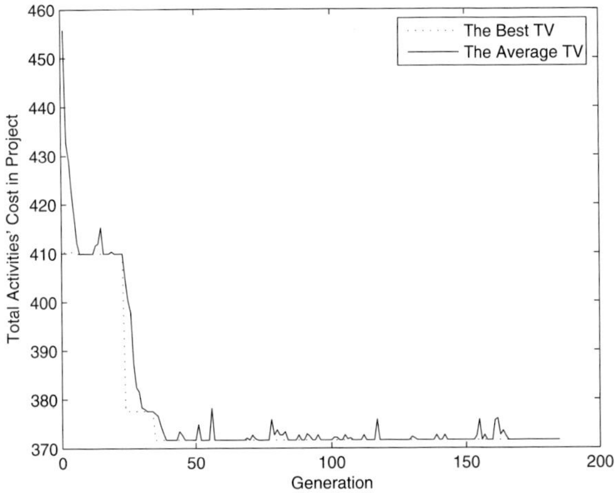


**Fig. 4.** The effect of the parameters of activity network on GA

## 5 Conclusion

Selecting suppliers for renewable resources is an important task in construction supply chain that has a direct effect on controlling progress, quality and cost of the construction project. This paper has considered the capacity of the renewable resources' suppliers as constraint for project scheduling and given out the selection model based on project scheduling with the objective of minimizing the activities' cost in project. To solve the problem, a hybrid genetic algorithm was designed. In practice, people often consider multiple objectives such as quality, customer service and credit besides progress and cost. This type of problems is one of which we will focus our mind on in the future.

## Acknowledgments

The work was supported by the National Science Foundation of China(7017015) and The Teaching and Research Award Fund for Outstanding Young Teachers in Higher Education Institutions of MOE, P.R. China.

## References

1. Weber C.A., Current J.R., Benton W.C.: Vendor Selection Criteria and Methods. European Journal of Operational Research,**50** (1991) 2-18
2. Liu X., Li H.Y., Wang Ch.E.: A Survey of Supplier Selection Models and Approaches. Chinese Journal of Management Science,**1** (2004) 139-148
3. Wang D.W., Yung K.L., Lp, W.H.: Partner Selection Model and Soft Computing Approach for Dynamic Alliance of Enterprises. Science in China(Series F),**6** (2002) 68-80

4. Wang D.W., Ip W.H., Yung K. L.: A Heuristic Genetic Algorithm for Subcontractor Selection in a Global Manufacturing Environment. IEEE Transactions on Systems Man and Cybernetics Part C-Applications and Reviews,**2** (2001) 189-198
5. Ip W.H., Huang M., Yung K. L. et al: Genetic Algorithm for a Risk-based Partner Selection Problem in a Virtual Enterprise. Computers and Operations Research,**2** (2002) 213-231
6. Dainty R.J., Geoffrey B., Millett S.: New Perspectives on Construction Supply Chain Integration. Supply Chain Management: An International Journal,**4** (2001) 163-173
7. Wang Y. W., Xue X. L.: Improving Construction Performance through Supply Chain Management. Journal of Harbin Institute of Technology(New Series),**5** (2004) 528-532
8. Liu, Z.Y., Wang, H.W.: GA-based Resource-Constrained Project Scheduling with the Objective of Minimizing Activities' Cost. Lecture Notes in Computation Science,**3644** (2005) 937-946
9. Kolisch R., Sprecher A.: PSPLIB-A Project Scheduling Problem Library. European Journal of Operational Research,**1**(1996) 205-216
10. Zhou M., Sun Sh. D.: The Principle and Application of Genetic Algorithm. Defence Industry Press(China) (1999)

# Time Based Congestion Control (TBCC) for High Speed High Delay Networks

Yanping Xiang[1], Jianqiang Yi[1], Dongbin Zhao[1], and John T. Wen[2]

[1] Key Laboratory of Complex Systems & Intelligence Science, Institute of Automation, Chinese Academy of Sciences, 100080 Beijing, China
{yanping.xiang, jianqiang.yi, dongbin.zhao}@ia.ac.cn

[2] Department of Electrical, Computer, and Systems Engineering, Rensselaer Polytechnic Institute, 12180 Troy, NY USA
wen@cat.rpi.edu

**Abstract.** High speed networks with high delays present a unique environment where TCP can not efficiently utilize the full bandwidth. In this paper, we present a simple and novel Time Based Congestion Control scheme (TBCC for short) that alleviates RTT unfairness while supporting TCP friendliness and bandwidth scalability. We provide the general framework for TBCC protocol modifications. Then, using a simplified design, we illustrate the scalability of TBCC for improving the efficiency, without sacrificing the fairness of TCP. We assess the RTT unfairness of TBCC and show that the RTT unfairness of TBCC can be firmly guaranteed to be no worse than that of unmodified TCP. Compared with similar protocols such as HSTCP and STCP, TBCC can guarantee the bandwidth scalability and achieve better fairness. The flexible framework of TBCC provides a whole class of design options for improving the performance of TCP in high speed networks.

## 1 Introduction

TCP increases its congestion window by one packet per Round-Trip Time (RTT) in congestion avoidance phase and reduces it by half at a loss event. In high speed networks, the congestion avoidance phase of TCP takes a very long time to increase the window size. And the effect of random packet losses on TCP cannot be ignored, since they may limit the TCP throughput more than the congestion losses do and may lead to a poor utilization of the large available capacity. The window increase rate is unnecessarily fixed at only one packet per Round-Trip Time (RTT), which makes TCP inefficient in the high speed environment.

*Related Work*: Several promising solutions have been put forward for solving the problem. These solutions can be classified into four main categories [1]: a) Tuning the network stack. [2], [3], [4] and [5] are some of the examples. Tuning the stack improves the performance significantly and is best used in conjunction with other solutions mentioned below. b) Opening parallel TCP connections between the end hosts ([6], [7], [8], [9], [10]). c) Modifications to the TCP congestion control. This category of research modifies the congestion response function of TCP. High Speed TCP [11], scalable TCP [12], FAST TCP [13], Bic-TCP [14] and H-TCP [15] are

D.-S. Huang, K. Li, and G.W. Irwin (Eds.): ICIC 2006, LNCS 4113, pp. 863 – 874, 2006.

some of examples in this area. d) Modifications to the network infrastructure or use of non-TCP transport protocol. Some schemes go beyond modifications only to TCP and use either UDP or rely on support from the network infrastructure. XCP [16], Tsunami [17], RBUDP [18], SABUL/UDT [19] and GTP [20] are some of the examples.

In this paper, we propose the TBCC which modifies the congestion response function of TCP at the sender-side and requires no additional support from the network infrastructure or the receivers. We focus on improving the TCP performance on high speed high delay links through a simple time based technique, wherein, the increase rate and decrease rate of congestion window are adaptively adjusted based on time intervals between two consecutive loss events. Compared with similar protocols such as HSTCP and STCP, TBCC can guarantee the scalability and achieve better fairness. In HSTCP and STCP, a larger window increases faster than a smaller window. Compounded with delay differences, RTT unfairness gets worse as the window of a shorter RTT flow grows faster than that of a longer RTT flow. The severe RTT unfairness of HSTCP and STCP comes from their adaptability, ironically, the very reason that makes them more scalable to large bandwidth [13] [14]. TBCC overcomes these limitations.

The rest of this paper is organized as follows: Section 2 gives model assumptions and simplifications. Section 3 provides the general framework for the TBCC scheme. In Section 4, we discuss one possible design of TBCC class and presents analyses pertaining to it. Conclusions and future work are summarized in section 5.

## 2 Assumptions and Simplifications

To simplify the analysis, various assumptions and simplifications which have been made in the analysis are summarized below:

- We assume that the sender always has data to send (i.e. a saturated sender). The receiver always advertises a large enough receiver window size such that the send window size is determined by the congestion window size [21].
- Since the slow start phase is very short. We focus on congestion avoidance mechanisms. The impact of slow start has been ignored.

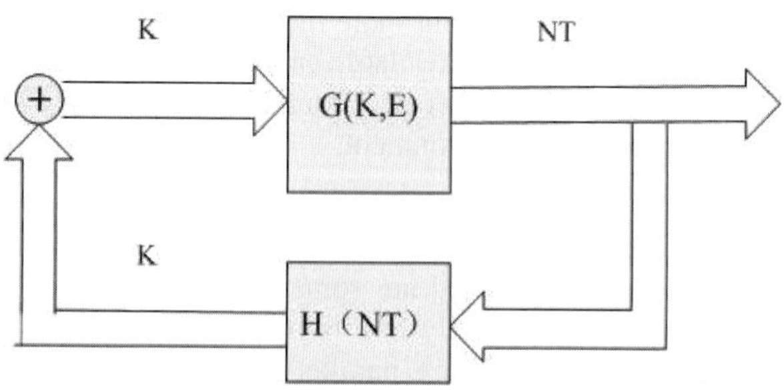


**Fig. 1.** The whole network can be considered as a time interval feedback control system

- We model congestion avoidance behavior in terms of rounds. A round starts with the back-to-back transmission of W packets, where W is the current window size. In this model, the duration of a round is equal to the Round-Trip time and is assumed to be independent of the window size. Also, it is assumed that the time needed to send all of the packets in a window is smaller than the Round-Trip time [21].
- We consider multiple losses in one window as one loss event.

## 3 Time Based TCP: The Framework

It is challenging to design a protocol that can satisfy all three criteria: RTT fairness, scalability, and TCP friendliness. We design TBCC protocol under the following criteria [1]: (a) the congestion response function should scale in high speed networks. (b) the TBCC flows should be fair to each other when they have the same RTT. (c) the unfairness of TBCC flows with different RTTs should be at least no worse than the unfairness between unmodified TCP flows with similar RTTs. (d) The TBCC flows should be fair to TCP flows under high loss rates.

In TBCC, we extend the existing AIMD [22] algorithms of TCP. A TBCC flow increases its congestion window by $k$ packets per RTT and decreases it by $e*W$, where $W$ is the current window size when a loss event is detected. It is the time interval between two consecutive loss events instead of window size or current sending rate that determine the congestion window increase rate $k$ and decrease rate $b$.

Suppose the network is shared by n flows, $K= [k_1, k_2 ... k_n]$, $E= [e_1, e_2... e_n]$, where, $K$ is the increase rates vector and $E$ is the decrease rates vector. The whole network can be considered as a time interval feedback control system, which is described in Figure 1, where, $NT= [t_1, t_2... t_n]$ is time interval vector. When $k_i$ increases or $e_i$ decreases, it is easier to get a loss event and $t_i$ decreases. When $k_i$ decreases or $e_i$ increases, it is more difficult to get a loss event and $t_i$ increases. So $t_i$ can be considered as a decreasing function of $k_i$ and increasing function of $e_i$. Here, we simplify the network and describe it by a simple binary function: $T=G(K, E)$. Since networks with larger bandwidth and RTTs correspond to longer time intervals. The increase rate $k_i$ should be an increasing function of time intervals $t_i$: $k_i = in(t_i)$. And the decrease rate $e_i$ should be a decreasing function of time intervals $t_i$: $e_i=de(t_i)$. So we get the feedback function: $[K, E]=H(NT)=[In(NT), De(NT)]$, where, $In(NT)=[in(t_1), in(t_2), \ldots, in(t_n)]$, $De(NT)= [de(t_1), de(t_2), \ldots, de(t_n)]$. The primal task of TBCC is to design the feedback function. In addition to satisfy the criteria mentioned above, the feedback function $H(NT) = [In(NT), De(NT)]$ should also be chosen appropriately to guarantee the convergence of $K$, $E$ and $NT$.

To meet the fairness criteria, the increase and decrease rates of different flows must be the same or be asymptotically the same. Consider the single bottleneck model. In synchronous loss environment, flows get loss events at the same time and the time intervals between losses of these flows are the same, even if they have different windows and RTTs. So these flows' increase rates and decrease rates, which are calculated by the feedback function $H(NT)$, are the same respectively. In random loss environment, suppose the mathematical expectation of the loss rate is $p$. When TBCC flows have the same RTT, their mathematical expectations of time intervals are the same. So the increase rates and decrease rates of these flows are statistically equal to each other respectively. When TBCC flows have different RTTs, flows with lager RTTs or smaller windows usually have lower throughputs and longer time intervals, which leads to lager increase rate and lower decrease rate to compensate its throughput. More detailed analysis can be seen in the sections below. It is confirmed that TBCC flows are fair to each other when they have the same RTT and the unfairness of TBCC flows with different RTTs is at least no worse than the unfairness between unmodified TCP flows with similar RTTs.

In TBCC, when the time intervals between two consecutive loss events is below a predefined threshold $t_0$, the increase rate and decrease rate are equal to that of TCP respectively. Since short time intervals correspond to high loss rate or short RTT, TBCC behaves exactly the same as TCP does under high loss rates.

## 4 A Design Choice

Several different design options are possible for choosing the appropriate feedback function *H (NT)*. Since we want to keep the design as close to that of TCP as possible, we only change the increasing method and set the decrease rate $e_i$ to a fixed value: *0.5*, which is equal to that of TCP. In this section, we first analyze the network model, then present one possible design of TBCC. We support this design with extensive analysis to understand the TBCC behavior.

### 4.1 Model Analysis

Since *E* is a constant vector, *G (K, E)* can be simplified as *G(K)*. In this part, we analyze the network model *G (K)* and give the steady-state relationship between *T* and *K*, where *K* is fixed. First, we set the parameters of the single bottleneck model and give some assumptions. The maximum bandwidth of a bottleneck link, which is shared by n flows ( $f_1$, $f_2$, …, $f_n$.), is fixed at *B(bps)*. The Round-Trip time (*RTT*) of these flows is set to *R1, R2… Rn* respectively. The packet size is set to *D (bytes)*.

In synchronous loss environment, the time intervals between two consecutive loss events of all flows are the same: $t_1=t_2=\ldots t_n= t$. So the increase rate of these flows is the same: $k_1 = k_2= \ldots = k_n = k$. The maximum number of packets across the bottleneck link per second is *B/(8D)*. Since $e_i$=*0.5,* the window increment between two consecutive loss events is a half of the maximum window size in steady-state. When a congestion event is detected, the numbers of packets sent per second by these flows are $2tk/R_1^2$, $2tk/R_2^2, \ldots, 2tk/R_n^2$ respectively. Thus, we obtain an equation:

$$\frac{2tk}{R_1^2}+\frac{2tk}{R_2^2}+,\ldots,+\frac{2tk}{R_n^2}=\frac{B}{8D}. \quad (1)$$

The relationship between *T* and *K* can be expressed as:

$$t=\frac{B}{16D(\frac{1}{R_1^2}+\frac{1}{R_2^2}+,\ldots,+\frac{1}{R_n^2})k}. \quad (2)$$

Let

$$U = \frac{B}{16D(\frac{1}{R_1^2} + \frac{1}{R_2^2} +,...,+ \frac{1}{R_n^2})} . \tag{3}$$

then we have

$$t = \frac{U}{k} . \tag{4}$$

We can see that $t$ and $k$ have an inverse relation in synchronous environment.

In random loss environment, we select a random flow $f_j$, its Round-Trip time is $R_j$ and increase rate is $k_j$. The time interval between two consecutive loss events is $t_j$. In [25], for random loss model the probability of the packet loss $p_i$ is given by

$$p_j = \frac{A_j(w_j^*, R_j)}{A_j(w_j^*, R_j) + B_j(w_j^*, R_j)} . \tag{5}$$

where $A_j(w_j^*, R_j)$ and $B_j(w_j^*, R_j)$ are the window increase and decrease functions respectively. And $w_j^*$ is the statistical equilibrium window.

For TBCC, $A_j(w_j^*, R_j) = k_j/w^*$ and $B_j(w_j^*, R_j) = 0.5\, w_j^*$. Substituting these values in the above equation, we can calculated the loss rate as

$$p_j = \frac{1}{1 + \frac{0.5 w_j^{*2}}{k_j}} \approx \frac{k_j}{0.5 w_j^{*2}} \qquad (\frac{0.5 w_j^{*2}}{k_j} >> 1). \tag{6}$$

Since $w_j^* \propto k_j \frac{t_j}{R_j}$, let $w_j^* = \theta k_j \frac{t_j}{R_j}$, where $\theta$ is a constant, we can get

$$p_j = \frac{1}{0.5\theta^2 k_j (\frac{t_j}{R_j})^2} . \tag{7}$$

$$\Rightarrow t_j = \frac{R_j}{\theta \sqrt{0.5 p_j} \sqrt{k_j}} . \tag{8}$$

Let $V = \frac{R_j}{\theta \sqrt{0.5 p_j}}$ then we have $t_j = \frac{V}{\sqrt{k_j}}$.

We can see that $t_j$ and $\sqrt{k_j}$ have an inverse relation in asynchronous environment.

### 4.2 Our Design

For our design, the decrease behaviours are equal to that of TCP. In this part, we give the increase behaviours by simple feedback functions:

$$k = in(t_A) = (t_A / t_0)^c . \tag{9}$$

$$t_A = r\,t + (1 - r)\,t_A . \tag{10}$$

where, $c$ and $r$ $(0<r<1)$ are predefined constants, $t_A$ is weighted average of $t$. So $K = In(NT) = [\, in(t_{A1}), in(t_{A2}), \ldots, in(t_{An}) \,]$. In this section, a weighted average method is used to avoid violent oscillation of $t$ and $k$. This method limits the oscillation, and smoothes the value of $t$ and $k$. If we choose $c$ and $r$ appropriately, $NT$ and $K$ can converge to stable values. This can be confirmed by the analysis and simulation below and the transient effect of $G(K)$ is ignored.

In synchronous loss environment, let the sequence of $t$, $t_A$ and $k$ are $t(1), t(2), \ldots, t(i), \ldots$; $t_A(1), t_A(2), \ldots, t_A(i), \ldots$ and $k(1), k(2), \ldots, k(i), \ldots$ respectively. Suppose the initial value of $t_A$ is $t_A(0)$, then we obtain

$$\begin{aligned} t_A(i) &= rt(i) + (1-r)t_A(i-1) = rt(i) + r(1-r)t(i-1) + \ldots + r(1-r)^{i-1}t(1) \\ &\quad + (1-r)^i t_A(0) \end{aligned} . \tag{11}$$

Consider (4), we can get

$$t_A(i) = r\frac{U}{k(i)} + r(1-r)\frac{U}{k(i-1)} + \ldots + r(1-r)^{i-1}\frac{U}{k(1)} + (1-r)^i t_A(0) \tag{12}$$

Substitute the above equation into (9), we have

$$k(i) = [\frac{t_A(i-1)}{t_0}]^c = (\frac{rU}{t_0})^c [\frac{1}{k(i-1)} + \frac{1-r}{k(i-2)} + \ldots + \frac{(1-r)^{i-2}}{k(1)} + (1-r)^{i-1} t_A(0)]^c . \tag{13}$$

and

$$k(i+1) = [\frac{t_A(i)}{t_0}]^c = (\frac{rU}{t_0})^c [\frac{1}{k(i)} + \frac{1-r}{k(i-1)} + \ldots + \frac{(1-r)^{i-1}}{k(1)} + (1-r)^i t_A(0)]^c . \tag{14}$$

Combining (13) and (14), we obtain that

$$k(i+1)^{\frac{1}{c}} = (1-r)k(i)^{\frac{1}{c}} + \frac{rU}{t_0}\frac{1}{k(i)} . \tag{15}$$

The above recurrent formula is convergent, when $c$ and $r$ satisfy certain condition. We give the empirical convergence condition by simulation as Fig. 2. When a $r$ is given, c < CM. In random loss environment, the process is similar and the convergence condition is: c < 2CM.

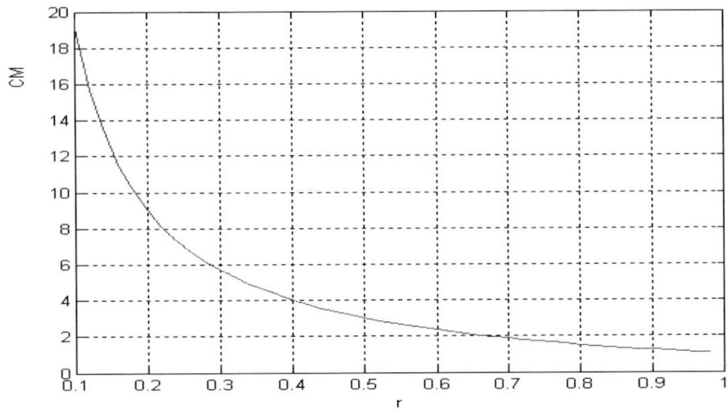


**Fig. 2.** The convergence condition: c < CM

To be more compatible with current TCP in high loss rate environment, we set $k$=1.0 when $t_A < t_0$. So it behaves exactly the same as TCP does under high loss rates.

## 4.3 Response Function

In this section, following a similar analysis in [14], we present a deterministic analysis on the response function of TBCC. Suppose that the loss events of flow *fi* are uniformly distributed with rate $p$. The total number of packets sent by a flow between its two consecutive loss events is $1/p$. Let $t$ denote the time interval between two consecutive loss events of a flow during steady state. The total number of RTTs between two consecutive loss events is $t/R$. So the average window size can be obtained as follows

$$w = \frac{1/p}{t/R} = \frac{1}{p}\frac{R}{t} \ . \tag{16}$$

Let R(p) denote the response function of a protocol, which is the average sending rate of the protocol in the unit of packets per RTT, in terms of a loss event rate $p$.

During steady state, $t$ and $k$ are invariant, $t_A = t$. So $k$ and $t$ can be calculated as:

$$t = \frac{\frac{2}{3}w}{k}R \ . \tag{17}$$

$$k = (\frac{t}{t_0})^c \ . \tag{18}$$

Combining (17) and (18), we obtain that

$$t = (\frac{2}{3}t_0^{\,c}Rw)^{\frac{1}{1+c}} \ . \tag{19}$$

Combining (19) and (16), we get

$$w = \frac{R^{\frac{c}{2+c}}}{(\frac{2}{3}t_0^{\ c})^{\frac{1}{2+c}} p^{\frac{1+c}{2+c}}} . \tag{20}$$

For TBCC, its response function is

$$R(p) = \frac{1}{R} \frac{(\frac{2}{3}t_0^{\ c})^{-\frac{1}{2+c}} R^{\frac{c}{2+c}}}{p^{\frac{1+c}{2+c}}} . \tag{21}$$

For HSTCP, STCP, and TCP, their response functions are of form [14]: $R(p) = \frac{1}{R}\frac{A}{p^d}$, where $A$ and $d$ are protocol dependent constants. The value of $d$ is between 0.5 and 1 [23]. The value of ($A$, d) for TCP [24], HSTCP [11], and STCP [12] is ($\sqrt{1.5}$, 0.5), (0.15, 0.82), and (0.08, 1), respectively. Set $t_0$ = *1.5 seconds*, $R$=0.1 *seconds* and $c$ = 3.2. The response functions of TBCC, HSTCP, STCP, TCP is shown in Figure 3 in a log-log scale.

In Figure 3, TBCC shows a similar scalability as HSTCP. In fact, the slope of TBCC's response function is determined by $c$. A larger $c$ corresponds to a larger slope, and the slope of TBCC is no larger than that of STCP and no less than that of TCP. The analysis results below indicate that the fairness criterion is firmly guaranteed and is not influenced by the slope of TBCC's response function. So we can design the response function more freely to obtain better performances. For HSTCP, STCP, and TCP, the RTT unfairness gets worse as the slope gets lager. HSTCP and STCP improved throughput and responsiveness over TCP at the cost of fairness [13] [14].

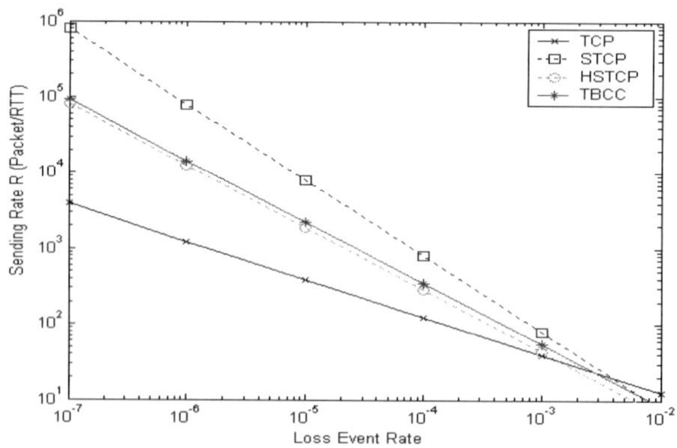


**Fig. 3.** Response Functions of various protocols

### 4.4 RTT Unfairness Analysis

We consider the RTT unfairness of TBCC under both synchronous loss model and random loss model. Let $w_i$, $t_i$, $T_i$ and $R_i$ denote the average window size, the time interval between two consecutive loss events, the average throughput and the RTT of flow $i$ ( $i$ =1,2) respectively.

In synchronous loss environment, $t_1 = t_2$. Since $1/p_i$ is the total number of packets sent by a flow between its two consecutive loss events, $1/p_i$ can be calculated as

$$\frac{1}{p_i}=\frac{3}{2}(\frac{t_i}{R_i})^2 k_i=\frac{3}{2}(\frac{t_i}{R_i})^2 in(t_i) \ . \tag{22}$$

Substitute the above equation into (16), we have

$$\frac{w_i}{R_i}=\frac{1}{p_i}\frac{1}{t_i}=\frac{3}{2}(\frac{t_i}{R_i})^2 in(t_i)\frac{1}{t_i} \ . \tag{23}$$

Therefore the RTT unfairness of the two flows, the ratio of their average throughputs, can be calculated as

$$\frac{T_1}{T_2}=\frac{(w_1/R_1)(1-p_1)}{(w_2/R_2)(1-p_2)}\approx\frac{(w_1/R_1)}{(w_2/R_2)}=(\frac{R_2}{R_1})^2 \ . \tag{24}$$

where (1- $p_i$) is approximated by 1, since $p_i$ is usually far less than 1.It is clear that TBCC has the same RTT unfairness as that of TCP under synchronous loss model. For TCP, HSTCP and STCP, throughput at the equilibrium point becomes proportional to $(R_2/R_1)^{1/(1-d)}$ and the exponent $1/(1-d)$ is 2.0, 5.56, and $\infty$ respectively [14].

In random loss environment, $p_1$=$p_2$. Consider the equation (6), we can get

$$\frac{w_i}{R_i}=\frac{\sqrt{k_i}}{R_i\sqrt{p_i/2}}=\frac{\sqrt{in(t_i)}}{R_i\sqrt{p_i/2}} \ . \tag{25}$$

Since $t_i=\frac{1}{p_iT_i}$, we have

$$\frac{T_1}{T_2}=\frac{(w_1/R_1)(1-p_1)}{(w_2/R_2)(1-p_2)}\approx\sqrt{\frac{in(\frac{1}{p_1T_1})}{in(\frac{1}{p_2T_2})}}\frac{R_2}{R_1} \ . \tag{26}$$

A flow with larger RTT usually achieves lower throughput and $in(t_i)$ is an increasing function. Suppose $R_1$<$R_2$, then $T_1$>$T_2$. The following inequality can be obtained

$$1<\frac{T_1}{T_2}<\frac{R_2}{R_1} \ . \tag{27}$$

TBCC successfully limits the RTT unfairness. The throughput of TBCC flows with longer RTT or smaller window is partly compensated by larger increase rate. For TCP, throughput at the equilibrium point becomes inversely proportional to its round trip time [1]. For HSTCP and STCP, the RTT unfairness is worse than TCP under random models [2] [3]. So ccompared with TCP, HSTCP and STCP, TBCC can get better fairness.

Note that, TBCC will satisfy the fairness criteria, if the feedback function $in(t)$ satisfies a loose constraint: the feedback function $in(t)$ should be a positive and increasing function of $t$.

### 4.5 Alternate Designs

Since the fairness is well guaranteed, the flexible framework of TBCC provides a whole class of design options for improving the performance of TCP in high speed networks. Under the framework, we could choose other feedback functions (such as logarithmic function) to achieve better performances. The decrease rate can also be a function of the time intervals or be set to a smaller value to avoid violent oscillation of the congestion window. We are currently in the process of evaluating other designs. Details will be made available in a technical report.

## 5 Conclusions and Future Work

In this paper, we have proposed a simple and novel Time Based Congestion Control scheme (TBCC) for high speed high delay links. The increase and decrease rate of congestion window is adaptively adjusted based on time interval between two consecutive losses instead of current window size or sending rate. TBCC modifies the behavior of TCP at the sender-side and requires no additional support from the network infrastructure or the receivers. Fairiness is well guaranteed and a whole class of design options is provided by the TBCC framework. We give one of the designs and support the design with extensive analysis. The preliminary analysis results indicate that TBCC can utilize the large available bandwidth efficiently and can achieve better fairness in high speed environment. Due to lack of space, rounded simulation results have not been included in this paper. They will be presented in a subsequent paper. We note that a number of other possibilities exist for alternate designs of general TBCC and more detailed analysis and simulation remain to be done in the future.

## Acknowledgments

This work was supported in part by NSFC Projects (No. 60334020, 60440420130) and the Outstanding Overseas Chinese Scholars Fund of Chinese Academy of Sciences (No. 2005-1-11).

## References

1. Bhandarkar, S., Jain S., Narasimha R. A. L.: Improving TCP Performance in High Bandwidth High RTT Links Using Layered Congestion Control. PFLDNet 2005, Lyon France (2005)
2. Semke, J., Mahdavi, J., Mathis, Ma.: Automatic TCP Buffer Tuning. Computer Communication Review, Vol. 28, n 4. (1998) 315-323

3. Weigle, E., Feng, W.: Dynamic Right-Sizing: a Simulation Study. Proceedings of IEEE International Conference on Computer Communications and Networks (ICCCN) ( 2001)
4. Tierney, B. L., Gunter, D., Lee, J., Stoufer, M., Evans, J. B.: Enabling Network-Aware Applications. IEEE International Symposium on High Performance Distributed Computing, Proceedings (2001) 281-288
5. Dunigan, T., Mathis, M., Tierney, B.: A TCP Tuning Daemon. Proceedings of the 2002 ACM/IEEE conference on Supercomputing (2002) 1-16
6. Ostermann, S., Allman, M., Kruse, H.: An Application-Level solution to TCP's Satellite Inefficiencies. Proceedings of Workshop on Satellite-Based Information Services (WOSBIS), Rye NY (1996)
7. Lee, J., Gunter, D., Tierney, B., Allcock, B., Bester, J., Bresnahan, J., Tuecke, S.: Applied Techniques for High Bandwidth Data Transfers across Wide Area Networks. Proceedings of International Conference on Computing in High Energy and Nuclear Physics, LBNL-46269, Vol. 7. Beijing China (2001)
8. Baru, C., Moore, R., Rajasekar, A., Wan, M.: The SDSC storage resource broker. Proc. CASCON'98 Conference, Toronto Canada (1998)
9. Long, R., Berman, L. E., Neve, L., Roy, G., Thoma, G. R.: An application-level technique for faster transmission of large images on the Internet. Proceedings of SPIE: Multimedia Computing and Networking 1995, Vol. 2417. San Jose CA (1995)
10. Sivakumar, H., Bailey, S., Grossman, R.: PSockets: The Case for Application-level Network Striping for Data Intensive Applications using High Speed Wide Area Networks. Proceedings of the 2000 ACM/IEEE Conference on Supercomputing (CDROM), IEEE Computer Society, Washington DC USA (2000) 38
11. Floyd, S.: HighSpeed TCP for Large Congestion Windows. RFC3649 December 2003
12. Kelly, T.: Scalable TCP: Improving Performance in HighSpeed Wide Area Networks. COMPUTER COMMUNICATION REVIEW, Vol. 33 (2). APR (2003)
13. Cheng, J., Wei, D. X., Low, S. H.: FAST TCP: motivation, architecture, algorithms, performance. Twenty-Third Annual Joint Conference of the IEEE Computer and Communications Societies (2004) 2490-2501
14. Xu, L., Harfoush, K., Rhee, I.: Binary Increase Congestion Control for Fast Long-Distance Networks. Twenty-Third Annual Joint Conference of the IEEE Computer and Communications Societies (2004) 2514-2524
15. Shorten, R. N., Leith, D. J., Foy, J., Kilduff, R.: Analysis and design of congestion control in synchronized communication networks. Proceedings of the 12th Yale Workshop on Adaptive and Learning Systems, Chatham USA (2003)
16. Katabi, D., Handley, M., Rohrs, C.: Congestion Control for High Bandwidth-Delay Product Networks. COMPUTER COMMUNICATION REVIEW, Vol. 32 (4). (2002) 89-102
17. README file of tsunami-2002-12-02 release. http://www.indiana.edu/anml/anmlresearch.html.
18. He, E., Leigh, J., Yu, O., DeFanti, T. A.: Reliable Blast UDP : Predictable High Performance Bulk Data Transfer", Proceedings of the IEEE International Conference on Cluster Computing (2002) 317
19. Sivakumar, H., Grossman, R., Mazzucco, M., Pan, Y., Zhang, Q.: Simple Available Bandwidth Utilization Library for High-Speed Wide Area Networks. Journal of Supercomputing, Vol. 34. (2005) 231-242
20. Wu, R.X., Chien, A.A.: GTP: Group Transport Protocol for Lambda-Grids. 2004 IEEE International Symposium on Cluster Computing and the Grid, CCGrid (2004) 228-238.

21. Yang, Y. R., Lam, S. S., General AIMD Congestion Control, Proc. of the ICNP 2000. Osaka: IEEE Computer Society (2000)187-198
22. Jacbson, V.: Congestion avoidance and control. ACM Computer Communication Review, Vol. 18 (1988) 314-329
23. Floyd, S.: HighSpeed TCP for large congestion windows. IETF, INTERNET DRAFT, draft-floyd-tcp-highspeed-01.txt (2003)
24. Floyd, S., Handley, M., Padhye, J.: A comparison of equation-based and AIMD congestion control. http://www.icir.org/tfrc/ (2000)
25. Golestani, S. J., Sabnani, K. K.: Fundamental observations on multicast congestion control in the Internet. Proc. IEEE INFOCOM (1999) 990-1000

# A DEA-Benchmarking Optimization Model and Method Based on the Theory of Maximum Entropy*

Yin-sheng Yang, Ning Li, Hai-cun Liu, and Hong-peng Guo**

School of Biological and Agricultural Engineering, Jilin University
(Nanling Campus), 5988 Renmin Street, Changchun 130022, P.R. China

**Abstract.** Benchmarking is a technique that engages and executes a series of measures to change indexes of the Decision Making Unit (DMU) to excellent by using the gap analysis information between the DMU and benchmark. In this paper, a DEA-Benchmarking model based on the theory of maximum entropy is proposed and the conception of Entropy-DEA efficiency is defined. According to the optimization model based on the theory of maximum entropy, the Entropy-DEA efficient DMUs is regarded as benchmarks, which have more advantages and direction than DEA efficient DMUs. The measure method and existence property of Entropy-DEA efficiency are all analyzed in this paper.

## 1 Introduction

DEA proposed by A. Charnes and W. W. Cooper et al. in 1978 is a non-parametrical optimization technique used to evaluate the relative efficiencies of DMUs. DEA can identify the relative efficient DMUs in multiple inputs and multiple outputs system by constructing a frontier which is composed of excellent DMUs and then measuring efficiency which is relative to that frontier by using the properties of convexity[6,7,8]. If the DMUs posited on the frontier, the DMU is denoted as DEA efficient, otherwise the DMU is inefficient.

Benchmarking is a technique which takes the relative efficient DMUs as study standard and obtains the improving information by using the comparison analysis between the improving DMUs and the benchmark[3]. The quantitative methods, such as statistical algorithm and regression analysis are often used when comparing the proceeding of benchmarking. However, because of the existence of random errors and approximation of statistical distribution, induce the absence of the methods mentioned above. The method also lacks of the ability of dealing multiple inputs and outputs system in gap analysis. The methods can't

* Supported by the National Science Foundation of China (No. 70571028).

** Corresponding author: Tel.:086-431-5095726, ghp@jlu.edu.cn

D.-S. Huang, K. Li, and G.W. Irwin (Eds.): ICIC 2006, LNCS 4113, pp. 875–882, 2006.

provide the effective information of reducing the distance between DMU and benchmarks. The effect of benchmarking is limited by the disadvantages of the methods mentioned above.

The procession of Benchmarking is introduced in section two. In section three, the conception of information entropy and the theory of maximum entropy are defined, and the way of constructing a DEA-Benchmarking optimization model based on the theory of maximum entropy is proposed. The measure method and existence property of Entropy-DEA efficiency are all analyzed in this section. The conclusion and prospect of the research in this field are showed in section four.

## 2 The Basic Procedure in Benchmarking

Benchmarking is a systemic and durative proceeding to improve the DMUs performance. First, we should identify the research field and corresponding indexes in the procedure comparing the performance of DMUs. Secondly, the excellent performance benchmarks in the field mentioned above should be selected. At last, we reach the goal of improving DMUs performance and reducing the distance between DMUs and benchmarks by comparing their indexes between improving units and benchmarks. In the course of analysis how to identify the distance between DMUs and benchmarks is the core of benchmarking. The DMUs should be evaluated and compared in the view of multiple inputs and outputs system. The application of DEA to the gap analysis is efficient, which can calculate the relative efficiency of multiple inputs and outputs DMUs.

## 3 DEA-Benchmarking Model and Method Based on the Theory of Maximum Entropy

To apply DEA to benchmarking can identify the unit with excellent performance as benchmarks in the view of technical and scale efficiency. A comprehensive evaluation method, DEA-Benchmarking, can be constructed by integrating the advantage of DEA in the aspect of dealing with multiple indexes and that of benchmarking in comparing and evaluation. The DEA-Benchmarking method can identify efficient benchmarks as the goal of the other inefficient DMUs in the system, identify corresponding benchmarks, and provide more accurate analysis and evaluation for additive DMUs. It plays an important role to perfect the function of the system. Two key procedures in the DEA-Benchmarking method are (1) to identify benchmarks by integrated DEA model and benchmarking; (2) to identify the improving information of its input and output indexes by using the gap analysis of DMUs and benchmarks.

The key technique of DEA-Benchmarking is to obtain accurate DMUs' improving information used to improve DMUs. DEA-Benchmarking model based on the theory of maximum entropy, with integrated the maximum entropy theory to DEA-Benchmarking, has been explored in this paper.

### 3.1 The Theory of Entropy

According to information theory, entropy is a measure to scale the system's degree of out-of-order. To a series of random events, the bigger the uncertainty of the system is, the bigger output information entropy value is. On the other hand, the smaller the entropy value is, the more ordered the system is. The necessity event's information entropy equal to zero, then equal probable event has the maximum information entropy. In the view of information science, entropy is a measure concerning the uncertainty of a system. If there is a random test with $n$ kinds of states $x_1, x_2, \ldots, x_n$ , which have corresponding occurrence probability denoted by $P_1, P_2, \ldots, P_n$ . Although the event with bigger probability has more chance to happen, we can't identify the certain result before the test, which is the uncertainty and out-of-order property of random events.

Shannon defined the uncertainty as the follows mathematic form:

$$S = -k_0 \sum_{i=1}^{n} P_i \ln P_i \tag{1}$$

where $S$ is defined as information entropy, $k_0$ is a constant connected with the units of measurement[1].

The value of uncertainty is connected with the result of test, where an event probability contribution has the maximum degree of uncertainty. This means the system is in the most disorder state. Taynes proposed the maximum entropy theory that if and only if the entropy is maximum values, the event happening probability is the only unbiased estimator when inducing is based on parts of the important information[2].

### 3.2 DEA-Benchmarking Model Based on the Theory of Maximum Entropy

All aspects of effective information of DMUs can be reflected by using the theory of maximum entropy to construct the weights of DMUs. An objective and quantitative management method can be provided by integrating the maximum entropy theory and DEA in benchmarking, which makes the benchmarking proceeding more effective[4,5].

The core technique of benchmarking is gap analysis, that is, to collect information from DMU or out of DMU, compare then, work out a plan and execute it. The procedure has direct influence on the effect of management and its power. A DEA-Benchmarking model based on the theory of maximum entropy is proposed by integrating the theory of maximum entropy and DEA model. The model can be described as follows:

This article assumes that there are $n$ DMU's , and each DMU has $m$ kinds of input indexes and $s$ kinds of output indexes, which are denoted respectively as $X_j = (x_{1j}, x_{2j}, \ldots, x_{mj})^T$ and $Y_j = (y_{1j}, y_{2j}, \ldots, y_{sj})^T$ , $j = 1, 2, \ldots, n$ . The $C^2GS^2$ model of DEA approach to assess the technical efficiency of the DMU-$j_0$ is determined by the following linear programming:

$$\begin{cases} \min \theta = V_{DMU_{j0}} \\ s.t. \begin{cases} \sum_{j=1}^{n} X_j\lambda_j + S^- = \theta X_0 \\ \sum_{j=1}^{n} Y_j\lambda_j - S^+ = Y_0 \\ \sum_{j=1}^{n} \lambda_j = 1, \lambda_j \geq 0, j = 1, 2, ..., n \\ S^+ \geq 0, S^- \geq 0 \end{cases} \end{cases} \tag{2}$$

If the optimal solution of programming (2) $\lambda^*, S^{*+}, S^{*-}, \theta^*$satisfies that $\theta^* = 1$, then the DMU-j$_0$ is DEA(C$^2$GS$^2$)week efficient. Under the above conditions, if the optimal solution also satisfies that $S^{*+} = 0, S^{*-} = 0$, then the DMU-j$_0$ is DEA(C$^2$GS$^2$)efficient.

The feasible solution corresponding of C$^2$GS$^2$ model is

$$T = \left\{ (X, Y) \middle| \sum_{j=1}^{n} X_j\lambda_j < X, \sum_{j=1}^{n} Y_j\lambda_j > Y, \sum_{j=1}^{n} \lambda_j = 1, j = 1, 2, ..., n \right\} \tag{3}$$

The problem of multiple objective programming in set $T$ is

$$\begin{cases} V - \min(f_1(X, Y), \dots, f_{m+s}(X, Y)) \\ s.t.(X, Y) \in T \end{cases} \tag{4}$$

where $f_k(X, Y) = \begin{cases} X_k, 1 \leq k \leq m \\ -Y_{k-m}, m+1 \leq k \leq m+s \end{cases}, X = (X_1, X_2, \dots, X_m)^T, Y = (Y_1, Y_2, \dots, Y_s)^T$,

**Lemma.** The sufficient and necessary condition when DMU-j$_0$ is DEA(C$^2$GS$^2$) efficient is that(X*,Y*)is the Pareto effective solution of multiple objective programming (4).

In practical production and application, though every event has corresponding happening probability, each kind of happening has different value and avail influence. To bring the subject value and significance into information measure, we put the weigh entropy into DEA model which can be described as follows:

$$\begin{cases} \min \omega^T X - \mu^T Y + \frac{1}{k}(\sum_{i=1}^{m} \omega_i \ln \omega_i + \sum_{j=1}^{s} \mu_j \ln \mu_j) \\ s.t. \begin{cases} \omega_i > 0, \mu_j > 0, i = 1, 2, ..., m; j = 1, 2, ..., s \\ \sum_{i=1}^{m} \omega_i + \sum_{j=1}^{s} \mu_j = 1 \\ (X, Y) \in T \end{cases} \end{cases} \tag{5}$$

where $k$ is a parameter which is bigger than zero.

**Definition 1.** *For a given parameter $k > 0$, if the optimal solution of programming (4) is denoted as $\bar{X}, \bar{Y}, \bar{\omega}_i, \bar{\mu}_j (i = 1, 2, \dots, m; j = 1, 2, \dots, s)$ , then the DMU identified by vector $(\bar{X}, \bar{Y})$is Entropy DEA efficient.*

**Theorem 1.** *If $(\bar{X},\bar{Y})$ is Entropy DEA efficient, the DMU must be DEA efficient.*

*Proof:* Based on the Lemma, we just need to prove that $(\bar{X},\bar{Y})$ is the Pareto effect solution of multiple objective programming (4). By using reduction to absurdity, we assume that $(\bar{X},\bar{Y})$ is not the Pareto effect solution of multiple objective programming (4), then there must be a vector $(X',Y') \in T$ which satisfies that

$$\begin{pmatrix} X' \\ -Y' \end{pmatrix} < \begin{pmatrix} \bar{X} \\ -\bar{Y} \end{pmatrix} \tag{6}$$

Because $(\bar{X},\bar{Y})$ is Entropy DEA efficient, there must be a group of weight vectors $\bar{\omega} = (\bar{\omega}_1, \bar{\omega}_2, ..., \bar{\omega}_m) > 0, \bar{\mu} = (\bar{\mu}_1, \bar{\mu}_2, ..., \bar{\mu}_s) > 0$ , and $\sum_{i=1}^{m} \bar{\omega}_i + \sum_{j=1}^{s} \bar{\mu}_j = 1$ satisfied the nonlinear programming (5), where $(\bar{X},\bar{Y},\bar{\omega},\bar{\mu})$ is the optimal solution of nonlinear programming (5), then

$$\bar{\omega}^T\bar{X}-\bar{\mu}^T\bar{Y}+\frac{1}{k}(\sum_{i=1}^{m}\bar{\omega}_i\ln\bar{\omega}_i+\sum_{j=1}^{s}\bar{\mu}_j\ln\bar{\mu}_j) \le \bar{\omega}^TX'-\bar{\mu}^TY'+\frac{1}{k}(\sum_{i=1}^{m}\bar{\omega}_i\ln\bar{\omega}_i+\sum_{j=1}^{s}\bar{\mu}_j\ln\bar{\mu}_j)$$

$$\bar{\omega}^T\bar{X} - \bar{\mu}^T\bar{Y} \le \bar{\omega}^TX' - \bar{\mu}^TY' \tag{7}$$

Left-handed multiply weight vector $(\bar{\omega},\bar{\mu})$ into (6), where $\bar{\omega} > 0, \bar{\mu} > 0$ , then

$$\bar{\omega}^T\bar{X} - \bar{\mu}^T\bar{Y} > \bar{\omega}^TX' - \bar{\mu}^TY' \tag{8}$$

There is an antinomy between the inequality (7) and (8), so $(\bar{X},\bar{Y})$ must be the Pareto effect solution of multiple objective programming (4), which also means the corresponding DMU is efficient. □

The Theorem 1 indicates the Entropy DEA efficient DMU must be DEA efficient DMU, but the contrary proposition is not true. So the Entropy DEA efficient is a more significant conception than DEA efficient.

### 3.3 The Measure of Entropy-DEA Efficiency

Although the Entropy DEA efficient has more application significance in application than DEA efficient, the DEA model based on maximum entropy (5) is a nonlinear programming, which brings a lot of inconvenience in calculation. We introduce Lagrange multiplication operator to discuss the solution of programming (5), then the programming (5) can be changed into an equivalent exponential programming problem which is a measure of DEA efficiency.

We introduce Lagrange multiplication operator $\lambda$ into programming (5), then a Lagrange function can be constructed as follows:

$$L_k(\omega,\mu,X,Y,\lambda) = \omega^TX - \mu^TY + \frac{1}{k}(\sum_{i=1}^{m}\omega_i\ln\omega_i + \sum_{j=1}^{s}\mu_j\ln\mu_j) + \lambda(\sum_{i=1}^{m}\omega_i + \sum_{j=1}^{s}\mu_j - 1)$$

Because the stationary point condition is $\frac{\partial L_k}{\partial \omega_i} = 0, \frac{\partial L_k}{\partial \mu_j} = 0$, we can obtain the formula as follows:

$$X_i + \frac{1}{k}(\ln \omega_i + 1) + \lambda = 0 \quad i = 1, 2, ..., m \tag{9}$$

$$-Y_j + \frac{1}{k}(\ln \mu_j + 1) + \lambda = 0 \quad j = 1, 2, ..., s \tag{10}$$

The other stationary point condition is $\frac{\partial L_k}{\partial \lambda} = 0$ , we can draw the criterion constraint as follows:

$$\sum_{i=1}^{m} \omega_i + \sum_{j=1}^{s} \mu_j = 1 \tag{11}$$

By associating calculate the formula (9), (10) and (11), we can obtain the formulas as follows:

$$\omega_i = Ce^{-kx_i} \quad i = 1, 2, ..., m$$
$$\mu_j = Ce^{ky_j} \quad j = 1, 2, ..., s$$

where $C = \dfrac{1}{\sum\limits_{i=1}^{m} e^{-kx_i} + \sum\limits_{j=1}^{s} e^{ky_j}}$

Put $\omega_i$ and $\mu_j$ into the formula of Lagrange function, we get the result :

$$L_k(\omega, \mu, X, Y, \lambda) = \omega^T X - \mu^T Y + \frac{1}{k}\left[\sum_{i=1}^{m} \omega_i \ln(Ce^{-kx_i}) + \sum_{j=1}^{s} \mu_j \ln(Ce^{-ky_j})\right]$$
$$= \omega^T X - \mu^T Y + \frac{1}{k}\left[\sum_{i=1}^{m} \omega_i \ln C + \sum_{i=1}^{m} \omega_i \ln e^{-kx_i} + \sum_{j=1}^{s} \mu_j \ln C + \sum_{j=1}^{s} \mu_j \ln e^{-ky_j}\right]$$
$$= \omega^T X - \mu^T Y + \frac{1}{k}\left[\ln C(\sum_{i=1}^{m} \omega_i + \sum_{j=1}^{s} \mu_j) - \omega^T X + \mu^T Y\right] = \frac{1}{k} \ln C$$

So the problem of calculate the function $L_k$ is equal to the formula as follows:

$$\max(\sum_{i=1}^{m} e^{-kx_i} + \sum_{j=1}^{s} e^{ky_j}) \quad (X, Y) \in T \tag{12}$$

Then we can draw the conclusions:

**Theorem 2.** *The solution of (5) is equal to the solution of (12).*

Using Theorem 1 and Theorem 2 , we can draw the conclusion below:

**Theorem 3.** *For all $k > 0$, the $\forall(X, Y)$ of the solution of programming (12) is Entropy-DEA efficient, that is DEA efficient.*

From now on, we can construct a mapping in $J^D$ for DEA efficient DMUs:

$$H : J^D \rightarrow R_1^+$$

$\forall(X, Y) \in J^D$ , define$H(X, Y) \triangleq \sum\limits_{i=1}^{m} e^{-kx_i} + \sum\limits_{j=1}^{n} e^{ky_j}$ as the exponential measure of DEA efficient DMU (X,Y).

### 3.4 The Existence of Entropy-DEA Efficient DMUs

**Theorem 4.** *Assume that* $(X_{j_0}, Y_{j_0})$ *is the maximum solution to* $\sum_{i=1}^{m} e^{-kx_i} + \sum_{j=1}^{s} e^{ky_j}$, *where* $(X,Y) \in \hat{T} = \{(X_1,Y_1),...,(X_n,Y_n)\}$ *and* $X = (X_1,X_2,...,X_m)^T, Y = (Y_1,Y_2,...,Y_s)^T$, *then* $(X_{j_0}, Y_{j_0})$ *must be DEA efficient.*

*Proof:* Based on the Theorem 3, we just need to prove $(X_{j_0}, Y_{j_0})$ is also the solution of

$$\max(\sum_{i=1}^{m} e^{-kx_i} + \sum_{j=1}^{s} e^{ky_j}) \quad \text{s.t.}(X,Y) \in T$$

In fact, because $(X_{j_0}, Y_{j_0})$ is the solution of

$$\max(\sum_{i=1}^{m} e^{-kx_i} + \sum_{j=1}^{s} e^{ky_j}) \quad \text{s.t.}(X,Y) \in \hat{T} \quad (\forall j = 1,2,\ldots,n)$$

Then

$$\sum_{i=1}^{m} e^{-kx_i^{(j)}} + \sum_{j=1}^{s} e^{ky_r^{(j)}} \leq \sum_{i=1}^{m} e^{-kx_i^{(j_0)}} + \sum_{j=1}^{s} e^{ky_r^{(j_0)}} \tag{13}$$

where $X_j = (x_1^{(j)}, x_2^{(j)}, ..., x_m^{(j)}), Y_j = (y_1^{(j)}, y_2^{(j)}, ..., y_s^{(j)})$

For $\forall(X,Y) \in T$, $\sum_{j=1}^{n} X_j\lambda_j \leq X$, $\sum_{j=1}^{n} Y_j\lambda_j \geq Y$, because of $\hat{T} \subset T$ , it also means

$$X_i \geq \sum_{j=1}^{n} x_i^{(j)}\lambda_j, \quad Y_r \leq \sum_{j=1}^{n} y_r^{(j)}\lambda_j, i = 1,2,...,m; j = 1,2,...s$$

Based on the convex property of function $e^x$, we can draw the conclusion as follows:

$$e^{-kX_i} \leq e^{\sum_{j=1}^{n}\lambda_j(-kx_i^{(j)})} \leq \lambda_1 e^{-kx_i^{(1)}} + \lambda_2 e^{-kx_i^{(2)}} + ... + \lambda_n e^{-kx_i^{(n)}}$$

where

$$\sum_{i=1}^{m} e^{-kX_i} \leq \sum_{i=1}^{m} \lambda_1 e^{-kx_i^{(1)}} + \sum_{i=1}^{m} \lambda_2 e^{-kx_i^{(2)}} + ... + \sum_{i=1}^{m} \lambda_n e^{-kx_i^{(n)}} \tag{14}$$

Because of

$$\sum_{r=1}^{s} e^{kY_r} \leq \lambda_1 \sum_{r=1}^{s} e^{ky_r^{(1)}} + \lambda_2 \sum_{r=1}^{s} e^{ky_r^{(2)}} + ... + \lambda_n \sum_{r=1}^{s} e^{ky_r^{(n)}} \tag{15}$$

Calculate the formula (14)+(15) and use the formula (13), we can draw the following conclusion:

$$\sum_{i=1}^{m} e^{-kx_i^{(j)}} + \sum_{j=1}^{s} e^{ky_r^{(j)}} \leq \lambda_1 \left(\sum_{i=1}^{m} e^{-kx_i^{(1)}} + \sum_{r=1}^{s} e^{ky_r^{(1)}}\right) + \lambda_2 \left(\sum_{i=1}^{m} e^{-kx_i^{(2)}} + \sum_{r=1}^{s} e^{ky_r^{(2)}}\right)$$
$$+ ... + \lambda_n \left(\sum_{i=1}^{m} e^{-kx_i^{(n)}} + \sum_{r=1}^{s} e^{ky_r^{(n)}}\right) \leq \lambda_1 \left(\sum_{i=1}^{m} e^{-kx_i^{(j_0)}} + \sum_{r=1}^{s} e^{ky_r^{(j_0)}}\right) + ... +$$
$$\lambda_2 \left(\sum_{i=1}^{m} e^{-kx_i^{(j_0)}} + \sum_{r=1}^{s} e^{ky_r^{(j_0)}}\right) = (\lambda_1 + ... + \lambda_n) \left(\sum_{i=1}^{m} e^{-kx_i^{(j_0)}} + \sum_{r=1}^{s} e^{ky_r^{(j_0)}}\right)$$
$$= \sum_{i=1}^{m} e^{-kx_i^{(j_0)}} + \sum_{r=1}^{s} e^{ky_r^{(j_0)}}$$

□

From the Theorem 4, we know that the solution of programming (12) must be in the set $\hat{T} = \{(X_1, Y_1), ..., (X_n, Y_n)\}$, which indicates that there at least exist a DMU in the evaluation DMUs is Entropy-DEA efficient, and the DMU is DEA efficient. It is an embodiment of relative efficiency of Entropy-DEA efficient.

## 4 Conclusions

The core of benchmarking needs some accurate quantitative methods to obtain efficient information, so we proposed a DEA-Benchmarking model with the maximum entropy and defined Entropy-DEA efficiency. The measure and the existence of Entropy-DEA efficient DMU were also strictly induced in this paper. The Entropy-DEA efficient DMU is a more complete and objective in the view of uncertainty of DMUs information, which has more advantage property over DEA efficient DMUs. In the proceeding of benchmarking, we accept the evaluation method based on Entropy-DEA efficiency and select the Entropy-DEA efficient DMUs as benchmarks for gap analysis between the indexes of DMUs and benchmarks, which have more accurate and operative property in management. The optimization method provides a more efficient means to search in select DEA efficient DMUs within feasible solution space.

## References

1. Fu Z.Y.:Information Theory: Basic Theory And Application. Beijing: Electron Industry Press (2002)35–51
2. Gu, R.Z.: The New Path of Multiple Objective Decision. System Engineering, Vol. 9,4.(1991) 1–8
3. Zhao, F.: Benchmarking.Beijing: The Textile Press of China, (2004)5–12
4. Robert, K., Niven: The Constrained Entropy and Cross-entropy Functions. Physica A. Vol. 334,(2004) 444–458
5. Diasparra, M.,Gzyl,H.:Entropic: Approach to Interior Point Solution of Linear Programs. Applied Mathematics and Computation. Vol. 143,(2003) 339–347
6. Yang, Y.H.: The Quantitative Method in Economy System. Changchun: Jilin science Technology Press.(2001) 285–327
7. Sheng, S.H.,Zhu,Q.,Wu, G.M.: DEA Theory, Methodology and Application. Beijing: The Science Press.(1996) 73–144
8. Wei, Q.L.: Data Envelopment Analysis. Beijing: The Science Press.(2004) 148–203

# A Two Step Approach for the Integrated Production and Distribution Planning of a Supply Chain

Ali Serdar Tasan

Department of Industrial Engineering, Dokuz Eylul University,
Bornova, 35100 Izmir Turkey
serdar.tasan@deu.edu.tr

**Abstract.** Since the production and distribution planning is one of the most important activities to support the global optimization of supply chains, they must be considered in an integrated platform. Most of the integrated production-distribution models consider transportation with a fixed per unit cost, without routing or transportation capacity issues. The aim of this study is to develop an efficient methodology which provides cost savings in logistics activities by considering production, inventory and distribution decisions simultaneously. Generally, finding optimum solution for such an integrated problem is not easy due to its combinatorial nature, especially when vehicle routing is taken into account. Therefore, a two step solution methodology is proposed in order to cope with these issues.

## 1 Introduction

A supply chain is a network of facilities and distribution options that performs the functions of procurement of materials, transformation of these materials into intermediate and finished products, and the distribution of these finished products to customers [1]. Logistics is the part of the supply chain that plans, implements, and controls the efficient, effective flow and storage of goods, services and related information from the point of origin to the point of consumption in order to meet customers' requirements [2]. It has been typically seen that logistics costs account for nearly 30% of the operating cost of an industry. To obtain cost savings in logistics, decisions have to be made by considering the cost elements together. Most studies on supply chain management (SCM) consider inventory point of view of the chain, is thus analyzed as a series of production-inventory decisions. Although it is correct, that approach neglects issues on the transportation between nodes of the chain, resulting missing important opportunities for cost savings and optimization.

The aim of this study is to develop an efficient methodology, which provides cost savings in logistics activities, by considering production, inventory and distribution decisions simultaneously in an integrated manner. Moreover this study concerns with shipment consolidation policy, which consolidates different product items produced and used at different locations and different times, into single vehicle loads in order to get the benefit of the economy of the scale.

D.-S. Huang, K. Li, and G.W. Irwin (Eds.): ICIC 2006, LNCS 4113, pp. 883 – 888, 2006.

## 2 The Integrated Production, Inventory and Distribution Problem

The integrated production, inventory and distribution problem is concerned with coordinating the production, inventory and delivery operations to meet customer demand with cost minimization objective. Companies become aware of their supply chain performance and the importance of their performance improvement, competitive advantage of the production, inventory, and distribution integration [3, 4, 5, 6, 7, 8]. In the literature, there are many studies for optimizing the integration of parts in the integrated production, inventory and distribution problem. Some of these studies address, production-distribution coordination [9, 10], and inventory-distribution coordination [11]. Many models have been studied for production, inventory and distribution problems [3, 12, 13, 14].

However, most of these integrated production-distribution models consider transportation element as a fixed cost, without routing or transportation capacity issues. Consideration of these models is only the demand allocation in distribution, and they answer only how much product transported from production plants to customers. Most of these models with few exceptions do not consider how these allocated quantities delivered by the vehicles. In many of these production-distribution models, the transportation cost per trip is simplified to be proportional to the amount of product shipped, instead of a fixed quantity shipped. Thus the optimal solution is to ship every item direct from the plants to destination distribution centers as soon as it has been produced [15].

## 3 Proposed Methodology

The aim of the proposed approach is the cost minimization of production, inventory and transportation simultaneously, while satisfying the demand requirements. The model is developed under the assumptions of; multiple production plants, distribution centers (DCs), products and time periods, and each vehicle can visit more than one DC during a trip and returns to its base plant at the end of each trip. Generally solving such an integrated problem optimally is not easy due to its combinatorial nature, especially when vehicle routing is taken into account. To cope with this issue a two step solution methodology is proposed in this study.

In the first step, not only production of plants is allocated to DCs to fulfill demand requirements among the time but also vehicles are assigned to plants assuring enough vehicle capacity required for shipments from production plants. The second step considers with the transportation of the allocated production to the DCs with lower transportation cost, involving consolidation and vehicle routing considerations.

### 3.1 Mixed Integer Programming Model

In the first step of the proposed approach a mixed integer programming model is developed for determining the production quantities and allocation of this production to demands, considering production, inventory and distribution issues. In order to satisfy the simplicity, direct shipments are assumed between production facilities and demand centers; the location consolidation and vehicle routing issues are handled by the second step of the methodology. Equations (1) to (10) formulate the mathematical model for the problem.

$$\text{MIN} \sum_{t\in T}\sum_{w\in W}\sum_{i\in I} a_{i,w}(t)\,p_{i,w}(t) + \sum_{t\in T}\sum_{w\in W}\sum_{i\in I} h_{i,w}(t)(sc_{i,w}(t)+sc_{i,w}(t-1))/2 + \sum_{t\in T}\sum_{w\in W}\sum_{j\in J} l_{j,w}(t)(sd_{j,w}(t)+sd_{j,w}(t-1))/2 + \sum_{t\in T}\sum_{i\in I}\sum_{j\in J} cd\ ds_{i,j}\,x_{i,j}(t) + \sum_{t\in T}\sum_{i\in I}\sum_{v\in V} c_v\,y_{i,v}(t) \quad (1)$$

$$sc_{i,w}(t) = sc_{i,w}(t-1) + p_{i,w}(t) - \sum_{w\in W}\sum_{j\in J} q_{i,j,w}(t) \qquad \forall i\in I, t\in T, w\in W \quad (2)$$

$$sd_{j,w}(t) = sd_{j,w}(t-1) + \sum_{w\in W}\sum_{i\in I} q_{i,j,w}(t) - d_{j,w}(t) \qquad \forall j\in J, t\in T, w\in W \quad (3)$$

$$scl_{i,w} \le sc_{i,w}(t) \le sch_{i,w} \qquad \forall i\in I, t\in T, w\in W \quad (4)$$

$$sdl_{j,w} \le sd_{j,w}(t) \le sdh_{j,w} \qquad \forall j\in J, t\in T, w\in W \quad (5)$$

$$0 \le p_i(t) \le PR_i \qquad \forall i\in I, t\in T \quad (6)$$

$$\sum_{w\in W} q_{i,j,w}(t) \le Capp\ x_{i,j}(t) \qquad \forall i\in I, j\in J, t\in T \quad (7)$$

$$\sum_{j\in J}\sum_{w\in W} q_{i,j,w}(t) \le \sum_{v\in V} Cap_v\,y_{i,v}(t) \qquad \forall i\in I, t\in T \quad (8)$$

$$\sum_{i\in I} y_{i,v}(t) \le 1 \qquad \forall v\in V, t\in T \quad (9)$$

$$x_{i,j}(t) = 0 \text{ or } 1, \quad y_{i,v}(t) = 0 \text{ or } 1 \qquad \forall i\in I, j\in J, v\in V, t\in T \quad (10)$$

Equation (1) is the objective function, which is the summation of production cost, inventory cost, and transportation cost (assuming direct shipments) and cost for vehicle usage. The Mixed Integer Programming model tries to minimize this objective function. Equation (2) and (3) are the constraints that provides production satisfies demand by determining production quantities as well as quantities hold in inventory over time horizon. Equation (4) and (5) are inventory capacity constrains while Equation (6) is production capacity constraint. Equation (7) determines the shipment from $i$ to $j$ by using a dummy capacity *Capp*. Equation (8) determines vehicle assignment decisions by satisfying vehicles' loading capacity. Equation (9) satisfies each vehicle assigned to only one plant during $t$. finally Equation (10) assures $x$ and $y$ values arc binary. In the formulation; $I$, $J$, $T$, $V$, $W$ are the sets of production plants, DCs, time periods, vehicles, product items respectively. $a_{i,w}(t)$ is unit production cost and $h_{j,w}(t)$ is inventory holding cost of product $w$ at $i^{th}$ production plant during $t$. $l_{j,w}(t)$ is inventory holding cost of product w at $j^{h}$ DC during $t$ and $cd$ is transportation cost per unit distance. $c_v$ is cost of assigning vehicle $v$ and $Cap_v$ is shipping capacity of vehicle $v$. $ds_{i,j}$ is distance from $i$ to $j$ and $d_{j,w}(t)$ is demand of $j^{th}$ DC for product $w$ during $t$. $PR_{i,w}$ is production capacity of product $w$ at $i^{th}$ plant. $sch_{i,w}$ is maximum and $scl_{i,w}$ is minimum level of inventory of product $w$ at $i^{th}$ plant respectively. $sdh_{j,w}$ is maximum and $sdl_{j,w}$ is minimum level of inventory of product $w$ at $j^{th}$ DC.

The decision variables in the proposed mixed integer programming model are; $p_{i,w}(t)$ is production quantity and $sc_{i,w}(t)$ is inventory of product $w$ at $i^{th}$ plant during $t$. $sd_{j,w}(t)$ shows inventory of product $w$ at $j^{th}$ DC during $t$ and $x_{i,j}(t)$ shows if there is shipment between $i$ and $j$ during $t$. $q_{i,j,w}(t)$ denotes quantity of product $w$ transported from $i$ to $j$ by $v$ during $t$ and $y_{i,v}(t)$ shows assignment of $v$ to $i$ during $t$.

### 3.2 Genetic Algorithm Based Vehicle Routing

This step uses the outputs of the first step as inputs and decides how the allocated product quantities transported to the DCs with vehicle routing consideration. Due to genetic algorithm's efficiency on solving the combinatorial problems, genetic algorithm (GA) based method is used to develop an efficient solution algorithm. Execution of this step is done by using GA Based Routing Application (GABRA) [16], which is continuously developing vehicle routing tool based on GA.

**Genetic Algorithms**

GA belongs to evolutionary algorithms which are based on Darwin's mechanics of the natural selection process. The Theory of Natural Selection, proposed by the British naturalist Charles Darwin, states that individuals with certain favorable characteristics are more likely to survive and reproduce and consequently pass their characteristics on to their offsprings. In nature, the genetic inheritance is stored in chromosomes, made of genes. Once in a while a mutation causes a change in the chromosomes. Due to natural selection, the population will gradually improve on the average as the number of individuals with the favorable characteristics increases. The GAs were invented by John Holland and his colleagues in the early 1970s [17]. The idea behind GA is to model the natural evolution by using genetic inheritance together with Darwin's theory. For more information, readers can refer to [18, 19, 20].

## 4 Illustrative Example

In order to illustrate the proposed methodology, an example with 3 production facilities and 36 DCs, where production facilities produce 3 different products with 10 time period is used. In the example, products are shipped by 8 vehicles with different capacities. The locations of the production facility and DCs are shown in the Fig. 1, where production facilities illustrated with circles and DCs with triangles. Additionally, the demands of DCs for different type of products as well as other variables related to production facilities and DCs change over time periods.

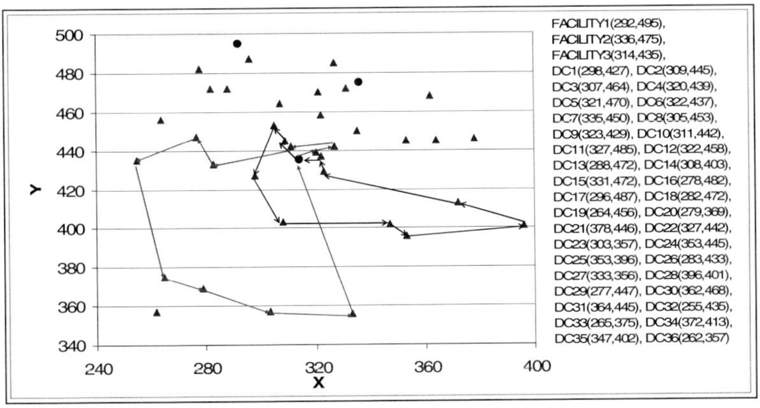


**Fig. 1.** Locations of the production facilities and DCs with their corresponding coordinates and routes from Facility 3 to served DCs during $4^{th}$ time period

In the first step of the proposed methodology a mixed integer programming model is formulated using the data and solved by LINGO software. Following, the solution from this step is used as the input for the proposed GABRA model. As an example of the solution, two routes for the shipments from facility 3 at the $4^{th}$ time period and the vehicle routes are found and shown in Fig 1. Similarly, all shipments from all facilities to DCs for all periods are calculated with their routes. In this study permutation type genetic representation, roulette wheel selection method, alternating edges crossover operator and reciprocal exchange mutation operator are used in the proposed methodology.

# 5 Conclusion

In this study, a methodology, which considers with production, inventory and distribution issues of a supply chain, is proposed. In addition to this integrated frame, routing and consolidation considerations are also taken into account. The originality of the study based on the concerned supply chain environment, which involves multi products, heterogeneous transportation vehicles with various capacities, as well as vehicle routing consideration. Due to the combinatorial nature of these kinds of problems, especially for vehicle routing considerations, optimally solving such an integrated problem is very difficult even for small sized problems. And much of real world problems can be modeled by huge sized models, in order to reflect their structure by developed models realistically. To deal with the combinatorial nature of this problem, a two step integrated methodology is proposed in this study. Additionally, an illustrative example is modeled and solved using the proposed methodology.

In conclusion, according to the results of various trials, proposed approach gives good quality solutions to the integrated production, inventory and distribution problem including routing considerations with heterogeneous vehicles. Furthermore, the structure of the proposed two step approach enables to handle huge sized problems, which represents most of the real world logistics systems.

## References


1. Ganeshan, R., Harrison, T.P.: An Introduction to Supply Chain Management. Working Paper Penn State University (1996)
2. Council of Logistics Management: http://www.clm1.org (2000)
3. Thomas, D.J., Griffin, P.M.: Coordinated Supply Chain Management. European Journal of Operational Research 94 (1996) 1-15
4. Fumero, F., Vercellis, C.: Synchronized Development of Production, Inventory, and Distribution Schedules. Transportation Science 33 (1999) 330-340
5. Brown, G., Keegan, J., Vigus, B., Wood, K.: The Kellogg Company Optimizes Production, Inventory, and Distribution. Interfaces 31 (2001) 1-15
6. Lee, H.L., Whang, S.: Winning the Last Mile of E-Commerce. MIT Sloan Management Review 42 (4) (2001) 54-62
7. Gupta, V., Peters, E., Miller, T.: Implementing a Distribution-Network Decision-Support System at Pfizer/Warner-Lambert. Interfaces 32 (2002) 28-45
8. Bloomquist, D., Graziosi, D., Lei, L., Ruszczynski, A., Liu, S., Zhong, H.: Practice Abstracts: Optimizing Production, Inventory, and Distribution for General Chemical Group. Interfaces 32 (2002) 67-68
9. Cohen, M.A., Lee, H.L.: Strategic Analysis of Integrated Production-Distribution Systems: Models and Methods. Operation Research 36 (1988) 216-228
10. Chandra, P., Fisher, M.L.: Coordination of Production and Distribution Planning. European Journal of Operational Research 72 (1994) 503-517
11. Chandra, P.: A Dynamic Distribution Model with Warehouse and Customer Replenishment Requirements. Journal of the Operational Research Society 44 (1993) 681-692
12. Vidal, C.J., Goetschalckx, M.: Strategic Production-Distribution Models: A Critical Review with Emphasis on Global Supply Chain Models. European Journal of Operational Research 98 (1997) 1-18
13. Baita, F., Ukovich, W., Pesenti, R., Favaretto, D.: Dynamic Routing and Inventory Problems: A Review. Transportation Research Part A: Policy and Practice 32 (1998) 585-598
14. Erenguc, Ş.S., Simpson, N.C., Vakharia, A.J.: Integrated Production/Distribution Planning in Supply Chains: An Invited Review. European Journal of Operational Research 115 (1999) 219-236
15. Daganzo, C.F.: Logistics Systems Analysis. Wiley New York (1991)
16. Tasan, A.S.: Genetic Algorithm Based Approach for Vehicle Routing. Working Paper (2006)
17. Holland, J.H.: Adaptation in Natural and Artificial Systems. The University of Michigan Press Ann Arbor Michigan (1975)
18. Reeves, C.R.: Modern Heuristic Techniques for Combinatorial Problems. Blackwell Scientific Press Oxford (1993)
19. Mitchell, M.: An Introduction to Genetic Algorithms. MIT Press Cambridge (1996)
20. Reeves, C.R.: Genetic Algorithms. In: F. Glover & G. A. Kochenberger(eds.): Handbook of Metaheuristics. Kluwer Academic Publishers NJ,USA (2002) 55–82

# An Enhanced Heuristic Searching Algorithm for Complicated Constrained Optimization Problems

Feng Yu, Yanjun Li, and Tie-Jun Wu

National Laboratory of Industrial Control Technology,
Institute of Intelligent Systems & Decision Making,
Zhejiang University, Hangzhou 310027, China
yjlee@iipc.zju.edu.cn

**Abstract.** In many complicated constrained optimization problems, intelligent searching technique based algorithms are very inefficient even to get a feasible solution. This paper presents an enhanced heuristic searching algorithm to solve this kind of problems. The proposed algorithm uses known feasible solutions as heuristic information, then orients and shrinks the search spaces towards the feasible set. It is capable of improving the search performance significantly without any complicated and specialized operators. Benchmark problems are tested to validate the effectiveness of the proposed algorithm.

## 1 Introduction

Intelligent algorithms such as evolutionary algorithms [1]-[6], ant colony algorithms [7] and immune algorithms [8], etc., have been widely used to solve complicated constrained optimization problems in recent years. In many real-world problems, the feasible space is much smaller than the search space. For this reason, solving complicated constrained problems using such methods would be inefficient [1],[2].

In most cases in actual optimization problems, getting one feasible solution is not difficult. Based on this information, this paper presents an enhanced heuristic search (EHS) algorithm to solve constrained optimization problems. Multi-point searching and elitist reserve scheme are used in the algorithm in order to guarantee the diversity of the solutions and the convergence of the algorithm. Theoretic analysis and simulation results indicate that this algorithm has higher efficiency than normal searching methods.

## 2 Problem Statement

The constrained optimization problem considered in this paper is formulated as

$$\begin{aligned} &\min f(\boldsymbol{X}) = f(x_1, x_2, \cdots, x_n) \\ &s.t.\ \ \boldsymbol{X} \in \boldsymbol{F} \triangleq \boldsymbol{G} \cap \boldsymbol{S} \\ &\quad \boldsymbol{G} \triangleq \left\{ \boldsymbol{X} \,\middle|\, g_j(\boldsymbol{X}) = g_j(x_1, x_2, \cdots, x_n) \le 0,\ j = 1, 2, \cdots, m \right\} \\ &\quad \boldsymbol{S} \triangleq \left\{ \boldsymbol{X} \,\middle|\, \underline{x_i} \le x_i \le \overline{x_i},\ i = 1, 2, \cdots, n \right\} \end{aligned} \quad (1)$$

where the objective function $f(\bullet)$ and constraints $g_j(\bullet)$ may possess various complex forms. The feasible space is defined by $\boldsymbol{F}$ . $\boldsymbol{S}$ defines the initial search space.

D.-S. Huang, K. Li, and G.W. Irwin (Eds.): ICIC 2006, LNCS 4113, pp. 889 – 894, 2006.

Without loss of generality, we assume that $\boldsymbol{F} \subset \boldsymbol{S}$. Then, for arbitrary solution $\boldsymbol{X}$, we define the candidate solution as $\boldsymbol{X}^c \in \boldsymbol{S}$, the feasible solution as $\boldsymbol{X}^{fea} \in \boldsymbol{F}$ and the infeasible solution as $(\boldsymbol{X}^{ufea} \in \boldsymbol{S}) \wedge (\boldsymbol{X}^{ufea} \notin \boldsymbol{F})$. We define the feasible reference solution $\boldsymbol{X}^r$ which provides heuristic information to start search.

To estimate the difficulty of generating feasible solutions, we define $\eta$ as:

$$\eta = |\boldsymbol{S}| / |\boldsymbol{F}|. \tag{2}$$

where $|\boldsymbol{S}|$ is the number of candidate solutions, and $|\boldsymbol{F}|$ is the number of feasible solutions. By $\eta \gg 1$ it means an intelligent algorithm is difficult to get feasible solutions. The work in this paper is to construct a search algorithm to solve the problem (1) for arbitrary $\eta$.

## 3 Theoretical Description

Suppose that one or more feasible reference solutions can be obtained (e.g., operating parameters of industrial processes and power supply networks). Based on this information, a new candidate solution could be generated towards feasibility and optimality, by dealing with the following two cases.

(i) The candidate solution is an infeasible solution. The candidate solution selects a reference solution randomly as heuristic information orienting the search of next candidate solution approaching ***F***. The search stepsize is adaptively set according to the degree of infeasibility of the candidate solution.

(ii) The candidate solution is a feasible solution. Then it will be guided towards the best reference solution with an adaptive stepsize. A large stepsize is chosen if the number of the feasible solutions occupy a large portion in the population, in order to avoid premature of the search process. Otherwise, a small stepsize is used in favor of local search ability.

The search process of the algorithm is described in detail as follows. Without loss of generality, we select the $i$th candidate solution $\boldsymbol{X}_{i,k}^c = \{x_{i,k}^c(1), x_{i,k}^c(2), \ldots, x_{i,k}^c(n)\}$, $(i = 1, 2, \ldots, N)$ during the $k$th iteration as an example. $N$ is the population size. The $j$th feasible reference solution $\boldsymbol{X}_{j,k}^r = \{x_{j,k}^r(1), x_{j,k}^r(2), \ldots, x_{j,k}^r(n)\}$ is used to guide $\boldsymbol{X}_{i,k}^c$ to move. The distance between $\boldsymbol{X}_{i,k}^c$ and $\boldsymbol{X}_{j,k}^r$ is defined by (3):

$$\begin{aligned} \boldsymbol{D}_{k+1} &\triangleq \boldsymbol{X}_{j,k}^r - \boldsymbol{X}_{i,k}^c = \{d_{k+1}(1), d_{k+1}(2), \ldots, d_{k+1}(n)\} \\ &= \{x_{j,k}^r(1) - x_{i,k}^c(1), x_{j,k}^r(2) - x_{i,k}^c(2), \ldots, x_{j,k}^r(n) - x_{i,k}^c(n)\} \end{aligned}. \tag{3}$$

After one iterative step, the $p$th element of $\boldsymbol{X}_{i,k+1}^c$ is calculated by (4):

$$x_{i,k+1}^c(p) = x_{i,k}^c(p) + \varphi(k+1)\alpha_{i,k+1}(p) d_{k+1}(p), \quad 1 \le p \le n. \tag{4}$$

where $\alpha_{i,k+1}(\bullet) \in [0,1]$ is a random number. We adjust the value of $\alpha_{i,k+1}(p)$ until $x_{i,k+1}^c(p)$ satisfies the condition: $\underline{x_i}(p) \le x_{i,k+1}^c(p) \le \overline{x_i}(p)$, where $\overline{x_i}(p)$ and $\underline{x_i}(p)$

are the upper and lower boundaries of the decision variable $x_i(p)$ respectively. $\varphi(\bullet)$ is the search stepsize and adjusted by

$$\varphi(k+1)=\begin{cases}\varphi(k)+\Delta\varphi & if\ Count(N_{fea}/N_{ufea}\geq 0.8)>10\ \ or\ \ Count(N_{ufea}/N_{fea}\geq 0.2)>10\\ \varphi(k)-\Delta\varphi & if\ Count(N_{fea}/N_{ufea}<0.8)>10\ \ or\ \ Count(N_{ufea}/N_{fea}<0.2)>10\\ \varphi(k) & otherwise\end{cases}. \quad (5)$$

where $N_{fea}$ and $N_{ufea}$ are the number of the feasible candidate solutions and the infeasible candidate solutions, respectively; $Count(\bullet)$ is a function denoting the times that the value of the expression in the bracket remains true up to this iteration; $\Delta\varphi$ is the increment of $\varphi$.

## 4 Simulations

The effectiveness of the proposed algorithm has been verified by a set of benchmark problems [1] listed in the Appendix of this paper. Three feasible reference solutions are known initially in each benchmark problem.

The simulation parameters are set as follows: $N=50$, the search stepsize $\varphi\in[1.0,3.0]$ with $\varphi(0)=2$, and $\Delta\varphi=0.08$. The algorithm will stop if the candidate solution is not improved obviously during 100 continuous iterative steps.

The convergence of the first benchmark problem [1] is shown in Fig. 1.

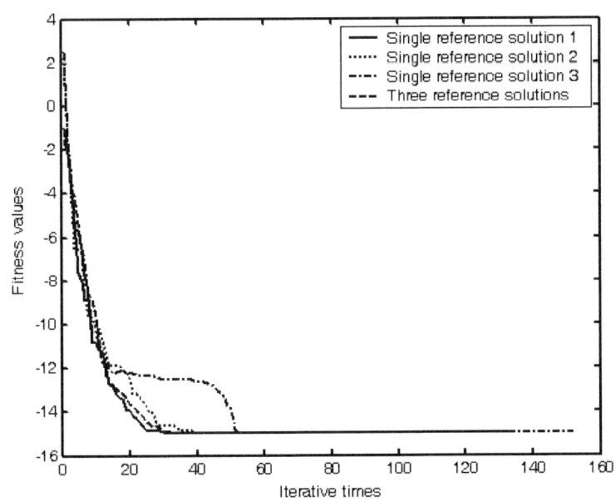


**Fig. 1.** The convergence curves of the first model for one and three reference solutions

In order to validate that the algorithm is insensitive to the initial feasible reference solutions, different initial reference solutions are tested in the simulations. The convergence rates of the second and the third benchmark problems with different number of reference solutions are similar to that of the first problem, and are omitted for the limitation of the paper's length.

**Table 1.** Known feasible reference solutions and their fitness

| | |
|---|---|
| G1: | $X_{1,1}^r$=(0.5,0.5,0.5,0.5,0.5,0.5,0.5,0.5,0.5,1,1,1,0.5); $f_1$=-1 |
| | $X_{2,1}^r$=(0.6624,0.5532,0.3992,0.4009,0.5469,0.2142,0.3767,0.2028,0.4433,0,0,0,0.4385); $f_2$=2.5316 |
| | $X_{3,1}^r$=(0.6655,0.5593,0.5808,0.4301,0.4420,0.3454,0.7835,0.1088,0.4254,0,0,0,0.4738); $f_3$=2.2096 |
| G2: | $X_{1,1}^r$= (580,1361,6000,182,295,218,286,395); $f_1$=7941.0 |
| | $X_{2,1}^r$= (580,1396.7,5166.5,182,295.99,218,285.77,395); $f_2$=7143.2 |
| | $X_{3,1}^r$= (579.86,1350.2,5996.5,182,295.14,218,286.83,395); $f_3$=7926.6 |
| G3: | $X_{1,1}^r$= (0,0,0,0,0,0,0); $f_1$=1183.0 |
| | $X_{2,1}^r$= (1.3581,0.24432,-0.096835,0.00030777,-0.20318,-1.461,0.36611); $f_2$=1157.4 |
| | $X_{3,1}^r$= (0.18066,1.8137,0.22965,1.656,0.022634,-1.4212,1.0768); $f_3$=904.4 |

**Table 2.** Statistical results obtained by our EHS against HM, SR and SMES

| Fun | | g1 | g2 | g3 |
|---|---|---|---|---|
| best | EHS | -15.000 | 7049.251 | 680.636 |
| | HM | -15.000 | 7149.9 | 680.91 |
| | SR | -15.000 | 7054.316 | 680.630 |
| | SMES | -15.000 | 7051.903 | 680.632 |
| mean | EHS | -15.000 | 7049.322 | 680.801 |
| | HM | -15.000 | 8163.6 | 681.16 |
| | SR | -15.000 | 7559.192 | 680.656 |
| | SMES | -15.000 | 7253.047 | 680.643 |
| worst | EHS | -15.000 | 7049.368 | 681.224 |
| | HM | -15.000 | 9659.3 | 683.18 |
| | SR | -15.000 | 8835.655 | 680.763 |
| | SMES | -15.000 | 7638.366 | 680.719 |

We compare our algorithm with three other existing algorithms: SMES [1], SR (stochastic ranking) [6] and HM (homomorphous maps) [1]. The feasible reference solutions and their corresponding fitness values $f$ are shown in Table 1 and the simulation results are shown in Table 2.

The benchmark problem in [9] is also tested by extending the size of the initial search space to 10, 50 and 100 times respectively while the feasible space maintains a constant size. The curves in Fig.2 show the relationship between the iterations and the convergence speed under the four cases. The same parameters are set in this simulation.

As is shown in Fig.2, the EHS algorithm demonstrates very good robustness against the change of search space size.

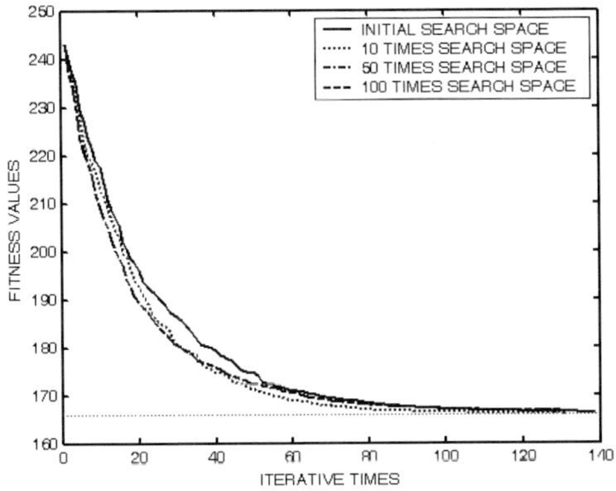


**Fig. 2.** Performance comparision by extending different sizes of the initial search space

# 5 Conclusions

A simple but effective algorithm for solving complicated constrained optimization problems is proposed in this paper. It can deal with such kind of problems with complicated feasible spaces for which most of the existing searching algorithms are difficult to even get a feasible solution. Benchmark problem simulation results show that the proposed algorithm is able to find optimal (or near-optimal) solutions quickly.

# Acknowledgement

The work is supported by the National 973 program of China (2002CB312200).

# References

1. E. Mezura-Montes, C.A.C. Coello.: A Simple Multimembered Evolution Strategy to Solve Constrained Optimization Problems, IEEE Trans. on Evol. Comput., Vol.9, (2005) 1-17
2. Z. Michalewicz.: A Survey of Constraint Handling Techniques in Evolutionary Computation Methods. Proc. of the 4th Annual Conference on Evolutionary Programming, MIT Press, Cambridge, MA, (1995) 135-155
3. S.E. Carlson.: A General Method for Handling Constraints in Genetic Algorithms. Proc. 2th Annual Joint Conference on Information Science, (1995) 663-666
4. J.C.B. Helio And C.C.L. Afonso.: A New Adaptive Penalty Schema for Genetic Algorithms. Informatino Sciences, Vol. 156, (2003) 215-251
5. K.C. Tan, T.H. Lee, D. Khoo And E.F. Khor.: Constrained Evolutionary Exploration via Genetic Structure of Packet Distribution. IEEE Proceedings of the 2001 Congress on Evolutionary Computation, Vol.1, (2001) 27-30
6. T. P. Runarsson, X. Yao.: Stochastic Ranking for Constrained Evolutionary Optimization. IEEE Trans. on Evolutionary Computation, Vol. 4, (2000) 284-294

7. C. Solnon.: Ants Can Solve Constraint Satisfaction Problems, IEEE Transaction on Evolutionary. Vol.6, ( 2002) 347-357
8. Yanjun Li, David J. Hill, Tie-Jun Wu.: Nonlinear Predictive Control Scheme with Immune Optimization for Voltage Security Control of Power System. Automation of Electric Power Systems, Vol.28, (2004) 25-31
9. http://www.sor.princeton.edu/~rvdb/ampl/nlmodels/cute/airport.mod

## Appendix: Test Function Suite

In the following formulas, $x^*$ and $f(x^*)$ are the global optimal solution and the corresponding objective function value, respectively.

g1: min $f(x) = 5\sum_{i=1}^{4} x_i - 5\sum_{i=1}^{4} x_i^2 - \sum_{i=5}^{13} x_i$

$s.t.$ $2x_1 + 2x_2 + x_{10} + x_{11} - 10 \le 0$, $2x_1 + 2x_3 + x_{10} + x_{12} - 10 \le 0$, $-8x_1 + x_{10} \le 0$

$2x_2 + 2x_3 + x_{11} + x_{12} - 10 \le 0$, $-8x_2 + x_{11} \le 0$, $-8x_3 + x_{12} \le 0$

$-2x_4 - x_5 + x_{10} \le 0$, $-2x_6 - x_7 + x_{11} \le 0$, $-2x_8 - x_9 + x_{12} \le 0$

$0 \le x_i \le 1 \quad (i = 1,...,9,13)$, $0 \le x_i \le 100 \quad (i = 10,11,12)$

$f(x^*) = -15$, $x^* = (1,1,1,1,1,1,1,1,1,3,3,3,1)$.

g 2: min $f(x) = x_1 + x_2 + x_3$

$s.t.$ $-1 + 0.0025(x_4 + x_6) \le 0$, $-1 + 0.0025(x_5 + x_7 - x_4) \le 0$, $-1 + 0.01(x_8 - x_5) \le 0$

$-x_3x_8 + 1250000 + x_3x_5 - 2500x_5 \le 0$, $-x_2x_7 + 1250x_5 + x_2x_4 - 1250x_4 \le 0$

$-x_1x_6 + 833.33252x_4 + 100x_1 - 83333.333 \le 0$

$100 \le x_1 \le 10000$, $1000 \le x_i \le 10000 \quad (i = 2,3)$, $10 \le x_i \le 1000 \quad (i = 4,...,8)$

$f(x^*) = 7049.25, x^* = (579.19, 1360.13, 5109.92, 182.0174, 295.5985, 217.9799, 286.40, 395.5979)$.

g 3: min $f(x) = (x_1 - 10)^2 + 5(x_2 - 12)^2 + x_3^4 + 3(x_4 - 11)^2 + 10x_5^6 + 7x_6^2 + x_7^4 - 4x_6x_7 - 10x_6 - 8x_7$

$s.t.$ $-127 + 2x_1^2 + 3x_2^4 + x_3 + 4x_4^2 + 5x_5 \le 0$, $-282 + 7x_1 + 3x_2 + 10x_3^2 + x_4 - x_5 \le 0$

$-196 + 23x_1 + x_2^2 + 6x_6^2 - 8x_7 \le 0$, $4x_1^2 + x_2^2 - 3x_1x_2 + 2x_3^2 + 5x_6 - 11x_7 \le 0$

$-10 \le x \le 10 \quad (i = 1,...,7)$ $f(x^*) = 680.6300573$,

$x^* = (2.330499, 1.951372, -0.4775414, 4.365726, -0.6244870, 1.038131, 1.594227)$.

# Further Research on Node Based Bottleneck Improvement Problem for Multicut

Xiucui Guan[1] and Jie Su[2]

[1] Dept. of Math., Southeast University, Nanjing, 210096, P.R. China
[2] Sch. of Bus., Renmin University of China, Beijing,
Sch. of Math. and Sys. Sci., Shandong University, Jinan, P.R. China
xcguan@163.com

**Abstract.** In this paper, we consider the node based bottleneck improvement problem for multicut (NBBIM). The objective is to upgrade a set of nodes with minimum cost such that there is a feasible multicut whose maximum weight is not more than a given value $D$ in the upgraded network. We first show that the problem is $\mathcal{NP}$-hard and MaxSNP-hard for $K \geq 2$ on general directed graphs, where $K$ is the number of source-terminal pairs. Then we present two polynomial algorithms for a special case of problem (NBBIM) on directed MSMT trees.

## 1 Introduction

Many recent studies have focused on network improvement problems in a node based upgrading model [6,7,8,3,4]. The aim is to enhance the performance of a given network by restrictively modifying some nodes. In a node weighted network $G = (V, E, c)$, the cost to upgrade a node subset $S \subseteq V$ is $c(S) = \sum_{v \in S} c(v)$, where $c(v)$ is the cost to upgrade the node $v$. Three nonnegative integers $w_0(e) \geq w_1(e) \geq w_2(e)$ are given for each edge $e$, where $w_i(e)$ represents the weight of the edge if exactly $i$ of its endpoints are upgraded. The edge weight function resulted from upgrading $S$ is $w_S(e) = w_i(e)$ for each $e = (u, v)$, where $i = |\{u, v\} \cap S|$.

Recently, Guan et. al. [4] considered the node based bottleneck improvement problem for the multicut (NBBIM for simplicity). Given a connected network $G = (V, E)$ with positive weights $w(e)$ on all edges and a set of 'source-terminal' pairs $\{(s_i, t_i)\}, i = 1, \cdots, K$, a *multicut* is a subset $X$ of edges whose removal disconnects each pair of source-terminal. Given a value $D$, a multicut $X \subseteq E$ is said to be *feasible* with respect to $D$ if $\max_{e \in X} w(e) \leq D$. Thus, the purpose of problem (NBBIM) is to upgrade a set $S$ of nodes with minimum cost such that there is a feasible multicut with respect to $D$ in the upgraded network. We mainly considered the problem for a directed MSMT tree defined below [4].

Given an undirected tree $T = (V, E)$ satisfying $V_s \cup V_t \supseteq V_l$, where $V_s$ is the set of sources, $V_t$ is the set of terminals and $V_l$ is the set of leaves of $T$, we assume that there are no edges connecting two sources or two terminals. We call $\overrightarrow{T} = (V, \overrightarrow{E})$ an orientated tree of $T$ if it satisfies the conditions as follows: (i) each source $s_i \in V_s$ has only out-arcs and each terminal $t_j \in V_t$ has only in arcs; (ii) $\overrightarrow{T}$ is a union of directed paths (not necessary disjoint) from each

D.-S. Huang, K. Li, and G.W. Irwin (Eds.): ICIC 2006, LNCS 4113, pp. 895–900, 2006.

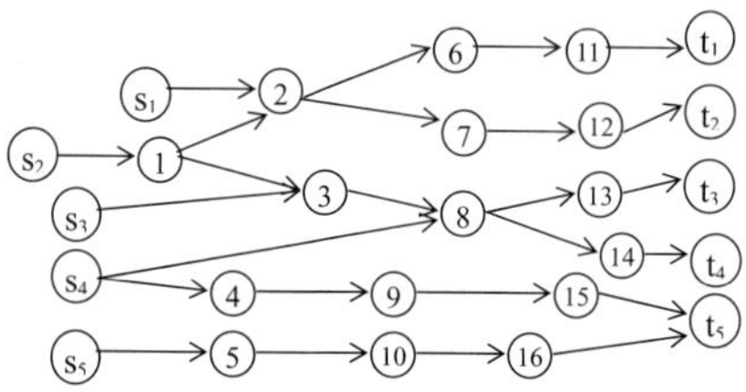


**Fig. 1.** A directed MSMT tree

source to all its reachable terminals (not necessary from every source to every terminal) and each arc of $\overrightarrow{E}$ must be lied on one of such paths (See Fig. 1). We call $\overrightarrow{T} = (V, \overrightarrow{E})$ a directed tree with multiple sources and multiple terminals (*MSMT tree* for simplicity) and we omit the arrow over $T$ and $E$ in the sequel.

In this paper, we first show that the problem (NBBIM) is $\mathcal{NP}$-hard and MaxSNP-hard for $K \geq 2$ on general directed graphs. We have proposed a general algorithm with time complexity $O(K \cdot n + 2^K \cdot (K^2 + n))$ for problem (NBBIM) on directed MSMT trees in [4], which is a polynomial algorithm when the number $K$ is upper bounded by a given value. Thus we turn to consider a special case of problem (NBBIM) on directed MSMT trees and propose two polynomial algorithms with time complexities $O(n^2 \log n)$ and $O(n^2)$, which only concern the number $n$ of nodes and are irrespective of the number $K$.

Given a value $D$, we can partition the edge set $E$ into four subsets according to how many endpoints of the edge must be upgraded in order to decrease its weight to be below the threshold $D$ [4]. An edge $e$ is *uncritical* if $w_0(e) \leq D$, *1-critical* if $w_0(e) > D \geq w_1(e)$, and *2-critical* if $w_1(e) > D \geq w_2(e)$. Finally, an edge $e$ is said to be *useless* if $w_2(e) > D$. Denote by $E^1$ and $E^u$ the set of 1-critical and useless edges, respectively. To simplify the narration, we make two assumptions [4]. Assume without loss of generality that $w_0(e) > D$ for any edge $e \in E$ and $\min_{e \in P_{s_i t_i}} w_2(e) \leq D$ for each pair of source-terminal $(s_i, t_i), i = 1, 2, \cdots, K$, where $P_{s_i t_i}$ is the path from source $s_i$ to terminal $t_i$.

In the remainder of the paper, the organization is as follows. We first analyze the complexity of problem (NBBIM) on general directed graphs in Section 2. Then we present polynomial algorithms for problem (NBBIM) on directed MSMT trees when there are no 2-critical edges in Section 3. Conclusions and further research are given in Section 4.

## 2 Complexity of Problem (NBBIM) on Directed Graphs

To consider the complexity of problem (NBBIM) for general directed graphs, we need to introduce a minimum multicut in node version. Given a connected graph $G = (V, E)$ with positive weights $c(v)$ on all nodes $v$ and a set of 'source-terminal' pairs $\{(s_i, t_i) | i = 1, \cdots, K\}$, a *minimum node multicut* is a set of nodes with minimum weights whose removal disconnects each pair of source-terminal. Note that the node multicut herein may contain sources and terminals themselves. Obviously, the set of sources and the set of terminals are two node multicuts.

Note that in directed graphs, the node version of the multicut problem can be easily reduced to the edge version [2]. Given a directed graph $G = (V, E)$, construct an auxiliary graph $H$ as follows. For each node $v$, add a new node $v'$ and an arc from $v$ to $v'$ with weight $c(v)$. The arcs of $G$ coming from $v$ are now coming from $v'$ and the arcs coming into $v$ remain the same; these arcs are given large weight $M$, say $M := c(V)$. The set of sources remains the same, while the set of terminals becomes $V_t' := \{t_i'\}$. As above, we can assume without loss of generality that an optimal cost or approximate edge multicut in $H$ does not include any edge of weight $M$, and hence there is a one-to-one weight-preserving correspondence of such cuts with the node multicuts in $G$. For the unweighted case, we can replace the weight-$M$ edges by $M$ parallel edges of weight 1 (or parallel paths, if we want a simple graph).

Obviously, if all the edges are 1-critical in the input network, then the problem (NBBIM) reduces to the minimum node multicut problem in directed graphs. Recall that minimum (edge) multicut is known to be $\mathcal{NP}$-hard and MaxSNP-hard for $K \geq 2$ in directed graphs [1]. Therefore, based on the reduction from the node version of the multicut to the edge version, we can easily conclude that

**Lemma 1.** *The problem (NBBIM) is $\mathcal{NP}$-hard and MaxSNP-hard for $K \geq 2$ in general directed graphs, where $K$ is the number of source-terminal pairs.*

Next we mainly consider the problem (NBBIM) for the directed MSMT tree when there are no 2-critical edges, and propose two polynomial algorithms.

## 3 Algorithms in the Case of Without 2-Critical Edges

Assume that there are no 2-critical edges in this section. Recall that if there are only 1-critical edges, we proposed a polynomial algorithm for the problem (NBBIM) in directed MSMT trees. Thus we intend to reduce the case of without 2-critical edges to the case of only 1-critical edges. Now introduce some concepts.

For any $v \in V$, let *parent*$(v) := \{u|(u, v) \in E\}$ and *child*$(v) := \{u|(v, u) \in E\}$. A *descendent* (an *ascendant*) of a node $v$ is defined as any other node reachable from (to) that node, that is, the node's children (parents) and all their descendants (ascendants). Given a directed MSMT tree $T$, for any $v \in V$, a *source* (*terminal*) *subtree* rooted at $v$, denoted by $T_v^s$ ($T_v^t$), is induced by $v$ and all its ascendants (descendants). For the node 8 in Fig. 1, the node set of source subtree $T_8^s$ is $\{8, 3, 1, s_2, s_3, s_4\}$ and of terminal subtree $T_8^t$ is $\{8, 13, 14, t_3, t_4\}$.

For any node $v \in V$, let *parent-edge*$(v) := \{e = (u, v)|u \in parent(v)\}$ and *child-edge*$(v) := \{e = (v, u)|u \in child(v)\}$. A node $v$ is said to be *feasible* if either *parent-edge*$(v) \subseteq E^1$ or *child-edge*$(v) \subseteq E^1$, and *infeasible* otherwise. Notice that if $v$ is feasible, then upgrading $v$ can make all the paths $P_{s_it_j} (\forall s_i \in T_v^s, \forall t_j \in T_v^t)$ traversing $v$ have an edge with upgraded weight not more than $D$. In Fig. 2, the edges labelled with $E^u$ are useless, and other edges are 1-critical. Then the infeasible nodes are $\{3, 8, 9, t_3, s_4\}$, which are shown in bold letters.

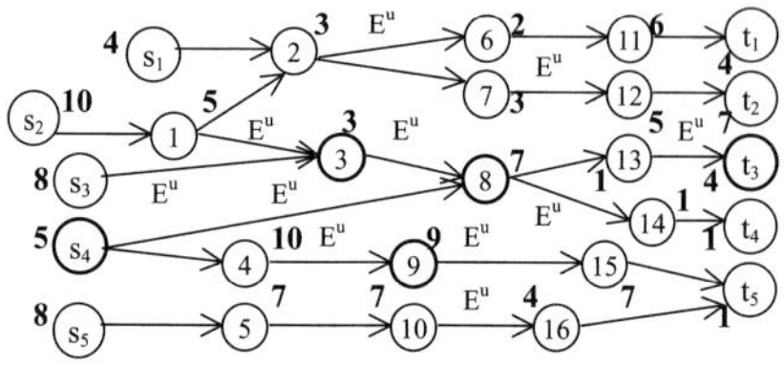

**Fig. 2.** A directed MSMT tree without 2-critical edges

In this section, we consider the problem (NBBIM) for the directed MSMT tree when there are no 2-critical edges. We present two polynomial algorithms for two cases according to whether there is a general cost for each node or not.

### 3.1 In the Case of General Cost on Each Node

Now we present a polynomial algorithm to solve problem (NBBIM) when there is a general cost on each node. The main idea is as follows. Based on the auxiliary graph $H$ obtained for the MSMT tree $T$ in Section 2, we first construct another auxiliary graph $H_2$, then find the minimum s-t cut for $H_2$.

**Algorithm 1.** *(Algorithm in the case of general cost on each node)*
*Input: an MSMT tree $T = (V, E)$, its auxiliary graph $H$ and the set $V_I$ of infeasible nodes. Output: a set $V'$ of nodes with the minimum upgrading cost.*
*Step 1: If $V_I \neq \emptyset$, go to Step 2; else go to Step 3.*
*Step 2: For any infeasible node $v \in V_I$, do*
*If there is an infeasible node $u \in parent(v)$, then add an arc $(u', v')$ to $H$;*
*else if there is an infeasible node $u \in child(v)$, then add an arc $(v, u)$ to $H$;*
*else choose any node $u \in parent(v)$, s.t., $(u, v) \in E^u$ $[u \in child(v)$, s.t., $(v, u) \in E^u]$, add an arc $(u', v')$ $[(v, u)]$.*
*Assign each added arc a large weight $M$. Denote the resulting graph by $H_1$.*
*Step 3: Add an ingoing node $s_0$ and an outgoing node $t_0$, add an arc from $s_0$ to each source $s_i \in V_s$ and an arc from each terminal $t'_i \in V'_t$ to $t_0$. Each added arc is given a large weight $M$. The obtained graph is denoted by $H_2$.*
*Step 4: Find the minimum $s_0 - t_0$ cut, denoted by $E'$, for $H_2$. Then $V' := \{v|(v, v') \in E'\}$ is the minimum cost upgrading set for the MSMT tree.*

Note that all the added arcs in $H_1$ and $H_2$ have sufficiently large weights so that they cannot belong to a minimum cut in $H_2$. Thus the minimum cut $E'$ in $H_2$ corresponds to a minimum node multicut $V'$ in $T$. Furthermore, all the auxiliary graphs $H$, $H_1$ and $H_2$ do not contain directed cycles. Then we can find the minimum $s - t$ cut in $O(|E||V|\log(|V|^2/|E|))$ operations by the algorithm presented in [5]. For the given MSMT tree $T = (V, E)$, let $n := |V|$ and $m := |E|$. Then $H$ has $2n$ nodes and $m + n$ arcs. In $H_1$, at most $2m$ arcs are added. In $H_2$, two more nodes and $|V_s| + |V_t| \leq n$ arcs are added. As a result, $H_2$ has $O(n)$ nodes and $O(3m + 2n)$ arcs, and the minimum cut can be obtained in $O((3m + 2n)n\log(n^2/(3m + 2n)))$ operations, that is, $O(n^2 \log n)$, since $m = n-1$ in a tree. Furthermore, all the auxiliary graphs can be constructed in $O(n)$ operations. Thus the complexity of Algorithm 1 is $O(n^2 \log n)$.

For example, A minimum $s_0 - t_0$ cut for the auxiliary graph $H_2$ corresponding to Fig. 2 is $E' := \{(2,2'),(13,13'),(14,14'),(t_5,t_5')\}$ and the minimum cost upgrading set is $V' := \{2,13,14,t_5\}$.

### 3.2 In the Case of Unit Cost on Each Node

We assume there is a unit cost on each node in this subsection. If there are only 1-critical edges, the problem (NBBIM) reduces to the *Minimum Cardinality Node Multicut* (MCNM) problem, in which we need to find a set $S$ of nodes with minimum cardinality $|S|$ whose removal disconnects each pair of source-terminal. Therefore, in the case that there are no 2-critical edges, we can similarly obtain the minimum cardinality upgrading set according to the algorithm for the problem (MCNM) in [4]. We also first introduce some concepts.

For each node $v$ and any node $u \in T_v^t$, the *depth* of $u$ from $v$ is defined to be the number of edges in the path from $v$ to $u$. Specifically, the depth of $v$ from $v$ is 0. For any node $v$, let $t(v) := V_t \cap T_v^t$ be the set of reachable terminals from $v$. For each node $v$, the *farthest common (feasible) ascendant* (denoted by *fca* and *fcfa*, respectively) of all its reachable terminals $t_j \in t(v)$ is the (feasible) node $x \in T_v^t$ of largest depth from $v$ that lies on each path from $v$ to $t_j$. Specifically, if $fca(v) = v_1$ and $v_1$ is infeasible, then $fcfa(v) = \bigcup_{u \in child(v)} fcfa(u)$. In the example given in Fig. 2, $fcfa(s_3) = s_3$ and $fcfa(s_4) = fcfa(8) \cup fcfa(4) = \{13, t_4, t_5\}$. Thus, the set of farthest common feasible ascendants is $V_{fcfa} := \{2, 1, s_3, 13, t_4, t_5\}$.

Notice that the set $V_{fcfa}$ is a feasible upgrading set, but a subset of $V_{fcfa}$ may still be a feasible one. Thus in Algorithm 2, we find a minimal feasible set from the set $V_{fcfa}$. More precisely, if a node $v$ can be removed from $V_{fcfa}$ such that the remaining node subset is still a feasible upgrading set, then $v$ is deleted.

**Algorithm 2.** *(Algorithm in the case of unit cost on each node)*
*Input: an MSMT tree $T = (V, E)$ and the set $V_{fcfa}$.*
*Output: a set $V_c$ of nodes with the minimum cardinality.*
*Step 1: Let $\overline{V} := V_{fcfa}$ and $V_c := \emptyset$.*
*Step 2: While $\overline{V} \neq V_c$, do*
*Choose arbitrarily a node $v \in \overline{V} \backslash V_c$.*
*Let $V' := (\overline{V} \backslash v) \cap T_v^t$. If $\bigcup_{v' \in V'} t(v') \supseteq t(v)$, then let $\overline{V} := \overline{V} \backslash v$; else put $V_c := V_c \cup v$.*

Take the MSMT tree shown in Fig. 2 as an example. We can obtain the minimum cardinality upgrading set $V_c := \{2, 13, t_4, t_5\}$ by Algorithm 2. Obviously, $1 \le |V_c| \le K$, where $K$ is the number of source-terminal pairs. Furthermore, Algorithm 2 can be done in $O(K \cdot n)$ operations, which can be relaxed to $O(n^2)$. In fact, the node multicut $V_c$ obtained from the algorithm is a minimum cardinality one by the primal-dual relationship between the minimum cardinality node multicut problem and the maximum cardinality node-disjoint path problem [4].

## 4 Conclusion and Further Research

In this paper, we consider the node based bottleneck improvement problem for multicut. We first show that the problem (NBBIM) is $\mathcal{NP}$-hard and MaxSNP-hard for $K \geq 2$ on general directed graphs. Then we consider a special case of the problem on directed MSMT trees when there are no 2-critical edges. We obtain an $O(n^2 \log n)$ algorithm when there is a general cost on each node, and present an $O(n^2)$ algorithm when there is a unit cost on each node. The two algorithms only concern the number $n$ and are irrespective of the number $K$.

Although we have solved the problem (NBBIM) on directed MSMT trees when there are no 2-critical edges, it is still a promising problem when there are only 2-critical edges. As other research topics, we can consider other improvement strategies for other cases of multicut problems, such as improving the multicut with upgrade costs on edges or under other node based upgrading models. All kinds of improvement problems can be considered on the directed or undirected graphs, especially on the trees.

## References

1. Costa, M.C., Létocart, L., Roupin, F.: Minimal Multicut and Maximal Integer Multiflow: A Survey. European J. Oper. Res. 162 (2005) 55–69
2. Garg, N., Vazirani, V.V., Yannakakis, M.: Multiway Cuts in Node Weighted Graphs. J. Algorithms 50 (2004) 49–61
3. Guan, X.C., Zhang, J.Z.: A Class of Node Based Bottleneck Improvement Problems. European J. Oper. Res. Available online 17 May (2005)
4. Guan, X.C., Zhang, J.Z.: Improving Multicut in Directed Trees by Upgrading Nodes. European J. Oper. Res. Accepted, (2005)
5. Hao, J.X., Orlin, J.B.: A Faster Algorithm for Finding the Minimum Cut in a Directed Graph. J. Algorithms 17 (1994) 424–446
6. Krumke, S.O., Marathe, M.V., et. al.: Approximation Algorithms for Certain Network Improvement Problems. J. Comb. Optim. 2 (1998) 257–288
7. Krumke, S.O., Marathe, M.V., Noltemeier, H., et. al.: Improving Minimum Cost Spanning Trees by Upgrading Nodes. J. Algorithms 33 (1999) 92–111
8. Krumke, S.O., Marathe, M.V., Noltemeier, H., et. al.: Upgrading Bottleneck Constrained Forests. Discrete Appl. Math. 108 (2001) 129–142

# Global Optimization Algorithms Using Fourier Smoothing*

Yuping Wang

School of Computer Science and Technology
Xidian University, Xi'an, 710071, China
ywang@xidian.edu.cn

**Abstract.** In this paper, a novel technique called Fourier smoothing technique, which can be used to improve any global optimization algorithm, is presented. This technique uses a properly truncated Fourier series as the smoothing function to approximate the objective function. This smoothing function can maintain the overall shape or basic shape of the objective function but eliminate its finer details. Thus it can eliminate many local minima but preserve the global minima, and make the search of optimal solution more easier and faster. To demonstrate efficiency of this technique, we integrate this technique into a simple optimization algorithm: Powell direct method. The simulation results indicate this smoothing technique can improve the Powell direct method greatly.

## 1 Introduction

If a function $f(x)$ has many local minimum points, looking for its global minimum point is a very difficult task. In recent years different kinds of effective global optimization algorithms have been proposed. For examples, evolutionary algorithms (e.g., [1]∼ [4]), filled function algorithms (e.g., [5]∼[6]) and tunneling algorithms (e.g., [7]) etc. In this paper a new technique called Fourier smoothing technique is presented. It can be used to any optimization algorithm to enhance its efficiency and performance. In this technique, a properly truncated Fourier series is as the smoothing function and used to approximate the objective function. The smoothing function can maintain the overall or basic shape of the primary function but eliminate its finer details. Thus it can eliminate many local minima but preserve the global minima, and make the search of optimal solution more easier and faster.

## 2 Smoothing Function

When we consider a global optimization problem of the following form:

$$\min\{f(x) \mid x \in [a_k, b_k]^n\}, \tag{1}$$

* This work was supported by the National Natural Science Foundation of China (60374063), and SRF for ROCS, SEM.

D.-S. Huang, K. Li, and G.W. Irwin (Eds.): ICIC 2006, LNCS 4113, pp. 901–906, 2006.

where the domain of $f(x)$ we are interested in is a bounded closed set $V = [a_k, b_k]^n$. Denote $c_k = b_k - a_k$ for $k = 1, 2, ..., n$ and $\frac{x}{c} = (\frac{x_1}{c_1}, ..., \frac{x_n}{c_n})$ Define

$$Z_m = \frac{1}{c_1 c_2 \cdots c_n} \underbrace{\int \cdots \int}_{V} f(x) \exp(-2\pi i m \cdot \frac{x}{c}) dx. \tag{2}$$

Then the Fourier series of function $f(x)$ is

$$f(x) \sim \sum_m Z_m \exp(2\pi i m \cdot \frac{x}{c}), \tag{3}$$

where the sum is taken for all $m = (m_1, ..., m_n)$ with integer entries([8]). We use a part of points generated so far to calculate the Fourier coefficients by some numerical methods such as Monte Carlo method ([9]), Number-theoretic method ([9]), etc. The Monte Carlo method calculates $Z_m$ in the following way. If we take $N$ independent samples $x^1, x^2, ..., x^N$ of $x$, an unbiased estimator for $Z_m$ is its sample mean:

$$\bar{Z}_m = \frac{1}{N} \sum_{k=1}^{N} f(x^k) \exp(-2\pi i m \cdot \frac{x^k}{c}), \tag{4}$$

where $x^k = (x_1^k, x_2^k, ..., x_n^k)$ for $k = 1, 2, ..., N$ and $\frac{x^k}{c} = (\frac{x_1^k}{c_1}, ..., \frac{x_n^k}{c_n})$ By the Strong Law of Large Numbers in probability theory, $\bar{Z}_m$ converges to $Z_m$ with probability one as $N \to +\infty$ ([9]). Define the smoothing function by the following way

$$f_t(x) = \sum_{\substack{m=(m_1,...,m_n) \\ \max\{|m_k|\} \le \lambda}} \bar{Z}_m \exp(2\pi i m \cdot \frac{x}{c}), \tag{5}$$

where $\lambda$ is a positive integer parameter and $\bar{Z}_m$ is defined by formula (4). If we denote $b_m(x) = \bar{Z}_m \exp(2\pi i m \cdot \frac{x}{c}) + \bar{Z}_{-m} \exp(2\pi i(-m) \cdot \frac{x}{c})$ for $m = (m_1, ..., m_n)$ with

$$0 < \max\{m_k | m_k \ge 0, k = 1, ..., n\} \le \lambda$$

and

$$b_0(x) = \bar{Z}_0 \exp(2\pi i 0 \cdot \frac{x}{c}),$$

then

$$b_m(x) = \frac{1}{N} \sum_{k=1}^{N} 2 f(x^k) \cos(2\pi m \cdot \frac{x - x^k}{c}) \tag{6}$$

for $m \ne (0, ..., 0)$, and

$$b_0(x) = \frac{1}{N} \sum_{k=1}^{N} f(x^k). \tag{7}$$

$$f_t(x) = \sum_{\substack{m=(m_1,...,m_n) \\ \max\{m_k | m_k \ge 0, k=1,...,n\} \le \lambda}} b_m(x). \tag{8}$$

## 3 Improving Powell Direct Method by Smoothing Technique

The smoothing technique can be integrated into any optimization algorithm to improve it. To demonstrate the improvement, in this subsection we use the smoothing technique to improve Powell direct method (briefly denoted as PDM) [10] as an example. The improved algorithm is called Smoothing Powell direct method (briefly denoted as SPDM).

**Algorithm 1 (Powell direct method—PDM)**

1. (Initialization). Given an initial point $x^1 \in R^n$, denote $e^i = (\overbrace{0, ...0, 1}^{i}, 0, ..., 0)$ for $i = 1, ..., n$. Let $d_i = e^i$ for $i = 1, ..., n$, and $k = 1$.
2. (Line search). Find $\lambda_k$ such that
$$\min_{\lambda \in R} f(x^k + \lambda d_k) = f(x^k + \lambda_k d_k)$$
and denote
$$x^{k+1} = x^k + \lambda_k d_k, \ f_{k+1} = f(x^{k+1})$$
for $k = 1, ..., n$. Denote $f_1 = f(x^1)$.
3. If k=n, go to step 4; otherwise, let $k = k + 1$, go to step 2.
4. If stop criterion is satisfied, let $x^* = x^{n+1}$, stop; otherwise, go to step 5.
5. Denote
$$\Delta = \max_{i=1 \sim n} (f_i - f_{i+1}) = f_m - f_{m+1}, \ \ \bar{f} = f(2x^{n+1} - x^1)$$
6. If
$$f_1 - 2f_{n+1} + \bar{f} \geq 2\Delta$$
let $x^1 = x^{n+1}$, $f_1 = f_{n+1}$, $k = 1$, go to step 2; otherwise, go to step 7.
7. Let
$$d_i = d_{i+1}, \ (i = m, m + 1, ..., n - 1), \ \ d_n = x^{n+1} - x^1$$
Find $\bar{\lambda}$ such that
$$f(x^{n+1} + \bar{\lambda} d_n) = \min_{\lambda \in R} f(x^{n+1} + \lambda d_n).$$
Let
$$x^1 = x^{n+1} + \bar{\lambda} d_n, \ \ f_1 = f(x^{n+1} + \bar{\lambda} d_n)$$
$k = 1$, go to step 2.

**Algorithm 2 (Smoothing Powell direct method—SMP)**

*First phase*

1. Generate a set of uniformly distributed points $\{Z^1, ..., Z^N\}$ in $[a_k, b_k]^n$ by the uniform distribution on $[a_k, b_k]^n$ or uniform design methods in ([9],[2], [11]), and calculate the initial smoothing function $f_l(x)$ by formulas (6) ∼ (8).

2. Using the best point among the points $Z^1, ..., Z^N$ as the initial point, we optimize the current smoothing function $f_t(x)$ by Powell direct method until the best solution found can not be improved further.
3. Modify the smoothing function by using the new points generated to get a new smoothing function, go to step 2.
4. If the several successive best solutions got in step 2 can not be improved, then stop; otherwise, go to the second phase.
   *Second phase*
5. Optimize the original function by Powell direct method using the final point got in step 2 as the initial point until the best solution can not be improved further.

## 4 Simulation Results

*Test problems*

$$F1(x) = -\sum_{i=1}^{n} \sin(x_i) \sin^{20}\left(\frac{i \times x_i^2}{\pi}\right),$$

where $n = 100$, $x_i \in [0, \pi]$, $i = 1 \sim 100$, $F1_{min} = -99.51$.

$$F2(x) = \frac{1}{n}\sum_{i=1}^{n}(x_i^4 - 16x_i^2 + 5x_i),$$

where $n = 100$, $x_i \in [-5, 5]$, $F2_{min} = -78.33$.

$$F3(x) = 1 + \sum_{i=1}^{n} \frac{x_i^2}{4000} - \prod_{i=1}^{n} \cos(\frac{x_i}{\sqrt{i}}),$$

where $n = 30$, $x_i \in [-600, 600]$, $i = 1 \sim 30$, $F3_{min} = 0$.

$$F4(x) = -20 \exp\left(-0.2\sqrt{\frac{1}{n}\sum_{i=1}^{n} x_i^2}\right) - \exp\left(\frac{1}{n}\sum_{i=1}^{n} \cos 2\pi x_i\right) + 20 + e,$$

where $n = 30$, $x_i \in [-32, 32]$, $i = 1 \sim 30$, $F4_{min} = 0$.

$$F5(x) = n \cdot A + \sum_{i=1}^{n}(x_i^2 - A\cos(\omega \cdot x_i)),$$

where $A = 10$, $\omega = 2\pi$, $n = 30$, $x = (x_1, ..., x_n)$, $x_1, ..., x_n \in [-5.12, 5.12]$, $F8_{min} = 0$.

$$F6(x) = \tfrac{\pi}{n}\{10\sin^2(\pi y_i) + \sum_{i=1}^{n-1}(y_i - 1)^2[1 + 10\sin^2(\pi y_{i+1})] + (y_n - 1)^2\} + \sum_{i=1}^{n} u(x_i, 10, 100, 4),$$

where $y_i = 1 + \frac{1}{4}(x_i + 1)$,

$$u(x_i, a, k, m) = \begin{cases} k(x_i - a)^m, & x_i > a, \\ 0 & x_i \in [-a, a], \\ k(-x_i - a)^m, & x_i < -a, \end{cases}$$

$n = 30$, $x_i \in [-50, 50]$, $i = 1 \sim 30$, $F3_{min} = 0$.

These test functions are all multimodal functions, where the number of local minima increases exponentially with the problem dimension ([3]). These test problems are challenging enough for performance evaluation. For example, the test function $F1$ has 100! local minima and the test function $F2$ has $2^{100}$ local minima.

*Results and comparison*

To identify any improvement due to smoothing technique, in simulations we use the Golden section method as the line search method for both PDM and SPDM, and use the same initial points on same test function for both PDM and SPDM. When solutions found in 30 successive iterations after 500 iterations can not be improved, the execution of both algorithms is stopped. We performed 50 independent runs for each of PDM and SPDM on each test function and recorded: The best function value found in 50 runs, denoted as $F_{min}$, the mean best function value in 50 runs, denoted as $F_{mean}$, the worst one among the 50 best function values found in 50 runs, denoted as $F_{max}$, the standard deviation of the 50 best function values found in 50 runs, denoted as $std$, and the mean CPU time (minutes) used on each function in 50, denoted as $CPU_{mean}$. The results are given in the Tables 1 and 2.

It can be observed from Table 1 that, as a local optimization method, PDM can not find a close-to-optimal mean best solution for most problems, and only for test function $F2$ it can find a close-to-optimal mean best solution. However, for all test functions, its improvement, SPDM, can find close-to-optimal mean best solutions. Moreover, the standard deviations of solutions found by SPDM are smaller or much smaller than those of solutions found by PDM. It can also be seen from Table 2 that both the best and worst solutions obtained by SPDM for each test function are very close to optimal ones. This illustrates that even for PDM, a local optimization method, its improvement by smoothing function method, SPDM, is very efficient and stable. Although SPDM uses more CPU

**Table 1.** Comparison of mean best solution, standard deviation and mean CPU time for PDM and SPDM

| | $F_{mean}$ | | $std$ | | $CPU_{mean}$ | |
|---|---|---|---|---|---|---|
| | SPDM | PDM | SPDM | PDM | SPDM | PDM |
| $F1$ | -99.4632 | -84.5451 | $4.26\times10^{-14}$ | 0.3710 | 616.58 | 578.17 |
| $F2$ | -78.3323 | -78.3323 | $6.09\times10^{-14}$ | $6.70\times10^{-14}$ | 249.55 | 233.38 |
| $F3$ | $6.70\times10^{-9}$ | 0.5937 | $1.89\times10^{-9}$ | 0.4268 | 51.044 | 80.597 |
| $F4$ | $2.29\times10^{-4}$ | 11.7765 | $2.26\times10^{-5}$ | 8.5217 | 43.857 | 69.508 |
| $F5$ | $1.98\times10^{-5}$ | 29.5547 | $3.87\times10^{-6}$ | 0.4755 | 36.115 | 58.075 |
| $F6$ | $1.16\times10^{-14}$ | 2.8039 | $7.78\times10^{-15}$ | 0.9169 | 196.65 | 242.99 |

**Table 2.** Comparison of the best and worst optimal solutions found by PDM and SPDM in 50 runs

| | $F_{min}$ | | $F_{max}$ | |
|---|---|---|---|---|
| | SPDM | PDM | SPDM | PDM |
| $F1$ | -99.4632 | -85.7981 | -99.4632 | -84.0456 |
| $F2$ | -78.3323 | -78.3323 | -78.3323 | -78.3323 |
| $F3$ | $2.9727\times10^{-9}$ | 0.0544 | $1.1512\times10^{-8}$ | 3.1174 |
| $F4$ | $1.7156\times10^{-4}$ | $2.7957\times10^{-7}$ | $2.8771\times10^{-4}$ | 19.3325 |
| $F5$ | $1.0936\times10^{-5}$ | 27.8169 | $3.0733\times10^{-5}$ | 29.8488 |
| $F6$ | $1.4021\times10^{-15}$ | $1.1202\times10^{-15}$ | $2.8115\times10^{-14}$ | 3.1094 |

time than PDM for $F1$ and $F2$, SPDM is unnecessary to use so much time because it has found the optimal solutions in much fewer than 500 iterations.

## References


1. Lee,C.Y., Yao,X.: Evolutionary Programming Using Mutations Based on the Levy Probability Distribution. IEEE Trans. Evol. Comput. **8** (2004) 1-13
2. Leung,Y.W., Wang,Y.P.: An Orthogonal Genetic Algorithm with Quantization for Global Numerical Optimization. IEEE Trans. Evol. Comput. **5** (2001) 41-53
3. Yao,X., Liu,Y., Lin,G.: Evolutionary Programming Made Faster. IEEE Trans. Evol. Comput. **3** (1999) 82-102
4. Fogel,D.B.: Evolutionary Computation: toward a New Philosophy of Machine Intelligence. IEEE Press, New York (1995)
5. Lucidi,S., Piccialli,V.: New Classes of Globally Convexized Filled Functions for Global Optimization. J. of Global Optimization. **24** (2002) 219-236
6. Ge,R.P., Qin,Y. F.: Globally Convexized Filled Functions for Global Optimization. Applied Mathematics and Computation. **35** (1999) 131-158
7. Oblow,E.M.: Stochastic Tunneling Algorithm for Global Optimization. J. of Global Optimization. **20** (2001) 195-212
8. Cartwright,M.: Fourier Methods for Mathematicians, Scientists and Engineers. Ellis Horwood Limited, Chichester England (1990)
9. Fang,F.T., Wang,Y.: Number-theoretic Methods in Atatistics. Chapman & Hall, London UK (1994)
10. Fletcher,R.: Practical Methods of Optimization. Wiley, Chichester England (1987)
11. Leung,Y.W., Wang,Y.P.: Multiobjective Programming Using Uniform Design and Genetic Algorithm. IEEE Trans. Systems, Man, and Cybernetics, Part C: Applications and Review. **30** (2000) 293-304

# Heuristics to Convex Quadratic Knapsack Problems in Sorted ADP*

Bin Zhang and Zhongsheng Hua

School of Management, University of Science & Technology of China,
Hefei, Anhui 230026, People's Republic of China
bzhang3@mail.ustc.edu.cn, zshua@ustc.edu.cn

**Abstract.** Approximate dynamic programming (ADP) was developed for solving large-scale optimization problems, and function approximation is an important method in the dynamic programming scheme. Continuous quadratic programming relaxation (CQPR) and the integral parts of the solutions to CQPR are two intuitionistic heuristics as function approximations in ADP for solving quadratic knapsack problems (QKPs). We propose a rule of ordering variables to sort the first variable to be solved in ADP, and develop a heuristic which adaptively fixes the variables according to the solution to CQPR of convex QKPs based the rule. By using the rule and heuristics, we propose a sorted ADP heuristic scheme for QKPs.

## 1 Introduction

The quadratic knapsack problem (QKP) consists minimizing a positive quadratic function subject to a linear capacity constraint. Denote by $\mathbf{x}^T$ transpose of a vector $\mathbf{x}$, QKP can be formally defined as follows.

$$\begin{array}{lll} \mathrm{QKP}(n,b_0,\mathbf{c}) & \min & \frac{1}{2}\mathbf{x}^T\mathbf{Q}\mathbf{x}+\mathbf{c}^T\mathbf{x}, \\ & \text{s.t.} & \mathbf{p}^T\mathbf{x}\le b_0, \mathbf{x}\in \mathbf{Z}_\mathbf{n}^+, \end{array} \tag{1}$$

with $\mathbf{Q}=(q_{ij})_{n\times n}$ is the symmetric quadratic coefficient matrix, $\mathbf{x}=(x_1, \cdots, x_n)^T$ is the decision vector, and $\mathbf{c}=(c_1, \cdots, c_n)^T$ is the linear coefficient vector. Vector $\mathbf{p}=(p_1,\cdots,p_n)^T$ with $p_i>0$ for $i=1, \ldots, n$ and scalar $b_0>0$ construct a linear capacity constraint. This paper focuses on convex QKP in which $\mathbf{Q}$ is positive semidefinite.

QKP may represent many practical situations such as capacity planning problems [1], and appears as a subproblem in several applications of set covering problem and complier design [2]. Current practical approaches for solving QKP are branch and

* Supported by Program for New Century Excellent Talents in University of China (Grant No.: NCET-04-0570), NSFC (Grant No.: 70571073) and the Specialized Research Fund for the Doctoral Programme of Higher Education (Grant No.: 20050358002).

D.-S. Huang, K. Li, and G.W. Irwin (Eds.): ICIC 2006, LNCS 4113, pp. 907 – 912, 2006.

bound algorithms [3]. These approaches can obtain the exact solution of QKP, but they are of little use if the size of QKP is large or QKP appears as a subproblem within general constrained quadratic programming. QKP can be solved by dynamic programming theoretically. However, because of their storage requirement and computation complexity, dynamic programming is usually impractical for large-scale problems. Many methods such as function approximation and Lagrangian multiplier methods have been proposed to contribute diverse ADP methodologies [4].

In this paper, we try to construct a sorted ADP heuristic scheme, which is based on ADP and a rule of ordering variables we have developed for sorting the first variable to be solved in ADP, and propose a new heuristic which adaptively fixes the variables according to the solution of CQPR.

## 2 The Sorted ADP Heuristic Scheme

We propose a rule of ordering variables to construct sorted ADP heuristic scheme.

### 2.1 ADP Concepts

To reformulate QKP$(n,b_0,\mathbf{c})$ in Eq. (1) as a dynamic program, we consider the subproblem QKP$(k,b,\mathbf{c}')$, which includes the *first* $k$ variables with the right-hand side $b$ and $k$-dimensional vector $\mathbf{c}'$. Denote by $F(k,b,\mathbf{c}')$ the optimal value of QKP$(k,b,\mathbf{c}')$, $x^{OPT}(k,b,\mathbf{c}')=(x_1^*,\cdots,x_k^*)$ an optimal solution to QKP$(k,b,\mathbf{c}')$. Denote by $D(k,b)=\{x_k \mid 0\le x_k \le \lfloor b/p_k \rfloor\}$ the set of possible integer values of variable $x_k$, where $\lfloor\ \rfloor$ is the floor operation. Taking the minimum of the preceding objective values gives the optimal value $F(k,b,\mathbf{c}')$ to the subproblem QKP$(k,b,\mathbf{c}')$. Thus dynamic programming recursion can be stated as a "forward sweep" process

$$F(1,b,\mathbf{c}')=\min_{x_1\in D(1,b)}\left\{\frac{1}{2}q_{11}x_1^2+c_1'x_1\right\}, \tag{2}$$

$$\begin{cases} F(k,b,\mathbf{c}')=\min\limits_{x_k\in D(k,b)}\{F(k-1,\ b-p_kx_k,\ \mathbf{c}'')+\frac{1}{2}q_{kk}x_k^2+c_k'x_k\}, \\ \text{where } c_i''=c_i'+q_{ki}x_k,\ \ \text{for } i=1,\ \cdots,\ k-1,\ \ \text{and } k=2,\ \cdots,\ n, \end{cases} \tag{3}$$

where $\mathbf{c}'=(c_1',\ \cdots,\ c_k')^T$, $\mathbf{c}''=(c_1'',\ \cdots,\ c_k'')^T$. Using

$$x_k^*\in\arg\min_{x_k\in D(k,b)}\{F(k-1,\ b-p_kx_k,\ \mathbf{c}'')+\frac{1}{2}q_{kk}x_k^2+c_k'x_k\}, \tag{4}$$

the optimal solution can be constructed in a bottom-up fashion

$$x^{OPT}(k,b,\mathbf{c}')=(x^{OPT}(k-1,b-p_kx_k^*,\mathbf{c}''),x_k^*), \tag{5}$$

with $c''_i = c'_i + q_{ki}x^*_k$, $i = 1,\cdots,k-1$ for $k = 2,\ldots,n$. The basic idea behind ADP is to approximate $F(k,b,\mathbf{c}')$ and construct an upper bound solution through Eqs. (3-5).

## 2.2 Rule of Ordering Variables

We develop a rule to order variables to sort the first variable to be solved in ADP, according to their profit-to-weight ratios.

Denote by QP($k,b,\mathbf{c}'$) the CQPR of the QKP($k,b,\mathbf{c}'$), which replaces $\mathbf{x} \in \mathbf{Z}^+_\mathbf{n}$ by $\mathbf{x} \in \mathbf{R}^+_\mathbf{n}$ in Eq. (1), which can be efficiently solved by using the Lemke algorithm [5]. Let $\mathbf{x}^{H_1}(k,b,\mathbf{c}') = (x_1,\cdots,x_k)$ be the optimal solution to QP($k,b,\mathbf{c}'$), $H_1(k,b,\mathbf{c}')$ be the corresponding objective value . Let $f(x_1,\cdots,x_k) = H_1(k,b,\mathbf{c}')$. If all variables of the solution $\mathbf{x}^{H_1}(k,b,\mathbf{c}')$ are integral, then let $x^{OPT}(k,b,\mathbf{c}') = \mathbf{x}^{H_1}(k,b,\mathbf{c}')$, the rule terminates with an optimal solution. Otherwise, let $S(k,b,\mathbf{c}') = \{i \mid x_i \text{ not integral}, i = 1,\cdots,k\}$ and, let $s$ be the size of $S(k,b,\mathbf{c}')$. For $\forall i \in S(k,b,\mathbf{c}')$, let $r^L_i$ be the augment of the function value when saving one unit resource, and $r^U_i$ be the decrease of the function value when expending one unit resource, then

$$\begin{cases} r^L_i = (f(x_1,\cdots,\lfloor x_i \rfloor,\cdots,x_k) - f(x_1,\cdots,x_i,\cdots,x_k))/(p_i(x_i - \lfloor x_i \rfloor)), \\ r^U_i = (f(x_1,\cdots,x_i,\cdots,x_k) - f(x_1,\cdots,\lceil x_i \rceil,\cdots,x_k))/(p_i(\lceil x_i \rceil - x_i)), \end{cases} \tag{6}$$

where $\lceil\ \rceil$ is the ceil operation, Denote by $z^L_i$ and $z^U_i$ the normalization of $r^L_i$ and $r^U_i$ as follows. ( $z^U_i$ can be obtained similarly.)

$$\begin{cases} z^L_i = 1/s, & \text{if } r^L_i = r^L_j \text{ for } \forall j \in S(k,b,\mathbf{c}'), \\ z^L_i = \dfrac{r^L_i - \min_{i\in S(k,b,\mathbf{c}')}\{r^L_i\}}{\max_{i\in S(k,b,\mathbf{c}')}\{r^L_i\} - \min_{i\in S(k,b,\mathbf{c}')}\{r^L_i\}}, & \text{otherwise.} \end{cases} \tag{7}$$

Taking the balance of the smallness of $r^L_i$ and $r^U_i$, the index of the first decision variable to be solved can be determined by $t \in \arg\min_{i\in S(k,b,\mathbf{c}')}\{z^l_i + z^u_i\}$.

## 2.3 The SADP-*H* Scheme

The basic idea of ADP heuristic scheme is to estimate $F(k,b,\mathbf{c}')$ in Eq. (3) by an upper bound $H(k,b,\mathbf{c}')$. By applying the rule of ordering variables, we construct the SADP-*H* scheme. We denote by $\mathbf{x}^H$ the corresponding solution of $H(k,b,\mathbf{c}')$, details of the SADP-*H* scheme are described in Fig. 1

*Step* 1. Using the rule of ordering variable to calulate $t \in \arg\min_{i \in S(k,b,\mathbf{c}')} \left\{ z_i^l + z_i^u \right\}$.

*Step* 2. Exchange parameters $q$, $c'$ and $p$ of $x_t$ and that of $x_k$.

*Step* 3. Calculate $D(k,b)$, and calculate $H(k-1, b-p_k x_k, \mathbf{c}'')$, for $\forall x_k \in D(k,b)$. Apply Eqs. (4-5) and calculate $x_k^*$. $c_i' \leftarrow c_i' + q_{ki} x_k^*$, for $i = 1, \cdots, k-1$, $b \leftarrow b - p_k x_k^*$, $k \leftarrow k-1$, and update $A'$, $G'$.

*Step* 4. If $(k = 1)$, calculate and output $x^*$; Otherwise go to *Step* 1.

**Fig. 1.** Main steps of SADP-*H* scheme

### 2.4 A Heuristic

Denoted by $H_1$, $H_2$ the objective value of CQPR and that of the integral parts of the solutions to CQPR, respectively, for more details of $H_1$, $H_2$, see [6]. The basic idea of adaptively fixing the variables is to adaptively reduce the number of variables ($H_3$) by the rule of ordering variables we have proposed. By applying the above rule, we can calculate $x_t$ and let $x_t^{H_3} = \lfloor x_t \rfloor$, update $c_i'' = c_i' + q_{ti} x_t^{H_3}$, for $i \neq t$, $\forall i \in S(k,b,\mathbf{c}')$. Let $H_3(k,b,\mathbf{c}')$ denote the corresponding objective value of $\mathbf{x}^{H_3}(k,b,\mathbf{c}')$. Thus, we get the upper bound solution of QKP$(k,b,\mathbf{c}')$ by

$$\begin{cases} \mathbf{x}^{H_3}(k,b,\mathbf{c}') = (x^{H_3}(k-1, b-p_t x_t^{H_3}, \mathbf{c}''), x_t^{H_3}), \quad k = 2, \cdots, n, \\ \mathbf{x}^{H_3}(1,b,\mathbf{c}') = \mathbf{x}^{H_2}(1,b,\mathbf{c}'). \end{cases} \tag{8}$$

## 3 Numerical Results

In this section, numerical results are provided for evaluating SADP-*H* scheme for QKPs. The test QKPs in our experiments are both randomly generated as well as the literature [6], we also construct *uncorrelated (UC)*, *weakly correlated (WC)* and *strongly correlated (SC)* random problems, and set computing time and solution quality as the performance criteria. In all computational studies, given problem size $n$, 10 test instances for each type problem (*UC*, *WC* and *SC*) were randomly generated, and we set $\varepsilon = 0$ for heuristic $H_1$, and report CPU computation times in seconds and perform all calculations in double-precision arithmetic. All computational experiments were conducted on a Dell PowerEdge 1500SC (1266MHz, dual processor) with Microsoft Visual C++ 6.0.

For small size problems (10 variables), we compare $H_2$, $H_3$, SADP-$H_1$, SADP-$H_2$, and SADP-$H_3$ with the optimal solution obtained by dynamic programming (DP). The solution quality and computing time of these six approaches are shown in Table 1. We record the gaps between the optimal objective values *OPT* to QKP and the objective value $v(X)$ resulting from our approaches, as $(v(X) - OPT)/|OPT| \times 100$. For large-scale QKPs, we compare the performance of the five approaches expect for DP, and report computational results for QKPs with 100 variables, shown in Table 2. For these large-scale QKPs, we report the gaps calculated by the optimal objective value to QP instead of *OPT*.

**Table 1.** Six approaches performance and comparison for QKPs with 10 variables

| Criteria | Type | DP | $H_2$ | $H_3$ | SADP-$H_1$ | SADP-$H_2$ | SADP-$H_3$ |
|---|---|---|---|---|---|---|---|
| | *UC* | 0 | 13.07 | 1.35 | 1.02 | 3.17 | 1.14 |
| Mean of gap | *WC* | 0 | 17.10 | 2.75 | 1.62 | 4.97 | 1.82 |
| | *SC* | 0 | 14.78 | 1.64 | 1.26 | 3.69 | 0.83 |
| Mean of | *UC* | 4.32 | 0.05 | 0.05 | 0.05 | 0.06 | 0.08 |
| computing | *WC* | 6.32 | 0.05 | 0.04 | 0.05 | 0.06 | 0.08 |
| time | *SC* | 2.62 | 0.05 | 0.05 | 0.05 | 0.05 | 0.08 |

**Table 2.** Five approaches performance and comparison for QKPs with 100 variables

| Criteria | Type | $H_2$ | $H_3$ | SADP-$H_1$ | SADP-$H_2$ | SADP-$H_3$ |
|---|---|---|---|---|---|---|
| | *UC* | 45.13 | 9.44 | 9.27 | 19.03 | 7.06 |
| Mean of gap | *WC* | 59.86 | 13.86 | 12.50 | 29.52 | 6.90 |
| | *SC* | 30.50 | 3.81 | 3.80 | 13.33 | 2.56 |
| Mean of | *UC* | 0.12 | 0.62 | 18.35 | 12.86 | 83.66 |
| computing | *WC* | 0.12 | 0.65 | 19.72 | 14.41 | 107.39 |
| time | *SC* | 0.14 | 1.31 | 33.18 | 29.01 | 256.10 |

The results in Table 1 show that the computation time of $H_2$ or $H_3$ is much shorter than that of dynamic programming, and $H_3$ is a promising heuristic in terms of both solution quality and computation time. As shown in Table 2, $H_3$ can solve large-scale QKPs in short computing times. SADP-$H_3$ is the leading approach for solving large-scale QKPs in terms of solution quality. In addition, in comparison with the results of ADP-*H* in [6], on average, SADP-*H* can achieve higher solution quality at the cost of more computation time.

The above observations are confirmed by statistical tests. Table 3 summarizes all pairwise comparisons on computing times and gaps between the five approaches, respectively, by applying a paired 2-tailed t-test for all randomly generated QKPs with 100 variables. In Table 3, "≈" indicates that there is no significant difference between the corresponding row and column approaches, while ">>" ("<<") indicates that the corresponding result to the row approach is significantly larger (smaller) than the corresponding result to the column approach at the 0.01 significance level, and ">" ("<") indicates the same comparison at the 0.05 significance level.

**Table 3.** Approaches comparison on computing time (gap) for QKPs with 100 variables

| | $H_3$ | SADP-$H_1$ | SADP-$H_2$ | SADP-$H_3$ |
|---|---|---|---|---|
| $H_2$ | << (>>) | << (>>) | << (>>) | << (>>) |
| $H_3$ | | << (≈) | << (<<) | << (>>) |
| SADP-$H_1$ | | | >> (<) | << (>>) |
| SADP-$H_2$ | | | | << (>>) |

## 4 Conclusions

Based on the numerical results, it can be concluded that: (1) the heuristic which adaptively fixes the variables according to the solution of CQPR for large-scale QKP is surprisingly strong. (2) SADP heuristic scheme is encouraging. It is flexible as it works with an arbitrary heuristic.

## References

1. Hua, Z.S., Banerjee, P.: Aggregate Line Capacity Design for PWB Assembly Systems. Int. J. Prod. Res. 38 (2000) 2417–2441
2. Ferreira, C.E., Martin, A., De, Souza C., Weismantel, R., Wolsey, L.: Formulations and Valid Inequalities for the Node Capacitated Graph Partitioning Problem. Math. Program. 74 (1996) 247–267
3. Hammer, P.L., Rader, D.J.: Efficient Methods for Solving Quadratic 0-1 Knapsack Problems. Infor, 35 (1997) 170–182
4. Cooper, L., Cooper, M.W.: Introduction to Dynamic Programming. Pergamon Press, Elmsford New York (1981)
5. Zhang, B., Hua, Z.S.: An Improved Lemke Algorithm for Convex Quadratic Programming with Equality Constraints. Journal of University of Science and Technology of China, 34 (2004) 668–677
6. Hua, Z.S., Zhang, B., Liang, L.: An Approximate Dynamic Programming Approach to Convex Quadratic Knapsack Problems. Comput. Oper. Res. (2006) 660–673

# Local Optima Properties and Iterated Local Search Algorithm for Optimum Multiuser Detection Problem

Shaowei Wang[1], Qiuping Zhu[1], and Lishan Kang[2]

[1] School of Electronic Information, Wuhan University, Wuhan, Hubei, 430079, P.R. China
[2] State Key Laboratory of Software Engineering,
Wuhan University, Wuhan,Hubei, 430072, P.R. China
{shwwang, qpzhu, kang}@whu.edu.cn

**Abstract.** Optimum multiuser detection (OMD) in direct-sequence code-division multiple access (DS-CDMA) communication systems is an NP-complete combinatorial optimization problem. The first contribution of this paper is the theoretical investigation of the OMD problem. Its fitness landscape is specified by a set of neighborhoods of all points of the search space. The number and the distributions of local optima are studied in detail. Investigation results give hints how to choose the modification operators and design more efficient random search heuristics for this problem. Then an efficient iterated local search algorithm is proposed for multiuser detection and simulation results show that it can provide rather good performance for cases where other algorithms perform poorly.

## 1 Introduction

From a combinatorial optimization viewpoint, the optimum multiuser detection (OMD) [1] in direct-sequence code-division multiple access (DS-CDMA) communication systems is an NP-complete problem [2]. Random search heuristics (RSH) are useful methods for such problems and many RSH multiuser detectors have been studied which exhibit better performance than other linear or nonlinear ones. Earlier works on applying RSH to OMD problem can be found in [3][4][5].The essence of OMD is to search for possible combinations of the users' entire transmitted bit sequence that maximizes the logarithm likelihood function (LLF) derived from the maximum likelihood sequence estimation rule [1], which is called fitness function or objective function in the RSH multiuser detectors[3][4][5]. Comparing with so much emphasis on the implementation details and the performance analysis of these algorithms, little attention has been paid on the analysis of statistical characteristics of the OMD problem in terms of combinatorial optimization.

Combinatorial optimization is concerned with finding "optimal", i.e., minimal or maximal values of a cost function. Local optima thus play an important role since they might be obstacle on the way to the optimal solution [6]. The number of local optima is a measure for the "ruggedness" of landscape [7]. On the other hand, the distributions of local optima provide the key information of jumping out the local optima and moving towards the global optimum. In this paper we formulate the fitness landscapes [8][9] of OMD problem by specifying a set of neighborhoods of

D.-S. Huang, K. Li, and G.W. Irwin (Eds.): ICIC 2006, LNCS 4113, pp. 913 – 918, 2006.

all points in the search space and taking the LLF as the objective function. Then we analyze the characteristics of local optima in the fitness landscapes, including the number of local optima and their distributions. Based on the analysis results, we propose an efficient iterated local search (ILS) [10][11] multiuser detector and compare its performance with others.

The remainder of this paper is organized as follows. In Sect.2, we state the OMD problem and construct its fitness landscape. Local optima properties of the fitness landscape are analyzed in Sect.3 by statistical analysis. In Sect.4, we propose an efficient iterated local search algorithm and compare its performance with other multiuser detection algorithms. A short conclusion is given in Sect.5.

## 2 System Model

Assume a binary phase shift keying (BPSK) transmission through an additive-white-Gaussian-noise (AWGN) channel shared by $K$ active users in a synchronous DS-CDMA system. The baseband received signal can be expressed as

$$r(t)=\sum_{k=1}^{K} A_k b_k s_k(t)+n(t) . \tag{1}$$

where $A_k$ is the signal amplitude of the $k$th user, $b_k$ is the transmitted bit of the $k$th user, $s_k(t)$ is the normalized signature waveform of the $k$th user, $n(t)$ is the white Gaussian noise with power spectral density $\sigma^2$. The sufficient statistics for demodulation of the transmitted bits $\mathbf{b}$ are given by $K$ matched filter outputs [12]

$$\mathbf{y}=\mathbf{RAb}+\mathbf{n} . \tag{2}$$

where $\mathbf{y}=[y_1,y_2,...,y_K]^T$, $\mathbf{b}=[b_1,b_2,...,b_K]^T$. $\mathbf{A}$ is the $K\times K$ diagonal matrix whose diagonal element is the $k$th user's signal amplitude $A_k$. $\mathbf{R}\in\mathbb{R}^{K\times K}$ is the signature correlation matrix of the signature waveform. $\mathbf{n}$ is the Gaussian noise vector with zero mean and autocorrelation matrix

$$E[\mathbf{nn}^T]=\sigma^2\mathbf{R} . \tag{3}$$

The optimum multiuser detection problem is to generate an estimation sequence $\hat{\mathbf{b}}=[\hat{b}_1,\hat{b}_2,...,\hat{b}_K]^T$ to maximum the objective function

$$f(\mathbf{b})=2\mathbf{y}^T\mathbf{Ab}-\mathbf{b}^T\mathbf{Hb} . \tag{4}$$

where $\mathbf{H}=\mathbf{ARA}$. It means to search $2^K$ possible bit sequences exhaustively and is proven to be NP-complete in [2].

## 3 Local Optima Properties of the OMD Problem

The fitness landscape of the OMD problem is dynamic because of the varieties of signal to noise ratio ( $SNR$ ) and the spreading factor. Our main purpose is to find out the corresponding changes of local optima and track it in order to design efficient modification operators for RSH algorithms.

First we study the properties of local optima under different spreading factors. Without loss the generality the packet size $M$ is set to 1. The number of active users is 10, 20 and 50 ( $K = 10, 20, 50$ ). The spreading factor is 31, 63 and 127 ( $SF = 31, 63, 127$ ). The load of the systems concerned is $L = K/SF$ and $SNR$ is set

**Table 1.** Number of local optima $N$ for different systems, $SNR = 6$

| Cases | $SF = 31$ $K = 10$ | $SF = 31$ $K = 20$ | $SF = 31$ $K = 50$ | $SF = 63$ $K = 10$ | $SF = 63$ $K = 20$ | $SF = 63$ $K = 50$ | $SF = 127$ $K = 10$ | $SF = 127$ $K = 20$ | $SF = 127$ $K = 50$ |
|---|---|---|---|---|---|---|---|---|---|
| $L = K/SF$ | 0.32 | 0.65 | 1.64 | 0.16 | 0.32 | 0.79 | 0.08 | 0.16 | 0.39 |
| $N\ (\times 10^4)$ | 0.40 | 3.17. | 47.51 | 0.12 | 0.47 | 24.01 | 0.02 | 0.08 | 1.81 |

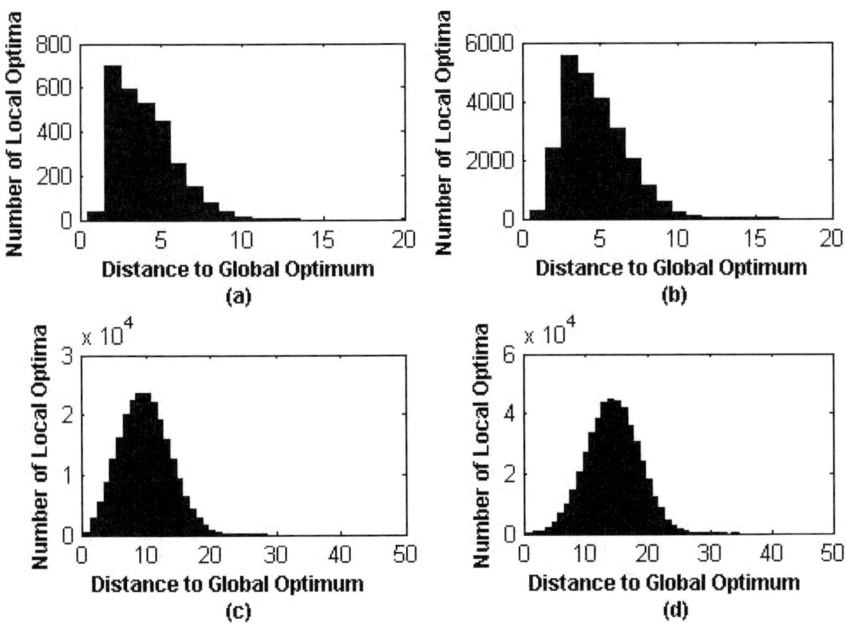


**Fig. 1.** Distributions of local optima in different systems, $SNR = 6$, (a) $K = 20$, $SF = 63$; (b) $K = 20$, $SF = 31$; (c) $K = 50$, $SF = 63$; (d) $K = 50$, $SF = 31$

**Table 2.** Number of local optima $N$ for different $SNR$ . $K = 50$ , $SF = 63$ .

| $SNR$ /dB | 2 | 4 | 6 | 8 | 10 |
|---|---|---|---|---|---|
| $N$ ($\times 10^4$) | 23.90 | 25.44 | 24.01 | 23.23 | 22.12 |

to 6. For each system $10^4$ instances are randomly generated to investigate the local optima properties. Since the global optima are not known for the problems in the analysis, the transmitted bits $\mathbf{b}$ are used instead which are likely to be the global optima of the instances, at least if the $SNR$ is not too small. Table 1 gives the number of local optima $N$ in different systems.

From Table 1 we can see that the local optima of the OMD problem increase with the load of systems. In other words, if the spreading factor is constant, the local optima increase with the number of users. By using curve fitting techniques, the number of local optima is approximated as

$$N \approx 2.48 \times 10^{-6} 2^{K} . \tag{5}$$

We can see that the local optima increase exponentially with the number of users $K$ in the same spreading factor case. Therefore, it becomes harder and harder to find out the optimum as the increase of users. Fig.1 gives the histograms of local optima (not including global optima) in four systems.

Then we investigate how the varieties of $SNR$ affect the properties of local optima. The number of active users is 50 and the spreading factor is 63. Table 2 shows the number of local optima is in the same order as the $SNR$ changes. It proves that the load of systems is the key factor which determines the number of the local optima.

## 4 Efficient Iterated Local Search for the OMD Problem

With the conclusions derived from the local optima properties, we propose an efficient ILS algorithm for the OMD problem. The algorithm can be outlined as follows.

1) The output of the conventional detector (CD) is taken as the initial search point, $\mathbf{b} = sign(\mathbf{y}) \in \{-1,+1\}^K$ . Perform local search and produce the local optima $\mathbf{b}_{\mathrm{L}}$ which is associated with $\mathbf{b}$ . The algorithm producing local optima is the $k-\mathrm{opt}$ local search proposed by Lim [5].
2) Flip $m$ bits of $\mathbf{b}_{\mathrm{L}}$ to generate a new start $\mathbf{b}$ . $m$ is decided as follows.

$$m = \mathrm{round}(\left|\mathbf{N}\left(\mu,\sigma^2\right)\right|) . \tag{6}$$

Here $\mathbf{N}\left(0,\sigma^2\right)$ is the distribution function of local optima of the system studied, round(X) is a function which rounds the elements of X to the nearest integers. There is litter probability that $m$ is greater than $K$ which is the length of solution vector. If this case happens, perform the function round( $\left|\mathbf{N}\left(\mu,\sigma^2\right)\right|$ ) until $1 \le m \le K$ . Then perform local search to produce new local optimum $\mathbf{b}_L$ .

3) Repeat the second step until the pre-assigned number of iterations is met.

Consider synchronous DS-CDMA systems with perfect power control and random binary sequences with length $L = 63$ are employed as spreading sequences. For asynchronous DS-CDMA systems, each symbol within the observation window can be considered as originated from a different synchronous user [11]. Therefore an asynchronous system is interpreted as an equivalent synchronous system and the ILS algorithm is available too.

The bit error rate (BER) performance of the conventional detector (CD), evolutionary programming detector (EP) [3], $k-\text{opt}$ detector [5], parallel interference cancellation (PIC) [13] and the proposed ILS is illustrated in Fig.3 by the curves of BER versus $SNR$ . The number of users is 20 and 50 ( $K = 20, 50$ ) in Fig.3 (a) and (b) respectively. It is obvious that ILS detector outperforms other detectors in BER performance.

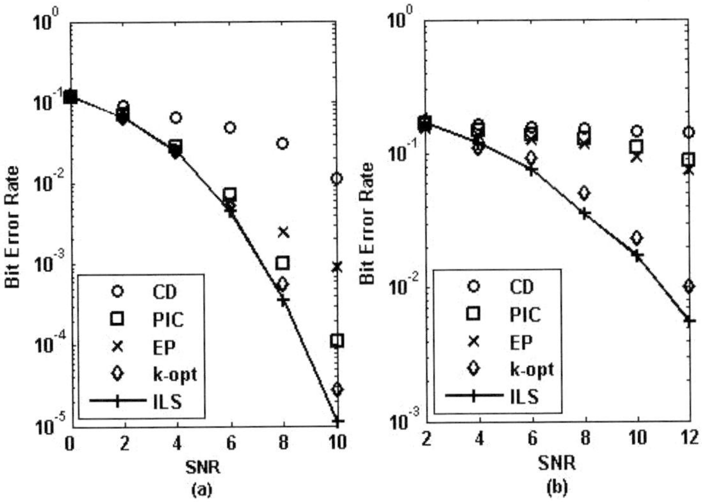


**Fig. 2.** BER against $SNR$ performance of ILS, $k-\text{opt}$ , EP, PIC and CD for $SF = 63$ . (a) $K = 20$ and (b) $K = 50$ .

## 5 Conclusions

This paper studies the local optima properties of the fitness landscape of OMD problem and proposes an efficient iterated local search multiuser detector. Using curve fitting techniques, we find that local optima increase exponentially with the load of active users. The local optima are approximately subject to Gaussian PDF, especially the number of users is large. The iterated local search multiuser detector which takes into account these properties can provide good performance for cases where other ones perform poorly.

## References


1. Verdu, S.: Minimum Probability of Error for Asynchronous Gaussian Multiple-access Channels. IEEE Transactions on Information Theory, Vol. 32(1) (1986) 85-96
2. Verdu, S.: Computational Complexity of Optimal Multiuser Detection. Algorithmica, Vol.4 (1989) 303–312
3. Lim,, H.S., Rao, M.V.C., Alan, W.C., Chuah, H.T.: Mulatiuser Detection for DS-CDMA Systems Using Evolutionary Programming. IEEE Communications Letters, Vol.7(3) (2003) 101-103
4. Hu, J., Rick S.B.: A Gradient Guided Search Algorithm for Multiuser Detection. IEEE Communications Letters, Vol.4(11) (2000) 340-342
5. Lim, H.S., Venkatesh, B.: An Efficient Local Search Heuristics for Asynchronous Multiuser Detection. IEEE Communications Letters, Vol.7(6) (2003) 299-301
6. Stadler, P.F.: Fitness Landscape. Lecture Notes in Physics, Vol.585, Springer-Verlag Berlin Heidelberg, (2002) 183-204
7. Palmer, R.: Optimization on Rugged Landscapes. Molecular Evolution on Rugged Landscapes: Proteins, RNA, and the Immune System. Edit by A.S. Perelson, S.A. Kauffman, (1991) 3–25
8. Weinberger, E. D.: Correlated and Uncorrelated Fitness Landscapes and How to Tell the Difference. Biological Cybernetics, Vol.63 (1990) 325-336
9. Peter, M., Bernd, F.: Fitness Landscape Analysis and Memetic Algorithms for the Quadratic Assignment Problem. IEEE Transactions on Evolutionary Computation, Vol.4(4) (2000) 337-352
10. Lourenco, H. R., Martin, O., Thomas, S.: A Beginner's Introdution to Iterated Local Search. Procedings of the 4th Metaheuristics International Conference, (2001) 1-6
11. Holger, H., Thomas, S: Stochastic Local Search: Foundations and Applications. Morgan Kaufmann Publishers/Elsevier, San Fransisco (2004)
12. Verdu, S.: Multiuser Detection. Cambridge University Press, Cambridge, U.K (1998)
13. Dariush, D., Marvin, K. S., Dan R.: Improved Parallel Interference Cancellation for CDMA. IEEE Transactions on Communications., Vol.46(2) (1998) 258-268

# Multi-objective Optimal Strategy for Individual Consumption-Investment with Fuzzy Coefficients

Jie Su[1,2] and Xiucui Guan[3]

[1] School of Business, Renmin University of China, Beijing, China
[2] School of Math. and Sys. Sci., Shandong University, Jinan, China
[3] Department of Mathematics, Southeast University, Nanjing, China
sujie@sdu.edu.cn

**Abstract.** The goal of this paper is to solve an optimal consumption-investment problem with fuzzy financial coefficients. A multi-objective fuzzy decision-making model for consumption-investment problem is proposed, based on the uncertainty in some economic factors, to maximize the consumption utility and to maximize the total profit in investment and to minimize the risk in investment. The fuzzy optimal consumption-investment strategy is characterized by maximizing the satisfactory grade of the decision-maker. Finally an effective algorithm is proposed to solve the problem and a numerical example shows the effectiveness and feasibility of this method.

## 1 Introduction

In practice, there is uncertainty in the financial market and consumable market, and one individual usually can not get the complete market information. The optimal consumption and investment problem under uncertain financial conditions has become a favorite topic in finance engineering.

Recently there has been many studies on optimal consumption-investment strategies with specific assumptions on the stochastic market conditions. Brennan et. al. [1] studied consumption and portfolio choice problems in settings with uncertain inflation. Leyva et. al. [2] solved an optimal consumption-investment problem in the context of an incomplete financial market. Clausa et. al. [4] considered the consumption and investment problem for a power utility investor in a continuous-time dynamically complete market with stochastic changes in the opportunity set. In addition, fuzzy characteristic is also a quite important token of the uncertain environment in financial market [7]. And a few papers have considered the portfolio problem under fuzzy factors [5, 6].

In this paper, we mainly focus on the decision-making model for the individual consumption-investment problem with fuzzy financial coefficients and propose an algorithm to obtain the optimal consumption-investment strategy.

The organization is as follows. In Sec.2, we establish the multi-objective fuzzy decision-making model for individual consumption-investment problem, and define the fuzzy optimal solution to the model by maximizing the satisfactory grade of the decision-maker. An effective algorithm for the problem is proposed in Sec.3, and a numerical example is given to illuminate the algorithm in Sec.4.

D.-S. Huang, K. Li, and G.W. Irwin (Eds.): ICIC 2006, LNCS 4113, pp. 919–924, 2006.

## 2 The Multi-objective Fuzzy Optimal Strategy

Suppose that there are one kind of non-risk portfolio and $n$ kinds of risk portfolios in a financial market, in addition there are $m$ kinds of consumables in a consumption market. One can consume and invest in two markets simultaneously. Let the total income be $\tilde{W}$, the revenue rate of non-risk portfolio be $r_0$, the expected revenue rate and risk rate of the $i$-th risk portfolio be $\tilde{r}_i$ and $\tilde{\sigma}_i$ $(i = 1, \cdots, n)$, respectively. Moreover, let the price and the least demand bound of the $j$-th consumable be $\tilde{a}_j$ and $\tilde{w}_j$ $(j = 1, \cdots, m)$, respectively. Note that $\tilde{r} = (\tilde{r}_1, \cdots, \tilde{r}_n)$, $\tilde{\sigma} = (\tilde{\sigma}_1, \cdots, \tilde{\sigma}_n)$, $\tilde{a} = (\tilde{a}_1, \cdots, \tilde{a}_m)$, $\tilde{w} = (\tilde{w}_1, \cdots, \tilde{w}_m)$ are fuzzy vectors and $\tilde{W}$ is a fuzzy number. Suppose the consumption utility function $U$ is a quadratic differential concave function on the quantity of consumables.

There are three aims to make a decision, to maximize the consumption utility and the total investment profit, and to minimize the total investment risk. Thus, we can obtain the multi-objective fuzzy decision-making model to individual consumption-investment problem as follows, where the fuzzy coefficients depend on some uncertain economic factors.

$$
\begin{aligned}
&\max_{x_0,x_1,\cdots,x_n,y_1,\cdots,y_m} && U(y) \\
&\max_{x_0,x_1,\cdots,x_n,y_1,\cdots,y_m} && \tilde{R}(x) = r_0 x_0 + \sum_{i=1}^{n} \tilde{r}_i x_i \\
&\min_{x_0,x_1,\cdots,x_n,y_1,\cdots,y_m} && \tilde{\Omega}(x) = \sum_{i=1}^{n} \tilde{\sigma}_i x_i \\
&\text{s.t.} && \sum_{j=1}^{m} \tilde{a}_j y_j + \sum_{i=0}^{n} x_i = \tilde{W}, \\
& && y_j \geq \tilde{w}_j,\ j = 1, \cdots, m, \\
& && x_i \geq 0,\ y_j \geq 0,\ i = 0, \cdots, n,\ j = 1, \cdots, m,
\end{aligned}
\tag{1}
$$

where variables $x_i$ and $y_j$ express the money of the $i$-th portfolio and the quantity of the $j$-th consumable, and $x = (x_0, \cdots, x_n)$ and $y = (y_1, \cdots, y_m)$.

Now us analyze the properties of the fuzzy optimal strategy to problem (1).

Firstly we introduce some symbols for convenience. For each membership grade $\lambda \in [0, 1]$, let $[e^l(\lambda), e^u(\lambda)]$ be the $\lambda$-level set of fuzzy number $\tilde{e}$. Suppose $Coe(\lambda) = \{(r, \sigma, w, a, W) | e \in [e^l(\lambda), e^u(\lambda)], e \in \{r, \sigma, w, a, W\}\}$. For any given $\lambda \in [0, 1]$, problem (1) can be transformed into the following problem:

$$
\begin{aligned}
&\max_{x,y,r,\sigma,w,a,W} && U(y) \\
&\max_{x,y,r,\sigma,w,a,W} && R(x) = r_0 x_0 + \sum_{i=1}^{n} r_i x_i \\
&\min_{x,y,r,\sigma,w,a,W} && \Omega(x) = \sum_{i=1}^{n} \sigma_i x_i
\end{aligned}
\tag{2}
$$

$$\text{s.t.} \quad \sum_{j=1}^{m} a_j y_j + \sum_{i=0}^{n} x_i = W,$$
$$y_j \geq w_j, \ j = 1, \cdots, m,$$
$$x \geq 0, \ y \geq 0, \ (r, \sigma, w, a, W) \in Coe(\lambda).$$

Denote the feasible region of problem (2) by $Set(\lambda)$.

It is quite difficult to optimize all the three objectives simultaneously. Hence the optimal values of the programs with just one objective will give the bounds to the optimal value of problem (2). More precisely, we have six mono-objective programs. We only list two programs below and omit four other programs, in which we replace $U(y)$ in problems below with $R(x)$ and $\Omega(x)$, respectively.

$$\max_{(x,y,r,\sigma,w,a,W)\in Set(\lambda)} U(y), \qquad \min_{(x,y,r,\sigma,w,a,W)\in Set(\lambda)} U(y).$$

Denote by $U_\lambda^u$, $U_\lambda^l$, $R_\lambda^u$, $R_\lambda^l$, $\Omega_\lambda^u$ and $\Omega_\lambda^l$ the optimal values, respectively.

Note that in most practical applications there is a situation that the investment profit contradicts the investment risk, and that the investment profit has some relationship with the investment risk: high profit always comes with high risk, low investment always brings low profit. So it is the key to decision making that how to deal with the relationship between risk and profit. Usually, a rational investor that avoids risk and seeks profit would choose an equilibrium point between profit and risk. Thus, according to invest mentality and the optimization theory of fuzzy programming problems [3], we introduce the concept of satisfactory grade to describe the behavior of the decision-maker.

**Definition 1.** *For any given membership grade* $\lambda \in [0, 1]$, $\beta(x, y, r, \sigma, w, a, W) = \min\{\beta_1, \beta_2, \beta_3\}$ *is called as the satisfactory grade of the decision-maker for the strategy* $(x, y)$ *with coefficients* $(r, \sigma, w, a, W) \in Coe(\lambda)$, *where* $\beta_1 = \frac{U(y)-U_\lambda^l}{U_\lambda^u-U_\lambda^l}$, $\beta_2 = \frac{R(x)-R_\lambda^l}{R_\lambda^u-R_\lambda^l}$, $\beta_3 = \frac{\Omega_\lambda^u-\Omega(x)}{\Omega_\lambda^u-\Omega_\lambda^l}$.

For any $\lambda \in [0, 1]$, to maximize the satisfactory grade, we transform problem (2) into problem (3) as follows:

$$\begin{aligned} \max_{x,y,\beta,r,\sigma,w,a,W} \quad & \beta \\ \text{s.t.} \quad & \beta_k \geq \beta, \ k = 1, 2, 3, \\ & (x, y, r, \sigma, w, a, W) \in Set(\lambda). \end{aligned} \tag{3}$$

Denote the optimal solution of problem (3) as $(x_\lambda^*, y_\lambda^*, r_\lambda^*, \sigma_\lambda^*, w_\lambda^*, a_\lambda^*, W_\lambda^*)$, and the corresponding consumption-investment strategy as $S(\lambda) = (x_\lambda^*, y_\lambda^*)$. Then we obtain a fuzzy set $\tilde{S}$ with membership function $S(\lambda)$ as below [3]:

$$\tilde{S} = \int_S \frac{\lambda}{S(\lambda)}, \qquad \text{for each } \lambda \in [0, 1].$$

Hence, we define the fuzzy set $\tilde{S}$ as the *fuzzy optimal strategy* for individual consumption-investment problem (1) with the optimal condition that maximizes the satisfactory grade of the decision-maker.

## 3 An Effective Algorithm for the Fuzzy Optimal Strategy

In this section, we propose an effective method for the fuzzy optimal consumption-investment strategy. First, based on the conclusion in [8], we can conclude that

**Theorem 2.** *For any membership grade $\lambda \in [0,1]$, the optimal objective values of problems (3) and (4) are the same.*

$$\begin{aligned}
&\max_{x,y,\beta} \beta \\
&s.t.\ \beta_1 \geq \beta, \\
&\qquad \{r_0 x_0 + \sum_{i=1}^{n} r_i^u(\lambda) x_i - R_\lambda^l\}/\{R_\lambda^u - R_\lambda^l\} \geq \beta, \\
&\qquad \{\Omega_\lambda^u - \sum_{i=1}^{n} \sigma_i^l(\lambda) x_i\}/\{\Omega_\lambda^u - \Omega_\lambda^l\} \geq \beta, \\
&\qquad \sum_{j=1}^{m} a_j^l(\lambda) y_j + \sum_{i=0}^{n} x_i \leq W^u(\lambda), \\
&\qquad \sum_{j=1}^{m} a_j^u(\lambda) y_j + \sum_{i=0}^{n} x_i \geq W^l(\lambda), \\
&\qquad y_j \geq w_j^l(\lambda),\ j = 1, \cdots, m;\ x \geq 0,\ y \geq 0.
\end{aligned} \tag{4}$$

*Proof.* Let $\beta^*$ and $\hat{\beta}$ be the optimal values of problems (3) and (4), respectively. If $(x, y, \beta, r, \sigma, w, a, W)$ is a feasible solution of problem (3), then we have

$$\sum_{j=1}^{m} a_j^l(\lambda) y_j + \sum_{i=0}^{n} x_i \leq W \leq W^u(\lambda),\ \sum_{j=1}^{m} a_j^u(\lambda) y_j + \sum_{i=0}^{n} x_i \geq W \geq W^l(\lambda).$$

Thus $(x, y, \beta)$ is also a feasible solution of problem (4),therefore $\beta^* \leq \hat{\beta}$.

On the other hand, suppose that $(\hat{x}, \hat{y}, \hat{\beta})$ is an optimal solution of problem (4), then we only need to show that there are $a_j^0 \in [a_j^l(\lambda), a_j^u(\lambda)]$ and $W^0 \in [W^l(\lambda), W^u(\lambda)]$ such that $(\hat{x}, \hat{y}, \hat{\beta})$ is a feasible solution to problem (5) below:

$$\begin{aligned}
&\max_{x,y,\beta} \beta \\
&\text{s.t.}\ \beta_1 \geq \beta, \\
&\qquad \{r_0 x_0 + \sum_{i=1}^{n} r_i^u(\lambda) x_i - R_\lambda^l\}/\{R_\lambda^u - R_\lambda^l\} \geq \beta, \\
&\qquad \{\Omega_\lambda^u - \sum_{i=1}^{n} \sigma_i^l(\lambda) x_i\}/\{\Omega_\lambda^u - \Omega_\lambda^l\} \geq \beta, \\
&\qquad \sum_{j=1}^{m} a_j^0 y_j + \sum_{i=0}^{n} x_i = W^0(\lambda), \\
&\qquad y_j \geq w_j^l(\lambda),\ j = 1, \cdots, m;\ x \geq 0,\ y \geq 0.
\end{aligned} \tag{5}$$

If $\sum_{j=1}^{m} a_j^l(\lambda)y_j + \sum_{i=0}^{n} x_i \geq W^l(\lambda)$, let $a_j^0 = a_j^l(\lambda), j = 1, \cdots, m$. Otherwise, it follows from the Mean Value Theorem that there exists $a_j^0 \in [a_j^l(\lambda), a_j^u(\lambda)]$ $(j = 1, \cdots, m)$ satisfying $W^l(\lambda) \leq \sum_{j=1}^{m} a_j^0 y_j + \sum_{i=0}^{n} x_i \leq W^u(\lambda)$.

Consequently, we have $\beta^* = \hat{\beta}$. □

Summarized from above, we describe an effective algorithm for solving fuzzy consumption-investment problem as follows:

**Step1:** For any given membership grade $\lambda \in [0,1]$, calculate the values $r^l(\lambda), r^u(\lambda), \sigma^l(\lambda), \sigma^u(\lambda), a^l(\lambda), a^u(\lambda), w^l(\lambda), w^u(\lambda), W^l(\lambda)$ and $W^u(\lambda)$.
**Step2:** Solve the six programs including (3)-(4), and obtain the bounds $U_\lambda^u$, $U_\lambda^l$, $R_\lambda^u$, $R_\lambda^l$, $\Omega_\lambda^u$ and $\Omega_\lambda^l$.
**Step3:** Solve the problem (5), and obtain the optimal solution $s(\lambda)$.

Now us analyze the complexity of this algorithm. For any membership grade $\lambda \in [0,1]$, there are six programs to solve in Step2, and one program in Step3. Furthermore, in practice, we just need to consider some finite useful membership grades, such as $\lambda = 0.7, 0.8, 0.9, 1$, etc. So this method is really effective.

## 4 Numerical Example

According to the algorithm above, we calculate the following example.

Suppose that in model (1), the certain coefficients are chosen as $r_0 = 0.05, U(y) = 0.2y_1 + 0.4y_2 + 0.2y_3$, and all the fuzzy coefficients are triangular fuzzy numbers, $\tilde{W} = (160, 180, 200), \tilde{r}_1 = (0.1, 0.2, 0.3), \tilde{r}_2 = (0.2, 0.3, 0.4), \tilde{\sigma}_1 = (0.2, 0.3, 0.4), \tilde{\sigma}_2 = (0.2, 0.4, 0.6), \tilde{a}_1 = (1.5, 1.6, 1.7), \tilde{a}_2 = (1.9, 2.1, 2.3), \tilde{a}_3 = (1.6, 1.8, 2.0), \tilde{w}_1 = (8, 10, 12), \tilde{w}_2 = (3, 4, 5), \tilde{w}_3 = (7, 8, 9)$. And the symbol $\tilde{e} = (e_1, e_2, e_3)$ denotes that the membership function of fuzzy number $\tilde{e}$ is

$$\mu_{\tilde{e}}(t) = \begin{cases} 1, & t = e_2, \\ (t - e_1)/(e_2 - e_1), & t \in [e_1, e_2], \\ (t - e_3)/(e_2 - e_3), & t \in [e_2, e_3], \\ 0, & t \in (-\infty, e_1) \cup (e_3, +\infty). \end{cases}$$

When $\lambda = 1$, we have the form of program (2) as

$$\begin{aligned} \max\ & 0.2y_1 + 0.4y_2 + 0.2y_3 \\ \max\ & 0.05x_0 + 0.2_1x_1 + 0.3x_2 \\ \min\ & 0.3x_1 + 0.4x_2 \\ \text{s.t.}\ & 1.6y_1 + 2.1y_2 + 1.8y_3 + x_0 + x_1 + x_2 = 180, \\ & y_1 \geq 10, y_2 \geq 4, y_3 \geq 8, x_0 \geq 0, x_1 \geq 0, x_2 \geq 0. \end{aligned} \tag{6}$$

Then the calculate results to program (6) are $U^u = 32.0952, U^l = 5.2, R^u = 42.36, R^l = 0, \Omega^u = 56.48, \Omega^l = 0$, and the optimal strategy to program (6) is $S(1) = (x_0, x_1, x_2, y_1, y_2, y_3) = (0, 0, 70.6, 10, 37.619, 8),\ \beta = 0.5$.

When $\lambda = 0.9$, we have the form of program (2) as

$$\begin{aligned}
&\max 0.2y_1 + 0.4y_2 + 0.2y_3 \\
&\max 0.05x_0 + r_1x_1 + r_2x_2 \\
&\min \sigma_1x_1 + \sigma_2x_2 \\
&\text{s.t. } a_1y_1 + a_2y_2 + a_3y_3 + x_0 + x_1 + x_2 = W, \\
&\quad y_1 \geq w_1, y_2 \geq w_2, y_2 \geq w_2, x_0 \geq 0, x_1 \geq 0, x_2 \geq 0, \\
&\quad r_1 \in [0.19, 0.21], r_2 \in [0.29, 0.31], \sigma_1 \in [0.29, 0.31], \sigma_2 \in [0.38, 0.42], \\
&\quad a_1 \in [1.59, 1.61], a_2 \in [2.08, 2.12], a_3 \in [1.78, 1.82], w_1 \in [9.8, 10.2], \\
&\quad w_2 \in [3.9, 4.1], w_3 \in [7.9, 8.1], W \in [178, 182].
\end{aligned} \tag{7}$$

The results to program (7) are $U^u = 32.8392, U^l = 5.1, R^u = 44.7156, R^l = 0, \Omega^u = 60.5825, \Omega^l = 0$, and the optimal strategy to program (7) is $S(0.9) = (x_0, x_1, x_2, y_1, y_2, y_3) = (0, 0, 77.356, 9.8, 3.9, 8.4590)$, $\beta = 0.536$.

Similarly, we could calculate the optimal strategy to program (2) with any given membership grade $\lambda \in [0, 1]$.

## 5 Conclusion

In this paper, we consider the optimal consumption-investment problem with fuzzy economic coefficients. Based on the satisfactory grade of the decision-maker, we define the fuzzy optimal strategy for individual consumption-investment. And an effective method is given to solve the problem and the numerical example shows the effectiveness and feasibility of the method.

## References


1. Brennan, M.J., Xia, Y.: Dynamic Asset Allocation under Inflation. Journal of Finance. **57** (2002) 1201–1238
2. Castaneda-Leyva, N., Hernandez-Hernandez, D.: Optimal Consumption-Investment Problems in Incomplete Markets with Stochastic Coefficients. SIAM Journal on Control and Optimization. **44** (2005) 1322–1344
3. Lai, Y.J., Hwang, C.L.: Fuzzy Mathematical Programming. Springer-Verlag (1992)
4. Munk, C., Sørensen, C.: Optimal Consumption and Investment Strategies with Stochastic Interest Rates. Journal of Banking and Finance. **28** (2004) 1987–2013
5. Tanaka, H., Peijun, G., Trksen, I.B.: Portfolio Selection Based on Fuzzy Probabilities and Possibility Distributions. Fuzzy Sets and Systems. **111** (2000) 387–397
6. Tanaka, H., Ishibuchi, H., Yoshikawa, S.: Exponential Possibility Regression Analysis. Fuzzy Sets and Systems. **69** (1995) 305–318
7. Zeng, J.H., Wang, S.Y.: A Model for Portfolio Selection Based on Fuzzy Decision-Making Theory. Systems Engineering-theory & Practice. **1** (2003) 99–104
8. Zeng, Q.N.: All-Coefficient-Fuzzy Linear Programming with Equations. System Engineering Theory and Practice. **9** (2000) 105–109

# On Auxiliary Algorithm for the Simplex Method by H. Luh and R. Tsaih

Wei Li

Hangzhou Dianzi University, Hangzhou 310018, China*
weilihz@126.com

**Abstract.** The interesting auxiliary algorithm for simplex method by Luh and Tsaih (Computers and Operations Research 29 (2002)) and its modified version by B. J. Chaderjian and T. Gao (Computers and Operations Research 30 (2003)) present an effective method to start an initial basic feasible solution from an interior feasible solution. We modify the algorithm in the above reference. By using QR decomposition, a much smaller $(n-m-k)\times(n-m-k)$ matrix, in stead of a $n\times n$ matrix, is handled in $k^{th}$ iteration. The QR factors at each iteration can be obtained from its predecessor cheaply by an updating process. This substantially improve the efficiency of the algorithm proposed by Luh and Tsaih.

## 1 Introduction

Numerous improvements have been added to the simplex method to make it more competitive with the interior point method over the past two decades[1,2,3]. Recently, Luh and Tsaih [4] present an effective method to start an initial basic feasible solution from an interior feasible solution. B. J. Chaderjian and T. Gao [5] propose its modified version. Numerical results on some randomly generated problems show that the method can lead to good starting feasible solutions near the optimal points for the simplex method. In this work, we offer some further improvements to the method.

Hsing Luh and Ray Tsaih [4] consider the linear programming problem

$$min\ c^T x$$

$$s.t.\ Ax \geq b, \quad x \geq 0\ .$$

where $x = (x_1, x_2, \ldots, x_n)^T \in R_n$, $A \in R^{m\times n}$, $c = (c_1, c_2, \ldots, c_n)^T \in R^n$, $b = (b_1, b_2, \ldots, b_m)^T \in R^m$. The paper presents a new effective search direction based on the interior point method to start an initial basic feasible solution. Bruce J. Chaderjian, Tangan Gao [5] provide a correction of a mathematical error, and modify the auxiliary algorithm proposed by Hsing Luh and Ray Tsaih. Numerical results on some randomly generated problems show that the method in [4] and its modified version in [5] can lead to good starting feasible solutions near the optimal points for the simplex method. Even though the algorithm is efficient, however, the algorithm can be modified obviously.

* This work was supported by the NSF of China (10371017) and NSF of HDU (KYS091504025).

D.-S. Huang, K. Li, and G.W. Irwin (Eds.): ICIC 2006, LNCS 4113, pp. 925–930, 2006.

We follow the notations used in [4]. In Step 5 of the Theorem the direction $v$ is defined as: $\forall i \in \Omega_1^k, A_i.g^{(k)} \geq 0$ and $\forall j \in \Omega_2^k, g^{(k)} \geq 0$ then $v = g^{(k)}$, where $\Omega_1^k = \{i | A_i.x^{(k)} = b_i\}$ and $\Omega_2^k = \{j | x_j^{(k)} = 0\}$ , the indices of the binding constraints at $x^{(k)}$. Otherwise, let $v = [I - A_q^T(A_q A_q^T)^{-1} A_q] g^{(k)}$, where $A_q = [a_1, \ldots, a_q]^T$, where $a_1, \ldots, a_q$ is a largest set of linearly independent vectors in the set $\{A_{i.}^T, e_j | i \in \Omega_1^k, j \in \Omega_2^k\}$.

However, the condition $\forall i \in \Omega_1^k, A_i.g^{(k)} \geq 0$ might be too strict to hold. The algorithm has not any guarantee with it. Thus, the direction used in the process is mostly $v = Mg^{(k)}$, where $M = [I - A_q^T(A_q A_q^T)^{-1} A_q]$. This direction $v$ is actually the same direction of $M(-c)$ if the set of vectors $\{A_i., e_j | i \in \Omega_1^k, j \in \Omega_2^k\}$ are linearly independent. To see this, notice that $h^{(k)} = \sum_{i \in \Omega_1^k} A_i.^T + \sum_{i \in \Omega_2^k} e_j = A_q^T \mathbf{1}$, where $\mathbf{1}$ is denoted a column vector, of appropriate dimension, with each component equals 1. Therefore, $v = Mh^{(k)} = [I - A_q^T(A_q A_q^T)^{-1} A_q] A_q^T \mathbf{1} = 0$, and hence $v = Mg^{(k)} = M \frac{h^{(k)} - c}{||h^{(k)} - c||} = -\frac{1}{||h^{(k)} - c||} Mc$. Thus, the possibility of $v = -Mc = 0$ cannot be ruled out which would lead to the failure of Step 6. In addition, although computational performance on some random test problems are encouraging, there lacks the guaranty for the finiteness of the auxiliary algorithm. The conclusion that $x^{(k)}$ is an optimal solution if and only if $x^{(k+1)} = x^{(k)}$ (see Theorem 1 in [4]) is valid only for $g^{(k)} = \frac{h^{(k)} - c}{||h^{(k)} - c||}$. Unfortunately, as discussed above, the mostly used direction is $M(-c)$. Obviously, $v = -Mc = 0$ does not implies that the current point $x^{(k)}$ is an optimal solution. Moreover, the direction used in the proposed method is in general the projection $-[I - A_q^T(A_q A_q^T)^{-1} A_q]c$. It is too expensive if we handle the matrix $(A_q A_q^T)^{-1}$ directly. The algorithm can be significantly improved if we handle a much smaller system in stead of $(A_q A_q^T)^{-1}$.

From the discussion above, we know that the process of generating a basic feasible solution from an interior point can be improved further. In this note , we present a modified auxiliary algorithm. The new algorithm begins at an interior feasible point, or any feasible solution on the surface of the polytope, and produce a basic feasible solution. An alternative approach using QR decomposition is constructed for computing the projection. In stead of $(A_q A_q^T)^{-1}$, we handle a much smaller system.

## 2 An Modified Auxiliary Algorithm for Simplex Method by QR Decomposition

We are concerned with the linear programming problem in the standard form

$$\begin{aligned} &min \;\; c^T x \\ &s.t. \; Ax = b, \quad x \geq 0 \; . \end{aligned} \tag{1}$$

and its associated dual problem

$$\begin{aligned} &max \;\; b^T y \\ &s.t. \; A^T y + z = c, \quad s \geq 0 \; . \end{aligned} \tag{2}$$

where $c, x, z \in R^n$, $b, y \in R^m$, $A \in R^{m \times n}$ with $m < n$, $rank(A) = m$.

Assume now that the QR factorization of $A^T$ ($A^T$ has full column rank) is known as $A^T = QR$, where $Q$ is an $n \times n$ orthogonal matrix, and $R$ an $n \times m$ upper-triangular matrix with nonzero diagonal entries. Partition $Q$ and $R$ respectively into

$$Q = [Q_1, Q_3], \qquad R = \begin{bmatrix} R_{11} \\ 0 \end{bmatrix}, \tag{3}$$

where $Q_1$ and $Q_3$ are, respectively, $n \times m$ and $n \times (n-m)$ matrices, and $R_{11}$ an $m \times m$ nonsingular upper-triangular matrix. Then it follows that

$$A^T = Q_1 R_{11} \ . \tag{4}$$

Using the preceding natation, it is easy to obtain the following result.

**Lemma 1.** *The orthogonal projection of any n-vector $v$ into $N(A)$, the null space of $A$, equals*

$$p = Q_3 Q_3^T v \ . \tag{5}$$

Now consider the dual problem (2). Denote by $N$ a subset of the $n$ indices, of $s$, and define $B \equiv \{1, \ldots, n\} \setminus N$. Assuming the cardinality of $N$ and $B$ more precisely by

$$N = \{N_1, \ldots, N_k\} \quad \text{and} \quad B = \{B_1, \ldots, B_{n-k}\} \ . \tag{6}$$

Then problem (2) can be written as

$$\begin{aligned} &max \ \ b^T y \\ &s.t. \ \ A^T y + I_N z_N + I_B z_B = c, \\ &\qquad z_N, z_B \geq 0 \ . \end{aligned} \tag{7}$$

Assume now that $n \times (m+k)$ matrix $[A^T, \ I_N]$ has full column rank, where $0 \leq k < n-m$, and the QR factorization of $[A^T, I_N]$ is known as $[A^T, I_N] = QR$. Partition $Q$ and $R$ into

$$Q = [Q_1, Q_2, Q_3], \qquad R = \begin{bmatrix} R_{11} & R_{12} \\ 0 & R_{22} \\ 0 & 0 \end{bmatrix}, \tag{8}$$

where, respectively, $Q_1, Q_2, Q_3$ are $n \times m, n \times k, n \times (n-m-k)$ matrices, $R_{11}$ and $R_{22}$ are $m \times m, k \times k$ nonsingular upper-triangular matrices. Then, using the preceding notation, the orthogonal projection of any n-vector $v$ into the null space of

$$[A^T, I_N]^T \tag{9}$$

can be expressed by (5).

Therefore, the orthogonal projection, $\triangle x$, of $-c$ into the null space of (9) can be expressed by $\triangle x = -Q_3 Q_3^T c$ . Reordering components of $\triangle x$ in accordance with the ordered set $N, B$ leads to its permuted version below:

$$\begin{bmatrix} \triangle x_N \\ \triangle x_B \end{bmatrix} \equiv \begin{bmatrix} I_N^T \\ I_B^T \end{bmatrix} \triangle x = \begin{bmatrix} I_N^T \\ I_B^T \end{bmatrix} (-Q_3 Q_3^T c) = - \begin{bmatrix} I_N^T Q_3 \\ I_B^T Q_3 \end{bmatrix} Q_3^T c \ . \tag{10}$$

Since $Q_3^T I_N = 0$, and hence $\triangle x_N = 0$. The only part needed in subsequent computations will be $\triangle x_B = -I_B^T Q_3 Q_3^T c$. Note that $Q_3^T c = Q_3^T(I_B c_B + I_N c_N) = Q_3^T I_B c_B$, thus we have

$$\triangle x_B = -(Q_3^T I_B)^T Q_3^T I_B c_B \ . \tag{11}$$

On the other hand, the same orthogonalization converts the left hand sise of (7) into the following matrix:

$$U = Q^T[A^T, I_N, I_B] = \begin{bmatrix} Q_1^T A^T & Q_1^T I_N & Q_1^T I_B \\ Q_2^T A^T & Q_2^T I_N & Q_2^T I_B \\ Q_3^T A^T & Q_3^T I_N & Q_3^T I_B \end{bmatrix} = \begin{bmatrix} R_{11} & R_{12} & Q_1^T I_B \\ 0 & R_{22} & Q_2^T I_B \\ 0 & 0 & Q_3^T I_B \end{bmatrix} \ . \tag{12}$$

When $k = n - m$, the preceding discussions will still apply if $Q_3$ is viewed as empty. Tableau (12) is termed *triangle form* ( of the equality constraint (7), associated with $B$ and $N$). In particular, a triangular form is termed *canonical* if $k = n - m$ or else $Q_3^T I_B c_B = 0$. The following results indicate that the subvector $\triangle x_B$ of the permuted projection can be determined from the associated triangular form.

**Lemma 2.** *$\triangle x_B = 0$ if and only if the triangular form (12) is canonical. In the other case, $\triangle x_B$ can be computed utilizing the south-east $(n - m - k) \times (n - k)$ matrix of (12).*

*Proof.* Clearly, if $k = n - m$, $[A^T, I_N]^T$ is a $n \times n$ matrix with full column rank, and hence the projection of $-c$ into the null space of (9) vanishes. If $0 \le k < n - m$, by (11), $Q_3^T I_B c_B = 0$ implies $\triangle x_B = 0$. Assume conversely $\triangle x_B = -I_B^T Q_3 Q_3^T c = 0$. Since it is also holds that $\triangle x_N = -I_N^T Q_3 Q_3^T c = 0$, we have $Q_3 Q_3^T I_B c_B = 0$. Premultiplying by $c_B^T I_B^T$ its two sides gives $c_B^T I_B^T Q_3 Q_3^T I_B c_B = \| Q_3^T I_B c_B \|^2 = 0$, implying $Q_3^T I_B c_B = 0$. Comparing (11) and (12) leads to the other half of the theorem.

Assume now that $N$ is empty $(k = 0)$ and $B = \{B_1, \ldots, B_n\} \equiv \{1, \ldots, n\}$. Let (12) be the associated triangular form. In this case, $Q_2 = \emptyset$ and hence $Q = [Q_1, Q_3]$. (12) and (11) are

$$U = Q^T[A^T, I] = \begin{bmatrix} Q_1^T A^T & Q_1^T \\ Q_3^T A^T & Q_3^T \end{bmatrix} = \begin{bmatrix} R_{11} & Q_1^T \\ 0 & Q_3^T \end{bmatrix} \tag{13}$$

and

$$\triangle x_B = \triangle x = -(Q_3 Q_3^T)c, \tag{14}$$

respectively. Obviously it holds that $\triangle x_B \neq 0$. If $\triangle x_B \geq 0$, together with $\triangle x_B \neq 0$, then program (1) is unbounded below. Suppose now that $\triangle x_B \not\geq 0$. We take $\triangle x_B$ as search direction. Starting from any nonbasic primal feasible solution , say, a relative interior solution $x^0 > 0$ on the face of dimension $n - m$, we move along $\triangle x_B$ until hitting the boundary. Thereby, a subscript $t$ is determined such that $\alpha = (\bar{x}_B)_t/(\triangle x_B)_t = min\{-(\bar{x}_B)_j/(\triangle x_B)_j \mid (\triangle x_B)_j < 0; j = 1, \ldots, n\}$ . Consequently, the boundary point reached on a face of dimension $n - m - 1$ is $\hat{x}_B = \bar{x}_B + \alpha \triangle x_B$ . Then, we update $N$ and $B$ by bring $B_t$ from $B$ to $N$, and form a new $\bar{x}_B$ from $\hat{x}_B$ conformably. Note that the only element $B_t$ that the $N$ includes is now represented by $N_1$ (k=1). The first iteration is thus complete.

We carry out a second iteration by computing the orthogonal projection of $-c$ into the null space of the coefficient matrix of current active constraints, i.e., $Ax = b$, $x_{N_1} = 0$ and move along it from the new point until reaching a point on some face of dimension $n - m - 2$. Such iterations are continued until $\triangle x_B$ vanishes with a canonical form reached, which means a vertex is reached, or otherwise $\triangle x_B \geq 0$, detecting unboundedness of (1). The system handled in the proposed method is the south-east $(n - m - k) \times (n - k)$ matrix of (12), which is much smaller than $(n \times n)$ matrix, especially when $m$ is large. Moreover, each triangular form, except for $k = 0$, can be obtained from its predecessor cheaply. Assume that for some $k$ satisfying $1 \leq k \leq n - m$, the $(k-1)$-th iteration has been done. Denote by (12) the triangular form, and by $B_t$ the index chosen from $B$ to $N$. Then the next triangular form results from (12) by bring the $t$-th column of $Q^T I_B$ to the end of $Q^T I_N$, and then eliminating the $(m+k+2)$ through $n$-th entries of this column via a single Household transformation if $k < n - m$. It is such a simple doing that makes the preceding process a promising one. The pricipal steps of the iteration process are stated below.

**Modified Auxiliary Algorithm**

Let $x^0$ be a interior solution to (1). This auxiliary algorithm produces a basic feasible solution, or detects unboundedness of (1).

1. Set $k = 0, N = \emptyset, B = \{1, \ldots, n\}$.
2. Determine Household transformations $P_1, \ldots, P_m$ such that $P_m \cdots P_1 A^T$ is upper-triangular. Denote $P_m \cdots P_1[A^T, I_N, I_B]$ by (12).
3. Stop if $Q_3^T I_B c_B = 0$.
4. Compute $\triangle x_B$ by (11).
5. Stop if $\triangle x_B \geq 0$.
6. Determine $t$ such that $\alpha = -(\bar{x}_B)_t/(\triangle x_B)_t = min\{-(\bar{x}_B)_j/(\triangle x_B)_j \mid (\triangle x_B)_j < 0; j = 1, \ldots, n\}$
7. Update $\bar{x}$ by $\bar{x}_B = \bar{x}_B + \alpha \triangle x_B$.
8. Update $B$ and $N$ by bringing $B_t$ from $B$ to the end of $N$, and rearrange columns and components of (12).
9. Set $k = k + 1$.
10. Stop if $k = n - m$.
11. Update (12) by eliminating the $(m + k + 2)$ through $n$-th entries of the column, indexed by $N_k$, via Householder transformation.
12. Go to Step 3.

Clearly, the preceding procedure terminates within $n - m$ iterations. Based on the precious discussions, we have:

**Theorem 1.** *The auxiliary algorithm terminates at either*

*1. Step 3 or 10, producing a canonical form and a primal basic feasible solution; or*

*2. Step 5, detecting lower unboundedness of (1).*

## 3 Conclusion and Future Work

The modified auxiliary algorithm proposed in this paper only concentrate on the process of producing a basic feasible solution from an interior feasible solution, since it can be easily cooperated with the simplex method if an interior feasible point is available. Obviously, any primal feasible solution $x^0$ can be used to get the auxiliary algorithm started. In fact, the number of iterations will less than $n - m$ if $x^0$ is a a boundary point of the polytope, since $N \neq \emptyset$ in this case.

As was suggested in [5] that the steepest descent direction $-c$ would provide another choice for the initial search direction if $x^0$ is an interior feasible point. We can use $-c$ as the initial search direction and then start the auxiliary algorithm after the boundary is hit.

The modified auxiliary algorithm has been experimentally implemented with a group random test problems. The computational results seem promising. We shall test it with the test problems used in NETLIB for further comparisons.

## References

1. Illés,T., Terlaky,T.: Pivot Versus Interior Points Methods: Pros and Cons. European Journal of Operational Research **140** (2002) 170–190
2. Paparrizos,K., Samaras,N., Stephanides,G.: An Efficient Simplex Type Algorithm for Sparse and Dense Linear Programs. European Journal of Operational Research **148** (2003) 323–334
3. Pan,P.-Q. : A Revised Dual Projective Pivot Algorithm for Linear Programming. SIAM Journal on Optimization **16** (2005) 49–68
4. Luh,H., Tsaih,R.: An Efficient Search Direction for Linear Programming Problems. Computers and Operations Research **29** (2002) 195–203
5. Chaderjian,B. J., Gao,T.: Comments on An Efficient Search Direction for Linear Programming Problems by H. Luh and R. Tsaih. Computers and Operations Research **30** (2003) 1255–1258

# Fast Discrimination of Juicy Peach Varieties by Vis/NIR Spectroscopy Based on Bayesian-SDA and PCA

Di Wu, Yong He*, and Yidan Bao

College of Biosystems Engineering and Food Science,
Zhejiang University, 310029, Hangzhou, China
yhe@zju.edu.cn

**Abstract.** Visible/Near-infrared reflectance spectroscopy (Vis/NIRS) was applied to variety discrimination of juicy peach. A total of 75 samples were investigated for Vis/NIRS using a field spectroradiometer. Chemometrics was used to build the relationship between the absorbance spectra and varieties. Principle component analysis (PCA) was executed to reduce numerous wavebands into 8 principle components (PCs) as variables of stepwise discrimination analysis (SDA). After execution of SDA through variables selection with 21 samples as validation set, the final results shown an excellent performance of 100% varieties discrimination which was better than the one only predicted by using partial least squares (PLS) model. The results showed the potential ability of Vis/NIRS coupled with SDA-PCA algorithm to discriminate the varieties of juicy peach. The analysis model was rapid, objective and accurate.

## 1 Introduction

In the Chinese fruit markets, as an important fruit, juicy peach is favored by many consumers. There are many varieties about juicy peach. Each variety has different efficacy and quality. However the study on variety discrimination is still seldom. Routine methods used to identify the variety of fruits are based on appearances and interior qualities. But these ways are somewhat subjective and biased and others are destructive methods which are involved a amount of considerable manual work. In this study, a method for variety discrimination of juicy peach was developed.

Recently, Visible and near-infrared spectroscopy (Vir/NIRS) technique is widely applied in many fields[1, 2] include the variety discrimination as its advantages like low cost, non-destruction, limited sample preparation and using in grading system. Optical method based on Vis/NIRS has been evaluated for non-destructive estimation of the internal attributes [3, 4]. As internal attributes are the important characteristics for variety discrimination [5], Vis/NIRS technique was applied availably in it.

The goal of the present study was to propose a novel method to discriminate varieties of juicy peach qualitatively and non-destructively by using Vis-NIRS technique coupled with chemometrics.

* Corresponding author.

D.-S. Huang, K. Li, and G.W. Irwin (Eds.): ICIC 2006, LNCS 4113, pp. 931 – 936, 2006.

## 2 Material and Methods

### 2.1 Fruit Samples and Vis-NIRS Analysis

Juicy peach samples were purchased at some local supermarkets. A total of 75 samples of 3 varieties included Mengyin juicy peach (from Shandong province in China), Fenghua juicy peach and Jinhua juicy peach (both from Zhejiang province in China) were divided into two groups both in PLS and PCA-SDA process: 54 samples for calibration and 21 samples for validation of the calibration performed.

All the 75 samples were scanned at opposite two positions along the equator (approximately 180°) by an average of 30 times in the range of 325-1075nm at 1.5cm-1 interval using a spectrophotometer (FieldSpec Pro FR A110070) Trademarks of Analytical Spectral Devices, Inc. equipped with a 150W halogen lamp as light source. The distance between sample's surface and lamp was 230mm meanwhile it between spectral probe and sample was 80mm. The visual angle of the spectrograph was 25°. Data were collected over the spectral range from 401-1000nm which means that the first 75 and the last 75 wavelength values were taken out because some noise which will affect the accuracy of data process appeared in these wavebands. Spectral data were converted into absorbance which is defined as the logarithm of the reciprocal of the reflected(R) energy (log (1/R)) and stored as ASCII datum for further data process. Thus, a total of 600 data points were collected for each sample. ASD View Spec Pro software was used to execute these processes mentioned above.

### 2.2 Chemometrics

*Pre-process of the optical data.* Original spectral data has much noise and other influences which will affect the establishment of model and the final predictive results. So the absorbance wavebands were then pre-processed using moving average smoothing (MAS), S. Golay 1st-Der, S. Golay 2ed-Der and multiple scatter correction (MSC) respectively. It had been proved that the high frequency noise could be eliminated by MAS. Meanwhile the light always travels the different path and distances both between surfaces of sample, lamp and spectral device as the scattering. A shorter light path related to a higher relative reflectance value, since less light was absorbed. So a parallel translation of the spectra was happened. That's why the S. Golay Der and MSC were tried to eliminate this disturbance as many as possible. All of the pre-processes and calculations were carried out using the Unscrambler V9.2 software.

*Partial Least Squares Regression Analysis (PLS).* PLS was introduced by Wold and Krishnaiah [6] and is commonly used in chemometrics when the predictor matrix is poorly conditioned. PLS regression is one of the standard calibration methods where the response variables ($X$-data) are projected onto a small number of latent variables (LV) that is used to explain most of the variation in both predictors and responses to simplify the relationship between $X$ and $Y$ for predicting with the smallest number of LVs. These LVs provide good predictive models for new responses, and LVs that explain predictor variation which are well represented by the observed values of the predictors [7]. PLS regression method is always used for application with response variables and multi-collinear predictor.

*Principal components analysis (PCA).* As reflectance data has many wavebands, these variables need to be simplified by variable reduction in order to make them more easily to interpreted. PCA [8] is a well-known reduction technique:

$$X = TP^{-1} + E\,. \tag{1}$$

Where X is the N×K spectral data matrix, T the N×A matrix of score vectors, P the K×A matrix of loading vectors, E the N×K residual matrix, N the number of objects, K the number of variables (which in our case is the number of wavenumbers), and A is the number of components calculated (principal components, PCs). The first principal component describes the greatest contribution amount of spectral information. In this paper, with the first 8 PCs, it is possible to extract more than 95% of the desired variance. So, before the calibration, the spectra variation of the data was analyzed by principal component analysis (PCA) and defective spectral was eliminated.

*Stepwise discrimination analysis (SDA).* The SDA is a linear discrimination method based on F-test for the significance of the variables. In each step one variable will be selected on the basis of its significance. Fisher [9] founded discriminant analysis (DA), and then it was ameliorated and evolved as SDA. With its satisfactory results in discriminating with different sedimentary environment, SDA was commonly applied in numerous fields such as socio-economics, medicine, psychology and geosciences.

## 3 Results and Discussion

Before further data processing, several pre-processes were applied separately and also combined. After compared with the final predictive results, the pre-process with 3 segments of Moving Average Smoothing and S. Golay 1st-Der (average number of leftside and rightside set as 1) is the best one.

### 3.1 Partial Least Squares Regression Analysis (PLS)

PLS model was build by calibration set and validation set. The correlation of calibration between Vis/NIRS measurements and the varieties was high with value of 0.962, with standard error of calibration (SEC) of 0.224. When the model was used to predict the unknown samples in the prediction set, prediction result was good ($r$= 0.847), standard error of prediction (SEP) 0.460 with a bias of 0.022, with nine factors (LVs). The discrimination result about discrimination of varieties was presented in Table1.

### 3.2 Principle Component Analysis (PCA)

*Clustering of varieties.* PCA was applied to enhance the feature of variety and reduce dimensionality. Each kind of samples was numbered individually. After pre-process, PCA was performed to obtain major principle components (PCs) on the spectral data. A resultant plot of discrimination could be created with first two PCs (PC1 as X-axis and PC2 as Y-axis). Although the PCs plot could display the clustering of varieties from multiple wavebands qualitatively, it is hard to achieve discrimination in this study as the PCs plot is shown in Fig. 1. So SDA was used for further data analysis based on PCs.

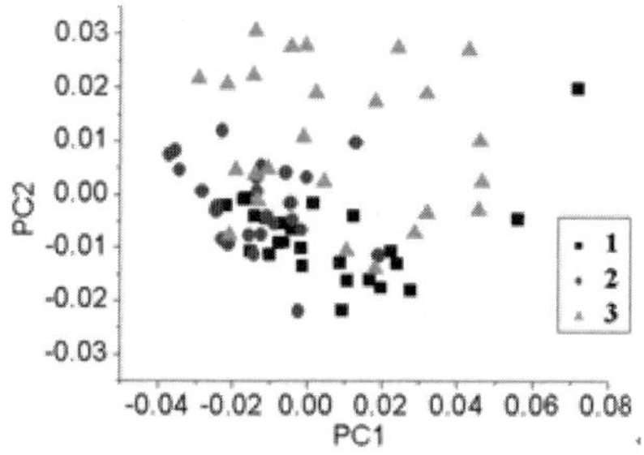


**Fig. 1.** Clustering of the PCA model with PC1 and PC2. 1- Fenghua juicy peach, 2- Jinhua juicy peach, and 3- Mengyin juicy peach.

*PCs obtained in PCA*. The PCs as the new response variables (X-data) were used to replace the original spectral absorbance data in order to make the process of SDA more simple, feasible and efficient. These PCs were orthogonal reciprocally and ranged by its contribution such as PC1 means the most important PC in this model and PC2 take second place. Fig.2 shows the contribution rate of the first 8 PCs. It was observed that these principal components are enough to explain more than 95% of the data variance.

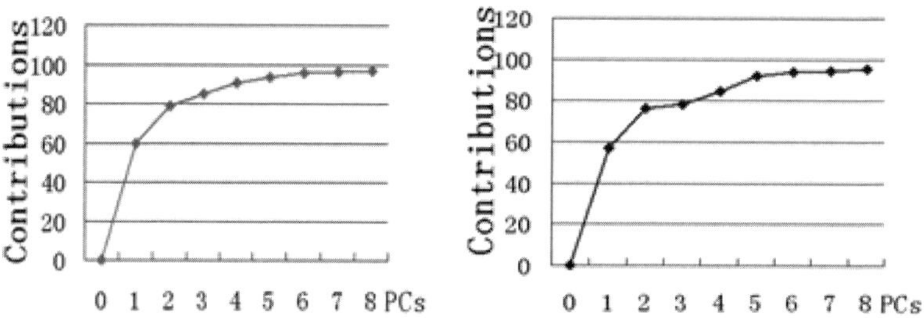


**Fig. 2.** Ability of explained variance of the first 8 PCs(Left: calibration, Right: validation)

### 3.3 The Stepwise Discrimination Analysis (SDA) Prediction Model

After the process of PCA, there was a matrix that contains 75 rows (as sample) and 8 columns (as 8 PCs) came into being. Imported this matrix into DPS software and defined as data-block in the software. The critical value $Fa$=1.90. The discrimination effects and results of prediction set are showed in Table 1.

The Stepwise Discrimination Analysis (SDA) in DPS needed to set the predicting samples as the number 0, and set other reality validation samples as the number of 1, 2, and 3 based on different varieties (i.e. 1 for 'Fenghua juicy peach', 2 for 'Jinhua juicy peach', and 3 for 'Mengyin juicy peach'). 21 unknown samples selected random were predicted by this model. The result was present in Table 1. The recognition rate is100 % and posterior validated possibility is excellent too (Table 1).

### 3.4 The Comparison Between SDA-PCA and PLS

By analyzing these two results shown in Table 1 based on SDA-PAC and PLS model individually, it could be made a conclusion easily that although PLS arithmetic was applied in numerous fields successfully, the SDA-PCA model was better than it in this study. The results predicted by SDA-PCA model are same as known numbers absolutely, but some results predicted by PLS have made a wrong discrimination or can not be judged to which variety easily. For example, the result predicted by PLS in line 9 of left Table1 is 2.709 but it's hard to charge that whether this sample is belong to variety 2 or 3. In addition, the result also predicted by PLS in line 5 of right Table 1 is 2.173, but the true variety number of this sample is 3, so the PLS model has made a wrong discrimination.

**Table 1.** Prediction results for unknown samples by SDA-PCA and PLS model. 1- Fenghua juicy peach, 2- Jinhua juicy peach, and 3- Mengyin juicy peach. A: Predictive sort number, B: Posterior probability, C: Deviation, D: Variety number.

| D | SDA-PCA | | PLS | | D | SDA-PCA | | PLS | |
|---|---|---|---|---|---|---|---|---|---|
| | A | B | A | C | | A | B | A | C |
| 1 | 1 | 0.96689 | 1.14 | 0.313 | 2 | 2 | 0.92479 | 1.871 | 0.356 |
| 1 | 1 | 0.99983 | 1.136 | 0.308 | 2 | 2 | 0.93844 | 2.49 | 0.321 |
| 1 | 1 | 1 | 0.884 | 0.352 | 2 | 2 | 0.99989 | 2.051 | 0.258 |
| 1 | 1 | 0.99282 | 1.297 | 0.333 | 3 | 3 | 0.99986 | 3.192 | 0.603 |
| 1 | 1 | 1 | 0.623 | 0.402 | 3 | 3 | 0.95966 | 2.173 | 0.409 |
| 1 | 1 | 0.99999 | 0.876 | 0.384 | 3 | 3 | 0.48921 | 2.489 | 0.296 |
| 1 | 1 | 0.9997 | 0.991 | 0.355 | 3 | 3 | 0.99998 | 3.455 | 0.701 |
| 2 | 2 | 0.98634 | 2.334 | 0.423 | 3 | 3 | 0.99045 | 2.948 | 0.377 |
| 2 | 2 | 0.97425 | 2.709 | 0.385 | 3 | 3 | 0.99973 | 2.936 | 0.353 |
| 2 | 2 | 0.84957 | 2.181 | 0.297 | 3 | 3 | 1 | 3.464 | 0.534 |
| 2 | 2 | 0.93963 | 2.664 | 0.33 | | | | | |

## 4 Conclusion

This study has shown that by using a set of juicy peach samples, Vis/NIRS spectroscopy coupled with SDA-PCA algorithm has demonstrated the ability to predict the peaches which were belong to different varieties with sufficient accuracy and non-destructive. After treated with pre-process, two algorithm model established by PLS and SDA-PCA were used to predict the varieties of unknown peach samples. PLS model is not suitable in this study because of its bad predictive ability and PCA model without SDA also failed to discriminate as the PCs plot couldn't distinguish the varieties intuitively. So the SDA-PCA model was proposed by the advantage of variable selection. The final results based on SDA-PCA model showed an excellent performance with high discrimination rate of 100%. Further study includes optimizing and standardizing this technique and making it industrialization. Meanwhile the number of peach samples needed to be expanded. More fundamental researches are also required to provide a physical-chemical background of spectroscopy.

## Acknowledgements

This study was supported by the Teaching and Research Award Program for Outstanding Young Teachers in Higher Education Institutions of MOE, P. R. C., Natural Science Foundation of China (Project No: 30270773), Specialized Research Fund for the Doctoral Program of Higher Education (Project No: 20040335034), and Science and Technology Department of Zhejiang Province (Project No. 2005C21094, 2005C12029).

## References

1. Li, W. J., Mckim, J.M., Martin, R.A.: Development of Near-infrared Diffuse Reflectance Spectroscopy for Rapid Screening and Authentication of Chinese Material Medical. Analytical Sciences, 117 (2001) 429-442
2. Steuer, B., Schulz, H., Lager, E.: Classification and Analysis of Citrus Oils by NIR Spectroscopy. Food Chemistry, 72 (2001) 113-117
3. He, Y., Li, X. L., Shao, Y. N.: Quantitative Analysis of the Varieties of Apple Using Near Infrared Spectroscopy by Principal Component Analysis and BP Model. In: Zhang, S.C., Jarvis, R. (eds.):AI2005:Advances in Artificial Intelligence. Lecture Notes in Artificial Intelligence, Vol. 3809. Springer-Verlag, Berlin Heidelberg Germany (2005) 1053–1056
4. Slaughter, D.C.: Non-destructive Determination of Internal Quality in Peaches and Nectarines. Transactions of the ASAE, 38(2) (1995) 617–623
5. He, Y., Feng, S. J., Deng, X. F., Li, X. L.: Study on Lossless Discrimination of Varieties of Yogurt Using the Visible/NIR-spectroscopy. Food Research International, 39(6) (2006) 645–650
6. Wold, H., Krishnaiah, P.R. (ed.): Academic Press, New York, (1966) 391–420
7. Ramadan, Z., Hopke, P.K., Johnson, M.J., Scow, K.M.: Application of PLS and Back-Propagation Neural Networks for Theestimation of Soil Properties. Chemometrics and Intelligent Laboratory Systems, 75 (2005) 23–30
8. Martens, H., Naes, T.: Mulutivariate Calibration, Wiley New York (1998)
9. Fisher, R.A.: The Use of Multiple Measurements in Taxonomic Problems. Annals of Eugenics, 7(2) (1936) 179-188

# Rolling Partial Rescheduling with Efficiency and Stability Based on Local Search Algorithm*

Bing Wang[1] and Tao Liu[2]

[1] Department of Automation, Shandong University at Weihai,
Weihai 264209, China
wangbing@sdu.edu.cn

[2] School of Automobile Engineering, Harbin Institute of Technology at Weihai,
Weihai 264209, China

**Abstract.** This paper discusses the single-machine large-scale rescheduling problem with efficiency and stability as criteria, where more disruptions arise during the execution of schedule. A rolling strategy is driven by disruption events and the reactive partial rescheduling (PR) is adopted at each disruption. Two types of PR sub-problem are designed respectively for the procedural and the terminal PR-horizons. A local search algorithm is used to solve the PR sub-problems. Computational results show that the rolling PR can greatly improve the schedule stability with little sacrifice in schedule efficiency and consistently outperforms the rolling RSR.

## 1 Introduction

A deterministic initial schedule is often produced in advance in order to direct production operations and to support other planning activities. However, unforeseen disruptions, such as rush orders, excess processing time, and machine breakdown etc, will arise during the execution of such an initial schedule. Under such dynamic environments, a new feasible schedule should be generated by rescheduling the unfinished operations.

Three types of reactive rescheduling strategies were used in the existing literatures [1]. Full rescheduling (FR), where all unfinished jobs are rescheduled to satisfy certain objective. Right-shift rescheduling (RSR), where all unfinished jobs are just slid to the right as far as necessary to accommodate (absorbing idle time) the disruption. Compromising FR and RSR, PR can provide a trade-off between solution quality and computational cost through considering only partial unfinished jobs.

The practical solution of rescheduling problem requires satisfaction of two often conflicting objectives: (1) to retain schedule efficiency, i.e. to keep the schedule performance less degraded as possible as we can, and (2) to minimize the cost impact of the schedule deviation. Wu et al. [2] addressed the rescheduling problem with efficiency and stability, where only one disruption occurs.

* Partly supported Science Research Foundation of Shandong University at Weihai (XZ2005001).

D.-S. Huang, K. Li, and G.W. Irwin (Eds.): ICIC 2006, LNCS 4113, pp. 937–942, 2006.

In order to deal with large-scale scheduling problems, Wang et al. [3] explored a rolling horizon scheduling strategy. In this paper, we extend this rolling strategy to deal with the large-scale rescheduling problem with efficiency and stability for single machine subject to more disruptions.

## 2 Single-Machine Rescheduling with Efficiency and Stability

Consider a single-machine scheduling problem with release time to minimize the makespan. There are $n$ jobs to be scheduled. A job denoted as $i$ has a release time $r_i$, a processing time $p_i$, and a tail $q_i$. These three parameters of each job are known a priori. For a solution $S$ of this problem, the makespan, which is denoted as $M(S)$, is defined as follows:

$$M(S) = \max_{i \in S} (b_i + p_i + q_i), \tag{1}$$

where $b_i$ is the beginning time of job $i$ in $S$. This problem is NP-hard [4].

A minimal makespan initial schedule $S^0$ can be generated without considering any disruptions. After a disruption occurs, at the moment $u$, when the machine returns to service, the release time of each unfinished job is updated as follows:

$$r_i{}' = \max (u, r_i). \tag{2}$$

In this paper, the stability of schedule is measured by the schedule deviation based on the initial schedule, which is denoted as, i.e. $D(S)$

$$D(S) = \sum_{i \in S} |b_i - b_i^0|, \tag{3}$$

where $b_i^0$ is the beginning time of job $i$ in $S^0$.

The rescheduling problem is to minimize (1) and (3). An optimization problem with such dual objectives can be converted into a single overall objective problem. Let the criteria be

$$\min_S J(S) = D(S) + M(S). \tag{4}$$

This single objective problem is also NP-hard [2].

## 3 PR Sub-problem at Each Disruption

For large-scale problems with more disruptions, FR strategy is neither beneficial nor needed because many operations are probably rescheduled more than one time. RSR strategy simply shifts the unfinished operations to the right without any consideration of objective optimality. Therefore, PR strategy will be a good alternative.

**Definition 1.** *The new schedule obtained through the previous rescheduling is referred to as the original schedule of the current rescheduling.*

In the following, we use $t$ to represent the rescheduling moment driven by a disruption. Obviously, the original schedule of the first rescheduling, when $t = 1$, is exactly the initial schedule. In this paper, at each disruption PR strategy decomposes all the unfinished jobs into two portions: the first portion is from the beginning jobs of the original schedule, which constitute the PR sub-problem and are totally rescheduled with respect to a certain criteria. Meanwhile RSR strategy is performed for the jobs of the remaining portion. Let $N$ be the set of all jobs. Let $\breve{N}_t$ be the set of finished jobs at $t$ and $\breve{S}(t)$ be the partial schedule of the original schedule for $\breve{N}_t$. Let $N'_t$ be the set of unfinished jobs at $t$, then $N = \breve{N}_t \bigcup N'_t$. At $t$, the moment when the machine return to service is denoted as $u_t$, the duration of the disruption is denoted as $D_t$.

**Definition 2.** *At $t$, the set of unfinished jobs involved by a PR sub-problem is referred to as a PR-horizon, denoted as $N_t$. The size of PR-horizon refers to the number of jobs in $N_t$, denoted as $|N_t|$.*

At $t$, let $\tilde{N}_t$ be the set of the remaining jobs in $N'_t$ except for $N_t$, i.e. $N'_t = N_t \bigcup \tilde{N}_t$. The number of jobs in $\tilde{N}_t$ is denoted as $|\tilde{N}_t|$. The global rescheduling consists of the PR for $N_t$ and the RSR for $\tilde{N}_t$. The global new schedule consists of the local new schedule for $N_t$ and the latter new schedule for $\tilde{N}_t$.

**Definition 3.** *Let the partial original schedule for $\tilde{N}_t$ be $S^0(\tilde{N}_t)$, a RSR solution $S^R(\tilde{N}_t)$ for $\tilde{N}_t$ is referred to as the $\triangle t$-RSR solution to $S^0(\tilde{N}_t)$ if the first unfinished job in $\tilde{N}_t$ is shifted to the right by $\triangle t$.*

In a general way, the original schedule at $t$ is the new schedule at $t-1$, denoted as $S(t-1)$, where the beginning time of job $i$ is denoted as $b_i(t-1)$. The partial schedule of $S(t-1)$ for $N_t$ is denoted as $S(N_t)$, whose completion time is denoted as $C(t-1)$. After PR, the new schedule for $N_t$ is denoted as $S^p(N_t)$, whose completion time is denoted as $C^p(t)$. The beginning time of job $i$ in $S^p(N_t)$ is denoted as $b_i^p(t)$. If $C^p(t) > C(t-1)$, the delay for PR-horizon is $\triangle C^p(t) = C^p(t) - C(t-1)$, else if $C^p(t) \leq C(t-1)$, the delay $\triangle C^p(t) = 0$. Let the $\triangle C^p(t)$-RSR solution for $\tilde{N}_t$ be $S^{pr}(\tilde{N}_t)$. Therefore, at $t$, the new schedule $S(t)$ consists of $S^p(N_t)$ and $S^{pr}(\tilde{N}_t)$. At $t$, two types of criteria for PR sub-problem are defined as follows based on PR-horizon $N_t$ respectively locating in the midst or the end of the original schedule:

$$\min_{S^p(N_t)} J_t = \{\sum_{i \in N_t} |b_i^p(t) - b_i(t-1)| + |\tilde{N}_t|[\triangle C^p(t)]\}, \qquad |\tilde{N}_t| > 0. \tag{5}$$

$$\min_{S^p(N_t)} J_t = \{\sum_{i \in N_t} |b_i^p(t) - b_i(t-1)| + M(S(t))\}, \qquad |\tilde{N}_t| = 0. \tag{6}$$

(5) is designed for $N_t$ locating in the midst of the original schedule. The objective of PR sub-problem is to minimize both the delay $\triangle C^p(t)$) and the schedule

deviation. Since the consideration of the delay for PR-horizon would make the new schedule inserted by less idle time, it is reasonable to use the number of later jobs as the weight for the delay in case more idle time greatly puts off later jobs. When $N_t$ locates in the end of the original schedule, the job set $\tilde{N}_t$ is empty and we directly consider the makespan in PR sub-problem (6).

## 4 Rolling PR Based on Local Search Algorithm

When more disruptions occur during the processing procedure, PR is driven by disruption events in a rolling mechanism. Let $l$ be the number of disruptions, the rolling PR is performed as follows:

Step 1. Minimize the makespan of the problem to generate the initial schedule $S^0$ without considering any disruption, denote $S(0) = S^0$, let $t = 1$;

Step 2. Implement the original schedule $S(t-1)$ until a disruption occurs, when the moment is noted as $d_t$;

Step 3. For a specified disruption duration $D_t$, calculate the moment $u_t$ for the machine returning to service, $u_t = d_t + D_t$, the release times of unfinished jobs in $N_t'$ are updated according to (2) (after the disruption, the interrupted job is resumed and included into $N_t'$);

Step 4. The first $k_t$ jobs from the beginning of $S(N_t')$ are included into the PR-horizon, $N_t$, note the completion time of $S(N_t)$, $C(t-1)$, calculate the number of jobs in $\tilde{N}_t$, $|\tilde{N}_t| = n - (|\breve{N}_t| + |N_t|)$ (Here $k_t$ is the specified size of PR-horizon);

Step 5. If $t \neq l$ and $|\tilde{N}_t| > 0$, the PR sub-problem is solved according to (5) and the solution $S^p(N_t)$, the completion time $C^p(t)$ as well as the delay $\triangle C^p(t)$ can be obtained. The new schedule $S^{pr}(\tilde{N}_t)$ is the $\triangle C^p(t)$-RSR solution to the original schedule for $\tilde{N}_t$. Thus the new schedule is $S(t) = S(\breve{N}_t) + S^p(N_t) + S^{pr}(\tilde{N}_t)$; If $|\tilde{N}_t| = 0$, the PR sub-problem is solved according to (6) and the solution $S^p(N_t)$ can be obtained. Thus the new schedule is $S(t) = S(\breve{N}_t) + S^p(N_t)$, which is exactly the original schedule of the next rescheduling. Let $t = t + 1$. If $t \leq l$, go to Step 2, else go to Step 6;

Step 6. The new schedule $S$ is exactly the last new schedule, i.e. $S = S(l)$. Calculate the schedule makespan $M(S)$ and the schedule deviation $D(S)$, the overall objective $J(S)$ defined as (4) can be obtained.

In this paper, since the size of PR sub-problem is limited, a local search algorithm based on all-pair exchange of jobs can be used to solve the PR sub-problems. The algorithm proceeds as follows:

Step 1. The initial solution $S^s(N_t)$ for local search is obtained by SPT [5] for $k_t$ jobs from PR-horizon $N_t$ with the updated release times. The objective function value $J_t^s$ was calculated according to (5) or (6);

Step 2. Let the solution of PR sub-problem be $S^p(N_t) = S^s(N_t)$, its objective function value is $J_t^p = J_t^s$, where the job in the $i$th position is denoted as $i$.

Do for $(i = 1; i < k; i++)$

For $(j = i + 1; j < k + 1; j++)$

Exchange the positions of job $i$ and $j$, then obtain the schedule $S^e(N_t)$, whose objective function value is denoted as $J_t^e$. If $J_t^e < J_t^p$, then $S^p(N_t) = S^e(N_t)$, $J_t^p = J_t^e$;

Step 3. If $J_t^p < J_t^s$, update $S^s(N_t) = S^p(N_t)$, go to Step2, or else go to Step4;

Step 4. $S^p(N_t)$ is the solution of the PR problem, stop.

## 5 Computational Results and Analysis

In the following testing, the initial schedule was generated by use of Schrage's algorithm [6]. All procedures were coded in C language and ran on a computer with Pentium 4-M CPU 1.80GHz. Three disruptions would occur during a run. The durations of disruptions range from five percent to ten percent of the processing time of the initial schedule. We assumed that the disruption would not occur among the last twenty jobs because the rescheduled jobs is too few to make rescheduling trivial in those cases.

Problems were randomly generated using a format similar to that used by Wang et al. [3]. The range parameter $\rho$ is used to control how rapidly jobs are expected to arrive for processing. When $\rho$ value is 0.20, jobs arrive rather rapidly so that almost no idle time exists in the initial schedule. However, the situation when $\rho$ value is 2.00 is the reverse. Therefore, the problems with these three $\rho$ values actually represent three situations where different amount of idle time exists in the initial schedule. We used a RSR solution as a baseline where our approach is compared. Testing was conducted to compare rolling PR with rolling RSR for each problem. The percentage improvements of rolling PR over rolling RSR were calculated as (RSR-PR)/PR. The size of PR-horizon was specified to be four types, which are 10-job, 20-job, 30-job, and 40-job. Figure 1 presents the average improvement percentage of efficiency (indicated by (D)) and stability (indicated by (M)). It is obviously shown that the schedule stability for PR was largely improved over that for RSR though the improvements of schedule efficiency was trivial in most cases. The improvements obviously get larger as the size of PR-horizon increases. The computational results also indicate that the

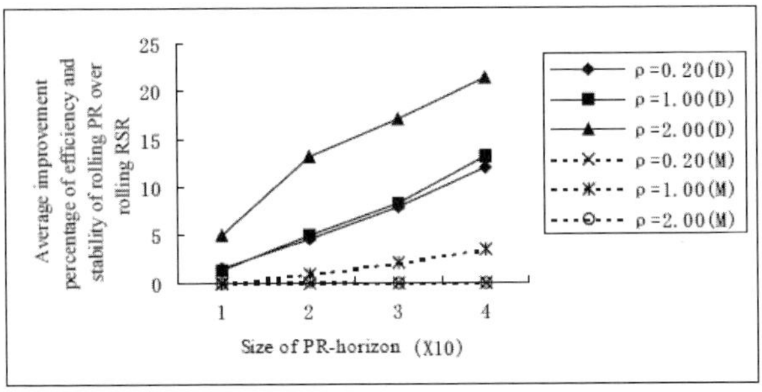


**Fig. 1.** Average improvement percentage of rolling PR over rolling RSR

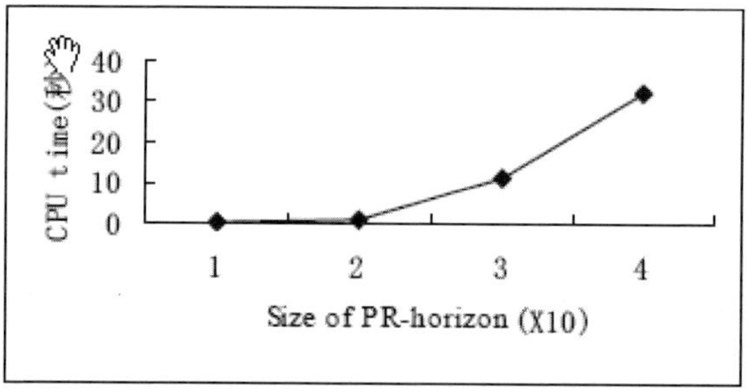


**Fig. 2.** CPU time of rolling PR for 200-job problems with 1.00 range parameter

improvements of schedule stability are larger when more idle time exists in the initial schedule. Figure 2 presents CPU time paid by rolling PR under different sizes of PR-horizon. It indicates that more CPU time should be paid for larger improvements achieved by rolling PR with larger PR-horizons.

## 6 Conclusions

Aiming at large-scale unfinished jobs and more disruptions during the execution of initial schedule, the rolling PR strategy driven by disruption events is adopted in this paper. The new schedule is required to satisfy dual objectives: efficiency and stability. Computational results show that the rolling PR can greatly improve the schedule stability with little sacrifice in schedule efficiency and consistently outperforms the rolling RSR. The rolling PR strategy is effective for large-scale dynamic rescheduling problems with more disruptions.

## References

1. Sabuncuoglu, I., Bayiz, M.: Analysis of Reactive Scheduling Problems in A Job Shop Environment. European Journal of Operational Research. **126**(2000) 567–586
2. Wu, D.S., Storer, R.H., Chang, P.C.: One-Machine Rescheduling Heuristics with Efficiency and Stability as Criteria. Computers in Operations Research. **20**(1993) 1–14
3. Wang, B., Xi, Y.G., Gu, H.Y.: Terminal Penalty Rolling Scheduling Based on An Initial Schedule for Single-Machine Scheduling Problem. Computers and Operations Research. **32**(2005) 3059–3072
4. Garey, M.R., Johnson, D.S.: Computers Intractability. Freeman, San Francisico, Calif. (1979)
5. Chu, C.B.: Efficient Heuristics to Minimize Total Flow Time with Release Dates. Operations Research Letters. **12**(1992) 321–330
6. Carlier, J.: The One-Machine Sequencing Problem. European Journal of Operational Research. **11**(1982) 42–47

# Sudoku Solver by Q'tron Neural Networks

Tai-Wen Yue and Zou-Chung Lee

Dept. of Computer Science and Engineering, Tatung University
Taipei, Taiwan, R.O.C
twyu@mail.cse.ttu.edu.tw, zzlee.tw@msa.hinet.net

**Abstract.** This paper presents a Sudoku solver based on the energy-driven neural-network (NN) model, called the Q'tron NN model. The rules to solve Sudoku are formulated as an energy function in the same form as a Q'tron NN's. The Q'tron NN for Sudoku can then be built simply by mapping. Equipping the NN with the proposed noise-injection mechanism, the Sudoku NN is ensured local-minima free. Besides solving Sudoku puzzles, the NN can also be used to generate Sudoku puzzles.

## 1 Introduction

Sudoku, also known as *Number Place*, is a logic-based placement puzzle. The puzzle is most frequently a $9 \times 9$ grid made up of $3 \times 3$ subgrids (called "regions"). To resolve a Sudoku puzzle successfully, each cell finally will contain a number from 1 through 9[1] subject to the constraints described below. Initially, some cells already contain numbers, known as "givens". The goal is to fill in the empty cells, one number in each, so that each column, row, and region contains the numbers 1 through 9 exactly once. Fig. 1 gives an instance of Sudoku puzzle.

The Sudoku was published anonymously by Garns (1979), who created the puzzle at age 74, and then promptly relegated to obscurity. It became popular in Japan starting somewhere between 1984 and 1986 under the name "nanpure," or Number Place. (Even today, in many Japanese publication, the puzzle is called Number Place, written in English.) The puzzle received a large amount of attention in the United States and Europe in 2005 after a regular Sudoku puzzle began appearing in the *London Times*. Sadly, Garns died in 1989 before getting a chance to see his creation as a worldwide phenomenon [10].

The general problem of solving Sudoku puzzles on $n^2 \times n^2$ boards of $n \times n$ blocks is known to be NP-complete [11]. This gives some indication of why Sudoku is difficult to solve, although on boards of finite size the problem is finite and can be solved by a deterministic finite automaton that knows the entire game tree. The popularity of Sudoku stimulated many Sudoku solvers to be born [17,18]. Most of Sudoku solvers were developed using 'algorithmic' approaches. For examples, it can be solved graph theoretically by translating the problem into a graphic search problem [4,19,20], or solved logically by reducing the problem into SAT [9]. Besides, building a Sudoku puzzle is another challenge. A proper Sudoku puzzle should contain a unique solution.

[1] Each cell can also be filled any one from nine different symbols, e.g., a through i.

D.-S. Huang, K. Li, and G.W. Irwin (Eds.): ICIC 2006, LNCS 4113, pp. 943–952, 2006.

| | | | | | | | | |
|---|---|---|---|---|---|---|---|---|
| | | | | | 7 | | 5 | 1 |
| 1 | 5 | | | | | | | |
| | | | | | 8 | 4 | | 6 |
| 9 | 8 | | | 2 | 4 | | 6 | |
| | 1 | | | | | | 4 | |
| | 6 | | 9 | 5 | | | 2 | 8 |
| 2 | | 5 | 6 | | | | | |
| | | | | | | | 9 | 3 |
| 4 | 9 | | 3 | | | | | |

**Fig. 1.** An instance of Sudoku puzzle

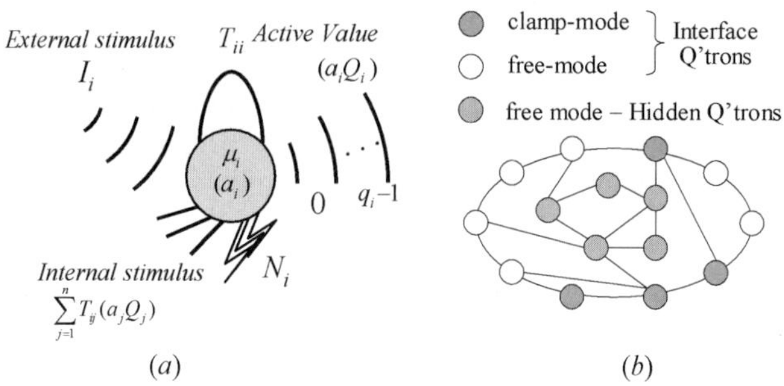


**Fig. 2.** (a) The Q'tron NN model; (b) The abstract Q'tron NN

Ironically, we found no neural network (NN) in this wonderland. Does solving Sudoku go beyond the capability of neural networks? The answer would be true if an effective local-minima escaping mechanism to keep NN's from being stuck at infeasible states does not exist. Specifically, to solve a constraint satisfaction problem, such as Sudoku, using an energy-driven NN, the NN can report a vaild solution usually when it has reached a global minimum of its corresponding energy landscape. This is because that any violation of constraints described by the rules is not tolerable.

This paper describes the technique to build a *Q'tron* (a shorthand of *quantum neuron*) NN to solve the underlying problems of Sudoku effectively, including puzzle resolution and puzzle generation. The Q'tron NN model, which is a significantly extended version of the Hopfield NN model [5,8], features in its local-minima escaping capability [6,13]. By constructing the NN as a *known-energy system* [13,14], it was shown that the *bounded noise spectra* for Q'trons in the NN can be systematically determined and, by injecting such pieces of random noise into Q'trons persistently, the NN will settle down if and only if it has reached a state whose energy is low enough. Roughly speaking, the NN seemingly knows whether or not an energy valley can be an acceptable solution by measuring its energy value[2]. Such an approach is considerably different from the concept of *simulated annealing*, which is, in fact, a *known-temperature* approach.

[2] In fact, an NN's energy is never measured. Instead, each Q'tron measures the force apply onto it.

Using that approach, the noise spectra for neurons are controlled by the current temperature of the system, which, in turn, is controlled by a carefully specified cooling schedule. Typical representatives of known-temperature approach include Boltzmann [1,2], Cauchy [7] and Gaussian Machines [3]. Further more, the known-energy property allows a Q'tron NN to function as an associative memory, i.e., feeding the piece of information available to the NN, a robust recall will then be responded by the NN provided that an admissible association is possible. This implies that we can interact with it the in a *question-answer* mode.

The organization of this paper is as follows: Section 2 gives a brief overview on the Q'tron NN model and describes the concept of known-energy systems. Section 3 presents the details to build the Q'tron Sudoku solver. Section 4 describes the operation modes of the Sudoku NN. We will show how the Sudoku NN can function versatilely to fulfill different requests, such as to solve a puzzle or to generate a puzzle. Section 5 demonstrates some experimental results. Finally, a conclusion is drawn in Section 6. Java applet and source code of the Q'tron Sudoku solver are now available at `http://www.cse.ttu.edu.tw/twyu/qtron/Sudoku`.

## 2 The Q'tron NN Model

The basic processing element of a Q'tron NN is called a Q'tron, a shorthand of a *quantum neuron*, which is schematically shown in Fig. 2(a). Let $\mu_i$ represent the $i^{th}$ Q'tron in a Q'tron NN. The output-level of $\mu_i$, denoted as $Q_i \in \{0, 1, ..., q_i - 1\}$ with $q_i$ ($\geq 2$). The actual output of $\mu_i$, called *active value*, is $a_i Q_i$, where $a_i > 0$ is the unit excitation strength, called *active weight*. In a Q'tron NN, for a pair of connected Q'trons $\mu_i$ and $\mu_j$, there is only one connection strength, i.e. $T_{ij} = T_{ji}$, and $T_{ii} < 0$ usually. The *noise-injected stimulus* $\hat{\mathcal{H}}_i$ for the Q'tron $\mu_i$ is defined as:

$$\hat{\mathcal{H}}_i = \mathcal{H}_i + \mathcal{N}_i = \sum_{j=1}^{n} T_{ij}(a_j Q_j) + I_i + \mathcal{N}_i, \tag{1}$$

where $\mathcal{H}_i$ denotes the *noise-free net stimulus* of $\mu_i$, which apparently is equal to the sum of *internal stimuli*, namely, $\sum_{j=1}^{n} T_{ij}(a_j Q_j)$, and *external stimulus* $I_i$. The term $\mathcal{N}_i$ denotes the piece of random noise fed into $\mu_i$, and $n$ denotes the number of Q'trons in the NN. In case that $P(\mathcal{N}_i = 0) = 1$, $i = 1, \ldots, n$, the Q'tron NN is said to run in *simple mode*; otherwise, it is said to run in *full mode*.

At each time step only one Q'tron is selected for level transition subject to the following rule:

$$Q_i(t+1) = Q_i(t) + \Delta Q_i(t), \tag{2}$$

with

$$\Delta Q_i(t) = \begin{cases} +1 & \hat{\mathcal{H}}_i(t) > \frac{1}{2}|T_{ii}a_i| \text{ and } Q_i(t) < q_i - 1; \\ -1 & \hat{\mathcal{H}}_i(t) < -\frac{1}{2}|T_{ii}a_i| \text{ and } Q_i(t) > 0; \\ 0 & \text{otherwise} \end{cases} \tag{3}$$

### 2.1 The Application Model

To make a Q'tron NN versatilely accessible, each Q'tron can either be operated in *clamp mode*, i.e., its output-level is clamped fixed at a particular level, or in *free mode*, i.e., its output-level is allowed to be updated according to the level transition rule specified in Eq. (2). Furthermore, the Q'trons in an NN are categorized into two types: *interface Q'trons* and *hidden Q'trons*, see Fig. 2(b). The former provides an interface for user's interaction, whereas the latter is functionally necessary to make the NN to a known-energy one[3]. We will assume that hidden Q'trons are always free unless otherwise specified. Interface Q'trons operated in clamp-mode are used to feed the available or affirmative information (a question) into the NN. The other free-mode interface Q'trons, on the other hand, are used to perform association to retrieve the missing or uncertain information (an answer).

### 2.2 System Energy — Stability

The system energy $\mathcal{E}$ embedded in a Q'tron NN, called *Liapunov energy*, is defined by the following form:

$$\mathcal{E} = -\frac{1}{2}\sum_{i=1}^{n}\sum_{j=1}^{n}(a_iQ_i)T_{ij}(a_jQ_j) - \sum_{i=1}^{n} I_i(a_iQ_i) + K; \tag{4}$$

where $n$ is the total number of Q'trons in the NN, and $K$ can be any suitable constant. It was shown that, to run a Q'tron NN in simple mode, the energy $\mathcal{E}$ defined above will monotonically decrease with time [13,14] and, hence, is stable. Therefore, if a problem can be reformulated as one that minimizes an energy function in the above form, then a Q'tron NN to solve the problem can be built simply by mapping[4]. Hopefully, the NN will autonomously solve the problem once it reaches a local/global minimum. However, the monotonic decrease nature of energy also implies that the Q'tron NN running in simple mode performs a greedy search. In case the overwhelming majority of local-minima of the NN corresponds to poor or, even worse, illegal solutions to the underlying problem, then the NN will be useless almost.

### 2.3 Known-Energy Systems

A Q'tron NN is said to be a known-energy system if, letting all Q'trons free, it will settle down with probability one onto a state whose energy lies within a prespecified *low-and-known* range, e.g., $\mathcal{E}^* \leq \mathcal{E} \leq \mathcal{E}^* + \frac{1}{2}(\frac{\Delta}{2})^2$ where $\mathcal{E}^*$ is the least possible energy of the system[5], and $\frac{\Delta}{2}(\geq 0)$ is called a *solution qualifier*

[3] The Sudoku solver does not need any hidden Q'tron. An example that needs hidden Q'trons can be found in [16].

[4] To solve a problem using the Q'tron NN model, the values of $q_i$'s and $a_i$'s usually can be determined intuitively from the problem' nature, and the values of $T_{ij}$'s and $I_i$'s are obtained by mapping the problem's cost function to Eq (4).

[5] $\mathcal{E}^*$ can be a energy value that is less than or equal to that of a global minimum.

[13], provided such a state does exist. Suppose that a state with energy lying within $[\mathcal{E}^*, \mathcal{E}^* + \frac{1}{2}(\frac{\Delta}{2})^2]$ always corresponds to a satisfactory and/or legal solution. Then, the NN settles if and only if it has found an appropriate solution. Typical constraint satisfaction problems have such a known-energy property, such as the Sudoku solver to be described in the next section, and, hence, can be solved based on the known-energy concept [12,13,14]. However, many combinatorial optimization problems, e.g., TSP and knapsack problems, are intrinsically 'unknown' in energy. The method to convert them into known-energy ones and, then, solved by incorporating with a solution refining scheme were described in [15].

### 2.4 Bounded Noise Spectra

To make the known-energy systems realizable, they must be able to escape from the local-minima corresponding to unsatisfactory and/or illegal solutions only. To this end, each Q'tron is allowed to have a bounded noise spectrum only, i.e., $\mathcal{N}_i \in [\mathcal{N}_i^-, \mathcal{N}_i^+]$. The values of $\mathcal{N}_i^-$ and $\mathcal{N}_i^+$ for each Q'tron can be systematically determined based on the value of the solution qualifier, i.e., $\frac{\Delta}{2}$. For example, if the energy function of a Q'tron NN is in an integer-programming type [13], we will have

$$\mathcal{N}_i^- = -\mathcal{N}_i^+ = \max\left(0, \frac{1}{2}|T_{ii}a_i| - \frac{\Delta}{2}\right). \tag{5}$$

One convenient way for computer simulation is to generate only *bang-bang noise*. In this way, the distribution of noise is specified by the so-called *noise ratio specification* (NRS) of a Q'tron. It is defined as:

$$\text{NRS}_i = P(\mathcal{N}_i = \mathcal{N}_i^-) : P(\mathcal{N}_i = 0) : P(\mathcal{N}_i = \mathcal{N}_i^+) \tag{6}$$

with $P(\mathcal{N}_i = \mathcal{N}_i^-) + P(\mathcal{N}_i = 0) + P(\mathcal{N}_i = \mathcal{N}_i^+) = 1$, where $\text{NRS}_i$ represents the NRS of $\mu_i$, and $P(\mathcal{N}_i = x)$ represents the probability that $\mathcal{N}_i = x$ is generated. Clearly, if a Q'tron NN runs in *simple mode*, then $\text{NRS}_i = 0 : 1 : 0$ for all $i$. We will assume that $P(\mathcal{N}_i = \mathcal{N}_i^-) \neq 0$ and $P(\mathcal{N}_i = \mathcal{N}_i^+) \neq 0$ for all $i$ if a Q'tron NN runs in full mode.

## 3 The Sudoku Solver

In this section, we describe how to build a Q'tron Sudoku solver based on the known-energy concept. Let's start with the puzzle representation.

### 3.1 Puzzle Representation

We will use a $9 \times 9 \times 9$ Q'tron cube to represent the Sodudo puzzle, and use $\mu_{ijk}$ to denote its $ijk^{th}$ Q'tron, where $i, j, k \in \{1, \ldots, 9\}$. Let $Q_{ijk} \in \{0, 1\}$ (hence, $q_{ijk} = 2$) represent the output of $\mu_{ijk}$, and let $Q_{ijk} = 1$ (=0) represent that the cell in the $i^{th}$ row and the $j^{th}$ column of the puzzle is (not) filled with the $k^{th}$ symbol. Since this is a pure constraint satisfaction problem, we don't associate with each Q'tron with a cost. Hence, let $a_{ijk} = 1$ for all $i, j, k \in \{1, \ldots, 9\}$.

### 3.2 Sudoku as an Integer Program

Based on the Q'tron representation defined above, the Sudoku rules can be described as the following integer program:

$$\sum_{j=1}^{9} Q_{ijk} = 1, \text{ for all } i,k \in \{1,\dots 9\} \tag{7}$$

$$\sum_{i=1}^{9} Q_{ijk} = 1, \text{ for all } j,k \in \{1,\dots 9\} \tag{8}$$

$$\sum_{i=1}^{3}\sum_{j=1}^{3} Q_{3m+i,3n+j,k} = 1, \text{ for all } m,n \in \{0,1,2\} \text{ and } k \in \{1,\dots 9\} \tag{9}$$

$$\sum_{k=1}^{9} Q_{ijk} = 1 \text{ for all } i,j \in \{1,\dots 9\} \tag{10}$$

where Eq. (7) to (9) require that each of the nine symbols must appear in each row, each column and each $3 \times 3$ subregion of the puzzle exactly once, respectively, and Eq. (10) requires that each cell must be filled with exactly one symbol.

### 3.3 Energy Function

By above, the Sudoku solver can then be one that minimizes the following energy function:

$$\mathcal{E}_{Sudoku} = \mathcal{E}_{row} + \mathcal{E}_{col} + \mathcal{E}_{rgn} + \mathcal{E}_{sym} \tag{11}$$

$$\mathcal{E}_{row} = \frac{1}{2}\sum_{i=1}^{9}\sum_{k=1}^{9}\left(\sum_{j=1}^{9} Q_{ijk} - 1\right)^2 \tag{12}$$

$$\mathcal{E}_{col} = \frac{1}{2}\sum_{j=1}^{9}\sum_{k=1}^{9}\left(\sum_{i=1}^{9} Q_{ijk} - 1\right)^2 \tag{13}$$

$$\mathcal{E}_{rgn} = \frac{1}{2}\sum_{m=0}^{2}\sum_{n=0}^{2}\sum_{k=1}^{9}\left(\sum_{i=1}^{3}\sum_{j=1}^{3} Q_{3m+i,3n+j,k} - 1\right)^2 \tag{14}$$

$$\mathcal{E}_{sym} = \frac{1}{2}\sum_{i=1}^{9}\sum_{j=1}^{9}\left(\sum_{i=1}^{9} Q_{ijk} - 1\right)^2 \tag{15}$$

Clearly, when a Sudoku puzzle is resolved, we must have $\mathcal{E}_{Sudoku} = 0$ or, more loosely, $0 \le \mathcal{E}_{Sudoku} \le \frac{1}{2}(\frac{\Delta}{2})^2$ as long as $0 \le \frac{\Delta}{2} < 1$. To solve combinatorial optimization problems, $\frac{\Delta}{2}$, called a solution qualifier, is an important factor to tune the solution quality. However, we don't have any flexibility to 'tune' the constraints of Sudoku. Therefore, we set $\frac{\Delta}{2} = 0$ for simplicity.

### 3.4 The Q'tron NN Construction

The energy function of the Sudoku cube is in the following form:

$$\mathcal{E}_{cube} = -\frac{1}{2}\sum_{i=1}^{9}\sum_{j=1}^{9}\sum_{k=1}^{9}\sum_{l=1}^{9}\sum_{m=1}^{9}\sum_{n=1}^{9}(a_{ijk}Q_{ijk})T_{ijk,lmn}(a_{lmn}Q_{lmn})$$
$$-\sum_{i=1}^{9}\sum_{j=1}^{9}\sum_{k=1}^{9}I_{ijk}(a_{ijk}Q_{ijk}) + K \quad (16)$$

Mapping Eq. (11) to Eq. (16), all parameters for the Sudoku solver can then be determined. In summary, $q_{ijk} = 2$, $a_{ijk} = 1$, $I_{ijk} = 4$, and

$$T_{ijk,lmn} = -\delta_{il} - \delta_{jm} - \delta_{kn} - \delta_{(i-1)/3,(l-1)/3}\delta_{(j-1)/3,(m-1)/3} \quad (17)$$

for all $i, j, k, l, m, n \in \{1, \ldots, 9\}$. In Eq. (17), integer division is used in subscripts, and $\delta_{ij}$ is the Kronecker delta function defined by

$$\delta_{ij} = \begin{cases} 0, i \neq j \\ 1, i = j \end{cases}$$

Furthermore, since $\mathcal{E}_{Sudoku}$ is in integer-programming type, the noise spectrum for each Q'tron can thus be determined from Eq. (5). Hence, $N^{+}_{ijk} = 2$ and $N^{-}_{ijk} = 2$ for all $i, j, k \in \{1, \ldots, 9\}$. We here have implicitly assumed that $\frac{\Delta}{2} = 0$.

## 4 The Operation Modes of Sudoku Solver

It can be shown that, to run the Sudoku solver in full mode with all Q'tron being set free, all states corresponding to a valid Sudoku configuration are stable, and all others are not. This implies that we have stored all valid configurations of Sodudo puzzle into the solver and, hence, allows us to perform recall in an associative sense.

### 4.1 Sudoku Solver as an Associative Memory

Suppose that the Sodudo solver is now in an arbitrary stable state. Now, consider a simple recall case. Suppose that we now want to recall a valid configuration of Sodudo puzzle with a single cell being set to a particular symbol, e.g., we need the cell in the $i^{th}$ row and the $j^{th}$ column to contain the $k^{th}$ symbol. A lazy method is to just clamp $\mu_{ijk}$ to level one, and set all other Q'trons free. Due to persistent noise, such an action will pump the system energy to very high and, hence, will render the system to become unstable immediately unless that the $ij^{th}$ cell already has the $k^{th}$ symbol in it. Consequently, Sodudo solver will settle down (with probability one) if and only if a successful recall has been done (refer to [14] for rigorous proof).

Although the lazy method is workable, its convergent behavior will be also lazy. A more effective method, called the diligent method, is to clamp all available information relative to that clamped cell to the solver. For example, we can set

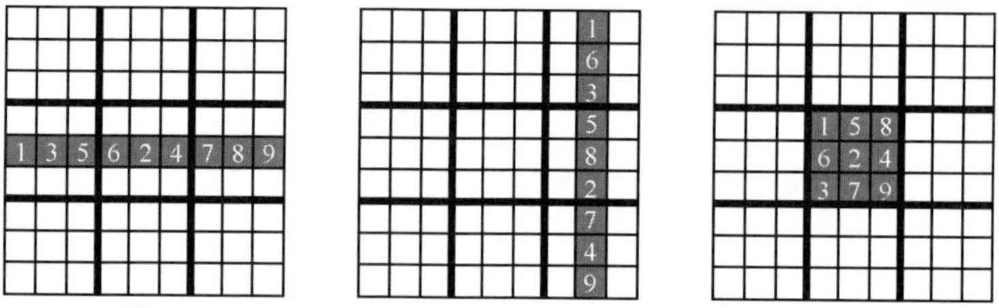

(a) (b) (c)

**Fig. 3.** To generate a valid Sudoku configuration by clamping an arbitrary (a) row, (b) column, and (c) 3×3 subregion, diligently

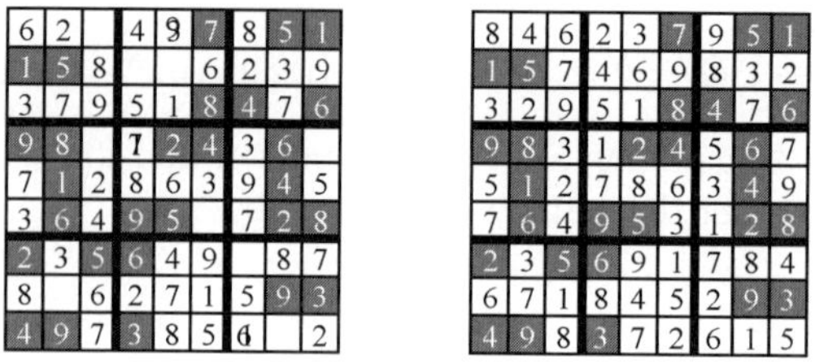

(a) (b)

**Fig. 4.** Experimental results of Sudoku solver ran (a) in simple mode, (b) in full mode

Q'trons $\mu_{\cdot jk}$'s, $\mu_{i\cdot k}$'s and $\mu_{ij\cdot}$'s, where $\cdot \in \{1, \ldots, 9\}$, and $\mu_{i'j'k}$'s such that $(i'-1)/3 = (i-1)/3$ and $(j'-1)/3 = (j-1)/3$, to clamp mode. Among them, only $\mu_{ijk}$ is clamped to level one, and the others are clamped to level zero. And, all the other Q'trons are set free. In the following, the diligent method will be used to feed cells' information into the Sudoku solver.

### 4.2 Puzzle Resolution

Sudoku puzzle resolution is a straightforward implication of the above discussion. Given a Sudoku puzzle, we can solve it by clamping all of the given symbols diligently as was described in the last subsection. The solver will then respond with a legal solution when it settles down provided that the given puzzle is not unsolvable.

### 4.3 Puzzle Generation

There are 6, 670, 903, 752, 021, 072, 936, 960 valid Sudoku configurations for the standard 9×9 grid [21]. Any valid Sudoku configuration can become a proper Sudoku puzzle, i.e., its solution is unique, by masking some of its cells blank conscientiously. First of all, we can generate a valid Sudoku configuration by freeing all Q'trons of the Sudoku solver, initializing its state arbitrarily and, then, running it in full mode. A valid Sudoku configuration will then be resulted when the solver settles down. Without losing the randomness nature, one can also arbitrarily select a row, a column or a 3 × 3 region and clamp the nine Q'trons in it diligently with nine different symbols for speed up, as shown in Fig. 3.

After a valid Sudoku configuration is generated, any Sudoku construction algorithm that ensures properness of the puzzle [21] can then be applied to determine the cells of 'givens' and, hence, the blanks. This final task can also be done by interacting with our Q'tron Sudoku solver iteratively. Specifically, we can determine whether a given Sudoku puzzle is proper by running the Sudoku solver under different initial conditions on free Q'trons multiple times, e.g., 10 times. If all of the tests get the same solution, then the given puzzle has high probability to be proper. There are two possible approaches based on the above such a properness test. One is in forward sense, while the other is in backward sense. The former starts from a small number of blank cells, which are randomly selected, and then marks more cells as blanks iteratively until it fails in the properness test. Contrarily, the later starts from a larger number of blank cells, and then changes some of them as givens iteratively until it passes the properness test.

## 5 The Experiments

Several experiments were performed on a digital computer, Pentium IV, to verify the effectiveness of the Q'tron Sudoku solver. Fig. 4(a) shows an experimental result obtained by running the solver in simple mode. In the figure, the symbols with dark background represent the givens of a Sudoku puzzle, which was generated by the solver itself, and the symbols in the other cells represent the solution reported by the solver when it settles down. Clearly, the solver is malfunctioned in the noise-free mode. More than that, solving the same puzzle with different initial conditions on free Q'trons, we did not get any legal solution on 1000 tests. Oppositely, Fig. 4(b) shows a legal solution obtained by running the solver in full mode with $NRS = 1 : 1 : 1$ for all Q'trons. In this instance, the solution is obtained within one second. This shows the local-minima-free escaping capability of the Q'tron NN approach.

## 6 Conclusions

This paper describes the details on building a Sudoku solver using the Q'tron NN model. The Q'tron NN model features in its local-minima escaping capability by incorporating it with a persistent noise-injection mechanism. In particular, if a problem can be formulated as an integer program in a standard form, then all of parameters of the Q'tron NN, including the bounded noise-spectra for Q'trons, can be systematically determined, and the so-built Q'tron NN will be a known-energy system. Sudoku is intrinsically such a problem. Hence, the Q'tron-NN strategy is readily applicable. As a known-energy system, the Q'tron Sudoku solver can thus serve as a versatile associative memory. This will allow us to interact with it in a question-answer sense. Hence, besides solving Sudoku puzzles, the Q'tron Sudoku solver can also be used for puzzle generation. Some experiments were demonstrated in the paper for verification. More information relevant to the Q'tron NN researches can be found at `http://www.cse.ttu.edu.tw/twyu/qtron`.

## References

1. Aarts, E., Korst, J.: Simulated Annealing and Boltzmann Machines. Wiley and Sons, Chichester, England (1989)
2. Ackley, D. H., Hinton, G. E., Sejnowski, T. J.: A Learning Algorithm for Boltzmann Machine. Cognitive Science, 9 (1985) 147-169
3. Akiyama, Y., Yamashita, A., Kajiura, M., Aiso, H.: Combinatorial Optimization with Gaussian Machines. Proceedings of IEEE International Joint Conference on Neural Networks, Washington , DC, 1 (1989) 533–540
4. Hayes, B.: Unwed Numbers - The mathematics of Sudoku: A Puzzle That Boasts 'No Math Required!'. American Scientist, 94 (1) (2006) 12-15
5. Hopfield, J. J.: Neural Networks and Physical Systems with Emergent Collective Computational Abilities. Proceedings of Natl. Acad. Sci. USA, 79 (1982) 2554-2558
6. Hopfield, J. J., Tank, D. W.: Neural Computation of Decisions in Optimization Problems. Biological Cybernetics, 52 (1985) 141-152
7. Jeong, H., Park, J. H.: Lower Bounds of Annealing Schedule for Boltzmann and Cauchy Machines. Proceeding of IEEE International Joint Conference on Neural Networks, Washington , DC, 1 (1989) 581-586
8. Lee, B. W., Sheu, B. J.: Modified Hopfield Neural Networks for Retrieving the Optimal Solution. IEEE Transactions on Neural Networks, 6 (1991) 137-142
9. Tjark, W.: A SAT-based Sudoku Solver. In Processing of The 12th International Conference on Logic for Programming, Artificial Intelligence and Reasoning (LPAR 2005), Montego Bay, Jamaica (2005)
10. Will, S.: Sudoku Easy. St. Martin's Press, New York (2005)
11. Yato T., Seta. T.: Complexity and Completeness of Finding Another Solution and Its Application to Puzzles. IPSJ SIG Notes 2002-AL-87-2. http://www-imai.is.s.u-tokyo.ac.jp/ ~ yato/data2/SIGAL87-2.pdf (2002)
12. Yue, T. W., Chen, M. C.: Q'tron Neural Networks for Constraint Satisfaction. Proceedings of Fourth International Conference on Hybrid Intelligent Systems (HIS'04), Kitakyushu, Japan (2004) 398-403
13. Yue, T. W.: A Goal-Driven Neural Network Approach for Combinatorial Optimization and Invariant Pattern Recognition. Phds Thesis, Department of Computer Engineering, National Taiwan University, Taiwan (1992)
14. Yue, T. W., Chiang S.: Quench, Goal-Matching and Converge – The Three-Phase Resoning of A Q'tron Neural Network. Proceedings of IASTED2002, International Conference on Artificial and Computational Intelligence, Tokyo, Japan (2002) 54-59
15. Yue, T. W., Lee Z. C.: A Goal-Driven Approach for Combinatorial Optimization Using Q'tron Neural Networks. Proceedings of IASTED2002, International Conference on Artificial and Computational Intelligence, Tokyo, Japan (2002) 60-65
16. Yue, T. W., Chen M. C.: Associativity, Auto-reversibility and Question-Answering on Q'tron Neural Networks. Proceedings of International Conference on Intelligent Computing 2005 (ICIC2005), Hefei, China (2005) 1023-1034
17. Sudoku Solver. Sudoku Solver by Logic. http://www.sudokusolver.co.uk/ (2006)
18. Scanraid Ltd. Sudoku Solver. http://www.scanraid.com/sudoku.htm (2006)
19. Wikipedia. Graph coloring. http://en.wikipedia.org/wiki/Graph_coloring (2006)
20. Wikipedia. Mathematics of Sudoku. http://en.wikipedia.org/wiki/Mathematics_of_Sudoku (2006)
21. Wikipedia. Sudoku. http://en.wikipedia.org/wiki/Sudoku (2006)

# A Simulation-Based Process Evaluation Approach to Enterprise Business Process Intelligence

Wen-An Tan[1,2], Anqiong Tang[1], and Wei-ming Shen[2]

[1] Software Engineering Institute, Zhejiang Normal University
JinHua, Zhejiang, P.R. China, 321004
twajsj@sohu.com

[2] Integrated Manufacturing Technologies Institute, National Research Council of Canada,
800 Collip Circle, London, ON, Canada N6G 4X8
weiming.shen@nrc-cnrc.gc.ca

**Abstract.** In order to discover and manage enterprise businesses effectively, enterprise decision makers need to understand enterprise business processes from various aspects using sophisticated process simulation and analysis tools. Based on ABM technology (Activity-Based Management), this paper presents intelligent business process analysis concepts and metric measurement models for six kinds of process flows within manufacturing enterprises: activity flow, product flow, resource flow, cost flow, cash flow, and profit flow. The proposed process flow analysis approach has been developed as a dynamic enterprise process analysis tool within a process simulation and optimization environment.

## 1 Introduction

Dynamic modeling and simulation of enterprise systems has been an active research topic of research for more than two decades [1]. There are a number of approaches, such as CIM-OSA [2], GRAI-GIM [3] and ARIS [4], which have been focused on the description of the enterprise model: describing the enterprise organization, its resources, business processes, functions and product data information model. The objective of research on enterprise business process simulation and optimization are to create an optimized enterprise model for instructing enterprise operation and management. Using process simulation and optimization technologies, computer-aided solutions can be obtained economically. Enterprise dynamic modeling has been the recent research focus for the development of flexible systems.

How do we analyze and evaluate enterprise processes effectively? This is important to enterprise process simulation and optimization. In different modeling environments, we usually have different information needed to analyze because of the different context of the meta-model [5]. The different managers take care of the different process characteristics of the enterprise system in different domains. An outstanding enterprise system should provide the analysis functions of various flows during process execution to assist enterprise decision-makers to understand their enterprise and make reasonable decisions.

Generally speaking, there are essentially three kinds of approaches to the monitoring and analysis of process execution. Thc first and simplest one consists of providing simple reports from the process execution database. Users can typically

D.-S. Huang, K. Li, and G.W. Irwin (Eds.): ICIC 2006, LNCS 4113, pp. 953 – 963, 2006.

access reports showing basic process statistics. A more sophisticated approach takes care of OLAP-style analysis. In this technique, execution data are periodically collected into a data warehouse, and users are offered a number of different ways to look at the data, including possible multidimensional analysis views. The third and most intriguing approach to process execution analysis involves the use of business intelligence, to provide users with explanations of process behaviours of interest as well as predictions on running and even yet-to-be process executions. The adoption of business intelligence causes a shift from the passive system behaviour of the previous two approaches to an active one, where it is up to the system to provide the user with information about problems and their causes. Some scholars call it *business process intelligence* (*BPI*) [6].

This study systematically introduces the six flows occurring during enterprise process execution: activity flow, product flow, resource flow, cost flow, cash flow, and benefit flow as based on ABM [7], and the related business process intelligent analysis functions. Activity flow is the primary flow in the enterprise process, and other flows can be derived according to the execution of activity. The rest of this paper is focused on the implementation of process flow analysis tool with BPI within a process simulation and optimization environment. It can be used for enterprise business reengineering and enterprise diagnosis.

## 2 ABM-Based Process Flow Analysis Technologies

When the business environment has changed, business information must change quickly with it. The TCM (Total Cost Management) [7] approach is based on the belief that an in-depth understanding and the continuous improvement of the business process are the driving forces behind effective management of costs. Today, ABC/ABM is widely adopted to address the above issues because they provide a complete picture of the profits and costs of doing business than traditional cost accounting methods.

Business Process Analysis is the foundation for business process improvement. In order to realize Business Process Analysis, an integrated enterprise process model framework should be determined first. Based on traditional ABC solutions, we offer the integrated capabilities in data management, analysis, cooperative control, and behaviour description. In our proposed solution, evolved from the SADT and COSMOS models and referenced with CIM-OSA, the proposed enterprise model is constructed to be a multi-dimensional framework containing the view dimension, the generality dimension, and the lifecycle dimension [8]. In the view-dimension, an enterprise can be effectively described from five aspects: process, infrastructure, behaviour, cooperation and information.

$$E_M = \langle P_M, I_M, B_M, C_M, I_{FM} \rangle \,. \tag{1}$$

where $P_M$: Process Model; $I_M$: Infrastructure Model; $B_M$: Behavior Model; $C_M$: Cooperation Model; $I_{FM}$: Information Model.

$P_M$ is the core of the enterprise model. It is a partial set of business activities with the relative resource supports, inputs, outputs, and controls. It can be described as:

$$P_M = \langle A, P, R, Control, Support, Input, Output \rangle. \tag{2}$$

where $A=\{a_1,a_2,\ldots,a_m\}$ is a set of activities; $P=\{Product_1,Product_2,\ldots,Product_j\}$ is a set of products; $R=\{r_1,r_2,\ldots,r_k\}$ is a set of resource types; *Control* is the tangible and intangible control relationships; *Support* is the relationship of resources for an activity, and $Support \subseteq A\times R$; *Input* is the relationship of input products to an activity, $Input \subseteq A\times P$; *Output* is the relationship of output products to an activity, $Output \subseteq A\times P$.

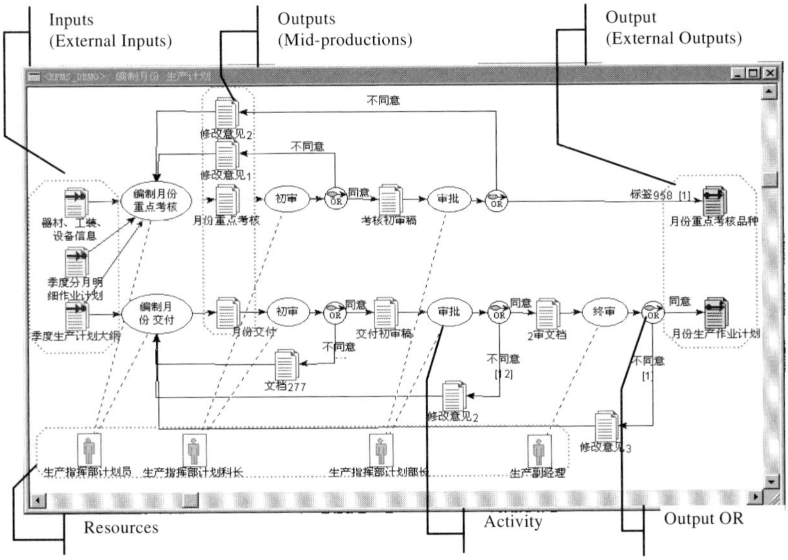


**Fig. 1.** A Process of Manufacturing Planning

Based on the proposed model framework, an example of the process of manufacturing planning is illustrated as Figure 1, which sequenced by three activities: Planning for Monthly MPS, Verifying, Examine and Approval, and with the supports.

## 2.1 Activity Flow

*Activity flow* represents the execution order of activities in the enterprise process life cycle. Execution order of activities includes activities time order and the structural relationship of activities. The latter can be defined in the structure of the process model. The former could be illustrated within the Gantt chart.

*Activity flow* embodies the parallelism among activities in enterprise processes, such as structure parallelism and run-time parallelism. *Activity flow* is the baseline of enterprise business processes. Other stream information can be derived from it. During process simulation, all activities are in initial state while initiating *activity flow* and other flow information. When an activity's input conditions or timing constraints are satisfied, its activity state changes to ready state. All activity ready events are stored in the activity ready pool. All activities of which has got their required resources will be activated, and their behaviour functions will be run. Each activity's real duration can be created by *random-number-generator* according to the defined duration and its probability distribution. The whole process of activity execution has been created within the *activity flow*. *Activity flow* analysis can be used to support enterprise concurrent engineering and computer supported cooperative work in business management.

### 2.2 Information Flow

***Product Flow.*** Like activity flow, *product flow* has two aspects. From the vertical aspect of the enterprise process, i.e., from the beginning to the end of one process, *product flow* indicates the generation relations between products. From the horizontal aspect, i.e., upon the input or output of one activity in the enterprise process, *product flow* shows its product heap state.

**Definition 1.** For $Product_i \in P$, the queue of continually varying product quantity is called the product heap quantity queue for $Product_i$ in its product lifecycle.

The product heap quantity queue in the horizontal product flow can be used to study "Zero Inventory" and "JIT". It reflects the attainability of the cooperative degree/balance between producer activity and consumer activity of a product. The generation of product's tree structure can be referred from the sub-process model by process tracking. It serves as a producing history supporting quality improvement and the tracking of products.

***Data Flow.*** Data flow is a time sequence to describe the data changes in the behaviour model and database or file system. It is ordered by time and used to verify process execution. Similar to the product flow, the data used and generated by the activities from start to stop of a process execution forms a horizontal data flow which can be used for analyzing the structure of the behaviour model. The data at one particular point varying over time is called a vertical data flow for analyzing the function of the behaviour model in an enterprise model. In reality, enterprise supply chain management is a spread of product flow and data flow management.

### 2.3 Resource Flow

*Resource flow* is the resource usage varying with time in the execution of enterprise processes. The resource consumption is defined in the specification of resource related with an activity. Thus *resource flow* can be calculated on the basis of *activity flow*. The difference between *information flow* and *resource flow* is that resources only support activity operations, but not be consumed and processed as information. Therefore, *resource flow* only focuses on the horizontal aspect, i.e., to calculate the consumption of all kinds of resources in an enterprise process at some time.

**Definition 2.** For resource $r \in R$, $ActsSupported(r)=\{x|x \in A \wedge <r,x> \in Supporting\}$ is called *Relative activity set* of resource *r*.

**Definition 3.** For $a \in A$, activity cloning set of activity *a* at *t* is:

$$ActiveClone(a, t) = \{LT\ (ISet(a)) \mid LT\ (ISet(a)) \leq t \leq LT\ (ISet(a)) + d\ (a)\} \quad (3)$$

where $d(a)$ is the duration of activity *a*; $ISet(a)$ is the input product set of activity *a*; *LT* is the last completion time of the products in $ISet(a)$ of activity *a*. We use *LT* to represent an element of activity cloning.

**Definition 4.** At time $t$, the consumption of resource $r$ occupied by activity $a \in$ A:

$$ResUsed\ (a,r,t)=card(ActivitClone\ (a,t))\ *NUsed(a,r) \tag{4}$$

where $card(ActivitClone(a,\ t))$ is the cardinal number of $ActivitClone(a,\ t)$, *i.e.*, the number of the elements in the set; $NUsed(a,r)$ is the consumption of resource $r$ when activity $a$ runs once.

**Definition 5.** The consumption of resource $r$ for all $r \in R$ in process $ps$ at time $t$ is:

$$NumOfRes\ (ps,r,t) = \sum_{i=1}^{n} ResUsed\ (a_i,\ r,\ t) \tag{5}$$

where $N$=$card(ActsSupported(r))$, i.e., the number of activities related to resource $r$; $a_i$ is $i$th activity related to resource $r$. The discrete order of the resource consumption varying with time is called the resource flow for $r$.

## 2.4 Cost Flow

*Cost flow* is a time order of the expense in a business process, such as salary, rent of machine and workshop and so on. In general, *cost flow* may be divided into resource usage cost and source product cost. It is used to show the consumed cost during the life cycle of a process.

**Definition 6.** For $r \in R$□$ResUnitCost$: R→$R^+$ is the unit cost relation on R. It is signed as $ResUnitCost(r)$.

**Definition 7.** *The effective cost* of $r$, $r \in R$, related to process $ps$ in $[t_1,t_2]$, can be calculated as follows:

$$Cost(ps,r,t_1,t_2)=ResUnitCost(r)\times\int_{t1}^{t2} NumOfRes\ (ps,r,\ t)dt \tag{6}$$

where $NumOfRes(ps,r,\ t)$ is the usage of resource $r$ in process $ps$. It could be got from formula (5).

**Definition 8.** *Total Resource Cost* is the cost consumption for all kinds of resource supporting activities during the execution of $ps$ in $[t_1$□$t_2]$ can be calculated as:

$$TResCost(ps,\ t_1,\ t_2)=\sum_{i=1}^{n} Cost(ps,\ r_i,\ t_1,\ t_2) \tag{7}$$

where $n$=$card(R)$ is the cardinal number of resource set related to process $ps$, *i.e.*, the number of resource classes defined in process $ps$; $Cost$ is the cost of one kind of resource used in process $ps$ in $[t_1,t_2]$.

**Definition 9.** *Source product set* in process $ps$ is :

$$SPS(ps)=\{p|p \in P \wedge (p\ \mathrm{IN}\ ps) \wedge \neg(\exists a\ (a \in \mathbf{A} \wedge \langle a,\ p\rangle \in Output))\} \tag{8}$$

For partial order set $\langle A \cup P,\ Input \cup Output\rangle$, $SPS$ is the maximal set of source products in process $ps$.

**Definition 10.** For source product $sp$ in process $ps$, $sp \in SPS$, there is a mapping function $SProdCost$: $P \rightarrow R^+$, which is called *unit cost function of source product*, signed as $SProdCost(sp)$.

**Definition 11.** In $[t_1,t_2]$, *Source Product Cost* in process *ps* can be calculated using the formula:

$$SouCost(ps,t_1,t_2)=\sum_{i=1}^{m} SProdCost(sp_i)\times NPurc(ps, sp_i, t_1, t_2) \tag{9}$$

where $m=card(SPS)$; $sp_i \in SourceProducts$ in process *ps*; $NumPurc(ps,sp_i,t_1,t_2)$ is the purchase quantity of source product $sp_i$ in $[t_1, t_2]$, it is a statistical value. In the simulation environment, source products are created by the generator of random numbers according to the specific distribution of source product arrival frequency.

**Definition 12.** *Process Effective Cost* in $[t_1 \square t_2]$ can be calculated as follows:

$$ProCost(t_1,t_2) = SouCost(ps,t_1,t_2) + TResCost(ps,t_1,t_2) \tag{10}$$

In process execution (via simulation or enactment), the consumption of source products and resource is recorded and collected, process effective cost can be calculated and thus cost flow is generated.

## 2.5 Cash Flow

*Cash flow* is the amount of cash varying with time in the process execution. A complete enterprise process model should consist of various sub-processes such as the main production plan, product design, manufacturing, finance management, human management, material purchase and product sales and so on. To analyze features of *cash flow*, a sale sub-process must be part of the process model. The end products in this sub-process are goods. In the specification of goods, the sale price must be specified.

**Definition 13.** The goods set in the process sale is a set of all end products, which can be described as:

$$Gds(Sale)=\{\, p \mid p \in P \wedge (p \text{ In } Sale) \wedge \neg(\exists a\,(a \in A \wedge \langle a, p\rangle \in Input))\} \tag{11}$$

For partial order set $<A \cup P, Input \cup Output>$, *Gds*(*Sale*) is its maximal number set in process *sale*.

**Definition 14.** To any goods $p \in Gds$, there exists a mapping relation, *Price*: $P \rightarrow R^+$, which is called *Goods price function* and let it be denoted by *Price*(*p*).

**Definition 15.** In $[t_1, t_2]$, the sale income of process *ps* can be calculated by:

$$Income(ps,t_1,t_2) = \sum_{i=1}^{m} Price(p_i)\times NSale(ps,t_1, t_2, p_i) \tag{12}$$

where $k=card\ (Gds)$; $p_i \in Gds$; $NSale(ps,t_1,t_2,p_i)$ is the sold amount of goods $p_i$ in $[t_1,t_2]$, which can be calculated from simulation or execution.

## 2.6 Profit Flow

**Definition 16.** To process *ps* in $[t_1, t_2]$, enterprise *Profit* can be calculated by:

$$Profit(ps,t_1,t_2)= Income(ps, t_1, t_2)- ProCost(ps,t_1, t_2) \tag{13}$$

where *Income* ($ps$, $t_1$,$t_2$) is the sale income in process $ps$ in [$t_1$,$t_2$]; and *ProCost*($ps$, $t_1$,$t_2$) is the cost of process $ps$ in [$t_1$,$t_2$]; They can be calculated by formula (10)&(12).

In this way, dividing execution time of enterprise process into $n$ time sections and calculating profits in each section, we can get cash flow in the enterprise process, as shown in Figure 6. Cash flow prediction is the key for the enterprise to make investment decisions and process reengineering. For a candidate investment project or a process to be improved, its economical lifecycle needs to be estimated first. Then it is necessary to calculate income and expenditure in each time section throughout its lifecycle. The balance in each time section forms cash flow for the investment.

During enterprise process execution, in addition to the investment and outcome for the process, enterprise profits are affected by the elements from outside circumstances, such as management and revenue policies. Therefore, *profit flow*, which describes actual profits for the enterprise, can be inferred from cash flow within outside effects. Its figure is the same as *cash flow*, except for external elements in the processes. With the progress in modern accounting, the calculation of *profit flow* is changing. It can be described in the behavior model.

# 3 Implementation and Applications

## 3.1 Architecture of Flow Analysis Tool with BPI

Based on the proposed process flow analysis techniques, a business process intelligence (BPI) analysis system containing six kinds of process flow reports and process flow analysis tools were implemented in an enterprise process simulation and optimization environment at the *Software Engineering Institute of BeiHang University* in China. It contains the calculations of the various flows such as activity flow, product flow, resource flow and cost flow, and the analysis of the various flows for the enterprise. Based on these tools, *business process intelligence* can be used to analyze the measurement data of the various flows and evaluate the enterprise process according to the enterprise decision model and the specified features to determine the direction for approaching the optimal solution of the enterprise process.

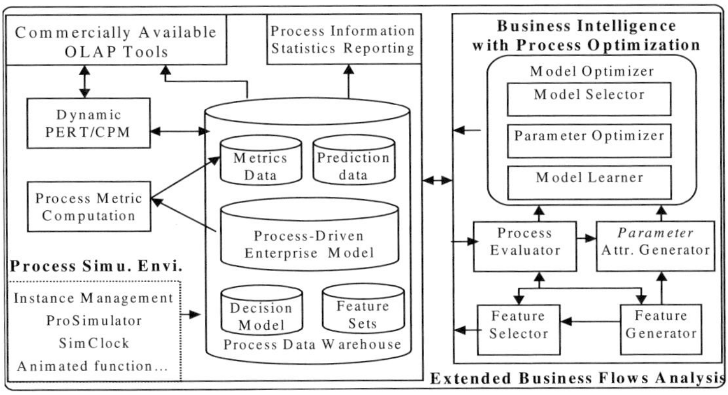


**Fig. 2.** Architecture of Business Process Intelligent Analysis

In Fig. 2, the Architecture of the Business Process Intelligent Analysis is divided into two aspects: Business process flow analysis is one of the basic functions implemented in the process simulation environment, which is responsible for metric data computation of process execution and process flow analysis and reporting. It needs the support of the dynamic PERT/CPM technique [9] to implement tasks scheduling and to forecast the duration of each activity in future. Another part is the business process intelligence which could help the managers to optimize process parameters and provide model learner and selection functions.

### 3.2 Business Process Flow Analysis (BPFA)

In the first part, *Process metric computation* is responsible for calculating the metric information of the process during process simulation. It provides data for *process flow analysis and reporting*.

The *dynamic PERT/CPM* technique uses a compound number compounded by one deterministic number and one non-deterministic number to define the duration, the earliest start time and the latest start time of activities in process models. During the process execution, the non-deterministic compound factor $i$ will be adjusted to approach to the real and exact value and used to calculate the earliest start time and the latest start time of future activities to forecast future events [9]. It supports *process flow analysis-OLAP*.

*Process flow information statistics reporting* is responsible for business statistics of process flow and for reporting the features according to the aforementioned flow definitions. It contains the following six flow statistics functions: activity flow, product flow, data flow, resource flow, cost flow, cash flow, and benefit flow.

*Commercially Available OLAP Tools* is the function of explanations and predictions on a wide variety of process flow metrics and behaviors. The underlying technology is data mining and the application of dynamic PERT/CPM. In order to implement the goal, we refer to reference [3] and analyze the classification of business process analysis and prediction problems from *scope, focus* and *status*.

*Process analysis* refers to the problem of detecting "interesting" behaviors of one or more process executions and of providing explanations for the situations in which such behaviors typically occur. *Process prediction* refers to the problem of providing analysts with information about the outcome of a running process instance, or even information about instances yet to be started, such as how many orders will be placed tomorrow or what will be the predicted total order value.

There are essentially two kinds of metrics that can be analyzed or predicted: generic and user-defined. Generic metrics are applicable to any process, and are needed in many analysis scenarios. On the other hand, user-defined metrics can relate aspects that are specific to a particular process or to a group of processes, and cannot be easily generalized.

Analysis on business process execution can be *targeted* or *untargeted*. In targeted analysis, we ask BPI to explain why a process metric has a certain value. In some cases, users are interested in finding "interesting" patterns in data that may be indicative of some characteristics of the process that they were not aware of.

Predictions about active instances are useful for various purposes. For example, they may indicate the likely outcome of the process execution or the expected completion time. If the prediction for an instance is such as it would not complete in time, then a specified user can be informed, so that he can try to correct the problem. In practical scenarios, this involves making telephone calls to the supplier asking him to speed up the delivery. However, even if it is not possible to react to an exception in order to avoid it, exception prediction information can still be used to take actions to reduce the damage caused by the exception.

### 3.3 Business Process Intelligence (BPI)

*BPI* based on Process Optimization could provide an enterprise with an intelligent measure for business evaluation. It is composed of *model optimizer*, *process evaluator*, *feature generator*, *feature selector*, and *parameter attribute generator*.

*Model optimizer* is the core technology. It contains *model learner*, *parameters optimizer*, and *model selector*. *Model selector* is used to assists the managers to select the most reasonable enterprise process model. In order to give a reasonable explanation for the metric information or future predication, it needs to discuss the task, metric scope, focus of prediction and status of the instances subject to the prediction with the relative data mining technology according to the decision model. It uses random generator to generate the parameter values for *model learner* according to the description files created by the *Parameters attribute generator*. *Model learner* receives the training set prepared by *process evaluator* as input. It applies its algorithm, a kind of *Fletcher Reeves* method to learn a model from this data set. Using this algorithm, it can learn to approach the local optimal solution (*LocBest*) along the direction of seeking optimization, and the local worst solution (*LocBad*) in the opposition direction. The area from *LocBest to LocBad* is taboo for the next seeking optimum, and it called a *Tabu-Area*. *Parameter optimizer* uses an expanded *Tabu Search* algorithm [8] to implement global optimization. In this algorithm, using the concept of *Tabu-Area* can speed up the process of seeking optimum. Using *Tabu Search* algorithm, we can get the track of model learn.

*Process evaluator* is the base to assist enterprise managers to analyze, evaluate and optimize business processes. It analyzes the metrics data generated by process simulation, and generates a total process evaluation value for business process according to the business features and decision model. *Feature selector* provides the definition/selection function of business process feature. After feature selection, only some of them like *duration, activity's resource usage*, and *requestedDeliveryDate* were found as the subset of relevant features. *Feature generator* is responsible for the generation of the feature attributes of process model, such as activity's duration, product's arriving-ratio. Here, the statistical process control (SPC) methods can be used to determine the process capability of sustaining stable levels of variability. The features can be predicted according to the value computed by *process evaluator*. *Feature generator* passes them back to create the training set. The attribute features in training set can be chosen by *feature selector*. *Parameter attribute generator* is used for generate parameter attribute description files in canonical format and map it into the specific formats required by the data mining algorithms.

## 4 Conclusions and Perspectives

This paper proposes intelligent business process analysis concepts, techniques, and architecture of extended business process flow analysis tool. The main contributions of this paper include:

- the metric measurement models for six kinds of process flows, and
- an approach that makes business process intelligence available to enterprise decision makers.

As an application software support tool, it can be effectively used for supporting business process intelligent analysis and business process reengineering in small and medium size enterprises. It is especially important in those application domains where the enterprise environment changes frequently. Our ongoing efforts are underway to address more functions for the proposed system in the simulation of a complex and large size enterprise processes. Our future works are to combine ontology [10], event queuing theory and cooperative schedule strategies with multi-agent technology [11]. Basic idea is to embed simulation algorithm and cooperation model into process model. The simulation of enterprise process will be implemented with a kind of the cooperative simulation of multi-agent systems among the sub-process models and agent-based process simulation in the sub-process model.

## Acknowledgements

The majority of the work presented in this paper was done by the first author during his Ph.D studies in BeiHang University, China. Appreciations should be given to Prof. Bosheng Zhou, the Ph.D supervisor and the team members in BeiHang University. This work was partially supported by the National Natural Science Foundation of China (Grant No. 69803003) and the Research Foundation for University Young Academic Leaders of Zhejiang Province of China (Grant No. SD200103).

## References

1. Cheng, M.Y., Tsai,M.H.: Reengineering of Construction Management Process, Journal of Construction Engineering and Management, 129(1) (2003)105–114
2. ESPRIT Consortium AMICE.: CIMOSA: Open System Architecture for CIM. Springer – Verlag, Berlin, (1993)
3. Doumeingts, G., Vallespir, B., Darricau, D., et al.: Design Methodology for Advanced Manufacturing Systems, Computers in Industry, 9(4) (1987) 271~296
4. Scheer, A.W.: ARIS-business Process Engineering. Springer –Verlag, Berlin, (1998)
5. Lucia, A.D., Pompella, E., Stefanucci, S.: Assessing the Maintenance Processes of a Software Organization: an Empirical Analysis of a Large Industrial Project, The Journal of Systems and Software, 65(2) (2003) 87-103
6. Castellanos, M., Casati, F., Dayal, U.: A Comprehensive and Automated Approach to Intelligent Business Processes Execution Analysis, Distributed and Parallel Databases, 16(4) (2004) 1-35

7. Ostrenga, M.R. , Ozan, T.R. , Mcllhattan, R.D., Harwood, M.D.: The Ernst & Young Guide to Total Cost Management. John Wiley & Sons, New York, (1992)
8. Tan, W.A., Li, S., Yang, F.: Zero-Time Enterprise Modeling with Component Assembly and Process Model Optimization Techniques, Proceedings of IEEE CIT2005/SOAIC2005, Shanghai, China, (2005) 1135-1139
9. Tan, W.A. , Zhou, B.S., Zhang, L.: Research on the Flexible Simulation Technology for Enterprise Process Model, Journal of software, 12(7) (2001) 1080-1087
10. Gruber, T.R.: A Translation Approach to Portable Ontologies. Knowledge Acquisition, 5(2) (1993) 199-220
11. Unite States of America, Department of Defense.: Defense Modeling and Simulation Office (DMSO). High Level Architecture Overview. www.dmso.mil, (Jun 1998)

# Multi-objective PSO Algorithm Based on Fitness Sharing and Online Elite Archiving

Li Wang[1], Yushu Liu[1], and Yuanqing Xu[2]

[1] School of Computer Science and Technology, Beijing Institute of Technology, 100081 Beijing, China
{alliexyq, liuyushu}@bit.edu.cn
[2] School of Chemical Engineering and Environment,Beijing Institute of Technology, 100081 Beijing, China
bitxyq@126.com

**Abstract.** A new technique for multi-objective PSO (Particle Swarm Optimization) based on fitness sharing and online elite archiving is proposed. Global best position of particle swarm is selected from repository by fitness sharing, which guarantees the diversity of the population. At the same time, in order to ensure the excellent population, the elite particles from the repository are introduced into next iteration. Three well-known test functions taken from the multi-objective optimization literature are used to evaluate the performance of the proposed approach. The results indicate that our approach generates a satisfactory approximation of the Pareto front and spread widely along the front.

## 1 Introduction

Many real-world problems belong to multi-objective optimization (MO) problems. Different with single-objective optimizations, competing goals give rise to a set of compromise solutions, generally denoted as Pareto-optimal. In the absence of preference information, none of the corresponding trade-offs can be said to be better than the others. What's more, MO problems always have large and complex search space. So using traditional methods to solve MO problems may result in high time-complex, thus, designing new efficient optimization algorithms become imminent and realistic.

Evolutionary algorithms have been proved very efficient in solving MO problems. In Ref.[1], [2], surveys of the existing variants and techniques for EAs are provided. Nearly all algorithms are able to find good approximations of the true Pareto front but the distribution of the obtained solutions vary among different methods [3], [4].

In the last years, several new nature-inspired algorithms have been developed. Particle swarm optimization (PSO) mimics the social behavior of flocks of birds to guide swarm of particles towards the most proved very efficient in solving a plethora of problem in science and engineering [5], [6]. Comparing with GA, PSO needs few parameters and has faster convergence rates. Although previous work has been done to deal with MO problems using PSO [7], [8], [9], [10], the research on PSO for MO problems is insufficient. In this article a new PSO technique for MO problems is proposed. Our approach integrates well-known online archiving techniques and fitness sharing from evolutionary algorithms into PSO. The results show that our approach generates satisfactory approximation of the Pareto front with evenly distributed solution along it.

D.-S. Huang, K. Li, and G.W. Irwin (Eds.): ICIC 2006, LNCS 4113, pp. 964 – 974, 2006.

The rest of this article is organized as follows: in Section 2 and Section 3, the overviews of the MO problem and PSO are given respectively. In Section 4, the implementation details of our method are briefly described, and the different comparison methods are sketched and preliminary results are reported in Section 5. Finally, the paper closes with some concluding remarks.

## 2 Multi-objective Optimization Problem

The multi-objective optimization problem can be expressed as follows:

$$\begin{aligned} &\min z = f(x) = (f_1(x), f_2(x), \cdots, f_q(x)) \\ &s.t. \quad g_i(x) \le 0, i = 1, 2, \cdots, m \end{aligned} . \tag{1}$$

Where $x \in R^n$ is the decision vector belonged to the feasible region $S$, which is described as follows: $S = \{x \in R^n \mid g_i(x) \le 0, i = 1, 2, \cdots, m\}$.

A decision vector $x_1 \in S$ is said to *dominate* a decision vector $x_2 \in S$ (denoted $x_1 \prec x_2$) iff:

- The decision vector $x_1$ is not worse than $x_2$ in all objectives, or $f_i(x_1) \le f_i(x_2) \forall i = 1, 2, \cdots, q$.
- The decision vector $x_1$ is strictly better than $x_2$ in at least one objective, or $f_i(x_1) < f_i(x_2)$ for at least one $i = 1, 2, \cdots, q$.

and $x_1$ *weakly dominated* $x_2$ (denoted $x_1 \preceq x_2$) iff:

- The decision vector $x_1$ is not worse than $x_2$ in all objective, or $f_i(x_1) \le f_i(x_2) \forall i = 1, 2, \cdots, q$.

A decision vector $x_1 \in S$ is called *Pareto-optimal* if there does not exist another $x_2 \in S$ that dominates it. Finally, and objective vector is called *Pareto-optimal* if the corresponding decision vector is *Pareto-optimal.*

## 3 Particle Swarm Optimization

PSO has been proposed by Kennedy and Eberhart in 1995 [11]. Years of study on the dynamics of bird flocking has resulted in the possibilities of utilizing this behavior as an optimization tool. In PSO system, multiple candidate solutions coexist and collaborate simultaneously. Each solution candidate, called a "particle", flies in the problem space looking for the optimal position to land. A particle, as time passes through, adjusts its position according to its own "experience", as well as according to the experience of neighboring particles.

Suppose the dimension of the searching space is *D*, the number of particle is *n*. Vector $\vec{x}_i = (x_{i1}, x_{i2}, \ldots, x_{iD})$ represents the position of the $i^{\text{th}}$ particle. $P_i = (p_{i1}, p_{i2}, \ldots, p_{iD})$ is the best position (*pBest*) of the $i^{\text{th}}$ particle searched by now and the whole particle swarm's best position (*gBest*) is represented as $P_g = (g_1, g_2, \ldots, g_D)$. Vector $\vec{v}_i = (v_{i1}, v_{i2}, \ldots, v_{iD})$ is the position change rate of the $i^{\text{th}}$ particle. Each particle updates its position ("flies") according to the following formulas:

$$v_{ij}(t+1) = w \times v_{ij}(t) + c_1 \times rand() \times (p_{ij}(t) - x_{ij}(t)) + c_2 \times rand() \times (g_j(t) - x_{ij}(t)). \quad (2)$$

$$x_{ij}(t+1) = x_{ij}(t) + v_{ij}(t+1). \quad (3)$$

Where $c_1, c_2$ are positive constant parameter called acceleration coefficients. $rand()$ is a random function with the range [0,1]. $w$, called inertia weight, is a user-specified parameter. A large inertia weight pressures towards global exploration while a smaller inertia weight pressures towards fine-tuning the current search area. Proper selection of the inertia weight and acceleration coefficients can provide a balance between the global and the local search. Equation (2) is used to calculate the particle's new velocity according to its previous velocity and to the distances of its current position from its own best historical position and its neighbors' best position, and the particle flies towards a new position according to Eq. (3). The performance of each particle is measured according to a predefined fitness function, which is usually proportional to the cost function associated with the problem. This process is repeated until user-defined stopping criteria are satisfied [12].

## 4 Proposed Approach and Implementation Details

PSO can not be immediately applied to MO problems, because there are essential distinctions between multiple and single-objective optimization problems. The successful application of GA in MO problems and the similarity between PSO and GA reflect that PSO is likely a method to deal with MO problems. However, there is a great distinction between PSO and GA. In GA, chromosomes share the information, which causes the whole community moves gradually into a better area, while in PSO the information is sent out by the best particle which is followed by other individuals to quickly converge to a point. Therefore, it may easily cause the swarms to converge to the local area of Pareto front if the PSO is applied directly to MO problems. It is obviously that the important part in multi-objective particle swarm optimization (MOPSO) is to determine the best global particle (*gBest*) for the population.

Coello et al.' proposal is based on the idea of having a global repository in which every particle will deposit its flight experiences after each flight cycle. Additionally, the updates to the repository are performed considering a geographically-based system defined in terms of the objective function values of each individual. This technique is inspired on the external file used with the Pareto Archive Evolution Strategy

(PAES) [7]. However, their approach only belongs to off-line elite archiving, and the elite of the archive has not been used to produce new particle in evidence because of its off-line mechanism. Therefore, in this paper a new MOPSO approach based on fitness sharing and online elite archive is proposed.

The main idea of fitness sharing is to distribute a population of individuals along a set of resources [14], [15]. Along with process of the iteration, the number of non-dominated in external repository also increase□at the same time, they have distributing characteristic in objective space. In order to spread the individuals along the Pareto front, the fitness sharing has been introduce to our approach. Fitness sharing will help to our algorithm to maintain diversity between solutions, particles within high populated areas in the objective space will be less likely to be follow.

Fitness sharing adjusts individual's fitness through a fitness sharing function, which is defined as:

$$Sh(d_{ij}) = \begin{cases} 1-\left(d_{ij}/\sigma_{\text{share}}\right)^{\alpha}, d_{ij} < \sigma_{\text{share}} \\ 0, \qquad\qquad \text{otherwise} \end{cases} . \tag{4}$$

where $d_{ij} = d\left(x_i, x_j\right)$ is the distance between individual $i$ and $j$. $\sigma_{\text{share}}$ is defined as the radius of the niche indicating the minimum distance between two solution peaks. Individuals derate each other's fitness while their distance is less than $\sigma_{\text{share}}$ . The niche count $m_i$ for each individual $i$ is calculated by summing the sharing function values over all the individuals:

$$m_i = \sum_{j=1}^{s} Sh(d_{ij}) . \tag{5}$$

The modified fitness $f_i^{'}$ of an individual $i$ can be gained from dividing the individual's raw fitness by the niche count:

$$f_i^{'} = f_i/m_i . \tag{6}$$

The technique of online elite archive for MOPSO is explained as follows:

*Definition.* Supposed that the particles is represented as $x_t^1, x_t^2, \cdots, x_t^N$ at the $t^{\text{th}}$ iteration, $p_t^i$ is the number of particles dominated $x_t^i$ , the rank of $x_t^i$ is defined as $R_t^i = 1 + p_t^i$.

After the $t^{\text{th}}$ cycle, the population of the particles is marked with $P(t)$ and the repository with $M(t)$. Firstly, having a fitness sharing assigned for each particle in the repository, particles form the repository which will guide to the others into the next cycle will be chose as *gBest* to be followed. They will be chosen according to a stochastic universal sampling method Roulette Wheel. Particles with higher levels of fitness will be selected over the less fit ones. This will allow them to explore places less explored in the search space. Secondly, execute the $t$+1 cycle: update the positions and velocities of the particles which form new population marked with $P'(t)$; According to the definition, calculate the ranks of the whole particles including $P'(t)$ and $M(t)$ and rank them form 1. Select $N$ particles corresponding to less $N$ ranks to act as the next evolutional population $P(t+1)$. If there are particles which have same rank compete to turn into next iterative, select the particles which have fewer particles surrounding their vicinity. Finally, the repository is updated with the particles whose rank is 1. In this way we maintain the repository as the Pareto front found so far, in the case where the number of the particles with the *rank*=1 is more than the size of the repository, we discard redundant particles with worst fitness sharing.

It is obviously that using online elite archive technique the elite from repository provide the *gBest* position for population in reason and participate in the next evolutionary population effectively. Which is explained particularly with Fig. 1.

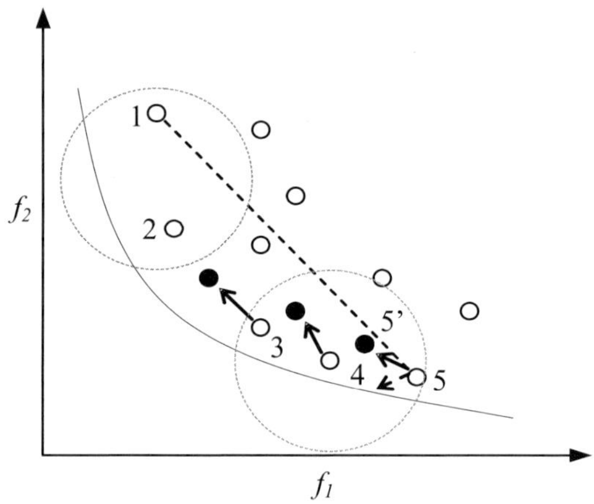


**Fig. 1.** The situation for lose the optimal solution and next population becoming bad

Suppose that there is population with ten particles, after the $t^{th}$ cycle, the distributing of particles in objective space is showed in Fig.1. In the repository there are five particles which tabs are from 1 to 5. It is intuitively clear that the density of the area which including the particle 1 and particle 2 is less than the ones including particles 3, 4 and 5, therefore, the fitness of particles 1 and particle 2 are greater according to fitness sharing. Assume that the particle 1 is be selected to act as the *gBest* position in terms of Roulette Wheel, then the next population after one iteration may lose the optimal solution and become bad if adopt off-line elite archiving.

For instance, to the particle 5, it is closer the real Pareto front than the particle 1, however, it will flight to the new position marked with 5' which is close to particle 1. The solution corresponding to new position 5' of particle 5 is dominated by the ones corresponding to particle 4. In the worst case where the particle 3 and particle 4 also close to the particle 1 like particle 5, the new solutions corresponding to particle 3 and

4 will be dominated by original solution, although they are not able to store in repository they will turn into next cycle acted as new particles if using off-line elite archiving. Which result in the bad population in next iteration and it is insignificance.

In order to overcome the above mentioned shortcoming, the elite from the repository is introduced into next evolutionary population using online elite archiving technique, that is, when executing the $t$+1 cycle the new population marked with $P'(t)$ updated by Eq. (2) and (3) will combine the population in $M(t)$ to produce the excellent particles for next iteration. Thus, the particle 3, 4 and 5 are reserved into next iteration in Fig. 1. In a word the badness particle has been eliminate in terms of online elite archiving thereby the algorithm can rapidly converge to the Pareto optimal front and spread widely along the front.

Our approach based on fitness sharing and online archiving is as followed:

Input: the multi-objective optimization problem
Output: the non-dominate of the archiving $M(t)$
Step1: $t = 0$.
Step2: Initialize the population $P(t)$. Initialize an array of particles $\vec{x}_0^i = (x_{i1}, x_{i2}, \cdots x_{in})(i = 1, 2, \cdots, N)$ with random positions and initialize the speed of each particle with 0. Evaluate each of the particles in $P(0)$, and store the position of the particles that represent non-dominated vectors in the repository $M(0)$.

Step3: If $\vec{x}_{t-1}^i$ is dominated by $\vec{x}_t^i$, the position of $\vec{x}_t^i$ is viewed as the *pBest* position of particle $i$ after each flight cycle, otherwise the *pBest* position of particle $i$ hold the line, that is , the *pBest* position is the position of $\vec{x}_{t-1}^i$ .Find the *gBest* position from repository according to fitness sharing.

Step4: Update the positions and velocities of the particles according to Eq. (2) and (3), which form new population $P'(t)$.

Step5: Form next population $P(t)$ according to online elite archive technique and update the repository with the particles whose *rank* is 1.

Step6: Evaluate each of the particles in $P(t)$.

Step7: While maximum number of cycles has not been reached do $t = t$+1, and goto Step3.

## 5 Test and Comparison

We have test our approach using three test functions proposed in [16]: ZDT1, ZDT2 and ZDT3. They have 30 variables and two objectives. Functions ZDT1 has convex Pareto front, ZDT2 has a non-convex Pareto front and ZDT3 has a non-convex and discontinuous Pareto front. We have compared them against two well knows techniques in MO literature. The techniques are: MOPSO [13], NSGA-II [3].

For this paper we have performed two set of experiments. In the first set of experiments we have set the heuristics to find only 30 non-dominated solutions per run, and in the second set 100 non-dominated solutions. To compare and obtain statistics for each test function, we performed 30 runs for each technologies used.

Set the parameters of our approach as the following: $c_1 = c_2 = 1.0$, $w = 0.729$. The value of $\sigma_{share}$ is specified in each set of experiments. In the first set the value is 0.04 and in the second set the value is 0.01.The parameters used by MOPSO in [13] are: a mutation rate of 0.5, 30 division for its adaptive grid, and a real number representation. NSGA-II used: a crossover rate of 0.8, a mutation probability of $1/x$, where $x$ is the number of variables for the given problem, and a real number representation with tournament selection.

The graphical results using our approach are showed in Fig. 2 to Fig. 4, the anterior figures with 30 non-dominated solutions and the latter figures with 100 non-dominated solutions. It is obviously that algorithm can rapidly converge to the Pareto optimal front and spread widely along the front even if using a small size repository.

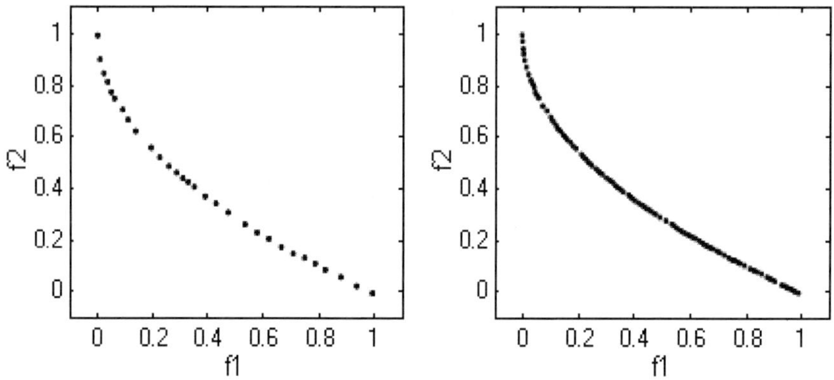


(a) 30 non-dominated solutions (b) 100 non-dominated solutions

**Fig. 2.** Pareto front obtained by our approach for function ZDT1

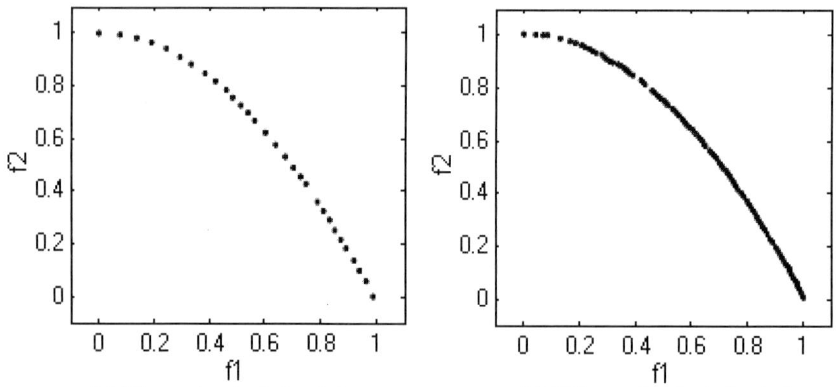


(a) 30 non-dominated solutions (b) 100 non-dominated solutions

**Fig. 3.** Pareto front obtained by our approach for function ZDT2

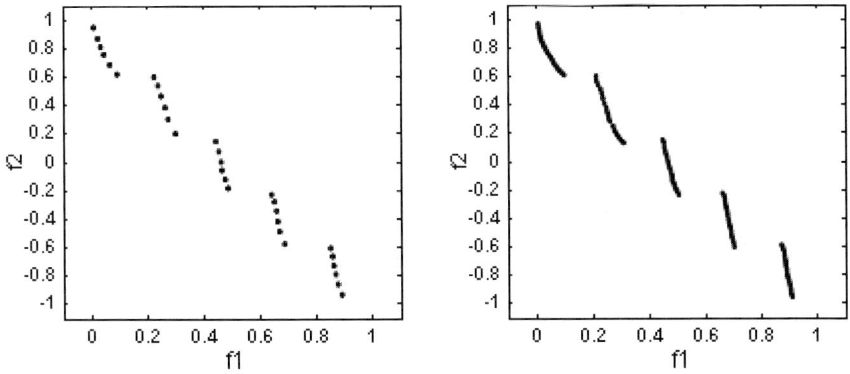


(a) 30 non-dominated solutions (b) 100 non-dominated solutions

**Fig. 4.** Pareto front obtained by our approach for function ZDT3

Fig. 5 shows the graphical with 30 non-dominated solutions using MOPSO in [13] for three test functions and the results show the algorithm concentrates all its solutions in a very small portion of the Pareto front.

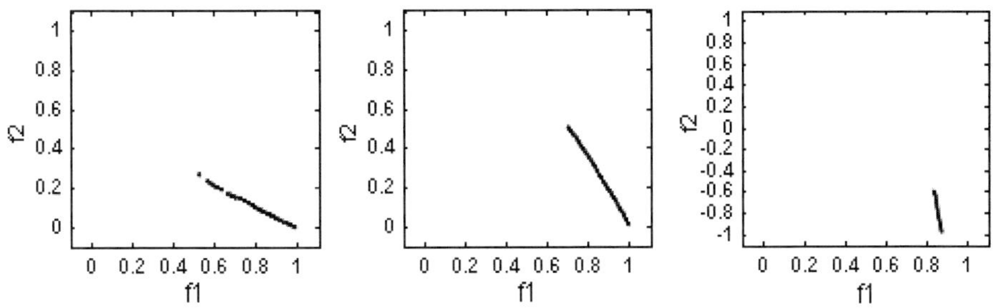


(a) ZDT1 (b) ZDT2 (c) ZDT3

**Fig. 5.** The graphical with 30 non-dominated solution using MOPSO in [13] for test functions

To measure performance of our approach against the MOPSO and NSGA-II techniques we chose S metric. In Table 1 to 6 we can observe the statistical results after executing each technique 30000 times.

As we can observe form Table 1 to Table 3, in the case where there are 30 non-dominated solutions in the repository, the consuming time of NSGA-II is more than the one of the else algorithms for all test functions. From a statistical point of view, for the ZDT1 test function, the performance of our approach is better than NSGA-II, even if MOPSO has the better values for the S metric, this is due to the fact that MOPSO is concentrating all its solutions in a very small portion of the Pareto front, not necessarily due to a better set of dispersed solution (see figure 5). For the ZDT2 and ZDT3 test function, a very similar situation as that presented with the ZDT1 test function can be observed. In the latter three tables, for 100 non-dominated solutions in the repository statistics show that all methods are very competitive for three test functions.

**Table 1.** Statistical results obtained from function ZDT1 with 30 non-dominated solutions

| Algorithm | S metric | | | | Average Time (s) |
|---|---|---|---|---|---|
| | Avg | Std | Max | Min | |
| MOPSO | 3.35694 | 0.03265 | 3.62460 | 2.87562 | 0.95634 |
| NSGA-II | 11.23695 | 0.35631 | 16.35872 | 8.36549 | 4.01395 |
| Ours | 10.36954 | 0.26314 | 12.36216 | 9.62318 | 1.35976 |

**Table 2.** Statistical results obtained from function ZDT2 with 30 non-dominated solutions

| Algorithm | S metric | | | | Average Time (s) |
|---|---|---|---|---|---|
| | Avg | Std | Max | Min | |
| MOPSO | 2.36957 | 0.13654 | 2.83612 | 1.98936 | 0.86357 |
| NSGA-II | 8.96513 | 0.49635 | 10.62351 | 7.26396 | 3.95136 |
| Ours | 7.92365 | 0.40268 | 9.36147 | 6.23956 | 1.42310 |

**Table 3.** Statistical results obtained from function ZDT3 with 30 non-dominated solutions

| Algorithm | S metric | | | | Average Time (s) |
|---|---|---|---|---|---|
| | Avg | Std | Max | Min | |
| MOPSO | 1.76235 | 0.05369 | 2.16320 | 1.52394 | 0.63942 |
| NSGA-II | 7.56349 | 1.13692 | 9.01653 | 7.03264 | 4.06987 |
| Ours | 7.96531 | 0.95873 | 8.62341 | 6.73652 | 1.56923 |

**Table 4.** Statistical results obtained from function ZDT1 with 100 non-dominated solutions

| Algorithm | S metric | | | | Average Time (s) |
|---|---|---|---|---|---|
| | Avg | Std | Max | Min | |
| MOPSO | 3.12654 | 0.06395 | 3.31569 | 2.92346 | 1.77856 |
| NSGA-II | 3.05892 | 0.04958 | 3.12596 | 2.98562 | 6.25896 |
| Ours | 3.06954 | 0.05126 | 3.20143 | 2.98236 | 3.15864 |

**Table 5.** Statistical results obtained from function ZDT2 with 100 non-dominated solutions

| Algorithm | S metric | | | | Average Time (s) |
|---|---|---|---|---|---|
| | Avg | Std | Max | Min | |
| MOPSO | 2.43598 | 0.12695 | 2.76315 | 2.25634 | 1.82563 |
| NSGA-II | 2.48653 | 0.13050 | 2.81324 | 2.16935 | 6.55632 |
| Ours | 2.44069 | 0.13008 | 2.69856 | 2.26891 | 2.96314 |

**Table 6.** Statistical results obtained from function ZDT3 with 100 non-dominated solutions

| Algorithm | S metric | | | | Average Time (s) |
|---|---|---|---|---|---|
| | Avg | Std | Max | Min | |
| MOPSO | 3.75562 | 0.12403 | 3.95117 | 3.42653 | 2.05691 |
| NSGA-II | 3.56987 | 0.11563 | 3.78563 | 3.36954 | 8.23640 |
| Ours | 3.49635 | 0.11264 | 3.56921 | 3.12953 | 3.69102 |

## 6 Conclusion

We have proposed an approach to incorporate the concepts of online elite archiving and fitness sharing to multi-objective optimization using PSO. The proposed technique had been tested using several multi-objective test functions and compared against two other multi-objective algorithm, From our results, we conclude that online elite archiving technique can reduce the computational cost without decreasing the quality of the results in a significant way. On the other hand, using a small size in the repository, algorithm can rapidly converge to the Pareto optimal front and spread widely along the front.

## References


1. Coello Coello, C.A.: A Comprehensive Survey of Evolutionary-based Multiobjective Optimization. Knowledge and Information systems 1 (1999) 269-308
2. Deb, K.: Multi-Objective Optimization Using Evolutionary Algorithms. Wiley-Interscience Series in Systems and Optimization. John Wiley & Sons, Ltd., 1edition (2001)
3. Deb, K., Agrawal, S., Pratab, A., Meyarivan, T.: A Fast Elitist Non-Dominated Sorting Genetic Algorithm for Multi-Objective Optimization: NSGA-II. In proceedings of the Parallel Problem Solving from Nature VI Conference, Paris, France (2000) 849-858
4. Knowles, J.D., Corne, D.W.: The Pareto Archived Evolution Strategy: A New Baseline Algorithm for Pareto Multi-objective Optimization. In Congress on Evolutionary Computeration (2000) 325-332
5. Laskari, E.C., Parsopoulos, K.E., Vrahatis, M.N.: Particle Swarm Optimization for Miniimax Problems. In Proc. of the IEEE 2002 Congress on Evolutionary Computation, Hawaii (HI), USA (2002) 1582-1587
6. Parsopoulos, K.E., Vrahatis, M.N.: Particle Swarm Optimization Method for Constrained Optimization Problems. Intelligent Technologied-Theory and Application: New Trends in Intelligence Technologies, Vol. 76 of Frontier in Artificial Intelligence and Application (2002) 214-220
7. Coello Coello, C.A., Salazer Lechuga, M.: MOPSO: A Proposal for Multi Objective Particle Swarm Optimization. In Congr. on Evolutionary Computation, Piscataway, New Jersey. Vol.2 (2002) 1051-1056
8. Hu, X.: Multiobjective Optimization Using Dynamic Neighborhood Particle Swarm Optimization. In Proceeding of the IEEE Congress on Evolutionary Computation, Honolulu, HI, USA (2002)
9. Parsopoulos, K.E., Vrahatis, M.N.: Particle Swarm Optimization Method in Multiobjective Problems. In Proc. of the ACM Symposium on Applied Computing , Madrid, Spain (2002) 603-607
10. Li, X.: A Non-dominated Sorting Particle Swarm Optimizer for Multiobjective Optimization. In Proc. of the Genetic and Evolutionary Computation Conf. Chicago, IL, USA (2003) 37-48
11. Kennedy, J., Eberhart, R.: Particle Swarm Optimization. In Proc. of IEEE Intl. Conf. on Neural Networks, Perth, Australia (1995) 1942-1948
12. Zeng, J.C., Jie, J., Cui Z.H.: Particle Swarm Optimization Algorithm. Beijing, Science Press (2004).

13. Coello Coello, C.A., Toscano Pulido, G., Salazar Lechuga, M.: Handling Multiple Objectives With Particle Swarm Optimization. IEEE Transactions on Evolutionary Computation, 8 (2004) 205-230
14. Goldberg, D.E., Richardson, J.: Genetic Algorithm with Sharing for Multimodal Function Optimization. In Grefenstette, J. editor, Proceedings of the 2nd International Conference on Genetic Algorithms, Hillsdale, New Hersey, Lawrence Erlbaum Assocaites (1987) 41-49
15. Deb, K., Goldberg D.E.: An Investigation of Niche and Species Formation in Genetic Function Optimization. In Schaffer, J.D., editor, Proceedings of the Third International Conference on Genetic Algorithms, George Mason University, Morgan Kaufmann Publishers (1989) 42-50
16. Eckart Zitzler, Kalyanmoy Deb, Lothar Thiele.: Comparison of Multiobjective Evolutionary Algorithms: Empirical Results. Evolutionary Computation 8 (2000) 173-195

# An Intelligent Algorithm for Modeling and Optimizing Dynamic Supply Chains Complexity

Khalid Al-Mutawah, Vincent Lee, and Yen Cheung

Clayton School of Information Technology, Clayton Campus, Monash University, Clayton, Melbourne, Victoria 3800, Australia
{Khalid.Al.Mutawah, Vincent.Lee, Yen.Ping.Cheung}@infotech.monash.edu.au

**Abstract.** Traditional theories and principles on supply chains management (SCM) have implicitly assumed homogenous cultural environment characteristics across the entire supply chain (SC). In practice, however, such an assumption is too restrictive due to the dynamic and non-homogenous nature of organisational cultural attributes. By extending the evolutionary platform of cultural algorithms, we design an innovative multi-objective optimization model to test the null hypothesis – the SC's performance is independent of its sub-chains cultural attributes. Simulation results suggest that the null hypothesis cannot be statistically accepted.

## 1 Introduction and Research Motivation

The globalization, dynamics, and frequent variations of customer demands on today's markets increase the needs of companies to form supply chains (SCs) and collaborative business partnerships [1],[2]. SCs are networks of autonomous business entities that collectively procure, manufacture, and distribute certain products in order to respond efficiently to customer demands and minimize the cost of all participating business entities. To achieve this, SC systems must coordinate and optimize the entire chain operations. In reality, however, SCs are often operating in dynamic and non-homogenous cultural environments. Therefore, current SCM systems need to adopt adaptive learning features and reasoning behaviour to reflect the dynamic changes.

This study is motivated by the fact that the paradigm of a Culture Algorithm (CA) naturally contains adaptive components in which the belief space can be used to store cultural attributes to influence the dynamic non-homogenous environment of the associated SC (residing in the population space) in a self-adaptive way. In section 2, we briefly review CAs and the Dempster-Shafer theory. Section 3 proposes a new approach that integrates belief functions and CAs with a Distributed Multi-objective Genetic Algorithm (DMOGA). A hypothetical scenario- *inspired from the trading agent competition f*or *Supply Chain Management (http://www.sics.se/tac) (TAC SCM)* -is presented and simulation results are given for validation of the proposed approach.

## 2 Literature Review

Several systems were developed to model the SCs complexity using a GA, for examples Truong and Azadivar [3] have integrated GAs into a hybrid optimization model,

D.-S. Huang, K. Li, and G.W. Irwin (Eds.): ICIC 2006, LNCS 4113, pp. 975–980, 2006.

while others use GAs and Pareto Optimal techniques [4]. Furthermore, Al-Mutawah, Lee, and Cheung have developed a Distributed Multi-objective Genetic Algorithm (DMOGA) to solve the SC optimization problem in [5]. One common limitation of DMOGA and other typical multi-objective optimization GAs is the inheritance process which restricts offspring experiences to the experiences transferred from their parents, thus ignoring the influence of other external sources. In real world problems, particularly in a distributed environment, SCs data are collected from heterogenous cultures, implying the need to co-opt other sources of influence as well. Measurement of the fitness values based on the individual's objective function alone is inadequate thus prompting the need to incorporate cultural variables.

### 2.1 Cultural Algorithms

CAs were developed by R.G. Reynolds to model the evolution of culture [6]. Reynolds defined culture as a group of beliefs that are acquired from a group of members, and subsequently influence the patterns of behaviour that are practiced by various members of the population. CAs were developed to model the evolution of the cultural component over time as it learns and acquire knowledge. Based on this approach we used CAs to drive a self-adaptation process within the DMOGA in Dynamic SCs.

### 2.2 Dempster-Shafer Theory (DS)

A means of quantitatively manipulating evidence was developed by Arthur Dempster in the 1960's, and refined by his student Glen Shafer [7]. The frame of discernment $\Theta$ is the set of mutually exclusive propositions of interest. Defined on the set of all subsets of $\Theta$ is the belief function *(bf)* that associates with every subset of $\Theta$ a degree of belief that lies within the interval [0,1] given that the *bf* must satisfy two conditions: $bf(\varnothing) = 0$ and $0 \leq \sum_{A \subseteq \Theta} bf(A) \leq 1$.

The DS method to calculate the total belief degree is termed belief (*Bel*) which measures the total evidence that support a hypothesis **A** without any ambiguity. The motivation for using DS theory is to provide a well-principled framework for combiningevidence from heterogenous sources with respect to competing hypotheses, where the SC attributes form the evidences whilst the cultural aspects form the hypothesis.

$$Bel(A) = \sum_{B \subseteq A} bf(B) \tag{1}$$

## 3 The Proposed Cultural Algorithm Based DMOGA Approach

The DMOGA approach utilizes GAs optimization technique, and decomposes a three sub chains SC into three subpopulations (supplier, manufacturer and retailer), each of which uses a local GA to optimize its attributes configuration (i.e. cost, sell price, time and capacity, quantity) based on an objective function (OBJ):

$$OBJ_{supplier} = Max\left(\sum ComponentsPrice - \sum ComponentCost\right) \tag{2}$$

$$OBJ_{manufacturer} = Max\left(\sum ProductPrice - \sum ManufacturingCost\right) \tag{3}$$

$$OBJ_{\text{Re}\,tailer} = Max\left(\sum Sale\ \text{Pr}\,ice - \sum (Delivery + Inventory)Cost\right). \tag{4}$$

Furthermore, a matchmaker model forms a population consisting of the best individuals of all subpopulations. The matchmaker population builds an individual comprising three segments each of which corresponds to an attribute configuration of a subpopulation. The matchmaker then runs a GA with crossover operation that exchanges segments rather than bits to optimize the entire SC configuration with the following OBJ:

$$OBJ_{\text{Re}\,tailer} = Max\left(\sum CustomerBi\,d - \sum (Supplier + Manufac. + \text{Re}\,tailer)Cost\right) \tag{5}$$

Accordingly, DMOGA produced good results as reported in [5]. The execution time is reduced as the three subpopulations run in parallel as threads and distribute the process of computing the optimal solution. Given that each sub chain possesses its own OBJs and constraints (e.g. capacity and time), the DMOGA reduces the conflicts of this multi-objective problem using the matchmaker model to a rational rate. The diversity of the sub chain culture, however, points out a doubt that is associated with the efficiency of this approach, as individuals might be influenced by external sources such as organisational culture. The goal of this paper is to use CAs to improve the efficiency of the DMOGA in identifying the optimal configuration of a dynamic SC. Prior analysis showed that the CA approach worked best in complex environment akin to SCs [8], [9].

The use of CAs based DMOGA (CA-DMOGA) can be approached by defining the problem as finding the most efficient sub chain configuration in a population of possible configurations. The sub chains configuration can be differentiated from each other depending on which sub chain segments are being used more by the matchmaker model. Here the population space (SP) of the CA contains the three subpopulations (see Fig. 1. next page). For the *acceptance function ()* we have implemented a decision tree (DT) to classify the matchmaker population based on the sub chains attributes (e.g. product type). Consequently, the DT generates rules and its corresponding confidence values. In our approach the highest confidence rules value is selected and normalized to comply conditions (1) and (2) of DS theory. These normalized values are then voted as *bf* to the belief space (BS) to *adjust the current beliefs*. The *influence function ()* calculates a belief degree using equation (3) according to the new voted beliefs.

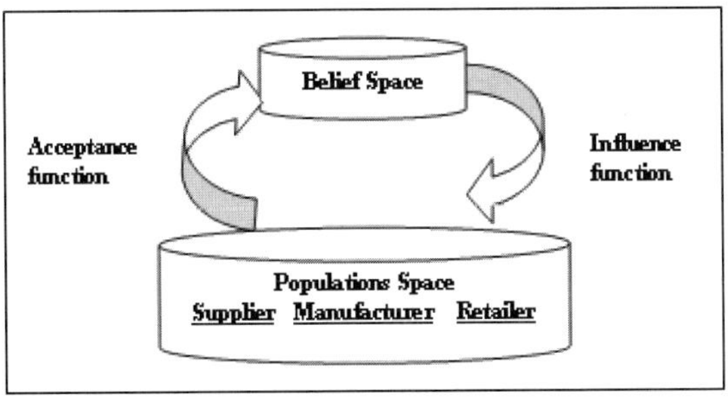


**Fig. 1.** Conceptual Model of a CA combined with DMOGA

Each sub chain compute a new fitness value based on both the OBJ and Bel values, and subsequently select the best fitness individual to create a new population for the next iteration until the maximum generation number is reached. The following is the pseudo code of the CA-DMOGA approach

```
Begin
n=0;
Initialize Subpopulation (n); //for all 3 sub chains
Initialize Belief Space (n);
Repeat Until Maximum Generation Number
  Evaluate Subpopulation(n); //Rank based on OBJ
  Run Matchmaker Model(n); // match the 3 sub chains
  Accept Subpopulation (n) into Belief Space;
  Adjust Belief Space(n); // update beliefs
  Influence Subpopulation(n) into Population Space;
  I=0;
  For I IN n loop
    fitness value = Rank_OBJ + Rank_Bel;
  End For loop;
  n=n+1;
  Select Subpopulation(n) from Subpopulation(n-1)
Repeat
end.
```

# 4 Implementation and Results

To judge the performance of the CA-DMOGA approach, we ran it on a simulated data of a hypothetical SC composed of three sub-chains. The output of this supply chain is three different personnel computers (PCs). Each PC is classified according to their capabilities, i.e. (Low, Med and High). There are 6 different manufacturers to assemble PCs, 6 retailers to store and distribute the PCs and two suppliers for supplying each component (e.g. Hard disk and memory).

## 4.1 Parameters Settings

The GA parameters are set according to the simulation values used in [5]. We randomly generated preferences for 50 customers. The simulation is implemented using the Evolver Optimizer[1] tool. Each generation was executed five times to assure results reliability. Furthermore, we ran the simulation with two test cases, A and B. Case A associates cultural variables using *bf*, whilst case B ignores the cultural aspects, i.e. depends only on individuals objective function ranking.

## 4.2 Results

The CA-DMOGA produced good results to acquire optimal or near-optimal solutions. Table 1 shows the observations for two performance variables i) the fitness value progress through generations, and ii) the individual organisms (chromosomes) fitness

[1]http://www.palisade.com

**Table 1.** Observation of Case A and Case B for Manufacturers

| *Case* | *Manufacturer GA Progress (i)* | *Value of Current Population (ii)* |
|---|---|---|
| A | 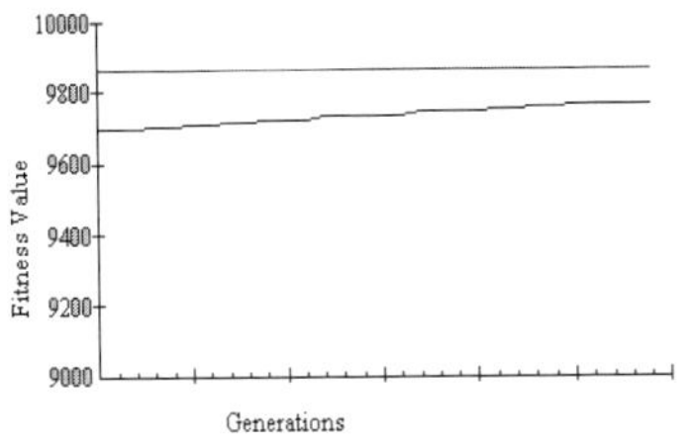  | 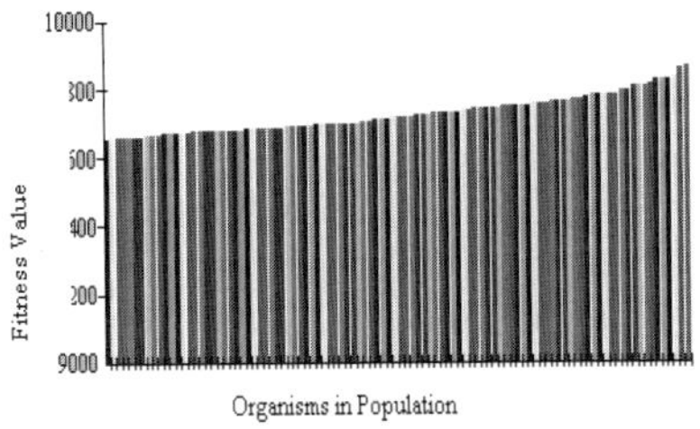  |
| B | 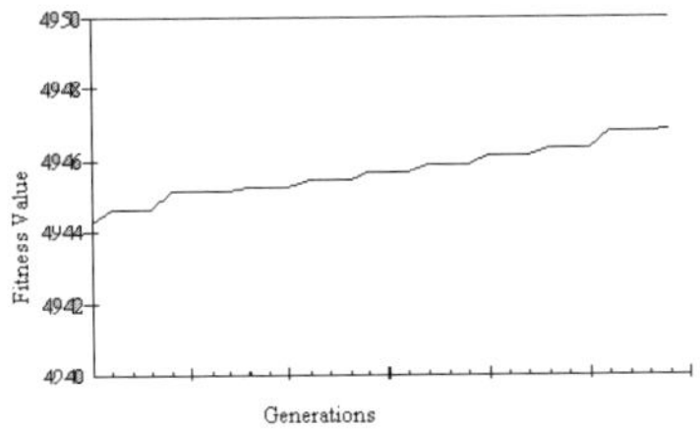  | 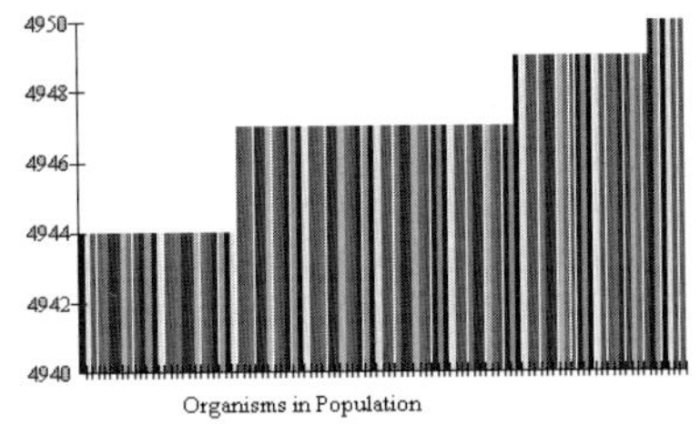  |

value. Figure (i) has two lines: the straight (red) line indicates the best achieved value after 1000 generations, and the curved (black) line indicates the average of all valid solutions. In case A the two lines are merging faster than case B where cultural aspects were ignored. Figure (ii) shows the fitness value of all individuals where it is obvious that individuals in case A have almost the same fitness values, whilst in case B there is a clear variation in the fitness values. We obtained the same observations for both retailers and suppliers.

# 5 Conclusion and Future Works

The results have proved the hypothesis that there is a positive correlation between cultural aspects and SCs attributes. Hence, the GAs learning process is faster when it incorporates cultural variables measurements in case **A**. We suggested an alternative extension to improve the original DMOGA approach – *and subsequently other typical genetic based implementation of Multi-objective optimization,* - to measure heterogenous cultural aspects with uncertainty in a dynamic SC. We applied the DS theory to handle uncertainties derived from organizational unit inter-relationships, and a CA to improve the Inter-evolutionary process. We proposed a method to construct the *bf* by measuring the confidence of the revealed patterns in a transaction level, to measure the cultural variables. To further improve the algorithm, our future initiatives include measuring the relationship between organization culture, and organization attributes and their effects on organizational performance using the CA-DMOGA approach.

Furthermore, we intend to incorporate *Electronic Supply Chain (e-SC)* organizations as case studies to identify how these organizations perform toward changes in organizational culture.

## References


1. S. Chopra , P. Meindl:Supply Chain Management: Strategy, Planning, and Operations. Prentice Hall College ,(2001)
2. Terry P. Harrison, Hau L. Lee, J. J. Neale: The Practice of Supply Chain Management. Kluwer Academic Publishing, (2003)
3. T. H. Truong ,F. Azadivar:Simulation Based Optimization for Supply Chain Configuration Design. presented at the Winter Simulation Conference, Piscataway, NJ (2003)
4. J. A. Joines, D. Kupta, M. A. Gokce, R. E. King, K. M.G.:Supply Chain Multi-Objective Simulation Optimization. presented at the 2002 Winter Simulation Conference ,(2002)
5. K. Al-Mutawah, V. Lee, Y. Cheung:Modeling Supply Chain Complexity using a Distributed Multi-objective Genetic Algorithm.presented at The 2006 International Conference on Computational Science and its Applications ICCSA'06, Glasgow, Scotland, (2006)
6. R. G. Reynolds:An Introduction to Cultural Algorithms. presented at Third Annual Conference on Evolutionary Programming, River Edge, NJ, (1994)
7. G. Shafer:A Mathematical Theory of Evidence. Princeton, New Jersey: Princeton University Press, (1976)
8. R. G. Reynolds , B. Peng:Cultural Algorithms: Modeling of How Cultures Learn to Solve Problems. presented at 16th IEEE International Conference on Tools with Artificial Intelligence (ICTAI 2004), Boca Raton, FL, USA, (2004)
9. R. G. Reynolds , B. Peng:Knowledge Learning in Dynamic Environments. presented at IEEE International Congress on Evolutionary Computation, Portland, OR ,(2004)

# Design of Data Association Filter Using Neural Networks for Multi-Target Tracking

Yang Weon Lee and Chil Woo Lee

Department of Information and Communication Engineering, Honam University, Seobongdong, Gwangsangu, Gwangju, 506-714, South Korea
Department of Computer Engineering, Chonnam University, Yongbongdong, Gwangju, South Korea
ywlee@honam.ac.kr, cwlee@chonnam.ac.kr

**Abstract.** In this paper, we have developed the MHDA scheme for data association. This scheme is important in providing a computationally feasible alternative to complete enumeration of JPDA which is intractable. We have proved that given an artificial measurement and track's configuration, MHDA scheme converges to a proper plot in a finite number of iterations. Also, a proper plot which is not the global solution can be corrected by re-initializing one or more times. In this light, even if the performance is enhanced by using the MHDA, we also note that the difficulty in tuning the parameters of the MHDA is critical aspect of this scheme. The difficulty can, however, be overcome by developing suitable automatic instruments that will iteratively verify convergence as the network parameters vary.

## 1 Introduction

Generally, there are three approaches in data association for MTT : non-Bayesian approach based on likelihood function[1], Bayesian approach[2,4,3], and neural network approach[5]. The major difference of the first two approaches is how treat the false alarms. The non-Bayesian approach calculates all the likelihood functions of all the possible tracks with given measurements and selects the track which gives the maximum value of the likelihood function. Meanwhile, the tracking filter using Bayesian approach predicts the location of interest using *a posteriori* probability. These two approaches are inadequate for real time applications because the computational complexity is tremendous.

As an alternative approach, Sengupta and Iltis[5] suggested a Hopfield neural network probabilistic data association (HNPDA) to approximately compute *a posteriori* probability $\beta_j^t$, for the joint probabilities data association filter (JPDAF)[7] as a constrained minimization problem. This technique based on the use of neural networks was also started by comparison with the traveling salesman problem(TSP). In fact $\beta_j^t$ is approximated by the output voltage $X_j^t$ of a neuron in an $(m+1) \times n$ array of neurons, where $m$ is the number of measurements and $n$ is the number of targets. Sengupta and Iltis[5] claimed that the performance of the HNPDA was close to that of the JPDAF in situations where the numbers of measurements and targets were in the ranges of 3 to 20 and 2

D.-S. Huang, K. Li, and G.W. Irwin (Eds.): ICIC 2006, LNCS 4113, pp. 981–990, 2006.

to 6, respectively. The success of the HNPDA in their examples was credited to the accurate emulation of all the properties of the JPDAF by the HNPDA.

However, the neural network developed in [5] has been shown the two problems. First, the neural network developed in [5] has been shown to have improper energy functions. Second, heuristic choices of the constant parameters in the energy function in [5] didn't guarantee the optimal data association.

The outline of this paper is as follows. In section 2 the Hopfield neural network used in [5] is briefly reviewed and some comments are made on the assumptions which used to set up the energy function in [5]. Then, the modified scheme of HNPDA is proposed as an alternative data association method for MTT. Finally, we present our simulation results in Section 4, and conclusions in Section 5.

## 2 Review of the Energy Function in the HNPDA and Comments

Suppose there are $n$ targets and $m$ measurements. The energy function used in [5] is reproduced below.

$$E_{DAP} = \frac{A}{2}\sum_{j=0}^{m}\sum_{t=1}^{n}\sum_{\tau=1 \tau\neq t}^{n} X_j^t X_j^\tau + \frac{B}{2}\sum_{t=1}^{n}\sum_{j=0}^{m}\sum_{l=0 l\neq j}^{m} X_j^t X_l^t + \frac{C}{2}\sum_{t=1}^{n}(\sum_{j=0}^{m} X_j^t - 1)^2$$
$$+\frac{D}{2}\sum_{j=0}^{m}\sum_{t=1}^{n}(X_j^t - \rho_j^t)^2 + \frac{E}{2}\sum_{j=0}^{m}\sum_{t=1}^{n}\sum_{\tau=1 \tau\neq t}^{n}(X_j^t - \sum_{l=0 l\neq j}^{m} \rho_l^\tau)^2. \quad (1)$$

In [5], $X_j^t$ is the output voltage of a neuron in an $(m+1)\times n$ array of neurons and is the approximation to the *a posteriori* probability $\beta_j^t$ in the JPDAF[7]. This *a posteriori* probability, in the special case of the PDAF[7] when the probability $P_G$ that the correct measurement falls inside the validation gate is unity, is denoted by $\rho_j^t$. Actually, $P_G$ is very close to unity when the validation gate size is adequate. In (1), A,B,C,D, and E are constants.

In the HNPDA, the connection strength matrix is a symmetric matrix of order $n(m+1)$. With the given energy function $E_{DAP}$ in (1), the connection strength $W_{jl}^{t\tau}$ from the neuron at location $(\tau, l)$ to the neuron at location $(t, j)$ is

$$W_{jl}^{t\tau} = \begin{cases} -[C+D+E(n-1)] & \text{if } t=\tau \text{ and } j=l \text{ “self feedback”}, \\ -A & \text{if } t\neq\tau \text{ and } j=l \text{ “row connection”}, \\ -(B+C) & \text{if } t=\tau \text{ and } j\neq l \text{ “column connection”}, \\ 0 & \text{if } t\neq\tau \text{ and } j\neq l \text{ “global connection”}. \end{cases} \quad (2)$$

The input current $I_j^t$ to the neuron at location $(t, j)$, for $t = 1, 2, \ldots, n$, and $j = 0, 1, \ldots, m$, is

$$I_j^t = C + (D+E)\rho_j^t + E\Big(n - 1 - \sum_{\tau=1}^{n}\rho_j^\tau\Big). \quad (3)$$

Clearly from (2)and (3), the input current $I_j^t$ but not the connection strength $T_{jl}^{t\tau}$ depends on the $\rho_j^t$ s, which are computed form the measurements that comprise the input data. Ironically, in the neural network for the TSP[9], only the connection strengths depend on the input data which, in this case, are the distances between pairs of cities.

In order to justify the first two terms of $E_{DAP}$ in (1), the authors of [5] claimed that the dual assumptions of no two returns form the same target and no single return from two targets are consistent with the presence of a dominating $X_j^t$ in each row and each column of the $(m+1) \times n$ array of neurons. However, these assumptions are not constraints on the values of the $\beta_j^t$'s in the original JPDAF. Those assumptions should be used only in the generation of the feasible data association hypotheses, as pointed out in [7]. As a matter of fact, there could be two $\beta_j^t$'s of comparable magnitude in the same row and in the same column as shown in Chapter 4 of [8]. Therefore, the presence of a dominating $X_j^t$ in each row and each column is not a property of the JPDAF.

The third term of $E_{DAP}$ is used to constrain the sum of the $X_j^t$'s in each column to unity *i.e.* $\sum_{j=0}^{m} X_j^t = 1$. This constraint is consistent with the requirement that $\sum_{j=0}^{m} \beta_j^t = 1$ in both the JPDAF and the PDAF[10]. Therefore, this constraint, by itself, does not permit us to infer whether the $\beta_j^t$'s are from the JPDAF, or from the PDAF. The assumption used to set up the fourth term is that this term is small only if $X_j^t$ is close to $\rho_j^t$, in which case the neural network simulates more closely the PDAF for each target rather than the intended JPDAF in the multitarget scenario. Finally, the fifth term is supposed to be minimized if $X_j^t$ is not large unless for each $\tau \neq t$ there is a unique $l \neq j$ such that $\rho_l^\tau$ is large. Unfortunately, this constrained minimization may not be possible as shown in [8]. This is consistent with the heuristic nature of the derivation of the energy function in [5], which could lead to the problems in the implementation of the HNPDA as discussed next.

## 3 Modified Scheme of HNPDA

### 3.1 Modification of Energy Equation

In Hopfield network, when the operation is approaching the steady state, at most one neuron gets into the ON state in each row and column and the other neurons must be in the OFF state. To guarantee the this state, we add the following constraints additionally for Hopfield network :

$$E_s = \frac{1}{2}\sum_{j=1}^{m}\sum_{t=0}^{n}\sum_{\tau\neq t}^{n} \omega_{jt}\omega_{j\tau} + \frac{1}{2}\sum_{t=1}^{n}\sum_{j=1}^{m}\sum_{l\neq j}^{m} \omega_{jt}\omega_{lt}. \quad (4)$$

By summing (4) and (10) in [11], we get the final energy equation for Hopfield network:

$$E_{HDA} = \frac{A}{2}\sum_{j=1}^{m}\sum_{t=0}^{n}\sum_{\tau\neq t}^{n}\omega_{jt}\omega_{j\tau} + \frac{B}{2}\sum_{t=1}^{n}\sum_{j=1}^{m}\sum_{l\neq j}^{m}\omega_{jt}\omega_{lt} + \frac{C}{2}\sum_{t=1}^{n}\sum_{j=1}^{m}(\hat{w}_{jt} - w_{jt})^2$$
$$+\frac{D}{2}\sum_{t=1}^{n}(\sum_{j=1}^{m}\hat{w}_{jt} - 1)^2 + \frac{F}{2}\sum_{j=1}^{m}(\sum_{t=0}^{n}\hat{w}_{jt} - 1)^2 + \frac{G}{2}\sum_{t=1}^{n}\sum_{j=1}^{m} r_{jt}\hat{w}_{jt}. \quad (5)$$

The first two terms of (5) correspond to row and column inhibition and the third term suppressed the activation of uncorrelated part( *i.e.* if $\omega_{jt} = 0$, then $\hat{\omega}_{jt} = 0$). The fourth and fifth terms biased the final solution towards a normalized set of numbers. The last term favors associations which have a nearest neighbor in view of target velocity.

### 3.2 Transformation of Energy Function into Hopfield Network

A Hopfield network with $m(n+1)$ neurons was considered. The neurons were subdivided into $n+1$ target's column of $m$ neurons each. Henceforward we will identify each neuron with a double index, $tl$(where the index $t = 0, 1, \ldots, n$ relates to the target, whereas the index $l = 1, \ldots, m$ refers to the neurons in each column), its output with $X_l^t$, the weight for neurons $jt$ and $l\tau$ with $W_{jl}^{t\tau}$, and the external bias current for neuron $tl$ with $I_l^t$. According to this convention, we can extend the notation of the Lyapunov energy function[12] to two dimensions. Using the Kronecker delta function

$$\delta_{ij} = \begin{cases} 1 \text{ if } i = j, \\ 0 \text{ if } i \neq j, \end{cases} \quad (6)$$

The Lyapunov energy function[12] can be written as

$$E_{HDA} = \frac{A}{2}\sum_{l}\sum_{j}\sum_{t}\sum_{\tau}\delta_{lj}(1-\delta_{t\tau})X_l^t X_j^\tau + \frac{B}{2}\sum_{l}\sum_{j}\sum_{t}\sum_{\tau}\delta_{t\tau}(1-\delta_{lj})$$
$$(1-\delta_{ot})X_l^t X_j^\tau + \frac{C}{2}\sum_{l}\sum_{j}\sum_{t}\sum_{\tau}\delta_{t\tau}\delta_{lj}(1-\delta_{ot})X_l^t X_j^\tau - C\sum_{l}\sum_{t}$$
$$\omega_{jt}(1-\delta_{ot})X_l^t + \frac{C}{2}\sum_{l}\sum_{t}\omega_{jt}^2(1-\delta_{ot}) + \frac{Dn}{2} - D\sum_{l}\sum_{t}(1-\delta_{ot})X_l^t$$
$$+\frac{D}{2}\sum_{l}\sum_{j}\sum_{t}\sum_{\tau}\delta_{t\tau}(1-\delta_{ot})X_l^t X_j^\tau + \frac{Fm}{2} - F\sum_{l}\sum_{t}X_l^t$$
$$+\frac{F}{2}\sum_{l}\sum_{j}\sum_{t}\sum_{\tau}\delta_{lj}X_l^t X_j^\tau + \frac{G}{2}\sum_{l}\sum_{t} r_{jt}(1-\delta_{ot})X_l^t. \quad (7)$$

We also can extend the notation of the Lyapunov energy function[12] to two dimensions:

$$\mathbf{E} = -\frac{1}{2}\sum_{l}\sum_{j}\sum_{t}\sum_{\tau}W_{jl}^{t\tau}X_l^t X_j^\tau - \sum_{l}\sum_{t}I_l^t X_l^t. \quad (8)$$

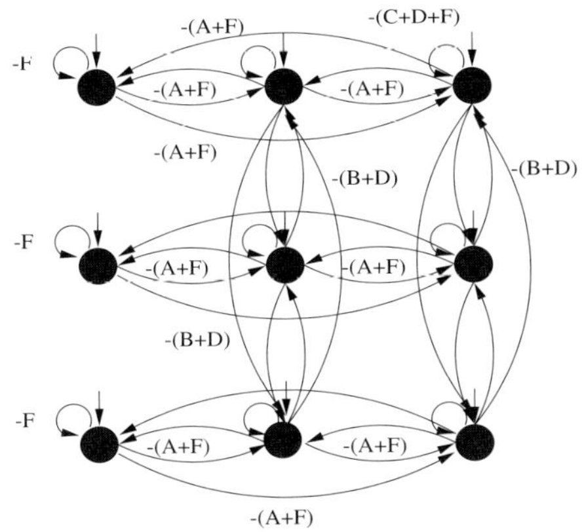


**Fig. 1.** Example of Hopfield network for two targets and three plots

By comparing (8) and (7), we get the connection strength matrix and input parameters each :

$$\begin{cases} W_{jl}^{t\tau} = -\big[A(1-\delta_{t\tau})+C\delta_{t\tau}(1-\delta_{ot})+F\big]\delta_{lj} - \big[B(1-\delta_{lj})+D\big]\delta_{t\tau}(1-\delta_{ot}), \\ I_l^t = (C\omega_{jt}+D-\frac{G}{2}r_{jt})(1-\delta_{ot})+F. \end{cases} \tag{9}$$

Here we omit the constant terms such as $\frac{Dn+Fm}{2}+\frac{C}{2}\sum\sum\omega_{jt}^2(1-\delta_{ot})$ . These terms do not affect the neuron's output since they just act as a bias terms during the processing.

Using the (9), the connection strength $W_{jl}^{t\tau}$ from the neuron at location $(\tau, l)$ to the neuron at location $(t, j)$ is

$$W_{jl}^{t\tau} = \begin{cases} -[(C+D)(1-\delta_{ot})+F] & \text{if } t=\tau \text{ and } j=l \text{ "self feedback"}, \\ -(A+F) & \text{if } t\neq\tau \text{ and } j=l \text{ "row connection"}, \\ -(B+D)(1-\delta_{ot}) & \text{if } t=\tau \text{ and } j\neq l \text{ "column connection"}, \\ 0 & \text{if } t\neq\tau \text{ and } j\neq l \text{ "global connection"}. \end{cases} \tag{10}$$

Fig.1 sketches the resulting two-dimensional network architecture as a directed graph using the (10). We note that only 39 connections of possible 81 connections are achieved in this 3 × 3 neurons example. This means that modified Hopfield network can be represented as a sparse matrix. In Fig.1, we also note that there are no connections between diagonal neurons.

With the specific values from (9), the equation of motion for the MTT becomes

$$\begin{aligned} \frac{dS_l^t}{dt} = -\frac{S_l^t}{s_o} - \sum_{\tau}\sum_{j}\Big[&\{A(1-\delta_{t\tau})+C\delta_{t\tau}(1-\delta_{ot})+F\}\delta_{lj} \\ &-\{B(1-\delta_{lj})+D\}\delta_{t\tau}(1-\delta_{ot})\Big]X_j^{\tau} \\ &+(C\omega_{jt}+D-\frac{r_{jt}}{2}G)(1-\delta_{ot})+F \end{aligned} \tag{11}$$

The final equation of data association is

$$\frac{dS_l^t}{dt} = -\frac{S_l^t}{S_o} - A\sum_{\tau=1,\tau\neq t}^{n} X_l^\tau - B(1-\delta_{ot})\sum_{j=1,j\neq l}^{n} X_j^t - D(1-\delta_{ot})(\sum_{j=1}^{m} X_j^t - 1)$$
$$-F(\sum_{\tau=1}^{m} X_l^\tau - 1) - C(1-\delta_{ot})(1-\omega_{jt}) - \frac{r_{jt}}{2}(1-\delta_{ot})G. \quad (12)$$

The parameters $A, B, C, D, F$ and $G$ can be adjusted to control the emphasis on different constraints and properties. A larger emphasis on $A, B$, and $F$ will produce the only one neuron's activation both column and row. A large value of $C$ will produce $X_l^t$ close to $\omega_{jt}$ except the duplicated activation of neurons in the same row and column. A larger emphasis on $G$ will make the neuron activate depending on the value of target's course weighted value. Finally, a balanced combination of all six parameters will lead to the most desirable association. In this case, a large number of targets and measurements will only require a larger array of interconnected neurons instead of an increased load on any sequential software to compute the association probabilities.

### 3.3 Computational Complexity

The computational complexity of the modified Hopfield data association (MHDA) scheme, when applied to the target association problem, depends on the number of tracks and measurements and the iteration numbers to be reached stable state. Suppose that there are $n$ tracks and $m$ measurements. Then according to the (12) for data association, the computational complexity per iteration of the MHDA method require $\mathcal{O}(nm)$ computations. When we assume the average iteration number as $\bar{k}$, the total data association calculations require $\mathcal{O}(\bar{k}nm)$ computations. Therefore, even if the tracks and measurements are increased , the required computations are not increasing exponentially . However JPDAF as estimated in [5] requires the computational complexity $\mathcal{O}(2^{nm})$ , so its computational complexity increases exponentially depending on the number of tracks and measurements.

## 4 Simulation Results

### 4.1 Data Association Results

To exactly test the data association capability of the MHDA method, predefined targets and measurements value are used to exclude any effects due to miss detection that are moderately occurring in real environment. An example of three targets and seven measurements is depicted in Fig. 2. In Fig. 2, large circles represent track gates and symbol * means plots of measurements and small circles on the some measurement's plots represent the plots of measurements which are associated with tracks by MHDA. During the iteration, Fig. 3 and 4 show how the distance and matching energy change respectively. In this example, the

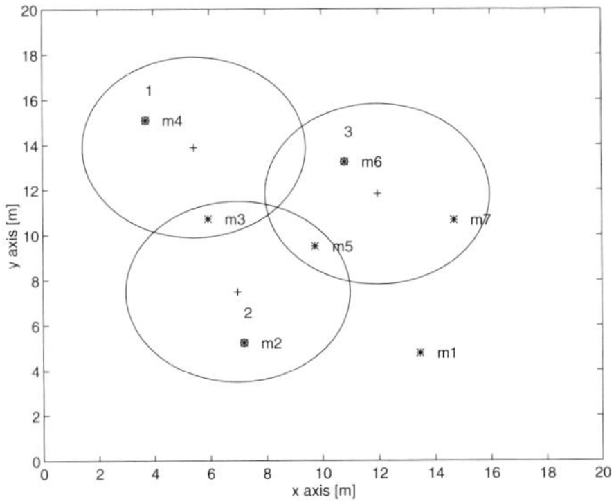


**Fig. 2.** Diagram of Hopfield network for three targets and seven plots

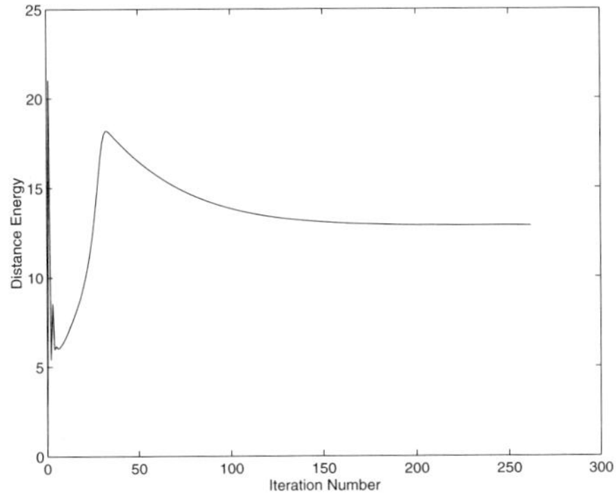


**Fig. 3.** Distance energy convergence for three targets and seven plots

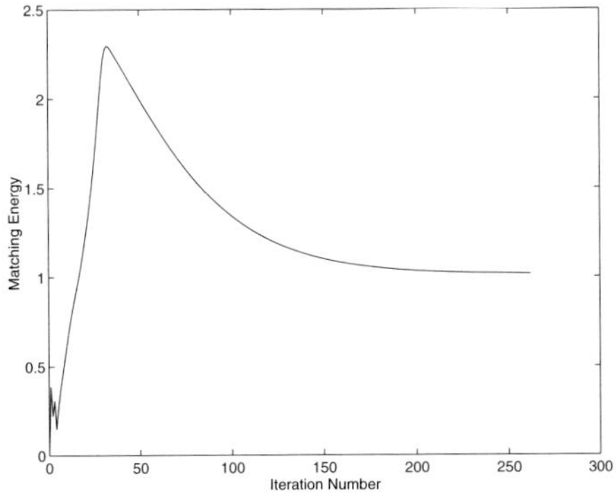


**Fig. 4.** Matching energy of Hopfield network for three targets and seven plots

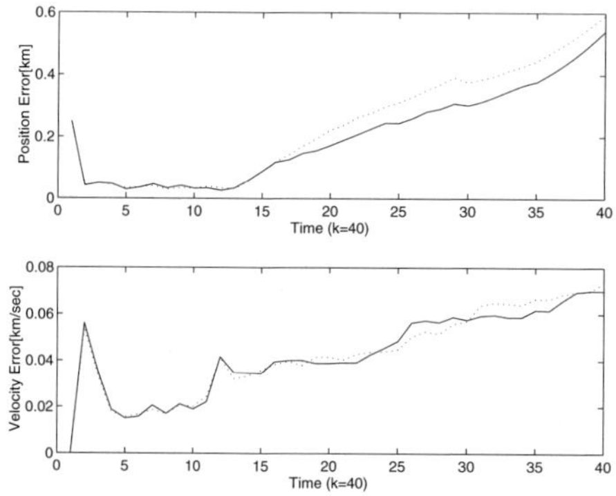


**Fig. 5.** RMS errors in X axis for target 8 : — MHDA ···HNPDA

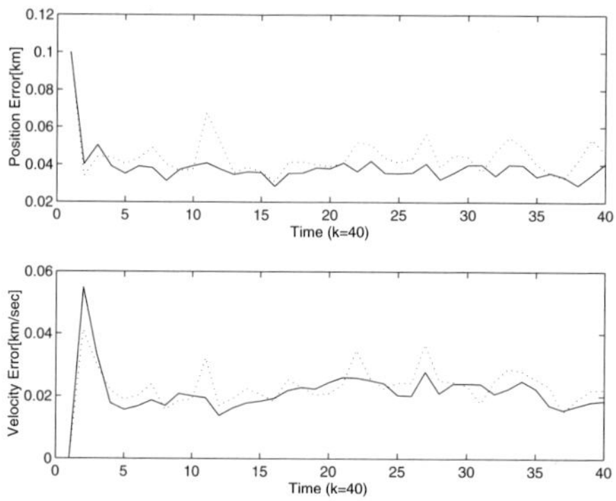


**Fig. 6.** RMS errors in X axis for target 9 : — MHDA ···HNPDA

association pairs are track 1 and measurement 4, track 2 measurement 2 ,and track 3 and measurement 6. Note that the results of data association is correct with respect to nearest neighbor. In the simulation, the constants $A = 50, B = 50, C = 100, D = 1000, F = 1000$and $G = 100$ appeared to be suitable for this scenario. $S_o$ was selected to be 1 $s$.

## 4.2 Sequential Tracking Results

The crossing, parallel and maneuvering targets whose initial parameters are taken from target 1,2,3,4,8 and 9 respectively in Table 1 in [11] are tested. In Fig. 5 and 6, the rms estimation errors for the maneuvering targets are shown. HNPDA can not track the dog leg maneuvering targets but the constant acceleration target. Table 1 summarizes the rms position and velocity errors for each target. The rms errors of the HNPDA about maneuvering targets have not been included since it loses track of one of targets. The performance of the MHDA is superior to that of HNPDA in terms of tracking accuracy and track maintenance.

**Table 1.** RMS Errors in case of ten targets

| Target | Position error ($km$) | | Velocity error ($km/s$) | | Track maintenance (%) | |
|---|---|---|---|---|---|---|
| $i$ | HNPDA | MHDA | HNPDA | MHDA | HNPDA | MHDA |
| 1 | 0.048 | 0.044 | 0.024 | 0.021 | 95 | 98 |
| 2 | 0.051 | 0.048 | 0.028 | 0.018 | 95 | 98 |
| 3 | 0.065 | 0.044 | 0.021 | 0.018 | 85 | 98 |
| 4 | 0.049 | 0.041 | 0.020 | 0.018 | 93 | 98 |
| 5 | 0.041 | 0.044 | 0.018 | 0.018 | 100 | 100 |
| 6 | 0.042 | 0.043 | 0.021 | 0.018 | 100 | 100 |
| 7 | 0.040 | 0.040 | 0.018 | 0.018 | 100 | 100 |
| 8 | - | 0.295 | - | 0.118 | 0 | 53 |
| 9 | 0.058 | 0.047 | 0.027 | 0.022 | 100 | 100 |
| 10 | 0.037 | 0.039 | 0.011 | 0.012 | 100 | 100 |

## 5 Conclusions

In this chapter, we have developed the MHDA scheme for data association. This scheme is important in providing a computationally feasible alternative to complete enumeration of JPDA which is intractable. We have proved that given an artificial measurement and track's configuration, MHDA scheme converges to a proper plot in a finite number of iterations. Also, a proper plot which is not the global solution can be corrected by re-initializing one or more times. In this light, even if the performance is enhanced by using the MHDA, we also note that the difficulty in tuning the parameters of the MHDA is critical aspect of this scheme. The difficulty can, however, be overcome by developing suitable automatic instruments that will iteratively verify convergence as the network parameters vary.

## Acknowledgements

This research has been supported by research funding of 'Center for High-Quality Electric Components and Systems', Chonnam National University, Korea.

## References

1. Alspach, D. L.: A Gaussian Sum Approach to the Multi-Target Identification Tracking Problem. *Automatica* , 11(1975) 285-296
2. Bar-Shalom, Y.: Extension of the Probabilistic Data Association Filter in Multi-Target Tracking. *Proceedings of the 5th Symposium on Nonlinear Estimation*, Sep.(1974) 16-21
3. Reid, D. B.: An Algorithm for Tracking Multiple Targets. *IEEE Trans. on Automat. Contr.*, 24(1979) 843-854
4. Reid, D. B.: A Multiple Hypothesis Filter for Tracking Multiple Targets in a Cluttered Environment. *Lockheed Palo Alto Research Laboratory Tech. Report* LMSC-D560254, Sept. (1977). (J. Basic Eng.,) 82(1960) 34-45

5. Sengupta,D., Iltis, R. A.: Neural Solution to the Multitarget Tracking Data Association Problem. *IEEE Trans. on AES, AES-25*, Jan.(1999) 96-108
6. Kuczewski, R.: Neural Network Approaches to Multitarget Tracking. In proceedings of the *IEEE ICNN conference*, (1987)
7. Fortmann, T. E., Bar-Shalom, Y., Scheffe, M.: Sonar Tracking of Multiple Targets Using Joint Probabilistic Data Association. *IEEE J. Oceanic Engineering*, OE-8, Jul. (1983) 173-184
8. Zhou, B.: Multitarget Tracking in Clutter : Algorithms for Data Association and State Estimation. PhD thesis, Pennsylvania State University, Department of Electrical and Computer Engineering, University Park, PA 16802, May (1992)
9. Hopfield, J. J., Tank, D. W.: Neural Computation of Decisions in Optimization Problems. Biological Cybernatics,(1985) 141-152
10. Fortmann, T. E., Bar-Shalom, Y.: *Tracking and Data Association.* Orland Acdemic Press, Inc., (1988) 224
11. Yang Weon Lee: Adaptive Data Association for Multi-target Tracking Using Relaxation. LNCS 35644, (2005) 552-561
12. Yang Weon Lee, Seo, J. H., Lee, J. G.: A Study on the TWS Tracking Filter for Multi-Target Tracking. *Journal of KIEE*, 41(4), (2004) 411-421

# Algorithm Analysis and Application Based on Chaotic Neural Network for Cellular Channel Assignment

Xiaojin Zhu, Yanchun Chen, Hesheng Zhang, and Jialin Cao

School of Mechatronics Engineering & Automation, Shanghai University
200072 Shanghai, P.R. China
mgzhuxj@staff.shu.edu.cn

**Abstract.** A new chaotic simulated annealing mechanism with transient chaotic neural network is proposed as an optimization algorithm, called Two-phase annealing method in transient chaotic neural network model (TPA-TCNN), and applied for the channel assignment problem. We use Kunz's benchmark test, a 25 cells channel assignment problem, to demonstrate TPA-TCNN algorithm. Comparing with the Chen and Aihara's transient chaotic neural network model and the chaotic neural network model generated by injecting chaotic noise into the Hopfield neural network (DCN-HNN), the TPA-TCNN model has a higher searching ability and lower computing time in searching the global minimum.

## 1 Introduction

Recently, various neural network algorithms have been considered for the channel assignment problems. Although these neural networks guarantee convergence to a stable equilibrium point due to their gradient descent dynamics, the main drawback is that they suffer from the local minimum problems when applied to the CAP.

To alleviate the shortcomings of the conventional networks described above, Aihara et al [1] created a chaotic neuron network (CNN). The efficiency and solution quality were both superior to the traditional Hopfield network. However, the convergence problems have not yet been satisfactorily solved. Then Chen and Aihara [2] developed a transiently chaotic neural network (TCNN) for solving combinatorial optimization problems. A salient feature of the TCNN model is that the chaotic neurodynamics are self-organizing in order to escape local minima.

Another approach for solving combinatorial optimization problems is the injection of chaotic noise into the network. Hayakawa et al [5] used the logistic map with different values of the bifurcation parameter as noise, and some values of the bifurcation parameter were found to offer better optimization ability.

In this paper, a new chaotic simulated annealing mechanism (TPA-TCNN) is proposed to solve the CAP .Comparing with the Chen and Aihara's TCNN and DCN-HNN; the TPA-TCNN model has a higher searching ability and lower computing time in searching the global minimum.

## 2 Problem Description

The channel assignment problem (CAP) must satisfy the three constraints:

(i) Co site Constraint (CSC): any pair of frequencies assigned to a cell should have a minimal distance between frequencies.

D.-S. Huang, K. Li, and G.W. Irwin (Eds.): ICIC 2006, LNCS 4113, pp. 991 – 996, 2006.

(ii) Co channel Constraint (CCC): for a certain pair of radio cells, the same frequency cannot be used simultaneously.
(iii)Adjacent Channel Constraint (ACC): the adjacent frequencies in the frequency domain cannot be assigned to adjacent radio cells simultaneously.

Gamst defined the compatibility matrix C=( $c_{ij}$ ), which is an n×n symmetric matrix, where n is the number of cells in the mobile network and $c_{ij}$ is the minimum frequency separation between a frequency in cell i and cell j. The number of channels needed for each cell is presented by the demand vector D=( $d_i$ ), where $1 \leqslant i \leqslant n$.

## 3 The Neural Network Model

### 3.1 Transiently Chaotic Neural Network (TCNN) Model

The TCNN model is defined as below:

$$v_i(t) = \frac{1}{1+e^{-y_i(t)/b}} . \quad (1)$$

$$y_i(t+1) = h \cdot y_i(t) + \alpha \cdot \left( \sum_{j=1, j \neq i}^{n} w_{ij} \cdot v_j(t) + I_i \right) - z_i(v_i(t) - I_0) \cdot \quad (2)$$

$$z_i(t+1) = (1-r) z_i(t) . \quad (3)$$

The parameters shown above are defined the same as in [2].

With some chosen parameters and initial neuron states, equation (1), (2) and (3) altogether determine the dynamics of the TCNN. A sufficiently large value of z is used such that the self-coupling is strong enough to generate chaotic dynamics to search for global minima. Clearly, when $z_i$ =0, the TCNN is reduced to the Hopfield neural network, and when the value of $z_i$ is fixed, the TCNN is equivalent to CNN.

### 3.2 Chaotic Simulated Annealing with Decaying Chaotic Noise (DCN-HNN)

The neural network with chaotic noise is defined as follows:

$$y_i(t+1) = hy_i(t) + \alpha\left(\sum_j w_{ij} v_j + I_i\right) + \gamma(z_i(t) - h)) . \quad (4)$$

$$v_i(t) = f(u_i(t)) = \frac{1}{1+e^{-u_i(t)/\varepsilon}} . \quad (5)$$

$$z_i(t+1) = a(t) z_i(t)(1 - z_i(t)) . \quad (6)$$

$$a(t+1) = (1-\beta) a(t) + \beta a_0 . \quad (7)$$

$$h = 1 - 1/a_0 . \quad (8)$$

Where $\gamma$ is the positive scaling parameter for the chaotic noise, $1 \le a_0 \le 2.9$. $0 < \beta < 1$ is a decay rate.

### 3.3 Two-Phase Annealing Method in TCNN Model (TPA-TCNN)

The dynamics of the TCNN can be classified into two phases, depending on the value of $z_i$ .The first phase is the "chaotic searching phase" with transiently chaotic dynamics for a relatively large z. the second phase is the "stable convergent phase" with convergent dynamics similar to the Hopfield neural network for a relatively small z.

In Chen's TCNN model, $z_i$ varies according to $z_i(t+1)=(1-r)z_i(t)$, which damps exponentially and could be called as exponential annealing method. Wang Ling [6] proposed a new damping method: $z(t+1) = z(t)/\ln[e + r_1 \cdot (1 - z(t))]$ to control the damping speed of $z_i$ .It helps to enhance the chaotic dynamics and short the converging time, and can be called as the logarithmic annealing method. $z_i$ could also varies as $z(t+1) = z(t) - r_2$ ,called linear annealing method.

To utilize the advantage of the methods above, a new annealing mechanism called two-phase annealing method consisting of the logarithmic annealing phase and the linear annealing phase is proposed. The logarithmic annealing method is used in the "chaotic searching phase" and the linear annealing method is used in the "stable convergent phase". It can take enough time to make use of the chaotic dynamics to escape the local minima, and converging as quickly as possible. The TPA-TCNN model is defined by the following equation:

$$v_i(t) = \frac{1}{1+e^{-y_i(t)/b}} . \tag{9}$$

$$y_i(t+1) = h \cdot y_i(t) + \alpha \cdot \Big(\sum_{j=1, j\neq i}^{n} w_{ij} \cdot v_j(t) + I_i\Big) - z_i(v_i(t) - I_0) . \tag{10}$$

$$z(t+1) = \begin{cases} z(t)/\ln[e + r_1 \cdot (1 - z(t))], & z \geq d \\ z(t) - r_2, & z < d \end{cases} . \tag{11}$$

Where d is the dividing point, and $r_1$ , $r_2$ are the damping factors of $z_i$ in the model.

## 4 Simulation Results

In this section, the implementation of the three algorithms used in CAP is discussed. The interconnection weight is defined as follows:

$$w_{ijpq} = -A\delta_{ip} - B_1\delta_{ip}(1-\delta_{jq})\alpha_{jq}(c_{ii}-1) - B_2(1-\delta_{ip})\alpha_{jq}(c_{ip}-1) . \tag{12}$$

And $I_{ij}$ can be defined as:

$$I_{ij} = Ad_i . \tag{13}$$

Where ① $\delta_{ij} = \begin{cases} 1, i = j \\ 0, i \neq j \end{cases}$ ② $\alpha_{ij}(x) = \begin{cases} 1, |i - j| \leq x \\ 0, |i - j| > x \end{cases}$

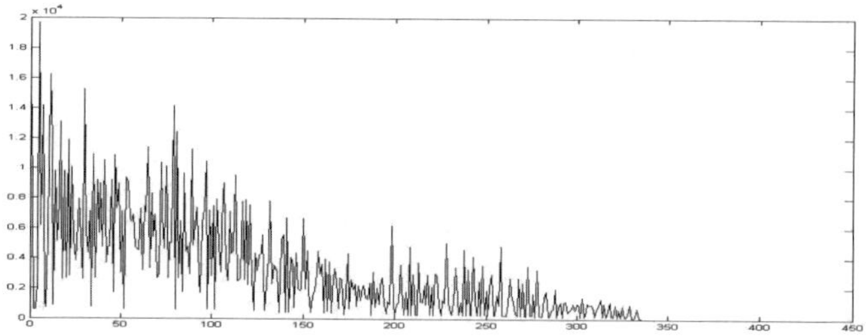

**Fig. 1.** Time evolutions of objective function in simulation of TPA-TCNN model for the Kunz testing problems

$$
C=\begin{bmatrix}
2&1&1&0&1&0&1&1&1&1&0&1&1&1&1&0&0&0&0&0&0&0&0&0&0\\
1&2&1&0&1&0&1&1&0&1&0&1&1&1&1&0&0&0&0&0&0&0&0&0&0\\
1&1&2&1&1&1&1&1&1&1&1&1&1&1&0&0&0&0&0&0&0&0&0&0&0\\
0&0&1&2&0&0&1&1&1&1&1&1&1&0&0&0&0&0&0&0&0&0&1&1&1\\
1&1&1&0&2&0&0&0&0&1&1&1&1&1&1&1&0&0&0&0&0&0&0&0&0\\
0&0&1&0&0&2&1&1&1&1&0&0&0&0&0&0&0&0&0&0&0&0&0&0&0\\
1&1&1&1&0&1&2&1&1&1&1&1&1&0&0&0&0&0&0&0&0&0&0&0&0\\
1&1&1&1&0&1&1&2&1&1&1&1&1&0&0&0&0&0&0&0&0&0&0&1&0\\
1&0&1&1&0&1&1&1&2&1&1&1&0&0&0&0&0&0&0&0&0&0&0&1&1\\
1&1&1&1&1&1&1&1&1&2&1&1&1&1&1&1&0&0&0&0&0&1&0&1&0\\
0&0&1&1&1&0&1&1&1&1&2&0&1&1&1&1&0&1&1&1&1&1&1&1&1\\
1&1&1&1&1&0&1&1&1&1&0&2&1&1&0&0&0&0&0&0&0&0&0&0&0\\
1&1&1&1&1&0&1&1&0&1&1&1&2&1&1&1&1&1&1&1&0&0&0&0&0\\
1&1&1&0&1&0&0&0&0&1&1&1&1&2&1&1&1&1&1&1&0&0&0&0&0\\
1&1&0&0&1&0&0&0&0&1&1&0&1&1&2&1&1&1&1&1&1&1&0&0&0\\
0&0&0&0&1&0&0&0&0&1&1&0&1&1&1&2&1&1&1&1&0&0&0&0&0\\
0&0&0&0&0&0&0&0&0&0&0&0&1&1&1&1&2&1&1&0&0&0&0&0&0\\
0&0&0&0&0&0&0&0&0&0&1&0&1&1&1&1&1&2&1&1&0&0&0&0&0\\
0&0&0&0&0&0&0&0&0&0&1&0&1&1&1&1&1&1&2&1&1&1&1&0&0\\
0&0&0&0&0&0&0&0&0&0&1&0&1&1&1&1&0&1&1&2&1&1&1&0&0\\
0&0&0&0&0&0&0&0&0&0&1&0&0&0&1&0&0&0&1&1&2&1&1&0&0\\
0&0&0&0&0&0&0&0&0&1&1&0&0&0&1&0&0&0&1&1&1&2&1&1&1\\
0&0&0&1&0&0&0&0&0&0&1&0&0&0&0&0&0&0&1&1&1&1&2&1&1\\
0&0&0&1&0&0&0&1&1&1&1&0&0&0&0&0&0&0&0&0&0&1&1&2&1\\
0&0&0&1&0&0&0&0&1&0&1&0&0&0&0&0&0&0&0&0&0&1&1&1&2
\end{bmatrix}
\qquad
D=\begin{matrix}10\\11\\9\\5\\9\\4\\5\\7\\4\\8\\8\\9\\10\\7\\7\\6\\4\\5\\5\\7\\6\\4\\5\\7\\5\end{matrix}
$$

(a) Comparability matrix C (b) Demand vector D

**Fig. 2.** Comparability matrix and a demand vector for the Kunz testing problems

**Table 1.** Results of 100 different initial conditions on Kunz's benchmark test problem

| | TCNN | DCN-HNN | TPA-TCNN | Results in[10] | Results in[9] |
|---|---|---|---|---|---|
| GM | 81% | 70% | 90% | 62% | 9% |
| NI | 381.57 | 410.49 | 356.38 | 279.9 | 294 |

Benchmark problem of mobile systems consisting of 25 cells in [4] is used to evaluate the TCNN, DCN-HNN and TPA-TCNN in this paper. Kunz's test problem is a practical CAP derived from traffic density data of an actual 24×21 km area around Helsinki, Finland. The compatibility matrix and demand vector are shown in Fig. 2.

The number of channels is taken to be a fraction of the 73 channels available for the entire 25 regions. The results are shown in table1.Fig.1 shows the time evolutions of the continuous energy function in TPA-TCNN model.

Table 1 summarizes the assignment results and shows the convergence rate compared with recently reported results. The assignment results show that the TPA- TCNN has a better performance in searching the global minimum then other algorithms. (GM=Rate of reaching the global minimum, NI=Number of iterations required for the network to converge).

## 5 Conclusions

In [3], Chen and Aihara showed that TCNN has a global attracting set, which encompasses all the global minima of an objective function when certain conditions are satisfied, thereby ensuring the global searching of TCNN. Despite the small search region of TCNN, it has a strong global searching capability. The searching ability of DCN − TCNN is also discussed in [7].

Terence Kwok and A. Smith proposed a unified framework for chaotic neural-network approaches to combinatorial optimization in [8].That is, they proposed a modified and more general form of the computational energy E, defined as:

$$E = -\frac{1}{2}\sum_i \sum_j \omega_{ij} x_i x_j - \sum_i I_i x_i + \frac{1}{\tau}\sum_i \int_0^{x_i} f^{-1}(\xi) d\xi + H(x_i, \omega_{ij}, I_i) \quad (14)$$

Equation (14) could be simply described as $E = E_{Hop} + H$ , where $E_{Hop}$ is the energy function of Hopfield neural network and H is the additional term. $E_{Hop}$ is a common term ,and the methods different from each other according to various H. In Chen's TCNN model, $H_{CA} = \frac{\lambda(t)}{2}\sum_i x_i(x_i - 1)$, which is a quadratic form. In DCN − TCNN model, $H_\eta = -\sum_i \eta_i(t) x_i(t)$, which is linear in form. Terence Kwok and A. Smith suggested that may be the reason for the different searching ability of the two methods. But it has not been proved yet. Many researchers have applied these methods to various NPC problems, and got different conclusions. We think, is due to the selecting of the parameters. The criterion of the parameter selecting and the evaluation of the neural network models will be the subject of future research.

## Acknowledgements

This work was supported by Shanghai Municipal Education Commission and Shanghai Education Development Foundation "Shu Guang" project (under Grant No.04SG41), the Scientific Research Foundation for the Returned Overseas Chinese Scholars, Shanghai Leading Academic Disciplines (under Grant No. T0103), and Shanghai Key Laboratory of Power Station Automation Technology.

## References

1. Aihara, K., Takabe, T., Toyoda, M.: Chaotic Neural Networks. Phys. Lett. A, Vol. 144, Issue 6/7 (1990) 333–340
2. Chen, L., Aihara, K.: Chaotic Simulated Annealing by a Neural Network Model with Transient Chaos. Neural Networks, Vol. 8, Issue 6 (1995) 915–930
3. Chen, L., Aihara, K.: Global Searching Ability of Chaotic Neural Networks. IEEE Transaction on circuits and systems, Vol. 46, Issue 8 (1999) 974–993
4. Kunz, D.: Channel Assignment for Cellular Radio Using Neural Networks. IEEE Transactions on Vehicular Technology, Vol. 40, Issue 1 (1991) 188–193
5. Hayakawa, Y, et al.: Effects of the Chaotic Noise on the Performance of Neural Network Model for Optimization Problems. Phys. Rev. E, Vol. 51, Issue 4 (1995) 2693–2696
6. Wang, L, Zheng, D.Z.: A Kind of Chaotic Neural Network Optimization Algorithm Based on Annealing Strategy. Control Theory and Applications, Vol. 17, Issue 1 (2000) 139–142
7. He, Y.Y.: Chaotic Simulated Annealing with Decaying Chaotic Noise. IEEE Transactions on Neural Networks, Vol. 13, Issue 6 (2002) 1526–1531
8. Kwok,T, Smith, A.: A Unified Framework for Chaotic Neural Network Approaches to Combinatorial Optimization. IEEE Trans. on Neural Networks, Vol. 10, Issue (1999) 978–981
9. Funabiki, N, Takefuji, Y.: A Neural Network Parallel Algorithm for Channel Assignment Problems in Cellular Radio Networks. IEEE Trans. Veh. Technol., 41 (1992) 430–436
10. Kim, J.S, et al.: Cellular Radio Channel Assignment Using a Modified Hopfield Network. IEEE Transactions on Vehicular Technology, 46 (1997) 957–967

# A Capacitated Production Planning with Outsourcing: A General Model and Its Algorithm

X. Liu and J. Zhang

School of Business Administration, Northeastern University, P.R. China
xliu@mail.neu.edu.cn

**Abstract.** This paper addresses a capacitated production planning (CPP) problem with outsourcing. Specially, the outsourcing problem considered in this paper has the following features: (1) all demands are met by production, inventory, outsourcing, and sale loss without postponement or backlog; (2) The goal of the solution to this problem is to minimize the total cost covering the production, setup, inventory holding, sale loss, and outsourcing activities; (3) different from previous studies which usually involved some special assumptions on the cost function for these activities, the cost function structure we consider in this paper are arbitrary and time-varying; and (4) we consider a general problem situation where the production, inventory, and outsourcing have a capacity limitation. It is likely that there is no solution in the model due to the consideration of such general cost functions and many constraints, hence we employ a Bellman/Ford algorithm for checking feasible solutions of the problem and resulting in a feasible solution region. After that, a proposed algorithm is applied for searching a global optimal solution with in the feasible solution region.

## 1 Introduction

In general, there are four strategies to cope with the capacitated production planning (CPP) problem in their production planning: (1) the customer demands are met on time by production or inventory, (2) the demands are met by postponement or backlog (i.e., the demands are met in the future), (3) the demands are un-met (i.e. giving up the market opportunity), and (4) the demands are met by "paying" an extra cost through outsourcing. Nowadays more and more firms prefer to take the outsourcing strategy due to its potentially high promise.

The outsourcing problem is complex and has considerable implication to business firm. During the past several years, outsourcing has emerged to be an important management issue. It is claimed that philosophically, outsourcing suppliers can achieve high quality but low cost because they are specialized in relatively a professional and business category. This claim has led many firm's managers to enter into various types of sub-contracts with their outsourcing suppliers. Some firms have achieved success with their outsourcing strategies, but others have experienced dismal failures (Rochester and Dougles, 1990; 1993). One explanation for this uncertainty on outsourcing is the lack of decision models and tools to help managers systematically analyze an outsourcing decision.

D.-S. Huang, K. Li, and G.W. Irwin (Eds.): ICIC 2006, LNCS 4113, pp. 997 – 1002, 2006.

In the CPP problem without consideration of outsourcing, Wagner and Whitin (1958) did the first study on un-capacitated model with an $O(T^2)$ algorithm. Since then, extensive studies have been reported. A dynamic programming shortest path algorithm with constant production capacity and concave production and inventory holding cost functions has been shown to be polynomial solvable in $O(T^4)$ time by Florian and Klein (1971). Recently, Van Hoesel and Wagelmans (1996) showed that this bound can be improved to be $O(T^3)$. Florian et al. (1980) showed that the general capacitated lot sizing problem is NP-hard. Liu (2004) presented a pseudo polynomial with $O(TD^2)$ for the CPP problem with the most general cost function structure without outsourcing.

There are a few studies on the outsourcing CPP problem using analytical approaches. Lee and Hsu (2004) proposed a framework of outsourcing capacity planning for an IC design house, which does not reach the level of algorithms. Liu et al. (2005) considered an outsourcing model with special cost functions structure and showed that the model can be resolved in strongly polynomial time. Yang et al. (2005) proposed an optimal production-inventory-outsourcing policy with an independent stochastic demand, but they have not discussed the cost function structure.

Let us call an outsourcing CPP problem with the cost function being arbitrary the general outsourcing CPP problem in this paper. The study presented in this paper was to formulate a general outsourcing CPP model and allowed sale loss problem. The goal of the study is to tradeoff among such activities as production, inventory, outsourcing, and sale loss, and to minimize the total cost aggregated from these activities. The remainder of this paper is organized as follows: In section 2, the general outsourcing model will be formulated. In section 3, a dynamic programming approach is presented for searching a global optimal solution in a feasible solution space. Section 4 concludes the paper.

## 2 A General Outsourcing Model

The outsourcing problem can be stated that each demand $d_t$ must be entirely delivered at a period $t$ at expense of the outsourcing cost. In other words, a demand must be satisfied by production and/or inventory from previous periods and/or outsourcing and/or sale loss. Note that the outsourcing here also includes the utilization of additional internal capacities of a company, e.g., acquiring additional personnel and facilities. In this paper, for our general outsourcing CPP model, we consider that demands, capacities, and cost functions are all time-varying, and can be linear, concave, convex, or arbitrary form. Further, we consider not only production capacity but also inventory capacity as potential limiting factors, and we set limits on different outsourcing levels. The total cost of production activities over a set of periods needs to be minimized.

The following notation will be used throughout this paper.

$T$ : The number of periods indexed from 1 to $T$

$d_t$ : The demand at period $t$

$c_t$ : The production capacity at period $t$

$\bar{b}_t$ : The inventory capacity at period $t$
$\bar{O}_t$ : The upper level of outsourcing quantity at period $t$
$\underline{O}_t$ : The lower level (the minimum level) of outsourcing quantity at period $t$
$\bar{L}_t$ : The upper level of sale loss quantity at period $t$
$p_t(\cdot)$ : The production cost function at period $t$
$h_t(\cdot)$ : The inventory cost function at period $t$
$m_t(\cdot)$ : The outsourcing cost function at period $t$
$z_t(\cdot)$ : The sale loss cost function at period $t$
$X_t$ : The production level at period $t$
$O_t$ : The outsourcing level at period $t$
$L_t$ : The sale loss level at period $t$
$I_t$ : The inventory level at the end of period $t$

In the above, $X_t$, $O_t$, $L_t$, and $I_t$ are decision variables, $t = 1,2,...,T$. We make the following assumptions.

- The outsourcing strategy is taken under contract with alliance companies, and each alliance company has limited capacity which should be constrained by an upper bound and a lower bound of outsourcing quantity at period $t$;
- Sale loss are allowed, and the upper bound is $d_t$ at period $t$;
- All cost functions can be linear, concave, convex, or arbitrary;
- (4) $d_t \geq 0$, $t = 1,2,...,T$;
- Without the loss of generality, the inventory levels at both the initial time and the end of the period $T$ are 0.

The general outsourcing model can be formulated below:

$$Minimize \sum_{t=1}^{T} \left[ p_t(X_t) + h_t(I_t) + m_t(O_t) + z_t(L_t) \right] \tag{1}$$

$$\text{subject to:} \quad I_t - I_{t-1} = X_t + O_t + L_t - d_t \qquad t = 1,2,...,T \tag{2}$$

$$0 \leq I_t \leq \bar{b}_t \qquad t = 1,2,...,T \tag{3}$$

$$\underline{O}_t \leq O_t \leq \bar{O}_t \qquad t = 1,2,...,T \tag{4}$$

$$0 \leq L_t \leq \bar{L}_t \qquad t = 1,2,...,T \tag{5}$$

$$0 \leq X_t \leq c_t \qquad t = 1,2,...,T \tag{6}$$

$$I_0 = I_T = 0 \tag{7}$$

In the above, expression (1) represents the minimization of the total cost aggregated from the setup, production, holding, sale loss, and outsourcing activities. The constraints (2) represent the material balance with which to determine the inventory levels from the previous decision. The inventory level is within the lower and upper bounds by constraints (3). The constraints (4) represent that any outsourcing level cannot exceed the lower and upper bounds within that period, which is given based on the outsourcing supplier capacity. The constraints (5) represent that the sale loss quantity is less than the upper bounds within that period. The constraints (6) represent that the production quantity is less than the maximum production capacity within that period. Finally, without the loss of generality, the constraints (7) represent the fifth assumption.

# 3 Algorithms Development

## 3.1 Model Transformation

In the above model, i.e., expressions (1) - (7), there are four kinds of variables, namely $X_t$, $I_t$, $O_t$ and $L_t$. Among them, the three kinds of decision variables $X_t$, $O_t$ and $L_t$ should be associated with one kind of variables in order to solve the model more effectively. Let us define a new decision variable $V_t$ for $O_t$ and $L_t$, i.e., $V_t = O_t + L_t$. This new variable is called the middle virtual production level (MVPL) hereafter in this paper. Let $\xi_t(V_t)$ be the cost of MVPL at period $t$, where $\underline{O}_t \le V_t \le \overline{O}_t + \overline{L}_t$, we have $\xi_t(V_t) = \min_{\underline{O}_t \le O_t \le \min\{V_t, \overline{O}_t\}} \{z_t(V_t - O_t) + m_t(O_t)\}$. The original model of the problem can be transformed into the following equations:

$$Minimize \sum_{t=1}^{T} [p_t(X_t) + h_t(I_t) + \xi_t(V_t)] \tag{8}$$

subject to:

$$I_t - I_{t-1} = X_t + V_t - d_t \qquad t = 1,2,...,T \tag{9}$$

$$0 \le I_t \le \overline{b}_t \qquad t = 1,2,...,T \tag{10}$$

$$\underline{O}_t \le V_t \le \overline{O}_t + \overline{L}_t \qquad t = 1,2,...,T \tag{11}$$

$$0 \le X_t \le c_t \qquad t = 1,2,...,T \tag{12}$$

$$I_0 = I_T = 0 \tag{13}$$

Let us define a new decision variable $Q_t$ for $X_t$ and $V_t$, i.e., $Q_t = X_t + V_t$. This new variable is called the virtual production level (VPL) in this paper. Let $\mu_t(Q_t)$ be the cost of VPL at period $t$, where $\underline{O}_t \le Q_t \le c_t + \overline{O}_t + \overline{L}_t$. We have $\mu_t(Q_t) = \min_{\max\{0, \underline{O}_t\} \le X_t \le \min\{Q_t, c_t\}} \{\xi_t(Q_t - X_t) + p_t(X_t)\}$. The above model can be transformed into the following equations:

$$Minimize \sum_{t=1}^{T} [\mu_t(Q_t) + h_t(I_t)] \tag{14}$$

subject to:

$$I_t - I_{t-1} = Q_t - d_t \qquad t = 1,2,...,T \tag{15}$$

$$0 \le I_t \le \overline{b}_t \qquad t = 1,2,...,T \tag{16}$$

$$\underline{Q}_t \le Q_t \le c_t + \overline{O}_t + \overline{L}_t \qquad t = 1,2,...,T \tag{17}$$

$$I_0 = I_T = 0 \tag{18}$$

### 3.2 Feasible Solutions Checking

Due to relatively more constraints in the above model, not all $I_t$ which lies in range from 0 to $\overline{b}_t$ are feasible solutions; or it may happen that none of $I_t$ is a feasible solution. It should be useful to find a so-called actual feasible solution region, denoted as $\Omega_t$, as the searching for an optimal solution within $\Omega_t$. This can reduce the searching space and improve the efficiency of the algorithm. It is also understood that $\Omega_t$ is represented by a lower bound and an upper bound. The upper bound of $I_t$, namely $u_t$, can be checked and obtained by using Bellman/Ford algorithm; similarly, the lower bound of $I_t$, namely $l_t$, can be done using Bellman/Ford algorithm as well. For more details about how to check the feasible solutions in a region, we refer the reader to Liu (2004).

### 3.3 A Dynamic Programming Approach

For the above model of the problem, i.e., equation (14)-(18), we propose a dynamic programming approach to searching the global optimal solution within $\Omega_t$. Let $f_t(I)$ be the minimum total costs of production, inventory, outsourcing and sale loss from period 1 to $t$, such that the inventory level at the end of period $t$ is $I$. Note that $I$ is bounded by its lower bound $l_t$ and its upper bound $u_t$. By definition, we have the following recursive equation:

$$f_t(I) = \min_{LOW(t,I) \le Q \le UPP(t,I)} \{h_t(I) + \mu_t(Q) + f_{t-1}(I - Q + d_t)\} \tag{19}$$

$$\text{where} \quad LOW(t,I) = \max(\underline{Q}_t, I + d_t - u_{t-1}) \tag{20}$$

$$UPP(t,I) = \min(c_t + \overline{O}_t + \overline{L}_t, I + d_t - l_{t-1}) \tag{21}$$

which are the minimum and maximum production levels at $t$ so that the inventory level at period $t$ is $I$. The initial condition is $f_0(0) = 0$. The optimal solution corresponds to $f_T(0)$. The complexity of the algorithm is $O(TD^2)$ as well.

## 4 Conclusion and Future Work

This paper presented a general outsourcing model. Due to various constraints on the production, inventory, sale loss, and outsourcing levels, the actual feasible solution space would be rather smaller compared with the theoretical feasible solution space. This situation may offer an opportunity in the sense that an actual feasible solution region can be developed first, and then the searching for an optimal solution can be performed over that region. After a series of model transformation, an algorithm for searching a global optimal solution is proposed. The algorithm has the same computational complexity as the one presented by Liu (2004), but in this paper, the model includes outsourcing case. Specialized outsourcing models may be solved with more efficient algorithms in the future.

## Acknowledgments

This research is partially supported by the National Science Foundation of China (Grant No. 70571077 and 70431003) and Key Laboratory of Process Industry Automation, Ministry of Education, China.

## References

1. Rochester, J., Douglas, D (Eds).: Taking an Objective Look at Outsourcing. IS Analyzer. 28 (1990) 1-16
2. Rochester, J., Douglas, D (Eds).: New Wrinkles in IS Outsourcing. IS Analyzer. 31 (1993) 1-18
3. Wagner, H.M., Whitin, T.: Dynamic Version of the Economic Lot Size Model. Management Science, 5 (1958) 89-96
4. Florian, M., Klein, M.: Deterministic Production Planning with Concave Costs and Capacity Constraints. Management Science, 18 (1971) 12-20
5. VanHoesel, C.P.M., Wagelmans, A.P.M.: An $O(T^3)$ Algorithm for the Economic Lot-Sizing Problem with Constant Capacities. Management Science, 42 (1996) 142-150
6. Florian, M., Lenstra, J.K., RinnooyKan, A.H.G.: Deterministic Production Planning: Algorithm and Complexity. Management Science, 26 (1980) 669-79
7. Liu, X.: Models and Algorithms for Capacitated Lot Sizing Problems. Ph.D Thesis. Université de Technologie de Troyes, France (2004)
8. LeeHsu, S.C.L.: Outsourcing Capacity Planning for an IC Design House. International Journal of Advanced Manufacturing Technology, 24 (2004) 306-320
9. Liu, X., Wang, C., Luo, X., Wang, D.: A Model and Algorithm for Outsourcing Planning. IEEE International Conference on e-Business Engineering, Beijing, China, 18-21 October (2005) 195-198
10. Yang, J., Qi, X., Xia, Y.: A Production-Inventory System with Markovian Capacity and Outsourcing Option. Oper. Res., 53 (2005) 328-49

# A Case-Based Seat Allocation System for Airline Revenue Management

Pei-Chann Chang[1], Jih-Chang Hsieh[2], Chia-Hsuan Yeh[3], and Chen-Hao Liu[1]

[1] Department of Industrial Engineering and Management, Yuan-Ze University, Ne-Li, Tao-Yuan, Taiwan, R.O.C
iepchang@saturn.yzu.edu.tw, s929510@mail.yzu.edu.tw

[2] Department of Finance, Vanung University, Chung-Li, Tao-Yuan, Taiwan, R.O.C
hjc@vnu.edu.tw

[3] Department of Information Management, Yuan-Ze University, Ne-Li, Tao-Yuan, Taiwan, R.O.C.
imcyeh@saturn.yzu.edu.tw

**Abstract.** Airline companies usually implement revenue management to increase profits. The revenue management can be performed through seat inventory management. The current system to book seats is first-come first-served. This approach tends to sell low-price seats because low-price requests often appear earlier. It also results in low revenue. In this paper, an expected dynamic probability method and a case-based seat allocation system are proposed to enhance the performance of the seat inventory management. Extensive studies are conducted to compare the performance of first-come first-served method, expected dynamic probability method, and case-based decision support system. The result indicates that the case-based seat allocation system outperforms the other methods.

## 1 Introduction

Revenue is one of the most important indices for the management of airline industry. The practical situations of the revenue management in airline companies are complicated. Many dimensions have to be considered such as customer behavior, demand forecasting, control system, revenue factors, variable cost factors, fare products, problem scale, and problem interfaces. Besides these dimensions airline companies also own two characteristics, i.e. high fixed cost and perishable products. However, seat selling is nearly the only revenue. Therefore every airline is dedicated to develop various strategies to raise the performance of seat selling. Donaghy et al. (1995) reported that revenue management has been successfully adopted by the airline industry after deregulation in the late 1970's. With introducing revenue management airline companies actually raised the net profit. For example, American Airline earned a net profit of 450 million to 500 million in 1989 and United Airline made 100 million to 200 million net profits in 1990.

In the open literature, airline revenue management problems can be classified as forecasting, overbooking, pricing and seat inventory control. In this paper, we concern the issues on seat inventory control to implement the revenue management. Seat inventory control is to allocate the seats with respect to several fare classes in order to reach maximal revenue. The past works were interested in finding the optimal

D.-S. Huang, K. Li, and G.W. Irwin (Eds.): ICIC 2006, LNCS 4113, pp. 1003 – 1011, 2006.

allocation. Many researchers have proposed their ideas such as Brumelle et al. (1990), Weatherford (1991), Sun (1992), Wollmer (1992), Weatherford et al. (1993), Shaykevich (1994), Young and Van Slyke (1994), Bodily and Weatherford (1995), Robison (1995), Belobaba and Rpbison (1996), Brumelle and Walczak (1997), Kleywegt and Papastavrou (1998), Li and Oun (1998), Subramanian et al. (1999), Lautenbacher and Stidham (1999). These works focused on applying operations research-based tools to obtain optimal solutions for seat inventory control. Too many mathematical techniques sometimes may be not suitable for the real case applications. Therefore we intend to propose a heuristic instead of optimal solutions in this paper.

McGill and Van Ryzin (1999) indicated that in the forty years airline revenue management has evolved from low level inventory control methods to advanced information systems. To meet the requirement of advanced information system, an artificial technique, case-based reasoning (CBR) is applied in this research. Case-based reasoning decision support systems lately are applied to many application areas. Malek (1998) developed a case-based reasoning operation system for the plastic moulding injection process. Göker et al. (1998) developed a case-based CAD/CAM help-desk support system, HOMER. Göker and Roth-Berghofer (1999) for computer aided design in Mercedes-Benz. Although there were some successful applications of CBR proposed, the application of CBR to seat allocation for the airline industry is still interesting and no effort was ever done.

## 2 Problem Definition

It can be mastered for airline companies to make the most effective use of seat allocation through controlling booking conditions, which involves assigning the total number of fixed seats with the goal of finding out appropriate passengers to make the whole benefit maximum. The optimal distribution of seat inventory management is considered as a booking control strategy to decide whether the request is accepted or not when the booking demand is achieved. Because the booking requests of different fare classes can be provided at the same cabin seats, how to allocate the booking number of passengers from different fare classes is the main problem to be studied in the research. The booking process has been viewed as a single time period in the past, in which the total demand quantity of each fare class was considered as a single variable; that is, only the possible accumulated demand sum from a certain fare class before the close of booking was considered. The existence of the uncertainty hidden between each different fare class has been ignored. This type of question is dealt with by dynamic planning in Lee and Hursh's strategy model, but when the scope of problems becomes too big, the solutions are usually not so easy to be found.

CBR is used in this research to solve the decision problem of seat allocation. The decision whether or not to accept the request is based on the booking information in the past and of the time being. The role of the airline company has been changed from passively selling tickets to passengers to actively deciding whether or not to sell the tickets. A decision system of seat allocation has been well built to provide a reference for solving related problems in realistic cases faced by the airline companies.

The main focus in this research is on the seat allocation problem for a single leg. When each fare level is fixed and the number of cabin seats is known, the seat allocation problem is investigated without considering the influences of other competitive companies. It is hypothesized that the booking demand is of specific environment and seasons, which does not have periodical changes and the factor of season is excluded in this research. The hypotheses for controlling the booking for a single leg are:

1. The booking demand of each fare class is independent, and the demand probability is known.
2. Only the interior seat allocation planning of a single airline company is considered; the influences of other competitive companies are not taken into consideration.
3. The influence of passengers' number is not considered for the changing expenses.
4. If a booking request is declined, it is considered as a benefit loss. The possibility of rebooking will not be taken into consideration; that is, the rebooking will be considered as a new booking request.

### 2.1 Current Operation System

The case study company in this research is a well-known airline in Taiwan. It was set up in 1989. Up to date this company cooperates with foreign airlines in order to raise global competition. The current seat allocation policy they are using to deal with the passenger requests is by the first come first served rule (FCFS). The booking process is operated by professional staffs. The demand of any passenger, any fare class will be accepted as long as any available seat remaining. In other words, the current system rejects the requests only when there is no seat available. This system is able to control the seat allocation effectively however it is possible to cause loss if the staffs make the wrong decisions. Moreover, FCFS tends to make low revenue. To prevent from the man-made errors and low revenue, an expected dynamic probability method and a case-based seat allocation system are developed in this paper.

## 3 Decision Model for Airline Seat Management

Two heuristic methods are developed in this research. One is the expected dynamic probability method (EDP) and the other is the case-based seat allocation system (CBSAS)

### 3.1 Expected Dynamic Probability Method

The EDP requires two types of information to accept or reject a request. The first is the request information of each period and the other is the information of available seat(s). A formula is used to decide whether each request should be accepted or rejected and the formula is as follows:

$$F_t^n + f_{s-1}^{n-1} \geq 0^n + f_s^{n-1} \tag{1}$$

where

$n$ denotes period,

$s$ denotes a seat,

$F_i^n$ denotes the revenue of request $i$ at period $n$,

$f_s^{n-1}$ denotes the revenue of seat $s$ is still available at period $n$-1.

Therefore the formula represents the revenue of a request must be greater than the revenue of not selling this seat at the next period. The request distribution can be described by probabilities for each period. Considering fares and probabilities together produces expected revenue. This formula actually is using the expected revenue to make decisions to accept or reject the requests.

## 3.2 Case-Based Seat Allocation System

To promote the revenue of seat allocation for the case study company, CBSAS is developed. The system is depicted as Figure 1. And the procedure of CBSAS is constituted of four steps. The first step is case representation. The second step is cases retrieve. The third step is case adaptation and the last step is case storage. The detailed description of the steps is reported as follows.

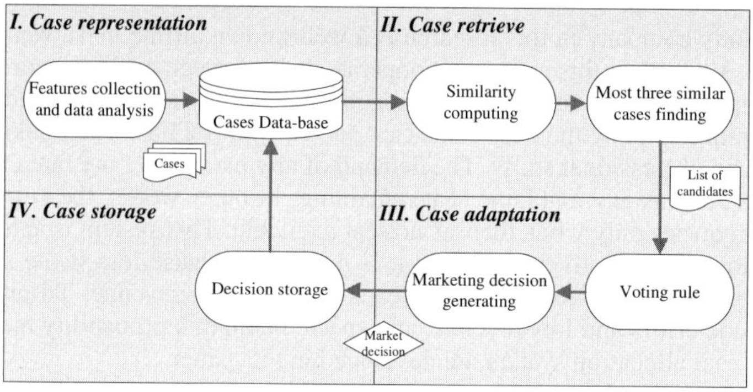


**Fig. 1.** Configuration of CBSAS

### 3.2.1 Case Representation

Each case is represented by five features, namely, period, fare class, arrival rate, available seats, decision. For example a case base is shown in Table 1.

**Table 1.** Case representation

| Period | Fare class | Arrival rate | Available seats | Decision |
|---|---|---|---|---|
| 20 | 3 | 2 | 100 | Accept |
| 15 | 2 | 1 | 30 | Accept |
| 3 | 1 | 1 | 0 | Reject |
| 1 | 3 | 5 | 6 | Accept |

### 3.2.2 Cases Retrieve

When a request shows, the CBSAS searches similar cases in the case base to make a decision whether the request should be accepted or rejected. As to how to measure the similarity, an idea comes from distance is proper. The shorter the distance between two cases is, the more similar the two cases are. Therefore distance is used to measure the similarity. Euclidean distance $S_{ij}(Q_i, C_j)$ between the request case and each case in the case base is calculated respectively.

$$S_{ij}(Q_i, C_j) = \sqrt{\sum_{k=1}^{4}(Q_{ik} - C_{jk})^2} \quad (2)$$

where

$Q_{ik}$ the *k*th feature of request *i*,

$C_{jk}$ the *k*th feature of case *j* in the case base,

$k$ index of features.

### 3.2.3 Case Adaptation

Similarities from the request to each case in the case base are calculated in the last step. The most three similar cases are retrieved. Then the voting rule is used to make a decision whether the request is to be accepted or not. The request is accepted if at least two decisions of the most three similar cases are "Accept" and vice versa.

### 3.2.4 Case Storage

Once the decision of the request has been made, it is also stored into the case base for the future use.

## 4 Numerical Experiments

Two scenarios are used to evaluate the proposed EDP and CBSAS. The first scenario is referred to the example in Lee and Hersh (1993). The second scenario is the real data from the case study company.

### 4.1 Scenario 1

The example from Lee and Hersh (1993) assumes four fare classes: 200, 150, 120, and 80. The number of booking period is 5. The request probability at each period is given in Table 2.

Ten simulations are executed. The results of each simulation and the average are shown in Table 3. The performance of current system is used as the benchmark. The percent improvement of EDP to FCFS and CBSAS are 12.4% and 16.9% respectively. It is evident that the proposed methods earn more revenue than the current system.

**Table 2.** Request probability at each period

| $P_k(t)$ | Period | | | | |
|---|---|---|---|---|---|
| | 1 | 2 | 3 | 4 | 5 |
| $P_1^n$ | 0.15 | 0.14 | 0.10 | 0.06 | 0.08 |
| $P_2^n$ | 0.15 | 0.14 | 0.10 | 0.06 | 0.08 |
| $P_3^n$ | 0.00 | 0.16 | 0.10 | 0.14 | 0.14 |
| $P_4^n$ | 0.00 | 0.16 | 0.10 | 0.14 | 0.14 |

**Table 3.** Simulation result by using example of Lee and Hersh (1993)

| # | FCFS | EDP | CBSAS | EDP(%) | CBSAS(%) |
|---|---|---|---|---|---|
| 1 | 38410 | 44110 | 43740 | 0.148399 | 0.138766 |
| 2 | 38050 | 41530 | 43820 | 0.091459 | 0.151643 |
| 3 | 39010 | 42770 | 44570 | 0.096386 | 0.142528 |
| 4 | 38310 | 42720 | 45150 | 0.115114 | 0.178543 |
| 5 | 38040 | 44290 | 45250 | 0.164301 | 0.189537 |
| 6 | 37800 | 41500 | 45350 | 0.097884 | 0.199735 |
| 7 | 38790 | 43230 | 44490 | 0.114462 | 0.146945 |
| 8 | 37070 | 43130 | 44480 | 0.163475 | 0.199892 |
| 9 | 39140 | 42710 | 44990 | 0.091211 | 0.149463 |
| 10 | 38080 | 44060 | 45440 | 0.157038 | 0.193277 |
| Avg. | 38270 | 43005 | 44728 | 0.123973 | 0.169033 |

## 4.2 Scenario 2

This example comes from the real data of the flight from Taipei to Hong Kong. There are two fare classes, 13800 and 10100. The number of booking periods is 6. The requests are summarized from the real data and modeled as four types of probability distribution.

*Type 1:* The request probability increases along with the booking period and the probability at each period is shown in Table 4.

*Type 2:* The request probability decreases along with the booking period and the probability at each period is shown in Table 5.

*Type 3:* The request probability increases first and then decreases. The request probability of each period is shown in Table 6.

*Type 4:* The request probability decreases first and then increases. The request probability of each period is shown in Table 7.

**Table 4.** Type 1 request probability

| $P_k(t)$ | Period | | | | | |
|---|---|---|---|---|---|---|
| | 1 | 2 | 3 | 4 | 5 | 6 |
| $P_1^n$ | 0.035 | 0.071 | 0.069 | 0.072 | 0.067 | 0.064 |
| $P_2^n$ | 0.235 | 0.245 | 0.262 | 0.271 | 0.267 | 0.265 |

**Table 5.** Type 2 request probability

| $P_k(t)$ | Period | | | | | |
|---|---|---|---|---|---|---|
| | 1 | 2 | 3 | 4 | 5 | 6 |
| $P_1^n$ | 0.051 | 0.123 | 0.154 | 0.134 | 0.147 | 0.156 |
| $P_2^n$ | 0.242 | 0.232 | 0.227 | 0.181 | 0.179 | 0.177 |

**Table 6.** Type 3 request probability

| $P_k(t)$ | Period | | | | | |
|---|---|---|---|---|---|---|
| | 1 | 2 | 3 | 4 | 5 | 6 |
| $P_1^n$ | 0.128 | 0.053 | 0.048 | 0.044 | 0.039 | 0.036 |
| $P_2^n$ | 0.243 | 0.276 | 0.284 | 0.284 | 0.276 | 0.268 |

**Table 7.** Type 4 request probability

| $P_k(t)$ | Period | | | | | |
|---|---|---|---|---|---|---|
| | 1 | 2 | 3 | 4 | 5 | 6 |
| $P_1^n$ | 0.043 | 0.002 | 0.037 | 0.059 | 0.053 | 0.057 |
| $P_2^n$ | 0.261 | 0.057 | 0.198 | 0.279 | 0.263 | 0.281 |

**Table 8.** Average revenue of each types of request probability

| Average revenue | FCFS | EDP | CBSAS |
|---|---|---|---|
| Type 1 | 3200940 | 3273830 | 3556880 |
| Type 2 | 3270870 | 3355600 | 3594250 |
| Type 3 | 3397410 | 3481030 | 3659000 |
| Type 4 | 3190580 | 3246080 | 3501750 |

The average revenue of each type is shown in Table 8. Both EDP and CBSAS perform better than the FCFS (the current system). In these numbers, it seems that no big gaps between FCFS v.s. EDP and FCFS v.s. CBSAS. However the result simply represents one flight. There are six flights each day. Therefore the annual revenue will be a meaningful number. It also indicates that the proposed EDP and CBSAS are effective.

In this paper, EDP and CBSAS are proposed to deal with the seat allocation problem in airline industry. Through the numerical validation, the proposed EDP and CBSAS are effective. In other words, both two methods earn more revenue than the current system.

## 5 Conclusion and Future Directions

Seat allocation directly relates to airline companies' benefits; therefore, how to promote passengers' demands and revenue management skills to increase the company's profits is a crucial issue. In order to make the passenger load factor and profit-gaining capacity higher, it is necessary to analyze the passengers' demands actively and control the seat allocation effectively. The research proposes two novel solutions for seat allocation planning, namely EDP and CBSAS. Through extensive numerical experiments, the proposed EDP and CBSAS are shown to be effective.

Several directions for future investigations can be suggested: 1. This research is based on a single-leg model; multi-leg problems can be further studied. 2. Only passengers of personal tickets are studied in the research. For further research, passengers of group tickets and those who purchase several tickets at the same time are suggested to be studied. 3. Building a database of passengers for research and analysis to study the customer's choice and purchasing model is recommended for effective airline yield management. 4. Magnificent results can be expected by applying the process of CBR proposed in the research to other industries.

## References


1. Belobaba, P.P., Weatherford, L.R.: Comparing Decision Rules that Incorporate Customer Diversion in Perishable Asset Revenue Management Situations. Decision Science. 27 (1996) 343–363
2. Bodily, S.E., Weatherford, L.R.: Perishable-asset Revenue Management: generic and multiple-price yield management with diversion. OMEGA. 23 (1995) 173–185
3. Brumelle, S., Walczak, D.: Dynamic Sllocation of Airline Seat Inventory with Batch Arrivals. Air Transport Research Group of the WCTR Society Proceedings, 3, Faculty of Commerce and Business Administration, University of British Columbia, Vancouver, Canada (1997)
4. Brumelle, S.L., McGill, J.I.: Airline Seat Allocation with Multiple Nested Fare Classes. Operations Research. 41 (1993) 127–137
5. Brumelle, S.L., McGill, J.I., Oum, T.H., Sawaki, K., Tretheway, M.W.: Allocation of Airline Seat Between Stochastically Dependent Demands. Transportation Science. 24 (1990) 183–192
6. Donaghy, K., McMahon, U., McDowell, D.: Yield Management: an overview. Int. J. Hospitality Management. 14 (1995) 139–150
7. Kleywegt, A.J., Papastravrou, J.D.: The Dynamic and Stochastic Knapsack Problem. Operations Research. 46 (1998) 17–35
8. Lautenbacher, C.J., Stidham, S.J.: The Underlying Markov Decision Process in the Single-leg Airline Yield Management. Transportation Science. 33 (1999) 136–146
9. Lee, T.C., Hersh, M.: A model for dynamic airline seat inventory control with multiple seat bookings. Transportation Science. 27 (1993) 252–265
10. Li, M.Z.F., Oum, T.H.: Seat Allocation Game on Flights with Two Fares. Division of Applied Economics, Nanyang Business School, Nanyang Technological University, Singapore (1998)
11. McGill, J.I., Van Ryzin, G.J.: Revenue Management: Research Overview and Prospects. Transportation Science. 33 (1999) 233–256
12. Pratte, N.: Automated Full Fare Protection System. AGIFORS Symposium Proceedings, 26, Bowness-On-Windermere, England (1986)
13. Robinson, L.W.: Optimal and Approximate Control Policies for Airline Booking with Sequential Nonmonotonic Fare Classes. Operations Research. 43 (1995) 252–265
14. Shaykevich, A.: Airline yield management: Dynamic Programming Approach. Master's thesis, Department of Operations Research, University of North Carolina, Chapel Hill, NC (1994)
15. Subramanian, J., Lautenbacher, C.J., Stidham, S.J.: Yield Management with Overbooking, Cancellations and No Shows. Transportation Science. 33 (1999) 147–167
16. Sun, X.: Airline yield management: A Dynamic Seat Allocation Model. Master's thesis, Faculty of Commerce, University of British Columbia, Vnacouver, Canada (1992)

17. Weatherford, L.R.: Perishable Asset Revenue Management in General Business Situations. Ph.D. thesis, Darden Graduate School of Business Administration, University of Virginia, Charlottesville, VA. (1991)
18. Weatherford, L.R., Bodily, S.E., Pfeifer, P.E.: Modeling the Customer Arrival Process and Comparing Decision Rules in Perishable Asset Revenue Management Situations. Transportation Science. 27 (1993) 239–251
19. Weatherford, L.R., Pfeifer, P.E.: The Economic Value of Using Advance Booking of Orders. OMEGA. 22 (1994) 105–111
20. Wollmer, R.D.: An Airline Seat Management Model for A Single Leg Route When Lower Fare Classes Book First. Operations Research. 40 (1992) 26–37
21. Young,Y., Van S. R.: Stochastic Knapsack Models of Yield Management. Technical Report 94-76, Polytechnic University, New York (1994)

# Feature-Weighted CBR with Neural Network for Symbolic Features

Sang Chan Park[1,2], Jun Woo Kim[2], and Kwang Hyuk Im[2]

[1] Graduate School of Culture Technology,
Korea Advanced Institute of Science and Technology (KAIST)
sangchanpark@kaist.ac.kr, apres@major.kaist.ac.kr,
gunni@major.kaist.ac.kr
[2] Department of Industrial Engineering,
Korea Advanced Institute of Science and Technology (KAIST)
373-1 Guseong-dong, Yuseong-gu, Daejeon, Korea 305-701

**Abstract.** Case-based reasoning (CBR) is frequently applied to data mining with various objectives. Unfortunately, it suffers from the feature weighting problem. In this framework, similar case retrieval plays an important role, and the *k*-nearest neighbor (*k*-nn) method or its variants are widely used as the retrieval mechanism. However, the most important assumption of *k*-nn is that all of the features presented are equally important, which is not true in many practical applications. Many variants of *k*-nn have been proposed to assign higher weights to the more relevant features for case retrieval. Though many feature-weighted variants of *k*-nn have been reported to improve its retrieval accuracy on some tasks, few have been used in conjunction with the neural network learning. We propose CANSY, a feature-weighted CBR with neural network for symbolic features.

## 1 Introduction

Case-based reasoning (CBR) is frequently applied to data mining with various objectives. CBR has common advantages over other learning strategies. It can be directly applied to classification without additional transformation mechanisms and has strength in learning the dynamic behavior of the system over a period of time. Unfortunately, it also has shortcomings to be applied to real world tasks. It suffers from the feature weighting problem. In this framework, similar case retrieval plays an important role, and the k-nearest neighbor (k-nn) method or its variants are widely used as the retrieval mechanism. However, the most important assumption of k-nn is that all of the features presented are equally important, which is not true in many practical applications. When CBR measures the distance between cases, some input features should be treated more important than other features.

Many variants of *k*-nn have been proposed to assign higher weights to the more relevant features for case retrieval. Though many feature-weighted variants of *k*-nn have been reported to improve its retrieval accuracy on some tasks [1],[2],[3], few have been used in conjunction with the neural network learning until Shin *et al.* proposed a hybrid approach of neural network (NN) and CBR named as MANN (Memory And Neural Network based learning) [4],[5],[6],[7]. We propose a CANSY,

D.-S. Huang, K. Li, and G.W. Irwin (Eds.): ICIC 2006, LNCS 4113, pp. 1012 – 1020, 2006.

an augmented MANN in symbolic domain. Value Difference Metric (VDM) presented by Stanfill and Waltz [8] is also augmented in this research. In various industries, we can survey customers' characteristics and preferences via questionnaire whose answers have symbolic features. Also, contextual data such as identity, location, entity has symbolic features. So, we adopted a modified VDM, which Scott Cost and Steven Salzberg [9] introduced, as the distance measure in symbolic domains.

## 2 MANN: A Numeric Feature Weighting Algorithm Using a Trained Neural Network

MANN adopts neural network and memory to realize an analogy to the human information processing system. After being trained, the neural network keeps its knowledge in the connection weights among the neurons. The neural network is expected to contain the intrinsic nature of the training dataset completely, and once the network is trained properly the training dataset itself is not utilized any more. However, the thinking process of human brain is apparently aided by the memory (the training dataset in the machine learning case) as well as the connection weights between neurons. In data mining 'memory' is realized in the form of database, which can store, query, and retrieve large amounts of data in a short time. Now database is the fundamental information resource in corporate information systems. It means that, with proper case retrieval methods, we can easily benefit from the abundant database. The approach uses the *k*-nearest neighbor (*k*-nn) method for case retrieval in CBR settings. *k*-nn assumes that each case $x = \{x_1, x_2, \ldots, x_n, x_c\}$ is defined by a set of $n$ features, where $x_c$ is $x$'s class value (discrete or numeric).

Given a query $q$ and a case library L, *k*-nn retrieves the set K of $q$'s $k$ most similar (i.e., of least distance) cases in L and predicts their weighted majority class value as the class value of $q$. Distance is defined as

$$D(x,q) = \sqrt{\sum_{f=1}^{n} W_f \times difference(x_f, q_f)^2} \cdot \quad (1)$$

where $w_f$ is the parameterized weight value assigned to feature $f$, and

$$difference(x_f, q_f) = \begin{cases} |x_f - q_f| & if \quad feature \ f \ is \ numeric \\ 0 & if \ feature \ f \ is \ symbolic \ and \ x_f = q_f \\ 1 & if \quad otherwise \end{cases} \cdot \quad (2)$$

## 3 Value Difference Metric (VDM)

In domains with symbolic features, the "overlap" metric is usually used, counting the number of features that differ [10]. However, it is observed that the overlap metric gives relatively poor performance in their learning tasks in symbolic feature domains. A new powerful metric for measuring the difference between two instances in domains with the symbolic features was proposed which was called value difference metric (VDM) by Stanfill and Waltz [8]. VDM takes into account similarity of feature values. The value difference metric is defined by (3).

$$\Delta(X,Y) = \sum_{i=1}^{N} \delta(x_i, y_i) \cdot \tag{3}$$

$$\delta(x_i, y_i) = d(x_i, y_i) w(x_i, y_i) \cdot \tag{4}$$

$$d(x_i, y_i) = \sum_{l=1}^{n} \left| \frac{D(f_i = x_i \cap g = c_l)}{D(f_i = x_i)} - \frac{D(f_i = y_i \cap g = c_l)}{D(f_i = y_i)} \right|^k \cdot \tag{5}$$

$$w(x_i, y_i) = \sqrt{\sum_{l=1}^{n} \left( \frac{D(f_i = x_i \cap g = c_l)}{D(f_i = x_i)} \right)^2} \cdot \tag{6}$$

$X$ and $Y$ are two instances. $x_i$ and $y_i$ are values of the $i^{th}$ feature for $X$ and $Y$. $N$ is the number of features and $n$ is the number of classes. $f_i$ and $g$ indicate the $i^{th}$ predicate feature and the class feature, respectively. $c_l$ is one of possible classes. $D(condition)$ is the number of instances in a given training dataset which satisfy the condition. $d(x_i, y_i)$ is a term for measuring the difference overall similarity between feature values $x_i$ and $y_i$. The term $\frac{D(f_i = x_i \cap g = c_l)}{D(f_i = x_i)}$ is the likelihood that an instance with $x_i$ of $i^{th}$ feature value will be classified as class $c_l$. $d(x_i, y_i)$ has a small value if two values give similar likelihoods for all possible classes and this means that two values are similar. Though Stanfill and Waltz used the value of $k$=2 in their equation, Cost and Salzberg observed that experiments indicated that equally good performance is achieved when $k$=1. We also used the value of $k$=1 for simplicity.

$w(x_i, y_i)$ measures the strength with which the $i^{th}$ feature constrain the values of the class. This measure represents the importance of each feature in classification. In our paper, we remove this term in order to give the same weight to features because the classification information is not given in clustering tasks. Our value difference metric in this paper is

$$\Delta(X,Y) = \sum_{i=1}^{N} \delta'(x_i, y_i) \cdot \tag{7}$$

$$\delta'(x_i, y_i) = d(x_i, y_i) = \sum_{l=1}^{n} \left| \frac{D(f_i = x_i \cap g = c_l)}{D(f_i = x_i)} - \frac{D(f_i = y_i \cap g = c_l)}{D(f_i = y_i)} \right| \cdot \tag{8}$$

## 4 CANSY : Feature-Weighted CBR with Neural Network for Symbolic Features

The learning system is consisted of three processes. The first process is evaluating the feature weight sets, which is extracted from the trained neural network. Before training the neural network, all of the symbolic features are transformed into binary features, which has $d$ original inputs ($x_i$, $i$=1,…,$d$), $E$ transformed binary input nodes ($b_i$, $i$=1,…,$E$), $M$ hidden nodes ($z_i$, $i$=1,…,$M$), and $c$ output nodes ($y_i$, $i$=1,…,$c$). Every output node represents one of possible values of the target feature, namely one of target classes. The number of output nodes is the number of possible values of the target feature.

When training of a neural network is finished, we obtain the feature weight set from the trained neural network using four feature weighting methods. The four feature weighting methods are Sensitivity, Activity, Saliency, and Relevance. Those methods calculate importance of each feature using the connection weights and activation patterns of nodes in the trained neural network.

- **Sensitivity**

Sensitivity of an input node is calculated by removing the input node from the trained neural network. A measure of sensitivity of an input feature is the difference of the error when the feature is removed and when it is left in place. The Sensitivity of an input feature $x_i$ is given by

$$Se_i = \frac{\left(\sum_L \left|P^o - P^i\right| / P^o\right)}{n}. \tag{9}$$

where $P^0$ is the normal prediction value for each training instance by the trained neural network and $P^i$ is the modified prediction value when the input i is removed. $L$ is the set of training data and $n$ is the number of training data.

- **Activity**

Activity of a node is measured by the variance of activation level for training data. When activity value of a node varies large according to its input value, the activity of the node is high. The activity of a hidden node $z_j$ is given by

$$A_j = \sum_{k=1}^{c} w_{kj}^2 \cdot \mathrm{var}\left(g\left(\sum_{l=1}^{d} w_{jl} b_l\right)\right). \tag{10}$$

where var() is the variance function. The activity of a binary input node $b_l$ is defined as

$$A_l = \sum_{j=1}^{M} w_{jl}^2 \cdot A_j. \tag{11}$$

and the activity of an input node $x_i$ is given by

$$A_i = \sum_{b_l \in x_i} A_l / n_i. \tag{12}$$

where $n_i$ is the number of values of $x_i$ input feature.

- **Saliency**

The saliency of a weight is measured by estimating the second derivative of the error with respect to the weight. They used the saliency measure to prune neural networks iteratively: that is, train to a reasonable error level, compute saliencies, delete low saliency weights, and resume training. The saliency of a binary input node $b_l$ is given by

$$Sa_l = \sum_{j=1}^{M}\sum_{k=1}^{c} w_{kj}^2 \cdot w_{jl}^2 \cdot \tag{13}$$

and the saliency of a input node $x_i$ is given by

$$Sa_i = \sum_{b_l \in x_i} Sa_l / n_i \cdot \tag{14}$$

- **Relevance**

It is reported that the variance of weights into a node is a good predictor of the node's relevance and that the relevance of a node is a good predictor of the increase in error expected when the node's largest weight is deleted. The relevance of a hidden node $z_j$ is given by

$$R_j = \sum_{k=1}^{c} w_{kj}^2 \cdot \mathrm{var}(w_{jl}) \cdot \tag{15}$$

and the overall relevance of a binary input node $b_l$ is

$$R_l = w_{jl} \cdot R_j \cdot \tag{16}$$

and the relevance of an input node $x_i$ is given by

$$R_i = \sum_{b_l \in x_i} R_l / n_i \cdot \tag{17}$$

**The second process** is constructing VDT (Value Different Tables) from the instances in the case base according to VDM, which defines the disances between different values of a given feature. For each feature, the value difference matrix is derived statistically based on the instances in the training dataset according to (18).
In fact, (18) is a simpler form of (8).

$$\delta(V_1, V_2) = \sum_{i=1}^{n} \left| \frac{C_{1i}}{C_1} - \frac{C_{2i}}{C_2} \right| \cdot \tag{18}$$

Where $V_1$ and $V_2$ are two possible values for the feature and $n$ is the number of classes. $C_{1i}$ is the number of times $V_1$ was classified into class i and $C_1$ is the total number of times value 1 occurred. The term $C_{1i}/C_1$ is the likelihood that an instance will be classified as class $i$ given that its $i_{th}$ feature has value $V_1$. Thus (18) computes overall similarity between two values by finding the sum of the difference of the likelihood over all classifications.

**The third process** is case-based reasoning using feature weights extracted from the trained neural network and VDT constructed by VDM. If a query is given, the distances between the query and the cases is

$$\Delta(q, x) = \sum_{i}^{N} w_i \delta(q_i, x_i)^r \cdot \tag{19}$$

where q is the query and x is a case from the case base, , qi and xi are the ith feature values of q and x, respectively. The system classifies the new instance following the closest cases from the case base. wi is the weight of the ith input feature. δ(qi,xi) is the distance between two values qi and xi of the ith input feature. r is usually set to 1 or 2 according to the case bases. In this paper, we set r = 1 for all of our experiments.

If a query is not contained existing case base, it becomes new case. Knowledge update manager (KUM) adds new case to case base and train neural network for new case. KUM takes the role of providing new cases for on-line learning. Old cases may just take unnecessary storage space in case base and delay searching similar cases. In a dynamic situation like manufacturing, old cases may even hinder CBR from correct prediction.

# 5 CANSY : Validation

To validate our system, we apply our methods to two datasets from the UCI machine learning repository. In this experiment, we created a neural network with one hidden layer. To train it, we applied the gradient descent algorithm with momentum & adaptive learning rate, which is implemented in MATLAB. Sensitivity, Activity, Salience and Relevance methods are used and for calculating the distance between two symbolic features. We compare the performance of our methods to that of the simple k-nearest neighbor (k-nn) algorithms without feature weighting. The experiments are repeated 10 times for each dataset and in every experiment. We evaluate the performance of all methods according to k, the number of nearest neighbors which, in our experiments, takes odd numbers from 1 to 15. Table 1 shows the experimental settings for the problems.

**Table 1.** Datasets and neural network settings

| | Datasets | | | | Neural Network | |
|---|---|---|---|---|---|---|
| **Problem** | **Training Instances** | **Test Instances** | **Attributes** | **Output Classes** | **# of Hidden Nodes** | **Training Goal** |
| **Monk's-1** | 124 | 432 | 6 | 2 | 2 | 0.01 |
| **Voting Records** | 300 | 135 | 16 | 2 | 4 | 0.01 |

## 5.1 Monk's Problem

The learning task is to generalize a binary classification, robots belong either to this class or not, with a subset of all 432 possible robots give classes. The domain has been partitioned into a train dataset and test dataset. The neural network has 2 hidden neurons. Table 2 shows the experimental results. 'Uniform' column shows the errors of the CBR without feature weighting, that is, pure *k*-nn. Because we experiment with uniform method once, 'Uniform' column has no variance. The next four columns show the mean errors and the variances of the errors of the four method of the CBR with the proposed symbolic feature weighting. Figure 1 shows the prediction accuracy of the feature weighting methods according to *k*. In this problem, the proposed weighting methods show better prediction accuracy than uniform method. The difference in the prediction accuracy of the four feature weighting methods-the Sensitivity, Activity, Saliency, and Relevance, is very small and the trend in the change of the errors according to k is also similar.

**Table 2.** The Monk's-1 problem – Mean errors and variances of weighting

| K | Uniform | Sensitivity | Activity | Saliency | Relevance |
|---|---|---|---|---|---|
| 1 | 0.1296 | 0.0576±0.0250 | 0.0215±0.0213 | 0.0231±0.0216 | 0.0234±0.0219 |
| 3 | 0.1759 | 0.1086±0.0114 | 0.0826±0.0130 | 0.0829±0.0139 | 0.0824±0.0147 |
| 5 | 0.2083 | 0.1273±0.0160 | 0.1012±0.0081 | 0.1014±0.0086 | 0.1016±0.0102 |
| 7 | 0.2269 | 0.1410±0.0061 | 0.1306±0.0077 | 0.1306±0.0075 | 0.1303±0.0076 |
| 9 | 0.2315 | 0.1435±0.0127 | 0.1289±0.0120 | 0.1308±0.0129 | 0.1306±0.0138 |
| 11 | 0.2315 | 0.1630±0.0043 | 0.1660±0.0016 | 0.1662±0.0015 | 0.1662±0.0015 |
| 13 | 0.2546 | 0.1667±0.0000 | 0.1667±0.0000 | 0.1667±0.0000 | 0.1667±0.0000 |
| 15 | 0.2500 | 0.1667±0.0000 | 0.1667±0.0000 | 0.1667±0.0000 | 0.1667±0.0000 |

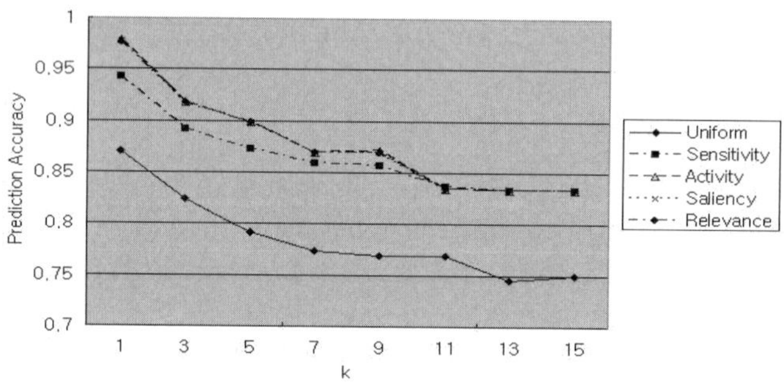


**Fig. 1.** The Monk's-1: Classification accuracy of feature weighting methods

## 5.2 Congressional Voting Records Database

This is the 1984 United States Congressional Voting Records Database. This data set includes votes for each of the U.S. House of Representatives Congressmen on the 16 key votes. All of the instances are classified into one of 2 classes, democrat or republican. We repeated the experiment 10 times and in every experiment and divided the 435 instances into a training dataset and a test dataset of 300 and 135, respectively. Table 3 is the experimental results. The neural network had 4 hidden neurons

**Table 3.** The Voting Records database – Mean error of feature weighting methods

| K | Uniform | Sensitivity | Activity | Saliency | Relevance |
|---|---|---|---|---|---|
| 1 | 0.0615±0.0201 | 0.0556±0.0172 | 0.0563±0.0168 | 0.0541±0.0178 | 0.0533±0.0143 |
| 3 | 0.0474±0.0117 | 0.0407±0.0106 | 0.0415±0.0062 | 0.0415±0.0062 | 0.0415±0.0062 |
| 5 | 0.0526±0.0118 | 0.0393±0.0093 | 0.0400±0.0080 | 0.0378±0.0107 | 0.0378±0.0107 |
| 7 | 0.0541±0.0111 | 0.0385±0.0104 | 0.0393±0.0086 | 0.0385±0.0109 | 0.0393±0.0105 |
| 9 | 0.0563±0.0157 | 0.0400±0.0112 | 0.0385±0.0115 | 0.0385±0.0104 | 0.0393±0.0099 |
| 11 | 0.0578±0.0147 | 0.0385±0.0120 | 0.0378±0.0128 | 0.0385±0.0115 | 0.0393±0.0121 |
| 13 | 0.0578±0.0125 | 0.0385±0.0120 | 0.0385±0.0120 | 0.0393±0.0105 | 0.0393±0.0105 |
| 15 | 0.0593±0.0126 | 0.0393±0.0105 | 0.0393±0.0105 | 0.0393±0.0105 | 0.0400±0.0112 |

We can scc that the four feature weighting methods outperform the pure k-nn in every datasets. Especially, when k is greater than 3, the difference in the prediction accuracy between the pure k-nn and proposed weighting method is very large. Figure 2 shows the prediction accuracy of the feature weighting methods according to k.

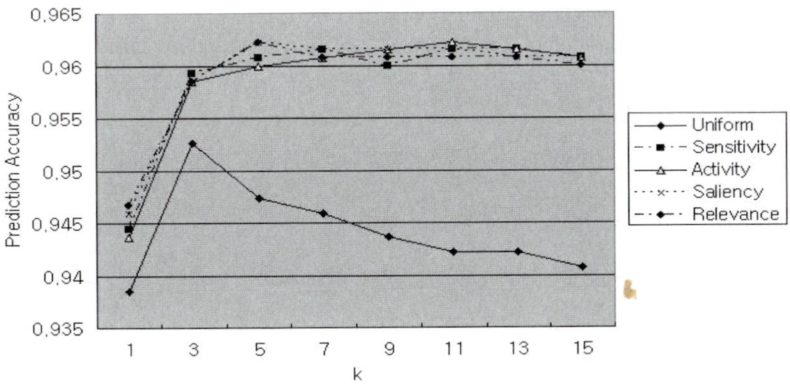


**Fig. 2.** The Voting Records: Classification accuracy of feature weighting methods

In pure k-nn, the prediction accuracy changes according to change of k. On the contrary, the four feature weighting methods prevent the decay of the prediction accuracy with the increase of k. The difference in the prediction accuracy of the four feature weighting methods is very small and the trend in the change of the errors according to k is also similar as you can see in Figure 2.

## Acknowledgement

This research is supported by KAIST Graduate School of Culture Technology.

## References

1. Wettschereck, D., Aha ,D. W.:Weighting Features, In Proc. ICCBR-95. A. Aamodt, M. Veloso, Eds (1995)347-358
2. Hastie ,T., Tibshirani, R.:Discriminant Adaptive Nearest Neighbor Classification, Int J IEEE Trans. Pattern Anal. Machine Intell., Vol. 18 (1996)607-616
3. Wettschereck, D., Aha, D.W., Mohri, T.:A Review and Empirical Evaluation of Feature Weighting Methods for a Class of Lazy Learning Algorithms, AI Rev., Vol. 11 (1997) 273-314
4. Shin, C.K., Yun, U.T., Kim, H.K., Park, S.C.:A Hybrid Approach of Neural Network and Memory-Based Learning to Data Mining, Int J IEEE Trans. on Neural Networks, Vol. 11, No. 3 (2000) 637-646
5. Yu, S.J., Shin, C.K., Park, S.C.:Memory-and Neural Network-Based Expert System: A Unified Approach, Encyclopedia of Microcomputers, Vol. 27, No. 6 (2001)287 - 303
6. Park, J.H., Im, K.H., Shin, c.K., Park, S.C.:MBNR: Case-Based Reasoning with Local Feature Weighting by Neural Network, Applied Intelligence, Vol. 21, No. 3 (2004)265 - 276
7. Im, K.H., Kim, T.H., Park, S.C.:Hybrid System of Case-Based Reasoning and Neural Nework for Symbolic Features, Lecture Notes in Computer Science, Vol. 3589 (2005)265 - 274
8. Stanfill,.C., Waltz, D.:Toward Memory-based Reasoning, Communications of the ACM. Vol. 29, No. 12 (1996) 1213-1228
9. Cost. S., Salzberg, S.:A Weighted Nearest Neighbor Algorithm for Learning with Symbolic Features, Machine Learning, Vol. 10 (1993)57-78
10. Ming, T. K.:Discretization of Continuous-Valued Attributes and Instance-Based Learning, Technical Report, No. 491, Basser Department of Computer Science University of Sydney, NSW 2006, Australia (1994)

# Object Detection Using Context-Based Cascade Classifier

Mi Young Nam and Phill Kyu Rhee

Dept. of Computer Science & Engineering Inha University
253, Yong-Hyun Dong, Incheon, Nam-Gu, South Korea
rera@im.inha.ac.kr, pkrhee@inha.ac.kr

**Abstract.** The face images are varying environment database from external illumination. Therefore we propose parallel cascade face detector. We define context image illumination and distinguish context using unsupervised learning. Many unsupervised method is available to distinguish varying illuminant images. This approach can be distribution face image and we can make the classifier for face image context. Therefore, in this paper, we parallel classifier that is strutted cascade classifier of two methods. In first classifier, we use sub-sampling feature extraction and in second classifier we use wavelet transformation method. We achieved very encouraging experimental results. Our method is enhancement varying illumination environment.

## 1 Introduction

Captured images are dynamic from CCD and PC Camera, so we propose the method that is robust changing illumination images. In this paper context is defined face illumination. As environment context changes, it is identified by the multiple context fusion, and the detection scheme is restructured. The detection scheme is restructured to adapt to changing environment and to perform an action that is appropriate over a range of the change. In this paper, propose method is to explore the possibility of environment-insensitive face detection by adopting the concept of parallel context classifier. Much research has been done to solve this problem [1,2 3,5,6].

Recently, the concept of context-awareness has been applied for robust face detection under dynamically changing environments [7]. In this paper, we propose parallel cascade classifier for the adaptive detection scheme using illumination, color, texture information. We employ K-means for the context modeling and awareness. Because K-means is the highest performance other unsupervised methods. This method is suitable to distinguish face images because that is uniformity distributed shape. It provides the capacity of the high level attentive process by the environment context-awareness in face detection.

The outline of this paper is as follows. In section 2, we will present the architecture of the proposed parallel cascade face detector. Proposed face detector system will be discussed in section 3 and 4. We will give experimental results in section 5. Finally, we will give concluding remarks.

## 2 Context Based Cascade Face Detection Architecture

In this session, we present environment modeling and identification using multiple contexts such as context from illuminant clustering.

D.-S. Huang, K. Li, and G.W. Irwin (Eds.): ICIC 2006, LNCS 4113, pp. 1021 – 1029, 2006.

### 2.1 Illumination Context-Awareness

Environment context is analyzed and identified using the K-means. It is hybrid method of supervised and unsupervised learning method. The idea is to train the network in two separate stages. First, we perform a statistical method to determine the Gaussians' parameters (j, j). In the second stage, the multiplicative weights $w_{kj}$ are trained using the regular supervised approach. Input pattern is vectorized for image size of 20x20 sizes, input node had mosaic of size of 10x10 pixels. 10x10 images is converted 1x100 vectors.

### 2.2 Parallel Cascade Face Detection Architecture

Fig. 4 shows context based face detection architecture. Context is divided five clusters. A Bayesian classifier is produced for each illumination context. We have modeling four Multi class based Bayesian classifiers are made in five groups for face.

#### 2.2.1 First Classifier Modeling

We extract face feature by sub-sampling that is made vector sum of 2 x 2, 3 x 3, 4 x 4 and 5 x 5 subset for face image size of 20 x 20.

We extracted 54-dimensional feature from facial images using sub-regions. Face in search window is encoded to 54-dimensional vector which including hierarchical intensity information.

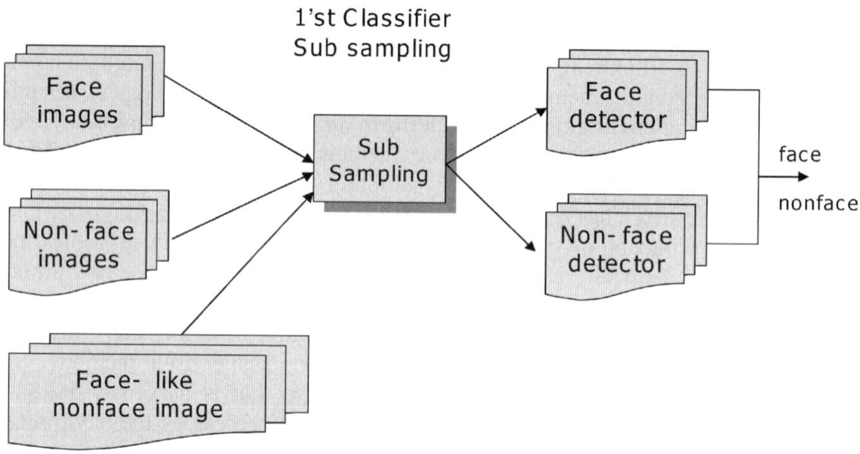


**Fig. 1.** A first classifier in cascade for face detection

#### 2.2.2 Second Classifier Modeling

We also take advantage of the information of frequency domain using Haar wavelet transform. It is organize the image into sub-bands that are localized in orientation and frequency. In each sub-bands, each coefficient is spatially localized. We use a wavelet transform based on 3 level decomposition producing 10 sub-bands. Generally, low frequency component has more discriminate power than higher. Also too high component has some noisy information. Then we use 3 level decomposition of Haar wavelet transform. The K-means is used for the texture context-awareness using Haar wavelet transform.

Table 1 and Table 2 are clustering result by using FART when feature extracting method is used gray law label value and Haar wavelet.

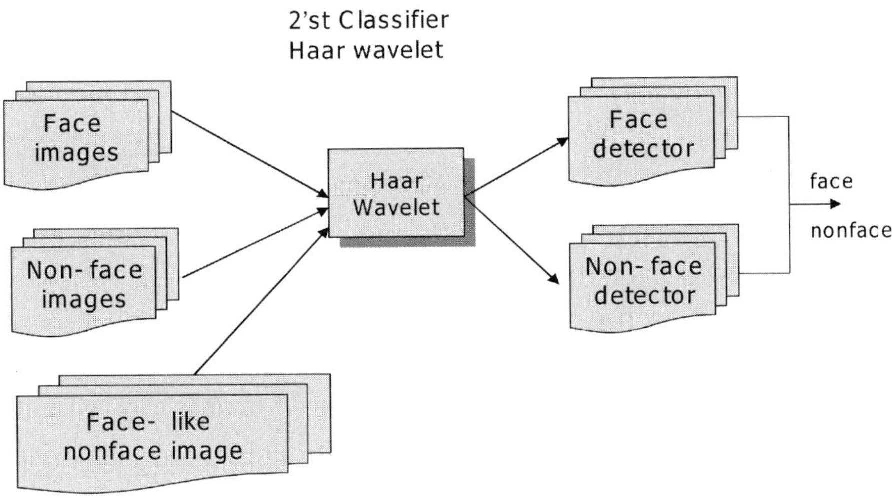


**Fig. 2.** A second classifier in cascade for face detection

**Table 1.** FART clustering result by using gray label features

| Cluster | 0 | 1 | 2 | 3 |
|---|---|---|---|---|
| Number of Image | 4 | 1 | 7559 | 68 |

**Table 2.** FART clustering result by using Haar Transform features

| Cluster | 0 | 1 | 2 |
|---|---|---|---|
| Number of Image | 3 | 7600 | 29 |

We used context modeling following database (as shown table 1). We distinguish FERET database structure to 3 layer illumination image. Next we have clustering, and we integrated nine clusters to six cluster.

| Light Direction | Brightness | Class | Count |
|---|---|---|---|
| Right | Bright | 1 | 500 |
| | Dark | 2 | 500 |
| | Normal | 3 | 500 |
| Left | Bright | 4 | 500 |
| | Dark | 5 | 500 |
| | Normal | 6 | 500 |
| Center | Bright | 7 | 500 |
| | Dark | 8 | 500 |
| | Normal | 9 | 500 |
| Total | | | 4,500 |

**Fig. 3.** K-means clustering results

Fig. 3 shows K-means clustering results in FERET face image database. We can see that data each cluster is equality. Therefore we decide that clustering algorithm is K-means.

## 3 Proposed Face Detection Schema

The specific task we are discussing in this paper is a robust face detector which is adaptive against changing illumination environments. The system consists of the multi-resolution pyramid, parallel cascade dace detector, finally detector results combination using cluster correlation. Clustering is made by k-means for varying illuminant face images.

In this paper, we proposed method, parallel cascade Bayesian classifier as shown in Fig. 1. The details will be discussed in the following.

In the proposed method, the feature space for face detection with multiple scales and varying illumination condition has been partitioned into subspaces properly so that face detection error can be minimized. However, the partitioning of multiple scales is very subjective and ambiguous in many cases. The multi-resolution pyramid generates face candidate region. Pyramid method based face detection is attractive since it could accumulate the face models by autonomous learning process. In our approach, the face object scale is approximated with nine steps. In this module, 20×20 windows are generated. A tradeoff must be considered between the size of multiple scales, view representation of the object and its accuracy. Finally, multi-context based Bayesian is in a multi classifier structure by combining several Bayesian classifiers. Each Bayesian classifier is trained using face images in each environment context category. Face candidate windows are selected using the multi-context based Bayesian classifiers, and finally face window is filtered by the merging process.

In the learning stage, the candidate face regions are clustered into 4 face models, 6 face-like non-face models, non-face models using combined learning algorithm [10], the threshold parameters of multiple Bayesian classifiers are decided. Initially, seed appearance models of face is manually gathered and classified for training the detector module. The detector with prior classes is trained by the initial seed data set.

## 4 Multiple Context Based Bayesian Classifiers

We show that illumination context based Bayesian face modeling can be improved by strengthening both contextual modeling and statistical characterization. Multiple Bayesian classifiers are adopted for deciding face and non-face.

Initially, seed appearance models of face is manually gathered and classified for training the appearance detector module. Each detector, Bayesian classifier here, with prior classes is trained by the training data set [11, 12]. Training set of faces is gathered and divided into several group in accordance with illumination contexts. Multi-resolution pyramid consists of nine levels by an experiment, and the offset between adjacent levels is established by four pixels. Each training face image is scaled to 20x20 and normalized using the max-min value normalization method, and vectorized. Since the vectorization method affects much to face detection performance, we have tested several vectorization methods and decided 54 dimensional hierarchical vectorization methods.

**Modeling of Face and Nonface**

We assume that distributions of face and nonface samples form the shape of Gaussian distribution. The likelihood of face and nonface can be modeled as multivariate normal distribution as (1).

$$p(\mathbf{x} \mid \omega_i) = \frac{1}{(2\pi)^{d/2} |\boldsymbol{\Sigma}_i|^{1/2}} \exp\left[ -\frac{1}{2} (\mathbf{x} - \boldsymbol{\mu}_i)^t \boldsymbol{\Sigma}_i^{-1} (\mathbf{x} - \boldsymbol{\mu}_i) \right]. \tag{1}$$

$\mathbf{x}$ is the $d$-dimensional feature, $\Sigma_i$ is the covariance matrix of the samples, and $\boldsymbol{\mu}_i$ is the $d$-dimensional mean vector.

**Choosing Face-Like Nonfaces and Post Processing**

We choose face-like nonface samples from 23 natural images. The method choosing face-like nonface samples is based on squared Mahalanobis distance from face class. In post processing, we eliminate overlapped face windows as the number of neighborhoods. We can preserver the location with more number of detection, and remove locations with less detections

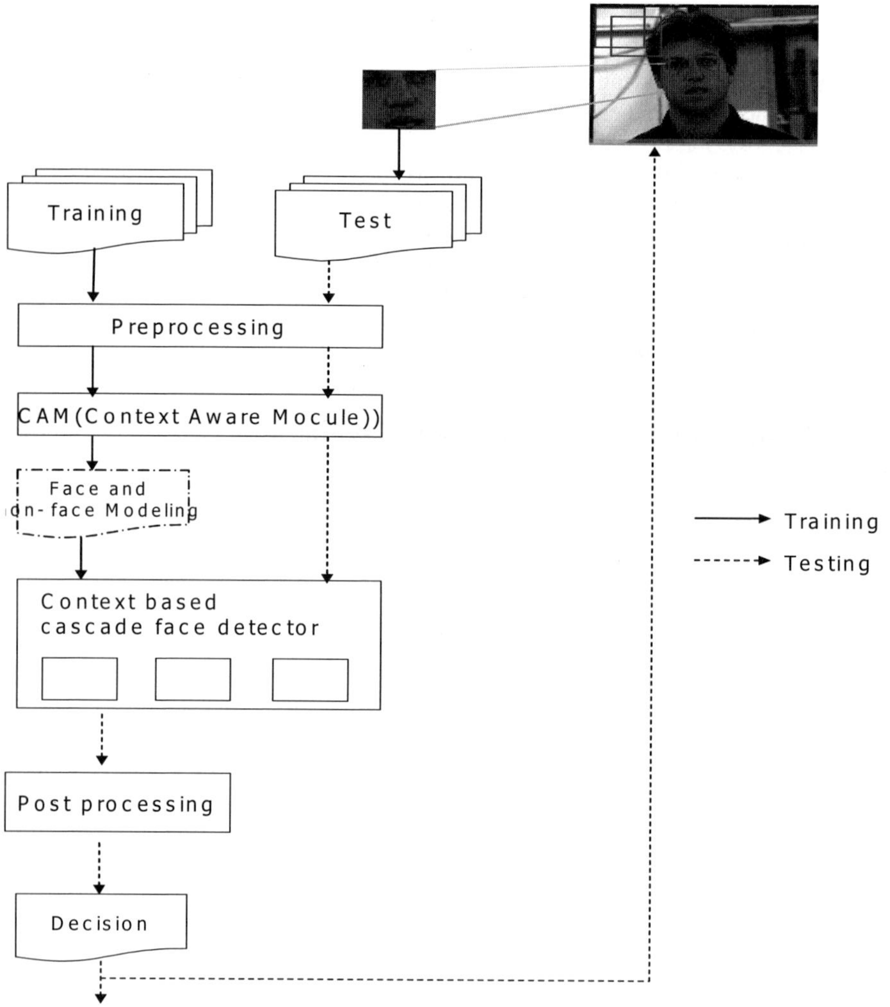


**Fig. 4.** Proposed face detection system architecture

## 5 Experiment

We used face images from feret database, and training image has size of 20x20. In this paper, vectorization use two methods from sub sampling and 3 levels Haar wavlet. The experiment has been performed with images captured in various environments 1000 images are captured. Fig.5 shows face detection in real-time image by using the proposed parallel cascade face detectors and single context-based Bayesian methods.

Face detection result shows Table 3-4. Images have size of 320 x 240 pixels and encoded. Each face is normalized into a re-scaled size of 20x20 pixels and each data is preprocessed by histogram equalization and max-min value normalization. Table 3 shows that the result of face detection between multi context-based Bayesian and single context based Bayesian in our lab gray images. Table 4 shows that the result of face detection between multiple context based Bayesian and single context based Bayesian in FERET fafb dataset.

**Fig. 5.** Examples face detection in color image

**Table 3.** The face detection our lab gray images

| Method | Total Image | Accept Rate | False Accept Rate |
|---|---|---|---|
| Context-based Cascade Bayesian | 1000 | 980 | 22 |
| Single Context Model | 1000 | 905 | 46 |

**Table 4.** Face detection result in FERET dataset normal images

| Method | Total Image | Accept Rate | False Accept Rate |
|---|---|---|---|
| Context-based Cascade Bayesian | 1196 | 1194 | 8 |
| Single Context Model | 1196 | 1130 | 40 |

Table 5 shows that the result of face detection between multiple context based Bayesian and single context based Bayesian in FERET fafc dataset include dark illuminant image.

**Table 5.** Face detection result in FERET dataset dark images

| Method | Total Image | Accept | False Accept Rate |
|---|---|---|---|
| Context-based Cascade Bayesian | 194 | 193 | 1 |
| Normal Context Model | 194 | 130 | 45 |

From Tables, we know that propose method is good face detection performance other method. In this experiment, illuminant images were considered. We classified varying illumination images into the image including a partially lighted face, good images into that including a nearly uniformly lighted face. Our proposed method is high performance more than other method, and is robust low resolution image and low lighting face images. Fig. 6 shows ROC graph in CMU 117 face images.

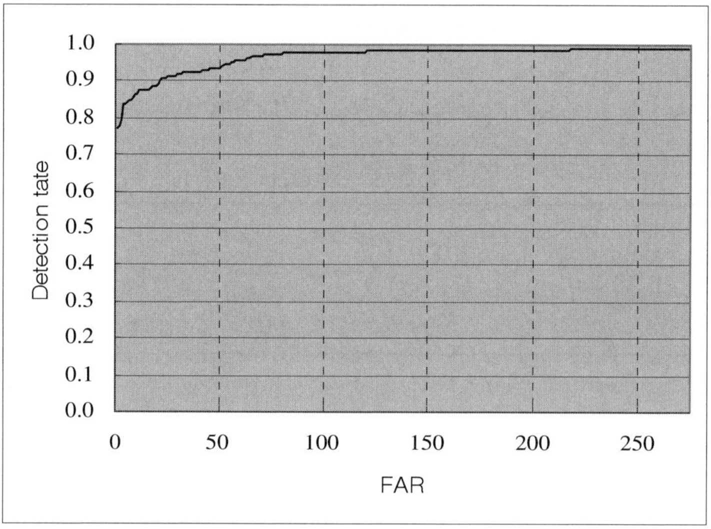


**Fig. 6.** ROC curve

# 6 Concluding Remarks

In this paper, we proposed a parallel cascade detection scheme by feature-based method with the capability of context-awareness. We define context that has been resolved by K-means because K-means clustering has the highest performance. That is clustering to priority probability in experimental result. For high performance face detection in varying environment, we proposed parallel cascade face detector. Parallel face detector is made integration single cascade face detector. And single face detector is construct two classifiers, they are sub-sampling based Bayesian face detector and wavelet based face detector. We can enhancement the face detection rate and reduce false detection rate.

## References


1. Yang, M.-H., Ahuja, N., Kriegman, D.: Mixtures of Linear Subspaces for Face Detection, Proc. Fourth Int'l Conf. Automatic Face and Gesture Recognition, (2000) 70-76
2. Yang, M.-H., Roth, D., Ahuja, N.: A SNoW-Based Face Detector, Advances in Neural Information Processing Systems 12, S.A. Solla, T. K. Leen, and K.-R. Muller, MIT,Press, (2000) 855-861
3. Erik B.K.L., Hjelmas.: Face Detection A Survey, Computer Vision and Image Understanding, Vol. 3, No.3 (2001) 236-274
4. Pham, T. V., et. Al.: Face detection by aggregated Bayesian network classifiers, Pattern Recognition Letters, 23 (2002) 451-461
5. Li, S.Z., Zhenqiu, Z.: FloatBoost learning and statistical face detection, Pattern Analysis and Machine Intelligence, IEEE Transactions on, Vol.26 (2004) 1112 – 1123
6. Liu, C.: Bayesian Discriminating Features Method for Face Detection. IEEE Trans. Pattern Analysis and Machine Intelligence, Vl. 25, No. 6 (2003) 725-740
7. Schneiderman, H. , Kanade, T.: Object Detection Using the Statistics of Parts, Int'l J. Computer Vision, Vol. 56, No. 3 (2004) 151- 177
8. Nam, M.Y., Rhee, P.K.: A Scale and Viewing Point Invariant Pose Estimation, KES2005 (2004) 833-842
9. Maio, D., Maltoni, D.: Real-time Face Location on Gray-scale Static Images. Pattern Recognition, Vol.33, No.9 (2000) 1525-1539
10. Viola, P., Jones, M.: Robust Real Time Object Detection. IEEE ICCV Workshop Statistical and Computational Theories of Vision, (2001)
11. Li, S.Z., Zhu, L., Zhang, Z.Q., Blake, A., et. Al.: Statistical Learning of Multi-View Face Detection, Proc. European Conf. Computer Vision, Vol. 4 (2002) 67-81

# Research on a Case-Based Decision Support System for Aircraft Maintenance Review Board Report

Ming Liu, Hong Fu Zuo, Xian Cun Ni, and Jing Cai

Civil Aviation College, Nanjing University of Aeronautics and Astronautics, Nanjing 210016, China
{Ming.Liu, Hong Fu.Zuo, Xian Cun.Ni, Jing.Cai}, lmnxc@163.com

**Abstract.** Aircraft Maintenance Review Board Report (MRB Report) is necessary one of the most important Continuing Airworthiness documents. Determination Maintenance interval in MRB Report depends mainly on experience and there isn't a rigorous and quick method. The paper proposes a multi-stage framework for determination maintenance interval using case-based reasoning (CBR), which uses fuzzy generalized nearest-neighbor matching (FNN) to retrieve case and fuzzy Group decision making to determine attributes' weight. An example illustrates the proposed approach and the average relative error is under 3.21%. Finally the developed civil aircraft CBR-MRBR decision support system is described. The method enriches the MRB Report developing method.

## 1 Introduction

Continuing Airworthiness documents require, when the aircraft Type Certificate is issued, the presenter should produce MRB Report. MRB Report is approved by the Regulatory Authority in establishing initial scheduled maintenance tasks and intervals for new types of aircraft and/or Power Plant. In the literatures, there are a few papers about how to determine maintenance tasks in civil aircraft MRB Report [1][2]. The method to determine maintenance tasks is mainly based on Maintenance Steering Group (MSG) logic method. The method to determine maintenance intervals mainly relies on the engineer experience. Most new products are improved from old ones, their structures, functions, working conditions, function failure and failure effects have certain similarities, and some products have standard systems. There isn't maintenance knowledge in the developing new aircrafts. Therefore analysts consult the experience of resemble aircrafts. The kind of idea is the same as case-based reasoning (CBR). CBR is a method of solving a new problem by using or adapting solutions to old problems. So the paper proposes to determine maintenance interval using CBR.

The paper is organized as follows. A multi-stage framework for determining intervals using CBR is briefly described in Section 2. In the section also, every stage about case representation, selection and adaptation & retention is presented in detail. An instance is given in Section 3. Section 4 describes the developing CBR-MRBR decision support system. Finally, some conclusions and future works are drawn in Section 5.

D.-S. Huang, K. Li, and G.W. Irwin (Eds.): ICIC 2006, LNCS 4113, pp. 1030 – 1039, 2006.

## 2 The Proposed Framework to Determine Maintenance Interval

The method for determining the scheduled maintenance tasks of Systems/ Power Plants (including components and APU's) MRB Report uses a progressive logic diagram. This logic is the basis of evaluating each maintenance significant item (MSI) including system, sub-system, module, component, accessory, unit, part, etc. Principally, the evaluations are based on the item's functional failures and failure causes. After determining the maintenance tasks, we propose a multi-stage framework based on CBR as shown in Fig.1.

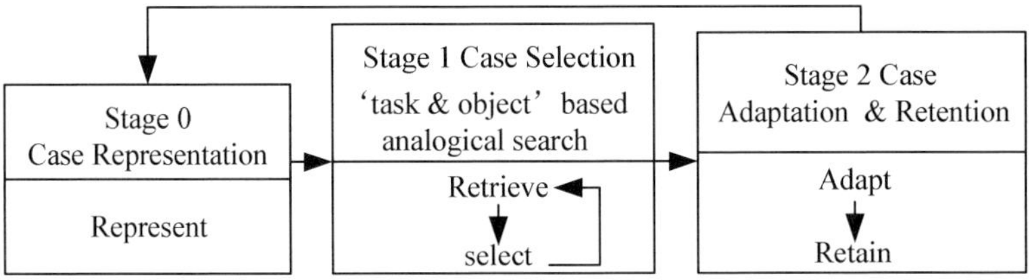


**Fig. 1.** A multi-stage framework for case-based reasoning decision analysis

### 2.1 Stage 0: Case Representation

Maintenance interval cases include plenty of MSG analysis knowledge. It is difficult to describe the whole knowledge in detail during case representation. Therefore we mainly research "task and object" based analogical case and pick up main attributes concerned with maintenance intervals. These attributes are divided into two classes:

①maintenance object knowledge: MSI NO., MSI name, structure, manufacturer, function.

②maintenance task knowledge:

Task category: Lubrication or Servicing; Operational or Visual Check; Inspection or Functional Check; Restoration; Discard.

Failure Effect Category (FEC): 5-evident safety; 6-evident operational; 7-evident economic; 8-hidden safety; 9-hidden economic.

These attributes should be preprocessed, such as one qualitative attribute has one kind of description. The MSI name is the case name and the case is stored in hierarchy, which is expressed as:

$$Case= (P_1, P_2 \ldots P_i \ldots P_m; I) . \tag{1}$$

Where $P_i = (a_{i1}^c, a_{i2}^c, \ldots a_{ij}^c, \ldots a_{in}^c; I_i^c)$ represents *i*th case, *n* is the total number of attributes in a case; $a_{ij}^c$ is the *j*th attribute value of the retrieved case *i*; $I_i^c$ is the interval attribute value of the *i*th retrieved case.

### 2.2 Stage 1: Case Selection

Stage 1 is concerned with the selection of relevant cases, which is a key step and hotspot matter of CBR research. 'Task and object' based analogical search includes case retrieval and selection, among which the well known methods for case retrieval [3][4][5][6][7] are: Nearest Neighbor, induction, knowledge guided induction and template retrieval. Nearest Neighbor is the most widely used in CBR applications. Considering the non-linear similarity, aircraft complexity and human fuzzy thought, we propose a fuzzy generalized nearest-neighbor (FNN) matching to compute case similarity.

#### 2.2.1 FNN Method to Determine Interval Similarity

Through plenty of data computations, we find, when computing attribute similarity, that there is a strengthened favorable effect when the attribute is important and the similarity measure on this attribute is high; there is an strengthened adverse effect when similarity measure is low and weight is important; it weakens the weighted similarity measure to prevent an unimportant attribute from dominating the overall similarity when the similarity measure on this attribute is high. Therefore, a Non-linear similarity formula is shown below.

$$l_i = \sqrt{[w_i \cdot s(a_i^t, a_i^c)]^k} \ . \tag{2}$$

Where $w_i$ is normalized for denoting the importance of the *i*th attribute towards the determination of overall similarity; $s(a_i^t, a_i^c)$ is pair-wise similarity measure of the *i*th attribute of target problem T and an case C. (low, medium, high) and (light, medium, important) are linguistic terms defined on $s(a_i^t, a_i^c)$ and $w_i$, respectively. The membership functions for the linguistic terms of $s(a_i^t, a_i^c)$ and $w_i$ are shown in Fig.2. *k* is the exponent of the distance function for the corresponding target and retrieved attribute values. *k* value is shown in table 1.

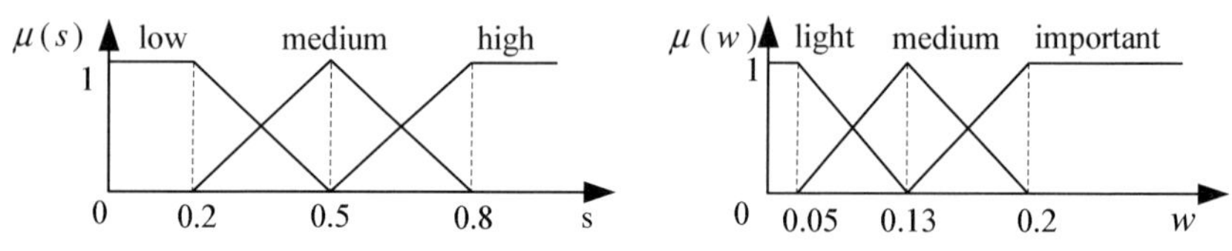


**Fig. 2.** Membership functions of the linguistic terms of the similarity measure(*s*) and weight(*w*)

**Table 1.** *k* value

| Rule *j* | If $w_i$; $s(a_i^t, a_i^c)$ | Then *k* |
|---|---|---|
| 1 | important; high | 1 |
| 2 | important; low / light; high | 4 |
| 3 | others | 2 |

(1) Calculation $s(a_i^t, a_i^c)$

$$s(a_i^t, a_i^c) = 1 - \frac{\left|a_i^t - a_i^c\right|}{(MAX_i - MIN_i)} \quad . \tag{3}$$

For quantitative/numerical attributes, $a_i^t$ and $a_i^c$ are the *i*th attribute of the target problem and the old case, respectively. $MAX_i$ and $MIN_i$ are the maximum and minimum values of the *i*th attribute respectively. For qualitative/symbolic attributes, $s(a_i^t, a_i^c)$ can be represented using the formula:

$$s(a_i^t, a_i^c) = \begin{cases} 1, a_i^t = a_i^c \\ 0, \text{otherwise} \end{cases} \quad . \tag{4}$$

(2) Determination weight $w_i$

The attribute weights can be determined by experts. To reflect all the options of the experts including, Administrator, Operator and Manufacturer, this study uses the fuzzy group decision making weighting method. The fuzzy weights of the attribute can be determined as follows:

$$\begin{cases} \tilde{w}_i = [w_{il}, w_{im}, w_{ir}], i = 1 \sim n \\ w_{il} = \min\{w_{ik}\}, \forall i, k = 1 \sim p, p = 3 \\ w_{im} = \text{geomean}\{w_{ik}\}, \forall i, k \\ w_{ir} = \max\{w_{ik}\}, \forall i, k \end{cases} \quad . \tag{5}$$

Where *n* denotes the total number of attributes, *p* represents number of experts, $w_{ik}$ is the weight of attribute *i* judged by expert *k*, $w_{il}$ denotes the minimum weight of attribute *i* judged by all of the experts, $w_{im}$ represents the average weight of attribute *i* judged by all the experts, and $w_{ir}$ is the maximum weight of attribute *i* judged by all the experts.

Next we should 'defuzzify' the fuzzy weight numbers into crisp values based on the concept of the Chen and Hwang method [8][9]. The crisp score of a fuzzy number $\tilde{w}_i$ is expressed as follows:

$\tilde{w}_i = [w_l, w_m, w_r]$, $0 < w_l < w_m < w_r$. The membership triangular function for $\tilde{w}_i$ is defined as follows:

$$\mu_{\tilde{w}_i}(x) = \begin{cases} \dfrac{(x - w_l)}{(w_m - w_l)}, w_l \le x \le w_m \\ \dfrac{(x - w_r)}{(w_m - w_r)}, w_m \le x \le w_r \\ 0, \text{ other} \end{cases} \tag{6}$$

The right score is determined using:

$$R_S = \sup_x [u_{max}(x) \wedge \mu_{\tilde{w}_i}(x)] \ . \tag{7}$$

The left score is determined using:

$$L_S = \sup_x [u_{min}(x) \wedge \mu_{\tilde{w}_i}(x)] \ . \tag{8}$$

Where a maximizing set and a minimizing set are:

$$\mu_{min}(x) = \begin{cases} 1 - x, 0 \le x \le 1 \\ 0, \text{otherwise} \end{cases} \ .$$

$$\mu_{max}(x) = \begin{cases} x, 0 \le x \le 1 \\ 0, \text{otherwise} \end{cases} \ .$$

the total crisp score of $\tilde{w}_i$ is determined using:

$$w_i^{'} = \frac{R_S + 1 - L_S}{2} \tag{9}$$

Next $w_i^{`}$ should be standardization disposal using:

$$w_i = \frac{w_i^{'}}{\sum_{i=1}^{n} w_i^{'}} \ . \tag{10}$$

(3) Overall similarity assessment
Similarity measures along qualitative attributes and quantitative attributes are aggregated to obtain a synthetic similarity. Aggregation of similarity measures of quantitative attributes is formulated as

$$f(w_i, s(a_i^t, a_i^c)) = \frac{\sum_{j=1}^{3} v_j l_j}{\sum_{j=1}^{3} v_j} \ . \tag{11}$$

$$S_A(T, C) = \sum_{i \in A} f(w_i, s(a_i^t, a_i^c)) \ . \tag{12}$$

For each rule, $v_j$ is determined by aggregating the truth values (i.e., membership values) of all linguistic terms through algebraic product, such as the first rule expression is

$$v_1 = \mu_{important}(\omega_i) \cdot \mu_{high}(s(a_i^t, a_i^c)) \ . \tag{13}$$

If $w_i$ is important and $s(a_i^t, a_i^c)$ is high, then $v_1$=1.

$f(\cdot)$ is a nonlinear function of $w_i$ and $s(a_i^t, a_i^c)$ .

$l_j$ is the weighted similarity measure adjusted by the user under the conditions prescribed in the premise of the *j*th rule.

$S_A(T,C)$ is an overall quantitative attributes similarity of the target problem T and an old case C, A is the set of quantitative attributes.

Aggregation of similarity measures of qualitative attributes is formulated as

$$S_L = \sum_{i=1}^{h} w_i \cdot s(a_i^t, a_i^c) \ . \tag{14}$$

Where $h$ is the total number of qualitative attributes.

The total similarity assessment function is then reformulated as

$$S(T, C) = S_L + S_A(T, C) \ . \tag{15}$$

### 2.2.2 "Task and Object" Based Analogical Case Selection

Case selection can be processed using the formula as:

$$S(T, C) \geq \omega, \ 0 \leq \omega \leq 1 \ . \tag{16}$$

Where $\omega$ is the similarity threshold value. The subset of "task and object" based analogical cases can be changed by varying the value of $\omega$. The maintenance task and object of the selected cases must be just the same as the target case, otherwise we omit the selected cases.

## 2.3 Stage Two: Case Adaptation and Retention

There are various ontological classifications of case adaptation methods based on different criteria [10][11][12], each adaptation method has its applicable qualification, it is difficult to provide a general guideline for formulating case adaptation rules. For maintenance interval matter, null adaptation applies if the retrieved case matches entirely with the target problem, which is a special instance. In most circumstances it is about imperfectness match and several cases are worthy references, so we adopt compositional adaptation policy.

After selecting similar cases using the above mentioned FNN methods, the similarity of target problem and case can be considered as the similarity of interval between target problem and case. Therefore, the interval of target problem can be received by resolving attribute similarity formulation (3). However, formulation (3) cannot be resolved when there is only one the most similar case. Therefore, for the selected similar cases, another method is adopted to calculate attribute similarity via formula (17), and then case similarity $S(T,C_j)$ is calculated.

$$s(a_i^t, a_i^c) = 1 - \frac{(a_i^t - a_i^c)}{a_i^t} \ . \tag{17}$$

Formulation (17) can be rewritten as adaptation formulation (18).

$$\begin{cases} I' = \dfrac{1}{n} \sum_{j=1}^{n} I_j \\ I_j = \dfrac{I_j^c}{S(T, C_j)} \end{cases} \ . \tag{18}$$

where $I_j$ is the interval calculated by the *j*th case, $I_j^c$ is the maintenance interval of the *j*th case, $S(T,C_j)$ is the similarity between target problem T and case $C_j$. The interval is disposed using formula (19):

$$I=INT(\frac{\grave{I}}{500}+0.5)\times 500 \tag{19}$$

The premise applying formula (19) shows that the task interval is 500 multiple which is in favor of the maintenance task pack. The formula can be changed with the actual need.

**Table 2.** Partial cases originality data

| C | NO. | MN | EM | ED | ET | EB | EB | EC | F |
|---|---|---|---|---|---|---|---|---|---|
| | *l* | *l* | *l* | *l* | *a* | *a* | *a* | *l* | *l* |
| 1 | 7220 | Fan section | CFM1 | CFM56-5B8 | 21600 | 6 | 5250 | 1F+4L,9H | 6 |
| 2 | 7220 | Fan section | CFM1 | CFM56-5B9 | 23300 | 6 | 5250 | 1F+4L,9H | 6 |
| 3 | 7220 | Fan Section | CFM1 | CFM56-5A4 | 22000 | 6 | 4995 | 1F+3L,9H | 6 |
| 4 | 7220 | Fan Section | CFM1 | CFM56-5A5 | 23500 | 6 | 4995 | 1F+3L,9H | 6 |
| 5 | 7220 | Fan Section | CFM1 | CFM56-5B5 | 22000 | 6 | 5250 | 1F+4L,9H | 6 |
| 6 | 7220 | Fan Section | CFM1 | CFM56-5B6 | 23500 | 5.9 | 5250 | 1F+4L,9H | 6 |
| 7 | 7220 | Fan Section | CFM1 | CFM56-5B4 | 26500 | 6 | 4995 | 1F+3L,9H | 6 |
| 8 | 7220 | Fan Section | CFM1 | CFM56-5B4 | 27000 | 5.7 | 5250 | 1F+4L,9H | 6 |
| 9 | 7220 | Fan Section | CFM1 | CFM56-5B1 | 30000 | 5.5 | 5250 | 1F+4L,9H | 6 |
| 10 | 7220 | Fan Section | CFM1 | CFM56-5B2 | 31000 | 5.5 | 5250 | 1F+4L,9H | 6 |
| 11 | 7220 | Fan Section | CFM1 | CFM56-5B3 | 33000 | 5.4 | 5250 | 1F+4L,9H | 6 |
| 12 | 7231 | Fan module | IAE | V2500-A1 | 25000 | 5.4 | 5074 | 1F+3L,10H | 6 |
| 13 | 7220 | Fan Section | CFM1 | CFM56-7B18 | 19500 | 5.5 | 5257 | 1F+3L,9H | 6 |
| 14 | 7220 | Fan Section | CFM1 | CFM56-7B20 | 20600 | 5.4 | 5257 | 1F+3L,9H | 6 |
| 15 | 7220 | Fan Section | CFM1 | CFM56-7B24 | 24200 | 5.3 | 5257 | 1F+3L,9H | 6 |
| 16 | 7220 | Fan Section | CFM1 | CFM56-7B26 | 26300 | 5.1 | 5257 | 1F+3L,9H | 6 |
| 17 | 7220 | Fan Section | CFM1 | CFM56-7B27 | 27300 | 5.1 | 5257 | 1F+3L,9H | 6 |
| 18 | 7220 | Fan Section | CFM1 | CFM56-5-A1 | 25000 | 6 | 4995 | 1F+3L,9H | 6 |
| 19 | 7220 | Fan Section | GE | CF34-8C1 | 12670 | 4.9 | 2335 | 1F,10H | 9 |
| 20 | 7220 | Fan Section | GE | CF34-8C5 | 13690 | 4.9 | 2335 | 1F,10H | 9 |
| 21 | 7221 | Fan wheel | RR | AE3007A | 7580 | 5.3 | 1608 | 1L,14H | 9 |
| 22 | 7220 | Fan Section | CFM1 | CFM56-7B22 | 22700 | 5.3 | 5257 | 1F+3L,9H | 6 |

Case NO.-C; MSI NO.-NO.; MSI Name-MN; Engine Manufacturer -EM; Engine Designation-ED; Engine take off thrust (lb)-ET; Engine Bypass ratio-EB; Engine Basic weight (lb)-EB; Engine Compressor stages-EC; FEC-F; *l* -qualitative attribute; *a* -quantitative attribute

# 3 Experiments

We have validated above methods using many tests. Now taking fan section in ATA72 (engine) as an example. At first one of maintenance tasks is determined as: detailed inspection of fan blades, that is, the maintenance task and object are "detailed inspection" and fan blade, respectively. The original data of partial retrieved cases are shown in Table 2; these cases are the same maintenance task category and object as the target problem. We selected$\omega$=0.90. Table 3 lists the CBR results of many tests. The average relative error is under 3.21%, then the interval is disposed using formula (19) and maintenance tasks are packed, so the result is reliant according to Table 3 and the maintenance interval error is entirely rational and receivable for the aircraft preliminary MRB Report.

**Table 3.** Test results

| Test | Case similarity | CBR Interval | Relative Error (%) |
|---|---|---|---|
| 1 | 0.9733 | 1027.484 | 2.748 |
| 2 | 0.9619 | 1039.6626 | 3.966 |
| 3 | 0.961 | 1015.9854 | 1.599 |
| 4 | 0.9453 | 1032.708 | 3.271 |
| 5 | 0.9827 | 1017.6354 | 1.764 |
| 6 | 0.9637 | 1037.8217 | 3.782 |
| 7 | 0.9541 | 1048.1826 | 4.818 |
| 8 | 0.9541 | 1030.2155 | 3.022 |
| 9 | 0.9541 | 1039.1991 | 3.92 |
| | Average relative error (%) | | 3.21 |

# 4 System Realizations

Using above CBR methods, we develop CBR-MRBR decision support system. The developing tool is Visual C++, Data Base (DB) uses Microsoft SQL Server and Case Base (CB) includes many air types' data. The structure of CBR-MRBR is shown in Fig.3.

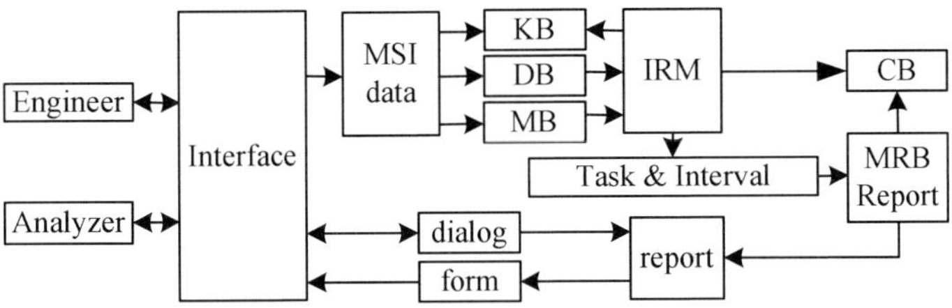


**Fig. 3.** CBR-MRBR Structure

System working process is as follows: in the prophase, the engineer and analyzer build MSI database, similar aircraft Case Base and Knowledge Base (KB) including MSG analysis knowledge; in the middle phase, the integration reasoning machine (IRM) determines MSI maintenance tasks using the knowledge in the KB and DB, then retrieves in the CB, and reasons to receive the satisfying maintenance interval, so develops the preliminary System MRB Report and stores the case in the Case Base. In the anaphase, CBR-MRBR creates or prints MRB Report and all kinds of forms according to users' requirements. What's more, alone with aircraft application data gathering, maintenance interval modeling is done which is stored in the model base (MB) and used to amend the maintenance interval previously. It forms a closed loop of producing MRB Report. Fig.4 is the interface of maintenance task result and Fig.5 is the interface of determination intervals.

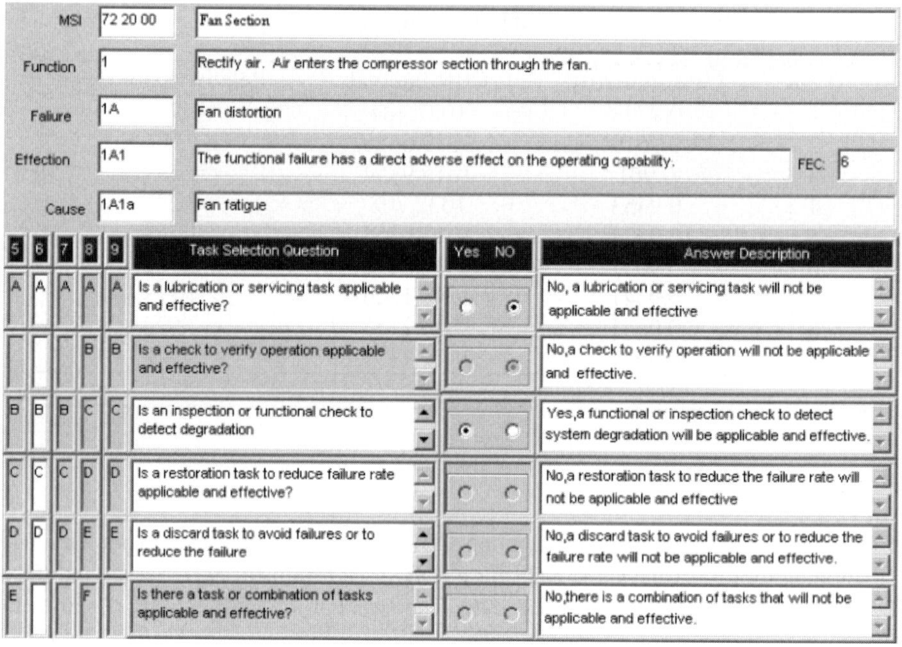


**Fig. 4.** Maintenance task result

## 5 Conclusions and Future Works

The paper proposed a multi-stage framework for determination maintenance intervals in aircraft MRB Report using CBR, which uses fuzzy generalized nearest-neighbor matching (FNN) to retrieve case and fuzzy Group decision making to determine attributes' weight. What's more, we adopted compositional adaptation policy to adapt cases. The approach applies especially to the detailed design period of developing new aircrafts without prototypes.

We illustrated the proposed approach in Engine fan section. The average relative error is under 3.21%, which is receivable for the aircraft preliminary MRB Report. Later we developed the CBR-MRBR decision support system, which realized the intelligence of computer-aided MRB Report and improved the efficiency of MRB Report job.

What's more, the maintenance tasks and intervals generated by the CBR-MRBR system should be submitted to the aircraft Industry Steering Committee for review and approval.

Future work will be focused on developing the whole MRB Report using CBR. The information needed to determine optimum intervals is ordinarily not available until the aircraft is put into service. The difficulty of establishing "correct" intervals for maintenance tasks is essentially an information problem and an issue that persists throughout the operating life of the equipment.

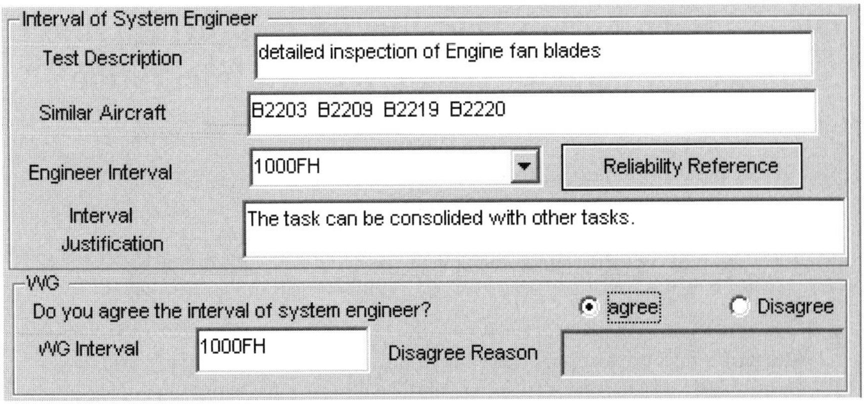


**Fig. 5.** Determine interval result

## References


1. Air Transport Association, Inc.: ATA MSG-3 Operator/Manufacturer Scheduled Maintenance Development. (2003) 15-47
2. Airbus Industry: A318/A319/A320/A321 Maintenance Program Development Policy and Procedures Handbook. (2001)
3. Liao, T.W. , Zhang, Z.: Similarity Measures for Retrieval in Case-based Reasoning Systems. Applied Artificial Intelligence. 12 (1998) 267~288
4. Watson, I., Mariri, F.: Case-Based Reasoning: A Review. Knowledge Engineering Review. 9 (1994) 327-54
5. Bergmann, R.: Experience Retrieval. Lecture Notes in Artificial Intelligence, Vol. 2432. Springer-Verlag Berlin Heidelberg (2002) 187-218
6. Cheng, C.-B.: A Fuzzy Inference System in Case-based Reasoning Systems: An Application to Product Design. Mathematical and Computer Modeling, 38 (2003) 385-394
7. San Pedro, J., Burstein, F.: A Framework for Case-Based Fuzzy Multicriteria Decision Support for Tropical Cyclone Forecasting. In: Proceedings of the 36th Annual Hawaii International Conference on System Sciences (2003)
8. Opricovic, S., TZENG, G-H.: Defuzzification within a Multicriteria Decision Model. International journal of uncertainty, 11 (2003) 635-652
9. Chen, S. J., Hwang, C.L.: Fuzzy Multiple Attribute Decision Making: Methods and Applications, Springer-Verlag (1992) 86-100
10. Mitra, R., Basak, J.: Methods of Case Adaptation: A Survey. International journal of intelligent systems, (2005) 20(6): 627-645
11. Chang, C.G., Cui, J.J., Wang, D.W., Hu, K.-Y.: Research on Case Adaptation Techniques in Case-based Reasoning. In: Machine Learning And Cybernetics, Vol. 4. Shanghai (2004) 2128-2133
12. Bergmann, R.: Experience Adaptation. Lecture Notes in Artificial Intelligence, Vol. 2432 (2002) 219-239

# Objects Relationship Modeling for Improving Object Detection Using Bayesian Network Integration

Youn-Suk Song and Sung-Bae Cho

Dept. of Computer Science, Yonsei University
134 Shinchon-dong, Sudaemun-ku, Seoul 120-749, Korea
corlary@sclab.yonsei.ac.kr, sbcho@cs.yonsei.ac.kr

**Abstract.** Object detection is very important to service robots. Many tasks for service such as delivery, cleaning, and health-care for elderly people are strongly related to objects. Conventional approaches for object detection are mainly based on the geometric models, because they have been applied to static environments. In indoor environments having uncertainty, they have limitation in some situations where interesting objects are occluded by other ones or small in the scene. Context information can be helpful to overcome these uncertain situations. In this paper, we adopt objects as context information to allow for service robots to predict the probability of interesting objects through observed ones. For this, an object relationship model based on Bayesian network (BN) and integration method are proposed. Experimental results confirm that the proposed method predicts the objects very well.

## 1 Introduction

The studies of object detection and scene understating using visual sensors for service robot are important. Conventional approaches mainly used in industrial environments mainly obtain the information from images based on predefined geometric models, so they have shown limitations in uncertain situations when objects are occluded by other ones or small [1]. Since the service robots reside in human environments such as home and office, it is very important to manage them. Knowledge-based approaches can be a good choice to manage these uncertain situations, because they can give robots context information to resolve the uncertainty. Bayesian network (BN) is well known as a good method to represent the degree of uncertainty of some facts in a probabilistic framework [2]. There are many relevant works as follows.

**Table 1.** Relevant works

| Researcher | Year | Context | Modeling method |
|---|---|---|---|
| Socher | 2000 | Voice | Bayesian network |
| Luo | 2003 | Location | Bayesian network |
| Song | 2005 | Object | Bayesian network |

In this paper, BN model is adopted to represent the relationship between objects and the probability of object being present for object detection for service robots. It can help service robots to detect objects.

D.-S. Huang, K. Li, and G.W. Irwin (Eds.): ICIC 2006, LNCS 4113, pp. 1040 – 1046, 2006.

## 2 Bayesian Network Modeling

Bayesian network is the DAG (directed acyclic graph) model to evaluate the belief of variables using the dependency between them based on the Bayes' rule. The nodes represent random variables while the edges denote the dependencies of them. The two nodes linked by an edge have the joint probability distribution respectively, in which the parent has prior probability, and the child has the conditional probability in the context of parent's states.

In many applications, BN has shown a good performance, but it is also known that the modeling process of BN has difficulties in several perspectives such as complexity of modeling according to scalability of domain and eliciting parameters for conditional probability [2]. For this, in the mid 1990's, Laskey *et al.* proposed the modularized design method under object-oriented paradigm for modeling military situation. They proposed the approach to integrate pre-designed Bayesian networks for the situations by integration methods like noisy-min [3].

We propose a novel BN structure based on a common-cause structure, binary-cross conditional probability table (CPT) setting method, and the method integrating the basic BNs with high-level BN using virtual nodes for object relationship modeling.

## 3 Object Relationship Modeling

To make object relationship, it is required to define the criteria of their relationship. Activities can be used for explaining the purposes of objects existence. Activity theory supports this idea. Our modeling process is composed of two stages: object-stage and activity-stage. In object-stage, the basic relationships called primitive BNs are defined between objects. They are small relatively, so it is easy to make them. Next stage, they are integrated for extending the object relationships if it is needed for reasoning. Fig. 1 shows the overall process of modeling.

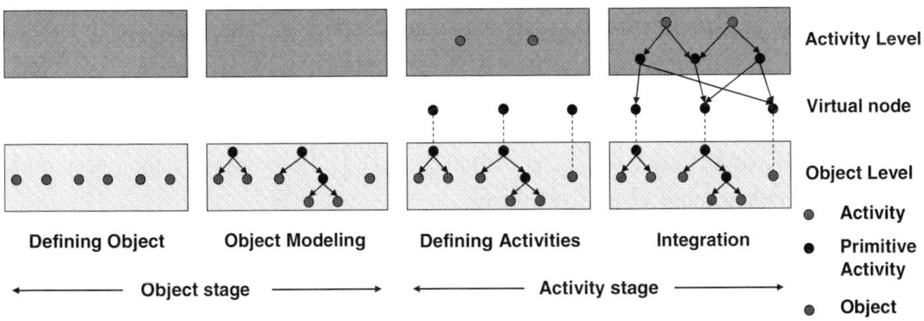


**Fig. 1.** Modeling Process

After explaining about the service robot and the domain in this section, the proposed BN model will be described.

### 3.1 Service Robot

We construct the BNs in the environments of 15 places and 29 objects. The environments are summarized in Table 2.

**Table 2.** Service environment

| Category | Contents |
|---|---|
| **Places (15)** | Lecture room, Meeting room, Seminar room, Computer room, Prof. of fice, Admin. office, Guard office, Lab., Hallway, Stair, Hall, Elevator, Toilet, Former Toilet, Rest room |
| **Objects (29)** | Table, Side Chair, Castor Chair, Lectern, Cabinet, Bookcase, Garbage can, Sink, Seat toilet, Wall clock, Air conditioner, Telephone, Desktop PC, Notebook PC, Mouse, LCD Monitor, Keyboard, Beam Projector, Projection Screen, Audio, Speaker, Microphone, Wall white board, Ca stor white board, Partition, Curtain, Water bucket, Door, Window |

The proposed BN models in this paper are used for predicting the probability of registered objects by the discovered ones. When the robot executes detection, he can decide whether it is needed to try further detection.

### 3.2 Activity Theory

Activity theory gives us theoretical background of our idea that uses activity as the criterion of defining objects relationship. Vygosky suggested the simple activity model 'subject-tool-object' in 1920s. It helps us to explain why the objects (tools) exist together, because they are used for the same purpose (activity). Activity also has the property that can be subsumed by other activities like goals. This property can be also used to make the relationship and promote us to use hierarchical structure (tree shape) for modeling.

### 3.3 Object Stage: Primitive Bayesian Network

The primitive Bayesian networks are tree structures that each node has one parent and binary state, and they are composed of four kinds of basic nodes: activity node $(A)$, class node $(C)$, object node $(O)$, and virtual node $(V)$. The summary for every node and the hierarchical relations are as follows.

- Virtual node: $V_k = Observed\ Object_j$, Adjusting relationship between objects
- Object node: $O_j$ can include $\{Object_1, Object_2, ...Object_{l-1}, Object_l\} \cup \{V_1, V_2, ...V_{w-1}, V_w\}$, Representing observed objects or probability of target objects
- Class node: $C_i$ can include $\{C_1, C_2, ..., C_{n-1}, C_n\} \cup \{O_1, O_2, ...O_{m-1}, O_m\}$, Criterion of detailed object relationship
- Activity node: $A_p$ can include $= \{C_1, C_2, ..., C_{n-1}, C_n\} \cup \{O_1, O_2, ...O_{m-1}, O_m\}$, Root node, Criterion of primitive activity BN

We define the relationship of objects as four types. They are described as follows:

- Equality: $P(X \mid Y) = P(Y \mid X)$
- Part-of: $P(Y \mid X) = P(X \mid Y) = 1$
- Inequality: $P(X \mid Y) \neq P(Y \mid X)\, and\, P(Z \mid X,Y) \neq P(Z \mid X), P(Z \mid Y)$
- Independence: $P(X \mid Y) = P(X)\ or\ P(Y \mid X) = P(Y)$

Equality relationship means that influences between two objects are equal. Part-of relation is the special case of equality. This is the case one object is the part of other one like door and door handle. Inequality relationship is the case that two objects have different influence to each other. That is, one object is necessary condition for the other one. In general the objects that are used with many other objects are necessary condition for another one, because they have little information according to information theory. Independence relationship means that there is no influence between objects, so it is not under consideration. Structures mentioned above are shown in Fig. 2.

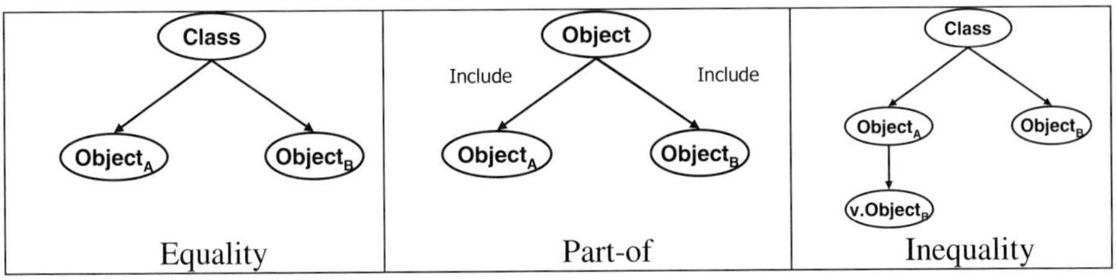


**Fig. 2.** Defined structures (v means virtual node)

We set the value of CPT of the BN model as follows.

$$\sum_{parent_i} P(child_j \mid parent_i) = 1 \text{ (child}_j\text{.parent}_i \text{ is the state of parent)} \tag{1}$$

$$P(child_{yes} \mid parent_{yes}) = P(child_{no} \mid parent_{np}) \tag{2}$$

In this way, we can keep the probability distributions of all nodes uniformly after belief-updating without evidences. This is important for prediction. Next formula explains about this.

$$\begin{aligned} P(Child_{yes} \mid Parent) &= P(Child_{yes} \mid Parent_{yes})P(Parent_{yes}) \\ &\quad + P(Child_{yes} \mid Parent_{no})P(Parent_{no}) \\ &= \alpha \times 0.5 + (1-\alpha) \times 0.5 \\ &= 0.5 \text{ ( we can use the same formula for } P(Child_{no} \mid Parent) \text{ )} \end{aligned}$$

Suppose $\alpha$ represent the probability of $P(Child_{yes}|Parent_{yes})$ and assign 1- $\alpha$ to $P(Child_{yes}|Parent_{no})$ (following to formula 1 ) then we can maintain the probability of all nodes as (0.5, 0.5) in the case that there are no evidences in the network having the uniform prior probability of activity node. This method allows us to just decide the value called as 'influence value' $P(Child_{yes}|Parent_{yes})$ to express the degree of relationship. If the influence value of child node has large one, it means it has large influence to other nodes belonged to the same class. This method is called binary-cross probability setting due to their formation when they are represented in the CPTs.

### 3.4 Activity Stage: Integration

If primitive BNs can be properly combined together, it becomes easier to extend and represent the object relationship. For this, we propose the method for integrating primitive BNs properly with high-level BNs (Activity BNs). This is efficient to make object relationship in the view point of reusability. Fig. 3 (left) shows the overall models.

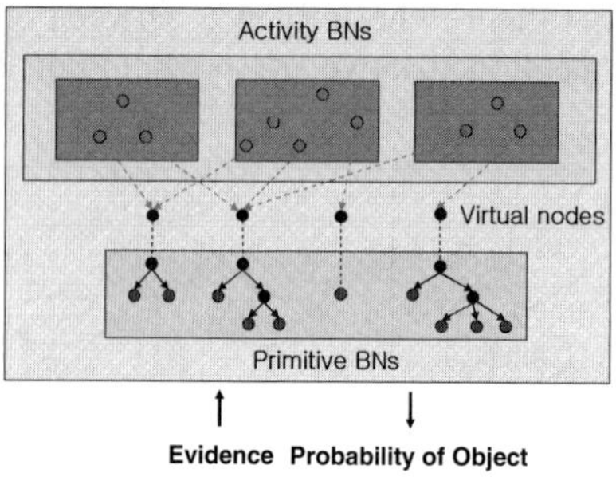


<PrimitiveBNs>
ComputerWorking; Studying; Sitting;
</PrimitiveBNs>
<ActivityRelation>
Presenting ComputerWorking 0.8;
Presenting Studying 0.7;
Studying Sitting 0.7;
</ActivityRelation>

**Fig. 3.** Left: Overall models. Right: scripts for integration (presenting)

ActivityRelation describes the Activity BN structure. The values of root nodes of Primitive BNs are used for influence value of virtual nodes, the leaves of activity BNs. The process of inference is as follows.

1. Compute *P(root node | Evidence)* of primitive BNs
2. Construct activity BN following to the scripts in the Activity Relation
3. Make virtual nodes that have influence value computed in step 1 as the child of corresponding activity nodes in the activity BN
4. Set the evidence to virtual nodes and update the belief
5. Set the prior probability of primitive BNs with the new values of activity nodes. ($Prior_{new}$= 0.5 + $Activity_{activityBN}$ – $\alpha$of v.$Activity_{activityBN}$, $\alpha$ is influence value)
6. Inference the value of interesting object

## 4 Experimental Results

Experiments are carried out to verify the performance of the proposed BN model in five different places (Computer room, Laboratory, Rest room, Conference room, and

Seminar room). We use BN model that represents the presenting-activity for detecting beam-projector existing in Conference room. It is designed by composing 5 primitive BNs: ComputerWorking, Audio working, Projecting, Studying and Sitting.

We assumed that the service robot would move from place to place and the objects are detected randomly, and recorded the values and hit rates to predict the probability of target objects being present in each place. Fig. 4 shows the results.

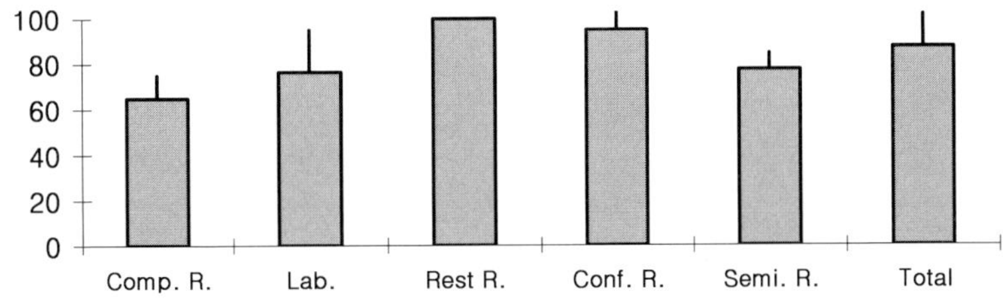


**Fig. 4.** Accuracy rates at each place

The probabilities of the beam-projector being present in each place were observed under a threshold of 70% (this value is the best one of our experiments) until the robot was able to find five objects. The overall results shows 87.25% of accuracy, that is reasonable, but it denoted also that a false-positive error is likely to occur in similar environments (especially Computer room) that contain many objects related to a beam-projector.

## 5 Conclusion

In this paper, we proposed the BN model for predicting target object when the service robot acts in indoor environment and the method to integrate them for making a large scale BN for efficient design. For efficient design, we design BN by combining small BNs for overall structure, and propose binary-cross parameter setting method. The experiments show the proposed BN has good performance.

For the future works, we will devise ensemble method of the results from diverse BNs for improving the performance, and study a way to make primitive BN relationship dynamically according to the situation.

## Acknowledgement

This research was supported by the Ministry of Information and Communication, Korea under the Information Technology Research Center support program supervised by the Institute of Information Technology Assessment, IITA-2005-(C1090-0501-0019).

## References

1. Murphy, K., et al.: Using the Forest to See the Trees: A Graphical Model Relating Features, Objects, and Scenes. Proc. Neural Info. Proc. System, Vol.16 (2003) 1499-1506
2. Pearl, J.: Probabilistic Reasoning in Intelligent Systems: Networks of Plausible Inference. Morgan Kaufmann, (1988)
3. Laskey, K. B., Mahoney, S. M.: "Network Fragments: Representing Knowledge for Constructing Probabilistic Models." Proc. of 13th Conf. Uncertainty in Artificial Intelligence, (1997) 334-341

# The Embodiment of Autonomic Computing in the Middleware for Distributed System with Bayesian Networks

Bo-Yoon Choi, Kyung-Joong Kim, and Sung-Bae Cho

Dept. of Computer Science, Yonsei University
134 Shinchon-dong, Sudaemoon-Ku, Seoul 120-749, South Korea
bychoi@sclab.yonsei.ac.kr, kjkim@cs.yonsei.ac.kr,
sbcho@cs.yonsei.ac.kr

**Abstract.** In this paper, we propose an intelligent middleware framework based on the concept of the autonomic computing. Because decisions for optimizing a system are highly dependent on the status of the system in the near future, predictions of the status can boost up the performance of system. Bayesian networks that are frequently used in the domain of user modeling are adopted as a diagnosis engine. Since there are many different kinds of behavioral patterns, it is impossible to model all of them into a single model. A Bayesian network is learned for each typical behavioral pattern. Experimental results show that the proposed method offers a promising way of intelligent middlewares.

## 1 Introduction

Component-based applications are independent of component's location and flexible in the change of its structure. When a user makes use of a process or takes a service from a server using internet at distributed environment, a middleware organizes a component set of applications for a user on real time to satisfy user's request. Meanwhile, it can optimize components structure of an application for improvement of the performance according to a user's environment. Such a process is called as autonomic computing [1], which is a skill for the development of an adaptive application reflecting immediately to changing system and updating its function by component insertion or deletion. It continuously optimizes itself to provide a service requested, given the state of a user's environment.

This paper proposes an intelligent middleware using Bayesian networks for autonomic computing, which is more flexible. Because Bayesian network is based on the probability theory, it can naturally deal with such uncertainties without any significant effort. Also, it can provide two directional inferences (forward and backward). Intelligent middleware consists of data collection, performance analysis and component configuration or reconfiguration. When a user operates a distributed application at the circumstance of distributed systems, the middleware collects information about the system and the component set. After processing collected data, they are inputted to the diagnosis engine and used as evidences of Bayesian networks in the diagnosis engine for the performance analysis and the system diagnosis. The inferred result from the learned Bayesian network can be used to make the decision of component swapping.

D.-S. Huang, K. Li, and G.W. Irwin (Eds.): ICIC 2006, LNCS 4113, pp. 1047 – 1052, 2006.

## 2 Diagnosis Engine Using Bayesian Networks

System resources and the user's behavior are considered as relevant information sources to infer future resource levels. System resources include the speed of the network, free memory, CPU usage, and the type of device. User behavior can be modeled from the history of application execution, whether the system is on or off, usage time, and the switching of tasks. Eric Horvitz *et al.* attempted to model the user's behavior patterns through activities on the desktop with the help of a camera and acoustic sensors [5]. Because our platform assumes the reconfiguration of middleware, the information sources for inference are at a relatively lower level than those of application reconfiguration.

```
/* n : Number of variables */
/* A[i,j] : Score gain when an edge from the jth node to the ith node is connected */
/* Score(B) : Score of Bayesian network structure B */
/* Score(B, j→i) : Return a score when B has an edge (j→i) */
/* Find_Max(A) : Return an edge (j→i) that has the maximum A[i,j] */
/* Min : minus infinity */
/* Ancestors(x_i) : A set of nodes that have a path from the node to x_i */
/* Decendants(x_i) : A set of nodes that have a path from x_i to the node */
/* Stop(); If all (i,j), A[i,j] ≤ 0 or A[i,j]=Min then True */
FOR i=1 to n { Pa(x_i) = φ ; }
FOR i=1 to n FOR j=1 to n
   IF i ≠ j THEN A[i,j]=Score(B, j→i) – Score(B);
WHILE(TRUE) {
   (i, j)=Find_Max(A);
   IF A[i,j]>0 THEN Pa(x_i) = Pa(x_i) ∪ {x_j} ;
   A[i,j]=Min;
   FOR a=1 to n FOR b=1 to n
      IF x_a ∈ Ancestors(x_j) ∪ {x_j} && x_b ∈ Decendants(x_i) ∪ {x_i}
      THEN A[a,b]=Min;
   FOR k=1 to n {IF A [i,k]>Min THEN A[i,k]=Score(B, k→i) – Score(B); }
   IF Stop()==True THEN break;
}
```

**Fig. 1.** Overview of the greedy search for Bayesian network

We use $< B, \theta_B >$ to denote a Bayesian network with a structure $B$ and probability parameters $\theta_B$. $P < B, \theta_B >$ denotes the joint probability distribution of all the variables of this network. A possible structure of a Bayesian network can be drawn as a directed acyclic graph. $B = (V, E)$, where the set of nodes $V = \{x_1, x_2, ..., x_n\}$ represents the domain variables and $E$, a set of arcs, represents the direct dependency among the variables. For each variable $x_i \in V$, the conditional probability distribution is $P(x_i \mid Pa(x_i))$, where $Pa(x_i)$ represents the parent set of the variable $x_i$.

$$P < B, \theta_B >= P(x_1, x_2, ..., x_n) = \prod_{i=1}^{n} P(x_i \mid Pa(x_i))$$

Bayesian probabilistic inference is one of the most popular models for inference and representation of environments with insufficient information [6][7]. Usually the structure is designed by an expert. To develop appropriate Bayesian networks for this specific problem given a little prior knowledge, learning is essential. Using a scoring function that returns a numerical value for the appropriateness of the given data in the Bayesian networks, search algorithms such as greedy and genetic algorithms attempt to maximize the score.

From an empty network with no edge, the greedy algorithm repeats the procedure of adding an edge that maximizes a score gain on the current structure and fixes the new structure as a current one until the structure converges. Though the algorithm can get stuck in the local minimum, it can perform well if the number of variables is relatively small. If the number of variables is large, a global search algorithm such as a genetic algorithm is a more appropriate choice. In this domain, we assume that relevant variables are selected by the expert and the learning procedure is conducted by the greedy algorithm. Figure 1 shows the pseudo code of the greedy search.

The intelligent middleware adopts the Bayesian network as a diagnosis engine for the performance analysis of distributed applications. A structure of Bayesian network is important to improve the efficiency of the diagnosis engine. It is difficult to develop highly efficient diagnosis engine using only one structure of Bayesian network which is suitable for various users. Therefore, the intelligent middleware creates Bayesian networks of the diagnosis engine dynamically according to the pattern of users' computer usage. For example, when a user executes a distributed application, the intelligent middleware collects data in advance about system environment and executed process list. Such data are used for learning Bayesian networks. The Bayesian network is maintained if the diagnosis engine produces good performance. Otherwise, when the engine does not work or the pattern of a computer usage is changed, Bayesian networks will be reconstructed again.

## 3 Experimental Results

Data were collected from a student and a programmer for two hours. After installing a monitoring program, they used their computers in the same way as usual. The monitoring program collected the usage patterns of specific programs and system resource information. The student played continuously an online game with the player of another computer and the programmer worked for programming and accessed steadily a database for inquiring data. In addition, they performed several kinds of programs and also their systems executed many basic processes for system management. Table 1 shows the details of the process executed by a user and a system.

A half of the data which present the proper change of a system state is used for training and the remaining is used for test. The purpose of the Bayesian network was to infer the future CPU load given the current CPU load and the user's current job list. From the preliminary study, the performance of a distributed application showed unexpected quality degradation when the CPU load was kept 100% for more than 5 seconds, but when the CPU load was kept 100% for less than 5 seconds, it did not affect the performance of the application. Sometimes the CPU load became the state of 100% for less than 5 seconds. In this case, most of the cases was the time when a user executed new process. It did not make a system problem or degrade the performance of the system. Otherwise, when the CPU load was kept 100% for more than 5 seconds, we could predict a system problem led to a system overload. In this paper, the Bayesian network infers the probability of the event that CPU is kept 100% for more than 5 seconds.

**Table 1.** List of process executed by a user and a system

| | List of processes |
|---|---|
| User 1 | SystemIdleProcess, System, smss, csrss, winlogon, services, lsass, ati2evxx0, svchost0, svchost1, svchost2, svchost3, svchost4, spoolsv ,ati2evxx1, explorer, V3monnt, V3monsvc, myLinker, DrVirus, ctfmon, msmsgs, trayapp, alg, LCDPlyer, wscntfy, CDSLicenseMng, conime, taskmgr, CpuUsage, ProcMon, TalesWeaver, InphaseNXD, IEXPLORE, skcbgm, npkagt, regsvr32, npkcsvc, npdownv |
| User 2 | SystemIdleProcess, System, smss, csrss, winlogon, services, lsass, svchost, spoolsv, explorer, MsgPlus, monsysnt, v3p3at, daemon, ctfmon, ProtHelp, ClientSM, conime, ahnsdsv, ahnsd, AszTray, monsvcnt, v3impro, msnmsgr, putty, TOAD, notepad, editplus, CpuUsage, ProcMon, EMEDITOR, IEXPLORE, v3syson, rundll32, npcopyv, npdownv, NPMON, logon, sucer, supdate, autoup |

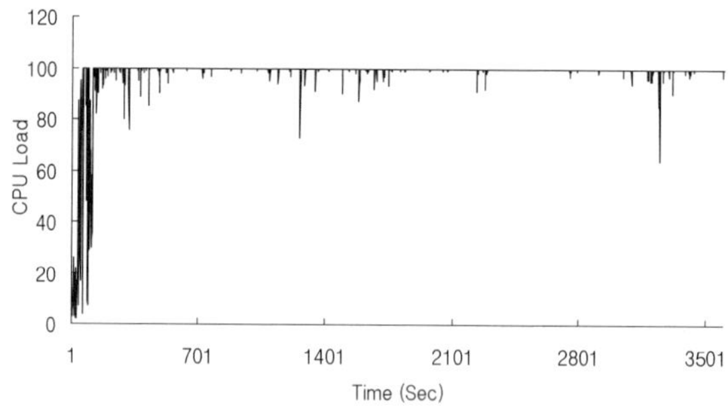


(a) user 1

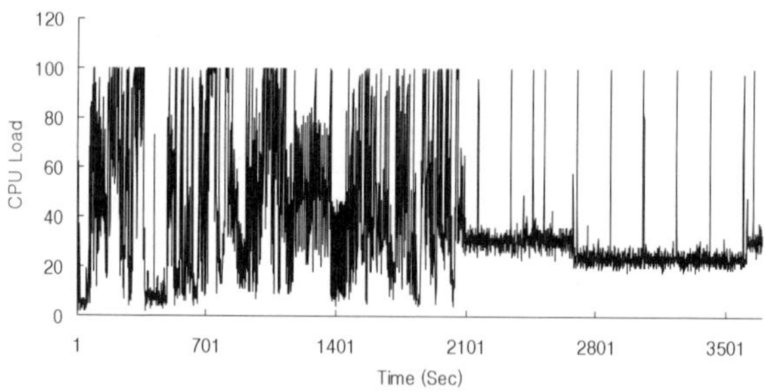


(b) user 2

**Fig. 2.** CPU load change in the training data (one hour)

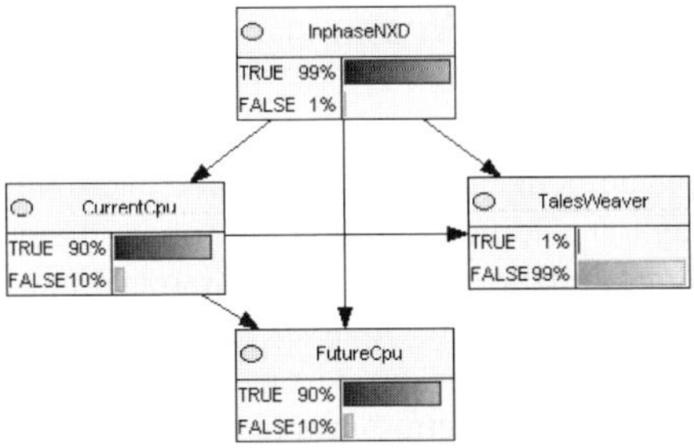


(a) user 1

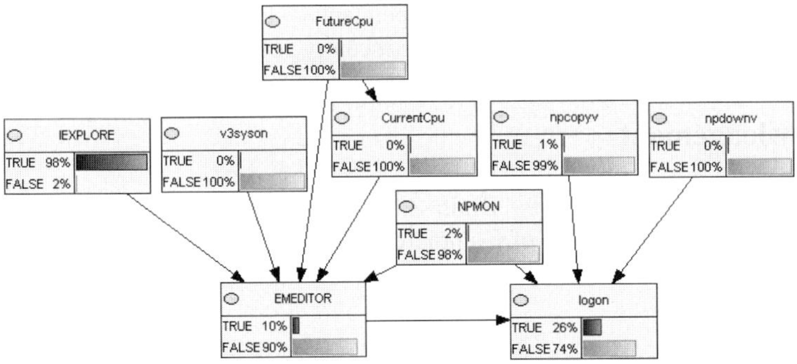


(b) user 2

**Fig. 3.** The structure of Bayesian networks

**Table 2.** Prediction accuracy of the Bayesian networks on the test data

| | CPU load is 100% | | CPU load is not 100% | | Accuracy | |
|---|---|---|---|---|---|---|
| | User 1 | User 2 | User 1 | User 2 | User 1 | User 2 |
| CPU load is 100% | 1275 | 17 | 83 | 3 | 93.88% | 85.00% |
| CPU load is not 100% | 81 | 5 | 2135 | 3572 | 96.34% | 99.86% |
| Total | 1356 | 22 | 2218 | 3575 | 95.41% | 99.77% |

Figure 2 shows the CPU load changes in the data of user 1 and user 2. Figure 3 shows the structure of the learned Bayesian networks of user 1 and user 2. The learned networks contain relatively small nodes because some nodes have no edge. The structures depend on the computer usage pattern of each user, which led to the different structures of Bayesian networks for user 1 and user 2. The Bayesian network of user 1 has four nodes. For user 2, the Bayesian network has nine nodes. Table 2 shows the prediction accuracy of the learned models. The Bayesian network for user 1 shows 95.41% prediction accuracy and the model for user 2 shows 99.77% prediction accuracy.

## 4 Conclusions and Future Works

In this paper, we have proposed a middleware framework for distributed applications. Because distributed environments are highly dynamic and contain uncertainties due to noise and network delays, it is crucial to develop robust diagnosis engines. Bayesian networks can model probabilistic dependencies among random variables provide a flexible two-directional inference mechanism (forward and backward inferences). Experimental results show that the proposed method is promising enough to estimate future states given evidence for selecting proper services. To deal with various situations, it is necessary to use more than one Bayesian network. In this context, the management of several Bayesian networks including construction, aggregation, and replacement has to be developed as an independent system module. It is also necessary to adapt previous learned models given the recently collected data.

## Acknowledgement

This research was supported by Brain Science and Engineering Research Program sponsored by Korean Ministry of Commerce, Industry and Energy.

## References

1. Jephart, J.O., Chess, D.M.: The Vision of Autonomic Computing. IEEE Computer, vol. 36, no. 1, January (2003) 41-50
2. Kon, F. et al.: Design, Implementation, and Performance of an Automatic Configuration Service for Distributed Component Systems. Software-Practice and Experience, vol. 34, (2004) 1-39
3. Diaconescu, A., Murphy, J.: A Framework for Automatic Performance Monitoring, Analysis and Optimization of Component based Software Systems. Proceedings of the 2nd ICSE Workshop on Remote Analysis and Measurement of Software Systems, (2004) 29-34
4. Heckerman, D., Geiger, D., Chickering, D.: Learning Bayesian Networks: The Combination of Knowledge and Statistical Data. Machine Learning. vol. 20, (1995) 197-243
5. Horvitz, E., Kadie, C. M., Paek, T., Hovel, D.: Models of Attention in Computing and Communications: From Principles to Applications, Communications of the ACM, vol. 46, no. 3, (2003) 52-59
6. Charniak, E.: Bayesian Networks without Tears. AI Magazine, vol. 12, no. 4, (1991) 50-63
7. Stephenson, T.: An Introduction to Bayesian Network Theory and Usage. IDIAP-RR00-03, (2000)

# Adaptable Designated Group Signature

Chunbo Ma and Jianhua Li

School of Information Security Engineering,
Shanghai Jiao Tong University, Shanghai, 200030, P.R. China
{machunbo, lijh888}@sjtu.edu.cn

**Abstract.** An adaptable designated group signature is presented in this paper. In contrast with traditional group oriented signature, the new one laid a strong emphasis on how to improve the signer's efficiency. In fact, this new type of designated group signature can be seen as a type of designated verifier signature. In contrast with the ordinary designated verifier signature, it does not designate one member but several members to independently verify the signature. The designated members, who can independently verify the signature, come into a group. This scheme can ensure the anonymity of the verifiers. This type of signature can be used in such system that the compute resource is limited, such as the broadcast protocols of the mobile telephone in the mobile networks.

## 1 Introduction

In distributed networks, the traditional group-oriented signature is that only when all members in an authorized subset of a given group operate collectively, they can generate, conform or deny a signature on behalf of the group. The key skill used in traditional group-oriented is secret sharing. The aim of this type of signature is to improve the signature security. In many applications, the signer should sign a same message for lots of members, and how to improve the signing efficiency comes to be a problem. For example, we hope a mobile telephone has broadcast function, that is, it can send its signature to several members in the mobile networks. In such situations, the compute resource is limited, so signing a same message one by one for all designated members overloads the signer.

If a signer wants a designated member to verify his signature, he can use designated verifier signature, such as Chameleon signature [10],[11]. If the signer wants several members to independently verify his signature, then he can sign the same message one by one for every member. But with this method, the efficiency is very low.

In practical networks, there exist several group models constructed by the members.

Firstly, in distributed networks, all users come into a group, that is, there is no member outside the group in this model. There is no member outsider the group wants to verify the signature, such as a small scale LAN.

Secondly, in distributed networks, the users in the different companies or institutions naturally come into different groups (this is the second model). In this condition, if the signer wants to provide such type signature service, he should have

D.-S. Huang, K. Li, and G.W. Irwin (Eds.): ICIC 2006, LNCS 4113, pp. 1053 – 1061, 2006.

effective ways to prevent the members outside the designated group from verifying the signature.

Thirdly, in distributed networks, the signer just wants several members to verify his signature no matter whether these members are in one natural group or not (third model). What the signer should do is that he should define a group for these members. Then he should find effect way to prevent the member outside the defined group from verifying the signature. We can see the third model as a generalizing for the first and second models.

The efficiency of a cryptosystem is not only in his arithmetic but also in the way to manage the public keys. To date, the ID based cryptosystem can be seen as the substitute for the traditional PKI. Generally speaking, it is much easier to manage the ID based cryptosystem than the traditional PKI. In traditional PKI, there is no relation between the identity of user A and its public key, and the public key just is a random string. When user B wants to send a message to A, B should get A's authenticated public key. In order to solve this problem, it is necessary to establish a public key list. The virtue of the ID based cryptosystem is that any user can get his public key from his identity information, such as his email address. So, it makes the public key management and authentication much easier.

In the ID based cryptosystem, if the verifier outputs "True", then it means:

a) The sender generates this signature with his private key, which is based on his identity.
b) The sender's ID has been authenticated by TTP (Trusted Third Party). With the certificate sent by TTP, the sender can generate his signature.

It is very important to complete above two aspects in the same time for the ID based signature scheme, because it avoids the certificate transmitting and saves communication bandwidth.

Considering the public key management, a novel ID based adaptive designated group signature is presented in this paper. In this scheme, before signing a message, the signer defines a group by embedding a group tab in the public key of the designated members. In contrast with the first and the second models, the signer can freely define a group containing the members he wants designated. In first and second models, the group is defined by the system. To any member, he can't get any information about other designated verifier from the published values. Then the anonymity is realized.

## 2 Related Works

Desmedt first presents the concept of group-oriented cryptography [1] in 1987. The problem he wants to solve is that when a sender encrypts a message for a group of members, how to make the members to decrypt the ciphertext by cooperation. This concept used in signature, then group-oriented signature comes. Generally speaking, the key skill of traditional group oriented signature is secret sharing. Papers [2],[3] are some researches about this type of signature.

Shamir first presents the concept of ID based cryptography [4], and designs the first signature based on ID. It can greatly decrease the complexity of public key authentication and in fact it is similar to email system. In his scheme, the private key mode reverses to that of traditional PKI. That is the private key is generated by the master key and member's public key. In order to preserve the private key secret, this process is kept secret. However, practical identity-based encryption (IBE) schemes were not found until Boneh and Franklin [5] published their work in 2001. The Boneh-Franklin scheme bases its security on the Bilinear Diffie-Hellman Problem, and is quite fast and efficient when using Weil or Tate pairings on supersingular elliptic curves or abelian varieties. From then on, the pairings come to be an important tools to construct cryptosystem, and lots of researches are published, such as [8],[9].

Chunbo Ma et al. present the concept of group inside signature [6]. In their scheme, any one in the same group with the signer can verify the signature generated by the signer. This type of signature can be transmitted by broadcast on the Internet. Embedding a group tab in the private key is the key skill to construct this signature. With this method, the efficiency of signing a message is improved enormously. This signature is corresponding to the first model.

Chunbo Ma et al. present another group-oriented signature in paper [7]. This signature is corresponding to the second model. In this scheme, any member in the designated group can independently verify the signature generated by the signer.

The member's group in paper [7] is naturally generated, and it may be a company or an institution on the Internet. It is necessary to embed a group tab in corresponding member's private key, in this aspect, it is similarly to that of paper [6]. The flaw of this method is that the signer can't designate several members in different groups to verify his signature.

## 3 Backgroud

### 3.1 Bilinear Pairings

Let $G_1$ be a cyclic additive group generated by $P$, whose order is a prime $q$ and $G_2$ be a cyclic multiplicative group of the same order $q$. Assume that the discrete logarithm in both $G_1$ and $G_2$ is intractable. A bilinear pairing is a map $e: G_1 \times G_1 \to G_2$ and satisfies the following properties:

a) ***Bilinear:*** $e(aP,bQ) = e(P,Q)^{ab}$. For all $P, Q \in G_1$ and $a,b \in Z_q$, the equation holds;

b) ***Non-degenerate:*** There exists $Q \in G_1$, if $e(P,Q) = 1$, then $P = O$;

c) ***Computable:*** For $P, Q \in G_1$, there is an efficient algorithm to compute $e(P,Q)$.

Typically, the map $e$ will be derived from either the Weil or Tate pairing on an elliptic curve over a finite field. Pairings and other parameters should be selected in proactive for efficiency and security [12].

### 3.2 General Scheme

The signature schemes are made of four algorithms which are the following:

***Initialize:*** given a security parameter, the key Generating Center (KGC) generates the system's parameters.

***KeyGen:*** given an identity ID, the KGC computes the private key $S_i$ and send it to its owner in a secure way.

***Sign:*** given a message $m$ and ID, the algorithm outputs a signature $(m, \sigma, ID)$.

***SignVer:*** given a signature $(m, \sigma, ID)$, the algorithm outputs True if $\sigma$ is valid, otherwise outputs error symbol $\perp$.

### 3.3 Security Notions

The accepted definition of security for signature schemes is *existential unforgeability under adaptive chosen message attack*, which is described in [ 13],[15].

**Definition:** We say that a signature scheme has against an existential forgery for adaptive chosen messages attacks property (EF-ACMA) if no polynomial bonded adversary has a non-negligible advantage in the following game.

The attacker performs a polynomial bounded number of requests as follows.

a) ***Setup****:* the challenger $\beta$ runs the Initialize algorithm and gives the system parameters to the attacker.

b) ***Attack phase*****:** the attacker $\alpha$ performs a polynomial bounded number of requests defined as follows.

   i. ***Key extraction queries.*** The attacker chooses $ID_i$ and the challenger responds with *KeyGen*( $ID_i$ ).

   ii. ***Sign queries.*** The attacker produces a query $(m, ID_i)$. The challenger computes $d_i$ and outputs *Sign*(**m,** $ID_i$ **).**

c) ***Forge phase****:* the attacker $\alpha$ gives a new *signature* $(m, \sigma^*, ID_j)$, where the private key of $ID_j$ was not asked in the Attack phase, and wins the game if the *Signature Verification* $(m, \sigma^*, ID_j)$ outputs True.

We define the advantage of the attacker $\alpha$ to be $Adv(\alpha) = \Pr[\alpha \text{ win}]$. We say that the signature is EF-ACMA secure if no polynomial bounded attacker has non-negligible advantage in the game described above.

***Discrete Logarithm Problem (DLP)*****:** Given two elements $P$ and $Q$, to find an integer $n \in Z_q^*$, such that $Q = nP$ whenever such an integer exists.

***Computation Diffie-Hellman Problem (CDHP):*** Given $P, aP, bP$ for $a, b \in Z_q^*$, to compute $abP$.

# 4 Designated Group Signature

Assume that there are $n$ users $a_0, a_1, a_2, \cdots, a_n$ in the distributed network. We denote the set of $a_1, a_2, \cdots, a_n$ by $A$. Let $a_0 \in A$ be the signer who wants to sign a message $m$ and sends it to certain user's group $B = \{a_1, a_2, \cdots, a_i\}$, where $i < 0 \le n$. The signer $a_0$ wants that only the designated members can independently verify his signature. The group $B$ is defined by signer $a_0$.

## 4.1 Initialize

Let $G_1$ be a GDH Group generated by $P$, whose order is a prime $q$ and $G_2$ be a cyclic multiplicative group of the same order $q$. A bilinear pairing is a map $e: G_1 \times G_1 \to G_2$. Define two cryptographic hash functions:

$$H_0: \{0,1\}^* \to G_1 \qquad H_1: \{0,1\}^* \times G_1 \to Z_q^* \tag{1}$$

There exist a KGC (Key Generating Center), whose function is to generate private keys for corresponding members.

## 4.2 Key Generation (KeyGen)

Let $ID_i$ denote the identity of $a_i \in A$. KGC selects $s \in Z_q^*$ uniformly at random, then $a_i$'s private key is $S_i = sH_0(ID_i)$ and the corresponding public key is $P_i = H_0(ID_i)$. Any member can compute the public key. The private key generated by KGC is sent to corresponding member in secure way. KGC publishes $sP$.

## 4.3 Designated Group Signature Generation (Sign)

The signer $a_0$ selects $r, k, t \in Z_q^*$ uniformly at random, and publishes the value $T_i = kH_0(ID_i)$, where $a_i \in B$. Then $a_0$ computes $h = H_1(m)$ and publishes $V_0 = tsP, V_1 = tkP$, $V_2 = rksH_0(ID_0)$ and $T_0 = kH_0(ID_0)$.

The signer $a_0$ performs the following computing.

$$\sigma = (r + h)sH_0(ID_0) \tag{2}$$

The signer $a_0$ generates the signature $(m, \sigma, V_0, V_1, V_2, T_0, \cdots, T_i)$ for the message $m$. This signature will be transmitted to the designated members by broadcast over Internet.

### 4.4 Signature Verification (SignVer)

The verification can be divided into two steps, the first step is to judge who can verify the signature, and the second step is how to verify it.

***1)Judge Verifier.*** The aim of this step is to judge who can verify the signature. Using the value $T_i = kH_0(ID_i)$, any one can perform the following step.

$$e(T_i, V_0) \stackrel{?}{=} e(S_i, V_1) \tag{3}$$

If the equation holds, then the corresponding member has the ability to verify the signature. The signer $a_0$ publishes $i$ values, that is, only $i$ members have the ability to go on verification.

***2)Verify Signature.*** The member $a_i \in B$, who passes above step, can perform the verification as follows.

$$e(\sigma, T_i) \stackrel{?}{=} e(V_2, P_i) e(hT_0, S_i) \tag{4}$$

If above equation hold, then the signature is valid.

## 5 Security

### 5.1 Correctness

***1)Judge verifier.*** To the equation (2), we have

$$e(T_i, V_0) = e(kH_0(ID_i), tsP) = e(sH_0(ID_i), tkP) = e(S_i, V_1) \tag{5}$$

Only the designated $a_i \in B$ has the corresponding $S_i$, so only $a_i$ himself can verify that whether he is fit for the next verification step or not. After confirming his verification ability, $a_i$ uses $T_i$ to perform the following step.

***2)Verify signature.*** To the equation (3), we have

$$\begin{aligned} e(\sigma, T_i) &= e((r+h)sH_0(ID_0), kH_0(ID_i)) \\ &= e(rskH_0(ID_i), H_0(ID_i)) e(hkH_0(ID_0), sH_0(ID_i)) \\ &= e(V_2, P_i) e(hT_0, S_i) \end{aligned} \tag{6}$$

With (2) and (3), we can see that only the designated member corresponding to $T_i$ can verify the signature.

### 5.2 Anonymity

With the equation (2), any $a_j \notin B$ can't distinguish who is the designated verifier, because he has no $S_i$ corresponding to $T_i$. The difficulty he gets $s$ from $S_j$, $sP$, $V_0$, $V_1$, and $V_2$ is equal to solving discrete logarithm on elliptic curves. For the designated verifier $a_l, a_i \in B$ and $a_j \neq a_i$, $a_j$ can't distinguish whether $a_i$ can verify the signature or not.

### 5.3 Unforgeability

**Theorem.** *Suppose the CDH assumption holds. Then our scheme is secure against existential forgery for adaptive chosen messages attacks (EF-ACMA).*

Suppose that there are challenger $\beta$ and attacker $\alpha$ in our game. The challenger receives a random instance $(P, aP, sP)$. His aim is to compute $asP$. The challenger $\beta$ will run the attacker $\alpha$ as a subroutine in the EF-ACMA game. Before we begin our proof, we have the following lemma.

**Lemma [14].** *Suppose $\alpha$ be a Probabilistic Polynomial Time Turing machine. Given only the public data, if $\alpha$ can find a valid signature $(m, h, \sigma)$ with non-negligible probability, then we can construct an algorithm $\beta$ to get two valid signatures $(m, h, \sigma)$ and $(m, h', \sigma')$ with non-negligible probability.*

We will use the lemma to prove the theorem.

***Proof.*** Suppose the attacker $\alpha$ can forge a signature by adaptive chosen messages attacks. Then, we can prove that the challenger $\beta$ can solve CDHP with non-negligible probability, i.e. given $aP$ and $sP$, the challenger $\beta$ can compute $asP$. In our signature scheme, the challenger $\beta$ will interactive with attacker $\alpha$ by simulating $H_0$, $H_1$, KeyGen, and Sign.

At the beginning of the game, challenger $\beta$ gives $\alpha$ the system parameters with the master public key $sP$. The attacker $\alpha$ designates a member $ID^*$ whose signature he wants to forge.

$H_0$ ***requests:*** Setup a empty list $L_0$. For a query $H_0(ID_i)$, if $ID_i \neq ID^*$, then the challenger $\beta$ chooses $b_i \in Z_q^*$ uniformly at random, puts the pair $(ID_i, b_i)$ in the list $L_0$, and answers $H_0(ID_i) = b_i P$. If $ID_i = ID^*$, then $\beta$ puts the pair $(aP, \perp)$ in the list. The $ID_i$ is queried only once.

$H_1$ ***requests*:** Setup a empty list $L_1$. For a query $H_1(m_i)$, the challenger $\beta$ chooses $h_i \in \{0,1\}^l$ uniformly at random, answers $H_1(m_i) = h_i$, and puts the pair $(m_i, h_i)$ in the list $L_1$. The $m_i$ is queried only once.

***Key extraction requests:*** For a query **KeyGen** $(ID_i)$, if $ID_i \neq ID^*$, the list $L_0$ must contain a pair $(ID_i, b_i)$. Then challenger $\beta$ answers **KeyGen** $(ID_i)$ with $b_i sP$. If $ID_i = ID^*$, then $\beta$ outputs $\perp$ and stop.

***Sign requests:*** For a query **Sign** $(m, ID_i)$, if $ID_i = ID^*$, the challenger outputs $\perp$ and reject the query. Otherwise the challenger $\beta$ chooses $r, k, t \in Z_q^*$ uniformly at random and computes. Request $H_0$, $H_1$, and **KeyGen**, the challenger can compute

$$\begin{aligned} &T_j = kH_0(ID_j) \;\; h = H_1(m) \;\; V_0 = tsP \\ &V_1 = tkP \;\; V_2 = rksH_0(ID_i) \quad T_i = kH_0(ID_i) \end{aligned} \tag{7}$$

where $a_i \in B$. The challenger $\beta$ computes

$$\sigma = (r+h)sH_0(ID_i) \tag{8}$$

and answers **Sign** $(m, ID_i)$ with $(m, \sigma, V_0, V_1, V_2, T_0, \cdots, T_i)$.

According the above description, the attacker $\alpha$ can't distinguish the simulation result from the practical. So we say the simulation is perfect.

After a polynomial bounded number of queries, the attacker $\alpha$ gives a valid signature $(m, \sigma, h, V_0, V_1, V_2, T_0, \cdots, T_i)$. Using the **lemma**, the challenger $\beta$ can get another valid signature $(m, h', \sigma', V_0, V_1, V_2, T_0, \cdots, T_i)$, where $h \neq h'$. Then we have

$$\sigma' = rsH_0(ID_i) + h' sH_0(ID_i) \tag{9}$$

and

$$\sigma = rsH_0(ID_i) + hsH_0(ID_i) \tag{10}$$

Subtracting the two equations $\sigma' - \sigma = (h' - h)sH_0(ID_i)$, and we have

$$sH_0(ID_i) = (\sigma' - \sigma)/(h' - h) = asP \tag{11}$$

In other words, given $aP$ and $sP$, the challenger $\beta$ can use $\alpha$ to solve CDHP if the attacker $\alpha$ has the ability to forge a signature. It is contradictory to our complex assumption.

## 6 Conclusion

This paper generalizes the result of [6] and [7], and designs a new type of signature: adaptable designated group signature. In the new scheme, the signer can define the group freely to make all members in the defined group can independently verify his signature. What the most different from the paper [6],[7] is that the designated group does not naturally come into being, but defines by the signer. In the instance that the signer should sign the same message for several members, this scheme can effectively improve the signing efficiency. In practice, this scheme can be used in the distributed networks, whose member has limited compute ability.

## References


1. Desmedt Y.: Society and Group Oriented Cryptography: A New Concept. Proceedings of CRYPTO 87, Lecture Notes in Computer Science ,(1988) 120-127
2. Pedersen, T. P.: A Threhold Cryptosystem Without a Trusted Party. Proceedings of EUROCRYPT'91, Lecture Notes in Computer Science ,(1992) 522-526
3. Shoup, V.: Practical Threshold Signatures. Advance in Cryptology-Eurocrypt'00, LNCS 1807, (2000) 207-220
4. Shamir, A.: Identity-based Cryptosystems and Signature Schemes. In Proc. of Cryptology-CRYPTO'84, (1984) 47-53
5. Boneh D, Lynn B, Shacham H.: Short Signatures from the Weil Pairing. Advances in Cryptology -- Asiacrypt'2001, Lecture Notes in Computer Science 2248, Springer-Verlag ,(2002) 514-532
6. Ma, C. B, Ao, F. L, He D. K.: Certificateless Group Inside Signature. Proceedings of ISADS'05, IEEE Computer Society, (2005) 194-200
7. Chunbo Ma, Jun Ao, Dake He: Broadcast Group Oriented Signature. Proceedings of ICICS2005. IEEE Computer Society ,(2005) 454-458
8. Kenneth G. Paterson.: ID-based Signature from Pairings on Elliptic Curves. Http://eprint.iacr.org/2002/004
9. Boneh ,D. , Boyen, X.: Secure Identity Based Encryption without Random Oracles. In Advances in Cryptology-Crypto 2004, LNCS 3152, Springer-Verlag, (2004) 443-456
10. Krawczyk, H,Rabin T.: Chameleon Signatures. In Proceedings of NDSS2000, San Diego, California, USA ,(2000) 143-154
11. Chunbo, Ma, Dake He.: A New Chameleon Multisignature Based on Bilinear Pairing. Proceedings of GCC'04, Lecture Notes in Computer Science3252. Springer-Verlag, (2004) 329-335
12. Boneh, D., Lynn, B., Shacham, H.: Short Signatures from the Weil Pairing. Advances in Cryptology -- Asiacrypt'2001, Gold Coast, Australia, Lecture Notes in Computer Science, 2248, Springer-Verlag, (2001) 514-532
13. Brickell, E., Pointcheval, D., Vaudenay, S., Yung M: Design Validations for Discrete Logarithm Based Signature Schemes. In PKC'2000, Lecture Notes in Computer Science, Springer-Verlag, Vol. 1751, (2000) 276-292
14. Pointcheval, D.,Stern, J.: Security Arguments for Digital Signature and Blind Signatures. J. of Cryptology, 2000, 13(3) 361-396
15. Pointcheval, D.,Stern, J.: Security Proofs for Signature Schemes. In Advances in Cryptology-EUROCRYPT'96, Lecture Notes in Computer Science, Springer-Verlag, Vol. 1070,(1996) 387-398

# Performance Analysis of Adaptive Digital FPU Transmission System in Fading Environment

In-hye Seo[1], Heau-jo Kang[1], and Tai-hoon Kim[2]

[1] Department of Computer Engineering, Mokwon University,
800, Doan-dong, Seo-gu, Daejeon, 302-729, Korea
{ihseo, hjkang}@mokwon.ac.kr

[2] Department of Computer Science and Communication Engineering, Kyushu University, Japan
taihoonn@empal.com

**Abstract.** Home and abroad, the M/W intermediary service bandwidth is between 3 and 30 GHz. However, recently the bandwidth is getting insufficient due to the increasing number of services and the capacities. Thus FPU (Field Pick UP) Transmission System, the mobile broadcasting intermediary link, needs to be evaluated in the system capacity by means of simulation in order to estimate whether or not the number of channels and the places are changeable when the bandwidth is rearranged in the future. In this paper, we have modeled of Digital FPU link system in M/W band portable digital wireless transmission system. Also, we analyzed digital FPU system performance adopt adaptive modulation scheme in variable channel environment.

## 1 Introduction

Home and abroad, the M/W intermediary service bandwidth is between 3 and 30 GHz. However, recently the bandwidth is getting insufficient due to the increasing number of services and the capacities. Besides, in line with the feature of radio wave propagation, the new telecommunication bandwidth is likely to be under 6GHz, and further, it seems essential to rearrange the channels of exiting services due to the government's switchover plan to the digital broadcasting television system and the next generation ITS & wireless LAN introduction[1][2]. Thus FPU Transmission System, the mobile broadcasting intermediary link, needs to be evaluated in the system capacity by means of simulation in order to estimate whether or not the number of channels and the places are changeable when the bandwidth is rearranged in the future.

In this paper, we have modeled of Digital FPU link system in M/W band portable digital wireless transmission system. Also, we analyzed digital FPU system performance according to fading channel characteristic through the Monte-Carlo simulation scheme. In here, fading channel model is used 3-ray multi-path fading model considering attenuation and time delay with Clarke & Gans channel model using doppler shift. And, digital FPU system was evaluated BER performance in Rummler's Two-ray multi-path fading channel, frequency non-selective fading channel and frequency selective fading channel for microwave transmission link channel.

D.-S. Huang, K. Li, and G.W. Irwin (Eds.): ICIC 2006, LNCS 4113, pp. 1062 – 1071, 2006.

# 2 M/W Band Digital FPU Wireless Transmission System

In this paper, we have modeled of Digital FPU link system in M/W band portable digital wireless transmission system.

Fig. 1 shows the block diagram of the digital transmission system for the [3][4].

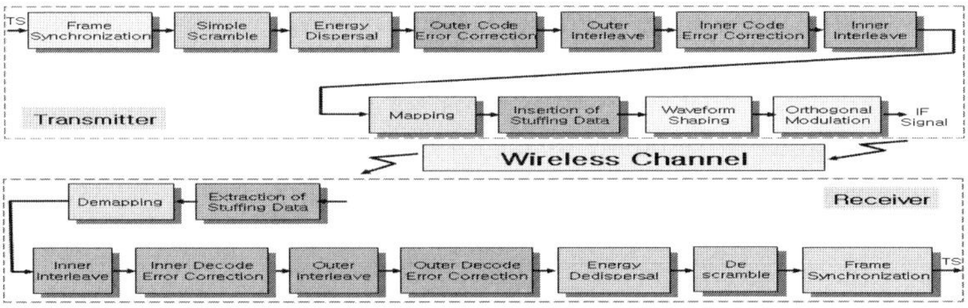


**Fig. 1.** Block diagram of FPU system

## 2.1 Access Bit Rate

**Table. 1** shows the Access bit rate and Fig.2 shows the block diagram of modulation signal in digital FPU.

**Table 1.** Connection bit rate (maximum rate/SNG)

| Band Efficiency [bit/symbol] | Modulation Mode code rate | TS+RS Rate [Mbit/s] | Stuffing S [symbols] |
|---|---|---|---|
| 6 | 64QAM (no inner code) | 79.056 | 0 |
| 5 | 64QAM (5/6 trellis ) of 32QAM (no inner code) | 65.880 | 0 |
| | | 59.648 | 112×16 |
| | | 44.736 | 380×16 |
| | | 33.552 | 581×16 |
| | | *29.824* | 648×16 |
| | | *22.368* | 782×16 |
| 4 | 32QAM (4/5 trellis) *or* 16QAM (no inner code) | 49.5435 | 71×16 |
| | | 44.736 | 179×16 |
| | | 29.824 | 514×16 |
| 3 | 16QAM (3/4 trellis) | 36.85712 | 80×16 |
| | | 33.552 | 179×16 |
| 2 | QPSK (no inner code) | 24.57142 | 80×16 |
| | | 22.368 | 179×16 |

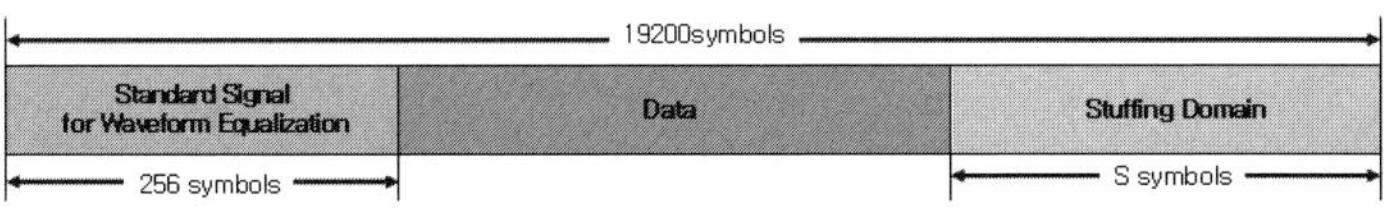


**Fig. 2.** Block diagram of modulation signal in digital FPU

In the event of not being able to transmit through 64QAM Trellis due to transmission channel problems, it can be presumed to transmit though QPSK of bandwidth efficiency $\eta \leq 4$. During its multi connection with other FPU and TSL, the connection by commonly used 64QAM trellis without any special rate change is desirable.

### 2.2 Insertion of Standard Signal for Waveform Equalization

Fig 3 shows multiplex system of standard signal for waveform equalization

The last Q(Quadrature) pluse of standard signal for waveform equalization is the symbol of confirmation that since other signs are BPSK, there is 180℃ phase uncertainty. The amplitude of standard signal for equalization needs to be the same with average amplitude.

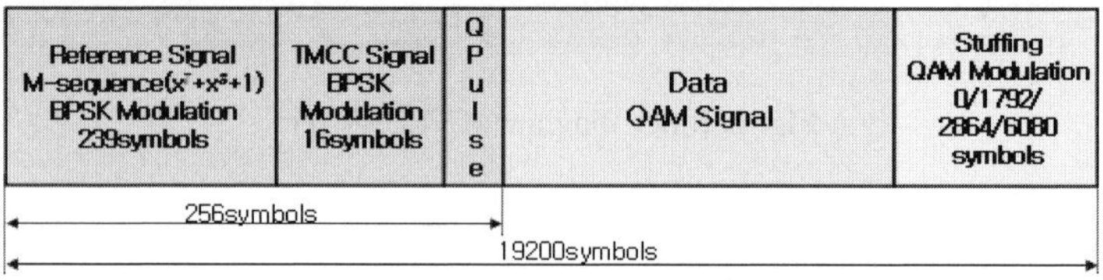


**Fig. 3.** Format of standard signal for waveform equalization

Table 2 shows mapping value of reference signal for waveform equalization in QPSK, 16QAM, 64QAM. Also, the amplitude of equalization standard signal equalize average amplitude.

**Table 2.** Mapping value of standard signal for waveform equalization

| Modulation Mode | Value | Mapping Value (I, Q) |
|---|---|---|
| QPSK | 0 | (+1, +1) |
| | 1 | (-1, -1) |
| | Q pulse | (-1, +1) |
| 16QAM | 0 | (+3, +1) |
| | 1 | (-3, -1) |
| | Q pulse | (-1, +3) |
| 64QAM | 0 | (+7, +1) |
| | 1 | (-7, -1) |
| | Q pulse | (-1, +7) |

## 3 Channel Model

### 3.1 Multi-path Fading Channel Model

In any wireless communication channel there can be more than one path in which the signal can travel between the transmitter and receiver antennas. The presence of multiple paths may be due to atmospheric reflection or refraction, or reflections from buildings and other object. Multi-path and/or fading may occur in all radio communication system[5].

To illustrate the basic approach to modeling fading channels, let us consider a mobile communication channel in which there are two distinct paths (or rays) from the mobile unit to a fixed base station, as illustrated in Figure Fig 4.

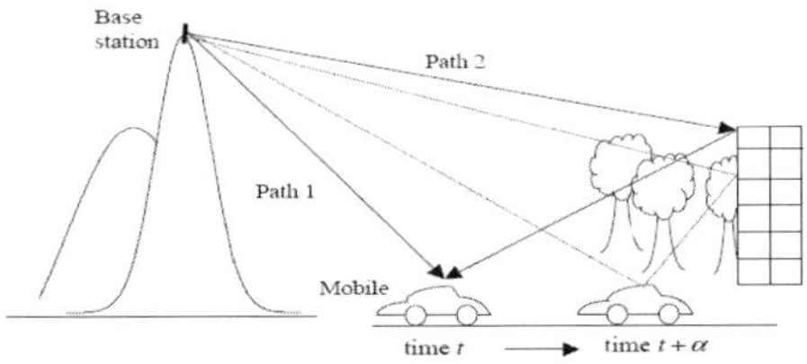


**Fig. 4.** Example of a multi-path fading channel

Fig 4 shows only two paths, it is easily generalized to N-paths. For the N-path case the channel output (the input signal to the mobile receiver) is

$$y(t) = \sum_{n=1}^{N} a_n(t)x(t - \tau_n(t)) \cdot \quad (1)$$

Where $a_n(t)$ and $\tau_n(t)$ represent the attenuation and propagation delay associated with the nth multi-path component, respectively. Note that the delays and attenuations are shown as functions of time to indicate that, as the automobile moves, the attenuations and delays, as well as the number of multi-path components, generally change as a function of time. In (1) the additional multi-path components are assumed to be caused by reflections from both natural features, such as mountains, and manmade features, such as additional buildings. Furthermore, each multi-path component or ray may be subjected to local scattering in the vicinity of the mobile due the presence of objects such as signs, road surfaces, and trees located near the mobile, the total signal that arrives at the receiver is made up of the sum of a large number of scattered components [6].

### 3.2 Clarke and Gans Channel Model

Clarke developed a model where the statistical characteristics of the electromagnetic fields of the received signal at the mobile are deduced from scattering. The model assumes a fixed transmitter with a vertically polarized antenna. The field incident on the mobile antenna is assumed to comprise of N azimuthal plane waves with arbitrary carrier phases, arbitrary azimuthal angles of arrival, and each wave having equal average amplitude [7].

Figure 5 shows a diagram of plane waves incident on a mobile traveling at a velocity $v$, in the $x$-direction. The angle of arrival is measured in the $x-y$ plane with respect to the direction of motion. Every wave that is incident on the mobile undergoes a doppler shift due to the motion of the receiver and arrives at the receiver at the same time. That is, no excess delay due to multi-path is assumed for any of the waves (flat fading assumption).

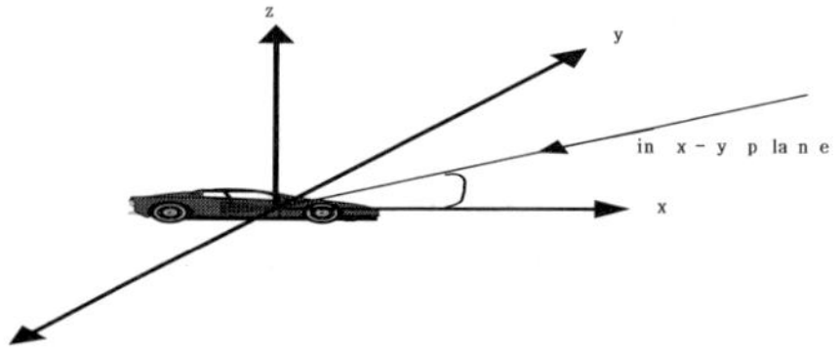


**Fig. 5.** Illustrating plane waves arriving at random angles

For the case of a vertical $\lambda/4$ antenna $(G(\alpha)=1.5)$, and a uniform distribution $p(\alpha)=1/2\pi$ over $[0 \sim 2\pi]$, the output spectrum is given as

$$S_{Ez}(f)=\frac{1.5}{\pi f_m\sqrt{1-\left(\frac{f-f_c}{f_m}\right)^2}}. \tag{2}$$

Where $f_m$ is the maximum doppler shift.

### 3.3 Rummler Fading Channel Model

One of the most widely used models for terrestrial microwave links operating in the frequency range of 4-6 GHz between fixed towers, was developed by Rummler[8].

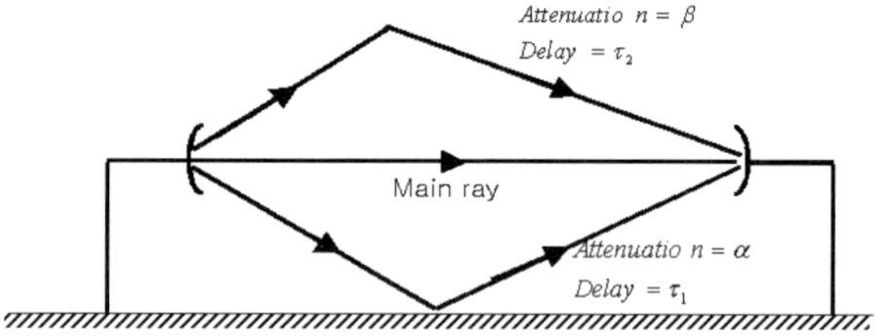


**Fig. 6.** Three-ray LOS channel model of Rummler

This model is based on a set of assumptions, and measured data is used to obtain numerical values of the model parameters. Given the geometry of the link and antenna parameters, Rummler hypothesized a three-ray model of the form

$$y(t)=x(t)+\alpha x(t-\tau_1)+\beta x(t-\tau_2). \tag{3}$$

Where $x(t)$ and $y(t)$ are the bandpass input and output, respectively. The amplitude response of the Rummler model is

$$|H(f)|^2=a^2[1+b^2-2b\cos(2\pi(f-f_0)\tau)]. \tag{4}$$

In this study, regarding the case that the value figure is regularize as 1, and the delaying time is 16[nsec], the regularized two-ray channel, in which the delaying signal 's amplitude b and notch frequency vary, will be modeled and used.

## 4 Simulation Results

This section analyzes each channel's capacity of FPU transmitting system focusing on the BER capacity according to the modulation method in both circumstances of frequency non-selective fading channels and frequency selective fading channels.

In order to consider 3-ray multi-path fading environment we will make the following assumptions:

1. The channel has three paths consisting of an unfaded LOS path and two Rayleigh components. The received power levels associated with each path, and the differential delays between the three paths, are simulation parameters.
2. The Rayleigh fading in the channel affects only the amplitude of the transmitted signal, The instantaneous phase is not affected.
3. The magnitude of the attenuation of each multi-path component is constant over a symbol interval and has independent values over adjacent intervals (no Doppler spectral shaping required).

Table 3 shows the FPU link simulation parameter. Table 4 shows the M/W transmission channel simulation parameter.

**Table 3.** FPU link simulation parameter

| Modulation Mode | TS [Byte] | Block Length [symbol] | Reference Signal Length | Band Efficiency [bit/symbol] | Bit rate [Mbit/s] | Stuffing [symbol] |
|---|---|---|---|---|---|---|
| QPSK | 204 | 19200 | 256 | 2 | 22.368 | 179×16 |
| 16QAM | | | | 4 | 29.824 | 514×16 |
| 64QAM | | | | 6 | 79.056 | 0 |

**Table 4.** M/W transmission channel simulation parameter

<table>
<tr><td>Channel Model</td><td>Fading</td><td colspan="5">Simulation Parameter</td></tr>
<tr><td rowspan="2">Clarke & Gans</td><td rowspan="2">Non-Selective</td><td colspan="2">Maximum Doppler Shift</td><td colspan="2">Frequency</td><td>Speed</td></tr>
<tr><td colspan="2">500 [Hz]</td><td colspan="2">18G</td><td>30km/h</td></tr>
<tr><td rowspan="3">3-ray Multipath fading</td><td></td><td>$P_0$</td><td>$P_1$</td><td>$P_2$</td><td>$\tau$ Delay</td><td>Comment</td></tr>
<tr><td>Non-Selective</td><td>1.0</td><td>0</td><td>0.2</td><td>0</td><td>Ricean Flat Fading</td></tr>
<tr><td>Selective</td><td>1.0</td><td>0</td><td>0.2</td><td>8</td><td>Ricean Frequency Selective Faidng</td></tr>
<tr><td rowspan="2">Rummler 2-ray Multipath Faindg</td><td></td><td colspan="3">Attenuation Coefficient</td><td>Band-width</td><td>Delay($\tau$)</td></tr>
<tr><td>Selective</td><td>0.2</td><td></td><td></td><td>10MHz</td><td>16 [nsec]</td></tr>
<tr><td>Modulation Mode</td><td colspan="6">QPSK, 16QAM, 64QAM</td></tr>
</table>

Fig. 7~8 shows the BER performance graph of FPU system in frequency non-selective fading channel environment. Fig. 7 shows the BER performance graph of FPU system in 3-ray non-selective Multi-path fading environment. Fig. 8 shows the BER performance by modulation mode of FPU system in Glarke & Gans fading environment.

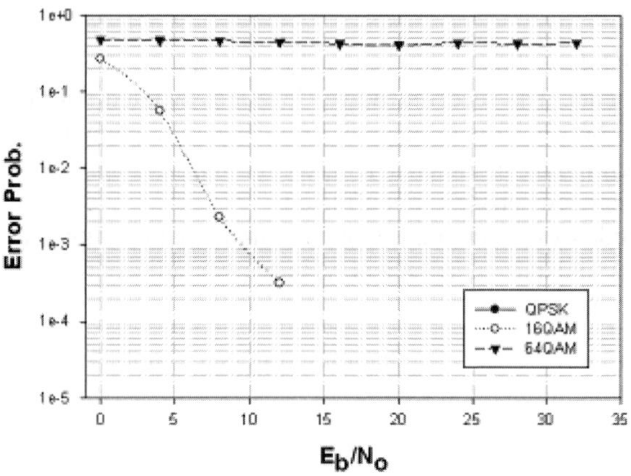


**Fig. 7.** BER performance of FPU system in 3-ray Non-selective multi-path fading environment

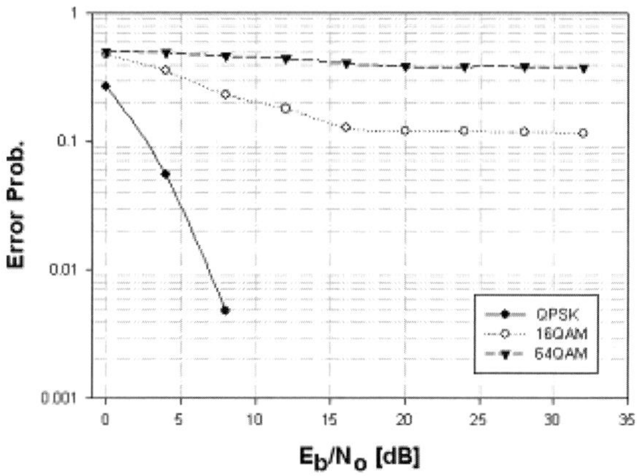


**Fig. 8.** BER Performance of FPU system in Clarke & Gans Non-selective fading environment (maximum doppler shift = 500 Hz)

As a simulation results, we observe that for a given Eb/No, the FPU-QPSK transmission system achieves a lower BER, than other modulation mode in Glarke & Gans frequency non-selective fading environment considered doppler shift. BER performance curve of multi-level modulation (more than 16QAM) undershoot at about $10^{-1}$ BER more than SNR=15dB. We could know that FPU-64QAM transmission system is not influence in the system performance even if increase SNR in frequency non-selective fading environment. But, Fig 7~8 show that the achievable BER performance is better in fading environments with multi-path, than in the fading environments with Doppler in 16QAM modulation mode.

Thus, the results of Fig 7~8 show that the achievable BER performance is better in fading environments with multi-path, than in the fading environments with doppler shift.

Fig. 9~10 shows the BER performance graph by modulation mode of FPU system in frequency selective fading channel environment. Fig. 9 shows the BER performance graph of FPU system in selective 3-ray Multi-path fading environment. Fig. 10 shows the BER performance of FPU system in Two-ray Rummler fading environment.

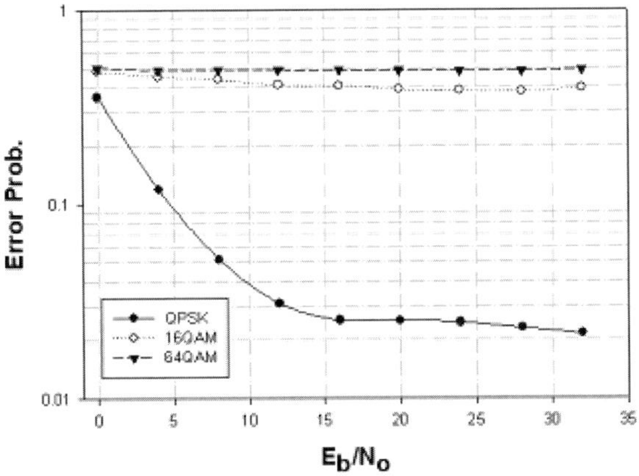


**Fig. 9.** BER performance of FPU system in 3-ray selective multi-path fading environment

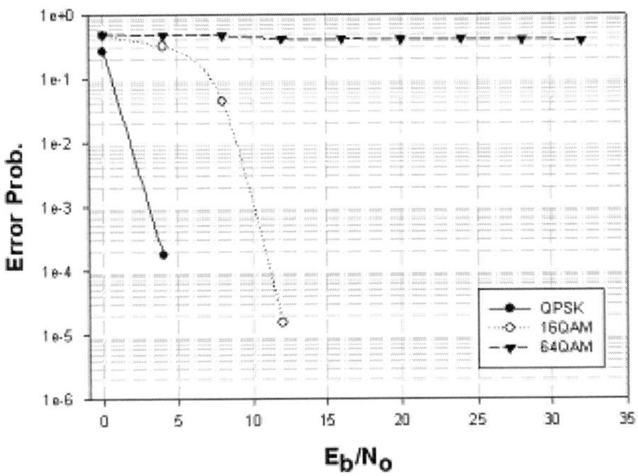


**Fig. 10.** BER performance of FPU system in Two-ray Rummler fading environment (attenuation coefficient = 0.2)

From the results of Fig. 9, we observe that for a given Eb/No, the FPU-QPSK transmission system achieves a lower BER, than 16QAM and 64QAM modulation mode in frequency selective 3-ray multi-path fading environment. But, BER performance curve of the FPU-QPSK transmission system undershoot at about $10^{-2}$ BER more than SNR=15dB in 3-ray multi-path fading environment.

From the results of Fig. 10, BER performance curve of the FPU-16QAM transmission system is about $10^{-5}$ at the Eb/No of 12dB when attenuation coefficient is 0.2 in Rummler channel environment

Thus, the results of Fig 9~10 show that the achievable BER performance is better in fading environments with attenuation coefficient, than in the fading environments with multi-path in frequency selective fading channel environments .

## 5 Conclusions

In this paper, we have modeled of Adaptive Digital FPU link system in M/W band portable digital wireless transmission system. Also, we analyzed digital FPU system performance adopt adaptive modulation scheme in variable channel environment

As a simulation results, we could know that the digital FPU system show that the achievable BER performance is better in multi-path fading environments, than in the fading environments considered doppler shift in the presence of frequency non-selective fading.

In the case of multi level modulation more than 16QAM modulation scheme, we could know that digital FPU system is not influence in the system performance even if increase SNR in frequency-selective 3-ray multi-path fading environment. But in the case of Rummler's fading environment, we could know that reception performance is changed clearly by attenuation coefficient of multi-path fading.

Therefore, we have come to know that it would be possible to draw the minimum SNR through the application of necessary SNR & degree of damping coefficient of a reflected wave and improvement method in order to meet the performance required in case that the transmission method of more than 16QAM is operated in M/W band.

## Acknowledgement

This research was supported by the Program for the Training of Graduate Students in Regional Innovation which was conducted by the Ministry of Commerce Industry and Energy of the Korean Government

## References

1. Korea Radio Promotion Association: A Study on the Policy of the Radio Spectrum Use (2004)
2. Korea Radio Promotion Association: A Study on the Pre-planing of Frequency Use (2003)
3. ARIB STD-B11
4. ARIB STD-B18

5. Bello, P. A.: Characterization of Randomly Time-Variant Linear Channels. IEEE Transactions on Communication Systems, Vol. 11, No. 4 (1963) 360-393
6. William H. T.: Shanmugan, K. S., Rappaport, Theodore S., Kosbar, Kurt L.: Principles Of Communication Systems Simulation with Wireless Applications. Prentice Hall
7. Rappaport, T.: Wireless Communications, Prentics Hall (1999)
8. Rummler, W. D., Counts, R. P., Lineger, M.: Multipath Fading Models for Microwave Digital Radio. IEEE Communication Magazine, Vol. 24, No. 11 (1986) 30-42

# A Component for Management System and Ubiquitous Environment

Malrey Lee and Kang Yun Jeong

Department of Computer Science, Chonbuk National University 664-14 1ga Duckjin-Dong Duckjin-Gu, Jeonju , 561-756, South Korea
mrlee@chonbuk.ac.kr

**Abstract.** Management system is based on agent is divided into two parts such as operational and collaborative customer management and analytical customer management for ubiquitous environment. This system is in charge of marketing automation and customer services which are included in operational and collaborative is developed. And the analytical engine part which can create report in using and analyzing data mining technology which is based on the rules with collecting customer information is developed, too. The operational customer management part takes part in various channels and customer check and it is consisted of many components which are necessary for communication. This was implemented through basis of specialized components and it supports the concept of ASP service. Through the development of a module, which helps to use existing data environment more effectively, it supports and creates an environment that users can use easily.

## 1 Introduction

The operational part takes part in various channels and customer check and it is consisted of many components which are necessary for communication. The collaborative part is combined with the application of customer check and it is consisted of components such as business automation, marketing automation, customer service, and support. The data problems which can be created in the real world should be indicated, and the tasks which can be solved before data analysis should be suggested, and finally the development of appropriate way of analyzing is necessary. The analytical which is the major part in this paper is consisted of many components which analyzes data using data mining technology. This system consists of the component module independently and reusable, so interface is comprised for user convenience. Also, it is organized to make easy customizing and maintenance of component module. It is guaranteed the high confidentiality in using tested technology and library component system in data analysis technology.

In section 2, we describe the related study; in section 3, describe the developmental environment of customer management system. Finally section 4 describes the result and future of the research.

D.-S. Huang, K. Li, and G.W. Irwin (Eds.): ICIC 2006, LNCS 4113, pp. 1072 – 1077, 2006.

## 2 Related Studies

Component management system is developed on customer-centered service[1]. This means that if we manage the existing customer well, it is possible to sell various products and more expensive products and it is the approach that the marketing fees for alluring new customers takes triple the amount of maintaining existing customer. Also, data base marketing and e-mail marketing can be a good means of maintaining existing customer. But without solving the convenience of customer, the trial through E-mail is questionable. This is the business centered thought but not a real component customer management. The realm of management system is included in internal process automation, operational automation, E-commerce, marketing automation, customer data warehousing construction, OLAP and data mining, call center, and e-service based on web; and the successful construction of them, the back office system and the integration with Legacy System are important and also they are technically difficult part[1,2]. Component management system based on agent analyzes various data which can be occurred on the web including web log data and it divides the data in the different way according to researchers. In this paper web data are divided into log data, customer data, and marketing related data according to the characteristic of acquiring data[5]. The primary problem in analyzing large capacity of data is time consuming in calculation. To solve this problem, hard ware point of view and soft ware point of view can be considered such as to extend the capacity of computer memory equipment and to use parallel/distributed computing utilizing many central processing units. Also, in statistical way, it abstracts sample from data base and utilizes similar information such as OLAP[3,4].

In this paper, I use summary for effectiveness of large capacity data. The original purpose of summary table is to manage the statistical summary information into the secondary table form and the summary table using this paper is utilized in saving structure the step by step information in using data analysis.

## 3 Component Composition

The component management system based on agents developed in this paper is divided into two parts such as operational/collaborative and analytical; and the system which is in charge of marketing automation and customer service in operational/ collaborative is developed. Operational system manages various channels and customer check and it is composed of components which are necessary in communication. Collaborative is the unified which is combined customer check application and it is composed of many components such as operational automation, marketing automation, customer service and support.

The role of engine part is to collect the information from customer and produce the report in using and analyzing data mining technology based on the rule which already collected the customer information. The analytical component is a core part of this paper and it is composed of component which is using data mining technology and analyzing data. The component which was developed in this paper is focused on the data which is analyzed in applying various analysis techniques and providing the analyzed information to the customer. The most important role in CM system is the data analysis technique for abstracting data and the use of information technique of abstracted information which can be provided effectively. So, the research on the development of data analysis technique and effective use of information technique are very important. The implemented system can be used easily with simple customizing procedure in using on the real web-site which is the same on shopping site. The problem in formatting and utilizing the result of data analysis is the consideration of business environment.

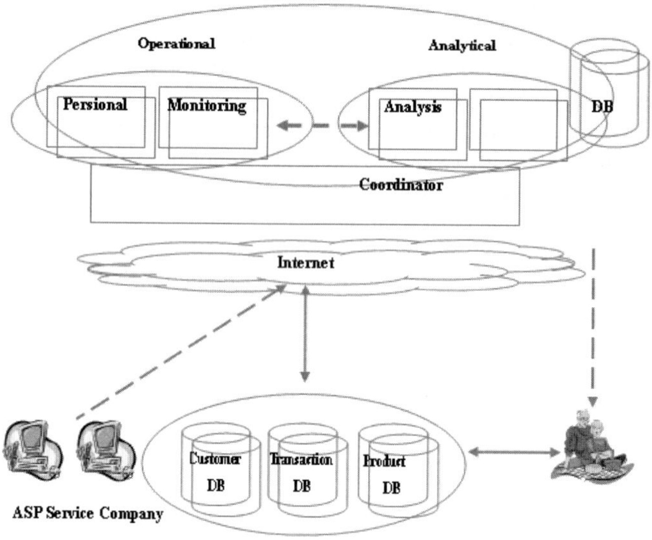


**Fig. 1.** Environment of Component

## 3.1 System Structure

The purpose of the general data analyzing applications is to analysis the data which is downloaded in various forms. For example, the data can be downloaded directly or it can be used in the saved file form. Recently, the analysis about the data which is saved in the data base is also possible. But we should know exactly the structure about table of data base to use the saved data in data base from application. In other words, without knowing the structure about table of data base which is saved, it is difficult to analyze the data. For example, the data base table is divided into many parts and it is essential to join the table to analyze the data. This figure shows the service to the customer through analysis procedure and provides the information about analysis and feedback to the business manager. As we can see, management system starts from constructing the data warehouse with collecting various data about customer. Data warehouse is not for saving the data but for utilizing data. So, before construction, we should consider the kind of data and the form of preparation to analyze the data. The content about data preparation is important in system design and implementation for analyzing data which is saved in data base and this is different from the application for analyzing general data.

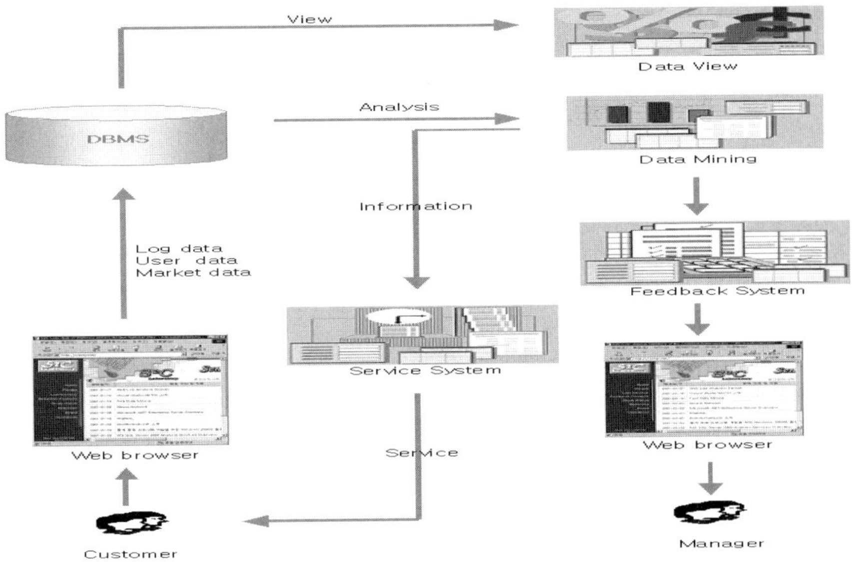


**Fig. 2.** Component System Structure

## 3.2 Component

The component which collects the information about customer and shares this information with each other is developed to construct the effective system in operational part. This is the most basic stage for valuable and much information which is scattered should be collected with the help of web, telephone and mail to support customer management in this stage. Operational component which is developed in this paper is for analyzing web log data and web site traffic management and effective analysis for site should be accomplished. Collaborative is composed of the component which can communicative effectively with the customer using information which is acquired from operational and analysis about customer. This is the stage for providing personalized service and also the value of CCM can be decided in this stage. So, this is the important part because the customer feels directly the concern of business to the customer. The component to support operational automation, marketing automation and customer service are developed in collaborative.

Analytical system is composed of the component which can abstract valuable information through data analytical procedure which is collected in operational part. The valuable information which has not known yet can be acquired to satisfy the customer request based on those information. So, the level of customer management is getting higher and the marketing strategy can be accomplished effectively. In this stage, the component to analyze data using data mining technology is developed. Analytical is the core part of this paper and it is composed of pattern discovery component, product and customer analysis component, multitude component, sorting and customer fractionation component, and customer value evaluation component.

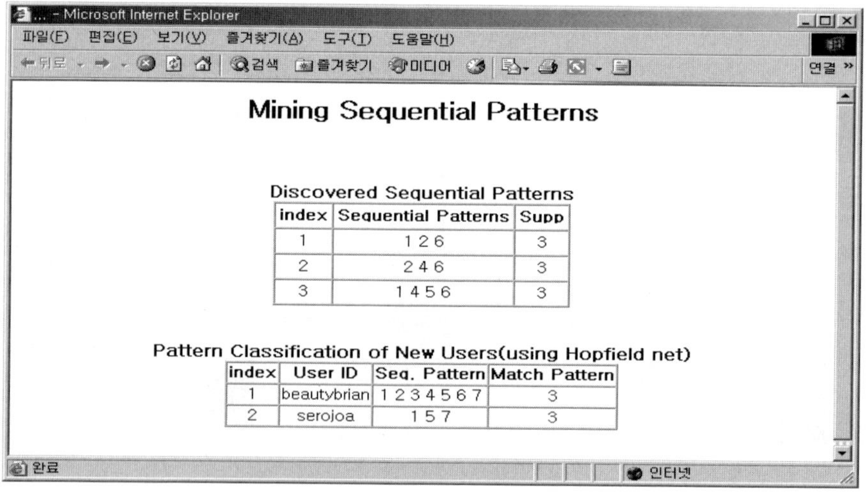


**Fig. 3.** Consecutive pattern and Sort

Figure 3 shows a scene which abstracts the consecutive pattern of customer visiting web site and sort new visiting customer pattern. All algorithm and to sort new customer, Hopfield network algorithm which is one of network techniques is used. Sorting customer according to visiting pattern is important information to provide personalized service.

The purpose of component management system is to maximize the benefit of business with strong relationship between customers based on the information about customer starting from the acquired data about customer. To do this, the understanding of economical value of individual customer is essentially required. The economical value of customer is varied from high income customer to low income customer.

## 4 Conclusions

In this paper, the system which is appropriate for small and middle business rather than large business was developed in ubiquitous environment. It is easy to use because it was developed on the basis of characterized component and also it was developed with low price for small and middle business. The necessity of comprehensive system for satisfying and solidifying customer desire has been increased. The system which was developed in this paper is helpful in the advancement of customer analysis ability, the improvement of management support ability, and the improvement of marketing achievement ability, and consequently, it contributes to elevate the marketing effect. The development of component which can use the various analysis techniques and the detailed strategy for developing more effective system to apply to the real business environment are necessary in the near future for ubiquitous environment.

## Acknowledgement

This work was supported by grant R01-2006-000-10147-0 from the basic Research Program of THE Korea Science & Engineering Foundation.

## References

1. David, B.: eCRM/What is eCRM?, Ovum, (2001)
2. Eisenfeld, B., Close, W.: Benefits to be gained from eCRM. Gartner, 12 (2000) 1-6
3. Peter, S., Manuela, V.: Multiagent Systems: A Survey from a Machine Learning Perspective. Autonomous Robots, 8 (2000) 345-383
4. Friedman, J. H.: Data Mining and Statistics : What's the Connection?, Proceedings of the International Conference on the Interface: Computing Science and Statistics, (1997)
5. Micheal, P. W.: Some Economics of Market-based Distributed Scheduling, In 18th International Conference on Distributed Computing System, Amsterdam, Holand (1998)

# A Novel Feature Extraction Approach to Face Recognition Based on Partial Least Squares Regression

Yuan-Yuan Wan[1,2], Ji-Xiang Du[1,2], and Kang Li[3]

[1] Intelligent Computing Lab, Hefei Institute of Intelligent Machines, Chinese Academy of Sciences, P.O.Box 1130, HeFei Anhui 230031, China
{yywan, du_jx}@iim.ac.cn

[2] Department of Automation, University of Science and Technology of China, Hefei 230027, China

[3] School of Electrical & Electronic Engineering Queen's University Belfast, UK

**Abstract.** In this paper, partial least square (PLS) regression is firstly employed in image processing. And a new technique coined partial least squares (PLS) regression, line-based PLS, is proposed for feature extraction of the images. To test this new approach, a series of experiments were performed on the famous face image database: ORL face database. Compared with newly proposed two dimensional principal component analysis (2DPCA), it can be found that the dimension of the feature vectors of the line-based PLS is no more than half of the 2DPCA's while the recognition rate can retain at the same high level. Thus, the feature extraction based on line-based PLS regression is a feasible and effective method.

## 1 Introduction

Partial least squares (PLS) regression is a recently proposed technique that generalizes and combines features from principal component analysis and multiple regression. It is particularly useful when we need to predict a set of dependent variables from a very large set of independent variables (i.e., predictors). In other words, PLS regression is competent for the situation that the number of independent variables (i.e., predictors) is larger than the number of samples. It originated in the social sciences, especially in economy [1], but it became popular first in chemometrics (i.e., computational chemistry [2] [3]) and in sensory evaluation [4]. However, up to now, this method has been rarely used in image processing. Hence, such kind of attempt was presented in this paper. It was first proposed as an algorithm akin to the power method used for computing eigenvectors but it was rapidly interpreted in a statistical framework[5][6].

In this paper, the PLS regression was employed to extract features from the image matrix. Firstly, the image matrix was transformed into a long vector. Afterwards, the PLS regression (also called 1DPLS in this paper) was directly used according to the class labels. Then considering the characteristic of the matrix itself, A little alteration without using that kind of transformation (called line-based PLS in this paper) was made. Finally, in order to evaluate the performances of above two methods, we respectively made a comparison with PCA and 2DPCA proposed by Jian Yang, David Zhang et al. [7]. For the sake of impartial comparison, the same database, a famous

D.-S. Huang, K. Li, and G.W. Irwin (Eds.): ICIC 2006, LNCS 4113, pp. 1078 – 1084, 2006.

face image database: ORL and the same classifier: nearest neighbor classifier for classification were utilized. Note that the evaluation results of PCA and 2DPCA were totally taken from [7]. So it was really very impartial. The final experimental results showed that both of those two kinds of approaches, 1DPLS and line-based PLS, were more superior respectively to 1DPCA and 2DPCA. They extracted more effective features from the images. Therefore, while keeping the recognition accuracy on the same high level, their dimensions of feature vectors were respectively less than that of 1DPCA or 2DPCA, actually only half of the dimension of 1DPCA or 2DPCA.

The remainder of this paper is organized as follows: In Section 2, the idea and algorithm of PLS regression is described. The experiments and analysis are discussed in Section 3. In the end, some conclusions are presented in Section 4.

## 2 Partial Least Squares Regression

### 2.1 Idea of the PLS Regression

Let $X \subset R^{I \times K}$ , $Y \subset R^{I \times J}$ respectively be predictor matrix and response matrix. The goal of the PLS regression is to predict Y from X, and at the same time, to describe their common structure. Different from the PCA, PLS regression tries to find components from X that are also relevant to Y. Specially the PLS regression is to search for a set of components (called latent vectors) and it performs a simultaneous decomposition of X and Y with the constraint that these components explain the covariance between X and Y as much as possible. This step generalizes the PCA. It is followed by a regression step where the decomposition of X is used to predict Y [8].

The PLS regression can decompose both $X$ and $Y$ as a product of a common set of orthogonal factors and a set of specific loadings. So, the independent variables are decomposed as $X = TP^T$ with $T^T T = I$ with $I$ being the identity matrix (some variations of the technique do not require T to have unit norms). Similar to the PCA, $T$ is called the score matrix and $P$ the loading matrix (in PLS regression the loadings are not orthogonal). Likewise, $Y$ is estimated as $\hat{Y} = TBC^T$ where $B$ is a diagonal matrix with the "regression weights" as diagonal elements (see below for more details on these weights). The columns of $T$ are the latent vectors. Note that $\widehat{Y}$ is only an evaluation of $Y$ .In general $\widehat{Y}$ is not equal to $Y$ [9].

In order to specify $T$ , additional conditions are required. For PLS regression, this amounts to finding two sets of weights $w$ and $c$ in order to create (respectively) a linear combination of the columns of $X$ and $Y$ such that their covariance is maximized. Specially, the goal is to obtain a first pair of vectors $t = Xw$ and $u = Yc$ with the constraints that $w^T w = 1$ , $t^T t = 1$ and $t^T u$ is maximal. When the first latent vector is found, it is subtracted from both $X$ and $Y$ , and then the procedure is reiterated until $X$ becomes a null matrix (please see the algorithm section for more details) [12].

### 2.2 PLS Regression Algorithm

The first step is to create two matrices: $E = X$ and $F = Y$. These matrices are then column centered and normalized. Before starting the iteration process, the vector $u$ is initialized with random values. (in what follows the symbol $\propto$ means "to normalize the result of the operation") [10].

Step 1. $w \propto E^T u$ (estimate $X$ weights).
Step 2. $t \propto Ew$ (estimate $X$ factor scores).
Step 3. $c \propto F^T t$ (estimate $Y$ weights).
Step 4. $u = Fc$ (estimate $Y$ scores).

If $t$ has not converged, then go to Step 1, if $t$ has converged, then compute the value of $b$ which is used to predict $Y$ from $t$ as $b = t^T u$, and compute the factor loadings for $X$ as $p = E^T t$. Now subtract the effect of $t$ from both $E$ and $F$ as follows $E = E - tp^T$ and $F = F - btc^T$. The vectors $t, u, w, c$ and $p$ are then stored in the corresponding matrices, and the scalar $b$ is stored as a diagonal element of $B$. If $E$ is a null matrix, then the whole set of latent vectors has been found. Otherwise the procedure can be re-iterated from Step 1 on.

### 2.3 PLS Regression and the Singular Value Decomposition

The iterative algorithm presented above is similar to the power method which finds eigenvectors. So PLS regression is likely to be closely related to the eigen and singular value decompositions, and this is indeed the case. For example, if we start from Step 1 which computes: $w \propto E^T u$, and substitute the rightmost term iteratively, we find the following series of equations:

$$w \propto E^T u \propto E^T Fc \propto E^T FF^T t \propto E^T FF^T Ew$$

This shows that the first weight vector $w$ is the first right singular vector of the matrix $X^T Y$. Similarly, the first weight vector $c$ is the left singular vector of $X^T Y$.

## 3 Experiments and Analysis

### 3.1 Database

The ORL database (htpp://www.cam-orl.co.uk) is utilized which contains images from 40 individuals, each providing 10 different images. For some subjects, the images were taken at different times. The facial expressions (open or closed eyes, smiling or non-smiling) and facial details (glasses or no glasses) also vary. The images were taken with a tolerance for some tilting and rotation of the face of up to 20 degrees. Moreover, there is also some variation in the scale of up to about 10 percent. All images are grayscale and normalized to a resolution of 92*112 pixels (so the size of image matrix is 112*92). Five sample images of one person from the ORL database are shown in Fig.1.

**Fig. 1.** Five samples images of one subject in the ORL face database

### 3.2 1D PLS

In the PLS regression, data table $X$ has $I$ rows and $K$ columns. Each row denotes a sample and each sample has $K$ features. But every sample in ORL is an image, in other words, a matrix. The most probable method is to transform the image matrix into a large vector. ($1\times10304$). Some experiments were performed based on this concept. At that time, $X$ was a big $I\times10304$ matrix and each row denoted a sample image in the database. And $Y$ was a $I\times1$ vector representing the corresponding class labels of all the samples. After fixing $X$ and $Y$, 1DPLS was employed. Then the latent vectors $T$ were gained which were the principal components of $X$ and simultaneously relevant to $Y$ (the class information). Afterwards $T$ could be used as the features extracted from source images.

Moreover, in order to test its performance, comparative experiments were made using PCA to extract features from $X$ . At first, an experiment was performed using the first five image samples per class for training, and the remaining images for test. Thus, the total number of training samples and testing samples was both 200. The trial result is shown in Table 1. Experiments respectively with $4, 3, 2, 1$ training sample(s) per class were also made. Corresponding results are shown in Table 1, too. Particularly, the performance of 1DPCA was tested by Jian Yang, David Zhang [7]. The same database and the same nearest neighbor classifier were utilized. Furthermore, for each trial, the number of training samples per class was also the same. Note that the values in parentheses denote the dimension of feature vectors for the best recognition accuracy. We can see that both 1DPCA and 1DPLS can gain the equivalent level of recognition accuracy, but the dimension of feature vectors for 1DPLS is less than half of the 1DPCA's.

The values in parentheses denote the dimension of feature vectors for the best recognition accuracy. Note that the best choices of the number of the components for the top recognition accuracy depend on the test data and are not known beforehand in a real problem.

**Table 1.** Comparison of the Top Recognition Accuracy (%) of 1DPCA versus 1DPLS

| #Training samples /class | 1DPCA | 1DPLS |
|---|---|---|
| 1 | 66.9 (39) | 67.22 (15) |
| 2 | 84.7 (79) | 81.25 (20) |
| 3 | 88.2 (95) | 88.93 (18) |
| 4 | 90.8 (60) | 90.42 (15) |
| 5 | 93.5 (37) | 93.5 (16) |

**Table 2.** Comparison of the Top Recognition Accuracy (%) of 2DPCA versus Line-based PLS

| #Training samples /class | 2DPCA | Line-based PLS |
|---|---|---|
| 1 | 76.7(112*2) | 75.56 (56*2) |
| 2 | 89.1 (112*2) | 88.4 (56*2) |
| 3 | 91.8 (112*6) | 92.5 (56*4) |
| 4 | 95.0 (112*5) | 96.25 (56*2) |
| 5 | 96.0 (112*3) | 95.5 (56*2) |

### 3.3 Line-Based PLS

The feature extraction based on 1DPLS seems available, but the matrix $X$ is so large that it enormously increases computing complication. So we attempted to use PLS in another way. Jian Yang, David Zhang extended 1DPCA to 2DPCA [7]. Liwei Wang and Xiao Wang demonstrated that 2DPCA was equivalent to line-based PCA [11]. So we tried to use line-based PLS. Since we all know that every pixel's gray is very close to the neighbor's. Consequently for every sample image, in other words, every sample matrix, we took out the first row and finally saved all the first rows as $X$ . An example is shown in Fig 2. $X$ is formed by all the first rows of the three matrices. Similarly, all the second rows were taken out and saved as $Y$ . Then PLS regression was used to extract the latent vectors $T_1$ using $X$ and $Y$ . It is obvious that $T_1$ is the right common structure which represents both $X$ and $Y$ . And iteratively $X$ denoted all the third rows and $Y$ presented all the fourth rows so $T_2$ was extracted. The procedure is re-iterated until no more rows are left.

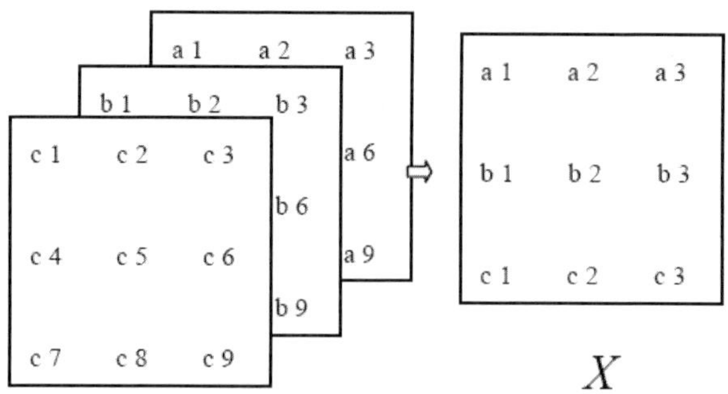


**Fig. 2.** Extract all the first rows and form a new matrix $X$

After the PLS regression process, a three dimensional matrix composed by $T_1, T_2, \cdots, T_n$ was obtained. At that time, every source image corresponded to a small matrix. If the size of source image matrix is 112*92, the number of the samples is 400 and two principle components are extracted from $X$ and $Y$ which correspond two rows, then the size of the small matrix mentioned previously is 56*2. Consequently we could use such kind of small matrix extracted by line-based matrix as the features of the source image.

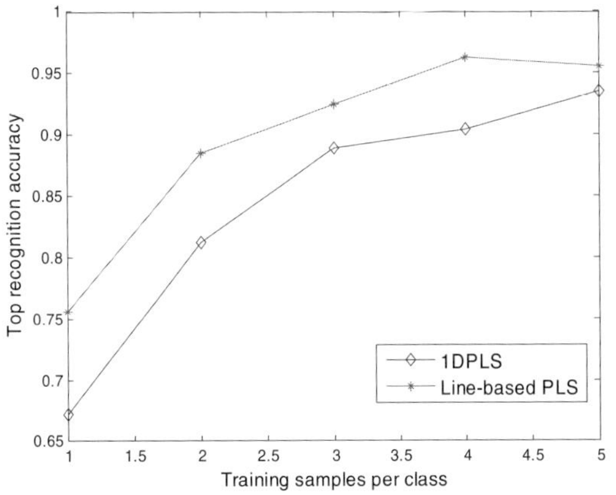


**Fig. 3.** Comparison of the Top Recognition Accuracy of 1DPLS versus Line-based PLS

Similarly to the 1DPLS, we compared line-based PLS with 2DPCA newly proposed by Jian Yang, David Zhang on PAMI [7], see Table 2. The data of recognition accuracy using 2DPCA is all taken from the previously mentioned paper. We used the same database (ORL) and the same classifier (the nearest neighbor classifier). Only the approaches are different. All the values in parentheses denote the dimension of feature vectors for the best recognition accuracy by 2DPCA and line-based PLS. So it is very rational and fair. From Table 2 it is obvious that line-based PLS can retain the same level of recognition accuracy of 2DPCA and simultaneously can sharply reduce the dimension of the feature vectors. Figure 3 also indicates that line-based PLS is even better than 1DPLS considering recognition accuracy.

## 4 Conclusion

In this paper, PLS regression was firstly employed in image feature extraction. In order to test its performance, some experiments were performed on the famous face image database, ORL. Moreover, corresponding comparison between PCA and PLS was also made. The experimental results showed that PLS could reduce more dimensions of feature vectors than PCA did, while keeping the recognition accuracy on the same level. Particularly, line-based PLS performed better than 2DPCA on reducing the dimension of the feature vector. From this point, we can see feature extraction based on PLS regression, especially line-based PLS, is a very useful and effective approach.

## References

1. Wold, H.: Estimation of Principal Components and Related Model by Iterative Least Squares. Multivariate Analysis. New York: Academic Press, (1966) 391-420
2. Frank, I.E., Friedman, J.H.: A Statistical View of Chemometrics Regression Tools. Technometrics, 35 (1988) 109-148
3. Martens, H., Naes, T.: Multivariate Calibration. London: Wiley (1989)
4. Anthony, R.M., Natasha, R., Nanch, J. L.: Interactions of Prefrontal Cortex in Relation to Awareness in Sensory Learning. Science, Vol.284 (1999 )
5. Helland, I.S.: PLS Regression and Statistical Models. Scandivian Journal of Statistics, 17 (1990) 97-114
6. Hoskuldson, A.: PLS Regression Method. Journal of Chemometrics, 2 (1988) 211-228
7. Yang, J., Zhang, D., et al.: Two-Dimensional PCA: A New Approach to Appearance-Based Face Representation and Recognition. IEEE Transaction on Pattern Analysis and Machine Intelligence, Vol.26 (2004) 131-137
8. Huang, D.S.: Systematic Theory of Neural Networks for Pattern Recognition. Publishing House of Electronic Industry of China, Beijing (1996)
9. Huang, D.S.: Radial Basis Probabilistic Neural Networks: Model and Application, International Journal of Pattern Recognition and Artificial Intelligence, 13(7) (1999) 1083-1101
10. Herve, A.: Partial Least Squares (PLS) Regression. Encyclopedia of Social Sciences Research Method (2003)
11. Wang, L.W., Wang, X., Zhang, X.R., Feng, J.F.: The Equivalence of Two-Dimensional PCA to Line-based PCA. Pattern Recognition Letters, 26 (2005) 57-60
12. Wang, H.W.: Partial Least-Squares Regression Method and Applications. National Defence Industrial University Press (1999)

# A Novel Feature Fusion Approach Based on Blocking and Its Application in Image Recognition

Xing Yan[1,3], Lei Cao[2], De-Shuang Huang, Kang Li[4], and George Irwin[4]

[1] Intelligent Computing Lab, Hefei Institute of Intelligent Machines, Chinese Academy of Sciences, P.O. Box 1130, HeFei Anhui 230031, China
xyan@iim.ac.cn, xyan@mail.ustc.edu.cn
[2] Artillery Academy of People Liberation Army, HeFei, Anhui 230031, China
[3] Department of Automation, University of Science and Technology of China, HeFei 230027, China
[4] School of Electrical & Electronic Engineering Queen's University Belfast

**Abstract.** According to the idea of canonical correlation analysis, a block-based method for feature extraction is proposed. The main process can be explained as follows: extract two groups of feature vectors from different blocks which belong to the same pattern; and then extract their canonical correlation features to form more effective discriminant vectors for recognition. To test this new approach, the experiment is performed on ORL face database and it shows that the recognition rate is higher than that of algorithm adopting single feature.

## 1 Introduction

Feature fusion has achieved delightful development in recent years. Feature fusion method aims at increasing the recognition rate. Obviously, the feature vectors extracted from different blocks of the same pattern always reflect the different features. Through combining them to get the correlations between them, it will not only keep the most effective discriminant information, but also eliminate the redundant information. Apparently, this is very important to the classification and recognition.

Canonical Correlation Analysis(CCA) is a statistical method of correlating two multidimensional variables, it deals with the mutual relationships between them. As a very important multivariate statistical analysis, CCA has been applied to many fields such as speech recognition, signal processing and computer vision etc.

In the CCA-based pattern recognition technique, Sun et al.[1] used CCA as a feature fusion method. They argued that the using of correlation features between two groups of feature vectors as effective discriminant information is not only suitable for information fusion, but also eliminates the redundant information within the features.

In this paper, a block-based method adopting the idea of CCA is proposed. At first, divide the image sample into two blocks and extract feature vectors respectively, then extract their canonical correlation features according to some definite criterions, and to form more effective discriminant vectors for recognition. This method uses canonical correlation variables between two groups of feature vectors belonging to different

D.-S. Huang, K. Li, and G.W. Irwin (Eds.): ICIC 2006, LNCS 4113, pp. 1085 – 1091, 2006.

blocks of the same pattern as more effective discriminant information. It will increase the recognition accuracy, and at the same time, decrease the feature dimensions.

The final experimental results on ORL standard face database show that recognition rate is higher than that of adopting the feature of the whole image. This algorithm can reflect the essential feature of the images.

The remainder of this paper is organized as follows: In Section 2, the theory and method of CCA are described. In Section 3, the block-based feature fusion method is presented. In Section 4, the proposed method has been tested on the ORL face database. In the end, some conclusions are presented in Section 5.

## 2 The Theory and Method of CCA

### 2.1 The Basic Idea

CCA was developed by H.Hotelling in 1936 [6]. Canonical correlation analysis can be defined as the problem of finding two sets of basis vectors, one for $X$ and the other for $Y$, such that the correlations between the projections of the variables onto these basis vectors are mutually maximized.

Given two zero-mean random variables X and Y, CCA finds a pair of directions $w_{11}$ and $w_{21}$ that maximize the correlation between the projections $u_1 = w_{11}^T x$ and $v_1 = w_{21}^T y$. In the context of CCA, the projections $u_1$ and $v_1$ are also referred to as canonical variates. Then the second pair of canonical variates $u_2$ and $v_2$ can be found, which is uncorrelated with $u_1$ and $v_1$ and meanwhile also maximize the correlation between $u_2$ and $v_2$.Repeat like this until all the canonical variates are extracted. According to studying the correlation of these canonical variates, the correlation between X and Y can be found indirectly.

### 2.2 The Theory of Feature Extraction Based on CCA

Given two zero-mean random variables $x = (x_1, x_2 ......x_n) \in R^n$ and $y = (y_1, y_2 ......y_m) \in R^m$, our goal is to extract the canonical correlation features between $x$ and $y$ using CCA.

Considering their linear combination

$$\begin{aligned} u &= w_1^T x = w_{11} x_1 + w_{12} x_2 + ......w_{1n} x_n, \\ v &= w_2^T y = w_{21} y_1 + w_{22} y_2 + ......w_{2m} y_m. \end{aligned} \quad (1)$$

we call $w_{1i}^T x$ and $w_{2i}^T y$ the ith pair of Canonical Variates(CV). Next we will discuss how to get CV. Suppose the covariance matrix of $z = \begin{pmatrix} x \\ y \end{pmatrix}$ can be denoted as

$$\Sigma = \begin{pmatrix} Var(x) & Cov(x,y) \\ Cov(y,x) & Var(y) \end{pmatrix} = \begin{pmatrix} \Sigma_{11} & \Sigma_{12} \\ \Sigma_{21} & \Sigma_{22} \end{pmatrix}. \tag{2}$$

The criterion function can be given as the following:

$$P = P_{u.v} = \frac{Cov(u,v)}{\sqrt{Var(u)Var(v)}} = w_1^T Cov(x,y) w_2 = w_1^T \Sigma_{12} \, w_2. \tag{3}$$

So the question can been converted to solving of generalized eigenvalue and eigenvector of Eqs.(4) and (5).

$$(\Sigma_{11}^{-1} \Sigma_{12} \Sigma_{22}^{-1} \Sigma_{21})w_1 = \lambda^2 w_1, \tag{4}$$

$$(\Sigma_{22}^{-1} \Sigma_{21} \Sigma_{11}^{-1} \Sigma_{12})w_2 = \lambda^2 w_2. \tag{5}$$

In order to get the solution, suppose that

$$H = \Sigma_{11}^{-1/2} \Sigma_{12} \Sigma_{22}^{-1/2}, G_1 = H^T H, G_2 = H^T H,$$

using Singular Value Decompose(SVD) on $H$ ,we obtain $H = \sum_{i=1}^{p} d_i \alpha_i \beta_i^T$ ,where $d_1^2 \ge d_2^2 \ge ... \ge d_p^2$ are the nonzero eigenvalues of $G_1$ and $G_2$, $\alpha_i$ and $\beta_i$ are the orthogonal eigenvectors of $G_1$ and $G_2$ respectively corresponding to the eigenvalue $d_i^2$. We call

$$w_{1i} = \Sigma_{11}^{-1/2} \alpha_i, w_{2i} = \Sigma_{22}^{-1/2} \beta_i \tag{6}$$

the $i$ th Canonical Vectors(CVR) of $x$ and $y$ respectively, and we call the linear combination:

$$u_i = w_{1i}^T x, v_1 = w_{2i}^T y \tag{7}$$

the $i$ th Canonical Variates (CV) of $x$ and $y$ respectively.

## 3 The Block-Based Algorithm

There are several conventional rules can be used to combine $u$ and $v$:

Max rule: DV=max($u, v$). (8)

Min rule: DV=min($u, v$). (9)

Product rule: DV=($u \cdot v$). (10)

$$\text{Mean rule: DV}=\frac{(u+v)}{2}. \tag{11}$$

The steps of this algorithm can be described as follows:

**Step 1:** Divide every pattern into two blocks.
**Step 2:** Extract two feature vectors(same or different) from the two blocks belonging to the same pattern respectively to form X and Y.
**Step 3:** Compute the CV, choose the first d pairs of CV to form u and v.
**Step 4:** Use the linear feature fusion strategy Eq.(11) to form the final Discriminant Vectors(DV).

## 4 Experiments and Analysis

### 4.1 Database

The ORL database (htpp://www.cam-orl.co.uk) is utilized which contains images from 40 individuals, each providing 10 different images. For some subjects, the images were taken at different times. The facial expressions (open or closed eyes, smiling or nonsmiling) and facial details (glasses or no glasses) also vary. The images were taken with a tolerance for some tilting and rotation of the face of up to 20 degrees. Moreover, there is also some variation in the scale of up to about 10 percent. All images are grayscale and normalized to a resolution of 92*112 pixels. Five sample images of one person from the ORL database are shown in Fig.1.

**Fig. 1.** Five samples images of one subject in the ORL face database

### 4.2 Experiments on the ORL Database

The experiment is performed using the first five image samples per class for training, and the remaining image samples for testing. Thus, both the number of training samples and that of testing ones are 200.

In the first experiment, firstly we divide the original training images into two blocks with the same size, from the top down, so the size of each block is 56*92. Then we extract the singular value feature vectors of each pair of blocks to make the two feature space of samples X and Y, at last we combine the two groups of features using CCA.

In this experiment, the 2DSVD[2] method is used to compute the orthonormal feature vectors from the two blocks of the training samples, 56*92 dimension singular-value feature vectors of original image will be reduced to 10*10 dimension respectively. Then we use CCA to extract the CVR and CV, we choose the first $d$ pairs of CV to form $u$ and $v$. Finally we use Eq.(11) to form the feature vectors. Since during this process, the CVR $w_1$ and $w_2$ have been gotten, to the testing samples, we utilize the CVR and Eq.(7) to form the CV and DV of the testing samples. Finally after employing the nearest-neighbor classifier, the recognition results are shown in Table 1.

In order to test its performance, the SVD method and the 2DSVD method based on single feature is given out. Recognition result is also given in Table.1 by taking the nearest-neighbor classifier.

In the second experiment, we use the same strategy to get X and Y. Here we also divide the images into two blocks with different sizes (20% to 80%, 40% to 60%, 50% to 50%, 60% to 40% and 80% to 20% ), the PCA method is used to compute the eigenface of each pair of blocks to make X and Y, then combine them using CCA.

In the last experiment, we divide the images into two blocks as well as before, then use the 2DPCA[4] method to extract the eigenface from the first ones of each pair of blocks and the orthonormal feature vectors from the second ones of each pair of blocks, after getting two feature space of samples X and Y, we combine them using CCA. Here we also divide the images into two different size blocks to get the top recognition accuracy.

In order to test the performance of the block-based method, the PCA and 2DPCA method based on single feature is also given out. Recognition results are also given in Table 2 and Table 3 respectively by taking the nearest-neighbor classifier.

**Table 1.** Comparison of recognition accuracy of SVD,2DSVD versus Block-based Method

| **Dimension** | 2 | 3 | 4 | 5 |
|---|---|---|---|---|
| **SVD** | 0.58 | 0.70 | 0.78 | 0.74 |
| **2DSVD** | 0.55 | 0.75 | 0.76 | 0.84 |
| **Block-based Method** | 0.54 | 0.83 | 0.85 | 0.88 |

**Table 2.** Comparison of recognition accuracy of PCA versus Block-based Method

| **Dimension** | | 2 | 3 | 4 | 5 |
|---|---|---|---|---|---|
| **PCA** | | 0.56 | 0.56 | 0.82 | 0.92 |
| **Block-based Method** | 20% to 80% | 0.73 | 0.89 | 0.90 | 0.92 |
| | 40% to 60% | 0.77 | 0.91 | 0.93 | 0.93 |
| | 50% to 50% | 0.75 | 0.90 | 0.91 | 0.92 |
| | 60% to 40% | 0.75 | 0.89 | 0.90 | 0.92 |
| | 80% to 20% | 0.76 | 0.91 | 0.92 | 0.92 |

**Table 3.** Comparison of recognition accuracy of 2DSVD,2DPCA versus Block-based Method

| **Dimension** | 2 | 3 | 4 | 5 |
|---|---|---|---|---|
| **2DSVD** | 0.55(*2) | 0.75(*3) | 0.76(*4) | 0.84(*5) |
| **2DPCA** | 0.64(*112) | 0.835(*112) | 0.905(*112) | 0.90(*112) |
| **Block-based Method** | 0.75(*2) | 0.85(*3) | 0.89(*4) | 0.90(*5) |

The values in parentheses denote the dimension of the feature vectors have to multiply by. For example, when the dimension of the feature vectors is 16(4*4), the recognition accuracy of our method is 89.0%.

### 4.3 Analysis

From Tables 1-3, we can see that, the recognition accuracy of our method is higher than the other methods which are based on single feature. From Fig.2-3, we can see that, our method can obtain much higher recognition rate when the feature dimension is very small, that is significant to application. So it suggests that the algorithm proposed in this paper is an efficient feature fusion method. Moreover, by using this method, the dimension of feature vectors decrease dramatically.

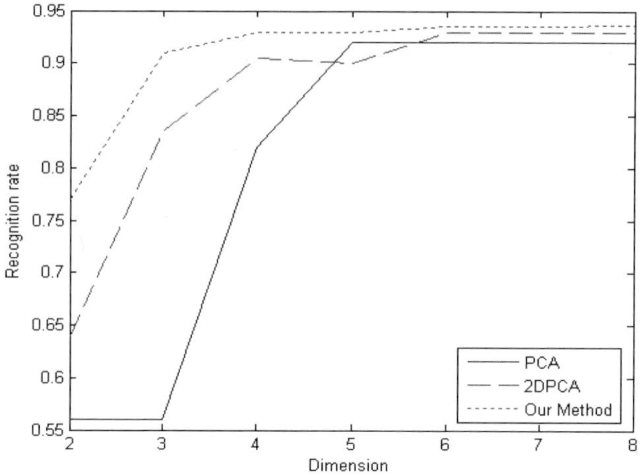


**Fig. 2.** Comparison of our method, PCA and 2DPCA

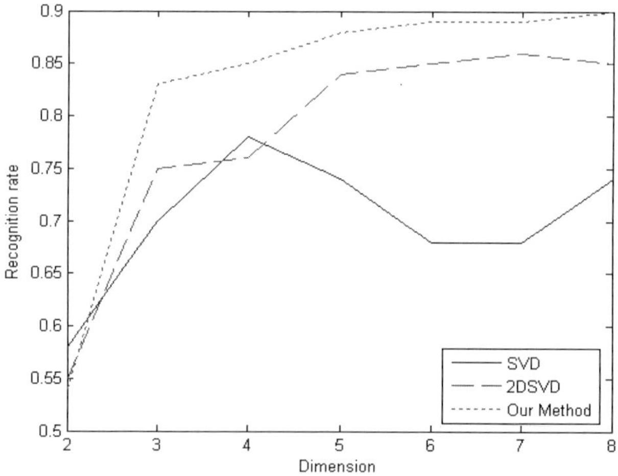


**Fig. 3.** Comparison of our method, SVD and 2DSVD

The reason why we divide the images into two blocks is that different blocks of image contain different information. Although the images were taken at different times, the facial expressions and facial details also vary, but the intrinsic features and their correlations are stable. The CCA method is good at extracting the correlation between two variables. Therefore by combining these features belonging to two blocks using CCA, we can extract the relationship (more effective discriminant information) between the two blocks, so it is expected that better recognition performance can be obtained and at the meantime, the redundant information within the features is eliminated.

## 5 Conclusion

In this paper, an approach based on blocking using CCA is proposed and applied to feature fusion and image recognition. Using of correlation features between two groups of feature vectors as effective discriminant information is not only suitable for information fusion, but also eliminates the redundant information within the features. This method uses canonical correlation variables between two groups of feature vectors belonging to different blocks of the same pattern as more effective discriminant information. It will increase the recognition accuracy, and at the same time, decrease the feature dimensions.

## References

1. Sun, Q. S., Zeng, S. G., Liu, Y., Heng, P.A., Xia, D.S.: A New Method of Feature Fusion and Application in Image Recognition. Pattern Recognition 38 (2005) 2437-2448
2. Liang, Y. X., Gong, W. G., Pan, Y. J., Li W. H., Liu, J. M., Zhang. H. M.: Singular Value Decomposition-Based Approach For Face Recognition. Optics and Precision Engnineering Vol.12 No.5 Oct (2004) 543-549
3. Weenink, D.: Canonical Correlation Analysis. Institute of Phonetic Science, University of Amsterdam. Proceedings Vol.25 (2003) 81-99
4. Yang, J, Zhang, D., etc: Two-Dimensional PCA:A New Approach to Appearance-Based Face Representation and Recognition. IEEE Transaction on Pattern Analysis and Machine Intelligence, Vol.26 No.1 January (2004) 131-137
5. James M.Lattin, J.Douglas Carroll, Paul E. Green: Analyzing Multivariate Data. China Machine Press. 313-345
6. H. Hotelling: Relations Between two Sets of Variates, Biometrika 8 (1936) 321-377
7. Huang, D.S.: Systematic Theory of Neural Networks for Pattern Recognition. Publishing House of Electronic Industry of China. Beijing (1996)
8. Huang, D.S.: Radial Basis Probabilistic Neural Networks: Model and Application. International Journal of Pattern Recognition and Artificial Intelligence, 13(7) (1999) 1083-1101
9. Huang, D.S., Ma, S.D.: Linear and Nonlinear Feedforward Neural Network Classifiers: A Comprehensive Understanding. Journal of Intelligent Systems. Vol.9 No.1 (1999) 1-38
10. Huang, D.S.: Application of Generalized Radial Basis Function Networks to Recognition of Radar Targets. International Journal of Pattern Recognition and Artificial Intelligence, Vol.13 No.6 (1999) 945-962

# A Social-Intelligence-Inspired Security Integrated Model for Network Information Flow

Qinghua Meng[1,2] and Yongsheng Ding[1]

[1] College of Information Sciences and Technology
Donghua University, Shanghai 201620, China
[2] Department of Computer Sciences and Technology
Weifang University, Weifang Shandong 261401, China
ysding@dhu.edu.cn

**Abstract.** Inspired by social intelligence of individual's avoiding harm and auto-protect himself, a security-ring model for network information flow is proposed. The model extends TCP/IP security protocols and controls dynamic security of network information flow in four layers. These layers can cooperate to build closed-secure-channels and form a closed security-ring. In the model, security-channels have different security grades. The information flows are transmitted, deal with transactions, and exchange secret in these channels. The model can guarantee static and dynamic securities for information flows.

## 1 Introduction

In the field of information security, in order to guarantee the confidentiality and integrality of information, people propose many security models, such as control matrix model, multi-grade security model, information flow model, noninterference model [1] et al. With more research work, security control policy of information flow has begun into the language. A. Labeled summarizes characters of information flow models based on languages [2], and has designed the JIF language supporting information flow theory by extending on java [3]. Also, V. Simonet presents another language Flow Calm [4].

These two kinds of languages do some explore in monitoring dynamic supervision and prevent covert channel. However, the language information flow at the actual application still faces following challenges [5]: 1) integrating information-flow controls with existing infrastructure; 2) escaping from the confines of pure noninterference; 3) managing complex security policies.

Social intelligence is a kind of capability that people can adjust their behavior under different and dangerous conditions to protect themselves [6]. Along with complication of application system, it is necessary that social intelligence should be introduced into information flow to ensure the confidentiality and integrity for data. If information flows have the social ability, not only information flows can smartly manipulate complex business, but also automatically protect themselves. This paper aims to meet the three challenges mentioned above, and proposes a integrate control model for information flow security.

D.-S. Huang, K. Li, and G.W. Irwin (Eds.): ICIC 2006, LNCS 4113, pp. 1092 – 1097, 2006.

# 2 The Integrated Security Model for Information Flow Security

## 2.1 The Security in Social Intelligence

The meaning of the security of social intelligence includes: 1) People can adjust their attitude and behavior according to particular circumstances to protect themselves and avoid attacks. To the feature, we call this as secure self-protect intelligence. 2) However they counter what complicated transactions, people always keep business to be correctly finished. To the feature, we call this as secure transaction-logic-integrity intelligence. These two kinds of social secure intelligence should be introduced to information flows security model, and provide some useful security mechanisms for handling complicated business. In addition, since information flows face with complicated and un-trusted environment, they must manipulate more and more fussy business. So, we can design flexible security policies according to secure self-protect intelligence and establish secure transaction processing mechanism according to secure transaction-logic-integrity intelligence for business.

## 2.2 The Integrated Security Model

In order to guarantee the integrated security of network information flow, we design a hierarchical control model, which is illustrated in Fig. 1. The main purpose of the model is to guarantee the dynamic security, transaction integrity security, self-adjusting, self-sensing, and self-recovering for information flows. These integrated secure measures provide a whole and closed solution for secure management. The function of each layer is as follows:

(1)*Security entrance layer*: This layer requires the user authentication, having a unique user ID, and specifies a security grade of the information flow. All operations of the information flow are done in the corresponding secure channel. According to the related national security standard, the secure channels of the information flow have six secure grades.

(2)*Social intelligence layer*: This layer monitors dynamic security features of information flow, implements the social intelligence feature to make flows to have the capability of self-judging and self-adjusting. Social intelligence layer can get some parameters from intelligence interface of information flows, and perceive dynamic security state and detect intrusions.

(3)*Business layer*: This layer is designed for satisfying business security. For requests of information flows, this layer response in forms of transaction, and then the transactions be submitted, processed, audited, and logged. If there are any errors and defaults, transaction processing immediately is roll backed. By this way, online recovery for business can be automatically finished.

(4)*TCP/IP security communication layer*: This layer main includes some conventional security technologies such SSL, HTTPS, IPSEC•SET etc.. These security methods work in network layer, transmitting layer, and application layer of TCP/IP reference model.

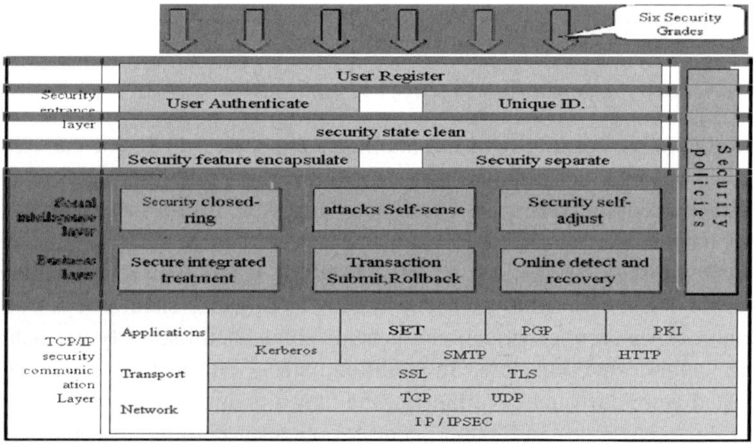


**Fig. 1.** Security Integrated Model for NIF

# 3 Closed-Security-Ring Mechanism for Network Information Flow

## 3.1 Social-Intelligence Inspired Closed-Security-Ring

Inspired by social intelligence, services providing to users should been full and integrated. So, an integrated service should be a logic closed-security-ring (see Fig.2). 1) *Closed-Security-Grade-Ring*. All behaviors from an information flow should have same security-grade. 2) *Closed-Transaction-Integrity-Ring*. Service providing for users should be a whole item, the transaction should be full completed.3) *Closed-Visiting-Path-Ring*. As an integral service, the nodes passed through should compose a closed-ring.

Based on social intelligence, secure channel is designed to implement closed logic-ring for information flow. The secure channel is a closed logic-accessing route, in which information flow can be transmitted, processed, and transactions can be fully carried out. Each channel has unique security grade, and owns the three secure closed-ring characters. These secure characters can prevent some attacks from outside.

## 3.2 Closed-Security-Ring Control Policies

*(1) Closed-Security-Grade-Ring*

For interviewed information flow sets ($NIF_1, NIF_2, \ldots\ldots, NIF_n$), the regulation is expressed as

$$SC_{\mathrm{NIF}_1} = SC_{\mathrm{NIF}_2} = \ldots = SC_{\mathrm{NIF}_n} . \qquad \textbf{\textit{Rule 1}}$$

*(2) Closed-Transaction-Integrity-Ring*

According to continuity and connection of transaction, directed graph $\mathrm{G} < N, T_{\mathrm{trans}} >$ is built along with the path of information flow. Where $N$ is MAC addresses or IP addresses of nodes where the information flow passes, $T_{trans}$ is the transmission time between neighboring nodes: $T_{\text{trans(i, j)}} = (T_{\text{timestamp( i)}} - T_{\text{timestamp( j)}})$. Where, $T_{\text{timestamp( i)}}$ is the timestamp when the information flow passes he node. Then the adjacent matrix $A(\text{G}) = (a_{\text{ij}})_{\text{n*n}}$ can be got from directed graph $\text{G} < N, T_{\text{trans}} >$. $A(G)$ should have features of symmetric matrix, i.e. the transposed matrix of $A(G)$ is itself:

$$A(\text{G})^{\text{T}} = A(\text{G}). \qquad \textbf{\textit{Rule 2}}$$

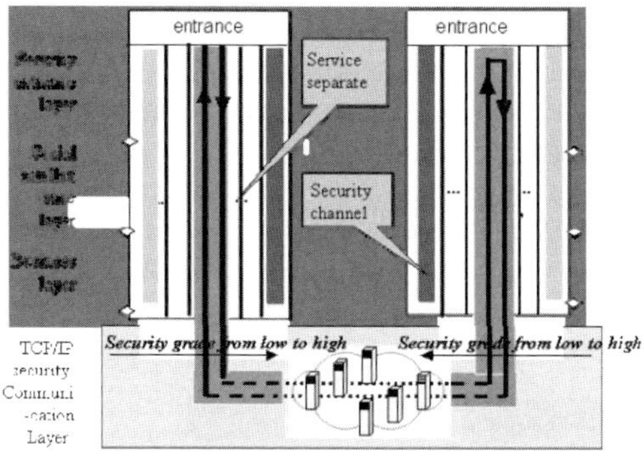


**Fig. 2.** Closed-Security-Ring

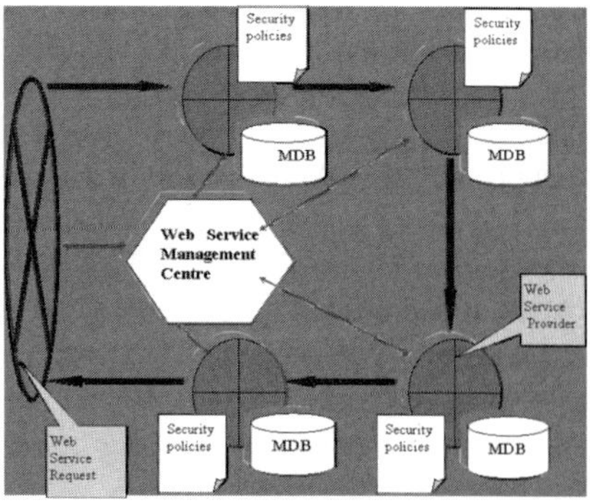


**Fig. 3.** Security integrated for Web Service

*(3) Closed-Visiting-Path-Ring*

Judge whether directed graph $\text{G} < N, T_{\text{trans}} >$ has a circuit. According to EULER circuit theorem, a directed graph has a circuit if and only if it is interconnected, i.e. the out-degree and in-degree of each node are equal. The Definition is given:

$$b_{ik} = \begin{cases} \text{counter}(T_{trans(i,j)}) \quad [\text{i, j} \in (1,\text{n})] \quad T_{trans(i,j)} \neq 0 \quad k = 0 \\ \\ \text{counter}(T_{trans(j,i)}) \quad [\text{i, j} \in (1,\text{n})] \quad T_{trans(j,i)} \neq 0 \quad k = 1 \end{cases} . \qquad \textbf{\textit{Rule 3}}$$

According to whether $b_{\text{i0}}$ equals $b_{\text{i1}}$, we can know whether behaviors of network information flows can compose closed-logic-ring.

*(4) Transform regulation*

Transform regulation for security grade of network information security class is : $\text{SC}_{(\text{NIF}_\text{i})} = (\text{SC}_{(\text{USER})}, \text{SC}_{\text{business }(\text{NIF}_\text{i})}, \text{Field}_{(\text{NIF}_\text{i})}, \text{OP}_{(\text{NIF}_\text{i})}, \cdots\cdots)$ .The related access relation for information flows is semi-order, which is only

$$\text{SC}_{(\text{NIF}_\text{i})} \geq \text{SC}_{(\text{NIF}_\text{j})}. \qquad \textbf{\textit{Rule 4}}$$

Information flow I can access flow j, but the flow I must reduce its security grade, making $SC_{(NIF_i)} \equiv SC_{(NIF_j)}$, then they may exchange their information or commonly tackle businesses.

## 4 A Case Study: A Security Framework for Web Service

In the framework (see Fig.3), each web service request has a security ID, and uses it to mark responding web services flow. Also, each web service provider has a security ID to mark its services, and handle different transaction according its security policy, finally write the logs into its management database (MDB). When web service flow start from the request, it will pass a serious of web service providers. As long as each provider finishes its task, it will send a recorder to the web service management center, which will check whether closed-security-ring is completed.

The security channel has three layers: message layer (see Fig.4), access control layer, and business layer. Message layer we includes XML Encryption, XML Signature, SSL et al. Access control layer includes Ws-Security, Ws-Policy, Ws-Privacy, and Ws-Trust et al. Business layer includes Ws-Coordination et al.

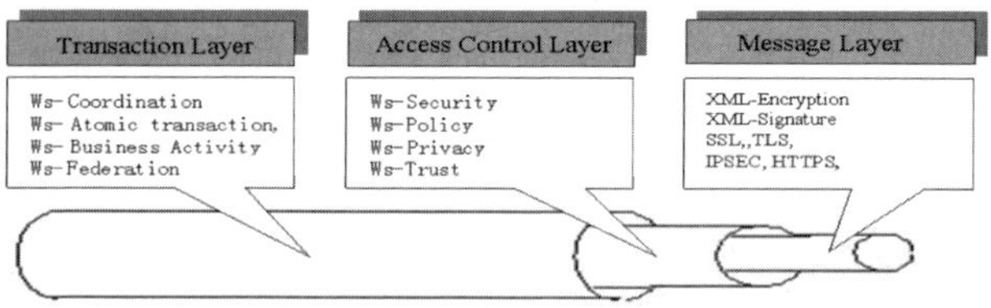


**Fig. 4.** Security channel for web service

For web service, security policy should be embedded into XML document, and be implemented by using related WS-policy specification. The detail syntaxes are omitted, and policies for web service flow (PFWSF) are shown in the following.

```
<wsp: Policy xmlns: wsp="..." xmlns: wsse="...">
  <wsp: PFWSF>
    <wsp: All wsp: Preference="100">
      <wsse: Security Token>
        <wsse: Token Type>wsse: Kerberosv5TGT</wsse: TokenType>
      </wsse: Security Token>
      <wsse: security channel>
     <wsse: Rule1 (Closed-Security-Grade-Ring);
     Rule2 (Closed-Transaction-Integrity-Ring);
     Rule3 (Closed-Visiting-Path-Ring);
     Rule4 (Transform regulation )/>
      </wsse: security channel >
  </wsp: PFWSF >
</wsp:Policy>
```

## 5 Conclusions

In order to ensure the whole security of information flows, based on social intelligence a network closed-security-ring model is presented. In the model, different security channels with security grades are designed, and information flows are transmitted, accessed, exchanging secret in the channels. Therefore, the channels can guarantee static and dynamic security for information flows.

## Acknowledgments

This work was supported in part by the National Nature Science Foundation of China (No. 60474037), and Program for New Century Excellent Talents in University (No. NCET-04-415).

## References

1. Goguen, J. A., Meseguer, J.: Security Policies and Security Models. Proceeding of IEEE symposium on Security and Privacy (SSP '82). IEEE Computer Society Press, Los Alamitos, Ca., USA (1982) 11-20
2. Sabelfeld, A., Myers, A. C.: Language-based Information-flow Security. IEEE Journal on Selected Areas in Communications, 21 (2003) 5-19
3. Myers, C. A., Nystrom, N., Zheng, L., Zdancewic, S.: Jif: Java Information Flow. http://www.cs.cornell.edu/jif (2001)
4. Simonet, V.: Flow Caml in a Nutshell. Proceedings of the First APPSEM-II workshop, Graham Hutton (2003) 152-165
5. Zdancewic, S.: Challenges for Information-flow Security. Programming Language Interference and Dependence, (PLID'04) (2004) 124-129
6. Ruyter, D., Saini, B., Markopoulos, P.: Assessing the Effects of Building Social Intelligence in a Robotic Interface for The Home. Interacting with Computers, 17 (2005) 522-541

# A Study on the Improvement of Military Logistics System Using RFID*

Mingyun Kang[1], Minseong Ju[1], Taihoon Kim[2], Geuk Leek[3], and Kyung Sung[4]

[1] Hannam University, Department of Multimedia Engineering, Postfach , 306 791
133 Ojeong-Dong, Daedeok-Gu, Daejeon, Korea
{Kang}card7s@paran.com, {Ju}nimpe2@naver.com
[2] San-7, Geoyeo-dong,Songpa-Gu, Seoul, Korea
Taihoonn@paran.com
[3] Hannam University, Department of Computer Engineering, Postfach , 306 791
133 Ojeong-Dong, Daedeok-Gu, Daejeon, South Korea
leegeuk@hannam.ac.kr
[4] Mokwon University, Department of Computer Education, Postfach , 302 729
800 Doan-Dong, Seo-Gu, Daejeon, Korea
Skyys04@mokwon.ac.kr

**Abstract.** Some of them are completely lost. The military distribution system may have an advantage of responding each situation but also causes waste of time and a budget. To address the problem this document took a look at the logistics system using RFID technology. But the document has its limitations, for use of RFID in a logistics system has yet to be developed and there're not sufficient data to prove the effect of the system.

## 1 Introduction

"There's no innovation in the army without logistics innovation," comments General Shinseki, the Chief of the General Staff, placing a top priority on logistics innovation. Considering the Republic of Korea Army (ROKA), when there is the need for supplies, the request is sent to the army division after passing through 5 steps, and again 3-step processing procedures.

The supplies are finally delivered to the soldiers after 7-step distribution procedures. That is, the military supplies go through 71-72 steps to be delivered from the division to the soldiers. In addition, though the division promises to secure required supplies when they are not in stock, the request in not made in an automatic manner. So the supplies appear to be depleted until the officials in charge of distribution check out them. Unlike officials in the higher divisions, the military units do not know about the schedule that the supplies are delivered.

Because there is no automatic system among a division, a logistics supply command, and a logistics command, it is hard to receive needed supplies even when they are in stock. To solve the problem this document analyzes the ubiquitous military distribution system using an RFID tag.

---

* "This work was supported by the Korea Research Foundation Grant funded by the Korean Government (MOEHRD)" (KRF-2005-041-D00576).

D.-S. Huang, K. Li, and G.W. Irwin (Eds.): ICIC 2006, LNCS 4113, pp. 1098 – 1102, 2006.

# 2 Logistics Information System

## 2.1 Overview

The manufacturing industry is an activity of procuring materials, making goods, and selling them to earn profits. While activities are laid on people, goods, and money at each stage, production is the outcome of the activity laid on goods, where physical distribution occurs. And the logistics information system supports such an activity. Physical distribution has to do with all the activities of an enterprise.

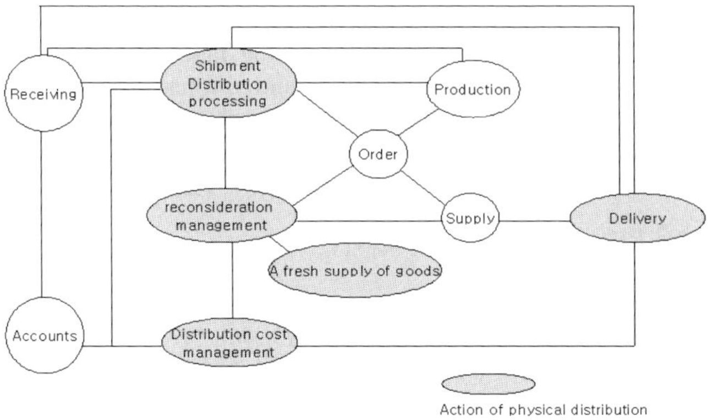


**Fig. 1.** Depicts the relationship of logistics information with activities of an enterprise

That is, logistics information system is a system that utilizes all the information regarding distribution and processes/delivers the information in order to facilitate every function of physical distribution. Logistics information is divided into the information arising from distribution activities and that arising from other activities but still influencing physical distribution. Figure.1 depicts the relationship of logistics information with activities of an enterprise. Since logistics information system of small- and medium-sized enterprises is closely related to non-distribution activities also, they should not only deal with distribution activity but also production activity, promoting a system integrated with all other the activities of supply [1].

## 2.2 Purpose of Logistics Information System and Distribution Service

Plans of logistics information system aims at enhancing the customer service and reducing the distribution costs. The two purposes conflict with each other. That is, they are in the trade-off relationship. Customer service includes factors of commercial distribution service and those of physical distribution service. Of course, they are closely related with each other to some measure. And this is the reason why their trade-off relation can matter. Still, let's take commercial distribution service for example. Keeping an assortment of goods based on the product line, designing pricing system according to the classes of customers, providing information on a product, and promoting products with various means evidently belong to the service with the nature of marketing. Though sometimes it is hard to tell some factors of the commercial distribution services from those of physical distribution, this document will exclude customer services considered belonging to original commercial distribution or marketing services but will include physical distribution services. Meanwhile, sales distribution is the flow of goods that starts with the contract of orders (a verbal or written contract). It begins with understanding the contents of an order and ends with delivering the goods to the right place [2].

### 2.3 The Role of RFID in Logistics Information System

During the war in Iraq, the U.S. had to open up 30,000 containers to verify their contents. Some of them are completely lost. The paper explaining the items was attached to the outside of the containers but it was destroyed by water or sand. Now smart labels are in use, solving the problem. Use of the label is being promoted in the FMCG supply chain also. So RFID technology and wireless barcode are drawing lots of attention, for they reduce costs in many areas such as distribution chain management and air/postal distribution [3], [4].

## 3 Logistics Management of ROKA

**Classification by Kinds:** Military supplies are classified according to the number of pieces, nature (expendables and non-expendables), unit prices (high and low), and so on. Of the various standards, classification based on their kinds is used most common. So let's take a close look at the way supplies are classified into Class□-Class □ according to their usage and nature. Class I is mainly food such as the staple/subsidiary food. Items of Class I include polished rice and barely. Class II is equipment such as clothing and individual outfits. Items of Class II include combat uniform, combat shoes, an entrenching tool, a bombproof helmet, etc. Class III is fuel such as light oil and gasoline. Class IV is construction materials including timber, cement, plywood, paint, a nail, etc. Class V is munitions such as gun cartridge and a cannon ball. Class VI is individual stuffs like a cigarette and they are provided now by Army Welfare Support Group. Class VII is represented by finished combat equipment including a rifle, a tank, and a vehicle. Class VIII is medical supplies such as various medicines and equipment. Parts of equipment belong to Class IX including a bolt, a nut, an engine, and a tire. Finally, the rest that belongs to none of the above-mentioned classes is Class X and equipment for public welfare service (a farming tool) is included in this category.

**Classification by Functions:** Military supplies are also divided by their functions such as fire power, movement, special weaponry, telecommunication and electronics, aviation and shipping, general equipment, supplies, munitions, and medical supplies (9 categories in total). Fire power involves firing equipment, a monitor, measuring devices for artillery. Movement has to do with various vehicles and parts needed to repair them. Anti-aircraft guns and missiles, an antitank guided weapon, and a ground-to-ground weapon belong to special weaponry. Telecommunication and electronics include wired/wireless telecommunications/detection (radar)/photograph devices. An airplane, a ship, and their parts belong to aviation and shipping category. General equipment means construction/power supply/river-crossing/service (laundry and bath trucks) equipment. Some of the articles not included in Class 5, 7, 8, and 9 are food, clothing, and stationery, which belong to supplies category. Various munitions, explosives, and their accessories come into the munitions category [5], [6].

# 4 Army Logistics System

ROKA logistics system is divided by the enterprises' delivery types. First, supplies could be directly sent to both a supply unit and a military unit that needs the articles. Or they could be delivered to a logistics supply command and then to a military unit which needs the articles. With respect to expendables, a unit can make a request for them while it reports the status of non-expendables every quarter to expect the demand.

Such system may require longer time, for the logistics supply command takes charge of the distribution but allows accuracy of an itemized statement and real-time service.

In the above mentioned logistics system a quarterly report replaces a request and a channel of logistics supply collects the reports. The flow of supplies is direct delivery from an enterprise to a unit but administrative procedures are done by a support unit, creating inconsistency. And supplies are divided by their use and kinds in the system.

Introduction of RFID technology to the logistics system as depicted in Figure 2 can prevent waste of a budget and other resources by prompt delivery and accurate management of supplies. In addition, though a division promises to offer required supplies when they are not in stock, the request in not made in an automatic manner so that the supplies appear to be depleted unless the official in charge of logistics system ask for the articles. Unlike officials in higher divisions, military units do not know about the schedule when the supplies are delivered. Because there's no automatic system among a division, a logistics supply command, and a logistics command, it's hard to receive needed supplies even when they are in stock. But the introduction of RFID technology can solve the problem, providing a network for the Ministry of National Defense, the Logistics Command, and a logistics supply command.

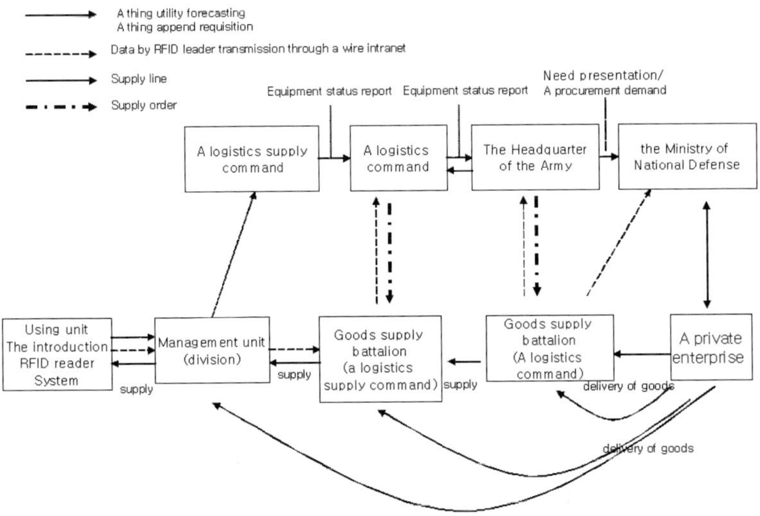


**Fig. 2.** Logistics System by RFID Technology

## 5 Conclusion

The distribution system of enterprises based on the Internet service today has allowed e-commerce to take root and automatic transportation system utilizing intellectual traffic control as well as trace technology has been applied to the system. Along with the development, the distribution system of the army has adopted cutting-edge technologies. The logistics system of ROKA is divided by the way of delivery: direct delivery from an enterprise to both a support unit and a unit that needs supplies and the deliver to a logistics supply command which sends the supplies to a military unit. Concerning expendables, a unit can make a request, but it makes a report of non-expendables to expect the demand. The logistics system may have an advantage of responding each situation but also causes waste of time and a budget. To address the problem this document took a look at the logistics system using RFID technology. But the document has its limitations, for use of RFID in a logistics system has yet to be developed and there're not sufficient data to prove the effect of the system. Though large-scale logistics companies are active in adopting RFID system, the analysis of the effect should be done in the near future.

## References

1. Sunil Chopra, Peter Meindl.: Supply Chain Management –Strategy: Planning and Operation-. Prentice Hall Press, (2001)
2. David, S. L.: Design and Managing the Supply Chain: McGraw-Hill Press, London (2001)
3. Yang, G. M., Bag, J. H., Gyeong, S. K.: Development of Quality Information System for the Improvement of Efficiency of Small Business: Journal of the Research Institute of Industrial Technology, 22 (2003) 423-437
4. RFID Executive Overview, Accenture (2004)
5. Sterman, J. D., Business, D.: System Thinking and Modeling for a Complex World. Irwin McGrw-Hill Press, London (2000)
6. Lee, S. Y.: A Study on The Improvement of Military Logistics System: Focus on the Clustering Group by Product Characteristics, National Defense University, Master's Thesis, (2004)

# Performance Improvement of Intelligent UWB-IR Communication System in Multipath Channel

Sang-Heon Lee[1], Nam-Sung Kim[2], Heau-Jo Kang[1], and Soon-Gohn Kim[3]

[1] Department of Computer Engineering, Mokwon University, 800, Doan-dong, Seo-gu, Daejeon, 302-729, Korea
{shlee, hjkang}@mokwon.ac.kr

[2] Department of Electronics, Daejeon Polytechnic College, 99-1, Gayang 2-dong, Dong-gu, Daejeon, 300-702, Korea
siluet@kopo.ac.kr

[3] Department of Computer Multimedia Science, Joongbu University, 101, Daehak-ro, Chuboo-myeon, Kumsan-Gun, Chongnam, 312-702, Korea
sgkim@joongbu.ac.kr

**Abstract.** Multipath fading causes decrease of system performance in wireless communication environment. Therefore, intelligent high-speed communication system which can effectively reduce ever-changing multipath interference is necessary in order to provide high quality data service. In this paper, we analyzed channel performance of intelligent UWB communication system in indoor radio fading environment that consider amplitude characteristic of channel. Also, we improved performance of system that it is decreased in fading environment employing rake receiver and convolution encoding techniques.

## 1 Introduction

Problem for frequency resources is very serious even though world each country's effort including advanced nation to maximize efficiency for confined frequency resources in present wireless communication area. By share and use existent communication system and frequency spectrum to solve this, Ultra Wideband(UWB or Impulse Radio : IR) communication method that can use frequency resources little more efficiently appeared. Such Ultra Wideband communication method does not give interference to another thing communication system existing in form such as baseband noise. It is profitable existing communication system in transmission speed because can adopt bandwidth by wideband. And Because unuse carrier wave used compulsorily in existing system, can reduce power dissipation of tranceiver and make simplify tranceiver[1],[2].

But, UWB technology is not enough development yet. It needs the new experimentations and the theoretical studies for efficient design of communication system. The best necessary studies are UWB channel modeling and performance evaluation for analysis of UWB technology [3], [4].

Therefore, in this paper, we analyzed channel performance of intelligent UWB communication system in indoor radio fading environment that consider amplitude characteristic of channel. Fading channel considered various channel environments by fading index m utilizing Nakagami-m distribution model with data through an UWB

D.-S. Huang, K. Li, and G.W. Irwin (Eds.): ICIC 2006, LNCS 4113, pp. 1103 – 1108, 2006.

radio signal experiment that announced in existing. Also, we improved performance of system that it is decreased in fading environment employing rake receiver and convolution encoding techniques.

## 2 UWB-IR System

### 2.1 Monocycle Pulse

For $p_{RX}(t)$ we consider an UWB-IR pulse that can be modeled by the second derivative of a Gaussian function $\exp(-2\pi[t/t_n]^2)$ Properly scaled. The UWB-IR pulse $p_{RX}(t)$ has duration $T_p$ and energy $E_p = \int_{-\infty}^{\infty} [p(t)]^2 dt$ [5],[6]. In this case the transmitted pulse is

$$p_{TX}(t) = t\exp\left(-2\pi\left[\frac{t}{t_n}\right]^2\right) \cdot \tag{1}$$

where the value $t_n$ is parameter for decision of pulse width. The value uses very little value as a few nano second. The received pulse can be modeled by the second derivative of a Gaussian function. The received pulse is

$$p_{RX}(t) = \left(1-4\pi\left[\frac{t}{t_n}\right]^2\right)\exp\left(-2\pi\left[\frac{t}{t_n}\right]^2\right) \cdot \tag{2}$$

where the value $t_n$ determine spectrum and time domain structure of signal.

The normalized signal correlation function corresponding to $p_{RX}(t)$ is calculated to give

$$\begin{aligned}\gamma_p(\tau) &= \frac{1}{E_p}\int_{-\infty}^{+\infty} P_{RX}(t)P_{RX}(t+\tau) \cdot \\ &= \left[1-4\pi\left[\frac{\tau}{t_n}\right]^2 + \frac{4\pi^2}{3}\left[\frac{\tau}{t_n}\right]^4\right]\exp\left(-\pi\left[\frac{\tau}{t_n}\right]^2\right)\end{aligned} \tag{3}$$

### 2.2 Indoor Wireless Channel Model

Nakagami distribution is generally characterized by two parameters, $m$ and $\Omega_s$ and its probability density function(pdf) has the following expression:

$$p(R) = \frac{2m^m R^{2m-1}}{\Gamma(m)\Omega_s^m}\exp\left(\frac{mR^2}{\Omega_s}\right), m \geq 0.5 \cdot \tag{4}$$

where $\Omega_s = R^2$ and $\Gamma(\cdot)$ is the Gamma function[7],[8].

# 3 Performance of UWB-IR System

## 3.1 Performance of UWB-IR System in AWGN Environment

When $N_u$ users are active in the multiple-access system, the composite received signal at the output of the receiver's antenna is modeled as

$$r(t)=\sum_{k=1}^{N_u} A_k s^{(k)}(t-\tau_k)+n(t) \cdot \tag{5}$$

in which $A_k$ represents the amplitude of the signal received from the $k$ th transmitter. The random variable $\tau_k$ represents the time asynchronism between the clock of transmitter and the receiver, and $n(t)$ represents other nonmonocycle interferences (e.g., receiver noise) present at the correlator input.

A transmitted signal passes through the transmitter and receiver antenna systems and propagation channel. We assume that $N_u$ transmitters are active in the multiple-access system and the transmitter and the receiver are perfectly synchronized. Then the total received signal is

$$\begin{aligned} r(t) &= r_{RX}(t-\tau)+n(t) \\ &= \sum_{j=-\infty}^{+\infty} \sqrt{E_s}\, p_{RX}\left(t - jT_f - c_j T_c - \delta\alpha_{[j/N_s]} - r\right)+n(t) \end{aligned} \tag{6}$$

The correlation receiver, under hypothesis of perfect synchronization, computes:

$$\beta_i = \sum_{j=iN_s}^{(i+1)N_s} \int_{\tau+jT_f}^{\tau+(j+1)T_f} r(t)v(t-jT_f-c_jT_c-\tau)dt \cdot \tag{7}$$

Decision is made according to the following rule:

$$\hat{\alpha}_i = \begin{cases} 0 & if \quad \beta \geq 0 \\ 1 & if \quad \beta < 0 \end{cases} . \tag{8}$$

Therefore, in AWGN environment, the bit rate of UWB-IR system is

$$P_b = \frac{1}{2} erfc\left(\sqrt{\frac{N_s E_p}{2N_0}} \sqrt{1-\gamma(\delta)}\right) \cdot \tag{9}$$

where $N_s E_p = E_b$, single data bit energy.

Results for different values of Ns are shown in Fig. 1. Where, Ns is the number of pulses transmitted for each bit in UWB-IR system. From the Fig. 1, IR system is satisfied reference BER($10^{-6}$) of the data service more than SNR= 11.45dB. And, system performance is improved by increase Ns.

Increase Ns means the bit rate decrease. As a result, we can satisfy required reception SNR and bit rate by we design Ns according to get quality of service.

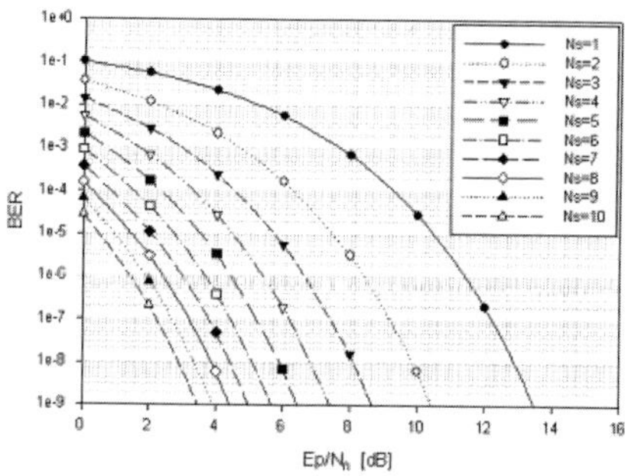


**Fig. 1.** UWB-IR system performance in AWGN environment

## 3.2 Performance Analysis of UWB-IR System in Indoor M-Distribution Fading Environment

Nakagami distribution reduces to Rayleigh for $m=1$ and to one sided Gaussian distribution for $m=1/2$. In addition, when $m>1$ it is possible to approximate Rice distribution using the following relation between Rice $k$-factor and $m$ Nakagami parameter [9],[10]:

$$k=\frac{\sqrt{m^2-m}}{m-\sqrt{m^2-m}}, m>1 \,. \tag{10}$$

From the analysis of $m$ parameter statistical characteristics, it is possible to conclude that the considered channel model assumes that in the first paths a single high energy contribution is predominant, so that a statistical description similar to Race distribution is used. The latest component instead are supposed to experiment fading conditions similar to Rayleigh channel or even worse.

Results for different values of m are shown in Fig. 2. From the Fig. 2, IR system is not satisfied reference BER ($10^{-6}$) of the data service even 30dB then m≥5.

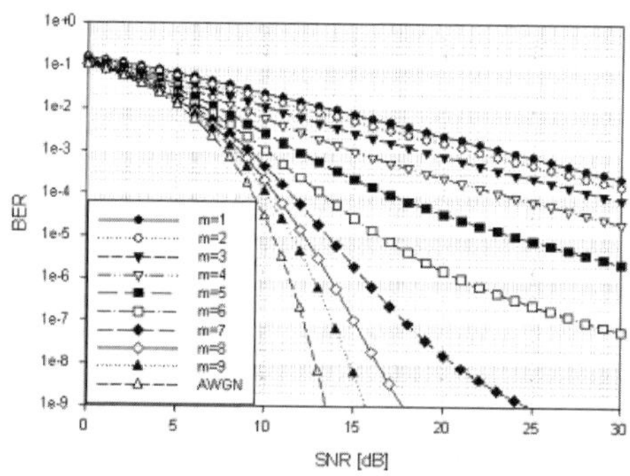


**Fig. 2.** UWB-IR system performance in fading environment

### 3.3 UWB-IR System Performance Improvement Using Convolution Coding and Rake Receiver in Indoor M-Distribution Fading Environment

In this paper, we analyzed performance of UWB-IR communication system that it is decreased in fading environment employing rake receiver and convolution encoding techniques.

In this section the performance of the system is evaluated using convolution encoding(R=1/2, k=7) and Rake correlation receivers with different complexity, i.e., equipped with three of fingers.

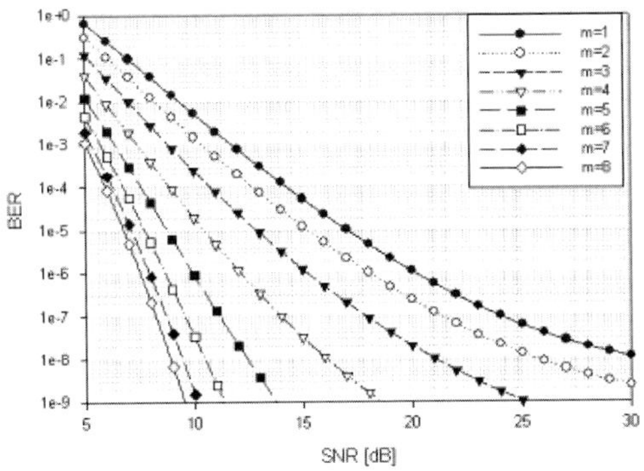


**Fig. 3.** Performance of UWB-IR system with convolution code and Rake receiver in fading environment(Ns=1)

Fig. 3 shows the performance of UWB-IR system with convolution encoding and Rake receiver in fading cnvironment.

From Fig. 2 and Fig. 3, we can know that the system performance is improved greatly by convolution encoding and Rake receiver in fading environment.

## 4 Conclusion

In this paper, we analyzed channel performance of UWB-IR communication system in multipath fading environment. Also, we improved performance of system that it is decreased in fading environment employing rake receiver and convolution encoding techniques.

According to the results, we could know that UWB-IR system performance is greatly by convolution encoding and Rake receiver in multipath fading.

## Acknowledgment

This research was supported by the Program for the Training of Graduate Students in Regional Innovation which was conducted by the Ministry of Commerce Industry and Energy of the Korean Government.

## References


1. Withington, P.: UWB Regulation & Applications. UWB Workshop, www.timedomain.com (2001)
2. Aetherwire & Location Inc., www.aetherwire.com
3. FCC Notice of Proposed Rule Making: Revision of Part 15 of the commission's Rules Regarding Ultra_Wideband Transmission System. ET-Docket, 98-153
4. Lee, Y. S., Kang, H. J., Lee, M., Kim, T. H.: A Study on the Effect of Interference on Time Hopping Binary PPM Impulse Radio System. ICIC2005/LNCS3645, Part 2, Hefei, China (2005) 665-674
5. Win M. Z., Scholtz, R. A.: Impulse Radio: How It Works. IEEE Comm. Lett., Vol. 2 (1998) 6-38
6. Ramirez-Mireles, F.: On Performance of Ultra Wideband Signals in Gaussian Noise and Dense Multipath. IEEE Trans. on Veh. Tec., Vol. 50 (2001) 244-249
7. Giuseppe D., Giovanni, R.: Simulation Analysis and Performance Evaluation of an UWB System in Indoor Multipath Channel. IEEE Conference on Ultra Wideband Systems and Technologies (2002)
8. Ganesh, R., Pahlavan, K.: Statistical Modeling and Computer Simulation of the Indoor Radio Channel. IEE Proc. Part I: Commun., Speech and Vision, Vol. 138, No. 3 (1991) 153-161
9. Cassioli, D., Win, M. Z., Molisch, A. F.: A Statistical Model for the UWB Indoor Channel. IEEE J. Select Areas Commun, Vol. 20, (2002)1247-1257
10. Nakagami, M.: The M-distribution, a General Formular of Intensity Distribution of Rapid Fading. In Statistical Methods of Radio Wave Propagation, W.C. Hoffman Ed., New York: Pergamon Press (1960) 3-36

# A Study on the Performance Improvement of UWB-IR System for Intelligent High Speed Multimedia Service

Heau-jo Kang and Man-ho Kim

Dept. of Computer Engineering, Mokwon University,
800, Doan-dong, Seo-gu, Daejeon, 302-729, Korea
hjkang@mokwon.ac.kr,
mhkim@mokwon.ac.kr

**Abstract.** Ultra-wideband (UWB) technology has been considered to offer an innovative solution for future short-range high-speed wireless communication. Interference suppression is important for the UWB devices to operate over spectrum with established narrowband systems. But it's difficult to secure a QoS of high quality because it coexists other system that was used same band. We need a adaptable change of the system that follow the changing channel environment. In this paper, derived monocycle pulse that application is possible within permission frequency band that establish in The Federal Communications Commission(FCC). Also, PPM modulated TH IR system simulator is designed in Two-path environment. It is analyzed monocycle pulse specific property and system performance using simulator.

## 1 Introduction

The problem for frequency resources is very serious even though world each country's effort including advanced nation to maximize efficiency for confined frequency resources in present wireless communication areas. By share and use existent communication system and frequency spectrum to solve this, Ultra Wideband(Ultra Wideband : UWB or Impulse radio: IR) communication method that can use frequency resources little more efficiently appeared[1],[2].

UWB system uses wide band signal, which power spectral density is over all band. It likes as a noise floor, so UWB system can be without interfering with other communication system. On February 2002, Federal Communications Commission (FCC) partially was allowed UWB technology to be used for commercial applications and thus the UWB based communication systems has been developed[3].

In this thesis, we have analyzed the performance of UWB Pulse Position Modulation(PPM) System which is provided high speed multimedia service. At first, the performance of UWB-IR System has been analyzed. Then, we have proposed PPM System's parameters which is considered the latest FCC proposal, and analyzed the BER performance of PPM system based on it in indoor multipath environment.

D.-S. Huang, K. Li, and G.W. Irwin (Eds.): ICIC 2006, LNCS 4113, pp. 1109 – 1114, 2006.

## 2 TH PPM UWB-IR System

Every transmitter sends $N_s$ pulses for each data bit. These pulses are located apart in sequential frames, each with duration $T_f$ . The modulation of the UWB-IR is generally binary pulse position modulation (BPPM) where the pulses corresponding to bit "1" are sent $\delta$ seconds later than pulses corresponding to bit "0". In the time hopping (TH) systems, a location of a pulse in each frame is determined by a user dedicated pseudorandom sequence. The transmitted signal for the $k$ th user is

$$S_{tr}^{(k)}(t) = \sum_{j=-\infty}^{\infty} w_{tr}\left(t - jT_f - c_j^{(k)}T_c - \delta D_{\lfloor j/N_s \rfloor}^{(k)}\right) \cdot \tag{1}$$

where the index $j$ indicates the frame number, $w_{tr}(t)$ represents the transmitted monocycle waveform, $t$ is the transmitter clock time, $T_f$ is the frame duration, $T_c$ is the chip duration of pseudorandom TH sequence, $c_j^{(k)}$ is the dedicated pseudorandom TH sequence of the $k$ th user with inter components, $\delta$ is on the order of pulse width $T_w$ and $D_{\lfloor j/N_s \rfloor}^{(k)}$ is the binary sequence of the transmitted symbols corresponding to the $k$ th user[4].

A transmitted signal passes through the transmitter and receiver antenna systems and propagation channel. We assume that $N_u$ transmitters are active in the multiple-access system and the transmitter and the receiver are perfectly synchronized. Then the total received signal is

$$r(t) = \sum_{k=1}^{N_u} A_k s_{rec}^{(k)}(t - \tau_k) + n(t) \cdot \tag{2}$$

where $A_k$ and $\tau_k$ are the channel attenuation and delay, corresponding to the $k$ th user, respectively, and $n(t)$ is the receiver noise. The receiver waveform can be written by the following equation[5].

$$w_{rec}(t) = \left[1 - 4\pi\left(\frac{t}{\tau_m}\right)^2\right]\exp\left[-2\pi\left(\frac{t}{\tau_m}\right)^2\right] \cdot \tag{3}$$

We assume that $w_{rec}(t)$ is the received signal. The energy and the normalized signal correlation function corresponding to $w_{rec}(t)$ can be expressed as[6][7]

$$E_w = \int_{-\infty}^{\infty} [w_{rec}(t)]^2 dt \cdot \tag{4}$$

and

$$\gamma_w(\tau)d\frac{1}{E}\int_{-\infty}^{\infty} w_{rec}(t)w_{rec}(t-\tau)dt > -1 \cdot, \tag{5}$$

where $\tau$ is arbitrary. If we express $w_{rec}(t)$ as (3), $\gamma_w(\tau)$ can be expressed as

$$\gamma_w(\tau)=\left[1-4\pi\left(\frac{\tau}{\tau_m}\right)^2+\frac{4\pi^2}{3}\left(\frac{\tau}{\tau_m}\right)^4\right]\exp\left[-\pi\left(\frac{\tau}{\tau_m}\right)^2\right]. \tag{6}$$

**Table 1** shows the parameters used in simulation.

**Table 1.** UWB-IR system parameter

| Symbol | Explanation | |
|---|---|---|
| $\alpha$ | Waveform width parameter | 0.714 ns |
| $T_p(T_p/2)$ | Waveform width | 1.875(0.938) ns |
| $\delta$ | PPM parameter | 0.4518 ns |

## 3 TH PPM UWB-IR System Model

In this section, we designed PPM modulated UWB-IR system simulator. And, we analyzed the characteristics of system using the UWB-IR system simulator.

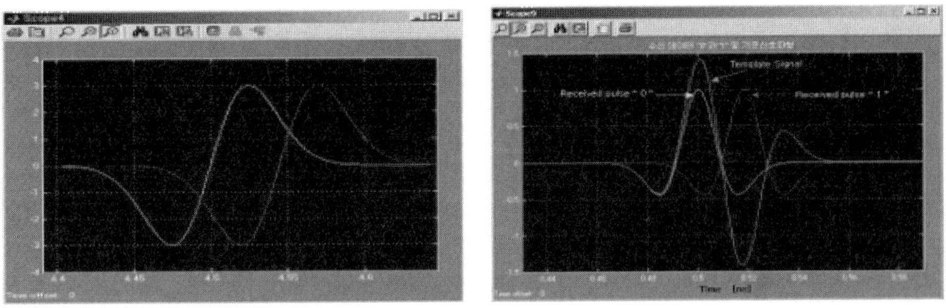


**Fig. 1.** Transmitted monocycle pulse signal and Received signal waveform "0", "1"

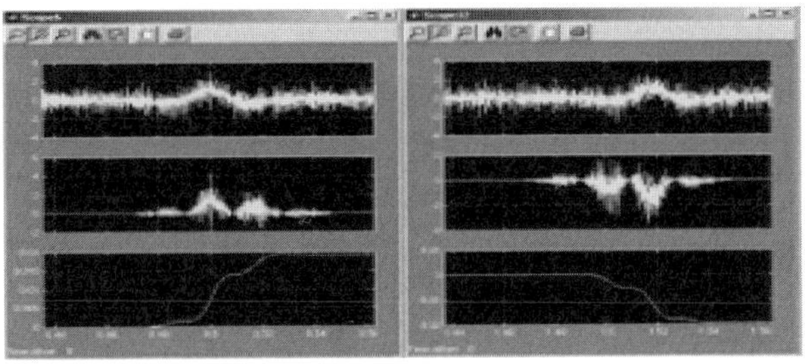

**Fig. 2.** Correlator output according to received signal waveform "0" , "1"

**Fig. 1** ~ **Fig. 2** illustrate signal waveform of transceiver and the process of the correlator output. In this modulation method, when the data symbol is "0", no additional time shift is modulated on the monocycle, but a time shift is added to a monocycle when the symbol is "1". In **Fig. 2**, when the data symbol is "0", correlator output would become a positive value, and when the data symbol is "1", correlator output would become a negative value.

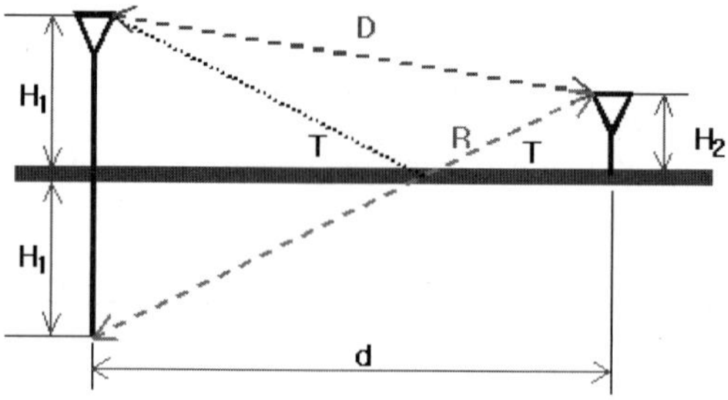


**Fig. 3.** Two-Path model

**Fig. 3** shows the deterministic Two-path model[8] considered in this paper. In this Figure, the path difference between the direct and indirect paths can be approximated as follows:

$$\Delta d \approx \frac{2H_1H_2}{d} \tag{7}$$

where $D$ and $R$ represent the distances of the direct and indirect paths, respectively, $d$ is the distance between the transmitter and receiver antennas are $H_1$ and , $H_2$ respectively.

Therefore, the time-delay difference between the two component is $t = 2H_1H_2 / cd$ , where $c$ stands for the speed of light.

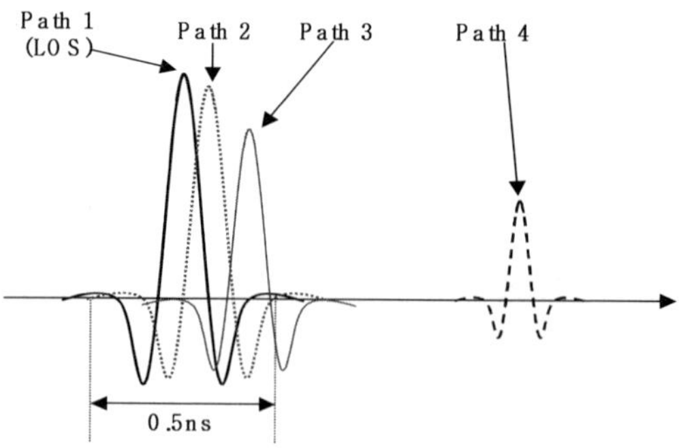


**Fig. 4.** Characteristics of indirect path to direct path according to path delay time

In the **Fig. 4**, Indirect path pulse that have bigger time delay A than $T_p/2$ that is half duration of direct path pulse escapes in related extent coming received direct path pulse(path 3, path 4). But, indirect path pulse that have smaller delay time than direct path pulse width same to path2 can act for cause of definite interference when received signal is detected by delay time. Specially, in case of indirect path pulse that have delay time $\triangle t$ or indirect path pulse that have delay time as $\delta$ that is PPM variation parameter, effect is expected to be big because give big change in amplitude of direct path pulse. **Fig. 5** shows performance of UWB-IR system according to when =1.2m.

**Table 2.** Path delay time in Two-path model

| d[m] | $H_1 = H_2[m]$ | | | |
|---|---|---|---|---|
| | 0.9 | 1 | 1.2 | 1.3 |
| 4 | 1.288 | 1.574 | 2.216 | 2.569 |
| 6 | 0.881 | 1.082 | **1.541** | 1.797 |
| 8 | 0.667 | 0.821 | 1.174 | 1.373 |
| 10 | 0.536 | 0.601 | **0.947** | 1.108 |
| 14 | 0.384 | 0.478 | 0.681 | 0.798 |
| 20 | 0.269 | 0.333 | **0.478** | 0.561 |

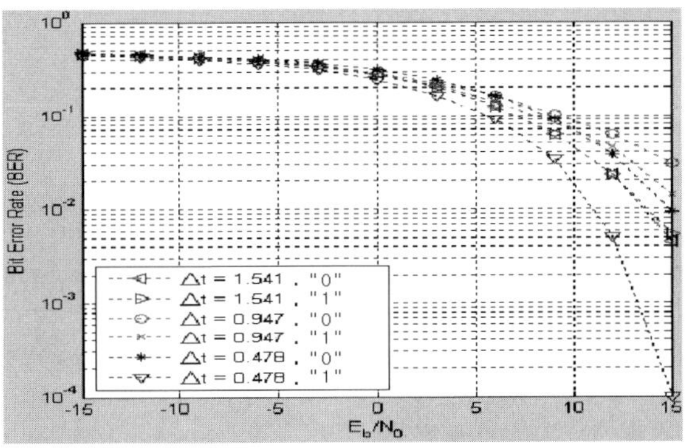


**Fig. 5.** Bit error rate of indirect path

# 4 Conclusion

In this paper, the effects of the interference environments on the performance of the time hopping binary PPM impulse radio (IR) system are presented. Based on the monocycle pulses available within the frequency of 3.1~10.6 GHz permitted for application by FCC, a PPM-modulated TH UWB-IR system simulator was designed in an Two-path environment. Using the simulator, the monocycle pulse characteristics and system performance were analyzed.

We consider the deterministic two-path model for indoor multipath environment. Consequently, it indicate that performance of PPM depends on time delay difference between the indirect path delay and the time interval of PPM, and to the indirect path gains.

## References

[1] P. Withington, "UWB Regulation & Applications". *UWB Workshop*, www.timedomain.com, 11. 2001.
[2] Aetherwire & Location Inc., www.aether-wire.com
[3] FCC Notice of Proposed Rule Making, "Revision of Part 15 of the Commission's Rules Regarding Ultra-Wideband Trans- mission System", *ET-Docket*, pp. 98-153.
[4] M. Z. Win and R. A. Scholtz, "Ultra-wide Bandwidth time-hopping spread spectrum impulse iadio for wireless multiple-access communication," *IEEE Trans. Commun.*, pp. 6792691, vol.48, no.4, April 2000.
[5] F. Ramirez-Mireles, "On the performance of Ultra-Wide Band signals in Gaussian noise and dense multipath," *IEEE Trans. Veh. Technol.*, vol.50, no.1, Jan. 2001.
[6] F. Ramirez-Mireles, "Performance of Ultra wideband SSMA using time hopping and M-ary PPM," *IEEE J. Select. Area Commun.*, vol.19, no.6, June 2001.
[7] Time Domain Corp., "Time-modulated ultra wide-band radio measurement & spectrum management issues", *Presentation Material at National Radio Science Meeting*, Boulder, USA, Jan. 1999.
[8] Kazimierz Siwiak and Alan Petroff, "A path link model for ultra wide band pulse transmissions", *The IEEE Semiannual Vehicular Technology Conference VTC2001 Spring*, May , 2001.

# A Vulnerability Assessment Tool Based on OVAL in System Block Model*

Geuk Lee[1], Il-seok Ko[2], and Tai-hoon Kim[3]

[1] Hannam University, Daejeon, Korea
glee@hannam.ac.kr
[2] Chungbuk Provincial University, Chungbuk, Korea
glee@hannam.ac.kr
[3] Kyushu University, Kyushu, Japan
taihoonn@empal.com

**Abstract.** OVAL (Open Vulnerability Assessment Language) is a standard language which is used to detect the vulnerability of local system based on the system characteristics and configurations. It is suggested by MITRE. OVAL consists of XML schema and SQL query statements. XML schema defines the vulnarable points and SQL query detects the vulnerable and weak points. This paper designed and implemented the vulnerability assesment tool with OVAL to detect the weak points in security countermeasure block. It has more readability, reliability, scalability and simplicity than traditional tools.

## 1 Introduction

The vulnerability assessment tool is a security tool to diagnose the computer system and detect the weakness in advance to keep the system's status safe. The vulnerability assessment tools are broadly classified as host-based assessment tool, network-based assessment tool and application assessment tool to detect the specific applications' attack-ability. Existing vulnerability assessment tools detect the system's weakness by executing the attack code such as exploit scripts [1]. But, individual tools don't have common criteria with vulnerability detection and vulnerability assessment scripts are implemented with various programming languages. So it is difficult to know which tools provide more correct diagnoses, as well as the prices to develop and maintain the assessment script gets higher. MITRE suggested the OVAL (Open Vulnerability Assessment Language) to overcome these limitations. OVAL is a standard language to assess the fragility of the local system based on the information of the system's characteristics and the configurations. Basically OVAL defines the weakness of CVE with XML schema. Using these XML schemas, it constructs and executes the query statements to detect the weak points.

This paper designed the host-based vulnerability assessment tool in the security countermeasure block with OVAL which has been proposed by MITRE.

* This work was supported by a grant from Ministry of Commerce, Industry and Energy.

D.-S. Huang, K. Li, and G.W. Irwin (Eds.): ICIC 2006, LNCS 4113, pp. 1115–1120, 2006.

# 2 System Block Model

## 2.1 Division of IT Systems

Implementation of any security countermeasure may require economic support. If your security countermeasures are not sufficient to prevent the threats, the existence of the countermeasures is not a real countermeasure and just considered as like waste. If your security countermeasures are built over the real risks you have, maybe you are wasting your economic resources.

First step is the division of IT systems into some. In this paper, we divide IT systems into 4 parts. But we think this partition is not perfect one and we are now researching about that.

Next step is construction of block matrix by using the parts of IT systems and common components we mentioned above (See the Fig. 1).

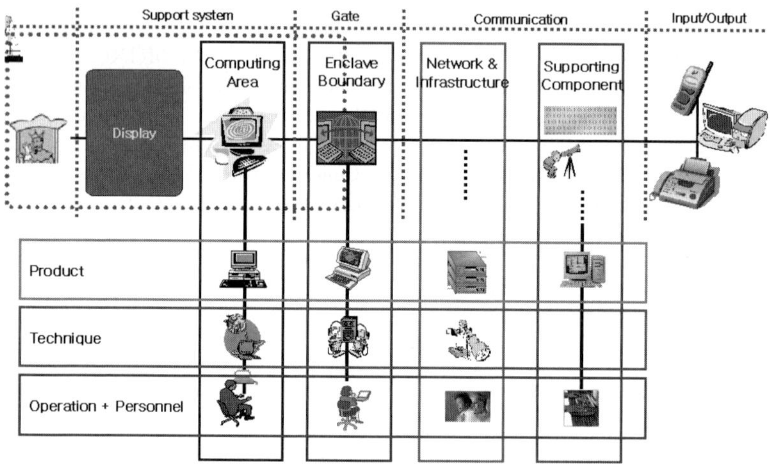


**Fig. 1.** Block matrix

Each cross point area of Fig.1 may be generalized and reduced into Block and matrix of Fig.2. Each Block may mean the area require security countermeasures or security method.

Next step is determination of security assurance level of IT systems. Security assurance level is related to the robustness. In the concept of our Block model, all cross point area should be protected by security countermeasures.

Robustness is connected to the level or strength of security countermeasures and this idea is expressed like as Fig.3. The last step may be building security countermeasures by using Block Region.

This block matrix can be applied to information engineering and system engineering. Next is the sample applied to design security countermeasures for IT systems.

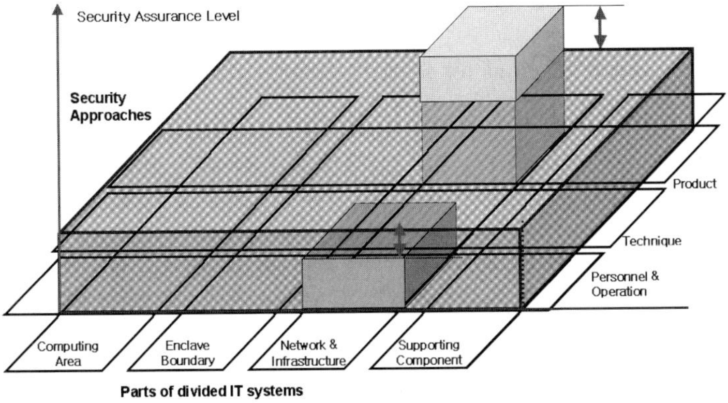


**Fig. 2.** Block Model for Security Countermeasures

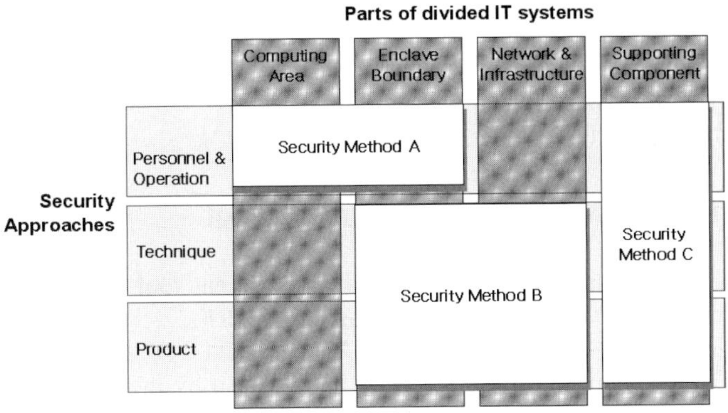


**Fig. 3.** Building security countermeasures by using Block Region

# 3 Vulnerability Assessment Tool

## 3.1 The Vulnerability Assessment Tool

The vulnerability assessment tool is a sort of security tool to keep the systems more safe by diagnosing the weak points in the computer systems in advance and providing the solutions and the proper patch information. It is also called as vulnerability scanner or security scanner. These scanners are classified as a host scanner and network scanner in accordance with the checking contents [2]. Host scanner is installed at each operator's platform. It searches the security problems which can be caused by the administrator's mistakes or mis-configurations [3]. The network scanner assesses the portable weak points which can be attacked by the external hackers.

The vulnerability scanner usually uses the detection scripts such as exploit to find weak points. But currently used commercial or free codes have a problem that the detection results are not reliable, because they apply some different criteria in the vulnerability assessment and the codes are made with different description languages with wide variety.

### 3.2 OVAL

OVAL is the common language for security experts to discuss and agree upon technical details about how to check for the presence of vulnerabilities on a computer system. The end results of the discussions are OVAL queries, which perform the checks to identify the vulnerabilities [1], [3]. OVAL queries are written in SQL and use a collaboratively developed and standardized SQL schema as the basis for each query. OVAL queries detect the presence of software vulnerabilities in terms of system characteristics and configuration information, without requiring software exploit code. By specifying logical conditions on the values of system characteristics and configuration attributes, OVAL queries characterize exactly which systems are susceptible to a given vulnerability. OVAL queries are based primarily on the known vulnerabilities identified in Common Vulnerabilities and Exposures (CVE), a dictionary of standardized names and descriptions for publicly known information security vulnerabilities and exposures developed by The MITRE Corporation in cooperation with the international security community. CVE common names make it easier to share data across separate network security databases and tools that are CVE-compatible. CVE also provides a baseline for evaluating the coverage of an organization's security tools, including the security advisories it receives. For each CVE name, there are one or more OVAL queries.

## 4 Design of Vulnerabilities Assessment Tool

In this paper, we designed the vulnerability assessment tool designed for RedHat Linux Platform with OVAL schema suggested by MITRE.

Data File consists of "INSERT DATA" part and "OVAL queries" part. In "INSERT DATA" part, the lists of data to be collected by the "System Information Collecting Module" are presented. In "OVAL queries" part, the conditions to detect the system's vulnerability based on the system information collected from input data using "query interpreter" module are described in the form of SQL query statements.

"Data File Verification Module" verifies whether the given data file is correct or not. "Log Management Module" deals with the errors which can be occurred in the system. "System Information Collecting Module" has two roles in the vulnerability assessment tool. The one role is to collect various system information such as configuration setting information, software installation information, file information and process information based on "INSERT DATA." And the other role is to update database status based on the collected data. Because the "OVAL Queries" part is described with SQL language, OVAL-based vulnerability assessment system should contain DBMS (Database Management System). In our design, we used SQLite as DBMS. It operates in a file-base.

System Data gathered by "System Information Collecting Module" is stored in database. OVAL Query statements are applied to this database to find corresponding vulnerabilities. Tables of database are constructed using OVAL schema of individual OS platform. In the RedHat-series Linux Platform, we designed the required schema; File Metadata Schema, Internet Server Daemon Schema, Passwd File Schema, Shadow File Schema, Process Information Schema, RPM Information Schema, Information for

Comparison with Susceptible RPM Versions Schema and Operating Platform Information Schema.

"System Information Collecting Module" plays two roles; 1) collecting the required system information to assess the vulnerabilities in the system, 2) reflect that information to the database. The data list which this module should collect is listed up in "INSERT DATA." OVAL uses this "INSERT DATA" part to reduce the time of collecting required system information. In other words, "INSERT DATA" part lists up not all the information of installed packages and files, but only the information items required to assess the vulnerability of the system. "System Information Collecting Module" consists of 8 sub-modules. Their names are taken after the corresponding schema. They are File Metadata Collecting Sub-module, Internet Server Daemon Information Collecting Sub-module, RPM Information Collecting Sub-module, RPM Version Comparison Sub-module, Password File Information Collecting Sub-module, Process Information Collecting Sub-module, Shadow File Information Collecting Sub-module and Operating Platform Information Collecting Sub-module.

## 5 Comparison with Traditional Tools

We designed and implemented the OVAL-based vulnerability assessment tool operating on RedHat Linux Platform in security countermeasure block. There are some other existing tools used in UNIX-like platform such as Tiger or SATAN. They have specific scripts and specific goals. Our design follows the standard guideline suggested in the MITRE. So our tool is very general-purpose assessment tool and has as similar benefits as OVAL concept. They are following:

- A simple and straightforward way to determine if a vulnerability exists on a given system
- A standard, common schema of security-relevant configuration information
- For each CVE entry, one or more SQL queries precisely demonstrate that the vulnerability exists
- Reduces need for disclosure of exploit code as an assessment tool
- An open alternative to closed, proprietary, and replicated efforts
- A community effort of security experts, system administrators, software developers, and other experts
- Freely available vulnerability content for public review, comment, or download from the Internet
- Industry-endorsed via the OVAL Board and OVAL Community Forum

## 6 Conclusion

Existing assessment tools only check the existence of the vulnerabilities by checking the checklists mainly listed in [4]. But the suggested tool can not only check the weak points but also define new checklists in the form of XML and SQL syntax.

Traditional tools only check the mainly weak points which have been aimed to by the attackers. But the suggested tool can check all the weak points registered in CVE list at once.

In this paper, first we divide IT systems into 12 blocks, and apply OVAL-based vulnerability methods to them. Because existing tools apply somewhat different description languages with wide variety each other, their detection results are not reliable. OVAL-based vulnerability methods are getting higher estimation by the security experts, so the tools on various OS platforms will be developed continuously in the future.

## References

1. Jung, H. K.: The Trends of International Standardization on Vulnerability Assessment of Computer Systems. The Trends in International Information Security, Korea Information Security Agency, Korea (2003)
2. Tai, H. K., Hwang, S. M., Kouich, S.: Security Countermeasure Design by Using Block Model. TELE-INFO 2006 Conference, Japan (2006)
3. Ragi, G.: Network and Host-based Vulnerability Assessments. http://www.sans.org, SANS Institute, February (2004)
4. UNIX Security Checklist V2. http://www.cert.org, AusCERT, October (2001)

# Bark Classification Based on Contourlet Filter Features Using RBPNN

Zhi-Kai Huang[1,2], Zhong-Hua Quan[1,2], and Ji-Xiang Du[1,2]

[1] Intelligent Computing Lab, Hefei Institute of Intelligent Machines, Chinese Academy of Sciences, P.O.Box 1130, Hefei, Anhui 230031, China
[2] Department of Automation, University of Science and Technology of China
huangzk@iim.ac.cn

**Abstract.** This paper proposed a new method of extracting texture features based on contourlet domain in RGB color space. In addition, the application of these features for bark classification applying radial basis probabilistic network (RBPNN) has been introduced. In this method, the bark texture feature is firstly extracted by decomposing an image into 6 subbands using the 7-9 biorthogonal Debauches wavelet transform, where each subband is fed to the directional filter banks stage with 32 directions at the finest level, then the mean and standard deviation of the image output are computed. The obtained feature vectors are fed up into RBPNN for classification. Experimental results show that, features extracted using the proposed approach can be more efficient for bark texture classification than gray bark image.

## 1 Introduction

Efficient recognition and identification the plant species from collecting databases is an important challenge. Specially, automatic plant recognition from color images is one of the most difficult tasks in computer vision because of lacking of proper models or representations for plant. Many plant barks show evident texture features, which can be used as one of useful features for plant recognition. Bark image has shown some texture properties. A great number of texture analysis methods have been proposed over decades, such as multi-channel filtering features, fractal based features and co-occurrence features [1],[2],[3], and these methods can capture different texture properties of the images at different levels. Many methods of texture features extracted which focus on the luminance components of the image; however, color has always been an important feature for image recognition and classification. Color-based image classification is inherently invariant to transformations in the image that are due to rescaling, translation, distortion, and rotation.

A simple architecture of a typical classification system, where there are two major tasks. The first one is feature extraction, where a set of features, called image signatures, is generated to accurately represent the content of each image; the second task is classification, where a suitable classifier should be chosen, the image features which will be classified were computed to classify image.

In this paper, we describe a system where color information is used for the contourlet-based for bark texture recognition, which can be viewed as a color extension

D.-S. Huang, K. Li, and G.W. Irwin (Eds.): ICIC 2006, LNCS 4113, pp. 1121 – 1126, 2006.

of gray bark image. Given a color bark image, each color component is passed through contourlet decomposition; Texture information that the mean and variance of each triplet coefficient vector per bandwidth with different orientations at various scales is captured in different directional subbands is grouped to form a set of subband features. Finally, the obtained contourlet filter feature vectors are fed up into radial basis function neural network (RBPNN) for classification and identification.

## 2 Features Extracted and RBPNN Classifier

Contourlet, firstly proposed by Do and Vetterli [4], is a new image representation scheme which owns a powerful ability to efficiently capture the smooth contours of image. Contourlets not only possess the main features of wavelets (namely, multiscale and time frequency localization), but also specially decompose the subband at each scale into different directional parts with flexible number [5].

The contourlet transform is implemented via a double filter bank named pyramidal directional filter bank (PDFB), where the Laplacian Pyramid (LP) is first used to decompose images into multiscale. This allows contourlets to efficiently approximate a smooth contour at different scales. The double filter bank design certainly allows the contourlet to be flexibly constructed. Then, followed by a Directional Filter Bank (DFB) to decompose subbands at each scale into directional parts. This contourlet transform can be implemented iteratively applying PDFB on the coarse scale of image, as shown in Figure 1.

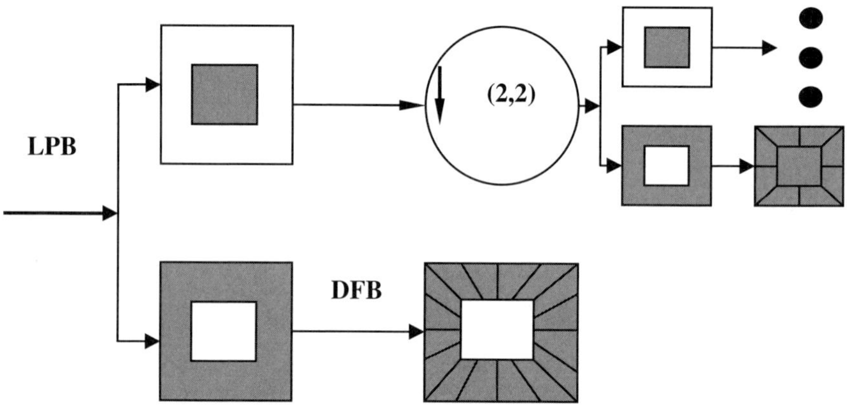


**Fig. 1.** Pyramid structure for the contourlet decomposition

A RGB color image is a multi-spectral image with one band for each color red, green and blue, thus producing a weighted combination of the three primary colors for each pixel. Consider the contourlet decomposition of a color image, which yields three sets of directional subband images, corresponding to the three color components. Subbands with orientation $\theta$ at scale $L$ are grouped together to form a triplet, denoted as $T_\theta^L = [R_\theta^L, G_\theta^L, B_\theta^L]$, which is the child of a parent triplet with same/similar orientation at scale $L+1$.

The features used in contour model are the mean and variance of each triplet coefficient vector per bandwidth, which these two features, can describe the statistical distribution of coefficients at each subband. After pre-processing and attribute extraction steps, features of the bark are introduced to the artificial neural network (ANN) for bark classification.

A neural network is composed of multiple layers of interconnected nodes with an activation function in each node and weights on the edges or arcs connecting the nodes of the network[11]. The output of each nodes is a nonlinear function of all its inputs and the network represents an expansion of the unknown nonlinear relationship between inputs, $x$ , and outputs, F(or y), into a space spanned by the functions represented by the activation functions of the network's nodes. In this paper, radial basis probabilistic network (RBPNN) has been used for recognition of bark texture image.

The RBPNN model is essentially developed from the radial basis function neural networks (RBFNN) and the probabilistic neural networks (PNN) [5], [6], [7], [8]. Therefore, the RBPNN possesses the common characteristics of the two original networks, i.e., the signal is concurrently feed-forwarded from the input layer to the output layer without any feedback connections within the network models. Moreover, the RBPNN avoids the disadvantages of the two original models to some extent. The RBPNN, shown in Fig.2, consists of four layers: one input layer, two hidden layers and one output layer. The first hidden layer is a nonlinear processing layer, which generally consists of hidden centers selected from a set of training samples. The second hidden layer selectively sums the first hidden layer outputs according to the categories to which the hidden centers belong. Generally, the corresponding weight values of the second hidden layer are 1's. For pattern recognition problems, the outputs in the second hidden layer need to be normalized. The last layer for RBPNN is simply the output layer, which completes the nonlinear mapping by carrying out tasks such as classification, approximation and prediction. In fact, the first hidden layer of the RBPNN has the vital role of performing the problem-solving task[9].

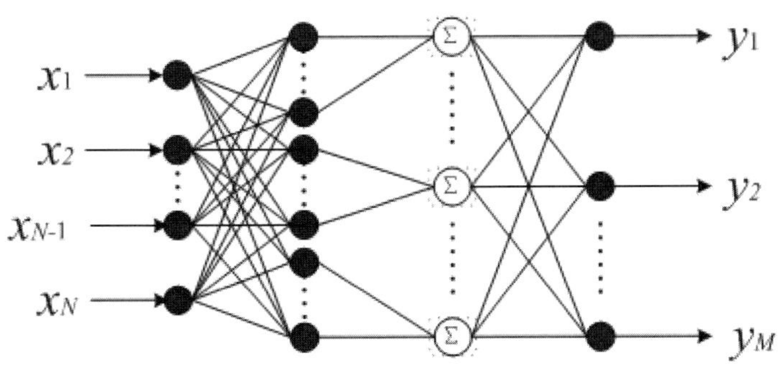


**Fig. 2.** The topology scheme of the RBPNN

Training of the network for the RBPNN used orthogonal least square algorithms (OLSA). The advantages of recursive least square algorithms are that it can fast convergence and good convergent accuracy. The detail algorithms has been addressed by D.S. Huang[7].

The architecture of the bark classification system would look something like the one presented in Figure 3.

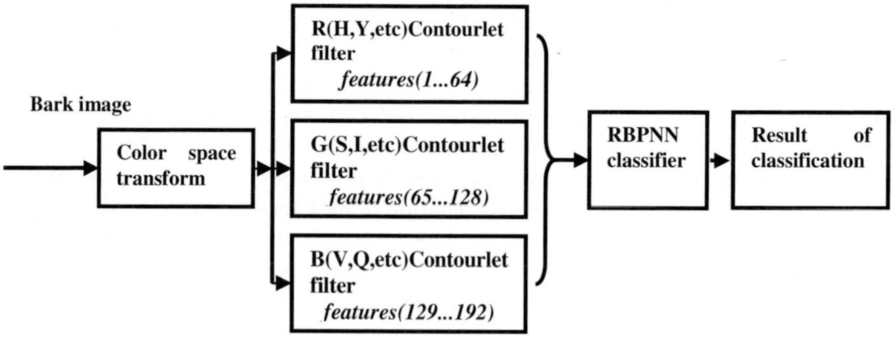


**Fig. 3.** Overall architecture of the bark classification system

# 3 Image Data and Experimental Results

## 3.1 Image Data and Features Chosen

Using a texture database from which we have collected more than 300 pictures of bark. These images were recorded at a resolution of 640 x 480 pixels, with a bit depth of 8 bits/pixel. Thus, 256 levels were available for each R, G, and B color plane. Some bark images are shown in Fig.4.

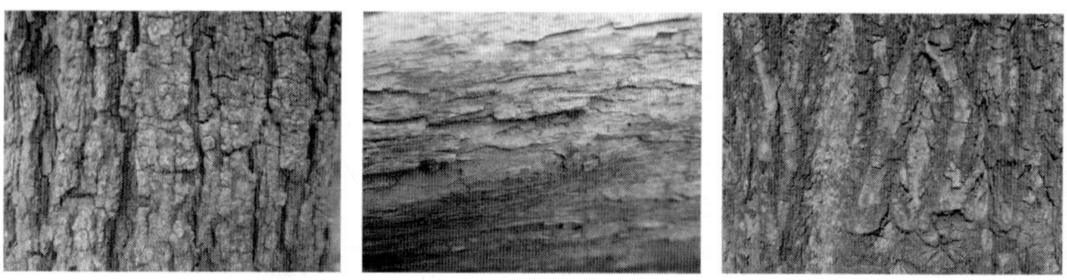

**Fig. 4.** Three kinds of original bark images

Randomly chosen about 50% of plant bark samples for each bark class form a testing set and the remaining samples form a training set. By this partition, there are 248 samples in the training set and 17 character samples in the testing set. In addition, because the trunk of the tree is cylinder and the two sides of the pictures are possibly blurred, so the particularity region-of-interests (ROI), we have select that is a relatively bigger ROI with the size of $350 \times 400$ pixels.

As we have discussed in section 2, the contourlet filter-based feature extraction method requires setting control parameters of contourlet filter. Hence a feature vector consists of different parameters will be obtained which contains the visual content of the image. To get the best result, the contourlet parameters were test for 6 subbands using the 7-9 biorthogonal Debauches wavelet transform, where each subband is fed to the directional filter banks stage with 32 directions at the finest level. In addition, we implemented a direct wavelet transform coder using the fully decimated 7-9 biorthogonal Debauches wavelet transform for comparison.

The RBPNN classifier has been used for bark image classification, at the same time, other classifier such as KNN classifier has been employed in our experiment so the classification results can be comparison. The k-nearest neighbor classifier labels an unknown object with the label of the majority of the k nearest neighbors. A neighbor is deemed nearest if it has the smallest distance, in the Euclidian sense, in feature space. For k = 1, this is the label of its closest neighbor in the learning set.[9]

The experiment has been made on a PC (PentiumIV-2.4GHz CPU, 512M RAM).The image features were calculated using subroutines written in Matlab 7.0 language [8]. Software for Classifier of RBPNN, we use a conventional C++6.0 programming environment. Totally seventeen bark classes are used for identification. These were: retinispora, maple, Sophora japonica, dogbane, trumpet creeper, osier, pine, phoenix tree, camphor, poplar and willow, honey locust, palm, gingkgo, elm, etc. Every type of bark has half images for training, others for testing. We used the" quantity average recognition rate" defined as below to compare the results.

$$Average\ Recognition\ Rate = \frac{Number\ of\ Bark\ Image\ \ Classified\ Truely}{Totat\ Number\ of\ Classified\ Bark\ Images} \cdot \%$$

The average recognition rates have been presented in Table 1.

**Table 1.** Average Recognition Rates used different features

| Texture methods | RBPNN | k-NN |
|---|---|---|
| Auto-correlation method(ACM) | 0.65 | 0.65 |
| Co-occurrence matrices method (COMM) | 0.72 | 0.75 |
| Histogram method(HM) | 0.62 | 0.62 |
| Contourlet filter method(CFM, color space) | 0.79 | 0.74 |
| Contourlet filter method(CFM, gray image) | 0.58 | 0.57 |

Comparing the Auto-correlation method (ACM), Co-occurrence matrices method (COMM), Histogram method (HM) and contourlet method, the average recognition rate of the contourlet filter method is 79%, higher than other features method. The Table 1 shows the texture images that are better classification by contourlets filter methods.

## 4 Conclusions

This paper proposed a new method of extracting texture features based on contourlet domain in RGB color space. The bark texture feature is firstly extracted by decomposing an image into 6 subbands using the 7-9 biorthogonal Debauches wavelet transform, where each subband is fed to the directional filter banks stage with 32 directions at the finest level, and then the mean and standard deviation of the image output are computed. The obtained feature vectors are fed up into RBPNN for classification. Experimental results show that, features extracted using the proposed approach can be more efficient for bark texture classification than others gray bark image because Contourlets possess not only the main features of wavelets, namely multiresolution and time-frequency localization, but they also show a high degree of directionality and anisotropy, this characteristic is suitable to expression texture image. In the future, more effective feature extracted methods will be investigated for bark classification; at the same time, compared the classification results using different classifier should be done.

## References

1. David, A. Clausi, Huang Deng.: Design-Based Texture Feature Fusion Using Gabor Filters and Co-Occurrence Probabilities, IEEE Transactions on Image Processing, Vol. 14, No. 7, July (2005) 925-936
2. Zheru Chi, Li Houqiang, and Wang Chao.: Plant Species Recognition Based on Bark Patterns Using Novel Gabor Filter Banks, IEEE Int. Conf. Neural Networks & Signal Processing Nanjing. China (2003) 1035-1038
3. Cunha, J.B.: Application of Image Processing Techniques in the Characterization of Plant Leafs, International Symposium on Industrial Electronics, Vol1, (2003)612-616
4. M. N. Do and M. Vetterli.: Rotation Invariant Texture Characterization and Retrieval Using Steerable Wavelet-Domain Hidden Markov Models, IEEE Trans. Multimedia, vol. 4, no. 4, Dec(2002)517-527
5. D. D.-Y. Po.: Image Modeling in Contourlet Domain, Master's thesis, University of Illinois at Urbana-Champaign, (2003)
6. D.S. Huang.: Radial Basis Probabilistic Neural Networks: Model and Application, International Journal of Pattern Recognition and Artificial Intelligence, 13(7), (1999)1083-1101
7. D.S.Huang.: Systematic Theory of Neural Networks for Pattern Recognition. Publishing House of Electronic Industry of China, Beijing, (1996)
8. M. N. Do.: Contourlet Toolbox , http://www.ifp.uiuc.edu/ minhdo/software/
9. Wen-Jyi Hwang, Kuo-Wei Wen.: Fast kNN Classification Algorithm Based on Partial Distance Search. Electronics Letters, Vol. 34, Issue 21, Oct (1998)2062-2063
10. D.S.Huang, Wen-Bo Zhao.:Determining the Centers of Radial Basis Probabilities Neural Networks by Recursive Orthogonal Least Square Algorithms,Applied Mathematics and Computation, vol 162, no.1(2005) 461-473
11. D.S.Huang.: Application of Generalized Radial Basis Function Networks to Recognition of Radar Targets,International Journal of Pattern Recognition and Artificial Intelligence, Vol.13, No.6, (1999)945-962

# Community for Ubiquitous Medical Information System*

Jaekoo Song[1], Minseong Ju[1,**], Sunho Kim[1], Hyoungjoo Han[1], and Kyung Sung[2]

[1] Hannam University, Department of Multimedia Engineering, Postfach , 306 791
133 Ojeong-Dong, Daedeok-Gu, Daejeon, Korea
nimpe2@naver.com
[2] Mokwon University, Department of Computer Education, Postfach , 302 729
800 Doan-Dong, Seo-Gu, Daejeon, Korea
Skyys04@mokwon.ac.kr

**Abstract.** This research aimed to provide smooth mutual interlock among systems by grouping classified class based systems and focused on easy scalability and modification. The basic model of the research was; each class contains its own applications and these services mutually interlock in complex platforms. The community considered in this research is a basis for providing combined management of medical equipments and applications within environment where compatibility is causing problems during migration, and is suitable for designing medical information system within the ubiquitous environment.

## 1 Introduction

Generally, when the ubiquitous computing environment is designed using each detailed technologies, array of these devices or services search cooperative target they require according to the need and provide temporary cooperation services. That is many of devices and services only process given number of situations and consideration for repetition of these phenomenon has been omitted. These phenomenons are problems often seen from all systems using ubiquitous system. In particular, there is an immediate need to solve these problems for medical services where lives of people are depended to these services. In the case of medical services, various medical accidents are occurring during offline status and the possibility of much more problems occurring during application of online medical diagnosis is high. This suggests that, there is a need to equip mutual security system structure to reduce conflicts between various medical systems that have been introduced and to maintain integrity of information.

Therefore, the researcher will design a class based community system that will categorize systems, as a means to design systematic medical information system in ubiquitous environment [1],[2].

## 2 Related Literatures

Ubiquitous Medical System has already been adopted by hospitals together with the introduction of POC. These technologies will support various types of medical system

* This work was supported by the Korea Research Foundation Grant funded by the Korean Government(MOEHRD)(KRF-2005-041-D00576).

** Corresponding author.

D.-S. Huang, K. Li, and G.W. Irwin (Eds.): ICIC 2006, LNCS 4113, pp. 1127 – 1132, 2006.

as the technology involved in basic infrastructure develops. A representing example is the u-Hospital, which utilizes RFID into medical system by using sensors. Massachusetts General Hospital of United States has already adopted RFID and GPS technology to identify location of medical equipments, doctors, nurses and patients. Also, diagnosis can be made remotely within normal households as "at home" medical services utilizing "at home" medical devices and internet develop [4].

The ubiquitous medical system utilizes existing systems that had been developed during the medical information process and has adopted sensors for diagnosing patients effectively [5]. However, countermeasures are being demanded for solving problems arising from compatibilities among equipments and data exchanges.

# 3 Designing and Evaluating MIC System

In this chapter, the author will design a community required to introduce systems reliably during the procedure of medical information transition. Various types of medical information system is being introduced as the ubiquitous environment develops, causing various compatibility problems. Therefore, class will be constructed between compatible systems and these classes will be combined to provide stability of medical information system. Suggested model has basic design as shown in Figure 2.

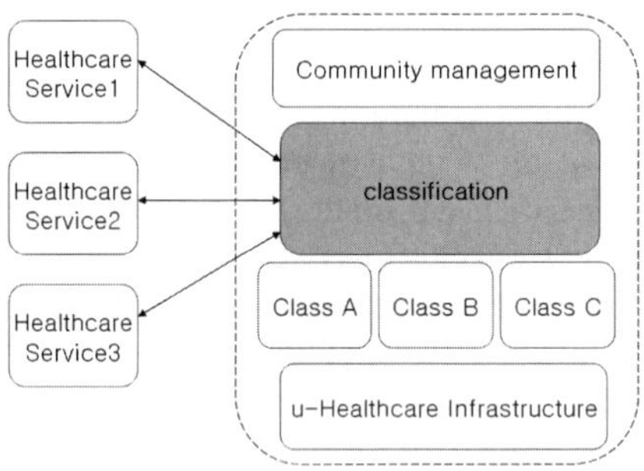


**Fig. 1.** The suggested medical community system

The suggested medical community system will classify healthcare services basing on the classification module. At this time, the classified healthcare service will be registered under the concerning class. Community management module will take role of applying and modifying standards applied by the classification module and will input standards to examine connection between each class. At this time, the basic infrastructure for supporting ubiquitous environment must have been structured and communication between each class will base on the wireless communication.

## 3.1 Medical Information Community System Information Classification

Standard classification of suggested medical community system is defined in the Table 1 to manage healthcare systems.

**Table 1.** Classifications for standard classification of the suggested medical community system

| Classification | Define | Example |
|---|---|---|
| Task and management | Provide tasks required to execute medical activities | CRM |
| Diagnosis system | System that is involved with medical activities directly | PACS |
| Additional system | Systems providing additional support during diagnosis | OCS, POS |
| Sensor based system | Used sensor system | RFID Mobile |
| Communication method | Cable or wireless method | POC |
| Data system | Stores information | ERM |

There are 6 classifications for standard classification of the suggested medical community system. System used to provide tasks required to execute medical activities are classified in to task and management system and systems that is involved with medical activities directly is defined as diagnosis system. Systems providing additional support during diagnosis, such as stock management and diagnosis delivery system, are defined as additional system and sensor driven systems such as RFID is defined as sensor based system. Communication method will be defined following cable or wireless method and lastly, system like ERM that stores information is defined as data system. Classified systems within the community system classification may alter depending on the situation. Specially, systems having high relativity in information processing will be treated as being the same Class, allowing easy construction of community.

### 3.2 Designing Suggested Medical Information Community System

Medical information community should be designed basing on virtual scenario. This is a countermeasure of the research trying to support various problems that may arise during the medical information processing through situational class bases. The scenario of this research will be creation of mobile device community between the medical information system within the hospital and the mobile devices of the patient when the patient visits the hospital.Following the scenario, the classification will under go procedures as shown in the Figure 2.

At this time, there is high tendency for the definition of work compatibility section to alter depending on the situational recognition. Therefore there is a need for the Community management to assign a standard by recognizing the situation. Specially, consideration for compatibility and data migration is necessary when a new system is introduced to the existing system. Result of classification of each class following the introduction of scenario is as follows in Figure 3.

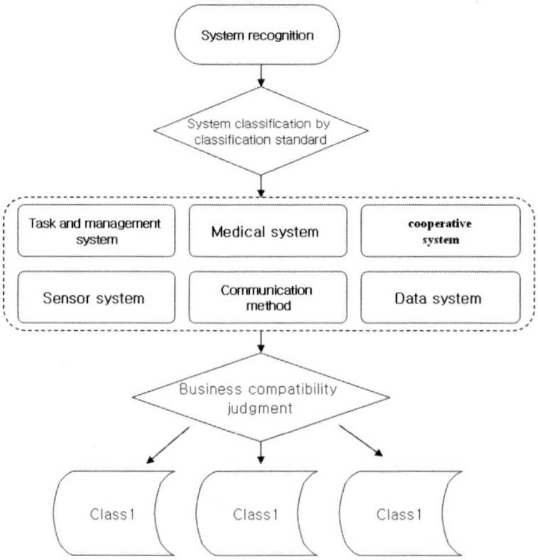


**Fig. 2.** Classification procedures

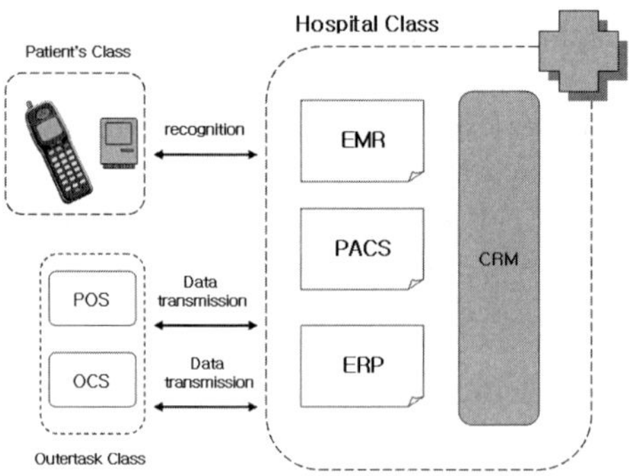


**Fig. 3.** Class structure for Medical Information system

In the classification of each class following scenario introduction, classes are classified in to Patient class, Hospital Class and Outer Task Class. With the consideration of portability and convenience, the Patient Class will consist of sensor based system and wireless communication method system based on the RFID mobile. The Hospital Class will be comprised of Electronic Medical Diagnosis Record (ERM), Medical Image Storing Information System (PACS) and the Enterprise Resource Management System (ERP), furthermore, the Outer Task Class will be comprised of Diagnosis Delivery System (OCS) and Stock Management System (POS).Cable and wireless communication between each class has been assumed to be possible following the result of medical information system class structures. Also, sensor information of Patient Class was assumed to provide required patient information to necessary systems within the Hospital Class.

### 3.3 Application of Class Based Medical Information Community System

By applying suggested medical information system to actual emergency medical situations, following structures as shown in <Figure 4> had been designed. Abnormal heart beat of patients with heart problems among Patient Class will be detected through sensor recognition and this information will be transmitted to the Hospital Class through mobile devices. At this time, sensor information will be analyzed, classified and transmitted to doctors then will trigger occurrence of emergency situation. After this, patient transfer will be ordered by communicating with ambulance while the emergency treatments will be executed through remote diagnosis system. Mutual interlock among systems plays an important role in complex situations like this. As a result of applying medical information community system suggested in this research, to a specific example, we were able to design class classification and structure where addition of class can be done easily. Furthermore, community classified in to class based can be simply expanded, provide environment that can cope with limited services while providing much effective services to users utilizing medical information as user unit gets recognized as a class.

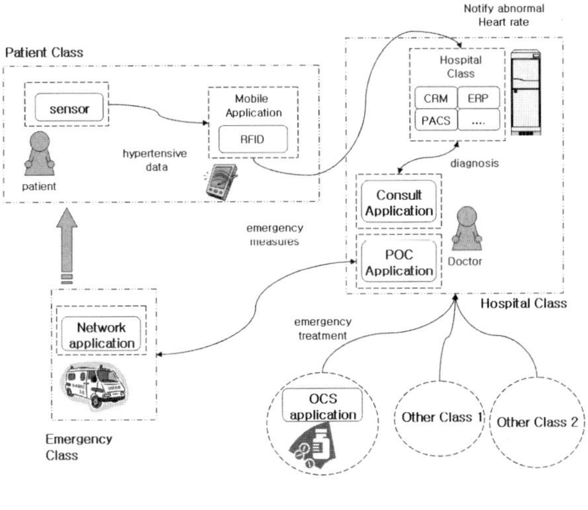


**Fig. 4.** Using of Medical information community system

### 3.4 System Evaluation

Various kinds of community method are being researched to design effective systems within the ubiquitous environment. The research aimed to provide smooth mutual interlock among systems by grouping classified class based systems and focused on easy scalability and modification. The basic model of the research was; each class contains its own applications and these services mutually interlock in complex platforms. The community considered in this research is a basis for providing combined management of medical equipments and applications within environment where compatibility is causing problems during migration, and is suitable for designing medical information system within the ubiquitous environment.

## 4 Conclusion

The class based community system suggested to design medical information system, allows expansion of possible service targets by designing class units for the complex structured medical information, reduces unnecessary waste of resources such as repeated by interlocking systems and will provide convenient managements by classifying individual users into objects. Lastly, further researches on community management module and security protection scheme for classes are required, to clearly define changes in classes following situational changes.

## References

1. Mohan, K.: PICO : A Middleware Framework for pervasive Compting. IEEE Persive Computing, 4 (2003) 342-358
2. Wang, B., John, B., Sandeep, K. S., Gupta: Supporting Persistent Social Group in Ubiquitous Computing Environments Using Context-Aware Ephemeral Group Service. Proc. 2nd IEEE International Conference on Pervasive Computing and Communications (PerCom), Orlando, FL (2004) 287-296
3. Martin, T., Jovanov, E., Raskovic, D.: Issues in Wearable Computing for Medical Monitoring Applications: A Case Study of a Wearable ECG Monitoring Device. In Proceedings of ISWC 2000, Atlanta, USA (2000)
4. Istepanian, R. S. H., Jovanov, E., Zhang, Y. T.: Guest Editorial Introduction to The Special Section on M-Health: Beyond Seamless Mobility and Global Wireless Health-Care Connectivity. In IEEE Transactions on Information Technology in Biomedicine, 8 (4) (2004) 405-414
5. Jovanov, E., Milenkovic, A., Otto, C., De-Groen, P. C.: A Wireless Body Area Network of Intelligent Motion Sensors for Computer Assisted Physical Rehabilitation. In Journal of Neuro Engineering and Rehabilitation, 2 (6) (2005) 241-262

# Design and Implementation of a Fast DIO (Digital I/O) and Motion Control System

Gyusang Cho[1], Jinkyung Ryeu[2,*], and Jongwoon Lee[3]

[1] Dept. of Computer Eng., Dongyang Univ., Youngju, Korea
[2] Dept. of IT Electronic Eng., Dongyang Univ., Youngju, Korea
[3] Dept. of Railway Control Eng., Dongyang Univ., Youngju, Korea
{gyusang, jkryeu, jwlee}@dyu.ac.kr

**Abstract.** High speed PC-based DIO (Digital I/O) system that consists of a master device and slave I/O devices is developed. The master device, which has PCI interface to a PC, controls all of serial communications, reducing the load on the CPU to a minimum. And the slave I/O devices, which are used as 16 bits input, 16 bits output, and 8bits input-output each, are connected from the master device to one slave, from the slave to the next slave, and to a maximum 64 slaves repeatedly. The master device has 2 rings which can take 64 slaves each. Therefore, total I/O points covered by the master are 2048 points. The slave features 3 types of input/output function interchangeability by DIP switch settings. Library, application, and device driver software for the DIO system that have a secure and a convenient functionality are developed.

## 1 Introduction

Many Digital I/O's such as switch input, AC input, relay output and TR output are required in the field of industrial machine, high-accuracy semiconductor instruments, chemical factory and steel factory. PLC (Programmable Logic Controller) [1] is used mostly in these types of I/O processes. In this case, there are some defects such as additional cost fir instruments and the necessities of another OS and of large space for implementing. Moreover, it is difficult to communicate with PC and the length of cable is getting longer. Because of these defects, PC-based I/O cards are used widely. But there also exist some problems such as using limited slots for many I/O cards [2].

Recently, PC-based I/O system using PC as main controller is used widely [3],[4]. Many merits of this method such as real-time controllability, development facility, reliability and scalability make the cost lower. The key criteria of performance in this type of system are wiring between the master device and the slave device, data transfer speed and interfacing PC with the master device.

One-to-one wiring between the master device and the slave device is general, but many I/O cards must be equipped on limited PC slots. In a study using USB for overcoming the defect [5], maximum 64 points can be used by connecting 4 slaves per one USB master port. But the above method has a problem that an additional USB master

* Corresponding author.

D.-S. Huang, K. Li, and G.W. Irwin (Eds.): ICIC 2006, LNCS 4113, pp. 1133 – 1138, 2006.

device is needed for many points. To overcome this demerit the USB HSIO (High Speed I/O) system which can distribute master and slave by adopting the structure having very high transfer speed and reduced routing was developed[6]. Continued on this research the PCI HSIO system which is more stable and faster than the existing systems and guarantees fixed access time was implemented [7].

In this research, we designed and implemented a DIO (Digital I/O) system which is much better in speed, number of available points and design facility than PCI HSIO [7]. In the body of this paper there are specific methods of design and implementation. The overview of the overall DIO system and the description about the method of hardware implementation for the master and slave devices having simple wiring structure and high operating speed are in Chap 2.

## 2 Overview of DIO System

### 2.1 Features of the System

Master device considers I/O of slaves just like accessing memory, so this helps to reduce the burden of CPU and to enhance the communication speed. And it is possible that make the system configuration in a simple form. By using RS-485 communication, it is possible to cut down wiring cost and simplify wiring problem [8].

System is consists of Master and Slave devices as shown in Fig. 1. Master device is installed on PC with PCI interface. The slaves are connected from the master device to one slave, from that slave to next slave, and to other slave, etc. PLX9030 [9] chip is used for PCI communication, and G9001 is used for master device, and G9002 is used for DIO slave devices.

The master device equipped with two G9001 chip can connect maximum 64 slaves each. One is called ring 0 and the other is called ring 1. So the maximum 128 slave can be used. RS-485 communications between the master and slaves have half-duplex way. With 20Mbps communication, the communication time for a slave is about 15.1 microseconds and 64 slaves (1024 points of I/O) can be updated within 1 millisecond.

### 2.2 Wiring and Scalability

The slave device is connected from the master device and another slave device is co nnected to the slave device, it can be repeated to maximum 64 slave devices in one rin g, in case of two rings the master can take 128 slaves. In general, a parallel I/O metho d has a strong point in a fast response, but the method has a weak point in wring all sl ave devices to a mater device. A serial I/O method takes advantages in a long distanc e communication and in total numbers of wire connection, but has disadvantages in the communication speed and load of computation time. Adoption of RS-485 com munication method gives a strong point of the serial and the parallel method, and it gi ves the system an enhancement of communication speed and simplicity in wring.

And, in our system, the way of slave connection is extensible. Several slave types, for example, DIO slave device for I/O device with G9002 chip, motion control slave device for CPU emulation device with G9004 and PCL device with G9003 chip, are operated on a master device. It is possible that, on the one hand, the system communicates with DIO devices, on the other hand, communicates with motion control devices.

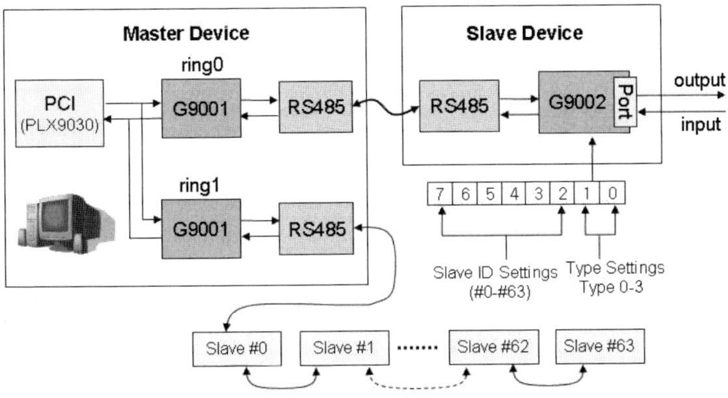


**Fig. 1.** Configuration of DIO system

# 3 Control of DIO System

## 3.1 Command and the Memory Map

On the master device the information for controlling the slave devices is document. Having the information about slave makes the master device easier to control slave. Slave device is not holds the information itself but take in charge of only input and output function. The every information on slave is documented on the master device memory. Table 1 show the information which are documented on the master.

Commands to control the master device and the slave device are can be documented on the master device's commands' data in 16 bits of 000-001h. #0100h is for make it have software reset, #1000h is for make it have all system communication, 1100h is for make it have all system communication except the allotted slave., 1200h-123Fh is for make it have assigned device's communication work by bit( 0001 0010 00## ####(#ID assign bit) ), 3000h I/O is for make it have start for communication, 3100h I/O is for make it have end the communication.

## 3.2 Slave Information

The information which is documented in the master device's memory is recorded after test communication for each slave devices. Upon response to the slaves the information about the type of device, the connection status and the I/O port are periodically renewed. The type of slave can be in four formats as shown in Table 2. The number of type is decided by the setting value. Each setting is organized to be set by the deep switch. According to this the port which is used in the control is decided and functioning input or output by the deep switch. When the slaves are connected to the master device the 8 bit information is saved in the memory slot 078h-0B7h as the value corresponding to the slave setting in Table 2.

Fig. 2 is the actual master device. Fig. 3 is the slave devices that are on operation. LED shows the condition of input and output.

**Table 1.** Memory map of the master device

| Address | Write | Read |
|---|---|---|
| 000-001 | Command | status |
| 002-003 | Invalid | Interrupt status |
| 078-0B7 | Device Info. 8bit for each device.<br>Device #0-#63 | Device Info. 8bit for each device.<br>Device #0-#63 |
| 0B8-0BF | I/O communication error flag<br>1bit for each device | I/O communication error flag<br>1bit for each device |
| 0C0-0FF | Input port change Interrupt settings<br>4bit for each device | Input port change Interrupt settings<br>4bit for each device |
| 100-1FF | I/O port data<br>8bit for each device | I/O port data<br>8bit for each device |

**Table 2.** Type number settings by DIP switch

| Type NO. | Setting | Port0 | Port1 | Port2 | Port3 |
|---|---|---|---|---|---|
| type0 | 00 | X | X | Output | |
| type1 | 01 | Input | X | X | Output |
| type2 | 10 | X | Input | Output | X |
| type3 | 11 | Input | | X | X |

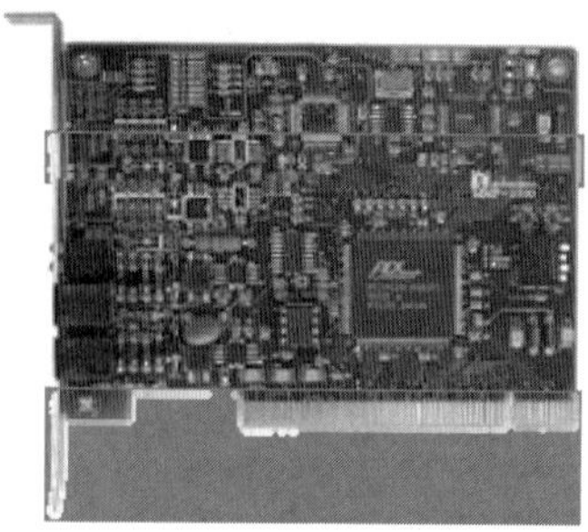

**Fig. 2.** PCI master device

**Fig. 3.** Slave devices for (a) DIO (b) motion control

## 4 Library Software for DIO System

Library routines for the DIO system are categorized to 4 groups, such as PCI setup and master initialization DIO, slave control, I/O, and ring setting.

PCI setup and master initialization category is consists of five functions. - *InitializePCI()* is used to prepare communication to open device driver DIO.sys, and *FinishPCI()* closes the communication to the driver. After initialization procedure, *StartComm()* and *StopComm()* start and stop I/O communication between the master

**Table 3.** Library functions for DIO system

| Category | Functions |
|---|---|
| PCI settings and initialization | InitializePCI(), FinishPCI(), StartIOComm(), StopIOComm(), Reset() |
| Slave Control | GetDeviceType(),GetAllDeviceType(),GetConnectedDevice(), ClearAllSlave() |
| Input/Output | WriteWord(),WriteByte(),WriteWordBitwise(),WriteByteBitwise(), ReadWord(),ReadByte(),ReadWordBitwise(),ReadByteBitwise() |
| Ring Control | SetRing(), GetRing() |

and the slave devices. *Reset()* is to reset the master device so that all the register of the master can be reset and all slave information can be reset.

Four functions are presented to slave control. *GetDeviceType()* returns the slave type value when the slave ID is assigned in the argument. *GetAllDeviceType()* write the type information of all connected slaves(#0-#63) to the slave type information array. *GetConncetionDevice()* returns the slave number and slave type that are currently connected. *ClearAllSlave()* clears the all slave information in the master devices.

Eight functions that are used to input and output are presented. That functions operates in word, byte, and bitwise. *WriteWord()* and *WriteByte()* writes in a word and in a byte to a specified slave respectively. *WriteWordBitwise()* and *WriteByteBitwise()* writes in a word and a byte to only specified bit to set 0 or 1 respectively. Each *ReadWord( )* and *ReadByte()* returns word and byte data for input. *ReadWordBitwise()* and *ReadByteBitwise()* reads the bit data in word and byte from the specified slave.

*SetRing()* is used to set ring number to 0 or 1, and *GetRing()* returns a current ring number.

## 5 Conclusions

In this study, we designed and implemented high speed DIO (Digital I/O) system which has master-slave type structure. Master device is PC-based I/O system with PCI interface. Slave devices can be distributed by using wiring the mater to a slave and a slave to another slave, hence long and complex cabling problem of the existing systems can be solved.

Very fast I/O and simple structure can be accomplished in out system by storing I/O and attribute information of a slave into the master device. As shown in Table 1, our system is superior to the existing methods in communication speed, number of slave's I/O points and applicability of the slave. In our system, the port of a slave can be used for input or output selectively. Therefore the cost of designing and implementing is reduced and the user's facility is improved.

Software is programmed to operate on Windows XP in this study. We fabricated a device driver with WDM type and programmed a library software having some functions such as PCI initialization of DIO system, initialization of the master device, slave control, I/O and ring selection/reset. And also we implemented an application program of dialogue type as an application example.

Under the situation that generalization of PC-based I/O controller and the design of software PLC are going on, high performance with low cost can be accomplished by adopting out system to accurate equipments, control instruments and process control in which digital I/O is required. Moreover, high performance program for controlling I/O which is suited to user's circumstances can be implemented by using the functions provided as library forms. Commercialization is anticipated by applying one up technique of our DIO system..

## References

1. Kelvin, E. T.: Programmable Logic Controller, IEEE Potential, 3 (1996)14-17
2. Juniper, M.: PC vs. PLC-The Debate Rages On Control Systems -Tonbridge, 13 (6) (1996) 33-34
3. Agostino, C.: Automation of Direct Reduction Plant Using PLC/PC. IFAC Symposium on Intelligent Components and Instruments for Control Applications, New York (2001) 341-346
4. Hankoo, P.: Application of PC-based Control System to Steel Manufacturing Process, Rolling 2001 : 4th Symposium, Japan (2001)
5. Jong W. L.: Distributed Industrial I/O Control System with USB. IEEK Summer Conference Proceeding, Vol. D. (2001) 2362-2364
6. Cho, G. S.: Distributed I/O Control System with USB. 2004 IEEK Summer Conference Proceeding Vol.V. (2004) 1477-1480
7. Cho, G. S.: Development of HSIO (High Speed I/O) System with PCI Interface. 2004 KIEE Summer Conference Proceeding, Vol. D. (2004)2628-2630
8. Motionnet User's Manual, Chapter 1~IV-4, NPM (2004)
9. PCI 9030 Data Book Version 1.4, PLX Technology, New York (2002) 1-198

# G.711-Based Adaptive Speech Information Hiding Approach

Zhijun Wu[1, 2] and Wei Yang[2]

[1] Department of Communication Engineering, Civil Aviation University of China, 300300 Tianjin, China
zjwu@cauc.edu.cn
[2] Network Research Center, Tsinghua University, 100084 Beijing, China
kaiw3816@163.com

**Abstract.** This paper presents an adaptive LSB (Least Significant Bit) algorithm to embed dynamic secret speech information data bits into public speech of G.711-PCM (Pulse Code Modulation) for the purpose of secure communication according to energy distribution, with high efficiency in steganography and good quality in output speech. It is superior to available classical algorithms, LSB. Experiments show that the proposed approach is capable of embedding up to 20 Kbps information data of secret speech into G.711 speech at an average embedded error rate of $10^{-5}$. It meets the requirements of information hiding, and satisfies the secure communication speech quality constraints with an excellent speech quality and complicating speakers' recognition.

## 1 Introduction

The basic concept of Information hiding is one data stream concealed into another one for a special purpose, i.e. data hiding (embedding) [1]. The research on information hiding covers several fields: watermarking, fingerprint, steganography, etc. Watermarking focuses on copyright protection of digital media, while fingerprint puts attention to authentication of authority, and steganography is for secure communication. The main idea of above mentioned research is data embedding, i.e. important secret information is incorporated in the transmitted public data stream by using a key with slightly distorting the original object [2]. Nowadays, there are most researchers putting their efforts on watermarking and fingerprint, few on the steganography, and no practical product by now. The distinct differences among them are expressed in real-time, communication quality, hiding (embedding) capacity, security, and robustness. The approach of secure communication has more severe requirements on the performances of data embedding than watermarking and fingerprint in the aspects of real time and hiding capacity.

LSB (Least Significant Bit) substitution for speech information hiding is a commonly used classical algorithm [3]. The drawback of LSB algorithm is that the LSB (or LSBs) of every octet speech information data must be cut out and embedded into secret speech information data bit, i.e. substitution. This operation will harm speech continuance, and the degeneracy of speech quality.

D.-S. Huang, K. Li, and G.W. Irwin (Eds.): ICIC 2006, LNCS 4113, pp. 1139 – 1144, 2006.

Chen Liang and etc. [4][5] proposed a speech hiding algorithm based on speech parameter model for secure communication. In this approach, the instantaneous pitch is utilized to determine the current embedding positions in DFT (Discrete Fourier Transform) frequency domain of public speech, and secret information data embedded by modifying relevant frequency coefficients. This approach is very similar to the way of watermarking, it has the constraint of hiding capacity and is weak to the attack by low rate speech coding, such as G.728 and G.729. Jerry D.Gibson and etc. [6] presented a data embedding approach of UniType, it embedded digital information into G.711 encoded speech signal for secure data communication. The data embed procedure is completed according to the probability based on certain hypothesis. The embedded error probability becomes big with the increase of embedding data rate, because there is no accurate statistical model for possible data sources.

ITU-T G.711 is a standard to represent 8 bit compressed pulse code modulation (PCM) samples for voice at the rate of 8000 samples/second and creates a 64 Kbps bit stream. It is primarily used in telephone for wider band speech communication. In telephone, there are two main algorithms defined in the standard, μ-law algorithm (used in America) and A-law algorithm (used in Europe and the rest of the world). Both are logarithmic, but the latter was specifically designed to be simpler for a computer to process.

We proposed an approach adopting the idea steganography to embed, transmit, and extract secret information for the purpose of secure communication based on the technique of speech information hiding [7]. This approach implements the algorithm of adaptive LSB speech information hiding to embed 2.4 Kbps MELP (Mixed Excitation Linear Prediction) secret speech into A-law G.711-based public speech [8]. Experiment on hiding capacity shows that this approach is capable of embedding up to 20 Kbps secret speech information into public speech. The scheme of adaptive LSB adopts the masking effect of strong voice suppress to the weak voice in HAS (Human Acoustical System). The number of being embedded is determined by the average energy of speech distributed in the frequency domain of speech spectrum, the bigger the average energy is, the more secret information can be embedded. This results in better adaptive hiding effect of hiding capacity and imperceptible.

## 2 Approach to Embed Secret Speech into G.711

The basis of proposed adaptive LSB approach is HAS, which specifies that the higher the speech segment occupies more energy it contains in the speech frequency domain. More energy means more redundancy can be used for secret speech information embedding.

Speech features has been changed after being coded by no-linear compress in A-law or μ-law, because the process of speech coding includes the operation of log compress and uniform linear quantization to speech sample points, which is composed of 8 segments. The value variation between neighbor sample points in each segment after log operation has distinct differences with the changes between original sample points. Calculation result of uniform linear difference value in 8 segments is 1, 1, 2, 4, 8, 16, 32, and 64 individually. Therefore, the power of noise generated by every bit changing of an 8 bits non-linear code word is very different from each other. The value of introduced noise power is determined by the position of quantization segment, which the current code word belongs to.

The basic operation of adaptive LSB algorithm is to change the lowest data bit in code word, and to substitute it with the data bit of secret information. Experiments show that only LSB change of 8 segments code word, the error (noise) introduced to the highest segment is 64 times than that of lowest segment, i.e. the noise power in highest segment is 36dB high than the lowest segment. According to HAS the speech signal energy congregate in the higher segment code word, in which more data bits can be embedded. Experiments above show that embed secret speech data bits into (i) higher segment code word introduces stronger noise, which damages to the quality of speech badly, resulting in bad hiding effect. (ii) lower segment code word changes the features of speech, leading to low hiding capacity. In order to solve this problem, optimal tradeoff between mask effect of acoustical system and noise power introduced by embedding must be taken to meet the requirement of information hiding in hiding capacity and imperceptibility for secure communication. Based on the analysis of non-linear compress feature and consideration of minimum noise power rule, the adaptive LSB embed and extract algorithm for G.711 scheme is presented in this paper.

## 2.1 Embedding Process

The procedures of embedding secret speech information into G.711 scheme (Fig.1) are as following.

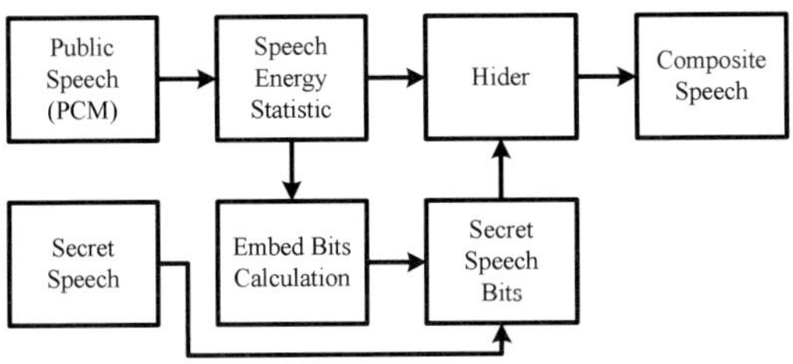


**Fig. 1.** Embed block-diagram

Public speech is PCM non-linear coding in A-law at a rate of 64 Kbps, secret speech is low rate type of compress scheme (in experiment adopts 2.4 Kbps MELP).

(i) Pre-processing. The pre-processing of sampled speech points adopts band-pass filter to eliminate the noise in low and high frequency. In experiments, the band-pass filter was designed as a Chebyshev window FIR (Finite Impulse Response) with bandwidth of 150Hz to 3800Hz.

(ii) Energy uniform. The processing of uniform balancing to speech energy for building up a short-time energy threshold.

(iii) Speech segment division. This process divides PCM speech after pre-processing into segment of $M$ length for energy statistic. The length of each segment is in a range of 50ms, which is determined by practical application.

(iv) Embedding. The operation of embedding is that the hider embeds $N$ bits secret speech information into G.711 scheme public speech by adopting the algorithm of adaptive LSB.

(v) Average energy calculation. The average energy of speech segment is calculated according the equation:

$$E_n = \sum_{i=0}^{M-1} s_n(i)^2 \Big/ M \tag{1}$$

Where $E_n$ is the average energy of speech segment, $M$ is the sample number of one segment, $s_n(i)$ is the $i^{\text{-th}}$ linear sample point value of $n^{\text{-th}}$ speech segment.

(vi) Embedding bits number calculation. Based on the value of $E_n$ and $s_n(i)$, the bits number *N* is computed according to the relationship of $E_n$ and *N*.

$$N=\begin{cases} 0; & 63 < s_n(i) < 128 \text{ and } E_n > \lambda \\ 2; & 0 < s_n(i) \le 63 \text{ or } 128 \le s_n(i) \le 191 \text{ and } E_n > \lambda \\ 3; & 32 \le s_n(i) \le 63 \text{ or } 159 < s_n(i) \le 191 \text{ and } E_n < \lambda \\ 4; & 0 < s_n(i) \le 31 \text{ or } 128 \le s_n(i) \le 159 \text{ and } E_n < \lambda \end{cases} \cdot \tag{2}$$

Where, threshold $\lambda$ is the average energy threshold of segment.

This operation guarantees to embed *N* bits secret speech information data into the LSB of public speech sample points.

Repeat the above steps circularly until all data bits of secret speech information, i.e. entire secret speech is embedded into public speech of G.711 scheme and generates the composite speech.

### 2.2 Extraction Process

The procedures of extracting to secret speech data bits are shown in Fig.2.

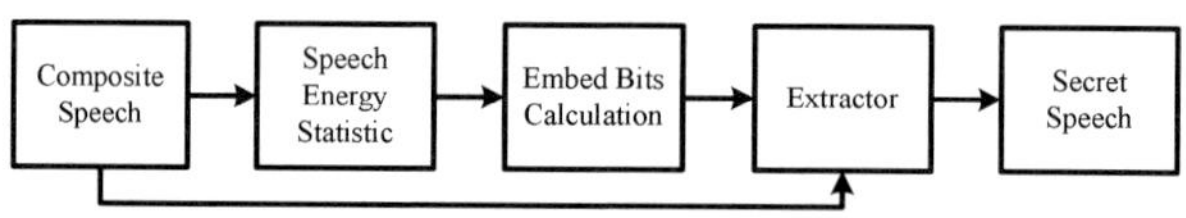


**Fig. 2.** Extract block-diagram

(i) Divide the composite speech into segments according to the same rule as embedding process.

(ii) Calculate the average energy $E_n$ of each speech segment according to equ. (1).

(iii) Compute the embed bits number *N* of secret speech information, depending on the equ. (2).

(iv) Extract data bits of secret speech information one-by-one based on above calculation of $E_n$ and *N*, and then code the extracted data bits into secret speech.

## 3 Experiment and Analysis

Experiments on embedding *N* bits of secret speech information data into G.711 scheme public speech by adopting algorithm of adaptive LSB and traditional LSB are conducted to test the hiding capacity and speech quality. Test result (Table.1) by adopting adaptive LSB algorithm shows that the average number of data bits embedded into each code word is 3 bits, while the traditional LSB algorithm is 2 bits. The change of speech quality is measured by the speech quality variation $\delta$, which is calculated according to the equation $\delta = E_{no} - E_{nc}$, where $E_{no}$ is the average energy of original speech segment and $E_{nc}$ the average energy of composite speech segment. Test result (Table.1) shows that the speech quality variation of adaptive LSB is 2.36, while traditional LSB is 3.94.

**Table 1.** Test result

| Test Items \ Algorithm | Traditional LSB | Adaptive LSB |
|---|---|---|
| Average hiding capacity $N$ | 2 | 3 |
| Speech quality variation $\delta$ | 3.94 | 2.36 |

Comparison of the composite speech spectrum of adaptive LSB algorithm with traditional LSB algorithm (Fig.3) shows that the latter has lower hiding capacity and more noise than adaptive LSB algorithm.

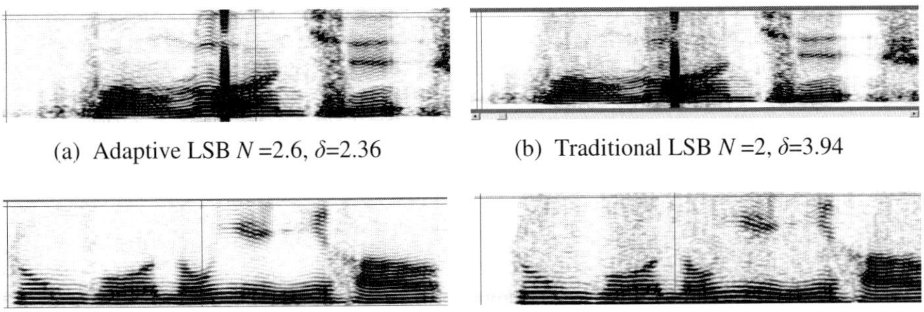

(a) Adaptive LSB $N$=2.6, $\delta$=2.36
(b) Traditional LSB $N$=2, $\delta$=3.94
(c) Adaptive LSB $N$=3.1, $\delta$=2.36
(d) Traditional LSB $N$=3, $\delta$=3.94

**Fig. 3.** Composite speech spectrum

Experiments on practical trial show that adaptive LSB algorithm is better than traditional LSB algorithm in the aspects of speech quality and hiding capacity.

## 4 Conclusion

The overall goal of this approach is to increase the data throughput of a given channel without increasing transmitted data rate or changing the transmission codes, network protocols or source compression method with a high security guaranteed.

This approach has the feature of multi-level security on the aspect of secret speech protection. First, it is difficult for eavesdropper to decode the secret speech without the knowledge of the secret speech coding scheme. Second, the encryption algorithm for secret speech is unlikely that the eavesdropper could de-encrypt this message. Third, G.711 scheme based telephone network is widely applied for voice communication, it is impossible to monitor all G.711 telephone calls. Four, this approach of data embedding offers the possibility of expanding the delivered data rate of many existing telecommunication links, both wired and wireless, without changing allocated bandwidth or source compression method. Therefore, this proposed approach can provide high security for secure speech communication.

This approach can be improved in two aspects: (i) need more complicated data set to test and improve the performance of this approach for the purpose of achieving optimal effect in practical application. (ii) improve the embed effect of speech quality and hiding capacity by adopting other novel algorithm, for example ABS (Analysis-by-Synthesis)-based algorithm.

## References


1. Petitcolas, F. A. P., Anderson, R. J., and Kuhn, M. G.: Information Hiding—A Survey. IEEE Trans. Proc. Thy, Vol. 87 (1999) 1062-1078
2. Voloshynovskiy, S., Deguillaume, F., Kovall, O., Pun, T.: Information-Theoretic Data-Hiding for Public Network Security, Services Control and Secure Communications. Proc. of TELSIKS 2003, Serbia and Montenegro, NIS (2003) 3-17
3. Moulin, P., O'Sullivan, J.A.: Information-theoretic analysis of watermarking. ICASSP '00 Proc. of 2000 IEEE International Conference on Acoustics, Speech, and Signal, Istanbul, Turkey, Vol.6 (2000) 3630 -3633
4. Chen, L., Zhang, X.: Speech Hiding Algorithm Based on Speech Parameter Model. Chinese Journal of Computers, Vol.26 (2003) 954-981
5. Chen, L. and Zhang, X.: Study of Information Hiding in Security Speech Communication. Journal of PLA University of Science and Technology, Vol.3 (2002) 1-5
6. Gibson, J.D., Kokes, M.G.: Data embedding for secure communications. MILCOM 2002. Proceedings, Vol. 1 (2002) 406 - 410
7. Moulin, P., Joseph, A., O'Sullivan: Information-theoretic analysis of information hiding. IEEE Trans. on Information Theory, Vol. 49 (2003) 563-593
8. Wu, Z., Hu, Y., Niu X., *et al.*.: Information Hiding Technique Based Speech Secure Communication over PSTN. The Chinese Journal of Electronics, Vol. 15 (2006) 108-112

# Mobile Phone Number Management System Using an X-internet Approach

Malrey Lee and Hye-Jin Jeong

Division of Electronic and Information Engineering, Chonbuk National University, 664-14 1ga Duckjin-Dong, Duckjin-Gu, Jeonju, Korea
mrlee@chonbuk.ac.kr

**Abstract.** Presently, the advanced computing capabilities of information communication hardware and equipment far exceed the ability of software that utilizes these features. Mobile phones have extraordinary features for multimedia and communications and are the prime example of current software limitations. The multimedia usage of mobile phones is limited in its speed because of the computations requirements for internet connection, poor user interface and battery power drainage, due to heavy computation requirements. While these devices are very convenient and portable, there are serious problems for users to fully utilize the data processing and communications capabilities. This paper proposes an improvement of mobile phone service by developing software based on an X-internet approach.

## 1 Introduction

Ubiquitous consists of a conversational logic that has developed in recent years as a concept, which connects people, objects, and space over time, and provides various types of information and communication equipment to be used as tools in the ubiquitous. When information terminals become intelligent tools, and the arrival of ubiquitous computing environments arrives in the near future, mobile virtual reality content-related technologies, which emphasizes mobility and interactivity will be in the spotlight[1]. There is no place for doubt that computers are becoming a type of leading equipment in information and communication tools. However, mobile phones are already equipped with various functions of leading tools compared to other devices even though many types of equipment are to be converted into multi-purposed, personalized, and computerized tools [2]. In recent years, mobile phones have increasingly decreased in size, but the performance becomes multi-functional tools. However, mobile phones may have some disadvantages as follows.

First, it is necessary to always connect to a certain network in order to receive wireless services. This will increase the battery exhaustion and calculation loads in the calculation process of encoding and decoding. Second, a mobile phone has some limitations in multimedia output speeds and interface performances. Third, a mobile phone has disadvantages in power because only a mobile phone can use services by connecting it to a network. Fourth, there is the possibility of loss due to the

D.-S. Huang, K. Li, and G.W. Irwin (Eds.): ICIC 2006, LNCS 4113, pp. 1145 – 1150, 2006.

miniaturized size and easy mobility. The loss of a mobile phone is also the loss of stored data. Fifth, certain frequent connections with a server to receive information will require not only a large amount of server resources and bandwidth, but also a long user's wait time [3]. Sixth, in the side of content providers (CP), it is difficult to develop contents, which satisfy requirements of various mobile communication companies, due to the increase in costs to supply it to the different platform required in each company and weakening in the ability of developments [4].

This paper attempts to use X-internet in order to improve these problems. X-Internet can improve the response speed of user interfaces using a storage function, which can save state information to a local section as much as is necessary, and a client can perform certain tasks without maintaining a connection to a server using a container and transfer the results of the work to the server after modifying and adding data.The objective of this study is to reduce costs with this minimum data transmission due to the fact that a certain level of data processing can be achieved in an off-line state by implementing this type of X-internet and use the minimum power and bandwidth. In addition, this study attempts to update the data used in a mobile phone using the Internet and save data when a mobile phone is lost.

In this paper, Chapter 2 introduces X-internet that is a basic idea in this study. Chapter 3 designs a system based on X-internet. Chapter 4 attempts to design another system using the system designed in Chapter 3. Finally, Chapter 5 presents the conclusion and future direction of the study.

## 2 Related Work

Most businesses desire to implement abundant UIs and complicate applications by maintaining the advantage of Internet. According to this requirement, this study proposes X-internet as an alternative method. This chapter investigates the concepts and characteristics of X-internet.

### 2.1 X-internet

At the beginning of the year 2000, the traditional Web based Internet presented some difficulties in satisfying the development of computers for clients and various requirements of users. Thus, X-internet that satisfies the performance of computers for clients and maintains the advantage of Web has become a new trend [5,6]. Executable Internet is a type of Smart Client (Engines and various other components) based internet system and able to intelligently presents applications. This means an application environment, which browses Rich UI applications like CS using the Smart Client based on Internet. In addition, the extended Internet support that the Smart Client provides include not only various developments and operational environments, such as Web browser, 4GL Tool, and independent modules, but also smart interfaces between the existing S/W component and the external equipment. Also, this system can be easily operated with the existing system and is a type of extended internet system, which can also be easily operated with external environments by supporting multi-OS environments, such as Windows, WinCE, Palm, and Embedded LINUX.

### 2.2 Necessity of X-internet

Although application programs for businesses are generally developed and implemented based on the Web, it is naturally considered that the UI, which is the last step to meet end users, is 'text based simple screens' and 'slow screen output speeds'. Huge efforts of developers are required to provide UIs, which are similar to the past CS, according to the needs of users. Based on the fact that IT architectures are considered as 'cost reduction' and 'functions and flexibilities' from the viewpoint of deploys and maintains for managing S/Ws, the former main frame presented low values in both cost reduction and functions and flexibilities. In spite of appearing with a down-sizing in Client/Server environments, it also presented low effects in 'cost reduction' due to the increase in the load of PCs, which is mainly caused by the intention of Fat Clients, even though it provided excellent functions. The appearance of the Internet makes it possible to cater to the intention of Thin Clients and to simplify the process of production. In addition, it is possible to perform certain desirable results in 'cost reduction' due to the fact that all application programs can be processed using a single browser (however, there were some gaps from the reality.). Conversely, it presented certain functional retrogressions compared to that of Client/Server systems [7].

### 2.3 Characteristics of X-internet

X-internet is a new technology, which can implement not only various functions in the basic C/S environment, but also applications in all device environments. In addition, it makes it possible to reduce the operation cost of networks due to the minimum data transmission compared to that of the existing Web browser. Moreover, X-internet is able to implement a smart user interface as the similar level as 4GL based on Web in XML and significantly reduce network traffics compared to the existing Web browser. Also, it can provide a platform, from which one is able to reduce the cost of development and maintenance [8].

X-internet provides various functions the same as CS by installing it locally to user's PC, notebook computer, PDA, and WebPad and easy deploys due to the centralized management in a limited area. The file size installed in a client is a very small size, which can be downloaded at one time. Because the required information or modified information is only communicated with a server without any retransmission of tag information, which is required to display it on the screen, it is possible to reduce bandwidths. In addition, the cost of the Internet can be reduced because off-line works are possible. Thus, this paper attempts to design and implement an X-internet based mobile phone service in order to update data through Internet and preserve data stored in a mobile phone when it is lost.

## 3 System Design

X-internet based wire and wireless internet services can provide a local power, which is able to process additional works, while the existing characteristics of PC, PocketPC, and mobile phone are maintained. In addition, it is possible to request certain services that existed in other places through networks by introducing XML Web services and transfer data through on-line during an off-line work. Moreover, data can be automatically distributed by up-loading it at a specific location, where data is up-loaded.

Thus, this study attempts to design and implement an X-internet based mobile phone service and to solve certain problems in data loss from the breakage or loss of mobile phones. In the system implementation applied in this study, the characteristics of X-internet can be achieved using .NET in an actual situation. Although it is not true that only .NET can implement the system, the implementation can be effectively achieved using MS .NET.

### 3.1 User

In the case of the X-internet based system, users can do work both on-line and off-line using the local file of mobile applications. Each user can access to desktops or mobile applications using their private key. Although this access is not allowed to connect a server, it is possible to add or delete new data using local files. This means that an off-line state is possible.

### 3.2 Updating Local Files

This system makes it possible to work in an off-line state using desktops or mobile applications. If data updating occurred in desktops or mobile applications, users can transmit the updated data to a Web Service Server using user's private key through on-line

(1) admin Service
Admin Service verifies a private key, which is belonged to individual users, in order to verify an accurate user when data is updated from users. If the user is verified, the updated data will be transferred to a Web Service Server.
(2) Web Service Server
The data transferred from the admin Service is loaded into database, and the updated data will be distributed to deploy areas whenever data is updated. In addition, this server can support the service, which is provided from a Web Service Server to users, in order to help easy updating the serviced data.
(3) Deploy area
It is easy to distribute without any installation processes for a particular management program. In addition, it presents an easy access through the Web and does not require management of a data updating process because the updated data will bc automatically restored as an updated version by comparing it to the update information of management programs when a certain reconnection is attempted by saving data onto a local section at the moment of the connection.

Users don't receive services from a server with a certain connection, but users can use the distributed services from a server in an off-line state from the loaded data in local files of desktops or mobile applications through an on-line. In addition, desktop applications can be used to continue the service when a mobile phone is lost or broken.

# 4 System Implementation

The characteristics of X-internet can be implemented using .NET, as shown in Figure 1. Although the implementation is not always performed, most of the characteristics can be effectively implemented using MS .NET. This paper presents the update in applications or desktop applications without a mobile phone for the phone number stored in a mobile phone in mobile services in which the updated data can be newly loaded in a mobile phone in applications or desktop applications. This means that any difficulty accessing lost data, which is stored in mobile phone locals, due to the breakage or loss of a mobile phone can be solved. A mobile phone system was configured in a local environment in order to manage mobile phone numbers because the test applied in an actual mobile phone is difficult.

## 4.1 Implementation of an Application Before Updating Data

A user application consists of a mobile application. The implementation applied in this paper was limited to a phone number management process.

In the deployment area of the Web Application, the data that is to be distributed to the User Application is managed in its version. In the case of the update of the data in a deploy area, the updated data will be automatically restored as an updated version by comparing it to the update information of management programs when a certain reconnection is attempted by saving data into a local section at the moment of the connection.

# 5 Conclusion and Future Work

Mobile phones are increasingly decreasing in size, but the performance becomes enhanced by multi-functional tools. However, it exhausts a large amount of battery and requires large loads in the calculation process of encryption and description. In addition, mobile phones have some limitations in multimedia output speeds and interface performances. Also, there is the possibility of loss due to the decreased size and easy mobility. The loss of a mobile phone could result in a loss of data. This paper designed and implemented a phone number management system among mobile services using X-internet in order to improve these problems. As a result, X-Internet can improve the response speed of user interfaces using a storage function, which can save state information to a local section as much as is required, and a client can perform certain works without maintaining a connection to a server using a container and

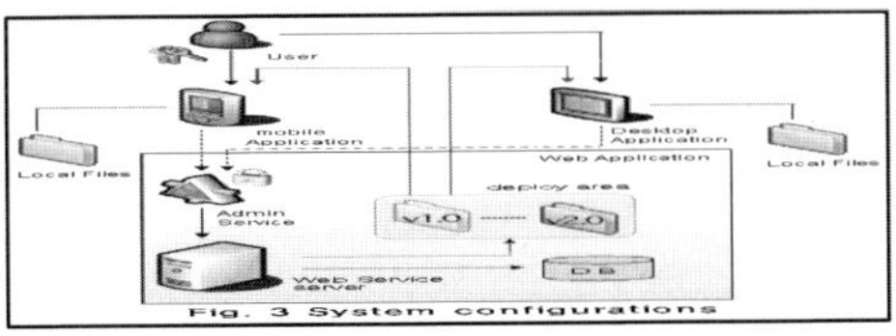


**Fig. 1.** System implementation

transfer the results of the work to the server after modifying and adding data. Thus, it is possible to provide customized services according to the personal characteristics and thus take a step further towards the age of ubiquitous.

However, X-internet was not executed in a Windows 98/ME system because it downloaded most of the application programs using BITS. Thus, a Windows 2000 or above is required. In addition, because it neglects most of the code access securities due to the fact that it is executed as a fully reliable local application system, technologies that can improve these problems are required in future studies. In addition, a verification process to identify an accurate user is required because data will be automatically updated when they access the system through on-line.

## Acknowledgements

"This research was supported by the MIC(Ministry of Information and Communication), Korea, under the ITRC(Information Technology Research Center) support program supervised by the IITA(Institute of Information Technology Assessment)" (IITA-2005-C1090-0502-0023).

## References

1. Baldonado, M., Chang, C. C. K., Gravano, L., Paepcke, A.: The Stanford Digital Library Metadata Architecture. Int. J. Digit. Libr. 1 (1997) 108–121
2. Bruce, K. B., Cardelli, L., Pierce, B. C.: Comparing Object Encodings. In: Abadi, M., Ito, T.: Theoretical Aspects of Computer Software. Lecture Notes in Computer Science, 1281 (1997) 415–438
3. Yan L., J.: Computer Science Today. Recent Trends and Developments. Lecture Notes in Computer Science, 1000 (1995) 7-12
4. Michalewicz, Z.: Genetic Algorithms + Data Structures = Evolution Programs. 3rd edn. Springer-Verlag, Berlin Heidelberg, New York (1996)

# Performance Analysis of Multimedia Communication System with Enhanced STTD Technique for USN

Byung-Hoon Woo[1], Yang-Sun Lee[2], Heau-Jo Kang[2], and Sung-Eon Cho[3]

[1] Dept. of Computer Mobile Communication, Jeonju Technical College, 1070, Hyoja-dong 2-ga, Wansan-gu, Jeonju-shi, Jeollabuk-do, 560-760, Korea
bhwoo@jtc.ac.kr

[2] Dept. of Computer Engineering, Mokwon University, 800, Doan-dong, Seo-gu, Daejeon, 302-729, Korea
{yslee, hjkang}@mokwon.ac.kr

[3] Department of Information Communication, Sunchon National University, Sunchon-shi, Chonnam, 540-472, Korea
chose@sunchon.ac.kr

**Abstract.** In this paper, the new STTD receiver for multimedia communication system in ubiquitous network environment is proposed and the performance of them is analyzed. For the multimedia systems that equip the transmit diversity for forward channel, it is well known that the Tx diversity technique is appropriate for the high rate communications. Adopting the proposed STTD receiver, at $10^{-2} \sim 10^{-4}$ in bit error rate, the SNR of 0.5dB ~ 2dB performance improvement in AWGN and Rayleigh fading environment has been achieved.

## 1 Introduction

The 3rd generation mobile systems (IMT-2000 : International Mobile Telecommunication-2000) are required to have high data rate and multimedia services. IMT-2000 is separated into the proposed asynchronous W-CDMA (Wideband-Code Division Multiple Access) by 3GPP(3rd Generation Partnership Project) and the synchronous IS-2000 evolved from PCS(Personal Communication Service) IS-95A/B. W-CDMA and IS-2000 are based on the DS-CDMA(Direct Sequence-Code Division Multiple Access) digital technology[1],[2].

In DS-CDMA system, many users transmit messages simultaneously over the same wireless communication channel, each using a specific spread spectrum PN(pseudo-random noise) code. At the receiver, a user's message can be extracted using a PN code pre-assigned to each user. The extraction of each user message is suffered by MAI(Multi-Access Interference) and multi-path fading. But the problem can be reduced by CCI(Co-Channel Interference) cancellation techniques and rake receiver[3],[4].

For the multimedia systems that equip the transmit diversity for forward channel, it is well known that the Tx diversity technique is appropriate for the high rate communications, such as personal communication of multimedia communication systems.

D.-S. Huang, K. Li, and G.W. Irwin (Eds.): ICIC 2006, LNCS 4113, pp. 1151 – 1157, 2006.

In this paper, we propose a STTD(Space Time Transmit Diversity) receiver that design of Tx diversity receiver without antenna mutual interference using CCI cancellation technique. The design of rake receiver using STTD receiver are proposed and analyzed in mobile environments. Finally, the performance of simulation using proposed new receiver were shown in figures and described.

## 2 Space Time Transmit Diversity(STTD)

Figure 1 shows the baseband representation of the two branch transmit diversity scheme. The scheme uses two transmit antennas and on receive antenna and may be defined by the following three functions[5];

- the encoding and transmission sequence of information symbols at the transmitter;
- the combining scheme at the receiver;
- the decision rule for maximum likelihood detection.

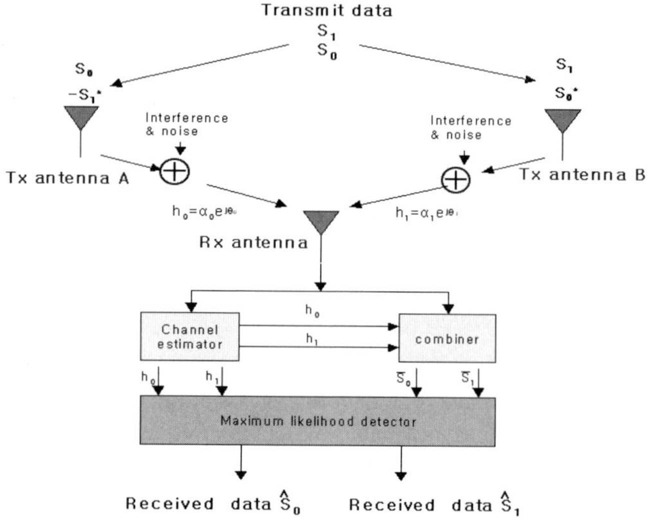


**Fig. 1.** Space time transmit diversity

## 3 System Model

In this paper, the transmitter and receiver system based on the proposed asynchronous IMT-2000(W-CDMA : Wideband CDMA) system standard by 3GPP is constructed as shown figure 2[6],[7]. In order to simulate, we assume that the wireless channel is AWGN, MAI and multi-path fading environment. The transmit data signal is NRZ(Non-return to zero) and system modulation is DS-CDMA/QPSK.

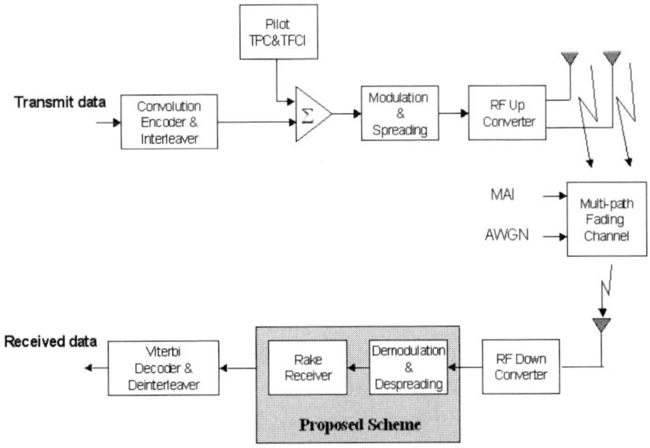


**Fig. 2.** W-CDMA system model

### 3.1 Co-channel Interference(CCI) Cancellation Technique

Here we assume that the cell-site transmits the same power for each user and that interfering signals share the same propagation path. Multi-access interference (MAI) can be modeled as Gaussian random variance. Based on the random sequence assumption, the variance of the interference component at the output of the matched filter, MAI is then given by

$$MAI = \frac{2}{3M} E_b \rho^2 . \tag{1}$$

where, $\rho$ is the instantaneous amplitude and $M$ is $PN$ code length. MAI of reference user in the reference cell is given by

$$I_{total} = (K-1)\frac{2}{3M} E_b \rho_2 . \tag{2}$$

where, $K$ is number of users in the reference cell.

If we consider the interference from other users, the equivalent $\gamma = SNR_{DS}$ (SNR: Signal-to-Noise power Ratio) of DS-CDMA can then be expressed as[8]

$$\gamma = \frac{E_b \rho^2}{\frac{2(K-1)}{3M} E_b \rho^2 + \frac{N_o}{2}} . \tag{3}$$

Where, $N_o/2$ is power spectrum density of AWGN.

In order to cancel antenna mutual interference in STTD receiver we use the CCI cancellation technique.

Signal to noise ratio $\gamma_{CCI}$ after correlation calculation between Sc and the PN sequence of reference user can be obtained as follows.

$$\gamma_{CCI} = \frac{1}{\left(3P_e \frac{2(K-1)}{3M}\right) + \left(\frac{N_o}{E_h}\right)}. \tag{4}$$

where, $P_e$ is bit error rate after correlation detection at the receiver with CCI non-cancellation.

### 3.2 Propose STTD Receiver

In this paper, we propose the new scheme of STTD receiver. Using two transmit antenna, the scheme provides mutual interference side effect caused by each antenna. So, we propose a STTD(Space Time Transmit Diversity) receiver that design of Tx diversity receiver without antenna mutual interference. Figure 3 shows a design of STTD receiver using CCI cancellation technique.

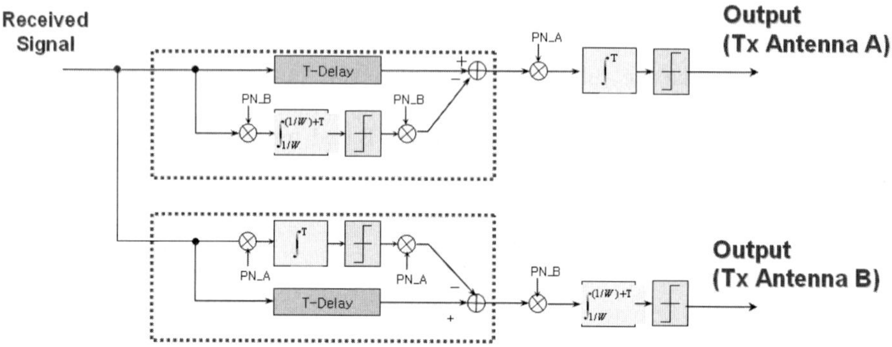


**Fig. 3.** Propose STTD receiver

## 4 Simulation

### 4.1 Simulation of the Proposed STTD Receiver

Block diagram of simulation for the proposed STTD receiver is shown in figure 4. The bit error rate of the proposed scheme are compared with that of transmit signals and received signals in AWGN and Rayleigh fading environment. Simulation parameter is given by table 1.

### 4.2 Simulation Results and Discussion

The simulation results of the DS-CDMA/QPSK using proposed STTD receiver are shown in figure 5 ~ figure 6. The BER curves of the proposed scheme are compared with that of typical and ideal case in AWGN and Rayleigh fading environment.

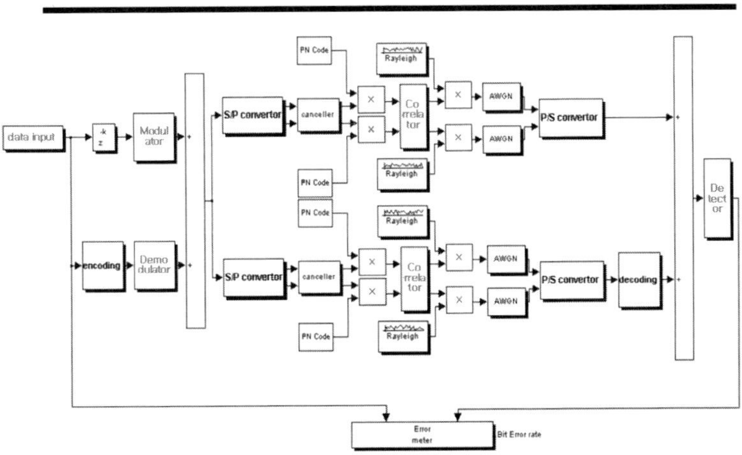


**Fig. 4.** Block diagram of simulation for the proposed STTD receiver

**Table 1.** Simulation parameter of the proposed STTD receiver

| Parameters | Values |
|---|---|
| Modulation Type | QPSK |
| Transmit antenna | 2 |
| PN length | 64 |
| PN chip duration | 1/64 [sec] |
| No. of user | 1 |
| Channel environment | Multi-path (Rayleigh fading) |
| Baseband transmission | NRZ(Non-return to zero) |
| No. of data | 10,000 ~ 20,000 |

Figure 5 shows the error performance of DS-CDMA/QPSK using proposed STTD receiver in AWGN environment. We observed that proposed STTD receiver gained about 0.5dB and 1dB when the bit error rate is $10^{-3}$ and $10^{-4}$, respectively.

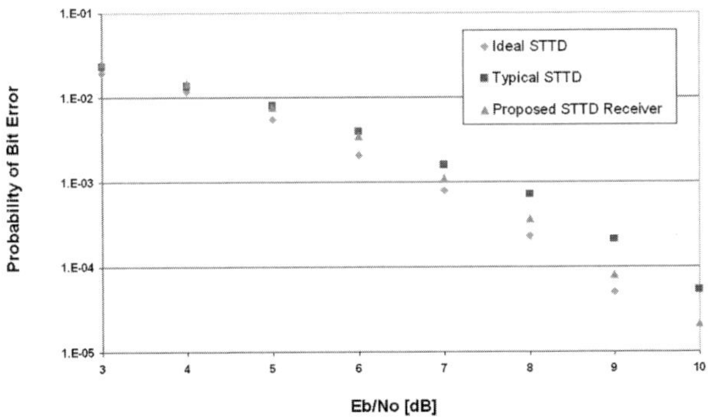


**Fig. 5.** Performance of the proposed STTD receiver in AWGN environment

Figure 6 shows the error performance of DS-CDMA/QPSK adopting the proposed STTD receiver, at $10^{-2}$ in bit error rate, the SNR of 2 dB performance improvement in Rayleigh fading environment has been achieved.

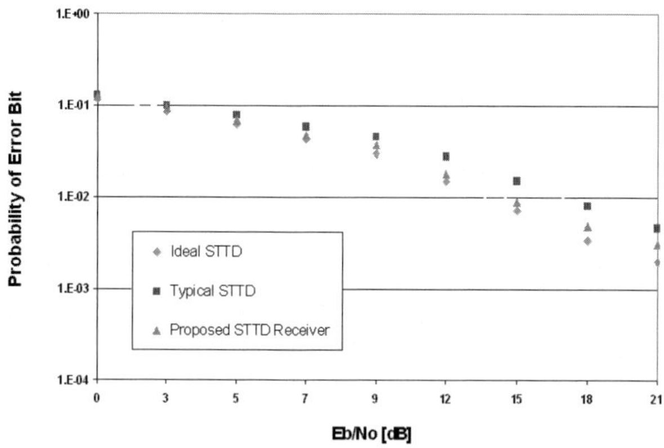


**Fig. 6.** Performance of the proposed STTD receiver Rayleigh fading environment

## 5 Conclusion

In this paper, the new STTD receiver for multimedia communication system is proposed and the performance of them is analyzed. For the multimedia systems that equip the transmit diversity for forward channel, it is well known that the Tx diversity technique is appropriate for the high rate communications. We propose a STTD(Space Time Transmit Diversity) receiver that design of Tx diversity receiver without antenna mutual interference using CCI cancellation technique. As the results of simulation, the proposed receivers have improved the performance of DS-CDMA/QPSK by increasing the total received signal to noise ratio. By adopting the proposed STTD receiver, at $10^{-2} \sim 10^{-4}$ in bit error rate, the SNR of 0.5 dB ~ 2 dB performance improvements in AWGN and Rayleigh fading environment has been achieved.

Consequently, the proposed STTD receiver will be a very effective method to improve the performance of mobile multimedia forward channel using transmits diversity.

## Acknowledgment

This research was supported by the MIC(Ministry of Information and Communication), Korea, under the ITRC(Information Technology Research Center) support program supervised by the IITA(Institute of Information Technology Assessment). (IITA-2005-(C1090-0501-0022)).

## References

1. Mohr, W., Onoe, S.: The 3GPP Proposal for IMT-2000. IEEE Commun. Mag., 12 (1999) 77-81
2. Bi, Q., Zysman, G. I., Menkes, H.: Wireless Mobile Communications at the Start of the 21st Century. IEEE Commun. Mag, 39 (1) (2001) 110-116
3. Sklar, B.: Digital Communications Fundamentals and Applications. Prentice-Hall International Editions, 1988
4. Woo, B. H., Kang, H. J.: BER Performance of Rake Receiver design for IMT-2000. APCC2000(Asia-Pacific Conference on Communications), 2 (10) (2000) 765-768
5. Alamouti, S. M.: A simple transmit diversity technique for wireless communications. IEEE J. on Select Areas in Commun., 16 ( 8) (1998) 1451-1458
6. 3GPP.: 3rd Generation Partnership Project. Technical Specification Group Radio Access Network, Working Group 1, Ts 25.213 V5.2.0, Spreading and Modulation, (2002)
7. 3GPP.: 3rd Generation Partnership Project ; Technical Specification Group Radio Access Network ; Working Group 1, TS 25.214 V5.2.0, Physical layer procedures, (2002)
8. Kerr, R., Wang, Q., Bhargava, V. K.: Capacity Analysis of Cellular CDMA. ISSSTA'92, 11 (1992) 235-238

# U-Logistic Services in Military Using RFID and Mobile Sensor Network*

Gilcheol Park and Seoksoo Kim**

Hannam University, Department of Multimedia Engineering, Postfach, 306 791
133 Ojeong-Dong, Daedeok-Gu, Daejeon, South Korea
sskim@hannam.ac.kr, gcpark@hannam.ac.kr

**Abstract.** Superiority in information technology became an important factor influencing success or failure of the national defense, and prompt delivery of information gathered from IT serves as a core factor in exhibiting combative power of the military. Furthermore, applications of these technologies can lead to increase in strategic capabilities like sensing and detection, exchanging and sharing advanced real time information and increasing community power of the strategic units. Therefore, the author wants to research core technology sector that can be developed and applied in preparation of ubiquitous national defense era. In particular, this paper aims to design Logistic system that is mobile sensor network and RFID based.

## 1 Introduction

Living environment of mankind is becoming more automated and intellectualized, and evolving into information and knowledge centered cultural society. Following these revolutions in information technology, superiority in information technology became an important factor influencing success or failure of the national defense, and prompt delivery of information gathered from IT serves as a core factor in exhibiting combative power of the military. , the basic fundamental of military system, as well as the paradigm of a war, is changing remarkably. Concept of mass destruction using conventional weapons is changing in to concept of precision attacks which only destroys core military targets in precise manner [1].

## 2 Related Works (Ubiquitous Computing)

The word, "ubiquitous," which is widely known to us means "Anywhere Anytime," "Coexisting" in Latin. It is generally used to express existence of natural resources like an object or air, or to symbolize existence of supreme power transcending time and space.

---

* This work was supported by a grant from Security Engineering Research Center of Ministry of Commerce, Industry and Energy.

** Corresponding author.

D.-S. Huang, K. Li, and G.W. Irwin (Eds.): ICIC 2006, LNCS 4113, pp. 1158 – 1163, 2006.

In the information technology sector, ubiquitous is accepted as a new type of IT environment or IT paradigm like the "ubiquitous computing" or "ubiquitous network." Simply, ubiquitous communication or ubiquitous computing does not mean adding a function to a computer or putting something in it but means insertion of a computer that matches the role of an object like a cup, a car, eyeglasses or shoes and allowing communication between objects. Presently, as specialized tasks or Internet can be accessed through wireless communication network using portable and convenient post PC products like PDA, Internet TV, Smart phones, etc, without the limitation of the time and space, it is forecasted that the ubiquitous computing will gradually grow in the future following development in technologies or products related to these devices [2]. The word "ubiquitous computing" originated from Mark Weiser, a researcher at the Palo Alto Research Center in the United States. Mark Weiser defined "ubiquitous computing" as an environment where users can acquire information needed from a network anywhere, anytime by actualizing communication network that does not have gap between cable, wireless or close range wireless network. Simply, he proposed actualization of network environment allowing connection to a computer attached to the network without the limitation of space and actualization of pocket size, computer built-in devices or humanized computer interfaces at the same time. In addition, Mark Weiser defined four characteristics of ubiquitous computing. First, a computer that is not connected to a network is not a ubiquitous computing. Second, as a humanized interface, it should be invisible. Third, computers must be accessible in reality not in virtual reality. Fourth, services must change following user environments (location, ID, devices, time, temperature, brightness, weather. Along with these characteristics, he has newly defined evolution of computers centering on the relationship between the computer technologies and the human. The 1$^{st}$ wave as an era of main frame where multi-users shared one high costing computer. The 2$^{nd}$ wave as an era of personal computer where a single user used a computer. In addition, he defined ubiquitous computing era as time when people can utilize information from a network without being aware of existence of various built-in computers, and forecasted that changed in these technologies throughout 2005-2020 will create renovated ubiquitous culture. Presently, we are stepping towards ubiquitous society. Mark Weiser has stated the importance of study on five types of issues such as visibility, complexity, simplicity, connectivity, invisibility, for materializing ubiquitous computing society [2].

# 3 Application in Military

## 3.1 Mobile Sensor Network

Sensor network will consist of various sensor nodes equipped with sensing function, information processing function and communication functions. These nodes will be assigned to a specific strategic mission and create ad-hoc network among them automatically to collect information from the real world and to provide application services by processing these data. Sensor network technology in the national defense sector can be used in the various types of field sectors. For example, large number of sensor nodes such as smart dust or miniature unmanned UAV, etc., can be assigned to the strategic location in the field to carry out surveillance and reconnaissance missions. It is noted that the number of sensor network will exceed ad-hoc network by far. These sensor nodes will be closely distributed in a small area executing broadcasting communications. Also, these sensors are by far smaller than the ad-hoc network nodes utilizing low power batteries thus replacement might not be easy. As fundamental units of the sensor network, sensor nodes will be assigned to strategic locations to collect data, process data and to transmit processed information to the upper level networks through the mobile communication devices. Sensor nodes are micro controller installed mini-computer systems. Thus, the operating system of the sensors nodes to process sensing applications and to communicate between nodes will run under sensor node hardware with limited hardware resources. The sensor node OS should be small, electric consumption should be minimal, and should be designed to manage process and memory efficiently while providing low power communication services among sensor nodes. Also, in order for the sensor network to service various types of tasks, general purpose hardware or software will not be used. Hardware and software can vary depending on the applications thus the operating system should be flexible and designed with modules to be effectively used for other types of hardware. Sensor nodes should be designed to withstand various types of external factors for it is difficult to maintain or repair sensor nodes once they have been assigned and the operating environment might be inferior. Lastly, simplicity of ad-hoc routing protocol used in forming sensor network and programming should be considered. These data will be transmitted between sensor nodes using RF signals by the radio equipments. Transmission and reception of RF signals will fall under the physical layer, the lowest level of the OSI model. As the low layer creating data links, MAC connected to the radio device will service data packet exchange among other nodes. Network protocol of sensor network should provide ad-hoc routing services and communication services to other sensor network and military communication network such as military communication satellite and TICN system. In order to provide these services, sensor network protocol requires few additional specifications in comparison to existing network protocols. Such as efficient power management, data centered, overall collection of data, attribute based address and location recognitions.

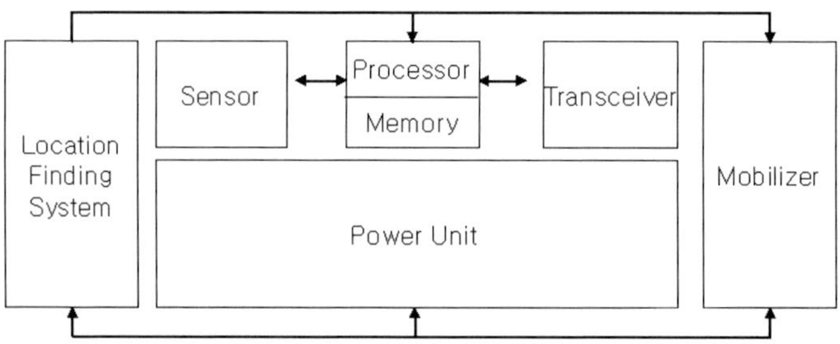


**Fig. 1.** Structure of Sensor node

Location searching technology is required to collect location of each sensors located within the sensor network, either through centralized or distributed method. Processing accurate location of sensor nodes will provide geographical information of the event occurrence, allowing routing and target detection functions based on the processed geographical information. These location data will become absolute or relative location information depending on the types of the application. Generally various measurement techniques utilizing supersonic or RF are being suggested for location measurement within the sensor network. Normally the location should be measured based on the arrival time, signal strength, direction and distance from the base. Due to the large number of applications that can be used within the sensor network, large types of sensors exist. Sensor can be largely classified in to 3 types; Passive, Passive0-Array and Active. Sensors such as vibration, illumination intensity, temperature, etc, falls under the passive sensors, bio-chemical, infrared, etc, falls under the passive-array sensors and radar, sonar, etc, falls under the active sensors. Presently active movements for standardization is under way and the author will commonly discuss low pricing, standard interface, network, smart sensing and actuation.

### 3.2 RFID

RFID is a core factor in constructing ubiquitous logistic support. In the ubiquitous logistic support, identification, location check, status check such as damages, usability measurement, route tracking, etc, of all weapon system will be processed in real-time without help of man. In addition, headquarter, militant units and logistic support units can acquire real-time information of the supplies suitable for the war situations, can request supply, operate repair systems, search the optimal route for supply and process priority supply orders in real-time. In the perspective of the combined war management, the ubiquitous logistic support will bring large impact.

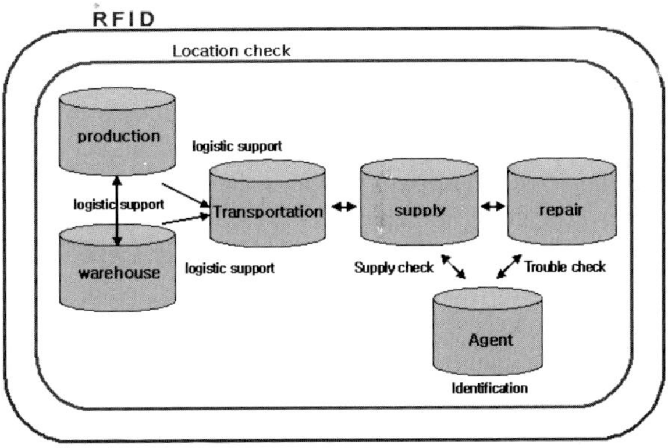


**Fig. 2.** Structure of U-Logistic

All weapon systems, vehicles, equipments, military facilities, supplies, parts, ammunitions, etc would be attached with wireless recognition tags and chips having functions for sensing, data processing, data saving and communications, for creation of ad-hoc network among them, to be connected to future military communication networks such as the military satellite communication and TICN system. RFID will utilize radio frequency for confirming materials, entry (or transfer) of staff, locations, or to identify categories. RFID system may function properly by combining reader, transponder and computer or any other devices that can process data [3].

The RFID reader contains electronic circuits that transmits and receives frequency from and to the transponder (or to tags). The microprocessor built-in to the reader will encode signals transmitted by the tags, will authenticate the data signals, may save this information in the memory devices and may transmit this information when necessary. The reader contains antenna for transmission and reception of signals. Antenna used to transmit and receive signals may either be attached to the circuit board directly or may be contained in the private case. Within the tag, custom built IC chips serves as an important part, controlling communication from and to the reader. The storage device within the chip is divided in to various sections. A section for storing certification number and other data and another section to receive signal activating tags from the reader for transmitting information of the tag. Within the tag, capacitor for synchronizing frequencies with the antenna attached to the chip is installed. Tags normally contain memory devices to store data per address and capacities ranging from 8bit to 16K BIT is normally used. Most of the RFID systems are custom designed and allotted with dedicated frequency and antenna size for smooth operation. Signals transmitted by the reader through the antenna have adequate size of signal range. When the tag passes through the signal range of the antenna of the reader, the tag will sense the signal transmitted by the reader and starts to transmit information stored within the tag to the reader. Generally, frequency signals transmitted by the reader to the tags contain timing information, providing enough electric force to activate the tag. When the tags transmit data to the reader, the reader alters this information to digital signals and decides authenticity of the information transmitted by the tags through the CRC checks. Tags are generally classified in to active and passive. Active types require batteries. It either receives operation power from external devices or from batteries attached to non-metallic case of the tag. Advantages of these types are reduction of unnecessary powers from the reader and possibility of extending signal recognition distance from the reader. For the disadvantages, operation time may be limited to the life of the batteries, can be used under optimal environment only and having higher costs than passive types. Passive type tags do not require internal or external power sources and can be operated using electric signals transmitted by the reader. For the advantages, passive tags are lighter and cheaper than the active tags and can be used for semi-permanently. On the other hand, the passive tags have disadvantages of having shorter recognition distance and requiring higher power loads for the readers. These tags can be classified in to 3 groups following the functionality. First, read and write, second, write once and read often, third, read only type. These types of tags can be applied to both the passive and active tags. Distribution and retail sectors can utilize status check and location detection function of the RFID ubiquitous network optimally. RFID tags attached to products (or box, transportations, fork lift, etc) allow efficient tracking of location of the product, stock management, customer management and automated transaction. As mentioned in the early part, utilization of RFID technologies in logistics support tasks, where large number of stocks is being maintained in comparison to private sectors and frequent miss delivery is occurring due to lack of inter-connection among producers and consuming troops, will greatly improve efficiency of the task. All military weapons, vehicles, military facilities, supplies, ammunitions, etc can be controlled through out processes such as production, supply, transportation, stock management, repair management and disposal, using a chip. Which means that the RFID installed military supplies, can be connected to the delivery route information to find the optimal path for delivery to the supply units, and the supply units can recognize the necessary supplies for each consuming units for future delivery of supplies. Using the communication between RFID chip and information system, adequate level of supply can be managed without the help of man hours. Also, supplied logistic support supplies would be connected to the repair system during the expected lifespan. Information such as location and status of the equipment will be used for calculating weapon system and utilization frequency in real-time. Efficiency of the equipment will be raised by assigning maintenance support units immediately when necessary [4], [5], [6].

## 4 Conclusion

In this paper, have discussed about the plans for applying recent u-Logistic technology to the military sector had been suggested. Particularly, the author have suggested plans for utilizing combined future information technologies such as mobile, wireless sensor network and RFID for the logistic supply in construction of u-Defense system. By utilizing these information technologies, combat power and strategic capabilities of the military can be enhanced greatly. In order to activate information based national defense, changing stereotype concepts to accept information technology environment is a must. With the information technology minds, we should successfully construct combined defense information system at the early stage and should operate these systems effectively. Also, aggressive investment in terms of fighting power improvement is required for the information technology based and scientific national defense, thus, limited defense budget should be effectively utilized to raise small but powerful advanced information technology units and the utilization of potentials of private sectors should be optimized to raise low cost- high efficient military power.

## References

1. David S. L.: Design and Managing The Supply Chain: McGraw-Hill, London (2001)
2. Ubiquitous. Korea Information Processing Society, 10 (2) (2003)
3. RFID Executive Overview. Accenture (2004)
4. Lee, S. Y.: A Study on The Improvement of Military Logistics System: Focus on The Clustering Group by Product Characteristics. National Defense University, Master's Thesis, USA (2004)
5. Bu, H. N.: A Logistics Annex Setup Plan of the Period of the Information. The Research Subject Which Ministry of National Defense RMA Hangs Out. Korea Development Strategy Researcher, Korea (2000)
6. Radio Frequency Identification homepage. http://www.aimglobal.org/technologies/rfid

# Web Based Learning Application for LMS*

Seoksoo Kim

Hannam University, Department of Multimedia Engineering, Postfach, 306 791
133 Ojeong-Dong, Daedeok-Gu, Daejeon, South Korea
sskim@hannam.ac.kr

**Abstract.** The Although a variety of standardization and Learning Management System (LMS) were produced to develop and effectively manage web contents in response to active diffusion of internet application, practical changes to assist online learners are not yet to be found. The core purpose of the LMS system proposed in this paper is to help learners pursue proactive and self-oriented education by allowing learners to proactively configure their own content, that is, learners no longer have to be restricted by prescribed sequence of lectures. In this paper, I would like to introduce a LMS that can support self-leading education by providing various types of learners at Virtual University with delicately organized educational contents for maximum efficiency. The system allows a learner to select a lecture or a chapter which has been presorted to meet his educational needs and intellectual ability.

## 1 Introduction

Online education systems and contents, when developed based on the SCORM (Sharable Content Object Reference Model) standard developed by Advanced Distributed Learning (ADL), can be implemented in other systems without needs for configuration and organization of contents can be easily edited. Content is composed of a SCO and SCO contains chapters which constitute contents. Based on the standardization of SCORM, maintenance of contents can be easily done and SCORM can be configured and customized by learners to meet their specific educational needs.[1,2] However, although contents are delicately divided, it is the administrators or contents producers who have the control over the organization of contents. In reality, learners have to follow prescribed steps regardless of their knowledge or level of educational competence. When it comes to a virtual college where levels of educational competence among learners greatly vary, it is very tough for instructors to offer contents that can meet individual educational needs. For instance, those with sufficient knowledge in a specific subject would not want to learn basic or introduction portion of the subject. Unlike offline education which requires face to face interaction, virtual university can give a variety of people an opportunity to take advantage of self-leading education by selecting contents that meet their specific educational needs.

* This work was supported by a grant No. (2004-GA-12) from Ministry of Commerce, Industry and Energy.

D.-S. Huang, K. Li, and G.W. Irwin (Eds.): ICIC 2006, LNCS 4113, pp. 1164 – 1169, 2006.

By selecting contents of their needs, learners can heighten their self-satisfaction and enjoy academic achievements at the same time[3,4]. This paper addresses the problem stated beforehand and presents relevant research and implementation of solutions that can allow learners to set their own difficulty of the contents they select.

"Open Education" can be possible within an environment where everybody can learn wherever they are and whenever they want. Today's highly developed computer network makes "Open Online Education" possible by combining the offline "Open Education" and benefits of internet technology. "Open Online Education" is considered a very effective means of education because it frees people from physical and time limitations that employees face: For example, employees can set their own time for education which makes it a proactive learning experience. Many researches done on this subject and numerous case studies assert that computer network, which has an ability to overcome space and time and help learners exchange information cooperatively, can establish learner-oriented educational system.[5,6]

Unfortunately, except for the fact that individuals can learn in their home instead of a classroom and set their own time instead of following a prescribed schedule, difference between online education and offline education is minimal. So far, the most common type of online education has targeted only at the majority of people and unilaterally delivers educational information to its learners. However, educational achievement can be possible when contents can be prescribed to meet specific educational needs of an individual. [7, 8]

## 2 Suggestions and System Requirements

As I have presented, the needs for standardization of online education has become increasingly important and SCORM has been positioning itself as the standard of online education. As of now, using search and category functions, reorganization and maintenance of contents became easy, however, service provider organizes contents for his learners to search and register a lecture of their choice. In this paper, I would like to present a solution that can allow learners to choose lecture contents for each subject [9, 10].

The figure 1 illustrates a SCORM based LMS which is supplemented with the self-leading type of process management service.

In fact, the LMS discussed in this paper is based on the implementation of features related to self-leading type of process management service because not all SCORM based LMS share same type of database organization and contents management implementation via meter information. The purpose of this paper is to build a system that can allow learners to choose contents of their educational level, learn to achieve educational goals, and move onto the next level. The system offers detailed information, such as completed courses and prerequisites of lectures that a learner has to know before registering a lecture. Once he selects a subject, the system illustrates subject contents that are categorized by chapter and difficulty. With the given information of the subject, he can confidently select his own contents to be studied. Organization of the proposed system is as follows:

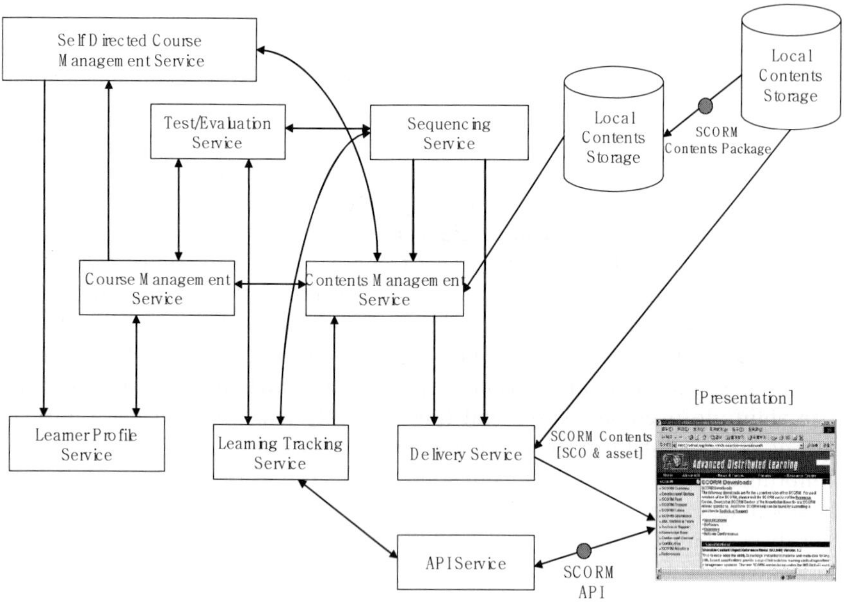


**Fig. 1.** LMS System Service Diagram

1) DB server which contains SCO information
2) Module which allows administrators and instructors to input detailed contents
3) Webpage module that can illustrate detailed information of each subject and its contents for learners to choose.
4) Module that can organize educational process for each subject according to the specific requirements and needs that a learner requests.
5) Module that can operate in conjunction with LMS and contents for learners to use.

# 3 System Organization

## 3.1 SOC Information Input Module for Administrators and Instructors

This module registers contents of lectures established by LMS administrators or instructors and inputs the registered contents. Detail contents information would possess the following information: learner's year in school, completed subjects, open lectures, available level, and grades after completion. The sequence the module's information input, as illustrated in a flowchart of the figure 2, starts off with the page where a learner's ability is confirmed and available categories, which can be registered, are displayed. For administrators, all available subjects are displayed and for instructors, categories in progress are displayed. When selecting specified category's subject, administrators and instructors can input or edit detailed information for each chapter. Once the input is completed, information stored in DB is renewed. If there are no errors, the system will direct to the categorical page and if there are errors, the system will direct do the contents registration page [11], [12].

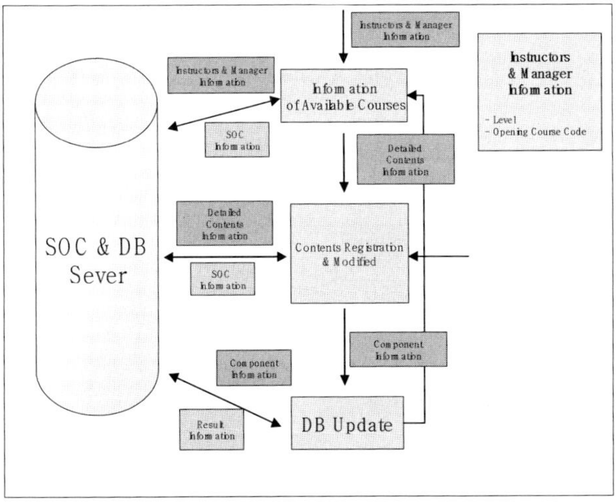


**Fig. 2.** Input Information Module Basic Flowchart

### 3.2 SCO & DB Servers

RFID is a core factor in constructing ubiquitous logistic support.

SCO & DB servers are database servers that contain required information for the proposed LMS. They basically manage information of contents and instructors and learners. 1) Detailed Contents Information, 2) Instructors Information, 3) Learners Information, 4) Information of Available Courses

Detailed contents and information of available courses are shared among instructors because it is not always just one instructor who makes up the entire contents for a course. Thus, learners can easily find out about other courses that are complementary to their selected courses. To determine competence level, points are given discriminately based on learner's occupation, major, depth of knowledge of the selected subject. As a learner completes a course and move on, he will gain points and eventually get to the higher level. Educational competence levels are A, B, C, and D and levels based on occupation are A for professionals, B for students, C and D for others based on their depth of knowledge and job descriptions.

### 3.3 Learning Process Request Module

Learning Process Request Module displays available subject for learners. Once a subject is chosen, the module will show detailed information for each chapter of the contents so that learners can choose that fits his level and complete his registration request. For those who do not want to organize the contents, instructors will determine basic organization contents.

Learning Process Request Module is activated once a learner requests course registration. Based on the information submitted to DB server, which includes major, year in school, and competence level, the module displays available courses and their information on the "Available Courses Page" and prerequisites for non-available

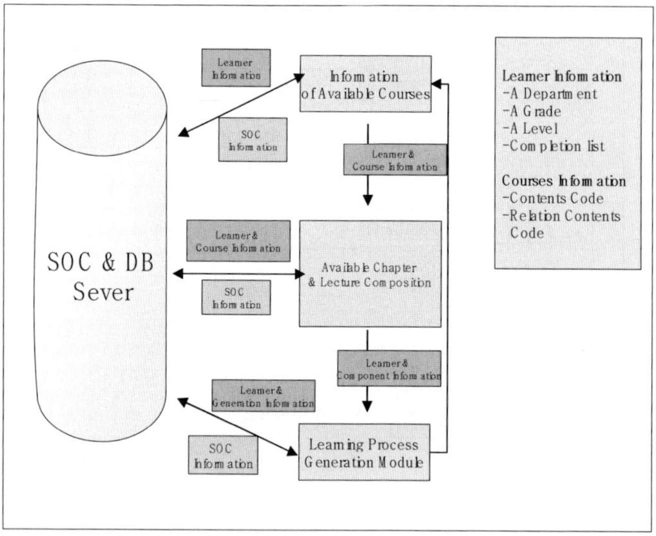


**Fig. 3.** Learning Process Application Module Basic flowchart

courses. If a course is selected, the learner is taken to the page where available chapters are displayed based on the contents information and his background information. There, only the available courses for his level are displayed for him to choose and organize. Once registered courses are confirmed be the learner, he can call up the subject organization page using information of selected subject and his background information. Based on the detailed contents information received from DB server, Learning Process Request Module generates contents sequence in the order requested by the learner and moves to the "Available Courses Page after storing the sequence into DB server.

### 3.4 Learning Module

Learning Module allows learners to take courses by displaying selected lectures. Learning Module displays categorized registered subjects using the learner's information. Once a subject is selected, available lectures are displayed. Lecture window is launched upon completion of lecture selection process.

## 4 Conclusion

The core purpose of the system proposed in this thesis is to help learners pursue proactive and self-oriented education by allowing learners to proactively configure their own content, that is, learners no longer have to be restricted by prescribed sequence of lectures. In general, most LMS cannot meet every individual's educational needs because they structure their programs by letting learners simply choose from a list of available lectures at prescribed level or difficulty. However the Self-Leading LMS eliminates such boundaries by allowing learners to choose contents and difficulty within the limit set by their own educational competence. Although a variety of standardization and Learning Management System (LMS) were produced to develop and effectively manage web contents in response to active diffusion of internet application, practical changes to assist online learners are not yet to be found. In this paper, I would like to introduce a LMS that can support self-leading education by providing various types of learners at Virtual University with delicately organized educational contents for maximum efficiency. The system allows a learner to select a lecture or a chapter which has been presorted to meet his educational needs and intellectual ability.

## References

1. Standard, http://www.onstudy.com/CyberNews/CyberNews_view.asp? (2002)
2. Scorm, http://www.edupd.com/learn/standard05.htm (2005)
3. XML : my.dreamwiz.com/aphise (2006)
4. Long, H. B.: Self-directed learning: Research and Application. Norman , OK: The Oklahoma Research Center for Continuing Professional and Higher Education, ( 1992)
5. Flora C.I. C.: Intelligent Assessment of Distance Learning, Information Sciences, 140 (1), (2002) 105-125
6. Willis, B.: Effective Distance Education Planning: Lessons Learned, Educational Technology, 38 (1) (1998) 57-59
7. Barry K., Rob, R.: An Affective Module for an Intelligent Tutoring System, ITS 2002, LNCS, Berlin Heidelberg, New York (2002) 23-63
8. Frasson, C.: LANCA: A Distance Learning Architecture Based on Networked Cognitive Agents, Intelligent Tutoring Systems, 8 (1999) 593-603
9. Critical Business Benefits of an LCMS. LCMS Council Panel at The Online Learning 2002 hall.com, (2002)
10. Hall, B. L., Cavalier, J.: E-learning Across the Enterprise:The Benchmarking Study of Best Practices. CA: Brandon-hall.com.(2000)
11. Banan, B., Miheim, W. D.: Existing Web-based Instruction Courses and Their Design. In B. H. Khan (Ed). Web-based Education. 381-388. Englewood Cliffs, NJ: Educational Technology Publication (1997).
12. Harasim, L.: Online Education: Perspective on a New Environment. New York (1990)

# Application of a Strong Tracking Finite-Difference Extended Kalman Filter to Eye Tracking

Jiashu Zhang[1] and Zutao Zhang[1,2]

[1] Sichuan Key Lab of Signal and Information Processing, Southwest Jiaotong University, Chengdu 610031, P.R. China
jszhang@home.swjtu.edu.cn
[2] School of Mechanical Eng., Southwest Jiaotong University, Chengdu 610031, P.R. China
ztxy130@sina.com

**Abstract.** Non-intrusive methods for eye tracking are important for many applications of vision-based human computer interaction, such as driver fatigue detection, eye gaze replacing the hand operating mouse, eye typing instead of manually depressing keys as a virtual keyboard, eye gaze correction for video conferencing, interactive assistant application for disabled users, etc. However, due to the eye motion be the high nonlinearity, the obstacles of robustness of external interference and accuracy of eye tracking, these tend to significantly limit their scope of application. In this paper, we present a strong tracking finite-difference extended Kalman filter algorithm, and overcome the modeling of nonlinear eye tracking. In filtering calculation, strong tracking factor is introduced to modify prior covariance matrix to improve the accuracy of the filter. The filter uses finite-difference method to calculate partial derivatives of nonlinear functions to eye tracking. The last experimental results show validity of our method for eye tracking under realistic conditions.

## 1 Introduction

Since eye tracking was first introduced by Mowrer in 1936, it has been gaining in popularity over the past decades as a window into observers' visual and cognitive process. For instance, researchers have utilized eye tracking to study behavior in such domains as driver fatigue detection [1,2,3], eye typing for helping users with movement disabilities interact with computers [4], eye tracking analysis of user behavior in WWW search [5], using eye tracking techniques to study collaboration on physical tasks for medical research, VR system for measuring inspection methods, and image scanning [6]. Above all applications, two types of human-computer interfaces utilize eye tracking, passive and active interfaces. Passive interfaces monitor the user's eye movements and automatically adapt themselves to the user. For example in driver fatigue detection, the researchers track the driver eyes to fatigue detection, because the human eyes express the most direct reaction when dozing, inattention and yawning. On the other hand, Active interfaces allow users to explicitly control the interface though the use of eye movements. For example, eye typing has users look at keys on a virtual keyboard to type instead of manually depressing keys as on a traditional keyboard [4,7]. Such active interfaces have been quite effective at helping users with

D.-S. Huang, K. Li, and G.W. Irwin (Eds.): ICIC 2006, LNCS 4113, pp. 1170 – 1179, 2006.

movement disabilities interact with computers. Not surprisingly, eye tracking has attracted the interest of many researchers, and eye trackers have been commercially available for many years [1,2,7,8].

In the past decades, many researchers have paid attention to the eye tracking in human computer interaction. There have been many methods that support non-invasive eye tracking. In [17], all of these eye tracking algorithms can be classified into two approaches: feature-based and model-based approaches. Feature-based approaches detect and localize image features related to the position of the eye. A commonality among feature-based approaches is that a criteria (e.g., a threshold) is needed to decide when a feature is present or absent. The determination of an appropriate threshold is typically left as a free parameter that is adjusted by the user. The tracked features vary widely across algorithms but most often rely on intensity levels or intensity gradients. For example, in infrared (IR) images created with the dark-pupil technique, an appropriately set intensity threshold can be used to extract the region corresponding to the pupil. The pupil center can be taken as the geometric center of this identified region. The intensity gradient can be used to detect the limbus in visible spectrum images [9] or the pupil contour in infrared spectrum images [10]. In [1,11,12,13 ], several active IR based eye trackers were proposed. The authors thought that eye tracking based on the active remote IR illuminations is a simple and effective approach. But most of them require distinctive bright pupil effect to work well because they all track the eyes by tracking the bright pupils. Qiang Ji et al. has also made significant improvement of eye tracking over existing techniques [1, 11]. However, their methods need IR eye detector, or bright pupils and steady illumination. Their eye tracking method using Kalman filtering is linear system estimation algorithm. In realistic driving environments, the eye motion is the high nonlinearity of the likelihood model, the stand Kanlman filter is no longer optimal.

On the other hand, model-based approaches do not explicitly detect features but rather find the best fitting model that is consistent with the image. For example, integrodifferential operators can be used to find the best-fitting circle [14] or ellipse [15] for the limbus and pupil contour. Michael Chau and Margrit Betke use correlation with an online template to eye tracking in [16]. The authors in [2] use the dynamic templates for eye tracking. After finding the eye templates, they are used for eye tracking by template matching. And the minimum value within the search area is the most matching position of the eye. The model- based approach can provide a more precise estimate of the pupil center than a feature-based approach given that a feature-defining criteria is not applied to the image data.

Eye tracking has not reached its full potential even though the general-purpose eye tracking technology has been explored for decades. The first obstacle to integrating these techniques into human-computer interfaces is that they have been too expensive for routine use. Currently, a number of eye trackers are available on the market and their prices range from approximately 5,000 to 40,000 US Dollars [17]. The second factor is that it's very difficult to model to eye tracking because of the eye motion being the high nonlinearity. The third factor is the robustness of eye tracking should be improved because of the variety of head and eyes moving fast, external illuminations interference and realistic lighting conditions. The accuracy of eye tracking can't satisfy the realistic requirement of HCI.

To tackle some of those problems, we propose a strong tracking finite-difference extended Kalman filter algorithm to eye tracking. In this paper, a strong tracking factor is introduced to modify prior covariance matrix to improve the accuracy of the algorithm. And the finite-difference method is presented to calculate partial derivatives of nonlinear functions to eye tracking. At the same time, we overcome the eye tracking modeling in nonlinear system. The last experimental results show that the average correct rate of eye tracking can achieve 99.4% on three video.

The organization of the paper is as follows. Strong Tracking Finite-Difference Extended Kalman Filter algorithm is given in next section. Section 3 gives STFDEKF based Eye Tracking algorithm and experimental results. Final conclusion is in section 4.

## 2 Strong Tracking Finite-Difference Extended Kalman Filter

Extended Kalman filter (EKF) is one of the most common and popular filtering approach in nonlinear target tracking and state estimation. It includes state estimation of a nonlinear dynamic system, parameters estimation for nonlinear system identification and dual estimation where both states and parameters are estimated simultaneously. However, EKF simply linearizes all nonlinear functions to the first order by using the Talyor series expansions. At the same time, EKF may cause more errors for the nonlinear system while estimating system state and its variance. Moreover, the linearization may lead to divergence of filtering process. In a non-linear mismatched model and limited applications scope, EKF filter will lead the divergence problem of state estimation. For these reasons, two improved EKF algorithms are introduced to tackle some of those problems.

### 2.1 Suboptimal Fading Extended Kalman Filter

In this section, an adaptive extended Kalman filter - a suboptimal fading extended Kalman filter (SFEKF) is presented. The derivation of the filter is presented in [18,19] in detail. SFEKF has the following good properties: 1) lower sensitivity to the statistics of the initial states and the statistics of the system and/or measurement noise, 2) stronger tracking ability to the suddenly changing states and bias no matter whether the filter operates in dynamic or stationary fashion, 3) acceptable computational complexity.

Considering a class of nonlinear discrete-time dynamical system,

$$x_{k+1} = f(x_k, u_k, v_k) \tag{1}$$

$$y_k = g(x_k, w_k) \tag{2}$$

where, $x_k$ is the state vector, $y_k$ is the measurement vector, $u_k$ is control input vector, $v_k$ is process noise and $w_k$ is measurement noise. $v_k$ and $w_k$ are statistically independent. The equations of mean and covariance are as follow.

$$\begin{aligned} &E[v_k]=q_k, \quad \mathrm{cov}[v_k,v_j]=Q_k\delta(k-j) \\ &E[w_k]=r_k, \quad \mathrm{cov}[w_k,w_j]=R_k\delta(k-j) \end{aligned} \tag{3}$$

The extended Kalman filter is based on the assumption that sensor noises and, propagation errors are driven by zero-mean, Gaussian-distributed, white, random process. Retaining only the first-order terms in the Taylor series expansion, one obtains

$$\begin{cases} x_{k+1} \approx f(\hat{x}_k,u_k,q_k)+F_x(k)(x_k-\hat{x}_k)+F_v(k)(v_k-q_k), \\ y_k \approx g(\overline{x}_k,r_k)+G_x(k)(x_k-\hat{x}_k)+G_w(k)(w_k-r_k), \end{cases} \tag{4}$$

where $F_x(k)$ and $F_v(k)$ are the partial derivatives of $f(\bullet)$ to $x$ and $v$, $G_x(k)$ and $F_w(k)$ are the partial derivatives of $f(\bullet)$ to $x$ and $w$.

So the suboptimal fading extended Kalman filter (SFEKF) is deduced as follows:

The predicted state estimation equations are

$$\overline{x}_{k+1}=f(\hat{x}_k,u_k,v_k) \tag{5}$$

$$\overline{y}_k=g(\overline{x}_k,r_k) \tag{6}$$

The predicted covariance estimation equations are

$$\overline{P}_{k+1}=\lambda(k+1)F_x(k)\hat{P}_kF_x(k)^T+F_v(k)Q_kF_v(k)^T \tag{7}$$

Where $\lambda(k+1)\ge 1$ is the suboptimal fading factor, which is used to fade the bypast datum and adjust predictable state estimation covariance matrix.

With this model in [20], $\lambda(k+1)$ can be directly determined as follows:

$$\lambda(k+1)=\begin{cases} \lambda_0, \lambda_0 \ge 1; \\ 1, \lambda_0 < 1; \end{cases} \tag{8}$$

where

$$\lambda_0=tr[N(k+1)]/tr[M(k+1)], \tag{9}$$

$$N(k+1)=V_0(k+1)-G_x(k)F_v(k)\bullet F_v(k)^T-G_w(k)R_kG_w(k)^T, \tag{10}$$

$$M(k+1)=G_xF_x(k)\hat{P}_kF_x^T(k)G_x^T(k). \tag{11}$$

$$V_0(k+1)=\frac{1}{k}\sum_{j=1}^{k}\gamma_j\gamma_j^T=\begin{cases} G_x(0)\hat{P}_0G_x(0)+G_w(0)^T, k=0; \\ \dfrac{\rho V_0(k)+\gamma_j\gamma_j^T}{1+\rho}, k\ge 1 \end{cases} \tag{12}$$

with $0 \le \rho \le 1$ is the preselected forgetting, it may be selected according to the real processes. For fast changing processes, a smaller $\rho$ should be selected, and vice versa. As that pointed out in [20], $\lambda(k+1)$ is insensitive to the value of $\rho$.

## 2.2 Strong Tracking Finite-Difference Extended Kalman Filter

Deriving the ideas in papers [21, 22], the authors proposed a finite-difference method to replace partial derivatives of nonlinear functions. From further improving the self-covariance and between-covariance, we obtain the algorithm based on strong tracking filter-difference enhanced kalman filter.

We adopt cholesky to decompose $Q_k$, $R_k$, $\overline{P}_K$, $\hat{P}_k$,

$$\begin{aligned} Q_k = S_v S_v^T, R_k = S_w S_W^T, \\ \overline{P}_k = \overline{S}_x \overline{S}_x^T, P_k = \hat{S}_x \hat{S}_x^T. \end{aligned} \tag{13}$$

central difference of partial derivative in non-linear function $Fx(k)$:

$$F_x(k) = \{f_{ij}\} = \left\{\left(f_i\left(x_{k,j} + \Delta x_{k,j}, u_k, q_k - f\left(x_{k,j} - \Delta x_{k,j}, u_k, q_k\right)\right)/2\Delta x_{k,j}\right)\right\} \tag{14}$$

Where $\Delta \hat{x}_{k,j} = h\hat{s}_{x,j}, h$ is the step adjustment coefficient; $\hat{s}_{x,j}$ represents the j column of $\hat{s}_x$, then

$$F_x(k)\hat{S}_x = S_{x\bar{x}} = \left\{\left(f\left(\hat{x}_k + hs_{x,j}, u_k, q_k,\right) - f_i(\hat{x}_k + hs_{x,j}, u_k, q_k)\right)/2h\right\}. \tag{15}$$

$$F_v(k)S_v = S_{xv} = \left\{\left(f_i\left(\hat{x}_k, u_k, q_k, +hs_{v,j}\right) - f_i\left(\hat{x}_k, u_k, q_k - hs_{v,j}\right)\right)/2h\right\}, \tag{16}$$

$$G_x\left(k\right)\overline{S}_x = S_{y\bar{x}} = \left\{\left(g_i\left(\overline{x}_k + h\overline{s}_{x,j,rk}\right) - g_i\left(\overline{x}_k - h\overline{s}_{x,j,rk}\right)\right)/2h\right\}, \tag{17}$$

$$G_w\left(k\right)S_w = S_{yw} = \left\{\left(g_i\left(\overline{x}_{k,rk} + hs_{w,j} - g_i\left(\overline{x}_{k,rk} - hs_{w,j}\right)\right)/2h\right)\right\} \tag{18}$$

The predicted covariance matrix, gain matrix and covariance estimate of suboptimal fading extended Kalman filter (SFEKF) are mended as follows

$$\begin{aligned} &\overline{P}_{k+1} = \lambda(k+1)F_x\left(k\right)\hat{P}_k F_x\left(k\right)^T + F_v\left(k\right)Q_k F_v\left(k\right)^T = \\ &\lambda\left(k+1\right)F_x\left(k\right)\hat{S}_x\hat{S}_x^T F_x\left(k\right)^T + F_v\left(k\right)\hat{S}_v\hat{S}_v^T F_v\left(k\right)^T = \\ &\lambda\left(k+1\right)S_{x\hat{x}}S_{x\hat{x}}^T + S_{xv}S_{xv}^T; \end{aligned} \tag{19}$$

$$K_{k+1} = \overline{P}_k G_x(k)^T \left[ G_x(k) \overline{P}_k G_x(k)^T + G_w(k) R_k G_w^T(k) \right]^{-1} = \tag{20}$$
$$\overline{S}_x \overline{S}_x^T \left( S_{y\overline{x}} S_x^{-1} \right)^T \left[ S_{y\overline{x}} S_{y\overline{x}}^T + S_{y\overline{w}} S_{y\overline{w}}^{-T} \right]^{-1} = \overline{S}_x S_{y\overline{x}}^T \left[ S_{y\overline{x}} S_{y\overline{x}}^T + S_{y\overline{w}} S_{y\overline{w}}^{-T} \right]^{-1};$$

$$\begin{aligned}
&\hat{P}_{k+1} = \\
&\left[ I - K_{k+1} G_x(k) \overline{P}_{k+1} \right] = \\
&\overline{S}_x \overline{S}_x^T - K_{k+1} G_x(k) \overline{S}_x \overline{S}_x^T = \\
&\overline{S}_x \overline{S}_x^T - \overline{S}_x \overline{S}_{y\overline{x}}^T K_{k+1}^T - K_{k+1} \overline{S}_{y\overline{x}}^T \overline{S}_x^T + \overline{S}_x \overline{S}_{y\overline{x}}^T K_{k+1}^T = \\
&\overline{S}_x \overline{S}_x^T - \overline{S}_x \overline{S}_{y\overline{x}}^T - K_{k+1} \overline{S}_{y\overline{x}}^T \overline{S}_x^T + \\
&K_{k+1} \overline{S}_{y\overline{x}} \overline{S}_{y\overline{x}}^T K_{k+1}^T + K_{k+1} S_{yw} S_{yw}^T K_{k+1}^T = \\
&\left[ \overline{S}_x - K_{k+1} \overline{S}_{y\overline{x}} K_{k+1} S_{yw} \right] \times \left[ \overline{S}_x - K_{k+1} \overline{S}_{y\overline{x}} K_{k+1} S_{yw} \right]^T
\end{aligned} \tag{21}$$

From before-mentioned deduction, we can infer to that all calculations of above include the process noise impact and the error problem of model linearization. The step number which nonlinear function is linearized also changes with last time covariance matrix, process noise and observation noise. The filter becomes very simple because of replacing partial derivatives calculation using finite-difference value. The new strong finite-difference Kalman filter (STFDEKF) has more accuracy and covariance estimation, and improves the robustness of target tracking. The last experiment results show that the STFDEKF can be used for the high nonlinear stochastic systems such as eye tracking.

## 3 STFDEKF Based Eye Tracking and Results

In this section, we develop the following eye tracking using STFDEKF. Because the eye motion is the high nonlinearity of the likelihood model, it's very difficult to model human eye movement dynamics. In our tracking system, the following nonlinear equation is used to model the eye movement dynamics.

$$x = x_0 + vt + \frac{1}{2} a t^2 \tag{22}$$

$$\dot{x}_{k+1} = v_0 + A_k \sin(\omega_k t) \tag{23}$$

$$a_{k+1} = \ddot{x}_{k+1} = A_k \omega_k \cos(\omega_k t) \tag{24}$$

where, the initial value $x_0$ and $v_0$ are zero. The acceleration $a$ follows the sine distribution, and $a$ will be considered process noise ( $v_k$ ), respectively $A_k = 0.08 m/s$ and $\omega_k = \pi rad/s$.

The proposed eye tracking experiment is developed in platform of *OPEN CV*. Our system uses a ViewQuest VQ680 video camera to capture human images. The experiment is tested on a Pentium III 1.7G CPU with 128MB RAM. Eye tracking based on the proposed method can reach 10 frames per second. The format of input video is 352×288. Fig.1 represents the eye tracking using STFDEKF algorithm. The *Correct Rate* of eye tracking is shown in Table.1.

Correct Rate of eye tracking is defined as in equation (25).

$$Correct \quad Rate = \frac{Total \quad Frames - Tracking \quad Failure}{Total \quad Frames} \tag{25}$$

The following experimental results evaluate the performance of our proposed method and other eye tracking methods in [1,2,3,11].

In order to qualitatively gauge performance and discuss resulting issues, we consider using the traditional measures of performance: the RMSE (Root Mean Square Error) and MSE (Mean Square Error). The simulation results of RMSE and MSE are depicted in Table 3.

**Table 1.** Result of eye tracking using STFDEKF algorithm

| | **Video 1 (without glasses)** | **Video2 (glasses)** | **Video3 (long hair)** |
|---|---|---|---|
| **Total Frames** | 1999 | 2941 | 2889 |
| **Tracking Failure** | 9 | 16 | 18 |
| **Correct Rate** | 99.45% | 99.35% | 99.4% |
| **Average Correct Rate** | | 99.4% | |

**Table 2.** Comparison of eye tracking algorithms

| Algorithm | Correct rate | remark |
|---|---|---|
| Templates Match | 99.1% | Refer to [2] |
| Kalman and mean shift algorithm | 99.1% | Refer to [11] |
| EKF tracking algorithm | 99% | |
| STFDEK algorithm in this paper | 99.4% | Refer to Table.1 |

**Table 3.** RMSE and MSE of eye tracking filtering algorithms

| Algorithm | RMSE | MSE |
|---|---|---|
| Kalman Filter algorithm | 0.13155 | 0.164661 |
| EKF tracking algorithm | 0.1222 | 0.0904 |
| STFDEK algorithm in this paper | 0.0989 | 0.0780 |

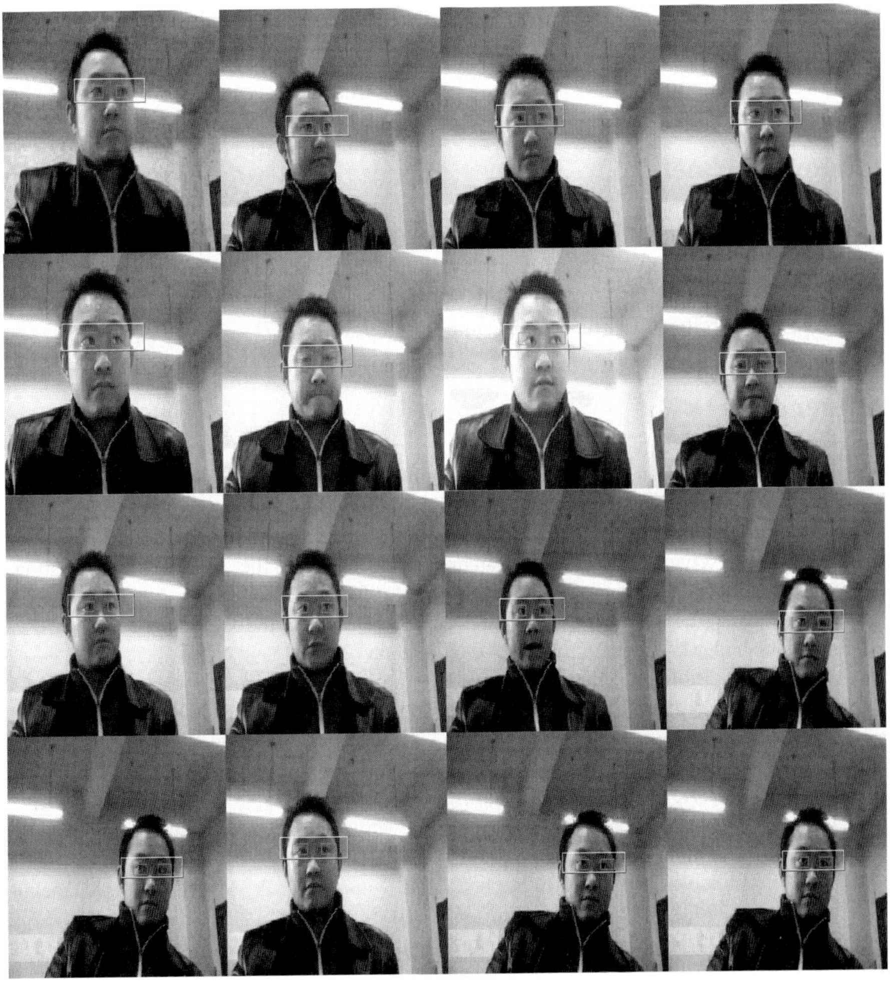

**Fig. 1.** Eye tracking using STFDEKF algorithm

The results of above experiments indicate that the proposed method has better performance. So we can use STFDEK algorithm for eyes tracking.

## 4 Conclusion

This paper proposes a new eye tracking method using strong finite-difference Kalman filter. Firstly, strong tracking factor is introduced to modify priori covariance matrix to improve the accuracy of the eye tracking algorithm. Secondly, the finite-difference method is proposed to replace partial derivatives of nonlinear functions to eye tracking. From above deduction, the new strong finite-difference Kalman filter becomes very simple because of replacing partial derivatives calculation using finite-difference value. The last experiment results show that STFDEKF has more accuracy and covariance estimation, improves the robustness of target tracking, and can be used for the high nonlinear stochastic systems such as eye tracking.

## Acknowledgement

This work is supported by the National Natural Science Foundation of China under Grant No. 60572027, by the Outstanding Young Researchers Foundation of Sichuan Province Grant No.03ZQ026-033□and by the Program for New Century Excellent Talents in University of China under grant No.NCET-05-0794.

## References

1. Ji, Q., Zhu, Z.W., Lan, P.L.: Real-Time Nonintrusive Monitoring and Prediction of Driver Fatigue, IEEE Transactions on Vehicular Technology, VOL. 53, NO. 4(2004)
2. Horng, W.B., Chen, C.Y., Chang, Y., Fan, C.H.: Driver Fatigue Detection Based On Eye Tracking and Dynamic Template Matching, Proceeding of the 2004 IEEE International Conference on Networking, Sensing & Control (2004) 21-23
3. Dong, W.H., Wu, X.J.: Driver Fatigue Detection Based on the Distance of Eyelid, IEEE Int. Workshop VLSI Design & Video Tech Suzhou (2005).
4. Majaranta, P., Raiha, K.: Twenty Year of Eye Typing: System and Design Issues, in ACM eye tracking research and applications symposium, New Orleans, Louisiana, USA(2002)15-22
5. Granka, L.A., Joachims, T.: Eye-Tracking Analysis of User Behavior in WWW Search,SIGIR '04, Sheffield, South Yorkshire, UK(2004)
6. Noton, D., Stark, L.: Scanpaths in Accadic Eye Movements while Viewing and Recognizing Patterns Vision Research, 11(1971)929-942
7. Ohno, T., Mukawa, N., Kawato, S,: Just Blink Your Eyes: A Head-Free Gaze Tracking System,CHI 2003, Ft. Lauderdale, Florida, USA(2003)
8. McCarthy, J.D., Riegelsberger, J., Sasse, M.A.: Commercial Uses of Eye Tracking,HCI (2005)
9. Zhu, J., Yang, J.: Subpixel Eye Gaze Tracking, in IEEE conference on Automatic Face and Gesture Recognition(2002)124-129
10. Ohno, T., Mukawa, N., Yoshikawa, A.:A Gaze Tracking System for Everyday Gaze Interaction, in Eye tracking research and applications symposium(2002)15-22.
11. Zhu, Z.W., Ji, Q., Fujimura, K.: Combining Kalman Filtering and Mean Shift for Real Time Eye Tracking under Active IR Illumination(2002)
12. Ebisawa, Y.: Unconstrained Pupil Detecting Technique Using Two Light Sources and the Image Difference Method. Visualization and Intelligent Design in engineering and architecture,pages (1995)79-89
13. Morimoto, C.H., Flickner, M.: Real-time Multiple Face Detection Using Active Illumination. Proc. of the 4th IEEE International Conference on Automatic Face and Gesture Recognition 2000, Grenoble, France(2000)
14. Daugman, J.: High Confidence Visual Recognition of Persons by a Test of Statistical Independence, IEEE Transactions on Pattern Analysis and Machine Intelligence, vol. 15, no. 11(1993) 1148–1161, 1993
15. Nishino, K., Nayar, S.: Eyes for Relighting, ACM SIGGRAPH 2004, vol. 23(2004)704–711

16. Chau, M., Betke, M.: Real Time Eye Tracking and Blink Detection with USB Cameras, Boston University Computer Science Technical Report No.12 (2005)
17. Li, D.H., Winfield, D., Parkhurst, D. J.: A Hybrid Algorithm for Video-based Eye Tracking Combining Feature-based and Model-based Approaches, Proceedings of the IEEE Vision for Human-Computer Interaction(2005)
18. Zhou, D. H., Xi, Y. G., Zhang, Z. J.: A Suboptimal Multiple Fading Extended Kalman Filter, to appear in Chinese J. Automation
19. Zhou, D. H.: Fault Detection and Diagnostics for A Class of Nonlinear Systems, Ph.D. dissertation, Shanghai Jiao Tong Univ., P.R. China(1990)
20. Zhou, **D.** H., Sun, Y. X., Xi, Y. G., Zhang, Z. J.: Extension of Friedland's Separate-Bias Estimation to Randomly Time-Varying Bias of Nonlinear Systems, IEEE TRANSACTIONS ON AUTOMATIC CONTROL, VOL. 38, NO. 8 (1993)
21. FAN W. B., LIU C.F. , ZHANG S.Z.: Improved Method of STRONG Tracking Extended Kalman Filter, Control and Decision (2006)
22. Zhou D. H., Wang Q. L.: Strong Tracking Filter of Nonlinear Systems with Colored Noise, j of Beijing Institute of Technology (1997)321-326

# Fast Affine Transform for Real-Time Machine Vision Applications

Sunyoung Lee[1], Gwang-Gook Lee[2], Euee S. Jang[1], and Whol-Yul Kim[2]

[1] Digital Media Lab., College of Information and Communications, Hanyang University
17 Haengdang-dong, Seongdong-gu, Seoul, 133-791, Korea
sunnykr@ihanyang.ac.kr, esjang@hanyang.ac.kr
[2] Image Engineering Lab., College of Engineering, Hanyang University
17 Haengdang-dong, Seongdong-gu, Seoul, 133-791, Korea
gglee@vision.hanyang.ac.kr, wykim@hanyang.ac.kr
http://vision.hanyang.ac.kr/

**Abstract.** In this paper, we have proposed a fast affine transform method for real-time machine vision applications. Inspection of parts by machine vision requires accurate, fast, reliable, and consistent operations, where the transform of visual images plays an important role. Image transform is generally expensive in computation for real-time applications. For example, a transform including rotation and scaling would require four multiplications and four additions per pixel, which is going to be a great burden to process a large image. Our proposed method reduces the complexity substantially by removing four multiplications per pixel, which exploits the relationship between two neighboring pixels. In addition, this paper shows that the affine transform can be performed by fixed point operations with marginal error. Two interpolation methods are also tried on top of the proposed method in order to test the feasibility of fixed point operations. Experimental results indicated that the proposed algorithm was about six times faster than conventional ones without any interpolation and five times faster with bilinear interpolation.

## 1 Introduction

In a few applications, such as machine vision, it is required that images are to be rotated, sheared, and scaled while preserving the image integrity. Thanks to the rapid rise of cost-performance efficiency of image acquisition systems, the major focus in machine vision is not only on accuracy, but also on the computational complexity for real-time imaging. The most time consuming, and therefore complex operations are (affine) image transforms including rotation and scaling. This problem is getting worse when the size of the input image increases, which poses a common problem for today's machine vision system.

Affine transform is applied for rotating, scaling, and shearing images, which generally needs four multiplications and four additions per pixel [1]-[6]. Image rotation is the most time consuming and tricky part, which eventually affects the quality of the rotated image. Image rotation process maps each discrete pixel in the transformed image to a spatial location in the input image and computes the intensity using interpolation [7][8]. Popular interpolation methods include the nearest neighbor and bilinear interpolations.

D.-S. Huang, K. Li, and G.W. Irwin (Eds.): ICIC 2006, LNCS 4113, pp. 1180–1190, 2006.

In implementing a rotation transform, there are non-separable and separable rotations. Non-separable rotation methods become impractical for high order models because of the increase of the reference pixels, which can lead to high computational complexity. To address this problem, a separable rotation method decomposes the rotation into two or more 1D transformations along the x and y directions. There are several decompositions: two-pass and three-pass algorithms [9][10][11]. The separable method can reduce the use of the memory because of accessing data in one row or column at one time and also reduce complexity when using high order interpolations. A multi-pass algorithm, however, requires intermediate data contraction, which may complicate implementation, introduce errors, and increase complexity. This may not fit in zero order interpolation and bilinear interpolation. It can not be a fast method for real-time operation and is going to be a great burden to process a large image.

In this paper, we showed a fast affine transform which reduces the complexity substantially by removing four multiplications per pixel by exploiting the relationship between two neighboring pixels. In addition, this paper showed that the affine transform can be performed by fixed point operations with marginal error in which its coefficients are in bounds. Lastly, we tried to combine the aforementioned two methods. To estimate the feasibility of the proposed methods, we used zero order interpolation and bilinear interpolation. The feasibility of the proposed methods is all evaluated by error analysis.

The remainder of this paper is as follows. Section 2 describes the affine transform of two dimensional images. In Section 3, our proposed methods, interpolation, and error analysis are explained and experimental results are given in Section 4. Finally, we summarize this paper in Section 5.

## 2 Affine Transform of 2D Image

A matrix **A** represents a 2D image affine transform such as rotation, scaling, and translation. A transformed pixel $\mathbf{v} = \begin{pmatrix} x' \\ y' \end{pmatrix}$ on an image **D** is acquired by a pixel $\mathbf{u} = \begin{pmatrix} x \\ y \end{pmatrix}$ of an original image **S** and transform matrix **A**:

$$\mathbf{v} = \mathbf{A}\mathbf{u} = \begin{pmatrix} a_{00} & a_{01} & a_{02} \\ a_{10} & a_{11} & a_{12} \\ 0 & 0 & 1 \end{pmatrix} \begin{pmatrix} x \\ y \\ 1 \end{pmatrix} = \begin{pmatrix} x' \\ y' \\ 1 \end{pmatrix} \tag{1}$$

Equation (1) is represented by two Equations in (2-a) and (2-b).

$$x' = a_{00}x + a_{01}y + a_{02} \tag{2-a}$$

$$y' = a_{10}x + a_{11}y + a_{12} \tag{2-b}$$

When all pixels of the original image **S** are transformed by Equations (2-a) and (2-b), we can obtain the transformed image **D**, where all the pixels on images **S** and **D** are represented as discrete integer values. Fig. 1-(a) shows an example of affine transform from image **S** to image **D**. Not all parts of image **D** is filled by the pixels of image **S**.

In general, the transform matrix **A** in affine transform has an inverse matrix $\mathbf{A}^{-1}$ shown in (3), where **u** is the original pixel and **v** is the transformed pixel. Affine transform with inverse matrix is applied in Fig. 1-(b).

$$\mathbf{u} = \mathbf{A}^{-1}\mathbf{v} = \begin{pmatrix} a_{00}' & a_{01}' & a_{02}' \\ a_{10}' & a_{11}' & a_{12}' \\ 0 & 0 & 1 \end{pmatrix} \begin{pmatrix} x' \\ y' \\ 1 \end{pmatrix} = \begin{pmatrix} x \\ y \\ 1 \end{pmatrix} \qquad (3)$$

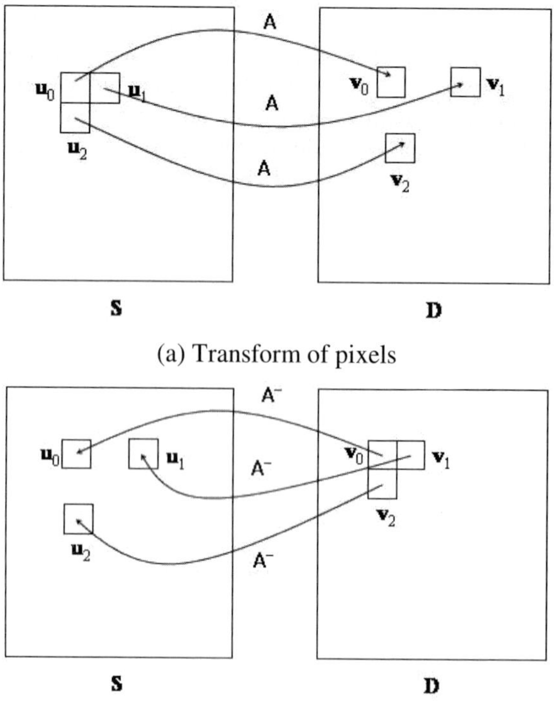


**Fig. 1.** Affine transform

As shown in Equations (2-a) and (2-b), when the pixel $\mathbf{u} = \begin{pmatrix} x \\ y \end{pmatrix}$ is rotated, four multiplications and four additions per pixel are required. If an image size is *MxN*, conventional affine transform needs 4*MN* additions and 4*MN* multiplications.

## 3 Proposed Fast Affine Transform Method

This paper shows three methods for fast affine transform: the first one removes four multiplications per pixel by using the relationship between two neighboring pixels and the second is the method that uses fixed point operations instead of floating point operations with marginal error. To further reduce the computational complexity, we combined the aforementioned two methods, which is the third.

### 3.1 Affine Transform by Removing Multiplications (ATRM)

Two neighboring pixels on image **S**, $\mathbf{u}_0 = \begin{pmatrix} x_0 \\ y_0 \end{pmatrix}$ and $\mathbf{u}_1 = \begin{pmatrix} x_1 \\ y_1 \end{pmatrix}$ are transformed to $\mathbf{v}_0 = \begin{pmatrix} x_0' \\ y_0' \end{pmatrix}$ and $\mathbf{v}_1 = \begin{pmatrix} x_1' \\ y_1' \end{pmatrix}$ of image **D** respectively, with affine transform matrix **A**. Fig. 2 shows the relationship between neighboring pixels after affine transform.

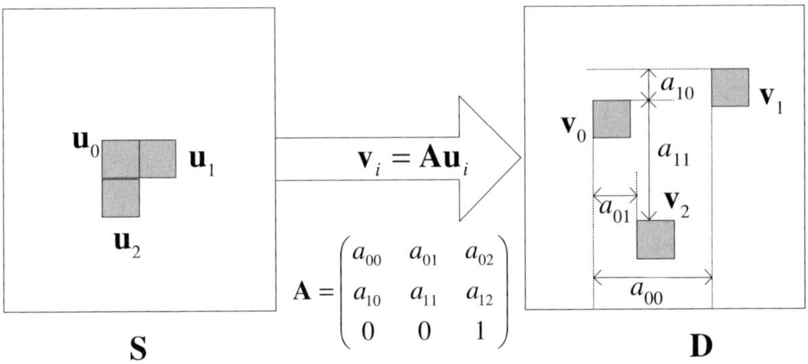


**Fig. 2.** Relation between neighboring pixels in affine transform

$\mathbf{v}_0$ and $\mathbf{v}_1$ follows:

$$\mathbf{v}_0 = \begin{pmatrix} x_0' \\ y_0' \end{pmatrix} = \begin{pmatrix} a_{00}x_0 + a_{01}y_0 + a_{02} \\ a_{10}x_0 + a_{11}y_0 + a_{12} \end{pmatrix} \tag{4}$$

$$\mathbf{v}_1 = \begin{pmatrix} x_1' \\ y_1' \end{pmatrix} = \begin{pmatrix} a_{00}x_1 + a_{01}y_1 + a_{02} \\ a_{10}x_1 + a_{11}y_1 + a_{12} \end{pmatrix} \tag{5}$$

The pixel $\mathbf{v}_1$ (5) can also be represented as (6).

$$\mathbf{v}_1 = \begin{pmatrix} a_{00}x_0 + a_{00} + a_{01}y_0 + a_{02} \\ a_{10}x_0 + a_{10} + a_{11}y_0 + a_{21} \end{pmatrix} \tag{6}$$

where, $x_1 = x_0 + 1, \quad y_1 = y_0$.

To estimate the relation between the pixels $\mathbf{v}_0$ and $\mathbf{v}_1$, we tried to subtract (4) from (6). The pixel $\mathbf{v}_1$ is therefore

$$\mathbf{v}_1 = \mathbf{v}_0 + \begin{pmatrix} a_{00} \\ a_{10} \end{pmatrix} \tag{7}$$

The pixels $\mathbf{v}_0$ and $\mathbf{v}_2$ are applied in the same way, where $\mathbf{v}_2$ is the neighboring pixel of $\mathbf{v}_0$ in *y* direction.

$$\mathbf{v}_2 = \mathbf{v}_0 + \begin{pmatrix} a_{01} \\ a_{11} \end{pmatrix} \tag{8}$$

Equations (7) and (8) show that the correlation of neighboring pixels can be exploited for fast affine transform. The transformed pixels can be calculated by neighboring pixels only with additions.

### 3.2 Affine Transform with Fixed Point Operations (ATFP)

A conventional affine transform generally requires real number operations, which are complicated in implementation. All the pixels of an image are represented by integer values and the pixels transformed by affine transform are represented by real numbers. After all, the pixels have to be represented in integer values. The conversion from a floating-point real value to an integer value is a great burden. In an Intel processor, the conversion speed of the process is much slower than other operations such as multiplication and addition with real numbers.

To reduce the computation complexity due to the conversion process, we tried to use fixed point operations in image rotation because it is faster than floating point operations. There are constraints to calculate fixed point numbers in image size as follows:

- Scaling: The sizes of input and transformed image should be within 8192×8192.
- Rotation: There is no limit in image size and rotation angle. But, the image should come full circle.
- Shearing: The coefficients of the shearing operation are within the area of –1/2 ~ 1/2. Because of distortion, shearing is applied in between 1/2 and –1/2 in most machine vision applications.
- Translation: The size of an image is within 8192×8192 before and after such operations as horizontal and vertical transfer.

In this paper, we used a process with 32 bit operations and fixed point numbers, which have 16 bit integer parts and 16 bit fraction parts. The fixed point number may be within $-2^{16} \sim 2^{16}-1$, whose error is between $-1/2^{17}$ and $1/2^{17}$. Floating point number (*d*), fixed point number (*f*), and integer number (*n*) are represented by Equations (9) and (10).

$$f = \text{int}(d \times 65536.0 + 0.5) \tag{9}$$

$$n = f >> 16 \tag{10}$$

where, >> is a shift to right bit

When the matrix **A** in (1) is for affine transform with floating point operations, the matrix of affine transform using fixed point number is **B**, which converts 32-bit floating point operations into fixed point operations with 16-bit integer part and 16-bit fraction parts by multiplying 65535 ($2^{16}$-1) value.

$$\mathbf{B} = 65535 \times \mathbf{A} = \begin{pmatrix} b_{00} & b_{01} & b_{02} \\ b_{10} & b_{11} & b_{12} \\ 0 & 0 & 1 \end{pmatrix} \tag{11}$$

where, $b_{ij}$ is a fixed point integer

Function $\text{n}_f(f)$ converts the fixed point number into a fixed point integer. The pixel **v** is represented by the conversion function $\text{n}_f(f)$, matrix **B**, and original pixel **u** in (12).

$$\mathbf{v} = \text{n}_f(\mathbf{Bu}) \tag{12}$$

### 3.3 Combined Affine Transform Method (CATM)

We proposed the fast affine transform method, which combines two methods: ATRM and ATFP. In the case of fixed point number, affine transform can also be calculated only with addition by exploiting the relationship between neighboring pixels, as well.

## 4 Experimental Results

### 4.1 Experimental Conditions

We have tested the conventional affine transform method and three proposed methods: ATRM, ATFP, and CATM. The sizes of test images with 256 grayscale values are 512×512, 1024×1024, and 2048×2048. To estimate the performance of the methods, we rotated the test images by 20 degrees. A Pentium-III 800MHz PC, Windows 2000 OS, and Microsoft Visual C++ 6.0 were used for this experiment.

### 4.2 Computational Complexity Results

Table 1 shows the complexity of six operations in the conventional method and three proposed methods for an *M×N–size* image. The operations (OP) are as follows.

- OP 1. Conversion of real number to integer
- OP 2. Multiplication of real numbers

- OP 3. Addition of real numbers OP 4. Multiplication of integers
- OP 5. Addition of integers
- OP 6. Shift operation

**Table 1.** Complexity of six operations

| | OP 1 | OP 2 | OP 3 | OP 4 | OP 5 | OP 6 |
|---|---|---|---|---|---|---|
| Conventional | $2MN$ | $4MN$ | $4MN$ | X | X | X |
| ATRM | $2MN$ | X | $2MN$ | X | X | X |
| ATFP | X | X | X | $4MN$ | $4MN$ | $2MN$ |
| CATM | X | X | X | X | $2MN$ | $2MN$ |

To evaluate the operation time, the operations are repeatedly executed 1 billion times. In Table 2, the operation time for OPs 1 through 5 are presented. We have tested the empty loop in order to estimate operation time without loop. It should be noted that the operation time for OP1 (conversion) is the longest as compared to the other operations as shown in Table 2. OP 2 and OP 3 are also complicated comparatively. Compared with the conventional method, ATRM can save operation time by not using OP 2 in Table 1. ATFP and CATM can substantially reduce the computational complexity due to not using OP1, OP2, and OP3 as well.

Table 3 shows the result of the average time when images are rotated by 20 degrees a total of 10 times. The results indicate that ATRM was about 30 percent faster than the conventional method and ATFP is about 80 percent faster. CATM is about 85 percent faster without any interpolation.

**Table 2.** Operation time with Intel Pentium III 800MHz Processor (1 billion times)

| | Operation time | Operation time without loop |
|---|---|---|
| Empty loop | 8552 | |
| OP 1 | 97590 | 89038 |
| OP 2 | 25426 | 16874 |
| OP 3 | 22763 | 14211 |
| OP 4 | 9454 | 902 |
| OP 5 | 9403 | 851 |

**Table 3.** Rotation time by 20 degrees for each image size

| | 512x512 | 1024x1024 | 2048x2048 |
|---|---|---|---|
| Conventional | 92.2 (100.0%) | 366.5 (100.0%) | 1469.1 (100.0%) |
| ATRM | 65.1 (70.6%) | 262.3 (71.6%) | 1058.5 (72.1%) |
| ATFP | 20.0 (21.7%) | 74.1 (20.2%) | 297.4 (20.2%) |
| CATM | 14.0 (15.0%) | 56.0 (15.3%) | 226.4 (15.4%) |

### 4.3 Subjective and Objective Evaluation Results

For testing, we have used an 4096x4096image with lattice. The image was rotated by 20 degrees and then rotated by -20 degrees in the conventional method and three proposed methods. Fig. 3 shows the results when zero order interpolation is used. Some pixels in all cases could not be recovered because the error of zero order interpolation has about 0.5 pixel values. We also used bilinear interpolation as shown in Fig. 4. All pixels were located at their original position after rotation, which indicates that our proposed methods have no error in using bilinear interpolation with reducing computational complexity.

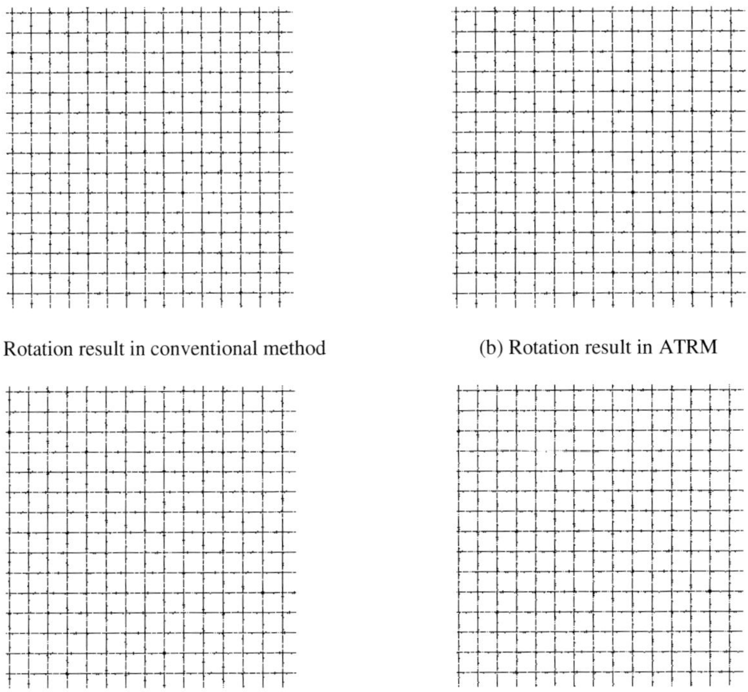

(a) Rotation result in conventional method

(b) Rotation result in ATRM

(c) Rotation result in ATFP

(d) Rotation result in CATM

**Fig. 3.** Rotational image with zero order interpolation

In order to evaluate the error of the proposed methods, we used RMS (Root Mean Square). Fig. 5 shows the RMS results by rotation degree in three images compared with the conventional method. The error between the conventional method and ATRM is close to zero in all cases while reducing complexity is about 25-30 percent. ATFP and CATM can substantially reduce computational complexity by 75-85 percent and their error is marginal at less than 0.035 and 0.07 pixel values respectively.

All the objectively measured errors are within the negligible level, which proves that all the proposed methods meet the rendering quality while reducing the computational complexity by up to 85 percent.

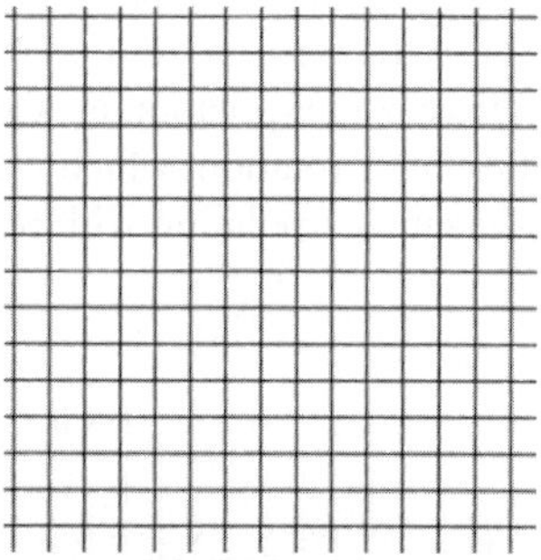

(a) Rotation result in conventional method

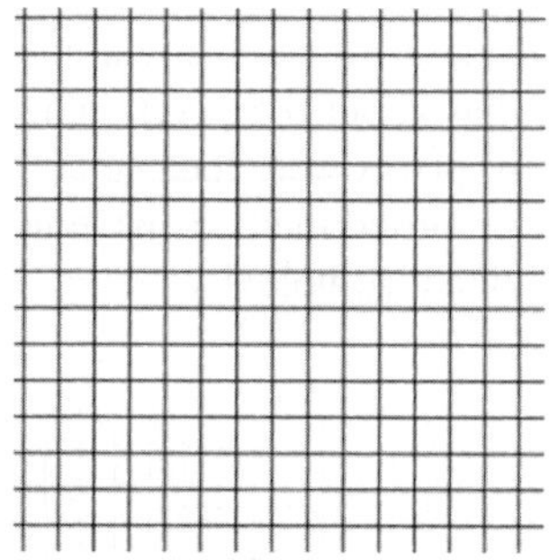

(b) Rotation result in ATRM

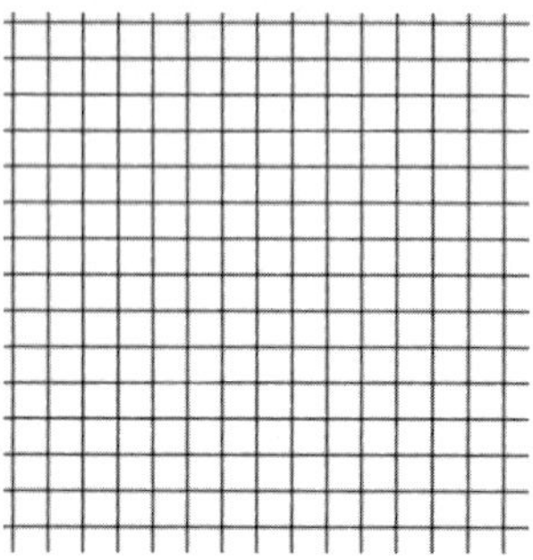

(c) Rotation result in ATFP

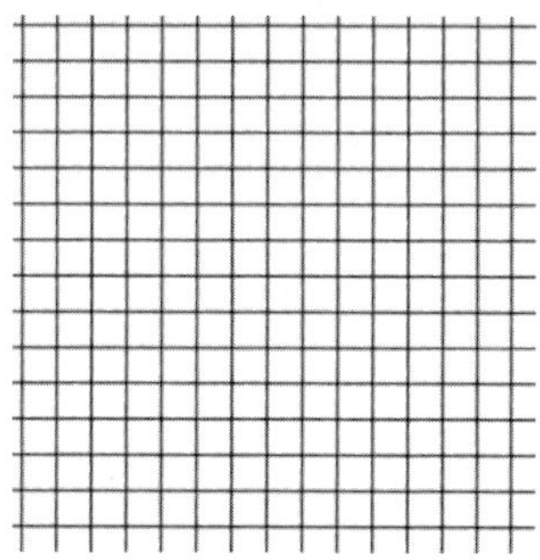

(d) Rotation result in CATM

**Fig. 4.** Rotational image with bilinear interpolation

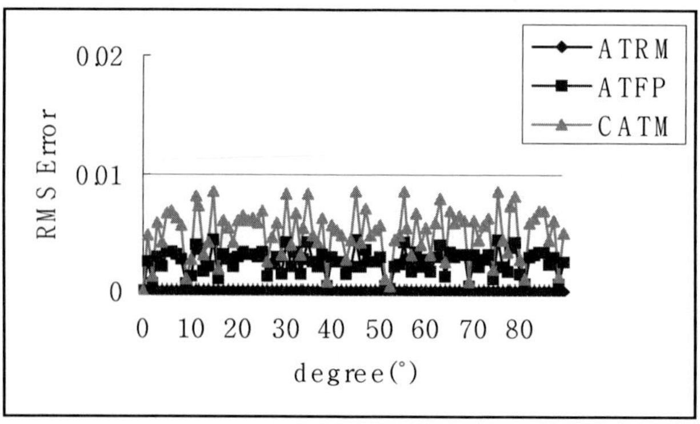


(a) RMS in 512x512 image

**Fig. 5.** RMS by rotation degree

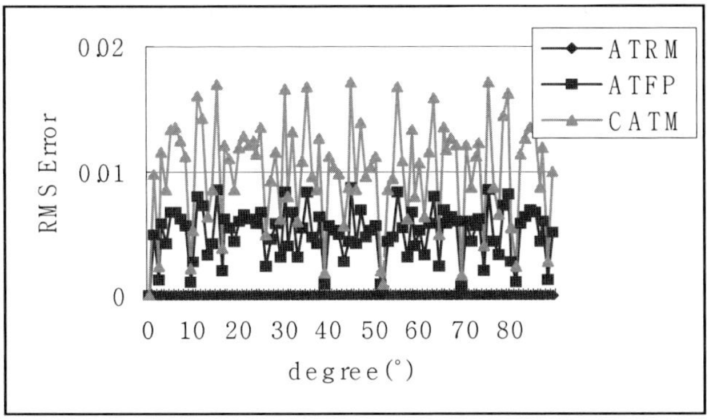


(b) RMS in 1024x1024 image

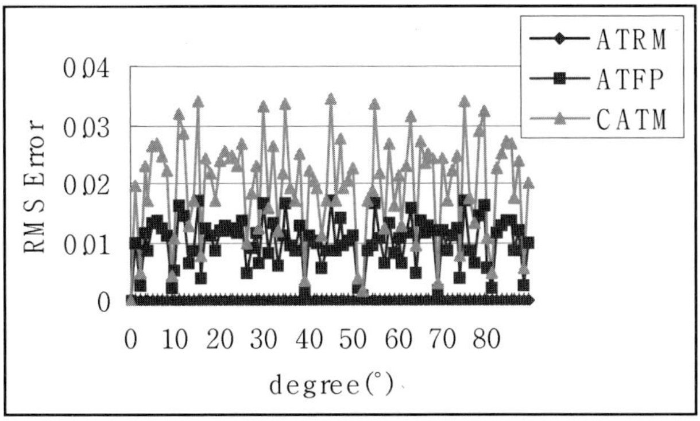


(c) RMS in 2048x2048 image

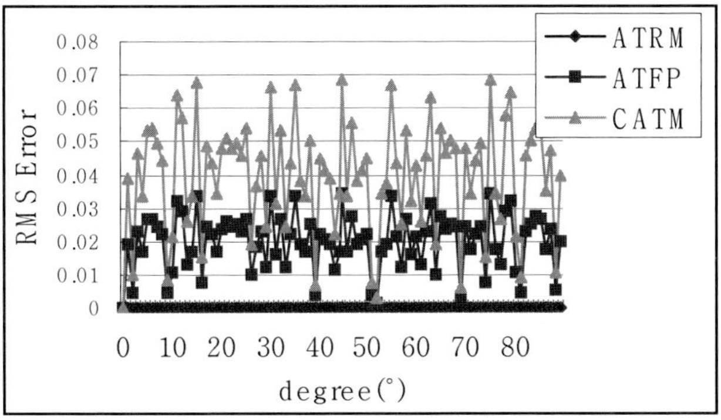


(d) RMS in 4096x4096 image

**Fig. 5.** (*continued*)

# 5 Conclusions

We have proposed fast affine transform methods. The first method removes four multiplications per pixel by exploiting the relationship between two neighboring pixels, which has no RMS error when compared with the conventional method. The second one performs fixed point operations with marginal error. Lastly, we tried to combine two methods. The proposed methods can reduce the computational complexity by up to 85 percent while their errors are within 0.07 values. As the result, the proposed method was about six times faster than conventional ones without any interpolation and five times faster with bilinear interpolation. Extending the proposed work in efficient hardware implementation would be one of the future directions that we intend to research.

## References


1. Rafael, C. G., Richard, E. W.: Digital Image Processing. Addison Wesley, Sep. (1993) 296-299
2. Donald, H., Baker, M.P.: Computer Graphics C Version $2^{nd}$. Prentice Hall (1997) 184-208
3. Milan, S., Vaclav, H., Roger, B.: Image Processing, Analysis and Machine Vision $2^{nd}$. PWS Publishing (1998)
4. Anil K.J.: Fundamentals of Digital Image Processing. Prentice Hall, (1989) 320-322
5. Davies, E. R.: Machine Vision. Academic Press, (1997) 663-675
6. Kenneth R. Castleman: Digital Image Processing. Prentice Hall, (1996) 115-137
7. Affine Transformations of Images : A least Squares Formulation
8. A Generalized Two Pass Approach to Image Geometric Transform Implementation, Theory and Ramifications
9. Convolution-based Interpolation for Fast, High-quality Rotation of Images
10. Fraser, D.: Comparison of High Special Frequencies of Two-pass and One-pass Geometric Transform Algorithms. Computer Vision, Graphics, Image Processing, vol. 46, (1989) 267-283
11. Paeth, A.W.: A Fast Algorithm for General Raster Rotation. in Proc Graphics Interface '86, (1986) 77-81

# Multi-modal Feature Integration for Secure Authentication

Hang-Bong Kang and Myung-Ho Ju

Dept. of Computer Eng., Catholic Univ. of Korea
#43-1 Yokkok 2-dong Wonmi-Gu, Puchon City, Kyonggi-Do, Korea
hbkang@catholic.ac.kr

**Abstract.** In this paper, we propose a new multi-modal feature integration for secure authentication. We introduce behavioral information as well as biometrics information for the person of interest to test his verification. For continuous authentication, temporal score integration method is presented that incorporates biometrics and behavioral features. The proposed method was evaluated under several real situations and promising results were obtained.

## 1 Introduction

Currently, various multi-modal biometric verification systems are proposed [1-3]. The goal of a multi-modal biometric verification system is to either accept or reject the person of interest based on the combination of his characteristics such as speech, face or fingerprints. The possible application areas of multi-modal verification systems are secure tele-shopping, tele-banking and controlled access to restricted environments such as an airport.

Even though the multi-modal verification system provides satisfactory results, it only provides meaningful verification result at the specified time instance. After some minutes passed by, the verification result is no longer meaningful. As stated in Altinok and Turk [4], if continuous biometrics is developed, we can get an appropriate verification result whenever it is needed. For example, a user is in front of the computer and has inputted his password to log on the computer. After identification check, the computer system does not check the user's identity any more for computer usage. If the user leaves the computer without logging out, somebody can use his account freely. So, it is necessary to check the person's identity continuously for secure computer usage.

However, successive execution of discrete biometrics system for secure authentication needs expensive computing costs and the cooperation of the person of interest. To relieve this burden, it is desirable to develop a biometrics system which provides secure verification result with cheap computing cost. One possible approach for continuous secure authentication is to add behavioral information for the person of interest to test his verification. Therefore, we propose a multi-modal feature integration method incorporating biometrics and behavioral features.

In this paper, we make three contributions. First, we introduce behavioral features in computing biometrics system. Second, we propose temporal integration of

D.-S. Huang, K. Li, and G.W. Irwin (Eds.): ICIC 2006, LNCS 4113, pp. 1191 – 1200, 2006.

biometrics and behavioral features to construct continuous multi-modal secure authentication. Third, our proposed system can provide an option of re-test as well as accept/reject at any time instance.

The paper is organized as follows. Section 2 discusses multi-modal features for secure authentication. Section 3 presents our proposed temporal integration of confidence scores for authentication. Section 4 shows preliminary experimental results of our proposed method.

## 2 Multi-modal Features

For secure computer usage, we use two kinds of features such as physiological and behavioral features of the person of interest. Physiological or biometrics features refer to the meaningful features in biometrics such as face, fingerprint, iris and speech. We classify these features as primary features and require these primary features sporadically. Behavioral features refer to the associated features with biometrics such as trajectory, movement and belongings of the person of interest. In this section, we will discuss multi-modal features for secure authentication.

### 2.1 Biometrics Feature

For face verification, the score of the candidate pattern with regard to the reference model is calculated first, and then compared with the threshold value. If the score is higher than the threshold value, the candidate is accepted. To compute facial features, we use PCA (Principal Component Analysis) and LDA (Linear Discriminant Analysis) methods. Usually, PCA outperforms LDA in the case of small training set, while LDA can outperform PCA in the case of lighting variations [5].

Both of these representations, PCA and LDA can be considered as a linear transformation from the original image vector to a projected feature vector. It is as follows.

$$Y = W^T X \,. \tag{1}$$

where Y is the d x N feature vector matrix, d is the dimension of the feature vector and N is the number of face images.

In PCA, the transformation matrix $W_{PCA}$ is composed of the eigenvectors corresponding to the *d* largest eigenvalues. The PCA basis vectors are defined as the eigenvectors of the covariance matrix.

In LDA, the transformation matrix $W_{LDA}$ is computed as

$$W_{LDA} = \arg\max_{W} \frac{W^T S_B W}{W^T S_w W} \,. \tag{2}$$

Where

$$\begin{aligned} S_B &= \sum_{i=1}^{c} N(x_i - \mu)(x_i - \mu)^T \\ S_W &= \sum_{i=1}^{c} \sum_{x_k \in X_i} (x_k - \mu_i)(x_k - \mu_i)^T \end{aligned} \,. \tag{3}$$

Marcialis et al.[6] pointed out that the fusion of PCA and LDA outperforms the individual verification algorithm based on PCA or LDA in ORL data set and Yale data set. However, in other data set, the fusion of LDA and PCA cannot outperform the individual algorithm. So, it is necessary to select the appropriate method in each instance.

Usually "sum" algorithm in the fusion of PCA and LDA can outperform individual algorithm in the specific data set [6]. However, it is not always the case on every data set. In other words, individual algorithm can outperform the fusion method sometimes. To handle this weakness, we use a majority voting method on PCA, LDA and the sum of PCA and LDA for person verification.

In majority voting, the decision of which majority of classifiers is used, is selected. Odd number of classifiers is usually required to break ties. In our proposed system, we use three classifiers consisting of PCA, LDA and the sum of PCA and LDA. This is shown in Fig. 1. For example, if LDA expert and the "sum" expert show the same class, the high score between two experts is used as verification score.

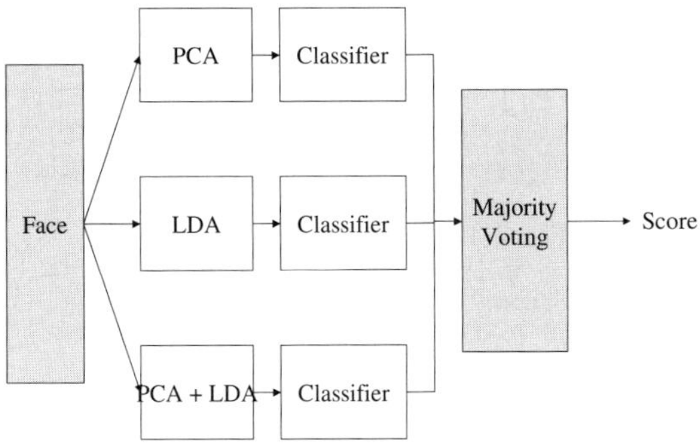


**Fig. 1.** Face Verification Scheme

## 2.2 Behavioral Feature

After verification of a person, it is necessary to track the admitted person's behavioral features continuously for secure authentication. For behavioral features, we estimate the face trajectory and its pose. To compute behavioral features, we use multi-modal face tracking system using color and edge information [7].

To represent multi-modal feature tracking, we adopt a dynamic Bayesian network (DBN). DBN is a powerful tool for modeling dynamic systems and allows a probabilistic way to determine a state in each time frame by integrating modalities such as the prior model of the state and observations. Fig. 2 shows a general DBN structure.

To construct DBN-based tracking, we must specify three kinds of information such as the prior distribution over state variables $p(x_0)$, the transition model $p(x_n \mid x_{n-1})$ and the sensor model $p(y_n \mid x_n)$. The transition model $p(x_n \mid x_{n-1})$ describes how the state evolves over time. In this paper, we only consider a first-order Markov process. The sensor model $p(y_n \mid x_n)$ describes how the evidence variables are affected by the actual state. The current state is evaluated as the posterior probability through the integration of multiple cues in DBN. In other words, the posterior probability of the state is evaluated as

$$p(x_n \mid y_n, x_{n-1}). \tag{4}$$

where $x_n$ and $x_{n-1}$ are the current and previous state, respectively. $y_n$ is the evidence of observed features such as color and edge information.

In our visual tracking, we use two features such as color and edge. For evidence variables in our framework, we use color likelihood $p(c_n \mid x_n)$ and edge likelihood $p(e_n \mid x_n)$ where $c_n$ and $e_n$ are the color and edge measurements at time $n$, respectively. The posterior probability like Eq. (4) is interpreted as

$$p(x_n \mid c_n, e_n, x_{n-1}) \propto p(c_n \mid x_n) p(e_n \mid x_n) p(x_n \mid x_{n-1}). \tag{5}$$

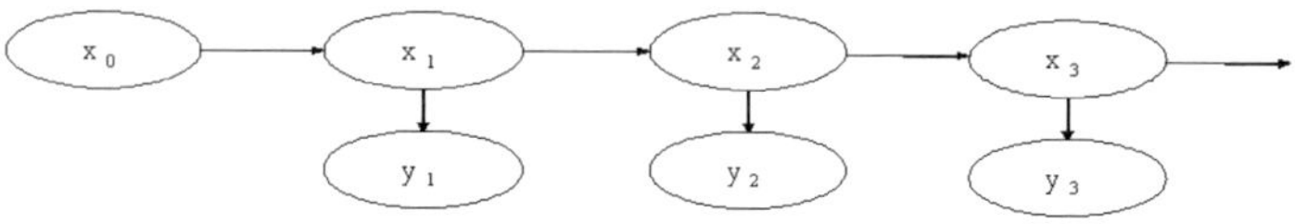


**Fig. 2.** Dynamic Bayesian Network

The color likelihood $p(c_n \mid x_n)$ is defined as

$$p(c_n \mid x_n) = \left[ \frac{1}{\sqrt{2\pi\sigma}} e^{-\frac{1-\sum_{u=1}^{m}\sqrt{p_i^{(u)} q^{(u)}}}{2\sigma^2}} \right]. \tag{6}$$

where $p_i^{(u)}$ is the $i^{th}$ object candidate's color distribution and $q^{(u)}$ is color distribution of reference object.

We use the edge likelihood as the one proposed by Nishihara [8]. The edge likelihood is computed as

$$p(e_n \mid x_n) = \left( \frac{1}{N_p} \sum_j \left| n(j) \cdot g(j) \right| \right). \tag{7}$$

where $\{n(i)\}_{i=1,\ldots,N_p}$ is the unit vector normal to the ellipse (object) at pixel j and $\{g(i)\}_{i=1,\ldots,N_p}$ is the intensity gradient at perimeter pixel j of the ellipse, and $N_p$ is the number of pixels on the perimeter of an ellipse.

Given the observation and transition models, the filtering distribution can be computed as two-step recursion as

$$\text{Prediction: } \begin{aligned} & p(x_n \mid y_{1:n-1}) \\ & = \int p(x_n \mid x_{n-1}) p(x_{n-1} \mid y_{1:n-1}) dx_{n-1} \end{aligned} . \tag{8}$$

$$\text{Filtering: } p(x_n \mid y_{1:n}) \propto p(y_n \mid x_n) p(x_n \mid y_{1:n-1}) . \tag{9}$$

where the prediction step follows from marginalization, and the new filtering distribution is obtained through a direct application of Bayes' rule.

Recently, sequential Monte Carlo methods known as particle filters, have gained a lot of popularity in the numerical approximation in DBN. Various particle-based filtering methods have been proposed already. As in particle-based filtering [9], we start from a weighted set of samples $\wp_{n-1} = \{x_{n-1}^i, w_{n-1}^i\}_{n=1}^N$ which is approximately distributed according to $p(x_{n-1} \mid y_{1:n-1})$ and sample candidate particles from an appropriate proposal distribution $x_n^i \sim q(x_n \mid x_{n-1}^i, y_n)$ , $i$ = 1..N. The new importance weights are

$$w_n^i \propto w_{n-1}^i \frac{p(y_n \mid x_n^i) p(x_n^i \mid x_{n-1}^i)}{q(x_n^i \mid x_{n-1}^i, y_n)} . \tag{10}$$

where $\sum_{i=1}^N w_n^i = 1$. The new particle set $\wp_n = \{x_n^i, w_n^i\}_{n=1}^N$ is then approximately distributed according to $p(x_n \mid y_{1:n})$.

From the current target state, the behavioral score is computed from the similarity between the reference model and current target model. The similarity is computed as Battacharria coefficient based on color histogram of each model. If the Battacharria coefficient is small, it shows that current tracked object is changed a lot from the initial state. Therefore, the biometrics score of the initial state is no longer meaningful for secure authentication.

In this case, we estimate the face pose to re-compute the biometrics score. The face pose estimation is performed by eigenspace analysis like [10]. The face image is projected into the eigenspace of each pose and then the probabilistic distance is computed. The estimated pose at time *t* is

$$P_t = \arg\min_k (I, P^k) . \tag{11}$$

where I is the face candidate and $p^k$ is the one of the face pose.

The accurate face pose estimation is important to compute the confidence score of face verification results because face verification is very difficult in some poses. Pose estimation score is computed from the distance between the pose average and the given image. Even though behavioral features do not have strong discrimination power in the verification or authentication, they would become meaningful if incorporated with biometrics features. We can sample these behavioral features densely along the time direction with cheap computing cost.

## 3 Temporal Integration

To measure continuous multi-modal biometrics, it is necessary to temporally integrate biometrics scores which are usually captured from multi channels discretely [4]. One possible approach to compute continuous authentication is to extend discrete value into the continuous distribution which has decreasing property along the time axis. However, this is not desirable in some situations. Fig. 3 shows two situations. In Fig. 3(a), the person of interest has checked his face for secure authentication and was still sitting in front of the computer like Fig. 3(b). The score for biometrics should be still meaningful after checking biometrics. But in Fig. 3(c), the person left the computer, so the score for his biometrics should be no longer meaningful for the secure computer usage. Therefore, decreasing property of the biometrics score should depend on the person of interest's behavior not along the time axis. In this section, we will discuss how to integrate biometrics features and behavioral features along the time direction for secure authentication.

(a) (b) (c)

**Fig. 3.** User Authentication

### 3.1 Biometrics Score

We analyze the face recognition results according to the various face poses. Fig. 4 shows the recognition result on 11 face poses. The recognition accuracy in frontal faces is the best. So, it is desirable to compute verification score at the frontal face pose.

Since successive execution of face verification requires expensive computing cost, we perform verification operation sporadically. The confidence of verification value decreased as the function of time along the time direction. Usually, we can express the verification score as

$$S_f = \begin{cases} f(b) & \text{initial state} \\ f(b)e^{-\lambda t} & \text{otherwise} \end{cases} . \tag{12}$$

where *f(b)* represents biometrics score from biometric feature ***b*** . This is shown in Fig. 5 (a).

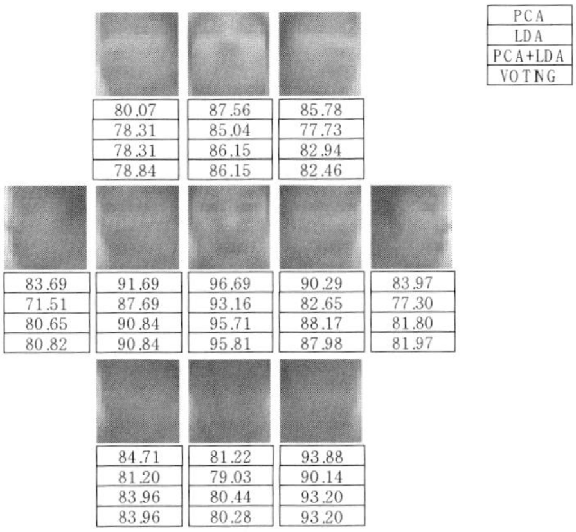


**Fig. 4.** Recognition Result on 11 Face Poses

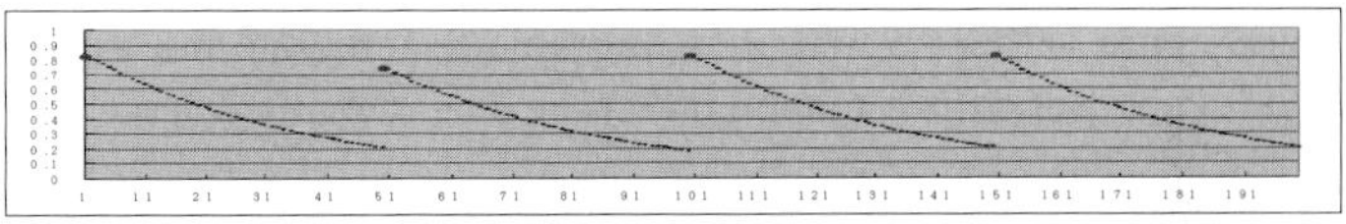

(a)

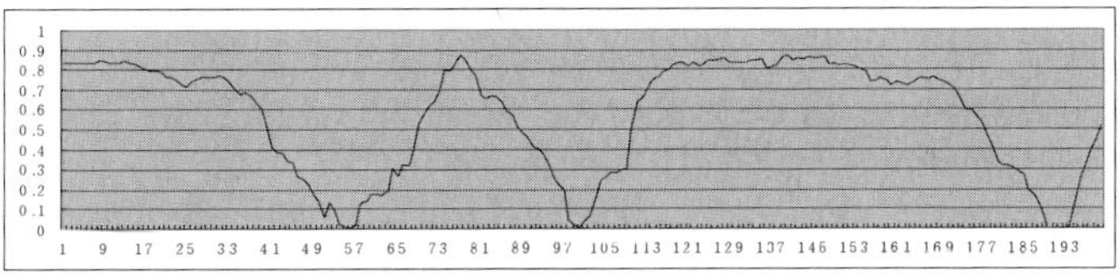

(b)

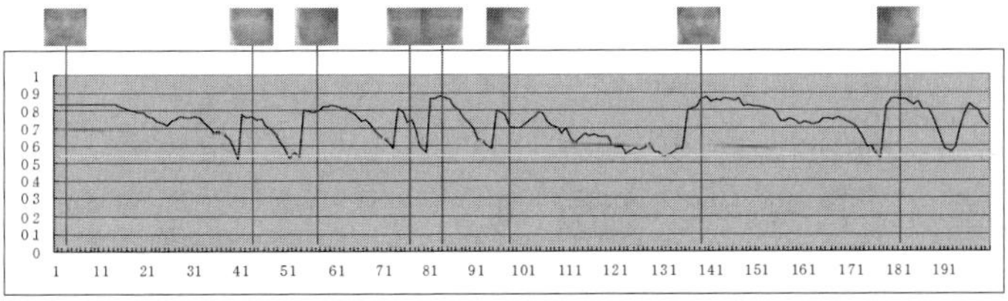

(c)

**Fig. 5.** (a) Biometrics Score, (b) Behavioral Score, (c) Pose Estimation is performed at red vertical lines

## 3.2 Behavioral Score

From the face tracking result, we can compute the behavioral score from Bhattacharyya distance

$$S_b(t) = 1 - d_b = 1 - \sqrt{1 - \rho[r, q]} \ . \tag{13}$$

where color histograms of each model at time instance $t$ are $r=\{r^{(u)}\}_{u=1,..,m}$ and $q=\{q^{(u)}\}_{u=1,..,m}$ , the coefficient is defined as $\rho[r,q]=\sum_{u=1}^{m}\sqrt{r^{(u)}q^{(u)}}$ . Fig. 5(b) shows the behavioral score. When the behavioral score is below than the threshold value, it is necessary to compute pose estimation of the tracked person like Eq. (11). The confidence score for pose estimation at time instance $t$ is represented as

$$S_p(t)=\frac{1}{\Lambda}\exp(-\frac{1}{\sigma^2}d(I,p_t)) \ . \tag{14}$$

where $\Lambda$ is the normalization factor and $d(I,p_t)$ is the distance between current target face and its estimated pose. In Fig. 5(c), the pose estimation is performed at the vertical red lines. After pose estimation, behavioral score is changed from $S_b(t)$ to $S_p(t)$.

### 3.3 Temporal Integration

For continuous secure authentication, it is desirable to integrate the biometrics scores with behavioral score along the temporal direction. The integrated score S is defined as

$$S(t)=\begin{cases} S_f & t=0 \\ S_f * S_b(t) & 0<t, S(t)>T \end{cases} . \tag{15}$$

When the score S(t) goes to the below the threshold value T, we estimate face pose and the pose estimation score $S_p(t)$ is replaced by the score S. After that, S(t) is computed according to Eq. (15). This is shown in Fig. 6. From the temporal integration of confidence score, we can make a decision such as *accept*, *reject* or *re-test* for the person of interest. The decision *re-test* refers to the state that the current biometrics state is a little suspicious because the person of interest's behavioral features are strange. By computing continuous biometrics, the decision *re-test* is possible.

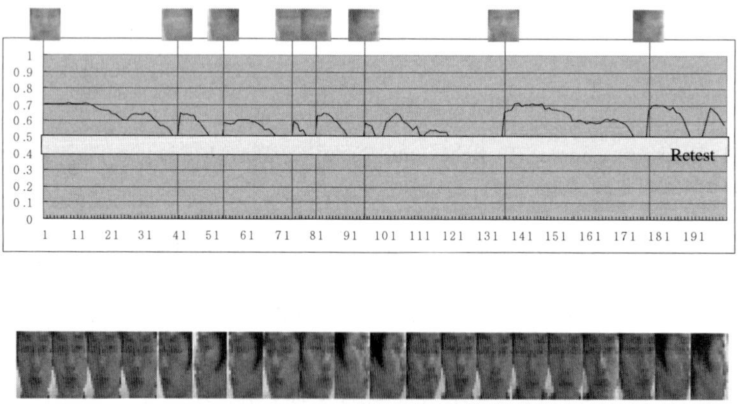


**Fig. 6.** Temporal Integration of Scores

## 4 Experimental Results

Our proposed secure authentication system is implemented on a P4-3.0 Ghz system. The system consists of a sensor input module, biometrics feature verification module, behavioral feature tracking and pose estimation module. This is shown in Fig. 7. We simulate our framework on the real situation. The test video sequence is that a person takes a verification test using face and password. Then, he moves his head and left the computer. First, a person of interest takes a verification test. The primary feature like biometrics score is computed at the verification stage. After that, secondary behavioral feature like face pose is estimated. Fig. 6 shows the confidence value along the time direction.

Based on the continuous score, the verification system can decide whether to *accept*, *reject* or *re-test* the person of interest. The score depends on the tracked face pose. For example, at the frame 54 in Fig. 6, the score level is low because the tracked face shows the side face and is different from the initial front face. At this point, the sensor should be operated to capture the biometrics features. Whenever the face is verified, the new score is generated. From this new score, the biometrics score for the face will be regenerated. If the score is in the yellow region in Fig. 6, re-test is required for secure authentication. When the score goes to the region below the re-test state, the screen saver is executed to lock the screen. From our method, we can obtain continuous biometrics score.

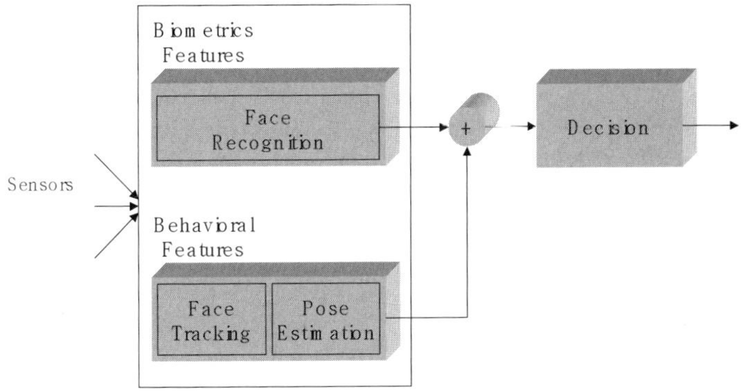


**Fig. 7.** Proposed System

## 5 Conclusions

In this paper, we proposed a multi-modal feature integration for secure authentication. To approximate inference of the DBN state, we used particle filters. We have presented results on the realistic scenario to show the validity of the proposed approach. Our proposed system shows a reasonable continuous biometric score for the verification the person of interest. Using the continuous biometric score, the system can determine whether the person of interest is in the state of *accept, reject or re-test*.

To improve the continuous biometrics system, efficient video-based verification methods should be developed. Real-time particle filtering method is also needed to deal with multi-channel information effectively.

## Acknowledgements

This study was supported by the department specialization Fund, 2006 of The Catholic University of Korea.

## References

1. Ross, A., Jain, A.: Multimodal Biometrics: An Overview, Proc. EUSIPCO (2004)
2. Sanderson, C., Paliwal, K.: Information Fusion and Person Verification Using Speech and Face Information, IDIAP Research Report, IDIAP-RR 02-33, IDIAP (2002)
3. Ross, A., Jain, A.: Multimodal Biometrics: An Overview, Proc. EUSIPCO (2004)
4. Altinok, A., Turk, M.: Temporal Integration for Continuous Multimodal Biometrics, Proc. Multi-modal user Authentication (2003)
5. Martinez, A., Kak, A.: PCA Versus LDA, IEEE Tans. PAMI, Vol23, No. 2 (2001)
6. Marcialis, G., Roli, F.: Fusion of LDA and PCA for Face Verification, Int. Workshop on Multiple Classifier Systems(MCS 2003), LNCS ( 2003)
7. Kang, H. –B, Cho, S.: Multi-modal Face Tracking in Multi-Camera Environments, LNCS 3691 (2005)
8. Nishihara, H., Thomas, H., Huber, E.: Real-time Tracking of People Using Stereo and Motion, Proc. SPIE, vol. 2183 (1994) 266-273
9. Nummiaro, K., Koller-Meier, E., Van Gool, L.: A Color-Based Particle Filter, First International Workshop on Generative-Model-Based Vision (2002) 53-60
10. Du, C., Su, G.: Face Pose Estimation based on Eigenspace Analysis and Fuzzy Clustering, LNCS 3174 (2004)

# Three-View Shape Recovery and Incremental Registration of 3D Point Sets

Jong-Hyun Yoon and Jong-Seung Park

Department of Computer Science & Engineering, University of Incheon,
177 Dohwa-dong, Nam-gu, Incheon, 402-749, Republic of Korea
{jhyoon, jong}@incheon.ac.kr

**Abstract.** This paper describes a shape recovery framework based on scaled orthographic factorization and incremental 3D point cloud registration. While the camera is moving freely in unknown environments, point features are automatically extracted and tracked. Using the tracked features in three consecutive frames, 3D locations are recovered and partial point subsets are immediately registered to the global point cloud. The advantage of the proposed incremental method is that the registration process does not rely on past frames for estimating the global 3D point cloud. The shape recovery and registration steps are combined as a single procedure that processes each input frame only once. All the internal steps are linear and non-iterative, hence the procedure is applicable to on-line interactive applications. Experimental results showing the feasibility of the presented approach are also provided.

## 1 Introduction

The multi-view shape recovery problem and the 3D point set registration problem are two most common problems in computer vision. Poelman and Kanade[1] proposed a robust factorization method to recover scene geometry and camera motion from given images using the paraperspective projection and the scaled orthographic projection. Their factorization method applies the singular value decomposition to a measurement matrix that consists of tracked feature points.

The Iterative Closest Point (ICP) algorithm[2] is the dominant method for 3D model registration that aligns a sequence of partially recovered point clouds. The ICP algorithm uses two point clouds and an initial guess for the relative rigid-body transform. It iteratively refines the transform by computing pairs of corresponding points in the point clouds and minimizing the error. Most approaches for the registration of point clouds are based on minimizing registration error using general-purpose nonlinear optimization[3]. For such approaches, a good initial estimate is critical for the fast convergence[4].

Recently, a framework for aligning a video stream onto 3D sensor data has been presented[5]. They compute 3D point clouds from a video through motion stereo-based camera pose estimation. Contrary to their approach, we have focused on recovery and registration of sparse feature points into a global point cloud with extremely low computational cost.

D.-S. Huang, K. Li, and G.W. Irwin (Eds.): ICIC 2006, LNCS 4113, pp. 1201–1206, 2006.

This paper presents a unified framework to automatically construct a 3D scene point cloud from the video frames. First, we detect point features on a given input frame. Then, the point features are tracked in the next consecutive frame. From the point correspondences for the three consecutive frames, 3D coordinates of the tracked points are estimated. Finally, the newly found points are registered to a global point cloud.

## 2 Shape Recovery Using Factorization

Assume $P$ feature points are tracked over $F$ frames whose image coordinates are $\{(u_{fp}, v_{fp})|f = 1, \ldots, F, p = 1, \ldots, P\}$. Using the factorization method, initially developed by Tomasi and Kanade[6], both the object shape and its motion can be recovered from a sequence of images without having to compute the depth.

The factorization method in shape and motion recovery is robust and fast. Unlike iterative methods, no initialization is required and convergence is virtually guaranteed. For each frame, let $(\bar{u}_f, \bar{v}_f)$ be the mean position of all feature points in the $f$'th frame. The following $2F \times P$ measurement matrix is built from the images coordinates: $\mathbf{W} = (w_{ij}),\ i = 1, \ldots, 2F, j = 1, \ldots, P$ . If $i \leq F$ then $w_{ij} = u_{ij} - \bar{u}_i$. Otherwise, $w_{ij} = v_{i-F,j} - \bar{v}_{i-F}$. By computing the SVD of $\mathbf{W}$ we decompose $\mathbf{W}$ into a $2F \times P$ matrix $\mathbf{O}_1$, a diagonal $P \times P$ matrix $\mathbf{\Sigma}$, and a $P \times P$ matrix $\mathbf{O}_2$ such that $\mathbf{W} = \mathbf{O}_1\mathbf{\Sigma}\mathbf{O}_2$. By choosing the first three columns of $\mathbf{O}_1$, the first $3 \times 3$ submatrix of $\mathbf{\Sigma}$, and the first three rows of $\mathbf{O}_2$, we set the $2F \times 3$ submatrix $\tilde{\mathbf{O}}_1$, the $3 \times 3$ submatrix $\tilde{\mathbf{\Sigma}}$, and the $3 \times P$ submatrix $\tilde{\mathbf{O}}_2$, respectively. Then, from the three submatrices, we build two matrices $\hat{\mathbf{R}}$ and $\hat{\mathbf{S}}$ by $\hat{\mathbf{R}} = \tilde{\mathbf{O}}_1(\tilde{\mathbf{\Sigma}})^{1/2}$ and $\hat{\mathbf{S}} = (\tilde{\mathbf{\Sigma}})^{1/2}\tilde{\mathbf{O}}_2$. Using metric constraints specified in [6], we compute a $3 \times 3$ matrix $\mathbf{Q}$ which satisfies $\tilde{\mathbf{R}} = \hat{\mathbf{R}}\mathbf{Q}$ and $\tilde{\mathbf{S}} = \mathbf{Q}^{-1}\hat{\mathbf{S}}$. Then we compute the rotation matrix $\tilde{\mathbf{R}}$ and the shape matrix $\tilde{\mathbf{S}}$ from the computed $\mathbf{Q}$. Let $\tilde{\mathbf{i}}_f$ and $\tilde{\mathbf{j}}_f$ $(f = 1, \ldots, F)$ be the row vectors of $\tilde{\mathbf{R}}$ and $\tilde{\mathbf{s}}_p$ $(p = 1, \ldots, P)$ be the column vectors of $\tilde{\mathbf{S}}$: $\tilde{\mathbf{R}} = [\tilde{\mathbf{i}}_1 \cdots \tilde{\mathbf{i}}_F\, \tilde{\mathbf{j}}_1 \cdots \tilde{\mathbf{j}}_F]^T$, $\tilde{\mathbf{S}} = [\tilde{\mathbf{s}}_1 \cdots \tilde{\mathbf{s}}_P]$. Then, $\tilde{\mathbf{i}}_f$ and $\tilde{\mathbf{j}}_f$ represent the orientation of the horizontal and vertical camera reference axes of $f$'th frame, respectively. The vector $\tilde{\mathbf{s}}_p$ is the coordinates of the $p$'th feature point with respect to its centroid.

A 3D point $\mathbf{s}_p$ is projected to an image position $(u_{fp}, v_{fp})$ on frame $f$ and the projection equations are: $u_{fp} = \tilde{\mathbf{i}}_f \cdot (\mathbf{s}_p - \mathbf{t}_f)$, $v_{fp} = \tilde{\mathbf{j}}_f \cdot (\mathbf{s}_p - \mathbf{t}_f)$ where $\tilde{\mathbf{i}}_f = (1/z_f)\mathbf{i}_f$ and $\tilde{\mathbf{j}}_f = (1/z_f)\mathbf{j}_f$. Since $\mathbf{i}_f$ should be a unit vector, the value $z_f$ can be determined from the inverse of the norm of $\tilde{\mathbf{i}}_f$. The orientation of the $f$'th camera is determined by the two unit vectors, $\mathbf{i}_f$ and $\mathbf{j}_f$, where $\mathbf{i}_f = \tilde{\mathbf{i}}_f/|\tilde{\mathbf{i}}_f|$ and $\mathbf{j}_f = \tilde{\mathbf{j}}_f/|\tilde{\mathbf{j}}_f|$. The third reference axis $\mathbf{k}_f$ is the direction of all orthographic projection rays, which is the cross product of $\mathbf{i}_f$ and $\mathbf{j}_f$, $\mathbf{k}_f = \mathbf{i}_f \times \mathbf{j}_f$. Hence, the rotation matrix for the $f$'th frame corresponds to $\mathbf{R}_f = \left[\mathbf{i}_f\ \mathbf{j}_f\ \mathbf{k}_f\right]^T$.

Since the orientation of the world reference frame could be arbitrary, the rotation $\mathbf{R}$ is determined up to a rotation of the whole reference system. To make the rotation matrix $\mathbf{R}$ unique, we can enforce the world reference system to be aligned with the first camera reference system. The alignment could be done simply by multiplying the transpose of the rotation matrix to all rotation matrices, so that $\mathbf{i}_1 = [1\ 0\ 0]^T$ and $\mathbf{j}_1 = [0\ 1\ 0]^T$.

When we place the origin of the world coordinate frame at the centroid of object points, the scaled orthographic projection equations can be rewritten as:

$$u_{fp} = \tilde{\mathbf{i}}_f \cdot \mathbf{s}_p + \bar{u}_f, \ v_{fp} = \tilde{\mathbf{j}}_f \cdot \mathbf{s}_p + \bar{v}_f.$$

Once the value $z_f$ is found, the camera translation $\mathbf{t}_f = [x_f\ y_f\ z_f]^T$ can be computed by $\mathbf{t}_f = -\mathbf{R}_f \tilde{\mathbf{t}}_f$ where $\tilde{\mathbf{t}} = [\bar{u}_f/z_f, \bar{v}_f/z_f, z_f]^T$. All the steps to compute $\mathbf{R}_f$ and $\mathbf{t}_f$ are deterministic and initial estimates are not required.

## 3 Registration of Point Sets

Each set of surface measurements should be transformed into a common coordinate frame. Making a complete object surfaces using partial measurements from different viewpoints is the shape registration problem. The ICP algorithm, introduced by Besl and McKay[2], is a general-purpose method for the accurate and computationally efficient registration of shapes.

The algorithm registers two point sets provided that the transform between the two sets is approximately known. Given a point set $P$ and a surface $Q$, the shape $P$ is positioned to be in the best alignment with the model shape $Q$. First, for each point $p$ in $P$, the closest point $q$ on $Q$ is found. Then, it evaluates the rigid transform $T$ that minimizes the sum of squared distances between pairs of closest points $(p, q)$. The rigid transform $T$ is applied to all points in set $P$. These steps are repeated until the change in mean-square error falls below a predefined threshold.

Multiple point sets are often required to capture the complete surface of an object. By extending the ICP algorithm, we compute the registration between pairs of overlapping point sets. When the number of point sets is greater than two, registration is achieved by pairwise registration of pairs of overlapping point sets. When some points are overlapped among more than two point sets, the pairwise registration does not compute the optimal result.

Our approach does not assume any hardware aided scan environment. An image capture device such as a hand-held camera can be moved freely along an arbitrary trajectory. In such cases, the global minimization cannot be used. Though the registration accuracy depends on surface shape, the registration error converges to zero as the number of points increases.

## 4 Experimental Results

Automatically detected features are tracked continuously until they are disappeared and also points from newly appeared parts are added and tracked. For each input frame, new 3D point subsets are computed in the structure recovery step using the current frame and the two previous frames. Three consecutive images provide a subset of new 3D points and the new subset is registered to the global point cloud.

**Fig. 1.** The cap image sequences (upper) and the sheep image sequences (lower)

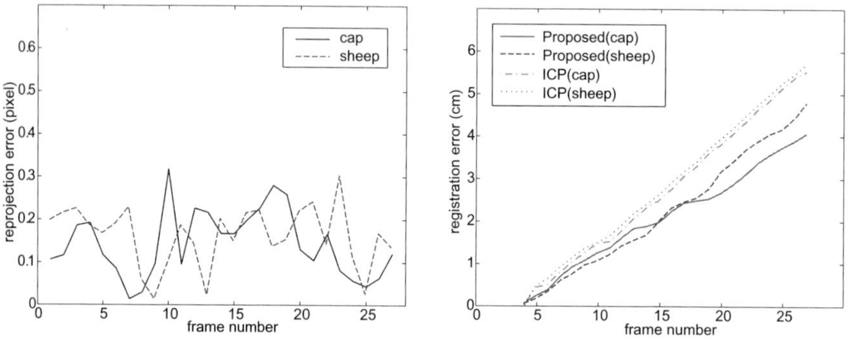


**Fig. 2.** Error of the recovered subsets (left) and error of the global point cloud at intermediate registration steps (right)

Extensive experiments have been performed on real image sequences. Fig. 1 shows two test image sequences of our test data, the cap sequence and the sheep sequence. The objects are arbitrary and unknown. Though their shapes are too complex to model by simple geometric primitives, our incremental registration results in Fig. 3 and Fig. 4 show that the proposed method is sound and practically feasible. The top row shows the point cloud of the first subset, the middle row shows the global point cloud after merging the second subset, and the bottom row shows the global point cloud after merging the third subset.

The recovery accuracy is shown in Fig. 2. The left figure is the error of the recovered subsets for the cap sequence and the sheep sequence. The right figure is the error of the global point cloud after each registration step. The error accumulation of the proposed method is less than that of the ICP method.

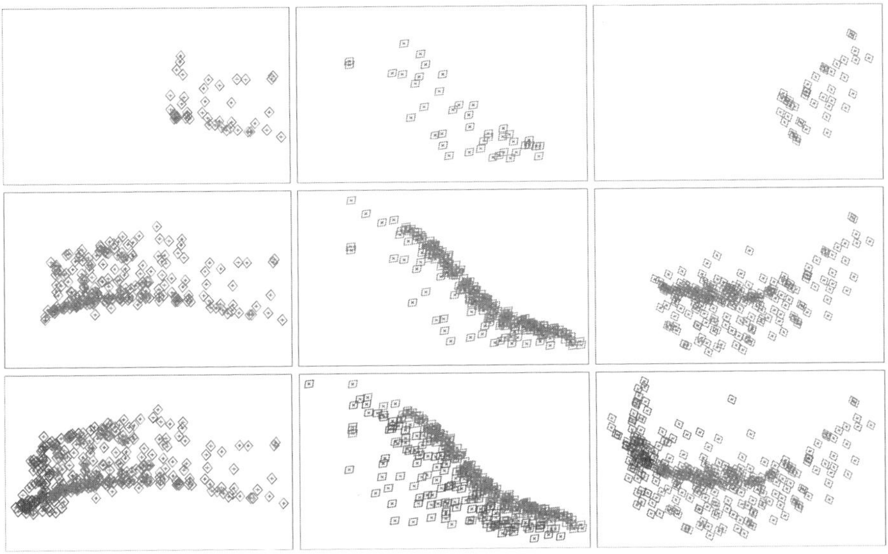

**Fig. 3.** The incremental registration results for the cap sequence

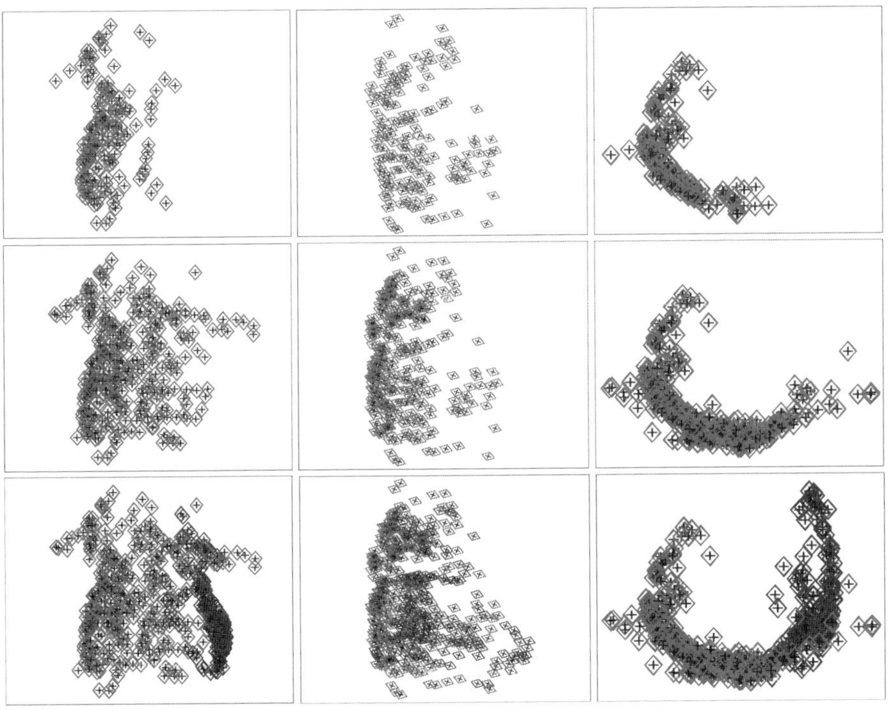

**Fig. 4.** The incremental registration results for the sheep sequence

Computational cost was measured for 27 frames in the cap sequence. For each input frame, the recovery step takes about 30 ms including the feature point tracking. The registration step takes about 20 ms for the cap sequence. Since our method is based on the sparse feature set, the number of points in the global point cloud hardly affects the registration time.

## 5 Conclusion

This paper has presented a unified approach for efficient recovery and registration of unknown 3D shapes from a sequence of frames. The proposed method is incremental which means that it does not rely on past frames for estimating 3D point locations and camera poses, and it is applicable to on-line interactive applications. The image features are continuously tracked and the 3D coordinates of features are found directly from a linear approximation. As soon as the 3D points are recovered, they are registered to the global point cloud using an efficient registration of 3D point sets.

Our future research includes a fast and implementation of the Delaunay triangulation to convert the global 3D point cloud into a mesh object applicable to real-time interactive applications. The corresponding textures for the mesh object should also be extracted for the realistic texture mapping. When new points are added to the global point cloud, the mesh object should be updated immediately for the real-time rendering of the mesh object.

## Acknowledgement

This work was supported in part by the Ministry of Commerce, Industry and Energy (MOCIE) through the Incheon IT Promotion Agency (IITPA) and in part by the Brain Korea 21 Project in 2006.

## References

1. Poelman, C., Kanade, T.: A Paraperspective Factorization Method for Shape and Recovery. In: Proceedings of the 3rd European Conference on Computer Vision (ECCV '94). (1994) 97–108
2. Besl, P.J., McKay, N.D.: A Method for Registration of 3-d Shapes. IEEE T-PAMI. 14 (1992) 239–256
3. Fitzgibbon, A.: Robust Registration of 2d and 3d Point Sets. In: Proc. British Machine Vision Conference. 2 (2001) 411–420
4. Krishnan, S., Lee, P.Y., Moore, J.B., Venkatasubramanian, S.: Global Registration of Multiple 3d Point Sets via Optimization-on-a-manifold. In: Eurographics Symposium on Geometry Processing. (2005) 187–196
5. Zhao, W., Nister, D., Hsu, S.: Alignment of Continuous Video onto 3d Point Clouds. IEEE T-PAMI. 27 (2005) 1305–1318
6. Tomasi, C., Kanade, T.: Shape and Motion From Image Streams under Orthography: A Factorization Approach. International Journal of Computer Vision. 9 (1992) 137–154

# An Efficient Arbitrary View Generation Method Using Panoramic-Based Image Morphing

Jang-Hyun Jung and Hang-Bong Kang

Dept. of Computer Eng. Catholic University of Korea
#43-1 Yokkok 2-dong Wonmi-Gu, Puchon City, Kyonggi-Do, Korea
hbkang@cahtolic.ac.kr

**Abstract.** In this paper, we propose a new arbitrary view image generation method using panoramic-based image morphing for large-scale scenes. The panoramic images are sampled with large step size. From these panoramic images, intermediate panoramic images are generated by bi-directional image morphing and finally arbitrary view images are generated by light field rendering. It is shown that an arbitrary view image with reasonably high quality is obtained using a few captured panoramic images.

## 1 Introduction

Image-based rendering (IBR) is a promising technique in generating a virtual 3-D world from real image data without an explicit 3-D model. One of key concepts in IBR is plenoptic function [1]. In particular, reasonable methods are "Lightfield" [2] and "Lumigraph"[3] which use the 4D plenoptic function with clever parameterization. However, these methods have limitations in viewing spaces. Specifically, the viewing space in "Lumigraph" and "Lightfield" are inside a 3D box, so they are not useful for large-scale scene rendering.

One of desirable approaches for large-scale rendering is suggested in Takahashi et al.[4]. They proposed a new plenoptic function which creates any view from any position in a wide area of a city. They densely captured panoramic images along one direction and then divided the stored panoramic images into vertical slits. After that, suitable slits were selected and assembled to generate images.

However, this method has its own limitations. First, it is very difficult to capture panoramic images densely. Secondly, this method is not suitable in the network environment due to the necessity of large bandwidth. In order to minimize these problems, we propose a new method to generate an arbitrary view image: first, we capture panoramic images sporadically and then from these stored panoramic images generate intermediate images by bi-directional morphing. After that, using light field rendering we generate an arbitrary view.

The paper is organized as follows. Section 2 discusses walkthroughs from panoramic images. Section 3 presents our proposed arbitrary view generation method using panoramic images morphing. Section 4 shows experimental results of our proposed method.

D.-S. Huang, K. Li, and G.W. Irwin (Eds.): ICIC 2006, LNCS 4113, pp. 1207 – 1212, 2006.

## 2 Walkthroughs from Panoramic Images

In this section, we discuss several capturing methods of panoramic images and present our new capturing method for walkthrough applications.

### 2.1 Capturing Panoramic Images

For walkthrough using panoramic images, numerous algorithms are proposed. They are plenoptic stitching [5], concentric mosaic [6], sea of images [7], and Takahasi's method [4] which used 4D light field rendering.

In plenoptic stitching [5], reference images of the environment are captured using omni-directional camera along several paths forming an irregular grid. In concentric mosaic [6], camera motion is constrained to planar concentric circles, and concentric mosaics are created by composing slit images taken at different locations along the circle. In sea of images [7], images are captured at every few inches in a large complex indoor environment and then novel images are reconstructed with high quality.

These methods are useful for the walkthrough applications in closed or small-scale space. For the navigation in large-scale scenes, the method proposed by Takahasi et al.[4] is more desirable. The capturing method of panoramic images is shown in Fig. 1(a). This method, however, requires a large number of panoramic images for high quality arbitrary view images. Therefore, its usage in network environment is limited due to the bandwidth. As shown in Fig. 2, the simulation service for virtual navigation at the end user computer is very difficult. In order to cope with this limitation, in our approach, we capture panoramic images sporadically, as shown in Fig. 1(b). After that, we generate a number of intermediate images from a pair of panoramic images by image morphing.

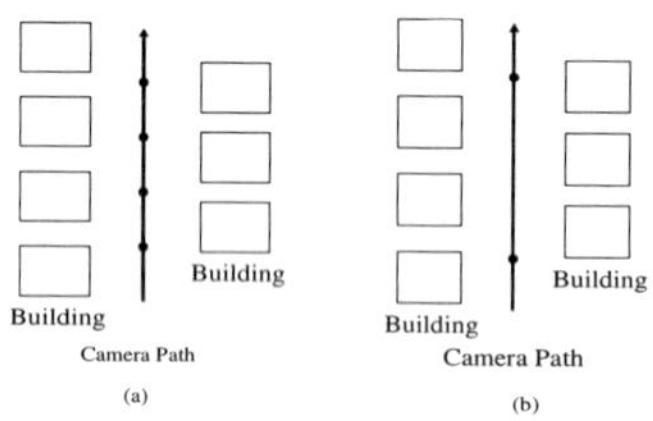


**Fig. 1.** Panoramic Image capturing

### 2.2 Panoramic Image Morphing

For images morphing, it is necessary to link corresponding points between a pair of images. Yan-fai [8] used a triangle-based panoramic image morphing method but it shows some problems in image morphing where the distortion of the object may occur depending on images. Thus, we use polygon-based panoramic image morphing instead for fast and easy implementation.

We first extract polygon-based corresponding points from a pair of images. For detecting corresponding points, we used two-frame wide baseline matching method proposed by Xiao and Shah [9]. Then, from the corresponding line segment, we compute morphing information based on feature-based morphing [10]. In this morphing, the relations between pixels inside the corresponding polygons in each image are computed.

After computing morphing information, we generate a number of intermediate images from a pair of panoramic images $C_n$ and $C_{n-1}$. Each intermediate image is generated by translating point x to point x'. The amount of distortion generated in making each intermediate image depends on the translation distance such as x'- x. So, we use bi-directional morphing like Fig. 3.

As shown in Fig. 3, left half of intermediate images generated from "left to right" morphing have better quality than right half of intermediate images. In addition, right half of intermediate images generated from "right to left" morphing have also better quality than left half of intermediate images of that morphing. So, we choose those better halves of intermediate images and combine them, making the final intermediate images.

Since we generate a number of intermediate images from a pair of panoramic images, we do not need to capture panoramic images densely. Furthermore, the distortions generated from morphing process are removed by linear interpolation process.

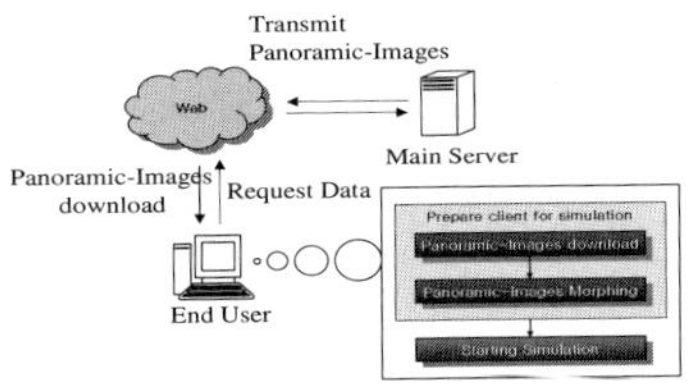


**Fig. 2.** Network Environment

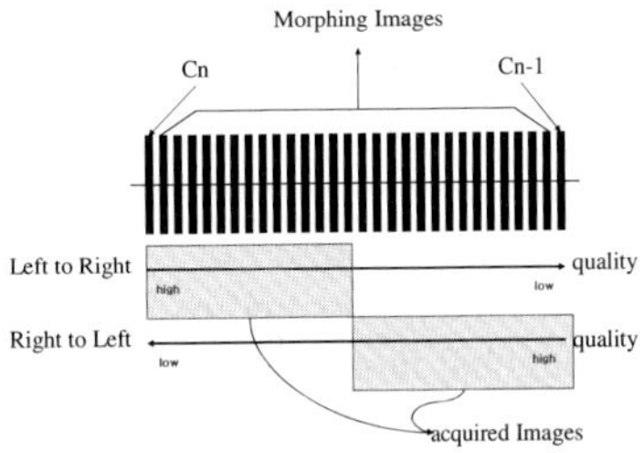


**Fig. 3.** Morphing images

## 3 Arbitrary View Image Generation

From the panoramic and intermediate images, we can generate an arbitrary view images using Takahasi's method [4]. Fig. 4 shows light field rendering which generates an arbitrary view image. However, serious vertical distortion occurs in Takahasi's method. To minimize the vertical distortion, we constrain the slit range using the information of the building location. This is shown in Fig. 5.

The range of ray slit from P to $C_n$ is $\alpha - \theta$. $\alpha$ and $\theta$ are computed as

$$\alpha = \arctan(\frac{x}{z}) \cdot \tag{1}$$

$$\theta = \alpha - \arctan\left( \frac{\tan(\beta) \times d_1 - d_2}{d_1} \right) \cdot \tag{2}$$

where x is the distance of x-direction from P to $C_n$, z is the distance from P to $C_n$ in z-direction, $d_1$ is the distance from $C_n$ to the building, and $d_2$ is the distance from $C_n$ to $C_{n-1}$.

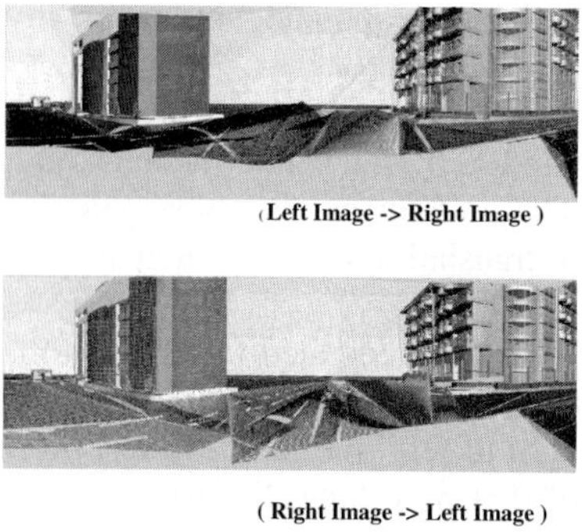


**Fig. 4.** Bi-directional Morphing

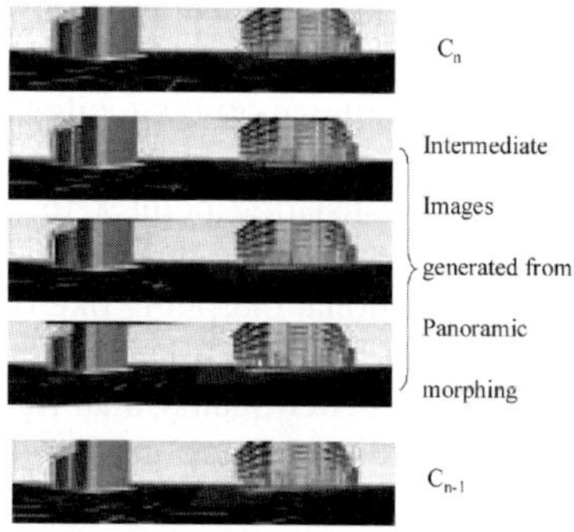


**Fig. 5.** Intermediate images from a pair of panoramic images $C_n$ and $C_{n-1}$

# 4 Experimental Results

We have implemented this system on Pentium IV 3GHz, Microsoft windows 2000 server and experimented using panoramic images for simulation. We modeled virtual city using 3D Max 5 and captured 26 panoramic images with capturing step size 0.03. The capturing step size refers to the distance between two captures and is normalized by the whole length of camera path. Then, we compute polygon-based correspondence points and execute bi-directional morphing. Fig. 6 shows the results of bi-directional morphing such as right-to-left and left-to-right morphing.

From the bi-directional morphing, we obtain 780 intermediate images. Fig. 7 shows a pair of captured images $C_n$, $C_{n-1}$ and intermediate images. To compare our method with Takahashi's method, we also generated a novel view from panoramic images captured with step size 0.001, 0.01, 0.02 and 0.03 using Takahashi's method. This is shown in Fig. 8. At the step size 0.001, the result shows good quality, but the image quality is degraded as the step size increases. At the step size 0.03, the result is very poor.

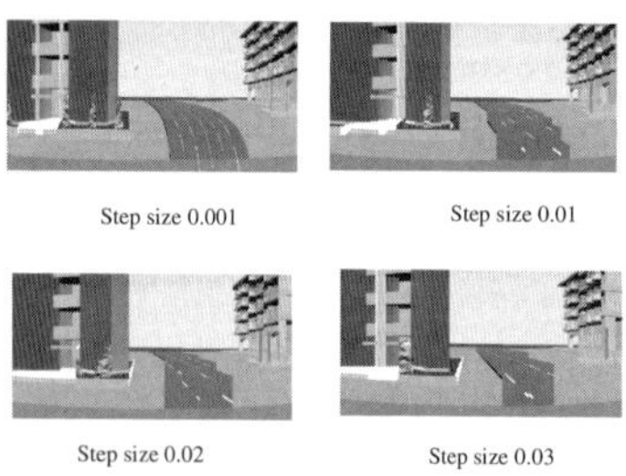


**Fig. 6.** A novel view with Takahasi's method

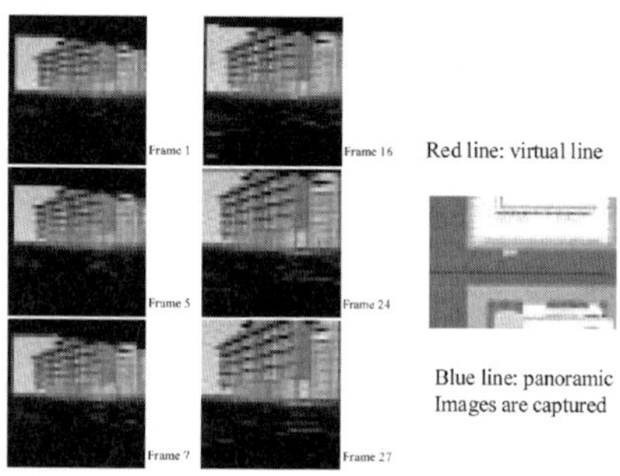


**Fig. 7.** An arbitrary view image sequence along the red line path with step size 0.03

We also generated a novel view using panoramic and intermediate images. Fig. 9 shows the reconstructed novel view with step size 0.03. In comparison with Fig. 8, our results show less vertical distortion. In Fig. 9, blue line is the camera path which captured panoramic images and red line is the virtual camera path. Along the red line, a number of arbitrary view images are generated. The image quality is reasonable.

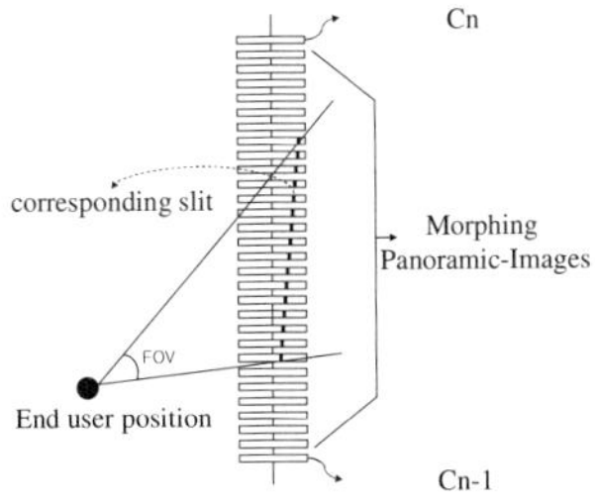


**Fig. 8.** Reconstruction a novel view

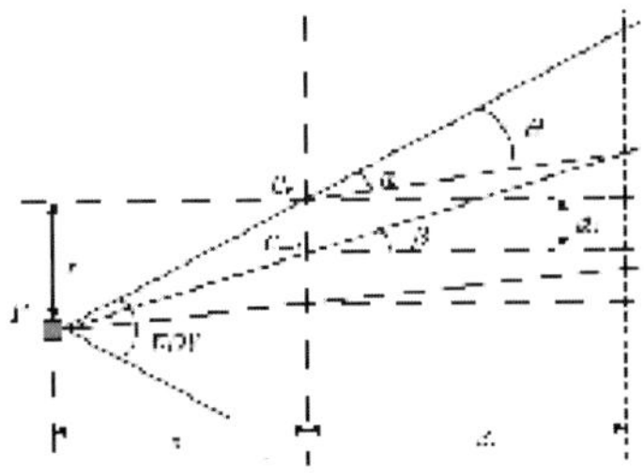

**Fig. 9.** Slit range

# 5 Conclusions

This paper proposed an efficient novel view image reconstruction from panoramic images captured with a large step size while reducing the amount of captured images. We first find polygon-based corresponding points between two panoramic images and then compute morphing information from corresponding line segment. Then we generate some intermediate images using bi-directional image morphing. To minimize the distortion, we apply linear interpolation method to the intermediate images. Even though a few panoramic images are used, a novel view is reconstructed with reasonable quality.

# Acknowledgement

This work was supported by the Catholic University of Korea, Research Fund, 2005.

# References

1. Chen, S.: QuickTime VR - an Image-based Approach to Virtual Environment Navigation. Computer Graphics Proceedings, Annual Conference Series, SIGGRAPH'95 (1995) 29-38
2. Levoy, M., Hanrahan, P.: Light Field Rendering. ACM SIGGRAPH (1996) 31-42
3. Gortler, S., Grzeszezuk, R., Szeliski, R., Cohen, M.: The Lumigraph, ACM SIGGRAPH (1996) 43-54
4. Takahashi, T., Kawasaki, H., Ikeuchi, K., Sakauchi, M.: Arbitrary View Position and Direction Rendering for Large-scale Scenes, IEEE CVPR (2000) 296-303
5. Aliaga, D., Carlbom, I.: Plenoptic stitching: A Scalable Method for Reconstructing Interactive Walkthroughs. ACM SIGGRAPH (2001) 443-450
6. Shum, H., He, L.: Rendering with Concentric Mosaics. ACM SIGGRAPH (1999) 299-306

7. Aliaga, D., Funkhouser, T., Yanovsky, D., Carbom, I.: Sea of Images. In Proceedings of IEEE Visualization (2002) 331-338
8. Yan-Fai, C., Man-Hong, F., Chi-Wing, F., Pheng-Ann, H., Tien-Tsin, W.: A Panoramic-based Walkthrough System using Real Photos. in Proceedings of Pacific Graphics'99 (1999)
9. Xiao J., Shah M.: Two-frame Wide Baseline Matching, in Proceedings of ICCV (2003)
10. Beier T., Neely, S.: Feature-based Image Metamorphosis, Computer Graphics (SIGGRAPH `92), Vol. 26, No. 2 (1992) 35-42

# Audio Content Analysis for Understanding Structures of Scene in Video

Chan-Mi Kang[1] and Joong-Hwan Baek[2]

[1] Multimedia Retrieval Lab. in School of Electronics and Communication Engineering, Hankuk Aviation University
happychan@mail.hangkong.ac.kr
[2] School of Electronics and Communication Engineering, Hankuk Aviation University
jhbaek@mail.hangkong.ac.kr

**Abstract.** In this paper, we propose a system to categorize audio in 7 classes. For classification features, we use the mean and variance of RMS, ZCR, fundamental frequency and frequency peak which are extracted from every frame of 25ms length. In addition to the audio content classification, we also perform speaker identification with the voice sequences extracted automatically using our proposed method. The accuracy of our proposed scheme reaches 93.8% in categorizing audio signal and 80% in the speaker identification process.

## 1 Introduction

Content-based video analysis aims at obtaining a structured organization of the original video content and understanding its embed semantics as human does. For a better understanding the video and for extracting more information from it, we focus on the audio signal to index the content of each scene.

The predominant approach of this research is to categorize the audio sequence into some parts: silence, voice, music, song, environmental sound and mixture component of them. Also, we focus on the voice sequences to index them by individual speakers. Four features are selected to classify audio signal, and 32 mel frequency cepstral coefficients (MFCC) are used along with Gaussian mixture model (GMM) to identify speakers.

## 2 Overview of the Proposed System

Figure 1 shows the flow chart of our proposed system. Assuming that the video is already segmented into shots and grouped in scenes [1], we propose a scheme for an automatic segmentation and annotation of audiovisual data based on audio content analysis. From the video segmented by shots and scenes, audio signal is extracted, then four kinds of audio features are calculated form the audio sequences; root mean square (RMS), zero-crossing rate (ZCR), fundamental frequency using temporal autocorrelation (TA) and frequency peak. After feature extraction, audio is classified to each corresponding class.

D.-S. Huang, K. Li, and G.W. Irwin (Eds.): ICIC 2006, LNCS 4113, pp. 1213 – 1218, 2006.

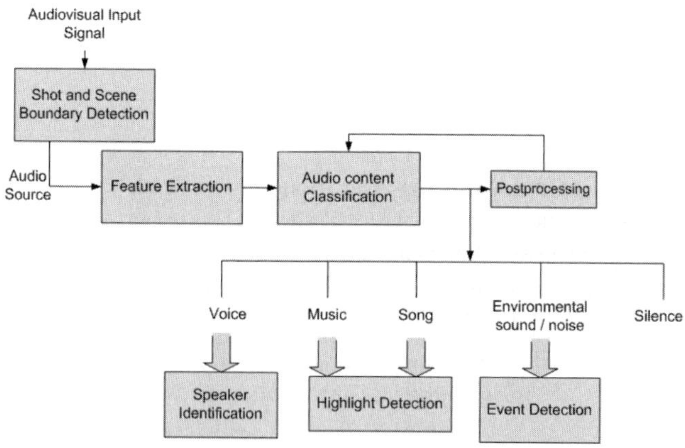


**Fig. 1.** Flow chart of the proposed system

## 2.1 Audio Features

In this paper, we use the statistical values of the RMS, ZCR, fundamental frequency and frequency peak of short time audio source for analysis of the sound characteristics. First of all, these features are calculated from each 25ms length frame.

The RMS efficiently and easily represents the volume of audio signals, and the computational cost is relatively low.

For discrete-time signals, a zero-crossing occurs when successive samples have different signs. The rate at which zero-crossing occurs is a simple measure of the frequency content of a signal. This feature can be used to distinguish voiced and unvoiced signals, because unvoiced speech components normally have much higher ZCR values than voice ones.

Numerous fundamental frequency estimation algorithms are available. In this paper, we use the temporal autocorrelation (TA) method as follow.

For a given frame index $l$, the normalized autocorrelation function of the signal is first estimated as

$$\Gamma_{STA}(m) = \frac{\sum_{n=0}^{N_w-1} s_l(n)\, s_l(n-m)}{\sqrt{\sum_{n=0}^{N_w-1} s_l(n)^2 \sum_{n=0}^{N_w-1} s_l(n-m)^2}} \quad (l \le m \le M; 0 \le l \le L-1) \tag{1}$$

where $s_l(n)$ is the audio signal in $l$th frame, $m$ is the lag index of the autocorrelation and $L$ is the total number of frames in s($n$). The fundamental period $T_0$ is then estimated as $T_0 = \arg\max[\Gamma_{STA}(m)]$, and the local fundamental frequency is the reciprocal of the fundamental period, $T_0$.

However, even though the temporal autocorrelation method produces exact pitch values in most cases, it may result in doubled pitch errors when the signal is highly periodic with short pitch periods [2]. For this reason, we use short-time frequency peak along with fundamental frequency to estimate the fundamental frequency.

Frequency peak is the frequency of the highest magnitude in short-time window which means the frequency containing the highest energy.

### 2.2 Audio Content Analysis

In this paper, we categorize the audio signal in seven classes: music, song, voice, environmental sound, silence and mixes of music, song with voice. Unlikely with other researches [3][4], we separate music and song which might be present in different kinds of scene. In dramas, songs are mostly used in highlight scenes to maximize emotional impression, while music appears through the whole video and enrich the atmosphere. Moreover, if the song class is not defined independently, the song clips have the risk to be identified as mixture of music and voice. Therefore, recognizing music and song separately is reasonable and needed.

In [3], Zhang et al. use the raw data itself of power, ZCR, fundamental frequency and spectral peak extracted from each frame for classification features. However, these raw data are very sensitive to noise and the frame including noise element might be misclassified. In this paper, to reduce the risk of misclassification in noisy frames, we assemble data from 20 frames, of which have 25 ms length for each, and calculate the mean and variance values to make feature vectors. The mean and variance values of each feature earlier expressed are used to categorize the audio signal with CART as classifier.

## 3 Speaker Identification

In this paper, we propose a speaker identification method to index scenes by character. The speaker identification is done based on the voice sequences, which are extracted using audio classification method described in section 2.2. Our proposed method consists in two steps; preprocessing to extract real speech portion, and extracting MFCCs to identify the speaker using GMM. In this paper, we extract 24 MFCCs to represent the short time speech spectra.

MFCC, which is one of the most typical features in speech or speaker identification fields, is computed from mel frequency filter to present voice spectrum. The signal converted into frequency and weighted by each mel-scale filter frequency response is calculated as $E_{mel}(n,l)$, in which $l$ denotes the order of mel filter at time $n$. The real cepstrum associated with $E_{mel}(n,l)$ is referred to as the mel-cepstrum and is computed for each $m$ coefficient as

$$C_{mel}[n,m] = \frac{1}{R}\sum_{l=0}^{R-1}\log(E_{mel}(n,l)\cos(\frac{2\pi}{k}lm)) \tag{2}$$

where $R$ is the number of filters [5].

To model enrolled speakers, we employ the GMM due to its successful application in the speaker identification area. The MFCCs from the voice sequence are inputted to the GMMs of all enrolled speakers, which are pre-trained to identify the current speaker.

Let $\boldsymbol{\theta}_i$ be the GMM model corresponding to the *i*th enrolled speaker and let **X** be the observation sequence consisting of *T* frames $\boldsymbol{x}_t$, $t$=1,…,*T*. Assuming that all observation frames are independent, the average log likelihood between **x** and $\boldsymbol{\theta}_i$ can be computed as

$$P(\mathbf{X} \mid \theta_i) = \frac{1}{T} \sum_{t=1}^{T} \log p(x_t \mid \theta_i) \tag{3}$$

where $p(\boldsymbol{x}_t|\boldsymbol{\theta}_i)$ is the probability of $\boldsymbol{x}_t$ belonging to $\boldsymbol{\theta}_i$. With these probabilities of $\boldsymbol{x}_t$ belonging to $\boldsymbol{\theta}_i$, an unknown speaker can be identified from a set of *N* speakers by choosing the one with the maximum likelihood.

## 4 Experimental Result

In this section, we examine the performance of our proposed algorithm. For sample data set, 1549 audio clips are used. These are digitized at 22 KHz with 16-bit precision in mono sound. Due to the insufficiency of samples, classification tree is trained by using 10-fold cross-validation. Performance of audio analysis and fully trained classification tree are described in Table 1. The classes are in alphabetical order; environmental sound, mixture of music and voice, mixture of song and voice, music, silence, song and voice which are indicated as numbers in the table. The classes in row are the true classes and those in column are predicted ones. As the table shows, our proposed algorithm shows a result as 93.8% of accuracy.

**Table 1.** Performance of audio content classification

| | *1'* | *2'* | *3'* | *4'* | *5'* | *6'* | *7'* | *Total* |
|---|---|---|---|---|---|---|---|---|
| 1 | 87 | 0 | 5 | 5 | 2 | 3 | 0 | 102 |
| 2 | 2 | 245 | 0 | 4 | 0 | 1 | 1 | 253 |
| 3 | 0 | 0 | 230 | 9 | 0 | 14 | 0 | 253 |
| 4 | 7 | 0 | 3 | 353 | 4 | 7 | 0 | 374 |
| 5 | 1 | 0 | 0 | 0 | 16 | 1 | 0 | 18 |
| 6 | 4 | 1 | 6 | 12 | 0 | 275 | 0 | 298 |
| 7 | 0 | 3 | 1 | 0 | 0 | 0 | 247 | 251 |
| **Total** | 101 | 249 | 245 | 383 | 22 | 301 | 248 | 1549 |

As discussed in Section 3.2 for speaker identification, first, MFCCs are extracted from the pure speech sequences. To choose the effective number of coefficients, we verify the classification result using variable number of MFCCs as shown in Table 2. We use 3 sample sets of 5 different speakers extracted from a drama (sample set 1 and 2) and a movie (sample set 3). It is shown a better consequence following to increasing numbers of coefficients, however the computing time also increases abruptly which intercepts us to continuing our experiment with larger value.

We assume that the number of components in GMM will affect the accuracy of identification. Therefore by changing the number of mixture components, we examine

**Table 2.** Accuracy of the speaker identification according to the number of MFCC in three sample data sets

| Number of Coefficients | Sample set 1 | Sample set 2 | Sample set 3 |
|---|---|---|---|
| 13 | 78.84% | 79.16% | 77.66% |
| 24 | 78.96% | 82.4% | 84.26% |
| 32 | 79.6% | 83.08% | 85.8% |

**Table 3.** Accuracy of the speaker identification according to the number of mixture components in GMM with 5 speakers from sample set 1

| Num. of Mixture co mponents | 10 | 11 | 12 | 13 | 14 | 15 | 16 | 17 | 18 |
|---|---|---|---|---|---|---|---|---|---|
| Accuracy (%) | 77.56 | 77.76 | 77.84 | 79.6 | 80.0 | 80.08 | 81.12 | 80.08 | 79.96 |

the classification result as in Table 3. The result with 16 components shows the best accuracy, however it shows same result with when the number of MFCCs is increased; the computational time increases more than two times, which decreases the effectiveness in our research.

Finally, based on the results above, we select 32 MFCCs and 16 mixture components, which correspond to the hidden node of GMM. We classify the voice sequences from the classification results described in section 2. We select 5 main characters of the sample video and build GMMs before performing the speaker identification. For testing our speaker models, 100 samples of each speaker are chosen. Because of the shortage of samples, we use 10-fold cross-validation to verify the result objectively. The result of our speaker identification scheme is shown in Table 4. The accuracy touches around 80% of average.

**Table 4.** Result of the speaker identification

| | *a* | *b* | *c* | *d* | *e* | *Total* |
|---|---|---|---|---|---|---|
| A | 74 | 13 | 6 | 7 | 0 | 100 |
| B | 7 | 88 | 1 | 2 | 2 | 100 |
| C | 9 | 10 | 67 | 5 | 9 | 100 |
| D | 0 | 1 | 3 | 89 | 7 | 100 |
| E | 1 | 6 | 8 | 10 | 75 | 100 |
| **Total** | 91 | 118 | 85 | 113 | 93 | 500 |

The cause of most of miss-classification is the tone of the speakers. In movies or dramas, characters change their tones according to each situation and emotion. Consequently, the MFCCs are changing, too.

## 5 Conclusion

In this paper, we propose a system to categorize audio in 7 classes, i.e. silence, music, song, voice, environmental sound, mixture of music and voice and mixture of song and voice. Unlike other researches, we separate music and song which take different part in drama or movie. For feature vector, we use the mean and variance of each RMS, ZCR, fundamental frequency and frequency peak which are extracted from every 25ms length frame. In addition to the audio content classification, we also perform speaker identification with the voice sequences that are automatically extracted.

The accuracy of our proposed scheme in categorizing audio signal reaches 93.8% and the speaker identification process shows around 80% of average accuracy. The misclassification in speaker identification mostly comes from the yelling voices inside voice sequences that have different coefficients with general voices. To overcome this defect, a post-processing method or a combination of video and audio is required.

## Acknowledgement

This work was supported by 2005 Hankuk Aviation University faculty research grant.

## References

1. Baek, J.S., Lee, S.T., Baek ,J.H.: Scene Boundary Detection by Audiovisual Contents Analysis. LNAI Vol.3809 (2005) 530-539
2. Kim, H.G., Moreau, N., Sikora, T.: MEPG-7 Audio and Beyond Audio Content Indexing and Retrieval. WILEY (2005)
3. Zhang, T., Jay, K., C.-C.: Audio Content Analysis for Online Audiovisual Data Segmentation and Classification, Speech and Audio Processing IEEE Transactions Vol.9 (2001) 441 – 457
4. Panagiotakis, C., Tziritas, G.: A Speech/music Discriminator Based on RMS and Zero-Crossings, IEEE transactions on Multimedia, Vol. 7 (2005) 155 - 166
5. Quatieri, T.: Discrete-time Speech Signal Processing Principles and Practice, Prentice Hall PTR (2002)

# Independent Components Analysis for Representation Interest Point Descriptors*

Dongfeng Han, Wenhui Li, Tianzhu Wang, Lingling Liu, and Yi Wang

College of Computer Science and Technology, Key Laboratory of Symbol Computation and Knowledge Engineering of the Ministry of Education, Jilin University, Changchun, 130012, P.R. China
handongfeng@gmail.com

**Abstract.** This paper presents a new interest point descriptors representation method based on independent components analysis (ICA). The aim of this algorithm is to find a meaningful image subspace and more compact descriptors. Combination the descriptors with an effective interest point detector, the proposed algorithm has a more accurate matching rate besides the robustness towards image deformations. The proposed algorithm first finds the characteristic scale and the location for the interest points using Harris-Laplacian interest point detector. We use Haar wavelet transform on the neighborhood of the interest points and get low frequency gradient feature vectors. Then ICA is used to model the subspace and reduces the dimension of the feature vectors. The experiments show the efficiency of the proposed algorithm.

## 1 Introduction

Interest point detection and representation are useful in computer vision applications such as matching [1], retrieval [2] and recognition [3]. The main idea is to find a set of interest points and compute their descriptors. Many approaches to interest point detection exist. The most popular methods are Harris [4] and SIFT [3]. Authors in [5] compares shape context, steerable filters, PCA-SIFT, differential invariants, spin images, SIFT, complex filters, moment invariants, and cross-correlation for different types of interest regions and finds the SIFT based descriptors perform best.

In this paper, we present a new representation for descriptors. This method is based on independent component analysis. The success of this method is combining an accurate interest point detector with a compact representation for point descriptors.

In section 2, the proposed algorithm is described. In section 3 and 4, experiments are given in detail. In the end, the conclusions and future work will be shown in section 5.

## 2 Independent Component Analysis Based Interest Point Descriptors

Using Harris-Laplacian detector [6], we can get some interest points associated with characteristic scale. The next step is to give the representation for the interest points.

* This work has been supported by NDSF Project 60573182, 69883004 and 50338030.

D.-S. Huang, K. Li, and G.W. Irwin (Eds.): ICIC 2006, LNCS 4113, pp. 1219 – 1223, 2006.

The standard SIFT descriptors perform best described in [5]. However, the construction of SIFT descriptors is complicated and the future dimension is high. So we use ICA to get the high-level description from low-level image features with low dimension.

### 2.1 Independent Component Analysis

In image understanding, it is often desirable to represent an image in a subspace to reveal some of intrinsic characteristics of the data and reduce the dimension, where linear representation is often used due to its computational and analytical properties. Independent component analysis (ICA) [7] has such property. Basically, one attempts to represent each image patch as a linear combination of 'basis' patches, such that the mixing coefficients are as sparse as possible. In other words:

$$X = AS = \sum_{i=1}^{n} a_i s_i \tag{1}$$

Where $X$ is the image patch, $a_i$ is the basis images. ICA attempts to seek mutually independent components $s_i$ . Most of the $s_i$ will be close to zero and only a few will have significantly non-zero values. Once obtaining $A$, we can compute its inverse, say $W$, and obtain the independent component by:

$$S = WX = \sum_{i}^{m} w_i x_i \tag{2}$$

Then we can represent image patch $X$ by $S$, and $S$ has a good property.

### 2.2 ICA Based Feature Descriptors

We first describe the input vectors used in training ICA. In order to make the patches less sensitive to the exact feature location and noise effect, we sample the pixels at a lower frequency. We extract a $64 \times 64$ patch centered over the interest point and perform the Haar wavelet transform on the patch. The sub-band LL ($32 \times 32$) is used to get the feature vector which is created by computing the vertical and horizontal gradient maps for the $32 \times 32$ patch. So the vector's length is $2 \times 32 \times 32$. We normalize the vector to unit magnitude to reduce the effects of illumination change. In Fig. 1, an example of above procedure is given.

Using Harris-Laplacian point detector, we extract 1,0000 interest points from a common image database and create the input vector for each interest point. The whole input vectors are used to train ICA and the transformation matrix $W$ in Eq. (4) can be computed.

ICA can linearly project high dimension vector onto a low dimension feature space. Further more, it has a more meaningful visual property compared to PCA.

Thus, the ICA based feature descriptors includes following steps:

Step1. Extract a $64 \times 64$ patch at the characteristic scale, centered over the interest point;

Step2. Rotate to its main orientation to a canonical direction and perform the Haar wavelet transform and get LL sub-band;

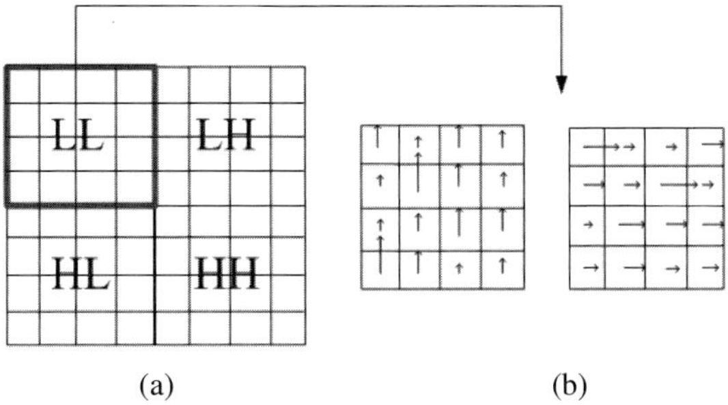


**Fig. 1.** An example of the creation input vectors. This figure shows an 8×8 patch, whereas our experiment use a 64×64 patch. (a) The input image patch centered over an interest point. (b) The vertical and horizontal gradient maps.

Step3. Compute the gradients of the LL sub-band and get the vertical and horizontal gradient maps and arrange the gradient maps and normalize it to unit magnitude;

Step4. use Eq. (4) to find the feature space for the 2×32×32 input vector;

The reduced feature space is the final interest point descriptors. In experiments, the dimension of feature space n=40 can get a high performance response.

# 3 Evaluation Criterion and Data Set

We use detection rate and false positive as the performance evaluation metric. They are defined as:

$$d = \frac{\#\, correct\ matches}{\#\, possible\ matches} \tag{3}$$

$$f = \frac{\#\, false\ matches}{\#\, detection\ points} \tag{4}$$

Two points $i$ and $j$ are correct match if the error in relative location is less than 2 pixels.

We use INRIA dataset for experiments. Images can be available on the Internet[1]. A significant amount of noise is added which includes blurring, scale, rotation, view point changes, zoom and illumination changes. We generate the detection ratio vs false positive graph by changing the threshold for ICA based algorithm and SIFT algorithm.

# 4 Experimental Results

## 4.1 Results for Different Image Deformations

In Fig. 2, we give the experimental performances of the proposed algorithm vs SIFT algorithm. The image deformations include scale & rotation and view changes. We find ICA based method is better than SIFT, especially under scale & rotation changes

---

[1] http://www.robots.ox.ac.uk/~vgg/research/affine/

and view changes. The reason for this phenomenon is that we use ICA to train the feature vectors. ICA perhaps has the ability to find a more instinct feature.

### 4.2 Running Time and Dimensions Choice

In Fig. 3, we compare the running time with SIFT. The range of dimensions changes from 10 to 40 with 5 intervals. The rate is computed by $Time(ICA)/Time(SIFT)$. For the choice of dimensions, we find an empirical choice with dimensions 40 can get a trade-off between precision and running time.

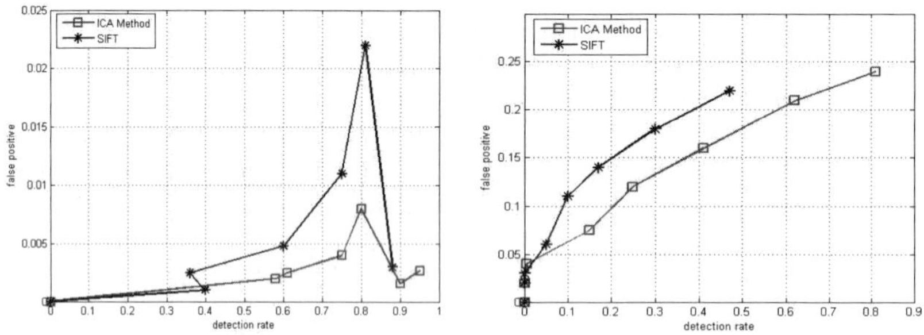


(a) (b)

**Fig. 2.** The performance curves for different image deformations. (a) Scale & rotation changes. (b) View point changes.

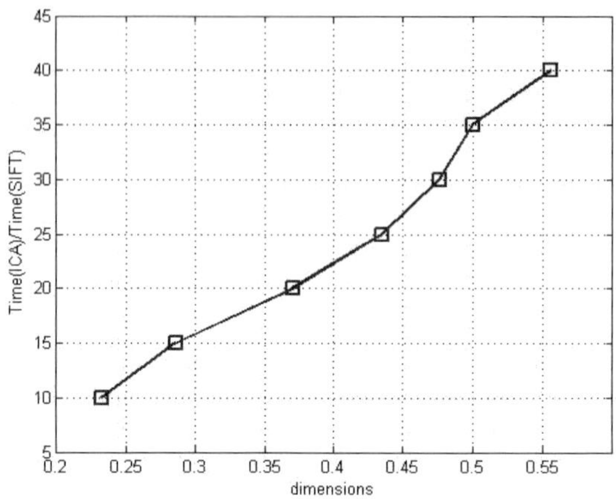


**Fig. 3.** The running time rate comparison for different dimensions

## 5 Conclusions and Future Work

In this paper, an interest point descriptors algorithm is presented. The main contribute of this paper is introducing ICA to local descriptors. We design an efficient interest point detector and a compact local descriptors representation.

In the future, we will explore the internal relationship between local descriptors and ICA. Some new applications based on ICA descriptors will be applied.

## Acknowledgments

This work has been supported by NSFC Project 60573182, 69883004 and 50338030. We also wish to acknowledge Y. Zhan, Y. Meng and Xu Yang for discussion on the validation proof and the paper format. Also Sun haibin, Zhenhua Zhang and other members of the Image&Graphics group at JLU provide much useful feedback on our algorithm.

## References

1. Tuytelaars, T., Van Gool, L.: Matching Widely Separated Views Based on Affine Invariant Regions", International Journal of Computer Vision, 1(59), (2004) 61-85
2. Sivic J., Zisserman, A.: Video Google: A Text Retrieval Approach to Object Matching in Videos. IEEE International Conference on Computer Vision, (2003)
3. Lowe, D.: Distinctive Image Features from Scale-invariant Keypoints. International Journal of Computer Vision, 2(60), (2004) 91-110
4. Stephens, M., Harris, C.: A Combined Corner and Edge Detector. In Alvey Vision Conference, (1988) 147-151
5. Mikolajczyk, K., Schmid, C.: A Performance Evaluation of Local Descriptors. IEEE Transactions on Pattern Analysis and Machine Intelligence, 27(10), (2005) 1615-1630
6. Mikolajczyk, K., Schmid., C.: Scale & affine Invariant Interest Point Detectors. International Journal of Computer Vision, 1(60), (2004) 63-86
7. Hyv ärinen, A.: Fast and Robust Fixed-point Algorithms for Independent Component Analysis. IEEE Transactions on Neural Networks, 10(3), (1999) 626-634

# New Color Correction Approach to Multi-view Images with Region Correspondence

Gangyi Jiang[1,3], Feng Shao[1,2], Mei Yu[1,3], Ken Chen[1], and Xiexiong Chen[2]

[1] Faculty of Information Science and Engineering, Ningbo University, Ningbo, 315211, China

[2] Department of Information and Electro. Engineering, Zhejiang University, Hangzhou, 310027, China

[3] National Key Laboratory of Machine Perception, Peking University, Beijing, 100871, China

**Abstract.** Color appearance of the same object between different viewpoints may be different due to inconsistent illumination or inevitable errors and noises resulting from imaging devices, which brings difficulties to the subsequent multi-view image compression and arbitrary viewpoint rendering. Thus, color correction is necessary for multi-view applications. In this paper, a color correction method of multi-view images is proposed based on region correspondence. Through expectation-maximum segmentation for reference image and current viewpoint image, mapping relationship is built with similar statistical model between two regions in the two images. Experimental results show that the proposed method can be used to correct the color of viewpoint images according to the color of the reference image, and preserve the visual impression of the viewpoint images simultaneously.

## 1 Introduction

Multi-view video coding and view generation have been two of the main technical areas in three-dimensional audio video (3DAV) [1,2]. Multi-view video coding is used to compress the multiple viewpoint video signals, and view generation is used to generate arbitrary viewpoint images for display purposes. However, due to inconsistent illumination or some undesired factors from imaging devices, color appearance of the same object between different viewpoints may be different, which brings much difficulty to the subsequent multi-view image compression and view generation. So, color correction of multi-view images is expected before a virtual intermediate view is generated and displayed.

Some simple correction algorithms (such as retinex[3] or global correction[4]) perform well for some classes of images but poorly for others because of the absence of region information. In [5], color, texture and geometry is used to acquire the region information, which results in high calculation complexity. In [6], color and texture segmentation is performed with expectation-maximum (EM) algorithm, which needs spatial grouping step. In this paper, a modified EM algorithm is given, and a new color correction method of multi-view images is proposed. Experimental results show that the proposed method is quite effective.

D.-S. Huang, K. Li, and G.W. Irwin (Eds.): ICIC 2006, LNCS 4113, pp. 1224 – 1228, 2006.

## 2 New Color Correction Approach to Multi-view Images

For one pixel $(x,y)$ in image and its color value $I(x,y)$, let $\pi_k$ denote prior probability of mixture components, $\Theta=(\theta_1,\theta_2,\ldots,\theta_k)$ is parameter vectors for mixture components. Here, Gaussian mixture model is used, and $\theta_k=(\mu_k, \sum_k)$ is mean and variance of Gaussian distribution. Then, probability density function of $I(x,y)$ is expressed as

$$P(I(x,y)|\Theta)=\sum_{k=1}^{K}\pi_k p_k(I(x,y)|\theta_k)\ . \tag{1}$$

To segment regions of image, an expectation-maximum (EM) algorithm is performed with two steps, that is, E-Step and M-Step.

**E-Step:**

$$p(k\mid I(x,y),\theta_k)=\pi_k^{'}p_k(I(x,y)\mid\theta_k)/\sum_{j=1}^{K}\pi_j^{'}p_j(I(x,y)\mid\theta_k) \tag{2}$$

**M-Step:**

$$\pi_k^{'}=\frac{1}{N}\sum_{i=1}^{N}p(k\mid I(x,y),\theta_k) \tag{3}$$

$$\mu_k^{t+1}=\sum_{i=1}^{N}x_i\,p(k\mid I(x,y),\theta_k)/\sum_{i=1}^{N}p(k\mid I(x,y),\theta_k) \tag{4}$$

$$\sum\nolimits_k^{t+1}=\frac{\sum_{i=1}^{N}p(k\mid I(x,y),\theta_k)(I(x,y)-\mu_k^{t+1})(I(x,y)-\mu_k^{t+1})}{\sum_{i=1}^{N}p(k\mid I(x,y),\theta_k)} \tag{5}$$

The E-step and M-step are iterated until convergence. The initial values in the above EM algorithm are calculated by $K$-means method. Traditionally, the clustering number is set manually, not adaptive to image content. To improve the implementation of EM algorithm, an adaptive clustering method in the EM algorithm is given in this paper. At the beginning, we assign the maximum clustering number $K_{max}$ and the minimum threshold $T_h$. EM algorithm is carried out to estimate the means and variances of $K_{max}$ clusters. If the means of two clusters are very approximate, that is $|\mu_i^t-\mu_j^t|<T_h$, then merge the two corresponding clusters and re-estimate the statistical parameters. We iterate the algorithm to estimate regions until no region mergence exists.

Lastly, a probability smoothing operation is performed for each pixel. If two pixels $I(x,y)$ and $I(x',y')$ have similar colors, they may be close in Gaussian distribution. Let $N(x,y)$ denote the neighborhood of $(x,y)$, $N$ be the total number of neighborhood pixels and $K_{cluster}$ be the clustering number. If $I(x,y)$ belongs to the region $K$, and its probability is larger than its neighborhood value, as described by

$$p(K\mid I(x,y),\theta_k)=\max\{p(k\mid I(x,y),\theta_k),0\le k<K_{cluster}\} \tag{6}$$

$$p(K\mid I(x,y),\theta_k)>>\sum_{(x',y')\in N(x,y)}p(K\mid I(x',y'),\theta_k)/N \tag{7}$$

For the current pixel (*x*,*y*), not belonging to the region *K*, a probability smoothing operation is performed to it, which is described as

$$p(k \mid I(x,y),\theta_k) = \frac{1}{N} \cdot \sum_{(x',y') \in N(x,y)} p(k \mid I(x',y'),\theta_k), \quad 0 \le k < K_{cluster} \tag{8}$$

After establishing probability model, region classification is automatically run by comparing probability value for every pixel in each region.

Let $I_c$ and $I_r$ be the reference image and the current viewpoint image, respectively. After region classification, $I_c$ and $I_r$ will be associated with a GMM denoted as $\{G_{c_i}(c_i;\mu_{c_i},\sigma_{c_i}) \mid 0<i\le K\}$ and $\{G_{r_j}(r_j;\mu_{r_j},\sigma_{r_j}) \mid 0<j\le K\}$. Mapping relationship such as $f(G_{r_j}) = G_{c_i}$ can be established. For *K* clustering number, there are (*K*!) types of mapping for the segmented regions between $I_r$ and $I_c$.

How to establish the best mapping relation will have large impact on vision impression of the corrected image. Here, we define a mapping function *f*(.) as the region correspondence in $I_r$ and $I_c$, using the similarity model in the respective regions as the mapping criterion. After obtaining the mapping function *f*(.) which maps Gaussian component from $\{G_{c_i}(c_i;\mu_{c_i},\sigma_{c_i}) \mid 0<i\le K\}$ to $\{G_{r_j}(r_j;\mu_{r_j},\sigma_{r_j}) \mid 0<j\le K\}$, we compute the corrected color of the pixel $I_c(x,y)$ in the current viewpoint image as

$$f(I_c(x,y)) = \frac{\sigma_{r_i}}{\sigma_{c_j}}(I_c(x,y) - \mu_{c_j}) + \mu_{r_i} \tag{9}$$

After the above operation is accomplished, all the viewpoint images will have consistent color appearances. To objectively evaluate the correction method, Euler distance between original image and corrected image is calculated. Firstly, *RGB* color space is transformed to normalized *rg* space, then Euler distance $D_{1,2}$ is denoted by

$$r = \frac{R}{R+G+B}, \quad g = \frac{G}{R+G+B}, \quad D_{1,2} = \sqrt{(\bar{r}_1 - \bar{r}_2)^2 + (\bar{g}_1 - \bar{g}_2)^2} \tag{10}$$

## 3 Experimental Results

In the experiments, multi-view video images, ‘golf1’ and ‘race1’, provided by KDDI Corp.[7], are used as test sets, in which the size of images is 320×240. The multi-view images were taken by a horizontal parallel camera configuration with eight viewpoints and 200mm camera interval. As an example, Fig.1 shows the ‘golf1’ multi-view video with eight original viewpoint images. Clearly, the color consistency among these eight original viewpoint images is poor because of lighting or imaging device. Thus, the color correction is necessary if these multi-view images will be used to render new virtual arbitrary viewpoint image. One camera view, which is close to the center of the camera setup, is chosen as the reference view. All other camera views are corrected so as to fit their color appearance to the chosen reference view.

Figs.2 shows the reference images, reference segmentation images, current viewpoint image, current segmentation images and the corrected images of 'golf1' and 'race1' test sets, respectively. The $5^{th}$ viewpoint image is considered as the reference image, while the other seven viewpoint images are corrected so as to get consistent color appearance with the reference image. From the figures, it is seen that the color appearance of corrected images is almost consistent with the reference images.

**Fig. 1.** Eight original viewpoint images of 'golf1'

(a) Reference image (b) Reference segmentation region (c) Current viewpoint image

(d) Current segmentation region (e) Corrected image (f) Comparison of Euler distances

**Fig. 2.** Color correction of 'golf1' multi-view images

In Fig.2(f), Euler distance between the reference image and original viewpoint image and Euler distance between the reference image and corrected image are compared. The corrected image's Euler distances are smaller than that of the original image, and Euler distances of the $2^{th}$, $3^{th}$, $4^{th}$ or $8^{th}$ viewpoint images is very close because of the color consistency between the original and the reference image.

## 4 Conclusions

Color inconsistency of multi-view images, simultaneously captured for a scene, is a major problem which is demanded to be solved in multi-view video systems, such as free viewpoint television and 3DTV. In this paper, we have proposed a color correction method of multi-view images based on region classification. We propose probabilistic segmentation, and model the set of regions as Gaussian Mixture Model. Experimental results show that the proposed method can be applied to correcting the color of viewpoint images on the basis of the color of reference image. In the future work, we will investigate how to effectively evaluate the correction method, speed up the correction process, and improve the accuracy.

## Acknowledgments

This work was supported by the Natural Science Foundation of China (grant 60472100), the Natural Science Foundation of Zhejiang Province (grant 601017, RC01057, Y105577), the Ningbo Science and Technology Project of China (grant 2004A610001, 2004A630002), and the Zhejiang Science and Technology Project of China (Grant 2004C31105).

## References

1. ISO/IEC JTC1/SC29/WG11, Survey of Algorithms Used for Multi-view Video Coding (MVC), MPEG2005/N6909, Hong Kong, (2005)
2. ISO/IEC JTC1/SC29/WG11, Report on 3DAV Exploration, document N5878 MPEG Meeting, Trondheim, Norway, (2003)
3. Rahman, Z., Jobson, D., Woodel, G.: Retinex Processing for Automatic Image Enhancement. Proc. of SPIE, Human Vision and Electronic Imaging, 2(4662) (2002) 390-401
4. Reinhard, E., Ashikhmin, M., Gooch, B. et al.: Color Transfer Between Images. IEEE Computer Graphics and Applications, 21(4) (2001)34-41
5. Fredembach, C., Schroder, M., Susstrunk, S.: Region-based Image Classification for Automatic Color Correction, Proc. IS&T 11th Color Imaging Conference, (2003) 59-65
6. Belongie, S., Carson, C., Greenspan, H., Malik, J.: Color- and Texture-based Image Segmentation Using EM and its Application to Content Based Image Retrieval. International Conferences on Computer Vision, (1998) 675-682
7. ISO/IEC JTC1/SC29/WG11, KDDI Multi-View Video Sequences for MPEG 2DAV Use, M10533, Munich, (2004)

# Research of Chaos Theory and Local Support Vector Machine in Effective Prediction of VBR MPEG Video Traffic


Heng-Chao Li[1,2], Wen Hong[2], Yi-Rong Wu[2], and Si-Jie Xu[3]

[1] Graduate School of Chinese Academy of Sciences, Beijing, 100080, P.R. China
lihengchao_78@163.com

[2] National Key Laboratory of Microwave Imaging Technology, Institute of Electronics, Chinese Academy of Sciences, Beijing, 100080, P.R. China
{whong, wyr}@mail.ie.ac.cn

[3] Graduate School of Southwest Jiaotong University, Chengdu, 610031, P.R. China
xsj928@163.com



**Abstract.** The highly bursty and time-variant characteristics of VBR MPEG video traffic make it more difficult to manage network resources, and lead to the significant reduction of network utilization. Dynamic bandwidth allocation scheme based on real-time prediction algorithms has been used to guarantee the Quality of Service (QoS). In this paper, chaos theory and local support vector machine in effective prediction of VBR MPEG video traffic is investigated. Experimental results show that our proposed scheme can effectively capture the dynamics and complexity of VBR MPEG video traffic.


## 1 Introduction

Multimedia applications such as video teleconferencing, home education, content-based image/video retrieval from large databases, and video-on-demand (VOD) have been emerged as major sources of traffic for a variety of high-speed networks. Since digital video demands large bandwidth requirements, several coding schemes (e.g. constant bit rate, variable bit rate) have been proposed to accomplish efficient video compression, which are generally based on MPEG standard in virtue of its generic structure and support for a broad range of applications. Among them, the variable bit rate (VBR) mode presents many advantages when compared to constant bit rate (CBR) one: (i) achieve shorter delay for the same average bit rate; (ii) guarantee the constant image/video quality. So most of MPEG video traffic are encoded and transmitted in VBR manner.

However, how to satisfy the corresponding Quality of Service (QoS) requirements such as low packet loss, guaranteed bandwidth and delay is a stringent problem, because the output rate of VBR encoders fluctuates according to video activity. If a static bandwidth allocation scheme based on peak rate is applied, a significant amount of bandwidth resource may be wasted. Consequently, the dynamic bandwidth allocation one is desirable according to the prediction of future video frame. And the more accurate the traffic prediction is, the more reliable the prevision of QoS is. Hence, modeling and prediction of VBR MPEG video traffic have become a critical issue and have received much attention in the literature [1-8].


D.-S. Huang, K. Li, and G.W. Irwin (Eds.): ICIC 2006, LNCS 4113, pp. 1229 – 1234, 2006.

Over the years, a variety of techniques have been developed to predict the VBR MPEG video traffic. Derived from the statistical analysis of VBR MPEG video traffic, the stochastic models such as first-order autoregressive (AR) [1], autoregressive moving average (ARMA) [2], and Gamma autoregressive (GAR) [3] were introduced to simulate the video sources. But most of them only can capture the short-range dependence of VBR traffic. The other type of technique is the online traffic prediction, which mainly includes adaptive filter algorithm [4], and neural network approach [5]. If the bandwidth reserved is at least equal to predicted value, only the errors in the prediction need to be buffered.

Nevertheless, the actual VBR MPEG video traffic exhibits high variability and long-range dependence (LRD) due to the evolution of scenes of different complexity and degrees of motion. The above-mentioned prediction techniques are still challenges for real-time video applications. Recently, Alkhatib and Krunz [6] investigate the chaotic behavior of VBR video traffic from the viewpoint of the sensitivity of the trajectories to initial conditions, the correlation coefficient, and the maximum Lyapunov exponent. The phase space characteristics of VBR video traffic are analyzed in [7]. The research of chaotic characteristics in VBR video traffic is also reported in our previous paper [8]. The results show that the frame sequence of VBR video traffic is chaotic. In this paper, chaos theory and local support vector machine in effective prediction of VBR MPEG video traffic is investigated. Experiments demonstrate that our proposed scheme can effectively capture the dynamics and complexity of VBR MPEG video traffic.

This paper is organized as follows. In Section 2, we briefly review the characteristics of VBR MPEG video traffic. Section 3 presents the proposed prediction algorithm of VBR video traffic, derived from the chaos theory and local support vector machine. In Section 4, the experimental results are given. Finally, Section 5 concludes this paper and expects the future work.

## 2 Characteristics of VBR MPEG Video Traffic

It is well known that MPEG is one of the most widely used video encoding standard due to its generic structure and support for a broad range of applications, whose encoder can compress a video signal at a constant picture quality, and produce a coded stream with variable bit rate. There types of frames are generated during compression, namely, I frame (Intra frame), P frame (Predictive frame), and B frame (Bidirectional Predictive frame). These frames are arranged in a deterministic periodic pattern called Group of Picture (GOP). The GOP pattern is characterized by two parameters: one is the frame distance $N$ between one I frame and the next I frame, the other is the frame distance $M$ from one I frame to the following P frame or two successive P frame. For instance, $M$=3 and $L$=12 will result in the following GOP pattern: IBBPBBPBBPBB. The video sequences of 'Star Wars' and 'Soccer' are selected as test benchmarks. The autocorrelation function and three-dimensional phase space are displayed in Figs. 1 and 2 (a)-(b) respectively.

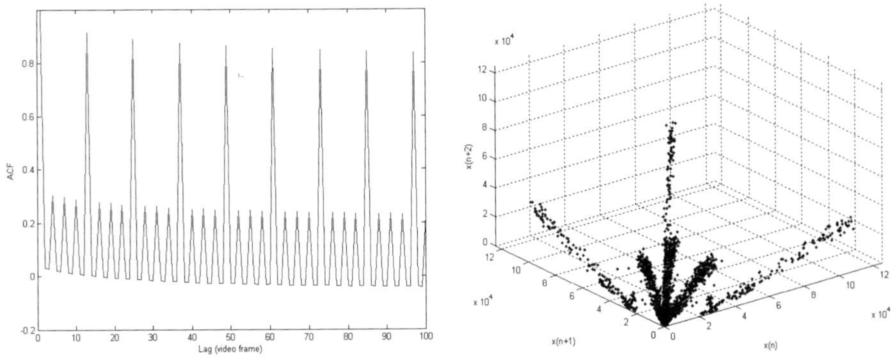


(a) (b)

**Fig. 1.** 'Star Wars': (a) autocorrelation function, (b) three-dimensional phase space

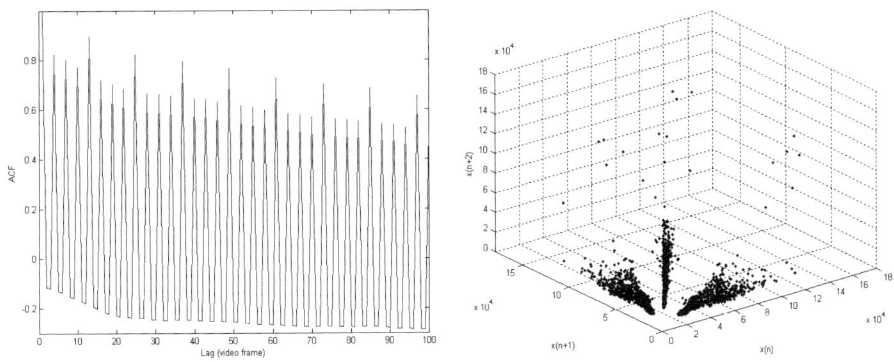


(a) (b)

**Fig. 2.** 'Soccer': (a) autocorrelation function, (b) three-dimensional phase space

From the Figs. 1 and 2 (a), we can see that the pattern between two I frame peaks is repeated with slowly decaying amplitude, which indicates the VBR video traffic is highly correlated and exhibit long-range dependence. Meanwhile, Figs. 1 and 2 (b) illustrate that VBR video traffic has the regular attractor, except several dissociative phase dots, who may imply the scene changes.

## 3 Proposed Prediction Algorithm of VBR MPEG Video Traffic

Chaos is the very complex behavior of a low-order dynamical system. It is possible to predict the chaotic time series if we can find the simple deterministic equation of chaos system. From the attractor reconstruction point of view, chaos theory and local support vector machine in effective prediction of VBR MPEG video traffic is investigated in this paper.

### 3.1 Phase Space Reconstruction

The important first step in predicting chaotic time series is the reconstruction of phase space of the time series. Such a reconstruction approach uses the concept of embedding a single-variable series in a multi-dimensional phase-space to represent the underlying dynamics.

According to the above-mentioned approach, for a scalar time series $\{x(t), t = 1,2,...,n\}$, the multi-dimensional phase-space can be reconstructed based on Takens' embedding theorem [9]:

$$X_i = \{x(i), x(i-\tau),...,x(i-(m-1)\tau)\} \tag{1}$$

where $i = (m-1)\tau + 1, (m-1)\tau + 2,...,n$, $\tau$ is the time delay; $m$ is the embedding phase space dimension, and the number of phase point is $N = n-(m-1)\tau$. If the time delay $\tau$ and the embedding dimension $m$ are selected appropriately, the reconstruction and the original system will have the same dynamic behavior.

### 3.2 Local Support Vector Machine

The basic idea of support vector machines (SVM) for regression is to map the data $x$ into a high dimensional feature space via a nonlinear mapping, and perform a linear regression in this feature space. The SVM training procedure amounts to solving the following convex QP problem, so the final regression solution has the following form:

$$f(x) = \sum_{i=1}^{l} (\alpha_i - \alpha_i^*) K(x_i, x) + b \tag{2}$$

where $\alpha_i$, $\alpha_i^*$ are Lagrange multipliers, and $K(x_i, x) = \phi(x_i)\cdot\phi(x)$.

Taken into account that SVM is suitable to the modeling of the small sample size datum, and combined with local methods, a new local prediction using support vector machine are given as follows [10]:

1. For a time series $\{x(t), t = 1,2,\cdots,n\}$, selecting the embedding dimension $m$ and time delay $\tau$, and reconstructing phase space based on expression (1).

2. Choosing Euclidian distance $\|\bullet\|$ as the distance metric in phase space, and finding the $k$ nearest neighbors $\{X_t^1, X_t^2, \cdots, X_t^k\}$ of $X_t$ through calculating the Euclidian distance between the query vector $X_t$ and the foregoing reconstruction vector $X_i$:

$$R(X_t, X_i) = \|X_t - X_i\| = \sqrt{\sum_{j=1}^{m} [x(t-(j-1)\tau) - x(i-(j-1)\tau)]^2} \tag{3}$$

where $i = 1,2,\cdots,(t-1)$.

3. Regarding each neighbor $X_t^l, l = 1,2,\cdots,k$ as a coordinate point in the input-space of support vector machine and $x(t_l + T), l = 1,2,\cdots,k$ as the target value, and training support vector machine to obtain support vectors and corresponding weight coefficients.

4. Calculating the prediction value $x(t+T)$ of the query vector $X_t$ based on local support vector machine prediction model obtained above.

5. Repeating the first four steps until the future values of different query vectors are all acquired.

The research results of reference [10] show that local support vector machine is insensitive to the selection of embedding dimension and the number of nearest neighbors, and also can save computational time and memory space compared to the global support vector machine.

## 4 Simulation Results

In this section, we select 2000 frames each of 'Star Wars' and 'Soccer' as the experimental data, which are frame-size traces generated from UC Berkeley MPEG-1 encoder software [11]. They represent a variety of video scenes such as action movie, and sports. The GOP pattern all are IBBPBBPBBPBB ($M$=3 and $L$=12).

For the experimental data, the first 1800 frames serve as the training set, and the remaining 200 frames as the test set. Considering that the local support vector machine is insensitive to the selection of embedding dimension and the number of nearest neighbors [10], and referring to the shapes of attractor, and the GOP pattern for VBR video traffic, we set the embedding phase space dimension $m$ to 12, which may be only larger than the minimal value. And the time delay $\tau$ is 1. The radial-basis function kernel is used as local learning machine to implement local prediction of VBR MPEG video traffic.

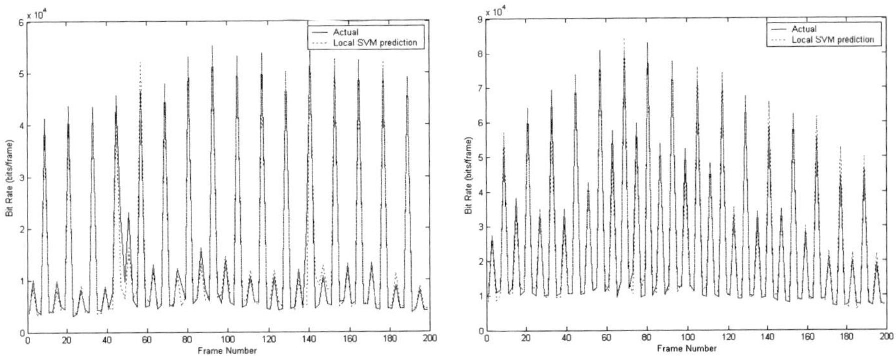


(a) (b)

**Fig. 3.** Predicted results: (a) 'Star Wars', (b) 'Soccer'

Simulation results of 'Star Wars' and 'Soccer' VBR video traffic using our proposed method are shown in Figs. 3 (a) and (b), respectively. As can be seen from Fig. 3, the predicted frame sequences are very close to the original and display no time delay. If a dynamic bandwidth allocation scheme based on prediction is applied, only the mild and stationary residuals need to be buffered for bandwidth reservation, and small buffers, less delay, and high channel utilization can be achieved.

## 5 Conclusions and Future Work

In this paper, we have proposed a new and effective prediction scheme of VBR MPEG video traffic. Combined with phase space reconstruction, local support vector machine is employed as the prediction model of VBR video traffic considering its good generalization performance, the absence of local minima, and computational advantage. Our experimental results demonstrate that our proposed scheme can effectively capture the dynamics and complexity of VBR MPEG video traffic. Further, we will carry out the corresponding network simulation and queue analysis to investigate the QoS (such as bandwidth allocation, time delay, jitter and packet loss).

## References

1. Maglaris, B., Anastassiou, D., Sen, P., Karlsson, G., Robbins, J.D.: Performance Models of Statistical Multiplexing in Packet Video Communications. IEEE Trans. Commun. 36 (1988) 834-843
2. Grunenfelder, R., Cosmas, J., Manthorpe, S., Okafor, A.O.: Characterization of Video Codecs as Autoregressive Moving Average Process and Related Queuing System Performance. IEEE J. Select. Areas Comun. 9 (1991) 284-293
3. Xu, S.G., Huang, Z.L.: A Gamma Autoregressive Video Model on ATM Networks. IEEE Trans. Circuits Syst. Video Technol. 8 (1998) 138-142
4. Adas, A.M.: Using Adaptive Linear Prediction to Support Real-Time VBR Video Under RCBR Network Service Model. IEEE Trans. Networking. 6 (1998) 635-644
5. Doulamis, A.D., Doulamis, N.D., Kollias, S.D.: An Adaptable Neural-Network Model for Recursive Nonlinear Traffic Prediction and Modeling of MPEG Video Sources. IEEE Trans. Neural Networks. 14 (2003) 150-166
6. Alkhatib, A., Krunz, M.: Application of Chaos Theory to the Modeling of Compressed Video. In Proc. IEEE Int. Conf. on Communications. (2000) 836-840
7. Chodorek, A., Chodorek, R.R.: An MPEG-2 Video Traffic Prediction Based on Phase Space Analysis and Its Application to On-line Dynamic Bandwidth Allocation. In Proc. 2nd Eur. Conf. Universal Multiservice Networks. (2002) 44-55
8. Li, H.C., Zhang, J.S., Wang, J.Y.: The Research of Chaotic Characteristics in VBR video Traffic. Tie Dao Xue Bao. 25 (2003) 56-60
9. Takens, F.: Detecting Strange Attractors in Turbulence. Dynamical Systems and Turbulence. (1981) 366-381
10. Li, H.C., Zhang, J.S.: Local Prediction of Chaotic Time Series Based on Support Vector Machine. Chinese Physics Letters. 22 (2005) 2776-2779
11. 2005. [Online]. Availabe: http://www3.informatic.uni-wuerzburg.de/~rose/

# A New Principal Curve Algorithm for Nonlinear Principal Component Analysis

David Antory[1], Uwe Kruger[2], and Tim Littler[3]

[1] International Automotive Research Centre, University of Warwick, Coventry, CV4 7AL, U.K.
D.Antory@warwick.ac.uk
[2] Intelligent Systems and Control Group, Queen's University Belfast, BT9 5AH, U.K.
uwe.kruger@ee.qub.ac.uk
[3] Energy Systems Research Group, Queen's University Belfast, BT9 5AH, U.K.
t.littler@ee.qub.ac.uk

**Abstract.** This paper summarizes a new concept to determine principal curves for nonlinear principal component analysis (PCA). The concept is explained within the framework of the Hastie and Stuetzle algorithm and utilizes spline functions. The paper proposes a new algorithm and shows that it provides an efficient method to extract underlying information from measured data. The new method is geometrically simple and computationally expedient, as the number of unknown parameters increases linearly with the analyzed variable set. The utility of the algorithm is exemplified in two examples.

## 1 Introduction

Redundant information is a common issue in industrial data. The analysis of such data provides an important basis to determine the performance of safety-critical systems, for example those found in the power, manufacturing and chemical industry. Data-driven analysis tools have also found applications in non-safety critical systems, for instance in addressing inefficient operation, detecting abnormal behavior and process faults.

In the proposed context, Multivariate Statistical Process Control (MSPC) has emerged as a suitable framework for data analysis [7,12]. MSPC commonly employs projection-based methods to remove redundant information in the data and produce a reduced set of score variables. However, these methods assume a linear relationship between the measured variables, an assumption that is often only satisfied when the data are recorded within a small operating regime.

To address this shortcoming, numerous nonlinear extensions of MSPC tools have been proposed [6,8,2,11,4]. Since PCA has received considerable attention in the literature based on its conceptual simplicity, this paper focuses in particular on the application of nonlinear PCA (NLPCA). Nonlinear extensions to PCA include principal curves [3] and autoassociative neural networks (ANN) [6]. Irrespective of which NLPCA implementation is considered, each method comprises a *projection* and a *self-consistency* stage.

Although a number of applications show the usefulness of principal curves, it is difficult to implement in practice if the number of analyzed variables exceed 3 [14],

D.-S. Huang, K. Li, and G.W. Irwin (Eds.): ICIC 2006, LNCS 4113, pp. 1235 – 1246, 2006.

despite the fact that principal curves offer a simple geometrical interpretation. In contrast, ANNs produce nonlinear score variables, irrespective of how many variables are analyzed, however, their geometry is difficult to interpret.

This paper proposes an alternative principal curve algorithm that does not suffer from the inherent limitations of the algorithm by Hastie and Stuetzle [3]. The new approach is based on the use of spline functions [13], which define the principal curve. For the new algorithm, the calculation of scores is described in the projection stage, whilst the determination of the spline parameters is based on the self-consistency stage.

This paper is organized as follows. A brief introduction to principal curves is given in Section 2 prior to a discussion of associated problems with the algorithm by Hastie and Stuetzle [3]. Section 4 gives a detailed description of the new algorithm and Section 5 presents two simulation examples to demonstrate the working of the new technique, followed by a concluding summary in Section 6.

## 2 Principal Curve Preliminaries

A principal curve is a non-parametric approach, whereby the nature of the data determines the shape of the curve. This is an iterative approach, whereby the initial curve is represented by the first principal direction of a linear PCA model of the data [10]. The curve at each successive iteration is a smooth or local average for a given set of points $\boldsymbol{x} \in \mathbb{R}^d$. The curve is initially segmented and a centre of gravity is obtained for each segment. The curve passes through each centre and the boundaries determine which segment a corresponding data point belongs to are updated, followed by re-computing each segment centre. This completes one full iteration step. The algorithm subsequently converges when the difference of two consecutive curves is negligible.

Figure 1 shows various curves designs for a given data set. Let $\xi(t) \in \mathbb{R}^d$ be a principal curve in a $d$-dimensional space, where $t$ is the curve parameter and $\xi^T(t) = \begin{pmatrix} \xi_1(t) & \xi_2(t) & \cdots & \xi_d(t) \end{pmatrix}$. For any data point, $\mathbf{x}$, let the *projection index* $\boldsymbol{t}_f(\boldsymbol{x})$ denote the largest parameter value $t$ for which the distance between $\mathbf{x}$ and $\xi(t)$ is minimized as follows:

$$\boldsymbol{t}_f(\boldsymbol{x}) = \sup\left\{t : \left\|\boldsymbol{x} - \xi(t)\right\|_2 = \inf_{\tau} \left\|\boldsymbol{x} - \xi(\tau)\right\|_2\right\} \tag{1}$$

The smooth curve $\xi(t)$ is a principal curve *if and only if*:

- $\xi(\cdot)$ does not intercept itself;
- $\xi(\cdot)$ has a finite length inside any bounded subset of $\mathbb{R}^d$; and
- $\xi(\cdot)$ is self-consistent, that is $\xi(t) = E\left\{\boldsymbol{x} \mid \boldsymbol{t}_f(\boldsymbol{x}) = t\right\}$.

Hastie and Stuetzle [3] summarized the principal curve algorithm, denoted here as HS algorithm, of a data set with a known probability density function as shown in Algorithm 1.

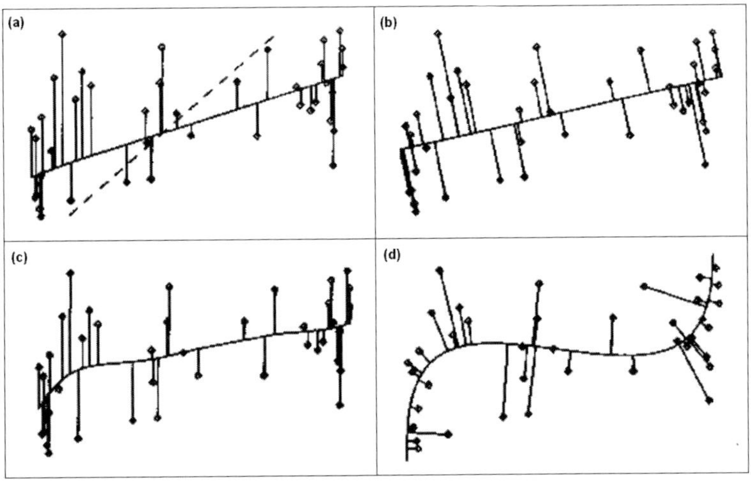


**Fig. 1.** Various types of curves in a 2D plane; (a) linear regression model, (b) linear principal component model, (c) nonlinear regression model and (d) principal curve model

1. Start with $\xi^0(t) = E(\boldsymbol{x}) + \boldsymbol{a}t$ where $\boldsymbol{a}$ is the *first linear principal component direction* of the covariance matrix of $\boldsymbol{x}$. Set $\boldsymbol{t}^0(\boldsymbol{x}) = \boldsymbol{t}_{\xi^0}(\boldsymbol{x})$ for each $\mathbf{x}$. Set $n$ = 1
2. Define $\xi^n(t) = E\left\{\boldsymbol{x} \middle| \boldsymbol{t}_{\xi^{n-1}}(\boldsymbol{x}) = t\right\}$ for each $n$
3. Set
   $\boldsymbol{t}_{\xi^n}(\boldsymbol{x}) = \max\left\{t : \left\|\boldsymbol{x} - \xi^n(t)\right\|_2\right.$
   $\left. = \min_\tau \left\|\boldsymbol{x} - \xi^n(\tau)\right\|_2\right\} \forall \boldsymbol{x} \in \mathbb{R}^d$
4. Compute $\Delta(\xi^n) = E\left\{\left\|\boldsymbol{x} - \xi^n(\boldsymbol{t}_{\xi^n}(\boldsymbol{x}))\right\|\right\}^2$, if $\left|\Delta(\xi^n) - \Delta(\xi^{n-1})\right| < \varepsilon$ *(threshold)* then stop
5. Otherwise $n = n + 1$ and repeat step (2) until *convergence*

**Algorithm 1.** HS principle curve

## 3 Problems with the HS Algorithm

Several authors have raised concerns with respect to the HS algorithm. For example, Kegl *et al.* [5] argued that a principal curve only exists for special densities such as radially symmetric or an annulus in a plane. Apart from that, it is unknown how the hypothetical HS algorithm behaves for a probability density for which a principal curve does not exist. Consequently, it is theoretically difficult to analyze the consistency and convergence rate of any estimation schemes for principal curves.

A study by Tibshirani [10] outlined a bias in determining the principal curve using the HS algorithm. Hence, new theoretical developments are required to address these problems [10,5,1]. Additionally, Zhang [14] outlined that the 2D concept of principal curves is difficult to extend to a $d$-dimensional space. This relates to the difficulty in associating a set of data points to a particular segment of the curve if $d$ exceeds 2 or 3.

The next section introduces a new algorithm that is (i) conceptually simpler, (ii) has a guaranteed convergence and (iii) is not restricted by any dimension $d$ in comparison to the HS algorithm.

## 4 Spline Principal Curve Algorithm

This section details the proposed spline principal curve algorithm. The curve is reconstructed by a number of smooth spline functions. Whilst this is a well-known area that has produced many research contributions, this paper brings this body of knowledge into a PCA framework to determine a reduced set of nonlinear principal components.

For simplicity, the introduction of the technique is based on two variables, denoted here as $x_1$ and $x_2$ and two spline functions only. This is not a restriction of generality, as the extension to include more variables and splines is straightforward, which is elaborated upon later on in this section. A graphical representation of an example curve:

$$\begin{pmatrix} x_1 \\ x_2 \end{pmatrix} = \begin{pmatrix} t \\ \sin(t) \end{pmatrix} + \begin{pmatrix} e_1 \\ e_2 \end{pmatrix} = \xi(t) + \boldsymbol{e} \tag{2}$$

is given below.

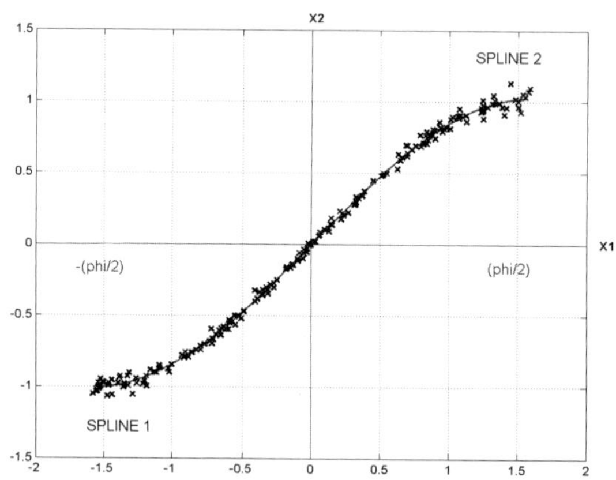


**Fig. 2.** Representation of $\xi(t)$ for 500 data points

In this example, $t \in [-\pi/2\ \pi/2]$ is a random variable and $e_1$ and $e_2 \in \mathcal{N}\{0,0.01\}$ are residuals, representing measurement uncertainty. Moreover, $\xi(t)$ is reconstructed here by two splines, that is Spline 1 for $x_1 \in [-\pi/2\ 0]$ and Spline 2 for $x_2 \in (0\ \pi/2]$. Note that a round bracket indicates an open interval, i.e. not including 0 in Spline 2, whilst a squared bracket represents a close interval, i.e. including 0 in Spline 1.

Subsection 4.1 summarizes some preliminaries regarding the spline functions used here. This is followed by introduction to an algorithm detailing the transformation from a higher to a lower dimensional space to produce nonlinear scores (*projection stage*) in Section 4.2. Subsection 4.3 gives an overview of how the spline functions are identified and utilised to transform the nonlinear scores back to the original data space (*self-consistency stage*). Section 4.4 discusses extensions of the proposed algorithm for more than 2 variables and splines including the determination of more than 1 principal curve. Finally, Section 4.5 provides a comparison between the new algorithm and the HS algorithm by Hastie and Stuetzle [3].

### 4.1 Preliminaries

The splines functions used in this work are third order polynomials of the form:

$$\xi_{ij}(t) = a_3^{(ij)} t^3 + a_2^{(ij)} t^2 + a_1^{(ij)} t + a_0^{(ij)} \tag{3}$$

where $j$ and $i$ denote the spline number and original variable, $x_i$, respectively, and $a_3^{(ij)} \cdots a_0^{(ij)}$ are the associated spline parameters. At any knot of two splines, the following condition must be met to guarantee a smooth curve:

$$\begin{bmatrix} t_j^3 & t_j^2 & t_j & 1 & -t_j^3 & -t_j^2 & -t_j & -1 \\ 3t_j^2 & 2t_j & 1 & 0 & -3t_j^2 & -2t_j & -1 & 0 \\ 6t_j & 2 & 0 & 0 & -6t_j & -2 & 0 & 0 \end{bmatrix} \begin{pmatrix} a_3^{(j)} \\ a_2^{(j)} \\ a_1^{(j)} \\ a_0^{(j)} \\ a_3^{(j+1)} \\ a_2^{(j+1)} \\ a_1^{(j+1)} \\ a_0^{(j+1)} \end{pmatrix} = \begin{pmatrix} 0 \\ 0 \\ 0 \end{pmatrix} \tag{4}$$

Here, $t_j$ is the parameter value for the $j$th knot. The spline functions, $\xi_{(\cdot)}^{(j)}$, are assumed here to be determined by one of the variables, for example $x_1$, as the parameter. This implies that the function $\xi_{1j}(\cdot)$ is equal to $x_1$ $\forall\ j$ and the function $\xi_{2j}(\cdot)$ depends on this parameter, i.e.

$$\xi_{(x_1)}^{(j)} = \begin{pmatrix} x_1 \\ \xi_{2j}(x_1) \end{pmatrix} = \begin{pmatrix} x_1 \\ a_3^{(2j)} x_1^3 + a_2^{(2j)} x_1^2 + a_1^{(2j)} x_1 + a_0^{(2j)} \end{pmatrix} \tag{5}$$

Given the definition of the principal curve above, the nonlinear score variables, $t$, can be obtained as:

$$t = \int_0^{x_1} \left\| \xi'_{(\hat{x}_1)} \right\|_2 dx_1 = \int_0^{x_1} \sqrt{1 + \xi_2'^2 (x_1)} dx_1 \tag{6}$$

where $(\cdot)'$ denotes the derivative of a curve and $\|\cdot\|_2$ is the norm of a vector. Given the assumptions imposed on a principal curve, outlined in Section 2, there is a unique solution to Equation (6). Furthermore, it is assumed that the function between $t$ and $x_1$ is bijective, so that $t$ can be expressed as a function of $x_1$ and $x_1$ can alternatively be formulated as a function of $t$. This implies that the $j$th spline function $\xi_{(x_1)}^{(j)}$ is equivalent to $\xi_{(t)}^{(j)}$. Next, the projection and the self-consistency stages of the new algorithm are outlined.

## 4.2 Projection Stage

The projection stage, i.e. transformation of a point $\boldsymbol{x}$ in the original variable space onto the principal curve, is carried out by defining the following orthogonal projection that is illustrated in Figure 3. The smallest distance between $\boldsymbol{x}$ and the curve $\xi(\cdot)$ is given by the error vector $\boldsymbol{e}$ that is orthogonal to the principal curve, i.e.:

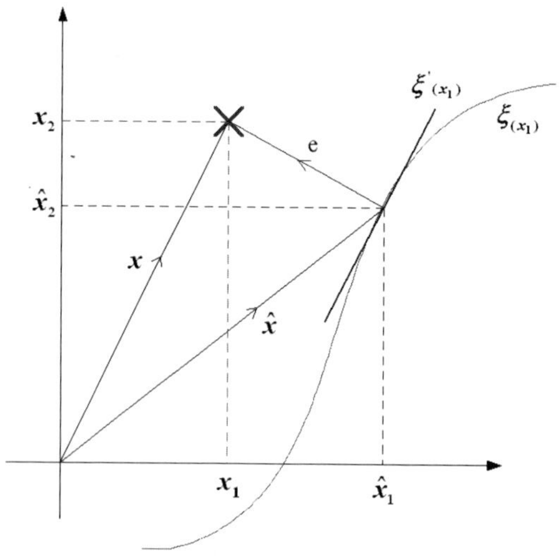


**Fig. 3.** Orthogonal projection of a data point, **x**, onto the principal curve

$$\xi'^T (\boldsymbol{x} - \xi) = 0 \tag{7}$$

Or

$$x_1 - \hat{x}_1 + \xi_2' (\hat{x}_1) (x_2 - \xi_2 (\hat{x}_1)) = 0 \tag{8}$$

where $\hat{x}_1$ and $\hat{x}_2 = f(\hat{x}_1)$ are the projections of $\mathbf{x}^T = (x_1 \ x_2)$ onto the principal curve. This has to be evaluated for each spline to determine the smallest distance of $\mathbf{x}$ from the curve. Equation (8) can be satisfied by application of the Newton-Raphson algorithm. After determining $\hat{x}_1$, such that $\mathbf{e}$ is minimized, the value of the score variable $t$ can now be determined as $t = \int_0^{\hat{x}_1} \left\| \xi'_{(\hat{x}_1)} \right\|_2 d\hat{x}_1$. This iteration represents the definition of the projection index $\boldsymbol{t}_f(\boldsymbol{x})$ to calculate $t$.

### 4.3 Self-consistency

Thus far, it is assumed that the principal curve is predetermined and comprises a number of 3rd order splines. Given the restriction to two variables, the values of the score variable can be obtained as previously discussed and the reconstruction, i.e. the transformation back to the original data space, is:

$$\begin{pmatrix} \hat{x}_1 \\ \hat{x}_2 \end{pmatrix} = \begin{pmatrix} \hat{x}_1 \\ \xi_j(\hat{x}_1) \end{pmatrix}; \quad \begin{pmatrix} x_1 \\ x_2 \end{pmatrix} - \begin{pmatrix} \hat{x}_1 \\ \xi_j(\hat{x}_1) \end{pmatrix} = \begin{pmatrix} \varepsilon_1 \\ \varepsilon_2 \end{pmatrix} \tag{9}$$

where $\varepsilon_1$ and $\varepsilon_2$ are residuals that are assumed to have the same variance as the original residuals $e_1$ and $e_2$ which is significantly smaller than the variance of $\hat{x}_1$ and $\xi_2(\hat{x}_1)$. Note that Equation (9) has to be evaluated for each spline function to guarantee that the length of the vector $\boldsymbol{\varepsilon}^T = (\varepsilon_1 \ \varepsilon_2)$ is minimal. The determination of the curve is discussed next.

To determine the set of parameters for each spline function, i.e. $a_3^{(21)} \ \cdots \ a_0^{(22)}$, the following optimization must be carried out:

$$\left\| E\left\{ \varepsilon\varepsilon^T \right\} \right\|_2^2 = \min_{\boldsymbol{a}} \left\| E\left\{ \left(\boldsymbol{x} - \xi(\hat{x}_1)\right)\left(\boldsymbol{x} - \xi(\hat{x}_1)\right)^T \right\} \right\|_2^2 \tag{10}$$

where $E\{\cdot\}$ is the expectation operator, $E\{\boldsymbol{\varepsilon\varepsilon}^T\}$ is the covariance matrix of $\boldsymbol{\varepsilon}$, $\|\cdot\|_2$ represents, in this case, the Frobenius norm of a matrix and $\boldsymbol{a}$ is vector storing the parameters for each spline. Based on Equation (4), including the constraints, produces a total of 5 unknown parameters for two splines. In this work, we propose the use of the genetic algorithm (GA) by Sharma and Irwin [9] to determine the unknown parameters using Algorithm 2. It should be noted that the preference of a GA over a gradient descent technique is based on the fact that the GA is less likely to determine a local minima and show convergence problems.

Next, it is shown how the proposed algorithm is applicable to cases including more than 2 recorded variables, which may require the determination of more than one principal curve to accurately represent the underlying relationships between these variables.

1. Find the initial parameters set by projecting the data points orthogonally to the $x_1$-axis and using a standard least squares technique.
2. Define boundaries for each parameter centred around the initial parameter set.
3. Establish an initial population (chromosomes) in the parameter space.
4. Compute the cost-function $\left\| \frac{1}{K-1} \sum_{k=1}^{K} \left( \boldsymbol{x}_k - \xi(\hat{x}_{k1}) \right) \left( \boldsymbol{x}_k - \xi(\hat{x}_{k1}) \right)^T \right\|_2^2$ for each chromosome, where $k$ is a sample index and $K$ represents the total number of samples.
5. Carry out crossover and mutation to establish the next generation (chromosomes).
6. Continue with Step 4 until the maximum number of generations is computed otherwise terminate optimisation

**Algorithm 2.** Definition of new principal curve algorithm

### 4.4 Extension of the New Algorithm to Include More Then 2 Variables and 1 Principal Curve

In cases that involve $d$ variables, the $j$th spline function is given by Equation (11)

$$\xi_{(\hat{x}_1)}^{(j)} = \begin{pmatrix} \hat{x}_1 \\ \xi_{2,j}(\hat{x}_1) \\ \vdots \\ \xi_{d,j}(\hat{x}_1) \end{pmatrix} \tag{11}$$

As before, the functions $\xi_{ij}(\cdot)$ are 3[rd] order polynomials and $\hat{x}_1$ as well as the score variable can be obtained using the Newton-Raphson algorithm and an extended version of Equation (6). For determining the score variable, Equation (6) becomes:

$$t = \int_0^{\hat{x}_1} \sqrt{1 + \sum_{i=2}^{d} \xi_i'^2(\hat{x}_1)} \, d\hat{x}_1 \tag{12}$$

If more than one principal curve is required to adequately reconstruct the $d$-dimensional data space, the information encapsulated in the first principal curve must be subtracted (deflated) from the original data set:

$$\begin{bmatrix} \boldsymbol{x}_1^T \\ \boldsymbol{x}_2^T \\ \vdots \\ \boldsymbol{x}_k^T \\ \vdots \\ \boldsymbol{x}_K^T \end{bmatrix}_1 = \begin{bmatrix} \boldsymbol{x}_1^T \\ \boldsymbol{x}_2^T \\ \vdots \\ \boldsymbol{x}_k^T \\ \vdots \\ \boldsymbol{x}_K^T \end{bmatrix}_0 - \begin{bmatrix} \xi_{(\hat{x}_{11})}^T \\ \xi_{(\hat{x}_{21})}^T \\ \vdots \\ \xi_{(\hat{x}_{k1})}^T \\ \vdots \\ \xi_{(\hat{x}_{K1})}^T \end{bmatrix}; \; \boldsymbol{X}_1 = \boldsymbol{X}_0 - \xi_{(\hat{x}_1)}^T \tag{13}$$

where the indices 0 and 1 refer to the original data and the residuals after the variation captured by the first principal curve has been deflated, respectively. Using the residual matrix $\boldsymbol{X}_1$, the next principal curve can be computed using Algorithm 2. If further curves are to be computed, determine $\boldsymbol{X}_2 = = \boldsymbol{X}_1 - {}_2\xi^T_{({}_2\hat{x}_1)}$ and obtain the 3rd curve and so on.

This produces an iterative algorithm that is similar to the NIPALS algorithm for linear PCA. Note that the principal curves successively determined are denoted by ${}_1\xi_{({}_0\hat{x}_1)}$ for the first curve, ${}_2\xi_{({}_1\hat{x}_1)}$ for the second curve and so on. Furthermore, the index 0 refers to the original data, whilst the indices 1, 2, … denote the data after 1, 2, … deflation steps.

The final issue that has not yet been addressed is how to determine the number of splines and particularly the knots between them. This paper proposes the following iterative design technique and suggests concentrating on this issue in future work. Note that the number of unknown parameters, $p$, is given by $m$ + 3, with $m$ being the number of splines.

The iterative technique commences by ranking the entries in the matrix $\boldsymbol{X}_0$ with respect to the values in first column, i.e. the values associated with the variable $x_1$. Then, two spline functions are defined by equally spacing the range defined by the observations representing $x_1$. Then apply Algorithm 2 to determine the parameters for each spline functions, followed by division of one of the spline functions, for example the spline covering the first section, into two, considering the parameters of the other spline function as known. Apply Algorithm 2 again to determine the parameters of the two remaining splines.

The performance of the increase in spline numbers is then benchmarked with the previous setting. If a significant reduction in residual variance can be felt for this region, a further division can be considered and so on. This division and subdivision is carried out until a satisfactory performance of the resultant principal curve is achieved with as few splines as possible.

### 4.5 Comparison with the HS Algorithm

The shortcomings of the HS algorithm are briefly summarized in Section 3. The most restrictive of these is the difficulty in determining a principal curve if the dimension of the data space exceeds 2 or 3. In contrast, the new algorithm does not suffer from this inherent limitation, as the minimum distance of each data point to each of the splines determines which spline a particular point is associated with.

As the number of splines can be altered, a large variety of smooth non-linear relationships between the recorded variables can be revealed. However, a more theoretical framework is required to investigate issues such as bias and consistency for the new algorithm, which is beyond the scope of this paper.

## 5 Examples

To exemplify the proposed principal curve algorithm two representative examples were prepared as simulation studies and are presented in this section. The simulated data comprised 200 observation points generated by a random number function, with a normal distribution $\mathcal{N}(0,1)$. A 2-dimensional example was chosen for simplicity, where the two generated variables, $x_1$ and $x_2$, represent the variable axes.

In both simulation examples variable $x_1$ was defined as $x_1 = t + 0.01e_2$ . In Example 1, $x_2$ was defined as $x_2 = -\arctan(t) + \sin(t)^3 + 0.05e_2$ , and in Example 2 $x_2 = \sin(t) + \cos(t) + t^2 + 0.13e_2$ . The sequences $e_1$ and $e_2$ were identically and independently distributed sequences of $\mathcal{N}(0,1)$.

Defining the knot between two splines as $x_1 = 0$, Figure 4 shows the principal curve algorithm applied to Example 1 simulation data, with the original data (x) and the projection data (+) over-plotted on the same axis. It is apparent that the principal curve determination, represented by the solid line in the middle of the data cloud, clearly approximates the optimal projection points of the original data.

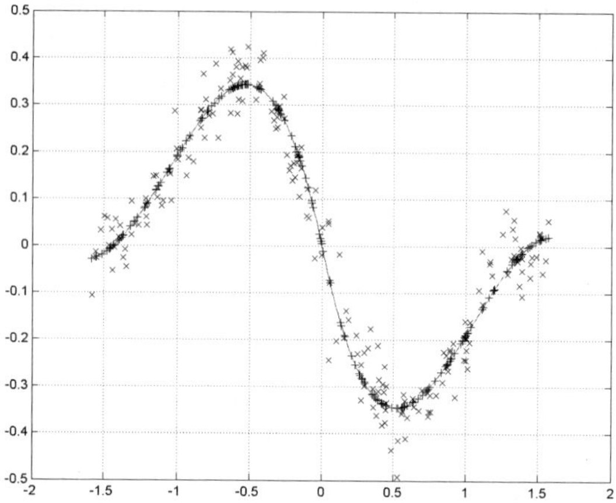


**Fig. 4.** Principal curve determination of Example 1

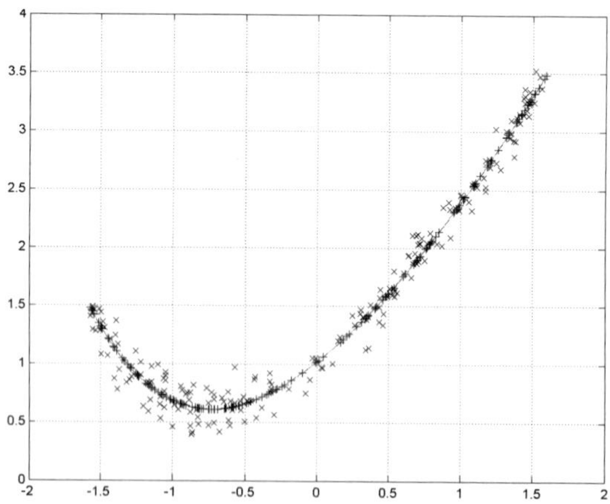


**Fig. 5.** Principal curve determination of Example 2

The same algorithm was used in Example 2, where the knot of two splines was also for $x_1 = 0$ (Figure 5). As in the previous example, the solid line principal curve determination provides a sufficiently accurate representation of the original data predominantly throughout the midpoints of the data cloud clusters.

## 6 Concluding Summary

This paper has proposed a new principal curve algorithm for nonlinear PCA using a polynomial model. Two 3rd order polynomial functions were used to produce a smooth spline curve capable of providing a robust determination of underlying data signature along the midpoints of the projected data.

In comparison to other contemporary techniques for nonlinear determination, such as artificial neural networks, the proposed algorithm has minimal complexity and is computationally expedient, as the number of unknown parameters grows linearly with an increase in the number of analyzed variables. The two simulation examples demonstrate that the spline principal curve determination provides an accurate representation of the underlying information contained within the simulated data. Further study is required to determine whether the proposed algorithm would equally provide faithful determination of simple measured data for a variable space that exceeds 2 or 3, although the groundwork is laid out in this paper.

As this paper forms part of ongoing research, further work is required to establish the broader capabilities of the proposed algorithm for more complex problems, for example in industrial processes, where latent underlying information in measured nonlinear data requires more than one principal curve to be determined. In comparison to the HS algorithm, the new algorithm provides a more general basis for principal curve determination in nonlinear PCA.

## References

1. Delicado, P.: Another Look at Principal Curves and Surfaces. Commun. Stat. Part. B Simul. Comput. 77 (2001) 84-116
2. Dong, D., McAvoy, T.J.: Non-Linear Principal Component Analysis – Based on Principal Curves and Neural Networks. Comp. Chem. Engng. 20 (1) (1996) 65-78
3. Hastie, T., Stuetzle. W.: Principal Curves. J. Am. Stat. Assoc. 84 (406) (1989) 502-517
4. Jia, F., Martin, E.B., Morris, A.J.: Non-Linear Principal Component Analysis with Applications to Process Fault Detection. Int. J. Syst. Sci. 31 (11) (2000) 1473-1487
5. Kegl, B., Krzyzak, A., Linder, T., Zeger, K.: Learning and Design of Principal Curves. IEEE Trans. Pattern. Anal. Mach. Intell. 22 (3) (2000) 281-297
6. Kramer, M.A.: Non-linear Principal Component Analysis using Auto-Associative Neural Networks. AIChE J, 37 (2) (1991) 233-243
7. MacGregor, J.F., Marlin, T.E., Kresta, J.V., Skagerberg, B.: Multivariate Statistical Methods in Process Analysis and Control. Proceedings of the 4th International Conference on Chemical Process Control, New York: AIChE Publ. No. P-67 (1991) 79-99
8. Qin, S.J., McAvoy, T.J.: Nonlinear PLS Modelling Using Neural Networks. Comp. Chem. Engng. 16 (4) (1992) 379-391
9. Sharma, S.K., Irwin, G.W.: Fuzzy Coding of Genetic Algorithms. IEEE Trans. Evol. Comput. 7 (4) (2003) 344 355

10. Tibshirani, R.: Principal Curves Revisited, Stat. Comput. 2 (1992) 183-190
11. Wilson, D.J.H., Irwin, G.W., Lightbody, G.: RBF Manifolds for Process Monitoring, IEEE Trans. Neural. Netw. 10 (6) (1999) 1424-1434
12. Wise, B.M., Gallagher, N.B.: The Process Chemometrics Approach to Process Monitoring and Fault Detection. J. Process. Control. 6 (6) (1996) 329- 348
13. Wold, S. (1974). Spline functions in data analysis. Technometrics, 16, 1-11
14. Zhang, F.: Identifying Nonlinear Variation Patterns in Multivariate Manufacturing Processes, Ph.D. Thesis, Texas A&M University (2004)

# Statistical Processes Monitoring Based on Improved ICA and SVDD

Lei Xie[1] and Uwe Kruger[2]

[1] National Key Laboratory of Industrial Control Technology, Institute of Advanced Process Control, Zhejiang University, Hangzhou 310027, P.R. China
leix@iipc.zju.edu.cn
[2] Intelligent Systems and Control Research Group, Queen's University Belfast, BT9 5AH, U.K.
uwe.kruger@ee.qub.ac.uk

**Abstract.** An industrial process often has a large number of measured variables, which are usually driven by fewer essential variables. An improved independent component analysis based on particle swarm optimization (PSO-ICA) is presented to extract these essential variables. Process faults can be detected more efficiently by monitoring the independent components. To monitor the non-Gaussian distributed independent components obtained by PSO-ICA, the one-class SVDD (Support Vector Data Description) is employed to find the separating boundary between the normal operational data and the rest of independent component feature space. The proposed approach is illustrated by the application to the Tennessee Eastman challenging process.

## 1 Introduction

With the development of instrumentation and automation, modern industrial processes present a large set of measured variables which are frequently recorded. These measurements provide useful signatures about the status of the process. In the last two decades, Multivariate Statistical Process Control (MSPC) technology has been proven to be efficient to extract information from the process data and to identify and diagnose the abnormal process behavior. Principal Component Analysis (PCA) is one of the most popular MSPC techniques. By identifying the linear correlation between the process variables, PCA projects the process data into the low-dimensional model space and residual subspaces. Hotelling's $T^2$ and SPE (squared prediction error) statistics are defined as the Mahalanobis and Euclidian distances in the model and residual subspaces, respectively. Violation of these statistics confidence limits indicates the abnormal process behavior. Although traditional PCA method has been applied to industrial processes successfully, it assumes that the process is operated under steady state and variables are normally distributed. These assumptions are not valid for many practical processes. Many improved algorithms have been proposed to address these problems, such as Dynamic PCA [1], Multiscale PCA [2], Nonlinear PCA [3] to name a few. The preparation of manuscripts which are to be reproduced by photo-offset requires special care. Papers submitted in a technically unsuitable form will be returned for retyping, or canceled if the volume cannot otherwise be finished on time.

D.-S. Huang, K. Li, and G.W. Irwin (Eds.): ICIC 2006, LNCS 4113, pp. 1247 – 1256, 2006.

However, these PCA based methods only employ second order statistical information. Independent component analysis (ICA), as a new signal processing technique, makes full use of high order statistical information, and can separate the statistically independent components from the observed variables. Li and Wang [5] used ICA to remove the dependencies among variables. Kano *et al.* [6] employed ICA to extract the independent variables from measured variables to detect fault, and obtained satisfying results. But their work did not concern random behaviors of ICA algorithms, i.e. the algorithms give different results according to different initial conditions [7]. For instance, the widely adopted FastICA algorithm [8] and the natural gradient algorithm [9] are carried out to optimize non-convex objective functions, i.e. negentropy and mutual information, but no global optimal solution is guaranteed.

In current study, we propose a novel PSO(Particle Swarm Optimization)-ICA based approach to address the global optimal analysis of independent component. PSO was first proposed by Kennedy and Eberhart [10] which simulates the simplified social life models. As a swarm intelligent technique and general global optimization tool, PSO has many advantages over other heuristic techniques such as it can be easily implemented and has great capability of escaping local optimal solution [11]. The constrained optimization problem, which is typically encountered with conventional ICA, is converted to an unconstrained problem with the orthogonal projection approach. Then the PSO is employed to solve the unconstrained problem and extract the independent components (IC) from the process data.

To monitor the independent components obtained by PSO-ICA, it is inappropriate to derive Hotelling's $T^2$ and SPE statistics as PCA does because the independent components do not follow the Gaussian distribution. In this paper, we employ the one-class SVDD (Support Vector Data Description) to find the separating boundary between the normal operational data and the rest of independent component feature space.

The remainder of this paper is structured as follows. Section 2 describes the proposed PSO-ICA algorithm in which a scheme is presented to convert traditional constrained ICA to a constraint free version. How to obtain the normal operation boundary in the IC feature space and to tune the parameters of SVDD is given in section 3. Section 4 gives monitoring results of the application to Tennessee Eastman process. Finally, section 5 concludes with an assessment of the suggested approach.

# 2 Independent Components Analysis Based on PSO

## 2.1 Independent Component Analysis Formulation

ICA is a statistical signal processing technique that transforms the observed data to the linear combination of source signals (or independent components) which are non-gaussian and mutually independent.

With the assumption of the existence of $m$ independent source signals $\mathbf{s}=[s_1,s_2,,s_m]^T$ and the observations of $n$ mixtures $\mathbf{x}=[x_1,x_2,,x_n]^T$, these mixtures being linear and instantaneous:

$$\mathbf{x} = \mathbf{A} \cdot \mathbf{s} . \tag{1}$$

where $\mathbf{A} \in \Re^{n\times m}$ matrix contains the mixture coefficients.

ICA problem can be formulated as the computation of a separating matrix $\mathbf{W} \in \Re^{m \times n}$ whose output is an estimation of the source signals $\mathbf{s}$ :

$$\hat{\mathbf{s}} = \mathbf{W} \cdot \mathbf{x} = \mathbf{W} \cdot \mathbf{A} \cdot \mathbf{s} \approx \mathbf{s} \tag{2}$$

where $\hat{\mathbf{s}}$ has zero mean and standard variation.

For the sake of computation efficiency, the mixed signals $\mathbf{x}$ is whitened first, i.e. the cross correlation between entries of $\mathbf{x}$ is eliminated:

$$\mathbf{z} = \mathbf{Q}\mathbf{x} \in \Re^{r} \tag{3}$$

where $\mathbf{Q} \in \Re^{r \times n}$ is the whitening matrix and $r \in [m, n]$ is the number of retained whitened signals. After the whitening process, Eq.(3) can be expressed as:

$$\hat{\mathbf{s}} = \mathbf{B}^{T}\mathbf{z} \tag{4}$$

ICA calculates the matrix $\mathbf{B} \in \Re^{r \times m}$ which maximizes the nongaussianity of the projection $\hat{\mathbf{s}} = \mathbf{B}^{T}\mathbf{z}$ under the constraint of $\|\mathbf{b}_i\| = \sqrt{\mathbf{b}_i^{T}\mathbf{b}_i} = 1$ and $\mathbf{b}_i \perp \mathbf{b}_j$ , $\forall 1 \le i \ne j \le m$, where $\mathbf{b}_i$ is $i$ th column of $\mathbf{B}$ , i.e. $\mathbf{b}_i$ is the solution of the following optimization problem:

$$\begin{aligned} \mathbf{b}_i &= \underset{a \in \Re^{r}}{\operatorname{argmax}} \ J(\mathbf{a}^{T}\mathbf{z}) \\ s.t. \ & \|\mathbf{a}\| = 1, \mathbf{a} \perp \mathbf{b}_1, \mathbf{a} \perp \mathbf{b}_2, \ldots, \mathbf{a} \perp \mathbf{b}_{i-1} \end{aligned} \tag{5}$$

$$J(\mathbf{y}) \approx [E\{G(\mathbf{y})\} - E\{G(\mathbf{v})\}]^{2} \tag{6}$$

where y is a standardized random vector, v is a Gauss white time series with the same deviation of y and E{.} stands for the expectation. G{y} is chosen to approximate the negentropy:

$$G(\mathbf{y}) = \frac{1}{a_1}\operatorname{logcosh}(a_1\mathbf{y}) \tag{7}$$

where $1 \le a_1 \le 2$ . Other choices of $G$ can be found in ref [4] and Eq.(7) is the most general-purposed and employed in this paper.

The objective function formulation in Eq.(6) is non-convex and the gradient based algorithm such as FastICA algorithm [8] and the natural gradient algorithm [9] are likely trapped at some local optimal solutions, thus the most nongaussian component maybe omitted. In the next section, a global optimization approach based on particle swarm is proposed to obtain the separating matrix **B**.

### 2.2 Particle Swarm Optimization

PSO is an algorithm first introduced by Kennedy and Eberhart in 1995 [10]. As an swarm intelligent algorithm, PSO imitates the social behavior of organisms such as birds flocking and fish schooling. Each solution of the optimization problem, called a particle, flies in the problem search space looking for the optimal position according to its own experience as well as to the experience of its neighborhood. The performance of each particle is evaluated using a predefined fitness function, which capturing the characteristics of the optimization problem. Two factors characterize a particle status in the $n$-dimensional search space: its velocity and position which are updated according to the following equations at the $j$ th iteration:

$$\begin{cases} \Delta \mathbf{x}_i^{j+1} = w \cdot \Delta \mathbf{x}_i^j + \varphi_1 r_1^j (\mathbf{p}_{id}^j - \mathbf{x}_i^j) + \varphi_2 r_2^j (\mathbf{p}_{gd}^j - \mathbf{x}_i^j) \\ \mathbf{x}_i^{j+1} = \mathbf{x}_i^j + \Delta \mathbf{x}_i^{j+1} \end{cases} \tag{8}$$

where $\Delta \mathbf{x}_i^{j+1} \in \Re^n$, called the velocity for particle $i$, represents the position change by this swarm from its current position in the $j$ th iteration, $\mathbf{x}_i^{j+1} \in \Re^n$ is the particle position, $\mathbf{p}_{id}^j \in \Re^n$ is the best previous position of particle $i$, $\mathbf{p}_{gd}^j \in \Re^n$ is the best position that all the particles have reached, $\varphi_1, \varphi_2$ are the positive acceleration coefficient, w is so called inertia weight and $r_1^i, r_2^j$ are uniformly distributed random numbers between [0, 1].

### 2.3 Particle Swarm Based Analysis of Independent Components

The standard PSO algorithm described in the pervious subsection can only handle unconstrained problem but the ICA optimization problem formulation Eq.(5) includes a set of constraints. In this section, a novel approach (PSO-ICA) is presented to convert the ICA problem to a series of constraint free problems which can be solved efficiently by PSO algorithm.

The presented PSO-ICA approach is described as follows:

(1) The separating vector $\mathbf{b}_1$ (the first column of matrix $\mathbf{B}$), corresponding to most nongaussian (interesting) component, is obtained by solving the following optimization problem with PSO algorithm:

$$\begin{aligned} \mathbf{b}_1^* &= \underset{\mathbf{a} \in \Re^r}{\operatorname{argmax}} \; J(\mathbf{a}^T z / \|\mathbf{a}\|) \\ \mathbf{b}_1 &= \mathbf{b}_1^* / \|\mathbf{b}_1^*\| \end{aligned} \tag{9}$$

Considering the gradient based approach has better convergence behavior, FastICA or the natural gradient algorithm can be involved to improve the accuracy the solution after the PSO algorithm.

(2) From $i$ =2 to $m$ (the predetermined number of independent components), repeat step (3)-(4).

(3) Define the following orthogonal projection matrix $\mathbf{M}_i$ as:

$$\mathbf{M}_i = \mathbf{I}_r - \sum_{j=1}^{i-1} \mathbf{b}_j \mathbf{b}_j^T \tag{10}$$

where $\mathbf{I}_r \in \Re^{r \times r}$ is the identity matrix.

(4) According to Eq.(5), the columns in **B** are orthogonal to each other. Therefore, $\mathbf{b}_i$ belongs to the orthogonal complement of the subspace Span{$\mathbf{b}_1$,$\mathbf{b}_2$, ... $\mathbf{b}_{i-1}$ } and can be defined as:

$$\mathbf{b}_i = \mathbf{M}_i\mathbf{a},\ \mathbf{a} \in \Re^r \tag{11}$$

The $i$ th separator vector $\mathbf{b}_i$ optimizes the following problem and is also obtained by PSO algorithm:

$$\begin{aligned} \mathbf{b}_i^* &= \underset{\mathbf{a}\in\Re^r}{\operatorname{argmax}}\ J(\mathbf{a}^T\mathbf{M}_i^T\mathbf{z}/\|\mathbf{M}_i\mathbf{a}\|) \\ \mathbf{b}_i &= \mathbf{M}_i\mathbf{b}_i^*/\|\mathbf{M}_i\mathbf{b}_i^*\| \end{aligned} \tag{12}$$

The $i$ th independent component is:

$$\hat{\mathbf{s}}_i = \mathbf{b}_i^T\mathbf{z} \tag{13}$$

When the number of PSO particles is large enough (20 ~ 50 are the most common [12]) in the PSO-ICA approach, global optimal solution is guaranteed with probability. Furthermore, PSO can also be performed in a distributed manner which can improve the efficiency of the presented PSO-ICA approach especially for the high dimensional problems.

## 3 Fault Detection with PSO-ICA and SVDD

For many industrial processes, most of the measured variables are usually driven by fewer essential variables, which are usually unmeasured or corrupted by measurement noise. In this work, the measurement data $\mathbf{X}_{NOC} \in \Re^{n\times l}$ ($n$ is the number of sensors, $l$ the number of samples) under normal operating condition (NOC) is analyzed by PSO-ICA,

$$\hat{\mathbf{S}}_{NOC} = \mathbf{W}_{NOC} \cdot \mathbf{X}_{NOC} \tag{14}$$

where $\hat{\mathbf{S}}_{NOC} \in \Re^{m\times l}$ denotes the $m$ underlying independent components and $\mathbf{W}_{NOC} \in \Re^{m\times n}$ is the separating matrix, both under NOC.

Note that the essential variables retrieved by PSO-ICA are not normally distributed, thus it is inappropriate to use the Hotelling's $T^2$ and SPE statistics in PCA to monitor the behaviour of the essential variables. As a kernel-based one-class classifer, SVDD [15] has been proven to be efficient to find the separation boundary between the target class (NOC) and the rest of the feature space.

### 3.1 Support Vector Data Description

The main idea of the SVDD is (i) to map the input vectors to a feature space and (ii) to find a hypersphere with the minimum volume which separates the transferred data from the rest of the feature space.

Given a data set containing $l$ target training examples, $\{ \hat{\mathbf{s}}_i \in \Re^m, i = 1,2,...,l \}$, the mapping $\Phi : \hat{\mathbf{s}} \to F$ is implicitly done by a given kernel $K : \Re^m \times \Re^m \to \Re$ which compute the inner product in the feature space, i.e., $\langle \Phi(\hat{\mathbf{s}}_i), \Phi(\hat{\mathbf{s}}_j) \rangle = K(\hat{\mathbf{s}}_i, \hat{\mathbf{s}}_j)$. The SVDD solves the following optimization problem:

$$\begin{aligned} &\min_{R,a,\xi} R^2 + \frac{1}{l \cdot \nu} \sum_{i=1}^{l} \xi_i \\ &s.t. \left\| \Phi(\hat{\mathbf{s}}_i) - \mathbf{a} \right\|^2 \le R^2 + \xi_i, \xi_i \ge 0 \end{aligned} \tag{15}$$

where a is the centre of the hypersphere in the feature space. $\nu > 0$ is the tuning parameter which controls the upper limit on the fraction of training error on target class and a lower bound on the fraction of support vectors [15]. $\xi_i$ represent the slack variables which allow the possibility that some of the training examples can be wrongly classified.

The dual problem of Eq.(15) is formulated as:

$$\begin{aligned} &\min_{\alpha_i} \sum_{i=1}^{l} \alpha_i K(\hat{\mathbf{s}}_i, \hat{\mathbf{s}}_j) - \sum_{i=1}^{l} \sum_{j=1}^{l} \alpha_i \alpha_j K(\hat{\mathbf{s}}_i, \hat{\mathbf{s}}_j) \\ &s.t. \;\; 0 \le \alpha_i \le C, \sum_{i=1}^{l} \alpha_i = 1 \end{aligned} \tag{16}$$

where $\alpha_i$ are called Lagrange multipliers. The minimization of Eq.(16) is a well-known quadratic programming problem which can be solved effieciently by sequential mimimal optimization (SMO) method [16]. The centre of the hypersphere **a** can be expressed as a linear combination of samples in the feature space, $\mathbf{a} = \sum_{i=1}^{l} \alpha_i \Phi(\hat{\mathbf{s}}_i)$. When a training sample $\hat{\mathbf{s}}_i$ satisfies the inequality constraint in Eq.(15) (the sample is located in the hypersphere), the corresponding $\alpha_i$ will be equal to 0. For training samples locate on or outside of the boundary, the constraint has to be enforced and the Langrange multiplier will become positive. When one sample obtains $\alpha_i = C$, the sample is regarded as an outlier and will not be accepted by the SVDD. For the sample $\hat{\mathbf{s}}_k$ on the boundary which corresponds to $0 < \alpha_i < C$, the radius $R$ is obtained as:

$$R^2 = K(\hat{\mathbf{s}}_k, \hat{\mathbf{s}}_k) - 2\sum_{i=1}^{l} \alpha_i K(\hat{\mathbf{s}}_i, \hat{\mathbf{s}}_k) + \sum_{i=1}^{l} \sum_{j=1}^{l} \alpha_i \alpha_j K(\hat{\mathbf{s}}_i, \hat{\mathbf{s}}_j) \tag{17}$$

Let $\mathbf{x} \in \Re^n$ be the new process observations to be monitored, then we have:

$$\hat{\mathbf{s}} = \mathbf{W}_{NOC} \cdot \mathbf{x} \tag{18}$$

Denote $D$ as the distance of $\Phi(\hat{s})$ to **a** in the feature space, i.e., $D = \left\| \Phi(\hat{s}) - a \right\|$. The decision function $f(z)$ is employed to determine whether $x$ stays in the normal operational region:

$$f(x) = \begin{cases} 1\,(NOC),\, D < R \\ 0 \quad otherwise \end{cases} \tag{19}$$

For kernel based approaches, the choice of the kernel function is a crucial step which need skills. Gaussain RBF (Radical Basis Function), polynominal, sigmoidal kernels are most widely used kernel types [17]. If the kernel family is predetermined, e.g., the RBF kernel, $K(\hat{\mathbf{s}}_i, \hat{\mathbf{s}}_j) = \exp(-(\hat{\mathbf{s}}_i - \hat{\mathbf{s}}_j)^T \gamma(\hat{\mathbf{s}}_i - \hat{\mathbf{s}}_j))$, the problem reduces to selecting an appropriate set of parameters for the classifiers. In ref[17] and [18], the parameters selection based on stochastic optimization are introduced and the swarm intelligent approach [18] is used in this paper.

## 4 Case study on Tennessee Eastman Process

The Tennessee Eastman process simulator was developed by Downs and Vogel [19]. The process consists of five major unit operations: a reactor, a product condenser, a vapor-liquid separator, a recycle compressor, and a product stripper. There are 12 manipulated variables and 41 measured variables. The simulator includes a set of programmed disturbances listed in Table 1 of ref [1]. The control system used for dynamic simulation is the self-optimization approach presented by Larsson et al. [20]. The process is used as a benchmark for evaluating different control strategies and monitoring methods. Kano et al. [21] compared the monitoring performance of the different multivariate statistical monitoring methods on this process. In this study, according to ref[22], the reference dataset to construct NOC model includes 2000 samples of 33 continuously measured variables which were recorded at 0.1 h interval.

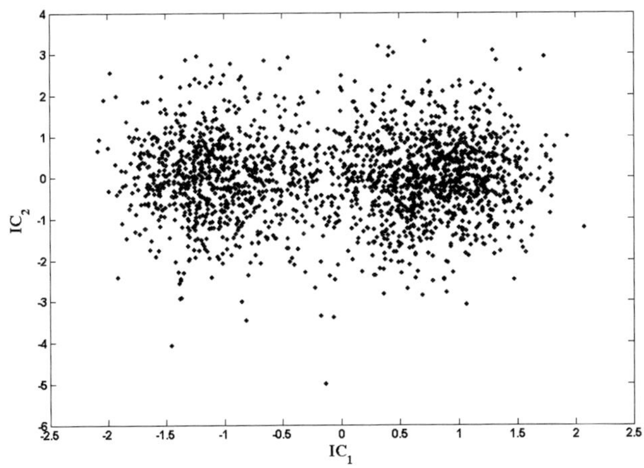


**Fig. 1.** The variations of first two independent components obtained by PSO-ICA

In current study, the number of retained whitened signals is 18 and the number of independent components is chosen as 3. Fig.1 illustrates the variations of first two independent components and Fig.2 shows the normal probability plot of the first independent component, both obtained by PSO-ICA corresponding to the normal operation condition. It is clear that the values of the independent components do not follow a Gaussian distribution. Therefore, it is not suitable to monitor the independent components with the $T^2$ statistic which bases on the Gaussian assumption.

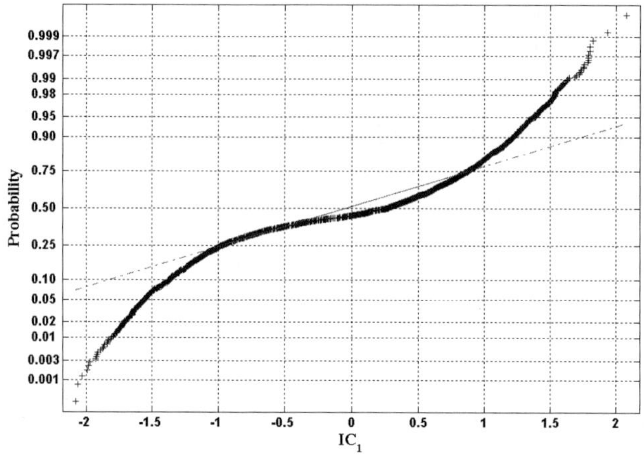


**Fig. 2.** The normal probability plot of the first independent componentic1density

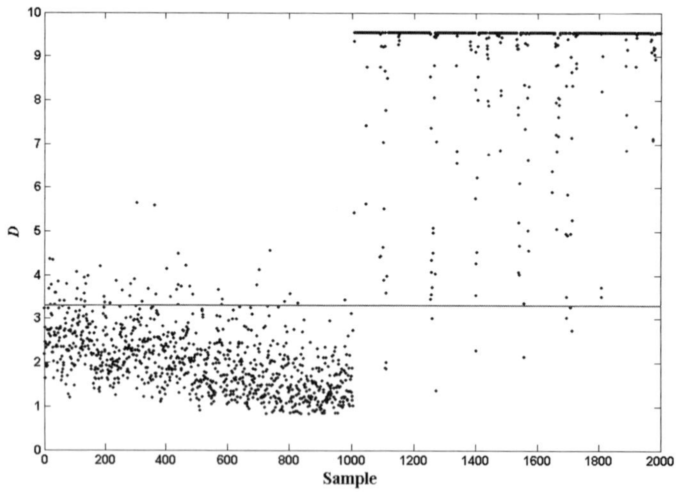


**Fig. 3.** The *D* monitoring chart of excessive feed composition variation

In order to describe the actual distribution of the indepenent compoents and obtain the boundary of the normal operational region. The presented SVDD approach is involved and the RBF kernel is employed to map the independent components to the high dimensional feature space. The corresponding pararmeters selected with the swarm intelligent approach are $\nu = 0.05$ (the relative false alarm rate is 5%) and $\gamma = 0.1$, respectively.

To demonstrate the capability of presented approach to detect abnormal behavior, excessive variation of the feed composition was simulated (disturbance type 8) to generate a fault dataset. The fault dataset also contains 2000 samples and the fault was injected after the 1000 sample.

The $D$ monitoring chart is shown in Fig.3. The solid line denotes the radius of the hypersphere in the feature space. It is evident that the last 1000 $D$ values produce an excessive number of violations. Therefore, the presented SVDD approach detects the out-of-control situation correctly.

## 5 Conclusion

A novel strategy has been developed for the monitoring of abnormal plant operation based on PSO-ICA and SVDD. Due to its ability of escaping the local optimal point, the proposed PSO-ICA can guarantee with probability that the most interesting essential variables are extracted from the process recorded variables. Support vector data description is involved to describe the nonGaussian distributed essential variables and determine the NOC boundary. The proposed approach has been evaluated by the application on the Tennessee Eastman challenging process.

## Acknowledgement

This work is partially supported by National Natural Science Foundation of China with grant number 60421002 and 70471052.

## References

1. Ku, W., Storet, R. H., Georgakis, C.: Disturbance Detection and Isolation by Dynamic Principal Component Analysis. Chemometrics and Intelligent Laboratory Systems. 30 (1995) 179-196
2. Bakshi, B.R.: Multiscale PCA with Application to Multivariate Statistical Process Monitoring. AIChE J. 44 (1998) 1596-1610
3. Kramer, M.A.: Nonlinear Principal Component Analysis Using Auto-associative Neural Networks. AIChE. J. 37 (1991) 233-243
4. Hyvärinen, A., Karhunen, J., Oja, E.: Independent Component Analysis, John Wiley & Sons, New York, (2001)
5. Li, R. F., Wang, X. Z.: Dimension Reduction of Process Dynamic Trends Using Independent Component Analysis. Computers and Chemical Engineering. 26 (2002) 467-473
6. Kano, M., Tanaka, S., Hasebe, S.: Monitoring Independent Components for Fault Detection. AIChE. J. 49 (2003) 969-976

7. Himberg, J., Icasso, A. H.: Software for Investigating the Reliability of ICA Estimates by Clustering and Visualization, in: Proc. IEEE Workshop on Neural Networks for Signal Processing (NNSP2003), Toulouse, France (2003) 259–268
8. Hyvärinen, A.: Fast and Robust Fixed-point Algorithms for Independent Component Analysis. IEEE Transactions on Neural Networks. 10 (1996) 626–634
9. Bell, A., Sejnowski, T.: An Information-maximization Approach to Blind Separation and Blind Deconvolution. Neural Computation. 7 (1995) 1129–1159
10. Kennedy, J., Eberhart, R.: Particle Swarm Optimization, In Proc. IEEE Int. Conf. Neural Networks, Perth, (1995), 1942-1948
11. Parsonpoulos, K.E., Varhatis: Recent Approaches to Global Optimization Problems through Particle Swarm Optimization. Natural Computing. 1 (2002) 235-306
12. Mendes, R.: Population Topologies and their Influence in Particle Swarm Performance. Ph.D thesis, University of Minho, (2004)
13. Johannesmeyer, M. C., Singhal, A., Seborg, D.E.: Pattern Matching in Historical Data. AIChE. J. 48 (2002) 2022-2038
14. Rick, C.: Simple and Fast Linear Space Computation of Longest Common Subsequence. Information Processing Letters. 75 (2000) 275-281
15. Tax, D.M.J., Duin, R.P.W.: Uniform Object Generation for Optimizing One-class Classifiers. Journal of Machine Learning Research 2 (2001) 15-173
16. Schölkopf, B., Somla, A.J.: Learning with Kernels: Support Vector Machines, Regularization, Optimization and Beyond. MIT press, Cambridge, 2002
17. Frauke, F., Igel, C.: Evolutionary Tuning of Multiple SVM Parameters. Neurocomputing 64(2005) 107-117
18. Xie, L.: Swarm Intelligent Tuning of One-class v-SVM Parameters. in: Proc. The First International Conference on Rough Sets and Knowledge Technology, ChongQing, China (2006)
19. Downs, J.J., Vogel, E.F.: A Plant-wide Industrial Process Control Problem. Computers and Chemical Engineering. 17 (1993) 245-255
20. Larsson, T., Hestetun, K., Hovland, E., Skogestad, S.: Self-optimizing Control of A Large-scale Plant: the Tennessee Eastman Process. Ind. Rng. Chem. Res. 40 (2001) 4889-4901
21. Kano, M., Nagao, K., Hasebe, S.: Comparison of Multivariate Statistical Process Monitoring Methods with Applications to the Eastman Challenge Problem. Computers and Chemical Engineering. 26 (2002) 161-174
22. Lee, J., Yoo, C., Lee, I.: Statistical Monitoring of Dynamic Processes Based on Dynamic Independent Component Analysis. Chemcial Engineering Science. 59 (2004) 2995-3006

# A Novel Personalized Paper Search System*

Sanggil Kang and Youngim Cho**

Department of Computer Science, The University of Suwon,
San 2-2, Wau-ri, Bongdam-eup, Hwaseong, Gyeonggi-do 445-743, South Korea
{sgkang, ycho}@suwon.ac.kr

**Abstract.** In this paper we propose a novel personalized paper search system using the relevance among user's queried keywords and user's behaviors on a searched paper list. The proposed system builds user's individual relevance network from analyzing the appearance frequencies of keywords in the searched papers. The relevance network is personalized by providing weights to the appearance frequencies of keywords according to users' behaviors on the searched list, such as "downloading," "opening," and "no-action." In the experimental section, we demonstrate our method using 100 faculties' search information in the University of Suwon.

## 1 Introduction

With the flood of publications, users often have a difficulty in finding their preferred papers. Also, users usually spend heavy surfing time to find relevant papers in the search list in which huge number of papers is cited. If according to user's individual interest, a paper search system can recognize highly relevant papers for user's queried keywords, then not only the search time can be saved but also the list can be reduced and more coincide with user's interest.

We propose a personalized paper search system using the relevance among a user's queried keywords and his/her behaviors on searched paper lists. Our system builds user's individual relevance network from analyzing the appearance frequencies of keywords in the searched papers. The relevance network is personalized by providing weights to the appearance frequencies of keywords according to users' behaviors on the searched list, such as "downloading," "opening," and "no-action."

In the experimental section, we demonstrate our method using 100 faculties' search information in the University of Suwon. Also, the performance of our method is compared with that of the conventional paper search system by surveying the satisfaction of users for both systems.

The remainder of this paper consists as follows. Chapter 2 introduces various personalization techniques. Chapter 3 explains the proposed personalized paper search algorithm in detail. In Chapter 4, we show the simulated results of our system. Finally chapter 5 will conclude.

---

* This work was supported by the Korea Research Foundation Grant funded by the Korean Government (MOEHRD)(R04-2003-000-10122-0).

** Corresponding author: +82-31-229-8214.

D.-S. Huang, K. Li, and G.W. Irwin (Eds.): ICIC 2006, LNCS 4113, pp. 1257 – 1262, 2006.

## 2 Related Work

Various personalization techniques can be classified into three possible categories such as the rule-based, inference method, and collaborative filtering. The rule-based recommendation is usually implemented by a predetermined rule, for instance, if - then rule. The inference method is the technique that a user's content consumption behavior is predicted based on the history of personal content consumption behaviors. Collaborative filtering (CF) technique recommends a target user the preferred content of the group whose content consumption mind is similar to that of the user. Because of the mature of the technique, CF has been attractive for predicting various preference problems such as net-news, e-commerce, digital TV, digital libraries.

Bollacker et al. [1] introduced a personalized CiteSeer digital library system which is an automatic paper search system. The system can track and recommend the similar papers whose topics are very relevant, using the content-based relatedness measures [3]. Torres et al. [2] improved the performance of the automatic paper search system by developing the hybrid recommender which is the combination of CF and content-based filtering [4].

However, the above literatures about digital library systems consider the topic of papers for analyzing the users' preferred papers. In this case, they can not recommend the papers whose topic is not relevant to the queried keywords request by a user but contents are relevant to them. In order to solve the problem, we consider the abstracts in the papers for providing a personalized paper search list according to the user's behavior on the papers and the relevance among keywords in the abstracts.

## 3 Personalized Paper Search Algorithm

### 3.1 Modeling Keyword Relevance Network

From abstracts in the papers retrieved by a user's query with a keyword, we can measure the relevance between nouns in the abstracts and the keyword. For example, if a user requests a query with a keyword through the search engine then the search engine retrieves every relevant paper with the keyword. Also, we can extract the abstracts from the retrieved papers by parsing them. From the extracted abstracts, we can compute the frequency of the appearance of each noun as in Equation (1).

$$freq(keyword, noun_i) = \sum_{a=1} n_{i,a} \quad (1)$$

where $n_{i,a}$ is the appearance number of noun $i$ from the $a^{th}$ retrieved. Also, $freq(keyword, noun_i)$ implies the strength of the relevance of the retrieved noun $i$ with respect to a keyword over all abstracts. The relationship of a keyword and the relevance strength for each noun can be modeled in the network form (called keyword relevance network in this paper) as viewed in Fig. 1.

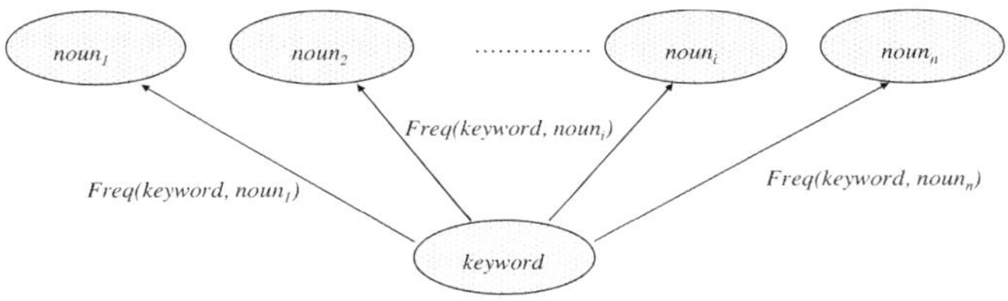


**Fig. 1.** The keyword relevance network

As seen in Equation (1), the strength of the relevance between the keyword and a noun depends on the appearance frequency in the abstracts. If the number of the appearance of a noun is large, it can be considered the noun is very relevant with the keyword. In the same way, each noun also can be a possible keyword queried by the user. However, if we take an account of keywords for the nouns appeared even a single frequency over all abstracts then the number of keywords for the user can increase exponentially as time passes. It causes the relevance network complicated. To avoid this situation, it is needed to decide the threshold of the frequency of the appearance for each noun as the qualification of being a keyword. Following the previous process, the generalized keyword relevance network among the keywords can be viewed as in Fig. 2. As seen in Fig. 2, all keywords queried by the user are fully connected to among them with the strength of the relevance to each connection.

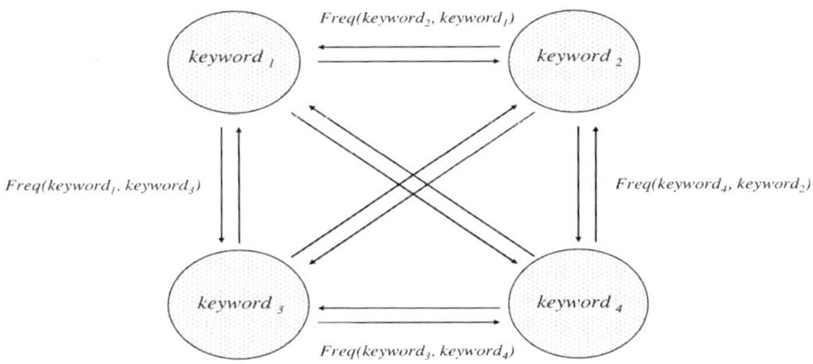


**Fig. 2.** The fully connected relevance network of keywords

### 3.2 Personalized Keyword Relevance Network

From the keyword relevance network in Fig. 2, we can not provide the personalized search list of papers because an identical list is showed for all users with the same queried keywords. In order to solve the problem, we modify Equation (1) by giving weights to the computation of the frequency of appearance of keywords according to the user's behaviors (actions) on the searched list, such as downloading, opening, and no-action.

$$freq(keyword_i, keyword_j) = \sum_{a=1} w_a n_{i,j,a} \tag{2}$$

where $w_a$ is the weight of the user's behavior for paper $a$ and $n_{i,j,a}$ is the appearance number of keyword $j$ from the $a^{th}$ retrieved paper by the query of keyword $i$. In general, the action of downloading papers from the searched list is understood that the user is very interested in the paper. From this point of view, the keywords in the paper can be considered more preferred than the other two actions, opening and no-action. In order to take this into the consideration, we give relatively large value of the weight $w_a$ for the action of downloading, compared to the other two actions. Therefore, the order of the values of the weight for the three actions is downloading > opening > no-action. The value of the weight for each action is also determined by the empirical experiment.

Equation (2) shows the relevance between two keywords. However, users often request a query with more than one keyword (called a set of keywords in this paper). The generalization of Equation (2) for various numbers of keywords can be expressed in Equation (3) which implies the strength of the relevance of keyword $j$ for the set of keywords.

$$freq(Set\_keyword, keyword_j) = \sum_{k=1}^{s} freq(keyword_k, keyword_j) \quad (3)$$

where *Set_keyword* is a set of queried keywords and $s$ is the number of the queried keywords. For the convenience, Equation (3) can be expressed in the normalized form as in Equation (4).

$$Nfreq(Set\_keyword, keyword_j) = \frac{freq(Set\_keyword, keyword_j)}{\sum_{j=1}^{J} freq(Set\_keyword, keyword_j)} \quad (4)$$

where $Nfreq(Set\_keyword, keyword_j)$ is the normalized strength of the relevance of keyword $j$ for the set of keywords. According to the value of the normalized strength of keyword relevance, the order of the searched papers in the list is determined.

## 4 Experiment

We implemented our personalized paper search system (PPSS) using Visual C++ in the Window NT environment. The My SQL server was used to implement the relevance DB in PPSS. In this experiment, we chose the values of weight of users' behavior for paper $a$, as in Equation (2), $w_a = 5$ for downloading, $w_a = 2$ for opening, and $w_a = 1$ for no-action, respectively. Also, the threshold of the frequency of the appearance for the qualification of being a keyword is 2. Those values were determined by empirical experience using 100 faculties in the University of Suwon, Korea. The information of their paper search behaviors had been collected during one month.

Fig. 3 shows the searched list of the ACM PORTAL for the queried keyword '*network*' by a faculty. As seen in Fig. 3, the 64,493 papers were found. It is a huge number of papers the user needed to look up for finding the most relevant papers of what the user was looking for. Fig. 4 shows the user interface of PPSS for the same keyword used in the ACM PORTAL. From the user's keyword relevance network viewed on the right bottom in Fig. 4, the normalized strength of the relevance for keyword "neural" is

0.47 which is the biggest relevant keyword to the 'network.' It means that the user had been interested in the papers with keywords 'network' and 'neural' during the period so he/she had acted the downloading or opening for those papers. For the user, our system placed the papers with the keywords having 'network' and 'neural' in their abstracts on the top positions in the searched list as seen on the right top in Fig. 4. By placing a user's possibly preferred papers on the early pages in the searched list, it can save time to surf the list and reduce the user's effort to find his/her preferred papers.

Also, we evaluated the performances of our system and the conventional search system by comparing the satisfaction of both systems for the 100 faculties. From Table, 98% (27 for "very satisfactory",71 for "satisfactory") out of 100 expressed their satisfaction for our system, while only 5% for the conventional system.

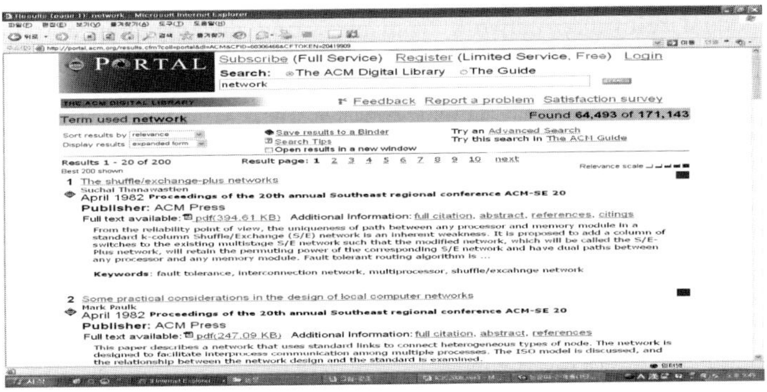


**Fig. 3.** The searched list obtained from the queried keyword 'network' by the conventional search engine

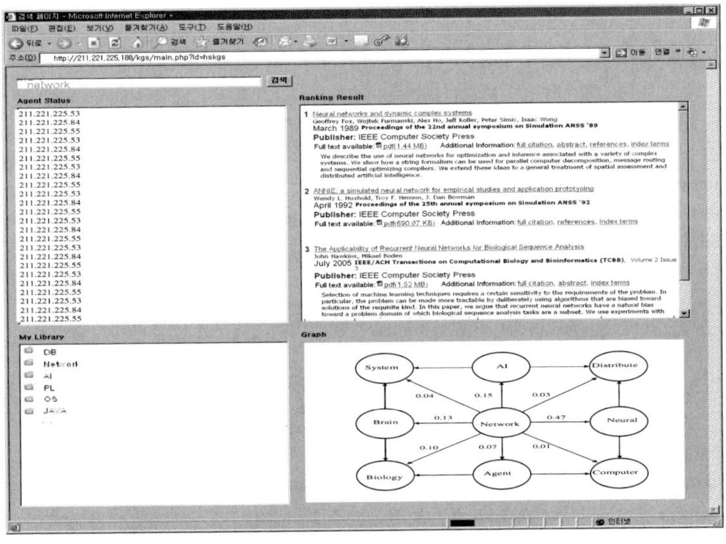


**Fig. 4.** Search result viewed on the user interface

**Table 1.** The result of the survey of the satisfaction of both systems for the 100 faculties

| Evaluation | System | |
|---|---|---|
| | The Conventional System | **PPSS** |
| very satisfactory | 0 | **27** |
| satisfactory | 5 | **71** |
| dissatisfied | 83 | **2** |
| very dissatisfied | 12 | **0** |

## 5 Conclusion

In this paper, we proposed a novel personalized paper search system by building user's individual relevance network from analyzing the appearance frequencies of keywords in the searched papers. As seen in the previous experimental section, we showed that users can save paper search time and reduce an effort to find their preferred paper by using our system. Also, as seen on the table in the previous section, our system can be a useful tool for searching users' preferred papers.

However, the values of the weights for users' behaviors, i.e., $w_a = 5$ for downloading, $w_a = 2$ for opening, and $w_a = 1$ for no-action was obtained from the exhaustively empirical experiment. The values might not be optimal for all users. For the further work of this paper, we need to develop an automatic algorithm for determining the values according to each individual user.

## References

1. Bollacker, K.D., Lawrence S., Giles, C.L.: A System for Automatic Personalized Tracking of Scientific Literature on the Web. Proc. ACM Conference on Digital Libraries (1999) 105-113
2. Torres, R., McNee, S.M., Abel, M., Konstan, J.A., Riedl, J.: Enhancing Digital Libraries with TechLens+. ACM/IEEE-CS Joint Conference on Digital Libraries (2004) 228-236
3. Bollacker, K., Lawrence, S., Giles, C.L.: An Autonomous Web Agent for Automatic Retrieval and Identification of Interesting Publications. Proc. The Second International Conference on Autonomous Agents (1998) 116-123
4. Kamba, T., Bharat, K., Albers, M.C.: An Interactive Personalized Newspaper on the Web. Proc. International World Wide Web Conference (1995) 159-170

# An Expert System for the Identification of Nonlinear Dynamical Systems

Grigorios Dimitriadis[1], Gareth A. Vio[1], and Dongfeng Shi[2]

[1] School of Mechanical, Aerospace and Civil Engineering, The University of Manchester, M13 9PL, UK
grigorios.dimitriadis@man.ac.uk
[2] Condition Monitoring Research Group, University of Nottingham NG7 2RD, UK

**Abstract.** This paper describes an Expert System that can detect and quantify the nonlinearity present in a given dynamical system and, subsequently, determine and apply the most suitable nonlinear system identification method. The internal workings, algorithms and decision making processes of the Expert System are discussed. For demonstration purposes the Expert System is applied to a nonlinear experimental test-rig. The results show that the Expert System is an automatic tool that will detect nonlinearity, choose the best class of model for the system under investigation and perform optimal parameter estimation, so that the resulting identified models are parsimonious and accurate.

## 1 Introduction

The identification of dynamical systems is increasingly becoming a necessity in every branch of engineering that deals with vibrating structures. There is now a consensus that, despite highly evolved modelling methodologies, the only way to estimate the true vibrational characteristics of a dynamic system is by system identification. The response of a system to a known input signal is measured and analysed in order to extract vibrational information, such as natural frequencies and dampings, or to create a mathematical model of the system. System identification for linear systems is at a highly advanced stage to the extent that entire aircraft can be identified during Ground Vibration Tests.

Currently, the identification of nonlinear dynamical systems is still at a preliminary stage, despite the large number of proposed methods, since none of these methods is paradigmatic. Nonlinear systems do not conform to the principle of superposition. A great number of system identification methodologies for nonlinear systems have been proposed, only a small number of which have been the object of extensive research. Such techniques include the NARMAX model [1], various Hilbert-Transform-based approaches [2,3], Voltera Series [4] and Restoring Force Surfaces [5]. A detailed description and theoretical analysis of all these methods is given in Worden and Tomlinson [6].

However, none of these widely used techniques have, as yet, been extended to be applicable to any general nonlinear system. The aim of the present work

D.-S. Huang, K. Li, and G.W. Irwin (Eds.): ICIC 2006, LNCS 4113, pp. 1263–1268, 2006.

is to attempt to create a logical framework to be used for the identification of nonlinear systems. It is assumed that no single identification method is general enough to work with a significant range of systems. Therefore, this framework is based on the development of an Expert System that will detect and quantify the nonlinearity present in a given dynamical system and, subsequently, determine and apply the most suitable nonlinear system identification method or methods.

## 2 Expert System

The Expert System is structured around the four standard tenets of nonlinear system identification: 1. Nonlinearity detection, 2. Model type selection, 3. Term selection and parameter estimation and 4. Model validation. The most crucial aspect is the capability to apply suitable excitation signals at each one of these stages. The Expert System must be able to choose the appropriate excitation signal for each method it attempts to apply, measure the resulting responses and perform the necessary calculations.

The nonlinearity detection stage is necessary in order to justify the subsequent application of nonlinear system identification techniques. Additional information that can be extracted at this stage includes the location of the nonlinearity and, if possible, its characteristics. Important characteristics of nonlinear functions that, if known, can facilitate the choice of model type, basis functions and parameter estimation techniques are:

- Damping or stiffness nonlinearity.
- Strength of nonlinearity at various excitation levels.
- Degree of nonlinearity. This refers mainly to nonlinear functions that can be approximated using polynomials. The degree of the nonlinear function is the maximum polynomial order required for accurate modelling.
- Odd or even nonlinearity.
- Continuity, i.e. whether the nonlinear function and its derivatives are continuous.
- Existence of hysteresis.

Once the existence of nonlinearity has been confirmed and some information has been obtained about the nonlinear function or functions in the system a model type can be chosen. Model type here refers to a number of possible options for the final identified model, including: 1. Frequency or time domain, 2. Ordinary Differential Equations or Regression Equations, 3. Polynomial or other basis functions.

For a general nonlinear system, once the model type has been chosen, there is a very large number of possible terms that can be included in the final model. Many techniques have been proposed for term selection but experience shows that each technique tends to select a different set of terms for the same system. Additionally, the selected terms can depend on the values of a number of sensitivity parameters. The Expert System applies as many methods as possible at this stage and correlates and compares the resulting selected terms in an effort to produce the best possible model. Terms that tend to be selected by many methods are more likely to be representative of the true system than terms that are only selected once.

Finally, the model validation stage ensures that the final identified model is accurate. The final stage of the identification process must ensure that the model is not a representation of a particular data set but of the original system and all of its characteristics. If the method validation stage fails then the Expert System returns to the model type selection stage.

The Expert System must also allow for the possibility of complete failure. The number of possible nonlinear functions is infinite while the number of basis functions and system identification methodologies is small. Additionally, various practical considerations can cause failure. For example, an insufficient number of exciters or response measurement sensors can render impossible any identification procedure. So can badly placed exciters and sensors or inadequate instrumentation.

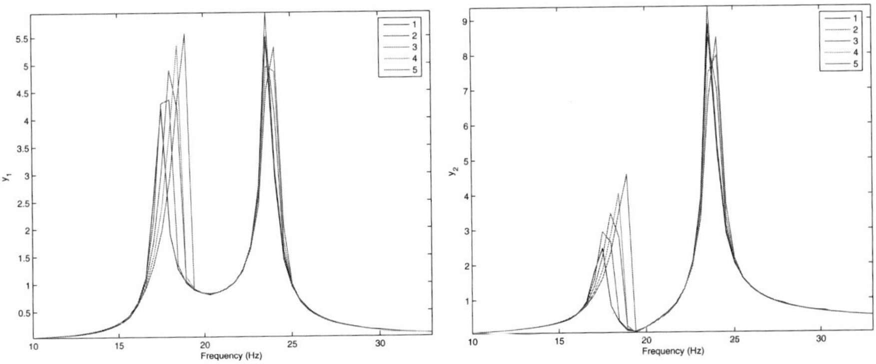


(a) Response 1 (b) Response 2

**Fig. 1.** Step-sine test results

## 3 Expert Knowledge

The Expert System is based around two types of knowledge: 1. Algorithms for the application of various methodologies and 2. Rules for taking decisions. The following is a list of all the algorithms in the Expert System's knowledge, including short descriptions.

- Short Time Fourier Transforms (STFT) of chirp responses. The Expert System applies chirp signals to the system under investigation, with various force levels. The responses are Short Time Fourier Transformed. The STFT plots are inspected for the existence of higher harmonics in the system responses.
- Hilbert Transform. The Expert System can calculate the Envelope of the responses of the system under investigation to random input.
- Stepped Sine testing. The system under investigation is excited by sine waves of increasing frequencies and amplitudes. The force amplitude is controlled so that it remains at the desired value at all test frequencies.

- First and Higher Order Frequency Response Functions. The Stepped Sine responses can be curve-fitted by sinusoids of orders from 1 to infinity. The Expert System can extract the true first order FRF and the diagonals of the higher order ones. This procedure yields good estimates for the order of the system (number of modes or generalised co-ordinates) and the orders of nonlinearity.
- Constant Level Identification [7]. The Expert System applies wide or narrow band chirp or random excitation to all of the system inputs. It then pinpoints time instances in the response time histories where each response has a certain value (level).
- Linear Direct Parameter Identification. The system is assumed to be linear and represented by a 2nd order Ordinary Differential Equation. The mass, stiffness and damping matrices are calculated for each of the Constant Levels. The model order used in this identification is the order determined by the Higher Order FRF procedure.
- Nonlinear Direct Parameter Identification. This method is a nonlinear extension of the Linear Direct Parameter Identification procedure. The nonlinear basis functions are chosen to be polynomial. The model order and orders of nonlinearity used are the ones determined by the Higher Order FRF procedure.
- Restoring Force Surface. If the system's mass matrix is known then it is used directly by the Expert System. If not, the mass matrix is assumed to be the unit matrix and the forcing matrix estimated by the Constant Level method is used.
- NAR(MA)X model. The Expert System can fit a NARX or NARMAX model to data from the system under investigation, given chirp or random input. The model order and orders of nonlinearity are chosen using the Higher Order FRF results.
- Model Structure Selection and Parameter Estimation. The following techniques are used: 1. Full Parameter Search, 2. Forward Selection, 3. Backwards Elimination and 4. Orthogonal Estimator

## 4 Demonstration of Expert System Performance

The Expert System is here demonstrated on a two-degree-of-freedom (DOF) mass-spring dynamical system. Nonlinear stiffness was implemented by means of a steel ruler under transverse loading. The Expert System was given control of the two exciters and was directly linked to the force gauges and accelerometers. The only information about the system that was required by the Expert System is the number of excitation positions and response sensors. A maximum limit to the amplitude of excitation was imposed to avoid damaging the rig or the exciters. Figure 1 shows the Frequency Response Functions obtained from the Step-sine tests for increasing force amplitude levels (from 1 to 5). It is clear that the frequency of the first peak increases significantly with excitation amplitude. The second peak also changes frequency although the effect is less pronounce. Figure 2 shows results from the Higher Order FRF analysis. The contour plots display the amplitude of the harmonics in the system response (in color) against frequency and for harmonics from 1 to 5. It can be seen that the third harmonic

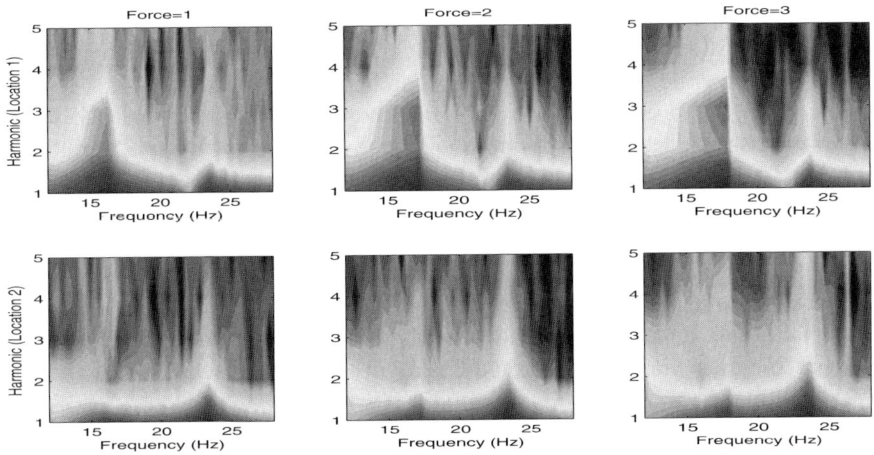


**Fig. 2.** Orders of non-linearity present in the two response locations for increasing force level

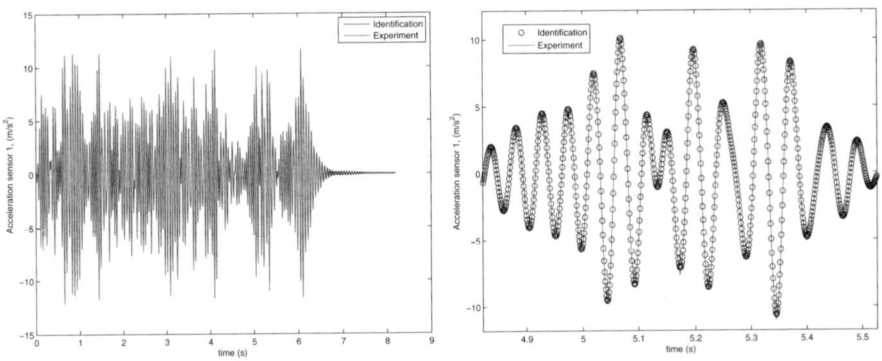


**Fig. 3.** Responses from the true system and identified model

is very prominent at response location 1 around 16Hz, which is the frequency of the first mode of the structure. This means that there is a strong nonlinearity at that location of order 3. This information was exploited by the Expert System for the rest of the identification process.

Figure 3 shows the very good agreement obtained between the acceleration responses of the true system and those of the identified model to a validation excitation signal. The left hand plot shows the full time history while the right hand plot zooms in on a narrow time range. The two sets of signals virtually coincide.

## 5 Conclusions

This paper presented an Expert System for the identification of nonlinear systems. The Expert System is an attempt to bring order into the nonlinear system identification process. The final objective is to deliver a parsimonious mathematical model of the dynamical system under investigation. It works by defining the key stages of the procedure and iterating between them if necessary. It takes advantage of numerous methodologies to accomplish the tasks in each of the stages and uses the results from many of them. The Expert System applies the excitation forces appropriate to each method and analyses the responses. Each stage ends with a set of recommendations that can be used to begin the next stage.

The Expert System is applied to a simple nonlinear dynamic system. The procedure is described step-by-step and the decisions of the system explained. It is shown that the nonlinearity is correctly detected, located and characterised and that the final mathematical model is an accurate representation of the true experimental system.

## References

1. Chen, S., Billings, S.A.: Representations of non-linear systems: the NARMAX model. International Journal of Control **49**(3) (1989) 1013–1032
2. Simon, M., Tomlinson, G.R.: Use of the Hilbert transform in modal analysis of linear and non-linear structures. Journal of Sound and Vibration **96**(4) (1984) 421–436
3. Feldman, M.: Nonlinear system vibration analysis using hilbert transform - i. free vibration analysis method freevib. Mechanical Systems and Signal Processing **8**(2) (1994) 119–127
4. Volterra, V., ed.: Theory of Functionals and Integral Equations. Dover, New York (1959)
5. Crawley, E.F., Aubert, A.C.: Identification of nonlinear structural elements by force-state mapping. AIAA Journal **24**(1) (1986) 155–162
6. Worden, K., Tomlinson, G.R.: Nonlinear vibrations. Sheffield University Press, Sheffield: (2000)
7. Dimitriadis, G.: Experimental validation of the Constant Level method for identification of nonlinear multi degree of freedom systems. Journal of Sound and Vibration **258**(5) (2000) 829–845

# Fuzzy Modeling of a Medium-Speed Pulverizer Using Improved Genetic Algorithms

Jian Zhang[1], Minrui Fei[1], Kang Li[2], and Qiang Zhu[1]

[1] Shanghai Key Laboratory of Power Station Automation Technology,
School of Mechatronics and Automation,
Shanghai University, Shanghai 200072, China
Jianzhang668@163.com, mrfei@staff.shu.edu.cn,
zhuqiang@dcs.saic.sh.cn

[2] School of Electronics, Electrical Engineering and Computer Science
Queen's University of Belfast, Belfast BT9 5AH, UK
k.li@ee.qub.ac.uk

**Abstract.** Based on the analysis of its operational mechanism, an improved nonlinear model is developed for a medium-speed pulverizer. This is achieved by identifying a group of constant coefficients for a set of nonlinear differential equations with the aid of an improved genetic algorithm. The main objective of this research is to convert the nonlinear model into a T-S fuzzy model composed of several linear models, enabling easy design of the control system for the pulverizer. The simulation results show a satisfactory agreement between the T-S fuzzy model response and the measured data, confirming the effectiveness of the proposed method. Moreover, the proposed modeling method can be easily applied to other nonlinear systems, given that their nonlinear differential equations are known "a priori".

## 1 Introduction

The medium speed pulverizer is the core unit of a pulverised coal preparation system. Fast pulverizer response is desired to maintain the boiler pressure and temperature in a thermal power unit. A mathematical model which adequately describes the dynamics of the pulverizer will help to control the device and to improve the pulverizer responses. So far, several pulverizer models have been developed [1][2][3]. However, these models are too complicated to apply, and it is very difficult to design a control system for the pulverizer with good performance due to the model complexity and nonlinearity.

In this paper, we first improve the mathematical model for pulverizers developed in [2] based on the analysis of the operation mechanism. The improved model contains twelve coefficients, and it allows more precise description of the nonlinear dynamic properties for the pulverizers. However, for such an intrinsically complex model, the analytical solutions of these model coefficients are difficult to obtain. To overcome this difficulty, an improved GA is employed. The above method is then employed to model a pulverizer of a power plant in Shanghai. Given the complexity of the obtained model, it is then converted into a T-S fuzzy model. In the fuzzy model, local dynamics in different state-space regions is represented by linear models.

D.-S. Huang, K. Li, and G.W. Irwin (Eds.): ICIC 2006, LNCS 4113, pp. 1269 – 1274, 2006.

The blended linear models can give a very precise approximation of the nonlinear system [4]~[8]. Thus, we can design controller with good performance for every linear system, and satisfactory controller for the whole nonlinear system using parallel distributed compensation (PDC).

## 2 Nonlinear Mathematical Model of Medium Speed Pulverizers

The objective of controlling a coal medium speed pulverizer is to regulate the amount of coal being ground so that a proper amount of pulverized fuel is fed to the burners to meet the load requirements while maintaining optimum operations [9]. The model in [2] describes the nonlinear dynamic characteristics of the pulverizer from the view of controller design. It is composed of three differential equations and three algebra equations [2].

$$\begin{cases} \dot{M}_c = W_c - K_{11}M_c \\ \dot{M}_{pf} = K_{11}M_c - W_{pf} \\ \dot{T}_{out} = (K_1T_{in} + K_2)W_{air} + K_3W_c - (W_{air} + W_c)(K_4T_{out} + K_5) \\ \Delta P_{mill} = K_8\Delta P_{pa} + K_9(M_{pf} + K_{10}M_c) \\ W_{pf} = K_{12}\Delta P_{pa}M_{pf} \\ P = K_6(\Delta P_{mill} - \Delta P_{pa}) + K_7 \end{cases} \tag{1}$$

where

$M_c$ mass of coal in pulverizer (kg)
$M_{pf}$ mass of pulverized coal in pulverier (kg)
$T_{out}$ outlet temperature of pulverizer (℃)
$\Delta P_{mill}$ pulverizer differential pressure (Pa)
$W_{pf}$ mass flow rate of pulverized coal out of pulverizer (kg/s)
$P$ consumed pulverizer power (MW)
$\Delta P_{pa}$ primary air differential pressure (Pa)
$W_c$ mass flow rate of coal into pulverizer (kg/s)
$T_{in}$ inlet temperature of pulverizer (℃)
$W_{air}$ primary air flow into pulverizer (kg/s)
$K_i$ $i$=1,2,3,…,12, constant coefficients.

The input variables are $W_c$, $\Delta P_{pa}$, $T_{in}$ and $W_{air}$. The output variables are $\Delta P_{mill}$, $T_{out}$, $W_{pf}$ and $P$. Equation set (1) is applicable to most pulverizers. The nonlinear dynamic properties of different pulverizers can be well described using different sets of values for the coefficients $K_1$ ~$K_{12}$.

In the practical operations, the air-coal ratio is always kept constant according to the load variety, and can not be regulated randomly. $W_{air}$ has a square relationship with $\Delta P_{pa}$. So $\Delta P_{pa}$, $W_c$ and $W_{air}$ can be unified into $W_{air}$. Then the input variables can be simplified into $W_{air}$ and $T_{in}$. In output variables, $P$ and $\Delta P_{mill}$ are the monitored parameters that can not be regulated as well. $T_{out}$ of pulverizer is an important parameter that should be controlled in the operation. So the output variables that should be regulated are $T_{out}$ and $W_{pf}$.

The following equation relates the primary air-flow into pulverizer $W_{air}$ and the primary air differential pressure $\Delta P_{pa}$ [10]:

$$W_{air} = \frac{1}{\sqrt{K_{pw}}}\left(\Delta P_{pa} / T\right)^{0.5} \tag{2}$$

where $K_{pw}$ is the correction coefficients; $T = T_{in} + 273.15$ is the Kelvin temperature of the primary air.

$$\Delta P_{pa} = K_{pw} T W_{air}^2 = K_{pw}\left(T_{in} + 273.15\right) W_{air}^2 \tag{3}$$

The ratio of coal and air is $K_{ca}$, that is, $W_c = K_{ca} W_{air}$.

According to the above analysis, the equation set (1) of the pulverizer model can be converted into the following mathematical model:

$$\begin{cases} \dot{M}_c = K_{ca} W_{air} - K_{11} M_c \\ \dot{M}_{pf} = K_{11} M_c - K_{12} \Delta P_{pa} M_{pf} \\ \dot{T}_{out} = -K_4\left(1 + K_{ca}\right) T_{out} W_{air} + K_1 T_{in} W_{air} + \left(K_2 + K_3 K_{ca} - K_5\left(1 + K_{ca}\right)\right) W_{air} \\ \Delta P_{mill} = K_8 \Delta P_{pa} + K_9\left(M_{pf} + K_{10} M_c\right) = K_8 K_{pw}\left(T_{in} + 273.15\right) W_{air}^2 + K_9\left(M_{pf} + K_{10} M_c\right) \\ W_{pf} = K_{12} \Delta P_{pa} M_{pf} \\ T_{out} = T_{out} \\ P = K_6\left(K_8 \Delta P_{pa} + K_9 (M_{pf} + K_{10} M_c) - \Delta P_{pa}\right) + K_7 \\ \quad = K_6\left(\left(K_8 - 1\right) K_{pw}\left(T_{in} + 273.15\right) W_{air}^2 + K_9 (M_{pf} + K_{10} M_c)\right) + K_7 \end{cases} \tag{4}$$

where $P$ and $\Delta P_{mill}$ are the monitored parameters and can not be manipulated.

## 3 T-S Fuzzy Model of Medium Speed Pulverizers

An improved GA can efficiently identify multiple coefficients in a set of equations [11]. We can obtain the whole mathematic model of a pulverizer by identifying the coefficients in equation set (2) using the improved GA. However, the model is a set of differential equations containing nonlinear terms. It is not convenient to design the controller for the pulverizer based on this nonlinear model.

To minimize the design effort and complexity , we try to use as few rules as possible while guaranteeing the accuracy when the nonlinear system is approximated by a T-S fuzzy model. Let the primary air differential pressure $\Delta P_{pa}$ and the primary air-flow into pulverizer $W_{air}$ be the premise variables of T-S fuzzy model. $W_{air}$ and the product of $T_{in}$ and $W_{air}$ are the input variables. $W_{pf}$, $\Delta P_{mill}$, $T_{out}$, $P$-$K_7$ are the output variables. Then we obtain the following T-S fuzzy model for the pulverizer:

Plant Rule $i$:
IF $\Delta P_{pa}$ is $P_i$ and $W_{air}$ is $W_i$,
THEN $\dot{x} = A_i x + B_i u$
$\quad\quad\; y = C_i x + D_i u \quad i = 1, 2, 3, 4$

where

$$x=\begin{bmatrix} M_c & M_{pf} & T_{out} \end{bmatrix}'; \qquad u=\begin{bmatrix} W_{air} & T_{in}W_{air} \end{bmatrix}'; \qquad y=\begin{bmatrix} \Delta P_{mill} & T_{out} & W_{pf} & D-K_7 \end{bmatrix}';$$

$$A_i=\begin{bmatrix} -K_{11} & 0 & 0 \\ K_{11} & -K_{12}\Delta P_{pa} & 0 \\ 0 & 0 & -K_4(1+K_{ca})W_{air} \end{bmatrix}; \quad B_i=\begin{bmatrix} K_{ca} & 0 \\ 0 & 0 \\ K_2+K_3K_{ca}-K_5(1+K_{ca}) & K \end{bmatrix};$$

$$C_i=\begin{bmatrix} K_9K_{10} & K_9 & 0 \\ 0 & 0 & 1 \\ 0 & K_{12}\Delta P_{pa} & 0 \\ K_6K_9K_{10} & K_6K_9 & 0 \end{bmatrix}; \quad D_i=\begin{bmatrix} 273.15K_8K_{pw}W_{air} & K_8K_{pw}W_{air} \\ 0 & 0 \\ 0 & 0 \\ 273.15K_6(K_8-1)K_{pw}W_{air} & K_6(K_8-1)K_{pw}W_{air} \end{bmatrix}$$

Membership functions for Plant Rule 1~4 are as follows:

$$\mu_1^1(\Delta P_{pa})=\frac{-\Delta P_{pa}+P_2}{P_2-P_1}; \quad \mu_2^1(W_{air})=\frac{-W_{air}+W_2}{W_2-W_1}; \quad \mu_1^2(\Delta P_{pa})=\frac{-\Delta P_{pa}+P_2}{P_2-P_1}; \quad \mu_2^2(W_{air})=\frac{W_{air}-W_1}{W_2-W_1};$$

$$\mu_1^3(\Delta P_{pa})=\frac{\Delta P_{pa}-P_1}{P_2-P_1}; \quad \mu_2^3(W_{air})=\frac{-W_{air}+W_2}{W_2-W_1}; \quad \mu_1^4(\Delta P_{pa})=\frac{\Delta P_{pa}-P_1}{P_2-P_1}; \quad \mu_2^4(W_{air})=\frac{W_{air}-W_1}{W_2-W_1};$$

$[P_1,\ P_2]$ are the high and low limits of $\Delta P_{pa}$ in operation; $[W_1,\ W_2]$ are the high and low limits of $W_{air}$ in operation.

Blending linear models (1)~(4) through the above nonlinear fuzzy membership functions $\mu_i^j\,(i=1,2;\, j=1,2,3,4)$, we get the T-S fuzzy model of the pulverizer as follows:

$$\begin{cases} \dot{x}(t)=\sum_{i=1}^{4} h_i\left[A_i x(t)+B_i u(t)\right] \\ y(t)=\sum_{i=1}^{4} h_i\left[C_i x(t)+D_i u(t)\right] \end{cases}, \qquad h_i=\frac{\mu_1^i\mu_2^i}{\sum_{i=1}^{4}\mu_1^i\mu_2^i} \tag{5}$$

The T-S fuzzy model is equivalent to the nonlinear model of the pulverizer represented by equation set (2). It is suitable for the controller design for the pulverizer. The outcome will be useful in improving the design of the operating procedures and the control strategies for medium speed pulverizers.

## 4 Simulation Research

To validate the T-S fuzzy model of the pulverizer, we model a real medium speed pulverizer.The data are measured from a pulverizer group that consists of five HP863-type pulverizers operating in a commercial power plant. The pulverizer exhibits significant variation in the operation during the data acquisition (DAQ) period.

Choosing appropriate $P_1$, $P_2$, $W_1$ and $W_2$, we can get the coefficient matrixes of the T-S fuzzy model for the pulverizer.

The T-S fuzzy model output variable values obtained from the simulation are show in Figs. 1~2 indicated by solid line. The observed values are indicated by dashed line.

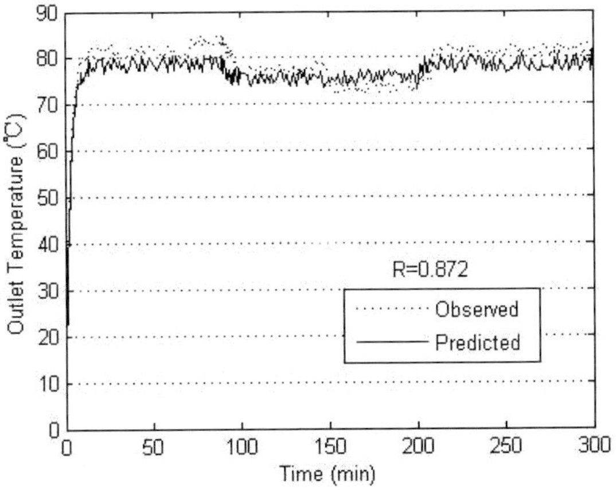


**Fig. 1.** Outlet temperature simulation

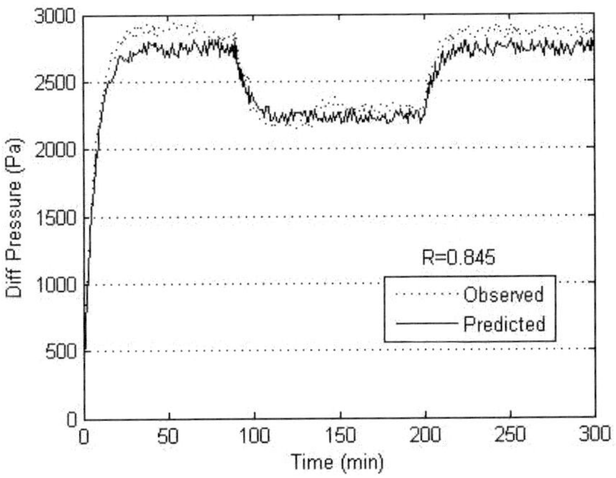


**Fig. 2.** Differential pressure simulation

The value of correlation coefficient $R$ is defined to indicate the correlation degree between the observed and predicted values [2]. These figures indicate that the T-S fuzzy model predictions agree well with the measured values during the whole process.

# 5 Conclusions

In this paper, a mathematical model has been developed to describe the nonlinear dynamic characteristics of a pulverizer. An improved GA has been employed to identify the optimum coefficients of the pulverizer model. Then the model is approximated by an equivalent T-S fuzzy model. We model the HP863 type pulverizer which currently is still in the service in a real power unit. The simulation results show that the model can give an accurate representation of the real pulverizer system. Thus it is possible to examine intermediate state variables which are difficult to measure in practice. The model also makes it convenient to design the control system for the nonlinear pulverizer.

## Acknowledgement

This work was supported by Key Project of Science & Technology Commission of Shanghai Municipality under grant 04JC14038 and 04DZ11008, Program for New Century Excellent Talents in University (NCET-04-0433), and Shanghai Leading Academic Disciplines (T0103).

## References

1. Zhou, G., Si, J., Taft, C.W.: Modeling and simulation of C-E deep bowl pulverizer. IEEE Transactions on Energy Conversion. 3 (2000) 312-322
2. Zhang, Y.G., Wu, Q.H., Wang, J., Matts, D., Zhou, X.X.: Pulverizer modeling by machine learning based on onsite measurements. IEEE Transactions on Energy Conversion. 4 (2002) 549-555
3. Tanaka, S., Kurosaki, Y., Teramoto, T., Murakami, S.: Dynamic simulation analysis of MPS mill for coal fired boiler and application of its results to boiler control system. IFAC Symposium of Power Plant and Control, Beijing, China (1997)
4. Takagi, T., Sugeno, M.: Fuzzy Identification of Systems and Its Applications to Modeling and Control. IEEE Transactions on System, Man, and Cybernetics. 1 (1985) 116-132
5. Wu, H.N., Zhang, H.Y.: Reliable mixed L-2/H-infinity fuzzy static output feedback control for nonlinear systems with sensor faults. Automatica. 11 (2005) 1925-1932
6. Lin, C., Wang, Q.G., Lee, T.H.: Improvement on observer-based H-infinity control for T-S fuzzy systems. Automatica. 9 (2005) 1651-1656
7. Chen, S.S., Chang, Y.C., Su, S.F.: Robust static output feedback stabilization for nonlinear discrete-time systems with time delay via fuzzy control approach. IEEE Transactions on Fuzzy Systems. 2 (2005) 263-272
8. Liu, H.P., Sun, F.C., Sun, Z.Q.: Stability analysis and synthesis of fuzzy singularly perturbed systems. IEEE Transactions on Fuzzy Systems. 2 (2005) 273-284
9. Li, K., Thompson, S., Peng, J.: Modelling and prediction of NOx emission in a coal-fired power generation plant. Control Engineering Practice. 12 (2004) 707-723
10. Huang, X.Y.: Operation and combustion regulation of boiler in power plants. Chinese electric power press, Beijing, (2003)
11. Leung, F.H.F., Lam, H.K., Ling, S.H., Tam, Peter K.S.: Tuning of the structure and parameters of a neural network using an improved genetic algorithm. IEEE Transactions on Neural Networks. 1 (2003) 79-88

# Least Squares Support Vector Machines Based on Support Vector Degrees*

Lijuan Li[1,2], Youfeng Li[1], Hongye Su[1], and Jian Chu[1]

[1] National Laboratory of Industrial Control Technology, Institute of Advanced Process Control, Zhejiang University, Yuquan Campus, Hangzhou, 310027, P.R. China
[2] College of Automation, Nanjing University of Technology, Nanjing, 210009, P.R. China
ljli@iipc.zju.edu.cn

**Abstract.** A modified least squares support vector machines (LS-SVM) approach, which treats the training data points differently according to their different degrees of importance, is proposed in this paper. On each data point, a support vector degree is defined and it is associated with the corresponding absolute value of Lagrange multiplier. The experiment of identification of pH neutralization process with polluted measuring data is shown in this paper and the result indicates that the method is effective in identification of nonlinear system. By contrast with the basic LS-SVM, the result also shows the priority of the presented new algorithm.

## 1 Introduction

Support Vector Machine (SVM) based on the principle of structural risk minimization was introduced by Vapnik [1], [2]. The theory has drawn much attention for the high generalization ability in classification and regression problems [3], [4]. Fuzzy Support Vector Machine (FSVM) is a modified SVM algorithm for data with noise or outliers [5]. Weighted errors are introduced into the cost function such that different points can make different contributions to the learning of classification function in [5]. Least Squares Support Vector Machine (LS-SVM) was developed by Suykens [6] in which analytical solutions can be obtained by solving linear equations instead of a quadratic programming (QP) problem. In [6], all the data points are support vectors and make the same contributions in the training.

In this paper, a concept of support vector degree is introduced in LS-SVM to distinguish different contributions of different data points. The support vector degree of a data point is determined by the absolute value of corresponding Lagrange multiplier, that is, those with larger absolute value are considered more

* This work was supported by the National Natural Science Foundation of China (60421002) and Priority supported financially by "the New Century 151 Talent Project" of Zhejiang Province.

D.-S. Huang, K. Li, and G.W. Irwin (Eds.): ICIC 2006, LNCS 4113, pp. 1275–1281, 2006.

important and vice versa. By the experiment of nonlinear system identification for a pH neutralization process with polluted measuring data, the result indicates the better performance of the proposed approach compared with the benchmark LS-SVM.

## 2 Least Squares Support Vector Machines

Given a data set $\{(\boldsymbol{x}_i, y_i)\}_{i=1}^N$, where $N$ is the total number of training data pairs, $\boldsymbol{x}_i \in \mathcal{R}^n$ is input vector and $y_i \in \mathcal{R}$ is output signal. According to the SVM theory of Vapnik [1], [2], the input space $\mathcal{R}^n$ is mapped into a feature space $\mathcal{Z}$ with a nonlinear function $\varphi(\boldsymbol{x}_i)$ being the corresponding mapping function. In the feature space, we take the form

$$y(\boldsymbol{x}) = \boldsymbol{w}^T\varphi(\boldsymbol{x}) + b \quad \text{with} \quad \boldsymbol{w} \in \mathcal{Z}, b \in \mathcal{R} \tag{1}$$

to estimate the unknown nonlinear function where $\boldsymbol{w}$ and $b$ are the parameters to be identified. The optimization problem is defined as follows

$$\min_{\boldsymbol{w},\boldsymbol{e}} J(\boldsymbol{w}, \boldsymbol{e}) = \frac{1}{2}\boldsymbol{w}^T\boldsymbol{w} + \frac{\gamma}{2}\sum_{i=1}^N e_i^2 \quad \gamma > 0 \tag{2}$$

$$\text{subject to} \quad y_i = \boldsymbol{w}^T\varphi(\boldsymbol{x}_i) + b + e_i \quad i = 1, 2, \ldots, N. \tag{3}$$

where $e_i$ is the error between actual output and predictive output of the $i$th data.

The LS-SVM model of the data set can be given by

$$y(\boldsymbol{x}) = \sum_{i=1}^N \alpha_i K(\boldsymbol{x}, \boldsymbol{x}_i) + b \tag{4}$$

where $\alpha_i \in \mathcal{R}$ $(i=1, 2, \ldots, N)$ are Lagrange multipliers, $K(\boldsymbol{x}, \boldsymbol{x}_i)$ $(i=1, 2, \ldots, N)$ are any kernel functions satisfying the Mercer condition [3]. The typical kernel functions are linear, polynomial, Radial Basis Function (RBF), MLP functions, *etc.* Analytical solutions of parameters $\alpha_i \in \mathcal{R}$ $(i = 1, 2, \ldots, N)$ and $b$ can be obtained from the equation

$$\begin{bmatrix} b \\ \boldsymbol{\alpha} \end{bmatrix} = \boldsymbol{\Phi}^{-1} \begin{bmatrix} 0 \\ \boldsymbol{Y} \end{bmatrix} \tag{5}$$

with $\boldsymbol{Y} = [y_1 \; y_2 \; \ldots \; y_N]^T$, $\boldsymbol{\alpha} = [\alpha_1 \; \alpha_2 \; \ldots \; \alpha_N]^T$ and the supposed nonsingular matrix

$$\boldsymbol{\Phi} = \begin{bmatrix} \mathbf{0} & \mathbf{1}^T \\ \mathbf{1} & \boldsymbol{\Omega} + \gamma^{-1}\boldsymbol{I} \end{bmatrix} \tag{6}$$

where $\mathbf{1} = [1 \; 1 \; \ldots \; 1]^T$, $\boldsymbol{I}$ is a $N \times N$ identity matrix and $\boldsymbol{\Omega}$ is a $N \times N$ symmetric matrix with the elements

$$\boldsymbol{\Omega}_{ij} = \varphi(\boldsymbol{x}_i)^T\varphi(\boldsymbol{x}_j) = K(\boldsymbol{x}_i, \boldsymbol{x}_j) \quad i, j = 1, 2, \ldots, N. \tag{7}$$

# 3 LS-SVM Based on Support Vector Degree

## 3.1 Definition of Support Vector Degree

In (2), all the errors $e_i$ are added in the same weight 1, *i.e.* all the data points make the same contributions to the training. However, in many applications, the data obtained are not so identically significant. Some data probably include noise whereas others are not polluted. Moreover, noise in different data is hardly equal. Those comprising larger noise would inevitably affect the precision of the function estimation. Even if all the data does not comprise noise, data points located at different positions of the function curve are also not uniformly significant. The points at the maximum and minimum of the function are generally more important than those at the smooth section. Therefore, different data points should be treated with different weights in the cost function. In benchmark SVM, data points with zero Lagrange multipliers are non-support vectors (non-SVs) and they are redundant, *i.e.* even without these points in the training set, the SVM would construct exactly the same function [3]. So these non-SVs can be ignored in the process of solving SVM. However, it is also not so exact that the support vectors (with nonzero Lagrange multipliers) are treated uniformly despite their unequal Lagrange multipliers. Those with smaller absolute values of Lagrange multiplier close to zero consequentially are not so important and can even be neglected whereas those with much larger values are so important that they should be emphasized in the training.

In LS-SVM, all the data points are support vectors because all the Lagrange multipliers are nonzero. To distinguish the different degrees of importance, a support vector degree $0 < s_i < 1$ is defined to each data point $(x_i, y_i)$, *i.e.* $0 < s_i < 1$ denotes the degree of the point $(x_i, y_i)$ belonging to support vectors set and the relatively larger $s_i$ denotes that the corresponding point belongs to support vectors set to a higher extent. On the other hand, the absolute value of Lagrange multiplier can evaluate the importance of the data point for contribution to the LS-SVM model, which has been pointed out in [7], and just based on which we can define the support vector degree of each point through the absolute value of corresponding Lagrange multiplier,

$$s_i = f(\alpha_i) = (1-\delta)\left(\frac{|\alpha_i| - |\alpha_{\min}|}{|\alpha_{\max}| - |\alpha_{\min}|}\right) + \delta \tag{8}$$

where sufficient small parameter $\delta > 0$ is the minimum of support vector degree $s_i$, $\alpha_{\min}$ is the Lagrange multiplier with minimum absolute value and $\alpha_{\max}$ is that of maximum.

## 3.2 LS-SVM with Support Vector Degree

Given a data set $\{(\boldsymbol{x}_i, y_i, s_i)\}_{i=1}^{N}$, where $N$ is the total number of training data pairs, $\boldsymbol{x}_i \in \mathcal{R}^n$ is input vector, $y_i \in \mathcal{R}$ is output signal, and $s_i$ is the corresponding support vector degree. Then, $s_i$ is introduced into the second term of (2) and optimization problem is defined as

$$\min_{\boldsymbol{w},\boldsymbol{e}} J(\boldsymbol{w},\boldsymbol{e}) = \frac{1}{2}\boldsymbol{w}^T\boldsymbol{w} + \frac{\gamma}{2}\sum_{i=1}^{N} s_i e_i^2 \quad \gamma > 0 \tag{9}$$

$$\text{subject to} \quad y_i = \boldsymbol{w}^T\varphi(\boldsymbol{x}_i) + b + e_i \quad i = 1, 2, \ldots, N \tag{10}$$

where parameters have the same meanings as those in section 2.

The final formulation of analytical solution is just as (5), but the matrix $\boldsymbol{\Phi}$ is

$$\boldsymbol{\Phi} = \begin{bmatrix} \mathbf{0} & \mathbf{1}^T \\ \mathbf{1} & \Omega + (\gamma \boldsymbol{S})^{-1} \end{bmatrix} \tag{11}$$

with $\boldsymbol{S} = \text{diag}\{s_1, s_2, \ldots, s_N\}$. The expression of estimation function is the same as (4).

From the above presentation, it is easy to find that, with all $s_i = 1$, the modified LS-SVM is just the same as benchmark LS-SVM, namely, the benchmark LS-SVM is only a special formulation of the proposed algorithm.

### 3.3 Procedure of the Modified LS-SVM

From (8) we know that support vector degree is determined by the absolute values of Lagrange multipliers. Then there comes a question: now that the Lagrange multipliers are calculated from the LS-SVM algorithm, how to get the values and compute the support vector degrees before the algorithm starts? To solve the problem, we first start the algorithm with the benchmark LS-SVM, namely all the $\{s_i\}_{i=1}^N$ are set to 1, and then the modified LS-SVM can be carried out. The procedure is designed as follows,

1. Train modified LS-SVM based on given data set $\{(\boldsymbol{x}_i, y_i, s_i)\}_{i=1}^N$ where initial values of support vector degrees $s_i|_{i=1}^N$ are set to 1 (*i.e.* benchmark LS-SVM), and the initial values of $\alpha_i|_{i=1}^N$ are obtained after the first training.
2. Calculate $s_i|_{i=1}^N$ based on (8) and update the data set $\{(\boldsymbol{x}_i, y_i, s_i)\}_{i=1}^N$.
3. Train the modified LS-SVM based on the renewed data set and get final Lagrange multipliers $\alpha_i|_{i=1}^N$ and the parameter $b$.

## 4 Experiments

The modified LS-SVM in section 3 is applied into the identification of pH neutralization process which is a system with strong nonlinearity, especially in the vicinity of pH$=9$.

The physical model of a pH process in a continuously stirred tank reactor (CSTR) consists of two parts, a linear dynamical part followed by a nonlinear static part [8]. The dynamical model is given by

$$\begin{cases} V\frac{dw_a}{dt} & = F_a C_a - (F_a + F_b) w_a \\ V\frac{dw_b}{dt} & = F_b C_b - (F_a + F_b) w_b \end{cases} \tag{12}$$

where $F_a$ and $F_b$ denote the inlet flow-rate of acid and base (cm$^3$/min), respectively, $C_a$ and $C_b$ are the inlet concentrations of acid and base (mol/l), the

**Table 1.** Parameter Values Used in The Model

| Parameter | Nominal Value |
|---|---|
| $F_a$ | $81\text{cm}^3/\text{min}$ |
| $C_a$ | 0.32mol/l |
| $C_b$ | 0.05mol/l |
| $V$ | $1000\text{cm}^3$ |
| $w_a(0)$ | 0.0435mol/l |
| $w_b(0)$ | 0.0432mol/l |

**Table 2.** Comparison of Root Mean Squared Error

| | $n=1$ | $n=2$ | $n=3$ | $n=4$ | $n=5$ | $n=6$ | Average |
|---|---|---|---|---|---|---|---|
| LS-SVM | 0.5053 | 0.4564 | 0.7617 | 0.4742 | 0.5053 | 0.6306 | 0.5556 |
| Modified LS-SVM | 0.3792 | 0.3401 | 0.5556 | 0.3414 | 0.3736 | 0.3779 | 0.3946 |

volume of the content in the reactor is denoted by the constant $V(\text{cm}^3)$, $w_a$ and $w_b$ are the concentrations of acid and base after the process of dynamical model (mol/l). Simultaneously $w_a$ and $w_b$ are the inputs of the static model

$$w_b + 10^{-y} - 10^{y-14} - \frac{w_a}{1+10^{pK_a-y}} = 0 \tag{13}$$

where $y$ is the pH value of the effluent, $K_a$ is the dissociation constant of the acetic acid with $K_a = 1.76 \times 10^{-5}$ and $pK_a = -\log_{10} K_a$.

By fixing the flow-rate $F_a$ at a specific value, the process is regarded as a single variable system with base flow-rate $F_b$ and pH value $y$ of the effluent being the input and the output, respectively. The data pairs $\{F_b(i), y(i)\}_{i=1}^N$ with $N$ being the number of samples are produced using the physical model with the parameter values given in Table 1. The input $F_b$ is the sum of a fixed value 515 $(\text{cm}^3/\min)$ plus an uniformly distributed random signal ranging in the interval [- 51.5, + 51.5]. The variable $y$ is the output including measured noise with standard deviation of 0.2. The sample period is 0.5min. The RBF function

$$K(\boldsymbol{x}, x_i) = \exp\{-\|x - x_i\|_2^2/\sigma^2\} \tag{14}$$

is employed as the kernel function of the LS-SVM in the experiment where $\sigma = 2.1$. The minimum $\delta$ of support vector degree $s_i$ is set to 0.1.

In the experiments, 400 data pairs are trained by the basic LS-SVM and the modified LS-SVM with $\gamma = 100$, respectively. 200 test data pairs are produced by the physical model with the sum of four sine waves of different frequencies being the input. We randomly carried out the experiments six times and the total root mean squared error (RMSE) over the test data is shown in Table 2 where $n$ is the serial number. The tracking results by basic LS-SVM and modified LS-SVM are showed in Fig.1 and Fig.2, respectively, where YYs are the physical model curves and YMs are the identified model curves.

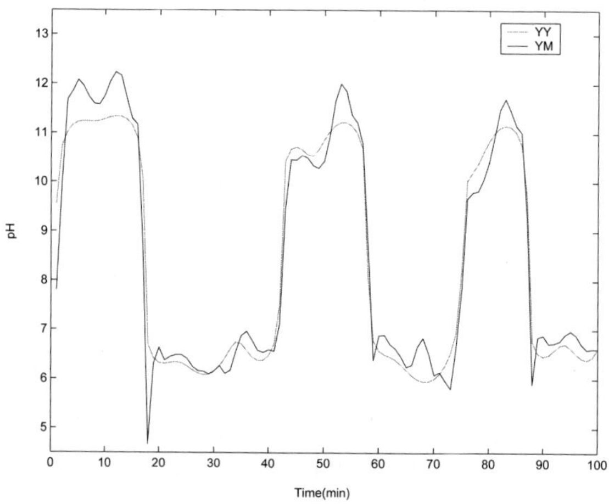


**Fig. 1.** Test result of LS-SVM model

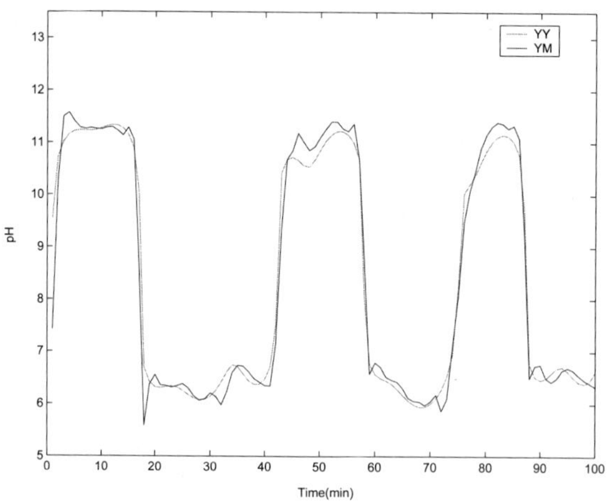


**Fig. 2.** Test result of modified LS-SVM model

It can be seen from Fig.2 that the modified LS-SVM can distinguish the significance of different data points and track the test curves effectively although the training data are polluted. Moreover, higher tracking precision is obtained in Fig.2 compared with Fig.1, especially in the vicinity of peak points.

## 5 Conclusions

In this paper, a modified LS-SVM algorithm based on support vector degree is presented which treats the data points differently according to the absolute values of Lagrange multipliers. A similar strategy, *i.e.* fuzzy support vector machines (FSVM) [5], has been proposed in which the member function corresponds to the support vector degree defined in section 3, but it has not given an effective method to determine the member function. Reference [9] tries to solve the problem turning out a quite intricate method in which a heuristic function needs to be ascertained beforehand. This paper gives a simple and effective approach to determine the parameters by associating each support vector degree with corresponding Lagrange multiplier. The simulation result of a pH neutralization process indicates the validity of the method.

## References


1. Vapnik, V.: Statistical Learning Theory. John Wiley, New York (1998)
2. Vapnik, V.: The Nature of Statistical Learning Theory. Spring-Verlag, Berlin Heidelberg New York (1995)
3. Smola, A. J., Schökopf, B.: A Tutorial on Support Vector Regression [online]. Available: http://www.neurocolt.com/tech_reps/1998/98030.ps.gz
4. Gestel, T. V., Suykens, J. A. K.: Benchmarking Least Squares Support Vector Machine Classifiers. Kluwer Academic Publishers, Netherlands (2001)
5. Lin, C., Wang, S.: Fuzzy Support Vector Machines. Neural Networks, 13 (2002) 464–471
6. Suykens, J. A. K., Vandewalle, J.: Least Squares Support Vector Machine Classifiers. Neural Processing Letters 9 (1999) 293–300
7. Suykens, J. A. K., Lukas, L., Vandewalle, J.: Sparse Approximation Using Least Squares Support Vector Machines. IEEE International Symposium on Circuits and Systems, Geneva, Swizerland (2000) 757–760
8. Nie, J. H., Loh, A. P., Hang, C. C.: Modeling pH Neutralization Process Using Fuzzy-neutral Approaches. Fuzzy Set and Systems 78 (1996) 5–22
9. Lin, C., Wang, S.: Training Algorithms for Fuzzy Support Vector Machines with Noisy Data. Pattern Recognition Letters 25 (2004) 1647–1656

# Staged Neural Modeling with Application to Prediction of $NO_x$ Pollutant Concentrations in Urban Air

Kang Li[1], Barbara Pizzileo[1], Adetutu Ogle[2], and Colm Scott[1]

[1] School of Electronics, Electronic Engineering & Computer Science
Queen's University Belfast, Stranmillis Road, Belfast BT9 5AH, U.K.
K.LI@qub.ac.uk
[2] ATU, QUESTOR centre, Queen's University Belfast
Stranmillis Road, Belfast, BT9 5AG, UK

**Abstract.** Addressing the drawbacks of widely used forward neural network growing methods in neural modeling of time series and nonlinear dynamic systems, a staged algorithm is proposed in this paper for modeling and prediction of $NO_x$ Pollutant Concentrations in urban air in Belfast, Northern Ireland, using generalized single-layer network. In this algorithm, forward method is used for neural network growing, the resultant network is then refined at the second stage to remove inefficient hidden nodes. Application study confirms the effectiveness of the proposed method.

## 1 Introduction

As a major pollutant in the air that affects human health, the nitrogen oxide ($NO_x$) emission problem has received a lot of public attentions and academic researches in the past decade [1][2]. Vehicle exhaust and other combustion emissions (including household heating systems, industrial combustors of different scales, etc) are the main sources of NOx in urban air. Most NOx is emitted in the form of nitric oxides (NO), but most of it is ultimately converted to $NO_2$ by reaction with ozone ($O_3$) in the atmosphere. Both for the air quality forecasting and for the development of control strategy and policy, it is important to identify the factors that control $NO_x$ concentrations and to develop a function (model) to predict the $NO_x$ concentration [2].

There exist two different general approaches in developing the prediction model. The first approach is to develop atmospheric diffusion models, and the second is the black-box models such as regressions models and neural networks [2]. The first approach requires detailed $NO_x$ emission data distributed over the studied area which is usually very difficult to obtain, and the modeling process is computationally quite demanding. The second approach is to develop a model to represent the correlations of possible inputs with $NO_x$ outputs, which is perhaps more computationally efficient. However the second approach heavily depends on the modeling method and the historic data quality and richness.

Among various black-box models, the generalized single-layer network (GSLN) represents a large class of flexible and efficient structures for modeling time-series and nonlinear dynamic systems due to their excellent approximating capabilities [3][4]. GSLNs, sometimes also called generalized linear discriminants, is a linear

D.-S. Huang, K. Li, and G.W. Irwin (Eds.): ICIC 2006, LNCS 4113, pp. 1282 – 1293, 2006.

combinations of some basis functions that are arbitrary (usually nonlinear) functions of the inputs. Depending on the set of basis functions used, various GSLNs have been proposed, such as the radial basis function (RBF) networks, polynomial neural networks and Volterra networks. If more than one type of basis functions is used in the network, a popular structure is the functional-link network (FLN). FLN is a simplified neural network structure that allows the user to integrate some types of known process dynamics into the model, and it is computationally capable as conventional feedforward networks.

One problem with GSLNs is that an excessive number of basis functions are considered initially, from which a small subset of candidate basis functions are selected, based on the parsimonious principle, which explains the data. To solve this problem, a number of approaches have been proposed, and the stepwise forward subset selection is perhaps the most widely used one [5][6][7]. Forward subset selection algorithms select one basis function at a time, which maximizes the reduction of cost function usually the sum-squared-errors (SSE) between the neural outputs and targets. This process is repeated until the desired number of, say n, basis functions have been selected. If n is unknown a 'prior', some other selection criterion may be applied, such as the Akaike's information criteion (AIC) [8], etc.

Although the forward approaches introduce one basis function each time based on largest improvement in model fit, the overall SSE is not minimized due to the linear correlativeness of the late introduced basis function and previously selection functions. This results in that the produced model is inefficient in the sense that it requires more than the smallest possible number of basis functions to achieve a specified SSE value [9]. This inefficiency can be improved by adopting a staged method which employs both forward neural construction and backward network refinement.

## 2 Problem Representation

Suppose $M$ candidate basis functions $\phi_i(t), i=1,2,\cdots,M$ are considered initially for neural network modeling, and a set of $N$ samples of experimental data is used for neural network training. This leads a regression matrix $\mathbf{\Phi}=[\boldsymbol{\phi}_1,\boldsymbol{\phi}_2,\cdots,\boldsymbol{\phi}_M]$ where

$$\boldsymbol{\phi}_i=[\phi_i(1),\phi_i(2),\cdots,\phi_i(N)]^{\mathrm{T}}, i=1,2,\cdots,M \tag{1}$$

is refereed to as a *candidate basis vector*. The problem becomes to select, say $n$, vectors denoted as $\mathbf{p}_1,\mathbf{p}_2,\cdots,\mathbf{p}_n$, from these above candidates to form the neural model of the form

$$\mathbf{y}=\mathbf{P}\boldsymbol{\theta}+\mathbf{e} \tag{2}$$

which fits the experiment data to minimizes the SSE

$$J(\mathbf{P})=\mathbf{e}^{\mathrm{T}}\mathbf{e}=(\mathbf{y}-\mathbf{P}\boldsymbol{\theta})^{\mathrm{T}}(\mathbf{y}-\mathbf{P}\boldsymbol{\theta})\rightarrow \min \tag{3}$$

where $\mathbf{y}=[y(1),y(2),\cdots,y(N)]^{\mathrm{T}}$ is targets. If $\mathbf{P}=[\mathbf{p}_1,\mathbf{p}_2,\cdots,\mathbf{p}_n]$ is of full column rank, the least-squares estimation of the regression coefficients $\boldsymbol{\theta}$ is

$$\boldsymbol{\theta}=(\mathbf{P}^{\mathrm{T}}\mathbf{P})^{-1}\mathbf{P}^{\mathrm{T}}\mathbf{y} \tag{4}$$

Note that there are $M!/n!/(M-n)!$ potential combinations of $n$ regressors out of the $M$ candidates. It is often a so big number that enumerating all possible combinations to identify the global optimal solution is computationally infeasible.

## 3 A Staged Algorithm

In this paper, a staged algorithm is used for both neural network growing and network refinement.

### 3.1 Forward Method for Neural Network Growing

Denote the regression matrix composing of the $k$ selected basis vectors

$$\mathbf{P}_k = [\mathbf{p}_1, \mathbf{p}_2, \cdots, \mathbf{p}_k], k = 1,2,\cdots,n \tag{5}$$

The corresponding SSE is then computed by substituting (4) into (3) as

$$J(\mathbf{P}_k) = \mathbf{y}^{\mathrm{T}}\mathbf{y} - \mathbf{y}^{\mathrm{T}}\mathbf{P}_k(\mathbf{P}_k^{\mathrm{T}}\mathbf{P}_k)^{-1}\mathbf{P}_k^{\mathrm{T}}\mathbf{y} \tag{6}$$

If $\mathbf{P}_k$ is of full column rank, then $\mathbf{W} = \mathbf{P}_k^{\mathrm{T}}\mathbf{P}_k \triangleq [w_{i,j}]_{k\times k}$ is symmetric and positive definite which can be decomposed as

$$\mathbf{W} = \mathbf{P}_k^{\mathrm{T}}\mathbf{P}_k = \tilde{\mathbf{A}}^{\mathrm{T}}\mathbf{D}\tilde{\mathbf{A}}, \tag{7}$$

where $\mathbf{D} = diag(d_1, \cdots, d_k)$ and $\tilde{\mathbf{A}} = [\tilde{a}_{i,j}]_{k\times k}$ is a unity upper triangular. Define

$$\mathbf{A} \triangleq \mathbf{D}\tilde{\mathbf{A}} = [a_{i,j}]_{k\times k}, a_{i,j} = \begin{cases} 0, & j < i \\ d_i\tilde{a}_{i,j} & j \ge i \end{cases} \tag{8}$$

Noting that $\tilde{a}_{i,i} = 1$ hence $d_i = a_{i,i}$ holds for $i = 1,\cdots,k$. From (7), there have

$$a_{i,j} = w_{i,j} - \textstyle\sum_{s=1}^{i-1} a_{s,i}a_{s,j} / a_{s,s}, i = 1,\cdots,k, j = i,\cdots,k \tag{9}$$

Define

$$\mathbf{a}_y \triangleq \mathbf{A}\boldsymbol{\theta} = \mathbf{D}\tilde{\mathbf{A}}\boldsymbol{\theta} = [a_{1,y}, \cdots, a_{k,y}]^{\mathrm{T}}. \tag{10}$$

and

$$\mathbf{w}_y \triangleq \mathbf{P}^{\mathrm{T}}\mathbf{y} = [w_{1,y}, \cdots, w_{k,y}]^{\mathrm{T}} \tag{11}$$

Left-multiplying $\mathbf{W} = \mathbf{P}_k^{\mathrm{T}}\mathbf{P}_k$ to both sides of (4) for $\mathbf{P} = \mathbf{P}_k$,

$$\tilde{\mathbf{A}}^{\mathrm{T}}\mathbf{a}_y = \mathbf{w}_y \tag{12}$$

Noting (8) and $\tilde{\mathbf{A}}$ is unity upper triangular, from (12) $\mathbf{a}_y$ could be readily computed as

$$a_{i,y} = w_{i,y} - \sum_{i=1}^{k-1} a_{s,i} a_{s,y} / a_{s,s}, i = 1, \cdots, k \tag{13}$$

Substituting (7) into (6) and noting (12) or $\mathbf{a}_y = (\tilde{\mathbf{A}}^{\mathrm{T}})^{-1} \mathbf{w}_y = (\tilde{\mathbf{A}}^{\mathrm{T}})^{-1} \mathbf{P}_k^{\mathrm{T}} \mathbf{y}$, therefore

$$J(\mathbf{P}_k) = \mathbf{y}^{\mathrm{T}}\mathbf{y} - \mathbf{y}^{\mathrm{T}}\mathbf{P}_k \tilde{\mathbf{A}}^{-1}\mathbf{D}^{-1}(\tilde{\mathbf{A}}^{\mathrm{T}})^{-1}\mathbf{P}_k^{\mathrm{T}}\mathbf{y} = \mathbf{y}^{\mathrm{T}}\mathbf{y} - \mathbf{a}_y^{\mathrm{T}}\mathbf{D}^{-1}\mathbf{a}_y$$

or

$$J(\mathbf{P}_k) = \mathbf{y}^{\mathrm{T}}\mathbf{y} - \sum_{i=1}^{k} a_{i,y}^2 / a_{i,i} \tag{14}$$

Supposing that one more basis vector $\mathbf{p}_{k+1}$ is selected, the SSE becomes

$$J(\mathbf{P}_{k+1}) = \mathbf{y}^{\mathrm{T}}\mathbf{y} - \sum_{i=1}^{k+1} a_{i,y}^2 / a_{i,i} \tag{15}$$

The *contribution* of the new basis vector $\mathbf{p}_{k+1}$ to the SSE reduction is

$$\Delta J_{k+1}(\mathbf{p}_{k+1}) = J(\mathbf{P}_k) - J(\mathbf{P}_{k+1}) = a_{k+1,y}^2 / a_{k+1,k+1} \tag{16}$$

where $a_{k+1,y}$ and $a_{k+1,k+1}$ are computed using (9) and (13) as the dimension $k$ increases by 1.

From (9) and (13), it reveals that if $\mathbf{p}_1, \cdots, \mathbf{p}_k$ are fixed, $\sum_{i=1}^{k} a_{i,y}^2 / a_{i,i}$ is a constant. Therefore, subject to that $\mathbf{p}_1, \cdots, \mathbf{p}_k$ is fixed, minimization of the SSE is equivalent to the maximization of $\Delta J_{k+1}$ as

$$\min\{J([\mathbf{P}_k, \phi)\} = J(\mathbf{P}_k) - \max\{\Delta J_{k+1}(\phi), \phi \in \{\phi_{k+1}, \cdots, \phi_M\}\} \tag{17}$$

where $\{\phi_{k+1}, \cdots, \phi_M\}$, referred to as the *candidate pool*, from which future basis vectors will be selected.

To find the best basis vector from the candidate pool, the contribution $\Delta J_{k+1}(\phi)$ for all the candidates needs to be computed using (16). To do this, $\mathbf{A}$, $\tilde{\mathbf{A}}$ and $\mathbf{a}_y$ is augmented as follows.

Suppose that $k$ regressors have been selected, $\mathbf{A}$ is augmented based on (9) as

$$\mathbf{A} = [a_{i,j}]_{k \times M}, a_{i,j} = \begin{cases} 0, & j < i \\ w_{i,j} - \sum_{s=1}^{i-1} a_{s,i} a_{s,j} / a_{s,s}, & i \le j \le M \end{cases} \tag{18}$$

where $w_{i,j} = \mathbf{p}_i^{\mathrm{T}}$ for $j \le k$, $w_{i,j} = \mathbf{p}_i^{\mathrm{T}} \phi_j$ for $j > k$. $\tilde{\mathbf{A}}$ is augmented based on (8) as

$$\tilde{\mathbf{A}} = [\tilde{a}_{i,j}]_{k \times M}, \tilde{a}_{i,j} = a_{i,j} / a_{i,i}. \tag{19}$$

Vector $\mathbf{a}_y$ is augmented based on (13) as

$$\mathbf{a}_y = [a_{i,y}]_{M \times 1}, a_{i,y} = \begin{cases} \mathbf{y}^{\mathrm{T}}\mathbf{p}_i - \sum_{s=1}^{i-1} a_{s,i} a_{s,y} / a_{s,s}, & i \le k \\ \mathbf{y}^{\mathrm{T}}\phi_i - \sum_{s=1}^{k} a_{s,i} a_{s,y} / a_{s,s}, & i > k \end{cases} \tag{20}$$

In addition, one more $M$-by-1 vector $\mathbf{b}$ is defined as

$$\mathbf{b} = [b_i]_{M\times 1}, b_i = \begin{cases} \mathbf{p}_i^{\mathrm{T}}\mathbf{p}_i - \sum_{s=1}^{i-1} a_{s,i}a_{s,i} / a_{s,s}, & i \le k \\ \boldsymbol{\phi}_i^{\mathrm{T}}\boldsymbol{\phi}_i - \sum_{s=1}^{k} a_{s,i}a_{s,i} / a_{s,s}, & i > k \end{cases} \tag{21}$$

Obviously

$$b_i = a_{i,i}, i = 1, \cdots, k \tag{22}$$

Compute contribution for all the left candidates based on (16) as

$$\Delta J_{k+1}(\boldsymbol{\phi}_i) = a_{i,y}^2 / b_i, \quad i = k+1, \cdots, M \tag{23}$$

Assume $\Delta J_{k+1}(\boldsymbol{\phi}_j) = \max\{\Delta J_{k+1}(\boldsymbol{\phi}_i), k < i \le M\}$, and $\boldsymbol{\phi}_j$ is selected as the ($k$+1)'th basis vector and redefine as $\mathbf{p}_{k+1} = \boldsymbol{\phi}_j$. The SSE is maximally reduced by $\Delta J_{k+1}(\boldsymbol{\phi}_j)$.

Interchanging $\boldsymbol{\phi}_{k+1}$ and $\boldsymbol{\phi}_j$, the candidate pool is updated as $\{\boldsymbol{\phi}_{k+2}, \cdots, \boldsymbol{\phi}_M\}$. Correspondingly, columns $k$+1 and $j$ of $\mathbf{A}$ and $\widetilde{\mathbf{A}}$ are interchanged as

$$\widehat{a}_{i,k+1} = a_{i,j}, \widehat{a}_{i,j} = a_{i,k+1}, \widehat{\widetilde{a}}_{i,k+1} = \widetilde{a}_{i,j}, \widehat{\widetilde{a}}_{i,j} = \widetilde{a}_{i,k+1}, i = 1, \cdots, k \tag{24}$$

where $\widehat{a}_{i,k+1}$ and $\widehat{a}_{i,j}$ denote the updated $a_{i,k+1}$ and $a_{i,j}$, respectively. To denote an updated element, a hat is applied to the affected elements in the following context.

Similarly, elements $k$+1 and $j$ should also be interchanged for both $\mathbf{a}_y$ and $\mathbf{b}$ as

$$\widehat{a}_{k+1,y} = a_{j,y}, \widehat{a}_{j,y} = a_{k+1,y}; \widehat{b}_{k+1} = b_j, \widehat{b}_j = b_{k+1}. \tag{25}$$

In addition, as the ($k$+1)'th regressor selected, a new row should be computed based on (18) and (19) for the ($k$+1)'th row of $\mathbf{A}$ and $\widetilde{\mathbf{A}}$, respectively, as

$$a_{k+1,i} = \mathbf{p}_{k+1}^{\mathrm{T}}\boldsymbol{\phi}_i - \sum_{s=1}^{k} \widetilde{a}_{s,k+1}a_{s,i}, \ \widetilde{a}_{k+1,i} = a_{k+1,i} / a_{k+1,k+1}, i = k+1, \cdots, M, \tag{26}$$

Furthermore, for both vectors $\mathbf{a}_y$ and $\mathbf{b}$, elements from the ($k$+2)'th to the last should be updated according to their definition (20) and (21), respectively as

$$\widehat{a}_{i,y} = a_{i,y} - \widetilde{a}_{k+1,i}a_{k+1,y}; \widehat{b}_i = b_i - \widetilde{a}_{k+1,i}a_{k+1,i}, i = k+2, \cdots, M, \tag{27}$$

This selection procedure is repeated as the number of selected basis vectors $k$ increases until the termination condition is satisfied. The regression coefficients for $n$ selected regressors are solved from the upper triangular linear equation system (10) as

$$\theta_k = a_{k,y} / a_{k,k} - \sum_{i=k+1}^{n} \widetilde{a}_{k,i}\theta_i, k = n, \cdots, 1 \tag{28}$$

As previously discussed, the SSE is not fully minimized for this forward network growing algorithm. Therefore, the second stage network refinement is introduced.

### 3.2 Neural Network Refinement

Suppose $n$ basis vectors have been selected in the forward network growing. For each basis vector, say $\mathbf{p}_i$, $1 \le i < n$ (the last selected one is always significant), the contribution $\Delta J_n(\mathbf{p}_i)$ is compared with $\Delta J_n^{-i)}(\boldsymbol{\phi}_j)$ (the maximum contribution of all candidates with $\mathbf{p}_i$ being removed from the selected $n$ basis vectors). If $\Delta J_n(\mathbf{p}_i) < \Delta J_n^{-i)}(\boldsymbol{\phi}_j)$, $\mathbf{p}_i$ is said insignificant, and will be replaced with $\boldsymbol{\phi}_j$, thus the SSE can be further reduced by $\Delta J_n^{-i)}(\boldsymbol{\phi}_j) - \Delta J_n(\mathbf{p}_i)$ without changing the number of hidden nodes.

To compute contribution for $\mathbf{p}_i$ and all the candidates $\boldsymbol{\phi}_{n+1},\cdots,\boldsymbol{\phi}_M$, an appropriate regression context should be re-constructed. This regression context include **A**, $\tilde{\mathbf{A}}$, $\mathbf{a}_y$ and **b** that are defined in above subsection.

Suppose a regression context with $n$ basis vectors being selected in the order of $\mathbf{p}_1,\cdots,\mathbf{p}_n$, the idea of re-construction of the regression context is to move $\mathbf{p}_i$ to the $n$'th position in the selected regression matrix $\mathbf{P}_n$ defined in (5) by consecutively interchanging two adjacent regressors $\mathbf{p}_x$ and $\mathbf{p}_{x+1}$ for $x = i,\cdots,n-1$. Denote the $n$ regressors in the new selected order as $\mathbf{p}_1,\cdots,\mathbf{p}_{x-1},\hat{\mathbf{p}}_x,\hat{\mathbf{p}}_{x+1},\mathbf{p}_{x+2}\cdots,\mathbf{p}_n$, where $\hat{\mathbf{p}}_x = \mathbf{p}_{x+1}$ and $\hat{\mathbf{p}}_{x+1} = \mathbf{p}_x$. The changes of **A**, $\tilde{\mathbf{A}}$, $\mathbf{a}_y$ and **b** are summarized as follows.

Based on (9), for columns 1 to $x$-1 of **A**, because

$$\left.\begin{array}{l} \hat{w}_{i,x} = \mathbf{p}_i^{\mathrm{T}}\hat{\mathbf{p}}_x = \mathbf{p}_i^{\mathrm{T}}\mathbf{p}_{x+1} = w_{i,x+1} \\ \hat{w}_{i,x+1} = \mathbf{p}_i^{\mathrm{T}}\hat{\mathbf{p}}_{x+1} = \mathbf{p}_i^{\mathrm{T}}\mathbf{p}_x = w_{i,x} \\ \hat{w}_{i,k} = w_{i,k}, k = i,\cdots,x-1,x+2,\cdots,M \end{array}\right\}, i = 1,\cdots,x-1 \tag{29}$$

therefore

$$\hat{a}_{i,x} = a_{i,x+1}, \hat{a}_{i,x+1} = a_{i,x}; \hat{a}_{i,k} = a_{i,k}, k = i,\cdots,x-1,x+2,\cdots,M, i = 1,\cdots,x-1 \tag{30}$$

that is, only columns $x$ and $x$+1 are interchanged, while the rest remains unchanged.

For the $x$'th row of **A**, noting $\hat{w}_{x,x+1} = \hat{\mathbf{p}}_x^{\mathrm{T}}\hat{\mathbf{p}}_{x+1} = \mathbf{p}_{x+1}^{\mathrm{T}}\mathbf{p}_x = w_{x+1,x}$, there have

$$\hat{a}_{x,x+1} = \hat{w}_{x,x+1} - \textstyle\sum_{s=1}^{x-1}\hat{a}_{s,x}\hat{a}_{s,x+1} / \hat{a}_{s,s} = w_{x,x+1} - \sum_{s=1}^{x-1} a_{s,x+1}a_{s,x} / a_{s,s}$$

Comparing with equation (9) gives

$$\hat{a}_{x,x+1} = a_{x,x+1} \tag{31}$$

Noting $\hat{w}_{x,x} = \hat{\mathbf{p}}_x^{\mathrm{T}}\hat{\mathbf{p}}_x = \mathbf{p}_{x+1}^{\mathrm{T}}\mathbf{p}_{x+1} = w_{x+1,x+1}$, therefore

$$\hat{a}_{x,x} = \hat{w}_{x,x} - \textstyle\sum_{s=1}^{x-1}\hat{a}_{s,x}\hat{a}_{s,x} / \hat{a}_{s,s} = w_{x+1,x+1} - \sum_{s=1}^{x-1} a_{s,x+1}a_{s,x+1} / a_{s,s}$$

or

$$\hat{a}_{x,x} = a_{x+1,x+1} + a_{x,x+1}a_{x,x+1} / a_{x,x} \tag{32}$$

For other elements in the $x$'th row of **A,** there have

$$\hat{a}_{x,j} = \hat{w}_{x,j} - \textstyle\sum_{s=1}^{x-1}\hat{a}_{s,x}\hat{a}_{s,j} / \hat{a}_{s,s} = w_{x+1,j} - \sum_{s=1}^{x-1} a_{s,x+1}a_{s,j} / a_{s,s}\,,\ \ j = x+2,\cdots,n\,,$$

or

$$\hat{a}_{x,j} = a_{x,j} + a_{x,x+1} a_{x,j} / a_{x,x}, \; j = x+2, \cdots, n \tag{33}$$

For the ($x$+1)'th row of **A**, it could be derived in a similarly way that

$$\left.\begin{aligned} \hat{a}_{x+1,x+1} &= a_{x,x} - (a_{x,x+1})^2 / \hat{a}_{x,x} \\ \hat{a}_{x+1,j} &= a_{x,j} - a_{x,x+1} \hat{a}_{x,j} / \hat{a}_{x,x}, \; j = x+2, \cdots, M \end{aligned}\right\} \tag{34}$$

For elements of **A** in row $x$+2, noting (29), for $j > x+1$, there have

$$\begin{aligned} \hat{a}_{x+2,j} &= \hat{w}_{x+2,j} - \textstyle\sum_{s=1}^{x+1} \hat{a}_{s,x+2} \hat{a}_{s,j} / \hat{a}_{s,s} \\ &= w_{x+2,j} - \textstyle\sum_{s=1}^{x-1} a_{s,x+2} a_{s,j} / a_{s,s} - \hat{a}_{x,x+2} \hat{a}_{x,j} / \hat{a}_{x,x} - \hat{a}_{x+1,x+2} \hat{a}_{x+1,j} / \hat{a}_{x+1,x+1} \end{aligned} \tag{35}$$

From (32), (33) and (34), it can be derived that

$$\frac{\hat{a}_{x,x+2} \hat{a}_{x,j}}{\hat{a}_{x,x}} - \frac{\hat{a}_{x+1,x+2} \hat{a}_{x+1,j}}{\hat{a}_{x+1,x+1}} = \frac{a_{x,x+2} a_{x,j}}{a_{x,x}} - \frac{a_{x+1,x+2} a_{x+1,j}}{a_{x+1,x+1}} \tag{36}$$

which means no change in row $x$+2 of **A**. Furthermore, it could be recursively derived that rows from ($x$+2) to $n$ of **A** have no change as well. That is

$$\hat{a}_{i,j} = a_{i,j}, \; j = i, \cdots, n, i = x+2, \cdots, n \tag{37}$$

Similarly as (33) and (34), for vector $\mathbf{a}_y$ only two elements are change as

$$\left.\begin{aligned} \hat{a}_{x,y} &= a_{x+1,y} + a_{x,x+1} a_{x,y} / a_{x,x} \\ \hat{a}_{x+1,y} &= a_{x,y} - a_{x,x+1} \hat{a}_{x,j} / \hat{a}_{x,x} \end{aligned}\right\} \tag{38}$$

For **b**, only both the $x$'th and the ($x$+1) 'th elements changed. From (22), we have

$$\hat{b}_x = \hat{a}_{x,x}, \hat{b}_{x+1} = \hat{a}_{x+1,x+1} \tag{39}$$

This operation continues for $x = i, \cdots, n-1$, $\mathbf{p}_i$ can be easily moved up to the $n$'th position and the contribution of $\mathbf{p}_i$ can then be computed based on (16) for $k = n-1$ as

$$\Delta J_n(\mathbf{p}_i) = \Delta J_n(\hat{\mathbf{p}}_n) = a_{n,y}^2 / a_{n,n} \tag{40}$$

where $\hat{\mathbf{p}}_n$ is $\mathbf{p}_i$ which has been moved to the $n$'th position. To compute the contribution of the remaining candidates, the following intermediate quantities need to be computed:

$$a_{s,y}^{(-i)} = a_{s,y} + a_{n,s} a_{n,y} / a_{n,n}, \; b_s^{(-i)} = b_s + (a_{n,n+1})^2 / a_{n,n}, \; s = n+1, \cdots, M \tag{41}$$

These are actually the values of the corresponding elements of $\mathbf{a}_y$ and **b** in case that regressor $\hat{\mathbf{p}}_n$ (which is $\mathbf{p}_i$ that has been moved to the $n$'th position) is pruned.

The contribution of all the candidates can therefore be computed based on (23) as

$$\Delta J_n^{-i)}(\boldsymbol{\phi}_s) = (a_{s,y}^{(-i)})^2 / b_s^{(-i)}, s = n+1, \cdots, M \tag{42}$$

Assuming $\Delta J_n^{-i)}(\phi_j) = \max\{\Delta J_n^{-i)}(\phi_s), s = n+1,\cdots,M\}$ , then the significance of $\mathbf{p}_i$ can then be easily checked. If $\Delta J_n^{-i)}(\phi_j) > \Delta J_n(\mathbf{p}_i)$ , $\widehat{\mathbf{p}}_n$ is said insignificant. In this case, the positions of $\widehat{\mathbf{p}}_n$ and $\phi_j$ are interchanged, the regression context is updated as follows.

For **A**, interchange columns $n$ and $j$, and re-calculate its $n$'th row as

$$\widehat{a}_{n,n} = b_j^{(-i)},\ \widehat{a}_{n,j} = a_{n,j},\ \widehat{a}_{n,k} = \widehat{\widehat{\mathbf{p}}}{}_n^{\mathrm{T}}\phi_k - \textstyle\sum_{s=1}^{n-1} a_{s,n}a_{s,k} / a_{s,s},\ k = n+1,\cdots,M, k \neq j \tag{43}$$

where $\widehat{\widehat{\mathbf{p}}}_n$ denotes $\phi_j$ which is now the new $n$'th selected basis vector to replace $\widehat{\mathbf{p}}_n$ . While, elements $n$ to $M$ of both $\mathbf{a}_y$ and **b** are updated respectively as

$$\left.\begin{aligned} &\widehat{a}_{n,y} = a_{n,y}^{(-i)}, a_{j,y} = a_{n,y} - \widehat{a}_{n,j}\widehat{a}_{n,y} / \widehat{a}_{n,n}, \\ &a_{s,y} = a_{s,y}^{(-i)} - \widehat{a}_{n,s}\widehat{a}_{n,y} / \widehat{a}_{n,n},\ s = n+1,\cdots,M, s \neq j \end{aligned}\right\} \tag{44}$$

and

$$\left.\begin{aligned} &\widehat{b}_n = b_j^{(-i)}, \widehat{b}_j = a_{n,n} - (\widehat{a}_{n,n+1})^2 / \widehat{a}_{n,n} \\ &\widehat{b}_s = b_s^{(-i)} - (\widehat{a}_{n,n+1})^2 / \widehat{a}_{n,n},\ s = n+1,\cdots,M, s \neq j \end{aligned}\right\} \tag{45}$$

If **A** is updated, the corresponding element of $\widetilde{\mathbf{A}}$ should be recalculated as in (19).

The above procedure is repeated in loops for $i = n-1,\cdots,1$ . If a basis vector is found insignificant and replaced with a candidate, the SSE is further reduced by $\Delta J_n^{-i)}(\phi_j) - \Delta J_n(\mathbf{p}_i)$ and the check loop is restarted again from $i = n-1$ . This neural network refinement procedure continues until no selected basis vector is found insignificant.

## 4 Neural Modeling of $NO_x$ Pollutant Concentrations in Urban Air

In this paper, the $NO_x$ concentration level in the urban air of Belfast area is studied. The following variables are considered to be associated with $NO_x$ concentration in the air and so included in the neural network : $u_1$- Ozone concentration; $u_2$- Wind direction; $u_3$- Wind speed; $u_4$- Temperature; $u_5$- Humidity; $u_6$- Total radiation; $u_7$-Traffic volumes. Data relating to all the variables mentioned above were obtained from many different governmental bodies.

The $NO_X$ concentration levels for the whole of 2005 for Belfast city centre were gathered from an online source provided by Department for Environment, Food & Rural Affairs (DEFRA). This data, representing hourly measurements of $NO_X$ levels, was processed and analyzed to identify the trends which may exist within its dynamics. During the processing stage, all unknown and invalid data points were replaced with appropriate mean values, calculated for each hour and for each day of the week. The processed data can be viewed in figure 1.

Analysis of this data revealed diurnal variations throughout the week, as shown in figure 2.

Human related emissions of Nitrogen Oxides result from the combustion of fuel in the likes of motor vehicles, Electric Utilities, and different Industrial, Commercial and Residual settings. According to DEFRA [11], vehicle exhaust fumes, accounting for 38% of all primary sources of $NO_X$ emissions, are the major contributor to $NO_X$ emissions in the UK.

To model this variable, traffic volumes were obtained from the Department of Road Development (DRD), a sub-department of the Department of the Environment (DOE).

Traffic counting apparatus cannot reliably detect vehicles moving with low velocities, and as a result direct traffic volumes for Belfast City centre are not available.

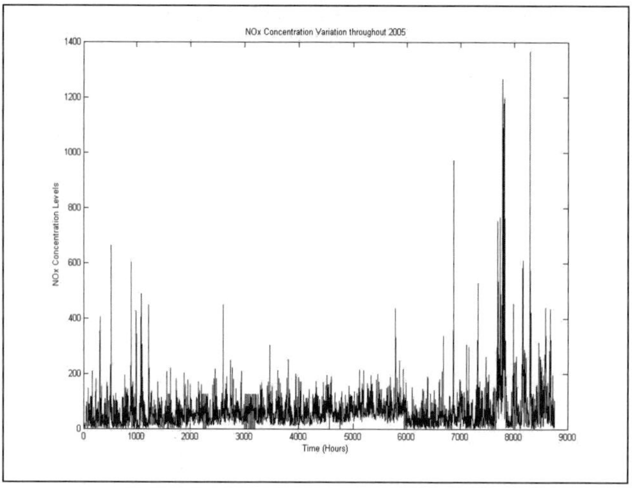


**Fig. 1.** Nox Concentrations throughout 2005

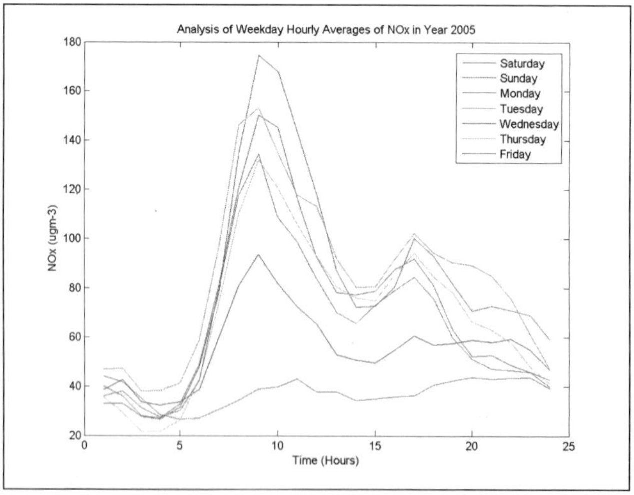


**Fig. 2.** Diurnal NOx Variation for each day of the week

However, traffic volumes on the major roads entering and exiting the city are available and data relating to these roads were obtained. The major roads used for this analysis are:

- M2 – measurements taken at York Street and Fortwilliam in both directions
- Sydenham bypass- measurements taken in both directions
- Westlink – Measurements taken at Divis Street and Clifton Street in both directions
- Lisburn Road – Measurements taken at Kings Hall in both directions.

The data obtained for these roads was sporadic over a 6 week period ranging from the end of August to mid October of 2005. The data was sporadic in that the time period during which the roads were monitored were all different, leading to complications in generating true representations of traffic data for any substantial period of time. To counteract this, statistical analysis was employed to develop average diurnal traffic levels for each day of the week for the roads being monitored. The collective analysis of these average traffic levels allows data to be reiterated for any length of dataset, providing a reasonable representation of traffic volumes in Belfast.

The data required for the different weather conditions included in this study were gathered through contacting the MET office. This data consisted of diurnal variations of the various weather conditions throughout Year 2005, measured at a weather monitoring site based at Belfast's Altergrove Airport.

Ozone concentration levels were obtained from an online source provided by the Department for Environment, Food & Rural Affairs (DEFRA). The data provides an hourly account of the Ozone levels at a Belfast monitoring site during the Year 2005.

The values of the variables differ significantly and then we need to get the rescaled values. The normalised values have zero mean and unit standard deviation.

Volterra polynomial neural network [10] was used to model the $NO_x$ concentration levels. All the variables were measured every hour, in total 998 data samples comprising the above 7 variables and the $NO_x$ concentration levels were used, among which 672 samples were used for neural network training and 336 samples were used for validation. Both forward method and the staged algorithm proposed above were used for neural modeling. The neural inputs include $u_1(t)$, $u_1(t-1)$, $u_1(t-2)$, $u_2(t)$, $u_2(t-1)$, $u_2(t-2)$, $u_3(t)$, $u_3(t-1)$, $u_3(t-2)$, $u_4(t)$, $u_4(t-1)$, $u_4(t-2)$, $u_5(t)$, $u_5(t-1)$, $u_5(t-2)$, $u_6(t)$, $u_6(t-1)$, $u_6(t-2)$, $u_7(t)$, $u_7(t-1)$, $u_7(t-2)$, $y(t-1)$, $y(t-2)$, where y is the $NO_x$ concentration levels.

**Table 1.** Comparison of neural network performance using two different methods

| Method | Selected terms | SSE |
|---|---|---|
| Forward | $y(t-1)$, $u_6(t)y(t-1)$, $u_1(t)$, $u_1(t-1)$, $u_7(t)y(t-1)$, $u_7(t)u_7(t-2)$, $u_4(t-1)y(t-2)$, $y^2(t-1)$ | 78.2423 |
| Refinement -1 | $y(t-1)$, $u_6(t)y(t-1)$, $u_1(t)$, $u_1(t-1)$, $u_7(t)y(t-1)$, $u_7(t)u_7(t-2)$, $y^2(t-1)$, $u_4(t-1)y(t-1)$ | 76.6423 |
| Refinement -2 | $y(t-1)$, $u_4(t-1)y(t-1)$, $y^2(t-1)$, $u_7(t)u_7(t-2)$, $u_7(t)y(t-1)$, $u_1(t-1)$, $u_1(t)$, $u_6(t-1)y(t-1)$ | 73.9348 |

Table 1 shows that results using forward method, both forward network growing and backward model refinement. Two loops of neural model refinement were performed, and it is obvious that the neural network performance were improved by using backward neural network refinement.

Figures 3 and 4 show the long term prediction performance of the final neural model obtained by the proposed network.

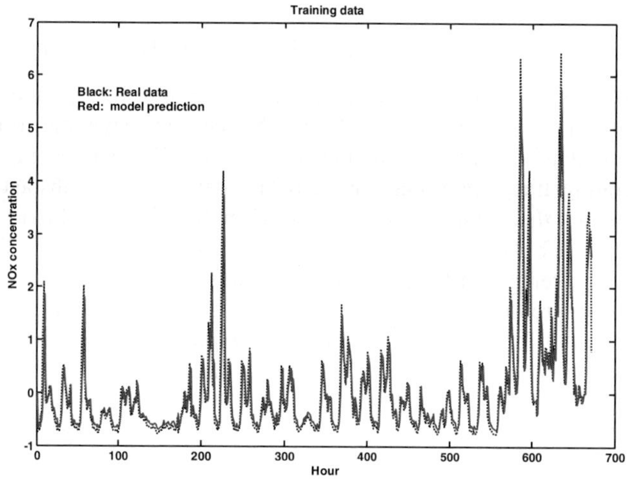


**Fig. 3.** Neural network prediction over training data

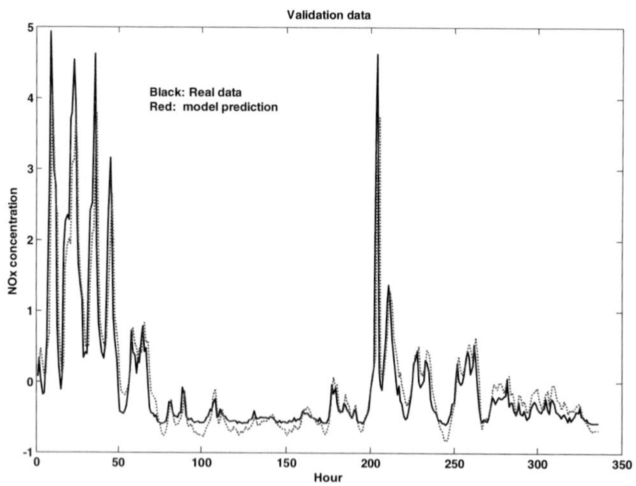


**Fig. 4.** Neural network prediction over validation data

## 5 Conclusion

A staged algorithm is proposed for modeling of pollutant concentrations in the urban air using generalized single-layer neural networks. To overcome the inefficiency of neural networks generated using forward network growing method, this paper uses a network refinement algorithm to modify the network obtained by the forward algorithm. The application results show the effectiveness of the proposed method.

## References


1. Li, K., Thompson, S., Peng, J.: Modelling and Prediction of NOx Emission in a Coal-fired Power Generation Plant. Control Engineering Practice, 12 (2004) 707-723
2. Shi, J.P., Harrison, R.M.: Regression Modeling of Hourly $NO_x$ and $NO_2$ Concentrations in Urban Air in London. Atmospheric Envrionment, 31 (1997) 4081-4094
3. Igelnik, B. Pao, Y.H.: Additional Perspectives of Feedforward Neural-nets and the Functional-link, IJCNN '93, Nagoya, Japan, (1993) 2284-2287
4. Adeney, K.M., Korenberg, M.J.: Iterative Fast Orthogonal Search Algorithm for MDL-based Training of Generalized Single-layer Networks. Neural Networks, 13 (2000) 787-799
5. Nelles, O.: Nonlinear System Identification. Springer-Verlag, Berlin Heidelberg New York (2001)
6. Chen, S., Billings, S.A., Luo,W.: Orthogonal Least Squares Methods and Their Application to Non-linear System Identification. Int. J. Control, 50 (1989) 1873-1896
7. Li, K., Peng, J., Irwin, G.: A Fast Nonlinear Model Identification Method, IEEE Transactions on Automatic Control, 50 (2005) 1211-1216
8. Akaike, H.: A New Look at the Statistical Model Identification. J. R. Statist. Soc. Ser. B. 36 (1974) 117-147
9. Sherstinsky, A., Picard, R.W.: On the Efficiency of the Orthogonal Least Squares Training Method for Radial Basis Function Networks. IEEE Trans. on Neural Networks, 7 (1996) 195-200
10. Liu, G.P., Kadirkamanathan, V., Billings, S.A.: On-line Identification of Nonlinear Systems Using Volterra Polynomial Basis Function Neural Networks. Neural Networks, 11 (1998) 1645–1657
11. Department for Environment, Food and Rural Affairs: Estimated Emissions of Nitrogen Oxides ($NO_X$) by UNECE Source Category, Type of Fuel and End User for Large Combustion Plants (LCPs) 1970 – 2004. e-Digest of Environmental Statistics, Published March 2006

# T-S Fuzzy Modeling Based on Support Vector Learning

Wei Li, Yupu Yang, and Zhong Yang

Institute of Automation, Shanghai Jiaotong University, Shanghai 200030, China
{wei_lea, ypyang, yangzhong}@sjtu.edu.cn

**Abstract.** This paper presents a satisfactory modeling method for data-driven fuzzy modeling problem based on support vector regression and Kalman filter algorithm. Support vector learning mechanism has been utilized to partition input data space to accomplish structure identification, then the complex model can be constructed by local linearization represented as T-S fuzzy model. For the ensuing parameter identification, we proceed with Kalman filter algorithm. Compared with previous works, the proposed approach guarantees the good accuracy and generalization capability especially in the few observations case. Numerical simulation results and comparisons with neuro-fuzzy method are discussed in order to assess the efficiency of the proposed approach.

## 1 Introduction

Fuzzy modeling, first exploited by Takagi and Sugeno [1], has been a powerful tool to handle a class of nonlinear, uncertain problems. So far, there have been many methods proposed to define fuzzy rule-based modeling, such as neuron-fuzzy method, a class of clustering-based methods, evolutionary computation methods [2],[3],[4],[5],[6]. But even now, to design a fuzzy model with good generalization ability in high dimensional space is still a challenging research topic.

As a powerful machine learning tool for pattern recognition problems, support vector machine (SVM) is known to have good generalization ability, that is due to its aim at minimizing an upper bound on the generalization error of a model, rather than minimizing the mean-square-error over the training data set [7],[8]. In addition, SVM can perform very well in the case of high dimension and few observations. Illuminated by this, researchers have proposed fuzzy modeling or classification methods based on support vector machine to improve fuzzy model's generalization capability. Yixin Chen [9] proposed a fuzzy classifier named positive definite fuzzy classifier (PDFC) utilizing positive definite reference function and SVM. The resulting PDFC related additive fuzzy systems to kernel machines and exhibited good generalization performance. Jung-Hsien Chiang [10] presented a SVM-based fuzzy modeling method and bridged the SVM and fuzzy basis function inference system. There is a common point that the above mentioned two approaches both use the support vectors as centers of antecedent membership function of fuzzy rules. If there exist noises in training samples, the model performance can be ruined directly by this. In this paper, we propose a new approach that can alleviate noise impact by using T-S fuzzy model and support vector learning mechanism.

D.-S. Huang, K. Li, and G.W. Irwin (Eds.): ICIC 2006, LNCS 4113, pp. 1294 – 1299, 2006.

The remainder of this paper is organized as follows. Section 2 describes the specified procedures of fuzzy rule-based modeling utilizing support vector regression and Kalman filter algorithms. In section 3, we provide numeric simulation to prove the approach's performance and make a comparison with existing method. Section 4 concludes this paper and gives future directions of this work.

## 2 Support Vector Learning Mechanism for T-S Fuzzy Modeling

Here, the remaining question is how to find a set of fuzzy rules from the given training samples so that the model possesses good accuracy and generalization ability. Motivated by statistical learning theory, support vector machine introduces "Margin Maximization" principal to guaranty the generalization ability, and involves the optimization of a convex cost function to avoid local minima [7]. The model constructed by support vector regression algorithm has an explicit dependence on a subset of the training points (the support vectors), that is, SVM has the sparse property. By configuring the proper parameters, the support vectors can be found from the area varying most drastically. Intuitionally, utilizing this property we can get the proper partition of input-output space for anticipant fuzzy system. Furthermore, the local areas between neighboring support vectors can be regarded as relatively smooth, so we apply linearization method to approximate them to some degree of accuracy. For the conjunction area, fuzzy operator can be chosen to make it smooth. Consequently, we use T-S fuzzy model to achieve this assignment.

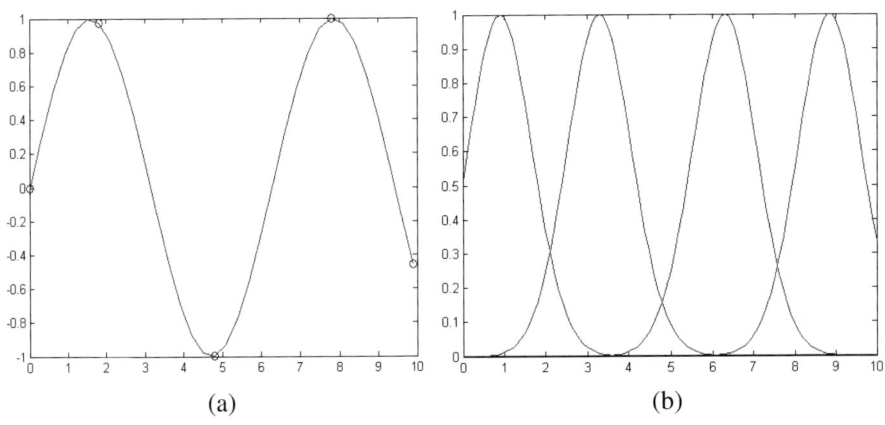

(a) (b)

**Fig. 1.** Example of the partition based on support vectors (a) Five support vector points (marked with circles) (b) Corresponding four fuzzy subspaces

Fig.1 shows a simple partition example using support vector points. Five support vectors are obtained by SVR for $Sin$ function which ranges from 0 to 10. Then the input space can be divided into four fuzzy subspaces. The corresponding fuzzy sets are characterized by Gaussian membership function in Fig.1 (b).

By choosing proper kernel function and solving a quadratic programming-regression problem [7], support vectors can be obtained, and then locating the geometric centers of neighboring support vector points makes antecedent parameters specified. The consequent parameters optimization problem could be solved by various optimization techniques. Generally, the weight vector $z_i$ can be obtained by minimizing the total approximate error

$$RMSE = \sqrt{\sum_{i=1}^{m} \frac{(y^i - \hat{y}_i)^2}{m}} . \tag{1}$$

Thus, a least squares solution (LS) is obtained by

$$Z = (X^T X)^{-1} X^T Y . \tag{2}$$

where $X = [x_1 \ldots x_m]^T, Y = [y_1 \ldots y_m]^T$ .Then, the existing stable-state Kalman filter algorithm is employed to solve $z_i$ as

$$\begin{cases} Z_{i+1} = Z_i + S_{i+1} X_{i+1}^T (y_{i+1} - (X_{i+1}) Z_i) \\ S_{i+1} = S_i - \dfrac{S_i X_{i+1}^T (X_{i+1}) S_i}{1 + X_{i+1} S_i X_{i+1}^T}, \quad i = 0,1,\ldots,m-1 \end{cases} . \tag{3}$$

where $S_i$ is called the covariance matrix. The initial conditions select as $Z_0 = 0$, $S_0 = \lambda I$, $\lambda$ is a positive large number and $I$ is the identity matrix. The whole procedure is described by the following algorithm.

*Algorithm 2.1: SVR and Kalman filter algorithm for T-S fuzzy model*

*Inputs*: A set of training samples { $(\vec{x}_1, y_1)$ ,..., $(\vec{x}_n, y_n)$ }, and Gaussian membership functions.
*Outputs*: A set of fuzzy rules parameterized by $\gamma_i, \sigma_i$, $z_i$, $m$ $(i = 1,\ldots,m)$. $\gamma_i$ and $\sigma_i$ contain the location parameters of the if-part membership functions of the $ith$ fuzzy rule. As to Gaussian function, $\gamma_i$ is the center and $\sigma_i$ is the width. $z_i$ ( $i = 1,\ldots,m$ ) is the Then-part of the $ith$ fuzzy rule, and $m$ is the number of fuzzy rules.
*Steps*:

1 Select a Mercer kernel $k$ , such as RBF kernel: $k(x, y) = \exp\left\{ -\|x - y\|^2 / 2\sigma^2 \right\}$ ;

2 Get support vector points utilizing SVR and partition the input data space;

1) Assign a positive number to $C$, set the initial value of $e$, and solve the quadratic program to get the support vectors { $(\vec{x}_1, y_1)$ ,..., $(\vec{x}_k, y_k)$ }, and $k$ is the total number of the support vectors;
2) Locate the geometric centers of neighboring support vector points in the input space, then specify the parameters $\gamma_i = {(x_i + x_{i+1})}/{2}$, ( $i = 1,...,m$ )□then specify the fuzzy rule number as $m = k - 1$.

3 Obtain the optimum consequent parameters $z_i$ utilizing Kalman filter algorithm formulated by (3) with specified matrix $S$, $X$;

4 Extract fuzzy rules. Choose Gaussian function as membership function, adopt product inference and height defuzzifier to get crisp output. Then evaluate the performance of the constructed model according to error curves and $RMSE$ for checking data set.

The resulting T-S fuzzy model using this method will have the following advantages:

- "Margin maximization" principle of SVM guarantees good generalization capability.
- The computation complexity mainly depends on the size of training set, so "curse of dimensionality" can be avoided.
- "Convex optimization" makes the solution be free of the local minima.
- Not use the support vectors directly, the influence of noise points can be lowered.

## 3 Numerical Simulation Results

In order to verify the efficiency of this proposed method, we design T-S fuzzy model using algorithm 2.1 to realize nonlinear function approximation and compare the model performance with ANFIS (adaptive network-based fuzzy inference system) [2] in terms of generalization, accuracy, complexity (number of fuzzy rules). Now we consider using the proposed method to model a two-input nonlinear function

$$Z = \frac{\sin(\sqrt{x^2 + y^2})}{\sqrt{x^2 + y^2}}. \tag{4}$$

From the grid points of the range $[-10,10]\times[-10,10]$ within the input space of the above equation, training and checking data pairs were obtained randomly. Training set size is increased from 200 to 1000, Checking set size is 1000. For SVR we use RBF kernel and specify parameter with $e = 0.07, C = 15$.For T-S fuzzy model we adopt Gaussian membership function $\mu_{A_i} = \exp[{-(x-\gamma)^2}/{2\sigma^2}]$ and $\sigma = 2.22$.

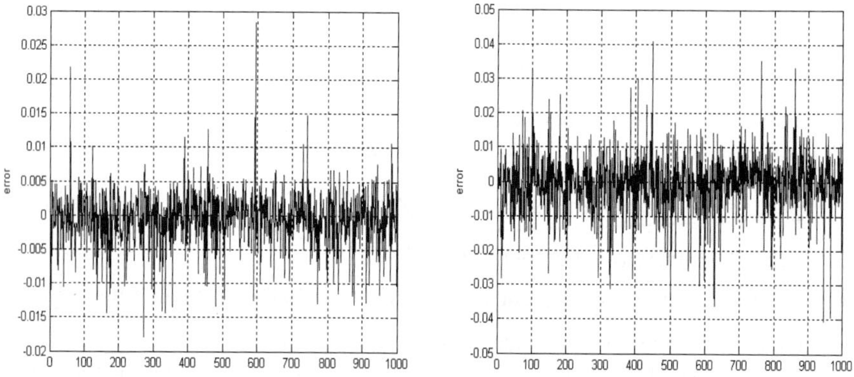


(a) (b)

**Fig. 2.** Error curve for checking data set (a) proposed model (b) ANFIS

The error curves in Fig.2 depict the approximate performance when checking set size is 1000.We apply 73 fuzzy rules with RMSE=0.0039717 using proposed model whereas 81 fuzzy rules with RMSE=0.0077822 for ANFIS. Besides the accuracy, it is seen that the error curve applying proposed model is less fluctuant.

**Table 1.** Model complexity for proposed method

| Training data set size | 100 | 150 | 200 | 250 | 300 | 500 | 1000 |
|---|---|---|---|---|---|---|---|
| Rule number | 38 | 43 | 49 | 52 | 55 | 59 | 73 |

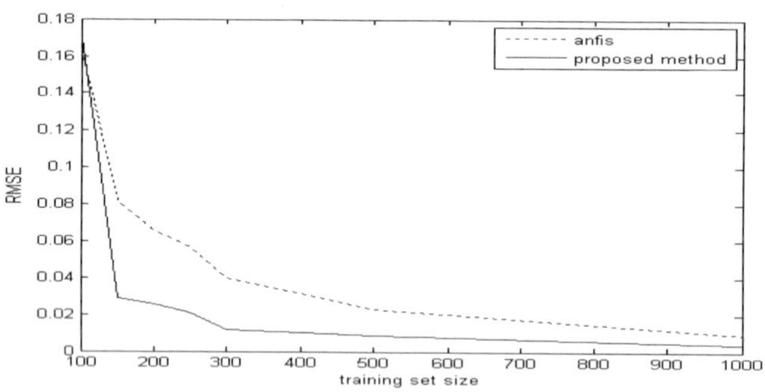


**Fig. 3.** RMSE compared with ANFIS when training set size increasing from 100 to 1000

Seen from Table 1, the complexity of T-S model constructed by proposed method is increasing with increment of training set size due to the fixed $e$ value. Nevertheless, the model complexity is not excessive compared with the ANFIS. Fig.3 shows the comparative result for the proposed method and ANFIS in terms of RMSE of checking data set when training data set size increasing from 100 to 1000. The ANFIS used here contains 64 rules, with 8 membership functions being assigned to each input variable. It is seen that the generalization ability of the proposed method is stronger than ANFIS in the case of few observations.

## 4 Conclusion and Future Work

A new fuzzy modeling method is proposed. Based on support vector regression machine, the partition of input data space has been achieved by using support vector points. The antecedent of rules can be specified easily by locating centers of local even areas. The consequent parameters are identified by Kalman filter method. The number of support vectors determines the number of fuzzy rules. Simulation solutions have shown the advantages of the proposed method. Comparatively, this method is more suitable to solve high dimensional problem, especially in the few observations case. As future work, the design of proper kernel function using some prior knowledge and kernel parameter optimization must be regarded. Further researches are also needed for the theoretical prove of the approximation ability of the resulting fuzzy system based on this approach.

## References

1. Takagi ,T., Sugeno, M.: Fuzzy Identification of Systems and Applications to Modeling and Control, IEEE Transactions on System. Man, Cybernetic(1985) 116-132
2. Jyh-Shing, Roger Jang, ANFIS: Adaptive-Network-based Fuzzy Inference System, IEEE Transactions on Systems, Man, Cybernetics (1993) 665-685
3. Chiu, S.: Fuzzy Model Identification Based on Cluster Estimation, Journal of Intelligent and Fuzzy Systems (1994) 267-278
4. Mohammad Fazle Azeem.: Structure Identification of Generalized Adaptive Neuro-Fuzzy Inference Systems, IEEE Transactions on Fuzzy Systems (2003)666-681
5. Bastian, A.:Identifying Fuzzy Models Utilizing Genetic Programming, Fuzzy Sets and Systems (2000)333-350
6. Witold Pedrycz.: Evolutionary Fuzzy Modeling, IEEE Transactions on Fuzzy Systems (2003)652-665
7. Vapnik, V.N.: The Nature of Statistical Learning Theory. New York: Springer-Verlag (1995)
8. A Tutorial on Support Vector Machines for Pattern Recognition, Christopher JC Burges, Knowledge Discovery and Data Mining, (1998)121-167
9. Yixin Chen,.:Support Vector Learning for Fuzzy Rule-Based Classification Systems, IEEE Transactions on Fuzzy Systems, (2003)716-728
10. Jung-Hsien Chiang.: Support Vector Learning Mechanism for Fuzzy Rule-Based Modeling:A New Approach, IEEE Transactions on Fuzzy Systems (2004)1-12

# The Research of an Intelligent Object-Oriented Prototype for Data Warehouse

Wenchuan Yang, Ping Hou, Yanyang Fan, and Qiong Wu

School of Telecom. Engineering, Beijing Univ. of Post & Telecom,
Beijing, 100876, P.R. China
yangwenchuan@buptsse.cn

**Abstract.** In this paper, we intend to do research and implementation of an intelligent object-oriented prototype for data warehouse. We design an intelligent prototype with object-oriented methodology, also we summarize some basic requirements and data model constructing for applying data warehouse in population fields. Finally, we introduce the research of an agent-based algorithm to process the special information in data mining on data warehousing, together with the corresponding rule for mathematic model. It is fitful to be used especially on statistic field.

## 1 Introduction

The analysis and research of Population statistics is an important work of government's population statistics, the population statistical data can benefit the developing of economy when it was processed and analyzed.

Data warehouse is the popular database technology in this field, depending on the definition of data warehouse by *W.H.Inmon*[1], The Data Warehouse is a subject-oriented, integrated, non-volatile, time- accumulate data set, which is fit for decision. It can help users processing the data, finding the inherent law and help designers guiding the decision-making and inspire the competitive advantages of the enterprise. Therefore, the guideline system for macro-economy monitor is also various and having many levels of structure. Now the general processing method is qualitative analysis: Experts select several primary agent as the candidates from all kinds of monthly statistical agent, which reflect macro-economy circulation state and are possibly got from Statistical Department.

The Chinese demography has begun since 80th, through three times census of the whole country, Nose-count of the 1% population every five years and the spot check of the population alteration situation of the 1‰ population every year; it has formed a perfect system of demographic investigation.

In the *Population Data Warehouse* (PDW) system, through applying the data warehouse technology in the demographic industry and providing the assistant decision-making support for the leader, it solves the problem described above well. Based on the abundant operational data, the population data warehouse provides the designers with supporting decision-making and analyzing forecast[2] [3].

D.-S. Huang, K. Li, and G.W. Irwin (Eds.): ICIC 2006, LNCS 4113, pp. 1300 – 1305, 2006.

## 2 Data Warehouse Architecture

The following figure 1 gives the system structure of "statistic data warehouse" based on the population data. It includes the subsystems of source database, ETL (which provides data extraction, transform and data loading), Meta database and Center Data Warehouse (including the corresponding data mart), also the subsystems of online analysis GUI[4].

The main functions of subsystems as below:

***(1) Source Database Subsystem***

The source data for census is the data that have been surveyed and investigated which includes microscopic and macroscopic data. In this figure, it includes the fifth census data, the fourth census data, the Nose-count data of 1% population.

***(2) ETL Subsystem***

In the data warehouse, the subsystem of ETL (data extraction, transform and loading) automatically extracts and translates data from the source database into the subject; it guarantees the refresh mechanism of data warehouse[5].

***(3) Meta Database Subsystem***

The main content of Meta database is primary based on the survey system of the country's statistics law. The Meta database is based on the statistic index. Its foundation is based on the various statistic reports and forms.

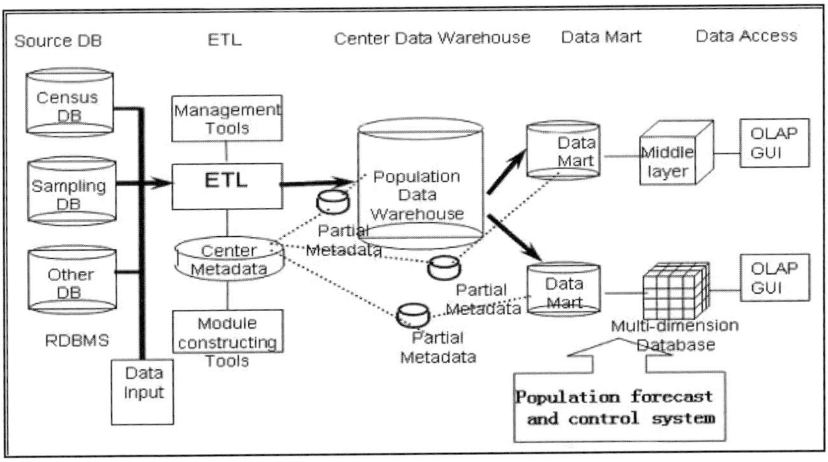


**Fig. 1.** The Population Data Warehouse System

***(4) Center Data Warehouse subsystem (including the corresponding data mart)***

The subject of data warehouse is the objective reflection of the development of the object. The subject comes from both statistic survey and the scientific checking. The population quantity, population structure and population quality are the subject of the warehouse[6] [7].

***(5) The OLAP GUI Subsystems***

With the supporting of OLAP server, PDW GUI users can use multi-dimension show and obtainment assisted by OLAP server, and can see metadata, subject, population theory model, multi-statistic-analysis, multi-dimension show, roll-up and drill down.

## 3 Mathematic Model

Because the economic fluctuation's anabiosis[8], expanding, shrinking and going to pot do not always happened in one month, however they are always developing step by step through the continuously evolvement of many economic variables in the different economic course. We do not know about the duration of every phase in the future economic fluctuation, and we also could not mark every phase clearly. However, we can ensure the order of the different economic variables, which participate in every phase of the economic fluctuation.

***(1) Diffusing Agent DA***

After classifying prosperity agent with the character of antecedence, consistent and lagging, we should take some proper action to synthesize every agent's fluctuation of each class, and then describe it by a measurable agent to review the process of fluctuation of macro-economy, so this agent is called Diffusing Agent.

In a certain kind of agent, comparing some agent's value of the current month to that of last month or several months ago, we record a sign "+" when the current value is bigger.

Otherwise we record a sign "--", and if their values are equal, we record a sign "+" of 0.5. The sign "+" is a symbol of diffusing state, and if we put the number of the sign "+" together in this kind of agent, and the value we get divides the general agent and then multiply 100, we can get the value of diffusing agent of this kind in the current month[9] [10].

We use $DA_t$ to describe the rate of increasing agent existing in "t" time period, the formula as follows:

If weigh of every variable ($W_i$ ) is equal, then we can get the following formula:

$$DI_t = \sum_{t=1}^{N} W_i I\left[X_t^i \geq X_{t-j}^i\right] \times 100 \tag{1}$$

$DA_i$ = (Diffusing number of variable at "t" clock)/(Total number of variable)*100

In the above formula, $X_t^i$ is a measurable value of variable agent's fluctuation at "t" clock of the number of I; $W_i$ is the distributed weigh of the agent of I; N is the total number of variable agent; I is a instruction function withthree values: 0, 1, 0.5.

How to determine the value of j? Base on comparative elements:

if compared to the last value, then j = 1,

if compared to the latest two values, then j = 2, and etc.

***(2) Colligation Index(CI )***

Colligation Index (CI) can quantitatively reflect the degree of economic outspread or shrink, and its fluctuation mode is similar with the mode of index fluctuation. Colligation Index is classified to 3 types: Antecedence Colligation Index (ACI), Consistent Colligation Index (CCI), and Lagging Colligation Index (LgCI).

Computing CI is relatively complex than DI, its computing steps as follows:

(1) Find change rate $C_i(t)$ of the single index i:

Assume index sequence $d_i(t)$, then changing velocity can compute as follows:

$$\begin{aligned} C_i(t) &= 100[d_i(t)\ d_i(t\ 1)]/\{[(d_i(t)+d_i(t\ 1)]/2\} \\ &= 200[d_i(t)\ d_i(t\ 1)]/[d_i(t)+d_i(t\ 1)] \end{aligned} \tag{2}$$

However, if $D_i(t)$ is a form of percent or a certain type of index, then:

$$C_i(t) = d_i(t) - d_i(t-1) \tag{3}$$

(2) Take standardization management for $C_i(t)$ on the same base line:

$$Y_i(t) = C_i(t)/\overline{C} \tag{4}$$

And,

$$\overline{C} = \sum_{i=1}^{n} |C_i(t)|/n \tag{5}$$

In the above formula, n is the number of indexes.

(3) Find colligation changing rate after standardization:

$$V(t) = \sum_{i=1}^{n} Y_i(t) \tag{6}$$

(4) Find initialization colligation index I(t):

$$CI(t) = [I(t)/CI_i] \times 100\% \tag{7}$$

$I_0(1)$ is the initialization colligation index of the first month of the basic year.

## 4 System Simulation

As shown in figure 1, we especially design the model of population and controlling aimed at the particularity of population data depending on these systems[11].

The model is used to the population data forecast, control calculation and finding and validating the corresponding population running rules from vast population data.

***(1) The Population Development Equation***

We especially designed the population development equation based on population data warehouse, the data analysis of population data warehouse and the corresponding generalized international standard[12].

$$\begin{cases} \dfrac{\partial P}{\partial r} + \dfrac{\partial P}{\partial t} = -\mu(r,t)p(r,t), t \geq 0, 0 \leq r \leq r_m \\ p(r,0) = p_0(r) \\ p(0,t) = f(t) \\ p(r_m,t) = 0 \end{cases} \tag{8}$$

p(r,t) is the function of age density
U(r,t) is the death rate of people with the age of $r$ at time $t$.
define p(r,0)=$p_0$(r) the initial density function
define p(0,t)=f(t) the number of infants born in a second as the infant birthrate.

We can get $p_0$(r) through population investigation data, and f(t) is the key of population forecast and controlling.

Through the further analysis of f(t):

$$f(t) = \beta(t)\int_{r_1}^{r_2} h(r,t)k(r,t)p(r,t)dr \tag{9}$$

[r1,r2]is the zone of raising a baby, h(r,t) fulfills

$$\int_{r_1}^{r_2} h(r,t)dr = 1 \tag{10}$$

$\beta(t)$ is the gross birthrate (or the times of bearing)

$h(r,t)$ is the model of bearing

We consecutively describe the population model herein before, in the practical calculation, we will use the discrete calculation method, and the technology of this aspect is mature and feasible.

***(2)Examples***

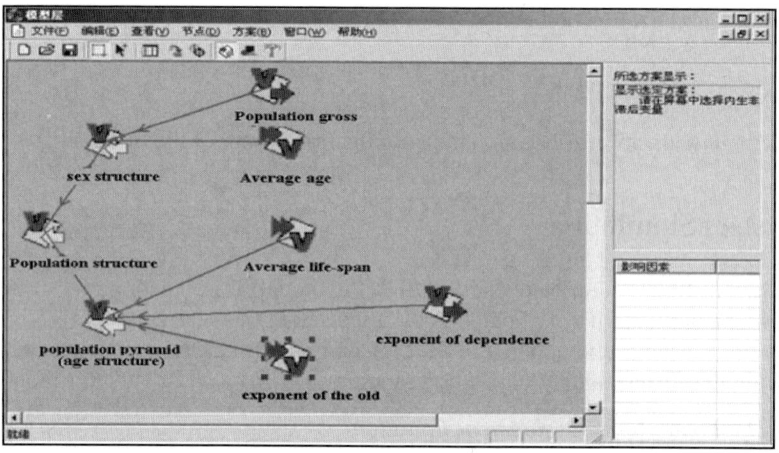


**Fig. 2.** The GUI for Population Forecast and Controlling Model

The development model of world population has three kinds based on the research of United Nation Population Fund. Chinese population development model approaches the eastern model, which has the determinative function to confirm the corresponding function of the above model.

Following is an example of population forecast and controlling model calculation based on the data warehouse, the figure 2 is the running interface figure of the system,

***Input data***

(1) Initialized population density (2) Infant birthrate

(3) Raise domain (4) Anticipative life of baby born

***Output data*** , including sometime for the future:

(1) Population gross (2) Average age

(3) Average life-span (4) The exponent of the old age

(5) The exponent of the dependence. (6) Population structure

(7)The age structure (population pyramid) (8) sex structure

(9)diathesis structure (needing diathesis parameter)

## 5 Conclusions

The macro-economy monitor system, which is based on data warehouse, has been applied in the first period e-government system in China. Now it can make early warning to government, and reflect in time the results of the adjustments in macro-economy. Also it can adjust in time the abnormal states in economic circulation for leaders, and take an assistant function for them to adopt essential adjustments.

## Acknowledgement

This work was supported in part by the Foundation of Beijing Nova Program under grant of 2005B41.

## References

1. Inmon W.H: Building the Data Warehouse, 2nd edition. John Wiley, (1996).
2. Samos J., Saltor F., Sistac J. and Bardes A.: Database Architecture for Data Warehousing-an Evolutionary Approach. In DEXA (1998): 746-756.
3. Inmon W.H.: Information Architecture for the 90's- Legacy Systems, Operational Data store, Data Warehouse. PRISM Tech Topic,(1993) Vol.1, No.13.
4. Inmon W.H.: The Operational Data Store. PRISM Tech Topic, (1993)Vol.1, No.17.
5. P.Valides-Perez: Principles of Human-computer Collaboration for Knowledge-Discovery in science. Artificial Intelligence, (1999)107:335-346.
6. Widrow B., Rumelhart D.E., and Lehr M.A.: Neural networks -Application in Industry, Business and Science. Communication of ACM,(1994)37:93-105.
7. Wang R., Storey V., and Firth C. : Framework for Analysis of Data Quality Research, IEEE Trans. Knowledge and Data Engineering,(1995)7:623-640.
8. Birman Alexander: Computing Approximate Congestion Probabilities for a Class of All-Optical Networks, IEEE JOURNAL ON SELECTED AREAS IN COMMUNICATIONS, (1996) 11:312-316.
9. Chung S., Kashper,A. and Ross K.W.: Computing Approximate Congestion Probabilities for Large Loss Networks with State-dependent Routing, IEEE/ACM Trans. Networking, (1993) 5:112-121.
10. Sridharan Ashwin: Congestion in All-Optical Networks, IEEE/ACM TRANSACTIONS ON NETWORKING,(2004) VOL. 12, NO. 2, APRIL.
11. Shortle John F.: Dynamic Call-Congestion Algorithms for Telecommunications Networks. IEEE TRANSACTIONS ON COMMUNICATIONS, (2003)Vol.51, No.5,MAY.
12. Romanow Allyn: Dynamics of TCP traffic over ATM networks. IEEE TRANSACTIONS ON COMMUNICATIONS, (2003)Vol.61, No.3, MAR.

# Improving Data Availability in Ad Hoc Wireless Networks*

Luciano Bertini, Orlando Loques, and J.C.B. Leite

Instituto de Computação, Universidade Federal Fluminense
Niterói, RJ, Brazil
{lbertini, loques, julius}@ic.uff.br

**Abstract.** This paper presents a data replication approach for ad hoc wireless networks which aims to improve data availability. Besides, the number of replications is minimized, helping to reduce energy consumption and, thus, the application lifetime. A mobile node replicates its data either when its energy is in a weak level or when it is in the imminence of loosing connection. For replica allocation, the Bayesian decision theory is used, but with fuzzy states modeling and fuzzy observations made on the system. The proposed approach presents features that make it suitable to be used in a mobile computing environment.

## 1 Introduction

This work presents an on-demand replication technique to improve data availability, designed to be embedded in a mobile computing system, based on ad hoc wireless networks. By on-demand we mean that replication is not triggered always that the data is updated, but only when certain conditions are met. This strategy aims to minimize the energy consumption of the mobile nodes. Considering that communication activities consume relatively large amounts of power, this improves the operational lifetime of the overall system. The distributed system model here adopted consists of an ad hoc network where the nodes are spread over an area that is much larger than the communication range of each individual mobile node. Under our assumptions, a data unit can become unavailable either because its owner node either looses connection or has not enough battery power to continue operating. Thus, to improve data availability, whenever there is a high probability of loosing the critical data being kept in a node it should be replicated in another mobile node, potentially with better conditions, chosen from its neighborhood. In principle, the best choice is impossible to be achieved, due to the impossibility of collecting a complete view of the global state in a distributed system.

In this work an approach based on Bayesian decision theory is adopted for decision making. The approach includes fuzzy modeling techniques, which are better suited to represent the properties of the system variables under consideration, and also avoids state explosion. Specifically, the decision model assumed

* This work was partially supported by CNPq and FAPERJ.

D.-S. Huang, K. Li, and G.W. Irwin (Eds.): ICIC 2006, LNCS 4113, pp. 1306–1313, 2006.

is based on two main random variables, that are directly related to node data availability: the Energy and the Connectivity of the nodes. Actually, the energy consumption occurs as sequences of random variables, including the consumption related to user's activity, exchange of messages, etc. In this way, it is possible to happen that a node with a lower level of energy achieves a greater battery lifetime than another node with a higher energy level. The connectivity of a node is also a random variable, because it depends on the physical trajectory being followed by its owner agent. When finding a node to replicate a data unit, the potentially best decision depends on a combination of both variables and on the current system state. Simulation studies have shown that the application of the proposed approach allows good results when compared to the optimum but unfeasible choice.

This paper is organized as follows. Section 2 presents some related work. Details of the system model and of the decision approach are presented in Section 3. Section 4 discuss some details of the simulation used to evaluate the technique. Section 5 presents some evaluation results, and, finally, in Section 6 we draw our conclusions.

## 2 Related Work

The work in [1] deals with the data replication issue in an ad hoc network. Replicas are created based on the current profile of each mobile node. This profile has information associated to three resources: energy, storage capacity, and the time that the user is willing to stay connected. In that work, each one of the three mentioned variables may be in one of three states: *weak*, *acceptable*, and *optimal*. The combinations of these variables allows to classify a mobile node in three general quality classes, accordingly to its current profile. When a mobile node profile decays to the *weak* class, it replicates its data in another mobile node with *optimal* or *acceptable* profile, as available. A similar mechanism is adopted in our approach. However, it should be noted that in the cited work, the choice is done directly, by consulting the set of profiles of the system nodes, without considering any kind of prevision or probabilistic-based technique. Although this technique allows for some energy economy, when compared to the usual replication scheme where replicas are updated each time they are modified, we see two weaknesses. The first is the fact that the users have to specify up to what time they intend to remain connected. As noted in [2], even for more general contexts, it does not seem realistic to design a data replication technique relying on the user's estimated connection time to infer the best node to place a replica. The second reason is that their target network topology is one-hop, which means that every node has to be in the communication range of the others.

Data replication methods can be classified in two categories: with periodic replica updates, or with aperiodic replica updates. Generally, the methods with periodic updates are simpler to implement, and these methods can be a first step toward the development of a more general aperiodic method. A replication method with periodic updates is presented in [3]. In this work, the mobile nodes where to allocate the replicas are chosen based on the access frequency to the data to be replicated. The node with the highest access to this data unit is chosen as a target to receive the replica; the goal is to minimize the network traffic. Although our method is aperiodic, it is relatively simple to implement and also minimizes network traffic. Besides that, our replication scheme takes into account the energy and connectivity levels of the target node in order to increase the availability of the data.

## 3 System Model

In our model, the system state is characterized by two variables: Energy and Connectivity. The energy of a node at some instant is modeled as a random variable, and is a strictly decreasing function. The variable Connectivity represents the degree of communication coverage of a mobile node in the ad hoc network, and depends not only on the number of mobile nodes that are in its communication range, but also on their signal power levels.

The Energy variable has a minimum and a maximum value, and it does not represent, actually, the energy level of the battery, but an estimation of its lifetime. The Connectivity variable is defined in a similar way. The values of both variables can be classified in $r$ levels, that would generate $r^2$ different states for each node. The mapping of these $r$ levels in just three fuzzy sets or states, such as *weak*, *acceptable* and *optimal*, avoids this state explosion. In this way, despite the number $r$ of levels, just nine states are required, as shown in table 1.

**Table 1.** System states

| State | Energy | Connectivity |
|---|---|---|
| $s_1$ | weak | weak |
| $s_2$ | weak | acceptable |
| $s_3$ | weak | optimal |
| $s_4$ | acceptable | weak |
| $s_5$ | acceptable | acceptable |
| $s_6$ | acceptable | optimal |
| $s_7$ | optimal | weak |
| $s_8$ | optimal | acceptable |
| $s_9$ | optimal | optimal |

A utility function determines the payoff value for each possible state, if some action is taken. Here, there is only one kind of action, that is, the transference of a data unity to another node. When a mobile node $j$ needs to replicate data, a decision making method is executed, and the result indicates to which mobile node $i$ the data will be sent. Therefore, for node $j$ and $n$ nodes, there are $n - 1$ possible actions.

For a discrete system, the utility function is defined as a matrix that relates the actions with the possible states. In this application, the aiming is to replicate the data on a node that will stay connected and alive the longer, assuring the highest expected availability for this data. Thus, it becomes natural to associate an increasing payoff as the node state goes from $s_1$ to $s_9$ (accordingly to table 1), where $s_9$ corresponds to the case of a node with the best combination of resources. The utility function is unique for all actions, differently from what occurs in the traditional Bayesian decision theory. In the latter, the probability functions are the same, but the utility function is different for each action.

Our model extends the classic Bayesian model including Fuzzy theory concepts, as in [4]. Let $x_k$ be the observation obtained from the system, taking a value from the set $X = \{x_1, x_2, \ldots, x_r\}$, where $r$ is the amount of discrete levels being considered for the variables. This set $X$ may be classified in fuzzy events, $\underset{\sim}{M}$, and these fuzzy events will have a membership function $\mu_{\underset{\sim}{M}}(x_k)$, $k = 1, 2, \ldots, r$.

The notion of probability of a fuzzy event is defined as follows:

$$Pr\left[\underset{\sim}{M}\right] = \sum_{k=1}^{r} \mu_{\underset{\sim}{M}}(x_k)\, Pr\left[x_k\right] \tag{1}$$

In our data replication approach, three fuzzy events, $\underset{\sim}{M}_1$, $\underset{\sim}{M}_2$, and $\underset{\sim}{M}_3$, describe the information, representing, respectively, *weak*, *acceptable* and *optimal.* These events must be orthogonal, meaning that the sum of the membership values for each fuzzy event, $\underset{\sim}{M}_i$, for every data point $x_k$, is equal to one:

$$\sum_{i=1}^{3} \mu_{\underset{\sim}{M}_i}(x_k) = 1 \tag{2}$$

Given the probability of a fuzzy event $\underset{\sim}{M}$ (equation 1), and using Bayes theorem [5], the posterior probability can be defined as:

$$Pr\left[s_i|\underset{\sim}{M}\right] = \frac{Pr\left[\underset{\sim}{M}|s_i\right] Pr\left[s_i\right]}{Pr\left[\underset{\sim}{M}\right]} \tag{3}$$

where

$$Pr\left[\underset{\sim}{M}|s_i\right] = \sum_{k=1}^{r} \mu_{\underset{\sim}{M}}(x_k)\, Pr\left[x_k|s_i\right] \tag{4}$$

Substituting equations 1 and 4 in equation 3:

$$Pr\left[s_i|\underset{\sim}{M}\right] = \frac{\sum_{k=1}^{r} \mu_{\underset{\sim}{M}}(x_k)\, Pr\left[x_k|s_i\right] Pr\left[s_i\right]}{\sum_{k=1}^{r} \mu_{\underset{\sim}{M}}(x_k)\, Pr\left[x_k\right]} \tag{5}$$

From equation 5, for an event $\underset{\sim}{M}_t$, the expected utility for each action $j$ can be calculated:

$$E(u_j|\underset{\sim}{M}_t) = \sum_{i=1}^{n} u_{ji} Pr\left[s_i|\underset{\sim}{M}_t\right] \tag{6}$$

In this last equation $u_{ji}$ is the profit associated to the *j-th* choice in the *i-th* system state. Finally, the best action to be taken will be the one with the best expected utility:

$$E(u^*|\underset{\sim}{M}_t) = \max_j E(u_j|\underset{\sim}{M}_t) \tag{7}$$

The previous equations include the system observation as a fuzzy variable. System states are also assumed to be fuzzy. Accordingly, the Energy variable is represented by the fuzzy sets $\underset{\sim}{E}_1$, $\underset{\sim}{E}_2$ and $\underset{\sim}{E}_3$, which are associated, respectively, to the states *weak*, *acceptable*, and *optimal.* The function $\mu_{\underset{\sim}{E}_i}(e_k)$ is the membership of the value $e_k$ of energy to the fuzzy set $\underset{\sim}{E}_i$. Thus, the probability of the fuzzy state $E_s$, mapped into $m$ discrete values, is:

$$Pr\left[\underset{\sim}{E}_s\right] = \sum_{k=1}^{m} \mu_{\underset{\sim}{E}_s}(e_k)\, Pr\left[e_k\right] \tag{8}$$

Using this value for $Pr\left[s_i\right]$ in equation 5, gives:

$$Pr\left[\underset{\sim}{E}_s|\underset{\sim}{M}_t^E\right] = \frac{\sum_{i=1}^{m}\sum_{k=1}^{r} \mu_{\underset{\sim}{E}_s}(e_i)\,\mu_{\underset{\sim}{M}_t^E}(x_k)\, Pr\left[x_k|e_i\right] Pr\left[e_i\right]}{\sum_{k=1}^{r} \mu_{\underset{\sim}{M}_t^E}(x_k)\, Pr\left[x_k\right]} \tag{9}$$

where $\underset{\sim}{M}_t^E$ is the observation relative to the variable Energy.

Similarly, an equivalent equation to 9 can be obtained for the variable Connectivity. Energy and Connectivity must be treated independently before calculating the joint probability, which is given by the product of both. This will generate the probabilities of states $s_1$ to $s_9$. The calculation of the expected utility $E\left(u_j|\underset{\sim}{M}_t\right)$ is the same as before, but using the nine values of the joint probabilities.

## 4 Simulation

We designed a simulator where each mobile node follows a movement pattern generated by the ns-2 simulator [6], and consumes energy at a random rate, which is periodically chosen from an uniform distribution. The initial energy value is chosen in such a way as to allow every mobile node to get without energy before the end of the simulation. For the connectivity, it is assumed that the higher is the number of neighbors, the higher is the connectivity level of this node. In a real system, the energy values from the neighbors can be piggybacked in messages exchanged by the application level or communication level entities. Also, the connectivity information would be directly obtained from the network interface. Data gathered for both variables through simulation is used to construct the probability density functions, each with $r$ discretization levels. These functions are represented in the form of tables in our simulator. The computational complexity of equation 9 is low, dependending only on $m$ and $r$. Also, the calculation is done just for those nodes that belong to the neighborhood of the node that is replicating the data.

In the simulation model, each mobile node has initially one data unit that is relevant to the other nodes of the network and, for this reason, it must be replicated if needed. With the purpose of measuring the effectiveness of our method, we compute the total number of data replications until the end of a simulation run. If one mobile node has one data unit and it receives a replica, when this node need to replicate it will have to send two data units. Thus, a non optimal decision generates more replication.

## 5 Evaluation Results

The generation of the scenarios was done using the tool *setdest* of ns-2, assuming an area of $1500m \times 300m$, range of transmission of $250m$ for each node, without obstacles. The experiments were done using 25, 50, 75 and 100 nodes; the maximum speeds for nodes were assumed to be equal to $1m/s$, $5m/s$, and $10m/s$, with pause periods of $50s$. For each combination of speed and number of nodes, 30 experiments were realized, each one with distinct initial spatial distribution, movement direction, speed for the nodes, and initial energies.

The method was compared against a low-cost random policy (RM), where the target for data unit replication is chosen randomly. A lower bound ($LB$) for the number of replicated data units was defined considering the best node where to send the data, that is, the node that will take longer to disconnect. Also, an upper bound ($UB$) was determined, always choosing the node that would certainly be the next to disconnect. For all the methods, the decision making process, called the decision period, runs every $1s$.

Figure 1 shows a plot for the 30 experiments, using a particular configuration for speed and number of nodes, to evaluate the effect of our Fuzzy-Bayesian (FB) policy in the total number of replicas generated in the system. As can be seen, our method produces good results as compared to the lower bound and is consistently better than the random policy. A similar pattern was observed for all other configurations of nodes and speeds.

Aiming to evaluate the methods, we defined a quality measure, *closeness*, that indicates how close are the results of a method (FB or RM) to the lower bound. This quality measure is computed as $cln = \frac{result-LB}{LB}$. For the number of nodes varying from 25 to 100 and node speeds from $1m/s$ to $10m/s$, we computed the closeness of the methods. Figure 2 shows that the FB policy is consistently better than RM, for maximum node speed of $5m/s$. It should be noted that we observed a similar behavior for node speeds of $1m/s$ and $10m/s$. In the figure, each point is the average of 30 experiments, and is shown with a 95% confidence interval. As a final point, we observed that the FB policy follows the same trend than LB, for different combinations of number of nodes and speeds.

We define that a fault has occurred when the disconnection of a node is not predicted by the method. This can be mitigated if the time granularity of the decision period is reduced, at the expense of an increase in the computational

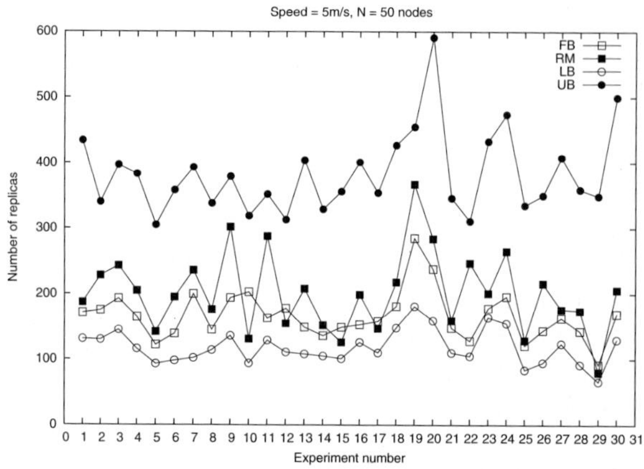


**Fig. 1.** FB *versus* RM method

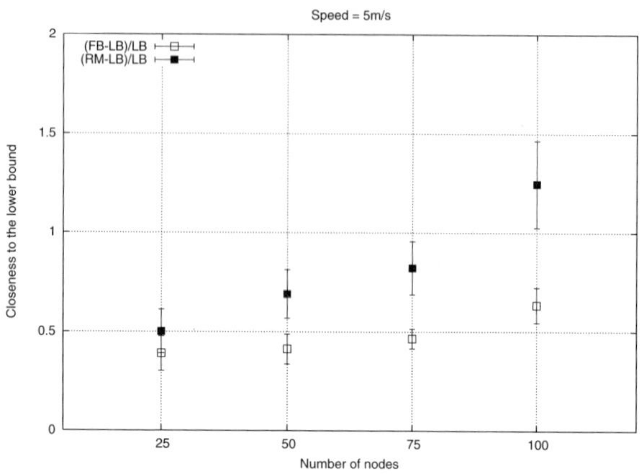


**Fig. 2.** Closeness: maximum speed $= 5m/s$

cost. With replication inhibited, to obtain an upper bound, we obtained a maximum of 55 faults. For the same scenarios, assuming decision periods of $1s$ and $20s$, the average number of faults were, roughly, 12 and 22, respectively. This shows the effectiveness of our approach.

## 6 Conclusion

In some mobile applications, based on ad hoc networks, data replication is essential, because the network may become disjoint at some time. The Bayesian-Fuzzy model here presented provides a sound technique to implement the required decision making process. Additional experiments we have been carrying out suggest that the FB method uses much less messages (circa 4%) than that required to implement a basic data duplication technique used to provide fault-tolerance [7]. This happens because, for keeping data consistency in the latter method, a replication is made every time that the data is modified. Clearly, this implies in a longer life-time for a system using only the FB method.

In order to cater for requirements of other mobile applications, additional characteristics could be included in our model. For example, for disaster recovery systems, we could try to avoid data replication in nodes that are physically too close to the original node, because a fatal accident could happen to both. For this same application, we could incorporate in our model groups of nodes with similar moving patterns [8]. This would reduce the unpredictability of the variable Connectivity. It should be pointed out that, in both cases, the method here presented would maintain its basic characteristics.

## References

[1] Malika, B., Valérie, Issarny.: A Middleware Service for Mobile Ad Hoc Data Sharing, Enhancing Data Availability. In ACM/IFIP/USENIX International Middleware Conference, Rio de Janeiro, Brazil, (2003) 493-511
[2] David, R., Peter, R., Gerald, J. Popek, G. H., Kuenning: Replication Requirements in Mobile Environments. Mobile Networks and Applications, 6 (2001) 525-533
[3] Takahiro, H.: Replica Allocation Methods in Ad Hoc Networks with Data Update. Mobile Networks and Applications, 8 (2003) 343-354
[4] AndréM, B., Leite, J. C. B.: Orlando Loques: Treating Uncertainty in Distributed Scheduling. Journal of Systems and Software, 63 (2002) 129-136
[5] Timothy J. R.: Fuzzy Logic With Engineering Applications. New York, NY, McGraw Hill, USA (1995)
[6] NS-2. The Network Simulator - Ns-2. http://www.isi.edu/nsnam/ns (2004)
[7] Guimarães, M.: Fault-tolerance and Economy of Resources in a Disaster Mitigation System (in portuguese). Instituto De Computação, Universidade Federal Fluminense, Niterói, RJ, Brazil, (2006)
[8] Huang, J. L., Chen, M. S., Peng, W. C.: Exploring Group Mobility for Replica Data Allocation in A Mobile Environment. In International Conference on Information and Knowledge Management, New Orleans, LA, USA (2003) 161-168

# Routing Algorithm Using GPSR and Fuzzy Membership for Wireless Sensor Networks

Kyung-Bae Chang, Dong-Wha Kim, and Gwi-Tae Park

Department of Electrical Engineering, Korea University, Anam-dong 5(o)-ga, Seongbuk-gu, Seoul, Korea
{lslove, assimila, gtpark}@korea.ac.kr

**Abstract.** In the wireless sensor networks, sensor nodes are generally clustered under the necessity. GPSR which Brad Karp et al. proposed, is routing algorithm that has follow advantages: GPSR is localized algorithm to find routes and sensor nodes have few data for routing. These features make GPSR be adapted to sensor networks. But, forwarding a packet is able to be failed because of geographic data error or mobility of sensor nodes. In order to improve such a problem, this paper proposes clustered GPSR by fuzzy membership.

## 1 Introduction

As mobile network becomes the guiding technology of ubiquitous era, there are a large number or researches trying to apply Ad-hoc network to mobile sensor network systems. However, a number of significant problem have come out since Ad-hoc network is different from mobile sensor network in various aspects. In routing algorithms for mobile sensor networks, such as DSR [4], DSDV [5] and AODV [3], the most critical problem is the flooding generated while searching routing a route and the increase of overhead caused by the flooding. As the number of nodes increases, the overhead due to the network searching also increases considering that a mobile wireless sensor network consists of a large number of nodes possessing restively short transmission distances.

To resolve these difficulties, GPSR was proposed by Brad Karp et al. [8]. Since GPSR doesn't take flooding in the route searching procedure, it has a highly reduced overhead. In addition, GPSR needs only routing information of neighbor nodes on the contrary to other IP address based algorithms. [8] Considering those advantages GPSR is much more applicable to mobile sensor networks. However, GPSR still has unavoidable problems such as errors of locating information or possible transmission failures due to moving nodes since it is used in a mobile sensor network.

A hierarchical routing algorithm using clustering technique can be used to resolve these problems. In addition, the use of clustering algorithm is reasonable since sensor nodes are actually grouped as needed in real cases.

Considering the necessity and rationality, researches on algorithms applying clustering techniques to mobile sensor networks are largely being conducted.

In this paper, Fuzzy logic is applied to enhance the routing algorithm in performance in a mobile sensor network. This paper indicates a method of increasing extensibility of mobile sensor network using a representative geographic routing algorithm,

D.-S. Huang, K. Li, and G.W. Irwin (Eds.): ICIC 2006, LNCS 4113, pp. 1314 – 1319, 2006.

GPSR, and a method of decreasing packet losses caused by errors of sensor locations and node moving using Fuzzy C-means algorithm (FCM) [7].

## 2 GPSR Algorithm and Communication Between Clusters

GPSR is a communication method between nodes using geographical information. Each communication node takes its location as its own address. Communication between neighbor nodes is realized with IDs recognizable in a lower layer. There are methods for route searching using geographical locations such as Greedy method and Perimeter (Face) method.

### 2.1 Greedy Forwarding

In Greedy method, a packet is forwarded in a direction from node x to node y which is geographically nearest to destination node of node x among neighbor nodes of node x.

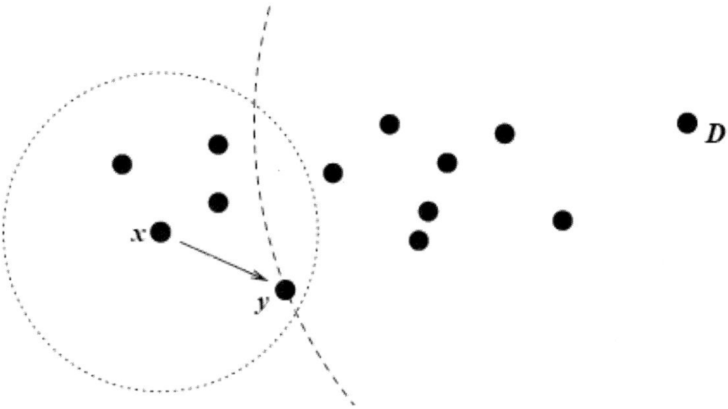


**Fig. 1.** Greedy forwarding method

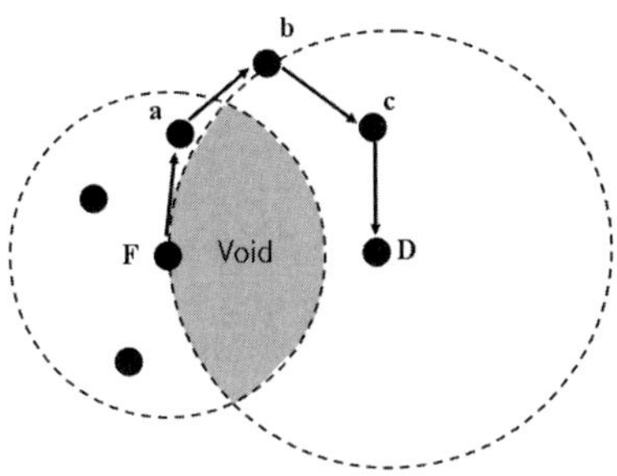


**Fig. 2.** Local minimum problem of Greedy method

However, Greedy method might cause local minima as shown in Fig. 2. In Fig. 2, since node F is located nearer to destination node D than neighbor nodes, a routing failure occurs because there is no nearer node for the packet to be forwarded, even though a route of F-a-b-c-D exists.

To avoid such routing failures shown above, a packet is forwarded using Perimeter method when it meets void as shown in Fig.2.

### 2.2 Perimeter Forwarding

Once a network is switched to Perimeter method, it prevents the links between nodes from being overlapped by constructing a planar graph using RNG or GG. [6], [10] In this procedure, a packet is forwarded from a start node F to its destination node D guided by the planar graph in clockwise direction as shown in Fig. 3.

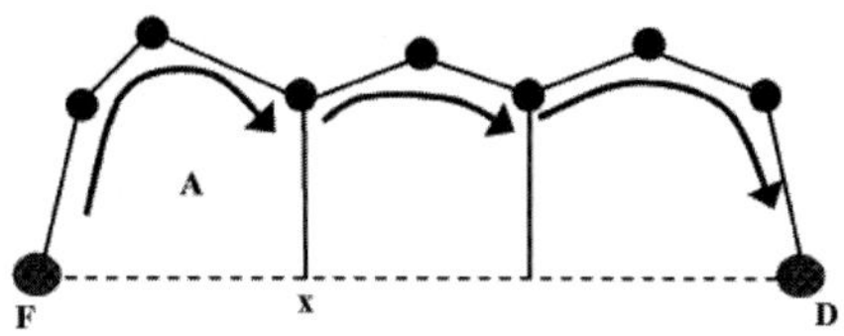


**Fig. 3.** Perimeter forwarding method

Routing is possible only using Perimeter [9] and GPSR uses both of Greedy and Perimeter methods for more optimized routing. First, a packet is forwarded with Greedy method and the network switches its mode to Perimeter method when it falls into local minimum.

While using Perimeter method, the network might be switched into Greedy method again when it finds a nearer node to the destination.

### 2.3 Clustering Method and Cluster Header

This section depicts the procedure after clusters constructed. The proposed method in this paper, routing method using clustering algorithm of Fuzzy C-means, is discussed in Section 3. A cluster is represented as its location of its cluster header and the cluster header contains information of its membership nodes and neighbor clusters (information of cluster headers locations) while clusters formed. Through this procedure, GPSR method is used to determine the route between cluster headers. Therefore, a cluster takes a roll as a communication node of GPSR method in the proposed method.

In the procedure of packet communication between clusters, a cluster header forwards a packet to a member node possessing the highest membership value to the destination cluster. In Fig. 4, Cluster A forwards a packet to node y to communicate with a neighbor cluster, Cluster B. Communication between clusters is realized in this way. If transmission from node y to Cluster B occurs, Cluster A forwards the packet to the node having the second highest membership value. At this step, a cluster to be forwarded is selected using Greedy method or Perimeter method. Using gateways are in general for communications between clusters in the routing methods applying clustering. The use of Fuzzy membership functions enables to avoid problems such as packet losses and packet delays caused by an abrupt shutdown of a gateway or an overload to the cluster. In the forwarding decision procedure of a cluster header, Reduce failing method can be added to Greedy method and Perimeter to reduce transmission delay caused by moving nodes described in Section 1.

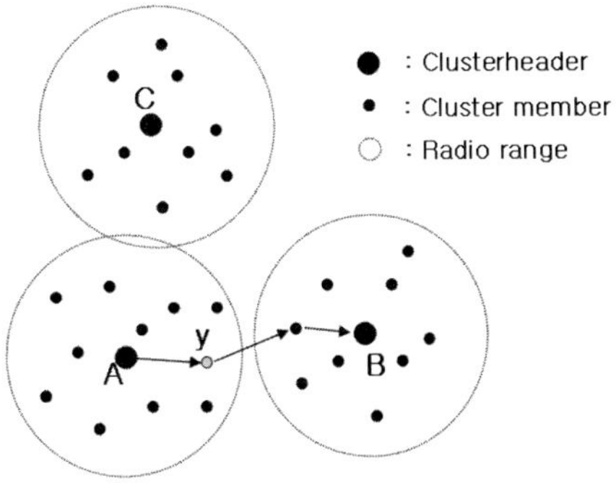


**Fig. 4.** Forwarding procedure between clusters

### 2.4 Reduce Failing Method

Nodes have the membership information of neighbor nodes. So, nodes get information of neighbor cluster headers from neighbor nodes. In addition, a cluster header has the membership information of member nodes.

Reduce failing is a method applying geographic method and ID method to reduce transmission failure due to moving nodes. In the example given in Fig. 5, Cluster header A forwards a packet to Cluster C with the ID information of node D using the membership information of node D after Cluster header A recognizes the transmission failure to node D.

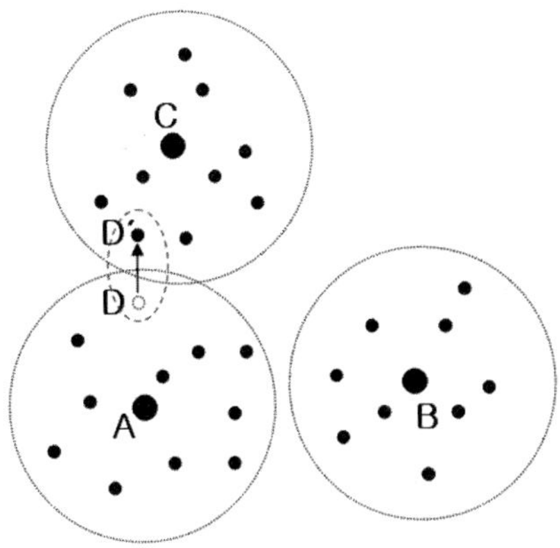


**Fig. 5.** Routing failure caused by moving nodes

For a network having larger mobility, Reduce failing method still can be applied with forwarding to the clusters possessing the largest and the second largest memberships. When the cluster which node D moves to is different from the cluster selected by membership method, the described method above is meaningless.

## 3 Generating and Maintaining Clusters

For an appropriate clustering method of mobile sensor networks, two possible approaches are considered in this paper. First is a method of selecting cluster headers and the second method is how to find memberships for each member.

First of all, a method of minimizing the change of cluster headers is considered. [1] Because the number of all clusters should be specified and a repeated calculations of cluster headers and nodes for membership functions in the case of applying Fuzzy c-means clustering. A frequent change of cluster headers might increase the amount of calculations for its member nodes and packet transmission delays might be occurred by information exchanges between the current and new cluster headers. [1] To prevent the mentioned problem by minimizing the change of cluster headers, Least Cluster Change method (LCC) proposed by Ching-Chuan Chiang et al. is considered. [2]

Secondly, Fuzzy C-means method is used to specify memberships of each node. [7] A membership $u_{ij}$ (membership of $x_i$ to Cluster $c_j$) is formed by (1)

$$u_{ij} = \frac{1}{\sum_{k=1}^{c} \left( \frac{\left\| x_i - c_j \right\|}{\left\| x_i - c_k \right\|} \right)^{\frac{2}{m-1}}} \tag{1}$$

c is the number of clusters nearby $x_i$ and $c_i$ is the location of near cluster headers. A value of 2 is used for variable m. Cluster headers are possible to attain the information of neighbor clusters and each node also updates the information and the memberships of its cluster by using the memberships of neighbor nodes. Using the information formed in the described way above, the routing method introduces in Section 2 can be realized.

## 4 Conclusion

GPSR is an algorithm highly applicable to a mobile sensor network with a large number of nodes since it takes less resources needed in nodes and doesn't cause overheads while route searching. However, in the case to sue GPSR to a mobile network with many frequent moving nodes, there is a possibility of packet transmission failures so that it might increase packet losses. In real applications, sensor nodes are generally grouped as needed and it makes a hierarchical routing method using clustering more reasonable than routing methods with even level nodes.

In this paper, for a more applicable routing to these characteristics of mobile sensor network, GPSR method is applied to the routing between clusters and ID method is used in each cluster. In addition, a method of enhancing transmission failures by using cluster memberships and IDs is proposed when a transmission failure is occurred by a node moving.

The methods of generating and maintaining clusters will be specified and the simulations for the performance evaluation of the proposed method will be conducted for further researches. Moreover, an enhancing method of Reduce failing with currently applying only simple memberships will be considered by applying a method of predicting moving clusters using membership gradients of nodes attained from information of memberships before and after updates.

## References


1. Jie, G., Guibas, L. J., Gershberger, J., Zhang, L., Zhu, A.: Geometric Spanners for Routing in Mobile Networks. IEEE Journal on Selected Areas in Communications, Vol. 23, No 1 (2005) 174–185
2. Chiang, C.C, Wu, H.K., Liu, W., Gerla, M.: Routing in Clustered Multihop, Mobile Wireless Networks With Fading Channel. Proc. IEEE SICON (1997) 197–211
3. Perkins, C., Royer, E.: Ad-hoc On-Demand Distance Vector Routing. In Proceedings the 2nd IEEE Workshop on Mobile Computing Systems and Applications (1999)
4. Johnson, D., Maltz, D.: Dynamic Source Routing in Ad Hoc Wireless Networks. Mobile Computing (1996)
5. Perkins, C., Bhagwat, P.: Highly Dynamic Destination-Sequenced Distance-Vector Routing(DSDV) for Mobile Computers. In Proceedings of ACM SIGCOMM (1994)
6. Toussaint, G.: The Relative Neighborhood Graph of a Finite Planar Set. Pattern Recognition, Vol. 12, No 4 (1980)
7. Bezdek, J.C., Hathaway, R.J., Sabin, M.J., Tucker, W.T.: Convergence Theory for Fuzzy C-Means: Counterexamples and Repairs. IEEE Trans. Syst., Man, Cybern., Vol. 17 (1987) 873–877
8. Karp, B., Kung, H.T.: GPSR: Greedy Perimeter Stateless Routing for Wireless Networks. Proc. Of the International Conf. on Mobile Computing and Networking (2000) 243–254
9. Bose, P., Morin, P., Stojmenovic, I., Urrutia, J.: Routing with Guaranteed Delivery in Ad Hoc Wireless Networks. Workshop on Discrete Algorithms and Methods for Mobile Computing and Communications (1999)
10. Gabriel, K., Sokal, R.: A New Statistical Approach to Geographic Variation Analysis. Systematic Zoology, Vol. 18 (1969) 259–278

# Autocontrol of Performance Measurement for RhombShape Achromatic Phase Retarder

Pei-Tao Zhao[1], Yin-Chao Zhang[1], Yue-Feng Zhao[1], Xin Fang[1], Jia Su[1], Jun Xie[1], Xiao-Yong Du[1], Guo-Hua Li[2], Fu-Quan Wu[2], and Han-Dong Peng[2]

[1] 863 Program Key Laboratory of Atmospheric Optics, Anhui Institute of Optics and FineMechanics, Chinese Academy of Sciences, Hefei, Anhui, China, 230031
[2] Laser Institute of Qufu Normal University, Qufu, Shandong, China, 273165
peitaozhao@163.com

**Abstract.** Achromatic retarder is an important optical device. Because of its important applied value, modern polarization technology and optical modulation demand high precision for the design and measurement of achromatic retarder. Based on the principle of polarizing modulation, this paper presented an autocontrol experiment system to measure the phase retardation for high precision achromatic retarder, whose shape is rhomb. The experimental results indicate that the principle of high precision achromatic retarder is correct and the measurement error is less than 1%, Since the autocontrol experiment system is convenient to operation, it can satisfy the demand of application.

## 1 Introduction

Achromatic retarder is such a device that can be used in wide spectrum in optical phase retardation. The phase retardation is a constant when the wavelength was changed. Modern polarization technology and optical modulation demand high precision for the measurement of achromatic retarder [1,2]. The precision of retardation is such a important parameter that can be indicated the performance of retarder is excellent or not, so optical staff are very concerned of the design and precision measurement for retarder. Currently, the major measurement methods include such as Compensating、Spectrum, Photo-Electricity Modulation, Phase Detection, Interferometry etc [3,4,5,6]. But in these methods the parameters are relational with the wavelength, so the reliability is low, and the operation are not convenient for their operation are manual operation. Following with the development of computer and autocontrol technology, measurement system must be realize intelligent and autocontrol. Based on the principle of polarizing modulation [7,8], this paper set up an autocontrol experiment system for measuring the phase retardation for high precision achromatic retarder, whose shape is rhomb. This measurement system has such excellence as convenient operation and high precision, so it can be used for achromatic phase retarder performance measurement and analysis.

## 2 Measurement Principle

The experiment system is indicated by Fig.1. Where $P_0$、$P_1$ are polarizer W is Wollaston polarizer and the transmission orientation of $P_0$ is horizontal, the transmission

D.-S. Huang, K. Li, and G.W. Irwin (Eds.): ICIC 2006, LNCS 4113, pp. 1320–1325, 2006.

orientation of $P_1$ can be at any positions, the angle formed with $P_1$ transmission orientation and horizontal is denoted by $\theta$, R is measurement sample: Special angle incidence high precision achromatic phase retarder.[9] During the process of measurement, the angle formed with the fast axis of $R_x$ and horizontal is $45^0$. The polarization state of incident beam can be changed into line polarized beam after passing the $P_0$ 、 $P_1$, and changed into ellipse or circle polarized beam after passing the $R_x$, and changed into two perpendicular line polarized beams. Suppose the angle formed with one beam's transmission orientation and horizontal is denoted by $\beta$, then the angle formed with other beam's transmission orientation and horizontal is denoted by $\beta + \pi/2$. The two detectors of intensity can be denoted by $I_1$ 、 $I_2$ separately.

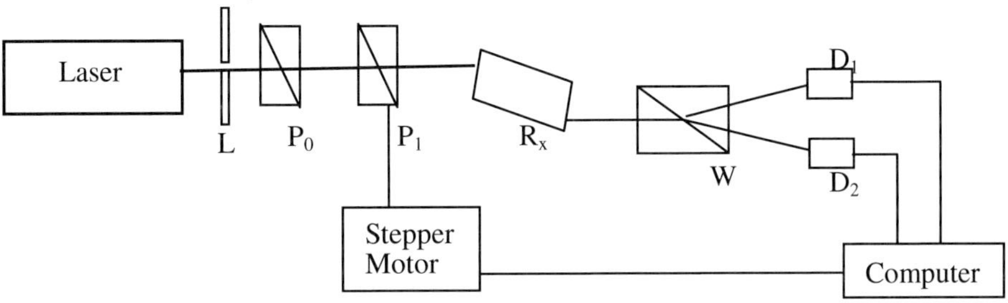


**Fig. 1.** Measurement Principle Sketch Map. Where the capital letter L is diaphragm, the $P_0$ and $P_1$ are polarization prisms. The polarization state of incident beam can be changed into line polarized beam after passing the $P_0$ 、 $P_1$, prism $P_1$ can be rotated by the stepper motor so the transmission orientation is alterable. After passing the phase retarder $R_x$, the polarization state of beam can be changed into ellipse or circle polarization. W is a beam-splitting polarized prism: Wollaston prism. After passing the Wollaston prism, the beam can be split into two beams and their intensities were detected by two detectors $D_1$ and $D_2$.

Where the Jones Matrix of $P_0$, $P_1$ , $R_x$ and W can be expressed as following:

$$J_{P_0} = \begin{bmatrix} 1 & 0 \\ 0 & 0 \end{bmatrix} \tag{1}$$

$$J_{P_1} = \begin{bmatrix} \cos^2\theta & \sin\theta\cos\theta \\ \sin\theta\cos\theta & \sin^2\theta \end{bmatrix} \tag{2}$$

$$J_R = \begin{bmatrix} \cos\frac{\delta}{2} & i\sin\frac{\delta}{2} \\ i\sin\frac{\delta}{2} & \cos\frac{\delta}{2} \end{bmatrix} \tag{3}$$

$$J_{W_1} = \begin{bmatrix} \cos^2\beta & \sin\beta\cos\beta \\ \sin\beta\cos\beta & \sin^2\beta \end{bmatrix} \tag{4}$$

$$J_{W_2} = \begin{bmatrix} \cos^2(\beta+\frac{\pi}{2}) & \sin(\beta+\frac{\pi}{2})\cos(\beta+\frac{\pi}{2}) \\ \sin(\beta+\frac{\pi}{2})\cos(\beta+\frac{\pi}{2}) & \sin^2(\beta+\frac{\pi}{2}) \end{bmatrix} \tag{5}$$

Based on the Principle of Matrix optics, we can get the expressions of two detectors intensity when the $\theta$ is $30^0$ and $\beta$ is $0^0$.

$$\begin{cases} I_1(\theta=30^0,\beta=0^0,\delta)=g_1(\frac{9}{16}\cos^2\frac{\delta}{2}+\frac{3}{16}\sin^2\frac{\delta}{2}) \\ I_2(\theta=30^0,\beta=90^0,\delta)=g_2(\frac{3}{16}\cos^2\frac{\delta}{2}+\frac{9}{16}\sin^2\frac{\delta}{2}) \end{cases} \tag{6}$$

In the same way, we can get the other expressions of two detectors intensity when the $\theta$ is $60^0$ and $\beta$ is $0^0$.

$$\begin{cases} I_1'(\theta=60^0,\beta=0^0,\delta)=g_1(\frac{1}{16}\cos^2\frac{\delta}{2}+\frac{3}{16}\sin^2\frac{\delta}{2}) \\ I_2'(\theta=60^0,\beta=90^0,\delta)=g_2(\frac{3}{16}\cos^2\frac{\delta}{2}+\frac{1}{16}\sin^2\frac{\delta}{2}) \end{cases} \tag{7}$$

It can be introduces a unitary parameter as the following expression:

$$I_N(\theta,\beta,\delta)=\left[\frac{I_1(\theta=30^0,\beta=0^0,\delta)I_2'(\theta=60^0,\beta=90^0,\delta)}{I_1'(\theta=60^0,\beta=90^0,\delta)I_2(\theta=30^0,\beta=0^0,\delta)}\right] \tag{8}$$

We can get the expression (9) after introducing expressions(6)、(7) into expression(8).

$$I_N(\theta,\beta,\delta)=\left[\frac{g_1g_2'(\frac{3}{8}\cos^2\frac{\delta}{2}+\frac{3}{16})(\frac{1}{8}\cos^2\frac{\delta}{2}+\frac{1}{16})}{g_1'g_2(\frac{3}{16}-\frac{1}{8}\cos^2\frac{\delta}{2})(\frac{9}{16}-\frac{3}{8}\cos^2\frac{\delta}{2})}\right]=\left[\frac{(\frac{3}{8}\cos^2\frac{\delta}{2}+\frac{3}{16})(\frac{1}{8}\cos^2\frac{\delta}{2}+\frac{1}{16})}{(\frac{3}{16}-\frac{1}{8}\cos^2\frac{\delta}{2})(\frac{9}{16}-\frac{3}{8}\cos^2\frac{\delta}{2})}\right] \tag{9}$$

It is easy to get the conclusion that unitary parameter is related to phase retardation $\delta$ and the angle $\theta$. We can get the phase retardation $\delta$ after getting the intensity of two detectors and the transmission orientation of incident beam.

## 3 System Intelligent Process

In order to realize the intelligent function, some special instruments are needed, such as industrial control computer、stepper motor、collection card etc.

The flow chart of intelligent process can be shown by the following chart:

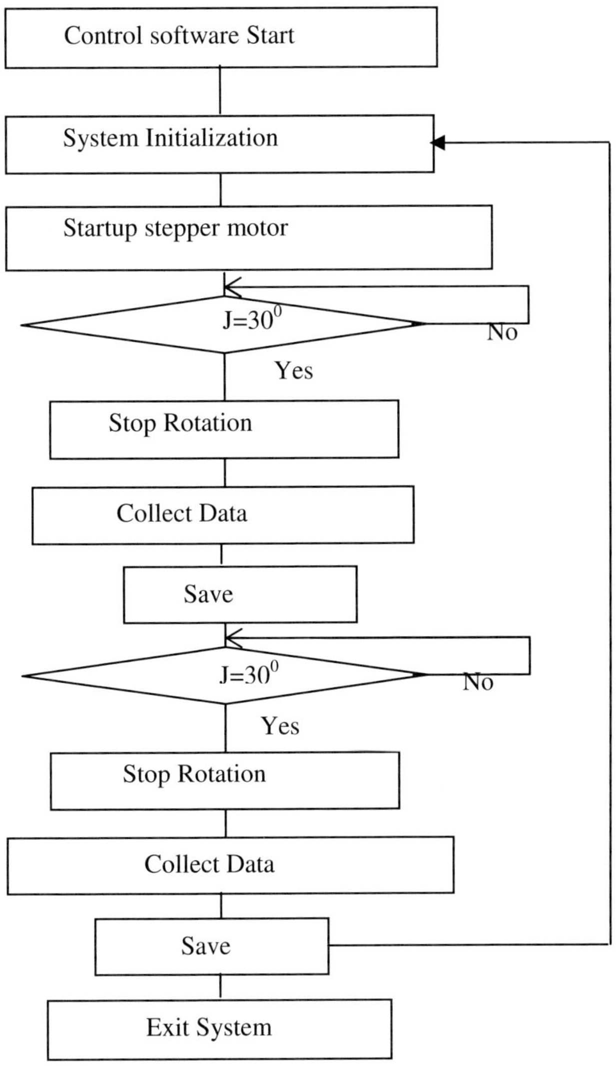


**Fig. 2.** Intelligent System Flowing. The controlling software compiled by Visual Basic language that can be used to control the rotation of the stepper motor and give an indication to data record to collecting.

System need to initialization at the beginning of the measurement, which include the stepper motor rotate to zero position and sweeping base line etc. Then the stepper motor receive an dictation to start rotating until it reaches the $30^0$ position, we can judge the position by a closed loop feed back controlling[10]. This method can eliminate error caused by the offset of $\theta$ angle for the lost step during the rotation process. Then collect card record the two detectors intensities for many times, the number of collecting times was set by soft controlling. Next progress is similar to the former. Stepper motor continue rotating $30^0$, thus the $\theta$ is $60^0$ and repeat the same action for the collection card. At last the collection data about two times of detectors were taken into the expression (5) and get the phase retardation. Considering the many times of collect data, we can adopt different method of data processing such as least square method and it can be realized in the soft controlling.

It need to point out that the value of angle $\theta$ adopt $30^0$,$60^0$ are not exclusively because of introduced the unitary parameter $I_N$. The intensities of two detectors are related to the angle $\theta$, so any value of the angle of rotation can be chosen and we can get the phase retardation according to the definition of $I_N$. Considering the performance of achromatic measurement, the wavelength of the incidence beam need to change after an whole process. So the following operations are the repetition of the former process.

## 4 Experiment and Conclusion

According to the designation of Fig.1, we set up an experiment system and choose the wavelength of incidence beam as 473nm, 532nm, 633nm, 650nm, 670nm. The performance curve of retardation was shown by Fig.3.

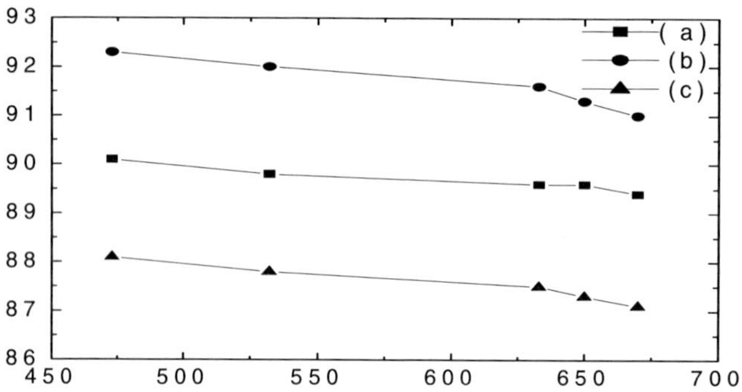


**Fig. 3.** Performance curve of high precision achromatic retarder Incidence angle: (a) $44.96^0$(b) $43.96^0$ (c) $45.96^0$

The intelligent measurement system can be used to measure the performance of achromatic rhomb shape phase retarder successfully and exactly. The result accorded with the design with the error is less than 1%. It must be pointed that the introduced unitary parameter played very important value, it can eliminate the influence of fluctuated laser power and the ratio of intensities of beam-splitting. The error of system were caused by the responsibility of non-matching in time for two detectors. It can be explained by the following expression:

$$\frac{g_1 g_2'}{g_2 g_1'} \neq 1 \qquad (10)$$

Where the $g_1, g_2$ are the responsibility of two detectors in the first time, $g_1', g_2'$ are the responsibility of two detectors in the second time. Because of the responsibility of non-matching in time that expressed by the (10), it can resulted the error of system. Considering the measurement stabilization of the two detectors is less 2%, so thatwe can get the following expression after analysis theoretically

$$\frac{g_1 g_2'}{g_2 g_1'} - 1 \leq 0.04 \qquad (11)$$

Since it reaches the high precision and can satisfy the demand of application, so it can be used to measure the rhomb shape retarder such as Fresnel Rhomb, Mooney Rhomb, Achromatic retarder AD-1and AD-2 and oblique incidence Fresnel Rhomb.

## References


1. Xu, G.B., Xu, X.G., Yu, X.Q.: High Isolation Broadband Optical Isolator with Fresnel Rhomb. Acta Optica Sinica, Vol.23 (2003) 997-999
2. Ding, H.B., Pang, W.N., Liu, Y.B., Shang, R.CH.: Polarization direction Modulation for Spin-polarized electrons with liquid crystal variable retarder. Acta Physica Sinica, Vol.54 (2005) 4097-4100
3. Jerrard, H.G.: Optical Compensators for Measurement Elliptical Polarization. Opt. Soc. Am, Vol.38 (1948) 35-59
4. Jin, G.F., Li, J.ZH.: Laser Metrology, Science Press Beijing (1998)
5. Nakadate, S.: High Precision retardation Measurement using Phase Detection of Young's fringers. Appl. Opt, Vol.29 (1990) 242-246
6. Shyu, L., Chen, C., Su, D.: Method for Measuring the Retardation of a Wave Plate. Appl. Opt , Vol.32 (1993) 4228-4230
7. Zhao, Q.L., Wu, F.Q.: Optical Phase Retardation Measurement by Normalized Polarizing Modulation. Acta Optica Sinica, Vol.22 (2002 ) 360-362
8. Zhao, Q.L., Wu, F.Q.: Testing Research of Achromatic Phase Retarder's Spectral Character. Spectroscopy and Spectral Analysis, Vol.23 (2003) 28-30
9. Zhao, P.T., Li, G.H., Wu, F.Q.: New Design of High Precision Achromatic Phase Retarder. Acta Optica Sinica, Vol.25 (2005) 980-983
10. Hao, D.Z., Song, L.K., Wu, F.Q.: Intelligentized Measurement of Wave Plate Phase Retardation with Beam-splitting Differential Method. Journal Optoelectronics Laser, Vol.16 (2005 ) 601-604

# Author Index

# Lecture Notes in Computer Science

For information about Vols. 1–4013

please contact your bookseller or Springer

Vol. 4127: E. Damiani, P. Liu (Eds.), Data and Applications Security XX. X, 319 pages. 2006.

Vol. 4121: A. Biere, C.P. Gomes (Eds.), Theory and Applications of Satisfiability Testing - SAT 2006. XII, 438 pages. 2006.

Vol. 4115: D.-S. Huang, K. Li, G.W. Irwin (Eds.), Computational Intelligence and Bioinformatics, Part III. XXI, 803 pages. 2006. (Sublibrary LNBI).

Vol. 4114: D.-S. Huang, K. Li, G.W. Irwin (Eds.), Computational Intelligence, Part II. XXVII, 1337 pages. 2006. (Sublibrary LNAI).

Vol. 4113: D.-S. Huang, K. Li, G.W. Irwin (Eds.), Intelligent Computing, Part I. XXVII, 1331 pages. 2006.

Vol. 4112: D.Z. Chen, D. T. Lee (Eds.), Computing and Combinatorics. XIV, 528 pages. 2006.

Vol. 4111: F.S. de Boer, M.M. Bonsangue, S. Graf, W.-P. de Roever (Eds.), Formal Methods for Components and Objects. VIII, 447 pages. 2006.

Vol. 4108: J.M. Borwein, W.M. Farmer (Eds.), Mathematical Knowledge Management. VIII, 295 pages. 2006. (Sublibrary LNAI).

Vol. 4106: T.R. Roth-Berghofer, M.H. Göker, H. A. Güvenir (Eds.), Advances in Case-Based Reasoning. XIV, 566 pages. 2006. (Sublibrary LNAI).

Vol. 4104: T. Kunz, S.S. Ravi (Eds.), Ad-Hoc, Mobile, and Wireless Networks. XII, 474 pages. 2006.

Vol. 4099: Q. Yang, G. Webb (Eds.), PRICAI 2006: Trends in Artificial Intelligence. XXVIII, 1263 pages. 2006. (Sublibrary LNAI).

Vol. 4098: F. Pfenning (Ed.), Term Rewriting and Applications. XIII, 415 pages. 2006.

Vol. 4097: X. Zhou, O. Sokolsky, L. Yan, E.-S. Jung, Z. Shao, Y. Mu, D.C. Lee, D. Kim, Y.-S. Jeong, C.-Z. Xu (Eds.), Emerging Directions in Embedded and Ubiquitous Computing. XXVII, 1034 pages. 2006.

Vol. 4096: E. Sha, S.-K. Han, C.-Z. Xu, M.H. Kim, L.T. Yang, B. Xiao (Eds.), Embedded and Ubiquitous Computing. XXIV, 1170 pages. 2006.

Vol. 4094: O. H. Ibarra, H.-C. Yen (Eds.), Implementation and Application of Automata. XIII, 291 pages. 2006.

Vol. 4093: X. Li, O.R. Zaiane, Z. Li (Eds.), Advanced Data Mining and Applications. XXI, 1110 pages. 2006. (Sublibrary LNAI).

Vol. 4092: J. Lang, F. Lin, J. Wang (Eds.), Knowledge Science, Engineering and Management. XV, 664 pages. 2006. (Sublibrary LNAI).

Vol. 4090: S. Spaccapietra, K. Aberer, P. Cudré-Mauroux (Eds.), Journal on Data Semantics VI. XI, 211 pages. 2006.

Vol. 4088: Z.-Z. Shi, R. Sadananda (Eds.), Agent Computing and Multi-Agent Systems. XVII, 827 pages. 2006. (Sublibrary LNAI).

Vol. 4079: S. Etalle, M. Truszczyński (Eds.), Logic Programming. XIV, 474 pages. 2006.

Vol. 4077: M.-S. Kim, K. Shimada (Eds.), Advances in Geometric Modeling and Processing. XVI, 696 pages. 2006.

Vol. 4076: F. Hess, S. Pauli, M. Pohst (Eds.), Algorithmic Number Theory. X, 599 pages. 2006.

Vol. 4075: U. Leser, F. Naumann, B. Eckman (Eds.), Data Integration in the Life Sciences. XI, 298 pages. 2006. (Sublibrary LNBI).

Vol. 4074: M. Burmester, A. Yasinsac (Eds.), Secure Mobile Ad-hoc Networks and Sensors. X, 193 pages. 2006.

Vol. 4073: A. Butz, B. Fisher, A. Krüger, P. Olivier (Eds.), Smart Graphics. XI, 263 pages. 2006.

Vol. 4072: M. Harders, G. Székely (Eds.), Biomedical Simulation. XI, 216 pages. 2006.

Vol. 4071: H. Sundaram, M. Naphade, J.R. Smith, Y. Rui (Eds.), Image and Video Retrieval. XII, 547 pages. 2006.

Vol. 4070: C. Priami, X. Hu, Y. Pan, T.Y. Lin (Eds.), Transactions on Computational Systems Biology V. IX, 129 pages. 2006. (Sublibrary LNBI).

Vol. 4069: F.J. Perales, R.B. Fisher (Eds.), Articulated Motion and Deformable Objects. XV, 526 pages. 2006.

Vol. 4068: H. Schärfe, P. Hitzler, P. Øhrstrøm (Eds.), Conceptual Structures: Inspiration and Application. XI, 455 pages. 2006. (Sublibrary LNAI).

Vol. 4067: D. Thomas (Ed.), ECOOP 2006 – Object-Oriented Programming. XIV, 527 pages. 2006.

Vol. 4066: A. Rensink, J. Warmer (Eds.), Model Driven Architecture – Foundations and Applications. XII, 392 pages. 2006.

Vol. 4065: P. Perner (Ed.), Advances in Data Mining. XI, 592 pages. 2006. (Sublibrary LNAI).

Vol. 4064: R. Büschkes, P. Laskov (Eds.), Detection of Intrusions and Malware & Vulnerability Assessment. X, 195 pages. 2006.

Vol. 4063: I. Gorton, G.T. Heineman, I. Crnkovic, H.W. Schmidt, J.A. Stafford, C.A. Szyperski, K. Wallnau (Eds.), Component-Based Software Engineering. XI, 394 pages. 2006.

Vol. 4062: G. Wang, J.F. Peters, A. Skowron, Y. Yao (Eds.), Rough Sets and Knowledge Technology. XX, 810 pages. 2006. (Sublibrary LNAI).

Vol. 4061: K. Miesenberger, J. Klaus, W. Zagler, A. Karshmer (Eds.), Computers Helping People with Special Needs. XXIX, 1356 pages. 2006.

Vol. 4060: K. Futatsugi, J.-P. Jouannaud, J. Meseguer (Eds.), Algebra, Meaning and Computation. XXXVIII, 643 pages. 2006.

Vol. 4059: L. Arge, R. Freivalds (Eds.), Algorithm Theory – SWAT 2006. XII, 436 pages. 2006.

Vol. 4058: L.M. Batten, R. Safavi-Naini (Eds.), Information Security and Privacy. XII, 446 pages. 2006.

Vol. 4057: J.P. W. Pluim, B. Likar, F.A. Gerritsen (Eds.), Biomedical Image Registration. XII, 324 pages. 2006.

Vol. 4056: P. Flocchini, L. Gąsieniec (Eds.), Structural Information and Communication Complexity. X, 357 pages. 2006.

Vol. 4055: J. Lee, J. Shim, S.-g. Lee, C. Bussler, S. Shim (Eds.), Data Engineering Issues in E-Commerce and Services. IX, 290 pages. 2006.

Vol. 4054: A. Horváth, M. Telek (Eds.), Formal Methods and Stochastic Models for Performance Evaluation. VIII, 239 pages. 2006.

Vol. 4053: M. Ikeda, K.D. Ashley, T.-W. Chan (Eds.), Intelligent Tutoring Systems. XXVI, 821 pages. 2006.

Vol. 4052: M. Bugliesi, B. Preneel, V. Sassone, I. Wegener (Eds.), Automata, Languages and Programming, Part II. XXIV, 603 pages. 2006.

Vol. 4051: M. Bugliesi, B. Preneel, V. Sassone, I. Wegener (Eds.), Automata, Languages and Programming, Part I. XXIII, 729 pages. 2006.

Vol. 4049: S. Parsons, N. Maudet, P. Moraitis, I. Rahwan (Eds.), Argumentation in Multi-Agent Systems. XIV, 313 pages. 2006. (Sublibrary LNAI).

Vol. 4048: L. Goble, J.-J.C.. Meyer (Eds.), Deontic Logic and Artificial Normative Systems. X, 273 pages. 2006. (Sublibrary LNAI).

Vol. 4047: M. Robshaw (Ed.), Fast Software Encryption. XI, 434 pages. 2006.

Vol. 4046: S.M. Astley, M. Brady, C. Rose, R. Zwiggelaar (Eds.), Digital Mammography. XVI, 654 pages. 2006.

Vol. 4045: D. Barker-Plummer, R. Cox, N. Swoboda (Eds.), Diagrammatic Representation and Inference. XII, 301 pages. 2006. (Sublibrary LNAI).

Vol. 4044: P. Abrahamsson, M. Marchesi, G. Succi (Eds.), Extreme Programming and Agile Processes in Software Engineering. XII, 230 pages. 2006.

Vol. 4043: A.S. Atzeni, A. Lioy (Eds.), Public Key Infrastructure. XI, 261 pages. 2006.

Vol. 4042: D. Bell, J. Hong (Eds.), Flexible and Efficient Information Handling. XVI, 296 pages. 2006.

Vol. 4041: S.-W. Cheng, C.K. Poon (Eds.), Algorithmic Aspects in Information and Management. XI, 395 pages. 2006.

Vol. 4040: R. Reulke, U. Eckardt, B. Flach, U. Knauer, K. Polthier (Eds.), Combinatorial Image Analysis. XII, 482 pages. 2006.

Vol. 4039: M. Morisio (Ed.), Reuse of Off-the-Shelf Components. XIII, 444 pages. 2006.

Vol. 4038: P. Ciancarini, H. Wiklicky (Eds.), Coordination Models and Languages. VIII, 299 pages. 2006.

Vol. 4037: R. Gorrieri, H. Wehrheim (Eds.), Formal Methods for Open Object-Based Distributed Systems. XVII, 474 pages. 2006.

Vol. 4036: O. H. Ibarra, Z. Dang (Eds.), Developments in Language Theory. XII, 456 pages. 2006.

Vol. 4035: T. Nishita, Q. Peng, H.-P. Seidel (Eds.), Advances in Computer Graphics. XX, 771 pages. 2006.

Vol. 4034: J. Münch, M. Vierimaa (Eds.), Product-Focused Software Process Improvement. XVII, 474 pages. 2006.

Vol. 4033: B. Stiller, P. Reichl, B. Tuffin (Eds.), Performability Has its Price. X, 103 pages. 2006.

Vol. 4032: O. Etzion, T. Kuflik, A. Motro (Eds.), Next Generation Information Technologies and Systems. XIII, 365 pages. 2006.

Vol. 4031: M. Ali, R. Dapoigny (Eds.), Advances in Applied Artificial Intelligence. XXIII, 1353 pages. 2006. (Sublibrary LNAI).

Vol. 4029: L. Rutkowski, R. Tadeusiewicz, L.A. Zadeh, J.M. Zurada (Eds.), Artificial Intelligence and Soft Computing – ICAISC 2006. XXI, 1235 pages. 2006. (Sublibrary LNAI).

Vol. 4028: J. Kohlas, B. Meyer, A. Schiper (Eds.), Dependable Systems: Software, Computing, Networks. XII, 295 pages. 2006.

Vol. 4027: H.L. Larsen, G. Pasi, D. Ortiz-Arroyo, T. Andreasen, H. Christiansen (Eds.), Flexible Query Answering Systems. XVIII, 714 pages. 2006. (Sublibrary LNAI).

Vol. 4026: P.B. Gibbons, T. Abdelzaher, J. Aspnes, R. Rao (Eds.), Distributed Computing in Sensor Systems. XIV, 566 pages. 2006.

Vol. 4025: F. Eliassen, A. Montresor (Eds.), Distributed Applications and Interoperable Systems. XI, 355 pages. 2006.

Vol. 4024: S. Donatelli, P. S. Thiagarajan (Eds.), Petri Nets and Other Models of Concurrency - ICATPN 2006. XI, 441 pages. 2006.

Vol. 4021: E. André, L. Dybkjær, W. Minker, H. Neumann, M. Weber (Eds.), Perception and Interactive Technologies. XI, 217 pages. 2006. (Sublibrary LNAI).

Vol. 4020: A. Bredenfeld, A. Jacoff, I. Noda, Y. Takahashi (Eds.), RoboCup 2005: Robot Soccer World Cup IX. XVII, 727 pages. 2006. (Sublibrary LNAI).

Vol. 4019: M. Johnson, V. Vene (Eds.), Algebraic Methodology and Software Technology. XI, 389 pages. 2006.

Vol. 4018: V. Wade, H. Ashman, B. Smyth (Eds.), Adaptive Hypermedia and Adaptive Web-Based Systems. XVI, 474 pages. 2006.

Vol. 4017: S. Vassiliadis, S. Wong, T.D. Hämäläinen (Eds.), Embedded Computer Systems: Architectures, Modeling, and Simulation. XV, 492 pages. 2006.

Vol. 4016: J.X. Yu, M. Kitsuregawa, H.V. Leong (Eds.), Advances in Web-Age Information Management. XVII, 606 pages. 2006.

Vol. 4014: T. Uustalu (Ed.), Mathematics of Program Construction. X, 455 pages. 2006.